D1737955

FRONT PAGE

A Collection of Historical Headlines from the *Los Angeles Times* 1881–1989

FRONT PAGE

A Collection of Historical Headlines from the *Los Angeles Times* 1881–1989

Introduction by OTIS CHANDLER

A Note from W. THOMAS JOHNSON

A Note from WILLIAM F. THOMAS

Text by Digby Diehl

Enlarged and Updated Edition

Harry N. Abrams, Inc., Publishers, New York

Editor: Darlene Geis
Assistant Editor: Anne Yarowsky
Designer: Patrick Cunningham

Enlarged and Updated Edition

ISBN 0-8109-3555-4

Published in 1990 by Harry N. Abrams, Incorporated, New York

A Times Mirror Company

Printed and bound in the United States of America

Contents

Acknowledgments

Thanks are due to the following people whose help made this book possible:

Martin Levin, who conceived the project; Leigh Kennicott Romero, who assisted in the preparation and research; John Weaver for his suggestions and criticism; Stanley Gordon for his *Los Angeles Times* chronology; John L. Snyder, manager of micrographics and records for the *Los Angeles Times;* Lois Markwith, Carolyn Strickler, and Darrell Kunitomi of the *Los Angeles Times* archives; Cecily Surace, director of the *Los Angeles Times* Research Library, and Tom Lutgen, Susanna Shuster, and Pat Cavanaugh of her staff; and my wife, Kay Beyer Diehl.

In addition, I would like to cite some references that have been particularly valuable in my work on this project:

Bowman, Lynn. *Los Angeles: Epic of a City.* Berkeley: Howell-North Books. 1974.

Caughey, John, and Caughey, LaRee. *Los Angeles: Biography of a City.* Berkeley and Los Angeles: University of California Press. 1976.

Halberstam, David. *The Powers That Be*. New York: Alfred A. Knopf. 1979.

Henstell, Bruce. *Los Angeles: An Illustrated History.* New York: Alfred A. Knopf. 1980.

Weaver, John D. *Los Angeles: The Enormous Village 1781–1981*. Santa Barbara: Capra Press. 1980.

D. D.

Introduction

OTIS CHANDLER
Publisher, 1960–1980

We often stand or fall on timing. The key elements of timing were just right when I commenced my publishership in 1960.

I inherited a good, primarily local editorial product and a very sound business from my father, Norman Chandler. Los Angeles at that moment was ready for a great newspaper—a reflection of the West's rising leadership and influence. A condition some writers chose to call the "Continental Tilt" was in full swing. Not only did the East-to-West tilt encompass the greatest voluntary migration in history, but also, within the space of a few years, it included the most dynamic explosion of education and cultural and scientific exploration this country has ever seen.

The time was right to build a newspaper that would bring to its readers a new kind of excellence in journalism—the best account of public affairs that we were capable of delivering; plus a recognizable picture of our environment and of ourselves, telling, as sensitively as possible, how people work, live, and have fun; plus an acknowledgment of an admirable attribute in all of us, the quest for self-improvement.

In short, the time was right to aim our newspaper at an audience of better-educated men and women with greater purchasing power and to bring our readers and advertisers together in a fast-growing marketplace on a scale much larger than ever before.

It was not necessary to start from scratch. I had already apprenticed for seven years in a carefully planned executive training program. It gave me an opportunity to work in the major departments of *The Times*—production, editorial, advertising, circulation, etc.—and to observe at close range where improvements could be made.

Fortunately, *The Times* already had in place a fine editor, Nick Williams. He had been named to the job in 1958, the same year I became marketing manager of *The Times*, and we often discussed changes that could be made in the years ahead.

Thus, when I became publisher in 1960, we were ready to proceed and began immediately to upgrade the editorial staff, to create new editorial sections, and to expand coverage throughout the paper.

I had two basic goals. One was to make *The Times* the best paper in the United States. The other was to make it the most profitable in the world.

The road to greatness, obviously, must be paved with more than good intentions. *The Times* would have to pay the massive bills for these major improvements.

It was clear that we faced gigantic costs required to upgrade our editorial staff, to hire and train better-qualified personnel in the advertising and circulation areas and the production departments, to develop additional office space, and to build larger and more modern production facilities. We needed to spend money on research and development to take advantage of new technology, including data processing and, later, microwave transmission to our Orange County satellite plant. It was important to pioneer, wherever possible, efficiencies that would make our operations more profitable.

It appeared to me that we must push forward on all these fronts at the same time: editorial improvements should not be delayed while we expanded and modernized the circulation and advertising departments, but neither should we count on larger revenues from circulation and advertising without sharpening the editorial product. It was another case of timing, and it meant a series of carefully synchronized actions to begin promptly and to take place over a period of years.

Our work inside the newspaper during those two

decades was accompanied by an incredible orchestration of events around the world, all covered fully in the pages of *The Times:* The Vietnam War, First Man in Space, Cuban Missile Crisis, Bay of Pigs, Student Riots, Racial Confrontations, Three Tragic Assassinations of National Leaders, A Landing on the Moon, The Beatles, The Manson Gang, Jogging, CB Radios, Coed Dorms, Gasoline Lines, Small Cars, Terrorist Bombings, Kidnappings, Air Hijackings, Watergate, Presidential Elections, Seizure of the U.S. Embassy in Iran.

During the twenty years spanned by those events, *The Times* launched one new section after another: TV TIMES, OPINION, OUTLOOK, SUNDAY CALENDAR, FOOD, TRAVEL, VIEW, BOOK REVIEW, YOU, FASHION, and the daily BUSINESS and CALENDAR sections.

We hired editorial stars—Jim Murray, Chuck Champlin, Art Seidenbaum, and a great many more.

We established eighteen foreign news bureaus covering the world from Hong Kong to Moscow, from Jerusalem to Peking. And at home we opened new offices in twelve cities.

In Washington we expanded our news bureau from a three-man office in 1960 to thirty-six staffers.

We inaugurated the *Los Angeles Times–Washington Post* News Service, an arrangement making our stories available to many newspapers around the world.

The Times's prestige and acclaim were dramatically enhanced during the two decades 1960 to 1980—first under Nick Williams and then under his able successor, William Thomas—with the awarding of seven Pulitzer Prizes (added to the three Pulitzers won in previous years).

Some highlights of the unparalleled growth from 1960 to 1980 can be seen in a few figures:

- *The Times*'s net revenues increased by $400 million, or 650 percent.
- Daily circulation increased by 520,000, or 104 percent.
- Sunday circulation increased by 400,000, or 45 percent.
- Advertising increased by over 87 million lines, or 110 percent.
- The total number of full-time *Times* employees during the twenty years increased by 1,900, or 40 percent.
- In Editorial, employees increased by 417, or 140 percent.
- Editorial operating costs increased by $27.5 million, or 820 percent.
- We made enormous progress in technological advancements. We bade good-bye to old-fashioned equipment such as Linotype machines, and we pioneered photocomposition. We also launched a daily Orange County edition and later an edition for San Diego County. Management representatives from the largest Eastern papers have beaten a path to our door to observe our advanced technology.
- In 1979 we launched a five-year, $220 million facilities expansion program—the biggest expenditure in the history of newspapering—to enlarge our Orange County satellite plant, to build a *new* San Fernando satellite operation, and to modernize *The Times*'s downtown Los Angeles plant.

We scored other noteworthy achievements, reaching our goal of making *The Times* the most profitable newspaper in the world and arriving high up on the list—some say right at the top—of the best newspapers in the nation.

A Note from

W. THOMAS JOHNSON

Publisher, 1980–1989

As we move into our second century, we think the future of the *Los Angeles Times* is nearly limitless. In the last hundred years, *The Times* has grown from a small but vigorous newspaper in a small but ambitious town into one of the nation's largest and most comprehensive newspapers in one of the great metropolitan areas of the world. Yet the next hundred years look even more promising.

We have the opportunity to build the *Los Angeles Times* into a newspaper without parallel. We accept the challenge. Our aim is excellence, and we intend to achieve it.

We do not know what news the front pages of *The Times* will bring us over the next hundred years, but we know what that news will demand of us: accuracy, thoroughness, fairness, clarity, and, always, the meaning of the news.

Modern life requires, and modern readers demand, that newspapers go beyond a mere recounting of what happened yesterday to explain, as best they can, the context of events and their implication for the future. The daily nature of our work makes it impossible for us to be historians, and we can't claim to be. What we must do, though, is catch history on the wing and provide as much explanation and analysis of events as is possible for us to discern. If you believe, as we do, that the success of American democracy depends upon an informed citizenry, then our work is cut out for us.

We move ahead from a strong base. We have more than eight hundred women and men on our editorial staff. Most of them work in Southern California, covering the news of our home territory from offices in Los Angeles, Orange County, and San Diego.

As our newspaper has grown, so have our responsibilities. We have five news bureaus in California, seven throughout the nation—including twenty-seven reporters and editors in Washington—and nineteen foreign correspondents. We foresee expansion of our news-gathering forces, for the world is becoming not less, but more, interdependent.

What we in the newspaper craft call "hard news"—the great events of the day, whether in Los Angeles, the nation, or abroad—is the heart of a newspaper. But a modern newspaper is much more than that. It is, in fact, concerned with every aspect of life: the arts, business, sports, entertainment, our changing styles of living, and, along the way, diversion to lighten our readers' days. We express our own views about public affairs on our editorial pages, and we provide space for commentary and the opinions of others.

I can't predict exactly what the newspaper in the decades ahead is going to look like. New technology—computers, lasers, satellites—will enable us to produce better newspapers more efficiently.

Rapidly changing communications technology will bring improvements in our format and in our content. We shall continue to be a medium of advertising—whose breadth, quality, and appeal is essential to the success of every metropolitan American newspaper—and of news in all its varied forms and aspects.

Our challenge in the coming years is to excel in everything we undertake. We look forward to doing just that.

A Note from

WILLIAM F. THOMAS

Editor and Executive Vice President, 1971–1988

The group sat loosely arranged around the table, taking one by one the day's events and subjecting them to mild debate as to relative importance and interest. These were editors, and the debate was mild because none of the subjects discussed was of overshadowing import. Most of the stories simply moved events already in progress a step or two farther along.

There were the latest developments in a sensational murder case already two days old and a deadlocked jury in another sensational manslaughter case. Both involved Hollywood personalities, which gave them some standing so far as interest was concerned anywhere in the world but especially in Los Angeles.

Then there was the convocation of cardinals to elect a pope, along with the latest in the interminable disarmament talks, a rail strike in Europe, another violent confrontation in Ireland.

Strong stuff. From this a front page was to be fashioned.

In the end, the murder case led the page, at least partly because the newspaper's own reporters had enterprisingly brought forth information whose basic importance was debatable but whose exclusivity was not. Also on the page were the manslaughter case, the convocation of cardinals, and the other stories mentioned above.

The murder was that of famed movie director William Desmond Taylor, linked, as the picture's caption of that day put it, in a "Sinister Drama of Mystery" with the beautiful actress Mabel Normand.

The manslaughter trial was that of Fatty Arbuckle, and all the events discussed were recorded on the front page of *The Times* of February 3, 1922.

This book takes us through one hundred and six years of history as reflected in these front pages, each composed in more or less the way the 1922 page was put together.

Some were easier than others, though. I selected the page from February 3 as an example because, unlike many of the pages presented here that were chosen because they record true historical landmarks, this page records a day on which the editors had to deal with events in mid-path, whose beginnings were past and whose endings were not yet clear.

There are many, many days like this, and that's when editors earn their pay, when years of experience in each one's particular field must help build a consensus that, taken day-by-day, reflects a newspaper's true personality and values, balancing the stories of short-term but obvious interest with those whose outcomes are important to the community and the world, yet are not impressive in the area of human interest.

The pages in this book represent more than a century of human history in snapshot form unique in their faithful reflection of the world as it was on the day they were published.

The record of events in these pages is at times fragmentary, at times incorrect in interpretation, for it lacks the polish of hindsight and the long view of history.

We see here reflected the speech mannerisms and the prejudices of the times, and as we sail through these pages we cannot fail to see, also in a way unique to this medium, the evolution of attitudes and language and values of the human society.

The history books can tell us how it all came out, and why. These pages tell us what it was like to be there.

1881–1989
A City, A Family, A Newspaper

The City room of the *Los Angeles Times* is a place where all the newspaper's millions of readers would feel the energy and excitement that surges through this great information center. Keyboards clatter. Reporters pore over their notes. Phones ring. In the wire room, the Associated Press, United Press International, Reuters, and other news services spew forth reams of teletyped information twenty-four hours a day. The feeling that you are present at the recording of events, the constant chronicling of history, pervades the room. Of course such a visit is not possible for every reader, but a bit of such city room excitement can be recaptured in the more than a century of front pages collected in this book.

These pages graphically portray a variety of phenomena at the heart of the American experience. They show us, in headlines and pictures, the sweep of events, issues, and ideas that have affected the lives of millions of Americans. From the minutiae of city life to crises of international scope, the events reported give us a sense of how daily life was lived in different eras, and, more important, how the people living in those eras perceived themselves. These pages also measure the growth of Los Angeles from cow-town days to its present stature as a major world metropolis.

From its inception in 1881 to the present, the *Los Angeles Times* has been a dynamic daily reflection of the society it chronicles. The history of the newspaper and the history of the city reveal an unusual record of cultural symbiosis. In these glimpses from the past, we see a familiar American story repeated: strong individualists with idealistic visions shaping a frontier outpost into an urban center. One of these early individualists was General Harrison Gray Otis, who, as its publisher, guided *The Times* into the twentieth century and established a publishing dynasty that continues with his great-grandson Otis Chandler. So this story is also the story of a newspaper family.

Examined individually, the front pages are frames snipped from the ongoing movie of history. They are a kind of Polaroid vision of the past, to be treasured for their candid immediacy. At any given hour, on any given day, the variety of events engaging the attention of the citizens of Los Angeles has been frozen in ink and paper and positioned according to social or political values of that moment. This collage could be said to resemble a medieval tapestry in its attempt at visual expression (and interpretation) of those events.

These front pages offer important historical information as well. Like artifacts from an urban archaeological dig, they are primary source material for history. But journalistic reportage is not history. The writing of history implies a perspective and depth of analysis that are not possible in the presentation of breaking news. Total immersion in a tiny piece of time is the limitation of a newspaper front page—and is also its value.

There were 38,351 front-page candidates for inclusion in this book without taking into account the additional special editions (statisticians and puzzle fans will note that an extra front page appeared each leap year). The criteria for selection included historical insight, local importance, nostalgic value, significance in the development of the newspaper, and the special appeal of certain events to the eccentric tastes of this book's editor.

Not all the selections in this book reflect events of national or international importance. In some cases, the headlines are about the first freeway, early smog attacks, or the opening of Disneyland. Stories about the various transportation systems, beginning with the electric trolleys and Union Station, all have impact on our lives today. Even the early advertisements and stories about subdivisions of the Lankershim tract in San Fernando Valley describe historical influences that have shaped the city of Los Angeles.

The fascinating jumble of diverse events presented on any day chosen at random is remarkable to read. For instance, on the day that George Bernard Shaw died, the Truman assassination plot dominated the headlines. Or on May 27, 1953, when Norris Poulson won the mayoralty of Los Angeles, the main headline of *The Times* reflected euphoria; but a more somber headline proclaimed that the Rosenbergs had just lost their plea for a stay of execution. A May 5, 1970, front page dramatized the war at home and abroad with twin pictures of the shootings at Kent State and the bombings in Cambodia.

On June 29, 1971, the editors must have thrown up their hands. Under the headline "Winners—Losers," the front page chronicled a mosaic of triumphs and defeats that transpired all in one day: Daniel Ellsberg was indicted, thirty death sentences were overturned, Joe Colombo had been shot, and Muhammad Ali was cleared of draft evasion charges.

The growth of the *Los Angeles Times* reflects a pattern familiar to the development of all newspapers in the United States. The papers were stirring spoons in the great melting pot: homogenizing, educating, acculturating forces. The first continuously published newspaper in America, the *Boston News-Letter*, did not appear until 1704, long after adequate printing facilities were available in the colonies. Following skirmishes with government censorship, the *American Weekly Mercury* (Philadelphia) began publication in the year 1719, as did the *Boston Gazette*. The first newspaper in New York, the *New-York Gazette*, appeared in 1725.

But the American press did not show significant growth until the westward movement of the mid-nineteenth century, of which General Harrison Gray Otis was a beneficiary. Between 1850 and 1880, the number of newspapers in the United States more than doubled to 850.

Social responsibility in American journalism developed less rapidly. The nineteenth-century papers were filled with shameless proselytizing, partisan politics, circulation-building theatrics, and the prejudices of the day. To paraphrase A. J. Liebling, freedom of the press belonged to those who owned one.

In the early decades of *The Times*, the paper's colorful prose was striking. There was little objectivity in those pages. Stories led the reader to one specific conclusion without a balanced presentation of the facts. Reading these stories now is amusing because their style runs contrary to present rules of journalism. Today journalists observe the inverted pyramid technique of reportage, with a summation of the essential information contained in the first paragraph followed by elaboration of the story. Our contemporary news is neater, more homogenized. There is an attempt to provide a balanced, objective view of the news and keep opinion clearly labeled.

In a few of the early front pages there are insensitive references to minority groups and political groups revealing attitudes that have shifted with history and politics. We see, for example, a nonchalance about our Russian allies before World War II that changes into absolute hysteria in the postwar era.

The major role that the *Los Angeles Times* played in the shaping of Los Angeles during the past century is clear. The paper is unique because it has had such a big voice. There have always been other newspapers in Los Angeles, but since its inception, *The Times* was an active force for the city: the fight for Owens Valley water; the location of the Union Station; the creation of the Music Center and the accompanying downtown revitalization. *The Times*'s drive to clean up the downtown area has made the urban core a tax-producing, lively business center rather than a decaying inner city. The battles against poverty and slums have not yet been won, but in recent years the *Los Angeles Times* has attacked urban problems with fervor.

Although these 106 years of front pages are separated into eleven chapters marked by decades, the real rhythms of change were established by the four family publishers, the present publisher, and their personalities. Those personal eras offer another way of looking at the pages of this book: Harrison Gray Otis (1882–1917); Harry Chandler (1917–44); Norman Chandler (1944–60); Otis Chandler (1960–80); and Thomas Johnson (1980–).

Harrison Gray Otis became editor in chief of the *Los Angeles Daily Times* in 1882 after the paper had survived eight months of rocky beginnings. He had considerable experience in the newspaper business, having apprenticed himself at age fourteen to the *Noble County Courier* in Ohio. Then came the Civil War and two acquaintanceships that would later insure Otis's welcome in the halls of power: his military service with Rutherford B. Hayes and William McKinley.

Otis made his first trip to California in 1874 and was immediately drawn to its possibilities. What made Otis's tenure as editor and publisher of the fledgling paper so successful were his outspoken personality and the daring of his dreams. His first editor, Charles Lummis, once remarked that the early *Times* reflected "the dominant personality of [only] one man."

Otis's editorial stands included eccentric notions

such as promoting ostrich farms and eucalyptus groves as well as opposing the monopolistic Southern Pacific Railroad and the closed union shop. He saw the need to develop business and was instrumental in creating the Merchants and Manufacturers Association and the Chamber of Commerce for those purposes. As the paper grew stronger, opposition from Otis's enemies grew with it. But Otis's views helped determine the attitudes of the business and political leadership of the city, and opponents were hard pressed to come up with a base of support.

In the mid-eighties, young Harry Chandler signed on as a clerk in the circulation department. He was a canny businessman, who, in addition to his *Times* duties, bought up independent paper routes and played one rival paper against another in favor of the *Los Angeles Times*. In a short time Chandler became circulation manager, and by the time of his marriage to Otis's daughter, Marian, he was the business manager and part of the firm.

Throughout Chandler's career as publisher, he was known for his thousand-dollar-a-plate luncheons in support of a wide variety of projects. It was Chandler who involved his father-in-law in San Fernando Valley real estate, who brought the first automotive-related industry to Southern California, and who underwrote one of the first ventures in the aviation industry.

Harry Chandler's son Norman, born in 1899, went through more than ten years of apprenticeship in circulation, advertising, and promotion before receiving the reins as the third family publisher in the early '40s. Norman inherited the paper at a time when old values were rapidly changing. His major contribution was his recognition of the need to broaden the editorial view. While remaining Republican in outlook, the paper nevertheless began to take a less personalized stance on the issues.

Norman Chandler also saw the implied threat to newspapers in the new television broadcasts, and he set about diversifying the parent Times Mirror Company in order to insure that there would always be revenue enough to run a quality paper.

He did not foresee the success of his son, Otis. A third-generation Angeleno, Otis loved sports and the outdoors. At Stanford University he became a world class shot putter. His first exposure to the paper—during summer vacations home from the university—did not impel him to publishing. Only after he returned from a stint in the air force and began a rigorous training program, including a successful time as a cub reporter, did he become convinced.

On April 12, 1960, Otis Chandler became the fourth publisher of the *Los Angeles Times*. Under Otis's leadership the next twenty years saw the most extensive changes in *Los Angeles Times* history. One of his first moves was taking an underrated newspaper, a mediocre newspaper, and ordering editor Nick B. Williams to make it the best newspaper in the United States. They expanded the editorial department and gave reporters greater freedom to pursue their own stories. Otis Chandler also increased both the size and number of foreign and domestic bureaus.

In 1963 Chandler, Nick Williams, and editorial pages director James Bassett went to Southeast Asia. Included in their journey was a fact-finding trip to Vietnam, stimulating the thorough coverage that garnered a Pulitzer for the paper and set a new standard of journalistic excellence. The riots in Watts in 1965 provided another challenge, which the paper met with award-winning coverage.

Otis Chandler was an early proponent of new technologies. By 1974, the old Linotype machines were replaced by photocomposition, a process one hundred times faster than setting metal type. Not content with mere technological progress, Otis Chandler set out to expand the readership of the newspaper by creating zone editions. The first began in the San Gabriel Valley, with two issues published weekly by a staff headquartered in that zone. Then, in 1968, the ten-acre Costa Mesa plant opened, publishing the first Orange County edition. It was the first satellite plant in the United States for a daily metropolitan newspaper; plans are underway for a second plant to be situated in the San Fernando Valley.

When Otis Chandler stepped down as publisher in 1980 in favor of Tom Johnson, he had, as his Washington bureau chief, Jack Nelson, expressed it, "lived up to his promise to spend the time and the money and the effort to make [the *Los Angeles Times*] the best newspaper in the country." Under Otis's publishership, *The Times* received seven Pulitzer Prizes, eleven awards presented by the Overseas Press Club, and nine citations from Sigma Delta Chi, the journalism society.

The *Los Angeles Times* has moved into its second century of publication, with computers and a technology that would have sounded like bizarre science fiction to General Otis. When publisher Tom Johnson and editor William Thomas are asked what the next hundred years hold, they say they are content to cope with the next hundred days. So let us not dabble in prognostication either, but rest content with this celebration of the past.

D. D.

1881–1890

LOS ANGELES DAILY TIMES.

VOL. I. LOS ANGELES, CALIFORNIA, SUNDAY MORNING, DECEMBER 4, 1881. NO. 1.

THE GOLDEN GATE.

A Breezy Letter from the Times Correspondent.

The Business Boom at the Bay.—The Dirty-Dolliver Case and Other Cases—The Belt Shore Road.

[Special Correspondence of the DAILY TIMES.]

San Francisco, Dec. 1.

A great deal has been said recently in San Francisco newspapers about the "business boom" which has struck the city. It isn't always safe to credit the statements of merchants about their business, but there are several signs of prosperity which furnish the unfailing index of good times. Chief of these is the amount of advertising in the newspapers. When merchants are pinched by dull times, as they were three years ago at this time, they do not feel like spending money for advertisements. Another and a surer evidence is the number of buildings going up in all parts of the city. Several costly business blocks are in course of construction, notable among which are the huge structures of Senator Fair and of James G. Phelan; but these do not speak so plainly of abundant means as the many elegant private residences which are building in the Western addition. Van Ness Avenue used to end at Clay street; beyond that toward North Beach it struggled away with only an occasional dilapidated house to emphasize its width and aristocratic pretentions. Now some of the costliest private mansions are going up on this avenue between Clay and Pacific streets, while beyond, on Sackson and Fillmore and Washington streets the crop of

NEW BUILDINGS

May be seen in every direction. This mania for building is not confined, however to any quarter. Far out on California street, as one rides by on the cable road he will see many evidences of the same enterprise. New styles of architecture have been introduced, so that the old monotony of square houses with the inevitable tiers of bay windows has been broken up. The visitor to the city, who has not been here for a year or two, should not fail to take a ride out on California street and notice these new departures in architecture. Above all he will be struck by the Swiss country house, with its many gables, its picturesque roofs, its casemented windows and its general Old World air. It will also be noticed that the decorative art craze has done good service in introducing colored glass casements for windows and other devices which add immensely to the general effect of the buildings. One of the French party from Yorktown, now in this city, was much impressed with the beauty and variety of the new buildings in San Francisco and prophesied that a few years would see it the handsomest city on the continent.

But it was well that this French guest didn't inspect the workings of our laws. The Guiteau trial at the East is doing much to damage our laws in the eyes of European nations;-our local judges and lawyers are doing fully as much to bring law on this coast into contempt. The Hope burglary case was a shining example of the way law may be twisted for the sake of a criminal who has money to lavish on ingenious counsel. An equally flagrant case is occupying the court at present. It is known as the Dolliver case. Dolliver is an old merchant of this city, wealthy, white-haired, patriarchial—the sort of man who would make a good-looking deacon in an aristocratic church. For a long time it seems that his chief amusement has been to inveigle young girls of ten or twelve years into his rooms on Kearney street and there take improper liberties with them. He threatened them with

TERRIBLE VENGEANCE

if they told where they had been or what he had done, and he propitiated them with money and sweetmeats. Some of the children told their mothers, the mothers told the police and, singular to relate, the police went vigorously to work and investigated the ancient nuisance. They obtained a cloud of witnesses, they got a detective to prosecute the case, but Dolliver, with the aid of his lawyers, obtained postponement after postponement until he almost wearied out the prosecution's witnesses. Meanwhile he was moving heaven and earth to buy off the chief witnesses. The police laid a trap for him and caught one of his emissaries in the act of offering $200 as hush money to the mother of one of the girls who had been abused. But even this did not seem to stagger the defence. They counted on the judge, and as events have shown it appears they did not count in vain. Rosenbaum is the judge and his recent rulings in this case have been town talk for several days. Although it is a criminal case he ruled that the evidence should be taken with closed doors and reporters be rigorously excluded. Officer Maroney who preferred the charge against Dolliver was not allowed in Court, so that the prosecution failed to get the benefit of any suggestions which he might have made during the progress of the case. The trial is now going on with closed doors and the defense is preparing to bring in witnesses to show that the case is a conspiracy against their venerable client.

Judge Rosenbaum who has so singularly set aside the usual proceedings of the law in this case, is a fine example of the evils of the appointive system for the judiciary. He owes his place to the personal friendship of Governor Perkins and he never showed any sign of fitness for the responsible position which he now fills. A political "worker" may be a necessary animal in a canvass, but he is not eminently qualified for the bench.

Another equally flagrant case of the use of money to control legislation is furnished by the action of the retiring board of Supervisors of this city. They have before them two applications for franchise by rival railroad companies. One is called the "Ocean Shore Railroad," and is the application of the Atchison, Topeka and Santa Fe road to get terminal facilities in this city. The other is called the "Bay Shore Railroad," and is a device of

SHREWD SPECULATORS

to get a franchise to belt the city with a continuous railroad line, thus excluding all other roads from crossing their track. No one supposes that they would ever build the projected road, for it wouldn't pay. But the franchise would make them all wealthy, as the Central Pacific would pay a good round sum for it, in order to get control of the lower portion of Townsend street, and to rule out all rival lines. The Bay Shore party boasted that they had secured eight Supervisors, but when the matter came to a vote it was indefinitely postponed. Then the schemers turned to the courts, and they are now trying to get an injunction against granting the franchise removed. Dr. Cogswell, who presented the new Montgomery street fountain to the city, brought the injunction, as he owns four entire squares of property on Townsend street, and the road, if built, would ruin his lots for all business purposes. The plan of the Bay Shore people is now to get the injunction removed, and then bring the franchise once more before the Supervisors, and there is a fair chance of a gigantic job being put up on the community, while not a single tax payer has the power to lift a finger to prevent the outrage.

Everything is dull here except the holiday trade, which is just fairly begun. Theatres are suffering from bad weather and bad plays. The Baldwin has a new leading man, Vinton, who seems to have so much confidence in his fine face and manly figure that he disdains acting; the result is very slender houses, as the play, "Impudence," is dull. There is plenty of room every night in that huge cavern, the California Theatre, although Mrs. Oates gives a good show. The "Mascotte" has been presented here at the Tivoli Concert Garden, which probably prevents many from going to see it again. Billy Emerson is the only theatrical man who is making any money. He turned his fiftieth performance on Monday night and every house has been crowded. He gives a rollicking minstrel show, changes the bill every way, puts all his own life and dash into the performance, and the result is a big success. The most melancholy failure is taking place opposite Emerson.

G. H. F.

CUTTING WHALES IN TWO.

The Steamship Newport Runs into a School of Them.

[New York Sun.]

The Newport, of the New York and Cuba Mail Steamship Company, ran into a school of sperm whales off the Delaware capes on the last southward trip. It was about 8 o'clock in the morning, and Captain John P. Sundberg says he could see millions of them from the deck. He estimated the width of the school at a half a mile, and its length at twenty miles. The sea was smooth, the sun was shining, and all the passengers were on deck. The vessel was steaming at fifteen knots. Some of the whales were seventy feet long. One of them, about sixty-five feet long, was struck by the bow of the steamship at right angles and about in the middle of the body. The shock nearly threw the passengers from their feet. At the moment of the collision the whale threw up its flukes and deluged the fore part of the deck. Commissioner Alden S. Swan, of the Brooklyn Bridge, who was looking over the prow, was among the passengers who got drenched. The whale, Captain Sundberg says, was cut in two, the fore part going to one side of the vessel and the after part to the other. The sea was colored with blood. The head was driven down into the water so far that when it came up it arose six feet above the surface in plain sight of those who were looking over the side. The shock threw the steam steering gear temporarily out of order, but otherwise the vessel was not damaged. A few minutes later a second whale was cut in two, almost in the same manner as the first had been. The head went to the port side, but the body passed under the bottom, and was struck by the propeller blades. The effect of this on the machinery alarmed the engineer in the engine-room, who thought the blades had struck a drifting spar. The course of the vessel was then changed, and she ran out of the school.

A Product of the Morgue.

[New York Telegram.]

Last week the habitues of the Paris Morgue were greatly puzzled by a curious India-rubber leg that lay exposed for recognition on one of the slabs. It appears that the body of an elegantly dressed woman, apparently aged about 50, had been found in the Seine, above the bridge of St. Clond, but the body was so decomposed that it could not be kept. It was remarked, however, that the left leg, amputated at the thigh, had been replaced by an ingeniously constructed India-rubber leg, which was exhibited in the hope that it might lead to the identification of the owner.

A canvas of the city and suburban towns of Alameda county is being made for the enforcement of the Sunday law, and the churches, temperance societies and Christian associations are banding together for war. The liquor men are also rallying their forces and will make a fight against the enforcement of the law.

A VIAL OF VITRIOL.

An Unknown Scoundrel Hurls it on a Crowd.

The Fiery Fluid Burns Men, Women and Children—A Fiendish Crime at a Carnival in Philadelphia.

[Philadelphia Times, October 22.]

An absolutely fiendish instance of malicious mischief that might have resulted in the life-disfigurement of hundreds of people occurred on Thursday night in the main Centennial building. Forty-two men, women and children were burned and had their clothing ruined by the vitriol-thrower. A full gallon of the terrible acid was emptied over the crowd assembled in front of the space north of the Roosevelt organ by some villains concealed in the north-east gallery, who followed up their work by sending the heavy bottle crashing to the floor, the splintered glass flying in every direction. They then escaped through the skylight to the roof of the building and thence to the ground. The act was done so quickly, and the result so instantaneous, that the victims scarcely realized what was the matter until sufficient time had elapsed to permit the scoundrels to make good their escape. The injuries inflicted were principally upon ladies, of whom the greater part of the audience was composed. Four ladies were terribly burned about the neck, arms and hands. A twelve-year-old boy was burned on the right cheek, neck, and back, and a babe in arms had its little face and arms seared and scarred by the terrible fluid. Trifling burns were inflicted on fifteen other ladies and three gentlemen. The greatest damage, however, from a pecuniary point of view, was done to clothing. No less than seven silk dresses were utterly ruined. Hats and bonnets were burnt and spotted so as to render them useless, and lace trimmings shared the same fate. It was just before the grand hop began, at 8 o'clock, that the

CRIME WAS COMMITTED.

The audience consisted of about 500 persons, who were seated and standing in front of the space formerly used for roller skating. The first intimation of what was coming was received by Mrs. Deery, a lady stopping at the Irving House, who, in company with her daughter, had come to witness the performance. Mrs. Deery felt a drop of something on her neck like scalding water, and, looking up, received another drop on her head. She called to her daughter to step aside, and as she did so, several other ladies moved out of the way also, leaving a clear space of about three feet square. A moment later a volume of liquid came pouring down, and striking the floor splashed over those nearest. The crowd broke, and as they did so a gallon bottle was thrown violently from the northeastern gallery, and flew into hundreds of pieces as it struck the floor. There was an immediate stampede for the different points of exit. A lady with a child in her arms received about an ounce of the scorching stuff upon her bonnet, and the fluid trickling down, fell upon the child's cheek. The little one writhed in agony, screaming loudly. A boy standing near was burnt on the forehead and started a scene of confusion by his loud outcries, which were followed by screams of pain from a dozen others. The victims finally became composed enough to go out of the building in a body, numbering over forty, and twenty of them proceeded to the drug store at Fourth street and Girard avenue. The remainder suffered only trivial injuries and went to their homes. Dr. Harshberger's store was soon surrounded by a

CURIOUS CROWD,

and filled with a very indignant one. The walk from the main building, although short, had given the acid time to do its work, and the application of ammonia as an antidote was of no avail. The most seriously injured were found to be the boy, the infant and its mother. Their faces and necks were painfully seared, and their hands spotted in places. Mrs. Chambers of Sixteenth and Arch streets, had an expensive lace fichu almost entirely burned away by the quick-working acid, and her silk dress and overskirt was burnt in great spots. A Mrs. May, living in the neighborhood, of Twentieth and Arch streets, had her lace bonnet completely spoiled, and Mrs. and Miss Deery suffered the ruination of their silk dresses and dolmans. Miss Deery was scarred on one side of her face. Two gentlemen had holes burnt in their hats and coats, and one of them had one shoe eaten through.

So suddenly was the deed committed that no one could form any theory either as to its perpetrators or their design. Yesterday morning a son of Mrs. Deery called on the Superintendent of the building to have an investigation made, but that individual was inclined to treat the matter very lightly. He neither made any apology, expressed any regret, or offered to make good the damage done. The only plausible theory seems to be that some scoundrels, out of pure mischief, must have made their way unobserved to the floor of the gallery by the circular stairway, where the acid jars used to generate electricity are kept. A gallon jar of undiluted acid was kept there to replenish these jars, and it was that with which the work was done. The fragments of the broken bottle had been carefully removed yesterday and an effort made to have the matter hushed up. An investigation of the gallery from whence the acid was poured showed plainly that the gallon bottle had been lifted up to the railing, which is about three-and-one-half feet high, and then tilted over. The bottle was carried fully fifteen feet, and the distance to the floor beneath from the point from which it was poured was about forty feet. It is an impossibility for the disaster to have been caused by an accident. There are unmistakable evidences in the blackened wood eaten partly away to show that the bottle was lifted on the railing. The police are not bothering themselves about the matter.

Ingersoll's Poesy.

[St. Louis Globe-Democrat.]

One of Colonel R.G. Ingersoll's tricks of rhetoric—that of writing graceful prose in unconscious blank verse—was pointed out a few days ago, when his attack on Christianity and Judge Black's reply appeared together. It requires no great stretch of imagination to detect the same peculiarity in the eloquent orator's diatribe in the North American Review. The following sentences are iambic pentameters which halt scarcely more than the labored productions of some poets:

We did not get our freedom from the Church.
The great truth that all men are by Nature free
Was never told on Sinai's barren crags,
Nor by the lonely shores of Galilee.
If the lot of countles millions is to be
Eternal pain—better a thousand times
That all the constellations of the shoreless vast
Were eyeless darkness and eternal space.
Better that all is should cease to be.
Better that all the seeds and springs of things
Should fail and wither from great Nature's realm.
Better that causes and effects should lose
Relation and become unmeaning phrases and
Forgotten sounds. Better that every life
Should change to breathless death, to voiceless blank,
And every world to blind oblivion and
To moveless naught.

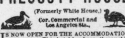

Los Angeles Daily Times.

VOL. I. LOS ANGELES, CALIFORNIA, SATURDAY MORNING, APRIL 15, 1882. NO. 114.

AFTERNOON DISPATCHES.

Captain Howgate, the Signal Service Thief, Escapes.

A Railroad From Jersey City to San Francisco Contemplated—Trouble on the Mexican Border.

WASHINGTON, April 14.—Captain Howgate made his escape to-day. He fled from the police, and the neighboring cities have been notified.

BOILER EXPLOSION.

A boiler explosion at Baltimore demolished the neighboring buildings and killed six men and wounded many others.

ENDORSING IRISH AGITATION.

The Land League Convention has adopted resolutions endorsing the Irish agitation and advising passive resistance.

ABSENTEES WANTED.

The Republican caucus of the House to-day is for the purpose of securing the presence of thirty Republican members now absent, as the Democrats are able to dictate the course of the House on the tariff and Chinese bills and in the contested election cases.

A NEW RAILROAD.

A bill was introduced in the Senate to-day for building a railroad from Jersey City to San Francisco.

DON'T KNOW WHICH WAY TO JUMP.

The Democrats are divided on the question of making tariff reform an issue of the campaign. Many are afraid to push it.

THE GRAVE OF THOMAS JEFFERSON.

The Senate passed the Indian Territory Railway bill. The House passed the Senate bill appropriating $10,000 for a monument over the grave of Thomas Jefferson.

EDMUNDS CONSIDERING.

The Senate Committee on Foreign Relations took up the Chinese bill today, but at the request of Senator Edmunds, who has been absent for several weeks, adjourned until Tuesday to give him time to consider it.

REVELATIONS ON A LAND GRANT.

The House Judiciary Committee has received a letter from James A. George, urging the forfeiture of the land grant to the Texas Pacific Railroad, which has lately been sold to the Southern Pacific. The grant was made to secure a competing line to the Pacific Coast, and comprises about 18,000,000 acres, and not a mile of the road has been built in the region covered by the grant. Mr. George declares that the grant was secured by bribery, and asked to be called as a witness.

THE LAST OF THE MOHICANS.

The *Critic* says Secretary Lincoln, the only member of the Cabinet appointed by President Garfield, will remain a short time longer and then he will be superseded by some one more in accord with the present Administration.

Another Double Tragedy.

CAMBRIDGE, Ohio, April 13.—John Nassett, a farmer, 65 years old, living five miles west of this place, to-day shot his son, E. Nassett, and then shot himself through the head, causing instant death.

Proving Guiteau Insane.

CHICAGO, April 14.—The attorney for Mrs. Scoville, in the proceedings to appoint a conservator for Guiteau's property, says that the case will certainly come up and insanity will probably be proved.

An Inspecting Tour.

FORTRESS MONROE, Va., April 13.—The President and party arrived to-day and inspected the Soldiers' Home and the Hampton Normal and Agricultural School for Indians. Later there was an informal reception at the hotel. The party left at five for Washington.

Crop Prospects.

MILWAUKEE, April 14.—The crop reports from important points in the West and Northwest show a materially decreased acreage in Minnesota, Iowa and Wisconsin, and a slight increase in Dakota and Manitoba. The ground is reported wet and cold, and seeding will be late.

A Terrible Storm.

MORGAN CITY, La., April 14.—A terrible storm last night devastated this section of the county. The destruction of stock, buildings, bridges, etc., is very heavy. A great loss of life is feared by the destruction of a gin house, where the flood refugees had collected.

The Anti-Polygamy Mormons.

INDEPENDENCE, Mo., April 14.—The Josephite Mormon Conference, which has been in session here for nine days, adjourned last evening to meet at Lamoni, Iowa, next autumn. The session has been harmonious and a large amount of business has been transacted.

The Mexican Blood Up.

SAN ANTONIO, April 14.—A telegram from Laredo announces that the Mexican authorities have stationed several companies of infantry along the Rio Grande, opposite the city, and refuse to allow Americans to cross. The trouble is caused on account of the United States authorities holding and refusing to give up cattle belonging to Mexicans that strayed across the river. The facts were reported to both governments.

New York Items.

NEW YORK, April 14.—The Chinese Minister visited General Hancock at Governor's Island yesterday. He was received with honors. A salute was was fired, etc.

The *Herald's* Paris reporters have failed to find Parnell. If in the city he keeps close.

The Union League Club (Republican), last night passed resolutions approving the veto of the Chinese bill.

A Buffalo Bank Closed.

BUFFALO, April 14.—The First National Bank closed its doors to-day. A large number of drafts issued to live stock dealers, drawn on the Fourth National Bank of New York, on the 4th instant and since that date, were yesterday dishonored in New York. The extent of the drafts unpaid cannot be ascertained now, but it is thought this will be a large failure. It will seriously affect a large number of cattle dealers who sent their drafts in payment for stock sold by them. It is believed the depositors will be paid in full.

Restraining the Liquor Traffic.

HARTFORD, Conn., April 14.—Both branches of the Legislature passed a bill restraining the traffic in intoxicating liquors. The present local option system will be retained.

The Knights of Honor.

SAN FRANCISCO, April 13.—The Grand Lodge of the Knights of Honor of California elected last evening the following officers: Grand Dictator, R. R. Webster; Grand Vice-Dictator, J.W. Ward, Jr; Grand Assistant Dictator, M. M. Stern; Grand Guide, H. L. Lusk; Grand Chaplain, G.W. Lemont; Grand Reporter, W. H. Money; Grand Treasurer, R. H. Warfield; Grand Guardian, S. American; Grand Sentinel, J. M. Linart; Grand Trustee, R. A. Johnson; Medical Examiner, Lee G. Rodgers.

He Preferred Sleeping in the Barn.

A few days since Mr. Grattan purchased a checker-board, and when he took it home in the evening he said to his wife:

"Well, Martha, we'll have a game or two before we go over to the social. I expect to beat you all to flinders, but you won't care."

"Of course not, and if I beat you why you won't care," she replied.

They sat down, and he claimed the first move. She at once objected, but when he began to grow red in the face she yielded and he led off. At the fourth move she took a man, chuckling as she raked him in.

"I don't see anything to grin at," he sneered, as he moved a man backward.

"Here! you can't move that way!" she called out.

"I can't, eh? Perhaps I never played checkers before you were born!"

She saw a chance to jump two more men, and gave in th· point, but as she moved he cried out:

"Put them men right back there! I've concluded not to move backward, even if Hoyle does permit it!"

She gave in again, but when he jumped a man her nose grew red and she cried out:

"I didn't mean to move there; I was thinking of the social."

"Can't help the social, Martha—we must go by Hoyle."

In about two minutes she jumped two men and went into the king row shouting:

"Crown him! crown him! I've got a king!"

"One would think by your childish actions that you never played a game before," he growled.

"I know enough to beat you!"

"You do, eh? Some folks are awful smart."

"And some folks ain't!" she snapped, as her king captured another man.

"What are you jumping that way for?"

"A king can jump any way."

"No, he can't."

"Yes, he can!"

"Don't talk back to me, Martha Grattan! I was playing checkers when you were in your cradle!"

"I don't care! I can jump two men whichever way you move!"

He looked down on the board, saw that such was the case, and roared out:

"You've moved twice to my once."

"I haven't!"

"I'll take my oath you have! I can't play against any such gambling practices!"

"Who is a gambler? You not only cheated, but you tried to lie out of it!"

Board and checkers fell between them. He could get on his hat quicker than she could find her bonnet, and that was the only reason why he got out of the house first.

A grocer found him sitting on a basket of cranberries at the door as he was closing up for the night, and asked him if he was waiting for his wife to come along.

"Well, not exactly; I stopped here to feel in my pocket for the key of the barn. I shall sleep on the hay to-night, and see if it won't cure this cold in my head.

A Financial Anecdote.

Theodore was a poor lad. One day, when he was very hungry, he espied a five-cent piece on the floor of the broker's office, which he was sweeping out. He had remembered stories wherein little boys had picked up a small piece of money, handed it to the great merchant or rich banker and been immediately taken into partnership. So Theodore stepped up to the door of the broker's private room and said, "Please, sir, here's a five cent piece I found on your floor." The broker looked at Theodore a moment and then said: "You found that on my floor, did you? And you are hungry, aren't you?" "Yes, sir," replied Theodore. "Well, give it to me and get out. I was looking around for a partner, but a boy who doesn't know enough to buy bread when he is starving to death would make but a sorry broker. No, boy, I can't take you into the firm." And Theodore never became a great broker. Honesty is the best policy, children, but it is not indispensable to success in the brokerage business.—*Boston Transcript.*

Dr. Bliss Gets Even.

The editor of the *Evening Critic* tells the following at his own expense:

He had been suffering for a week past with a carbuncle on his neck. Yesterday he called at Dr. Bliss's office to have it lanced. Bliss cut and slashed so vigorously that poor Buell fairly howled in pain. "In heaven's name, Bliss, are you trying to murder me?"

"Oh, no!" was the phlegmatic reply. "You said in your paper last summer, during Garfield's illness, that I was squeamish in using a knife. I'm only showing you that I am not," and he cut harder than ever.—*Buffalo Advertiser.*

What a very funny world this is! Eastern Republican journals charge the Democrats with the *disgrace* of having passed the Chinese bill, while Democratic papers lay the blame at the door of the Republicans. Turn we to the West! Democratic publications claim for their party the *honor* of having passed the bill, while those of a Republican tendency make the same claim for their party.

Eureka *Leader*: "Ive hurt my leg," said a damsel who fell on the ice at the rink the other night, to a gentleman who went to her assistance, "and there is a lump on it. Just feel it." The man's face assumed the color of the rainbow, and he whispered that he wouldn't just then, cause the old woman was over the way a lookin'.

SOUTHERN CALIFORNIA.

What a Gentleman Observed in an Eight Months' Residence.

The Climate—Variation of Thermometer—The Winter's Drouths—Products—Markets—Health, Etc.

IT is the purpose of the writer to answer some questions asked by persons at a distance as to Southern California. A residence of eight months has given some opportunities of observation, and he can speak only of Los Angeles and what he has known of it since July 1st, 1881.

The question of climate stands first of all. Is it what was expected? No. In the absence of definite report on this point an uncomfortable heat was anticipated. No advantage was hoped for to one coming from an altitude of over 5,000 feet above the tides, and from a higher altitude by nearly six degrees, and yet the advantage was most decided, and a most happy sense of relief experienced. A daily statement shows an average variation of 19 degrees from morning until noon. Throughout the month of July the highest mercury was 84 degrees, the lowest 50. Throughout the month of August the variation was three degrees higher than the month preceding. The average was much increased by the marked heat of the 6th, 7th and 8th days of this month. On the 6th the mercury rose to 102 degrees at 1 P. M. This with the two following days were decidedly hot and uncomfortable, and yet the evenings and nights were not sultry. Thus out of 60 there were only three that could be called really hot days. The almost invariable winds from the coast, springing up in the morning from the south and bearing around to the west in the after part of the day, delightfully modified the heat that would otherwise have been intense.

Is it cold in winter? Yes, at least colder than had been anticipated. To one who expects to find fires and winter clothes no longer necessary, California will furnish a surprise. When the mercury falls to the neighborhood of 30 degrees there must be ice, and this is sometimes the case. Frosts are not unfrequent, but when orange trees will bloom and flowers flourish out of doors in winter the cold cannot be intense. The average variation from dawn until noon throughout the month of January was 20 degrees; the highest mercury was 70 degrees, the lowest 30 degrees. On the 12th of January we had a light fall of snow which disappeared in less than two hours. Thus it will be seen that both in summer and in winter we have colder weather than many imagine to be possible in Southern California.

Are not the droughts a serious drawback? A dry year in any part of the country must be attended with more or less of distress to certain interests. Once in five, some say once in each seven years, there is such a drought as permits on profitable vegetation outside of water lines. But in this respect California resembles other States whose reputation for profitable culture is well assured. There are Western States where it is safe to say that once in three years the crops are almost totally destroyed, either by drought on the one hand, or immoderate rains on the other. Southern California has never suffered from floods upon her growing or maturing crops. Comparison in this respect is very favorable to this State, there being an increased certainty of a crop. The living streams of the Coast Range of mountains furnish unfailing irrigation to a large scope of country within the lines of which there is no such thing as failure. Outside of water limits there is the possibility of losing a crop once in five years, and four crops out of five in any country is an excellent showing.

Is there a diversity of products in the country? It is quite within the bounds of truth to say that there is no section of equal breath upon the whole continent where a greater variety of things can be produced. In the list of both citrus and deciduous fruits we omit scarcely any from the list. The apple flourishes beside the orange; the apricot and the Bartlett pear grow quite as well as the lemon; the peach, the nectarine and the fig grow side by side. The English walnut, the almond and the olive find here grateful surroundings.

The ocean front is not considered favorable to the growing of wheat, owing to the liability to rust, but back in its sheltering valleys very fine crops are raised. Barley is the great grain product of the country, and the hay made from it in its unripened state as well as the ripened grain itself, constitute a valuable feed for all kinds of stock. This is harvested early enough to permit a crop of corn to be grown on the same space the same year. Under favorable conditions may be seen corn that would compare well with that raised on the dark loamy fields of Illinois.

The question is asked, Have you a market? Happily, at last, we can answer, yes. Until about one year ago San Francisco was the chief market, and transportation was so high as to leave but a trifling margin fo the producer. All this is changed by the Southern Pacific railroad, that has opened toward the East a market for everything that can be raised. Our oranges and lemons are now in competition with like fruits from other parts of the world.

By this it will be seen that the railroads are making such concessions as will permit the producer to reap the reward of his labors. These are considerations that fully justify the large onpouring of people from all parts of the country, who find in this genial climate a gratifying union of pleasure and profit.

The question of health has induced perhaps a larger percentage of immigration than any other single cause. As a last resort invalids who have tried the most favored health resorts of the world turn to Southern California as their last earthly hope. Alas! in many cases no climate can do more than to bring temporary relief and prolong the life beyond what could be hoped for in climates more violent. In instances, not a few, where death seemed inevitable, this climate has wrought a cure. As to the absolute certainty of benefit in any given case, no one can say in advance. With abundance of fruit and the chance to be in the sunshine and open air so much of the time, the probabilities are in favor of benefit to almost any case of chronic sickness. However, an actual trial must be made, and, where it is practicable this should be done before a permanent removal is made.

COAST NOTES.

Eighteen hundred barrels of flour have been shipped from Gridley to Texas, and orders for 2,000 more have been received.

The Union Pacific is so crowded with emigrants and other passengers along the line that the road is short of cars to carry them.

The Democratic Central Committee of Sacramento county, will hold a meeting on the 15th inst. at the Capital Hotel, Sacramento.

A street railroad operated on the San Francisco cable plan is to be constructed between Butte City, M. T., and Walkerville, the coming season.

Thomas Nurse, a farmer living three miles from Ione, was killed on the 5th instant, by W. Kirkendall, a neighbor. A dispute about land led to the killing.

The last of the four robbers who broke into a freight car at Lovelock, Nev., was arrested recently. The other three pleaded guilty and were sent to State Prison.

Three Chinamen of Stockton were arrested recently for fishing with a seine, near Bum's cut-off. One of them paid $65 fine and the other two were discharged.

The Alta miners of Gold Hill, Nev., raised a purse of $22, on the last payday, for the family of Malachi Curran, who was accidentally struck in the eye with a pick by a fellow-miner.

Utah potatoes now command ninety cents a bushel at retail in Salt Lake. This is the highest price that has ruled there for ten or fifteen years, and is caused by the great demand in California and Colorado.

Charley Callahan was arrested in Bedford, M. T., last week on the charge of carrying concealed weapons. His lawyer cleared him by making the plea the Colt navy Charley was carrying was too big to be concealed.

The Chinese servants of Olympia, W. T., have struck for higher wages. The citizens intend to hold a meeting to arrange a schedule of prices. A movement is also on foot to bring white labor to take the Chinamen's places.

A diminutive babe, weighing eight ounces, was born to a miner's wife in Candelaria recently. Its face is about the size of a horse chestnut, and a ring worn upon the little finger of its mother was easily pulled over the babe's foot and drawn nearly up to its knee.

On the Stanford vineyard ditch, at Vina, says the Chico *Enterprise*, there have been seventy-five white men at work until last week, receiving one dollar a day and board. These have all been discharged and one hundred and thirty-five Chinamen hired to take their places at one dollar a day and board themselves.

Grass Valley last week sent a praying and singing band up to Nevada City to reclaim sinners in the streets. This missionary crusading effort of Grass Valley on behalf of its rival city was not received in the spirit it deserved, for the unrighteous turned out a band of hoodlums to jeer at the missionaries, and they would have laid hands on the Christians but for the interference of the police.

Half a century ago the average of a Minister in a French Cabinet was sixty-five. Twenty-five years ago it fell to sixty. The new Cabinet is the youngest that has been known in France. Its oldest member is only sixty-two, its youngest thirty-five. M. Gambetta, its chief, is only forty-three. The twelve Ministers count between them six hundred and twelve and a half years, giving an average of a little over fifty-one years for each Minister.

At a crowded French country theatre a woman fell from the gallery to the pit, and was picked up by one of the spectators, who, hearing her groaning, asked her if she was much injured. "Much injured!" exclaimed the woman, "I should think I am. I have lost the best seat in the very middle of the front row."

The custom of leading marriage notices with the names of the high contracting parties separated by a dash, gives sometimes a curious combination. Among the notices in a Philadelphia paper on Saturday were three headed, "Birch—Twiggs," "Fort—Reed," and "Price—Given."

LOS ANGELES DAILY TIMES.

VOL. IV. LOS ANGELES, CALIFORNIA, WEDNESDAY MORNING, NOVEMBER 7, 1883. 132.

Let the Bird Loose!

APPOMATOX!

The Dose the Democrats Got Yesterday

In Massachusetts, New York, Pennsylvania, Connecticut,

And all Along the Republican Line.

"THIS FINISHES BUTLER."

See the Republican Majorities:

Massachusetts, : :	17,000
New York, : : :	30,000
Pennsylvania, : :	8,000
Minnesota, : : :	18,000

And Then There are Connecticut and Nebraska in the Same Column.

The Old Dominion is Captured by the Readjusters.

The Democratic Column: New Jersey, Maryland and Mississippi.

A GOOD BEGINNING FOR 1884.

MASSACHUSETTS.

THE OLD BAY STATE REPUDIATES BUTLER.

WORCESTER, Nov. 7.—The election is passing off quietly, with every indication of a large vote. The Republicans are especially active and confident. In the Eighth Ward, a warden pro tem. was elected and found to be a minor after two or three hundred votes had been cast. At first it was feared the mistake would be fatal, but the law decisions are that the ballots cast will be rejected in counting. The indications point to the largest vote ever known.

BOSTON, Nov. 6.—The weather to-day throughout the State is favorable for a very heavy vote. In this city at 1 o'clock in ward 4 the vote stood: For Butler, 153; Robinson, 274. In ward 10 at 11 o'clock the Republican majority was 575. In ward 24 it was considered that half the votes cast at 10 o'clock were Republicans.

In Newton indications are for a Republican majority.

In Waltham the Republicans are claiming a majority.

In Dedham at 10 o'clock Robinson had 270, against Butler's 101.

In Malden, at noon Robinson was 100 to 600 for Butler.

In Lowell, at 10 o'clock the vote stood: Butler, 1,050; Robinson, 259.

Gloucester, at the same time, Butler, 691; Robinson, 122.

At Fall River the total vote, 6,000, will be close, and the Republicans claim they will be able to reduce Butler's majority to 800.

Precinct 5, ward 11, of Boston, which gave Bishop 253 last year, shows at noon 500 plurality for Robinson.

Returns from precincts and various wards show considerable Republican gains over last year. An unprecedented number of votes were cast early in the day. One ward, which had many colored voters, at 11 o'clock showed a total of 602 for Robinson, and 359 for Butler.

BOSTON, Nov. 6.—Sixty-one towns, including Lynn, Lowell, Fall River, Taunton, Newburyport and Fitchburg, give Robinson, 29,978; Butler, 26,579; majority for Robinson, 3299. Lowell gives Butler, 1092 majority against 1527 last year.

SALEM, Nov. 6.—Largest vote for years. Appearance indicate that Butler's majority of last year will be materially cut, if not entirely wiped out. The Republicans claim the city by 100 majority against last year's majority of about 400 for Butler.

BOSTON, Mass., Nov. 6.—The first complete return received is that of Ward 3: Butler, 47; Robinson, 39; Republican gain of 4 over last year.

The complete vote of Boston, as given by the Journal, is: Butler, 32,165; Robinson, 25,954. Butler's majority, 6,211. Last year Boston gave Butler 30,357; Bishop, 17,005; Almy, 218. If these figures are substantiated by later returns, they will doubtless give the State to the Republicans.

BOSTON, Mass., Nov. 6.—At Republican headquarters Chairman Lodge said the State has undoubtedly gone Republican.

Ward six of Lowell, Butler's home, gives Butler 816; Robinson, 719; Butler's loss, 97.

Salem, which last year gave Butler a majority of 392, has gone for Robinson by 25 majority.

Lynn gives Butler a gain of 93 on his vote of a year ago, while Fall River shows a Republican gain over last year of 636.

BOSTON, Nov. 6.—Butler's plurality in Boston is six thousand behind last year's. Eighty-five cities and towns heard from indicate that the vote of the State will be: Robinson, 155,000; Butler, 135,000; scattering, 3000. The Republicans claim 30,000 majority on the State ticket. They elect seven out of the eight Governor's Counsellors, twenty-seven of forty Senators, and 160 out of 240 representatives.

BOSTON, Nov. 6.—Two hundred and thirty two cities and towns give Butler 124,404; Robinson, 129,807. The same towns in '82 gave Butler 112,100 and the Republicans 93,591. The indication are that Robinson will carry the State by ten thousand majority. Chicopee, Robinson's home, which gave Butler last year a majority of 256, gives Robinson a majority of 24. Lieut-Governor Ames is undoubtedly elected, in many places running ahead of his ticket. The excitement in the city is intense, crowds packing the streets in a solid mass.

BOSTON, Nov. 6.—Butler is defeated in Massachusetts by 15,600.

BOSTON, November 6.—The indications at this hour are that Massachusetts has elected a Republican Governor by 17,000 majority, and has three-fourths of the whole legislative machinery.

BOSTON, Nov. 6, midnight.—The Globe, Democratic organ, concedes the election of Robinson by 10,000 majority. Other papers claim the majority to be 20,000. The Boston Traveler says that Lt-Gov. Ames is elected by 25,000 majority.

BOSTON, Nov. 6.—The Senate, as far as the returns indicate, stands 16 Republicans, 7 Democrats, with 17 districts to hear from.

NEW JERSEY.

PROBABLE DEMOCRATIC SUCCESS.

Trenton, Nov. 6.—Middlesex Co. gives Abbett 300 majority. Democratic Assemblymen are elected in the 1st, 2d and 3d districts. Princeton City gives Dixon for Governor 48 majority; Vanderbilt (Dem.) for Senator, 83 majority, and [illegible]

NEW YORK.

THIRTY THOUSAND REPUBLICAN MAJORITY.

NEW YORK, Nov. 6.—The weather is fine and indications of a large vote. 178 of the 688 election districts in this city give Carr (Rep.) for Secretary of State, 17,103; Maynard (Dem.), 1?,650. For Attorney General O'brien (Dem.) has 21,630; Russell (Rep.), 15,356. These figures show that Maynard has been cut, as it was promised he would be, by the liquor dealers.

ALBANY, Nov. 6.—The election is quiet. A heavy vote was polled early. In the Republican wards Carr is being freely cut and the indications are that Maynard will run ahead of his ticket in the city.

Brooklyn, Nov. 6.—In this city, 100 districts give Maynard, 24,131; Carr, 22,448; Chapin, 25,081; Davenport, 21,275; majority for Maynard, 1683.

New York City, Nov. 6.—Three hundred and sixty-three districts out of 688, give Carr, 35,117; Maynard, 45,870; Gates, 217; Beecher, 250; Russell, 30,508.

Brooklyn, Nov. 6.—One hundred and thirty-five districts give Maynard, 30,519; Carr, 29,543; Chapin, 22,617; Davenport, 28,073; Maynard's majority, 106.

New York City, Nov. 6.—Returns show an apparant majority for the Democratic State ticket of 4700, excepting Maynard, who runs 1000 behind. The Democrats claim that Low is beaten by 3000 in Brooklyn.

New York City, Nov. 6, 9:56 p. m.—The Fifth Senate district complete gives Murphy, 11,805; Hovey, 6047.

New York, Nov. 6.—Four hundred and forty eight city election districts give Hess, 41,130; Reilly, 46,000; O'Brien, 10,009.

Brooklyn, Nov. 6.—In this city the vote for Mayor, as far as counted, Hendrix leads by 2692.

New York City, Nov. 6.—The Ninth Senate district complete gives Fitzgerald, 10,947; Cullin, 1155.

Brooklyn, Nov. 6.—Returns indicate the election of Willard Bartlett for Supreme Court Justice.

Brooklyn, Nov. 6.—Kernan and Jacobs, (Dem.) and Daggett, (Rep.) are elected Senators. The following is the total vote of Brooklyn for Secretary of State and Comptroller: Maynard, 46,991; Carr, 47,266.

Brooklyn, midnight, Nov. 6.—Figures received up to this hour indicate the election of Hendrix. Complete returns may change this result by morning. The Democrats have elected their county ticket, and claim 10 out of the 12 assemblymen. The Democratic Aldermen at large are elected, and the Republican candidate in the Second District. In the First and Third Districts the Democrats claim to have won. In Rockland county, Maynard's majority, 439; Nelson (Dem.), for Senator, 440 majority. Assemblyman in doubt.

Brooklyn, N. Y., Nov. 7, 12:30 a. m.—Sixty-four districts heard from: Hendrix, 14,482; Low, 13,760.

Brooklyn, Nov. 7, 2:30, a. m.—118 districts give Low, 44,138; Hendrix, 33,510. Low's majority, 6,282. There are 212 election districts in the city.

New York, Nov. 6.—New York has gone Republican by 30,000.

PENNSYLVANIA.

EIGHT THOUSAND REPUBLICAN MAJORITY.

PITTSBURG, Nov. 6.—The day is close and warm and threatening rain. The election is passing off quietly. No disturbance is reported up to noon. A very light vote was polled.

PHILADELPHIA, Nov. 6.—The weather to-day is fine and the indications are that a much larger vote will be polled in the State than anticipated by party managers. The contest in the State presents no other issue than the regular one between the Republicans and Democrats. The candidates on the State ticket are J. B. Niles (Rep.) and Robert Taggart (Dem.), for Auditor General, and Wm. Livezy (Rep.) and Joseph Powell (Dem.), for State Treasurer. The Greenback and Prohibition parties both have candidates in the field for these places, but their vote is so small as not to be a factor in the fight. It is agreed between the leaders of the Democratic and Republican sides that the comparison of figures shall be made with last year's election for Governor. The combined vote of Beard (Rep.) and Stewart (Ind.) will be set against that of Pattison (Dem.), so that the gains for the Democrats to-day will mean, as against the full Republican vote, that the Democrats will have to gain some 4000 on the full vote in order to elect their ticket to-day.

In this city the interest centers chiefly on the Controllership. S. Davis Page has been indorsed by the Committee of One Hundred for that office, while Harper E. Jeffreys is running as a straight-out. As the Committee of One Hundred is a large factor in municipal politics here, the election of Page is expected.

New York, Nov. 6, 11:10 p. m.—The returns come in very slowly from Pennsylvania, and nothing definite is known up to this hour.

Philadelphia, Nov. 6.—At 11:30 o'clock only 24 counties out of 67 had been heard from. These show net Republican gains of 4564.

Philadelphia, Nov. 7, 1:15 a. m.—The Republican State ticket has 20,000 majority in Philadelphia. Estimated majority in the State, 8000.

CONNECTICUT.

THE REPUBLICANS SWEEP THE LEGISLATURE.

Hartford, Conn., Nov. 6.—Hartford goes Republican by 300, electing a Senator and two Representatives. Hartford county elected a Republican sheriff. Republicans claim the Legislature by 40 majority joint ballot, and probably 9 out of the 12 Senators. Republican sheriffs are elected in Hartford, Tolland, Middlesex, Fairfield and New London counties.

Hartford, Nov. 6, 8:15 p. m.—The Republicans carry Hartford by 600 majority.

Hartford, Conn., Nov. 6.—Returns received at 8 o'clock show that the Republicans have carried the Legislature by probably forty majority on joint ballot, and probably have nine of the twelve Senators. This will make the next Senate stand fourteen Republicans to ten Democrats.

Hartford, Nov. 6.—The Senate will now stand 15 Republicans and 9 Democrats—a Republican gain of 2; House, Republicans 101, Democrats 9—Republican gain 11.

MARYLAND.

BALTIMORE DEMOCRATIC SAME AS BEFORE.

BALTIMORE, Nov. 6.—The election in this State to-day is for Governor, State Comptroller, Attorney General and members of the Legislature, excepting one-half the Senate, who hold over, all county Judges, and in Baltimore, the Judge of the Court of Appeals, Clerk of the Supreme Court, Sheriff, State's Attorney, three Judges of the Orphans' Court and City Surveyor.

Baltimore, Nov. 6.—Returns from several wards indicate that McLane's (Dem.) majority in this city will be 7000.

VIRGINIA.

MAHONE CLAIMS THE LEGISLATURE.

PETERSBURG, Va., Nov. 6.—Mayor Jarrett addressed a Readjuster meeting last night. He called upon the blacks and whites to observe proper order to-day and avoid all difficulties. He was followed by Attorney General Blair and other speakers. Among those on the platform was Senator Mahone. In the interest of a quiet election to-day all bar-rooms were closed last night. An extra police force is on duty. The Readjusters distributed yesterday afternoon circulars calling on the negroes to avenge the death of the six negroes killed at Danville, at the ballot box to-day by voting the Readjusters' ticket.

SENATOR MAHONE AT THE POLLS.

PETERSBURG, Va., Nov. 6.—The election is passing off quietly. Both parties are polling a heavy vote. The Democrats claim that if they get four hundred negro votes they will carry the city. Senator Mahone visited the different precincts.

WASHINGTON, Nov. 6.—The Virginia election and the possibility of trouble in connection therewith, is the all-absorbing topic of discussion here to-day. At Alexandria two-thirds of the vote was polled, at noon, without disturbance.

DANVILLE, Va., Nov. 6.—After the Mayor's proclamation, announcing arrangements for preserving the peace, and stating that those arrangements were deemed complete and reliable, Witcher, acting chairman of the Liberal Coalition party, and George C. Cable, chairman of the Democratic party, requested the Mayor, as an additional means of preserving the peace, to forbid any assembly of men of either party, white or colored, at any public speaking, parade or procession, till the 8th inst. These orders were issued by a [illegible] received by City Sergeant Wood last night, stating that he (the Governor) sent troops to Danville from Richmond. Capt. Wood replied, after consulting with leading citizens, that it was not necessary to send troops. This morning the Richmond Light Infantry Blues and a section of the Richmond Howitzers, came from Richmond. A piece of artillery was planted on the main street, near the Arlington Hotel. The Coalition judges of election having declined serving, others were appointed. Very few negroes voted. Not more than a dozen votes were given at one ward where they have large registered majority.

Richmond, Va., Nov. 6.—The election in this State passed off quietly; no trouble in this city or Danville. Nothing definite is known of the result of the election, which is claimed by both parties.

The negroes refused to vote in Richmond and Danville, fearing trouble.

Richmond, Va., Nov. 6.—The Democrats have carried Winchester, the first time in seven years. The Democrats expect to have a majority in the Senate, and possibly in the House of Delegates. Neither side, however, has as yet received information enough to justify any positive statement.

Richmond, Va., Nov. 6.—The election in this State was the most exciting since '69, when the Conservative party was organized. Half the Senate and the entire House of Delegates were elected to-day. This Legislature reapportions the State for Congressional representation and elects most of the heads of the State departments. The new Senators vote for a successor to U. S. Senator Mahone. The race issue was never before so strongly marked.

Richmond, Va., Nov. 8.—The Democratic majority in this city is 2611. Thirteen cities in the State all show Democratic gains, except Norfolk.

Petersburg, Nov. 6.—Mahone claims from returns received up to midnight that the Readjuster party has gained 4 counties and the city of Norfolk; that they will have a continual majority in both branches of the Legislature.

MINNESOTA.

TWELVE TO EIGHTEEN THOUSAND REPUBLICAN MAJORITY.

ST. PAUL, Nov. 6th.—The election in this State to-day is for Governor, Lieutenant-Governor, Secretary of State, Treasurer, Attorney-General and Railroad Commissioners. Each county also elects a portion of their officers. It is a beautiful day and an unusually large vote is being polled, with the main fight between the candidates for Governor. The Republicans renominated the entire present State officers, with Governor Hubbard at the head of the ticket. The Democrats have nominated for Governor, N. A. Bierman, a Norwegian, and as a large proportion of the Republican voters of this State are of that nationality, the Democrats hope to make a close fight for that office. Governor Hubbard had a majority of 20,000 last time, and leading Republicans claim 10,000 for him this time. Few Democrats concede more than 5,000.

St. Paul, Minn., Nov. 6.—68 towns heard from in Minnesota, up to 10 o'clock p. m., outside of St. Paul and Minneapolis, give Hubbard (Rep.) for Governor 2044 majority over Birman, the Democratic candidate. In these towns much scratching was done on the balance of the ticket, but they show a Republican majority varying very little from that for Governor. The Secretary of the Central Republican Committee estimates from present returns that Hubbard's majority will not be less than 12,000. The balance of the Republican ticket is elected by 18,000 majority.

St. Paul, Minn., Nov. 6, 11 p. m.—One hundred and one towns give Hubbard (Rep.) 2290 majority over Birman (Dem.). Eighty-seven towns give Gilman (Rep.) 2600 majority over Frazer (Dem.); Van Daumbach (Rep.) for Secretary of State, has 2700 majority over Greenhahn. The Republican candidate for Attorney General has 2900 majority over Willlis.

NEBRASKA.

THE STATE TRUE TO HER EARLY PRINCIPLES.

Lincoln, Neb., Nov. 6.—Weather is fine and a good vote will be polled. Reports will be made on the vote for Supreme Judge and comparisons with last year, when Dawes lacked one thousand of a majority over the Democrats and Anti-monopolists.

Omaha,—10, p. m. Owing to the universal scratching of tickets in all parts of the State, reports will be very late.

Scattering reports indicate a Republican majority of six to eight thousand. The returns are coming in slowly and will not be complete until morning.

MISSISSIPPI.

THE DEMOCRATS SWEEP THE STATE OF COURSE.

Memphis, Tenn., Nov. 6.—Meager election returns from Mississippi indicate a sweeping Democratic victory, so far as heard from. Election was quiet.

Memphis, Nov. 7, 12:25 a.m.—The Democrats had no opposition in the State except in a few districts, where the Republicans and Democrats combined on a fusion ticket against the Independents, and Democratic and fusion tickets were elected.

KANSAS.

AN UNIMPORTANT ELECTION.

St. Louis, Nov. 6.—A dispatch from Topeka, Kansas, to the Associated Press here says there will be but meagre election returns from Kansas to-night. Only county officers and judges are to be elected, but as there are three or four tickets each county will take till morning to count the votes.

PRESS COMMENTS.

"This Finishes Butler"—Massachusetts Has Spoken in Earnest.

BOSTON, Mass., Nov. 6.—The Herald says: "This finishes Butler. Massachusetts has spoken in earnest, and with a full voice, 'Never more be officer of mine.' It is true he has not been able permanently to injure Massachusetts, for his power is limited and her institutions are strong. The disgrace was in electing him. The State will survive and look back with shame upon this wild Butler frolic, when Butler is dust. The Democrats of Massachusetts will rue the day when, in defiance of principle and honor, and for the hope of spoils, they allowed such a demagogue to capture their party. The great victory achieved is not a victory for party, but for all citizens who love the State and approve decency in office. All honor to the Democrats who refused to bow the knee to the demagogue."

"THE APPOMATOX OF BUTLERISM."

The Journal says, editorially: "What Appomatox was to the Confederacy, the election yesterday was to Butler and Butlerism. Both man and thing have been annihilated. For such result done, the people, not only of Massachusetts, but of both parties throughout the country, should be profoundly thankful, because the one man in this country who could rally about him the ignorant and vicious element has been cast down for the last time."

THE BAY STATE VICTOR.

Reception to Governor-elect Robinson at Springfield City Hall.

SPRINGFIELD, Mass., Nov. 6.—The reception to Governor-elect Robinson at Springfield City Hall, at 10 this evening, was an unprecedented ovation for this locality. He came from Chicopee by special train, and was escorted to the hall by the band and a committee, and introduced as the first Governor of Massachusetts ever elected from Hampden county. As soon as Robinson had finished there was a general handshaking for a few minutes, and then 2,000 people escorted Robinson through the main street to the depot, and as he took the train the band played "Auld Lang Syne."

THE THUNDERS OF VICTORY.

WORCESTER, Mass., Nov. 6.—A salute of one hundred guns was fired by the Republicans to-night.

A gentleman of Santa Barbara has in his cabinet of curiosities several sets of false teeth exhumed from the graves of aborigines on the Santa Barbara Islands. They are formed each from a shell, which was fashioned to fit the roof of the mouth, and could be adjusted outside of the gums. These false teeth are perfectly formed and easily [illegible]

PACIFIC COAST NEWS.

[illegible]

SAN FRANCISCO, Nov. 6.—Mrs. Leavitt, the temperance lecturer, at a meeting of the International Lodge of Good Templars last night, declared that most of the present incumbents of offices of trust were either heavy drinkers or the enemies of prohibition. She dwelt severely on Governor Butler, styling him an "cock-eyed blackguard and an enemy of temperance." "President Arthur," she said, "is a very heavy drinker. Many a night before he was nominated Vice President, he would sleep the sleep of the drunken in low grog-shops in New York. Even now, when he complains of afternoon headaches, it is whisky that is the trouble." Mrs. Leavitt closed her remarks by advocating woman's rights, that the obtaining of them would have the effect of producing total abstinence in the land.

THE STRANGLER EXCEPTS.

Counsel for Le Roy, the strangler and murderer of Nicholas Sherrett, has filed a bill of exceptions in the Superior Court. The case is to be carried to the Supreme Court.

BLIGHTED AFFECTIONS, PERFIDY AND PHOTOGRAPHY.

SAN FRANCISCO, Nov. 6.—In the matter of the application of the defendant in the case of Sarah Althea Hill vs. Wm. Sharon for an order allowing him to inspect a certain document alleged to be in the possession of plaintiff, which she claims to be a marriage contract between the parties, came up for hearing before Superior Judge Finn this morning. An order was made by the Court and plaintiff given until Thursday at 12 o'clock to produce a photographic copy of the marriage contract.

ARCHBISHOP REARDON ARRIVES.

SAN FRANCISCO, Nov. 6.—Archbishop Reardon arrived this evening.

IS HANGING NOT PLAYED OUT?

SAN FRANCISCO, Nov. 6.—In the appealed case of the People vs. Collins, sentenced to be hanged for the murder of Wm. T. Cummings, Sept. 1st, 1879, in the Eureka stage robbery, the Supreme Court has affirmed the rulings of the lower court, and Collins will have to undergo the supreme penalty of the law.

THE RAILROAD COMPANY MUST ANSWER FOR EXTORTION.

SAN FRANCISCO, Nov. 6.—Superior Judge Finn, in the case of Rudolph Armstrong vs. C. P. R. R. Co. to recover damages for alleged extortion, decided that the Court had jurisdiction in actions of this character, and that the case must be placed on the calendar for trial.

GATHERING THEM IN.

SAN FRANCISCO, Nov. 6.—General Kelton received this evening the following from General Crook:

Silver Creek, Arizona, Nov. 6.—Fourth Chief Cuyetena, ten men and one woman have arrived. I leave to-morrow for San Carlos with ninety Chiricahuas.

(Signed,) RAFFERTY, Captain.

SHOCKING MURDER IN OREGON.

ALBANY, Ogn., Nov. 6.—Yesterday afternoon this city was startled by the announcement that the wife of J. J. Findlayson had been murdered. E. E. Holdsworth, Justice of the Peace, and Young, the Coroner, were summoned, and empaneling a jury, elicited the following facts: Last Saturday Mr. Findlayson went to Brownsville and returned to-day about noon and found his wife had been murdered during his absence. The deceased had been killed by an axe and a pocket-knife. An examination showed that she had been stabbed twenty-five times, her skull had been mashed with an axe, the back sinking its entire length into her head. After hearing the evidence the jury returned a verdict that the woman had been murdered, in their opinion, by her stepson Charles Benson Findlayson, aged 15 years. The boy left on Saturday evening and has not since been heard of. His shirt, with blood on the sleeve, was found in his room, as was also a bloody knife found near the deceased, with which she was murdered. It was identified as belonging to him.

THE MISSOURI CYCLONE.

Seven Persons Killed—Two Hundred Buildings Damaged—Loss, $200,000.

KANSAS CITY, Nov. 6.—A Journal Springfield special says: This city was visited this afternoon by a very destructive cyclone. The loss amounts to fully $232,000. Seven persons were killed and many injured. St. Mary's Catholic Church was among the buildings wrecked. The path of the storm was only a few yards in width, but it swept everything in its way. Thirty buildings were destroyed and two hundred damaged. Five of those killed were women.

SURRENDERED CHIRICAHUAS.

The Renegades Give Up—Geronimo's Son and Chatto's Family.

SAN FRANCISCO, Nov. 6.—Adjutant-General Kelton received a dispatch from General Crook confirming the surrender of the Chiricahuas to Lieutenant Hunter, at Silver Creek, Arizona. The Indians are stated to have come to the reservations before, but were obliged to scatter to the mountains to avoid an attempt of Mexicans to surround them. Geronimo's son and Chatto's family are among the submissives.

A SLOUGH OF CRIME.

Another Settler Murdered in Mussel Slough.

HANFORD, Cal., Nov. 6.—Mussel Slough is the scene of another excitement, on account of the slaying of McAuliffe, who was yesterday placed in possession of the Cockrell tract by Marshal Drew, and was found dead this morning with a bullet-hole through his heart.

The President's Views.

Washington, Nov. 6.—There is the best authority for saying that the Washington Capital article, professing to give President Arthur's views, was produced without information from him, and the statement that he is of opinion that New York State is hopeless for the Republicans next year, is the reverse of the truth. The President is anxious to see the Bourbons overthrown in Virginia, and believes New York will be a Republican State in 1884. So much of the article in question as relates to the President's views about Virginia is not so far out of the way as that about New York and Indiana.

Ashes to Ashes.

RALEIGH, N. C., Nov. 6.—On Sunday night, near Sanford, a negro man and his wife went to church, leaving in their house three children. Three hours later house and children were in ashes.

CONDENSED TELEGRAMS.

Two more pension claim agents at Washington have been disbarred.

For seducing a young lady at Kerville, Tenn., an ex-church elder was killed.

Kate Townsend was murdered in New Orleans Saturday by a man named Sykes.

Train robbery near Danville, Ill.

The Clyde (O.) bank has closed its doors and the cashier is missing.

The great Mullan tunnel in Montana is completed.

Cree Indians are committing depredations in Dakota.

A whale sixty-two feet long is ashore at Burnett's Island, off the eastern coast of Maryland.

The Czar will arm the Russian troops with repeating rifles of the latest American pattern.

Fifty houses have been destroyed at Santiago de Cuba by a storm.

A stage was robbed by a single highwayman Saturday, near Copperopolis.

Gamblers have gained a victory in the Oregon Courts.

Mormons are leaving Utah in considerable numbers for Arizona.

Fire destroyed fifteen tons of hay near Santa Barbara.

The heaviest frost of the season occurred in Napa county Saturday night.

An eleven-year-old boy was found murdered Friday at Princeton, Wis.

Another important capture of counterfeiters has been made in Indiana.

Civil suits are to be brought by the Government against the [illegible]

LOS ANGELES DAILY TIMES.

VOL. V...NO. 286. LOS ANGELES, CALIFORNIA, WEDNESDAY MORNING, NOVEMBER 5, 1884. FIVE CENTS.

The Times.

...—Temple, Main and New High.

IS IT VICTORY! IT IS VICTORY!

It begins to look like it! Since ...r question and article printed on the second page headed ...it Defeat?" the returns ...m to justify the claim of a Republican victory. The latest dispatch from ...w York, dated 3:30 this morning, says ... have won there.

Hallelujah! We proclaim our joy, ...declare our complete satisfaction, ...sing our political hosannas. We ...ve met the enemy and they are ours; ...se, foot and dragoons, guns and ammunition, baggage and plunder. Let ...heavens rejoice, let the earth be ...d. This morning the hearts of the ...t people in America are as jubilant ...they were on the day when the news ...hed from ocean to ocean that ..."Great Rebellion" had collapsed, ...that Gen. Lee was a prisoner. ...eed, in all of its most important ...tures, this victory is *similar* to that; ...it is a triumph of intelligent patriots ...r their country's foes. In tones not ...be misunderstood the American people have declared that the Democratic ...ty cannot be trusted with the reins ...the Government. The past, with its ...wers of tears, its chorus of agonies, ...rivers of blood and its mountain of ...', is too vividly in mind. Will the ...mocrats take the hint without another ...k? Possibly not. They declared ...t the Vermont election was a mere ...al matter, that the Maine election ...a severe rebuke to Blaine, that ...Ohio election was a Republican defeat, and a brilliant augury ...a Democratic victory; and it would ...but another illustration of the thick...ss of the Democratic hide, of Democratic regard for the truth, and of Democratic apprehension of American politics, American feeling and American ...dencies, if they were to affirm that ...ugh Blaine and Logan are *really* ...ted, yet the fact is devoid of political ...nificance, inasmuch as from end to ...d of the country there have been *immense Democratic gains*, and that the ...rty is *everywhere* in splendid spirit ...d panting for the fray.

THE COUNTY TICKET

Amid the sound of the roar of the cannon and the joyful hallelujahs that fill ...e air over the probable election ...the glorious Republican leaders, ...laine and Logan there mingles ...no less grateful strain of ...hanksgiving over the almost cer...tain election of the entire Republican county ticket. The voice ...f the people has at last been heard ...nd Los Angeles county is redeemed. There will be such an exodus from ...hat old Democratic ruin, the Court ...ouse, on the 1st of January, ...885, that will be ever memorable in the annals of the ...unty. The battle is won, and ...

Let the great guns thunder! Let the drums beat!
Swelling the roar of the turbulent street,
For we honor the proudest banner to-day
That floats o'er a nation's holiday.
The sign of a century's sure increase,
Of the patriot's pride, of his children's peace,
On greenest branch of humanity's tree,
The full-blown flower of Liberty!
Symbol of deeds by the martyrs done
In the cause oft lost, yet forever won,
By valley and mountain, by city and sea,
The ideal banner of Liberty!

VICTORY ASSURED!

Definite Returns from New York.

Republican Plurality in the State 6,000.

Blaine Carries Indiana by 4,000 Majority.

New Jersey Carried by the Democrats.

Michigan Stands by the Republicans.

Ohio Rolls Up a Republican Majority of 35,000.

California Still True to the Republican Cause.

Colorado, Kansas and Iowa Republican.

Elkins Says New York is Safe.

SAN FRANCISCO, Nov. 4.—*To Col. H. H. Boyce:* A dispatch just received from Elkins says that the indications show New York for Blaine by 10,000 to 15,000. Connecticut safe; New Jersey and Indiana not enough reports to figure. No news from Markham's district. This city all right, and returns so far of State. Large gains. JAMES R. FINLAYSON, Secretary.

New York All Right.

NEW YORK, Nov. 5, 2 a. m.—Cleveland's ...

THE ELECTORAL VOTE

A Probability of Blaine Receiving 233.

CLEVELAND CONCEDED 168.

New Jersey and Connecticut Democratic.

BLAINE CARRIES NEW YORK.

Indiana Also Probably Safe for the Republicans.

THE ELECTORAL COLLEGE.

How It Is Divided Between Blaine and Cleveland.

ELECTORAL VOTES FOR BLAINE.

California	8
Colorado	3
Illinois	22
Iowa	13
Kansas	9
Maine	6
Indiana	15
Massachusetts	14
Michigan	13
Minnesota	7
Nebraska	5
Nevada	3
New Hampshire	4
New York	36
Ohio	23
Oregon	3
Pennsylvania	30
Rhode Island	4
Vermont	4
Wisconsin	11
Total	233

ELECTORAL VOTES FOR CLEVELAND.

Alabama	10
Arkansas	7
Delaware	3
Connecticut	6
Florida	4
Georgia	12
Kentucky	13
Louisiana	8
Maryland	8
Mississippi	9
Missouri	16
New Jersey	9
North Carolina	11
South Carolina	9
Tennessee	12
Texas	13
Virginia	12
West Virginia	6
Total	168

NEW YORK.

Associated Press Dispatches to The Times.

NEW YORK, Nov. 4.—Fifty five election districts out of 712 in New York city give Blaine 5,648 votes, Cleveland 10,887, Butler 181, St. John 22. One hundred and twenty-eight election districts in New York State outside cities of New York and Brooklyn give Blaine 29,273, Cleveland 25,574, Butler 489, St. John 153. Net Democratic gain, 2,698. Fourteen election districts in New York State outside ...

THE HOME VOTE.

Los Angeles County Redeemed From Misrule.

MARKHAM ELECTED TO CONGRESS.

Indications that the Whole Republican County Ticket is Elected—The "Invincible" Bites the Dust.

Sixth Congressional District.

Special Dispatch to The Times.

SANTA ANA, Nov. 4.—Garden Grove Precinct—Kohler 36, Del Valle 36, Martin 35, Smith 37, Brousseau 36, Barham 39, Potts 39, Sepulveda 40, Miles 37, Levy 36, Brown 36, Broaded 37, Cutler 67, Nadeau 36, Buxton 36, Ross 40, Edgerton 38, Markham 38, Edwards 39, Cheney 38, Brunson 39, Gard 32, Dunsmoor 36, Montano 35, Ward 38, Hammond 39, Holton 38, Gephard 38, Fisher 38, McFarland 39, Wright 39, McPherson 34. R. T. HARRIS.

SANTA ANA, Nov. 4.—Westminster precinct—Kohler 37, Del Valle 36, Martin 32, Smith 37, Brousseau 35, Barham 37, Potts 33, Sepulveda 38, Miles 37, Levy 34, Brown 34, Broaded 34, Cutler 37, Nadean 35, Buxton 35, Ross 41, Edgerton 74, Markham 75, Edwards 79, Brunson 76, Cheney 79, Gard 71, Dunsmoor 80, Montano 72, Ward 76, Hammond 77, Holton 77, Gephard 77, Fisher 74, McFarland 76, Wright 76, McPherson 69.

OHIO.

COLUMBUS, Ohio, Nov. 4.—The Secretary of State's report for Ohio in 1883 does not give the number of voting places correct. At the October election there were 2,017 voting places in the State. We will compare with Garfield's vote in 1880, when the majority was 34,227, and also with Robinson's vote in October, 1884, when the Republican majority was 11,187.

COLUMBUS, Nov. 4.—Seventeen wards and precincts in Ohio show a net Republican gain of 268 over 1884 and a net Democratic gain of 14 over 1880.

MISSISSIPPI.

JACKSON, Miss., Nov. 4.—Blaine carries Jackson by a majority of 250. Returns from other precincts in Hinds county will give Cleveland a small majority. Hancock's majority in Hinds county was 1381. The Democratic ticket has a majority of about 250 in Rankin county, which gave Hancock a majority of 647. Returns from the State are coming in slowly, and show a very light vote, but of unquestionable Democratic tendency. Yazoo City cast 296 votes, 6 of which were Republican.

COLORADO.

DENVER, Col., Nov. 4.—The election in this city passed off quietly. The polls closed at 7 o'clock. Returns received at this hour (9:30) are meagre and unimportant. It is generally conceded that Blaine's majority in the county is 1,000 to 1,500; the State, 2,500 to 3,000. The Republicans probably elect the Governor by a good majority. Congressman in doubt. Both parties claim the Legislature.

FLORIDA.

JACKSONVILLE, Nov. 4.—A special to the Times-Union from sixteen counties indicate that the Democrats have elected their entire National, State and Congressional tickets. Weather favorable and a very heavy vote polled.

NORTH CAROLINA.

WILMINGTON, N. C., Nov. 5.—Returns from many counties remove all doubt as to the result in this State. The Republicans concede the State to the Democrats on both the Presidential and State ticket. Democrats claim their majority will not be less than 10,000. There seems to be little doubt that the Democrats have eight out of nine Congressmen, a gain of one.

TRAMP! TRAMP! TRAMP!

An Extraordinary Feat, in Fact, Two Extraordinary Feet

MARCHING TOWARDS THE SETTIN' SUN.

The Longest Tramp on Record—From Chillicothe, the Ancient Capital of Ohio, to the City of the Angels.

[SPECIAL CORRESPONDENCE OF THE TIMES.]

DENVER, Col., Oct. 25.—Yes, this is a big country. You will glibly assent to this hackneyed proposition; and assenting will have no more genuine conception of the fact than a hog has of hoopskirts. Now, don't fly off and fancy I am asserting anything por cine of your intelligence, for I am not. The simile simply implies that we are all innocent of knowledge in matters whereof we have had no experience. Oh, yes, it is true that you have been clear across the continent, from Boston to 'Frisco; and after those seven or eight mortal days on the cars you reckon you ought to know how wide this country is. Well, my dear sir or dear madam, I assure you that you haven't the remotest idea. You know that it takes four pretty good-sized digits to denote the number of miles; that it takes a week of discomfort to overcome those miles, and about here your knowledge runs up against a wall. At least a third of the week you slept—the sleep, I hope, of the just—and the other two-thirds you were thinking of everything else but the extent of Uncle Sam's territory.

There used to be an embryonic notion in my head that the United States was a tolerably sizable patch of land. I thought I knew all about it, and felt greatly in sympathy with the Fourth of July orator ...

... perience. They never will recover, for they struggle on in yearly anticipation of recurring catastrophes, bad or worse. It is a pitiful thing to see the air of desolation and despair which broods over them. Enterprise is paralyzed, business is at a stand-still. Part of the wrecked buildings have been shifted, propped up; part lie as the waters left them. There is no inducement to repair, to build up, to wipe out the scars. Over ten per cent. of the population of little Lawrenceburg—the worst sufferer by the flood—have moved away. That, of course, represents all who *can* move. Owners of property who have their all invested here will hang on, no doubt, to the bitter end, for they cannot "sell out." The river, now an innocent, narrow silver ribbon, has sealed the fate of every town along its banks from Marietta to Louisville.

The Ohio and Mississippi Railroad, which marked my line of march from Chincinnati to St. Louis, leaves the Ohio at Aurora, Ind., and shoots off across the State toward Vincennes. This part of the State is, I trust, a poor sample of the whole; for it is about as rich as the seven lean kine of Pharaoh. The villages are mostly shanty appendages to noisy and unfinished saw-mills; the people themselves are tattooed with the marks of "fever 'n' ager."

At Vincennes, right on the bluff bank of the Wabash, stands a building whose associations are of wide interest. The natives commonly call it "the Pigeon Roost," because of its present proprietor, W. F. Pigeon, editor of the Democratic Daily Sun. The house is large, two-storied, brick, well built and well preserved. There is nothing of the antique about its look, and your eyes open in wonder when you are told that this is the old Harrison mansion—the home of William Henry Harrison before and during the glorious, hard-cider, Tippecanoe-and-Tyler-too campaign of 1840; such a campaign as the country never saw before and will probably never see again. The house stands nearly as it did in those old days of the ...

LOS ANGELES DAILY TIMES.

VOL. VIII—NO. 145. LOS ANGELES, CALIFORNIA, THURSDAY MORNING, NOVEMBER 19, 1885. FIVE CENTS.

The Times.

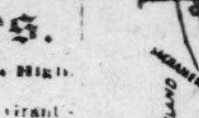

MAP OF THE ATLANTIC AND PACIFIC RAILROAD AND CONNECTIONS

HAPPY SAN DIEGO.

The Ambitious Little City Wild With Joy

OVER THE CALIFORNIA SOUTHERN ROAD.

Whose Final Completion is Celebrated by the Citizens with a General Jollification.

WASHINGTON.

BULGARIA'S TURN.

Prince Alexander Defeats the Servians.

HEAVY FIGHTING AND VARIED RUMORS.

THE LOAN EXHIBIT.

HOT SHOT

In the Camp of the Fruit Shippers' Union.

THE DOMINION.

THREE VICTIMS.

Oregon Chooses a Senator.

REFORMED HEBREWS.

GRANT'S MEMOIRS

THE BRITISH IN BURMAH

FINANCIAL AND COMMERCIAL.

LOS ANGELES DAILY TIMES.

VOL. IX---NO. 39. LOS ANGELES, CALIFORNIA, WEDNESDAY MORNING, JANUARY 20, 1886. FIVE CENTS.

A FIERCE FRESHET.

Los Angeles River on a Rampage,

TEARS AWAY BRIDGES,

And Inundates a Considerable Portion of the City Along Its Banks.

THREE LIVES SACRIFICED.

And Many Narrow Escapes—Accidents and Incidents of the Flood—Homeless People Cared for.

LOS ANGELES suffered yesterday the fourth severe flood recorded here in twenty-four years. The Los Angeles river, swollen by the heavy rains of Sunday and Monday, or by a cloudburst in the mountains, became an irresistible torrent, sweeping away bridges and inundating a large part of the lowlands in the south-central part of the city. Not less than two thousand acres of land, devoted to homes, orchards and vineyards, were flooded. Upon the larger part of this territory the damage is inconsiderable, as the waters spread so widely that they lost their destroying force. But in the more circumscribed area between Aliso street and First, and broadening from the point of overflow to a width of two city blocks, the full strength of the current was experienced. This section was occupied mainly by small frame houses which had sprung up since the flood of February, 1884, when the place was swept in a similar manner. The flood of yesterday, it is claimed, rose two feet higher than that of 1884, and the greater suddenness of its coming made the damage proportionately greater. Some of the buildings were swept away entirely and the ground upon which they had stood was swept away after them. Other buildings were floated down and lodged, and still others were undermined and tilted over.

Up to this hour three deaths are known to have occurred as the result of the flood. Many rumors were current yesterday as to further loss of life, but they could not be traced to any reliable source.

It is difficult at this time to estimate the financial loss, but a rough calculation is made as follows, not vouching for more than approximate correctness:

Southern Pacific R. R. Co:		
Upper bridge	$15,000	
Lower bridge	1,000	
Damage to road-bed	500	
		$16,500
San Gabriel Valley R.R.Co:		
Bridge	2,000	
Depot and road-bed	1,500	
		3,500
City of Los Angeles:		
Downey Avenue bridge	6,000	
Aliso Avenue bridge	3,000	
First Street bridge	6,000	
		15,000
City and County:		
Macy Street bridge		500
Central Railway Co:		
Boyle Heights bridge	2,000	
Downey Avenue bridge	500	
		2,500
Private property		20,000
		$58,000

This comprehends nothing for depreciated real estate by reason of the flooding, or for lands entirely washed away by the torrent. If these could be aggregated with the more tangible losses, they would show startling figures—perhaps $100,000 to $125,000 as a grand total.

A circumstantial account of the flood, as gathered by TIMES reporters, is given below:

AN ANGRY TORRENT.

How the River Rose in an Hour and Demolished Things.

Some people—especially those who had suffered an uncomfortable experience in the flood of 1884—went to bed Monday night with an uneasy feeling. They considered that the ground was already thoroughly soaked, and the hard rain then falling must necessarily run off and make trouble. Their worst fears were realized between 4 and 5 o'clock yesterday morning, when the Los Angeles river suddenly became an angry, turbid stream and went roaring down, bank full. A great mass of driftwood was borne upon the crest of the oncoming flood, and this, lodging against the upper Southern Pacific railroad bridge, was the first cause of trouble. The higher the driftwood piled the higher rose the tide, until it swept over the top of the bridge. At that point the water was at least ten feet above the normal level of the river. Unable to withstand the tremendous pressure thus brought against it, the bridge gave way in almost its entire length, and the riven timbers went down on the flood. This occurred about 6 o'clock, and within an hour and a half after the time when the rise was first noticed.

Below the bridge on the west side of the river the Southern Pacific Railroad track skirts along the edge of the bluff, where the roadbed has been excavated. The force of the current was directed against the embankment at this point and ate away the hard gravel until the track was left in a state of suspension in many places and became totally impassable.

A SECOND BRIDGE ATTACKED.

The freight of driftwood, now liberated from its upper lodgment and augmented by the timbers of the Southern Pacific bridge, bore down upon the new bridge of the San Gabriel Valley railway, the next obstacle in its way. Both approaches were carried away and the waters, thus finding vent, left the structure uninjured. About 100 feet of the embankment at the east end is gone, and the gap at the west end is about half as wide. Below this bridge again, on the west side, the river bank was aligned by the track of the San Gabriel Valley railway. Efforts at rip-rapping had been made, with rocks, trees, and sundry bags of sand piled up against the railroad embankment, but these slight impediments availed nothing against the seething tide hurled against them. About three hundred feet of the track was here undermined and the new-made earth upon which the snug little depot building stood was dissolved like so much sugar.

DOWNEY AVENUE BRIDGE.

Some of the piles in the street railroad bridge, attached to and apparently forming a part of the Downey Avenue bridge, must have been washed out in the early stages of the flood. The first car left the East Los Angeles terminus at 4:05 a. m., and reached the bridge at 4:15. There were three passengers (all men) on the car, besides the driver. When about a hundred feet out on the bridge, it was noticed that the bridge was swaying. Two of the passengers, who were on the rear platform, stepped off. They did this just in time, for, a moment later, a section of the bridge went down, and the car with it. The driver, Orville Robinson, and one passenger, a Frenchman named Sion, remained on board, and the car, striking the water right side up, made a not very bad impromptu ferry boat. The horse was either promptly cut loose or succeeded in disengaging himself, for he swam away and made a safe landing near the soap works, a few hundred yards below. The car lodged about midway between the soap works and the bridge, and the conductor and passenger climbed to its roof to keep out of the wet. But it was

NOT A VERY SAFE LANDING PLACE.

The rushing waters were on every hand, and the men were in imminent danger of being washed away at any moment. A crowd collected on the river bank, manifesting a keen interest in the imperiled men. Vain efforts were made to pass a rope to them, but nobody was able to give them any substantial assistance, until Police Officer Arguello came along on horseback. "I can get them out," he said.

"Do you think so?" asked Mayor Spence, who was one of the party on the bank.

"I am sure I can."

"Then go it."

Arguello drew his feet out of the stirrups and reined his horse into the river. The animal breasted the flood sturdily, and was soon beside the car. One of the men on the roof was taken on behind the officer and ferried to shore. Then a second trip brought the other off. The rescued men were thoroughly drenched and chilled, but withal happy and thankful for their deliverance.

OTHER DESTRUCTION.

It was half-past 8 o'clock when the shipwrecked street-car passengers reached terra firma, and, before that time, a section of about sixty feet of the Downey avenue bridge, near the east end, had gone out with a crash.

Then the San Gabriel Valley depot, whose support had been melted away, toppled over and dove into the river. It floated for a moment, intact, till it reached the Downey avenue bridge, when it collapsed and a hundred feet of the bridge went to pot with it. A part of the depot timbers lodged below, near the anchored street car. Later in the day, when the flood had partially subsided, the depot safe was found there, partly buried in sand. It was dug up and the contents rescued, not much damaged.

At a point just below the Downey avenue bridge, on the west side, the river

FIRST BROKE OVER ITS BANKS,

running across the lands occupied by York, and thence making its way through the Hollenbeck tract, occupied mostly by small dwellings. Neidt's Soap Factory was provided with a bulkhead formed of casks filled with rocks, and imbedded in solid phalanx about the building. This bulkhead resisted the encroachment of the water, and even became stronger as the sand banked up against it.

The overflow was not very destructive in this section, as the full force of the current was diverted into the opposite bank. On the east side, a Mexican cabin was carried off, and the fortunes of a German, who had recently located on the river bank and paid $600 for two lots, upon which to build a bath house, were wrecked. Both building and land were incontinently taken down the stream.

THE SECOND BRIDGE

of the Southern Pacific Railroad, which spans the river at this point, was badly crippled, a section near the middle sinking down to medium-water line. The incoming train from the East, arriving at 2 p. m., stopped on the east side, and some of the passengers managed to crawl across.

HOLLENBECK AND SABICHI TRACTS.

An inspection of this locality showed considerable damage from the overflow, but no buildings actually washed away. In St. John's street, Wm. Mayo lost twenty-five yards of fence and had his house damaged. Wm. Holly suffered damages to the extent of $100.

In Georgia street two houses owned by Mrs. Brown, and unoccupied, were damaged.

In Leroy street a strong current was running at noon.

In Bline street, No. 74, the southernmost house, had five feet of water on the floor. Mr. Noll, at No. 72, suffered considerable loss in damaged furniture. Richard Degener, No. 70, was damaged to the extent of $300. His chickens were drowned. At No. 66, Miss H. S. McLellan and sister lost $500. Of their effects they saved only the clothes they had on. Kutz, No. 50; Evarts, 46, and Curran, 64, were all flooded and damaged.

In Ann street Joe Juaneme's house was flooded to the eaves.

The flood through this section, as stated, was

NOT VERY TURBULENT,

and, without washing away any buildings, passed on, inundating the Sherer place, the Cline place and other properties contiguous. Encountering an impassable barrier in the graded approach to the Macy street bridge, a good share of the overflowing waters were here turned back into the bed of the stream. At this point the channel is narrower than at any other along the river after it issues from the hills, and here the troubled waters lashed themselves into fury. The middle pier of the bridge was undermined and sank about three feet, making a corresponding sag in the superstructure. But the old "covered" bridge proved the city's stand-by, after all. It furnished yesterday, and is now, the only means of crossing the river. Transit was barred, however, a good share of the time yesterday, as it was thought the bridge was not safe and might go down at any minute. Pedestrians who chose to chance it were allowed to pass, and, late in the afternoon, a few saddle horses and a light buggy or two were allowed to cross.

A STRICKEN SECTION.

Where the Greatest Damage was Done.

The portion of the flooded district in which the worst effects of the overflow were felt was that section bounded by Alameda, Georgia and Macy streets, which includes First, Guadalupe, Banning, Turner, Sepulveda, Ducommun, Sainsevain, Aliso, Lazard, Weill, Rose, Hewitt, Garey, Center, Vignes, Amelia and Lafayette streets. This portion of the city is densely populated with small homes, and nearly all were overflowed and near the river more or less damaged. The Aliso tract lies within this boundary, and here it was during the flood of 1884 that about thirty-five houses were washed away, and Front street, which lies directly along the official river bed, was entirely obliterated. The amount of suffering caused in this district by the disastrous flood of two years ago will be remembered by all who were residents of the city at that time; and while the citizens did all that was possible for the unfortunate people at that time, still a large proportion were left with little more than the desolate, wave-washed spot that they had once called home. Most of these owners in the Aliso tract, near the river-bed, made up their minds at that time that they would make no further effort to re-establish their homes, but the action of the municipal authorities in building a so called levee encouraged them to try once more, and quite a number of new houses were put up by persons whose limited means did not justify the expenditure, while many more made improvements, under the assurance that they would be protected in the future. These people have once more seen their property devastated, and if there ever was a time for the charitable people of this city to open their hearts and their purses, it is in these cases.

STATEMENT OF AN EYE WITNESS.

The people of the Aliso tract retired on Monday night feeling some uneasiness as to the river, but still hoping that nothing serious would occur. As the rain poured down in torrents the roaring of the rising river did not tend to calm them, but when, about 11 o'clock, the storm ceased and the clouds broke, they felt easier, as they thought the worst was over. What afterwards happened may perhaps be best described by the statement of an eye-witness, Mrs. A. Moore, who resides on Banning street. She said: "I was feeling very anxious all night about the river, but my husband looked out several times and assured me that everything was all right and there was no danger. After midnight we noticed that there was considerable water in the yard, but concluded that it was only the surface water which had gathered from the tremendous showers. But shortly after four o'clock the increased roaring sound of the river led us to look out again, and to our horror we found the water pouring in on every side. In a few minutes there were several feet of water in the yard, and it came over the porch and began to come into the house. Oh, it was dreadful! We went out and shouted for wagons, but none appeared, and all the other families were in the same fix we were. We could see, as daylight came, the houses nearer the river breaking down and floating off, and the people making frantic efforts to escape and shouting for help. We did not know but our turn would come next, and we were very much frightened. It was long past daylight before there was much effort to rescue the people in our neighborhood, and then the water was so deep that the wagons could not reach us. At 9:30 a police officer rode with great difficulty into our yard and tried to reach our house, but the current was too strong and the water too deep. The animal went down and the officer fell off. By good luck he escaped drowning, and managed to get out into shallow water; and then there was no more help for us until the water went down. Oh, it was a terrible night for us, and I hope never to see its like again."

DROWNING OF TWO PERSONS.

In this neighborhood there were certainly two persons drowned, and probably more. Mrs. Kate Lytle, a lady who resided on Center street, corner of First, saw that in all probability her house would be swept away, as it afterwards was, and made a desperate effort to escape. She stepped out and was soon waist deep in the water, but managed to avoid being carried down by the strong current by clinging to a small tree. Officer Weed made a determined effort to save her, but just as he was about to succeed, a small house came floating down and struck the unfortunate woman. She was knocked over, and was seen no more. At last accounts the body had not been recovered.

The house where Mr. Whitney, a hard-working man in the employ of the soap company, lived, was in imminent danger of being carried away, and Deputy Sheriff Martin Aguirre, with great bravery, came to the rescue. He took two children out and got them to a place of safety, and then came back for the third. This was a little girl 8 years old, named Theresa Whitney. He was lifting her onto his horse when a piece of fence came drifting along and struck the animal, throwing him off his feet. Aguirre's feet got tangled in the stirrup and the child clung to his neck. He placed the little one on the piece of fence and was carried by the current down to Seventh street before he was able to save himself and his horse. When he got back the child was gone. About 3 p. m. a boy passing along the bank where the water was rapidly receding, saw a little foot protruding from the mud. He raised the body and notified Officer Gilbert, who found that it was the missing little girl. The remains were carried to the store of Schatto & Son, on First street, where the grief-stricken parents and brother and sisters of the deceased soon arrived almost heart-broken. Deputy Coroner Oakley was notified, and an inquest was held, of course showing that the cause of death was accidental drowning.

Many other persons had narrow escapes. Mr. J. L. Wilson in an effort to save some goods in a house on Weill street, fell into the current, and had he not been thrown a rope by an officer on horseback, he must inevitably have been drowned. Arthur Harris, a lad ten years old, fell into the stream near Center street, but his father jumped in and caught him before he was borne down. Mrs. Sinclair also had a narrow escape from being crushed to death by a passing house.

THE DAMAGE TO PROPERTY.

At about 7:30 a. m. a reporter of the TIMES, who had been aroused by the ringing of the alarm bells and the blowing of steam-whistles, hastened to the scene of the disaster. Even at that early hour the streets were crowded with people, and every wagon was pressed into service in the district below Alameda street. People were anxiously inquiring for the safety of friends, loads of furniture were being hauled out, and flood sufferers, many of them wet to the skin, in their desperate effort to escape, were to be seen huddled together in places provided by the many citizens who threw open their doors to all who needed relief. Alameda street was practically a river about three feet in depth, and down Sainsevain and Ducommun streets came streams which materially increased the flow. But at Alameda, corner of First street, swelled by the current which came down the latter thoroughfare, there was a raging torrent. Teams with great difficulty crossed here, and yet much effective work was done.

All the streets east of Alameda street were more or less under water, and some were nothing more than branch rivers, the streams being from two to five feet in depth. The Macy street, or, as it is better known, the covered bridge, was found to be all right, but the tremendous torrent and the debris piled against it soon caused it to sag, and it sunk in the center between three and four feet. It was in about the same condition it was at the last flood, and certainly bore the strain well. It became necessary to forbid all persons from driving over it with teams, and thus the only means to get to the east side was on foot. The structure shook occasionally as the great waves struck it, and probably nothing could have saved it from going down had the river not commenced falling. The current rushed under the bridge and struck with great force, rebounding and striking the opposite bank. The remnants of the municipal levee soon disappeared, and nothing was left but the soft sand banks, which were cut away as if with a knife. The Aliso street horse railroad bridge was the first to succumb to the accumulated debris and the rush of water, and the principal portion of it was washed away. The approach to the Aliso street public bridge was then cut away for about 250 feet on the western side of the river, but the bridge itself was not damaged at all. The First street bridge was treated in a similar manner, the approaches on both sides being cut away, but the structure itself was not damaged. Towards morning Officer Fouck was on duty in the neighborhood of First street, just before the river had cut away the bank. A Spanish woman, terrified at the rapidly rising waters, made an attempt to cross the bridge. Fouck, seeing her danger, rushed to the rescue, but before he could get her across, the approaches on both sides were cut off. He remained on the bridge several hours, until the river receded and he was able to swim his horse ashore, while his charge was helped across by the assistance of men who came to the rescue.

INDIVIDUAL LOSSES.

On the Aliso tract the work of destruction proceeded. A store belonging to Mrs. Dunn, a sufferer by the flood of 1884, was floated from the corner of Center and Weill streets to First street, and both store and contents (a stock of groceries) were almost ruined. The loss is estimated at $2500. Two houses belonging to Mrs. Margaret Moore, one on Weill street and one on Turner street, were carried away, and three small houses on Center street belonging to Alfred Moore, her husband, also floated off. Mr. Moore was a heavy sufferer by the flood of 1884, and this second loss comes very hard upon him. He states that his total loss this time will reach $3000.

Mr. Bonfillio, an Italian, was preparing to start an extensive laundry on Center street, and had the framework for a building already up. This building and a quantity of lumber and other material on the ground was washed away. Loss about $1500. Two small houses on First street, belonging to Swedes, their names no one seeming to know, were washed away. The property recently sold for $1400. One of the houses was occupied by Mrs. Lida Johnson, and she escaped with difficulty.

One of the hardest losses was that of a widow lady named Mathews. Her house and home was located at the corner of Banning and Center streets, and all she had in the world was swept away. The loss is said to be total. The property was valued at $1500.

Two houses belonging to a man by the name of Allen, located near the foot of Center street, were carried down the stream. They were valued at $600.

The grocery store of Schatto & Sons, 551 First street, was inundated and the stock of groceries damaged to the extent of $400.

The fences around Mrs. McGlen's place, near the river, were destroyed. Loss about $100.

Mr. Moody's house on Center street was entirely washed away. Loss $500.

A house belonging to Mr. Naze, the other side of Center street, was undermined on all sides and narrowly escaped. Damage $250.

Mr. Monet, corner of Weill and Franklin streets, lost a house valued at $300.

Mr. Luse, corner of Lazard and Center streets, lost a house; value, $300.

A house belonging to Mr. Franklin, located on Lazard street, was washed away; loss, $400.

Catherine, a Spanish butcher, lost a house valued at $400.

A man whose name could not be learned, but who was formerly engineer in the Nadeau Block, lost a shanty valued at $50.

August Lust lost a house near the levee valued at $250.

Mrs. Bigelow's place, south of First street, was badly flooded. A number of trees and vines were washed away, and the damage is hard to estimate. The water was about two feet deep in the house, damaging the furniture considerably. No attempt was made by the family to leave the house. None of her other tenement houses were washed away, but all were flooded. The damage will, all told, not be over $1500.

A house belonging to a Mrs. Clark, on First street, went down. Loss $1000.

A small house located near Aliso avenue had a most extraordinary career. It was carried down the current, and, although meeting many obstacles, was safely landed in the middle of First street, a distance of several blocks. The contents were unharmed, and all the owner will have to do will be to move it back to its old location.

W. F. White, a hard-working teamster, had his house on First street damaged probably to the extent of $400.

A house belonging to a Mrs. Snyder was floated for some distance down the stream. It was valued at $400.

J. Hitchcock's house was damaged to the extent of $800.

A man by the name of Kip had a woodyard, and lost his whole stock, valued at $2000.

A house built by E. Nittinger, and owned at present by Mrs. Gray, located on Center street, was damaged considerably.

A widow by the name of Norris had two houses damaged, probably to the extent of $500.

Dr. Bangerter's house on Weill street was also injured—just how much it is hard to tell.

J. E. Ellis, on Turner street, had furniture damaged to the extent of $200.

P. T. Bonton lost a fence worth $100.

T. B. Brant lost a chicken house and a lot of thoroughbred poultry valued at $150.

Mrs. Picquelo, on Georgia street, had seven feet of water in her house and her furniture is ruined.

A. F. Bland, on First street, estimates the damage to his furniture at $250.

T. B. Bell, who lives in a rented house on Vignes street, had three feet of water in the house, and places his loss at $150, his furniture in three rooms being nearly ruined.

The Los Angeles Soap Works was not injured materially.

The Los Angeles Gas Works, on Aliso avenue, escaped with a thorough wetting down.

The Los Angeles Cracker Company protected their building with sand bags, and no injury was done by the water.

Not a vestige is left of the levee built by the city last summer, at a cost of $10,000.

All the streets from Vignes to Alameda were under water, but no very serious damage was reported. In most cases it amounted to little more than a thorough irrigation of the yards.

About twelve families residing on the Aliso tract lost everything they had except the clothes they wore when they left.

J. T. Williams, who resides in San Francisco, lost a house on Turner street valued at $500.

Houses and portions of houses are lodged along the banks for several miles.

The damage to a number of other houses was considerable, but, owing to the water and mud, it was impossible to reach them or to obtain any information concerning them.

The zanja on the Aliso road broke early in the morning and helped to swell the flood on Aliso avenue. Howard, Keller and Mission streets were all partially under water.

SOUTH OF FIRST STREET

the flood constantly broadened. It poured through the orchard of Mrs. Bigelow, and ran down Geary, Hewitt and Rose streets to Georgia street. In these lower localities the water in no place attained a depth of more than two or three feet. No buildings were destroyed or moved from their foundations, but a vast amount of damage in a small way was accomplished. Tasty little dooryards, with their lawns and flower-beds, were all plastered over with slickens to the depth of three inches or a foot, according to circumstances. Fences were broken down and rubbish was scattered everywhere. From Georgia street the flood poured into Alameda street, and thence directly southward. Here and there one could see evidences of civilization in parts of furniture, tin cans, bags, barrels and baskets scattered by the wayside. A lace curtain was wrapped about a shade-tree, and the elliptical top of a centre-table was lodged between the pickets of a fence.

The Bliss place and a portion of the Wolfskill place were swept over. The cellar under the eastern part of the old Wolfskill mansion was filled with water, and the adobe wall on that end fell in. The old Keller vineyard and other places below were all under water. At Seventh street the flood spread out to fully

TWO-THIRDS OF A MILE

in width, covering the entire section from Alameda street to the river. There was a report that five children had been drowned on Seventh street, but this, when run down, proved to have been founded on the fact that the family of an Italian named Gaberdini had taken refuge at the house of Mr. Kiefer, and consequently were missed from their home.

It is said that the flood continued down Alameda street about five miles and then discharged into the river bed. How much damage was done in that locality cannot now be stated. Coroner McFarland, who drove up from Compton yesterday, reports that he saw signals of distress displayed at several places on the way.

The track of the Southern Pacific Railroad was washed so much in portions of Alameda street that a red flag was displayed between the rails as a danger signal.

Mr. Butler, a farmer living three miles below town, lost fifty hogs by the flood.

THE DEATH ROLL.

Drowning of a Little Girl—Bravery of Deputy Sheriff Martin Aguirre.

Coroner McFarland held an inquest upon the body of Theresa Whitney, a little girl who was drowned on First street yesterday morning at about 6 o'clock. The body was found by Joseph Armijo and another man who were looking for salvage on the west side of the river, nearly a mile below First street. They saw a shoe sticking out of the mud and sand, and upon digging down found the body of the little girl, which was only ten feet from the edge of the river bed. F. A. Valdez and Armijo took the body to a grocery store on First street, and from there it was conveyed to the morgue, when a jury being empanneled and testimony heard, a verdict of drowned was returned. The testimony of Deputy Sheriff Martin Aguirre, which explains the whole accident, is hereby appended in a condensed form. Mr. Aguirre was down in the worst flooded district early yesterday morning, and had already made three trips to the house, No. 626 First street, and carried away an equal number of children on his horse. He returned a fourth time, and was handed the deceased little girl through the window. He placed it in front of his saddle, and turned to get ashore. Ahead of him there was a picket fence, which was giving way. The horse got hit by the fence, and being much exhausted, rolled over twice. Aguirre was hit by the pommel of the saddle twice, and began spitting blood. He grabbed the fence, which had a barbed wire at the top, cutting his hands severely. He got the child to the fence, telling her to hold on. His horse then sank, and Aguirre's foot being caught in the stirrup, he sank with him, and when he came up again he was a long way from the fence and banked up against some willows. He then pulled off his clothes, which were lost, and having caught the horse, he mounted him and returned towards the fence, but when he got there the child had disappeared.

Aguirre was seriously hurt, which did not prevent him from doing his utmost afterwards to be useful to the flooded people. His conduct is deserving of great commendation. Another version of Aguirre's brave exploit will be found under the sub-heading, "Drowning of Two Persons."

DIED OF FRIGHT.

An old Scotchman named Lewis M. Sifford, who had been camping for over a year in the river-bed, a short distance above the East Los Angeles crossing, was found dead about daylight yesterday morning, a few feet from the door of his rude tent. He was not drowned, but appears to have died from over-excitement or fright, caused by the approach of the surging waters, which he could hear but not see, as he was partially blind. He was about 65 years old, alone, and lived in a miserable condition, supporting himself by collecting old clothes from the city dumping-grounds, fixing them up and selling them. He also gathered up the major part of his food from the offal heaps, and was helped by the charitable to some extent. He was found by Hugh McCafferty, an old man tenting near by, who dragged the body to higher ground to keep it out of the water, which was then fast closing in over the spot where the poor old Scotchman fell and expired. His miserable tent presented a curious conglomeration of old clothes, old bedding, boulders, tin cans, broken bits of food, and odds and ends picked up here and there. The body was guarded by some of the neighbors till afternoon, when mounted officer Fouck came upon the scene and took charge of the corpse. Deputy Coroner Oakley notified Coroner McFarland early in the day, and that official came up from Compton, but found his hands so full of sad business that he was unable to recover the body last night. It will be brought in this morning after an inquest is held on it where it lies.

The third life lost was that of Mrs. Kate Lytle, an account of whose drowning will be found in another place.

INCIDENTS AND ADVENTURES.

Notes of the Flood—Down Stream on a Raft.

John Whitesides and his wife (colored) lived at 213 Banning street. They have six children, ranging in age from four to sixteen. In the flurry of getting out, their two boys, Charlie, aged sixteen, and Willie, aged twelve, took the wrong direction and found they were getting into deep water. They then attempted to get back to the house, but were swept down the by current. At this moment a section of a house floor came along and they climbed upon it for a raft. Down stream they went at steamboat speed, the current sometimes carrying them under and the water almost strangling them. The younger boy was nearly exhausted and must have lost his hold had not his brother clung to him with a grip of desperation. At Seventh street the raft was carried into an eddy, and the boys were able to wade ashore. This adventure probably gave rise to the report that two men were carried down the river on a raft and upset and drowned.

Notes.

Three horses broke their legs yesterday by falling into holes, and all were killed.

Poultry coops innumerable floated down the river yesterday.

There is a break of 1000 feet at the railroad bridge at Tejunga.

Special Officer Tyler kept a sharp lookout for thieves, who were quite ready to avail themselves of the opportunity to plunder.

Among the deeds yesterday deserving special mention was that of an expressman, who rescued a man whose life was in danger, and refused any compensation. The man offered him $20 if he would go back and take out two trunks, but he declined, saying that he was only seeking to save life.

Right below the covered bridge the current was thrown back to the west side with such force that immense waves were formed, and early in the morning the sight was a grand one.

The roar of the river could be heard all over the city last night.

The San Gabriel Valley Railroad officials take a good-natured view of the situation. Their depot is now located somewhere near Florence.

J. G. Estudillo, who was born at San Gabriel and has lived in Southern California all his life, says that twenty-five years ago half of the district bordering on the river east of Alameda street was looked upon as a marsh.

Hundreds of people visited the flooded district yesterday.

A large delegation from the Santa Ana Valley is forcibly detained in this city.

The failure of the Santa Monica train to come in yesterday occasioned considerable surprise. The Santa Monica line has long been known as "Old Reliable."

The Wolfskill adobe wall on Alameda street fell yesterday.

Yesterday there were rumors all over town that Officers Jackson and Weed had been drowned. Both turned up all right. Officer Jackson had been up all night, and in the morning went to bed. His failure to "show up" caused the alarm.

The San Gabriel Valley Railroad Company expect to get trains through to-morrow, or at most the day after.

The excursionists who arrived day before yesterday may consider themselves fortunate. A day later and they would have had another picnic.

Two houses on Alameda street below Jefferson, occupied by Mexicans, were washed away yesterday.

Several people walked in from Pasadena yesterday.

The sun came out in good shape at about 10 o'clock yesterday, and, with the exception of two light showers in the afternoon, the weather was pleasant.

All the zanjas are out of order, as usual. For that matter, a few hours' rain demoralizes the zanjas.

The ladies were out in force yesterday, and many of them braved mud and rain to see the sights.

The heaviest losers by this flood are unfortunately the people who could least afford to lose.

The Signal Service gives the total rainfall for the twenty-four hours ending at 7:07 o'clock last evening at 1.96 inches.

The Second Street Cable-road Company report that the only damage done to their road was by water at the Pearl street crossing and at the Spring street terminus. They expect to be in running order by this noon. $200 will cover the damage done.

J. E. Lacy, whose place was on the corner of Turner and Vignes streets, devised a sort of raft on which to ferry his wife and two children across to the opposite corner, so that they might escape thence to terra firma. A rope was employed for towing purposes. When the raft neared its destination the force of the current swung it around against a tree, upsetting it and throwing the passengers into the water. Mr. Lacy jumped in and rescued them. The water, he says, was three feet deep.

Fred and Billy Stoermer worked nobly at the First street bridge.

Officer Lemon shot a horse that had broken one of its legs in the melee.

One hundred and fifty feet of the City Water Company's twenty-two inch main, leading around the point of the bluff near the San Gabriel Valley bridge, was washed away. Fortunately a smaller conduit was left intact, and the city in the midst of a flood was not left without a drink of water. The pipe suppling the east side is also broken.

The wagons of the City Ice Company and the Excelsior Soda Works, under the direction of Superintendent Thos. Strohm, were engaged from 6 o'clock in the morning until noon in removing the residents of the flooded district to *terra firma*, and the patrons of the company will surely excuse the non-delivery of ice and soda, in view of the humane work in which the teams were engaged.

A flurry of excitement was raised yesterday afternoon by a report that telegraphic information had been received of a cloudburst on the Tejunga, which was in a wild state, and that the supplemental flood might be expected down about midnight (last night). The telegram was credited to Senator Maclay, of San Fernando. There was no truth in the report.

No telegraphic dispatches were received from any quarter, as the barren telegraphic columns of the TIMES to-day attest.

THE SUFFERERS.

How the Kind-hearted Took Them In and Cared for Them.

There were a great many homeless people in the city yesterday, and others still who had homes that were not tenable. A purse of about $200 was raised by private subscription, and, the Council being appealed to, appropriated $250. It was also found that about $200 remained in the relief fund of the flood of 1884, which was available.

A GENEROUS GIFT FROM A PHILANTHROPIC SAN FRANCISCAN.

Yesterday morning E. A. Schreck, of the firm of Boericke & Schreck, San Francisco, proprietors of the leading homœopathic pharmacy on the Pacific Coast, went down to the river, and after seeing the distress caused by the loss of so many homes in the flood, he decided to donate a liberal sum of money for the relief of those who had been rendered destitute. He accordingly addressed a gracious letter to the committee (consisting of Frank A. Gibson, C. H. Dunsmoor, E. T. Wright, L. H. Boyce, Mrs. R. M. Widney, Mrs. J. D. Bicknell and Mrs. F. A. Gibson), expressing his sympathy in fitting terms, and informing them that he had, earlier in the day, arranged with Dr. Isaac Fellows to pay to the proper person the sum of $100 for the benefit of the sufferers. The committee acknowledged receipt of the generous gift in an appropriate letter. Mr. Schreck did a generous thing in a handsome way.

Several homeless families found accommodation in the Sisters' Hospital. About twenty refugees, large and small, collected at Police Headquarters, and subsequently went to the rooms of the Young Men's Christian Association. During the day about forty of the sufferers collected at the latter place. Late in the afternoon all were transferred to the Tabernacle on South Main street. There roaring fires were kept burning in two of the large heaters, and the unfortunate people were made as cosy as possible in a place so resembling "all out doors."

J. B. Dutton, a newcomer from Kansas, and E. L. Atherton devoted themselves to caring for the temporal wants of the unfortunates. Rev. Mr. Dorsey and wife were also assiduous in their attentions, and other people called and interested themselves in the good work, among the number Mayor Spence and his wife. Provisions were sent in, and, about 6 o'clock, a good supper of meat, bread, coffee and cakes was served smoking hot, and it was eaten with a relish by the weary and bedraggled people, many of whom had not tasted food before all day. Blankets and quilts were also provided in abundance, and each family was allowed to bunk down, either on the floor or on cots, as they chose. When a reporter called at the tabernacle, about 8 o'clock he found some of the children already tucked up in their beds, and others running around enjoying the picnic. The older people were more serious. Some of them had lost their all.

Following is a list of the unfortunates:

Ignez Schneider, wife and four children. House, 125 Weill street, washed away. Saved only the clothing upon their persons. Loss $600.

M. Maehl, wife and four children (oldest 11, youngest 3); residence, 125 Turner street. Water was already in their house when they left, at 5 a. m. Loss, $100 on furniture.

Henry Lawrence, wife and two children. House, No. 124 Turner street, swept away. Lost furniture to the value of $250, including a new sewing machine.

John Whiteside, wife and six children (colored), 213 Banning street; lived in a rented house; saved household effects, except clothing and provisions left in an outbuilding. Loss $50.

N. Pollich, wife and six children, ranging in age from ten months to thirteen years. House, 124 Banning street, still standing, but foundation undermined and building canted over. Loss on furniture not great.

Mrs. M. Cook, whose residence is in the warehouse on the end of Macy-street bridge, left because it was becoming unsafe; four children; husband in the country.

Mrs R. M. Mathews (widow) and two children, 13 and 16 years of age, saved only clothing upon their persons, and lost house, lot and furniture, all their worldly possessions, valued at $1000. This family is deserving of substantial assistance.

Albert Hamilton, wife and three children, 36 Banning street, took refuge in the Tabernacle because they could not find room at a hotel, and were afraid of another cloudburst. Loss not great.

SHUT OFF.

No Mails nor Trains to nor from Anywhere.

Owing to the extent and fierceness of the storm and flood, communication with the outside world is entirely cut off. No mails arrived from the East day before yesterday, none from any direction yesterday, and there will be none to-day. How soon they may be resumed, it is at present impossible to state. The wires, both telephone and telegraph, are all down, so there is no present medium of intelligence. No trains will run in either direction to-day, unless the bridge for east-bound traffic be risked for the passage of a train, which is hardly probable. The California Southern train, due here at 9:10 Sunday night, was at noon yesterday hesitating whether to cross this bridge or not. The passengers walked in, and the train backed to San Gabriel, where it still lies. It met a two-foot torrent across the track at El Monte. The upper Southern Pacific Railroad bridge and some thousand feet of track are gone, and it will take considerable time to repair this damage. Even the telephone line to East Los Angeles is down. Council has ordered temporary repairs of the city bridges so as to admit of foot travel at once.

THE FLOOD OF '84.

Reminiscences of the Disastrous Overflow Two Years Ago.

The great flood of 1884 occurred Sunday night, February 17th. The season had been dry up to within two weeks of the date of the flood, and the rain was at first heartily welcomed. It continued, however, until Sunday the 17th, when it came down in torrents. Cloudbursts occurred Sunday morning in the Tejunga and Verdugo cañons, and at 2 p. m. the water reached town and a general alarm was given. From that time until evening it swept over the whole district bounded by Macy, Georgia and Alameda streets and portions of the Sabichi and Hollenbeck tracts near the Southern Pacific depot. The Southern Pacific railway bridges were both knocked out of shape. The approach on the east side to the East Los Angeles bridge was washed away, but the bridge itself was not materially damaged. Both the Aliso avenue and First street bridges were completely destroyed and the covered bridge sank two or three feet in the center. About forty houses, nearly all on the Aliso tract, were carried away. The agricultural implement establishment of Rees & Wirsching, together with a full stock of goods, was carried down, the loss in this case amounting to $12,000. The Aliso street car bridge was also wrecked. George Stoltz, a milkman, was drowned in the Arroyo Seco, and this was the only life lost during the flood. The body was recovered several weeks later. The railroads were washed out everywhere and there was no communication with the North or East for two weeks. The total loss in the city was estimated at $150,000. The City Council immediately took measures to prevent the recurrence of the flood, and, under the direction of the City Surveyor, a wing-dam of sand-bags was built just below the covered bridge. A few days later the river rose again and carried away every vestige of the dam, but did not overflow the city.

The sufferers by the flood of 1884 received prompt relief from the charitable people of Los Angeles. A relief committee was appointed by the Council, and liberal contributions of money and clothing were made for the benefit of the destitute people. Miss Louise Rial being in the city, tendered a benefit for the relief fund, and a large addition was made to it by this means.

In the country the whole district from the Cerritos rancho to New River was under water, and bridges and roads were washed out everywhere. There were three separate floods during 1884, but the first was the most disastrous to the city.

THE FLOOD OF 1861-2.

Which Played Some Curious Freaks, Did Some Harm and Some Good.

The flood of 1861-62 began with the rain on Christmas eve, 1861, and continued almost without intermission until January 17, 1862, on which last day, 3 o'clock p. m., fell tremendous torrents of water, accompanied by loud claps of thunder and vivid lightning. For many years this rain of December-January (1861-62) was the heaviest that had fallen. The city dam was damaged; some adobe houses fell; travel on the roads was considerably impeded; the southeast gales delayed the arrival of the Brother Jonathan at San Pedro. At El Monte San Gabriel river made a new channel, entering near the town of Lexington. On the Santa Ana, at Anaheim, the overflow was rather advantageous than otherwise to the vineyards. Some thirty miles higher up, by accessions of torrents from the mountain creeks of San Bernardino, on the night of January 17th, the flood destroyed the thriving New Mexican settlement of Agua Mansa (Gentle Water). There was no loss of life, the sleeping inhabitants having timely alarm by the bells of their church; but every former sign of culture was obliterated by the waste of sand which the rush of waters spread over the whole valley, and five hundred souls, houseless, were turned out upon the surrounding hills.

Villa Excursion Postponed.

Owing to the rain, the grand fifty-cent excursion and auction sale at Sierra Madre Villa, has been postponed to Monday next, January 25th, at 1 o'clock p. m.

LOS ANGELES DAILY TIMES.

VOL. IX....NO. 63. LOS ANGELES, CALIFORNIA, SATURDAY MORNING FEBRUARY 20, 1886. FIVE CENTS.

RATTLED RATES.

The Railway War Fairly Inaugurated,

RATE CUTTING CUTS ALL AROUND.

The Atchison Determined to Fight It Out—The Other Lines Show No Signs of Yielding.

Associated Press Dispatches to The Times.

CHICAGO, Feb. 19.—The overland railway war, growing out of the collapse of the Transcontinental Association, was inaugurated to-day in a thoroughly [illegible] way, both as to passenger and freight traffic. All lines running west and southwest from this city having California connections were booking passengers to-day to San Francisco at $60 for first-class unlimited, $60 for first-class limited, $42 for second-class and emigrant. In the matter of contracting for freight, no rates are quoted, but the agents have been given carte blanche to secure business at any figure, and it is known that very large reductions are being made. The Atchison, Topeka and Santa Fé did not announce its rate until this morning, awaiting until the initiative had been taken by the Union and Southern Pacific Companies. The officials of the Atchison Company assert that the war has been forced upon them against their wishes, and owing to their claim to what they deemed an equitable percentage of the overland traffic.

THE ATCHISON COMPANY'S DEMANDS.

The First Vice-President of the Atchison Company to-day, speaking of the situation, said that the company had given notice of its intention to withdraw from the Transcontinental Association December 4th, 1885, for the reason that the association was not being conducted upon what they deemed proper business principles. The Atchison Company had purchased an unfinished railroad in Southern California, …

G. A. R.

Second Day of the Encampment at Sacramento

SACRAMENTO, Feb. 19.—The second day's session of the Department Encampment of the Grand Army of the Republic began this morning at Odd Fellows' Hall. Fully two hundred and fifty delegates were present. The entire morning session was occupied in transacting routine business, among other things being the consideration of the report of the General Committee of Management appointed by the Department Commander to take charge of the arrangement for the National Encampment. On motion of E. S. Solomon, the petition of Col. J. D. Stevenson to Congress for a pension was indorsed, and this constituted the work of the morning session.

During the session this afternoon a communication was read from Gen. Ransom Post, of Flagstaff, Arizona, stating that that post had recently lost all its property by fire, and requesting assistance. A collection was immediately taken up, and over $100 contributed.

AFTERNOON SESSION.

At 3:30 the nomination and election of officers was taken up. An hour and a quarter was occupied in the nominating speeches. Gen. W. H. L. Barnes was first placed in nomination. Then he, in an eloquent speech, nominated Col. W. R. Smedberg. The nominations of Col. Stuart M. Taylor, J. H. Barbour and Gov. Geo. Stoneman, followed in order.

The first ballot consumed about an hour, and resulted as follows: W. R. Smedberg 61, Stuart M. Taylor 56, J. H. Barbour 43, W. H. L. Barnes 37, and Gov. Stoneman 10. Total, 207; necessary to a choice, 104. There being no election a recess was taken until 8 p. m.

In the evening session Smedberg was elected Commander on the fifth ballot receiving 109 votes.

WOMEN'S RELIEF CORPS CONVENTION.

The Women's Relief Corps Convention met at 2:30 this afternoon and elected department officers as follows: President, Mrs. Betsy Jane Russell of Appomattox Corps, Oakland; Senior Vice President, Mary Jordan, Warren …

CONGRESS.

An Investigation Demanded, in the Senate,

OF THE DEATH OF CAPTAIN CRAWFORD.

Bills Passed Removing Political Disabilities—Another Discussion in the House on the Silver Question.

Associated Press Dispatches to The Times.

WASHINGTON, Feb. 19.—In the Senate Mr. Manderson offered a resolution directing the Secretary of State and the Secretary of War to inquire and report to the Senate the facts surrounding the killing of Captain Emmet Crawford, said to have been slain on or about January 10, 1886, by Mexican troops, and to report what steps were being taken for the punishment by the Mexican government of those guilty of the alleged outrage; also whether reparation and indemnity should not be made to those who suffered, and an ample explanation and apology be given to the United States for the apparently gross insult. In offering the resolution Mr. Manderson said it was due to the United States, not less than to the relations of the deceased, that inquiry should be made as to the killing of Capt. Crawford. Mr. Manderson read the official report of Lieut. Maus on the subject, and maintained that if the facts were there correctly set forth, they constitute a very severe reflection on the Mexican troops. Mr. Manderson paid a high tribute to the courage and soldierly devotion of Capt. Crawford and animadverted with severity on the course pursued by the Mexicans. He expressed a hope that the United States would compel reparation, if necessary by force, from the Mexican government, in case that government should prove to be in any way responsible for the conduct of its troops in this instance.

Mr. Butler objected to the present consideration of the resolution.

Mr. Edmunds said that the custom of …

SENSATIONS

Piling Up on the Heels of the Trial.

Yesterday was a big day for sensations. Aside from the conclusion of the long and famous Perkins-Baldwin trial, with a verdict for plaintiff as big as the jury dare make it, there were other startling developments. Mrs. Hunter was Miss Perkins's principal witness to prove the engagement. On this account the defense concentrated their fire on her, and brought a whole drove of Colton cattle to swear away her character. She appeared a thorough lady on the stand, and told a perfectly straightforward story. But the horrible attack upon her preyed on her mind, naturally inclined to melancholy, and already saddened by the recent death of her mother and brother. Last Wednesday morning she left her home four miles west of this city, left her nursing babe, and nothing has been seen nor heard of her since. It is believed that she has wandered off in her agony and probably perished.

While the jury was out deliberating on a verdict yesterday afternoon, Lucky Baldwin was making a new move which is generally deemed to indicate that he is "rattled." He transferred a part of his property to other hands! There was filed in the Recorder's office a conveyance of his Santa Anita tract to H. A. Unruh for $350,000. The description will be found under real-estate transfers elsewhere. At the same time, it is understood, he deposited with the Wells Fargo Express Company here the necessary papers to be filed in San Francisco conveying the Baldwin Hotel and other San Francisco property to his little Lulu Dram. It is stated by able legal authority that such a transfer would not hold good against Miss Perkins's judgment. It is understood that the present Mrs. Baldwin is even now taking steps for a divorce.

A Bad Runaway.

At a quarter to 6 o'clock last evening Mr. Holgate and three men in his employ were riding on a gravel wagon at the eastern end of Downey avenue, when the team was frightened by a loose animal coming up behind, and ran away. The loose boards on the bed of the wagon …

CROOKED WORK.

Assessments Levied on Jail Architect Hall

BY A LOCAL SYNDICATE OF JOBBERS.

Startling Development Before a Special Session of the Supervisors Yesterday—Holcomb, the Nervy Witness.

For several days the circumambient air has been loaded with strange rumors. So highly spiced, indeed, were these stories, that they caused people to turn aside temporarily from the all-prevailing Perkins-Baldwin sensation, and talk about those notable personages, Tom Mott and General Bouton. The report ran that John Hall, the architect of the new county jail, had been tampered with by "the lobby," and had been made to give up $1000 in blood money. This coming to the ears of prominent citizens and county officials, caused the holding of a prolonged meeting Wednesday night, at which indisputable evidence of crookedness was adduced. A special session of the Board of Supervisors was called for 10 o'clock yesterday morning. The proceedingings yesterday took the form of an official investigation, the witnesses all being placed under oath and their testimony being taken down in shorthand by Frank W. Cherry. The small space in the Supervisors' room available for spectators was filled. Supervisors Macy, Lindley, Foord, Ross and Hinds were present, constituting the entire Board, with President Macy in the chair.

District Attorney Holton conducted the examination on the part of the Supervisors, assisted by W. T. Williams, Esq., and Judge Morgan appeared apparently for Mott and Bouton.

JOHN HALL,

being first sworn by County Clerk Dunsmoor, testified, in substance, as follows: "I am an architect by profession. Some time ago I submitted plans for the county jail. I was successful and my plans were adopted. While the plans were with the board I had no negotiations with anybody outside to secure their adoption. The morning after the plans were adopted, Mr. Bouton took me by the arm and said that some friends up in Temple Block …

[illegible]

LOS ANGELES DAILY TIMES.

VOL. X----NO. 22. LOS ANGELES, CALIFORNIA, TUESDAY MORNING, JUNE 29, 1886. FIVE CENTS.

WASHINGTON.

France Mustn't Meddle with the Panama Canal.

MR. MORROW'S ANTI-CHINESE EFFORTS.

Alleged Probable Change in the Cabinet—Legislation Asked Against Bad Wines—The Lincoln-Grant Bridge.

Associated Press Dispatches to The Times.

WASHINGTON, June 28.—The Chair laid before the Senate a conference report on the Postoffice Appropriation bill, stating that the committee was unable to agree (question being on subsidy provision).

Mr. Plumb moved that the Senate insist on its amendment (the subsidy appropriation), and ask a further conference. After debate the amendment was agreed to—yeas, 33; nays, 12; the Democrats voting with the Republicans in the affirmative were Messrs. Brown, Call, Eustis.

After an executive session the Senate adjourned.

A MONUMENTAL BRIDGE.

Senator Spooner to-day submitted amendment to the Sundry Civil Appropriation bill to appropriate $10 000 to enable the Secretary of War to prepare suitable plans, drawings and specifications, and to ascertain and estimate soundings, site and foundation for piers, and cost of the Lincoln-Grant monumental bridge, with suitable approaches, from Observatory Point in this city across the Potomac River to Arlington Gate.

House of Representatives.

WASHINGTON, D. C., June 28.—Under a call of States a bill was introduced by Mr. Randall to reduce and equalize duties on imports, to reduce internal-revenue taxes, and to modify the laws in relation to the collection of the revenue.

Mr. King, of Louisiana, introduced the following:

"WHEREAS, The French government gave its assurance to the government of the United States that the project of De Lesseps was a private enterprise, for which the French government was in no wise responsible; and

WHEREAS, The extraordinary expenditures of the Panama Canal Company have caused it to appeal for aid to the Government of France, to assist it by authorizing a loan of 600,000,000 francs for the purpose of continuing the work of construction, and

WHEREAS, It is reported that the French Government has recently recommended to the Chamber of Deputies to grant the necessary authorization; and

WHEREAS, Such authorization will identify the French Government with the enterprise;

Resolved, That the United States will view with great solicitude and disfavor this contemplated action of the French government, or any other measure calculated to identify it with the Panama Canal, as such action is opposed to the policy of the American people, as expressed by the Chief Executive of the United States at the inception of this canal, and which policy is now most emphatically repeated and reiterated by the United States.

Resolved, That the Secretary of State be requested to send to Congress, without delay, all correspondence bearing on this subject of such importance and fraught with such danger to national interests.

A PETITION FROM THE WINE MEN.

A petition, signed by the most prominent importers of foreign wines, dealers in domestic wines and wholesale grocers of New York, has been forwarded to Senator Warner Miller, to be presented to Congress. The petitioners represent that the existing law (section 3328 of the Revised Statutes) taxing imitation and spurious wines has not been enforced, for reasons which officers of the government may explain.

It is generally understood that this law can be made to operate by additional legislation and with such changes as Congress, in its wisdom, may decide to be proper. The enforcement of this law would prevent the loss of revenue to the Government, and would, by reason of stamps affixed to packages, benefit the public by enabling consumers and physicians to distinguish between pure and spurious wines.

MORROW GETS IN HIS WORK.

The House resumed discussion of the Sundry Civil Appropriation bill. Mr. Morrow of California moved to amend the bill by increasing from $5500 to $10,000 the appropriation to meet expenses incurred under the Chinese Immigration act, and by adding a provision requiring the Secretary of the Treasury to cause to be prepared preliminary and return certificates identifying more particularly than at present the Chinese to whom they are granted. He went on to point out defects in the present law, declaring that the law was evaded in a most shameful manner. The certificates now used, instead of preventing the introduction of Chinese labor, are an aid to immigration. Defects in the law exist in privileges accorded to certain classes of Chinese by treaty to come and go at pleasure. Chinese laborers are constantly coming to the country under pretense of belonging to one or the other of the classes. The condition of the Pacific Coast, so far as the Chinese question is concerned, is worse than ever before, and if Congress knew the whole truth on that question, the Burlingame treaty would not be in existence one hour. He presented a petition prepared under auspices of the Knights of Labor of the Pacific Coast, and signed by fifty thousand persons, asking that some action be taken which would forever prohibit Chinese immigration. After debate Morrow's amendment was adopted without division.

RANDALL KICKS IT OVER.

In the afternoon session Mr. Randall, of Pennsylvania, stated that he had understood that the vote on Morrow's amendment, which was adopted this morning, would not be taken until afternoon. He, therefore, asked unanimous consent that the vote be annulled. This was agreed to, and then Morrow's amendment was rejected—74 to 91.

Changes Probable.

WASHINGTON, Monday, June 28.—It is stated on good authority that a change in the Cabinet is contemplated. Garland is to resign before October, and Bissell, of New York, the President's former law partner, is mentioned as his successor, to keep the geographical composition of the Cabinet harmonious.

It is said that ex-Senator Davis, of West Virginia, will be called to the Treasury Department.

THE CANADIAN PACIFIC.

First Through Train from Montreal to Vancouver.

MONTREAL, June 28.—The first through train to Vancouver on the Canadian Pacific Railroad left here at 8 p. m. Many of the most prominent men in the city, including representatives of all commercial bodies, and thousands of other citizens, witnessed its departure, and the field battery fired a salute of fifteen guns.

A POUNDING HAIL.

Heavy Storm Damage to Crops in Dakota.

ST. PAUL, Minn, June 28.—A Grafton, Dakota, special to the Pioneer Press says: A strip of country twenty miles long by two miles wide, around Inkster, was pounded bare of crops by a terrible hail storm Saturday. The Norwegian church near Grafton was blown to kindling wood. The damage to crops is estimated at $50,000.

THE STRIKES.

Trains at Last Moving Out of Chicago.

CHICAGO, June 28.—Winchester rifles rested on the shoulders of the Pinkerton men as they made their appearance at the Lake Shore freight yards this morning. The first thing they attended to was to drive every one from the tracks. The strikers and their adherents congregated just outside of the right of way, excitedly discussing the situation. Deputy Sheriff Gleason appeared at Forty-first street, shortly after 10 o'clock this morning, accompanied by six deputies. This is the first time since the strike began that any representative of the Sheriff has appeared on the ground. The deputy read the Riot Act at four points along the line, and the police and deputies then began to clear the tracks.

THE BLOCKADE RAISED.

CHICAGO, June 28.—The Lake Shore Railway Company has at last succeeded in raising the freight blockade. At 12:15 the switch engines which had been busy in the yards making up a train steamed into the side tracks and the regular engine coupled to the freight train. The special police, with their Winchester rifles ready, stood by on the alert. Their guns were too much for the crowd, and not one attempt was made to interfere with the movement. Other trains soon followed, reached South Chicago in safety, and passed the Indiana State line, and proceeded eastward without molestation. The officials of the road now think the strike ended.

OUR G. A. R. VISITORS.

The Committee on Entertainment Meets.

The general Committee of Arrangements for the reception of Grand Army visitors who may pass through Los Angeles whilst traveling to and fro' the Grand Army Encampment, to be held in San Francisco, in the early part of July, met in the Mayor's court room yesterday, at 4 p. m. Chairman I. R. Dunkelberger, of Frank Bartlett Post, was in the chair. There were present, also, J. R. Fletcher and E. A. Weed, of the same post; F. W. Tyler, of Gelcich Post; A. M. Thornton, A. W. Barrett and J. C. Oliver, of Stanton Post, and Abbot Kinney, E. F. Spence and M. L. Wicks, of the Citizens Committee.

The Committee on Hall reported that two halls could be obtained. On motion, the old Armory Hall, on Requena street, was ordered rented, at a cost of $150, for a period beginning on the 6th of July and ending on the 20th of September. The committee was also empowered to hire two janitors for that length of time, at the rate of $2 per day; and to make all final arrangements in regard to lighting the hall and renting seats.

Abbott Kinney was requested to notify the Pomological Society, and all fruit growers of Southern California, to send exhibits, and that they would be authorized to issue and distribute in the Hall pamphlets describing and advocating their several districts. It was urged that the best time to forward exhibits of fruits would be from the 15th of August to the close of the entertainment.

The Finance Committee was increased to six, and reinforced by adding the names of Geo Gebhardt, Wm. H. Workman and F. J. Gilmore.

I. W. Hellman was made treasurer of the General Committee, and it was moved that no money shall be drawn except as approved by the majority of the Finance Committee, and the warrants shall be countersigned by E. A. Weed, Secretary, and approved by I. R. Dunkelberger, Chairman.

The meeting then adjourned to meet at 4 p. m. on the 6th of July, at Old Armory Hall, if not convened before that time by the Chairman.

PERKINS VS. BALDWIN.

Money is No Object, but Time Seems to be.

S. M. White telegraphed Wm. T. Williams yesterday that the writ of prohibition issued by the Supreme Court restraining Judge D. P. Hatch from hearing the motion for a new trial in the case of Perkins vs. Baldwin had been dissolved during the day. As the case then stood, nothing prevented Judge Hatch from listening to the motion, which was set for this morning, in Department No. 2 of the Superior Court. It seems, however, that "Lucky" was not yet deprived of all his artillery, for, late yesterday afternoon, the Sheriff received a new alternative writ of prohibition from the Supreme Court to serve upon Judge Hatch. It stated that H. A. Unruh, on behalf of E. J. Baldwin, had represented to the Supreme Court that Judge Hatch, of Santa Barbara county, assumes to hold court in Los Angeles, and to hear and determine this motion for a new trial, without having been requested to do so by a Superior Judge of this county, notwithstanding the objections of the defendant. Unruh is afraid that, if Judge Hatch proceeds to hear and determine the motion, great and irreparable injury will be done the defendant, and he therefore prays, on behalf of his employer, for a writ of prohibition. For these reasons the Supreme Court command Judge Hatch to refrain and desist from further proceeding in the case of Louise C. Perkins vs. E. J. Baldwin, now pending in the Superior Court of this county, and that he show cause, at the Supreme Court-room, on the 29th day of June, 1886, at 2 p. m., why he should not be absolutely restrained and prohibited from any further proceedings in the case. The writ was served by Major George E. Gard, and Judge Hatch will not hear the case to-day.

AMUSEMENTS.

ZAMLOCH, THE CONJUROR.—A very fair sized audience was assembled at the Grand Opera House last evening to witness the performance of the so-called Austrian conjuror and exposer of Spiritualism. Zamloch is a parlor magician of the conventional type, in appearance a dapper little gentleman, smooth spoken, and fond of indulging in small witticisms which raise an easy laugh and assist in destroying the attention of the spectators. His tricks, as shown last night, comprise nothing that may be called new; for in the line of prestidigitation there is hardly anything new under the sun, but they are performed with an ease and dexterity which stamp the magician as an old practitioner.

The programme promises an entire change each night, and, judging from the performance of last evening, it will likely be quite entertaining. Not the least diverting act of the evening was the distribution of presents, given to the fortunate holders of numbered tickets found in the envelopes handed at the door on entering. Over a hundred gifts were distributed in this way, comprising articles of glassware, crockery, dress and household furniture and utensils. The gravity with which the long procession of people moved up to the stage and received their unexpected gifts was sometimes disturbed by the laughter of the spectators; as, for instance, when a well-known physician received a sack of potatoes, another a ham, another a sack of flour, and yet another a huge wash tub and wash board. The most valuable of the gifts consisted of a china tea set of forty-four pieces and a piece of silk eighteen inches long, which were duly presented and carried away.

A Good Man Gone.

The writer of the justly famous hymn: "When I can read my title clear to mansions in the skies," has long since been laid to rest, but the truth of his words are applicable to-day in this land of schemes and lotteries. When you can read your title clear, buy a lot, and not before. The Bonito tract gives each purchaser a perfect title without flaw. Furthermore, the Bonito tract is a straight land purchase, and no scheme, and lots are sold at a safe and reasonable price, so that no one need fear to invest even all of his savings. Think of it! Large lots, 52 3 by 128 feet, on Washington street, for $150. There are only eighty of them, and they are going fast. This is the best offer ever made in this town. It will pay to read the advertisement.

Examinations.

The entrance examinations for the University of Southern California begin to-morrow.

PACIFIC COAST.

An Alleged Seducer Gets His Billet.

NO ONE TO BLAME FOR THE BOILERS.

Alleged Apache News—Killed by a Tarantula—Sentenced for Life—Drowned at San Diego—Etc.

Associated Press Dispatches to The Times.

SAN FRANCISCO, June 28.—The report of the investigation of the boiler explosion on board the steamer Mariposa last February, outside the port of Honolulu, whereby three men were killed, was filed to-day by Government Inspectors with the supervising inspectors. The report concludes as follows: "Under the foregoing testimony and facts we cannot attach any blame to the chief engineer or his assistants, in connection with the accident."

TYLER ON TRIAL.

When the trial of George W. Tyler, on an indictment charging him with preparing a false affidavit signed by Isabella Clark, a witness in the celebrated Sharon case, came up before Judge Wilson and a jury to-day. W. B. Tyler, attorney for his father, asked leave to withdraw the motion argued and submitted on Friday last to dismiss the indictment, stating that testimony would be introduced for the defense. The court complied with Tyler's request. W. B. Tyler then addressed the jury for the defense, and said he expected to prove that, in April, 1884, the only time defendant ever saw Isabella Clark, she was of sound mind, and capable of comprehending what was said to her. Witness then testified on this point.

SENTENCED FOR LIFE.

Larry Huff, who was convicted of murder in the second degree for killing Matthew T. Eddy, proprietor of the Amador House, was to-day sentenced to imprisonment at Folsom for life.

A SOCIALIST SOAKED.

Francis Martin, one of the socialists arrested on the 16th of May, on the charge of obstructing the streets, today pleaded guilty, and was sentenced to thirty days in the county jail.

Coast Elections.

SAN JOSE, June 28.—The election on the question of issuing bonds to the sum of $300,000, for the purpose of public improvements, to-day, resulted in the defeat of the proposition; 1626 votes being polled, of which 763 were against the bonds.

ANTI PROHIBITION.

SEATTLE, W. T., June 28.—Elections were held throughout the Territory under the local option law to-day. There was a large vote polled with but little excitement. Prohibition was defeated in Seattle by a majority of 1030. All the larger towns in the Territory except Tacoma, Chehalis and Centralia give heavy majorities against prohibition.

The Arizona Operator Again Heard From.

CALABASAS, A. T., June 28.—A. L. Peck returned from Magdalena, this morning, where his niece, who was captured from the Apaches, now is. She says there is a renegade Mexican with the Apaches, who worked for Peck at Minas Prietas, in Sonora. It was through his intercession that Peck's life was saved. This renegade told Peck's niece that if he had known that the woman who was murdered was Peck's wife, her life would have been spared as his had been.

The recaptured girl says Geronimo is wounded in the shoulder, but not very badly, and that nine bucks left the camp where she was recaptured about two days before.

Shot Her Betrayer.

SACRAMENTO, June 28.—Jacob Kline, a member of the First Artillery band, was shot and instantly killed last night by Teenie Wiezel, at the corner of Ninth and J. streets. The girl, who is 20 years old, says Kline seduced her, and she shot him because he refused to marry her. She was arrested and taken to prison.

STONEMAN SURPRISES HIMSELF.

Gov. Stoneman has decided not to interfere in the case of Uzza F. French, who murdered his brother-in-law, named Wells, at Olcta, Amador county, in 1884, and is to be hanged at Stockton to-morrow.

Drowned in Bayncilmate.

SAN DIEGO, June 28.—A young German named Chas. Rheinachrem, quartermaster on the steamer Santa Rosa, was standing in a small boat under the steamer, this morning, when a falling boom struck him on the head and threw him into the water. The body has not been recovered.

Died of a Tarantula Bite.

FRESNO, June 28.—Leonard Downing, six years old, out with a party of campers, was bitten by a tarantula on the thigh, Saturday last. Before treatment could be procured the child died.

CANADA.

The Fisheries Law Not to be Relaxed.

TORONTO, June 28.—The Mail's Ottawa correspondent denies, upon the highest authority, the statement that the Dominion Government, at the instance of the imperial authorities, has relaxed its measures for the protection of Canadian fisheries. On the contrary, there has been no interference of any kind on the part of the home government; and the Dominion Government is determined, in the future as in the past, strictly to enforce the law against United States fishing vessels found violating it.

OFFICIALLY VERIFIED.

OTTAWA, June 28.—It is officially learned that no change has taken place in the policy of the Dominion government in reference to the protection of Canadian fisheries in the line of a less vigorous enforcement of the law. The recent circular to collectors of customs was merely to make plain certain matters of interpretation. It is now, as it has always been, the policy of the Government that any United States fishing vessel found fishing, or preparing to fish, or known to have fished, in Canadian waters shall be seized at once and without warning. Twenty-four hours' warning is applicable solely to United States fishing vessels found hovering within limits.

For Parnell.

NEW YORK, June 28.—The Parnell Parliamentary Fund Committee held its next to last meeting at the Hoffman House to-night. Nearly $10,000 was subscribed. Joseph J. O'Donohue cabled from Paris that he had instructed him to pay in $1,000 for himself, and expressed that the generous support, given by the American people gave great courage to Parnell and Gladstone.

TELEGRAPHIC BRIEFS.

Mr. Laird of Nebraska mounted Commissioner Sparks's policy, in the House, yesterday.

Preparations for Judge Davis's funeral, at Bloomington, are completed. The funeral will take place this afternoon, at 3 o'clock.

The steam yacht Corsair, bearing the Presidential party, arrived at Washington, yesterday, from her cruise down the Potomac river and Chesapeake Bay.

The names of Prince Murat and his son have been stricken from the rolls of the French army because they belong to the former reigning family.

The Senate has confirmed Evan Long as Chief Justice of New Mexico. A. M. Phleger was confirmed as Postmaster of Bodie; and W. J. Bryan ditto at San Francisco.

ELECTRIC ROADS.

Their History and General Method of Operating.

In view of the fact that Los Angeles has two electric street railroads in process of construction, and that it is proposed to give the city a service of considerably over a dozen miles of electric lines, information as to "how the old thing works" will be found interesting. Very few people have even an approximately lucid idea of the method by which the subtile spark becomes a motive agent; and you will hear folks speak of cables pulled by electricity, etc., enough to break Edison's heart.

The first electric railway built in the world was the handiwork of Thomas Davenport, a Vermont blacksmith, who began his experiments in 1834 with an electro-magnet weighing four pounds, from which a weight of 150 pounds could be suspended. In 1835, at Springfield, Mass., he built a small circular railway, on which he placed an electro-magnetic engine. The same year he exhibited in Boston for two weeks. The first electric railway on a useful scale was that of Siemens, exhibited at Berlin in 1879. It was a narrow-gauge, half a mile long, carried about twenty-five persons each way, and its maximum speed was twenty miles an hour. An electric railroad, a mile and a half long, has been running in a suburb of Berlin since 1881, and has never failed to carry its daily traffic. In the neighborhood of the Giant's Causeway, on the coast of Ireland, an electric railway six miles long has been in successful daily operation since November 5th, 1883. The electricity is supplied by a waterfall on the river Bush. The steepest grade is 200 feet to the mile. The road is paying 12 per cent. dividends, and it is proposed to extend it six miles. The electric railway on the beach at Brighton, England, has handled a heavy traffic for the past year without hitch or delay, the cars running incessantly twelve hours a day. The electric railway last opened in Great Britain runs between Newry and Bessbrook, a distance of three miles. The dynamos here also are worked by waterfall. The electric railway at Blackpool, England, two miles long, was opened last September. There are short electric lines on the Continent, including one two miles long in the suburbs of Vienna. The application of power from stored electricity has not yet been perfected, but it is likely to play a most important part in the electric world. Since March, 1882, an electric railway, using Faure accumulators, has been in operation at Breuil-en-Auge, France, with great practical success. Public experiments with the accumulators in the streets of London, Paris and Berlin have been very encouraging. In America the first electric railroad was opened to the public at Saratoga in 1883. One, operated on the Daft system, began its trips at Coney Island in the summer of 1884, and about the same time an electric railroad was put in use on the East Cleveland horse railroad. The most practical electric railway in this country is that running in one of the suburbs of Baltimore. It has a maximum grade of 275 feet to the mile. Some of the L roads in New York are getting ready to use the electro-motor. Its application to them, Edison says, is now only a question of the draughtsman's work.

THE METHOD OF WORKING.

The system adopted by Col. C. H. Howland for the 12-mile network of electric roads, for which he was granted a franchise some months ago, is the aerial one. In the successful Baltimore road, the wire which transmits the power from the central station to the car is laid in a trough along the center of the track, where, over it, a fifth wheel of the dummy runs. This is unsightly, and a great obstruction to the street. In the aerial system; a naked wire is suspended on poles parallel to the track, and carries the mysterious current from the engine-house out along the road. Upon this suspended wire runs a tiny box, called the contact carriage, which contains two 6-inch brass wheels, to take up the electricity from the wire. From this contact carriage, a flexible cable runs to the motor in the car. The current passes down this cable, and through the convolutions of a coiled wire in the motor. Here, by mechanical contrivances, the electricity is made to give back the power which the dynamo consumed at the central station, with a loss of only 30 per cent. The revolution of the armature of the motor acts by gearing on the axles of the dummy wheels. The motor on the dummy is similar in appearance to the generator, only not quite so large. Any person who has seen the dynamos at the electric light works, see in them facsimiles of the motor. The control of the motor (that is, its stopping and reversal), is done by a simple lever switch, and so simple and easy that a child five years old can control it. The lever throwing the brushes on the commutator, either forward or back, reverses the course of electricity through the motor. The electric current is generated at the central station, where a complete power plant, boilers, engine and dynamos, with necessary automatic devices for controlling the current, are placed.

The electric current is then conveyed by the overhead wire to the motor, whence, after performing its work, it is returned by the car track to the dynamo.

The motor is not on the same axle with the driving-wheel, but is connected to it by intermediate gearing.

As the motor revolves at a high speed and the car-wheels at a comparatively low speed, it is necessary to "gear down" within the limit of speed as allowed by law. The average speed of cars propelled by electricity is 12 miles an hour, but they can be easily run at 30 miles an hour.

A PLEASANT AFFAIR.

High School Alumni Reception to the Class of '86.

The reception given by the High School Alumni to the graduating class of '86, at New Armory Hall last night, was a very pleasant event. The hall was filled with bevies of gaily-dressed maidens and ladies, escorted by the *fine fleur* of Los Angeles' young men. George W. Williamson was the very efficient floor manager, and the committees were constituted as follows:

Executive committee—Mrs. John Bloesser, Alice Fitch, L. A. Mendelson, Arthur Bent.

Reception committee—Mrs. H. M. Caystile, Fannie Kalisher, Mary Foy, Florence Potts, Theodore Savage, T. E. Rowan, Jr., Albert Lang, Wm. Bachelder.

The following is the programme of the exercises that took place, which, owing to want of space, cannot be commented upon:

1. Instrumental duet, Alice Fitch and Minnie Hamilton.
2. Address to Class of '86, Margaret F. Philipson, President.
3. Response by Herman Lichtenberger.
4. Vocal solo, Miss M. D. Brown.
5. Essay, L. A. Mendelson.
6. Instrumental solo (selected), Mrs. E. Jennings.
7. Recitation, Miss Agnes McLain.
8. Vocal solo, Marcus Snook.
9. Essay, "Old Maids," Miss A. Mathews.
10. Selection, High School Quartette.

After the exercises dancing became in order and was kept up for several hours with great good will by the alumni, the Class of '86 and all their admiring friends.

Ripe Cantaloupes.

The TIMES was presented yesterday with some ripe cantaloupes, which are rather scarce yet in Southern California at this time of the year. Only one or two, so far, have been seen in the market. The specimens now at this office were received from J. G. McCallum, of 131 Main street, whose son raised them on his ranch at Palm Valley, four miles south of Seven Palms station, on the Southern Pacific railroad. The climate of Palm Valley is an exceptional one, some fruits ripening there as much as two months earlier than in any other part of the State. Palm Valley has been reveling in ripe cantaloupes for the last three weeks.

Under Advisement.

The motion to dismiss the information for assault with a deadly weapon pending against J. C. Gormley was heard yesterday by Judge Cheney, and taken under advisement.

One-fifth Sold in Two Days.

The Southern California Land Company deals only in first-class enterprises. One-fifth of the Williamson tract sold in two days!

Incorporated.

The St. Vincent Hotel Company was incorporated yesterday. Capital stock, $100,000.

FOREIGN.

The G. O. M. on the Masses and the Classes.

BR'ER LABOUCHERE'S LITTLE LIBEL.

Bavaria's Regent Inaugurated—Another Dory to Cross the Atlantic—The Comte de Paris's Manifesto.

Associated Press Dispatches to The Times.

LIVERPOOL, June 28.—Gladstone, this afternoon, addressed the electors of Liverpool in Hengler's Circus. He was received with boundless enthusiasm. The circus was crowded to its utmost capacity, 5,000 persons being present. Hundreds of people, unable to gain admittance, crowded around the outside. Mr. Gladstone said the enthusiasm in favor of home rule surpassed anything he had witnessed during his life. The Liberal party, he said, was, as a rule, not supported by dukes, 'squires, clergymen of the established church, officers of the army, and so forth. The question was whether the masses were able constitutionally to overbear the classes; because it had always been shown that wherever truth, justice and humanity were concerned, the masses were in the right and the classes in the wrong. Parliament, he said, had been paralyzed because of the Irish question, and it would remain paralyzed unless some measures of justice were passed.

Field Wouldn't Have It.

LONDON, June 28.—When the case of Cyrus W. Field against Labouchere, editor of Truth, for libel, was called for hearing, the Attorney General, on behalf of Labouchere, withdrew the plea of justification and expressed Labouchere's regret for publishing the article, and stated that he and Sir Henry James, Field's counsel, had agreed upon the amount that would be paid by Labouchere in satisfaction of the costs, and asked the Judge to discharge the jury. It is understood that for several days Labouchere's counsel has been wanting to have the case settled by his making an apology and retraction, and not paying anything for costs. This Field refused to accept.

Bavaria's Regent.

MUNICH, June 28.—Prince Luitpold was to-day formally made Regent of Bavaria, to administer the affairs of the kingdom during the occupation of the throne by King Otto, the insane successor of Ludwig. The ceremony was performed in the throne room of the residence schloss, in the presence of the ministry and a majority of Parliament.

The Compte's Manifesto.

LONDON, June 28.—The manifesto of the Count of Paris has been placarded in many towns throughout France. It was mailed to every elector in the republic. The Royalists will organize their campaign on the basis of the manifesto.

Nice to Have in the Family.

BUCHAREST, June 28.—A servant in a family in this city to-day murdered his master and mistress and their five children, stole 100,000 francs, and then fled to Bulgaria.

Two More Fools.

LONDON, June 28.—Two men sailed for New York from the Clyde to-day, in a boat 19 feet long. They took provisions for two months.

A Costly Fire.

EDINBURGH, June 28.—Balruddery mansion, at Dundee, owned by Martin White of New York, was destroyed by fire to-day. Loss, $250,000.

THE TELEPHONE.

Wonderful Development of its System.

The telephone has become so much of an indispensable institution to the United States that the growth of its use has been very much lost sight of, just as always occurs in all matters without which people cannot do. In Los Angeles county this development has been perhaps greater than anywhere else, and accomplished in such a manner that anyone unacquainted with the extent of the telephone system of this section, could not possibly make an approximately correct guess of its extension. The telephone was practically unknown here four years ago. To-day its use is an indispensable necessity to business and professional persons and for those who live in the suburbs to be without a telephone is almost as bad as to be in the woods. There are actually in use to-day in Los Angeles county 550 telephones, necessitating over 400 miles of wire. Of this considerable network, 210 miles are employed to connect the city with the outside towns in the county. A steadily increasing demand for telephonic communication by the owners of business houses and private residences is one of the remarkable features of the system. As an instance of the popularity of the instrument, it may here be mentioned that E. N. Snider, the present manager, has registered no less than 100 new subscribers since the time he assumed charge of the office, and they have all been connected with the Central office. On the 23d inst. communication was established with Florence, Vernon and Lynwood, and two or three other towns will be connected within a short date with the city.

In the Central operating room business has been increasing space, so that at present no less than eight operators are at work there. Though there have at times been complaints made of the insufficiency of the service at that office, this state of affairs has now ceased to exist. One of the causes of the improvement is no doubt the increase of the staff. Another is the introduction of a fine new multiple switch-board which when in operation will do much to remedy the constantly increasing business necessitates frequent editions of books containing all the names of subscribers. Though it is not long since that a catalogue was printed, the necessities of the telephone system of Los Angeles demand a new one and this may be expected by the 1st of July.

FOUND AT LAST.

Peter Lercher's Body Discovered in a Grain Field.

It will be remembered that early in May—about the 7th—Peter Lercher, of this city, brother of Joseph Lercher, of the Eintracht saloon, disappeared. He was last seen near Fulton Wells, crazed by drink. A reward was offered, and searching parties were sent out, but in vain. Yesterday, however, a farmer, a mile from Fulton Wells, raked up the body in his grain field. Lercher was lying upon the ground, with his coat under his head, and it is supposed died of alcohol and exposure. An inquest will be held to-day.

Picking Up Fire Points.

Chief Engineer Walter S. Moore, of the Los Angeles fire department, got home Sunday after a week's absence up north. Having secured leave of absence from the Fire Commissioners, he went at his own expense to inspect the fire departments of San Francisco and other northern cities. He was present at the Antisell fire and other big blazes, and got many valuable points.

Day School.

On Monday and during vacation, Professor Lawson will receive day pupils at his High School rooms, 11 and 12 Schumacher block. Reduced rates to High School pupils. To those deficient in any branch, this will afford an excellent opportunity to "study up." All desiring to become proficient in book-keeping, penmanship or arithmetic, cannot do better that attend his school.

To Open.

The Belmont, on the hills, at the end of the Second street cable road, opens to-morrow.

Pomological Society.

The County Pomological Society meets at Anaheim to-morrow.

THE WHITE SCALE.

A Startling Statement as to its Increase.

Some weeks ago Council appointed a special committee—Messrs. Breed, Willard and Stearns—to see it the Fruit Pest Inspectors had earned their salaries. The committee has been investigating the matter very carefully, and commends the inspectors for faithful work, but finds that they have been unable to compete with the scale-bug, which the committee finds *is much more numerous than it was last year.* The concluding portion of the committee's report follows, and further interesting matter on the same subject will be found in the Council proceedings.

"It is just what condition the orange orchards would be in at this time if no steps had been taken to destroy the pest we are unable to say. But if, as many scientific men assure us and as we believe, these bugs are destructive to orange trees, it does not take much of a mathematician to figure out the length of time it will take these prolific bugs to go away with every orange tree in the city limits; provided, of course, that they are allowed to increase and multiply in the future as they have during the past year. As the orange tree is one of our chief attractions and figures, to some extent in the price of corner lots, such a result is not very desirable and ought to be, if possible, avoided.

"Your committee is of the opinion that by far the greater portion of the people are not aware of the magnitude and increasing danger which threatens not only our fruit trees, but our entire vineyards as well. We attribute this fact to the policy adopted by parties interested to keep the matter as quiet as possible.

"We believe that the true status of the matter should be known, and the sooner the people are made aware of it the better it will be for the pecuniary interests of the people and the future prosperity of the city. If there is any way of destroying these pests we would urge the necessity of taking up arms at once and moving as a body against them. With this end in view we would recommend

First—That the City Attorney draft an ordinance to amend an ordinance governing this matter, in such a way as will enable the Inspectors to not only compel the owners of infected trees to commence to clean them, but to prosecute their work to an actual finish.

Second—That the Police Commissioners be requested to appoint sufficient Inspectors to do the work thoroughly and afterwards to see that they do it.

Third—That the Supervisors be requested to appoint more Inspectors, and, in order to prevent confusion and promote harmony among the Inspectors, we would suggest that the Board of Police Commissioners and the County Board of Horticultural Commissioners consult together in regard to the districts assigned to the different Inspectors.

Silver Wedding.

A large number of the friends of Mr. and Mrs L. Dennis gave them a surprise party at the residence of Dr. C. E. Clacius, corner of Figueroa and Pico streets, last Saturday night. The pleasant gathering was in honor of the twenty-fifth anniversary of the wedding of Mr. and Mrs. Dennis, and a thoroughly enjoyable evening was passed.

Free 'Bus.

Free 'bus daily to Co-operative Nursery tract. No. 236 No. Main street. Horse cars will run within one block by October 1st.

Call and See the List

Of subscribers to the Co-operative Nursery Tract. The names mount way up in the hundreds. 236 N. Main street. Free 'bus daily.

One-fifth Sold in Two Days.

The Southern California Land Company deals only in first-class enterprises. One-fifth of the Williamson tract sold in two days!

Double Your Money.

Buy a lot in Wiesendanger's city tract. Free ride—9, 11:30, 3, 6:30 p. m., from 23 N Spring.

One-fifth Sold in Two Days.

The Southern California Land Company deals only in first-class enterprises. One-fifth of the Williamson tract sold in two days!

Best Value for Least Outlay.

Wiesendanger city tract. Free ride from 23 N. Spring street.

At 6:30 p. m Every Evening.

Free ride from 23 N. Spring to Wiesendanger city tract; also 9, 11:30 and 3 p. m.

A Fine Business for Sale.

Please read John C. Bell's, the auctioneer's advertisement, in another column.

THE WEATHER.

LOCAL BULLETIN.

LOS ANGELES SIGNAL OFFICE, June 28.—At 4:07 a. m. to-day the thermometer registered 59; at 12:07 p. m. 80, and at 7:07 p. m. 67. Barometer for corresponding periods, 29.94, 29.96, 29.93. Maximum temperature, 82.0; minimum, 57.0. Weather at 7:07 p. m., clear.

People's Store's Stocktaking Sale.

All-linen table linen sold to-day at 19c.

Gents' brown lace straw hats to-day 10c.

Half-wool dress goods to-day 6c.

42 inch all-wool plaid dress goods 25c.

Special sale of Lonsdale muslin to-day.

Special sale of bleached sheeting to-day.

Men's bathing suits to-day 85c.

Children's lace caps 25c.

A sale of embroideries 10c. A sale of linen laces 5c, worth 15c. A sale of Oriental laces. Boys' blue or brown sailor suits, two pieces, $2. New shapes in hats and bonnets received by express to-day.

All-linen napkins 25c a dozen.

White embroidery dress patterns, 10 yards of material and 9 yards of embroidery to match $2.50. Ladies' lace Oxfords 95c Ladies' opera-toe slippers 75 cents. Ladies' gray cloth top shoes $1.75. Ladies' curacoa kid button shoes $1.25. Children's spring heel shoes, 5 to 8, 75c. Infants' slippers, 8 different styles, 45c. Misses' curacoa kid low-cut shoes 95c. Ladies', boys', misses', and children's spring heel canvas shoes. Apron check ginghams 6c. Extra grade checks 7 cents, worth 10c a yard. 500-bone corsets 95c, regular price $1.75.

PEOPLE'S STORE.

Ready-Made Suits.

H. Mosgrove & Co. are offering immense bargains in ready-made traveling and walking suits, made from the newest summer fabrics and in the latest styles, also a fine line of plain and embroidered lawn and muslin suits at most reasonable prices. 21 S. Spring st.

Nevada Shoulder Cape,

At the only Cloak and Suit House. A new line of Nevadas, in cut velvet, dice material and corded Sicilian silk, for the low price of $10 each. 21 S. Spring st.

Japanese Embroidered Scarfs.

Don't fail to visit Mosgrove's to-day and see his new line of embroidered scarfs at $2.50 each; former price $5. 21 S. Spring st.

John C. Bell has removed his office to No. 48 Temple Block.

Consult Mrs. Dr. Wells for all diseases of women. Prompt relief for female irregularities. Two hours each day devoted to electro-thermal and medicated baths. Consultation free. 341 Spring street.

Excursion East.

June 8th and 22d, July 20th, via Salt Lake, the Home of the Saints.

BAKER & DANISON,

304 N. Main street, Los Angeles.

For choice fresh cows, call on Niles, on Washington, near Main street.

Gentlemen's clothes cleaned or dyed and repaired at short notice at MARTEEN'S, No. 9 Aliso street.

Running sixteen hours a day to accommodate the great rush and increasing busin No. 9 Aliso street.

Honey Case Shooks

For sale by George E. Dickson, agent Capital Box Factory. Office with Harrison & Dickson, 221 N. Los Angeles street.

Swiss Dressing Sacks.

100 dotted Swiss dressing sacks will be offered to-day at Mosgrove's for 50c each. 21 S. Spring st.

Profits in Seedling Oranges.

Col. B. D. Wilson once sold $1800 worth from a single acre. Three years ago Mr. Dalton, now deceased, sold $300 from a quarter of an acre.—Herald editorial, June 19. Above orange grove is adjoining the Co-operative Nursery tract. The old trees on the Wolfskill tract return $1200 to $1500 per acre profit.—Editorial Rural Californian, June number. Can you now hesitate in buying lots in the Co-operative Nursery tract, containing 14-year-old trees? You can get yearly more than the price of each lot from the fruit. This is a forced sale, remember. Nothing equals it in the market. Call at 236 N. Main street. Free 'bus.

Electro-Magnetism, the New Means of Cure.

Dr. E. Robbins's Electro-Magnetic Institute, corner First and Spring streets, entrance on First street, is now fitted up, at considerable expense, with everything that is necessary to cure chronic and so-called incurable diseases, by the finest electrical apparatus in the world. Turkish and Russian baths; also electric sulphur baths. Dr. Robbins has had several years' experience in the Australian colonies, San Francisco, Salt Lake City, Denver and three years in Los Angeles, and hundreds of leading citizens can testify to the wonderful effects of electricity in curing cases of chronic diseases when all else had failed, and therefore no persons suffering should try the new remedy before abandoning all hope. After every treatment the patients are treated with the Massage treatment, by persons of their own sex. The Doctor diagnoses disease without explanation from the patient, free of charge. His office hours are 8 till 12, 1 to 5.

Eastern Prices Have Come to Stay at McDonell's Drug Store, 271 North Main Street.

The enormous profits once realized by the drug store trade are a thing of the past. We sell our goods at genuine Eastern prices. For instance, we will sell you—

Best gum camphor, 25c a pound, regular price 60c.

Colgate's Cashmere Bouquet Soap, 25c per cake, regular price 35c.

Hoyt's German Cologne, 15c, regular price 25c.

Warner's Kidney and Liver Cure, $1 per bottle, regular price $1.25—and all other goods at genuine Eastern prices.

Prescriptions compounded at the new Schedule of prices. Remember! McDonnell, the Druggist, Ross Block.

Those P. P. P. P.'s.

They mean just what they say—Popular Pullman Palace Parties. Don't forget it. July 5th we start East by a round-trip, first-class excursion, good for three months. Don't be persuaded to go any other way, when our rate is so low. Call at 114 First street, Nadeau Block. S. J. MATHES, Manager Sigler P. P. P. P.'s.

Ladies.

Consult Mrs. Dr. Wells, whose specialty is diseases of women, and treatment entirely new. Prompt relief in female irregularities. Two hours each day devoted to electro, medicated and hot-air baths. Consultation free. 341 Spring street.

Ice-cream given away at Brown's Restaurant, 26 N. Main street, with dinner every day from 11 a. m. to 4 p. m.

Ghirardelli's Eagle chocolate is the most popular brand in the market.

Special Notices.

Royal Templars of Temperance Council will meet at 127 South Spring street on WEDNESDAY, JUNE 30th, at 8 p. m., for the transaction of important business. All are expected to be present. J. P. LAMOREE, Financial Secretary.

Soap Bubble Party.—Under the auspices of the ladies of Epiphany Mission (Episcopal) at Crescenta Hall, East Los Angeles, on the evening of THURSDAY, JULY 1. All are invited.

To the Republican Club (Colored) of Los Angeles—Greeting: You are hereby notified of a special meeting of the members and all those wishing to become members, to be held at Emigration Hall, 57 North Spring street, opposite Courthouse, on THURSDAY EVENING, JULY 1, 1886. JAS. MARCHLOR, President; CHAS. COUNCELLOR, Secretary.

Stanton Post, G. A. R., meets every Friday evening at Masonic Hall, 12½ S. Spring st. Visiting comrades cordially invited. J. M. GUINN, Post Commander. S. C. SIMONDS, Adjutant.

Mrs. Elizabeth Mills, Metaphysical, who will teach the science of healing. All diseases successfully treated. The poor treated free. Office 203 S. Fort st.

David Elterich of New York, and lately of San Francisco, will please communicate with his brother concerning his father's estate. Any information concerning him will be thankfully received by LOUIS ELTERICH, 18 Chrystie st., New York; or H. ASCHE, 10 Geary st., San Francisco.

Stockholders' Meeting.—The annual meeting of the stockholders of the Los Angeles Savings Bank will be held at the office of the bank on TUESDAY, JULY 6, 1886 (the first Tuesday in July), at 10 a. m., for the purpose of electing a Board of Directors and transacting such other business as may be brought before the meeting. J. V. WACHTEL, Secretary.

Mrs. Elsie Reynolds—Materializing séances on Sunday and Wednesday evenings at 306 South Spring street.

The Drawing for the $1000 diamond ring will take place positively on the 1st of July, at 2 o'clock, at the Old Armory Hall, Requena st., opposite United States Hotel. Few tickets left.

WANTED—HELP.

WANTED—Two men for mill work at Los Angeles Box Company, 310 E. Fifth st.

WANTED—Good man willing to work 10 hours a day; fair education; some business experience. Address S. S., Times office.

WANTED—Responsible agents to sell the Culelia Self-acting Fire Extinguisher and other popular specialties. FRANCISCO & CO. 24 S. Spring st.

WANTED—To rent—House of three or four rooms convenient to street car. Address S., Daily Times.

WANTED—General employment and intelligence office. Males and females wishing employment and others wanting help can save time and expense by calling on Mrs. E. H. MOORE, 21 South Main street. Always in demand for canvassers.

WANTED—SITUATIONS.

COMPANION—Competent lady desires to take charge of house for furnished rooms, or as companion. Address 20 S. Fort st.

AUCTIONEER—First class salesman with experience and dry goods open for engagement in city or country. H. H. MATLOCK, 113 S. Main st., Los Angeles.

NURSE—Reliable woman desires position to take care of an invalid. Address 703 Hill st.

GOVERNESS—Young lady, graduate of Mills Seminary, desires position as governess. Address E. L. H. 176 Ninth st., Oakland, Cal., or R. W. Poindexter, Los Angeles.

A FIRST-CLASS dressmaker, cutter and fitter, a stranger in the city, wishes to find a few more engagements by the day; best of reference given. Call or address Mrs. A. C. M., cor. S. Spring and Fifth sts.

BOOKKEEPER—Situation wanted as bookkeeper or copyist by a competent young lady; best of references. Address A. C. M., Times office.

WANTED—MISCELLANEOUS.

WANTED—To buy a second-hand guitar. Apply to or address M. C., 141 S. Fort street.

WANTED—First-class pens, not to cost much; must be cheap. Send card, stating size and price, to GEO. A. HOWARD, 304 Fort st.

WANTED—To buy or lease, a quite or a daily paper; moving and locations. Address with particulars to H. B., care of Times office.

WANTED—A child to board; mother's care. 353 S. Los Angeles st.

TO LET—ROOMS.

TO LET—Three rooms, partly furnished, 517 6th st.

426 S. SPRING ST.—Handsomely furnished rooms, with or without board.

182 WALL ST. (near Seventh)—Furnished rooms for housekeeping.

THE OCCIDENTAL has been recently repaired and refitted. Special rates for summer months. Also day board. In to-day's paper.

517 SIXTH ST.—To let, 4 or 5 rooms, partly furnished.

409 S. PEARL ST.—Pleasant furnished rooms; lovely yard; half block from street cars.

220 S. FORT ST.—St. Helena House, sunny rooms, neatly furnished; first class location.

FOR EXCHANGE.

TO EXCHANGE—A stock of millinery, valued at $500, for lot. Address S. H. O. L., Times office.

FOR SALE—CITY PROPERTY.

FOR SALE—The best lots in the new Second Street Tract by J. T. BROWN, 18 Georgia street.

TO LET—Or sale, house of 4 rooms, cor. King and Charity, near Washington.

FOR SALE—Handsome villa lots on Euclid Hill, Boyle Heights, 100x200, at $1000 each. Apply 23 S. Spring st.

FOR SALE—Choice lot in the Childs tract, 25x165 feet on Flower st., at a bargain, $3500; 2 lots on Main st. near Washington, cheap; bargains on Upper Main st., Johnson Mansion 25 rooms; 2 good buys in business lots at Pasadena; beautiful home on Pearl st.; cheap. BEN E. WARD, 31 North Spring st.

FOR SALE—House of 5 rooms, with basement, well of delicious cold water, windmill, tank, etc., including 3 good sized lots, laid out to trees, small fruit, etc., for the low amount of $2250; but as the owner is now in the East and wishes to use the money for other purposes, it is offered for one week only at this bargain. Call early and avail yourself of this bargain at PIERCE BROS.' Livery Stable, 11 Truman st., East Los Angeles.

FOR SALE—Two fine lots 60x140 on Aliso avenue; $400 each. Apply at 182 Wall st.

FOR SALE—Very cheap; 9 room house, one block from omnibus line; price $2800. Call on C. C. COOK, 13 Court st.

FOR SALE—West End property, 17 beautiful residence lots on Seventh and Ninth sts. and Western ave., near the terminus of the Seventh street cable line and Lake Pearl, are offered for sale. Price and terms very reasonable. Apply to J. S. O'NEIL, on the premises.

FOR SALE—COUNTRY PROPERTY.

FOR SALE—80 acres very choice fruit land, near the lovely village of Tustin; 10 acres in prunes, 6 acres in muscat grapes 4 ye rs old, 6 acres in deciduous fruit, well divided if desired. E. B. MILLAR, corner Spring and Franklin, or E. K. EDWARDS, Santa Ana. my16 4t 8u

FOR SALE—Fine ranch, 515¼ acres, all improved, at Pasadena, in a good suburb; fine lots of water all piped; price only $20,000; can always go East next week; will trade part in city property. BEN E. WARD, 31 North Spring st.

FOR SALE—Ten acres just south of city limits; frontage on three streets, 80 rods on Main st. just the place to subdivide; $400 an acre; easy terms. Apply at 182 Wall st.

FOR SALE—A delightful place of 5 acres; beautiful garden and orchard; a good house, first-class in every respect. Apply to CHAS. VICTOR HALL, 10½ S. Spring st.

FOR SALE—10 or 15 acres in raisin vineyard in bearing, at a bargain. Address O. H. Times office.

FOR SALE—"Cosey Nook," one of the prettiest country homes in Southern California; five and a half acres in fruits of all kinds; two-story cottage of seven rooms, finished in plain woods and hard finish; all necessary outbuildings, stable, etc.; windmill, deep well, excellent water; convenient to stores, schools, churches, railroad, etc.; just the home for a family of taste looking for a rural health retreat. Address or call upon E. A. SAXTON, Anaheim.

FOR SALE—40 acres, join city, elegant residence, bearing fruits and vineyard; abundance of pure water free; owner says it is rich, deep, mellow loam soil; no rocks, no gravel, no adobe; improvements cost $6400; title, United States patent; all for $7500. Inquire of CHAS. CHARBOCK, 13 Court st.

FOR SALE—LIVE STOCK.

FOR SALE—Fresh Jersey cows, from $60 upward; kind and gentle; also poultry eggs for hatching. Apply to WM. NILES, fancy stock raiser, Washington st., near Main. my1Sodlm

FOR SALE—1 Jersey cow and calf at 115 E. Pico st.

FOR SALE—A gentleman's fine driving team; fast roadster; will sell pair or one or both. Apply to PICKIT & KELLY, 302 N. Main st.

FOR SALE—Reliable family horse and two-seated surrey; can be seen at Central Stables, 125 and 127 Requena st.

FOR SALE—A good family old horse for $65 at Cooper's Livery stable, on Requena st., near Los Angeles st.

FOR SALE—Poland China hogs; finest in Southern California. Apply to JOHN CARALERIS, Sepulveda Station, or write Los Angeles P. O.

FOR SALE—MISCELLANEOUS.

FOR SALE—Picket fence-front; cheap. 331 S. Hill.

FOR SALE—A good second-hand top buggy at Cooper's Stable, on Requena st.

FOR SALE—Cheap; 3 horses, 1 family cow, 2 carts, 1 buckboard, 1 wagon, double and single harness. Ventura Stables, 24 Los Angeles st.

FOR SALE—Cheap; a new Wheeler & Wilson sewing machine, $25; also hat-racks, mattresses and other articles of household furniture. Apply at 52 N. Workman st., East Los Angeles.

FOR SALE—Iron Sulphur Water, by the leading grocers and druggists.

ROOMS AND BOARD

ROOMS AND BOARD—Three nicely furnished rooms, good table, with a beautiful view; home cooking. 255 Fort Hill.

ROOMS AND BOARD—The Occidental has been thoroughly repaired and refitted. Special rates for summer months. See adv. in to-day's paper.

KIMBALL MANSION, strictly first-class, fine suites and large single rooms, modern improvements, without board; or business centers, terms reasonable. New High st., near Temple.

TO LET—Two nicely furnished rooms with board at 120 hill st., between Second and Third.

TO LET—Sunny furnished rooms, with board, at summer prices; table boarders accommodated. 141 S. Fort st.

BUSINESS OPPORTUNITIES.

WANTED—An intelligent man, willing to call on a good business man who might be interested in an important matter. Address E., this office.

WANTED—Capable business man of good character, with a capital of from $500 per month. Address, with references, Box 8. Good salary and prompt investments of advertiser. Address E. G. J., this office.

WANTED—A competent person to take an interest in and to cooperate in a profitable business at a summer resort near Pasadena. Address Dr. T. NICHOLS, Pasadena.

FOR SALE—The candy kitchen at 15 W. First st. Apply on premises.

FOR SALE—One-half interest in a good paying business in East Los Angeles. Apply to ADAMS & SON, 75 N. Spring.

MONEY TO LOAN.

TO LOAN—$500. I. S. MALTMAN, 168 N. Main st. Room 9.

MONEY TO LOAN—On mortgage. C. W. MORTIMER, attorney-at-law, 74 Temple Block.

$100,000 TO LOAN on first-class real estate security; mortgages bought and sold. J. VIELE, 55 North Spring st.

BORROWERS OF LARGE SUMS, having first-class real estate security, should call on GEO. D. ROWAN, 38 Nadeau block.

MONEY TO LOAN—In sums to suit on good real estate security; mortgages bought and sold. McKOON & BRODTBECK, No. 19 N. Spring st.

MONEY TO LOAN—Large or small amounts; long or short time. LAMB & GRIFFIN, 19 W. First st.

TO LET—MISCELLANEOUS.

TO LET—Country property—To invalids or persons wanting a good home, with mountain air, in the best four months—A gentleman going to the seaside would like to rent his house and furnishings to a good family; within four miles beyond Pasadena. Apply to Mrs. NITTINGER, Employment Office, or to E. P. T., Box 116, Pasadena.

TO LET—Store in Covina, Los Angeles county. A good opening for a live general merchandise store. Apply to the owner here. Address E. K. RIGHMOND, Covina, Citrus Postoffice.

TO LET—Drug store; a good stand, new building; also good room for restaurant. McCOYE & CUSHMAN, 33 N. Spring st.

TO LET—A ranch of thirty acres, six miles from courthouse, at the Cahuenga foot hills; fruit trees, and grove, house of five rooms, etc. Apply at 240 S. Fort st.

TO LET—HOUSES.

TO LET—House of 5 rooms, hard finish; fruit tree on lot and good water. Inquire 79 Date st.

TO LET—House 319 Temple, 5 rooms. Apply on premises.

TO LET—Furnished house of five rooms and bath-room. 119 North Hill street, opposite Temple.

TO LET—A six-room cottage on Downey ave., in best part of East Los Angeles; furnished or unfurnished. Inquire 19 Hellman st., south of Downey ave.

EXCURSIONS.

PHILLIPS'S Popular Pleasure Parties going East leave June 1 and 29, Aug. 19, Oct. 5. Lowest rates and best accommodations. Call on or address A. PHILLIPS & CO., 124 N. Main st., Los Angeles.

ALL ABOARD!—Violet's select overland excursion No. 9 leaves Tuesday, July 6. Lowest rates and best accommodations. Call on or address O. H. VIOLET, Manager, St. Charles Hotel.

WARNER BROS. & CROSBY popular excursions East every fifteen days. For points East every two weeks. Lowest rates, and through cars always. Apply to WARNER BROS. & CROSBY, 30 N. Main st., Los Angeles.

WALTER'S next excursion East leaves Los Angeles July 26th. A fine party and good accommodations guaranteed. Inquire M. WALTERS, 34 N. Spring st.

The Los Angeles Times.

SIXTH YEAR. VOL. XI. NO. 148. LOS ANGELES, WEDNESDAY MORNING, MAY 11, 1887.—TEN PAGES. PRICE: Single Copies 5 Cents. By the Week, 3 Cents.

Amusements.

THE PAVILION.
Corner Fifth and Olive streets.
McLAIN & LEHMAN.................Managers.

THE GREATEST MUSICAL
EVENT OF THE SEASON.
AMERICAN OPERA
—BY THE—
NATIONAL
—OPERA—
COMPANY

THEODORE THOMAS..........Musical Director.
CHAS. E. LOCKE..........General Manager.

4 —NIGHTS— —AND MATINEE.— 4

Commencing Monday, May 16, 1887.

305—PEOPLE—305

Comprising Eminent Artists, Unrivaled Thomas Orchestra, Magnificent Ballet, Grand Choruses and Elaborate Mise-en-scene.

—REPERTOIRE:—
Monday, LAKME..........Delibes.
Tuesday, LOHENGRIN..........Wagner.
Wednesday, FAUST..........Gounod.
Thursday Matinee..........
THE MERRY WIVES OF WINDSOR...Nicolai.
Thursday, AIDA..........Verdi.

SCHEDULE OF PRICES:

Subscription season ticket (entitling holder to choice of seat, and is transferable)	$15 00
Single Nights:	
Main floor, first fifteen rows	4 00
" " next seven rows	3 00
" " next six rows	2 00
" " side of hall under balcony	1 50
First balcony, first two rows	4 00
" " third row	3 00
" " fourth and remaining rows	2 00
Second balcony, first row	4 00
" " next two rows	3 00
" " remaining five rows	2 00
General admission	1 00

Subscription list closes Wednesday evening, May 4th.

☞Subscription list closes Wednesday evening, May 4th. Seats will be allotted for subscribers only at Turnverein Hall, Thursday morning at 10 o'clock, and Friday and Saturday at the office of McLain & Lehman, No. 3 Market st.

Single night seats will be on sale on Monday morning, May 9th, at 10 a.m. No extra charge for reserved seats.

Arrangements are being made to have excursion trains run from all surrounding towns.

For further information address or call on
McLAIN & LEHMAN,
No. 3 Market st.

GRAND OPERA HOUSE.
H. C. WYATT..........Manager
—FIVE NIGHTS ONLY!—
Commencing, Tuesday, May 10th.
First apppearance of Mr. and Mrs. Geo. S.
KNIGHT.
Direct from their success at the Bush-st. Theater, San Francisco.

Tuesday....May 10 Thursday..May 12 Saturday.....May 14	"OVER THE GARDEN WALL." Musical Farce-comedy.
Wednesday...May 11 Friday..........May 13	"RUDOLPH," BARON VON HOLLENSTEIN. Master Character Play.
Saturday........May 14 Matinee.	"OTTO." A German Comedy-drama.

MIRTH! MUSIC! PATHOS!
A Superb Company of Talented Artists.
Wonderful Scenic Effects.
☞Seats now on sale.

WASHINGTON GARDENS
OSTRICH FARM & ZOOLOGICAL GARDENS.
Grand Promenade
CONCERTS
Every THURSDAY afternoon.
Every SUNDAY afternoon.
—BY—
MEINE'S MILITARY BAND
AND DOHS'S ORCHESTRA.
Forty breeding OSTRICHES always on view.
Admission..........Twenty-five and Ten Cents.
Take the Main-street cars.
CAWSTON & FOX, Prop'rs.

BATTLE OF GETTYSBURG
CYCLORAMA!
Open daily from 10 a.m. to 6 p.m., and from 7:30 to 10 o'clock every evening. Take the South Main-street cars to the immense Pavilion especially erected to exhibit this decisive battle of the late Civil War. Take your opera glasses.

FREE EXHIBITION
OF PAINTINGS,
In oil and water color, crayon drawings, etc., at the Los Angeles School of Art and Design, Callaghan block, corner Spring and Third streets. These pictures are by the artists C. Dalton Bond and L. E. Garden, from London, England, and have been exhibited at all the principal galleries of Europe. Open from 9 to 1 and 2 to 4 daily, except Mondays. See advertisement, page 6. Admission free.

DO NOT FAIL TO PASS A PLEASANT hour inspecting the new and beautiful assortment of Los Angeles, Pasadena and other views, at TABER'S branch view department, in Nadeau House, adjoining parlor.

Safe Deposit Bank.

FOR RENT—AT FROM $3 TO $20 PER year, safe deposit boxes in absolutely fire and burglar proof chrome-steel vault; inspection invited. THE CHILDRESS SAFE DEPOSIT BANK, 37 South Spring st.

MAGNOLIA—
Keep your eye on this town.

Real Estate.

THE LOS ANGELES
AND CALIFORNIAN
LAND COMPANY,
25 —— TEMPLE STREET —— 25

"ROWENA."
WHERE IS IT?
"ROWENA."
WHERE IS IT?
"ROWENA."
WHERE IS IT?

1 ACRE.
21-2 ACRES.
5 ACRES.

WHERE ARE THEY?
"ROWENA."
WHERE ARE THEY?
"ROWENA."
WHERE ARE THEY?
"ROWENA."

"ROWENA."
WHERE IS IT?
"ROWENA."
WHERE IS IT?
"ROWENA."
WHERE IS IT?

1 ACRE.
21-2 ACRES.
5 ACRES.

WHERE ARE THEY?
"ROWENA."
WHERE ARE THEY?
"ROWENA."
WHERE ARE THEY?
"ROWENA."

"ROWENA."
WHERE IS IT?
"ROWENA."
WHERE IS IT?
"ROWENA."
WHERE IS IT?

1 ACRE.
21-2 ACRES.
5 ACRES.

WHERE ARE THEY?
"ROWENA."
WHERE ARE THEY?
"ROWENA."
WHERE ARE THEY?
"ROWENA."

LOS ANGELES AND CALIFORNIAN
LAND
COMPANY
25 - TEMPLE- -STREET,- 25
LOS ANGELES.

For Sale.

Real-estate Bargains.

FOR SALE—
ONE LOT ON RAYMOND ave., Pasadena. Buyer of this can realize 50 per cent. profit in thirty days.
FINE CORNER, VERNON ave., near Seventh-st. cable. This is cheap.
40 ACRES ON CORNER. Great speculation. $750 per acre.
5 ACRES, ADAMS ST., 12 acres, Adams st. Both near Ellis tract.
A BEAUTIFUL CORNER on Hope st., cheap, and most liberal terms.
MACKEY & BURNHAM,
37 S. Spring st., Childress Bank Room.

FOR SALE—VERY DESIRABLE; 4¼ acres in Highland Park; streets on three sides of it; price $6800. A. M. CROTHERS, 9 N. Main st.

FOR SALE—CHEAP FOR CASH, THIS week only, three lots, Nos. 50, 51, 52, Wiesendanger tract, Budlong ave.; also, two lots in Waverly tract, on Vermont ave., $550 down, balance in three and nine months, at 8 per cent. interest. For further particulars address P. O. Box 1054, or call at 120 S. Spring st.

C. B. HOLMES, REAL ESTATE, LOAN and investment agent. Choice acre and city property for sale. Investments made. Loans negotiated; 12 per cent. net, per annum, secured on loans. Best of references. Give me a call, at 6½ N. Main st., Los Angeles.

FOR SALE—THE GOLDEN OPPORtunity—Ten acres of choice land, well improved, near the University and street car line, at a bargain if sold within 30 days; also, choice lots at the University, cheap. Address Thomas Lloyd, University Postoffice, Cal.

CHEAP LOTS—NEAR THE CENTER of business, on easy terms—near the new depot of the A., T. and S. F. R. R. Call and see them, and secure a bargain before they are closed out. JAMES T. BROWN, 18 Georgia st.

PARTY WISHING TO EXCHANGE Los Angeles or Santa Monica property for a fine, entirely new piano or organ will please state what make preferred, and location and price of property. Address G. H., this office.

FOR SALE—$1000 CASH AND $75 PER month and interest; two-story, 12-room house, suitable for boarding or lodging; $5000. BYRAM & POINDEXTER, 27 W. First st.

FOR SALE—FOR THIS WEEK, AT $185 per front foot, with $3000 improvements, northwest corner Fort and Eighth sts. J. H. BARNWELL.

GEO. B. HOGIN, NO. 9 N. MAIN ST., offers for a few days half interest in business property; a decidedly good thing; small amount of cash required.

MAGNOLIA—
Keep your eye on this town.

MAY 11TH.
Auction sale at Rosemont.

For Sale—City Property.

FOR SALE—50 FEET FRONT, ON Colorado st., Pasadena, between Fair Oaks ave. and Raymond st., right opposite The Carleton.
Also, for sale or exchange for property in Los Angeles county: 2 lots in Jamestown, Dak.; 20 lots in Fargo, Dak.; ½ section near Bismarck, Dak.
Apply to P. ROBERTSON,
Santa Monica, Los Angeles Co., Cal.

FOR SALE—LOTS IN THE BLISS tract, very near A., T. & S. F. new depots; very cheap, and very easy terms.
MACKEY & BURNHAM,
37 S. Spring, Childress Bank Room.

FOR SALE—A CHOICE PIECE OF business property, northwest corner of Los Angeles and Second sts.; 56 feet on Los Angeles, by 120 on Second. DAVIS & BUTRICK, sole agents, 29 S. Spring st., room 3, upstairs.

FOR SALE—NEW 10-ROOM HOUSE, corner lot, finely improved; daily increasing in value. Rent pays over 15 per cent. on price. Buyers can deal solely with the owner by addressing Box 224, city.

FOR SALE—A NEW 5-ROOM HOUSE, with closets, etc., on the most desirable part of Boyle Heights, at a bargain, for a few days; terms easy. Apply to OWNER, 39 N. Spring st., room 13.

FOR SALE—ELEGANT LOTS ON Ocean ave., Santa Monica. Also, fine lots near Belmont Hotel. A. J. VIELE, room 23, Schumacher block.

FOR SALE—NEW 16-ROOM DOUBLE house; bath, closets, etc. Lot, 60x165. No. 626 Flower, between Seventh and Eighth sts. A. D. BOYD.

FOR SALE—CHOICE LOTS ON BOYLE Heights for $250 each. ROCHESTER, HUNTINGTON & LAYTON, 31 W. First st.

FOR SALE—FINE LOT ON VIRGIN st., near Pearl st.; $950. ROCHESTER, HUNTINGTON & LAYTON, 31 W. First st.

MAGNOLIA—
Keep your eye on this town.

For Sale—Country Property.

FOR SALE—BARGAINS.
207 acres choice alfalfa, corn and fruit land, near Santa Ana; artesian water.
Also 20 acres, 6-year-old vineyard, ½ mile from street railroad, and 1½ miles from Tustin; choice location.
Also 600 acres fine fruit and grain land in beautiful Beaumont.
A. J. VIELE, room 23, Schumacher block.

FOR SALE—46 ACRES OF VINEYARD, adjoining the townsite of Glendale, at a bargain for a few days; would subdivide to advantage.
210 acres, near Florence; 100 in alfalfa, balance in corn and barley; $125 per acre.
Verdugo land cheap.
Lots on Figueroa st. and in Childs tract.
MISSOURI AND CALIFORNIA LAND CO.,
Room 12, Lichtenberger block.

FOR SALE—FOR A FEW DAYS ONLY, in town of Anaheim, fine tract level land, all under ditch, plenty water, forty acres grapes, five acres general orchard—400 walnut trees, 500 great gum trees; splendid brick house, 12 rooms, outhouses, etc., etc. Price only $230 per acre. Cheapest place in the county. See it at once. GEORGE W. BURTON, 106 N. Spring st.

FOR SALE—120 ACRES, OR ANY portion of it. The best located tract near Los Angeles city limits. High, level, beautiful view: easy to reach. Suitable for subdivision or fine residences. Come and see this bargain today. 25 W. First st. WIESENDANGER & BONSALL.

FOR SALE—LANDS IN LOS ANGELES county, from $7 to $25 per acre, with water for irrigation; terms easy. JOHN J. JONES & CO., 283 N. Main st.

GEM OF THE VALLEY—TUSTIN. See bargains in real estate of H. FAIRBANKS & CO., Tustin, Cal., in another column.

MAGNOLIA—
Keep your eye on this town.

MAY 11TH.
Auction sale at Rosemont.

For Sale—Live Stock.

FOR SALE—FIFTY DOLLARS WILL buy a good, fresh milch cow, if taken at once. Apply to J. JACQUES, coal and wood yard, 1514 S. Main st. A number of fine graded Jersey cows and two-year-old heifers for sale cheap, if taken quickly. Apply to W. DENBY, Cienega ranch, Washington st., near Sentous Bros.' slaughter-house.

FOR SALE—CHEAP. A NUMBER OF good fresh milch cows, graded Jerseys, a thoroughbred Jersey bull (registered), a number of 2-year- heifers, ¾ Jerseys; also 5 good work-horses, 2 spring wagons, etc.; or will exchange stock, etc., for city lots. For price and for further particulars, address W. D., Box 545, city.

FOR SALE—TWO PONIES; ONE 800 pounds, the other about 600 pounds; both safe for ladies or children to ride or drive. Also, ¾-seat open road wagon, built by Brewster, New York; will sell low for cash. Apply at 20 Walnut ave., three blocks south of Washington Gardens.

FOR SALE—FRESH FAMILY COWS, from $50 upwards; very kind and gentle. WILLIAM NILES, 16 Court st., or E. Washington, near Main-st. cars.

FOR SALE—A FINE, FRESH JERSEY cow. H. ELLIOTT, cor. Jefferson st. and Vermont ave.

FOR SALE—SPAN BLACK HORSES. POWELL, HASKELL & CO., 11 N. Spring st.

MAGNOLIA—
Keep your eye on this town.

Personal.

PERSONAL—MASSAGE. MRS. GREY, St. Helena House, Fort st., room 17.

MAGNOLIA—
Keep your eye on this town

For Sale.

For Sale—Miscellaneous.

FOR SALE—40 TONS GOOD FEED oats, in lots of not less than one ton, by F. M. KEACH, merchandise broker; office, 242 N. Main st.; telephone 235.

FOR SALE—CHEAP; A CHICKERING piano, in good order. Apply to FRANK ENGLER, maker, tuner and repairer, 217 New High st.

FOR SALE—CHEAP, ON ACCOUNT of departure; a fine Cabinet Grand Upright piano. Inquire at 462 S. Los Angeles st.

FOR SALE—THREE SECOND-HAND organs—$50, $75 and $100. POWELL, HASKELL & CO., 11 North Spring st.

FOR SALE—LIGHT SECOND-HAND spring wagon; price, $30. 23 Gallardo st., one block from covered bridge.

FOR SALE—CLOSING OUT TREES and plants cheap. FORSYTH & BALDWIN, No. 8 W. Second st.

FOR SALE—ONE NEW SAFE, VERY cheap. One lot in Howes tract. Room 40, Downey block.

FOR SALE—ELEGANT BIRTHDAY cards, by OLMSTED & WALES, 19 W. First st.

MAGNOLIA—
Keep your eye on this town.

FOR SALE—A TON OF TYPE, SUITable for Babbit metal. Apply at Times office

Wants.

Wanted—Help.

WANTED—EXPERT ABSTRACTER and searcher of record; must be experienced in the work in Southern California. Apply with reference, P. O. Box 893.

WANTED—100 TEAMSTERS AND shovelers. Apply to E. C. BURLINGAME, railroad contractor, No. 7 Beaudry ave.

WANTED—A DRESSMAKER, AND an apprentice to learn dressmaking, at MRS. BORLAND'S, No 1 S. Fort st.

WANTED—TWO EXPERIENCED MAchine hands, to make shirts. Troy Shirt Factory, Schumacher block.

WANTED—BOY TO WASH DISHES in small restaurant. Apply at 502 Downey ave., East Los Angeles.

WANTED—FOUR FARM HANDS AT once. SHATTO & MALTMAN, room 1, Law Building, Temple st.

WANTED—TWO MEN TO DEVELOP water, by Southern California Investment Company, 9 Main st.

WANTED—SALESMEN AND SALESladies; experienced people only. PEOPLE'S STORE.

WANTED—FIRST-CLASS PATTERNmakers. Apply at BAKER IRON WORKS.

MAGNOLIA—
Keep your eye on this town.

WANTED—PAINTERS, TODAY, AT Thatcher & Cleland, 28 N. Los Angeles st.

WANTED—PANTALOON MAKERS, at SHORT BROS.', 131 S. Spring st.

WANTED—A GIRL FOR GENERAL housework. 462 S. Los Angeles st.

WANTED—BUSHELMAN, AT SHORT BROS.', 131 S. Spring st.

WANTED—BOY, AT SHORT BROS.', 131 S. Spring st.

Wanted—Situations.

WANTED—WATCHMAN'S POSITION in Southern California, by an experienced expolice officer, with ten years service on night police; can be relied upon in any emergency; married; temperate; best references. Address WATCHMAN, P. O. Box 862.

WANTED—ONE MONTH'S TRIAL free. A competent young man wishes position with mercantile house as book-keeper or assistant in office; good references; moderate salary, only, expected. Address RELIABLE, Times office.

WANTED—BY MAN AND WIFE, situation in hotel or lodging-house; good references; experience; no children; man to clerk, wife housekeeper. Address D. B. BOON, Pasadena.

WANTED—SITUATION IN A DRUG store, by an experienced and competent druggist. Address W., No. 526 Fort st.

MAGNOLIA—
Keep your eye on this town.

Wanted—To Rent.

WANTED—A SMALL, FURNISHED house, or 4 or 5 rooms, for housekeeping, centrally located; would occupy and care for some person's house who may desire to be absent for the summer; references exchanged. E. G. NORTHUP, Nadeau House.

WANTED—HOUSE OF SIX TO EIGHT rooms, in a central location, by May 1st. Address 34 S. Spring st., Los Angeles.

MAGNOLIA—
Keep your eye on this town.

Wanted—Agents.

WANTED—AGENTS FOR NEW, FAST-selling books and Bibles. Apply to F. A. HUTCHINSON, 39 N. Spring st., Los Angeles, Cal.

WANTED—LIVE AGENTS, BY A leading publishing house; booming books; extra terms. J. B. WOOD, 402 Downey ave.

MAGNOLIA—
Keep your eye on this town.

Wanted—Miscellaneous.

WANTED—FOR A NEAT JOB OF kalsomining or patching, leave your order at No. 20 Second st., between Main and Spring. Prices reasonable. Need not take up your carpets or move furniture. ELLIOTT & BOULWARE.

WANTED—GENTLEMAN AND WIFE would like to take charge of a good house in town while owners are at the seaside; references given. Address H. E. W., postoffice, Los Angeles.

WANTED—A PAIR OF GOOD CARriage horses, between 5 and 7 years old; must weigh about 1100 pounds. Apply to E. A. ALLEN, Lamanda Park.

WANTED—TO EXCHANGE AN EXpress wagon for low covered wagon. Address, stating where wagon can be seen, S. A. M., P. O. Box 389, city.

WANTED—THE PEOPLE TO KNOW that corns, bunions, warts, moles and tumors are removed at 108 N. Main st., near U. S. Hotel.

WANTED—TO EXCHANGE 119 ACRES of land near Los Angeles, for house and lots in the city. G. A. MILLARD, 134 N. Main st.

MAGNOLIA—
Keep your eye on this town.

Business Opportunities.

FOR SALE—STOCK OF HARDWARE, fixtures, tinners' and well-pipe tools. On account of sickness, the undersigned will sell, at a bargain, the hardware stock, fixtures, tinners' and well-pipe tools in the store of E. J. Chamberlain, in the thriving town of Santa Ana. The business house is one of the oldest in the town, and has a well-established trade. Address THEO. F. WORTH, manager for E. J. Chamberlain, Santa Ana, Cal.

FOR SALE—LONG LEASE AND FURniture of one of the best paying hotels in Los Angeles; satisfactory reasons for selling. Also, one Alden fruit evaporating works, all in running order; two grocery stores, one crockery and glassware store, one bakery, one meat market, one bookstore, one hardware store. A. J. VIELE, room 23, Schumacher block.

FOR SALE—RARE CHANCE—HOTEL business; small investment. GEO. B. HOGIN, No. 9 N. Main st.

FOR SALE—PAYING RESTAURANT. A. J. VIELE, room 23, Schumacher block.

MAGNOLIA—
Keep your eye on this town.

Rooms and Board.

A FEW PLEASANT ROOMS, WITH board, at Hermosa Vista, South Pasadena. Tourists leave L. A. & S. G. V. R. R. at Raymond Station and take street cars west.

TO LET—WITH BOARD, SUITE OF pleasant rooms, suitable for man and wife or two gentlemen. Apply at 123 S. Hill st.

MAGNOLIA—
Keep your eye on this town.

TO LET—ROOMS, SINGLE OR EN suite, with or without board, at 238 S. Hill st.

141 S. FORT ST., DESIRABLE SUNNY rooms, en suite or single, with board.

To Let.

To Let—Rooms.

TO LET—TWO FURNISHED ROOMS, in new house; private family; easy walking distance from center of city; close to street-car line; meals next door; prices very low. Call at 3 Myrtle ave., near corner Seventh and Wall sts.

TO LET—FURNISHED ROOMS, WITH or without board, by the week or month; special rates given to permanent tenants. NORWOOD HOUSE, corner Sixth and Hill.

TO LET—COR. THIRD AND GRAND ave., one block from Second-st. cable line, a nicely-furnished front room, well lighted, with two windows, one a bay-window.

TO LET—ROOMS, FURNISHED OR unfurnished, en suite or single; new building; central, with all conveniences. 520 S. Hope st.

TO LET—THREE UNFURNISHED rooms, suitable for housekeeping, to parties without children. Call 1 to 4 p.m. 346 S. Fort.

TO LET—ROOMS, AT SUMMER RATES, in Ontario; elegantly-furnished rooms, single or en suite. MISS FREEMAN, Ontario, Cal.

TO LET—2 UNFURNISHED ROOMS for small family; no children. C. E. RICHARDSON, Times office, or 69 Rosas st.

TO LET—NEWLY-FURNISHED rooms, with bath and parlor, en suite or single. 53 S. Olive, near Second st.

TO LET—A FIRST-CLASS FIRST-floor front room, with bath, at 643 S. Hill st., to a couple of gentlemen.

TO LET—NICELY-FURNISHED rooms, with or without board, at the New Denison, 316 S. Main st.

TO LET—FIRST-CLASS, SUNNY, FURnished rooms, at 123 Courthouse st., cor. Olive.

220 S. FORT ST., HELENA HOUSE sunny rooms; neatly furnished; first-class.

TO LET—ROOMS AND BOARD, AT the new and elegant house, 506 Fort st., cor 6th.

MAGNOLIA—
Keep your eye on this town

TO LET—FURNISHED ROOMS, WITH board, at MRS. BROWN'S, No. 539 S. Hill.

MAY 11TH.
Auction sale at Rosemont.

TO LET—TWO BEAUTIFUL FRONT rooms, furnished. 127 S. Fort st.

TO LET—FOUR FURNISHED ROOMS for housekeeping. 203 S. Hill st.

TO LET—AT 140 S. FORT ST., pleasant, furnished rooms.

TO LET—31 N. OLIVE ST., TWO front rooms, unfurnished.

To Let—Houses.

TO LET—IN SANTA MONICA, A house of 8 rooms, with bathroom; range, with hot and cold water; will sell furniture, or rent furnished. Address Lockbox 27, Santa Monica, Cal.

TO LET—HOUSE; SIX, ELEGANT rooms; finest view in city; near corner of Courthouse and Fort sts. R. C. GLOVER, Hillside Home, 31 N. Fort st.

MAGNOLIA—
Keep your eye on this town.

MAY 11TH.
Auction sale at Rosemont.

TO LET—COTTAGE ON SECOND ST. Apply west of engine-house.

To Let—Miscellaneous.

TO LET—A 3-ACRE ORCHARD, WITH house of 4 rooms, two blocks from street car; terms profitable. Apply to REV. C. A. NOLTE, Rouland st., third block west of Figueroa.

TO LET—FURNISHED HOTEL; ALSO new hotel, not yet completed. Inquire of POMEROY & GATES, 16 Court st., Los Angeles.

MAGNOLIA—
Keep your eye on this town.

Excursions.

PHILLIPS' POPULAR PLEASURE parties going East leave here May 12 and 26. Call on or address A. PHILLIPS & CO., 134 N. Main st., Los Angeles.

DENVER AND RIO GRANDE EXCURsions—Parties East May 4th, 18th and June 1st, Call on or address GEORGE D. PHILLIPS, 263 N. Main st.

MAGNOLIA—
Keep your eye on this town.

WARNER BROS. & CROSBY EXCURsions east and west. 302 N. Main st.

Money To Loan.

MONEY TO LOAN ON REAL-ESTATE mortgages, or will discount real-estate contracts where enough has been paid to make them good security. Loans made on any first-class security. Rooms 7 and 8, University Bank Building, 117 New High st.

$100,000 TO LOAN, AT LOWEST rate of interest. A. J. VIELE, room 23, Schumacher block.

MONEY TO LOAN ON MORTGAGE. MORTIMER & HARRIS, attorneys-at law, 78 and 78a, Temple block.

Dressmaking.

WANTED—SEWING AND DRESS making to do by middle-aged lady, at home or party's residence. Address MRS. S., Times office.

MRS. C. W. MERRY, DRESSMAKING parlors, 604 Downey ave., East Los Angeles.

MAGNOLIA—
Keep your eye on this town.

Strayed or Stolen.

STRAYED OR STOLEN—ONE ALL-white horse, 12 years old, and one sorrel horse, hind feet white, and white forehead. Bring to A. ABBOTT, adjoining Pico House, and get liberal reward.

MAGNOLIA—
Keep your eye on this town.

Unclassified.

OWNERS OF LARGE AND SMALL tracts, suitable for farm, orchard or vineyard, will find it to their interest to leave the same for sale with JOHN J. JONES & CO., 283 N. Main st., Los Angeles.

SKALPERS! R. J. PRYKE & CO., 212 N. Main st.; members American Ticket-brokers' Association. Railroad tickets bought, sold and exchanged; 20 to 50 per ct. saved by buying from them.

R. R. TICKETS BOUGHT, SOLD AND exchanged. Cut rates to all points. Member Guarantee Ticket Brokers' Association. L. H. WHITSON, 30 S Spring st.

MILK BUSINESS FOR SALE—A good paying business. For particulars address P. O. Box 50, Ventura, Cal.

SALVATION MEETINGS, NOON AND night, Nadeau basement, cor. First and Spring.

MAGNOLIA—
Keep your eye on this town.

Come and See This Today—10 a.m., 2 p.m.

Lots 50x150, close to Los Angeles city limits, $100 each; half-acres, $280, 62x330 feet. Also, 100 acres in 5-acre tracts; high, beautiful; suitable for subdivision or fine residences; very cheap. 25 West First street. Wiesendanger & Bonsall.

Lovely Lordsburg.

Maps are now ready at the office of John C. Bell, the auctioneer, 17 Temple block, over the County Bank.

Booth in Burbank.

Booth's subdivision of lot 1, block 101, adjoining the town of Burbank: 43 lots, 50x179 feet, at $150 each. These lots are in one of the finest locations, being on Providencia avenue and Second street. The books are now open, and maps can be had at office. George W. Booth, 134 North Main street.

The Choicest Spot on Earth—Lordsburg.

Maps now ready. Can be had of John C. Bell, the auctioneer, No. 17 Temple block, third story, over the County Bank.

In Their New Quarters.

Crandall, Crow & Co. are now at 133 and 135 West First street, with full line of stoves, mantels and grates.

Large assortment of traveling and tourists' shirts at Eagleson & Co.'s. 50 North Spring st.

THE UNION PACIFIC.

IT IS COMING DOWN FROM UTAH TO LOS ANGELES,

Crossing the Sierra Madres by Way of Millard's Cañon—A Santa Fe Promotion—Reduction of Fares to Pasadena, Etc.

Last year when Charles Francis Adams, the able but close-mouthed president of the Union Pacific Railroad, passed through this city, he was interviewed by a representative of THE TIMES. Among the queries fired plump at the railway magnate was this: "Doesn't your road intend shortly to extend the Southern Utah to a junction with the Atlantic and Pacific, or to Los Angeles itself?" or words to that effect. President Adams answered dryly—for even railroaders sometimes take a little poetic license—"Oh, no. We are perfectly satisfied with what we have."

The belief has prevailed with those best posted that, notwithstanding President Adams's coy disclaimer, the Southern Utah will be pushed to Southern California. Its present lower terminus is in Southern Nevada.

THE TIMES is happy to be able to state, this morning, upon authority, that this desirable consummation is about to come true; that the Southern Utah Railroad is to be pushed on down to Los Angeles; and that the chief engineer and the locating engineer of the Union Pacific are now in this county making the necessary arrangements thereto. They have located a feasible pass through the Sierra Madres by way of Millard's cañon, which will let them out from the Majave Desert into the San Fernando Valley. This route will, they claim, materially shorten the distance from Los Angeles to Chicago, making it 110 miles less than by any present line. The Union Pacific line from the present terminus will run down across the great desert, intersect the Atlantic and Pacific somewhere between Daggett and Waterman, and come from the Point of Rocks (a promontory on the Mojave River below Lane's crossing) direct to the mountains, whose walls it will scale by the natural ladder of Millard's cañon.

The benefit to Los Angeles of having a third great transcontinental line enter her gates is too obvious to need extended comment. There will be further particulars in a few days.

A HAPPY PROMOTION.

The following circular is self-explanatory:

A., T. & S. F. RAILROAD COMPANY,
GENERAL FREIGHT DEPARTMENT,
TOPEKA (Kan.), May 1.

Circular No. 105.

Mr. C. A. Parker is hereby appointed assistant general freight agent, vice J. O. Phillippi, resigned, to engage in other business. Appointment to take effect from this date.

J. S. LEEDS, General Freight Agent.
Approved:
WM. F. WHITE, Traffic Manager.

Mr. Phillippi resigns to accept the presidency of the Topeka Investment and Loan Company, vice P. I. Bonebrake, cousin of Maj. George H. Bonebrake, of this city, resigned to devote his attention to his duties as president of the Central National Bank.

C. A. Parker, the new assistant general freight agent, is a very brilliant young man. He was formerly chief clerk of the freight department; afterward St. Louis passenger agent of the Atchison, Topeka and Santa Fé, which position he resigned to accept the place of contracting agent at Chicago for the Mexican Central Railroad. He was there about a year, and then resigned to become chief clerk of the freight department of the Atchison, Topeka and Santa Fé. He is now promoted in the natural order of that business-like policy so long followed by the Santa Fé system.

REDUCTION OF FARES ON THE LOS ANGELES AND SAN GABRIEL VALLEY.

A noteworthy reduction in fares on the Los Angeles and San Gabriel Valley Railway took place yesterday.

The Pasadena commutation (thirty rides, good for a period of four months) is reduced from $7.50 to $6.

The Pasadena round-trip (ticket good if used within thirty days from issue) is reduced from 65 cents to 50 cents.

The Azusa round-trip is reduced from $1.60 to $1.50.

This will be hailed as the best of good news by people all along the line of the new road.

THE NEW BRIDGE.

Several bents of the new Arroyo Seco bridge, on the main-line cut-off of the Los Angeles and San Gabriel Valley road, are up, and work is being pushed. Materials are supplied at the western end where the track has been extended up to the wash.

SPIKES.

John L. Truslow, western ticket and passenger agent of the Atchison, Topeka and Santa Fé, got back yesterday from a trip into the country.

H. B. Wilkins, general freight and passenger agent of the California Central and California Southern lines, went home to San Diego last night, after a few busy days here.

THE SECRET STRING.

Some Interesting Matter About the Porter Ashe Case.

Mrs. E. B. Crocker, the grandmother of little Alma A. Ashe, the child over whom so much fuss was made last week, and Mrs. Porter Ashe, the mother of Alma, went North the other evening, and it is reported that they were to pick the little Alma up at Merced and take her to Europe, where they will keep her until she is of an age when she will be competent to say whether she will live with her father or her mother. It is further said that this step is taken with Ashe's knowledge, and that it was part of the contract, which was entered into on the morning when the habeas corpus matter was disposed of in such a mysterious way. Mrs. Crocker, Porter Ashe and one attorney for each brought this arrangement to a close, and the bottom of the sensation of the day was knocked out. The other attorneys on both sides knew nothing of this settlement at the time, and the chances are that they are still in the dark. The gossips, who keep posted in such matters, say Mrs. Crocker and little Alma are already on their way to Europe, or will be in a few days.

The Times.

SEVENTH YEAR. VOL. XIII. NO. 169. LOS ANGELES, MONDAY, MAY 21, 1888. PRICE: Single Copies 5 Cents. By the Week, 3 Cents.

"Times" Advertising Rates.

Line Schedule.

FROM AND AFTER NOVEMBER 1, 1887, the following line rates will be charged for advertising in the LOS ANGELES TIMES:

SMALL CLASSIFIED ADVERTISEMENTS ("Wanted," "For Sale" etc.), 5 cents per Agate line for each insertion, or $1.00 per line per month, payable at the counter.

BY THE MONTH.

DISPLAYED ADVERTISEMENTS, in preferred or fixed positions (fifth or eighth pages), 3½ cents per Nonpareil line for each insertion. Same taking run of the paper (inside), 2½ cents per Nonpareil line for each insertion. Higher rates for shorter periods. (One inch contains 12 Nonpareil lines; one column, 280 Nonpareil lines.)

READING NOTICES, in leaded Nonpareil, per line, each insertion, 15 cents. Professional cards, per Agate line, 2½ cents for each insertion. Marriages and deaths, free. Funeral notices, 15 cents per line.

MIRROR ADVERTISING RATES—Transients, per square (six lines), per week, $1.00. Regulars, per square, per month, $1.50. Professional cards, per line, per month, 25 cents. Reading notices, in Nonpareil, each insertion, per line, 15 cents.

THE TIMES

Can be found on sale at the following places: LONDON—American Exchange, 449 Strand. PARIS—American Exchange, 35 Boulevard des Capucines. BERLIN—American Exchange, Unter den Linden strasse. NEW YORK—Hoffman House News Stand. CHICAGO—Palmer House News Stand. ST. LOUIS—E. T. Jett, 804 Olive street. KANSAS CITY—B. Glick, 21 E. Fifth street. SAN FRANCISCO—J. C. Scott, 23 Third street, and Smith's book store, 225 Kearney street.

Address (Telephone No. 29)

THE TIMES-MIRROR COMPANY,

TIMES BUILDING,

N.E. cor. First and Fort sts., Los Angeles, Cal.

Amusements.

GRAND OPERA HOUSE.

H. C. WYATT.......................Lessee and Manager

ONE WEEK—Monday, May 21—ONE WEEK

Engagement of the Eminent Tragedian,

—FREDERICK—

WARDE

Supported by an Efficient Dramatic Company.

HUDSON AND O'NEIL.......................Managers.

—REPERTOIRE.—

Monday......................"VIRGINIUS."
Tuesday......................"GALBA, THE GLADIATOR."
Wednesday......................"GASTON CADOL."
Thursday......................"VIRGINIUS."
Friday......................"DAMON AND PYTHIAS."
Saturday Matinee......................"GASTON CADOL."
Saturday Night......................"RICHARD III."

Thursday Evening, "VIRGINIUS."

BENEFIT OF MANAGER H. C. WYATT.

PRICES—Dress Circle and Parquet, $1. Gallery, 50c.

HAZARD'S PAVILION, Cor. Fifth and Olive streets.

McLAIN & LEHMAN.......................Lessees and Managers

One week and Saturday matinee, commencing

Monday.......................May 21, 1888

The great Military Drama,

DRUMMER BOY

—OR THE BATTLE FIELD OF SHILOH—

A piece fraught with instruction to the mind and eye, as shown the past twenty years to immense audiences in all parts of the United States.

Thrilling War Scenes! Magnificent Tableaux! Perfect representation of life in camp, field and prison.

Popular prices.......................Fifty and Twenty-five Cents

No extra charge for reserved seats. Seats now on sale at McLain & Lehman's office, No. 3 Market street, opposite Courthouse.

BANCROFT MUSIC HALL.

218 S. Main st. New Panorama Building.

SEIFERT-KOHLER

CONCERTS

Wednesday and Thursday Evenings, May 23d and 24th, at 8 o'clock.

AND ONE CONCERT MATINEE,

Thursday, May 24.......................at 3 p.m.

EMIL SEIFERT, The celebrated Violinist and Concert Master from Berlin, has become famous in Europe and America for his poetic conception, broad tone and deep feeling.

HEINRICH KOHLER. The eminent Pianist from London, now on a tour of the world, is master of the instrument, and ranks among the world's greatest pianists.

SIGNOR CARLO MODINI Has a high tenor voice of superb quality, great power and brilliancy.

ALBERT GEMUENDER, Solo Violoncellist.

Tickets now on sale at Bancroft's, 218 S. Main st. Secure reserved seats without extra charge. Evening Concert, $1. Matinee, 50c. 24

CALIFORNIA DIME

MUSEUM

North Main Street, near First.

THE POPULAR FAMILY RESORT.

A Host of Novelties. New Features. New Freaks.

CAKO—The Arctic survivor, and his rare collection of Arctic curios.

NANNARB—The Fire King.

EVERETT'S Superb Shadowgraphs.

THE WILD MAN, from the island of Ceylon, entirely covered with hair.

KING KALKASA—The wonderful Jap Juggler.

In Theater—The STAR SPECIALTY COMPANY, in a choice and novel stage performance.

Doors open from 10 a.m. to 10 p.m.

ADMISSION.......................TEN CENTS

Reserved Seats Ten Cents Extra. 6-18

ARMORY HALL.

Tuesday, May 22d, at 8 o'clock P.M.

MRS. JULIA WARD HOWE,

The eminent Boston Poet and Philanthropist.

—WILL—

LECTURE

Subject: "IS POLITE SOCIETY POLITE?"

Tickets.......................Fifty Cents.

For sale at the bookstores and at the door.

WASHINGTON GARDENS

OSTRICH FARM AND ZOOLOGICAL GARDENS!

Open Daily. The Only

BABY OSTRICHES

In Los Angeles, now on exhibition. The Greatest Attraction in California.

Admission.......................Twenty-five Cents.

D. PEARL, Lessee and Manager. Telephone 766.

PANORAMA.

—SIEGE OF PARIS!—

MAIN AND THIRD STREETS.

This magnificent work of art is now open daily, including Sundays, from 9 a.m. to 10 p.m. J. C. CAMERON, Esq., will deliver a refined historical lecture hourly upon the painting. Admission, 50c.; children, 25c.

Special Notices.

W. J. COLVILLE WILL LECTURE in I.O.O.F. Hall, Spring st., Whitsunday, May 20th, at 2:30 p.m. Subject: "The Descent and Gifts of the Holy Spirit." 7:30 p.m.: "Saul of Tarsus." Choice music and flowers. Admission, 10 cents. Lectures on "Theosophy" in Bartlett's Hall, First st., Monday, Tuesday and Wednesday, 8 p.m. "Lessons in Spiritual Science or Practical Metaphysics," in I.O.O.F. Hall Tuesday, Wednesday and Thursday, 2:30 p.m. Admission, 25 cents. 20

ALEX GIBSON & CO., LEADING furniture auctioneers and valuators. If you want to dispose of your furniture don't sacrifice it. Send for us and we will obtain highest values under keen competition buyers. ALEX GIBSON & CO., 109 West First st. We also value for buyer or seller.

SPECIAL NOTICE TO BUILDERS and proprietors. Plans and specifications for cottage, $15; plans and specifications for 2-story residence, $25; plans and specifications for entire block, 1 percent. Furnished by J. FRIEDLANDER & CO., architects, 104 N. Main st., room 3. 6-2

EXCELSIOR STEAM LAUNDRY, office, 15 W. Second st.; work called for and delivered to any part of the city. Telephone 367.

Wants.

Wanted—Situations.

WANTED—AN ENGLISH CLERGYman will give private lessons to pupils of either sex in English, classics, languages, arts, etc. Address REV. ALPHA, care Mrs. C. L. Patrick, 211 Third st. 24

WANTED—SITUATION BY GERman girl; speaks English; position as chambermaid, waitress or housework. 75 Earl st., between Eighth and Ninth. 21

WANTED—A POSITION AS BOOKkeeper or assistant, clerk or salesman, by a thoroughly competent young man; can give city reference. Address M 21, Times office. 24

WANTED—A SITUATION BY A first-class colored cook, in hotel, restaurant, boarding-house; pantry cook preferred. Address M 16 Times office. 22

WANTED—A LADY WOULD LIKE to keep house for a gentleman, or where she would be comparatively independent. Address M 6, Times office. 24

WANTED—SITUATION TO DO cooking or general housework in private family; no washing; good references. Address or telephone 358. 21

WANTED—EMPLOYMENT IN A grocery or produce store by a man having some knowledge of that business. Address N. NANDEY city P O. 21

WANTED—A GOOD HAND WISHES lunch or dinner job, to do pantry work, or help the cook. 23

WANTED—A STEADY, SOBER MAN wishes employment to take care of garden and horses, and be of general utility. 23

WANTED—A SITUATION BY A competent German cook or housework in private family. Address M 13, Times office. 21

WANTED—SITUATION IN A PRIvate family by two girls, one as cook and one as second girl. Address 39 E. Fifth st. 21

WANTED—A SITUATION AS CHAMbermaid in hotel or private family. Address 159 S. Los Angeles st., room 12. 21

WANTED—SITUATION IN GROcery store, by a young man who is willing to work; good references. Apply 41 Clover st. 21

WANTED—SITUATION FOR TWO as waitresses. Apply 121 Wilmington st. 22

WANTED—A SITUATION BY A young man to take care of horses and garden, etc.; is a good driver. Address M 15, Times office. 22

WANTED—SITUATION BY TWO waitresses. Address 121 Wilmington st. 22

Wanted—Help.

WANTED—FEMALE—WOMAN cook, restaurant, city, $30 month and room; woman cook, country hotel $35 and room; woman cook, private family, $30; woman cook, private family, $25; girl to do second work, $20; girl to do second work, $15, 3 in family; girl to do general housework, $30; girl to do general housework, $25; girl to do general housework, $20; 2 girls to do general housework, $25, and second work, $25, together; laundry woman, hotel, country, $25, board and room; nurse girl, $20 month; nurse girl for child, $15 month.

MALE—Colored waiter $25, board and room, free pass; cook, country restaurant, $60 and room; cook, city restaurant, $40 and room; second cook, city restaurant, $40 and room; pantry man, $30 and room; 2 drillers; 2 teamsters, $31 and found; 5 shovelers, city; 7 men for railroad work; man to take contract to chop from 500 to 1000 cords of 4-foot white oak wood. C. D. ADAMS & CO., 38 N. Main st., room 9, telephone 930. 21

WANTED—THIS MORNING—FIELD engineer; 6 teamsters for canal, free pass; teamster in city, $30 and board; large boy to pick fruit; references; man to skin 4 mules $1 50 and board. I also want the address of every man and woman in the city that wants work; no registry; see caution; do not be foolish enough to pay any of the leeches 50 cents for registering your name. F. A. POOLER, 209 E. First st. 21

WANTED—A GOOD GIRL FOR cooking and down-stairs work; call at southeast corner of Washington and Toberman sts., on 2-horse car line; wages $30. Address M 19, Times office. 21

WANTED—A GOOD COLORED GIRL for cooking and down-stairs work; wages $20. Address M 19, Times office. 21

WANTED—A WOMAN WHO UNderstands the duties of a lady's maid. Apply N., 850 S. Olive st., between 2 and 4 p.m. 22

WANTED—A GOOD COMPETENT girl for general housework. 317 S. Hope st., between Fourth and Fifth. 21

WANTED—A WORKING HOUSEkeeper. Apply at 122 S. Hill st., from 9 to 12 a.m. 20

WANTED—FIRE INSURANCE SOlicitor for leading agency. Address, with references, M 14, Times office. 6-1

WANTED—AGENTS FOR FASTselling books, bibles and albums; liberal terms. I. B. WOOD, 44½ South Spring st. 6-14

Wanted—To Rent.

WANTED—TO RENT FOR THE summer—a set of parlor-furniture, by gentleman and wife; no children; furniture must be in good condition; excellent care guaranteed; references given. Address M 17, Times office. 21

WANTED—UNFURNISHED ROOM and chance to keep and care for a horse near Fort and First st. Address K 60, Times office.

Wanted—Partner.

$1000—I WANT A MAN THORoughly acquainted with manufacturing line with the above capital, as a partner; none but principals who can fill the bill treated with. JOHN WHYTE, P. O. box 13, Pomona, Cal. 30

Wanted—Real Estate.

WANTED—TO BUY A RESIDENCE in good location, and pay some cash and exchange 10 or 20 acres of finest orange land in Lugonia, with good water right. Apply at office of W. P. McINTOSH, 13 S. Main st. 24

WANTED—FROM 3 TO 5 ACRES building ground not more than 3½ miles from center of the city; elevated position preferred. Address P. O. Box 1011; state price per acre. 21

WANTED—6, AND IF POSSIBLE 8, lots in Euclid Heights tract. They must form a compact body. Address L. L., Times office. 21

Wanted—Miscellaneous.

WANTED—EVERYBODY TO PATronize Mrs. E. C. Freeman's home bakery, where home-made salt-rising bread, pies and cakes; also Boston brown bread and beans hot, on Saturday and Sunday mornings. 407 S. Spring st.

WANTED—TYPEWRITERS TO BUY No 2 Remington typewriters; also machines adjusted or repaired; ribbons, papers and other supplies. ELIAS LONGLEY, room 1, Wilson block, 24 First st. 6-13

WANTED—PHÆTON, OR BUGGY and harness, suitable for 750 pound pony. Address, stating lowest cash price, H., P. O. box 534. 21

WANTED—A BAT LIVE OR DEAD; pug and fox terrier pups for sale. BIRD STORE, 405½ S. Spring st. 27

WANTED—TO BUY AN ESTABlished grocery, or partnership in same, to cost from $1000 to $2000. Address M 10, Times office. 22

WANTED—$5000 TO $10,000 FOR ONE to two years; best of security. Address P. O. box 880

WANTED—TO BUY A GOOD PIANO, upright preferred; cash. J. S., P. O. Box 8. 25

Auctioneers.

A. L. TEELE, Business Manager. BEN O. RHOADES, Auctioneer.

BEN O. RHOADES & CO., GENERAL auctioneers; will make special sales of real estate, live stock and general merchandise in any part of the State; 25 years' experience; satisfaction guaranteed; offices corner Second and Fort sts., Los Angeles, Cal.; P.O. Box 1287. 6-17

Rental and Collection Agency.

HOUSES RENTED, RENTS COLlected; full charge of property, including payment water tax, making repairs, on terms customary in large cities. Reliable, prompt and systematic. Property-owners dealing with tenants will find it advantageous to deal with me. Call or write for circulars and rates. A. L. TEELE, Real-estate and Insurance, Second and Fort sts. 6-17

Business Opportunities.

FOR SALE—BUSINESS OPPORTUNIties.

Hotels—40 rooms $4000, 30 rooms $4000, 21 rooms $3500.

Rooming Houses—33 rooms $4000, 7 rooms $550, 8 rooms $500.

Restaurants—One at $25 000, one at $900, one at $700.

Groceries—One at $2 00, one at $ 50, one at $125.

Bakeries—One at $[illegible], one at $2[illegible], one at $[illegible].

Half-interests—One at $2750, one at $800, one at $750.

Saloons—One at $2000, one at $1 00, one at $500.

Leases—Ground rent, 50x100, 5 years, $1000; store, 3 years, $500; meat market and fixtures, $150; gasoline business, $700; jewelry store, $2800; stationery business, $[illegible].

D. B. MACQUARRIE & CO., Business Chances, 7 S. Main st. 24

GROCERIES—$600 TO $4000.

Stationery—$500 to $3000.
Drugs—$[illegible]00 to $7000.
Lodging-houses—$600 to $3000.
Cigar stores—$50 to $3000.
Saloons—$500 to $[illegible].
Boots and shoes—$2000 to $8000.
Partnerships—$100 to $5000.

We can find you any business. PACIFIC BUSINESS CHANCE AGENCY, 34 N. Spring st. 21

FOR SALE—BUSINESS OPPORTUNIties.

One-half interest in one of the best paying business chances in this city; long established; immense trade, wholesale and retail; staple articles; full value in sight; long lease and low rent. We have investigated this business and can guarantee it A1. D. B. MACQUARRIE & CO., Business Chances, 7 S. Main st. 24

CORNER GROCERY FOR SALE.

Fine stock of goods, first-class location; business increasing every day; no bonus asked for good will. Apply to STAUNTON & MATTHEWS, 21 N. Spring st.

FOR SALE—CHEAP, TO GOOD TENant, the furniture, fixtures and entire contents of the Carlton Cafe and hotel, dining-room and kitchen, and 32 rooms completely and handsomely furnished; purchaser given good lease. Apply to MITCHEL & CREIGHTON, attorneys, room 10, Allen block. 6-16

$10,000—THE SUBSCRIBER wants a party with the above amount of capital to join him in completing the distribution of a domestic water system in the most prosperous and thriving city in Southern California, outside of Los Angeles; none but principals need apply. Address box 13, Pomona, Cal. 22

FOR SALE—ON ACCOUNT ON SICKness, real-estate office, furniture, safe, lease of ground, and good will, in live town; only $50 needed; no humbug. Address P. O. box 54, San Buenaventura, Cal. 24

FOR SALE—RESTAURANT, NEAR corner of First and Main sts.; rent $50; 3 years' lease; place clearing $200 per month; owner selling on account of sickness; this place will stand a thorough investigation. Apply to M J NOLAN & CO., 7 S. Main st. 22

FOR SALE—GROCERY STORE ON Main st., near Second; rent $100 per month, 2 years' lease; doing business of $100 per day. Invoice stock and sell at cost. Apply to M. J. NOLAN & CO., 7 S. Main st. 22

FOR SALE—GROCERY STORE ON Main st.; rent $35 per month; one year's lease; doing a nice business; stock and fixtures, $300; this is a bonanza for some one with a limited capital. Apply to M. J NOLAN & CO., 7 S. Main st. 22

FOR SALE—AT A BIG BARGAIN—a well-established bakery business, with house, lot, good oven and all necessary fixtures; weekly sale, $30 to $100. Address or call at COMPTON BAKERY, Compton, Cal. 6-14

FOR SALE—TO THE RIGHT PARties a half interest in an established and paying wholesale commission business; cash capital of $2500 required. For full particulars address K. 44, S. Spring st., till June 1. 6-1

$500 ONLY REQUIRED—BILLIARD Parlor, 4 tables, paying handsomely; low rent; long lease. Inquire immediately at STEWART'S Exchange, room 16, Allen block. 21

FOR SALE—JEWELRY BUSINESS; will sell stock and fixtures low, watches, jewelry, spectacles, etc.; to be closed out in a few days; address OWNER, corner Sixth and Spring sts. 21

FORSALE—HAYLOCK HOUSE, FULL all the time. Address ISAAC HAYLOCK, Sr., Compton, Cal., or A. O. DAMAN, 9 North Main st., Los Angeles. 6-12

NOTICE TO PRINTERS—WANTED to sell a half interest in a job printing business; very small capital needed. Box 416, Pasadena. 21

FOR SALE—CIGAR-STAND. APPLY at No 2 S. Los Angeles st. 22

FOR SALE—CIGAR STAND. APPLY at 312½ S. Spring st. 21

Money to Loan.

$1,000,000 TO LOAN AT R. G. LUNT'S LOAN AND INSURANCE AGENCY, No. 20 W. First st., Los Angeles. Agent for the GERMAN SAVINGS AND LOAN SOCIETY of San Francisco.

Loans effected on city and country property, in sums of $1500 and upward, at lowest rates, from one to five years. Building loans effected. Mortgages, city and county bonds purchased.

Estates managed, rents collected and taxes paid. APPLY DIRECT AND SAVE EXPENSES.

Insurance Department—Capital represented, $75,000,000. Doing the largest business on the Pacific Coast. Losses promptly paid.

MONEY TO LOAN—$10 TO $20,000. NOTES AND MORTGAGES DISCOUNTED. Loan on real estate (improved and unimproved), chattels, contracts, leases, crops, etc. CRAWFORD & McCREERY, Room 13, northeast corner First and Spring sts., Los Angeles National Bank building. 26

MONEY TO LOAN—IN SUMS TO suit, on good improved inside property in Los Angeles. McCONNALL & MERWIN, 13½ N. Main.

MONEY TO LOAN—IN SUMS TO suit, on good improved inside property in Los Angeles. BYRAM & POINDEXTER, 19 W. First street.

TO LOAN—$2500 TO $3000 ON INSIDE improved property. R. A. CRIPPIN & SON, basement California Bank building. 26

MONEY TO LOAN—$100 UP; MORTgages and notes discounted. R. NANCE, room 83 No. 36 S. Main st.

Excursions.

EXCURSIONS TO BEAUMONT every Tuesday and Saturday on the 8:30 train. Round-trip ticket, good for two days, Los Angeles to Beaumont and return, $2; Pomona and Ontario to Beaumont and return, $1.50. Colton to Beaumont and return, $1. For particulars inquire of the Southern California Investment Company, 9 N. Main st., Los Angeles. 6-16

BURLINGTON ROUTE EXCURSIONS east; see large advertisement in reading column. J. B. QUIGLEY, Agt., C. B. & Q. R. R., 112 N. Spring.

SCENIC LINE EXCURSIONS — EXcursions over the Denver and Rio Grande Railway, "The Scenic Line of the World," will leave Los Angeles, going via Salt Lake City and Denver, as follows: May 17th and 31st, June 14th and 28th, July 12th and 26th, August 9th and 23d. Passengers are furnished mattresses, pillows, blankets, curtains, etc., free of charge. A competent conductor accompanies each party. For further particulars call on or address J. H. HENRY, manager, 110 N. Spring st., Los Angeles, Cal.

GEORGE F. COTTERAL & CO.'S EXcursion east and west, via Sacramento, Salt Lake City and Denver; parties east leave Los Angeles May 22d and 29th, June 12th and 26th, July 10th and 24th. Call on or address GEORGE F. COTTERAL & CO., 236 North Main st.

PHILLIPS'S POPULAR PLEASURE parties going east leave here May 10th and 31st, June 14th and 28th, July 12th. Call on or address A. PHILLIPS & CO., 34 N. Main st., Los Angeles, Cal.

EXCURSIONS — WARNER BROS.' semi-monthly; May 17th, June 7th, 21st, July 5th, 19th. Lowest rates to all points east. 302 N. Main st.

Lost and Found.

LOST BEAUTY FOUND—MALVINA Cream and Lotion and Malvina Ichthyol Soap beautifies the complexion; a safe and never-failing cure for freckles, pimples, tan and all discolorations and eruption of the skin. We hereby certify that we have seen many original testimonials which leave no doubt as to the merits of the above preparations. We also testify that many cures have been effected in this city. REDINGTON & CO., LANGLEY & MICHAELS, Wholesale Druggists, San Francisco.

For sale and recommended by all druggists. We will positively refund the money for every package of Malvina preparations bought of us if a cure is not effected. C. H. HANCE, Druggist, 77 N. Spring st.; R. W. ELLIS & CO., Druggists, 27 S. Spring st. Trade supplied by F. W. BRAUN & CO., wholesale druggists, 127 and 129 New High st., Los Angeles.

LOST—CORNER OF SECOND AND Olive sts., an oxidized chain, with scent bottle. Return to office of Dr. Wells, 23 S. Spring st., and get reward. 21

LOST—REWARD FOR RETURN OF bunch of keys lost May 12th. CHILDRESS SAFE DEPOSIT COMPANY. 21

Commission Merchants.

E. S. M. JUDSON, SHIPPING AND commission merchant. Butter, eggs, cheese, etc.; new potatoes in carload lots for shipment east a specialty. No. 253-255 S. Spring st. 6-17

STANLEY & HENRY, SHIPPING and commission merchants; all classes of farm produce; dairy produce a specialty. 38 N. Los Angeles st.; telephone 384.

For Sale.

For Sale—City Property.

BUSINESS MEN, ATTENTION!

Great bargain in first-class business property on west side of Main st., opposite the million-dollar hotel, for a few days only. Apply to STAUNTON & MATTHEWS, 21 N. Spring st.

FOR SALE—ONE OR TWO NICE lots, very close to Figueroa st., and just off of Washington st.; first class improvements in neighborhood; will be sold at a bargain. As this is the very best inside property, it will be well for persons wishing a good location on street car to look at it. T. WISENDANGER, 23 W. First st.

FOR SALE—BUSINESS CORNER LOT, near hotel, in Downey City, with store and 7 living rooms; good location for bake shop or other business; $2500; easy terms. LEWIS & PINKHAM, 119 W. First st., Los Angeles. 25

$350—50x155, MONTANA TRACT. $45—50x200, Inglewood, near hotel. $400—Corner on Main st. For sale only by C. B. HOLMES, 9 N. Main.

FOR SALE—OR LEASE—LOT S. W. corner of First and Hewitt sts. Inquire at room 3, 29½ S. Spring. 21

For Sale—Houses.

FOR SALE OR EXCHANGE.

A LOVELY HOME ON BOYLE HEIGHTS.

Elegant house, 14 rooms, with all modern conveniences. Beautiful grounds and fine stable.

Call and see views and plans of dwelling and get prices at

DOBINSON & FAIRCHILD'S, 124 W. SECOND ST. 6-13

FOR SALE—ONE OF THE FINEST homes in the city on the finest street in the city; house of 8 large rooms, bath, pantries, closets, every modern convenience, electric bells, hot and cold water, finely decorated; must be seen to be appreciated; nicely improved lot, situated on the northeast corner of Ellis and Bonsallo aves; price $12,000. Apply on the premises.

$1200 ON THE INSTALLMENT plan; $200 cash; balance $20 per month; immediate possession given; 4 new houses in the City View tract, Boyle Heights, 1¼ miles from Plaza, three minutes' walk from station rapid transit road; beautiful view. ROCHESTER & CALKINS, 9½ S. Fort st. 6-19

FOR SALE—11-ROOM NEW HOUSE, with electric bells and all modern improvements, worth $8500; will be offered for $7500, for the next few days, on very easy terms. Apply to W. P. McINTOSH, 13 S. Main st. 24

FOR SALE—$2800—DON'T MISS THIS; 5-room house on Temple st., near Beaudry ave; $1000 cash, balance 6 months; for short time only. ALFRED DAY, JR., 28 N. Spring st., room 3. 21

$2300 WILL BUY THE CHEAPest and best house for the money ever offered in this city, and in the most beautiful location; must be sold. W. E. MASON, 16 S. Main street. 22

FOR SALE—A BARGAIN—NEAT cottage of 6 rooms, bath, closets, etc., furnished or unfurnished; lot 70x205 on Union ave., near Temple; No. 1 location; fine view. Address box 719. 6-8

FORSALE—$1800; EASY TERMS; NEW four-room cottage; also fine lot, Judson tract, covered with fruit; and large lot on York st., third west of Figueroa, where see OWNER. 23

FOR SALE—A BEAUTIFUL COTtage; 5 rooms; fine Eastlake finish; bath, closets, etc.; call and see and make offer; must sell. Apply on premises to owner. 107 Walnut ave. 24

FOR SALE—THE BIGGEST BARGAIN ever offered. Six-room cottage, Eleventh st., near Pearl; $2400, ⅓ cash. ROYAL, 105 W. First st.

For Sale—Country Property.

CHEAP LANDS.

SYNDICATES, CAPITALISTS, COLONISTS AND SETTLERS.

DR. E. T. BARBER of Lancaster, Los Angeles county, Cal., offers 40,000 acres of land for sale, in tracts of 20 acres and upward, at $8 to $50 per acre, with terms liberal and title perfect.

Antelope Valley has raised the premium wheat of the world, and grown sugar-beets at the rate of 218 tons to the acre, and barley hay which has netted $22.50 per acre profit, grown 8 crops of alfalfa in one year, and parsnips 71 inches in diameter, and is competent to compete with Spain for raisins, and France for champagne.

This land can be covered with mountain water, and has good surface and artesian water, and much of it a sub-soil irrigation.

It has now good railroad facilities, and four transcontinental railways are expected in the near future to cross this part of the valley.

No blizzards, no cyclones, no fogs, no malaria. Antelope Valley is the hope of the poor man, a boon to men of moderate means, and a bonanza to the keen-sighted business man. Send for map and description.

I WILL SELL FOR CASH FIVE ACRES on Hill ave., Pasadena, with cottage, orchard, lawn and flowers; 2 extra shares of water stock, marked Rodgers on Pasadena map. Price, $4000. Also, lots 2 and 3, block 18; lot 27, block 20, Brooklyn Heights. Price, $1000.

W. B. HUFF, 16 N. Spring st., P. O. box 455, Los Angeles. 22

FOR SALE—2000 ACRES LAND FOR sale, in whole or in part, in San Diego county; beautifully located and suitable for subdivision; all well improved, with house and outhouses, thriving orchard, 100 acres sown in alfalfa and 1000 acres sown in grain, looking well; balance good pasture lands, with abundant supply of surface water 6 to 12 feet, with stock and farming implements; price $110,000; will take part cash and part Los Angeles city property. Call or address A. WORKMAN, 230 Boyle ave., city.

FOR SALE—SMALL FARMS IN THE famous Santa Clara Valley, Ventura county, at from $25 to $75 per acre, grazing and fruit land, splendidly watered, in large tracts at $10 per acre; easy terms. Apply to SANTA CLARA VALLEY LAND AND WATER COMPANY, 51 North Spring st., Los Angeles. 6-18

FOR SALE—OR EXCHANGE FOR LOS Angeles or San Bernardino city property, 1180 acres, in tracts of from 40 to 160 acres, at prices from $15 to $40 per acre; near California Central Railroad, between Los Angeles and San Bernardino. M. KELLEHER, room 8, No. 25 N. Main st., Los Angeles, Cal. 6-7

FOR SALE—A BARGAIN—MUST BE sold in 10 days; 40 acres fine orange land, at Orange Thorpe, near Fullerton, on Santa Fe Railroad; abundance of water; only $150 per acre. Apply to OWNER, 125 N. Grand ave., near Temple. 29

FOR SALE—BEAUTIFUL LOTS IN Inglewood. $2400 will buy 12 lots and ¼ interest in a well. Address STETSON & HOUSER, Inglewood, Cal. 21

FOR SALE—VERY CHEAP—10 ACRES of land at Anaheim. J. F. KEARNEY, 411 Buena Vista st. 26

FOR SALE—A HANDSOME LOT IN Alhambra; prettiest place in the county for a home; only $900, half cash, worth $1500. Address P. E., Times office.

FOR SALE—A SMALL RANCH OF 5 acres, on the installment plan. Address 16 S. Main st. SMITH & SCHAUMWAY. 6-13

FOR SALE—50 ACRES OF CHOICE damp land near Compton at $200 per acre; a bargain. Address K 5, Times office.

For Sale—Live Stock.

FOR SALE—$190 WILL BUY HORSE, harness and buggy if taken by the 22d; worth $250. ALFRED DAY, JR., 28 N. Spring st., room 3. 21

FOR SALE—ONE BRIGHT BAY ROAD horse, 7 years old; is very fast; can be seen at Washington Garden stable, corner Hill and Washington sts. 22

For Sale—Miscellaneous.

1000 WASHINGTON NAVEL ORANGE TREES.

One year bud, three-year-stock, 2½ to 4 feet high, price, 80c.

These trees are a choice lot and now growing fast. For further particulars call on

6-2 J. P. QUINETTE, 116 West First st.

FOR SALE—SECOND-HAND ORGANS at a great bargain for a few days only. One George Price organ, $50, as good as new; 1 New England organ for $80, and 1 fine Estey for $90; also new upright piano for $250. POWELL, HASKELL & CO., 11 N. Spring st. 21

FOR SALE—WALL PAPER DECORAtions, etc., cheap; biggest stock in the city. 102 South Los Angeles st., Germania Wall Paper House. 6-19

FOR SALE—A NEW SAFE, MACNeale & Urban make, with burglar-proof Comer box. GEORGE E. PRATT, 48 N. Spring street. 28

FOR SALE—ABOUT 4000 BRICKS AT $6 per M.; lot, 50x14, fronts on Main, bet. Adams and Washington sts., at $75 per foot. A. C. DAMAN, 202 S. Main st.

FOR SALE—HALF OR WHOLE INterest in a printing office, for sale, cheap; good business, cheap rent. Address P. O. box 1066. 28

For Sale.

For Sale—Miscellaneous.

FOR SALE—AT THE TIMES OFFICE, old newspapers, at very low rates, in large quantities.

FOR SALE—GASOLINE STOVE, WITH furniture. No. 216 S. Olive st. 23

SEA-SIDE OUTFITS, FURNITURE, stoves, etc. GASS & RENSHAW'S, 14 Third st. 8

FOR SALE—LOVELL'S AND OTHER libraries at the Panorama Bookstore.

FOR SALE—4 ENGINEERS' TRANsits. 49 S. Main st., room 26. 21

FOR SALE—OLD PAPERS, CHEAP at Times business office.

Personal.

PERSONAL—WANTED, EVERYBODY to know that I have the largest and best assorted stock of wood, iron and slate mantels; also mantel and grate tiling. An early inspection is solicited before buying elsewhere. at H. BOHRMAN, manufacturer, 414 S. Spring st., bet. Fifth and Sixth.

PERSONAL—A STENOGRAPHER wishes board in the family of a business man, where her services as amanuensis might be taken as payment for board. Address L 26, Times office. 21

PERSONAL—SPEED OF 125 TO 150 words per minute in 3-months' course of shorthand; also type-writing taught. Rooms 4 and 5, 115 W. First st. 23

PERSONAL—IF IRA W. NEWLAND will communicate with Dr. R. E. Newland, at the New Carleton Hotel, San Diego, Cal., he will hear that which will be to his advantage.

PERSONAL—A GOOD SEAMSTRESS and dressmaker wants work, either at home or in private families. Address 386 Grand ave., near Fifth st. 22

PERSONAL—MME. MORRIS HAS removed to her new parlors, 136 S. Spring st.; dresses cut, fitted, stitched and draped for $3; suits made from latest styles at moderate prices; all work guaranteed. 23

MME. HART, THE WONDERFUL FORtune-teller, reveals the past and future, 20½ S. Fort st., room 1. Office hours from 10 a.m. to 5 p.m. 24

PERSONAL—AN EXPERIENCED dressmaker would like cutting and fitting by the day; will bring draping form. Address MRS. E. J WINN, No. 214 W. Second st. 6-14

PERSONAL—SITUATION AS STENographer, type-writer and office clerk; satisfactory references given. Address M 20, Times office. 21

PERSONAL—STYLISH DRESSMAKing and draping a specialty, at 318 S. Main st. Chicago Emporium of Fashion. 21

PERSONAL—NOBLE BROTHERS, rubber stamp makers, seals, etc.; 104 N. Main st., cor. of Requena. 6-2

MRS. DURANT, CLAIRVOYANT, from Boston; unites separated lovers; reliable in all affairs of life. 28 S. Main st., room 20. 24

PERSONAL—MISS M. KARNS, LATE of New York, has opened the Palace Dressmaking Parlors, 36 S. Main, rooms 7 and 9.

PERSONAL—MRS. BORLAND, DRESSmaking, 38½ S. Spring st., has removed to 120 W. First st., upstairs.

FASHIONABLE DRESSMAKING—Fine dresses a specialty and warrant satisfaction. 827 Temple st.

PERSONAL—MIRON, ARMSTRONG & CO., cement coping, walls & walks. 33 S. Spring.

PERSONAL—A COMPETENT NURSE at 47 S. Olive st.

For Exchange.

FOR EXCHANGE—AN ELEGANT 2-seat canopy top family carriage, with shafts; light enough for one horse; new; cost $280; for a horse and light open buggy. A. L. TEELE, corner Fort and Second. 24

FOR EXCHANGE—15 ACRES ADjoining city; all in fine fruit, old trees; house, barn, windmill; want improved city property; cheap lots for sale on Central ave. JOHN A. PIRTLE, 21 North Spring st.

FOR EXCHANGE—THE FINEST IMproved farm in Eastern Kansas for first class property in Los Angeles or good acreage. Call and see photograph and description at No 117 W. First street. 21

FOR EXCHANGE—NICE FOUR-ROOM house and corner lot for good vacant lots or acre property. R. VERCH, room 80, Temple block. 25

FOR EXCHANGE—HOUSES, LOTS, ranches, eastern property, stocks, bonds, notes, mortgages, horses, diamonds, etc. Come and trade. J. C. WILLMON, 133 W. First st.

FOR EXCHANGE—40 ACRES FINE land toward ocean from Los Angeles, to exchange for city property; will pay some cash difference. SHERMAN & SHORT. 24

FOR EXCHANGE—PROPERTY IN Santa Fe Springs for one or more lots in the Euclid Heights tract. Will pay some difference. Address Z. O., Times office. 21

FOR EXCHANGE—10 ACRES OF IMproved land in Santa Ana Valley for 10 acres unimproved land near Burbank. Address MR. BURTON, No 117 W. First st., city. 22

FOR EXCHANGE—A FINE CITY RESidence for an improved foothill fruit ranch; state location and full information about ranch. Address L 44, Times office.

FOREXCHANGE—CITY LOTS, CLOSE in, for trade. J. M. TAYLOR & CO., 271 N. Main st. 23

FOR EXCHANGE—NEW WHEELER & Wilson sewing machine for good second-hand buggy. Address K 94, Times office. 21

FOR EXCHANGE—SOME CHOICE lots on Angeleno Heights for a house. Address 111 Bellevue ave. 24

FOR EXCHANGE—LOTS FOR ROOMing-houses. DOMESTIC SEWING MACHINE COMPANY, 113 West First st.

FOR EXCHANGE—PROPERTIES OF all descriptions. J. M. HIXSON, 16 S. Spring street. 22

Unclassified.

$50 REWARD—$25 FOR THE RETURN of a jump-seat cloth-cushion and canopy top surrey, harness and small bay mare, about 13 hands high; natural depression on left ham, lolls tongue and slobbers profusely; stolen from front of Christian Church, Wednesday night, May 16th. $25 for arrest and conviction of thief. J. B. JONES, room 42, Downey block, Los Angeles. 19

TO THE PUBLIC—HAVING PURchased the restaurant at No. 165 Upper Main st., notice is hereby given to all persons having claims, to present them on or before the 22d of May, or they will be disallowed. An excellent cook and good attention to future business is assured. SAM LEE. 21

SKALPERS! R. J. PRYKE & CO., 212 N. Main st., members American Ticket Brokers' Association. Railroad tickets bought, sold and exchanged; 20 to 50 per cent. saved by buying from them.

PERSONAL—A GERMAN MIDWIFE of 20 years' experience will furnish a private home to ladies in confinement, with best medical attendance. A No. 1 references furnished. Call at 234 Castelar st., near College st.

HOP LEE, CHINESE LAUNDRY, 21 Winston st., corner alley, Los Angeles, Cal. Washing, ironing, polishing and fluting done in the best style; satisfaction guaranteed; give me a trial. 6-2

UNION IRON WORKS—STEAM ENgines and boilers, oil and water tanks, iron and brass casting and finishing, 306 to 312 East First st. Telephone 323. tf5-15

FOR FIRST-CLASS ALFALFA PASturage, apply to Dickson Bros.' stable, 126 Requena st.; stock taken out Saturdays and Tuesdays.

LUNE ON CHONG & CO., LABOR contractors, 117 Anabiasa st., below Alameda, Los Angeles, Cal. LOO QUONG, Proprietor.

TOURISTS' PHOTOGRAPHIC VIEW depot; only exclusive view house in Southern California. 413 N. Main st., opp. Plaza.

TO LET—FRONT SUITE OF TWO beautiful office rooms, Newell block, Second st., between Spring and Main.

SELL YOUR CAST-OFF CLOTHING TO M. STARR, 129 Aliso st. Particular attention to misfits. Send postal.

Rooms and Board.

SUMMER RATES! SUMMER RATES! THE WINONA, 215 Temple st. First class family hotel, near business center; elegantly furnished rooms at $12, $15, $20, $22.50 and $25 per month with or without board; special rates given to families; no Chinese cooking; hot and cold baths.

TO LET—PENN VILLA, BOYLE Heights; large, pleasant furnished rooms with or without board at one-half the usual price during the summer months. Inquire of the owner, JAMES W. STRONG, 113 W. First st. 0

SANTA BARBARA BOARD—FURnished rooms with board, single or en suite, at the Diamond House, De la Vina st.; excellent location; terms reasonable, street cars leave the house for the beach and railroad depot. P. O. Box 181.

THE PARKER, 324 W. FOURTH ST., BEtween Hill and Olive; rooms with board; for gentlemen, without board if desired.

WANTED—A FEW BOARDERS, PRIvate family; reasonable prices; 1633 S. Main street. 26

FIRST-CLASS ROOMS, WITH BOARD, at the ARDMOUR, 5?8 Fort st., corner Sixth.

Strayed or Stolen.

STRAY MARE TAKEN UP BY A. PRATT, south end of Lemon st., Los Angeles, Sunday, May 13th; light bay, with strip in face; mane and tail light; had on headstrap with long piece of halter attached. 25

ONE FOR EVERY 300.

Alarming Increase of Saloons in the City.

A Tough Showing for the Democratic License Mongers.

Are They Putting Up Corruption Money for "Dive" Votes?

The Police Board Turning Out Saloon Licenses by the Wholesale—Over 200 "Joints," or One Ginmill for Every 300 Souls.

The phenomenal increase in the number of saloons throughout the city during the past three or four months has caused no end of comment among the thinking men of both political parties. This increase has been without precedent since the advent of the Democratic police administration, and has caused no little alarm among the law-abiding portion of the population, who see in this increase of drinking places and groggeries a great and constantly growing menace against the peace of the community. According to City Clerk Teed, there are now about 200 saloons in the city of Los Angeles. There may be a few more, but for the sake of simplifying matters, it will be put down at 200 even. On a basis of 60,000 population, this would be one saloon for every 300 of the population, a thing out of all reason, on common business principles. The saloon license is $50 per month, with a prospect of its being raised to $100 in the near future. The rent will average, at the very lowest calculation, at least $150 per month more. Help and incidentals will foot up $150, making $250 expense, without counting the cost of the liquor and interest on the capital invested, which, if the place does any business at all, will certainly go up to $250, making $500 per month before a dollar profit is made. Now, very many of these new saloons have been opened in places where, if every man, woman and child who passed the doors were to spend the price of a drink every time they passed, it would not make up

THE TOTAL EXPENSE,

and in some cases would not pay the license and buy the liquors. Another peculiar feature is the fact that it is no uncommon thing for two saloons to open adjoining one another, or across the street, where the legitimate profits of the business, great as they are, would not support one place. There must, of course, be some explanation of this extraordinary state of affairs, as it is well known that men do not run saloons, or, for that matter, any other sort of business, from purely philanthropic motives. They run the concerns for the money that there is in them, and if they did not get good pay from some source, for the business is not a pleasant one, they would get out of it. Now, the next subject to be considered is where the money comes from to make up the deficit, for there must be a shortage in some cases, as the following instance will show: A TIMES reporter, in looking up this subject, called at a fairly respectable place, and remained for two hours by the watch, during which time but 25 cents was spent in the place, and that was expended by the reporter for beer for himself and a couple of hangers-on about the place, and the bar-keeper, and the latter then returned the compliment by "setting 'em up," making ten glasses of beer dispensed in two houses, with total cash receipts of 25 cents. There was no particular reason for this being an especially dull day, and it may be put down fairly as an average. Now, the next subject to be considered is, who makes up the difference. It is a well known fact that the saloon has always been a powerful factor in the municipal politics of the country, and it must be confessed that the Democratic party has always catered to that interest, as well as that of gambling, both classes being proverbially liberal in the expenditure of coin for campaign purposes. And, while this proposition holds good, in a general sense, it will also be admitted without argument that nowhere in the country has this interest been more systematically fostered and utilized than on the Pacific Coast. In San Francisco it has brought down to such a point that it approximates very closely

AN EXACT SCIENCE,

and it is by the study and application of this science that the "Blind Boss" Chris Buckley has made himself such a factor in the politics, not only of the city, but of the entire State, a fair illustration of which was given at the recent meeting of the State Convention in this city. Every saloon is good for at least 15 votes, if properly manipulated, and by the judicious distribution of his groggeries in San Francisco the "Boss" holds the key to the situation in every precinct in the city, a fact which was proven by the solid 104 delegation voting as a unit whichever way the Boss indicated. This is the situation as regards San Francisco. Now as to Los Angeles. It is well known that Buckley has had an eye on Los Angeles ever since the phenomenal increase in the population and consequent importance of the city attracted the attention not only of the State of California, but of the entire Union, and there has been a systematic effort on the part of the "Boss" to introduce his tactics into this city, in which effort he has been assisted by a small gang of local politicians, commonly denominated the "hoodlum wing" of the Democratic party, who bow at the shrine of the Boss and contribute to the coffers of the machine. This wing, through the San Francisco influence, has been able, to a certain extent, to control the entire party, and the decent members who had political aspirations have been whipped into line by the threat that rebellion would be punished by political extinction, and they have succumbed, smothering the pangs of conscience and principle for the sake of a few empty honors—for instance, the chairmanship of a convention, or the head of a committee. But to return to first principles, the saloon in politics, and the methods by which it is utilized. Some time since, it will be remembered,

A PLOT WAS EXPOSED

by THE TIMES, by which it was proposed to purchase two of the county officers, so as to secure the control of the registration of the county, and by this means capture the county for the Legislature and the election this fall. Fifty thousand dollars was appropriated for this purpose, but the scheme fell through, because of the incorruptibility of the Republican office-holders and the honesty of at least one prominent Democrat, who declined to be a party to the infamous transaction. That this statement is a fact is well known, and there has never been any effort on the part of the Democrats to disprove it, as they were afraid to let the inside facts come out, and the whole matter was quietly smothered. But the $50,000 was appropriated for this purpose, and the question arose as to the best disposition to make of it. The Buckley gang had got a foothold in the Turf Exchange (that was before the concern was indicted), and it was proposed to inaugurate the San Francisco plan in Los Angeles—plant saloons throughout the city where they would do the most good. A saloon, it was argued, was good for 10 to 20 votes at the very least, and 100 saloons properly worked would swing from 1000 to 2000 votes, and possibly more, at least enough to carry the election, which was the object sought to be obtained. There have been 85 saloon licenses granted in this city since the 1st of February, when the Police Board became wholly Democratic, and they are being added to almost every day. The following is a list of the licenses issued, as copied from the official permits in the possession of the City Clerk:

THE OFFICIAL LIST.

Singer & Kuhl, 25 South Main, February 8th.
Rufus R. Brown, 152 South Spring, February 1st.
James A. Smith, 808 North Alameda, February 1st.
Eichhorn Bros., 300 Downey avenue, February 1st.
J. G. Kenyon, 25 North Los Angeles, February 2d.
W. H. Dillard, 257 East First, February 7th.
John King, 26 Aliso, February 6th.
Herald & Vellquite, New Main and Alameda, February 6th.
W. J. Stephenson, 316 North Main, February 8th.
Stewart & Bates, 780 San Fernando, February 8th.
Seifreid & McKee, 622 San Fernando, February 8th.
Ferdinand Guendre, Sainsevain and Alameda, February 11th.
Graham & Luckman, 614 San Fernando, February 11th.
J. H. Whitney, 138 East First, February 8th.
Merrick & Hall, 160 South Los Angeles, February 11th.
August C. Strelow, 113 North Los Angeles, February 11th.
H. A. Marcellus & Co., 960 North Main, February 13th.
Joseph Greutz, 152 North Alameda, February 14th.
G. Groseman, 205 Upper Main, February 14th.
Jerue & Eddy, 136 South Main, January 18th.
Schafer & Salter, 605 East First, February 17th.
Andrew Fuhrberg, 207 Commercial, February 18th.
P. Ballade, 740 and 742 South Main, February 21st.
Robert Stewart, 252 New High, March 1st.
Bunker & Doll, 174 East First, March 1st.
Champion & Myers, 21 and 23 North Los Angeles, March 1st.
John P. Rafferty, 311 Aliso, March 1st.
Silverberg & Ott, 115 South Spring, March 3d.
Antonio Save, 29 North Los Angeles, March 2d.
John Fosney, 517 East First, March 5th.
E. S. Fanchon, 152 East First, March 5th.
Scotto & Villa, 11 East First, March 7th.
Charles Friece, 114 East Second, March 7th.
Rendle & Mohr, 202 San Fernando, March 8th.
D. J. Harmer, 134 South Spring, March 8th.
W. H. Brown, 257 East First, March 10th.
Haley & Newman, 4 San Pedro, March 10th.
Fred Ahrens, Second-street Park, March 16th (change).
Gaggioni & Johnson, City Garden, March 15th (renewal).
Peter Bissero, 178 East First, March 17th.
J. Malloy, 3 West First, March 17th.
H. F. Wescott, 91 Ducommun, April 1st.
Albert Meinzeininger, 44 North Alameda, April 2d (change).
William Guenther, Turner's Hall, Spring, April 2d.
Charles Alexander, 6½ North Main, April 3d.
Aug. P. Clos, 144 North Alameda (no license issued).
Frank Esperance, Sainsevain and Alameda, April 5th (change).
James D. Gilman, 120 San Fernando, April 4th.
Paul Navarro, 29 San Pedro, April 4th.
F. H. Olding, 40 Wilmington, April 3d (change).
F. F. Frazier, 130½ West First, April 7th.
Kohler & Eugert, 13½ West Third, April 7th.
George Guirre, Panorama building, South Main, April 10th.
G. M. Thorp, 59 North Los Angeles, April 11th (change).
Chase, Finn & Co., Nadeau Hotel, April 12th (change).
Lucknow & Schmidt, 20 North Main, April 10th (change).
Jo Ketto, Commercial and Los Angeles, April 13th (change).
N. A. Covarrubias, Los Angeles street, April 12th.
Files & Schades, 360 South Spring, April 13th.
John Hewberger, 312½ South Spring, April 13th.
John Fisher & Co., 138 East First, May 4th (change).
Staten & Co., 758 South Main, May 2d.
Otto Rosenthal, 614 San Fernando, May 5th (change).
Blind & Plant, 614 Downey avenue, May 5th.
G. Frederick, opposite Second-street Park, April 26th.
F. Pettit, 112 West Second, May 4th.
Henry Stuber, 127 West First, May 5th.
James Mascott, 13 Aliso, May 7th.
Peterson & Lawler, 201 New High, May 4th.
H. W. Gerke, 630 East First, May 4th (change).
Charles Smith, Sixth and Olive, May 2d (change).
H. Luckman, 46 North Main, May 9th.
A. E. Bernard, 960 Alameda, May 3d (change).
Crowley, Baker & Co., Hollenbeck block, May 12th.
John McManes, 7 East First, May 9th (change).
Schnaatfeger & Zimmerman, 133 East First, May 9th.
William Schumacher, 4 North Main, May 9th (change).
Herald & Valchner, Main and Alameda, May 9th (change).
A. Greenwald, 500 East First, May 14th (change).
Richard Bros., 316 North Main, May 10th (change.)
John Rall & Co., 45 Wilmington, May 14th (change).

From the above, it would appear that there have been numerous "changes of proprietors," but as an offset, there have been a number of applicants refused licenses, because they desired to go into the residence portion of the city, a special effort appearing to have been made in that direction, as will be remembered by all those who have kept track of the proceedings of the Police Board during that time.

ANOTHER CURIOUS COINCIDENCE.

In this connection, another fact is worth recalling. During January, there was an investigation of the saloon of John King, on Aliso street, by the Police Board, during which it was sworn to by a dozen officers that his place was one of the worst in the city. In the course of the investigation, it came out that there were other equally hard places, and, after a very full hearing, extending over two days, the following licenses were ordered revoked:

E. M. Myers, 21 and 23 North Los Angeles, January 5th.
G. G. Brown, 115 Marchessault, January 5th.
Bates & Bonner, 112 North Los Angeles, January 5th.
W. H. Dillard, 257 East First, January 5th.
John King, 26 Aliso, January 5th.
J. G. Kenyon, 25 North Los Angeles, January 5th.
J. Dupuy, 29 North Los Angeles, January 5th.
W. H. Dillard, March 5th.

In reference to the list of licenses granted since February 1st, it will be seen that of those revoked, King, Kenyon, Dillard and Myers were granted new licenses. This may be only a coincidence, but, in view of all the facts and surroundings, it is a singular one, anyway. That the saloon is to be worked by the Democratic party at the coming election is a self-evident fact, in view of the preceding statements, and the matter will require watchful attention on the part of the Republicans to prevent its success. The danger signal is displayed, and it behooves the Republicans to act upon the timely warning, not by starting more saloons, and thus increasing the existing evil, but by watching and curbing those that exist.

PART II.
Pages 9 to 12.

The Times.

Sunday

EIGHTH YEAR. LOS ANGELES, SUNDAY, APRIL 7, 1889.—TWELVE PAGES. PRICE: Single Copies 5 Cents; By the Week, 3 Cents

THE LITTLE TYCOON.

PLOT OF WILLARD SPENSER'S POPULAR COMIC OPERA.

Its First Production in This City at the Grand Opera-house Tomorrow Night—A Good Libretto and Charming Music.

Tomorrow evening, at the Grand Opera-house, will mark the initial production in Los Angeles of Willard Spenser's justly-styled perpetual comic opera success, *The Little Tycoon.*

It is not often that a light opera combines a witty libretto and a fine score. Gilbert and Sullivan succeed at it usually, but the librettist is too frequently an important person in the preparation of comic opera. *Erminie,* in spite of the fact that its beautiful music made it a wonderful success, has the stupidest of stupid librettos. The synopsis of *The Little Tycoon* given herewith is prepared for the purpose of making the opera intelligible to the people who are to hear it this week at the Grand Opera-house. There is a good deal of charming music in the opera and half a hundred people in the company to sing it.

General Knickerbocker.

Mr. Spenser's opera opens on the deck of an ocean steamer returning from Europe. The passenger list includes "Gen. Knickerbocker," the aristocratic descendant of an old New York family; "Violet," his charming daughter, whom he wishes to marry a title; "Alvin Barry," a young Wall-street broker, who loves and is loved by "Violet;" "Rufus Ready," a lively young American, "Alvin's" college friend; "Lord Dolphin," an ideal descendant of effete monarchical institutions, whose conversational ability is limited to the monosylables, "Oh, ah!" with varying inflections, and whom the tuft-hunting "Gen. Knickerbocker" has chosen to be his daughter's husband; "Teddy," the Milesian valet of "his ludship;" a chorus of tourist-maidens, chaperoned by "Miss Hurricane," a Bostonese schoolmistress, and including "Violet's" vivacious friend, "Dolly Dimple;" and a chorus of college tourists under the leadership of the irrepressible "Rufus."

After the opening chorus, in which are related the delights of ocean travel in these days of steamships as compared with the discomforts of the old time sailing vessels, the company turns it attention to looking for the whale, which, their guide books say, is due to appear at this particular point in the voyage. This furnishes occasion for a solo by Rufus, with all hands in the chorus:

We'll watch for the blowing whale
O'er the starboard taffy-rail;
We'll follow his trail, and put salt on his tail, Yo ho! Yo ho! Yo ho!

The tourist maidens enters with alpen stocks and recount their travels in a vivacious chorus, which is brought to an end by the entrance of Rufus, who bears the shocking information that Violet's father has locked her up to prevent her from seeing Alvin. Dolly opportunely finds a duplicate key and releases Violet, who dejectedly appears and sings her sorrows:

Doomed am I to marry a lord;
Was ever destiny so sad?
Doomed to be too much adored,
To weep and never more be glad.
Doomed to know I yet must live,
To wed a lord when oh, my heart
To Alvin only I can give,
Must we part?

"Rufus," much moved by her melancholy, announces in a spirited recitative his determination to circumvent "Old Knick-er-bocker" and unite the lovers. In this determination the college tourists join heartily and sing their college cry, which is as profoundly intellectual as college cries usually are:

We are up to snuff! [*All sneeze.*]
For we're immensely high-toned
—high-toned, high-toned!
Kala-ma-zoo, zoo, zoo, zoo, zoo, zoo-o-o-o,
—Kal-a-ma-zoo, zoo!

It is then announced that the girls, with "Miss Hurricane's" amiable collusion, have hit upon a plan for enabling "Violet" to elude her father and the hateful lord. Whereupon "Violet" and the chorus sing the waltz-song that is generally considered the bright particular gem of the opera:

Love comes like a summer sigh,
Softly o'er you stealing.
Love comes, and you wonder why
To its shrine you're kneeling.
Love comes and the days go by
While your fate Love's sealing—
Love some day must come to all.
—Come to all, come to all,
Love some day must come to all,
Come to all!

Exit "Violet" and enter her father, looking for her. He threatens to incarcerate her on a bread and water diet. In a song he explains that "when he was a boy" daughters never thought of disobeying paternal mandates or of choosing a husband in defiance of paternal choice. Upon the heels of this song Lord Dolphin and his valet, "Teddy," enter and circle about the stage with the eccentric step known as the Dolphin dance, "Teddy" meanwhile singing:

Oh! heel and toe we always go,
We always go together,
In rain or shine, in hail or snow,
And never mind the weather.

The "General" is in ecstasies of admiration over the movement, but the chorus denounces it as a fatal step, and deplores the fact that it "has a fascination all its own," which may lead to disastrous results. In a song they

Violet, the Little Tycoon.

make an analogy between the lureful Dolphin dance and the equally lureful step into matrimony.

The stage is cleared to give "Alvin" and "Violet" an opportunity to declare their mutual, undying affection in a duet. "Lord Dolphin," "Teddy" and "Gen. Knickerbocker" enter and surprise them, but before "Violet" can be taken away to her stateroom, "Rufus" and the collegians come, disguised as hob-goblins, and manage to separate the girl from her father and his lordship. The enemy driven from the field, the lovers have another chance, and sing "Love Reigns," at the end of which the hob-goblins and the tourist maidens reappear to give joyful voice to the "Kal-a-ma-zoo" song. "Violet" is taken to Miss Hurricane's room to be disguised in boy's clothing. "Teddy" appears and bewails the fate that led him to leave Ireland to become a nobleman's factotum. Incidentally he hints that,

I've a mighty saycret kapin',
That if I should revale,
Would shtop Miss Vi'let's waypin'
An' make Lord Dolphin quail.
He'd pull shtroke in a galley;
But then I'm not so green
For I'd lose my place as valet,
If I'd lake out what I've seen.
Oh, for me bogs, an' me fogs, an' me hogs,
An' me dogs, an' me clogs, an' me nate little frogs!
Oh, for me togs, an' me grogs, an' me nogs,
An' me jogs, an' me illegant cabin of logs!
Arrah! Arrah!

The steamer reaches port, and the custom-house officers come on board to inspect the luggage, or to inspect the "blindfold" fees presented by the worldly-wise tourists. "Gen. Knickerbocker," assisted by the chorus, explains the working of the inspection system:

Oh, don't you see how
We hold our breath when they begin,
With not so much as a word or bow,
To clean us out and scoop things in,
Unless some gold we show.
Oh, what a go!
An elevated man, on the elevated plan,
Keeps all he gets and gets all he can.

This is followed by a general musical moaning and lamentation by the victims of a high protective tariff. "Gen. Knickerbocker," to temporarily dispose of "Alvin," has him arrested as a smuggler. "Violet," in boy's clothing, betrays herself by her tearful solicitude for her lover, and is recaptured by her father, who exults over his fine diplomacy. The girl, encouraged by the chorus, declares her eternal affection for "Alvin," and the curtain falls.

Miss Hurricane.

The second act opens in "Gen. Knickerbocker's" villa at Newport. "Violet," sadly gazing out to sea, deplores her unhappy situation in a song, "Sad Heart of Mine." Her father enters and sneers at her tears. Presently two footmen enter, one from each side of the stage, with cards on waiters. The footmen meet and bow at the same time to the General, who is surprised to discover that each card announces the arrival of "Lord Dolphin." "Ah! I see," he exclaims, "too deeply in love for one card!"

But immediately the Dolphin dance strikes up. From one side of the stage enter "Lord Dolphin" and "Teddy" in their characteristic attitudes. From the opposite side enter "Alvin" and "Rufus" disguised so as to look exactly like the other pair. Meeting the astounded General, "Dolphin" and "Alvin" each raise an eyeglass and ejaculate: "Oh, ah!" After an amusing dialogue it is decided to settle the question of identity by drawing lots. "Violet" prepares the slips of paper and contrives to give "Alvin," whom she has recognized, the winning one. The real lord is politely shown out and the lovers left alone together, but the "General" soon returns and discovers the trick played upon him. A lively trio, "Oh, You Incense Me," follows, which is interrupted by the entrance of the versatile collegians, who, this time, are disguised as brigands. They fail, however, to prevent the angry father from bearing away his daughter. The baffled rescuers admit that they have been checkmated, and, since all their violent schemes have failed, they resolve upon diplomacy. After they disappear "Violet" enters with a bunch of daisies in her hand and sings "Tell Me Daisy," which is another of the most successful numbers in the opera:

Tell me daisy, true now,
Tell me daisy, do now—
Pretty petals falling;
On the last one calling.
Yes, no, yes, no—say, which?
Yes, no, yes, no—nay, which?
Anxious heart this proves me—
Yes! that, ah! he loves me!

A change of scene leads to the final episode of the story. After the incident of the brigands, "Gen. Knickerbocker" has been surprised and delighted by the notification that the "Great Tycoon of Japan," accompanied by his suite, will do him the honor to call upon him that very evening. The "General" has had his garden and conservatory hastily and gorgeously arranged for the reception of his royal guest, and when the time arrives the stage is darkened for an instant and is illuminated again to disclose the preparations for the reception. Dolly and the tourist maidens enter, disguised as Japanese maidens, and announce the coming of "Sham, the Great Tycoon." Incidentally they hint that something is to turn up that will throw "Lord Dolphin" completely out of the contest for "Violet's" hand. The "Tycoon's March" strikes up, and, in great state, "Alvin," disguised as the "Tycoon," enters, accompanied by "Rufus," who personates "Gull-Gull," the court interpreter.

The never-failing collegians form the attendant cortége. A supposedly characteristic Japanese chorus is sung, and "Gull-Gull" flatters the "General"

The Heel and Toe Step.

into singing a song of his own composition entitled "The American Eagle." The "Tycoon" shows great admiration, and the "General," his head completely turned, agrees to grant any request he may make. The "Tycoon" immediately asked for the hand of "Violet," whom he wishes to make the "Little Tycoon." Disregardful of the prior claim of "Lord Dolphin," the "General" consents. Just then the "Marchioness of Pullhimback," "Lord Dolphin's" mother, enters and seizes her son, who it appears has been making his matrimonial arrangements without her consent.

"Alvin" presently discloses his identity, but the "General" is so delighted with his persistence and his diplomacy that he finally consents to "Violet's" marrying him, and all ends happily.

And she will be the Little Tycoon,
Yes, yes, yes, yes,
The Little Tycoon.

CAST OF CHARACTERS.

"Gen. Knickerbocker" (one of the old-time Knickerbockers), R. E. Graham.

"Alvin Barry" (a young Wall-street broker, afterwards the Great Tycoon), J. Aldrich Libby.

"Rufus Ready" (Alvin's college friend, afterwards "Gull Gull," interpreter to the Great Tycoon), Lloyd Wilson.

"Lord Dolphin" (suitor for the hand of Violet), J. W. McGovern.

"Teddy" (Lord Dolphin's valet), Joseph Mealey.

"Montgomery" (Gen. Knickerbocker's footman), W. S. Reeves.

Custom-house officers, J. Mulholland, James Steer.

"Captain," George Lechler.

"Miss Hurricane" (chaperone to tourist maidens), Hattie Arnold.

"Dolly Dimple" (Violet's school friend), Mamie Cerbi.

"Violet" (Gen. Knickerbocker's daughter, afterward the Little Tycoon), Catharine Linyard.

Large chorus of tourists, maidens, college tourists, hobgoblins, brigands, sailors and Japanese masqueraders.

A Secret.

Out from the deeps of the air gather the clouds,
Their whistling battalions sweeping the sky
Of winter. Silently, yet steadily,
On they come, their Marshal—the wind—blowing
His trumpet, sweeping the seas with his breath.
The leaves of the forest catch the sound of
His coming, and his couriers run through
Their leaves with a tremulous step, and all
Ashiver they stir at the touch, as if
Each had a heart in its breast. Grand army
Of clouds, ye cover the field of the sky,
And then let your batteries loose on the
World. Ye have hidden redoubts, ye have paths
That we cannot discern, and forces that
Take us with swiftest surprise, sometimes in
This land of the sun—sometimes on the verge
Of the summer. Where gather ye then your
Soldiers gay, your army of raindrops
Which sometimes descend just to tickle the
Earth with their lances, then withdraw, with bright
Banners of rainbows, to hide from the sun?
Where away do ye wander as summer
Draws near? O, luminous mountains with heads
Sky-pillowed and bold, are ye so far-visioned
Ye see what keepeth the calm of our summer,
The sheen of her skies from the storm? Hear ye
Who saith "Depart" to winter's storm-clouded
Battalions, so that o'er the blue eye of
Summer there never is seen the eyelid
Of cloud fringed with tear-drops of rain? Ah, yes,
I think ye know somewhat of the secret.
We, da sea and mountains, ye are lovers
Together of the summerland fair, and
Her eye that is shining with laughter, her
Breath that is sweet with the flowers, and her
Garments with orange-scent laden, ye love
As a mother doth love her babe in its
Cradle, and we, you could tell the secret
Of her sun-shining summer and calm.

ELIZA A. OTIS.

An Impression.

One day, says the Philadelphia American, Dr. McCosh, when president of Princeton College, came into the mental philosophy class, and said: "Ah, young gentlemen, I have an impression! Now, young gentlemen," continued the Doctor, as he touched his head with his fore finger, "can you tell me what an impression is?" No answer. "What! No one knows? No one can tell what an impression is?" exclaimed the Doctor, looking up and down the class. "I know," said young Alan A[illegible], "an impression is a dent in a soft place." "Young gentlemen," said the Doctor, removing his hand from his forehead and growing red in the face, "you are excused for the day."

PART II.
Pages 9 to 12.

The Los Angeles Sunday Times.

EIGHTH YEAR. LOS ANGELES, SUNDAY, JUNE 16, 1889.—TWELVE PAGES. PRICE: Single Copies 5 Cents. By the Week 3 Cents.

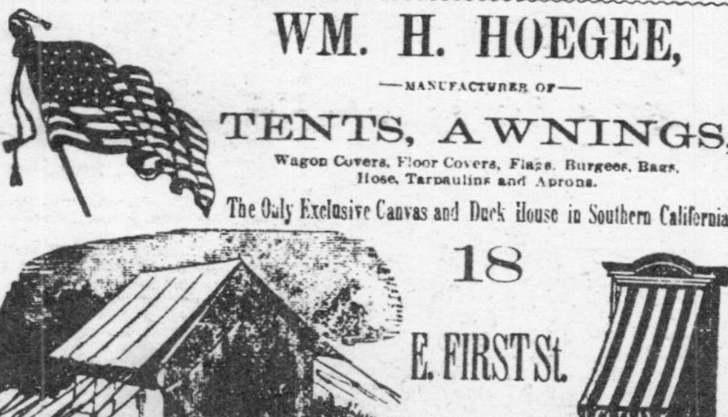

"DOPE FIENDS."

A TOUR OF INSPECTION THROUGH CHINATOWN.

Views of Mongols as They Appear at All Stages of the Game—How They Burn and Smoke the Drug, and How It Fascinates Them.

It has been well said that "knowledge is power." Hence the deduction that all knowledge, be it good or evil, is of benefit in some way to society. It is true that moralists and teachers of the gospel have cried down the publication in newspapers of the doings of the criminal classes, while men of the world have with one voice declared that the surest preventive of vice of all kinds is the exposure of its votaries in the daily press. Muzzle the press or

No. 1—Ready to Smoke.

wipe it out of existence and human nature sinks to the level of the brute creation. Murder, robbery and mob law run riot with each other, and the whole country is given up to evil-doers.

Conspicuous among the criminal classes of this country are the Chinese. The tendency of the Chinese to crime is especially great, and is well worthy the closest consideration of the moralist, the philanthropist, the philosopher and the historian, to say naught of the politician and lawmaker. The inner life of the Chinese is replete with mystery and superstition. Within the past century France has thrown off the yoke of tyranny; England and Germany, obeying the law of compulsion, have become limited inside of absolute monarchies, while Russia and China alone of the great powers of the Old World still adhere to the ancient and tyrannical rule of Czar and Emperor. Christianity and civilization have exerted but little influence with the people of these two nations, where slavery blooms and liberty perishes. Crime seems to be closely connected with the character of the Chinese, who, lacking in a sufficient degree of moral restraint, are generally but too willing, for a suitable consideration, to enter into any wicked scheme.

In this country the Chinese character is but little known, and many of the [illegible] and [illegible] awful [illegible] [illegible] from the eyes of the Caucasian. The full extent and nature of the crimes committed in California by the Chinese

No. 2—Cooking the pill.

are commonly unknown, except it may be to the special detectives and the press reporters, who have superior sources of information. A detailed recital of these crimes would make a volume equaling in dramatic incident any of the old romances, dreams or tragedies; rivaling in plot and sensation the record of the dreadful "Council of Ten," or the dark and cruel acts of the Inquisition. All of the crimes in the calendar, from misdemeanor to murder, have at divers times in the past been committed within the Chinese quarters of this city, and in a majority of these the identity of the felon has remained undiscovered. A trip through the filthy dens occupied by this strange people will convince the most casual observer that the Chinaman's facilities for covering up his tracks are greater than any other class of people. Even the shrewdest detectives are fooled and humbugged at will, and, unless a majority of the inhabitants of Chinatown desire to turn the criminal over to justice, the officer might just as well give up.

Not only do the Chinese revel in crime, but they delight to draw the detested white race down to their level, and that they have succeeded with certain classes in this country there is no doubt.

The Chinese criminal, be he high or low, is thoroughly devoted to the "bamboo," or opium pipe; and when he isn't "burgling" or doing something worse, he devotes his leisure

No. 3—Something Wrong.

hours to "hitting the dope" or training his white brother in the way he should not go.

The opium habit was first introduced on this coast about 30 years ago, and it is hard today to find a white criminal, male or female, on this coast who is not a victim of the terrible opium habit.

The Legislature has fought this evil for years, and yet "John" goes on year after year adding victims to his death-dealing practice. Opium fiends are more numerous among the criminal classes than any other, although during the past few years the habit has reached out and has secured a strong foothold among the better classes. Chinese servants have taken the opium layout into the families of the upper crust, and it is not an uncommon thing to see its deadly signs on the cheeks and in the watery eyes of society's votaries. Young men and women, too, who have nothing to do but seek new pleasures, make willing victims, and the almond-eyed master of the kitchen is only too glad to give them the first lesson.

Much has been said on the subject of opium smoking, but it is a subject that will never be exhausted, and is always interesting to even those who have visited "opium joints," as the smoking places are called.

A few nights ago the TIMES artist, armed with his flash camera, and followed by a reporter and several sightseers visited Chinatown. To reach an opium "joint" one has to wend his way through dark passage ways, braving a stench that has been aptly likened to "a mixture of sandalwood and fish." The party was determined to get a few opium views, and they were successful, as the cuts in this article will prove.

The first joint entered was a filthy little room, 8x10. Three or four "fiends" were sleeping in bunks that decorated the walls. A "layout," composed of a bamboo pipe, a small glass lamp, a steel wire about the length and size of a knitting-needle, a horn box for liquid opium, a pair of shears and a few matches, spread out on a common mat, rested on a larger mat, on which the fiend reclined. All of them except one had smoked themselves into a death-like sleep, and he was just preparing to partake of the deadly drug. The artist adjusted his camera and flashed the cap, with the result shown in picture No. 1.

The subject has probably just returned from a hard day's work in the home of some highly-respectable family, and from the self-satisfied smile on his ugly face it will be seen that he has made up his mind to enjoy himself. He has lighted the lamp and is just preparing the "pill." To make this simple operation plain to the un-

No. 4.—Trying again.

initiated it will be necessary to describe the pipe.

The pipe is made of a large bamboo, about eighteen inches long and one inch in diameter. It is [illegible] the other. The bowl is placed about eight inches from the closed end of the bamboo. The bowl is made of light wood and the top is covered with skin, which is stretched as tight as a drumhead. In the center a small hole, just large enough to receive the wire or knitting-needle, is made. The smoker dips this needle into the liquid opium and gathers up a drop about the size of a pea, which he carefully burns and carefully rolls on the bowl until it is "cooked," or ready to be smoked. He then places it over the small hole in the bowl and runs the hot needle through it into the bowl. He is now ready to smoke. The bowl is placed to the lamp, with the open end of the bamboo in the heathen's mouth, and he takes three or four long puffs. Cut No. 2 shows him in the act of cooking the pill.

This is the most difficult feature of smoking, and a good "cooker" is in great demand among the white females who smoke opium. In this cut John is about ready to smoke his first pill, but before he is ready for the interesting operation he discovers that something is wrong with the pill, and it will be seen by examining cut No. 3 that the fear of losing his smoke has thrown a look of disappointment over his face that is truly painful.

For a few moments he struggles

No. 5—The ninth pipe.

with the unruly bamboo, and the TIMES party look on with more than passing interest. It is a study to watch the fellow's face when he puts on his big horn eye-glasses, and goes to work on the pipe in earnest. Cut No. 4 shows him in the act of adjusting the pill a second time, and as he put the pipe to his lips and drew a long satisfactory whiff the party filed out.

Before he drops off to sleep, as has his partner, who is by his side, he will probably cook and inhale a dozen or twenty pills, according to the length of time he has been a victim of the habit.

Another joint was entered, and an old saddle-colored rascal was caught in the act of smoking his ninth pipe. It will be seen that he is growing quite drowsy, and is about ready to drop the bamboo and dream about the beauties of his distant home.

After visiting several other joints, the artist succeeded in getting a fiend who was on his last pill. His whole body shows that the drug has gained perfect control over him. In a few seconds he will drop the pipe, and for hours he will be in a deep sleep.

It is said who have experienced the sensation that the most beautiful dreams come to the smoker and for hours after he awakes he walks about in a kind of trance that makes him forgetful of his earthly surroundings. There is no other dissipation that is so fascinating, and when it once gets a hold on a person there is no human power that can shake it off. The victim is lost to this world, for when he is not smoking he is wandering about in a kind of drunken stupor that unfits him for any kind of business, or he is

No. 6.—Almost gone.

sleeping with his fairy-like dreams that draw him back to the pipe time after time, until death steps in and relieves the world of a vagabond who is much lower in the scale of humanity than the vilest drunkard that ever crawled out of the gutter.

And the Chinese are introducing this death-dealing habit into happy homes every day.

THE "RAZOR-BACK.

A Style of Hog Peculiar to Florida and Other Parts.

A correspondent of the Jacksonville Times-Union asks the editor of that paper the following question:

> Can you show to the people wherein they will be benefited by the utter extinction of the "razor-back," when he is the only hog in Florida proof against cholera and other infectious diseases?

To which the editor responds:

> The inquiry recalls a conversation held yesterday with an old-time Florida "cracker." He declared that the war waged against the "razor-back" was founded in ignorance; that it is not the fault of the "razor-back" that he is long, lean, lank and larcenous, but the fault of his master. He had taken up the half-starved animals from their range of sand (on which they were forced to subsist) and, after feeding them on corn, as other hogs are fed, had made large, fine stock of them. The owner himself would hardly know the breed, after two or three generations. Their sides fill out, their humped-up backs take on a straight, horizontal line, and even their snouts contract several inches. Take Kentucky thoroughbreds, hogs, cows or horses, turn them loose on Florida sand for a hundred years, and we should soon see nothing but scrubs and razor-backs. Let our razor-back owners pay half the attention and feed half the food to the home article that the "imported" stock gets, and the change would soon surprise everybody.

In order to demonstrate its "perfect fairness to all sections," including Florida, THE TIMES goes out of its way to give an illustration of the able "razor-back" hog, taken from life, and also an illustration of what the animal can be made by tender care, generous feeding and civilized culture. Look on this picture:

The "razor-back"—"Sibboy thar!"

And then look on this:

The "razor-back" renewed, regenerated and disenthralled.

THE TIMES now considers that it has done its duty by Florida. Bring on the next country with a grievance!

A Permanent Retirement.

[Pasadena Star.]

Gov. Waterman announces that he is a candidate for renomination. This will be a surprise to the State, as he had declared that he did not wish to be reelected. It requires no prophet to declare that he will be retired permanently at the close of the present term.

Written for The Times.

Johnstown.

Fire and flood. God! what a sight.
Maddened humanity; vain is their flight;
Husbands and wives torn rudely asunder,
Little children in terror and wonder,
Helpless call.
Like an avalanche onward rushing,
Man and beast together crushing;
Homes of plenty, homes of care,
Wildly sweeping, where, O, where?
Chaos all.

No time for thought, no time for prayer:
A lightning stroke from a sky all fair.
What does it mean, that cry from the street?
What says the rider who comes so fleet?
"Fly for your lives!"
In fancied security men turn and say,
"He is crazy, poor fellow," and go their way.
Horse and rider dash swiftly along:
Unheeding, they hear, O, hapless throng;
Not one survives.

Self-sacrificed, a hero he
Who dies to save humanity;
When years go by this Paul Revere
Will still call forth a pitying tear
From eyes now dim
With weeping o'er some loved and lost,
Who might have fled the holocaust
Had they but heeded that hoarse cry
From throat in vain grown parched and dry—
God pity him!

God pity him? Nay, he is blest,
And all who share his quiet rest.
God help the living, no need, the dead;
Help those who still have tears to shed—
Tears all so vain.
Theirs to carry a breaking heart;
To smile and cover up the smart
Until life's little farce is played,
And they, in robes of peace arrayed,
Forget all pain.

ELLEN F. PRATT.

Another Nursery Rhyme.

DEDICATED TO CHARLES A. GARDNER.

It's lady-bugs, is it, ye want?
Then divil a bit need ye wait:
Me orchard is full of the bastes,
As ye'll see when ye open the gate.

Me apricot trees they have stripped,
Eating all of the leaves save the bones;
The fruit they have gobbled up clean,
And now they are at work on the stones.

You may talk of *icerya* and sich
Horrible names for the new-fangled scale,
Or anything else ever made
From a microbe up to a whale.

But if ever there lived on the earth,
A creature more false to its name,
Than this same un-ladylike bug,
I'd like ye to show me the same.

J. A. C. K.

IN SOCIETY.

THE SEASON KEEPING UP MOST ADMIRABLY.

A Fancy Dress Party and a Reception That Were Largely Attended and Greatly Enjoyed—Notes from Santa Monica, Alhambra and Coronado.

A delightful fancy-dress party was given at the residence of Mr. and Mrs. S. A. Rendall, corner of Ninth and Alvarado streets, last Friday evening. A glittering assemblage, elegant costumes, fine music, brilliant illuminations and an elegant collation, presided over by a gracious and attentive hostess, gave spirit to the occasion and made the hours pass swiftly by. After the grand march of all the characters, which took place at 9:45, a minuet was danced by eight of the chief participants. Songs, recitations and instrumental music followed, and finally a carpet dance was indulged in, and the festivities did not conclude till a late hour. The fair hostess was congratulated by every one present on the successful result of her careful preparations and tasteful arrangement of all the details incident to such an arduous undertaking.

The following is a list of the guests present in costume and the characters assumed by them:

"Napoleon," Gen. Mathews; "Empress Josephine," Miss Julia Rendall; "King Edward of Scotland," James Garrison; "Queen Elizabeth," Mrs. A. Andrews; "Duke of Wellington," Mr. Paine; "Marie Antoinette," Miss Stella Norris; "Sir William Wallace," Charles Lantz; "Lady Marion," Miss Alta Fry; "Robert Bruce," Dr. W. H. Dukeman; "Lady Helen," Miss Bessie Tillotson; "Lord Guilford," William Veazy; "Lady Jane Grey," Miss Anna Williams; "King Ferdinand," W. J. Hughes; "Queen Isabella," Miss Maggie Cowper; "Brutus," Mr. Mills; "Portia," Miss Anna Pendleton; "Lord Byron," Mr. Humphreys; "Lady Byron," Miss Florence Riley; "King Otho of Greece," Dr. West Hughes; "Lady Loretta," Miss Grace Lowell; "Prince Rupert," Mr. Cal. Foy; "Queen of Muses," Miss Kate Fleming; "Sir Walter Scott," Mr. Wahls; "Lady Rebecca," Miss Huntley; "Romeo," Prof. Williams; "Juliet," Miss Helen Mar Bennett; "Lysander," Harry Veazy; "Lady Hermia," Miss Grace McNab; "Don Carlos," Theodore Coulter; "Spanish Princess," Miss Zoe Ballard; "Othello," F. E. Lowrey; "Desdemona," Miss L. Veazy; "Ophelia," Miss Cora Foy; "Bertram," E. W. Lowell; "Helena," Miss Clara Cook; "Beethoven," Prof. J. H. Brenner; "Perdita," Miss Julia Off; "Mary, Queen of Scots," Miss Anna McNab; "Longinius," M. Pendleton; "Maid of Athens," Miss Lulu James; "Page," Miss Mabel Rendall.

The following guests were not in costume:

Dr. W. L. Graves and wife, Prof. Dozier and wife, Dr. Dozier and wife, Mr. Flint and wife, Dr. Pepper and wife, H. Jevne, wife and daughter; Mr. Riley and wife, J. A. Fairchild and wife, B. [illegible] and wife, J. Johnston and wife, [illegible] wife, St. Louis, [illegible]; Judge [illegible], wife and daughter, Washington, D.C., Mr. Mullen, wife and daughter; Mrs. Lawton and daughter, Miss Dodge, San Francisco; Mr. Barclay and wife, J. M. Elliott and wife, G. A. Dobinson and wife, G. F. Conant and wife, Mr. Allen and wife, Miss Clark and many others.

THE MYSTICS.

The members of Al Malaikah Temple A.A. O.N. M.S. planned a theater party at the Grand last Monday evening in honor of the opening of Nat Goodwin, one of their brothers, but Mr. Goodwin failed to put in an appearance, and the Nobles made up their minds to entertain their lady friends, who had been engaged to attend the theater, in Masonic Temple. A light banquet had been prepared to be partaken of after the theater, and the Nobles engaged a band and dancing was kept up until 10:30 o'clock, when their magnificent banqueting hall was thrown open, and a most pleasant hour was spent at the table. Among those present were: Mr. and Mrs. W. H. Perry, D. E. Miles, J. C. Haskell, Mr. and Mrs. J. D. Bicknell, Freeman G. Teed, Mr. and Mrs. J. R. McManis, Mr. and Mrs. Hervey Lindley, Mr. and Mrs. J. A. Bennett, Dr. and Mrs. Salisbury, Mr. and Mrs. George M. Holton, Dr. Orme, A. G. Bartlett, W. A. Morgan, J. F. Bandhodlt, Col. C. C. Allen, George Gillson, D. W. Field, Mr. and Mrs. W. B. Scarborough, Mr. and Mrs. J. T. Jenkins, Mr. and Mrs. T. J. Weldon, Mr. and Mrs. A. J. Packard, Mr. and Mrs. H. M. Maggee, A. H. Palmer, Mr. and Mrs. S. K. Lindley, James Beck, Dr. and Mrs. Cochran, C. O. Scott, J. D. Urmston, F. Jorden, Mr. and Mrs. F. C. Woodbury, R. W. Kinney, Mr. and Mrs. H. M. Russell, T. H. Ward, Mr. and Mrs. G. W. Lawrence, Dr. and Mrs. Baldwin, H. S. Parcels, Mr. and Mrs. H. Z. Osborne, A. H. Donecker, Dr. Burbank, Mr. and Mrs. M. R. Higgins, O. W. Baldwin, Mr. and Mrs. T. J. Carver, Miss Farquhar, Miss Brown, Miss Florence Perry, Miss Kate Fleming, Miss Hattie Chapman, Miss Holcomb, Miss Ward, Miss Field, Miss Clark, Miss Bandholdt, Miss Cameron, Miss Watson, Miss Bicknell, Miss Ragland, Miss Whitley, Miss Hortense Whitley, Miss Monroe, Miss Donecker, Miss Carver, Mrs. Holmes, Mrs. G. W. Baldwin, Mrs. O. F. Baldwin, Mrs. Ross, Miss Annie Yokum, Miss Renney.

THE FORMAN RECEPTION.

Tuesday afternoon Mrs. Charles Forman gave a reception at her residence on Pico street. The affair was one of the most notable of the season, and was attended by a large number of friends and acquaintances of the hostess. The grounds are among the finest in the city and presented an appearance long to be remembered by those who were fortunate enough to be present. The house was handsomely decorated, the parlors being fairly loaded with rare flowers and beautiful ferns. Among those present were: Mrs. Doria Jones, Miss Constance Jones, Mrs. W. H. Spencer, Mrs. John Plater, Mrs. William Pridham, Mrs. C. E. Thom; Mrs. S. B. Caswell, Mrs. Banning, Mrs. W. W. Ross, Mrs. Perry W. Ross, Mrs. Lankershim, Mrs. John Mansfield, Mrs. Charles de Szigethy, Baroness Reguiat, Miss Emma Childs, Miss Stoneman, Miss Silent, Miss Northam, Mrs. Dupuy, Miss Dupuy, Miss Banning, Mrs. J. S. Owens, Miss Sadie Miles, Mrs. W. R. Briggs, Mrs. John Vosberg, Mrs. J. B. Slauson, Mrs. A. S. Shorb, Miss Shorb, Mrs. T. A. Greaves, Miss Ruth Stephenson, Mrs. Dewey, Miss Dewey, Mrs. E. F. Spence, Miss Kate Spence, Mr. R. M. Widney, Mrs. A. T. Kang,

PART II.
Pages 5 to 12.

The Los Angeles Sunday Times.

EIGHTH YEAR. LOS ANGELES, SUNDAY, SEPTEMBER 1, 1889.—TWELVE PAGES. PRICE: Single Copies 5 Cents. By the Week, 3 Cents.

ARID LANDS.

How Reclaimed by the Use of Water.

Irrigation in the Earliest Times.

THE SYSTEMS USED IN EUROPE.

Crude Methods Employed on the Western Slope.

SOUTH CALIFORNIA'S ARID LANDS.

Progress Made and Some of the Results Achieved.

THE SOUL OF PLANT LIFE.

Millions of Acres May "Blossom as the Rose."

OUR GOVERNMENT DESERT LANDS.

A Statement by Register Patton for the Information of the Arid Lands Committee.

No section of the world can be more interested in the reclamation of arid lands by irrigation than California, for though there are Territories east of us which contain a larger area of land which is useless without artificial moisture, yet, even in these cases, the increased business property of such Territories would mean increased wealth for our manufacturers, merchants, and population in general.

Senator Stewart's proposition, properly carried out, means the reclamation of from 50,000,000 to 160,000,000 acres of barren land at a cost of perhaps $60,000,000. Reckoning on only 25,000,000 acres, and the value with water at $50 an acre, this would mean the creation of value of $1,250,000,000.

PRESENT INVESTIGATION.

[illegible]nce of the present Government inquiry into the matter of irrigation is due to the passage by the Forty-ninth Congress of a law, appropriating $100,000 for the purpose of investigating the extent to which the arid region of the United States can be redeemed by irrigation, the selection of sites for reservoirs, the making of maps, etc.

On February 7th of this year Senator Stewart of Nevada introduced a resolution in the Senate, providing for the appointment of a special committee of seven members, to be known as the Committee on Irrigation and Reclamation of Arid Lands, to investigate thoroughly during the recess, and report in December. The resolution was passed on the 14th, and the committee appointed, and the same Congress appropriated $250,000 to enable the Geological Survey to carry out its work, on the extended scale shown to be necessary.

On August 1st, the committee began its work at St. Paul, Minn. The committee then visited Montana, Idaho, Salt Lake, Nevada and California. After leaving this State, the committee will visit Arizona, New Mexico, Southwest Texas, Colorado and Northwestern Texas, where the committee will close its work.

ANCIENT IRRIGATION.

Tradition asserts that Noah constructed a zanja from Mount Ararat, to water his vineyard. In nearly all Oriental countries, the most ancient records tell of extensive canals and aqueducts, to convey water long distances, many of which already existed in prehistoric times. There are, in Armenia, extensive districts, which were already abandoned to desolation at the earliest historical epoch, but which, in a yet remote antiquity, had been irrigated by a complicated and highly artificial system of canals, the lines of which can still be followed, and there are, in all the highlands, where the sources of the Euphrates rise: in Persia, in Egypt, in India, and in China, works of this sort, which must have been in existence before man had begun to record his own annals. A single year's cessation of irrigation in the delta of the Nile, where no rain falls, and there are no springs, would transform the most fertile of soils to the most barren of deserts, and render uninhabitable a territory that irrigation has made capable of sustaining as dense a population as has ever existed in any part of the world. The irrigation enterprises of the ancient Egyptians were of the most stupendous character. The capacity of Lake Moeris, an artificial reservoir, has been estimated at 3,686,[illegible] cubic yards, and the water received by it at high Nile at 465 cubic yards to the second.

MODERN IRRIGATION.

Modern India affords us the most conspicuous example of irrigation on a grand scale, and it is here more than anywhere else in the world that it is conducted according to one great systematic scheme. In most other countries irrigation is merely an incident. It permits the cultivation of certain crops, which, indeed, add greatly to general and individual wealth, and if it were withdrawn the general prosperity would doubtless suffer. In many parts of India irrigation is the very condition of existence, both of the Government and the people. More than half of the revenue of India comes directly from the products of the soil,

OUR ARID GOVERNMENT LANDS.

MAP PREPARED BY UNITED STATES LAND REGISTER H. W. PATTON,

Of the Los Angeles Land District, for the Information of the Arid Lands Committee of the United States Senate, Showing the Quantity, Character and Location of Arid or Desert Lands Susceptible of Irrigation, Within the District, Together with Descriptive Text, Giving Facts and Statistics and Embodying Important Recomendations.

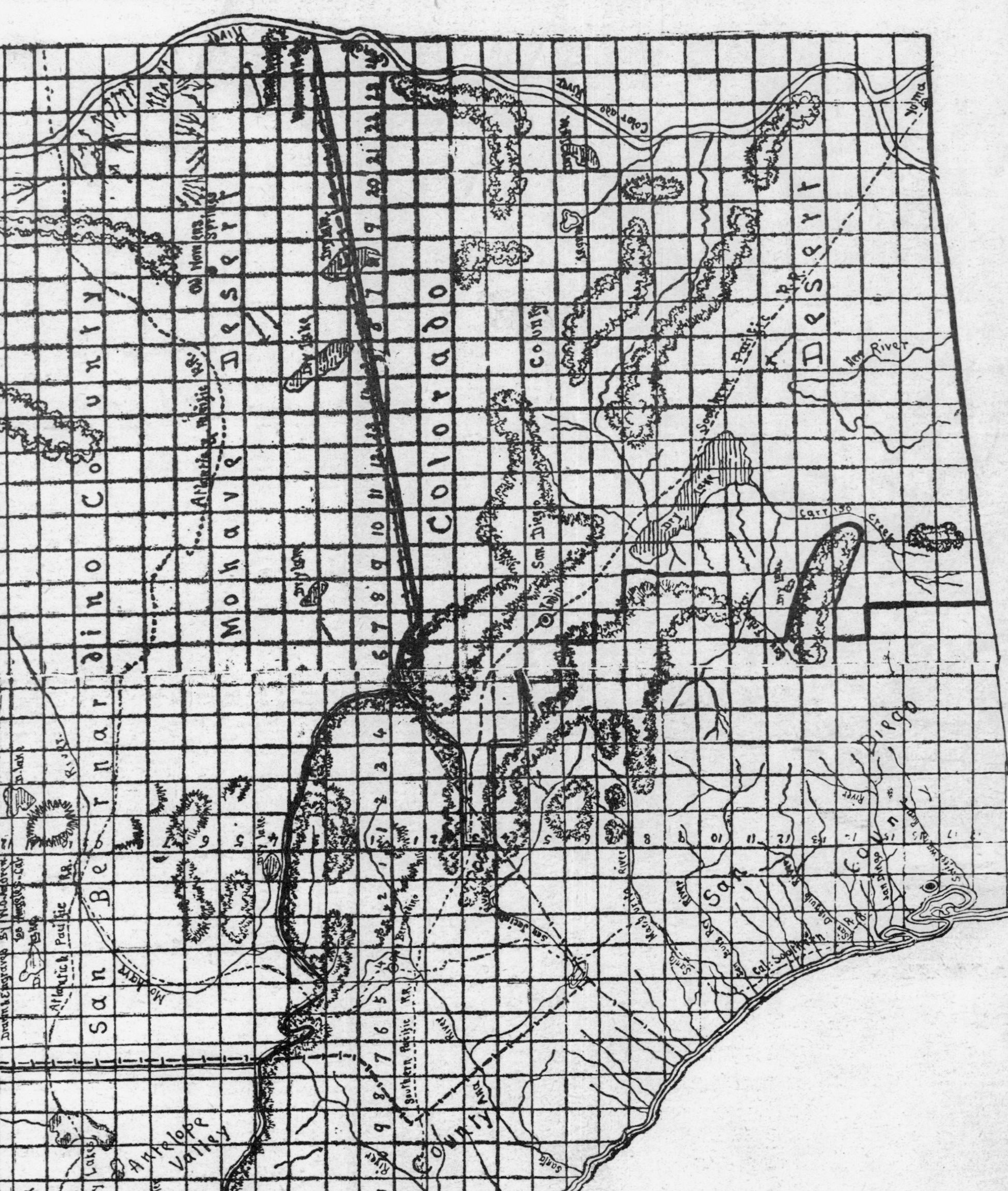

Lines marked thus, —|—|, are county borders. Desert-land borders thus, ———. Railroad lines thus, – – – – –.

and the country is so vast—800,000 square miles, with a population of 200,000,000—that a generally good harvest has not sufficed to preserve large districts from the most dreadful ravages of famine.

Thomas Stevens writes of the great India irrigating canals: "I do not remember anything that impressed me more favorably as a genuine economic enterprise the whole world round than the canal system of India. People go into raptures over the Taj, the Elephanta caves and the other wonders that are to be seen in India, but to me the most wonderful of all were the canals that have practically rescued the teeming millions of the peninsula from famine.

"Whole districts have undergone a complete change. The now thriving city of Jacobadad stands on a plain which, previous to the construction of the Begari Canal, was a verdureless waste, the hottest place in all India, and supposed to be quite uninhabitable. The thermometer climbs up to 145 in the shade at Jacobadad, but since the canal put life into the desert several thousand people have made the desert their home."

Irrigation in Australia is still in the experimental stage, but public, private and Governmental attention is being strongly directed to the necessity of this method of agricultural enterprise. The Chaffee Bros. of San Bernardino have undertaken to expend $1,250,000 in clearing, leveling, irrigating and improving 50,000 acres in Victoria, having made an agreement with the Victorian Government to that effect. Their enterprise is now well under way.

Notwithstanding the fact that Italy has a large rainfall, distributed throughout the year, irrigation is extensively practiced in that country. The main canals of Italy date from very ancient times. Recently, legislation on the matter of irrigation has been full and decisive, irrigation districts having been formed.

In England, irrigation on a large scale was attempted as far back as the sixteenth century, but it was not until 70 years ago that the system was fairly established as an important branch of agriculture. Of late years, what are called water meadows have become a common feature in many counties, also in Southern Scotland. A recent writer says:

> Some peculiar methods have been introduced, as that of irrigating by currents of liquid manure, the sewerage of Edinburgh being distributed on this principle with the most beneficial results over the meadows that lie below the level of the city. The grass grown upon the meadows thus watered has to be cut once a month from April to November, and it is described as remarkably tender and succulent, admirably adapted as a milk-producing food for cows.

In Spain artificial irrigation is an absolute necessity to a successful diversified agriculture, if not to any kind of valued cultivation. Spain resembles California in many physical conditions. Irrigation in Spain is a legacy left by the Moors. The customs of that remarkable people remain, in some provinces, almost untouched, since their departure, the efforts of rulers and the progress of events having been powerless to change them. Some of these regulations are very peculiar. In some places the water and land are, so to speak, married without the possibility of a divorce. When the land is sold, the water that irrigates it goes with it, neither can be sold separately, and the irrigator cannot even dispose of his privilege of water. At other places the land has no rights, and the farmer buys the water at an exchange, where he can purchase the use of water in an irrigating channel for twenty-four hours, beginning at 6 o'clock in the evening. In other places there is a daily water auction.

Irrigation is practiced in France under a great variety of physical circumstances. There we also find an attempted complete Governmental control of irrigation and water right matters under a comparatively liberal form of government. The Government of France has in late years specially encouraged irrigation in a variety of ways, but the necessity for and value of irrigation in that country was not sufficiently appreciated by past generations to bring about a general sentiment in favor of national encouragement to irrigation enterprise.

EARLY ATTEMPTS ON THIS COAST.

The Spaniards found the early Peruvians using irrigation much as it was used in Spain. The same practice was observed by Cortez among the Aztecs, and it has been found that all the native races of the Pacific Coast knew of the advantages of irrigation and utilized that knowledge. This was specially the case among the Pueblo Indians of New Mexico, the Aztecs and Toltecs, the Mayas and the residents of Nicaragua, who are said by this means to have been able to pluck well-filled corn, only 40 days after planting the seed. In Arizona the remains of very extensive irrigation works are found over a large area, the population of these sections, now desert, having evidently once been very dense. So well were their canals constructed, that modern engineers have in several cases adopted the same lines.

CALIFORNIA'S PHYSICAL FEATURES.

Across the northern end of the State is a belt of mountains. Along the eastern edge the great Sierra Nevada range protects the land lying at its western foot from the cold winds and blizzards of the great central plains. From the western edge of the northern belt extends southward the Coast Range, which joins the Sierra near Tehachepi. Between these two great mountain ranges lies the great basin of the Sacramento and San Joaquin rivers—practically one valley—400 miles from north to south, and 40 or 50 miles from east to west. The San Joaquin Valley is chiefly formed of two plains which slope toward each other, with the San Joaquin River in the center. The soil throughout the San Joaquin Valley is of the best and most readily worked description. The extent of low, flat lands in the Sacramento Valley is much less than in the San Joaquin. This valley is considerably below the river banks. There are also here two plains, apparently flat, but really sloping toward the river, in the center. Southern California is quite distinct in its geographical features from the rest of the State; light rainfall along the coast; rainfall rather than heavy snow in the mountains; mountain ranges too low to husband [illegible] late in spring, as in the [illegible]

The  Times.

Pasadena Edition.

BY MAIL, $9 A YEAR. WEDNESDAY MORNING, JANUARY 1, 1890. BY CARRIER: { PER MONTH, 85c; PER YEAR, $10.

IN PASADENA

THE TIMES is served regularly by carrier, at an early hour every morning, to the residences and business places of citizens, at the same price charged in Los Angeles.

The Pasadena Edition is now published every day, and the matter on this page runs through the entire issue; so that Pasadena and her advertisers get the full benefit of the Times circulation.

The Times.

PASADENA DAILY EDITION.

BRANCH OFFICE, NO. 26½ E. COLORADO ST.

EDITORIALS.

1890.

MANY happy returns of the day.

THE year is dead. Long live the year!

THE diary and good resolution now start bravely off.

THE year past will be a dark one in history. Floods, accidents, fire and disaster seem to have been uncommonly prevalent.

HO, for the tourney! If the sun shines this morning as it should, Sportsman's Park, on Los Robles avenue, will not hold the crowd.

THE roads are in running order again, showing a remarkably recuperative faculty on the part of railroad men. Even experts gave them another week to get things in shape.

THE belated eastern mail was delivered late last night, bringing much delayed information, joy and sorrow, to many. Tons of Christmas presents, it is said, still linger in the Cajon Pass, paying tribute to Jupiter Pluvius at the gates of his particular paradise.

THE ball at the Raymond last night was the brilliant success that was expected, and was the most brilliant assemblage of dancers seen in Pasadena for a long time. Many of the costumes were very beautiful, and the general effect was striking in the extreme.

THE mistakes made in 1889 can be corrected in 1890. It is never too late to mend. This morning dawns on a season of rich promise. A full harvest is assured. The city looks well, is improving every day; in fact, things are moving forward, and 1891 will find Pasadena richer and better in every way. These are the signs of the times.

PASADENA CITY COUNCIL.

Meeting of the Board of Trustees Yesterday.

The Board of Trustees meet in adjourned session yesterday morning and transacted the following business:

The minutes of the last meeting were read and approved.

The committee on streets and alleys reported in favor of closing Fulton street.

A resolution to this effect was passed.

A resolution of intention to widen Main street, between Fair Oaks and Raymond avenues, was passed.

The bid of J. P. Mushrush to grade Fair Oaks avenue was accepted [illegible] and award of contract were passed and ordered published.

The Committee on Fire and Water was instructed to direct the contractor to place the fire hydrants in accordance with contract.

Bids to grade Marengo avenue between California and Glenarm were opened and read as follows:

O. S. Picher, W. P. Forsyth and Adam Becker, 28 cents per lineal foot; J. P. Mushrush, 32 cents per lineal foot, or 15½ cents per cubic yard.

The bid of O. S. Picher et al. was accepted and contract awarded.

Committee on Streets and Alleys recommended that temporary ditches be dug on Lake avenue to drain stormwater. Recommendation rejected.

The City Engineer was instructed to examine and report as to the condition of the grade of Colorado street, between Fair Oaks and Terrace drive. Also of the condition of the grade and the street-car line on Fair Oaks, between Union and Dayton streets.

The Attorney reported that the city had the right to abate the nuisance at the corner of Raymond and Kansas streets, and the Superintendent of Streets was instructed to close the sidewalk in front of the lot on Raymond and Kansas.

A resolution was passed prohibiting parading and the use of musical instruments on the sidewalks or in the streets, without special permit from the Marshal, which will place all such applicants under police regulation.

The Attorney was instructed to keep a record of all street work.

The Clerk was instructed to formally notify the Attorney and City Engineer, as well as all others connected in any way with the city government, of all actions taken by the board, and all instructions given.

The Superintendent of Streets was instructed to procure and place the necessary poles for the United States mail boxes, still to be erected.

The Committee on Fire and Water was instructed to report on fire-alarm matters at the next meeting.

A communication from L. Lion & Son in regard to the purchase of horses for the fire department was read and placed on file.

A communication from W. E. Arthur in behalf of Mrs. E. A. Foote, asking for damages sustained by storm water, was read. Referred.

A communication from A. W. Berry, asking for a rebate on taxes in the sum of $17.27, was read, and, on motion, ordered paid.

A petition for rebate of taxes from the West Coast Lumber Company for $2.17, and one from the L. W. Elinn Lumber Company for $1.27, were received, and ordered paid.

Committee on Fire and Water asked for further time in which to report on the contract with the Electric Light Company.

The Council then adjourned to meet Saturday, January 4.

PERSONALS.

W. S. Gilmore is again about, after several days of illness.

James G. Rossiter will open a law office soon in Pasadena.

James L. Patterson of Calico registered at the Webster yesterday.

C. S. Harrison of Oakland is a visitor in the city. He is the cousin of President Harrison.

J. B. Mitchell of La Mar, Iowa, arrived from the East on Monday evening to remain during the winter.

Hancock Banning of Los Angeles was out from town yesterday on business and was exchanging New Year compliments with friends.

TODAY'S RODEO.

THE TOURNAMENT—ARE YOU READY?—GO!

Horses, Men, Bicycles, Boys, Girls, Ponies and Burros—The Great Event After Days of Excitement.

For the last two days the grounds of the Sportsman's Park on North Los Robles avenue have been crowded with those who propose entering the now famous tournament. The ground has been put in shape by Superintendent of Streets Vore, and a fine race-track awaits the flyers this morning.

Yesterday fast horses went round the track like mad, Mr. Volkmar, Mr. Senter, Dr. Rowland, Mr. Vore and Whit Elliott putting their horses over the hurdles in great shape. Dr. F. F. Rowland's proved herself a noble jumper, taking the high fence like a bird; indeed the hurdle prepared was a mere bagatelle for her. On the center several gentlemen, notably Mr. Livingstone and Dr. Sherk, practiced at the rings, and will undoubtedly take the prizes for that event unless some one else does. Col. Volkmar, U.S.A., spent an hour or so on the track, while a number of members of the Valley Hunt Club were on hand, overseeing and preparing for the sport today. Some facts regarding the hunt, under whose auspices the tournament is given, may interest the reader. The club was gotten up to encourage manly and womanly sports, especially cross-country riding after greyhounds, a jack-rabbit or coyote being supposed to be before the dogs.

The club officers are: Charles Frederick Holder, president; Clarence S. Martin, vice-president; F. N. Cole, secretary; Ernest May, treasurer; Robert Vandevort and Dr. Ward B. Rowland, master of hounds. The membership is about 75, including the following active members: W. U. Masters, Mrs. W. U. Masters, J. H. Outhwaite, F. F. Buell, Mrs. F. F. Buell, H. H. Suesserott, T. D. Barnum, Mrs. T. D. Barnum, C. F. Holder, Mrs. C. F. Holder, J. Vandevort, R. Vandevort, P. Martin, S. E. Locke, Mrs. S. E. Locke, C. A. Scharff, N. E. Swartwout, Mrs. N. E. Swartwout, Dr. J. M. Radebaugh, Miss Hulbert, C. A. Barnes, Miss M. Green, R. H. Lindsay, W. Browning, B. M. Wotkyns, Mrs. B. M. Wotkyns, W. Wotkyns, Mrs. W. Wotkyns, W. L. Wotkyns, Mrs. W. L. Wotkyns, Clarence S. Martin, O. Stewart Taylor, Mrs. O. Stewart Taylor, Miss Wotkyns, Miss Peck, L. Blankenhorn, Mrs. L. Blankenhorn, E. H. May, Mrs. E. H. May, Misses M. Greenleaf, Shorb, T. Greene, Mary Cole, Fanny Cole and E. S. Reed; T. M. Livingston, F. D. Goodhue, Miss Ada Swartwout, B. Scoville, G. S. Cole, Conway Campbell-Johnston, A. G. Campbell-Johnston, Miss C. Hill, Mrs. J. W. Mitchell, Dr. Charles P. Murray, Mrs. Charles P. Murray, Mrs. J. F. Crank, Miss M. Bradley, Miss E. Bradley, Mrs. J. W. Hugus, Mrs. W. A. Kimball, W. R. Staats, W. Graves, Mrs. W. Graves, Dr. F. F. Rowland, Mrs. E. R. Hall, Miss Cooley, J. de Barth Shorb, Jr., Dr. F. F. and Mrs. Rowland, Mr. and Mrs. Daggett, Mr. and Mrs. George F. Granger, Mr. J. M. Ball, Dr. and Mrs. H. H. Sherk, Dr. and Mrs. W. B. Rowland, Count von Schmidt, Artero and Mrs. Bandini, Mr. and Mrs. Liddle, Mr. Keyser, Mr. Leitheid, Rev. and Mrs. Ottman, Mrs. Crane.

It will be seen from this that the hunt has a social side, including ladies in its organization, a feature which the gentlemen members consider most delightful. The club has a meet once a month, at which 20 or more dogs are used and much sport had. At midday the riders repair to some spot previously selected and here a fine luncheon is spread, and a hunt breakfast under blue skies enjoyed. The club has had but one accident, that not a serious one, which is remarkable, as the pace is harder than any foxhunters take in the East. The club gives an annual ball and, in short, does everything it can to encourage horseback riding and a love for outdoor life. The tournament which the club gives is simply following out this idea, and to afford the people, old and young, some holiday amusement, and establish something permanent in this line. The custom is one which finds place among all the hunt clubs of the East, and from the interest taken is evidently going to be a success here. The hunt owns among its members some of the finest grey and staghounds in the country, those of Mr. Outhwaite, Dr. Rowland, Mr. J. de Barth Shorb, Jr., and Mr. Bandini being the best known. The club has also a pack of fine foxhounds which are used at hunting the fox, coyote and wild cat. They came from the famous Rose Tree Hunt in Medea, Pa. The meets of the hunt and the exciting sport have often been described in THE TIMES, and the St. Nicholas of November has an illustrated article telling the complete story of a day with the hunt club.

PROGRAMME.

The order of exercises today will be as follows:

1. Men's foot race.
2. Boys' foot race for 15 years and under.
3. Men's foot-race, 220 yards.
4. Hurdle race, 120 yards.
5. Orange race.
6. Bicycle race.
7. Boys' foot race, 16 years and over.
8. Boys' pony race, ¼ mile.
9. Burro race.
10. Girls' pony race.
11. Bronco race, ½ mile.
12. Polo game on burros. Pasadena vs. Raymond.
13. Half mile dash for horses.
14. Tug of war.
15. Knights' ring tourney.

The first event will start promptly at 10 p. m., entrance on Los Robles avenue, and, as the programme is a long one, the races will be pushed as much as possible. The prizes are many and handsome, there being two or three, it is believed, for each event, a list of which was given in THE TIMES of yesterday. The various societies of the city, the Pickwick Club and Bicycle Club have coöperated with the Hunt Club to make the event a success.

TOURNAMENT TIPS.

Dr. Rowland's mare Fanny is the best jumper in the field, so far. She spins the hurdles like a bird. Undue influence was brought to bear upon the gentleman who was to have ridden her, and another lucky person will take his place.

All the old chaps who looked on at the tournament practice yesterday wished they were young again.

Mamie Gertrude Pierce is the favorite for the little girls' pony race. If that pony gets started he will come in with the diamond and pearl brooch.

Miss Pierce rides the famous pony Bob, and her rose is the Maréchal Niel.

Clayton Raymond is on deck this morning, and don't you boys forget it.

Mr. Masters's "Bob" showed up in good form yesterday. Mr. Senter proposes to bring him in near the front today.

Buy your tickets at Wetherby & Kayser's, before you go to the grounds, and save time.

The charge of horses at the rings is a pretty sight.

The flat race will not be flat. Some runners are down for it.

The best place to see the entire proceeding will be the grand stand.

A judges' stand has been placed opposite the grand stand.

The victors will have the prizes given them at the grand stand immediately after the event.

Odds of 40 to 1 are offered that the burro "Mr. Maginty" will either win the race or eat up the grand stand.

An "Anxious Inquirer" asks if a burro rider can dismount and carry the burro—until he is rested. Decidedly no!

Burros with ears having a spread of more than 15 square feet, may cinch the ears under the saddle, so they will not catch the wind.

A Duarte tug of war team is coming down. Good for Duarte.

The Pickwick Club offers two challenge cups for foot-races, one for 220 yards and the other for a mile.

Bring all the flowers you can. Poppies, roses, all of them, and pile them up on the stands—on the judges' stand and everywhere.

Mr. H. R. Hertel donates a fine silk manicure case as a prize.

A foot-ball team will have a game.

Hurdle race—Taking the last hurdle.

Knights riding at the rings.

Tug o' war—At the tournament.

Death.

George L. Johnson, son of Mrs. John Wyatt, died Monday night at the temporary home of Mrs. Wyatt, on Oak Knoll. The body was removed Tuesday to their home at Lamanda Park, where the funeral will take place today (New Year's), at 10 o'clock, Reynolds Bros. officiating.

THE RAYMOND BALL.

Masked Figures—Brilliant Assembly at the Hotel Last Night.

The Raymond masquerade ball terminated the carnival festivities at the great hotel last night, and was the success of the season.

A large number of invitations were extended, and the result was a crush of no ordinary dimensions. By 8 o'clock masked figures began to come in, and an hour later the parlors were well filled with a curious assemblage. Here was Mrs. Jarley talking to Mephistopheles, Richard in a quiet confab with Hamlet, a fairy laughing with Mr. Rox, while captains of the guards, dominoes, kings, princes, goblins, dukes and many more, mingled in the throng as natural as life. The maskers were formed in a line shortly after 9 and marched into the ballroom, making a most impressive, not to say remarkable appearance, and one that was appreciated by the lookers-on. A large number of guests from Los Angeles were present, and the invited guests from Pasadena were: Mr. and Mrs. Hurlbut, Miss Hurlbut, Mr. and Mrs. Seymour E. Locke, Miss Greenleaf, Mr. and Mrs. Webster Wotkyns, Mr. and Mrs. Leddle, Miss McBride, Mr. and Mrs. O. S. Taylor, Mr. and Mrs. C. F. Holder, Mrs. J. B. Holder, Mr. and Mrs. Crane, Mr. and Mrs. Louis Blankenhorn, Mr. and Mrs. Daggett, Mr. and Mrs. Walter Wotkyns, Mr. and Mrs. Buell, Mr. and Mrs. Scoville, Mr. and Mrs. Granger, Mr. and Mrs. Hugus, Mr. and Mrs. Devereaux, Mrs. Kimball, Mrs. Mitchell, Mr. and Mrs. May, Dr. and Mrs. Channing, Miss Channing, Mrs. Outhwaite, Miss Boyle, Mr. J. W. Outhwaite, C. S. Martin, Mrs. Cooley, Judge Van Doren, C. W. Bell, Mr. Frank Polley, [illegible] W. U. Masters, Mr. [illegible] Mr. and Mrs. [illegible] and wife, Dr. W. B. [illegible] and wife, C. A. Scharff, Mr. and Mrs. Charles Walter Stetson, Mr. John Ball, Mr. Livingstone, Mr. Suesserott, Dr. J. H. Radebaugh, Dr. H. H. Sherk, Mr. Staats, George F. Granger and wife, Miss Dexter and many more. The ball was a decided success in every way, the costumes being rich and in many cases marvels of beauty. A Pasadena lady was the belle of the occasion, while Seymour E. Locke carried off the honors for the sex.

The "Times" cup.

COMPANY B.

Preparations for Service in the National Guard.

On Monday evening Company B had a very satisfactory drill in facings, salutes and other tactics of the civil drill.

At the conclusion of the drill Capt. Buckley appointed as a permanent committee on Armory, First Lieut. Hamilton; Second Lieut. Cambell and H. J. Vail.

Also, a committee to select honorary members as follows: First Lieut. Hamilton, Second Lieut. Cambell, A. G. Buchanan, J. G. Rossiter and W. P. Hyatt.

There were 63 members in attendance, which was all but three of the enrolled membership.

Several new applications are in for membership. The company is popular and is growing.

The company was dismissed at 9:30 to meet again on Monday evening in the Wooster Hall, when it is hoped all will be in attendance.

A group of prizes.

W.C.T.U.

The W.C.T.U. will hold the regular monthly mothers' meeting Thursday at 3 p.m. at the Baptist Church. Subject: "Social Purity."

There will be a meeting of the Charity Organization Society on Friday morning at the office of the secretary, No. 48 East Colorado street. Time of meeting, 1 o'clock.

BREVITIES.

It is thought the overland traffic will be resumed today.

Something new at last—New Year. This is Riggins's joke—no charge.

The Webster seems to be popular, judging from its liberal patronage.

The mud dries slowly, owing to the extreme humidity in the atmosphere.

A new sensation is promised in a few days. It will open some one's eyes.

Company B has become a fixture—one of the real live institutions of Pasadena.

The Santa Fé was opened to Los Angeles last evening, and people are again happy.

The Y.M.C.A. gives a reception today, to which all young men are cordially invited.

Business is certainly on the "pick up," as the man said who found that pocket-book with $27 in its inside pocket.

The military company will have but $700 available for Armory rent, after paying all other necessary expenses from the State fund.

Cases in the police court were postponed yesterday until after New Year's, owing to the absence of District Attorney McLachlin.

The City Marshal says the Salvation Army will be obliged to cease pumping the bass drum, in accordance with the ordinance passed yesterday.

Mrs. Robinson continues to draw the masses with her eloquent sermons at the Tabernacle. The lady is accomplishing a great deal of good.

The first train to bring overland passengers arrived Monday evening about 7.30. The passengers were transferred in the Cajon Pass, walking about a mile.

Old Pluvius tried hard to shed a few tears Monday evening, but didn't make a "blooming" success of it. He may be holding back for a flood of them.

Local trains were running between South Pasadena and San Bernardino yesterday. There will probably be more regularity in the movements of trains today.

The Sons of Veterans have changed their camp from the A.O.U.W Hall, above the old library building, on Dayton street, to the Odd Fellows' Hall, in the Doty building.

Prof. Pierce, the lightning (?) expressman, was seen hauling a wagonload of mail up from South Pasadena yesterday morning. His outfit kept pace with the speed of the mail trains during the week past.

As an evidence of our increasing prosperity is mentioned the fact that a Pasadena real-estate man had a turkey which he could not get into the oven of his stove. He took it to the Raymond, where the obliging *chef* took care of it for him.

In spite of the fact that there has been a vast amount of rain, mud and all that was disagreeable during the holiday season, the Pasadena merchants report having done a big trade. The trade was confined to the city, as people were unable to reach Los Angeles.

The mail service of the Pacific Coast is in able hands; at least it looks so. A carload of very important mail arrived in Pasadena Monday evening from the East, and Pasadena got her share. The balance passed through to South Pasadena, to within six miles of the Los Angeles postoffice, and there it remained about twenty-four hours.

The first shipment of bonded goods overland through San Diego to the City of Mexico was made on Saturday.

LINES OF TRAVEL.

S. G. V. RAPID TRANSIT R'Y.

Passes given to parties building (subject to approval of the directors) along the line of its road.

LEAVE MONROVIA FOR LOS ANGELES.	LEAVE NO. 9 ARCADIA ST. FOR MONROVIA.
7:00 a.m. and 9:05 a.m.	7:40 a.m. and 11:0 a.m.
1:15 p.m. and 4:15 p.m.	3:00 p.m. and 5:0 p.m.

LEAVE ALHAMBRA FOR LOS ANGELES.	LEAVE ALHAMBRA FOR MONROVIA.
7:27 a.m. and 9:32 a.m.	8:18 a.m. and 11:23 a.m.
1:42 p.m. and 4:42 p.m.	3:33 p.m. and 5:26 p.m.

SUNDAYS: Leave Los Angeles at 8:40 a.m. and 4:40 p.m. Leave Monrovia at 8:00 a.m. and 4:00 p.m. Time between Los Angeles and Monrovia, one hour.

INTERMEDIATE STATIONS: Soto Street, Batz, Ramona, Alhambra, Mayberry, Lake Vineyard, San Marino, San Gabriel, Sunny Slope, Chapman, Baldwin, Arcadia.

E. F. SPENCE, Pres. F. Q. STORY, Gn. Mgr.

SOUTHERN CALIFORNIA RAILWAY CO. (SANTA FE ROUTE.)

On and after SUNDAY, OCT. 27, 1889, trains will leave and arrive at First-street depot as follows:

LEAVE.	LOS ANGELES.	ARRIVE.
*8:30 a.m.	Overland	*4:30 p.m.
*8:52 a.m.	S Diego Ex, Coast Line	*8:00 a.m.
*4:40 p.m.	S Diego Ex, Coast Line	*1:00 p.m.
†8:30 a.m.	S Diego Ex, via S B'd'no	
	S Diego Ex, via Riverside and Orange	
*8:52 a.m.	Santa Ana	†6:50 p.m.
†10:30 a.m.	Santa Ana	*8:00 a.m.
†4:00 p.m.	Santa Ana	*10:15 a.m.
*4:40 p.m.	Santa Ana	*1:00 p.m.
†10:30 a.m.	Riverside v a Orange	†6:50 p.m.
*8:30 a.m.	Riverside via San Bernardino	*9:55 a.m.
*4:00 p.m.	Riverside via San Bernardino	*4:20 p.m.
†10:30 a.m.	Colton via Orange	†6:50 p.m.
*8:30 a.m.	Colton via San Ber'dno.	*9:55 a.m.
*4:00 p.m.	Colton via San Ber'dno.	*4:20 p.m.
*8:30 a.m.	San Bernardino	*9:55 a.m.
*4:00 p.m.	San Bernardino	*4:20 p.m.
†10:30 a.m.	San Bernardino via Orange	†6:50 p.m.
†7:45 a.m.	Pasadena	†7:40 a.m.
*8:30 a.m.	Pasadena	†8:50 a.m.
†12:30 p.m.	Pasadena	*9:55 a.m.
*4:00 p.m.	Pasadena	†2:50 p.m.
†5:05 p.m.	Pasadena	*4:20 p.m.
†6:20 p.m.	Pasadena	*6:10 p.m.
†12:30 p.m.	Duarte Accommodation	†7:40 a.m.
†6:20 p.m.	Duarte Accommodation	†2:50 p.m.
†10:00 a.m.	Port Ballona	†8:55 p.m.
*10:00 a.m.	Redondo Beach	*8:25 a.m.
*5:00 p.m.	Redondo Beach	*3:55 p.m.
†8:30 a.m.	San Jacinto	†6:50 p.m.
†10:30 a.m.	San Jacinto	
†4:40 p.m.	Escondido	†1:00 p.m.
*8:30 a.m.	Redlands and Mentone	*9:55 a.m.
*4:00 p.m.	Redlands and Mentone	*4:20 p.m.

*Daily. †Daily except Sunday.

Train leaving Los Angeles at 8:30 a.m. connects at San Bernardino for all points south to Oceanside. Trains leaving Los Angeles at 10:30 a.m. and arriving at 6:50 p.m. connect at East Riverside for all points south to Oceanside.

Depot at foot of First street.

K. H. WADE, General Manager.
S. B. HYNES, General Passenger Ag't.
WILLIAMSON DUNN, General Agent.
City ticket office, 29 North Spring street.
CHAS T. PARSONS, Ticket Agent.

SOUTHERN PACIFIC COMPANY. (Pacific System.)

IMPORTANT CHANGE OF TIME. THURSDAY, NOVEMBER 28, 1889.

Trains leave and are due to arrive at Los Angeles (New Arcade Depot), Fifth street, daily, as follows:

Leave for.	DESTINATION.	Arr. from.
*3:50 p.m.	Banning	*10:04 a.m.
5:10 p.m.	Banning	10:00 p.m.
9:00 a.m.	Colton	8:57 a.m.
*3:50 p.m.	Colton	*10:04 a.m.
2:10 p.m.	Colton	4:20 p.m.
5:10 p.m.	Deming and East	10:00 p.m.
5:10 p.m.	El Paso and East	10:00 p.m.
12:35 p.m.	Long Beach	11:55 a.m.
9:30 a.m.	L. Beach and San Pedro	8:20 a.m.
5:10 p.m.	L. Beach and San Pedro	4:15 p.m.
10:40 p.m.	Ogden and East	7:25 a.m.
	Ogden and East	4:10 p.m.
10:40 p.m.	Portland, Or.	7:25 a.m.
9:00 a.m.	Riverside	8:57 a.m.
*3:50 p.m.	Riverside	*10:04 a.m.
2:10 p.m.	Riverside	4:20 p.m.
	Riverside	10:00 p.m.
9:00 a.m.	San Bernardino	8:57 a.m.
*3:50 p.m.	San Bernardino	*10:04 a.m.
2:10 p.m.	San Bernardino	4:20 p.m.
	San Bernardino	10:00 p.m.
9:00 a.m.	Redlands	*10:04 a.m.
*3:50 p.m.	Redlands	10:00 p.m.
1:40 p.m.	San Fran & Sacramento	7:25 a.m.
10:40 p.m.	San Fran & Sacramento	4:10 p.m.
9:30 a.m.	Santa Ana and Anaheim	8:57 a.m.
5:08 p.m.	Santa Ana and Anaheim	[illegible]
1:40 p.m.	Santa Barbara	[illegible]
7:25 a.m.	Santa Barbara	[illegible]
9:27 a.m.	Santa Monica	[illegible]
[illegible]	Santa Monica	[illegible]
[illegible]	Santa Monica	[illegible]
*6:10 p.m.	Santa Monica	[illegible]
4:28 p.m.	Tustin	9:08 a.m.
*11:00 a.m.	Whittier	*8:15 a.m.
4:28 p.m.	Whittier	9:08 a.m.

*Sundays excepted. ‡Except Monday.

Local and through tickets sold, baggage checked. Pullman sleeping-car reservations made and general information given upon application to J. M. CRAWLEY, Ass't G. P. Ag't, No. 208 N. Main st.

CHARLES SEYLER, agent at depot.
A. N. TOWNE, General Manager.
T. H. GOODWIN, G. P. & T. Agent.

PACIFIC COAST STEAMSHIP CO.

Goodall, Perkins & Co., general agents, San Francisco.

Northern Routes embrace lines for Portland, Or., Victoria, B. C., Puget Sound, Alaska and all coast points.

SOUTHERN ROUTES.

Time Table for December, 1889:

LEAVE SAN FRANCISCO.

For	
Port Harford, Santa Barbara	S. S. Corona, Dec. 3, 11, 19, 27; Jan. 4.
San Pedro, San Diego	S. S. Mexico, Dec. 7, 15, 23 and 31.
For Redondo	S. S. Eureka, Dec. 1, 9, 17, 25 and Jan. 2.
San Pedro and Way Ports	S. S. Los Angeles, Dec. 5, 13, 21 and 29.

LEAVE SAN PEDRO.

For	
San Diego	S. S. Mexico, Dec. 1, 9, 17, 25 and Jan. 2.
	S. S. Corona, Dec. 5, 13, 21 and 29.

LEAVE SAN PEDRO.

For	
San Francisco	S. S. Mexico, Dec. 3, 11, 19, 27 and Jan. 4.
Port Harford, Santa Barbara	S. S. Corona, Dec. 7, 15, 23 and 31.

LEAVE SAN PEDRO AND REDONDO.

For	
San Francisco	S. S. Eureka, Dec. 4, 12, 20 and 29.
and Way Points	S. S. Los Angeles, Dec. 8, 16, 24 and Jan. 1.

Cars to connect with steamers leave S. P. R. R. depot, Fifth street, Los Angeles, as follows: With the Mexico and Corona at 9:50 o'clock a.m.; with Los Angeles and Eureka, going north, at 5:10 o'clock p.m.

Passengers per Los Angeles and Eureka, via Redondo, leave Santa Fe depot at 5:00 p.m.

Plans of steamers' cabins at agents' office, where berths may be secured.

The steamers Los Angeles and Eureka will call regularly at Newport pier for and with freight and passengers.

The company reserves the right to change the steamers or their days of sailing.

☞ For passage or freight as above, or for tickets to and from all important points in Europe, apply to

W. PARRIS, Agent, Office, No. 8 Commercial St., Los Angeles.

Legal.

Proposals for Bridge Materials.

OFFICE OF BOARD OF SUPERvisors of Los Angeles county, California. Sealed proposals will be received by this board until 1 a.m., January 10, 1890, for lumber to be used in the construction and repair of bridges in Los Angeles county, same to be delivered f. o. b. on cars at Los Angeles, San Pedro and Redondo Beach, or in the yards at Los Angeles, in such quantities as may be required.

Also for such bolts, iron and rods as may be needed by the county. Also proposals to furnish nails and spikes for bridge work in such quantities as may be required.

The board reserves the right to reject any or all bids.

By order of the Board of Supervisors.

CHARLES H. DUNSMOOR, Clerk.
By C. W. BLAKE, Deputy.

Stockholders' Meeting.

NOTICE—THE ANNUAL MEETing of the stockholders of the Southern California Insurance Company for the election of directors, amending the bylaws and for the transaction of such other business as may properly come before the meeting, will be held at the company's office, No. 211 North Main street, in the city of Los Angeles, State of California, on Wednesday, January 15th, 1890 at 1:30 p.m. D. E. MILES, Secretary.

Notice.

THE STOCK BOOKS OF THE Southern California Insurance Company for the transfer of stock will be closed from the 5th day of January, 1890, until after adjournment of stockholders' meeting, to be held January 15th, 1890. D. E. MILES, Secretary.

Notice.

THE ANNUAL MEETING OF THE Los Angeles Cemetery Association for the election of trustees and such [illegible] business as shall come before said association, will be held at the office of the [illegible] No. 117 New High street, room 16 on [illegible] the 6th day of January, 1890, at 2 o'clock [illegible]. All stockholders and owners of [illegible] "Evergreen Cemetery" are entitled to [illegible] said meeting. A. FOLSOM, [illegible]. December 16, 1889.

1891–1900

PART I.
PAGES 1 TO 8.

The Los Angeles Times.

SOUTHERN CALIFORNIA PROGRESS.
THE STORY OF A DECADE.

TENTH YEAR. LOS ANGELES, JANUARY 1, 1891.—ANNUAL TRADE NUMBER: TEN CENTS.

1880 : : 1890.

THE ADVANCE OF A DECADE.

Wonders That Ten Years Have Wrought in Los Angeles County.

From Cattle Range and Sheep Pasture to Orchard, Vineyard and Villa Home.

Three Times the Population and Four Times the Assessed Wealth of Ten Years Ago.

The Rapid Growth of Our Horticultural Industry—Big Profits from Small Tracts.

LOS ANGELES THE SECOND CITY IN THE STATE.

How It Has Grown from a Sleepy Spanish-American Town to a Handsome City of Over 50,000 People.

A Great Railroad Center—Eleventh in the United States in Street Railroad Mileage and Fifth in Cable Roads.

The Other Counties of Southern California—Practical Information About Lands and Crops—Health and Climate, Education, Banking, Commerce, Real Estate, Buildings, and Other Solid Statistics—Ten Millions of Fruit Trees Growing in the County—Nearly 500,000 Boxes of Oranges Will Be Shipped This Season—Population of County, 1880, 33,779; 1890, 101,400—The Era of Production.

MARVELOUS is the only word that fitly describes the progress of the county of Los Angeles during the past ten years.

In 1880 the county was composed mainly of a number of large Spanish grants, upon which cattle grazed and sheep browsed. The traveler could ride for half a day, in many directions, without encountering any sign of civilization. Farm houses were few and far between. The main industries were the production of wool and hides. There was one railroad—the Southern Pacific—which had not yet been completed through Arizona to a junction with the eastern lines. Passengers for the east had to go north and east by way of Lathrop and Ogden. Outside of the city of Los Angeles, towns in the county were very few and very small. Oranges were grown, sufficient for home consumption. Other fruits were mostly imported from the north. The population of the county was 33,379, of whom 11,311 were within the city limits, leaving only 22,068 in the whole county outside, and this included the present county of Orange. Los Angeles city was a quiet, sleepy place, the buildings largely of adobe, and only one—the Baker block—that would attract attention. A few miles of horse-car line carried passengers, every twenty minutes or so, through the main streets of the city. The railroad depot was a shed, a mile out of town.

How is it now?

Los Angeles county, exclusive of Orange county, which fertile and thickly-populated section was segregated two years ago, has a population of 101,400, more than three times the population of 1880, including Orange. The city has grown from 11,311 to 50,394. There are at least 5000 more inhabitants just outside the city limits, on the south, west and northeast, so that during the decade it has quintupled in population and has supplanted Oakland as the second city in this great State. Towns which in 1880 did not exist are now cities with several thousand population, such as Pasadena, with 5870, and Pomona with 3000. A score of other flourishing little towns, with several hundred population apiece, have sprung into being on land which ten years ago was given over to sage-brush and jack-rabbits. Among these are Azusa, Burbank, Garvanza, Glendale, Inglewood, Long Beach, Monrovia, Redondo, Sierra Madre and Whittier. We have two transcontinental railroads, and more coming. Our fruit industry has grown to be one of almost national importance. The introduction of water has increased the value of land from $5 to—in some cases—$500 an acre. Where, in 1880, sheep and cattle ranged, are now seen orchards of oranges, lemons, olives, apricots, peaches, walnuts, and vineyards planted with the choicest wine-grapes of Europe. Our horticulturists grow rich on ten acres of land. Over 10,000,000 fruit trees are now growing in the county. Last year Los Angeles county shipped East 368,275 boxes of oranges. The export for this year will be greater yet, and hundreds of thousands of trees are set out in nursery. The assessed wealth of the county (including Orange) in 1880 was $16,697,591. This year (exclusive of Orange) it is $69,475,025 and this, be it remembered, three years after the culmination of a wild real-estate boom, the reaction from which has unduly depressed values. As recently as five years ago there were only four banks in Los Angeles City, with a capital and surplus of $1,100,000 and deposits of $3,128,000. Today the banks of Los Angeles county have a capital and surplus of $5,101,814 and deposits of $10,119,486. In 1880 there were 5445 children enrolled in the county schools. Today there are 19,059, and in the city 8288—more than there were in the county in 1880.

The transformation which has taken place in the city during the past ten years is, if possible, more wonderful than that which has occurred in the county. A large and beautiful city, with handsome buildings and paved streets has grown up in these ten years, and chiefly within the past five. In place of muddy highways, in which, during wet weather, horses sank up to their knees, we have seventy-five miles of paved and graveled streets within the city limits. We have completed a magnificent courthouse, a city hall and a high school building, and built a score of great business blocks, which would do credit to any of the large cities of the Union. Hundreds of beautiful private residences have been erected in the city at a cost of $10,000 apiece and upward. We have one of the finest systems of cable railroads in the United States, with forty-five miles of single track, and costing $2,000,000. There are other cable, horse and electric lines of equal length, and work is commenced on a new belt electric road which will encompass the entire city, with several branches. The city has voted half a million dollars for an interior sewer system. Ten lines of railroad center in the city. Electric lights turn night into day and make Los Angeles look like a fairy spot from a distance. Our public library excites the envy and surprise of other cities. Our two handsome theaters attract the leading dramatic companies on the road. Our Chamber of Commerce maintains an exhibit in this city and another in Chicago. There are 1000 manufacturing establishments of various descriptions in the city. Los Angeles, which, ten years ago, was known to the world only as a sleepy, picturesque Spanish-American town, is now the Mecca of tourists and health-seekers from all parts of the world. It has become a favorite meeting place for conventions of some of the leading societies of the country.

How did this great change come about? What magician's wand worked this wonderful transformation?

The question is not easily answered, except by saying that the intrinsic merit was here; it had but to become known; it became known, and intelligent people, who recognize a good thing, hastened to take advantage of it.

Thirty years ago, in 1860, the assessed wealth of the county was $3,065,330. That was evidently something of a boom year, for five years later, in 1865, the assessment was only $1,905,380. Then it gradually rose to $12,085,110 in 1874 and $20,665,294 in 1882. From this date there was a rapid rise, until, in 1888, the assessment reached the enormous sum of $102,944,061. This was the climax, and the depression consequent upon the boom brought us to our present figures of $69,475,025, which is twice the assessment of 1885.

In 1872 the letters of Nordhoff to a New York paper, afteward published in book form, first attracted wide attention to the advantages of climate and soil possessed by this section. At that time there was no railroad to Los Angeles, the journey most of the way from San Francisco having to be made by stage or steamer. This was a great obstacle to those in poor health and even to many pleasure-seekers. In 1876 the railroad was completed from San Francisco, and there was something of a boom, which is shown by an increase of nearly fifty per cent. in the assessed valuation of the county between 1875 and 1876. This advance was, however, nipped in the bud by a disastrous bank failure and a small-pox epidemic, and business continued very dull for five or six years. Many old residents were discouraged about that time, and a mining excitement breaking out in Arizona in 1880, hundreds of Angeleños sold their property for whatever it would bring—which was then very little—and followed the Southern Pacific, which had been just opened into the Territory. Tucson was largely settled in that year by Los Angeles people. In 1880 the population of Tucson was 6994 and of Los Angeles 11,311, and many believed that in 1890 the former would be the larger city. It certainly looked that way, for a time, but how things have changed since then! Today the "ancient and honorable pueblo" on the Santa Cruz has a population of a little more than 5000, of whom two-thirds are Mexicans, while the City of the Queen of the Angels contains over 50,000 Americans within her borders. The lucky ones in 1880 were those who could not sell their Los Angeles property.

And the future? He would indeed be a bold prophet who, in view of what has already been accomplished, should attempt to picture Los Angeles county and city in the year 1900. Certain it is that we have only just started on the path of progress. The horticultural industry, which is destined to make this county one broad expanse of beautiful, productive homes, embowered in flowers and foliage, is yet in its infancy. But a small proportion of our arable land has been placed under cultivation. Within ten miles of this city are thousands of acres, now devoted to grazing or the raising of hay, which will, ten years hence, support a dense population. The past year has introduced our fruits to thousands of Eastern homes, which will demand them regularly henceforth. During the next ten years our manufacturing industries will be largely increased. Petroleum will be developed in the neighborhood of the city — perhaps within the city limits. Natural gas will also be found, and perhaps the water of the Los Angeles River made to turn the wheels of a score of factories. A railroad will bring us cheap coal and rich ores from Utah, and smelters will align the river bed. From Los Angeles to the ocean will be, not a city, but a succession of beautiful villa homes, each surrounded by from five to twenty acres of productive land.

In 1900 Los Angeles will be a city of at least 100,000 people, and many old-timers will be telling of the big bargains in real estate which they might have picked up in 1890.

Let those who think we take too roseate a view of the future peruse the facts presented in this issue, and then say whether we are not too conservative rather than too sanguine. Then let them go over the county in person and examine its resources, and they will exclaim, with the Queen of Sheba, that the half has not been told about this, THE EMPIRE COUNTY OF THE GOLDEN STATE

1890 : : : 1891.

WHILE BEARING TRIBUTE TO OUR MATERIAL PROSPERITY,

THE OLD YEAR PRESENTS HIS INFANT SUCCESSOR.

"1890:" "Here, take him, Angelina! You've prospered so since I arrived that it's hard to tell what you'll have attained ere he's as old as I am."

THEN AND NOW.

Los Angeles Advertisers of 1880 and of 1890.

STRIKING CONTRASTS SHOWN

The Changes of Ten Years—Old Houses Still Running—New Ones Established—Notable Expansions.

A GLANCE through the files of the city newspapers of 1880—when Los Angeles was a city one-fifth its present size—brings to mind the mutations of time with emphasis.

As a theme of interest in this year of our Lord, a retrospect has been made of the advertisers who were wont to make their wares or professions known in the last census year before the one now on the field of action, and as the reviewer turns the yellow and musty files he is impressed with the shortness of life and the constant change that goes on in business as in all other things of the world, natural and artificial.

As this newspaper was not in existence ten years ago, we have drawn upon our esteemed contemporaries for the facts shown in this article.

We find that P. W. Dooner, attorney at law, was holding forth in the Downey block, as he has ever since.

H. K. S. O'Melveny was then a practicing lawyer with rooms in the Strelitz block. He was afterward a Superior Judge, and is now retired, rich in learning and honors.

G. A. Dobinson was then an attorney at law with an office in the Downey block—at that time the home of the fraternity. He has since forsaken the thorny path of litigation for the more peaceful one now occupied as an insurance agent, with a fine suite of offices on Broadway, finding time meanwhile to do the drama for this journal with satisfaction to all.

Phineas Banning was then printing an advertisement in the paper as forwarding and commission agent at Wilmington. He has gone to join the great majority, and his sons are his successors in the business out of which he amassed more than one fortune.

The Farmers and Merchants Bank was then doing business in the present Southern California Insurance Company's building, with I. W. Hellman as president, as he is today. But he now lives in San Francisco, and is the president of the great Nevada Bank of that city.

J. S. Slauson was then president of the Los Angeles County Bank, since retired with an ample fortune, but apparently younger than he was ten years ago. His old bank, however, is still one of the solid institutions of the city, and its present president, John E. Plater, has filled the position with the greatest ability—having few peers as a banker in this city of banks. Mr. H. L. Macneil, then its cashier, has since retired, and now goes into the directories as a capitalist.

The Commercial Bank was then in existence, with J. E. Hollenbeck as president, and E. F. Spence as cashier. The mutations of time changed the institution into the First National Bank—sent its honored president to his long sleep on the hillside at Evergreen, and made its then cashier president, as he now is. The years have been kind to the bank and its officers, President Spence having served the city as its Mayor, and in other important capacities, and the bank grown to be one of the staunch institutions of the State.

Lewis Bros. were then in the shoe business at Nos. 57 and 59 Spring street, as their successor, Meyer Lewis, now is, the numbers of the streets having all been changed since that time. Mr. Lewis has prospered with the city, and is now one of our wealthy men, with ample capital to fight boycotters and to hold his own in the fierce competition that has grown up.

The City of Paris was then the great dry goods emporium of the city, and was running a two-column ad. in the papers, being located at Nos. 53 and 55 Main street, about opposite the St. Charles Hotel, and Eugene Meyer & Co. were its proprietors. Mr. Meyer has since removed to San Francisco, and become the manager of one of that city's great banks, and the old house is still here with a great establishment on Spring street, under other managers.

Osborne's Overland Transfer was then on the field of action, but has since changed hands and been merged into other companies.

The Pico House was then in the heart of the city and advertised itself as the only first-class hotel. Its fortunes have been varied in the last ten years and the city has grown away to the southward of it, until it is scarcely more than a monument of the past.

B. C. Whiting was then United States Court Commissioner and one of the city's most honored citizens. He has since gone to the realm of shadows.

E. Martin & Co. were then the great wholesale liquor men of the city, with C. C. Lips as manager, and one of the substantial men of the city. The fortunes of the house waned and its manager one day took his own life in a moment of insanity.

Mrs. V. Ponet was the city's most popular milliner, but has retired from trade with an ample fortune, which she and her husband, then an undertaker, enjoy in the shape of rentals from big business blocks and other revenue-producing properties.

Walter S. Maxwell was advertising grain sacks at No. 13 Court street. He became later the city's coal king, but retired with the great boom, and is not now actively engaged in business, other than looking after the magnificent Lanfranco estate.

W. H. Northcraft was then an auctioneer, but has since gone to other fields.

S. M. Perry was then in the plumbing business, as he is now.

J. G. Eastman's card as attorney at law was then running in the papers, and he was the Beau Brummel of the city, but he fell from his high estate to die in the gutter, one of the most awful specimens of utter degradation this town has ever known.

The *Express* was then owned and edited by Col. J. J. Ayers, who afterward became State Printer, and is now one of the editors and proprietors of our contemporary, the Herald.

F. J. Gillmore was advertising a great dollar store at No. 25 Spring street. He has since retired with a fortune and gone into politics, having served several years as chairman of the Republican County Committee.

The Queen Shoe Store was then in business at the same stand it is today.

A. M. Lawrence was then in the cigar and tobacco business, but afterward became the secretary of the Board of Trade, and died a few years ago, universally regretted, as he proved himself possessed of sterling qualities.

Maskell & Mercadante were then fruit merchants at No. 131 Main street. Mr. Maskell is now a grocer in the southern portion of the city, and Mercadante is still doing business near the old stand, but on First street.

Drs. Joseph Kurtz, K. D. Wise and Henry Worthington were each in business, as they are now.

L. Jacoby was the leading clothing man in Temple block and advertising great bargains. Since then the house has become Jacoby Bros., and in addition to the great retail business handled by them, they conduct the largest wholesale business in the South, occupying a building on Los Angeles street.

Messrs. Bonebrake and McManus were then in the buggy business, and the Express relates the fact that they did, on January 22d, dispatch a train of twelve buggies overland to Santa Barbara, drawn by teams.

Maj. Bonebrake has since become one of the town's greatest bank presidents and has grown wealthy, no doubt, beyond his wildest dreams at that time.

George Pridham was then conducting a cigar store in the Temple block. He has since become a great cattle rancher in Arizona, and is said to have amassed a fortune.

Fred Dohs was then advertising his business as a barber, but has since forsaken the music of the "rattler" razor to become leader of the city band.

Henry C. Roberts of Azusa was advertising a bee ranch for sale. He still lives at that flourishing suburb and the years deal lightly with him.

D. M. Graham was in the land and loan brokerage business in the Commercial Bank building. He later became one of the solid men of Pasadena, where he died.

H. S. Orme was printing his card in the papers as physician and surgeon then, as now.

Woodhead & Gay were the best-known fruit merchants of the city, and grew wealthy in the business, though beginning in the most modest and humble way. The transferred their business to Porter Bros. & Co. later, Mr. Gay going into the real-estate business and Mr. Woodhead becoming a political reformer, with but moderate success. He owns much fine property in the city, and has kept his fortune well in hand.

Preuss & Pironi were then druggists at the location now occupied by C. H. Hance. Mr. Preuss became the Nasby of the city under the administration of President Cleveland, and Mr. Pironi conducts a great wine business on Alameda street.

G. G. Green of New Jersey was advertising his "August Flower" with no idea, presumably, that he would ever see Los Angeles, but he has since become a large owner of property in Pasadena, and at Altadena has built a magnificent residence, which he occupies every winter.

St. Mary's Hospital of San Francisco was telling of its advantages through our city papers, Dr. James Murphy being mentioned as its visiting surgeon. He died a few years ago and was followed to his long home by the tender thoughts of thousands of patients all over California.

Joe Bayer was the proprietor of Congress Hall, a place long since changed into a store basement, but the genial Bayer still conducts a business on Main street.

Dr. Nadeau, still a city physician, was then Coroner.

The Kimball mansion on New High street was the swell private hotel of the city. The place where it once stood has been cut down and the big hill behind its location walled with granite.

The Los Angeles and Ventura stage line advertised that its stages would leave the Temple-street stables every morning, but now the location of the stables is the site of the Lawyer block, and the passenger goes to Ventura by the cars of the Southern Pacific.

V. Dol was conducting the Commercial restaurant on Main street—then *the* restaurant of the city. He also grew wealthy, and owns brick blocks along with many other old-time advertisers, but now conducts the Maison Doreé on First street, near THE TIMES office.

W. C. Furrey was in the stove and hardware business at No. 19 Los Angeles street, but in that year removed to his present location on Spring street, opposite the old Courthouse.

E. Naud was advertising his wool warehouse on Alameda street. He, too, has gone to the place of shades, and his estate has become the food for lawyers and others.

Eugene Germain was then in the commission business, as he still is, the firm having been incorporated and become the Germain Fruit Company, with E. Germain as president. He likewise owns more than one brick business block, and counts among the city's rich men.

H. J. Woollacott, "long with Alex McKenzie," announces the opening in this year, of his present establishment on Spring street. He has grown wealthy and can walk down Spring street and look at his buildings towering up into the glorious climate and see his name in gilt letters on the windows of a big bank as one of its directors, all of which has come about since 1880.

Chapman & Paul, the stove men, were then in business as they are yet.

Some of the lawyers of the city, other than those already mentioned were A. Glassell, A. W. Hutton, W. D. Stephenson, Bicknell and White, John F. Godfrey, A. M. Stephens, C. E. Thom, Thomas B. Brown, J. G. Howard, H. T. Hazard, F. H. Howard, Brunson & Wells, Graves and Chapman and P. C. Tonner. Of these all are still practicing their profession yet except A. Glassell retired with a competency, W. D. Stephenson, gone over to the majority, as has also that loyal friend and soldier John F. Godfrey. Capt. C. E. Thom afterward served as the city's Mayor, but has retired from practice and takes time to look over his big blocks of brick and mortar with an admiring eye. J. G. Howard has also gone before that Judge from whom there is no appeal. Henry T. Hazard is now our Mayor, for the second term. Judge Brunson is of a new firm and the resident attorney for the Southern California Railway.

Miss L. J. Hammond was a milliner at No. 31 Spring street. She, too, has retired and reaps the rents from handsome Spring-street building.

Dillon & Kenealy were then in the dry goods business, with a big store on Main street, opposite Temple block. They retired from business some years ago with a competency.

The Wright House on South Main street was then a popular private hotel, but has since made way for a big pile of brick and mortar.

R. Bills was the owner of the largest truck line in the city, since merged into a corporation known as the California Truck Company.

Fred Linde, who is still in the jewelry business, had a store at No. 71 Main street.

Bryant Howard & Co. were the paint and oil house of the city, since merged into the house of Whittier, Fuller & Co.

J. Kiefer & Co. have not changed from the business and the location they occupied ten years ago.

H. Newmark & Co. were then wholesale grocers, but were succeeded in the interim by M. A. Newmark & Co., who conduct the great store on Los Angeles street.

The other great grocery house was that of Hellman, Haas & Co., recently transformed into the firm of Haas, Baruch & Co. by the retirement of H. W. Hellman, who became the manager of the Farmers' and Merchants' bank upon I. W. Hellman's removal to San Francisco.

The St. Elmo Hotel was then called the Cosmopolitan, with Hammel & Denker, proprietors, who also conducted the United States Hotel at that time, since rebuilt. Mr. Hammel recently followed the long list of pioneers who sleep under the daisies.

The Philadelphia Brewery, then but a nucleus of the present great establishment on Aliso street, was operated by D. Mahlstedt, since deceased, having retired with a fortune and become the owner of a large number of houses in different portions of the city.

The New York Brewery was then a landmark at Third and Spring streets, and under the management of Phil Lauth was long one of the institutions of the town. It made way for the march of improvement which has made such great headway in that part of the city.

H. M. Mitchell was then an attorney at law with an office in Downey block. His tragic death at the hands of a friend when on a hunting excursion on the 7th of December last is so recent as to be well remembered by all newspaper readers.

S. C. Hubbell's shingle as attorney at law also swung in the breeze, but he has since become one of the town's solid men and retired from the practice of his profession.

B. F. Coulter, the great Dry Goods merchant, was then established at No. 32 Baker block, but some years ago moved to Second and Spring streets, supposed at that time to be away out of town. His foresight, however, was better than his critics', as the growth of the city has been steadily in that direction.

F. Adam advertised his merchant tailoring establishment at No. 13 Spring street and still holds out there under the new number.

E. K. Chapin was making public the fact that he had opened a store at Santa Monica Cañon, at that time *the* resort of the seaside seekers. He is now one of the leading merchants of the city of Santa Monica.

T. H. McNally was also advertising a stage line to Santa Monica Cañon.

Louis Lewin & Co. were then in the book and stationery business, but were succeeded later by Messrs. Lazarus and Melzer, Mr. Lewin becoming a partner in the house of M. Levy & Co.—they still do business on Los Angeles street.

The "Sisters Hospital," then as now called the Los Angeles Infirmary, was located on San Fernando street opposite the present railway station. In the interim their beautiful hospital on Beaudry avenue has been built and occupied, where the faithful Sisters still smooth the brow of pain and comfort the stricken heart of the moaning sufferer.

H. Siegel, the hatter, announced the opening of his establishment at the corner of Main and Commercial streets.

Dotter and Bradley was the big furniture house of the city, but the business has since been incorporated as the Los Angeles Furniture Company, of which Gov. Markham is president, Mr. Dotter still being active in the business. Mr. Sid Lacy was then announced as being in charge of the carpet department, but has since become a great political boss and sachem of the Iroquois tribe of Democrats.

A. S. McDonald was then in the shoe business very near his present location on Spring street.

L. Polaski & Son were in the clothing business at the corner of Main and Commercial street in the apartments now occupied by the Farmers & Merchants Bank. The head of the firm has since retired and Polaski Bros., his sons, still conduct one of the great merchant tailoring establishments of the city.

E. W. Noyes announced himself in the press as "the war-horse auctioneer" and his musical voice is still heard upon our streets calling upon the moneyed public to call around and buy horses and other live stock free from blemish and sound in every limb.

The St. Charles Hotel was being conducted by J. A. Brown, who, later on, retired and opened a big restaurant on Main street, near the old Courthouse, where he did business until a short time ago.

H. Slotterbeck conducted the gun-making establishment in the Temple block, over the door of which his [illegible]

DECENNIAL ANNIVERSARY NUMBER—THE STORY OF A DECADE.

THE DEVELOPMENT OF LOS ANGELES FROM THE ERA OF ADOBE.

The Los Angeles Times

A RED-LETTER DAY IN THE LIFE OF "THE TIMES" NEWSPAPER—UPWARD AND ONWARD.

A STRIKING RECORD OF RESULTS IN THE TASK OF UPBUILDING A CITY AND A STATE.

ELEVENTH YEAR. FRIDAY, DECEMBER 4, 1891.—TWENTY-FOUR PAGES. PRICE :

THE STORY OF A DECADE

LOS ANGELES IN 1881 AND 1891.

A STRIKING EXHIBIT of Growth and Progress.

THE TIMES from its Birth to the Present.

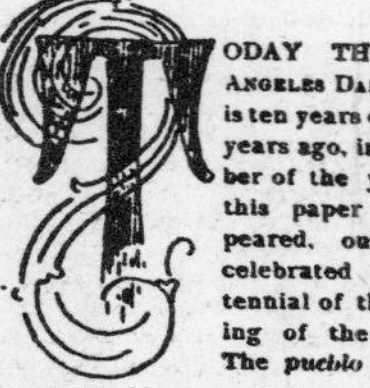

ODAY THE LOS ANGELES DAILY TIMES is ten years old. Ten years ago, in September of the year that this paper first appeared, our people celebrated the centennial of the founding of the Mission. The *pueblo* was thus a century old when the paper started, but for all that the history of THE TIMES covers the history of Los Angeles as a modern American city. The first number of THE TIMES was the *avant courier* of the Los Angeles of today, which is as different from the Los Angeles of 1881 as today's issue of this paper is from the modest four-page sheet which first sought the patronage of Angeleños on December 4, 1881.

It is given to few journals to chronicle such wonderful changes during the first decade of their existence as THE TIMES truthfully sets forth in regard to Los Angeles today. Other western journals have seen cities spring up in the wilderness within that space of time and become large centers of population. American energy, backed by American resources, accomplishes wonders. Ten-year-old cities, with populations of from 20,000 to 50,000, no longer excite special comment in the Great West; but where is there another instance of a venerable, slow-going city, that had already passed its 100th birthday and which seemed destined to slumber on till the end of time, being suddenly transformed into a busy American metropolis whose name and fame have extended to the ends of the earth? It is this marvelous change from the old to the new that makes the history of Los Angeles during the past ten years so fascinating, and, as aforesaid, the history of modern Los Angeles is the history of THE TIMES. The two are indissolubly linked together. Their birth was, in fact, almost simultaneous, for within a few months of the date of this journal's first appearance the Southern Pacific Railroad had been completed through to the East, thus giving the first great impetus to the growth of the city as an independent commercial center, free from the overweening influence of the chief city of the State, to which hitherto all roads had led as, in olden times, all roads led to Rome.

In the following pages will be found a truthful, unvarnished account of the growth of Los Angeles during the past ten years; a narrative of the most important events affecting the material progress of the city during that period; a description of Los Angeles as it was in 1881 and as it is today, and a comprehensive report of the manner in which the resources of the county are being developed. It is upon these resources that the faith of Angeleños in a future growth equaling, if not exceeding, that of the past, is based. The rise and progress of the city is shown from the time—only a short ten years ago—when the county was covered mainly with large Spanish grants, upon which cattle grazed and sheep browsed; when the traveler could ride for half a day in many directions without encountering any sign of civilization; when farm houses were few and far between, and the main industries were the production of wool and hides; when towns outside of Los Angeles in the county were few and very small; when most of our fruits were imported from the North; when the only line of railroad to the East ran by way of San Francisco; when the population of the city was only 11,000, and of the whole county outside—which then included what is now Orange county—only 33,000. Today we have in the county, not including Orange, considerably over 100,000 population, and within the city limits at least 55,000, placing Los Angeles in the position of the second city in the State. A score of flourishing towns, with populations of several thousand apiece, have sprung up in places where not a house stood ten years ago. Where, in 1881, sheep and cattle ranged are now seen orchards of oranges, lemons, olives, apricots, peaches, walnuts, and vineyards of choice wine, raisin and table grapes, the product of which finds ready sale in every quarter of the globe. Over 10,000,000 fruit trees are now growing in the county, and our exports of oranges alone from Los Angeles county will this season amount to 500,000 boxes. The assessed value of the city's wealth has increased seven fold, and the banks of the county hold deposits to the amount of $12,000,000. A large and beautiful city has grown up within these ten years, and chiefly within the past five. In place of muddy highways we have graded and paved streets; in place of one-story adobe structures we have magnificent business blocks and public buildings that would challenge admiration in any of the largest cities of the country; in place of a few modest cottages we have hundreds of beautiful private residences, costing from $10,000 upwards; in place of a few miles of horse-car line, carrying passengers every twenty minutes or so, we have one of the finest cable railroads in the United States, with nearly fifty miles of track, costing $2,000,000, and an electric system which, when completed, will be as long. Eleven lines of railroad center here; electric lights turn night into day; over a thousand manufacturing establishments, great and small, are busy; two handsome theaters furnish a constant round of entertainment, and, during the winter season, a dozen large hotels throughout the county are crowded with guests from all parts of the world.

While the narration of these wonderful changes, merely as a story, would prove interesting—more interesting than much fiction—the main purpose of this publication by THE TIMES would be missed did we not refer to the causes which have made such a transformation possible, and which cannot fail to render the improvement constant. It was no chance freak of the goddess of Fortune that selected Los Angeles as the scene of this great drama of development in the Southwest.

CLIMATE, SOIL and LOCATION are the three factors which have produced the Los Angeles of today, and which will make the Los Angeles of 1900, with a population of 150,000. The first of these features—our "glorious climate"—has been so frequently enlarged upon that we shall here pass the subject over with the simple statement that the climate of Southern California is always with us—a never-diminishing factor of positive value—and it is now generally admitted, by experienced travelers and by experts to be the finest climate in the world. Another reason for skipping the subject is the impression which obtains in some quarters that climate is about all that Southern California has to offer. The old joke about our charging so much an acre for climate is still popular in the East. In this issue of THE TIMES the climatic question is shelved. The question of the preëminence of Southern California in this respect is no longer an open one—is no longer a subject for debate. It is fully proven.

While the climatic question is thus disposed of without elaboration, we present ample facts in today's issue regarding the second secret of Southern California's greatness—*the soil*—to fully prove to the satisfaction of every unprejudiced reader that land in this section at from $100 to $300 an acre is worth the price, with the climate thrown into the bargain. Here are presented facts showing the wonderful material development that has taken place throughout the county during the past three or four years. On every hand goes forward the planting of orchards and vineyards and alfalfa fields and berry patches; the drying of fruits, the making of cheese and butter, and other forms of rural productive industry. Records of profit made from the soil remarkable though truthful, are given. They are not confined to any particular crop, but take a wide range. Scarcely a product that can be named but has proved a bonanza in some cases, when planted in the right soil and given the right kind of attention. A fact abundantly established, and which proves beyond any other the intrinsic value of our lands, is that it is possible not only to support a family in comfort on ten acres of Southern California soil, but even to grow rich thereon; while five acres, rightly handled, in many cases furnish a family all the necessaries and reasonable luxuries of life.

Climate and soil would not, however, have sufficed to create the Los Angeles of today were it not for its *advantageous geographical location*, near the ocean, at the western end of the shortest line across the continent, and at the foot of the low mountain passes across which all future railroads coming to the State from the East must, as a question of economy, be constructed. The two transcontinental lines which are here at present are but the harbingers of others that are to come. Steamship lines from our neighboring ports will, ere long, carry the bounteous products of Los Angeles county to Asia and Australia, and, when the Nicaragua Canal is opened, through that great interoceanic highway to Europe, laying down the products of our soil in London at less expense than it now is to ship them to New York.

The progress of Los Angeles during the past ten years, as recorded in these pages, has been great; but he is indeed blind who does not see that this progress has but just begun. With more fruit trees planted during the past twelve months than were growing a year ago; with nine-tenths of our markets yet untouched; with hundreds of thousands of fertile acres within the county yet unimproved, it needs no high order of prophetic vision to see in the Los Angeles of 1900 a city thrice as large, thrice as populous and thrice as wealthy as that of today. Unless there should come some unforeseen cataclysm of nature, changing the entire conditions of this region, Los Angeles will, at the end of this decade, contain a population of 150,000 and the county one of 500,000, while THE TIMES will print every day in the year as many copies as it does of this annual number which we now present to an intelligent and discriminating public.

PAST AND PRESENT.

Los Angeles Ten Years Ago and Today.

A WONDERFUL TRANSFORMATION

From a Slow-going Semi-Mexican Town of Adobes to a Flourishing American Metropolis of Brick, Stone and Iron.

FTER GIVING A description of Los Angeles as it was in 1881, a short glance at the principal events of the century which intervened between the founding of the Mission and that year will be appropriate. The changes which took place during the first century of the existence of Los Angeles were far less important and striking than those which have transpired since 1881. During the first century Los Angeles crawled; during the past decade it has advanced at railroad pace. The progress of the past ten years has been more than ten times as great as that of the previous hundred.

HISTORICAL.

Founding of the Pueblo—The First Century's Record.

The *pueblo de Nuestra Senora la Reina de Los Angeles* was founded September 4, 1781, by a colony of twelve Mexican soldiers and their families, most of them having served their time at San Gabriel, which had been established ten years before. Its beautiful location, midway between the mountains and the sea, its delightful climate and the fertility of its soil are said to have earned it the name, or it may have been named after the other *pueblo de Los Angeles* in Mexico, from which country the founder of the city came.

Over forty years passed before the first American arrived. He was a man named Chapman, who was brought in as a prisoner, but soon fraternized and afterwards married into a Spanish family. In 1824 a Scotchman opened the first general store on the American plan. In 1831 the opening of the Santa Fé trail created a new outlet to the East and was the means of developing an extensive trade, as the opening of the Santa Fé railroad was, to a far greater extent, fifty-five years later. The old pueblos of Santa Fé and Los Angeles have thus been linked together in trade for over half a century.

How many of the non-resident readers of this article are aware that Los Angeles was once the capital of California? It attained to that dignity in 1835. The Mexican war being inaugurated in 1846, Commodore Stockton and Capt. Frémont marched into Los Angeles and raised the Stars and Stripes. Don Pio Pico, who still lives here, hale and hearty at the age of 90, was then Governor of California, under appointment from the Mexican government. Frémont and Stockton went north, leaving Lieut. Gillespie in charge with but seventeen men. There was soon a general revolt, and in September Lieut. Gillespie, after being in a state of siege for several days on Fort Hill, surrendered Los Angeles to the Mexicans, on condition that he and his men be permitted to march unmolested to San Pedro, where they were taken on board a merchant ship. On January 10, 1847, Commodore Stockton and Gen. Stephen W. Kearney recaptured the town, and on the 14th Frémont rejoined them with his forces, after effecting a treaty with the Mexicans under Gen. Andreas Pico at the Cahuenga Pass, west of the city. On January 16 Frémont became Governor of California, establishing his headquarters in the two-story adobe building at the corner of Aliso and Los Angeles streets. About this time the seat of government was removed to Monterey, and Kearny, in compliance with instructions from Washington, became Governor. On April 7 Col. Mason superseded Frémont as commander in Los Angeles, and on May 9, 1847, Gen. Kearney arrived and took command. Three days later Capt. Frémont left for the north.

The first Protestant preacher in Los Angeles was Rev. J. W. Brier, of the Methodist Episcopal Church, who arrived here in 1852, with an ox team, and held his first service in the adobe residence of Col. J. G. Nichols. Today his denomination has a dozen churches and a large university in the city. The first mayor of Los Angeles was elected in the same year. Two years later the first brick house—a one-story building—was erected at the corner of Main and Third streets. In 1859-'60 this building was occupied by Capt. Winfield Scott Hancock. The first English-speaking school was taught by Rev. Dr. Wicks in 1850. The first American child born in Los Angeles was Gregg Nichols on April 15, 1851. The first newspaper was started on May 17, 1851. It was called "The Los Angeles Star."

Fifty years ago the population of Los Angeles was greater than that of Chicago. In 1854 the population was 4000, of whom but 500 were Americans. In 1860 in had only risen to 4500. The first telegraph line was constructed in that year. In 1868 the first railroad was built, twenty-three miles in length, from Los Angeles to San Pedro. In 1874 the first attempt was made to utilize our horticultural resources by the establishment of a fruit-drying factory.

The year 1876 was a disastrous one for Los Angeles. There was a bank failure, a drought and an epidemic of smallpox. On the other hand, the Southern Pacific Railroad was completed from San Francisco to Los Angeles, giving the city communication with the rest of the world. Shortly afterward railways were completed to Santa Monica and Santa Ana, and the Southern Pacific was rapidly extended east.

On September 4, 1881, Los Angeles celebrated her centennial anniversary with great enthusiasm, over 30,000 people being in procession, the native Californian population taking an important part in the ceremonies. This brings us down to the date of the founding of THE TIMES.

AS IT WAS.

What Los Angeles Looked Like in the Year 1881.

A quiet, slow-moving, half-way frontier town was Los Angeles early in 1881. The census of the previous year had given it a population of 11,311, and it had certainly not increased since then, for there was quite an exodus to Arizona, which Territory had been brought into prominence by the discovery of the Tombstone mines and the extension eastward of the Southern Pacific railroad, then fast approaching a junction with the eastern lines. Tucson, the other old *pueblo* on the Santa Cruz, had a population of 6994, and was booming, while Los Angeles was decidedly dull. Hundreds were endeavoring to dispose of their property here at any price in order to go and make their fortunes in the mining country. Arizona was largely settled up at that time with Los Angeles people. The fortunate ones were those who were unable to sell their property here, although they did not see it in that light. You could have exchanged property in Los Angeles for property in Tucson on even terms then, while today fifty feet on Congress street, Tucson, would scarcely bring enough to pay one year's taxes on fifty feet of Spring-street property, for Los Angeles now has a population of over 55,000, while Tucson has only about 5500. Most of the wanderers have come back home, like the Prodigal Son, convinced that irrigation ditches are safer to base estimates of wealth upon than are holes in the ground.

As the year wore on the Southern Pacific effected a junction at Deming, giving Los Angeles a direct through line to the East, shorter and with much easier grades than that from San Francisco. The mining business in Arizona also brought many thousands of dollars to Los Angeles, whence most of the supplies for that Territory were drawn, as they are, to a great extent, now. This instilled a little life into the drowsy pueblo, and by the beginning of December, when the first number of THE TIMES appeared, there was a perceptible improvement in business. In its second issue THE TIMES noticed that rooms and houses were all taken, and that stores were engaged as soon as the corner-stone was laid. Many new buildings were being built, and old settlers were expressing the belief that "Los Angeles never had a brighter future before it than now." On the 24th of that month a leading editorial was published on "The Need of Manufactories," in the course of which the rapid development of the business resources of the city was referred to. The article continued:

> General business has been so prosperous, the demand for our produce in Arizona and New Mexico has been so active, the opportunities for successful speculation in land have offered so many inducements to the capitalist, and money has commanded such a high premium for safe investments on real estate and personal securities that but few of our citizens have given thought to the more important consideration of inaugurating manufacturing ventures in Los Angeles. It cannot be denied but that the City of Angels is now enjoying a season of business prosperity almost without parallel in her history. Every mercantile and commercial enterprise of any importance is accomplishing wonders in the way of business success. The city is increasing rapidly in the way of population and influence, and is speedily assuming all the attributes of metropolitan existence. Still, in the minds of certain people, there is a doubt as to the permanency of this prosperity. Some people naturally regard it as only a boom, and with a decline in the demand for our produce, or with the evil of a dry season to curtail our harvests, they reasonably expect a corresponding falling off in the volume of our business, in the number of new buildings, in the amount of real estate transactions and in the immigration to our city and county. While we are sanguine enough to doubt that either of the causes enumerated would produce general disaster in business and financial circles, as some think, still we believe that Los Angeles should begin to consider measures that would tend to avert any such dire calamities. There should be some balance wheel that will prevent seasons of booms and depressions, and will create a steady and certain condition of business prosperity. That balance wheel is undoubtedly manufactures.

In the light of events that have transpired it is amusing to read of the dire forebodings as to the effect of a reaction from the "boom" then prevailing. What an innocent little boomlet it was! The croaker was evidently here in 1881, with his mouldy maunderings about dry seasons and overproduction. He is here yet, although irrigation has made us to a great extent independent of dry seasons, and the markets of the world yet clamor for our products. The remarks about factories are, however, still pertinent, although we have established scores of manufacturing enterprises during the past ten years.

It must not be supposed, from the reference to the wonderful business done, that stores were carrying on a business then that bore any sort of comparison to that of today. In December, 1881, a peddler went into one of the leading dry goods stores of the city and selected seven pieces of prints which he wanted to buy. The proprietors complained that this would deplete their stock of those goods, and persuaded him to take only half a piece of each! The Los Angeles retail merchant princes of today were yet in embryo in 1881.

The change in the appearance of Los Angeles during the past ten years has been so remarkable that persons who visited it then and who return now can scarcely recognize it as the same city. In 1881 the Spanish quarter, with its low, one-story adobe houses, was still an important part of the city, and adobe houses and stores were numerous elsewhere. The residences were nearly all of the cottage order, and few business buildings rose above two stories. The only blocks of importance were those named after Baker, Temple and Downey, the first-named being really the only building in the city of any architectural pretensions. In the last-named was located the office of this paper.

Much business yet clustered about the Plaza, around the little park in the center of which was a handsome row of well-trimmed cypress trees. The business center was then at the Temple Block, the business quarter being bounded on the north by the Plaza and on the south by First street. Where the Nadeau Hotel now stands was a German butcher shop, in an adobe building, back of which was a horse corral and hay yard. Adjoining on Spring street on the south was a planing mill. Spring street, south of First, had more bare lots than residences and no stores, for business had not then begun to move so far south. Property on Spring street, between First and Second, was sold at $150 a foot, which was considered a very high price. At two other corners of First and Spring were a saloon and a coal-yard. The Wilcox Block on North Spring, where Jevne's grocery now is, was the only good business building on Spring street. Where the Phillips Block now stands was an old one-story adobe building used as a city jail.

On First street there was no business east of Los Angeles street, the road being very bad. Los Angeles street was then, as now, the principal wholesale business street. Main street was then the leading residence street. I. W. Hellman, Gov. Downey and John Jones had fair residences there. On Broadway—then Fort street—were a few cottages. There were a few scattering residences out to the west as far as Pearl street. Even at that time Figueroa was considered a fine residence street, there being residences here and there as far south as Adams street, and on the latter street a number of houses had been built around the Longstreet tract, of a character that was then considered superior. The houses on other streets in the neighborhood were mostly shanties. Below Eighth street most of the town was planted in barley. Acreage in the Morris Vineyard tract, between Pico and Washington, near Main, was offered at $800.

Up Temple street, near Bunker Hill avenue, was a deep cut. Here an old frame and muslin building, called the Pavilion, stood almost alone. There were scarcely any buildings on the hills west of Bunker Hill avenue. Lots were offered this side of the hill at $100 apiece, without finding many buyers. Second street, west of Hill, was nothing but a wagon track. Beaudry was trying to supply the hills with water, which he succeeded in doing after a time.

East of Main, both north and south of First street, there was quite a settlement of small buildings. Mrs. Woodworth's residence, at the corner of San Pedro and Second, was then a stylish place. Orchards and vineyards, in patches of from two to ten acres, covered much of this section.

The only bridge in the city, in December, 1881, was that at Aliso street, the Downey avenue bridge having been built very shortly afterward. East Los Angeles was a small settlement, consisting chiefly of Downey avenue, then recently laid out. Lots on the avenue were valued at about $100 apiece, and one groceryman was slowly starving to death. On Boyle Heights there were half a dozen houses, chief among which were the residences of Cummings, Hollenbeck and W. H. Workman. Where the Cummings Hotel now stands a Spaniard kept a little flour and plenty of whisky. Teams stopped there as the "last chance" this side of Downey.

The Pico House and St. Elmo—then called the Layfayette House—were the principal hotels. There were no paved streets in the city, which, during the rainy season, were in a horrible condition, horses and vehicles often sinking knee-deep into the foul-smelling mixture of black mud and offal, which was churned by the vehicles and hoofs into the consistency of a sticky paste. The "sidewalks" were little better in most places, consisting mostly of gravel, which after a long rain got so mixed with the soil that you could not tell one from the other. This state of affairs continued to prevail, even on Main and First streets, until 1887, when a serious attempt was begun to pave the city.

The show places of those days were the home of O. W. Childs on Main street and the Wolfskill orange orchard. The street-car system was confined to a single horse railroad, running every twenty minutes from the San Fernando depot to Washington Gardens. The railroads were the Southern Pacific to San Francisco, and its lines to Santa Monica, San Pedro and Santa Ana.

The leading agricultural industry was the raising of sheep and cattle. Immense bands of sheep kept the hills bare of herbage. The great complaint throughout the country was that there was "no water." Since then bountiful streams have been conducted on the plains from mountain cañons and tunnels, and more is constantly being developed, yet some people complain that this is a waterless region. Los Angeles was the center of what orange-growing business there was. THE TIMES of that year claimed that there were 356,135 orange trees growing within a few miles of the city. The Wolfskill orange orchard, where the Arcade depot now stands, was famous all over the country. Some of the orange trees, forty years old, are still standing in the home place of Mr. Wolfskill, near the depot.

The climatic and other attractions of Southern California had been made widely known in 1872 by Charles Nordhoff, and quite a number of Easterners began to visit and winter here. The stream was, however, a tiny one compared with that at present. There were no special arrangements made for the comfort of visitors. The Nadeau, the Westminster, the Raymond, the Arcadia and the Coronado hotels had not then been thought of.

They were crying for a Federal building in December, 1881. The cry still goes up. State division was talked of a little even then, and "Los Angeles" was suggested as a good name for the baby, which has not yet been born. The City Council was urged to have the houses numbered. A reduction in fruit rates to the East had just been secured. Several more reductions have since been given and the end is not yet. The city library boasted of from seventy-five to eighty visitors every evening, and that 990 books had been given out during the previous month. As many as that are sometimes issued in a day now. The Chamber of Commerce was considering the obtaining of an appropriation of $200,000 from Congress for the improvement of Wilmington harbor. That and a good deal more has since been secured, but the appetite of Wilmington harbor grows with the getting, and it now asks for millions where it then wanted hundreds of thousands. But then, its business has increased in the same proportion. There were 1924 pupils enrolled in the public schools of the city in 1881. The city assessment amounted to $7,627,632, and the tax levy to $75,749. It takes a good deal more to make the municipal mare go now-a-days. THE TIMES was saying it "would like to see" a first-class theater, a fire-alarm system, streets and sidewalks repaired, and a paper with larger circulation than THE TIMES. We have two first-class theaters, a fire-alarm system and excellent streets and sidewalks, but the paper with a larger circulation than THE TIMES is not yet here.

Pasadena—then still generally known as the "Indiana Colony"—consisted at that time of four corners and a post-office. Five acres on what is now the city of Pasadena were sold in December, 1881, for $40 an acre. Santa Monica was already quite a promising little place. In one respect it was ahead of the present time, for it had a wharf and steamship communication. A hotel was there, known as the "Jones and Baker."

As to prices of real estate in 1881, a glance through THE TIMES will give the best idea of that. One of the largest sales of the year was that of the Cardona building, a large two-story [illegible] block standing on a lot 81 feet [illegible]

The Los Angeles Times

THE COUNTY CONVENTION CONTINUED ITS LABORS YESTERDAY. — CORBETT DEFEATED SULLIVAN IN THE TWENTY-FIRST ROUND.

ELEVENTH YEAR. TWELVE PAGES. THURSDAY MORNING, SEPTEMBER 8, 1892. 5:00 O'CLOCK A. M. PRICE: SINGLE COPIES, 5 CENTS; BY THE WEEK, 3 CENTS

CORBETT WINS

John L. Sullivan no Longer Champion.

The Californian Knocks Him Out in Twenty-one Rounds.

The Huge Bruiser Pounded to Jelly and Streaming With Blood.

Corbett Finishes Fresh and Without a Mark—Sullivan Says He Has Fought Once too Often in the Ring.

By Telegraph to The Times.

NEW ORLEANS, Sept. 7.—[By the Associated Press.] The laurels have shifted and John L. Sullivan has had some new sensations. So has James J. Corbett. One has been knocked off the pedestal of the pugilistic championship and the other has climbed into his place. The California heavyweight, Corbett, has knocked out the champion, John L. Sullivan, and won besides some $35,000. Furthermore, it appeared to spectators, if the truth be told, as though Corbett won easily.

The impression left by the rapid spectacle is that Sullivan was at no moment in the path of success, and the physical evidences of this were apparent at the finish. Corbett, the winner, at the moment of his victory, was keen, quick and alert in every round. Although marked by bruises and blood, his face was aglow with a steady interest. His face wore a half smile, and he was ready to attack his foe with a ferocious force, so that had that foe been able to rise there were conditions of victory.

Sullivan was reeking with blood, smashed, bruised, jellied and nearly, if not quite, insensible. These were the evidences of defeat and it was when these had been established that the laurels shifted and a new man had been born in the championship.

Why was Sullivan dethroned? He, himself, had contributed to the causes of his own downfall. If his life had known no excess Sullivan would have been able to fight and struggle more effectively to retain his prestige. He is not relatively so good a man at 34 as hundreds of other men at that age. His face is furrowed, not alone by years, but by his methods of living. His ponderous body also bore traces, not alone of time, but of easy living. His condition was not comparable with that of his foe. It could not be. There was a cumulation of age and wide freedom which could not be trained away without impairing the man. Sullivan, too, has been over-confident. He had been contemptuous of the needful measures for his perfect condition. He was Sullivan, and Sullivan could not lose in battle. Corbett has taught him otherwise, and now he is starting with eight years less of life's inevitable wear. Had he conserved his powers and perfected the methods of their use, charging his heart meanwhile with confidence, he would have become king of his kind. His was the

The victor and vanquished.

capital of brawn and muscle upon which to build up the fortune of victory and reputation.

It may not be carelessly said that Corbett at 26 years of age is a better man than Sullivan was at that age, but assuming that they were equally good men at equal ages, the analysis of this victory comes back to the fact that, while some men of 34 may whip some men of 26 the elder man, to be the victor, must not have added his own methods of depletion to those which the silent years so surely employ.

Sullivan came forward tonight into the glare of twenty electric lights, his senses fed by the shouts of those who will flout him now. If the majority believed in him, why should not the champion believe in himself? So while they yelled with worshiping plaudits he sat down in his corner, and with easy interest scanned the powerful fellow opposite.

Somehow there is a homage in the eager attention the trainers bestow upon their champion, and tonight, while Sullivan enjoyed this, his heavy form sunk down. As he sat awaiting for the preliminaries those who scanned him

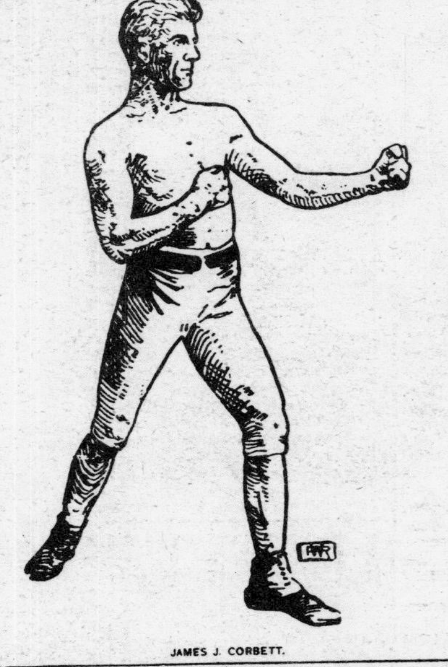
JAMES J. CORBETT.

closely saw welts of flesh on his abdomen rolling far over the edge of his firmly drawn belt. It should not have been the obesity of age, for the man tonight should be in the prime of his years. It was the distention surely following wine suppers and hot dinners of rich food. While sitting thus under the eyes of hundreds whose scrutiny was sharpened by their money being on the result, Sullivan was in turn studying his foe. In the opposite corner, out of which all victors in the Olympic Club have gone to victory, sat a beautiful specimen of human flesh and bone. Sullivan saw a smiling and confident face; he saw a neck that had poise and strength; he saw a chest deep enough to hold a bellows; he saw a pair of browned shoulders where piles of muscles crept and glided beneath the skin. He beheld, outstretched upon the ropes, while the trainers did their service, a pair of arms as long as those of a windmill, bunched with lithe driving muscles with the blood and nerve of youth. The champion beholds a foe whose figure was clean cut and rounded in its lines. There was no adipose to clog his lungs or harden the freedom of his actions. Like a racer was Corbett, trim, solid, balanced physically at every point, unless, indeed his long legs seemed a trifle light for the muscular shoulders and body. But those who doubted the power of lithe underlimbs could not know how like steel they had been tempered to bend without breaking under stress and tension. Doubles Sullivan learned later what iron thews lay along the slender columns that held up the man.

When the fight began Corbett came up prancing, verily prancing. He teetered about Sullivan like a carpet amateur, and while the crowd laughed, Sullivan smiled as though amused. So did Corbett. But one of them grew terribly serious before the night had grown much older, while the other continued with a smile on his face, and is smiling yet. As they came up to the second round the crowd was treated to what has gone down into history as "the Sullivan rush." His awful right flew out, but finding lodgment only for an instant, a glancing shot on the back of the catlike fellow, who wheeled suddenly and slammed his left on the big man's stomach. The crowd yelled. The cheers for his foe's cleverness nettled the champion, though he smiled in a derisive way while Corbett laughed in his face. The spectacle was new to old-timers. Never before had they seen any man laugh in Sullivan's face.

So it went on. There was an onslaught by the champion, but there was no teetering then. Straight and swift as lightning Corbett's left shot forth and landed with a shock on Sullivan's jaw. Sullivan would brook no such liberties. To be sure he had not yet landed a blow of any moment on Corbett, but after such an affront he would kill his presumptuous foe. The big fellow's jaw closed, his lower lip became pushed up against its fellow, and the crowd cried, "See Sullivan's mug now!" Corbett heeded the injunction. Again his right shot away and returned and—could it be?—blood stained Sullivan's nose and trickled over his lips.

Surely now he would grind Corbett to atoms, and he tried, but away flew Corbett's left and right, landing squarely on the damaged nose again and again. The blows splashed the blood over Sullivan's face until it was dripping with fluid. Could this be? Sullivan receiving such indignities and permitting his assailant to live? Yet so it was.

Another time the men lined up and Sullivan's face bore the prophecy of defeat. His eyes were anxious; his face was pale; it had a surprised and troubled expression, and the conviction was being forced on the crowd that there was a possibility that Sullivan was to go down. Corbett continued to land on Sullivan's stomach, jaw and three times on his bleeding nose, that was growing pulpy. Again and again Sullivan led but failed and lurched forward with the force of his unlanded blows. Could it be that he was becoming weak while Corbett was unruffled? And so it was, and so it continued from round to round until, in the fifteenth, the bleeding champion betrayed clearly the outcome of it all. It was only a matter of time.

When for the twentieth time the men stood up, hope had gone from Sullivan's face. Defeat was putting its iron in his heart. He knew it and showed it. There came a clinch and a break, and as Sullivan heavily backed away Corbett rained his face with blows until it was a mass of blood and bruises. His body was smeared with blood, he seemed heavy, and led no more, but waited only for the end. And all the time Corbett was smiling in his face.

The end was in the next, the twenty-first round. Sullivan hugged Corbett's neck, but it cost him dearly, for the fresh, agile fellow again spattered blood from Sullivan's nose. The big fellow responded as best he could, and tried to clinch. Corbett shoved the champion off. He staggered back and then began the final strokes. Corbett felt victory in his reach, and followed his man, slamming right and left on his nose, jaw, neck, eyes and mouth. Finally with a terrible swing, he knocked Sullivan clear off his feet, and a moment later the champion that was lay flat on his back, still more or less covered with blood, and as he lay there his great frame was a dire picture of the fall of the great. The count of the referee began and Sullivan moved, rolled over, got on one knee and both hands, and essayed to rise, while Corbett advanced to punch him more should he succeed. But it was useless. The great bulk of what had been the champion reeled and again went down, and the "Ten and out!" of the referee told the battle was over.

A more pitiable sight than was the champion has seldom been seen in a prize ring. Corbett leaped up then and helped to lift Sullivan to his chair. Sullivan could not recognize him. His head rolled helplessly. Corbett shook his hand and he did not know it. His star had set; a new one had risen.

BEFORE THE FIGHT.

Intense Excitement Everywhere—The Men at the Ringside.

NEW ORLEANS, Sept. 7.—[By the Associated Press.] The excitement which has prevailed in this city has had no parallel since the Italian assassins were lynched eighteen months ago. There has been no subject of conversation discussed in any quarter save the fistic event of the evening, in which every portion of the country is more or less deeply interested. It apparently effected the outside world as deeply as it did the participants in the battle. Both Sullivan and Corbett were known to be in prime condition, and the greatest fight of the series was looked forward to by all with keenness. There was a universal move in the direction of the Olympic Club even before the evening began to fall. Business men, lawyers and journalists took their dinners down town and had their vehicles ordered early. They were willing to wait at the club, but they were unwilling to waste time in going down. At 6 o'clock carriages were already heading down Canal street, which was crowded with people, and vehicles were passing down the intersecting streets, the carriages reaching the scene of battle. Down in the neighborhood of the club for blocks and blocks carriages were strung along the curbstones and every street corner had a crowd.

The Sullivan poople came to the club first. They took a carriage at the hotel before 7 o'clock and drove leisurely down with a string of hacks. Sullivan looked strong and determined. He walked with a jaunty air and came in so easy with a line of people entering at the time that few noticed him.

Big Jim Corbett followed in the wake of the champion, coming in fifteen minutes later. When his party pulled up in front of the door the street was cleared and an avenue opened into the building. Corbett came in first with a light step and his face wreathed in smiles. The first sign of the contest for the championship of America came in the person of Police Captain Barrett, who went into the ring at five minutes before 9 o'clock. The scales upon which the gloves were weighed were laid beside the center of the post. Ex-Mayor Guillotte, who acted as master of ceremonies, entered the arena a few minutes later and made a speech, warning the spectators not to violate any of the rules of the club.

Sullivan entered the ring first. He was dressed in green trunks and black shoes and socks. He looked in perfect condition. Corbett followed a moment later, looking pale and finely drawn beside his bulky antagonist. He wore an air of confidence, however. He smiled and nodded to his acquaintances around the ring, though he was said by some people to be a little nervons.

Police Captain Barrett stepped to the center of the ring and presented Prof. John Duffy with a beautiful silver ice bowl and ladel. John Donaldson and Billy Delaney were announced as Corbett's seconds with Bat Masterson as timekeeper. Charles Johnson and Jack McAuliffe were the seconds for John L. Sullivan. Frank Moran was his timekeeper. In the toss for corners Corbett won and chose the lucky one that Dixon and McAuliffe fought in.

Gloves were weighed and found to be according to law and they were given to the fighters. In the parley which was held in the center of the ring, Corbett looked entirely out-classed in point of build, though his friends relied upon his cleverness to win the battle. The pivot blow and back heeling were barred by mutual consent, and the men after agreeing to fight fair went to their corners to get ready for the fray.

POINTS OF THE MORNING'S NEWS.

BY TELEGRAPH.

No cases of cholera have occurred in New York city and the scare is subsiding, but reports from Hamburg show no abatement of the disease....The poet Whittier is dead....Sensational testimony was brought out in the McWhirter inquest at Fresno....Vermont has gone overwhelmingly Republican....The American Bankers' Association is in session in San Francisco....More Christians have been massacred in China....Nancy Hanks trotted a mile in 2:07 on a regulation track at St. Paul....Senator Cullom made a great speech at Joliet, Ill.

IN AND ABOUT THE CITY.

A day of surprises in the Republican County Convention....The Colonels won the opening game of the Oakland-Los Angeles series....Native Sons to leave for Santa Barbara today....Meeting of the Southern California World's Fair Association....The city flooded with "green goods" circulars.

THE BATTLE BY ROUNDS.

How the Californian Outfought and Conquered the Champion.

NEW ORLEANS, Sept. 7.—[By the Associated Press.] It was 9:10 o'clock when the men stepped to the center of the ring. They shook hands and time was called.

First round—Both men stopped, lightly countering, and Sullivan immediately became the aggressor. He made a left lead, but was stopped. Corbett danced all about his opponent, eyeing him closely. Sullivan made a rush, but Jim backed away. Sullivan also attempted a left-hander, but Jim cleverly avoided it. Sullivan looked vicious as he played for an opening. He next attempted a right-hand stomach punch, but the blow fell short. Sullivan tried to corner Jim, but the latter slipped away. The gong sounded and not a blow had been landed by either man.

Second round—Sully was still the aggressor. He upper cut Jim and touched him again with his left hand a little later. Jim eyed his man closely, and when Sullivan rushed the Californian would slip away. Sullivan landed a heavp right on the shoulder, but received a stomach punch in return.

Third round—Corbett ducked away from a heavy lunge. Sully followed him about the ring trying for his stomach. Jim's head missed a heavy left hander, and Sully looked vicious. Jim landed two heavy stomach punches and Sully missed a vicious right. Each hit the other on the head. Corbett then stepped out of harm's way, but came back quickly and landed his left on the stomack. He also planted a heavy blow on the champion's ear, sending his head back. Both men were fighting hard when the gong sounded. Sullivan was ringing wet with perspiration.

Fourth round—Sullivan missed with his left, but he chased Jim around the ring, and finally landed a light left. Corbett stepped up close, attempting to punch the stomach, but John was guarding with the right. The champion followed up his man all over the ring, but received a heavy left-hand swing for his pains. Jim landed with both hands on Sullivan's head as the round ended, and the champion went to his corner with a sneering smile.

Fifth round—Sullivan stepped to the center with a smile, and Corbett touched his nose with his left. The champion tried to land his left on the stomach and the men clinched, Sullivan landing his first heavy right. Sullivan missed a fearful left-hander and staggered forward from the force of the blow. Tha men boxed cautiously for an opening, and the champiou seemed eager for hot work. He followed his antagonist all around the ring. The first blood came from Sullivan's nose. The fighting was fast and furious, and Sullivan nearly fell on the ropes from left-hand jabs on the head. As the round ended Corbett landed a heavy right on the champion's head.

Sixth round—Both men landed light lefts and Sullivan's nose was bleeding again. The champion was beginning to look tired, for he missed with his right as he aimed for the jaw. Corbett took plenty of time and used the entire ring to maneuver in. He landed a light stomach punch and hit the champion in the face. A little later there was a heavy exchange of lefts on the head, and Sullivan seemed angry. He slapped his opponent with his left hand, but Corbett landed with blows on the head and ran away. The men walked to the center of the ring and it began to look as if some of the fight was out of Sully. Jim landed a heavy left on Sullivan's head and the champion went to his corner, looking tired.

Seventh round—Corbett walked right up to Sullivan and barely avoided a left-hand punch. The champion kept trying his hardest for a right on the jaw, but the foxy Corbett was not there. The champion landed two light blows on the head, and Corbett sent in hot shot from his left. He jabbed Sullivan continually on the nose in this round and blood flowed freely. Jim was cheered to the echo for his skillful fighting. Sullivan was forced on the ropes by a heavy right on the jaw, and, as the gong sounded, received a heavy left on the jaw.

Eighth round—Sullivan landed a light left on the stomach and received a left on the mouth. Jim was now the aggressor. Sullivan hit Corbett in a clinch and the audience yelled "foul." Both exchanged heavy lefts, but Jim cleverly ducked a mighty right. Jim, after a narrow escape from another right, sent his left in the champion's stomach, forcing him to the ropes. Jim landed a heavy left on the mouth, which brought blood and a smile from the champion, who looked fatigued.

Ninth round—Sullivan was puffing when he came up this time. Both exchanged good lefts. Sullivan received a light one on the ear and got another on the nose, but evened up matters a little with his right. Jim landed a heavy left on the nose and both men hugged each other in a clinch. Sullivan was missing many of his blows now, although when he did land his blows were twice as heavy as those of his antagonist. Jim had much the best of Sullivan.

Tenth round—Sullivan attempted to land a left, but the blow fell short. He followed his opponent, however, and

The Times

ANOTHER PIECE OF QUEER LEGISLATIVE WORK HAS JUST COME TO LIGHT.

THE WORLD'S COLUMBIAN EXPOSITION WAS OPENED BY THE PRESIDENT YESTERDAY.

TWELFTH YEAR. TWELVE PAGES. TUESDAY MORNING, MAY 2, 1893. 4:05 O'CLOCK A.M. PRICE:

TODAY'S BULLETIN —OF— The Times.

MAY 2, 1893.

(BY TELEGRAPH.) The President pressed the gold button and formally opened the World's Columbian Exposition yesterday.... High water reported along the Mississippi River and in Ohio ... May day in Europe passed with few riots.... California cherries sent to the Duke de Varagua ... The revolution in Cuba ... Public debt statement.

IN AND ABOUT THE CITY.

Time for sentence in the Bentley case postponed for ten days.... Return of the delegates from the Transmississippi Congress.... Verdict of the Coroner's jury in the Irene Mansfield case.... The Los Angeles street improvement discussed in the Council ... The Southern Pacific has inaugurated an aggressive policy.... Dissatisfaction among county employees over the reduction of salaries.... News from neighboring counties.

WEATHER INDICATIONS.

For Southern California: Fair weather; slight changes in temperature; westerly winds.

BIRD'S-EYE VIEW OF THE WORLD'S COLUMBIAN EXPOSITION.

A GOLDEN KEY

Unlocks the Wonders of the World.

The Engines at the World's Fair in Motion.

THOUSANDS OF WHEELS

Turn in Response to the Magical Button.

"OLD GLORY" FLOATS ON HIGH

Director-General Davis's Review of the Work.

ADDRESS BY THE PRESIDENT

Descendants of Columbus Join in the Ceremonies.

A TRIBUTE TO WOMANHOOD.

The Woman's Building Formally Dedicated and Opened.

A VAST CROWD IN ATTENDANCE.

A Terrible Panic and Many Casualties Narrowly Averted in Front of the Grand Stand During the Exercises.

By Telegraph to The Times.

CHICAGO, May 1.—[By the Associated Press.] The electric age was ushered into being in this last decade of the nineteenth century today, when President Cleveland, by pressing a button, started the mighty machinery and rushing waters and revolving wheels in the World's Columbian Exposition. No exhibit of the fair that is to attract thousands to this city, from far and near, for the next six months, can be more marvelous than the magic effect following the solemn opening of the fair today. Of the multitude of visitors—some estimate the number as high as two hundred thousand—probably not one fully realized the full import of the effect that was to come from the arrangement so cleverly devised for the opening of the exposition. It was known in a vague way that the President was to press a golden key, and that an electric communication with the machinery was to start the fair, but no one realized how intricate was this machinery, how infinite the ramifications if that electric spark, until the great fountains threw up their geysers seventy feet into the air, and the rumble and hum of the wheels in the Manufactures building, and the clatter of the machinery in all parts of that area of a mile square or more, told the story of final consummation of scientific thought. The lifeless was started into being on every hand; draped statuary shed its veil and revealed to the world the artistic labors of the past eighteen months, and in a moment all that had been apathy and inertia and inactive through the long hours of the morning sprang into animated existence and thrilled the multitude and crowned the triumph of the exposition. In previous expositions the possibilities of electricity had been limited to the mere starting of engines in machinery halls, but in this exposition it was made to do the duty of thousands of servants, and from the great Corliss engine down to the minutest acts, where power and touch are requisite, the magic of electricity did the duty of the hour.

THE LINE OF MARCH.

Thousands View the Notables on the Way to the Exposition.

CHICAGO, May 1.—[By the Associated Press.] Jupiter Pluvius held an uplifted and threatening fist over Chicago this morning. The skies were sodden, and a bleak and chilled mist filled the atmosphere. The bunting throughout the city was damp and listless, and a general tone of gloom pervaded the air and streets of Chicago. These were the weather conditions, but they counted for nothing, and at an early hour the people were astir, the bustling, eager, spirit of the great West, bounding through every artery of this, its capital city. The consummation of this great enterprise took place today, when the myriad of wheels began turning at Jackson Park in response to the touch of the Nation's Chief Executive upon the golden key that reached out through an electric train to the mighty engines which are the World's Columbian Exposition's vital moving energy.

In the great circle of events which today made Chicago a festal city, the first point of interest centered at the Auditorium Hotel, where large numbers gathered for a glimpse of Columbus's descendant, the Duke de Veragua, who, with the members of his family and committees of prominent officials of the national, State and municipal governments, took carriages about 9 o'clock, and, under a military escort, drove to the Lexington Hotel, at Michigan avenue and Twentieth street, and joined President Cleveland and the members of his Cabinet, and from which point the procession to the park was to start.

The ducal party was arrayed in all the glories of the Spanish court costume, brilliant in color, rich with gold-lace and bright with the decorations of the orders of nobility, with swords, knee-breeches, silk stockings and all the trappings of the Spanish court. The assembled multitude set up a shout as the party appeared and entered the carriages and drove rapidly to the Lexington Hotel.

CHRISTOPHER COLUMBUS.

Meantime the city at large seemed to be going in a body to the White City by the lake. Nine big steamers, from early morning, were plying from Van Buren street to the fair grounds, heavily loaded. Every cable car was thronged to the tail board. The elevated cars groaned with their loads of humanity. The steam cars reaped a harvest, and the great Michigan boulevard was thronged with private carriages and conveyances of all sorts.

Soon after 9 o'clock President Cleveland and his associates appeared at the entrance to the Lexington Hotel, and were conducted to carriages. When all was in readiness the procession moved in the following order:

Platoon of mounted police.
Two companies of United States cavalry.
Chicago Hussars.
Troop of Illinois National Guard.
World's Fair managers occupying six carriages.
President Cleveland and the chairman of the Columbian Commission and the presidents of the World's Columbian Exposition.
Five carriages containing the President's Cabinet and fair officials.
The Duke de Veragua and party in five carriages.
Thomas F. Bayard, Ambassador to Great Britain, Maj.-Gen. Schofield, Admiral Gherardi, Gov. Altgeld and Mayor Harrison.

Down Michigan avenue, cheered by the thousands that lined the curb, clattered and rumbled the cavalcade. It turned into the Grand boulevard at Thirty-fifth street, into Washington Park at Fifty-first street and from the park into Midway Plaisance, which is now a medley of all nations, and from it into the great White City, and to the Administration building, where the ceremonies of the day took place.

Passing through the building, the notables came out upon the platform at the east side, looking out upon the Grand plaza and Court of Honor. The plaza was black with people, the whole scene forming one of the most remarkable and enchanting in history.

THE MAGICAL BUTTON.

The Exposition Springs into Life at the Touch of the President.

Opening Address of Director-General Davis—The Wonders That Have Been Accomplished in the White City.

CHICAGO, May 1.—[By the Associated Press.] The officials and invited guests not in the procession were seated on the platform, and as the head of the Nation walked down the main aisle to his place at the outer edge, a tumult of cheers shook the air. He and those accompanying him were soon seated, and shortly after 10 o'clock the opening ceremonies began with Prof. John K. Paine's "Columbian March," followed by prayer by Chaplain Milburn of the United States Senate.

Then Miss Jessie Couthoui, a dramatic reader, recited a rhymed prophecy by W. A. Croful of Washington.

After the orchestral overture, Director-General Davis, as master of ceremonies, made the opening address, as follows:

Ladies and gentlemen: The dedication of these grounds and buildings for the purpose of an international exhibition took place on the 21st of last October, at which time they were accepted for the object to which they were destined by the action of Congress. This is not the time or place, neither will it be expected of me, to give a comprehensive resumé of the strenuous efforts which have been put forth to complete the work to which we invite your inspection today. I may be permitted to say, however, a word in praise and gratitude to my co-officers and official staff, who form the great organization which has made the consummation of this great work possible. This exposition has not been the conception of any single mind; neither is it the result of any single effort, but the grandest conception of all minds and the best obtainable results of the efforts put forth by all the people who in any manner have contributed to its creation.

The great commanding agencies through which the Government authorized this work to proceed are: A national commission consisting of 108 men and alternates, selected from the several States and Territories, and presided over by Hon. Thomas W. Palmer of Michigan; a corporation of the State of Illinois, known as the World's Columbian Exposition, consisting of forty-three directors, which is presided over by E. N. Higinbotham of Chicago, and a board of lady managers, consisting of 115 women and alternates, selected from the several States, and presided over by Mrs. Potter Palmer of Chicago. To these great agencies, wisely selected by Congress, each performing its special function, the gratitude of the people of this country and the cordial recognition of all these friendly foreign representatives is due.

To perfect from these agencies an efficient organization was our first duty, and it was successfully accomplished at the outset through committees, and subsequently by the great executive departments, and through these departments a systematic, vigorous and effective work has progressed. Through the Department of Administration, the Department of Finance, the Department of Works and the great exhibit departments the plan and scope of a grand international exposition were worked out.

The Department of Finance, which is composed of members of the Illinois corporation, has, with disinterestedness remarkable, with courage undaunted, successfully financed the exposition and provided for the great work, which has cost upward of $20,000,000.

The Department of Works and its many bureaus of artists, architects, engineers and builders have transformed these grounds, which twenty-one months ago were an unsightly, uninviting and unoccupied stretch of landscape, into the beauty and splendor of today. They have conspicuously performed their functions, and these grand avenues, these Venetian waterways, the finished landscape, fountains and sculptures and colonnades, and these grand palaces stand out as monuments to their genius and skill, supplemented by the labor of that great army of skilled artisans and workmen, all citizens of this republic.

The chiefs of the great departments who have exploited this mighty enterprise and gathered here the exhibits forming the picture that is set in this magnificent frame have confirmed the wisdom of their selection. No State or Territory of the Union has escaped their voice; there is no land on the globe that has a language but has been visited and the invitation of the President of the United States personally presented.

Fortunately at the inception of this enterprise our Government was, and still is, at peace with the whole world. Commissioners were sent to Europe, Asia, Australia, British North America and the islands of the seas, so that today the whole world knows and is familiar with the significance of the great peace festival we are about to inaugurate upon this campus, and all the nations will join in celebrating the event which it commemorates.

This inclosure, containing nearly seven hundred acres and covered by more than four hundred structures, from the small pavilion, occupying an ordinary building site, to the colossal structure of the Manufactures and Liberal Arts building, covering over thirty acres, is filled and crowded with a display of the achievements and products of the mind and hand of man such as never before have been presented to mortal vision. The habits, customs and life of the people of our own and foreign lands are shown, and those stately buildings on the north are filled with historical treasures and natural products from our several States.

The artistic, characteristic and beautiful edifices, the headquarters of foreign commissions, surrounding the gallery of fine arts, which in itself will be an agreeable surprise to the American beholder, constitute the grand central zone of the social and friendly amenities among the different peoples of the earth.

• WORLDS • COLUMBIAN • COMMISSION •

Surrounding this grand plaza where we stand, and reaching from the north pond to extreme south, is the great mechanical, scientific, industrial and agricultural exhibition of the resources and products of the world. These have been secured from the four quarters of the globe, and placed in systematic order under the supervision of these great departments, and, while all the material upon the grounds is not yet in place, I am gratified to be able to present to the President of the United States at this time an official catalogue containing the description and location of the exhibits of 4000 participants in the exposition. The number of exhibitors will exceed sixty thousand when everything is in place.

The citizens of our country are proud and always will be proud of the action of the Congress of the United States of America in authorizing and directing this celebration to take place, and for its appropriations of more than five millions of dollars in its aid, and for the unswerving support and encouragement of the officers of the Government.

To the various States of the Union we are largely indebted for active and substantial support. A sum in excess of six millions of dollars has been raised and expended by the States and Territories for official use in promoting their own interests, conjointly with the general success of the exhibition. To the foreign nations who have representation upon our grounds, and the hundreds of official representatives of the foreign governments who are present on this occasion, we bow in grateful thanks. More than six millions of dollars have been officially appropriated for these commissions in furtherance of their participation in the exposition, and the great nations of Europe and their dependencies are all represented upon these grounds, and also the governments of Asia and Africa and the republics of the Western Hemisphere, with but few exceptions, are represented.

To the citizens and corporations of the city of Chicago, who have furnished $11,000,000 as a contribution, and, in addition, have loaned the management $5,000,000 more, are due the greatest acknowledgments of our own people and the honored guests who share with us the advantages of this great international festival.

To the tens of thousands of exhibitors who have contributed a larger amount than all the others combined, we are under the deepest obligations for interest and co-operation.

To the women of Chicago and of our land, whose prompt, spontaneous and enthusiastic coöperation in our work [illegible]

The Times

LOS ANGELES

XIIITH YEAR.—10 PAGES. TUESDAY MORNING, JUNE 26, 1894. PER WEEK, 20c. PER MONTH, 85c. | FIVE CENTS

THE MORNING'S NEWS —IN— The Times.

ASSOCIATED PRESS REPORTS BRIEFED.

(BY TELEGRAPH:) France mourns for Carnot—The remains of the dead President taken from Lyons to Paris—Rioting at Toulon, Dijon, Grenoble and other places—Italians attacked and their shops wrecked—Messages of condolence from crowned heads and America—The candidates for the Presidency—Santo and his record....The strike against the Pullman Car Company under way—An attack on a train in Oklahoma....The two Milton stage-robbers confess their crime—Highwayman Keener killed himself after being shot....The sunken tug at New York—Forty-five persons are still missing—The captain's story....Racing at Sheepshead Bay and elsewhere....President Cleveland interviewed on the financial conditions....The record of one day's crimes and casualties in Chicago....Election frauds in St. Paul—1000 votes said to have been bought....The O. R. & N. receivership—The Southern Pacific and Santa Fe....A town wrecked by a cyclone—Damage to the railroads by floods....Emma Juch, the prima donna, married at Stamford, Ct.....Edison sustains serious injuries by a fall.

Dispatches were also received from San Francisco, New York, Louisville, Ky.; Wichita, Kan.; Galveston, Danville, Ind.; Chicago, Pittsburgh, New Orleans, St. Louis, Cincinnati and other places.

THE CITY.

Divorce proceedings commenced against John Bryson, Sr., the millionaire, by his wife, alleging cruelty and infidelity....Merchants appear before the Council to protest against the license tax....A lively debate over the oil-well complaints....Judge Ross decides the Atlantic and Pacific land-grant case in favor of the government....New Superintendent of Schools elected by the Board of Education—Teachers' salaries fixed for the ensuing year.

SOUTHERN CALIFORNIA.

Pasadena getting uneasy about the water supply....Another suit against the Riverside Banking Company....Trespanting statistics for San Bernardino county....A sensational divorce suit at Riverside....Redlands vital statistics....Probably fatal accident at Long Beach.

ONE DAY.

Chicago and Its Tragedies for Twenty-four Hours.

Murder, Poison, Drownings, Fatal Falls and Other Casualties—A Husband and a Rival Kill Each Other.

Associated Press Leased-wire Service.

CHICAGO, June 25.—The following is a brief resume of accidents and crime in this city for the past twenty-four hours:

Mrs. Carrie Donigan, wife of an ex-police officer, was almost murdered by her husband in front of their home. He fired point blank at her and inflicted wounds which it is believed will prove fatal. The tragedy is attributed to domestic differences. Donigan escaped.

Edward Otto was drowned in the Calumet River at Riverdale last night while bathing. The body was recovered.

In a free fight on the banks of the Desplaines River, near River Forest, Theodore Victor was stabbed fatally.

Passengers on a Cottage Grove avenue cable train were startled by seeing two men in a desperate struggle on the promenade. Pistol shots punctuated the combat and when the men were separated both were found to be badly hurt. The combatants were Joseph la Rochelle and August Bender, the latter being the assailant. It is claimed La Rochelle had alienated his wife's affections. Both men were locked up pending investigation.

Flossie Martin, aged 6 years, the daughter of a fireman, while playing in the engine-room, fell from the observatory tower, a distance of fifty feet, and was instantly killed. The mother, who accompanied the child, was with great difficulty restrained from throwing herself from the tower.

August Duholz, his wife and six children, were poisoned by eating ice cream. It is thought the three youngest children will die. The poisoned articles were purchased from an Italian street merchant.

Peter Peterson died at the County Hospital from injuries received in a saloon brawl over the question of pay for the drinks. He was shot in the head by Adolph Gleasmon, the proprietor of the saloon.

While at work on a new building Fred Desmors, a carpenter, was overcome by the heat and fell to the ground, a distance of twenty feet. He died soon after reaching the hospital.

James Davis sat on the Wisconsin Central Railroad track in a drunken stupor as the east-bound train appeared. The engineer blew his whistle, but he awoke to find his leg cut off below the knee. He died soon after.

John Victa, a Pole, was drowned in the lake at the foot of North Water street while bathing. He leaves a widow and nine children.

While John Williamson was driving last night his horse took fright and ran away. Williamson was thrown out on his head and probably fatally hurt.

Christopher Goghinson, a brakeman on the Fort Wayne, was instantly killed while making a coupling. He was caught between the drawheads and squeezed to death.

Emma Juch Married.

STAMFORD (Ct.,) June 25.—Miss Emma Juch, the prima donna, and Francis L. Wellman, assistant district attorney of New York, were married this afternoon and immediately started on a wedding trip, the destination of which is secret.

Two Hundred and Thirty Bodies.

CARDIFF, June 25.—Two hundred and thirty bodies have been recovered from the Albion colliery at Gilfynd, the scene of Saturday's explosion.

FRANCE'S LOSS

Europe and America Sympathize.

Messages of Condolence from Crowned Heads.

The United States Congress Adjourns Early.

RIOTING IN FRENCH CITIES.

Italian Shops Wrecked and Set on Fire.

The Assassin Now Said to Be a Swiss by Birth.

Carnot's Remains are Taken Back to Paris.

CANDIDATES FOR PRESIDENT.

The Electoral Congress to Meet at Versailles Wednesday—Santo Confined to a Cell at Lyons—Press and Other Comment.

Associated Press Leased-wire Service.

PARIS, June 25.—(By Atlantic Cable.) The announcement of the death of President Carnot was formally made in the Chamber of Deputies today by Premier Dupuy, and in the Senate by M. Challemel-Lacour. The Chamber of Deputies was thronged to the utmost, and there was great excitement when Premier Casimir-Perier entered. Every person present arose, and remained standing while the President of the Chamber of Deputies read M. Dupuy's letter making the formal announcement of the death of President Carnot, and adding that the whole of France was stupefied by the abominable crime. Dupuy also said:

"From all parts, expressions of emotion and sorrow are arriving. France weeps at the loss of the loyal servant and upright citizen who carried with honor and firmly the national flag, and who awakened in Europe feelings which show how great is the ordeal through which we are now passing. The republic will ever remember President Carnot. All of our sympathies are with the family which mourns his loss, and which, like him, is worthy of France. The whole country joins in the indignation felt at the crime."

M. Casimir-Perier, after he had finished reading, said: "The Chamber of Deputies and France associate themselves with these words. Let us bow respectfully before the tomb which closes over a life of devotion to the fatherland and to the republic. France remains brave and strong in the day of national mourning."

The Chamber of Deputies then adjourned.

Crowds of people during the morning and this afternoon have surrounded the palace where all the foreign ambassadors and ministers, Senators and Deputies, called during the day. The majority of the Deputies, after calling at the Elysees Palace, assembled at the Palace Bourbon, where meetings of all parties were held during the afternoon. The Senate and Chamber of Deputies will assemble in electoral congress at Versailles at 1 p.m. on Wednesday next, for the purpose of electing a successor.

The police inquiry late this afternoon resulted in obtaining the following facts in regard to the assassin's movements previous to the crime: Santo missed the train running direct to Lyons from Cette on Saturday, and had to go to Montpelier and thence to Vienna. From there he was unable to pay his fare on the train to Lyons, and, having only 60 centimes in his pocket, was obliged to walk thirty miles. He arrived at Lyons the same afternoon.

When the police rescued the prisoner from the mob, after he had stabbed the President, his clothes were torn to shreds, and it was found necessary to sew them together at the police station. Santo was confined in a cell in the prison of the Palace of Justice at Lyons. The body of the late President will possibly be placed on a train for Paris tonight, and may arrive in this city early tomorrow morning.

The Senate was crowded this evening when the President, M. Challemel-Lacour, made an address expressive of the Senate's feeling at the death of M. Carnot. "Europe," he said, "is appreciating the nobleness and strength of his character, and shares in France's grief."

The speaker then voiced the sentiment and condolence with the family, saying: "If any man's innate goodness should have guarded him from hatred and fanaticism, it was President Carnot. The crime has strengthened our energetic resolve to defend the fundamental rules of society and to prevent outrages upon human life."

AT PARIS.

PARIS, June 25.—The deepest sorrow, dismay and anger prevail throughout France over the cowardly assassination of President Carnot. Telegrams of sympathy are pouring in from all points. The newspapers of all shades of opinion deplore the assassination. Throughout France flags are at half-mast, and public buildings are draped.

MARIE FRANCOIS SADI-CARNOT.

[The above picture is from a heliograph by Dujardin, the heliograph being taken from a photograph by Pierre Petit. The heliograph was presented by Carnot to Leon Phillipe, the French Under Secretary of Agriculture, whose presence at the Irrigation Congress in this city last October will be remembered. The picture was presented by Phillipe to the French colony in this city about six months ago and has been placed in the custody of Vice-Consul Loeb.]

Mme. Carnot, accompanied by three sons, arrived at Lyons this morning. She proceeded immediately to the Prefecture, where the body of the late President reposes in state. The death chamber was cleared, and the family was left alone. They remained a long time in prayer before the bier. Then the widow was led away by the sons, all weeping bitterly. Later the remains were photographed. It is stated that Mme. Carnot does not desire the body embalmed, and wishes it removed immediately from Lyons to this city to lie in state in the chapel of the Elysee Palace.

The remains of the murdered man are clad in a dress suit, and across his breast is the grand cordon of the Legion of Honor, of which, as chief of State, he was grand master. High officers of the President's military household and Sisters of Charity watched the remains throughout the night. The Prefecture is surrounded by troops, and a strong detachment is guarding the building in which Giovani Santo, the assassin, is confined.

On the boulevards scenes of the greatest excitement have been witnessed today. The police had difficulty dispersing the crowds of angry people who assembled at different points calling for vengeance against the murderer and his supposed accomplices. Several Italian flags, displayed out of sympathy with France's loss, draped with crape, were hooted at, and at least one was torn into shreds. In every quarter fierce demonstrations against Italian residents have taken place. Nearly all Italian cafes and restaurants have been closed. But if the feeling against Italians is strong, the sentiment of hatred with which the majority regard the Anarchists is still stronger. Murderer Santo has boldly asserted that he is an Anarchist. It is reported that the police are convinced that the assassination of Carnot is the result of a plot.

The weapon used by the murderer was a long, triangular blade of the stiletto pattern. Upon the blade are engraved the words, "Record of Toledo." The sheath of the weapon is of velvet, with red and black stripes. President Carnot's last words were: "Thank you, my friends, thank you." It is believed that ex-Premier Casimir-Perier, now President of the Chamber of Deputies, has the best chance of succeeding the late President. Challemel Lacour, President of the Senate; Caviagnac, Depuy, Brisson, Constans and Gen. Saussier are also mentioned.

The government will propose to the chamber that Carnot be accorded a national funeral. Santo was born at Motta Visconti, northwest of Pavia, in December, 1873. He is a baker, and was tried in Milan in 1892 for breach of the peace, but was acquitted. Santo delivered Anarchist lectures of the vilest character before going to Switzerland last year. There no longer seems to be much doubt that the assassination was the result of an anarchistic conspiracy to avenge the deaths of Valliant and Emile Henri. Twenty detectives have gone to Gette, where Santo was recently domiciled, to track down his supposed accomplices.

AT LYONS.

Italian Cafes Wrecked by the Mob—The President's Remains.

Associated Press Leased-wire Service.

LYONS, June 25.—(By Atlantic Cable.) The mob this evening set fire to several of the Italian cafes. A commissary of police begged the crowd to respect the affliction of Mme. Carnot, but the rioters replied with shouts of, "We will avenge Carnot."

Were it not for the presence of the overwhelming force of troops stationed in and about the city, there is little doubt that the mob would have attacked the Palace of Justice and wrought vengeance upon the murderer. Mourning emblems are worn by nearly every man, woman and child in the city, and no dwelling seems too poor to display the emblems of grief.

During the day a mob, including a number of members of the various gymnastic societies who had arrived in this city to take part in the fetes, began to gather about the Cafes Casti, Nattosi and Maderni and about the Italian quarter. Another large crowd gathered about the hall where the well-known Italian Harmonic Club meets, and most serious disorder was apprehended. Threats were heard on all sides against Italians and Anarchists. Several of the Italian wineshops were attacked and partly wrecked and the Italian cafes mentioned were stoned and otherwise damaged in spite of the efforts of the police and military. The sidewalks in front of the Italian cafes were strewn with wreckage.

Some of the more hot-headed men proposed an attack upon the Italian quarter and the proposition was received with wild cries of approval and in a moment an enormous mob, at the head of which was carried a French flag, was en route to that part of the city given over to the Italians. Before the police could intervene to prevent, the terrible mob had attacked all shops belonging to the foreigners and sacked them. The proprietors and their families were forced to flee for their lives. Meantime another large band marched through other streets and by threats compelled every Italian who kept a cafe to close his place of business. The crowds in the Rue de la Republique became threatening and refused to obey orders to disperse. It was finally found necessary to command cuirassiers to charge the crowd.

The Associated Press correspondent has been able to obtain the details of the last moments of President Carnot. When the President regained consciousness, after fainting at the Prefecture, he asked for a pen, but when it was placed in his hand he was too weak to write. A little while before he died the President whispered for Col. Chamoine, one of the leading officials of his military household. The colonel approached him, and the dying mand pressed his hand and said: "Je suis touche, bien touche." ("I am wounded, badly wounded.")

The body of M. Carnot was this evening placed on a train that will convey it to Paris. After prayers for the dead had been offered, the casket containing the remains was carried out and placed on a gun-carriage. While this was being done salutes of the artillery were fired, trumpets were sounded and drums were beaten. All civil and military honor was shown the dead. The square in front of the Prefecture was densely thronged, as were all the streets leading to the railway station. Troops and gendarmes kept the route clear.

The procession that followed included all the civil and military authorities of Lyons and a large number of delegations from different cities and towns. Every man along the line of march removed his hat as the body passed by him. The people who had heretofore stood reverent and mute before the nation's martyr, when the body had passed gave vent to their pent-up excitement and rage. Everywhere could be heard cries of "Long live Carnot, and death to his murderer."

Upon the arrival of the cortege at the railway station the casket was tenderly lifted from the carriage and conveyed into a saloon carriage. The remains were attended to by the officers of M. Carnot's military household, who had accompanied him to Lyons. In another carriage were Mme. Carnot and her three sons. A large crowd was assembled about the station and as the train started on its journey for Paris, many signs of deepest emotion were displayed.

The troops are still held in reserve under arms at their barracks. A company of infantry is also held in reserve in a house adjoining the Italian Consulate, to be ready to support the police in case of attack. At the request of the local authorities the Italian Consul has removed the Italian flag from outside the consulate.

As the night advanced the rioting in the city became more general, and it appeared that the mob would take full possession of the cafes in the Guillotierie quarter, where the disturbances were particularly violent. Thousands of men and boys paraded the streets and attacked and sacked every Italian store they came across. Much of the loot obtained by the rioters consisted of liquors, part of which was drunk, while what was not so disposed of was either poured into the streets and set on fire or

[Continued on second page.]

AT IT AGAIN.

Dissatisfied Labor on the Warpath.

The Fight Against Pullman is Already Organized.

A Passenger-train Attacked in Oklahoma Territory.

A Mass-meeting at Lincoln Park, Denver, to Discuss the Tarsney Affair—The Mine Employees in Michigan.

Associated Press Leased-wire Service.

NORTH ENID (Okla.,) June 25.—The trouble at Round Point is getting to be more serious. Last night a mob attacked the south-bound passenger train with a hot fusillade of bullets. More than a hundred shots were fired. Mr. Fossett of Kingfisher, standing on the car platform, had his hat shot off and received scalp-wounds; another passenger was struck in the throat by a bullet. A newspaper man named Johnson was hit in the leg with a heavy charge of buckshot. The deputy marshals did not fire a shot. Marshal Nix says all the power of the Territory will be required to put down the lawlessness.

THEIR CHEERFUL TASK.

CHICAGO, June 25.—At noon tomorrow the American Railway Union will begin its fight against the Pullman Palace Car Company. Vice-President Howard said: "We are going to bankrupt George M. Pullman in a short time. We have shut up his works at Ludlow and St. Louis, and shall be able to close his last door at Wilmington by next week. He will be rendered completely helpless inside of ten days unless he comes to terms."

Attorney Reynolds, speaking today for Mr. Pullman, said:

"The Pullman Company is prepared to stand by its original position in this matter to the end. Personally I have not the least doubt as to what the outcome will be. It will beyond question result in a victory for the unemployed. We have about 750 men working in the shops at Wilmington, Del., where the American Railway Union made an unsuccessful attempt to organize the employees. There are no indications at present that the strikers will be able to draw the men at this point into the fight.

The Pullman Company tonight issued a statement regarding the strike and proposed boycott. After reviewing the situation, and stating that the strikers have already deprived themselves of more than $200,000 in wages, the document concludes with the statement that the boycott is threatened because the company will not agree to submit to arbitration the question as to whether or not it shall operate its shops at Pullman under a scale of wages which would cause a daily loss to them.

Anticipating the boycott against Pullman cars by the American Railway Union, the general managers of all roads which have terminals in Chicago, practically decided today that all Pullman cars will go out with trains or trains will remain in the depots until they can go with their [illegible] Pullman equipment. This decision [illegible] at the general manager's session which was called together in special meeting for the purpose of considering the proposed boycott.

Resolutions were adopted at the meeting condemning the boycott and asserting the intention of the roads represented to act unitedly in resisting the proposed move of the union. Twenty-five hundred railroad men attended a mass-meeting held tonight to consider the Pullman strike. The proposed boycott was heartily indorsed, and speeches by President Debs and others were enthusiastically received. The speakers were emphatic in their condemnation of the Pullman Company, and confident of success.

O, THE WOMEN!

PUNXSUTAWNEY (Pa.,) June 25.—Since the men attacked the trainload of coal and iron police at Adrian last night, the women have put on the warpaint. At Walsten, early today, they massed and charged upon the worktrain, but before any serious damage was done the guards drove them off. At noon Capt. Clark of the coal and iron police in Adrian was pounced upon and beaten by women. Stones were thrown at General Manager Fisher's train last night and both the engineer and fireman were hurt.

DYNAMITE AT NEW HAVEN.

CONNELLSVILLE (Pa.,) June 25.—The striking cokers seriously damaged Bosum Run railroad bridge on the outskirts of New Haven last night with dynamite. The railroad is a branch of the Southwestern Pennsylvania over which coke from the Trotter works is transported.

TOO HARD WORK.

PITTSBURGH, June 25.—The laborers employed in the thirty-five and forty-inch mills of the Homestead Steel Works have struck, and the departments are idle. The men formerly worked in gangs of ten, but lately the number has been reduced to six. The strikers claim that this reduction made the work too hard, and they quit, to force the company to restore the gangs to their former size.

AT ST. LOUIS.

ST. LOUIS, June 25.—The employees of the Pullman carworks in this city struck today.

TWO HUNDRED OUT.

LUDLOW (Ky.,) June 25.—Two hundred employees of the Pullman company struck today in pursuance of orders from Chicago.

EVICTION AT THE PANHANDLE.

PITTSBURGH, June 25.—Two hundred families in the company houses at the Panhandle mines, Paynter's Run, have been evicted. The firm refused to sign the scale.

FIFTEEN HUNDRED IDLE.

IRONWOOD (Mich.,) June 25.—There are 1500 Gogebic Range mine employees idle now, in consequence of the action of the receivers of the Colby mine in closing that property this morning. A mass of non-union miners from the first district opposed the strike, which has been called for Tuesday afternoon. They want to

The Times — LOS ANGELES — Midsummer Number.

XIVth YEAR.—36 PAGES. THURSDAY MORNING, AUGUST 15, 1895.—TRIPLE SHEET. PER WEEK, 20c. PER MONTH 85c. FIVE CENTS

SOUTHERN CALIFORNIA IN SUMMER.

THE LAND WE LIVE IN.

TOO many non-residents are unfamiliar with our Southern California summers. Some of those who have passed a winter in this section, and enjoyed it, make the mistake of jumping at the conclusion, in view of the sunny atmosphere of December, and the pleasant temperature of that season, that if the winters are so warm and balmy, the sumers must certainly be hot and sultry. They picture long, unclouded summer days, when the land is scorched and dry, and the whole region lies cradled in heat, burning in the continuous glare of a hot and unbroken sunshine.

But this is a mere fiction of the imagination. The term semi-tropical, as applied to California, is in fact incorrect; it has certainly been a misleading term, for it by no means implies the existence of extreme heat; it denotes, rather, the absence of cold—a year without its winter.

The Times proposes to present to non-resident readers, who are naturally desirious of learning the truth about Southern California, a simple picture of her summer temperature and aspect. We will describe as well as we may the peculiar characteristics of our summer months, which in no other land can be fully duplicated.

One great charm of Southern California's summer is her sea-breeze, born of the ocean and the desert, moving gently across the land. Behind the mighty bulwark of the mountains which guard the coast valleys and plains lies the great desert region. Here the air is hot and the temeparture is high. "And here," as is well spoken by T. S. Van Dyke, "it is easy to see whence comes the sea-breeze, the great glory of the California summer. It is passing us here, a gentle breeze of six or eight miles an hour. It is flowing over this great ridge directly into the immense basin of the Colorado Desert, 6000 feet deep, where the temperature is probably 120 deg., and perhaps higher. For many leagues on either side of us this current is thus flowing at the same speed, and is probably half a mile or more in depth.—About sundown, when the air over the desert cools and descends, the current will change and come the other way and flood these western slopes with an air as pure as that of the Sahara and nearly as dry. The air, heated on the western slopes by the sun, would, by rising, produce considerable suction, which could be filled only from the sea, but that alone would not make the sea-breeze as dry as it is. The principal suction is caused by the rising of heated air from the great desert. This cannot flow over eastward, because a still greater volume, equally hot, is rising from the fiery furnace of Arizona, nor on the north, for there lies the great desert of the Mojave. . . . The greater part must flow over in a high stratum upon the west, that being the coolest place surrounding it. It soon reaches the ocean, and once over that, its course is easy to determine. It is quickly cooled off and descends, to be carried back again by the suction produced by the air rising from the desert and on the western slopes of the country. Hence, instead of being a wind born of the sea, the sea-breeze is here a mere undertow, a vast returning wave of air, most of which, in its circuit, reaches the desert and mingles with its dry breath. All over Southern Califonia the conditions of this breeze are about the same. . . . Hence, these deserts, which at first seem to be a disadvantage to the land, are the great conditions of its climate, and are of far more value than if they were like the prairies of Illinois."

How this delightful, continuous breeze fans the land and filters the air into delicious coolness! The sultriness of the all-pervading sun flees before it. There is no prostrating heat, no heavy moisture in the air to saturate us with discomfort. The dry desert currents as they seek the ocean absorb all of that and help to establish the rare climatic conditions of Southern California's summer.

And these conditions not only bring us comfort but they bring us health. In the warmest days of summer one finds a pleasant temperature in the shade. These cooling breezes search us out there and fan us. The air is rarely pulseless, and it seems to possess an element of coolness which, when out of the immediate presence of the sun's rays, is always perceptible. The average summer-day temperature is from 60 to 80 deg. It is rarely that the thermometer climbs to the nineties in the coast regions, but when it does, owing to the dryness of the atmosphere, the heat has little of the oppressiveness which belongs to such temperature in more humid regions.

The uninterrupted procession of bright days is never wearying. The dry summer atmosphere is bracing. With the cool, golden dawns you awake with fresh strength, for the night air is like a tonic. The heat of the day lies mostly in the heat of its noon. But even then you miss the element of sultriness common to more easterly climes, and, unless in direct contact with the sun's rays, you are not disposed to complain of discomfort.

Soon after noon fresh breezes begin to stir. There is something delicious in their breath. You feel as if they had lips drawing out everything tending to sultriness in the air. They are at home with the sunbeams and mingle with them to temper their heat. The whole land seems to breathe a sigh of content as they blow softly o'er it, and there is a sense of fresh joyousness in nature. Every leaf is astir as if clapping its small hands in delight. Every flower exhales greater fragrance, and nods upon its stalk as if a new joy were born. The veranda is delightful and full of airy refreshment. You do not breathe in heat, but coolness. You need not wait for the sun to sink lower in the west before taking your carriage drive, for the onward motion stirs a current of cool air that brings you perfect satisfaction. It may be that it is midsummer, the season when the cicada's song at the East seems like the sizzle of hot flame, but to judge by your feelings you would dream that it were a dewy morning in June, that season of enchantment when the world along the Atlantic borders seems fairest and fullest of beauty.

And then when the summer night drops down, and the curled silver leaf of the new moon is hung from the clear azure of the west, that delicious breeze, born of land and sea, that "great undertow" of pure air, cool and dry, floods everything, and makes the perfection of California's summer days and nights.

Oh, the comfort of it all! You may have lived a score or two of years in Southern California, but you never forget to welcome this delightful visitant, nor to be thankful for the balmy and delicious nights that follow the warmest days. And when you seek your night's rest, with windows all open to admit the fragrant air, you will want at least one blanket through the summer months, and then how you can sleep! There is refreshment and strength in every breath you draw. Nature is like a great alembic filled with new wine which the night distills. If you chance to wake at midnight, you may hear the note of the mocking-bird in the tree near your window, for he breaks forth into song at all hours for the very gladness of being. And sometimes the old chanticleer in your barnyard will arouse you by his cheerful crow, as if his life were too full of content and comfort for him to keep silent until the morning.

Another feature of the Southern California summer, aside from its equable temperature, is its uniform calm—the almost entire absence of strong winds. California does not breed cyclones. She does not beget the thunderstorm or tempest. She has no dangerous winds at any season. In summer the sea breeze blows often at the rate of eight or ten miles an hour, just enough to bring comfort without setting the dust awhirr. Sometimes along our high mountain tops we see the lightning's play and hear the reverberations of the distant thunder. These thunderstorms gather upon the deserts, and we upon the coast borders get the merest edge of these summer showers as they are lifted up over the high mountain barriers which guard this coast region and shut it off from the desert heat.

Aside from these rare visitations, our summers are absolutely rainless; for six or seven months no rain falls, but clear skies, a pleasant and equable temperature, and a breeze-stirred calm are the delightful features of our summer months.

Occasionally we have fogs, but not like those which breed the murky and sultry atmosphere on the Atlantic Coast. These fogs have been described as "a bank or cloud arising from the sea in peculiar conditions of the respective temperatures of the air and water. The bank is about one thousand feet thick, lies out on the water all day, and moves in at evening—when it comes in at all, for often it does not come in. Sometimes it comes before sundown, generally a little after. It rolls out again soon after sunrise. . . . The elevation of the lower edge of this bank varies from sea level to 1200 feet, though sometimes it is much higher. When it is high the lower levels are dry all night, and it appears like a dry, cloudy night, but the hills that reach into it will have their chaparral wet with it."

You may stand upon the high elevations and watch this fog roll outward, like a vast, tossing, billowy ocean. The sun shines clearly upon the upper heights while yet the lower world is buried. Soon, like mighty promontories, the lower hills rise above the cloud-like mass, then appear long lines like ocean waterways, through which may sometimes be caught the shimmer of green valleys, and then with a swift, seaward rush, the great white sea sweeps outward, and soon the whole land is flooded with sunlight. Then the day shines bright through all its remaining hours. This fog mass, a thousand feet in depth, has sucked in all the miasma lurking in the air, washed the heavens free of dust, and left the day divinely calm and bright.

From the mountain summits above can be seen vast canyon chasms lying between tall spurs, their cool green levels thousands of feet below the commanding heights where the electric car is gliding. Below lies a world which has grown ghost-like in the moonlight. A silver sea is at your feet, in whose vast depths are immersed towns and cities, the lower hills, the wide stretch of vineyards and orchards, the world of men, and even earth's greatest ocean. But you are under the stars, with the still glory of the summer night about you.

You are nearer the silent blue of heaven, where summer in Southern California has undreamed-of charms. The coniferous forests are near, and the "Garden of the Gods" throws wide open its rocky doors for you to behold its wonders. A thousand figures in stone fill this mountain garden, and everywhere hold the eyes, but after all you rejoice most of all in the delicious atmosphere which you breathe, and the balm and refreshing coolness which environ you.

"But tell us something of the general aspect of the country in summer," says the impatient reader. "Without any rain for six months it must be bare and brown, dusty and forbidding. What have you to relieve the eye or to vary the dull monotony of the scene?"

These inquiries can perhaps best be answered by giving a pen-picture of the scene as viewed from the higher ridges of the Sierra Madre, 3500 feet above sea level.

The view is a typical one, and if the reader can behold it in fancy he may comprehend the general appearance which Southern California presents in summer throughout her whole extent. It is a picture to hold the eye and to fill the mind with wonder.

Broad valleys stretch out into vast, dim distances, mountain-guarded, sea-bordered and color-flecked. It is six months since rain has fallen, with the exception of a few light showers. In the great valleys the fields are turning brown. The pastures look bare. The harvest fields are tawny. The great San Gabriel Valley looks like a wide checker-board, marked by lines of green. There are patches of the brightest emerald, where perhaps the fifth or sixth crop of alfalfa is growing, affording the most luscious feed for cattle. There are great orchards of apricots, prunes and plums, of peaches and almonds and walnuts, of nectarines and pears, and other fruits. Here, too, are orange and lemon groves, and fig trees dotting the land with beauty and lifting the cool emerald of their leaves above the plains. There are fields of ripening corn, and vegetable gardens, and vast vineyards which give a June face to the landscape. Extensive lines of eucalypti and pepper stretch out in every direction, and the broad-leafed fan-palm casts its cool shadows upon the ground. The long water-courses, showing their white sands, thread their ways between banks lined with sycamores and willows. There are low, moist lands where there are thick jungles of wild bloom, and the deep canyons below you are a sea of green. From this height you cannot see the gardens, full of fragrant blossoming, which everywhere surround the valley homes. The rose bushes are full of bloom and climb to the very housetops. Great hedges of geranium glow with color like the sunset. There are banks of lilies, and the white snow of the elder, which here becomes a tree in stature.

Descend, and you will find beautiful homes steeped in the fragrance of the blossoming honey-suckle, or in the purple bloom of the wisteria. You may see century-old oaks casting beyond their vast circumference cool, thick shadows upon the warm earth.

And here the magnolia blossoms, and the rubber tree spreads its polished leaves to the sun. The acacia shimmers in the sunlight, the banana droops its long, pointed leaves, the aloe is here, and the pampas grass shows its swaying spines upon the plain. The dull browns of the pastures and hillsides only serve to vary the picture, and with all this greenness intermingled, they are not forbidding.

The soil is rich and deep, and where irrigation is used the land is kept looking green and summery throughout the year. Go into the towns and cities and you will find everywhere velvet lawns and gardens that know no end of blossoming. You will meet with the faces of hundreds of new flowers. Such as you knew at your old home you will scarcely recognize here. You will think of your geranium that you nursed in its little pot in the south window, and find it here a giant with its thick arms thrown about the very apex of the roof and with the birds building their nests amid its branches.

Though it does not rain in summer, every month of the year has its harvest. The farmer may even gather his strawberries every month, dig his potatoes in December, and partake of fresh fruits of one kind or another every day in the year.

Another charm of the summer is that you are never fearful that a storm will interfere with your plans for work or pleasure. Sunshine is your birthright in Southern California through the long summer, and you never weary of it. The sky is so intensley blue—so "deeply, darkly, beautifully blue"—that there is a charm and glory about it that appeal to your higher nature. It is never brazen, as if it were out of temper and were meditating you harm. It is flooded with cheerfulness and soft airs and the glamor of light and beauty; it is infinite in depth, and your soul expands in the presence of its immensity.

The summer in Southern California is also full of bird life. The valley

Midwinter Number.

The Times

LOS ANGELES

[THREE SHEETS—WITH COVER.]

Vth YEAR. [75 CENTS PER MONTH, OR 2½ CENTS A COPY.] WEDNESDAY MORNING, JANUARY 1, 1896.—40 PAGES. PRICE TEN CENTS.

LOS ANGELES OF TO-DAY.

LOOKING SOUTHWEST.

LOOKING SOUTHEAST.

BIRD'S-EYE VIEWS OF LOS ANGELES FROM COURTHOUSE TOWER.

NATURE must have been in her most genial mood when she molded the spot where Los Angeles now stands, and perfected its environment. Her endeavor must have been to give a fit setting to the city of the future, which, with prophetic eye, she saw, down the dim vistas of Time, standing, as it stands today, a city of beautiful homes, of inviting loveliness, and of unlimited possibilities.

There is probably no city in the United States that is better known throughout the country as a desirable place of residence than is Los Angeles of today, with its enticing charms of climate, its wonderful business activity, its modern residences of constantly varying architectural design, set, each in its delightful garden of bloom and fragrance, amid nodding palm and pepper, with clinging vines and flowering bush, and generous expanse of greensward, fresh in December as in June, and as fragrant at the old year's close as is the sweet Maytime of an eastern summer.

The idyllic charms of her climate and of her natural surroundings, Los Angeles has, with rare wisdom, been able to emphasize. The stranger coming here is first attracted by the marvelous charm of climatic beauty. Such skies as are above us in December, day succeeding day, flooded with golden sunshine, every leaf glinting with its sheen, every flower and blade of grass luminous with its mellow fullness, the warm color stealing into the face of every blossom and the languorous air breathing its perfume about him, the newcomer is at once intoxicated with the place, and, if circumstanced so that he may, he promptly begins to look about him to find a location for a home. As he begins to study the city, the desire to become one with us grows upon him, for culture, wealth and refinement have supplemented nature, and have built along the lines of modern advancement, every day pushing farther and farther into the background the primitive past, with its sleepy old Spanish regime, and transforming with modern life everything that is a part of the life of the Los Angeles of today. Everything that is about and within us has changed, excepting the soil beneath our feet and the all-pervading sunshine. Even the hills that environ the city have put on new faces. These beautiful slopes of the Sierra Madre foothills have, to some extent, been planted with trees. Forests of eucalypti are already beginning to show their green fronts where once the hills were bare. Other hills are home-crowned, these elevations offering the most beautiful sites for residences that can be found anywhere in the world.

The perspective is unparalleled in its charm.

Climb, for instance, the long and beautiful slope of Angeleno Heights. Eighteen years ago it was a bare, solitary elevation, covered with a rich growth of wild mustard or rank weeds and grasses. Not a home was there. The heights were outside the city limits, and people then had not begun to dream of the development that was coming. Sometimes a lover of the beautiful would climb the slope that he might enjoy the wide prospect that was afforded him from the summit, and look away over the wide, unpeopled intervale of low, rolling hills and vast extent of valley to the sea, the silver of whose surf he could easily discern along the distant line of shore, and beyond that, to the blue crest of Catalina, lying upon the ocean's breast forty miles away. It was a picture to fill the eye and thrill the hearts of Nature's lovers, yet very few people enjoyed it in those days, or thought of climbing that waste of hill for such purpose. But today Los Angeles occupies those heights, and upon them some of her most beautiful residences may be found, while a broad network of streets covers them, and to the rear of them the electric car rushes, and to the front the cable climbs the hill of Temple street; new homes are all along its line, schoolhouses and churches and business blocks lining the way and creeping up the slopes, until now, looking from the heights, humanity confronts the beholder everywhere, and the solitary place is not there, but is far outside its old landmarks.

So, too, all the western hills have been built up within this period. The squirrel and the gopher have retired and given place to happy children; the schoolhouse is in the field where the wild oats grew; the church is where the yellow mustard waved, and the college stands on what a few years ago was virgin pasture land for cattle.

Over the hills in all directions climbs the cable or the electric car, and where it goes the home has been swift to follow. The Westlake Park region, the home of the quail and the gopher a few years since, is now one of the loveliest residence portions of Los Angeles. A decade ago and the throb of the city's life was hardly felt there. But today the beautiful lake reflects not only the outlines of the hills and the trees, but palatial homes without number. The stir and movement of the city's life is here: the long lines of shining track glitter for miles in the sun, and the pulse of the business center throbs along the way, which is no longer remote from the city's heart.

Eighteen years ago and we occasionally heard Pico Heights spoken of in connection with the charm of its natural surroundings. But it lay "out in the country" and wore a rural aspect, and formed no portion of the city's life. But today it is thickly peopled, and Los Angeles has thrust out her busy streets into its very heart, and every few moments the electric car whizzes past us with its thronging freight of humanity coming and going, for the city is there upon those heights, with all of its modern life and progress, as it is upon Boyle Heights also, where scarce two decades ago Nature brooded in quiet reverie, and lay drowned in the unbroken sunshine.

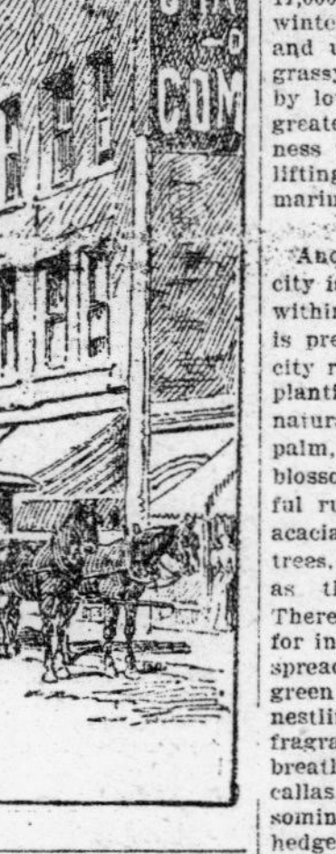

BROADWAY FROM FIFTH STREET.

The expansion of the city is simply marvelous, and the progressive life of the whole land is represented here. It is no mad craze that is behind our growth, but men have come here full of faith in our future, determined to make of this section the most desirable place for homes that the world offers. It is young, progressive American life that is with us, and the best that the country has to give of wealth and culture and progress she has poured in upon us. We have somewhat of Boston's culture, New York's business activity, New England's love of education, Chicago's push and vim, the broadness of the Great West, and the determination and pride which spring from all of these, and from which combination greatness is sure to be evolved.

Los Angeles is no longer content to sit in the valley where she was planted by her founders. The Los Angeles of today, with her population of more than eighty thousand, stands with head erect, queen of the hills no less than of the valley, looking away to the sea and the mountains, enveloped everywhere in a nineteenth-century atmosphere and ready to challenge the world in the race of progress. In the whole country you will find no city with a larger proportion of beautiful homes, no city of its size with more churches and educational institutions, or with better facilities for advancement than Los Angeles. A few months' stay here develops an unquestioning faith in her future which kindles the spirit of enterprise and makes men eager to work for her upbuilding. Men love to work where there is the promise of reward and a sure foundation upon which to rear the structures of their hopes, and here they work without question or doubt, and watch with pleased eyes the gradual evolution of a city which is almost without its peer in the history of the country.

The new Los Angeles—the Los Angeles of today—in which her people take so much pride, is hardly more than a decade and a half old. It is almost entirely within this period that the old life has been gradually slipping away, gliding like a swift-moving panorama from before our eyes. Within the past decade the most rapid changes have transpired, and Los Angeles has come into the fullest touch with the world. A cosmopolitan city, there is nothing provincial in its life, and it is now without the slightest touch of the frontier element. You can give your children as good an education here, as far as our public schools are concerned, as in Boston. The best dramatic talent of the country seeks us here; much of our pulpit talent is of a high order, and a better regulated public library can nowhere be found than that of which Los Angeles boasts.

With the vanishing of the old adobe comes to us the full tide of modern thought and progress. Art has its home with us, and there are those among its devotees whose names may yet become household words throughout the whole land. Music has her gifted representatives, and literature her followers whose names are familiar to almost every fireside in America. Modern architecture is here molding and building our homes, answering all the demands of wealth, refinement and ease, adding beauty to utility, blending the practical with the ideal as they could nowhere else be blended. For what home is complete without its setting, and where can the natural environment be made so perfect as in this land of soft airs and almost unfailing sunshine, where December tells the story of June, and the bees and the butterflies all hum the same story; where Nature sings her winter songs in rippling brooks or in the fuller anthem of the rolling river; where she crowns our winter hills with golden poppies, and our gardens with lilies and roses; where, at the opening of the year, we may breathe the breath of the heliotrope, and the fragrance of the orange is wafted to us, and the voice of the robin and the mockingbird fills our ears, and the lark rises in gladness and paves a pathway of song to the skies, and the butterfly's wings are a-flutter, and the bees wake to musical murmurings, and the caterpillar crawls lazily in the sun. Where plants and trees leap into growth and in a little season envelop every new home in pleasant shade and the fragrance of abundant blossoming.

All this has been considered, and it has influenced men of culture and home-seekers from all sections of the country, and, indeed, from all parts of the world, to come hither and help us build the Los Angeles of today, which, aside from the climate and the soil, has no resemblance to the Los Angeles of two decades ago. Gone are the walls of sun-dried bricks and the red-tiled roofs, and in their place stands the modern mansion, complete in all the details of architectural skill. Vanished are the cobble-stone pavements and the muddy streets; they have given place to the well-paved road and the pavements of artificial stone. The old *carreta* has been supplanted by the cable and electric car, and even the gaslight has vanished, and for it we have substituted the clear blaze of the electric light. Our parks have been improved and beautified, and there is an atmosphere of cleanliness about the residence portion of the city that is inviting and assuring to the home-seeker.

On every side of the city is beauty. The majestic mountain ranges, with their higher snow-capped peaks rising 11,000 feet into the clear azure of our winter skies, guard us upon one hand, and upon the other, across the level grassy plains, broken here and there by low, billowy hills, lies the world's greatest ocean, giving its touch of coolness to our summer atmosphere, and lifting through all the winter its marine-blue face toward the skies.

Another attractive feature of the city is the vast amount of tree growth within its limits. Modern Los Angeles is pre-eminently a garden city, and a city rich in its wealth of trees. Tree-planting follows home-building as naturally as day succeeds night. The palm, the orange and the pepper, the blossoming magnolia and the beautiful rubber and umbrella trees, the acacia, together with numerous other trees, are planted for shade, as well as the rapidly-growing eucalyptus. There are streets, like Adams street, for instance, that are overarched with spreading boughs, and back, across the green lawns, are the beautiful homes nestling in green vines, fanned by fragrant winds that have caught the breath of hundreds of roses and odorous callas, and purple heliotrope and blossoming pinks and violets. There are hedges of scarlet geraniums, and banks of sweet alyssum, and great walls of climbing fuchsias, that glow like a sunset cloud. Perhaps you hear the tinkle of a fountain and look into a clean pool to find the water lilies looking into the winter's face, and casting smiling glances at the gay poinsetta. What wonder that life in such portions of the city is like a sweet idyl set to the harmony of color and fragrance? The birds twitter amid the thick vines, the flies buzz softly in the sunshine, and Nature has everywhere a thousand hints of gladness. She is in love with the Los Angeles of today, and looks at her with complacent eyes, as if she would say, "Go on in your work of improvement and I will do my part. Plant your flowers and your trees and I will do my best to make them thrive. You shall have my most delightful airs and my mellowest sunshine, for I mean that here the race shall attain to its ideal homes, which are the highest means of its advancement. Never in all the world were such homes as you may have here, nor such beauty of bloom and fragrance."

As if we heard such a voice, the beautiful homes multiply, and the city is beginning to take pride in what it has accomplished in home-building, and more frequently we see reared the costly and elegant mansions, in the midst of ample grounds that afford abundant space for trees and flowers.

We take pride, too, in the way in which our business is housed. Vanished are nearly all the rude, one-story structures that ten years ago sheltered a large population of the business of Los Angeles. Trade is becoming aristocratic and is adopting all modern ways and methods. The metropolitan structure is in demand, and five and six-story buildings, solidly built of brick or stone, are naturally slipping into the business sections, and there are whole blocks upon our business streets that present their imposing fronts, and where behind their high walls business goes on and on.

Another attractive feature of Los Angeles is the number of delightful resorts which are close at her door. The old Los Angeles had little to offer in this line save what Nature afforded. But public and private enterprise has wrought in many directions. It has harnessed the lightning, and now, like a swift steed, it not only bears us along the valleys, but to the summits of some of our high mountain peaks. The electric car is at home with us in the upper air, 5000 feet above sea-level. Here the most inviting of hostelries have been built, and the world-worn traveler finds rest and fresh delight. He may breathe the mountain air and the balsamic atmosphere of piney woods. He may enjoy the quiet and soothing influence of Nature, with the world of busy activities at his feet. Towns and cities are below him, and the busy marts of trade are full in view, but not a sound from them all disturbs him. Nature nurses him and he is at rest in her lap.

Or, if he likes more primitive quarters, let the patient donkey be brought, and up over the mountain's sides, and athwart its mighty shoulders he may ride to Wilson's Peak, where the white tents beckon him, and the mockingbird often breaks out at midnight into the fullness of song. And here the cedars and the pines grow tall and stately, and you may look out over deep-mouthed canyons and a wilderness of peaks on one hand, and see God's world about you, while man's world lies below.

Or, if you do not care for the mountains, Los Angeles will send you by rail to the seashore, where the comforts of the modern hotel will greet you, and all the delights which the seaside affords. And over the channel lies Catalina, like an emerald upon the deep.

MAIN STREET, LOOKING EAST, SHOWING POSTOFFICE IN FOREGROUND.

CORNER FIRST AND SPRING STREETS.

The Los Angeles Times

Regular Edition—12 Pages

XVth YEAR. [75 CENTS PER MONTH; OR 2½ CENTS A COPY.] WEDNESDAY MORNING, NOVEMBER 4, 1896. PRICE 3 CENTS ON RAILWAY TRAINS ON OCEAN STEAMERS 5c

McKINLEY AND HOBART WIN.

A Magnificent Victory for the Republican Ticket and the National Honor.

New York Puts Up a Wonderful Majority of Three Hundred Thousand, and Illinois is Well in Front.

GREAT GAINS MADE IN SOUTHERN AND WESTERN STATES.

Maryland, West Virginia and Tennessee March Proudly in Line—New England is Solid and Shows a Remarkable Increase of Strength Over the Last Election—A Majority of the Electoral Vote Certain at an Early Hour, with Ultimate Prospects of a Total of Three Hundred and Twenty-six—Congress Will not Be Dominated by Silver if Appearances Can Be Trusted—How the Candidates Passed the Day—Democrats Greatly Disappointed by the Returns.

(BY ASSOCIATED PRESS WIRE.)

The Result.

FOR M'KINLEY.	Votes.	FOR BRYAN.	Votes.
CONNECTICUT	6	ALABAMA	11
DELAWARE	3	ARKANSAS	8
ILLINOIS	24	COLORADO	4
INDIANA	15	FLORIDA	4
IOWA	13	GEORGIA	13
KENTUCKY	13	IDAHO	3
MAINE	6	KANSAS	10
MARYLAND	8	LOUISIANA	8
MASSACHUSETTS	15	MISSISSIPPI	9
MICHIGAN	14	MONTANA	3
MINNESOTA	9	NEVADA	3
NEBRASKA	8	S. CAROLINA	9
N. HAMPSHIRE	4	TEXAS	15
NEW JERSEY	10	UTAH	3
NEW YORK	36		
NORTH DAKOTA	3		
OHIO	23		
OREGON	4		
PENNSYLVANIA	32		
RHODE ISLAND	4		
SOUTH DAKOTA	4		
VERMONT	4		
WEST VIRGINIA	6		
WISCONSIN	12		
Total	276	Total	103

Undecided States.

CALIFORNIA	Votes	9
MISSOURI	"	17
NORTH CAROLINA	"	11
TENNESSEE	"	12
VIRGINIA	"	12
WASHINGTON	"	4
WYOMING	"	3

NEW YORK, Nov. 3.—At 8 o'clock Gen. Osborne, secretary of the Republican National Committee, gave out the following bulletin:

"Reports show that we have carried Maryland and West Virginia. New York gives us about 300,000 majority. Iowa will probably give 80,000 plurality. Maryland, 10,000; Tennessee, 20,000; Massachusetts, 100,000. Illinois will give a majority. We are confident of Kentucky. McKinley and Hobart are elected without any doubt."

M'KINLEY CONGRATULATED.

Garret A. Hobart Sends a Splendid Message to the Leader.

(BY ASSOCIATED PRESS WIRE.)

CANTON, Nov. 3.—At 9 o'clock Maj. McKinley received a telegram of congratulation from his associate on the national ticket as follows:

"Congratulations with all my heart on the glorious achievement under your magnificent leadership. The manhood of the republic has asserted itself, and the nation's honor and integrity will never again be assailed by the same forces, Mrs. Hobart joins me in congratulation.

(Signed) "GARRET A. HOBART."

WE HAVE 'EM.

Iowa, Indiana, Kentucky, Minnesota and Illinois are Safe.

CHICAGO, Nov. 3.—At 8 o'clock Vice-chairman Payne of the Republican National Committee, made the following announcement, which he also wired to Mr. Hanna: "We have Chicago by about 60,000. Returns from Iowa, Indiana, Kentucky, and Minnesota indicate that those States are safe for McKinley."

THE ELECTORAL VOTE.

Two Hundred and Eighty-four Sure for McKinley.

(BY ASSOCIATED PRESS WIRE.)

WASHINGTON, Nov. 3.—At 11 o'clock sufficient returns had been received at the Republican Congress headquarters to show that McKinley had received 284 electoral votes, and Bryan 69 votes, while 94 were in doubt, some through a question as to what the returns indicate, and others from lack of definite returns. The States voting for McKinley are:

Connecticut	6
Delaware	3
Illinois	24
Indiana	15
Iowa	13
Kentucky	13
Maine	6
Maryland	8
Massachusetts	15
Michigan	14
Minnesota	9
Nebraska	8
New Hampshire	4
New Jersey	10
New York	36
North Dakota	3
Ohio	23
Pennsylvania	32
Rhode Island	4
South Dakota	4
Tennessee	12
Vermont	4
West Virginia	6
Wisconsin	12

The States for Bryan:

Alabama	11
Arkansas	8
Colorado	4
Florida	4
Georgia	13
Idaho	3
Louisiana	8
Mississippi	9
South Carolina	9

In doubt or returns indefinite:

California	9
Kansas	10
Missouri	17
Montana	3
Nevada	3
North Carolina	11
Oregon	4
Texas	15
Utah	3
Virginia	12
Washington	6
Wyoming	3

KENTUCKY'S SPLENDID WORK.

LEXINGTON (Ky.,) Nov. 3.—Later news from the State indicates that McKinley will carry the State by a much greater majority than Bradley carried it in 1895 for Governor. The State will probably give McKinley 25,000 or 30,000.

The result is a great surprise to the free-silver leaders, and the size of the result is a surprise to the sound-money men. Not much news has been heard from the western part of the State where free-silver is strongest, but the increased Republican majorities in the central and eastern portion puts the State beyond question into the sound-money column.

THE DEMOCRATS IN HIDING.

They Lock the Doors on the Republican Landslide—The "Poppies."

WASHINGTON, Nov. 3.—Chairman Faulkner of the Democratic Congress Committee, Senator Gorman and a few other notables are locked in Democratic headquarters receiving the news. They refuse admittance to all, including the newspaper men.

Senator Butler, chairman of the Populist Committee is also receiving the returns behind closed doors. The Republicans are bulleting the returns at Republican Congressional headquarters, and are keeping open house. Chairman Babcock claims a McKinley landslide.

THE MAN AND THE ELEPHANT.

G. O. P. (in background:) "Say, Samue', I didn't do a ting to that platform, did I?"

THEY WERE SURPRISED.

CHICAGO, Nov. 3.—Chairman Jones and other members of the Democratic Executive Committee, including Committeeman Johnson of Kansas and Campau of Michigan, received returns in Chairman Jones's office, where an Associated Press wire had been run. Chairman Washburn of the Populist National Committee was also present, as were also Senators Teller of Colorado and Tillman of South Carolina.

The first returns received at Democratic national headquarters were from Rutland, Kan., and gave a vote of 2111 for Bryan and 71 for McKinley.

The early returns from the eastern States showed Republican gains in about every instance. But little interest, however, was manifested in the returns admittedly Republican. The first surprise came from Baltimore, which showed a big majority for McKinley, indicating that the State had gone Republican. Every report from the Middle and Western States was eagerly watched for, and much gratification was expressed at the first report from Michigan. This was from Gratiot county, giving Bryan 800 plurality. This county gave Harrison a plurality of 1376 in 1892.

"We have no reason to lose heart," said Chairman Jones after reading returns from New York and other eastern States. "All this early stuff is what we have been expecting."

The first really bad news began to come in about 7:30 o'clock in the returns from States south of the "line." Early returns from both Tennessee and Kentucky showed large Republican gains, as did the first returns from Illinois outside of Cook county. Two precincts in Bloomington, the home of Vice-President Stevenson, gave McKinley 200 plurality. The returns from Michigan, however, were more encouraging. At 8:30 p.m., Chairman Campau claimed that State by 25,000.

At 9 p.m. Chairman Campau of the Campaign Committee expressed great confidence with the result. Returns from Ohio, Michigan and Indiana look very well for us, said he, especially State Committee, claimed the State of from the two former States. The only thing we are surprised at so far are the returns from Illinois, outside of Cook county. These seem to indicate that the State has gone for McKinley. The returns from Baltimore look rather bad, but we expected early returns to be unfavorable.

"I have seen no unfavorable reports from any State that we have ever claimed, except from Kentucky," said Chairman Jones at 11 o'clock. "The reports from that State indicate a larger defalcation than we had anticipated, but we do not concede that State by any means. We can lose Kentucky and will then have enough electoral votes to win."

At 11 p.m. Chairman Jones received a message from State Chairman Martin, stating that Indiana was absolutely certain for Bryan. Private telegrams from Michigan indicate large Democratic gains and the Democratic Committee based their hopes of Bryan's election upon the results in these two States.

BILLY BOY'S STATE.

A Majority of Over Seven Thousand for McKinley.

(BY ASSOCIATED PRESS WIRE.)

LINCOLN, Nov. 3.—At 10 o'clock Chairman Post of the Republican Nebraska for McKinley by a majority of from 7000 to 8000.

"We have," said he, "received very scattering returns, and it is impossible to give anything like accurate figures. Complete returns have been received from only 85 precincts in the State and we have neither footed up totals or made comparisons in them. The returns, however, indicate gains sufficient to warrant the claims made."

Judge Post said the principal gains were in the country precincts.

Telegrams to Bryan say that Saline county is conceded to Bryan by the Republicans by a majority of 300; that Crete gives Bryan 337 to 336 for McKinley; Grant, Bryan 247, McKinley 290; Lexington, Bryan 180, McKinley 200; Snyder, Bryan 121, McKinley 90; Springfield, Bryan 120, McKinley 65.

MEAGER BUT SATISFACTORY

OMAHA, Nov. 3.—At midnight returns from Nebraska precincts are still very meager, but indicate that McKinley has carried Nebraska. Eighty-seven precincts in Nebraska outside of Omaha give McKinley 10,476, Bryan 9080; in 1892, Republicans, 9714; Democrats, 7665. Not only does the count seem to be retarded by slow counting, but the total vote polled is much heavier than two years ago.

STILL HOPING.

LINCOLN (Neb.,) Nov. 3.—Bryan's intimate friends report at midnight that he did not consider the case as definitely lost, but on the contrary he considered that there was still ground for hope of his success. He had expected that the first returns, being from the larger cities, would be against him. He left orders that the principal bulletins be sent to his rooms, and he read them there, manifesting especial interest in reports from Nebraska.

In case of the verification of the report of his defeat, it is reported to be Bryan's intention to issue an address urging the maintenance of the silver cause as the paramount issue for the next campaign.

At 12 o'clock the correspondents at the Bryan house awaiting reports were served with lunch, and at 12:30 o'clock the library was closed and no more bulletins were received. Bryan was asleep, and no one was allowed to see him.

M'KINLEY A WINNER.

PARIS, Nov. 3.—The French newspapers are devoting much space to the Presidential election in the United States. The Gaulois remarks in the financial world McKinley's success is no longer doubted, but "we Europeans expect nothing from either candidate."

NEW YORK SIGHTSEERS.

The Tin-horn Fiend Collapsed When McKinley Gained.

(BY ASSOCIATED PRESS WIRE.)

NEW YORK, Nov 3.—There were little squads of sight-seers in Printing House Square all day long, looking at the elaborate preparations making by the newspapers for the display of the returns. Shortly after 5 o'clock the crowd began to gather, however, and by 6 o'clock the people were massed all the way from the cable tracks in Park Row to the eastern end of the City Hall. It was a noisy, but good-humored crowd, and the majority was evidently for Bryan, as was shown by the applause when portraits of the candidates were thrown on the screens.

Bryan was rapturously cheered, while Maj. McKinley's picture scarcely evoked a sound. The tin-horn fiends were largely in evidence, but the people who had made early purchases of horns were evidently Bryanites, for at 7 o'clock, when the tide was strong for McKinley, hardly a horn was heard.

OVER A MILLION PLURALITY.

CLEVELAND (O.,) Nov. 3.—Chairman Hanna says McKinley will have over a million plurality on the popular vote.

A JOY FOREVER.

McKinley and Hobart Will Tame the Tammany Tiger.

(BY ASSOCIATED PRESS WIRE.)

NEW YORK, Nov. 3.—McKinley and Hobart carried the city, and the news at midnight, which told how the votes had been cast in the various Assembly districts called out many expressions of delight.

When the results were so far known as to announce that Black, Republican candidate for Governor, had run behind his electoral ticket about 9000, which idicates his having about one-half the plurality given McKinley, expressions of surprise could be heard.

But such a result was naturally to be expected on account of many Democrats voting the Republican national ticket and refusing to vote the State ticket. Still more comment was made on the Lieutenant-Governor, which pointed to his having about 3000 plurality.

General results in the city were known early. All the streets of the city and squares where unique devices were employed by the newspapers were thronged, and this concourse kept up a continual din. In the early hours the confusion could have been understood to havet been intended for any candidate, city, State or national. But when the later hours rolled around the clamor increased, but it took up the universal sound that makes McKinley's name.

SEWALL CONCEDES DEFEAT.

He Finds Comfort in the Size of Billy's Vote.

BATH (Me.,) Nov. 3.—Arthur Sewall, Democratic Vice-Presidential candidate, was interviewed by an Associated Press representative.

Said he: "We will be under a government controlled by syndicates for the next four years, as well as by injunction. Mr. Bryan received 140 electoral votes, which shows there are some honest men in the country."

All the Election News.

THIS EDITION OF THE TIMES, issued at 4:30 a.m., is published for regular subscribers. It will be followed by

Later Editions at 10 a.m. and 12 m.,

which will be sold on the streets by newsboys. Each of these editions will contain the very latest

ELECTION NEWS

Received up to the hour of sending them to press—Further returns from Los Angeles County, the Sixth District and the State of California are expected early in the day.

Sinnle Part . . . Pages 1 to 12.

The Los Angeles Times

XVIth YEAR. [At the Counter... 3 Cents.] [By the Month.....75 Cents.] WEDNESDAY MORNING, MARCH 3, 1897. PRICE {On Streets and Trains / At All News Agencies} 5c

The Morning's News in The Times

IN BRIEF.

The City—Pages 5, 6, 7, 8, 9, 12.

Jubilation over the Harbor Board's decision....Park Superintendent loses his star....Charles Hess turns on the gas....Council will appropriate money for the unemployed....Janes goes to prison....Road to be built in Elysian Park....Work of the courts.

Southern California—Page 11.

Miner killed at Good Hope mine....A Santa Barbara bride's lonely wedding journey....Pomona city campaign....Hobo speculations in San Bernardino....San Pedro celebrates....Green held for trial in Santa Ana....San Diego hears the harbor news.

Financial and Commercial—Page 10.

Strength imparted to the New York stock market by the issue of $50,000,000 3 per cent. 100-year Lake Shore refunding bonds....Improvement in Jersey Central....Dullness of London 'change. Wheat takes an upward spurt, then drops back again....London wool brokers ridicule the idea of Boston wool dealers cornering the market....Grain and produce quotations....General business topics.

Weather Forecast.

SAN FRANCISCO, March 2.—For Southern California: Rain Wednesday; brisk southerly, probably shifting to westerly, winds.

Pacific Coast—Page 5.

Dredger job passes the California Senate—Big grist ground by the legislative mill....The Oregon legislative fiasco comes to an end....Southern and Central Pacific settlement....Rich gold strike near Yuma....The Arizona Legislature....Races at Ingleside.

General Eastern—Pages 1, 2, 3, 5.

Harbor fight decided in favor of San Pedro....McKinley and Hobart's entry at Washington—The President-elect dines with the President—Cleveland suffering from gout....Immigration bill vetoed....The Sundry Civil Bill amended by the Senate so as to hold the Southern Pacific's claim in escrow. House and Senate proceedings....Sensational incident in the Kansas Legislature....Burlington road arranges to run weekly tourist excursions between Boston and Los Angeles.

By Cable—Pages 2, 5.

Salisbury further outlines the powers' Cretan policy—Union of Crete with Greece forbidden—Autonomy with Turkish suzerainty of the island is agreed upon—Mutiny of gendarmes at Canea—Greece notified to withdraw her troops from Crete....Bayard's farewell banquet....A London actress joins the Salvation Army.

Greeks Ordered to Vamose.

ATHENS, March 2.—Representatives of the powers presented a joint note this afternoon to the Greek government. It declares Crete will be converted completely into an autonomous state under the suzerainty of the Sultan, and demands that Greek vessels and troops be withdrawn within six days.

Enforcing the Food Law.

SAN FRANCISCO, March 2.—Food Inspector Dockery has sworn to complaints against thirteen well-known merchants, who are charged with selling adulterated food supplies. The health authorities will cause the arrest of all local merchants who sell impure food.

VICTORY!

San Pedro Gets the Deep-water Harbor

And Uncle Collis is Given the Marble Heart.

The Government Won't Build Him a Breakwater.

THE OLD MAN IS CRUSHED.

Aging Sadly Under His Many Reverses.

He Tried to Run a Bluff on Secretary Lamont.

But Daniel Would not Listen to the Old Sinner.

THE HARBOR BOARD'S REPORT.

Commissioner Morgan Did not Sign it, but All the Others Did—Every Point at Issue Decided in Favor of San Pedro.

[BY THE TIMES' SPECIAL WIRE.]

WASHINGTON, March 2.—[Special Dispatch.] The California Deep-Water Harbor Commission has submitted its report to the Secretary of War, recommending San Pedro as the harbor on which the government appropriation shall be expended.

The old man of the railroads (Collis P. Huntington) is ageing rapidly. The government refused to make him a present of a few million dollars he owed, and now this ungrateful country declines to give him three millions for a harbor in the open sea.

It is learned from inside authority that Huntington went twice to Secretary Lamont and urged him to begin work at Santa Monica.

"But the commission has not reported," answered the Secretary.

"It will decide in favor of Santa Monica," replied the old man, but the bluff did not work.

The people's harbor goes to the people's site, and Uncle Collis feels very desolate. One of his engineers is reported as saying they might as well burn the long pier.

In addition to particulars as sent out by the Associated Press, the following provisions of the report are of interest:

The break-water is to be built opposite the entrance to San Pedro Harbor and immediately east of Point Firmin. It is to be 8500 feet at mean low water and 8532 feet twelve feet lower, to be increased if found practicable, without exceeding an aggregate cost of $2,900,000.

The depth is to be from twenty-four to fifty-two feet at mean low water, the sub-structure to be below the plane of mean low water, thirty-eight feet wide at the level and ninety feet twelve feet below the super-structure. The sub-structure is to contain 2,069,623 tons of stone, weighing not less than 130 pounds per cubic foot; the super-structure shall contain 221,025 tons. The Santa Catalina stone is recommended.

The length of the protection by the break-water at the six-fathoms line is 6200 feet; five-fathoms line, 6800 feet; four-fathoms line, 7300 feet.

The center of the entrance to the present harbor falls 2800 feet inside of a line drawn at right angles to the east arm of the break-water at its east end.

By extending the jetties, it is stated that the total cost of opening a twenty-four foot channel at San Pedro would be less than the cost of the Santa Monica pier.

Every point at issue is decided in favor of San Pedro, as against Santa Monica. The victory is a complete one, and the specifications such that a magnificient harbor is assured.

THE BOARD'S REPORT.

Signed by All the Commissioners Except Morgan.

WASHINGTON, March 2.—The board appointed by the President some months ago to examine and decide upon the location of a deep-water harbor for the commerce of Southern California at San Pedro or Santa Monica, today made its report to the Secretary of War. It definitely defines the harbor at San Pedro at an estimated cost of $2,901,787.

Richard P. Morgan of the commission did not sign the report, but by the wording of the law under which the board acts, the findings of the majority of the members is final.

The report cites in detail the operations of the board, then makes a comparison of the two harbors for the purposes named. At each place, it says, good deep water anchorage in six to eight fathoms of water can be obtained. At either place the necessary accessories for the convenient transfer of business from shipping to land can be constructed.

In determining which will be the more useful, five different considerations were reviewed: Convenience for construction, accessory works, approaches from the sea and from the land, availability as a harbor of refuge and capacity for extension and enlargement as the demands of commerce may require.

After a careful examination of all these considerations, the board finds that the greatest advantages are with San Pedro. While the physical advantages of the San Pedro location led to its selection, the report says the advisability of that choice is materially strengthend by consideration of the extensive improvements of its interior harbor, already made, conditionally provided for or contemplated as an object of future appropriations. If the choice did fall to Port Los Angeles the present statute would then authorize improvements at San Pedro to the amount of $392,000, and the same statute unqualifiedly directs the Secretary of War, at his discretion, to cause surveys and estimates to be made for future improvements at the same location.

In concluding the report, the board says: "It is the judgment of this board that the best public policy, in the interest of economy and for the attainment of a deep-water harbor for commerce and refuge, demands concentration of the expenditures at one point, with a corresponding cumulative excellence of results, rather than a dispersion and weakening of results by divided expenditures at two locations. This conclusion is strengthened by the fact that the selection of San Pedro undoubtedly involves materially less ultimate expenditure than is certain to be incurred in the maintenance of two harbors. Preponderance of physical advantages leads to the selection of San Pedro as in line with the requirements of the best public policy."

The improvement contemplated is a stone breakwater beginning about twenty-one hundred feet from the shore and extending in a straight line 300 feet, thence 3 deg. curve, about eighteen hundred feet, thence in a straight line 3700 feet to the end, making the total lengh of the breakwater 8500 feet.

KEPT HIS VOW.

Why a Celebrated Ohio Hermit Let His Hair Grow.

[BY ASSOCIATED PRESS WIRE.]

WOOSTER (O.,) March 2.—Christian Shank, aged 60 years, who has for many years lived in a miserable hovel in an isolated section of this country and who was known as the Sugar Creek hermit, is dead. He had allowed his hair to grow until it hung almost to his waist, while his whiskers were almost as long. Unlike most hermits, Shank was tidy about his person and kept his hair braided like a school girl, permitting it to hang down his back.

A few days ago as a party of hunters were going by his hovel, Shank was found sick with pneumonia. He was removed to the hospital where, to an attendant a few moments before his death, he told why he never cut his hair.

When a young man his sweetheart jilted him because he allowed a barber to cut his hair, and he then made a vow never to again cut his hair or trim his beard until she married him. The maiden married another and Shank died without having broken his vow.

New York's Racing Law.

ALBANY (N. Y.,) March 2.—The Court of Appeals has decided that the Percey Gray racing law is constitutional and the methods of book-making allowed by the racing commission are in accordance with the law. The cases decided were appeals from the people from a dismissal of actions brought against President Lawrence, of the Westchester Racing Association and Joseph Sturgess, bookmaker.

IT WAS "A PROUD DAY," AS MRS. MURPHY SAYS.

The Times artist tries to make a cartoon to fit the occasion, but having attended the jollification at the Jonathan Club, can only picture his remembrance of the various incidents of the day.

THIS BEATS RANDSBURG.

WONDERFUL GOLD MINES FOUND NEAR YUMA.

Samples of Ore Brought in That Assay 'Way Up in the Thousands. A Big Rush from Yuma to the New Eldorado.

[BY THE TIMES' SPECIAL WIRE.]

YUMA (Ariz.,) March 2.—[Special Dispatch.] Great excitement prevails here regarding fabulous strikes being made in the Sierra Madre Mountains, eighty miles from Yuma. A low average for rock being brought in from there is $2000 per ton, and from that up to $4000. A ledge of this kind of rock, three miles long and from four to eight feet wide on top, is reported, and as a result all classes of men are developing the gold fever and are either rushing to the scene of the great strike or sending some one in their stead.

It is probable that such an excitement will be developed as has not been known in the West for years. The place already has a store, and a stage line is carrying passengers from Sentinel, on the Southern Pacific Railroad, to the scene of excitement, forty miles distant.

LOADING FOR CUBA.

Another Alleged Filibustering Expedition Fitted Out.

[BY ASSOCIATED PRESS WIRE.]

NEW YORK, March 2.—The World this morning says: Passing coasters observed four suspicious-looking craft, two tugs, a schooner and a barge, lying off Barnegat until the storm with its fuzz of snow became so thick as to shut off the vision. A steamer with a single funnel, a black hull and two masts rigged as derricks, emerged from the gloom of the morning, signalled the tugs, which answered understandingly, and they presently came about and tied up against the sailing vessel, which in turn was made fast to one of the tugs and had no sail spread. The whole proceeding looked like the start of a carefully-planned filibustering expedition for Cuba.

It was learned that Maj. Castroverdi, a young and dashing Cuban patriot, who was formerly with Maceo, disappeared a week ago last Sunday. He went south to lead an expedition from some point on the coast, his friends in the Cuban junta say. His outfit will comprise his stores, rifles, ammunition and a few picked men. The point from which he is to sail is kept secret. No one about the junta would say he knew of the arrangements for the expedition.

A tug called the Volunteer, which is said to tie up ordinarily when not running about, at the foot of Bridge street, Brooklyn, left the old logwood house at Green Point. In tow of the tug was the barge Relief, upon whose deck crouched in shadows more than a score of Cubans, mostly young men, and many, judging from appearances, of the adventuresome and daring class that are always pressing the officials of the junta for a chance to strike a blow for Cuba libre.

Thus the flotilla lay until the mysterious steamer came out of the horizon on the southward. In addition to her many cases of arms, etc., the schooner is said to have had on board nine or ten men who climbed aboard the steamer.

From appearances, Maj. Castroverdi's $1000 expedition headed for the mouth of the San Juan River, is already on its way.

Uhl is Popular.

BERLIN, March 2.—A petition for the retention here of Edwin F. Uhl, United States Ambassador, signed by a number of prominent Americans in this city, has been cabled to President-elect McKinley.

Carnegie's Illness.

GREENWICK (Ct.,) March 2.—Andrew Carnegie, who is seriously ill with pleurisy, is improving. Unless unexpected complications set in, it is expected that Carnegie will speedily recover.

SANTA FE LAND TITLES.

GREAT EXCITEMENT AT THE ANCIENT CAPITAL.

The Supreme Court Decision Has Made Property-holders Uneasy. Talk of Resort to Firearms to Protect Real Estate Holdings.

[BY THE TIMES' SPECIAL WIRE.]

SANTA FE (N. M.,) March 2.—[Special Dispatch.] Threats of shotgun and rifle were heard when the decision of the United States Supreme Court became known today, for by it the city of Santa Fé has absolutely no title to the land upon which it stands and that which it has passed by deed to private citizens.

The town claims to have received its consent to existance from the King of Spain, at a period which latter-day historians claim antedates the settlement of St. Augustine.

The decision created an immense sensation, and those who saw their security only in victory for the city, were thoroughly alarmed. They were later made easier by the statement that they would not be disturbed in their rights by claim-jumpers, and, indeed, it would have been risky and foolish to attempt such a thing.

It now remains for the city to acquire title under the general statutes of the country, which is a singular proceeding, as the place has been in existence as a settlement since 1559, at which time it was the commercial cross-roads of this section of the country and was the hub around which trade revolved up to the construction of railway trunk lines.

A JEALOUS SUITOR.

Arrested for Murdering His More Favored Rival.

[BY ASSOCIATED PRESS WIRE.]

EVANSVILLE (Ind.,) March 2.—Nicholas Trautvetter, a young farmer 19 years old, was found dead, lying in the road a few miles from this city. Young Trautvetter was found to have three bullet holes through his head and one through the body and had been dead some little time when found. He had left home in a buggy with another young man to call upon a young lady. He failed to return at his usual hour and his folks became uneasy and organized a search.

When the remains were found the young man who had been with him was sought, but had not been found at last accounts. Messengers were at once dispatched to Boonville for the Sheriff and Coroner and an effort will be made to track the murderers down, for there is every evidence that it is a case of murder. It is not known that young Trautvetter had any enemies, but the young lady he was waiting upon is very popular in her neighborhood and had other young men besides Mr. Trautvetter enamored of her, and it may be that his death is the result of jealousy on the part of some of the less favored suitors.

LATER:—Robert Moore has been arrested charged with the crime. Trautvetter and Moore were suitors of Miss Phoebe Schiek. Trautvetter had been with Miss Schiek, and was on his way home when shot to death. As Trautvetter traversed the country road, Moore joined him. Moore claims that some unknown person shot Trauvetter from ambush. Moore the nhastened home and told the story to his father, who aroused the neighborhood and then sought the murdered man.

The Valley Road.

SAN FRANCISCO, March 2.—Grading on the San Joaquin Valley Railroad has reached a point opposite Oleander, nearly seven miles south of Fresno, on the Hanford ranch. This portion of the road will be ready for track laying as soon as the culverts and bridges are constructed. The grading camp will be removed to Kings River and grading will be carried on between that point and Oleander. The bridge building party will be moved to Kings River within a week.

A FALL DOWN.

Dredger Job Passes the Senate.

Senator Smith's Gallant Fight Did not Avail.

Los Angeles Members Voted with the Majority.

Bulla's Five-blocks Bill Endorsed by Business Men—The Torrens Land-Transfer Bill Goes to the Governor—Legislative Notes.

[BY THE TIMES' SPECIAL WIRE.]

SACRAMENTO, March 2.—[Special Dispatch.] No such bitter fight has been made in the Senate as that made tonight over the dredger job. For nearly three hours, invective and argument poured out in a continuous stream, and at least one man made a reputation that he may be proud of.

Langford, Gillette and others attacked this proposition which, under the guise of dredging the Sacramento River and reclaiming swamp and overflowed lands, means biennial demands on the State Treasury for the Lord knows how much money. But it remained for Senator Smith of Bakersfield to show up in all their glaring sophistry the arguments in favor of the bill and expose what he called the most "audacious scheme ever presented to the Legislature of this State."

Smith's denunciation was pronounced even by friends of the bill, to be a masterly effort.

The Los Angeles members, for reasons best known to themselves, but certainly not for lack of knowledge concerning this nefarious proposition, for the Times correspondent has repeatedly called attention to it, chose to vote for the bill. Men who will have reason in future to look back on their votes with satisfaction because they voted against this scheme, are Senators Beard, Braunhart, Gillette, Holloway, Jones, Larue, Mahoney, Pedlar, Smith, Stratton, Withington and Langford. The vote stood ayes, 27; nayes, 12.

The lobby and floor of the Senate were crowded with people who hung breathless on the words of the speakers, and the roll calls upon the motion to postpone action for tonight and on the passage of the bill, were followed with the keenest interest.

The bill is a precedent that will prove a sorry one for the State of California, and only the signature of Gov. Budd is needed to make it a law.

BULLA'S FIVE-BLOCKS BILL.

It Is Urged by Business Men—Legislative Notes.

[BY THE TIMES' SPECIAL WIRE.]

SACRAMENTO, March 2.—[Special Dispatch.] Members of the Los Angeles delegation are receiving telegrams reading as follows: "We believe the present street-railway law works a detriment to our section by keeping capital from investing in this class of securities. Senate Bill 392, while giving adequate protection to the public, will tend to prevent irresponsible attacks on legitimate enterprises."

These telegrams are signed by such prominent citizens as W. J. Brodrick, H. Newmark, S. H. Mott, T. L. Duque, M. S. Hellman, T. E. Rowan, J. S. Slauson, W. Gillelen, H. J. Woollacott, J. W. A. Off, F. C. Howes, Frank P. Flint, J. M. Elliott, W. C. Patterson, J. A. Graves, E. T. Wright, G. B. Barham, Security Loan and Trust Company, by M. W. Stimson, president; Union Bank of Savings, by M. W. Stimson, president; H. Jevne, A. H. Naftzger, H. J. Fleishman, F. A. Gibson, J. M. Johnston, J. Schoder, L. C. Schiller, John Wigmore & Sons Co., Harper & Reynolds Co., H. W. O'Melveny and J. V. Wachtel.

Senate Bill 392 is Bulla's five-block bill, and these indorsements of the measure will strengthen it materially with country delegates.

Capt. Cross, in one of his belligerent moods, this afternoon moved that the second day of March appear on the journal as the day for "cinch" bills against corporations and joint stock companies. This scorcher was called forth by the passage of a bill giving the Railroad Commissioners power to order switches, sidetracks and stations put in wherever they might deem fit, and by Shanahan's income-tax bill, which came up for amendment.

The Railroad Commission Bill was opposed by Valentine and Cutter, as giving dangerous power to the commissioners. Capt. Cross declared, with a bang of his fist on his desk, that Commissioner Larue had been lobbying here two weeks for the bill, to his personal knowledge.

Mead defended the bill as in line with the Constitution.

Cross wanted street car and stage lines exempted from its provisions, but the amendment was lost, ayes, 22, nayes 49. Cutter gave notice of reconsideration.

Belshaw added fuel to the fire by introducing a joint resolution that no action be taken by Congress with respect to the Pacific Railroad debts, but that the laws of the land be allowed to take their natural course.

On the other side of the Capitol "cinch" bills were in favor of corporate or combine interests. The dredger job came up for consideration and Aram

The Los Angeles Times

XVIIth YEAR. PRICE { SINGLE PART—TWELVE PAGES AT THE OFFICE COUNTER..... } 3 CENTS. WEDNESDAY MORNING, FEBRUARY 16, 1898. ON STREETS AND TRAINS AT ALL NEWS AGENCIES } 5 CENTS

BLOWN UP.

Great Battleship Maine a Mass of Ruins.

Wrecked as She Lay in the Harbor of Havana.

Force of the Explosion Broke All Windows Ashore.

OVER ONE HUNDRED KILLED.

Two Hundred Missing and Many are Wounded.

Theories as to the Cause of the Terrible Disaster.

Admiral Manterola Thinks That a Grenade Was Thrown.

THE SCENE AN AWFUL ONE.

Wildest Consternation at Havana. The Spanish War Vessels' Boats Sent to Assist—De Lome Leaves Washington—Amazon Caught.

[ASSOCIATED PRESS NIGHT REPORT.]

HAVANA, Feb. 15. — [By Central American Cable.] At a quarter of 10 o'clock this evening a terrible explosion took place on board the United States battleship Maine in Havana harbor. Many were killed or wounded. All the boats of the Spanish cruiser Alfonso XIII are assisting. As yet the cause of the explosion is not apparent.

The wounded sailors of the Maine are unable to explain the disaster. It is believed that the battleship is totally destroyed. The explosion shook the whole city. The windows were broken in all the houses.

The correspondent of the Associated Press says he has conversed with several of the wounded sailors, and understands from them that the explosion took place while they were asleep, so that they can give no particulars as to the cause.

CAPT. SIGSBEE CABLES.

Says Public Opinion Should Be Suspended Till Further Report.

[ASSOCIATED PRESS NIGHT REPORT.]

WASHINGTON, Feb. 15.—The Secretary of the Navy received the following telegram from Capt. Sigsbee:

"Maine blown up in Havana harbor at 9:40 and destroyed. Many wounded, and doubtless many killed and drowned. Wounded and others on board Spanish man-of-war and Ward Line steamer. Send lighthouse tender from Key West for crew and few pieces of equipment still above (water.) No one had other clothes than those upon him. Public opinion should be suspended until further report. All officers believed to be saved. Jenkins and Merritt not yet accounted for. Many Spanish officers, including representatives of Gen. Blanco, now with me and express sympathy.

(Signed,) "SIGSBEE."

The officers referred to in the above dispatch are Lieut. Friend W. Jenkins and Assistant Engineer Darwin R. Merritt. From the wording of the dispatch, the Navy Department thinks it is possible that they were on shore at the time of the accident. The Secretary of the Navy received another dispatch from Key West at the same time with the above, but its contents were not made public.

The orders for the lighthouse tenders were at once sent to Key West in plain language, thus avoiding the delay that would have arisen from the use of a cipher.

Capt. Dickens, after carrying out the instructions of Secretary Long with regard to relief measures for the survivors of the Maine, went at once to the White House where the President was aroused and informed of the disaster. President McKinley received the news calmly and expressed his deep sorrow, but said nothing further except that he was thoroughly satisfied with the measures adopted by the Navy Department.

Secretary Long retired at 4 a.m. and gave orders that all further dispatches from Havana should be transmitted to Capt. Dickens. It is learned that Secretary Long's dispatch from Key West, which was not given out, was merely from Capt. Forsyth, confirming the message of Capt. Sigsbee.

CABLEGRAM FROM LEE.

Cause of the Explosion is Yet to Be Investigated.

[ASSOCIATED PRESS NIGHT REPORT.]

WASHINGTON, Feb. 16.—Secretary Day received the following dispatch from Gen. Lee:

"The Maine blew up at 9:40. The explosion occurred well forward under men's quarters, consequently many were lost. It is believed all officers saved, but Jenkins and Merritt not accounted for. Cause of explosion yet to be investigated. Captain-General and army and navy officers rendered every assistance. Sigsbee and most of his officers on board steamer City of Washington. Others on Spanish gunboat and in the city. Am with Sigsbee, who has telegraphed Navy Department.

(Signed,) "LEE."

SIGSBEE NOT WOUNDED.

More Than Two Hundred Men are Missing.

[ASSOCIATED PRESS NIGHT REPORT.]

HAVANA, Feb. 15.—[By Central American Cable.] The report that Capt. Sigsbee was wounded is inaccurate. Capt. Sigsbee, with other officers, went in a small boat to the Ward line steamer City of Washington. Two officers and more than two hundred of the crew are missing. Some of the crew who were able to support themselves by swimming were saved by the boats.

Six of the wounded crew and one of the officers have been taken to the Military Hospital by Gen. Blanco's orders.

CONSTERNATION AT HAVANA.

Thousands of People Flock to the Wharves.

[ASSOCIATED PRESS NIGHT REPORT.]

HAVANA, Feb. 16. — [By Central American Cable.] The wildest consternation prevails in Havana. The wharves are crowded with thousands of people. It is believed the explosion occurred in a small powder magazine. At 10:45 what remains of the Maine is still burning. Capt. Sigsbee and the other officers have been saved. It is estimated that over one hundred of the crew were killed, but it is impossible as yet to give exact details.

Admiral Manterola has ordered that boats of all kinds should go to the assistance of the Maine and her wounded. The Havana firemen are giving aid tending carefully to the wounded as they are brought ashore. It is a terrible sight. Gen. Zolano and the other generals have orders from Capt.-Gen. Blanco to take steps to help the Maine's crew in every way possible. The correspondent of the Associated Press has been near the Maine in on of the boats of the cruiser Alfonso XIII, and seen others of the wounded who corroborate the statement of those first interviewed that they were asleep when the explosion occurred.

Capt. Sigsbee says the explosion occurred in the bow of the vessel. He received a wound in the head. Orders were given to the officers to save themselves as best they could. The latter, who were literally thrown from their bunks in their night-clothing gave the necessary orders with great self-control. At 1:15 o'clock the Maine continues burning.

The first theory was that there had been a preliminary explosion in the Santa Barbara (magazine) of powder or dynamite below the water. Admiral Manterola believes that the first explosion was of a grenade that was hurled over the navy yard.

SECRETARY LONG'S ACTION.

[ASSOCIATED PRESS NIGHT REPORT.]

WASHINGTON, Feb. 16.—Paymaster Charles W. Littlefield, who is given in the list of officers on the Maine, has recently been replaced by Paymaster Ryan. Littlefield is now in Washington.

The Maine was built in New York in 1890 at a cost of $2,588,000. She had a steel hull and a complement of 874 men. Secretary Long received Capt. Sigsbee's dispatch but a few minutes before the Associated Press dispatches were handed him. He received the news with apparent calm, and his first act was to comply with Capt. Sigsbee's request that assistance be sent from Key West. He wired Capt. Forsythe at Key West to proceed with the naval tender Fern to Havana Harbor.

Secretary Long then sent for Capt. Dickens, and the two discussed Capt. Sigsbee's brief telegram. No other naval officers were present, and besides the Secretary and Capt. Dickens the naval colony here is ignorant of this disaster, the greatest which has befallen the American navy since the disaster in Apia many years ago. The Secretary is inclined to believe that most of the officers of the Maine were on shore at the time of the accident, as it was still early in the night. While neither the Secretary nor Capt. Dickens is inclined to discuss the probable cause of the accident, several suggestions were ventured. They believe that it may have been caused by a fire in the bunkers, heating the bulkhead near a magazine, or that an accident may have occurred while inspecting high explosives for torpedoes. Of course, this is mere speculation, and the Secretary is anxiously waiting a more detailed report from Capt. Sigsbee.

Later the Secretary sent another telegram to Key West, directing that the tender Mangrove also be sent to Havana.

THE WRECKED BATTLESHIP.

[ASSOCIATED PRESS NIGHT REPORT.]

WASHINGTON, Feb. 15.—The Maine was a battleship of the second-class, and was regarded as one of the best ships in the new navy. She was built at the Brooklyn navy yard, and was 318ft. long, 57ft. broad, 21.6ft. mean draught, and 6682 tons displacement. She had two 10-inch vertical turrets and two military masts, and her motive power was furnished by twin-screws, with triple expansion engines, having a maximum power of 9293, capable of making a speed of 17.8 knots. She carried four 10-inch and six 6-inch breech-loading guns in her main battery, and seven 6-pounders and eight 1-pounder rapid-firing guns, and four Gatlings in her second battery, and four Whitehead torpedoes.

The commander of the Maine, Capt. Sigsbee, is popular in the Navy Department. For four years he was chief of the Hydrographic Office.

THE INCIDENT CLOSED.

[ASSOCIATED PRESS DAY REPORT.]

NEW YORK, Feb. 15.—A special from Washington says that a cable dispatch received by the Secretary of State from Minister Woodford at Mad-

(CONTINUED ON FIFTH PAGE.)

ALL IN DOUBT.

Efforts to Trace the Clara Nevada.

Capt. O'Brown Says He Did not Pass the Steamer.

What One of the Owners Says of the Wreckage.

H. W. Heinsch of Los Angeles Arrested on Board the Alice Blanchard—Ten Carloads of Burros to Be Shipped North.

[ASSOCIATED PRESS NIGHT REPORT.]

SEATTLE (Wash.,) Feb. 15. — Capt. O'Brown of the steamer Rasalie, which arrived here last night from Alaska, said this afternoon that the published statement that the Rosalie passed the Clara Nevada December 9, was untrue. On Tuesday night, December 8, he saw a vessel which resembled the Clara Nevada just south of Douglass Island. He was not positive that it was the Clara Nevada. It might have been the United States gunboat Wheeling, the Clara Nevada not having reached Juneau when he left.

W. W. McGuire, one of the owners of the Clara Nevada, states that when the steamer was overhauled new life-preservers were put on and the name "Hassler" was entirely effaced from the vessel. He thinks there must be some mistake about the reported picking up of wreckage with the word "Hassler" on it, at Seyward City.

RUMORS CONFLICT.

[ASSOCIATED PRESS DAY REPORT.]

SEATTLE (Wash.,) Feb. 15.—No further news has been received concerning the reported loss of the steamer Clara Nevada, in Alaskan waters. Owing to the many conflicting rumors, hopes for her safety have not yet been abandoned. On account of the remoteness of the scene of the reported disaster, it is impossible to get anything authentic. Unless some unexpected steamer shall arrive, no definite news is expected before next Thursday.

The last report received was that brought down by the steamer Excelsior, which arrived early this morning. Capt. Donaldson said that just before he left Juneau the steamer Coleman arrived and reported that wreckage and bedding marked "Haseler" had been washed ashore at Seward. He said:

"The Clara Nevada was formerly a government vessel, known as the Hassler, and I have no doubt but that she is at the bottom of the sea, at least such of her and her effects as were not burned, for the Seward citizens report having seen a blaze on the water."

The Excelsior arrived at Juneau five hours after the steamer Rosalie, which reported passing the Clara Nevada.

REPORT NOT BELIEVED.

[ASSOCIATED PRESS DAY REPORT.]

SEATTLE (Wash.,) Feb. 15.—W. W. McGuire, one of the owners of the Clara Nevada, says that in the absence of urther confirmatory news, he believes that the report of the steamer's loss is untrue.

February 3, Purser Beck wrote from Juneau as follows: "Arrived at 6 a.m., after a very windy trip from Wrangel. Will arrive at Skaguay Friday night and start home Sunday morning, February 6."

"It will be noticed," said McGuire, "that the Clara Nevada is reported to have been due at Juneau on her return trip February 5."

ANOTHER DENIAL.

[ASSOCIATED PRESS DAY REPORT.]

SEATTLE (Wash.,) Feb. 15.—W. H. Daly, one of the crew of the steamer Rosalie, which arrived here last night from Alaska, does not think the steamer Clara Nevada is lost. He said that the Rosalie passed the Nevada last Wednesday morning, February 9, near Juneau, for which place she was headed. The Clara Nevada answered the Rosalie's signal, and passed on, seemingly in no trouble.

SAYS SHE FOUNDERED.

VICTORIA (B. C.,) Feb. 16.—The steamer Islander, which has arrived here, brings further details of the reported loss of the steamer Clara Nevada. The news was conveyed to Juneau, shortly before the Islander, sailed by Capt. Lathom of the steamer Coleman. He says the Clara Nevada foundered with all on board opposite Seaward City in Berner's Bay, where she was running for shelter.

George Beck, a resident of Seaward City, was an eyewitness of the disaster. He was standing on the beach when he saw a small steamer battling with the wind. Suddenly there was a flash and the steamer burst into flames, foundering in a few seconds. She had on board twenty-five passengers and crew. Fifteen passengers, who went North on the Clara Nevada and returned on the Islander, say her boilers gave much trouble on the northward voyage, and once the steamer took fire, but it was extinguished before serious damage was done. They say the steamer was undoubtedly wrecked by the boilers bursting.

The Rustler of Juneau has gone to look for survivors.

H. W. HEINSCH ARRESTED.

His Wife Accuses Him of Failing to Provide.

[ASSOCIATED PRESS NIGHT REPORT.]

SAN FRANCISCO, Feb. 15.—Late last night H. W. Heinsch of Los Angeles was arrested in his berth on the Alice Blanchard, which was realy to sail for the Klondike. Heinsch's wife had accused him of having for the past two years failed to provide for their eight-year-old boy. At the City Prison Heinsch put up cash bail of $40, and was released. When his case was called today in Police Judge Joachimsen's court Heinsch failed to appear.

He was at one time a shoe merchant in Los Angeles, but, it is said, he failed over two years ago, his liabilities amounting to $40,000.

RAILROAD TO BE RUSHED.

[ASSOCIATED PRESS DAY REPORT.]

MONTREAL, Feb. 15.—C. H. Wilkinson, representing the British Yukon Company, says the construction of a railroad through the White Pass for the head of Lynn Canal to Lake Bennett will be begun immediately by his company. The road, which will be forty-five miles in length, will be completed within ninety days of the beginning of the work.

WALKING TO DAWSON.

[ASSOCIATED PRESS DAY REPORT.]

LOGAN (Utah,) Feb. 15.—An individual giving his name as Benjamin Caldwell, who has just arrived here, claims to be walking from Denver to Dawson City on a wager made by Mil-

(CONTINUED ON FIFTH PAGE.)

Points of the News in Today's Times.

SUMMARY.

	No. of Words.	No. of Cols.
Associated Press night report, including commercial, 14,340 words, Times exclusive dispatches, 1345 words; day report, 10,500 words—total.	26,485	22

The City—Pages 5, 6, 7, 8, 9, 12.

Everett's bondsmen must make good his stealings....Validity of the Police Court sustained....Trouble impending over insurance rates....Politics playing a part in the investigation of Policeman Hiriart....License of the Van Nuys Hotel bar revoked....A domestic difficulty in Dogtown lands Carl Klotz in jail....Boiler Inspector triumphs in his contest with the fire department. A woman found guilty of using canceled postage stamps....Rev. Burt Estes Howard does not expect to be pastor of Unity Church....Detectives admit that they have captured a few burglars....Failure of a Broadway carriage dealer....Landlords' Association resolves to patronize conduit companies only....Impressive ceremonies at Father Meyer's funeral....Merchants and manufacturers oppose the anti-scalping bill....Two children hurt in a Broadway runaway....Subscriptions coming in for La Fiesta.

Southern California—Page 11.

Pasadena non-partisans open the municipal campaign....Orange County Supervisors will not give prisoners cheaper meals....San Diego Common Council meets....Changes in Santa Barbara Board of Trade....Redlands prepared for Washington's birthday. Hill murder trial at Ventura....Mr. Flagler at Riverside....Water claims at San Bernardino.

By Cable—Pages 1, 2, 3.

Battleship Maine blown up in Havana harbor—Probably a hundred seamen killed....Edhem Pasha to investigate Bulgarian outrages....Lord Neville sentenced to five years' penal servitude. Spanish populace enraged because of the apology made for De Lome's letter. Germany's fruit decree to be published. More sensations in the Zola trial. Cecil Rhodes's railway scheme.

Financial and Commercial—Page 10.

Rush of shorts to cover in the Chicago wheat pit....Sharp rally in stocks at New York....Cattle at Chicago and Kansas City strong....London stock markets dominated by politics....Petroleum dull....Available supplies.... California dried fruits....Coast produce.

General Eastern—Pages 1, 2, 3, 5.

Senate discusses the Kansas Pacific sale....Boston Congregational minister fears a Mormon war....Slimly-attended Cabinet meeting....Five men crushed under falling walls at Pittsburgh. Peace reported in Nicaragua....Labor Arbitration Bill in the Senate. Luther G. Billings dismissed from the navy....Cuban Gen. Gomez confident of victory....Secretary Wilson reports on the striking development of tobacco culture in Florida....Senator Tillman stirred up....Santa Fé restrained from boycotting....Silver leaders in the three parties lining up for battle. Kansas Pacific sale to be made today. Rich placer strike in Mexico....Prospect of more strikes in New England mills....Preacher Brown thinks the Chicago association was uncharitable to condemn him....Former Los Angeles man arrested at El Paso for bigamy, jumps his bond....Trusted bank employé at Chicago goes wrong....Republican victory at Pittsburgh....Number of fishermen lost on Lake Erie. Schaefer accepts Ives's challenge. Chicago engineers report the Nicaragua Canal feasible.

Pacific Coast—Page 3.

Important ruling at Tacoma on rights of aliens....Clara Nevada may be safe....Poor outlook for the sealing fleet....Rich gold strike in Trinity county....Many consumptive patients in insane asylums....Gunboat Pinta ready for the naval reserve....Y.M.C.A. State Convention....Regular Klondike in Arizona....Weather and crop bulletin....Murder on Koatenai Lake....Ten carloads of burros for Alaska....Terrible blizzard raging on the Alaskan coast....Big gun for San Diego covered with Cuban legends....Great times on the Mexican border....Big sale of dried fruit to German firm....Sailor pugilist shot at Angel's Samp....Wealthy sea captain dies at Sacramento....San José woman kills herself.

At Large Pages—1, 2, 3.

Dispatches were also received from Cleveland, O.; London, Berlin, Washington, Pittsburgh, New Orleans, Zenobia, Miss., Chicago, Denver, New York, San Francisco and other places.

SPIRITED TALK

Pacific Railroad Debate is Resumed.

Harris's Resolution of Inquiry Again Taken Up.

He Denounces the Plan to Sell the Road.

House Devotes Time to Consideration of Bills and Joint Resolutions—An Order for Consideration of the Loud Bill.

[ASSOCIATED PRESS NIGHT REPORT.]

WASHINGTON, Feb. 15.—A resolution of inquiry offered yesterday by Mr. Harris of Kansas, precipitated a spirited discussion of the Pacific Railroad question in the Senate today. The resolution called upon the Attorney-General for the reasons which induced him to abandon his plan of redeeming the first-mortgage bonds of the Kansas Pacific branch of the Union Pacific, and having the road operated by a receiver.

Mr. Harris denounced the present plan to sell the road at the bid of the Reorganization Committee, as defrauding the government of nearly $7,000,000. Mr. Foraker of Ohio explained the view taken of the matter by the administration, showing the President was convinced that the Reorganization Committee proposed to pay for the road all that it was worth. The resolution was finally passed in amended form.

The House put in a busy day. The time was devoted to the consideration of bills and joint resolutions presented under the call of committees, and sixteen of more or less public importance were passed.

An order was entered for the consideration of the Loud Bill relating to second-class mail matter on March 1, 2 and 3, and the order for the consideration of the Bankruptcy Bill which begins tomorrow was modified, so that the final vote shall be taken Saturday instead of Monday, as arranged last week.

FIFTY-FIFTH CONGRESS.

REGULAR SESSION.

[ASSOCIATED PRESS DAY REPORT.]

WASHINGTON, Feb. 15.—SENATE.—Mr. Pettus of Alabama offered and secured the passage of a resolution requesting the President, if not incompatible with the public interest, to inform the Senate what action has been taken in reference to the murder of Segundo N. Lopez, a citizen of the United States, on the 11th of April, 1896, in the district of San Diego del Valla Maguerralia, Cuba, by soldiers of Spain, commanded by Col. Estruch.

The resolution introduced yesterday by Mr. Harris of Kansas, directing the Attorney-General to furnish the Senate information as to the agreement reached by the government with the Reorganization Committee of the Union Pacific Railroad Company, concerning the Kansas Pacific branch, was laid before the Senate.

Mr. Chandler said he had no objection to the resolution, but did not approve of the preamble, which included a press dispatch.

Mr. Harris replied that he might not insist upon the preamble after he had made a statement. The Union Pacific, he said, for a long time had attempted to influence Congress and officials of the administration to scale down the debt of that company to the government about 50 per cent. Until a year ago last January, the company had been unsuccessful. At that time they made arrangements with Cleveland's administration, by which the road was to be disposed of with a loss to the government of about $28,000,000. Mr. Harris then outlined the reasons why that arrangement was not carried into effect. Public sentiment was aroused from Maine to California, the demands of the people being that they should not be swindled out of the enormous sum mentioned.

When the present administration came into power, the question was grappled with and the government finally obtained every cent due the United States from the Union Pacific on the main line.

"We were all very glad," said Mr. Harris, "that the government received its just due, and nobody more sincerely congratulated the administration upon the successful negotiation of the transaction than myself. It was also hoped that the government would get the full amount of the debt due from the Kansas branch. If the Reorganization Committee should decline to pay the full amount due—about $13,000,000—it was the understanding that the government would redeem the first-mortgage bonds and have the road operated by a receiver."

A competent receiver would develop the value of the property, which Mr. Harris believed was worth quite $30,000,000. The Reorganization Committee, Mr. Harris said, had evidently succeeded in securing from the Attorney-General such concessions as have been outlined in the Associated Press dispatches, and the government was going to stand idly by and see the enormous sum of $6,500,000 interest due sacrificed.

"It is particularly significant," said Mr. Harris, "that the statements of the Reorganization Committee and the officials of the Union Pacific regarding the value of the main line have been proved by subsequent events to be untrue."

LYING OR STEALING.

[ASSOCIATED PRESS NIGHT REPORT.]

WASHINGTON, Feb. 15.—As was said once by the Senator from Missouri (Mr. Vest,) "When they speak they lie; and when they are silent they steal."

Mr. Harris then discussed the value of the Kansas Pacific road and said that, having a civil engineer on the line, his information was that of an expert. He said that during the last eleven years the line had earned an amount equal to 4 per cent. on $30,000,000. He further said that on the 5th

HE WAS POPULAR.

Country People Come in Crowds to the Funeral of Gutierres.

[BY DIRECT WIRE TO THE TIMES.]

ALBUQUERQUE (N. M.,) Feb. 15.—[Exclusive Dispatch.] The funeral services over the body of the dead lawyer and ranchman, Frank A. Gutierres, who was shot and killed Sunday morning by Manuel D. Gonzales, took place this morning at the Church of Immaculate Conception, Rev. Mandalori officiating.

The church building and the street for half a square in front were crowded with people, for the dead man was very popular with the country people, and they came in droves. The procession was one of the largest ever held in this city. Burial was in Santa Barbara Cemetery. The preliminary hearing of Gonzales will take place before Justice Duran tomorrow morning.

Sunday Deed is Void.

ST. LOUIS, Feb. 15.—The appeal of Hill, Fontaine & Co. of St. Louis from the decision of the United States Circuit Court of Arkansas in their suit against Henry C. and Laura Hite, to foreclose a deed of trust, resulted in affimative judgment in favor of the defendants in the Court of Appeals Monday, that court holding that the deed was void because executed on Sunday.

The Times

LOS ANGELES

XVIITH YEAR. PRICE { SINGLE PART—TWELVE PAGES AT THE OFFICE COUNTER..... } 3 CENTS. MONDAY, MAY 2, 1898. ON STREETS AND TRAINS AT ALL NEWS AGENCIES } 5 CENTS

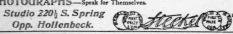

AMERICAN NAVAL VICTORY.

Dewey's Fleet Wipes Out the Spanish Squadron in Manila Bay.

Three and Probably More of the Dons' Cruisers Burned and Sunk in the First Naval Battle.

SPANISH OFFICIALS BREAK BAD NEWS GENTLY IN MADRID.

Details Only From Spanish Sources, but Even These Do Not Indicate Any Serious Damage to the American Ships—Captain of a Spanish Cruiser Goes Down With His Ship—Populace of Madrid Becomes Exasperated and Dangerous to the Government—Belief in London and Washington That Spain Has Had Enough and Will Give Up Cuba to Save Her Other Colonies—Dewey Probably Will Resume Operations and Finish the Job in Order to Seize Manila and Procure Coal for His Vessels.

[BY DIRECT WIRE TO THE TIMES.]

LISBON, May 2.—[By Atlantic Cable.] Dispatches received here from Manila show that the American fleet has been victorious; that two of the Spanish cruisers have been destroyed; that the captain of one of them was killed, as well as many marines; that the Spanish fleet finally retired, and that the Americans effected at least one landing.

Two brisk engagements were fought. In the first the Spanish vessels were seriously damaged, but not fatally. The American vessels then began to maneuver for position. The Spanish believed that they were retiring, and great excitement followed.

Dispatches were sent to Spain that a victory had been won; that the Americans had been routed. An hour later, however, the Americans again began to press closer to the Spanish, and opened fire with their heavy guns. In this engagement it was that Spain met defeat.

The first shell from the Baltimore struck the Maria Christiana and set her afire. Efforts were made to quench the flames, but in vain. When it became evident that she must burn, and that there was danger of her powder magazines exploding, Admiral Montejo left the ship, transferring his flag to the cruiser Isla de Cuba.

Just as the admiral left the vessel, another bomb struck on the deck of the Maria Christiana, killing Capt. Cardarzo and wounding several marines.

While it is not clear that the Spanish squadron has suffered a crushing defeat, the dispatches leave in doubt the intensely interesting question whether the American squadron has suffered material damage.

All news thus far comes from Spanish sources, but it seems evident that Commodore Dewey has not captured Manila.

Unless he is able to make another attack and capture the town, he will be in an awkward position, having no base upon which to retire and recruit.

SPANISH VERSION.

[BY DIRECT WIRE TO THE TIMES.]

NEW YORK, May 2.—[Exclusive Dispatch.] Accounts of the battle between Admiral Dewey's fleet off Manila are all from Spanish sources. The Spanish control the cable from Manila, and nothing favorable to American arms would be allowed to pass through it. The significance of the Spanish version of the fight is in the fact that it admits the loss of three of the finest Spanish ships, and does not mention the loss of an American ship. It seems plain that Dewey has practically destroyed the Spanish fleet. It will be several days before his report of the battle can be received.

THE PRESIDENT'S INSTRUCTIONS.

[BY DIRECT WIRE TO THE TIMES.]

NEW YORK, May 2.—[Exclusive Dispatch.] A special to the World from Washington says that the President himself prepared Commodore Dewey's instructions as follows, according to a Cabinet officer tonight: "Proceed to Manila, come to anchor about eight miles off and watch for the Spanish fleet. If you can engage them out of range of the shore batteries, destroy them. Then try to occupy the city, but keep a safe range from the shore batteries. If the fleet has left, try and find it. If impossible, make a landing, using your own discretion, and guided by the advice of a pilot. You can destroy the batteries, but have no unnecessary bombardment."

DETAILS OF THE BATTLE.

Admiral Montejo Practically Concedes His Utter Defeat.

[ASSOCIATED PRESS NIGHT REPORT.]

MADRID, May 1, 6:20 p.m.—[By Atlantic Cable.] Advices from Manila say that the American squadron, under Commodore Dewey, appeared off the Bay of Manila at 5 o'clock this morning and opened a strong cannonade against the Spanish squadron and forts protecting the harbor. The Spanish second-class cruiser Don Juan de Austria was severely damaged and her commander was killed. Another Spanish vessel was burned. The American squadron retired, having also sustained severe damages. A second naval engagement followed, in which the American squadron again suffered considerable loss and the Spanish warships Mindanao and Ulloa were slightly damaged.

OFFICIAL REPORT.

[ASSOCIATED PRESS NIGHT REPORT.]

MADRID, May 1, 8 p.m.—The following is the text of the official dispatch from the Governor-General of the Philippines to the Minister of War, Gen. Correa, as to the engagement off Manila:

"Last night, April 30, the batteries at the entrance to the forts announced the arrival of the enemy, forcing a passage under the obscurity of the night. At daybreak, the enemy took up positions, opening with a strong fire against Fort Cavite and the arsenal. Our fleet engaged the enemy in a brilliant combat, protected by the Cavite and Manila forts. They obliged the enemy, with heavy loss, to maneuver repeatedly.

"At 9 o'clock, the Americans took refuge behind the foreign merchant shipping on the east side of the bay. Our fleet, considering the enemy's superiority, naturally suffered a severe loss. The Maria Christiana is on fire and another ship believed to be the Don Juan de Austria, was blown up. There was considerable loss of life. Capt. Cadarzo, commanding the Maria Christiana, is among the killed. I cannot now give further details. The spirit of the army, navy and volunteers is excellent."

BERMEJO'S CONGRATULATIONS.

[ASSOCIATED PRESS NIGHT REPORT.]

MADRID, May 1.—The Spanish warships Mindanao and Ulloa were slightly damaged. During this engagement the Cavite forts maintained a steadier and stronger fire upon the American squadron than in the first engagement.

Admiral Bermejo, the Minister of Marine, has expressed himself as highly pleased with the heroism of the Spanish marines, and has telegraphed congratulations to Admiral Montejo and the valorous crews of the Spanish squadron under the fire of superior warships.

TWO SPANISH SHIPS BURN.

[ASSOCIATED PRESS NIGHT REPORT.]

MADRID, May 1, midnight.—An official telegram received at a late hour from the Governor-General of the Philippines says: "Admiral Montejo has transferred his flag to the cruiser Isle de Cuba from the cruiser Reina Maria Christiana. The Reina Maria Christiana was completely burned, as was also the Cruiser Castilla, the other ships having to retire from the combat, and some being sunk to avoid their falling into the hands of the enemy."

GREAT ENTHUSIASM.

[ASSOCIATED PRESS NIGHT REPORT.]

MADRID, May 1, 9 p.m.—The news from the Philippines has produced greatly increased enthusiasm, especially in view of the fact that the American squadron was obliged to retreat. Notwithstanding the severe damage, the Spanish ships suffered, naval officers here consider that future operations by the American squadron will be conducted under great difficulty, owing to their having no base where they could repair and recoal, or obtain fresh supplies of ammunition. Another account says the Mindana and Ulloa were severely damaged in the second engagement.

BERMEJO FEELS JOYFUL.

MADRID, May 1, 10 p.m.—Admiral Bermejo, Minister of Marine, joined the Cabinet council this evening and informed his colleagues that the Spanish forces had gained a victory in the Philippines. He asserted that he found difficulty in restraining his joyful emotions. The official dispatch does not mention the destruction of any American vessel, although it says that the United States squadron finally cast anchor in the bay beyond the foreign merchantmen.

MADRID GREATLY EXCITED.

MADRID, May 1, 11:30 p.m.—The town is greatly excited by the serious news from the Philippines, and there is an immense crowd gathering in the Calle de Sevilla. The civil guards on horseback were called out to preserve order, and all precautions have been taken.

SPANIARDS LAMENTING.

LONDON May 2.—Dispatches from Madrid dated 2:20 a.m., say the city is now tranquil although the mounted guards are patrolling all the main streets. At the theaters, cafés and in front of the newspaper offices last evening, the people loudly lamented the unpreparedness of Manila to resist the American warships, whose attack had long been expected. The Madrid authorities are determined vigorously to suppress all street demonstrations.

SPAIN'S CRUSHING DEFEAT.

LONDON, May 1.—While it is quite clear that the Spanish squadron has suffered a crushing defeat, the dispatches leave unclear the intensely interesting question whether the American squadron has suffered material damage.

All news thus far comes from Spanish sources, but it seems evident that Commodore Dewey has not captured Manila. Unless he is able to make another attack and capture the town, he will be in an awkward position, having no base upon which to retire and to refit.

Probably, therefore, the United States squadron will be obliged to make for San Francisco as the entrance to Manila Bay was heavily mined with torpedoes.

Commodore Dewey displayed great pluck and daring in making for the inner harbor. Acording to private advices received from Madrid, the United States cruisers Olympia, Raleigh and two other vessels, the names of which are not given, entered the harbor.

No dispatches give details as to the vessels actualy engaged on either side.

It appears to be incorrect that the ships anchored behind the merchantmen are on the east side of the harbor. It should be the west side.

Probabilities point in the direction of the second engagement having occurred, through the Spaniards trying to prevent the landing of the American wounded.

Reliable details cannot be had until Commodore Dewey's squadron is able to communicate with Hongkong. There is, however, a suspicious frankness in the Spanish dispatches that savors of the intention to break unwelcome news to the Spaniards. It is not likely, however, that Commodore Dewey will renew the attack.

MONTEJO ADMITS DEFEAT.

[ASSOCIATED PRESS NIGHT REPORT.]

MADRID, May 1. (via Paris, May 1.)—The time of the retreat of the American merchantmen was 11:30 a.m. The naval bureau at Manila sends the following, signed "Montejo, Admiral:"

"In the middle of the night the American squadron forced the forts and before daybreak appeared off Cavite. The night was completely dark. At 7:30 o'clock the bow of the Reina Maria Christiana took fire and soon after the poop also was burned. At 8 o'clock, with my staff, I went on board the Isle of Cuba. The Reina Maria Christiana and the Castilla were then entirely enveloped in flames.

"The other ships have been damaged, retired into Baker Bay. Some had to be sunk to prevent their falling into the hands of the enemy. The losses are numerous, notably Capt. Cardarzo, a priest and nine other persons."

WENT DOWN WITH HIS SHIP.

[ASSOCIATED PRESS NIGHT REPORT.]

LONDON, May 2.—The Madrid correspondent of the Financial News telegraphs this morning as follows:

"The Spanish Ministry of Marine claims a victory for Spain because the Americans were forced to retire behind the merchantmen. Capt. Cardarzo, in command of the Reina Maria Christiana, went down with the ship. The Spaniards fought splendidly. There is the greatest anxiety for further details."

DONS DISILLUSIONED.

[BY DIRECT WIRE TO THE TIMES.]

LONDON, May 1.—[Exclusive Dispatch.] A dispatch received from Madrid late tonight indicates that the public there is at last awakening to the fact that Spanish arms have really suffered a terrible reverse in the Bay of Manila. There was a loud demand from the street crowds for an explanation of the fact that so many warships had been lost in a great Spanish victory. A large force of Civil Guards was called out to overcome the crowds, who were undoubtedly on the verge of rioting.

HEAR THE EAGLE SCREAM

REJOICING AT WASHINGTON OVER DEWEY'S VICTORY.

News From the Philippines Affords the Greatest Satisfaction to the Administration — Prediction Is Made That Spain Will Quit.

[ASSOCIATED PRESS NIGHT REPORT.]

WASHINGON, May 1.—Washington is rejoicing tonight. Not since the dark days of the great civil conflict of a third of a century ago have the people of this city been so profoundly moved by war news as they were this evening. General rejoicing over the victory of Admiral Dewey was the order of the night. The streets were crowded and the people greatly excited.

Thus far no official advices have been received by the government, but the Asociated Press dispatches were transmitted to the President and officials of the administration as rapidly as they were received.

The President, in company with several of his advisers, read the bulletins in the library of the White House early in the evening, but later in the night he went to his office on the second floor of the Exectuve Mansion, where, until a late hour, he continued to peruse every dispatch with deepest interest.

Officials of the Navy Department were reticent in discussing the conflict in the absence of official information, but they made no pretense of concealing their great gratification. It has been known for days at the Navy Department that a conflict at Manila was inevitable, and while no great fear of the result was expressed, there was yet a deep concern in the heart of every official until tonight's news removed some of the weight from their minds.

When Secretary Bliss was shown the first dispatch, briefly recounting the victory of the American squadron, he unhesitatingly expressed his gratification at the result.

Secretary Alger declared that it was "a clean, glorious victory," but in common with other officials of the administration, declined to make extended comment upon it.

The absence of any statement of specific injury to the American vessels in the Madrid advices was construed as a convincing indication that they had not suffered appreciable injury and this was especially pleasing to naval students of the news.

Not only was the preservation of the American ships and men considered in itself a happy outcome, but was commented upon as indicating clearly that Admiral Dewey and his associate officers and men under their command had discharged splendidly their several duties in directing and executing the fight.

In this connection it was pointed out

[CONTINUED ON FIFTH PAGE.]

ON TO TAMPA.

Campfollowers Hurrying to the Front.

Pioneer Corps Nearly Ready to Start for Cuba.

To Relieve the Necessities of Reconcentrados.

LANDING PLACE A SECRET.

Matanzas May Not Be the Point of Invasion.

Possible Debarkation on Coast of Pinar del Rio.

Sampson May Have to Slay a Few More Mules.

GENERAL FORWARD MOVEMENT

Expected to Take Place Early This Week — Bombardment of Cuban Forts Predicted—Army and Navy Orders—Naval Movements.

[BY DIRECT WIRE TO THE TIMES.]

WASHINGTON, May 1.—[Exclusive Dispatch.] Nothing has happened today to change any plan with regard to the invasion of Cuba. Army and navy officers, newspaper correspondents, Cuban guides, and the host that usually follows an army, are hurrying down to Tampa, whence the pioneer corps will start on its mission. Primarily the expedition is to open a way for food for the reconcentrados and arms for the insurgents. Its secondary purpose is to establish a base of supplies for the army corps that are to follow.

Wednesday is the day generally supposed to be the time for the sailing of the troop transports. Reports sent out a week ago gave "early next week" as the time. Later "Tuesday or Wednesday" was fixed as the time. Newspapers here in the East, which mentioned Wednesday as the day of sailing have been denounced as traitors by newspapers which guesssed earlier or later dates. The fixing of Wednesday agitated war officials, so that it is concluded it is about the right time.

THE LANDING PLACE.

The idea that Matanzas is to be the landing place is not as strong as it has been. The weakening is due to the fact that no effort has been made to preserve secrecy with regard to what Admiral Sampson did to its batteries.

Tonight there is a suggestion among well informed men that the troops will land at some point in Pinar del Rio province, which is west of Havana. Matanzas is sixty or more miles east of the capital, and no harbor in Pinar del Rio is within 100 miles of the Havana province city, where the Spaniards say Sampson slew a mule.

The confusion in Spanish minds produced by conflicting stories from this city will not displease the War Department. There are no large numbers of insurgents in Pinar del Rio, so the suggestions that American troops will land there are slightly suspicious.

PRESIDENT NOT PERTURBED.

Prepartaions for the invasion appear to be so well in hand that there was but little doing at the White House or the Army and Navy departments. Secretary Long visited the President and went to church with him. Later the President went for a walk. If he is at all agitated about what was likely to happen to Commodore Dewey's fleet, he did not betray it.

Secretary Long had nothing to give out. In fact there is neither confirmation nor denial of rumors to be had from any official source, nor from the War or the Navy Department.

TAR-HEEL REBELLION ENDED.

During the day a report was received at the Navy Department that the rebellion in North Carolina had been suppressed This rebellion was led by the commander of the Tar-heel Naval Reserves. On Saturday Lieut. Moore of the navy, was sent to Wilmington to take charge of the monitor Nantucket, which was loaned to North Carolina for the use of the reserves. She was needed to guard the navy yard at Port Royal, S. C. Commander Morton refused to turn her over to Moore. He ran up the State flag, and put himself in rebellion. Correspondence between the Navy Department and the Governor of North Carolina brought about an understanding and Morton hauled down his flag.

STATE PRIDE REBUKED.

Manifestations of State pride are

Points of the News in Today's Times.

[THE BUDGET—This morning's fresh telegraphic budget, received since dark last night, includes the principal Associated Press (or night) report, many exclusive Times dispatches, these together making 15,000 words or about 15 columns. In addition is a day report, not so fresh, of about 7000 words—the whole making a mass of wired news aggregating the large volume of 21 columns—A large proportion of it relates to the existing war. A summary follows:]

The Los Angeles Times

XVIIITH YEAR. SINGLE PART—SIXTEEN PAGES AT THE OFFICE COUNTER...... PRICE 3 CENTS — FRIDAY MORNING, OCTOBER 13, 1899. — ON STREETS AND TRAINS AT ALL NEWS AGENCIES 5 CENTS

Baron Farrar Dead.

LONDON, Oct. 12.—Baron Thomas Henry Farrar, of Abinger Hall, one of the most distinguished British authorities on trade and finance, and at one time permanent secretary to the Board of Trade, died suddenly this morning, in his eighty-first year.

Smith Shoots Shoemaker.

SANTA ROSA, Oct. 12.—Fred Smith, a blacksmith of this city, is locked up in the County Jail. After an altercation with a young man named Charlie Shoemaker, Smith fired four times at him with a revolver. The fourth bullet struck Shoemaker in the neck, inflicting a wound which may prove dangerous.

[SOUTH AFRICA.]

BOER ADVANCE

HAS BEGUN.

The Campfires Burn on Laing's Neck.

Natal Invaded and Heights of Ingogon Occupied.

Little Republics Defy the Might of Great Britain.

Free State Burghers Take a Cape Colony Town.

Chamberlain's Reply to the Ultimatum Deems it Impossible to Discuss Latter's Terms—The United States Neutral.

[ASSOCIATED PRESS NIGHT REPORT.]

JOHANNESBURG, Oct. 12.—[By South African Cable.]—War was declared yesterday. The formal declaration occurred at 10 o'clock this morning.

Cut the Border.

[ASSOCIATED PRESS NIGHT REPORT.]

VRYBURG (Cape Colony,) Oct. 12.—Afternoon.—A body of Boers have cut the border fence, advanced to the railroad and cut the telegraph wires. Two thousand Boers are now occupying the railroad line.

Armored Train Destroyed.

[ASSOCIATED PRESS NIGHT REPORT.]

CAPE TOWN, Oct 13, 9:45 a.m.—A dispatch from Vryburg says that an armored train has been destroyed. It is feared that much loss of life will result. The news has been unofficially confirmed.

Laing's Neck Occupied.

[A. P. EARLY MORNING REPORT.]

LONDON, Oct. 12.—A special from Ladysmith says: "The Boers occupied Laing's Neck the moment the ultimatum expired. They are now pouring into Natal and Ingogon Heights have been occupied."

British Make Reply.

[ASSOCIATED PRESS NIGHT REPORT.]

LONDON, Oct. 12.—Following is the text of the British reply to the Boer ultimatum:

"Chamberlain to Milner, High Commissioner, sent 10:45 p.m., October 10, 1899—Her Majesty's government has received with great regret the peremptory demands of the South African Republic, conveyed in your telegram of October 9. You will inform the government of the South African Republic in reply that the conditions demanded by the government of the South African Republic are such as Her Majesty's Government deems it impossible to discuss."

FIVE POINTS THREATENED.

Therefore the British Cabinet Will Have to Guess Hard.

[ASSOCIATED PRESS NIGHT REPORT.]

LONDON, Oct. 13.—[By Atlantic Cable.] When the Cabinet meets at noon today it is evident that the Boer advance will be in full swing. Judging from present appearances, the Boers are preparing for a simultaneous invasion at five separate points, Laing's Neck, Kimberley, Vryburg, Mafeking and Lobastsi. Therefore it is almost impossible to guess the plan of campaign.

A dispatch from Durban, dated Thursday morning at 8 o'clock, announces that the Boers have seized Albertine Station and demanded the keys, which were delivered to them by the station master, who reached Ladysmith on a trolley car. The excitement at Ladysmith is increasing, and the troops are ready to act at a moment's notice.

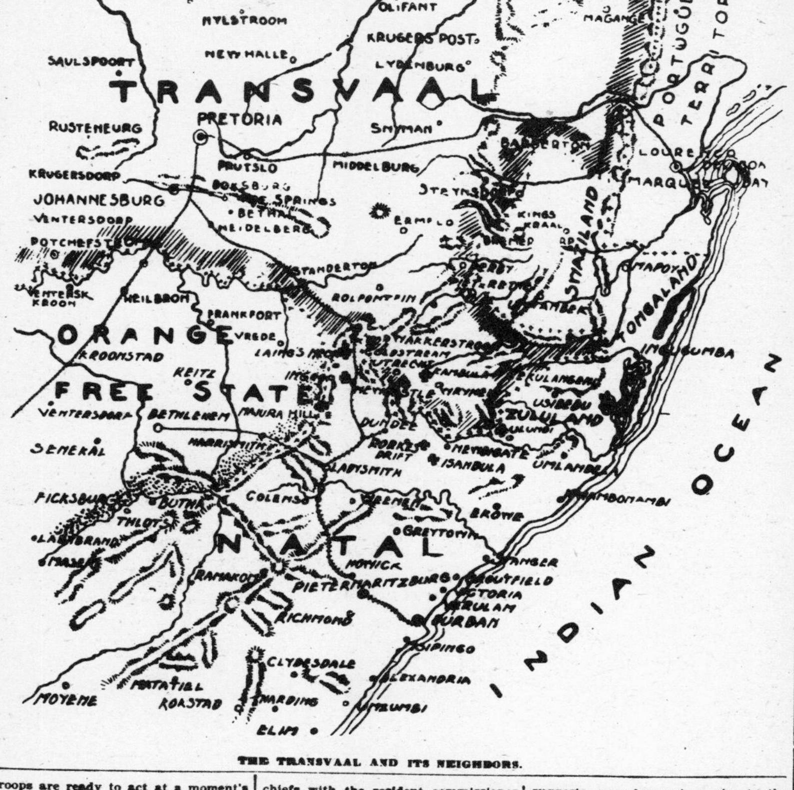

THE TRANSVAAL AND ITS NEIGHBORS.

FREE STATE'S ALLIANCE.

[ASSOCIATED PRESS NIGHT REPORT.]

LONDON, Oct. 12.—In reply to the formal inquiry of Sir Alfred Milner, Governor of Cape Colony and British High Commissioner in South Africa, President Steyn announces that the State will make common cause with the Transvaal.

WILL LACK COFFEE.

[ASSOCIATED PRESS NIGHT REPORT.]

CAPE TOWN, Oct. 12.—It is learned here that the Free State traders have have heavily commandered and have refused to import more goods, and it is expected that the Boers will shortly find difficulty in obtaining coffee and sugar. The telegraph wires have been cut at Maribogo, forty mils south of Mafeking.

JINGOES TOOK POSSESSION.

[ASSOCIATED PRESS NIGHT REPORT.]

LONDON, Oct. 12.—Although a considerable minority of the English public regard the war with a grave misgiving, it is practically impossible for this feeling to get voice at the present juncture.

An attempt of the Peace and Arbitration Association to hold a meeting at Bristol last evening occasioned an extraordinary scene. Directly the doors were opened, the jingoes crowded into the hall, sang patriotic songs, waved Union Jacks and refused any hearing to the orators, finally taking possession of the platform and passing a vote of confidence in the government.

CODE MESSAGES REFUSED.

[ASSOCIATED PRESS NIGHT REPORT.]

LONDON, Oct. 12.—The Eastern Telegraph Company (limited) announces that no code messages will be accepted for Cape Town.

SITTING ON IT.

[ASSOCIATED PRESS NIGHT REPORT.]

LONDON, Oct. 12.—The Daily Mail's correspondent at Lobastsi, telegraphing Wednesday, says: "The Boers are on the border, preparing to cross at 3 o'clock today. A messenger sent to the Boers asking them to spare the women and children has been detained."

DESTROYING DOCUMENTS.

[ASSOCIATED PRESS NIGHT REPORT.]

LONDON, Oct. 12.—The Daily Mail's correspondent at Pietermaritzburg says: "It is rumored at Newcastle that the destruction of documents incriminating President Kruger and other members of the Executive Council has commenced at Pretoria."

CAPE TOWN NOTES.

Panic at Vryburg—Free State and the Basuto Warriors.

[ASSOCIATED PRESS NIGHT REPORT.]

CAPE TOWN, Oct. 12.—[By Atlantic Cable.] The reply of the imperial government to the Transvaal's ultimatum is published here. It was accompanied by instructions to Conyngham Greene, diplomatic agent at Pretoria, to ask for his passports. The reply was publicly read by a magistrate at the evening parade of the town guard here, and evoked loyal and enthusiastic demonstrations. Cecil Rhodes has arrived at Kimberley.

A panic has broken out at Vryburg, and a hurried exodus has begun, owing to British refugees from the Transvaal declaring that a large force of Boers was advancing on the town. The rumor that Nawcastle has been occupied by the Boers is without confirmation.

Mr. Hofmeyer and other prominent members of the Afrikander bund have issued a circular appealing for subscriptions for the relief of the widows and families of burghers killed in the Transvaal.

The position of the Orange Free State at the present juncture is peculiar. While the Transvaal has virtually declared war, technically Great Britain and the Free State are on friendly terms.

It is alleged that the Free State Board has been endeavoring to induce the Basutos to cross the Caledon River and consent to a conference. It is the belief that they favor the Transvaal, but it is said the Basutos ridicule the idea.

At a late meeting of the paramount chiefs with the resident commissioner of Maseru, the chief was most pronounced in asserting the firm loyalty of the Basutos, and although pleasant words have been exchanged, the authorities are confident that an alliance between the Boers and Basutos is impossible.

CAMPAIGN HAS BEGUN.

Report of Entrance of Natal by the Burghers Confirmed.

[ASSOCIATED PRESS DAY REPORT.]

LONDON, Oct. 12.—[By Atlantic Cable.] All kinds of rumors are telegraphed from South Africa regarding the Boer movements. Apart from the advance of the Volksrust and Van Reenan commandos, reports have arrived of the concentration of the Utrecht and Vryheir commandos toward the drifts along the Buffalo River, east of Dundee.

One of the special correspondents at Ladysmith expresses the opinion that a Boer commando of some 200 men visited Newcastle Tuesday, made purchases and then withdrew. These, he suggests, may have given rise to the reports regarding the occupation of Laing's Neck.

Official confirmation of the announcement that the Orange Free State burghers have entered Natal by way of Van Reenan's Pass, is at hand. It leaves no further room for doubt that acts of war have already been committed, and that the campaign has begun.

News of an invasion on the northern border is also generally accepted as reliable. It seems improbable, therefore, that a clash between the forces of Britons and Boers can be long delayed, if, indeed, it has not occurred already.

This morning's dispatches furnish ample details of the situation on the frontier and enable a clearer exposition of the military status. It now seems that the Boers intend to act in two columns, those from the Transvaal working from the north, and those from the Orange Free State working from the west, with the object of keeping the British forces at Ladysmith and Dundee occupied, while

(CONTINUED ON THIRD PAGE.)

Points of the News in Today's Times.

[INDEX TO THE NEWS BUDGET:—Volume: Fresh A. P. Night Report and exclusive Times specials received by wire since dark last night, about 12 columns. Financial and Commercial, about 3 columns. Day Report (not so fresh) about 11 columns. Aggregate, 26 columns. The Index (for both telegraphic and local news) refers to general classification, subject and page.]

HIGH TRIBUTE

TO VOLUNTEERS.

President Expresses the Nation's Welcome.

Minnesota Boys Made to Feel They Did Their Duty.

Would not Stack Arms While Country Needed Them.

Telling Speech on the Growth of the American Domain.

Century Drawing to a Close Has Been a Most Memorable One—Increase of Territory Despite the Omnipresent "Auntie."

[ASSOCIATED PRESS NIGHT REPORT.]

MINNEAPOLIS, Oct. 12.—From a platform in front of the Minneapolis Exposition building, President McKinley this afternoon voiced the nation's welcome to the Thirteenth Minnesota Volunteers, just returned from the Philippines, and delivered an address to thousands of cheering people.

The President and his party were driven to the Exposition building directly after having reviewed the long parade from the reviewing stand on Nicollet avenue. About the platform in front of the building where Gen. Harrison was nominated for President of the United States by a convention presided over by William McKinley, were massed the returned volunteers. Behind them was a crowd whose numbers could scarcely be estimated. The cheering broke loose as soon as President McKinley, Gov. Lind and Gen. Summers of the Second Oregon Volunteers appeared on the platform. Dr. Cyrus Northrup, president of the University of Minnesota, presided over the exercises, and the invocation was pronounced by Bishop Isaac W. Joyce of the Methodist Episcopal Church.

Mayor Gray spoke the words of greeting to the soldiers and distinguished guests on behalf of the city, and Gov. Lind on behalf of the State. The Governor paid a strong tribute to the returned volunteers.

President McKinley was greeted with cheers that continued for several minutes, and throughout the delivery of the address the applause was frequent. He said:

"I have come from the capital of the nation that I might give the nation's welcome to a regiment of the nation's defenders. I have come to speak the voice of gratitude which comes today from every American heart that loves the flag. I have come to bid you welcome because you did your duty, and that is the highest tribute that can be paid to any soldier anywhere, and I do not think the members of this regiment, or the regiments constituting the Eighth Army Corps in the Philippines realize the importance and heroism of their action after the treaty of peace was signed and ratified. I want to say to you men, and to Col. Summers—Gen. Summers now, because of his gallantry—that the officers and men of the Eighth Army Corps sent to Washington a message telling me that they would stay in the Philippines until I could create a new army and send it there to take their places.

"I come to bid you welcome and give you the honor of the nation because you sustained the flag of the nation; because you refused to stack arms; refused to sound retreat. And you have come back, having a high place in the hearts and affections of the American people and gratitude that will continue for all time. You have also by your your services added much to the cause of humanity, added much to the advancement of the civilization which has so characterized the century just now fading away."

NATIONAL EXPANSION.

[ASSOCIATED PRESS DAY REPORT.]

MINNEAPOLIS, Oct. 12.—Continuing, the President said:

"The century now drawing to a close has been most memorable in the world's progress and history. The march of moral and intelligent advancement has been onward and upward. The growth of the world's material interests is so vast that the figures would almost seem to be drawn from the realm of imagination rather than from the field of fact. All peoples have felt the elevating influences of the century. Humanity and home have been lifted up. Nations have been drawn closer together in feeling and interest and sentiment. Contact has removed old prejudices at home and abroad and brought about a better understanding which has destroyed enmity and promoted amity.

"Civilization has achieved great victories and to the gospel of good-will there are now few dissenters. The great powers, under the inspiration of the Czar of Russia, have been sitting together in a parliament of peace, seeking to find a common basis for the adjustment of controversies without war and waste. While they have not made war impossible, they have made peace more possible and have more emphasized the universal love of peace. They have made a gain for the world's repose, and Americans, while rejoicing in what was accomplished, rejoice also for their participation in the great cause yet to be advanced, we trust, to more perfect fulfillment.

"The century has blessed us as a

The Los Angeles Times

XIXth YEAR. SINGLE PART—FOURTEEN PAGES AT THE OFFICE COUNTER........ PRICE 3 CENTS | TUESDAY MORNING, DECEMBER 26, 1899. | ON STREETS AND TRAINS AT ALL NEWS AGENCIES | 5 CENTS

MOTHER EARTH SHOOK.

TOWN OF SAN JACINTO ALMOST RUINED BY THE QUAKES YESTERDAY.

Southern California Rocked by an Invisible Force, and People Awakened from Their Slumbers in the Early Morning Hours.

Seismic Disturbance Generally Felt, but Serious Damage Reported at Few Places—Walls Cracked, Chimneys Toppled, Windows Broken, Dishes Smashed and Clocks Stopped—Six Indians Killed and Many Hurt by Falling Adobe Walls.

Christmas morning in Southern California was ushered in with one of the severest earthquakes this section of the Pacific Coast has experienced in many years. It occurred at an hour, 4:25 o'clock in the morning, when most people were in bed, but, sleeping or waking, few persons in the convulsed region failed to notice it.

The sleeping populace was not literally shaken out of bed, but many nervous individuals tumbled out in great haste when the heaving began and scrambled for doors and stairways. But aside from the early-rising record, nothing was smashed in this city and vicinity. From the interior, however, notably from San Jacinto, Hemet and other points in Riverside county come more serious reports. Both of the towns named suffered severely through demolishment of buildings, but fortunately no lives were lost in those villages, nor was anybody injured, though many persons had narrow escapes.

But the temblor did not spend its fury without finding some human victims. From the Saboba Indian reservation, Riverside county, comes the report that six aborigines were killed and four fatally injured by the collapse of an adobe building in which they were holding a dance in honor of the natal day of the Savior of the world. This brings to mind a similar disaster many years ago, when San Juan Capistrano Mission was partially destroyed during the Easter festivities, many Indian worshipers being buried in the ruins.

In this city the quake was quite pronounced, but not as much damage was done by it as by the one last summer, which did some slight injury to the City Hall and broke plate-glass windows in various business blocks. The City Superintendent of Buildings, after examining the City Hall carefully yesterday morning, found only a few slight cracks in addition to those caused by the last previous earthquake. A slight crack was also noted in the Courthouse tower. No damage of any consequence resulted to any other building, and aside from stopping of clocks and upsetting of top-heavy articles, the effect of the earthquake was untraceable after the vibrations ceased.

One citizen in the West End, whose house was recently robbed by burglars, was awakened by the pounding of the window weights against their cases, when the earthquake came. He thought burglars were again trying to get into the house, and started up, revolver in hand, to give them a warm reception. While he was tip-toeing through the parlor in search of the imaginary burglars, his little son emerged from his sleeping-room and said: "Papa, the burglars are under my bed; I felt them shaking it." By this time the old man observed that the whole house was shaking, and that he was gunning for an earthquake instead of burglars.

George E. Franklin, local forecast official of the Weather Bureau, took probably as accurate an observation of the temblor as any one in the city. Mr. Franklin usually goes to his office in the Wilson Block shortly before 5 o'clock in the morning to send to Washington his daily report of local conditions for the preceding day, but for some time past he has been engaged industriously in preparing an especially fine brand of holiday weather, and was on hand yesterday morning at 4 o'clock.

The local representative of "Old Probs." said last night:

"There were three distinct shocks, two faint and one severe and prolonged, and they began at 4:25 o'clock. The time from the beginning of the first until the end of the third was probably twenty seconds, although it seemed much longer.

The motion seemed to pass from a little west of south to a trifle east of north, and seemed undulating in its progress, like the motion of a ship at sea. A subdued roar or crunching sound accompanied the shock."

The Weather Bureau is on the fourth floor of the Wilson Block, and the building swayed for some time after the tremors occurred. In Mr. Franklin's office the locked doors of a bookcase were burst open and a tin box on top of a cabinet was moved several inches. Appleton's Geography, edited by Profs. Newberry of Columbia College and Hitchcock of Dartmouth, says in reference to earthquakes:

"The most general explanation is to be found in the breaking of the earth's crust under the same contraction that squeezes out lava from volcanoes, and folds the region of weakness into mountain ranges, and the shrinking of the crust on the cooling interior. The strata bend very gradually, and the rock is put into a condition of strain until it suddenly yields with a violent concussion."

There is no seismograph in this part of the State, and no accurate record of temblors is kept by the local Weather Bureau.

CENTERED AT SAN JACINTO.

The earthquake seemed to center at San Jacinto, and the business portion of that town, lining one side of a block with two-story brick buildings, is in ruins. The shock was felt at 4:29 o'clock a.m. It is generally conceded to have lasted nearly one minute.

Every brick building on the main street is practically demolished. Roofs, fronts, backs and sides fell in, and the shock was violent. Everybody was terrified, and within a few minutes a majority of the population were on the streets, hastily clad, and inquiring the extent of the disaster, the noise of falling walls and roofs creating general alarm. In frame buildings not damaged by the shock, bureaus and washstands were toppled over, and the temblor awakened everybody. Vibrations seemed to be west to east. The business street is lined with bricks, and stores are totally or badly wrecked.

No one was hurt. Some of the buildings knocked down were occupied, and some escapes were almost miraculous. One woman rushed to a door to escape from a building. The key had fallen to the floor, and while she was hunting for it the walls in the hallway toppled in. Had exit been effected it would have meant certain death.

Electric wires are down, and one of the power-houses has fallen in. The walls of the County Hospital, erected recently at a cost of $10,000, are badly damaged. The principal losses are estimated as follows, but it is impossible to state how much the total amounts to in dollars and cents:

Hards & Daggett, general merchandise, $1000, building, $1500; Dallis building, $3000; Jones building, $500; Vawter building, $3000; McBeath Block, $2000; Daggett's building, $3000; S. Pigous, $500; Indian Agency, $8000; McKin and Chambers' drug store, $6000; S. Kries building, $4000; bank building, $1000; J. W. Ryan building, $1000; Domingoni building, $3000; L. A. Wright's drug store, $1000; S. Mead's building and goods, $1000; E. D. Mead, hardware, $1000; Durett's building, $1500; Freeman's store, $2000; Col. Ritchey, $2000; Baker's store, $1000. The minor losses amount to considerable.

At Hemet the hotel was damaged to the extent of $10,000; Bingham's flour mill, $2000. The fire walls of Webber's brick store fell out, the plate-glass windows were smashed, and the entire stock of goods is on the floor in a heap. The chimneys of the hotel fell, many of them crashing through the roof. One fell upon the bed of Frank Robinson, bruising him badly. The verandas are all down, and the walls badly cracked. The rear wall of the Johnson Block fell outward, and the whole building was badly demolished. The third story of the Hemet mills is down, and the second story walls fell in. Prugh's grocery store fixtures were all shaken down, and he has his goods piled on the floor. The new Whittier Block was but slightly damaged. The front of Parker's store fell out, and the shelving was shaken down. There are but two chimneys left in town.

The shock was severe at Corona, but no special damage is reported, aside from slight wall cracks. The shock was also severe at Moreno, and brick buildings there were damaged. Following the main shock were three minor ones.

The gables of Highland Asylum were cracked and the chimneys shaken down.

At the Saboba Indian Reservation six squaws were killed by falling walls, two fatally injured and many seriously hurt. They were mostly old and were present at a dance. They were horribly crushed by the adobe walls.

The shock caused dry artesian wells to flow larger streams than ever before.

It is said that rumblings had been heard for several days about Tauquitz Peak, in the San Jacinto range, supposed to be an extinct volcano. Between San Jacinto and Hemet geysers of hot sulphur water appeared yesterday, and the fumes are so strong that no one can get near the geysers.

The streets of San Jacinto are being cleared of débris and merchants are moving their stocks into warehouses and frame structures. Preparations are already being made for the rebuilding of most of the ruined structures.

EASY AT PASADENA.

Clocks on the walls of Pasadena houses and stores stopped at 4:25 o'clock yesterday morning, showing the time the earthquake came along. The shock was quite long, but not violent, and hardly any damage is reported. In the west wing of Hotel Green, the largest building in the city, a riveted steel structure, one closely-knit frame from one end to the other and from top to bottom, considerable creaking was heard, but not the least crack in the walls or ceilings is to be seen. The plastering was not disturbed a hair's breadth. A crack opened in the ceiling of Odd Fellows' Hall, and a few minor happenings like that have been noted: but it was not much of a shake in this vicinity.

COVINA [illegible] BROKEN.

At Covina the earthquake occurred at 4:27 o'clock, but aside from the breaking of some china which was shaken from shelves, no damage is reported.

POMONA'S EXPERIENCE.

The shock awakened the people of Pomona at 4:25 o'clock a.m., and was of a number of seconds' duration, the vibrations apparently being from east to west. The earthquake was the most severe experienced in that section in recent years, but the extent of the damage was the shaking down of plastering in many places. Books and other loose articles were tumbled from racks and shelves.

RIVERSIDE'S QUAKE.

Some damage was done to walls, windows, chimneys and crockery at Riverside, but it will not aggregate much. The shock is described as having been quite severe, and of several seconds duration, the vibrations being from east to west, and then apparently up and down. It occurred at 4:30 a.m., and created a stir among people in tall buildings, many of whom made their way to the street in less than their accustomed time.

LIGHT AT SAN BERNARDINO.

It is reported from San Bernardino that the earthquake occurred there at 4:25 a.m., and was of about one minute duration, moving slowly from south to north. The sound of the earthquake was heard at least a half minute before the shock was felt. No damage was done in any part of the city. One cap stone on top of the High School building, about forty feet from the ground, which had been previously loosened, fell to the ground. The quake as a whole was not severe.

DAMAGE AT REDLANDS.

Redlands felt the shock at 4:25 o'clock, and it was quite severe. The rumbling noise usually accompanying temblors was less marked and of shorter duration, but the agitation itself was of longer duration. The length of time is variously given at from eight to twelve seconds, and the vibration was from east to west, being decidedly marked. The damage done was but slight, considering the severity of the shake as determined by the sensation of the people. The damage was principally to the following buildings:

At the residence of A. K. Smiley, in Cañon Crest Park, southwestern part of the city, two large chimneys were toppled over at the roof line, and the roof damaged by the falling bricks. The plastering was cracked some in several of the rooms.

The greatest damage to a public building was sustained by the new Columbia building, recently erected by K. C. Wells, president of the Union Bank. About midway from the front to the rear of the building the individual wall is joined to the party wall of that and the building next east. The walls are parted and spread about two and a half inches. The new Knights of Pythias Castle Hall is on the second floor of the building, and there the plastering was cracked all over the main hall, and several square yards of plastering shaken off the curved wall and ceiling on the north end.

The big plate-glass windows in the store front of Meserve's clothing-house were shifted one-eighth to one-quarter inch. The plate-glass window in the front of the Great American tea store was cracked from top to bottom, near the middle, and separated about one-eighth of an inch. Considerable chinaware was shaken from the shelves and smashed in falling. The arch-topped plate glass in the front of John W. Edwards's grocery, Fisher building, which had been cracked horizontally at the base of the arched portion, was shaken from the sash and fell, cutting a hole through the floor of the show window.

One of the service wires from the sub-station of the electric company was snapped, and the lights went out.

The west wall of the carhouse of the Redlands Street Railway Company was cracked.

SEVERE AT SANTA ANA

At Santa Ana the earthquake was the severest that has visited that section for many years. The vibrations lasted about thirty seconds, and were from west to east. The earth began to rock at 4:27 o'clock, and in a very short time hundreds of people were out of their beds and on the streets. Clocks were stopped all over the city, pictures were shaken from the walls, and in several instances dishes were broken in cupboards. Several brick buildings in the business portion of the city showed the effects yesterday in the shape of cracked walls. At the Rossmore and Richelieu hotels guests in the third story were almost rolled out of bed. A disagreeable desert wind prevailed throughout the valley, the past week, and atmospheric conditions became strained.

EARLY AT ANAHEIM.

The heaviest earthquake shock ever known at Anaheim occurred yesterday at 4:15 a.m. It lasted fully twenty seconds, and was violent from the beginning. Lodging-houses were emptied and in a few minutes some of the streets filled with shivering people, scared from their beds. The walls of a number of buildings were slightly cracked, but no serious damage was done.

ORANGE.

Reports from Orange are to the effect that a severe shock was felt there shortly after 4 o'clock a.m., which is considerably earlier than other points were shaken. The temblor lasted about twenty seconds there. No damage has been reported.

SAN DIEGO'S SHOCK.

The most severe shock of earthquake experienced in San Diego in fourteen years, took place at 4:25 a.m. yesterday, and was accompanied by a loud rumbling noise. The taller buildings in the city were severely shaken up, and plaster was shaken off, and a few broken articles of household furniture were reported, but no serious damage was done. A high wave struck the beach on the ocean front soon after the shock, but no damage resulted to shipping. A slighter shock followed the first one a few seconds later. In the heart of town people fled to the streets from upstairs apartments. At Coronado Beach loose articles were rattled and people awakened.

NO DAMAGE AT PERRIS.

Perris experienced the earthquake yesterday morning at 4:20 o'clock, but no damage was done at that point other than some cracked plastering in brick buildings, and the stopping of clocks.

THREE SHOCKS AT NEEDLES.

At Needles three earthquake shocks passed, traveling northeasterly, between 4:25 and 4:32 yesterday morning. Windows were rattled and buildings shaken, sleepers awakened and strangers startled, but no damage is reported. It was the severest shock felt on the desert in a long time.

REDONDO AWAKENED.

The disturbance awakened many people at Redondo, but, so far as reported, did no damage. A few clocks were stopped. At least one of the residents of the cottages on the beach noted the action of the waves at that time. Feeling the shock he listened to the surf, thinking there might be a big undulation on the ocean's surface. Apparently the earthquake had not the slightest effect on the sea. As far as the observer could determine the waves rolled in exactly as if the earth had not trembled.

SANTA MONICA UNDAMAGED.

The shock aroused many from their early morning slumber at Santa Monica, but caused only slight damage or none at all. Cracks which were noticed in some of the brick buildings after the earthquake provoked many amusing discussions, some people contending that the seismic movements had caused them, and others arguing that they had existed for years.

LONG BEACH FELT IT.

Long Beach felt the shock at 4:20 a.m., and it was more or less severe there, the vibrations lasting about fifteen seconds. The shock was heavy enough to shake down pans and other loose articles in the stores and houses. It stopped the clocks in the Julian Hotel.

WELDON'S BLOODY CHRISTMAS.

FARM-HAND KILLS CARPENTER OVER POKER.

[A. P. NIGHT REPORT.]

CLINTON (Ill.,) Dec. 25.—At 3 o'clock today, at Weldon, ten miles southeast of here, Harry Summers, Jr., of Weldon, a carpenter, and "Doc" Marcum, a farm-hand in Piatt county, engaged in a quarrel in a poker-room. Marcum shot and killed Summers.

Marcum, who was drunk, is a Kentuckian, about 25 years old. His victim was about 30 years of age, and peaceable. He had a family, while Marcum is unmarried, and has been in Weldon but once before. The murderer was placed in jail here this afternoon.

Weldon has about six hundred population, and is the town in which Postmaster John A. Pace killed Hon. W. H. Taylor, December 28, 1895. The murder today being three days before the fourth anniversary of the killing of Taylor, who was at that time a member of the Legislature, the citizens were greatly excited, and Marcum was hurried to Clinton, as it was feared an attempt would be made to lynch him.

FATAL FREE FIGHT.

ONE MAN KILLED, SEVERAL WOUNDED.

[A. P. NIGHT REPORT.]

RICHMOND, (Va.,) Dec. 25.—At Virgilania, Halifax county, today, a man named Loftis entered the depot and fired several times at Turner, the operator. Turner returned the fire and killed Loftis. Friends of the dead man attacked Turner. A general fight followed, and Turner received a terrible gash in the throat, while several other men, two of whom will probably die, were wounded.

At last accounts a mob was threatening to lynch Turner, but he was being guarded in the depot by armed friends. The Sheriff has gone to the scene.

Severe Storms in Ohio.

CLEVELAND (O.,) Dec. 25.—A furious snowstorm accompanied by a forty-five-mile gale has been raging throughout Northern Ohio and over Lake Erie for the past twenty-four hours. The thermometer registers 16 deg. below zero. In this city street-car traffic is badly impeded as a result of the heavy snowdrifts piled on the tracks. Trains on the trunk-line railroads are nearly all late.

Points of the News in Today's Times

[INDEX TO THE NEWS BUDGET:—Volume: Fresh A.P. Night Report and exclusive Times specials received by wire since dark last night, about 13 columns. Day Report (not so fresh) about 7 columns. Aggregate, 20 columns. The Index for telegraphic and local news refers to general classification, subject and page.]

[SOUTH AFRICA.]

TAKE A TURN

AT THE ENEMY.

Buller Expected to Get to Work Soon.

Ladysmith Probably Will First Receive Attention.

Methuen Stands by and Sees Boers Intrench.

Military Men Look for an Attack at Colenso.

Publication of Letters Which Escaped the Censor—Irritation and Fussiness of Martinets Exhausting the Patience of Soldiers.

[BY DIRECT WIRE TO THE TIMES.]

LONDON, Dec. 25.—[Exclusive Dispatch.] Unless all signs fail, Tommy Atkins has eaten Christmas dinner as quietly as an ordinary English householder. The War Office has issued a series of casualty lists from Cape Town, Modder River, Pietermaritzburg and Ladysmith, but otherwise has not thrown new light upon the military situation. The Ladysmith lists show that typhoid fever and dynsentery are more effective than the Boers' artillery in reducing the strength of the garrison, day by day. The military staff seems to have chosen an unsanitary, as well as an indefensible, position at Ladysmith before the opening of the campaign, when a much stronger site for a camp might have been selected at Colenso or Estcourt, with superior water supply.

Buller and White have been obliged to pay penalties for the original blunders of engineers, who recommended Ladysmith and Glencoe as sites for the British camps when the Tugela line was the natural line of defense in Natal, with a station in reserve at Mooi River. The concentration of their forces is now an undertaking of great difficulty, as is evident from the reports of Buller's battle, which are still coming in ten days after Long's artillery was lost.

It is clear that Buller will renew the attempt to relieve Ladysmith while Roberts is on the sea. He is receiving reinforcements and fresh batteries, and ought to be in a position to reopen hostilities in a week or ten days, unless he waits for a siege train. The movements of the battalion arriving at Cape Town are now concealed by authority, but Buller is evidently taking fresh troops and replacing artillery, while Methuen is forced to stand by and watch the Boers, while they extend their rifle trenches and strengthen their position in front of Modder River.

Buller is justified in this course if Ladysmith, as is generally believed, is in a more critical condition than Kimberley. About eleven thousand troops will arrive during the next eighteen days at Cape Town, before Roberts can assume command. With this body of reinforcements, Buller will not have facilities for setting every column again on the offensive, but he will at least have sufficient strength for maneuvering against Colenso, and attempting to turn the enemy's position there. This is what military men in London are now expecting him to do within a fortnight.

One reassuring sign is the publication of mail letters from Ladysmith, Estcourt and other points in Natal, which evidently have not been submitted to the military censor. This budget of correspondence deals in a critical spirit with the blunders made by the staff, and the irritation and fussiness of the martinets in repeatedly changing camp and exhausting the patience of the soldiers. They also contain evidence that the British field artillery is distinctly inferior, not only to the Boer guns in range, but to the guns of almost every important European power. This campaign is bringing out many unpleasant revelations of which full political use will be made when the Liberal opposition learns the true points for an attack.

BOER REPORT ON TUGELA RIVER BATTLE

GEN. SCHALKBERGER'S ACCOUNT OF BRITISH DEFEAT.

Forces Rolled Back Like a Spent Wave, Leaving Ridges of Dead and Dying Humanity Behind—French and German Attaches Praise the Tactics of the Transvaal Forces.

[A. P. DAY REPORT.]

PRETORIA, Sunday, Dec. 17.—[By South African Cable.] Over five hundred British prisoners, captured at the battle of Stormberg, have arrived here. They have been taken to Waterfall to join the other prisoners.

An official account of the Boer casualties at Tugela River says thirty men were killed or wounded. Gen. Schalkberger's report of the battle, dispatched from the head laager, December 16, says:

"Friday, at dawn, the long-expected arrived. The Pretoria detachment

The Times

XIXth YEAR — SINGLE PART—SIXTEEN PAGES. AT THE OFFICE COUNTER......PRICE 3 CENTS — LOS ANGELES — FRIDAY MORNING, NOVEMBER 23, 1900. — ON STREETS AND TRAINS AT ALL NEWS AGENCIES 5 CENTS

EAST AND WEST HAVE JOINED HANDS.

The National Irrigation Congress a Glorious Success in Its Unity—Strong Principles Evolved.

[BY DIRECT WIRE TO THE TIMES.]

CHICAGO (Ill.) Nov. 22.—[Exclusive Dispatch.] Though the papers read before the National Irrigation Congress today were splendid, yet they were less interesting to those who have long been advocating national irrigation than were the discussions. These latter, reflecting a wide public sentiment, show how thoroughly men from all over the country have gotten together upon the great principles of national irrigation, differing only upon the mere details. Senators, Congressmen, lawyers and professional men, more than two dozen, discussed this problem, the chief point of discussion being as to whether the Federal or the State government should distribute the water.

The strong current of sentiment in the convention is evidently in favor of concentrating energy on the things the West absolutely agreed on, which are expressed in the motto adopted by resolution: "Save the forests and store the floods." George H. Maxwell strongly urged this policy, and it was plain that he struck a responsive chord in the audience.

A striking feature of the discussion has been the evident interest and knowledge on the subject displayed by eastern men in attendance. J. C. Brady of the Wheeling Hinge Company of Wheeling, W. Va., said that the West had not itself awakened to the magnitude of this great question. The West, he said, should ask for $5,000,000 a year for water storage.

The sentiments expressed in the discussion show that there was also an enthusiastic approval of the fundamental idea of uniting the ownership of land and water by making the ownership of water appurtenant to land, and making beneficial use the basis of measure and limit of the right to water for irrigation. Also that the public lands should be held for home-builders after they had been provided with water for irrigation.

The western delegates were surprised at the character and enthusiasm of the eastern delegates, and the latter are surprised that the West has not enlightened the East on this problem long ago and been less modest in their demands at Washington.

Hon. Thomas Knight of Kansas City gave one of the best thoughts. Agriculture was but one good result from this policy, vast mining and other industries would be made possible after the desert had become a land of homes. Whenever a dollar can be made, after an irrigation development which could not have been made before, that dollar should be credited to the wisdom of this irrigation policy.

On committees the following California men were chosen: Permanent Organization, Charles B. Boothe, Los Angeles; Resolutions, Scipio Craig, Redlands; Credentials, A. D. Bishop, Orange; Rules and Order, President F. L. Ferguson, Pomona College.

GOV. ROOSEVELT'S INTEREST.

[BY DIRECT WIRE TO THE TIMES.]

CHICAGO, Nov. 22.—[Exclusive Dispatch.] "The problem of the development of the Greater West is in larger part a problem of irrigation. I earnestly believe in the nation's government giving generous aid to the movement."

With these words, conveyed by letter, owing to inability to be present in person, Vice-President-elect Theodore Roosevelt placed himself on record last evening as being heartily in sympathy with the aims of the National Irrigation Congress. His letter, read at the meeting at the Auditorium, went even further than this, for it contained his practical promise of assistance in the effort which will be made from now on for government aid to irrigation, and his appeal to all "far-sighted citizens" to interest themselves in a movement which will benefit the entire nation.

Gov. Roosevelt's letter was all the more welcome because it was directly in line, as regards its point of view, with the feeling of the congress, as developed in the discussions which had lasted all through the day. It was a paper on the construction of great storage reservoirs by the government for the general use of entire districts of farmers, read by Capt. Hiram Chittenden, Engineer Corps, U.S.A., which started the discussion, and perhaps half the delegates to the congress found a chance to support the project with strong words. Gov. Roosevelt's letter in part is as follows:

"I believe to the last the vital necessity of preserving the forests, especially throughout the plain and Rocky Mountain regions. The problem of development of the Greater West is in a large part the problem of irrigation. I earnestly believe in the national government giving generous aid to the movement, for it is not possible and would not be wise to have this storage work done merely through private ownership, and owing to peculiar necessities of the case, much of the work must be done by the national and not by any State government.

"We are just getting to understand what is involved in the preservation of our forests. Not only is an industry at stake which employs more than half a million of men, the lumber industry, but the whole prosperity and development of the West, and, indeed, ultimately of the entire country, is bound up with the preservation of the forests. Right use of the forests means the perpetuation of our supply of wood and water. Therefore we cannot be satisfied with anything short of expert, responsible management of the national forest reserves and other national forest interests.

"The forest reserves must be cared for by the best-trained foresters to be had, just as the storage reservoirs must be built and maintained by the best engineers. There is the same need of trained skill in handling forests in your best interests as there is in building great dams which will some day bring population and abounding prosperity to the vast stretches of the so-called desert in the West.

"Without pretending to outline definitely a working scheme, I venture to point out that without the attainment of the following objects your plans must measureably fail:

"1. Government study of streams upon which your plans depend.

"2. Government construction and control of great irrigation plants.

"3. The preservation of forests by the extension of a forest reserve system, hence of government control of the forests.

"4. National protection, use of forests under expert supervision.

"5. I urge you to see to it that private owners of forests in the West and East alike understand that timber can be cut without forest destruction (the Department of Agriculture will tell them how) and that ownership of water rights in arid country and of forest lands anywhere, entails public as well as private duties and responsibilities."

The Resolutions Committee was instructed to embody the salient points of Capt. Chittenden's argument in their report.

At the afternoon session, Col. H. B. Maxson, secretary of the congress, made his annual report.

"SAVE THE FORESTS: STORE THE FLOODS."

MOTTO SUGGESTED FOR THE IRRIGATION CONGRESS.

Numerous Interesting Papers Presented Yesterday—Movement to Have Committee Set Forth Aims and Purposes of the Gathering.

[BY THE NEW ASSOCIATED PRESS—P.M.]

CHICAGO, Nov. 22.—The National Irrigation Congress got down to business today. President Eldwood Meade of Wyoming presided. Scipio Craig of California made a motion that the motto of the congress be "Save the Forests and Store the Floods," and that a committee on resolutions be instructed to draft a memorial setting forth the objects of the congress, and showing the importance of the reclamation of the arid lands in the United States and to report Saturday. Capt. Hiram M. Chittenden of the United States Engineer Corps delivered an address.

Capt. Chittenden said in part:

"The industrial growth of any country and its capacity for a high civilization depend in an eminent degree upon its agricultural development. In the western portion of the United States this development is limited by the

(CONTINUED ON FIFTH PAGE.)

News Index to The Times This Morning

CLASSIFIED NEWS SYNOPSIS.

THE CITY.—Damage by flood in and around the city and Southern California....Work of repairing streets under way....Work on Federal Building soon to be under way....Examination of Yglesias, slayer of Perez, begun....Mayor's statement regarding Mr. Silver's soundness on water question....Ninth Ward Republican meeting....Mrs. Creede declared a mercenary adventuress and family allowance denied her....Brisk oil development work in Sunset field....Still agitating for pure milk....Factories damaged by fire...Panson House reception....Death of an Ex-Assemblyman.

SOUTHERN CALIFORNIA. Fire in Long Beach....Light at San Pedro on Chilean bark mystery....High tide's freaks at Terminal Island cause damage....San Diego State Normal School's needs investigated....Different story about Victor cutting affray. Riverside fruit shipments....Ventura woman shoots her husband....Aged German found dead in Orange county.

PACIFIC COAST. Seattle man's eight-year boycott of street cars called off....Child burned to death near Millville....Wronged husband traces wife to Phoenix to find elopers gone. Money secured on incendiary fire returned to insurance company....Ex-convict shoots a prison guard....Storm damage to railroads is immense.

CHINA. Allied forces may again take the field....Danger of an uprising against the Emperor....United States fears Kwang Su may be killed.

FOREIGN. BY CABLE. Czar of Russia reported dead....Kruger given an ovation at Marseilles....Sir Arthur Sullivan dies at London....Active campaign in the Philippines....Boers defeated with heavy loss by lancers. Pope Leo returns to his bed....Colombian rebels crushed.

SPORTS. Lawyer Witte offers big purse for bout between Corbett and Jeffries at Cincinnati....Three knockouts and a draw at Stockton....Mounce pilots three of Jennings's horses to victory at Tanforan.

GENERAL EASTERN. East and West join hands in National Irrigation Congress....Particulars of Salt Lake road organization....Needham soon to begin work for San Diego Harbor appropriation....Congressman Steele talks of coming session....Colorado Springs recovering from windstorm.

MILLIONS IN IT INSURE SUCCESS.

Launching of the Great Salt Lake Road Enterprise Which Means So Much to Los Angeles.

[BY DIRECT WIRE TO THE TIMES.]

SALT LAKE (Utah,) Nov. 22.—[Exclusive Dispatch.] After an all-night and all-day session, the Los Angeles and Salt Lake Railway has been fully organized. The Empire Construction Company was formed at the same time for the purpose of equipping and building the road, and in the process of organization is a development company to look after the development of the resources of the country traversed by the railroad.

Never in the history of Utah has so important a project been started, a project that is of even greater importance to California. Salt Lake has been filled with men of millions, mining experts, engineers and contractors, and in the long session of the magnates a wonderful amount of business was cleaned up.

Senator W. A. Clark and J. Ross Clark left for Los Angeles today. They will be followed tomorrow by Vice-President T. E. Gibbon and Charles Clark of Missouri. They go to Los Angeles to effect the transfer of Terminal property to the new company, after which the articles of incorporation will be filed.

The Los Angeles and Salt Lake Railway has a capital stock of $25,000,000, of which $2,500,000 is paid up. The officers and directors are W. A. Clark of Montana, president; R. C. Kerens of St. Louis, first vice-president; J. Ross Clark of Los Angeles, second vice-president; T. E. Gibbon of Los Angeles, third vice-president and general counsel; T. F. Miller of Los Angeles, secretary; W. S. McCornick, Reed Smoot, Thomas Kearns of Salt Lake; E. W. Clark of Ophir, Utah; Charles W. Clark of Montana; Perry S. Heath of Muncie, Ind.; George B. Leighton of St. Louis, directors. F. K. Rule of Los Angeles is treasurer, but not a director. Other incorporators are Charles Clark of St. Louis, David Keith, C. O. Whittemore of Salt Lake, W. B. Clark of Kansas City, Richard Kerens, Jr., A. H. Handlan and S. A. Bemis of St. Louis.

The officers and directors of the Empire Construction Company are J. Ross Clark, president; George B. Leighton, vice-president; H. E. McKee of Los Angeles, secretary. W. A. Clark, W. S. McCornick, David Keith, Reed Smoot, R. C. Kerens, T. E. Gibbon and T. F. Miller, directors. This company is incorporated for $10,000,000, of which $100,000 is paid up. The organization of a development company is left to a committee consisting of Messrs. Keith, Kerens, Gibbon and McCornick.

The route is not specifically stated as to the main line, but it is to be built by the best and most practicable route. The line of railway will run from Salt Lake to Los Angeles, with branches to Deep Creek and to Cedar City, the former being the great gold and silver section, and the latter the coal and iron lands. The company will also build many spurs and branches in and around Los Angeles, San Pedro and other points, so as to form a network of feeders at the western terminus.

The headquarters of all the companies will be at Los Angeles, with a branch office at Salt Lake. Work on the San Bernardino extension and at other points in California will be pushed with vigor, and later on work will be commenced at the Utah end. The Pioneers' Square being assured for the passenger terminal gives the new road an entrance to the heart of the business center of Salt Lake, and nearer all points of commerce and interest than any other railroad depot.

The Times correspondent has just left Messrs. Gibbon, Kerens, Leighton and others, and they are delighted at the prospects. Mr. Gibbon says: "The line will be built as quickly as money can build it. There is not one barrier to overcome before the people of the City of Saints can become acquainted with those of the City of Los Angeles by making a twenty-four hour trip over the new road. Eminent success has crowned the efforts of all who have in any way been working for this project. It is a great day for Los Angeles."

CONTINUED ON FOURTH PAGE.

1901–1910

The Times
LOS ANGELES
XXTH YEAR — TWO PARTS—EIGHTEEN PAGES AT THE OFFICE COUNTER ... PRICE 3 CENTS — WEDNESDAY MORNING, JANUARY 23, 1901. — ON STREETS AND TRAINS AT ALL NEWS AGENCIES 5 CENTS

BRITAIN MOURNS THE DEATH OF ITS SOVEREIGN.

PASSING OF VICTORIA.

Good Queen's End Was Peaceful.

Died Surrounded by the Royal Family.

Recognized Most of Them Before She Expired.

The Body Will be Taken to Windsor—King Goes to London.

[BY DIRECT WIRE TO THE TIMES.]

NEW YORK, Jan. 22.—[Exclusive Dispatch.] The Sun's cable from East Cowes, England, says Queen Victoria is no more. She passed away, without pain or suffering, at Osborne House at 6:30 o'clock this evening. King Edward VII rules in her stead. England is silent with grief.

A glimpse of the last moments of the beloved sovereign which the nation, and the world also, so earnestly craved has been vouchsafed by a representative of the stricken family. We are permitted to know not only the brief but eloquent facts stated in the frequent bulletins, but some few details which make very human this deathbed of the most illustrious sovereign of her time.

It was when the cold, gray day dawned that the renewed decline of the vital powers warned the watchers that their struggle against nature could not much longer succeed. The Queen was then completely unconscious, and from moment to moment the exhaustion of the small remaining store of vitality became perceptibly greater. Shortly after 9 o'clock the doctors sent a summons to all members of the family and also to the rector of the royal chapel. Before they all arrived, there took place that prudential phenomenon which Nature sometimes grants to the dying. The Queen became conscious and free of all suffering.

It was under these circumstances of precious memory that the last interviews with her children and grandchildren took place. The world will never know and has no right to know what took place then. The Queen received them all singly and by twos and threes within the next four hours. She recognized most of them. Then the curtain of unconsciousness fell for the last time and physicians made known that the Queen was dying. All assembled and remained until the very end.

It was so quiet and peaceful and gentle that it was difficult to realize that the shadow of death was present. Nothing more can be said of those last moments. Even the fierce light which beats upon a throne did not penetrate that chamber, and the tender memories of the last hours belong to those who mourn Victoria, not as Queen, but in the dearer relationship of the family.

The circulation of all manner of imaginative reports during the past three days led the authorities at Osborne House to authorize the publication of these simple facts. In addition to the foregoing, the Queen was attended throughout her illness by two nurses and four dressers, in charge of Miss Soal, who is matron of the sanatorium in Osborne Park. They had long been her personal attendants when Her Majesty was at Osborne. The Queen was nourished throughout her illness only with warm milk, invalids' prepared food, champagne and brandy. She was never fed artificially.

GUARDING THE EVENT.

The doors of the wing of the palace where the Queen lay were kept locked during her illness, so she was entirely isolated from the rest of the establishment. The strictest precautions were taken Saturday, Sunday and Monday nights that in case of sudden death no unauthorized person should communicate the fact to the Prince of Wales in violation of strict traditions. The Earl of Clarendon, the Lord Chamberlain, and Arthur Balfour, First Lord of the Treasury, arrived just in time to perform this duty. Balfour did not see the Queen.

The most significant point of the present situation is the statement of the authorities of the court, that absolutely no preparations have been made for any feature of the elaborate proceedings now forced upon the nation. One would imagine that the great age of the sovereign would have led to some consideration of the inevitable problem now presented. It is only another evidence of the marvelous hold that the Queen had upon the affections of all classes, including, of course most of all, those personally attached to her. They simply refused to consider the possibility of her death.

CLOUDS ROLLED AWAY.

Within an hour of the Queen's death the vicinity of Osborne House was deserted, and it was difficult to believe one was almost in the presence of the first great event of the new century. Then came one of those little signs which even Englishmen are sufficiently superstitious to notice. The day had been damp and chill and heavily overcast. Presently, when the tragedy had been enacted, the evening became mild, the clouds rolled away, and the stars shone brightly. It is now the traditional "Queen's weather," but the phrase has become a mournful memory.

While the court is not prepared for the great public functions attendant upon a change of sovereigns, it, of course, is settled that the body will be taken to Windsor and buried beside that of the Prince Consort at Frogmore. The funeral will certainly be delayed more than a week. It has not yet been decided whether the body will lie in state in Osborne House or be removed immediately to St. George's Chapel, Windsor.

THE KING.

The King will go to London early in the morning, where a meeting of the Privy Council will be held in the course of the day. The German Emperor will accompany him. The latter's future movements have not been decided upon. The remainder of the palace party will stay at Osborne House until the further arrangements are decided.

The new sovereign remains tonight under the same roof as his dead mother, the chief mourner among a larger gathering of children than often meets around a parent's deathbed anywhere in the world. They are in their own secluded world, inside the gates of Osborne lodge.

IN DEATH'S CHAMBER.

SOVEREIGNTY ENDED.

[BY THE NEW ASSOCIATED PRESS—P.M.]

COWES (Isle of Wight,) Jan. 23.—[By Atlantic Cable.] Queen Victoria is dead, and Edward VII reigns.

The greatest event in the memory of this generation, the most stupendous change in existing conditions that could possibly be imagined, has taken place quietly, almost gently, upon the anniversary of the death of the Queen's father, the Duke of Kent.

The end of this career, never equaled by any woman in the world's history, came in a simply-furnished room in Osborne House. This most respected of women, now dead, lies in a great four-posted bed, a shrunken atom, whose aged face and figure are a cruel mockery of the fair girl who in 1837 began to rule over England.

Around her, at the end, were gathered almost every descendant of her line. Well within view of her dying eyes there hung a portrait of the Prince Consort. It was he who designed the room and every part of the castle. In scarcely audible words, the white-haired Bishop of Winchester prayed beside her, as he had often prayed with his sovereign, for he was her chaplain at Windsor. With bowed heads, the imperious ruler of the German empire and the man who is now King of England, the woman who has succeeded to the title of Queen, the Princes and Princesses, and those of less than royal designation, listened to the bishop's ceaseless prayer.

Six o'clock passed. The bishop continued his intercession. One of the younger children asked a question in shrill, childish treble, and was immediately silenced. The women of this royal family sobbed faintly and the men shuffled uneasily.

At exactly half-past 6 o'clock Sir James Reid held up his head, and the people then knew that England had lost her Queen. The bishop pronounced the benediction. Those who were now mourning went to their rooms. A few minutes later the inevitable element of materialism stepped into this pathetic chapter of international history, for the court dames went busily to work ordering their mourning from London.

The wheels of the world were jarred when the announcement came, but in this palace at Osborne everything pursued the usual course. Down in the kitchen they were cooking a huge dinner for an assemblage, the like of which has seldom been known in England, and the dinner preparations proceeded just as if nothing had happened.

The body of Queen Victoria was embalmed and will probably be taken to Windsor Saturday. The coffin arrived last evening from London.

CHARACTERISTIC THOUGHTS.

An incident characteristic of the Queen's solicitude for others occurred two days ago, when, in one of the intervals of consciousness, she summoned strength to suggest to her dressers who had been acting as nurses, to take the opportunity of getting some fresh air. Monday she asked that her little Pomeranian spaniel be brought to her bedroom.

It was thought that the Queen was dying about 9 o'clock in the morning and carriages were sent to Osborne cottage and the rectory to bring all the Princes and Princesses and the Bishop of Winchester to her bedside. It seemed then very near the end, but when things looked the worst the Queen had one of the rallies due to her wonderful constitution, opened her eyes and recognized the Prince of Wales, the Princesses and Emperor William. She asked to see one of her faithful servants, a member of the household. He hastened to the room, but before he got there the Queen had passed into a fitful sleep.

Four o'clock marked the beginning of the end. Again the family was summoned, and this time the relapse was not followed by recovery.

THE PRINCE AFFECTED.

The Prince of Wales was very much affected when the doctors at last informed him that his mother had breathed her last. Emperor William, himself deeply affected, did his best to minister comfort to his sorrow-stricken uncle, whose new dignity he was the first to acknowledge.

From all parts of the world there are still pouring into Cowes messages of condolence. They come from crowned heads, millionaires, tradesmen and paupers, and are variously addressed to the Prince of Wales and the King of England.

Emperor William's arrangements are not settled. His coach will arrive here today (Wednesday,) but it is believed that he will not depart until after the funeral. Several other royal personages are likely to be present at the funeral.

The record of the last days of the reign of Victoria is not easy to tell. The correspondent of the Associated Press was the only correspondent admitted to Osborne House, and his interview with Sir Arthur John Bigge, private secretary to the late Queen, was the only official statement that had been given out. For several weeks the Queen had been failing. Monday week, she summoned Lord Roberts, and asked him some very searching questions regarding the war in South Africa. Tuesday, she went for a drive, but was visibly affected. Wednesday she suffered a paralytic stroke, accompanied by intense physical weakness. It was her first illness in all her 81 years, and she would not admit it. Then her condition grew so serious that, against her wishes, the members of the family were summoned. When they arrived her reason had practically succumbed to paralysis and weakness.

"BLOOD IS THICKER THAN WATER."

England, across the breadth of land and sea
Columbia sends her tribute to that worth
That maketh royal royalty of earth.
She, whom we mourn as dead, can never die
As long as England's flag floats in the sky.
Where'er it flies men will recall the trust
Her people gave to her, the wise and just.

Victoria, above thy bier we do not weep
That thou hast entered into rest and sleep,
That thy long loyalty is crowned at last
With joy. That age and weeping all are past.
We mourn that earth, which needs such royalty
As was thine own, has lost so much in thee.

C.

News Index to The Times This Morning

CLASSIFIED NEWS SYNOPSIS.

THE CITY. Gamblers boldly defying the law....Work begun on new temporary postoffice....Talk of cut in passenger rates....Courthouse jobs distributed....Supervisors requested to reduce telephone tax....Wife objects to husband taking ax to bed with him. Arthur Odell gets ten years in San Quentin....City rests its case in big water suit....New Police Commissioners learning the ropes....Dr. Bacon snaps his fingers at City Council.

SPORTS. Favorites fall by wayside at Tanforan Park....Sharkey wants another try at the championship. Honors paid to memory of Queen Victoria....Oil-land values increasing.

SOUTHERN CALIFORNIA. Pasadena youth confesses to robbing dentist's safe....Ontario improvements. Dog-cat aquatic duel at San Pedro. Death from accident at Elsinore. Stabbing at Santa Ana....Whittier electric-railway franchise sold....Former wife shoots Tia Juana rancher. Doctors' suit non-suited at Riverside.

PACIFIC COAST. Legislature adjourns out of respect to dead Queen. Senate begins passing bills....Coyote Scalp Bill again bobs up....President Wheeler addresses legislative committees on needs of State University. Assembly adopts resolution for investigation of Paris Commission—Hurry for new Franchise Bill over—Senator Rowell wants investigation of oil land locations....W. L. Walker's family removed by giant powder....License of Iaqua's captain suspended....Arizona Legislature listens to Governor's message.

GENERAL EASTERN. Election of Senators in many States....Uprising of Indians in Creek Nation....Grand Operahouse burned in Cincinnati. British sloop burned by Venezuelan gunboat....Suppression of billboard nuisance in Chicago....Gould-Rockefeller railroad combine....Chicago's record of crime....Rev. Ed Davis goes on the stage....Battle with safe-blowers in Kentucky.

FOREIGN, BY CABLE. Death of Queen Victoria—Messages of condolence from the whole world—Albert Edward ascends to the throne....Kruger leaves The Hague for Utrecht....Inadequacy of England's navy.

WASHINGTON. Californians talk for San Pedro inner harbor....Salt Lands Bill goes to President....Cabinet reads report of Philippines Commission....Senate approves supplementary treaty with Spain.

THE WEATHER. The weather report in detail is printed daily on the "Liner" page, including "comparative temperatures" at widely-separated points.

The Los Angeles Times

In One Part: 16 Pages.

XXth YEAR. PER WEEK....20 CENTS PER MONTH....75 CENTS | $9 A YEAR. SATURDAY, SEPTEMBER 7, 1901. ON ALL NEWS STANDS TRAINS AND STREETS | 5 CENTS

THE PRESIDENT TWICE SHOT, BUT LIVES.

Dastardly Attempt to Assassinate the Chief Magistrate of the Nation at the Pan-American Exposition.

One Wound in Stomach Serious, But Doctors Say Patient Will Recover.

Would-Be Assassin Says His Name Is Czolgosz and That He Is An Anarchist.

[BY THE NEW ASSOCIATED PRESS—P.M.]

BUFFALO (N. Y.) Sept. 6.—Just a brief twenty-four hours ago the newspapers of the city blazoned forth in all the pomp of headline type "The Proudest Day in Buffalo's History."

Tonight, in sackcloth and ashes, in somber type, surrounded by grewsome borders of black, the same newspapers are telling in funereal tones to a horrified populace, the deplorable details of "The blackest day in the history of Buffalo."

President McKinley, the idol of the American people, the nation's Chief Executive and the city's honored guest, lies prostrate, suffering the pangs inflicted by the bullet of a cowardly assassin, while his life hangs in the balance.

Out on Delaware Avenue, at the home of John C. Milburn, president of the Pan-American Exposition, with tears on her face, and with a heart torn by conflicting hopes and fears, sits the faithful wife, whose devotion is known to all the nation.

It was a few moments after 4 o'clock this afternoon, while the President was holding a reception in the Temple of Music on the Pan-American grounds, that the cowardly attack was made, with what success time alone can tell.

Standing in the midst of thousands, surrounded by every evidence of good will, pressed by a motely throng of people, showered with expressions of love and loyalty from enthusiastic multitudes, all eager to clasp his hands—amid these surroundings—and with the ever-recurring plaudits of an army of sight-seers ringing in his ears, the blow of the assassin came, and in an instant pleasure gave way to pain, admiration to anger, jolly turned to fury and pandemonium followed.

Tonight a surging, swaying, eager multitude throngs the city's main thoroughfares, choking the streets in front of the principal newspapers, scanning the bulletins with anxious eyes, and groaning or cheering in turn at each succeeding announcement, as the nature of the news sinks or buoys their hopes.

THE PRISONER.

Down at police headquarters, surrounded by the stern-faced inquisitors of the law, is a medium-sized man of common-place appearance, with his gaze fixed on the floor, who presses his lips firmly together and listens with an air of assumed indifference to the persistent stream of questions, arguments, objurgations and admonitions with which his captors seek to induce or compel him to talk.

WILLIAM M'KINLEY.

THE CRIME.

It was just after the daily organ recital in the splendid Temple of Music that the dastardly attempt was made. Planned with all the diabolical ingenuity and finesse of which anarchy or nihilism is capable, the would-be assassin carried out the work without a hitch, and should his designs fail and the President survive, only to Divine Providence can be attributed that beneficent result.

The President, though well guarded by United States Secret Service detectives, was fully exposed to such an attack as occurred. He stood at the edge of the raised dais upon which stands the great pipe organ at the east side of the magnificent structure. Throngs of people crowded in at the various entrances to gaze upon the Executive, perchance to clasp his hand, and then file their way out in the good-natured mob that every minute swelled and multiplied at the points of ingress and egress to the building.

The President was in a cheerful mood and was enjoying to the full the hearty evidence of good will which everywhere met his gaze. On his right stood John C. Milburn of Buffalo, president of the Pan-American Exposition, chatting with the President and introducing him especially to persons of note who approached. Upon the President's left stood Private Secretary Cortelyou.

It was shortly after 4 o'clock, when one of the throng which surrounded the Presidential party, a medium-sized man, of ordinary appearance, and plainly dressed in black, approached as if to greet the President. Both Secretary Cortelyou and Mr. Milburn noticed that the man's hand was swathed in a bandage, or handkerchief; reports of bystanders differ as to which hand. He worked his way amid the stream of people up to the edge of the dais until he was within two feet of the Chief Executive.

The President smiled, bowed and extended his hand in that spirit of geniality which the American people so well know, when suddenly the sharp crack of a revolver rang out loud and clear above the hum of voices, the shuffling of myriad feet and vibrating waves of applause that ever and anon swept here and there over the assemblage.

There was an instant of almost complete silence. The President stood stock still, a look of hesitancy, almost of bewilderment on his face. He then retreated a step, while a pallor began to steal over his features.

The multitude, only partially aware that something serious had happened, paused in surprise, while necks were craned and all eyes turned as one to the rostrum where a great tragedy was being enacted.

Then came a commotion. Three men threw themselves forward as with one impulse and sprang toward the would-be assassin. Two of them were United States Secret Service men who were on the lookout and whose duty it was to guard against just such a calamity as had here befallen the President and the nation. The third was a bystander, a negro, who had only an instant previously grasped the hand of the President. In an instant the assassin was borne to the ground. His weapon was wrested from his grasp, and strong arms pinioned him down.

PANDEMONIUM.

Then the multitude which thronged the edifice began to come to a realizing sense of the awfulness of the scene to which they had been unwilling witnesses. A

(CONTINUED ON THIRD PAGE.)

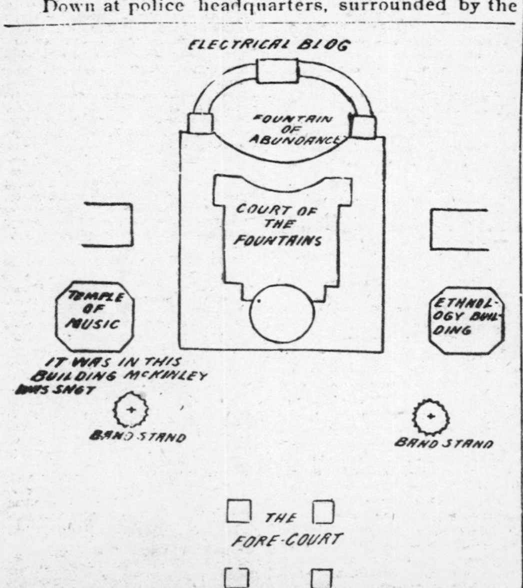

DIAGRAM OF EXPOSITION GROUNDS IN VICINITY OF TEMPLE OF MUSIC.

THE PRESIDENT AS HE RODE THROUGH THE STREETS OF LOS ANGELES LAST MAY.

BULLETINS OF CONDITION.

The Chief Magistrate Was Resting Easy at Last Accounts.

[NEW ASSOCIATED PRESS—P.M.]

BUFFALO, Sept. 6.—The following bulletin was issued by the President's physician at 10:40 o'clock p.m.:

"The President is rallying satisfactorily, and is resting comfortably." 10:15 p.m. Temperature 100.4 deg.; pulse, 124; respiration, 24. (Signed)

"P. M. RIXEY,
"M. B. MANN,
"R. E. PARKE,
"H. E. MYNTER,
"EUGENE WANTSIN."

(Signed by George B. Cortelyou, Secretary to the President.)

AT 1 A. M.

BUFFALO, Sept. 7.—The President's physician issued the following bulletin at 1 o'clock:

"The President is free from pain and resting well. Temperature, 100.2; pulse, 120; respiration, 24."

AT 3 A. M.

BUFFALO, Sept. 7.—At 3 a.m. the following bulletin was issued:

"The President continues to rest well. Temperature, 101.6; pulse, 110; respiration, 24. (Signed)

"P. M. RIXEY.
"GEORGE CORTELYOU,
"Secretary."

AT 6 A. M.

BUFFALO, Sept. 7.—The President's physicians issued the following bulletin at 6 a. m.:

"The President has passed a good night; temperature 102; pulse 110; respiration 24."

WIRE FROM WIGGINS.

[BY DIRECT WIRE TO THE TIMES.]

BUFFALO (N.Y.) Sept. 6.—To Gen. H. G. Otis, Los Angeles: The President was shot twice by an Armenian Pole at the public reception at the Temple of Music at 4:15 o'clock while shaking hands, the assailant having a revolver covered with a handkerchief. One shot entered the breastbone, the other entering between the apex of heart and stomach, perforating the stomach, not affecting intestines. Wound not considered dangerous unless peritonitis sets in. The President is conscious. Was moved to Mr. Milburn's residence, where Mrs. McKinley awaits him. She was not present at the tragedy. Dr. Roswell Parke in charge. Assassin Fred Nieman overpowered immediately and removed with great difficulty from mob. Reason given by assassin: "I am an anarchist and did my duty."

The fair is in darkness; everything suspended.

FRANK WIGGINS.

HE TRUSTED THE PEOPLE.

The President Would not Heed Attorney-General Griggs's Warnings.

[NEW ASSOCIATED PRESS—P.M.]

NEW YORK, Sept. 6.—Former Atty.-Gen. Griggs in discussing at Paterson, N. J., the shooting of President McKinley, said: "I warned him against this very thing time and time again. I asked him for the country's sake and his own to have a bodyguard when he went out. He refused. He laughed at me. He insisted that the American people were too intelligent and too loyal to their country to do any harm to their Chief Executive. He had supreme confidence in the people."

The Times — Los Angeles

Two Parts: 22 Pages. GENERAL NEWS SHEET—14 PAGES.

XXIIID YEAR. PER WEEK, 20 CENTS. PER MONTH, 75 CENTS. $9 A YEAR. TUESDAY, FEBRUARY 9, 1904. ON ALL NEWS STANDS, TRAINS AND STREETS 5 CENTS.

WEATHER FILLS HOSPITALS.

NEW YORK, Feb. 8.—A record-breaking number of patients crowd the hospitals, owing to several days of warm, changeable weather. At Bellevue there are 973 patients, 113 more than the place is supposed to accommodate. As many of the convalescents as can be moved are taken from medical wards and placed in the surgical. Colder weather is expected to alleviate conditions shortly.

LOCAL WEATHER REPORT

YESTERDAY: Maximum temperature, 60 deg.; minimum, 42 deg. Wind, 5 a.m., northeast, velocity 9 miles; 5 p.m., southwest, velocity 9 miles. At midnight the temperature was 44 deg.; clear.

TODAY: At 3 a.m. the temperature was 42 deg.; clear.

Forecast for Los Angeles and vicinity: Fair, though with considerable cloudiness; snow in mountains; continued cold; fresh southerly winds.

San Francisco and vicinity: Clearing; fresh west winds.

[The complete Weather Report, including Comparative Temperatures, will be found on page 8, Part 1.]

POINTS OF THE NEWS IN TODAY'S ISSUE OF The Times

INDEX.

SYNOPSIS.

THE CITY. Ten-story skyscraper for Fourth and Broadway....Sheriffs and constables make it warm for elusive Mrs. Osburn....Spanish farmer leases 3500 acres of land and corners the raindrops....Cahuenga annexation scheme killed off....Mother tries to drown her children....J. B. Solomon robbed at church door....Former labor union agitators forced to go to work....Fight against liquor shop at west end of Third-street tunnel....Ruskin's birthday celebrated....Close finishes at races. King Ballerino throws his money around recklessly....Stableman's skull cracked by pitcher....Col Green loses $20,000 in Baltimore fire....Fine trainload of Oakland visitors arrives. Council makes everybody happy by report on franchise question....Bond issue for $50,000 detention hospital to be submitted....New license schedule proposed....Law against vacant lots wanted....Storm drain bonds not to be cancelled....Mrs. Rose Porter re-arrested....Trial of Mrs. Dixon for robbery begun....Monrovia Telephone Company gets franchise....Willis J. Benedict cleared of burglary charge....J. Greenwald fined $50 for selling lottery ticket.

SOUTHERN CALIFORNIA. Sunday music barred from Pasadena parks. Opening eyes of blind pigs in Ventura county....Jackson fairly treated, but obstinate, says Whittier City Attorney. Moving Gen. Fremont's former headquarters in Santa Barbara....Salt Lake family's fearful trip to San Bernardino. Colton heiress elopes....Larger chapel for Pomona College....Whittier bonds sell at premium....Separated Santa Barbara pair's scrap .... Monrovia preacher dies in church....Four burglaries in Redondo....Bond-issue talk in Santa Monica....Too much hypnotism in Orange....Hollywood schoolsite indorsed....More murder mystery in Riverside.

GENERAL EASTERN. Great fire at Baltimore; flames raged twenty-seven hours; insurance companies hard hit; striking incidents of fiery conflict; twenty thousand thrown out of employment; State and national relief measures....New York automobilist kills aged woman, then tries to escape. Fickle weather fills New York hospitals....New York's fire danger....Decided improvement in dried-fruit business....Chicago Aldermen won't stand cut in their pay....Nat Goodwin's stage manager victim of leap-year proposal....Wins race with death. Basket-ball girls stop street fight. Sixteen prominent clubmen go to jail for illegal liquor selling.

FOREIGN, BY CABLE. Japan opens war on Russia; troops landed at Mesampho; Seoul to be occupied; China in the melee; firing reported east of Koje Island; scenes in St. Petersburg; text of Russian reply. Japan seizes Russian transports. Kaiser guest of Ambassador Tower.

SPORTING. Long-priced horses win at Oakland races....New Orleans races.

WASHINGTON. Senator Hanna is slightly worse....Bill for relief of Baltimore introduced....Proceedings of Congress: Senate approves Lewis and Clark exposition appropriation; House against aid to St. Louis Exposition; Urgent Deficiency Bill; Money lost to Los Angeles postoffice; Diplomatic Appropriation Bill....Miss Brewer weds. Emerson's grandson honored....Interstate Commerce Commission and immigrants.

PACIFIC SLOPE. Heavy freight charges on California exhibit at St. Louis Exposition....Murder at Woodland....Philippines lack made-up lumber....Contest over large estate....A light on mysterious life rafts....Private Magee's heavy sentence....Gov. Pardee makes requisition....Capitalist kills himself....Grayson case dropped. Fireman held for manslaughter....The rains boom planting....Stove explodes, injuring two....Killed by falling beam. One clergyman calls another a liar. Indians get drunk, then fight with fatal results....Miners buried by landslide....Tramp locked in box car saved from death by starvation....Diamond thief arraigned....First woman negro student.

JAPAN DECLARES FOR WAR.

Her Troops Occupying Korea, Where They Have Been Preceded in the Northern Districts by the Russians—She Wins First Blood.

[BY THE ASSOCIATED PRESS—P.M.]

PORT ARTHUR, Feb. 9.—Japanese torpedo boats attacked the Russian fleet here during the night and three of the Russian ships were badly damaged. The Japanese, who thus scored the first success of the war, escaped undamaged.

ATTACKED WITH MINES.

[BY THE ASSOCIATED PRESS—P.M.]

ST. PETERSBURG, Feb. 9.—Admiral Alexieff's official report of the attack by the Japanese is as follows: "I most respectfully inform Your Majesty that at or about midnight of February 8-9 Japanese torpedo boats made a sudden attack by means of mines upon the Russian squadron in the outer roads of the fortress of Port Arthur, in which the battleships Retvisian and Ceasaravitch and the cruiser Pallada were damaged. An inspection is being made to ascertain the character of the damage. Details are following for Your Majesty."

DECLARATION OF WAR.

[BY DIRECT WIRE TO THE TIMES.]

LONDON, Feb. 9, 5 a. m.—[Exclusive Dispatch.] The Foreign Office has received official notice from Japan that the country is at war with Russia.

JAPANESE LAND AT MASAMPHO.

[BY DIRECT WIRE TO THE TIMES.]

BERLIN, Feb. 9.—[By Atlantic Cable.] A dispatch received here from Port Arthur says news has been received there that Japanese troops have been landed at Masampho.

SEOUL TO BE OCCUPIED.

[BY THE ASSOCIATED PRESS—P.M.]

LONDON, Feb. 9.—The Cheefoo correspondent of the Daily Mail cables that six Japanese transports are landing troops at various ports in Korea, from Masampho and Fusan, on the south, and Kunzan, Mokpho and Chemulpo, on the west.

Seoul is to be occupied and the landing is being covered by the torpedo division. The main body of the Japanese fleet, the correspondent concludes, will sail in the direction of Port Arthur.

GUNNERY EAST OF KOJE.

[BY THE ASSOCIATED PRESS—P.M.]

LONDON, Feb. 9.—In a dispatch from Tokio, a correspondent of the Daily Mail says the Jiji Shimpo has received a telegram from Fusan, Korea, declaring that the firing of guns was heard to the east of Koje Island (about twenty-five miles southwest of Fusan) at 8 o'clock Saturday morning.

RUSSIANS TAKE NORTHERN KOREA.

[BY DIRECT WIRE TO THE TIMES.]

NEW YORK, Feb. 9.—[Exclusive Dispatch.] The Herald this morning publishes the following:

NAGASAKI, Saturday—Russia procured transports, and dispatching her fleet from Port Arthur, some days ago, escorted vessels loaded with full divisions of troops and landed them near the Yalu River, thus occupying Northern Korea.

The Japanese fleet also moved its ships to Masampo, where, during the morning, files of marines took possession of certain Russian merchant vessels, including the Shilka and the Manchuria, and one ship which had been chartered by the Russian government and was engaged in loading up with a cargo of coal and stores for Port Arthur. The Japanese encountered no resistance, and the steamers have now been placed under a guard. It is reported that two other Russian vessels had been taken outside and escorted to Sascho.

PERMITS TO THE PRESS.

NAGASAKI, Monday, 6 p. m.—The War Department is issuing permits to correspondents. Baron von Rosen will leave Tokio February 11, and will sail by the French steamer Yana February 12. It is reported that the ice is two feet thick at Port Arthur, and that this affects the movements of torpedo boats, but it is probably only on the shoals and shore waters. A letter received from there indicates that the harbor was quite open up to January 31. The Japanese naval reserve has been called out.

RUSSIAN FLEET WILL FIGHT.

NAGASAKI, Monday, 9:20 p.m.—From a Russian source news comes that their fleet will fight. For months past many colliers have cleared from Kusatsu for Cheefoo, but have invariably landed their coal at Port Arthur. The Russian steamer Argun was due at Nagasaki today from Dalny, but has not yet arrived.

TALK WITH OUR AMBASSADOR.

[BY DIRECT WIRE TO THE TIMES.]

NEW YORK, Feb. 9.—[Exclusive Dispatch.] The Herald's St. Petersburg correspondent, cabling Monday, says: "I have just had a conversation with the United States Ambassador as to how the taking-over of the Japanese interests by the United States would be construed. He said: 'Such a charge could only be handed to the care of the representative of a power known to be neutral—England, being biased, could not undertake it. It is a pity the Russians should imagine that the Americans have an unfriendly feeling toward them, my opinion—and I have a large correspondence with the United States—is that such a feeling does not exist.' "

FRENCH TO LAND IN CHINA

[BY THE ASSOCIATED PRESS—P.M.]

LONDON, Feb. 9.—The Paris correspondent of Daily Mail says France has agreed with other powers to land troops in China directly hostilities begin, in order to insure the neutrality of the Middle Kingdom.

CHINESE COURT TO FLEE.

[BY THE ASSOCIATED PRESS—P.M.]

LONDON, Feb. 9.—In a dispatch from Tien-Tsin, a correspondent there of the Standard says a Russian force is expected at Kalgan Pei Chi Li, 110 miles northwest of Peking and near the Great Wall, and that preparations are making for the flight of the Chinese court and the removal of the imperial treasure, as it is feared that Russia will descend upon Peking.

LOOKS FOR GOLD AT THE START.

RUSSIA NEGOTIATING WITH A FOREIGN SYNDICATE.

Loan of Large Proportions is Desired—Muscovites Are Accused of Deliberately Precipitating a Crisis. Landed a Full Division of Troops in Northern Korea—Probable Line of Action.

[BY THE ASSOCIATED PRESS—P.M.]

LONDON, Feb. 9.—[By Atlantic Cable.] Russia is negotiating with a syndicate of French, Belgian and Dutch bankers, cables the Brussels correspondent of the Standard, for a loan of $200,000,000.

UTMOST ACTIVITY.

TROOPS MOVING FROM TOKIO.

[BY THE ASSOCIATED PRESS—A.M.]

LONDON, Feb. 8.—[By Atlantic Cable.] The Tokio correspondent of the Standard reports the utmost activity on the part of the authorities, who are rapidly conveying troops to ports of embarkation. The people are calm and confident, and there is no excitement.

Cabling from Tokio, the correspondent there of the Daily Telegraph, gives a report that Russian troops have already crossed the Korean frontier, and that an official declaration of war is expected momentarily.

LINE OF ACTION.

A correspondent of the Daily Mail at Seoul says he learns that Japan has warned non-combatants to withdraw from Song Ching and all Japanese women, children, north of Chong Ju to come south. This is supposed to indicate Japan's intention to strike through Northern Korea in the direction of Harbin and the Manchurian Railroad.

The correspondent of the Times at Tokio cables that the Russian gunboat Mandjura, which is in dock at Nagasaki, will probably not be able to leave that port before hostilities begin.

Baron de Rosen will leave Tokio, February 12, the correspondent continues, after an audience with the Emperor. There are indications that Russia is moving toward the Yalu River. The Japanese residents have nearly all withdrawn from Manchuria and Wiju.

HAYASHI POINTS OUT.

Baron Hayashi, the Japanese Minister, has informed the Associated Press that military steps contemplated by Japan for the preservation of its interests in the Far East already have commenced.

The Minister was careful to point out, however, that this does not mean actual hostilities, but strategic action through pouring Japanese troops into Korea and Manchuria. This, he stated, is now in progress.

Baron Hayashi calculated that forces adequate to meet any emergency will have been fully disembarked within two or three days. He regards the breaking-off of the negotiations tantamount to war, and does not look for any formal declaration. The Minister reiterates the statement that the Russian reply was not delivered, and declares his belief to be that it never was sent.

RUSSIA PRECIPITATED CRISIS.

[BY THE ASSOCIATED PRESS—P.M.]

LONDON, Feb. 9.—In a dispatch dated Nagasaki, February 6, and which was delayed by the censor, a correspondent of the Daily Telegraph asserts that Russia deliberately precipitated the crisis by secretly dispatching a few days ago from Port Arthur

(CONTINUED ON THIRD PAGE.)

In Two Parts—First News Sheet—12 Pages

The Los Angeles Times

Twenty-third Year.

EASTERN TEMPERATURES (Max.:) Boston, 44; New York, 46; Buffalo, 42; Washin ton, 52; Pittsburgh, 48; Cincinnati, 58; Chicago, 54; St. Paul, 46; Kansas City, 66; Jacksonvi le, 68.

PER ANNUM, $9.00. {Per Week, 20 Cents. / Per Month, 75 Cents.

WEDNESDAY MORNING, NOVEMBER 9, 1904.

On All News Stands, Trains and Streets, 5 CENTS

IT WAS A FAMOUS VICTORY.

Roosevelt and Fairbanks Receive Largest Electoral Vote Ever Given National Candidates.

[BY DIRECT WIRE TO THE TIMES.]

ESOPUS N. Y.) Nov. 8.—At 8:30 p.m. Judge Parker sent this telegram to the President:

ROSEMONT, ESOPUS (N. Y.) Nov. 8, 8:30 p.m.—The President, Washington: The people by their votes have emphatically approved your administration, and I congratulate you.

[Signed] ALTON B. PARKER.

Returns from Ulster county, Esopus township, Parker's home district, show that Roosevelt polled 173 votes against 159 for Parker.

THE PRESIDENT RESPONDS.

[BY THE ASSOCIATED PRESS—P.M.]

WASHINGTON, Nov. 8.—President Roosevelt's reply to Judge Parker's telegram was as follows:

"Alton B. Parker, Rosemont, N. Y.: I thank you for your congratulations."

GREATEST OF LANDSLIDES.

[BY DIRECT WIRE TO THE TIMES.]

CHICAGO, Nov. 8.—[Exclusive Dispatch.] Theodore Roosevelt was first; there was no second. The national election today developed the greatest Republican landslide and the most crushing Democratic defeat since 1872, when President Grant cut the electoral vote of Horace Greeley to 80.

Theodore Roosevelt and Charles Warren Fairbanks will receive for President and Vice-President respectively the largest electoral vote ever cast for a national ticket. The Parker candidacy was metaphorically "burned to a crisp." It was a political holocaust.

NO NORTHERN STATE DEMOCRATIC.

Parker did not carry a single Northern State, and the Democratic pluralities were cut frighttully in the "Solid South." Even Winfield Scott saved Massachusetts and Vermont when he went down with the Whig party in 1852, but Parker's candidacy has a counterpart only in that of Horace Greeley, who is the only other Democratic Presidential nominee that ever failed to carry a Northern State.

In the Middle West the greatness of the victory is shown by these figures:

Wisconsin went Republican by 100,000 and La Follette has been re-elected for a third term as Governor; Roosevelt and Deneen (for Governor) carried Illinois by upward of 200,000; Indiana has gone Republican by 40,000 and the Republicans control both branches of the Legislature.

MAJORITY IN CONGRESS 56

The Republicans will control the lower branch of Congress by a majority of at least 56. Incomplete returns show a gain of one Congressman in Delaware, three in Illinois, one each in Iowa, Massachusetts, Michigan, Minnesota, Nebraska, New Jersey and Ohio and five in New York. Returns received up to midnight show that the Fifty-ninth Congress will stand: Republicans, 226; Democrats, 159; and Union Labor 1. A gain of one is indicated in the Senate, the chances being that Thomas H. Carter (Rep.) will succeed Paris Gibson (Dem.) in Montana.

CHICAGO'S POLITICAL SENSATION

The political sensation in Chicago was the defeat for Congress of William Preston Harrison, brother of Mayor Harrison, in the Eighth District. Charles McGavin, the Republican nominee, was elected by a conceded plurality of 5120 in a district that was considered Democratic by 8500. The defeat of W. P. Harrison is regarded as the beginning of the end of Mayor Harrison as a controlling factor in the Cook county Democracy.

VOTE OF CONFIDENCE. IN ADMINISTRATION.

[BY DIRECT WIRE TO THE TIMES.]

NEW YORK, Nov. 8.—[Exclusive Dispatch.] It is more than a Republican landslide, it is an avalanche. Theodore Roosevelt has been elected President by probably a greater plurality of the popular vote than was ever cast for a nominee for President and by a larger majority of the electoral college than was ever given before.

The people have decided, as they always have done in affairs in this country, and they have decided in unmistakable terms in favor of the administration at Washington and against any change in existing business conditions. The result is a vote of confidence in President Roosevelt of a most emphatic character.

New York State, contrary to general expectations, was not doubtful about anything. It was not doubtful about the Presidency, baceuse it will give Roosevelt a plurality aggregating 200,000. The result will seem to indicate wreckage of the Democratic party, as reorganized at St. Louis on a "safe and sane basis." Under the leadership of Parker, it would seem that the party was only united on the surface.

But under the surface the party has not ben united. Bryan leaders apparently were loyal, but the minor leaders for weeks have been working to insure the defeat of Parker in order to bring about a new reorganization of the party, looking to nominating Bryan for President in 1908.

In the other hand, many followers of Hearst have been engaged in slaughtering Parker, and the candidacy of Thomas E. Watson on the Populist ticket has been used as a mask under which an anti-Parker propaganda has been conducted throughout the country.

The effect of this is shown in the returns of Indiana, New Jersey, New York, Connecticut and Illinois. The word seems to have gone around secretly to Bryan men in every section of the country to defeat Parker because he was the candidate of David B. Hill and various gold Democrats in the East, so that the party could once more be reorganized on radical lines and make a fight against the trusts four years hence.

The knowledge of this appears to have inspired Parker to take the stump and made his serious charge against President Roosevelt and Cortelyou, in the hope that it would swing the radicals back into line, but he made the move too late if it ever could have availed, which is not probable.

ELECTORAL VOTES.

ALSO PROBABLE PLURALITIES.

[BY DIRECT WIRE TO THE TIMES.]

NEW YORK, Nov. 8.—[Exclusive Dispatch.] The World's returns show that the electoral college will stand: Roosevelt, 332; Parker, 144; necessary to choice, 239. Roosevelt's majority, 174.

STATE.	ROOSEVELT.	ESTIMATED PLURALITY.	PARKER
Alabama			11
Arkansas			9
California	10	30,000	
Colorado	5		
Connecticut	7	25,000	
Delaware	3	5,000	
Florida			5
Georgia			13
Idaho	3		
Illinois	27	200,000	
Indiana	15	60,000	
Iowa	13	150,000	
Kansas	10		
Kentucky			13
Louisiana			9
Maryland			8
Maine	6	33,000	
Massachusetts	16	80,000	
Michigan	14	100,000	
Minnesota	11	100,000	
Mississippi			10
Missouri	18		
Montana			3
Nebraska	8	30,000	
Nevada	3		
New Hampshire	4	18,000	
New Jersey	12	65,000	
New York	39	250,000	
North Carolina			12
North Dakota	4	25,000	
Ohio	23		
Oregon	4		
Pennsylvania	34	300,000	
Rhode Island	4		
South Carolina			9
South Dakota	4	45,000	
Tennessee		25,000	12
Texas		25,000	18
Utah	3	8,000	
Vermont	4	30,000	
Virginia		25,000	12
Washington	5		
West Virginia	7		
Wisconsin	13	50,000	
Wyoming	3		
Total	332		144

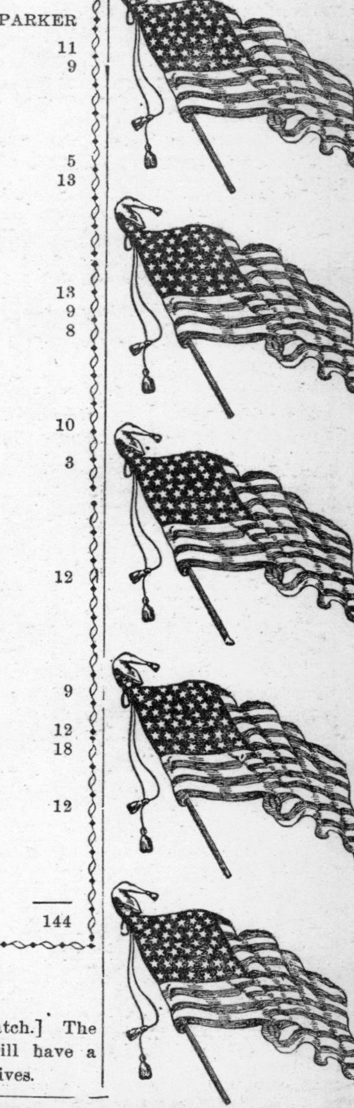

HOUSE MAJORITY OF 40.

[BY DIRECT WIRE TO THE TIMES.]

NEW YORK, Nov. 8.—[Exclusive Dispatch.] The latest returns indicate that the Republicans will have a majority of 40 in the next House of Representatives.

Editorial Section.
PART II—MAIN SHEET—12 PAGES.

Los Angeles Daily Times

California del Sur.
NEWS OF THE SOUTH.

XXIVTH YEAR. TUESDAY, JANUARY 31, 1905. PRICE 3 CENTS

MRS. WELLS' GOLD SPIKE UNITES SALT LAKE LINES.

Last Rail to Close Gap in Newest Steel Pathway Across Desert Laid Yesterday Afternoon—Strange and Stirring Scenes at the Front.

BY HARRY C. CARR.

[STAFF CORRESPONDENCE OF THE TIMES.]

SIDING NO. 31, ON THE SALT LAKE RAILROAD, IN THE DESERT, TWENTY MILES ACROSS THE NEVADA LINE, Jan. 30.—The last spike was unceremoniously whacked into the last tie of the Salt Lake road at 3:15 o'clock this afternoon by a bullet-headed Greek born in the shadow of the Acropolis.

Alas, 'twas not golden, but molded of humble Pittsburgh pig iron.

With the horror of his kind for a poseur, Chief Engineer Tilton cut out all the programme.

Had it not been for the wife of General Manager Wells, it all would have been as devoid of sentiment as buying stale bread.

She sent on a tiny spike of gold, not larger than a man's thumb nail. After the Greek had the last rail whacked in place, Mr. Tilton guiltily fished the gold trinket out of his vest pocket, and punched it into the last tie.

The Greeks and Austrians on the Nevada end set up a yowl, answered by a melancholy whoop from the Mexicans who built the California side.

IT'S A TEMPORARY TRACK.

A car can now run direct from Los Angeles to Salt Lake City.

Before the road is open to regular traffic, several changes will be made. About twelve miles of the present track will be abandoned. A shorter piece of track, through a tunnel and some difficult rock cuts, will be substituted for the track now running into Las Vegas Valley.

When this addition is patched on, there will be ceremonies. Although the soil, untouched by plow, lie mile after mile in the bottoms, ready to be taken by whomever wills.

Towns are already springing up, headed by the frontier grog shop. Lots are being staked out, houses going up, water developed.

In this vastness, there is room for a nation.

THREE MONTHS' CHANGE.

Three months ago, not a living soul was in all this wilderness; as far as the eye could reach was only an aching desolation, homes for coyotes, jackrabbits and rattlesnakes.

Miners sometimes ventured through, but it cost a fortune to mine. A man at the head of Death Valley, now made accessible, had to pay $7 a barrel for his water, $80 per ton for barley. Frequently, in sandstorms, the barley would be eaten up by the transportation teams before they could get back from civilization with the load.

The riches laid bare are tremendous as of Solomon's mines; but they are not for the pioneers, whose hard work and bitter suffering has at last shackled the desert in bands of steel. These are already folding up their tents to steal away.

Every train is taking out stock and horses; rusty Fresno scrapers are being packed on flat cars; soiled tent ing the stillness of the desert; Fresno scrapers and braying mules.

Following came the track layers, with the great engines tumbling out ties in enormous bundles, rails shooting out with incredible swiftness; then the ballasting crews, the "surfacing gangs" embedding the ties in firm earth.

Behind these the trains bearing pile drivers to replace the temporary bridges, each gang a class, a stratum of society, a little world unto itself.

Came the commissary department dropping kitchens and dining-rooms in the wilderness; came the operating department, drawing complete little railroad office bureaus in condemned cars to be switched onto sidings with telegraph lines, train masters, stenographers, clacking train orders, flimsy train slips, filing cases, boyish clerks, detail maps, train dispatchers.

Came after these, the crawling freights, the gangs to dig wells, the carpenters to build section houses, the painters and the plasterers. And at last the ubiquitious drummer bearing samples of the finest article for sale on this earth.

A CHEERING LIGHT.

About two week ago, the man who sits atop of the track-laying machine saw a faint smoke over a hill toward California; he gave a loud whoop; the end was in sight; the smoke came from the funnels of the engines pushing the road in from the Golden State.

Since that day the road has been rushed through with astonishing swiftness; the day's work has run from a mile and three-quarters to two miles a day.

ACTUAL MEETING PLACE.

The actual meeting of the builders took place this afternoon about four miles out from Siding 31 and about twenty miles across the Nevada line, on a rise overlooking a famous mirage of Forty-niner days, known as Dry Lake.

> The story in figures and plain data:
>
> Miles of track from Los Angeles to Salt Lake City, 778.6.
>
> Miles of desert section just completed, 300.
>
> Tons of steel used, 1,027,752.
>
> Cost of building road so far, $42,000,000.
>
> Cost of equipment, $7,000,000.
>
> Prevention of freshet washouts, more than the cost of track laying.
>
> Place where the gap was connected, Dry Lake, Nev., about twenty miles from the California State line.
>
> Time occupied in building road, eighteen months.
>
> Date of opening traffic, about next June.
>
> Terminals of track, Caliente, Nev., and Daggett, Cal. Salt Lake road uses Santa Fé track west from Daggett to Riverside and Oregon Short Line east from Caliente to Salt Lake City.
>
> Work yet to be done, shoo-fly tracks, wash-out guards, depot building.
>
> Principal desert towns, Daggett, Caliente, Kelso, Cima, Good Springs, Las Vegas.

picket lines of the teams, the solitary isolated tents where vile liquor is sold to the workmen, pitfalls where their hard-earned money is torn from them.

Toward California, the line from the joining place cuddles quickly into the low burrow-like hills, scoots in under a bleak rough mountain of almost solid rock and disappears.

Toward Nevada, it lies straight and level and gleaming, pointed straight for

The Climax of the Building of the Newest Transcontinental Railroad Line.

line will then have been in constant use for several months, the Salt Lake City Council and maybe the Council of this city will get up an official golden spike laying.

THE FIRST TRAIN.

The first train that crossed the gap was not a millionaire's palace on wheels, but the battered-up old track-laying machine, which has suffered the stress and storm of the desert in its awful heat and freezing storms.

Although the pioneers who have forced this road through the trackless wilderness have got their orders from day to day in five different languages, the end of it was characteristically and deliciously Yankee.

And a part of which was The Times correspondent, the only newspaper man on the ground.

It was one of the biggest events in desert railroading since the building of the first transcontinental line.

It opens to the world a territory of fabulous richness. The valleys through which the new road runs are almost rotten with ore.

Already there are signs of a mad mining rush. Prospectors are hurrying to the scene even on the construction trains, sitting with their ore picks among bridge materials and mule collars on the cars.

Tiffany has turquoise mines within sight of the roadbed; the famous Providence mines lie near; Ivanpah lies a white patch in the valley to the left.

Splendid agricultural lands, virgin homes are coming down in rumpled heaps; toil-worn workers are drawing their pay checks and going away.

In three months a dozen towns have spurted up; in three weeks they will have gone again; the valley, now crawling with innumerable teams and dotted with men in every direction, will look like a sawdust circus ring the day after.

There are other roads to be built and other hardships to be suffered. The vanguard has moved on; the sheltered folk may now whirl in where the pioneers have tramped so wearily and reap the prizes.

HOT AS HADES.

Eighteen months ago, a gang of Greeks and Austrians began working in the pitiless heat of Caliente on the Nevada Desert, following the survey lines.

It was so hot that twenty-two of them dropped senseless in one day. At night, men stripped to the skin, moaned and turned in their effort to sleep, running rivers of sweat, until the hell next day.

Meanwhile gangs of Mexicans and Americans were starting the other end of the road at Daggett, Cal., an old town created many years ago as a trading post for the old Calico mines.

They worked through picturesque vividly painted valleys, out past the old Roach camp, standing like a sentinel to Death Valley.

First came the engineers with their transits; then the graders with giant steam shovels, powder blasts disturb-

The road here winds out from the Nevada end around the range of low hills, hiding Las Vegas Valley from the California line.

The rails of the two ends were spliced at the entrance of a deep cut.

To the south and east lay the low saucer-like valley with the mirage of dry lake sheltered in the shadow of the hills. There is a little water in it since the rains, but in the peculiar deceptive light of the desert it seems to be rippling with cool depths of sweet blue water.

The hills behind the mocking lake stand roseate with changing colors, that miraculous kaleidoscope of nature to be found nowhere but in the mountains of these western deserts. A hillside flashes bright crimson in the sun slashed with a ghastly spear, half a mile long by two city blocks wide, of leprous white—the track of some frightful cloudburst sweeping vegetation, rocks and earth before it.

To the west lies the hot, shaggy interminable desert, its flat rough skin humped in the distance into low rolling hills, its middle distance scarred by the dotting camps of the contractors standing out white and glaring, the the line of symmetrical hills, veers around them and is seen no more.

One of these dreary God-forsaken mountains figures in the recent prospectus of a new boom town as "heavily wooded heights." The fact is, even sage brush refuses to grow there.

The long vista is broken by antlike moving specks in the far distance, where scores upon scores of grading teams are at work; by the blur to the south, where stand the long row of house cars, the administration buildings and bunk rooms of the station now known as siding 31, soon to be called Good Springs.

In a general way the roadbed follows one of the old Forty-niner trails which ran from water hole to water hole through the parched desert.

Every mile of the route has been punctuated by heart aches, hopes that were blasted, struggling ox teams that sank moaning to die, suffering untold, tantalizing lakes mocking afar off the argonauts dying of thirst.

THE OLD TRAIL.

The old "Salt Lake trail" where they

(Continued on Twelfth Page.)

FOURTH "DIP" IS ARRESTED.

Quartette of Clever Pickpockets Now in Limbo.

Remaining Member of Gang Taken at San Diego.

Companions Confess and Plunder is Recovered.

The fourth member of the quartette of professional pickpockets who a few days ago robbed a San Bernardino man on a Santa Fé train and who have committed nearly all the really big "dip" jobs reported here since Christmas, has been captured. With him the detectives have recovered many stolen watches and other jewelry.

The man, whose name is not known here, was arrested in San Diego and thither went Detective Talamantes yesterday to bring him back. It is known that the prisoner was a pal of the three men arrested last Thursday and identified by several of their victims.

Names given by the three men are John Downey, William Burns and J. Harrison, but under other names two of them served terms in San Quentin penitentiary. The third is believed to be a professional crook from the East. The detectives had started an investigation into his record, when a complete confession by all of the men rendered it unnesessary.

TELL OF CRIMES.

The confession came unexpectedly. The men told their connection with various crimes committed here; told where they had secreted their booty and who was their companion.

In their confession the prisoners told the officers that their companion had gone to San Diego and that two suit cases, containing the proceeds of several robberies, would be shipped to him there.

Telling of the robbery on the Santa Fé train, the men say they held other passengers off while the man captured in San Diego searched their victim. Later they divided the money. As to robberies on street cars en route from the depots, the crooks told how they spotted their victims, surrounded them and then jostled and robbed them before they recovered from their confusion.

MORE BOOTY FOUND.

When the three men were arrested they were searched and it was supposed $70 found in their pockets was all the money they had. It was known they had stolen several hundred dollars.

While the men were talking to the detectives Sunday, one of them dropped a remark about having some money. They were stripped and the officers found nearly $600 in currency concealed in their clothing.

More than $200 was sewed in the lining of Harrison's coat. Burns had nearly $300 in $20 bills sewed in the waistband of his trousers. The money had been folded, ironed smooth and then placed in the waistband. Only the fact that the stitching was crude led to the discovery.

Two of the prisoners have agreed to plead guilty when their cases come to trial. Their confessions have been taken down and can be used as evidence against them.

The steamer David Evans, owned by the Pacific Shipping Company of San Francisco, ran aground near Point No Point while bound to San Diego from Everett with a cargo of lumber and piles. The vessel is not badly damaged. High winds and a strong tide carried the craft ashore.

In Two Parts, Complete—28 Pages

Part I—General News Sheet—16 Pages

The Los Angeles Times

Twenty-fifth Year.

PER ANNUM, $9.00 | Per Month, 75 Cents, or 2 1-2 Cents a Copy.

THURSDAY MORNING, APRIL 19, 1906.

On All News Stands, Trains and Streets. | 5 CENTS

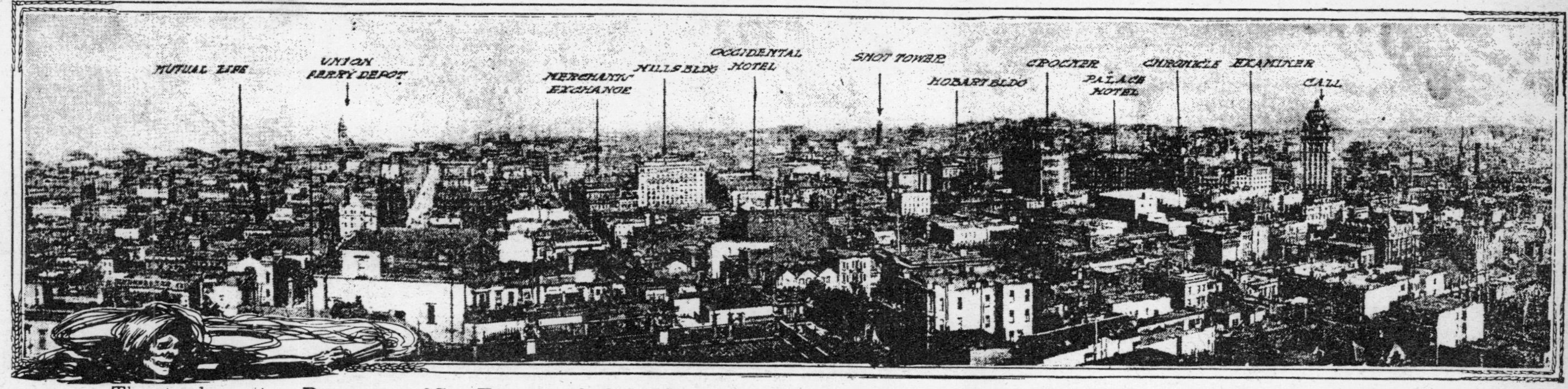

The stricken city. Panorama of San Francisco before the catastrophe, showing principal buildings that are partially or wholly destroyed.

HEART IS TORN FROM GREAT CITY.

San Francisco Nearly Destroyed By Earthquakes and Fire—Hundreds of Killed and Injured—Destruction of Other Coast Cities—California's Greatest Horror.

By the Associated Press—P. M.

SAN FRANCISCO, April 19.—It looks now as if the entire city would be burned, following the great quake of yesterday. The government is furnishing tugs to convey news to Oakland, but the confusion is so great that they cannot be relied upon. It will be impossible to send full details for several days.

The latest reports from Leland Stanford University indicate that the magni[illegible] stone buildings of that institution have suffered severe damage. Many of the buildings were ruined by cracks, which split them from cornice to foundation. The buildings are practically intact. Only a few structures collapsed in Berkeley, the earthquake shock being slight there.

At 10 o'clock at night, the fire was unabated, and thousands of people are fleeing to the hills and clamoring for places on the ferry boats.

The damage is now believed to have reached $200,000,000 and 50,000 people are thought to be homeless.

Under the fierce heat of the sun today, 29 bodies lay in Washington Square, where they were taken at the order of the Mayor when the morgues and Hall of Justice basement held all that could be cared for.

At 10 p. m. last night the newspapers ceased all effort to collect news, and the Associated Press force is compelled to act independently.

THE PRESIDENT'S MESSAGE:

The President sent the following telegram to Gov. Pardee, Sacramento:

"Sir: Rumors of great disaster from an earthquake in San Francisco, but know nothing of the real facts. Call upon me for any assistance I can render.

(Signed) THEODORE ROOSEVELT, Washington, April 18."

The President later sent the following additional telegram to Gov. Pardee:

"It was difficult at first to credit the catastrophe that has befallen San Francisco. I feel the greatest concern and sympathy for you and the people, not only of San Francisco, but of California in the terrible disaster. You will let me know if there is anything that the national government can do.

(Signed) THEODORE ROOSEVELT."

Gov: Pardee sent the following in reply:

"Owing to interruption of telegraphic communication extent of disaster in San Francisco not yet known here, but no doubt calamity is very serious. People of California appreciate your kind inquiry and offer of assistance. State troops doing patrol duty, and if federal assistance is needed will call upon you.

Signed, "GEO. C. PARDEE"

TOSSING SIX HOURS ON SEISMIC WAVES.

SAN FRANCISCO, April 18.—[Special.] During six hours of mortal dread and nameless terror San Francisco was today tossed upon the seismic waves of the most disastrous earthquake known to the history or the traditions of America's west coast. In the mad confusion and helpless horror of this night uncounted bodies of dead men and women are lying in morgues and under unuplifted walls. It is believed that nearly 1000 lives have been lost. The number cannot fall far short of that, and it may prove to be much grea[illegible] Fire and flame have added to the destruction, the ruin and despair. The material losses are beyond computation. Wounded and hurt inexpressibly the chief city of the West lies at this hour humbled to the dust, blackened, battered and charred, her glory of yesterday but a hideous dream, and the moans from her stricken heart filling the pitying world.

The first shock came while still the mighty city lay deep in slumber, weary with the revelries and pleasures of the night before. In the quiet homes, in the crowded hotels, men had not yet awakened to the strifes and endeavors of the new-dawned da[illegible]. The stars had but waned, and the morn was just b[illegible]g through the mists and fogs that hung in gray [illegible]oss the waters of the placid bay and over the wait-[illegible]. In through the Golden Gate were blowing the [illegible]g winds with the greeting of the sea to the green-clad heights and flower-strewn fields that skirted the shores and stretched away into the dim distances beyond. The sailors still slept in their hammocks in the harbored ships. A few wan-eyed wanderers of the night were stealing through the streets, a few early toilers were astir. But that was all.

Then came the rumble of deep thunder from the mighty bowels of the startled earth. The city shook like an aspen leaf, and her gray highways suddenly cracked and split as though the batteries of Satan and his upper hell had been ope[illegible] against them from underneath. Along shore th[illegible] warped and creaked, and the rakish shacks of the [illegible] fell like stacks of cards. The hills of San [illegible]mont, the Oakland heights and the dim [illegible] rocked like forests in the wind. The w[illegible]

THE WEATHER.

BRIEF REPORT.

YESTERDAY — Maximum temperature, 73 deg.; minimum, 49 deg. Wind 5 a. m., east; velocity, 1 mile; 5 p. m., west; velocity, 7 miles. At midnight the temperature was 60 deg.; clear.

TODAY—At 2 a. m. the temperature was 58 deg.; clear.

POINTS OF THE NEWS

IN TODAY'S ISSUE OF

INDEX.

SYNOPSIS.

THE CITY. Los Angeles stunned by tidings of sister city's doom, sympathy and money freely offered, nearly $50,000 raised and $100,000 pledged in day: two cities closely connected in business, names of concerns directly affected: panic-stricken crowd besieges telegraph office in vain effort to reach loved ones, and many take trains toward scene of terror: The Times beats all other papers an hour with the news. Horse Show opens brilliantly, with classy equines prancing and society a-sparkle....Mary Powers gets judgment for $500 against man who fell in love with her photograph....Passers of forged checks arrested....City Council places ban on skyscrapers....Maguire defeats Keniston at billiards....Stanford may take Occidental's coach. Quarantine-breaker Kindgren has inning with Health Office....Fund to send Miss Sutton abroad grows....Looloos 3, Seattle 2....Ex-preacner Wylie and Green woman held on ugly charge.

SOUTHERN CALIFORNIA. See page 3, Part I.

CALIFORNIA'S CALAMITY. At 10 o'clock last night fires following earthquake shocks which practically left all San Francisco in ruins were still burning fiercely in that city and the monetary loss at that hour was estimated at $200,000,000....With 500 or more persons killed by falling buildings to accentuate their fears, citizens of the stricken metropolis and surrounding bayside were fleeing to the hills for safety or crowding the ferry-boats, an avenue of escape which, more than once became dangerously congested....Gen. Funston last night telegraphed to the War Department that 100,000 persons are homeless and that thousands of tents and such quantities of provisions as can be taken into the city are urgently needed....Federal troops are aiding the police in maintaining order and several looters have been shot....The area covered in San Francisco alone by flames up to 6 o'clock last night was about eight square miles; insurance companies say they will pay losses in full...Mayor Schmitz has appointed Committee of Safety composed of prominent citizens, an[illegible] one of the questions most needin[illegible] answer is how to supply stricken [illegible] with water—In the ruin by ea[illegible]ake and consequent fire, Sa[illegible] Francisco's finest and most note[illegible] public buildings and commercial structures went down in destruction, as [illegible] also hundreds of buildings of an inferior class, taking hundreds of lives—Cities within a radius of many miles of the metropolis were affected by the shocks, and to some of them the blow dealt was terrific, the loss at Salinas alone being $2,500,000—Two hundred patients at Agnews insane asylum perished when the walls of that institution crumbled—All costumes and scenery of Metropolitan Opera Company destroyed—San Maeto water mains broken; Spring Valley flooded—Goldstein, Bowen & Co. offer entire store and contents for use of city—All wharves on San Francisco side of bay have caved in—Twenty persons killed in collapse of Terminal Hotel—Banks, though not fireproof, stand fire well.

Editorial Section.
PART II—LOCAL SHEET: 16 PAGES.

Los Angeles Daily Times

California del Sur.
CITY AND COUNTRY.

XXVITH YEAR. THURSDAY MORNING, JUNE 13, 1907. On All News Stands, Trains and Streets. | 5 CENTS

OWENS RIVER BONDS CARRIED BY OVERWHELMING MAJORITY.

LOS ANGELES yesterday declared for the $23,000,000 bond issue for the Owens River enterprise by the magnificent vote of ten to one. The total vote was 24,051. For the bonds, 21,923. Against the bonds, 2,128. The vote was the largest ever cast in a special election in this city. The opposition was surprisingly weak. The Third Ward led with a majority of seventeen to one in favor of the bonds. The issue was ratified in every precinct.

HOW THEY VOTED THE WATER IN.

Los Angeles electors indorsed the Owens River aqueduct project yesterday by the heaviest vote and the largest majority ever polled here in a special election. Every ward, every precinct, ratified the bonds; the ratio ranged all the way from six to one to ninety to one.

A June rain greeted the early voters as the polls opened. It proved a good omen; a deluge of affirmative ballots followed, for the city went wet, soaked, waterlogged. There wasn't a dry spot within a mile of a polling place.

Manufacturers, merchants, real estate men, Tammany chieftains and Rough Riders vied with each other in marshaling their forces to bring the silent voter to the polls. Captains of industry and precinct bosses rode in the same automobile. Rough-necked leaders of the Royal Arch came to the polling places with a clean shave and a dozen hangers-on each. The chiefs stood guard to see that the trailers voted "straight."

The perfect organization of the Campaign Committee included each of the 143 precincts in the city. At every booth a minute man of this committee stood guard. Few of these were called into action during the day, for the reason that the opposition was cowed, overawed by the tramp, tramp, tramp of the early voters who marched to the polls to register in favor of the bonds.

It was the opportunity of the independent citizen to express his opinion of the campaign of misrepresentation that had sought to brand as tricksters and grafters the men who have made Los Angeles.

Mayor Harper and the Democratic administration made good in keeping the Sixth, Seventh and Eighth Wards in line. It was among the laboring men in these wards that the knockers had worked hardest; it was here that they hoped to poll the votes that would defeat the bonds.

But these voters repudiated the knockers just as effectively as did the business men of the West End. In the Sixth Ward the opposition expected to make the best showing, and in this ward the rout was most complete. If not a vote had been cast for the bonds outside the Sixth Ward yesterday the issue would still have received the two-thirds majority necessary for ratification.

Councilman Barney Healy worked valiantly all day to save the reputation of the Eighth Ward. He made a good showing, but not good enough to keep his bailiwick from trailing along at the rear of the procession. The bonds carried in this ward by a ratio of six to one, but this was the lowest of the day. The Third Ward led the parade with a vote of seventeen to one.

Thirty minutes after the polls opened in the morning it was apparent that it was only a question of majority. The few "antis" who appeared were as lonesome as a ham sandwich at a picnic of the sons of Levi.

From Highland Park there came early reports that the opposition was making slight headway; this proved to be mainly a false alarm, but the First Ward made a showing that compares rather unfavorably with that of the bailiwicks west of the river. This ward attained the distinction of polling a greater per cent. of its registered vote than any of the others.

Councilman Blanchard came to the City Hall late in the afternoon. He wore a happy smile, but he had left his voice somewhere among the voting booths of his favorite Ninth Ward.

"I've been talking for two days to break up a band of knockers over at First and Chicago streets," he explained in a hoarse whisper. "I guess I caught cold last night, but we routed 'em. The Ninth Ward is going to ride in the front seat of the water wagon."

In this he was disappointed, for the bonds carried on Boyle Heights but by a vote of nine to one.

Chief Engineer Mulholland voted early, but he left the active campaigning to the committee. He expressed perfect confidence in the intelligence of the average citizen and his estimate of the majority in favor of the bonds was remarkably accurate.

Engineer Lippincott went to the headquarters of the Campaign Committee in the evening to listen to the returns.

Active boomers of the Owens River project, who, with automobiles and hard work, aided in bringing the bond campaign to a glorious close yesterday. In the auto at the top, from left to right, J. M. Schneider, president of the Merchants' and Manufacturers' Association; W. D. Stephens, president of the Chamber of Commerce; William Mulholland, chief engineer of the Los Angeles aqueduct; M. Lissner, secretary of the Owens River Campaign Committee; J. O. Koepfli, president of the Municipal League. Below, Fred A. Hines and Matthew S. Robertson and their lieutenants, who brought out a large vote in the forty-ninth precinct.

part in the day's campaign. He [illegible] the chief [illegible] mained at home comforting his wife whose father died early yesterday morning. But his lieutenants worked

Early in the evening the Mayor sent a message of congratulation to the Campaign Committee.

Lively interest in the outcome of

capitalists. Last night City Clerk Lelande sent telegrams announcing the result to twenty-two eastern addresses. Each was in response to a telegraphic

"Never before was so great an interest evidenced in a bond election," said Mr. Lelande yesterday, "from the inquiries which I have received I

CORONER HOLDS UP DRAMATIC FUNERAL.

Boy, Without a Physician Until Too Late, Dies of Lockjaw and Investigation Comes—Case of Christian Science.

Prof. Charles A. Kunou, supervisor of manual training in the Los Angeles public schools, and his son, Erhard, who died of tetanus after being attended by Christian Science practitioners. The Coroner stopped the funeral and will investigate.

ERHARD A. KUNOU, the 13-year-old son of Prof. Charles A. Kunou, supervisor of manual training in the public schools, died Monday night of tetanus. The father is a Christian Scientist, and the little sufferer was treated by Christian Science practitioners. A physician was not called until the afternoon of the day on which death came.

Coroner Lanterman stopped the funeral yesterday afternoon, and an investigation of the circumstances surrounding the death will be made today.

Frenzied with grief, the father has been prostrated since his son died. He blamed himself yesterday for not calling a physician in time. Like a crazed man he paced his room, sobbing in despair. Too late he realized that his son's life might perhaps have been spared had the proper remedies been applied.

Ten days ago Erhard, with companions, was playing near his home, No. 1051 South Flower street. The lad stepped on an upturned rusty nail,

(Continued on Third Page.)

TOTAL VOTE OF CITY BY WARDS.

Ward.	The Vote Yesterday on $23,000,000 Bond Issue for Aqueduct. Yes.	No.	Total	Total Vote of Last Mayoralty Election, Dec. 4, 1906.	Vote on First Owens River Bond Issue of $1,500,000, Sept. 7, 1905. Yes.	No.	Total	Vote on Purchase of Water Company and $2,000,000 Bond Issue, Aug. 28, 1901. Yes.	No.	Total
1	2,018	300	2,318	2,357	293	108	1,107	489	160	649
2	2,141	239	2,380	3,160	1,028	104	1,132	627	149	776
3	2,062	118	2,180	3,033	1,183	50	1,233	691	138	829
4	3,858	254	4,112	5,201	1,972	84	2,056	1,012	246	1,258
5	3,611	288	3,899	4,394	1,600	64	1,654	713	135	846
6	4,315	485	4,800	6,072	1,879	149	2,028	1,020	126	1,146
7	1,811	180	1,991	3,282	963	87	1,050	864	128	992
8	565	94	659	1,008	449	65	514	394	105	499
9	1,542	170	1,712	2,390	714	44	758	494	62	556
Total	21,923	2,128	24,051	31,387	10,787	785	11,542	6,284	1,267	7,551

In Two Parts, Complete—24 Pages

Part I—Telegraph-News Sheet—12 Pages.

The Los Angeles Times

Twenty-Seventh Year

MINIMUM TEMPERATURES: LOS ANGELES, 56; Boston, 36; New York, 40; Washington, 32; Pittsburgh, 38; Cincinnati, 38; Chicago, 42; Kansas City, 36; St. Paul, 46; Jacksonville, 66.

PER ANNUM, $9.00 | Per Month, 75 Cents, or 2 1-2 Cents a Copy.

WEDNESDAY MORNING, NOVEMBER 4, 1908.

On All News Stands, Trains and Streets. | 5 CENTS.

SWEEPING VICTORY FOR TAFT AND PROSPERITY.

YES, THE PEOPLE RULE.

TAFT ELECTORAL VOTE OVER THREE HUNDRED.

Estimates Give Republican Popular Plurality As Million and Half.

Downfall of Tammany in New York and Republican Victory in City Is Sensation of Election—Bryan's Only Gains Are in West—Gompers and Unionism Fail Completely.

BY WALTER WELLMAN.

[BY DIRECT WIRE TO THE TIMES.]

CHICAGO, Nov. 3.—[Exclusive Dispatch.] Taft has carried the country and Bryan has lost his third battle for the Presidency.

The next House of Representatives is Republican and the Republican party will remain in control of all branches of the government after March 4 next.

Returns up to this hour indicate that Taft has 306 votes in the electoral college, and Bryan 177. Taft has sixty-four more than the number required to elect, but falls a little short of Roosevelt's total of 336 four years ago.

Taft has a plurality of the popular vote in the entire country of about 1,500,000 against Roosevelt's 2,545,000 in 1904. Of the States called doubtful or debatable in the campaign, Taft has carried nearly all.

He has won New York by a plurality of about 190,000, due to the amazing downfall of Tammany and the Democracy in the greatest city in the country.

Taft has actually carried the city of New York.

Thanks also to the Democratic collapse in New York City, Gov. Hughes is re-elected by about 45,000 over Chanler.

"DOUBTFUL" STATES WERE SURE.

Ohio, upon returns up to this hour, appears to have given Taft a substantial plurality.

Indiana is close and tonight was claimed by both parties, but the plurality for Taft is indicated at from 5000 to 15,000 by the latest returns.

Maryland, confidently claimed by both parties before the election, has given Taft a small plurality, though the Democrats still claim the State.

West Virginia, also deemed doubtful, turns up with a Taft plurality of about 20,000.

The latest returns indicate that Nebraska is a sort of Democratic island in the western Republican sea, Bryan's plurality in his home State being estimated at 8000.

Kansas gives Taft a small plurality, the size of it being in doubt at this hour.

WEST FAILED TO "SLIDE."

Upon meager returns, Colorado, Nevada and Montana are for Bryan. The much-talked-of Bryan landslide in the West has not materialized. Taft's pluralities in Illinois, Wisconsin, Iowa, Minnesota, Michigan and other States of this region are much reduced from the Roosevelt figures of 1904, but are still comfortably large.

The Democrats have won Governorships in Michigan and Rhode Island and the contest between Johnson (Dem.) and Jacobson (Rep.) in Minnesota is very close. Gov. Cummins has apparently beaten Lacey for United States Senator in Iowa.

There are no breaks in the solid South. Missouri, Kentucky, Tennessee, North Carolina and other States, in which some thought Taft had a chance, returning the normal pluralities.

Meager returns from the Pacific Coast indicate a Taft sweep in all those States except Nevada.

BRYAN SLOWLY IMPROVING.

Bryan has made a much better race for the Presidency than he did in either of his other campaigns, gaining both in electoral and popular votes, but has made no serious inroads upon the great Republican fortress.

He has done better in the West than in the East. In the West he has won his own State and other States which were for Roosevelt, but in the East he has made no headway and the majorities against him there are almost as large as they were in 1900.

UNIONISM PROVES FAILURE.

One conspicuous factor of the result is the obvious failure of organized labor to make effective warfare upon Taft. The Gompers movement has failed almost everywhere. It apparently made no serious impression upon the Republican majorities in such cities as New York, Buffalo, Albany, Troy, Cincinnati and Cleveland, where it threatened to do so much. It did throw enough votes to Bryan in Ohio and Indiana to make great reductions of the former Republican majorities, without affecting the results.

In view of this failure of that part of organized labor led by Mr. Gompers, the country will probably conclude that all efforts to make a political factor of organized labor in the United States must be ineffective, in the future.

Bryan's only chance to win in States like New York, Ohio and Indiana lay in his labor allies, and these proved ineffective.

SECOND TIME IN NEW YORK.

New York City affords one of the greatest surprises of the election. Instead of giving Bryan the 100,000 plurality so confidently claimed by Bosses Murphy and McCarren, Taft has actually carried the metropolis.

This is the second time a Republican candidate for President has carried New York City, McKinley having a plurality of 61,000 in 1896. Four years later Bryan carried the city by 28,000, and in 1904 Parker carried it by 48,000. Two years ago Chanler carried it for Lieutenant-Governor by 139,000, and this year the Democratic leaders felt sure of from 90,000 to 110,000 for Bryan. Even the Republicans conceded the city to Bryan by 75,000, and probably there are

(Continued on Sixth Page.)

PORTRAITS OF NEXT PRESIDENT AND VICE-PRESIDENT OF UNITED STATES.

William Howard Taft and James Schoolcraft Sherman,
chosen yesterday by the people of the country to steer the ship of state for four years, beginning next March.

HARDEST BLOW.

BRYAN'S STATE IS DOUBTFUL.

REPUBLICAN COMMITTEE WILL NOT CONCEDE IT.

Late Figures, However, Point to a Decisive Victory for the Democratic Leader in Nebraska by About Five Thousand Plurality—His Friends Make Large Claims.

[BY DIRECT WIRE TO THE TIMES.]

LINCOLN (Neb.) Nov. 3.—[Exclusive Dispatch.] W. J. Bryan has carried Nebraska by not less than 5000 and his plurality may run as high as 20,000. The latter figure is claimed by the Democratic State Committee, but is probably excessive.

The Republican State Committee does not concede Bryan a victory in his home State, and says returns from the country precincts, many of which will not be received until tomorrow will offset the admitted Democratic gains in the towns and cities. Such figures as have been received, however, point to a Democratic victory for at least the national ticket and probably State officers. Gov. Sheldon has run ahead of Judge Taft in a number of cases, and with A. C. Shallenberger, Democrat, for Governor, running behind Bryan, Sheldon may pull through.

Bryan's greatest gain was in Lincoln, which he carried, overcoming a normal Republican plurality of 1600. Eighteen out of twenty-one precincts in Lincoln gave Bryan 3883 and Taft 3244, a plurality for Bryan of 639. The remaining three precincts will not greatly change these figures. Bryan carried his home precinct by 111 to 54.

GAINS IN LINCOLN.

The gain for the Democrat national ticket in Bryan's home town was steady and decisive. The ward in which he formerly lived, the banner Republican ward of the city and which never in Mr. Bryan's political career gave anything but a handsome Republican majority, today was nearly evenly divided.

The Bryan workers throughout the day were aggressive and confident and the vote polled here was the largest in the history.

As an offset to the early Democrat celebration, the new returns from country precincts showed a very slight Democrat gain or none at all. One precinct in Saunders county showed a Republican gain, and this, the Republicans said, was as expected, that Bryan would gain in the cities and towns, but would lose in the agricultural districts.

As the night advanced and the country precincts began to come in the outlook was better for the Republicans. One precinct in Buffalo county gave Taft a gain over McKinley eight years ago of fifty-four and a gain for Bryan of but fifteen. In none of the country precincts was there any falling off in the Republican vote, but the gain was hardly in proportion to the Democratic gain in the towns and cities.

THE ELECTORAL COLLEGE.

	Taft.	Bryan.
Alabama	..	11
Arkansas	..	9
California	10	..
Colorado	..	5
Connecticut	7	..
Delaware	3	..
Florida	..	5
Georgia	..	13
Idaho	3	..
Illinois	27	..
Indiana	15	..
Iowa	13	..
Kansas	10	..
Kentucky	..	13
Louisiana	..	9
Maine	6	..
Maryland	8	..
Massachusetts	16	..
Michigan	14	..
Minnesota	11	..
Mississippi	..	10
Missouri	..	18
Montana	..	3
Nebraska	..	8
Nevada	..	3
New Hampshire	4	..
New Jersey	12	..
New York	39	..
North Carolina	..	12
North Dakota	4	..
Ohio	23	..
Oklahoma	..	7
Oregon	4	..
Pennsylvania	34	..
Rhode Island	4	..
South Carolina	..	9
South Dakota	4	..
Tennessee	..	12
Texas	..	18
Utah	3	..
Vermont	4	..
Virginia	..	12
Washington	5	..
West Virginia	7	..
Wisconsin	13	..
Wyoming	3	..
Total	306	177

OUT OF THE WAY.

BRYAN'S DEFEAT PLEASES DEBS.

SOCIALISTS REJOICE AT DOWNFALL OF GOMPERS.

"Elimination of Hearst, et al., Paves the Way for Further Normal and Healthy Growth of Our Party," Says "Red" Editor in Discussing the Campaign.

[BY DIRECT WIRE TO THE TIMES.]

CHICAGO, Nov. 3.—[Exclusive Dispatch.] The elimination of Hearst, Bryan and Gompers from the political field and consequent gains for the Socialists was the way the Debs party leaders analyzed the returns tonight.

At the headquarters of the Socialist party tonight a group of leaders sat until early this morning, but returns throughout the country were slow in coming in, which made it difficult to form a correct idea of the growth of the movement.

The large slump in the vote in Chicago and Cook county was expected and did not disconcert the leaders. The vote of four years ago was not regarded as a Socialist vote, while the leaders declared that the vote of today might be accepted as reflecting the genuine strength of the party in the city.

The insignificance of the labor vote as represented by the American Federation of Labor was pleasing to the Socialists. Since the beginning of the campaign they have been bitter in their opposition to Samuel Gompers and his programme.

"The results remove Bryan, Hearst and Gompers from the political field," said A. M. Simons, managing editor of the Daily Socialist, as he watched the returns. "I do not mean that it will eliminate Gompers from the industrial field, where he has proved himself useful, but it proves that his political activities were futile and ill-advised. There were almost as many labor unions throughout the country which indorsed the Socialist party as indorsed the Gompers programme.

"Some Socialists believe that the election means the death knell of the Democratic party, but I do not view it in that light. The Solid South will hold the Democratic party together for several years to come, although I look for labor to unite solidly under the Socialist banner in some districts within the next two years."

"How do you account for the slump in Chicago with a daily organ which you did not have four years ago?" was asked.

"A factor which contributed to the slump in Chicago was the fact that the party did not make as active a campaign as it might have done. The 'Red Special' was quite an undertaking, which limited our campaign fund in other directions. On the whole we are well satisfied with the results, which indicate a healthy growth in the movement as far as we can judge from the returns received up to this hour."

INTRENCHED.

CONGRESS IS SAFE.

Republicans Keep a Majority.

Many of the Old Members Are Re-elected by Good Margin.

"Uncle Joe" Cannon, Again a Victor, Begins Fight for Gavel.

Sereno Payne Will Introduce New Tariff Bill at Coming Session.

[BY DIRECT WIRE TO THE TIMES.]

CHICAGO, Nov. 3.—[Exclusive Dispatch.] Early returns indicate that Congress is still heavily Republican with a majority on division of fifty-eight. The probable Republican membership in the Sixty-first House is 223, while the Democrats show but 168.

Most of the old members have been returned, the spectacular fight of "Uncle Joe" Cannon being the most interesting, owing to the fierce contest that has been made upon him all over the country. His battle for the Speakership has already begun, and it is likely that his enemies will renew their contest to keep him from wielding the gavel, now that their efforts to defeat him have failed.

Tawney of Minnesota has pulled through, and McCleary, after a two years' absence, has been chosen.

John Dalzell, Rep[illegible] from the Thirtieth [illegible] trict, won after a har[illegible] Edward F. Duffy. [illegible] he had 2500 votes to spare, although the returns have not been tabulated as yet.

The election of Sereno E. Payne, chairman of the Ways and Means Committee, means that he will introduce the new tariff bill, and that the same influences which controlled during the life of Mr. Dingley will very largely prevail.

In Wisconsin a very good fight was fought by the Socialists in the Fifth Milwaukee District, but it was found impossible to defeat the Republican.

In the First Michigan District, William D. Mahon, the leader of the street car men, gave his opponent on the Republican ticket a gallant contest, but he was not in receipt of the votes necessary to make him a winner. His Chicago friends were particularly anxious to put him over, and sent a fund of $1500 for his campaign, but it did not avail.

CONGRESSIONAL RESULT.

[ASSOCIATED PRESS NIGHT REPORT.]

CHICAGO, Nov. 4.—The returns giving the results in the Congressional districts, as far as they have been received up to 2 o'clock this morning, giving the following elections of Congressmen:

ALABAMA.

George W. Taylor, S. H. Dent (full term,) O. C. Wiley (unexpired term,) Henry D. Clayton, William B. Craig, James Thomas Heflin, Richmond P. Hobson, John L. Burnett, William Richardson, Oscar W. Underwood, all Democrats.

ARKANSAS.

Robert B. Macon, William A. Oldfield, John C. Floyd, William B. Cravens, Charles C. Reid, Joseph T. Robinson, R. Minor Wallace, all Democrats.

CONNECTICUT.

At Large, Joseph Q. Tilson, E. Stevens Henry, Nehemiah D. Sperry, Edwin W. Higgins, Ebenezer J. Hill, all Republicans.

DELAWARE.

At Large, William H. Heald, Republican.

FLORIDA.

Stephen M. Sparkman, Frank Clark, D. H. Mays, Democrats.

GEORGIA.

Charles G. Edwards, James M. Griggs Dudley M. Hughes, William C. Adamson, Leonidas F. Livingston,

(Continued on Fourth Page.)

PRESIDENT VERY HAPPY.

Sends "Hearty Congratulations" to Mr. Taft and Other Candidates.

[ASSOCIATED PRESS NIGHT REPORT.]

WASHINGTON, Nov. 3.—The President sent the following dispatch to Taft tonight:

"I need hardly say how heartily I congratulate you, and the country even more."

He also sent the following to Governor Hughes:

"Accept my hearty congratulations."

The following was sent to Representative Loudenslager:

"Accept my hearty congratulations."

No statement was made by the President tonight on result of election.

In Two Parts Complete—26 Pages.

Part I—Telegraph-News Sheet—16 Pages.

The Los Angeles Times

Twenty-Eighth Year.

MAXIMUM TEMPERATURE: LOS ANGELES, 69; Denver, 58; Detroit, 66; Duluth, 58; Omaha, 60; Cincinnati, 64; Chicago, 70; Kansas City, 62; St. Paul, 68; St. Louis, 62.

PER ANNUM $9.00 { Per Month, 75 Cents, or 2½ Cents a Copy.

TUESDAY MORNING, SEPTEMBER 7, 1909.

On All News Stands, Trains and Streets. } 5 CENTS.

"I HAVE THE OLD POLE," WIRES PEARY.

THE WEATHER.

BRIEF REPORT.

FORECAST—For Los Angeles and vicinity: Fair, light northwest wind. For San Francisco and vicinity: Fair, with fog in morning; moderate west wind.

Sunrise, 5:31; sunset, 6:11; moon rises 11:42 p.m.

YESTERDAY—Maximum temperature, 69 deg.; minimum, 59 deg. Wind, 5 a.m., southwest; velocity, 2 miles; 5 p.m., southwest; velocity, 12 miles. At midnight the temperature was 62 deg.; high fog.

TODAY—At 2 a.m. the temperature was 61 deg.; high fog.

[The complete weather report, including comparative temperatures, will be found on page 15, Part I.]

The Times

Total Reading Matter Today........81 Cols.
Total Advertising Matter..........101 Cols.

INDEX TO PARTS AND PAGES.

POINTS OF THE NEWS

IN THIS ISSUE.

The City.

A report reached Los Angeles last night from Sacramento that the State Board of Equalization has decided to raise the assessed valuation of Los Angeles property 33 1-3 per cent. or more than $140,000,000.

President Diaz telegraphs to a friend in this city that he will be unable to visit Los Angeles with President Taft.

Harper E. Bennett, whose trial on a charge of poisoning his wife will begin this morning, gives out a remarkable interview in the County Jail.

Dr. Locke's plan of appointing a nonsectarian commission to introduce the reading of the Bible in the public schools is indorsed at a meeting of Methodist ministers.

The port of Los Angeles may become the center of a rate war between the Hill and Harriman interests when the new Hill steamer begins its trips between Southern California and northern points next month.

Police Capt. Broadhead is returned to duty at Central Police Station pending the action of the Police Commission this evening.

Cruisers and torpedo boats of Uncle Sam's navy will arrive at Santa Monica today to take part in the celebration over the completion of the municipal pier.

Thousands take advantage of the legal holiday yesterday to take outings in the public city parks and many associations hold picnics.

Many drivers are arrested for not complying with the new city ordinance providing for two lights on every vehicle.

The conference of the German Methodist Church, which opens in this city tomorrow evening, promises to be an exceedingly interesting one.

Southern California.

Burglars operate by the wholesale during holiday at Pasadena; plan to reform moving picture business.

Largest swordfish of season, caught off San Clemente yesterday, is reckoned to be 200 years old.

Through oversight in water ordinance, Long Beach may have to pay several thousands yearly more than it expected.

Cloudburst washes out track in four places between Ethnac and Minifee; Elsinore branch also suffers.

Auto turns turtle in Orange county mountains and banker and son-in-law are pinned beneath machine.

Brentwood car stops on boy's hand at Sawtelle; Los Angeles lad victim of curious accident.

Heart of Ventura county unanimous for good roads; proposes to expend $100,000.

Hollywood Board of Trade passes resolution favoring consolidation with Los Angeles.

Pacific Slope.

Portland minister jumps overboard to save son and drowns while boy is rescued.

Chinese Six Companies demand investigation of constable's killing of Chinese cook.

Easterner returns after many years to locate rich ledge near Nevada City as he left it.

Two men lost in Arizona ice caves rescued when nearly frozen to death.

Reno telephone girl poisoned by bottle of port wine sent to her by messenger.

General Eastern.

Message received from Commander Peary that he has reached the North Pole.

Mrs. Peary overcome with joy at receipt of message from husband announcing his success.

Two Chicago cranks write letters threatening life of President during his visit to city.

Eastern railways have figures compiled showing that $100,000,000 has been added to their burden by recent legislation.

Great crowd at DeKalb, Ill., picnic sees aeronaut fall thousand feet.

Dr. Cook wires New York newspaper that he has promised to submit his data to faculty of University of Denmark.

Washington.

Department of Far Eastern Affairs reorganized by new appointments.

Scientists accept Peary's statement that he found pole without hesitation; plan great ovation.

Foreign.

Italy filled with enthusiasm by aerofete which opens at Brescia today. Many special trains leaving Rome.

Britons admit at last that American discovered North Pole; hope Shackelton will find South.

Paris enjoys profound sensation at news of Peary's discovery of pole.

Cook says he's glad Peary found pole; only friendly rivalry, he says; will confirm facts.

Twelfth division of Spanish army ordered to Morocco to fight Moors.

Prominent merchant of Amoy, China, found dead; warrant issued for American citizen.

BUBONIC IN CHINA.

During the fortnight ended last Saturday, there were ninety-four bubonic and thirty-five cholera deaths in Amoy, China.

PEARY AT POLE FINDS NO TRACE OF COOK.

Explorer Reaches Top of World After Lifetime of Endeavor.

For Second Time Within a Week the World Learns That an American Has Attained the Goal of Centuries—Most Remarkable Coincidence in History Recorded When Naval Officer Reports Discovery.

[ASSOCIATED PRESS NIGHT REPORT.]

SOUTH HARPSWELL (Me.) Sept. 6.—Commander Robert E. Peary announced his success in discovering the North Pole to his wife, who is summering at Eagle Island here, as follows:

"Indian Harbor (via Cape Ray) Sept. 6, 1909.

"Mrs. R. E. Peary, South Harpswell, Maine.

"Have made good at last. I have the old pole. Am well. Love. Will wire again from Chateau.

[Signed] "BERT."

In replying, Mrs. Peary sent the following dispatch:

"South Harpswell (Me.) Sept. 6, 1909.

"Commander R. E. Peary, Steamer Roosevelt, Chateau Bay.

"All well. Best love. God bless you. Hurry home.

[Signed] "JO."

ST. JOHNS (N. F.) Sept. 6.—Commander Robert E. Peary, who announced today that he had discovered the North Pole on April 6 of the present year, found no trace of Dr. Frederick A. Cook, who reported that he had made the same discovery in April of the preceding year. This news reached here tonight through Capt. Robert Bartlett of the Roosevelt, Peary's ship.

While Peary does not expressly repudiate Dr. Cook's contention in so many words, his statement may have an important bearing upon determining the extent of Dr. Cook's explorations.

The Roosevelt was in good condition and the crew all right, Capt. Bartlett wired, and he reported that the schooner Jeannie carrying supplies for the expedition had met them off the coast of Greenland.

Coming south the Roosevelt passed Etah and Upernavik, where Dr. Cook had preceded Peary.

The Roosevelt tonight is bound for Chateau Bay, Labrador, with Peary and party on board, where she is due tomorrow, Chateau Bay lies northwest of Castle and Henley Islands, on the northern shore of Belle Isle Straits and due east of Belle Isle.

DOUBLY DISCOVERED.

[ASSOCIATED PRESS NIGHT REPORT.]

NEW YORK, Sept. 6.—Peary has reached the North Pole. It has been doubly discovered. From the bleak coast of Labrador, Commander Peary today flashed the news that he had attained his goal in the Far North, while at the same moment in Denmark, Dr. Frederick A. Cook was being dined and lionized by royalty for the same achievement.

Yankee grit has conquered the frozen north, and there has been created a coincidence such as the world will never see again. Two Americans have planted the flag of their country in the land of ice which man has sought to penetrate for four centuries, and each ignorant of the other's conquest, has sent within a period of five days a laconic message of success.

Here are the various messages received today announcing Peary's victory:

"Indian Harbor, via Cape Ray, Sept. 6, 1909.

"The Associated Press, New York:

"Stars and Stripes nailed to North Pole.

[Signed] "PEARY."

"Indian Harbor, via Cape Ray, N. F., Sept. 6, 1909.

"Herbert L. Bridgeman, Brooklyn, N. Y.:

"Pole reached. Roosevelt safe.

[Signed] "PEARY."

"Indian Harbor, via Cape Ray, Sept. 6, 1909.

"The New York Times, New York:

"I have the pole, April 6. Expect arrive Chateau Bay Sept. 7. Secure control wire for me there and arrange expedite transmission big story.

[Signed] "PEARY."

LEAVES NO DOUBT.

Cook, in his first message to his countrymen, was brief but non-committal. Peary was even briefer, but specific.

"Stars and Stripes nailed to the pole," he said.

Five days ago, on September 1, Dr. Cook sent out from the Shetland Islands the first message of his success, a message which has aroused a storm of controversy around the world. Today Robert E. Peary, lost from view in the land of ice and unheard from since August, 1908, startled the world by a similar message sent from Indian Harbor, Labrador. There was no qualification; it left no doubt.

With but a word from Peary, the world waits for details, but none will be available until he arrives at Chateau Bay, Labrador.

Both the Old and the New World were apprised of Peary's great achievement practically at the same moment, and the excitement which followed attests to the high pitch of interest

(Continued on Fifth Page.)

LOYAL WIFE.

BEST NEWS IN WORLD, CRIES MRS. PEARY.

[BY DIRECT WIRE TO THE TIMES.]

EAGLE ISLAND (Me.) Sept. 6.—[Exclusive Dispatch.] "Glory, mamma, mamma, papa has been heard from."

Seizing the message containing the news of Peary's discovery, Miss Marie A. Peary, sixteen-year-old daughter of Commander Robert E. Peary, rushed upstairs to bear the glad and wonderful tidings to her mother, who only a few minutes before, had gone to her room with a headache.

An hour and a half later, Arthur Palmer, the storekeeper at West Harpswell, arrived at Eagle Island with a personal telegram from the intrepid Arctic explorer to his wife and family.

Mrs. Peary was not slow in coming downstairs when she heard the news, and when asked for an interview, said:

"What do you want me to say? God bless you, I'll say anything. I'm tickled to death."

Mrs. Peary prepared the following short message for publication:

"You have brought me the best news possible. I can't find words to express my feelings. Mr. Peary's twenty-three years of work and hardship have been crowned with success. God bless him."

In discussing the trip of her husband, Mrs. Peary said:

"Mr. Peary left New York July 6, 1908, and left Sydney the last week in July. He was reported several times from Labrador, and on September 17, I received a dispatch from him dated at Etah, August 17, 1908.

"This telegram, which never before has been made public, was as follows:

"'ETAH, Aug. 17, 1908.—Arrived Cape York July 23. Roosevelt went to Etah to overhaul and trim for the ice. With Eric visited Eskimo settlement to secure Eskimo dogs and material for equipment. Thirty-five walrus killed by party. Rejoined Roosevelt at Etah with Eric August 11, 1908. Coaled Roosevelt. Left supplies for relief of Cook, not yet returned. Put two men in charge. Sent Cook's companion (Francke) home disabled. Whitney remains through the winter to hunt muskoxen and bear. Unusually stormy season, but no ice yet. Snowing furiously now, plenty of it from Littleton Island and Sabin north. All depends on ice conditions beyond. Have good supply Eskimo dogs and walrus meat. All well on board. Expect to steam north some time tonight. Love ROBERT E. PEARY.'"

About this time several other newspaper men arrived at the island and when they asked for Mrs. Peary she herself opened the door and said:

"All are welcome. There is plenty of room on Eagle Island today."

Continuing her story about Mr. Peary's trip she said:

"Nobody knows of the sacrifices he has made. We have been married for twenty-one years and I have been waiting for him all that time. Now I want to wait on him. This is the last trip that he will make into the frozen north. I wintered north with Mr. Peary in 1891 and 1892, but since that time have only been on summer trips with him. I will join Mr. Peary at Sydney. We then will go either to New York or Washington. Mr. Peary still is on duty and will have to report at the Navy Department at once. I cannot tell what our plans will be after that.

"This is Mr. Peary's seventh trip into the Arctic regions. In 1886 he went on his first expedition to study ice conditions and see if there was any particular route to the pole. In 1891 and 1892 and 1894 and 1895, he made trips north. In 1896 and 1897 he went north to establish depots and stock them with supplies for his next trip, on which he started in 1898, and from which he returned in 1902. Another trip was made in 1905, from which he returned the following year and now he has achieved success on his seventh and last trip."

DISTINGUISHED EXPLORER FINDS NORTH POLE.

Commander Robert E. Peary,

United States Navy, who yesterday announced that he had discovered pole after lifetime spent in effort. This picture was taken of Peary on a former expedition.

EPOCH-MAKING.

PEARY'S VICTORY WINS WASHINGTON PLAUDITS.

Scientists Unite in Praise of American Naval Officer Who Has Also Planted Stars and Stripes on "Top of the World."

[ASSOCIATED PRESS NIGHT REPORT.]

WASHINGTON, Sept. 6.—"Should an American first of all place the Stars and Stripes at that coveted spot, there is not an American citizen at home or abroad but would feel a little better and a little prouder of being an American."

Commander Robert E. Peary almost three years ago thus prophetically outlined his view of the value and interest attached to the achievement he announced in his dispatch today.

The news of Peary's feat, following lose on the heels of Dr. Cook's planting the American flag at the same spot, evoked enthusiastic plaudits in Washington.

"Such wonderful achievements as this make epochs in the history of the world," declared Capt. Veeder, in charge of the United States Naval Observatory.

"Peary adds still another name to the long list of American heroes," said Prof. Asaph Hall of the observatory.

"The energy he has displayed, his persistence and the intelligence he has brought to bear on this great problem are worthy of all commendation."

Those persons who had associated with Peary here spoke of him today as a man of wonderful capacity for doing things and they instantly accepted the statement that he had discovered the pole.

TOOK COURSE LIKE COOK'S.

The courses taken by Commander Peary and Dr. Cook did not differ very materially, according to Prof. Henry Grannett, the geographer.

"It seemed to me that Peary was being delayed when he left a year or so ago," said Prof. Grannett.

"Peary's plan was to get up to the northwestern cape of Grant Land, where he made his former headquarters, before the ice closed in. He had been previously to the vicinity of Lady Franklin Bay, and then northwest along the coast for quite a distance before proceeding away from land and starting out for the pole. I should say he took about the same course this time.

"Dr. Cook started at Etah and crossed over into Grinnell Land to some point on the north coast near where Peary started. Their courses seem to have varied little."

Peary's attainment crowns the work of expeditions that he has led for a number of years. His last expedition was in 1906, when by means of the little Arctic steamer Roosevelt, and by journeying on sledges, he succeeded in reaching 87 deg. 6 sec. north latitude. This was accomplished April 21, 1906, after a zigzag journey in the Arctic Ocean, exactly two years to a day before Dr. Cook reached the pole. He regarded that expedition as simplifying the task by 50 per cent. and his failure to reach the pole was attributed by him to the fact that the winter was not normal, being a particularly open season throughout the northern hemisphere. He believed he could have reached the pole then in spite of the open season if he had known actual conditions northward as he subsequently knew them.

An exploration following him, according to Commander Peary, could not easily attain the pole, but could make deep-sea soundings throughout the central polar ocean and delineate the unknown gap in the northeast coast line of Greenland from Cape Morris Jessup to Cape Bismarck.

Commander Peary's last public appearance at Washington was when President Roosevelt presented to him, December 15, 1906, the Hubbard medal of the National Geographic Society. It was then that Peary declared that man and the Eskimo dogs are the only two mechanicisms that could meet all the contingencies of Arctic work.

Prof. Willis L. Moore, in discussing the achievements of Cook and Peary, said it was entirely probable that the data of one would not check up with that of the other, because of the moving ice, and that Peary may not have found April 6 last any trace indicating

(Continued on Second Page.)

BANNS AT DINGWALL.

First Royal Marriage in Scotland Since the Reformation, Prince Miguel's.

[ASSOCIATED PRESS NIGHT REPORT.]

DINGWALL (Scotland) Sept. 6.—The proclamation of the banns at Dingwall of the marriage September 15, at Tulloch Castle, of Prince Miguel of Braganza and Miss Anita Stewart, constitutes the first announcement of a royal marriage in Scotland since the reformation.

Prince Miguel is the son of the pretender to the Portuguese throne; Miss Stewart is the only daughter of Mrs. James Henry Smith of New York, by her first marriage.

THE RED HAND.

THREATEN LIFE OF PRESIDENT.

TWO CHICAGO CRANKS WRITE WARNING LETTERS.

Extraordinary Precautions to Be Taken During Visit of Mr. Taft, Although Police Profess to Take no Stock in Communications—Bodyguard to Be Imposing.

[BY DIRECT WIRE TO THE TIMES.]

CHICAGO, Sept. 6.—[Exclusive Dispatch.] Two letters, threatening the life of President Taft during his visit in Chicago, now in the hands of Capt. Porter of the Secret Service, have stirred up the police officials, with the result that efforts will be made to make the Chief Executive of the nation the most guarded President that ever came to Chicago.

Capt. Porter was inclined today to belittle the threats, although he began making preparations immediately to prevent the possibility of an attack on President Taft. The letters, he declared, were from cranks. He refused to reveal the contents or signatures.

The President will arrive in the care of good Secret Service men. These will be reinforced by the best operatives of the local headquarters, and a heavy guard of city detectives and policemen. One of the new methods to be employed in guarding the President is the plan of Capt. Porter, to have all Mr. Taft's protectors face the crowd at all times, instead of turning their backs on the multitudes, as has been the common practice on previous occasions. His men in this way, he believes, will be able to intercept the possible use of firearms or missiles of any sort.

As soon as the policemen arrive at the La Salle Street Station, Capt. Porter will assume charge of the bodyguard. The President will be taken to one of the rooms of the station, where the Reception Committee will meet him. Introductions will be censored by Capt. Archie Butt, his personal aid, to prevent the possibility of a straggler sifting through and gaining communication with the President. Those to be introduced will present their cards to Capt. Butt, who will in turn introduce them to Mr. Taft.

Regarding the visit of Mr. Taft to Chicago, and the arrangements made to escort him about the city, Capt. Porter said:

"It is true we have received a couple of threatening letters about the President. I believe they are from cranks. We are making no effort from this office to ascertain who wrote them. So far as I am concerned, I don't care about them. Whatever preparations we are making cannot be given in detail at this time.

COOK PROUD OF PEARY.

If Explorer Sent Dispatch He Is Convinced It Is True.

[BY DIRECT WIRE TO THE TIMES.]

NEW YORK, Sept. 7.—[Exclusive Dispatch.] The Herald this morning publishes the following:

[Copyright 1909 by the New York Herald Company.]

COPENHAGEN, Monday: "If Mr. Peary sent a dispatch from Indian Harbor, Labrador, that he has discovered the North Pole I am sure he has accomplished his life's ambition. I am proud of him and join with my fellow-countrymen in three cheers. The dispatch as read to me sounds like Peary, and knowing the man, his pluck and endurance, I have expected him to win his way to the 'Big Nail,'" said Dr. Frederick A. Cook when told that Mr. Peary had sent a dispatch to the President. Dr. Cook added: "I am not a doubting Thomas. I have always admired Mr. Peary's courage and have been impressed by his ability, and can only say three cheers for him and the Stars and Stripes." The announcement has created a great sensation in Copenhagen and at 1 o'clock crowds are discussing the wonderful coincidence that two plucky Americans have won their way to the farthest north.

AGAIN.

HARRIMAN RELAPSES

Has Bad Attack of Indigestion.

Nurses Hurriedly Summoned From New York to His Arden Home.

Patient's Condition not Such as to Cause any Immediate Alarm.

Presence of Noted Surgeons Revives Talk of Operation Soon.

[BY DIRECT WIRE TO THE TIMES.]

TURNER (N. Y.) Sept. 6.—[Exclusive Dispatch.] E. H. Harriman suffered a relapse Sunday. His condition early today was so grave that hurried messages were telephoned from the house on the top of Tower Hill, Arden, to New York, for trained nurses to be sent out on the first train from the city. The messages were sent by Dr. Lyle, Harriman's personal physician, to Miss Taylor, superintendent of the St. Luke's Hospital, Central Registry. In response, two nurses were dispatched, and arrived here at Turner station about 10 a.m., and were immediately whizzed to the hill-top in one of the Harriman automobiles.

"We hope for the best," was the answer Dr. Lyle gave in reply to inquiries at the Harriman home as to the condition of the little railroad king. "Mr. Harriman suffered a sharp attack of indigestion late Sunday night, but I do not think his condition is such as to cause any immediate alarm. I telephoned to New York for nurses because—well—because Mr. Harriman is a sick man, and it is only natural that a sick man should require the services of nurses." Dr. Lyle would not explain why the man who had been sick since he arrived here two weeks ago had not required the services of nurses earlier. Continuing his statement, however, he added:

"Mr. Harriman is resting comfortably tonight."

Although it was reported that Dr. C. E. Brewer, visiting surgeon to Roosevelt Hospital, New York, and Dr. Walter B. Janes of New York were both at the Harriman home, Dr. Lyle would neither deny nor confirm the story of their presence there. At the offices of these two specialists in New York it was said that both were "out of town," but that they were expected back tomorrow.

MAY HAVE CANCER.

It is believed here that both the noted surgeons are in the Harriman home, with the result that the stories of an operation are being revived. The character of the disease for which any operation would be necessary is still a matter of the wildest guesswork. The fact, however, leaked out here tonight that last week, presumably subsequent to the issuance of the Harriman statement, in which he admitted that Drs. Brewer, Janes and Crile had examined him, he had submitted to a searching examination by Drs. Wyeth and Hancock, noted in New York as specialists on cancer.

Another item of information gleaned here today was regarded as most significant in respect to the condition of Mr. Harriman. This was the fact that the first thing this morning the railroad magnate's unmarried daughters, the Misses Mary and Carol Harriman, telephoned to the young woman in charge of the Sunday-school of St. John's (Harriman's) Church at Arden, saying:

"We are very sorry, but we shall not be able to attend the picnic today.

The sudden relapse of the railroad magnate has brought back on the run to this village a corps of newspaper men and telegraph operators, even larger than that which departed hence last Monday.

EXCITEMENT AGAIN REIGNS.

Once more the villages at the foot of the Harriman mountain are buzzing with unwonted life, once more the Harriman army is mounting guard at all the approaches to the fastnesses, and once more a condition of siege is apparent, with the Harriman people trying to keep secret the goings on in the castle and the newspaper men discovering them in spite of all.

Dr. Lyle would add nothing to his earlier statement that it was merely indigestion. He insists that there is not the lightest cause for alarm. In view of the fact that no official bulletins as to Mr. Harriman's condition are issued, and no official statement is made in respect to the presence of the surgeons in the home, the sensational reports circulated here cannot be disproved. He may not be nearly so sick as the disconnected facts about the presence of nurses and doctors would seem to indicate, but no one beyond those in attendance on him know, and they won't tell.

PICNIC POSTPONED.

[ASSOCIATED PRESS NIGHT REPORT.]

ARDEN (N. Y.) Sept. 6.—E. H. Harriman is not as well as he was a week ago on the day that his personal reassurance led the newspapers of the country to abandon the watch main-

(Continued on Fifth Page.)

II. Editorial Section
LOCAL SHEET: 14 PAGES

Los Angeles Daily Times

California del Sur.
CITY AND COUNTRY.

XXVIIITH YEAR | FRIDAY MORNING, SEPTEMBER 24, 1909. | On All News Stands, Trains and Streets. | 5 CENTS

NEW ERA.

GREAT LANKERSHIM RANCH SOLD, LOCAL SYNDICATE TO SUBDIVIDE.

Two and a Half Millions for Forty-eight Thousand Acres in San Fernando Valley—Soon Open to Home-makers.

THE GREAT Lankershim ranch of 48,000 acres, in the heart of the fertile San Fernando Valley, has just been purchased for $2,500,000 by a syndicate of local capitalists which will proceed to subdivide and sell it in small parcels to home-makers. This is the largest and most notable real estate transaction ever made in Southern California. The ranch just sold is the largest undivided piece of property in Los Angeles county, having a length of fifteen miles and a width of more than six and one-half miles.

A number of surveyors will go into the field soon, and towns will be laid out, a boulevard running the entire length of the ranch will be constructed, together with fifty or sixty miles of parallel and lateral roads.

Homes for at least 25,000 persons will be possible under the plans of the purchasers, the small ranches to be placed on the market affording abundant opportunity for the support of this number from the products of the soil. As the southern boundary of the ranch is but a few miles from Los Angeles, a tremendous addition to the "back country" of this city is thus assured within a very few years.

The purchase includes not only the land, but all the property of the Los Angeles Farming and Milling Company. This takes in the company's big milling plant in this city, the warehouses, live stock, engines, wagons, harvesting machinery, and all other appurtenances of the ranch. The Farming and Milling Company will continue the operation of the ranch for another year.

A partial list of the members of the syndicate which has purchased the property is as follows: J. F. Sartori, president; Maurice S. Hellman, vice-president, and W. D. Longyear, cashier of the Security Savings Bank; Stoddard Jess and W. C. Patterson, vice-presidents of the First National Bank; James H. Adams and James R. Martin of James H. Adams and Company; O. J. Wigdall, vice-president of the Home Savings Bank; W. H. Allen, R. C. Gillis, E. J. Marshall, E. E. Hewlett and J. S. Torrence. There are a number of other purchasers—good citizens who have been enthusiastic and successful developers of Southern California Henry W. O'Melveny will be the attorney for the new owners.

Mr. and Mrs. I. N. Van Nuys, Who Have Relinquished the Vast Property.

For forty years Mr. Van Nuys was associated in the management and ownership of the immense ranch, his wife being the daughter of the late Isaac Lankershim, who bought the land from Pio Pico and the De Celises in the late '60's.

The transaction just completed does not include the Encino ranch, which occupies a comparatively small area adjoining the Lankershim ranch, and which is owned by outside interests.

It was stated yesterday by one of the members of the purchasing syndicate that it has two purposes in mind. One, of course, is to make money; the other is to afford an opportunity for home-makers to secure desirable land close to Los Angeles at a reasonable price instead of being forced to go to distant points and pay more for property less desirable.

With these objects in view, the syndicate will build highways and establish towns, making of the vast territory one great community of ranches of varying size, to be sold in parcels to suit the buyers. The town of Van Nuys, to be named in honor of the man who for so many years has controlled the destinies of the big ranch, probably will be the first to be established.

MUCH WORK FOR SURVEYORS.

While possession of none of the land will be given to the purchasers before November 1 of next year, it is understood that locations will be listed some time before that date, selections to be made from maps that will be prepared soon. It is said the surveyors will have work for a year or two in laying out the roads, the townsites and the boundaries of the various sections.

No company has yet been organized for the handling of the property of the syndicate, and it is not known at this time just what plan will be followed n placing the land on the market.

It is proposed to call the new company, which will own and handle the property, The Los Angeles Suburban Homes Company.

CHANCE FOR SMALL RANCHERS.

In the last two or three years lands f similar nature in this section of the tate have been bringing prices so igh as to oblige persons seeking acreage for plain farming to go up into he fertile San Joaquin or Imperial 'alleys or to distant points on the 'acific Coast.

Within a very short time, according the plans of the new owners, an pportunity will be afforded for thousnds to obtain at a fair price such nds as they desire, close to Los Anles—so close that a trolley car could ake the run in from thirty-five to ty minutes, the time dependent on the portion of the big tract seted upon.

The great domain which has just anged hands comprises more than e-half of the tillable land in the fer San Fernando Valley. It is boundon the south by the town of Lanshim, only a short distance from Angeles through Hollywood and Cahuenga Pass. The soil is uniformly rich and deep and of an alluvial character. It is declared to be of the best in Southern California for alfalfa, small fruits, and diversified farming. It is the largest single body of fertile, level land in this part of the State, and said to be the largest single body of land lying so near a big city, in the United States.

The northern boundary of the Lankershim ranch is near the town of Chatsworth, while to the west are the foothills of the Santa Monica Mountains, and to the east the level floor and slightly rolling hills of the remainder of the great valley.

EMPIRE UNDER PLOW.

Of the 48,000 acres of the ranch, 31,000 were plowed in summer fallow or in grain last year. Some 2000 to 3000 acres, suitable to the cultivation of strawberries and other fruits, never have been plowed or planted. Only a small proportion of the entire area is of a nature that precludes its cultivation.

The crop of the Los Angeles Farming and Milling Company for the current year was approximately 300,000 bags of wheat and barley.

In the production of wheat the ranch is notable in Southern California. It is about the only one that has been continuously and successfully operated along these lines. Under the terms of the sale, the Farming and Milling Company will continue to operate the ranch for the next year, by which time the work of subdividing will be well under way, the small ranchers will be pouring in and the broad reaches of wheat and barley will be giving way to the march of the fruit tree and to development along many other lines.

Where for more than thirty years has been only a broad, uninterrupted expanse of wheat fields and only the gang plow turned the soil, there will spring up homes and churches and schools and stores.

WATER ABUNDANT.

Throughout a great part of the ranch there is an abundant supply of water close to the surface, and the owners express the assurance that they will have no difficulty in obtaining all that is needed for irrigation and domestic purposes.

Though the ranch long has been noted for grain growing, it is by no means simply an expanse of waving wheat and barley. Along the county road that runs through it for miles are low hills and vales that are covered with ancient live-oak trees. There are acres and acres of these beautiful trees, the landscape being dotted as on the "Lucky" Baldwin ranch at Santa Anita. These charming spots, it is believed, eventually will be acquired by wealthy persons in quest of villa sites or for the less pretentious but beautifully environed country home.

TWO RAILROAD LINES.

Already there are excellent transportation facilities, the Coast line of the Southern Pacific running through a section of the ranch, while the Chatsworth Park branch also traverses it practically from end to end.

PAGES FROM PAST.

EARLY HISTORY OF BIG RANCH.

HELD BY LANKERSHIM FAMILY OVER FORTY YEARS.

Pioneer, Now Dead, Whose Name It Bears, Once Part Owner of Entire Valley—Rare Ability of I. N. Van Nuys in Conducting Business Makes It Wonderful Success.

History of the long-gone past in Los Angeles is recalled by the sale of the extensive Lankershim ranch. Going back a period of over fifty years, it is recalled that the San Fernando Valley was owned in undivided half-interests by the late Gov. Pio Pico and the De Celises, two of the best-known families of Spanish origin in California.

In 1868, the late Isaac Lankershim, a pioneer merchant and miller of California, bought out the Pico interest in the valley. He was associated with capitalists of San Francisco, and they organized under the corporate name of the San Fernando Farming and Homestead Association. The joint holdings of Pico and De Celis ran up to 120,000 acres at that time, used exclusively as grazing for cattle and sheep. Immense flocks of both ranged over the rich valley at will.

In 1870, I. N. Van Nuys became associated with Mr. Lankershim, Van Nuys taking charge of the farming interests in the valley. It soon became desirable that the land should be segregated, and an understanding to this end was reached between Mr. Lankershim and the De Celises.

A well-known pioneer character, a civil engineer, one John Reynolds, was employed to segregate the ranch into subdivisions, according to quality of the land. If Reynolds had been let alone he would be still in the valley running lines, and would have had the whole county subdivided into city lots. Mr. Lankershim was of too practical a turn of mind to let this go on. The

Isaac Lankershim,

late pioneer California merchant and miller, and an early owner of the great ranch, who began its development.

matter was handled by the late Anson Brunson, one time judge of the County Court here, who was attorney for the Lankershim interests in the division of the estate.

THE RANCH DIVIDED.

It soon became apparent that De Celis wished to have the upper end of the ranch, including the portion now embraced by Chatsworth and the Porter ranches. Lankershim saw that, though there were advantages in the upper part of the valley, the lower part was better suited for general farming purposes. An agreement was entered into, mutually acceptable to both of them, to run a line through the valley from east to west, the De Celises taking the upper portion and Isaac Lankershim and his associates the lower part of the valley.

The soil in this lower part of the valley is most excellent, and the Lankershim holdings embraced 59,500 acres. For several years after the subdivision it was still used for a range for sheep and cattle.

In 1874 I. N. Van Nuys, who was in charge of the ranch, concluded that it would be profitable to undertake fruit growing on a portion of the land. Mr. Van Nuys was born and raised on a farm near Dansville, a town not far from Rochester in the western part of New York. He had come to California in 1865, settling in the northern part of the State, and to Los Angeles in 1870, where he became associated with Mr. Lankershim.

FIRST SUCCESS.

The first crop of wheat was put in in 1874, not a very large area, but the experiment proved entirely successful. In the winter of 1875-6 a much larger area was broken up and seeded to wheat, the result astonishing every one and far surpassing the most sanguine expectations. In cutting the grain in the summer the heads reached as high as a horse's back. Many acres yielded from ten to twenty sacks each.

The question was what to do with the grain. The Southern Pacific Rail-

J. Benton Van Nuys,

assistant general manager Los Angeles Farming and Milling Company and active head of operation of the big ranch.

road had within the last three years been built up the valley, and connected with the road coming down through the San Joaquin Valley from San Francisco. In 1869 a railroad had been built from the harbor at Wilmington to the crossing of Alameda and Commercial streets in this city. The Southern Pacific had become possessed of this piece of road, and had brought its main line down to connect therewith.

But there was more wheat on the San Fernando than would be ground in the mills of Los Angeles in three years. Two ships were chartered, carrying a total of between 2000 and 3000 tons of wheat. They were in the offing off San Pedro and, according to the charter provisions, the first ship was to be loaded in thirty days or the San Fernando people would be obliged to pay heavy demurrage. Every team on the ranch was set hauling wheat to the San Fernando sta-

(Continued on Ninth Page.)

RECORD DEAL ON MAIN.

Foreign Capitalist Pays Nearly a Quarter Million for Peoples' Theater Site.

One of the largest and most important deals in Los Angeles business property consummated this year was put through yesterday when John C. Mordough, a retired banker and lumber merchant, of the City of Mexico, purchased through the agency of R. A. Rowan & Co., the property at Nos. 521-523-525 South Main street, known as the Peoples Theater building. H. J. Woollacott, the seller, received $225,000 for his holding, or at the rate of over $3600 a front foot.

The site is improved with a three-story brick building, containing two stores and the Peoples Theater on the ground floor, and a rooming-house on the two upper floors. The lot fronts 61½ feet on Main and extends back 165 feet to an alley. The present rents are said to be $15,000 a year, which will pay Mr. Mordough 6 per cent. on his investment.

Mr. Mordough came to Los Angeles first with the Shrine convention in 1907, as one of the delegates of the Anezeh Shrine of the City of Mexico. He was so impressed with the bustling and hustling way of the city, that he immediately made a loan of $50,000 on a Broadway lot. Since then he has visited the city frequently and has loaned through R. A. Rowan & Co., several hundred thousand dollars.

Mr. Woollacott, the seller, purchased the holding many years ago, while it was still residence property, at $800 a front foot. He erected the present building four years ago at a cost of $46,000.

PRICES CUT.

WAR ON RATES ALONG COAST.

SLASH COST OF OCEAN TRIPS FROM LOS ANGELES.

Steamships of Rival Lines Running to and from San Francisco Announce New Schedule and Further Reduction Is Expected—Pacific Mail and St. Croix Involved.

War in earnest has been declared on the Pacific Coast Steamship Company by Schubach & Hamilton, of Seattle, which firm will publish a first-class rate of $6.35 from San Francisco to Los Angeles on the steamer St. Croix.

The rate is a cut of $3 under that declared by the Pacific Coast Company some days ago. A dispatch from San Francisco received last night, says:

"Beginning Monday the St. Croix will leave San Francisco alongside the Pacific Coast Company's crack steamers the President and the Governor and will carry passengers first class to Los Angeles for $6.35. The round trip rate will be $11.50. We shall have an intermediate rate of $5.35, $9.50 for the round trip, and a one-way steerage rate of $4.35. The St. Croix will make two round-trips each week, sailing Mondays and Thursdays, and will make a little money at the rates published."

It is said that the St. Croix may be operated for what it costs to purchase the coal for one of the Pacific Coast Company's new steamers, and apparently, Schubach & Hamilton have entered a fight to a finish. It is expected the Pacific Coast Company will not only meet the St. Croix's cut but will go under it.

Whatever the final outcome of the rate war, the traveling public will be benefited both by low rates and by augmented steamer service between the North and the South.

MYSTERIOUS.

ELOPES WITH HIS OWN WIFE?

YOUNG WIFE DISAPPEARS WHILE TAKING A WALK.

Had Recently Left Her Husband for Cruelty—Mother Is Prostrated With Grief—Husband Is Also Missing—Evidence That She Intended to Return When She Left.

A puzzling enigma was presented to the police yesterday when relatives of Mrs. Sadie Clark Sinclair, 16 years old, reported that she had suddenly disappeared while taking a walk Sunday. Her kin declare she has either been kidnaped or "done away with."

Behind her mysterious disappearance lies a story of domestic unhappiness and a separation from her husband less than three weeks ago. One strange feature of the case is that her husband, Harry H. Sinclair, whom she had left, cannot be found.

Mrs. C. F. Clark, the girl's mother, is prostrated with grief and fear over her daughter's disappearance. On this account, other relatives are exerting every influence to find Mrs. Sinclair.

Sinclair was the girl's first sweetheart. They were married January 20. Her aunt, Mrs. James P. Maxcy, who lived next door to the Sinclair home at No. 401 North Lake Shore Drive, declares he abused her. She deserted her home and fled to the parental roof at No. 1202 West Second street, September 3.

Her husband is said to have attempted to induce her to return to live with him but she refused.

"She seemed so happy to get home," said Mrs. Maxcy, yesterday. "She sang around the house and smiled for the first time in months. She did not want to ever have anything to do with her husband again."

Sunday, about 1:30 o'clock in the afternoon, the girl went out for a walk. Her mother suggested that she should change her waist as the one she was wearing was slightly torn.

"This is all right," she replied. "I am going only a few blocks and no one will see me."

That was the last time she was seen by the family. Her friends argue that there is plenty of evidence to establish the fact that she did not intend to go away when she left the house. She wore no coat and left all her jewelry, including a diamond ring, in her room.

A search was made for her but no trace of her movements was found. Her aunt then began making inquiries for Sinclair. She ascertained that he had left his employment as a workman at the new Huntington residence Saturday.

"Sinclair had always seemed to be jealous because Sadie thought so

(Continued on Fourteenth Page.)

PARTY TICKET.

REPUBLICANS INDORSE SMITH AS CANDIDATE.

Two Thousand Delegates Approve of Him As Party Candidate.

Convention Refuses to Set Its Seal on Present City Board of Education and Voices No Choice Therefor. Lively Contest Over Aspirants for Assessor and Auditor.

THE FOLLOWING candidates for city offices were indorsed by the delegates to the Republican city convention at Shrine Auditorium last night, the greatest gathering of its kind ever assembled in Los Angeles:

Mayor—George A. Smith.
City Clerk—Harry J. Lelande.
City Treasurer—Reuben Heffelfinger.
Tax Collector—E. E. Johnson.
City Assessor—Robert L. Hayhurst.
City Auditor—E. E. Bostwick.
City Attorney—Leslie R. Hewitt.

Councilmen—First Ward, Charles J. Letts; Second Ward, W. E. McKee; Third Ward, S. C. Dodge; Fourth Ward, Percy W. Ross; Fifth Ward, W. H. O'Connell; Sixth Ward, H. H. Yonkin; Seventh Ward, Henry H. Lyon; Eighth Ward, Bernard Healy; Ninth Ward, R. E. Wirsching.

The only great uproar in the convention of nearly 2000 delegates, there being some absentees, was caused by the proposal to indorse the present Board of Education for renomination. This was followed by a lively contest over the approval of candidates for the positions of Auditor and Assessor.

Nothing more was needed to prove that there were no "strings" on the delegates, for in these matters the convention simply tore loose, and did exactly as it pleased.

When the chairman ruled against the opponents of the indorsement of the Board of Education, arbitrarily, as many believed, the matter was brought up for further action, and on a call for division it was proved that the great majority was against the indorsement.

The only two administrative offices about which there was any question were those of Assessor and Auditor.

It had been understood generally that the present Assessor, Walter Mallard, was to be indorsed, but many of the delegates were opposed to such action. The name of Mallard was proposed, and it was thought nominations would

R. E. Wirsching

of the Ninth Ward, indorsed as candidate for Council.

squabbles that broke out from time to time, afforded an abundance of life.

There was a good deal of fun, too, for delegates and spectators. When one of the speakers, reaching the climax of his address, talked his false teeth out of place and was forced to grab them to prevent their forcible collision with the floor, the thousands in the hall were forced to roar, and at times when the presiding officer, because of the size of the hall and his unfamiliarity with names, got proper names twisted, there was some hilarity.

On the whole it was a delightful gathering of party men, and women, too, who are sincerely interested in politics, and especially party politics, and who, by their presence testified to the fact that the Grand Old Party cannot be snuffed out of existence by the shoutings of a few self-constituted leaders of an opposing element. Some of these leaders were bold enough to enter the convention hall, and even to go onto the floor and mingle with the delegates, in an effort to aid their own cause.

CALLED TO ORDER.

It was 8 o'clock when Chairman McGarvin, of the Republican City Central Committee called the great throng to order. It required no second effort to

D. C. McGarvin,

chairman of the Republican City Central Committee, who called the convention to order.

close, but a man from the Sixth Ward created a stir by presenting the name of Robert L. Hayhurst, who a few days ago announced that he had stepped out of the race, and another delegate proposed the name of Fred Stein.

ANOTHER BREAK.

In the case of Auditor, where many thought that P. C. Mulqueeny might be selected, there was another break. Mulqueeny's name was not mentioned, while friends of E. E. Bostwick and Ethan R. Allen proposed them for the place.

These two contests called for a vote by secret ballot, the result of which was as follows:

For Assessor—Hayhurst, 1083; Mallard 654; Stein, 194.

For Auditor—Bostwick, 1646; Allen, 274.

The main floor of the big auditorium was jammed with delegates, the only vacant seats being those arranged for less than a hundred delegates who failed to attend, while the first balcony was filled wtih spectators, including a large number of women.

In the delegations from the various wards were seen the faces of many Republicans, who in recent years have not taken the trouble to attend conventions. They turned out last night to prove that their party spirit is strong, and that they resent any attempt to break down the ranks. Some familiar faces were not seen, to be sure, but there were many new ones, among them those of young men who are keen for the principles of the grand old party, and who cannot be stampeded by the shouts of the enemy.

ANIMATED SCENE.

The big hall had been decorated with American flags and banners for the occasion and it presented an animated scene as the hundreds of delegates and visitors filed in. A band in the balcony played before the gathering was called to order, and at intermissions during the session, while the speeches from platform and floor, and the little

Percy W. Ross,

of the Fourth Ward, who was indorsed for the Council.

bring about composure for the serious business of the evening. The hum of conversation subsided and the delegates who were in the aisles sought their seats.

In the first silence, D. C. Casselman gained recognition and proposed R. W. Richardson, well-known attorney, for permanent chairman. In doing so he alluded to the great gathering as "genuine delegates to a genuine convention." Several delegates seconded the motion and the choice, on motion of Casselman, was made enthusiastically by acclamation. Mr. Richardson was escorted to the platform by Casselman and Col. George N. Black, who were named a committee by Chairman McGarvin.

CHAIRMAN'S ADDRESS.

Mr. Richardson said in part:

"It was in the wisdom of the fathers, born of the experience of the ages then past, to establish for this republic a representative form of government safe from the arbitrary rule of monarchies and the extremes of mob democracy. Fads and fancies, results of misguided sentiment, would annul this great principle.

"Republicans, constituting a large

(Continued on Eighth Page.)

In One Part, Complete—18 Pages.

The Los Angeles Times

Twenty-Ninth Year

PER ANNUM, $9.00 | Per Month, 75 Cents, Or 2½ Cents a Copy. | MONDAY MORNING, JANUARY 10, 1910. | On All News Stands, Trains and Streets. | 5 CENTS.

THE WEATHER.

BRIEF REPORT.

FORECAST—For Los Angeles and vicinity: Cloudy, unsettled; light northeast wind, changing to south. For San Francisco and vicinity: Unsettled, with showers.

Sunrise, 6:59; sunset, 5:02; moon sets early in evening.

YESTERDAY—Maximum temperature, 67 deg.; minimum, 41 deg. Wind 5 a.m., northeast; velocity, 9 miles; 5 p.m., southwest; velocity, 6 miles. At midnight the temperature was 48 deg.; cloudy.

TODAY—At 2 a.m. the temperature was 46 deg.; cloudy.

[The complete weather report, including comparative temperatures, will be found on page 8.]

Total Reading Matter Today........62 Cols.
Total Advertising Matter..........64 Cols.

INDEX TO PARTS AND PAGES.

POINTS OF THE NEWS.

IN THIS ISSUE.

The City.

First flight of an aeroplane here was made yesterday by Glenn H. Curtiss, who drove his biplane nearly a mile at Aviation Park while thousands witnessed its flight; Aviation Week begins today.

Barney Oldfield at Ascot Park, after repeated failures in attempt to lower world's record for a mile, defies death and lowered world's five-mile record on dirt track; won $1000 side bet.

All motorcycle records from thirty to 100 miles were shattered yesterday at the Coliseum; Jake De Rozier, winner of the century event, gets most of the honors.

Police Department here receives news that many eastern crooks have headed for Los Angeles to look for easy plunder during this week; several pockets picked and homes entered already.

Suspicion was raised in Coroner's mind that the death of boy in Hotel Berkeley was not altogether due to natural causes; received mysterious telephone message; will make thorough investigation.

Southern California.

By death of Pasadena woman wife of eastern milkman comes into fortune.

San Bernardino man loses way in awful storm, wanders for hours on desert in blizzard and has feet frozen; wife heroic in emergency.

Chief of Police Dishman arrested at Hollywood on charge of exceeding speed limit in auto; will come up for trial today.

Long Beach will hold another annexation election.

Riverside man who has option on stock of Home Telephone Company offers it to city, but may turn it over to the Sunset.

Young rancher of Fallbrook, San Diego county, may die of gunshot wound accidently inflicted.

Pacific Slope.

Congress will allow $125,000 to deepen San Diego harbor entrance; refuses other grant to dredge middle ground.

Gov. Sloan of Arizona to make trip to Washington and will ask government to bridge the Colorado river at Yuma.

Trial of Binger Herrmann, ex-Congressman and Land Office Commissioner, begins today in Portland; charged with conspiracy to defraud.

Robbers loot Sacramento ostrich farm of $2000 to $3000 of fine plumes; police without clues.

District Attorney Fickert cannot find grand jury evidence in Calhoun or trolly cases.

Olga Nethersole, actress, appeals to Governor Gillett for pardon for Percy Pembroke, boy bandit.

Ki Ki, the man monkey, loses wife and child when affinity appears.

Oregon rancher has fierce battle with pet deer and finally kills it.

California State Board of Health extends quarantine in diphtheria cases.

General Eastern.

Member of John D. Rockefeller, Jr.'s Bible class suggests that instructor's public activity may result in his nomination for Congress.

Nebraska Railway Commission puts prohibition license on selling liquors on trains in State.

Pennsylvania man welcomes sixty-ninth grandchild and hopes to see more.

Woman leopard trainer is badly mutilated by one of her animals; assistant twists tail and saves life.

Texas farmer kills wife and two children and badly wounds niece with hatchet; cuts own throat with pocketknife.

Forty-five "lonely Christians" respond to unique advertisement placed by church in Chicago paper.

Thirty shipwrecked sailors who narrowly escape death are being brought to New York.

Chicago Italian who receives "Black Hand" letter says he will not disobey its orders.

Washington.

Cardinal Gibbons is greeted by prominent men during annual visit to St. Patrick's parish.

Pinchot-Ballinger controversy seems to have checked instead of urging conflict in Congress with "insurgents;" Speaker complimented by Senate.

American Civic Association opens headquarters to fight for national park at Niagara Falls, regulation of billboards and abatement of smoke nuisance.

Denied at German Embassy that there is any danger of a tariff war with United States; would play into hands of France and England.

Representative Fitzgerald will fight Senate's action in Pinchot-Ballinger investigation resolution.

Gifford Pinchot will make lengthy reply to President's letter of dismissal, and will present it Tuesday.

Secretary Ballinger orders removal of four Oklahoma Indian Service officials for neglecting schools.

Foreign.

Mob of Nova Scotian coal miner strikers attack police in attempt to wreck colliery machinery and get whipped; ten ringleaders arrested.

President Madriz of Nicaragua grieves over death of Gen. Diaz, and orders court proceedings for punishment of those who caused Americans to die.

Gen. Booth, of the Salvation Army, believes that destruction of the world by fire will occur soon.

J. M. Barrie, noted English author and playwright, is reported in very ill health.

Italian village is sliding to destruction and inhabitants desert homes.

HOSPITAL DROPS INTO MINE.

VIENNA, Jan. 9.—The sudden cave-in of an abandoned mine at Raibl, in Corinthia yesterday, completely engulfed a small hospital building. Not a vestige of the hospital remains. Seven inmates of the hospital, including Surgeon Wessely and his family, perished.

BRITISH POLITICS.

READY FOR ELECTION.

Campaign Closes in Excitement.

King Edward Will Dissolve Parliament Today, and Vote Is Next.

Saturday to Be Big Day for Battle of Ballots in the Kingdom.

Great Issues of Fight Boiled Down by Leaders to Two Questions.

[BY DIRECT WIRE TO THE TIMES.]

LONDON, Jan. 9.—[Exclusive Dispatch.] By a stroke of the pen, King Edward will dissolve Parliament tomorrow and the writs for the general election will go out to the London and ordinary boroughs, the counties and the district boroughs. Both sides have only a few days left in which to burn up the powder remaining in their magazines. One or two boroughs probably will go to the polls Friday, but Saturday will be the big day for the London boroughs and the ordinary boroughs.

Out of the great debate of the campaign, in which the landlords have been rated as "fattened parasites" and as "the few who monopolize the land of the country," the questions at the bottom of the present upheaval in England have been boiled down to two, which, as the Liberal press puts it, contain the whole gist of the controversy.

These two questions, crystallized by Lloyd George and John Burns, out of the [illegible] and confusion of the discussion, are, in the words of these men, the following:

Lloyd George. The question you have got to decide is whether the people are going to make their wishes known through elected representatives or whether they are going to depend upon the House of Peers.

John Burns: The Chancellor of the Exchequer was confronted with two policies—to tax the poor through their necessities, or to tax the rich through their luxuries and their superfluities. He chose the latter.

To these questions, avoiding refinements of economic speciosities, the Liberal orators have clung all through the campaign.

BALFOUR FACES CONTEST.

[ASSOCIATED PRESS NIGHT REPORT.]

LONDON, Jan. 9.—A. J. Balfour, leader of the opposition in the House of Commons, will not enter the new Parliament without a contest. At the last moment the Liberals have nominated Sir Hugh Bell to oppose for Balfour's seat for the city of London. Sir Hugh Bell has no chance of election, but the Liberal party considered that it might adversely influence their prospects if both Mr. Balfour and Mr. Chamberlain were returned unopposed.

To secure a majority in the new Parliament, the Unionists must win 170 seats from their opponents. That there will be many renewals of allegiance to Unionist seats is not doubted. The long list of seceding Liberals who have been won over to tariff reform indicates there may be great surprises in the elections. Many

(Continued on Thirteenth Page.)

SKIMMING OVER THE GROUND IN MECHANICAL FLIGHT.

Curtiss Biplane Flying at Aviation Camp,

yesterday afternoon in the first flight in the West—The center picture shows the aeroplane about twelve feet in the air in the initial attempt up the stretch in front of the grand stand. Above the machine is flying at about thirty-five feet from the ground as it made its dip in starting on the long flight. Below is Mrs. Curtiss at the wheel of the biplane while her husband stands beside her.

DIES IN RED-LIGHT RESORT.

Nephew of Judge Moore, Rock Island Owner, Expires of Heart Disease While "Sporting."

[BY DIRECT WIRE TO THE TIMES.]

CHICAGO, Jan. 9.—[Exclusive Dispatch.] Nathaniel F. Moore, son of J. Hobart Moore, and nephew of Judge W. H. Moore of the Rock Island lines, was found dead in a disorderly resort in the South Side "red-light" district at 4 o'clock this morning. His body was removed to his late residence, No. 1104 Lake Shore drive, in a private ambulance this afternoon by the police.

According to his friends, young Moore had suffered from heart disease for some time, and the physicians who were called said that there was every reason to believe that this had caused his death. There were no marks on the body.

Moore, who was 26 years old, was married in New York to Miss Helen Fargo, daughter of a wealthy family.

IT'S DONE AT LAST.

GLENN CURTISS FLIES OVER AVIATION PARK.

Famous Sky Pilot Drives His Biplane Nearly a Mile at Greatest Height of Sixty Feet—Spectators Satisfied of Success.

THE first flight in an aëroplane west of the Great Plains, was made by Glenn H. Curtiss, at Aviation Park yesterday afternoon, at 3:20 o'clock, and as his machine rose gracefully in the air thousands of persons on the grounds, including aviators, employers, concessionaires, and visitors who had filtered in through the gates, cheered lustily.

It marked an epoch in the affairs of the West, for a flight had never before been made on the Coast, and native sons were skeptical of its accomplishment until they actually set eyes on the performance.

Three flights were made by Curtiss, his longest being a trifle more than a mile, at a maximum height of about sixty feet, and the other attempts were but a few hundred feet each to try out the ground.

In the longer flight Curtiss attempted to completely circle the aërodrome but when about three-quarters of the way around, his propellor splintered—just a trifle—but enough to cause the machine to wobble slightly, and Curtiss shut off his engine and sailed to the ground unharmed.

Curtiss was enabled to alight near the great tent in which the aëroplanes are housed, and when he stepped from the machine in an unconcerned manner, he quietly remarked, "I broke my propellor, but I don't know where." Then he carefully examined the wooden fan and found a slight split on one blade, seemingly of no account. So nicely was the machinery adjusted that Curtiss had been enabled to feel the break and immediately take the necessary steps to alight.

The incident showed how delicate is the mechanism of the air craft and how great must be the skill necessary to balance and control the erratic flyers. The group of spectators about Curtiss wondered and marvelled.

Curtiss first tried his machine up the slight incline in front of the grand stand, going to the left on the course. He steered against the wind and rose about a dozen feet in the air, sailing in all about 150 feet.

The second attempt was made from the head of the stretch. Curtiss sent his machine slightly down grade, and going at about twenty miles an hour left the ground and flew about 250 to 300 feet.

The aviator seemed satisfied with the test of the air-currents and the ground, and gave the signal for a more extended trial. He faced about to-

(Continued on Fourth Page.)

READY TO START.

EXHIBITION FLIGHTS TODAY'S PROGRAMME.

THE Executive Committee has scheduled the following flights for today, the events being in the nature of try-outs and exhibitions, rather than contests:

Glen Curtiss, biplane.

Charles F. Willard, biplane.

Louis Paulhan, Bleriot monoplane.

H. Paulhan, Farman biplane.

Charles K. Hamilton, Curtiss biplane.

Clifford B. Harmon, Curtiss biplane.

Messrs. Miscarol and Masson, trials with Paulhan's machines.

Other machines, notably the Gill-Dosh machine, and the Beachey-Knabenshue biplane, are to be tried out, but the aviators are not yet chosen. The two local machines, Edgar S. Smith's monoplane, and the Klassen monoplane, also are to be tried.

Tomorrow's events are to be similar, and by Tuesday the contests are to begin, as it is likely that all the machines will be in the best working order.

It is calculated that for the first two days the novelty of seeing flying will be sufficient to draw the crowds, and that it would be folly to put on races when the exhibitions are what is wanted to educate the crowd up to the possibilities of the machines.

Opening day is expected to be the banner day of the fore part of the

(Continued on Fifth Page.)

COUGH CURES 'APPENDICITIS'

Boy on Operating Table Gives Up Needle, and Knife Is Stayed.

[ASSOCIATED PRESS NIGHT REPORT.]

PITTSBURGH, Jan. 9.—Surgeons at Kittaning, Pa., had placed Norman Barnett, the little son of George Barnett, on the operating table today to cut out his appendix. Just as the knife was ready the lad was seized with a fit of coughing, which cured him. He coughed up a needle, which is believed to have caused his illness. He is rapidly recovering.

CREEL REACHES NATIVE SOIL.

LAREDO (Tex.) Jan. 9.—Señor Enrique Creel, Governor of the State of Chihuahua, who had been at Washington on a diplomatic mission, passed through here today en route for Mexico City. Beyond the mere statement that his mission had been successful, the Ambassador was guarded in his speech. When the train reached Nuevo Laredo, on the Mexican side of the Rio Grande, a representative gathering of citizens, including municipal and Federal officials, greeted Señor Creel.

SENILITY OR INSPIRATION?

GEN. BOOTH SAYS END APPROACHES.

WORLD'S WICKEDNESS INVITES DESTRUCTION.

Aged Head of Salvation Army Joins Ranks of Prophets of Earth's Dissolution—All Nations Banded Together to Work Evil, He Declares. Will Be Burned, of Course.

[BY DIRECT WIRE TO THE TIMES.]

LONDON, Jan. 9.—[Exclusive Dispatch.] Gen. Booth, head of the Salvation Army, has taken upon his shoulders the mantle of those sad prophets who from time to time have predicted imminent dissolution of the world because of its wickedness. Addressing a meeting tonight, he said:

"We have a world setting God Almighty at naught and rushing forward reckless of His wishes and threatenings as to their fate. Notwithstanding all that has been done in years gone by, men and women still pursue their wickedness today in all the nations of the earth.

"Not only one nation, but all nations, seem banded together as one great people of rebellion, transgression and wickedness, until some think—I believe with a considerable degree of probability—that we may be approaching rapidly the end of all things, with similar results, but far surpassing in magnitude anything that has gone before: that all things may be wound up, but that instead of there being a deluge of water sweeping the world and its inhabitants, there will be destruction by fire."

OLD SOL KILLS CRIME GERMS.

So Declares Chicago Chief, Who Plans New City Jail With Maximum of Sunshine.

[BY DIRECT WIRE TO THE TIMES.]

CHICAGO, Jan. 9.—[Exclusive Dispatch.] Chicago is to have a new City Jail that will be a model for all jails, according to plans now in the hands of Assistant Chief of Police Herman F. Schuettler. The new jail has been planned entirely by the assistant chief, who has planned and built eleven police stations in Chicago.

Instead of being in the damp and unsanitary basement, all cells—150 in number—will be on the top floor of the building. Then instead of the regulation dark roof, Assistant Chief Schuettler has provided for a heavy glass roof, so that every cell constantly will be bathed in sunlight, making the cells cheerful and sanitary instead of breeding places for disease.

"Sunshine kills crime germs," declared the chief.

The roof of the building, instead of being a wasted space, is to be devoted to an exercise room for prisoners and a place where those being detained unnecessarily may spend a large part of the daylight.

ROOSEVELTIAN.

BALLINGER USES AX

Indian-Service Men Removed.

A Superintendent and Three Supervisors in Oklahoma Punished.

Secretary Remedies Disgraceful Conditions Found in Schools.

Improper Activities for Employees of Government Charged.

[ASSOCIATED PRESS NIGHT REPORT.]

WASHINGTON, Jan. 9.—Secretary Ballinger of the Interior Department today suspended from office Superintendent John D. Benedict of the Five Civilized Tribes of Oklahoma, and three supervisors, after an investigation that has disclosed a "disgraceful condition" affecting the material welfare of the schools.

As a result of the investigation which the Interior Department has been carrying on for some time, and which will be continued, other officials in the Indian service may suffer a fate like that of Superintendent Benedict and the three supervisors suspended.

The investigation that resulted in today's action was begun by re[illegible] charging the suspended officials [illegible] well as others, with activities imp[illegible] for government employés.

The suspended supervisors are C[illegible] Ballard of the Choctaw schools at [illegible]Alester; Frederick M. Umholtz of Chickasaw schools at Ardmore, Walter Falwell of the Creek sch[ools] at Muskogee.

WILL BE ALLOWED ANSWER.

Before any further action is taken in their cases, the four men will be allowed to answer the charges before the Secretary of the Interior.

From the report, it appears that Superintendent Benedict is connected with certain business interests in Oklahoma that have dealings with the Indians. This relationship, it was believed, was wholly incompatible with his service as superintendent.

It was reported, also, that Benedict had permitted the schools to fall into a disgraceful condition, and that the supervisors have neglected their duties in matters affecting the material and moral conditions of the schools.

Oscar H. Lipps, supervisor of Indian schools, who has been sent to Oklahoma, notified the department today that he has relieved Superintendent Benedict, pending the investigation. The duties of the suspended supervisors will be performed temporarily by detailed clerks of the Indian office.

Superintendent Benedict had been connected with the Indian service for ten years.

ACCUSED OFFICIALS MAKE FULL DENIAL.

[ASSOCIATED PRESS NIGHT REPORT.]

OKLAHOMA CITY, Jan. 9.—John D. Benedict and other accused Indian officials made a full denial of the charges of Secretary Ballinger when interviewed tonight. They hint that politics might be held responsible for the accusations, and that Supervisor Oscar H. Lipps' methods were nothing less than "sneaky."

"I have had an idea that something of the kind would happen for some time," said Superintendent Benedict, when interviewed at his home in Muskogee. "It has been brought to my attention in more ways than one that other fellows are after my job, so I telegraphed to Washington last week that should there be any charges against my administration, I might have a chance to answer them. I received a reply that I would be given full opportunity to prepare and present my answer.

"I have no idea what is referred to by 'disgraceful conditions.' It is probable that Lipps came to Oklahoma expecting to find the schools in the same condition as government reservation schools. Government buildings used for schools under my direction are dilapidated, and many of our teachers have left us to teach in the State schools.

"Mr. Lipps did not come to see me and ask about matters, but went to each one of the schools without meeting the Supervisors. It is an easy matter for any one to go to any school and, by quizzing the pupils about conditions and the treatment accorded them, render an unfavorable report.

"In regard to my connection with Indian affairs which renders it wrong for me to hold official position, I think there must be some mistake. The only position that I hold that could in any way have a bearing on the situation is that to which I was appointed by Gov. Haskell, on the State text-book board. I would consider this an advantage and calculated to help in my regular work."

MANY AT TENEMENT FUNERAL.

NEW YORK, Jan. 9.—Had Isaac Finkelstein, who died in a tunnel of his own digging under Ludlow street, been a great man, he could have had no more spectacular funeral than that held over his body in the miserable tenement where he lived. Ten thousand persons attended out of curiosity, and for four hours they filed through the little room where the body lay.

OHIO GAS COMBINE CREATED.

CLEVELAND (O.) Jan. 9.—Plans for a new $30,000,000 company to swallow up the East Ohio Gas Company and the Columbia Gas Company, whose aggregate capital is about $21,000,000, was announced here today by M. B. Bailey, president of the East Ohio company.

The Los Angeles Times

For Liberty and Law, Equal Rights and Industri[al Freedom]

ANNUM, $9.00 | Per Month, 75 Cents. Or 2½ Cents a Copy. — SATURDAY MORNING, OCTOBER 1, 1910. — On All News Stands, Trains and Streets, | 5 CENTS

UNIONIST BOMBS WRECK THE TIMES; MANY SERIOUSLY INJURED

Terrific Explosion at 1 o'Clock This Morning Starts Fire Which Engulfs Score of Employes in Great Newspaper Plant---Many Victims ---Great Property Loss.

Many lives were jeopardized and half a million dollars' worth property was sacrificed on the altar of hatred of the labor unions 1 o'clock this morning, when the plant of the Los Angeles Times was blown-up and burned, following numerous threats by the laborites.

Not quite as many of the employes were on duty as would have been the case earlier in the night, when all departments were work-ng in full blast, but even so, the murderous cowards knew that fully 0 people were in the building at the time.

With the suddenness of an earthquake, an explosion, of which -v, snappy sound left no room to doubt of its origin in dyna-re down the whole first floor wall of the building on Broad- back of the entrance to the business offices. In as many four or five other explosions of lesser volume were heard. -e time it took to run at full speed from the police station ner of First and Broadway, a distance of less than half a ne entire building was in flames on three floors. Almost in the s-ne instant flames and smoke filled the east stairway on First street, driving down in a frenzied panic those employes of the com-posing room who had been so fortunate as to reach the landing in me.

Elbowing past the last of these fugitives, men fought their way to the first floor with flash lights and handkerchiefs over their -ces. There efforts were unavailing, the blistering hot smoke and e lurid light of the flames almost upon them and licking down at -em fiercely, drove the would-be rescuers back, hurriedly.

Although they could hear clearly the cries of distress, the groans screams of the men and women who, mangled and crippled by -ing debris from the explosion, lay imprisoned by the flames, about be cremated alive.

Along the windows of the editorial and city rooms, on the south ide of the building, through a choking volume of black smoke, could be seen men and women crowding each other about the windows of the third floor. The cries for ladders went up, frantic.

A fire wagon drove up at full speed. Groans greeted it when it was seen that it was but a hose wagon instead of the hook and ladder truck.

"Nets; get nets, nets!" was the yell.

A policeman came running up from headquarters, carrying a short ladder, pathetically inadequate. Some one called him a fool. But the ladder saved the live of Lovelace, the country editor, who jumped upon it and escaped with broken leg and some minor burns.

Other fire apparatus thundered up. The nets were jerked out in less time than it takes to tell, but by that time the fire had surged through the building with such rapidity that it was impossible to approach the reddening walls with them, and those unfortunates who had not jumped with Lovelace were doomed.

In less than four minutes from the time the explosion was heard the entire building was ablaze.

The Work of Demons

It reeked little to the man who placed the bombs which wrecked a splendid newspaper plant that 100 men were at work on the various floors, busily engaged in getting out the great newspaper. That the instant that the bombs were exploded their lives were in peril; that as a result of the hellish work lives were probably lost and other lives precious to wives, children and relatives were in deadly peril.

The bombs were planted by experienced hands. They did the work for which they were intended, at least temporarily, to cripple a great newspaper.

At 1 o'clock the Times plant was humming in every department. Forms were being closed up, sterotyped and sent down to the press room. An hour later the great presses would run at lightning speed to print the many thousands of papers which carriers were waiting to serve to their customers.

A second hell broke loose. A deafening detonation, a sickening uplift of men's hearts and lungs, then vivid tongues of flames, dense, stifling smoke which obscured the electric lights on every floor.

One instant busy occupation, lights, the whirr of machinery, the next, black midnight, smoke that overpowers, flames that shot their wicked tongues from basement to roof.

Trapped on all floors, the men of the Times, picked men they were, preserved their coolness in the midst of this appalling scene.

But it would seem that there was no escape. The murderers had planned with hellish cunning. The broad stairways were filled with deadly smoke almost as soon as the echo of the dynamite bomb had died away. The building was on fire on every side. But there was a way out for brave men, and they took the desperate chance.

The explosion caught the working force unawares and many were buried in the ruins, while others jumped from windows, fell through the elevator chutes or climbed down fire escapes after receiving terrible injuries from flying timbers and debris.

A few in the building escaped uninjured.

Most of the injured were employed in the composing, stereotyping and press rooms, the greater number of those in the editorial rooms having finished their tasks and gone home.

The explosions were heard throughout the business district, and scores of persons going home in the 1 o'clock cars jumped out and joined the thousands of citizens who were pouring from downtown houses and hurrying to the fire.

Within five minutes the scene of the explosion presented a terrible spectacle, as the big building had burst immediately into flame and was doomed.

Great excitement seized the multitude and word quickly passed that scores of doomed persons were within the seething furnace. Desperate attempts were made by policemen, firemen and citizens to rescue those within, but the flames drove them back.

The terrible spectacle of persons attempting to escape from windows in the upper stories was turned to a horror when they were seen to leap to the ground. One man was seen framed in a window casing; he threw up his hands and fell backward into the seething caldron behind and beneath him.

Men poured from doors dragging broken limbs and holding battered heads and bodies. Those who tottered forth were seized by eager hands and borne to places of safety.

Men begged to be permitted to dash into the burning building, but officers with drawn revolvers and riot guns forced them back and cleared the streets. A few moments later the flames licked up the woodwork of the structure, the walls began to fall and electric wires fell, sputtering to the pavements, and endangered those in the vicinity.

Wives and mothers of men employed in the great building, scenting the horror from afar, rushed frantically to the lines and emplored for news from their loved ones. As each new form came tottering from the holocaust he was seized by scores of hands and hugged to suffocation if uninjured and lifted tenderly to safety if hurt.

As each well-known face appeared to this little group of Times women he was greeted with tears of joy, which mingled with the bitter salt of anguish when no news of others was received.

The injured were quickly carried or driven to the receiving hospital, and scores of persons, men and women, volunteered to aid the surgeons in dressing the wounds.

For those in the wreck there was no aid; God only could care for their souls. Human agencies were of no avail.

With eyes glued on the red flames, the great crowd gazed in sorrow and amaze at the dastardly deed and its terrible consequences. A murmur of anger ran through the rows and rows of faces.

The street at First and Broadway was quickly cleared of people and scores of lines of hose were rushed through the lanes, but the building and those buried within were beyond saving, and the water was turned to adjoining structures.

Fearing a riot by gloating unionites, police carefully patrolled the neighborhood, but the cowards and murderers were gone.

Harry Chandler, assistant manager of the Times, had left the building a few minutes before the explosion. He rushed to rescue his imprisoned employes, but was driven back with the others. He gathered his faithful about him, and with tears streaming down his face thanked God for those who were saved.

"The hounds!" he cried. "My poor men!" Then he hurried to the receiving hospital.

It may seem strange to say it that there was no panic; that no pandemonium broke out; that men fought and trampled one another to save their own lives.

No, these brave, the victims of the foulest plot of the foul union labor ruffians, shouted encouragement. Those temporarily overcome with the deadly smoke reached out a hand and helped their brothers. The women came first. There were shouts of "This way!"

Through the smoke, to the sound of the crackling flames, they plunged to the rear of the composing room.

OUT OF THE JAWS OF DEATH

The escape from the city room and telegraph room on the third floor is little short of miraculous. In the former were Harvey Elder, assistant city editor; Mr. Lovelace, country editor; William E. Tribit, deskman. The reporters had all gone. Harry E. Andrews, managing editor, had left the city room a short half hour before the dynamiting.

In the telegraph room were H. D. Crane, assistant telegraph editor; R. L. Sawyer, chief telegraph operator, and Mr. McQuoddy, an operator. R. M. Whitney, telegraph editor, had left for home only a few minutes before.

When the explosion took place every man in both rooms sprang to his feet. One remarked sorrowfully, "That's the end." He felt the union laborites had done their worst. The men in the telegraph room ran into the city room, and the five stared blankly Then came the glare of flames and the smoke. Immediatel-- escape was cut off from the stairway leading to the pavement. Flames shooting him into the air cut off escape by the library and thence to the job department. The entire front of the building was a mass of thick, black smoke. It rushed into the city room, putting it into darkness: it choked the brave men fighting for their lives. One shouted, "The fire escapes."

But in that dense darkness no window could be seen. All seemed to be doomed.

McQuoddy and Tribit fought their way to the Broadway front, striking against tables, overturning chairs. Sawyer appeared for a moment when a fierce glare lighted up the room, walking in the center, searching a way. Verily that stray gleam was providential. It showed a window.

Tribit owes his life undoubtedly to the fact that he held his handkerchief over his mouth. As the men appeared at the windows they heard the crowd in the street shout, "Don't come down!"

They thought it was instructions to wait until ladders could be placed against the building, but it was death to stay.

Fighting, gasping, staggering, they groped their way to the window before which the fire escapes were located, and taking chances with the flames which were curling up, they climbed down to the pavement.

Lovelace and Elder probably became confused. They mistook the location of the fire escapes. They reached a window, climbed out and hung by their hands on the ledge until a shout ordered them to let go. A life net had been spread below them. But as Elder hung, the flames bit into his flesh. When he was picked up his face and hands were black. It was later discovered that his leg was broken. Lovelace was not touched by the flames, but his leg was badly injured. Both men were taken with others rescued from the burning building to the receiving hospital. Later Elder and Lovelace were conveyed to the California hospital.

CHIEF'S STATEMENT

CHIEF GALLOWAY, AT 3 O'CLOCK THIS MORNING, SAID:

"THAT THE BUILDING WAS WRECKED BY DYNAMITE SEEMS CERTAIN FROM ALL MY MEN CAN LEARN. THERE ARE ABOUT 100 PATROLMEN ON DUTY AT THE FIRE NOW, AND MOST OF THE DETECTIVES. WE HAVE FOUND SOME THINGS THAT SEEM TO US TO POINT TO THE AUTHORS OF THIS CALAMITY. WHETHER THEY WILL END IN ANY REAL RESULT IS IMPOSSIBLE TO TELL NOW, BUT I DO KNOW THAT WHETHER THEY DO OR NOT THE POLICE WILL KEEP AT IT WITHOUT REST UNTIL THIS WHOLE MATTER IS LAID BARE."

INJURED

E. B. ASPINALL, linotype operator. Cut over left eye; nose cut; right wrist strained.

S. W. CRABILL, foreman composing room. Burned and cut with flying glass.

WILL LATTA, sterotyper. Burned arms and back.

U. S. G. PENTZ, linotype operator. Jumped from window; wrist broken.

G. RICHARD, cut.

M. WESTON, cut on shoulders.

RANDOLPH ROSS, lynotype operator. Jumped from second story window; abrasion left knee; ankle sprained.

CHARLES VON VELSEN, fireman. Cut on left hand.

MRS. J. B. ULRICH, fell down elevator.

CHARLES E. LOVELACE, editorial staff. Jumped from third floor window; injuries perhaps fatal.

AUGUST KOTSCH, compositor. Slightly burned.

J. F. LINK, glass cuts on head.

CHURCHILL HARVEY-ELDER, burned over body and head; broken right leg; will probably die.

RICHARD GOFF, slight burns and cuts.

MISSING

J. C. GALLIHER, 40, linotype operator, married and five children.

W. G. TUNSTALL, 45, linotype operator, married.

FRED LLEWELLYN, 36, operator, married.

JOHN HOWARD, 45, printer, married and one child.

GRANT MOORE, 42, machinist, married and three children.

ED. WASSON, 35, printer, married.

ELMER FRINK, 25, operator, married.

EUGENE CARESS, 35, operator, married and one child.

DON E. JOHNSON, 36, operator, married.

ERNEST JORDAN, 32, operator, married and one child.

FRANK UNDERWOOD, 48, printer, married and one child.

J. WESLEY REAVER, stenographer.

R. L. SAWYER, 34, telegraph operator, married and two children.

HARRY L. CRANE, 38, assistant telegraph editor, married and one child.

CHARLES GULLIVER, 35, compositor, married.

A PLAIN STATEMENT

By the Managing Editor of The Times

The Times building was destroyed this morning by the enemies of industrial freedom by dynamite bombs and fire.

Numerous threats to do this dastardly deed had been received.

The Times itself cannot be destroyed. It will be issued every day and will fight its battles to the end.

The elements that conspired to perpetrate this horror must not be permitted to pursue their awful campaign of intimidation and terror. Never will the Times cease its warfare against them.

Gen. Otis, the principal owner of the Times, is on his way home from Mexico and will arrive here this afternoon.

The Times has a complete auxiliary plant from which this issue was printed on its own presses.

The management is under great obligations to The Herald for hearty assistance and to the Examiner for friendly offers.

The Times will soon be itself again. All business will be conducted at the Times Branch Office, 531 South Spring street.

A further statement cannot be made at this hour in the presence of frightful death and destruction.

Harry Chandler, assistant general manager of the Times, happened to be on the street when the explosion occurred and immediately took command of the situation.

They can kill our men and can wreck our buildings, but by the God above they cannot kill The Times.

HARRY E. ANDREWS,
Managing Editor of The Times.

WANT ADS WILL BE TAKEN AND ALL BUSINESS WILL BE TRANSACTED AT THE TIMES BRANCH OFFICE, NO. 531 SOUTH SPRING STREET, AND IN A TEMPORARY OFFICE ON NORTH BROADWAY, OPPOSITE THE RUINS OF THE OLD BUILDING.

All Business for THE TIMES

Will be Transacted at Their Branch Office 531 SOUTH SPRING ST.

WINSLOW HOMER, NOTED ARTIST, DIES; AGED 74

PORTLAND, Me., Sept. 30.—Winslow Homer, the famous artist, died at his home in Scarborough yesterday, aged 74. He had been ill for four weeks.

Homer had practically lived the life of a hermit in his Scarborough studio for several years past. His long life work many years ago won for him a conceded place as one of the ablest and most original of American artists.

In the later years of his life he worked largely in water colors, winning a place of prominence in this department of his art. His works are all notable for their fine sense of color, great truth to nature and virile sentiment.

Born in Boston in 1836, Homer came of stout New England stock. Both his grandfathers and grandmothers had lived in Massachusetts about the middle of the seventeenth century. He showed his talent when less than 6 years old, and at the age of 20 had opened a studio in Boston and begun his independent career.

In 1859 he settled in New York. Two years later he was commissioned by a firm of publishers to make sketches of scenes at the inaugural of Lincoln and at the front, and he crossed the Potomac with the first volunteers. During the next three years he saw much of army life and painted a series of popular army pictures from his observations.

"Prisoners at the Front" was with others of a like nature exhibited at the Paris salon in 1867.

Homer's more notable works include: "Life Line," 1884; "Eight Bells," 1885; "Fog Off the Banks," 1886; "Undertow," 1887, and "High Seas," 1894.

N. Y. DEMOCRATS SELECT DIX FOR STANDARD BEARER

State Chairman Finally Agrees Run for Governor of the Empire State

FULL TICKET IS NOMINATED

When Independence League Is Mentioned It Is Greeted with a Storm of Hisses

ROCHESTER, N. Y., Oct. 1.—A state convention that will go into political history as one of the most remarkable in the history of the Democratic party closed this morning by nominating John A. Dix, chairman of the party's state committee and a wealthy Washington county business man, to run on a progressive platform of the widest type.

Regarding the platform, there was from the first little or no division of opinion.

But the candidate was not chosen until Charles F. Murphy, leader of Tammany hall, who by virtue of his 213 delegates was in a position to control the convention, had canvassed the merits of no less than fourteen others.

"I said I would give them an upstate candidate, and I've done it," was Murphy's comment following the nomination.

[Associated Press]

ROCHESTER, N. Y., Sept. 30.—John A. Dix of Washington county was chosen candidate for governor by the Democratic convention tonight, while 400 delegates to the convention waited two hours in their seats for the formation of the slate.

The chief cause of delay was in the difficulty of filling second place. Mr. Dix had been selected and the other places on the ticket had been settled to the apparent satisfaction of those who gathered in the rooms of Ch[arle]s F. Murphy, the Tammany leader, [ear]lier in the evening.

Mr. Dix yielded tonight to the soli[c]itation of the leaders and agreed to run. The rest of the slate was arranged as follows:

Lieutenant governor — Thomas F. Conway, Clinton county.

Secretary of state—Edward Lazanski, Kings county.

Comptroller—Martin H. Glynn, Albany.

State treasurer—John J. Kennedy, Erie.

Attorney general—Thomas J. Carmody, Yates.

Associate judge court of appeals—Frederick Colin, Chemung.

Mr. Glynn refused the nomination for comptroller and William Sohmer of New York was substituted in his place.

Mr. Conway said he was reluctant to accept the nomination for lieutenant governor. It was said he felt his county was too near that of Mr. Dix to make him a logical candidate.

When the leaders left the rooms of Mr. Murphy at 2:30 this morning, after a vain effort to agree on a candidate, the majority of them were for the state chairman, Dix. Unanimity of opinion, however, was prevented mainly by Mr. Dix refusing to run.

"I do not see how I could accept the hanor," he declared. "I am afraid it would leave sore spots all over the state."

Every influence was brought to bear upon the unwilling choice. Several of his relatives, his wife, his brother-in-law and his nephew, all of whom were here with him, were sought out and urged to try persuasion. But when the convention met this afternoon for the first session of the day, Mr. Dix was still undecided. Pale and haggard, showing the strain under which he was laboring, he called the convention to order. The address of Permanent Chairman Herbert X. Bisse[ll], the reading of the platform, the report of the committees and the adoption of the routine resolutions held the delegates until 3:45, when the convention took a recess until 7:30 p. m.

The conference in Mr. Murphy's room was resumed almost immediately. Four hours later a committee consisting of National Democratic Committee Chairman Mack and John E. McCocey, the Brooklyn leader, left the room and went to Mr. Dix's suite. There they told the chairman that the leaders still held to their opinion that he should run. Then Mr. Dix capitulated.

Within five minutes the committee returned to the conference and announced his decision. Soon Dix himself came out of his room.

"Yes," he said, "you may shake [my] hand," smiling like those wh[o con]gratulated him. "But," he said, ["I] don't know whether you should [con]gratulate me or not."

"He has shown himself a big m[an]," was the comment of Edward M. S[hep]ard. Mr. Shepard was the firs[t to] abandon his own candidacy in f[avor] of Mr. Dix. Mr. Dix had made [it a] condition of his acceptance that al[l] other candidates should promise their support. From how many h[e re]ceived this pledge could not be a[scer]tained.

1911–1920

Editorial Sheet—The State and Coast.

Part II—The City and Its Environs

The Los Angeles Times

Population: { By the last Federal Census (1910)—319,198 / By the last School Census (1911)—360,000

XXXTH YEAR. MONDAY MORNING, NOVEMBER 6, 1911.—6 PAGES. PRICE: { Single Copies, on Streets and Trains, 5 Cents / Per Month, Per Copy, Delivered, 2½ Cents

Across the Continent.

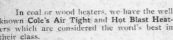

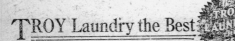

MASSED THOUSANDS HAIL END OF RODGERS' FLIGHT.

Unparalleled Ovation Given First Aviator to Span the Country by Aeroplane—Crowd Goes Mad With Joy and Bird Man Is Literally Mobbed—Forty-nine Days Is Total for Four Thousand, Two Hundred Miles.

WHEN Calbraith P. Rodgers, the first aviator to fly across the American continent, alighted at Tournament Park in Pasadena at 4:04 o'clock yesterday afternoon, 10,000 people deserted grand stand and bleachers and rushed to greet him.

No number of policemen could have held them back. Fences were no more than strips of tissue paper before them. Men, women and children, of all conditions in life, elbowed and fought and struggled to get to the birdman, and have a look at him, to attempt to seize him by the hand.

And all yelled. They yelled at the tops of their voices. They yelled and scarcely knew what they were doing. History was made and recorded as never before in aeronautics. And Rodgers in the supreme moment was a hero of heroes.

His biplane was surrounded by a black mass of humanity. When he was finally extricated from the surge of admirers, so enthusiastic that for the time being the world held nothing else for them, and placed into an automobile and driven twice around the race course, the yelling and cheering broke forth anew. Every feet, craning their necks to catch sight of him. The silence was absolute.

Then the aeroplane reappeared over the tops of trees. Some boys were the first to shout. The crowd took it up. Another instant and the cheers were ear-splitting. Someone begun to ring a huge bell mounted on the judges' stand beside the race course, and to this din Rodgers came flying straight for the park.

A THRILLING SIGHT.

"Oh, oh!" was heard, and, "I tell you that is thrilling," and, "Look, look!" There were exclamations on all sides.

The aviator circled once around the course at a high altitude. His aeroplane swerved and tilted, rhythmically, and with all the grace of a gigantic white bird, dipping first from right to left, then from left to right, until those who stood directly underneath it seemed as if he must certainly be going to turn clear over.

He started to circle the grounds a second time, coming constantly lower, and the excitement knew no bounds. Then there was a third round, and he came gently to ground in the center of the polo field, hardly more than a dozen yards from a

The Bird Man Who Conquered a Continent

The Triumphant End of Calbraith P. Rodgers's Flight Across North America,

At Tournament Park, Pasadena, yesterday afternoon. Thousands went literally mad in the tremendous enthusiasm of the greeting extended the first aviator ever to make the ocean-to-ocean flight. Above is Rodgers's aeroplane snapped in the air as he was descending above the park. In the center picture the aviator is telephoning the news of his arrival to the Associated Press, whence it was flashed to every city in the country almost in Rodgers's own laconic words. Holding the telephone is D. M. Linnard, of the reception committee. On the left is Mrs. R. D. Davis, wife of the Pasadena Board of Trade, who presented Rodgers with a great bouquet of California chrysanthemums, and on the right Miss Irene Grosse, prominent in local society, who also formally greeted the bird man. Below is the aeroplane immediately after descending, showing the crowds roped back from it. On the right is a glass bottle, carried by Rodgers during the entire flight and which was in every one of his eleven accidents. It is nearly the only thing about his machine that was not broken at one time or another.

piece of white canvas that had been placed for a mark. The aeroplane took its wheels as prettily as it had flirted with the air, and rolled along for about twenty feet, then came to a standstill.

The grand stand and bleachers were already empty. There was one mad, wild dash for the spot, and nothing short of a concrete wall could have checked it. All dignity was thrown aside. It was every person for himself.

The police and members of the Reception Committee fought about the aviator to preevnt him from fairly being crushed. An attempt was made to fence him off with a rope, but it was futile. He and the mass of struggling people of which he was the nucleus made gradually across the field to where an automobile in which were seated Mrs. E. D. Davis, wife of the president of the Board of Trade, and Miss Irene Grosse, a charming society woman of the city. Mrs. Davis presented the airman with an immense bouquet of chrysanthemums.

DRAPED WITH THE FLAGS.

He was helped into the car and aken twice around the race course, hen draped with an American flag y Edward T. Off, president of the 'ournament of Roses Association.

From the park he was taken to the

possible attention was shown him, except to allow him personal comfort.

BEAUTIFUL LANDING.

The landing was spectacular and perfectly timed. Ten minutes before his arrival, announcement was received from watchers on Mt. Wilson that he was coming. Two or three minutes before the hour he was sighted. His own advance agent, L. Peters, was the first to see him.

Peters suddenly leaped out into the clear space of the polo grounds reserved for the landing and, shading his eyes, looked intently at the sky. A minute later, "There he is," was heard everywhere. Every other spectator was pointing out to his neighbor a small horizontal black streak about as long as a lead pencil, against the blue heavens.

It grew steadily in size, but was always horizontal, slanting neither up nor down.

A yell went up from the grand stand, a yell that was deafening. Then came silence. The crowd watched the birdman come on. His aeroplane had first appeared in the southeast, but gradually it veered across the sky, until he was due south, and then southwest. As the side of his craft was turned toward the park, the rear rigging of the machine came into view, like a little body separated from the rest.

By this time he was back of the grand stand, and all were on their

(Continued on Sixth Page.)

Coats Off.

WORKING MEN TO THE FRONT

They Will Close Offices to Aid Campaign.

Citizens' Committee to Meet and Plan Battle.

House-to-House Canvass to Register Voters.

Between now and Thursday, when the registration closes, the city will have been raked with a fine-tooth comb and practically everyone qualified to be an elector will have his or her name upon the Great Register.

The Good Government Organization now has 300 deputies in the field, this army having been started out last Friday, and by Wednesday night there will be 700 deputies registering voters. Most of these deputies are volunteers who work some portion of the day or night; others are devoting their entire time to it. Frank P. Doherty, who has charge of the work, reports that the registration is between 3000 and 4000 daily.

After the registration has been concluded, the real campaign work will start. On Thursday morning the thorough organization of the city into Alexander precincts will be under way. In this work, as in the registration, the Good Government Organization has the effective aid of the Citizens' Committee of One Hundred. The members of this committee are old campaigners who are aroused to the peril and are bending every effort to get out a vote which will overwhelm the Socialists.

OFFERS OF HELP.

Bradner W. Lee, chairman of the Citizens' Committee of One Hundred, stated last night that he is preparing to divide the Committee of Twenty-five into sub-committees and start them at work. He said that this would be accomplished at a meeting of the Executive Committee this afternoon, when the assignments will be given out.

He declares that he had never seen such enthusiasm as these men show in any campaign of which he has had charge. He has been constantly in receipt of telegrams, telephone communications and verbal offers from men he has met on the street, asking him to suggest anything they might do to help in the fight. Hard working men of small affairs have begged him not to hesitate, for they declared they are ready to take off their coats, close their offices and go to work for the good of the city.

"It is going to be a red-hot campaign," he said, "with a good chance to win. But the people must not grow over confident. This fight depends on getting out the vote. I don't want to mislead anyone with the idea that it is going to be an easy victory.

"The vote is going to be tremendously large, and I would not attempt an approximation. There are changes by reason of death, removals and transfers. To offset this, families have come into the city who are entitled to register, but who were not eligible at the time of the primaries. We are going after these.

"It's a campaign full of ginger, one of the greatest Los Angeles will have seen, and we are going to get every vote possible. I never saw such workers as we have or such eagerness on the part of men to lend their assistance."

GETTING VOTERS.

The Woman's Progressive League is doing yeoman work and has a campaign planned that will bring to the support of the Alexander ticket thousands of women who did not intend to vote. Twenty automobiles will start out this morning loaded with deputies who will cover the southwestern portion of the city.

The members of the Los Angeles Realty Board are working like Trojans and accomplishing tremendous results. Not content with being on the citizens' committees, many have become registration deputies and are adding to the multitude of votes for Alexander.

The realty men have a reputation for getting what they go after and they are heart and soul in this campaign. W. N. Garland, who is a deputy registrar, signed up sixty women who

(Continued on Second Page.)

Humming.

PROGRESSIVE LEAGUE IN FOREFRONT OF CAMPAIGN.

THE WOMAN'S PROGRESSIVE League's headquarters in the Merchants' Trust building yesterday hummed with industry. The force of campaign workers was augumented by many business women who volunteered their services for filing and detail work. These women, who are unable to leave their occupations during the week, gladly labored Sunday and their experience was a great help to the league.

Twenty automobiles donated for the purpose will leave the league headquarters at 9 o'clock this morning, each machine containing from four to five deputies. They expect to add the names of many hundreds of women to the great register.

A portion of the districts they will cover will be Vermont to Western; Santa Barbara to West Adams; Washington to Wilshire, and Hoover to Second avenue.

Four deputies have been assigned to the Shriners' Household Show at the Auditorium; four have been detailed at the Woman's City Club and one deputy will be at the Ebell Clubhouse at 1:30 this afternoon to register members and friends.

Mrs. C. B. Nichols and Mrs. J. E. Barton have been sworn in as registration deputies and they will cover their districts in taxis. The league reports that since Wednesday 2700 women have been registered by deputies. At headquarters yesterday the registration was heavy.

There is a call for contributions to finish the whirlwind campaign. Women who are unable to work and others interested in the fight for a free city are asked to send their contributions to the league.

Mrs. John D. Hooker yesterday was made a member of the league, which has a large membership. Each member is doing her full duty and constantly adding to the large army of women who will vote the Alexander ticket December 5.

A forty-foot banner inscribed

(Continued on Second Page.)

In Three Parts Complete—34 Pages.

Part I—Telegraph News Sheet—10 Pages.

The Los Angeles Times

For Liberty and Law, Equal Rights and Industrial Freedom

BY THE YEAR, $9.00. { One Month, postpaid, 75 Cents. Three Months, postpaid, $2.25. | TUESDAY MORNING, APRIL 16, 1912. | PRICE: { Single Copies, on Streets and Trains, 5 Cents. Per Month, Per Copy, Delivered, 2½ Cents.

FIFTEEN HUNDRED LIVES LOST WHEN TITANIC PLUNGES HEADLONG INTO DEPTHS OF THE SEA.

Men of World-Wide Prominence Go Down With Ship After Women and Children Are Taken Off in Lifeboats—Only Six Hundred and Seventy-five People Saved Out of Total of Twenty-two Hundred on Board Ill-fated Vessel—Newest and Greatest Liner in World, Built at Cost of Ten Million Dollars and Embodying Latest Scientific Principles, Sinks as Quickly as Wooden Fishing Smack After Collision With Iceberg Off Coast of Newfoundland.

[BY DIRECT WIRE TO THE TIMES.]

NEW YORK, April 15.—[Exclusive Dispatch.] The greatest marine disaster in the history of the world occurred last Sunday night when the Titanic, of the White Star Line, the biggest and finest of steamships, shattered herself against an iceberg and sank with 1500 of her passengers and crew in less than four hours.

Out of nearly 2200 persons that she carried only 675 were saved and most of these are women and children. They were picked up from small boats by Cunarder Carpathia which found, when she ended her desperate race against time, a sea strewn with the wreckage of the lost ship and the bodies of drowned men and women.

Not a name of those saved had reached the offices of the White Star line or the Cunard line at midnight, though every effort was being made to get in communication with the vessel that bore the survivors. It is probable that these names will be received in the morning. All night a crowd of anxious relatives and friends of the Titanic's passengers were massed in front of the line's offices at No. 9 Broadway.

There were 325 first cabin passengers on the Titanic, of whom 128 were women and 15 children. In the second cabin there were 285 persons, including 79 women and 8 children, and in the steerage the complement of 710 was divided almost equally, it is believed, between women and men, with a small percentage of children.

The numbers are enough to indicate that if the women and children were saved, very few men could have survived the disaster, as there were almost enough women and children aboard to make up the 675 sur-

The Annihilated Leviathan.

The large picture shows the vitals of the White Star liner "Titanic," which crashed to its doom Sunday night. Attention is called to the myriad of water-tight compartments, designed especially to prevent the very catastrophe which overtook the ill-fated steamer. The small picture shows the vessel, the largest in the world, as she looked as she hit the iceberg.

vivors. The crew numbered 860, bringing the total of those known to be aboard up to 2180, but it is understood that at the last minute before sailing several got aboard, making the total up to a full 2200.

Capt. E. J. Smith of the Titanic is believed to have gone to the bottom with his vessel.

Among the 1320 passengers of the giant liner were Col. John Jacob Astor and his wife, Isidor Straus, Maj. Archibald W. Butt, aide to President Taft, George B. Widener and Mrs. Widener of Philadelphia, Mr. and Mrs. Henry S. Harper, William T. Stead, the London journalist, and many more whose names are known on both sides of the Atlantic. The news that few besides the women and children were saved has caused the greatest apprehension as to the fate of these.

When the Titanic plunged headlong against a wall of ice at 10:40 p.m. on Sunday night, her fate established that no modern steamship is unsinkable, and that all of a large passenger list cannot be saved in a liner's small boats. The White Star line believed that the Titanic was practically invulnerable and insisted until there was no doubting the full extent of the catastrophe that she could not sink. The great ship was the last word in modern scientific construction, but she found the ocean floor almost as quickly as a wooden ship.

On her maiden trip, the Titanic, built and equipped at a cost of $10,000,000, a floating palace, found her graveyard when, swinging from the westerly steamship lane, south of the Grand Banks of Newfoundland, to take the direct run to this port, she hurled her giant bulk against an iceberg that rose from an immense field that drifted from the Arctic. Running at high speed into that grim

(Continued on Sixth Pag

Rescued.

LIST OF SURVIVORS OF TITANIC DISASTER.

[BY DIRECT WIRE TO THE TIMES.]

NEW YORK, April 15.—[Exclusive Dispatch.] The White Star officials tonight gave out this list of persons saved, the list of survivors of the Titanic disaster being sent to them by wireless from the Carpathia.

Mrs. Jacob P. —(possibly Mrs. John Jacob Astor.)
Mrs. Harry Anderson.
Mrs. Edward W. Appleton.
Mrs. Rose Abbott.
Mrs. G. M. Burns.
Miss D. D. Cassebier.
Mrs. W. M. Clark.
Mrs. B. Chibinance (Chibnaits.)
Mrs. E. G. Crosby.
Miss Rose Crosby.
Miss Jean Thayer.
Mrs. K. F. Andrews.
Miss Linette Panhart.
Miss E. W. Allen.
Mr. and Mrs. D. Bishop
H. Blank.
Miss A. Bassine.
Mrs. James Baxter.
George A. Bayton.
Mrs. C. Barnelli.
Mrs. J. M. Brown.
Miss G. C. Bowen.
Mr. and Mrs. R. L. Beckwith.
Mrs. Henry B. Harris.
Mrs. Alexander Halverson.
Miss Jean Hoppach.
Miss Marguerite Bayss.
Mr. and Mrs. Edward Kimberly (Kimball.)
A. A. Kennyman.
Miss Emile Kenechin.
Miss G. F. Longley.
Mrs. A. M. Leader.
Miss Bertha Lavery.
Mrs. Ernest H. Lines.
Miss Neary C. Lines.
Mrs. J. Lindstrom.
Gustave Lesneur.
Miss Georgette Amadill.
Madame Meliteard.
Mrs. G. M. Tucker, Jr., and maid.
Mrs. J. D. Thayer.
Mr. Thayer, Jr.
Hugh Wollner.
Miss Anna Ward.
Mrs. S. M. Warner.
Richard M. Williams.
Miss Helen A. Wilson.
Miss Willard.
Miss Mary Wicks.
Mrs. George D. Widener and maid.
C. Rolmane.
Master Allerson and nurse.
Mrs. Kate T. Andrews.
Mrs. J. Stuart White.
Miss Maria Young.
Mrs. Thomas Potter, Jr.
Mrs. Edna Roberts.
Countess of Rothes.
Miss Lucile Fortune.
Mrs. Henry Sharper.
Mrs. William Carter.
Mr. and Mrs. L. Henry.
Mrs. Graham. (Possibly Mrs. William Graham.)
Robert Douglas.
Mrs. P. P. Smith.
Hilda Slayton.
Mrs. Earle.
Mrs. Susan P. Rogerson.
Miss Emily B. Rogerson.
Mrs. Arthur Rogerson.
Bruce Ismay.
Mrs. J. Stewart.
Mrs. W. A. Hooper.
Mr. Nile.
J. Flynn.
Miss Lucile Carter.
William Carter.
Miss Cummins.
Mrs. Florence Mare.
Miss Alice P. Phillips.
Mrs. Paula Munge.
Miss Rosie ——.
Mrs. Jane ——.
Mrs. Phillis ——.
Miss Bertha ——.
(Last names were missed.)

The foregoing was received by wireless at Cape Race station from the steamer Carpathia. In spelling and initials it does not correspond with the list as cabled from London today.

Mistakes were due to the hurried wireless transmission and relays. In one instance, Mrs. L. Y. B. Harris is named in the wireless list. On the passenger list as announced here there was a Mrs. Henry B. Harris only, and there were a number of similar discrepancies.

Flashes and Kernels.

The News in The Times This Morning.

CONDENSED AND CLASSIFIED.

INDEX: TITLES — PAGES — PARTS

SUMMARY.

THE SKY. Clear. Wind at 5 p.m., south; velocity 5 miles. Thermometer, highest, 66 deg.; lowest, 48 deg. Forecast: Fair Tuesday; light south wind. For complete weather report see page 13, Part II.

THE CITY. An abject apology is to be made today by the Mexican Vice-Counsel at San Diego to the United States government, through Dist.-Atty. McCormack, here, for the arrest and short imprisonment of a secret service officer at Tia Juana recently, who at the time was the guest of the Mexican officials, but was suspected of being a spy for the insurrectos.

The father and mother who abandoned their baby in the Pacific Electric depot a few days ago were arrested yesterday, and gave as their excuse that they were unable to care properly for the infant and get along financially.

The president of the Central Labor Council here has resigned and gone to San Francisco, and his place has been filled by another. It is believed the retiring official was fearful of becoming involved in the dynamite investigation.

Following Santa Monica, several other adjacent cities have asked to be counted in on the Owens River water supply, if possible.

Call to Colors.

ARMY AND NAVY ORDERED TO BE READY TO INVADE MEXICO.

President Taft and Advisers, Convinced That Intervention Is Inevitable, Instruct to Prepare for Action.

Arms and Ammunition Already Sent to United States Representatives in Southern Republic for Citizens to Use in Defense and Prevent Massacre When Troops Cross Border—Step Will Not Be Taken Without Consent of Congress.

[BY DIRECT WIRE TO THE TIMES.]

WASHINGTON (April 15)—[Exclusive Dispatch.] President Taft and his advisers are convinced that intervention in Mexico by the United States is inevitable.

No announcement to this effect has been made at either the White House or the State Department, but it became known today that secret orders have been issued to the various corps of the army to get ready for an invasion.

To the navy divisions orders have been issued directing that supplies for men and ships be assembled at the various naval stores. The Atlantic and Pacific fleets are ready for war in other respects.

While President Taft will not move any troops until he has authority from Congress to do so, he will be prepared to strike the instant that authority is given. The President does not believe that when he asks Congress for authority to send an army into Mexico for the purpose of restoring peace and order, thus protecting the lives and property of Americans in that country, that Congress will hesitate.

GETTING ORDNANCE READY.

The orders sent to the various corps of the army were to get ready. The ordnance department since that order was issued has been working at top speed finishing field guns and mounts, getting small arms in shape, manufacturing ammunition and purchasing considerable of the latter from the manufacturers. The medical department has been gathering supplies as has the quartermaster's department. These supplies are being assembled at depots in the various divisions.

The railroads have been communicated with a number of times regarding the transportation of troops to the Mexican border. The five army transports at Newport News, Va., have been in shape for months to load with troops and supplies. The mobile army in the United States is being reinforced by the sending home of four regiments from the Philippines. Two regiments of cavalry and two of infantry are now en route or will be in a few days, from the Philippines to the United States. Two of these regiments have been ordered to the Department of Texas, and two to the Department of the Columbia.

President Taft will not make any recommendations to Congress just now. He will wait and see what effect the note acting Secretary of State Wilson sent at his orders to Ambassador Wilson will have on the Mexican government and the rebel chieftains. The orders to the Mexican people through the United States representatives in that country were mandatory, the reports that there is to be no intervention to the contrary nothwithstanding.

NO MORE WANTON KILLING.

It became known at the White House today that President Taft will not tolerate any longer the wanton killing of Americans and the destroying of their property. He has demanded their protection from both combatants in Mexico, and now he intends to see that this is carried out.

In official circles here, that part of acting Secretary Wilson's note to President Madero and Gen. Orozco, "that intervention was not contemplated by the United States," is regarded merely as diplomatic language, for it is known that intervention will be the order unless both parties to the conflict heed the warning.

President Taft is now convinced that Gen. Pascual Orozco, the rebel leader in Chihuahua, is doing his utmost to bring about intervention. The President does not want to interfere in the affairs of Mexico, and he would rather Orozco was the victor than take such steps, but if Orozco continues to order the execution of Americans and the confiscation of their property as a means of forcing intervention, President Taft will take the step.

Further evidence that the administration is preparing for such a contingency as intervention was

(Continued on Second Page.)

In Three Parts—32 Pages

PART I—TELEGRAPH SHEET—16 PAGES

The Los Angeles Times

1781-1912.

See Page 1, Part II.

For Liberty under Law, Equal Rights and Industrial Freedom

WEDNESDAY MORNING, NOVEMBER 6, 1912.

PRICE: { Yearly, $9; Monthly, 75 Cents, postpaid. Delivered, average cost per copy, 2½ Cts. 5c

DEMOCRACY TRIUMPHS IN THE NATION; ITS VICTORY IN THE STATE INDICATED.

Triumphant.

WILSON AND MARSHALL WIN ON A LANDSLIDE.

Democrats in Power Again for the First Time in About a Quarter Century.

Both Houses of Congress Will Probably Be Democratic—Of the Lower House No Doubt Exists at All. Incomplete Figures Indicate Upper Will Also Be Lost to the Republicans.

[BY DIRECT WIRE TO THE TIMES.]

CHICAGO BUREAU OF THE TIMES, Nov. 5.—[Exclusive Dispatch.] Woodrow Wilson of New Jersey has been elected President of the United States. Thomas R. Marshall of Indiana has been elected Vice-President. For the first time in twenty years the Democratic national ticket has triumphed.

From all indications it has been a landslide. Both Houses of Congress will probably be Democratic. The House is overwhelmingly Democratic, while the incomplete returns indicate that the Legislatures elected at yesterday's polls will elect enough Democratic Senators to give the Democrats a majority of the upper branch of Congress.

Incomplete returns received up to midnight establish the election of Wilson. With no complete figures from western States, the returns show that the "Solid South," adhering to its Democratic traditions, and the Eastern States in which Wilson has won, have given him more than the requisite 266 votes in the Electoral College.

MIDNIGHT RETURNS.

At midnight, the returns show that fifteen southern States, exclusive of Missouri and inclusive of West Virginia, have yielded 165 electoral votes for Wilson. Three New England States, Connecticut, Maine and Massachusetts, have given him thirty-one more electoral votes; Delaware has contributed three and New York has given the Democratic candidate its forty-five votes. Indiana has apparently gone Democratic by a large plurality, while Missouri, the "Mysterious Stranger" that appeared in the Republican ranks in 1904 and 1908, has given its electoral votes to the Democrats.

Counting only States from which practically complete returns, though unofficial, had been given up to midnight, Wilson has 277 electoral votes—266 are sufficient to elect. Roosevelt has apparently carried Illinois with its twenty-nine electoral votes, while on the face of the incomplete returns Taft has swung Rhode Island, New Hampshire and Vermont, with thirteen electoral votes.

STORY OF THE RETURNS.

The story of the returns can be told succinctly—the Republican vote divided by Taft and Roosevelt equalled a Democratic plurality for Wilson. This was the way it ran in most of the Eastern States, although the returns showed slashings on both sides in many instances.

Roosevelt and Taft are now engaged in the race for second place, both on the popular and the electoral vote. The returns up to midnight are still too incomplete to indicate which will run third. Taft has exhibited a strength in many sections that was hardly looked for by the politicians—the effect of the prosperity and the "let well enough alone" campaign.

THREE-CORNERED FIGHT.

Old Republican strongholds have been smashed into smithereens by the three-cornered fight. Staid New England, which manifested a tendency to wander towards Democracy in the Congressional elections two years ago, demonstrated the same inclination yesterday so far as the bulk of its

(Continued on Second Page.)

Woodrow Wilson,

Governor of New Jersey, and ex-president of Princeton University, who was yesterday elected the twenty-eighth President of the United States. He was born in Staunton, Va., December 28, 1856, and was graduated from Princeton in 1879. He is the author of a number of histories and political works.

Anticipated.

CALIFORNIA FOR WILSON IS DEMOCRATIC CLAIM.

Available Returns This Morning Show Safe Lead for the Democrats.

Hiram Johnson Snowed Under in His Home City and County—Bull Moose Lead South of Tehachepi Pass and on Coast Apparently Overcome by the Vote Elsewhere—Idaho and Utah Appear to Be for Taft.

[BY DIRECT WIRE TO THE TIMES.]

SAN FRANCISCO BUREAU OF THE TIMES, Nov. 5.—[Exclusive Dispatch.] Indications are that Wilson has carried California by a safe plurality over Roosevelt. Returns from south of Tehachepi showing Roosevelt's lead are expected to be more than offset by results in the northern counties.

Gov. Hiram W. Johnson, Roosevelt's running mate on the Bull Moose ticket, failed to carry his own precinct, city or county.

Reports from counties north and east of Sacramento indicate heavy majorities for Wilson.

Calculating on partial returns from 310 precincts out of 455, Los Angeles Progressive leaders claim a plurality of 25,000 in Los Angeles. This claim is based on returns giving Roosevelt 10,326, Wilson 7380, Debs 2455, Taft 29. Returns coming in from northern counties clearly indicate that the Roosevelt plurality claimed in the south will be offset by the overwhelming vote for Wilson.

Returns from 100 scattering precincts in the city give Roosevelt 4428, Wilson 5141, and Debs 1577. If the proportion continues, Wilson will leave the city with 15,000. Reports from the Sacramento Valley make the prospect even brighter for the New Jersey Governor. Eldorado county gives him 800 plurality and nearly every other rolls up a large vote. In the San Joaquin he is also running ahead, but apparently the coast counties are with the Bull Moose.

WASHINGTON IN DOUBT.

Among the States of the Pacific Coast, Washington is the only one in which the Bull Moose is ahead, but even there the issue is yet to be decided. Elsewhere the third-termer is running second or third. Idaho and Utah appear safe for Taft, but Wilson has swept the States of the West. He carried every county in Arizona and may have a majority in Nevada. In Oregon returns from only ten precincts show a close race there. Woman suffrage is running even.

BIRTHPLACE REBUKES JOHNSON.

Hiram W. Johnson failed to carry his own precinct, city, county or State, in today's election. Sacramento county, the Governor's birthplace and present home, went Republican by nearly 5000 on most of the State ticket two years ago, but Johnson failed even to carry it by more than 800. Today, according to indications, the county has gone against him by about 3000, and this in spite of the fact that the State administration is in undisputed possession of the city government of the city and county Republican organizations of the State printing house and all the State departments located here, with one or two minor exceptions. The Roosevelt campaign here was well financed also, while the Democrats had little to spend.

Reports from the Sacramento Valley and the counties to the north and east show heavy majorities for Wilson.

CURRY'S BIG LEAD.

Charles F. Curry, former Secretary of State, who defeated Frank Devlin, vice-president of the Lincoln-Roosevelt League, for the Republican nomination from this district, which was carved out for Devlin's special benefit, is running like a scared deer and

(Continued on Seventh Page.)

A Change.

HOUSE IS DEMOCRATIC; MAYBE SENATE ALSO.

Returns Indicate Many New Faces Will Be Seen in the Halls of Legislation in Washington — Wilson Is Sure to Have Plenty of Backing to Put Into Effect and Practice the Policies for Which He Stands.

[BY DIRECT WIRE TO THE TIMES.]

CHICAGO BUREAU OF THE TIMES, Nov. 5.—[Exclusive Dispatch.] The next House of Representatives, the sixty-third in the history of the nation, will be overwhelmingly Democratic. Early returns indicated there would be 277 Democrats, 148 Republicans and ten of other parties, mostly Progressives, in the new lower Congressional body.

This would mean a Democratic flat majority of 119 votes over all opposing party strength.

In the Senate, there is little upon which to base more than a guess, as returns regarding completion of State Legislature are coming in slowly. It is indicated, however, that Illinois will send to Washington two Democratic United States Senators.

The Senate from scattering reports may be divided this way: Democrats, forty-eight; Republicans, forty, and doubtful, eight.

In the doubtful list are included several Progressives, who have a chance of election.

There is nothing uncertain about the next House of Representatives. All the Southern States have accorded their usual quota of Democratic members, whereas the Wilson landslide in various eastern and northern sections will add to the former majority of the party.

It looks as if Indiana will send a solid Democratic delegation to the lower body. This will mean the defeat of Edgar D. Crumpacker, lone surviving Representative of the G. O. P.

Joseph G. Cannon is not yet under the wire in the Danville district in Illinois, but his old friend, Champ Clark, galloped in easily in the Ninth Missouri District.

This undoubtedly means that Mr. Clark will be honored again with the Speakership.

So far as the Senate is concerned it may be several days before anything like a correct division by party may be learned.

Republican Senators whose terms expire March 3, next year, are: W. E. Borah, Idaho; J. Bourne, Oregon; F. O. riggs, New Jersey; Norris Brown, Nebraska; H. E. Burnham, New Hampshire; W. Murray Crane, Massachusetts; Shelby M. Cullom, Illinois; William Lorimer (seat declared vacant,) Illinois; Charles Curtis, Kansas; Joseph M. Dixon, Montana (now a Progressive;) R. J. Gamble, South Dakota; S. Guggenheim, Colorado; W. S. Kenyon, Iowa; Knute Wilson, Minnesota; H. A. Richardson, Delaware; William Alden Smith, Michigan; Noel Sanders, Tennessee;

(Continued on Eighth Page.)

Philosophic.

COLONEL WIRES FELICITATIONS.

CONGRATULATIONS TO WILSON FROM ROOSEVELT.

Statement from Oyster Bay Shortly Before Midnight Expresses Confidence in Eventual Triumph of Progressive Cause, Professes Contentment and Good Humor.

[BY A. P. NIGHT WIRE TO THE TIMES.]

OYSTER BAY (N. Y.) Nov. 5.—Shortly before midnight Col. Roosevelt made the following statement:

"The American people by a great plurality have decided in favor of Mr. Wilson and the Democratic party. Like all good citizens, I accept the result with entire good humor and contentment. As for the Progressive cause, I can only repeat what I have already so many times said: the fate of the leader for the time being is of little consequence, but the cause itself must in the end triumph for its triumph is essential to well-being of the American people.

[Signed]

"THEODORE ROOSEVELT."

At the same time he issued his statement, Col. Roosevelt sent the following telegram to Gov. Wilson:

"The American people by a great plurality have conferred upon you the highest honor in their gift. I congratulate you thereon.

"THEODORE ROOSEVELT."

THEY LIKE HIM BACK HOME.

RICHMOND (Va.) Nov. 5.—[By A. P. Night Wire.] Gov. Wilson's birthplace, Staunton, Va., gave him 632, Taft 287, Roosevelt 65.

Gratitude.

WILSON THANKS PARTY LEADERS.

FIRST PUBLIC MESSAGE SINCE TOLD OF ELECTION.

Newly-Elected President Asks Democrats and Progressives of Whatever Alliance to Lend Help in Fulfilling People's Hope that Judgment and Peace May Prevail.

[BY A. P. NIGHT WIRE TO THE TIMES.]

PRINCETON (N. J.) Nov. 5.—Responding to a telegram from the Democratic national chairman, asserting that Gov. Wilson unquestionably was elected, the Democratic candidate sent a dispatch to Mr. McCombs as follows:

"I deeply appreciate your telegram and wish to extend to you, and the members of the Campaign Committee, my warm congratulations on the part you have played in the organization and conduct of a campaign fought out upon essential issues.

"A great cause has triumphed. Every Democrat, every true Progressive, of whatever alliance, must now lend his full force and enthusiasm to the fulfillment of the people's hope, the establishment of the people's right, so that judgment and peace may go hand in hand."

This was Gov. Wilson's first utterance of a public character following his acceptance of the reports that he had been elected.

THE REDDING DISTRICT IS SAFE FOR WILSON.

[By Federal (Wireless) Line to The Times.]

REDDING (Cal.) Nov. 5.—[Special Dispatch.] This section of the State according to early returns has gone for Wilson.

Herculean.

WILSON FACES BIG CONTRACT.

MAINTENANCE OF PROSPERITY IS HIS CHIEF TASK.

Democratic Victory Is Fully Discounted by Officials in Washington—Attaches Say President Taft Has Had No Hope of Success Since the Party Split at Chicago.

[BY DIRECT WIRE TO THE TIMES.]

WASHINGTON BUREAU OF THE TIMES, Nov. 5.—[Exclusive Dispatch.] The government of the United States has been turned over to the Democrats, who will find it prosperous as never before in its history, but filled with elements of distrust, revolt and fault-finding. The incoming administration faces a tremendous task in keeping up the record set by the Republicans, who leave the government with clean hands and a knowledge of work well done. The best evidence of sound prosperity is the fact that business men everywhere have no fear that that prosperity will suffer, at least not before the Democratic Congress begins work upon the tariff. The fine business condition prevailing throughout the land is on a solid base.

Washington never saw such crowds on election night as gathered this evening in front of the newspaper offices and paraded Pennsylvania avenue. Many anxious eyes were focussed on the early bulletins forecasting the election of Gov. Wilson, and later bulletins were patiently awaited in the faint hope that completed returns might change the trend of the landslide. The change of administration on March 4, with the Democrats in control of the distribution of patronage, means a great deal to Republican office-holders in Washington

(Continued on Fourth Page.)

Rout.

VICTOR BERGER IS BEATEN; HE SAYS SO HIMSELF.

[BY DIRECT WIRE TO THE TIMES.]

MILWAUKEE (Wis.) Nov. 5.—[Exclusive Dispatch.] "It seems that I am beaten. I will do my duty to the last minute and return to my paper in Milwaukee."

This statement was made by V. L. Berger, Milwaukee's lone Socialist Congressman.

Tonight spelled the complete wiping out of the shame of Milwaukee, its domination by the red flag.

Milwaukee city last spring ousted the Socialists. The county was still Socialist, but the fusion plan which defeated the Socialists in the city was again successful and carried with it defeat to Berger, leader and father of the Milwaukee Socialist element. The only Socialists now left in office in Milwaukee are the few Aldermen from solid Socialist wards who escaped the spring deluge.

Tidings.

MRS. WILSON BREAKS NEWS TO HUSBAND WITH A KISS.

Wife of President Taft Is Cheerful and Apparently Happy that She Will Have Executive More to Herself Within a Few Months — Mrs. Marshall Wires Congratulations to Princeton.

[BY FEDERAL (WIRELESS) LINE TO THE TIMES.]

NEW YORK BUREAU OF THE TIMES, Nov. 5.—[Special Dispatch.] Mrs. William H. Taft followed the course of the voting from the bulletins received at the New York home of the President's brother, Henry W. Taft, where she spent the day. Early in the forenoon she received a telegram from her husband, sent from Cincinnati. She replied in a message which she told reporters was "not worth publishing, it being of no significance." Mrs. Taft seemed in excellent spirits. One of her closest friends in this city said: "Much as she may feel that her husband was entitled to re-election, she will be very glad to have him more to herself. Mr. Taft and Mrs. Taft have made great sacrifices to represent the manhood and womanhood of the United States, in the White House."

A PLEASING FAMILY SCENE.

Mrs. Wilson and the Wilson girls were more excited over the returns than the President-elect. The wife and daughters of the Governor presided over the bulletin room and all the reports passed through their hands before reaching the man of the moment at Princeton.

As the big clock in the library of the Wilson home chimed out the hour of 10, Mrs. Woodrow Wilson placed her hands upon the shoulders of her husband and kissed him.

"My dear, I want to be the first to congratulate you," she said.

The Governor was standing with his hands folded and his back to the open log fire. It was the first definite word that he was the President-elect of the United States. The bulletins that removed all doubt of the verdict were given to Mrs. Wilson by Jack Mendelson, the telegrapher who received the news off the leased wire.

Next to congratulate the Governor were his three daughters, Misses Margaret, Jessie and Eleanor Wilson. Bubbling over with happiness, the President-elect fondly embraced each of his daughters.

"Dad," said the youngest of the girls, rushing into the Governor's study when the eastern landslide was told, "you are elected."

"That's very interesting," was Wilson's only comment.

Asked for a statement, Mrs. Wilson said her husband would be chosen by the electorate. "He is the finest husband in the world and, of course, he will be the best of Presidents," said the gratified wife of the Democratic victor.

Figures Tell.

AN ELECTION FORECAST THAT WAS WELL DONE.

[BY DIRECT WIRE TO THE TIMES.]

NEW YORK BUREAU OF THE TIMES, Nov. 5.—[Exclusive Dispatch.] The New York Herald says: We trust our readers will pardon an allusion to the New York Herald-Los Angeles Times forecast of this Presidential election. If ever a prediction was verified by the actual event, the Herald's prophecy that Gov. Wilson would be elected President, that there would be a tremendous increase in the Democratic House of Representatives, and that William Sulzer would be elected Governor of New York, was borne out by the balloting of yesterday. This result is the best answer that can be made to the carping critics who almost daily brought out their stock jokes about straw votes being a parlor game to amuse children. The forecast, the most elaborate ever made in this country, was conducted conjointly with the Herald, the Chicago Record Herald, the Cincinnati Enquirer, the St. Louis Republican, the Los Angeles Times, the Boston Globe and the Denver Republican.

We felicitate each of our contemporaries on the gratifying result of an absolutely serious and honest endeavor to indicate the result of the election. It was something worth doing well and it was well done.

Pictorial Cream Sheet (II).

The Advancing City and Tributaries. *California and the Coast—14 Pages*

The Los Angeles Times

XXXIIND YEAR. THURSDAY, NOVEMBER 6, 1913.—EDITORIAL SECTION. POPULATION { By the Federal Census (1910)—319,198 / By the City Directory (1913)—462,427

GLORIOUS MOUNTAIN RIVER NOW FLOWS TO LOS ANGELES' GATES.

Inquiry.

LOS ANGELES INVESTMENT COMPANY INVESTIGATED.

Federal Authorities Act Under Orders from Washington Chiefs.

Complaints that Misleading Statements Have Been Sent Through the Mails by Officials of Elder's Companies to Cause Scrutiny of Books and Possible Reorganization—Stockholders to Be Protected.

FOLLOWING a secret investigation by the Federal authorities of complaints to the effect that officers of the Los Angeles Investment Company have sent misleading statements of the financial condition of the concern through the United States mails, it is believed the affairs of the company will be brought to a crisis today. The investigation was ordered by United States Attorney-General McReynolds and Postmaster-General Burleson.

The plans of the government officials are twofold. One is to co-operate in every way with leading financiers of the city who, it is declared, wish to reorganize the investment company and safeguard the stockholders. The other is to examine books, documents, transfers and instruments of every description to ascertain whether fraud has been practiced by any of the officers of the company.

It was admitted by the Federal authorities yesterday that C. A. Elder, president and general manager of the company, is under fire. He has been generally held responsible for the remarkable rise of the Los Angeles Investment Company since its incorporation in 1899. So now he will be looked to to explain various matters that have caused the stock to drop from more than $4.50 a share to a quotation of $1.26 yesterday.

A level-headed and well-informed business man at the head of a large local financial concern, who has had occasion to look in a general way into the affairs of the Los Angeles Investment Company, stated last night that he believed the complaints made to Washington were due to enemies jealous of the success achieved by the company; that the concern was solvent: had been exceptionally well managed as a business enterprise, and that the more thoroughly the investigators go into the affairs of the concern the better it will be for the company. In other words, that if those who have been authorized by the government to make an investigation would do it well and thoroughly and then give the company the benefit of their findings, everybody financially interested would feel that a real service had been done the company, because it would permanently stop the loose talk started by enemies that has been current on the street for some weeks past.

ELDER NOT ALARMED.

Mr. Elder is not alarmed by any investigations. He said yesterday that he has been fighting jealous competitors for many years and expects to continue fighting as long as he lives. He attributes all his troubles to his enemies—and as to this he is probably right. He is certainly game and faces the situation bravely.

He declared he was unable to say whether the present condition of the company which he virtually brought into being is under attack by stock jobbers, by adverse banking interests or by men unfriendly to him personally.

The government officials usually pursue their course in silence. They do not talk copiously for publication and as a rule do not start an investigation so far-reaching in its outcome as this one without carefully weighing the results.

Beyond confirming the fact that United States District Attorney Schoonover and several postoffice inspectors are about to examine the books of the Los Angeles Investment Company, nothing could be learned at the Federal Building yesterday. One government official said that the Federal grand jury may finally be given the case with the aid of expert accountants, but that the ordinary method of laying a complaint before the United States Commissioner may be sufficient.

With President Elder have been associated Secretary W. D. Deeble and Treasurer G. M. Derby. The three have been associated for more than eighteen years.

THEIR STATED CONDITION.

In one of the late statements the capital stock is placed at $5,000,000 and surplus at $12,000,000 or more. In June there were 19,145 stockholders. The company first occupied a little back room on Broadway and then moved to Hill street, where spacious offices were used until it moved into its present magnificent building at Eighth street and Broadway known as the Los Angeles Investment building. Until a short time ago the Globe

(Continued on Eighth Page.)

See the first water, several feet deep, come dashing down the cascade!

Remarkable photograph taken from the speakers' stand a minute and a half after Gen. Chaffee opened the gates. This view is exactly as the camera caught it, without so much as the touch of a pencil added. The front of the "water wall" was black from the dust and sediment that had accumulated at the head of the cascade.

Realization.

SILVER TORRENT CROWNS THE CITY'S MIGHTY ACHIEVEMENT.

Forty Thousand People Loose Pent-Up Enthusiasm of Six Years as Rolling Flood Bursts from Mouth of the Completed Aqueduct.

FROM the mountain fastnesses of the snow-capped Sierras, through the world's longest man-made conduit of steel, cement and solid granite, sparkling water poured in a mighty torrent from the aqueduct's mouth at 1:15 o'clock yesterday afternoon.

It gurgled and splashed its cheerful message of good health, great wealth, long life and plenteous prosperity to Los Angeles and her people. It dashed in ever-increasing volume down the rocky cascade and flowed blithely on down the open conduit to San Fernando reservoir.

Then the 40,000 people who had assembled in the magnificent amphitheater provided by nature at the head of San Fernando Valley, gave vent to pent-up enthusiasm. It was the moment of their victory, the reward for their faith and courage through the years while the aqueduct was being planned and constructed.

Forty thousand hearts beat a little faster for this was the culmination of a project daringly conceived, boldly executed and successfully completed. Almost in the flash of an eye there had been delivered to the people of this city an asset worth more than $100,000,000, four times its cost. It brought assurance of metropolitan grandeur and future prosperity such as but few cities of the world can hope to attain.

Thrilled by the spectacle of the coming waters, exulting in the triumph of them all, 40,000 people cheered long and lustily. Shout after shout went up until the hills rang again and again in echoing response. It was a fitting time for celebration and jubilation and all the people responded unreservedly. Cheering, hand-clapping and noisy congratulations continued for twenty minutes, while the murmur of the onrushing water sang a comforting and harmonious obligato to it all.

CENTER OF IT ALL.

In the center of the great crowd, one of them, stood William Mulholland, who has given of himself and of his best in unswerving loyalty to build the aqueduct for the people. Through the long years of toil and planning, fighting against obstacles, boring through mountains and bridging deep canyons, Mulholland has continued his work without excitement or flurry.

All through the celebration exercises, when men high up in public affairs and representatives of the city's citizens heaped unstinted and well-deserved encomiums upon him, he remained the calm, efficient engineer. Without a tremor he gave the signal for opening the gates, calmly confident that the water would come forth at his bidding.

But in that supreme moment when came the full realization that the battle had been fought and won, when the people were cheering and exulting, emotion overcame him. High officials, many of them among his closest friends, clapped him on the back and congratulated him, but for a moment he could not answer. For a brief period he was living in review the long years of struggle and work. When he did speak it was to say briefly and modestly: "We knew it could be done and there it is."

It was the biggest and most heartfelt celebration ever held in Los Angeles. By automobile and train, people poured through the various thoroughfares to the amphitheater at the foot of the cascade where some time the 150-foot drop will be utilized to produce electrical energy. When the salute announcing the arrival of Mulholland and other distinguished guests was fired the big stand was filled with people. Thousands of others were massed about the platform in every direction. Along the banks of the cascade and high up the mountainsides men and women were awaiting the big event.

The band played "America" and as the people thrilled to the music and the occasion everybody felt, in his heart, that it was to be a grand celebration. When Ellen Beach Yaw's wonderful soprano rose higher and higher in that great proscenium the enthusiasm increased and continued to grow while Congressman Stephens, President Kinney of the Chamber of Commerce and ex-Gov. Pardee pictured in words of eloquence the significance of the completed aqueduct.

Joseph D. Radford, chairman of the Celebration Committee, spoke briefly of the early history of the aqueduct. "We had our doubts in the beginning," he said. "Then we came to believe that not only must the city have water, but that we could get it by spending money and building a great conduit. Then people began to ask where a man could be found who was big enough to tackle the job and put it through. We found him. He was right here in our midst. We decided that Bill Mulholland was the man and we have never changed our minds. Here he is."

As the great engineer advanced to the front of the platform, then, indeed, did the celebration become jubilantly vociferous. Hats waving in air and eager throats shouting heartfelt, even affectionate, reception, the multitude cheered and applauded the man whom they put on the job and who had made good for them.

MULHOLLAND'S ADDRESS.

"In the few remarks that I shall make," began Mulholland, "I speak not for myself alone, but for my associates in this great work. It has been a close partnership and we have worked together. Therefore we appear jointly and this expression is on behalf of all of us.

"This is a great event, fraught with the greatest importance to the future prosperity of this city. I have been already overwhelmed and honored. What greater honor can any man ask than to have the confidence of his neighbors? You have given me an opportunity to create a great public enterprise and I am here to render my account to you.

"It was your own fidelity and unfaltering courage that made the work possible, and I want to thank you. This period in my life is one of great exaltation. The aqueduct is completed

(Continued on Fourth Page.)

PROGRAMME FOR TODAY OF THE AQUEDUCT CELEBRATION.

AT 10 o'clock a.m. the industrial parade will move through the downtown streets, starting from Temple and Spring streets. Full details as to route and participants will be found elsewhere in this issue of The Times.

12:00 m. to 12:45 p.m.—Band concert, Sunken Garden, Exposition Park.

12:15 p.m.—Official party will leave Chamber of Commerce for Exposition Park.

12:30 to 2:30 p.m.—Informal reception; music; State Exposition Building.

1:00 p.m.—Exercises open with music by the band.

1:05 p.m.—Address, "Exposition Park as a State Institution" (Lee C. Gates, representing the Governor in front of State Exposition Building.

Music by the band.

1:20 p.m.—Dedication of aqueduct memorial fountain site—Sunken Garden. Address, United States Senator Works.

1:35 p.m.—Laying corner-stone of the State (Seventh Regiment) Armory (auspices the Masonic Order.)

Music by the band.

2:00 p.m.—Address, officially opening the Los Angeles County Museum of History, Science and Art—Hon. John D. Fredericks.

2:30 p.m.—Athletic games on Exposition Park infield playground. (Special automobile parkings at games.)

8:00 to 11:00 p.m.—Reception to distinguished guests at Museum of History, Science and Art, by Board of Governors—by invitation.

In Three Parts—22 Pages

PART I—TELEGRAPH SHEET—10 PAGES

The Los Angeles Times

1781 1914

Liberty Under Law—Equal Rights—True Industrial Freedom

MONDAY MORNING — JUNE 29, 1914 — PRICE 2½ CENTS {Delivered to Subscribers — Yearly, $9; Monthly, 75 Cents, postpaid. On Streets, Stands and Trains, 5 Cents.

THE HEIR TO AUSTRIAN THRONE ASSASSINATED.

Decisive.

UNCLE SAM INTERVENES IN SANTO DOMINGO.

Cruiser Fires on Federals to Prevent Bombardment of Puerta Plata.

Acting Under Instructions of the State Department United States War Vessel Silences a Battery Whose Operations Were Threatening the Lives of Americans and Other Foreigners.

[BY DIRECT WIRE—EXCLUSIVE DISPATCH.]

WASHINGTON BUREAU OF THE TIMES, June 28.—The United States today intervened in the revolution in Santo Domingo in order to protect Americans and foreigners in the besieged city of Puerta Plata.

Under instructions from the Navy Department, the gunboat Machias on Friday entered the harbor at Puerta Plata and with her guns silenced the main battery of the Federal artillery, which was bombarding the city. Secretary of Navy Daniels tonight gave out this statement of the occurrence:

"Acting under instructions from the department to protect lives and property of Americans and foreigners at Santa Domingo during the struggle that is now going on between the forces of President Bordas and the revolutionists, Capt. Russell of the South Carolina, who is in charge of the American naval vessel at Santo Domingo, ordered the United States steamer Machias to enter the inner harbor at Puerta Plata at 5 o'clock Friday afternoon, and opened fire with her main battery on the Bordas artillery, which had begun a bombardment of the city, although warned not to do so.

"Only a few shots were needed to put an abrupt end to the bombardment.

"The conditions existing at Puerta Plata for the past month have been increasingly intolerable and in this time the belief has become well established in official and diplomatic circles here that American intervention would be inevitable in order to protect its own nationals and those of other governments. This, it was believed, was the only step which could prevent intervention by some other government. The forces of the Santo Domingo government, which is headed by President Bordas, have been besieging Puerta Plata for about six weeks. The city is held by the rebel leader, Arias, who has proclaimed himself provisional President of the republic. Both sides in the fighting have appeared to be absolutely careless of the safety of the foreigners in the beleaguered city. The British Consul was wounded by the fire of the besiegers and other foreigners have been killed. The loss from destruction of foreign property in the city has been considerable.

"Several times President Bordas has been warned by the United States Minister that the bombardment of Puerta Plata must cease because of the danger involved to American and foreign citizens and their property. The President has made promises to discontinue the bombardment, but failed to do so. In the last week the administration decided that Bordas must be forced to carry out his promise and orders were sent to Capt. Russell, in command of the American vessel off Santo Domingo, to compel the artillery to cease firing. In accordance with his instructions, Capt. Russell sent a message to Bordas that if the bombardment, which had been held up for several days, was renewed American guns would silence his fire. It was upon the failure of Bordas to discontinue firing at the end of the period fixed by Capt. Russell that orders were given to the American gunboat to proceed into the inner harbor and silence the Federal guns."

THE WORLD'S NEWS IN TODAY'S TIMES.

THE HEART OF IT

EPITOMIZED, CLASSIFIED AND INDEXED.

Leading Events of Yesterday: (1) Archduke of Austria Assassinated. (2) United States Intervenes in Santo Domingo. (3) Carranza Asks More Time. (4) Chicago Contractors Revolt Against Business Agents. (5) The Balkan Situation.

INDEX.

SUMMARY.

THE SKY. Partly cloudy. Wind at 5 p.m., west; velocity, 9 miles. Thermometer, highest, 88 deg.; lowest, 64 deg. Forecast: Fair. For complete weather report see last page of Part I.

THE CITY. According to Long Beach Councilmen, a Los Angeles engineer yesterday made a remarkable statement in which city officials of the beach town are accused of attempted bribery.

The City Prosecutor will today present to the City Council an ordinance providing that women convicted of certain offenses shall be examined by city health officers and confined and treated if found afflicted with certain ailments.

A circular has been spread broadcast about the proposed site of the Florence Crittenton Home, opposing its location and quoting, as a means of disposing of unfortunate women, "Let her be stoned with stones, that she die."

A former auditor with a large corporation, now in jail charged with issuing fictitious checks, lives in the past, unable to conceive events after March, 1913.

Simultaneously with news that a former chief deputy county recorder has been driven out of Mexico with a woman, his one-time wife was married here. The police are seeking him.

Twenty thousand snakes and cats, spiders and toads, were turned loose Friday by school children who have used them in nature-study work. The pets have made startling appearances about town.

An "absent member" of the Board of Public Utilities will be removed from office Wednesday if he does not tender his resignation before that time.

While three women were joking as to what they would do if a burglar should enter, a thief stole jewelry in an adjoining room and the "lookout" was at the window, according to a police report yesterday.

SOUTHERN CALIFORNIA. The director of the Mt. Wilson observatory suggests that, because of the variability of the sun's heat, vegetation may hereafter be evolved by varicolored glass.

Shippers of inland counties are planning to secure a refund from the railroads on haul-back charges.

Citrus growers of the Porterville district are planning to form a league to protect against pests.

PACIFIC SLOPE. Many conductors on the Oregon-Washington Railroad have been caught "knocking down" fares.

Former Assistant Secretary of State Loomis declared the proposed Colombian treaty was an attempt to loot the Federal treasury.

Extension of the workmen's compensation act is proposed in the State of Washington.

GENERAL EASTERN. Chicago contractors have been forced by the blackmailing tactics of labor unions to seek contracts in other cities, and a revolt against their methods is threatened.

Many cyclonic disturbances are reported in the East, and the heat wave continues.

President of a hardware company in Detroit was killed by a highwayman.

WASHINGTON. The United States was forced to intervene in Santo Domingo to protect the lives of foreigners and other citizens in the city of Puerta Plata.

MEXICO. Villa is reported on his way to Mexico City, and it is said that the Federals have abandoned the city of Aguas Calientes.

Members of a new Cabinet for Carranza have been named and it is said Calderon will be Minister of Foreign Relations.

FOREIGN. The assassination of the Archduke of Austria may cause a disruption of the dual empire.

The reader who would do justice to himself will not depend wholly upon the foregoing Summary, comprehensive though it is, but will take in the complete news reports, which necessarily cannot be luminously summarized, epitomized or classified.

Principals in Tragedy of the Dual Empire.

Francis Ferdinand and wife.

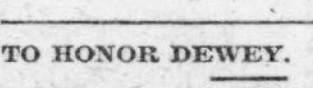

Francis Joseph.

Archduke and relatives.

In the upper panel are shown Francis Ferdinand and his wife, victims of assassins, in the second panel are Archduke Charles Francis Joseph, the heir presumptive, and the Princess Zita, his wife, and in the lower panel is the aged Francis Joseph, the present Emperor.

Expectant.

THE HEIR PRESUMPTIVE.

WED BOURBON PRINCESS IN GENUINE LOVE AFFAIR.

Marriage Was an Event of Note and Was Celebrated All Over Empire—Charles Francis Joseph Is the Eldest Son of the Late Archduke Otto.

[BY DIRECT WIRE—EXCLUSIVE DISPATCH.]

NEW YORK BUREAU OF THE TIMES, June 28.—By the tragic death of Archduke Francis Ferdinand, Charles Francis Joseph will become the heir presumptive to the Austrian throne. He is the eldest son of the late Archduke Otto Francis Joseph.

The heir presumptive was born in Parsenberg on August 17, 1887. He will, therefore, be 27 years old next August. Up to the present his life has been without special incident, except that he has always been granted all the favors and privileges of precedence, due to the ever strong likelihood that he would eventually be placed on the throne.

The marriage of Charles Francis Joseph, which took place on October 21, 1911, was an event of note and much celebration in Austria, especially in view of the fact that he took as his bride, Zita, Princess of Bourbon of Parma, a woman of his own rank. Princess Zita, who is talented and well versed in diplomatic and government affairs, comes from an illustrious family. She is the thirteenth child of the late Duke of Parma and his second wife, Marie Antonia, Princess of Portugal. She was born May 9, 1892. She has twenty-three brothers and sisters.

Emperor Francis Joseph highly approved of the marriage of Charles Francis Joseph and the Princess, and attended the ceremony and the reception which followed. The marriage was the outcome of a genuine love affair, and the couple have since been exceedingly happy. The heir presumptive is studious, fond of travel and occasionally goes on hunting trips.

Emperor Francis Joseph, at the time of the marriage, presented the royal bride with a diamond coronet arranged in five tiers, each of which can be taken off and worn as a separate ornament. One child, a son, Francis Joseph Otto, was born of the union.

Prior to his marrying Princess Zita, Charles Francis Joseph was often engaged by rumor to many young women of note in European capitals. It was once reported that the Kaiser had essayed to play the role of matchmaker between him and his daughter, the then Princess Victoria Luise.

Charles Francis Joseph is a major in the Thirty-ninth Regiment of Infantry and a member of the Eleventh Regiment of Prussian Hussars, the Thirteenth Regiment of Bavarian Infantry and is a member of the Order of the Black Eagle and St. Hubert.

FLAG FLIES AT NIGHT.

Stars and Stripes Over White House Interpreted as Wilson's "No Surrender" Defiance to Advisers.

[BY DIRECT WIRE—EXCLUSIVE DISPATCH.]

WASHINGTON BUREAU OF THE TIMES, June 28.—Vivid flashes of lightning during the heavy rainstorm in Washington tonight revealed the Stars and Stripes flying from the top of the flagstaff on the White House. The flag is supposed to fly there when the President is in the White House, but only between sunrise and sunset. Rumors spread over the city that President Wilson had nailed his flag to the mast and that such was his answer to his advisers who insist that he must surrender in his campaign for trust legislation and permit Congress to adjourn.

However, newspaper men who called up the White House and inquired the why and wherefore of the unusual display of Old Glory were promptly assured that the flag had been left up through the mistake or oversight of a servant. Five minutes later when the lightning flashed the flag no longer waved, and only the black line of the flagstaff stood out against the sky.

TO HONOR DEWEY.

Admiral of the Navy May Occupy Bridge of Olympia on Passage Through Canal.

[BY DIRECT WIRE—EXCLUSIVE DISPATCH.]

WASHINGTON BUREAU OF THE TIMES, June 28.—In arranging for the largest and most interesting naval display ever known, which is to be exhibited at the Panama Pacific exposition at San Francisco, beginning early next year, Secretary of the Navy Daniels has decided that the old cruiser Olympia shall share honors with the battleship Oregon and that Admiral George Dewey, like Rear Admiral Charles E. Clark, shall have opportunity again to stand on the bridge from which he directed the successful fighting in 1898.

Neither Dewey or Clark has visited his ship since they surrendered their commands shortly after the termination of the Spanish American war. Rear Admiral Clark already has accepted the invitation of Secretary Daniels to command the Oregon on her voyage, leading the American navy and the visiting squadrons of the world from Hampton Roads through the Panama canal and up to San Francisco. On the Oregon will be the president, Secretary Daniels and other members of the cabinet. Within a few days Secretary Daniels will extend a formal invitation to Admiral Dewey to make this cruise if he desires, or at any rate to visit the Olympia after it is moored at the naval exhibition wharf.

TO MARRY NAVY MEDICO.

Engagement of Indianapolis Girl to Surgeon on President Wilson's Yacht Is Announced.

[BY A. P. NIGHT WIRE.]

INDIANAPOLIS, June 28.—The engagement of Miss Dorothy Layman, daughter of Mr. and Mrs. Charles A. Layman of this city, to Dr. Robert Cathcart Ransdell, United States navy, who is attached to President Wilson's yacht, U.S.S. Mayflower, was announced here yesterday.

The wedding is to take place in New York, July 15.

BULLETS FATAL TO BOTH.

President of Detroit Hardware Company Kills Supposed Highwayman and Is Shot to Death Himself.

[BY A. P. NIGHT WIRE.]

DETROIT (Mich.) June 28.—John Burbank, president and treasurer of a local hardware company, was shot and killed late last night by an alleged highwayman, whose body was found a block away from the place where Burbank fell.

Burbank is believed to have shot and killed his assailant after he himself had receive four bullet wounds, which proved fatal. The alleged assailant has not been identified. A revolver was found by each body.

DATE FOR M'CARN TRIAL.

Federal Attorney in Hawaii Is Charged With an Attack Upon Opposing Counsel in a Suit.

[BY PACIFIC CABLE.]

HONOLULU, June 28.—The trial of Jeff McCarn, United States District Attorney for the Territory of Hawaii, indicted by the Territorial grand jury for assault with a deadly weapon, was set yesterday for September 8, in the territorial court.

Mr. McCarn will plead Monday to an indictment on the same charge returned by the Federal grand jury.

The offense charged in both instances is an alleged attack, with a pistol on Claudius McBride, opposing counsel in a suit. The men had an altercation in a corridor of the Federal building.

WOOLEN MILLS FAIL.

[BY A. P. NIGHT WIRE.]

MARTINSBURG (W. Va.) June 28.—Receivers were appointed by Judge R. W. Dailey at Romney yesterday for the Crawford Woolen Mills Company of Martinsburg. The liabilities are placed at $160,000 and assets at about the same amount.

Lawless.

ARCHDUKE AND WIFE SHOT AFTER ESCAPING BOMB.

Anarchist in Bosnian Capital Adds to List of Tragedies of Hapsburgs.

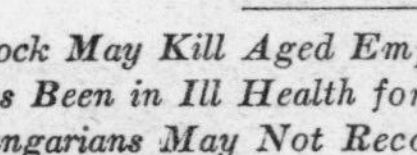

Shock May Kill Aged Emperor Francis Joseph, Who Has Been in Ill Health for the Last Few Months. Hungarians May Not Recognize Succession and Rupture in Dual Empire Is Feared.

[BY ATLANTIC CABLE AND A. P.]

SERAJEVO (Bosnia) June 28.—Archduke Francis Ferdinand, heir to the Austro-Hungarian throne, and the Princess of Hohenberg, his morganatic wife, were shot dead today by a student in the main street of the Bosnian capital, a short time after they had escaped death from a bomb hurled at the royal automobile. They were slain while passing through the city on their annual visit to the annexed provinces of Bosnia and Herzegovina.

The Archduke was struck full in the face and the Princess was shot through the abdomen and throat. They died a few minutes after reaching the palace, to which they were hurried with all possible speed.

Those responsible for the assassination took care that it should prove effective, as there were two assaults, the first with a bomb, and the second with a revolver. The bomb was thrown at the royal automobile as it was proceeding to the Town Hall, where a reception was to be held. The Archduke saw the missile hurtling through the air and warded it off with his arm. It fell outside the car and exploded, slightly wounding two aides de camp in a second car and half a dozen spectators.

It was on the return of the procession that the tragedy was added to the long list of those that have darkened the pages of the recent history of the Hapsburgs. As the royal automobile reached a prominent point in the route to the palace, an eighth-grade student, Gavrio Prinzipe, sprang out of the crowd and poured a deadly fusillade of bullets from an automatic pistol at the Archduke and Princess.

ESCAPE LYNCHING.

Prinzipe and a fellow-conspirator, a compositor from Trebinje, named Gabrinovics, barely escaped lynching by the infuriated spectators. They finally were seized by the police, who afforded them protection. Both are natives of the annexed province of Herzegovina.

The first attempt against the Duke occurred just outside the Girls' High School. His car had restarted after a brief pause for an inspection of the building, when Gabrinovics hurled the bomb. This was so successfully warded off by the Archduke that it fell directly beneath the following car, the occupants of which, Count Von Boos Waldeck and Col. Merizzo, were struck by slivers of iron.

Archduke Francis Ferdinand stopped his car, and after making inquiries as to their injuries and lending what aid he could, continued his journey to the Town Hall. There the burgomaster began the customary address, but the Archduke sharply interrupted and snapped out:

"Herr Burgomaster, we have come here to pay you a visit and bombs have been thrown at us. This is altogether an amazing indignity."

After a pause the Archduke said:

"Now you may speak."

On leaving the hall the Archduke and his wife announced their intention of visiting the wounded members of their suite at the hospital on their way back to the palace. They were actually bound on their mission of mercy when, at the corner of Rudolf Strasse and Franz Josef Strasse, Prinzipe opened fire.

PRINCESS IS SLAIN.

A bullet struck the Archduke in the face. The Princess was wounded

(Continued on Second Page.)

Destroyer.

MANY VIOLENT DEATHS IN HAPSBURG FAMILY.

BY HECTOR ALLIOT.

VIOLENT death seems to be the destroying angel of the Hapsburgs.

It is only through what might well be termed a miracle, that the life of the Francis Josef, Emperor of Austria, and King of Bohemia and Apostolic King of Hungary, has been spared.

In war, he escaped twice, and four times fate saved him from the attacks of assassins.

But if his own life was spared, he was the victim of terrible catastrophes: His wife, his brother, his only son having been destroyed by sudden and violent death.

Now comes the tragedy of Serajevo, Bosnia, which destroys the strongest hope of Austria, Archduke Ferdinand and Princess Hohenberg.

Beyond the great drama, useless and inhuman act of violence, which eliminates suddenly two human lives, soon to be called upon by the ordinary rule of life to take the place of one of the ablest sovereigns of Europe, there is the international and local question of succession.

The old adage, "The King is dead! Long live the King!" still obtains in Austria.

And here comes one of the greatest complications of sovereignty ever presented in monarchial Europe.

In 1854 Francis Josef married Elizabeth, daughter of the Duke of Bavaria, who was justly celebrated during her life for her extraordinary beauty. In 1857 was born to them the Crown Prince Rudolph, who in time married Princess Stephanie, daughter of the King of the Belgians.

On the last day of January, 1889, Prince Rudolph committed suicide at Mayerling, a country house near Vienna, under romantic and mysterious conditions never clearly ellucidated. His only daughter, Elizabeth, became the Countess of Windischgratz and his widow married Count Lonyay in 1900.

Emperor Francis Josef then recognized as his heir apparent his nephew, Francis Ferdinand, a great disciplinarian, distinguished officer and zealous churchman.

Unfortunately for the succession, however, he had followed the very democratic matrimonial notions of the House of Hapsburg for a generation.

An old legend says that Viennese are very susceptible to feminine charm and that archdukes and archduchess are thrice Viennese, amply confirmed by a dozen morganatic unions of the royal house.

Ferdinand's marriage of Countess Sophie Chotek was a confirmation of the old saying which caused and will now occasion serious complications.

The Emperor elevated Sophie Chotek to the rank of Princess and she was officially known as Princess Hohenberg, but according to the constitution of Austria her children were deprived of the right of succession.

Arch-duke Charles Francis Joseph, who married a few years ago the beautiful Princess Zita of Bourbon, becomes the heir presumptive of Austria-Hungary, according to the constitution of Austria, but the historical sequence in the occupancy of the throne of Hungary, accepted in 1867, does not recognize the ban placed upon royal children born of morganatic unions.

This fundamental constitutional difference may lead to endless and bloody conflict between the two most important members of the Osterreichisch-ungarisches Reich, whose discording elements have for years been difficulty held in leash.

On December 2, 1848, Emperor Ferdinand abdicated the throne of Austria in favor of his nephew, Francis Josef I, who was crowned as the one who could preserve the lustre of the crown and unite all countries and races, composing the empire into one "great body politic."

The herculean task of bringing together the seven main divisions of the empire, each one of a different race, speaking its own language, and governed by ancient autonomic customs and laws, was successfully accomplished by the venerable head of the Hapsburg House, still retaining at the advanced age of 83 the reins of the dual government of Austria-Hungary.

Through sixty-six years of reign, Francis Joseph has experienced every form of sorrow that a monarch could be expected to experience.

Brave as the famed lion, the Emperor met in battle the greatest personal dangers, his life was attacked three times, Bohemia and Hungary caused him for thirty years an endless chain of trouble and worry as the sovereign of the dual monarchy.

German-Austrians, Czechs, Poles, Southern Slavs, Ruthenes, Italians and Rumanians, Bohemians and Hungarians constitute the strange mosaic of heterogeneous elements cast together by the fall of the Roman Empire, yet retaining with extraordinary tenacity their own language, their customs and their intense love of tribal liberty of action.

For half a century the first gentleman of Europe and its greatest diplomat managed to hold together, notwithstanding the crushing defeat of Sadowa, which gave the German element the ascindancy in Austria, the revolution and compromise in Hungary, the troubles in Bohemia and among the Czechs, the master hand over his own dominions.

Rudolph, beloved of all Austria, was the ideal Crown Prince Ferdinand with his stern demeanor, his high standing among army men and in the church, seemed to be able to hold with a firm hand the "lustre of the crown" given by his ancestor to Francis Josef in 1848.

What may be the power of Charles Ferdinand, 26 years old, a youth, especially known for his fondness of life and its pleasure and whose greatest European renown so far is that he selected for spouse a clever and beautiful princess.

In her veins, however, flows the old blood of the Bourbons and Austrian Empresses have like the immortal Theresa, often managed to tame the free Czech, the Magyar and the Roumanian.

In Three Parts—18 Pages
PART I—TELEGRAPH SHEET — 8 PAGES

The Los Angeles Times

1781 1914

Liberty Under Law—Equal Rights—True Industrial Freedom

MONDAY MORNING — AUGUST 3, 1914

PRICE 2½ CENTS { Delivered to Subscribers — Yearly, $9; Monthly, 75 Cents, postpaid. On Streets, Stands and Trains, 5 Cents.

GERMANY HITS FIRST BLOW BY INVADING FRANCE.

Full Pocketbook.

HALF BILLION DOLLARS FOR NATIONAL BANKS.

Uncle Sam Has It Ready to Distribute Throughout the Country.

McAdoo Goes to New York With Full Authority Under the Aldrich-Vreeland Act to Loan Vast Sum on High-Class Security—Secretary Declares the United States Is in Excellent Shape to Take Care of Itself.

[BY A. P. NIGHT WIRE.]

WASHINGTON, Aug. 2.—Conferences at the White House and Treasury Department at which the foreign and domestic aspects of the financial situation were discussed, culminated late today in the departure for New York of Secretary McAdoo and Comptroller of the Currency Williams.

These two men have all the government authority to put in operation the plan which Congress designed years ago for such situations as the present by which the national banks of the country can obtain $500,000,000 in currency under the Aldrich-Vreeland Act with which to face any condition and meet any obligations.

Mr. McAdoo before he left declared that he considered the country to be in excellent shape to take care of itself and there was not the slightest reason for any feeling of alarm.

President Wilson, who discussed the situation at luncheon with Secretary McAdoo, is confident that any condition which arises can be meet without great difficulty.

Mr. McAdoo may return to Washington late tomorrow in time to meet representatives of clearing house associations of Chicago and St. Louis now en route to the capital at his invitation.

In official circles here the feeling was evident that any unusual strain will be manifest first in New York, and both the President and Mr. McAdoo were anxious that the highest government financial authority be on the ground.

Before Mr. McAdoo left Washington the treasury shipped out about $100,000,000 of the Aldrich-Vreeland currency, which will be in the vaults of the sub-treasury tomorrow ready for the New York banks.

EMERGENCY CURRENCY.

The emergency currency in most essentials is like that of the national banks, but can be issued on the security of high-class commercial paper or State and municipal bonds. Commercial paper used for this purpose must be approved not only by the bank, which asks for currency in exchange, but by the particular association of which the bank is a member. In addition the security must be available to the government. Tomorrow Mr. McAdoo and Mr. Williams probably will scan securities offered by New York banks for emergency and facilitate in every way its movement from the subtreasury to the banks.

It would not surprise officials in Washington if Mr. McAdoo used his influence in New York to keep the New York Stock Exchange closed for some time. No direct proposal of this kind could be made, but he is expected to show the government does not look kindly upon the reopening of the exchange at this time and the speculation which may follow.

There has been no call from outside New York for Aldrich-Vreeland currency, and it was not believed here

(Continued on Fourth Page.)

THE WORLD'S NEWS — THE HEART OF IT — IN TODAY'S TIMES.

EPITOMIZED, CLASSIFIED AND INDEXED.

Forcmost Events of Yesterday: (1) Germany Invades France. (2) French Aeroplane Brought to the Ground Over German Borders. (3) England Calls Out Naval Reservists. (4) Russia Invades Germany. (5) American Tourists Abroad to Be Aided. (6) Proclamation of America's Neutrality Due Today. (7) Railroad Strike Situation.

INDEX.

SUMMARY.

THE SKY. Clear. Wind at 5 p.m., southwest; velocity, 5 miles. Thermometer, highest, 84 deg.; lowest, 60 deg. Forecast: Fair. For complete weather report see last page of Part I.

THE CITY. A son of the fire chief was drowned in four feet of water in a plunge, while 200 bathers disported about him.

Police who investigated another "poison needle" tale branded all such stories "bunk" and bred of hectic sex literature.

A salesman who was dragged from his car by a fire warden and made to fight a grass blaze will sue for damages.

A huge wave hurled an attorney from a sailing craft outside the harbor and he was drowned.

The Los Angeles Baldheaded Club plans to capture for next year the national convention of the Baldheaded League of America.

A Courthouse watchman 60 years old, friend of elopers to Santa Ana, ran away and was married.

A bride 82 and a groom 63, who came here on their honeymoon, declared they are happy.

More than 500,000 voters are registered as Republicans and 100,000 more will be in the ranks by the November elections.

A white woman who has mothered a little Indian boy refused to turn him over to Federal officials.

In answer to citizens who object to nudity and near-nudity a member of the Edenite sect quoted scripture.

SOUTHERN CALIFORNIA. A church worker is accused at Long Beach by three boys of questionable actions.

An aviator at Venice, after flying upside down, was precipitated into the water when he swerved to prevent landing in the crowd.

Imperial Supervisors have adopted a plan to protect autoists on the mountain roads.

PACIFIC SLOPE. German steamer arrived at San Francisco with a crew of German reservists, who will go to Fatherland via New York.

Stillwater man killed a farm hand whom he accused of paying attention to his wife.

Man arrested at Santa Clara for burglary found to have a valise full of love letters from girls all over the country.

GENERAL EASTERN. Unofficial reports received from Washington indicate the managers of the western railroads will heed the President's plea for peace instead of disastrous strike.

Austrian reservists in the East have been ordered to get ready to respond to a call to rally around the colors.

WASHINGTON. President Wilson and the Cabinet, after a lengthy session, decide to put $500,000,000 in emergency currency at the service of the banks of the country.

Steps are being taken by the State Department to aid Americans abroad who are temporarily embarrassed by the war situation, although it has not been decided what form this aid will take.

It is probable a proclamation of neutrality by the United States will be issued by the United States today.

Secretary McAdoo went to New York to confer with bankers over the financial situation.

FOREIGN. Germany yesterday invaded France without a declaration of war, and the Kaiser's troops are reported to have been defeated in an engagement near Nancy.

Russia invades Germany and a detachment of Cossacks is said to have been driven back in the first engagement.

The reader who would do justice to himself will not depend wholly upon the foregoing Summary, comprehensive though it is, but will take in the complete news reports, which necessarily cannot be luminously summarized, epitomized or classified.

Figure in Opening Clash on French Soil.

Typical French Soldiers.

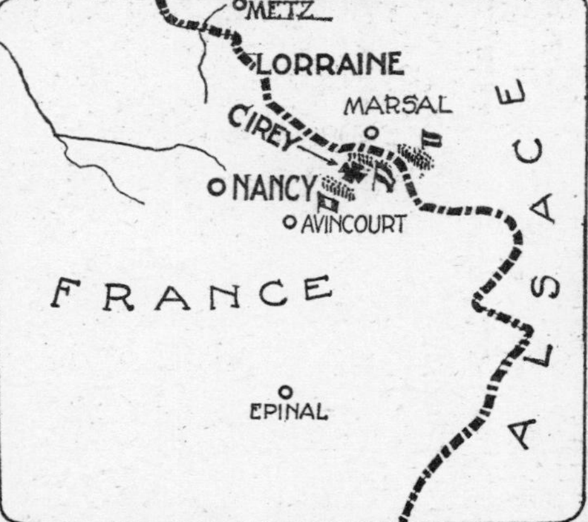

Tower and gateway at Nancy.

Ready for Kaiser's Invasion.

In the upper panel is shown two typical French soldiers of whom thousands are gathered on the border awaiting the coming of the German hosts. In the lower left hand panel is a map of the district where the clash occurred, the cross showing Cirey, near whose fortifications the Germans crossed, and in the right panel is the tower and gate of Nancy, the French city now threatened by the Germans.

Suspense.

ENGLAND ON DEFENSIVE; WAR PARTY IS ACTIVE.

Naval Reserves Called, Arms Policy to Be Announced Today.

Censors Take Charge of All Cable Offices, Telephones to Continent Are Stopped Entirely, National Banking Act to Be Suspended—Question of Supporting France on Everyone's Lips.

[BY ATLANTIC CABLE AND A. P.]

BELFORT (France) Aug. 2.—The Germans opened fire on the French posts at Petit Croix today. Details of the engagement are not known.

TOKIO, Aug. 3.—Russia has seized a German steamer at Vladivostok.

CETTINJE, Aug. 2.—King Nicholas has signed a decree for the mobilization of the Montenegrin army. It is said that Montenegro has a secret military agreement with Servia.

LONDON, Aug. 3.—A late dispatch from Paris says that two officers and twenty men of a German patrol were killed at Longwy and that the German attack was repelled.

BERLIN (Via Brussels) Aug. 2.—The small cruiser Augsburg has sent the following report to Berlin by wireless: "Am bombarding the naval harbor at Libau and am engaged with the enemy's cruisers. The naval port of Libau is in flames."

Libau is one of the principal seaports of Russia and is located on the Baltic Sea, one hundred miles or more north of the German coast. It is fortified and used as an arsenal by the navy.

The German protected cruiser Augsburg is of 4,280 tons displacement and her chief armament consists of twelve 4.1-inch guns. Her crew aggregates about 400 men.

LONDON, Aug. 2.—This Sunday has been a day of the greatest suspense England has known in a century. For hours the Cabinet was in council at Whitehall, and the whole country believed it to be wrestling with the question of whether Great Britain should take up arms in support of her partners of the triple entente.

No statement was made officially concerning the Cabinet's deliberations except that the Premier would make an announcement in the House of Commons tomorrow and the Cabinet would hold another meeting in the morning.

The government took three measures for defense today, none of them inconsistent with the policy of remaining outside the conflict, if that should be her policy. The naval reserves and naval marine pensioners were called out by proclamation; the territorials, who had just assembled at the training camps for annual practice, were ordered back to their headquarters; the Home Secretary prohibited air flights over the entire kingdom and territorial waters, except by military craft.

All these measures are purely defensive. Great Britain would feel obliged to take them with a great war raging close to her shores, even if there was no question of her participation.

CABLES CENSORED.

Censors took charge of all the cable offices in the kingdom tonight. All code messages were prohibited even to Australia. Telephonic communication with the continent was stopped entirely. The Brussels telephone, which was the last line working, is silent tonight.

The King issued a proclamation declaring a moratorium for a month and the suspension of the banking act tomorrow appears assured. Parliament probably will pass a bill for a loan for defensive purposes to the amount of $250,000,000. A rise in price of foodstuffs is expected tomorrow, although the Board of Trade has issued a reassuring statement that there is a wheat supply of four months in the country.

The newspapers of England are confronted with the possibility of a paper famine. Most of them depend upon the Scandinavian countries for stock and have only a few weeks'

(Continued on Second Page.)

Hostilities.

DEFEAT OF KAISER'S ARMY REPORTED NEAR NANCY.

[BY ATLANTIC CABLE AND A. P.]

LONDON, Aug. 2.—German forces today began the invasion of France without, so far as is known, a declaration of war having been made. The German detachments entered French territory, moving in the direction of Paris.

One German force crossed the French frontier near the village of Cirey between Nancy and Strassburg, and another German detachment, probably the Twenty-ninth Infantry, last night invaded the Grand Duchy of Luxemburg, neutral territory between Belgium and Germany, and continued its march on the French fortified town of Longwy. A dispatch from Brussels says there was good reason to believe that this force, later in the day, entered France.

The German force of 20,000 men which came into France near Cirey, which is forty miles from Nancy, is reported to have been repulsed with heavy losses, but this has not yet been confirmed.

Apparently the German army is duplicating the first movement of the Franco-Russian war. It was on August 2, 1870, forty-four years ago today, that the French and Germans clashed in the first battle of that war at Saarbrucken, where the Prince Imperial, under the orders of the Emperor, received his famous "baptism of fire."

It would appear today that Germany is taking the fullest possible advantage of her supposed superiority in rapid mobilization over France.

PLANS OF KAISER.

The plan of the German Emperor, according to military observers here, is to vanquish or attempt to vanquish, France in the interval, before Russia will be able to create serious trouble on her northern frontier. It is supposed that Russian mobilization will take about three weeks.

All telegraphic and telephonic communication between Brussels, and Luxemburg has been severed.

By the treaty of London, signed in 1867, the Grand Duchy of Luxemburg was declared neutral territory. Its integrity and independence were guaranteed.

Longwy is a fortified town of France on the Belgium frontier forty miles northwest of Metz in Germany.

A trainful of German soldiers arrived at the station at Luxemburg during the night.

The troops seized the station and the bridges on the Treves and Trois Vierges line in order to insure the regular passage of military trains across the Grand Duchy.

SOLDIERS IN BARRACKS.

After these seizures the soldiers proceeded to the barracks. The major of the Luxemburg volunteers protested against the violation of neutrality, but in reply, the Germans asserted that the railway belonged to them and that they had the right to do what they liked in Luxemburg.

A telephone dispatch from Brussels today said it was reported there that Germany had declared war on France and that the French Ambassador, Jules Gambon, had left the German capital.

This report could not be confirmed.

The French Embassy issued today the following statement:

"French territory has been invaded at Cirey and German troops are marching on the fort at Cirey. This act has been committed without a declaration of war. The German Ambassador is at present in Paris."

Germany declared today that she was unable to answer the question put by the British Ambassador at Berlin as to whether she is prepared to respect the neutrality of Belgium.

This statement appears in a communication issued by the French Embassy.

The neutrality of Belgium has been guaranteed by Great Britain and she is bound to protect Belgium for her own safety as Belgium under German rule would be a never-ending menace to England.

New Warfare.

REPORTS FIGHT IN MIDAIR.

LONDON HEARS GERMAN DIRIGIBLE WAS DESTROYED.

Berlin Dispatch Declares Two Million Men Have Been Called to the Colors and that the Proclamation of Martial Law Has Stopped All Socialist Opposition.

[BY ATLANTIC CABLE AND A. P.]

LONDON, Aug. 3.—The Standard publishes a report that a French aviator, Roland Garros, met and engaged a German airship in midair, rammed and destroyed it. The Standards fails to give the source of its story.

The Standard's Berlin correspondent sends a message from Boxtel, The Netherlands, that 2,000,000 men have been called to the colors.

Many of the railway lines, says the correspondent, are reserved exclusively for the transport of the troops. The men are in excellent spirits, all of them singing. The authorities have taken over the control of all the necessaries of life, as well as petrol, all motor cars and most of the horses in the country.

The proclamation of martial law has entirely crushed the Socialist opposition. All lighthouses have shut off their lights.

Czar.

RUSSIA INVADES GERMANY, COSSACKS ARE REPULSED.

[BY ATLANTIC CABLE AND A. P.]

BERLIN, Aug. 2.—An official statement issued today says:

"In consequence of a Russian attack on German territory, Germany is in a state of war with Russia. The French reply to the German representations is of an unsatisfactory character.

"Moreover France has mobilized and an outbreak of war with France must therefore be reckoned with any day or any moment."

Another statement declares Russia has invaded Germany during a time of peace, "in flagrant contradiction of Russia's peaceful assurances."

The Russian column which crossed the frontier at Schwinden was accompanied by artillery. Two squadrons of Russian Cossacks are riding in the direction of Johannesburg in East Prussia, fifteen miles from the frontier.

The Russian patrol which entered near Eichenreid attacked the German guard at the railroad bridge over the Warthe. The attack was repulsed. Two Germans were slightly wounded.

The above information was given out by the Imperial staff. The staff at the same time said that the invasion near Schwinden showed that war had actually begun.

AVIATOR DROPS BOMBS.

A French aviator has been dropping bombs from an aeroplane in the neighborhood of Nuremburg, Bavaria, according to an announcement made by the military authorities today. In making this announcement the authorities added that this action was a crime against the rights of men, as there had been no declaration of war.

Emperor William came to Berlin this afternoon from Potsdam. He traveled in an open automobile and was greeted on the streets of the capital by tumultuous cheering.

His Majesty was followed in other automobiles by the Crown Prince, Prince Henry of Bavaria, his brother, and other Princes.

Later in the afternoon Dr. Von Bethmann-Hollweg, the Imperial Chancellor, drove to the imperial palace. He was heartily cheered by the populace.

ENTHUSIASM AT BOURSE.

The receipt of war news at the bourse gave occasion for enthusiastic patriotic demonstrations.

A telegram received here from Koenigsberg says a Russian patrol has entered Eydtkuhnen, on the Russian border.

It advanced to Bilderweitschen, near Eydtkuhnen, where it destroyed the local postoffice.

The enemy, according to this intelligence, crossed the border at several points.

In Three Parts—24 Pages.
PART I—TELEGRAPH SHEET—10 PAGES

The Los Angeles Times
1781 1915
Liberty Under Law—Equal Rights—True Industrial Freedom

SATURDAY MORNING, MAY 8, 1915
PRICE 2½ CENTS { Delivered to Subscribers. } { Yearly, $9; Monthly, 75 Cents, postpaid. On Streets, Stands and Trains, 5 Cents.

OVER A THOUSAND LIVES PROBABLY LOST WHEN THE GERMANS SANK THE LUSITANIA.

"Strict Accountability."

SUSPEND JUDGMENT, SAYS PRESIDENT WILSON.

Executive Faces Necessity of Making Good War Zone Protest to Germany.

United States Authorities will Make a Thorough Inquiry into the Number of Americans Lost on the Lusitania and will Include in Whatever Representations are Made Some Other Grievances.

BY JOHN CALLAN O'LAUGHLIN.

[BY DIRECT WIRE—EXCLUSIVE DISPATCH.]

WASHINGTON BUREAU OF THE TIMES, May 7.—Official and diplomatic Washington is stunned tonight by the destruction of the Lusitania and the terrible loss of life which occurred as a consequence thereof. President Wilson and Secretary Bryan are exceedingly anxious that the country shall observe the advice of Capt. Sigsbee when his ship, the Maine, was destroyed in Havana Harbor, and "suspend judgment" until all the facts are officially established.

It is their firm intention to hold Germany to a "strict accountability" for the loss of any American lives, and they may deem it imperative, if no Americans were drowned or killed, to make a protest to the Berlin government against a practice which they hold to be contrary to the law of nations. But they realize that any excitement that may sweep over the country will be exceedingly embarrassing to the administration, and they are anxious that the people shall be calm and leave to Washington the determination of the character of the representations to be made to Germany.

BRITISH TO MAKE INQUIRY.

The British government will make a thorough probe and will establish the facts. The United States will not participate in this inquiry, but if any Americans have been lost it will institute an independent investigation. It will pursue the same course with reference to the American passengers of the Lusitania as it followed when Leon C. Thresher, a passenger on the torpedoed British steamer Falaba, was drowned. No representations were made to Germany with reference to Thresher, because the President, understanding the superheated frame of mind of the German government, deemed it advisable to postpone bringing the question of indemnity up until a more opportune time.

This government, however, has been brought face to face with the necessity of making good the language it used in protesting against the Berlin decree establishing a "war zone" about the British Isles.

There is not the slightest doubt that Germany will enthusiastically welcome the news of the destruction of the Lusitania, while at the same time regretting that innocent neutrals were drowned, killed or wounded. But it will claim they took the risk of traveling on the Lusitania when they were warned not to do so.

THE REPRESENTATIONS.

It is possible that in the representations which will be made to Germany President Wilson will group the following incidents:

(1.) The death of Thresher, the American lost on the Falaba.

(2.) The aeroplane attack on the American tank steamer Cushing.

(3.) The torpedo attack on the American tank steamer Gulflight and the resultant death of her captain and two of her crew.

(4.) The drowning of any American passengers on the Lusitania.

According to experts on international law the United States has the right to protest against destruction of the Lusitania on the following grounds:

That of common humanity.

That admission by the United States of such a practice might justify the use of the practice against the United States.

That American citizens, under a rule laid down by Chief Justice Marshall, have the right in their persons and property to be safeguarded from death or destruction.

That under the Declaration of Paris, to which Germany is a party, "neutral goods, with the exception of contraband of war, are not liable to capture under enemy's flag."

That it was the duty of the attacking warship under the rules and regulations issued by the German government on August 3, 1914, to see that the passengers and crew of the Lusitania, Falaba and Gulflight were taken off the vessel before they were destroyed and placed in safety.

WILSON HEARS NEWS.

President Wilson had just finished luncheon and was about to leave the White House for a drive when he heard of the sinking of the Lusitania. At the Cabinet meeting less than an hour before, the torpedoing of the American steamer Gulflight with the death of three Americans had been discussed and a party of Cabinet members had gathered for luncheon at a near-by hotel, where the news was taken to them. All the Secretaries immediately hurried back to their offices.

The President's first question was whether any lives had been lost, and his relief was evident when he was told that the first dispatches indicated that all were saved. He abandoned his ride to keep in touch with the State Department, which soon after transmitted to him Ambassador Page's cablegram, which was the first official information to reach the gov-government. The President kept to his study for the remainder of the afternoon, reading dispatches as the Secretaries brought them in. He made no comment and White House officials said none would be forthcoming, if at all, until after all the facts were known.

CAME AS A SHOCK.

Even though it had been feared that the liner might be attacked, to the President and his official family the news was a shock and a surprise.

For some hours officials silently and gravely scanned the news dispatches, and eagerly awaiting some official advices from London or the American Consulates scattered along the region of the disaster, withheld their comment, merely expressing the hope that no Americans had been lost. The tension of the first few hours, however, in all branches of the government was unconcealed. It probably has not been equaled since the Mexican crisis reached its height just a year ago.

The State Department and the executive offices were deluged with a setady stream of inquiries, many of which came from the diplomatic colony.

After dinner the President returned to his study and spent the evening reading the dispatches.

Two Views of Ship that Was.

The Cunarder, Lusitania.

The upper picture shows the wonderful ship in dock in New York. A notion of her size is obtained in this picture by comparing the leviathan with the pier and the luggage and baggage piled thereon. The lower panel, a side view of the Lusitania under full steam.

SCORE BOOKED FROM PITTSBURGH.

[BY A. P. NIGHT WIRE.]

PITTSBURGH, May 7.—According to steamship agents here, twenty persons from the Pittsburgh district had booked passage on the Lusitania. In the number were eight first cabin, nine second cabin and three third cabin passengers. C. G. Andrews, manager of the J. J. McCormick agency, stated he was not at liberty to give the names of some of the first cabin passengers, as he had promised to withhold their names. He said, however, that among the number were several prominent steel and iron manufacturers bound for Europe to close contracts.

PHILADELPHIANS ABOARD VESSEL.

[BY A. P. NIGHT WIRE.]

PHILADELPHIA, May, 7.—S. M. Knox, president of the New York Shipping Company, Camden, and William Sterling Hodges, Paris representative of the Baldwin Locomotive Works, were among the prominent Philadelphians who were passengers on the Lusitania. Mr. Knox went abroad on business. Mr. Hodges was accompanied by his wife and two small sons.

Harry J. Keser, vice-president of the Philadelphia National Bank, and widely known in financial circles, was another passenger. Paul Compton, who was accompanied by his family, is vice-president of the Surpass Leather Company.

Rescued.

BRETHERTONS OF LOS ANGELES AMONG THE PASSENGERS SAVED.

[BY A. P. NIGHT WIRE.]

NEW YORK, May 7.—According to a cablegram received tonight by the Cunard line, Cyril H. Bretherton of Los Angeles, Cal., and his wife and two children, who were passengers on the Lusitania, are safe.

Many inquiries were made for Mr. Bretherton. Prior to sailing he made a lengthy visit in New York. His friends remained at the Cunard offices for hours, waiting to hear some news of him. They were rewarded late tonight when a cablegram was received by the Cunard line reading that the Bretherton family was safe.

Among the last messages received at the Cunard offices were several stating that individuals were safe. In these messages were the names of George Kessler, a New York wine agent; Miss Jessie Taft Smith, Braceville, O.; Mrs. H. B. Lassetter, wife of Gen. H. B. Lassetter, and their son, P. Lassetter of London. Mrs. Lassetter and her son were booked for Sydney, Australia.

Among those for whom anxious inquiries were made at the Cunard line's offices tonight were Dr. T. Houghton of Troy, N. Y., said by the officials of the company to be the son of a former New York State Supreme Justice. Dr. Houghton was on his way to Belgium to take charge of the war hospital at La Panna. He went as the representative of Mme. Adepage, head of the Belgium relief in this country. Dr. Houghton had a premonition of disaster and persuaded her to allow him to go in her stead. Before embarking he made his will.

REVISED LIST OF PASSENGERS.

A revised list of the passengers, made public by the line tonight, showed there were 1251 passengers in all on board. The crew numbered between 700 and 800, making a total of more than 2000 on the steamer.

The list made public showed the various nationalities of the passengers as follows:

First cabin—Great Britain, 179; United States, 106; Greece, 3; Sweden, 1; Mexico, 1; Switzerland, 1.

Second cabin—Great Britain, 521; United States, 65; Russia, 3; Belgium, 1; Holland, 3; France, 5; Italy, 1; unknown, 2.

Third class—Great Britain, England, 204; Ireland, 39; Scotland, 13; Russia, 59; United States, 17; Persia, 18; Greece, 3; Finland, 1; Scandinavia, 4; Mexico, 1.

The Lusitania is the third big trans-Atlantic liner lost since the war started. The two others were the White Star liner Oceanic, wrecked off the north coast of Scotland September 8 last, and the North German Lloyd steamer Kaiser Wilhelm der Grosse, converted into a German auxiliary cruiser, which was sunk by the British cruiser Highflier, August 27.

A fourth big steamer, the mammoth Cunarder Aquitania, was severely damaged in a collision with the Leyland liner Canadian off the Irish coast in the latter part of last August.

Ruthlessness.

FIVE TO SIX HUNDRED SURVIVORS LANDED ALONG THE IRISH COAST.

Two Torpedoes Fired, Without a Note of Warning, into the Steel Sides of the Huge Cunarder.

Passengers at Luncheon, Confident that the Swift Atlantic Liner Could Elude Any War Craft Afloat, Taken Completely by Surprise — England's Fastest Merchant Vessel Submerged in Fifteen Minutes.

[BY ATLANTIC CABLE AND A. P.]

QUEENSTOWN, May 8, 4:24 a.m.—Survivors of the Lusitania who have arrived here estimate that only about 650 of those aboard the steamer were saved and only a small proportion of those rescued were saloon passengers.

LONDON, May 8.—Only a few of the first-class passengers on board the Lusitania, sunk today by a German submarine, were saved. Most of them remained on board, thinking the great ship would stay afloat. Trawlers arriving at Queenstown have about one hundred bodies on board.

WASHINGTON, May 8.—A dispatch to the State Department early today from American Consul Frost at Queenstown stated that the total number of survivors of the Lusitania was about 700. The Consul's dispatch gave a partial list of American survivors, but did not say definitely whether any Americans had been lost.

LONDON, May 8, 5:58 a.m.—Signals have been received at Queenstown that an armed trawler believed to be the Heron and two fishing trawlers are bringing in 100 more bodies. The Cunard line agent states that the total number of persons aboard the Lusitania was 2160.

LONDON, May 8, 4:42 a.m.—The Times' Queenstown correspondent says that some of the survivors who have arrived there report that Alfred Vanderbilt was drowned. Inquiry failed to develop any trace of Charles Frohman, who is believed lost.

LONDON, May 8.—The Cunard liner Lusitania, which sailed out of New York last Saturday with more than 2000 persons aboard, lies at the bottom of the ocean off the Irish coast.

She was sunk by a German submarine, which sent two

(Continued on Ninth Page.)

Passengers.

LUSITANIA SURVIVORS LANDED AT QUEENSTOWN.

[BY ATLANTIC CABLE AND A. P.]

QUEENSTOWN, May 8.—Among the survivors of the Lusitania who have arrived here are:

A. T. Mathews, Montreal.
S. Abramowitz.
Miss Catherine Kaye.
G. B. Lane.
W. G. E. Meyers.
J. T. Trimmins.
Mrs. A. F. Witherbee.
Lady Mackworth.
Mrs. Henry Adams, Boston.
Robert Rankin, New York.
Samuel Sharp.
M. G. Byrne, New York.
Emily Davis.
Annie Walker.
E. Housnell.
A. B. Cross.
Philip Young, Montreal.
W. A. F. Vasser, London.
George Steele.
Cyrus Crosley.
James Parker.
R. Colebrook.
The Rev. H. C. H. Morris.
Mrs. Fish and two children.
Miss R. Martin.
F. J. Gautlett, New York.
Miss May Maycock.
Violet Henderson.
Uno Marderud.
Thomas D. Levin.
D. A. Thomas, Cardiff, Wales.
T. J. M. Evans.
A. R. Clarke.
W. G. Burgess.
J. H. Charles and daughter, Toronto.
Miss Loneq, New York.
John Herris.
Miss Holland.
Miss Josephine Brandell, New York.
F. K. A. Perry.
O. H. Grab.
C. G. Mosley, New York.
J. H. Brooks, New York.
A. M. Jeffry.
M. Cairns.
O. H. Hammond, New York.
A. Manley.
H. Heath.
Miss North.
Miss Winter.
George Duguid.
Daniel Moore.
John W. McConnell, Memphis, Tenn.
Miss Sharpe.
Miss Conner.
H. M. Daly.
Patrick Cliffe.
James Bohan, Toronto.
Mrs. Cyrus Crosley.
Capt. Turner.
First Officer Jones.
Second Officer Lewis.
Rev. H. W. Simpson.
Miss Minnie Webb.
John Ellis.
George Ward and wife.
Mr. and Mrs. Charles of Toronto.
John Freeman.
Mrs. Doherty and infant.
Miss Jessie Murdock.
Philip Young, Montreal.
Wallace D. Phillips.
Robert Stockton.
Robert J. Ewart.
Guy Chambers.
George Stevens.
Miss G. Hardy.
G. Reiddy.
Joseph Marichal and wife and two daughters.
M. Sternchie.
John J. Balba.
Joseph Levinsef.
Mrs. Burnside.
J. Scott.
J. Hooke.
Elsie Hooke.
E. Sampson.
D. O. Harris.
Dorothy Dodd.
Mrs. Irene Paynter of Liverpool.
Margaret Balbantyne.
Richard Lionel Taylor of Montreal.
Huntley Henderson.
Mrs. Merilein.
Arthur Vadster.
E. A. Duckworth.
John Moore.
O. Bernard, Boston.
R. Gardner.
Herbert Ghiberdot.
Frances Jenkins.
John Ferereszewich.
H. Edgar Birmingham.
H. D. Whitecombe.
R. Dyer.
Woodward Walter Dawson.
Rev. H. L. Gwyer and wife.
Thomas Ostevan.
Mrs. Andrew Lurdon and infant.
N. N. Allen.
Patrick Shattery.
Mr. Byington.
Mr. Brooks.

(Continued on Third Page.)

In Three Parts—26 Pages,
PART I—TELEGRAPH SHEET—12 PAGES

The Los Angeles Times
1781 1916

FRIDAY MORNING. MARCH 10, 1916.

Liberty Under Law—Equal Rights—True Industrial Freedom

PRICE 2½ CENTS

PUNISHMENT, NOT INTERVENTION, WILSON'S PLAN

Villa's Rear Guard Halts Pursuit of United States Troops

The Great War.

FRENCH GAIN ON MEUSE.

Drive Germans Out with Bayonets.

Battery Fire Stops the Invaders Debouching from the Corbeaux Wood.

Teutons Capture the Village of Forges, a New and Commanding Position.

Kaiser's Aviators the Victors in Several Engagements Over City of Verdun.

[BY ATLANTIC CABLE AND A. P.]

PARIS, March 9.—Further progress for the French in the Corbeaux wood is reported in the official statement issued by the War Office tonight as well as a German repulse along the front from Douaumont to Vaux.

The French official statement issued today says:

"In the Argonne our artillery has continued its bombardment of the enemy's routes of communication, notably in the Eastern Argonne and in the region of Montfaucon and Nantillois.

"West of the Meuse the enemy attempted several counter-attacks during the night to regain ground lost yesterday. Two abortive attacks were preceded by an intense artillery preparation directed against Bethincourt. The attacks were stopped by our batteries, which prevented the enemy from debouching from the Corbeaux wood. The renewed efforts of the enemy have not been able to dislodge us from the large stretch of territory which we have reconquered and consolidated.

"East of the Meuse the struggle is being carried on with great bitterness since yesterday. At the end of the evening and during the night, between Douaumont and the village of Vaux, the Germans directed several powerful attacks. In spite of the intensity of the artillery fire and the violence of the infantry assaults the enemy was unable to make any impression on our line and has been completely repulsed. Some detachments of German infantry, which had penetrated the village of Vaux, were driven out immediately at the point of the bayonet by a counter-attack.

"In the Woevre there has been an intermittent bombardment on both sides without any infantry action. In Lorraine a surprise attack, west of the Le Pretre forest, resulted in the capture by us of twenty prisoners."

ATTACK ON FORGES SWEEPS FRENCH BACK.

[BY ATLANTIC CABLE AND A. P.]

BERLIN, March 8 (via London, March 9.)—The attack on the village of Forges on the west bank of the Meuse, which resulted in the capture by the Germans, was rendered necessary by the fact that the French positions overlapped those of the Germans by several kilometers to the north. From the ridges of the Cote de l'Oie the French heavy artillery was able to take the Germans from the flank and rear. In the earlier phases of the operations the crown prince confined his attack to the eastern bank of the river.

At Forges there is a promontory which forces the Meuse to make a sharp bend toward the east. The German attack swept the French back from the river about two miles.

The loss of Fresnes is a serious

(Continued on Fourth Page.)

THE WORLD'S NEWS IN TODAY'S TIMES.

THE HEART OF IT.

The Foremost Events of Yesterday: (1) Mexico. (2) The Verdun Battle. (3) Railway Men to Demand Eight-hour Day. (4) Congress. (5) Wall Street's Recovery from War Alarms.

INDEX.

SUMMARY.

THE SKY. Clear. Wind at 5 p.m., southwest, velocity 6 miles. Thermometer, highest, 89 deg.; lowest, 63 deg. Forecast: Fair and continued warm Friday. For complete weather report see last page of Part I.

THE CITY. Attorney George P. Adams gave an able review of points in the trial of the Scott libel case against the Times-Mirror Company.

A woman who gave her property to cover her husband's defalcation and whose son was spirited away was refused a divorce.

A prominent church worker who accuses her husband of misconduct admitted in court her love for another man.

A Pittsburgh steel magnate was seriously ill in a hospital here, suffering with throat trouble.

A man of 72 eloped with a nurse and married in spite of the opposition of his relatives.

Ventura officers, fearing a lynching, rushed the slayer of a family of three to a jail cell here.

A French Legion of Honor soldier, who is also noted professor, spoke to the Alliance Francaise.

SOUTHERN CALIFORNIA. Long Beach City Commissioners have indicated that they propose to clean the harbor channel in a few days.

A Los Angeles woman was found wandering in the mountains back of Pasadena.

PACIFIC SLOPE. California grape and fruit men agreed to accept the administration tax on unfortified wines.

Seattle man in Los Angeles is sued by wife for maintenance.

Floods in Washington State tie up railroads.

Mrs. Eleve Morgan of Los Angeles flees to San Francisco to avoid detectives.

GENERAL EASTERN. Six men were killed and several wounded in an explosion in a colliery at Wilkesbarre.

Much colder weather is promised in Chicago and the East.

WASHINGTON. Three new coast guard cutters will be constructed this year.

Articles of war, over hundred years old, revised by the Senate.

Congress indignant at border outrages, and may compel Wilson to act.

MEXICO. The American troops which crossed the border in pursuit of Villa's bandits are reported to have been checked by rear guard action.

American machine guns at Columbus fail to act.

Only few troops on Coast available for border duty.

American troops on the border are reported to be on the qui vive to go on Villa's trail in Mexico.

THE GREAT WAR. The Situation to Date: Germany at war with Portugal.

Continuation of the fighting at Verdun.

Russians in the East renew offensive against the Germans.

COMMENT ON THE SITUATION.

Fighting between the French and the Germans northwest and north of Verdun has in no wise slackened. Particularly violent have been the attacks of the Germans to the north of Verdun, around Douaumont, the village of Vaux and Fort Vaux, but according to Paris they went for naught. The Germans were thrown in solid formation against trenches of the French bordering the foot of the ridge dominating Fort Vaux, which the latest German official report said the Germans had captured, but the French drove back the attacking forces with "enormous losses." Northeast of the fort, the Germans essayed an assault against the village of Vaux, from which they previously had been driven by the French, but here also they were repulsed with heavy casualties. To the west of the Meuse, midway between Bethincourt and the river, the French have continued on the offensive in the Corbeaux wood, and are officially reported to have driven the Germans from almost all of that point salient.

The attention of Washington and the administration is again centered on Mexico. America has virtually and practically invaded Mexico, intervened, so to speak, but the movement of United States troops across the border, for various reasons, goes by another name in diplomatic parlance. This much is said to be sure: The administration is back of every action so far taken by Col. Slocum.

HINT TO READERS: It is a mistake to jump at the wrong conclusion that all, or even the greater part, of the more important news is to be found on the first page, which cannot contain it. Consult the Index and the Summary, then read the entire paper—all the parts—and thus get all the news of the day.

Co-operation.

CARRANZA CONSENTS TO AMERICAN TACTICS.

United States Cavalry May Pursue Villa and His Bandits Until Captured.

Sanction of the De Facto Government to Invade Mexican Territory Already Obtained by the Washington Administration—In a Sense this Action May be Regarded as Actual Intervention.

BY JOHN CALLAN O'LAUGHLIN.

[BY DIRECT WIRE—EXCLUSIVE DISPATCH.]

WASHINGTON BUREAU OF THE TIMES, March 9.—Punishment, not intervention. This in a nutshell is the policy of the President as a result of the wanton assault made by a column of Mexicans, under the command of Villa, upon the town of Columbus, N. M.

With the consent of the representatives of the Carranza government and, it is said, with the approval of Gen. Carranza, American cavalry is to pursue Villa's bandits until they have been killed or captured. This will necessitate pursuit upon Mexican soil. In a sense such action will be intervention. In the larger sense it will not have this aspect. It is not the intention of the administration to seek to pacify Mexico, which would be the cause of intervention. It is merely the intention to kill or capture the bandits who committed the depredations upon American soil. Those who may be apprehended, even including Villa, will be turned over to Gen. Carranza for punishment. This would mean their immediate execution.

WASHINGTON STIRRED.

Official Washington was deeply stirred by the outrage perpetrated by Villa on Columbus. There were mutterings in the Senate and House and preparations are being made by Senator Fall of New Mexico to force instant action through a Congressional resolution. The administration, however, does not propose to be driven by Congress. It intends to act itself in order that its purpose to secure punishment and redress may be understood both in the United States and Mexico. At the same time the President realizes he cannot shut off a debate, which will open up the entire Mexican question. To prevent it becoming embarrassing he deemed it wise to reach an immediate decision.

As a matter of fact, American troops had crossed into Mexico without waiting permission from Washington; indeed, in violation of the orders heretofore even not to leave American soil. From Gen. Funston, who is in command of the situation, there came late this afternoon a dispatch enclosing a report from Gen. Pershing of El Paso. The latter stated that "Five troops of cavalry are in pursuit with orders not to go more than two miles beyond the border."

The further statement was made that "Slocum recommends cavalry be sent if any number of troops are to go after Villa."

Col. Slocum is in command of the detachment that followed Villa from Columbus.

President Wilson, it is understood, is determined to bring Villa to swift punishment. To rely on Gen. Carranza with the small force he has available is to accomplish nothing. Such reliance was placed upon Carranza when seventeen Americans were taken from a train in Chihuahua a few weeks ago and shot. But it is also realized by the President that to intervene will be to do precisely the thing which Gen. Villa aimed to bring about when he led the attack upon Columbus.

The President does not propose to fall into any such trap. The question he has had to consider is first, whether there should be intervention and, second, how to capture and punish Villa and his

(Continued on Fifth Page.)

U.S. Cavalry on the march.

Villa crosses and recrosses the border.

The upper panel, Villa in motion. The middle, a map of the region he invaded in New Mexico. The third panel, American cavalry in motion. United States cavalrymen are in pursuit of Villa and his outlaws and at late accounts were engaged in a pitched battle with them.

The Expected.

MURDER, ARSON, THEFT, BY VILLA IN AMERICA.

Outlawed Bandit Crosses the Border and Kills Sixteen Citizens.

Cries of "Death to the Gringoes" in Columbus, N. M., Drowned by the Rifle Fire of United States Troops Who Continued Their Pursuit of the Marauders into Mexico to Avenge Uncalled-for Attack.

[BY A. P. NIGHT WIRE.]

COLUMBUS (N. M.) March 9.—Francisco Villa, outlawed Mexican bandit, raided United States territory today. With 1500 men he attacked Columbus, killed at least sixteen Americans and fired many buildings before he was driven back across the international border.

At least 250 troopers of the Thirteenth United States Cavalry followed the Villa band into Mexico. Reports to Col. H. J. Slocum late today stated that Villa had made a stand fifteen miles south of the border, where spirited fighting ensued. In this engagement an unnamed private was killed and Capt.-Adjt. George Williams was wounded.

The raid to American territory proved costly to the bandit chieftain. The bodies of eighteen Mexican bandits, including Pablo Lopez, second in command, had been gathered and burned before noon and troopers reported an undetermined number of dead still lying in the brush.

"DEATH TO AMERICANS."

Led to the attack under the slogan, "Death to the Americans," Villa's followers fought with desperation. Just before dawn they crept along ditches skirting the United States cavalry camp and rushed the sleeping town, firing heavily.

The first volley brought American troopers into almost instant action. While a portion of the raiders engaged the cavalrymen, others detailed by the bandit chieftain began applying the torch and shooting American civilians who ventured from the buildings. Lights in homes and public buildings immediately became targets for snipers posted at Villa's direction. Other bandits, creeping close to American homes, enticed a number of civilians into the open with English spoken invitations. A number of fatalities are attributed to this ruse.

Stores were looted, oil was poured upon frame structures and the match applied by still other bandits. The postoffice was raided, furniture smashed, but the looters secured only one small registered package.

Many civilians barricaded themselves in their homes and fired at the Mexicans as they darted through the streets.

The fighting in the town ended almost as suddenly as it began. Less than two hours after the first shot was heard Villa's buglers sounded the retreat and the raiders began a disordered flight, closely followed by American troopers.

CAVALRY ON BORDER.

Three troops of cavalry were posted on the boundary tonight and a battalion of infantry with a squadron of the Eighth Cavalry from Fort Bliss left El Paso late today to reinforce the troops here. With these forces, Col. Slocum said he could handle any further attack which Villa, in desperation, might decide to make.

THE CASUALTIES.

The casualties of the Thirteenth Cavalry in the fight were seven killed and five wounded.

Villa's total losses in the day's fighting were estimated in excess

(Continued on Fifth Page.)

Qui Vive.

ANOTHER ATTACK IS FEARED BY AMERICANS ALONG BORDER.

Military Headquarters Hears that Bandits have Already Crossed at Another Point—Force which Invaded Mexico Compelled to Halt in Its Pursuit—Main Body of Outlaws now Thought to be Making for Boca Grande River.

[BY A. P. NIGHT WIRE.]

COLUMBUS (N. M.) March 9.—A report reached here tonight and was relayed to military headquarters at Hachita, N. M., that a Villa force had appeared on the American side of the border, west of here with the apparent intention of attacking the Seventh United States Cavalry border guard near that point.

SAN ANTONIO (Tex.) March 9.—Maj. Frank Tompkins, commanding the detachment of American troops, which pursued Gen. Villa and his bandits into Mexico after the attack early today on Columbus, N. M., has returned to the border, after engaging in three running fights with the Mexicans, who finally made a stand which stopped the advance of the American soldiers. This information was conveyed tonight to Maj.-Gen. Frederick Funston, commanding the Southern Department, United States army, in an official report on the situation from Col. H. J. Slocum, in command at Columbus.

"All peaceful as a summer morning at this writing," was the way Col. Slocum described the situation in Columbus tonight.

Following is the text of Col. Slocum's report, as given out by Gen. Funston at Fort Sam Houston:

"When Villa troops fell back before daylight, we followed them with a dismounted line. At the same time I sent Maj. Tompkins with three troops mounted to attack. Tompkins followed them for about five miles into Mexico, having three running fights with them and they finally made a stand with their entire force and stopped Tompkins's advance and he returned here. We had one corporal killed in the pursuit. The Mexicans dropped considerable material and loot that they had gotten in town. I am reliably informed that it was Villa who made the attack with 1500 men, leaving about

(Continued on Second Page.)

2d EDITION—5 O'CLOCK A.M.

The Los Angeles Times

1781 1916

"Sail on, sail on, sail on, and on and on."

2c

Liberty Under Law—Equal Rights—True Industrial Freedom

FRIDAY MORNING, NOVEMBER 10, 1916.

PRICE 2½ CENTS { Delivered to Subscribers } At All Hotels and on Railway Trains, 5c. On Streets and News Stands, 2 Cents.

WILSON CARRIES CALIFORNIA AND WINS RE-ELECTION.

Eight Hours.

TO ENJOIN GOMPERS.

Santa Fe Protests Adamson Act.

Petition Describes Measure as Unworkable for the Railroads.

Recitation of Circumstances Under Which Congress Passed Bill.

[BY A. P. NIGHT WIRE.]

KANSAS CITY (Mo.) Nov. 9.—A petition enjoining the Federal District Attorney and "labor leaders" from putting the Adamson eight-hour bill into effect was filed in the Federal District Court of Kansas City, Kan., late today in the name of the Atchison, Topeka and Santa Fe Railway.

The bill calls attention to agreements with train employees, none of which, it says, contemplate that the employee shall work a fixed number of hours, but that, owing to the nature of train service, the trip, in terms of hours or mileage, as preferred by the men, is the basis of compensation.

The bill recites the circumstances surrounding the passage of the Adamson law and claims that it is a mere arbitrary increase in wages. The law, says the bill, is unconstitutional and void because it is not a regulation of interstate commerce, that it is a mere experiment intended as a basis for further legislation, that it deprives the company of its liberty of contract and right of property without due process of law, and that it is unworkable and uncertain.

The bill devotes considerable space to explaining why the company considers the law unworkable. It concludes with a statement that the railroad is willing to guarantee employees against loss pending final decision as to the legality of the law.

The court is asked to indicate what steps it shall take "by way of keeping special accounts, giving bond, or otherwise, for the purpose of assuring complete protection to all its employees." On the other hand, the complainant says that if preliminary and final injunction be denied and this complainant be compelled, under fear of penalties of the said act, to adopt at its own peril some construction of the act involving the payment of increased wages to considerable numbers of its employees, and if the act shall subsequently be declared to be invalid, the loss thereby sustained by this complainant can never be repaired in any way.

DELAY SAILING OF SUBMARINE.

Failure of Cargo to Arrive Changes Plans of Capt. Paul Koenig.

[BY A. P. NIGHT WIRE.]

NEW LONDON (Ct.) Nov. 9.—The German submarine Deutschland will not start her homeward trip tomorrow, as was originally planned. Tonight it was stated her departure might be delayed until next week. Failure of some of the cargo to arrive here on time is the reason assigned for the delay. Capt. Paul Koenig tonight was made an honorary member of the local lodge of the Order of Herman's Sons, 1400 members being present at the ceremony. He was presented with a gold charm and a silver loving cup.

TRUMBULL ATTACK ON ADAMSON LAW.

[BY DIRECT WIRE—EXCLUSIVE DISPATCH.]

CHICAGO BUREAU OF THE TIMES, Nov. 9.—Political attacks

(Continued on Second Page.)

THE WORLD'S NEWS — THE HEART OF IT — IN TODAY'S TIMES.

The Foremost Events of Yesterday: (1) California Elects Wilson. (2) German Submarines Break the British Blockade. (3) Mexico. (4) Suit Filed to Enjoin the Adamson Law. (5) Belgium.

INDEX.

SUMMARY.

THE SKY. Clear. Wind at 5 p.m., west; velocity 6 miles. Thermometer, highest, 81 deg., lowest, 53 deg. Forecast: Fair Friday. For complete weather report see last page of part I.

THE CITY. A threatening demonstration by job-hungry Democrats caused the Registrar of Voters to place special guards over the ballots.

It developed that the European war, in which one plaintiff was killed and another lost, has ended damage suits against the Pacific Electric.

Forgotten but not gone is the predicament of a man discovered in the County Jail, after a fifteen months' fruitless wait for trial.

A French marquis arrived to study trade conditions: he will complete a world tour in the interest of commercial development.

The Barrett "double murder" preliminary hearing opened with attorneys charging a conspiracy to ruin the defendant.

Five boys, members of prominent families, were arrested as the gang that held up and robbed a Japanese and assulted a policeman.

PACIFIC SLOPE. The State of California, it is officially admitted, has gone for Wilson.

The vote of Oregon went largely to Charles Evans Hughes.

GENERAL EASTERN. Over $10,000,000 will be distributed by the will of the late James Hobart Moore, who died in Wisconsin.

Charles Evans Hughes was in conference at the Hotel Astor with leading Republicans.

WASHINGTON. President Wilson will return to Washington on Sunday night.

Possibilities of the Democrats controlling Congress are indicated by the late returns.

MEXICO. Ten British refugees have left Chihuahua City and have arrived at Juarez.

Another battle with Villa forces is reported near Santa Rosalia.

FOREIGN. The official banquet of the Lord Mayor of London was given last night.

THE GREAT WAR. The Situation to Date: The Russians have made a further advance in the Dobrudja, recapturing a town.

The Bulgarian army is on the retreat, according to a statement from Bucharest.

Premier Asquith in a speech in London declared England does not want peace until her war sacrifices will not have been in vain.

COMMENT ON THE SITUATION.

German artillery has defeated several attempts of the French to make gains on the Somme front according to announcements from Berlin. German and Austrian forces have captured hill positions in Rumania it is declared and the invasion of Hungary by the Czar's army is proceeding. Meanwhile the Italians continue their successes on the Carso plateau, having captured a total of twenty guns of large caliber. Intermittent bombardments have been kept up, hindered somewhat by the bad weather. The British are discharging gas bombs east of Armentieres.

The exodus of ten wealthy British residents of Chihuahua city is reported and they have arrived at Juarez. The situation is believed to be serious as the relatives of several of the Mexican generals are seeking asylums on the American side.

EIGHT BILLION FRANCS ASKED BY M. RIBOT.

[BY ATLANTIC CABLE AND A. P.]

PARIS, Nov. 9, 4:30 p.m.—Alexander Ribot, Minister of Finance, today introduced in the Chamber of Deputies a bill appropriating for the first quarter of 1917 8,539,000,000 francs for general purposes, including the war, and 934,000,000 francs for supplementary appropriations. The daily expenditures of France now exceed 105,000,000 francs.

M. Ribot announced in the Chamber that the second national loan amounted to 11,500,000,000 francs, of which 55 per cent. was in French money and 45 per cent. in converted bonds. There were 3,000,000 subscribers to the loan.

HINT TO READERS: It is a mistake to jump at the wrong conclusion that all, or even the greater part, of the more important news is to be found on the first page, which cannot contain it. Consult the Index and the Summary, then read the entire paper—all the parts—and thus get all the news of the day.

Johnsonism.

VOTE OF CALIFORNIA SETTLED THE CASE.

Wilson has a Safe Lead Here, but there will be a Recount.

[BY DIRECT WIRE—EXCLUSIVE DISPATCH.]

DOUBLE-CROSSED by the treachery of the Johnson political machine, Hughes failed to carry the State of California, whose thirteen electoral votes were necessary for his election.

Late last night the Associated Press gave out the following results from 5834 of the 5870 precincts in the State:

Hughes, 462,539.
Wilson, 465,669.
Wilson plurality, 3131.

There will be a recount of these votes as the result of bitter charges of fraud. The totals may eventually be changed. But as they stand now the day has been lost.

Because of the closeness of the vote there is a distinct possibility of a split in the electoral vote of the two parties. This is predicted both by Frank Jordan, the Secretary of State, and by Chester Rowell.

Francis J. Heney has run ahead of the other electors on the Democratic ticket. A. J. Wallace, a Republican Presidential elector, was heavily scratched by the radical wets because he is a leader of the Prohibition movement. Two women electors were also scratched on many tickets. These scratches may cause a split electoral vote.

Mr. Jordan announced last night that he would invite members of both parties to witness a careful canvass of the ballots, in view of the peculiar and critical predicament.

The nine Southern California counties gave Hughes a splendid plurality of 27,403. Hughes's total vote for the counties south of the Tehachepi Pass was 198,804; Wilson's vote in the south was 171,401.

San Francisco gave Wilson a plurality of 15,109. The fact that San Francisco also gave Johnson a plurality of 72,052 shows plainly enough the story of a treachery that will go down into the annals of history along with the story of Benedict Arnold and Judas and other characters who couldn't remember which side they were on. After accepting the support and campaign money from the National Republican Committee the Johnson political machine stuck a knife into Hughes and shamelessly flouted him.

To say the least, Mr. Johnson's position and standing among the Republican Senators in Washington will be one of peculiar and painful embarrassment.

Yesterday morning Hughes seemed again to be winning the battle. As the early returns came in Hughes was tearing up the Wilson plurality like a snow plow clearing up a railway track.

Last night, however, Wilson began to gain again as the returns came in from the mountain districts in the northern part of the State.

As the figures now stand, he has over 3000 plurality with only thirty-six precincts yet to be heard from. It will be some time before some of these voting places give their returns. They are in the mountain fastnesses of the high Sierras and out in the desert. Some of them are cut off by recent snowstorms from all contact with civilization; trails drifted over and impassable; telephone wires down.

Up there in the snow they probably think their few votes do not matter much. They little realize that the whole civilized world has been waiting with bated breath to hear what marks were on the ballots they dropped last Tuesday. Ships out on the great war blockade have been anxiously tuning their wireless to hear from them. In war offices of Europe the votes of these mountain hamlets have been waited for as anxiously as the news from the trenches. For forty-eight hours these back country districts have been the center of a world's anxious attention—and they did not know it.

The number of missing precincts has now been reduced to so small a

(Continued on Fourth Page.)

The Double Cross.

JOHNSON MACHINE IS BLAMED FOR TREACHERY.

Republican Leaders Send Indignant Telegrams of Protest Demanding to Know Why Hiram Johnson did not Make Good His Promise to Deliver the Whole Progressive Vote to Hughes.

[BY DIRECT WIRE—EXCLUSIVE DISPATCH.]

SACRAMENTO, Nov. 9.—Twenty mountain counties in Northern California are in a tremor of excitement tonight over the electrifying announcement that the result of their votes in the election Tuesday may decide who shall be the next President of the United States. Special officers have been sworn in at many places to guard the ballots already delivered to the county clerks; posses of Republicans are watching these special officers, many of whom are deputy United States marshals. Posses of Democrats are watching the Republicans, who are watching the marshals, who are in turn watching the County Clerk's office in which precious ballots are stored.

Dissatisfied with the estimates sent out by the news agencies, there has been an attempt tonight to get something more definite on the votes of the mountain counties, especially those in which there are scattered precincts. Telegraphic requests went to the county seats of most of the smaller counties for official reports from the county. Reports from San Joaquin county show Hughes running ahead where attention was paid to this feature.

MANY SPLITS.

Nearly every northern county reports that there was an unprecedented amount of split tickets for Presidential electors voted. During the last two years there has been a constant agitation over nonpartisanship in California, especially among the Progressives. They objected to combination voting on the ballot; as they had no candidate of their own in California this year, thousands of them seem to have wandered aimlessly through the Republican and Democratic lists.

Two Democratic electors, Mrs. Virginia Spinks and Mrs. Mary Marshall Wiley, have apparently run not less than 1500 votes behind their tickets. If the Wilson majority on the head of the ticket is not more than 2000 the two women are pretty certain to be nosed out by the heads of the Republican list.

Republican and Democratic leaders are complaining alike about the defects in the present election laws, which make no provision for the tabulating of the votes before the official count takes place. Several discrepancies have already been detected, and in some of the counties the totals now announced are only estimates.

Most of the replies received show discrepancies in the figures already published, but the totals are not enough to affect materially the results.

MACHINE ALARMED.

A sudden interest in the result of the Presidential vote was manifested from the Governor's office late this afternoon. The members of the State machine seemed to awaken suddenly to the fact that the probable loss of the State by the Republicans was being charged in the East to Gov. Johnson and Chester Rowell. Hot telegrams were arriving asking some explanation of the difference between the vote for Gov. Johnson and that of Mr. Hughes. Johnson and Rowell had pledged themselves to swing practically the whole progressive vote to Hughes in return for generous campaign contributions from the National Committee. As Rowell was in direct charge of the Republican campaign he is charged with the loss of the State. The case of Rowell is especially aggravating because Fresno county with its big Republican registration, gave a majority of more than 2000 to Wilson and the Republican candidate for Congress was also beaten badly.

RECALLS ROSCOE CONKLING.

Veteran Republicans recall the election when the defeat of Blaine in New York was charged to Roscoe Conkling. They say that the treachery of Johnson is even more marked than that of Conkling.

The administration seemed to awaken when too late to the fact that the loss of California to Hughes was the most severe blow to its prestige that it could possibly receive. The charge is made freely here that the administration retains control of the State's finances, but that it sacrificed a Republican President in order to do so. The assertion made by the stalwarts before the primary that Rowell and Johnson sought control of the Republican party in the State for the purpose of wrecking it seems fully justified by the results of the Presidential election.

Supreme interest in the result of the vote for Presidential electors has caused reports of all other contests to be side-tracked. It is impossible still to determine who has been elected to the Assembly in at least one-third the northern districts. The only returns received from the northern counties are on the "wet" and "dry" fight and on Presidential electors.

Estimates tonight indicate that about 75 per cent. of the registered vote of the State was cast in the general election. In Sacramento county the actual vote for Hughes is not more than one-third the Republican registration. For the whole State Hughes polled about 55 per cent. of the registered Republican vote, while Wilson has polled nearly twice the total Democratic registration. This loss for Hughes and gain for Wilson is explained in part by the number of mongrel Republicans who registered as intending to affiliate with the Republican party in the November election in order that they might vote for Johnson for United States Senator on the Republican ticket. These registration figures indicate that not half the Johnson supporters who registered as Republicans voted for Hughes for President.

THE INVESTIGATION NEEDED.

THERE is much talk of investigating the vote in this State and that. The Democratic State Committee is offering a reward for the detection of any attempt at election frauds; and in other parts of the country Republicans are making similar moves. But the ONE GREAT INVESTIGATION demanded at this time—one that should be undertaken by the Republicans of the Nation as well as those of the State—is an inquiry as to what Hiram Johnson and his accomplices did to the Republican ticket in California. Who passed the word "Johnson and Wilson" down the line of Johnson's adherents? How was the betrayal of Hughes in California brought about? How did it happen that Hiram Johnson received a majority of 200,000 for United States Senator while Hughes lost the State? What is needed is a sort of coroner's inquest to ascertain the facts and circumstances of the murder of the Republican party of California in the house of its own campaign committee by those who professed to be its leaders. A political crime unparalleled has been perpetrated in California—a crime against the Republicans of the Nation. Let not the guilty go unpunished!

Comment.

"CALIFORNIA DID IT," CHICAGO "TRIBUNE" SAYS

Declares We are "Champion Boob State" of American Republic, Demanding Right to Make Trouble Which may Bring Us a Japanese Governor Some Day—Insists We Have Voted Against Own Interests.

[BY DIRECT WIRE—EXCLUSIVE DISPATCH.]

CHICAGO BUREAU OF THE TIMES, Nov. 9. — Under the caption, "Nobody at Home in California," the Chicago Tribune in the morning will say editorially:

"California is the State which every now and then causes the rest of the nation to wonder how the trouble it makes can be safely handled. California hates the Japanese. It offends and insults the Japanese. It pays no attention to the treaty obligations of the United States.

"Several times California in a stubborn and belligerent mood has almost put the alternative of war or humiliation up to the rest of the nation. Some day, when Japan is ready, a California offense will result in the seizure of the Philippines and Hawaii. California makes the trouble and expects the rest of the country to protect it. It may make a war and drag the rest of the country into it. California is our junker State in all except willingness to strengthen the ability of the Federal government to meet the trouble it may make and is perfectly willing to make.

"California ought to have given the Republican ticket a great majority. A State which demands the privilege of making trouble ought to be willing to meet it. It ought to be willing to take ordinary precautions against consequences.

"California now seems to be concerned chiefly for the right to bluster. The moral condition of some little rotten spot in the interior of the United States can be understood. But California presents a long coast line which it demands that the United States defend. It wants a Pacific navy. It seems to have voted for a pacific navy.

"How a State which, when it is not scared to death itself, is scaring the rest of the nation to death could have given even two votes in a precinct to the administration, which maintains Josephus Daniels as schoolmaster of the American navy, is a question beyond normal intelligence.

"By giving President Wilson the vote it did, California, with its record and Wilson's record, presented itself as the champion boob State of the American Republic.

"The only thing needed for the perfection of the irony, was that the workers who want Japs excluded, in order that American standards of comfort shall not be lowered, should have tried to deliver the State to the administration, which has tried to break down national courage.

"California, which wants everything for itself, is inclined in the direction of an administration, which blindly says that America demands nothing for itself that it does not demand for the rest of humanity. What a sweet vaporing of magnanimity for California to snuff up eagerly—California, which wants nothing more for itself than it wants for the Japanese!

"The State, which has put the nation on the edge of war several times, kept it in suspense for forty-eight hours in this election, when the issue was one which should have been decided in this outpost State in two hours.

"Some day California may have a Japanese Governor—for a while. The rest of the nation eventually will annul his commission, but he may be there for a while.

"If California gets its Japanese Governor, there may be men in California who will recall that in a time of national emergency they voted for the candidate of the party which wishes to be just as sweet to the rest of humanity as it is to California.

"One of Kipling's characters, a chaplain with a burr under his tongue, quoted:

"'Quem Deus vult perdere, prius dementat.'

"Translated, means: 'When people insist upon getting it in the neck they are first made dead from the neck up.'"

Feat.

GERMAN SUBMARINES BREAK THE BLOCKADE.

Several Teuton Undersea Boats Slip Through Lines During Recent Raid and are Believed to Have been Active During the Past Week, Sinking Ships in the English Channel.

BY ARTHUR S. DRAPER.

[BY ATLANTIC CABLE AND DIRECT WIRE—EXCLUSIVE DISPATCH.]

LONDON, Nov. 10.—German submarines have been operating extensively in the English Channel and off the southern coast of France. They broke through the British blockade and ring of defenses under cover of the recent raid by German warships.

This information came today from reliable sources. The raid carried out by enemy warships in the shipping route between the Thames and Holland on November 1, this report says, was a blind to get half a dozen or more U-boats through the channel. That it succeeded is evidenced by the unusual activity of submarines in these waters during the last few days. Their roll of victims this week has been exceptionally high.

The British naval authorities have learned of this fact and are making strenuous efforts to trap some of the raiders, it is said. The channel patrol has been augmented and a watch is being kept night and day for any sign of the submarines reported to be operating off the coast. The few critics who share knowledge of the presence of the enemy submersibles express the opinion that by now most of them must have escaped and returned to their bases. The continued sinking of vessels in this region, however, suggests that a few raiders are still operating in the channel or slightly to the north.

VIOLATION OF NEUTRALITY.

[BY WIRELESS AND A. P.]

BERLIN, Nov. 9 (via Sayville.)—Reports from Christiania say that a Russian torpedo boat destroyer shelled a German submarine on November 2 while the Russian vessel was between two and a half and three miles from the Norwegian town of Homoen, near Vardoe, and while the submarine was from three to four miles distant from the Norwegian coast. The Norwegian government, according to the dispatch which was received by the Overseas News Agency, has instructed the Norwegian Minister at Petrograd to protest against this new alleged violation of neutrality.

THREE STEAMERS SUNK.

[BY ATLANTIC CABLE AND A. P.]

LONDON, Nov. 9.—Lloyd's announces that the British steamers Sheldrake, Skerries and Sunnyside have been sunk.

The Sheldrake was a vessel of 2697 tons and was owned in London. The Skerries, a vessel of 4278 tons, was last reported as having sailed from Antofagasta, Chile, August 29, and having touched at Newport News September 18 on a voyage to Barrow in England. Available shipping registers do not contain the steamer Sunnyside, but there is a steamer of 447 tons named Sunnieside mentioned. Her home port is Sunderland.

Of the 437 passengers on the Peninsular and Oriental line steamship Arabia, which was sunk in the Mediterranean by a submarine Monday, 198 have been landed at Malta and eighty-four at Port Said.

The steamship Suffolk Coast of Liverpool, 780 tons gross, has been sunk. The crew was landed.

MADAWASCA IS ASHORE.

[BY PACIFIC CABLE AND A. P.]

SANTIAGO (Chile) Nov. 9.—The British steamship Madawasca is ashore at Corral Bay.

The Madawasca, 4210 tons gross, is owned in London. She sailed from Calcutta September 4 for Peru, touching at Newcastle, New South Wales, on October 5.

Flash.

TUMULTY INFORMS PRESIDENT OF NEWS.

White House Secretary Sends Wireless to Executive on the Result.

[BY A. P. NIGHT WIRE.]

NEW YORK, Nov. 9.—President Wilson carried California and has been re-elected.

Fifty hours after the polls closed in California Republican Chairman Rowell conceded the State to the President. Thus the thirteen votes needed to assure the President a majority in the Electoral College dropped into the Democratic column and apparently ended the suspense and anxiety of an election which has been unparalleled in American political history.

Republican Chairman Willcox, when informed that the President carried California, only replied: "I have nothing to say."

TUMULTY NOTIFIES WILSON.

Secretary Tumulty at the summer White House at Shadow Lawn, sent the news by wireless to President Wilson on board the yacht Mayflower en route to Rhine Cliff, N. Y.

The California returns showed that, with only forty-eight districts missing, the President's plurality in the State was 2970.

Barring some wholly unexpected turnover in the incomplete States leaning toward Wilson, or a change on a recount, California's acquisition to the Democratic column gave the President 269 electoral votes without New Mexico's three. In New Mexico at midnight the President was leading by 2639 votes, with 158 districts missing, and it was not believed this advantage could be overcome by Mr. Hughes.

CONCESSIONS.

Conceding West Virginia, New Hampshire and Minnesota to Mr. Hughes—and he was in the lead in all three—only gives him 259 votes, seven less than the required majority. With 272 votes in sight, President Wilson had six to spare for a possible split of electors in California or a sudden reversal in New Mexico.

At Republican national headquarters it was admitted that, after conferences between George W. Wickersham, former Attorney-General of the United States; Everett Colby of New Jersey; Mr. Hughes, Chairman Willcox and George W. Perkins of Baltimore, preparations were being made to begin legal proceedings for recounts in States where the results were close. Chairman Willcox included California, New Mexico, North Dakota, New Hampshire and Minnesota in his list of States where recounts undoubtedly would be demanded.

Democratic headquarters was not behind the Republicans in preparing for legal developments.

Chairman McCormick conferred with Alton B. Parker, former Democratic candidate for President; Morgan J. O'Brien, Delancey Nicoll and John B. Stanchfield, all prominent New York lawyers. It was evident that if the election was to be taken into the courts the legal giants of both parties were being marshaled for such a battle royal as the United States never has seen.

"Any contest," declared a statement issued by Democratic headquarters, "is an insult to the intelligence of the American people."

It probably will still be another day before the full results are known from any of the four States left in the doubtful column, and certainly not until there has been an official count in New Hampshire and possibly in Minnesota. As Mr. Hughes is leading in Minnesota and West Virginia, and a change in these States could in no wise affect the result, there may be no demand for extraordinary haste to bring about the recount demanded.

Virtually all the States where the result is close are carried in the Hughes column and for that reason the Democrats profess to be not apprehensive that any overturning could come from a recount.

TUMULTY HAPPY.

[BY A. P. NIGHT WIRE.]

ASBURY PARK (N. J.) Nov. 9, 11:30 p.m.—Secretary Tumulty wired formal notification to the President of his re-election. The message was wirelessed to the President aboard the Mayflower. It was as follows:

"I am here surrounded by the loyal Democrats of Old Monmouth, and beg leave to send you our greeting and congratulations. The cause you have so nobly represented has at last triumphed and we greet you. Our hearts, our thoughts, and our affections go to you."

Secretary Tumulty waited for the flash from the Associated Press that President Wilson had carried California. When it came a shout of joy went up inside the executive offices, and Secretary Tumulty, who had told the President he would not congratulate him until the definite news was known, sent a wireless message to the Mayflower giving his congratulations.

Representatives.

HOUSE CONTROL IN DOUBT; DEMOCRATS CLAIM IT

[BY A. P. NIGHT WIRE.]

NEW YORK, Nov. 9. — The Democrats, assured of control of the next Senate, may retain control of the House by holding ten seats in twenty-one Congress Districts yet to be heard from. Early today the division of members already elected was as follows: Democrats, 210; Republicans, 200; Progressives, 2; Independent, 1; Socialist, 1.

In the twenty-one districts not yet reported are the following, which are Democratic in the present Congress:

Two each in Missouri and Indiana; three in West Virginia, and one each in Washington, Michigan and Pennsylvania. Eleven of the missing districts are Republican, as follows:

Two in Nebraska; three in West Virginia; three in Washington, and one each in New Mexico, Ohio and Wyoming.

If these districts should hold to their present political status in the returns yet to come, the Democrats would have the slender majority of five in the next House.

ALEXANDER'S LEAD CONCEDED IN IDAHO.

[BY A. P. NIGHT WIRE.]

BOISE (Idaho) Nov. 9.—Gov. Moses Alexander (Dem.,) who has a lead of 830, is conceded re-election by Republican managers in Idaho, although the complete count from numerous precincts is still missing. Alexander polled 60,840, and his opponent, D. W. Davis, received 60,010 votes.

President Wilson carried the State by about 15,000 votes, and all State offices, except those of Treasurer, Superintendent of Instruction and State Mine Inspector, fell to the Democrats, who also will control both houses of the next Legislature. The constitutional amendment favoring prohibition was carried by a large vote.

Later Dispatches

With fresh news marked "30"

Presidential.

NEWS OF THE ELECTION RECEIVED AT VERDUN.

[BY ATLANTIC CABLE AND A. P.] (30)

FORT VAUX ON THE VERDUN FRONT, Nov. 8 (via Paris.)—News of the Presidential election in the United States was communicated by wireless telegraph to the correspondent of the Associated Press in Fort Vaux today, and created intense interest amid the activities of defense preparations and under a very sever German bombardment.

The correspondent reached the fort, which is the most advanced fortified point of the French lines at Verdun, around the walls of which shells were then falling and thickly increased throughout the day. Within the garrison the French were engaged in restoring the fort to its original condition and strength.

Evidence was discovered in the shape of a programme drafted by the German commander, Von Engel Brechten, dated October 21, for strengthening the position so as to permit Germans to prepare for a further attack on Verdun. Th[illegible] comprised the erection of barricades in the interior in o[illegible] mit of its defense in sections, also the constructio[illegible] and galleries, the erection of barbed wire entan[illegible] excavations of a tunnel, forty feet of which [illegible]

DESTINY

The Los Angeles Times

"Sail on, sail on, and on, and on."
1781 1917

In Three Parts — 22 Pages.
PART I—TELEGRAPH SHEET—12 PAGES

FRIDAY MORNING, APRIL 6, 1917.

Liberty Under Law — Equal Rights — True Industrial Freedom
PRICE 2½ CENTS { Delivered to Subscribers { At All Hotels and on Railway Trains, 5c. On Streets and News Stands, 2 Cents.

WAR WITH THE GERMAN EMPIRE IS ON IN EARNEST.

Austria-Hungary Expected to Offer Peace Proposal to the President.

Opportunity.

NO PART AS MEDIATOR NOW OPEN TO WILSON.

Executive, However, may Play Important Role in Terminating War.

BY JOHN CALLAN O'LAUGHLIN.
[BY DIRECT WIRE—EXCLUSIVE DISPATCH.]

WASHINGTON BUREAU OF THE TIMES, April 5.—On high authority it may be said that Austria-Hungary, through her Embassy in Washington, is about to present a peace proposal to President Wilson.

The proposal contemplates the opening of negotiations with all the belligerents with a view to securing a "durable peace."

It is suggested in connection with the proposal that the President should play a prominent part in bringing the warring nations to the council table. There is no intention that he shall act as mediator—the United States now is regarded as an enemy by Germany and as having precisely the same status as Great Britain, France, Italy, Russia and Japan.

No offers as a basis of peace are said to be contained in the proposal.

Germany does not appear as one of the responsible principals in urging peace. She is, according to the statement of the President, in a state of war with this country and formal proclamation to this effect will be made tomorrow.

Therefore, Germany has used her ally to sound out the United States.

NO GUARANTEES.

As the proposal contains no guarantees, according to the information in the possession of the authorities here, it is not likely to be accepted by the President or appeal to the governments at London, Paris, Rome, Petrograd and Tokio.

The object of the proposal is believed to be that which has been apprehended for some time—division in American counsels. In spite of the fact that the United States is at war with Germany, the Teutonic governments are hopeful of moving in such fashion as to make ineffective American aid to the Allies. By constantly harping on peace, they hope to encourage the pacifists and thereby prevent the dispatch of troops to Europe and make half-hearted

(Continued on Sixth Page.)

THE WORLD'S NEWS — THE HEART OF IT — IN TODAY'S TIMES.

Covering the Globe.

The Foremost Events of Yesterday: (1) Congress. (2) Mexico. (3) The Battle at Rheims. (4) The Peace Movement. (5) The California Legislature. (6) Mobilization.

INDEX.

SUMMARY.

THE SKY. Clear. Wind at 5 p.m., southwest; velocity 12 miles. Thermometer, highest, 84 deg.; lowest, 60 deg. Forecast: Fair Friday. For complete weather report see last page of Part I.

THE CITY. Because of revelations purporting to show the Welland Canal conspiracy was hatched here, it was declared two Los Angeles Germans and a woman may be indicted in New York.

It developed that if battle comes anywhere on this continent as a result of Germany's war against the United States, hundreds of local women will be ready to pilot motor cars for the government.

Clarence A. Tolle, a law student, was convicted of manslaughter as a result of having driven an auto into a crowd, killing two persons.

Prominent business and professional men launched a movement to establish a Morris Plan bank here.

Through a court decision the city gained forty-five acres of valuable land, the key for the entrance of another railroad.

Arresting two alleged wholesale auto thieves, officers declare a woman's scout work had built up a big business in larceny.

SOUTHERN CALIFORNIA. Pasadena holds its city election and selects Commissioners and Freeholders.

San Diego reports more women enlisting for the navy than men, and a special plea is sent out for an increase in the applicants for sea warfare.

Whale canning season closes and Capt. Look proposes to go north to hunt for the mammals of the sea.

PACIFIC SLOPE. Lassen Peak is reported in violent eruption.

Legislature considers budget system for State finances.

Tie-up of San Francisco Bay ferry service threatened by hour demands of masters, mates and engineers.

GENERAL EASTERN. An emissary from Russia declared the great need of his country after the war will be foreign capital.

Thomas A. Edison is said to be working on a new war device.

WASHINGTON. Three and a half billion dollars will be raised by the United States to finance the war for the first year.

The most tremendous resources the world has ever seen will be thrown into the scale with the entry of the United States.

MEXICO. Mexicans are said to be approaching the borders of the United States.

German officers are said to be drilling Obregon's army.

FOREIGN. The American legion undergoing training in England are said to be delighted at the prospect of the United States entering the war.

THE GREAT WAR. The Situation to Date: Russians recapture positions in sharp fighting in Northern Galicia.

The Russians in a momentous operation, driving from Persia, have captured the Mesopotamian frontier towns.

The Turks are making a stand against the Slavs to prevent them from crossing the Diala River.

COMMENT ON THE SITUATION.

The Germans and French have met in a sanguinary engagement northwest of Rheims, where the Germans with a picked force attacked on a front of about a mile and a half between Sapigneul and the Godat farm. The exact result of the battle is beclouded by conflicting reports. Paris admits the Germans occupied portions of the French first-line trenches, but says the attack failed completely over the greater part of the front; that the French troops reoccupied almost immediately the captured positions and that counter-attacks for the recapture of elements still held by the Germans are in progress. Berlin says the Germans inflicted a sanguinary reverse on Gen. Nivelle's troops in this region, and that 800 men were made prisoner. On the battle front in the region of St. Quentin there have been only artillery duels between the French and German forces. On their part of the line the British have captured the villages of Basse-Boulogne and Ronssoy, northeast of Peronne. Here the Germans suffered heavy casualties by being caught in their own entanglements, and raked by the fire of the British machine guns. Additional gains for the British east and northeast of Metz-en-Couture also are chronicled by the British War Office.

Ominous reports from Mexico that Mexican troops are moving toward the American frontier have been received. It is also stated that German officers have been drilling troops under Obregon, which are said to have designs to overthrow Carranza.

HINT TO READERS: It is a mistake to jump at the wrong conclusion that all, or even the greater part, of the more important news is to be found on the first page, which cannot contain it. Consult the Index and the Summary, then read the entire paper—all the parts—and thus get all the news of the day.

When Congress Acts.

Hostilities!

RESOLUTION ADOPTED BY THE LOWER HOUSE.

Both Branches of Congress Have Now Declared for State of War.

[BY A. P. NIGHT WIRE.]

WASHINGTON, April 6.—The resolution declaring that a state of war exists between the United States and Germany, already passed by the Senate, passed the House shortly after 3 o'clock this morning by a vote of 373 to 50.

President Wilson will sign the resolution as soon as Vice-President Marshall has attached his signature in the Senate. It formally accepts the state of belligerency forced by German aggressions and authorizes and directs the President to employ the military and naval forces and all the resources of the nation to bring war against Germany to a successful termination.

Without roll calls the House rejected all amendments, including proposals to prohibit the sending of any troops overseas without Congressional authority.

Passage of the resolution followed seventeen hours of debate. There was no attempt to filibuster, but the pacifist group under the leadership of Democratic Leader Kitchin prolonged the discussion with impassioned speeches. Kitchin declared his conscience would not permit him to support the President's recommendation that a state of war be declared.

Miss Rankin of Montana, the only woman member of Congress, sat through the first roll call with bowed head, failing to answer to her name, twice called by the clerk.

On the second roll call Miss Rankin rose and said in a sobbing voice, "I want to stand by my country, but I cannot vote for war."

For a moment then she remained standing, supporting herself against a desk and as cries of "Vote, vote," came from several parts of the House, she sank back into her seat without voting audibly. She was recorded in the negative.

The fifty who voted against the resolution were:

Almond, Bacon, Britten, Browne, Burnett, Carey, Church, Connolly of Kansas; Cooper of Wisconsin; Davidson, Davis, Decker, Dill, Dillon, Dominick, Esch, Frear, Fuller of Illinois; Haugen, Hayes, Hensley, Hilliard, Hull of Iowa; Igoe, Johnson of South Dakota; Keating, King, Kinkaid, Kitchin, Knutson, La Follette, Little, London, Lundsen, McLemore, Mason, Nelson Randall, Rankin, Reavis, Roberts, Rodenburg, Shackleford, Sherwood, Sloan, Stafford, Van Dyke, Voigt, Wheeler and Woods of Iowa.

Cheers greeted the announcement of the result. A few minutes later Speaker Clark signed the resolution and the House then adjourned to meet again Monday and take up the administration's recommendations for war legislation.

WASHINGTON, April 5.—The House debated the war resolution all of today and far into the night, and although passage was assured before adjournment, the leaders predicted that a vote could not be reached until early morning.

For the most part the discussion proceeded with an air of unemotional acquiescence, scores of members making brief speeches to put themselves on record as reluctantly accepting war as the only course of honor.

During the day the debate revealed an unexpected strength in the minority opposing the resolution. Confident predictions of not more than a dozen votes against it gave place tonight to reports that the opposition might muster upwards of a hundred on the final roll call and supporters of the resolution conceded that the number to vote in the negative probably would be more than fifty.

EFFORTS OF KITCHIN.

This surprising accession to the minority ranks was attributed to the efforts of Democratic Leader Kitchin, who took the floor and in a dramatic speech announced that he could not with a clear conscience vote for war. Supporters of the President's course were not concerned over the defection, however. Sure of a great majority, they permitted the roll call to be delayed only so that everyone might be heard.

Shortly before midnight, after the debate had continued for more than thirteen hours, those in charge of the resolution predicted that a vote would be taken soon after 1 o'clock. There was no certainty that it might not be hours later, however. Mr. Kitchin's opposition drew an immediate following from among the group who have opposed preparedness.

Late in the night Representative Britten presented an amendment designed to prohibit the use of troops in Europe, Asia or Africa, without the approval of Congress, except troops volunteering for such service.

DRAWS FOLLOWING.

Mr. Kitchin's opposition drew an immediate following from among the group who have opposed preparedness and armed neutrality and tonight many of them who had sat silent and glum in the rear of the chamber throughout the day moved down in front and spoke against the resolution. One of the most earnest speeches in behalf of the President's course came from Republican Leader Mann, who declared Germany had deliberately affronted this country and that only war could save the national honor.

Administration leaders until today had paid little attention to reports that Representative Kitchin would oppose the reso-

(Continued on Second Page.)

POSTERS DENOUNCE ARMY CONSCRIPTION.

[BY A. P. NIGHT WIRE.]

QUEBEC (Que.) April 5.—Posters denouncing conscription in Canada, printed in English and French, were posted during the night on shop windows, fences and other conspicuous places throughout the city.

SENATORS HANGED IN EFFIGY.

[BY A. P. NIGHT WIRE.]

SAN ANSELMO (Cal.) April 5.—The six United States Senators who voted yesterday against the war resolution were hanged in effigy here tonight by former residents of Missouri, Wisconsin and Oregon. After being pronounced dead, the dummies were cut down and burned while the crowd sang "America."

RED CROSS WAREHOUSES.

[BY A. P. NIGHT WIRE.]

WASHINGTON, April 5.—Establishment of six enormous warehouses for use by the Red Cross mobilization centers for supplies being collected by that organization were announced today. They will be at Boston, New York, Chicago, Denver, San Francisco and New Orleans and will be made headquarters for their respective divisions.

BEHAVE, BE SAFE, FOREIGNERS TOLD.

[BY A. P. DAY WIRE.]

WASHINGTON, April 5.—Official announcement was made today that foreigners in the United States who conduct themselves properly will suffer no loss of property or liberty as a result of a declaration of a state of war.

In Two Parts—20 Pages
PART I—TELEGRAPH SHEET—12 PAGES.

The Los Angeles Times

"Sail on, sail on, and on, and on."

WEDNESDAY MORNING, VOL. XXXVII. JUNE 5, 1918.

Liberty Under Law—Equal Rights—True Industrial Freedom

AMERICANS BRILLIANTLY HALT HUN RUSH ON PARIS.

Eleven Atlantic Vessels Toll of Raider U-Boats.

Subsea Prey.

FOE'S SUBMARINES STILL OPERATING NEAR COAST.

American Destroyer Stops Attack on a French Ship; Naval Squadron Searching Atlantic Ocean.

[BY A. P. NIGHT WIRE.]

WASHINGTON, June 4.—The official list of vessels sunk by the U-boats as given out tonight by the Navy Department included seven schooners and four steamers. The statement follows:

"The latest reports received by the Navy Department indicate that the following vessels have been sunk as a result of enemy submarine activity off this coast:

"Schooner Edna, 325 tons.

"Schooner Hattie Dunn, 436 tons.

"Schooner Hauppauge, 1500 tons.

"Schooner Edward H. Cole, 1791 tons.

"Schooner Isabel B. Wiley, 776 tons.

"Schooner Jacob M. Haskell, 1778 tons.

"Steamship Winneconne, 1869 tons.

"Steamer Carolina, 5093 tons.

"Schooner Edward R. Baird, Jr., 279 tons.

"Steamship Herbert L. Pratt, 7200 tons; raised and towed to port.

"Steamship Texel."

Enemy submarines still were operating off the American coast today. A French tank steamer, the Radioleine, first trans-Atlantic craft to be attacked by the raiders, was rescued from destruction at 9:30 o'clock this morning by an American destroyer, sixty-five miles off the mainland coast.

The same destroyer found the coasting schooner Edward R. Baird, Jr., sinking after having been bombed in the same vicinity, making seven schooners and four steamers known officially to have been sunk by the raiders.

Announcement by the Navy Department of these facts late tonight disclosed that the raid in American waters had not ended with yesterday's tale of destruction, upsetting the theory that the raiders probably were speeding homeward. Coast patrol vessels had not acted on the theory. They now are closing in from all directions on the scene of the raider's last exploit, scouring the sea for further trace of enemy U-boats as they come.

Secretary Daniels directed tonight that brief report from the destroyer be made public. The destroyer herself, with two survivors from the Baird, a 279-ton craft hailing from Wilmington, Del., was still hunting for the enemy.

The announcement, which, naval officers said, contained all the department knew about today's activities of the raiders, follows:

"The Navy Department has received a dispatch from a United States destroyer that at 9:30 o'clock this morning she interrupted an attack by an enemy submarine on the French steamer Radioleine, about sixty-five miles off the Maryland coast. The destroyer also took on board two men from the Edward Baird, Jr., which was bombed and sinking.

"A later report was received stating that the Radioleine had arrived at an Atlantic port."

Reports from survivors who were aboard the vessels also established the fact during the day that at least two submarines have been at work in American waters. They are the U-37 and the U-151, and a report to the Navy Department shows that one of them, at least, had stores to last her three months.

Members of Congress who conferred with Secretary Daniels today were convinced that everything possible was being done that could be done without lessening American efforts to crush the enemy in France.

NO MILITARY DAMAGE DONE.

Secretary Daniels believes that the main purpose of the raid is to create a demand upon the part of the American people for the return of American craft that are fighting submarines abroad. If so, the German effort to crush United States participation in the war has again met with flat failure. The troops have gone forward without delay. The raiders have created panic among coastwise shipping, but they have done no military damage whatever.

The picking up of a floating mine off the New Jersey shore was announced today by the Navy Department. Undoubtedly it was dropped by one of the enemy U-boats. Possibly the raider was closely pursued and thought to lay a trap for her pursuer.

THE DAY'S NEWS SUMMED UP.

THE SKY. Partly cloudy. Wind at 5 p.m., southwest; velocity, eight miles. Thermometer, highest, 71 deg.; lowest, 65 deg. Forecast: Wednesday fair, moderate westerly winds. For complete weather data see last page of this section.

THE CITY. Local exemption boards prepared to register all young men who have become 21 years old since June 5, 1917, today.

The Santa Monica Vigilance Corps adopted a resolution pledging its members not to buy the Los Angeles Examiner. The Riverside City Council urged the public library there to bar disloyal newspapers.

The Shipping Board ordered an immediate investigation of the government navigation school here, following complaints of students. Capt. Deering denied the charges.

A Los Angeles woman announced her plan to charge admission to her wedding and donate the proceeds to the Red Cross.

The Watts City Council closed the "Country Club" after citizens testified to having secured strong drinks there.

The District Attorney was asked to investigate unusual facts in connection with a visitor's death here.

Well-known psychiatrist announced that a colony to treat morons will be located in Southern California.

The campaign for War Savings Stamps, which will be opened next week, was outlined at a meeting of 800 women workers.

Two more units of the Woman's Land Army will be sent out tomorrow, the leader of the movement here announced.

The acting superintendent of a Long Beach shipyard was arrested on a charge of making pro-German remarks.

Two plans for electing City Council in future, will be placed on the ballot at the next election, it was indicated.

Superintendent of Schools Shiels announced that the summer sessions will start on July 1.

SOUTHERN CALIFORNIA. One Hundred and Forty-fifth (First Utah) Field Artillery, arrives for five-day stay at Santa Ana.

Five hundred entries have been recorded for the Better Baby Conference to be held at Pasadena.

Fearing flood damage to lands Duarte citizens seek to curb operations of gravel company on San Gabriel River.

PACIFIC SLOPE. War session in reality is held by Arizona Legislature; Senator Sutter doesn't like Gov. Hunt, and says so; bill to pay Campbell for services as Governor fails to pass.

Two Angeleno educators join faculty of Stanford University for summer course which is to continue twelve weeks.

Union Iron Works at Alameda plans to begin work at once on ten new shipbuilding berths at its plant.

President of Guatemala sends 10,000 francs as donation to Red Cross following work of organization during earthquake at his capital.

WASHINGTON. Navy Department Department reports toll of submarine raiders in American waters is eleven boats; four of them steamers and the others small sailing craft; tonnage loss is light.

Washington learns raiding submarines received daily messages by wireless while near the coast; search for wireless on mainland is under way.

GENERAL EASTERN. New York shipping circles report fifty-eight persons missing from liner Carolina, sunk by submarine; no other casualties; sixteen die when lifeboat turns over.

Battle reports from France encourage Wall-street traders; material gains are registered by entire list; shipping issues share in advance of prices.

Survivors from U-boat raid landed at Atlantic City are cared for by bathers, among whom small boat pulls to shore; women wear overalls of sailors.

FOREIGN. Refugees from Aisne and Marne districts in France are crowding into Paris; American Red Cross feeds and cares for several thousand daily.

Harry Williams describes furious struggle raging along Marne; Americans like football players on side lines, eager to enter the game.

Allies' aerial raids over German cities causing panics; Cologne suffers heavily, deaths number 146 and injured more than 150.

THE GREAT WAR. The German advance has been stopped at every point. Where local gains were made yesterday by the Germans the Allies more than offset by retaking several important positions.

American troops have covered themselves with glory by their action in the past several days. Gen. Pershing reports that American troops, rushed in lorries to Chateau Thierry, manned their machine guns and organized their positions within an hour and cleared the Germans from the line. After stopping the onward rush of the Huns the Americans counter-attacked and drove the foe farther backward.

PRICE 2½ CENTS { Delivered to Subscribers. { At Hotels and on Railway Trains, 5c. On Streets and News Stands, 2 cents.

RECORD TOTAL OF NEW SHIPS.

America and England Give Kaiser's Raiders Food for Thought.

[BY A. P. NIGHT WIRE.]

WASHINGTON, June 4.—On the heels of the German submarine raid in the North Atlantic, the Shipping Board announced tonight that production of new vessels in May was the greatest of any month in the history of the nation.

There were completed and delivered to the Shipping Board forty-four ships, totaling 263,571 tons, three times the output of January and twice that of February.

Production for the first five months of the year is well along toward 1,000,000 tons, which officials expect to be passed this month. Production in the United Kingdom to May 1 was a total of 659,420 tons. The British output for May has not yet been received here.

ON WEST FRONT.

SUMMARY OF SITUATION.

From drives on wide fronts the German offensive in France has deteriorated into isolated attacks along the area between Soissons and Chateau Thierry and eastward on the Marne in the general direction of Rheims.

Although in these attacks the enemy still is using large effectives and great numbers of guns, he is being held almost everywhere from further progress and on various sectors compelled to assume the defensive against vicious blows delivered by the American, French and British troops.

WHERE YANKEES HELPED.

The Americans on the sectors where they are alone or brigaded with Allied troops everywhere are fighting with a spirit of abandon that places them rightly in the category of veterans. Near the Neuilly Wood, which lies northwest of Chateau Thierry and at the point where the drive has brought the enemy nearest Paris, the Americans have beaten off a strong German attack, and on the Marne at Jaulgonne, some six miles northeast of Chateau Thierry, fighting shoulder to shoulder with the French, they have aided in forcing the first contingent of the enemy to cross the Marne again to seek refuge on the northern bank of the stream. In this last engagement the Germans suffered severe casualties and also left 100 prisoners in the hands of the defenders of the line.

SOME FOE GAINS.

Between the Aisne and Ourcq rivers the Germans have captured Pernant, and to the south of that village the French have ceded a little terrain. In the Ourcq Valley they also took the town of Neuilly-la-Poterie, seven and one-half miles northwest of Chateau Thierry, in fighting during which the place changed hands several times. In the region between the Oise and the Aisne the Germans have been unable to advance anywhere. The losses of the Germans near Pernant were extremely heavy, owing to the stubborn defense of the French.

There is only moderate activity along the line held by the British in Flanders and Picardy, where patrol activity and bombing continue. On the Amiens front the Germans are heavily bombarding British positions.

KILL FOE, NOT GET PARIS, GERMAN AIM.

TEUTON WRITERS ARE TELLING READERS TAKING CAPITAL SECONDARY MATTER.

By George F. Stewart.

[ATLANTIC CABLE—EXCLUSIVE DISPATCH.]

ROTTERDAM, June. 4.—German military critics are urging the public not to think in terms of Paris and the other places to which their greedy eyes turned.

"The sole object of all the German movements," writes Capt. Salzemann in the Vossische Zeitung, "is the destruction of the enemy's armies. It is not to be denied," he continued, "that the possession of Paris would be of great importance, but the object of the present operations is not Paris, though it can easily become the objective.

"At the present moment the objective is beating the armies of the enemy. Where they are beaten is a matter of indifference. The attack on the Lys was a daring experiment, as was the attack on the Chemin des Dames. At the same time they were examples of the highest wisdom, of which only great army commanders are capable."

Rotterdam's Monday Kolnische Zeitung records the death of Gen. Von Buchana, commanding the German Twenty-eighth Infantry Division. He was hit by a shell splinter while standing on the banks of the Marne, which his division was the first to reach.

Freemen.

EAGER TO JOIN FRAY.

Pershing's Men at Battle Field.

American Troops Tense, Anxiously Awaiting Word to Enter Arena.

Outnumbered French Fight Like Lions to Hold Back Hun Divisions.

BY HARRY A. WILLIAMS.

[The Times Own War Correspondent in France.]

[SPECIAL CABLE.]

WESTERN FRONT IN FRANCE, June 3.—The eighth day of the furious struggle now raging beyond the Marne marks the longest sustained combat ever fought.

The battle fury is undiminished. Billows of gray break unceasingly upon the thin blue line.

The French are outnumbered six to one, but, fighting like lions, one French soldier is equal to several Huns.

The German legions seem limitless and the fighting has resolved into the sole question of whether the Allies can kill off Huns as fast as they come.

Foch must keep back his reserves until the German plans are fully revealed. Other Hun hordes may strike elsewhere at any time, and this counts against the Allies moving their forces at will.

The American troops, eager to take the plunge into the arena, gather here on the side lines, tense as football players waiting for the signal to charge.

PATHETIC SCENES.

Pathetic scenes are met everywhere. War refugees fill the roads leading southward from the battlefield. Some of them lost their homes once before when, in 1914, the Hun swept over the same district. Many of these now wear a look of hopeless despair.

One little girl, hungry and tired, trudged down the road with a big, yellow rooster clasped to her bosom. That was her family, all that was left of father, mother and loved ones of home. Both father and mother were killed by the Germans and her home wrecked.

Beware of the German propaganda that ruined Russia, threatened Italy and persists in England. The propaganda preceded the present drive. It's part of the war offensive. Stamp out propagandists as you would vipers. Over here they showed what to do in the Bolo Pasha case.

It is criminal to tolerate traitors in any country when the mothers are giving their first-born to prevent fulfillment of what the propagandist is striving to bring about.

IRISH GIVEN A CHANCE TO SHOW PATRIOTISM.

LORD LIEUTENANT CALLS FOR FIFTY THOUSAND VOLUNTEERS.

[BY ATLANTIC CABLE AND A. P.]

DUBLIN, Monday, June 3.—The proclamation issued tonight by the Lord Lieutenant, asking for 50,000 voluntary recruits and therafter 2000 to 3000 monthly to maintain Irish divisions, was issued as an opportunity for Ireland to avoid the application of the conscription law passed by Parliament. The text of the proclamation follows:

"In pursuance to our promise, we now make our offer which, if successful, will insure that Ireland will play her part fully and freely in the world struggle for liberty. The offer is that Ireland voluntarily furnish the number of men required to establish her equitable ratio compared with other parts of the empire.

"In order to establish that ratio, Ireland can be fairly asked to raise 50,000 recruits before October 1 to replenish Irish divisions in the field, and thereafter raise from 2000 to 3000 recruits per month to maintain those divisions."

EX-VICE-PRESIDENT FAIRBANKS PASSES.

[BY A. P. NIGHT WIRE.]

INDIANAPOLIS (Ind.) June 4.—Charles Warren Fairbanks, former Vice-President of the United States and former United States Senator from Indiana, died at his home here at 8:55 o'clock tonight.

Death was due to interstitial nephritis, which has been a chronic ailment with him, but not regarded as particularly serious until recently.

All members of the former Vice-President's family except Maj. Richard Fairbanks, who is in France, were at his bedside.

BRITISH DESTROYER SUNK.

[BY ATLANTIC CABLE AND A. P.]

LONDON, June 4.—A British destroyer was sunk last Friday. The Admiralty announcement says there were no casualties.

Where America Gave Hun Heavy Blow

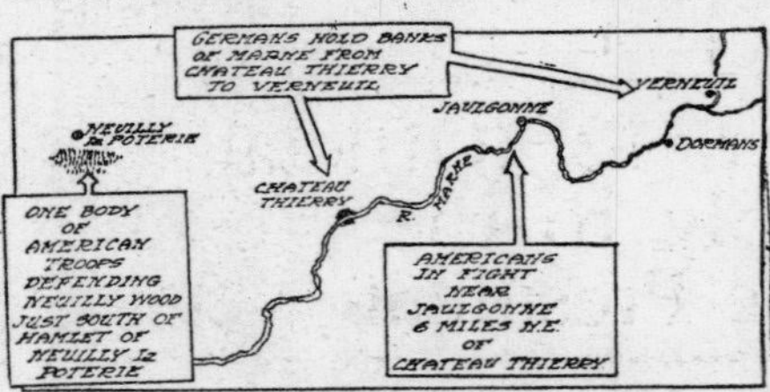

LOCATION OF AMERICANS ON MARNE IS DEFINITELY FIXED.

OFFICIAL statement from the French War Office definitely places for the first time American forces standing with the French and British in the path of the new German rush. One body of Americans is mentioned as defending Neuilly Wood. This little patch of forest lies just to the south of the hamlet Neuilly la Poterie and is eight miles west of Chateau Thierry and about seven miles due north of Nanteuil, which is situated on the north bank of the Marne River below Chateau Thierry.

The Americans participating in the fighting near Jaulgonne are about six miles northeast of Chateau Thierry and at about the middle of the German line along the Marne. The Germans now hold the bank of the Marne from Chateau Thierry to Verneuil.

The Logical Result.

AID OF AMERICA MAKES ALLIED TRIUMPH SURE.

Supreme War Council Gives Out Significant Official Statement.

[BY ATLANTIC CABLE AND A. P.]

LONDON, June 4.—The Supreme War Council, which has had under advisement the entire war situation, has expressed in an official statement made public tonight full confidence in the outcome of the war, with the aid of the American forces.

Complete confidence in Gen. Foch also is expressed and tribute is paid to President Wilson for his co-operation in the work of transporting and brigading American troops.

"The Supreme War Council held its sixth session under circumstances of great gravity for the alliance of free peoples," says the statement. The German government, relieved of all pressure on the eastern front by the collapse of the Russian armies and people, has concentrated all its efforts in the west. It now is seeking to gain a decision in Europe by a series of desperate and costly assaults upon the Allied armies before the United States can bring its full strength effectively to bear.

"The advantage it possesses in its strategic position and superior railway facilities has enabled the enemy command to gain some initial successes. It will undoubtedly renew its attacks and the Allied nations may be still exposed to critical days.

"After a review of the whole situation, the council is convinced that the Allies, bearing the trials of the forthcoming campaign with the same fortitude they have ever exhibited in defense of the right, will baffle the enemy's purpose and in due course bring him to defeat. Everything possible is being done to sustain and support the armies in the field.

"The arrangements for unity of command have greatly improved the position of the Allied armies and are working smoothly and with success. The Supreme War Council has complete confidence in Gen. Foch. It regards with pride and admiration the valor of the Allied troops.

"Thanks to the prompt and cordial co-operation of the President of the United States, the arrangements, which were set on foot more than two months ago for the transportation and brigading of American troops will make it impossible for the enemy to gain victory by wearing out the Allied reserve before he has exhausted his own.

"The Supreme War Council is confident of the ultimate result and the Allied peoples are resolute not to sacrifice a single one of the free nations of the world to the despotism of Berlin. Their armies are displaying the same steadfast courage which has enabled them on many previous occasions to defeat a German onset. They have only to endure with faith and patience to the end to make victory for freedom secure. The free peoples and their magnificent soldiers will save civilization."

NORTHERN CALIFORNIA MAY RECRUITS 1007.

[BY A. P. NIGHT WIRE.]

SAN FRANCISCO, June 4.—The army recruiting office here announced today that total enlistment in Northern California for May numbered 1007. San Francisco supplied 402 recruits. Sacramento was next with 88 and Fresno supplied 74.

Enemy's Admission.

GERMAN DRIVE STOPPED, BERLIN REPORT SHOWS.

[BY A. P. NIGHT WIRE.]

WASHINGTON, June 4.—Virtual admission that the third German drive in the west has been brought to a halt was seen here in tonight's official statement from Berlin. The brief announcement, without claim of advances, served to convince officers here that for the present at least Gen. Foch has fought the enemy to a standstill without the loss of any point of strategic value and without serious inroads on his reserves.

American troops aided in the fighting. Presumably they are part of Gen. Pershing's main units originally posted farther to the north. It may be, however, that they are a part of the reinforcements that have been rushed over since the German high command determined to force the war to a conclusion in the hope that a decisive victory could be won before the American army arrived in France.

GERMAN PRISONERS OF WAR IN RUSSIA FREE FOR WEST.

[BY A. P. NIGHT WIRE.]

WASHINGTON, June 4.—German soldiers who have been held prisoners in Russia now are returning home in large numbers, the State Department was advised today in dispatches from Moscow. Most of the men were reported in good physical condition and it was estimated that 70 per cent. of them would be ready for active duty within a month.

According to the dispatches, three trains, each carrying from 400 to 1000 Germans, are passing through Orsha daily. The men are being exchanged for Russian prisoners who are in poor health. Most of the latter, the State Department was informed, are suffering from tuberculosis and many die en route home.

Tried and Not Found Wanting.

OUR MEN AT THE MARNE INFLICT SEVERE LOSSES.

Repeated Attacks of Enemy at Nearest and Most Critical Point as to the Capital are Beaten Off.

[BY ATLANTIC CABLE AND A. P.]

WITH THE AMERICAN ARMY IN PICARDY, June 4.—American troops co-operating with the French west of Chateau Thierry, north of the Marne, the nearest and most critical point to Paris reached by the enemy, have brilliantly checked the onrushing Germans, beaten off repeated attacks and inflicted severe losses.

WASHINGTON, June 4.—Terse announcement is made in Gen. Pershing's evening communique of the actions announced today by the French War Office, in which Americans by a brilliant counter-attack repulsed the Germans near Chateau Thierry and French and American troops drove back an enemy force which had crossed the Marne farther south.

The communique says: "In the fighting northwest of Chateau Thierry our troops broke up an attempt of the enemy to advance to the south through Neuilly Woods and by a counter-attack drove him back to the north of the woods. On the Marne front a German battalion which had crossed at Jaulgonne was counter-attacked by French and American troops and forced to retreat to the right bank. It sustained severe losses in killed and prisoners."

AMERICANS RUSH FROM LORRIES TO FIRING LINE.

[BY ATLANTIC CABLE AND A. P.]

WITH THE FRENCH ARMY ON THE MARNE, Monday, June 3.—American machine gunners only an hour or so after their arrival on the banks of the River Marne, the 31st of May, took a most active part in the defense of Chateau Thierry, which then was menaced with imminent capture by the Germans.

Scarcely had the Americans alighted from their motor lorries when they were ordered into Chateau Thierry with a battalion of French colonial troops.

The Americans immediately organized their defenses and by rapid action and excellent shooting caused the approaching enemy to hesitate.

In order to mask their movements, the Germans used smoke grenades, rendering shooting difficult for the defenders, and at the same time opened a severe bombardment on the town.

The enemy started across the bridge, but when many had reached the center of the structure a terrific explosion behind them heralded the destruction of the central arch.

Dozens of the Germans were hurled into the water, while the few that reached the south side were captured.

The Americans, who held the south end of the bridge and banks of the river, covered the whole operations and protected the French troops while crossing before the explosion.

The French officers fighting with them declare that the Americans displayed wonderful qualities of coolness and courage in the most difficult situation and in the course of the trying struggle in the streets, while afterward they, with their machine guns, prevented all attempts of the enemy to repair the bridge.

FIRST AMERICAN WOUNDED ARRIVE AT NICE.

[BY ATLANTIC CABLE AND A. P.]

NICE (France) Monday, June 3.—The first batch of wounded American soldiers who had been amalgamated with French troops arrived at Nice today. They were sent to the American hospital here.

The Main Offensive.

FIFTY GERMAN DIVISIONS FAIL TO GAIN AT MARNE.

BY WILBUR FORREST.

[ATLANTIC CABLE—EXCLUSIVE DISPATCH.]

WITH THE FRENCH ARMY IN FRANCE, June 4.—The German advance has slowed down perceptibly, due largely to the fact that, despite the fresh divisions thrown into the battle line between Soissons and Rheims, it has found itself held fast on the flanks and able to advance only slightly in the center.

The theory, however, that the Germans were making only a test conflict on this particular front, with a view of carrying out the main assault elsewhere, was generally dissipated today with the absolute confirmation of the fact that they have already thrown fifty divisions, including their best troops, against numerically inferior Franco-British forces.

At the present time this main assault grows less threatening and the situation on the flank is no longer critical. The general situation has brightened. The Marne is a barrier which the enemy will find difficult. Another factor, even more important, is Foch's reserves who today are resting on their arms within striking distance and now are at the immediate disposal of the inter-Allied commander-in-chief.

There is certain to be an ebb and flow in a great battle such as this. I saw French reserves on the road today flowing forward in a perfectly evident state of mind that would pump confidence into the darkest pessimist. They were advancing to meet the Boche horde and their song and shout as they marched indicated clearly that there was unbeatable confidence in their ranks.

I saw the ebb of the battle from a concealed position on a high bluff which sloped back forming the south bank of the Marne. Just across the river the enemy had occupied the same sort of sloping hills during the night, and was today advancing along the river bank under heavy fire from French guns on our side.

To the right from our position could be seen squatty little villages on the river's edge now occupied by the Germans. On the hills behind it was an open wagon road frequently dotted with enemy wagons, which were closely following the infantry skirmishers who were fighting a scant mile away.

To the left was the ragged edge of the timber line held by the French. The black puffs of enemy shells were exploding along this line. Marking the bare, rolling hillside in front was a small, ten-acre wood seemingly held by no one. French airplanes cruised about fearless of the enemy's anti-aircraft fire.

Suddenly, in white puffs French shells were seen, pecking the open ground behind the isolated woods towards another fringe of trees where the enemy lines receded sharply back from the river. It was the enemy's skirmishers advancing to the isolated woods. They reached it and the artillery fire which had been pecking the open ground was concentrated on the woods.

This small view of the great battle was in the center. On the enemy's flank he is facing forces who will make him pay for every foot with heavy loss. The Marne and the reserves face him in the center now, and the next stage of this great open warfare fighting can be looked forward to with confidence.

SUNDAY MORNING VOL. XXXVII. OCTOBER 13, 1918.

Liberty Under Law—Equal Rights—True Industrial Freedom

GERMANY THROWS UP HER HANDS

WASHINGTON, Oct. 12—(Official Associated Press Bulletin.)—The German government in its reply to the recent note sent by President Wilson, accepts the terms laid down by the President in his address of January 8 and subsequent addresses.

Anglo-Americans Hurl Enemy Back of Valenciennes Defenses.

Where Allies are Fast Drawing in Fatal Circle

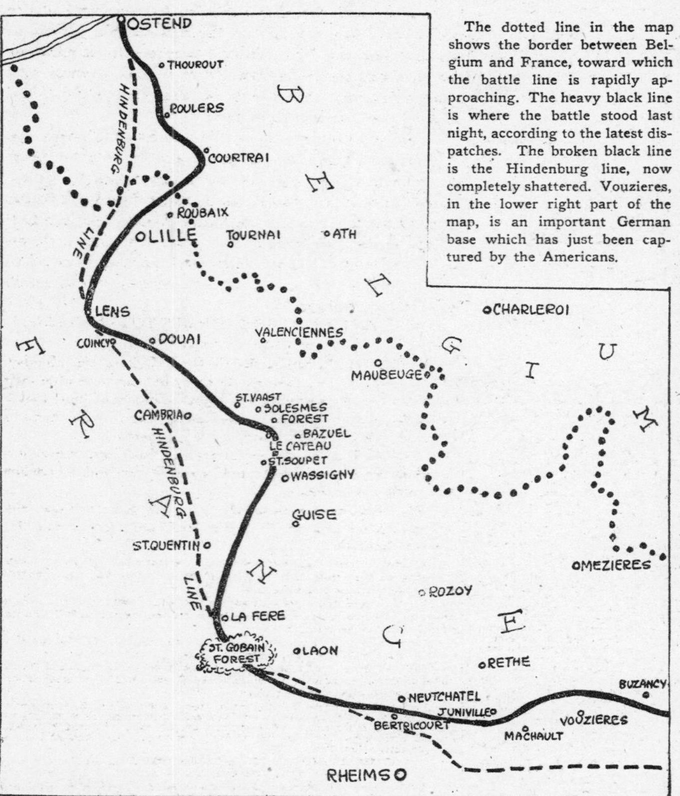

The dotted line in the map shows the border between Belgium and France, toward which the battle line is rapidly approaching. The heavy black line is where the battle stood last night, according to the latest dispatches. The broken black line is the Hindenburg line, now completely shattered. Vouzieres, in the lower right part of the map, is an important German base which has just been captured by the Americans.

ENEMY SAYS HE ACCEPTS OUR PEACE TERMS.

Berlin Declares Willingness to Evacuate Invaded Territory as Prerequisite to Ending the War and, Further, that this Proffer Represents Both German People and German Government.

[BY A. P. NIGHT WIRE.]

WASHINGTON, Oct. 12.—The German government, in its reply to the recent note sent by President Wilson, accepts the terms laid down by the President in his address of January 8 and subsequent addresses. The text of the German reply was received tonight.

In answer to the inquiry of President Wilson, the note says that the "responsibility for this step toward peace has been formed by conferences and in agreement with the great majority of the Reichstag." The Chancellor says he speaks for the German people, and he asks the President to secure the appointment of a mixed commission to arrange for evacuation.

The official text of the German note had not been received here at a late hour tonight. It was announced there would be no official comment, at least until it arrived.

Germany's reply to President Wilson's inquiry, intercepted as it was being sent by the great wireless towers at Nauen and forwarded here tonight in an official dispatch from France, declares Germany is ready to accept President Wilson's peace terms, evacuate the invaded territory as a prerequisite to an armistice, and that the bid for peace represents the German people as well as the government.

Although on its face the text of the German note seems to be a complete acceptance of President Wilson's terms, the people of the United States and the Allied countries should be cautioned against accepting it as such a compliance of the President's demands as will mean immediate cessation of hostilities.

A wireless dispatch sent out from Nauen, the great German wireless station, picked up and forwarded to official diplomatic sources here tonight, purports to give the text of Germany's answer to President Wilson's inquiry to Chancellor Maximilian on Germany's peace proposal. On its face it seems a complete acceptance of President Wilson's terms.

HERE IS TEXT OF GERMAN REPLY—IT SPEAKS FOR ITSELF.

In reply to the question of the President of the United States of America, the German government hereby declares:

The German government has accepted the terms laid down by President Wilson in his address of January 8 and in his subsequent addresses on the foundation of a permanent peace of justice. Consequently, its object in entering into discussions would be only to agree upon practical details of the application of these terms. The German government believes that the governments of the powers associated with the government of the United States also take the position taken by President Wilson in his address. The German government, in accordance with the Austro-Hungarian government, for the purpose of bringing about an armistice, declares itself ready to comply with the propositions of the President in regard to evacuation.

The German government suggests that the President may occasion the meeting of a mixed commission for making the necessary arrangements concerning the evacuation. The present German government, which has undertaken the responsibility for this step toward peace, has been formed by conferences and in agreement with the great majority of the Reichstag. The Chancellor, supported in all of his actions by the will of this majority, speaks in the name of the German government and of the German people.

BERLIN, Oct. 12, 1918.

[Signed] SOLF,

State Secretary of Foreign Office.

As President Wilson was in New York today and reserved comment on the note, his views cannot be stated now, and none of his official family here in Washington cared to speak for him.

(Continued on Sixth Page.)

UNCONDITIONAL SURRENDER SURE.

McAdoo Declares Max's Reply, if Authentic, is that and Nothing Else.

[BY A. P. NIGHT WIRE.]

CHICAGO, Oct. 12.—The text of Germany's reply to President Wilson's inquiry was communicated by the Associated Press tonight to William G. McAdoo, Secretary of the Treasury, just before he delivered a Liberty Loan address at a crowded mass meeting.

Mr. McAdoo told the audience the text of the reply and added:

"What the government demands, based on President Wilson's messages and speeches, is unconditional surrender, and if the text of this reply is authentic it means just that."

OFFICIAL REPORTS

SUMMARIES BY WAR OFFICES.

[BY ATLANTIC CABLE AND A. P.]

LONDON, Oct. 12.—British forces advancing east of Lens have captured several villages of importance, Field Marshal Haig reports in his official statement tonight.

The text of the statement says:

"There was local fighting today along the line of Selle River between Le Cateau and Solesmes. Northwest of Solesmes steady progress has been made throughout the day toward the valley of the Selle.

"The enemy rear guards have been driven out of the villages of St. Vaast, St. Aubert, Villers-en-Cauchies and Avesnes-le-Sece. Farther north we cleared the west bank of the Sensee Canal at Arleux and Corbehem, both of which villages are in our possession. We are closely approaching the line of the canal west of Douai.

"In the sector east of Lens we captured Montigny, Harnes and Antay. On the whole of this front there was sharp local fighting in the course of which we inflicted numerous casualties on the German rear guards and took prisoners."

PARIS, Friday, Oct. 11.—The official communication of the eastern theater, describing operations of October 10, says:

"Despite the very bad weather the Allied armies continue their progress to the north. The Serbian forces are in contact south of Nish with large German forces, including con-

(Continued on Sixth Page.)

RETIRE ON BIG SCALE.

Huns Driven from Vast Area.

Explosions in Germans' Rear Indicate Continued Retreats.

Allies Capture the Largest Ammunition Dump Ever Taken in War.

[BY ATLANTIC CABLE AND A. P.]

WITH THE ANGLO-AMERICAN FORCES ON THE VALENCIENNES FRONT, Oct. 12, 11 a.m.—The British again attacked southwest of Douai this morning, stormed and took Brebieres and passed through to the eastward. They are now within slightly more than a mile of Douai itself. A stiff rear-guard resistance by enemy machine gunners is being overcome.

WITH THE ANGLO-AMERICAN FORCES ON THE VALENCIENNES FRONT, Oct. 12.—Since the beginning of the present operations the Americans have captured forty-six officers and 1900 men and since joining the British fighting forces they have secured 3000 prisoners and 60 cannon.

There was every evidence to-12.—There was every evidence today that the Germans were preparing to make a strong stand on the Valenciennes line, which now has been reached. east of the River Selle, by the Anglo-American forces.

The evacuation of the city of Valenciennes itself was started three weeks ago. Prisoners captured today said they had orders to hold on to the last and to kill as many Britons and Americans as possible.

It is expected the German resistance will continue and will grow more determined until the first phase of the withdrawal in the Douai sector is completed. There are indications that the enemy also is contemplating withdrawals on a large scale elsewhere.

The Germans had to do quick work in the preparation of the Valenciennes lines, which, it appears, they intend trying to hold. It seems, in a general way, to run from Valenciennes to Vendegies, east of the River Escaillon, on the high ground south of Bermerain, along the high ground between Escarmain and Solesmes, along the high ground east of the River Selle, east of Le Cateau to Morlain, thence east of Andigny, west of Remnicourt, through the Piquerval wood and thence possibly southeast to Vandencourt on the Oise.

It is obvious that this is only a temporary line, for explosions are in progress east of it. It is known that the military offices that were formerly in Le Cateau were moved to Maubeuge and Charleroi and guns have been seen moving back to the eastward.

In Douai there have been several fires, while in Denain and in the southern and northern outskirts of Lille explosions and fires have been observed. Villages northeast of Douai are burning, including Maitaing, Marquette, Merchicourt and Marcq.

Notwithstanding the Germans having adopted a defensive line, the attacks by the British and Americans are continuing.

GERMAN REPLY READ TO ARMY.

Haig Warns Troops not to Allow Peace Reports to Destroy Victory.

[BY ATLANTIC CABLE AND A. P.]

AMERICAN ARMY HEADQUARTERS IN FRANCE, Oct. 12, 10 p.m.—Germany's reply to President Wilson's note was received by wireless at army headquarters tonight. It was not communicated to the fighting lines until much later.

LONDON, Oct. 12 (via Montreal.)—Field Marshal Haig on October 7 issued an army order calling attention of his officers and men to the circulation of false rumors to the effect that peace was at hand, with the evident object of discouraging the troops and diverting them from the great task of overthrowing their enemies.

Field Marshal Haig urged the troops to realize now more than ever that it was necessary to concentrate their energies upon the great goal all hoped for, namely, the attainment in the near future of a decisive and happy result.

California Man in German Prison.

[BY A. P. DAY WIRE.]

WASHINGTON, Oct. 12.—The War Department announced today that Allen Hauser of Laurel, Cal., is in the German prison camp at Rastatt.

Spanish Parliament to Meet.

[BY ATLANTIC CABLE AND A. P.]

SAN SEBASTIAN, Friday, Oct. 11.—Both houses of the Spanish Parliament will meet on October 22.

WOULD OUST KAISER FOR PEACE.

[BY ATLANTIC CABLE AND A. P.]

PARIS, Oct. 12.—The tendency is remarked in certain German circles, says a dispatch from Geneva to the Temps, to represent the eventual fall of Emperor William as a concession which the Germans would be disposed to allow to the Allies if they demanded it.

Such talk appears, above all, the message adds, to be an attempt to bring about an event which many Germans judge to be inevitable and even desirable.

ZURICH (Switzerland) Oct. 12.—Neutral travelers arriving here from Germany report that rumors that Emperor William may abdicate appear to take greater consistency day by day. The arrivals add that the unpopularity of the German Crown Prince has considerably increased in Germany.

DOUAI'S FALL NEAR; HAIG MILE OFF

[BY ATLANTIC CABLE AND A. P.]

BRITISH HEADQUARTERS IN FRANCE, Oct. 12.—(Reuter's.) British advance posts now have been pushed to within little more than a mile of the outskirts of Douai. The advance from here has to be very cautious, however, as many ground mines have been encountered and there is good reason to believe the town itself is honeycombed with death traps.

Considerable gains of ground were made by the British last night northeast of Cambrai. Near St. Vaast, between Cambrai and Solesmes, the advancing troops encountered considerable opposition. The enemy has dug in and wired his positions and his artillery was disposed to dispute the British progress.

At one or two points the British infantry has fallen back a trifle to give its batteries a clear field to deal with the stiffened enemy resistance.

Germans apparently are growing extremely anxious regarding the intentions of the British in Flanders. This is indicated by the numbers of low-flying airplanes, which they have out in reconnoitering work and constant raids all along the line.

WITH THE BRITISH ARMY IN FRANCE, Friday, Oct. 11.—The enemy today began an attempt to slow up the Anglo-American advance on the main battle front. All the bridges across the River Selle from Le Cateau southward were blown up and the Germans seem to have been digging in furiously along the line of the high ground some 2000 to 4000 yards east of the river, which already has been crossed by the British and Americans at several places. Apparently the Germans intend to make a stand here.

In this locality all of today's operations have been devoted to gaining the river crossings and establishing a firm footing on the east bank. There has been sharp machine-gun fighting and the Germans have poured a heavy fire on the west bank of the river.

As soon as the Americans and the cavalry entered St. Souplet south of Le Cateau, they came under a heavy fire from the German gun concentration.

(Continued on Second Page.)

THE DAY'S NEWS SUMMED UP

OCTOBER 13, 1918.

THE SKY. Clear. Wind at 5 p.m., southwest; velocity, 10 miles. Thermometer, highest, 91 deg.; lowest, 62 deg. Forecast: Sunday fair. For complete weather data see last page of this section.

THE CITY. New and still more rigid anti-influenza regulations were promulgated by the Health Advisory Committee. Nine more deaths, indirectly due to the malady, and 471 new cases were reported.

Leslie M. Shaw, former Secretary of the Treasury, was notified by cable of the death from pneumonia of his daughter, Miss Erma Shaw, on her way to France for Red Cross work.

The whole city turned out to aid the Liberty Loan Committee roll up a big total for Liberty Day.

Miss Charlotte Sibley, prominent in society, was married to an army man, but not the one to whom her engagement was recently announced.

SOUTHERN CALIFORNIA. Sixteen men from Throop College, recently at Presidio Training Camp, offered army commissions.

Balloon gas bag breaks at altitude of 3000 feet. Cadet drops and lands practically uninjured.

PACIFIC SLOPE. State Council of Defense plans to stop waste of irrigating waters and use all to increase production of crops.

Three celebrations held at Camp Lewis Liberty Day to boost Fourth Loan. Deaths from disease decreased. Ten soldiers go to West Point.

Ten thousand women will distribute new food regulation cards to California homes beginning Monday, October 28.

GENERAL EASTERN. Gale-fanned flames sweep Lake Superior district, wiping out towns, farms, forests and causing number deaths. Duluth menaced.

President Wilson accorded greatest ovation ever given President of United States as he leads Liberty Day bond parade in New York.

Secretary McAdoo appeals to rich and poor of nation to make supreme effort to make Liberty Loan success. Declares even if Kaiser quits money needed to get our soldiers back.

Two are mortally wounded and many others are injured in street battle between negroes and whites in Brooklyn.

WASHINGTON. Liberty Day celebrations throughout country bring uncounted millions to Liberty Loan. Estimated last night that half required amount now subscribed. Twelfth district now has little over 51 per cent. of quota.

Influenza is spreading on Pacific Coast and in Middle West; decreasing in East. Conservation of doctors and nurses urged by Surgeon-General.

85c Per Month
DELIVERED TO SUBSCRIBERS

Daily, at Hotels, on Railway Trains, 5 Cents.
Daily, on Streets and News Stands, 3 Cents.
Sunday, in Los Angeles and Suburbs, 7 Cents.
Sunday, Outside Territory, Per Copy, 10 Cents.

In Two Parts—16 Pages

PART I—TELEGRAPH SHEET—8 PAGES

MONDAY MORNING, VOL. XXXVII. NOVEMBER 11, 1918.

Liberty Under Law—Equal Rights—True Industrial Freedom

PEACE

WORLD WAR ENDS AS GERMANY SIGNS ARMISTICE!

[Extraordinary Service Bulletins by the Associated Press.]

WASHINGTON, Nov. 11th, (Monday)---The world war will end this morning at 6 o'Clock, Washington time, 11 o'clock Paris time. The armistice was signed by the German representatives at midnight. This announcement was made by the State Department at 2:50 o'Clock this morning.

The announcement was made verbally by an official of the State Department in this form: "The armistice has been signed. It was signed at 5 o'Clock a. m. Paris time and hostilities will cease at 11 o'Clock this morning, Paris time."

The terms of the armistice, it was announced, will not be made public until later. Military men here, however, regard it as certain that they include:

Immediate retirement of the German military forces from France, Belgium and Alsace-Lorraine.

Disarming and demobilization of the German armies.

Occupation by the Allied and American forces of such strategic points in Germany as will make impossible a renewal of hostilities.

Delivery of part of the German high seas fleet and a certain number of submarines to the Allied naval forces.

Disarmament of all other German warships under supervision of the Allied and

(Continued on Second Page.)

In Three Parts—28 Pages
PART I—TELEGRAPH SHEET—14 PAGES

The Los Angeles Times

TUESDAY MORNING, VOL. XXXVIII. JULY 1, 1919.

Liberty Under Law—Equal Rights—True Industrial Freedom

Liquor Ban is to be Rigorously Enforced; War Beer not Stopped.

NATION RUN FROM SEA.

Wilson Signs Bills on Way Home.

First Time in History an Executive has Made Laws Away from America.

Pretty War Brides on Presidential Ship; Due to Arrive Monday.

[BY A. P. NIGHT WIRE.]

ON BOARD THE U.S.S. GEORGE WASHINGTON, June 30.—(By Wireless to the Associated Press.) At her present rate of progress, the George Washington will arrive at Hoboken at noon, Monday.

The bills awaiting the President's signature and documents relating to much other government business were soon spread on the President's desk. In addition there were a number of army and navy court-martial reports and several reports from the Department of Justice.

This, the first time in history that such operations of receiving and signing bills in mid-ocean had occurred, was commented upon on board as marking another record breaking advance in modern methods of communication.

The President signed the railroad appropriation bill, the Indian bill, some minor measures and other documents which needed signature to become law before July 1, in mid-ocean at 8 a.m., Greenwich time, today.

A pouch containing the bills was dispatched on the eastbound transport Great Northern from New York on June 24. This morning the Great Northern met the George Washington and the important papers were sent on the President's ship.

Techically, the President was on American territory when he signed measures.

RUSH TO WASHINGTON.

The President's ship was 357 miles out at noon today, running sixteen knots an hour, which indicates her arrival in port about Monday noon.

It is expected the Presidential party will proceed direct to Washington, without stopping at New York, and that the President's first official utterance in America is likely to be when he in person will present before Congress a detailed statement of the proceedings of the Peace Conference. He carries with him copies of the treaty.

President and Mrs. Wilson are enjoying the balmy air and sunny breeze on an ideal passage. They spent much of the day on the upper deck. The President wore his customary tweed cap and Mrs. Wilson a blue tam-o'-shanter.

At 11 o'clock in the morning the alarm sounded for boat drill and the President went through the maneuvers with the rest, taking a place with his wife and the others in a lifeboat. The President complimented Capt. McCauley on the smartness of his crew in manning the boats and having everything prepared.

WAR BRIDES ON WILSON SHIP.

[BY A. P. DAY WIRE.]

ON BOARD THE U.S.S. GEORGE WASHINGTON, Sunday, June 29.—(By wireless to the Associated Press.)—Several thousand returning American soldiers and a score of

(Continued on Third Page.)

CHRISTIAN SERVICE HELD IN COLISEUM.

[A. P. FOREIGN CORRESPONDENCE.]

ROME, June 15.—On the very site where once Christians were offered as the prey of wild beasts to amuse the Roman populace in the Rome coliseum, a Christian service has at last been held. It was celebrated recently in memory of the Boy Scouts of the Italian army, who had done messenger service at the front and were killed in action.

FIELD ARTILLERY ON BORDER ASK DISCHARGE.

PETITION OF 406 NONCOMMISSIONED OFFICERS AND MEN ADDRESSED TO CONGRESS.

[BY A. P. NIGHT WIRE.]

EL PASO, June 30.—Immediate discharge from the army is asked by 406 noncommissioned officers and enlisted men of the Eighty-second Field Artillery stationed here, in a petition which they forwarded to Washington tonight.

The petition is addressed to the Senate and House Military Affairs committees.

Referring to conditions on the Mexican border, the petitioners declare:

"We are reminded of the unsettled conditions prevailing on the Mexican border. We wish to bring to your attention the offer of Gov. Hobby, (of Texas) of two brigades of troops, 7000 men, for border service. The refusal of the offer indicates the War Department's intention to hold us for all emergencies arising along the border, even though our enlistments have expired."

"Conditions on the border are such that it is impossible to discharge the men enlisted for the war emergency," said Brig.-Gen. James B. Erwin, commanding the border district tonight.

The Ninety-sixth Aero Squadron passed through here today on its way from Aberdeen Md., to Columbus, N. M., for duty in connection with the border patrol. Official announcement that a dirigible was to be sent here for border patrol and observation work was made today.

ST. LOUIS BARTENDERS SERVE IN MOURNING.

[BY A. P. NIGHT WIRE.]

ST. LOUIS, June 30.—War-time prohibition will be enforced to the letter in St. Louis unless official instructions are received to the contrary, Federal officials here announced late today. All policemen were ordered to report violators to the Federal authorities.

More than 50,000 persons were served at cafes tonight, it was estimated. In the downtown saloons, all bartenders wore black neckties and mourning bands, and the mirrors were festooned with crepe.

SEVERAL KILLED IN MONTANA WINDSTORM.

[BY A. P. NIGHT WIRE.]

MINOT (N. D.) June 30.—A windstorm which bordered on a tornado swept Northeastern Montana and Northwestern North Dakota late last night and early this morning, killing several, injuring many others and causing great damage to buildings both in towns and in rural sections.

Wires are all down west of Minot and only meager details are available tonight.

THE DAY'S NEWS SUMMED UP

THE SKY. Clear. Wind at 5 p.m., southwesterly; velocity, 12 miles. Thermometer, highest, 77 deg.; lowest, 58 deg. Forecast: For Los Angeles and vicinity: Tuesday, fair, except cloudy or foggy in the morning near the coast. Not so warm east portion. Gentle westerly winds.

For complete weather data see last page of this section.

THE CITY. Booze had a jolly end in the Southland, and it was the "wettest" day in its history; over $100,000 spent for booze in the city.

Asking co-operation in securing protection for the lives and property of Americans in Mexico, a distinguished army officer described that country as a sink of crime.

Southern California Dental Association opened its convention and famous oral surgeons praised war work.

New salary schedule of phone company made strikers regret quitting, and their desire to return may disrupt one union.

At a meeting of prominent business men a programme was outlined for the entertainment of visitors which is calculated to attract to Los Angeles people from all over the world.

Last-hour advices from all over the Southland indicated a heavy majority for the $40,000,000 highway bond issue at the polls today.

SOUTHERN CALIFORNIA. Last of wooden ships contracted for the government goes down the ways at Los Angeles Harbor.

Daughters of Revolution at Pasadena place memorial tablet on Old Mission Mill.

Opposition to bond issue at Long Beach becomes so strong that an attempt is made to postpone election.

Fiesta at Santa Barbara opens with elaborate [illegible].

PACIFIC SLOPE. International Brotherhood of Electrical Workers call out all operators and linemen in Washington and Oregon.

Canadian aviator announces several British planes will attempt to cross the Pacific, starting from San Diego.

FOREIGN. With nine different wars in progress, the Ukraine—"No Man's Land"—presents a problem for European stability.

Hundred reported dead, thousands injured and many villages and towns razed, by earthquake that centers in region around Florence, Italy.

For the first time in history President Wilson transacts government business in midocean. Many war brides on executive's ship, due to arrive Monday.

Allied task not completed with signing of peace, President Poincare warns French. Says ships and importations needed. Defensive pact to be announced in Paris.

Eighteen Americans killed and twenty-four wounded in fight with anti-Kolchak forces in Siberia.

Former Crown Prince again is reported to have escaped from his island refuge in Holland.

WASHINGTON. Fall and Borah attack peace treaty and League of Nations in senate and Hitchcock defends it.

Owing to high bids on Pacific Coast for fuel oil for fleet, Navy Department forced to commandeer supply, and will fix price later.

Congress fails in its recess plan and adjournment is postponed until today to pass final appropriation bills needed July 1 to provide government funds.

Department of Justice announces that, pending court decisions, beer of 2¾ per cent, and light wines of similar alcoholic content may be sold. [illegible] ban on solid.

MUST GET FLEET OIL.

Pacific Dealers are Given Orders.

Bids Considered Excessive, Navy Department Commandeers Product.

Protest is Made to Carranza Against Stopping American Drilling.

[BY A. P. NIGHT WIRE.]

WASHINGTON, June 30.—Forced to abandon the plan to maintain a large naval force in the Pacific or to commandeer enough fuel oil to supply the new fleet, the Navy Department today placed navy orders with west coast concerns for sufficient gasoline and fuel oil to supply the demands of the large naval force recently ordered to the Pacific.

An effort was made recently to get the fuel required by contract but the prices bid for the lower grade of fuel oil required were almost double those asked by contractors on the east coast, regardless of the considerable difference in transportation cost.

Under the navy orders placed today the west coast concerns will be required to supply the navy's demands and to accept a price to be fixed later after the Navy Department has carefully investigated the cost of production and delivery at Pacific Coast points.

PROTEST TO CARRANZA.

[EXCLUSIVE DISPATCH.]

WASHINGTON, June 30.—The State Department filed a protest with the Mexican government on April 2 of this year, it was learned today, against the refusal of the Carranza authorities to permit American oil companies to drill wells in their own lands. The Mexican government has just replied to this protest declaring that no permits, provisional or otherwise, would be granted to companies that "had not complied with the laws," which compliance would constitute admission that the Mexican government owned the lands legally acquired by the companies.

It was pointed out in official circles that the reply of Carranza was not made until after the Juarez incident, when American troops crossed the border and drove the Villistas out of the city. Since then Carranza has ordered troops to the oil fields to prevent forcibly the oil companies from drilling wells or doing other construction work in connection with the production of oil.

DRIVEN OUT BY TROOPS.

Advices from Mexico City report that several drilling crews of different American companies have been driven out by the soldiers under direct orders issued by Carranza. These orders were transmitted by the petroleum department to the War Department on May 16 and contain specific instructions to the military commanders at Tampico and Tuxpam.

This is interpreted here to be an overt act of confiscation.

The controversy between the Mexican and United States governments over Mexico's avowed determination to seize the oil properties belonging to American citizens and companies has reached another crisis. It is the subject of comment in official circles here, although no formal statement regarding the situation has been given out. The ordering of troops forcibly to prevent drilling is cited as another example of Carranza's truculent attitude which has invariably followed the granting of any favor by the American government.

GERMAN INFLUENCE AT WORK.

The Mexican government until now has respected the protests made by the United States, Great Britain, France and Holland against the seizure of oil lands, but has engaged in a continuous campaign to coerce the American companies into admitting that the Mexican government owns the lands. Such an admission would have the effect of making the protests of the State Department meaningless.

It has been definitely established, according to Mexican advices, that German influence is still behind the Carranza determination to force foreigners out of the oil fields and to confiscate their properties. German agencies have been steadily at work since the signing of the armistice to secure the Mexican oil and other trade for Germany. State Department officials are said to have information of this effort on the part of Germany and of Carranza's approval and aid in furthering the effort. The exclusion of Mexico from the League of Nations has been a feature of this "entente" between Germany and Mexico.

CANADIAN WHEAT TO BE SENT TO GREECE

[BY A. P. NIGHT WIRE.]

TORONTO, June 30.—Wheat in all Canadian elevators has been commandeered by the board of grain supervisors in order to provide Greece with 15,000,000 bushels within the next twelve months, it was announced tonight. No shipments can be made at present without permits from the board.

Yellow Fever Outbreak Checked.

[BY CABLE AND ASSOCIATED PRESS.]

SAN SALVADOR, [illegible] Strict sanitary [illegible] Union and San [illegible] have checked [illegible] fever.

JOLLY END IS DEMON'S.

Bereft Crowds in "Full" Mourning.

Dying Gurgles Acclaimed by Throngs at Vernon and Wet Beach Areas.

Roads Guarded, but Disorder is Absent; Jails Become Temples of Sorrow.

Los Angeles went dry last night after the "wettest" day in its history. It was said that one-quarter of a million dollars was a conservative estimate of the last day's booze bill for Los Angeles county, including Venice and Vernon. More than $100,000 was spent yesterday in the city of Los Angeles, where crowds besieged the city's seventy-five retail and wholesale wine and beer stores, and carried away arm-loads, trunk-loads, automobile-loads of 14 per cent goods of every description.

Big crowds filled the streets all day yesterday and last evening, and every cafe and hotel with a liquor license did a land office business. The City Jail was early turned into a temple of sorrow and at midnight the line of sorrowing drunks was coming stronger than ever. For the most part the crowd took their bereavement good-naturedly, and only minor disorders were reported at the score of "wakes" held in the city and county.

MANY "WAKES" HELD.

The old Baker block on North Main street, once the center of the city, and in the past years the true Bohemia of the city, was the scene of what was perhaps the largest, and undoubtedly the most picturesque farewell party and wake staged for John Barleycorn in Los Angeles last night.

Two bands, a traveling jazz band, that moved from studio to studio, and a confusion of pretty women, gaily colored lanterns, and artists of all sorts and descriptions held sway.

Exactly at midnight a pageant, "The Rise and Fall of John Barleycorn" was staged in the spacious hall of the building. There were seven scenes, beginning with the stone age, and ending with the mournful year of 1919. Beautiful cabaret girls, dancing, poetry, song and everything that old John ever claimed for his own were represented in the pageant, was written by Carl Claussen and Betty Murphy and staged by the artists of the olr Baker block.

The Eagles also had a sad wake, their ceremony including Tiny Kick, he of the 14-per cent, short-lived career, as well as his father John Barleycorn.

While a large audience gathered around the coffin, surrounded by candles stuck into the mouths of empty bottles, and some of the mourners reinforced themselves with long, bitter draughts of the things that was about to pass out, Bernard Mullen delivered a sad, sad oration.

"The youngster and his father came to the end of their career from a solar plexus blow delivered by a bunch of long hairs while the boys were away in trenches," the speaker said. "But costly flowers and empty beer bottles bring no condolence to the dead," he added, with a sob.

Down under the sidewalk in Jake's cafe, where the old Rathskeller was found in the ancient days, a cabaret girl was singing "Should Auld Acquaintance be Forgot," as the clock struck 9.

At McKee's a few solemn parties were clustered around the tables. They, like Brutus of old, had come to bury John and not to praise him, so there was no weeping or wailing or gnashing of teeth.

At Jahnke's, the New China, the Maple and the few remaining others, when the clock struck 9 the beer steins gave way to glasses of milk, the dancing went on and poor old John was soon forgotten.

[illegible] thousand automobiles visited

(Continued on Eighth Page.)

Farewells to Booze Said in Los Angeles.

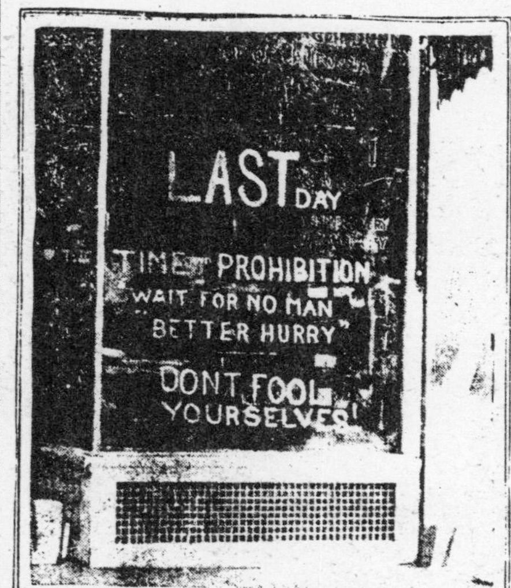

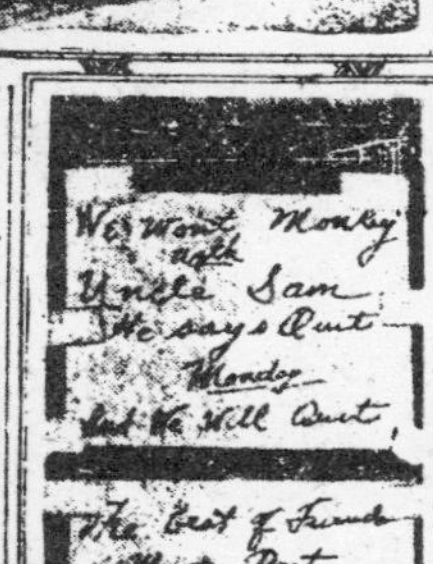

Reminders to Thirsty,

Noted by the photographer in a dry journey about town. Above, a "Word to the Wise," painted upon the window of the Union Wine Association, at 516 South Main street. In the center is shown not a few heeding the sign. Below, graphic warnings to the thirsty upon the windows of the Old Plantation Distillery Company, at 108 South Broadway.

LIQUOR STOCKS GONE; CAFES TO STAY OPEN.

DEALERS QUIT; SAY 2¾ BEER "AIN'T, THAT'S ALL, IT AIN'T."

All of the downtown restaurants and cafes serving beer and wine with meals will be hard hit by wartime prohibition, but for the present at least all will remain open on strictly a food-and-soft-drinks basis. McKee's Cafe will continue its cabaret, and dancing will continue at Jahnke's Tavern.

All of the restaurants have been preparing for the "drouth" for many months and believe that they can survive on a dry basis by increasing the volume of their food business. The restaurants have been on a beer-and-wine basis since April 1, 1918, when the "kick" was taken out of the liquor business in Los Angeles.

Henry Laub, president of the Old Plantation Distilling Company, at 108 South Broadway, commenting on the inauguration of prohibition yesterday said:

"All of the seventy-five wholesale and retail beer and wine stores in Los Angeles sold out their stocks today. The demand far exceeded the supply. We are

(Continued on Second Page.)

THIRSTY FIND ROAD BLOCKED.

Locked in Jam of Traffic on Boulevard, Never Get to Beach Oases.

Deputy Sheriffs Clark, Ledbetter and Bennett, stationed on the Venice road to insure order among pilgrims to beach oases, reported to the Sheriff's office late last evening that traffic on Washington boulevard was so heavy that the thoroughfare was practically blocked, and many a thristy wayfarer would not reach Venice until too late to slake his thirst.

The officers found two automobiles overturned on Inglewood road, a mile from Washington boulevard, but no traces of the cars' former occupants. One of the machines had been stolen from Ben R. Conrad, of 2742 Malabar street.

NOTHING IS KNOWN OF CYCLOPS IN GERMANY.

[BY CABLE—EXCLUSIVE DISPATCH.]

BERLIN, June 29 (via Copenhagen, June 30.)—After official inquiry into questions raised by the lost United Stateh collier Cyclops story, the German Admiralty today authorized the following statement:

"It is absolutely untrue that the United States collier Cyclops is in any German port. The German government has no information concerning the fate of the vessel, except it has heard it has vanished. No submarines were in the vicinity of where it disappeared and our records show nothing whatever concerning this vessel."

LETTISH TROOPS ARE CLOSING IN ON RIGA.

[BY CABLE AND ASSOCIATED PRESS.]

COPENHAGEN, June 30.—Lettish troops are within nine miles of Riga and the Germans are evacuating the city, according to a dispatch received by the Lettish press bureau from Libau.

DRY BULLETINS.

[BY A. P. NIGHT WIRE.]

MILWAUKEE, June 30.—Milwaukee saloonkeepers are ready to obey the mandates of the war-time prohibition law. It is estimated that 6000 proprietors and bartenders are affected.

BOSTON, June 30.—Hotels, restaurants and saloonkeepers made preparations today for the "wettest" night in their history. Statisticians said 5825 bartenders, porters, bottlers, brewery workers and wine clerks would lose their jobs.

BALTIMORE, June 30.—In a statement today announcing the local government policy regarding the enforcement of the war-time prohibition law, United States District Attorney Samuel K. Dennis said that light wines and beer containing 2¾ per cent. alcohol or less may be sold in Baltimore after today. The statement was made after a conference with the police board.

The Statement by Attorney-General as to Prohibition.

[BY A. P. NIGHT WIRE.]

WASHINGTON, June 30.—The statement of Atty.-Gen. Palmer, tonight, announcing that the Department of Justice will take no action, pending decisions in present litigation, against persons manufacturing or selling beer and wines containing 2 3-4 per cent. or less of alcoholic content, follows:

After today, it will be unlawful to sell for beverage purposes any distilled spirits and any beer, wine or other intoxicating malt or vinous liquor, except for export. This prohibition will continue under the terms of the law "until the conclusion of the present war and thereafter until the termination of demobilization." As long as the law thus remains in force, it must be obeyed, and I intend that the Department of Justice shall do its utmost to perform the duty which the Congress has placed upon it.

This law has been held to be constitutional and valid by the Circuit Court of Appeal, sitting in New York. It plainly makes unlawful the sale of whisky, brandy and other distilled spirits and wine.

The only controversy that has arisen is as to whether the sale of beer containing so little alcohol as not to be in fact intoxicating is prohibited. The government's contention has been that the act prohibits the manufacture and sale of beer containing as much as ½ of 1 per cent. of alcohol, but the interpretation of the act is not free from difficulty, and I am endeavoring to have the question settled by the courts at the earliest possible moment. My course, with respect to beer containing less than 2 3-4 per cent. of alcohol — which it is claimed is not intoxicating— will depend upon the ruling which will soon be made by the District Courts, in which cases are now pending, or in which other cases may be brought. I have no power to grant amnesty to any who may see fit to manufacture or sell beer pending an authoritative judicial construction of the law, and I am sure that brewers and dealers generally understand that the pendency of litigation will be no protection against prosecution for offenses under the law.

But with respect to whisky, brandy and other distilled spirits, wine and beer containing more than 2 3-4 per cent. of alcohol, and other intoxicating malt or vinous liquors, the prohibition is beyond controversy, and but one course is open to the Department of Justice. All persons found selling such liquors must be arrested and prosecuted. The District Attorneys will cause warrants to be issued for all offenders as to whom evidence is furnished by the bureau of investigation, the agents of the Internal Revenue Bureau of the Treasury Department, lo-

(Continued on Second Page.)

COURTS TO FIX POLICY.

Palmer Waits Rule on Intoxicants.

Prohibition may not Stop Manufacture, Sale of 2¾ Per Cent. Beverage.

Warning Given that Whisky is Legally Dead; House Acts on Enforcement.

[BY A. P. NIGHT WIRE.]

WASHINGTON, June 30.—As war-time prohibition took effect tonight, the Department of Justice announced that its agents throughout the country would not attempt tomorrow to stop the sale of 2¾ per cent. beer.

This eleventh-hour development, a flat reversal of an earlier ruling today by the department, was due to the uncertainty as to how the Federal District Court of New York might rule on a pending claim by brewers that beer containing that much alcohol was not intoxicating.

But while this uncertainty existed as to beer of lighter alcoholic percentage than that sold generally heretofore, full warning was given that with respect to whisky and all beverages as to whose intoxicating powers there was no doubt, every government legal agency would be set to work in a determined effort to prevent their manufacture and sale.

CONGRESS MAY ACT.

How long the sale of 2¾ per cent. beer might continue would depend ordinarily upon the speed of the courts, but Congress meanwhile will step to the front in an effort to complete the effectiveness of the war-time law.

Exactly what they have refused heretofore to do, prohibition members of the House will now attempt —passage of a straight, clear-cut bill for enforcement of war-time prohibition.

When word spread tonight that the Attorney-General by his ruling had permitted beer saloons and breweries to remain in operation, members of the Judiciary Committee counted noses to find a sufficient number ready to go to the front to den and separation of the enforcement measures so as to get through at once a bill that would stop the sale of all beer containing more than ½ of 1 per cent. alcohol.

Congressional leaders, it was said, refused to abandon plans for a recess beginning probably tomorrow, in order to put the bill through as an emergency measure, and the whole question of prohibition will be held up until next Monday, at the earliest. There were indications tonight that a hard fight would be made in behalf of an amendment to be offered by Representative Igoe, Democratf of Missouri, would permit the President to set aside the war-time act in so far as it relates to light wines and beer.

BOLD STROKE.

While the Attorney-General's staff was wrestling with the question of intoxicating and nonintoxicating beer, the Judiciary Committee sent to the House its report in which the bold assertion was made that anything over ½ of 1 per cent. alcohol was intoxicating within the purview of the general law construction, and that Congress, and not the courts, should fix the alcoholic percentage of all beverages, sale of which is restricted by prohibition statutes.

Atty.-Gen. Palmer in his statement as to the policy of the department, called attention to the fact

(Continued on Eighth Page.)

WYOMING SEIZES LIQUOR.

[BY A. P. NIGHT WIRE.]

CHEYENNE (Wyo.) June 30.—While the celebration marking the approach of State-wide prohibition was at its height here early tonight, Gov. Carey issued orders to the newly-created State prohibition department to seize at midnight all liquor left in the hands of saloonists throughout the State. The same orders were issued to prosecuting attorneys and sheriffs in all counties.

In practically all saloons here early tonight the stock of whiskey and other liquors had became so low as to make it improbable that a large amount would be left at midnight. The beer supply was exhausted.

Citizens of the city were joined by many from Colorado and Western Nebraska in today's celebration. Saloons were crowded throughout the afternoon and night. There had been no marked disorder up to an early hour tonight.

OBSERVE WET FUNERAL, REPRIEVE

[BY A. P. NIGHT WIRE.]

KANSAS CITY (Mo.) June 30.—Wet celebrants in Kansas City paused a moment and pondered early tonight over the news from Washington that a temporary respite had been granted light wines and beer and then decided that the ceremony could be carried on either as a funeral rite or to observe an eleventh-hour reprieve for the liquor business.

Francis M. Wilson, United States District Attorney, declared he had received no instructions to permit the sale of wine and beer and that, until such instructions were received, persons who sold beverages after midnight tonight, which did not comply with the letter of the law, would be prosecuted.

Editorial Section
VIEWS, NEWS, PICTURES.

Los Angeles Sunday Times

Part II: 16 Pages
THE CITY AND SUBURBS.

VOL. XXXIX. SUNDAY MORNING, MARCH 14, 1920. POPULATION: By the Federal Census—(1910)—319,198 By the City Directory—(1920)—671,659

LOS :: ANGELES :: THE :: MECCA :: FOR :: WORLD'S :: PRETTY :: GIRLS.

Universal Lure of the Films Puts City's Average in Feminine Beauty Far Ahead of That of Any Other Metropolis in America or Abroad.

BY LEE SHIPPEY

Genevieve Knapp, East Orange, N.J.

Dolores Rouse, San Francisco.

Ruth Maurice, Salt Lake City.

Alice Trumhold, Washington, D.C.

Mildred June, St. Louis.

"Extras" waiting outside film studio.

Jeanie Klipper, Wichita, Kansas.

Ludmila Daiger, Bohemia.

NOT FILM STARS BUT ONLY PRETTY NOVICES

The reason Los Angeles has a higher proportion of beautiful girls than any other city in the world is that every day pretty girls from far and near come here in the hope of getting in motion pictures. So many of these girls come that the field is overcrowded, and many have to seek other occupations—but they all add to the charm and loveliness of the city. These are all girls who have come to Los Angeles recently to "break into the films."

Jessie Willingmyre, Atlantic City.

Margaret Chaput, Boston, Mass.

Mary Ryan, Denver.

Margaret Long, Duluth, Minn.

"BY GEORGE!" exclaimed the Easterner, gazing admiringly about the cafeteria, "Los Angeles has more beautiful girls to the square block than any other town on earth. I've seen Paris and Brussels and Nice and Vienna but, man, this Los Angeles! Right here in this ordinary cafeteria there is a higher percentage of beauty, among the young women, than I ever saw in the Ambassadeurs, in the Champs Elysees. Every one of those girls at the serving tables is a peach, the cashier is a vision, and even those two gathering up soiled dishes are mighty pretty girls. What's the answer?"

"Motion pictures," replied the Los Angeles man across the table. "Probably they all came here to become queens of the films. They come here from all over the country—all over the world, in fact—and those who imagine beautiful faces alone will win them fame and fortune are the saddest of all. Most of the girls who have something inside their heads get along pretty well, but the others would do a lot better if they stuck to the dear old farm. The studio offices are full of thrilling telephone girls, stunning stenos, fascinating file clerks and dazzling desk polishers, all of whom came here to crowd Pickford off the screen. The companies really are awfully good to the girls and do all they can to aid them to live right while here, or to get back home, in many instances. But such throngs come in daily that it would ruin even picture companies to undertake any such general policy—besides which, it would take up all their time. So, many of the girls have to take any sort of job they can get and the chances are that even the waitress, who throws your hot cakes at you in the beanery into which you occasionally sneak when no one is looking, along toward the end of the month, used to be a village belle in Tonganoxie, Kan., but came to Los Angeles because people told her she looked just like Theda Bara."

MECCA FOR BEAUTIES.

What the cafeteria diner said is true. Beyond controversy, Los Angeles has a higher percentage of beautiful girls than any other city in the world. All great cities attract pretty girls, as Paris attracted Manon, and Los Angeles has more than its share of those because of its location and climate. But the fact that it is the greatest—and— much the greatest—motion-picture center, is what draws them by the thousands, from far and near. In one group of nine "extra" girls, all beauties, in one casting office the other day, one was from Russia, one from Wales and all the others from different States. All had come here solely in the hope of working in pictures.

Probably there is not a village in America which has not at least two or three seriously film-struck girls, and not a city which has not its hundreds or thousands, according to its sizes. The studios do not encourage any of those girls to come here. They discourage them. But they cannot stop them. Many of the girls are so seriously smitten that neither family objections nor inadequate funds can stop them. One girl recently arrived with a story of having tramped from Spokane, Wash. Her pluck so interested one big producer, that, sight unseen, he promised she should have work.

AS TO "FILM SCHOOLS."

"Schools" which hold out alluring promises tempt many of these film-struck girls, and they, very often, are the ones, who have to seek other lines of employment after coming here—and being separated from their money by the "schools." Just as many "literary agents" for years have been encouraging would-be writers who have no natural gifts to start with, some of the "schools" encourage girls to come here who never ought to leave home.

About all a "school" can teach a girl—or a man—about the art of acting for the films is how to make up. For the rest, they must study in the school of experience, work as "extras," and be classed simply as "atmosphere." The best of the schools, or booking agencies, frankly admit that to their "pupils." For, just as there are good literary agents as well as bad ones, there are trust-

(Continued on Twelfth Page.)

They watch the liner advertisements.

Sophie Dalmatova, Warsaw, Poland.

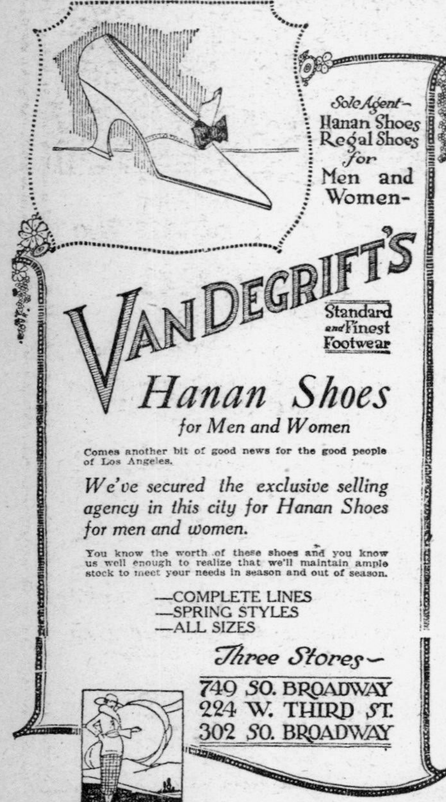

NEED CHINESE, SAY BIG FARMERS.

Urgent Demand for Bonded Coolies Voiced by Fruit and Cotton Growers to Relieve Acute Labor Shortage; Plan is Opposed by Stock Raisers.

Large employers of labor in Southern California favor suspension of certain immigration restrictions to the end that Chinese coolies may be brought into this country under contract and subject to compulsory return after a period of years, as a means of relieving the acute shortage of certain kinds of farm labor, according to a careful survey just completed by The Times.

Almost without a dissenting voice the 15,000 citrus fruit growers of the State favor the importation of coolie contract labor. The cotton growers are agreeable to the plan, by a large majority, and farmers pursuing other lines of agriculture are heartily in favor of it. A great many influential men look upon the idea with disfavor, but a large number admit that they are opposed to it only because they do not feel the need of Chinese laborers in their particular branch of farming.

In the main the hog, cattle and horse breeders appear to be less in favor of coolie labor than men engaged in other agricultural pursuits. This is because the Chinaman never was and never will be a live-stock man. He is at his best, like the Japanese, where he can plow, and hoe and dig and pick. He is a good potato farmer and a splendid vegetable gardener, as well as a fine fruit and cotton picker. Many of the ranchers who express their views in the following comments declare that they'd like to see enough Chinese brought in to break the Japanese's grip on the garden business in Southern California. The views of many prominent farmers, stockmen and fruit growers follow:

Los Angeles County.

City Manager Grant M. Lorraine of Alhambra, says: "I feel that I am qualified to speak from the farmers' standpoint, as I developed 6000 acres in Sacramento Valley. The Japanese must be discouraged from further production. Present labor conditions are disheartening to the white farmer. Therefore something must be done to call the white man back to the soil, and if Chinese coolie help will help him carry on his farming, and bring it again to a paying basis, bring them in."

Frank R. Richardson, representing the Richardson ranching interests in San Gabriel, states that members of the Richardson family are truck gardeenrs on a large scale, and raisers of poultry, and that they believe anyone who has had their experiences in securing help, will welcome coolie labor. He remarked: "Ranchers will welcome any conditions to relieve the present shortage of labor, and consequent shortage of production."

Robert Deverenx, orchardist, for many years in Southern California, says: "Having worked for many years with hundreds of Chinese, I am heartily in favor of importing them to carry on farm work in this country in accordance with the bonding plan. The Chinaman is one of the most honest laborers known—he has no ambition to own land for himself, and works unquestioningly and faithfully."

POMONA VALLEY.

Sentiment in the Pomona Valley is dividend on the question of importing coolie labor even for a limited time. The men who actually pay the wages favor the return of coolie labor, while those who are not direct employers of labor express strong convictions against letting down the bars.

Dr. J. G. Biller, of Spadra, near Pomona, chairman of a committee of the Los Angeles County Farm Bureau appointed some six months ago to investigate the Japanese situation in the county, says: "Our committee went into the question of coolie labor thoroughly and the conclusion reached was that it is a question which the farm bureau should leave strictly alone at present. We found that there is plenty of American labor if it can only be got to work on the farms. We also found there are many phases to be considered in the matter of introducing coolie labor, and after each phase was carefully sifted the conclusions appeared to justify our action.

A. B. Hill of Pomona, for years one of the most extensive grow[ers] of peaches and apricots, there, sa[ys]: "By all means let the coolies c[ome] in. Anything is better than w[hat] we face today. The labor such we can hire is disgustingly poor demands high wages and the we pay the less we get out I have found coolies to b faithful workmen, and hon reliable. They are not con thinking and talking strik

(Continued on Tenth Page.)

Southern California Interests

Editorials—News—Business—Society—The Drama

The Los Angeles Times

VOL. XXXIX. WEDNESDAY MORNING, MARCH 31, 1920.—PART II: 14 PAGES. POPULATION { By the Federal Census—1910—310,198 By the City Directory—(1920)—671,629

MARY PICKFORD AND DOUGLAS FAIRBANKS ARE SECRETLY MARRIED HERE.

CAR REVISION IS SWEEPING.

Rerouting of Yellow Lines Announced by Company.

Effective May 1 to Aid the No-Parking Ordinance.

Extensive Changes on Nearly All Main Divisions.

Making numerous changes in the routing of cars on many city lines, the revised routing schedule of the Los Angeles Railway, worked out at the suggestion of the State Railroad Commission and published for the first time in The Times today, is by far the most sweeping traffic revision ever conceived by the company. Officials say it will probably go into effect about May 1, or as soon thereafter as traffic changes to be adopted in connection with the anti-parking ordinance, which goes into effect April 10, can be brought about.

One of the important changes is that the Grand avenue cars will be taken off Seventh street entirely, and will cross from Grand to Broadway on Eleventh street. The West Adams cars will be hooked up with Lincoln Park via Hill street to First street. The Washington-street line hooks up with the Garvanza line instead of Maple avenue. The West Jefferson cars will go via Grand avenue to Seventh street, and east to Mateo street, instead of going north on Spring street to the Plaza. Eagle Rock City and Hawthorne cars will go south on Broadway from First street instead of on Spring street. University and Central avenue cars will cross the business district on Fifth instead of Second street. Brooklyn avenue cars hook up with Hooper avenue instead of Ninth street.

The complete rerouting system, as announced yesterday by the Los Angeles railway, is as follows:

ANGELENO AND CROWN HILL.

Route: Douglas street and Kensington road via Douglas to Edgeware, Bellevue, Beaudry, Alpine, Figueroa, Boston, Bunker Hill, California, Hill, Temple, North Broadway, First, Hill, Fifth, Olive, Sixth, Flower, Third, Boylston, Crown Hill, Columbia, Second, Loma Drive to First.

AVENUE 20.

Regular service abandoned. Tripper service morning and evening to and from the Southern Pacific shops.

BROOKLYN AND HOOPER AVENUE.

Route: Fifty-first and Ascot via Ascot avenue, private right of way, Hooper, Twentieth, Tennessee, Twelfth, Main, Macy, Brooklyn, Evergreen, Wabash to city limits.

EAGLE ROCK AND HAWTHORNE.

Route: From Eagle Rock City via private right of way, Avenue 28 to Dayton, San Fernando road,

(Continued on Fourth Page.)

FAMOUS FILM ROMANCE IS CROWNED BY NUPTIALS.

Bride, Cut Off from Own Church, Has Dr. Brougher, Baptist, Perform Ceremony; will Tour Europe.

Mary Pickford and Douglas Fairbanks are married. The ceremony was performed at 10:30 p.m. last Sunday by Dr. J. Whitcomb Brougher, pastor of Temple Baptist Church, at his residence, 1331 West Fourth street. Yesterday strenuous efforts to keep the news secret for at least another week failed because a telephone leaked. Mr. and Mrs. Fairbanks are at the former's home in Beverly Hills, where they entertained many friends at a belated wedding dinner last evening.

The license was issued last Friday evening at a small and very secret dinner at Mr. Fairbanks's residence. Both the motion-picture stars said at that time that, for business reasons, publicity would necessitate postponing their marriage. License Clerk R. S. Sparks for this reason agreed to help keep the news from an expectant world.

Mrs Fairbanks, by her own statement, published recently, voluntarily severed her connection with the Catholic church by her remarriage after her divorce from Owen Moore, obtained at Minden, Nev., the 2nd inst.

Monsignor P. Harnett of St. Vibiana's Cathedral stated last evening that Mary Pickford, by remarrying, is no longer a regular communicant of the Catholic church: that her second marriage forbids this. He stated, however, that she will not necessarily be excommunicated from the Catholic church.

By her marriage, however, Miss Pickford, a British subject, becomes an American citizen, making unnecessary her contemplated naturalization.

MARY'S REASONS.

At the little dinner last Friday Mr. Fairbanks had as his guests the present Mrs. Fairbanks, Dr. Brougher, Mr. and Mrs. Robert P. Fairbanks, brother and sister-in-law of the host, and Mr. Sparks. When Mr. Sparks had received his invitation to the dinner he had been informed that there was a possibility that his official services would be needed. He, therefore, took the necessary documents to Mr. Fairbanks's home.

And there was almost a wedding then and there. The plan to marry at once was abandoned only after Miss Pickford had advanced these three reasons against it: That she did not want to be married on Friday: that she was dressed in black and it was altogether inappropriate, and that Sunday was the best day to be married, anyhow.

So the ceremony was conducted, as quietly as possible, after chuch last Sunday at the home of Dr. Brougher, a friend of long standing.

Robert Fairbanks and Marjorie Daw stood up with the principals. Mrs. Charlotte Smith, mother of the bride, was present with Mrs. Robert P. Fairbanks, Mr. and Mrs. John Fairbanks, Mrs. Brougher and her mother, Mrs. Isabelle Morse; Mr. Sparks, Dr. Henry Miles Cook, assistant to Dr. Brougher in the pastorate of the Temple Baptist Church: Bennie Zeidman and J. Whitcomb Brougher, Jr.

HER WEDDING GOWN.

The bride was gowned in white tulle over white satin, with an apple-green binding and a spray of apple-green trimming at the belt. Her only jewel was a pearl sautoir.

Miss Daw was in pink Georgette crepe. Mrs Smith wore beaded white Georgette.

"They were as nervous as any couple I ever saw married," said Mr. Sparks yesterday of the film stars, who have enacted exactly similar scenes before a thousand cameras.

The double ring ceremony was used, and afterward Dr. Brougher read Ephesians v: 27-33, from a Bible given to Mr. Fairbanks by his mother, Mrs. Ella A. Fairbanks, at her death.

The clergyman yesterday said of the wedding: "In many respects it was the most solemn and serious ceremony I have ever performed."

Immediately after the ceremony the wedding party left Dr. Brougher's home by motor car.

The marriage license records show Mrs. Fairbanks is 26 years old, and that he is 36. Her name is given in the license as Gladys Mary Smith Moore, and his as Douglas Elton Fairbanks. Both, the records show, have been married before.

TELLTALE FAUX PAS.

Elaborate precautions were taken to guard against publicity. Since Miss Pickford obtained her divorce, rumor had persisted that a marriage to Mr. Fairbanks was imminent. He had been out in the Arizona desert "on location" at the time the court granted the separation from Owen Moore at Minden. But, when Miss Pickford arrived in this city a few days later, Mr. Fairbanks also hurried here. Then "America's Sweetheart" gave out a statement that while she understood that remarriage would mean excommunication from the Catholic church, she did not have to worry about that, as she was not going to be married again.

But the expectant world, nevertheless, waited with its fingers crossed. And when a faux pas by some hello girl in a telephone exchange spilled the news yesterday, the nuptial secret found ears ready and alert.

A certain telephone rang and a man's voice said: "Hello! I want to ask you to keep Doug and Mary's marriage secret for a while longer."

"Whom are you calling?" was the delighted answer.

"Heavens!" said the man's voice. "Is this the wrong number? Isn't this Mr. So-and-So?"

And the beans were spilled.

LONG EXPECTED.

Though nothing in cinema land has roused such interest since the Chaplin-Harris marriage secret transpired, the wedding of Mr. Fairbanks and Miss Pickford was a surprise only in respect to its circumstances. It was perhaps the most generally-expected event in the motion-picture world and was fraught with greatest interest because of the major prominence of the two stars.

Sunday night's event, indeed, has been looked for confidently since the unexpected announcement of Miss Pickford's divorce. At that time it was said that the marriage to Mr. Fairbanks would probably take place in London or Paris and that Mr. and Mrs. Fairbanks would perhaps live abroad for a time. With these rumors were coupled reports that, after making one more picture, Barrie's "Hop o' My Thumb," Mary Pickford would leave the screen.

Mr. Fairbanks's first wife, who was Miss Anna Beth Sully of Providence, R. I., and who married him July 11, 1907, was granted a final decree of divorce by the Supreme Court of New York, March 5, 1919. The papers mentioned as co-respondent an unknown woman. Under the terms of the decree the first Mrs. Fairbanks has the custody of her son, Douglas Fairbanks, Jr.

Mr. and Mrs. Fairbanks gave a dinner last evening at the Fairbanks home at Beverly Hills, where they formally announced their wedding and received the congratulations of their friends. Bride and groom seemed very happy, indeed. Mr. Fairbanks was asked, "Are you happy?" "Oh, gosh!" He replied in the enthusiastic Fairbanks manner. He looked it and so did his blond bride.

WON'T QUIT PICTURES.

"I shall remain in motion pictures," said Mrs. Fairbanks. "Just

(Continued on Second Page.)

Mr. and Mrs. Douglas Fairbanks,

The latter formerly Mary Pickford. The photograph was made at their delayed wedding dinner at the Fairbanks home at Beverly Hills last night.

STEELINK, I.W.W., GUILTY.

Criminal Syndicalism Conviction Means Red Organization is Put Outside Law.

Nicholas Steelink and the I.W.W. in California were convicted of criminal syndicalism by a jury yesterday in Judge Willis's court. The verdict of guilty was reached on the first ballot and the jury was out of the courtroom but twelve minutes.

This verdict, handed to the court by Foreman E. R. Brooks while spectators in the crowded room waited in silence, was reached following an excoriation by Dist.-Atty. Woolwine of the I.W.W. agitators, anarchists and seditionists in general, and Steelink, the defendant, and J. H. Ryckman, of defense counsel, in particular.

Strongly condemning Mr. Ryckman for his utterances in public meetings, in which he extolled the "freedom" of Russia and criticised this country, Mr. Woolwine said that "he is a lucky man that he is not tarred and feathered and driven from this community by an indignant people—it would serve him right."

After court adjourned, Mr. Woolwine issued the following statement:

"The conviction of Nicholas Steelink by a Los Angeles county jury of true Americans is a victory, not only for the citizens of this community, but for the nation at large. The issues in this case involved treason of the most diabolical character. There should be no resting place in the United States for such traitors and, as prosecuting officer of this county, it will at all times be my endeavor to see that destructionists and plotters against the government are as speedily brought to justice as the means at my command will permit and as rapidly as evidence is gathered upon which to found prosecution."

TALK TO JURY.

In his address to the jury Mr. Woolwine said, in part:

"Ryckman knows all about these anarchistic propositions; he has been in every case in which a villainous crime of dynamiting and treason has been involved in the county of Los Angeles for years; he is there lending aid and comfort to the enemies of this government, and sustaining and upholding those who would crush innocent lives in the dark hours of the night.

"Let me tell you something as an American citizen: he wants to go to Russia. You know that it is a monument to the tolerance and the mercy of the people of this great country of ours and it is a monument to Americanism that you men were able to sit there and listen quietly to the denunciation of your beloved country. It is a monument to the institutions of this great country that a man situated as I am, feeling what I felt in my heart as he drew an unfavorable comparison to this great country of ours and soviet Russia, and I sat there saying nothing.

"These miserable fellows believe in free love, too—free love that absolutely destroys every vestige of the home, destroys everything that goes to make a great republic, a great country, because you cannot have a great country and a great republic and a great democracy without those influences that are found at the fireside and at the knee of a mother in lawful wedlock.

"These human fiends have been fanning the flames of discontent, as they say in their sacrilegious song books, and as they tell you in these songs that advocate murder. That is the reason the government is after them.

THE DESTROYERS.

"Sabotage is just a polite term. Don't you know that this great government of ours was in a scrimmage for all kinds of foodstuffs, people were starving to death and babies were dying in their mothers' arms for the lack of nourishment, and these fellows went about destroying the foodstuffs of this country, and destroying the lumber of this great country of ours, 42,000,000 feet in one night?

"And these fellows set about, you know, to destroy property in this State—they say with a great deal of pride there that they have destroyed—that is what it means—$8,000,000 worth a year.

"You have no idea. There may be tens and tens or hundreds of millions that you never have been able to fix upon them in the way of forest fires and fires of incendiary origin, all over the State of California. You can not find these things out.

"Do you know, I never have seen

(Continued on Thirteenth Page.)

BLAST THREAT SIGNED I.W.W.

Woman Gets Note that Home will be Blown up if She Doesn't Move.

"If you do not move within ten days we will place a bomb under your house and blow it to pieces—I.W.W."

This letter, written with a typewriter and mailed at the main postoffice on March 23, was received yesterday by Mrs. Santiago Rodriquez of 625 South Western avenue. It was turned over to Police Detectives Brown and Barnett for investigation.

Police officers who interviewed Mrs. Rodriquez say no motive for the letter can be discovered. She told them that she has no enemies in the city.

The letter will be turned over to the Federal authorities.

WOULD DIVORCE CANFIELD.

Wife Who Said She'd Wait Sues Master Forger, Now Three Years a Convict.

When a wise old warden said not so long ago that prison walls sever all bonds of love for criminals; that a woman never waits longer than three years for a sweetheart who has been sent to the penitentiary, he perhaps didn't expect to have proof right at hand.

However, his little bit of philosophy was proved true yesterday when Mrs. Elsa Canfield filed suit for divorce from Leonard C. Canfield, who is now serving an eight-year sentence in San Quentin for forgery. Mrs. Canfield bases her action for divorce upon her husband's conviction of a felony.

Canfield, one of the most accomplished forgers who has even been called before the local courts, was given his eight-year sentence by Judge Craig February 23, 1917. Mrs. Canfield said at the time that she would wait for her husband. But three years have elapsed, and now, through her attorney, Robert J. O. Culver, she intimates that she does not care to keep a faithful vigil of five years more for her husband.

Canfield was arrested on the charge of forging the name of Justin E. Cook, a trust company notary, to a fictitious instrument used to defraud Miss Carolina Schurtz of Pasadena, out of $5000. This was in 1914. For two years following his arrest he was confined in the County Jail, although he almost succeeded in an audacious attempt to forge a jail bond by using a fraudulent seal. Later six charges were placed against him and he pleaded guilty to the charge of forging Miss Schurtz's name. When he pleaded guilty to this charge the other five were dropped.

During his confinement in the County Jail Mrs. Canfield called on her husband every day for two years, establishing a record in jail annals for devotion. She always brought him some little gift, generally something to eat. Shortly after Canfield was arrested he said regarding his faithful little wife:

"If I could only be alone with Mrs. Canfield for a few moments, so that she might know everything, it would be so much easier. I have tried to make her happy, and if a wrong has been done it was not done intentionally."

Throughout her husband's trail Mrs. Canfield, who had engaged attorneys to defend him, denied that he was guilty and declared that any confession which he might have made was a "lie."

"He was a good husband and provided me with everything that I wanted," she declared on one visit to the jail. "But he obtained his money honestly and we will be able to prove it."

But he could not; now, after a three-year vigil, Mrs. Canfield, in her divorce complaint, charges him with having been convicted of a felony, and on these grounds alone she asks for the divorce.

ROCKEFELLER'S MILLIONS FOR EDUCATION HERE.

Tentative Plans Outlined for Use of Part of Oil King's $100,000,000 Christmas Gift to Humanity.

Tentative plans for the expenditure here of part of John D. Rockefeller's recent $100,000,000 Christmas gift to humanity were outlined yesterday afternoon at a conference at the California Club between Dr. Wallace Buttrick and Dr. Abraham Flexner, representing the Rockefeller general education board, and a group of prominent Southern California business men, including Henry M. Robinson, president of the First National Bank of Los Angeles, former chairman of the Federal Coal Commission and former member of the United States Shipping Board, and H. W. O'Melveny. Dr. Buttrick is president and Dr. Flexner secretary of the Rockefeller general education board, under the direction of which Rockefeller's immense gifts for the advancement of education are being dispersed.

The conference lasted more than two hours and covered a general discussion of educational needs in this territory. Dr. Buttrick and Dr. Flexner previously had spent three days inspecting educational institutions here and in Pasadena.

"No definite announcement as to subjects discussed can be made at this time," said Mr. Robinson after the conference. "You may say it was simply a luncheon of Los Angeles and Pasadena men to Dr. Buttrick and Dr. Flexner at which questions relating to the possible application of funds of the General Education Board in this region were discussed."

"We are making a tour of inspection," added Dr. Buttrick. "We have spent three days here and are much interested. We leave for San Francisco on a similar mission tonight."

The Rockefeller General Education Board, of which Dr. Buttrick and Dr. Flexner are the principal executive officers, has charge of the greatest individual philanthropy now being carried on in the world. In 1916, it was thought to be doing great work for the progress of education when it announced a gift of $3,000,000 to three universities. That same year it announced two other immense gifts, one being $8,000,000 to the University of Chicago for medical research, said to have been

(Continued on Fourth Page.)

F. A. SEIBERLING ARRIVES.

F. A. Seiberling, president of the Goodyear Tire and Rubber Company, arrived here yesterday to be present at the League of the Southwest convention to discuss the development of the Colorado River, which meets tomorrow. He is staying at the Beverly Hills Hotel, where he will be joined by his family tomorrow and remain for one week.

Mr. Seiberling expressed himself as being delighted to be back in Los Angeles again and particularly gratified with the progress made on the Goodyear tire and cotton plants being erected at Ascot Park. The organization, he said, is looking forward to opening the rubber plant in June and in getting started with the actual manufacture. He will address the league convention on some phase of the influence of the development of the Colorado River on the agricultural future of Southern California and Arizona.

"I am heartily in favor of this idea of concentrating all the available forces on some definite plan of developing the great Colorado River basin," he said. "My understanding is that this convention will seek to do this very thing, and if it succeeds its work will be of great benefit to the entire West. This project is so vast in its scope that it will take perhaps ten years to accomplish anything of constructive importance, so it stands to reason that there is need of getting together at once on a definite programme which may be presented to Congress."

Mr. Seiberling, who came here by way of Phoenix, spoke of the remarkable cotton development in the Salt River Valley of Arizona. This prosperous territory, he said, is relatively as important to Los Angeles as is the Imperial Valley in being tributary to and a feeder of local industries.

EXTRA

WEDNESDAY MORNING, VOL. XXXIX. NOVEMBER 3, 1920.

HARDING AND SHORTRIDGE WIN

PHELAN IS SNOWED UNDER FOR UNITED STATES SENATE; LEGISLATURE IS REPUBLICAN

Samuel M. Shortridge was elected United States Senator yesterday, according to latest returns, by a plurality of at least 30,000 votes over his Democratic opponent, Senator James D. Phelan. Mr. Shortridge carried Los Angeles city and county by about 15,000 votes and Southern California as a whole by about 30,000. The vote is estimated to have been the heaviest ever cast for United States Senator in the State.

Returns from 1228 precincts, some complete and others incomplete, as reported at midnight, gave Shortridge 54,943 votes and Phelan 46,533. Phelan does not seem to have carried more than seven or eight counties in the State. He has an estimated plurality of 7500 in San Francisco and 1500 in Sacramento.

Shortridge ran three to one ahead of Phelan in San Bernardino and San Diego counties and was averaging about two to one in all the others.

Kern county is close with Shortridge slightly in the lead, while San Luis Obispo county seems to have given Phelan a slight plurality.

The vote for the Prohibition and Socialist candidates for United States Senator was so slight that it was not reported in the early returns.

Despite the lavish use of money by the Phelan supporters for literature, paid workers and automobiles, the Republicans of the Southern counties heeded the plea of Senator Harding to give him a Republican Congress to hold up his hands.

While the Anti-Japanese land law carried by a big majority the electors of the State refused to be fooled into believing that Phelan would be able to do more to keep the Japanese out of California than Shortridge, and the expected support for Phelan from that source failed to materialize.

The election of Shortridge is generally regarded by Republicans of the State as a well deserved reward for thirty years of valiant service for the Republican party in the State. He has always been a regular Republican, and his very regularity caused former Progressives like Chester Rowell, J. F. Neylan and Marshal Stimson to oppose him. He was attacked as a remnant of the Old Guard. The result shows that he was a pretty substantial remnant.

Mr. Shortridge has pledged himself to work with President Harding and the Republican majority to enact Federal laws which will keep the Japanese out of California, also to help formulate a League of Nations to promote and preserve peace.

HIGHER COURTS.

For the associate justiceships of the Second District Court of Appeal Judge Craig was leading by a safe margin at 1 o'clock this morning with Judges Weller and Works close to a tie for the second place. Judge Weller had a margin of a few votes over Works.

For associate justice of the State Supreme Court Warren Olney, Jr., and W. A. Sloane were elected without opposition, as was Frank G. Finlayson for presiding justice of the Appellate Court, Second Division.

STATE LEGISLATURE.

Little interest was manifested in the State legislative contests yesterday, compared to the primary election. One reason for this was

(Continued on Second Page.)

ANTI-JAP LAW WINS.

Carries State by a Big Majority.

Single Tax is Beaten by Its Usual Margin; May Not be Revived Soon.

Community Property Law is Apparently Rejected in the South.

Incomplete returns from about 1200 precincts in the State indicate that the anti-Japanese land law initiative has carried by a big majority, possibly by 300,000. The heaviest majorities were given in the cities of Los Angeles and San Francisco, but the anti-Japanese spirit was manifested in every part of the State.

In Los Angeles city and county the amendment received a majority of possibly 50,000. Its majority in San Francisco will not be less than 30,000. Judging from the early returns, it is doubtful if the amendment was beaten in a single county in the State.

Under the terms of the initiative Japanese are forbidden to lease agricultural land, either for themselves or as guardians for minor children. It does not prohibit them the right to own land and buildings for residential purposes or to own and occupy business property for commercial purposes. These rights are guaranteed to the Japanese by treaty rights, which take precedence over State laws.

PROHIBITION ENFORCEMENT.

Scattered returns fail to indicate clearly whether the prohibition enforcement act has been sustained or beaten. Returns from 624 precincts, partially complete, give 4724 votes for the act and 4625 against it. San Francisco has not given the majority against the act that was expected from the former wet majorities piled up in that city

Los Angeles, on the other hand, has not proved nearly as dry as was expected. The partial returns indicate that the vote in this city is close. Present indications are that the enforcement act will be sustained by a slight vote, as the country precincts are inclined to vote dry.

This law was passed by the Legislature for the purpose of enabling the State authorities to enforce the Eighteenth Amendment. It was referendumned by the "wet" interests.

SINGLE TAX BEATEN.

Single tax has been beaten by the customary majority. The amendment was repudiated in Southern California by a vote of at least three to one. Meager returns from the north indicate that it has not carried a single county in the entire State. The indicated adverse majority is about 350,000.

ANTI-SINGLE TAX INITIATIVE.

The amendment to increase the number of signatures necessary to place an initiative measure on the ballot from 8 per cent to 25 per cent has apparently carried in Los Angeles city and county by a small plurality. The votes in the northern part of the State, however, are generally against the amendment.

The proponents of the amendment are still hopeful, however, that the vote in Southern California will be big enough to overcome the northern adverse majorities.

COMMUNITY PROPERTY.

Early returns indicate that the community property act has been rejected in Southern California. Returns from about 300 Los Angeles

(Continued on Third Page.)

ELECTION RETURNS.

Following are 3 o'clock a.m. election returns in Los Angeles city and county, except as otherwise indicated:

PRESIDENT.
(1783, State.)

Harding	180,321
Cox	62,484

U. S. SENATOR.
(1220 precincts.)

S. M. Shortridge	54,943
J. D. Phelan	46,533

CONGRESS.
Ninth District—
(184 precincts.)

C. F. Van de Water	10,511
C. H. Randall	5,362

SUPERVISOR.
Second District—
(38 precincts.)

J. H. Bean	1,279
G. W. Lyons	1,159

Fourth District—
(179 precincts.)

R. F. McClellan	2,531
B. L. Farmer	2,011

APPEALS COURT.
(441 precincts.)

Gavin Craig	10,418
Lewis Works	7,667
Dana Weller	7,673

SUPERIOR COURT.
(Long Term.
(15 precincts.)

A. L. Stephens	538
F. R. Willis	584
Sidney Reeve	426
C. S. Crail	605
F. H. Taft	346
Charles Monroe	403
J. W. Shenk	456
L. R. Hewitt	550
W. J. Wood	479
Louis Myers	455
Grant Jackson	390
C. S. Burnell	457
J. W. Hanby	395
C. E. Cryer	356
L. F. Thompson	225
Minor Moore	195
Ruben Schmidt	210

SUPERIOR COURT.
(Short Term.)
(15 precincts.)

J. W. Summerfield	151
Hartley Shaw	424

STATE SENATOR.
Twenty-ninth District—
(2 precincts.)

Dwight Hart	81
J. F. Fitzpatrick	72

(Continued on Second Page.)

VAN DE WATER IS VICTOR.

Bean and McClellan Ahead for Supervisors; Incumbent Judges Winning.

For Congress in the Ninth District 184 precincts in Los Angeles city and county, incomplete, compiled at midnight last night, gave Van de Water 10,511 and Randall 5632. A midnight statement from his campaign committee claimed the district for Mr. Van de Water by 20,000 votes.

Throughout the citrus districts of the county, especially in Pomona, Covina, Monrovia and the eastern portion of Pasadena, Van de Water, the Republican candidate for Congress in the Ninth District, was holding a two-to-one lead in the early election returns. This is accounted for by his stand on the protective tariff issue, the citrus growers being strongly in favor of tariff relief from the next Congress. Van de Water also held a decided lead in a majority of the Long Beach precincts, making it apparent that the beach city was supporting him over Charles H. Randall, his Democratic-Prohibition opponent. Early reports from Glendale and Highland Park also favored the Republican candidate, who apparently was duplicating the vote of the other Republican candidates on the State and national tickets in these sections of the Ninth District. Randall's main strength appears to be in Los Angeles city.

At the Republican County Central Committee headquarters, in the Stowell Hotel, Chairman Bartlett expressed satisfaction over the returns in the Ninth District, which he said assures the election of Van de Water.

Congressman Osborne is far ahead of his Socialist opponent, Upton Sinclair, in the Tenth Congress District.

FOR JUDGES.

The first figures indicated the election of a majority of the ten incumbent Superior Court judges, although two of the seven attorneys making the race had polled a heavy vote in the earlier hours. Judge Albert Lee Stephens, duplicating his heavy primary vote, held the lead in the Superior Court contest, with Judges Louis W. Myers, Frank R. Willis, Charles Monroe, Grant Jackson, Charles S. Crail, Leslie R. Hewitt, John W. Shenk, Fred H. Taft and Sidney Reeve all showing strong support. George E. Cryer, Walton J. Wood and Charles S. Burnell maintained a position well up with the leaders, early indications giving Cryer and Wood a good chance of success in the final count. Ira F. Thompson, J. Walter Hanby and Ruben S. Schmidt were too far down in the list to warrant belief in their election.

FOR SUPERVISOR.

Supervisors Bean and McClellan, heavily supported in the early balloting, appeared safe for re-election in the Second and Fourth Supervisorial districts, respectively. George W. Lyons, opposing Suprvisor Bean, and Councilman Bert Farmer, opponent of Supervisor McClellan, both developed considerable support in portions of their districts, but in the main the advantage remained with the incumbents in a majority of the precincts. Boyle Heights and East Los Angeles were strong for Bean and McClellan showed great strength at Long Beach.

FOR DISTRICT ATTORNEY.

The re-election of Dist.-Atty. Woolwine, who ran unopposed, was conceded by an increased majority shortly before the polls closed. The name of State Senator Charles W.

(Continued on Second Page.)

Warren G. Harding, President-Elect.

BULLETINS.

Eight hundred and ninety precincts in Southern California, incomplete, compiled at midnight last night, gave Harding 109,973; Cox, 34,506.

NEW YORK, Nov. 3.—At 12:30 o'clock this morning with actual returns far from complete, Harding was certain of 275 votes in the Electoral College from the following States:

Connecticut, Delaware, Idaho, Illinois, Iowa, Kansas, Maine, Massachusetts, Michigan, Nebraska, New Hampshire, New Jersey, New York, Ohio, Oregon, Pennsylvania, Rhode Island, Vermont, Washington, Wisconsin and Wyoming.

COLUMBUS (O.) Nov. 2.—Returns received and tabulated at 11 o'clock tonight from 2338 out of 7145 precincts in Ohio showed Senator Harding leading Gov. Cox for President by 111,122. The returns gave Harding 358,798; Cox, 247,657.

HARDING NOT EXULTANT.

"Make Me Capable of Playing Part," is Prayer of Next President.

[BY A. P. NIGHT WIRE.]

MARION (O.) Nov. 2.—Convinced by early returns of his election to the Presidency, Warren G. Harding issued a statement tonight saying that, instead of being exultant over the result, he was "more given to prayer to God to make me capable of playing my part."

Coincident with the Senator's statement, Harry M. Daugherty, a member of the Republican campaign committee, made this statement here:

"It is the greatest victory in American politics, clearly foreshadowed and predicted. It is more than a partisan victory, as the result was contributed to by millions of Democrats.

"The women of the nation have quickly vindicated the conferring of the suffrage privilege, as they sensed correctly the issues and rallied to the cause of America and American institutions. The Republican party is fully conscious of the great responsibilities implied in this popular verdict and will faithfully keep its obligations."

WILL VISIT PANAMA FIRST.

The Senator's trip to Texas will begin Friday night or Saturday morning, and Mr. Harding will arrive at Point Isabel, Tex., near Brownsville, next Monday. He plans to spend about twelve days there, and then leave for Panama by way of New Orleans.

His stay in the Canal Zone will last about a week, during which he will make a first-hand study of local conditions and particularly of the tolls system for American ships. He has advocated throughout the campaign a repeal of these tolls, and it is expected he will collect information on that policy.

Leaving Colon about December 1, he will land at New Orleans and will travel by train to Bedford, Va., where he speaks December 5 at an Elks' celebration. Afterward he is to return to Marion, to remain, under present plans, most of the time until March 4. He may take a trip, during this interim, however, to some southern resort.

As President-elect, Mr. Harding still would be a United States Senator, but his friends say he probably would remain away from Washington and devote his attention to the choice of a Cabinet and formulation of his administration policies. Election of a Republican Governor in Ohio would enable him to resign from the Senate on January 1, when the term of Gov. Cox expires, and when the new Governor would appoint a Republican successor to the vacancy.

HARDING LEADS NEW JERSEY.

[BY A. P. NIGHT WIRE.]

TRENTON (N. J.) Nov. 3.—Harding Coolidge were leading by 39,120 votes in New Jersey when the poll for 387 districts out of the State's 2046 had been counted at 2 o'clock this morning. The vote in 397 districts was: Harding, 73,617; Cox, 34,497; Debs, 831.

PROBABLE ELECTORAL VOTE.

STATE	Harding	Cox	1916 Wilson	1916 Hughes	STATE	Harding	Cox	1916 Wilson	1916 Hughes
Alabama	..	12	12	..	Nebraska	8	..	8	..
Arizona	..	3	3	..	Nevada	x	..	3	..
Arkansas	..	9	9	..	New Hampshire	4	..	4	..
California	13	..	13	..	New Jersey	14	..	..	14
Colorado	6	..	6	..	New Mexico	3	..	3	..
Connecticut	7	..	..	7	New York	45	..	..	45
Delaware	3	..	..	3	North Carolina	..	12	12	..
Florida	..	6	6	..	North Dakota	5	..	5	..
Georgia	..	14	14	..	Ohio	24	..	24	..
Idaho	4	..	4	..	Oklahoma	..	10	10	..
Illinois	29	..	..	29	Oregon	5	..	..	5
Indiana	15	..	..	15	Pennsylvania	38	..	..	38
Iowa	13	..	..	13	Rhode Island	5	..	..	5
Kansas	10	..	10	..	South Carolina	..	9	9	..
Kentucky	..	13	13	..	South Dakota	5	..	..	5
Louisiana	..	10	10	..	Tennessee	..	12	12	..
Maine	6	..	..	6	Texas	..	20	20	..
Maryland	x	..	8	..	Utah	x	..	4	..
Massachusetts	18	..	..	18	Vermont	4	..	..	4
Michigan	15	..	..	15	Virginia	..	12	12	..
Minnesota	12	..	..	12	Washington	7	..	7	..
Mississippi	..	10	10	..	West Virginia	8	..	1	7
Missouri	x	..	18	..	Wisconsin	13	..	..	13
Montana	4	..	4	..	Wyoming	3	..	3	..
Totals						346	152	277	254

Total electoral vote, 531; necessary for choice, 266.

(x) Doubtful States. Total, 33.

SWEEPING VICTORY FOR REPUBLICANS; END OF DEMOCRACY

BY ARTHUR SEARS HENNING.

[EXCLUSIVE DISPATCH.]

CHICAGO, Nov. 2.—Harding and Coolidge were swept into office in the Presidential election by the greatest landslide in political annals.

With 25,000,000 or more Americans participating the Democratic candidates, Cox and Roosevelt, were buried beneath an avalanche of unprecedented pluralities from coast to coast.

The vote of the people constitutes the most complete repudiation of the policies of a President in the history of the republic. The silent vote on which the Democratic managers relied for the election of Cox was cast overwhelmingly for Senator Harding.

At 10:30 o'clock tonight Gov. Cox's newspaper, the Dayton (O.) News, conceded the election of Harding, the Democratic candidate reserving comment until later. Half an hour later Democratic National Chairman White conceded the defeat of Cox.

Incomplete returns at the hour of going to press indicated that Harding had won not less than 358 of the 531 votes in the electoral college, on which basis he would have a majority of 185 over Cox. This breaks the record of the Republican landslide of 1904, which gave Theodore Roosevelt an electoral college majority of 139 over Parker.

TREMENDOUS MAJORITY.

It looks as if Harding had won not only a plurality from ocean to ocean, but a tremendous majority of the total popular vote of the nation, as did McKinley, Roosevelt in 1896 and 1900, Roosevelt in 1904 and Taft in 1908.

The Republicans simply mopped the country. It is doubtful if the complete returns will show that Cox carried a single State outside of the Democratic stronghold comprised in the solid South and the border States. Even in the border States, Cox appears to have made a poor showing. He carried Kentucky by approximately 15,000, but it looks as if Harding had won Missouri, West Virginia and Maryland.

With from 5,000,000 to 10,000,000 women voting for President for the first time and with wholesale defections of men voters from the Democratic party, the Republicans rolled up the most phenomenal pluralities in the experience of the politicians.

MILLION IN NEW YORK.

Harding swept New York by a plurality of 1,000,000 or more, according to estimates based on incomplete returns. He even carried teh Democratic stronghold of New York City. The million margin took the breath away from the prophets of a Harding plurality of 500,000 in New York, but it was only the beginning of a tale of stupendous victory that beggared the wildest claims of the most optimistic Republicans. Still more remarkable was the performance of Gov. Al Smith of New York, Democrat, who appears to have been re-elected despite the Republican tidal wave.

Illinois smashed all records by sending Harding over the line with something like 700,000 or 800,000 more votes than Cox. The Harding plurality in Chicago alone, where the Democrats are strong is in excess of 300,000.

Pennsylvania delivered a Republican plurality conservatively estimated at 750,000. Returns from Massachusetts indicated that the Bay State had indorsed Harding to the tune of at least 300,000 plurality, while Gov. Coolidge estimated that

(Continued on Second Page.)

VERDICT JUST, SAYS HAYS.

"We Are Grateful," Declares Chairman of Republican National Committee.

[BY A. P. NIGHT WIRE.]

NEW YORK, Nov. 3.—Will H. Hays, shortly after midnight, said:

"Once more the American people in a real crisis have rendered a and just verdict. Certainly in this instance they have spoken in unmistakable terms. America is still first. There is a new glory to the Stars and Stripes. Hourly the majorities increase. Both the popular and electoral majorities of Harding and Coolidge will be entirely unprecedented. We will have a majority of not less than fourteen in the Senate and an overwhelming majority in the House. We are grateful."

MARION (O.) Nov. 2.—Senator Harding's statement follows: "Assuming that the early returns are wholly dependable, I do not hesitate to say that I am pleased. Of course I am happy to utter my gratitude. But I am not exultant. It is not a personal victory. It is a renewed expression of confident Americanism and a national call to the Republican party.

"It is all so serious, the obligations are so solemn that instead of exulting I am more given to prayer to God to make me capable of playing my part and that all these calls to responsibility may meet the aspirations and expectations of America and the world.

"I am sure the people who have voted the Republican ticket will understand my feeling that I should make no unstudied statement of policies at this time beyond the expression made throughout the campaign."

COLORADO BY 40,000.

[BY A. P. NIGHT WIRE.]

DENVER, Nov. 2.—Rush Holland, State chairman of the Republican party, in a statement tonight, declared that Harding had carried Colorado by 40,000; that Samuel D. Nicholson, Republican candidate for the United States Senate, and the entire State ticket had carried by 30,000.

He asserted that Congressmen Timberlake, Vaile and Hardy had been re-elected, and that early returns from the western district pointed to the defeat of Congressman E. T. Taylor and election of Merle Vincent, Republican.

COOLIDGE'S PREDICTIONS.

[BY A. P. NIGHT WIRE.]

NEW YORK, Nov. 2.—Senator Weeks of Massachusetts, received a message from Gov. Coolidge, predicting that the Republican plurality outside the city of Boston would be not less than 40,000.

Later Mr. Weeks predicted that Senator Harding would carry New York State by 750,000, and would have a majority of 250,000 in Greater New York City. Connecticut would give the Republican candidate a 75,000 majority, he said. He also claimed Kentucky and Indiana, the latter by 100,000.

CONCEDES IDAHO.

[BY A. P. NIGHT WIRE.]

BOISE (Idaho) Nov. 2.—James P. Pope, Democratic State Chairman, conceded Idaho to Harding tonight, with but seventeen precincts of the 825 in the State reported complete. These precincts gave Cox, 740; Harding, 1592.

WYOMING CLAIM.

[BY A. P. NIGHT WIRE.]

CHEYENNE (Wyo.) Nov. 2.—Republican State Chairman T. B. Kennedy, in a statement at 9 o'clock tonight, said Wyoming was carried for Harding by a majority of at least 8000, out of a total vote of approximately 60,000.

WHERE COX IS STRONG.

[BY A. P. NIGHT WIRE.]

COLUMBUS (S. C.) Nov. 2.—Unofficial returns indicate that out of 60,000 votes cast in three-fourths of the counties in South Carolina today, Gov. Cox's vote was more than 50,000. Gov. Cooper and Senator Smith were re-elected without opposition, and seven Democratic Congressmen were returned, six unopposed.

Harding Wires Congratulations to Gov. Coolidge.

[BY A. P. NIGHT WIRE.]

MARION (O.) Nov. 2.—At 11 o'clock tonight Senator Harding sent the following telegram to Gov. Coolidge:

"My heartiest congratulations over the great Republican victory to which your strength added so materially. You are to expect to play a full part in the coming Republican administration. Good wishes."

To Will H. Hays, Republican national chairman, Mr. Harding telegraphed:

"My gratitude along with congratulations on your capable and successful management of a great campaign."

1921–1930

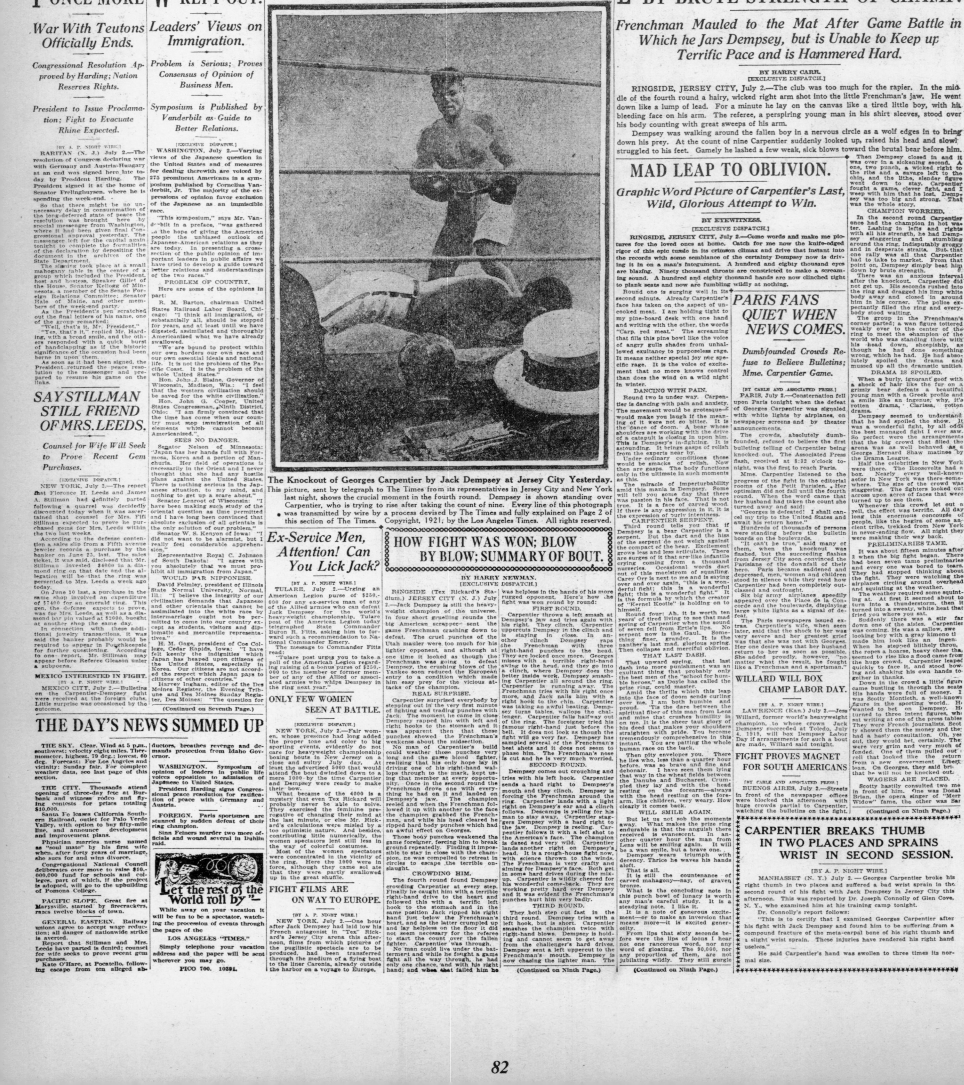

In Eleven Parts—138 Pages
PART I—TELEGRAPH SHEET—10 PAGES

The Los Angeles Times

"Sail on, sail on, and on and on."

GREATER SOUTHERN CALIFORNIA STRAIGHT AHEAD

SUNDAY MORNING, VOL. -- XL. JULY 3, 1921.

Liberty Under Law—Equal Rights—True Industrial Freedom

PEACE HERE ONCE MORE

War With Teutons Officially Ends.

Congressional Resolution Approved by Harding; Nation Reserves Rights.

President to Issue Proclamation; Fight to Evacuate Rhine Expected.

[BY A. P. NIGHT WIRE.]

RARITAN (N. J.) July 2.—The resolution of Congress declaring war with Germany and Austria-Hungary at an end was signed here late today by President Harding. The President signed it at the home of Senator Frelinghuysen, where he is spending the week-end.

So that there might be no unnecessary delay in consummation of the long-deferred state of peace the resolution was brought here by special messenger from Washington, where it had been given final Congressional approval yesterday. The messenger left for the capital again tonight to complete the formalities of the declaration by depositing the document in the archives of the State Department.

The signing took place at a small mahogany table in the center of a group which included the President, host and hostess, Speaker Gillet of the House, Senator Kellogg of Minnesota, a member of the Senate Foreign Relations Committee; Senator Hale of Maine, and other members of the week-end party.

As the President's pen scratched out the final letters of his name, one of the group remarked:

"Well, that's it, Mr. President."

"Yes, that's it," replied Mr. Harding, with a broad smile, and the others responded with a quick burst of handclapping as if the historic significance of the occasion had been borne in upon them.

As soon as it had been signed, the President returned the peace resolution to the messenger and prepared to resume his game on the links.

SAY STILLMAN STILL FRIEND OF MRS. LEEDS.

Counsel for Wife Will Seek to Prove Recent Gem Purchases.

[EXCLUSIVE DISPATCH.]

NEW YORK, July 2.—The report that Florence H. Leeds and James A. Stillman had definitely parted following a quarrel was decidedly discounted today when it was ascertained that counsel for Mrs. Fifi Stillman expected to prove he purchased gems for Mrs. Leeds within the two last weeks.

According to the defense contention a sales slip from a Fifth avenue jeweler records a purchase by the banker on June 25, last. The sales ticket, it was said, disclosed that Mr. Stillman invested $4000 in a diamond ring on that date and the allegation will be that the ring was persented to Mrs. Leeds a week ago today.

On June 10 last, a purchase in the same shop involved an expenditure of $7400 for an emerald ring. This gen, the defense expects to prove, was for Mrs. Leeds, as well as a diamond bar pin valued at $2000, buoght at another shop the same day.

In connection with these additional jewelry transactions, it was said the banker probably would be required to appear in Poughkeepsie for further questioning. According to one report, Mr. Stillman may appear before Referee Gleason unler a subpoena.

MEXICO INTERESTED IN FIGHT.

[BY A. P. NIGHT WIRE.]

MEXICO CITY, July 2.—Bulletins on the Carpentier-Dempsey fight were received at the foreign clubs. Little surprise was occasioned by the outcome.

WANT JAPS KEPT OUT.

Leaders' Views on Immigration.

Problem is Serious; Proves Consensus of Opinion of Business Men.

Symposium is Published by Vanderbilt as Guide to Better Relations.

[EXCLUSIVE DISPATCH.]

WASHINGTON, July 2.—Varying views of the Japanese question in the United States and of measures for dealing therewith are voiced by 275 prominent Americans in a symposium published by Cornelius Vanderbilt, Jr. The majority of the expressions of opinion favor exclusion of the Japanese as an immiscible race.

"This symposium," says Mr. Vanderbilt in a preface, "was gathered in the hope of giving the American people the unbiased outlook of Japanese-American relations as they are today. In presenting a cross-section of the public opinion of important leaders in public affairs we have tried to develop a guide toward better relations and understandings of the two races."

PROBLEM OF COUNTRY.

Here are some of the opinions in part:

R. M. Barton, chairman United States Railroad Labor Board, Chicago: "I think all immigration, or substantially all, should be stopped for years, and at least until we have digested, assimilated and thoroughly Americanized what we have already swallowed.

"We are bound to protect within our own borders our own race and our own essential ideals and national life. It is not the problem of the Pacific Coast. It is the problem of the whole United States."

Hon. John J. Blaine, Governor of Wisconsin, Madison, Wis.: "I feel that the western civilization should be saved for the white civilization."

Hon. John G. Cooper, United States Congressman, Ninth District, Ohio: "I am firmly convinced that the time has come when our country must stop immigration of all elements which cannot become Americanized."

SEES NO DANGER.

Senator Nelson of Minnesota: "Japan has her hands full with Formosa, Korea and a portion of Manchuria. Her field of operations is necessarily in the Orient and I never thought that she had any hostile plans against the United States. There is nothing serious in the Japanese situation, to my mind, and nothing to get up a scare about."

Senator Lenroot of Wisconsin: "I have been making such study of the oriental question as time permitted and I have long been convinced that absolute exclusion of all orientals is the only solution of our problem."

Senator W. S. Kenyon of Iowa: "I did not want to be alarmist, but I really feel considerable apprehension."

Representative Royal C. Johnson of South Dakota: "I agree with you absolutely that we must prohibit all immigration from Japan."

WOULD BAR NIPPONESE.

David Felmley, president of Illinois State Normal University, Normal, Ill.: "I believe the integrity of our civilization demands that Japanese and other orientals that cannot be assimilated into the white race by intermarriage ought not be permitted to come into our country except as students, visitors and diplomatic and mercantile representatives."

H. M. Gage, president of Coe College, Cedar Rapids, Iowa: "I have felt keenly the indignities which Japan has heaped upon citizens of the United States, especially in Korea. Our citizens are not accorded the respect which Japan pays to citizens of other countries."

Harvey Ingham, editor of the Des Moines Register, the Evening Tribune and Des Moines Sunday Register, Des Moines: "The question for

(Continued on Seventh Page.)

THE DAY'S NEWS SUMMED UP

THE SKY. Clear. Wind at 5 p.m., southwest; velocity eight miles. Thermometer, highest, 79 deg.; lowest, 60 deg. Forecast: For Los Angeles and vicinity: Sunday fair. For complete weather data, see last page of this section.

THE CITY. Thousands attend opening of three-day fete at Burbank and witness rodeo and flying contests for prizes totaling $10,000.

Santa Fe leases California Southern Railroad, outlet for Palo Verde Valley, with option to buy fifty-mile line, and announce development and improvement plans.

Physician marries nurse named as "soul mate" by his first wife when, after forty years of marriage, she sues for and wins divorce.

Congregational National Council deliberates over move to raise $10,000,000 fund for schools and colleges, part of which, if the project is adopted, will go to the upbuilding of Pomona College.

PACIFIC SLOPE. Great fire at Marysville, started by firecrackers, razes twelve blocks of town.

GENERAL EASTERN. Railway unions agree to accept wage reduction; all danger of nationwide strike is averted.

Report that Stillman and Mrs. Leeds have parted is denied; counsel for wife seeks to prove recent gem purchases.

Kate O'Hare, at Pocatello, following escape from ten alleged abductors, breathes revenge and demands protection from Idaho Governor.

WASHINGTON. Symposium of opinion of leaders in public life voices opposition to admission of Japanese to United States.

President Harding signs Congressional peace resolution for ratification of peace with Germany and Austria.

FOREIGN. Paris sportsmen are stunned by sudden defeat of their ring champion.

Sinn Feiners murder two more officials and wound several in Dublin raid.

"TIMES" KNOCKOUT PHOTOGRAPH SENT BY WIRE.

The Knockout of Georges Carpentier by Jack Dempsey at Jersey City Yesterday. This picture, sent by telegraph to The Times from its representatives in Jersey City and New York last night, shows the crucial moment in the fourth round. Dempsey is shown standing over Carpentier, who is trying to rise after taking the count of nine. Every line of this photograph was transmitted by wire by a process devised by The Times and fully explained on Page 2 of this section of The Times.

Ex-Service Men, Attention! Can You Lick Jack?

[BY A. P. NIGHT WIRE.]

TULARE, July 2.—Urging an American Legion purse of $250,000 for any ex-service man of any of the Allied armies who can defeat Jack Dempsey for the world's heavyweight championship, Tulare post of the American Legion today telegraphed State Commander Buron R. Fitts, asking him to forward such a recommendation to National Commander Emery.

The message to Commander Fitts read:

"Tulare post urges you to take a poll of the American Legion regarding raising of a bonus purse of $250,000 to the member or former member of any of the Allied or associated armies who whips Dempsey in the ring next year."

ONLY FEW WOMEN SEEN AT BATTLE.

[EXCLUSIVE DISPATCH.]

NEW YORK, July 2.—Fair women, whose presence had long added the proper tone and color to big sporting events, evidently do not care for heavyweight championship boxing bouts in New Jersey on a close and sultry July day. At least the advertised 5000 that would attend the bout dwindled down to a mere 1000 by the time Carpentier and Dempsey were ready to make their bow.

What became of the 4000 is a mystery that even Tex Rickard will probably never be able to solve. They exercised the feminine prerogative of changing their mind at the last minute, or else Mr. Rickard's calculations were misled by a too optimistic nature. And besides, contributing little numerically, the women spectators lent still less in the way of colorful costumes.

Most of the women spectators were concentrated in the vicinity of the ring. Here the 1000 were in force, although they came sol ate that they were partly swallowed up in the great shuffle.

FIGHT FILMS ARE ON WAY TO EUROPE.

[BY A. P. NIGHT WIRE.]

NEW YORK, July 2.—One hour after Jack Dempsey had laid low his French antagonist in "Tex" Rickard's Jersey City arena this afternoon, films from which pictures of the pugilistic spectacle are to be produced, had been transferred through the medium of a flying boat to the liner Caronia, already outside the harbor on a voyage to Europe.

HOW FIGHT WAS WON; BLOW BY BLOW; SUMMARY OF BOUT.

BY HARRY NEWMAN.
[EXCLUSIVE DISPATCH.]

RINGSIDE (Tex Rickard's Stadium,) JERSEY CITY (N. J.) July 2.—Jack Dempsey is still the heavyweight champion of the universe. In four short gruelling rounds the big American scrapper sent the game Frenchman crashing down to defeat. The cruel punches of the Utah mauler were too much for his lighter opponent, and although at one time it looked as though the Frenchman was going to defeat Dempsey, the crushing blows of the Yankee soon reduced the European entry to a condition which made him easy prey for the vicious attacks of the champion.

REAL SURPRISE.

Carpentier surprised everybody by stepping out in the very first minute of fighting and trading punches with Jack. The moment he came in close Dempsey rapped him with left and right hooks to the stomach and it was apparent then that those punches showed the Frenchman's weakenss about the midsection.

No man of Carpentier's build could weather those punches very long and the game blond fighter, realizing that his only hope lay in driving one of his right-hand wallops through to the mark, kept using that member at every opportunity. Once in the second round the Frenchman drove one with everything he had on it and landed on Dempsey's jaw. The champion reeled and when the Frenchman followed it up with another to the face the champion grabbed the Frenchman, and while his head cleared he ripped hard body punches which had an awful effect on Georges.

Those body punches weakened the game foreigner, forcing him to break ground repeatedly. Finding it impossible to stay in close with the champion, he was compelled to retreat in circles to escape the terrible onslaught.

CROWDING HIM.

The fourth round found Dempsey crowding Carpentier at every step. Finally he caught him with a terrible right-hand drive to the heart and followed this with a terrific left hook to the stomach and in the same position Jack ripped his right hand just below the Frenchman's heart, and as the latter crumpled up and lay helpless on the floor it did not seem necessary for the referee to start the count over the fallen fighter. Carpentier was through.

No man could live under the batterment and while he fought a game fight all the way through, he had only one chance, and with his right hand; and when that failed him he was helpless in the hands of his more rugged opponent. Here's how the fight was won round by round:

FIRST ROUND.

Carpentier throws a left smash at Dempsey's jaw and tries again with his right. They clinch. Carpentier uppercuts Dempsey in the clinch and is staying in close. In another clinch Dempsey raps the Frenchman with three right-hand punches to the head. They are locked once more. Georges misses with a terrible right-hand swing to the head, and they go into a clinch, where Dempsey does the better inside work, Dempsey smashing Carpentier all around the ring. Carpentier is running away. The Frenchman tries with his right once more, and Jack nails him with a right hook to the chin. Carpentier was taking an awful beating. Dempsey turns tables, wallops the challenger. Carpentier falls halfway out of the ring. The foreigner tried his famous right-hand just before the bell. It does not look as though the fight will go very far. Dempsey has sampled several of the Frenchman's best shots and it does not seem to phase him. The Frenchman's nose is cut and he is very much worried.

SECOND ROUND.

Dempsey comes out crouching and tries with his left hook. Carpentier sends a hard right to Dempsey's mouth and they clinch. Dempsey is forcing the Frenchman around the ring. Carpentier lands with a light right on Dempsey's ear and a clinch follows. Descamps is yelling for his man to stay away. Carpentier staggers Dempsey with a hard right to the jaw. Dempsey is reeling. Carpentier follows it with a left shot to the American's face. The champion is dazed and very wild. Carpentier lands another right on Dempsey's head. It is a rough-house fight now, with science thrown to the winds. The Frenchman is very crafty and aiming for Dempsey's face. Both get in some hard drives during the mix-up. Carpentier is wildly cheered for his wonderful come-back. They are working pretty hard over Dempsey and it was evident the Frenchman's punches hurt him very badly.

THIRD ROUND.

They both step out fast in the third round. Dempsey tries with a left hook, but is short. Carpentier smashes the champion twice with right-hand blows. Dempsey is holding and cannot seem to get away from the challenger's hard drives. Dempsey sent a left uppercut to the Frenchman's mouth. Dempsey is now chasing the lighter man. The

(Continued on Ninth Page.)

EUROPE'S RING IDOL BEATEN DOWN BY BRUTE STRENGTH OF CHAMP.

Frenchman Mauled to the Mat After Game Battle in Which he Jars Dempsey, but is Unable to Keep up Terrific Pace and is Hammered Hard.

BY HARRY CARR.
[EXCLUSIVE DISPATCH.]

RINGSIDE, JERSEY CITY, July 2.—The club was too much for the rapier. In the middle of the fourth round a hairy, wicked right arm shot into the little Frenchman's jaw. He went down like a lump of lead. For a minute he lay on the canvas like a tired little boy, with his bleeding face on his arm. The referee, a perspiring young man in his shirt sleeves, stood over his body counting with great sweeps of his arm.

Dempsey was walking around the fallen boy in a nervous circle as a wolf edges in to bring down his prey. At the count of nine Carpentier suddenly looked up, raised his head and slowly struggled to his feet. Gamely he lashed a few weak, sick blows toward the brutal bear before him.

Then Dempsey closed in and it was over in a sickening second. A one, two punch, a wicked right to the ribs and a savage left to the chin, and the lithe, slender figure went down to stay. Carpentier fought a game, clever fight, and I weep with him that he lost. Dempsey was too big and strong. That was the whole story.

CHAMPION WORRIED.

In the second round Carpentier once had the champion in hot water. Lashing in lefts and rights with all his strength, he had Dempsey staggering and stumbling around the ring, indisputably groggy and in desperate straits. But that one rally was all that Carpentier had to take to market. From that point on, Dempsey simply beat him down by brute strength.

There was an anxious interval after the knockout. Carpentier did not get up. His seconds rushed into the ring and dragged his limp white body away and closed in around him in his corner. The police expectantly filled the ring and everybody stood waiting.

The group in the Frenchman's corner parted; a wan figure tottered weakly over to the center of the ring to meet the champion of the world who was standing there with his head down, sheepishly, as though he had done something wrong, which he had. He had absolutely spoiled the drama and mussed up all the dramatic unities.

DRAMA IS SPOILED.

When a burly, ignorant goof with a shock of hair like the fur on a grizzly bear defeats a beautiful young man with a Greek profile and a smile like an ingenue, why, it's rotten drama, Clarissa, rotten drama.

Dempsey seemed to understand that he had spoiled the show. It was a wonderful fight, by all odds the best managed fight I ever saw. So perfect were the arrangements that the big crowd that filled the arena was as well behaved as a George Bernard Shaw matinee by the Drama League.

Half the celebrities in New York were there. The Roosevelts had a box. Nearly every well-known actor in New York was there somewhere. The size of the crowd was staggering. The fighters looked out across upon acres of faces that were turned up to see them.

Whenever this crowd let out a yell, the effect was terrific. All day long this enormous concourse of people, like the hegira of some ancient tribe, trekked from New York in never-ending flow. All night they were making their way back.

PRELIMINARIES TAME.

It was about fifteen minutes after 3 when the big fight began. There had been seven tame preliminaries and every one was bored to tears. They had stopped thinking about the fight. They were watching the airplanes circling around overhead and squinting at the weather.

The weather required some squinting at. At first it seemed about to turn into a thunderstorm, then it turned into a sweaty, white heat that fried you where you sat.

Suddenly there was a stir far down one of the aisles. Carpentier was coming. He was a sallow, swe looking boy with a gray kimono tl made him look like an ingen. When he stepped blithely throu, the ropes a hoarse, heavy cheer tha, seemed to rise like a flood came from the huge crowd. Carpentier leaped quickly to face it, and stood bowing and shaking his own hands together in thanks.

Down in the crowd a little figure came bustling in through the seats His hands were full of money. I was Scotty Montieth, a well-known figure in the sporting world. He wanted to bet on Dempsey. He turned to three intent figures, who sat writing at one of the press tables They were French journalists. Scotty showed them the money and they had a hasty consultation. Oh, yes oui, they would bet, certainly. They were very grim and very much offended. One of them pulled out a roll that looked like the return from a new government Liberty loan. On Georges, they said bri that he will not be knocked out.

WAGERS ARE PLACED.

Scotty hastily consulted two me in front of him. One was Donal Brian, the opera singer of "Merr Widow" fame, the other was Sar

(Continued on Ninth Page.)

MAD LEAP TO OBLIVION.

Graphic Word Picture of Carpentier's Last, Wild, Glorious Attempt to Win.

BY EYEWITNESS.
[EXCLUSIVE DISPATCH.]

RINGSIDE, JERSEY CITY, July 2.—Come words and make me pictures for the loved ones at home. Catch for me now the knife-edged rigor of this epic tussle in its crimson climax and drive that instant into the records with some semblance of the certainty Dempsey now is driving it in on a man's integument. A hundred and eighty thousand eyes are blazing. Ninety thousand throats are constricted to make a screaming sound. A hundred and eighty thousand hands are now clinched tight to plank seats and now are fumbling wildly at nothing.

Round one is surging well in its second minute. Already Carpentier's face has taken on the aspect of uncooked meat. I am holding tight to my pine-board desk with one hand and writing with the other, the words "Carp. red meat." The screaming that fills this pine bowl like the voice of angry gulls shades from unhallowed exultancy to purposeless rage. It means neither special joy nor specific rage. It is the voice of excitement that no more knows control than does the wind on a wild night in winter.

DANCING WITH PAIN.

Round two is under way. Carpentier is dancing with pain and anxiety. The movement would be grotesque—would make you laugh if the meaning of it were not so bitter. It is the dance of doom. A bear whose shoulders are working with the drive of a catapult is closing in upon him. This is Dempsey's in-fighting. It is astounding. It brings gasps of relish from the experts near by.

Under ordinary conditions those would be smacks of relish. Now then are gasps. The body functions only in the ultimate in such moments as this.

The miracle of imperturbability amid this mania is Dempsey. Some will tell you some day that there was passion in his face. That is not true. It is a face of carved wood. If there is any expression in it, it is the expression of burly intentness.

CARPENTIER SERPENT.

Third round tells you that if Dempsey is a bear Carpentier is a serpent. But the dart and the hiss of the serpent do not weigh against the compact of the bear. Excitement grows less and less articulate. There are surges of it that are like infantile crying coming from a thousand nurseries. Occasional words dart out of this maelstrom of squalling. Carey Orr is next to me and is saying over and over again, "this is a wonderful fight; this is a wonderful fight; this is a wonderful fight." It is the formula by which the creator of "Kernel Kootie" is holding on to himself.

Round four: Ah, it is worth ten years' of tired living to see that mad spring of Carpentier when the sound of seven fell from Ertle's lips. No serpent now is the Gaul. Something finer, grander. It is the panther's last mad, glorious spring. Then collapse and merciful oblivion.

THAT LAST DASH.

That upward spring, that last dash into more punishment was an exultant thing that probably only the best men of the "school for humble heroes," as Doyle has called the prize ring, could master.

Amid the thrills which this leap into the face of doom sends curling over me, I am both humble and proud. 'Tis the dare between the spiritual fiber of this man from Lens and mine that crushes humility in on me. It is the sheer taut glory of his deed that makes your shoulders straighten with pride. You become tremendously comprehensive in this instant. You are patting the whole human race on the back.

Then pity envelopes you. There he lies who, less than a quarter hour before, was so brave and fine and debonair. I have seen them lying that way in the wheat fields between the Danube and Bucharest. Crumpled they lay and with the head resting on the forearm—always with the head resting on the forearm, like children, very weary. How clearly it comes back.

WILL SMILE AGAIN.

But let us not sob the moments away. What makes the prize ring endurable is that the anguish there received is evanescent. In another quarter hour the man from Lens will be smiling again. It will be a wan smile, but a brave one.

Dempsey wears triumph with decency. Thrice he waves his hands aloft.

That is all.

It is still the countenance of carved mahogany—nay, of graven bronze.

What is the concluding note in this punch bowl of lunacy is worth any man's careful study. It is a steadying note. I like it.

It is a note of generous excitement—or to make an inversion that means more—it is excited generosity.

From lips that sixty seconds before were the lips of loons I hear not one rancorous word, nor any word of gloating. The 90,000, nor any proportion of them, are not jubilating wildly. They still gurgle

(Continued on Ninth Page.)

PARIS FANS QUIET WHEN NEWS COMES.

Dumbfounded Crowds Refuse to Believe Bulletins; Mme. Carpentier Game.

[BY CABLE AND ASSOCIATED PRESS.]

PARIS, July 2.—Consternation fell upon Paris tonight when the defeat of Georges Carpentier was signaled with white lights by airplanes, on newspaper screens and by theater announcements.

The crowds, absolutely dumbfounded, refused to believe the first bulleting telling of Carpentier being knocked out. The Associated Press flash, received at 8:32 o'clock tonight, was the first to reach Paris.

Mme. Carpentier listened to the progress of the fight in the editorial rooms of the Petit Parisien. Her optimism did not fail until the fourth round. When the word came that her husband had taken the count she turned away and said:

"Georges is defeated! I shall cancel my trip to the United States and await his return home."

Hundreds of thousands of persons were standing before the bulletin boards on the boulevards.

"It can't be true," said many of them, when the knockout was flashed, but the succeeding flashes from Jersey City soon convinced the Parisians of the downfall of their hero. Paris became saddened and depressed, men, women and children stood in silence while they read how Carpentier had been completely outclassed and outfought.

Six big army airplanes speedily appeared over the Place de la Concorde and the boulevards, displaying large white lights as a signal of defeat.

The Paris newspapers issued extras. Carpentier's wife, when seen later, said that the shock to her was very severe and her greatest grief was that she was not with Georges. Her one desire was that her husband return to her as soon as possible. She added proudly, however, "no matter what the result, he fought like a Frenchman and a sportsman."

WILLARD WILL BOX CHAMP LABOR DAY.

[BY A. P. NIGHT WIRE.]

LAWRENCE (Kan.) July 2.—Jess Willard, former world's heavyweight champion, to whose crown Jack Dempsey succeeded at Toledo, July 4, 1919, will box Dempsey Labor Day if arrangements for such a bout are made, Willard said tonight.

FIGHT PROVES MAGNET FOR SOUTH AMERICANS

[BY CABLE AND ASSOCIATED PRESS.]

BUENOS AIRES, July 2.—Streets in front of the newspaper offices were blocked this afternoon with huge crowds partial to Carpentier, watching the bulletins on the fight.

CARPENTIER BREAKS THUMB IN TWO PLACES AND SPRAINS WRIST IN SECOND SESSION.

[BY A. P. NIGHT WIRE.]

MANHASSET (N. Y.) July 2.—Georges Carpentier broke his right thumb in two places and suffered a bad wrist sprain in the second round of his fight with Jack Dempsey in Jersey City this afternoon. This was reported by Dr. Joseph Connolly of Glen Cove, N. Y., who examined him at his training camp tonight.

Dr. Connolly's report follows:

"This is to certify that I examined Georges Carpentier after his fight with Jack Dempsey and found him to be suffering from a compound fracture of the meta-carpal bone of his right thumb and a slight wrist sprain. These injuries have rendered his right hand useless."

He said Carpentier's hand was swollen to three times its normal size.

DEATH CAR CRASHES INTO AUTO; MAN HELD

LATEST EDITION---5 CENTS.

The Los Angeles Times

"Sail on, sail on, and on and on."

TUESDAY MORNING, VOL. -- XL. NOVEMBER 15, 1921.

Liberty Under Law—Equal Rights—True Industrial Freedom.

NEW SENSATION IN ARBUCKLE CASE!

SCRAPPING NAVY TO COST AMERICA HALF BILLION.

Few Vessels of Pacific Fleet Will Go to Junk Pile, Officials at Harbor Declare.

[BY A. P. NIGHT WIRE.]

WASHINGTON, Nov. 14.—The actual cost to the United States of the scrapping of the present naval building program, naval officials estimated today, would be between $400,000,000 and $500,000,000, exclusive of any salvage plan. In his statement to the conference Secretary Hughes said the work already done had cost $330,000,000, but these figures do not include costs incident to abandonment of the ships now building.

Assistant Secretary Roosevelt said today that the American program would save the government about $200,000,000 in naval expenditures. The figure is the difference between the total cost of completion of the ships, about $600,000,000 and what scrapping would cost. Included in the scrapping costs are allowances for reimbursement of contractors for work they were compelled to do in their yards in preparation for building the huge craft.

WILL AWAIT AGREEMENT.

There is no intention by the government to stop work on the new ships until an agreement actually is reached by the conference and ratified by the governments.

That was made plain today. Construction of the great majority of the vessels is proceeding slowly, however, the division of available building funds averaging about $2,000,000 a year per capital ship involved. The only ships on which work has been halted, pending developments, are the two at New York navy yard. Stoppage there, it was said, does not involve probability of damage suits for breach of contract.

In any case, it was added, expenditures in progress on ships that may be ordered scrapped, are of such a nature that they could not be saved.

MATERIALS ORDERED.

The bulk of the $2,000,000 a year for each ship is for materials ordered and which would have to be paid for in any case. Only in one or two cases is there a large labor force at work on actual building.

One phase of the program naval officers have been struck with is its probable effect on the three great shipbuilding plants doing most of the new ship construction. Those plants, it was said, were engaged almost entirely on government work and those ships which would be scrapped under the plan. All three, it was predicted, would in all probability be forced to close. They are the plants of the New York Shipbuilding Company, Fore River (Mass.) Company and the Newport News Company.

Expert naval officers expect the Hughes plan to be adopted with only minor alterations.

The Washington conference will spell the end for battle cruisers as naval weapons, in opinion of many naval officers. It is not alone, it was said today, that the American proposals for naval reductions seem to tend toward elimination of the craft from future fleets; but aircraft developments and the battle of Jutland are held by some naval experts to have answered in the negative theories

(Continued on Second Page.)

TO WORK IN SECLUSION.

Big Five Reach Decision.

One to Take Disarmament Problem, Another Far Eastern Question.

[BY A. P. NIGHT WIRE.]

WASHINGTON, Nov. 14.—Real work of the armament negotiations was transferred today from the open conference to the more secluded precincts of the committee room.

After a debate which developed widely separated views on the advisability of giving publicity to the negotiations, the Big Five, comprising chief delegates of the United States, Great Britain, France, Italy and Japan, settled on the committee plan as the only acceptable solution.

To one committee, whose membership will be identical with that of the full conference, was assigned the task of working out a solution for Far Eastern questions. Another, composed of the delegates of the five great powers, was created to take over negotiations on the main topic of armament limitation. Since only delegates of the five powers are qualified to act on armament limitation in the conference, the result in each case will be to resolve the delegates into a "committee of the whole."

BEHIND CLOSED DOORS.

Although no official would make a prediction prior to the assembling of the "new committees," the presumption everywhere tonight was that the meeting would be held behind closed doors and the public would get a glimpse of the proceedings only when, in their capacity as committeemen, the delegates have an important decision to report to the conference.

The committee plan was said to have been agreed to as the most direct method of attack on the problems before the conference, since it would permit greater liberty of confidential expression between representatives of the various governments and would obviate much of the procedure that would be necessary should the sessions continue in the open. Another argument used by those who favored the proposal was that it would facilitate such modifications of program as might become necessary through changes in the personnel of the various delegations and in the diplomatic situation generally confronting the conference.

LAST OPEN SESSION.

One result of the decision may be to make tomorrow's open session of the conference, the last of those which precede the period of actual decision of the questions on which the negotiations hinge. The most optimistic officials do not expect officials to report without long study and debate.

It is pointed out that there is no injunction against an open committee meeting, but the likelihood of such a development is generally conceded to be remote at the present stage of the negotiations.

An additional result, at least, at the beginning, will be to permit the whole body of delegates to deal with subjects before the conference, instead of leaving the decisions to the "big five" or the "big nine." Creation of subcommittees are provided in the plan, however, should that step be found advisable.

COMMITTEE OF WHOLE.

The decision to create the armament committee of the whole was reached at a meeting of the heads of the delegations of the five powers and was adopted for the handling of Far Eastern questions also at a later meeting of the heads of all nine delegations. It also was agreed that at tomorrow's open

(Continued on Second Page.)

FLEE TO BORDER AS WAR HITS LOWER CALIFORNIA.

Refugees Report Tijuana Under Martial Law; New Fighting in Hills Impending.

[EXCLUSIVE DISPATCH.]

SAN DIEGO, Nov. 14.—Civil war prevails in Lower California. Tijuana is under martial law and in the barracks on the eastern edge of the town lie the bodies of fifteen Mexican Federal troopers killed in yesterday's battle with the rebels.

Gov. Ybarra has arrived and established headquarters in Tijuana, and, with Gen. Rodrigues, military commander for the territory, has taken personal command of the troops. The Governor is making every effort to stop what is now acknowledged as an uprising big enough to be termed a revolution.

Reports of the fighting and efforts of the authorities to stop the rebel advance have come out of Mexico with the bands of refugees who hourly are seeking protection on the United States side of the line.

The battle yesterday was staged in San Antonio Canyon, about six miles from Tijuana, and this morning Federal soldiers, including a troop of cavalry which arrived early in the day from the direction of Tecate, started over the hills in several directions. It is believed that Federal troopers have sighted and reported several groups of armed men and that an attempt is now being made to engage them all in battle.

GUNS GUARD TIJUANA.

Four machine guns, the entire artillery equipment of the Tijuana garrison, have been taken to the hilltops nearest the town and are standing guard against any attempt to invade the city. Business is suspended and stores are closed. All the money in possession of Federal authorities has been brought here and every preparation has

(Continued on Third Page.)

NEED SHIPS TO HAWAII.

Pat Argument by Angelenos.

Shipping Board Members Convinced by Leaf and Fredericks.

BY ROBERT B. ARMSTRONG.
[EXCLUSIVE DISPATCH.]

WASHINGTON, Nov. 14.—Los Angeles today convinced the Shipping Board and the Emergency Fleet Corporation that it was in deadly earnest in seeking the establishment of a freight and passenger steamship line from Los Angeles to Hawaii. This action was taken when the board heard all the Pacific ports for allocation of Shipping Board vessels for development of Pacific Coast shipping.

Seattle, Portland, San Francisco and Los Angeles made definite propositions. When the hearing was at an end the experts and executive officers of the fleet corporation said the proposals of Portland and Los Angeles were by far the clearest and cleanest cut yet presented. The board will take no action on any of the applications until November 28, the intervening time being given to the steamship companies proposing to operate the ships in which to file statements of financial condition and proof of their responsibility and ability to operate successfully.

LEAF MAKES PROPOSAL.

Los Angeles' proposal was made by Earl M. Leaf, vice-president and secretary of the Los Angeles Steamship Company. He was introduced to the board by Capt. John D. Fredericks, vice-president of the Chamber of Commerce, and made the formal application. He declared that the Los Angeles Steamship Company had purchased the steamships Harvard and Yale from the Navy a year ago, paying more than $1,500,000 for them and spending a like amount on their rebuilding. He stated that they were in successful operation between Los Angeles and San Francisco, making eighteen knots an hour and

(Continued on Third Page.)

PITY THE POOR EX-HUN.

What Do We Get Out of Disarmament Plans, Is Hopeless Wail From Germany.

[BY CABLE AND ASSOCIATED PRESS.]

BERLIN, Nov. 14.—The Nationalist press discovers in the proposals of Secretary Hughes only "American egoism" and "lies, hypocrisy and dishonesty." The newspapers declare that Germany cannot "expect the slightest relief from French cruelty, carried on with a revolver on the hip along the Rhine."

Some newspapers express the belief that the delegates greeted the proposals with approval in order to gain time "to put something over on each other."

The liberal press is silent, but the radical Rote Fahne (Red Flag) says it is evident that the "four oppressed peoples"—Russia, Germany, Japan and Siberia—will be the sacrificial offerings to the commercial imperialism of America and England."

"Whether England wishes or not," it adds, "her Japan-hating dominions will force her to go with the United States. These dominions are a bigger trump card in the hand of Secretary Hughes than the billion pounds of war debt England owes."

The Pan-German Tages Zeitung thinks the American program of a ten years' naval holiday probably will result in a race to construct fighting submarines and airships and real disarmament is still far away.

The Taeglische Rundschau says: "Despite Quaker help and milch cows it means for us nothing but hypocrisy, lies and dishonesty. It is laughable to see England, America and Japan seeking to save each other from injury, while they are secretly planning later sabotage for the whole program."

The Allgemeine Zeitung sees the prospect of an American and British agreement and says it is certain France will be given a free hand in dealing with Germany.

The Kreuz Zeitung says President Harding's words sound like those of former President Wilson, but President Harding has a more workable scheme.

REMEMBER THIS
BY H. M. STANSIFER

The devil can run a mile while some good people are cranking up.

BIG MERGER COMPLETED.

New $25,000,000 Corporation Will Make West Independent of Eastern Steel and Iron.

[BY A. P. NIGHT WIRE.]

SAN FRANCISCO, Nov. 14.—Announcement was made here today of the closing of a deal between Utah and California capitalists which contemplates a $25,000,000 iron, coal and steel merger, the primary aim of which, it was said, will be to make the entire West industrially independent of eastern steel and iron.

The details as given out by L. F. Rains, president of the Carbon Fuel Company of Salt Lake City, here in connection with the merger, call for the single industrial management of the coal, coke and iron industries and deposits of the Utah mineral region, and the providing of raw materials from that section for finished steel products.

At the head of the merger is Wigginton E. Creed, president of the Pacific Gas and Electric Company and president of the Columbia Steel Company of Pittsburg, Cal. With him and Mr. Rains are associated A. C. Ellis, Jr., president of the Utah Coke and Coal Company; W. W. Armstrong, president of the National Copper Bank of Salt Lake City; Duncan MacVichie, capitalist; Capt. Radditz, president of the Tintic Standard Mining Company, and L. B. McCormick, all of Salt Lake City.

CALIFORNIANS INTERESTED.

The Californians include A. C. Denman, Jr., president of the Southern California Iron and Steel Company; William R. Staats, Russell McD. Taylor, S. K. Rindge, A. W. Grier, E. G. Pratt, C. G. Henderberger, all of Southern California, and Joseph Sloss, J. D. Grant, D. H. Blotchford, A. E. Boynton, W. C. Hammon and Herbert Fleishhacker of San Francisco.

Mr. Rains, founder of the plan, declared here tonight all details of the merger, including contracts for several phases of the work, have been signed, and that only certain legal and technical phases of the project remained to be finished. It had not been decided, he said, whether the new organization would be incorporated under California or Utah laws, and so far the merger is nameless.

Mr. Rains said the value of properties drawn into the merger approximated $10,000,000. The remaining $15,000,000, he said, represented capital investment to be spent in development work in iron, coke and coal deposits in Utah and in other amalgamation development work.

KEEP MONEY IN WEST.

An effect of the corporation's activities, he declared, would be to keep in the West $150,000,000 annually, which he said Pacific Coast and Rocky Mountain industrial firms were forced to spend each year in the East for eastern iron and steel products. With the manufacture of iron and steel products in the West, he pointed out, western firms would be enabled to obtain their products cheaper, also.

SCRAPPED SHIPS DON'T COUNT--KATO

Japanese Admiral Refuses to Discuss Counter-Suggestions on Hughes Plan.

[BY A. P. NIGHT WIRE.]

WASHINGTON, Nov. 14. — "It isn't the scrapped ships that count; it's the ships afloat," declared Admiral Baron Kato today in answering questions put by Japanese correspondents concerning the American proposals.

"Isn't it true, Admiral," he was asked, "that the ratio of scrapped warships under the Hughes proposition is rather disadvantageous to Japan considering the present inferior naval position of our country? Aren't they asking too much?"

The admiral responded:

"Why talk about scrapped ships. You should know that what really counts is the number of fighting ships left afloat and not the number of those to be abandoned."

The admiral declined to commit himself as to the probable Japanese counter-suggestions, but it is understood that although Japan is almost certain to favor the American proposals as a whole, it is probable they will be the subject of a serious discussion.

"Naturally," said one Japanese naval expert, "we cannot swallow in one mouthful, this most momentous project which is destined to so vitally affect the future of our empire. Therefore, we may have counter-suggestions or proposals."

The American plan was termed large and generous as well as practicable. The primary question interesting the Japanese, however, is understood to be whether an eventual ratio for Japan of 60 per cent in capital ships as compared with the United States and Great Britain will be regarded as sufficient defensive strength. In favor of its efficiency, it is said, is the circumstance that Japan's great distance from the other countries concerned makes it less imperative

(Continued on Second Page.)

LATEST NEWS

Bandit Wounded; Accomplice Kills Manager of Oil Station

CHICAGO, Nov. 14.—A bandit was shot down and captured by a policeman in a Standard Oil filling station tonight. But while he was being taken, an accomplice, firing from a stolen auto at the side of the station, killed William Frank, a submanager taking the place of regular employees who sought a few hours of relief. This was his first time at that station. Police believe the wounded bandit and his companion are the two men who climbed into the automobile of John Gundinger, forced him to take them to the Western-avenue road, took his money and watch, put him out of the car and fired two shots at him as they drove away.

Marble and Tile Works Destroyed by Fire

A fire which started at the Joe Musto & Sons Marble and Tile Works at Soto and Lugo streets at midnight last night was still burning early this morning, firemen and police estimating the damage to be around $200,000. Night Watchman Blankenship, who reported the fire, stated that he was awakened by the crackling of flames and found the large plant ablaze. The origin of the fire is undetermined. The plant is reported to house several valuable works of art tile and statuary.

Missing Arbuckle Case Witness Found

CHICAGO, Nov. 14.—Miss Betty Campbell, long sought as an important witness in the Fatty Arbuckle case, was found tonight in her home on Sheridan Road. Miss Campbell, 20 years old, was a member of the party at which Virginia Rappe met her death. She denied she had attempted to hide from the San Francisco authorities. "I do not believe Virginia Rappe was killed by Fatty or that he had anything to do with her death," the girl said.

Former Publisher and Lawyer Passes

TUCSON, Nov. 14.—John T. Hughes, aged 47 years, pioneer, former publisher of the Arizona Daily Star and prominent criminal lawyer of Arizona, died here at his home tonight after a long illness.

SHOT, DIES IN AUTO CRASH.

Man Wounded in Fracas With Speed Officer Thrown from Car While Being Rushed to Hospital.

Herman Goldstein, aged 31 years, a traveling salesman from New York, was shot by a motorcycle officer at Culver City at midnight during an asserted fracas over a speeding charge and several persons who were in the machine with Goldstein were slightly hurt in a collision fifteen minutes later while ostensibly en route to a hospital.

Police and deputy sheriffs are investigating the tangled details of the case. The substance of the story told by witnesses early this morning is that Paul Forman, a jeweler at 222½ East Fifth street, was driving Lieut. Harry K. Leventen of the U.S.S. Connecticut to a train. He admitted he was speeding through Culver City. In the machine also were Goldstein and Miss Juanita Hawkins of 325 West Fifty-seventh street, a manicurist.

Motorcycle Officer W. A. Minor of Culver City darted after the speeding automobile. There was an argument, in which Forman was struck in the face and Goldstein was shot. Officer Minor asserts he was set upon by the three men and his motorcycle was kicked into a ditch. His revolver was accidentally discharged, he claimed. He did not know anyone had been shot.

The four persons in the careening machine sped at nearly sixty miles an hour east on Washington street. Forman claims he was racing to the hospital with Goldstein, who was unable to talk, but was conscious at that time. At Hoover and Washington streets the auto, in attempting to make a turn, collided with a machine driven by Dr. A. Gottlieb, 605 Consolidated Realty Building. Both machines were wrecked. Miss Hawkins was lacerated on the face. Goldstein was thrown from the machine. He was dead when examined at the Receiving Hospital.

Fred W. Mattehy, 59 years old, of 2719 Rimpau avenue, who was in the doctor's car, was severely cut and bruised.

Beyond slight bruises, the other persons in the second accident were not injured.

Police Surgeon Crossan stated that Goldstein might have sustained a broken neck in the second accident. The bullet entered the right side of his neck.

Harry Wagner of the Hayward Hotel stated he was a witness to the collision at Washington and Hoover streets. He said he observed the motorcycle officer coming after the speeding machine. He was told by Officer Minor, he said, that the occupants of the car had not only resisted arrest, but had attacked him.

Forman was held at the County Jail on a charge of reckless driving and resisting an officer. Miss Hawkins and Lieut. Leventen, who were first detained as material witnesses, were later released on their own recognizance.

Officer Minor was not held by the police. He submitted a report on the case.

AGUILAR ARRESTED FOR JUMPING BOND.

[BY A. P. NIGHT WIRE.]

EL PASO, Nov. 14.—Candido Aguilar, son-in-law of the late President Carranza of Mexico, and Antonio Moreno, former Mexican army colonel, were arrested at San Antonio on charges of "jumping bonds" in the Federal court here, it was learned at the local marshal's office today.

FILM CLOWN'S TRIAL STARTS WITH A CLASH

BY OTIS M. WILES.
[EXCLUSIVE DISPATCH.]

SAN FRANCISCO, Nov. 14.—A heated controversy between Gavin McNab, chief counsel for Roscoe (Fatty) Arbuckle in his trial on a charge of manslaughter, which opened here today, and Dist.-Atty. Brady ended in a vociferous declaration from the District Attorney that he will resign if Mr. McNab is able to prove a statement he made at the close of the afternoon session.

Attorney McNab was questioning one of the prospective jurors. He asked him if he would take into consideration as evidence in the case the fact that witnesses for the prosecution had been threatened with imprisonment in the County Jail if they refused to make certain affidavits.

Dep. Dist.-Atty. U'Ren attacked Mr. McNab's statement as untrue. Mr. McNab replied that such tactics had been used by the prosecution. He declared he would bring seven witnesses into court to prove his statement.

"If you can prove it I'll resign immediately," Dist.-Atty. Brady retorted, as he leaped to his feet and waved a clenched fist at the defense attorney.

Seven prospective jurors were questioned during the day. Two were excused and five were temporarily passed.

QUESTIONED CLOSELY.

For an hour and forty-five minutes John C. Medley, the first venireman called, was lambasted with questions fired at him by Gavin McNab, chief counsel for Arbuckle, and Dep. Dist.-Atty. U'Ren.

At the close of his questioning the following salient points concerning the type of jury that will finally be chosen to judge Arbuckle guilty or innocent were well defined:

The prosecution will prevent any motion-picture fans from sitting on the jury. It will challenge all veniremen who have read with avidity the published reports of the Arbuckle case. It will oppose the choosing of any who aspire to political office during a Democratic administration, to any one who has any acquaintances among the motion-picture profession.

HOSTILE TO CLUB WOMEN.

The defense is hostile to all San Francisco clubwomen. It is eager to learn if any of the women called for jury service is a member of the women's vigilante committee, which apparently is after Fatty's scalp. It is opposed to all veniremen who may take into consideration that during the reported Arbuckle party in the St. Francisco Hotel, following which Miss Rappe died a tragic death, the Prohibition Enforcement Act was violated.

The first clash between the staid old Scotchman, Gavin McNab, and the District Attorney forces occurred shortly after the case was called. Attorney McNab referred to the Women's Vigilante Committee as a mob. Dep. Dist.-Atty. U'Ren was on his feet immediately. He objected to the word "mob."

"I'll change mob to vigilance," McNab replied.

The deputy District Attorney again entered an objection. He declared there was no vigilance committee in San Francisco.

"I'll change vigilance to Vigilante, then," McNab retorted.

McNAB A WINNER.

He won his point, the first legal victory of the trial.

Attorney McNab, in questioning Mr. Medley, made reference to witnesses which were kept incomunicado in the homes of attaches of Dist-Atty. Brady. He began to call the roll of all the leaders of the San Francisco women's clubs, and asked the juror if he knew any of them.

Dist.-Atty. Brady, who had been gently caressing his white locks, leaped to his feet.

"Are we trying Arbuckle, the defendant—or are we trying the climate of San Francisco, the women of the city or the dead girl?" he shouted.

McNab and the District Attorney were quarreling directly among themselves. Judge Louderback scolded them, told them to address the court. But McNab was permitted to continue with his busy calling the roll of the club women, leaders whose names are now dragged into the case.

Mr. Medley rejected, for cause, August Fritze, a San Francisco broker, was called next. Arbuckle was playing with a knotted rubber band. Occasionally he laid it aside to flip paper wads or to twiddle his thumbs. Tiring of this, he resumed playing with the rubber band.

At the counsel table with Arbuckle were his battery of attor-

(Continued on Third Page.)

ANGLO-JAP PACT HIT.

Peking Greets Northcliffe.

Secret Agreement Negotiated by British in Tokio, Publisher Hears.

BY PATRICK GALLAGHER,
Staff Correspondent "The Times."
[BY CABLE—EXCLUSIVE DISPATCH.]

PEKING, Nov. 14.—Americans, British and Chinese have been combining in public receptions given in honor of Lord Northcliffe, who is spending a few days here while on tour of China and other oriental countries.

No European in recent years has received such reception from the Chinese and European residents as that which greeted the London publisher upon his arrival in Peking. It was estimated that more than 50,000 persons thronged the streets for a glimpse of the Briton, who is credited here with being the strongest British influence against the Anglo-Japanese alliance, which is viewed with so much hostility by China.

Lord Northcliffe spent several hours today at the Rockefeller Institute, where he greeted newspaper correspondents from America and Europe. He took occasion to criticise the proposed Anglo-Japanese alliance and at the same time said he had heard that the British Foreign Office has been conducting secret negotiations with Japan on the alliance.

RUMOR MAY BE TRUE.

"There have been persistent rumors in Tokio, as well as in Peking, that the British Foreign Office has been negotiating a secret agreement with Japan," said Northcliffe. "This may be true. Past experience with Anglo-Japanese agreements is sufficient to give rise to the belief that anything is possible with secret diplomacy. The fact that the two nations may have agreed or are seeking to agree upon an amended alliance should occasion no great surprise.

"But," he continued, "it will be a serious mistake on the part of Great Britain if the treaty shall be signed first and then announced to the world. It will be an equally serious mistake on the part of Tokio. There is no question regarding the attitude of China regarding the treaty and both the signatory parties will have some trouble explaining their action at Washington."

FAVORED BY MILITARY.

Lord Northcliffe declared the proposed alliance was favored only by the militaristic classes of Great Britain and Japan. "The Anglo-Japanese agreement may easily be construed as inimical to the interest of the United States," he said. "Any agreement that has even the remotest chance of involving the United States in disputes with Great Britain should be carefully avoided. In fact almost any conceivable alliance between Japan and Great Britain is not favored by progressive Japanese, is detested by British and Americans in the Far East, as well as by the Chinese, and is opposed by Australians, New Zealanders and other parts of the empire. Only the Japanese militarists favor the pact and that for obvious reasons."

Lord Northcliffe has been several weeks in the Orient, having spent some time in Tokio and other Japanese cities before coming here. While in Japan he permitted his opposition to the Japanese alliance to become generally known without diminishing in any apparent degree the welcome shown him in the Mikado's kingdom.

Since his arrival in China he has been showered with honors as much by the native governments as by Europeans and Americans here.

In Three Parts—32 Pages
PART I—TELEGRAPH SHEET—16 PAGES

The Los Angeles Times

"Sail on, sail on, and on, and on."
Liberty Under Law—Equal Rights—True Industrial Freedom.
FRIDAY MORNING. VOL. -- XLI. FEBRUARY 3, 1922.

CONVENE TO NAME POPE.

Cardinals Meet in Seclusion.

Extra Precautions Taken to Keep Record of Voting Strict Secret.

Prelates Cut Off from Rest of the World Till Task is Accomplished.

[BY CABLE AND ASSOCIATED PRESS.]

ROME, Feb. 2.—Majestic stateliness attended the solemn immuring in the Vatican today of the Sacred College, comprising for the moment fifty-three cardinals. Every detail of the sacred rites was observed, and although the time fixed for the closing in of the cardinals was 3:30 this afternoon, so long was the ceremonial that darkness had enshrouded the huge basilica of St. Peter's and the Vatican palaces before the doors were finally barred and bolted, and the preliminaries were complete for the grave task of the election of a new Pontiff.

The fifty-three cardinals present in Rome are now in the Vatican. Even Cardinal Marini, who is suffering from influenza, was conveyed there. He did not participate in the ceremonies of the afternoon, but remained in bed, resting preparatory for tomorrow, when the first ballot will be taken.

STRICT SURVEILLANCE.

At the huge bronze doors surveillance of those passing within was of the strictest nature. A giant German-Swiss sergeant of the guard allowed nobody to enter unless provided with a white pass is-

(Continued on Fourth Page.)

JAPS MAKE CONCESSION TO CHINESE DEMANDS.

Arms Conference Expected to End Saturday Following Plenary Session to Adopt Treaties.

[BY A. P. NIGHT WIRE.]

WASHINGTON, Feb. 2.—Japan met China part way today on the latter's request for abandonment of the celebrated "twenty-one demands" program of 1915. Taking the center of the stage as the final scene of the Arms Conference began, the Japanese announced their government was ready to give up Group 5 of the "demands," which China has held was calculated to rob her of hen sovereignty, and to make further concessions regarding economic privileges and political and military preferences in Manchuria and Mongolia.

Tomorrow China is to reply in a statement that is expected to end the Far Eastern questions, and on Saturday the Washington conference probably will adjourn sine die after a plenary session for formal adoption of the Far Eastern treaties.

JOINT DECLARATION.

Consideration of the "twenty-one demands," the last topic remaining on the Far East agenda, began in the Far Eastern committee after hope of an adjustment of the Chinese Eastern Railway situation had been abandoned and a resolution adopted merely declaring arrangement for "better protection" of the road should be worked out in the near future through diplomatic channels. The powers other than China appended a joint declaration of China's responsibility for fulfillment of her obligations to foreign stockholders of the road.

Japan's statement on the "demands" was presented by Baron Shidehara, who argued that the Chinese request for abrogation of the treaties and agreements resulting from the 1915 program could not be supported by a plea of

(Continued on Fourth Page.)

LIQUOR ACT DECLARED NOT VALID.

Van Ness Measure in New Jersey Unconstitutional, Court's Decision.

[BY A. P. NIGHT WIRE.]

TRENTON (N. J.) Feb. 2.—Declaration today by the Court of Errors and Appeals that the severe State Prohibition Enforcement Act was unconstitutional brought both wet and dry forces to their toes. Developments of the afternoon included:

Announcement by the Anti-Saloon League of New Jersey that a substitute for the Van Ness Act immediately would be introduced.

Orders from Assistant State Prohibition Director Surtees to prosecutors that evidence of violations of the Van Ness Act immediately should be transferred to Federal prohibition authorities.

Reports that saloon owners, especially in Atlantic City, had shown marked activity since the court decision had become known.

Declaration in Jersey City by Gov. Edwards, elected on a wet platform, that it was up to the prohibition forces to worry, not him, and that he did not think they would "be able to put over anything as radical as the Van Ness Act."

Speculation ran high on the fate of those already apprehended for violation of the act.

From Atlantic City came word that County Prosecutor Gaskill had expressed belief that ten men indicted there would not be brought to trial unless the Federal authorities took over the cases.

Two-cent Stamp Counterfeited; First in Years.

[EXCLUSIVE DISPATCH.]

NEW YORK, Feb. 2.—The first counterfeit 2-cent postage stamps to come to light in twenty-seven years were discovered here today by a collector. It is an engraving said to be the first in stamp counterfeiting history. Two spurious issues which were circulated in 1895 were typographed.

The new counterfeit to the casual glance seems familiar enough, but comparative examination quickly exposes poor workmanship and reveals many points at variance with the original. The head of George Washington is shorter, the nose has a hook, the eyes seem to glance furtively to the side instead of straight ahead, and the quene appears carelessly knotted.

CRISIS IN GERMANY.

Railroad Strike Effective.

Coal Shortage Acute and Industries Are Forced to Slow Down.

Nation Virtually Isolated; Marooned Foreigners Seek to Escape.

BY GEORGE SELDES.

[BY CABLE—EXCLUSIVE DISPATCH.]

BERLIN, Feb. 2.—With the first day of Germany's railroad strike not quite over, all wheels throughout the nation are ceasing to move. Almost every railroad has ceased to operate and the coal shortage, which already has been affecting the nation, is reaching an acute stage. Nearly all industries are being forced to curtail their activities and as a result the country is facing one of the most serious crises since the founding of the republic.

Today Germany virtually is isolated by land from the rest of Europe, not even the international expresses being permitted to leave the stations at Berlin. Thousands of foreigners are marooned and are wondering how they can reach the seaboard.

AMERICANS DESPERATE.

Inasmuch as the Entente stopped all airplane traffic in Germany some months ago, Germany today is resorting to wagons and automobiles for transportation. Desperate Americans are paying hundreds of dollars for taxis to take them to Bremen and Hamburg, where they had booked passage for the United States.

Without claiming that their position is right, government officials are taking the most remarkable measures ever known here to break the strike. Under President Ebert's proclamation yesterday, which establishes a condition just below martial law, the police today arrested two of the committee of thirty-five, who voted to strike and the rest are in hiding "for their self-protection," as they announce.

STRIKE FUND SEIZED.

Government agents likewise raided the strike headquarters and confiscated the hundreds of thousands of marks in the treasury on which the strikers had hoped to subsist. The police and militia are everywhere guarding and patroling the railroad property, especially in Saxony, where, if anywhere, the strike might take a revolutionary turn.

While the strike apparently is completely successful, the government is making no effort to compromise. The officials admit that the workers are entitled to the higher wages demanded, but claim the Entente budget makes impossible an increase in pay. The locomotive brotherhood, which called the strike, has demanded an increase in wages commensurate with the increased cost of living, pointing out the devaluation of the German mark and the fact that wheat and meat, which are largely imported, make necessary at least a 40 per cent increase over the wages of a year ago when marks were sixty to the dollar.

Delays to trains or entire stoppage of service have been reported from all sections. In the Essen, Elberfeld, Munster and Erfert districts, traffic is at a complete standstill.

The strike has extended to Cassel and Chemnitz. Traffic between Berlin and Leipsic has been stopped and Berlin's city and suburban lines are at a standstill.

ARBUCKLE ABANDONS HOPE.

No Longer Expects to Clear Himself Before World; Jury Deadlocked, Chance of Verdict Wanes.

[EXCLUSIVE DISPATCH.]

SAN FRANCISCO, Feb. 2.—Fatty Arbuckle has given up hope of trying to clear himself in the eyes of the world. The jury trying him for manslaughter in the death of Virginia Rappe is still out, still deadlocked; and the hope he had that it might agree upon a verdict has waned and died.

Many hours have passed since the eleven men and the woman filed out of Judge Louderback's court yesterday, and although all sorts of rumors have trickled out of the jury-room, there has not been one authentic report.

It is variously reported that they are eleven to one for acquittal, seven to five for acquittal, seven to five for conviction, and ten to two for conviction. Each partisan has his own information.

BREAKS UNDER STRAIN.

The nervous strain that affects everybody in the courtroom grows with the hours. Arbuckle broke under it last night, weapened and called for a doctor.

He is full of fun today, full of stories, full of chuckles; but one

(Continued on Third Page.)

THE DAY'S NEWS SUMMED UP.

THE SKY. Clear. Wind at 5 p.m., west; velocity, 5 miles. Thermometer, highest, 56 deg.; lowest, 41 deg. Forecast: For Los Angeles and vicinity: Friday fair. For complete weather data, see last page of this section.

A digest in Spanish of day's most important news will be found on the third page of this edition of The Times.

THE CITY. Investigators for The Times located four witnesses who saw the suspected slayer of William Desmond Taylor, internationally known film director, before and after fatal shot was fired.

C. H. Wheeler, one of the dry agents sent from San Francisco to "clean up Los Angeles," was arrested on warrant from District Attorney's office charging assault on two counts; other officers are sorght.

California Citrus League called meeting of persons interested in orange industry for next Monday, to discuss stringent rules recently promulgated by State Department of Agriculture governing shipments of fruit.

Harold Thompson, 18-year-old Los Angeles boy, was frozen to death in blizzard raging through Sierra Madre Mountain and two companions severely injured while on hiking trip through the peaks.

Six of the Navy's newest submarines were found defective and ordered to the Atlantic Coast to be overhauled.

Three special excursion trains brought tourists from Idaho, Montana and the western part of North Dakota, the first excursions of the kind since 1917.

PACIFIC SLOPE. Bay City Treasury agent for ewelve years, and successful stager of many narcotic raids was transferred to New Orleans.

Three men started yesterday in an attempt to reach ice-capped peak of Mt. Rainer, a feat that has never been accomplished.

Texas Governor with the announcement of his withdrawal from the American party and his candidacy to the United States Senate, also announced dissolving of American party.

Secretary of State Veterans' Welfare Board announced approval of 150 ex-service men's applications for financial aid in purchasing land under recent Land Purchase Act.

Arbuckle jury, unable to agree, was locked up for night: film comedian lost hope of clearing self in eyes of world.

Ceremony of driving golden spike on completion of Alaskan railroad has been deferred until summer visit of President Harding.

GENERAL EASTERN. Miners' officials seek to revive "one big union" idea; want aid of railway crafts to fight wage reductions.

More than score of miners were asphyxiated in mine of Frick company following explosion that intombed them.

Notice was served on James A. Stillman that his wife would file tomorrow, motions for more expense money.

WASHINGTON. According to Department of Commerce figures a decrease of 18,000,000 in the population of soviet Russia as compared with prewar figures has been reported by Moscow.

State Department announced that a new commercial treaty with Bulgaria was being drafted. Wednesday's dispatches from Sofia announced ratification of treaty draft by Bulgarian Parliament.

Sine die adjournment of Arms Conference expected Saturday, according to information given delegates last night. Hope to finish Far Eastern treaties today.

Senator Spencer came to defense of Senator Newberry over attack made against him by Senator Reed.

Arms Conference expected to hold plenary session and adjourn Saturday; Japs make concessions to China.

Number of Annapolis graduates to receive commissions will depend on action of Arms Limitation Conference.

Foreign debt refunding bill struck obstacles in House when President Harding objected to some terms inserted by Senate.

FOREIGN. Cardinals assembled in secret conclave to elect successor to Pope Benedict XV. Extra precautions were taken to guard secrecy of balloting.

Crisis faced by Germany as railway strike proves effective; marooned foreigners seek escape from country.

New crisis arose in Irish affairs when Premier Sir James Craig of Ulster and Michael Collins came to hitch over boundaries.

High costs of necessities driving Paris students to face battle of the before careers really open.

German officials worried over great activity of American oil men in gathering leases in foreign fields.

Life is not salvage to be saved out of the world, but an investment to be used in the world.

NEW IRISH FUSS STARTED.

North and South at Loggerheads Over Boundaries and Free State is Making Threats.

[BY CABLE—EXCLUSIVE DISPATCH.]

DUBLIN, Feb. 2.—The Irish Free State is on the verge of an open break with the Ulster government over the boundary question. The crisis developed this afternoon at the resumption of the negotiations which began so auspiciously in London between Sir James Craig and Michael Collins.

At the end of a three-hour conference the Ulster Premier and the head of the provisional government found themselves perhaps hopelessly apart on the problem of readjusting the border line.

Mr. Collins insisted on incorporating in the southern government comparatively large areas which had been regarded as absolutely vital to the existence of the north.

TO FORCE ISSUE.

It is learned from an authoritative source that the provincial government plans to use every agency to compel the north to yield on this issue. It hesitates to re-establish the boycott against Belfast, which was removed only a few days ago, and to refuse to cooperate in operating the railway, telephone and other government services.

The southern leaders seem confident that they have it in their power to render Ulster almost impotent.

One high provisional official asserted that Ulster must come across on this issue, and that the south is going to make it do so.

OFFICIAL STATEMENT.

An official statement was made by Col. Spencer, secretary of the Ulster Cabinet. It says:

"The discussion between Michael Collins and Sir James Craig was almost entirely confined to the subject of the boundary commission.

"Owing to the fact of Mr. Collins's' stand on the boundary commission and the Irish delegation's agreement with Prime Minister Lloyd George that large territories were involved in the commission, and not merely the boundary line, as Sir James Craig was given to understand privately by several British ministers and from statements by Mr. Lloyd George, in the House of Commons, no further agreement was reached."

WRITER ARRESTED.

[BY CABLE AND ASSOCIATED PRESS.]

BELFAST, Feb. 2.—Michael Tobin, Belfast correspondent of the Dublin Freeman's Journal, was arrested today by officers of the Irish republican army in Westport, County Mayo, and is detained in a local barracks for reporting a sermon by Archbishop Gilmartin denouncing the recent outrages in Belfast.

Tobin, who is prominent as a newspaper man, has been ordered sent to Dublin.

THREE OF FAMILY KILLED BY POISON.

[BY A. P. NIGHT WIRE.]

SANTA ROSA, Feb. 2.—Father, mother and son lost their lives from botulinus poisoning caused by eating home preserved beans, according to physicians in attendance on Mr. and Mrs. Joseph Pastores and Joseph Pastores, Jr., all of Healdsburg.

The parents died during the night, while the son died at noon today.

Linked in Sinister Drama of Mystery.

Mabel Normand, who was questioned in connection with the case.

William D. Taylor

Photodiagram of Killing. Cross Marks the Spot where Body was Found

The Taylor Home

Figure in Taylor Killing Case.

The photodiagram reconstructs the actual slaying, according to the police theory. Taylor was shot by a man, who lurked in the shadows between the door and the piano at the right, as he re-entered the house from the curb.

FRIENDS EXPRESS SORROW.

From all quarters of the motion-picture world, from many of the biggest producers in the profession, came testimonials of William Desmond Taylor's worth as a friend. Two of his closest friends issued statements on the film director's murder. One was Jesse L. Lasky, first vice-president of the Famous Players-Lasky Corporation, and with whom Mr. Taylor was closely associated.

"I have lost a friend," said Mr. Lasky, "a man who won that place, not only for his own personal qualities, but also for the manner in which he discharged his professional duties. William D. Taylor's loyalty to the firm he worked for was proverbial. Never had he been late to any engagement; never had he balked at a task because it was too hard. And when a slump in the industry demanded personal sacrifice, William D. Taylor was the first to offer himself. A man of finer ideals I have never known.

"The Lasky studio plans to adequately recognize Mr. Taylor's funeral. The exact nature will be determined when the Motion Picture Directors' Association announces the date of burial.

"The Famous Players-Lasky Corporation proposes to enter actively into the plans for the detection of the murderer. Resources of time and money will be drawn upon to hasten the time when the murderer of our friend is brought to justice."

Charles Eyton, general manager of the Famous Players-Lasky Corporation, was one of Mr. Taylor's oldest and firmest friends.

"Through a cowardly assassin's bullet I have lost the best friend I have ever had. I have known Bill Taylor for nine years and we have worked side by side for the

(Continued on Second Page.)

TAYLOR MURDER SUSPECT TRACED TO, FROM HOUSE.

Asked Oil Station Man the Way to Slain Director's Home; Seen Leaving, Boarding Car.

Tracing the movements of a man suspected of being the slayer of William Desmond Taylor, internationally known film director, who was shot to death in his Alvarado-street apartments Wednesday night, investigators for The Times last night located four witnesses who saw the man before and after the tragedy. Actuated by motives of revenge due to jealousy, the police believe, the murderer fired the fatal shot as near as can be calculated a few minutes before 7:45 p.m., as Mr. Taylor was sated at his writing desk or just as he returned and closed the door when he returned from escorting Mabel Normand, acress, to her car.

Between 7:45 and 7:50 p.m., just after the report of the revolver was heard, Mrs. MacLean, wife of Douglas MacLean, the actor, who lives near the Taylor home, saw a man leaving the Taylor apartments. He was described as being about five feet nine or ten inches tall, of medium build and roughly, but not shabbily, dressed in dark clothes and a plaid cap.

Shortly before 6 o'clock a man answering this description stopped at the Hartley service station, Sixth and Alvarado streets, and inquired where W. D. Taylor resided. Floyd Hartley, 331 South Bonnie Brae street, and L. A. Grant, in charge of the station, were in the place at the time.

The circumstances recited by both of these witnesses tally to the minutest detail. The inquirer was 26 or 27 years old, they said, weighed about 165 pounds, wore a dark suit, probably of blue serge, and a light hat or cap. He had dark hair and was of medium complexion.

They directed him to the Alvarado Terrace Apartments and he left the oil station. He walked toward the apartments. That was the last they saw of him.

SEEN BY CARMEN.

Maryland street runs east and west at the rear of Mr. Taylor's apartment. It is a street car stop on the West First-street car line, but passengers board cars there at only rare intervals, possibly for months.

E. W. Dascomb, conductor, R. S. Woodard, motorman, s' that a man answering the scription boarded their ca either 7:54 or 8:27 p.m. were not certain which trip it ... but took notice because of the infrequency with which passengers are taken on the Maryland-street stop.

"I took particular notice of this passenger on that account," said Conductor Dascomb. "It was an inbound trip. This fellow was about five feet and ten inches tall, fairly weel dressed, as I remember, weighed about 165 pounds, and his hat or cap was of a light color. I remember that he wore something tan, but I don't recall whether it was his coat or vest. I can't remember where he got off, but I think I would know him again."

DESCRIPTIONS TALLY.

Motorman Woodard recalled that Mr. Grant, in charge of the oil station, had mentioned the circumstance of a man inquiring for Mr. Taylor, and of the similarity in descriptions. The descriptions given by Mrs. MacLean, Mr. Woodward and Mr. Dascomb tally so closely that authorities believe there is little doubt but what the three people saw the same man.

It is believed that the slayer had no automobile. Persons residing in the vicinity have taken special

(Continued on Second Page.)

TELLS OF VISITING TAYLOR.

Mabel Normand Explains Call on Friend and Says He Helped Her Into Her Car When She Left.

BY GRACE KINGSLEY.

Mabel Normand, seen at her home at Seventh street and Vermont avenue yesterday, was much agitated over the murder of her old friend, William D. Taylor. She gave a clear and frank statement of all her movements Wednesday afternoon and evening. J. A. Waldron, the Mack Sennett studio manager, was with her all day, answering phone calls and receiving messages, Miss Normand stated.

Continuing, she stated that she spent the afternoon downtown, attending principally to income tax matters and to her banking. She then called her home from the bank at Sixth and Main streets and asked if there were any messages for her. Her maid said: "Mr. Taylor has been trying to get you all the afternoon, and we told him that you were out. We told him you were downtown."

"He had been trying to get some books for me that I wanted," said Miss Normand. "We always discussed books a great deal. He told the maid he had got one of the books at Parker's and was sending it by his chauffeur. He said that he had obtained the other book I wanted at Robinson's, and left word with the maid for me to stop at his house and get it.

"I went and bought 5 cents' worth of peanuts, but the man didn't have any change; so I went to the drug store in the Pacific Electric Building and got the change. I bought a lot of magazines and papers, among others a Police Gazette. I ate the peanuts on the way, and we drove out to Mr. Taylor's, and when I got out I told my chauffeur to clean the car. Then I went up on the steps. I heard Mr. Taylor talking to somebody over the phone, underneath the stairs, and I hesitated about going in until he had finished. Then I entered. He had been talking to Mrs. Marjorie Berger, who has charge of the income tax business for many of the picture folk, including myself.

"He came in and said, 'Gee, I am glad to see you.' I said, 'I just came up for the book.'

"I arrived at his house about five minutes after 7. We talked about books. I looked around his drawing-room, and told him I thought he had changed his house furnishings. He said, 'You haven't been here for so long you forget.' I hadn't been to his house before in two months. He said, 'The Victrola is the only thing new.'

"His servant, Henry, had been arrested for some sort of misconduct, and he was saying that perhaps he would have to go down to court tomorrow (that's today) to see about it. Henry came in, and I said to Mr. Taylor, 'Have you had your dinner?' He said, 'Yes, have you had yours?' I said, 'No, but I am tired, and I'm going home now. I have a studio call for 7 o'clock tomorrow morning.' I've been going to bed very early every night—haven't been anywhere since I began work on my present picture.

"We were talking about the cameramen's ball next Saturday night, and he said he had a box, and I said I had one. He told me whom he was going to take and wanted to know whom I was going to take.

"Henry went out and talked to my chauffeur as my chauffeur cleaned up the car. Henry was telling my chauffeur what a nice man Taylor was to work for.

STOOD OUTSIDE DOOR.

"Finally Mr. Taylor said 'Well, if you're tired why don't you go home and rest and I will call you up this evening.' I asked Mr. Taylor who lived in the different bungalows in the court, and he told me. We stood outside two or three

(Continued on Second Page.)

LATEST MORNING EDITION

DESTINY

"Sail on, sail on, and on and on."

The Los Angeles Times

GREATER SOUTHERN CALIFORNIA STRAIGHT AHEAD

SATURDAY MORNING. VOL. XLII. FEBRUARY 17, 1923.

Liberty Under Law—Equal Rights—True Industrial Freedom.

Mystery in Shooting Near Sawtelle

NEW CLEW IN SHOTGUN MURDER

FAIL TO FIND VICTIM AFTER HUNT IN DARK

Reports of a violent quarrel, two shots and a despairing cry of "O my God" sent police officers last night to an isolated clump of woods near the intersection of Sawtelle Boulevard and the Pacific Electric Venice line.

C. A. Bell of La Belle Apartments, 630 West Fourth street, reported that he had his car parked on the road when he and a woman companion were startled by the sound of a quarrel, apparently between two men hidden by the trees.

According to Bell, both men began to curse loudly and suddenly one of them fired a shot.

Then came a cry of "O my God" and a groan, followed by a second shot. Bell said that a voice from the darkness then called out to him:

"Get out of here, or I'll give you some of this lead, too."

Without waiting, Bell turned his car around and notified the police. Officers E. L. Chaffee and J. T. Teel of the Wilshire Police Station were unable to discover any signs of a struggle.

It was learned that several residents living within a quarter of a mile of the scene had heard two shots at about 10:30 p.m.

Latest News

Viviani's Wife Succumbs

PARIS, Feb. 17.—Mme. Rene Viviani, wife of former Premier Viviani, died at 11 o'clock last night after an illness of only a few hours.

Woman Hurt by Auto Dies

Mrs. M. Jacqumin, 85 years of age, of 4403 Vermont avenue, who was run down by an automobile yesterday afternoon, died early this morning at the Westlake Hospital. Police of the University Station are investigating.

Washington Pacts Ratified

ROME, Feb. 16.—The Senate today adopted the treaties drawn up at the Washington Armament and Far Eastern conferences. It also ratified the Treaty of Santa Margherita between Italy and Jugo-Slavia.

Capture Slayer of Father

LONDON, Feb. 16.—Two sons of Dr. Thomas O. Higgins, who was assassinated last Sunday night, tracked the leader of the gang who murdered their father and arrested him, according to the Dublin correspondent of the Daily Express. The prisoner's name is given as Byrne.

Boy, 14, Kills Father

CENTER (Ala.) Feb. 16.—Bert Nolen, 50 years of age, was shot and killed by his 14-year-old son Heron at his home a few miles from here this afternoon, according to local officers. The son, who was lodged in jail here, is quoted as saying he acted in protection of his mother and himself.

Seek Insane Man's Brother

Police here were requested last night by the San Bernardino police to locate John Casey, believed to be the brother of William Casey, who yesterday tried to hang himself in the San Bernardino City Jail, according to the report. William Casey had been arrested and placed under observation on suspicion of insanity. His brother is believed to be a contractor in this city.

LINES MUST HAVE GOOD EQUIPMENT

[EXCLUSIVE DISPATCH.]

WASHINGTON, Feb. 16.—Atty.-Gen. Daugherty announced yesterday that an order issued by Judge Foster of New Orleans, directing the Texas and Pacific Railroad Company to provide proper equipment to "insure and protect the safety of employees, the traveling public and the United States mails," was entirely in accord with the policy of the department to enforce all laws relating to the railroads of the country.

For more than a month, the Attorney-General said, he had investigated conditions on this particular road, and when it was found that equipment apparently was defective and insufficient, he directed that legal action be instituted.

When representatives of the various railroad brotherhoods and the Interstate Commerce Commission several months ago called the attention of the department to what appeared to be an evasion of the inspection laws by common carriers engaged in interstate commerce, Mr. Daugherty ordered an examination of all evidence collected bearing on the subject.

TUTENKHAMUN TOMB OPENED; NOT DISTURBED

BY H. V. MORTON

[BY CABLE—EXCLUSIVE DISPATCH.]

[Copyright, 1923, Public Ledger.]

LUXOR, Feb. 16.—One of the most wonderful sights ever witnessed by Egyptologists was seen by the excavators of King Tutenkhamun's tomb today when the inner chamber was opened and they peered into the darkness. Around the great sarcophagus lay a mass of precious objects, vases, urns, statuettes and boxes with the dust of thirty centuries on them.

The lights of three powerful electric torches flickered like white moons in the pitch darkness, illuminating sections of the painted walls where the weird gods of Egypt were pictured tending the soul of the king on its journey to the Shades.

Although twenty persons were present there was not a single sound in the dim tomb. The lights focussed on the break in the wall leading to the death chamber. Hearts beat fast as the excavator-in-chief was bidden to look at that which no human eye had seen for 3000 years. No matter how little superstitious a man may be, the act of breaking the rest so carefully guarded through the centuries must cause an emotion which time can never efface. Lord Carnarvon was pale as he stepped slowly into the darkness and was lost in the shadows of ancient Egypt.

SECRECY ENFORCED

This peep into the mummy chamber of the Pharaoh took place amid great secrecy. Not one tourist was present and no correspondent, not even those favored by the excavators, entered the tomb.

The preparations for opening the chamber began at 8:30 o'clock this morning. The impressions of the seals on the inner doorway were taken by Dr. Alan Gardiner and Prof. James H. Breasted of Chicago. The glaring electric lights were tested and the last of the timber work made ready.

The mats on which the life-sized statues of the king had stood were brought out. The statues themselves had been encased to prevent damage.

The party of twenty arrived at 1:15 o'clock for the great event. It included Howard Carter, whose twenty years of work is now crowned with success, Sir William Garvin, Lord Carnavon, Inspector Engelbash in charge of antiquities in Upper Egypt, Director George Lacaus of Egyptian antiquities, and Soliman Pasha, Undersecretary for Public Works. Lady Evelyn Herbert, Lord Carnavon's daughter, was the only woman present.

CHISELS SPEAK

The door of the outer chamber was reopened at 1:30 o'clock. Cane chairs were taken into the tomb for visitors. The men removed their coats because of the stifling heat which they would experience below, and at last the party entered. A dramatic period of suspense and excitement followed. Howard Carter could be heard making a speech to the assembly in the depths of the tomb and there was a sound of hand-clapping at the close. Then at exactly twelve minutes to 2 came the first knock on the wall sealing the mummy chamber. Piercing the wall with chisels had begun.

I cannot exaggerate the indescribably weird effect of this knocking within the depths of the earth as it echoed in the still hot hush of the afternoon through the silent valley which had so long kept its royal secret.

A hawk hovered over the tomb like a spirit of the old gods.

"Chip, chip, chip," sounded the

(Continued on Second Page)

BRITISH DEBT FUNDING PLAN IS APPROVED

[BY A. P. NIGHT WIRE.]

WASHINGTON Feb. 16.—Congressional approval of the British debt funding settlement virtually was completed tonight when the Senate passed the House funding bill. The vote was 70 to 13.

The bill was returned to the House for adjustment of amendments not relating to the plan for funding the British debt of $4,604,000,000 over a term of sixty-two years at reduced interest, but providing that settlements with other debtor nations must have the approval of Congress instead of the President.

OPPOSITION LIMITED

The opposition consisted of four Republicans, Senators Borah, Idaho; France, Maryland; La Follette, Wisconsin, and Norris, Nebraska; and nine Democrats, Ashurst, Arizona; Gerry, Rhode Island; Heflin, Alabama; Hitchcock, Nebraska; McKellar, Tennessee; Reed, Missouri; Trammel, Florida; Walsh, Massachuetts and Walsh, Montana.

Forty-six Republicans and twenty-four Democrats voted for passage of the bill. The Republicans were: Ball, Brockhart, Bursum, Calder, Cameron, Capper, Colt, Couzens, Curtis, Dillingham, Ernest, Fernald, Frelinghuysen, Gooding, Hale, Harreld, Johnson, Jones (Washington,) Kellogg, Keyes, Lenroot, Lodge, McCormick, McCumber, McKinley, McLean, McNary, Moses, Nelson, New, Oddie, Page, Phipps, Poindexter, Reed (Pennsylvania,) Shortridge, Smoot, Spencer, Stanfield, Sterling, Sutherland, Townsend, Warren, Watson, Weller, and Willis.

The Democratic supporters were Bayard, Broussard, Caraway, Dial, Fletcher, George, Glass, Harrison, Jones (New Mexico,) King, Myers, Overman, Owen, Pittman, Pomerene, Ransdall, Robinson, Sheppard, Shields, Smith, Stanley, Swanson, Underwood and Williams.

The vote was not reached until after 7 o'clock and after a continuous session of eight hours and a total of four days of debate.

The bill was passed a week ago today by the House after one day's discussion and goes to conference with a certainty of enactment before Congress adjourns. Chairman McCumber of the Finance Committee, Senator Smoot, Republican, Utah, a member of the Finance Committee and also of the Allied Debt Commission and Senator Williams, Democrat, Mississippi., were

(Continued on Second Page)

POLES PUSH LITHUANIAN FORCE BACK

[BY CABLE—EXCLUSIVE DISPATCH.]

WARSAW, Feb. 16.—Engagements between Polish and Lithuanian troops in disputed Lithuanian territory resulted in wounding twelve Poles and several Lithuanians before the latter retreated. Most of the southern area is now Polish controlled but the Lithuanians are demolishing bridges and roads wherever they are forced to retreat.

The Polish government has sent a sharp warning to Lithuania that the latter government will be held to strict accountability for all acts of irregular troops operating in the disputed zone.

PARIS, Feb. 16.—The Allied Ambassador's Council gives Lithuania sovereignty in the Memel district, that part of Germany sequestered by the Allies.

KILLED AFTER FLEEING GAS

Doctor Driven From Barricaded Room in Nevada Hotel and is Shot in Gun Fight

[BY A. P. NIGHT WIRE]

RENO (Nev.) Feb. 16.—After deputy sheriffs and a score of persons had narrowly escaped death during a hail of bullets, Dr. J. Perry Tyson, 50 years of age, of San Jose, was shot and killed by Deputy Sheriff J. W. Carter at Wadsworth, near here, this afternoon, when gas from tear bombs forced him to fleet from his barricaded room.

Tyson, who is said to have been insane, was reported to have been attempting to incite a revolt against the whites among the Piute Indians of the Pyramid reservation.

BARRICATED IN ROOM

Justice of the Peace Ingalls of Wadsworth notified the Sheriff of Washoe county of Tyson's appearance on the reservation this morning after the physician had threatened him with a revolver.

The Sheriff's officers, arriving at Wodsworth, found Tyson locked in his room in a hotel, where he had gone after declaring he would kill the first man who entered. Attempts to inject ether through the keyhole of the room were given up when Tyson sent a volley of bullets through the door.

Unable to get near the window to throw tear bombs into the room, officers tossed the bombs against the door. The fumes finally drove Tyson from the room to the hallway, where, after exchanging shots with the officers from a window, a bullet from the gun of Deputy Carter hit him in the back of the head. He died instantly.

Tyson was formerly a practicing physician of Reno. After a disturbance here a year ago he was charged with insanity, but his son, Howard Tyson, of San Jose appeared in his father's behalf and he was placed in his care.

Tyson leaves his widow in San Jose and six children.

We're Never Too Busy to Stop and Rubber

FEEL ALONG UNDER THE SEAT OF THAT ROYAL THRONE AND SEE IF YOU CAN FIND ANY WADS OF GUM!
THE TOMB OF THE GREAT KING TUTENKHAMUN LUXOR, EGYPT
THEY'VE FOUND KING TUT'S FALSE TEETH!
NO MEN WANTED
RUSH ORDER
SPECIAL CORRESPONDENT
THIS BUSY OLD WORLD OF OURS
TELEGRAM
NO ADMITTANCE EXCEPT ON BUSINESS!
GALE

OPEN HEARING IS ASKED FOR BY CRONKHITE

[BY A. P. NIGHT WIRE.]

WASHINGTON, Feb. 16.—Revelations which "will shock the conscience of the country" were promised tonight by Maj.-Gen. Adelbert Cronkhite, war commander of the Eightieth Division, in his first public statement regarding the circumstances surrounding his recent enforced retirement from the active roll of the Army.

Repeating his charge that he was taken out of active service because of the attention he was giving to investigation of the death of his son, Maj. Alexander P. Cronkhite, mysteriously killed in 1918 at Camp Lewis, Wash., the general asserted that in what he had done he was only "performing the duty to which I was assigned by the President."

TRUE FACTS BURIED

He had been given no opportunity, he added, to place the true facts before the authorities, and, contrary to established regulations, had been denied even the right of appearing before a retiring board.

"The facts in this whole unfortunate affair, when they come to light," he said, "will shock the conscience of the country, and unless something happens to me they surely will come to light."

A Senate investigation into the case already has been requested by Jennings C. Wise, who served in the Eightieth Division as a lieutenant-colonel, and by others of Gen. Cronkhite's friends. Tonight no decision on the request had been reached by the Senators interested, although action on the nomination of a successor to Gen. Cronkhite still was being withheld at the request of Senator Glass, Democrat, Virginia, in whose State the Eightieth Division trained.

During the day Senator Reed, Republican, Pennsylvania, to whom Col. Wise addressed his request for an investigation, replied to the Colonel's letter with a promise that the case would receive careful consideration. Senator Reed added, however, that he had not yet decided whether to present a resolution of inquiry

In his statement tonight, Gen. Cronkhite emphasized that he believed President Harding had been "misled" into signing the retirement order and that the "grave irregularities" he charged in connection with the case of Maj.

(Continued on Second Page)

GUERRILLA WARFARE DEVELOPS IN RUHR; SOLDIERS AMBUSHED.

BY JOHN CLAYTON

[BY CABLE—EXCLUSIVE DISPATCH.]

[Copyright, 1923, Chicago Tribune, Inc.]

RECKLINGHAUSEN, Feb. 16.—Guerrilla warfare, such as has raged in Ireland since the armistice, is developing in the Ruhr. Bands of young men, operating secretly, already are making organized attempts to kill French officers I learned from French sources tonight.

Seated in his office at French headquarters, Gen. Laignelot, commanding the Forty-seventh Division, described how narrowly he had escaped death a few nights ago.

Several of these youngsters lay in wait and fired from behind a tree. The general was leaving headquarters to walk to town and as he stepped from the door several shots were fired. The bullets missed the general, but one struck a French sentry.

Attacks made on French soldiers by gunmen in ambush leads the French authorities to believe the movement is growing and that they may face organized guerrilla tactics already.

A French soldier was wounded last night at Westerhold. The shot was fired by an unseen adversary.

Gen. Laignelot's assailant was given a severe grilling by French military intelligence officers, who refuse to divulge the result, but it is reported that the prisoner made a statement admitting the presence of an organized defense body to oppose the French by individual killings.

ESSEN STORM CENTER

[BY CABLE AND ASSOCIATED PRESS.]

ESSEN, Feb. 17.—Essen was the storm center today in the Ruhr, where the friction between the French and the Germans has increased because of Thursday night's shooting of two French soldiers by security police in a cafe brawl.

In retaliation for this shooting, Gen. Fournier ordered a battalion of French infantry to occupy the German police barracks. The chief of police was arrested, all the files and documents at police headquarters were taken by the French and disarming of the police was begun.

The shooting of the French soldiers occurred when eight of them, off duty, entered the cafe. The waiters refused to serve them because of the boycott against the French started last Monday night and fighting immediately began.

The director of the Essen electric light plant, Herr Buszmann,

(Continued on Second Page)

New Year's Eve Jewel Robbery Suspect Nabbed

[BY A. P. NIGHT WIRE.]

NEW YORK, Feb. 16.—John F. Derby, alias Marshall of Albany, was arrested tonight as the ringleader of a gang which, last New Year's Eve, robbed Mrs. Irene Schoellkopf of Buffalo, of $500,000 of jewels as she was leaving a midnight watch party at the apartment of Frank Barrett Carman, an actor-artist.

Detectives declared his arrest meant solution of the jewel theft.

TUSCAN PRINCE IS FOUND

Coast Guard Cutter Snohomish Taking Off Crew of Vessel, Which is Total Loss

[BY A. P. NIGHT WIRE]

SEATTLE, Feb. 16.—The steamship Tuscan Prince, whose whereabouts and fate were unknown since 4 a.m. yesterday, was found this afternoon at Village Point, Vancouver Island, a wreck but with all on board alive.

Word of the discovery of the Tuscan Prince, for whom dozens of craft have been searching since she flashed, "We are going to drown," was received here in dispatches from the Coast Guard cutter Snohomish. The Snohomish took of fourteen of the crew of forty-three and is to remove the others in the morning.

The Snohomish, the message said, in returning tomorrow after completing rescue of the crew of the Tuscan Prince, will pick up that of the steamship Santa Rita. Santa Rita men, said to be short of wood, have been camped at Carmanah Point, Vancouver Island, since she hit on a rock early yesterday while attempting to go to the aid of the steamer Nika, which burned to the water's edge.

The fourteen men taken to the Snohomish were carried in the surf boat of the Canadian life-saving station at Bamfield Creek.

The Snohomish reported that the Tuscan Prince, a 420-foot steel steamer of British build and registry, was a total loss.

The Snohomish expected to take the crews of the Tuscan Prince and the Santa Rita to Port Angeles, where she last night set ashore the thirty-four officers and men of the Nika.

SEEN BY FISHERMAN

Discovery of the Tuscan Prince was preceded by reports today that a Japanese fisherman at Ucluelet had seen a large steamer ashore on Village Point.

Finding of the Tuscan Prince clears up a series of marine mysteries that had taxed the ingenuity of wireless operators and Coast Guard officers since the Nika reported herself rudderless at 4:30 Wednesday afternoon. While listening for messages from the Nika and the Santa Rita the radio operators ashore caught two messages sent by the Tuscan Prince, neither of which gave her position.

PISTOL BULLET FOUND IN BODY OF REMINGTON

Two men were being sought late last night as the slayers of Earle Remington, widely known electrical engineer and aviator, whose body was found early yesterday morning in the driveway of his home at 1409 South St. Andrews Place.

The theory that two men and not one, as had been thought earlier in the day, had fired the fatal shots that ended the popular society man's life, was accepted by Captain of Detectives George Home following the finding of a bullet hole under the dead man's heart.

Shotgun wounds in Mr. Remington's body led the police to believe at first that only one man was responsible for the murder. The finding of the bullet indicated that while one slayer fired a double-barrelled shotgun at Mr. Remington, the second slayer attacked him with a revolver.

Aside from this fact, no startling new clews were revealed by the homicide squad in their investigation of the murder, according to Captain of Detectives Home. Many persons were interviewed at Central Station during the evening hours, but none of them was of much assistance to the investigation, according to the police.

SEES WIFE'S ATTORNEY

Among those who held a long conference with Capt. of Detectives Home was Attorney J. L. Geisler, counsel for Mrs. Remington and who for the last two weeks had been arranging a property settlement for Mrs. Remington in her proposed divorce action against her husband.

"I have just had a long interview with Mrs. Remington," said Mr. Geisler, "and I am convinced she knows nothing of the murder which she has not already divulged to the authorities. She has requested me to assist the police in their investigation as much as I possibly can, which I have offered to do."

Following this statement and at the close of his long conference with Mr. Geisler, Capt. of Detectives Home and Detective Sergeants Jarvis and Herman Cline hurriedly left Central Station on a mission, the nature of which they would not divulge, and had not returned at a late hour.

DOMESTIC CLASHES

Shadows of the underworld late yesterday afternoon fell on the mystery surrounding the slaying of Remington, and mingled with reports of a bitter domestic clash of recent date between the slain man and his beautiful and socially well known wife, Mrs. Virginia Lola Stone Remington.

Less than two weeks ago Mrs. Remington discussed divorce proceedings with Dep. Dist.-Atty. Buron Fitts and later retained Attorney H. L. Geisler. Then she went to San Francisco to visit friends and only returned to this city two or three days ago. No divorce action had been filed before she left the city and no papers had been drawn up, according to the attorneys.

Shortly after Remington had been shot down by a hidden assassin or assasins as he stepped from his automobile in the driveway of his home, about 11:30 o'clock Thursday night, the information was in the hands of the police that he had had recent dealings with a bootlegger and had purchased a quantity of whisky. The name of the whisky-dealer was also supplied to the investigating police and a search put under way at once.

Reconstructing the incidents of the murder, Captain of Detectives George Home and Detective Sergeant Herman Cline yesterday searched the driveway and the yard of the beautiful Remington home for possible clews. They learned that Remington, returning to his home, drove into his driveway about 11:30 p.m. He had previously telephone to Mrs. Remington that he was going to the ranch he owned near Chino and would return at a late hour.

According to Capt. Home, Remington must have stepped from the right-hand door of his small coupe and then walked around the back of the machine.

As he reached the rear of the automobile the slayer, or slayers, the police believe, stepped from behind a hedge and attracted the victim's attention. Then they must have whispered some message to Remington and fired one shot from a double-barreled, sixteen-gage shotgun.

BRIEF CASE SHIELD

In an effort to protect himself Remington raised a large brief case, stuffed with business papers and clutched in both hands, over his heart. The birdshot fired at close range struck the brief case, passed through the papers and lodged in Remington's coat. A second shot struck the edge of the case, cut through the leather and pierced Remington's chest just above the heart. The revolver was probably discharged at the same time by a second assailant. He staggered a dozen steps toward the house and fell across the sidewalk. Physicians who examined the body yesterday declared he died before he struck the sidewalk.

Charity Dawson, a negro maid, who has attended Mrs. Remington for more than twelve years, was the first to discover the body of her master. She opened the rear door of the house about 7 o'clock yesterday morning and then ran screaming to her mistress. The police were at once notified and Dr. J. D. O'Brien was called. The physician arrived before the police and pronounced the man dead. The body was removed to the Booth & Boylston undertaking establishment.

NEIGHBORS HEAR SHOTS

Neighbors interviewed by the first officers to reach the scene of the murder said they had heard the shot but believed the sounds were caused by the backfire of an automobile. They stated that the shots came at about 11:30 p.m. and that an automobile door was slammed a short time later and an automobile driven away from somewhere near the Remington home.

Late yesterday afternoon the police interviewed Mr. Fitts, then they called at the Remington home and questioned Mrs. Remington. Capt. Home and Detective Cline conducted the questioning. Little could be learned from Mrs. Remington, who was under the care of a physician and watched over by her sister-in-law, Miss Blanche Remington, and her brother, T. E. Milster. Both stated that Mrs. Remington was under the care of her physician and was in a serious condition from shock.

A short time after the police arrived at the Remington home, a member of the family telephoned for Attorney Geisler and requested that he be present at the interview. He admitted before leaving his office that he had been retained by Mrs. Remington some time before and "discussed her domestic matters" at great length.

STATEMENT BY ATTORNEY

The attorney declared he had not been requested to file divorce papers, but stated that he had been informed by Mrs. Remington of "some trouble" between the couple. He declared that he could not discuss the case as he had not seen Mrs. Remington since the discovery of her husband's body.

From R. H. Moore of 1422 South St. Andrews Place, Detective Cline learned that two mysterious automobiles were seen in front of the Remington home about 7 o'clock Thursday night. One machine, according to Mr. Moore, was a small coupe and was occupied by a woman. The second machine containing two men drove up to the first machine and then both cars circled the block several times before driving away. A complete description of both automobiles and the two men and the woman is in the hands of the police.

No one in the neighborhood could be found who saw any one lurking about the Remington home or in the driveway during the late evening.

A dog owned by Mrs. L. Betts of 1407 South St. Andrews Place,

(Continued on Second Page)

In Three Parts—44 Pages
PART I—TELEGRAPH SHEET—18 PAGES

DESTINY

The Los Angeles Times

"Sail on, sail on, and on and on."

GREATER SOUTHERN CALIFORNIA STRAIGHT AHEAD

FRIDAY MORNING. Vol. XLII. AUGUST 3, 1923.

Liberty Under Law—Equal Rights—True Industrial Freedom

HARDING DIES SUDDENLY OF APOPLEXY; CALVIN COOLIDGE NOW IS PRESIDENT

SAN FRANCISCO, Aug. 2.—President Harding died at 7:30 o'clock tonight, stricken by apoplexy after having almost won his fight against broncho-pneumonia and other complications.

The end came suddenly and without warning while Mrs. Harding, truly faithful until death, sat by his bedside reading to him. Two nurses were the only other persons in the room, and there was no time for a last word from the nation's leader either to his wife or to the republic he served.

A shudder shook his frame weakened by seven days of illness, and worn by a trip of 7500 miles from Washington to Alaska and return as far as this city, he collapsed and it was over. Mrs. Harding only had time to rush to the door and call "Find Dr. Boone and the others quick," meaning the physicians.

Brig.-Gen. Sawyer, personal physician to the President, was in a near-by room, but when he hurried to the President's bedside medical skill was useless.

COOLIDGE TAKES OATH OF OFFICE; IS SWORN IN BY HIS FATHER AT FARM HOME IN VERMONT

[EXCLUSIVE DISPATCH]

PLYMOUTH (Vt.) Friday, Aug. 3.—Vice-President Calvin Coolidge received the news of the death of President Harding and of his own elevation to the Presidency at ten minutes before midnight, standard time. The new President was sworn in at 2:47 o'clock this morning by his father, John C. Coolidge, who is a notary public. Mr. Coolidge will leave for Washington immediately.

Mr. Coolidge received the first news of the death of President Harding through telegrams from George C. Christian, Jr., secretary to President Harding and from the New York Times, whose telegram reached him at the same moment as the notification from Mr. Christian.

ISSUES STATEMENT

Mr. Coolidge issued the following statement:

"Reports have reached me, which I fear are correct, that President Harding is gone. The world has lost a great and good man. I mourn his loss. He was my chief and my friend. It will be my purpose to carry out the policies which he has begun for the service of the American people and for meeting their responsibilities wherever they may arise.

"For this purpose, I shall seek the co-operation of all those who have been associated with the President during his term of office. Those who have given their efforts to assist him I wish to remain in office, that they may assist me.

"I have faith that God will direct the destinies of our nation."

OATH BY FATHER

Questioned concerning the time when he would assume office, Mr. Coolidge said:

"It is my intention to remain here until I can secure the correct form for the oath of office, which will be administered to me by my father who is a notary public, if that will meet the necessary requirements. I expect to leave for Washington during the day.

The following telegram was sent to Mrs. Harding:

"Plymouth, Vt., Aug. 3, 1923.
"Mrs. Warren G. Harding,
San Francisco, Cal.
"We offer you our deepest sympathy. May God bless you and keep you.
[Signed]
"CALVIN COOLIDGE.
"GRACE COOLIDGE."

The telegram announcing the death of the President was as follows:

"Palace Hotel, San Francisco, Cal.
"Aug. 2, 1923.
"Mr. Calvin Coolidge,
"Plymouth, Vt.
"The President died instantly and without warning and while conversing with members of his

(Continued on Second Page)

MRS. HARDING BRAVE

Mrs. Harding was as brave and strong after the end as she had been faithful to the end. Although not strong, and still affected by her illness of nearly a year ago, she declared she could not break down and she did not break down in the hour of her greatest grief.

The news of the President's death, the saddest news that telegraph wires can carry, was flashed at 7:51 o'clock as soon as a statement could be prepared. It was phrased in these words:

"The President died instantaneously and without warning and while conversing with members of his family at 7:30 p.m. Death was apparently due to some brain envolvement, probably an apopletic stroke.

"During the day he had been free from discomfort, and there was every justification for anticipating a prompt recovery.

[Signed]
"C. E. Sawyer, M.D.
"Ray Lyman Wilbur, M.D.
"C. M. Cooper, M.D.
"J. T. Boone, M.D.
"Hubert Work, M.D
"August 2, 1923, 7:35 pm."

In a second official statement issued at 8:02 p.m., the statement was made that death had been caused by a stroke of apoplexy.

MESSAGE TO COOLIDGE

Within a few minutes telegrams were sent to Calvin C. Coolidge, Vice-President of the United States, upon whom now devolves the duties and responsibilities of government. Mr. Coolidge was at his summer home in Vermont and undoubtedly will take the oath of office some time tomorrow.

The best explanation of the death of the Chief Executive may be found in these words by Lieut.-Commander Joel T. Boone, assistant to Dr. Sawyer, as the President's physician:

"The President had a most splendid afternoon," he said. "When I left the room for dinner, I commented, 'Doesn't he look splendid?'

"Then, all at once, he just went like that—"

Dr. Boone snapped his fingers "just like that; something snapped—that's all."

The last words of the President were spoken an instant before the

(Continued on Second Page)

Bay Stater Who Becomes President

[Copyright, Underwood & Underwood]

Calvin Coolidge, of North Hampton, Mass., who has shared the responsibilities and burdens with Mr. Harding of this great nation as Vice-President, now succeeds to the Presidency.

Character Sketch of President Harding

Late Drawing by Artist

NEW PRESIDENT TAKES POST AUTOMATICALLY

Calvin Coolidge, Vice-President of the United States, who automatically succeeds to the Presidency through the death of President Harding, is a native of Plymouth, Vt., and is 51 years of age. He has been long in the public service.

Geography, not infrequently a major consideration in the nomination of a candidate for "second place on the ticket," played less part than history in the nomination of Calvin Coolidge of Massachusetts for Vice-President of the United States by the Republican national convention in 1920 as his stepping stone to election as the thirtieth President.

From actual observation at the time and scene of that selection it may be stated beyond fear of contradiction that there was less talk of giving the necessary geographical balance to the ticket when his name went before the convention than there was of the achievements of the man and what he stood for.

In the commonwealth of Massachusetts where he was best known and had spent more than twenty years in public office before he achieved national prominence the name of Calvin Coolidge was a synonym for independence, rugged honesty, simplicity of habits, courage, inflexible devotion to duty and the austere virtues generally associated with the pioneer stock from which he sprang. It had become a synonym also for success at the polls, for he had never been defeated for office and, generally speaking, in each successive election at which he was a candidate the returns had shown increased pluralities.

NOT A HAND-SHAKER

Politicians in Massachusetts marveled at this for Coolidge never was a "hand-shaker." He was admittedly the poorest kind of a mixer and he appeared to shun rather than seek the publicity so eagerly sought by most men in public life, apparently living up to a homely adage of his own: "Let men in public office substitute the light that comes from the midnight oil for the limelight."

When the Republican national convention was held in June, 1920, only a few months had elapsed from the time when overnight Calvin Coolidge, then serving his first term as Governor of Massachusetts, became the talk of the nation for the important part he had played in "breaking" the police strike in Boston.

POLICEMEN'S STRIKE

What he did in that grave crisis to stay the forces of disorder, to uphold American institutions and vindicate the principles of law won him commendation from Gov-

(Continued on Second Page)

BODY TO GO EAST TODAY

[BY A. P. NIGHT WIRE]

SAN FRANCISCO, Aug. 2.—The body of President Harding will leave San Francisco on a special train at about 7 o'clock Friday evening and go directly to Washington by way of Reno, Ogden, Cheyenne, Omaha and Chicago. This announcement was made tonight after a conference participated in by the four members of the President's official party in San Francisco, and was approved by Mrs. Harding.

The car will be lighted at night and at all times two soldiers and two sailors, a part of a naval and military guard of sixteen enlisted men, will stand at attention guarding the coffin.

The train will make no stops en route, except those necessary for its operation. The body of the President will be borne in the rear car, probably the same in which he made the trip from the capital to the Pacific Coast.

The train will carry the Presidential party as composed during the trip across the country to Alaska and also Gen. Pershing, Attorney-General Daugherty and Mr. and Mrs. E. E. Remsberg and family. Mrs. Remsberg is a sister of the President. The body will not be taken from the hotel except to go directly to the train, and there will be only the simplest private ceremony at the hotel before it is moved

"TIMES" TO PUBLISH HARDING'S SPEECHES ON HIS LAST TOUR

In the belief that the speeches of President Harding on the tour which has just ended so tragically would prove of great and permanent public interest and value, The Times preserved the type of its printed text of the principal addresses and will shortly issue them in convenient newspaper form for the benefit of the public. The President's last public address, which was delivered in his stead by Secretary Christian in this city yesterday, will be included in this publication. A further announcement will appear in The Times soon.

Hughes Feels Harding Loss as Irreparable

[BY A. P. NIGHT WIRE.]

WASHINGTON, Aug. 3.—Secretary Hughes, the ranking official of the Federal government in Washington, early today issued a statement expressing his grief at the death of President Harding and saying that the country had suffered "an irreparable loss."

"No words can express the grief into which we are plunged by this calamity," said Mr. Hughes. "The nation has suffered an irreparable loss.

"A quiet, brave, strong leader has fallen, overborn by the burden he was carrying. He was not only an able and faithful public servant, but one of nature's noblemen; a true-hearted, generous spirit. He has left with the people he loved a rare evample of gentleness in high office and of the most conscientious and unselfish devotion to public duty."

FATHER PROSTRATED BY NEWS OF DEATH

[BY A. P. NIGHT WIRE.]

MARION (O.) Aug. 2. — Dr. George T. Harding, aged father of the President, is almost prostrated at the death of his son.

Just as soon as the news of the President's death reached here a messenger went to the home of the President's father.

Mr. Harding had just retired for the night and was only awakened after several minutes.

HOLLYWOOD MASONS GET LAST PRONOUNCEMENT

Harding's Final Speech Is Read by Christian Before 10,000 at Bowl

The last official pronouncement of the late President was made in Hollywood yesterday. His private secretary and most intimate friend, George B. Christian, Jr., read to an audience of 10,000 persons assembled in the Bowl a speech he had intended to deliver in person. The last public address, coming from the President's pen, was a talk on fraternalism, world peace and an appeal for a more general observance of the teachings of Christianity as taught by the Man of Sorrows.

The occasion for the address was the presentation on behalf of Marion (O.) Commandery of Knights Templar to the Hollywood Commandery of the International Traveling Beauseant of the Order. In return for the compliment, Hollywood Commandery, through Past Grand Commander Benjamin F. Bledsoe, presented a morocco-bound certificate, and gold credential giving to the President an honorary membership in the California organization.

The long-to-be-remembered occasion gave to the city of Hollywood the appearance of the Holy Grail. More than 2000 plumed Knights of the Temple wended their way through its streets to a shrine in Hollywood Bowl there to engage in one of the most beautiful and impressive ceremonies ever made possible for members of the Masonic order in California. The recent illness of the President made it necessary several days ago to change the plans arranged and give to the Chief Executive's secretary the place on the program to have been taken by his Chief.

Preceding the ceremonies at the Bowl a street parade, inspiring in its glittering pageantry, made its way through the main thoroughfare to Highland avenue where, at the entrance to the bowl, it passed a reviewing stand supporting the officers of the Grand Commandery

(Continued on Fourth Page)

DESTINY

In Twelve Parts—182 Pages

PART I—TELEGRAPH SHEET—14 PAGES

The Los Angeles Times

"Sail on, sail on, and on and on."

GREATER SOUTHERN CALIFORNIA STRAIGHT AHEAD

SUNDAY MORNING. Vol. XLII. SEPTEMBER 2, 1923.

Liberty Under Law—Equal Rights—True Industrial Freedom

ALL TOKIO IN FLAMES; DEATH TOLL STAGGERING

ITALIAN FLEET MOVES TO BLOCKADE GREEK PORTS

Athens Navy Rides at Anchor in Harbor Fearing to Venture Out for Action

[BY CABLE—EXCLUSIVE DISPATCH]

PARIS, Sept. 1.—The Italian main fleet is reported to have established a virtual blockade of all Greek ports. The Athens navy, consisting of four obsolete hulks, is anchored in the harbors and will not attempt to put to sea for fear of encountering Italian warships, resulting in a naval battle. All Greek shipping is remaining in port pending the stabilization of the situation. Complaints already are being received from American relief workers that the supply of food for Near East refugees at Lemnos and other islands is cut off and soon will be exhausted, resulting in starvation for thousands.

Naval experts point out that if Italy continues to hold Samos with the Dodecanese Islands she practically controls the Dardanelles and the Black Sea entrance.

SEAPLANES ACTIVE

[BY CABLE—EXCLUSIVE DISPATCH.]

ROME, Sept. 1.—Italian seaplanes are now scouting over the Greek coast. Italian sailors have seized the wireless station on the Island of Fatmos. Premier Mussolini met with his Cabinet this afternoon and informed the members that about ten casualties resulted from the shelling of Corfu.

Italian sailors have occupied the small islands of Paxos and Antipaxos, just south of Corfu.

TROOPS LANDED

[BY CABLE—EXCLUSIVE DISPATCH.]

LONDON, Sept. 1.—The latest report from Athens states that 5000 Italian troops from naval vessels have landed at Corfu. The Greek garrison, numbering about 150, have fled to the interior. The Greek Prefect and ten Greek officers have been taken prisoner. The victims of the battle number thirty-one, of whom twenty-one were refugees. The population of Corfu is incensed. The port of Tarento, Italy, is very active, with garrison troops embarking on transports

(Continued on Seventh Page)

Mussolini Sends New Ultimatum to Jugo-Slavia

[BY CABLE—EXCLUSIVE DISPATCH.]

BELGRADE, Sept. 1.—Premier Mussolini has extended the Italian ultimatum on the Fiume question until the 15th inst., to give Jugo-Slavia time to accept in full Italy's demands.

The first ultimatum, issued on August 8, expired at midnight last night. Jugo-Slavia's answer, giving all the concessions possible, was found unsatisfactory, Italy giving fifteen more days for the Jugo-Slavs to come to terms.

Jugo-Slavia's delegate on the Fiume commission has been recalled to Belgrade and will arrive here Sunday noon from Rome. He will go into immediate conference with the Premier and the Cabinet.

TOBACCO HARVEST BEGINS

JANESVILLE (Wis.) Sept. 1.—The work of harvesting Wisconsin's tobacco crop has started in the southern section of the State, and will be well under way in all localities before another week, with a promise of more than a fair crop.

The Four Horsemen Are Riding!

YOKOHAMA IN RUINS AS TEMBLOR ROCKS EAST COAST OF NATION

Tidal Wave Reported to Have Destroyed Ships; Seven Hundred Persons Killed in Collapse of Tower; Imperial Palace Is Ablaze

[BY CABLE AND ASSOCIATED PRESS]

OSAKA, Sept. 2.—With the exception of the Shiba Road, the whole of Tokio is burning in the fire that followed Saturday's earthquakes. Part of the Imperial Palace at Tokio is reported to be ablaze.

[BY A. P. NIGHT WIRE]

SAN FRANCISCO, Sept. 1.—Tokio is afire, many of the buildings of the city have collapsed, the water system is destroyed, the loss of life is heavy, all traffic has been suspended and the flames are spreading to surrounding towns, according to a message received here tonight by the Radio Corporation of America from the superintendent of the company's station at Tomioka regarding the great earthquakes of today. At 8:20 o'clock tonight, the Radio Corporation received a message from its station at Tomioka which said that 700 persons were reported killed when the twelve-story tower at Asakusa fell.

Many boats sank in a tidal wave in the Bay of Suruga. Most of the houses at Numazu collapsed, the message said. In Tokio the imperial railway station was swept by fire and the Imperial Theater collapsed. The railway station at Ueno burned.

It is rumored the Imperial Palace is in danger.

Communication with Japan, interrupted by the earthquake at noon, Tokio time, today, still was virtually at a standstill twenty-six hours later. The only means of obtaining intelligence from the Island Empire since the shocks has been through the Tomioka station of the Radio Corporation, located in an isolated position 144 miles from Tokio.

TIDAL WAVE REPORTED

Each of the brief messages emanating thence brought word of greater severity or wider spread disaster.

Most of Tokio was reported burning with many important buildings collapsed.

Yokohama was badly damaged by the shock and succeeding fire.

A tidal wave, with heavy damage and many vessels lost, was reported from the bay of Suruga. Fires had broken out in towns as far as eighty-four miles from Tokio and the disaster appeared general all along the east coast of Japan.

The only survivor so far reaching the radio station said the number of dead in Tokio alone was "incalculable."

The Radio Corporation of America here tonight received from its station at Tomioka, Japan, a first-hand story of the earthquake and fire in Tokio from a refugee. The refugee said that at the first shock fires broke out at various places in the city.

BUILDINGS BURNED DOWN

The flames originated in the Mitsukoshi Department Store and spread to the Metropolitan Police Board's building and the Imperial Theater. These were burned to the ground as were many other large buildings.

The city, the refugee said, is still in flames and the fire is spreading from Senju to Shinagawa. The flames can be seen seven miles away from Tokio. All railway bridges are destroyed and in many places there is no traffic at all.

The refugee said the number of dead and injured was incalculable.

The Radio Corporation's superintendent said he obtained his information today on the earthquake from a morning paper at Sendai, a large seacoast town about 200 miles north of Tokio. Tomioka is about 144 miles north of Tokio.

The message read:

"Severe earthquake Tokio and vicinity at noon yesterday; railway station near Tokio collapsed and no means to reach Tokio. Heavy damage in Tokio. Water

(Continued on Second Page)

AMERICAN SHIPS ORDERED TO SPEED TO YOKOHAMA TO HELP TEMBLOR SUFFERERS

[BY A. P. NIGHT WIRE]

WASHINGTON, Sept. 1.—After communication with President Coolidge, the Navy Department tonight ordered the commander of the Asiatic Fleet to rush vessels to Yokohama for relief of sufferers from the earthquake in Japan.

Reports of the earthquake and fire in Yokohama caused unusual anxiety here today because of the large number of Americans who make their home there.

It is estimated that more than a thousand citizens of the United States who have business connections in Tokio live in the section reported affected by the conflagration. More than half of all Americans in that part of Japan are said to have chosen Yokohama as their place of residence. It is only a half hour's ride from the capital.

The American Navy maintains a hospital at Yokohama, but there are believed to be only one or two patients there. The personnel consist of one doctor, one pharmacist, two nurses and seven enlisted men of the Medical Corps.

Concern over the fate of the Americans in Yokohama is the more intense because, in previous earthshocks there, the section occupied by the foreign colonies has been most severely shaken. This section is on higher ground than most of the remainder of the city.

It is believed here that the American Naval Hospital, if it escaped destruction, will become one of the principal centers of relief work.

IN THE GREATER SUNDAY "TIMES" TODAY

THE SKY. Clear. Wind at 5 p.m., west velocity, 9 miles. Thermometer, highest, 80 deg.; lowest, 59 deg. Forecast: For Los Angeles and vicinity: For complete weather data, see last page of this section.

SPANISH. A digest in Spanish of the most important news events of the day will be found on the eleventh page of this section of The Times.

LOS ANGELES HARBOR NEWS. Latest news of the arrivals and sailings of vessels in and out of Los Angeles Harbor will be found on Page 11, Part IV.

THE CITY. Visiting Chicago lawyer denounced tendency to sympathize with criminals.

Members of Crime Crusher squad of policemen reported that suspect invited them to take part in a bold hold-up, accused was held.

Legal protest was made against proposed election for Culver City; plan for fraudulent voting alleged.

Marriage License Bureau showed large increase in permits issued over August of 1922.

Superdreadnaughts Idaho and Nevada will arrive here at dawn today.

Centenarian Club conducted twelfth reunion at Sycamore Park.

Woman was sought by police after man acquaintance accused her of aiding bandits in hold-up and robbery.

Chief Dep. Dist.-Atty. Fricke announced that the De Coo case would be given to the grand jury Tuesday.

It was announced that change in parking law will be sought that busses will not be hindered in loading and discharging passengers at curb.

Five new Superior Court judges were sworn in and assumed new duties.

PACIFIC SLOPE. Bank teller at Long Beach was accused of faking hold-up to cover asserted manipulation of funds.

Forest fire burning over more than 400 acres in Santa Ynez Valley threatened to get beyond control.

Alfred Noyes, the poet, cabled he will return to Pasadena to join the teaching staff of the California Institute of Technology.

Southern California Chamber of Commerce secretaries conducted their monthly meeting at Oxnard.

MEXICO. Mexico named Alberto J. Pani, secretary of foreign relations, as new ambassador at Washington.

Gen. Angel Flores, civil governor of Sinaloa, announced candidacy for Presidency of Mexico.

GENERAL EASTERN. Pony express riders following old trail were far ahead of schedule as they covered more than half of State of Kansas.

WASHINGTON. More wars predicted at Army War College as commandant stressed need of national preparedness.

FOREIGN. Earthquakes, flames and tidal wave brought tremendous loss of life and property to Tokio, Yokohama and other Japanese cities. Imperial Palace in the capital was burned and many ships on coast were reported lost. Seven hundred persons were killed in collapse of one tower.

Chinese leader suggested commision to eliminate bandit activities in provinces.

Old leaders of war days at head of 400,000 Fascisti seized Nuremburg and raised imperial flag, declaring dictatorship.

Government in business was proved failure as Philippine National Bank showed enormous deficit.

FEATURES. California is Artists' Haven. Canyon Vacations No Snap. Beach Seen as Real Mirror to Human Nature. Old Apartments Have Lure of Romance. Writer Says Beauty Not Even Skin Deep. Los Angeles Has Its Own Stradivarius. Pierre Key's Music Article. Of Arts and Artists, by Anthony Anderson. The New in Stores and Homes. Fraternal Affairs. Women's Work and Clubs.

LITERARY PAGE. Conducted by Thomas F. and Lillian C. Ford. Parlor Radicals Satirized. Ten Dullest Authors Described. Fiction and Drama Reviewed. Publishers' Advance Notices Summarized.

STAGE AND SCREEN. Frances White Tells Ambitions. Pictures Displease New York Critic. Veteran Actress Recalls Experiences. Noted Director Describes Color Values. Intimate Doings of Players. Coming Events on Stage and Screen. Pilgrimage Play Soon to Close.

SOCIETY. Events Past and Planned. Society's Diversions; Activities of Hosts and Hostesses During the Past Week.

AUTOMOBILES. Murphy Admires Italy's Racing Bowls. New Production Mark Seen. Automobile Club Selects Site for New Branch. Many Car Dealers Fail. Lake Tahoe Trip Entrances. Motor Law Changes Effective. Angeles Takes Durant's Place in Race. Armored Tank Protects Messengers. Big Advances Predicted in Automotive Industry. Novel Baggage Carrier Described. Auto Equipment Examination Urged. Harry McPherson Thrums Motor Lyre.

REAL ESTATE AND INDUSTRIAL. Record Construction Program Planned. How Organized Labor Raises Building Costs Described. Court Test of Zoning Ordinance Welcomed. Travel Rush Unprecedented. Old District Comes to Life. Accidents in Building Trades Deplored. Contractor Builds King Tut Residence. Electric Needs Detailed. Manchester to be Boulevard. Wholesale. Homesites Novel Idea. Segunda Sales Set Record. Gigantic Expansion Program at Harbor. Monrovia Gets New Plants.

ILLUSTRATED MAGAZINE. John Steven McGroarty's page. Frank G. Carpenter. Describes Esthonia. Barnum's Biography Continued. Letters of a Japanese Schoolboy. Harry L. Foster Describes Malaya. Ida M. Tarbell Tells More About Lincoln. Up From a Death Cell, by John W. Kane. Another Chapter in Life of the Potters. Stories by Sir Phillips Gibbs, Charles Collins, Frederick Arnold Kummer, Jacques Futrelle and Mrs. Wilson Woodrow. The How in Houses. Good Short Stories From Everywhere. What the Insane Think About. The Married Life of Helen and Warren. Care of the Body.

FARM AND TRACTOR. Cover, "Farm Bred." King Cotton Resumes Southwest Throne. Walnut Growers Mass. County Farm Herd Wins Sweepstakes. Farm News of Great Southwest. Citrus Men Meet. Center of Produce Trade Pictured. Roto Depicts Sugar Beet and Lima Bean Harvests. College Livestock Judging Course Successful. Cattle Royalty at State Fair. Livestock Bulletin. Pointers in Culling Layers. Poultry Men Organize. The Garden Beautiful.

ROTOGRAVURE. Pictures to delight nimrods. Headliners and Kings. The So-called Summer Girl, by W. E. Hill. When a Nation Mourns Its President. Peggy Hamilton's Fashion Page. With the Fleet. In "The Wayfarer." Modern Mermaids.

COLORED COMICS. The Gumps, Winnie Winkle, Harold Teen, Gasoline Alley.

THE JUNIOR TIMES. The Ice Cream Mine, by Jane Corby. Wonderful Stories of Oz, by L. Frank Baum. Our Puzzle Gym. Boy Scout Membership Grows. "Times" Junior Club Page. Aunt Dolly's Letter Box. The Fireside Corner. Suggestions. Buddie and His Friends. Buttons and Fannie. Many Enter Aunt Dolly's Contest.

JUDGE PRAISES GIRL FOR ARREST OF MAN

[EXCLUSIVE DISPATCH.]

NEW YORK, Sept. 1.—Miss Theda King, 21 years of age, of 7 East Forty-fifth street, was complimented by Magistrate Oberwager in Yorkville Court for her work in effecting the arrest of Mannie Seaman, 25, a valet, 239 East One Hundred and Nineteenth street. The young woman was leaving her apartment last Wednesday when she saw Seaman at the door on the second floor. He left when he saw her, saying he had been looking for a man, but Miss King, seeing splinters about the door, followed him to the street. "Mister, you're a burglar," she said when she caught up with the young man. When Seaman protested Miss King smiled and asked him to go back to the house. Then she turned him over to a policeman. Seaman, charged with attempted burglary, was held for the grand jury, and Magistrate Oberwager told Miss King that he would request Commissioner Enright to reward her.

If we had more charity in business and more business in charity, there would be less suffering in the world.

IMPERIAL GERMAN FLAG RAISED IN NUREMBURG

Leaders of War-Crazed Days Lead 400,000 Fascisti in Seizure of City and Railroads

BY SAMUEL SPEWACK

[B_ CABLE—EXCLUSIVE DISPATCH]

BERLIN, Sept. 1.—"As we triumphed over Napoleon fifty years ago so will we crush Poincare," shouted 400,000 Fascisti who poured into Nuremburg this morning and declared a dictatorship in the mediaeval city. The imperial flag was hoisted and the city authorities driven out. The railroads were commandeered and a line of sentries flung about the picturesque home of Meistersanger.

Ludendorff, Hindenburg, Admiral Scheer, Gen. Hoefer, Prince Von Schoenich, Prince Oscar of Prussia, Prince Ludwig Ferdinand of Bavaria, Archduke Von Cobourg—these relics of German imperialism surrounded by old officers of the War Staff in spiked helmets and gold swords—rode at the head of their apparently war-crazed followers.

Tonight is the eve of the victory of Sedan and they had come to gloat over their memories and to promise themselves another victory over the French and to sneer at the German Republic.

COUP IS RUMORED

None of the leaders would comment on the situation tonight, but the rumor everywhere is that a coup is planned. Meanwhile Berlin authorities made public for the first time the capitulation terms announced five days ago.

After dispatches had appeared in Vorwaerts announcing that the workers were returning to the mines in the Ruhr a cautious statement was issued this morning stating that the government had decided to leave the question of Ruhr passive resistance to the local bodies in the occupied territories.

"Demoralization has set in among the workers and the government does not want to cause unnecessary suffering," was the roundabout explanation by the Foreign Office of the fact that the government had thus wiped out a whole series of decrees declaring passive war with the invaders.

However, no matter how diplomatically couched, the government officials finally had to concede that the statement meant that work would now be resumed in the Ruhr.

STATEMENTS CAREFUL

It was explained privately that in the face of the Fascisti demonstrations the government could not afford to wave the red flag of capitulation in front of the fanatic nationalists.

Stresemann, in his speech at Stuttgart tomorrow, will probably be even more cautious than the Foreign Office and will probably demand from the French the return of the railroads, the sovereignty of the Ruhr and the release of political prisoners. But between the lines there will be a plea for immediate pac.

Dspite Fascisti opposition Stresemann still sees hope of reparation and Ruhr settlements shortly and he points to the French fear of Italian expansion in the Mediterranean as a new factor. He believes the French government will follow the lead of the industrialists and liquidate the Ruhr so that it can turn its attention to Italy's expansion project.

MEXICO NAMES NEW ENVOY

Alberto J. Pani, Secretary of Foreign Relations, to be Ambassador at Washington

[BY A. P. NIGHT WIRE]

MEXICALI (Lower California) Sept. 1.—Alberto J. Pani, Secretary of Foreign Relations under the Obregon administration and formerly first secretary of the Mexican Embassy at Washington and later Minister to France, will be appointed Ambassador to the United States, according to radio advices received from Mexico City tonight by Jose Inocente Lugo, Governor of the northern district of Lower California.

BY JACK STARR-HUNT

[EXCLUSIVE DISPATCH]

MEXICO CITY, Sept. 1.—President Obregon, in an exceptionally jovial mood, received foreign correspondents today and again declared that he considered the restoration of diplomatic relations between the United States and Mexico as the greatest event in the recent history of this nation.

President Obregon would not discuss Mexico's probable ambassador to the United States, limiting himself to the statement that this subject had not yet been taken up. Contrary to his usual policy, President Obregon volunteered the fol-

(Continued on Seventh Page)

M'CLATCHY BROTHERS SPLIT

C. K. Outbids V. S. and Gets Both Sacramento and Fresno "Bees" for Large Sum

SACRAMENTO, Sept. 1.—Reports of a break between V. S. and C. K. McClatchy, owners of the Sacramento Bee and Fresno Bee, were confirmed today by the announcement that V. S. McClatchy has sold his half interest in the two newspapers to his brother. The price for the half interest is reported to have been in excess of $1,000,000.

Sale of the two newspapers was effected through the C. K. and V. S. companies and the James McClatchy Publishing Company.

Sealed bids of the brothers for each other's interest were opened at a local bank at 11 o'clock yesterday morning, it is understood, after all necessary arrangements for transfer of stock had been completed.

DEAL ANNOUNCED

C. K. McClatchy declined to add to an announcement which appeared in the Sacramento Bee today and which set forth simply that V. S. McClatchy had sold his half interest "to the C. K. Company, of which Charles K. McClatchy, editor of the Sacramento Bee, Mrs. Charles K. McClatchy and Carlos K. McClatchy, editor of the Fresno Bee, are the three stockholders.

"No other person holds any stock whatsoever. There will be no changes in policy.

"C. K. McClatchy, after a brief rest, will devote all his time to special writing, while Carlos K. McClatchy, in addition to news and editorial work, will represent the owners in all departments as general manager of the two papers.

"W. H. James, assistant to the publisher, heretofore, becomes the business head of the publications as business director, in full charge of all business and mechanical departments. G. C. Hamilton becomes the auditor of both papers.

"J. Earl Langdon will be in charge of news and editorial departments on the Sacramento paper as managing editor, while H. R. McLaughlin will be in similar capacity on the Fresno Bee."

CAUSE OF BREACH

Dissension between the two brothers was seen some months ago by close friends, it is said, and the breach was reported to have been widened since the return of C. K. McClatchy from Europe. Predictions of dissolution had been freely made in Sacramento and the State since the first of the year.

Anti-Japanese articles written by V. S. McClatchy, as publisher of the Sacramento Bee, were said to have been rejected by the editorial department, under the direction of his brother, unless advertising rates were paid. V. S. McClatchy is reported to have retaliated by issuing an order that all of his

(Continued on Third Page)

JURIES WORRY CITIZENS

[EXCLUSIVE DISPATCH.]

TOMBSTONE (Ariz.) Sept. 1.—A session has been conducted here of a committee of Douglas and Bisbee residents that has been looking into the question of why Cochise county trial juries refuse to convict criminals, even on the best of evidence. They are acting on information furnished by County Attorney Ross, whose remonstrance is supported by Superior Judge Lockwood.

"JOHNSON!" SOBS CROCODILE

New York "World" Commiserates Senator on His Famous Letter to McClatchy

[EXCLUSIVE DISPATCH]

NEW YORK, Sept. 1.—Referring to the famous McClatchy letter of Hiram Johnson, senior Senator from California, an editorial-page article in the New York World of this morning says:

"Mr. Hiram Johnson . . . has written himself to his undoing. He has, . . . like the beggar in his rags, exhibited his sores in the market place. Alas for man's inhumanity to man! . No alms drop into his uplifted hands. Not even a word of compassion to soothe his sufferings. . . .

"The pity is, we do not know what to do with it. We want to help Mr. Johnson, we should like to anoint his sores and bind up his wounds, but who can wrestle against fate? Only a few short weeks ago Mr. Johnson was marshalling his hosts for the coming battle. He was the pride and the hope of the serried legions of Isolation. Mr. Harding had furnished him with an issue that again was to fire the patriotic heart and make even the supine rise to that clarion call. Once more liberty—liberty, what political bunk has been spilled in thy name!—was threatened. The superstate was assuming shape—a most horrifying and terrific shape—and black ruin loomed. The sacred birthright of the fathers was to be bartered for a mess of World Court. Senator Moses had cast his mantle about Senator Johnson. Senator Johnson's disciples to the number of 4000, not including the overflow and those who did not have the price of a ticket, had to fortify themselves with a dinner before they felt themselves strong enough to listen to his words of warning and dire prophecy. All was as merry as a collector for an installment house making his rounds.

"There might have been some reason for Mr. Johnson to oppose Mr. Harding—an unsuccessful venture, we are inclined to think—but on what ground can he fight Mr. Coolidge? Mr. Coolidge is a more adroit politician that Mr. Johnson and, to use a technicality, he 'holds the edge.' He has the advantage of position. He will profit by Mr. Harding's mistakes. Will he make mistakes of his own? That remains to be seen, but he has been placed on guard. A man of Mr. Coolidge cautious temperament is more likely to avoid mistakes than to blunder into them. What can Mr. Johnson offer that Mr. Coolidge cannot match? Something new in progressivism, or an up-to-date design in conservatism? We are inclined to think that Mr. Coolidge will be prepared to book all orders and guarantee early spring delivery. If Mr. Johnson satisfied himself last June that he could not hold California against Mr. Harding, in August he must be convinced that his chances against Mr. Coolidge are even worse. Having lost the West he has now been forsaken by the East. Mr. Moses has handed New England over to Mr. Coolidge and eighty-eight votes are gone beyond recovery.

"Meantime, we suggest to Mr. Hiram Johnson and other ambitious statesmen that hereafter they write their strictly confidential letters in invisible ink."

In Three Parts—48 Pages
PART I—TELEGRAPH SHEET—20 PAGES

The Times
LOS ANGELES

"Sail on, sail on, and on and on."

WEDNESDAY MORNING. Vol. XLIII. JANUARY 23, 1924.

Liberty Under Law—Equal Rights—True Industrial Freedom

CAPTAIN AND TWO LOST IN GALE WITH TACOMA

American Cruiser Breaks Up Off Vera Cruz, and Rest of Crew is Saved by Rebel Navy

[BY A. P. NIGHT WIRE]

WASHINGTON, Jan. 22.—Death of Capt. Herbert G. Sparrow of the wrecked cruiser Tacoma at Vera Cruz, and two radio operators of the ship, due to an accident aboard the Tacoma during a norther, was reported to the State Department tonight in a cable message from Consul Wood at Vera Cruz. The message gave no details but said that Capt. Sparrow and the two operators lost their lives while in the performance of their duties.

Last reports to the Navy Department said that Capt. Sparrow and forty-eight men were on the Tacoma, the remaining 278 men of the crew having been taken off by the cruiser Richmond, now off Tampico. The cruiser Omaha and six destroyers are due at Vera Cruz tomorrow from Panama waters and it is expected that they will pick up the rescued.

The Tacoma more than a week ago, during a norther preceding the present storm, went aground broadside in an exposed position on a reef sixteen miles outside Vera Cruz. Three naval tugs, which had been sent from American Gulf ports to her assistance, were compelled yesterday by the present storm to seek refuge within the breakwater at the port and it is assumed that they are safe.

REBELS SAVE CREW

Consul Wood's message, which was sent from Vera Cruz at 2 p.m. today, was made public by the Navy Department as follows:

"I am profoundly distressed to announce the death of the captain of the U.S.S. Tacoma and also of two radio operators through an accident on board the ship during a norther while in performance of duty. Particulars will follow."

The Navy Department did not expect additional advices as to the conditions aboard the Tacoma before tomorrow when the light cruiser Omaha and six destroyers, delayed by the heavy storm on the Mexican coast, are expected to reach Vera Cruz.

Before Consul Wood's message arrived a wireless message signed by Adolfo De la Huerta, had been received from Vera Cruz, by his personal representative, Alvarez Castillo, saying that the Tacoma had been completely sunk in the storm, but that Mexican naval transports, by his direction, had put to sea and saved the remainder of the crew of the Tacoma.

Navy Department officials had expected the Tacoma would be destroyed in the renewal of the norther, which was driving her farther on the reef where she struck during a similar storm several days ago while attempting to enter Vera Cruz Harbor at night.

REPORTS LACKING

It was assumed from Consul Wood's message that the death of Capt. Sparrow and his two men

(Continued on Page 2, Column 5)

LABORITES IN OFFICE

Cabinet is Named by Macdonald

Premier Takes Portfolio of Foreign Affairs; Three Peers in Group

Government is Impotent to Force Its Policies, Has No Majority

[BY CABLE—EXCLUSIVE DISPATCH]

LONDON, Jan. 22. — Ramsay Macdonald, leader of the English Labor party, and a new Labor Cabinet today assumed administration of the government of Great Britain and its far-flung dominions.

Mr. Macdonald's accession to power came after Prime Minister Stanley Baldwin, whose government was dethroned yesterday, presented his resignation to King George and, following the British custom, advised that ruler to call upon the leader of the dominant party in the House of Commons to form a new government. King George immediately called Mr. Macdonald into conference.

The Labor leader accepted the King's invitation to form a new government, and Europe's last stronghold of conservatism had fallen before the onslaught of followers of newer political ideas.

CABINET NAMED

The leaders of the Labor government went into session almost immediately, and this afternoon officially announced the new Labor Cabinet, which is as follows:

Ramsay Macdonald, Premier and Secretary for Foreign Affairs.

John Robert Clynes, Lord Privy

(Continued on Page 2, Column 6)

THE DAY'S NEWS SUMMED UP

THE SKY: Clear. Wind at 5 p.m., southwest; velocity, 9 miles. Thermometer, highest, 70 deg.; lowest, 53 deg. Forecast: For Los Angeles and vicinity: Fair. For complete weather data see last page of this section.

THE CITY. Former chamber president, declaring harbor is city's greatest asset, exhorted Advertising Club to work for "ship-minded" Los Angeles. Page 10, Part II.

Counsel for Horace Greer prepared to ask dismissal of charge of assault with intent to kill, declaring corpus delicti not proved. Page 1, Part II.

Oil portrait of J. A. Graves, financier, was completed by Arthur Cahill, California artist. Page 9, Part II.

Southwest Museum announced plans for campaign for $3,000,000 with which to erect two new buildings and establish endowment to meet increasing demands on institutions. Page 1, Part II.

Witnesses to attack on Charles Chaplin in Hollywood cafe flock to film comedian's defense. Page 1, Part II.

Prefect of discipline at Loyola College charged he was forced to sign $5000 check at a party. Page 2, Part II.

The cause of President Coolidge was espoused by seventeen Civil War veterans, voters for Lincoln. Page 1, Part II.

Announcement was made that Clara Barton Hospital would be converted into a nonprofit institution and that capacity for patients would be trebled by erection of new building. Page 1, Part II.

Ezra Meeker, aged pioneer traveler over the old Oregon trail, started from San Francisco for this city to aid in reproducing early day adventures for screen. Page 23, Part II.

Record-breaking influx of tourists to Southern California was predicted for next summer by traffic manager of Northern Pacific. Page 24, Part II.

Motion Picture Producers, Inc., at first meeting, elected officers and passed resolution to work to better films. Page 1, Part II.

PACIFIC SLOPE. Convicted former City Manager of Ontario was planning plea for parole from prison. Page 12, Part I.

Episcopal churches opened convention at Porterville with large number of delegates attending from several sections of State. Page 12, Part I.

GENERAL EASTERN. Lila Lee, screen actress, was named by mother as having signed notes to buy $40,000 liquor. Page 6, Part I.

Witness for State in prosecution of head of Anti-Saloon League was attacked by dry leaders' attorney in legal tilt on dry law activities. Page 11, Part I.

MEXICO. American cruiser Tacoma sank at Vera Cruz in norther, with loss of captain and two radio men. Rebel troops have gotten in rear of Obregon forces at Guadalajara; more munitions were sold Federals by American government. Page 1, Part I.

WASHINGTON. Administration Senators indicated they would support move to cancel Teapot Dome naval oil lease as committee inquiry continued. Page 1, Part I.

President Coolidge let it be known that he was opposed to any compromise on Mellon's plan to reduce surtaxes to 25 per cent. Page 1, Part I.

FOREIGN. Soviet officials arranged for great national funeral for Nicolai Lenin, whose death was announced. Page 1, Part I.

Ramsey Macdonald, Labor Premier of England, took over power and named his Cabinet. Page 1, Part I.

SPORTS. San Diego seeks motor speedway. Page 1, Part III.

Willie Hoppe defeated Jake Schaefer at billiards. Page 1, Part III.

Louis Disbrow to race at Ascot Speedway Sunday. Page 1, Part III.

Culver City race track to reopen Saturday. Page 1, Part III.

George Marks, Pancho Villa to battle for world's flyweight title. Page 2, Part III.

REMEMBER THIS
BY H. M. STANSIFER

Often the man who is very frank with you does not like it if you return the compliment.

Is This the End?

Russian Prince to Take Job at Ford Factory

[BY CABLE—EXCLUSIVE DISPATCH]

PARIS, Jan. 22.—Prince Orloff, one of the few surviving relatives of the late Czar Nicholas of Russia, is going to Detroit, supposedly to work for Henry Ford.

Ford's representative at Bordeaux has booked passage for Prince and Princess Orloff and Judge Sokoloff.

After learning the gentle art of turning out tin lizzies, the Prince will return to Bordeaux where he will act as interpreter between capricious Fords and French owners.

Invention May Give Vision to Undersea Ships

[BY CABLE—EXCLUSIVE DISPATCH]

PARIS, Jan. 22.—French naval experts are watching the invention of Prof. Guglielmo Motti, Italian savant, who, experimenting with Civita Vecchia, discovered a new law for light traversing water, enabling submarines to see clearly under water regardless of the depth.

It is realized here that perfection of the device will enable submersibles to escape from sunken nets and drags, and even dodge depth charges and follow in the wake of surface vessels.

Filipino Senate Passes Measure Over Wood Veto

[BY CABLE AND ASSOCIATED PRESS]

MANILA, Jan. 22.—The House of Representatives of the insular Legislature today passed, over the veto of Gov.-Gen. Leonard Wood, a bill appropriating $50,000 for the relief of sufferers from typhoons.

It is expected that the Senate will take similar action. Gen. Wood vetoed the bill because the measure placed the distribution of the funds in the hands of the insular Secretary of the Interior instead of with the Governor-General.

Sinclair Oil Stock Takes Gigantic Drop

[EXCLUSIVE DISPATCH]

NEW YORK, Jan. 22.—Sinclair Oil stock dropped $11,796,214 in value on the New York Stock Exchange today, as a result of the exposures in Washington.

The stock closed on Monday at $26.37½. It fell to $22.75, a loss of $3.62½ a sharefi but rallied $1 a share in late trading. There are 4,491,892 shares outstanding. Bonds of the various Sinclair companies also were weak, and suffered material losses.

WILLIAM C. RALSTON

[BY A. P. NIGHT WIRE]

SAN FRANCISCO, Jan. 22.—William C. Ralston, former subtreasurer of the government mint here, member of the State Legislature and Republican candidate for Governor in 1914, died here today. Double pneumonia was the cause of death.

TEAPOT DOME OIL LEASE CANCELLATION FAVORED

Administration Leaders in Senate to Support Move to Invalidate Deal; Prosecution Hinted

BY ROBERT BARRY
[EXCLUSIVE DISPATCH]
[Copyright, 1924, Public Ledger.]

WASHINGTON, Jan. 22.—As President Coolidge was giving notice today of Federal prosecutions of any frauds developed in the Teapot Dome naval oil reserve lease administration leaders in the Senate advised the Democrats that they would support the Caraway resolution for cancellation of the lease, if it were altered so as to direct the Attorney-General to institute suit for revocation.

Senator Caraway, Democrat, of Arkansas, will move in the Senate tomorrow that the Committee on Public Lands and Surveys shall be discharged from further consideration of the resolution of revocation and that the Senate proceed to its immediate consideration. He gave formal notice of that this afternoon.

An imposing array of attorneys, corporation officers and agents of Harry F. Sinclair, who obtained the Teapot Dome reserve from A. B. Fall when he was Secretary of the Interior, descended upon the committee room today in the wake of the sensational testimony yesterday by "Archie" Roosevelt, until Saturday an officer of one and a director of many of the Sinclair companies.

ATTORNEY IN REBUTTAL

E. T. Stanford, personal counsel for Sinclair, was the best witness in rebuttal of the Roosevelt testimony. To the mysterious loan of $100,000 to Fall, the uncashed McLean checks, Wahlburg's "six or eight cows" and Roosevelt's story of canceled checks for $68,000 to Fall's ranch foreman, Stanford added to the picture a $100,000 house on Long Island.

It was for the purchase of that house, Sinclair's attorney testified, that Col. James W. Zeveley obtained a loan of 3500 shares of Sinclair Consolidated Oil Corporation stock — a transaction which G. D. Wahlburg, Sinclair's private secretary, declared yesterday had aroused his suspicion of something wrong; his suspicion that "somebody might have lent money to Fall."

There was no $68,000 check to the foreman of Fall's ranch at Three Rivers, N. M., Stanford said. Moreover, the sleek attorney, with piercing light blue eyes, whose smiling exchanges with Senator Walsh of Montana, verged very close to sneers, asserted that Sinclair did not leave for Europe "in a great hurry," as Mr. Roosevelt testified, but was obliged to go to Germany and France on business,

(Continued on Page 2, Column 4)

GERMAN GOLD BANK URGED

Expert Budget Committee Creates Plan to End Financial Chaos of Teuton Nation

[BY CABLE AND ASSOCIATED PRESS]

PARIS, Jan. 22.—The experts committee, which under the chairmanship of Brig.-Gen. Charles G. Dawes, is dealing with the German budget, today took the most important step yet made toward a settlement of the reparations question, in the opinion of members of the Reparations Commission. This was when the committee decided to report in favor of establishing a German gold bank as the first essential to stabilization of German money and balancing the German budget.

Great significance is attached to the fact that the communique announcing the decision of the committee was referred to Dr. Hjalmar Schacht, president of the Reichsbank, who gave it his approval. This is taken as justifying the assumption that the German banker and the experts are in accord on this point at least.

The experts tonight were still reticent as to the decision reached, because the details remain to be worked out but satisfaction over this early agreement on one of the vital points of the problem was apparent on the faces of the delegates as they came out of the council room.

The decision of the experts, if it is approved by the Reparations Commission, amounts to a recommendation for an international loan, part of the funds to guarantee the gold value of the money of the new bank along with German-owned foreign money.

The coupling of German capital abroad with an international loan for this purpose is regarded as a clever expedient to induce Germany to make an effort to get back into that country capital exported abroad.

Foreign co-operation in the management of the bank as recommended by the committee, also is regarded as an important feature that would give confidence to money issued by the bank since outside participation would amount to insurance against new inflation. That the experts consider they have made a wide step forward, is indicated by the fact that they purpose to transfer the seat of their activities from Paris to Berlin a week from tomorrow.

The intention of the committeemen has been to get well along with the problem between themselves before undertaking the German end of their task.

Today's decision took Paris by surprise. The apparent slowing down in the work of the committee after its whirlwind commencement had brought about the impression that the commission was falling into the usual European

(Continued on Page 2, Column 3)

GREAT NATIONAL FUNERAL IS ARRANGED FOR LENIN

Russia in Mourning as Death of Premier and Revolutionary Leader is Announced

[BY CABLE—EXCLUSIVE DISPATCH]

MOSCOW, Jan. 22.—Nicolai Lenin, dictator and Premier of Red Russia, whose life aim was world revolution, died last night at his country villa in the village of Gorky, twenty miles from Moscow.

Announcement of his death was made this morning at the gathering of the All-Russia Congress, at which delegates from all parts of the country were assembled.

The body will be brought to Moscow tomorrow and will lie in state until Saturday, when there will be a great national funeral with the old revolutionary chiefs forming a guard of honor.

The public announcement of the Premier's death was withheld until the All-Russian Soviet Congress met this morning and only tonight did the wires carry to all corners of the soviet federation word of the event, which even Lenin's political opponents declare saddens the nation.

In the interest of science, an autopsy was performed this afternoon by eleven doctors, including the German specialist, Prof. Foerster. It disclosed, according to the official bulletin, marked changes in the blood vessels of the brain and fresh ruptures of these vessels which were the direct cause of death.

The death certificate was signed by four professors, four doctors and Health Commissar Semashko.

Another official bulletin, not signed, but dated the Kremlin, says the All-Russian Congress of Soviets "will take steps in the near future to secure the work of the government without interruption, and soviet power standing firm guard over the conquests of the revolution."

PARTY DIVIDED

Lenin's death, which the official announcement said was entirely unexpected, in view of recent improvement shown in his condition, comes at a time when party differences are being aired, and when the other soviet leader best known internationally, Leon Trotzky, is ill and for reasons of health out of state affairs temporarily.

The government is arranging for an impressive funeral at Moscow Saturday. Even before the public generally knew of the Premier's death, all arrangements for a great ceremony were completed. There will be nation-wide mourning and meanwhile party differences will be submerged.

Felix Djerjinsky, Commissar for the Interior, is chairman of the committee on funeral arrangements, which comprises many other prominent Communists. Trotzky is not among those named. From 6 o'clock tomorrow evening the public will be permitted to view the body.

THEATERS CLOSED

All theaters and places of amusement in Moscow have been ordered closed until after Saturday and tonight great crowds gathered in the neighborhood of the Pravda offices awaiting extra editions.

The announcement of Lenin's death was dramatic. The Congress had just assembled, when M. Kalinin, President of the republic, slowly stepped to the platform. He looked haggard and worn. Immediately the vast audience sensed a tragedy.

By Kalinin's side was M. Zinoviev, Lenin's closest friend and assistant in the old days of his exile and now one of the strongest trio in Russia. Zinoviev's eyes were red with weeping.

Kalinin bade the delegates stand and then spoke, calling Lenin by

(Continued on Page 3, Column 5)

REDS LINKED AT INQUIRY

Senators Given More Evidence

Agent of State Department Tells Committee About Soviet Agitation

Documents Offered Showing Hand of Bolshevists in Movement Here

[BY A. P. NIGHT WIRE]

WASHINGTON, Jan. 22.—The American and Russian Communist movements and official parties were linked together in testimony and documents submitted by State Department officials today to the Senate Foreign Relations Subcommittee investigating the question of recommending American recognition of the Russian Soviet government.

Through many documents obtained by government agents, some in radical raids, A. W. Kliefoth, assistant chief of the State Department's Eastern European division, and Robert F. Kelley of its intelligence office, sought to prove that the American and Russian Communists operated in close co-operation and toward a common goal. The aim, according to some of the papers presented, was "an armed uprising" in this country designed "to destroy the Bourgeoisie government."

Copies of code cablegrams and other communications set by the third Communist Internationale executive committee at Moscow, whose officers also were high officials of the soviet government, to the Communist party leaders in this country were presented to the Senate committee.

RUTHENBERG NAMED

Charles E. Ruthenberg of Chicago was named by Kliefoth as a prominent Communist leader and the witness presented many Communist documents, including official bulletins, which had been bared previously in the Michigan syndicalism trials of Ruthenberg and others.

While the committee was hearing testimony, Senator King, Democrat, Utah, delivered an address on the floor of the Senate reviewing conditions in Russia upon the basis of his visit there last summer. He denounced the Communist program and Bolshevik rule, but urged establishment of American trade relations, if confiscated American property should be restored or compensated for and other American interests protected. This would aid Russia's recovery, he argued.

ORDERED BY MOSCOW

The State Department officials told the Senate committee that the Communist party of America was organized at Chicago in 1919 under specific instructions from the Third Internationale. A "plenipotentiary representative" of the Russian party also was sent here and identified as John Moore, alias J. Ballim. Papers submitted by the government witnesses told of orders to form a "legal" party in America but also to retain an "unseen underground" Communist organization to press the workers' revolutionary movement.

"It is clearly established that the Workers' party of America was formed by the Communist party for its purpose," said Mr. Kliefoth in commenting on the many documents presented. Some of these, he added, were seized in a raid on 170 Bleecker street, New York City in December, 1921.

The Workers' party, the witnesses said, was proved by documents presented to have been organized in New York, December 23, 1921. There were 108 delegates present, according to the testimony, for the most part from foreign working men's groups.

ADOPT RED PROGRAM

A second convention of the new party was said to have been held at New York in December, 1922, where a program declared to have been framed by Ruthenberg was adopted. He was identified as a member of the American Communists' executive committee.

Cablegrams in code from Russian officers of the Third Interna-

(Continued on Page 2, Column 8)

FIRM STAND ON SURTAX

Coolidge Against Compromise

President Backs Mellon in Plan to Cut Rate to 25 Per Cent

Possibility of Veto Seen if Favorable Measure is Not Passed

[EXCLUSIVE DISPATCH]

WASHINGTON, Jan. 22.—Advocacy by Republican House leaders of a compromise on surtax rates has failed to influence President Coolidge.

Regardless of legislative developments the President proposes to continue to urge a reduction of the maximum surtax rates to 25 per cent as recommended by Secretary of the Treasury Mellon.

Reiteration of this position at the White House today was accompanied by an assertion that the President will not change his attitude even if Congress passes a measure in compromise form. It was added, however, that the President could not decide in advance just what course he would pursue in connection with the signing or vetoing of such a bill.

VETO POSSIBLE

While an impression prevailed in some quarters that the President might go so far as to veto a tax bill merely because of unsatisfactory surtax rates, it was regarded as more probable that he would sign the bill as the best that could be obtained and at the same time issue a statement expressing his dissatisfaction with certain features of the bill. Republican leaders in Congress are confident that the President will not deprive small taxpayers of reductions in their tax rates merely because men of large income are not given the amount of reduction which the President believes is essential for the stimulation of industrial activities.

The tax reduction was among the topics discussed at today's Cabinet meeting. The President made it clear to his advisers that he stands squarely with Secretary Mellon for the treasury tax bill and against fundamental changes.

DIFFERENT PURPOSE SEEN

The President recognizes that perfecting amendments are necessary in the case of all legislation. He regards a change in surtax rates as a fundamental change. He believes that those seeking this change do not have the same purpose in mind as the framers of the treasury bill.

There was little change in the situation in connection with the proposed compromise in surtax rates. Republican House Leader Longworth stood by his declaration that the House will not pass a bill with a maximum surtax rate of 25 per cent and that a compromise should be reached in the Ways and Means Committee at a higher figure. Representative Green, Republican, Iowa, chairman of the Ways and Means Committee, was believed to continue firm in his position that a compromise is necessary and his attitude made it seem impossible for the advocates of the 25 per cent rate to obtain the votes of a majority of the committee. At the same time it seemed doubtful if the Democrats would be willing to accept a compromise rate which will be satisfactory to the Republicans.

Republican members of the Ways and Means Committee were

(Continued on Page 2, Column 7)

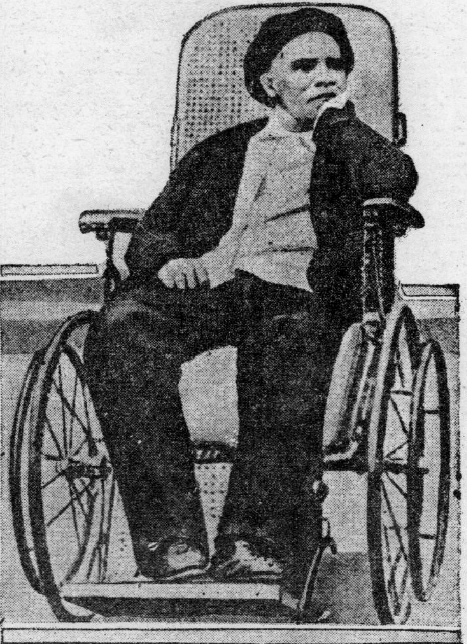

Last Photograph of Nicolai Lenin

Dictator of soviet Russia shown in wheel chair shortly before his death, which occurred as nation was expecting return to his duties.

DESTINY

The Los Angeles Times

"Sail on, sail on, and on and on."

FRIDAY MORNING, JUNE 6, 1924.

SUNDAY, 10 CENTS. DAILY, 5 CENTS.

In Two Parts—40 Pages

PART I—TELEGRAPH SHEET—20 PAGES

GREATER SOUTHERN CALIFORNIA STRAIGHT AHEAD

Liberty Under Law—Equal Rights—True Industrial Freedom.

BIDS JAPAN GOOD-BY

Woods Leaves to Wild Banzais

Thousands at Station Cheer Departing Ambassador as Nation's Friend

Mass-Meeting Protests Ban; America-Bound Ships Jammed in Rush

BY RODERICK MATHESON

[BY CABLE—EXCLUSIVE DISPATCH]

TOKIO, June 5.—The departure of former Ambassador Cyrus E. Woods today was an event formidably rivaling a great celebration nearby before the main entrance to the imperial palace, where Prince Regent Hirohito was receiving an address of congratulations from the citizens of Tokio, presented by the Mayor. A considerable portion of the 500,000 people jamming the center of the city left the imperial celebration to gather at the Tokio station and the former Ambassador was forced to leave his motor car some distance away and walk to the station through a lane which the police had forced through the crowd.

The crowd cheered uninterrupted for fifteen minutes, forcing the former Ambassador to bow time and again. At least 20,000 were jammed within the station itself, filling the steps and platforms. There was a continuous glare of flashlights for ten minutes and a score of police were unable to hold the crowds back. Hundreds of hands were stretched out to shake farewell.

Mr. Woods and his party had extreme difficulty in boarding the train, so great was the crush. The banzaiing continued until the train rounded the first curve. Mr. Woods was forced to hold his mother-in-law between his arms before him to protect her from the handshaking officials and diplomats.

REASSURES PEOPLE

The platform after the departure of the crowd was covered with flowers intended for presentation to Mr. Woods, and considerable Japanese footgear was lost in the confusion. Mr. Woods's parting statement follows:

"In leaving Japan, which I do with such deep regret, I am glad of this opportunity to express my most sincere thanks for the attitude of friendliness and helpfulness which the people and press of Japan have displayed toward me. On my part, I assure them that on my return to America, I shall continue to devote myself no less than here to the cause of concord between the countries which are so vital a necessity to the world's welfare."

Now that the former Ambassador is leaving it is possible to state

(Continued on Page 2, Column 4)

TRUE BILLS NAME BOYS

Charge Murder and Kidnaping

Crimes Punishable by Death Laid to Franks Slayers in Grand Jury Action

Confessions Are Disclosed; Woman Accuses Youths in Suit for $100,000

[BY A. P. NIGHT WIRE]

CHICAGO, June 5.—A plan by two rich youths, both brilliant students, to kill for excitement and to kidnap for a ransom which they did not need, was disclosed tonight in the detailed confession of Nathan Leopold, Jr., who with his boon companion, Richard Loeb, was named in true bills charging murder and kidnaping for ransom in connection with the slaying of 13-year-old Robert Franks. The confession which was presented to the grand jury today was made public tonight by Robert E. Crowe, State's Attorney.

The true bills were voted against Leopold and Loeb late today by the grand jury which has spent three days investigating the slaying and kidnaping two weeks ago of the Franks boy, son of a Chicago millionaire.

The grand jury heard seventy-one witnesses and the last evidence presented was the confession of one of the boys read from stenographic notes.

TO SEEK BONDS

State's Attorney Crowe issued no statement in connection with the grand jury's action, except that "indictments have been decided upon."

The true bills were made returnable tomorrow, it was reported, in view of pending writs of habeas corpus for the release of the confessed slayers, also returnable tomorrow. Arguments on the writs will be heard, it is expected, after the indictments are returned. It was reported that efforts will be made to seek bonds for the boys, but the State is expected to resist such efforts.

The true bill for murder against each of the boys was reported to contain ten counts and that for kidnaping for ransom was said to contain sixteen. The true bills were voted two weeks to a day from the time the body of the boys' victim was found stuffed into a culvert in a South Side swamp.

The only other important event of the day in connection with the case came with the filing of a suit for $100,000 damages against Leopold and Loeb by attorneys for Mrs. Louise T. Nohley. According to her counsel, the woman said the youths attacked her when she went automobile riding with them. Assistant State's Attorneys said they knew of the charges but were little concerned in view of the much graver charges which the boys are expected to face.

Investigation of possible connec-

(Continued on Page 2, Column 6)

The Opportunity of a Lifetime!

THE DAY'S NEWS SUMMED UP

THE SKY. Clear. Wind at 5 p.m., southwest. Velocity, 10 miles. Thermometer, highest, 72 deg.; lowest, 58 deg. Forecast: For Los Angeles and vicinity: Fair. For complete weather data, see last page of this section.

FEATURES. Radio, Page 3, Part II; Women's Pages, Clubs and Society, Pages 6 and 7, Part II; Markets and Financial, Pages 15, 16, 17, 18 and 19, Part I; News of Southern Counties, Page 9, Part I; Oil News, Page 18, Part I; Pictures, Page 8, Part I; Comics, Page 14, Part I.

SERIAL, Page 10, Part I.

NEWS IN SPANISH, Page 10, Part I.

SHIPPING NEWS, Page 15, Part I.

THE CITY. Rupert Hughes and Gene Stratton Porter clashed on film censorship in talks before session of General Federation of Women's Clubs. Page 1, Part I.

Judge sentenced scion of rich to five years and gives his pal in crime, orphaned in childhood, an opportunity to learn a trade at Ione. Page 8, Part II.

Trio were released in Federal Court as mentally incompetent in "Bond of Honor" fraud case. Page 8, Part II.

Fund of $3000 was asked of the Council by City Prosecutor for support of families of men sent to jail for failure to support. Page 8, Part II.

Sabotage indicated in damage done open-shop building jobs in new Country Club Drive district. Page 19, Part II.

Revenue reports show gain of million for April in attendance at film houses over same month a year ago. Page 3, Part II.

Joseph J. Lanzit, convicted for attempt to kill his wife with bomb, was sentenced and taken to San Quentin. Page 19, Part II.

Police arrested five men in raid revealing cache of auto theft gang in mountain garage. Page 19, Part II.

"Baby" bandit gang, composed of four boys ranging from 12 to 15 years of age, was rounded up by police after leader confessed to hold-up of woman's studio. Page 8, Part II.

Parrot and mocking bird fought two-day duel to death, with squeaks and squawks as their only weapons. Page 2, Part II.

Net was drawn closer about aide of death student bandit; desire to get funds for "wild party" was ascribed by police as reason for hold-up attempt. Page 1, Part II.

Leading citizens made plans for $1,500,000 drive for Harbor Y.M.C.A. for service men to aid that endeavor throughout Southern California. Page 10, Part II.

PACIFIC SLOPE. Dairy association official announced damage from hoof-and-mouth disease in State has been small; that harm is more psychological than material. More free territory recommended by State and Federal authorities. Page 5, Part I.

Casa Grande, Ariz., planned monster celebration over passage by Congress of Gila River dam bill. Page 4, Part I.

Bishop Nichols of the California diocese of the Episcopal church died in San Francisco after lingering illness. Page 4, Part I.

GENERAL EASTERN. Republican leaders at Cleveland were informed that former Gov. Lowden of Illinois was acceptable to President Coolidge as running mate. Page 1, Part I.

Slayers of Franks boy were named in true bills returned by grand jury as kidnapers and murderers, each crime punishable by death. Page 1, Part I.

Prohibition party national convention had before it resolutions to disband which were expected to be decided on floor today. Page 5, Part I.

Shrine council in session at Kansas City granted petition of Akron, O., for new temple and denied all others for territorial reasons. Page 1, Part I.

WASHINGTON. Senate passed bill appropriating funds to bring Navy up to standard. Page 1, Part I.

FOREIGN. Thousands of Japanese gathered at Tokio station to bid goodby to former Ambassador Cyrus Woods. Mass meeting in protest against Exclusion Act conducted. Page 1, Part I.

REMEMBER THIS

BY H.M. STANSIFER

Our ability to own is limited to our own ability.

PROVIDE VACATION

[LOCAL CORRESPONDENCE]

INGLEWOOD, June 5.—Inglewood City Fathers are generous, according to their action taken today. All employees on a monthly salary basis are granted two weeks' vacation on full pay, provided they have been in the employ of the city a year or more.

MINISTRY IS REFUSED BY M. HERRIOT

Rejects Premiership as Millerand Remains Firm in Serious Crisis

[BY CABLE—EXCLUSIVE DISPATCH]

PARIS, June 5.—Edward Herriot, Mayor of Lyons, refused tonight to form a Cabinet under President Millerand when the President refused to resign.

France is passing through her most serious political crisis since 1877 when Marshal MacMahon refused to abandon his post when faced by the victorious Gambetta party.

It is generally believed tonight that President Millerand will seek to have some substitute form a Cabinet with a view to postponing definite action until Saturday, when he will issue a decree closing the Chamber of Deputies, which then need not be convened until next January.

It is expected that Francois Marsal, Poincare's Minister of Finance or Maginot, former Minister of War, will attempt the task of lasting until Saturday night, after which, with the Chamber recessed, the government could remain in power, thanks to the laws of Presidential decree which Poincare jammed through the last parliament through a majority of the national bloc.

It was announced that M. Millerand will continue conversations with other political leaders tomorrow, seeking to find some one willing to constitute a Cabinet which will tide over the next two days as the constitution provides that the Chamber must be in session at least a week. The present session started the last Sunday and lasts to Saturday night, and whoever is Premier can decree of cloture without vote and then goven the republic until January, when the Chamber officially and automatically reconvenes.

The wildest rumors are seething in the capital that the Millerand-Maginot combination is contemplating a coup d'etat and the establishment of a dictatorship, but the left leaders ridicule the reports, asserting it is impossible for the President to ignore the will of the people.

Fatal Accident to Send Driver to Prison Cell

[BY A. P. NIGHT WIRE]

SAN FRANCISCO, June 5.—Victor Johnson was given a sentence in the Superior Court here today of from one to ten years in the State prison after being convicted of manslaughter in connection with an automobile accident in which Hans Lahti, a passenger in Johnson's car, was killed.

According to the evidence, Johnson was intoxicated and was driving at high speed on the wrong side of the street when the accident occurred.

FINDS OLD GOLD PIECE

[EXCLUSIVE DISPATCH]

MARIPOSA, June 5.—A $20 gold piece bearing the date of 1847 was found near the Sebastopol mine near Bootjack, when Jesse Mollan was prospecting. The coin has the appearance of having been buried for many years. The gold piece was struck by the prospector's pick and was but little damaged.

LOCAL REALTY MAN NAMED

B. L. Clogston Elected Section Leader at National Conclave; Coolidge Makes Address

[EXCLUSIVE DISPATCH]

WASHINGTON, June 5.—Burt L. Clogston of Los Angeles this afternoon was unanimously elected head of the subdivision section of the National Association of Real Estate Boards, now in convention in Washington. Mr. Clogston has made a specialty of subdivisions in Southern California and his election without opposition is a signal recognition of real estate men of Southern California, and a national compliment to Mr. Clogston personally.

The real estate men of the country were urged by President Coolidge in an address today to conduct their business with a view to mutuality of advantage to both buyer and seller.

"The deal in which one side 'gets the best of it' is not good business," the President said. "It doesn't promote more business or produce confidence in business generally. Formerly there was a curious notion that if one side in a business transaction profited, the other must necessarily lose. If that were true, all business would be under suspicion and wise people would stand aloof from it.

"The truth is that when two parties enter into a transaction by which each exchanges something which he needs less for something he needs more, both sides are benefited. That is the ideal basis of all trade and commerce, and it is the real basis of most transactions.

"It is particularly the opportunity and duty of real estate men to maintain such a standard. As a result their service is that of a middle man, bringing buyer and seller together. They will in the long run prosper if they are guided by the aim to render a real service to both sides. The transaction whose sole motive is the brokerage fee, whether or not it is earned by genuinely benefiting the principals, it is not commendable."

The real estate men had gathered on the south lawn of the White House and in opening his address the President greeted them as the "purveyors of cheer, confidence and soundly based optimism."

"You are in a very literal sense the sellers of America," he added. "You have sold it so well that it is recognized everywhere as the best buy in the world.

"Your profession has given largely to leadership of the better housing and better home movement throughout the country. Therein it has done much for the advancement of the community. We cannot hope that good citizens will come from bad homes. There will always be exceptions, but on the whole the quality of citizenship cannot be expected to rise much above the character of the home from which the citizens come.

"The ownership of a home, the feeling of independence that comes with possession of a bit of the earth, are among the most powerful incentives to high civic interest and usefulness. You can represent one of the strong practical forces working to make ours a nation of home-owning families."

Huge Fund for Road Building Passes House

[BY A. P. NIGHT WIRE]

WASHINGTON, June 5.—Expenditure of $165,000,000 by the Federal government for highway construction would be authorized under a bill passed today by the House and sent to the Senate.

The money would be available July 1, 1925. Appropriations now on hand extend to that date.

A two-year building program is contemplated under the measure for rural post roads, forest roads and trails.

JAPAN ACTS TO BEAT EXCLUSION ACT DATE

[BY CABLE AND ASSOCIATED PRESS]

TOKIO, June 6.—The difficult problem of returning Japanese residents of the United States, who are at present in Japan, to America before the exclusion act becomes effective on July 1 has called forth government action. The government has arranged with shipping companies for three special ships to reach America before that date.

JACK FROST WON'T LET GO

Coal Man Still Rules in Chicago Instead of Those "Perfect Days" the Poet Wrote of

[EXCLUSIVE DISPATCH]

CHICAGO, June 5.—The much-heralded "perfcet days" of June is anathema to Chicagoans, who still have the coal man to contend with. Cold, blustery days have followed those that were chilly, damp and rainy since Old Man Winter officially released his frigid hold on this section several weeks ago.

Truck gardeners and florists of the back yard and suburban variety are impatiently but hopefully watching for signs of germination before searing winds of autumn blow again.

Meanwhile Weather Forecaster Henry F. Cox is being submerged with letters and telephone calls asking whether there is going to be any warm weather at all. He has hopes for the future, but none for the present.

Disturbances, Cox says, moving across the country with a rapidity usually found in the month of March, are the reasons for the continued unseasonable temperature.

"Storms moving across the country with unseasonal rapidity do not give the sun a chance to warm up the air," said the weather man. "For real warm weather we must have at least two or three days of sunshine, but the disturbances follow each other so fast that the temperature is pulled down by the succeeding disturbance before the mercury gets fairly on its way upward. The tendency from now on, however, will be toward rising temperatures, and we may even have as warm a June as last year."

COOLIDGE WILLING TO HAVE LOWDEN AS RUNNING-MATE

President Indicates Illinois Man Is Acceptable but Refuses to Dictate Selection

[BY A. P. NIGHT WIRE]

CLEVELAND, June 5.—President Coolidge has passed the word that former Gov. Lowden of Illinois would be acceptable to him as his running mate. There is every reason to believe that Mr. Lowden, who was the choice of the old-line party leaders for first place in 1920 will not resist a draft. This word came to Cleveland today and crystallized the sentiment already running strong toward Lowden.

It was plain that President Coolidge in disclosing his approval of Lowden, had not departed from his hands-off policy and was still leaving it to the convention, so long as no attempt was being made to put on a running mate to represent the insurgent wing of the party. The President, it was carefully pointed out, was simply making it known that he would regard Lowden as acceptable, if the convention chose to pick him.

All this fitted in with a rapidly rising tide for the former Illinois Governor which today had entirely drowned out the talk for Charles G. Dawes of Chicago, and puts Secretary Hoover out of the running, if he ever was in it, for Mr. Hoover had publicly declared he did not want the place.

NORTHWEST FOR HIM

Delegates and committeemen arriving from the States of the Northwest where the La Follette strength is openly admitted as a factor to be reckoned with, added to the rapidly growing sentiment for Lowden.

They declared that Lowden was the man who could do the ticket most good in the agricultural States west of the Mississippi, and who would draw strength from the rural vote which otherwise might be attracted elsewhere.

If the committeemen and delegates already on the ground were to pick out a Vice-Presidential nominee now it undoubtedly would be Lowden.

As preconvention details steadily are being cleared away, the mahcinery which will nominate the ticket next week is beginning to gather momentum.

Principal contests among delegates have been disposed of; organization selections for national committee officers are being made; last-minute touches have been added to the arrangements for the sessions beginning Tuesday; delegates are beginning to arrive and the preconvention period has now reached the stage of the ticket scramble.

TICKETS MUCH SOUGHT

The center of interest in Cleveland tonight is a great burglar-proof, bomb-proof steel and concrete vault over in the Federal Reserve Bank Building which contains the thousands of coveted pasteboards which are many thousands too few to satisfy all. Everybody who has anything to do with distributing tickets is going to have a fresh crop of enemies by Tuesday. Even the party leaders of the highest position cannot get enough tickets to meet the demands upon them.

It was definitely made known today for the first time with official sanction that the name of Hiram Johnson will not be presented to the convention and that no votes are expected to be cast for him from the floor as will be done for Senator La Follette. State Senator George H. Bender, Johnson's manager in Ohio, announced that there would be no nomination of the California Senator and that he stood by his previous release of his delegates. William M. Butler, President Coolidge's manager, said he had been advised that the two Johnson delegates chosen in Illinois would cast their votes for Coolidge.

SEEK NEW TREASURER

Before the National Committee completes its reorganization, it will choose a treasurer to succeed Fred W. Upham of Chicago. Charles D. Hilles, National Committeeman from New York, who has been discussed for the place, said today he was not a candidate and would not have it under any circumstances.

Carmi Thompson, one of the Ohio leaders also discussed for the place, said he appreciated the honor of being considered, but

(Continued on Page 2, Column 2)

STAGE SET FOR FINALS IN ORATORY

Parade to White House is on Program; President to Preside at Contest

[EXCLUSIVE DISPATCH]

WASHINGTON, June 5.—R. E. L. Saner, president of the American Bar Association, arrived here this afternoon from Dallas, Tex., to act as temporary chairman at the final meeting in the national oratorical contest tomorrow night. Mr. Saner will introduce President Coolidge, who will make an address and preside throughout the rest of the meeting.

In addition to the chairman and the contestants the following will be on the stage: Secretary of State Hughes, Gen. Pershing, John T. Tigert, United States Commissioner of Education; Frank B. Noyes, president of the Associated Press; W. L. McLean, publisher of the Philadelphia Bulletin; F. L. Thompson, publisher of the Birmingham Age-Herald; Victor F. Lawson, publisher of the Chicago Daily News, and E. Lansing Ray, publisher of the St. Louis Globe Democrat.

The awards will be made by Chief Justice Taft.

All of the seven finalists now are in this city, and with them have come approximately 400 supporters. Escorted by hundreds of high-school pupils the finalists will march down Pennsylvania avenue tomorrow afternoon to the White House, their steps quickened by nine brass bands. The largest of these bands is the twenty-five unit Boys' Industrial Band of Birmingham, which holds the Alabama championship and which came here solely for this occasion.

The contest will begin tomorrow evening at 8:15 o'clock, Eastern standard time. The entire program will be broadcast by stations WCAP, Washington; WEAF, New York and WJAR, Providence, R. I.

CANADA LINE RUM BATTLE IS REPORTED

Dry Agents Hurt, Liquor Smugglers Captured in Fray, Quebec Hears

[BY A. P. NIGHT WIRE]

QUEBEC, June 5.—An unknown number of American revenue agents have been injured and several rum runners have been captured in a ten-day battle at the border over the possession of a ship's cargo of whisky which was being smuggled toward New York City, according to reports today from Sully township in Temiscouata county.

The smugglers are said to be Canadians. An unverified report is that ringleaders of the smugglers' crew are mobilizing lumberjacks for an attack upon the American authorities in revenge for the arrest of two of the prisoners.

Details concerning the conflict are lacking, for it is being waged in the thick forests which fringe the international border in the Temiscouata region. It is known, however, that huge quantities of liquor have been cached in the timber fastnesses for smuggling into the United States.

Canadian and American revenue and customs agents, as well as inspectors of the Quebec Liquor Commission, invaded the region recently to hunt for the liquor and block its passage across the line.

It has been established definitely that the liquor came from St. Pierre Miquelon after having been smuggled by schooner from abroad and landed on the rocky coast north of Maine.

WASHINGTON HAS NO WORD OF RUM FIGHT

[BY A. P. NIGHT WIRE]

WASHINGTON, June 5.—Both at the Treasury and the prohibition unit knowledge was denied today of any rum running battle along the Canadian border. No reports had been received of such an incident, it was stated.

TOO MUCH RELIGION

[EXCLUSIVE DISPATCH]

MODESTO, June 5.—That his wife is animated and saturated with religion and is a member of the Holy Rollers and that she no longer cares for the plaintiff, are assertions made in a divorce complaint filed in the Superior Court by Paul Little, naming Rose Baker Little as defendant.

AMNESTY BILL SIGNED

[BY CABLE AND ASSOCIATED PRESS]

HAVANA (Cuba) June 5.—The amnesty bill canceling indictments and ending sentences against a number of persons was signed today by President Zayas.

NAVY PLANS APPROVED

Senate Quickly Passes Bill

Measure to Bring Sea Power Up to Standard Now Goes to the President

Large Sum Appropriated to Build New Cruisers and Improve Old Ships

[BY A. P. NIGHT WIRE]

WASHINGTON, June 5.—The bill authorizing construction of eight scout cruisers and conversion of several coal burning battleships into oil burners was passed by the Senate tonight. Action was taken in the time required for the clerk to read the title.

The measure was recommended by the Navy Department as necessary to bring the American Navy up to the standard established as a part of the country's naval policy. It already had passed the House and now goes to the President.

Not a voice was raised in opposition to the measure which authorizes construction and repair work estimated to cost at least $111,000,000. In addition to the construction of the eight 10,000-ton cruisers, costing $11,100,000 each, exclusive of armament, and the conversion into oil burners of six first line battleships, the Navy Department would have authority to proceed with the building of six gunboats costing $700,000 each for use in Chinese waters. The repairs to the battleships would include additional protection against aircraft and submarine attacks.

Efforts made unsuccessfully in the House to incorporate a provision for gun elevation on thirteen battleships were not renewed in the Senate.

Several Senators who have expressed opposition to the construction measure were not on the floor when the vote was taken, and there was said to be a possibility that reconsideration of the vote might be attempted tomorrow.

FIRE-SETTER PHANTOM IS FIRED UPON

Mystery Figure Reported Third Time as Possible School-Blaze Suspect

By a "Times" Staff Correspondent

VENICE, June 5.—For the third time Special Officer Eddie Codoni, a patrolman in the Villa City district, has turned in a report about a mysterious woman wandering along Grand Canal avenue and attempting to set fire to structures there. His last encounter was tonight when Sheriff Traeger, Undersheriff Biscailluz, Deputy Hunter and Detectives Burnett and Watson were lying in wait nearby watching for a reappearance of the phantom figure in the hope that it might lead to an explanation of the Hope Development School fire at Playa Del Rey.

Codoni fired seven shots into a vacant house. The officers nearby made a quick investigation, but were unable to corroborate his statement that he had seen the woman inside.

The first encounter, according to Codoni's reports, occurred the night following the Playa Del Rey fire. He said he fired several shots at the woman when he saw her setting fire to a house. The next encounter occurred Wednesday night, he said, when she hid beside a house and attempted to shoot him as he passed on his regular rounds. Again, he said, he shot several times. Walking with his half-brother, H. Krukow, tonight, he said he saw her inside the vacant house and began firing immediately.

Sheriff Traeger conferred with the local police as Codoni was making his third report. A full investigation is under way.

SHRINE VOTES ONE TEMPLE

Imperial Council Grants Akron (O.) Petition; Others Denied for Territorial Reasons

[EXCLUSIVE DISPATCH]

KANSAS CITY, June 5.—The granting of one petition for a new temple to Akron, O., was announced today in the report of the dispensations committee of the Imperial Council of the Shrine, in session in the Orpheum Theater.

Akron's temple will be known as Tadmor. Its mother temple is Al Koran of Cleveland, that is, its territory will come out of that now under Al Koran.

OTHERS DENIED

The territorial reason was the outstanding one for denying all the other petitions. The other petitions were Kansas City, Kan., for a temple to be known as Kedra; Topeka, Kan., for a temple to be known as Amena; Ottumwa, Iowa, for a temple to be known as Hazah; Council Bluffs, Iowa, for a temple to be known as Makalla; Ada, Okla., for a temple to be called Delphi; Cumberland, Md., for a temple to be called Alighan; Johnstown, Pa., for a temple to be called Jericho.

The report of the committee was adopted by the council, closing the subject of petitions until the next convention.

Nearly 100 men from Akron, waiting anxiously outside the convention doors, shrieked with delight and began a wild war dance when the news of their petition's acceptance reached them. Runners were sent at once for a band which the delegation brought with them. One hundred and forty came from Akron to boost the petition. They paraded late this afternoon.

FIRST POTENTATE

Robert E. Lee, first vice-president of the Firestone Rubber Company, will be the first illustrious potentate of the Akron temple, everyone seems to agree. The first ceremonial will be in September. The petition was signed by 1000, and twenty-four temples were represented.

In the cheering group in front of the Orpheum Theater, E. W. (Tex) Edward of Hella Temple, Dallas, Tex., towered. He has been one of the principal workers for the new temple and none shouted so loud as he to every passerby:

"Shake, Akron has a temple."

In Three Parts—40 Pages
PART I—TELEGRAPH SHEET—16 PAGES

The Los Angeles Times

"Sail on, sail on, and on and on!"

GREATER SOUTHERN CALIFORNIA STRAIGHT AHEAD

FRIDAY MORNING, JUNE 13, 1924. SUNDAY, 10 CENTS. DAILY, 5 CENTS.

Liberty Under Law—Equal Rights—True Industrial Freedom.

FORTY-EIGHT DIE IN WARSHIP BLASTS

COOLIDGE AND DAWES NAMED TO LEAD REPUBLICAN TICKET

"Hell and Maria" General Is Selected as President's Running-Mate After Lowden Declines Nomination Accorded Him by National Convention

[EXCLUSIVE DISPATCH]

CLEVELAND, June 12.—Calvin Coolidge of Massachusetts, for President; Charles Gates Dawes of Illinois for Vice-President.

The Republican National Convention named this ticket today for the Presidential election campaign, nominating Gen. Dawes at 10:30 o'clock tonight in the final scene of one of the most extraordinary and dramatic episodes in the history of the party.

The selection of Gen. Dawes was the second nomination for Vice-President formally made by the convention. The delegates, giving full rein to their enthusiasm, had nominated former Gov. Frank Ofl Lowden of Illinois, ignoring his reiterated assertions that he would not serve if chosen.

Then amidst indescribable confusion among the antagonistic groups of leaders on the platform and the excited and bewildered delegates on the floor, the convention hesitated in the face of a warning by William M. Butler, President Coolidge's campaign manager, of the danger of choosing an unwilling candidate and in the face of another and still more emphatic declination wired by Mr. Lowden a few minutes after he had been declared tho nominee.

A recess of the convention was taken during which the convention telegraphed a final appeal to Mr. Lowden to accept and Mr. Lowden again in a formal telegram positively refused to serve.

Mr. Lowden's message follows:

"Telegram just received. I am deeply grateful for the action of the convention. However, I have said a thousand times, I think, that I would decline if nominated and I must keep my word. To yield now would mean the loss of my self-respect. I shall do what I can for the Republican success as a private citizen, but I cannot accept a place on the ticket."

REFUSAL ACCEPTED

When the convention reassembled after the recess, shortly before 10 o'clock, Mr. Lowden's telegram was read and his declination formally accepted. Then the roll was called again, the Coolidge forces having decided during the recess to concentrate on Secretary of Commerce Hoover, while the other leaders and delegates who had put Lowden over had agreed to get behind Gen. Dawes. The roll call was a neck-and-neck race between Dawes and Hoover for a time, but finally with Illinois, two thirds of New York, Pennsylvania and other big delegations plumping for Dawes, the Chicago banker came under the wire with 682 1-2 votes to 237 1-2 for Hoover.

Senator James E. Watson of Indiana, himself a candidate for Vice-President, then appeared on the platform and moved that the nomination of Gen. Dawes be made unanimous. He did this with a flourish of old-time Republican enthusiasm, asserting that with Coolidge and Dawes the G. O. P. would sweep the country next November.

DAWES TO RUN

In the meantime, Gen. Dawes had been reached at the old Dawes family home at Marietta, O., and to the telephoned notification of his nomination had replied that he would accept. This word was brought to the platform and soon afterward the convention adjourned without delay, with the

(Continued on Page 4, Column 1)

GET MILLION IN HOLD-UP

Robbers in Raid on Mail Train

Seventy Guards and Members of Crew Overpowered by Gang of Bandits

Huge Hoard of Securities and Cash Carried Off; One of Brigands Wounded

[BY A. P. NIGHT WIRE]

CHICAGO, June 12.—Forty pouches of registered mail containing bonds and currency valued at more than a million dollars were stolen by train robbers when they held up a Chicago, Milwaukee and St. Paul mail train near Rondout, Ill., thirty miles north of Chicago, at 10:30 o'clock, central standard time, tonight.

The train stopped at Buckley Road crossing, two miles this side of Rondout. Before it came to a stop two of the robbers boarded the engine and covered the engineer and fireman with revolvers. In the meantime the three men who were on the tender uncoupled the locomotive. The robbers in the cab forced the engineer to drive the locomotive to Rondout, two miles down the track.

The train was en route from Chicago to St. Paul and its first scheduled stop was Milwaukee.

RIDE BLIND BAGGAGE

Three of the robbers rode "blind baggage" or just back of the tender of the locomotive of the train, according to Lawrence Benson, chief of the railroad's special agents.

"As the train approached Rondout, the robbers pulled the airbrakes, which brought the train to a stop," he said.

"The robbers were strung along

(Continued on Page 10, Column 2)

Most of the war makers are too old for active military service.

COOLIDGE IS NOMINATED

Given All but 44 of Total Vote

La Follette and Johnson Do Not Figure Strongly at Convention

President Given Ovation in Cleveland by Wildly Cheering Thousands

[EXCLUSIVE DISPATCH]

CONVENTION HALL, CLEVELAND, June 12.—Calvin Coolidge of Massachusetts today was nominated as the Republican candidate for President amid scenes befitting such a tribute for a tried and trusted party leader. It was a personal ovation as well as a nomination. This convention came to Cleveland to nominate Calvin Coolidge and it was determined to make a job of it. As heretofore in the proceedings of this gathering, the mere mention of his name was enough to rouse the delegates to frenzied and vociferous demonstrations.

Underneath it all was a deep-seated feeling which was the result of mature thought and careful analysis that the White House incumbent was the symbol of the re-dedication of the Republican party to principles both economic and political which will have their influence in the party councils for many years to come.

The vote follows:

Coolidge, 1065.

La Follette, 34.

Hiram Johnson, 10.

Senator La Follette received 28 votes from his home State of Wisconsin and six from North Dakota. Senator Johnson received 10 votes from South Dakota.

S. X. Way of South Dakota moved to make the nomination unanimous, but Wisconsin's 28 voted "no."

BURTON PLEASES

Marion LeRoy Burton's nomi-

(Continued on Page 8, Column 1)

Rushing Dead and Maimed to Hospital Ship

Rescuers conveying victims from chamber of doom on U.S.S. Mississippi to small boats for transportation to U.S.S. Relief is shown at the upper left. At the upper right the victims of the catastrophe are being carried aboard the Relief. At the upper left in lower group is Lieut. T. E. Zellars; at right Ensign Marcus Erwin; at bottom left Ensign McCrea. All of these were killed. At bottom right is Ensign H. D. Smith, who was hero of rescue work in disaster killing forty-eight.

LIST OF BLAST DEAD IN WORST NAVY DISASTER

Following is the official list of dead in the U.S.S. Mississippi disaster as announced late last night on board the U.S.S. New Mexico:

U.S.S. MISSISSIPPI OFFICERS AND MEN

THOMAS EDWARD ZELLARS, 25 years of age, lieutenant, junior grade, commanding officer of the turret.

ENSIGN MARCUS ERWIN, Jr., junior gunnery officer.

PAUL HOLTON CHRISTENSEN, seaman, first class.

LAWRENCE HENRY WILLIS, seaman, first class.

VERNON BRUMFIELD, coxswain.

ANDREW RUBIN KINNEY, seaman, second class.

ALBERT DARAZIO, seaman, second class.

BRIGHAM FOSTER SMITH, gunner's mate.

LESLIE MALONE, gunner's mate, first class.

DOYLE SHAW, seaman, first class.

EDWARD HOMER HUFFMAN, seaman, first class.

JOHN ALBERT McCORMICK, seaman, second class.

STANLEY JOSEPH SERYMAS, ———, rating unknown.

ALBERT LEONARD LAWSON, seaman, first class.

FRED GRAHAM EVER, seaman, second class.

WILLIAM HOWARD WARD, gunner's mate, third class.

JAMES THOMAS WOOD, F.L.C.

GEORGE ALLEN BYERS, boatswain's mate, first class.

JAMES DURWARD HOLLIDAY, seaman, first class.

PHILLIP CUNNINGHAM CLARKE, seaman, first class

WALLACE WALTHAM KEYES, boatswain's mate, second class.

FREDERICK WILLIAM ZACHARIAS, seaman, first class.

(Continued on Page 3, Column 5)

FLAMES AND GAS SPREAD DEATH IN MISSISSIPPI GUN TURRET

Explosion Creates Shambles as TNT Is Ignited; Cause Is Mystery; Injured Rushed to Port Where New Convulsion Rocks Craft

Three officers and forty-five enlisted men were killed, nine others probably fatally injured and a score more hurt in various degree in the explosion of nearly two tons of TNT compound in Gun Turret No. 2 on the U.S.S. Mississippi off Los Angeles Harbor yesterday afternoon.

There were two separate blasts. The first was that of 1800 pounds of powder and the charge of the fourteen-inch rifle No. 4 while gun crews in Turret No. 2 were engaged in secret practice on the San Clemente drill grounds, forty-five miles from the harbor.

The second came when the hand of a dead man being carried out by rescuers dropped on the firing switch of Gun No. 5 as the dreadnaught dropped anchor four hours later near the hospital ship Relief in the harbor proper. The shell was hurled out to sea, missing the outgoing liner Yale by a few hundred feet.

Immediately after the accident the naval officials in charge of the battleship division and the ship clamped down a rigid censorship. Shore leave was denied members of the Mississippi's crew; all officers were instructed to say nothing. Newspaper men were prevented from visiting the wrecked craft; it was only on receipt of direct orders from Admiral Eberle, acting Secretary of the Navy, that a casualty list was forthcoming. The only official announcement which was made public was in the shape of a meager message sent to the Navy Department at Washington; at Los Angeles Harbor every possible attempt was made to keep news from leaking out save that approved by censors on the U.S.S. New Mexico.

But late last night a naval board of inquiry, headed by Capt. Yates Sterling, commanding officer of the U.S.S. New Mexico, was ordered by Vice-Admiral Henry S. Wiley to convene at 10 o'clock this morning to investigate the catastrophe.

On the arrival of the Mississippi in the harbor, rescue work amid the wrecked turret was still going forward; it was not until a late hour that the full death toll became known. And this rescue work carried its own danger, for in the explosion in the harbor, the recoil of the heavy rifle crushed to death four of the rescuing squad.

GREATEST DISASTER

The story of this greatest of naval disasters, for it eclipses all three other similar events in the Navy, best can be told chronologically. The story, compiled from such information as could be gleaned, follows:

For several days the Pacific Fleet has been engaged in mock warfare and target practice. The crashing boom of its guns has resounded for many miles along the Pacific Coast. Windows in Los Angeles, Santa Barbara and San Diego have rattled, chimneys have quivered and the populace, alarmed, has telephoned to points of information for the latest news of another earthquake.

Yesterday was one such day. The battleships Mississippi, Tennessee, Idaho and California, comprising a division under the command of Rear-Admiral William V. Pratt, who, it will be remembered, headed the naval board of inquiry on the wrecking of seven destroyers at Honda Bay, September 8, 1923, left Los Angeles Harbor yesterday for the San Clemente drill grounds for secret practice.

PROUDLY ON WAY

The California towed behind it a giant target; it was to be the objective for the mass firing of the thirty-six fourteen-inch rifles of the other three superbattlers.

On the way to the target ground—fifteen miles north of San Clemente Island—the crew of the Mississippi proudly polished their guns and prepared for the fray; for they were the champions of the fleet; and of their ship Gun Turret No. 2 held all records for speed and accuracy in target practice.

They reached the firing grou[nd] a few maneuvers and they v[...] lined up. In the distance—tiny specks—were the Calif[ornia] and its target. Officers sprai[...] range finders; others do[...] glasses and searched the seas. [Ex]perts made mental computatio[ns of] distance and elevation; and r[...] barked commands resou[nding] throughout the ship.

At full speed they pl[owed] through the waves, for this ta[rget] practice was to be against e[very] handicap the Navy could mu[ster].

SHELLS BROUGHT UP

In Gun Turret No. 2, situa[ted] above and slightly aft of Gun Turret No. 1, forward of the ship, were the eighty-odd men comprising the gun crews for Guns Nos. 4, 5 and 6. Part of these eighty-odd men were stationed at the guns themselves; the remainder of the crews were occupied in the handling rooms and in the twin tunnels leading from the ammunition stores.

In command of the turret was Lieut. Thomas Edward Zellars, a Long Beach man. With him were Ensigns Marcus Erwin, J. J. Levasseur and James McCrea, the last two being observers from the U.S.S. New Mexico detailed to witness the target practice.

The monster shells were brought

(Continued on Page 3, Column 1)

SURVIVE BY MIRACLES

Only Two Escape From Turret

Seamen Dive Into Hatch as Flashes Token Blasts Rending Comrades

Sudden Coming of Disaster and Resultant Horror Stifle Memories

Eighty-six men were assigned to gun turret No. 2 of the dreadnaught Mississippi yesterday afternoon when more than 4000 pounds of TNT compound, exploding, made of its interior a tangled mass of twisted steel and shattered humanity.

Of those assigned, forty-six were in the gun turret proper. The remainder were engaged in handling ammunition from the magazines. Of the forty-six only two escaped; they saved their lives by diving down a forty-foot hatchway which automatically closed on their heels and left several comrades who followed them to die like rats in a trap. Four other seamen were killed during the second explosion.

And these two, their brains shocked into incomprehension, as yet can hardly tell a coherent story of what occurred; and the immediate happenings just before the flashes of light which they saw may always remain a blank in their memory.

Naval officials last night thus found themselves at a loss to account for just what happened; they say it may never be known.

J. F. Caviezel, seaman first-class, living at 5712 Baltimore avenue, Los Angeles, and Robert McAvin, seaman first-class, whose home is in San Francisco, were the Caviezel was at the left of the gun crew who were in the turret.

Both are members of the crew of the U.S.S. New Mexico and were acting temporarily as observers on the Mississippi. At the time of the explosion McAvin was

(Continued on Page 3, Column 4)

In Three Parts—48 Pages

PART I—TELEGRAPH SHEET—18 PAGES

The Los Angeles Times

"Sail on, sail on, and on and on."

WEDNESDAY MORNING, JULY 22, 1925.

DAILY, 5 CENTS. SUNDAY, 10 CENTS.

Liberty Under Law—Equal Rights—True Industrial Freedom

BERLIN NOTE WELCOMED

London Hopeful for Amity

British Regard Document as Real Effort to Gain European Peace

French Express Displeasure; Answer Paves Way to Fall Conference

BY JOHN STEELE

[BY CABLE—EXCLUSIVE DISPATCH]

LONDON, July 21.—The German reply to the French security note, which was made public tonight, is regarded by the British as a genuine attempt on the part of the Germans to clear up the outstanding difficulties and to create a situation in which real progress toward European pacification can be made.

The note evidently was very carefully prepared to include all the objections raised by various German individuals and parties to the Allied proposals. Many of these objections were merely details, which will be capable of quick disposal when the conference which the German note foreshadows takes place, but the others are vital and the purpose in raising them so early in the game is to allow full consideration by the Allies before the time for bargaining comes.

The chief of these vital objections is one against Clause 16 of the Versailles Treaty which would allow the French to march across German territory to assist their eastern allies. Germany also raises the point that it would be in an anomalous position if it entered the League of Nations as a disarmed nation, while all the other members were fully armed.

Berlin points out that the covenant of the League provides for eventual all-around disarmament, and suggests that some arrangement be made to tide over the period until that ideal is accomplished.

It is not believed here that the conference is likely to get under way before October. There will be a further exchange of notes, discussing details, clearing away misunderstandings and preparing the ground for the success of the conference.

FUNDAMENTAL IDEAS GIVEN BY STRESEMANN

[BY CABLE AND ASSOCIATED PRESS]

BERLIN, July 21.—Three fundamental ideas underlie the German reply to the French note on the proposed security pact, Dr. Stresemann, the Foreign Minister, explained to the correspondents today. First, the relation of the pact to existing treaties; second, Germany's position on arbitration treaties, including guarantees, and

(Continued on Page 2, Column 5)

SCOPES CONVICTION PAVES WAY FOR LEGAL STRUGGLE

Tennessee Supreme Court to Get Evolution Case as Result of 'Guilty' Verdict in Dayton

[BY A. P. NIGHT WIRE]

DAYTON (Tenn.) July 21.—The trial of John T. Scopes on a charge of teaching evolution theories in the public schools in violation of the Tennessee law ended today in a verdict of guilty. The minimum fine of $100 was imposed by the court and bail for an appeal was fixed at $500.

The entire testimony yesterday of William Jennings Bryan was stricken from the record today by Judge John T. Raulston, who held that the cross-examination by Clarence S. Darrow of Mr. Bryan on Bryan's biblical views had nothing to do with the case.

Defense counsel then agreed to have the jury brought back into court and return its verdict.

The scene of the "evolution test" will be shifted from Dayton to Knoxville, where, under the regular order of procedure, the Tennessee Supreme Court will hear cases from this circuit the first Monday in September.

MAKES SURETY BOND

The defendant made a surety bond for his appearance in Rhea County Circuit Court the first Monday in December, when the Supreme Court, it is expected, will have passed upon the case.

After both defense and State counsel had agreed this morning that the defendant should be convicted, the jury returned a verdict in less than ten minutes.

The defense then moved for a new trial and when this was overruled, Scopes's attorneys made the other customary legal motions to complete the record and send the case on its way to the Supreme Court.

The beginning of the end of the case that has covered a wide variety of subjects was noted soon after court convened this morning. Attorneys on the contending sides of the issue announced they had decided to forego argument and submit the case at once to the jury.

Judge John T. Raulston, before retiring to his chamber to prepare his charge, expunged Mr. Bryan's testimony from the record.

FEARS ERROR

"I fear that I may have committed error yesterday in my overzeal to ascertain if there was anything in the proof that was offered that might aid the higher court in determining whether or not I had committed error in my former decrees," said the judge. "I have no disposition to protect any decree that I make from being reversed by a higher court, because, if I am in error, I hope that somebody will correct my mistake.

"I feel that the testimony of Mr. Bryan can shed no light upon any issues that will be pending before the higher court.

"The lawsuit now is whether or not Mr. Scopes taught that man descended from a lower order of animals. It isn't a question of

(Continued on Page 2, Column 1)

EVOLUTION TRIAL COST IS $25,000

Expert Witness Expenses in Case Greatest Items; Court Fees $300

[BY A. P. NIGHT WIRE]

DAYTON (Tenn.) July 21. — A misdemeanor case, carrying as a penalty to the guilty offender a fine of $100 and costs of the trial, brought an expenditure to the defenders of John Thomas Scopes of approximately $25,000. The actual court costs are estimated at well over $300 or more than treble the fine assessed by the court.

By far the greatest expense of the trial, however, has been the cost of bringing expert witnesses, who were not allowed to testify, from different parts of the country, defraying their railroad fare, their hotel bills and maintaining a home for them in Dayton after their arrival here. Members of the defense counsel today estimated that cost to approximate between $20,000 and $25,000.

Attorneys on both sides of the case, it has been announced, bore their own expenditures and served without fees.

The cost of the court to be assessed to the defendant include two sessions of the grand jury at an estimated cost of $50 a session; a preliminary hearing and incidentals, including the issuance of papers and their service, estimated at $25; the cost of the trial jury and other officers of the court fixed at $225

The completion of the record for its presentation in the higher courts will add several thousand dollars to the defense expenses, it is estimated. In addition to the actual court expenses another expenditure of several hundred dollars was borne by the county in preparing the court for the trial.

SUIT SETS NEW MARK FOR SPEED

Case Settled Within Five Minutes When Railroads Confess Judgment

[BY A. P. NIGHT WIRE]

CHICAGO, July 21.—Speed records and precedents were believed to have been smashed today when within five minutes in Federal Judge Wilkerson's court a suit for $30,000 against three railroads, instigated by the Oklahoma State Shippers' Association, was filed, the railroads confessed judgment and each deposited a check for $10,000 in the hands of Jacob I. Grossman, Assistant District Attorney. The roads were the Atchison, Topeka and Santa Fe, Chicago, Burlington and Quincy and the Chicago, Rock Island and Pacific, which had maintained a discriminatory rate on canned goods from Colorado to points in Kansas and Oklahoma, after the Interstate Commerce Commission had ruled against the rate.

Similar action is to be started in Nebraska against the Union Pacific; in the eastern district of Missouri against the Missouri Pacific and the St. Louis and San Francisco; in Colorado against the Colorado and Southern and in the eastern district of Oklahoma against the Midland Valley Railroad.

TEXTBOOK ROW NEAR

Evolution Fight in California

Education Board to Decide What Works May be Used in State

Teaching of Darwinism as Theory Permissible But Not as Fact

[EXCLUSIVE DISPATCH]

SAN FRANCISCO, July 21.—The State Board of Education will decide Thursday morning precisely what text-books on evolution may be taught in the schools of California. The basis of selection will be whether the text presents evolution simply as a theory or as a fact. If the book says that evolution is a fact the board, sitting in solemn conclave at the Fairmont Hotel, will consign the volume to the bottom of the bay and points south.

Caught between two fires, the board has declared that evolution as a theory is permissible. One by one the text-books will come up for judgment, and the main fight is expected to develop over the "suspended list."

There are approximately sixty of these books. The board has previously looked them over and labeled them "doubtful." They were not definitely barred, but the board appointed a committee of educators, headed by President W. W. Campbell of the University of California, to examine the books. That was last April, and the committee duly turned in a favorable report. So far, however, the board has not adopted the texts as official.

Maynard Shipley, president of the Science League of America, will be present in person Thursday morning to insist that these books be given an official rating. Representatives of the fundamentalists are also expected to be on hand, fighting against their adoption. Advance indications are that the session will be a warm one.

BIOLOGY TEXT-BOOK

"The suspended list" is said to include Gruenberg's text-book on biology. Some of the scientists are greatly amused because this book, called doubtful by California, is one of the only two text-books that were permitted to be taught in Tennesee after the passage of the famous evolution law of that State.

Maynard Shipley sees a far-flung plot to put a similar law on the statute books of the State of California. He declares that the present move against the text-books is only the first step in the campaign. He appeared before the board at this morning's session with a statement that he read and then had the statement incorporated in the record of the proceedings.

Other statements and letters to the board also were read at today's session and incorporated into the record. Many of them were just as vehement in advocating the other side of the question, and a letter from the San Joaquin Valley Baptists' Association asserted that that organization had 6000 members and 60,000 adherents to back up the views stated therein.

The Glendale Presbyterian Church, with a membership of 300 assembled for the annual meeting, passed the following resolution:

"Resolved: That we enter our emphatic protest to the California State Board of Education against the reported decision to allow the Darwinian or evolutionary theory to be taught in the public schools of the State.

"In view of the fact that the Bible has been ruled out of our schools, we demand that no other theory of the origin of man be taught our children."

HIGHLIGHTS OF STATEMENT

Highlights from the statement introduced this morning by Maynard Shipley on behalf of the Science League of America follow:

"We hold that the State Board of Education has no interest in the question of whether the textbooks used in our public schools are in conformity or in conflict with the Bible or with any other sacred writings of any religious creed whatever.

"If the objections to any text-

(Continued on Page 2, Column 4)

"When Shall We Three Meet Again?"

CALIFORNIA AID ASKED

Santa Barbara's Need Shown

Appeal for $1,100,000 Fund to Help City Made by State Association

Development Body Directs Campaign of Relief for Earthquake Victims

[BY A. P. NIGHT WIRE]

SAN FRANCISCO, July 21.—Dr. Henry S. Pritchett, president of the Carnegie Foundation, and chairman of the Santa Barbara Relief Fund Committee, issued an appeal today through the California Development Association for a public fund of $1,100,000 to be used in the reconstruction of hospitals, for temporary school buildings, and for the rehabilitation of charitable agencies, community work and Red Cross relief in Santa Barbara.

The appeal is confined to California, Santa Barbara having refused national help. The development association adopted a resolution to act as the directing agency to raise the funds.

It was announced that the reconstruction of the business section of Santa Barbara and the Santa Barbara Mission will be taken care of through other means.

LETTER STARTS DRIVE

The California Development Association resolved to undertake the mission of raising the sum asked for after receiving the following letter from the Santa Barbara Relief Fund Committee:

"On the morning of June 29, Santa Barbara was visited by a severe earthquake, similar to that which proved so destructive to the city of San Francisco nineteen years ago. The business portion of the city suffered great loss. A large number of buildings were destroyed and many others were so badly injured that they must be taken down. Many homes of the poor as well as of the well-to-do were shattered. The charitable institutions of the city and its schools need the immediate expenditure of large sums of money in order to carry on their work during the period of emergency. Individuals in distress must be helped and the Red Cross must be put in possession of funds for the relief of such cases. All these facts are well known to you through the personal inspection of the city, which your board of directors has been good enough to make.

STATE AID PLEDGED

"No appeal for nation-wide assistance in the face of this disaster, has hitherto been made for two reasons: First, the extent of the disaster and the amount necessary to meet emergency needs could not be known without careful investigation. Secondly, at a meting of the board of directors of the Los Angeles Chamber of Commerce, Thursday, July 2, 1925, at which were present representatives from the San Francisco Chamber of Commerce, California Development Association, Los Angeles Clearing-house Association, Southern California Investment Dealers' Association and the Los Angeles Stock Exchange, the representatives of the city of Santa Barbara were advised that it was the common judgment of all these groups that such aid as was needed in Santa Barbara should be given by California. These representatives believed that the great State of California would prefer to care for its own.

"The committee whose names are signed hereto, including the Mayor of the city, was therefore appointed by the City Council to study the nature and extent of these injuries to public institutions, to public health and sanitation and to individuals which were beyond the resources of our citizens during this emergency period. This work has been most conscientiously done. The details of the whole study have been submitted to your board of directors and have led to the following conclusions:

"For emergency aid and the reconstruction of hospital buildings, for the building of the Associated Charities and for similar agencies; for temporary buildings to house pupils so that they can enter school in the autumn; for community health and sanitary emergency work, and for Red Cross relief, the sum of $1,100,000 is the minimum amount with which these pressing needs can be met and for which there is no other method of financing. With this assistance Santa Barbara will go forward with courage to take up the vastly greater burden of many millions of dollars of reconstruction that will fall upon her citizens.

"It is the opinion of all civic bodies that have been consulted that the California Development Association, reaching through its membership every community in the State, is pre-eminently the agency to undertake to raise this sum.

FOR HONOR OF STATE

"We, therefore, earnestly request that you will undertake this helpful and sympathetic service for the honor of California and for the encouragement of the community that is seeking bravely to meet the demands of a great emergency suddenly thrust upon its by an overwhelming disaster.

"We are, most sincerely,

"Dr. Henry S. Pritchett, chairman, president Carnegie Foundation; F. F. Peabody, vice-chairman, Cluett Peabody Co.; E. F. MacDonough, secretary, secretary of the Santa Barbara Chamber of Commerce; C. M. Andera, Mayor of Santa Barbara; E. B. Babbitt, major-general, United States Army; Dr. Rexwald, George Owen Knapp, president Union Carbide and Carbon Company; Harold S. Chase, George S. Edwards, Bernhard Hoffman, W. E. Erwin."

FORD BID FOR SHIPS FAVORED

Acceptance of Offer by Board Expected Although Action is Deferred

[BY A. P. NIGHT WIRE]

WASHINGTON, July 21.—Although action was deferred by the Shipping Board today, indications were that with little delay it would approve the recommendation of President Palmer of the Fleet Corporation for accepance of Henry Ford's bid of $1,706,000 for the 200 vessels offered for scrapping.

With four members present, the board discussed the recommendation at considerable length, but decided to resume consideration of the question Thursday, when additional commissioners are expected to be in the city.

Counsel for the board attended today's meeting and gave their opinions as to the legality of the Ford offer in relation to the advertisement of sale. Indications were that this was found satisfactory, while no question was said to have been raised as to the procedure of negotiation, which has been protested by the Boston Iron and Metal Company of Baltimore, but declared by the board's counsel to have been regular.

Although Ford in his offer expressed a hope that, if the ships were awarded him, some now on the Atlantic Coast might be substituted for several in the list of 200 offered, no change in the list was recommended by Palmer, and the board is expected to make no change on the ground that to do so would alter the basis of the entire sale and be contrary to the advertisement.

FREIGHT SHIPMENTS OF VALLEY SHOW GAIN

[EXCLUSIVE DISPATCH]

HARLINGEN (Tex.) July 21.—According to a statement just issued by W. M. Hundley of Harlingen, district freight agent of the Gulf Coast Lines, the total shipments of fruit and vegetables from the lower Rio Grande Valley of Texas during the season just closed were 13,649 cars. The freight car lot movement totaled 12,393 cars; the express car lot movement 421 cars and the less than car lot express movement 835 cars. Included in these figures are 760 car lots of citrus fruit. These figures compared to shipments for the season before show a decided gain. Freight shipments last season were 11,638 and express car lot shipments 267 cars.

RELIEF FUND IS GROWING

Over Thirteen Thousand Dollars Now on "Times" List for Santa Barbara Charities

The Times will receive, acknowledge by publication and deliver to the authorized agents of the California Development Association any sums sent to this paper as contributions to the $1,100,000 fund to be raised by the association for emergency and charitable work in stricken Santa Barbara.

The Times itself started the fund with a donation of $10,000 and takes this occasion to urge all loyal Californians, individuals, organizations, companies, etc., to give to the extent of their abilities. The need is urgent. Santa Barbara has pluckily refused eastern help in the belief that California will take care of her own. Let her be not disappointed!

Make checks payable to the Santa Barbara Fund and send them to The Times, Los Angeles, Cal.

Up to 4 p.m. yesterday the fund was as follows:

Previously acknowledged	$11,090.00
Sid Grauman	1,000.00
A. P. Giannini	1,000.00
R. B. Williamson	100.00
F. G. Calkins	100.00
Richard Luby	50.00
L. H. Applegate	25.00
Austin J. Mummert, M.D.	25.00
Martin Abernethy	25.00
Mrs. Mabel H. Bradshaw	10.00
Henry J. Kramer	10.00
Jeanie H. Guidinger	10.00
Ann Walker Pierce	10.00
Cornelia C. Smith	10.00
Helen Jennings Silver	10.00
Dr. F. E. Chamberlain	5.00
Stephen G. Snuggs	5.00
S. J. Neugroschl	5.00
Caroline S. Forsyth	2.00
Total	$13,492.00

Donations in generous sums were received by The Times in increasing numbers for the emergency relief of Santa Barbara's charitable institutions yesterday, the second day of the drive for a fund of $1,100,000 launched by the California Development Association to place the Channel City's humanitarian agencies on an operating basis again.

Santa Barbara's charities were among the heaviest sufferers of the recent earthquake, which disabled the city's charitable organizations and institutions to such an extent that they have been unable to minister a helping hand to the city's needy ones for more than three weeks. The city, itself, has chosen to care for its own civic and business losses, but the city is powerless to aid the charities.

Stress was laid upon the seriousness of the situation concerning the charities—the hospitals, orphanages, social centers and the like—yesterday by the leaders in the drive for the $1,100,000 emergency fund, a fund that is being sought for immediate relief to a most worthy cause. They emphasized that the restoration of these agencies is California's duty, and the duty of Californians alone. The care of the needy of a stricken California city is California's own trust.

OUR DUTY

"It is as much the duty of citizens of Los Angeles to come to the aid of the real sufferers of the Santa Barbara earthquake as if it were our own city," one of the officials of the drive stated.

"Those who are to benefit through the fund are the ones most worthy of being benefited. They cannot turn elsewhere, except to their own California kin, for assistance. And if California fails in this duty—and remember, Los Angeles is a most integral part of California—then those of Santa Barbara who need real help cannot hope for any assistance whatever."

In the meantime, while awaiting financial help from the only source from which it can be obtained, inmates of some of Santa Barbara's institutions are existing in tents and temporary buildings, under congested and uncomfortable conditions, and are deprived of the moderate conveniences that were theirs before the earthquake descended upon their city.

GIVE $1000 EACH

The two largest contributions yesterday came from two of the city's leading citizens. A. P. Giannini and Sid Grauman each subscribed $1000 to the growing fund. Mr. Giannini is president of the board of directors of the Bank of Italy and of the Bancitaly Corporation. Mr. Grauman is one of the leading motion-picture impresarios in the West, builder of many beautiful film theaters and operator of

(Continued on Page 2, Column 5)

THE DAY'S NEWS SUMMED UP

THE SKY. Clear. Wind at 5 p.m., southwest; velocity, ten miles. Thermometer, highest, 77 deg.; lowest, 62 deg. Forecast: For Los Angeles and vicinity: Fair. For complete weather data, see last page of this section.

FEATURES. Radio, Page 3, Part II. Women's Pages, Clubs and Society, Page 6, Part II. Markets and Financial, Pages 13, 14, 15, 16, 17, Part I. News of Southern Counties Page 10, Part II. Oil News, Page 17, Part I. Pictures, Page 8, Part I. Comics, Page 12, Part I.

NEWS IN SPANISH, Page 7, Part I.

SHIPPING NEWS. Page 17, Part I.

THE CITY. Senator Bingham on visit to Los Angeles airport predicts great future for development of aviation here, advantage being with city for greatest western terminal. Page 1, Part II.

Court is scene of near-riot when hundreds of witnesses cause uproar in Maywood trial. Page 7, Part II.

Run of grunion at beaches forecast for tonight, tomorrow and Friday. Page 7, Part II.

The mysterious disappearance of R. D. Donohoe, stock salesman, is revealed when Mrs. Donohoe is reported to have threatened her husband's employer if he failed to produce the missing spouse. Page 2, Part II.

Cal E. Stone, victim of despondency, suffers serious injuries in leap from eighth-story window of Alexandria and lights on fire escape of sixth floor. Page 18, Part II.

Wilshire Congregational Church officers will extend olive branch to members voting 67 to 2 for ousting Pastor Frank Dyer. Page 1, Part II.

Transit experts urge development of proposed system as greatest present need of city at Biltmore luncheon. Page 5, Part II.

Task of re-counting votes in Councilmanic election begins in election contest filed by defeated candidate. Page 1, Part II.

Wanda Hawley will marry Jay Stuart Wilkinson, her business manager on the 30th inst. Page 1, Part II.

Five arrested and two huge stills seized in raid conducted by Federal dry agents. Page 2, Part II.

Skipper of tanker, who rose from seaman to captain in six years, lays luck to being born on Sunday. Page 1, Part II.

Investigators convinced fatal duel and suicide in Imperial county is result of quarrel over woman. Page 2, Part I.

PACIFIC SLOPE. Statewide appeal for $1,100,000 fund to aid Santa Barbara is issued by California Development Association. Page 1, Part I.

State Board of Education must decide what text-books on evolution are suitable for use in California schools. Page 1, Part I.

Gov. Hunt reiterates defiance of Legislature in letters stating river parley will be unofficial. Page 3, Part I.

GENERAL EASTERN. Real battle opens over evolution with contemplated appeal to Tennessee Supreme Court following conviction and fining of Scopes. Page 1, Part I.

Inquiry into gigantic bootleg ring seeks to disclose if banks are involved in financing the ring's operations extending into twenty-nine States. Page 4, Part I.

Aged New York philanthropist, desiring to give away millions for the benefit of society, asks suggestions on how best to dispose of the money. Page 3, Part I.

WASHINGTON. Shipping Board expected to accept Henry Ford's bid for vessels ordered to be scrapped. Page 1, Part I.

FOREIGN. British interpret Berlin note on security pact as sincere attempt to reach agreement. Page 1, Part I.

Two Australian aviators are first to greet the American fleet steaming 120 miles off coast of New South Wales. Page 1, Part I.

Success of French bond issue leads to debt meeting of ministers with indications of action on funding by fall. Page 2, Part I.

REMEMBER THIS BY H. M. STANSIFER

He is making the greatest progress who observes how small his past achievements have been.

Nations' League Building Shaken by Earthquake

[BY CABLE—EXCLUSIVE DISPATCH]

GENEVA, July 21.—A violent earthquake shook the League of Nations' and other buildings in Geneva at 1 o'clock this afternoon and in the League buildings shook paintings of the founders of the League from the walls.

AIRPLANES WELCOME FLEET

Australian Flyers First to Greet American Armada Nearing Shores of Island Continent

BY JACK MYERS

[BY CABLE—EXCLUSIVE DISPATCH]

MELBOURNE (Australia) July 21.—The mighty United States fleet which is nearing Australian shores to pay a visit of good will received its first visible greeting from Australia today when two seaplanes met it while it was steaming 120 miles off the New South Wales Coast. The planes circled over the warships and then returned to shore.

Admiral Coontz, in command of the fleet, evidently appreciated the compliment, for he sent a message to the Australian Air Board describing the flight as magnificent and congratulating the airmen.

REVIVE FEATURE

A feature of the program of entertainment arranged in both Sydney and Melbourne is hospitality in private homes for thousands of officers and sailors. This feature of the 1908 visit is being revived for this occasion, and it is believed it will do more than all the public functions together to give the visitors a real insight in Australian life and promote abiding friendship.

Melbourne is already dressed in gala fashion. The streets and buildings are decorated and everything is pointing toward a wonderful reception when the Americans arrive on Thursday.

BEARS PEACE MESSAGE

Discussing the visit, the Melbourne Age says:

"This mighty naval force brings across the Pacific from a wonderful republic a message of peace and good will. The visit of 1908, which Roosebelt described as one of the great achievements of his career, gave impetus to Australia's interest in America even greater than impetus of America's interest in Australia. The American influence has encouraged Australians to believe in themselves. This experience has intensified our national consciousness."

In Three Parts—40 Pages
PART I—TELEGRAPH SHEET—16 PAGES

DESTINY

The Los Angeles Times

"Sail on, sail on, and on and on."

THURSDAY MORNING, JULY 30, 1925.

DAILY, 5 CENTS.
SUNDAY, 10 CENTS.

Liberty Under Law—Equal Rights—True Industrial Freedom

GEORGIA FOR EVOLUTION

Measure to Ban Theory Beaten

Lower House Overwhelms Measure to Prohibit Teaching in State

Sponsor of Bill Denounces Darwin Followers as "Smart Alecks"

[BY A. P. NIGHT WIRE]

ATLANTA (Ga.) July 29.—An amendment designed to prohibit the teaching of evolution in the common schools of Georgia today was voted down overwhelmingly by the State House of Representatives.

The amendment was offered to the general appropriations bill and provided that any teacher or school teaching or permitting to be taught a theory of evolution in contradiction to the Bible's account of the creation of man would be cut off from receiving State funds. The amendment related only to the common schools.

Representative Lindsay of Dekalb county, author of the amendment, stated after the amendment's crushing defeat that he would not offer an antievolution bill.

In the viva voce vote the "noes" drowned out the "ayes."

Speaking in behalf of the amendment, Representative Lindsay referred to the University of Chicago as the source of new theories "which for the last twenty-five years have overwhelmed this country" and which "culminated a short time ago in one of its graduates taking the life of a little boy as a scientific experiment."

He said:

"No man's education—no system of education that is founded on things other than the fundamentals of Holy Writ can endure.

"I don't want any smart Aleck trying to teach my child that man descended from a tadpole or a monkey.

"My child shall not be subject to the inroads of scientists. We must protect them from the poison that is being injected.

"When a man gets so smart that he can't believe the Bible he is just too smart to know that he's a fool."

BOY URGES STATE TO BAR EVOLUTION

[EXCLUSIVE DISPATCH]

SACRAMENTO, July 29.—An appeal was made today to Gov. Richardson by Golen Harvey, an Oakland High School boy, to prohibit the teaching of evolution in the public schools of the State.

"Please don't let evolution be

(Continued on Page 4, Column 5)

DRY CHIEFS APPOINTED

Names of Aides Withheld

Andrews Selects Number of Administrators Under Reorganization

Motorized Border Patrol to Wage War on Smugglers and Rum-Runners

[BY A. P. NIGHT WIRE]

WASHINGTON, July 29.—Striding forward with the construction of the Treasury's new prohibition enforcement machine, Assistant Secretary Andrews has definitely decided on seven or eight of the men to fill the posts of prohibition administrators under the reorganization.

The names of the men were withheld. It was said tonight, however, that they were regarded by the Treasury as among the best available and that each had agreed to a personal sacrifice to join with Mr. Andrews in his effort to carry out the terms of the Volstead Act.

PLANS BORDER DEFENSE

In furtherance of his basic plan to choke off the liquor supply at its source, Mr. Andrews proposes to erect a line of defense on the north and south borders that will dovetail in with the interior prohibition organization.

The assistant secretary began consideration today of a plan to reinforce the Customs Service border patrol to take care of the new defense areas.

Mr. Andrews apparently is committed to a completely motorized border patrol system.

Treasury officials have estimated that the government loses between $10,000,000 and $15,000,000 a year through smuggling and the plans under study would be aimed to prevent the illegal entry, not only of liquor, but of many articles of merchandise on which tariff duties are levied as well as the smuggling of narcotics and aliens.

BORDER POINTS OPEN

Long stretches of the American border are unguarded because of the small number of customs agents who can be assigned to the Dakota - Montana - Idaho - Washington areas, as well as along the Rio Grande and Southern California districts.

On the north, the smuggling of wheat and cattle has in the past been a serious problem.

The southern problem has been largely that of the smuggling of liquor, narcotics and aliens. Mr. Andrews feels that more men and

(Continued on Page 2, Column 5)

THE DAY'S NEWS SUMMED UP

THE SKY: Clear. Wind at 5 p.m., Southwest. Velocity, 11 miles. Thermometer, highest, 80 deg.; lowest, 62 deg. Forecast: For Los Angeles and vicinity: Fair. For complete weather data, see last page of this section.

THE CITY. Southern California Edison Company announces four-year $37,000,000 power program, with work on Shaver Lake tunnel to start in winter. Page 1, Part II.

Enthusiastic fans pay enviable tribute to Mary Pickford on her appearance at court in kidnaping trial. Page 1, Part II.

The California committee to attend the tri-State conference on Colorado River water issues will leave Los Angeles Tuesday for the scene of the conference. Page 1, Part II.

Santa Barbara charities declared in immediate need of aid in caring for the unfortunates of the community whose condition was rendered more serious by the disaster. Page 1, Part II.

Dispute over the possession of 3-year-old Thomas Dudley Arkle, heir to a $200,000 Kentucky estate, resulted in an asserted attack on two deputy sheriffs by Mrs. Maggie-Belle Drake, grandmother of the boy, and another woman. Page 2, Part II.

Rush Meadows, convicted of bond-forgery charges, is sentenced to two years, and fined $5000. Page 5, Part II.

Film actor dies after leg is amputated, as result of injury suffered in automobile accident. Page 2, Part II.

Mother instigates police inquiry by expressing fear daughter of Tom Mix faces kidnaping. Man is questioned and released. Page 2, Part II.

Constance Talmadge asks restoration of citizenship lost through marriage to Greek subject. Page 7, Part II.

Actual work on building huge government breakwater at Los Angeles Harbor has started. Page 1, Part II.

Gambling charges brought by women referred by City Council to Public Welfare Committee. Page 5, Part II.

More than 100 film stars will participate in Greater Movie Season parade through downtown streets tomorrow. Page 5, Part II.

Andrew Pepall, accused embezzler of funds from Ontario treasury, who was arrested at Long Beach, is freed on $300,000 bail. Page 2, Part II.

SPORTS. Jack Dempsey, heavyweight boxing champion, and his manager, Jack Kearns, come to settlement. Page 1, Part III.

San Francisco wins second straight over Vernon, 10 to 1, at Washington Park. Oakland defeats Los Angeles, 6 to 5; Salt Lake wins from Sacramento, 23 to 11, and Seattle defeats Portland, 7 to 5. Page 1, Part III.

Vincent Richards, United States tennis star, defeats Gerald Patterson of Australia in straight sets at Seabright tournament. Page 1, Part III.

Tommy Milton and Peter Kreis, American racing drivers, announce intention of leaving next week for Italian Grand Prix. Page 3, Part III.

GENERAL EASTERN. Evolution wins victory in Georgia when State House of Representatives votes down measure to prohibit teaching of theory in public schools. Page 1, Part I.

Station throngs pay silent homage to memory of William J. Bryan as body is carried toward national Capitol. Page 1, Part I.

President Coolidge mingles with members at reunion of Essex county Men's Republican Club in Massachusetts. Page 7, Part I.

Three die and society patrons of Chicago's smartest hotel are thrown into a panic as the result of a master hold-up in which the bandits escaped with $10,000 taken from the cashier's office of the Drake Hotel. Page 3, Part I.

WASHINGTON. Assistant Secretary Andrews selects a number of prohibition administrators under the reorganization of the department; the names of the men are withheld. Page 1, Part I.

Formal exchange of ratifications on nine-power treaty concerning China being prepared. Page 6, Part I.

FOREIGN. Ambassador Bancroft's death stirs Japanese leaders and press to words of high praise. Page 3, Part I.

Prince of Wales leaves South Africa for visit to South America. Page 4, Part I.

There must be something wrong with the life that can be happy only when it forgets.

How Our Union Terminal at Plaza Will Look

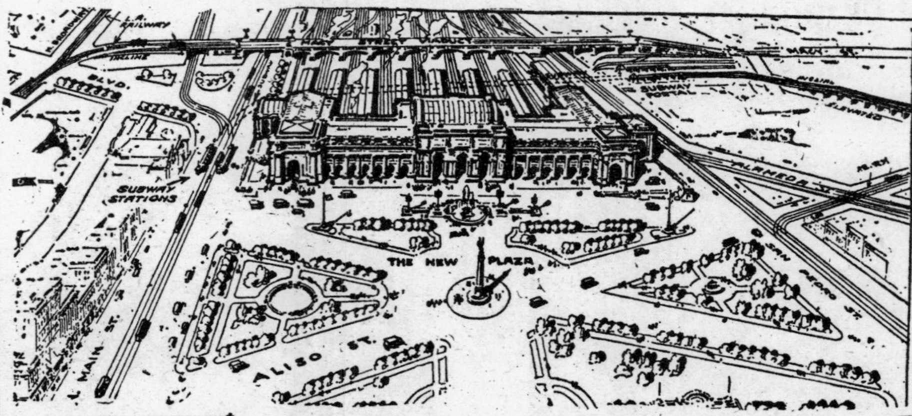

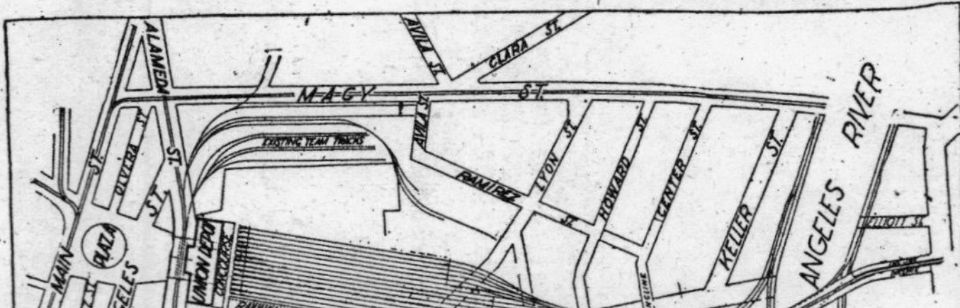

Projected Joint North End Railway Station and Its Approaches

The top picture, by Charles H. Owens, Times staff artist, shows the station as planend, in its setting adjacent to the Plaza. Below is the Railroad Commission map showing the rail approaches to the new terminal.

MUSSOLINI TO UNDERGO OPERATION

Premier May Submit to Knife While Guest of Italian Monarch

[BY CABLE AND ASSOCIATED PRESS]

PARIS, July 29.—In diplomatic circles in Paris the report is in circulation that Premier Mussolini of Italy may soon undergo a surgical operation for the removal of ulcer of the duodenum, that portion of the small intestine which is conjoined to the stomach. Information from the same sources is to the effect that the operation will be performed in strict secrecy, as Mussolini and his lieutenants do not desire that anyone should know of it until a satisfactory recovery could be reported.

When Mussolini passed through a crisis a few months ago with severe hemorrhages, specialists disagreed as to the advisability of an operation, fear being expressed on the one hand that, owing to the weakness of the patient, grave consequences might ensue. It was, therefore, decided to submit the Fascist chief to a rigorous food regimen, so as to bring about, if possible, cicatrization of the ulcer. This however, having been unsuccessful, it has been decided to resort to surgery.

The present moment, as the reports go, is considered opportune, both because Mussolini, under a diet, has become much stronger, and is, therefore, more capable of undergoing an operation, and also for the reason that the country is tranquil. Parliamentary work has been suspended, and there is an absence of political activities.

In some quarters the belief is held that an operation may be performed on the Premier when he is a guest of the King at San Rossore Palace.

Two Killed, One Injured When Airplanes Fall

[BY A. P. NIGHT WIRE]

PHILADELPHIA, July 29.—Logan R. Black, 22 years of age, and Roger Bispham, 19, both of Woodmont, Pa., were killed today in an airplane fall at the Pitcairn flying field, Bryn Athyn. Bispham was a passenger in Black's machine. When it was about 150 feet in the air the plane went into a sideslip and fell.

[BY A. P. NIGHT WIRE]

PITTSBURGH, July 29.—Lieut. Thomas Cagel, U.S.M.C. aviator, was injured seriously today when his plane crashed near Universal, Pa. The wrecked airship caught fire and Cagel was burned. Another occupant of the plane escaped with minor hurts.

Belgian Debt Mission Sails for America

[BY CABLE AND ASSOCIATED PRESS]

BRUSSELS, July 29.—The mission to Washington to discuss settlement of Belgium's debt to the United States left this morning for Cherbourg to sail for New York on the steamer Olympia tomorrow.

Former Premier Theunis and Baron Cartier de Marchienne, Belgian Ambassador to the United States, head the delegation.

BRYAN TRAIN NEAR CAPITAL

Silent Grief, Flowers and Hymns Betoken Love of South for Commoner as Cortege Passes

[BY A. P. NIGHT WIRE]

ON BOARD THE FUNERAL TRAIN EN ROUTE TO WASHINGTON; BRISTOL (Va.-Tenn.) July 29.—Kind hearts tonight kept watch over the body of William Jennings Bryan and tender hands ministered to the comfort of his widow as the train bearing the burdened casket moved out of Tennessee into Virginia on its journey to Washington.

Early on the morrow the funeral party with the body is expected to reach Washington, where his countrymen wait to bestow last honors. In the national Capital, where Mrs. Bryan and her daughter, Mrs. Ruth Owen, were to await the coming of the other daughter, Mrs. Grace Hargreaves and her brother, William Jennings Bryan, Jr., final plans for the funeral and burial in Arlington Cemetery Friday had yet to be completed.

Mrs. Bryan, sitting upright near her husband's casket, was overwhelmed by the crowds of men and women who appeared along many hundreds of miles of the Commoner's last journey to do silent homage to the dead.

Leaving Dayton early in the day after the friends of his last days and spectators of his last great fight had demonstrated their regard in every form of service, the body of the fundamentalist champion was witnessed throughout the day by throngs of sorrowing friends who showed their grief in unmistakable emotion. At Chattanooga and at Knoxville, hundreds were admitted into the rear compartment of the special Pullman to view the set face of the fallen leader.

At Chattanooga, where in transferring the special car from one train to another a halt of an hour was made, city officials, civic organizations and the public joined in a demonstration of esteem for which Mrs. Bryan returned grateful thanks.

In the small towns traversed by the funeral train the inhabitants flocked to the track-side. Stores were closed and flags flew low in token of respect. In many villages observers estimated that the crowds were in excess of the normal populations. At Knoxville, where Mrs. Bryan permitted a waiting crowd to view the body, many evidences of love and devotion were shown to both herself and Mr. Bryan.

The Knoxville Chamber of Commerce presented her with a Bible, attached to which was a ribbon bearing an inscription of one of the Commoner's favorite quotations:

"I have enough religion to live by, and to die by."

From the citizens of Lenoir City, a colorful bouquet of simple garden grown blossoms, told of the deep feelings of the givers, a penned message announcing:

"A token of our appreciation of his upright life and fearless defense of truth."

The Associated Bible Classes of Knoxville presented a large wreath of roses with a resolution expressing sorrow over the death of their Bible leader.

At Jefferson City roadside watchers expressed their tribute in song. A male quartet from Carson-Newman College stood at the door where the Christian leader's body lay and sang one of Mr. Bryan's favorite songs. As the train slowly drew away, the crowd joined in with the singing. From the train a large sign could be seen. It read:

"We honor the memory of William Jennings Bryan."

TENTATIVE PLANS FOR FUNERAL MADE

[BY A. P. NIGHT WIRE]

WASHINGTON, July 29.—Tentative arrangements for the funeral of William Jennings Bryan here

(Continued on Page 4, Column 4)

SECESSION PLOT NIPPED IN MEXICO

Disgruntled Statesman Launches Unsuccessful Plan in Chiapas State

BY JACK STARR-HUNT

[BY CABLE—EXCLUSIVE DISPATCH]

MEXICO CITY, July 29.—A secessionist movement in the southeastern part of the State of Chiapas has been stopped, it was learned today, by opportune action of the Federal government and the patriotism of residents. It was proposed to form an independent republic and ultimately join the Guatemala Union.

It was rumored that certain Chiapas politicians, led by Luis Ramirez Corso, defeated candidate for the governorship, planned the movement. The rumor was not published here at the special request of high government officials, and this afternoon it was announced that the plan had failed. The secessionists named a delegation, it was said, to ask aid and support from the United States and the American Minister at Guatemala City was approached.

Discussion of the matter came up in the "session permanente" of the Congressional committee and Corso is said to have resigned as Deputy from Chiapas as a result. There was a similar rumor on foot six months ago.

CONGRESSIONAL PARTY WELCOMED IN JAPAN

[BY CABLE AND ASSOCIATED PRESS]

TOKIO, July 29.—A party of Congressmen arrived here this morning aboard the United States transport Chaumont, to remain until Saturday as guests of the Japanese government. The Chaumont will depart for the United States on Saturday.

Bryan Casket Placed on Train at Dayton

[Telepix Photo, Copyright, 1925, P. & A. Photos]

Start of the Last Journey

Above is shown the flag-draped casket containing the body of William Jennings Bryan being placed aboard a special car at Dayton, Tenn., to start its journey to Washington. The body of the Commoner was accompanied by a military guard of soldiers, sailors and marines.

PLAZA SITE FOR UNION DEPOT HERE APPROVED

Interstate Commerce Commission Decides in Favor of Joint Terminal for All Railroads

[EXCLUSIVE DISPATCH]

WASHINGTON, July 29.—The Interstate Commerce Commission today made public its decision approving the Plaza site for the projected Los Angeles union railway terminal, thereby crowning with success that city's ten-year fight for an adequate joint station for its transcontinental railways and for the elimination of the death-trap grade crossings on its downtown streets.

The decision is an approval rather than an order and leaves to the California Railroad Commission the actual executive task of bringing it about. However, as the State Railroad Commission has been equally active with the city of Los Angeles in urging the Plaza terminal, there is no doubt as to the attitude and action of that body.

A possible loophole for appeal on the part of the railroads affected—the Santa Fe, Southern Pacific, Union Pacific and Pacific Electric—is seen in the fact that the United States Supreme Court at one time denied the jurisdiction of the California Railroad Commission in the case. However, the same decision put jurisdiction in the hands of the Interstate Commerce Commission for final adjudication. As that body has now declared in favor of the Plaza site it is not regarded as likely that an appeal will be successful.

The decision further denies the application of the Southern Pacific and the Union Pacific for permission jointly to use the Alameda-street trackage, and the Central Station as a permanent terminal (Finance Docket No. 3569.) It likewise advises the abandonment of rail traffic, both freight and passenger, on Alameda street, except for necessary switching. All of the findings are declared to be in the interest of the "public convenience and necessity." Commissioners Hall and Cox dissented.

The findings, which involve a cost to the affected railroads of about $10,000,000, if carried out, are as follows:

"Upon a consideration of all the facts of record we find:

"(1.) That the present and future public convenience and necessity permit the abandonment of operation of all passenger and freight-train service, except industrial freight-switching service, on the main line of the Southern Pacific on Alameda street from College street to East Fifteenth street, inclusive, in the city of Los Angeles, Cal.

"(2.) That neither the present nor future public convenience, and necessity require or will require the construction or extension by applicants of new or existing main lines of railroad in the city of Los Angeles, Cal., as described in the application in Finance Docket No. 3569.

ON PLAZA SITE

"(3.) That the present and future public convenience and necessity require and will require:

"(A.) The extension by defendants of their respective main lines of steam railroad in the city of Los Angeles, Cal., so as to reach and properly serve any union passenger station and terminal within that portion of said city bounded by Commercial street, North Main street, Redondo street, Alhambra avenue, and the Los Angeles River, which they or any of them may construct and establish in accordance with a lawful order of the Railroad Commission of California, and,

"B.) The extension of their respective main lines so as properly to provide for the rearrangement of passenger and freight routes incidental to the convenience and proper operation of such passenger station and terminal.

"(4.) That the extensions referred to in the preceding paragraph are reasonably required in the interest of the public convenience and necessity and that the expense involved therein will not impair the ability of defendants to perform their respective duties to the public.

"(5.) That, in addition to the abandonment of service on Alameda street as above authorized, the present and future public convenience and necessity permit the abandonment by defendants of such portions of their respective main lines of steam railroad in the city of Los Angeles, Cal., or of the operation of all or any portion of present interstate train service thereon as may be incidental to the rearrangement of passenger and freight routes, of tracks, and of terminal facilities, made necessity or proper in connection with the construction and establish-

(Continued on Page 2, Column 7)

RAILROADS IN SILENCE

Will Not Discuss Plaza Ruling

City Attorney Stephens Sees Victory in Long-Fought Terminal War

Next Move Up to the State Railroad Commission, Which Favors Plan

Civic interests yesterday received with general enthusiasm word from Washington of the Interstate Commerce Commission's decision in favor of a union railway station at the Plaza, unification of freight terminal facilities and elimination of many grade crossings by steam and electric rail lines here.

Railroad representatives retired behind the judicial front of withholding comment until after digesting the full text of the decision and declined to discuss the situation on their plans for a possible application for a rehearing.

"It looks like the end of the ten years' battle to me and I think that we have won," was the comment of City Attorney Stephens, who has in recent years directed the fight of the city to have the railroads build a union passenger station in the north end.

SAYS WE'VE WON

"We have fought this thing through every court in the land," stated Mr. Stephens. "We have gone to the United States Supreme Court and back again. It has been a clean fight and we have won. I hope that the railroads will not force us into court again. They must know by this time that we hold the winning hand and I hope and believe that for the good of the city, for the betterment of passenger service, and for the welfare of the Southland the railroads will bow to the wishes of the people and without further court action go to work and build the union passenger depot on the Plaza site.

"Press reports regarding the action of the Interstate Commerce Commission which I have so far seen are meager, and I have not had time to study the findings of that body. However, my offhand opinion is that the way has been cleared for the building of the union depot at the Plaza site.

"The joint application of the Southern Pacific and the Union Pacific railroads to use a passenger terminal outside the Plaza area has been denied by the commission. The commission has also held that the union passenger station on the Plaza site is necessary and reasonable and the commission also makes it plain that the railroads should follow this course but that the order should come from the State Railroad Commission.

"Some time ago the United States Supreme Court held that the State Railroad Commission did not have the authority to order the railroads to construct a union depot on the Plaza site.

"It was while the State Railroad Commission was fighting the case

(Continued on Page 2, Column 2)

STATE RAIL BODY TO ACT

Immediate Steps to Compel Erection of Plaza Union Depot Here Planned by Commission

[EXCLUSIVE DISPATCH]

SAN FRANCISCO, July 29.—The California Railroad Commission will take steps immediately to compel erection of a union station by the railroads running into Los Angeles, it was announced today at the commission's offices following a decision of the Interstate Commerce Commission approving the proposal and giving the State body the power to order execution.

Whether the action will take the form of a reopening of the old case, which was carried to the Supreme Court at Washington, or a new proceeding entirely, has not yet been determined.

The legal status of the case is that the Supreme Court has decided that the State body has the authority to compel erection of a union station provided the Interstate Commerce Commission did not find that such action would impair the funds of the railroad necessary to enable them to function as interstate carriers, explained Attorney Carl Wheat for the State body. With the Interstate Commission at Washington finding in favor of the project, the State commission now will consider its next step.

Commissioner Harley W. Brundige, who is more actively interested in the Los Angeles case than any of the members of the State body, is ill at his home in Oakland. When informed by the Los

(Continued on Page ?, Column 6)

In Three Parts—40 Pages
PART I—TELEGRAPH SHEET—16 PAGES

The Los Angeles Times

"Sail on, sail on, and on and on."

MONDAY MORNING, MAY 10, 1926.

SUNDAY, 10 CENTS. DAILY, 5 CENTS.

Liberty Under Law—Equal Rights—True Industrial Freedom.

BRITISH ARMY ON MOVE TO GUARD VITAL INDUSTRIES

Day Full of Anxiety as Possibility of Unions' 'Second Line' Being Called Out

[BY CABLE AND ASSOCIATED PRESS]

LONDON, May 9.—The British government utilized the greater part of Sunday in developing its preparations to combat the general strike, which has been in progress for nearly a week, and which seems no nearer settlement than the day it began.

Troop movements went along with a vim. Soldiers, all steel helmeted, passed through the city's main thoroughfares at intervals on their way to outlying districts and various vital points where the government deemed their services might be needed. The early morning Sabbath calm was broken as 158 motor trucks heavily loaded with food and convoyed by sixteen armored cars and flanked by cavalry rumbled from Hyde Park.

Sunday was full of anxiety for the authorities because the rest day gave labor's second and third lines of defense an opportunity to discuss the situation with their striking comrades; hope springing from the pulpit and other peaceful sources that some way would be found, before another Sabbath came, to end the struggle which already has brought deprivation and suffering to millions.

CHALLENGE DENIED

For so great an unheaval there has been little disturbance or disorder; even at the mass meetings held today, there was little evidence that so mighty a battle was being fought. J. H. Thomas, once Minister of the crown in the MacDonald Cabinet, and recognized leader of the labor men in the present strike, addressing strikers at Hammersmith, spoke earnestly and dispassionately, reiterating that no challenge to the constitution was involved.

On the other hand, the Earl of Balfour, ever high in the councils of government, in a signed statement in the British Gazette, the official government organ, described the general strike as "an attempted revolution," the success of which would bring ruin, swift, complete and irresistible, upon the country.

One of the questions still undecided by the union leaders is whether to call out what is known as the second line of defense, and, if necessary, the final reserve, the third line of defense. Many of the second-line workers continue to walk out on their own initiative, but without instructions from the Trades Union Congress. This line includes seamen, electricians gas and water workers, as well as unionists employed in various essential or municipal services

ACT INDEPENDENTLY

While a limited number of electricians in London and other cities went out during the week,

(Continued on Page 2, Column 6)

RIOT MARKS FETE DAY TO JOAN OF ARC

Paris Royalists Strive to Usurp Limelight in Doing Honor to Maid of Orleans

[BY CABLE AND ASSOCIATED PRESS]

PARIS, May 9.—Joan of Arc Day national fete was marred in Paris by a conflict between the police and royalist forces in which 118 policemen were injured. Two policemen were taken to a hospital and four others were unable to return to duty. About forty of the Camelets du Roi, a royalist organization, for the most part young students, were injured.

The clash grew out of the refusal of Minister of the Interior Durand to permit formal processions for the purpose of placing wreaths on the two monuments to the Maid of Orleans, one in the Place Sainte Augustin and the other in the Place des Pyramides, abutting the Rue Rivoli. Two hundred and twenty-one arrests were made but thirty-one persons were released after examination of their credentials.

Despite the mobilization of a vast force of police and republican guards, the royalists planted floral tributes at the bases of both statues, forcing their way through the police cordon and battling with canes against night sticks.

CATHOLICS SIDE WITH BRITISH GOVERMENT

[BY CABLE AND ASSOCIATED PRESS]

LONDON, May 9. — At a high mass at Westminster Cathedral today, Cardinal Bourne called upon Catholics to remain on the side of the government in the present strike movement. "It is necessary," he declared, "that Catholics should face clearly the fact that there is no pustification for a general strike All are bound to uphold and assist the government which lawfully constitutes the authority of the country."

BOMB TEARS UP CHURCH

Bay City Edifice Dynamited

Fiend Makes Second Attempt Within Three Months to Demolish Building

Roar of Detonation Results in Near Panic as Scores Quit Bed for Street

[EXCLUSIVE DISPATCH]

SAN FRANCISCO, May 9.—With a roar that aroused the neighborhood for blocks around and sent scores of startled residents flying to the street in their night attire, a dynamite bomb early this morning exploded at St. Peter and St. Paul's Church, in Filbert street, in what was the second attempt within less than three months to wreck the edifice.

Sleeping in the parish house at the time of the explosion, not more than fifty feet away, were Father Oreste Trinchieri, pastor of the church, Father Rafael Piperni and several others. They were uninjured.

PLANTED AT ENTRANCE

The bomb was planted at the front entrance to the building and exploded shortly after 3 a.m. It tore a hole in the concrete more than a foot deep, shattered marble walls and windows in the vestibule, splintered wooden wainscoating and loosened a heavy door.

The instrument, comprising from three to five sticks of dynamite bound together with wire, was identical in construction to the bomb planted at the church on the morning of January 31, last.

Detectives who were summoned immediately are sure that both explosions were set by the same person. But whether it is the vandalism of a religious fanatic or of some enemy of the church who is using too light a charge of explosive in a serious aim to wreck the building is undetermined.

Undaunted by the incident, Father Trinchieri conducted his Sunday masses as usual. Many churchgoers, who did not know of the explosion until they reached the place, feared to attend mass and departed upon seeing remnants of the wreckage.

Father Trinchieri referred to the explosion in his sermons and expressed his agitation in no small way. He characterized the incident as "an insult to the people of his congregation."

IDENTITY SURMISED

Ever since the previous explosion, Captain of Detectives Matheson has been working upon a definite suspicion as to the identity of the bomber.

"We have a conclusive idea of the guilty person's identity," he said, "but we have been unable to determine h's whereabouts"

The bomb of last January was lodged in an alley at the rear of the church, and, like today's, was exploded early on Sunday morning. The previous explosion did little damage to the church aside from blowing a small hole in the concrete and shattering windows of not only the church but neighboring apartment-houses.

Flyer Justifies Faith of Ford and Rockefeller

[P. & A. Photos]

First to Wing His Way Over North Pole

In honor of Edsel Ford, who, with John D. Rockefeller, Jr., made his Arctic flight possible, Lieutenant-Commander Richard E. Byrd named his plane the Josephine Ford, for Edsel's daughter. In the center he is shown tinkering with the motor of the giant triple-engined craft. The insert at the upper left is Lieutenant-Commander Byrd, while below is the Arctic pilot shaking hands with Mr. Rockefeller when he left New York. They are on board Vincent Astor's yacht.

BYRD FLIES OVER NORTH POLE AND BACK TO BASE

Flyer Makes Accurate Observations While Circling Arctic Goal; Trip Takes Fifteen Hours

BY LIEUTENANT-COMMANDER RICHARD E. BYRD
[BY WIRELESS—EXCLUSIVE DISPATCH]
[Copyright, 1926, by the New York Times]

KINGS BAY (Spitzbergen) May 9.—America's claim to the North Pole was made certain tonight when, after a flight of fifteen hours and fifty-one minutes Floyd Bennett, my pilot, and I returned safely from a flight to the North Pole. We circled it several times and verified Admiral Peary's observations completely.

We were favored by continued sunlight, and there was never the slightest fog, enabling me to use my sun compass and bubble sextant and obtain the most accurate observations possible.

There were three magnetic compasses in the plane, but all of them deviated eccentrically after reaching high latitudes. Bennett declared that when he was piloting the magnetic compasses were wholly useless and would swing almost a quarter turn, returning very slowly.

BOTH AT CONTROLS

Without the sunlight, navigation would have been almost impossible. Bennett and myself alternated in the piloting, Bennett refilling the gasoline containers while I piloted and navigated.

I found that the Bumstrad sun compass worked perfectly, even when held in the hand, so when I was in the pilot's seat I held the joystick in one hand while getting direction from the sun compass held in the other.

When we were within sixty miles of the pole the oil system of the right-hand motor began leaking baldly and it seemed necessary to choose between proceeding with two motors or attempting a landing to make repairs.

In the neighborhood of the pole numerous stretches of smooth ice were visible and a landing was favored by Bennett but, remembering difficulties in starting at Kings Bay, I veoted this proposal.

MOTOR HOLDS UP

Both of us agreed, however, to continue the flight to the pole even if we went on with only two motors. To our surprise the right hand motor continued to work effectively, despite the ruptured tank, and when the Fokker returned to Kings Bay all three motors. To our surprise the right-

The Josephine Ford, after making three circles over Kings Bay, landed at the take-off runway and taxied to her original starting position.

We hurried a mile and a half to the shore where a motorboat rushed us to the Chantier. The crew aboard her went wild with joy, waving flags and their caps. Many of the crew completely broke down with emotion and with tears streaming from their eyes embraced us.

FEAT CULMINATION OF BOYHOOD DREAM

[BY A. P. NIGHT WIRE]

NEW YORK, May 9.—When Commander Byrd set sail from New York, April 6, the occasion marked the realization of a dream which had been with him since boyhood days—an expedition of his own into the Arctic regions.

With him was Floyd Bennett, chief petty officer in the naval air service, who flew over 3000 miles with the commander last year when the two accompanied the MacMillan party in the North. He became Byrd's "right-hand" man and the two of them planned to share the most dangerous and important work of the expedition.

"Bennett is a man of the greatest energy, endurance and skill, both as a navigator and as a mechanic," Byrd wrote of him. "I would not like to be in the Arctic without him and I would take him before any other man in the world."

In outlining his plans, the commander said that after reaching Kings Bay, the airplane would be ready for the flights while William C. Haines, the United States Weather Bureau official, studied and reported on weather conditions.

Here the skill of Lieut. G. O.

(Continued on Page 3, Column 5)

RADIO MUTE ON WILKINS

Trio Believed at Point Barrow

Remainder of Party Confident Wireless Silence Due to Air Conditions

Plane Carries Gasoline for Ten Hours and Food for Three Weeks

[EXCLUSIVE DISPATCH]
[Copyright, 1926, by North American Newspaper Alliance]

FAIRBANKS (Alaska) May 9.—Safely over the Endicott Mountains and a clear sky ahead was the last message radioed from the Detroit Arctic expedition's monoplane Detroiter at 11 a.m. Saturday. Those of the expedition who remain at Fairbanks are reasonably confident Capt. George H. Wilkins, Maj. Thomas G. Lanphier and Lieu. Charles W. Wiseley safely arrived at Point Barrow within five and one-half hours of the time they hopped off here and that the silence of the radio is due to atmospheric conditions. Messages were coming in clearly from the States, but there were blind spaces in the northern air last night.

Both Robert Waskey, the expedition's radioman at Barrow, and Capt. Wilkins had sending sets. Howard Mason, the radioman here, listened at Esther Creek, thirteen miles from here, while Signal Corps men of the military telegraph station here listened on three Fairbanks sets. Down at Nenana, forty miles away, another operator was listening in but not a signal was heard.

TRAVELS LIGHT

The Detroiter will have aboard about 500 gallons of gasoline when it hops off toward the pole of relative inaccessibility. This will be sufficient for more than ten hours of flight. The big three-engined Fokker will travel light, not an ounce of surplus baggage being aboard during the push out over the unknown Arctic Sea. Capt. Wilkins will be in the navigator's seat beside Wiseley, the pilot. Maj. Lanphier, who will fly as observer, is carrying a camera. Stowed under the cockpit and in the baggage compartment in the rear of the cabin will be the scant equipment of the three explorers.

There will be sleeping bags, fur clothing, mukluks, a collapsible boat to be used in crossing open leads in case of a forced landing; and Mannlicher rifles which shoot a hollow-nosed copper bullet that will kill a polar bear.

The collapsible boat weighs less than ten pounds, and is constructed of rubberized fabric and is inflalted by means of a small bellows.

RATIONS TAKEN ALONG

There are enough rations on the Detroiter to sustain three men for three weeks. This food consists of pemmican which is strips of venison or other meat dried in the sun, mixed with fat or fruits and compressed into cakes. It is highly prized by explorers, because of the small space it occupies. If

(Continued on Page 2, Column 7)

ANGELENO UNDER KNIFE ON LIMITED

S. W. Mudd Operated on as Train Speeds Across Western Kansas

[BY A. P. NIGHT WIRE]

KANSAS CITY (Mo.) May 9.—As his special car, attached to the Golden Gate Express, sped across Western Kansas toward Kansas City this morning, Seeley W. Mudd, mining engineer of Los Angeles, was operated on for abdominal trouble.

The operation was decided upon when examination by physicians indicated he otherwise might not live until the train reached St. Louis, where he was to be taken to a hospital. His brother, Dr. Harvey G. Mudd, is chief surgeon of the hospital.

Dr. Rae Smith of Los Angeles performed the operation with the aid of Dr. Donald Frish, also of Los Angeles, two other assistants and four nurses.

The physicians decided to perform the operation with the train in motion so that they would lose no time in getting to St. Louis so Mr. Mudd could receive hospital treatment. The engineer was requested to slow down slightly and to take every precaution to prevent a jarring of the coach on the curves.

The special car arrived in Kansas City late today and was held here until 10 o'clock. Bulletins said the patient was resting easily and that the operation had been successful, although Mr. Mudd's condition was still grave.

At 10 o'clock the car was attached to a train due in St. Louis early tomorrow morning. Mr. Mudd will be taken to the hospital as soon as the train arrives, it was said.

LOWER DECK PASSENGERS DIE IN CRASH

Undetermined Number Go Down With Ship in Dnieper River Collision

[BY CABLE AND ASSOCIATED PRESS]

MOSCOW, May 9.—An undetermined number of passengers in the lower cabins of the steamer Bielormss went down with the vessel today after it collided with a barge soon after leaving Gomel. The steamer plied between Gomel and Kiev on the River Dnieper.

A rescue squad saved all of the passengers who were on the deck.

BATHER STUNNED BY DIVE, DROWN

[BY A. P. NIGHT WIRE]

SANTA ROSA, May 9.—Ralph Foresti, 21 years of age, business man of this city, drowned today in the municipal tank. A doctor's examination disclosed he had been stunned from a dive, striking his head on the bottom and suffocating.

THE DAY'S NEWS SUMMED UP

THE SKY: Clear. Wind at 5 p.m., Southwest; velocity, 9 miles. Thermometer, highest, 68 deg.; lowest, 50 deg. Forecast for Los Angeles and vicinity: Fair. For complete weather data, see last page of this section.

FEATURES. Radio, Page 5, Part II; Women's pages, Clubs and Society, Page 8, Part II; Markets and Financial, Pages 13, 14 and 15, Part I; News of Southern Counties, Page 10, Part I; Pictures, Page 8, Part I; Comics, Page 4, Part III.

SERIAL. Page 3, Part III.

NEWS IN SPANISH. Page 16, Part I.

SHIPPING NEWS. Page 15, Part I.

THE CITY. Rockliffe Fellows's face disfigured in mysterious auto crash. Page 1, Part II.

Four die and several injured in week-end traffic. Page 3, Part II.

Agitators for carpenters' strike consider revising demands to include wage increase. Page 9, Part II.

As straw hat day nears dealers launch plan to use native raw material in making our own. Page 1, Part II.

Katherine Grant, beauty prize winner, who has long been ill, will seek health in country. Page 10, Part II.

Mrs. Pettingell expected to testify at autopsy that local stock exchange president died of heart seizure. Page 1, Part II.

Last group oratory final to be held at San Diego today. Page 1, Part II.

Tanker Java Arrow, decorated in Japan for heroic rescue of Japanese seamen, pays brief call here. Page 2, Part II.

Week-end raids by police and Sheriff's officers numerous; seventy-six persons held on liquor and vice charges. Page 7, Part II.

SPORTS. U. S. C. athletes prepare for Coast Conference meet. Page 1, Part III.

Hollywood Stars defeat Oaks in double-header baseball game. Page 1, Part III.

Angels win double-header from Portland. Page 1, Part III.

Driver escapes death in Ascot auto race. Page 1, Part III.

PACIFIC SLOPE. Radio silent on outcome of Capt. Wilkins's flight into Far Arctic. Page 1, Part I.

San Francisco church dynamited for second time within three months. Page 1, Part I.

GENERAL EASTERN. Byrd flies over North Pole and back to Spitzbergen. Page 1, Part I.

Walter S. Ward, New Yorker, twice freed in Sailor Peters's slaying case, mysteriously disappears. Page 1, Part I.

Throng cheers as motorship maneuvers in New York Harbor. Page 4, Part I.

FOREIGN. London's streets filled with British troops on move to guard vital industries. Page 1, Part I.

Premier Baldwin repeats peace negotiations futile until general strike is called off. Page 2, Part I.

French and Spanish gain successes as Riffian war begins again. Page 6, Part I.

REMEMBER THIS by H. M. STANSIFER

You rob yourself when you bribe your own conscience.

CALIFORNIA POWER LINE KILLS RADIO

Federal Supervisor Finds Muting of Signals Due to High-Tension Leakage

[EXCLUSIVE DISPATCH]

WASHINGTON, May 9.—An electric line carrying 60,000 volts has been found to be the major cause of complaints received in the office of one of the Commerce Department's radio supervisors in California. In his report of a trip which took him through twenty-two towns and cities in one section of California he states that faulty or dirty insulators, power line substations and other equipment were causing the complete blanketing of reception of even the more powerful near-by stations during the tests made ta the time of his trip.

Road dust and other dirt settling on insulators is at low ebb during the winter months when seasonal rains wash the insulators. Even more serious power-line interference is to be expected in the summer months when dirt accumulates on the insulators and allows the current to "slop over," or leak.

With the completion of several new substations which are now in process of construction much of the trouble from this source will be eliminated, the supervisor believes.

MEXICO MAY REVISE RULE ON CLERICS

Constitutional Authority Sought for Ministers to Serve Own Nationals

[BY CABLE—EXCLUSIVE DISPATCH]

MEXICO CITY, May 9.—Foreign Minister Saenz announced today that officials of both the Foreign Office and the Ministry of the Interior are carefully studying the religious articles in the Constitution to ascertain whether foreign ministers of the Gospel of any creed may be allowed to remain here to exercise their ministerial office for their nationals only.

Saenz's statement followed the arrest of Rev. H. Dobson Peacock, British dean of the American Episcopal Cathedral here and an order for his deportation. Dean Peacock, who was given a six-day reprieve pending investigation, was allowed to return to his home from the British Legation yesterday.

Saenz said the constitutional study is a result of a request for a ruling by both the British and French governments. Foreign residents see the possibility of being left without opportunity for religious worship.

Coolidges Are Senators' Hosts on River Trip

[BY A. P. NIGHT WIRE]

WASHINGTON, May 9.—President and Mrs. Coolidge sailed on the yacht Mayflower today for an overnight cruise down the Potomac River, after attending morning services at the First Congregational Church.

Guests on the Mayflower were Senator Ransdell, Democrat, Louisiana; Representative and Mrs. Scott Leavitt, Montana; Representative and Mrs. Royal Johnson, South Dakota; Representative Will R. Wood, Indiana; Representative and Mrs. Cleveland A. Newton, Missouri, and Secretary and Mrs. Everett Sanders, all Republicans.

WARD MYSTERIOUSLY GONE

Rich Baker's Son, Twice Freed in Peters Slaying Case, Feared Victim of Violence

[BY A. P. NIGHT WIRE]

NEW YORK, May 9.—The disappearance since May 5 of Walter S. Ward, wealthy baker's son, acquitted three years ago on a plea of self-defense of a charge of first-degree murder for killing Clarence M. Peters, was reported to the police today by his brother, Ralph D. Ward.

The missing man is a son of George S. Ward, former head of the Ward Baking Company.

Ralph Ward said his brother had not been heard from since he left New York for Baltimore on a business trip. He said the family feared foul play.

Walter Ward's automobile was found abandoned in Trenton, N. Y., last Thursday night by Trenton police. The windshield was broken and a large rock was found in the front seat. Ralph Ward declared last night, however, that the car had been stolen and that reports of his brother's disappearance were "bunk." At Walter Ward's apartment a maid said he had stepped out "a few hours before."

When Trenton police found Ward's car, the floor and rear seat were strewn with clothing and papers. A search of all the Trenton hospitals and hotels was made, but the young man could not be found. At the request of the Trenton police, Thomas A. Downey, secretary of the Electruck Corporation of New York, of which the missing man was president, went to Trenton to aid in the search.

Ward's acquittal in 1923 followed a long legal battle in which he was twice indicted on a first-degree murder charge for the killing of Peters, whose body was found on a lonely road near the Kensico reservoirs in Westchester county, New York, on May 20, 1922.

Ward surrendered to the authorities two days after the body had been identified as Peters of Haverhill, Mass., a former sailor. Ward said he had killed the man in self-defense when he was threatened with death if he did not pay $75,000 to a blackmail gang to which, he said, Peters belonged.

He was freed January 22, 1923, by Supreme Court Justice Seeger, but upon order of Gov. Smith, an extraordinary grand jury convened. A second indictment for first-degree murder was returned on July 26, 1923, but Ward was acquitted September 28, 1923, on his thirty-second birthday.

WILD CHEERS GREET BYRD

Amundsen Among First to Embrace Flyer on Return from Pole Hours Ahead of Schedule

[BY CABLE—EXCLUSIVE DISPATCH]

KINGS BAY (Spitzbergen) May 9.—Lieutenant-Commander Richard E. Byrd, U.S.N., and his companion, Chief Petty Officer Lloyd Bennett, today flew to the North Pole and returned to their base here. They had not been expected to return from the airplane dash to the pole before 8 o'clock tonight. At 5:25 p.m. a tiny speck was seen in the distance by the eager watchers here.

As the speck grew larger and larger the American ship Chantier and the Norwegian ship Heimdal ran their flags up to the top masts and started their sirens to screeching, for it was realized that the flyers were returning. It was hard for the crowds to believe, but it was true.

The giant Fokker airplane circled the flying field at a distance of nearly 2000 yards, landing lightly on the spot from where it had started this morning, shortly after midnight.

The throng rushed toward the flyers before their propellers had stopped and lifted Commander Byrd from his machine amid wild cheering. Capt. Roald Amundsen and his partner in the projected dirigible flight over the pole, Lincoln Ellsworth, were among the first to welcome Commander Byrd and his companion.

Capt. Amundsen embraced the pair and called for three cheers. Questions were hurled at the flyers, the first men to reach the North Pole by airplane.

"Did you reach the pole? Did you find land?" were the queries.

But the flyers only smiled, too tired to reply. They were borne on the shoulders of the crowd to the ship Chantier, which brought them and their planes to Spitzbergen.

On the Chantier the crew went wild with joy and the band on the Heimdal struck up "The Star Spangled Banner."

Commander Byrd told this correspondent: "We flew three times in a circle over the pole, then dropped the American flag, with an account of our flight, in a box."

Commander Byrd also told Lieut. Risser Larsen of the Norge's crew that he was sure he had reached the pole, and it is generally agreed here that he did.

Asked if he had found new land, Commander Byrd said he had found none, affirming Capt.

(Continued on Page 3, Column 6)

In Three Parts—44 Pages
PART I—TELEGRAPH SHEET—18 PAGES

The Los Angeles Times

"Rail on, sail on, and on and on."
GREATER SOUTHERN CALIFORNIA
WEDNESDAY MORNING, MAY 19, 1926. SUNDAY, 10 CENTS. DAILY, 5 CENTS.
Liberty Under Law—Equal Rights—True Industrial Freedom.

WET LEADS FOR SENATE IN PENNSYLVANIA RACE

Strongholds of Senator Pepper and Gov. Pinchot Yet to Report as Vare Forges Ahead

[BY A. P. NIGHT WIRE]

PHILADELPHIA, May 19 (Wednesday)—Returns from 5075 districts gave Vare a lead of 73,164 over Pepper. The vote was: Vare, 411,093; Pepper, 337,929; Pinchot, 211,434. Vare's lead decreased as returns came from outside Philadelphia.

PHILADELPHIA, May 18.—Representative William S. Vare, running on a platform of prohibition-law modification, led his opponents for the Republican nomination for United States Senator from Pennsylvania in returns tonight from 3752 districts out of 8281 in the State in today's primary election. Senator George Wharton Pepper, candidate for the forces led by Secretary of the Treasury Mellon, and classed as a dry, was running second, with Gov. Pinchot, independent dry, third. Representative Vare's plurality over Senator Pepper was 73,952.

This vote included more than half of Philadelphia, the Vare stronghold which was conceded by the other candidates to give the Representative a substantial plurality. Senator Pepper based his hopes on Allegheny county and Western Pennsylvania, while the Governor looked for his greatest strength in the rural counties and the mining regions.

The figures were: Vare, 311,392; Pepper, 237,440; Pinchot, 146,219.

Returns from 3452 districts for Republican Governor gave: Beidleman, 314,158; Fisher, 258,713; Phillips, 26,248; Tener, 16,352.

In the Democratic gubernatorial contest returns from 1652 districts gave Bonnewell 17,189; Shull, 13,887; Porter, 10,557.

DESPERATE BATTLE

Today's State-wide primary election followed the most desperate campaign since the days of Cameron, Quay and Penrose.

Today's battle centered in Republican fights for the Senatorial and gubernatorial nominations. Two issues, attracting national attention, prohibition and party control, predominated in the contests.

The three candidates, Gov. Pinchot, Representative Vare and Senator Pepper each pledged support of President Coolidge and his administration.

While the President remained silent on his attitude toward each, Secretary of the Treasury Mellon entered the contest as a supporter of Senator Pepper, speaking, with James J. Davis, Secretary of Labor, at a political meeting in Pittsburgh.

The prohibition issue was stressed by Representative Vare and Gov. Pinchot, the former as an advocate of modification of the Volstead Act and the latter as a supporter of even stricter enforcement laws. Senator Pepper, while classed as a dry, declared it was not the paramount issue of the campaign, and asked support on the basis of his record in the Senate.

William S. Vare

Senator Pepper declared Repre-

(Continued on Page 2, Column 6)

THE DAY'S NEWS SUMMED UP

THE SKY. Clear, wind at 5 p.m., southwest; velocity, ten miles. Thermometer, highest, 75 deg.; lowest, 58 deg. Forecast for Los Angeles and vicinity: Fair. For complete weather data, see last page of this section.

THE CITY. Aimee Semple McPherson, Angelus Temple evangelist, believed drowned while swimming at Venice. Page 1, Part I.

Ninety-seven traffic violators receive jail sentences in Municipal Judge Chambers's court. Page 1, Part II.

Engineer counters railroad's arguments of excessive expense to build union depot on Plaza site. Page 1, Part II.

Spanish Consul Orfile, unwitting sponsor of Miss Ortero as a princess, resigns post. Page 1, Part II.

More than 400 prizes will be awarded in this week's Times ad-writing contest. Page 1, Part II.

N. H. Archdeacon is appointed deputy collector of internal revenue. Page 2, Part II.

Lawrence Hughes, ice cream maker, finds he is not father of "twins" born year ago. Page 2, Part II.

Mr. and Mrs. Thomas J. Lockhart celebrate sixty-second wedding anniversary today. Page 22, Part II.

Plumbers' convention favors State-wide sanitation code. Page 13, Part II.

Four hundred policemen may lose jobs if department budget is reduced further. Page 1, Part II.

School children observe Good-Will Day with costume pageants. Page 22, Part II.

Police request for two armored automobiles to combat desperadoes forwarded to City Council. Page 3, Part II.

SPORTS. Lee is hero of day as Hollywood Stars nose out Missions. Page 1, Part III.

Hoff's charges denied by A.A.U. Page 1, Part III.

Angels lucky to beat Seals in north. Page 1, Part III.

Fifteen Trojans nominated to go east for competition in I.C.A.A.A.A. meet. Page 1, Part III.

PACIFIC SLOPE. Strike disorders break out in Oakland, where nonunion carpenters are slugged. Page 1, Part I.

San Francisco police, firemen and citizens join in search for lost babe. Page 3, Part I.

GENERAL EASTERN. Wet candidate leads in Pennsylvania Senatorial race. Page 1, Part I.

Flyer loses life in storm which causes heavy damage in Chicago suburbs. Page 1, Part I.

Secretary Hoover in Health Congress address demands that standards of normal child be formulated. Page 6, Part I.

Gen. Pershing will present silver cup to winner of oratorical contest at Washington finals. Page 7, Part I.

Great growth of electric light and power business stressed at national convention. Page 5, Part I.

Hundreds of settlers in Minnesota join fight on forest fires to save homes. Page 5, Part I.

Many social functions planned for Crown Prince of Sweden and consort on arrival in New York next week. Page 5, Part I.

Illinois prison-system executives star witnesses in grand jury investigations in two counties. Page 4, Part I.

Gov. Smith backs liquor referendum in New York State. Page 9, Part I.

WASHINGTON: White House indicates understanding is that Senate will await French action on debt pact before passing on it. Page 3, Part I.

Completion of Hougen farm relief bill near. Page 4, Part I.

Catholic Welfare conference sees danger to America in Mexican church stand. Page 8, Part I.

FOREIGN: Commission preparing for disarmament session has its first meeting. Page 1, Part I.

New plunge of franc value menaces Briand Cabinet. Page 3, Part I.

Marshall Pilsudski fast is losing hold on Poland. Page 3, Part I.

Three English spies sentenced to prison by French court. Page 3, Part I.

Capt. Karl Boy-Ed, war-time German attache at Washington, denied passport visa for return to America. Page 3, Part I.

Fascism's system for solution of class war and labor disputes approved by Cabinet. Page 8, Part I.

REMEMBER THIS
BY H. M. STANSIFER

The difference between failure and success is often the difference between invest and investigate.

FLYER DIES IN STORM

Ford Plane Pilot Killed in Crash

Heavy Damage Caused by Rain, Hail and Wind in Northern Illinois Towns

Westbound Airmail Sent from Chicago by Train; Many Homes Wrecked

[BY A. P. NIGHT WIRE]

CHICAGO, May 18.—Ross Kirkpatrick, 30-year-old aviator of the freighter "Maiden Dearborn" of the Ford Motor Company air service, was killed at Summit, on the southern city limits, during a storm this evening which caused a forced landing. His plane, on landing, struck soft ground, causing it to nose into the earth. Damage estimated from $100,000 to $200,000 was caused by the storm, which extended east from Summit to Harvey, where more than 300 homes were wrecked.

The plane was due here to meet the transcontinental flyer at Maywood field for the transfer of mail bound west from Chicago.

MAIL GOES BY TRAIN

The regular mail plane did not leave the air-mail field for the west tonight because of the storm conditions, the mail going by train to Iowa City, where it was planned to send it by plane if the weather permitted.

Kirkpatrick was one of the best pilots who participated in the 1920 flight from Mitchell Field, Long Island, to Nome, Alaska. He was commander and pilot of plane No. 4 in the flight. His home was at Dearborn, Mich.

The Ford plane, the first of the all-metal planes put in service by the company, carried a cargo of mail from Detroit.

Kirkpatrick was crushed when the fuselage telescoped against the motor while he was strapped in his seat.

AUTOS ROLLED IN DITCH

In Harvey a heavy hailstorm accompanied the wind, which, besides blowing over houses, knocked down trees and telephone poles and rolled several automobiles into the ditch. No other near-by towns were seriously damaged and the storm in Harvey lasted but fifteen minutes.

In the central section of the State, near Danville, wind did considerable damage, uprooting trees and small buildings being blown down in many places.

Severe hail, wind and rainstorms were reported from near-by towns. Hailstones of large size tore fruit and growing orchards into shreds.

PLANE CARRYING FORD PARTS FOR CHICAGO DEALERS

[EXCLUSIVE DISPATCH]

CHICAGO, May 18.—Ross Kirkpatrick, pilot of the Ford plane, Maiden Dearborn, who was killed when his plane was caught in a storm this afternoon, was carrying interorganization mail and a quantity of automobile parts for Chicago dealers. He had just brought his machine into the suburbs of Chicago when a miniature tornado broke, spinning the plane around like a kite and smashing it to the ground so forcibly that the motor dug a large hole in the ground.

Apparently Kirkpatrick made a herculean effort to bring his plane down to a perfect landing, but one of the wings hit the ground first and shivered it.

No one witnessed the accident. His body was found, still strapped in the driver's seat, about an hour after the accident. Two young men passing the spot after the rainstorm saw the wreckage in the field and notified officials of the Checkerboard flying field.

Physicians were rushed to the spot, but Kirkpatrick was dead when they got there. His head and body were badly crushed. The body is at an underaking establishment in Argo, Ill., where an inquest will be conducted tomorrow.

ONE KILLED BY STORM IN INDIANA

[BY A. P. NIGHT WIRE]

INDIANAPOLIS, May 18.—One man was killed and small buildings suffered heavily in a hailstorm of almost cyclonic proportions which swept Northwestern and Central Indiana tonight. William Arnold, a farmer, was struck by lightning at Fort Wayne.

Many thousands of dollars' damage was done near Lafayette, Ind., where telephone poles were uprooted and garages and barns wrecked. The storm in that area hit with particular violence at the Purdue University Experimental Farm, where sheds, chicken houses and other buildings were blown down.

Sizable hailstones pelted downtown Indianapolis, where damage apparently was confined to broken windows.

KIRKPATRICK LEFT HERE FOR EAST EIGHT MONTHS AGO

Ross Kirkpatrick left Los Angeles eight months ago to accept a position in the engineering department of the Ford Motor Company at Detroit. He was well known in army and navy aviation circles, having served in both branches of the service during and after the World War as a lieutenant. He was at one time in charge of Mitchel Field, N. Y., and led the Army Air Service's planes in their first flight to Alaska, and he participated in the first transcontinental flight.

Shortly after the beginning of the war he enlisted and was assigned to an aviation school in the northern part of the State where he received his training. At va-

(Continued on Page 3, Column 6)

Pardon Us if We're Not Wildly Enthusiastic

GALE

FEAR OF HIDDEN STRENGTH STALKS AT ARMS SESSION

Potential Power of Nations May Form Chief Stumbling Block; American Stand Pleases

[BY CABLE AND ASSOCIATED PRESS]

GENEVA, May 18.—Nations will fear to disarm themselves because other nations, actually weaker but potentially stronger, in the long run can conquer them—that is the supreme stumbling block to disarmament which loomed today at the opening session of the preparatory commission.

France mentioned it: Belgium, overwhelmed in the great war, emphasized its anxiety, and Premier Mussolini's spokesman even declared: "If you do not take account of every kind of potential military strength in a country, then you show a desire to weaken a weak state and strengthen a strong one."

From the United States came a message which evoked considerable favorable comment, as manifesting sincere determination to cooperate in the huge problem of disarmament, and as showing sympathetic knowledge of the questions facing other nations, which make the limitation of armaments difficult, though not impossible.

ZEAL URGED

In the first place, as if meeting in advance any lukewarmness on the part of the others or any disposition to temporize with or postpone definite action, Hugh S. Gibson, chairman of the American delegation, urged all to devote their "earnest and continuous attention" to the work undertaken.

He expressed the opinion that constructive achievement in the limitation of land armaments lies in the conclusion of regional agreements, rather than in an effort to work out a plan applicable to the whole world.

This seemed to be interpreted tonight as meaning that the United States does not wish to intervene, except helpfully, in any European arrangement for land armament reduction. Special attention was paid to Mr. Gibson's words that America would welcome steps tending to a further limitation of competitive naval construction, as a supplement to the Washington conference. Some Europeans see in these words an American desire to obtain a reduction in submarines, which question was not treated at Washington.

SPECIFIC TASKS

Mr. Gibson's statement that it is important to consider not only general abstract principles, but also make an endeavor to isolate as many concrete questions as possible and deal with them directly and practically, was deemed to put the American position close to that enunciated by Viscount Cecil, Great Britain, who pleaded several times for concentration on limitable armaments.

The task, Mr. Gibson said, is beset with obstacles and difficulties, but he is convinced that progress can be made if they approach the task with readiness to understand each other's problems and patience to seek solutions.

"We have no right to disappoint our peoples," he exclaimed. "They have suffered too much, and their lives are crowded with fears of future wars."

Viscount Cecil frankly declared that England's responsibilities to her overseas possessions or mandated territories are the measure of

(Continued on Page 8, Column 4)

SECRETARY OF MINERS RAPS STRIKE

International Federation Officer Calls General Walkout Sheer Folly

[BY CABLE AND ASSOCIATED PRESS]

LONDON, May 18.—Severe criticism of the general strike was voiced today by Frank Hodges, secretary of the International Miners' Federation since 1925. In a press interview he characterized the strike as "a disaster motivated by blind passion to try out a machine which, though perfect on paper, took no account of simple human nature and economic forces."

He declared that the gigantic effort of the Trades Union Congress was a mere toy in the presence of the economic facts and social forces by which it was confronted.

[BY CABLE AND ASSOCIATED PRESS]

MOSCOW, May 18.—The soviet agency announces that A. J. Cook, secretary of the British Miners' Federation has accepted "with deepest thanks," the money given by the soviet miners to aid the strikers in the British Isles. The news agency adds that Mr. Cook has requested that the money be transferred immediately to England, "as the miners' need is very great."

Previous dispatches from Russia announced that the sum collected for the British miners in soviet Russia amounted to about $1,000,000. The money was offered to the British Trades Union Congress during the recent general strike, but was said to have been declined.

BAY CITIES' STRIKERS RIOT

Disorders Break Out in Oakland Carpenter Warfare; More Nonunion Workers Slugged

[EXCLUSIVE DISPATCH]

SAN FRANCISCO, May 18.—Simultaneously with new acts of violence in San Francisco, mob riots broke out in Oakland today for the first time during the strike of union carpenters, called in the bay area on April 1. In San Francisco four nonunion carpenters were beaten, one was kidnaped and two strike sympathizers were arrested.

In Oakland three nonunion men were slugged, one of them being seriously injured.

Following the two disturbances in Oakland Chief of Police Drew set about to maintain law and order by appointing Capt. J. Frank Lynch to head a flying squad of ten automobiles, each carrying two armed policemen, to constantly patrol vicinities in which buildings are under construction and to put down disorder with "all force necessary."

Riots in San Francisco began at noon when twenty or thirty automobile loads of strike sympathizers passed in procession in front of jobs at Twenty-second and Dolores streets, Pacific avenue and Laguna street, and Twenty-third and Mission streets, yelling oaths against nonunion carpenters employed at these places.

The automobiles did not stop and posses of police arrived in each instance to find groups of frightened nonunion workers, but no trace of the mobs.

KIDNAP WORKER

The first outbreak of violence was at Sixteenth and Capp streets, within a stone's throw of the union labor temple, where, after exchanging blows with nonunion carpenters on the job, a gang of twenty strike sympathizers in automobiles kidnaped Erickson, one of the men later injured, and took him to union headquarters.

The second instance of violence in this city occurred shortly after 5 o'clock at Twenty-second and Mission streets, where a mob of fifty men assembled and began jeering nonunion carpenters. Patrolman William Rusch, passing on his beat, was able to disperse the gathering before the arrival of a posse from the Mission-street station. He arrested John Lavin, strike sympathizer, after a struggle, and charged him with rioting.

During the day R. H. Stevenson, manager of the Crocker estate, which is constructing buildings at Geneva avenue and Toyan street, in the Crocker-Amazon district, appeared at police headquarters with three nonunion carpenters,

(Continued on Page 3, Column 5)

MILLIONS IN FUND GIVEN TO CHARITY

Kresge Foundation of $25,000,000 to be Used for Philanthropy

[BY A. P. NIGHT WIRE]

NEW YORK, May 18.—Establishment of a $25,000,000 fund for philanthropic and educational purposes by Sebastian S. Kresge, chain-store owner, was announced today on behalf of the Kresge Foundation, which will administer the endowment.

A gift of 500,000 common shares of the S. S. Kresge Company, valued at current market prices in excess of $22,000,000, has been made by Mr. Kresge to the foundation.

Under trust provisions, the shares will be held intact, but will be utilized as collateral for occasional bond issues. The first of these will be for $10,000,000, the proceeds to be devoted mainly to the purchase of real estate.

Through his banking representatives, Mr. Kresge indicated that he will make additional gifts to maintain a perpetual fund for charity. The Kresge Foundation was formed two years ago with a fund of $2,000,000 set aside by Mr. Kresge.

THREE-CENT CHECK

[EXCLUSIVE DISPATCH]

SAN ANTONIO (Tex.) May 18. A check for $0.03 was received by W. G. Hatcher, State Treasurer, in payment of gross receipts tax for the quarter ending March 31, the check being dated New York and signed by the Fleischmann Transportation Company. So far as known, this is the smallest check ever received by the department, Hatcher said.

AIMEE SEMPLE M'PHERSON BELIEVED BATHING VICTIM

Angelus Temple Pastor Last Seen Swimming Off Beach at Venice; Crowds Vainly Seek Body

Aimee Semple McPherson, pastor of Angelus Temple and widely-known evangelist, was reported drowned while swimming at Venice yesterday afternoon.

Up to a late hour last night the body had not been recovered. Police, life guards and members of Mrs. McPherson's congregation patrolled the beach throughout the night hoping to find a trace of the missing evangelist who was first reported missing by her secretary, Miss Emma Schaffer.

At Angelus Temple, where the evangelist's mother, Mrs. Minnie Kennedy, conducted the evening services, continuing a travelogue on Europe where her daughter left off the night before, the tears and sobs of 5000 followers belied their oft repeated words as they took their seats, "Aimee will come back to her temple."

What hope had been entertained by the faithful flock for the return of their pastor was blasted at the close of the service when the mother, having "carried on" heroically, announced: "Aimee has not come back—we know she is with Jesus. Pray for her."

Miss Emma Schaffer, secretary to Mrs. McPherson, told the police that she and Mrs. McPherson had driven to the beach yesterday afternoon for a customary dip in the ocean. Mrs. McPherson went into the water for a few moments, came out for a while and went back. While Mrs. McPherson was in swimming the second time Miss Schaffer had to go to the hotel a few steps away to telephone. The last she saw of the evangelist she was only a short distance out in the water, swimming.

"I'M ALL RIGHT!"

"She smiled, waved her hand to me and called out something—I thought it was 'The water's fine—I'm all right, honey!'" Miss Schaffer said.

The secretary came out from the hotel in a few moments. Mrs. McPherson was nowhere to be seen. She was not in the water, she was not about the beach—she was not in the little beach tent the couple had erected. She was gone.

It was then that the search was instituted, a search that up to a late hour last night had brought nothing but silence to the thousands who sat in Angelus Temple praying for her.

The fact that Mrs. McPherson was considered an unusually good swimmer and a powerful one led life guards and beach police to believe that the evangelist had either suffered a fainting spell or was seized with cramps while in the water.

The water was unusually quiet. There was no heavy seas and no rip tide was reported. Only a handful of persons were on the beach at the time. No one heard an outcry.

CALMLY TELLS STORY

Calmly, with her Bible under her arm and reiterating "we must hope and pray," Miss Schaffer told her story to the police. She said that during the past few weeks Mrs. McPherson and she had been going down to the beach of an afternoon occasionally. They drove down to the Ocean View Hotel, at Rose avenue and Ocean Front, Venice. Miss Schaffer does not swim.

Mrs. McPherson donned her swimming suit in the hotel and she and her secretary went out to a strip of open beach in front of the hotel a few steps away. They set up a small beach tent and fell to reading, discussing some papers and lounging.

As Mrs. McPherson went into the water the second time one of a couple standing near the water remarked to her, "Oh, the water is awfully cold" Mrs. McPherson replied that she was not afraid of cold water, and plunged in.

Considerable time appears to have elapsed from the time Miss Schaffer returned to the beach after being in the hotel and the time the alarm was sounded. Miss Schaffer said it naturally did not occur to her at once that Mrs. McPherson may have drowned. Her first thought was that she probably had strolled down the beach toward the center of Venice. She was due back in Los Angeles at 4:30 p.m. and so the secretary boarded a tram and rode to Venice. Her search there being futile she rode back, hunted around the hotel and then hurried up toward Santa Monica.

BECOMES ALARMED

When she failed to find her employer there, Miss Schaffer first became really alarmed. She rushed back to the Ocean Park bathhouse and told what had happened. Four men, Jimmy Green, Bob Foster, Reo Barbour and George Wolf, the latter a municipal life guard, manned a rowboat and cruised around the spot where Mrs. McPherson had been swimming. They found no trace of her. The opinion was commonly expressed that if Mrs. McPherson had gone down there it would be practically impossible to recover her body for some time.

About that time a woman, whose identity was not learned, called the Venice police and told them Mrs. McPherson had disappeared. Officers were sent to the

(Continued on Page 2, Column 1)

Reported Victim of Beach Tragedy

[Tibbals Studio, Rochester, N. Y.]

Aimee Semple McPherson

In Two Parts—44 Pages
PART I—TELEGRAPH SHEET—22 PAGES

The Los Angeles Times

"Sail on, sail on, and on, and on."

GREATER SOUTHERN CALIFORNIA STRAIGHTAHEAD

FRIDAY MORNING, SEPTEMBER 24, 1926. DAILY, 5 CENTS. SUNDAY, 10 CENTS.

Liberty Under Law—Equal Rights—True Industrial Freedom

STORM DEAD INCREASED

Florida's Losses Still Mount

Water and Debris Yield More Bodies as State Checks Its Toll by Cities

Several Ship Crews Missing; Disease Danger Grows; Relief Succeeding

MIAMI, Sept. 23. (AP)—Additional surveys and rechecks made today in the storm-devastated southeastern coast of Florida showed 365 known dead, 1100 injured, probably 500 seriously, in hospitals, and property loss of approximately $165,000,000.

As compiled by W. H. Comes, in charge of the bureau of missing persons here: Col. L. S. Lowry, Jr., leader in the rescue work at Moorehaven; the Associated Press, and the Miami Daily News the deaths by cities and towns were as follows:

Moorehaven, 126; Miami and immediate vicinity, 109; Hollywood and immediate vicinity 54; Hialeah 22; Fort Lauderdale 193; Dania 11; Fulford 8; Seaboard Park 7; Ingleside 3; Hallandale 2; Homestead 2, and Pompano 2.

An accurate check of the dead at Clewiston and Progresso remained to be made.

LOSSES ESTIMATED

Property loss was given as follows: Greater Miami district, including Miami Beach, Coral Gables and Cocoanut Grove, $100,000,000 estimated by Miami Chamber of Commerce.

Hialeah, $15,000,000, estimated by Mayor Grethen.

Hollywood and Dania, $25,000,000 to $35,000,000 estimated by J. W. Young, developer of Hollywood.

Fort Lauderdale, $25,000,000 to $35,000,000, estimated by city officials.

Searchers and divers still were at work in Biscayne Bay and at Moorehaven and it was expected that when their work was finished there would be large accretions to the death list. Col. Lowry estimated that there were at least 100 more dead at Moorehaven with the possibility that some bodies will not be recovered until the flood waters have receded a week or more hence.

Searching parties found seven more bodies at Miami and the fatality list was increased by two more with the deaths at Coral Gables of a small girl and a man who had been injured.

An unidentified man's body was recovered from the sunken schooner Evelyn D., which foundered in the harbor with a liquor cargo valued at $70,000.

OTHERS MISSING

Divers were sent into the Nohab, formerly the private yacht of the German Kaiserin, which ended its existence as a supper club anchored in Biscayne Bay. The captain and six of the crew of this craft are missing.

Eleven persons, seven of them children, were rescued today from a caved-in apartment-house, where they had lain in darkness since last Saturday night. None was injured, but their plight was described as pitiable.

(Continued on Page 2, Column 5)

SURPLUS AT NEW MARK

Mellon Boosts Tax Estimate

Treasury Chief Expects Total to Pass $185,000,000 for Fiscal Year

Talk on Reduction Prospects Refused by Secretary as Premature

WASHINGTON, Sept. 23. (AP)—Increasing tax receipts flooding into the Treasury impelled Secretary Mellon today to boost his original estimate of a $185,000,000 surplus for this fiscal year. He was unwilling to predict what the eventual surplus might be, however, and maintained it was too early to talk of tax reduction.

"The administration is as anxious as others to cut taxes to the lowest safe limit," said Mr. Mellon, "but we have got to look to future years. We are enjoying tax returns now on unprecedented prosperity, and any change in this would wipe out the anticipated margin."

OLDFIELD PLAN HIT

He described as impossible the proposal of Chairman Oldfield, of the Democratic Congressional Campaign Committee, that the surplus of $370,000,000 of last year be added to the probable surplus for this fiscal year and a total cut of approximately $500,000,000 in taxes be made.

This would cut the annual government revenue below its regular needs, the Secretary said. Receipts and expenditures must be balanced annually, he added, and the surpluses of two years could not be added to make a permanent annual reduction. Furthermore, he pointed out that the $370,000,000 surplus of last fiscal year had all been applied toward reduction of the public debt.

RECEIPT PREDICTIONS

The Treasury predicted today that income-tax receipts for September would total $440,000,000 or $15,000,000 more than previously estimated. This will bring the total of income-tax collections for this quarter to more than $500,000,000, or almost $100,000,000 about a year ago.

This will be partly offset, however, by a drop of about $80,000,000 this quarter in miscellaneous tax receipts under the new law. Altogether the Treasury believes $200,000,000 less will be collected this year than last year from the miscellaneous taxes.

Customs receipts since July 1, last, already are $10,000,000 above the collections a year ago.

ELOPING ARCHITECT ELUDES AUTHORITIES

JOHNSTOWN (Pa.) Sept. 23. (AP)—Frank Lloyd Wright, Chicago architect, and Mme. Olga Milanoff, named in habeas corpus proceedings here late yesterday, have eluded the authorities and escaped, taking with them the woman's child by a former marriage, Attorney Jackson of Chicago said here today.

When New World's Champion Was Made in Philadelphia Yesterday

[Copyright, 1926, by P. & A. Photos]

Gene Tunney Takes Lead Over Dempsey in First Round

The top picture shows the champion at the left just after the challenger had rocked him with a right to the jaw in the first round. A moment later they went into the clinch shown below. The top picture shows Referee Reilly in the background. These pictures were sent from Philadelphia to San Francisco over the wires of the American Telephone and Telegraph Company and were rushed to Los Angeles in a Times airplane piloted by Arthur Goebel. Goebel left Crissey Field at 8:40 p.m. and landed at Clover Field, Santa Monica, in just under five hours—remarkable time for a night flight.

FIVE HURT IN HEAVY OHIO WINDSTORM

Damage Set at $75,000 as Tornado Sweeps Over Columbiana County Town

EAST LIVERPOOL (O.) Sept. 23. (AP)—Five persons were injured, one probably fatally, and approximately $75,000 damage done today when a windstorm struck at two points in Southern Columbiana county.

Four were injured in a suburban settlement seven miles north of East Liverpool and another near Wellsville, about two miles distant, and property damage resulted at Summitville, seventeen miles southwest.

Two terrific wind and rain storms apparently met in the suburban zone north of here. Wreckage was strewn along the Lincoln Highway as well as the Wellsville, Lisbon and Salinesville-Summitville road.

SANDUSKY (O.) Sept. 23. (AP)—A tornado twisted its way along a twelve-mile stretch of Lake Erie near here today, whisked through the center of Huron, nine miles from here, and disappeared into Lake Erie.

The damage at Huron was placed at between $10,000 and $20,000. Barns were unroofed and trees uprooted in the vicinity. A house was wrecked at Bloomingville and a half a dozen other homes unroofed.

RADIO MAN TAKES ISSUE WITH EDISON

Disputes Statement That Broadcasting Has Failed for Musical Purposes

CHICAGO, Sept. 23. (AP)—Radio dealers are "making much more money than phonograph dealers, and the public, in general, is entirely satisfied with the advancement in radio, "Frank Reichmann, vice-president of the Broadcast Listeners' Association, told Thomas A. Edison tonight in a telegram instigated by statements attributed to the inventor that the radio for musical purposes had failed.

"A newspaper quotes you as making certain statements detrimental to the entire radio industry," the telegram read. "I positively cannot believe that a man of your intelligence and experience could be so badly misinformed as to publicly condemn a tremendously growing and healthy American industry.

"Actually the best modern radio devices give distinctly better music than the finest phonographs. Radio dealers have made money and they are making money, certainly much more than phonograph dealers, and they are going to continue to make money on radios.

"Generally, the public is entirely satisfied with advancements in radio, as evidenced by the increase in our business alone of 500 per cent over last year. We will be very glad to send you a modern radio set for test. Please wire confirmation my impression that you never made statement attributed to you."

Maissaye Boguslawski, member of the faculty of the Chicago Musical College, also came to the defense of radio today with the statement that "radio will supplant the concert halls and operahouses within a few years."

UTAH SEISMOGRAPH REGISTERS TREMOR

SALT LAKE CITY, Sept. 23. (AP)—Prof. H. G. Mitchell, in charge of the seismograph at the University of Utah, reported today that a slight earth tremor was recorded here at 2:14 p.m. yesterday. The shock lasted eight minutes. He thought it was in California.

GENE TUNNEY DETHRONES DEMPSEY AS FISTIC KING

Record Crowd of 132,000 Fans Sees Champion Deposed in Ten-Round Bout Via Decision Route

BY ALAN J. GOULD

RINGSIDE, SESQUICENTENNIAL STADIUM, PHILADELPHIA, Sept. 23. (AP)—Gene Tunney, the fighting Marine, is the new heavyweight champion of the world. He dethroned Jack Dempsey, king for the last seven years, tonight, by smashing his way to decisive victory in a ten-round match that went the limit and furnished one of the greatest upsets in boxing history.

Dempsey, only a shell of his old fighting self, was outboxed and outfought from start to finish, groggy and bleeding in a one-sided battle that was decided in a driving rain before a record crowd of 132,000 spectators.

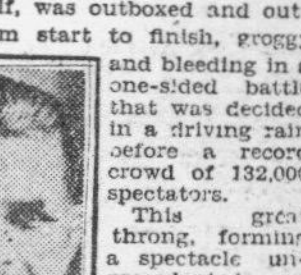

This great throng, forming a spectacle unprecedented in sports annals, paid close to $2,000,000 to witness a match that fell far short from the sensational heights expected of it.

Astounded at first by the amazing slowness, the lethargy and lack of old fighting fire in the champion's attack, the dripping throng cheered on he challenger as he steadily hammered and battered his way to triumph, piling up points that gave him an overwhelming margin and earned him the unanimous decision of the judges.

MASTERFUL FIGHT

Tunney, reaching the pinnacle of a fighting career that started when he was a buck private in the ranks of the marines, fought a masterful battle, outgeneralling Dempsey at nearly every turn as well as outpunching the champion. The battling product of sidewalks of New York's Greenwich Village, at the age of 28, fairly won his laurels and cleanly demonstrated his right to the purple robes of pugilism.

But the handsome, rugged challenger dethroned a man who came to the end of the championship trail with few weapons and less stamina to defend his place at the top.

Dempsey entered the ring a 4-to-1 favorite, backed as heavily as any champion in history. Experts had proclaimed him fit, in spite of his three-year layoff, but except for a gallant stand and a few flashes of his old self, he was outclassed.

TIGER MAN TAMED

Dempsey was far from the furious fighter, the "Tiger Man" who smashed his way to sensational victories over Jess Willard, Georges Carpentier and Luis Firpo. Gone was the devastating punch, the furious aggressiveness that marked him as one of the most feared men in the ring.

Instead he seemed in a daze from the start, unable at any time to sustain his attack for more than a few seconds. Occasionally, he connected with long left or right hooks to the head and body, but these no more than jarred the challenger temporarily. Always Tunney came back, punching with rights and lefts from the shoulder, rocking Dempsey's head with short but powerful punches.

It was Tunney's terrific right-hand blows to the head, chin and ribs that decided the battle. This blow, delivered like a ram rod, broke up Dempsey's rushes, opened cuts about his face and finally, in the last round, closed his left eye completely.

SORRY SIGHT

Dempsey was a sorry sight in the final round as Tunney, realizing victory and the goal of his fighting career was in his grasp, threw caution to the winds and lashed the champion about the ring. Gamely Dempsey, weaving and bobbing, bored in, but he only succeeded in taking a steady stream of punishment. One eye closed, blood dripped from a gash under the title-holder's right eye, his mouth was cut and he was reeling, his knees wobbly under the furious shower of Tunney's attack.

Desperately as Tunney tried, however, he could not bring Dempsey down. The champion, as he had done throughout the fight, absorbed his beating without giving much ground. In a final wild rally, he called his own guns into play, the weapons that had knocked out most of the men he ever faced, but this time they weren't loaded.

GREAT OVATION

The crowd gave Tunney a tumultuous ovation before the judges' decision was announced. There was no doubt as to what it would be. Dozens of the more enthusiastic climbed into the ring and a squad of police had to

(Continued on Page 11, Column 8)

GRAFT TRAIL SEARCHED

Daugherty Case Quest Pushed

Government Follows Partly Obliterated Course in Tracing $200,000

Bank Records in King Check Transaction Declared to Have Disappeared

NEW YORK, Sept. 23. (AP)—Over a partly obliterated paper trail, the government today pursued its tracing of $200,000 reputed graft money from German ownership to its asserted final resting place in the pockets of Harry M. Daugherty and Thomas W. Miller, Attorney-General and Alien Property Custodian respectively of the Harding administration.

During the morning session prosecution completed its attempt to show that of $441,000 paid John T. King, Republican leader, to "help and speed" claims for $7,000,000 of impounded enemy interests in the American Metal Company through government offices, $50,000 went to Miller.

The rest of the day was given over to testimony tending to show that $150,000 of the money King received from Richard Merton, German metal magnate, sent to this country to effect the claims, went to Daugherty. At the close of the day's session, evidence had been given through witnesses and documents concerning some $22,000 of this account.

It was in tracing this latter amount that the government attorneys had to follow a trail which they asserted had been mutilated by the defendant or his associates in an effort to destroy evidence of guilt.

BROKER TESTIFIES

James Watson, a New York broker, was called to testify that on October 4, 1921, King sold through a special account, opened for that single transaction, although he had three other accounts with the firm, Liberty Bonds to the face value of $24,000. He received for these, at his request, a cashier's check from the Seaboard National Bank of New York, which amounted, after deduction of commission, to $22,163.81.

Government transportation papers were introduced to show that on October 12, Daugherty and Jesse W. Smith, his confidential adviser, went to Ohio, and records of the Fourth National Bank of Cincinnati were shown revealing that on October 14, the King check was received there for payment, indorsed by the Midland National Bank of Washington Courthouse, O., of which Daugherty's brother, Mal S. Daugherty, is president.

Miss Vera V. Veall, assistant cashier of the Midland Bank, was called in an attempt to show how the King check had come to the bank where she was employed.

RECORDS MISSING

Her testimony revealed that both the Daughertys and Smith had had regular accounts in the bank and that King had never had one there. She testified, however, that all documents which might show who had cashed the King check there or to whose account it had been deposited, had disappeared. The government contends that these records were willfully destroyed as being incontrovertible evidence that the King money went to the former Attorney-General.

Miss Veall said that one sheet of the remittance letter accompanying checks sent to the Cincinnati bank on October 13 was missing, that the individual ledger sheets relative to the bank accounts of both Daugherty

(Continued on Page 2, Column 6)

THE DAY'S NEWS SUMMED UP

FEATURES. Radio, Page 5, Part II; Women's Pages, Clubs and Society, Page 6, Part II, Markets and Financial, Pages 17, 18, 19, 20, 21, Part I; Oil News, Page 21, Part I; Pictures, Page 8, Part I; Comics, Page 12, Part II.

NEWS OF SOUTHERN COUNTIES, Page 13, Part II.

STORY OF ELIZABETH, Page 10, Part I.

NEWS IN SPANISH, Page 16, Part I.

SHIPPING NEWS, Page 16, Part I.

THE SKY. Clear. Wind at 5 p.m., West, velocity, 6 miles. Thermometer, highest 77 deg.; lowest, 57 deg. Forecast: Fore Los Angeles and vicinity: Fair. For complete weather data, see last page of this section.

THE CITY. Papers of doctor who killed self link Mrs. McPherson to Ormiston, according to officials. Page 1, Part II.

W. C. T. U. leaders arrive to prepare for opening of convention. Page 1, Part II.

Plaza site is recommended for union rail station. Page 1, Part II.

Beatrice Lillie, musical comedy star, is sued for $100,000 as love thief. Page 2, Part II.

Annexation of Bell to city is held void. Page 1, Part II.

Burglars get $75,000 in women's finery by cutting way into shop through roof. Page 3, Part II.

South American actor tells of perils in motion-picture work in his country. Page 7, Part II.

Red Cross launches drive here for speedy collection of $50,000 for Florida relief. Page 3, Part I.

State flower and horticultural exhibition opened at Montebello. Page 1, Part II.

Dairymen's Association official here lauds co-operation as panacea for farmer's ills. Page 3, Part II.

Mayor Cryer signs ordinance of intention for Tenth-street opening and widening. Page 1, Part II.

Sixteen bids received and opened for grading and bridging in San Gabriel dam rail line project. Page 1, Part II.

SPORTS. Gene Tunney dethrones Jack Dempsey as world's heavyweight ring champion. Page 1, Part I.

Oaks in late rally to tie score, but Angels win. Page 14, Part I.

Cincinnati Reds and Phillies in fifteen-inning tie game. Page 14, Part I.

SLOPE. Three kiled when truck runs away down steep Yosemite grade. Page 6, Part I.

GENERAL EASTERN. More dead are discovered in Florida as cities check losses. Page 1, Part I.

Government pursues partly obliterated paper trail in Daugherty case graft quest. Page 1, Part I.

WASHINGTON. Geneva conference's action on American reservations to World Court entry may reopen fight in Senate. Page 1, Part I.

Secretary Mellon boosts original estimate of $185,000,000 surplus for fiscal year. Page 1, Part I.

Gov. Ritchie forces adoption of wet plank by State Democratic convention. Page 2, Part I.

Federal report points to increase of California autos. Page 2, Part I.

Rear-Admiral Fullam succumbs in Washington. Page 5, Part I.

FOREIGN. Oratorical finalists' party entertained at Mexico City luncheon. Page 3, Part I.

War of nations forecast in China as rival powers increase forces. Page 4, Part I.

Armistice brings lull in Nicaragua revolutionary struggle. Page 9, Part I.

REMEMBER THIS BY H. M. STANSIFER

The fellow who keeps pulling on the oars seldom rocks the boat.

ANOTHER SCHOOL MAY BAR STUDENT AUTOS

SALEM (Or.) Sept. 23 (Exclusive) The antiautomobile epidemic which has struck the University of Oregon threatens to descend on students of the Oregon Agricultural College as well. The question of prohibiting students from taking their autos to school will come up before the board of regents of the agricultural college at its next meeting, according to Secretary of State Kozer, member of the board. Kozer has received a number of letters asking that this action be taken. The university has just notified parents that it is not advisable for students to bring cars to school.

WORLD COURT ENTRY BAR FEARED IN WASHINGTON

Action on Reservations at Geneva May Necessitate Submission of New Protocol to Senate

WASHINGTON, Sept. 23. (AP)—American entry into the World Court will have to be reconsidered by the Senate in the judgment of a number of informed officials in the Capitol if the member powers adopt the recommendations submitted to them by the Geneva advisory conference on the American reservations.

In the absence of official advices from Geneva any authorized expression of views was lacking, but an undercurrent of feeling was discernable that the whole question of American participation in the work of the Court had been greatly complicated.

Initiative now rests with the powers participating in the Geneve discussion as the report of the conference, as adopted today, is merely of an advisory character. It recommends to the powers a formula of reply to the inquiry of the Washington government as to whether American signature of the World Court protocol on the basis of the reservation attached by the Senate would be satisfactory.

The powers are not committed to accept the advice of the Geneva delegates, each being free to formulate whatever reply to Washington it deems best and the next move expected is the decision of the individual powers on the nature of these replies.

Should the powers accept the advice of the Geneva gathering and transmit identical replies holding that American signature of a supplemental protocol as well as of the original protocol, was necessary, it is said in some quarters that President Coolidge must of necessity submit the new protocol drafted at Geneva to the Senate, if he believed it desirable that the United States should enter the Court on that basis.

These observers say he would be without authority to exchange ratifications without further advice and consent of the Senate, but whether the administration would take that course or merely drop the whole matter was a question on which no official cared to advance a prediction.

However, there apparently was no doubt in any quarter that the sup-

(Continued on Page 2, Column 7)

SNOW FALLS AS MERCURY GOES DOWN

Montana Blanketed When Thermometer Registers 22 Deg. Above Zero

HELENA (Mont.) Sept. 23. (AP)—Snow fall with freezing temperatures was reported generally over Montana today. Helena and Havre, with the mercury hovering around 22 deg. above zero, were the coldest points, while Helena also recorded the heaviest fall of snow, upward of four and one-half inches.

Great Falls reported three inches. The ground was covered at Billings, Yellowstone Park and Miles City.

The freezing temperatures extended into Wyoming and into Idaho.

SPOKANE, Sept. 23. (AP)—The earliest snowfall in the forty-five years' history of the Spokane Weather Bureau, arrived here today and covered the ground to the depth of .01 of an inch. The temperature was 31 deg. above zero at its lowest at 6:30 a.m.

CHICAGO, Sept. 23. (AP)—Snow tonight in Northern Minnesota probably will be one phenomenon of a general visitation of rain and cold weather upon the Central and Northwest, the Weather Bureau announced today.

CRASH INJURIES FATAL

MESA (Ariz.) Sept. 23. (Exclusive) Mrs. Amelia Gibbs has died here of injuries received in an automobile collision east of this city. The driver of the machine in which she was riding, C. W. Ogle, has been held for investigation.

AERIAL BASE FOR SAN DIEGO

West Coast Lighter-Than-Air Station Pledged by Warner and Moffett in Southern City

SAN DIEGO, Sept. 23. (AP)—San Diego is to get the proposed West Coast lighter-than-air base when Congress appropriates funds for carrying out the project. The sum of $20,000,000 has been estimated as necessary for the base.

This was the announcement made here otday by Edward P. Warner, assistant Secretary of the Navy for Aviation, and Rear-Admiral William Moffett, chief of the Bureau of Aeronautics, at a luncheon given in their honor and in subsequent interviews.

Speaking at the luncheon, Admiral Moffett said:

"The terrain, climatic and wind condition at San Diego for the operation and experimentation of lighter-than-air craft are unsurpassed by any other city in the world. If experiments in the field of lighter-than-air operation are to be carried out under the most advantageous conditions, and they should be, for the huge airships are as fragile as an eggshell in their present state of construction, these experiments must be conducted in a place where ideal conditions exist."

The admiral said that Congress is loath to appropriate money at present for the construction of additional naval aviation bases and predicted that it may be at least five years before actual work on the proposed San Diego airship base is started. He said that conditions at the Lakehurst, N. J., lighter-than-air base are far from ideal as compared with San Diego.

Admiral Moffett announced that the special service squadron comprised of PN-10 planes probably will leave Philadelphia next month for San Diego via the Panama Canal. This squadron, formerly in command of the late Commander John Rodgers, later may attempt a flight to Honolulu.

Fifteen Parts — 214 Pages
PART I—TELEGRAPH SHEET—16 PAGES

The Los Angeles Times

"Sail on, sail on, and on and on."
SUNDAY MORNING, MAY 22, 1927.
DAILY, 5 CENTS. SUNDAY, 10 CENTS.
Liberty Under Law—Equal Rights—True Industrial Freedom

CARQUINEZ SPAN OPEN

Coolidge Gives Signal

Mile Link Signal Victory Over Intricate Problem of Engineering

Costly Structure Provides Direct Route on to Redwood Highway

BY FLOYD HEALEY
"Times" Staff Correspondent

CROCKETT (Cal.) May 21. (Exclusive)—Three thousand miles away from here, in Washington, President Coolidge pushed a little button on his desk today, as if to summon an office boy. On such seemingly insignificant trifles hang the destinies of commonwealths.

When the electrical impulse thus motivated reached the Pacific, a target flickered, levers clattered from slot to slot, a steel cable whined through an eyelet, guns roared and a mass of multicolored silk whipped into the blue, never stopping until the western sun, mirrored through the Golden Gate, thirty miles away, softly burnished its opening folds.

FULFILLMENT OF DREAM

Human throats distended with a mighty shout of acclaim—not alone to Old Glory high above their heads, but to the visual fulfillment of a dream. Carquinez Strait Bridge, one of the greatest engineering achievements of modern times, fourth of the greatest bridges in the world and longest suspended highway span of all, had been dedicated.

The electrical contact between "Cal" and "Cal" had been twofold; it also marked congratulations from the shepherd of forty-eight great States to the most ambitious of his flock on another of its "impossible" attainments.

To the physical eye, Carquinez Bridge, is just a bridge, although a rather long one.

To the introspective eye it is to be a major link in a traffic chain whose benefits will lap the entire State like the waves which wash below it. That which becomes a lasting benefit to California reflects its blessing the length of the Pacific Coast; hence, that which the Pacific Coast achieves commands the attention of the world at large, for the coastal slope undeniably moves "downstage" in the arena of world affairs. There is the

(Continued on Page 3, Column 1)

HERO OF SKIES CASUALLY DESCRIBES ADVENTURE

Lindbergh Gets Bath at Home of Ambassador Herrick and Tells of Fighting Storm

[Copyright, 1927, by Chicago Tribune]

PARIS, May 22. (Exclusive)—At 1 o'clock this (Sunday) morning Capt. Lindbergh, with M. Weiss, veteran French pilot, escaped from the hangar at Le Bourget and stealthily crossed the air field aboard an automobile and was whirled to Paris by roundabout roads to escape the glut of cars on the main highway. M. Weiss stopped at the Arc de Triomphe en route to Mr. Herrick's house, near the Trocadero and "Slim" got his first glimpse of the tomb of the Unknown Soldier flickering in the flame.

Parmely Herrick, the Ambassador's son, welcomed Capt. Lindbergh at the embassy, escorting him to a room where a hot bath was awaiting him. "Lindy" swallowed a glassful of port and then a glass of milk and took a bath, combed his hair and donned a pair of Mr. Herrick's white flowered silk pajamas, blue embroidered silk bath robe and Moroccan leather slippers.

STILL HAS FULL

Capt. Lindbergh received the interviewer in the bedroom on the bed, when he arrived to deliver his mother's telegram of congratulations.

"I have fuel enough for another 500 miles, maybe 1000 miles, left in the tanks," he said. "I encountered no trouble on the trip. I did expect bad weather on the Newfoundland banks, but it was all right. After I passed that I ran into 1000 miles of bad weather over the ocean. That was last night. I struck sleet squalls, rain and fog. I flew at anywhere from ten feet to 10,000 feet altitude.

"When I ran into bad weather I had to try to ride over it or duck under it and I managed to avoid most of the sleet which would have weighted the plane. My compass worked fine. You know I studied navigation, although I don't pretend to be a navigator.

"I hit right over the Irish coast and recognized Cork and then veered over the Irish Sea over England and saw Plymouth, I guess it was. Then I crossed the channel and hit the French coast near Cherbourg. I just took a chance, driving straight inland toward Paris, according to what the map and compass showed me to be the direction.

"I was nearly to Paris and could see the lights before it got real dark. I saw a big flare at Mont Valerian and picked up the Eiffel Tower and saw the Seine reflected and the lights of the city. I made lots of altitude going over Paris.

"I never saw any ships on the At-

(Continued on Page 4, Column 3)

LINDBERGH'S PAL HURT

A. J. Edwards in Plane Crash

Ryan Company Executive's Craft Turns Turtle at Rogers Port

City Shares in Tribute to Ocean's Conquerer; Rich Offers Sent

Athrill with pride and admiration, Los Angeles yesterday paid vociferous tribute to the daring of Capt Charles Lindbergh, the slim and engaging young aviator who conquered the Atlantic in a California-built plane.

A flood of congratulatory telegrams from the city flashed over the cables to Paris and the young flyer even as word reached here that he had conquered the Atlantic wastes in his small gray monoplane, built for him at San Diego.

But one thing marred the city's joy, Arthur J. Edwards, general sales manager of the Ryan Airlines Corporation of San Diego, builders of the staunch little craft which carried Lindbergh to success in one of the

(Continued on Page 2, Column 7)

Sitting on Top of the World!

LINDBERGH REACHES PARIS AMID RIOT OF VAST MOB

Screaming Thousands Fight for Glimpse of American Flyer After Dash Across Ocean

[Copyright, 1927, by Chicago Tribune.]

PARIS, May 21. (Exclusive)—Slim Lindbergh arrived at 10:18 o'clock tonight, after flying from New York to Paris in 33 hours 10 minutes. "Am I in Paris?" were the pilot's first words as the French aviators and mechanics dragged him from the cockpit of the Spirit of St. Louis. "You're here," he was told as the mob jabbered in French, which was not in the least understood by the bewildered American. Enthusiasts hoisted the exhausted pilot on their shoulders and tried to fight their way across the field. The French pilots, however, spirited Capt. Lindbergh to the hangar, rescuing him from the mob, and then dashed away to Paris with him aboard an automobile across the aviation field.

Meantime the crowd picked up an American who had fallen and been trampled on by the mob and carried him on their shoulders to the administration building where American Ambassador Herrick, French officials and the welcome committee were awaiting him.

GET WRONG MAN

"Let me go, I am not Lindbergh," shrieked the American, but the sturdy Frenchmen carried him upstairs.

Ambassador Herrick, glancing at the man's dishevelled business suit, wilted collar and torn necktie, realized it was a mistake, and waited an hour for Capt. Lindbergh, fruitlessly.

The exultant yell that went out from the 40,000 Gallic throats when the plane finally picked its way through the obscurity to earth, was only a prelude to the wild dash out to the field and into the glare of the projectors, toward the shining Spirit of St. Louis. The historical gendarmes were trampled under foot as the mob streamed a full third of a mile toward the still moving plane. Capt. Lindbergh must have seen them start, for on landing he turned the nose of his ship away from the stampeding thousands, directly toward the group of military hangars, missing them only by 100 yards. He then turned his craft about and started to taxi straight into the crowd.

NEAR RIOT STARTS

"Mon dieu! mon dieu! He cannot see, the projectors have blinded him," many yelled in terror, while those in the lead scattered only to be forced forward again by the thousands pushing behind them. But finally the monoplane came to a full stop on the fringe of the terrified mob which then threw fear to the winds and surged around it, under it and over it. The door of the fuselage was yanked open and the grinning pilot was hauled forth and carried off.

But the riot had only begun. Fathers held youngsters, whose lives they risked, dragging them up there to kiss, feel or touch some part of the great bird that came down among them so wonderfully. Others hopped into the pilot's seat and stared in wonderment at its neatness and tidiness, especially the three neat little bundles hanging in back of the pilot's seat, reliably rumored to contain a change of linen. They greedily eyed the maps and instruments that helped him to gain his objective, but all refrained, if reluctantly, from annexing souvenirs.

Then, howling still, they began to dash in hundreds, as many as could took hold of the plane and shoved it toward the airport where its pilot apparently was being carried ahead in triumph.

WANT TO SEE HIM

But losing sight of Capt. Lindbergh in the blinding glare of the flood lights, they dropped the work of pushing the plane toward the administration building where Ambassador Herrick and all the nabobs were waiting to tell Lindbergh how proud they were. But Mr. Herrick and aides stood around, greeted the wrong man, came to the window,

(Continued on Page 2, Column 1)

PRESIDENT REJOICES

Coolidge Cables to Lindbergh

High Praise Voiced for His Remarkable Flight Over Uncharted Course

Navy, Army and All Other Washington Officials Join in Encomiums

WASHINGTON, May 21. (Exclusive)—News that Capt. Lindbergh successfully had driven his single-motored gray monoplane into Paris was received with jubilation and cheers in the national capital.

President Coolidge and high officials vied with each other in praising the achievement of the air-mail pilot and in congratulating him on his record-making flight. Crowds in the streets cheered as newsboys rushed extras down Pennsylvania avenue with the news that the lone pilot's attempt to make a nonstop flight from New York to Paris had been successful.

President Coolidge in a message of congratulation transmitted to the captain through the American Embassy at Paris, asserted that the flight "crowns the record of American aviation."

HIGH PRAISE VOICED

Secretary of State Kellogg termed the flight a "great step forward in the advancement of aviation." High naval officers and officials expressed unbounded admiration for the heroic captain and termed his feat "one of the greatest triumps in the history of the world." Arrival of dispatches that the airman had arrived safely crowned a day during which confidence that he would reach Paris remained unshaken throughout the day. From the time that Lindbergh first was reported off the coast of Ireland until he dropped into the French metropolis at 4:21 p.m., Washington time, naval officials expressed confidence that he would reach his goal. Crowds of officials were gathered at the Navy information office all day. Other officials, headed by the President, were kept advised constantly by the news services of the progress of the flight and their attempts to locate the aviator

The President received the news while cruising on the Potomac in the

(Continued on Page 2, Column 5)

MOTHER HAPPY BUT CALM

"There's No Use Trying to Find Words to Express My Joy," Declares Mrs. Lindbergh

DETROIT, May 21. (Exclusive)—"I am grateful. There is no use attempting to find words to express my happiness." These were the first words of Mrs. Evangeline Lodge Lindbergh, mother of the intrepid flyer, as she received word that her famous son had safely landed his plane in Paris. The mother waited the word of her son's victory or death in their modest home on Ashland avenue. It is a frame dwelling set far back from the street. Through the back yard runs Fox Creek, up which motor boats constantly sped while the mother awaited the word which she has been hoping for since early Friday morning.

"Somehow I felt all through that he would win. I was as confident as any mother could have been under the circumstances, and yet there were times when the difficulties which I knew he was facing depressed me. I am happy that it is over, more happy than I can ever tell. He has accomplished the greatest undertaking of his life, and I am proud to be the mother of such a boy," Mrs. Lindbergh continued.

TEARS IN HER EYES

Mrs. Lindbergh is the type of woman that possesses that faculty for perfect control of her emotions. She has been more composed that most Detroiters during the time her son was preparing for the flight. But when the news was flashed across the Atlantic today of his victory and she was called upon to discuss his feat, tears appeared in her eyes. She did not cry, but as she talked with a reporter under the cherry trees in her front yard, tears were distinctly visible.

"What is there for me to say, other than that I am happy?" was her question.

She was standing beneath the trees, which are banked by a bed of varicolored tulips in the front lawn when word came that Capt. Lindbergh had won in the great race across the sea. She wore a green dress and green hat as she chatted with newspaper men. She smiled throughout the interview, the same smile which she wore throughout the day as she went about her household duties.

"All through these hours that I have been awaiting word from my boy, everyone has been very kind to me. The boys and girls in my class have been particularly kind. They were naturally interested in the flight, but out of regard for my feelings were very careful not to discuss it in my presence. It is all too wonderful. I do not know how I could be more happy than I am today," she continued.

CLASSES AS USUAL

Mrs. Lindbergh, who teaches chemistry at the Cass Technical High School, conducted her classes on Friday.

"It was far better that I should spend the time in the classroom This occupied my mind and did not give me the opportunity to think so much about Charles," she said.

There was considerable commotion outside the home throughout the

(Continued on Page 2, Column 6)

MESSAGE OF DOUMERGUE LAUDS FEAT

French President Sends Nation's Congratulations; Coolidge Replies

WASHINGTON, May 21. (AP)—President Doumergue of France, in a message of congratulation to President Coolidge tonight viewed the successful trans-Atlantic flight of Capt. Lindbergh as the dream of Nungesser and Coli come true.

In reply, President Coolidge said that, while he and the entire country rejoiced in Lindbergh's success it had not forgotten to share France's sorrow in the loss of Nungesser and Coli.

In his cablegram, President Doumergue said:

"On the morrow of the attempt of our aviators whose misfortune was so keenly felt by the kindly hearts of your countrymen, Charles Lindbergh made true the dream of Nungesser and Coli and by his audacious flight brought about the aerial union of the United States and France. All Frenchmen unreservedly admire his courage and rejoice in his success. I congratulate you most heartily in the name of the government of the republic and of the whole country."

President Coolidge's reply follows:

"I thank you for your cordial message, which I share with the American people I rejoice in the success of the young man who so courageously set forth on his lonely flight, but neither I nor the people of the United States forget to share in the sorrow of France in the recent loss of your two brave aviators. It is largely due to the genius of France that aviation has progressed so rapidly and as it brings us closer as measured by ours, so it must increase our heritage of sympathy and understanding."

IN THE GREATER SUNDAY "TIMES" TODAY

Italian Flyer Plans Atlantic Flight Today

TREPASSEY (N. F.) May 22. (AP) As the first hint of dawn creeps on the eastern horizon Commander Francesco De Pinero, Italian four-continent flyer, will hop off in the Santa Maria II on his long jump to Casdelo Branco, near Horta, Azores, he announced this morning.

LONDON, May 22. (Exclusive)—No news has been received from the British aviators, Carr and Gillman, on their nonstop flight of 4150 miles to Karachi, India. A message received in London at 12:30 this morning from Constantinople stated that they had not been sighted at Constantinople or in its environs at 7 p.m.

"DAYLIGHT SAVING" FOUNDER HONORED

LONDON, May 21. (AP)—A memorial to William Willett, founder of "daylight saving," was dedicated today by Marquis Camden in Potts Wood, Chiselhurst, near the churchyard where Willett is buried.

HEADS COMMANDERY

MOBILE (Ala.) May 21. (Exclusive) Philip S. Myers of Mobile, has been elected Eminent Grand Commander of the Grand Commandery, Knights Templar of Alabama. Montgomery was chosen as the city for the sixty-eighth annual conclave.

PLANE CHIEF NOT SURPRISED

Ryan Organization Head Receives Arrival News With "I Told You So" Attitude

GARDEN CITY (L. I.) May 21. (Exclusive)—Benjamin F. Mahoney, 26 years of age, president of the Ryan Air Lines of San Diego, Cal., received the news of Lindbergh's arrival over France in his room at the Garden City Hotel with an "I told you so" attitude. This young man, who has been interested in flying for five years and is a pilot as well as the head of a company building planes, has never for a moment doubted the success of the venture. He is mature beyond his years, as is the pilot who came to him for a plane with which he could fly the Atlantic.

In 1922 he entered into partnership with T. C. Ryan, a California pilot, for whom engineers had already designed the plane known as the Ryan M-1, of which the "Spirit of St. Louis" is a modification.

In the ideal flying conditions of California their venture prospered from the first. They established the first regular schedule passenger service in America, which is in operation throughout the year between Los Angeles and San Diego.

Nine months ago Mahoney bought out his partner and now owns all the stock in the company. It is an organization of young men in which he is the youngest. To William H. Bowlus, 29, of Kentucky, superintendent, and Donald Hall, 27, designer and chief engineer for the Ryan company, Mahoney gives most of the credit for building the first plane to fly to Paris. Bowlus is a flyer and test pilot of several years' experience.

They had never heard of Lindbergh until they received a message from him in St. Louis March 28, last, asking them for a ship that would fly the ocean. After working all night, they wired him that they could. He started at once for San Diego. The Ryan organization went into action and sixty days later "Slim" Lindbergh took the air in his machine. It is believed that this job constitutes a record in speed and efficiency. The mechanics and those who directed them worked sixteen and twenty hours daily.

From the first it was decided that the Wright whirlwind air-cooled 200-horsepower motor was the only engine for the job and Mahoney, as soon as the decision was made to build the ship, ordered his motor by long-distance telephone to Paterson, N. J. D. C. Peterson of the Wright company said that the engine selected was a stock model which had received only the usual ten-hour block tests accorded to all their engines.

Tonight, with George Stumpf, representing the St. Louis backers of Capt. Lindbergh who raised $25,000 to finance the flight, awaited a direct cable from Capt. Lindbergh. Mahoney refused to discuss plans for the future. Lindbergh, he says, has no strings on him to prevent him from being a free agent, but Mahoney believes that the young flying man may decide to cast in his lot with the Ryan organization. If he does it is likely that he may set out against other long-distance obstacles and records.

Like the men behind the plane, the backers whose money helped put the flight over are young men. H. H. Knight is a broker, 28 years of age. Harold Bixby of the Chamber of Commerce of St. Louis, A. B. Lambert and Stumpf himself have known Capt. Lindbergh for several years. When he decided that he wanted to make the try they said they would help him.

SHORTRIDGE SILENT OVER NEW JURIST

Department of Justice Announces Post in North Will Soon be Filled

WASHINGTON, May 21. (Exclusive) The Department of Justice indicated today an appointment of a United States district judge will be made in the near future for the Northern California vacancy.

No recommendation has been received yet from Senator Shortridge but in view of the department's statement it is assumed that a recommendation will be received soon.

The Northern California bar is understood to be bombarding the department with demands that the vacancy be filled in the immediate future because of the congested condition of the calendar.

FLYING LOG OF PARIS DASH

The flying log of Lindbergh's plane follows:

7:52 a.m. (Friday)—Left New York for Paris.
9:05 a.m. (Friday)—Sighted over East Greenwich, R. I.
9:40 a.m. (Friday)—Sighted over Halifax, Mass.
12:25 p.m. (Friday)—Reported over Meteghan, N. S.
1:05 p.m. (Friday)—Reported over Springfield, N. S.
1:50 p.m. (Friday)—Over Milford, N. S.
3:05 p.m. (Friday)—Passing over Mulgrave, N. S., and Straits of Canso for Cape Breton.
5 p.m. (Friday)—Cleared Nova Scotia at Main-Dieu, the easternmost tip.
7:15 p.m. (Friday)—Passed St. John's N. F., and headed over broad Atlantic.
6:30 a.m. (Saturday)—Independent wireless says a vessel reports Lindbergh 200 miles off Irish coast.
8:10 a.m.—Cape Race, N. F., has wireless from Dutch ship that Lindbergh was 500 miles off Irish Coast.
2:50 (Greenwich time)—London Press Association dispatch says Lindbergh sighted 100 miles off Ireland.
10 a.m. (Eastern Daylight time)—Radio Corporation says its Paris office reports plane over Valencia.
10 a.m. (E.D.T.)—Halifax received a wireless dispatch that Lindbergh had passed over Valencia.
12:30 p.m. (E.D.T.)—Belfast, Ireland, reports Lindbergh over Dingle Bay, Ireland.
2:06 p.m. (E.D.T.)—Valencia, Ireland, government wireless says collier Nogi sights airplane near Dingle.
2:18 p.m. (E.D.T.)—Cork, Ireland, says Civic Guard reports Lindbergh plane passing over Smerwick Harbor, Ireland.
3:02 p.m. (E.D.T.)—New York-French Cable Company says official advices report Lindbergh over Bayeux, France, at 8 p.m. French time.
3:30 p.m. (E.D.T.)—Reported over Cherbourg, France.
5:21 p.m. (E.D.T.)—Lands safely at Le Bourget Field, Paris.

In Three Parts — 44 Pages
PART I—TELEGRAPH SHEET—22 PAGES

DESTINY

The Los Angeles Times

"Sail on, sail on, and on and on."

THURSDAY MORNING, AUGUST 4, 1927. C DAILY, 5 CENTS. SUNDAY, 10 CENTS.

Liberty Under Law—Equal Rights—True Industrial Freedom

NAVAL MEET HOPE DIES

Conference Will End Today

Japanese Compromise Fails; Proposal for "Holiday" Not Acceptable

Final Session Nears Close; Britain and America at Odds Over Cruisers

GENEVA, Aug. 3. (AP)—After trembling for a day on the brink of a precipice, the tripartite naval conference at the solemn hour of midnight crashed to the bottom of the abyss. Its delegates mutually and sorrowfully agreed that no pact could be reached to limit further the armaments of Great Britain, the United States and Japan at this time.

The final session, it was authoritatively stated tonight, will be held tomorrow afternoon at 3 o'clock. This announcement was made after tonight's meeting of the plenipotentiaries to consider the Japanese compromise proposals.

The decision to adjourn the conference tomorrow was brought about by the inability of both Great Britain and the United States to accept clearly the Japanese compromise as a basis of discussion for settling the cruiser question, which was the crux of the whole conference.

COMPROMISE DISCUSSED

When the private meeting of the delegates opened at the villa of Hugh S. Gibson, chief American delegate, presiding, the Japanese proposal was immediately brought up for discussion. W. C. Bridgeman, principal British representative, and his colleague, Viscount Cecil—all accounts of the meeting agree here—were not quite clear as to whether the Japanese compromise could be acceptable to them. This compromise virtually meant a naval holiday for Great Britain until the United States could catch up with her in naval construction. The British delegates, however, indicated that if the compromise were acceptable to both the United States and Japan, more time would be required to look into it further.

In the Japanese plan the word "authorized" was employed to emphasize that Great Britain and Japan would only finish their authorized cruiser program. Mr. Gibson asked Mr. Bridgeman what he understood this word to signify, adding:

"Does it mean approved and authorized?"

Viscount Cecil answered that it meant "authorized." After further duelling, Mr. Gibson asked:

"Does it mean the Birkenhead plan?"

Mr. Bridgeman is understood to have answered: "Yes."

"Then that means 458,000 tons for Great Britain by 1931," said Mr. Gibson.

TOO HIGH FOR AMERICA

Mr. Gibson added that this was higher than the United States could possibly go and that it would mean that America must build up to that figure. Mr. Bridgeman's reply was that the British did not wish to speak in terms of total tonnage. Mr. Gibson insisted that the United States could only build up to 400,000 tons as a maximum in cruisers, and declared that there was no advantage in signing a treaty to authorize the British building program.

All the British statesmen remarked

(Continued on Page 2, Column 6)

SACCO AND VANZETTI MUST DIE AS LAST PLEA FAILS

Gov. Fuller Decides Pair Convicted for Murder Had Fair Trial; Death Due Wednesday

BOSTON, Aug. 3. (Exclusive)—Gov. Alvan T. Fuller announced tonight at the State House that Nicola Sacco and Bartolomeo Vanzetti had a fair trial and that there was no justifiable reason for giving them a new trial for the murder of a paymaster and his guard at South Braintree, Mass., on April 15, 1920. The Governor declared in his opinion that he found no sufficient justification for executive intervention.

The reprieve of the condemned men expires next Wednesday, and the Governor's refusal to exercise clemency removes their last hope of escaping execution. They have already been moved to the death house in the State's prison.

"I believe with the jury," the Governor said, "that these men, Sacco and Vanzetti, were guilty and that they had a fair trial."

ADVISERS AGREE

President A. Lawrence Lowell of Harvard University, President Samuel Stratton of the Massachusetts Institute of Technology, and former Judge of Probate Robert Grant, the Governor's advisory commission, arrived unanimously at a decision that agreed wholly with that of the Governor.

The inquiry of the Governor was concerned, he explained, with these questions:

"Was the jury trial fair?"

"Were the accused entitled to a new trial?"

"Are they guilty or not guilty?"

He declared eleven living members of the jury were of the opinion that the men had a fair trial. Discussing the charges of prejudice against Judge Webster Thayer, Gov. Fuller cleared the presiding judge and said he saw no evidence of prejudice in his conduct of the trial.

He found nothing to support the charge that conditions in the courtroom were prejulicial to the defendants, nor could he see any warrant for the assertion that the jury was unfair.

TRIAL HELD FAIR

Having read the record and examined witnesses himself Gov. Fuller was of the opinion that the trial was fairly conducted.

Discussing the petition for a new trial on the basis of newly discovered evidence, the Governor further upheld Judge Thayer in refusing a new trial on the ground of asserted new evidence furnished on behalf of the defense. He also pointed out that the Supreme Judicial Court had read the affidavits containing the new matter and had refused to sustain the contention of counsel for the men.

The Governor discarded entirely the confession of Celestino Madeiros, self-confessed murderer of a Wrentham bank cashier, now in the death house awaiting execution. Madeiros had declared that he and the Morelli gang of Providence took part in the South Braintree hold-up and murders and that Sacco and Vanzetti had nothing to do with the case.

BELIEVES THEM GUILTY

As to the most vital question of all—whether Sacco and Vanzetti were guilty—the Governor said he reviewed the evidence in the case of Vanzetti, found guilty of an attempted robbery executed in Bridgewater on December 24, 1919, and for which he was convicted subsequently by Judge Thayer and sentenced to from twelve to fifteen years. He stressed the point that Vanzetti, who took the stand with Sacco in their joint trial, had not testified on his own behalf at his first trial. His conclusion was that Vanzetti was guilty and that he had had a fair trial.

The Governor then discussed the South Braintree crime and pointed out that both men were armed when arrested; that they lied when ques-

(Continued on Page 3, Column 4)

HEIRESS WED TO CHINESE

Bride Member of Noted Family

Miss Agassiz and Oriental Student Married in New York's City Hall

Bride Descendant of Famed Copper Mine Scientist; Dine in Chinatown

NEW YORK, Aug. 3. (Exclusive)—Miss Vaudine E. G. Agassiz, 21-year-old descendant of Alexander D. Agassiz, famous scientist and discoverer of the Calumet and Hecla copper mines of Michigan, long the richest copper property in the world, was married this morning to Nai Jan Chuck, 23-year-old Chinese student of this city. Deputy City Clerk J. J. McCormick performed the ceremony in the marriage-license chapel at City Hall.

Immediately after the wedding, the couple went to the bride's home, a studio apartment, where it is said she had been living alone for the past year. She describes herself in the marriage license as a typist. A private supper for twenty friends was held at 7 o'clock last night in Chinatown, where the "surprise" marriage was announced.

SILENT ON FAMILY

Miss Agassiz said this afternoon that she is "related to Agassiz, the scientist," but she refused to divulge her father's name. The wedding, she explained, was to have been a "secret" and she did not want "folks" to read of it in the newspapers.

At the bridegroom's residence this afternoon Lengby Ling, his cousin, asserted that the couple had known each other some time, but had never announced an engagement. Chuck, he said, was a graduate of the New York University school of commerce and had been in New York for the past four years. His home is in Shanghai, he added, where his guardian is an older brother, T. N. Chuck, exporter and importer.

Chuck had intended returning to China to live very soon, possibly joining his five brothers in the exporting business, Ling said. He believed that Miss Agassiz had proposed to accompany him. Ling knew nothing of Miss Agassiz's family connections except that her father was "an author" and reputed to be prominent in the financial world.

MADE MILLIONS

Alexander D. Agassiz, to whom the present Mrs. Chuck says she is related, died in 1910, after a life devoted to science, and the amassing of a fortune of several million dollars. He was the most prominent marine zoologist of his time, a deep-sea explorer, and discoverer of the submarine desert 5000 miles in length, just off the west coast of South Africa. His father, Louis Agassiz, was the founder of the Museum of Co-operative Zoology at Harvard University and Alexander Agassiz, after his copper-mine investigations, became curator of the museum.

The Hecla copper mining properties were just about to be abandoned in 1865, when Alexander Agassiz agreed to investigate their condition. In four years he had put them into working condition, and received a large share of stock for his services. The mines were consolidated later with the Calumet mines, which he also improved and the

(Continued on Page 2, Column 6)

"Let Me Do the Choosing, Mr. President!"

ILEANA REJECTS AMERICANS

Rumanian Princess Turns Down Nine Proposals Despite Offers of Love, Cows and Flivver

BUCHAREST (Rumania) Aug. 3. (AP)—Since Queen Marie announced that she would not object to Ileana marrying an American, provided she really loved him, the 18-year-old Princess has received nine proposals of matrimony from lonesome youths in different parts of the United States.

One swain in a rural district of Indiana promised not only to honor, love and obey Europe's pretty Princess if she married him but pledged her his ten-acre farm, six cows, an automobile, two buggies and a sleigh.

Another admirer, this one in New York State, wrote that he had no title, fortune or fame to offer her, but would give her all his love and devotion and in addition a cozy home.

A third American who sought the royal hand and heart, said that having seen Her Highness during her visit to the United States, he was sure she was just the girl for him and that he believed he could make her happer than if she became a queen.

Ileana, however, has rejected all these and the other proposals, declaring she will not marry for at least five years. She now is president of the Young Women's Christian Association of Rumania and plans to devote all her time to betterment of the welfare of the girls of her country. She desires also, now that her father is dead, to stay at her mother's side and give the Queen all the help and encouragement possible.

Although she has rejected the proposals, Ileana has nothing but friendly feelings for the American boys.

"I like them for their gallantry and chivalrous attitude toward womankind," she said today. "They were all just lovely to me when I was in America, especially the military cadets."

SIXTEEN DIE IN KENTUCKY MINE BLAST

Bodies Reported Found and Rescuers Search for Other Victims

CLAY (Ky.) Aug. 3. (AP)—Sixteen miners were reported killed late today in the West Kentucky Coal Company's mine near here, where exactly ten years ago sixty-seven lost their lives in one of the greatest mine disasters in the State.

Today's explosion came late in the afternoon as the 250 miners were partly out of the shaft and late tonight the exact number of dead had not been determined, but from the mine, a mile from here, it was reported that fifteen bodies had been found in addition to that of J. W. Meyers, 52 years of age, whose body was brought to the surface.

Rescuers hastened on, hoping to find and save miners who might still live, and left the other bodies for the time being.

First reports said today's explosion was caused by a faulty "shot."

CAMPBELL PROFFERED ENVOY POST

Arizona Reports Former Governor May be Next Ambassador to Mexico

PHOENIX, Aug. 3. (AP)—The Arizona Gazette will say today that private telegraphic advices from Washington declare that Thomas E. Campbell, former Governor of Arizona, has definitely been tendered the post of Ambassador to Mexico and has taken the matter under advisement. The tender is said to have been made shortly after Campbell's return from Seville, Spain, where he represented the United States at the Spanish World's Fair. The report said Campbell had requested thirty days to consider the offer.

Canada Sojourn Period Extended

WASHINGTON, Aug. 3. (Exclusive) Now effective United States motorists visiting Canada are privileged to remain within the Dominion for sixty days instead of thirty days as heretofore, under the original permit. In addition to sixty days for which the first permit may be procured an additional thirty-days extension is provided for, after the expiration of the first period.

An announcement to this effect was made here today at the national headquarters of the American Automobile Association on the receipt of telegraphic dispatches from the Canadian Automobile Association which concluded negotiations which led the Canadian Minister of Customs and Canadian Customs Commissioner to make the change in the period of the "original permit."

TWO SHIPS IN HEAD-ON COLLISION

Word of Crash in Texas Channel Given by Radio; Damage Details Lacking

GALVESTON, Aug. 3. (AP) — The British steamship Hornby Castle and the American steamship Cody were in head-on collision late today in the Houston ship channel, about thirty miles from here. Except from radio advices received here, little is known of the damage.

The Hornby Castle, which was struck full on the bow, is proceeding to Galveston with a tug, and is believed to have been badly damaged about the superstructure. Damages to the Cody have not been ascertained. As soon as word of the collision was received, tugs were dispached from here. The Hornby Castle is known to be badly damaged forward, and is not able to anchor.

The Cody had only a small amount of cargo aboard, while the Hornby Castle was about half loaded.

Bowles, Retired Rear-Admiral, Called by Death

BARNSTABLE (Mass.) Aug. 3. (AP)—Rear-Admiral Francis T. Bowles, retired, died early today at his summer home here.

Admiral Bowles chose a naval career rather than the newspaper field which had occupied his family since his father founded the Springfield Republican. He played a large part in the transformation of the wooden navy to one of steel and gave the first twin screws to an American war vessel.

Retiring from service in 1903, he became head of the Fore River Shipbuilding Corporation. Re-entering government service during the World War, he aided in building the "bridge of boats" to Europe.

Phone by Radio for 7500 Miles

BERLIN, Aug. 3. (AP)—The longest distance ever attained in commercial radio phoning—a stretch of 7500 miles—was achieved tonight when wireless telephony was successfully inaugurated between Berlin and Buenos Aires, Argentina, via the Nauen Radio Station.

Greetings were exchanged between German and Argentine government officials.

Ford Delivers Giant Airplane

DETROIT, Aug. 3. (AP)—A giant Ford trimotored transport, one of the largest types of airplane now built in America, fitted as an aerial delivery truck, took off at the Ford airport this morning for Cleveland en route to New York for delivery to a typewriter company which will use it to deliver products to purchasers. The plane was the first freight carrier of its kind to be built for service outside the regular Ford air lines.

The plane will fly to New York on a test flight and from there to Hartford, Ct., where it will start on the first delivery trip to Havana, Cuba.

Gasoline Only Fourteen Cents in Twin Cities

ST. PAUL, Aug. 3. (AP)—Gasoline prices were reduced 2 cents a gallon at virtually all service stations in the Twin Cities today.

The new price, including a 2-cent State tax, is 14 cents a gallon.

RE-ELECTION OF COOLIDGE CHAMPIONED BY HOOVER

Nation Deluges President With Pleas to Leave Way Open for Accepting Candidacy

PALO ALTO, Aug. 3. (AP)—Herbert Hoover, Secretary of Commerce, commenting today on President Coolidge's announcement that he does not choose to be a candidate for re-election in 1928, declared:

"I regret the suggestion in the President's statement. However, I still believe as I stated in Chicago two weeks ago, that President Coolidge should be renominated and re-elected."

RAPID CITY (S. D.) Aug. 3. (Exclusive)—Gray clouds that rolled away from the Black Hills today leaving a land of sparkling sunshine and green peace, found a mental corollary in the atmosphere of the President's office where his sudden dramatic announcement yesterday that he will not be a candidate for President next year left a reaction of political peace.

While his announcement formed the great topic of discussion around the executive office and town, the President contributed nothing to it. He saw an unusually small number of visitors, worked a short time and started away on what seemed another, and more real, vacation.

PLEAS POUR IN

While the whole country was marveling at his action, the only announcements from the President were that on the 10th inst. he will go to Rushmore Mountain to assist in the dedication work of carving the great stone faces of four Presidents there, and that on the 15th inst. he will go to Hermosa, his church town, and press a button which will start the great white way, an electric light affair, at Elizabeth, Tenn.

Hundreds of telegrams poured into the executive offices from party and business leaders in the nation, most of them deploring his action and urging him to reconsider and not put himself in a position where he can not be drafted as a candidate. It also was represented that a change of governmental policies or a long period of uncertainty could work incalculable harm to business.

The upshot of the situation appears to be that while it is considered here that the President has taken himself out of the Presidential picture next year, it is not so accepted throughout the country.

There are two political viewpoints emerging as a result of the announcement, one represented by Chairman Butler, who does not think the President is eliminated, and the other by those who know him well and have studied his methods for years, that his decision is final and irrevocable. This opinion prevails here.

UP TO PARTY

Senator Capper, who rode home with the President yesterday after the announcement, said later that he did not discuss it with the President but that he could not see that the announcement materially changes the situation, that responsibility is placed squarely with the Republican party as to its choice of a nominee next year. This seems to represent the attitude of many political leaders. Reactions from personal contact with Mr. Coolidge often are misleading, seldom enlightening, as this situation proves.

The shrewdest politician in this State, Senator Norbeck, who has been close to the President for weeks, was one of the most surprised men in the country yesterday. He had utterly mistaken the President's mind, misjudged his acts. The most experienced political men in the West have dropped in to see the President during the summer. Without exception they have come away with the idea that he was a candidate in a potential sense, that he would say nothing and permit the nomination to be given to him. What has happened?

(Continued on Page 2, Column 3)

MORE PLAN ISLAND HOP

Fifteen Sign for Hawaii Trip

Entry List May be Increased by Mail Applications Not Yet Received

Wife to Accompany Texan on Scheduled Dash for Dole Prize

SAN FRANCISCO, Aug. 3. (Exclusive)—At least fifteen airplanes, ranging from one wing to three, will answer the starter's gun in the $35,000 Dole flights to Honolulu the 12th inst. The official list as it stands was given today by Frank A. Flynn, local secretary of the National Aeronautic Association, who is in charge of preparations. There may be more as all entries mailed prior to midnight will be considered official.

The entries, as they stand now, are:

Maj. Livingston G. Iving, Berkeley, who will fly alone in a monoplane.

Arthur C. Goebel, Los Angeles, who will fly alone in a monoplane.

John A. Pedlar, Flint, Mich., who will pilot a biplane, carrying Miss Mildred Doran, Caro, Mich., school teacher, as a passenger, and W. R. Lawing, chief aerographer and meteorologist at the naval air station, North Island, San Diego, as navigator.

Frederick A. Giles, Detroit: expected to fly alone in a monoplane.

Charles W. Parkhurst, Lomax, Ill., with Ralph C. Lowes, Jr., Peoria, Ill., as navigator, in a biplane.

Lieut. Norman A. Goddard, naval reserve, San Diego, in a monoplane with Lieut. K. C. Hawkins, reserve, San Diego, as navigator.

Capt. William H. Erwin, Dallas, Tex., in a monoplane with his wife, Mrs. Connie Erwin, as a passenger.

Capt. Arthur V. Rogers, Los Angeles, in a monoplane, with Leland A. Bryant, Los Angeles, navigator.

Bennett Griffin, Oklahoma City, in a monoplane, with Al Henley, Bartlesville, Okla., as navigator.

Capt. James L. Giffin, Long Beach, in a triplane, with Theodore S. Lundgren, Los Angeles, as navigator.

Frank L. Clark, Los Angeles, in a

(Continued on Page 2, Column 4)

WALL STREET RIDES STORM

Near-Slump of Prices Caused by President's Announcement Quickly Checked

NEW YORK, Aug. 3. (AP)—The stock market today successfully rode out the storm of selling which arose in the wake of President Coolidge's unexpected announcement that he did not choose to be a candidate in 1928. Prices of leading issues crashed 3 to 16 points in the first few minutes of trading, when the lowest prices of the day were recorded, but the losses were substantially cut in half or wiped out altogether.

Early selling came principally from two sources—from bear traders who had been seeking an excuse to attack the market in the belief that the recent rapid advance to record high levels had weakened its technical position, and from professional operators who have been sponsoring the bull movement and desired to cash in part of their paper profits pending a more complete diagnosis of the market's reaction to the Coolidge announcement. Contrary to expectations in some quarters, there was no extensive forced liquidation by small speculators and investors, tending to confirm the view that it has been a "rich man's market."

Powerful financial support was quickly supplied after the opening break. The quickness and decisiveness of the recovery led to extensive short covering and stimulated a resumption of pool operations which carried more than a score of rails and specialties to record high levels. Trading was in unusually heavy volume, the day's sales running above 2,750,000 shares.

MARQUIS LANSDOWNE LEAVES $5,220,000

LONDON, Aug. 3 (Exclusive)—Marquis Lansdowne, former Foreign Minister, Governor-General of Canada and Viceroy of India, left property valued at more than $5,220,000, according to an announcement today. He died in June. His famous residence in Berkeley Square, which is occupied by Gordon Selfridge on long leases, is left to his son, the present Marquis.

Will Rogers Remarks:

BEVERLY HILLS, Aug. 3.—[To the Editor of The Times:] I think Mr. Coolidge's statement is one of the best worded acceptances of a nomination ever uttered by a candidate. He spent a long time in the dictionary looking for that word choose instead of "I will not." It doesn't take much political knowledge to know that a man can get more votes running on the people's request, than he can running on his own request. Mr. Coolidge is the shrewdest politician that ever drew government salary.

Yours,
WILL ROGERS.

THE DAY'S NEWS SUMMED UP

REMEMBER THIS

A dictatorship is the ideal form of government for people who had rather say, "Yes, sir" than to think.

All the News All the Time
LARGEST HOME-DELIVERED CIRCULATION
LARGEST ADVERTISING VOLUME

Los Angeles Times

In Three Parts—44 Pages
PART I—TELEGRAPH SHEET—22 PAGES

Equal Rights
Liberty Under the Law

True Industrial Freedom

Vol. XLVII. WEDNESDAY MORNING, MARCH 14, 1928. C DAILY, FIVE CENTS SUNDAY, TEN CENTS

200 DEAD, 300 MISSING, $7,000,000 LOSS IN ST. FRANCIS DAM DISASTER

Plane Views Give Idea of Magnitude of Catastrophe

Left—Air view of the wrecked St. Francis Dam at a point just below the dam. Right—Santa Paula, as seen from the air. Directly in the path of the raging torrents, portions of the city were inundated. [Photographs taken by Harry C. Anderson, Times staff photographer.]

THOUSANDS RUSH TO AID IN WORK OF RESCUE AND RELIEF

Red Cross Directs Gigantic Task of Succor in Devastated Area; Water Board Appropriates $25,000; Food and Shelter Needed Immediately

"TIMES" FLOOD RELIEF FUND

The Times will receive, acknowledge by publication and turn over to the proper authorities any contributions sent in care of this paper for the relief of the flood victims of the San Francisquito disaster. The Times announces a contribution of $1000 of its own to start this fund. The need for quick relief is very urgent and all able to do so are urged to subscribe at once and in as large sums as possible. All checks sent to The Times should be made payable to The Times Flood Relief Fund. Receipt is acknowledged of a check for $500 from Anita M. Baldwin. A telegram from Robert J. Foster at Louisville, Ky., states that $100 is being telegraphed by him to this paper for the fund.

Southern California mobilized yesterday on a wide-spreading front for the victims of the St. Francis Dam disaster. Shelter and food for homeless survivors are badly needed. Red Cross chapters of Los Angeles county, and of Ventura and Kern counties, responding quickly to the cry for help, last night had made much headway in the establishment of temporary housing for the hundreds whose homes had been destroyed and in the opening of kitchens for hungry survivors as well as for the hundreds of men employed in rescue work. The Salvation Army also was on hand aiding in the humanitarian work.

Men plowed through mud and debris as rescue work went on in the devastated area. Where once bloomed flowering trees and other vegetation, bodies of those trapped in the rushing wall of water lay exposed on slimy banks. Group here and there struggled through lanes blocked by clogging timbers, uprooted trees and mud-caked debris, pushing and pulling portable camp kitchens in an effort to get warm food to the sufferers, many of whom were stranded and shivering on small shoals in the middle of turbulent streams.

The work of the rescuers was disheartening. Many bodies were buried underneath tightly packed mud. Victims were trapped while they slept, clad only in night clothes. Hurled along on the twisting flood, their bodies were buffeted about making identification in many cases almost impossible. Dance halls, drug stores and almost every available place where rescue work could be conducted were commandeered. First-aid stations and morgues were established in all central points.

RED CROSS ON JOB

Before dawn the local committee of the Red Cross had established headquarters at Newhall where first aid and nursing service from the Los Angeles corps reported for duty. A hundred-bed hospital completely equipped to care for patients was loaded on trucks and reached the Newhall station early yesterday morning.

The Board of Water and Power Commissioners answered the call of the stricken people by appropriating $25,000 for relief work among the sufferers of the flood. The resolution was transmitted to the City Council and approved.

More than 300 members of the Los Angeles Police Department were dispatched by Chief Davis to the areas most seriously affected. All of these men were reported to have reached their destination before noon yesterday. Special details were rushed in fast cars to the stricken country about Saugus and Piru. Squads were deployed down the Santa Clara River co-operating with hundreds of county and State officials and other volunteers.

Members of the American Legion and details of police officers were rushed from Bakersfield to the Saugus district.

Linemen working on the restoration of wires between Saugus and Santa Barbara worked at a frenzied pace and completed their jobs early yesterday morning so that they could volunteer for relief work. More than 500 men left for different parts of the flooded sections to assist Red Cross nurses and doctors in rescue work.

Citizens of Oxnard and Fillmore reported late yesterday afternoon that immediate Red Cross aid is not needed in their districts

(Continued on Page 2, Column 7)

FLOOD AREA IN CONTROL

Army of Deputies Rule Region

Health Crews Working to Prevent Epidemic of Typhoid Fever

Ridge Route Traffic Turned Back at Burbank and North Hollywood

Every available man from the Los Angeles County Sheriff's office, from the County Health Department and from the motorcycle divisions of both Los Angeles and Kern counties and from the State Motor Patrol was dispatched to the scene of the flood during early morning hours yesterday and by nightfall the work of maintaining traffic control and of imposing the stringent sanitary measures deemed necessary was going smoothly but with energy.

Typhoid and contagions often present after flood disasters were being guarded against by the use of antityphoid serum and the enforcement of pure drinking water regulations.

The entire area around the Santa Clara Valley was under semimilitary control by deputy sheriffs, aided by volunteer citizens and members of the American Legion, and no one not included in the great

(Continued on Page 5, Column 3)

PARTIAL LIST OF PERSONS DEAD, INJURED AND MISSING IN FLOOD

The following is a partial and best obtainable list of identified dead, unidentified dead, missing and injured in the St. Francis Dam break.

As well as the below listed persons the authorities are searching for hundreds of missing men, women and children in San Francisquito Canyon, Fillmore, Saugus region, Piru, Ventura, Santa Paula, Castaic, Oberg, Camulos and other sections.

According to figures from improvised morgues in the stricken area and from the Sheriff's office and police department approximately 200 bodies of men, women and children have been recovered of which in the neighborhood of seventy-five have been identified.

THE DEAD

Identified dead at morgue at Newhall:

Earl Pike.
W. Y. Weinland.
Marion Casper.
Mrs. Ruth Hoppe.
Mrs. Ray Rising.
Mrs. Nell Hanson.
Kenneth Coe.
John Parker.
Dick Pike.
C. J. Mathews, 2 years of age.
Mrs. H. E. Holt.
Sol J. Byrd.
Roland Errarchuo, 14 months.
Three children of Mrs. Ray Rising.
Thelma Mathews.
Vida Mathews.
Mrs. C. J. Mathews.
Eddie Price.
Griffith Hughes.
Rosario Ruiz.
Mrs. Rosie Errarchuo.
Will W. Nelson, Jr.
Mrs. Nora Coe.
Home Coe.
Eugene Frazier.
Mrs. Rita Kennedy.
May Mathis, 6.
Eugene Kennedy, infant.
Ethel Cochrane.
Francis Garcia.
Tootsie Garcia.
M. J. Garcia.
Joy Hughes.
Alberta Isaac.
Maxie Brosky.
George Mann.
Mrs. Louise Burns.
Margaret Ely.

Identified dead in morgue at Piru:

Edward Locke.

Identified dead in morgue at Fillmore:

Clinton Anderson, foreman, Edison Company.
Keith Anderson.
Olvin Gureber.
H. Peterson.
Nick Nondlock.
George Bersolo.
Mrs. Ethel Boardman.
Mrs. .... Savala.
Mrs. .... Koffer.
Mrs. J. Carrillo.
Eight children of Mrs. J. Carrillo.
M. Miyachi, Japanese.
Mrs. .... Tatley.
Two girls and two boys, children of Charles Rogers.
Oscar Doty.
John Kingston.

Of the above dead, six were employed by the Edison company in a camp near Piru with 170 other men. Eighty of them have been accounted for.

IDENTIFIED DEAD IN MORGUE AT SANTA PAULA:

Mrs. S. A. Whitehead.
L. G. Robertson.
Mattilda Samaniego.

IDENTIFIED DEAD IN MORGUE AT MOORPARK

Elizabeth Torres.
Gordon Cummings.
Mrs. Gordon Cummings.
Bruce Lee.
Mrs. Ida Kelly.
Phillis Kelly, 7.
Delores Kelly, 4.
Mrs. D. Stevens.
Earl Cowden.
Mrs. G. R. Bordman.

IDENTIFIED DEAD IN MORGUE AT OXNARD:

Jeff Johnson.

UNIDENTIFIED DEAD

Newhall, six.
Fillmore, thirty.
Santa Paula, forty-seven.
Moorpark, nine.
Ventura, seven.

UNACCOUNTED FOR

In and around Santa Paula—One hundred and fifty.

KNOWN INJURED

Selma McCauley, Fillmore. She is in Santa Paula Hospital, not expected to recover from being battered by debris and due to exposure.

C. H. Hunick.
Bernard Ramos.
Miguel Ruiz.
Cecille Frazer.
Mrs. Lena Fraser.
Charles D. Fraser.
L. R. Ruiz.
Lester Johnson.
Louis Heptins.
John Peiffer.
Curtis Randall.
Albert Davis.
Mrs. Mary Nichols.
Chester Smith.
Mrs. A. L. Garcia.
Benjamin Dornaleche.
Van Dornaleche.
Tenase Ramos.
Mrs. F. Fraser.
L. M. Steenblock, Galt, Iowa.
Everett Goold, Victor, Colo.
L. F. Bennett, Fresno.
"Mazu" Anderson, no address.
H. A. Whitaker, Los Angeles.
E. Gilroy, San Francisco.
William Davis, Los Angeles.
B. G. Barworth, Los Angeles.
Albert M. Hill, Tony, Wyo.
Samuel Ucurso, Visalia, Cal.
Russell Roth, Bakersfield.
J. P. Toomey, Los Angeles.
J. R. Duke, no address.
G. E. Cameron, no address.
C. R. Kerr, Lindsay, Cal.
Peter Bozette, Los Angeles.
Herbert Anthony, Exeter, Cal. (broken right leg.)
Roy D. Purdy, Sawtelle, Cal.
R. A. Newell, Bakersfield, Cal.
Chris H. Kline, Tulare, Cal.
S. J. Hurst, Maryland.
G. E. Kanawayer, Fresno.
Oliver Crocker, Kansas City.
W. B. Smith, Picayune, Miss.

C. H. Hanick, A. Ramus, Miguel Ruiz, Bell Frazier, L. R. Ruiz, James J. Erracchuo, Chester Johnson, Louis Hepkins, John Peiffer, Curtis Randall, Albert David, Mary Nichols, Chester Smith, Mrs. A. L. Garcia, Ben Dernaleche, George McIntyre, Oscar Fountain and Charles Frazier. All went to their own homes or the residence of friends.

THE SHERIFF'S OFFICE LAST NIGHT POSTED THE FOLLOW-

(Continued on Page 2, Column 6)

The index to today's issue of "The Times" will be found on Page 5, this part.

SCORES MORE THOUGHT BURIED IN DEBRIS OF WILD WATERS

Darkness Halts Rescue as Crews Sight Other Bodies; Hundreds of Homes Crushed by Fatal Torrent and Many Bridges Washed Away

Approximately 200 persons dead, 300 others unaccounted for, and property damage estimated at $7,000,000, according to the latest available figures, is the toll of the disaster following collapse of the St. Francis Dam Monday night which released an avalanche of water upon the sleeping residents of San Francisquito Canyon and the Santa Clara River Valley and left death and destruction in its wake.

Of those listed among the missing, officials engaged in rescue work believe that many will be found safe. Because of the confusion created by the establishment of morgues at widely separated places it is believed that duplications in the compilation of the number of unidentified dead has taken place.

That the death toll will continue to grow higher, however, is the conclusion of rescue crews who stopped work last night because of darkness and the inaccessibility of many canyons and crevices were other bodies are believed to be lodged.

Many bodies, which could not be taken out last night, were sighted by searchers and will be removed this morning.

FEAR MANY MORE ARE DEAD

Officials in charge of the rescue and body recovering work, last night estimated that probably fifty additional victims at least will be found today.

Property damage throughout the area laid waste by the disaster is estimated at $7,000,000, which is admittedly only a rough guess and it will be several days before an accurate survey can be made.

The magnitude of the death-dealing torrent that plunged entire families to their deaths and swept all their possessions away was emphasized in the estimated figures on the number of dwellis emphasized in the estimated figures on the number of dwellings destroyed.

Approximately 400 houses located in the San Francisquito Canyon in the sixteen-mile gorge between Piru and the dam site, are wiped out.

Not a standing timber is left as a marker to indicate some once prosperous little farms that dotted the valley.

HOMES NOW MASS OF WRECKAGE

Three hundred houses at Santa Paula, in the southern section of the town, were caught in the flood and swept into a mass of wrecked and tangled timbers as the wall of water rushed from the dam down through the Santa Clara River bed. Thirty or forty houses were wrecked at Fillmore and fifteen at Piru, nine miles south of there.

All bridges excepting the State highway bridge at Montalvo and the Saticoy bridge were wiped out.

The Los Angeles Bureau of Power and Light suffered the heaviest single loss in the disaster in the St. Francis Dam and power plant No. 2, located at the foot of the giant basin. The city's loss will approximate $3,000,000.

The balance of the damage is in the homes and ranches of the San Francisquito Valley and the valley of the Santa Clara River, to which the downrushing flood was diverted near Castaic, in public utility lines destroyed, highways and bridges washed out and live stock drowned.

The loss in the Santa Clara Valley is estimated at more than $3,000,000. A mile of paved highway between Piru and Castaic is washed out. Two of the largest ranches in that district, owned by T. M. Storke, publisher of the Santa Barbara Daily News, and Gwyn Thurmond, were swept by water.

Immense pieces of the dam carried along by the force of the water, were found half a mile and more downstream, according to Lieut. Earl H. Robinson of the National Guard Aero Corps, who made an air survey of San Francisquito Canyon yesterday. Lieut. Robinson reported that the pumping stations and ranch houses in the path of the flood seem to be wiped out.

The collapse of the dam still is a mystery to the engineers of the Water Bureau who constructed it, and an investigation has been launched to attempt to fix the cause of the tragedy.

William Mulholland, chief engineer of the Water Bureau, ar-

(Continued on Page 2, Column 1)

ENGINEERS FIX BLAME

Dam Break Held Due to Fault

Mountain on West Side Grew Weak and Caused Flood, Mulholland Says

Others State Structure Was Last Word in Project of Gravity Type

The Board of Water and Power Commissioners yesterday started an investigation into the cause of the collapse of the St. Francis Dam and late in the afternoon Chief Engineer Mulholland and Assistant Chief Engineer Van Norman of the water department returned from an all-day visit to the dam and reported to the board. These engineers said the direct, immediate cause of the collapse was the giving way of the mountain on the west side of the canyon.

Due to causes unknown, possibly a fault in the mountain structure or to rains, the mountain on the west side of the dam had become weakened. The west side of the dam was the first to go, and it caused the anchorage of the dam on that side to give way. This was not a part of the dam proper, but a 1500-foot dike or secondary dam which acted as an abutment or anchorage for the main central arch of the dam, which still stands. As the west-side dike gave way, water poured through into the canyon.

On his return from his trip to the scene of the disaster, Chief Engineer Mulholland of the Municipal Water Department issued the following statement:

"I would not venture at this time to express a positive opinion as to the cause of the St. Francis Dam disaster.

"Mr. Van Norman and I arrived

(Continued on Page 6, Column 4)

All the News All the Time
LARGEST HOME-DELIVERED CIRCULATION
LARGEST ADVERTISING VOLUME

MADISON 2345
The Times Telephone Number
Connecting All Departments

Los Angeles Times

EQUAL RIGHTS
LIBERTY UNDER THE LAW
TRUE INDUSTRIAL FREEDOM

In Two Parts — 40 Pages
PART I—TELEGRAPH SHEET—20 PAGES

MADISON 2345
The Times Telephone Number
Connecting All Departments

Vol. XLVIII. WEDNESDAY MORNING, OCTOBER 30, 1929. C DAILY, FIVE CENTS

SCRAP WON BY WALKER

Hudkins Loses to Champ

Title-holder Retains Crown by Decisive Victory in Wrigley Field Bout

Crowd of 21,370 Fans Sees Monarch Earn Verdict from Challenger

BY PAUL LOWRY

The Bulldog chewed the Wildcat to pieces in a fight that was swift and one-sided, and thoroughly demonstrated his right to be called middleweight champion of the world.

Trained to the pink, Mickey Walker not only retained his title but repulsed the challenge of Ace Hudkins as only a real champion could repel it.

Walker was the real Walker last night at Wrigley Field and a crowd of 21,370 persons who paid $150,265 for the privilege saw him handle the Wildcat as no other man has handled this rip-tearing, savage flailer who fought his way up the ladder from the ranks of the newsies.

But for the second time in his career Hudkins has now been turned back by the Bulldog of Rumson, N. J. There was some question about the decision the champion gained over the Wildcat at Chicago a year ago last June—but there was none last night.

LOSES BUT ONE ROUND

Walker won every round but one. And the session the title-holder failed to win was even—the eighth. Twice Walker staggered Hudkins with terrific lefts and rights to the head, and just before the last bell the Wildcat, exhausted from his own efforts and the punishment the champion had afforded, nearly fell as he missed a blow to the face.

Nobody but Hudkins, with the heart of a lion, would have survived Walker's punishing blows and retained his feet, but upright he stayed, and each time came back with rallies of his own.

"Come on and fight, come on," was his snarl, as badly hurt he surged forward with lowered head and invited the champion to slug it out with him.

GENERAL THROUGHOUT

But Walker, cool and collected, was the general of that bout in the vast confines of the ball park, and he fought it out along his own carefully planned lines.

He led when he wanted to. He made the Wildcat force the fighting when it pleased him. He took the play away from the Wildcat on a notion.

Hudkins's usual boring-in tactics were of no avail against the champion. He leaped in as he has of old against the Colimas, the Bakers, the

(Cont'd on Page 11, Part II, Col. 8)

Will Rogers Remarks:

BEVERLY HILLS, Oct. 29. [To the Editor of The Times:] What's the matter with this for a laugh? When the stock market goes down Mr. Morgan, Lamont, Charley Mitchell and Mr. George Baker hold a meeting and let everybody see 'em in this huddle. Then the market perks up.

I was just thinking what a great idea it would be if we could just get these boys to room together for six months. There is no telling to what heights the market might go.

Just think what a calamity if these forgot where they were to meet some day to inspire confidence.

Yours,
WILL ROGERS.

LAKE STORM SINKS SHIP

Twelve Perish, Sixty Saved

Steamer Wisconsin Founders Due to Gales in Second Tragedy of Week

Radio Reports Reveal Battle Against Rising Water as It Floods Engines

By a "Times" Staff Representative

CHICAGO, Oct. 29. (Exclusive)—Twelve more persons perished on Lake Michigan today when the lake, stirred by a gale, reached out for the second time within a week in a lashing fury that dragged to the bottom the steamship Wisconsin, one of the largest of the Goodrich Transit Company's fleet, a few miles off Kenosha, Wis.

The loss of the Wisconsin followed exactly seven days the sinking of the Grand Trunk Railway's giant car ferry, Milwaukee, with fifty-two persons aboard.

A valiant captain gone down with his ship in a fifty-mile gale, eight others of the crew drowned and three more missing and given up for dead, sixty saved in wild night rescues—thus begins the obituary of the ill-fated Wisconsin.

ENGINES FLOODED

Hours of pumping against an ever-rising flood in the rocking, plunging hold of the leaking ship until the fires were quenched, the en-

(Continued on Page 2, Column 5)

PILOT FOILS ICY STORM

Airplane Arrives in Albuquerque

Snowfall Forces It Down on Mesa in New Mexico, Causing Day's Delay

Five Men Stay in Old House Overnight, Then Take Off; Aviator Wins Praise

ALBUQUERQUE, Oct. 29. (Exclusive)—Lost for more than twenty-four hours while marooned on a bleak New Mexico mesa, Western Air Express trimotored liner No. 113 escaped today from the snow-swept stretch where it was forced down Monday and landed at Albuquerque with its crew of three and two men passengers chilled, but safe.

Caught in a blinding swirl of snow Monday at 10:15 a.m. the plane was forced down near Trechado, seventy-five miles southeast of Gallup, N. M. The crew and passengers found refuge in an abandoned ranch house.

The passengers were Dr. A. W Ward of San Francisco and W. E Merz of Mt. Vernon, N. Y. The crew is composed of James E. Doles, chief pilot, of Los Angeles; Allen C. Barrie, co-pilot, of Burbank, and R. L. Britton, steward, of Los Angeles.

FIRE BUILT IN HOUSE

Immediately after landing the five men discovered they were without food or water, but they found shelter in the abandoned ranch house, where a fire was built and they spent the night as comfortably as they could while the storm howled outside.

"We left Holbrook, flying east," Doles said, "and were about one hour out when we had to dodge a storm. I nosed her down toward St. Johns. Suddenly the storm seemed to break over us all at once, and a landing became a necessity.

"I found a small spot, and it looked safe, so I got down there as snappily as possible. I thought the weather would clear later in the afternoon, but it got worse.

"During the afternoon a woman, who had seen us land, called and said we could find a house a mile or so away. The weather was not clearing as we expected, so we decided to dig in and all moved over to the house.

"I built a big fire, and we tried to be as comfortable as possible, but we nearly froze. The storm, meanwhile, was increasing. We had nothing to eat or drink. The light lunches all had been consumed and the water bottles emptied.

"About 1:30 o'clock this afternoon I saw a chance to get away and we took it. It started to snow just as we took off."

MOTORS ALL RIGHT

Doles said that motor trouble did not figure in the forced landing at all, the wretched weather alone being responsible.

Dr. Ward praised Doles's ability as pilot, and gave him the credit of bringing the passengers, crew and ship through safely.

"The storm we encountered was terrific," Dr. Ward said. "It just smothered us all at once. Doles did the right thing; nothing could have passed through it. He saw a place to land and his work was masterful as he put the big ship down in that rough, isolated country.

"The woman who came over to see if we were all right said her name was Bessie Mason. She directed us to the house, and when it became apparent that the storm wasn't going to break, we went there for the night.

"The snow was about a foot deep this morning, and my appetite was deeper than that."

PILOT PRAISED

As Dr. Ward turned to a substantial meal spread before him, his fellow-passenger, Mr. Merz, took up the conversation in a complimentary vein. He is a veteran air-traveler, and he expressed great confidence in Doles's flying technique.

"We had a good time last night sitting before that fire kidding each other about what might have been. It is a real experience," he said.

When the trimotored ship landed at the Western Air Express field here it brought to an abrupt halt a search in snow-filled skies almost as widespread as that of a few weeks ago for the ill-fated T.A.T. liner City of San Francisco, which crashed on Mt. Taylor with a loss of eight lives.

Some apprehension was felt for a while for Pilot Lamar Nelson, one of the searching flyers, but after battling with the weather for several hours around Flagstaff and San Francisco Peaks, he landed at Williams, according to a telegram received here.

MENINGITIS KILLS TWELVE

MEXICO CITY, Oct. 29. (AP)—The Health Department has rushed doctors and nurses to the town of Jiquilpan, Michoacan, where twelve persons are reported to have died from cerebral-spinal meningitis.

He's Strong for "Suspending" Chiefs!

MUSICIANS' UNION SHOWS EVILS OF CLOSED SHOP

Complete and Selfish Control of Field Redounds to Disadvantage of Public and Public Movements

(This is the thirtieth of a series of articles on the Los Angeles open-shop war. Others will follow daily.)

For reasons which are not far to seek, the closed shop enjoys its greatest strength and influence in Los Angeles in the professional amusement field of music and the stage. This is partly because the force of local public sentiment for the open shop has never fully been brought to bear on the situation, the vocations involved not being integral parts of the city's industrial life, but chiefly because the great majority of professional performers come here from the closely unionized amusement centers of the East. Where, as in the case of motion pictures, an amusement industry has grown up in the open-shop atmosphere, the opposite is true, as will appear in a later article.

The history of the local musicians' union, the Musicians' Mutual Protective Association, is a rather one-sided one and is of interest chiefly as illustrating the disadvantages to the public of a thoroughly closed shop in any line of activity. The professional musicians here are very nearly 100 per cent unionized and, with a few notable exceptions, the union membership comprises the ablest talent. There have been a few nonunion commercial bands and orchestras, but their way has been made difficult by every device known to unionist ingenuity and many of them have ultimately been forced out of existence or into the union.

It is not to be assumed that the rank and file of unionized musicians share in or even sympathize with the arrogant methods of their union's officials. On the contrary there are many instances in which the players themselves would have been glad to defy union orders but for the fact that the organization literally controls their bread and butter.

One of the first examples to come to public notice of the peculiar characteristics of this union's officials was in 1913 when the local Shriners put on a show to raise money for charity. The Shrine Band had a very essential and important part in the program. At the last moment and too late to make any other arrangements, the union forbade the thirty union members of the band to participate, calling them out, in fact, just as the parade was forming. No reason was

(Continued on Page 10, Column 1)

PREMATURE EXPLOSION KILLS THREE

Victims Were Union Men Believed Making Bomb to Wreck Theater

HOT SPRINGS (Ark.) Oct. 29. (Exclusive)—Three men, members of the International Alliance of Theatrical Stage Employees Union were killed tonight by the premature explosion of nitroglycerine with which the police believe they intended to wreck the Princess Theater here. There has been a wage dispute between the owners of the theater and its union employees for several weeks.

The victims of the explosion are: Roy V. Pugh, 45 years of age, W. W. Sickel, 45, and Spencer Bryant, 38, a union painter and decorator. Pugh held membership in the Tulsa local of the union and Sickel was a member of the Seminole local. Both, however, were said to be in the employ of the Orpheum Theater at Tulsa, Pugh as stage manager and Sickel as electrician. Bryant, it is said, was a former union motion-picture operator.

From a letter found in Pugh's coat the police learned that it was Bryant who had written for Pugh and Sickel to come to Hot Springs.

DALADIER GIVES UP GHOST

French Socialist Fails to Organize Government; Briand or Tardieu to Get Post

[Copyright, 1929, by the Chicago Tribune.]

PARIS, Oct. 30. (Exclusive)—Smacked in the face by the Socialists, whose national council, convoked from the four corners of France, today voted 1590 to 1450 against participating in any "bourgeois" government, Edouard Daladier, leader of the more conservative Radical Socialist party, gave up the ghost early this morning. After a call on President Doumergue to inform him of his difficulties in forming a radical government, he announced he had definitely given up the task of forming a ministry.

The way now therefore seems to be open for the re-establishment of Raymond Poincare's old concentration Cabinet, with either former Premier Briand or Andre Tardieu as Premier and Henry Cheron back in his old job as Finance Minister.

The situation seems to be in the hands of M. Briand and he either can form a ministry himself or let M. Tardieu or some other Center leader take the responsibility of presiding over the Cabinet, while he retains his old post in the Foreign Office.

The vote of the Socialists against participation in a bourgeoise government was a hard blow to M. Daladier and his Radical Socialist colleagues, who had promised the Reds a revolutionary program if they took part in the government, which was to lower the taxes of the poor, raise the taxes of the rich, cut down armament expenditures, raise the expenditures for social welfare and release all Red political prisoners.

MAGNATE'S FALL HELD SUSPICIOUS

Death Plunge of Union Tobacco Head Coincident With Stock's Drop

NEW YORK, Oct. 29. (Exclusive) Albert Schneider, 60-year-old president of the Union Tobacco Company, died today in a six-story plunge from his eleventh-floor apartment in the Hotel Beverly. His friends and hotel officials insisted his death was accidental. If such, police pointed out, it was strangely coincident with an amazing depreciation in the quoted value of the stocks in the large tobacco companies he heads.

Webster-Eisenlohr, Inc., stock on the New York Stock Exchange, selling at a high for the year of more than $133 some months ago and at $68 a week ago, hit a bottom of $4 yesterday and again today. The company is a $12,500,000 corporation of the Schulte chain. Union Tobacco stock, which sold up $20 a share earlier in the year, was down to around $1 a share on the curb today.

Yet, according to Louis Morrell, a Beverly Hotel waiter, Schneider was leaning out a window of the apartment into which he moved alone last February trying to repair a radio aerial when the waiter entered with his breakfast this morning.

Morrell told investigators he saw Schneider lose his balance and fall outward. Dropping the tray, the waiter asserts he reached the window in time to seize Schneider's left foot. Struggling briefly to drag the tobacco magnate back through the window, Morrell's hold was broken and Schneider fell to the street below, dying instantly.

CHICAGO MAN SHOOTS SELF IN KANSAS CITY

KANSAS CITY, Oct. 29. (AP)—Believed a victim of the falling market, John Schwitzgebel, said to be a representative of Chicago Lloyds, shot himself here today in his room at the Kansas City Club. His condition is critical.

Charles Schwitzgebel, a brother, and a department head of the Commerce Trust Company, said he had no explanation unless the insurance man "had been caught in the market."

Brakeman Dies in Rail Collision

ROSEVILLE, Oct. 29. (AP)—Fred Frith, a Southern Pacific brakeman, was killed and two other trainmen, Conductor E. E. Larison and Switchman Max Langston, were injured today when a rolling caboose collided with a switch engine in the yards here.

Frith was thrown from the rear platform and the caboose passed over his body. Larison's arms were fractured and Langston received severe lacerations and bruises.

WILBUR DISAPPROVES RIO GRANDE COMPACT

WASHINGTON, Oct. 29. (AP)—The Interior Department today disapproved the proposed Rio Grande River compact being considered by the Senate Irrigation Committee. Secretary Wilbur notified the committee his department cannot sanction it because the commission which formed the compact failed to apportion the Rio Grande waters among Colorado, New Mexico and Texas, the States party to the proposal.

STOCKS DIVE AMID FRENZY IN 16,410,000-SHARE DAY

Combined Financial Giants Finally Halt Plunge Toward Chaos as Bankers Ease Up on Credit

MANY BILLIONS GO IN LIMBO

NEW YORK, Oct. 29. (Exclusive)—The effects of Wall street's October bear market is shown by valuation tables prepared tonight which place the decline in the market value of 240 representative issues on the New York Stock Exchange at $15,894,818,894 during the period from the 1st inst. to today's close.

Since there are 1279 issues listed on the New York Stock Exchange, the total depreciation for the month may be placed conservatively at several times the loss for the 240 issues.

NEW YORK, Oct. 29. (Exclusive)—An incredible stock market tumbled toward chaos today despite heroic measures adopted by the nation's greatest bankers.

Wall street throbbed with excitement all day and tonight the men who guide its destiny are wondering whether they have won a hard-fought victory in their back-to-the-wall battle to stem the unprecedented and frenzied liquidation pouring in from the four corners of the country.

Selling of stocks broke all previous records, reaching 16,410,030 shares at the close. Losses of 10, 20, 30 points or more were piled on top of the staggering breaks of yesterday, threatening the credit structure of the country. There was no quarter. The wolves ranged through Wall street.

It was a day of tremendous activity with climaxes punctuating every hour. Only an erratic rally in the last hour saved the market from utter chaos. It was then the bankers and investment buyers dipped into a grab bag filled with hornets and sought furiously to rally prices. They succeeded after a fashion, but no one, as yet, knows the full temper of this history-making market.

TREMENDOUS PLUNGE

Last Thursday's 12,894,600-share record was passed in a swirling cloud of sell orders soon after midday as the clogged tickers clattered on into a new mathematical world. Before the rally prices were driven down recklessly as much as $45 a share as blocks of 50,000 of blue chips stocks came crashing into the market.

A few minutes before the close a vicious attack was launched on United States Steel to feel the temper of the market. Steel gave way to a low for the day, but true to its name failed to crack and snapped back in the last minute. Nevertheless this bellwether of the market suffered a $12 loss, carrying it into new low territory.

Stout resistance met the traders in other quarters as bullish news seeped into the turbulent market. United States Steel declared a $1 extra dividend. American Can announced a similar extra dividend.

SENTIMENT CHANGES

Sentiment changed suddenly on the floor and there was a wave of optimistic feeling among the brokers. Old traders "felt it in their bones" the worst was over. Heavy buying for cash made its appearance, and although unexplained, helped to restore confidence. Brokers were declaring that frenzied selling had run itself out. Stocks rose easily for a time, but fluctuations at the close were still highly erratic and nervous. Another day should tell the story.

The street does not expect to recover from such a devastating setback in a hurry. Bankers in San Francisco, following the lead of New York, formed a pool to support stocks. Reports from Central States cities indicate that bankers are taking steps to shut off some of the liquidation from the New York market.

The optimists saw hope in the catch-as-catch-can rally in the afternoon. Yesterday there was no rally. When a stock tumbled it stayed down. Today when a stock hit what should be bottom somebody was likely to pounce on it. There still are bank accounts in New York and so long as there are cashiers' checks there will be bargain hunters.

PETS SLAPPED DOWN

The leaders were hit on the belt today and the rich man's pets took a wallop along with the stocks the little trader "used to own." American Can slid down $16, American Foreign Power shed $22.50, Johns-Manville took it on the chin for $17. Sears, Roebuck was hit for $16.25.

There were many others in the same company.

Among the more volatile stocks

(Continued on Page 2, Column 2)

AIRSHIPS TO DOCK HERE

Sea Line Building Plans Given

Los Angeles and Akron Will be Sites for Gigantic Zeppelin Hangars

Mooring Masts to be Set Up in Hawaiian Islands and Philippines

AKRON (O.) Oct. 29. (AP)—A gigantic construction program of Zeppelins, hangars and mooring masts for the newly formed Pacific Zeppelin Transport Company was announced today by Paul W. Litchfield, Akron rubber magnate and chairman of the board.

Litchfield said the construction program will be started as quickly as possible with the intent of beginning Zeppelin passenger and express service between the Pacific Coast and Hawaii and the Philippines by 1932. He added that by that time "we probably will be constructing a hangar on the Atlantic Coast" for the first trans-Atlantic dirigible transport line.

HANGARS TO BE BUILT

For the Pacific service about $15,000,000 will be spent to construct two dirigibles of 600,000 cubic feet helium gas capacity, an enormous hangar at Akron, a similar hangar at Los Angeles, and mooring masts in Hawaii and the Philippines. The Goodyear-Zeppelin Corporation of Akron will build the dirigibles and assemble them in the projected Los Angeles hangar.

The same company now is building two Zeppelins for the United States Navy, which will be the largest dirigibles in the world. The passenger Zeppelins will carry eighty passengers and ten tons of express or similar cargo.

Announcement of the Pacific Zeppelin Transport Company's building program came within forty-eight hours after the organization of the firm.

Stock of the company was taken equally by the Goodyear organization, the National City Bank of New York and the banking houses of Grayson M. P. Murphy Company and Lehman Brothers of the same city.

WILL NOT COMPETE

"The Pacific airship line will not be a competitor of any other air, land or water transportation company, but rather will serve as an ally to all such American organiza-

(Continued on Page 2, Column 6)

CRASH MAROONS TOURISTS

Hundreds of Americans in Paris Ruined by Stock Debacle Seek Aid to Return Home

(Copyright, 1929, by the Chicago Tribune)

PARIS, Oct. 29. (Exclusive)—Panic scenes resembling those of the first days of the World War in August, 1914, were being re-enacted here today with hundreds of suddenly impoverished Americans ruined by the series of Wall-street market crashes seeking financial aid and steamship accommodations home.

Various brokerage offices maintaining cable stock quotations from New York were jammed with crowds of men and women helplessly watching the ticker whittling away the fortunes they had amassed during the upward drive of the market in the last couple of years.

Owing to the difference in time the brokerage offices here are open from 3 p.m. to 8 p.m., and many customers and speculators dash back in evening clothes and women in decollette gowns to get a last glimpse of the quotation board and learn they have sunk another step toward poverty.

BANKS CAUTIOUS

Branches of American banks and travel agencies have been besieged by tourists seeking to cash checks, drafts, I. O. U.'s, or anything to raise money, and all have been instructed to be extremely cautious about advancing funds and generally they insist on cabling banks in the United States for assurances that the checks are good before passing over the money.

Many of the wealthy class of visitors are frantically trying to sell valuables which they purchased here a few weeks ago, when they were still comparatively rich, and jewelers declare that more than half of their recent customers are desperately trying to return the gems purchased before the crash for half what they paid for them.

Classified advertisements in newspapers contain offers from formerly rich American women offering to sacrifice robes, coats and even lin-

(Continued on Page 2, Column 6)

THE DAY'S NEWS SUMMED UP

FEATURES. Radio, Page 7, Part II; Women's Page, Clubs and Society, Page 6, Part II; Markets and Financial, Pages 14 to 19, Part I; Oil News, Page 20, Part I; Pictures, Page 8, Part I; Comics, Page 12, Part I.

NEWS OF SOUTHERN COUNTIES. Page 13, Part I.

NEWS IN SPANISH. Page 10, Part I.

SHIPPING NEWS. Page 6, Part I.

SPORTS. Mickey Walker retains world's title by defeating Ace Hudkins in Wrigley Field fight. Page 11, Part II.

Lom certain to be dangerous against Trojans at Coliseum Saturday. Page 11, Part II.

Coach Knute Rockne denies report that he will be forced to quit job for balance of season because of illness. Page 11, Part II.

Arnold Statz wins baseball players' golf championship. Page 12, Part II.

THE CITY. Oil conservation pact signed at Santa Fe Springs. Page 1, Part II.

Shuler defense in Cryer case indicated. Page 2, Part II.

Monterey Road improvement protest denied by Council after heated session. Page 1, Part II.

Eleanor Boardman admits cash accounts for income-tax return were false. Page 3, Part II.

Chest campaign divisions reported on by Chairman Kerr. Page 10, Part II.

Island university head describes Hawaii as laboratory of races. Page 1, Part II.

Manufacturing in State totaling $5,000,000,000 is forecast by State chamber leaders. Page 3, Part II.

Japanese motor liner Asama Maru pays first call at harbor. Page 1, Part II.

Council reverses action on Hollywood five-finger plan paving; cement concrete adopted instead of Willite. Page 5, Part II.

Pantages's "hope" for new trial blasted by affidavit of juror. Page 1, Part II.

PACIFIC SLOPE. Air liner "lost" in New Mexico is flown into Albuquerque safely after storm forces landing and twenty-four-hour delay. Page 1, Part I.

California gasoline tax shows 16.15 per cent gain for quarter. Page 2, Part I.

GENERAL EASTERN. Financial giants battle chaos as wild stock market breaks all sales records. Page 1, Part I.

Twelve drown, sixty rescued in sinking of steamer in Lake Michigan storm. Page 1, Part I.

Pacific Zeppelin Transport Company reveals extensive building plans including large Los Angeles hangar. Page 1, Part I.

Dr. John Roach Straton dies in sanatorium. Page 3, Part I.

Kahn declines post as G.O.P. committee treasurer. Page 5, Part I.

WASHINGTON. Max Thelen presents final arguments in Los Angeles union station case to Supreme Court; justices impressed. Page 3, Part I.

Senator Watson is forced to leave Senate for rest as he faces physical collapse. Page 4, Part I.

President Hoover grieves over death of Senator Burton whom he praises highly. Page 4, Part I.

Grain growers first to form selling association under Farm Aid Act; Legge pledges $100,000 000 for capital. Page 5, Part I.

Grundy surprises Senate committee with attack on small State's tariff bill obstruction. Page 5, Part I.

FOREIGN. Hundreds of Americans stranded in Paris by stock crash. Page 1, Part I.

Deladier fails to form Cabinet. Page 1, Part I.

Three British industries face wage disputes as Parliament prepares to open. Page 19, Part I.

Mark Requa forecasts return of pastoral hardships as penalty for waste. Page 10, Part I.

REMEMBER THIS

Many a man never gets very far because he stops so often to pat himself on the back.

Fireman Killed in Train Wreck

CHATTANOOGA (Tenn.) Oct. 29. (AP)—Forrest Aderholt, fireman on No. 43, passenger train on the Alabama-Great Southern Line, was killed and several passengers injured when five cars and the engine of the train left the tracks at New England, Ga., twelve miles from here early today.

All the News All the Time
LARGEST HOME-DELIVERED CIRCULATION
LARGEST ADVERTISING VOLUME
MADISON 2345
The Times Telephone Number
Connecting All Departments

EQUAL RIGHTS

Los Angeles Times

LIBERTY UNDER THE LAW — TRUE INDUSTRIAL FREEDOM

In Two Parts — 44 Pages
PART I—TELEGRAPH SHEET—22 PAGES
MADISON 2345
The Times Telephone Number
Connecting All Departments

Vol. XLIX. FRIDAY MORNING, JUNE 6, 1930. C DAILY, FIVE CENTS

LOS ANGELES CITY POPULATION 1,231,730; LOS ANGELES COUNTY'S TOTAL 2,199,557

CANNON EXIT BALKS QUIZ

Lobby Committee Left Flat

Bishop Tells Senators He Will be at His Office to Receive Subpoena

Caraway Return Awaited to Decide Course With Defiant Churchman

WASHINGTON, June 5. (AP)—Left talking to themselves today by Bishop James Cannon, members of the Senate lobby committee await the return of Chairman Caraway to determine what they are to do about the defiant churchman.

Calling back over his shoulder that he will be in his office if the committee wants to subpoena him, Bishop Cannon walked out of the committee room while Senator Blaine, Republican, Wisconsin, was asking him questions.

The bishop remained with the committee only long enough to declare he was no longer a voluntary witness and that he will answer no more questions whatever unless subpoenaed. He previously had refused to tell the committee of his 1928 activities against Alfred E. Smith's candidacy.

APPLAUSE AND HISSES

Senator Walsh, Democrat, Montana, indignantly replied the bishop was not excused, but even as he spoke the defiant witness picked up his lone crutch and stalked from the room amid applause and hisses.

Walsh later termed the incident "plain contempt of the Senate," but beyond that he did not indicate what recommendation he will make to the lobby committee for future action.

Senator Walsh adjourned the committee until next Wednesday with the understanding that Chairman Caraway will not return until Tuesday. However, it is reported tonight Senator Caraway is on his way to the city. The committee chairman has taken the position in public statements that Bishop Cannon need not testify.

BORAH JOINS LAUGHTER

When Cannon made his dramatic exit Walsh and Blaine were the only members of the committee of five present. A few minutes later, however, Senator Borah, Republican, Idaho, entered and joined in the laughter as he looked across the table at the empty witness chair. It was the first time a quorum had been present.

Refusing to quit because of the lack of a witness, Senator Walsh read into the record reports made by the Virginia anti-Smith Democrats. After going through the records, Walsh said they do not show

(Continued on Page 15, Column 5)

Will Rogers Remarks:

BEVERLY HILLS, June 5. [To the Editor of The Times:] Headlines in all the papers say "authorities having trouble rounding up twelve escaped lunatics." The main trouble is recognizing 'em. I bet they get a different twelve back in.

Papers also been commenting on the novel way that the State of Nevada "executed a man for committing murder." The novelty of that was that a prisoner was executed in any way for just committing murder.

Mr. Hoover has had to tell the Senate treaty investigators that even a President of the United States has the right of some private correspondence. They asked Bishop Cannon to show his marriage and preaching license.

Yours,
WILL ROGERS.

CRISIS SEEN IN SPENDING

Hoover Warns of Tax Increase

Veterans' Bills in Congress if Passed Would Cause Boost in Rates

Override of Veto Indicates Both Senate and House "Soldier-Conscious"

BY LAURENCE M. BENEDICT
"Times" Staff Correspondent

WASHINGTON, June 5. (Exclusive—Unless the spending orgy on Capitol Hill is halted Congress will face the necessity of voting a tax increase.

The administration sent out warning to that effect today to Congressional leaders. If President Hoover's vetoes of bills liberalizing payments to war veterans are to be ineffective, as was the case Monday, when both Houses overrode his disapproval of the Spanish-American War pension bill, then there is no alternative but increased taxation, according to Treasury officials.

The Senate Finance Committee is putting the finishing touches on

(Continued in Page 15, Column 4)

THE DAY'S NEWS SUMMED UP

FEATURES. Radio, Page 21, Part I; Women's Pages, Clubs and Society, Pages 6-8, Part II; Markets and Financial, Pages 16-20, Part I; Oil News, Page 20, Part I; Pictures, Page 10, Part I; Comics, Page 17, Part II.

NEWS IN SPANISH. Page 22, Part I.

SHIPPING NEWS. Page 21, Part I.

NEWS OF SOUTHERN COUNTIES. Many schools in Southern California announce commencements. Glendale debates returning $400,000 collected as assessments. Deputy Sheriff runs amuck at Banning. Bandits rob branch of California Bank at San Gabriel. Mexican imports double at Calexico. Pasadena to vote on light fund. Page 14, Part I.

SPORTS. Upsets feature first round of Southern California golf championship. Page 13, Part II.

Stars drop third straight to Angels. Page 13, Part II.

National gymnastic meet at Olympic tonight. Page 13, Part II.

THE CITY. Population of city of Los Angeles is 1,231,730, an increase of 655,057 in ten years; county of Los Angeles, including the city, is 2,199,557, an increase of 1,263,102, for the decade. Three world records set by figures. Page 1, Part I.

Veterans of Second Division in reunion here relive stirring days on front twelve years ago. Page 1, Part II.

Lewis's fate may be in jury's hands late today. Page 2, Part II.

Corner-stone of new Edison building laid. Page 1, Part II.

Tragic sinking of Ameco will be lifted by Fitts. Page 2, Part II.

Heavy demands on facilities of county General Hospital disclosed in report. Page 1, Part II.

Dr. Michelson to direct measurements of speed of light in Orange county. Page 1, Part II.

All but four St. Francis Dam disaster claims settled. Page 5, Part II.

THE WEST. Bay City cafe "set-up" dry test case dismissed. Page 6, Part I.

Hoover given indorsement by Bay City G.O.P. committee. Page 7, Part I.

GENERAL EASTERN. One drowns as air liner with fifteen people hits water. Page 5, Part I.

Indiana G.O.P. refuses to renominate Supreme Court justice opposed by drys. Page 7, Part I.

Friend of Lincoln observes 100th birthday. Page 15, Part I.

WASHINGTON. Hoover warns Congress present spending orgy will mean tax increase. Page 1, Part I.

Bishop Cannon, walking out on Senate lobby committee, balks inquiry. Page 1, Part I.

Coast harbors and rivers get large sum from War Department. Page 5, Part I.

Laws to make liquor buying illegal urged as Senate gets batch of dry bills. Page 6, Part I.

Unity on land problems urged by Hoover commission. Page 9, Part I.

Tariff bill strikes snag in Senate and is sent back to conference. Page 11, Part I.

Britten urges air base survey trip for House subcommittee. Page 11, Part I.

Dawes lauds War Mothers in Cambridge address. Page 15, Part I.

Borah assures Hoover he will push naval treaty in Senate. Page 15, Part I.

MILLIGAN PROPERLY ELECTED

WASHINGTON, June 5. (AP)—A unanimous decision that Representative Jacob L. Milligan, Democrat, was properly elected to the seat from the Third Missouri District was reached late today by a House Elections Committee. Milligan's election had been contested by H. F. Lawrence, his opponent.

A Star Who Always "Doubles" for Herself!

ZEPPELIN ON LAST LAP OF ROUND TRIP

Spends Only Half-Hour at Seville After All-Night Battle With Storms

FRIEDRICHSHAFEN (Germany) June 6. (Friday) (AP)—The Graf Zeppelin reported by wireless at 6 a.m. mid-European time (midnight E.S.T.,) that it was flying over Mallorca, largest of the Balearic isles, and about 650 miles from Seville as the Zeppelin has flown.

SEVILLE, June 5. (AP)—A bedraggled Graf Zeppelin and a wobbly, storm-shaken group of passengers made port here between storms today and in half an hour whirred away toward Friedrichshafen, seventh and last stop of their historic tricontinent voyage of nearly 18,000 miles.

After flying around for several hours over Southern Spain Dr. Hugo Eckener, master, directed the huge craft to its depot, discharged passengers, literally snatched supplies from the ground and made off for home in just thirty-one minutes, demonstrating the express nature of the passenger craft.

It was a pale, haggard party of air adventurers that arrived after being tossed about in storm after storm during the last night of their journey here. They had little sleep last night, but gamely asserted the experience was worth their discomfort.

Dr. Eckener said the airship stood the terrific weather splendidly. It showed no sign of damage. The German skipper posed in a cabin window but did not go aground.

San Francisco Chamber Voices Ban Opposition

SAN FRANCISCO, June 5. (AP)—Assailing the bill as discriminatory, the board of directors of the San Francisco Chamber of Commerce today recorded its opposition to the Harris bill before the House of Representatives which would place Mexican immigration on a quota basis.

A resolution passed by the board declared the measure to be unjust because it singles out Mexico alone from among the nations in the Western Hemisphere.

Ritchie to Have Mayor as Rival

BALTIMORE, June 5. (AP)—Gov. Ritchie faced a fight today for a fourth term with the announcement of Mayor Broening of Baltimore that he will seek the Republican nomination.

Gov. Ritchie, a Democrat, is an avowed wet. Mayor Broening stated he will run on the State party platform adopted.

CENSUS RETURNS

Kansas City, Mo., 392,640; increase of 68,250, or 21.9 per cent.

Ferndale, Mich., 20,796; increase 18,156, or 687.7 per cent.

Wyandotte, Mich., 28,294; increase 14,443, or 104.3 per cent.

Waukesha, Wis., 17,174; increase 4616, or 36.7 per cent.

Kenosha, Wis., (revised,) 49,844; increase 9372, or 23.1 per cent.

Racine, Wis., (revised,) 67,515; increase 8922, or 15.2 per cent.

Dayton, O., (revised,) 200,763; gain of 50,000, or about 30 per cent.

Virginia, Minn., 11,957; increase 2065, or 16 per cent.

East St. Louis, Ill., 74,315; increase 7575, or 11.5 per cent. (Final revision.)

Maplewood, Mo. (St. Louis suburb,) 12,629; gain of 5198, or 70 per cent.

EDUCATION HOME PLANNED

SACRAMENTO, June 5. (Exclusive)—The education of poor girls is the aim and purpose of Louisa E. Vance Home for Girls, which will be established at Selma, Fresno county, according to articles of incorporation filed today with Secretary of State Jordan.

KANSAS CITY HAS 392,640 POPULATION

Increase of 68,250, or 21.9 Per Cent, Reported; County Total 463,956

KANSAS CITY, June 5. (AP)—With the close of all ward books in the Kansas City (Mo.) census, E. J. Price, supervisor, today announced the city's population at 392,640, an increase of 68,250, or 21.9 per cent.

Complete figures probably will be announced next week as five days must elapse to allow absentee citizens to be counted, Mr. Price said.

The population figure for Jackson county, including Kansas City, was announced as 463,956, the county's increase since 1920 being 96,110.

ATTACHE SHIFT ANNOUNCED

WASHINGTON, June 5. (AP)—The detachment of Capt. Joseph V. Ogan as naval attache to Tokio about September 24, next, and the assignment of Capt. Isaac C. Johnson, Jr., now commander of submarine Division Twelve, as attache, was announced today by the Navy Department

FIFTH IN THE UNITED STATES; NINETEENTH IN THE WORLD

The just-determined census total for this city indicates that Los Angeles is now the fifth city of the United States, being exceeded only by New York, Chicago, Philadelphia and probably Detroit and is the nineteenth city of the world. According to the best available figures the populations of the world's largest chief cities, those having over 1,000,000 residents, are approximately as follows:

1—London	7,742,212	
2—New York	6,148,785	(1930 est.)
3—Berlin	4,013,588	
4—Chicago	3,335,000	(1930 est.)
5—Paris	2,838,416	
6—Osaka	2,333,800	
7—Tokio	2,218,400	
8—Philadelphia	2,064,200	(1928 Federal est.)
9—Buenos Aires	2,042,296	
10—Moscow	2,025,947	
11—Rio de Janeiro	2,004,000	
12—Vienna	1,868,328	
13—Leningrad	1,614,008	
14—Shanghai	1,539,000	
15—Hangkow	1,500,000	
16—Calcutta	1,327,547	
17—Detroit (1930 figures not yet available.)		
18—Peking (Peiping)	1,297,719	
19—Los Angeles	1,231,730	
20—Budapest	1,217,325	
21—Bombay	1,176,000	
22—Sydney	1,101,000	
23—Hamburg	1,079,092	
24—Cairo	1,064,567	
25—Sao Paulo	1,040,000	
26—Glasgow	1,034,000	

LOS ANGELES SETS THREE NEW WORLD RECORDS FOR RAPIDITY OF GROWTH

Beats All Municipalities for Numerical Increase for Decade and for Fifty-Year Period; Now Fifth City of America and Nineteenth of Whole Earth

The 1930 population of the city of Los Angeles is 1,231,730, it was officially announced here last night by E. K. Ellsworth, chief of the field division of the United States Census Bureau.

The 1930 population of the county of Los Angeles, Mr. Ellsworth announced, is 2,199,557. This figure includes the city of Los Angeles. Excluding the city, the county has a population of 967,827.

The population figure for Los Angeles city represents an increase of 655,057 since 1920, when the city's census showed 576,673 people resident here. This is a relative increase of 113.59 per cent.

This numerical increase constitutes a world record for all cities. In other words, Los Angeles has actually added more persons to its total of bona-fide residents in the last ten years than any other city of any size in the world has done in the same period.

Los Angeles has also set two more world records in its growth over a period of fifty years. In 1880, with 11,183 residents, Los Angeles was 199th in the population list of United States cities. In 1930, with 1,231,730, she is the fifth city of the country, assuming that the advance estimate of 1,500,000 for the city of Detroit is approximately correct, giving that city fourth place. In this fifty-year period the population of Los Angeles has increased numerically by 1,220,547—and by 10,914.31 per cent.

The numerical increase in the total population of Los Angeles county is 1,263,102 over its 1920 population of 936,455, a relative increase of 134.88 per cent. The county outside the city of Los Angeles shows a numerical increase of 608,045 persons over the 1920 total of 359,782, a relative increase of 168.7 per cent.

NOW FIFTH CITY

Since 1920, when Los Angeles was the tenth city of the United States, she has outdistanced Cleveland, St. Louis, Boston, Baltimore and Pittsburgh and has taken Cleveland's place as the fifth city. Los Angeles is now exceeded in population only by New York, Chicago, Philadelphia and probably Detroit, of the cities of this country.

The Los Angeles population of 1,231,730 is nearly equal to the combined totals of San Francisco, Seattle and Portland, which aggregate 1,287,522.

Of the great cities of the world Los Angeles now stands in nineteenth place—assuming Detroit to be the fourth American city. Ahead of her are the four American cities named and London, Berlin, Paris, Osaka, Tokio, Buenos Aires, Moscow, Rio de Janeiro, Vienna, Leningrad, Shanghai, Hangkow, Calcutta and Peiping (Peking.) Of the world cities of over 1,000,000 population, Los Angeles now apparently is ahead of Budapest, Bombay, Sydney, Hamburg, Cairo, Sao Paulo and Glasgow. The latest available population figures for these several cities appear elsewhere in this issue.

POPULATION BY DISTRICTS

Population figures for each of the five census district in the county were announced by the five local census supervisors last night as follows:

Central District—A. C. Munson, supervisor, Los Angeles city, 434,669; county outside of city; none; total, 434,669. The district roughly is bounded by Sunset Boulevard, Manchester avenue, Alameda street and Angeles Mesa Drive.

Northern District—C. E. Chenoweth, supervisor, Los Angeles city, 124,627; county outside of city, 220,154; total, 344,781. The district generally lies north of Sunset Boulevard to the county line, including Glendale, Pasadena, Palmdale, Van Nuys and San Fernando Valley.

Eastern District—W. E. Ballentine, supervisor, Los Angeles city, 192,521; county outside of city, 212,900; total, 405,421. The district includes the territory roughly east of Alameda street to the county line embracing Alhambra, South Pasa-

(Continued on Page 2, Column 1)

THE CENSUS AT A GLANCE

Los Angeles city population, 1930, 1,231,730.
Numerical increase since 1920, 655,057. (World record for this decade.)
Percentage increase since 1920, 113.59.
Numerical increase since 1880, 1,220,547. (World record.)
Percentage increase since 1880, 10,914.31. (World record.)
City's position among U.S. cities; Fifth (assuming Detroit estimate correct.)
City's position among world cities; Nineteenth.
Cities outdistanced since 1920 census: Cleveland, St. Louis, Boston, Baltimore, Pittsburgh.
Only U.S. cities now larger than Los Angeles: New York, Chicago, Philadelphia and probably Detroit.
Los Angeles county population, 1930, including city, 2,199,557.
Numerical increase since 1920, 1,263,102.
Percentage increase since 1920, 134.88.
Los Angeles county population, 1930, excluding city, 967,827.
Numerical increase since 1920, 608,045.
Percentage increase since 1920, 169.
California State population, 1930 (est.) 5,426,000.
Numerical increase since 1920 (est.) 2,000,000.
Percentage increase since 1920 (est.) 58.3.
State's position among States of Union: Sixth.
States outdistanced since 1920: Michigan, Massachusetts.
Only States now more populous than California: New York, Pennsylvania, Illinois, Ohio, Texas.
New Congressmen for California (est.) Five to nine.
New Congressmen for L. A. county (est.) Two.

Los Angeles county has the city showing the largest percentage of increase of any city of any population in America—Beverly Hills with 2485.5 per cent increase since 1920—the only city of more than 25,000 in the 1920 census list having a greater than 100 per cent increase in the 1910-1920 decade to repeat that more-than-100-per-cent-increase performance in 1920-1930—Long Beach—and the largest number of towns in any county in America to report in excess of 100 per cent increases since 1920—eighteen. California leads the country in number of cities over 10,000 to show over 100 per cent increases in the last ten years, with fifteen—of which twelve are in Southern California and ten in Los Angeles county.

HOW THE STORY WAS TOLD

Dramatic Scene at Chamber of Commerce Dinner to Receive Population Totals

It was an anxious little company of about forty men who gathered in an upstairs room of the Chamber of Commerce last night to hear computed and announced figures of the United States census of 1930 that would disclose Los Angeles' new population standing among the cities of the world. The field division chief of the United States Census Bureau at Washington was there. So were the five Federal census supervisors who conducted the big count in Los Angeles county. They held in their inside pockets the totals of population for their districts. Officials of the chamber and newspaper men completed the party.

In all but silence they ate a repast that the chamber had provided for them on assembling at 6:30 p.m. Finally Chairman Harry Baskerville of the chamber's census committee rose and said:

"This is rather an auspicious occasion. We are all a-tiptoe waiting for these figures. We believe that the general plan of procedure has been good. We believe that the percentage of error was reduced to a minimum. On behalf of the Chamber of Commerce I wish to thank you supervisors for the work you have done. Irrespective of what the figures will be, we believe they will be the right ones." (Applause.)

Baskerville introduced E. K. Ellsworth, field division chief of the Federal Census Bureau in Washington, who called upon the five supervisors to give the figures for their districts, saying:

"The population figures to be given out here tonight are practically the same as the ones that will be given out in Washington. There may be a few errors but they will change the total but very slightly."

Supervisors Chenoweth of Glendale Kincaid of Hollywood, Munson of Los Angeles, Ballentine of Monrovia and DeCoudres of Long Beach arose and chalked on a blackboard their district's totals for the city the county outside of the city and then the total of the two, which was the total for their district. When DeCoudres, the last man, had chalked up his total, Secretary Guy C. Marion of the committee wrote down amidst applause the 1,231,730 five-district total for the city, the 967,827 total for the county outside of the city and the 2,199,557 total for the county.

Another gesture and he chalked down the city's ten-year gain of 655,057, or 113.59 per cent, and the county's gain of 1,263,102, or 134.88

(Continued on Page 2, Column 6)

1931–1940

GIVE ME A LIFT BUDDIE!
DOGGONE IT! MY LIGHTS HAVE GONE OUT—THANK GOODNESS THE MOON SHINES!
MAIL
COAST TO COAST NIGHT AIR-LINE SERVICE FOR PASSENGERS TO OPEN SOON.

IS MY BROTHER HERE!
TWO PAPERS SOUTH!
PAPERS READ IN SCHOOL BY MORE MEN THAN GIRLS.

WHAT'CHA TEARING UP THE PAPER FOR?
TO SEE IF THERE'S ANY WIRE IN IT SAP!
THE WORLD'S FIRST WIRELESS NEWSPAPER FOUNDED BY "TIMES".

The Weather

FORECAST FOR LOS ANGELES AND SOUTHERN CALIFORNIA: Fair today and tomorrow with rising temperature. Maximum and minimum temperatures for yesterday: 66-53.

Los Angeles Times

Twelve Parts — 140 Pages

PART II — LOCAL SHEET — 10 PAGES

Vol. L. SUNDAY MORNING, MARCH 29, 1931. CITY NEWS—EDITORIAL

ARE GANGSTERS BUILDING ANOTHER CHICAGO HERE?

Police Officially Deny It; Admit Privately Only a Leader Is Lacking; the Plain Facts

"Booze barons of other climes are just bootleggers in Los Angeles. Gangsters can never build another Chicago here."

So say the police—publicly. Privately they admit that we have here much the same set-up as prevailed in Chicago a few years ago. In their strictly unofficial opinion, the principal thing which now stands between Los Angeles and something at least approaching the Windy City's sorry plight is the absence, so far, of organized leadership for our budding gangland. Such an underworld leader, for example, as Big Jim Colosimo, who started the present liquor dynasty of Chicago, or a man of the organizing ability, determination and utter lack of scruple of Al Capone, who already is dickering for a California "estate."

The well-informed of our police department recognize the danger and point the warning. Asked what can be done now to nip in the bud the growing peril, they point silently but eloquently to the fetters of political interference, espionage and harassment which encumber their activities.

In the meantime the "pots" are simmering on a thousand hills and moonshine, Scotch, bourbon and beer pour into Los Angeles from all directions.

The gangs are forming and dead men mark the gathering. Bullets, booze and corruption are boon companions. Organization and war chests are lacking, but through the reek of pistol smoke and the spray of spurting blood a western Capone may emerge.

Records disclose and investigation proves that the stage is set. The market for liquor is present. The supply is also with us. Bootleggers are here by hundreds. But no outstanding leader has been developed in gangland.

From minor gangster killings such as we are having now came the underworld rule of Chicago when above the ruck of smaller figures loomed Al Capone, "Mops" Volpe, George (Bugs) Moran and others. Organization came to the liquor business. War chests filled with gold and Chicago surrendered to the liquor barons.

SIMILAR BEGINNINGS

So with Chicago in mind a check of the liquor situation in Los Angeles, an investigation of police reports and information gathered from experienced officials coupled with the tales told by the liquor dealers themselves indicate that the curtain may be going up. The stage setting is complete and the actors are here. They only await a leader.

Flaming guns from "Little Italy" less than two weeks ago slew Dominic Di Ciolla, owner of whisky stills, friend of public officials and the man who would be king of gangland. He died, as others died before him in Chicago and here, because of his inability to dominate the bootleg business and his efforts to rule without a flood of gold to buy his way.

And before Di Ciolla four others died to gangsters' guns, while five were wounded and three kidnaped. So through the smoke of pistols the police are peering to catch a glimpse of the expected leader who will weld the liquor racket together, collect a war fund, strike down and kill his rivals and reward with lavish hand the officials who protect him—a la Chicago.

"They cannot live in Los Angeles," say the police for public consumption, but in private they are watching fearfully for the looming figure of a leader and shudder as their efforts to control the situation are blocked by stupid politicians and inefficient police administration.

August Polambo, racketeer, liquor dealer, still-man, comes near to having been the man first to attempt organization among the Italian bootleggers of the north end. He died at the wheel of his automobile with his brains spattered on the windshield. A charge of buckshot from a sawed-off shotgun finished him.

Police records disclose that Palombo opened a speak-easy on Ord street and then not only refused to "pay-off" but undertook to control all bootlegging in his district. Then he died and five other Italians were arrested, tried for murder—and acquitted.

But in Palombo's day, July of 1928, the liquor racket in Los Angeles did not present the fruitful field of today for a real leader. Then liquor was high, the supply not so great, and most of the dealers were making money.

FLOOD OF BOOZE

Today, and all police officials and others know the facts although they seldom admit them, thousands of new faces have appeared in the liquor racket, hundreds of new stills have capped the surrounding hills, alcohol by the truck load is being poured into the city, imported whisky by the ship load is being dumped on our shores from Oceanside to San Pedro and prices have come down to a point where little or no profit remains for the poor bootleggers.

Alcohol, the backbone of the local liquor business, may be had in any quantity delivered at home for $4 a gallon or $20 for a five-gallon tin. Less than a year ago the price ranged from $45 for the cheaper grades to $75 per five-gallon tin.

Wholesalers today purchase Bourbon whisky over the rail of the booze ships at $19 to $26 per case and sell to retailers at $35 to $45 a case. Then with the whisky cut three-to-one the bootlegger sells to the trade for $50 a case.

Scotch, mostly manufactured here from Scotch malt, can be turned out for $22 a case, bottles, labels and all and is sold for $35 to $45 a case. At the rail of the rum ships the real stuff calls from $17 to $20 a case.

One gallon of alcohol makes five cases of gin and now bootleggers

(Continued on Page 2, Column 3)

Some Leading Figures in the Story of Southern California's Budding Gangland

Silver and Di Ciolla are two of the several local bootlegger victims of gang wars here. Sheldon and Frank are accused of kidnaping Zeke Caress and shooting a policeman. Tony and Frank Cornero, the former now in a Federal prison, brothers, are the leading wholesalers of bootleg liquor in Southern California. The bedside court scene shows, left to right, the wounded gangster, James (Well-Fed) Murphy, Judge Turney, Morris Fulton and Joseph ("Cockeye") Herring, now in San Quentin.

MAX SILVER, KILLED

RALPH SHELDON

DOMINIC DI CIOLLA, KILLED

LOUIS FRANK

TRIAL OF A GANGSTER, AT VICTIM'S BEDSIDE.

FRANK CORNERO

TONY CORNERO

by Harry Carr

THE town of Hemet is agitating the plan to mark the graves of Ramona and Alessandro—the two Indians from whose tragedy Mrs. Helen Hunt Jackson got the idea for her novel. Doubtless Mrs. Jackson would be amazed. There was no Ramona. The killing of Juan Diego was an incident such as novelists clip from news dispatches whereupon to hang stories.

In a larger sense she obtained the material for the novel "Ramona" from another tragedy locked among skeletons in the closet of an old California family, a tale that never has been told and probably never will be.

THE GREAT TACTICIAN

Commemorating the military glory of Frederick the Great, the ex-Kaiser has presented a miniature of his army of tin soldiers to The Netherlands Army Museum.

Frederick represented the highest point of European army efficiency. Yet he probably was the only great commander who had no interest in war and hated the whole business. Being a man of enlightened sense and without romantic illusions about soldiers, it was he who invented the military drill as we know it, and was the first to maneuver troops under fire. His place in military history is that of a great tactician rather than a strategist.

THE MERCIFUL RAINS

The Middle West is uneasy over the prospect of another dry season, the snowfall for the winter having been almost as insufficient as the last spring rains.

The truth is that nature made no provision for the condensed population areas which have grown up within the past half-century. Every time the rains do not come on express train schedules we glare at the cloudless sky as though it were a personal outrage.

The recent experiments with the tree rings found in the rafters of prehistoric dwellings in the Southwest indicate that we have been expecting entirely too much of nature. There have been droughts that have lasted for as long as twenty years; there was one period of insufficient rainfall that lasted, approximately, from the year 500 to the year 900.

In fact, the prehistoric history of the world can be read in a series of tragic migrations—of whole populations moving out of areas rendered arid when the

(Continued on Page 2, Column 5)

TRIALS NEARING IN "JAKE" CASE

Health Board Clears Way for Prosecutions

Steps clearing the way for court action in the cases of some fourteen druggists and heads of wholesale supply houses accused by the State of having distributed poisonous Jamaica ginger were taken yesterday when the State Department of Public Health held a series of private hearings.

Dr. Giles S. Porter, chief of the State Department of Public Health, and Prof. M. E. Jaffa, in charge of the Bureau of Foods and Drugs, conducted the hearings. The State

(Continued on Page 2, Column 5)

THOUSANDS TO RALLY FOR EASTER SUNRISE SERVICES

Throngs From All Over Southland Will Join in Pilgrimages to Early Morning Rites Commemorating Resurrection With Gatherings Scheduled at Many Centers

Southern California once more is making elaborate preparations for its crowning annual festival, the celebration of the resurrection of the Savior of the world which will be observed next Sunday with scores of Easter sunrise services to be conducted on hill tops, in bright glens and by the seaside for hundreds of thousands of worshipers.

Hollywood Bowl, Mt. Rubidoux and the Tower of Legends service at Glendale again take rank as the major focal points of public worship on Easter morning and it is estimated that more than 100,000 devotees will attend these programs, in addition to the throngs that will gather at Van Nuys, Canoga Park and other inland cities aand seaside resorts.

Much larger crowds are expected at the various services because of the fact that, on account of construction work, there will be no sunrise service this year at the Coliseum. Early street car and bus service to all points of worship will be provided by the transportation companies.

HOLLYWOOD BOWL

The civic committee in general charge of the Hollywood Bowl sunrise service announces that the program will begin at 5:15 a.m. This hour precedes actual sunrise by twenty minutes.

"The start of the service has been advanced so that the first numbers on the program, which are of an introductory nature, shall anticipate actual sunrise," said Dana Bennett, general chairman of the civic committee.

Silhouetted against the dim skyline heralds in Grecian garb will sound a welcome blast to the rising sun. Taking up the echo, Hollywood's symphonic group, the People's Orchestra of 100 musicians, under direction of Jay Plowe, will swing into the measures of Weber's "Euryanthe" overture. After invocation, "The Holy City" will be sung by Gordon Berger. As the sun tops the eastern crests of the mountains, flooding the Bowl with light, the "Singing Cross" will render the hymn, "Christ, the Lord, Is Risen Today." The cross will be comprised of 250 young persons who will be stationed in the depths of the huge concert shell and who, at sunrise, will doff their dark apparel and stand revealed in pure white.

Scripture reading by Dr. J. George Dorn of Hollywood Luther-

(Continued on Page 3, Column 1)

SHOCK OF BLAKE'S DEATH PROVES FATAL FOR SON

Two days after his father, Charles H. Blake, representative of the Southern California Hotel Men's Association, died at his desk in the office of the Chief of Police, J. Raymond Blake died in the California Lutheran Hospital late Friday night. He had been in ill health some time. The shock of his father's demise is believed to have proved fatal.

His mother, Mrs. Amanda Blake, was confined to her bed in her home at 1118 West Eighty-fourth street, suffering a complete collapse as the result of the unexpected deaths of both her husband and son. Mr. Blake was 44 years of age. He leaves, besides his mother, a sister, Mrs. Ruth A. Sapp.

Funeral services, with full police honors, were conducted yesterday at the W. A. Brown chapel for Mr. Blake, Sr., with members of the Police Commission, Acting Chief Finlinson and his executive staff, and a host of friends present. Interment was in Inglewood Cemetery. Mr. Blake, a resident of Los Angeles for thirty-five years, had been in charge of the Southern California Hotel Men's Association bureau of investigation at Chief Steckel's office since it was established in 1922.

Repairing — Refinishing — Upholstering
THE REEDCRAFT CO.
2718 WEST SEVENTH STREET

All the News All the Time

LARGEST HOME-DELIVERED CIRCULATION
LARGEST ADVERTISING VOLUME

MADISON 2345
The Times Telephone Number
Connecting All Departments

Los Angeles Times

EQUAL RIGHTS

LIBERTY UNDER THE LAW — TRUE INDUSTRIAL FREEDOM

In Two Parts — 36 Pages
PART I — TELEGRAPH SHEET — 18 PAGES

TIMES OFFICES
100 North Broadway
619½ South Spring
And Throughout Southern California

VOL. L. FRIDAY MORNING, JULY 10, 1931. C DAILY, FIVE CENTS

DUCE VOICES PEACE AIM

Stimson Told of Italy's Choice

Mussolini Cites Arms Cut as National Objective in Talk With Secretary

World Economic Recovery Declared Dependent on Success at Geneva

ROME, July 9. (AP)—Premier Mussolini informed Secretary of State Stimson in an interview today that peace and disarmament have been chosen as the objectives of Italy.

"There are two roads," the Duce declared after the two statesmen had conferred together for some time, "a road toward war and a road toward peace. I told Mr. Stimson today that I have chosen the road toward peace."

Italy, he said, will go to the disarmament conference at Geneva next February "with a sincere desire for peace." In order to solve the world economic problem, he said, it also is necessary "to solve the political crisis and that of morale."

"The success of the disarmament conference," Mussolini said, "is indispensable so that peoples may have faith in their governments. The people must not be disillusioned. The date of the conference must not be postponed."

AID TO RECOVERY

He and Secretary Stimson agreed, he said, that European tranquillity would insure economic recovery. "Secretary Stimson told me," he said, "and I agreed with him, that if Europe is tranquil, we are going ahead toward certain economic recovery."

In explaining that Italy has chosen the road toward peace the Premier declared that "Mr. Stimson and I find ourselves in accord in choosing that road."

The Secretary spent an hour with Mussolini this afternoon in the Premier's office in the Palazzo Venezia. The two statesmen talked alone and afterward Mussolini briefly told newspaper men about the conversation, but he added much from his own thoughts without indicating specifically what was, and what was not, expressed during the conversation with the Secretary.

ARMS COURSE URGED

At the disarmament conference, to which he said Italy will go with a "spirit of perfect loyalty and sincerity," the Premier insisted that arms reduction should be discussed on the basis of general principles rather than guns and tons.

"Italy is disposed to accept the lowest figure of armament—even a limit of 10,000 rifles for all Italy, provided no other nation has more," he said. "Of course, if any other nation had more such a reduction would be placing Italy in the posi-

(Continued on Page 2, Column 5)

DEBT ENVOY SELECTED

Gibson Will Act as Observer

All of Nation's Diplomatic Force Will Be Exerted at London Parley

Ambassador to Belgium Has Full-Knowledge of Hoover Moratorium Views

WASHINGTON, July 9. (AP)—The full force of American diplomatic prestige today was thrown into the adjustment of unsettled details of the intergovernmental debt moratorium.

President Hoover selected his close friend and adviser, Hugh S. Gibson of Los Angeles, Ambassador to Belgium, to serve as official observer for the United States on the experts' committee to which further negotiations have been consigned.

He will be assisted by Frederick Livesey, assistant economic adviser of the State Department, who is on his way to London, where the experts will meet next week. Livesey is an authority on reparations and war debts.

GUEST OF HOOVER

Until today, State Department officials, including Acting Secretary Castle, had indicated American participation in the experts' sessions would be perfunctory. At most, officials had said, Treasury experts would participate.

In May and early June, Gibson was a house guest of President Hoover. He had many talks with the Chief Executive on the European situation. Speaking recently at Brussels, he said he participated in the development of Mr. Hoover's moratorium proposal.

The Ambassador will enter the London meeting with a full knowledge of the President's hopes that the good will manifest in the debt proposal will advance the cause of international disarmament.

NOT IN DEFAULT

Gibson served as delegate to the League of Nations preparatory disarmament conference and is being mentioned prominently as a delegate to the forthcoming general disarmament conference at Geneva.

In announcing Gibson's appointment Castle made it clear the American government is confident an arrangement will be reached so that Germany will not be in technical default when conditional reparations payments fall due the 15th inst.

He reiterated a previous statement by the administration that the moratorium plan was considered morally effective when an agreement was reached with France on Monday.

Since the President's proposal was first made, State Department officials said tonight, the United States has proceeded on the assumption that Germany will not be required to pay the annuities due the 15th inst., either under a general acceptance of the President's

(Continued on Page 2, Column 6)

THE DAY'S NEWS SUMMED UP

FEATURES. Radio, Page 18, Part I; Women's Pages, Clubs and Society, Pages 6 and 7, Part II; Markets and Financial, Pages 13 to 17, Part I; Oil News, Page 16, Part I; Comics, Page 12, Part I.

DRAMA. Page 5, Part II.

NEWS IN SPANISH. Page 17, Part I.

SHIPPING NEWS. Page 10, Part I.

NEWS OF SOUTHERN COUNTIES. Naval officer's wife reported as suicide at Coronado. Pasadena City Director to urge creation of Mayor's office there. Ventura small boy lost in mountains overnight found. Co-ordinated program for fire prevention outlined at Upland meeting. Third annual conference on child delinquency opens at Whittier. Page 6, Part I.

SPORTS. Percy Allis leads in Canadian open with 67. Page 9, Part II.

Cubs recall Barton; Moore to rejoin Angels. Page 9, Part II.

British lead Czecho-Slovakians in Davis Cup play. Page 9, Part II.

Junior Olympic boys leave on South American tour. Page 10, Part II,

THE CITY. Construction of bridge across Westlake Park to join both ends of Wilshire Boulevard urged in City Engineer's report. Page 1, Part II.

Mayor's special harbor rate committee to hold first meet today. Page 1, Part II.

Politician's red auto revealed as clew that led to still raid and jailing of two. Page 12, Part II.

School report of last year shows Los Angeles attendance gains 4 per cent. Page 8, Part II.

Grand jury quizzes members of Sheldon acquittal jury and finds no basis for rumors of intimidation. Page 8, Part II.

Huntington Park delegation asks Supervisors for blanket assessed-valuation cut. Page 12, Part II.

Newly organized Thirty-two Club will boost re-election of President Hoover. Page 13, Part II.

THE WEST. Seattle-Tokio flight abandoned as Robbins and Jones land near Nome. Page 1, Part I.

Rolph may save Los Angeles dime murderer of woman from gallows. Page 1, Part I.

Finance Director Vandegrift rejects all bids on 1932 license plates due to rumors of "fixing" award. Page 2, Part I.

Gov. Rolph's office expenditures more than twice amount allowed in budget. Page 3, Part I.

California grape acreage control campaign reported successful. Page 9, Part I.

GENERAL EASTERN. Strike of oil producers declared in midcontinent area. Page 1, Part I.

Rudy Vallee forsakes vagabond-lover role for that of home lover. Page 2, Part I.

Business and professional women launch attack on two foes—man and old age. Page 4, Part I.

Chicago police judge retracts order of imprisonment for Mexican Consul; Mexico may demand apology. Page 5, Part I.

WASHINGTON. Hugh S. Gibson chosen by Hoover as official observer to London war debts moratorium parley. Page 1, Part I.

Officials investigate charges rich convicts buy summer camp vacations from Federal prisons. Page 3, Part I.

Senate investigators find irregularities in Alabama election of Bankhead over Heflin. Page 7, Part I.

Los Angeles city finances for 1929 analyzed in Census Bureau report. Page 9, Part I.

FOREIGN. Mussolini orders Italy to choose between Catholic Action Society and Fascist party. Page I, Part I.

Mussolini tells Stimson of Italy's desire for peace and disarmament. Page 1, Part I.

Kaye Don smashes own world record by averaging 110 miles an hour in speed boat. Page 1, Part I.

German slums fertile field for seed of Red revolution. Page 2, Part I.

Gandhi writes he does not intend to make visit to America. Page 4, Part I.

Narcotics treaty revised draft presented Geneva conference; approval uncertain. Page 8, Part I.

Success is the final test of character.

No Time to Play With Matches!

FIRE PERILS BEAUTIES OF YOSEMITE

Blaze at El Portal Races Over 1500 Acres and May Sweep Into Scenic Valley

SAN FRANCISCO, July 9. (Exclusive)—Fire tongues stretched toward Yosemite National Park today. A blaze which got a foothold near El Portal at the western entrance to the park seared 1500 acres and lapped into Ned's Gulch. Wind direction and velocity will be the determining factor in the extent of the spread, according to advices to United States forestry offices here. Under proper conditions the flames will be swept toward the floor of the valley.

Seventy-five men of the forestry service and another 100 from the Yosemite Lumber Company are fighting the flames. They reported them creeping up the gulch toward park timber.

This fire was the severest reported during the day, although humidity and continued hot weather in the interior keep the menace of other fires constantly alive.

There were two small fires in San Luis Obispo county and two others in Calaveras county. At Horneout Creek, Butte county, 4000 acres of grass were burned and a small fire was controlled near Standard City, Tuolumne county.

Tonight a new area fell prey to flames. Modesto reports told of an 80,000-acre grazing land fire in Stanislaus county moving slowly toward Patterson. An emergency call for workers was sent out.

The fire broke out on the Kling ranch near the old Phoenix mine. Ranger Seager, Mt. Oso lookout, believes it was started by a carelessly thrown cigarette. The flames followed Purto Creek, crossed into Santa Clara county and crept up Orestimba Creek. Fencer, barns and outbuildings on one ranch have been destroyed and it is believed some cattle have perished.

MADERA COUNTY FIRE CAUSES ONE DEATH

FRESNO, July 9. (AP)—Brush, grass and forest fires which for a week have burned about 100,000 acres in half a dozen places in Central California, took their first life today when Irving Young, 21-year-old fire fighter of Madera county, was killed when his fire truck overturned as he was driving to a grass fire in the Dairyland district, Madera county.

MICHELSON'S WILL GOES TO PROBATE

Scientist's Estate Valued at $37,500 and Widow Gets Major Share

CHICAGO, July 9. (AP)—An estate valued at $37,500 was left by Prof. Albert A. Michelson, Nobel prize winner in physics, who died May 9 at Pasadena. His will, showing $7000 in personal property and the remainder in real estate, was admitted to probate today

His widow, Mrs. Edna S Michelson, is bequeathed two houses here and a fifth of the residuary estate. Each of the three daughters, Mrs. Madeline Maher of Chicago, Mrs. Dorothy M. Dick of Provincetown, Mass., and Mrs. Beatrice M. Foster of Dahlgren, Va., receive a fifth, and the remaining fifth is to be divided among two sisters of the physicist and Miriam Julie Michelson of San Francisco.

Manila Press Hurls Charge at Professors

MANILA, July 10 (Friday) (AP)—The Manila Bulletin, American-owned newspaper, says today "compulsion" has been used by professors and teachers of one of the largest private schools in the city by telling their students a certain percentage will be deducted from their grades unless they attend an independence parade scheduled for Sunday.

The parade will be in the nature of a demonstration for Senator Hawes of Missouri and Senator Pittman of Nevada, who have declared for immediate independence for the islands.

Bay City Sights "Ma" Kennedy

SAN FRANCISCO, July 9. (AP)—Mrs. Minnie Kennedy-Hudson, mother of Aimee Semple McPherson, who recently was married in the Northwest, appeared and disappeared in San Francisco today.

Mrs. Hudson walked into a hotel here, admitted her identity and asked for mail.

There wasn't any mail, so she walked out again, and that was the one and only time San Francisco got a glimpse of the newlywed and knew who she was. Her husband wasn't with her.

MRS. WILSON SEES SITE OF MEMORIAL

GENEVA, July 9. (AP)—Mrs. Woodrow, has just four mottoes he keeps on her return from Pozman, Poland, today inspected the site of the new League of Nations headquarters building where the Palace of Peace is under construction. The entrance to this new home of the League will be a huge gateway memorial to Woodrow Wilson.

BERKELEY EDUCATOR DIES

GRASS VALLEY, July 9. (AP)—Mal P. Stone of Berkeley, 77 years of age, retired educator, died here last night.

Will Rogers Remarks:

BEVERLY HILLS, July 9. [To the Editor of The Times:] Editorials have been blaming France for not falling over themselves to cancel the debt. Well, France received $95,000,000 more than she pays out to England and the United States. France is better off today than all of them. Why? Because of hard work and watching the pennies. France is a good deal like Amos on the radio: "Now wait a minute Andy; that scheme of ours sounds mighty big and fine now, but in the end where is we gettin' off?" The United States is exactly like Andy. Anything comes up: "Oh, sho, sho, send it over c.o.d. We will pay fur it, or sumpin'. Come on Vanilla, les go fishin'."

Yours,

WILL ROGERS.

SPEED-BOAT RECORD SET BY KAYE DON

British Sportsman's Old Mark Tumbles in Tests at Lake Garda, Italy

GARDONE (Riviera, Italy) July 9. (AP)—Kaye Don, British sportsman, broke his own world's speed-boat record today by piloting the Miss England II over a measured course at a rate of 110.223 miles an hour. Don set the previous record of 103.49 miles an hour in Argentina earlier this year.

KAYE DON.

Don made two runs over the Lake Garda course at speeds of 107.878 miles per hour and 112.569 to smash the record.

Today's record-breaking run marked the end of nearly three months of efforts here by the British sportsman. He brought the Miss England here May 5 to compete in the international speed-boat regatta sponsored by Gabriele D'Annunzio, but motor trouble balked every attempt he made then to set a new record.

A new engine was installed in the boat last week, and other mechanical adjustments were made. On Saturday he averaged 109.43 miles an hour over a measured course but motor trouble prevented him from making the run in the other direction as required in record attempts. Today, with perfect conditions, prevailing, Don brought his boat to the course and ten minutes later had established his new mark.

TRACES OF YOUTH, LOST DAYS, FOUND

Hope Revived That Boy May Be Rescued From Wilds Above Sonora

FRESNO, July 9. (AP)—Hope that 12-year-old David Fargo of Los Banos, lost in the wilds fifty miles above Sonora since last Saturday, has been able to survive the hardships of almost a week in the mountains and might yet be found alive flared up again today with the discovery of a place where the boy is believed to have spent last night, the Republican learned tonight.

The discovery was reported at Sonora this afternoon by Sheriff Dambacher, who has persisted in the belief that the boy had not succumbed to exposure nor had met with an accident. The discovery was made by a party under Dambacher, who had set two bloodhounds on the trail believed to be that of the lad. The dogs led the way to a spot under a tree only about one and one-half miles from the camp of R. H. Fargo, father of the boy, on Niagara Creek. Evidence was plain, Dambacher reported, that some person had spent either last night or the one before at that spot.

SHOT KILLS R. L. HENRY

HOUSTON (Tex.) July 9. (AP)—Former Representative R. L. Henry, 67 years of age, died today of a bullet wound in the head. He was found wounded in his home, a pistol near by.

OIL TIE-UP IMPENDS

Producer-Strike Move Gains

Shutdown of Wells Under Way in Oklahoma Field Due to Low Prices

Kansas Operators to Confer Tomorrow on Proposal for Like Action

OKLAHOMA CITY, July 9. (AP)—A producers' strike against low prices for crude oil gathered momentum in the midcontinent area tonight.

A shut-down in wells is under way in the Oklahoma City oil field, with the possibility there will be a complete cessation in this rich pool and that the suspension will be extended to other fields of Oklahoma and Kansas.

Midcontinent purchasing companies tonight generally had reduced prices to from 10 to 22 cents a barrel, unprecedented figures.

Operators of the Oklahoma City field will meet tomorrow to consider a proposal for closing all wells until the industry becomes stabilized.

At Wichita, Kan., more than a score of operators agreed to call a meeting of Kansas producers for Saturday to consider shutting in all wells in that State "until such time as there is a demand for crude."

SHUTDOWN ORDERS

In advance of the Oklahoma City conference, operators began ordering the cutting off of production. Twenty-six wells of the Anderson-Pritchard Production Company, with a potential output of 392,962 barrels daily, were ordered shutdown after today's runs. Several other companies followed suit.

The movement has not extended to Texas, where ineffectual attempts have been made by State officials and many operators to enforce a curtailment of the feverish development in the new flush area of East Texas.

The Texas situation will be dealt with at a special session of the State Legislature called to convene next Tuesday. Stringent conservation laws to prevent ruinous overproduction will be presented for enactment.

BLAME FOR CRASH

Oil men blame the huge production thrown on the market from East Texas for the crash in crude prices.

Operators at the Wichita meeting declared the average price of 18 cents a barrel for Kansas crude is far below the cost of pumping and said:

"There is no longer any use or sense in playing horse. Shut down everything and stop every drop of Kansas oil from going on the market and it will get far better results than the present proration plan."

Challenge Given to Tariff Foes

WASHINGTON, July 9. (AP)—Senator Watson, the Republican leader, today challenged Senator Robinson, the Democratic leader, to "assume the leadership in a fight to make a 'serious revision' of the present tariff law."

Replying to a recent criticism of the Hawley-Smoot tariff by the Arkansas Democrat, Watson in a statement issued through the Republican National Committee said: "Facts show there has been no 'slaughter' of either our export or import trade because of the tariff."

Rocket Expert Off to Africa

TRIPOLI (North Africa) July 9. (AP)—Dr. Darwin O. Lyon, New York professor and interterrestrial rocket enthusiast, left here today for the Plain of Misola in the African Desert, where he will attempt to shoot an experimental rocket to the moon sometime near the end of this month.

A rocket constructed by Dr. Lyon, exploded prematurely in the Italian Alps last February, injuring three of his assistants.

Life Rules Told by Centenarian

ALAMEDA, July 8. (AP)—Nathan M. Jacobs, 104 years of age tomorrow, has just four mottos he keeps and on these he bases his claims to longevity.

"Be moderate; be contended; keep a clear conscience and don't worry over trifles," he said.

Jacobs was born in London in 1827. He has spent seventy-eight years in California.

Nine Millions Left by Phelan

SAN FRANCISCO, July 9. (AP)—The estate of the late James D. Phelan, former Mayor and United States Senator, was valued at $9,459,887 in an appraisal filed in Superior Court today.

POPE HURLED CHALLENGE BY MUSSOLINI'S ORDER

Duce Calls on Italy to Decide on Allegiance to Catholic Action Society or Fascist Party

ROME, July 9. (Exclusive)—Premier Mussolini took the step today in the Italo-Vatican controversy of calling on the people of Italy to decide between allegiance to him and allegiance to the Pope. No one in Italy can longer wear the black shirt and belong to any club or group depending on the Catholic Action Society.

Il Duce instructed Secretary Giurati of the Fascist party to notify all federal secretaries of the party that by his orders the former admission of the compatibility of belonging to the Fascist party and Catholic Action associations at the same time is revoked.

MUSSOLINI'S REPLY

The announcement of this step was made just after today's meeting of the Council of Ministers and constitutes Mussolini's reply to the Pontiff's encyclical telling the Fascists to give reserved allegiance to Fascism through taking a silent exception to the oath they are called upon to swear.

The measure carries the fight between the Pope and Il Duce to another phase, and it is likely to be far-reaching. Thousands of persons who now adhere to both Fascism and the Catholic Action will be called upon to make a decision and Il Duce will know shortly whether the great mass of the Italian people are on his side or the Pope's. It is a sort of plebiscite that has been precipitated.

TREATY END SEEN

Denunciation of the Concordat and Lateran Treaty with the Vatican by the Fascist government is freely predicted as the next step in the controversy.

Already tonight's newspapers announce that several groups of Young Fascists have withdrawn adherence from the Catholic Action youths' clubs.

Many other groups will also be affected. University students can no longer belong to Catholic student clubs and also to the Fascist student association.

CALLS FOR SHOWDOWN

The effect of Mussolini's move, which comes five days after the publication of the Pontiff's encyclical condemning Fascism is to remove all equivocation between the position of the church and the position of the state, for it is now flatly promulgated by the leader of Fascism that there is no compatibility between his principles and those of the Pope as given expression in the Catholic Action Society. The blow will be a severe one to the Pope, for he has repeatedly designated the Catholic Action as the "very apple of his eye."

The measure also gives evidence of Mussolini's belief that despite papal denials the Catholic Action is full of former members of the old Popular party.

MUST RENOUNCE

The clubs and associations dependent upon the Catholic Action Society are said to have a total membership of more than 300,000, all of who must either leave the Catholic Action or renounce all connection with Fascism. There is no indication yet as to whether today's measure is preliminary to a denunciation of the Concordat by the Fascist government, although the impression is gaining ground on both sides now that this instrument is insufficient and dodges issues which are unescapable between Fascism and the church.

One section of the Fascist opinion apparently continues to take a calm view of the Vatican offensive, holding that the Pope made a mistake and misjudged the situation through having been deliberately misled by his advisers.

WOUNDS SPIRIT

Another section of Fascism declares that the Pope's encyclical has wounded Italian spirit at home and discredited the country abroad, and that the only solution now is denunciation of the Concordat.

"With the Lateran Treaty Fascism wanted to solve the question between the church and the state, but since this desire for peace is flouted by Vatican hostility, only one solution is possible, and Fascism is ready to face the consequences of this step before Italy and the whole world," says the Messaggero today.

USED POPE'S WORDS

On the other hand, it will be difficult for the masses of Italian peo-

(Continued on Page 2, Column 3)

FLYERS TO TRY AGAIN

Attempted Trip to Tokio Fails

Robbins and Jones Forced to Land Near Nome With Hopes Undimmed

Plans for Second Effort Call for Heavier Engine to Be Installed in Plane

NOME (Alaska) July 9. (AP)—Plans for another attempted Seattle-Tokio flight were announced tonight by Reg L. Robbins and Harold S. Jones, Texas aviators, less than fourteen hours after they had been forced down on Solomon Beach, thirty miles east of here, early today following a successful refueling flight from Seattle.

Arising at 5:30 p.m. after a long sleep, Robbins said a larger engine will be placed in the Fort Worth for the next attempt.

At 3:50 a.m., (6:50 a.m. Pacific standard time) today, the two men set the Fort Worth down at Solomon, twenty-six hours and fifty-three minutes after taking off from Seattle early yesterday.

USE SAME PLANE

The same refueling plane will be used, Robbins said. The two men had completed nearly half of their 5100-mile proposed nonstop flight when heavy winds made the Fort Worth unwieldly after a 300-gallon refueling, and the landing was necessary. The four men, Robbins and Jones and the crew of the refueling ship, James Mattern and Nick Greener, flew here later in the trimotored refueling plane from Solomon, going to bed within a short time.

WEATHER WORSE

Late today the weather became worse here, with no flying possible between Nome and Fairbanks, traversed less than twenty-four hours ago by the two planes.

"We are sorry we were unable to continue the flight," Robbins said. "We tried as hard as we could, but could not manage the plane after loading 300 gallons of gasoline. We could not keep it in line long enough to take aboard a full load of 435 gallons of gasoline.

"It's tough, but we couldn't see any other way out. The weather was bad and visibility nil. We would have killed ourselves outright in attempting to get through, so we decided to land at Solomon."

Failure to reach their objective was a blow to crews of both the Seattle-Tokio plane and its refueling mother-ship. Three hours after the landing at Solomon, when the flyers brought their ships to the Nome landing field, they were unanimous in saying it was a "terrible blow."

CHICAGOANS PASS SECOND PAY DAY

CHICAGO, July 9. (Exclusive)—Cook county's 4500 employees passed their second payless pay day today. Commissioner Kavanaugh, chairman of the Finance Committee of the County Board, said there is no hope of paying county employees in cash before October 1, next.

DIME SLAYER OF WOMAN MAY DODGE NOOSE DEATH

SACRAMENTO, July 9. (Exclusive)—Benjamin J. Brown, who murdered a young Los Angeles mother for $2.20 in 10-cent pieces, and who now is in San Quentin awaiting execution for the crime, may escape the noose. This was indicated here today by Gov. Rolph as he took steps to reduce the number of slayers scheduled to be hanged at San Quentin and Folsom on the 17th inst. by granting two reprieves.

While he made no direct statement of his intention in the matter, the Governor intimated he has been giving Brown's plight serious consideration and may shortly commute his death sentence to imprisonment for life.

Underlying the Governor's deliberation of the case, it was hinted, is the fact that Brown was sentenced to die for the crime while Emery Ells, who paid the twenty-two dimes as hire for committing it, and who was declared equally guilty by the prosecution during the trial, received only life imprisonment.

Brown murdered Mrs. Merle Ells, 22 years of age, in Los Angeles November 5, last, as she slept in bed with her 18-month-old child at the home of her sister. He was tracked down quickly by detectives and, climaxing a twelve-hour grilling, confessed declaring Ells had hired him to murder the woman and had paid him $2.20 in dimes as "deposit" against a fee of $2000.

Throughout the grilling of Brown, Ells had steadfastly denied complicity in the crime, but when confronted with his hireling's confession corroborated the story in every detail.

The two were tried jointly before Superior Judge Schauer; and court attaches and spectators alike were dumfounded when the jury returned separate verdicts, prescribing the noose for Brown, the hireling, and life for Ells, the instigator.

Slayers reprieved by the Governor today are Pedro Magsaysay, a Fresno Filipino, and U. Tanaka, a Los Angeles Japanese, both under sentence to hang on the 17th inst., along with Charles Simpson, San Francisco "torch murderer;" William Burkhart, Los Angeles wife-slayer, and Fred Mott, convicted of killing a radio salesman in Los Angeles.

All the News All the Time

LARGEST HOME-DELIVERED CIRCULATION
LARGEST ADVERTISING VOLUME

MAdison 2345
The Times Telephone Number
Connecting All Departments

Los Angeles Times

EQUAL RIGHTS
LIBERTY UNDER THE LAW
TRUE INDUSTRIAL FREEDOM

In Two Parts — 32 Pages
PART I—TELEGRAPH SHEET—16 PAGES

TIMES OFFICES
100 North Broadway
619½ South Spring
And Throughout Southern California

VOL. LI. C WEDNESDAY MORNING, MARCH 2, 1932. DAILY, FIVE CENTS

LINDBERGH SON SEIZED BY KIDNAPERS

JAPAN DRIVES FOES BACK ALONG SHANGHAI FRONT

Fall of Tachang Reported as Air Raid Smashes Nanking Rail; New Army Pushes South

SHANGHAI, March 2. (Wednesday.) (AP)—Japanese troops drove the Chinese army at Shanghai into retreat today and were reported to have occupied Tachang, four miles west of Kiangwan.

Six Japanese airplanes at about the same time bombed and assertedly cut the Shanghai-Nanking railway near Kunshan, thirty-five miles west of Shanghai, in pursuance of a threat to destroy it if the Chinese continued to bring in reinforcements.

On the north thousands of fresh Japanese reinforcements, just off ships in the Yangtze River, were attempting to advance southward for a great encircling movement.

The Chinese Nineteenth Route Army and a Chinese force in Nantao, south of Shanghai, were reported to be in retreat, the army drawing back toward Chenju.

Chapei, devastated battleground of the conflict's beginning more than a month ago, took the heaviest punishment of fire and shell thus far. Flames devoured huge areas of shattered buildings.

Japanese guns hammered Chinese positions with their powerful explosives. Chinese guns replied in kind, their heaviest ordnance, placed on railway cars in western Chapei, thundering above the lesser pieces.

JAPAN LANDS 10,000

The battle shook everything within miles. Throughout Shanghai's residential district houses and apartment blocks rattled. The flashes of the heavy guns were visible over most of the city.

Beyond Chapei along the Kiangwan front action also picked up with the coming of dawn, although to a lesser degree. The entire area was under fog and smoke.

Despite Chinese denials, strong and apparently authenticated reports said the Japanese succeeded in landing a force of approximately 10,000 men in the vicinity of Liuho yesterday.

FIGHTING SOUTHWARD

Although communications with Liuho, twenty miles north of Shanghai, were shattered, it seemed the Japanese had landed on the south bank of the Yangtze River and were fighting their way southward. Whether they were troops of the Eleventh or Fourteenth Japanese divisions, both expected to come here, was not specified.

They were thought to have come ashore in armored barges while a destroyer squadron in the Yangtze shelled the shore line to cover their landing.

Japanese headquarters announced that during yesterday's action the whole line between Kiangwan and Miaochungchen, a distance of about two miles, had been advanced from three-fourths of a mile to a mile, and long before daybreak the Japanese storm troops continued the forward movement.

The Japanese apparently were carrying out their original plan to break through at Kiangwan and

(Continued on Page 6, Column 1)

TOKIO READY TO PARLEY

China Insists on Truce First

League Plan for Shanghai Six-Power Conference Depends on Nanking

Direct Armistice Efforts in Clash Zone Given Approval

GENEVA, March 1. (AP)—Japan formally notified the League of Nations Council tonight she accepted the League's proposal for an international conference at Shanghai to terminate the Sino-Japanese conflict there. A Chinese spokesman informed the Associated Press nis government has accepted a peace proposal submitted by representatives of the great powers at preliminary negotiations already conducted at Shanghai. But while the fighting continues, the spokesman said China's representatives in Geneva will withhold formal acceptance of the Council's peace plan.

The Council's proposal calls for a conference of the great powers and representatives of China and Japan at Shanghai. The United States has indicated its willingness to participate in this conference.

Ambassador Matsudaira formally presented Japan's acceptance of the Council's program to Sir John Simon, British Foreign Secretary. Sir John urged on the Ambassador, who is Tokio's representative at London, the necessity of putting an immediate stop to the hostilities. Matsudaira promised to do his utmost to achieve that end.

JAPAN DEMANDS VICTORY BEFORE PEACE PARLEY

[Copyright, 1932, by the Associated Press]

TOKIO, March 1. (AP)—Acceptance of the League of Nation's proposal for an international conference at Shanghai to end the Sino-Japanese

(Continued on Page 6, Column 2)

"Criminal Procedure!"

HOUSE WETS GAIN POINT

Vote on Control Plan Looms

WASHINGTON, March 1. (AP)—A House vote on considering a bill to give control of liquor to the States was assured today.

The wet bloc obtained 145 signatures to a petition to withdraw from the Judiciary Committee a resolution to bring this about. A vote will be taken the 14th inst. on the question whether the measure will be placed on the calendar of the House for its consideration.

In previous Congresses 218 petitioners, one more than a majority, have been necessary to discharge a committee from consideration of a

(Continued on Page 9, Column 1)

Will Rogers Remarks:

BEVERLY HILLS, March 1. [To the Editor of The Times:] On one column of our morning papers the war had been called off. But they hadn't notified the other column. The Japanese says they don't want China, and it's a cinch the Chinese don't want Japan. The Japanese say if the Chinese would get back twenty miles from Shanghai that they would quit fighting. The Chinese say if the Japanese would go on back home where they belong they would quit fighting. So nobody really knows what they are fighting over. It's almost like a civilized European war in that respect.

Yours,
WILL ROGERS.

INJUNCTION BILL VOTED

Measure Passed to House 75-5

WASHINGTON, March 1. (AP)—The Norris bill to curb the use of injunctions in labor disputes and outlaw so-called "yellow dog" contracts was passed by the Senate, 75 to 5, today and sent to the House.

The vote followed years of effort by organized labor to obtain such legislation.

The five votes against the bill were cast by New Englanders. The final ballot came at the end of more than a week of debate in which every amendment opposed by those sponsoring the legislation was rejected.

In addition to its labor clauses the bill carries a provision to protect the freedom of the press by authorizing jury trials and transfer of judges in cases of contempt of court.

Senator Reed of Pennsylvania announced he was voting for the bill "with a good deal of shame" because of "the condition in which it leaves the Senate."

RIGHTS ALSO LOST

He said he was "convinced that the court of equity should not be converted by the injunction method into a police court" and was opposed to the "yellow dog" contract, but felt some provisions of the bill will take away from labor more rights than the measure protects.

Reed expressed the hope certain provisions will be changed by the House.

Senator Johnson of California replied he was voting "with a feeling of pride and exultation because this Congress has done a measure of justice to the workers." He added: "At last we have seen the day when Congress has dared to legislate against a Federal injunction outrageously invoked against labor."

Senator Borah of Idaho said he felt the most important provision of the bill was that outlawing "yellow dog" contracts, which bind a worker not to join a union, and expressed confidence it will "put an end" to that form of bargain.

The bill declares the right of lador to organize, declares the "yellow dog" contract contrary to public policy and outlaws it by mak-

(Continued on Page 8, Column 1)

ABDUCTORS CARRY BABY FROM CRIB OUT NURSERY WINDOW

Note Found at Scene by Maid Who Discovered Crime Three Hours After Putting Boy to Bed; Three States Take up Search

NEW YORK, March 2. (Wednesday)—Charles Augustus Lindbergh, Jr., 20-months-old son of Colonel and Mrs. Charles A. Lindbergh was kidnaped sometime between 7:30 and 10 o'clock last night from his crib in the nursery on the second floor of his parents' home at Hopewell, N. J., near Princeton. His disappearance was discovered at 10 p.m. by Miss Betty Dow, his nurse. Entering the nursery, she discovered that the baby was not in his crib. She thought at first that he had rolled out and crawled under some furniture. But when she went to search the room she observed that a window was open and a ladder placed against it. She rushed down stairs immediately and notified Colonel and Mrs. Lindbergh. They hurried to the nursery, convinced themselves that the baby actually was gone, and Colonel Lindbergh telephoned the Hopewell police.

When Chief of Police Harry H. Wolf of Hopewell arrived at the house, he sized up the situation and telephoned without loss of time to State police headquarters at Trenton.

Every sign indicated that the kidnapers had taken advantage of the isolated nature of the section and had executed their plans with the greatest possible caution.

The Lindbergh home, built for them while they were on their flight to the Orient last summer, is a rambling two and one-half story structure that sets back about half a mile from the Stoutsbury-Wertsville highway. The site was selected for its complete privacy and there are no other houses near. On nearly all sides are stretches of dense woodland.

FAMILY AT DINNER

Apparently the kidnaping occurred while Col. and Mrs. Lindbergh were at dinner. The maid, and a butler and his wife were the only other occupants of the house. It is believed the kidnapers parked their car on the highway, walked half a mile through the woods to the house, placed a ladder in position against the wall and gained entrance to the nursery through the window, which either had been left unlocked or was readily jimmied.

Search of the ground at the base of the ladder showed footprints but no shoeprints. The kidnapers apparently had either doffed their shoes or wrapped them carefully in sacking.

Possibility that a woman figured in the kidnaping developed, police said, when a minute examination of the grounds around the Lindbergh home revealed feminine footprints, along with those of a man.

As soon as State police arrived on the scene Col. Lindbergh joined them in searching the woods adjacent to the house, hoping that some tracks of the kidnapers might be found. The colonel went out hatless in a leather jacket such as he uses frequently for flying. But after searching for more than half an hour and finding no clews they returned again to the house.

Col. Lindbergh would not discuss the events of the evening with newspaper men.

"You'll have to excuse me," he told them. "I'm sure you'll understand how I feel."

Mrs. Lindbergh, though greatly shocked by the baby's disappearance, was reported to be "bearing up as well as might be expected."

Within a few minutes after word of the kidnaping reached State police headquarters at Trenton all available troopers were ordered out to search automobiles along the highway and an alarm was flashed over the police teletype system in New Jersey, and adjacent States.

The alarm read:

"Col. Lindbergh's baby kidnaped from Lindbergh home at Hopewell between 7:30 and 10 p.m. Boy, nineteen months, dressed in sleeping suit. Search all cars."

A check was made on all of the men employed in some recent construction work on the building, in the belief that they alone would know exactly where the night nursery was located in the rear of the residence overlooking the gravel driveway.

Aviators throughout the nation volunteered their services, and tomorrow will fly over the country in an attempt to find the abductors or their hide-out. Army and Navy planes, as well as all craft at Roosevelt, Curtiss, Wright, Floyd Bennett, Newark and other near-by air fields were placed at Col. Lindbergh's command.

Shortly after midnight the Princeton police sent over the network of wires the first message containing anything approaching a definite clew. It read as follows:

"Information received that two men in blue or black sedan bearing New York license plates stopped a man working on highway and asked to be directed to the Lindbergh home in Hopewell."

Relayed to every outpost, this message gave the searchers their first indication of the possible description of the kidnapers' car. It was so vague, however, that they did not permit it to stop them from questioning the occupants of cars of other descriptions.

New York police received the alarm at 10:45 o'clock and a few minutes later Pennsylvania authorities also were notified.

Efforts to reach the Lindbergh home met the response: "No one has time to talk now."

The chief operator at the Hopewell telephone exchange said that although the Lindbergh home had a private telephone she had been instructed by Col. Lindbergh to "keep my telephone line clear all night." She said he had asked particularly that no calls from newspapers be put through till morning.

IN SECLUDED SPOT

The Lindbergh home is in a secluded spot in the Sourland Hills and is reached from Hopewell only by rough hirt roads, which wind through scrub and woodland. The home itself is backed by dense woods, but to the front and on each side there is open country and a quarter mile from the house is a natural landing field, which Col. Lindbergh had improved to assure safety in taking off and descending on his flights.

The only neighbors of the Lindberghs are farmers. Col. and Mrs. Lindbergh, seeking complete privacy, picked the site from the air and their home was built while they were on their trip to the Orient last fall. Hopewell is between fifteen and twenty miles south of Trenton and about five miles northeast of Princeton.

Col. Lindbergh had been scheduled to speak tonight at a dinner in this city of New York University alumni but he did not appear.

As soon as the alarm reached headquarters in New York Capt. James Cooper, in charge of the telegraph bureau, notified Commissioner Edward P. Mulrooney and Chief Inspector John O'Brien, Commissioner Mulrooney raced to headquarters and ordered nothing left undone to assure the capture of the kidnapers' automobile if one was used. Special police cars were shot out to help the

(Continued on Page 2, Column 1)

KIDNAP BILL VOTE NEAR

Death Provided as Penalty

Early Passage of Measure, Making Crime Federal Offense, Predicted.

Lindbergh Baby Abduction Considered by Author as Spur to Action

WASHINGTON, March 1. (Exclusive)—Immediate pressure for early passage of the measure making kidnaping a Federal offense punishable by death is held certain to be the result of the kidnaping of Col. Charles A. Lindbergh's son.

Senator Patterson of Missouri recently introduced a bill to this effect. It provides a death penalty. The measure would give authority to the government when the kidnaped person is removed from one State to another. The bill was approved unanimously two weeks ago by the Senate Judiciary Committee and its supporters are confident that it will be adopted by the Senate.

A companion bill, introduced by Representative Cochran of Missouri, chairman of the committee on expenditures, has been before the Judiciary Committee in that branch for about ten days. The hearings are scheduled for completion soon and the portents, before news of the Lindbergh kidnaping became known, were for a favorable report.

SHOCK TO SENATOR

"It is a shock to me to hear of this outrage," said Senator Patterson of the Lindbergh case. "I hope the child will soon be returned to its parents. This filthy act will aid us in passing the needed legislation and I am sorry it will not be retroactive, so that the Lindbergh kidnapers can be dealt with by the Federal government."

On January 23, last, a telephone message was received from Chicago to the effect that there was a plot to kidnap Gen. Charles G. Dawes, who had just been appointed president of the Reconstruction Finance Corporation.

Mr. Patterson then said that this information came from a newspaper correspondent. It created excitement in Washington official circles, although the general refused to take it it seriously. However, it spurred the efforts of those behind the legislation.

LIST OF KIDNAPINGS

As a result, when the House Judiciary Committee began hearings Col. Isham Randolph of Chicago, head of the "Secret Six" of that city, and former Representative Cleveland A. Newton of St. Louis came to Washington to urge early action. Mr. Newton gave the following list of kidnapings which he said had taken place:

California, 25; Indiana, 20; Illinois, 49; Kansas, 8; Michigan, 26; Oklahoma, 9; Wisconsin, 8; Nebraska, 6; Massachusetts, 15, and New Jersey, 10.

Representative Cochran declared the government was powerless and said this act would undoubtedly result in the early passage of his bill in the House.

THE "TIMES" TODAY—NEWS SUMMED UP

Welsh Students Tear Down Flag

CARNARVON (Wales) March 1. (AP)—Welsh Nationalist students today haupled down the Union Jack from historic Carnarvon Castle and tore it to shreds in the market place.

Their action was a reprisal for the government's refusal to accede to the Welsh Nationalist request that the red dragon flag of Wales should fly over the castle today, St. David's Day.

Farm Products at Lowest Prices

CHICAGO, March 1. (AP)—Wholesale butter and egg prices were the lowest they have been at this time of the year since the beginning of the twentieth century.

Extra grade butter sold wholesale at 21 1-4 cents a pound, and first quality eggs at 12 1-4 cents a dozen.

ALIEN BAN AS MEMBER BASIS VOTED

House Committee Passes Measure in Apportioning of Representatives

WASHINGTON, March 1. (AP)—The Sparks resolution proposing a constitutional amendment to exclude aliens in the apportionment of Representatives among the States was approved today by the House Judiciary Committee by a 12-to-7 vote.

The resolution is identical to one reported to the last House, which failed of action. The committee added an amendment requiring ratification in seven years.

The proposed amendment would read:

"Aliens shall be excluded from the count of the whole number of persons in each State in apportioning Representatives among the several States according to their respective numbers."

Middle West's March Leonine

CHICAGO, March 1. (Exclusive) With a load of sleet, snow, rain and wind, March blew into the Middle West today.

The storms rode down on this section on cold, blustery gales, driving temperatures down to below the freezing point. Colder weather is in store for tomorrow, according to the weather forecast tonight.

AMERICAN-FINNS ORGANIZE

HELSINGFORS (Finland) March 1. (AP)—An American-Finnish society was established last night at a meeting of prominent citizens to further industrial, cultural and social collaboration of Finns and Americans.

MORE COFFEE DESTROYED

RIO DE JANEIRO, March 1. (AP) The government destroyed 102,866 sacks of coffee during the week ended February 27.

Scores Homeless as Fire Rages in Jersey Town

PENNS GROVE (N. J.) March 1. (AP)—Fifty to sixty small homes were burned or damaged and a church and six stores were destroyed by a fire in Western Penns Grove Borough today.

About 200 persons were rendered homeless.

The damage was estimated by authorities at close to $500,000.

Full Story of the Olympic Games in Special Olympic Games Section of This Issue

All the News All the Time

LARGEST HOME-DELIVERED CIRCULATION
LARGEST ADVERTISING VOLUME

MADISON 2345
The Times Telephone Number
Connecting All Departments

In Two Parts — 32 Pages

PART I — TELEGRAPH SHEET — 16 PAGES

TIMES OFFICES
100 North Broadway
619½ South Spring
And Throughout Southern California

VOL. LI. C SATURDAY MORNING, JULY 30, 1932. DAILY, FIVE CENTS

SEVENTEEN WORDS TODAY TO OPEN TENTH OLYMPIAD

Vice-President Curtis Ready for Ceremony Starting World's Greatest Athletic Drama

The President's Greeting

President Hoover, through Vice-President Curtis, yesterday sent the following message to participants and guests of the Olympic Games:

"Will you please extend my cordial greetings to all those gathered at Los Angeles for the opening of the Olympic Games, and also my hearty welcome to our visitors from abroad. I deeply regret that I am unable to be present, for I had looked forward with eagerness to the pleasure of seeing these wonderful sports and also to visiting my home State. In the years since the Olympic Games were held in America for the first time, at St. Louis, they have grown steadily in the interest of all the Nations, until today they occupy at least as great a significance in our world as the original Olympic Games occupied in the ancient world when Greece was at the height of its glory. They have become a positive force for international acquaintance and understanding and good will. They teach that the hardest competition may be accompanied by good humor, and that rivalry may be expressed with good sportsmanship. I warmly hope that the Games may be in every way successful. Especially do I send my encouragement and best wishes to our own American athletes."

BY JEAN BOSQUET

"I proclaim open the Olympic Games of Los Angeles, celebrating the Tenth Olympiad of the modern era!"

These seventeen words, spoken by Charles Curtis, Vice-President of the United States, today at Olympic Stadium will usher in the greatest event of the Southland's history, the Olympic Games, spawn of the ancient Greeks, dedicated to the God Zeus—and hope of a world at peace.

Vice-President Curtis will make the short speech because Herbert Hoover is too deeply swamped in his labors. And the Vice-President cannot say more about the stupendous program which he unfolds. The sacred protocol of the Games prevents it. He must doff his famous silk "topper" and say only the seventeen words, which have been the same since 1896, when the Games were revived, and which will always be the same.

WORLD AT ATTENTION

A watching world will stand virtually at attention as the man from Kansas speaks the prescribed words, a world whose eyes and thoughts are focused upon Los Angeles.

Vice-President Curtis will be speaking from the Tribune of Honor at the Stadium. He will have witnessed the great parade of nations which is a part of every opening ceremony of the Olympiads. In this mighty parade will have passed almost 2000 athletes representing two-score nations. And not only the multitude at the Stadium, but the radio ears of the world will hear his words.

The crashing utterance of a ten-gun salute from American field pieces situated near the Stadium will follow the opening address.

FLAME TO FLARE UP

Then Vice-President Curtis will press a silver button near his chair. At the instant of his movement, a light will flare upward from the top of the great peristyle at the Stadium's main entrance, as the Olympic Torch bursts into flame in the traditional manner of the ancient Greeks summoning the athletes of the world to the Games.

Meanwhile, a vast chorus of voices and a massed band will have started a wave of sound in the Stadium. The Olympian hymn, with all its tradition and import, will fill the air of the vast amphitheater. The old Greeks will have been cham-

(Continued on Page 3, Column 5)

CUSTOM OF GAMES KEPT BY HOOVER

President Breaks Bread in Spirit With Olympic Contenders Across Nation

WASHINGTON, July 29. (AP)—President Hoover today broke bread, in a spirit of hospitality and fellowship, with athletes assembled for the Olympic Games in Los Angeles.

Representative Englebright of California presented a loaf of bread to the Chief Executive at the White House, explaining it was a custom for the reigning head of the nation acting as host to the athletes "to partake of the same bread at his own table that the competitors at the Games eat at their training table."

Englebright said the bread had been sent by airplane in order that the historic custom, established in the last century, could be continued.

Mr. Hoover replied that he appreciated the gesture, gladly would accept the bread, and placed it on his luncheon table in order that he might join in some way with the Olympic athletes.

NEW CHILEAN REGIME RECOGNIZED BY CUBA

HAVANA, July 29. (AP)—Cuba extended recognition today to the provisional government of Chile.

THOUSANDS SEEK GOLD

MEXICO CITY, July 29. (AP)—The gold rush that resulted from recent placer findings in the State of Sinaloa has attracted more than 1000 families to that district, it was reported today.

AIMS VOICED BY HOOVER

Rehabilitation Goal Cited

Plans for Pushing Nation Toward Better Times Have Nine Points

Slums Replacement, Rail Activity and Help for Agriculture Sought

WASHINGTON, July 29. (AP)—Plans for a concerted push toward national economic rehabilitation—reaching from coast to coast and into every industry—were outlined in a nine-point program today by President Hoover.

Speaking quietly, the Chief Executive counted off to newspaper men one point after another of a project upon which he and administration leaders are at work.

Quickly he enumerated plans to replace slum districts, stimulate programs for railway replacement and repair, broaden live stock and feeder loans, expand credit facilities and speed up the movement of agricultural commodities.

CALL FOR ACTION

When these variegated efforts are further advanced, the President said, the "business and industrial" committees, composed of prominent men in each of the twelve Federal districts, will be called into conference "with a view to establishing united and concerted action on a broad front throughout the country."

Should all these leaders come to the national capital simultaneously, the gathering might well establish a new high in efforts to improve the nation economically. The committees concerned were formed on the President's suggestion after a group of business men in New York banded together for co-ordinated effort.

Mr. Hoover said he spoke today of his ideas and efforts because of "some erroneous speculation" concerning conferences held by him, Secretaries Mills and Lamont, directors of the Reconstruction Finance Corporation, and others.

OUTLINES ACTIVITIES

Threading through almost the entire woof of the program, he then outlined activities of the $3,800,000,000 Reconstruction Corporation, the directorate of which he completed yesterday with the naming of Charles A. Miller of Utica, N. Y., who will be its president.

As the first point in his program, the President spoke of better organizing the corporation's new $1,500,000,000 powers for financing self-liquidating projects. An engineer of standing, he said, will be appointed as chairman of a board of engineers to advise the corporation as to how employment may be stimulated through early orders of material.

The Chief Executive's mention of a slum-cleaning campaign was his

(Continued on Page 2, Column 6)

A Real League of Nations!

LAST BONUS BAND OUSTED; HOOVER PRAISES TROOPS

Veterans Quit City as Camps Burn; Quiz Ordered and Reds Seized; White House Under Guard

WASHINGTON, July 29. (AP)—With one final gas and fire attack Federal troops late today swept away the last vestiges of the bonus army encampments in downtown Washington and heard their job pronounced well done by their Commander-in-Chief, President Hoover.

Confident that order at last had been restored after riotous clashes and hand-to-hand battles between police and veterans, the cavalry was returned to Fort Myer, Virginia, and the infantry taken in trucks to the Washington Quartermaster Depot, a temporary war structure several blocks from the White House, where it was quartered for the night.

Just as the tear-gas and torch-bearing troopers and doughboys were firing their last veteran shanty and scattering the few straggling bonus seekers in all directions, President Hoover announced to the nation that the riotous challenge to the government authority had been "met swiftly and firmly."

Maj.-Gen. V. H. Moseley, deputy Chief of Staff, said the military phases of the troubles were over.

"It is now a job for the District of Columbia police force," he added. "Of course, the troops will continue to lend a hand where the police need assistance. But the task is to keep the campers from drifting back into the city and to prevent crowds from congregating.

"The campers are leaving Washington in large numbers and a part of our troops have been withdrawn, as there will no longer be need for large patrols of soldiers."

Like Secretary Hurley and Maj.-Gen. Douglas MacArthur, Chief of Staff, Gen. Moseley emphasized that after the Army took charge of the situation yesterday not a civilian nor a soldier was injured, so far as the War Department has been able to learn.

HOOVER ORDERS INQUIRY

"Government cannot be coerced by mob rule," the President said, emphatically. He ordered a grand jury investigation of yesterday's clashes.

Thirty-six radical members of the "bonus expeditionary force" had been arrested by police as they left a meeting in an abandoned church in Southeast Washington. About seventy-five more of their number were escorted out of the city and a general exodus of hundreds of veterans made headway through the day and evening.

District of Columbia officials called the grand jury inquiry to start Monday.

The Red Cross formally offered transportation home to women and children of the marchers.

HOOVER'S STATEMENT

The President announced the Justice Department is pressing its inquiry into the violence resulting in the call for troops and expressed the hope the culprits will be taken speedily to trial in the civil courts. The text of his statement follows:

"A challenge to the authority of the United States government has been met swiftly and firmly.

"After months of patient indulgence, the government met overt lawlessness as it always must be met if the processes of self-government are to be preserved. We cannot tolerate the abuse of constitutional rights by those who would destroy all government.

"No matter who they may be government cannot be coerced by mob rule.

"The Deparment of Justice is pressing its investigation into the violence which forced the call for army detachments, and it is my sincere hope that those agitators who inspired yesterday's attack upon the Federal authority may be brought speedily to trial in the civil courts. There can be no safe harbor in the United States of America for violence.

"Order and civil tranquillity

(Continued on Page 2, Column 1)

PARIS DEFIED BY BERLIN

Threat to Arm Reaffirmed

Germany Notifies France It Will Gird Self Unless Others Disarm

Von Papen Assures America He Plans No Dictatorship; Hitler Troops Mass

BERLIN, July 29. (AP)—Chancellor von Papen assured the United States in a trans-Atlantic broadcast tonight that neither he nor his ministers are maneuvering for a German dictatorship.

His address, in which he assailed the Versailles Treaty, took on added significance because of two factors. Germany is embroiled in the campaign for the Reichstag elections Sunday, and she is involved in a new difference with France.

A few hours before the Chancellor went on the air, his Foreign Minister, Baron Konstantin von Neurath, told the French Ambassador that when Defense Minister von Schleicher threatened the other day to arm Germany if the other nations do not disarm, he spoke for every member of the German Cabinet and for the whole German nation.

FOR DEFENSE ONLY

The Treaty of Versailles limits Germany's armed forces to the number needed to preserve interior order.

The Von Papen radio speech, sponsored by the International Radio Forum founded by Ira Nelson Morris, American diplomat, was in English, a language the Chancellor learned when he served the old imperial government at Washington.

The treaty of Versailles, Von Papen said, is the main cause of the fatherland's distress; it fosters radicalism both of the Right and of the Left.

"But whereas National Socialism (the Fascist movement led by Adolf Hitler) aspires to national regeneration," the Chancellor declared, "Communism is directed against the cultural foundation of our national social life and is, therefore, a revolutionary movement and a danger to the country and the world."

CIVIL WAR THREATENED

Referring to the political events of the last few weeks, the Chancellor said "the outside world does not quite realize that Germany was endangered by an aspect of civil war due to extremist tension."

The Communists, he continued, had built powerful fighting units throughout Prussia and the recent disorders were due mainly to their illegal activities, which no government could continue to tolerate

(Continued on Page 2, Column 5)

RECEIVER FOR JULIAN APPOINTED

Promoter Reiterates His Story of Being "Broke;" Tells of Insurance

OKLAHOMA CITY, July 29. (AP) C. C. Julian, who built up an oil fortune from a "shoestring," returned today from Canada and heard a receiver appointed for what remains of his personal wealth.

Julian reiterated he is "broke," and answered questions propounded on behalf of creditors with "I don't remember," but said he has life insurance totaling $205,000.

The creditors asked a continuance until September 9 to permit investigation.

Julian was adjudicated bankrupt in Federal court after stating he is penniless and owes $3,057,436.

The promoter said "the books ought to show" what went with the millions of dollars of assets of the C. C. Julian Oil and Royalties Company while he was trustee. A. M. Betts, counsel for John W. Harreld, receiver of the company, said the books might be investigated.

Railway Sues Truck Owner

MUSKOGEE (Okla.) July 29. (AP) They used to sue the railroad but now:

The Fort Worth and Denver Railroad sued W. J. McFarland, truck line operator, today, for $61,401, asserting a truck broke an underpass at Oklaunion, Tex., August 3, 1930.

Passing over the underpass a train was wrecked, one person was killed and several injured. The amount asked was paid out for personal damages and repairs.

Chevaliers Balk Reconciliation

PARIS, July 29. (AP)—Maurice Chevalier and his wife, Yvonne Vallee, who are seeking a divorce by mutual consent, met today at the Palace of Justice for a formal attempt at reconciliation. It was unsuccessful.

Congress Asked to Note French Film Decree

PARIS, July 29. (AP)—Representatives of American motion-picture interests in France issued a statement today expressing the hope that the American Congress will remember the "unfair" limitation imposed upon American film imports whenever French imports to the United States are under consideration.

The statement was prompted by yesterday's Presidential decree barring from France talking pictures in which the speech is not synchronized with the film in this country. The Americans said that while it does not actually fix a quota the decree nevertheless limits the exhibition of foreign films to ten theaters and reserves the right to limit the day-to-day release of films synchronized in France.

Two Reds Go to Gallows Still Cheering Cause

BUDAPEST (Hungary) July 29. (AP)—Cheering for Communism, Emmerich Sallai-Hollaender and Alexander Fuerst, Communists sentenced to death for participating in a conspiracy to overthrow the government, went to the gallows today a few hours after a court-martial had condemned them.

Both men were active in the Bela Kun Communist regime in Hungary in 1919. They were Jews.

Hoover Signs 523 Measures

WASHINGTON, July 29. (AP)—President Hoover wrote his signature 523 times during the last session of Congress in making effective bills and resolutions passed by the legislators.

The President wielded his veto power eight times, the most notable instance being his rejection of the Wagner-Garner relief bill. He employed the pocket veto on one measure.

UTAH CATTLEMAN DIES

SAN FRANCISCO, July 29. (AP)—Charles Clayton, 59 years of age, of Ogden, Utah, one of the West's best-known cattle dealers, died here last night.

BOLIVIANS RAID FOE'S GARRISONS

Two Attackers Killed as Paraguayans Repulse Drive on Border Forts

ASUNCION (Paraguay) July 29. (AP)—Bolivian forces made attacks today on two Paraguayan garrisons along the border between the two countries, an official bulletin said today.

One detachment attacked Fort Corrales and was driven off without losses. Another was repulsed by the garrison of Fort Coronel. In that skirmish two Bolivians were killed and one was wounded. One Paraguayan soldier also was wounded.

The bulletin said a Bolivian airplane had been sighted over the Paraguayan Fort Boqueron at noon yesterday.

Arizona Loses on Train Limit

PHOENIX, July 29. (AP)—The State of Arizona lost today the first round of its fight to maintain constitutionality of its train limit law. J. E. Morrison, special master in chancery, in his report to the Federal court, held the law, which limits passenger trains passing through the State to fourteen cars, and freight trains to seventy cars, to be unconstitutional on every point raised by the railroads, in its effect on interstate commerce.

Liquor Damages Awarded Wife

ST. PAUL, July 29. (AP)—The Minnesota Supreme Court today ordered payment of damages by liquor sellers to a woman whose husband became crippled after drinking moonshine. The court held Mrs. Mary Benes was entitled to $3300 damages awarded her in a suit against Thomas and Annie Wrabek, who were asserted to have sold liquor to friends of Joseph Benes, 68 years of age, in January, 1929.

Cholera Pushes Into Manchuria

MUKDEN (Manchoukuo) July 30. (Saturday) (AP)—Cholera, now epidemic in China, is spreading to many sections of Manchuria.

Serious outbreaks were reported today in numerous cities. The worst is at Gungliao, where 500 cases and 130 deaths have been recorded.

SERVICES CONDUCTED FOR BETROTHED PAIR

BERKELEY, July 29. (AP)—Joint funeral services were conducted here today for Dr. Roger Miller Jones, former professor of Greek at Johns Hopkins University, and Mrs. Muriel Thoma, who were drowned in Pyramid Lake, Nevada, last Monday. They were to have been married the next day.

THE "TIMES" TODAY—NEWS SUMMED UP

FEATURES. Radio, Page 8, Part I; Women's Page, Page 5, Part II; Markets and Financial, Pages 9 to 11, inclusive, Part II; Oil News, Page 9, Part I; Comics, Page 6, Part II.

CONTRACT BRIDGE. By Milton C. Work. Page 5, Part II.

DRAMA. Page 7, Part I.

NEWS IN SPANISH. Page 8, Part I.

SHIPPING NEWS. Page 12, Part II.

FINANCIAL. Sinclair outlines status in connection with Richfield Oil purchase. Tide Water Associated reports 10 cents a share earned in second quarter. Continental Oil also reports profits in second three months. Page 9, Part II.

Stocks continue to forge ahead despite profit-taking activities. Page 9, Part II.

NEWS OF SOUTHERN COUNTIES. Searching parties are out in the San Bernardino Mountains, seeking a woman, two girls and a youth missing more than thirty-six hours. Two seaplane pilots killed and three men rescued when giant craft crashes in ocean off Del Mar. Republican women at Redlands indorse campaign of Senator Shortridge for re-election at luncheon given in his honor. Page 6, Part I.

SPORTS. Parade of Olympic stars today will be epic. Page 9, Part I.

Finns send defi on Nurmi. Page 9, Part I.

Earth never has seen such display of power in Games. Page 9, Part I.

THE CITY. Fifteen thousand attend colorful exercises dedicating new State Building and witness presentation of flying cross to Amelia Earhart by Vice-President Curtis. Page 1, Part II.

Throngs greet Vice-President Curtis, who arrives in city to open Olympic Games; guest at many events. Page 1, Part II.

Subpoenas issued for panel of thirty drawn for new grand jury. Page 1, Part II.

Harbor officials to open convention here today. Page 1, Part II.

Women's place in sports outlined in closing session of Recreation Congress. Page 1, Part II.

Record crowd at municipal airport sees March Field planes reviewed by Chief of Army Air Corps. Page 1, Part II.

Seven hundred police officers receive instructions from Mayor and Chief for special duties during Olympic Games. Page 3, Part II.

Gallaher sentenced to prison for oil fraud. Page 2, Part II.

Influx of Shriners from San Francisco convention slated to begin this morning. Page 5, Part II.

Former hotel man leaps ten floors to death from downtown building. Page 3, Part II.

Two racing-dog owners jailed for contempt in refusing to testify against Culver City group; case dismissed. Page 3, Part II.

Navy fleet at anchor here for Olympic Games period swelled by arrival of nine craft today. Page 2, Part II.

Man and boy killed and several persons injured in series of traffic accidents. Page 8, Part II.

GENERAL EASTERN. New York business man and close friend of President denies Hoover has made and lost fortune in investments in recent years. Page 2, Part I.

Bonus army chiefs to organize "khaki shirts" in Johnstown, Pa. Page 2, Part I.

Eastern leaders for Hoover campaign appointed. Page 4, Part I.

WASHINGTON. Troops oust last of bonus army; Hoover lauds speed in ending crisis. Page 1, Part I.

Hoover tells of plans to rehabilitate nation's business. Page 1, Part I.

United States and thirty-three other nations to open polar year scientific studies in Arctic Monday. Page 3, Part I.

Senator Harrison opens Democratic campaign over radio with attack on Hoover. Page 4, Part I.

FOREIGN. Germany reaffirms threat to arm unless France disarms. Page 1, Part I.

British Dominions may adopt series of independent trade agreements instead of empire preference program. Page 4, Part I.

French view expressed Washington will be scene of world economic conference in the autumn. Page 4, Part I.

Remember This

Only those with small minds try to belittle others.

WOMEN TO ATTEMPT ENDURANCE FLIGHT

VALLEY STREAM (N. Y.) July 29. (AP)—A refueling endurance flight in an effort to capture the women's record for sustained flight will be started here August 8 by Mrs. Frances Marsallis, formerly of Centerville, Tex., and Louise Thaden of Baltimore.

PIONEER LUMBERMAN DIES

PETALUMA, July 29. (AP)—George W. Moore, 73 years of age, former Michigan State Senator and pioneer lumberman of Bandon, Or., died here last night.

COW'S STOMACH WORKS FOR ALL WORLD TO SEE

ST. PAUL, July 29. (AP)—Betty, cow with a window, munched grass as usual today and felt very well.

A veterinarian placed a glass, 2 by 3 inches, in Betty's side so the effect of foods on digestive action might be studied conveniently. The glass is mounted on a silver plate.

D. E. Hale of Chicago, animal and poultry specialist, owns the cow. A local anesthetic was used in the operation.

"The window allows stomach contents to be taken out any time for laboratory work without pain or discomfort to the cow," he said. "And it will be a great aid to science because the digestive action can be studied at any time to prove nutrition theories.

"Penn State College had a cow with a hole in its side which was there nine years. It died last spring from old age.

"But so far as we can find out this is the first cow in the world to have a real window with a transparent cover for protection."

WILL ROGERS REMARKS:

BEVERLY HILLS, July 29.—[To the Editor of The Times:] Too bad, this affair in Washington. Personally, I think the whole idea of this pilgrimage was ill-advised and no doubt did their cause harm, but they have their side of it, too. They have the same right there as any other "lobbyist." They at least were not paid, they were doing it for themselves, which placed 'em right away about 90 per cent higher in public estimation than the thousands of "lobbyists" that are there all the time.

But no matter how you feel about the whole thing, you have got to admire the fine way that big body of hungry men acted while they were there. They hold the record for being the best behaved of any 15,000 hungry men ever assembled anywhere in the world. They were hungry and they were seeing our government wasting thousands and millions before their eyes, and yet they remained fair and sensible. Would 15,000 hungry bankers have done it, 15,000 farmers, 15,000 preachers? And just think what 15,000 club women would have done to Washington even if they wasn't hungry. The Senate would have resigned and the President committed suicide.

It's easy to be a gentleman when you are well fed, but those boys did it on an empty stomach. So we at least owe 'em a vote of thanks. And it was too bad their fine record was marred at the finish by somebody blundering.

Yours,

WILL ROGERS.

All the News All the Time
LARGEST HOME-DELIVERED CIRCULATION
LARGEST ADVERTISING VOLUME

MAdison 2345
The Times Telephone Number
Connecting All Departments

Los Angeles Times

EQUAL RIGHTS · LIBERTY UNDER THE LAW · TRUE INDUSTRIAL FREEDOM

In Two Parts — 32 Pages
PART I — TELEGRAPH SHEET — 16 PAGES

TIMES OFFICES
100 North Broadway
619½ South Spring
And Throughout Southern California

VOL. LI. CC WEDNESDAY MORNING, NOVEMBER 9, 1932. DAILY, FIVE CENTS

ROOSEVELT IS ELECTED PRESIDENT; M'ADOO SENATOR FOR CALIFORNIA

BOURBON NOMINEE WINS EASILY IN CALIFORNIA

Carries Los Angeles County and Bay District by Big Margin; Wright Act Repealed

Five thousand and ninety-nine precincts out of a total of 10,547 in California give for President: Franklin D. Roosevelt, 583,357; President Hoover, 383,485.

State-wide returns from yesterday's election in California show the following results:

Gov. Roosevelt carried the State over President Hoover by a majority between 300,000 and 400,000.

William G. McAdoo, Democratic nominee for United States Senator, was elected over Tallant Tubbs, Republican, and Rev. R. P. Shuler, Prohibition candidate.

Five, possibly six, of the eight Congressional seats from Los Angeles county seem likely to be occupied by Democrats in the next national legislature.

The Wright prohibition-enforcement act was repealed and its companion measure No. 2, providing State control of liquor, carried, both by big votes.

In Los Angeles county Harry M. Baine, incumbent Supervisor in the Third District, was elected over Robert M. Allan. In the Fifth District Henry W. Wright, incumbent and chairman of the board, was defeated by Roger Jessup.

Judges Fleming, Stafford and Guerin were recalled, and William J. Palmer, William S. Baird and Charles L. Bogue elected as their respective successors. All the incumbent judges nominated at the primaries were returned to the bench.

State Proposition No. 3, abolishing the trust deed, was defeated.

No. 4, allowing the State to place in the general fund its half of highway transportation taxes, was defeated.

No. 5, permitting race-track betting, carried.

No. 9, transferring county school taxes to the State, was defeated.

No. 11, permitting Huntington Beach to drill for oil on her tidelands, was defeated.

No. 13, amending the State boxing law, carried.

Gov. Roosevelt won California's twenty-two electoral votes by a majority over President Hoover which may reach 400,000.

The Democratic nominee ran more than 125,000 ahead of the President in Los Angeles county, where the principal vote of the State was registered, and while the Roosevelt victory in San Francisco was smaller in actual figures, the Governor of New York carried the Bay City more than two to one over Hoover.

Alameda county, which had been confidently listed in the Republican column, went over to Roosevelt substantially. Sacramento gave Roosevelt a lead of almost two to one.

Orange and Riverside counties, on the basis of incomplete returns, gave a small majority to Hoover.

The city of Los Angeles went overwhelmingly Democratic, as did many other sections of the county, although Pasadena, Pomona and several smaller communities in the State gove Hoover a majority.

The San Joaquin Valley returned large Democratic majorities, Fresno county going almost three to one for Roosevelt. A close race developed in San Bernardino county, with Roosevelt holding a slight lead. The Democratic nominee apparently carried Imperial county by more than two and one-half to one and also ran ahead in San Diego county.

EIGHTY PER CENT VOTE

Throughout California yesterday the largest vote in the State's history was cast and early tabulations indicated that the total might exceed 2,250,000, which is approximately 80 per cent of the full registration.

Approximately 1,000,000 Los Angeles county voters went to the polls, voting percentages in many city and county precincts running as high as 85 per cent of the registration total.

The total vote for the State four years ago was 1,796,283.

The unprecedented number of voters flocking to the polls in all sections of California yesterday and the unusually large size of the ballot contributed to congestion at most of the voting places throughout the day, and in hundreds of polling places extra ballot boxes were called for.

Registrar of Voters Kerr had calls for more than 1200 boxes in addition to the number supplied the 3568 polling-places in the city and county and when the extra ballot receptacles proved inadequate, election officials were forced

(Continued on Page 2, Column 1)

THE INDEX

The news index which customarily appears on Page 1 of The Times will be found on the second page today.

TOGA FOR DEMOCRAT

McAdoo Elected U. S. Senator

Big Margin Over Tubbs and Shuler Is Maintained Throughout State

Five Bourbons Ahead for Eight Congress Seats From This County

For Senator, 4458 precincts out of 10,547 in the State gave the following: McAdoo, 285,106; Tubbs, 199,694; Shuler, 173,029.

William Gibbs McAdoo, former Secretary of the Treasury and the man chiefly credited with responsibility for maneuvering Gov. Roosevelt's nomination by the Democratic National Convention at Chicago, was elected United States Senator from California yesterday though by a vote that fell considerably below that given the Democratic President-elect in this State.

He defeated Tallant Tubbs, Republican nominee, and Rev. R. P. Shuler, Prohibitionist nominee, by a wide plurality, however, and carried most of the fifty-eight counties of the State.

McAdoo's heaviest vote was in Los Angeles county, where Shuler was a poor second and Tubbs a poorer third.

In San Francisco city and county, the home of Tubbs, the Republican nominee had a lead of approximately two to one over the successful Democratic candidate, and the San Francisco vote of Tubbs was about seven to one over Shuler's in that area.

FOR CONGRESS

Victory for five and possibly six Democratic nominees for the House of Representatives from Los Angeles county was indicated, the only apparently sure Republican triumph in this county occurring in the Fifteenth District, where Sheriff Traeger, Republican, defeated John M. Costello, Democratic nominee.

In the Eleventh District, Representative Evans, Republican incumbent, took a belated lead over Albert D. Hadley, Democratic nominee, but this race was so close as to remain in doubt on the basis of incomplete returns.

John H. Hoeppel, Democrat, held a substantial lead over Assembly-

(Continued on Page 2, Column 8)

Our Next Chief Executive

Franklin Delano Roosevelt

ELECTION RETURNS

Following are Los Angeles city and county returns from yesterday's election as compiled up to 1 o'clock this morning.

PRESIDENT	
(3943 Precincts out of 3568)	
Hoover (Rep.)	291,530
Roosevelt (Dem.)	424,361
Thomas (Soc.)	18,064
Upshaw (Proh.)	6,242
Harvey (Lib.)	2,735
UNITED STATES SENATE	
(2840 Precincts out of 3568)	
McAdoo, William G (Dem.)	250,173
Shuler, Robert P. (Proh.)	177,872
Tubbs, Tallant (Rep.)	128,524
COUNTY SUPERVISOR	
Third District	
(550 Precincts out of 640)	
Allan, Robert M.	31,264
Baine, Harry M.	50,153
Fifth District	
(610 Precincts out of 699)	
Jessup, Roger W.	37,464
Wright, Henry W.	27,408
CONGRESSIONAL	
Eleventh District	
36 Precincts out of 487)	
Evans, Williams E. (Rep.)	1,112
Hadley, Albert D. (Dem.)	981
Hartranft, Marshall V. (Lib.)	507
Twelfth District	
(120 Precincts out of 415)	
Cannon, Richard M. (Proh.)	1,088
Hoepple, John H. (Dem.)	7,106
Houser, Frederick F. (Rep.)	2,968
Thirteenth District	
(216 Precincts out of 519)	
Higgings, George D. (Lib.)	2,543
Kramer, Charles (Dem.)	18,388
Randall, Charles H. (Rep.)	16,176
Fourteenth District	
(174 Precincts out of 388)	
Campbell, William D. (Rep.)	9,292
Ford, Thomas F. (Dem.)	13,149
Fifteenth District	
(260 Precincts out of 485)	
Costello, John M. (Dem.)	20,313
Traeger, William I. (Rep.)	24,614
Sixteenth District	
(105 Precincts out of 512)	
Dockweiler, John F. (Dem.)	11,311
Woodworth, Clyde (Rep.)	8,057
Seventeenth District	
(169 Precincts out of 334)	
Colden, Chas. J. (Dem.)	16,375
Debs, Ernest E. (Lib.)	1,561
Henning, A. E. (Rep.)	8,064
Eighteenth District	
(28 Precincts out of 398)	
Burke, John H. (Dem.)	601
Henderson, Robert (Rep.)	5[illegible]
Hinshaw, William E. (Ind.)	42
SUPERIOR COURT	
(450 Precincts out of 3568)	
Office No. 5	
Ambrose, Thomas L.	29,953
Gates, Walter S.	44,516
Office No. 12	
Johnson, Charles P.	24,607
Pacht, Isaac	48,383

(Continued on Page 2, Column 1)

FULL DEMOCRAT CONTROL OF CONGRESS ASSURED

Scant Majority in Senate Gained; Watson, Bingham, Glenn Lose Victories Swell House Total

WASHINGTON, Nov. 9. (AP)—The same avalanche of votes that carried Franklin D. Roosevelt to victory virtually had assured the Democrats today of comfortable majorities in both House and Senate beginning March 4, next.

By 3 a.m. the Democrats had won three seats now held by Republicans, sufficient to give them a bare control of the Senate, and were leading in most of the other contests.

Several old-timers in the Senate Republican ranks already were beaten or dangerously close to defeat. James E. Watson, Republican leader; Hiram Bingham of Connecticut, and Otis Glenn of Illinois were all three out of the race. Reed Smoot, Senate dean; Thomas of Idaho, Jones of Washington, Moses of New Hampshire, and Oddie of Nevada were among those trailing their opponents.

Republicans had won only three seats, in Oregon, Vermont and North Dakota, while the Democrats had added sixteen to their thirty-one holdovers.

The Democrats also added fifteen Republican scalps in the House to the two they acquired in Maine last September, as they headed for a real working majority.

Representative Ruth Pratt of New

(Continued on Page 3, Column 7)

Will Rogers Remarks:

BEVERLY HILLS, Nov. 8.—[To the Editor of The Times:] If your side lost don't take it too much to heart. Remember there is always this difference between us and Italy. In Italy Mussolini runs the country. But here the country runs the President.

As I dispatch this little message along late in the evening it looks like the only thing can beat the Democrats is honest counting.

Certainly brought out a big vote. There was actually women went to the polls that didn't have a new hat. Humiliation couldn't even stop 'em.

Yours,

WILL ROGERS.

MAYOR VOTE OF O'BRIEN SETS MARK

Tammany Choice Victor in New York City Race With Lead of 616,736

NEW YORK, Nov. 8. (AP)—Surrogate John P. O'Brien was elected Mayor by a plurality of 616,736 on the basis of complete returns tonight, breaking the record James J. Walker set with a half million in 1929.

The Democratic candidate polled a total of 1,055,768 votes, to 439,032 for Lewis H. Pounds, Republican, and 248,425 for Morris Hillquit, Socialist.

Despite his record breaking plurality, however, O'Brien trailed his party's Presidential and gubernatorial nominees — Roosevelt and Lehman.

A huge vote registered for Joseph V. McKee, who has been Mayor since Walker resigned September 1, last, in the course of a removal hearing before Gov. Roosevelt, surprised most observers in view of the difficulties confronting his supporters.

It was necessary to write his name on a roll in the voting machines, a process not easily comprehended by many voters, and McKee publicly had discouraged the move.

Nevertheless he received 103,078 votes in 2321 precincts, including four in Manhattan.

O'Brien takes office January 1 next.

London Asserts Dry Law Doomed

LONDON (Wednesday) Nov. 9. (AP) The Daily Mail's reaction to the American election came out this morning in an editorial entitled "Prohibition Doomed." Results of the election were received too late for comment in other papers.

VOTE RECORD MAY BE BROKEN; SOUTH SOLIDLY DEMOCRATIC

New York and Other Key States Annexed by Totals Which Indicate Complete Bourbon Control in Both Houses of Congress

[BY THE ASSOCIATED PRESS.]

The people have voted for a change at Washington.

By a popular and electoral plurality that may establish a new record, they have elevated Franklin D. Roosevelt to the Presidency.

The Republican reverse, one of the greatest in this generation for any party, apparently has put both Senate and House into the hands of the Democrats by wide majorities.

HOW THE STATES VOTED

The following table, compiled by the Associated Press, shows the vote of the States with the indicated electoral vote up to the hour of going to press with this edition of The Times:

State	Total Dists.	Dists. Reptd.	Popular Vote Hoover	Popular Vote Roosevelt	Indicated Elec. Vote Hvr.	Indicated Elec. Vote Rvt.	In Doubt
Alabama	2,126	790	12,525	84,347	..	11	..
Arizona	468	170	7,344	15,753	..	3	..
Arkansas	2,100	317	2,840	29,239	..	9	..
California	10,547	2,824	231,589	337,941	..	22	..
Colorado	1,549	130	14,441	17,306	..	..	6
Connecticut	169	153	276,944	273,500	..	..	8
Delaware	226	143	27,341	22,203	..	..	3
Florida	1,272	554	26,279	80,314	..	7	..
Georgia	1,811	1,060	11,541	156,060	..	12	..
Idaho	819	155	16,539	23,718	..	4	..
Illinois	7,222	3,003	847,923	1,252,706	..	29	..
Indiana	3,691	1,270	307,142	378,464	..	14	..
Iowa	2,435	946	165,038	227,415	..	11	..
Kansas	2,676	943	119,930	147,141	..	9	..
Kentucky	4,184	....	......	......	..	11	..
Louisiana	1,452	292	4,997	65,465	..	10	..
Maine	632	598	162,637	125,381	5	..	..
Maryland	1,371	1,048	132,285	243,607	..	8	..
Massachusetts	1,707	1,183	454,814	512,066	..	17	..
Michigan	3,417	1,165	244,424	260,026	..	..	19
Minnesota	3,716	480	84,800	117,589	..	11	..
Mississippi	1,590	401	1,664	41,248	..	9	..
Missouri	4,233	1,718	148,513	325,174	..	15	..
Montana	1,442	83	7,394	11,548	..	4	..
Nebraska	2,038	[illegible]67	63,809	118,002	..	7	..
Nevada	234	135	3,974	8,761	..	3	..
New Hampshire	294	274	87,646	84,903	4	..	..
New Jersey	3,415	474	59,215	111,034	..	16	..
New Mexico	798	78	4,445	9,225	..	3	..
New York	8,837	8,252	1,795,185	2,438,101	..	47	..
North Carolina	1,829	977	85,552	292,565	..	13	..
North Dakota	2,240	139	9,450	14,571	..	..	4
Ohio	8,678	2,100	251,830	271,909	..	26	..
Oklahoma	3,311	1,782	79,982	266,347	..	11	..
Oregon	1,783	454	21,551	28,459	..	..	5
Pennsylvania	8,199	5,820	1,070,975	933,918	..	..	36
Rhode Island	229	200	96,954	119,136	..	4	..
South Carolina	1,209	828	1,690	83,423	..	8	..
South Dakota	1,931	769	47,789	80,626	..	4	..
Tennessee	2,255	1,763	74,742	150,016	..	11	..
Texas	254x	134	34,455	153,950	..	23	..
Utah	812	151	12,891	17,470	..	..	4
Vermont	248	248	77,664	54,751	3	..	..
Virginia	1,686	1,265	67,280	158,144	..	11	..
Washington	2,682	447	42,358	63,088	..	8	..
West Virginia	2,340	817	120,498	140,909	..	8	..
Wisconsin	2,899	1,652	200,889	403,528	..	12	..
Wyoming	667	100	2,145	3,308	..	..	3
Totals	119,721	48,953	7,621,914	10,854,355	12	431	88

xCounties.

Popular vote majority does not elect; a total of at least 266 electoral votes is necessary to elect.

Incomplete returns compiled by the Associated Press at 1 a.m., still inconclusive as to many States, show totals which if borne out by later figures would give the following electoral vote: Hoover, 59; Roosevelt, 472. Necessary to elect, 266.

President Hoover, watching the mounting returns with increasing favor to his opponent in forty States, sent to Gov. Roosevelt, shortly after 9 p.m., this telegram:

"I congratulate you on the opportunity that has come to you to be of service to the country."

The President-elect shortly before had told workers in the New York party headquarters:

"I hope all of us will do what we can to restore this country to prosperity."

The Roosevelt sweep, carrying him to the White House as the third Democrat to sit there since the Civil War, carried to victory many a minor candidate for State and Congressional office and shook some of the principal Republican strongholds in the country.

WET ACTION UNCERTAIN

The Roosevelt-Garner ticket was acclaimed on a platform advocating repeal of the Eighteenth Amendment and immediate modification of the Volstead law to legalize the manufacture of beer and wine. How completely or how soon this program might be put into effect, if at all, hung, however, on the Congressional and Senatorial elections.

The returns showed a large number of candidates whom wet or dry organizations had classified as for repeal or revision had been elected to the new House, which meets thirteen months hence. Five of seven Senators who had been definitely elected are recorded for repeal.

From the outset of the vote tabulating, all indicators pointed toward Roosevelt's election. And when New York with her vital block of forty-seven electoral votes was listed in the Democratic column, Republican hopes were shaken.

SOUTH AGAIN SOLID

The South, successfully invaded by Hoover in 1928, was once more solidly Democratic. In addition, Roosevelt was amassing commanding leads in many key States and leading by narrower margins in others.

When the President conceded that the day was lost, Gov. Roosevelt was leading in all but eight States, with an electoral count of 438. The Hoover States at the time were Michigan, which had been wavering back and forth through the compilation, Pennsylvania, Connecticut, Vermont, New Hampshire, Maine, and Delaware.

KENTUCKY CONCEDED

Kentucky does not begin counting until tomorrow, but its vote has been conceded to the Democrats. Barring upsets, it would raise the total to 453, or nine more than the record Hoover set in 1928.

Texas was giving the Democratic candidate a lead of more than six to one; in Virginia he was ahead by more than two to one; his advantage in Florida was three to one and in North Carolina four to one.

In addition, the border States of Tennessee, Maryland and Kentucky, which went to Hoover four years

(Continued on Page 3, Column 1)

HOOVER CONGRATULATES ROOSEVELT ON VICTORY

PALO ALTO, Nov. 8. (AP)—In a briefly worded telegram, President Hoover tonight congratulated Franklin D. Roosevelt saying, "I congratulate you on the opportunity that has come to you to be of service to the country."

While a gathering of friends and neighbors of the Hoovers lingered in the living-room of the home, one of the Chief Executive's secretaries handed to newspaper men the following message to the New York Governor:

"Hon. Franklin D. Roosevelt, Biltmore Hotel, New York City.

"I congratulate you on the opportunity that has come to you to be of service to the country, and I wish for you a most successful adminstration. In the common purpose of all of us I shall dedicate myself to every possible helpful effort."

The President sent the telegram from his study after watching the returns pile up increasing majorities for his opponent.

SET OFF FIREWORKS

When the announcement of the President's conceding came, shortly after 9:30 p.m., a throng of Stanford University students filled his driveway. They waited opportunity to stage a rally for him.

Shortly, the Chief Executive, with Mrs. Hoover by his side, appeared on the front balcony of their pueblo dwelling and a burst of cheering that lasted for four minutes was started.

Large powder candles were set off, lighting the driveway and the crowd bright as day.

Smoke from the candles swirled upward, almost completely enveloping the President and first lady, but they stood smiling, until the smoke diminished.

YELLS FOR HOOVER

Some one in the college called for "another yell for the President and Mrs. Hoover" and a "siren" consisting of a whistle or two and a "boom, rah, President and Mrs. Hoover," was given.

Secretary Wilbur, president on leave of Stanford University, who was with Mr. Hoover when he signed the telegram to Roosevelt, shook hands with him and offered his condolences.

Later, standing in the doorway of the Hoover home, while Mr. and Mrs. Hoover were on the balcony, the Secretary of the Interior, told newspaper men:

"I am sorry. He made a great fight."

PLANS NOT KNOWN

After the college cheer had been given, the cheer leader called for quiet, and when a silence had fallen so complete that the hiss of the powder candles could be heard, the President said:

"I thank you for your fine loyalty and I deeply appreciate this very hearty greeting. Trank you."

The President spoke with very

(Continued on Page 7, Column 1)

Remember This

Nothing is clear to the intelligence of one who is prejudiced against understanding.

All the News All the Time
LARGEST HOME-DELIVERED CIRCULATION
LARGEST ADVERTISING VOLUME

MAdison 2345
The Times Telephone Number
Connecting All Departments

Los Angeles Times

EQUAL RIGHTS
LIBERTY UNDER THE LAW
TRUE INDUSTRIAL FREEDOM

In Two Parts—22 Pages
PART I—TELEGRAPH SHEET—12 PAGES

TIMES OFFICES
100 North Broadway
619½ South Spring
And Throughout Southern California

VOL. LII. R SATURDAY MORNING, MARCH 11, 1933. DAILY, FIVE CENTS

SCORES PERISH IN SOUTHLAND QUAKE

BANKS TO REOPEN TODAY BY ORDER OF ROOSEVELT

Essential Needs to Be Cared For; Normal Resumption in Majority of Cases Presaged for Monday

BY KYLE D. PALMER
"Times" Staff Correspondent

WASHINGTON, March 10. (Exclusive)—Reopening of the nation's banks tomorrow for all essential needs of the people was made possible by President Roosevelt today in an executive order which presaged resumption of normal banking operations by a majority of national and State banks on Monday.

New currency just turned out of the government Bureau of Engraving and Printing is being shipped to Federal Reserve banks in all sections of the United States, and while the total sum represented—known to run into hundreds of millions of dollars—has not been disclosed, one authority today said that the new money is "going out in bales."

President Roosevelt believes that the banking outlook is excellent and that measures taken by his administration to relieve the financial stringency will prove immediately effective and lead to a definite turn toward permanent improvement.

RAPID PROGRESS

He is represented as feeling that under the circumstances, and the tremendous labor imposed upon it, the Treasury Department is making rapid progress in getting the banks in operation.

Licensing of banking institutions prepared to open either with or without Federal or State restrictions is provided in the Presidential order which permits State as well as national banks to qualify.

The first step toward gradual return to normal banking will be taken tomorrow when Federal Reserve banks in the twelve national districts open for restricted transactions. Member banks will thus be able to draw the amount of cash required to meet their immediate needs.

MONDAY OPENING

Resumption of more general banking operations, to be made possible in all probability by 10 o'clock Monday morning, will proceed coincidentally along two lines.

The first will permit national banks and many State banks known to be solvent to open for the transaction of all business except the payment of gold.

The second will enable State banks not included in the Federal Reserve system to resume business, on the same basis when certified to the Secretary of the Treasury by State banking superintendents.

State bank superintendents in determining the conditions under which such certification is justified will be required to follow the same procedure and recognize the same standards as are applied to member banks by the Federal Reserve authorities.

CHECK MAY DELAY

Particular stress is laid upon the fact that many banks which may not open their doors simultaneously with the general resumption of banking are not to be considered as insolvent or as "shaky" in any manner, the sole reason for the delay in some cases being due to the inability of the supervising authorities, whether Federal or State, to

(Continued on Page 4, Column 6)

WORK ARMY PLANNED

Mobilizing of Idle Roosevelt Idea

Half-Million Men Would Be Recruited to Push Public Projects Program

Organization of Jobless on Military Lines Purpose of Chief Executive

WASHINGTON, March 10. (Exclusive)—Plans for organizing an American army of 500,000 or more unemployed on military lines so that an orderly system of giving them work on his $500,000,000 public construction program can be followed out, will be included by President Roosevelt in his next message to Congress, it was revealed today.

The message was to have been given to Congress tomorrow, but the President now believes that he should hold it up until his message asking far-reaching powers to economize is acted upon or at least well on the way.

Mr. Roosevelt plans to swing the efforts of three departments—War, Agriculture and Interior—behind his unemployment relief project, which contemplates the use of Federal bond moneys in forestry and road work, new buildings, power development and flood control.

IMPORTANT FEATURE

The President's advisers stressed as important today that the program is intended in all of its phases to incur no eventual loss of revenue to the government, and in many cases he expects the various projects to bring in revenue sufficient to pay off the principal and interest of the bond issues as they become due. The bonds would have long-term maturities, it was declared.

In the case of the forestation pro-

(Continued on Page 4, Column 3)

PRESIDENT MAPS CUTS

Reduction Set at $500,000,000

Roosevelt's Special Message Tells Plan to Slash Pay and Veterans' Fund

Strong Opposition Develops Against Dictator Move; Showdown Due Today

By a "Times" Staff Correspondent

WASHINGTON, March 10. (Exclusive)—With vitally needed machinery for reopening the country's banks set in motion President Roosevelt sent a special message to Congress today asking for legislation designed to cut approximately $500,000,000 from government costs and thus pave the way for balancing the budget.

As in the banking emergency he asked for a widening of executive powers under which he may exercise dictatorial authority in administering governmental functions.

It is estimated that a saving of $400,000,000 will be accomplished in pensions, allowances and compensation to veterans if the proposed legislation is approved by Congress and that an additional $120,000,000 will be saved in salary cuts for government officials and employees.

Democratic leaders who met today to consider the economy measure announced that they expected approval by Congress tomorrow afternoon but the evidences of opposition—not present in the quick enactment of the bank relief bill—were so widely and so strongly indicated as to promise a real struggle when the program is submitted to a vote.

In his direct and bold attack on the veterans' allowances and his proposal to reduce the public pay roll, President Roosevelt at the very outset of his administration has put to the test the ability of the Democratic leadership to whip the Seventy-third Congress into a disciplined and effective body responsive to the executive authority.

Rebellion already has developed among some elements of the new Democratic membership. If the administration succeeds in this great initial struggle, the task of accomplishing other needed reforms and reliefs will be comparatively easy.

DETERMINED TO SLASH

Calling for courageous, frank and prompt action with respect to the finances of the government, and warmly commending the Congress for its expeditious handling of the banking emergency, President Roosevelt's second message to the newly organized Senate and House left no question of his determination to slash costs of the Federal governmental institution

National recovery, he said, depends on maintenance of the credit of the United States. Drawing attention of Congress to the fact that the Senators and Representatives, as well as himself, are pledged to

(Continued on Page 4, Column 1)

ROOSEVELT TENDERS OFFER OF GOVERNMENT ASSISTANCE IN MESSAGE TO GOV. ROLPH

WASHINGTON, March 10. (AP)—President Roosevelt tonight extended the facilities of the government to Gov. Rolph of California, to relieve distress in the path of the earthquake.

After being up every night this week holding conferences on the banking emergencies, the Chief Executive had retired before news of the temblor reached here. His aides awakened him as reports of destruction mounted.

Stephen T. Early, the President's secretary, gave the Associated Press the following message from Mr. Roosevelt to Gov. Rolph and asked that a reply be transmitted to him:

"News dispatches report serious catastrophe in Los Angeles area:

"Wires are down and cannot get any confirmation. If there is anything needed that the government can do, wire me at once. Trust preliminary reports are exaggerated. Will be glad to be kept in touch with situation."

Red Cross headquarters awaited word from regional headquarters at San Francisco before swinging its huge resources into action to relieve distress.

Naval communications was informed soon after midnight that the relief resources of the ships stationed at Long Beach had swung into action and at that time were coping with the situation satisfactorily.

These communications confirmed dispatches from Los Angeles that some reports of hundreds killed in Long Beach were exaggerated. The Navy radio did not attempt, however, to estimate the dead or injured.

PAINLEVE ALSO ASKS PAYMENT

French Statesman Takes Cue From Herriot on War Debt Settlement

PARIS, March 10. (AP)—Former Premier Painleve, following former Premier Herriot's similar proposal yesterday, urged today that France pay the debt interest which was due the United States last December as a timely gesture.

Writing in the Petit Parisien he urged the payment of about $20,000,000 "not to help America—she will save herself—but to dispel the artifically magnified cloud between America and us so as to realise a firm accord among France, Great Britain and the United States."

He said this would make "democracies safe" in the world and "avert the direst perils."

TROOPS NIP FOOD MARCH IN AUSTRIA

Machine Guns and Barbed Wire Placed in Streets Group of 1200 Dispersed

VIENNA, March 10. (AP)—Federal troops and gendarmes occupied Neunkirchen, near the industrial center of Wiener Neustadt, this morning after a report that unemployed were organizing a hunger march from Ternitz.

Machine guns and barbed wire were placed across the highways. A group of 1200 marchers was easily dispersed.

The situation in Vienna was quiet and the streets presented a normal appearance.

Most of the morning newspapers did not even mention the presence of troops here. The newspapers, however, are under strict regulation.

MEXICO CITY POST URGED FOR DANIELS

Former Navy Secretary Seriously Considered, but Decision Yet in Doubt

WASHINGTON, March 10. (AP)—Josephus Daniels, North Carolina publisher, is under serious consideration for appointment as Ambassador to Mexico.

At the same time, it was emphasized at the White House that no decision has been made on selection of an Ambassador to the neighboring country and that several other names remain under consideration.

Daniels, war-time Secretary of the Navy when Mr. Roosevelt was his assistant, also has been in mind for head of the unified national transportation agency which Mr. Roosevelt plans.

HOOVER TO LEAVE SOON FOR COAST

Former President Keeps Plan to Make Journey to California by Ship

NEW YORK, March 10. (AP)—Herbert Hoover, who has remained in New York since the inauguration of his successor in the White House, will probably leave for the West the first of next week.

Lawrence Richey, secretary to the former President, said tonight:

"We expect to leave within a few days. We probably will stay over until the first of the week."

He explained there was no change in the original plan for Mr. Hoover to go to California by boat, via the Panama Canal.

Navy Man Made Guam Governor

WASHINGTON, March 10. (AP)—Capt. George A. Alexander, commander of the U.S.S. Medusa, was ordered today by Secretary Swanson to duty as Governor of Guam and commandant of the naval station.

Capt. Fred F. Rogers, commander of Destroyer Division 8, was ordered to Tokio as naval attache.

WOMAN WHO KILLED MATE GETS LIFE TERM

SALT LAKE CITY, March 10. (AP)—Mrs. Elizabeth Droubay, 40 years of age, found guilty by a jury in District Court here last week of fatally shooting her husband, Capt. C. Edson Droubay of the Salt Lake City Fire Department, today was sentenced to life imprisonment by District Judge Thurman.

MORE THAN THOUSAND INJURED; FIRE SWEEPS NEAR-BY TOWNS

Bluejackets Land at Long Beach to Rescue Victims; Damage Totals Millions as Buildings Fall; Panic Grips Throngs in Streets

(Full Page of Pictures on Page 3, Part I)

Death and destruction rode into Southern California at 5:54 p.m. yesterday when an earthquake twisted an dtore at practically every city and hamlet south of the Tehachapi Mountains.

Long Beach, Compton, Watts, Huntington Park, Huntington Beach and Santa Ana according to midnight reports, bore the brunt of the shake.

But Los Angeles got its full share as buildings shook and twisted, roofs collapsed, walls crashed into the streets, and injured person began to cry for medical assistance.

No complete list of dead and injured and no full estimate of the property damage to Southern California could be made last night.

Known dead, according to a late tabulation, amounted to fifty-four men and women. Authorities however stated that the toll will without question exceed this figure.

In Long Beach at midnight 25 bodies had been recovered but few identified. Under the wreckage of buildings other dead must be buried, the searching police and firemen said.

Los Angeles added many dead to the Long Beach list and in all a record of fifty-four dead was compiled at midnight.

Injured crowded the hospitals both in Los Angeles and all southern communities. No check was made, according to the police, will be near the number of persons who received medical attention. The total, however, is estimated at somewhere around 1500.

A death list of twelve was reported from Huntington Park, with a score or more injured, some seriously.

MILLIONS IN DAMAGE

Property damage into the millions, according to local officials, will be piled up when the final count is taken. The lists of wrecked buildings continued to pour in during the night from the Los Angeles industrial districts, as well as from all near-by communities.

Fire added its destruction in the wake of the quake and in many cases broken water mains prevented the fire departments of the various affected communities from putting up much of a fight.

All of the fire equipment in Los Angeles was out of the hundreds of fire houses for the first time in the history of the local fire department. No serious fires were reported from this city, but in Huntington Park, Huntington Beach, Watts, Compton and Santa Ana fires raged for hours, causing huge losses.

In Long Beach alone 4000 marines and sailors were sent ashore from the Battle Fleet and assisted the police in treating the injured, searching for the dead and fighting fire.

CITY HALL CRACKS

All of the major buildings in Long Beach withstood the first shock and the following quakes that for more than an hour rocked Southern California at intervals.

In Los Angeles there came no reports of major buildings being seriously damaged, although the City Hall, the largest building in the city, and many other large modern structures were cracked and twisted.

When the earthquake struck it came with a roar and a crash that sounded like an explosion. Within a minute the downtown streets swarmed with persons fleeing from the buildings and with pedestrians running for vacant lots and other points where they thought to find safety. Many were struck down by flying bricks and bits of building materials which seemed to spring from the huge downtown structures. Broken glass from plate windows filled the streets.

Roofs, walls and other portions of many of the older buildings, particularly in the industrial section of the city, crashed into the streets before the full force of the first quake had expended itself.

MANY LEAP FROM WINDOWS

With the first shock hardly over the scream of ambulance sirens began to split the air while fire apparatus rushed through the downtown streets in response to the hundreds of calls which followed the

(Continued on Page 2, Column 1)

LIST OF DEAD AND INJURED

The known death toll from the earthquake reached fifty-four at 10 o'clock last night and it was expected the number will be increased as reports keep coming from the areas hit hardest. Twenty-five of these deaths were accounted for in Long Beach, with only one body positively identified.

The known death list and locations where they were killed follows:

Alberto Rivas of 10622 Hickory street, Watts, hit by falling bricks at One Hundred and Third and Graham streets. Another man, unidentified, was buried under a brick wall at Beach and One Hundred and Third streets.

The dead reported at Santa Ana:

Mr. and Mrs. Jack Ellison of 2501 Ivy Drive, Oakland, killed by falling bricks at the Hotel Rossmore.

Earl Adamson, killed by flying bricks.

At San Pedro U. W. Murray, 23, fireman on the U.S.S. Marblehead, was killed.

At Hermosa Beach, a Mrs. Moore, 60, dropped dead at home from heart disease.

At Bellflower two were reported killed:

Mrs. Irene Campbell, 714 Ardmore street.

Mrs. Frank Ball.

At Compton eight known dead included:

Dr. Ashley Firkins, dentist.

William D. Marshall, 212 Spruce street, died on way to hospital.

——— Wade and infant son.

Unidentified man, guest Young Hotel.

Unidentified man, guest Young Hotel.

Unidentified woman.

Unidentified man.

Known dead at Garden Grove:

Virginia Pollard, 16 years of age, killed by falling brick as she was rushing from the high school building.

Frank Tobias, 1853 Crenshaw Boulevard, killed in a broom factory, Ninety-second and Beach street. Body at Graham.

Long Beach:

Flora Weeden, 23, 12[illegible] South Greenwood, Montebello, killed at Anaheim and Cherry, Long Beach.

Huntington Park:

Edna Greenmayer.

Albert Oleson, 2913 Liberty street, Southgate.

Unidentified woman.

Los Angeles:

Jayne Boyer, 3 years of age.

——— Hayes, killed at Florence and Compton avenues.

Mrs. Ralph Swenson, 39, 3462 Walnut street, Huntington Park, killed in the 6500 block on Pacific Boulevard, Huntington Park.

H. Lobes, employee Chrysler Motors, 5965 Pacific Boulevard. Killed by falling bricks.

Dottie Martyne, 30, Boulevard Hotel, Huntington Park. Hit by debris as she ran from hotel. Body at Wheat-Hulberson mortuary.

William C. Van Noy, 65, 2432½ Flower street, Los Angeles. Injured in Walnut Park and died in Huntington Park Hospital.

Although the list of injured was expected to reach into the hundreds, the unofficial lists compiled

(Continued on Page 2, Column 7)

SANITATION EMPLOYEES MOBILIZED

County Health Officer Orders Workers to Meet for Earthquake Duty

Dr. J. L. Pomeroy, Los Angeles County Health Officer, issued orders last night for the mobilization of all sanitary officers in the department to meet this morning at 8 a.m. at Huntington Park Health Center, 6810 Malabar street, Huntington Park.

"The entire personnel and nursing staff," Dr. Pomeroy stated, "will be on call for assignments as needed." In this emergency, it is urgent as a humanitarian measure that the strength and skill of the department be ready—mobilized—and to this end, because of disrupted means of communication, each member is urged to heed this notice and to pass the word along to others in the department where possible.

"Our quarantine officers also are to meet this morning at Huntington Park Health Center for assignment to sections where needed," Dr. Pomeroy added.

Late last night it was learned that 125 sanitary officers were available for call. Radio announcements, it was expected, would by this morning have reached the entire personnel. Twenty alternate positions in the sanitary division were to be held in reserve throughout the night and twenty special quarantine officers were being mobilized for relief work. Few calls, however, for quarantine assignments had been received last night up to 10:10 p.m.

The need for sanitary officers was sensed and Dr. Pomeroy made the announcement so that all men might be in readiness for an unexpected emergency.

Help Offered by Washington

OLYMPIA (Wash.) March 10. (AP) Gov. Clarence D. Martin, in a telegram sent tonight to Gov. Rolph of California, said the "people and government of Washington, as sympathetic neighbors, stand ready to help relieve your distress in whatever way possible."

"We are shocked and grieved by press reports of the disastrous earthquake in Southern California," the telegram said.

THE "TIMES" TODAY—NEWS SUMMED UP

Remember This

There is more pleasure in pursuit than in possession.

Mayor Porter in Proclamation Urges Courage

Mayor Porter late last night issued the following proclamation:

"Complete assurance is given the public that all facilities of the city government are definitely and fully prepared for action in the event of the necessity for further relief in Southern California.

"Thousands of policemen, firemen, sailors of the Pacific fleet, Marine Corps at San Pedro, members of the American Legion, Salvation Army, Red Cross and hundreds of citizens have volunteered their services will remain on constant duty until all danger has safely passed. Hospitals and other relief institutions are prepared for any emergency.

"As Mayor of Los Angeles, I urge our people to continue with the strong spirit of courage which they have so far evidenced, and extend deep felt thanks to many volunteers and to the Mayors of the various cities who have proferred their aid."

Flood Case Has Legislative Echo

SACRAMENTO, March 10. (AP)—An echo of the Flood will case in San Mateo county last year was heard in the Legislature today when the Assembly passed a bill providing a judge may not direct a verdict or dismiss a suit, except in certain cases.

In the Flood case Superior Judge George H. Buck gave a directed verdict for the defendant, but a check of the jury showed them eleven to one for the plaintiff. Judge Buck was defeated for re-election soon afterward.

Second Missile Sent President

WATERTOWN (N. Y.) March 10. (AP)—Postoffice inspectors were attempting today to trace the sender of a second package containing a shotgun shell addressed to President Roosevelt, intercepted in the Postoffice here Monday night.

The parcel was described as similar in most respects to the missile sent from here to the President shortly after the attempted assassination of Roosevelt last month.

Kansas Hoarders May Be Exposed

TOPEKA (Kan.) March 10. (AP)—With little debate the House of Representatives adopted today a resolution to expose the identity of hoarders of currency.

The resolution if adopted also by the Senate, would provide that banks and trust companies should prepare "for public inspection" a list of depositors who between January 1 and the 4th inst. withdrew currency in excess of $500 without re-depositing it.

Will Rogers Remarks:

BEVERLY HILLS, March 10. [To the Editor of The Times:] Say, didn't the Rockefellers (through their hired man, Mr. Aldrich) throw a custard pie right in the face of the Morgan banking outfit. Why if the Chase National turns "square" and removes itself from security companies, (that's the banks' roulette wheel) it will be a death blow to modern banking. Imagine a bank just having to live on interest alone. Removing their security or holding companies is like taking the loaded dice away from a crap shooter.

Yours,
WILL ROGERS.

BEDLAM IN HOSPITAL AS INJURED ARRIVE

The earthquake . . . suddenly the Georgia-street Receiving Hospital becomes a beehive. . . . Phones ring continuously. . . . Gertrude Stewart and Belle Tucker stand by their posts at the switchboard as the building quakes. . . . Call after call . . . Screenching sirens are heard outside. . . .

The ambulances return with their cargo of broken bodies . . . Victim after victim is brought in. . . . Every ambulance in the city pressed into service to pick up injured. . . . In they keep coming. . . . The girls still answering calls.

It is not long before the hospital is full to overflowing. . . . There is no favoritism. . . . They are treated in the order in which they arrive. . . . There are only four operating rooms. . . . Only two doctors are on duty when the tragic quake strikes. . . . Victims lying on the floor. . . . Groaning and crying in pain.

Surgeons arrive and volunteer their services . . . Nobody is complaining about being overworked . . . The activity becomes increasingly greater . . . A little girl is brought in . . . Jane Doe is the name given her . . . She is unconscious . . . She looks to be about 4 years of age . . . She is a pretty little thing with blond hair . . . Her arm is crushed at the elbow . . . This means an amputation . . . There she lies pale awaiting her turn on the operating table.

Over there lies a woman . . . She looks to be 60 . . . Her hair is gray . . . Her face is the same color—earthquakes seem to do that to people . . . In a room adjoining is John Doe . . . He is dead . . . His head is caved in by a falling brick.

In the victims keep coming. . . . Always the screeching ambulance siren is heard. . . . The phones keep ringing. . . . Now they are frightened relatives. . . . They inquire about their missing ones.

The street outside is filled with inquiring people . . . They all want to know the same thing . . . Is he or she here? . . . The inquirers become so numerous another reception room must be opened on the second floor.

Doctors continue to work feverishly repairing these innocent humans . . . They can only give them emergency treatment and ease pain . . . Those with minor hurts are dispatched home as quickly as possible . . . Those with broken bones and bad hurts are sent away to hospitals.

By 10 p.m. 1000 persons had received care. Unceasing labor marked the hours after the tremor had thrown thousands into a frenzy. The small staff of the hospital was taxed to the limit and beyond . . . at the rate of 700 an hour thereafter the injured arrived.

The majority were not seriously hurt, hundreds were hurt and bruised by falling chimneys, other hundreds by jumping from buildings, others from being struck by falling articles within the home, bookcases and furniture. While the injured were receiving attention, thousands of relatives and friends mingled with the hundreds of injured in the streets in front and near the institution. Bedlam existed . . .

The day shift was recalled to the hospital by Dr. Wallace Dodge, chief surgeon. More doctors more nurses were summoned hastily . . . the night shift then was dispatched to the stricken cities, Long Beach, Compton, South Gate and Huntington Park. It was estimated 300 volunteer surgeons in various parts of the city were giving first aid to the injured. As calls came in the nearest volunteer doctors were assigned to the cases. Everything was done to relieve the sufferers.

The switchboard was taxed to capacity. Operators were flooded with calls all through the night without respite.

'All the News 'All the Time
LARGEST HOME-DELIVERED CIRCULATION
LARGEST ADVERTISING VOLUME

MADISON 2345
The Times Telephone Number
Connecting All Departments

Los Angeles Times

EQUAL RIGHTS
LIBERTY UNDER THE LAW — TRUE INDUSTRIAL FREEDOM

In Two Parts — 36 Pages
PART I — TELEGRAPH SHEET — 18 PAGES

NRA MEMBER U.S. WE DO OUR PART

TIMES OFFICES
100 North Broadway
619½ South Spring
And Throughout Southern California

VOL. LIII. C WEDNESDAY MORNING, DECEMBER 6, 1933. DAILY, FIVE CENTS

GOLD BASIS HELD VITAL

Chamber Group Urges Return

Western Unit of National Body Asks Roosevelt Move to Stabilize Money

Annual Meeting Favors Trade Pacts With Other Nations to Encourage Exports

BY FLOYD J. HEALEY
"Times" Staff Representative

SACRAMENTO, Dec. 5. (Exclusive)—Return to the gold standard, though it means a reduction in the base content, as a means of stabilizing world currency, was urged upon President Roosevelt in a resolution adopted today at the final session of the annual meeting of the western division, United States Chamber of Commerce.

The resolution urges on the President to determine "scientifically" a new gold base "at the earliest possible date" and asks that he "proclaim such gold standard as a permanent and definite standard for the country until altered conditions make changes necessary."

AID TO TRADE

In addition, the resolution asks the President to "reconcile our basis of currency with the major currencies of the world as quickly as possible to the end that national and international stability and confidence may be restored and trade and industry stimulated."

Among other resolutions adopted were:

That reciprocal trade agreements or commercial treaties be consummated by this nation with others "to encourage the export of American products by making possible increases of non-competing imports."

AID MERCHANT MARINE

That continued government aid be given the American merchant marine "for the maintenance of regular and dependable service to and from foreign countries in amount and for a time sufficient to tide over the period until these lines may be self-supporting."

That the government abandon "transportation of freight and passengers in competition with privately owned American steamship lines."

That a "reasonable appropriation" be made by the Department of Commerce "for compilation and limited distribution" to offices of the customs service in each district every month "of the quantity and value of import and export shipments," because such statistical information is "essential" to the development of foreign trade and elimination of appropriation has stopped this service of the past. By confining the distribution to customs districts offices, the cost will be materially lessened but the figures will be available there for business men who need them.

PROTESTS URGED

That "protests" be filed against bills pending in both houses of the Congress "containing proposed radical changes in the present Federal Food and Drugs Act," which would put foods, drugs and cosmetics all in one general category, on the ground that foods and drugs should be considered as a separate entity.

That Congress pass laws prohibit-

(Continued on Page 2, Column 3)

It's About Time for the Next Course!

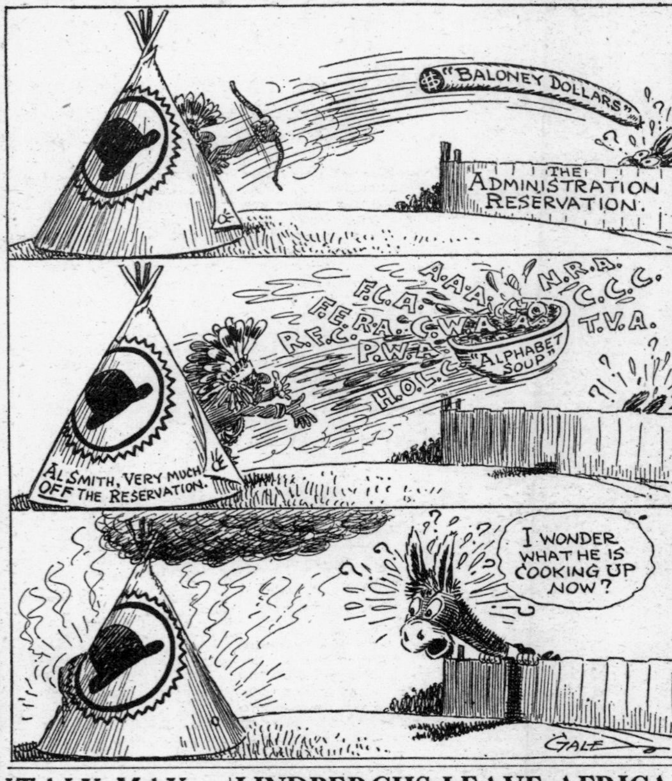

ITALY MAY QUIT LEAGUE, WORLD TOLD

Radical Reformation in Shortest Possible Time Demanded by Council

ROME, Dec. 6. (Wednesday) (AP)—The grand council of the Fascist party in a secret midnight meeting decided that Italy will remain in the League of Nations only if it is "radically reformed in the shortest possible time."

The meeting was presided over by Premier Mussolini.

Reform must be applied to the League's "constitution, working system and objectives," said a resolution voted by the council and communicated officially to the press.

Bitter articles in the Italian press in recent weeks and Mussolini's own denunciation of the League before the National Council of Corporations in November led many to believe the country would withdraw.

The council decided Italy will pay $1,000,000 to the United States on war debt interest due the 15th inst., as a token of good faith.

ANGELENO HURT IN ARIZONA

HOLBROOK (Ariz.) Dec. 5. (AP)—L. Whitney of 776 San Pedro street, Los Angeles, is in a serious condition here today, the result of a collision between his coupe and a truck three miles west of Holbrook. H. Frank, also of Los Angeles, and two other occupants of the car were uninjured.

LINDBERGHS LEAVE AFRICA IN HOP TO SOUTH AMERICA

Wife at Radio as Couple Head Across 1900 Miles of Atlantic After Many Unsuccessful Starts

BATHURST (Gambia) Dec. 6. (Wednesday.) (AP)—Col. Charles A. Lindbergh lifted his heavily laden red monoplane into the air at 2 a.m. today (6 p.m. Tuesday, Pacific standard time,) and with Mrs. Lindbergh at the radio headed across 1900 miles of open sea toward South America.

After a score or more unsuccessful attempts to lift the plane in an almost dead calm, he was helped on his way by a light breeze from the interier which rippled the surface of the lower Gambia River.

For four days the Lindberghs had been balked by inability to lift the heavy load of fuel required for the longest hop yet attempted in their aerial survey tour of Atlantic Ocean airways. Excess fuel and baggage were jettisoned.

The colonel was informed that weather indications insured a bright, clear tropical night for the take-off.

The German steamer Westfalen, which had been in Brazil obtaining supplies, was due to return to its mid-Atlantic post yesterday, affording further security for the Lindberghs on their long flight.

By veering slightly northward off a direct course to Natal, Brazil, they can also stop at St. Paul's Island, a French possession in mid-Atlantic.

Calculations based on the known speed of Col. Lindbergh's plane, fixed the approximate time of a

(Continued on Page 2, Column 2)

SNOW, RAIN AND WINDS RIP NORTH

Shipping Menaced and Air Traffic Disrupted in Oregon and Washington

SEATTLE, Dec. 5. (AP)—Menacing shipping and disrupting air traffic, a storm of snow, rain and high winds howled across the Pacific Northwest today.

Heavy downfalls of rain soaked the Oregon and Washington coastlines, with winds as high as 90 miles an hour halting shipping on the Columbia and in at least two ports breaking ships away from their moorings.

Heavy snow closed mountain passes on the inland empire and blanketed a wide area of Western Montana, Northern Idaho, Eastern Oregon and Washington. The Spokane airport was virtually closed in by the weather, with all ships grounded.

With a southeasterly gale lashing the Grays Harbor area, the steamship Yoneyama Maru was towed back to her moorings undamaged after being blown loose by the wind, and at Astoria, Or., part of a terminal dock was destroyed when the German steamer Este was swept away. After narrowly missing the steamer Oregonian, the Este was anchored in the Columbia Channel.

Thore Hassing, 65 years of age, was crushed by a falling tree blown down in the North River District of Grays Harbor county.

Wilkins Leaves for Antaractic

DUNEDIN (N. Z.) Dec. 5. (AP)—The expedition of Sir Hubert Wilkins, Lincoln Ellsworth and Bernt Balchen set sail today for the Antarctic, their first destination the Bay of Whales.

Aboard the Wyatt Earp is Balchen's monoplane, completely overhauled during the stay here, in which he is confident of making a successful exploring flight over the Weddell Sea.

Godowsky's Wife Taken by Death

NEW YORK, Dec. 5. (Exclusive) Mrs. Frieda Godowsky, wife of Leopold Godowsky, the composer, died today in her apartment at the Hotel Ansonia. She was 53 years of age and had recently returned from the west coast, where she had spent the summer with her husband.

AGRARIAN LEADER SHOT

MATAMOROS (Mex.) Dec. 5. (AP) An agrarian leader was shot and killed when two agrarian factions clashed in Ebanito, near here, today. Federal troops were sent to prevent further fighting.

OUSTER DUE ON INSULL

Greece Will Ask Him to Leave

Residence Permit of Former Utilities King Expires at End of Year

High Authorities Believe Extending Stay Would Hurt American Ties

ATHENS, Dec. 5. (AP)—It was learned reliably tonight that the Greek government will request Samuel Insull, former Chicago utilities magnate, to leave Greece at the expiration of his police permit the 31st inst.

Insull, it was explained, has no passport.

The government is said to be prepared to furnish a laissez passer for any country which Insull desires to enter from Greece.

WONT HURT TIES

This action would be the result of the Greek government's decision to do all possible to avoid disturbing friendly relations with the United States, which has made repeated representations desiring his extradition to face criminal charges in Chicago in connection with the bankruptcy of his utilities concern.

A member of the Greek Senate deposited with that body today an interpellation asking the Greek government what it has decided about Insull's return.

The Senator said he believed it is necessary to forbid Insull to remain further in Greece because of misunderstanding which might lessen the friendliness of Greco-American relations.

REFUGE INSECURE

There are other indications Insull's refuge in Greece is becoming insecure. Foreign Minister D. Maximos told the Associated Press the government will not deny any legal measures facilitating the return of the 73-year-old former utilities king.

The Minister pointed out, however, the government is unable to turn Insull directly over to the United States after Greek courts have twice denied his extradition in extended trials based on provisions of the newly arranged extradition treaty.

Maximos said nothing had been done about renewing Insull's residence permit, adding nothing had been brought up against Insull by competent Greek authorities, therefore no decision had been taken.

Einstein Plea to World Court Stirs Interest

THE HAGUE, Dec. 5. (AP)—A report that Prof. Albert Einstein had lodged a complaint against Prussia with the Permanent Court of International Justice to recover his confiscated fortune aroused interest here today.

It was pointed out that the court deals only with cases between states and could not accept a complaint from an individual.

Tornadoes Kill One, Hurt Five

SHREVEPORT (La.) Dec. 5. (AP) Tornadoes striking in widely separated sections of North Louisiana tonight claimed one life and resulted in five injured Negroes being brought to Charity Hospital here for treatment.

Mrs. J. C. Manasco, was killed east of Many, Sabine county.

Peak Explorer Frozen to Death

AMECAMECA (Mex.) Dec. 5. (AP) Edmundo Cordova, an explorer attempting to reach the highest peaks of the snow-covered mountain Ixtaccihuatl, died today from the intense cold.

Byrd Flagship at Wellington

WELLINGTON (N. Z.) Dec. 5. (AP) Rear-Admiral Richard E. Byrd's Antarctic flagship arrived in the harbor late tonight.

Will Rogers Remarks:

BEVERLY HILLS, Dec. 5.—[To the Editor of The Times:] Talk about the "noble experiment." "The noble experiment" is just starting. Every State is in doubt as to how their liquor will be handled. Say it's not how the State will handle its liquor, it's how the folks will handle theirs. States are going to have scandal over the sale of it, and politicians will fight over the taxes of it. But anyhow, the first week will be the hardest.

Yours,

WILL ROGERS.

DRY ERA END PROCLAIMED ON UTAH'S RATIFICATION

Roosevelt Calls on Nation to Ban Bootlegger and Saloon's Return; Huge Liquor Imports Authorized

WASHINGTON, Dec. 5. (Exclusive)—National prohibition ended this afternoon at 3:32 o'clock (mountain time, or 2:32 Pacific Coast time.) when a convention in Utah formally ratified the Twenty-first Amendment to the United States Constitution, and thus repealed the Eighteenth Amendment.

The end of the dry age was celebrated in many parts of the land, although in some of the States the suddenness of the Volsteadian departure prevented the adoption of laws and regulations legalizing and controlling the liquor traffic.

In twenty-eight States the rule of prohibition lives on by State decree.

Official proclamation heralding the termination of prohibition were signed by President Roosevelt and Acting Secretary of State Phillips. But their acts were no more than formalities, for actually the Eighteenth Amendment was a dead letter at the instant the action taken by the convention in the Utah city of the Mormon fathers was completed.

DELAY AVERTED

So anxious had these western citizens been to claim for their commonwealth the honor of accomplishing the actual repeal of the Eighteenth Amendment that they had planned to delay their action until night.

But when Pennsylvania and Ohio had acted speedily Utah hesitated no longer.

The President in his proclamation, signed at 6:55 p.m., gave the news of repeal and then delivered an injunction on "all citizens of the United States . . . to co-operate with the government in its endeavor to restore greater respect for law and order."

He pleaded that the people make their liquor purchases only through such dealers as have been licensed by State or Federal government.

"Observance of this request," he said, "which I make personally to every individual and every family in our nation, will result in the consumption of alcoholic beverages which have passed Federal inspection, in the break-up and eventual destruction of the notoriously evil illicit-liquor traffic, and in the payment of reasonable taxes for the support of government and thereby in the superseding of other forms of taxation."

WARNS AGAINST SALOON

The President warned that the Twenty-first Amendment imposes on the government the duty of protecting dry States from inundation by wet States. He asked that the "repugnant conditions" which existed prior to the adoption of the Eighteenth Amendment, and those existing since, shall not be the price of the return to individual freedom.

"I ask especially," he added, "that no State shall, by law, or otherwise, authorize the return of the saloon either in its old form or in some modern guise."

Voicing a determination that the day of the bootlegger is done, the President said he trusted "to the good sense of the American people that they will not bring upon themselves the curse of excessive use of intoxicating liquors, to the detriment of health, morals and social integrity."

The President's proclamation canceled nuisance taxes totaling $220,000,000, which had been imposed by Congress subject to termination on the repeal of prohibition.

Mr. Roosevelt had been swimming in the White House pool prior to the signing of the proclamation, and there were reports which White House attaches refused to discuss that the President had signed the document while in his swimming suit.

NATION HEARS QUICKLY

Mr. Phillips's proclamation, signed immediately after he had received telegraphic notice from Salt Lake City that Utah had become the thirty-sixth State to ratify, was the formal announcement that the Twenty-first Amendment had been approved.

As quickly as the news of Utah's action had been flashed over the country—and it was flashed by radio and telegraph and telephone with greater celerity than the news of any other event in many years—the people in nearly a score of States hastened to experience tasting a drink of legal liquor. It was

(Continued on Page 6, Column 1)

PLUG ON TAX LEAK FIXED

Change Asked in Revenue Law

House Subcommittee Strikes at Rich and Personal Holding Companies

Ways and Means Group Lets Lower Bracket Alone, but Proposes Single Rate

WASHINGTON, Dec. 5. (AP)—Striking at large incomes and personal holding companies organized to save taxes, a House Ways and Means subcommittee today recommended changes in the revenue law to bring in an estimated additional $237,000,000 to the government.

The full committee, headed by Representative Doughton, Democrat, of North Carolina, met and received the report of the subcommittee, but took no action pending hearings to be held later. The proposals are designed to simplify the present law and plug up holes through which wealthy persons have avoided taxes.

RUM TAX LATER

Liquor taxation was left to be handled in a separate bill after recommendations from President Roosevelt and joint discussions by the House and Senate tax committees.

The subcommittee did not disturb the lower income brackets, but proposed a single normal rate of 4 per cent on all net income instead of the present 4 per cent on the first $4000 and 8 per cent on the balance.

Other recommendations included higher surtaxes with only twenty-seven brackets, against the existing fifty-seven; increased rates on dividends and partly tax-exempt interest; a 35 per cent tax on the "undistributed adjusted net income" of personal holding companies, abolition of consolidated returns, and withdrawal of the right of partners to offset against their income losses sustained by partnerships.

The new surtax schedule proposed rates ranging from 4 per cent on net income between $4000 and $6000 to 59 per cent on all over $1,000,000. Present rates range from 1 per cent on between $6000 and $10,000 to 55 per cent on more than $1,000,000.

Othe changes and estimated revenue from each include:

Slashing by 25 per cent of allowances for depreciation and depletion in determining net income, for the years 1934, 1935, and 1936—$85,000,000.

A graduated scale for determining capital gains or losses from the sale of property by an individual, according to the length of time he has held the property—$30,000,000.

HITS HOLDING COMPANY

Personal holding company tax of 35 per cent—$25,000,000.

Dividends paid by a corporation out of earnings or profits accumulated or out of increase in value of property accrued before March 1, 1913, to be subjected to the surtax as in the case of any other dividend received by a stockholder—$6,000,000.

ROLPH OUSTED AS MEMBER OF WAR VETERANS BOARD

NEW YORK, Dec. 5. (AP)—The National Executive Committee of the National War Veterans' Association, Inc., today made public a resolution expelling Gov. Rolph of California from its national advisory board.

The resolution was adopted yesterday. It charged "that Gov. Rolph's proven gubernatorial unfitness so obviously demonstrated by his actions and statements in connection with the San Jose lynchings has likewise made him unfit to be continued in an advisory or in any other capacity in or with this organization."

The resolution also urged "that the good citizens of the State of California, in order to save their own reputations as law-abiding citizens of the fair State of California of our beloved United States, should take immediate steps to impeach their present nominal Governor."

The resolution was presented to the committee by Dr. George Paston, past National Commander, who appointed Rolph to the advisory board.

COUNTY INVESTIGATION OF LYNCHING LAUNCHED

SAN JOSE, Dec. 5. (Exclusive)—County authorities today inaugurated an official investigation into "certain phases" of the lynching of Tom Thurmond and John Holmes by a mob for the murder of Brooke Hart, San Jose youth, on November 9.

Dist.-Atty. Fred L. Thomas assigned a deputy to the investigation. Sheriff William J. Emig, recovered from injuries received during the lynching, was also instructed to cooperate with the District Attorney's office in a "full and searching" inquiry. No time limit was fixed for the inquiry.

The Sheriff said today he does not believe he would be able to recognize anyone he saw in the mob the night of the lynching, but will do his best to aid the District Attorney in the investigation.

RUM FLOWS IN QUIETLY

Repeal Hailed in Sane Style

Anticipated Rush for Legal Drink Fails to Materialize; Brands Plentiful

Police Report Arrests for Drunkenness Exceed Those One Month Ago

Los Angeles went back to legal consumption of liquor during the middle of yesterday afternoon but with nothing in evidence like the wild night which nearly fourteen years ago ushered in the advent of prohibition.

Hundreds of gallons of wines, whisky, brandy and other strong liquors were rushed to more than 10,000 retailers in Southern California during the afternoon but the anticipated rush to purchase failed to materialize and drinkers took the repeal in a quiet and orderly manner that surprised authorities.

LACK OF PATRONAGE

Apparently there was no shortage of the most select liquors but there was a lack of patronage, according to police, and early predictions of an unusual evening in celebrating the resurrection of John Barleycorn were without foundation.

Drug stores and other retailers reported an unusual business later in the fact that hotels, restaurants, cafes and cabarets were not permitted to serve anything stronger than beer and wine.

Many toasts to the repeal of the Eighteenth Amendment and the ratification of the Twenty-first Amendment were drunk in homes, clubs, cafes, hotels and speakeasies but there was a lack of zealous appreciation and police reports brought information that there was little if any increase in drinking over that of the last few months.

It was a quiet night in Hollywood. Hotels and fashionable clubs were filled to capacity with the bright spots humming to the advent of repeal but there was an apparent lack of excitement.

NOTHING UNUSUAL

It appeared that the crowds took the death of prohibition as a matter of course and drank in the usual way.

There were numerous private parties, most of them informal gatherings, where guests and hosts joined in a cocktail, a highball, or a glass of wine, as a memento of prohibition's passing, but drinking was restrained.

An unexpected and somewhat ironical situation developed in many of the drinking places in Hollywood when the management halted the use of strong drinks at 11 p.m.

In one of the more popular drinking places the management announced the following regulation and his words brought exclamations of surprise and consternation.

"The mangement requests that the following announcement be made," roared the loud speaker system in the cabaret. "It is our understanding that repeal of the Eighteenth Amendment became effective at 11 p.m. tonight. Therefore, this house wishes to comply with all provisions of the new law.

HARD LIQUORS BARRED

"Accordingly, we must respectfully request that all drinks other than beer or wine be removed from the tables. No hard liquors will be permitted to be consumed in this cafe from now on."

Police records in Los Angeles showed a general tendency to observe the new regulations. There were 111 drunk arrests reported up to midnight. Eight others were arrested for being drunk in an auto and five held for driving while intoxicated.

As a comparison police records show that on November 6, a month back, there were eighty-three drunk arrests; twenty-three arrested for being drunk in an auto and no arrests for driving while intoxicated.

IN LONG BEACH

Down at Long Beach, where liquor was sold legally for the first time in thirty-three years, a single arrest for drunkenness was reported from the hour of repeal at 2:32 p.m. until midnight. There was no public demonstration to welcome the overthrow of the dry laws. An old city ordinance prohibits drinking in public places, dance halls and streets. Police reported numerous inquiries as to proper legal procedure in purchasing and consuming the newly legalized beverages.

San Pedro police reported that residents of that section and the harbor district apparently were taking repeal without undue note. One arrest for drunkenness was reported and police reported he was not a celebrant of repeal.

QUIET AT SANTA MONICA

Santa Monica, on account of an election, was one of the driest spots in the Southland for more than two hours. Notification of repeal did not reach holders of retail licenses until 5 p.m. and the general municipal election polls did not close until 7 p.m. Chief of Police Webb directed that his organization enforce the new State liquor law which prohibits sale of liquor containing more than one-half per cent alcohol on election day.

When word was flashed from Washington to the Southland that the prohibition amendment had

(Continued on Page 6, Column 3)

THE "TIMES" TODAY—NEWS SUMMED UP

Remember This

The quickest way to make dreams come true is to wake up.

All the News All the Time

LARGEST HOME-DELIVERED CIRCULATION
LARGEST ADVERTISING VOLUME

MADISON 2345
The Times Telephone Number
Connecting All Departments

Los Angeles Times

EQUAL RIGHTS — LIBERTY UNDER THE LAW — TRUE INDUSTRIAL FREEDOM

In Seven Parts—148 Pages

PART I — TELEGRAPH SHEET — 14 PAGES

TIMES OFFICES
100 North Broadway
619½ South Spring
And Throughout Southern California

VOL. LIII. C TUESDAY MORNING, JANUARY 2, 1934. DAILY, FIVE CENTS

COLUMBIA WINS, 7-0

Stanford Upset in Rose Bowl

Lions Score Touchdown in Second Quarter With Barabas Tallying

Invaders Make Plucky Stand to Keep Goal Clear of Stanford Invasions

BY BILL HENRY

When Californians can find only a pale, flat word like "unusual" to describe a whole season's rainfall spilling in on us in a single day there ought to be a lot of fine comprehensive languag left in the dictionary with which to describe Columbia's stunning 7-to-0 football win over Stanford in the soggy Rose Bowl yesterday afternoon.

But the only guy who could think of the right words, however, was Mr. Claude (Tiny) Thornhill, master mind of the Stanfords, and Tiny's words wouldn't go through the mails.

Playing on a water-logged gridiron that only twenty-four hours previously was nothing but a large damp body of water with a few miscellaneous bits of lumber sticking out of the wet at either end, the sure-footed, cagey Columbians made one magnificent drive for a touchdown and then for the rest of the afternoon hurled back the desperate muddied Stanford giants in a series of goal line stands the equal of which hasn't been seen in the long and spectacular history of the Rose Bowl.

When the Lions and, by the way, nobody had warned us that they were sea lions, edged into Stanford territory early in the second period it took them just exactly two plays, plus a penalty and a fumble tossed in just to make it exciting, to make victims out of Stanford and suckers out of a lot of experts.

MONTGOMERY STARS

Capt. Cliff Montgomery built up the situation beautifully in the opening quarter. He had the Stanford giants as uneasy as a herd of elephants trying to trample a mouse with his swooping, sky-rocketing slants off tackle and around the ends. Trying to nail him was about as simple as lassoing a hiccough.

Finally he snatched a Stanford punt out of the slime and swerved his way thirteen yards to the Stanford 46-yard line.

Time out for a little heavy thinking was followed by one of those unimportant-looking plays when Barabas crashed into a Stanford stone wall but gained five yards anyway when the eagle-eyed officials discerned the fact that the stone wall was offside.

They lined up again and Montretrieved it for a 1-yard loss. be another one of those wild zigzags around right end but suddenly, just as they thought he was zigging, zagged back and chucked a long forward pass diagonally down the field where two burly young men were legging it just as fast as they could go.

It was a great play, a great toss and Mad Anthony Matal, the redheaded Columbia end, made a great catch, hugging the porkhide to his devoted bosom as Bobby Grayson, only inches away from him, hurled

(Cont'd on Page 13, Col. 8, Part II)

SHIFT MADE IN CABINET

Morgenthau New Treasury Head

Woodin Resigns Position and Acting Secretary Receives Title

Letter Exchange Spikes Tale of Friction on Roosevelt Gold Policies

WASHINGTON, Jan. 1. (AP)—President Roosevelt today gave evidence of his satisfaction with the progress of the administration's financial and moneta y programs under the direction of Henry Morgenthau, Jr., by giving his old friend and neighbor the title as well as the responsibilities of Secretary of the Treasury.

After more than a month as acting head of the department, Morgenthau was promoted to full membership in the Cabinet following the resignation of Secretary Woodin, who went on leave of absence in mid-November to seek rest and recovery from a persistent throat infection.

CONTINUE POLICIES

Thus Morgenthau assumed the portfolio with his own policies and ideas already in operation. His only comment was that they will be continued unchanged. The development left his old post of Undersecretary vacant, arousing speculation as to who will be appointed. It was made plain that it will not be Earle Bailie, whom Morgenthau brought into the department on a temporary basis as his chief fiscal adviser. Antagonism to Bailie, led by Senator Couzens, Republican, of Michigan, has developed on Capitol Hill because of his previous banking connections.

When Woodin left the Treasury, Mr. Roosevelt announced that he had declined to accept the Cabinet officer's resignation and hoped for his return after a few months. In the intervening period, it became apparent from Morgenthau's vigorous administration, as well as from other things, that eventually Woodin would withdraw completely. His resignation was submitted to the President in a letter from Tucson, Ariz., December 13.

WOODIN RESIGNS

"It is with great regret that I am compelled to tender you my resignation as Secretary of the Treasury, to take effect at your convenience any time before January 1," he said. "The state of my health will not permit me to remain in this position."

"That you feel you must definitely leave the Treasury post by the end of the year is, of course, a great sorrow to me," said Mr. Roosevelt in reply, "but I am even more saddened by the thought that the throat is still giving trouble.

"I know, however, that it is of the highest importance that you shelve official cares, and that with your fine courage and constitution you will soon get wholly well. Remember that when that day comes you are wanted in the service of the country."

FRICTION DISCOUNTED

An echo of the repeated denials that Woodin was out of sympathy with the administration policies which preceded and followed his withdrawal in November is seen in a paragraph of the President's letter which said:

"Henry Morgenthau, Jr., will go

(Continued on Page 2, Column 1)

"Fore!"

SAFEGUARD OF DEPOSITS NEAR TOTAL

Bank Insurance Covers 97 Per Cent of Accounts, President Hears

WASHINGTON, Jan. 1. (AP)—President Roosevelt was informed tonight that 97 per cent of the nation's bank depositors will be insured under the new deposit insurance which becomes effective tomorrow.

Walter J. Cummings, chairman of the Federal Deposit Insurance Corporation, reported to Mr. Roosevelt deposits in 13,423 banks will be insured.

He said only 141 banks had been found ineligible and predicted a number of them may be insured by making certain corrections.

Thus, tomorrow for the first time in American history depositors of sums up to $2500 will be insured against loss.

After July 1 this insurance will be increased to $10,000.

"I congratulate you," wrote President Roosevelt in response to the report of Cummings, E. G. Bennett and J. F. T. O'Connor, "because you have in these few months accomplished with complete success a gigantic task which the pessimists said could not possibly be done before January 1. That 97 per cent of the bank depositors of the nation are insured will give renewed faith. I am also happy to know of the fine co-operation given to you by the Reconstruction Finance Corporation."

Will Rogers Remarks:

BEVERLY HILLS, Jan. 1.—[To the Editor of The Times:] **Everybody comes to California. They see a lot of great wide rocky sandy creek and river beds, with not a hot water bottle full of water in 'em, and they are a big joke. They wonder what they are for. Well, yesterday they showed what they were there for, us old settlers (that have been here five or ten years) never saw anything like it. We are so tickled to see rain out here that we put on a big parade in honor of it.**

I am writing this before I go to the big game today. I am about half mad because Nicholas Murray Butler didn't come out here with his team. Somebody ought to have told him it was a Republican convention, that's his principal relaxation.

Yours,
WILL ROGERS.

French Plane, Southern Cross, Sets Sea Record

SAINT LOUIS (Senegal) Jan. 1. (AP)—Another "Southern Cross"—this time a French seaplane—proved itself a fit namesake of its trans-Atlantic and trans-Pacific predecessors today by setting a nonstop seaplane flight record of 2663 miles.

The new Southern Cross was flown from Berre, France, here to Saint Louis as a test, preparatory to flying the South Atlantic to South America. It is designed to operate in the South Atlantic air-mail service, soon to be inaugurated on a regular basis by Air France, the consolidated French aviation company.

The longest seaplane nonstop flight was made last September 8 by six United States Navy ships which flew in mass formation from Norfolk to Coco Solo, C. Z., a distance of 2059 miles.

LOCOMOTIVE SUFFERS IN CRASH WITH AUTO

LITTLETON (N. H.) Jan. 1. (AP) Edward Splude's automobile and a locomotive contended for the right of way at a crossing here today and, contrary to the general rule, the outcome was not a complete victory for the locomotive. Splude was slightly hurt and his car was demolished, but a locomotive wheel was broken, disabling it several hours.

FIFTEEN DIE IN CHICAGO'S BITTER COLD

Midwest and East Feel Grip of Sub-zero Weather and Drifting Snows

CHICAGO, Jan. 1. (Exclusive)—Cold of bitter intensity, icy winds and drifting snows ushered in the New Year to the northern section of the Middle West and Far West today. It was the tenth day of frigid weather for this section and the third major cold wave of the winter for the East, which has been punished by storms and cold for a month.

Fifteen deaths were reported from the cold tonight and hundreds of persons were sent to hospitals suffering from frost bite, exposure or accidents due to ice and snow.

Throughout Southern Canada, Northern Minnesota, Wisconsin and Michigan the cold wave drove the mercury so far below the zero mark that people had to search for it.

Many points in those sections reported temperatures ranging from 50 to 60 degrees below zero. Elsewhere throughout the Middle West the mercury hovered slightly below or at the zero mark, while a subzero wave was just beginning in the East.

On most of the highways in the affected area thousands of frozen automobiles had to be abandoned and motor cars wer stalled on snow-clogged roads. Trains are running behind schedule in many sections.

Milk Drivers in Strike Beaten

PHILADELPHIA, Jan. 1. (AP)—Violence broke out anew today in the taxicab and milk wagon drivers' strikes.

Three drivers for one milk company were beaten. One of the victims, Richard Atkins, 21 years of age, was found unconscious in his wagon and taken to a hospital suffering from a fractured skull and other injuries.

Police ascribed the attacks to resentment of strikers against efforts by the company, the Harbison Dairies, and its drivers to adjudicate their disagreement as directed by the Regional Labor Board.

Creek Inundates Eastern Village

ILION (N. Y.) Jan. 1. (AP)—Steele Creek went on a sudden and short-lived rampage today, and covered approximately one-fifth of this village with a four-foot depth of water.

At least 150 cellars were flooded and as many furnace fires extinguished.

THIRTY-SIX ON DEATH ROSTER IN RECORD 8.27-INCH DELUGE

Upward of Thirty-five Injured During Downpour; Thousands of Men Put to Work Removing Wreckage Left in Wake of Torrents

As the heaviest twenty-four-hour rainstorm in the history of the local United States Weather Bureau began to taper off, Los Angeles and Southern California yesterday turned to the task of counting the loss in human life and property destruction while thousands of men were put to work clearing away the wreckage left in the wake of the unprecedented storm.

Up to nightfall yesterday the list of dead whose bodies were recovered stood at twenty-nine a list that was expected to be added to as the rescue crews and workmen probed the wreckage and debris. In addition there were seven deaths in traffic accidents due to the storm, bringing the total to thirty-six.

The list of injured had reached upward of thirty-five the injuries ranging from broken bones to exposure, sprains and bruises.

The heaviest list of dead and injured came from the foothill areas at the foot of the burned-over section in the recent brush fire, including portions of La Crescenta, Montrose and North Glendale.

RAINFALL FIGURES

The official figures on the rainfall in Los Angeles yesterday afternoon for the storm showed 8.26 inches of rain. This brought the season's total to 11.98 inches, as compared with a normal total for this time of year of 4.81 inches. Last year at this time the total was 1.99 inches.

The twenty-four hours' total showed 7.25 inches, which is the heaviest precipitation in twenty-four hours in the history of the local office of the United States Weather Bureau, dating from 1877.

Portions of Southwestern Los Angeles, Culver City and Venice, as well as the area northeast of Long Beach were under water as the streams, washes and storm-drain systems carried the water from the higher regions down into the lowlands.

VICTIMS TRAPPED

Deaths and injuries resulted from the terrific rush of waters from the mountains and foothills catching people in their homes near washes that had burst from their confines. Even persons afoot fleeing from their homes at the warning of oncoming floods was heard were caught in the swirl of muddy waters, knocked over and beaten into unconsciousness by boulders and debris and drowned. Several were drowned when they drove their automobiles into washes after bridges were washed out.

Probably the greatest single disaster that took its toll of dead and injured occurred at the American Legion Hall at Montrose Boulevard and La Crescenta when a wall of water, sweeping down off the burned area on the mountains above, tore into the hall upon some twenty-five men, women and children who were being cared for by the Red Cross.

As one victim, who, with his family, had been driven from their home earlier in the evening, put it: "As the black demon of roaring water hit, the building quivered for a few minutes, then the wall went out and we found ourselves tossing about, fighting rocks, boulders and debris as we were swept on and on."

It was here that Mrs. Myrtle Adams, chairman of the La Crescenta Valley Red Cross, met her death. She was in charge of the refugee headquarters when the wall of water engulfed the place. Her body was recovered.

SURVEY OF HAVOC

A survey of the general picture of havoc wrought by the storm showed many roads and highways strewn with boulders and debris, some 1500 homes in the Venice area and along Ballona Creek under water, as well as the low area northeast of Long Beach suffering from inundation.

Scores of bridges were out, Chief County Flood Control Engineer Eaton listing thirty-nine in his district that were either washed out

(Continued on Page 3, Column 1)

FLOOD TOLL RUNS HIGH

Twenty-nine Die by Drowning

Coroner's Office Compiles List of Those Trapped in Raging Waters

More Than Dozen Missing; Traffic Deaths Excluded in Fatality Tally

Official figures of the Coroner's office at a late hour yesterday fixed the number of known dead from actual flood waters at twenty-nine. Many of these are unidentified. The figure did not include seven persons killed in traffic accidents attributed directly to the heavy rain. More than a dozen persons were reported as missing and several of these were believed unquestionably to have been drowned. Those injured in the flood waters, some seriously, numbered more than a score.

LIST OF DEAD

The official flood-water death list as arranged by the Coroner follows:

Elwood Plumb, 55 years of age, Long Beach, body recovered near the Selig Zoo in Los Angeles.

Frank Geraghty, 25, 11203 Tiara street, North Hollywood. Body at the Orrell & Steen mortuary, Van Nuys.

Marylin Ghoslin, 4, 912 Glen Oaks Drive, Glendale. Body at the Aycock & Durr mortuary, Glendale.

Mrs. J. E. Moore, 3106 South San Gabriel Boulevard, San Gabriel. Boddy at DuBois Funeral Home, San Gabriel.

J. E. Moore, 3106 South San Gabriel Boulevard. DuBois Funeral Home.

Marpha Moore, 11, daughter of Mr. and Mrs. Moore. DuBois Funeral Home.

Sherman Hubbard, 3106 South San Gabriel Boulevard, San Gabriel. DuBois Funeral Home.

"Toots" Hubbard, 18, sister of Sherman Hubbard, same address. DuBois Funeral Home.

Mrs. Dorothy Hartman Carter, 40, 110 North Sierra Vista avenue, Monterey Park. Body at Turner & Stevens mortuary, Pasadena.

Chester Herrera, 12, One Hundred Sixty-seventh and Hoover streets, drowned when a raft on which he was playing overturned.

Body of 6-months-old girl found near Verdugo Road and Apache Way, Glendale. H. E. Davis mortuary.

John Doe, 35, body found near Glenoaks and Gessell avenue, Glendale.

Clyde Powell, 26, found near C.W.A. Camp No. 9, Tujunga. Bade & Son mortuary, Tujunga.

John Doe, 16, found near Pacific and Glen Oaks, Glendale. Aycock & Dunn mortuary.

John Doe, 70, found near Riverside Drive and Van Nuys Boulevard, Van Nuys. Van Nuys Funeral Home.

John Doe, 19, found in Glendale. Aycock & Durr mortuary, Glendale.

Jane Doe, 45, Glendale. Aycock & Durr mortuary.

AT TEMPORARY MORGUES

Ten bodies were laid out in the Sparr Heights Community House at Montrose and at the La Crescenta Women's Club where temporary morgues were established.

Identified dead are:

Mrs. Myrtle Adams of 2425 Granada avenue.

Mrs. Phillys L. Reihl of 2635 Piedmont avenue.

Mrs. Margaret Smith, 52, of 4318 Rosemont street, who died of heart disease.

Clark Harmon, 35, Montrose.

Sam Wilson, 10, 2636 Piedmont street.

Unidentified are:

Jane Doe, 2½ years of age.
Jane Doe, 9 years of age.
Jane Doe, 50 years of age.
Jane Doe, 40 years of age.
John Doe, 12.

At a late hour yesterday the Glendale police reported that the bodies of two unidentified men had been located in silt near the bridge at Doran street and San Fernando Road.

TRAFFIC VICTIMS

Those killed in traffic accidents due to the rain were listed as follows:

John D. McDonald, 2, 702 Pannes street, Compton.

J. C. Doty, a sailor from aboard the U.S.S. New York.

Viola Wygart, 32, 735 Alabama street, Huntington Park.

(Continued on Page 10, Column 5)

RAIN TOTALS

Following is the rainfall, in inches, reported from various Southern California points up to 6 p.m. yesterday:

	Storm	Season	Last Year
Los Angeles	8.27	11.99	1.99
Alhambra	10.11	15.12	2.36
Altadena	11.39	16.35	1.89
Anaheim	5.04	7.30	2.38
Arcadia	13.36	17.99	2.23
Ash Mountain	2.04	7.55	..
Bakersfield	.54	1.21	1.24
Bell	7.15	9.94	2.13
Bellflower	5.14	7.18	2.28
Beverly Hills	9.88	14.90	1.97
Buena Park	4.69	6.70	2.62
Camarillo	3.53	7.56	1.00
Canoga Park	6.20	7.62	1.48
Carlsbad	1.56	4.23	5.53
Carpinteria	3.54	8.07	1.40
Claremont	9.57	13.30	3.09
Covina	12.28	16.06	2.72
Garvanza	13.36	17.46	2.00
Duarte	15.86	19.41	2.15
El Monte	11.96	15.13	1.70
El Segundo	4.72	7.10	2.36
Escondido	2.44	5.41	7.84
Fullerton	6.21	8.95	2.74
Gardena	4.57	7.53	2.67
Garden Grove	4.81	6.66	2.76
Girard	6.42	8.29	1.16
Glendora	15.40	20.61	2.46
Hanford	.70	1.15	.45
Hermosa	4.54	6.50	2.39
Huntington Park	7.23	10.26	2.09
Inglewood	5.73	8.78	2.05
Laguna Beach	2.96	4.71	2.61
Lindsay	.60	2.14	2.11
Long Beach	2.75	4.25	3.43
LaVerne	11.31	15.93	3.04
Lomita	5.14	7.71	3.58
Maywood	7.25	10.30	2.11
Manhattan Beach	4.36	6.05	2.16
Monrovia	12.98	17.45	2.48
Montebello	7.26	10.84	1.80
Monterey Park	11.05	15.39	2.23
Mt. Wilson	13.95	20.00	1.81
Newport Beach	3.24	5.21	3.42
Oceanside	2.68	4.76	4.15
Olive	5.65	8.48	2.45
Orange	5.38	8.28	2.60
Oxnard	3.75	6.99	.93
Palos Verdes	4.72	6.52	3.01
Pasadena	12.86	17.25	2.14
Pico	7.99	11.12	2.08
Placentia	6.90	..	..
Pomona	10.25	13.63	3.29
Puente	6.27	9.99	2.41
Redlands	2.65	4.98	4.04
Redondo Beach	3.22	5.19	2.20
Rosemead	13.44	17.02	2.20
San Clemente	3.00	5.10	4.27
San Diego	.67	..	..
San Dimas	12.91	17.50	3.32
San Fernando	7.55	10.60	1.69
San Gabriel	14.86	18.82	2.27
San Juan Capistran	3.55	5.93	4.08
San Marino	13.90	18.30	2.41
San Pedro	2.07	3.53	2.00
Santa Barbara	4.35	8.59	3.08
Santa Maria	1.52	4.11	1.37
Santa Monica	5.89	10.30	1.69
Sequoia Nat'l Park	3.01	15.64	..
Sierra Madre	13.50	18.45	2.17
South Pasadena	14.11	18.79	1.96
Torrance	4.82	6.70	3.33
Van Nuys	6.54	8.43	1.55
Whittier	7.50	11.06	4.91
Yorba Linda	5.16	7.77	2.61
Victorvilla	.48	1.53	1.67
Walnut Park	12.41	16.95	2.04
West Orange	5.75	9.05	2.59

BEDOUINS INJURE JEWS

JERUSALEM, Jan. 1. (Jewish Telegraphic Agency)—Attacked by a band of Bedouins, armed with sticks and stones, four Jewish tractor drivers were wounded today, two of them seriously.

TRANSPORT MAINTAINED

Schedules of Various Major Services Disrupted but No Travelers Marooned

Nearly all the major transportation systems reported yesterday that their service and schedules had been disrupted due to the unprecedented rainstorm but all continued in service, with minimum delay, by rerouting trains or electric cars and supplementing them with emergency bus schedules.

The storm affected service to the North, South and East and tied up travel temporarily to many adjacent cities and towns, but where it was impossible to resume normal travel last night the regular schedules were being maintained with auxiliary bus services and no travelers were definitely marooned or greatly inconvenienced.

Traffic on the Southern Pacific Coast lines was halted yesterday with damage to tracks and the bridge over the Verdugo wash between Burbank and Glendale, holding southbound trains at Saugus and Burbank. Passengers were taken to Los Angeles by bus and northbound Southern Pacific trains were leaving on schedule over the Union Pacific tracks via Colton, Santa Fe tracks to Barstow and thence on the company's own lines to the north by way of the inland route.

Officials said all repair crews of the Southern Division were at work on the damaged tracks and bridge between Glendale and Burbank, but that arrangements were complete to carry the seven special trains allocated to care for northbound traffic over the Union Pacific and Santa Fe tracks if the repairs were not completed in time.

A later announcement made by Southern Pacific officials revealed that excursionists and Rose Bowl football spectators would be taken from here to their homes in the East and North by two Sunset Limited trains, two Larks and one Owl West Coast Limited.

Any passengers who wished to leave last night for northern or eastern points from Glendale were taken by bus to Los Angeles where departure times for the Sunsets were given as 6:45 p.m. and 6:55 p.m. The Larks left at 8:30 p.m. and 8:40 p.m. and the Owl, as did the other four trains, departed on time at 6 p.m.

Passengers on Santa Fe trains Nos. 7, 9 and 13 from Chicago arrived in San Bernardino as scheduled, but due to submerged tracks and intermittent washouts en route to Los Angeles were thrown off their respective scheduled arrivals here of 6:30 a.m., 7 a.m. and 7:15 a.m. to a bunched arrival of 1 p.m. Train No. 24 for Chicago, due to depart here at noon did not leave until 1:30 p.m. Santa Fe trains from Los Angeles to San Diego were delayed on their north and south runs. That line, however, suffered only slight interruptions. Beginning at 2 p.m. trains were dispatched on time.

Officials of the Union Pacific Railway reported only one slight delay

(Continued on Page 2, Column 1)

THE "TIMES" TODAY—NEWS SUMMED UP

Remember This

A young man thinks everybody's crazy except himself. An old man knows everybody's crazy including himself.

Rockefeller, Ill, Drops Old Rule

TARRYTOWN (N. Y.) Jan. 1. (Exclusive)—John D. Rockefeller, ill in his Pocantico Hills mansion, today was unable to issue his usual New Year's message of cheer and confidence to the world. The 94-year-old oil king, stricken with a severe cold several weeks ago, also was obliged to forego all New Year's Day gaiety, being confined to his room all day.

CHILI QUAKE LEAVES DAMAGE

COQUIMBO (Chili) Jan. 1. (AP)—A strong earthquake ushered in the new year today. Only slight damage was reported, however, and there were no casualties. The quake occurred at 4:00 a.m.

OUT TODAY

Regular monthly subscribers of the Los Angeles Times will receive as part of today's issue the four pictorial magazines comprising the 1934 edition of the Annual Midwinter Number. These magazines, together with the pictorial Tournament of Roses section, will be inclosed in a decorated wrapper and mailed postpaid to any address in the world for 25 cents. By using the order blank inserted in last Sunday's issue of The Times subscribers may send copies away and have them charged to their subscription accounts. Copies of the Annual Midwinter Number will also go on sale today at principal news stands throughout Southern California.

All the News All the Time
LARGEST HOME-DELIVERED CIRCULATION
LARGEST ADVERTISING VOLUME

MAdison 2345
The Times Telephone Number
Connecting All Departments

Los Angeles Times

EQUAL RIGHTS · LIBERTY UNDER THE LAW · TRUE INDUSTRIAL FREEDOM

In Two Parts — 32 Pages
PART I — GENERAL NEWS — 24 PAGES

TIMES OFFICES
100 North Broadway
And Throughout Southern California

VOL. LIV · C · FRIDAY MORNING, JANUARY 4, 1935. · DAILY, FIVE CENTS

Lindberghs Tell of Kidnaping; State Asks Hauptmann's Death

WITNESSES DEFY INQUIRY ON GAMBLING

Deadlock Faced by Grand Jury

Four Must Appear in Court for Refusal to Testify; One Denies Pay-offs

Defied by most witnesses, the grand jury met an apparent impasse yesterday as it continued its investigation of gambling operations in Los Angeles county.

At least, such was the belief of observers last night in the light of comment by Dr. John P. Buckley, foreman pro tem. With the conclusion of the session, Dr. Buckley said:

"We had hoped some witnesses would give direct testimony in this matter. They failed to do so. This failure to obtain the desired testimony from these witnesses, of course, will materially hamper our investigation."

Before the jury during the day went six witnesses, four of whom will have to appear in court next Tuesday, along with Nola Hahn, and show cause why they should not be cited for contempt for having refused to testify. Hahn, co-proprietor of the Club Continental, similarly had refused to testify at Wednesday's session.

WITNESSES NAMED

Witnesses summoned yesterday included Homer (Slim) Gordon, proprietor of an Altadena night club; Walter Lipps, one of his employees; Milton (Farmer) Page, known in Los Angeles gambling circles for years; Moe Morton, associated with the Clover Club; Harry Leonard, said to be an employee of a local night club, and Alfred Freitas, former night-club operator.

Also in the group was Solomon Zemansky, loan company official.

None made any secret of what had developed in the jury's chambers.

ZEMANSKY STATEMENT

Explaining he had not taken the oath of secrecy as the jury called him to be questioned, Zemansky announced he had refused to testify and had read into the jury records the following statement:

"On the advice of my attorney I refuse to answer any and all questions in these proceedings on the ground that under Section 2065 of the Penal Code it might have a

(Cont'd on Page 2, Col. 2, Part II)

Officer 'Tags' Former Teacher

PALO ALTO, Jan. 3. (AP)—Ben Hickey, newest and youngest member of the Palo Alto Police Department, has realized the ambition of every school boy.

He motioned to the curb an automobile which had just passed through a twenty mile zone at thirty miles an hour and handed a ticket to William Carr McInnes, his former history instructor at Palo Alto High School.

Congress Begins Session Ready to Revamp New Deal

Marching Orders Waited as Houses Organize Mid Colorful Scenes; Forcing Vote Made Harder

BY W. B. FRANCIS
"Times" Staff Correspondent

WASHINGTON, Jan. 3. (Exclusive)—Waiting for marching orders from President Roosevelt, the Seventy-fourth Congress assumed office today prepared to overhaul many phases of the New Deal and confronted with the threat of radical legislation by organized minorities. Aside from swearing in new members and tightening House rules to strengthen administration control, neither branch attempted to transact business.

Instead, the Senate and House informed President Roosevelt through the visit of a top-hatted committee that the national legislature was ready for work and would be pleased to receive any communications from the White House.

MESSAGE TODAY

Following the custom revived last year, President Roosevelt planned to address a joint session of the two chambers at 12:30 tomorrow afternoon when he will read the

Wirephotos of the opening of Congress will be found on Page 16, Part I, of this issue of The Times.

annual message describing "the state of the Union," and outlining in broad terms the nature of the new legislative program.

The President denied himself to callers today and spent virtually all of his time putting finishing touches on the message he will deliver tomorrow.

The scheduled election of Representative Joseph W. Byrns of Tennessee as Speaker of the House and the induction of twelve new Senators were high points in the day's proceedings.

GETS HUGE VOTE

Byrns was named to succeed the late Henry T. Rainey of Illinois with 316 votes to ninety-five for Republican Leader Snell, nine for Representative Schneider, Wisconsin Progressive, and two for Representative Lambertson, Republican, of Kansas.

Among new Senators were Theodore Bilbo, Democrat, Mississippi; Edward R. Burke, Democrat, Nebraska; Vic Donahey, Democrat, Ohio; Francis T. Mahoney, Democrat, Connecticut; Sherman Minton, Democrat, Indiana; A. Harry Moore, Democrat, New Jersey; George L. Radcliffe, Democrat, Maryland; Lewis B. Schwellenbach, Democrat,

(Continued on Page 5, Column 1)

ANN HARDING WINS BATTLE

Husband Fails to Contest Motion to Obtain Sole Care of Daughter

RENO, Jan. 3. (Exclusive)—Ann Harding, blonde film star, today was granted exclusive custody of her 6-year-old daughter, Jane, at a closed hearing in the chambers of Judge Thomas F. Moran.

Her motion for exclusive custody

Ann Harding will have sole custody of daughter in future.

to change conditions of the divorce decree granted her in 1932 was based on changed conditions and on the allegation that the father was not the proper person to have even partial custody.

The only witness for Miss Harding was Lily Evendeen Burgess, a former governess.

Harry Bannister, the father and ex-husband, was unrepresented, and did not file any answer.

CHILD PLAYS IN LIBRARY

While the motion for sole custody was being heard the child played in the adjoining law library, pushing stick gum through a mail slot and climbing the ladder to the book shelves, carefully watched all the time by Police Lieutenant Holly of Los Angeles, who had been specially detailed here.

The motion filed today stated conditions had changed since the di-

(Continued on Page 24, Column 3)

Ellsworth Hop Halted by Snow

[Copyright, 1935, by the North American Newspaper Alliance, Inc., and the New York Times Co.]

SNOW HILL ISLAND (Weddell Sea, Antarctica) Jan. 3. (By wireless)—Lincoln Ellsworth, leader of the Ellsworth trans-Antarctic flight expedition, and Bernt Balchen, pilot, took off in the airplane Polar Star at 3 p.m. (P.S.T.) today on their projected flight across the Antarctic continent, but encountered snow and were forced to return to their base two hours later.

DUST STORM TAKES LIVES OF TWO BOYS

Pair Lost Near Own Home

Bodies Found Frozen After Mercury Suddenly Drops to Below Zero

ST. PAUL, Jan. 3. (AP)—A mid-winter dust storm that brought death to two boys, a near blizzard and temperatures that dipped sharply, as much as 56 deg. in less than twelve hours, were included in the weather fare of three Northwest States in the last thirty-six hours.

The dust storm came with suddenness accompanied by a 43 deg. temperature drop in the Huron (S. D.) area. Sweeping out of the northwest, it caught 11-year-old Edwin, Walter and his 6-year-old brother Melvin as they were returning from a visit with neighboring children a quarter of a mile away.

Unable to find their way home in the darkness and dust, with the mercury standing at 3 below zero, they fell, exhausted, and froze to death. Their bodies were found today.

In North Dakota, meanwhile, the Grand Forks area was experiencing a near blizzard as a twenty-six-mile wind swirled new fallen snow in the faces of those who ventured out.

Minnesota escaped both snow and dust but had the greatest temperature drop, 56 deg. in about twelve hours at Pipestone. The low point was 3 below.

Montana experienced similar temperature drops.

SEVEN FISHERMAN ADRIFT ON ICE

BARRIE (Ont.) Jan. 3. (AP)—Seven fishermen were set adrift on ice cakes in Lake Simcoe tonight when strong winds broke up the ice. The provincial police planned to remove the men when the wind subsides.

GREAT BEAR LAKE REPORTS 76 DEG. BELOW

EDMONTON (Alta.) Jan. 3. (AP)—A new low for cold weather in the coldest region in Canada was established at Great Bear Lake New Year's Day, when the temperature dropped to 76 deg. below zero, the official weather bureau announced today.

The previous record was held by Mayo, Yukon Territory, when on December 20, 1933, the mercury dropped to 68 below.

RAIN HEADED SOUTH FROM NORTH AREA

SAN FRANCISCO, Jan. 3. (Exclusive)—Light rain north of the Bay district, caused by a depression moving eastward from a point 300 miles west of Cape Mendocino tonight, will be followed by general showers tomorrow from this and a second depression behind it, the Weather Bureau predicts.

During the day, there was a trace of rain at Eureka, Redding and Sacramento. In San Francisco .10 of an inch fell.

Rain for Los Angeles and vicinity is forecast for today and tomorrow by the United States Weather Bureau. The storm is due over this section from a low-pressure area that is rolling in from off the coast of Central California.

Moderate temperatures will continue today and no frost is predicted, the bureau forecast says.

Light Temblor Jars San Jose

SAN JOSE, Jan. 3. (AP)—A light earthquake shook San Jose at 9:36 this morning.

It was recorded at Ricard Observatory at Santa Clara University and Lick Observatory at Mt. Hamilton, the third slight quake in five days. No damage was reported.

Massacre Case Jurors Retire

KANSAS CITY (Mo.) Jan. 3. (U.P.)—A Federal jury deliberating conspiracy charges against six defendants accused of plotting the Union Station massacre of five persons retired for the night shortly after 10 p.m.

Judge Otis told the jurors to resume their work at 9 a.m. tomorrow.

Daughter of Oil Man Disappears

TYLER (Tex.) Jan. 4. (Friday) (AP)—Mrs. Johnnie Fay Oxford, 19-year-old daughter of a wealthy oil man, was reported missing early today. Officers said she was last seen after driving a Negro maid to her home.

First photograph of Col. Charles A. Lindbergh on witness stand in Flemington, N. J., yesterday at the trial of Bruno Richard Hauptmann on the charge of murdering Lindbergh's baby son.
[Picture copyright, 1935, (AP) Wirephoto]

SPECTATORS SOB AS ANNE KEEPS NERVE

Colonel Relates Crash Outside

Accused Man Unshaken by Accounts of Baby's Loss; Prosecution Aim Shown

BY HARRY FERGUSON
[Copyright, 1935, by the United Press]

FLEMINGTON (N. J.) Jan. 3. (U.P.)—Col. and Mrs. Charles A. Lindbergh today told a sympathetic world—a world which had waited thirty months for the story—about the murder of their son.

They told it calmly—displaying that same courage which enabled them to live sanely through the tragedy.

Thirty feet across the courtroom from them sat Bruno Richard Hauptmann, on trial for his life. He was the same granite-faced prisoner today that he always has been, but when court recessed at 4:07 p.m., his clothing was damp with perspiration.

If this man is guilty, he took part of his punishment today.

Tears were shed, but they didn't come from the eyes of Anne Morrow Lindbergh. Not even when Atty.-Gen. David T. Wilentz walked slowly toward the witness chair and held before her a torn and stained scrap of cloth—the shirt which on the evening of March 1, 1932, she wrapped around the child she never saw again.

GULPS BACK GRIEF

Her hands trembled, but she gulped back her grief, paused a moment and said:

"Yes, that is the shirt."

Somewhere in court a woman

(Continued on Page 3, Column 1)

ACTOR GIVEN JAIL TERM

Francis Lederer Sentenced at Tulare on Charge of Auto Speeding

TULARE, Jan. 3. (AP)—Francis Lederer, handsome leading man of the films, was sentenced to five days in the County Jail today for speeding at seventy miles an hour near here early in December. He immediately gave notice of appeal and was freed on $500 bail.

Lederer asked Justice of the Peace

Francis Lederer, who was sentenced to jail yesterday for speeding.

Rush for leniency, but it was denied. Both the actor and Miss Mary Loos of Santa Monica, with him at the time of the arrest, denied they were traveling as fast as charged. Lederer said he was on his way to Hanford to lecture at a woman's club when arrested.

Mexico Liquor Taxes Boosted

MEXICO CITY, Jan. 3. (U.P.)—Mexican citizens felt the heavy hand of modification of their drinking habits today.

President Cardenas, fulfilling promises made in his campaign, decreed increased taxes on the sale, manufacture and importation of all alcoholic liquors and announced restrictions on the number of saloons allowed to operate throughout Mexico.

Huey Buys Radio to Tell World of Cancer Cure

NEW ORLEANS, Jan. 3. (U.P.)—Senator Long said tonight that Louisiana State University doctors have discovered a cure for cancer and that he has bought radio station WDSU in New Orleans for $100,000 to broadcast the cure to the world.

He gave no details of the discovery, but said he will make a speech about it on the floor of the United States Senate Monday night.

The "Kingfish" has been talking about his "university on the air" for weeks. Political observers believe he will make it a propaganda machine, with which to campaign for the Presidency in 1936.

BRITON SAYS GUARD FIRED ON HIS SHIP

ST. GEORGES (Bermuda) Jan. 3. (AP)—A United States Coast Guard cutter fired seven times at the British motor vessel Casanova outside territorial waters, the Casanova's master charged today at the end of a chase down the storm-swept Atlantic from the Rhode Island coast.

Her supplies running low, the Casanova, registered at St. John's, N. F., was here for fuel oil. The cutter Thetis had trailed her into port after seizing her off Rhode Island and then releasing her on orders from Washington.

Hitler Assails Foreign "Lies"

BERLIN, Jan. 3. (AP)—Nazi notables, hastily and mysteriously assembled here, tonight heard Reichsfuehrer Hitler scathingly assail "stupid and impertinent lies" spread abroad concerning the Nazi regime.

The leader said predictions of the Nazi's collapse and consequent catastrophe after the Saar plebiscite January 13 will "fail to turn our Saar brethren from their determination to return to the Reich fold."

St. Paul Garage Strike Starts

ST. PAUL, Jan. 3. (U.P.) — The strike of 1200 mechanics, greasers and washers in Twin Cities garages was called at midnight.

Herman Husman, union leader, declared arbitration ended.

Michael Johannes, Minneapolis police chief, ordered 400 men to duty in twelve-hour shifts. St. Paul police planned similar precautions.

Feet Frozen on Mountain Trip

SAN FRANCISCO, Jan. 3. (AP)—James Wright was in a hospital here tonight with badly frost bitten feet after a fight for his life near the summit of Mt. Whitney, highest peak in the continental United States.

FIRST LADY AIDS JUNIOR

Letter From Mrs. Roosevelt Declared Not Request for Leniency

ORANGE (Ct.) Jan. 3. (U.P.)—Mrs. Franklin D. Roosevelt has written Prosecutor Torrance a letter asking a continuance for her son, Franklin D. Roosevelt, Jr., who faces a speeding charge here, Torrance told the United Press tonight.

The prosecutor received the letter, written on White House stationery, today.

Torrance also received a telegram from Franklin D., Jr., saying he would be unable to appear in court today and requesting a postponement of his case until Saturday.

CLASSES AT STAKE

Torrance at first interpreted Mrs. Roosevelt's letter as "a request for leniency" but later he said this was a misconstruction. She merely asked that the case be continued until 5 p.m. Saturday so that her son could appear in court without missing his college classes.

Torrance said he would telegraph young Roosevelt notifying him to be present in court Saturday if possible; if not, on Monday.

ARRESTED LAST MONTH

He was arrested here late last month charged with speeding between seventy-five and eighty miles an hour along the Boston Post Road with his brother John.

The case attracted wide attention and Torrance has received scores of letters. Many of the letters are anonymous and some obviously are from cranks.

Some of the letters berate the defendant for recklessness, while others defend him.

Debt Installment Paid by Mexico

WASHINGTON, Jan. 3. (AP)—A check for $500,000 was presented Secretary Hull today by Pablo Campos-Ortiz, charge d'affaires of the Mexican Embassy, as the first installment of Mexico's approximately $7,000,000 debt to the United States.

Will Rogers Remarks:

HOLLYWOOD, Jan. 3.—[To the Editor of The Times:] You hear people say, "what is this new deal anyhow." Well, there was a headline today that explains it. "Wall Street anxiously await the presidents message."

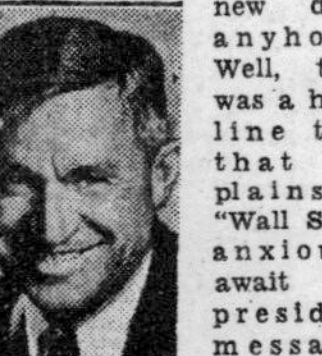

Well, in the "old deal" it was the president that was anxiously awaiting till Wall Street sent him the message to read. If Arizona, Texas, or Arkansas hear something whizzing over your heads, it won't be a plane, its Dixie Howell passing some autographed footballs back to friends in Tuscaloosa.

Yours,
WILL ROGERS.

EXCLUSIVELY IN "THE TIMES"

Gone is the day when news pictures are delivered by mail! Wirephoto has arrived in a blaze of glory! And, through its magic, The Times yesterday published exclusively:

The first photograph of the wreckage of the steamer Lexington in New York Harbor (on the street at 9 p.m. Wednesday, shortly after the actual collision.)

The first photograph of Bruno Richard Hauptmann entering the Flemington (N. J.) courtroom to stand trial for the murder of the Lindbergh baby.

The first photograph of courtroom spectators watching selection of the Hauptmann jury.

The first photograph of the first four jurors chosen to determine Hauptmann's fate.

The first photograph of Premier Mussolini reviewing troops of the international Saar police before their departure for the Saar Valley region.

The first photograph of Great Britain's contingent of the same troops marching to embark at Dover, Eng.

The first photograph of young revolutionaries arrested near Mexico City in connection with anti-religious outbreaks.

From all parts of the world they come, abreast of the news itself. They appear in The Times first in the new Night Pictorial Edition, out at 6 p.m., and are carried in all subsequent editions. The Times is the only California newspaper south of San Francisco where you can find Wirephoto.

THE "TIMES" TODAY—NEWS SUMMED UP

Remember This

If you are good at riddles, try solving that of life itself.

Hymnals Stolen From Convent

PHILADELPHIA, Jan 3. (AP)—The nuns of St. Francis Xavier convent are wondering what manner of man it was who robbed them.

Fifty hymn books were his sole plunder.

All the News at the Time

LARGEST HOME-DELIVERED CIRCULATION
LARGEST ADVERTISING VOLUME

MAdison 2345
The Times Telephone Number
Connecting All Departments

Los Angeles Times

EQUAL RIGHTS
LIBERTY UNDER THE LAW — TRUE INDUSTRIAL FREEDOM

In Two Parts—36 Pages

PART I — GENERAL NEWS — 18 PAGES

TIMES OFFICES
100 North Broadway
And Throughout Southern California

VOL. LIV — THURSDAY MORNING, MAY 2, 1935. — DAILY, FIVE CENTS

STATE'S NEW TAXES TOTAL $76,000,000

Budget Basis Agreed on

Joint Legislative Group Sets Figure, but May Have to Raise It

BY CHESTER G. HANSON
"Times" Staff Representative

SACRAMENTO, May 1. (Exclusive)—The joint tax steering committee named to plan a program of taxation to balance the State budget for the next two years, today established a tentative base on which it hopes to build its recommendations.

The tentative program arrived at after considerable study embraces such salient points as a State income tax lower than the one proposed by the administration, increase in the sales tax but exempting foodstuffs, a graduated automobile license-plate tax, increased inheritance tax and a higher liquor revenue.

TOTAL $76,000,000

All totaled, the new tax proposals will reach approximately $76,000,000, the committee announced. Nearly $100,000,000 in new revenue is needed to balance the 1935-37 budget.

Senator Duval, chairman, described the new plan as "something to shoot at," and stressed that it is not final.

Overcoming vigorous discussion with a 7-6 vote, the committee expressed favor toward an increase of the sales tax to 3 per cent with foodstuffs exempted. This operation, coupled with plans to extend the tax to rented and stored property, would add about $27,000,000 to State revenues, the committee estimated.

NOTICE SERVED

Assemblymen Williamson, San Francisco, and Riley, Long Beach, served notice that the lower house will not approve any sales-tax measure without foodstuffs exempted, and Senator Jespersen, Atascadero, reminded the committee that a sales-tax repeal petition is in the Secretary of State's office.

Jespersen said he thinks an election, with the possibility of repeal of the State's principal source of revenue, can be averted if the exemption is granted.

Senators Rich, Marysville, and

(Continued on Page 2, Column 5)

Chute Lands Pilot Killed in Air Crash

CHATEAUROUX (France) May 1. (AP)—A dead man dangling from an open parachute floated down out of the skies here today after two army planes engaged in maneuvers collided in midair.

One of the planes cut the other in two, throwing Pilots Herve and Henigue and Observer Quenebaud from the cockpits of the ships.

The observer was killed in the fall to earth, but the pilots' parachutes opened. Herve landed safely. Henigue was dead. Apparently he was killed in the collision and his parachute opened of itself.

Will Rogers Remarks:

SANTA MONICA, May 1.—[To the Editor of The Times:] The great argument with all Americans who want to join in with Europe and help set the world right was that any one that was in favor of it was pretty narrow minded and selfish. In plain words, its the dumb folks that are "agin" it. Well, read todays papers, the Premiers of Canada, Australia, South Africa and New Zealand have never been considered anything but intelligent, yet they notified England to quit messing around on the opposite bank of the English Channel. So the American dumb ones are in pretty good company.

Yours,
WILL ROGERS.

NEW CURES DISCOVERED

Harvard University Reports Remedies for Diphtheria and Other Diseases

PHILADELPHIA, May 1. (AP)—Concentrated in the bodies of human mothers, a new store of remedies against some of the major diseases has been discovered at Harvard University.

The remedies come from substances evidently concentrated by the mother's body as a protection for her child. They include protectives for measles, scarlet fever, diphtheria and infantile paralysis.

DATA GIVEN PHYSICIANS

They were described by Charles F. McKhann, professor of pedriatrics and communicable diseases at Harvard, to the American College of Physicians meeting here.

These substances are called antibodies, the name given by the medical profession to a great number of chemicals of unusual nature which living bodies form for their own protection against disease.

Dr. McKhann said the antibodies found so concentrated in omthers probably had their source in her own exposure at some time in her life to the ills for which they were the protection. They are extracted from the placenta.

TESTS GIVEN

Dr. McKhann said that the measles extract had been given to 1258 persons exposed to this malady and that it "proved highly effective in preventing the disease, or else was followed by a much milder form of measles."

The cause of chronic arthritis and of acute "inflammatory rheumatism" was traced to probable lack of vitamin C in experiments on guinea pigs, reported by Dr. James F. Rhinehart, assistant professor of pathology, University of California.

Vitamin C is most abundant in green leafy vegetables and fresh fruits. The guinea pigs developed ills similar to both the human forms when their vitamin C was low.

N.R.A. GIVEN TEN MONTHS EXTENSION

New Deal Plan Disregarded

Two-Year Lease on Life Refused by 16-to-3 Vote in Senate Committee

BY WARREN B. FRANCIS
"Times" Staff Correspondent

WASHINGTON, May 1. (Exclusive)—A ten-month extension of the National Industrial Recovery Act, major concession to foes of the Blue Eagle program, was voted today by the Senate Finance Committee in a desperate attempt to avoid drawn-out controversy and accelerate Congressional procedure.

In complete disregard for the wishes of Secretary of Labor Perkins and Donald R. Richberg, acting chairman of the Industrial Recovery Board, the body refused by a vote of 16 to 3 to give the N.R.A. a two-year lease on life and decided instead to recommend passage of a bill making basic changes in the present law and limiting the code system to April 1, 1936.

WHITE HOUSE CONFERENCE

The action followed a significant White House conference Monday at which President Roosevelt was told the present Congressional situation precludes all hope that a two-year extension can be effected before the present law expires June 16, but members of the committee refused to disclose the Chief Executive's attitude toward the compromise plan.

CALLS FOR CHANGES

The joint resolution postponing the expiration date of the law will require fundamental modification of policies, substantially in accordance with the desires of principal Congressional critics of the N.R.A., prohibiting price-fixing except in natural resource industries and exempting from code regulation all individuals and firms engaged in "wholly intrastate" business or commerce.

Continuing all current codes for a period of thirty days, the measure will require the President to order a review of every existing agreement and modify clauses which are in conflict with the two new basic principles. Unless previously reviewed, codes not in operation would expire automatically on July 15.

ARGUMENTS WILL BE MADE TODAY ON N.R.A.

WASHINGTON, May 1. (AP)—A brief upholding the constitutionality of the National Industrial Re-

(Continued on Page 2, Column 7)

Franco-Russian Treaty Ready for Signing

PARIS, May 1. (AP)—French officials announced today that France and Russia had reached agreement on the text of their mutual assistance pact.

The soviet Ambassador, Vladimir Potemkin, called on Foreign Minister Laval, who has been instrumental in negotiating the agreement, at the Foreign Office this evening, leading to the belief the signing might take place tonight.

Potemkin emerged, however, to explain that the great May Day celebration at Moscow made it difficult to communicate with Russian officials, thus delaying the signing.

Chain Letter Mail Deluge Growing Here

Postmaster Briggs shows Peggy Mulligan part of the deluge of mail in the send-a-dime chain letter scheme, which poured into the Los Angeles postoffice yesterday. Postal officials estimated that 200,000 letters were handled here in the day's business. "Times" photo

Send-a-Dime Letters Swamping Postoffice

Gaining overnight momentum, Southern California's latest of quick wealth pastimes—the dime chain-letter craze—whirled merrily on yesterday, to swell Los Angeles' postmen's mail bags with an estimated total of 200,000 dime letters for the twenty-four-hour period.

The increased mail delivery, first reflected yesterday, was believed to give only a rough picture of the chain-letter ramifications, for by far the most popular form of distribution was hand-to-hand circulation.

SIGNS OF TOPPLING

So far-reaching had the criss-cross of chains become that the whole fantastic pattern showed signs of toppling from its own weight, but persistent reports of friends, or friends of friends, receiving hundreds and even thousands of dimes acted as a spur to keep the financial merry-go-round still turning. A few admitted they have received appreciable sums.

Postoffice officials estimated that yesterday morning's mail delivery carried 33,000 of the send-a-dime missives, and of this total 14,000 went through the Hollywood substation, where the letters were being showered in greatest numbers.

MORE GET WORK

Postmaster Briggs announced that the normal increase in mail deliveries in recent weeks has made it necessary to give more work to temporary employees, and that the craze, if it continues, will require a still greater increase of work.

With stenographers busy typing chain letters for themselves and friends, the working efficiency of many offices was reported at low ebb and at least in one instance, at the Paramount Studios, orders were issued forbidding workers to write or mail the dime letters during work hours.

During the last week mail deliveries at the studio have jumped 300

(Continued on Page 2, Column 5)

ROBLES CASE LINKS THREE

Suspects Reported Held in Jail Incommunicado, but Not Booked

TUCSON (Ariz.) May 1. (U.P.)—Three men reportedly were arrested in connection with the June Robles kidnaping investigation tonight and held incommunicado in the City Jail. Arrests are credited to the Department of Justice, but the only statement was from Gus Wollard, police chief, who said "they have not been booked." The suspects are understood to be Mexican-American cattlemen.

The Federal grand jury will meet secretly tomorrow to receive information the government has spent a year gathering in connection with the case.

Frank Flynn, United States District Attorney for Arizona, said the case might be finished tomorrow, "and then the story will be public."

GRAND JURY GIVEN ROBLES EVIDENCE

TUCSON (Ariz.) May 1. (AP)—The Federal grand jury met today to hear evidence in the June Robles kidnaping, with government agents indicating the man who actually abducted the girl is now dead.

However, it was reported on good authority that three other men were involved in the imprisonment in a desert grave for nineteen days of the little girl and the efforts to obtain $15,000 in ransom money. The parents of the child declared no ransom was paid.

Italy Increases African Force by 30,000 Men

ROME, May 1. (U.P.)—Italy is rushing another 30,000 men to Africa shortly, bringing her total forces around Abyssinia to 105,000 men.

The reinforcements will include two additional army divisions, the Twenty-fourth and Twenty-seventh, detailed for duty in the Italian colonies of Eritrea and Somaliland, bordering Abyssinia, with which Italy is having a dangerous frontier dispute.

Inquiry to Open on Civil Service

SACRAMENTO, May 1. (AP)—A committee of nine headed by Senator Young, Los Gatos, was appointed today by President Hatfield of the Senate to conduct an inquiry into State civil service.

Although Senators declined to comment openly, it was known that a flood of protests against the discharge of State employees about to be blanketed in under permanent civil service lay behind the investigation.

SNOW FALLS IN IOWA AND MINNESOTA

ST. PAUL, May 1. (Exclusive)—Minnesota's May flowers were given a severe setback here today when winter returned to cover the ground with better than two inches of snow.

In the Twin Cities automobile and street-car traffic was handicapped severely by the sticky snow, borne on a hard wind.

The Twin Cities had a hard rainfall in the morning, but at noon the rain changed to snow and the temperature dropped to 34 deg. The United States Weather Bureau tonight predicted rain tonight and Thursday with slightly rising temperature.

Sioux City, Iowa, is reported to be the storm center, with Alexandria and Springfield, Minn., and Fargo, N. D., having steady rains.

Influenza Takes Two More Lives at Point Barrow

POINT BARROW (Alaska) May 1. (U.P.)—Epidemic influenza killed two more residents of panic-stricken Point Barrow tonight, raising the death toll to seven in two days.

Others are near death and there is no appreciable check in the intensity of the epidemic. It is feared the disease may spread east and south into communities where no medical attention is available. Point Barrow has 380 Eskimo and ten white residents.

GUARD INSULTER PUNISHED

SAN QUENTIN, May 1. (AP)—Coney Hurd, 29 years of age, Negro San Quentin prison convict, was ordered into solitary confinement today for "insulting a guard."

REGULAR

THREE HELD IN SPY QUIZ

Japanese Arrest Suspects; Retired American Navy Officer Among Them

TOKIO, May 2. (Thursday) (AP) Rengo (Japanese news agency) said today in a dispatch from Taihoku, Formosa, that three foreigners, including one retired United States naval lieutenant, are held for investigation on suspicion of espionage in connection with the detention of a small yacht.

The report said the procurator of the local court at Giron, on the east coast of Formosa, is handling the case.

The United States Embassy here lacked information on the detention and expressed doubt as to the American identification.

A court at Takao, Formosa, last Saturday ordered the confiscation of the Dutch tanker Juno and fined its skipper 2000 yen (about $750) following the tanker's detention on suspicion of espionage earlier this month.

Another foreign vessel, a small yacht manned by Prenchmen and Germans, was detained Saturday on similar charges. The officials expressed suspicion because the yacht previously had been under investigation after entering a fortified zone near Keelung.

'Error' Hanging Guard Suggested

SACRAMENTO, May 1. (AP)—A special Senate committee investigating the recent "mistake hanging" of Rush Griffin, Los Angeles Negro, today suggested a legal precaution against the possible recurrence of such an "accident."

The committee suggested that the Supreme Court be required automatically to review 2each case in which the death penalty has been decreed, with the clerk of the court required to notify the prison board of the decision.

BUREAU CHIEF PROMOTED

DENVER, May 1. (AP)—J. C. Newman, chief of the United States Bureau of Investigation in Denver, has been promoted to take charge of the bureau at San Francisco, it was announced here today.

Vast War Power of Soviet Shown in Army Parade

Nearly 700 Planes Zoom Overhead and 300 Tanks Rumble in Moscow Demonstration

MOSCOW, May 1. (AP)—Soviet Russia, professing peace, paraded her military might today in May Day exercises. Wave on wave of gray-clad warriors passed before Joseph Stalin in Red Square and nearly 700 military planes zoomed overhead by the most imposing display Russia ever has given of her aerial power.

"War danger has obliged us to increase the strength of our frontiers," Klement Voroshiloff, Commissar for Defense, told the marching men. "The principal desire of soviet Russia is peace for the whole world."

DIFFERENT ARMY

The troops, standing at attention before the parade, heard Voroshiloff assert: "Our country is doing everything possible to prevent war and our strong army appears to be the best argument to this end. If war is imposed upon us, the enemy will find there is a difference between the Czar's army and our Red army."

The somber walls of the Kremlin formed the background, with Ambassador William C. Bullitt and the United States Embassy staff viewing the parade from the diplomatic stand at one side of the mausoleum.

HUGE AIR FORCE

The air parade included all types of airplanes, from giant bombers to swift pursuit ships. The soviet air force, which had been something of a mystery due to the fact that figures indicating its actual strength have rarely been published, brought out for public display fast bimotored bombers with retractable landing gear which flew low over the heads of spectators at impressive speed. Foreign observers counted approximately 400 biplane fighting machines and 135 heavy bombers.

Most of the tanks, estimated to number 300 in the parade, were of a heavy type mounting large guns. In addition, there were hundreds of small armored motor cars.

Mechanized artillery machine-gun detachments turned out an impressive show of force, while the cavalry and infantry paraded for an hour.

RUSSIA TO INCREASE NAVY 300 PER CENT

LONDON, May 2. (Thursday) (U.P.) A Warsaw dispatch to the Daily Express today reported that Josef Stalin, dictator of soviet Russia, has approved a plan to increase Russia's navy 300 per cent in three years.

If Russia is unable to do the necessary building within the time limit, orders will be given to United States, British and Italian shipyards, according to the report.

QUIET REIGNS ON MAY DAY

Four Killed in Preliminaries

Demonstrations Abroad and in United States Carried Out Peacefully

BY THE ASSOCIATED PRESS

Despite preliminary clashes which took four lives, May Day passed peacefully enough in continental Europe, birthplace of the international Labor Day custom.

The United States, which has a Labor Day of its own in September, likewise witnessed an orderly series of demonstrations in the industrial centers.

Two killings were reported in the pre-May Day scrimmages in Spain, and one each was reported from Bulgaria and France.

SWASTIKA FLAG

In Vienna a huge swastika flag was strung to a high church steeple by agile Nazis. It took government steeplejacks three hours to bring it

Details of local May Day affair on Page 1, Part II.

down. Amnesty was granted 600 political prisoners; 500 other persons were arrested in a bombing, and free goulash was doled out to the hungry.

With squads of mobile guards posted at strategic points, Paris was quiet. London's preparations for Monday's jubilee overshadowed labor picnics.

New York Socialists and Communists marched in separate parades, with more than 150,000 in the two lines. The entire police force of 16,000 was on duty, but had little to do besides direct traffic.

BOSTON FIGHTS

Fist fights occurred in Boston and two men were injured when 300 marchers were showered with fruit and water-filled bags.

In Washington Communists dis-

(Continued on Page 2, Column 2)

Humane Pound Bill Shelved by Committee

SACRAMENTO, May 1. (AP)—The Wagner humane pound bill, described as "designed to provide a toehold for the introduction of stringent anti-vivisection laws," was tabled by the Assembly Committee on Public Health and Quarantine today.

The bill, by Assemblyman Wagner of Oakland, includes as its principal provision a clause prohibiting poundmasters from disposing of dogs and cats to universities or medical laboratories for purposes of experimentation.

Proponents argued that the measure is not an anti-vivisection bill and is designed primarily to stop an asserted "bootleg" traffic in impounded animals.

STATE LAND RELIEF BILL HELD BACK

SACRAMENTO, May 1. (AP)—The Merriam-indorsed plan of State production-for-use policy contained in a bill introduced by Senator Swing, San Bernardino, was kept today in the Senate Committee on governmental efficiency when the committee refused to vote it out without favorable recommendation.

There was no discussio non the merits of the bill and Swing made no motion to get the bill before the Senate. It was indicated the committee will take no further action.

The measure was the outgrowth of conferences between the Governor, Winslow Carleton, director of Federal-State unemployment co-operatives and Republican leaders in the Senate.

The bill would have provided lands, plants, machinery and other facilities to put the unemployed to work on co-operative projects.

Provisions of the measure include that there would be no competition with private industry.

CLOUDS BOMBED FOR RAIN IN TEXAS DUST REGION

DALHART (Tex.) May 1. (AP)—Tex Thornton, Amarillo explosive expert, this afternoon began a series of bombings from the ground as the first of his efforts to produce rain from the clouds over Baldies, four miles northwest of here.

Thornton said he will set off the blasts every twenty minutes, using T.N.T. and solidified nitroglycerin jelly.

FARMERS DOUBTFUL

As he went to work, doubting but hopeful Panhandle farmers and ranchers gathered to watch the unusual attempt. Some in the crowd wore masks for protection against sand clouds which whipped across the plains.

A few minutes after the first bomb was set off, the wind quieted and rain clouds seemed to range closer.

MOISTURE-LADEN

The weather man said the barometric pressure dropped, indicating clouds in this area are moisture-laden.

Thornton announced that tomorrow he will send bombs to the clouds' ceiling with gas balloons.

DENVER HAS CHANGE WITH MUD SHOWER

LIBERAL (Kan.) May 1. (AP)—The southwestern region where dust storms arise began May the way April ended—with more dust.

Denver varied the thing a bit, mixing rain and dust in a mud shower.

Outside the 18,000,000-acre dust belt, Mrs. Dora Cleland, 41 years of age, died at Muskogee, Okla., of pneumonia which her physician said was rendered critical by flying dirt particles.

Bennie Kershman, 9, of Booker, Tex., died at Beaver, Okla., today of pneumonia, apparently caused by dust.

The deaths brought to nine the total attributed to dust in Oklahoma within the last five days and increased the list of "more than twenty compiled here at dust storm headquarters of the Red Cross."

Thunderstorms Rumble in North

SAN FRANCISCO, May 1. (Exclusive)—Local thunderstorms swept the upper Sacramento Valley today and another trough spilled some moisture crossing the Tehachapis.

Eureka had a trace of rain, Redding .32 and San Luis Obispo .01 of an inch.

Blaine Son's Widow Dies

SACRAMENTO, May 1. (AP)—Mrs. Beryl Whitney Blaine, 51 years of age, member of a pioneer California family and daughter of the late J. P. Whitney, died here today following a brief illness.

Mrs. Blaine was the widow of James G. Blaine, son of the statesman of the 80's.

THE "TIMES" TODAY—NEWS SUMMED UP

Remember This

You will grow old too soon if you get wise too late.

All the News All the Time
LARGEST HOME-DELIVERED CIRCULATION
LARGEST ADVERTISING VOLUME

MAdison 2345
The Times Telephone Number
Connecting All Departments

Los Angeles Times

EQUAL RIGHTS · UNDER THE LAW · TRUE INDUSTRIAL FREEDOM

In Two Parts — 30 Pages
PART I — GENERAL NEWS — 18 PAGES

TIMES OFFICES
202 West First Street
And Throughout Southern California

VOL. LIV | SATURDAY MORNING, AUGUST 17, 1935. | DAILY, FIVE CENTS

ROGERS-POST ARCTIC DEATH CRASH RELATED

Mussolini's Stand Balks Ethiopia's Peace Overtures

Emperor Offers Concessions but Il Duce Won't Disclose Aims; Rome Envoy Quits Parley

PARIS, Aug. 16. (AP)—Ethiopia offered Italy economic concessions tonight but Premier Mussolini's unwillingness to tell France and England exactly what he wants balked efforts to avert a war.

In a message from Ethiopia to the tri-power conference Emperor Haile Selassie emphasized that he will not accept a military occupation.

His offer climaxed long deliberations by Premier Laval of France, Anthony Eden of Great Britain, and Baron Pompeo Aloisi of Italy as the talks formally were opened.

A British spokesman said Aloisi was pressed for a "frank statement" of what Mussolini wants. He declined to give it but instead quit the meeting and telephoned Il Duce, "into whose lap the whole thing has now been dumped," the spokesman asserted.

OFFERS MADE

Through his minister to Paris Haile Selassie laid the following proposal before the three powers:

(1.) A guarantee of the security of the Italian colonies of Somaliland and Eritrea and of the security of Italians living in Ethiopia.

(2.) The granting to Italy of economic facilities for mining, road building and railway operations in Ethiopia.

(3.) The possibility of even more extensive agricultural concessions to Rome.

After a full meeting of all three delegations, Laval announced the day had been devoted to analyzing diplomatic documents, presumably treaties involved in the dispute, and that further discussions would be held tomorrow.

EMPEROR ORDERS RECRUITING OF OFFICERS

Copyright, 1935, by the Associated Press

LONDON, Aug. 16. (AP)—Reversing his previous orders, Emperor Haile Selassie today instructed Dr. Warqnex C. Martin, Ethiopian Minister to Great Britain, to recruit foreign former commissioned and non-commissioned officers for service in his army.

It was understood that a shortage of qualified officers able to handle the expansion of Ethiopia's military forces prompted the order.

The men chosen will be given commands depending on their experience. All will be selected from the Ethiopian legation's list of 2000 applicants from a score of foreign countries.

Further applications are being refused and the legation will not consider any men unless they are experienced at least as non-commissioned officers.

SCOUTS OFF FOR EAST

SEATTLE, Aug. 16. (AP)—A delegation of 247 Boy Scouts from Fresno and San Joaquin Valley counties, California, left here today on a 1:45 p.m. train for the East, traveling by way of Glacier National Park. They will visit New York and Washington.

TUNA FLEET SEIZURE HIT

United States and Japan Notified of Action by Mexican War Boat

California's high seas tuna fleet of fifteen clippers has been seized by a Mexican war boat, radio flashes from Lower California waters disclosed yesterday.

International complications began immediately. Both the Japanese and American governments were called upon for aid. The State Department telegraphed Ambassador Josephus Daniels to investigate thoroughly. With eight Japanese vessels involved, the Japanese Ambassador at Washington was notified.

WARSHIP ASKED

Officials of the American Fishermen's Tunaboat Association and the California Fish Canners' Association sent protests to Washington and asked that an American war vessel be sent to protect their interests, if necessary.

The radio messages said the clippers valued at $1,500,000 had been seized in the vicinity of Magdalena Bay, 800 miles south of San Pedro, on the seaward side of Lower California.

Queries directed to Mexico City officials were met with the answer that information would have to come from the Mexican Fish and Game Commission office in San Diego.

BOATS REPORTED FREED

A call placed there late yesterday afternoon contained the assurance from Juan Duarte, acting head of

(Continued on Page 8, Column 1)

Hoover Spends Day in Chicago

CHICAGO, Aug. 16. (Exclusive)—Former President Herbert Hoover spent today in Chicago on his way from New York to his home in Palo Alto, Cal. He left late tonight after a series of meetings with old friends which were said to have little political significance.

Interspersed with these personal visits, however, was a forty-five-minute conference with Mrs. George B. Simmons of Missouri, who catapulted to fame after her speech ridiculing the A.A.A. at the Springfield Grass Roots conference.

They Died in Lonely Arctic—but Millions Grieve for Them

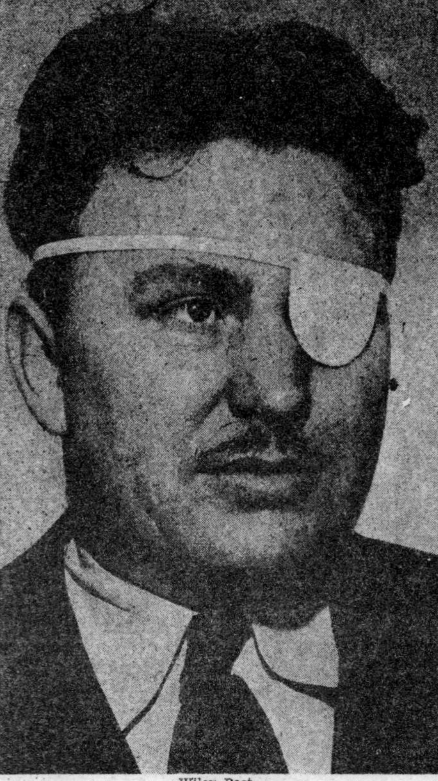

Wiley Post

Will Rogers

FAMILY WILL MEET TODAY

Mrs. Rogers and Daughter Speed to Rendezvous as Will, Jr., Flies East

All originally foreordained to be separated for the remainder of the summer, Will Rogers's loved ones last night were looking forward to being united again this morning in their common grief over the loss of the humorist, who crashed to instant death late Thursday night in the frozen tundra of the Alaskan wilds.

While the widow and daughter Mary sought seclusion in the Down-easter Express from Maine to New York, the son, Jimmy, awaited them there and the other, Will, Jr., was winging his way eastward through the night to complete what is left of the family circle.

SOLE SPOKESMAN HERE

On the broad shoulders of Will, Jr., there had rested throughout the day the responsibility of being sole spokesman here for the bereaved group.

Mrs. Rogers and Mary received news of the tragedy while at Skowhegan, Me., where the daughter was

(Continued on Page 2, Column 4)

Pair on World Flight, Post Friend Reveals

OKLAHOMA CITY, Aug. 16. (AP)—Harry Frederickson, Oklahoma City oil man and close friend of the late Wiley Post, revealed tonight the famous flyer and Will Rogers were on a leisurely flight around the world at the time of their fatal Alaskan crash.

Rogers, said Frederickson, had arranged to pay all expenses of the tour, which was planned as an aerial vacation.

"They planned to fly when they wanted to, and stop where and as long as they wanted to," said the oil man, who was one of the backers of Post in his solo, record-breaking trip around the world.

Frederickson said he talked to Post at Burbank, Cal., just before his take-off toward the north.

Frederickson explained Mrs. Post's decision not to accompany her husband and the humorist as being due to the somewhat crowded interior of Post's ship.

Mrs. Post never intended to make the 'round-the-world flight, Frederickson said, and changed her mind about the flight to Alaska after considering the cramped seating arrangement her presence would necessitate.

The trip was to have taken some two months.

"Probably not more than a dozen

(Continued on Page 2, Column 2)

Cobb Pays Tribute to Humorist for His Greatness

BY IRVIN S. COBB

(Two of the world's greatest humorists, Will Rogers and Irvin S. Cobb, were close friends for more than twenty years. Distraught and heart-broken by the death of his friend, Cobb yesterday wrote this tribute exclusively for The Times.)

Already today I have tried feebly enough to express my sentiments about Will Rogers.

The trouble is, there are a thousand things in my heart that I would like to say, but there is a lump in my throat that keeps them back.

Little men need eulogies.

Men of the moral, mental and spiritual stature of Will Rogers do not need them.

The words of their mouths, the works of their hands, the impresses of their souls are the everlasting markers for the living monuments that throb in the breasts of those who knew them and loved them.

To this rare group Will Rogers belonged. A personality so vivid, a wit so keen, a kindliness so great as his must live as long as there lives a single one of us who called him friend.

House Passes Bill to Obtain Post's Airplane

WASHINGTON, Aug. 16. (AP)—A Senate-approved bill for purchase by the Smithsonian Institution of Wiley Post's famed world-girdling plane, Winnie Mae, was passed today by the House.

A minor amendement will require Senate action before the bill is sent to the White House.

An appropriation of $25,000 was authorized.

Studio Cancels Preview to Pay Respect to Star

Out of respect to Will Rogers, a preview planned for last night at Grauman's Chinese Theater by Twentieth Century-Fox Studio was postponed. More than 1000 had been invited to see the film.

Friends of Rogers working for Twentieth Century-Fox Studio immediately cancelled all social engagements. The flag at the studio was ordered flown at half mast.

FOG BLAMED FOR DEATHS

Hospital Head Tells How Bodies of Rogers and Post Were Cared for

BY DR. HENRY W. GREIST
Director Presbyterian Hospital

Copyright, 1935, by the Associated Press

BARROW (Alaska) Aug. 16. (AP)—Victims of the fog which clung yesterday to the flat barren tundra, Will Rogers, noted humorist, and Wiley Post, world-circling flyer, crashed to their deaths in a shallow stream fifteen miles southwest of here at 8:15 o'clock last night.

Their bodies, brought here by Staff Sergeant Stanley R. Morgan, Signal Corps operator here, in a launch, were taken to the Presbyterian Hospital and the wounds dressed today by Charles D. Brower, "the king of the Arctic," whom Rogers was flying to visit; Sergt. Morgan, a school teacher and myself.

Then they were taken to the Presbyterian Mission warehouse to await instructions from Mrs. Post and Mrs. Rogers.

Forced down by fog at Harding

(Continued on Page 8, Column 2)

In Memoriam

For many years readers of The Times have begun their days with a reading of "Will Rogers Remarks." His humorous, pithy, philosophical comments have made the nation chuckle and have been a ray of sunshine through some of the darkest days in recent world history. In its customary place of honor on Page One Mr. Rogers's article appeared for the last time Friday morning. Here are

Will Rogers's Last Remarks—

FAIRBANKS (Alaska) Aug. 15.—[To the Editor of The Times:] Visited our new emigrants. Now this is not time to discuss whether it will succeed or whether it won't. Whether it's a farming country or whether it is not and to enumerate the hundreds of mistakes and confusions and rows and arguments and management in the whole thing at home and here. As I see it there is not but one problem now that they are here and that's to get 'em housed within six or eight weeks. Things have been a terrible mess. They are getting 'em straightened out but even now not fast enough. There is about 7 or 8 hundred of 'em. About 200 went back. Also about that many workmen sent from the transient camps down home (not C.C.C.) and just lately they are using about 150 Alaskan workmen. Paid regular wages but it's just a few weeks to snow now and they have to be out of the tents. Both workmen and settlers. Plenty food and always has been and will be. They can always get that in but it's houses they need right now and Col. Hunt in charge realizes it. You know after all there is a lot of difference in pioneering for gold and pioneering for spinach.

Yours, WILL ROGERS.

Plane Hits River as Engine Falters While Taking Off

Joe Crosson, Who Warned Against Dash to Barrow, Risks Same Peril to Get Bodies Back to States

Copyright, 1935, by the Associated Press

POINT BARROW (Alaska) Aug. 16. (AP)—Death, reaching through an Arctic fog, overtook Will Rogers, peerless comedian, and Wiley Post, master aviator, when their airplane faltered and fell into an icy little river near this forlorn outpost of civilization last night.

They had just taken off for a ten-minute flight from their river position to Point Barrow. Fifty feet in the air their motor missed fire. The plane heeled over on its right wing and plummeted to the river bank.

The lives of both Rogers and Post were crushed out instantly as the impact drove the heavy motor back through the fuselage.

RUNS FIFTEEN MILES

A terrified Eskimo ran fifteen miles to Point Barrow with the news. Sergt. Stanley R. Morgan of the United States Army Signal Corps dashed to the scene, recovered the bodies and flashed word of the tragedy that shocked millions throughout the world today.

Tonight Joe Crosson, famed Alaska pilot, flew here through fog and low-hanging clouds and after only a short stop hopped off again with the bodies of Rogers and Post for Fairbanks, first leg of the tragic return trip to the United States.

LINDBERGH WORD WAITED

Crosson said he will proceed from Fairbanks to Juneau, where it was believed a Pan American Airways transport plane will take over the task of carrying the bodies either to Seattle or California.

No definite plans could be learned pending word from Col. Charles Lindbergh, who arranged the plane trip, and the Post and Rogers families.

Decision to bring the bodies out by plane was made when the Coast Guard cutter Northland reported that it was making only slow progress against the ice pack off Wainwright and would be unable to reach Point Barrow for several days.

REMOVAL BY PLANE

Word was received here late today that the widows of Rogers and Wiley had authorized the removal of the bodies of the two victims from Barrow to Juneau by airplane. Authorization also was given for embalming the bodies prior to their removal.

Rogers and Post took off from Fairbanks for Barrow yesterday in the face of poor flying conditions. The flight was beset by difficulty, and they had to alight at Harding Lake, fifty miles away, until the fog lifted. Once again the fog settled down and they had to find the little river on the peninsula south of here, and land at the Eskimo camp to ask directions to Barrow where Rogers wanted to visit Charles Brower, known as "the King of the Arctic" because he has lived in the Arctic fifty-one years. He is a trader and operates a whaling station near by.

ENDS PLEASURE JAUNT

The tragedy ended a pleasure jaunt on which Post, himself carrying a passport for a projected flight to Siberia, had been piloting Rogers throughout Alaska, the Yukon and Northwest Territories of Canada.

It occurred during the height of the short Arctic summer—Barrow is more than 300 miles inside the Arctic circle, at the end of Alaska's northernmost point.

Behind the flyers when their dash to the top of Alaska ended in the shallow Arctic stream lay miles upon miles of barren, treeless tundra traversed by the Colville and its few and winding tributaries, and behind the tundra, they had crossed the Endicott range, northernmost mountain barrier of the many ranges of grim and forbidding mountains cut up by the Yukon, Koyukuk and Notak rivers.

Barrow itself is a tiny spot of civilization on the end of Point Barrow, inhabited by about a dozen white persons, and several hundred natives.

PLUNGES FIFTY FEET

En route to this northernmost Alaskan settlement, the flyers battled fog and finally sat down Post's pontoon-equipped monoplane on the river and asked the natives the way to Barrow.

Then, as reported to Sergt. Stanley R. Morgan, Army Signal Corps operator at this lonely post, by the native witnesses, the two noted flyers took off, but the engine missed fire and as Post banked his plane to the right, the machine plummeted out of control and dived nose-first fifty feet, smashing into two feet of water.

The right wing was torn off by the impact, the motor was driven back into the body of the plane, and the two men were killed, apparently instantaneously.

When Morgan, summoned by an Eskimo runner, arrived by launch at the wreck scene, he said today, he found the trim little scarlet low-winged monoplane a

(Continued on Page 3, Column 7)

THE "TIMES" TODAY—NEWS SUMMED UP

Remember This

In the old days at least there were fewer conveniences for starting trouble.

GIRL'S RITES CONDUCTED

NORTH HOLLYWOOD, Aug. 16. Funeral services for Miss Dorothy M. Anderson, 16 years of age, daughter of Capt. Arthur E. Anderson, member of the Los Angeles Fire Department for twenty years, were conducted today at the Steen Mortuary. Interment followed at Forest Lawn Memorial Park in Glendale.

The Weather

FORECAST FOR LOS ANGELES AND SOUTHERN CALIFORNIA: Rain today and probably tomorrow. Moderate temperature. Maximum and minimum temperatures for yesterday: 60—50. Complete weather report on Page 24, Part I.

Los Angeles Times

In Two Parts — 48 Pages

PART II — LOCAL NEWS — 24 PAGES

VOL. LV — FRIDAY MORNING, FEBRUARY 14, 1936. — C — CITY NEWS—EDITORIAL—SOCIETY—THE DRAMA

STARS' RADIO CODE STUDIED

Scientists Tell of Messages

New Equipment Aiding in Decoding of Strange Hisses From Skies

Radio messages from the stars are being decoded by California Institute of Technology scientists, it was disclosed in Pasadena last night.

The messages, say the scientists, are not from intelligent beings but consist of short-wave radio impulses that originate in the heat-tormented death dances of stellar atoms.

SIGNALS POWERFUL

Dr. G. W. Potapenko and D. F. Folland, both of Caltech, have discovered that nature's mysterious cosmic radio signals bring to the earth forty times the energy brought by starlight per spectrum band.

This discovery, say those who heard Folland describe preliminary results, may supply another master key for solution of such problems as the relation of gravitation and electricity and the origin and annihilation of matter.

The investigators point out that until these messages from the stars are translated further all theories of the structure of the universe will remain incomplete.

NEW EQUIPMENT USED

With elaborate equipment recently built in the Caltech shops the physicists are listening in on the hisses broadcast from the heavens. Dr. Potapenko explained that the radio waves from beyond the sola system are received when special short-wave receivers are tuned to 14.6 meters, or more than 20,000 kilocycles.

It is believed the celestial broadcasting station is situated in the center of the galaxy, the star cluster to which the sun belongs. This cluster contains some hundred billion stars, each comparable in size to the sun. From the earth, the galaxy is visible as the Milky Way.

ANTENNA POINTING CITED

Some signals, Dr. Potapenko said, are received when the antenna is pointed in the general direction of the Milky Way but that results are better when the antenna is aimed at the galaxy center. This center of the watch-shaped swarm of stars, in which the earth is but a point, is situated between the constellations Sagittarius and Ophiuchus.

"Many stars," said Dr. Potapenko, "have extremely high temperatures. The theory is that the electrons in these stars are in state of high agitation and thus radiate energy which can be picked up by a sensitive receiver."

The signals, discovered by Dr. Karl G. Jansky of the Bell Telephone Laboratories in New York City, are destined, according to research workers, to compete with cosmic rays in attracting the attention of the greatest scientists.

EL SEGUNDO SENDS 1000 TO "TIMES"

While El Segundo yesterday sent the largest per capita delegation yet to visit the New Times Building, the South Santa Monica Bay cities of Manhattan Beach, Hermosa Beach, Redondo Beach and Palos Verdes today expect to eclipse all daily figures for tours of the modern newspaper plant.

With a population of little more than 4000, El Segundo yesterday was represented by a delegation of approximately 1000 residents, who thronged The Times Building from 2:30 to 9:30 p.m. They came in busses and private cars, and, guided by escorts, got a real picture of the production of a metropolitan newspaper.

At 3:45 p.m., the El Segundo Women's Community Chorus, under direction of Mrs. A. H. Hughes, gave a radio program over station KHJ. Mrs. Leora Ridley was the accompanist.

Residents of the South Santa Monica Bay cities are scheduled to begin their tour of the building early this afternoon and continue throughout the day and evening.

At 9 p.m., on the stage of The Times auditorium, musical organizations of the four cities will combine for a forty-five minute program of music and song. The program will be open to the public.

Editor Visitor

Gen. C. B. Blethen, Seattle publisher, on visit to Los Angeles, urges greater fortifications for west coast. Times photo

MORE COAST FORTS URGED

Visiting General-Publisher Hits Defenses Being Built at Far-Away Posts

That United States coast defenses should be strengthened immediately in place of fortifying advance Pacific posts was the opinion expressed last night by Gen. C. B. Blethen, publisher of the Seattle Times.

Gen. Blethen, who with Mrs. Blethen is staying at the Biltmore for a month's vacation in Southern California, gave as the solution for weakened defenses the establishment of division posts along all shorelines.

QUICK ACTION VITAL

"With such posts placed at regular intervals, and with the interdependence of aircraft, artillery and infantry, immediate mobilization of an adequate defending force would be possible, whereas now our vast undefended areas on both coasts offer easy access for attack," he said.

The publisher urged the immediate appropriation of funds for all three services for installation of modern coast defense equipment on the basis of preparedness, although of the opinion that the United States is virtually immune from attack.

He recommended further that Federal funds "now being spent in aimless fashion on various work projects" be turned to this end.

BACKS BORDER PATROL

Regarding Los Angeles police patrolling northern border counties to stem the influx of indigents, Gen. Blethen said the city is quite right in taking such steps to solve an increasingly difficult problem.

Business, he said, is greatly improved and is hampered in the Northwest only by the present marine strike.

"Your splendid city also is apparently prosperous," he said in conclusion, "but it has grown so much since I was last here in 1930 that I feel the need of some sort of airship to find my way about."

Retired Doctor Taken by Death

Dr. Chett McDonald, 70 years of age, former instructor in the Kansas City Medical College and for years county Coroner at the Missouri metropolis, died last night at his home, 133 South Peck Drive, Beverly Hills.

Dr. McDonald came to Beverly Hills seven years ago, after retiring from active professional duty in Kansas City. He leaves his widow.

Plans for the funeral service were not completed last night.

INJURY FROM BOAR'S ATTACK PROVES FATAL

Infection resulting from a wound received February 5 when a boar on his ranch charged him, hooking a tusk in his leg, caused the death at General Hospital last night of William Mennetz, 52 years of age, a farmer of 3001 Pioneer Boulevard, Artesia. The rancher was charged by the boar while feeding the animal.

MEXICO PAID HIGH TRIBUTE

Daniels Relates School Gain

Envoy, Here With Wife, Says Illiteracy Sharply Cut; Nation Social Minded

The most significant thing in Mexico today is her ambitious educational program.

That was the expression last night of Josephus Daniels, Ambassador to Mexico for the United States as he ridded himself of political friends and admirers and settled down to serious discussion.

Ambassador Daniels and his wife arrived in Los Angeles from the opening of the California Pacific International Exposition at San Diego, and are stopping at the Biltmore.

BUILDING SCHOOLS

"Education will do for Mexico what education has done for the United States," said Mr. Daniels. "She is building 1000 schools a year for five years, and in the sixth year plans to build 2000 schools.

"Twenty-five years ago Mexico was 85 per cent illiterate," he added. "Today this has been brought down, I think, to 53 per cent illiteracy.

LIVING STANDARDS RISE

"As a consequence of her educational progress, living standards throughout Mexico are improving, wages are going up and the average Me[illegible] today is far better off than ever before."

"The world is witnessing a very interesting thing in Mexico," he said. "Of the sixteen millions of people in Mexico, fourteen millions are Indians or mestizos. They have a strong voice in government.

GOVERNMENT BY INDIANS

"In other words, we are watching the progress of a country governed by Indians—the first time in the history of mankind that this has been a fact.

"Of course there are Communists in Mexico, as elsewhere. But Mexico is not a Communistic country. As President Cardenas said to me only a little while ago, the first thought of a Mexican is to get himself a little land, where he can raise his family and support himself.

SOCIAL-MINDED NATION

"That certainly is not a Communistic idea. Mexico is rather a Socialistic country—and in saying that, the term Socialistic needs to be defined. She is very social minded. Her people are constantly trying to improve their condition of living. They want to obtain the education of their children and obtain ownership of land. To that extent they know the value of co-operation, but they are not seeking to gain something for nothing by force and violence."

GOOD NEIGHBOR POLICY

The "good neighbor" policy of the United States toward her southern neighbors is reflected in the sincere attitude of the Mexican people of good will and friendship toward the people of the United States, Mr. Daniels said.

Commercial exchange between the United States and Mexico is increasing at a rapid pace, Mr. Daniels said, indicating improving living conditions across the border. It may also indicate, he said, that capital investment from the United States, welcomed by Mexico, is having its effect on business development.

LEAVE TOMORROW

Ambassador and Mrs. Daniels will leave tomorrow morning to return to Mexico City. Today the Ambassador will address a Democratic luncheon at the Biltmore.

Sheriff Biscailuz and party will leave for Mexico City at the same time the Ambassador and Mrs. Daniels begin their return trip, but plan to stop en route.

Badger, on Lawn, Chews Leg of Radio Officer

Radio Officer Fitzpatrick is a strong advocate of a course in animal training for police officers.

With his partner, Officer Howard, Fitzpatrick answered a call last night to investigate a mad dog report at 342 North Hobart Boulevard. Arriving they found a small animal digging up the lawn.

Fitzpatrick climbed from the machine and shouted in an attempt to scare the animal, but it refused to scare. Instead, it rushed at the officer and affixed its teeth in the calf of his leg.

Officer Howard came to the rescue and fired four shots into the animal's body. At the Hollywood Receiving Hospital, where Fitzpatrick was treated for a badly lacerated leg, they found the dog wasn't a dog but a badger which apparently had been driven from the hills by recent rains.

Envoy to Southern Republic Arrives in City

Josephus Daniels, war-time Secretary of the Navy and now United States Ambassador to Mexico, arrived in Los Angeles with Mrs. Daniels last night. In the photo, left to right, are Sheriff Biscailuz, Capt. Bert Hastings, Mrs. Daniels and Ambassador Daniels. Sheriff Biscailuz and party will escort Ambassador and Mrs. Daniels part way to Mexico City when they leave tomorrow morning. Times photo

Loyola Teacher Killed as Auto Strikes Train

A group of young law students gathered in a classroom at Loyola University last night and for half an hour they awaited arrival of their instructor.

But they waited in vain, not knowing that Prof. Daniel F. McSweeney, 31-year-old law teacher, of 5120 West Boulevard, lay dead—killed in an automobile crash near Corona.

Prof. McSweeney, who practiced law outside his classroom as well as teaching, had gone to Corona on legal business in the afternoon. He was returning to meet his class at 6 o'clock.

SIDESWIPES TRAIN

Near Corona the slippery highway was suddenly blocked by a fast-traveling Santa Fe freight train. About 150 feet from the crossing, according to Capt. Raymond King of the California Highway Patrol, Prof. McSweeney applied the brakes on his car.

Skidding dizzily, the car turned completely around and swung broadside into the freight train. Prof. McSweeney died almost instantly. His body was removed to a Corona mortuary.

In addition to Loyola class duties, he engaged in law practice with Melvin J. Keane and Elza C. Mowry.

Besides his widow, he leaves a daughter, 4 months of age.

WOMAN KILLED

Another traffic victim yesterday was Mrs. Kathleen Harding, 44, of Pacoima. She was killed instantly when the automobile in which she was riding with her husband, Otto Harding, was struck head-on by another machine on San Fernando Road one mile north of San Fernando.

Prof. D. F. McSweeney

The other car was driven by Miss Marion Martine, 31, nurse, of 851 North Mt. Virgil street, Long Beach, who suffered chest and back injuries. She was booked on a charge of negligent homicide and sent to the General Hospital prison ward.

Police reported the accident took place when Miss Martine suddenly swerved to the wrong side of the road, forcing one machine from the

(Continued on Page 5, Column 3)

Bones Unbroken in Mishap

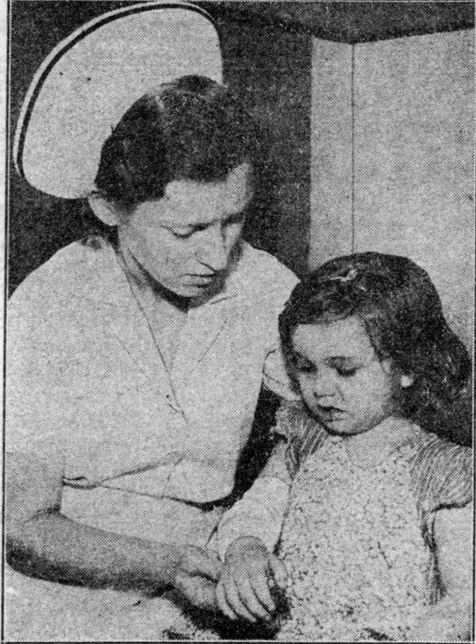

How it feels to have your arm caught between the rollers of an electric laundry wringer is tearfully told above by Dona Ercanbrack, 3 years of age, as she is comforted by Nurse Alta Mae Stuart at Georgia-street Receiving Hospital. Doctors say no bones were broken. Dona is a daughter of Mr. and Mrs. H. Ercanbrack of 1509 Venice Boulevard. Times photo

JINX CASE JUROR DIES

Defense Counsel, Prosecutor and Judge Ill, Witness Missing During Trial

Ill luck in United States District Judge Yankwich's court at the trial of Gustavo Carrillo, charged by the government with using the mails to defraud, reached a climax yesterday when one of the jurors, John W. Opie, 81 years of age, died.

For two weeks the case has dragged along, having to be postponed frequently because of serious heart attacks of defense attorney, E. Neal Ames, hunt for a missing witness, Dr. A. L. Lanning, and finally the fatal illness of the juror. To add to the bad-luck story, the government's prosecuting attorney, Hal Hughes, yesterday was suffering from influenza and Judge Yankwich was reported convalescing from a mild attack of ptomaine poisoning.

The defendant will be called into court today and it is expected that the court will rule a mistrial.

He is charged with having used the mails to enrich himself by $3000 from investors in a Mexican treasure hunt scheme, declaring that he knew where 200 bars of gold worth $3,000,000 had been buried in the interior of Mexico during a revolution. He proposed to unearth the golden cache, transport it to the United States border, sell the gold and divide with the investors.

NAVY'S AIR TERMINAL EXPEDITED

Revised plans for the improvement of the naval airport on Terminal Island make probable the beginning of that project within a short time, Mayor Shaw said yesterday.

He submitted to Lieut.-Col. Donald H. Connolly, Works Progress Administrator, the new plans for the work which would cost a total of $539,193 and would give more than 1000 men jobs for three or four months.

Connolly said the project has in principle already been approved by the Federal authorities, but was not started because the project did not provide work for enough men in proportion to its cost.

By arrangement of the Navy and city to share some of the cost, Mayor Shaw said, the revised plans, submitted yesterday, are expected to meet the approval of W.P.A. officials as soon as they receive the approval of the Bureau of Aeronautics.

The job includes dredging, ramps, piling and other construction to make the airport more usable by navy airplanes and seaplanes.

Orra Monnette Regains Health; Leaves Hospital

Orra E. Monnette, vice-president of the Bank of America National Trust and Savings Association, was released from the Cedars of Lebanon Hospital yesterday and returned to his home a well man.

Dr. P. G. White, his physician, said the 62-year-old banker has entirely recovered. Suffering from a toxic condition, he was admitted to the hospital February 5.

Besides being an author of several books, Monnette, a resident of Los Angeles thirty years, has spent twenty years as president of the Board of Library Commissioners.

CITY POLICE PATROLS HALT 1000 AT STATE'S BORDERS

Anti-Vagrant Drive Ruled Valid as Epic Councilman Asks End; Round-up Nets 308 Felons

The Los Angeles police border patrol searching out vagrants and criminals has turned back at State lines more than 1000 penniless transients with a resultant decrease in crime, begging and pilfering in the city, it was disclosed yesterday.

At the same time City Attorney Chesebro gave the City Council a ruling to the effect that the action of Chief of Police Davis in setting up the border patrol is legal.

Snow and rain combined with the police patrol in stemming the tide of indigents at far-flung border points, decreasing the influx of itinerants at all northern gateways.

STOP 662 AT ARIZONA

Showing the effectiveness of the blockade, first statistics from border patrol records were released by Deputy Chief of Police Homer Cross.

Along the Arizona border 662 itinerants have been stopped during the past week. On the Oregon border 312 were halted, and on the Nevada border fifty-one were discouraged from entering California. The total for the first week of operation was 1031.

MANY CHANGE MINDS

Cross said there is no means by which the department may determine how many hundreds of transients changed their minds about coming to California to escape inclement weather elsewhere. The figures, he said, only show those actually halted at the borders and turned back.

Within Los Angeles, Chief Davis declared crime already has decreased 25 per cent since the drive on vagrants and beggars began a week ago. He asserted that at least half the offenses committed in Los Angeles during winter months are by winter migrants.

ARREST 1470 HERE

Of the 1470 persons arrested in Los Angeles on charges of evading railroad fare, vagrancy or begging, between January 8 and February 8, a total of 308 were found to have previous felony records and 295 previous misdemeanor records. Chief Davis said a goodly number of them are "wanted for offenses ranging from murder to parole violation."

The ruling of City Attorney Chesebro, upholding the legality of the police border patrol, followed an effort in the City Council to force recall of the patrolmen.

CALLS DAVIS MUSSOLINI

Councilman Christensen, an Epic leader, offered the motion calling upon the Police Commission to "order the recall of the James E. Davis Foreign Legion." In the motion, Councilman Christensen referred to Chief Davis as a "Los Angeles edition of Mussolini."

Several Councilmen were on their feet seeking to reply to Christensen, when Councilman Gay ruled the motion was entirely out of order. Councilman MacAlister said he could not understand Christensen's attitude "when vagrants from other States are coming into Los Angeles and taking relief money and other benefits from our own citizens, who need protection."

Councilman Hyde said the most

(Continued on Page 5, Column 3)

DOLLAR DAY TRIPS FREE

Bargains Offered Tomorrow Will Draw Record Throng, Executive Predicts

Offering one of the greatest arrays of values ever presented in a single sales event, Los Angeles will present to its Southern California radius of buyers tomorrow a downtown Los Angeles Dollar Day that promises to eclipse all previous efforts in Dollar-Day history, according to an announcement made by Dain Sturges, executive secretary and general manager of Downtown Business Men's Association.

GREAT VALUES

"We feel that this day will be an occasion of outstanding shopping values for every purchaser," said Sturges.

"Millions of dollars' worth of merchandise has been assembled to care for every household and personal need. Not only will the dollar be featured in this event, but there will be found bargains galore at every price line. Values in this sale embrace all types of merchandise and attractions will extend to a wide range of goods that will be specially priced."

FREE CAR RIDES

Through arrangements made with the local transportation companies by the downtown merchants' Dollar-Day committee, shoppers will be able to ride downtown free tomorrow between the hours of 9 and 11 a.m.

RUDDERLESS YACHT SLIPS INTO HARBOR

Craft Damaged in Severe Storm Wednesday Makes Port Under Own Power

A rudder snapped off by turbulent seas, and its crew and passengers thoroughly drenched from mountainous waves, the yacht reported in distress late Wednesday off Newport beach limped into port under its own power early yesterday.

Robert S. McClelland, president of an ice company and owner of the yacht, brought the boat in by running each of the twin-screw propellers alternately, a procedure which allowed the craft to be steered after a fashion despite the loss of its rudder.

Staff members of a Vermont and Washington branch bank were with McClelland.

They had sailed for Santa Catalina Island and were well into the middle of the channel when the rudder broke.

CLUB HONORS COMPOSER

A dinner of the Opera and Fine Arts Club was held last evening at the Royal Palms Hotel, 360 Westlake street, in honor of Carrie Jacobs Bond, noted composer, and Maurice Frank 1936 impresario for the Hollywood Bowl Grand Opera Festival to be held in June.

County Relief Staff Cuts Off 100 Employees

More than 100 persons were released from employment by the Los Angeles County Relief Administration. They were a part of 345 dismissed since February 1 because of the reduction in the case load of the administration.

The administration now has 1145 administrative employees. For each 1000 reduction in the number of persons on relief thirty administrative workers are dismissed, Assistant Director Pomeroy said.

COURTHOUSE BOND ISSUE WILL GO BEFORE VOTERS

To obtain funds for the new county Courthouse and other county buildings the Board of Supervisors yesterday voted to place a $4,000,000 bond issue on the ballot May 5, the date of the Presidential primary.

The new Courthouse, to be located between the present Hall of Justice and Sunset Boulevard, is to cost between $6,000,000 and $6,400,000.

The other buildings, which will be in outlying communities, will cost in the neighborhood of an additional $2,200,000.

If the $4,000,000 bond issue is approved, the Supervisors hope to obtain another $3,825,000 from the Public Works Administration.

Still another $600,000 the county already has in its possession in the form of a county law library fund. This would bring the grand total to $8,425,000.

If the bonds are voted and the Federal grant is not forthcoming, the bond issue will automatically be voided.

Next Monday the Supervisors will vote whether to place a $2,200,000 bond issue for a new unit of Olive View Sanatorium on the same ballot.

'All the News 'All the Time

LARGEST HOME-DELIVERED CIRCULATION
LARGEST ADVERTISING VOLUME

MAdison 2345
The Times Telephone Number
Connecting All Departments

Los Angeles Times

EQUAL RIGHTS
LIBERTY UNDER THE LAW — TRUE INDUSTRIAL FREEDOM

(Copyright, 1936, by the Times-Mirror Company)

In Ten Parts — 132 Pages
PART I — GENERAL NEWS — 16 PAGES

FINAL EDITION

VOL. LV | CCC | SUNDAY MORNING, MARCH 8, 1936. | SUNDAY, TEN CENTS

Rhineland Seized by German Troops; France Places Army on War Footing

COURT SMITH WILL DIRECT SAN QUENTIN

Holohan Post to Be Taken

Promotion Leaves Opening at Folsom With Three Mentioned for Job

SAN QUENTIN, March 7. (U.P.)—Court Smith, bluff and brawny peace officer who at present directs the affairs of Folsom State Prison, was named warden of San Quentin Prison, the largest penal institution in America, late today.

Smith was chosen to succeed James B. Holohan, whose formal resignation becomes effective April 15.

ONLY ONE CONSIDERED

Smith was the only person considered by the State Board of Prison Directors, meeting here today, to take Holohan's seat on top of the "San Quentin powder keg," as the retiring administrator often referred to the prison which houses more than 5000 convicts.

The new warden will come to San Quentin after presiding for nine years over one of the nation's toughest prisons, the penal institution maintained by California in the Sacramento Valley for its second offenders.

FOLSOM POST VACANT

No one yet has been named to take Smith's place at Folsom. Fred Esola, a former United States marshal in San Francisco, and Charley Larkin, present deputy warden at the Repressa institution, are among those considered. C. I. Plummer, an investigator on Dist.-Atty. Buron Fitts's staff at Los Angeles, also has been mentioned.

San Quentin's new boss came to Folsom as its warden in 1927.

He was greeted with a riot—the bloody Thanksgiving Day riot of 1927. Twelve prisoners and guards were killed before Smith, refusing to give in to the convicts at a time they appeared to have control, smashed the revolt.

Since then Folsom has been relatively quiet.

OFFICIAL DISCHARGED

Holohan was beaten and his skull was fractured in January, 1935, when four prisoners attempted a break. Although he returned to duty later his health was poor.

Then a month ago United States secret service agents uncovered a gigantic counterfeiting plot which had its origin within the prison.

A prison official was discharged, and another suspended as the board of prison directors met to investigate. Holohan told the board a week or so ago he would resign as soon as the "mess" was cleaned up.

Today he presented his formal resignation. The board, recruited to full strength today for the first time in three years, accepted his

(Continued on Page 5, Column 2)

Fourth Try

Dorothy Lee, film actress, who is married again.

DOROTHY LEE WED IN EAST

Film Actress' Fourth Mate Brother-in-Law of Philip K. Wrigley

CHICAGO, March 7. (Exclusive) Dorothy Lee, film actress, and A. G. Cox Atwater, vice-president of the William Wrigley, Jr., Company and a brother-in-law of Philip K. Wrigley, were married today at Crown Point, Ind., by Justice of the Peace Harvey T. Minas. Following the ceremony the couple, both of whom designated the Ambassador Hotel in Chicago as their home, left for an unannounced destination.

Although Miss Lee is only 25 years of age, the venture is her fourth into matrimony. Her real name was given as Marjorie Millsap Duffield, and she stated that her father, Homer C. Millsap, is a Los Angeles attorney.

She was divorced from Marshall Duffield, former California football star, in Reno last November. Previously she had been married to, and divorced from, James Fidler and Bob De Forest.

Atwater, who is 28 years of age, was divorced less than a month ago by Mrs. Betty Ann Bergmann Atwater, to whom he was married on March 15, 1932. Mrs. Atwater was given custody of their infant daughter and a private financial settlement was arranged outside of court. The present Mrs. Atwater and her husband met last year while he was on a business trip to the coast.

Frozen Trapper Tells of Doing Surgery on Self

WILLIAMS LAKE (B. C.) March 7. (AP)—From a hospital cot Dan Crawley, a trapper, related today how he operated upon himself to save his life as he waited for several days in a cabin in the wilderness for help.

With a jackknife Crawley cut away parts of both frozen feet when gangrete set in after his partner, Ted Vachon, had left him in their cabin forty-five miles from Blue River to summon medical aid.

A plane brought him to a hospital here.

HOOVER SAYS TAXES PERIL TO FREEDOM

New Deal Ideas Condemned

Roosevelt and Aides Failed in Re-employing Jobless, ex-President Feels

COLORADO SPRINGS (Colo.) March 7. (AP)—Former President Hoover charged tonight the New Deal had laid groundwork for an ever-increasing tax burden, yet failed in the "outstanding" governmental job of re-employing the jobless.

Addressing the Young Republican League of Colorado, Mr. Hoover asserted again the American system of liberty is endangered by present administration policies and told his young listeners "certainly your freedom and your opportunities in life are being mortgaged."

Every seat in the Municipal Auditorium, 3200, was filled by an enthusiastic throng who applauded the former President's remarks. The address was broadcast nationally.

LAW APPROVED

One item in administration legislation did come in for favorable comment.

"The New Deal regulations of stocks and security promotion in

The full text of former President Hoover's address at Colorado Springs, Colo., will be found on Page 11, this section.

various aspects have the right objectives," said Mr. Hoover. "They were hastily and poorly formed without proper consideration by Congress. But they point right."

After indicting the administration's "planned economy" as endangering the Constitution, charging it with waste and ill-founded financial policies, the former President asked:

"What of the taxes that will ooze from this spending and debt all your lives?"

TAXES INEVITABLE

"Do not mistake. The new taxes of today are but part of them. More of them are as inevitable as the first of the month. The only alternatives are repudiation or inflation. No matter what nonsense you are told about corporations and the rich paying the bill, there will be two-thirds of it for the common man to pay after the corporations and the rich are sucked dry."

He said that election day, 1932, the American Federation of Labor reported 11,600,000 unemployed.

"Today, after three years of the New Deal," he said, "they report 11,600,000 unemployed. To get these people back on jobs was the outstanding job of our government. It was the excuse given for all these doings.

DEBT INCREASED

"But the grim fact remains that it has failed in its primary purpose. And $15,000,000,000 will be added to the national debt before the New Deal is over."

Asserting that President Roose-

(Continued on Page 11, Column 8)

PARIS CALLS FOR PENALTY

Soldiers Sped to Frontier

France Ready to Fight to Drive Nazi Force Out of Demilitarized Zone

PARIS, March 7. (AP)—French officials declared that tonight France is ready to use her army, supported by her allies, to compel Germany to evacuate the Rhineland, but that France first will exhaust the peaceful methods possible under the League of Nations.

This declaration followed an order by military authorities that all fortifications along the northeast frontier be garrisoned immediately with their full quotas of troops.

ASKS LEAGUE ACTION

The order was issued shortly after the French government decided to do its utmost under the League of Nations' covenant to compel Germany to take its troops out of the Rhineland.

Authorities said that, despite the military order, which includes the cancellation of all army leaves, the next military class will not be called to the colors before its time nor will any of the recently demobilized classes be called to duty.

The government announced the troops will go into the 150 miles of fortifications along the German frontier on a full war footing.

GAPS BEING FILLED

Not onl, are the fortifications being manned, but the gaps between the famous steel and cement pill boxes are being filled with troops.

A government spokesman said that Germany's occupation of the previously demilitarized zone is not "simply symbolic" and that Germany's forces in the Rhineland are equal to those on the French side of the frontier.

The spokesman said its military measures will not be increased "until after the League Council shall have formally pronounced Germany's violation of the treaty."

MEANS EVEN FORCE

French officials said the word "utmost" means everything that the League of Nations and the Locarno Treaty signatories may decide, even force if that is found necessary after all other means fail.

The government asked that Germany be punished for sending troops into the area ordered demilitarized by the Treaty of Versailles.

It was announced that Premier Sarraut will go before his Cabinet

(Continued on Page 7, Column 4)

A few minutes after Reichsfuehrer Hitler had told the Nazi Reichstag at Berlin yesterday that the Locarno Treaty is dead and had ordered 25,000 troops into the Rhineland, the camera caught the Nazi chief as he saluted the officers of his army. This retouched radiophoto was telephotoed to London and transmitted to New York by radio, thence to Los Angeles by Wirephoto. (AP) Wirephoto

HITLER SAYS TREATY DEAD

Has New Plan of Security

Peace Gesture Made as He Sends 25,000 Men Into Forbidden Area

Copyright, 1936, by the United Press

BERLIN, March 7. (U.P.) Adolf Hitler ordered 25,000 German troops into the demilitarized Rhineland adjoining the borders of France and Belgium today, thereby wiping out the last vestige of the repressive clauses of the Versailles Treaty.

At the same time, the Fuehrer offered France and Belgium, his former enemies, twenty-five years of peace in Western Europe, during which time the three powers would agree not to make war on one another.

BOLD STROKE

Hitler announced his bold stroke first to the stunned diplomatic representatives of the powers, and then to a madly-cheering Reichstag.

Because of France's new military alliance with Russia, he said, the Locarno Treaty which guarantees the frontiers of Germany, France and Belgium—and the Rhineland—has ceased to exist. Therefore the Versailles Treaty has likewise become non-existent.

WAR OR PEACE

Hitler's speech was one of the most amazing in modern diplomatic history. Almost every word came with telling impact as he laid down a program which gave Europe, now torn by dissension, the outright alternatives—war or peace.

As his gesture to show that Germany feels free and equal to every nation on earth, he started nineteen battalions of infantry and thirteen detachmets of artillery moving into the Rhineland—symbolic of Germany's military might if she has to fight.

HITLER'S PROPOSALS

On the side of peace, in addition to the offer of a twenty-five-year pact to France and Belgium, with The Netherlands joining if she chooses, Hitler made these proposals:

Germany is willing to reenter the League of Nations; she is ready to negotiate a nonaggression pact or pacts with all her neighbors, east and west; she is ready to establish with France and Belgium demilitarized zones on both sides of the borders, as deep as those two countries wish; she proposed an air defense treaty in Western Europe under which the powers would pool their forces to blow any aggressor into submission.

PERPETUAL THORN

Hitler was surprisingly conciliatory towards Poland, whose Versailles Treaty corridor to the sea cutting off East Prussia from the Fatherland has been a perpetual thorn in the German side.

"It is certainly regrettable that Poland's access to the sea passes through former German territory," he said, "but it would be unreasonable to deny the right of such a nation to her access to the sea."

Speaking of Russia, he was frank.

"The soviet union not only controls one-sixth of the earth," he

(Continued on Page 6, Column 1)

PEACE HOPE ADVANCED

London Diplomatic Circles Believe France Can Ease Situation

LONDON, March 7. (AP)—Neutral diplomatic circles, after a careful study of Adolf Hitler's memorandum, believe the situation created today by the German militarization of the Rhineland is far from desperate if France remains calm and does not demand forceful action.

Prime Minister Baldwin and Foreign Secretary Anthony Eden discussed the situation at the Prime Minister's country residence after Eden had talked over Hitler's bold move with the French and Italian ambassadors and the Belgian Charge d'Affaires.

CABINET DELAYS MEETING

Attempting to set an example by avoiding snap judgments which might turn the situation toward war, the Cabinet put off its meeting until Monday in order to weigh carefully all factors and developments and to study Hitler's proposal.

Military observers generally agreed Hitler's action came at a moment embarrassing to Britain, both diplomatically and militarily, because of the Italo-Ethiopian precautions.

BRITAIN'S POSITION

With about 175 warcraft in and near the Mediterranean, together with between 300 and 400 airplanes and between 30,000 and 40,000 troops in Egypt, Britain is in a poor condition to assert its voice in Western European affairs, observers believe.

If any of these ships, planes and troops were withdrawn for concentration at home, it would likely give Mussolini a freer hand in Ethiopia, and perhaps endanger the vital Suez Canal link to the Far East.

Italy Indifferent to Hitler Move in Rhineland

ROME, March 7. (AP)—Italy, although a guarantor of the Locarno Pact, met the news of Germany's remilitarization of the Rhineland today with the determination to do nothing about it.

Well-informed Italians picked up the pieces of the European jigsaw puzzle, swept over Europe by Adolf Hitler's denunciation of the Locarno Pact, and reassembled them in what they considered the following key position:

Italy will not rush to aid France and England to drive German troops out of the Rhineland zone, even though her obligations under the Locarno Pact bind her to do so.

There is much doubt in Rome if France and England will invoke the Locarno Pact against Germany.

If they should, however, Italy can always answer: "Why should we help nations employing sanctions against us?"

BELGIANS END LEAVES OF ABSENCE

BRUSSELS, March 7. (AP)—Leaves of absence of all Belgian troops stationed in eastern frontier garrisons were canceled tonight by the Belgian government.

The military order was announced in newspapers after Premier Paul van Zeeland had conferred with King Leopold and participated in conference with British, French and Italian ambassadors to Brussels.

The government sought to keep the population of the capital calm after the Reichstag speech of Adolf Hitler by broadcasting appeals urging the people not to accept alarming reports.

HITLER ACT BRINGS JOY

Germans Parade and Sing as Leaders Review Jubilant Marchers

Copyright, 1936, by the United Press

BERLIN, March 8. (Sunday) (U.P.)—Jubilant Germans paraded and sang in the streets until the early hours of the morning, celebrating Fuehrer Hitler's defiance of the powers in sending an estimated 25,000 troops into the demilitarized Rhineland.

HITLER HONORED

The celebration started last night and lasted for many hours. Its high point started at 10 p.m. when a stream of flame poured through the Brandenburg gate down the Wilhelmstrasse as 20,000 excited Nazis honored the Fuehrer in a torchlight parade.

Led by Hitler's goose-stepping, black-coated and black-helmeted elite guards with fixed bayonets, representatives of all Nazi men's organizations proudly and triumphantly surged through cheering, waving crowds to salute Hitler, Paul Joseph Goebbels and other Nazi dignitaries standing on the Chancellory balcony in the blaze of a searchlight.

LEADER SERIOUS

Hitler, wearing a brown leather coat, saluted confidently, but serious and unsmiling, as the throngs swung past to the tune of his favorite Badenweiller march.

An hour later, the paraders dispersed through Wilhelm Square with deafening cheers for Hitler and a full-throated rendition of "Deutschland Ueber Alles" and the Horst Wessel song, Nazi anthem.

In a two-minute radio broadcast to the Rhineland at 10:15 p.m., Paul Goebbels, who is Propaganda Minister, insisted that the reoccupation is really a "gesture of peace," foreshadowing a new and better future not only for Germany, but for all Europe.

Ann Rork Getty Files Divorce Suit in Nevada

LAS VEGAS (Nev.) March 7. (AP) Ann Rork Getty sued Jean Paul Getty, multimillionaire oil man, for divorce today, charging extreme cruelty. The case will be heard Monday morning.

She asked custody of their children, Eugene Paul, 3 years of age, and Gordon Peter, 2.

The couple were married in New York City September 1, 1931, and again at Cuernavaca, Mex., December 2, 1932, because they were not satisfied with the legality of the New York marriage.

Danzig Nazis in Clash With Jews

DANZIG FREE CITY, March 7. (U.P.)—Several persons were injured today in a clash between Jews and members of the Hitler Youth Organization.

The Hitler Youth members gathered outside a synagogue where a memorial service was being conducted for Jewish war dead and sang anti-Jewish songs.

Lord Beatty Loses Ground

LONDON, March 7. (U.P.)—The condition of Admiral of the Fleet Lord Beatty "gives rise to increased anxiety," his physicians said in a bulletin issued shortly before 9 p.m.

Lord Beatty, commander of the British Fleet in the battle of Jutland, has been ill for some weeks. He is 65 years of age.

London 'Times' Sees War Peril in Hitler Move

LONDON, March 8. (Sunday) (AP) The London Sunday Times, usually the mirror of official British thought, expressed frank alarm today at Adolf Hitler's abrogation of the Locarno pact and his remilitarization of the Rhineland:

"It is difficult not to think," the paper said, "that in Europe's dangerous drift since 1932 yesterday's events mark the most grave and most alarming and perhaps an irrevocable stage."

The Times admitted that Germany was "weighed down by fear," particularly fear of Russia, but it flayed Hitler for tearing up treaties and castigated what it called his "strike first, talk afterward" methods.

Operation Halts Girl's Laughing

WESTON (W. Va.) March 7. (AP)—Ten days of spasmodic laughing ended today for Teresa Hawkins.

The 18-year-old brunet business college student rested comfortably after an abdominal operation to relieve a psychoneurotic condition.

She had been laughing and giggling since February 26, when the attack seized her while she watched a show.

BRUNO ASKS FOR HOFFMAN; REPRIEVE DEAD LINE NEAR

TRENTON (N. J.) March 7. (Exclusive)—Informed that he has only five days left in which to win a second reprieve from electrocution, Bruno Richard Hauptmann late today abandoned his calm complacency again and pleaded for another death house interview with Gov. Hoffman.

"If I could talk to the Governor again," Bruno was quoted as saying, "maybe I could convince him to act right away.

Lloyd Fisher, Hauptmann's chief counsel, visited the State prison this afternoon and in a twenty-minute conference told the convicted German carpenter that the Governor's reprieve pow[illegible], under the New Jersey law, cannot be exercised in his behalf after Thursday, March 12.

"I also told Hauptmann about the new evidence uncovered this week," Fisher said. "He was particularly interested in the eye-witness who placed Isidor Fisch on the murder scene. He also wanted to know all about Dr. John F. (Jafsie) Condon's attempt to identify a prisoner in Florida after he already had identified Hauptmann as the ransom recipient.

"He hasn't given up hope by a long shot."

Meanwhile the political aspects of the Governor's new inquiry into the Lindbergh kidnaping case continued to occupy the attention of members of the Legislature.

Assemblyman Basil B. Bruno, Monmouth county Republican, indicated that his resolution for an inquiry of the Governor's use of Motor Vehicle Department employees in the Lindbergh case will have vigorous support from both Democrats and Republicans when the lower house meets again Monday night.

IN THE GREATER SUNDAY "TIMES" TODAY

Remember This

If only we could hear the truth about war from the lips of the slain!

Registration Dead Line Near

March 26 is the last day to register, if you expect to vote at the important Presidential primary May 5.

Because the old registration has been voided, you cannot vote at all unless you have registered since January 1, 1936.

Although the closing day for registration draws near, more than 250,000 people have failed to register.

Regardless of party affiliation, you should register, so you may vote on the selection of your officials, the imposition of taxes and the expenditure of public money—your money.

Go to the office of Registrar of Voters Kerr, 242 South Broadway, or your local City Hall, or telephone Kerr's office, MUtual 9211, and ask for the address of the nearest deputy registrar.

If you have a friend who isn't registered, take him along. Don't delay. Do it now.

ALL THE NEWS ALL THE TIME

LARGEST HOME-DELIVERED CIRCULATION
LARGEST ADVERTISING VOLUME

MAdison 2345
The Times Telephone Number Connecting All Departments

Los Angeles Times

EQUAL RIGHTS — LIBERTY UNDER THE LAW — TRUE INDUSTRIAL FREEDOM

IN TWO PARTS — 42 PAGES
Part I — GENERAL NEWS — 20 Pages

TIMES OFFICES
202 West First Street
And Throughout Southern California

VOL. LVI | CC | THURSDAY MORNING, DECEMBER 10, 1936. | DAILY, FIVE CENTS

KING'S ABDICATION SET FOR TODAY

FOURTEEN DIE IN BLAZING CRASH OF AIR LINER

Noted Europeans Among Victims as Craft Falls Into English Houses

Illustration on Page 20, Part I

CROYDON (Eng.) Dec. 9. (AP)—The most disastrous air liner crash in England's history brought death today to fourteen persons aboard a K.L.M. Dutch Line passenger ship which ripped the roofs from two houses and fell in flames four minutes after it left the runway at Croydon Airdrome en route to Amsterdam.

Three escaped from the twisted wreckage.

The Air Ministry tonight ordered thorough investigation after the K.L.M. Line announced it did not know the reason for the ship going down almost immediately after the take-off in dense fog.

The dead include Juan de la Cierva, autogyro inventor, Baron Gottfried Meyern-Hohenburg of Germany, former husband of the Viennese actress, Luli Deste, and Admiral Arvid Lindman, former Swedish Secretary of State.

STEWARDESS ESCAPES

The stewardess, Fraulein Von Bon Gertman, saved her life by jumping a second before the air liner struck the ground. She suffered only slight burns.

The two other survivors are Walter Schuberk, German passenger, and Wireless Operator Von Bemmel.

KILLED ON BIRTHDAY

Baron Meyern-Hohenburg ironically was killed on the anniversary of his birth. His former wife, the actress Deste, was to leave Germany for Hollywood tomorrow and the Baron had planned to see her.

The plane took off with visi-

Turn to Page 2, Column 4

DEATH TAKES LOTTIE PICKFORD

Heart Ailment Fatal to Actress

Lottie Pickford, film actress and sister of Mary Pickford, died at 11 o'clock last night at her home, 577 Burlington avenue, Brentwood Heights, West Los Angeles. She was 41 years of age.

In private life Miss Pickford was Mrs. John Lock. She had not been active in motion pictures for several years. For the last two years she had been in ill health, suffering from a heart ailment, and had been seriously ill for the last three months. Recent reports were that she was on the way to recovery.

At her bedside when she died were her sister Mary, her husband, and her daughter, Gwynne Pickford.

With the passing of Lottie, Mary Pickford lost the last remaining member of her immediate family, her mother and her brother Jack having died within recent years.

Wallace Tells Farm Plans

Promises Economic Parity With Industry for Agriculturists

PASADENA, Dec. 9. (Exclusive)—Economic parity for the nation's farmers and industry, based on a better program than that of the Agricultural Adjustment Administration, which was held unconstitutional by the United States Supreme Court, was promised tillers of the soil today by Secretary of Agriculture Wallace.

Addressing the opening session of the national convention of the American Farm Bureau Federation, which filled the Civic Auditorium to capacity, Secretary Wallace outlined an eleven-point program for agriculture.

TALKS AT PICNIC

Later in the day the Cabinet member delivered another address before a crowd of 8000 in Brookside Park, within a stone's throw of the famous Rose Bowl, described as the largest farmers' picnic on record.

Not to raise the price of meat, but to feed the throng, thirty beeves were butchered for the mammoth barbecue.

The eleven-point program outlining future policies of the Roosevelt administration was prefaced by a commentary from Secretary Wallace on the warm and sunny setting for the con-

Turn to Page 14, Column 1

Alaskan Plane Overdue on Trip

JUNEAU (Alaska) Dec. 9. (AP) Bad weather between Cordova and Anchorage today caused some anxiety for the safety of Pilot Don Glass, his co-pilot and four passengers.

Names of the passengers were given as Mrs. Wilson F. Erskine, Kodiak, Alaska, daughter of Capt. and Mrs. Louis Lane of San Francisco; William Evans of Seattle; Lorraine Cozac of Juneau, and Cecil M. Wells of Anchorage, Alaska.

Glass left here in his amphibian plane at 10 a.m. Tuesday and has not been reported.

Race Track Charges Fly at Hearing

State Board Accused of Using Favoritism; Santa Anita Also Hit

Figures—from millions of dollars to pennies—were cited in a long chain of testimony at the Assembly Audit-Finance Committee hearing on horse racing in the State Building yesterday.

Fifty persons prominent in racing circles heard of million-dollar stock-selling plans. They heard of multimillion-dollar wagering totals at tracks. And they heard lengthy arguments about breakage—the odd pennies above any 10-cent multiple which are deducted from payments on winning bets and retained by track operators.

Track promoters who have been denied licenses and horse breeders and owners restricted in stall space at tracks charged favoritism by the California Horse Racing Board and discrimination by the Santa Anita management.

OIL MAN TESTIFIES

A. T. Jergins, Long Beach oil man, traced the history of applications for a race-track license made by himself, Norman. H. Church, owner of the Northway Stables; Charles E. Cooper, owner of the Cooper Stables of the San Luis Rey breeding farm, and others.

"I am not a horseman and have no interest in horses whatever," Jergins laughed in introducing himself on the stand. Then he testified more than an hour.

Assemblyman Leon M. Donihue, committee chairman, and Assemblyman Ralph Evans heard Leo R. Friedman, committee counsel, fire a barrage of questions designed to lay a background for possible committee recommendations to the State Legislature.

HANDLING OF BREAKAGE

In the morning, they appeared especially interested in testimony regarding handling of breakage.

In the afternoon they heard Jergins and Robert Muckler, secretary of his group, charge that they had lived up to all requirements for a license set by the California Horse Racing Board but had been denied permits.

Further, they insisted, the board members kept secret their

Turn to Page 2, Column 3

Einstein's Wife Critically Ill

NEW YORK, Dec. 9. (Exclusive)—Mrs. Albert Einstein, the scientist's wife, is critically ill of a heart ailment, it was reported today.

She has been confined to her bed for three weeks, attended by three special nurses and several doctors.

HIS LOVE THROWS EMPIRE INTO TURMOIL

King Edward of Great Britain, whose love for Mrs. Wallis Warfield Simpson has upset the nation. Announcement of his abdication is awaited throughout England and her dominions. (AP) photo

Cabinet Told Ruler to Quit

Monarch Who Was Never Crowned Decides to Yield Throne for Mrs. Simpson; Empire Speculates on His Successor

LONDON, Dec. 10 (Thursday.) (U.P.)—Britain and her dominions beyond the seas awaited the announcement today that Edward VIII—the King who never was crowned—had decided to give up his throne so he can marry Mrs. Wallis Warfield Simpson.

Press, public and most members of Parliament confidently expected that Prime Minister Baldwin will inform the House of Commons this afternoon that the King has decided to abdicate.

CABINET TOLD OF DECISION

A source, usually reliable, told the United Press last night that Baldwin had communicated the King's decision to an emergency meeting of the British Cabinet.

The United Press understood, from a source of information that invariably has been correct in the constitutional crisis, that the King's decision was made as early as Tuesday night. Baldwin was so informed.

Lending considerable credence to the reports that Edward will abdicate within the next few hours was the fact that word went forward last night to churches throughout Great Britain to offer prayers for a new monarch Sunday.

SERVICES ALREADY PLANNED

It is understood that many churches and religious societies already have had preliminary meetings to plan such services.

The London Daily Mail appeared on the streets this morning with a banner line in large, heavy type, which read: "Abdication Feared Today."

Then shortly before midnight, the government-controlled British Broadcasting Company announced over the radio that the consensus among members of the House of Commons is that Prime Minister Baldwin will issue a statement tomorrow which will be a grave one.

MAY YET CHANGE MIND

Persons close to the court said the only possibility that Edward would keep his throne rested in the chance that he might have an eleventh-hour change of mind. Powerful pressure, it was said, is being brought on him from several sources. The King visited his mother, Dowager Queen Mary, in Windsor Castle yesterday—perhaps to say good-by, perhaps to inform her of his momentous decision.

The Princess Royal also was present, and the meeting took place under conditions of greatest secrecy.

The King wanted to leave Fort Belvedere without being seen. In this he was aided by a thick fog which hung over the countryside clouding the windows of his car so that its occupants could not be seen from the outside.

TAKES PRIVATE ROAD

The royal machine quietly glided down a bridle path and thence into a narrow, private road. Newspapermen who have watched the estate on a twenty-four-hour schedule for more than a week were not aware of his departure.

Two dispatch riders, on motorcycles, raced from No. 10 Downing street, home of Baldwin, toward the King's country estate at Fort Belvedere at 2:30 a.m. today. One of them was carrying a large tin box, on which was affixed a great red seal. Members of Baldwin's staff helped fasten the big box on the motorcycle, indicating how impor... sidered it. It was presumed to have ... taining to Edward's abdication.

EMERGENCY MACHINE

The second motorcycle ...
case the first one's machin...
mile journey to Fort Bel...

Last night, at ab...
of the Cabinet, a d...
dere and delivere...
out of the g...
royal truck-
out of F...
lights la...

T...
Norm...
woul...

PP...

Japan Cabinet Given Warning

Privy Council Attacks Premier and Aide for Foreign Policies

TOKIO, Dec. 9. (AP)—The Japanese Privy Council warned the government today it is displeased with the nation's foreign policy.

Premier Koki Hirota and Foreign Minister Hachiro Arita were called before the plenary session of the Council and attacked "from every direction for an hour and a half."

One councillor asked whether the government was prepared to make a grave decision, which was interpreted as an intimation the Cabinet may be forced to resign. The answer, observers said, was noncommittal and equivocal.

ARITA APOLOGIZES

After a lengthy grilling by the Privy Council, Arita expressed apologetic regret for the state of Japan's diplomacy in every nation mentioned by the councillors.

Emperor Hirohito, who attended the Privy Council meeting,

Turn to Page 2, Column 2

MRS. SIMPSON DISCUSSES DIVORCE WITH ATTORNEY

CANNES (France) Dec. 9. (U.P.) Mrs. Wallis Simpson today discussed details of her divorce at a long conference with her London attorney, Theodore Goddard, and reports spread that she is planning some startling action in the British empire's crisis.

Goddard admitted to the United Press that he had consulted the former Baltimore belle about her decree nisi from Ernest M. Simpson, London ship broker.

The decree was handed down October 27 at Ipswich but cannot become absolute until April 27, except by special legal action.

The conversation between Goddard and Mrs. Simpson in the pinkstone villa of Mr. and Mrs. Herman L. Rogers, where she sought seclusion four days ago after fleeing from England, was believed to have a direct bearing upon the impending climax of her romance with King Edward VIII.

Speculation as to what transpired in the conference took two paths:

(1.) King Edward has decided definitely to abdicate and efforts are being made to speed up the final divorce decree to permit an early marriage to Mrs. Simpson.

(2.) Mrs. Simpson has decided to give up Edward for his sake and the good of the empire and wants to rescind her decree nisi, thus making it impossible for him to marry her.

The swiftly moving events at the Rogers villa, Le Vieux, were

Turn to Page 8, Column 3

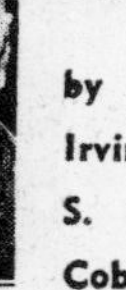

OBSERVATIONS

by Irvin S. Cobb

SANTA MONICA, Dec. 9.—On December 15, right on the dot as usual, the European powers will pay us the customary installments, with interest as accrued to date, on their debts to us—not war debts, as some still erroneously call them, for those loaned sums of incredible size we long ago charged off to universal good will and the cause of common humanity; but peace debts, the same being money borrowed from us after hostilities had ceased so that they might restore wasted lands and rehabilitate shattered industries and quicken hope amongst despairing peoples.

Thus will the world be given renewed proof that great governments are as ready as any decent individuals would be to discharge their pledged obligations, both financial and moral; to maintain their self-respect, to preserve their national honor and finally to show their gratitude for the country which, in the hour of their supremest need, came to the rescue, first with its man-power and its billions, and then with more and yet more of its billions.

And now, Egbert, it's your turn to think up one!

Repairman Must Die for Killing His Stepdaughter

HAZLEHURST (Ga.) Dec. 9. (AP)—Lawrence Ward, 51-year-old itinerant repairman accused of "stomping" his 14-year-old stepdaughter to death because she had a date, was convicted of murder today and sentenced to die.

Judge Gordon Knox fixed the execution date at January 29.

IN THE 'TIMES' TODAY

THURSDAY, DECEMBER 10, 1936

REMEMBER THIS

More buyers can afford to spend dimes than dollars.

ALL THE NEWS ALL THE TIME

LARGEST HOME-DELIVERED CIRCULATION
LARGEST ADVERTISING VOLUME

MAdison 2345
The Times Telephone Number
Connecting All Departments

IN TWO PARTS — 36 PAGES
Part I — GENERAL NEWS — 18 Pages

TIMES OFFICES
202 West First Street
And Throughout Southern California

VOL. LVI | CC | SATURDAY MORNING, FEBRUARY 6, 1937. | DAILY, FIVE CENTS

President Asks Fifteen-Judge Supreme Court in Shake-up

CARGO MOVES AGAIN AT WATER FRONT

First of the eighty-two ships strike-bound for weeks in Los Angeles Harbor to be unloaded yesterday was the Norwegian boat Hoyanger, signalizing end of the West Coast walkout. (AP) photo

Plan Designed to Add Youth and Swiftness

BY WARREN B. FRANCIS
"Times" Staff Correspondent

WASHINGTON, Feb. 5. (Exclusive) — President Roosevelt today in an epoch-marking message to Congress proposed a radical reorganization of the nation's judicial system embodying fundamental reforms in the methods of administering justice and expansion of the United States Supreme Court.

In his surprise message, the President carried out previous hints he would "do something" to the judiciary by calling for a far-reaching housecleaning of the Federal bench and giving vent to bitter criticism of both the present courts and the existing judiciary machinery. The plan outlined in

Other news and comment on proposed expansion of Supreme Court appear on Pages 6 and 7, Section I.

his communication constitutes the most radical shake-up in the judicial branch of the government in generations.

Calling for an overhauling of the "hierarchy" of courts from top to bottom, Mr. Roosevelt proposed:

(1.) Infusion of new blood in the Federal bench by appointment of not more than fifty new district judges and expansion of the Supreme Court to fifteen justices.

SHIFTING JUDGES

(2.) Greater flexibility through establishment of a mobile force of district judges who would be assigned to relieve congestion in various places.

(3.) Streamlined means of handling cases involving the constitutionality of Federal laws.

The purpose of the plan, as well as the keynote of the message, is to bring about better administration of justice. The President based his suggestions on the need for greater "equality," "certainty" and speed in handling litigation in Federal courts. He informed Congress his aim is "to strengthen the administration of justice and to make it a more effective servant of public need."

PERMANENT CHANGE

Supplementing his recommendations with a plea for action from Atty.-Gen. Cummings, the President submitted the draft of a bill which embraces most of his ideas.

Carefully prepared to cover several important technicalities, the legislation would have a permanent, not merely temporary, effect on the size of the judiciary, although there would be definite limitations on expansion of the different tribunals. The Supreme Court would be fixed at fifteen members, while the district courts could not be expanded beyond twice their present size.

Under the bill, the President

Turn to Page 7, Column 7

Auto Strike Chiefs Still Deadlocked

Lewis and Knudsen Reported Unwilling to Yield in Views

Illustration on Page 16, Part I

DETROIT, Feb. 6. (Saturday) (U.P.)—Gov. Murphy's strenuous attempt to bring the differences between General Motors and the United Automobile Workers in a small, informal conference of "top men" failed to bring peace nearer, the United Press was told early today.

The larger conference will be resumed at 10 a.m.

After twenty-three hours of persistent negotiations between three representatives of each group, with Murphy sitting in as special mediator for President Roosevelt, virtual stalemate was reached on a technical but vital point—the number of plants in which the U.A.W. shall be recognized as sole bargaining agent for the workers.

CONFERENCE TODAY

Murphy adjourned the larger conference yesterday and called William S. Knudsen, General Motors executive vice-president, and John L. Lewis, chief of the Committee for Industrial Organization and strike strategist, to his apartment late last night.

Lewis reportedly was unwilling to compromise further and Knudsen was understood to have explained that he was unable to raise the figure to which General Motors was willing to go.

SHORT MEETING

The meeting lasted only a short time. It was described as cordial but unfruitful.

From a participant in the formal conferences that occupied yesterday, it was learned that conferees with Gov. Murphy exerting pressure from the White House, hoped to achieve a compromise solution of Lewis's collective bargaining demands.

BASIS OF PEACE

But slight progress had been made on this, the most vital point of the union's demands, in three days of parley.

It was indicated strongly that settlement rested on ability of Knudsen and Lewis to come to terms on one question: to how many plants General Motors would grant the union sole collective bargaining rights.

Lewis is reported to be holding out for sole rights to represent the workers in all twenty of the plants which the U.A.W.A. has been able to close with sit-down strikers. According to the same authoritative sources,

Turn to Page 3, Column 3

NEW STORM AT SEA SWEEPS TOWARD COAST

Repetition of Thursday Gale Forecast as North Digs at Wind and Flood Debris

SAN FRANCISCO, Feb. 5. (AP)—A rapidly falling barometer presaged a possible repetition of yesterday's slashing southwest gale which swept in from Hawaii and covered much of Northern California with wind wreckage and flood debris.

The new storm was reported 1000 miles off the Pacific Coast this morning, and rain which started falling in San Francisco late today was believed the precursor of the disturbance by Thomas Read, United States meteorologist.

Train, automobile and airplane traffic to the north was operating on delayed schedules.

TRAINS STORM-BOUND

Fourteen trains were storm-bound in various California and Oregon towns until this afternoon. Twelve Southern Pacific passenger trains, held at Klamath Falls and Ashland, Or., and Redding, Delta, Gerber, Weed and Dunsmuir in California were routed over the company's Cascade route.

The Siskiyou route was blocked by derailment of an engine attached to a snowplow at White Point station near the Siskiyou summit. One of the trains held since yesterday noon at Delta was a ten-car special in which 100 members of the Monte Carlo Ballet Rousse are engaged in a national tour.

SLIDES BLOCK TRACKS

The Southern Pacific also attached snowplows to east and west bound trains over the Sierra to clear the way through a number of small snowslides. Because roads from Reno west to Northeastern California counties were virtually closed, the railroad decided to run daily stub trains to communities as far north as Klamath Falls over the line which ordinarily has only triweekly service.

Twenty snowslides between Keddie and Belden in the Feather Canyon blocked main line tracks of the Western Pacific Railroad. The eastbound Scenic Limited was held at Oroville pending clearing of tracks, and the westbound train was held at Portola.

RAINS ADD TO PERIL

Railroads reported the snow was the heaviest in thirty years in the mountain regions. Snowplows succeeded in removing that obstacle from the tracks, but yesterday's gale placed trees across the tracks and the trains

Turn to Page 2, Column 6

Gas Blast Kills Six

Others Believed Dead in Explosion and Fire at Louisville

LOUISVILLE (Ky.) Feb. 5. (Exclusive)—Effects of the flood took a new toll of life and property damage here today in a terrific gas explosion that is believed to have killed at least six persons, injured many more and shattered a three-story brick building at Floyd and Market streets.

Two explosions of gas that had accumulated in the building during the flood were followed by flames that spread rapidly before a high wind. The fire enveloped an apartment house adjoining the shattered building and is believed to have taken a heavy loss of life there. It is not known how many victims had been trapped in the apartment house.

WINDOWS SHATTERED

The blasts broke windows for a block around the brick building. The structure housed a drug store, tire shop, chain grocery store and several small shops.

The building is on the eastern edge of the downtown business section, an area that was partly flooded.

The explosion and the fire was the third in twenty-four hours as a result of gas leaks caused by the flood, although this was by far the most disastrous of the fires.

This new destruction came while President Roosevelt's flood commission was here inspecting the damage previously done and planning for rehabilitation.

RELIEF PROMISED

Describing Louisville as the hardest hit spot in the flood zone, Works Progress Administration Director Harry L. Hopkins, chairman of the commission, pledged full Federal aid for the rehabilitation of

Turn to Page 2, Column 4

Harbor Busy as 5000 Men Back on Job

Eighty-two Ships Tied Up by Strike Resume Activities

Illustration on Page 16, Part I

The metallic, rhythmic roar of moving cargo filled Los Angeles Harbor's twenty miles of transit sheds for the first time in ninety-nine days yesterday.

Smoke poured from the forest of funnels and clouds of steam etched the tracks of criss-crossing cranes and switch engines as 5000 men bent to the task of setting in motion the port's eighty-two strike-bound ships and their 234,000 tons of freight.

Twenty-two vessels were being worked by 1500 longshoremen who will double their working strength to 3000 this morning.

MEN BOARD SHIPS

Long queues of seamen, loaded down with sea bags and suit cases, trudged up the gangways of mist-shrouded ships from dawn to dark and last night 3000 seafaring personnel were aboard sixty-two long-idle United States flag vessels.

The local situation received a severe setback last night when, after a long day of wrangling between themselves and operators, all unlicensed personnel refused to return to work on intercoastal vessels which are owned on the east coast.

These eleven ships include vessels of the Grace, Panama-Pacific, Calmar, Luckenbach and Isthmian lines.

PACT SIGNED

All these lines except Panama-Pacific already have signed the west coast agreement but the seamen refused to return to any of the east coast vessels until Panama-Pacific joins, with the further stipulation by west coast union leaders that they be given jurisdiction over east coast personnel operating on the Pacific Coast.

Picket lines were established by east coast seamen late yesterday around the Panama-Pacific liner California and the Grace liner Santa Rosa.

It is expected these vessels and probably the other east coast carriers will be picketed again today. It is doubtful, however, that longshoremen will recognize the picket lines.

COMPROMISE MADE

The deck hands' strike, which has tied up the port's towboat fleet for five days, was to end at midnight last night as two of the operators, Wrigley and Rohl-Connolly, made a compromise settlement with the Inland Boatmen's Union.

The workers gained a sixty-hour week, cash for overtime and a compromise monthly wage of $150. Relative gains are also expected for licensed tug officers.

At San Francisco smiling maritime workers, ninety-nine days without pay envelopes, flocked

Turn to Page 3, Column 1

ESPEE VESSEL CALLS FOR AID

Rudder Reported Lost Off Virginia Coast

NEW YORK, Feb. 6. (Saturday) (U.P.)—Radio Marine reported early today that the S. S. El Occidente, freighter of the Southern Pacific Steam Ship Lines, sent out a distress call at 12:50 a.m., reporting a damaged rudder.

The vessel gave her position as about 100 miles due east of Norfolk, Va., and asked that a Coast Guard boat be sent to stand by. The damaged rudder made it impossible to steer the ship, the message said. She was drifting southwest in a heavy sea which was moderating.

Lindberghs Visit Vatican Museum

ROME, Feb. 5. (AP)—Col. and Mrs. Charles A. Lindbergh devoted another day today to sight-seeing in the Eternal City, after postponing their take-off for Tripoli on a flight presumably to Cairo, Egypt.

The American flyer's orange and black touring monoplane waited while he and Mrs. Lindbergh visited the Vatican Museum and the Sistine Chapel in privacy guarded by Italian police.

Moscow Rioting Report Called Error

MOSCOW, Feb. 6. (Saturday) (U.P.)—Reports published in London today to the effect that Josef Stalin had surrounded the Kremlin with 1000 bodyguards after serious street rioting proved to be without foundation upon investigation.

Nor was there any verification for reports that a conference of all soviet marshals had been summoned.

Calm prevailed and there were no disturbances of any kind.

Southland Gets Showers

Unsettled Weather Predicted for Today and Tomorrow

Light showers began falling in Los Angeles yesterday as the southern fringe of a widespread storm dipped down over Southern California.

Continued unsettled weather today and tomorrow with occasional rain is forecast by the United States Weather Bureau. Moderate temperatures with gentle shifting winds are predicted.

Precipitation yesterday in Los Angeles was measured at .45 of an inch up to midnight.

FAIRLY GENERAL

This increases the season's total fall to 10.45 inches, almost three times the amount received at this time last year — 3.68 inches. Normal is 8.42.

Reports from outlying points showed that the rain was fairly general but comparatively light over most areas near Los Angeles.

Turn to Page 2, Column 7

DEMAND FOR NEW JUDICIARY DENOUNCED AND DEFENDED

WASHINGTON, Feb. 5. (AP)—President Roosevelt's demand that the judiciary be made over stirred a strange mixture of joy and anger on Capitol Hill today.

Statements poured from legislators' offices in a steady stream. They ranged from the comment of Senator Guffey, Democrat, of Pennsylvania, that "I'm 100 per cent for it," to the cry of Representative Snell, Republican, of New York, that it was "the beginning of the end of everything."

Study of the Senate comment showed that, of those who discussed the President's proposals publicly, about two were friendly to it for every one critical.

Less than half of the Senators were willing to make any statement disclosing their view, however.

COMMENTS

Some of the Congressional comment follows:

SENATOR ROBINSON, Democrat, Arkansas, majority leader: "The program of the message is in no sense a violent innovation. It looks to dispatch in the decision of cases. It appears likely that the substantial recommendations will receive favorable consideration by the Senate."

SENATOR VANDENBERG, Republican, of Michigan, a leading minority spokesman: "I am opposed to tampering with the Supreme Court directly or indirectly, and particularly to any scheme for packing it."

SENATOR BORAH, Republican, of Idaho, one of the Constitution's leading defenders in Congress: "Some things are all right and some I cannot see my way clear to support. I would not care at this time to discuss increasing the Supreme Court—but it will be discussed."

NORRIS TELLS FAITH

SENATOR NORRIS, Independent, of Nebraska: "The President's message has very graphically called the attention of the country to the unfortunate condition that exists in our judiciary. I commend and agree with every word he has said in that respect. I doubt, however, the wisdom of the remedy suggested by the President. The whole subject is a perplexing one, and I hope and believe that Congress will be able to solve it."

SENATOR BANKHEAD, Democrat, of Alabama: "The message contained some very fine suggestions and contained nothing to indicate it was directed at the Supreme Court. The question of possible revival of the N.R.A. and A.A.A. in modified form is not tied up with this suggestion at all."

CRITICISMS

REPRESENTATIVE SNELL, Republican, of New York, House minority leader: "The adminis-

Turn to Page 6, Column 7

POPE SUFFERS MORE PAIN

VATICAN CITY, Feb. 6. (Saturday) (AP)—Pope Pius's rest was disturbed by pain early today, the fifteenth anniversary of his election as head of the church, Vatican sources said.

An official statement last night declared the Pontiff's overworked heart was returning to normal and his painful leg ulcer had almost completely healed.

IN THE 'TIMES' TODAY

SATURDAY, FEBRUARY 6, 1937

REMEMBER THIS

To grow old outside is human, to keep young inside is divine.

ORCHESTRA LEADER PAUSES TO TAKE PUNCH AT REVELER

Ben Bernie, orchestra leader at the Cocoanut Grove, stepped down from his rostrum and into a pugilistic role for a moment last night.

With a barely perceptible movement that hardly any revelers observed, he struck a man in uniform on the dance floor.

Bernie himself said the man was a naval lieutenant, but none wearing such a uniform, or any other uniform, could be found around the Ambassador a few moments later.

"I lost my temper over a remark he made," said Bernie, refusing to identify the man and finally declaring that he did not know the individual.

Persons near by said they understood the recipient of the blow to have made some remark about the big black cigars which the orchestra leader usually smokes.

"It was annoying," said Bernie. "Please forget it."

And shortly afterward Bernie left the orchestra and did not return.

None could identify the uniformed man, who was reputed to have been a lieutenant-commander from the fleet. Nor could anyone say who accompanied the gentleman.

"It was a quick punch and I regret it deeply," said Bernie.

Attendants at the Grove, waiters and others, were unwilling to discuss the matter. All they would say was there was no fight, no commotion.

"Nothing happened," said Jimmy Manos, maitre d'hotel.

Prince Michael Reported Well

FLORENCE (Italy) Feb. 5. (AP)—Michael, 15-year-old Crown Prince of Rumania, is completely recovered from an appendicitis operation and a touch of influenza, it was officially announced today. He will be able to leave the hospital tomorrow.

OBSERVATIONS

By Irvin S. Cobb

SANTA MONICA, Feb. 5.—I may be wrong—I remember I was wrong one other time in my life—but, as this innocent bystander understands the situation, should I find an uninvited and unwelcome individual on my business premises and he's standing up or strolling around and I invite him to leave and he doesn't leave, I am perfectly within my legal rights when I bounce him out on his head, even though I muss him up considerable in the process.

But on the other hand, should the intruder have the forethought to sit down and remain firmly seated, then there is nothing I can do except moan aloud.

Of course, it's possible that, were the issue carried to the Supreme Court, that tribunal might go even back beyond hoss-and-buggy days—in fact, as far back practically as Magna Carta—and decide that a man's house is still his castle. To be sure, if while we're waiting for guidance the trespasser keeps right on with his sit-downing, and my business goes plum' to thunderation, that'll be just my bad luck, won't it?

ALL THE NEWS ALL THE TIME
LARGEST HOME-DELIVERED CIRCULATION
LARGEST ADVERTISING VOLUME

MAdison 2345
The Times Telephone Number
Connecting All Departments

Los Angeles Times

EQUAL RIGHTS
LIBERTY UNDER THE LAW — TRUE INDUSTRIAL FREEDOM

IN TWO PARTS — 54 PAGES
Part I — GENERAL NEWS — 28 PAGES

TIMES OFFICES
202 West First Street
And Throughout Southern California

VOL. LVI — CCC — FRIDAY MORNING, MAY 7, 1937. — DAILY, FIVE CENTS

ZEPPELIN BLAST KILLS THIRTY-FIVE

BLASTS SEND GIANT BALLS OF FLAME SPURTING FROM AIRSHIP

Before the eyes of hundreds of horrified spectators, the giant dirigible Hindenburg exploded in mid-air with a terrific roar over the Lakehurst Naval Air Station yesterday at the completion of a trans-Atlantic journey from Germany. This remarkable picture was taken as one of several explosions sent giant balls of fire into the air from the descending gas bag. The huge Zeppelin was wrecked just as it was about to make fast to the mooring mast which is seen in the photograph.

(AP) Wirephoot. Copyright, 1937, by Philadelphia Public Ledger.

Giant Dirigible Blazing Wreck

Airship Blows Up on Its Arrival at Lakehurst Airport From Germany; Passengers Leap From Burning Ship

LAKEHURST (N. J.) May 6. (AP)—Germany's great silver Hindenburg, the world's largest dirigible, was ripped apart by an explosion tonight that sent her crumpling to the naval landing field a flaming wreck with horrible death to about a third of those aboard her.

Exactly how many died was still in dispute as the flames licked clean the twisted, telescoped skeleton of the airship that put out from Germany seventy-six hours before on its opening trip of the 1937 passenger season.

The American Zeppelin Company, through its press representative, Harry Bruno, placed the death toll at thirty-four of the ninety-seven aboard. The company listed twenty

Other news and wirephotos of the Hindenburg disaster will be found on Pages 2, 3, 8, 9, 10 and 16 of this section of The Times.

of the thirty-six passengers and forty-three of the sixty-one-man crew as the disaster's survivors.

Allen Hagaman of Lakehurst, who was watching the landing at the mooringg mast, also was killed, raising the known toll to thirty-five.

ESTIMATES RANGE TO FORTY

These figures were at slight variance with unofficial estimates of the number of dead which ranged up to forty.

In the crowded hospitals in neighboring communities many of the survivors were in critical condition, a number suffering from excruciating burns.

Some were so gravely injured, among them Capt. Ernst Lehman, that the last rites of the Roman Catholic Church were administered to them.

Lehman, skipper of the ship's 1936 flights, made the ill-fated flight as an observer. Capt. Max Pruss, the commander, was listed among the injured survivors.

CAUSE OF BLAST MYSTERY

What caused the fearful blast, just at the moment the great craft was being moored, no one knew. The explosion occurred at the rear and some observers believed a spark of static electricity following a mooring rope from the ground set off the highly inflammable hydrogen. Other reports indicated a backfiring motor might have sent a flash of flame into a minute gas leak.

Storms and buffeting headwinds had delayed the huge ship far behind her schedule for the maiden trip, and she nosed down in the early evening to keep the unexpected rendezvous with disaster.

The ground crew of sailors, soldiers and marines moved out into the field to handle her landing ropes.

PASSENGERS IN GAY MOOD

Lower she nosed, her Diesel motors throttled down. Passengers, gayly waving at the crowd, lined the long lounge windows which show like transparent slits in the great silver belly of the ship.

The spider-like web of landing ropes snaked down the little trap doors in the nose. Men of the ground crew grabbed them at the wooden crossbars.

It was 6:23.

Then came the terrific explosion, and brilliant red flames suddenly splashed out toward the stern and the rudder that bore the red-and-black Nazi swastika. The detonation tore the ship as if it were made of paper. The tail dropped earthward.

CRUMPLES DOWN IN FLAMES

The blunt nose bobbed up, hung a moment in the air and then crumpled toward the field, flames running along its sides and its fabric flaking off in big chunks.

Passengers and men of the crew were hurled through the silvered walls of the Hindenburg to the sandy loam below. The crowd receded in a panicky surge to the shouts of "run for your lives." Navy men dashed into the flaming debris to make rescues.

Collapsing in a tangled mass of girders and aluminum beams, the ship was torn by a series of additional explosions, lesser in force than the first shattering blast. And the flames roared up in a red and yellow wall to envelop the ship.

The flames burned well into the night, despite the efforts of fire departments to quench them.

BLAST IN SHIP'S STERN

The explosion occurred in the No. 2 gas cell toward the stern of the ship, according to State Aviation Commissioner Gill Robb Wilson, who called the blast strange. The hydrogen gas billowed into fierce flame as the explosion plummeted the ship to the airfield. Ground spectators said crew members in the stern of the ship never had a chance to escape.

Spectators shrieked and screamed as the explosion, apparently in the stern of the envelope, shattered the ship and she collapsed, falling in burning wreckage to the ground.

Even after the first stunning explosion sent the ship

Turn to Page 2, Column 1

C.I.O. Joins Film Strike

Labor Council Offer Rejected by F.M.P.C.; Shows to Be Picketed

The Hollywood film studio strike definitely still is on.

This fact was made clear yesterday by Charles Lessing, business agent for the striking Federated Motion Picture Crafts, who said his organization is not at all satisfied with the proposal of the Los Angeles Central Labor Council to end the current walkout.

"The strike will continue until the producers agree to a closed, or union, shop program," Lessing said.

It appeared that the powerful Committee for Industrial Organization will take a hand, both locally and nationally, in the motion-picture strike, after a conference of Lessing and Verne Murdock of the F.M.P.C. and C. H.

Turn to Page 4, Column 6

"In The Times Today," index and summary of news and features, will be found on Page 2, Part 1. Irvin S. Cobb's Observations" appear on Page 4, Part 1.

JURY QUIZZES MRS. SHELBY IN TAYLOR DEATH MYSTERY

Mrs. Charlotte Shelby, mother of Mary Miles Minter, yesterday dramatically denied that she murdered William Desmond Taylor.

She made her first denial before eighteen interested members of the Los Angeles county grand jury and told about it later to a crowd of newspapermen in the corridors of the Hall of Justice.

DAUGHTERS QUIZZED

"I was asked if I murdered Taylor and I had to tell them no," she asserted with gestures.

She paused for breath and continued:

"They asked me if I had any idea who did it and I had to say no again."

Mrs. Shelby was the last of three witnesses to appear before the grand jury during the day. She was preceded by her two daughters, Mrs. Margaret Fillmore and Mary Miles Minter, former screen star.

NEW CLEWS HINTED

But despite Mrs. Shelby's statements that she was unable to throw any light on the reopened investigation of the fifteen-year-old murder of the motion-picture director, Dep. Dist.-Atty. Eugene Williams, head of the bureau of investigation, engaged with Dist.-Atty. Fitts yesterday in presenting the evidence to the jurors, indicated that new material had been developed which may lead to a final solution of the case.

"Testimony given yesterday, together with other information already in our possession, is going to lead to a complete recapitulation of the entire case," he declared. "The grand jury is obviously interested in what they heard and want the investigation continued."

Williams indicated that sev-

Turn to Page 12, Column 1

AGE-PENSION MEASURE VOTED

Assembly Unanimous on Liberalizing Bill

SACRAMENTO, May 6. (AP)—By unanimous vote of 79 to 0, the Assembly tonight passed the Hornblower bill liberalizing old-age pensions.

Under provision of the bill, the necessity of giving a lien on real property is removed, pensioners need not take the pauper's oath and it requires the payment, in full, of the $35 monthly pension without deductions for rent, if they are living rent-free.

Also, it permits pensioners to receive gifts or earn up to a total of $15 additional a month before any deduction may be made from the pension allowance. The bill now goes to the Senate. (Other reports on yesterday's action in the Legislature will be found on Page 14, Part I.)

Survivor Tells Leap to Safety

Blasts Felt Only Slightly, Says One Aircraft Passenger

A survivor's account of the crash of the Zeppelin Hindenburg is given here by one of the passengers of the airship who suffered relatively few injuries.

BY HERBERT O'LAUGHLIN

Copyright, 1937, by the North American Newspaper Alliance, Inc.

LAKEHURST (N.J.) May 6. (Exclusive)—I was in my cabin, in the forward section of the Hindenburg, packing my belongings in preparation for the landing that seemed only minutes away, when I felt a slight tremor shaking the ship. That was an explosion that rent the tail of the airship, the first of the three that tore the dirigible apart, but its effect where I stood was like that of an air pocket.

Hearing people run past my door, I joined them to find the cause of the tremor. As I walked toward the promenade deck, a second tremor occurred.

There was very little confusion among the passengers, no screaming, hardly any noise. Nobody knew what had happened and people were just curious.

When I reached the promenade deck the nose of the ship was about twenty feet above the

Turn to Page 10, Column 2

TENTATIVE LIST OF MISSING AND KNOWN CRASH SURVIVORS

LAKEHURST (N. J.) May 6. (Exclusive)—A tentative list of passengers still missing in the Hindenburg disaster and believed dead was compiled tonight as follows:

Rudolf Anders, Dresden.

R. Herbert Anders, Dresden.

Birger Brinck.

Hermann Doehner, Mexico City.

Donald Curtis, Chicago.

Edward Douglas, New York.

Fritz Erdman.

Otto C. Ernst, Hamburg, Germany.

Mrs. Ernst.

Moritz Feibusch, San Francisco.

John Pannes, New York City.

Emma Pannes, New York City.

Otto Reichold, Vienna.

Ludwig Felber and Walter Bernholzer, members of the crew, died of burns in hospitals. They were the only crew members identified among the dead.

Hans Hugo, Leonard Jacobson, Ray Stahler, William Stett and Franz Werner, crew members, were listed as missing and believed dead.

LIST OF KNOWN SURVIVORS

Capt. Ernst Lehman, severe burns.

Capt. Max Pruss, severe burns.

Capt. Albert Sammt, burns.

Franz Herzog, German naval officer, critical burns.

Col. Nelson Morris, Chicago, injuries unknown.

Hans Vinhalb, injuries unknown.

Albert Summitt, injuries unknown.

Theodore Ritter, injuries unknown.

Philip Mongone, New York, injuries unknown.

George Hirschfeld, Bremen, Germany, injuries unknown.

William Leuchtenberg, injuries unknown.

Hans Hugo, injuries unknown.

Adolph Fischer, injuries unknown.

Carl Otto Clemens, Bonn, Germany, injuries unknown.

Mrs. Gertrude Adelt, injuries unknown.

Turn to Page 2, Column 8

ALL THE NEWS ALL THE TIME

LARGEST HOME-DELIVERED CIRCULATION
LARGEST ADVERTISING VOLUME

MAdison 2345
The Times Telephone Number
Connecting All Departments

Los Angeles Times

IN TWO PARTS — 34 PAGES
Part I — GENERAL NEWS — 18 Pages

TIMES OFFICES
202 West First Street
And Throughout Southern California

VOL. LVI | CC | SATURDAY MORNING, JULY 3, 1937. | DAILY, FIVE CENTS

Amelia Earhart Lost in Pacific; Radio Flashes Faint SOS

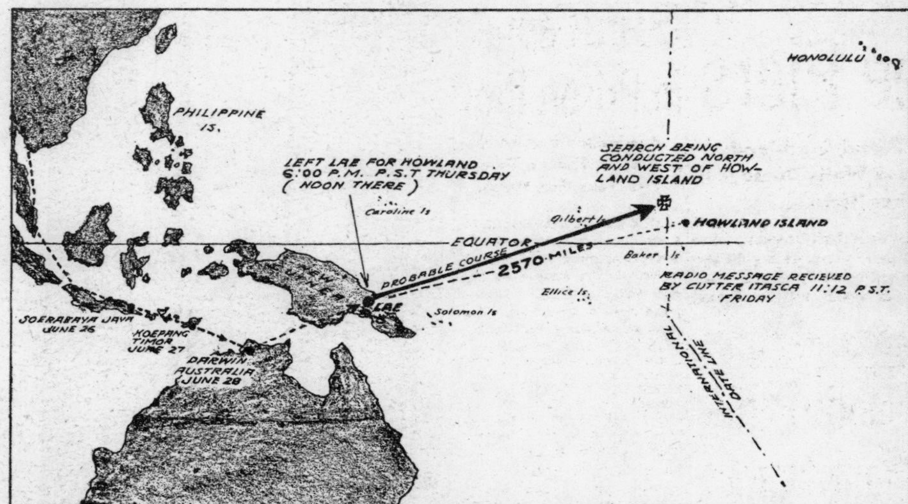

ROUTE OF MISSING FLYERS AND SCENE OF SEARCH

The probable course taken by Amelia Earhart and Navigator Frederick J. Noonan on their flight from Lae, New Guinea, to Howland Island, tiny sand spit in mid-Pacific, and the area in which their lost plane is being hunted by a Coast Guard cutter is shown by this map, drawn by Charles H. Owens, staff artist of The Times.

Plane Joins Ship Hunt for Flyers

Faint radio signals indicating that Amelia Earhart was still afloat somewhere in the vicinity of Howland Island at 1 a.m. today were picked up by Los Angeles radio amateurs and the British steamship Achilles. Repeated "SOS" calls followed by Miss Earhart's call letters "KHAQQ" were heard.

The Achilles was several hundred miles west of Miss Earhart's supposed position, too far to give her any quick assistance.

HONOLULU, July 3. (Saturday) (AP)—Amelia Earhart, who started a world flight "just for fun," was lost today in the vast equatorial Pacific where sea and air searchers desperately sought her fuelless land plane which missed tiny Howland Island and plunged into the shark-infested ocean.

While the Coast Guard cutter Itasca sought aviation's first lady by sea, a Navy flying boat sped toward Howland Island on a 1532-mile flight to seek her by air. The Itasca was searching an area 100 miles northwest of Howland.

SHIP JOINS HUNT

The Navy minesweeper Swan joined the hunt from a position halfway between here and Howland, where it had been stationed to give any possible aid to Miss Earhart on the next leg of her flight.

The flying boat itself was undertaking a hazardous night flight to join the search. Carrying a crew of eight, it took off from Pearl Harbor and headed directly for the tiny island, which the veteran aviatrix and her navigator mysteriously missed.

Lieut. W. W. Harvey, piloting the plane, was expected to reach the searching area in about thirteen hours which would give several hours of daylight to survey hundreds of square miles of sea.

SEARCH OCEAN

Throughout the night, the Itasca, stationed at Howland originally to assist the aviatrix and Noonan, scoured the waters within a 100 mile radius of the island, watching for distress flares.

Radio stations through the Pacific area listened for some word from the missing plane, which went ominously silent at 11:12 a.m., Pacific standard time, yesterday, after reporting only thirty minutes' fuel supply remained.

The aviatrix then was believed nearing Howland after a flight of 2570 miles from Lae, New Guinea, the longest and most hazardous hop of her adventure, which was to end at Oakland, Cal.

POSITION UNKNOWN

In the glare of a rising sun, officers of the Itasca said, she apparently overshot the island, a mere sandspit a mile and a half long and only two feet above the water, and was forced down a short time later.

The Itasca, only vessel within several hundred miles of Howland, was aiming at what was frankly only an estimated position since the last radio report from the daring woman flyer did not give her position. The message said only that she had but thirty minutes' fuel left and had not sighted land.

A few minutes before this the Itasca received a message in which Miss Earhart said she was 100 miles from the Coast Guard vessel, but did not give her position.

The next nearest land is Baker Island, a similar mid-Pacific dot forty miles south of Howland. Outside of these virtual sandbars there is nothing but water for hundreds of miles.

Paul Mantz, Miss Earhart's aviation adviser in Burbank, Cal., said the plane could float

Turn to Page 2, Column 1

Miss Earhart's Signals Heard

Operators 'Jnable to Tell Location of Plane in Pacific

Repeated radio calls of "SOS—KHAQQ" flashed across the Pacific Ocean last night indicating that Amelia Earhart and her 'round-the-world navigator, Capt. Fred Noonan, were still afloat at 1 a.m. today.

"SOS" was the international distress call and "KHAQQ" are the call letters of Miss Earhart's plane.

SIGNALS WEAK

The signals, weak and faltering, were picked up by Los Angeles Radio Amateurs Walter McMenamy of 749 Burnside avenue and Carl Pierson of 1171 Montecito Drive. Pierson is chief engineer of the Patterson Radio Corporation.

The amateur operators said the signals were so weak and there was so much interference that they were unable to distinguish whether Miss Earhart was reporting a position at sea. Once McMenamy caught the letters "Lat." for latitude, but was unable to decipher the figures that followed.

HEARS ITASCA

Amateur Listener Guy H. Dennis of 1195 Crenshaw Boulevard reported he could hear the Coast Guard cutter Itasca, searching for the Earhart plane, repeatedly calling KHAQQ on its radio up to 11:30 p.m. The Itasca's calls then suddenly ceased, he said

Miss Earhart's plane carried a portable hand-cranked generator which would supply power for her radio as long as she was afloat.

EARHART RESCUE REPORT DENIED

Navy Radio Calls Rumor Unfounded

SAN FRANCISCO, July 3 (Saturday) (U.P.)—Navy Radio informed the San Francisco Coast Guard headquarters early today that reports of the rescue of Amelia Earhart and Frederick J. Noonan in the South Pacific appeared to be unfounded.

The Coast Guard also indicated it doubted the report of the rescue, broadcast in Honolulu by radio station KGU.

German Sentenced in France as Spy

NANCY (France) July 2. (AP)—A German charged with seeking information on French motorized troops was sentenced as a spy by a military court today to six years in prison. He was listed as Willy Bohm, 45 years of age.

Indian Hunted as Child Slayer

Picture of Suspect Identified in Inglewood and Search Opened Throughout West for ex-Convict

Positive identification of Fred Godsey, 34-year-old quarter-blood Cherokee Indian and convicted felon, as "Eddie the Sailor" who promised rabbit hunts to young girls in Centinela Park, Inglewood, intensified the man hunt last night for the murderer of Madeline and Melba Everett and Jeanette Stephens a week ago today in the Baldwin Hills.

Pictures of Godsey, obtained by The Times and turned over to investigators, were identified by Al Blythe of 6107 Long street, recreational worker in the park, as the man he saw on Wednesday and Friday of last week playing with the three children who later were the victims of a murderer.

OTHER WITNESSES

Three other witnesses said that Godsey "looks exactly like the man" known as Eddie the Sailor who lured the children from the park, and as a result of this information obtained exclusively by The Times every law enforcement agency in a dozen western States joined in the search for this man.

Tomorrow 500 Legionnaires from Inglewood and Los Angeles will begin a two-day systematic search of every cellar and garage in the suburban town, hoping that some clew to the whereabouts of this new suspect may be picked up. Citizens will be questioned and service station operators shown pictures of Godsey.

TELETYPE BROADCAST

The exclusive information obtained by The Times was turned over to Dist.-Atty. Fitts and Sheriff's investigators yesterday with the result that the whole western half of the United States received teletype broadcasts asking that the manhunt for the Inglewood slayer concentrate on Godsey.

Police in Butte, Mont. ,from where Godsey is believed to have mailed a post card to his estranged wife in Salt Lake City, and to Couer d'Alene, Idaho, which is believed to be his destination, were asked to be on the watch for the suspect.

CALIFORNIA VISITOR

Godsey is known to have made frequent visits to California where he has relatives and friends living in Inglewood, San Pedro and Santa Monica. His sister, Mrs. Elizabeth Arth, wife of Alexander H. (Tubby) Arth, a former bartender, now serving a county jail sentence at Road Camp No. 3 in Mint Canyon, is said to have lived in Inglewood at one time and later in Los Angeles.

The fact that Godsey, who enjoyed being known as "Freddie the Sailor," also enjoyed dislocating his right wrist and laying the palm of his hand back on his forearm, a feat which "Eddie the Sailor" performed for little girls in Centinela Park, convinced investigators that they needed this man to round out their investigation.

"Not one man in 10,000 can dislocate his wrist in that manner," said Autopsy Surgeon Wagner.

Fitts, Chief Investigator Eu-

Turn to Page 3, Column 1

O'Donnell Oil Bill Signed

Governor Approves Other Measures Before Dead Line

SACRAMENTO, July 3. (Saturday) (AP)—As the hour of midnight brought an end to the period in which Gov. Merriam could sign bills passed by the Legislature, approval of scores of measures was announced, one of the most important being the O'Donnell bill which supersedes the Olson bill governing development of the State's tidelands oil fields.

The Olson bill was restricted to the Huntington Beach field but the O'Donnell measure applies equally to all holdings of the State.

ACT'S PROVISIONS

Generally regarded as among the most important legislation enacted by the fifty-second session, the O'Donnell Act provides the State must receive a minimum royalty of 30 per cent on all wells producing 200 barrels a day and 40 per cent when they exceed 1000 barrels.

The Governor left about 367 bills to die by the pocket veto route. Among those which perished was the Pierovich bill to legalize pari-mutuel betting on greyhound races.

Among the measures which received the Governor's approval in a hectic day of bill signing to beat the midnight deadline were special appropriation measures carrying millions of dollars for various State purposes and the support of institutions.

MONEY FOR U.C.

These included $1,000,000 for the University of California and a building construction program involving expenditures of $6,781,550.

The Governor slashed $455,888 from the appropriation for the University of California. He signed a bill appropriating $150,000 for control of social diseases without reducing it.

Supreme Court, Appellate Court and Superior Court judges can retire at 70 years of age on half-salary under the terms of the Clark-Peek bill which was among those signed by the Governor. The new law empowers the Governor to retire judges without their consent for inca-

Turn to Page 5, Column 1

Isolation of Paralysis Germ Told

Dr. E. C. Rosenow Discloses Epochal Research Here

Isolation of the germ which causes infantile paralysis, science's first major step in conquest of the dread disease, was announced last night in Glendale by Dr. Edward Carl Rosenow, professor of experimental bacteriology at the Mayo Foundation for Medical Education and Research at Rochester, Minn.

Addressing 100 physicians, surgeons and medical research workers at the Oakmont Country Club, Dr. Rosenow said that his work with spinal fluid taken from nurses who contracted the disease at the Los Angeles General Hospital in 1934 enabled him to isolate the micro-organism.

NEED OF SERUMS

Bits of muscle and swabs from the nose assisted in his work, Dr. Rosenow said.

Proof of isolation was obtained, he explained, when he injected the micro-organism into rabbits and later recovered it.

Asked what steps must be taken to fight the disease, now that isolation of the germ has been accomplished, Dr. Rosenow said that a serum must be developed, similar to serums used to combat ravages of other contagious ailments.

Already, the 62-year-old bacteriologist said, a composite vaccine has been prepared.

PRELIMINARY TESTS

"Preliminary tests indicate that favorable results should be forthcoming," he said. "It should be possible to immunize specifically and raise the resistance of patients and keep it at a high level and thus prevent recurrences."

Dr. Rosenow said that most important evidence of the streptococcal nature of the disease has been its reproduction in its essential respects.

"By the use of a small number of rabbits and mice, in three groups of experiments, we have produced the main symptoms of this disease as it now exists," he explained.

NINETEEN-YEAR STUDY

Dr. Rosenow has been studying infantile paralysis for nineteen years. His isolation of the germ was speeded by the epidemic at the General Hospital here in 1934 and his studies made more comprehensive because of availability of patients to study.

He paid special credit to the invitation of Dr. Hugh Jones, the generosity of the Mayo foundation and the co-operation of Dr. O. J. Sloan, Dr. E. T. Remmen and to everyone connected with the Physicians' and Surgeons' Hospital in Glendale, where 118 of the nurses suffering with the disease were taken for treatment.

Mattern Asks Permit for North Pole Flight

WASHINGTON, July 2. (AP)—James Mattern, flyer, asked the government's permission today to make a nonstop flight across the North Pole from Oakland, Cal., to Moscow. The Texan announced he will fly some time during August in his tri-motored monoplane.

Revised Court Bill Submitted

Measure Given Senate Provides for Three Roosevelt Appointees

WASHINGTON, July 2. (AP)—A Democratic substitute for the Roosevelt court bill went before the Senate today with an explanation by Senator Robinson, majority leader, that it would permit three appointments to the Supreme Court within the next six months.

Robinson said the bill, based upon the theory of one appointment to the court a year, would permit two new justices to be added within that time in addition to an appointment to fill the existing vacancy. One justice could be added now, addition to filling the vacancy.

Court bill foes quickly denounced the substitute as "just as bad" as the original. They met the proposal with demands that it be sent back to committee for study—a move which would sidetrack the entire issue.

"I think the bill should go back to committee," Senator Wheeler, Democrat, of Montana, leader of the opposition, said. "I don't think a bill of this importance should be written on the floor of the Senate.

"As far as I am concerned,

Turn to Page 4, Column 4

FRANCE THREATENS TO AID LOYALISTS IN REBELLION

LONDON, July 2. (AP)—Britain promptly rejected tonight a proposal of Italy and Germany that the naval patrol of Spanish coasts be abandoned and belligerent rights be accorded both parties in the Spanish civil war.

Backing up the refusal, France made clear tonight that she and Great Britain will supply arms, munitions and airplanes to the Spanish government unless Italy and Germany change their attitudes toward neutrality in Spain.

"Resumption of normal commercial relations" would be permitted, French Foreign Office sources disclosed, and would mean immediate reopening of the French frontier to the Spanish central government.

Insurgent Generalissimo Francisco Franco's frontier, it was said, would remain closed because he still would be viewed officially as the leader of an insurrection against Spain's legitimate government.

British rejection was considered to bring the whole European controversy over control to a stalemate. The subcommittee adjourned until next week, when other nations in the full committee will be called in for a review of the situation, which diplomats admitted was grave.

Russian-Japanese Crisis Eased by Troop Withdrawal

MOSCOW, July 3. (Saturday) (U.P.)—Soviet Russia yielded early today to a threat of Imperial Japanese military pressure and agreed to withdraw its armed forces from disputed island groups in the channel of the Amur River which forms part of the boundary between the far eastern territory of the U.S.S.R. and the Japan-sponsored state of Manchukuo.

Announcement of the settlement, which is believed to have averted the most serious threat of a new Russo-Japanese war in more than thirty years, was made by Japanese Ambassador Mamoru Shigemitsu after a new conference with Foreign Commissar Maxim Litvinoff which lasted half an hour. A Russian government communique confirmed the agreement and said the order for withdrawal of gunboats and troops has already gone out.

The soviet government has agreed to withdraw immediately its patrols or troops from the disputed islands — the Bolshoi and Sennufu groups—and to remove its gunboats from their vicinity, Shigemitsu said.

Evacuation News Gives Relief to Tokio

TOKIO, July 3. (Saturday) (AP) Russia's agreement to evacuate her forces from the disputed Amur River islands was received today with intense relief throughout Japan.

Cabinet ministers expressed their deepest satisfaction that possible war had been averted

IRELAND ADOPTS CONSTITUTION

Near-Independent Status Approved

DUBLIN, July 3. (Saturday) (U.P.)—Adoption of the "all but Republican" constitution, which would give the Irish Free State a near-independent status, by a majority of 3 to 2 was indicated early today in returns from Thursday's elections.

De Valera Wins Seat in Dail

DUBLIN (Irish Free State) July 2. (AP)—President Eamon De Valera and William T. Cosgrave, former President and opposition leader, were re-elected to the Dail (Parliament) as the Irish Free State tonight continued counting its election returns.

Lord Mayor Alfred Byrne won his Dublin constituency with 12,085.

French Strike Averted

PARIS, July 3 (Saturday)(AP) Threat of a nation-wide shutdown of hotels, restaurants and cafes was averted early today as employers and workers signed an agreement on working conditions.

OBSERVATIONS

by Irvin S. Cobb

SANTA MONICA, July 2.—While the optimists amongst us are celebrating the glorious Fourth—and hoping to survive until the convalescing fifth—there's a different kind of party going on. Those Liberty Leaguers who thus far have escaped falling into the hands of the taxidermist, along with a scattering handful of imperfectly embalmed old line Republicans and badly stuffed Bourbon Democrats, will insist on thinking of it as ex-independence day, their idea of a proper observance being not to commemorate the birth of freedom but to hold memorial services on account of its recent demise. In fact, they've been weeping at the grave for several months already.

Somebody or some group of somebodies is forever deploring the death of American freedom. Usually these despairing ones accuse the party in power. Once in a while they vary the routine and blame an individual politician for the murder.

But, somehow, our liberties decline to stay buried. They're like sassafras sprouts. Plow them under, dig 'em up, harrow 'em out, burn the roots, and in a year or two, they spring right up again.

Maybe we made a mistake in not choosing the sassafras sprout as the national flower.

IN THE 'TIMES' TODAY

SATURDAY, JULY 3, 1937

RADIO. Page 10, Part I.

CHURCH NEWS. Page 2, Part II.

COMICS. Page 14, Part II.

FASHIONS, CLUBS, SOCIETY. Pages 5 and 6, Part II.

FINANCIAL. Pages 6, 7, 8 and 9, Part I.

OIL. Page 9, Part I.

PUZZLE. Page 15, Part I.

DRAMA. Page 7, Part II.

SHIPPING. Page 13, Part II.

WEATHER. Page 16, Part II.

PICTORIAL PAGE. Page 18, Part I.

FINANCIAL. Local retail trade shows irregular trend in week. March of Finance. Transamerica Corporation boosts dividend. Wheat futures recede on profit taking. Late buying lifts stock prices. Page 6, Part 1.

THE SOUTHLAND. Ventura to dedicate $125,000 bridge today. Food poisoning believed cause of San Diego boy's death. Page 15, Part II.

SPORTS. Budge beats Von Cramm in straight sets. Page 9, Part II.

Padres defeat Angels as fight features game. Page 9, Part II.

Del Mar race track opens today. Page 9, Part II.

THE CITY. Cherokee Indian now sought as suspect in killing of three Inglewood girls. Page 1, Part I.

Hunt sentenced to three years in prison. Page 1, Part II.

James, rattlesnake slayer, wins new respite from gallows. Page 3, Part II.

Conroy found sane in wife slaying. Page 16, Part II.

City's three-day heat wave tempered by ocean breezes. Page 1, Part II.

Brush fire imperils Olive View Sanitarium before being brought under control. Page 1, Part II.

Councilman Kujaneck of San Gabriel indicted in bribery inquiry. Page 3, Part II.

THE WEST. Governor signs many bills before midnight dead line. Page 1, Part I.

Body of woman recovered from near wreckage of plane in Utah. Page 3, Part II.

GENERAL EASTERN. Steel workers protected by troops, return to mills through picket lines. Page 11, Part I.

Truck drivers' holiday causes seven papers to suspend publication. Page 11, Part I.

WASHINGTON. Substitute Supreme Court bill submitted to Senate. Page 1, Part I.

Joint tax returns by husbands and wives urged. Page 4, Part I.

Chicago strike riot film viewed by Senate committee. Page 11, Part I.

Federal deficit shows increase over estimates. Page 4, Part I.

FOREIGN. Amelia Earhart lost in South Pacific. Page 1, Part I.

France meets Italo-German proposal with threat to arm Spainish loyalists. Page 1, Part I.

Soviet to recall troops easing border crisis with Japan. Page 1, Part I.

REMEMBER THIS

He is in a bad way who is unconscious of his faults.

ALL THE NEWS ALL THE TIME
LARGEST HOME-DELIVERED CIRCULATION
LARGEST ADVERTISING VOLUME
MAdison 2345
The Times Telephone Number
Connecting All Departments

Los Angeles Times

EQUAL RIGHTS
LIBERTY UNDER THE LAW — TRUE INDUSTRIAL FREEDOM

IN TWO PARTS — 38 PAGES
Part 1 — GENERAL NEWS — 18 Pages
TIMES OFFICES
202 West First Street
And Throughout Southern California

VOL. LVII C MONDAY MORNING, DECEMBER 13, 1937. DAILY, FIVE CENTS

JAPANESE ADMIT SINKING U. S. SHIP

Heavy Seas Rip Out Three Piers

Fierce Ground Swells Pound Southland; Homes Undermined and Walls Damaged; Property Loss at Beaches High

Giant ground swells pounded Southland beaches yesterday and last night, ripping out three piers, damaging several others, wrecking two boats and beaching several more, undermining homes, smashing sea walls and demolishing shore line sidewalks.

Beaches around Santa Monica Bay were littered with wreckage as roaring waves frothed shoreward, driven by mountainous swells.

Damage estimated at $20,000 was suffered at the beach settlement of Sandyland, near Santa Barbara, where beach cottages were undermined and partially wrecked.

The phenomenon of swirling surf and battering waves followed in the wake of the sixty-six-hour storm that drenched the Southland. Rainfall in Los Angeles for the storm was 2.49 inches. It fell between 8:20 a.m. Thursday and 2 a.m. yesterday, according to Federal meteorologists.

CAPS OF SNOW

Bright sunshine took the place of the murky sky which brought the season rain total to 2.52 inches, far above last year's 1.48 inches at this time, and approaching the 2.90 normal for this date.

Planes again are taking off from the major airports after two days of suspended schedules.

Cloud banks hovered over the mountain ranges, however, and the higher peaks of Los Angeles and San Bernardino county ranges received their first caps of snow.

SNOW REPORTED

Hail fell in San Bernardino during the morning and a light snow also was reported in Big Bear Valley. The snow there melted quickly.

Maximum temperature in the city was 69 deg.; minimum was 57 deg.

A brisk northwest wind arose late in the afternoon and fair weather was forecast for today and tomorrow. Light morning frosts are predicted in wind-protected spots, but somewhat higher daytime temperatures are expected.

While the storm and floods in Northern and Central California were receding, Imperial Valley—dry when the rest of the Southland received rain—reported scattered showers early yesterday morning.

PIER DAMAGED

They brought .06 of an inch and raised the season total to .57 as compared with .77 at the same time last year.

At Bakersfield the storm ended leaving a storm and season total of .49 of an inch.

Hammered by the towering swells, which gained greatest force shortly after 4 a.m. when the tide reached five feet, two

Turn to Page 7, Column 1

Floods Peril Many Homes

Red Cross Officials Say 5000 Persons Feel Water's Effects

SAN FRANCISCO, Dec. 12. (AP)—American Red Cross officials said today the homes of about 5000 persons had been flooded or threatened with inundation in Northern California as the result of the area's worst storm in years.

A. L. Schafer, Pacific area manager, said relief already is being provided for 200 families, but that no definite count of the homeless is available.

TEMPERATURE FALLS

"Our survey indicates, however," he said, "that close to 5000 people have been driven from their homes or are fighting desperately to keep the waters from their doors."

Field Representative Milton Rendahl reported temperatures are dropping rapidly and might settle to 15 deg. above zero at Downieville, Sierra mining town in which most of the houses were swept away or damaged by flood waters.

MILLIONS LOST

He said the homeless are being cared for in houses still standing and that provisions are adequate.

The flood, which in many

Turn to Page 7, Column 4

Scientist Arrested in Hit-Run Killing

NEW YORK, Dec. 12. (Exclusive) — Dr. John E. Toole, 41 years of age, Yale graduate and well-known urologist, was arrested today on a charge of homicide. The arrest followed an all-night investigation into the death of Miss Mary McCormack, 60, who was hit, dragged more than 100 feet and killed by a hit-and-run motorist at 10 o'clock Saturday night.

Dr. Toole denied responsibility for the death of the woman.

Convicts Slay Guard Captain in Prison Riot

Barricaded Bad Men Kill Captive as Troops Fire Tear Gas Bombs

COLUMBIA (S. C.) Dec. 12. (AP) A machine gun company of National Guardsmen fired tear gas shells today to subdue six convicts who stabbed a prison guard captain to death and barricaded themselves in the captain's office in a desperate attempt to escape from the State penitentiary.

The victim, Capt. Olin Sanders, was stabbed five times after the felons had defied a dramatic two-hour plea by Gov. Johnston to give themselves up.

SHOUTS THROUGH DOOR

The Governor shouted to them through the door of their barricaded refuge, urging them to release their captive and submit to avoid bloodshed and obviate the necessity of calling out the National Guard.

"Get us a car. Open the gates. Otherwise it'll be too bad for Sanders," one of the felons retorted.

Two hours later the khaki-clad troopers arrived. Another plea was made by Adjt.-Gen. James C. Dozier, in command of the Guardsmen. Again the convicts refused.

MAKES LAST EFFORT

Gov. Johnston made one final effort to persuade them.

"If you boys will walk out of there and let Capt. Sanders walk out first I'll see that nothing goes against your record," he promised.

A hoarse rumble of defiance replied, and Gov. Johnston signaled the Guardsmen.

"Go ahead, boys — let them have it."

A barrage or tear gas brought quick surrender. Gasping and choking, the desperadoes came out with their hands up.

VICTIM SUCCUMBS

On the floor, bleeding profusely, lay Sanders, stabbed with an instrument sharpened like an ice pick. He died in a hospital a few minutes later.

Prison officials said Sanders was unarmed at the time of the attack because strict prison rules forbade carrying a gun into the prison yard.

Guards said he had "checked" his gun with the office force just a few minutes before the incident.

Stricken Babies Pronounced Cured

CHICAGO, Dec. 12. (AP)—Four babies stricken by a mysterious epidemic diarrhea that brought swift death to eleven infants in St. Elizabeth's Hospital were pronounced cured today.

Three others ill with the malady were described by doctors as "improved very considerably."

SUNK IN PERILOUS CHINESE WATERS

The U.S.S. Panay, American gunboat which was sunk by bombs while transporting refugees from embattled Nanking. (AP) Wirephoto

Sloan Donates $10,000,000

General Motors Head Endows Foundation for Research

NEW YORK, Dec. 12. (AP)—Alfred P. Sloan, Jr., chairman of the General Motors Corporation, today announced the donation of $10,000,000 in securities as an endowment to an economics research foundation bearing his name.

The foundation was organized in the summer of 1936 but union labor troubles in the automotive industry delayed plans for its operation and financing.

PURPOSE OF FUND

Sloan said more than 10.000 shares of General Motors common stock are involved, but the transaction is entirely a personal matter, having "nothing whatsoever to do with General Motors Corporation or my official relationship with same."

He said the foundation proposed to concentrate on the "promotion of a wider knowledge of basic economic truths generally accepted as such by authorities of recognized standing and as demonstrated by experience, as well as a better understanding of economic problems in which we are today so greatly involved and as to which we are so importantly concerned."

TURNS BACK PART

"Having been connected with industry during my entire life," he said, "it seems eminently proper that I should turn back, in part, the proceeds of that activity with the hope of promoting a broader as well as a better understanding of the economic principles and national policies which have characterized American enterprise down through the years."

Roosevelt Daughter Enters Hospital

SEATTLE, Dec. 12. (AP)—Mrs. Anna Roosevelt Boettiger, daughter of President Roosevelt and wife of John Boettiger, publisher of the Post-Intelligencer, entered Providence Hospital here tonight. The hospital said she was "under observation."

It was understood here Mrs. Boettiger was taken ill en route to Washington, D. C., and brought back to Seattle today.

Ex-Rail Executive Dies

SAN DIEGO, Dec. 12. (AP) — Ellzy W. Adams, 78 years of age, retired secretary of the Chicago, St. Paul and Milwaukee Railroad, died of cerebral hemorrhage here today.

BRITAIN AROUSED BY THREE JAPAN ATTACKS ON GUNBOATS

LONDON, Dec. 12. (Exclusive)—Three attacks on British gunboats in the Yangtze River by Japanese artillery and bombing planes set Whitehall buzzing with activity tonight.

Prime Minister Chamberlain and Foreign Secretary Eden were informed immediately when the news reached the Admiralty Office from China. Capt. Eden got in touch with his Foreign Office experts and after a long telephone talk with the Prime Minister, orders were sent out to the British authorities on the spot to rush a full report to London.

A meeting of the ministers, it is suggested in diplomatic sources here tonight, will likely be held when detailed information is received to decide what action Great Britain should take. A statement is expected to be made before a committee of the House of Commons tomorrow afternoon by the Foreign Secretary or Chamberlain.

A stiff protest supplementing that already made to the Japanese by the British consular and naval authorities at Shanghai will probably be sent to Tokio by the British government, according to sources close to Whitehall.

It is understood the protest will demand stringent steps to prevent further incidents, full compensation, a formal apology and punishment of those responsible. The Japanese government will be asked to act without wasting time.

The explanation of the Japanese authorities that today's shelling of the British warships, resulting in the death of one sailor and the wounding of several others, including an officer, was a "mistake" aroused indignation here.

Liner Begins Rescue of 600 Marooned Hoover Passengers

MANILA, Dec. 13 (Monday.) (AP)—Some 600 passengers of the ill-fated liner President Hoover began boarding a rescue vessel early today after being marooned thirty-six hours on Formosan islands, where the great ship piled up in darkness Saturday morning.

Officials of the Dollar Line, operators of the $8,000,000 luxury liner, said another company vessel, the President McKinley, is taking the passengers aboard and will bring them here. They did not know how long the transfer will require, but expected the President McKinley here late Wednesday afternoon or night.

The United States destroyer Barker, one of two warships which sped 500 miles from here to aid the liner, reported in messages heard at Shanghai that the vessel was not in immediate danger.

OBSERVATIONS

by Irvin S. Cobb

LA BABIA (Mex.) Dec. 12.—Just above the international line, I met up with him. Except that he was undersized for a Texas cowhand, he seemed orthodox in all regards—wore "cattlelin' clothes," as they call the customary regalia of chaps and neckerchief and wide-antlered hat down here on the border, and rode as though he'd been born on a wall-eyed plug. But his superimposed southwestern drawl carried a rich cockney accent. It turned out he'd started life as an exercise boy for an English racing stable. Kindly providence had brought him 6000 miles to tell me this one:

"'Erb was a jockey, syme as me. 'E turned up missin' one dye. We couldn't get 'air or 'ide of a trace of 'im. Finally three of 'is pals went to the morgue thinkin' 'e might be there amongst the unidentified dead. The morgue keeper was most obligin'. 'E started bringin' out 'is collection. Pretty soon one of the lads sings out, 'This party 'as been a bit knocked abaht by a motor car or somethin' so the fyce ain't wot it was, but it might be poor old 'Erb at that. 'Ere 'e is on number 4 slab.'"

"'In fourth place, eh?' speaks up me friend Egbert, wipin' awye a tear. 'That would be 'Erb. 'E never finished inside the money.'"

Gunboat Goes Down in River

Seaman Killed, Score Injured as Tokio Bombs Strike Refugee-Crowded Vessel; Three Other American Steamers Sunk

TOKIO, Dec. 13. (AP)—Foreign Minister Koki Hirota expressed "profoundest apologies" today for the sinking of the United States gunboat Panay.

The Foreign Minister called on United States Ambassador Joseph C. Grew to convey the Japanese government's regrets.

News of the Panay incident was suppressed in Japan.

The Japanese also accepted responsibility for sinking several Standard Oil Company boats.

A Navy communique pledged immediate steps to place direct responsibility for the incident.

SHANGHAI, Dec. 13. (Monday) (U.P.) — The United States gunboat Panay was bombed and sunk in the Yangtze River at a point about twenty-five miles upstream from Nanking late Sunday, according to official reports radioed to Shanghai. One American sailor aboard was killed. His identity is not known here. The commanding and executive officers of the vessel were injured.

THREE STEAMERS ALSO SUNK

Three Standard Oil Company steamers, loaded with refugees and accompanying the Panay, also were sunk, Ambassador Nelson T. Johnson notified the State Department in Washington.

The injured officers of the Panay are:

Lieutenant-Commander J. J. Hughes, leg broken.

Lieut. A. F. Anders, executive officer, injuries undetermined.

All members of the Embassy staff at Nanking aboard the Panay were rescued.

From fifteen to twenty persons were wounded. About 100 persons were aboard, including eleven American civilians.

CRAFT FLEEING WAR ZONE

The Panay, a vessel of the United States Yangtze River patrol, was steaming upriver from Nanking in an effort to escape from the spreading war zone around the Chinese central capital, which was invested by more than 200,000 Japanese soldiers.

Up to noon today only meager details of the disaster had arrived. It was known that at least eleven American civilians, three or four Italians, a number of Chinese employees of the United States Embassy in Nanking and other noncombatants were aboard. The crew was reported to number fifty-six.

MAROONED IN ATTACK

Survivors from the sunken vessels were marooned in Hohsien when Japanese attacked the town, Johnson informed the State Department.

He said he received this information in a message from Dr. H. B. Taylor, American Episcopalian missionary at Anking, who had been in communication with George Atcheson, Jr., second secretary of the American Embassy at Nanking, who was one of the survivors.

The ship carried two secretaries of the United States Embassy, George Atcheson Jr. and J. Paston Hall, as well as a large group of foreign refugees.

Other Americans known to have been aboard included Weldon James of Greenville, S. C., manager of the United Press office in Nanking; Norman Alley of the Universal News Reel; Eric Mayell of the Fox Movietone News Reel, and Roy Squires of Seattle, Wash.

DISASTER NEWS PHONED

The first news of the disaster reached Kiukiang, a port above Nanking, by telephone.

"The Panay has been bombed and sunk at mileage 221 above Woosung," the message said.

"Fifty-four survivors have been brought ashore. Many of them are badly wounded. They are at Hoshien in Anhwei Province.

"The British gunboat Bee is proceeding to this point to assist in rescue efforts and bring the survivors to Wuhu.

"The United States gunboat Oahu is taking on fuel at Kiukiang and will depart shortly for Wuhu to render assistance.

EMBASSY SECRETARY SAFE

"It is known that Secretary Atcheson of the United States Embassy in Nanking is safe. Lieutenant-Commander J. J. Hughes of New York City, commander of the Panay, suffered a broken leg."

The message did not indicate whether the ship was bombed by an airplane but it was assumed that this was the case. Japanese airplanes have been bombing Chinese vessels on which Chinese soldiers were evacuating Nan-

Turn to Page 6, Column 1

IN THE 'TIMES' TODAY

MONDAY, DECEMBER 13, 1937

REMEMBER THIS

A clever hostess can say sarcastic things without giving offense.

ALL THE NEWS ALL THE TIME
LARGEST HOME-DELIVERED CIRCULATION
LARGEST ADVERTISING VOLUME
MAdison 2345
The Times Telephone Number Connecting All Departments

Los Angeles Times

EQUAL RIGHTS
LIBERTY UNDER THE LAW — TRUE INDUSTRIAL FREEDOM

IN TWO PARTS — 42 PAGES
Part I — GENERAL NEWS — 22 Pages
TIMES OFFICES
202 West First Street
And Throughout Southern California

VOL. LVII | CC | FRIDAY MORNING, MARCH 4, 1938. | DAILY, FIVE CENTS

Known Deaths Reach Seventy as Storm Flood Waters Recede

Scores Missing, Thousands Driven From Ruined Homes; Crews Begin Digging Out

Sodden and battered, the Southland yesterday emerged from a near-record deluge and counted sixty-seven known dead, with scores missing.

Receding rivers which rampaged down upon the lowlands Wednesday began giving up their victims yesterday and rescuers feared that the total death list might near the 100 mark.

Authorities, hampered by disrupted communications, progressed slowly in the search for bodies and check of property damage, believed to be tremendous.

Forty-seven identified bodies had been recovered at a late hour last night and twenty others were unidentified.

The unprecedented five-day storm which dumped 11.06 inches of water on the Los Angeles area brought the season's total rainfall to 21.73 inches as compared with 17.85 inches to date last season and a normal of 11.20 inches.

LONESOME METROPOLIS

Fair weather was forecast for today and tomorrow with snow in the mountains.

Los Angeles, for a time yesterday, was a lonesome metropolis, unable to communicate by

Other storm and flood news, including three full pages of pictures, will be found on Pages 2 to 10, Part I, inclusive.

rail, bus, airplane, telephone or telegraph with the outside world.

More than 3700 storm refugees in Los Angeles and Orange counties were quartered by relief agencies in theaters, schools, public halls and camp sites. Fifteen hundred homes in Los Angeles were declared uninhabitable.

A break in the Hoover Dam main power line left many sections of the Southland without electricity while others suffered from water shortage and failure of gas service.

CREWS CLEAR HIGHWAYS

City and county road crews of more than 1500 men began clearing miles of highways and city streets while traffic officers posted hundreds of detour signs directing traffic around washouts of roads and bridges.

School pupils will troop back to classes today after a two-day holiday, all schools save ten and those in the San Fernando Valley having been directed to reopen.

Tremendous losses of life and property were spared by the county's $50,000,000 investment in its vast flood control system, which was put to its severest test.

DAMAGE TO RANCHES

Damage to ranch lands and orchards was much less than anticipated, the greater losses being reported in strawberry acreages, avocado groves and small truck farms.

Co-ordination of city, county and Federal agencies on immediate reconstruction and repairs was sought by the City Council in session yesterday.

The Board of Supervisors announced it will seek State and

Turn to Page 2, Column 1

Death List at Latest Tabulation

At an early hour this morning the death list reached a total of forty-nine identified and twenty-one unidentified, with scores still reported as missing in the flood area. The identified dead were:

Carmen Alvidrez, 10 months of age, North Hollywood.

Warren H. Atherton, 2006 Los Encinos avenue, Glendale.

S. M. Bathgate, San Juan Capistrano.

Three Castro children, first names unknown, Wood, Orange county.

William Campbell, Riverside.

P. E. Caye, 24, sailor, U.S.S. Chicago.

John Croft, 50, 1135 West Seaside Boulevard, Long Beach.

Tiburcia Casas, 11, Atwood, Orange county.

Mrs. J. F. Daley, 70, San Bernardino.

Santaro Fujihara, 45, 7855 Whitsett Drive, North Hollywood.

Mrs. Fujihara, 40, same address.

John Doe Fujihara, 10, same address.

John Gentry, Riverside.

William V. Gray, 32, of 156 Mariposa street, Long Beach.

Walker Gray, 50, Griffith Park watchman.

Antonia Hurtado, a girl, 12, Anaheim.

Charles B. Hughes, 85, Santa Ana.

Mrs. Henry Lackey, Claremont.

Lydia Hernandez, 6 months, Anaheim.

Melba Lackey, 6, Claremont.

Malcom Massey, 19, Riverside.

Jimmy McDonell, 14, San Bernardino.

Jack Lackey, an infant son.

Mrs. Rogers Montano of Richfield, Orange county.

Carmelita Montano, 9, same address.

Wesley Munn, Santa Ana.

Charles E. Parks, San Juan Capistrano.

Mrs. Joseph Randall, 34, of 1952 Landa street, Los Angeles.

Leonard Travis Randall, 6, same address.

A Mr. Riggs of Atwood, Orange county.

Romando Ritana, 12, La Jolla, near Atwood.

Phillip R. S. Stevenson, Los Angeles.

Mrs. Lenora Swanson, 47, Anaheim.

Lynn Stewart, 24, of 52 South Daisy avenue, Long Beach.

W. E. Stone, 68, of 1337 West Ninety-fifth street.

Theresa Varragan, 19, of Atwood, Orange county.

Rudolph Varragan, 12, Atwood.

Baby Varragan, 3, Atwood.

Mrs. Rachel Whitman, 26, of 10524 Seabury Road.

Donald Whitman, infant boy, same address.

Fred Wilke, 919 Yolo street.

Jason Welborn, 2½, 4117 Camelia street, North Hollywood.

R. H. Wessing, 344 South Sixth street, San Jose.

Chuck Yount, sailor, U.S.S. Pennsylvania.

John Zeunigo, 10, Fullerton.

Bill McCarthy, 66, Ventura.

Eliseo Ayala, Ventura.

ANNOUNCEMENT!

Because wires were down most of the day The Times goes to press with only partial reports of the Associated Press, United Press and other press services which regularly serve this newspaper.

Telephonic contact with points in Los Angeles county and other portions of Southern California was made throughout the day and a full report of storm toll and damage is presented.

Because of wire trouble much telegraphic material so familiar to Times readers is missing. Crews of men worked throughout the day to re-establish contact with the outside world but only partial success met their efforts.

Through the courtesy of the Transradio Press Service, Inc., The Times is able to present a short-wave radio bulletin service received by that organization. This covers in brief form important news events throughout the world, and The Times wishes to acknowledge its gratitude to Transradio Press for its courtesy.

SCENE TYPICAL OF INUNDATED SOUTHLAND

Venice, which used to be a city of waterways, reverted to its former state, only more so, as a result of the Southland's record deluge. This picture is representative of all Southern California lowlands in the path of the flood.

Leon Miller aerial photo

Men Search Snowdrifts for Air Liner

Crews Press Hunt for Nine Missing in Mountain Wilds

More than 200 grim men last night pressed the search for a Los Angeles-bound air transport lost with nine persons aboard in the wilderness near 8000-foot-high Huntington Lake, fifty miles northeast of Fresno.

Scant news of their hunt—thus far unsuccessful—trickled through to Burbank, home base of Transcontinental and Western Air, Inc., operators of the ship which was bound to Albuquerque, N. M., by way of the Southland last Tuesday night.

PHONE LINES DOWN

Only the radio, linking Union Air Terminal at Burbank with the Fresno flying field, brought infrequent bulletins on the search. Telephone lines were down between the two cities.

Bad weather grounded a small fleet of Army Reserve, civilian and air-line planes at Fresno.

Without this aerial aid, searching parties wandered doggedly through the Sierra Nevada country around the Huntington and Shaver lakes area where numerous reports indicated the TWA craft was last seen on the stormy night of March 1.

Just one chance in a thousand still exists, air-line officials admitted, that Pilot John D. Graves could have effected a safe, pancake landing of his eleven-ton Douglas in some secluded valley sloping down to the San Joaquin.

LIST OF VICTIMS

Hope waned for these passengers who flew with Capt. Graves, First Officer C. W. Wallace and Hostess Martha Wilson:

H. N. Salisbury, TWA captain, of Kansas City, Mo.

Tracy Dirlam, Stanford University senior of Mansfield, O.

Mary Lou Dirlam, sophomore at Stanford, and Tracy's sister.

Mr. and Mrs. L. B. Walts of Bieber.

Victor Krause, Kansas City, Mo.

HEARD SHOTS FIRED

Only two clews appeared plausible to the weather-weary searchers who slogged up the mountains through slushy snow that sometimes reached their knees. A jagged peak above Huntington Lake showed a 300-foot-long scar which might, they believe, mark the place where the ship plunged to earth. The peak was reported almost inaccessible because of washouts.

Hopes that some of the nine persons might have survived the crash were aroused when Bud Rhodes of Fresno, who was at his cabin at Bass Lake, in the general area in which the plane is believed down, told TWA officials he heard what he believed was a plane crash late Tuesday night, followed two hours later by two shots.

He said the shots might have

Turn to Page 11, Column 1

Palm Springs Celebrities Ask for Help

Isolated by the raging floodwaters of the Whitewater River, hundreds of motion-picture celebrities and wealthy society and businessmen and women in Palm Springs yesterday appealed to Los Angeles for aid.

Earl Coffman, proprietor of the Desert Inn, anxious to supply children of the district with sufficient certified milk, chartered an airplane from the Paul Mantz Air Service to rush fresh supplies to the marooned vacationists this morning.

Stanley Hicks, pilot, is expected to take off with the plane with 400 pounds of food, including milk, bread, butter and meat

Five hundred candles also will be provided for the residents and fifty copies of the Los Angeles Times to give them first-hand information on latest news of the flood.

Isolation of 300 Arouses Fears

Many Families Driven From Their Homes by Rampaging Rivers

Grave fears were expressed over the condition of 300 persons marooned at Camp Baldy and near-by camps in San Antonio Canyon last night when all communication lines were down and roads were washed out.

Several houses and power substations are known to have been demolished.

Authorities were checking reports that eight persons were drowned and that Camp Baldy resort buildings were washed out.

BARRACKS WRECKED

Floods wrecked all but two barracks housing 150 men in a Bear Canyon transient camp and no food has been transported to them since Wednesday.

William Vernon succeeded in getting a message out from this camp, saying there were no danger and no loss of life there but property damage was heaviest of any storm on record.

ROAD WASHED OUT

The main road was washed out at Hogback, preventing travel to Camp Baldy, Bear Canyon, Icehouse Canyon, Snowcrest and other resorts.

M. A. Bard, theater manager, telephoned from the base of San Antonio Canyon to his brother, Arthur Bard, in Los Angeles, and said he had turned back after hiking seven miles with a rescue party because deep mud made further progress impossible.

Sisters of King Zog Open Charity Drive

NEW YORK, March 3. (TP)—The three sisters of King Zog of Albania today contributed $100 to start the 1938 citizens' appeal for the Salvation Army in Brooklyn. The Princesses visited the Brooklyn Nursery Hospital today to inspect the nursery and made their gift upon leaving.

Aerial View Shows Ruin in Vast Area

Riverside and Orange Counties Hardest Hit, Flying Reporter Finds

BY JAMES BASSETT, JR.

Noah, peering from the crow's nest of the Ark, must have seen water—a plentiful world of it.

But his low vantage point gave no perspective. Even had he taken his voyage in modern times he could not have visualized the panorama of desolation vouchsafed a Times reporter and cameraman yesterday.

From 3000 feet, a scene unfolds that groundlings can never grasp. Disaster, gutted farmlands, ruined roads, shattered communications, wrecked railroad lines—all leap into sharp-etched reality from that altitude.

SCENES OF MISERY

For two hours a United Air Lines Mainliner winged tirelessly over 250 miles of flooded Southland, across Los Angeles county to Riverside, then to San Bernardino, south along the rampant Santa Ana River to the wasted coastlands north of Newport Beach, and finally back over inundated Anaheim and Fullerton to Burbank.

As it sped, a kaleidoscope of human misery shifted beneath the plane.

Whipping over deserted schools, where playgrounds gleamed wetly under the first sunlight in days, the ship headed toward Riverside county from Burbank. Los Angeles can congratulate herself: Riverside and Orange took the brunt of the waters. Low-lying, they held the flood like gargantuan saucers.

HOW DISASTER BEGAN

One saw how the disaster began. Out of the mists of the Sierra Madres appeared little canyon streams, swollen and rushing. They flowed briskly southward. Then they reached the broad Santa Ana River—sometimes only a dusty tract where sagebrush grows. From 3000 feet the Santa Ana today looks like the muddy Mississippi at 10,000.

Resembling veins on a leaf, the streams and rivers fan toward the Pacific. Death and destruction lie in their wake.

Probably Foothill Boulevard can't offer ten miles without a washout or a wrecked bridge. Toward Riverside, one bridge in three seemed to have caved in. Hard-put, motorists desperately rerouted themselves along the railroad tracks at one point.

CARS PILE UP

Funny how drivers react to such situations. Like all-observant gods, the airplane watchers could observe the crawling cars far below. And a half hour before a motorist reached a barrier that finally ended his unhappy trip, they knew what disappointment awaited him.

At each ruined bridge and at every washed-out highway segment, scores of automobilists lingered—frustrated.

The Santa Ana River, follow-

Turn to Page 2, Column 8

Planes Attempt to Drop Food

Two Hundred Men Without Provisions at Big Tujunga

One unidentified man was reported dead and three were ill in the Sheriff's Boys' Club Camp in Big Tujunga Canyon last night, with two airplanes attempting to drop parcels of food on the provisionless encampment.

Five men of the original nine living at the camp were said to be in good health.

CHILDREN ISOLATED

At Camp No. 8 one man and two children were cut off from outside communication, and at Wildwood Lodge twenty-four men and women were marooned. The latter had a four-day supply of foodstuffs on hand.

In Trail Canyon, just off the main road of the Big Tujunga Canyon, nineteen men have taken refuge on the property of Deputy Sheriff Harry Pulfer, where provisions are adequate, and thirty other persons isolated in the canyon have a four-day food supply.

HUNDREDS TOIL

With water in the bottom of the Big Tujunga standing at more than six feet, 200 men working on the State Relief Administration project are reported without food or shelter. The State shacks, according to reports, have been swept away by the flood.

Check on Aqueduct Shows Little Damage

Despite failure of commercial telephone and telegraph lines of communication between Los Angeles and San Bernardino and points east, the Metropolitan Water District yesterday afternoon established communications along its entire construction front by means of a 500-mile combination short-wave radio and telephone hook-up.

Messages received over this communication system in the office of F. E. Weymouth, general manager of the water district, disclosed that there had been little damage to the Metropolitan Aqueduct in spite of the torrential rains which swept Southern California.

What Family Salvaged on Short Notice

Warned to evacuate their San Gabriel River home on short notice, here is what members of the family of Arthur Millier, Times art critic, chose to take Wednesday night.

Mother: four pieces old New England silverware and a Spanish shawl—"in case we needed to sell something," she explained—and Aldous Huxley's latest book, "Ends and Means."

Daughter Mojave, 10 years of age: three costume dolls, a bottle of cheap perfume and her 10-cent store jewelry.

Arthur, Jr., 14: harmonica.

David, 8: the Teddy bear he can't sleep without.

Dad: carton of cigarettes and old pair military hair brushes.

Gov. Croy's Wife Marooned

Visiting the Southland for the winter, Mrs. Helen Croy, wife of Gov. John Croy of Alaska, has become marooned with friends at Camp Rincon, a few miles above San Gabriel Dam No. 1.

This was disclosed yesterday by Robert D. Pearson of 334 South Westlake avenue, who expressed fear that the party's food supply may be too meager for a long isolation.

Pearson and his wife took Mrs. Croy, with Mrs. Shirley Morgan of 324 South Cliffwood avenue, Brentwood Park, and County Probation Officer Ethel Cummings to the cabin Sunday.

Envoy Wilson Greeted by Hitler

BERLIN, March 3. (TP)—The new United States Ambassador to Germany, Hugh Wilson, presented his credentials to Chancellor Hitler today.

Wilson told the German Chancellor that he brought President Roosevelt's best wishes for the prosperity of Germany.

Chancellor Hitler assured Ambassador Wilson that he and the German government will do everything possible to help improve relations between the United States and Germany.

Dead Hunted at Riverside

Silt-Covered Land to Be Searched for Bodies of Storm Victims

Riverside authorities today will begin the grim search through silt-covered lands adjoining the Santa Ana River bed for the bodies of an unknown number of persons who lost their lives in the city's greatest flood tragedy.

With estimates of the dead as low as five and as high as fifteen, Sheriff's and Coroner's deputies will scan a devastated area of several miles for traces of the victims of the drownings when a wall of water swept marooned motorists from a section of Mission Boulevard as they sought safety.

LIGHTNING KILLS YOUTH

Malcolm Massey, 19 years of age, was killed by lightning near Corona, bringing the known storm dead in the Riverside area to three.

Bodies of two flood victims were recovered but neither was identified. Both were men about 25.

CARING FOR HOMELESS

Scores of families driven from their homes were cared for by relief agencies while preparations were made for permanent housing. The West Riverside district, where scores of homes were surrounded by the swirling torrents of the Santa Ana River, set up a shelter at the schoolhouse. All the district's utilities were out of order.

Riverside was in darkness for ten hours during an interruption of electrical service.

Suspects Accused of Storm Looting

First arrests on suspicion of storm looting came last night when Frasimo Corral, 23 years of age, of 1705 East Fourth street, and Benny Garcia, 30, of 116½ South Mission street, were lodged in Van Nuys Jail.

Radio Officers Hargreaves and Kilain reported they found the pair looting an auto lodged against a bridge after being carried down the Big Tujunga Wash.

IN THE 'TIMES' TODAY

FRIDAY, MARCH 4, 1938

REMEMBER THIS

Success is won with a will, not with a wish.

ALL THE NEWS ALL THE TIME
LARGEST HOME-DELIVERED CIRCULATION
LARGEST ADVERTISING VOLUME
MAdison 2345
The Times Telephone Number
Connecting All Departments

Los Angeles Times

EQUAL RIGHTS
LIBERTY UNDER THE LAW · TRUE INDUSTRIAL FREEDOM

IN TWO PARTS — 46 PAGES
Part I — GENERAL NEWS — 22 Pages
TIMES OFFICES
202 West First Street
And Throughout Southern California

VOL. LVII · CC · FRIDAY MORNING, SEPTEMBER 30, 1938. · DAILY, FIVE CENTS

FOUR-POWER PEACE PACT SIGNED

TWENTY-SIX KILLED, 200 HURT IN DIXIE TORNADO

Property Damage Heavy When Raging Storm Sweeps Over Charleston, S. C.

CHARLESTON (S.C.) Sept. 29. (AP)—A raging tornado dipped furiously into Charleston early today, killing at least twenty-six persons, injuring between 200 and 300, and damaging hundreds of thousands of dollars worth of property.

Hours after the destructive twister struck, searchers dug into the ruins of wrecked buildings, and it is feared additional bodies will be recovered.

Hospitals listed fifty-three victims seriously hurt. Others were given first aid for comparatively minor injuries.

STORM STRIKES

This historic city was thrown into confusion as the storm, which lasted scarcely a minute, broke down power and communication facilities, and blocked streets with uprooted trees, poles and dangerous live wires.

Identified victims of the storm were:

Mrs. Ruth Mehrtens, 26 years of age.
Irvin H. Mehrtens, 3.
Miriam Ziegler, 14.
Floyd Singletary, 9.
Audie T. Redmond, 35.
S. L. Westcoat, 65.
C. F. Heathington, 54.
Marion H. Josey, 45.
Grace Belle Josey, 36.
Mary Belle Josey, 18.
Walter Franklin Josey, 5.
Gardenia Driggers.
Barbara Graham, 17.
Christina Oliver.
Eva Reeves, James Island.

Two companies of National Guardsmen were mobilized hastily to aid civilian authorities in handling the situation. They later were augmented by soldiers from near-by Fort Moultrie and marines from the navy yard, instructed by President Roosevelt to make their services available.

LANDMARKS DAMAGED

In Washington the President directed the War and Navy departments and the Works Progress Administration to render all possible aid.

Many of Charleston's landmarks, known to thousands of tourists, were damaged. Included were St. Michael's Episcopal Church, St. Philip's Church, a short distance away, both of which date to pre-Revolutionary times, and the quaint little Huguenot Church, only one of its denomination in the United States.

HOMES SHATTERED

Also damaged was the Dock-street Theater, one of the country's oldest, the ancient city market building and the historic City Hall.

Colleges and schools escaped unscathed, but many of the fine old homes overlooking the famous battery suffered shattered windows and damaged roofs.

Meteorologist J. E. Lockwood

Turn to Page 10, Column 6

Bowron Aims Ax at Board

Civil Service Heads Expected to Fall; Vice Squad Rejected

Mayor Bowron's official ax was poised over the heads of the Civil Service Commission last night as it was learned that the new Mayor is devoting most of his time to obtaining a new commission.

Bowron interrupted his selection of the new commission long enough yesterday to grab the new Mayoralty broom and sweep out of his office a so-called vice squad that had begun to use the place as a base of operations for conducting raids on vice and gambling resorts around the city.

SENT BACK TO DUTY

"It is not my purpose to have vice raids conducted out of this office," said Bowron as he directed that a squad of detectives assigned to his office be returned to their posts in the police department.

Bowron also directed that tips as to vice and gambling operations be turned over to Chief of Police Davis for action, thus effectively disposing of reports that Davis is being ignored in the vice clean-up.

EIGHTEEN RESIGN

Disclosure that the ax will fall first on the Civil Service Commission came in the course of a press conference at which he announced that thus far eighteen members of commissions in response to his request had sent in their resignations. To date he has not acted on any.

"I am devoting nearly all my

Turn to Page 6, Column 1

Squirrel Cuts Lights for 800 Homes

PADUCAH (Ky.) Sept. 29. (AP)—A gray squirrel jumped from a tree to a power line with these results:

The squirrel was burned to death.

Three power lines were severed.

Eight hundred homes were without lights for several hours.

Total damage, $500.

FIRST PICTURE OF HISTORIC EUROPEAN PEACE MEETING

Here is the first photograph of yesterday's Munich peace conference to arrive in America. It shows, left to right, Field Marshal Goering of Germany, Nazi Fuehrer Hitler, an unidentified man, Count Ciano of Italy, Premier Mussolini of Italy, Premier Daladier of France and Prime Minister Chamberlain of Great Britain. (AP) Radio Wirephoto

Dewey to Run for Governor

New York G.O.P. Nominates Prosecutor by Acclamation

SARATOGA SPRINGS (N.Y.) Sept. 29. (U.P.)—New York District Attorney Thomas E. Dewey accepted the Republican nomination for Governor tonight with a blunt declaration to the convention which nominated him by acclamation that to have refused would have been "shirking the bigger job, the harder fight."

Dewey, "drafted" after less than a year as prosecutor of New York county, promised to continue his efforts to break the alliance between gangsters and politicians.

DEWEY'S PLEDGE

He said as Governor he could do a larger job in his war on crime, adding:

"I specifically promised my assistants (district attorneys) would not be chosen by Al Marinelli, Charles Schneider or any of the other district leaders who are now selecting my opponent at the Democratic State convention.

"BUILD, NOT TEAR DOWN"

"That promise has been kept and the record shows what its results have been. In that office there is now a staff of seventy-two able, energetic, high-principled lawyers.

"They can and will keep on do-

Turn to Page 5, Column 2

POPE BROADCASTS PLEA TO PRAY FOR WORLD PEACE

CASTEL GANDOLFO, Sept. 29. (AP)—Pope Pius directed the world's faithful today to turn to "the invincible power of prayer" to save the world from the "threat of unexampled slaughter and ruin."

The Pope's voice was weak and toward the end it quivered as the aging pontiff broadcast his plea from his summer palace over the Vatican's own radio station.

He spoke in Italian over the world-wide hook-up that carried his voice to Europe and the Americas and gave his benediction in Latin at the end.

PASTORAL LETTER

Translations of his words in English, German, French, Czech and other languages were broadcast immediately after he concluded.

"The Pope's message was in the form of a pastoral letter addressed to the bishops, faithful and clergy. He read it to them under the shadow of the meeting at Munich where the heads of Western Europe's four most powerful governments were meeting to try to save Europe from war.

The Holy Father called for prayers that the "sentiments and action" of all concerned should correspond to their "reiterated words of peace" and which would be "suited to foster peace and establish it upon the secure basis of law and gospel teachings."

PONTIFF'S APPEAL

The Pope said:

"While millions of men are still living in dread because of the imminent danger of war and because of the threat of unexampled slaughter and ruin, we gather into our paternal heart the trepidation of our children and we invite the bishops, clergy, the religious and the faithful to unite themselves with us in the most undaunted and insistent prayer for the preservation in justice and in charity of the peace.

"To this unarmed but invincible power of prayer let people have recourse once yet again so that God, in whose hands rest the destinies of the world, may

Turn to Page 4, Column 3

County's Total Registration Near 1,500,000 for New Record

While hundreds of clerks remained at their posts until midnight last night registering crowds of voters, Registrar of Voters Kerr estimated the registration for the November 8 election may reach 1,500,000—one of the largest in the history of the county.

Registration closed promptly at midnight as scores of persons sought last-minute registration at Kerr's office on South Broadway.

DEPUTIES BUSY

In various parts of the downtown section, a squad of deputy registrars were busy accommodating voters who had moved since their last registration, or had just become of age, or had completed one year's residence in the State.

Kerr—nearing the end of one of the heaviest years in the history of his office—pointed out that voters must have voted either in the August primary or vote in the November election in order to keep their names in the registration books.

OFFICIAL COUNT

It will be several days before an official count of the registration can be made, he said, due to the heavy registration brought about mainly because of the $30 every Thursday and single tax amendments which will appear on the ballot.

Despair Grips Czech Nation

Roosevelt Mediation Suggested as Last Hope in Crisis

PRAGUE, Sept. 30 (Friday) (U.P.)—Czechoslovak leaders early today turned in desperation to President Roosevelt, anxious for him to mediate a settlement of the Sudeten crisis and save the republic from dismemberment dictated by the "big four" conference in Munich.

The Munich peace agreement had not reached Prague early today, but President Benes and the government of Premier Gen. Jan Syrovy awaited it with deep pessimism, believing Czechoslovakia is being called upon to pay an exorbitant price for European peace.

CABINET DETERMINED

Having informed Britain and France yesterday it agrees to the original Anglo-French plan of territorial revision which the former Czech government approved on September 21, the Syrovy Cabinet appeared firmly determined to resist further sacrifices.

From the man in the street to the highest political personalities of the nation everyone is depressed and downcast. There is an evident impression everywhere the Czechs would rather fight, even alone, than have amputation forced upon them.

HOPE IN ROOSEVELT

Political circles said President Roosevelt offers Czechoslovakia's great hope in the nation's hour of need because he has openly expressed an interest in the Czech people and their fate.

Any offer by him to mediate or arbitrate would be acceptable

Turn to Page 3, Column 5

Trachoma Attacks Twelve of Family

SANTA ROSA, Sept. 29. (AP)—Health officers discovered a family of twelve persons all infected with trachoma today, some so seriously they may go blind, and expressed fear the infection already was being spread to transient camps about the State.

Edward Vaughan, 54-year-old father of ten children ranging in age from 16 years to 8 months, already has lost the sight of his left eye, and that of his right one is threatened, Dr. H. M. Every, eye specialist of Sonoma county, reported.

The family is camping in a tent at Sebastopol, where health investigators reported finding them living in squalor and extreme poverty.

PICKETS REDOUBLE WATCH ON PRIEST HELD SEVEN WEEKS

VULCAN (Mich.) Sept. 29. (U.P.) One hundred and fifty pickets milled about the rectory of St. Barbara's Catholic Church today determined to resist any new attempt to liberate Rev. Simon Borkowski, whom they have held a prisoner for nearly seven weeks.

The pickets are his parishioners. Two months ago his superiors ordered him to transfer to the Salvatoriam Seminary at St. Nazianz, Wis., but the parishioners were determined to keep him. When he attempted to leave August 14 they established a twenty-four-hour picket line and told him he would never get away.

They lost him for a time yesterday but got him back after rioting in which at least five men were beaten, two severely.

Sudetenland Given to Hitler

Compromise Plan Adopted at Munich Calls for Nazi Troops to Begin Occupying Czech Territory Tomorrow

MUNICH, Sept. 30. (Friday.) (U.P.)—Britain, France, Germany and Italy early today signed a compromise agreement for surrender of Czechoslovakia's strife-torn Sudeten areas to Germany without bloodshed.

Details of the plan were immediately sent to Czechoslovakia which, if it refuses to accept the terms, must face Germany without any help from France or Great Britain.

In Prague officials refused comment pending arrival of the text of the agreement but their complete pessimism was apparent.

RACE TO HEAD OFF WAR

The agreement of the "big four," racing against time to head off a general war, came only twenty-four hours before the October 1 "zero hour" fixed by Adolf Hitler for an invasion of the Sudetenland.

Germany's occupation of the Sudeten border areas with a "token force" of Nazi troops will begin Saturday—the day

Full page of pictures on Page 22, Part I.

that millions had looked forward to with fright as the day of war—and will be completed by October 10.

An international police force of British, French and Italian patrols will move into the German areas farther in the interior and take over authority pending plebiscites—on the lines of the Saar voting—which must be held within two months.

CLAIMS OF OTHER MINORITIES

In an annex to the plan of surrendering the Sudetenland to Hitler, the four powers specified that the claims of the Polish and Hungarian minorities under Prague's rule must be settled within three months—either by plebiscites or direct agreements. Pending this Great Britain and France will stand by the previous offer to guarantee the new boundaries of Czechoslovakia.

Then, when the Polish and Hungarian questions are satisfactorily out of the way, Germany and Italy will join Britain and France in a formal guarantee of the "new Czechoslovakia's" integrity, pledging themselves against any further dismemberment.

WEARY AND DEJECTED

Announcement of the signing of the agreement was made by Prime Minister Neville Chamberlain of Great Britain at 12:30 a.m. as he emerged, weary and dejected, from the brownstone Fuehrerhaus where the four statesmen had worked through the day and most of the night.

The decision of peace or war under the plan they devised no longer rests with Fuehrer Adolf Hitler, but is up to President Eduard Benes and the Czech government.

The conferees of the four western powers—Hitler, Chamberlain, Premier Benito Mussolini of Italy and Premier Edouard Daladier of France—were confident that Czechoslovakia would be prevailed upon to accept the decisions.

Czechoslovakia has indicated that she will vigorously oppose any settlement involving the use of an international "police force," insisting that any minorities settlement must be by means of consultation, but it was generally believed the Prague government will submit under Anglo-French pressure.

MUSSOLINI GOES HOME

Britain and France will be able to tell Prague that, in the nine hours of historic consultation here, they have prevailed on Hitler to moderate his warlike demands and ultimatums and compromise in a plan of peaceful settlement.

Two representatives of the Czech government left Munich early today for Prague with copies of the proposals and Prime Minister Chamberlain reportedly planned to remain in Munich until 4 p.m. in anticipation of a Czech answer.

Mussolini, who played a major role in bringing about the eleventh-hour escape from a war that threatened the lives of millions, left for home immediately after the conference aboard his special train. Chamberlain and Daladier planned to fly back to Paris and London to report to their Cabinets.

PROVISIONS OF PLAN

The compromise plan provides:

(1.) The evacuation of the predominantly Sudeten German regions of Czechoslovakia will begin Saturday and must be completed within ten days, meaning their occupation by German forces.

(2.) The agreement is among Germany, Britain, France and Italy and Czechoslovakia is not included in it.

(3.) The Czechs must evacuate the regions without destroying any property, including factories, railroad lines and communications lines. The Czech government is "held responsible for the evacuation without damage to the installations."

(4.) The conditions and terms of the evacuation will be laid in detail by an international commission to be com-

Turn to Page 2, Column 3

IN THE 'TIMES' TODAY

FRIDAY, SEPTEMBER 30, 1938

RADIO. Page 14, Part I.
COMICS. Page 11, Part II.
FASHIONS, CLUBS, SOCIETY. Pages 5, 6, 7, 8, 9, Part II.
FINANCIAL. Pages 18, 19, 20, 21, Part I.
OIL. Page 18, Part I.
PUZZLE. Page 16, Part I.
DRAMA. Pages 16, 17, Part I.
SHIPPING. Page 21, Part I.
WEATHER. Page 14, Part I.
PICTORIAL PAGE. Page 22, Part I.

FINANCIAL. Pacific Telephone reports eight months' earnings; March of Finance; Chicago grain prices irregular; Stocks continue upward climb. Page 18, Part I.

THE SOUTHLAND. Proposal to bring in outside W.P.A. labor for prison work protested at Chino. Throngs join in prayer for peace at Santa Monica. Page 10, Part II.

SPORTS. Chicago Cubs rout Pirates, 10-1. Page 13, Part II.

Gene Mako in triple victory. Page 13, Part II.

Loyola plays College of Pacific tonight. Page 13, Part II.

THE CITY. Mayor Bowron's ax poised over Civil Service Commission. Page 1, Part I.

Community Chest donors to be asked for fifth more than last year. Page 1, Part II.

Friday Morning Club today will formally receive Sartori library gift. Page 1, Part II.

European peace prospect discussed in message from Sproul, en route home after trip abroad. Page 4, Part I.

All-school hobby show under way today and tomorrow. Page 1, Part II.

Guaranty Liquidating Corporation control suit goes to trial today. Page 3, Part II.

Norma Shearer agrees to payment in settlement of government tax suit. Page 1, Part II.

Sturzenacker's hopes for yacht cited in oil investigation. Page 1, Part II.

WASHINGTON. Gen. Arnold appointed chief of Army Air Corps. Page 13, Part I.

President asks Americans to join with Roosevelt family in prayers for peace. Page 3, Part I.

Radio station's license periled over "Beyond the Horizon" broadcast. Page 10, Part I.

THE WEST. Downey still supports $30 pension plan after conference with President. Page 5, Part I.

Use of liftboards in handling cargo allowed by ruling of arbiter in port dispute. Page 9, Part I.

Bay area's union row flares anew with closing of drug house over hot boxcar. Page 9, Part I.

GENERAL EASTERN. Twenty-six killed when tornado strikes Dixie. Page 1, Part I.

New York Republican gubernatorial nomination. Page 1, Part I.

Pickets seek to prevent new attempt to liberate priest held seven weeks. Page 1, Part I.

FOREIGN. Powers sign pact giving Sudeten areas in Czechoslovakia to Hitler. Page 1, Part I.

Gen. Ugaki resigns as Japan's Foreign Minister. Page 13, Part I.

Pope broadcasts call for peace prayers to world. Page 1, Part I.

REMEMBER THIS

None need condemn himself to ignorance to preserve hope.

ALL THE NEWS ALL THE TIME
LARGEST HOME-DELIVERED CIRCULATION
LARGEST ADVERTISING VOLUME
MAdison 2345
The Times Telephone Number

Los Angeles Times
EQUAL RIGHTS — LIBERTY UNDER THE LAW — TRUE INDUSTRIAL FREEDOM

IN THREE PARTS — 44 PAGES
Part 1 — GENERAL NEWS — 30 Pages
TIMES OFFICE
202 West First Street

VOL. LVIII CCC FRIDAY MORNING, SEPTEMBER 1, 1939. DAILY, FIVE CENTS

GERMAN ARMY INVADES POLAND

British Mobilize Army and Fleet

London, Standing Firm Behind Poland, Speeds to Full War Footing as She Hears With Gravity Latest Hitler Moves

LONDON, Sept 1 (Friday.) (AP)—(6:46 a.m.)—(Passed Through British Censorship)—Great Britain, standing pat on her pledge to fight for Poland's independence, received the news of Germany's latest moves in the European crisis with the deepest gravity today as the nation moved swiftly toward a full war footing.

An immediate Cabinet meeting was expected to survey the implications both of Germany's eleventh-hour 16-point proposal to Poland and Hitler's early morning order to the German army on the Polish border to meet force with force.

Government offices, after a night marked by intense activity, were empty of officials authorized to speak when news of Hitler's instructions to the army were received. But this, together with the radio announcement of the German aerial attack on Polish cities and the German navy's blockade of the Polish port of Gdynia, created a stir among those on duty.

SPEEDY ACTION

Attention was attracted particularly by the speed with which the army order and harbor blockade followed the German broadcast which said Hitler had proposed to Poland hat Danzig be returned to the Reich and that a plebiscite be held to decide whether Pomorze (the Polish Corridor) should be Polish or German territory.

Meanwhile, with the British fleet mobilizing swiftly under the order issued yesterday and the entire army reserve called up, Britain began the evacuation of 3,000,000 women, children and infirm from the danger areas.

TRAINS REMOVE MANY

Suburban trains ran on skeleton schedules so that the rolling stock would be available to handle the exodus from London. Many of the London underground stations were closed except to those being evacuated.

It was learned authoritatively that the British position is that the proposals broadcast from Germany last night "are not a reply to any British proposals" and that the 16 points reached Poland last night for the first time.

Official sources said Germany still has given no answer of any kind to the British note asking for clarification of points in a previous communication from Hitler.

ONE OF TWO THINGS

Speaking purely privately a British informant said he thought Hitler's radio bombshell means one of two things:

1.—An attempt to show the world Hitler has made a magnanimous offer which the Poles

Turn to Page 6, Column 3

Henry Tells of War Work

'Times' Man Declares Britons Cheerful in Midst of Preparation

BY BILL HENRY
Times Staff Representative

LONDON, Aug. 31.—Dark clouds that hung like a pall over London this morning held more than rain.

War threat thunderbolts followed one another so rapidly that only so courageous a race as the British could swarm over sandbagged and partially darkened streets as they're doing tonight on the eve of a day which may bring anything.

At noon the government announced the evacuation of children from population centers and two hours later came an announcement that the stock exchange was closed until further notice.

Two hours later mobilization of the entire navy, regular army and reserves and the Royal Air Force and volunteer reserve was ordered.

Two hours later came the mobilization of air raid precaution units and official scrutiny of all press dispatches. Despite official emphasis on the precautionary nature of these moves, the feeling still persists that a definite showdown has arrived.

The government either feels

Turn to Page 7, Column 4

Windsor Telegraphs Hitler for Peace

LONDON, Sept. 1 (Friday) (U.P.)—The News Chronicle said in an undated dispatch today that the Duke of Windsor sent a personal telegram to Adolf Hitler early this week begging him to make every possible effort to keep peace.

Hitler did not reply.

Pact Ratified by Germany and Russia

Approval by Supreme Soviet Unanimous as Treaty Reasons Told

MOSCOW, Aug. 31. (U.P.)—Russia and Germany tonight ratified their momentous nonaggression treaty which creates a new alignment in world power politics.

Reports from Berlin, meanwhile, indicated that a Russian mission was on the way to Berlin possibly to reach a military alliance with the Reich.

Ratification of the nonaggression pact was effected here by the Supreme Soviet of the U.S.S.R. and was given in Berlin at the same time by the German government.

The vote of the Supreme Soviet was unanimous.

The vote was taken at 8:45 p.m. after Premier and Foreign Minister V. M. Molotoff, who summoned the high parliamentary body in special session to approve the agreement, had explained the reasons which caused Josef Stalin to reverse the whole trend of his foreign policy.

SPEAKS FOR HOUR

Molotoff spoke for nearly an hour.

"In the present world situation it is hard to overestimate the significance of the Soviet-German treaty," Molotoff said.

"This treaty is a turning point in the relation between Germany and the Soviet Union. Only yesterday we were enemies in the field of foreign policy. Today, however, we no longer are enemies. The political art in diplomacy is not to increase the number of enemies but to decrease them and make yesterday's enemies today's friends and maintan relations with them.

"History shows that the hostility between Germany and the Soviet Union was harmful to both. The peoples of the Soviet Union and Germany need a peace treaty."

NO REASON TO REFUSE

After explaining the negotiation of a trade pact between the Soviet Union and Germany, Molotoff said that "when the German government expressed a desire to improve political relations as well, the Soviet government had no grounds for refusing."

Molotoff then explained how the Soviet government could bring itself to dealing with an opposed ideology.

"Voices are now being heard testifying to a lack of understanding of the most simple reasons for improvement of political relations between the Soviet Union and Germany which has begun," he said. "For example,

Turn to Page 4, Column 3

LATE BULLETINS

WASHINGTON, Sept. 1 (Friday.) (U.P.)—President Roosevelt announced early today that he had received official word that Germany had invaded Poland. He was advised officially by the American Ambassador at Warsaw and William C. Bullitt at Paris. The President immediately directed that all navy ships and all American army commands be notified at once by radio of the developments.

GLEIWITZ (Germany) Sept. 1 (Friday) (A.P.)—An army ambulance carrying wounded soldiers arrived at the emergency hospital here today at 9:10 a.m. (12:10 a.m., P.S.T.) The men, carried in a wagon, were on stretchers. It could not be ascertained where the ambulance came from. Early today Gleiwitz residents reported artillery fire was heard "in the distance" a few miles from the Polish-Silesian border.

BERNE (Switzerland) Sept. 1 (Friday.) (A.P.)—The Neue Zurcher, Zeitung's correspondent in Berlin, wrote today: "It is declared here categorically that the Fuehrer's proclamation amounts to opening a state of war. Military operations were begun at 6 a.m. along the entire German-Polish frontier."

BRUSSELS, Sept. 1 (Friday.) (AP) (Passed by British Censor)—The Belgian Cabinet early today ordered the third stage of mobilization effective immediately as a precautionary move.

LONDON, Sept. 1 (Friday.) (A.P.)—A Reuters dispatch from Paris said: "The following is given with all reserve: According to unconfirmed reports received here the Germans have begun an offensive with extreme violence on the whole Polish front."

LONDON, Sept. 1 (Friday.) (A.P.)—Reuters (British news agency) said today in a Warsaw dispatch that the ocial Warsaw radio announced German troops had launched a full scale attack against towns in the Polish Corridor.

LONDON, Sept. 1 (Friday.) (U.P.)—Evacuation of the "first hundred" of London's school children began at 5:30 a.m.

LONDON, Sept. 1 (Friday.) (A.P.)—The British Parliament was summoned to meet today at 5 p.m. (8 a.m., P.S.T.)

PARIS, Sept. 1 (Friday.) (A.P.)—Edouard Daladier, Premier and War Minister of France, informed that German troops crossed the Polish frontier today, summoned an urgent meeting of his Cabinet for 10:30 a.m. (1:30 a.m., P.S.T.) It was probable that Parliament would be called tomorrow.

BERLIN, Sept. 1 (Friday.) (U.P.)—Notices mobilizing downtown civil air defense members appeared in the windows of downtown restaurants and shops about 9 a.m.

Eleventh-Hour War Moves Told in Brief

BY THE ASSOCIATED PRESS

Developments leading Europe to the brink of war last night and early today included:

BERLIN—Hitler orders German army to "meet force with force," declares Poland dangerous territory for foreigners, and orders naval blockade of Polish port of Gdynia; sharp border clashes occur along Polish-German frontier; Hitler publishes 16-point plan for settlement of quarrel with Poland; plan far less drastic than previous demands but still provides for immediate return of Danzig; proposes plebiscite for Polish Corridor; press announces Poland has "rejected" proposals; Hitler may address world today through Reichstag.

LONDON—Britain mobilizes fleet, calls up entire army reserve, brings air force to wartime strength, imposes censorship, restricts food buying and begins to evacuate 3,000,000 women and children from congested areas in sweeping preparations for war; German spokesman indicates German proposals not final.

WARSAW—Krakow and other Polish cities bombed by German warplanes. Poland's Foreign Office formally charges aggression by Germany. Both moves follow statement by Polish government spokesman that Hitler's terms are unacceptable.

PARIS—Cabinet in special meeting reaffirms pledge to help Poland; reported without confirmation Italy has proposed six-power peace conference for next Tuesday.

MOSCOW—Russian Parliament unanimously ratifies German-Soviet nonaggression pact after Premier Molotoff says British-French-Russian mutual assistance pact negotiations ran into insurmountable obstacles.

ROME—Mussolini continues frantic last-hour efforts for peace, but splits army command for actual war.

Poles Spurn Berlin Terms; Troops Move

Warsaw Determined to Hold Corridor and Retain Danzig Rights

WARSAW, Aug. 31. (AP)—The conditions of Fuehrer Hitler's proposals for settlement of the Polish-German dispute, such as immediate return of Danzig to Germany, are inacceptable to Poland, a government spokesman said tonight.

The spokesman emphasized that Poland is determined to keep Pomorze (the Polish Corridor) and her rights in the Free City of Danzig.

"WILL NOT YIELD"

Of Hitler's proposal for a plebiscite in Pomorze, one reaction here was: "Germany can begin with Czechoslovakia if she is interested in a plebiscite."

In reply to Hitler's "terms" as announced by the German radio tonight, it was stated Poland will insist upon full restitution of her rights in Danzig.

Danzig is under Polish customs administration, and certain Polish customs and railway functions have been reported taken over by Nazis in the past few days.

HOPE FADES

"Hitler insists on Poland yielding Danzig and Pomorze as a preliminary to negotiations," the spokesman said. "Poland has not given up Danzig and Pomorze, and will not.

"Britain, in a second reply to Hitler, has maintained her unyielding position without change."

He emphasized that Poland always has been interested in a peaceful settlement, but that the conditions of the proposals cannot be accepted.

As the spokesman disclosed that the government had refused to send a mission to Berlin to talk with Hitler, as the Fuehrer proposed, hope for peace faded.

TEN HELD IN PLOT

Sir Howard William Kennard, the British Ambassador, called upon Foreign Minister Joseph Beck to reiterate Britain's stand in support of Poland in case of aggression against her, it was reported.

It was reported that 10 Germans had been arrested on charges of plotting to dynamite

Turn to Page 8, Column 4

Polish Raid Takes France By Surprise

Attack News Arrives as Papers Continue Hope

PARIS, Sept. 1 (Friday.) (AP)—Havas (French news agency) said today that the Polish Embassy here had announced that "Germany violated the Polish frontier at four points."

The report caught Paris by surprise on a sunny morning when newspapers were proclaiming that "French and British firmness can still save peace."

An hour after the first report was received there still was no official reaction.

Dutch Steamer Takes 500 Americans Home

AMSTERDAM, Aug. 31. (AP)—With the departure of 500 Americans for New York today aboard the Dutch steamer Johan Van Oldenbarnevelt, all Americans wishing to leave The Netherlands now have gone. United States Consul Frank Lee announced.

The 500 aboard the Dutch ship came from all parts of Europe.

Battles Rage Along Border

Cities Bombed as Fuehrer Orders Troops to "Meet Force With Force" on Frontier; Harbor Blockaded and Neutral Ships Warned

WARSAW, Sept. 1. (U.P.)—Germans bombed Warsaw at 9 a.m. today (11 p.m. Thursday) (P.S.T.) Simultaneously the Polish government announced today that Germans had bombed five other places, including the railroad station at Czew and the town of Rypnic, as well as the town of Putzk near Czew.

The Warsaw Foreign Office immediately charged Germany with aggression against Poland.

Military circles said that "apparently general fighting has begun at most parts of the frontier."

BERLIN, Sept. 1. (Friday) (AP)—The German army was ordered to "meet force with force," and Poland was declared dangerous territory for foreigners by Adolf Hitler at 5:30 a.m. today (8:30 p.m. Thursday, P.S.T.)

At the same time a naval blockade of the Polish port of Gdynia was announced.

The Fuehrer proclaimed his action was because of alleged Polish violations of the German frontier.

Shortly after this, Nazi Leader Albert Forster of Danzig announced the Anschluss of Danzig and Germany, and Hitler made formal acceptance of

Additional news and pictures on European crisis will be found on Pages A to 9 inclusive.

Danzig, proclaiming German law in effect there and terminating the old Versailles Treaty constitution.

Simultaneously, dispatches from Warsaw reported that a number of Polish border towns had been bombed by German army planes, and that the sirens were blowing in Warsaw as its inhabitants awaited an attack by German bombers.

Neutral ships in the Baltic were warned they entered Danzig Harbor or near-by harbors at their own peril.

The announcement said military operations necessitated these measures.

HITLER ADDRESSES REICHSTAG

Four and a half hours after casting the die, the Fuehrer appeared before a specially called session of the Reichstag and in a speech broadcast throughout the world defended his course and declared Germany is prepared to meet "bomb with bomb" in the settlement of the Polish question.

"I have decided to speak to the Poles in the same language they are speaking to us," he said, referring to Polish mobilization.

The German Chancellor promised to be the "first soldier of the Reich."

GOERING NAMED SUCCESSOR

He named Field Marshal Hermann Goering as his successor, "should anything happen to me in this struggle."

"From now on I belong to my people as never before," he said.

Should, he continued, anything happen to "my friend Goering," the next in line to carry on the Fuehrer's duties is Minister Rudolph Hess."

"If anything should happen to Hess, then the Senate shall be called to appoint the most worthy of the people."

Hitler's command was issued as the order of the day to the army massed on Polish frontiers from

Turn to Page A, Column 2

IN THE 'TIMES' TODAY

FRIDAY
SEPTEMBER 1, 1939

REMEMBER THIS

You can't preserve hope in the ice box of ignorance.

ALL THE NEWS ALL THE TIME
LARGEST HOME-DELIVERED CIRCULATION
LARGEST ADVERTISING VOLUME
MAdison 2345
The Times Telephone Number

Los Angeles Times

EQUAL RIGHTS
LIBERTY UNDER THE LAW — TRUE INDUSTRIAL FREEDOM

IN THREE PARTS — 46 PAGES
Part I — GENERAL NEWS — 30 Pages
TIMES OFFICE
202 West First Street

VOL. LIX — CCC — TUESDAY MORNING, APRIL 9, 1940. — DAILY, FIVE CENTS

GERMANS INVADE DENMARK; NORWAY AT WAR WITH NAZIS

Deportation Bill Vetoed by President

Penalties Provided in Alien Ouster Measure Declared Too Harsh

WASHINGTON, April 8. (AP)—President Roosevelt vetoed the Starnes alien deportation bill today, maintaining that its penalties for alien spies and saboteurs were "superfluous" and that its application to narcotic addicts was too harsh.

The bill would require the deportation of alien spies, saboteurs, narcotic peddlers and addicts.

When the measure was before the House, Representative Starnes (D.) Ala., explained that his bill made such deportations mandatory while under present law deportation is discretionary with the Labor Secretary.

TEXT OF MESSAGE

The text of the President's message vetoing the Starnes bill follows:

"I am returning herewith, without my approval, a bill to provide for the prompt deportation of aliens engaging in espionage or sabotage, alien criminals, and other undesirable aliens.

"This bill provides for the deportation of three classes of aliens, irrespective of whether they entered the United States before or after passage of the act.

"In the first group are aliens who have been convicted or have voluntarily admitted in writing that they have engaged in espionage or sabotage affecting the national defense or the foreign relations of the United States, since entering into the United States.

HELD SUPERFLUOUS

"I am in full accord with the view that the government should be empowered to deal firmly and effectively with persons guilty of espionage or sabotage. With that end in view, several months ago I instructed the Federal Bureau of Investigation of the Department of Justice to co-ordinate and take charge of the investigation of offenses of this character, in conjunction with the military and naval intelligence services. A few days ago I approved a bill that substantially increased the maximum penalties that may be imposed on persons convicted of such crimes.

"Ample authority is found in the existing law for the depor-

Turn to Page A, Column 1

Roosevelt Will Rush to Capital

HYDE PARK (N.Y.) April 9. (AP) — President Roosevelt communicated with the State Department by telephone early today over the Northern European crisis. Aides awakened him with the news shortly before 4 a.m. and he immediately got in touch with Washington. Meanwhile, a secretary set about making arrangements, if feasible, to have a special train rushed here to return the President to the capital as soon as possible.

County Voters Show Gain

Registration Total for Primary Election Discloses G.O.P. Increase

Registration figures for the May 7 Presidential primary election, released yesterday by Registrar of Voters William M. Kerr, show:

1.—A total county registration of 1,547,527.

2.—A gain over the November, 1938, registration of 31,459 and a gain over the November, 1936, registration of 150,921.

3.—A slackening of wide Democratic gains from 1936 to 1938.

REPUBLICAN GAIN

From 1936 to 1938 the Democratic registration gained an imposing 97,833 to a Republican gain of 3109. The current figures show that from 1938 to date the Democrats have gained 16,330 to the Republicans' 11,781.

Los Angeles city shows a total registration of 853,212, including 263,164 Republicans and 534,858 Democrats.

REGISTRATION DIVIDED

Of the total county registration 771,725 are men, 775,802 are women. Corresponding figures in the city show 428,400 men and 424,812 women.

The county registration, bro-

Turn to Page A, Column 6

Hull Notified by Envoy of Oslo's Action

Mrs. Harriman Cables News Norway Considers Self at War With Reich

WASHINGTON, April 8. (AP)—Mrs. J. Borden Harriman, American Minister to Norway, notified the State Department tonight that the Norwegian Foreign Minister had informed her that Norway is at war with Germany.

The State Department issued the following statement:

"The American Minister to Oslo, Mrs. J. Borden Harriman, telegraphed to the Department of State tonight that the Foreign Minister has informed her that the Norwegians fired on four German warships coming up Oslo Fjord and that Norway is at war with Germany.

BRITISH REQUEST

"In response to a request by the British Minister to Norway, the American Legation at Oslo has been authorized to take over British interests in Norway if he is forced to evacuate."

The Norwegian Minister to the United States, Wilhelm de Morgenstierne, was in conversation with the State Department shortly before midnight.

The department, where a night watch has been maintained constantly since the outbreak of the European war, stirred quickly to activity. Officials there hurried to their offices.

WHITE HOUSE LIGHTS

Across the street, lights burned in the White House executive offices although President Roosevelt was at his Hyde Park home.

There was no comment from officials here as to whether the President would take immediate steps to issue a proclamation under the Neutrality Act adding Norway to the list of belligerents.

Such action undoubtedly would be coupled with a proclamation forbidding American ships to enter Norwegian waters. The present "combat zone" from which these vessels now are banned ends just south of Bergen, Norway.

OFFICIAL NEWS WAITED

When the State Department issued its dispatch from Mrs. Harriman, the Norwegian Minister said he had received no direct word yet from the government at Oslo.

At that time the State Depart-

Turn to Page 3, Column 3

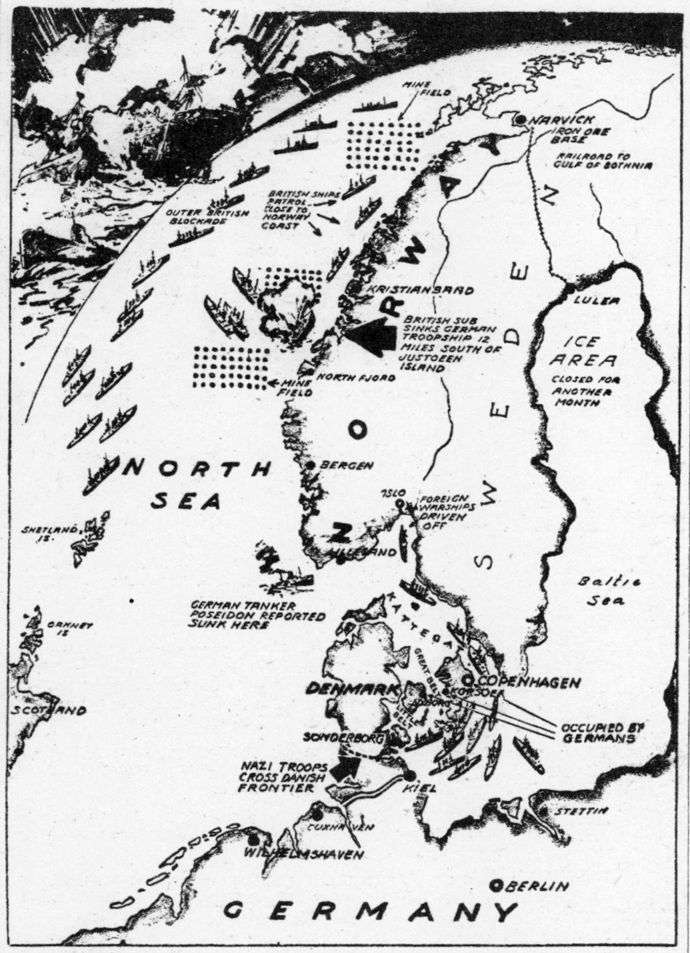

NEW WAR ARENA—Here is where Germany in a lightning stroke brought both Denmark and Norway into the European war situation last night. The map was prepared by Times staff artists.

Oslo Bombed; Troops Landed

Danish Forces Retreating Before Enemy; Armed Transports Reach Copenhagen; Other Key Cities Expected to Fall Quickly

Illustrated on Page B

PARIS, April 9. (A.P.)—The Oslo radio announced today that the Norwegian capital had been bombarded several times from the air and that the government had ordered that it be abandoned by the civilian population within two days.

NEW YORK, April 9 (Tuesday.) (A.P.) Swedish radio reports picked up here early today said that Sweden had ordered general mobilization.

LONDON, April 9 (Tuesday.) (U.P.)—Germany invaded Denmark today and was reported to be carrying out rapidly a bloodless occupation of the little Scandinavian kingdom.

Simultaneously it was announced that Norway is "at war" with Germany.

The Norwegian stand, it is understood, is based on a declaration by the government that Norway automatically would be "at war" with any power which invaded Norwegian territory.

German warships entered the Oslo Fjord early today and had a brisk engagement with Norwegian craft and shore batteries.

This act was considered a "start of war."

TROOPS MASS NEAR HOLLAND

Stockholm reported that the Norwegian radio, as heard in the Swedish capital, said that "German troops have landed on the south coast of Norway." (Mrs. J. Borden Harriman, American Minister to Norway, informed the State Department in Washington that she had been told by the Foreign Minister that Norway is at war with Germany.)

Travelers reaching Oldenzaal, Holland, from Germany reported heavy concentrations of German troops near the frontier.

An Oslo radio report said the Norwegian government had abandoned its capital and is moving to Hamar.

German troops were said to have occupied Bergen and Trondheim.

The radio also stated that the Norwegian government had ordered general mobilization.

The German invasion of Denmark, the British Exchange Telegraph Co. reported, was carried out by land and sea. German warships were reported to have landed troops at Nyborg on Fuehnen Island and at Korsoer in Zeeland.

Three large German ships, reportedly transports, were in the Copenhagen harbor and troops were landing.

COMMUNICATIONS CUT OFF

Ordinary communications between London and Copenhagen were interrupted.

Fragmentary messages, however, indicated that the Germans were swarming in with such speed that occupation of key centers in the little Danish state might be completed within 24 hours.

A Danish garrison at Sonderburg was reported retreating

Turn to Page 2, Column 1

British Sink Nazi Ship; 300 Troops Lost in Sea

OSLO, April 8. (AP)—The European war came to neutral Norway with smashing suddenness today as the British navy, only a few hours after sowing mines in Norwegian territorial waters, fired two torpedoes into the 5261-ton German transport Rio de Janeiro just four miles off the southeast coast.

Of 500 German infantrymen, cavalrymen and airmen aboard, 300 were killed and drowned. All of 80 horses on the ship also were lost.

BODIES FLOATING

Tonight only a huge blot of oil, tangled wreckage and floating bodies showed the spot where the Rio de Janeiro went down.

Following news of the Rio de Janeiro's sinking it was reported here tonight that possibly 200 men were lost from a ship believed to be the German tanker Poseidon, which sank after an explosion about noon today off Lillesland, on Norway's southern coast.

Norwegian residents at Lillesand and Kristiansand, where survivors of the Rio de Janeiro were landed by Norwegian schooners, said those who were brought ashore wore green uniforms of the German army.

LEAP OVERBOARD

Norwegian fishermen said the Germans began jumping overboard into the Skaggerak, entrance to the Baltic Sea from the North Sea, when the first British torpedo struck. Then the second torpedo was fired and many Germans were killed by flying debris as they swam in the water.

The German steamer Kreta re-

Turn to Page 2, Column 4

Nazis Announce Two Invasions

German Radio Tells Reasons for Attacks on Norway and Denmark

LONDON, April 9. (Tuesday.) (AP)—A special announcement of the German radio intercepted today by Reuters, British news agency, said German troops had invaded Denmark and Norway.

The agency only shortly before carried a dispatch from Paris saying that the radio at Oslo, Norway's capital, had announced the landing of German troops at Norwegian ports at 3 a.m.

Reuters said that the following announcement was made by the German radio:

"The high command of the German army announces that in order to counteract the actions against Denmark and Norway (apparently the Allied mine laying along the Norwegian coast) and to prevent a possible hostile attack against these countries, the German army has taken these two countries under its protection."

"The strong forces of the German army have therefore invaded these countries this morning."

A German navigation service broadcast, intercepted by Reuters, said that all of Sweden's important harbors on the Skagerrak, arm of the North Sea, had been mined early today by Germany.

British Dynamite Barges Seized by Rumania on Danube

BUCHAREST, April 8. (AP)—Detention of a fleet of dynamite-laden British barges, charged by Germans with being designed to blow up a narrow Danube gateway and block a German supply line, today electrified Southeastern Europe with the fear war soon might spread to this quarter of the world.

Rumanian police, acting on a tip said to have been supplied by the pro-Nazi Iron Guard, halted the fleet near Giurgiu, Danube River port whence Germany ships much-needed Rumanian oil supplies.

Aboard were tons of dynamite.

Germans alleged the British planned to blockade the spot in the Danube known as the Iron Gate by sinking the barges and wrecking the narrow channel where the river cuts through the Carpathian barrier between high cliffs. The Iron Gate is 280 miles up river from Giurgiu.

Official British quarters, acknowledging the barges were loaded with explosives, insisted they were to be used only for destroying Allied river craft in case of a German invasion of Rumania.

The only official British statement on the matter was a communique saying merely that Ru-

Turn to Page 3, Column 7

Archbishop of Paris, Cardinal Verdier, Dies

PARIS, April 9. (AP)—Jean Cardinal Verdier, archbishop of Paris, died today.

War Crisis at a Glance

Latest developments in the war crisis involving Denmark, Norway and Germany:

1.—German troops invade Denmark by land and sea, troops entering the capital and rapidly occupying strategic points in the interior.

2.—Norway reported at war with Germany after Nazi troops landed on coast and four German warships repulsed by gunfire in attempt to invade water entrance of Oslo.

3.—British submarine sinks German transport off Norway with loss of 300 German soldiers. German tanker also reported sunk by submarine.

4.—German air raiders bombed British naval base at Scapa Flow.

IN THE 'TIMES' TODAY

TUESDAY APRIL 9, 1940

REMEMBER THIS

A silly world naturally follows the latest craze.

ALL THE NEWS ALL THE TIME
LARGEST HOME-DELIVERED CIRCULATION
LARGEST ADVERTISING VOLUME
MAdison 2345
The Times Telephone Number

Los Angeles Times

EQUAL RIGHTS
LIBERTY UNDER THE LAW — TRUE INDUSTRIAL FREEDOM

IN THREE PARTS—44 PAGES
Part I—GENERAL NEWS—28 Pages
TIMES OFFICE
202 West First Street

VOL. LIX — C — THURSDAY MORNING, JULY 11, 1940. — DAILY, FIVE CENTS

LOS ANGELES POPULATION 1,496,792

British Grimly Wait Start of Blitzkrieg

Swarms of Enemy Planes Routed in Raid Believed Prelude to Threatened Invasion; 37 German Aircraft Shot Down or Disabled

LONDON, July 11 (Thursday.) (AP)—England, on guard and ready, watched through the dawn today without any indication along the coastal no man's land of Nazi invasion which Commons was warned last night might come at daybreak.

Britons speculated whether this warning, by Sir Edward Grigg, Undersecretary of State for War, was the authorized first word that the zero hour is near.

DEFENDERS ON ALERT

Most members of Parliament, however, took the statement as only an indication that Britain's defenses are ready and the next German move is awaited.

Sir Edward said:

"Tonight thousands of our soldiers will be on the alert, waiting for an attack which may come in several places at dawn."

He spoke while the thunder of bombs and the rattle of machine-gun fire still signaled the greatest air fight of the war over England—an attack which Sir Edward said might be only a prelude to the worst.

British battle planes and coastal guns drove the Germans off late in the day after shooting down or disabling 37 of the raiders.

EXPECT BLOW ON COAST

Some members of Parliament took the undersecretary's statement as implying only the need for increased watchfulness hour by hour along the coastal no man's land where the next blow is expected—soon.

Two explosions were heard over a wide area in Southeastern England today after a plane had passed over. Fires broke out, but were dealt with quickly.

Acknowledging the loss of two British planes, the Air Ministry reported that in incessant dogfights throughout the day 14 German bombers and their guardian fighter craft, sprung at England from close-range bases in France and the Low Countries, were shot out of the sky. Another 23 were reported "so severely damaged that they were unlikely to reach home."

STRIKE AT DEFENSES

The raiders concentrated on breaking down coast defenses and smashing shipping out of the narrow Straits of Dover.

The British said "a few persons" were killed by high explosives inland.

At times at least 150 planes battled simultaneously along the coast—the Germans trying for hits on ships and attempting to break through British defenses for inland attacks.

Unlike raids of weeks ago when the bombers came a few at a time without fighter escort, today's raiders brought whole flights of fast, light, fighting planes to ward off the British Spitfires and Hurricanes.

One squadron of nine big bombers was guarded by 50 lighter

Turn to Page 3, Column 1

Petain Given Nazi Warning

Totalitarian Shift Too Late to Avoid Penalties of Defeat

BERLIN, July 10. (U.P.)—The German press significantly warned France today that her conversion to totalitarian principles came too late to save her from the consequences of military defeat and that she must bear full responsibility for "her mistakes and crimes."

The warnings made plain that France must not expect to obtain more beneficial terms from Germany through establishment of the authoritarian regime now being formulated under the aegis of Marshal Henri Philippe Petain at Vichy.

BEAR RESPONSIBILITY

The unanimity with which German newspapers presented this viewpoint appeared to indicate a faithful reflection of the official German attitude.

The comment of the Essener National Zeitung, newspaper of Marshal Hermann Goering, was typical:

"France must bear the full responsibility for its mistakes and crimes," the National Zeitung said. "Germany has gained the dominant role in Europe. A France may exist beside her but not the France of yesterday which has been defeated and which must be satisfied with the role assigned to her."

The Frankfurter Zeitung declared that "no tardy recognition of the truth can free the nation from responsibility. The damage is done."

RECALL FORMER VIEWS

An authorized German spokesman said that "we observe as detached spectators and in no way interfere with the proceedings at Vichy."

The spokesman said that "practically the same gentlemen are involved who, two weeks ago, were making almost opposite statements."

The press gave no hint of what "role" Germany will assign to France but insisted that it would be a "different France" and that Germany alone will determine the conditions of French existence.

President Pledges No Aggression

New Defense Funds Asked but Stand Taken Against Sending Army to Europe

BY WARREN B. FRANCIS
Times Staff Correspondent

WASHINGTON, July 10. A definite pledge that American forces will not be called upon to participate in any overseas war was given Congress today by President Roosevelt along with a request for another $4,848,171,957 in cash and credit for further strengthening of the national defense.

Mr. Roosevelt declared unequivocably that the United

For text of President Roosevelt's defense message turn to Page 4, Part I.

States will not take part in any war of aggression or intervene with man power in the European conflict and has not been asleep concerning its own safety.

But he also reasserted with equal vigor that this country intends to compel respect for the Monroe Doctrine and that he will adhere to his principle of "hemisphere defense."

ANSWER TO REPUBLICANS

The special message, third on the subject of defense needs in less than three months, obviously was designed to combat the Republican platform, which hung a "war party" label on the New Dealers, and to stamp out dissension within Democratic ranks. It also was a reply to accusations the administration has neglected to take precautions.

Mr. Roosevelt's demand was broken down only generally. In his role of Commander-in-Chief of the naval and military forces, he asked for $2,161,441,957 in immediate appropriations and contract authorization of $2,686,730,000, stating these sums are urgent.

The chief objective of the latest program is speedy acquisition of 19,000 more airplanes and of equipment for—but not a peacetime Army of the same size—a 2,000,000-man fighting force.

OBJECTIVES OF PROGRAM

In asking Congress to raise the total defense outlays and authorizations this session to approximately $10,000,000,000, Mr. Roosevelt gave only an outline of the way the money and credit will be used. Further information is expected tomorrow, while detailed explanations will be given the House Appropriations Committee at hearings scheduled to begin July 22.

The President listed five principal objectives of his newest program. They are: speeding the naval building plan "to meet any possible combination" of foes; to provide all equipment needed for an Army of 1,200,000

Turn to Page 5, Column 2

Los Angeles City Population—1940
District / Supervisor / Population
11 K.H. Hicks—S.F. Valley 110621
13 H. Bejack—Hollywood 369388
14 K.D. Chri— Down town 302591
15 G. Hat— 323131
16 F.A.H— Venice 240219
17 C. Kell— arbor 210142
CITY OF — Total 1,496,792
1238048
258744
20.9%
THE FIR
City 1930
1 New Y
2 Chic
3 Phil
4 Detroi
5 L.A.

THE FIGURES—E. B. Lewis, local area manager of Census Bureau, points out to Mayor Bowron the old and new census figures and the percentage gain for Los Angeles. Times photo

Gain of 258,744 Made in Decade

Increase of 20.9 Per Cent Declared Largest of Any Major Municipality in Nation; Officials Expect Mark to Pass 1,500,000

Population of the city of Los Angeles is 1,496,792—so close to the anticipated 1,500,000 mark that subsequent rechecks are certain to boost it past that total!

The 1940 census figure was released last night by E. B. Lewis, Census Bureau area manager for Los Angeles County, who reported to members of the Citizens' Census Committee at a dinner meeting in the Chamber of Commerce Building.

The figure is for the city only, reports from parts of the county not being complete.

It means that the city of Los Angeles has gained 258,744 in population since 1930 — an increase of 20.9 per cent over 1930's 1,238,048.

IN FIFTH PLACE

The new mark keeps Los Angeles in fifth place among cities of the nation and boosts it from 19th to 17th in the roll of world metropolises.

Detroit, although gaining by only 3.18 per cent with a numerical increase of 49,887, keeps the fourth spot among United States cities with a population of 1,618,549.

Assurance of the 3208 additional population needed to reach the 1,500,000 mark was seen in the fact that the figure released is technically "preliminary," although official. In 1930, it was pointed out, further checks and tabulations boosted the preliminary figure by 6318.

COUNTY FIGURES

Although last night's disclosures were limited to population within the city, the addition of the Los Angeles city figure to the nearly complete county total provided a gauge for close-range estimates on the county-wide growth.

With 48 communities outside the city already tabulated at a total of 892,608, addition of Los Angeles' figure brings the county total to 2,389,400 to date.

Figuring from the fact that the county's fast-growing suburbs have shown an average increase of 22 per cent or more, and using 22 per cent as a conservative estimate for the increase in a few remaining enumeration districts, the county total should reach approximately 2,800,000, it was estimated.

ESTIMATED INCREASE

This would be an increase of 591,508 over the 1930 mark of 2,208,492.

The 2,389,400 already tabulated, it was noted, is above the complete county total of 2,208,492 in 1930.

Because of regulations in the Census Bureau in Washington,

Turn to Page C, Column 1

Census at a Glance

Los Angeles city population, 1940	1,496,792
Numerical increase since 1930	258,744
Percentage increase since 1930	20.9%
Numerical increase since 1880	1,485,609
Percentage increase since 1880	13,284.45%
City's position among United States cities	5th
City's position among world cities	17th

Only United States cities larger than Los Angeles are: New York, Chicago, Philadelphia and Detroit.

Leaders Hear Growth News

Only One Man Calm at Census Dinner, and He Knew Figures

Tension filled the Chamber of Commerce board room last night as 50 members of the Citizens' Census Committee, Mayor Bowron and Census Bureau officials waited for the biggest news of the moment—the 1940 census figures for Los Angeles.

Only one man was placid. He was E. B. Lewis, area manager for Los Angeles County for the United States Census Bureau.

He knew the figures.

PAST RECALLED

An undertone of conversation, with census estimates predominating, hummed through the soup, salad, entree and dessert. Then Harry H. Baskerville, chairman of the citizens committee and head of the research and statistical committee of the chamber, tapped a bell.

In preliminary comments he harked back to 50, 40, 30, 20 and 10 years ago.

"In 1920," he said, "the chamber had to come to the rescue in the census. Ten years later the Director of the Census came to Los Angeles because he had been informed that he had not allowed enough men and materials to count the population.

"We showed him the city and he forthwith tripled his supply requisition."

MASTER OF CEREMONIES

As master of ceremonies, Baskerville introduced Mayor Bowron and James L. Beebe, past president of the chamber, who represented President J. L. Van Norman. Both expressed their appreciation to the committee for the aid they gave the census-takers.

"I thought for a while they were going to miss me," the Mayor said, "but they finally got me counted, adding that much to the population, anyway."

WORK PRAISED

He particularly lauded the work of Guy E. Marion, manager of the chamber's research department, for efficient handling of the committee's work and for "keeping the census men working."

Baskerville read census estimates from the Department of Water and Power, the Chamber of Commerce, the Los Angeles Realty Board, the California Taxpayers' Association and Registrar of Voters William M. Kerr.

The strained expectant air in

Turn to Page, A Column 4

Japanese Ask Apology in Marine Arrest Row

New Diatribe Loosed by Press Against America Over Arrests of Gendarmes in Defense Zone

SHANGHAI, July 10. (AP)—Anti-American agitation based on the recent arrest of Japanese gendarmes by United States marines culminated tonight in a mass meeting at which Japanese residents demanded an official apology for the "insult."

It was a sober gathering, however, devoid of extravagant speeches, and some observers gathered the impression that Japanese officials are beginning to soft-pedal the excitement.

Domei, the Japanese news agency, did not mention the meeting.

FRESH DIATRIBE

The newspaper Tairiku Shimpo, however, printed a fresh diatribe against the United States marines for their "senseless cruelty" and said 11 gendarmes had been injured through rough handling during their five-hour detention.

Col. Dewitt Peck, United States marines commander, said only three of the 16, arrested while armed and in civilian clothing in the United States defense area of the International Settlement, were bruised badly enough to require iodine treatment.

AGREEMENT VIOLATION

Rear Admiral Moriji Takeda, Japanese naval garrison commander, was quoted by newspapers as saying the marines were barbarous in their action.

Col. Peck suggested that discussion turn back to the real issue, which was why the gendarmes entered the defense zone in violation of previous agreements.

The British steamer Shenking, which the Japanese navy seized here yesterday, still was detained at Woosung. The Shengking's failure to halt when a Japanese warship chased it was character-

Turn to Page 3, Column 6

Mercury Climbs to 91 Degrees

Solar Radiation Blamed by Weather Bureau for Warmth

Yesterday's Temperatures

6 a.m.	72	12 noon	88
7 a.m.	76	1 p.m.	89
8 a.m.	83	2 p.m.	87
9 a.m.	88	3 p.m.	86
10 a.m.	90	4 p.m.	84
10:30 a.m.	91	5 p.m.	82
11 a.m.	89	6 p.m.	80

Blame it all—those wilted collars and wilted personalities of yesterday—on just plain old solar radiation.

That's what caused the mercury column to rise to the 91-degree mark by 10:30 a.m. yesterday in Los Angeles, with foothill cities and other communities reporting even higher maximum temperatures.

HEAT PROSTRATION

In Pasadena one heat prostration was reported. Harry Buckwalter, a carpenter working on a new house, collapsed and was treated at Huntington Memorial Hospital. His address was given as 1754 Locust St. and his age as about 50.

Yesterday's maximum of 91 degrees was Los Angeles' hottest day since last May 9, when the thermometer atop the new Federal Building registered 94 degrees.

Yesterday's early morning minimum was 65 degrees.

TODAY'S PROSPECTS

The weather man predicted slightly cooler conditions today with gentle to moderate west and northwest winds prevailing off the coast.

Sierra Madre reported a reading of 101 degrees. At Santa Anita it was 97, Arcadia, 98; Monrovia, 92, Duarte, 95; Union Air Terminal, Burbank, 105; Azusa, 100; Glendora, 101; Santa Ana, 97, and Laguna Beach, 96.

Knox Confirmed as Navy Chief as Senate Casts Vote of 66 to 16

WASHINGTON, July 10. (U.P.)—President Roosevelt's national solidarity Cabinet became an accomplished fact today when the Senate confirmed the nomination of Col. Frank Knox, 1936 Republican Vice-Presidential candidate, as Secretary of the Navy. The vote was 66 to 16.

A few hours earlier, another Republican—Henry L. Stimson of New York—took the oath as Secretary of War. Stimson, who had served in two Republican Cabinets, was approved by the Senate yesterday, 56 to 28.

BIPARTISAN CABINET

Confirmation of the two Republican leaders gives the United States its first bipartisan Cabinet since the Lincoln administration. Mr. Roosevelt's revamped Cabinet also includes two former Republicans—Secretary of Agriculture Henry A. Wallace and Secretary of Interior Harold L. Ickes.

The Stimson-Knox nominations were approved after vitriolic criticism by isolationists and intended victims of Mr. Roosevelt's ill-starred 1938 political purge. Opponents charged that both nominees are interventionists and that in naming them to the key defense posts the President is forming a war Cabinet.

THREE-DAY DEBATE

Debate on the two appointments lasted three days.

Stimson succeeds Harry L. Woodring, who resigned a few hours before his successor's nomination was announced by Mr. Roosevelt June 20.

Knox, 66, replaces Charles

Turn to Page, A Column 4

Pair Who Traded Mates Remarry

ATLANTA, July 10. (AP)—The Ralph Forrester-Claude Smith marital wheel reached three-quarter cycle today with one remarriage canceling out one of two divorces.

Four years ago, Jessie and Ralph Forrester were divorced. At the same time, a court dissolved the wedding bonds of their friends, Mildred and Claude Smith. Then Jessie wed Claude, Mildred married Ralph.

The swap broke down some time ago when Ralph and Mildred were divorced. Monday Jessie and Claude followed suit.

Today the original Forrester line-up was restored when Jessie and Ralph remarried.

F. D. Roosevelt Jr. Declines Offer of Motion-Picture Part

Franklin D. Roosevelt Jr., son of the President, had a chance yesterday to become a full-fledged motion-picture actor, but turned it down.

As a guest of Douglas Fairbanks Jr., Roosevelt and his bride visited the Columbia Studio and were taken on a set where Fairbanks is performing.

Ben Hecht, producer-director of the picture, was introduced, looked Roosevelt over and said he had a part that would be just suited for him.

"No, thanks," replied Roosevelt. "This all looks too complicated for me. I'm afraid I could not come up to it."

Mr. and Mrs. Roosevelt have been honeymooning and they came to Hollywood to visit James Roosevelt, who now is in the picture business. The couple left last night for Washington to see the President.

Experts Miss Guesses on Los Angeles Population

Census-guessing, a pastime which has occupied a good many Angelenos during the last few days, is officially ended with the announcement last night of the preliminary figure—1,496,792—for Los Angeles.

If you missed it by a few hundred thousand, don't feel too badly. Here's what a few experts guessed.

Registrar of Voters William M. Kerr, 1,664,514.

Paul V. Lane, research engineer of the California Taxpayers' Association, 1,550,000.

George J. Eberle, statistician, 1,549,899.

Los Angeles Chamber of Commerce, 1,400,000.

Department of Water and Power, 1,455,000.

Glenn Willaman, secretary of the California Real Estate Association, 1,600,000.

Prof. Thurston Ross of the University of Southern California, 1,320,000.

IN THE 'TIMES' TODAY

THURSDAY JULY 11, 1940

REMEMBER THIS

He thinks to advise others who has failed to advise himself.

THE WEATHER

UNITED STATES WEATHER BUREAU FORECAST FOR LOS ANGELES AND SOUTHERN CALIFORNIA: Clear this morning becoming partly cloudy this afternoon and evening. Tomorrow generally clear. Maximum and minimum temperature for yesterday: 67-51. For complete United States weather report turn to Page 12, Part I.

Los Angeles Times

IN THREE PARTS — 34 PAGES

Part II — LOCAL NEWS — 16 Pages

TIMES OFFICE
202 West First Street

VOL. LX C TUESDAY MORNING, DECEMBER 31, 1940. CITY NEWS—EDITORIAL—SOCIETY

Six-Million-Dollar Arroyo Seco Parkway Opened

BY THE WAY

With BILL HENRY

Along about this time of the year, when 1940's bustle is just disappearing through the portals that divide the present from the past, editors fall victim to an epidemic of summing up—listing the big news stories of the year, the outstanding personalities, and so on. That's fine—as far as it goes!

SQUAWK OF THE YEAR—But what about the squawk of the year? What about my yelp as a long-suffering listener to the radio? I go home weak and exhausted from what is laughingly referred to as "my slavery" at the office and turn a dial in optimistic hope of being fascinated and entertained. What do I get? I get a lot of argufiers, 'sputifiers, questioners, hecklers and similar disturbers of the peace, all wrangling like a lot of fishwives. It sounds like a glorified Pershing Square Spit'n Argue session. Are you with me?

ENTERTAINMENT—If I could always be sure of a little good light entertainment on my radio I'd, almost be willing to call off my campaign for Bill Henry' outsize coffee cups. Besides, I now not only have an outsize java-swizzler at home for my exclusive use but have received a handsome hand-painted receptacle which is alleged to be a Bill Henry coffee cup, from Mr. Luke Andrews, a fellow-toiler. I think I'll take this over to the Lotus Cafe and let it be kept on the shelf there as the old-fashioned barber shops used to keep personal shaving mugs.

CAMPAIGN—As for the campaign of the S.R.R.C. (Society for the Regulation of Roadside Clocks) nothing much seems to be happening except that Mabelouise Billings remembers that they had similar trouble with the timepieces in an institution whose inmates were a bit balmy. When she asked one of them why the clocks didn't seem to keep time accurately an inmate proved that he was completely gone by remarking, "Well, lady—if those clocks were right, they wouldn't be here, would they?"

ODDS AND ENDS—Lots of people prefer Fibber McGee to Jack Benny . . . Leach Cross, ex-lightweight boxer, is still practicing his profession of dentistry in New York but says business is just like pulling teeth . . . Norman ("Trial of Mary Dugan") McLeod is going to help dedicate Hancock Hall at S.C. this week . . . He's quite a lad in the National Geographic Society . . . Does anybody know where the MacFarland Twins' Orchestra is playing now? . . . Marcel Herbelin knows a rugged individualist who attended a Christmas turkey dinner on the promise that he could eat a hamburger . . . Yes, I've had too much turkey in my day, too . . . A college president the other day offered this definition:

An economist is a man who can tell you what to do with your money after you have already done something else with it.

LEGAL RECOURSE—Just in case you feel that you may be driven to desperation by neighborhood celebrants tonight, By the Way's "What to Do About It" Dept. assures you that you have a right to make a citizen's arrest. Just step up to the guy who is bothering you and say, "I place you under arrest." Unless you outweigh him by 40 pounds it might be easier to call a policeman and, striking an attitude, say, "Officer, I order you to arrest that man." The officer has to do it. However, you'll have to appear to support your charges and if you can't do so it'll cost you plenty for false arrest. Maybe it would be better to just pull the covers up over your head and forget it. Apparently that is Mr. Ito's plan, for he says:

Whistle and horn are announcing New Year,
From bed I am jumping—giving big cheer;
Mrs. Ito is warning not to make noise,
She say important for maintaining poise.

I not giving hoot who hearing me shout,
When New Year come in, and old one go out;
I hope better days approaching for all,
Democracy making Dictator crawl!

QUEEN MEETS QUEEN—Sun Goddess Joan Leslie, left, as she met Beth Howley, senior honor student and "Sweetheart" of University of Nebraska as latter arrived.

Times photo

'Cornhuskers' Sweetheart' Finds Muffler Useless Here

Special Trains Arrive With Hundreds of Rooters to Be Greeted by Sun Goddess at Union Station

Illustrated on Page B.

Bundled in a warm winter coat, Beth Howley, "Nebraska's sweetheart," yesterday arrived in Los Angeles as an advance delegate of the hordes of Cornhuskers expected for the New Year's Day football game and the Tournament of Roses.

Fresh from snow-blanketed Nebraska, the visitor was greeted by a blazing California sun and by the Southland's Sun Goddess, Joan Leslie, and two princesses, Marilyn Hare and Jamie Ann Heise.

VISITOR SHEDS COAT

Under the warming rays, Miss Howley soon shed her coat and even her muffler as she posed for photographers at Union Station in a ceremony in which she was made an honorary member of the sun goddess' court.

"I know I shouldn't let anyone know," Miss Howley confided to friends, "but I also brought along my umbrella—just in case. The thing that surprised me most on my first trip here was that contrary to stories told me by acquaintances who have journeyed here for the first time the skies were actually clear."

Miss Howley, who traveled aboard the Union Pacific Los Angeles Limited, was accompanied by Dr. Helen Hosp, dean of women at the university. The visitor will be the sole rider on the Nebraska float in the Tournament of Roses.

BAND ARRIVES

The Cornhuskers' 120-piece R.O.T.C. band and more than 500 Nebraska students and rooters, led by L. E. Gunderson, secretary of the university board of regents, and Ellsworth DuTeau, alumni secretary, arrived later in the day on Southern Pacific special trains, which were delayed in Phoenix while the students staged a passing rally.

Stanford's band, also uniformed in red and white, arrived shortly afterward with two special trains of Bay District rooters, but the two musical organizations did not meet.

MORE TRAINS ON WAY

At 8 a.m. today, another 1000 Nebraska rooters will arrive on two special trains of the Union Pacific.

Two extra Santa Fe trains of Nebraska fans will arrive at 8 a.m. today at the old Santa Fe depot, First St. and Santa Fe Ave., marking the first use of the old terminal since the opening of Union Station in May, 1939. Three more special trains from Palo Alto are scheduled to arrive today.

Nebraska student and alumni headquarters are at the Rosslyn.

GOVERNOR NOT COMING

Governor-elect Dwight Griswold of Nebraska reported from his home in Gordon, Neb., last night that he is not planning to attend the New Year's Day football classic in the Rose Bowl.

Similarly, Governor R. L. Cochran of that State said in Lincoln that he has no plans to come west.

Rose Parade Floats Rushed

Hundreds Feverishly Pasting Final Blossoms; Traffic Setup Given

PASADENA, Dec. 30.—As busy as a beehive was this city today as hundreds of men and women and school children, too, rushed the preparations of floats to be paraded before enraptured spectators in the 52nd annual Tournament of Roses New Year's Day.

From all sections of California came blossoms to be transformed into figures of beauty for "America in Flowers"—theme of the world-famed procession. Float makers, their fingers sticky with mucilage, worked feverishly to glue the multicolored petals into place in time for the starting trumpet call Wednesday morning.

GIVES TRAFFIC SETUP

Meanwhile, Chief of Police Charles H. Kelley announced that he is confident that the ever-present traffic problem has been ironed out.

"We'll avoid snarls this year and I believe traffic will be handled smoothly," he said. "Our setup, with the exception of numerous improvements, will follow much the pattern of last year."

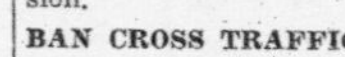

Traffic from the Rose Bowl last year set a new record when every car was emptied from the parking area in 50 minutes.

Officials this year, with the aid of officers from Los Angeles, Los Angeles County Sheriff's office and California State Highway Patrol, expect to be able to handle 2,000,000 persons without confusion.

BAN CROSS TRAFFIC

A departure from last year's plan will be the elimination of cross main artery traffic in handling inflow and outflow crowds before and after the parade. Wherever possible officers will shunt short-cut seekers back on to main marked routes, Chief Kelley asserted.

Chief Kelley for the fourth consecutive year will direct air traffic from a T.W.A. airliner. It will be the Pasadena police executive's last New Year's Day task inasmuch as he retires in April of 1941.

Parkway traffic, a brand new factor this year, will be parked south of Colorado St. between Broadway and Hill Aves. Traf-

Turn to Page 2, Column 5

THEY'LL RIDE—Left to right, Barbara Brantingham, Evelyn Dinsmoor and Audree Smith, who will ride on the Long Beach float in Tournament of Roses parade tomorrow.

Parade Bands Must Change Tune Near Radio Microphones

Music War Cause of Elaborate System to Avoid Broadcast of 'Forbidden' Pieces

Because of the dispute between the American Society of Composers, Authors and Publishers and the radio and networks, bands marching in the Pasadena Tournament of Roses tomorrow must refrain from playing bars of "forbidden" music within range of a radio microphone.

This was the decision reached yesterday by Alex Petry of the National Broadcasting Co.

"Music composers and publishers have installed recording instruments throughout the United States in an effort to catch the radio stations napping," he said.

If so much as one or two bars of a selection controlled by ASCAP go on the air, the N.B.C. spokesman said, the network is subject to a fine of $250 a station. Approximately 150 stations will be "hooked up" for the parade broadcast.

Worried tournament officials,

Turn to Page 2, Column 3

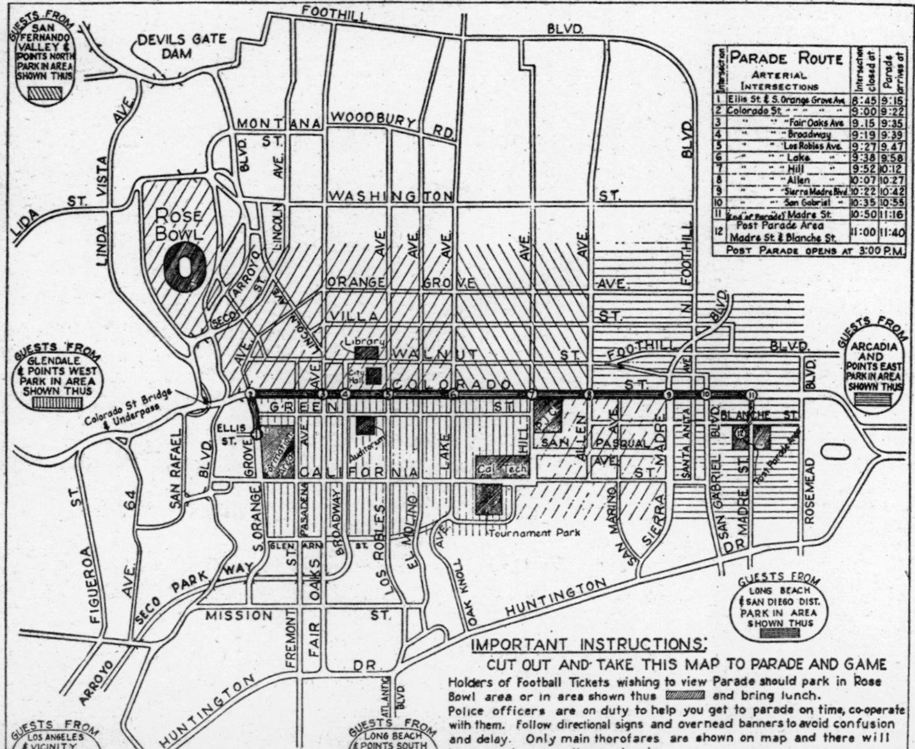

Intersection	PARADE ROUTE ARTERIAL INTERSECTIONS	Intersection closed at	Parade arrives at
1	Ellis St. & S. Orange Grove Ave.	8:45	9:15
2	Colorado St. " " " "	9:00	9:22
3	" " " Fair Oaks Ave	9.15	9:35
4	" " " Broadway	9:19	9:39
5	" " " Los Robles Ave.	9:27	9.47
6	" " " Lake "	9:38	9:58
7	" " " Hill "	9:52	10:12
8	" " " Allen "	10:07	10:27
9	" " " Sierra Madre Blvd.	10:22	10:42
10	" " " San Gabriel "	10:35	10:55
11	(End of Parade) Madre St.	10:50	11:16
12	Post Parade Area Madre St. & Blanche St.	11:00	11:40
	POST PARADE OPENS AT 3:00 P.M.		

FOR MOTORISTS—Here's information on procedure for those who attend Rose Tournament and football game.

Immoral Show Ban Urged

Archbishop Cantwell Asks Change in Laws to Forbid Obscenity

A communication urging the City Council to change city ordinances relating to the operation of stage shows in Los Angeles "so as to free our people from the prurient spectacles" was forwarded to each Councilman yesterday by Archbishop John J. Cantwell.

Writing as a citizen, "and particularly as a guide to the many thousands of my coreligionists who look to me for moral direction, my interest has been deeply aroused and I turn to the city fathers for aid," he wrote.

The Archbishop drew attention to the code covering issuance of show permits, and stated:

POLICE POWER

"Evidently the Police Commission is vested with no discretionary power to reject an application, no matter how undesirable the 'show' or the applicant may be, for, after making the investigation, it is required mandatorily to issue a permit.

"Subdivision "g" of Sec. 23.12 of the City Charter," the letter stated, "plainly declares that the board cannot revoke its permit, once given, unless a court of competent jurisdiction has first convicted the permittee of an indecent display. Again the board is an automaton, and with the uncertainty of jury trials the result of prosecution might merely increase the drawing power of the obscene presentation."

CHANGE NECESSARY

After stating that it is apparent that change in the ordinances on shows is necessary, the letter stated:

"No fouler stain can rest upon any city than that arising from laws which do not adequately control, but rather make possible, and even tend to encourage lewd and indecent public displays upon which unscrupulous promoters fatten, youthful minds are poisoned and morals corrupted.

"I feel sure that, on inquiring into this matter, your honorable body will amend the sections in question in such manner that not only youth but the older mem-

Turn to Page 2, Column 3

Rose Queen Unties Ribbon

Ceremony Featured by Speeding Motorcade on Great Traffic Way

Illustrated on Page B.

Six miles of six-lane highways, important to traffic, history and national defense, yesterday received official benediction of the men who built them and the people who will use them.

They are the glass-smooth miles from the Figueroa St. tunnels in Los Angeles to Glenarm St., Pasadena.

They cost $6,000,000 and they parallel the $8,000,000 flood control project which is designed to curb the sometimes angry waters of the sometimes "mojado" Arroyo Seco.

They are, in fact, aptly named the Arroyo Seco Parkway.

PASSAGE OPENED

At high noon, just 33 months after an earlier Tournament of Roses Queen formally broke ground for the impressive boulevard, Sally Stanton, Queen of the 1941 Pasadena festival, untied the red silk ribbon that barred passage along the road.

It was really open now.

As Governor Olson had remarked a few moments before, commuting motorists "will travel over it from one end to the other in seven, eight or perhaps nine minutes . . . from the very heart of Los Angeles, through Highland Park and South Pasadena, to the very heart of Pasadena . . . in easy, nerve-free comfort and safety."

Everyone had glowing words for the project at the dedication ceremonies attended by more than 1000 persons.

ARMY NEEDS ROADS

Maj. Gen. Jacob E. Fickel, commanding general of the Southwest Air District of the Army Air Corps, declared: "The Army wants good roads. Their use would be imperative in times of emergency. This is such a road."

Lawrence W. Barrett, chairman of the California Highway Commission, said: "This great modern freeway represents a standard of modern highway building . . . and is the beginning of a great era of modern highway construction in California."

MOTORCADE MOVES

Appropriately, the Arroyo Seco Parkway was "baptized" by the passing over its well-marked lanes of a fast motorcade. At the conclusion of a band concert on the downtown City Hall steps, the procession swung smartly into line through the Figueroa St. tunnels.

First came the Third Coast Artillery—three-inch anti-aircraft guns, searchlights, trucks—rolling at 40 miles an hour.

Behind them sped official cars

Turn to Page 3, Column 3

TODAY'S FAMOUS BIRTHDAYS

BY DURWARD HOWES

TUESDAY, DEC. 31

CHARLES CORNWALLIS, 1738-1805. English general who gained more fame in defeat than in victory; it was he who surrendered at Yorktown in 1781 in the last great battle of the American Revolution.

MICHAEL J. KELLY, 1857-94. Popular baseball hero whose prowess is immortalized in the song, "Slide, Kelly, Slide;" although he was not dependable as a catcher, pitcher, or infielder, at bat and on base he seemed to have a sixth sense which told him what each member of the opposing team was going to do next.

GEORGE CATLETT MARSHALL, 1880. Chief of Staff of the United States Army; he is one of the few men to attain that high post without having graduated from West Point; his genius for organization was responsible for his appointment, since it is his principal job at the moment to co-ordinate the work of the various departments planning national defense.

STANLEY REED, 1884. Associate Justice of the United States Supreme Court; although it was President Roosevelt who appointed him to that high post, it was President Hoover who persuaded him to leave his Kentucky law practice and come to Washington as attorney for the Federal Farm Board; under the New Deal he served as an R.F.C. attorney and later as Solicitor General.

1941–1950

ALL THE NEWS ALL THE TIME

LARGEST HOME-DELIVERED CIRCULATION
LARGEST ADVERTISING VOLUME

MAdison 2345
The Times Telephone Number

EQUAL RIGHTS

Los Angeles Times

LIBERTY UNDER THE LAW — TRUE INDUSTRIAL FREEDOM

IN THREE PARTS — 42 PAGES

Part I — GENERAL NEWS — 24 Pages

TIMES OFFICE
202 West First Street

VOL. LXI — CCC — MONDAY MORNING, DECEMBER 8, 1941. — DAILY, FIVE CENTS

JAPS OPEN WAR ON U.S. WITH BOMBING OF HAWAII

City Springs to Attention

Los Angeles, Stunned by Sudden War Start, Turns Wholeheartedly to Defense Task; 'They Started It, We'll Finish It,' Motto

Los Angeles was a city alert yesterday as every man and woman, electrified by the news that Japan had struck at this country 2400 miles westward in the Pacific, took his or her stand solidly for total defense.

Stunned at first, incredulous that Japan actually had bombed Pearl Harbor defenses, the city was set buzzing as the news flashed through the streets.

Traffic lanes jammed, telephones clattered incessantly and the downtown area swarmed with curious citizens.

'WE'LL FINISH IT'

Then came a reaction as truly American as apple pie.

Minutes after news of the Japanese attack was heard, defense and law enforcement agencies began operating. Citizens attached to defense groups mobilized. The city shrugged off its amazement. The word was:

"They started it—we'll finish it!"

Soldiers and sailors, their leaves canceled, were ordered to report immediately to their stations. This they did with the least confusion. All officers and men in the services were ordered to report for duty henceforth in uniform. No more mufti. It's war.

FAREWELL SCENES

There were farewell scenes in train and bus depots. Mothers, fathers and sweethearts came to wish their loved ones luck. But they were calm, those going and those staying.

Everywhere the import of war was apparent.

From San Diego to the Oregon border fighter planes of the 4th Interceptor Command waited on flight lines—ready to go.

Anti-aircraft crews, artillery and machine guns pointing skyward, guarded Southland aircraft factories. All members of the Aircraft Warning Service were ordered to report to their headquarters and all observation posts were directed to be manned at all times.

Complete black-out of the harbor area including San Pedro, Wilmington and a major part of Long Beach was ordered early today by Capt. Richard B. Coff-

Turn to Page F, Column 7

Japanese Aliens' Roundup Starts

F.B.I. Hunting Down 300 Subversives and Plans to Hold 3000 Today

A great man hunt was under way last night in Southern California as the Federal Bureau of Investigation agents sought 300 alien Japanese suspected of subversive activities.

As soon as war is declared against Japan, judged a certainty today when Congress meets, 3000 additional Japanese aliens are to be rounded up and placed in protective custody by government agents, The Times learned.

SUSPECTS ROUNDED UP

During the afternoon and night, close to 200 suspicious Japanese were rounded up by police, deputy sheriffs and special officers working under the direction of F.B.I. agents.

In West Los Angeles 18 were grabbed, 18 were taken into custody at Newton police station, 7 in Hollywood, 4 at Wilshire, between 30 and 40 went through the University station, 4 at Pasadena, 4 at Santa Monica, 3 at Hawthorne, 5 at Inglewood, 30 at Hollenbeck station, and on through the list of Los Angeles police stations and outlying cities.

In Santa Ana 15 were taken in custody for questionir Some cameras and 18 guns, mostly shotguns, were confiscated at their homes.

NAMES WITHHELD

The F.B.I. issued orders prohibiting the publication of the names of those held until further orders from Washington.

Raids throughout Los Angeles,

Turn to Page F, Column 4

F.D.R. Will Ask Congress Action Today

President to Make Plea Personally on Move to Answer Japan Attacks

WASHINGTON, Dec. 8 (Monday.) (AP)—Bombs from Japan made war on the United States today and as death tolls mounted President Roosevelt announced he will deliver in person today a special message to Congress.

In the background as the Commander-in-Chief went before the joint session of the House and Senate was a government report of "heavy" naval and "large" losses to the Army.

ACTION UNCERTAIN

Whether Mr. Roosevelt will ask for a formal declaration of war by this country, to match the action taken in Tokyo, was left uncertain after a hurriedly summoned meeting of his Cabinet

NEW YORK, Dec. 7. (AP)—All three major networks — National Broadcasting Co., Columbia Broadcasting System and Mutual Broadcasting System—will carry President Roosevelt's message to Congress at 12:30 p.m. (E.S.T.) 9:30 a.m. (P.S.T.) tomorrow.

and Congressional leaders of both parties tonight at the White House. Also uncertain was whether that declaration might extend to Japan's Axis allies, Germany and Italy.

It was clear from a statement made by the participants, however, that Congress would be requested to adopt a resolution of some nature, and equally clear that it would quickly give its approval. A request for governmental power equivalent to that under a war declaration was expected as a minimum.

WITHOUT WARNING

War came suddenly to the United States early yesterday afternoon. Without warning, and while Japanese diplomats

Turn to Page A, Column 7

Lindbergh Keeps Silent

WEST TISBURY (Mass.) Dec. 7. (AP)—Charles A. Lindbergh, visiting at Seven Gates farm in this Martha's Vineyard Island village, refused tonight to see newspapermen or accept any messages.

Berlin Shy About Aid to Tokyo

BERLIN, Dec. 8 (Monday.) (AP)—Obligated under the three-power pact to go to Japan's assistance if Japan is "attacked," Germany referred early today to hostilities in the Pacific as "clashes."

A special communique failed to clarify Germany's intentions, but termed President Roosevelt a "war incendiary."

"The warmonger Roosevelt has reached his aim," said the Berlin statement.

"Driven by blind hatred against the Reich of Adolf Hitler, he sent weapons and materials to British campaign areas and finally gave his fleet orders to fire on German warships.

"So Roosevelt ran after war like a demon until the Pacific Ocean also is inflamed. Dollar imperialism overcame the good sense of a wide circle of North American people."

Attacks Precede War Declaration

Tokyo Notifies Envoys After Surprise Raid Upon Pearl Harbor Base

TOKYO, Dec. 8 (Monday.) (AP) Japan went to war against the United States and Great Britain today with air and sea attacks against Hawaii followed by a formal declaration of hostilities.

Japanese Imperial headquarters announced at 6 a.m. (1 p.m. Sunday, P.S.T.) that a state of war existed among these nations in the Western Pacific, as of dawn.

Shortly afterward Domei announced that "naval operations are progressing off Hawaii, with at least one Japanese aircraft carrier in action against Pearl Harbor," the American naval base in the islands.

U.S. ENVOY NOTIFIED

Japanese bombers were declared to have raided Honolulu at 7:35 a.m. Hawaii time (10:05 a.m. Sunday, P.S.T.)

Premier-War Minister Gen. Hideki Tojo held a 20-minute Cabinet session at his official residence at 7 a.m., and shortly afterward it was announced that both the United States Ambassador, Joseph C. Grew, and the British Ambassador, Sir Robert Leslie Craigie, had been summoned by Foreign Minister Shigenori Togo.

The Foreign Minister, Domei said, handed to Grew the Japanese government's formal reply to the note sent to Japan by United States Secretary of State Cordell Hull on Nov. 26.

REJECT HULL'S TERMS

(In the course of the diplomatic negotiations leading up to Sunday's events, the Domei agency had stated that Japan could not accept the premises of Hull's note.)

Toll Feared High in Attack Against Isles

Field Near Honolulu Takes Brunt of Bombing; Naval Battle Reported

HONOLULU, Dec. 7. (AP)—War struck suddenly and without warning from the sky and sea today at the Hawaiian Islands. Japanese bombs took a heavy toll in American lives.

Cannonading offshore indicated a naval engagement in progress.

Wave after wave of planes streamed over Oahu in an attack which the Army said started at 8:10 a.m., Honolulu time, and which ended at around 9:25, an hour and 15 minutes later.

COUNT 50 PLANES

Witnesses said they counted at least 50 planes in the initial attack.

The attack seemed to center on Hickam Field, huge Army airport three miles northwest of Honolulu, and Honolulu, where the islands' heaviest fortifications are located.

The planes streamed through the sky from the southwest, their bombs shattering the morning calm. Most of the attackers flew high, but a few came low, five down to under a hundred feet elevation to attack Pearl Harbor.

WARSHIPS HIT

An oil tank there was seen blazing and smoking. An unconfirmed report said one ship in the harbor was on its side and four others burning.

Army officials said some Japanese planes had been shot down in the Honolulu area.

Planes which did not bomb Pearl Harbor apparently headed for Hickam Field. But there the attackers apparently did not confine themselves to the heavily fortified areas. From Wahiawa, a town of 3000 population about 20 miles northwest of Honolulu, came reports that 10 or more persons were injured when enemy planes sprayed bullets on the streets.

FROM PLANE CARRIERS

Unconfirmed reports said the attackers came from two airplane carriers.

United States destroyers were seen steaming full speed from Pearl Harbor, and spectators reported seeing shell splashes in the ocean, indicating an engagement between United States and Japanese ships.

Several fires were started in the Honolulu area, but all were immediately controlled.

ESTIMATE OF CASUALTIES

There was no immediate statement by military officials here as to whether any servicemen were killed or injured, or as to property damage at military and naval posts.

(Soon after this dispatch was telephoned, a tight censorship was imposed on dispatches from the Hawaiian Islands. In Wash-

Turn to Page A, Column 1

Air Guards, Attention!

To chief observers: All observation posts: A.W.S. (Aircraft Warning System) You are directed to activate your observation posts immediately and to see that the post is fully manned at all times.

By order Brig. Gen. William O. Ryan, Commanding Gen., 4th Interceptor Command.

Fleet Speeds Out to Battle Invader

Tokyo Claims Battleship Sunk and Another Set Afire With Hundreds Killed on Island; Singapore Attacked and Thailand Force Landed

BY THE ASSOCIATED PRESS

Japan assaulted every main United States and British possession in the Central and Western Pacific and invaded Thailand today (Monday) in a hasty but evidently shrewdly-planned prosecution of a war she began Sunday without warning.

Her formal declaration of war against both the United States and Britain came 2 hours and 55 minutes after Japanese planes spread death and terrific destruction in Honolulu and Pearl Harbor at 7:35 a.m., Hawaiian time (10:05 a.m., P.S.T.) Sunday.

The claimed successes for this fell swoop included sinking of the United States battleship West Virginia and setting afire of the battleship Oklahoma.

WAKE CAPTURED AND GUAM BOMBED

From that moment, each tense tick of the clock brought new and flaming accounts of Japanese aggression in her secretly launched war of conquest or death for the land of the Rising Sun.

As compiled from official and unofficial accounts from all affected countries, including such sources as the Tokyo and Berlin radios, the record of Japan's daring all-or-nothing gamble ran like this:

United States transport Gen. Hugh Scott, carrying lumber, sunk, 1600 miles from Manila;

Liner President Harrison, now a transport, seized or sunk in the Yangtze River near Shanghai;

British colony of Hongkong bombed twice;

Small United States garrison at Tientsin, China, disarmed and presumably captured;

United States island of Guam bombed, surrounded and oil reservoir and hotel set afire.

Honolulu bombed a second time;

Shanghai's International Settlement seized; United States gunboat Wake captured there and British gunboat Peterel destroyed;

United States island of Wake captured;

Many points throughout the Philippine Islands bombed;

Northern Malaya and Thailand (Siam) invaded and Singapore and Bangkok bombed.

The first United States official casualty report listed 104 dead and more than 300 injured in the Army at Hickam Field, alone, near Honolulu. An N.B.C. observer in Honolulu reported the death toll at Hickam was 300.

There was heavy damage in Honolulu residential districts and the death list among civilians was large but uncounted.

GERMANS CLAIM SEA BATTLE ON

The German radio reported that a sea battle between the Japanese navy on one side and the British and United States on the other was in progress in the Western Pacific, with a third United States warship hit in addition to the West Virginia and Oklahoma.

The British command at Singapore announced the Japanese invasion and said empire forces are engaging the foe.

There was little news of United States defensive actions, except the report that a number of the attacking planes at Honolulu had been shot down in dogfights over the city;

Turn to Page A, Column 1

Latest War Bulletins

NEW YORK, Dec. 8. (AP) N.B.C. said today the United States aircraft carrier Langley was reported unofficially in Manila to have been damaged in action with Japanese forces.

Radio Tokyo, as heard by the N.B.C. listening post in Los Angeles, reported that Japanese bombers had attacked the island of Palawan in the Philippines.

NEW YORK, Dec. 8. (U.P.) The British radio today quoted Tokyo broadcasts as saying that Germany probably will declare war on the United States within the next 24 hours.

WASHINGTON, Dec. 7. (AP)—The White House announced tonight that during President Roosevelt's conference with legislative leaders and members of the Cabinet he received word from Gen. Douglas MacArthur that "enemy planes were over Central Luzon in the Philippines."

N.B.C.'s listening post here tonight heard a Tokyo radio report that 63 American soldiers guarding the American Consulate in the international settlement at Tientsin had been captured and disarmed. The report, quoting the Japanese Army Bureau, did not mention the Consulate staff.

MANAGUA (Nicaragua) Dec. 7. (U.P.)—Nicaragua tonight declared war on Japan.

NEW YORK, Dec. 7. (U.P.)—The Berlin radio, heard by the United Press listening post here, said Tokyo had announced a

Turn to Page A, Column 3

IN THE 'TIMES' TODAY

MONDAY DECEMBER 8, 1941

REMEMBER THIS

No nation is free that cannot earn its own living.

9 A.M. FINAL

Los Angeles Times

LIBERTY UNDER THE LAW — EQUAL RIGHTS — TRUE INDUSTRIAL FREEDOM

9 A.M. FINAL

VOL. LXI | THURSDAY MORNING, DECEMBER 11, 1941. | DAILY, FIVE CENTS

AXIS DECLARES WAR ON AMERICA

City's Black-out Called Success

Southland Plunged Into Darkness as Army Reports Presence of Unidentified Aircraft; Searchlights Seen and Gunfire Reported

Full Page of Pictures on Page B

A gigantic black-out, covering the area from Bakersfield south to San Diego and eastward to Boulder City and Las Vegas, Nev., went into effect shortly after 8 o'clock last night on orders from the Army 4th Interceptor Command. It continued until 11:03 p.m.

As Los Angeles went dark amidst considerable confusion and uncertainty, the Interceptor Command announced: "This is not a practice black-out."

A yellow signal, indicating the approach of enemy air raiders, was flashed on the State-wide police teletype at 7:35 p.m. Police said this signal indicated the presence of unidentified airplanes approaching Los Angeles from the sea but did not necessarily mean they were enemy.

FORT GUNNERS SCRAMBLE TO POSTS

Anti-aircraft and machine gunners scrambled to their weapons at Ft. MacArthur, which was promptly placed on an "alert" basis.

Reports that the sound of gunfire was heard could not be verified from listening posts along the beach or at the harbor.

Definite indication that the Interceptor Command meant business by calling for the black-out was contained in a statement from a spokesman who said:

"There are planes over and south of Los Angeles that are unidentified. The area will remain blacked out until we can identify them."

PLANES SENT UP TO INVESTIGATE

When asked if Army planes had been sent aloft to contact these aircraft, the spokesman said:

"You can assume there have been."

Thousands of Angelenos, listening with straining ears for sounds of aircraft, were unable to distinguish sounds of motors, however.

A few minutes after the black-out was ordered, the flashing of what appeared to be Army searchlights was visible in the higher portions of Los Angeles, 25 miles from the water front.

Headquarters of the 4th Interceptor Command, calling the black-out a success, said they had a report that unidentified airplanes were in the vicinity of Los Angeles.

Chronologically, the black-out swung into motion thusly:

7:35 p.m.—The Police Department switchboard received

Turn to Page 6, Column 6

Tokyo Claims Three Ships Sunk in Hawaii

Washington Discloses Admiral Kidd Killed in Sunday Attack on Harbor

LONDON, Dec. 11. (AP)—A Japanese naval communique reported by Reuters and credited to the German official news agency, D.N.B., said today an American destroyer, a submarine and another ship had been destroyed by direct hits off Hawaii. The communique also claimed that at least 81 United States planes were destroyed in Japanese attacks yesterday on the Philippines, 45 in air combats and 36 others on the ground.

WASHINGTON, Dec. 10. (AP)—The Navy today announced that Rear Admiral Isaac Campbell Kidd was killed in action in the attack on Pearl Harbor, Hawaii, Sunday.

Kidd was flag secretary and aide on the staff of the commander-in-chief of the Pacific Fleet, Admiral Husband Kimmel.

Admiral Kidd reported for duty as chief of staff and aide commander of battleships of the Battle Force on Feb. 3, 1940, and

Turn to Page A, Column 4

New Black-out Set for Tonight

Swiftly on the heels of last night's black-out in the Los Angeles area, Army and city officials announced that a second black-out will be held tonight.

Tonight's black-out, a trial affair for the purpose of further acquainting air-raid wardens with their duty, will be held at a time to be determined later today.

The practice black-out was decided on at a meeting of Army,

Turn to Page A, Column 2

Dictators Cry 'We'll Win'

Hitler and Mussolini Announce Action Simultaneously at Berlin and Rome; News Was Expected by Washington

BY THE ASSOCIATED PRESS

Germany and Italy declared war against the United States today, with Premier Mussolini telling cheering crowds in Rome that "it is an honor to fight together with the Japanese" while Adolf Hitler declared the war would determine history for hundreds of years to come.

"Italian men and women, once again I tell you in this great hour: We shall be victorious!" Il Duce shouted from the balcony of the Palazzo Venezia in Rome.

Washington had already discounted both declarations by the Axis powers with the official comment "so what?" and it appeared that the European dictators were offering Japan moral support rather than any possibility of actual fighting aid.

SPEAK AT SAME HOUR

In Berlin Hitler told the Reichstag:

"This has become the greatest year of decision by the German people—and your greatest decision stands before us. We'll win this war!"

The two dictators began their addresses almost simultaneously, at about 5 a.m., P.S.T.

Both had been foreshadowed, a Japanese spokes-

Turn to Page A, Column 7

War Needs Money!

It will cost money to defeat Japan. Your government calls on you to help now.

Buy Defense Bonds or stamps today. Buy them every day, if you can. But buy them on a regular basis.

Bonds cost as little as $18.75. Stamps come as low as 10 cents. Defense Bonds and Stamps can be bought at all banks and postoffices, and stamps can also be purchased at retail stores and from your newspaper carrier boy.

The Times urges all Americans to support your government with your dollars.

LATEST WAR BULLETINS

LONDON, Dec. 11. (AP)—The Berlin radio today quoted the Japanese as saying the American aircraft carrier Lexington had been sunk off Malaya.

MANILA, Dec. 11. (6:15 p.m. local time, 2:15 a.m. P.S.T.) (AP) Japanese parachute troops were reported today to have have landed at an airport six miles from Illagan, in Isabella Province 80 miles south of Aparri, and the Filipino constabulary was organizing to repel them.

TOKYO, Dec. 11. (Official radio received by (AP)) — The navy section of Japan's imperial headquarters declared today a United States destroyer and submarine were sunk and a transport ship was damaged heavily in the Japanese bombing attack yesterday on Cavite and Manila Bay.

SINGAPORE, Dec. 11. (AP)—Heavy Japanese air attacks have rendered unserviceable a number of Northern Malaya airdromes but the situation of the British forces in that sector is unchanged, a communique said today. It added that no further Japanese attempts to land at Kuantan, 200 miles above Singapore, had been made since the initial landing yesterday.

NEW YORK, Dec. 11. (AP)—The German radio broadcast a dispatch from Tokyo today that a black-out of the Japanese capital and the district surrounding it had been ordered by Japanese military authorities.

TOKYO, Dec. 11. (Official radio received by (AP))—A Japanese army communique declared Japanese landing forces occupied the capital of Guam today, capturing 350 Americans including Capt. George G. McMillin, Governor, and other officers. These, the communique said, included the Vice-Governor and commandant of the naval station. They said 25 Japanese found interned on the island were released.

BERLIN, Dec. 11. (Official radio received by (AP)) — The German high command said today the Russians had suffered heavy losses in eastern front fighting, but still described the

Turn to Page A, Column 4

U.S. Mops Up Japs at Luzon

Filipinos and Americans in Stiff Fight as Enemy Gains Foothold at Some Points in Isle; Large Nippon Warcraft Left Blazing After Hits

MANILA, Dec. 11. (4:45 p.m. local time, 12:45 a.m. P.S.T.) (AP)—Japanese forces which landed on the coasts of Luzon Island are being disposed of and mopped up by United States and Philippines troops, a United States Army spokesman declared today.

MANILA, Dec. 11. (AP) — A successful bomber attack which left a 29,000-ton Japanese battleship "blazing fiercely" and the repulse by Philippine soldiers of a light Japanese attack about 110 miles northwest of Manila were reported today by a United States Army spokesman.

"The situation is completely in hand," the spokesman said.

He declared a United States Army bomber late yesterday attacked a Japanese battleship of the Hirinuma class about 10 miles northeast of Northern Luzon Island coast.

THREE DIRECT HITS MADE

"The bomber secured three direct hits and two very close alongside," he said. "When the bomber left the battleship was blazing fiercely."

(Jane's Fighting Ships, authoritative naval manual, does not list a Hirinuma but lists a 29,330-ton Haruna as one of four ships of the Kongo class, laid down in 1911-'12 and refitted in 1926-'30.)

On land, the spokesman said, there have been no major developments since yesterday with the exception of light attacks by Japanese ground troops in the vicinity of Lingayen, a port on the Gulf of Lingayen on the western coast of Luzon. A Philippine army division stopped this thrust, he said.

(The mention of Lingayen placed the Japanese land forces nearer Manila on Luzon than at any time thus far. Previous action on Luzon has centered north of Vigan, about 200 miles north of Manila. However, the Japanese have been reported on Lubang Island, 50 miles off the entrance to Manila Bay.)

BATTLE STILL RAGING

Meanwhile, United States and Filipino troops were battling the Japanese who landed along the 160-mile coastline between Vigan and Aparri.

The Philippine army received reports that the Japanese had been checked at Aparri, on the northern tip of the island 250 miles from Manila.

The Cavite naval base and Manila itself counted probably

Turn to Page A, Column 4

ALL THE NEWS ALL THE TIME
LARGEST HOME-DELIVERED CIRCULATION
LARGEST ADVERTISING VOLUME
MAdison 2345
The Times Telephone Number

Los Angeles Times

EQUAL RIGHTS
LIBERTY UNDER THE LAW — TRUE INDUSTRIAL FREEDOM

IN THREE PARTS — 36 PAGES
Part I — GENERAL NEWS — 18 Pages
TIMES OFFICE
202 West First Street

VOL. LXI — CC — TUESDAY MORNING, FEBRUARY 24, 1942. — DAILY, FIVE CENTS

SUBMARINE SHELLS SOUTHLAND OIL FIELD

Noble Pleads Jap Case at Hearing Here

Attack on Pearl Harbor Justified, He Says at Un-American Acts Inquiry

Inured to shocking testimony by months of hearings on un-American activities, the Assembly investigating committee at its hearing in the State Building yesterday was all but floored when they heard from the lips of Robert Noble, founder and leader of the Friends of Progress, a declaration that he thought that in their attack on Pearl Harbor "the Japanese did the proper thing under the exigencies of the time."

Prior to that the committee had wrung from Noble the admission that he had received a dishonorable discharge from the United States Navy after he ran away and had been arrested for desertion.

DESERTION EXPLAINED

He shrugged it off, however, with an explanation that he then was only 19, was ill and, anyway, he did not want to fight against the Germans in the first World War. He was really a pacifist then, he said.

Another statement credited to Noble by an earlier witness was that Gen. MacArthur and his men were "not heroes but fools."

PRESIDENT 'TRIED'

Noble later denied a statement credited to him in which he urged people not to buy Defense Bonds or Stamps. He said it would have been foolish for him to have done so because it would not have done any good. Asked if he had purchased any himself, he said he had not.

Ellis O. Jones, a codirector with Noble in the Friends of Progress meetings, held weekly in a downtown hotel auditorium, admitted that the organization had conducted a mock trial of President Roosevelt on charges of being "traitorous to the American people and had gotten them into war." Jones acted as "chief justice" and at the conclusion of

Turn to Page 13, Column 3

President Pledges to Take Offensive

Roosevelt Assures Nation Pacific Fleet Intact and Engaging Foe; Promises Destruction of Jap Militarism

BY KYLE PALMER
Times Staff Representative

WASHINGTON, Feb. 23.—On a rugged note of confidence, with a certain promise that the nation's enemies soon will be on the defensive, in a pledge to victory that held no proviso or reservation, President Roosevelt tonight gave his answer to critics of his administration and told the American people what they must face in the way of sacrifice and service before the war is won.

Speaking from the White House to a radio audience that listened throughout the world and encompassed the vast spread of oceans and continents which he discussed, the President analyzed the war strategy of friend and foe, told of the mighty prep-

Turn to Page 6, Part I, for full text of President Roosevelt's talk.

arations that are being made for victory, and spiked many of the false rumors which are being circulated about our war efforts and losses.

LOSSES SUFFERED

Reiterating a pledge he made to the people on Dec. 9, in which he said the government would keep the public informed of events, good or bad, Mr. Roosevelt said on their part the people must have confidence that the government will keep nothing from them which can be published without aiding the enemy.

We have suffered and will continue to suffer losses in the Atlantic and in the Pacific, Mr. Roosevelt said, but, he added:

"Speaking for the United States of America, let me say once and for all to the people of the world: We Americans have been compelled to yield ground, but we will regain it. We and the other United Nations are committed to the destruction of the militarism of Japan and Germany.

STRENGTH INCREASING

"We are daily increasing our strength. Soon we, and not our enemies, will have the offensive; we, not they, will win the final battles, and we, not they, will make the final peace."

Germany, Italy and Japan, he pointed out, "are very close to their maximum output of planes, guns, tanks and ships," while "the United Nations are not—es-

Turn to Page 5, Column 1

Desperate Stand Taken in Burma

Last Line of Defense Before Rangoon Pounded With Terrific Intensity

LONDON, Feb. 23. (U.P.)—Burma's defenders are making a desperate stand east of the Sittang River, last defense barrier before Rangoon, but the Japanese are pressing their attacks with "utmost intensity" and are aided by reinforcements fresh from the conquest of Singapore, Far East advices said today.

CLAIM NEW LANDINGS

(Vichy and Rome radio reports said that Japanese reinforcements had landed on the west coast of the Gulf of Martaban, south of Rangoon. If true, the troops could have come by sea from Singapore through Malacca Strait and Martaban Gulf and would be in position to flank Rangoon by driving up one or more mouths of the Irrawaddy River.)

(Chungking advices said Saturday that a large Japanese convoy had been observed steaming up the gulf.)

(An American Volunteer Group officer told United Press Correspondent Karl Eskelund at A.V.G. headquarters in Southwest China that telegraphic communication with Rangoon had been cut and that fall of the city was a matter of days.)

R.A.F. REPORT

The All-India Radio heard an R.A.F. communique broadcast from Rangoon today saying that the military situation was unchanged but that violent fighting continued between the Bilin and

Turn to Page 3, Column 7

Japs on Bali Shut Off From Fleet

Enemy Ships Smashed by Bomber Assaults; Drive Deeper Into Burma

Times Pacific War Summary

Three Japanese columns, reinforced by divisions released by the fall of Singapore, were driving deeper into British Burma yesterday but in the Netherlands Indies the Nipponese appeared to have been stopped, for the moment at least, on their partly won bases off the eastern and western ends of Java.

Batavia said that planes and warships of the United Nations had smashed a Japanese invasion fleet which landed troops on Bali, off the tip of Eastern Java, and Washington reinforced this by announcing that the United States Army Air Force in the Netherlands Indies since Jan. 1 has sunk at least 9 enemy vessels and damaged 24 others. The Bali invaders were cut off by the Jap fleet losses.

It was admitted, however, that the Japanese hold the important Denpasar Airdrome and other strategic points on Bali and that their conquest of Southeastern Sumatra is virtually complete.

The situation in the Far East yesterday as summarized from United Press and Associated Press dispatches was:

EAST INDIES—It seemed certain that the Japanese invasion fleet suffered heavily. Estimates ranged from 5 to 15 Jap ships were sunk, most of them victims of airplanes. The Japanese apparently captured the Denpasar Airdrome in good condition since the communique said that American planes bombed it yesterday, damaging the runways and field.

BURMA — London admitted the prospects in Burma were gloomy but it was asserted that combined forces of Indian, British and American-volunteer fighter planes had established air superiority over the battle front, which apparently was along the Sittang River, just west of the vital Rangoon-Lashio Railway.

PHILIPPINES—There was little change in the situation on the Bataan Peninsula where Gen. Douglas MacArthur's durable Filipino and American troops again had fought the Japanese to a standstill.

Japs Control Bali Airport

BANDOENG (Dutch East Indies) Feb. 23. (AP)—The Japanese enemy has overrun part of Bali and controls the airport at Denpasar, on the southeast of the island near its only good harbor, but his entire invading fleet has been destroyed, damaged or dispersed and his landing troops are isolated, the Dutch announced tonight.

Thus was summed up the first phase of the invader's thrust at the near approaches to the Java keystone in the Allied arch—a thrust in which Japanese sea power suffered, under co-ordinated American-Dutch bomber and warship fire, its gravest wounds

Turn to Page 3, Column 3

Japanese Make Direct Hit North of Santa Barbara

No Lives Lost and Little Damage Inflicted by First Enemy Assault on Soil of United States Since War Started in December; Witnesses Declare Submersible Fired 16 Shots From Mile Offshore

In the first attack upon United States soil since this war began, an enemy submarine rose out of the sea off the rich oil fields at Ellwood, 12 miles north of Santa Barbara, shortly after 7 p.m. yesterday and pumped 16 shells into the tidewater fields, but caused only superficial damage.

A single oil well derrick was reported by eyewitnesses to have been hit, but there were no casualties in human life.

Choosing the dramatic instant of the halfway mark in President Roosevelt's fireside chat, the commander of the presumably Japanese submarine opened fire from his deck guns at 7:15 p.m.

Three of the shells dug up the sands off the Bankline Oil Co. refinery. The only damage in the raid was the destruction of rigging and pumping equipment of a well about a quarter of a mile from the beach. Loss was estimated at several thousand dollars.

NAVY BEGINS HUNT FOR SUB

One of the shells whistled three miles inland to the Tecolote ranch where it exploded. Another missile gouged out a five-foot-wide crater on the Staniff ranch near by. The other salvos fell short of their marks, it was asserted, and dropped into the sea.

Navy planes roared over the channel a short time later and counteroperations were begun.

Four Japanese and one Italian were taken into custody

Illustrated on Page B

by Ventura County Sheriff's authorities last night shortly after the attack. Two Japs were said to have been riding around the city during the blackout in a station wagon, armed with guns. For more than two hours after the raid, brilliant yellow flares burst over darkened Ventura. Authorities said it was clearly an effort to signal the enemy.

RAIDER LAST SEEN HEADED SOUTH

When last reported, about 8:30 p.m. by a minister at Montecito, the submarine was slipping out of the Santa Barbara Channel in the direction of Los Angeles. The clergyman, Rev. Arthur Basham of Pomona, who was visiting there, said he observed the "pigboat" flashing signal lights, apparently to someone on shore.

The Ventura County Sheriff's office received reports that flares had been sighted lighting the skies at several points along the coast in Ventura County near Hueneme.

At 7:58 p.m. upon orders of the Fourth Interceptor Command all radio stations in Southern California abruptly left the air. A few minutes later the coast line was completely blacked out from Carpinteria to Goleta. The blackout area covered a distance of about 25 miles. The yellow alert flashed simultaneously in police headquarters in Los Angeles.

The "all-clear" signal light was flashed in Los Angeles at 12:11 a.m., four hours and 13 minutes later.

SANTA BARBARA BLACKED OUT

Air-raid sirens screamed in Santa Barbara and within a few moments the entire city was dark.

At 12:20 a.m. today the all clear was sounded.

First report of the submarine reached the Sheriff's office from Mrs. George Heaney on San Marcos Pass, northwest of Santa Barbara. She informed authorities that she heard the first gun report shortly after 7 p.m. With field glasses, she said she sighted the submarine. It was lying about a mile offshore.

The next report came from Bob Miller of the Bankline Oil Co., who gave a similar report. By this time, the guns of the submarine were speaking repeatedly and shells shrieking overhead.

F. W. Borden, superintendent of the Bankline plant, gave this eyewitness account of the raid to the 11th Naval District.

"At 7:10 P.W.T., one large submarine came to the surface

Turn to Page A, Column 3

Shelling of Oil Field Described by Eyewitness

Restaurant Man First Believed Explosions Caused by Army Conducting Target Practice

"Their marksmanship was rotten!"

Thus did Lawrence Wheeler, proprietor of a roadside inn situated in the heart of the Ellwood oil fields, describe the shelling of the fields by enemy submarine deck guns last night.

"It started about 7:15 p.m.," he said. "I know it was about that time because we were serving dinners to customers and listening to the President's speech, and he was about halfway through.

HEARD LOUD REPORT

"Suddenly we heard a loud report, followed in a few moments by another. Some soldiers who were in my place said it was probably just target practice.

"We heard a bit later that the oil fields were being shelled. I went outside and ran over to a point whence I could see the ocean. It looked like a submarine, about a mile offshore, cruising slowly down the coast and firing at regular intervals.

"I could see the flashes as the gun went off.

AIMED AT PLANT

"The submarine seemed to be aiming at the Barnsdall Oil Co.'s main absorption plant, located almost on the beach.

"They missed with all their shots at this plant, though some of the shells landed fairly close, throwing up geysers of dirt and sand near the building.

"One shell hit a well and blew the pumping plant and derrick to bits.

"That was the only real damage they did.

"There must have been 20 or 25 men working in the field at the time. Nobody was injured.

NOTIFIED SHERIFF

"One of their shots whistled over my inn, which is a good mile from the shore line, and burst up the canyon on the Hollister estate across the highway.

"We notified the Sheriff's office and they said planes would be here in 10 minutes.

"It seemed to me as if the enemy vessel was firing a 5 or 6-inch gun. Their shooting wasn't very good, because that absorption plant was a beautiful target and they didn't hit it."

CUSTOMERS CALM

Mrs. Wheeler added this account:

"I saw the explosions. At first they were very faint. I thought it was the Army practicing but then I heard a shell fly overhead and strike in a canyon inshore from our place."

Wheeler said there was no panic among his customers.

"We immediately blacked out the place," he said. "One shell landed about a quarter of a mile from here and the concussion shook the building but nobody was scared much."

Suspicious Lights Flashed Here After Submarine Attack

Flashlights in the hands of suspicious persons, possibly signalers, were reported to police last night shortly after a Japanese submarine dropped shells near Santa Barbara.

Six calls were received by the police complaint board, telling of the blinking flashlights in various parts of the city. One witness said he saw one or two persons at the end of the Venice pier with flashlights.

Policemen were dispatched to the locations given, but in all instances the suspicious persons were gone.

During the radio blackout coincident with the shelling, hundreds of phone calls were received by the board inquiring whether residence lights should be doused. Callers were reminded that one of the rules during an alert was not to use the telephone.

IN THE 'TIMES' TODAY

TUESDAY FEBRUARY 24, 1942

ALL THE NEWS ALL THE TIME

LARGEST HOME-DELIVERED CIRCULATION
LARGEST ADVERTISING VOLUME

MAdison 2345
The Times Telephone Number

Los Angeles Times

EQUAL RIGHTS
LIBERTY UNDER THE LAW — TRUE INDUSTRIAL FREEDOM

IN NINE PARTS — 118 PAGES

Part I — GENERAL NEWS — 16 Pages

FINAL EDITION

VOL. LXI — CCC — SUNDAY MORNING, MARCH 22, 1942. — SUNDAY, 10 CENTS in 100-mile zone 12 CENTS Elsewhere

Japs Open New Bataan Offensive

Japanese Here Begin Exodus

Nation's Greatest Mass Evacuation Starts as Vanguard of 35,000 Southland Nipponese Moves to Owens Valley Concentration Center

America's greatest mass evacuation began yesterday as 86 Japanese aliens and American-born citizens arrived in Manzanar, new evacuees' city in Owens Valley, from Los Angeles.

They are the forerunners of some 35,000 of their race who will be moved out of Southern California, first to the Owens Valley camp and later, after classification as to industrial ability, to inland concentration centers.

Eventually, a total of more than 170,000 Japanese, Germans and Italians will be evacuated from coastal communities.

DEWITT VISITS CAMP

The arrival of the first contingent of Los Angeles Japanese at Manzanar was preceded by an inspection visit by Lieut. Gen. John L. DeWitt, chief of the Western Defense Command, who flew down from his San Francisco headquarters with members of his staff to look over the huge establishment now rising in the remote valley.

He expressed himself as pleased with the progress made at the camp, where hundreds of carpenters and other artisans are building houses, assembly halls, a hospital and other facilities for the 10,000 evacuees who will soon people Manzanar.

GROUP OF ARTISANS

The first contingent of Japanese to leave Los Angeles in compliance with Gen. DeWitt's orders was comprised of plumbers, painters, nurses, cooks, waiters, bakers and stenographers, all of whom left voluntarily to aid in preparing the evacuation center for the thousands of others who will be taken there in the near future.

With the small amount of their worldly possessions they were able to take packed into neat bundles, this group climbed into three busses and a truck in the playground of the Maryknoll School, Third and Hewitt Sts., and waved good-by to more than 200 of their friends and relatives who had gathered to see them off.

MOVE SWIFTLY

Here and there, traditional Oriental stoicism cracked and there were a few tears, but for the most part, the voluntary evacuees evinced little emotion.

Headed by Army cars, the little motorcade proceeded swiftly through the city and out on the highway leading toward Manzanar.

Tomorrow morning, approximately 1000 Japanese will leave for the evacuation city on a special train and in busses, while a huge motorcade, again under the convoy of the Army, will depart from the Rose Bowl in

Turn to Page 13, Column 1

Plane Plants Work Lauded

Truman Committee Turns Critical Guns on War and O.P.M. Chiefs

Praise for aircraft manufacturers and criticism of the War Department and the Office of Production Management highlighted a report released here yesterday by a subcommittee of the special Senate (Truman) committee investigating the aviation industry.

After inspecting Southland air plants and hearing testimony here since last Monday, Senators Mon C. Wallgren, Harley M. Kilgore and Joseph H. Ball told newsmen "the airplane plants have done a marvelous job considering the conditions under which they have had to work."

SHORTAGES EXIST

They pointed to the mushrooming expansion of the industry and acknowledged that temporary shortages exist as the result of inevitable lag where the manufacturers—serving largely as assembly plants—depend on thousands of items delivered from almost every State in the Union.

In this connection the subcommittee criticized the War Department and the O.P.M. for "failure . . . to realize soon enough the necessity of expanding the production of suppliers of parts."

TEXT OF STATEMENT

The full statement follows:

"The subcommittee has visited most of the airplane plants in the Los Angeles area. It has ascertained the number of airplanes being delivered and has found that deliveries of completed airplanes are increasing each month.

"The airplane manufacturing plants are, and of necessity must be, principally assembly plants. They assemble thousands of items which are manufactured in almost every State in the Union by thousands of plants. Some of the suppliers of such parts

Turn to Page 12, Column 5

EASTWARD, HO—Uprooted by grim requirements of war, the first contingent of Japanese is shown waiting to board busses for journey to concentration camp at Manzanar. Vanguard of an army of 35,000 Nipponese in Southland, they went voluntarily. Times photo

Sales of Sugar Face Week Ban

Government Orders Halt on April 27 in Rationing Setup

CHICAGO, March 21. (AP)—All sugar sales in the United States will be halted at midnight April 27 for approximately one week, government officials announced today after they had set six days in April and May for the nationwide sugar rationing registration.

John E. Hamm, acting chief of the Office of Price Administration, reported that sugar will be off the market on April 28 and will not be available to buyers again until about May 5.

Hamm explained that the ban was ordered as a step preparatory to sales under rationing, which will go into effect as soon as the moratorium on sales ends.

Earlier, dates were fixed for the national registration—biggest in the history of the United States and involving every man, woman and child in the country.

Frank Bane, field chief of the O.P.A., announced that individual or family consumers will register May 4, 5, 6 and 7 at public elementary schools, and that wholesalers, retailers, bakers, confectioners and other industrial users will register April 28 and 29 at high schools.

The periods for recording the data concerning 131,000,000 Americans were scheduled at a conference of rationing administrators from the 48 States.

Bane reported that it had not

Turn to Page 12, Column 6

Unions' Grip on Farmers and Consumers Related

Thurman Arnold Accuses Organized Labor of Destroying Independent Businessmen

WASHINGTON, March 21. (AP)—Attacking organized labor in terms seldom, if ever, used by a New Deal official, Thurman Arnold, Assistant Attorney General, accused the unions today of a long list of misdeeds which, he asserted, are preventing the efficient use of men and machines and hampering the distribution of civilian necessities.

He charged organized labor with injuring or destroying independent businessmen, holding farmers and consumers "at its mercy," impeding the distribution of housing and food and of "undemocratic procedures" within itself.

NO RIGHTS RESPECTED

On the witness stand of the House Judiciary Committee, he said a pending bill to require the registration of labor unions was insufficient to protect the public from the practices which he alleged. "No other group in our society" could do anything like the things of which he complained and escape punishment, he said.

"Today, under Federal law, there is no right of the farmer which labor is bound to respect, there is no right of the consumer which labor is bound to respect and there is no right of the small businessman which labor is bound to respect," he asserted.

Arnold added that all three groups are "entirely subject to the will of the labor union . . . People complain to us and we have to say to them that there is nothing we can do." Arnold is in charge of antitrust prosecutions for the Justice Department.

LAWS INADEQUATE

He said that State laws are inadequate to meet the situation, explaining that even if an employer were successful in obtaining an injunction against a labor organization, the labor organization could boycott the employer's goods in another State.

"Independent businessmen all over the United States are completely at the mercy of organized labor groups," Arnold said.

In discussing a proposal that both labor union and trade association finances must be made public, Arnold declared that he could not "see any reason why contributions should not be made public and I can see every reason why they should."

NO NEED SIGHTED

Arnold's testimony capped a week of hearings by several committees or subcommittees on labor's relation to the war effort. They were aimed mostly at determining whether legislation should be enacted to outlaw the closed shop and suspend the overtime pay provisions of the wage-hour law for the duration of the war.

In the face of strong agitation for such action, the chairman of one committee, Senator Thomas (D.) Okla., said today that the hearings had demonstrated no

Turn to Page 8, Column 5

MacArthur Warns About False Hopes

Australians Reminded Modern War Requires More Than Courage

BY HAROLD GUARD

MELBOURNE, March 21. (U.P.)—Australia tonight heard Gen. Douglas MacArthur's grim warning that success against Japan hinges upon "careful preparation . . . sufficient troops and sufficient material."

After a welcome here that this Down Under continent accords only to heroes, the American commander closeted himself with his United States and Australian military associates. He began drafting plans to carry into execution his assigned duty—that of carrying back the war to Japan and striking hard enough to relieve the pressure upon his defenders of Bataan who sent him off with a pledge they would fight to the last man before yielding to Japan.

WARNS AUSTRALIANS

It was expected MacArthur and the American and Australian staffs will meet with Prime Minister John Curtin at Canberra shortly, possibly Sunday.

The general's first act was to warn Australia against overconfidence and airy optimism with a sharp reminder "modern war requires something more than courage and willingness to die."

MacArthur's realistic declaration was backed by Curtin who asserted the task facing Australia and America "is to hold what territory we still command and to fight back until the territory already occupied by the Japanese is recovered and liberated."

GROUNDWORK LAID

MacArthur found the groundwork for American-Australian co-operation already well advanced. Lieut. Gen. George H. Brett, his vice-commander, already is drafting plans to unify the Australian and American air forces on a basis of operating together in the same squadrons.

However, many major matters of strategy, co-ordination, supply and materiel as well as what were called "certain important political questions arising from MacArthur's appointment and other events of the past few days"—presumably the controversy between Curtin and Prime Minister Churchill—must be ironed out.

A far-reaching shake-up of the Australian army command is expected in which Maj. Gen. Thomas Blamey, who led Australian troops in the Middle East, may assume command of all Australian land forces under MacArthur.

Tonight MacArthur was in seclusion. American sentries stood guard around the hotel. They carried side arms but no rifles.

Turn to Page 3, Column 5

Foe Loses Two More Cruisers

Yamashita Launches Long-Expected Attack on Luzon With Sea Blockade and Bombardment; MacArthur Acclaimed by Throngs at Melbourne

Times Pacific War Summary

While MacArthur's airmen blasted a new gap in the Japanese invasion fleet off Australia yesterday, damaging two more enemy cruisers, the long-anticipated full-scale offensive apparently was launched against the defenders of Bataan Peninsula in the Philippines.

Enemy warships were seeking to blockade all of the unoccupied islands of the Philippines and batteries ashore hammered heavily at Manila Bay fortifications. Gen. Wainwright, who succeeded Gen. MacArthur as commander of the dauntless American and Filipino defenders, reported to the War Department that Gen. Yamashita's renewed assault on the peninsula appeared certain.

Meanwhile, Gen. MacArthur, arriving in Melbourne, received the tumultuous welcome of a hero, but, even while the cheers were ringing, the supreme commander of the Allied forces in the Southwest Pacific was warning Australia and the United States that his success there will depend primarily on the resources placed at his disposal by the United Nations.

Other developments yesterday in the Pacific as summarized from Associated Press and United Press dispatches, included:

AUSTRALIA — Prime Minister John Curtin reported that two more Japanese cruisers have been damaged, one probably sunk, by American and Australian airmen at Rabaul, bringing the toll of enemy ships sunk or damaged to 28 within the past two weeks. Australian planes also started big fires in raids on the island of Yamdena in the Timor group.

EAST INDIES — The Navy Department in Washington announced that the American gunboat Asheville presumably was lost in action south of Java, and it was feared that about 185 officers and men had perished with their ship.

BURMA — Strong Japanese forces were reported massed for a drive through the Sittang River defenses near Toungoo toward the Irrawaddy, on the Burma flank where Chinese troops and the American commander Gen. Joseph Stilwell already have gone into action.

U.S. Gunboat Lost in Action

Asheville, Attacked by Enemy South of Java, Carried About 185 Men

WASHINGTON, March 21. (U.P.) The United States gunboat Asheville, attacked by the enemy south of Java, is missing and presumed lost, the Navy announced tonight.

Ships of this type normally carry a complement of about 185 officers and men.

The Asheville, a 1270-ton vessel launched in 1918, was operated with the special service squadron of the Asiatic Fleet.

NAVY COMMUNIQUE

Text of Navy communique No. 59, based upon information received up to 5 p.m., P.W.T.:

"Far East—Early this month the United States gunboat Asheville was attacked by the enemy south of Java.

"The Asheville has been reported missing for some days and must be presumed to be lost.

"The next of kin of the personnel of the Asheville have been notified."

Sinking of the Asheville brings to 18 the number of naval vessels officially reported as lost. The losses include one battleship, one cruiser, seven destroyers, three submarines, a Coast Guard cutter and four miscellaneous.

It does not include the battleship Oklahoma, capsized at Pearl Harbor.

MINE SWEEPER LOST

In addition, the Navy said unofficially some time ago that a mine sweeper had been lost in the evacuation of Cavite naval base, Philippine Islands. Thirteen of the 18 losses were by enemy action.

The Japanese have claimed capture or destruction of several gunboats formerly used on the Yangtze River as part of the Asiatic Fleet, but these losses never have been confirmed.

The Asheville apparently was lost in the Battle of Java which cost the United States the cruiser Houston and the destroyer

Turn to Page 3, Column 6

Guns Shatter Lull at Bataan

WASHINGTON, March 21. (AP) The long-smoldering Philippine fighting front burst into flame today and the American-Filipino defenders braced for a new full-scale Japanese offensive.

While patrols skirmished sharply on the Bataan Peninsula, enemy batteries hammered at the Manila Bay fortifications, the War Department reported.

Japanese warships, including cruisers and destroyers, scouted around the islands, seeking to

Turn to Page 2, Column 3

IN THE 'TIMES' TODAY

SUNDAY MARCH 22, 1942

Submarine Off United States Sunk by American Bomber

NEW YORK, March 21. (AP)—With depth charges and machine-gun fire, an American bomber destroyed an Axis submarine off the Eastern United States coast, Lieut. Gen. Hugh A. Drum, commander of the eastern Army forces, disclosed tonight.

After depth charges had scored two direct hits on the conning tower, the plane pilot reported "the submarine was a clay pigeon . . . it looked as if we had struck an oil well."

"Destruction of the submarine was complete," Gen. Drum said. "The sea was covered with oil and debris. It is considered improbable that there could have been any survivors."

FOUR CHARGES DROPPED

Four depth charges were dropped by the bomber, which spotted the sub from about two miles away while the plane was bound home from a photographic mission, the general said.

Second Lieutenant E. H. Epperson of Scott City, Kan., the bomber's pilot, declared:

"We could see the conning tower clear of the water. We made four runs over the submarine and dropped one depth charge on each run. The first two were direct hits on the conning tower.

"Crippled by the first hit, the submarine was a clay pigeon for the following runs. The third blast was a 'short,' the fourth was an 'over' (a near miss.)

DESTRUCTION COMPLETE

"It looked as if we had struck an oil well. The submarine disappeared from sight. My report reads: 'Complete destruction of enemy submarine.'"

The co-pilot, Second Lieutenant Barney L. Johnson of Ft. Worth, Tex., said the bombing was from an altitude of 100 feet.

"We were on a photographic mission," Johnson said. "We went immediately to the submarine to launch our attack. There is no question about it. The submarine was destroyed."

In addition to the depth charges, the plane machine-gunned the U-boat, Corp. Clifton A. Cyr of Spokane, Wash., was the gunner.

"I gave the sub four bursts of

Turn to Page 6, Column 3

Five Die in Army Bomber Crash

Two Others Pulled From Wreckage Burned Badly

MEMPHIS (Tenn.) March 21. (AP)—Five men were killed when a two-motored Army bomber crashed and burned near the Municipal Airport today.

Two others were pulled from the flaming wreckage, badly burned.

The plane took off from the airport and crashed into the underbrush a quarter-mile from the airport.

Maj. A. D. Perley, commander of the Army Air Corps detachment here, identified the dead as:

Second Lieutenant J. F. Simpson, pilot.

Second Lieutenant J. P. Treadaway.

Second Lieutenant F. E. Budenholzer.

Second Lieutenant R. C. Jones.

Technical Sergeant V. A. Costlow.

The injured:

Lieut. Edward C. Huggs, 22, of Arkadelphia, Ark. His condition was undetermined.

Sergt. Richard Gemiem. His condition was reported as critical.

Plots to Kill MacArthur Disclosed by Gen. Casey

LONDON, March 21. (AP)—Brig. Gen. Hugh J. Casey, who accompanied Gen. Douglas MacArthur from Bataan to Australia, said today that MacArthur had had a number of escapes "from deliberate plots to kill him" by captured Japanese and from attempts by guerrillas and snipers to capture him.

The Japanese believe it a disgrace to be taken prisoner and as a result fight to the last, but Americans have a few prisoners, he added.

Gen. Casey also told of the amazing escape from the Philippines. The group roared away from Bataan in four speedboats under the noses of Japanese land forces and made rendezvous with two Flying Fortress-type bombers on an unnamed island two days later.

The boats, 70 feet long, were assembled at various points on Bataan. The odyssey started at dusk on March 11. The boats shot seaward through the night and tore through a moderate sea with no signs of pursuing Japanese ships or aircraft the first night.

The Japanese obviously had expected MacArthur to leave in a submarine.

Casey said throughout the next day the boats pressed on and just before night they saw the silhouette of a Japanese destroyer on the horizon. The speedboats, however, were not observed and the destroyer vanished in the blackness of the night. The next morning the party reached the island and climbed wearily aboard the huge bombers for the second leg of their trip to Darwin.

ALL THE NEWS ALL THE TIME
LARGEST HOME-DELIVERED CIRCULATION
LARGEST ADVERTISING VOLUME
MAdison 2345
The Times Telephone Number

Los Angeles Times

EQUAL RIGHTS
LIBERTY UNDER THE LAW — TRUE INDUSTRIAL FREEDOM

IN EIGHT PARTS — 132 PAGES
Part I — GENERAL NEWS — 30 Pages
FINAL EDITION

VOL. LXI — CCCC — SUNDAY MORNING, NOVEMBER 29, 1942. — SUNDAY, 10 CENTS in 100-mile zone 15 CENTS Elsewhere

260 Die in Boston Night Club Fire

Reds Kill 10,000 in New Nazi Rout

Soviets Free 300 Areas in Surprise Push

Russians Put Five German Divisions to Flight in Northern Drive

MOSCOW, Nov. 29 (Sunday.) (AP)—The Russians announced today that a surprise offensive on the northwest front had killed 10,000 German troops, routed five divisions, "liberated more than 300 populated places" and broken wide gaps in German fortifications less than 90 miles from the old Latvian border.

A special communique issued by the Soviets said that the Red army had broken through a "strongly fortified defense zone of the enemy" and that in the area of the town of Velikie Luki, which is 90 miles from Latvia, "the German front has been broken over a distance of 30 kilometers (about 20 miles.)"

RAIL LINE BROKEN

The Russians have, in fact, pushed on to the west of Velikie Luki, for the communique said the rail line between Velikie Luki and Novosokoliniki, 25 miles to the west of that city, had been broken, as well as the line from Velikie Luki to Nevel, 35 miles southwest of Velikie Luki.

The Russians, who usually broadcast their communiques without fanfare, announced this one with jubilation and singing.

All programs were interrupted.

The radio announcer then repeated several times that "This is Moscow calling" in a particularly triumphant tone and followed it by reading the recital of victories slowly and emphatically.

NAZIS ADMIT DRIVE

Songs were sung over the radio after the text was read.

The Germans already have broadcast that heavy operations were in progress on the northwest front but the Russians kept silent until the paean of triumph early today.

In sum, the Russians announced these victories in their new offensive while the Red army was cutting deeper into the German lines in the Stalingrad fighting:

About 10,000 enemy dead left on the battlefield;

Four infantry divisions and one tank division of the Ger-

Turn to Page 2, Column 3

R.A.F. Deals North Italy New Blows

LONDON, Nov. 29 (Sunday.) (AP)—Home-based bombers of the R.A.F. took the long road over the Alps to attack Northern Italy again last night, it was announced today.

It was the first such foray by the R.A.F. since the night of Nov. 20, when Turin was subjected to a devastating assault which the British described as the heaviest raid ever made on Italy.

Last night's attack was the seventh of the month on Northern Italy and marked the 11th time that R.A.F. bombers have made the 1500-mile round trip across the Alps since Oct. 22, when the British launched their new offensive against Italian targets with a powerful raid on Genoa.

The size of the force which participated in last night's raid and the specific targets were not immediately revealed.

Nine Axis Ships Sunk

British Subs Also Damage Cruiser and Three Other Vessels

LONDON, Nov. 28. (AP)—Nine more Axis supply ships, including a tank carrier, have been sunk in the Mediterranean by British submarines fighting attempts to rush men and provisions to German and Italian troops now forced back within 15 miles of Tunis.

Announcement of this destruction of Axis ships and supplies urgently needed by the Nazi defenders of Tunis and Bizerte came from the British Admiralty at the same time that enemy sources described the mounting scale of the Allied assault on the North African siege ports.

In addition to the nine cargo vessels sunk, the British reported they had damaged three other supply ships and an Italian destroyer of the Trione class that was escorting the relief convoy. The date of the sinkings was not given.

Among the ships sunk was a large twin-funneled passenger liner which was intercepted off the coast of Sicily. Another was a small tanker laden with benzine. A second tanker which previously had been damaged by aircraft was found burning and was sunk by torpedoes, the Admiralty said.

The tank-landing craft, of me-

Turn to Page 8, Column 4

First French Ship to Escape Toulon Docks

Nazi Reprisals Hinted as Reports Say Vichy Cabinet Dismissed

LONDON, Nov. 28. (U.P.)—Arrival at Barcelona of a French submarine from Toulon bolstered hope today that more submarines and perhaps surface units had escaped the scuttling of the French fleet and might join Allied naval forces in North Africa.

The submarine, which was given 24 hours to leave Barcelona or be interned, is the first French warship known definitely to have escaped Toulon. It is believed that, rather than undergo internment, it might attempt the run down the Spanish coast to Gibraltar, 550 miles away, or cross to any one of several Allied ports in French North Africa. The closest is Algiers, 260 miles due south.

THREE SHIPS INTACT

Radio Vichy reported tonight that three destroyers are intact in Toulon. During the fighting, the broadcast said, two persons were killed and 27 were wounded in the Toulon fortress.

Allied authorities, taking hope that other fleet units might have escaped, announced they are prepared to give all assistance needed by any French warship seeking haven from the Axis.

British warships cruised likely areas of the Mediterranean in search for French ships, which would have to weave their way through waters dangerously infested with Axis submarines.

CRUSHED HITLER HOPES

The scuttling of the French fleet, which the Nazis said had been complete, crushed Adolf Hitler's last hope of making some advantage of the North African situation and left the Italian fleet, if it dares emerge for battle, exposed to the full attention of British naval units.

The internal political situation in France, as a result of Hitler's

Turn to Page 8, Column 2

French Fleet Scuttle Order Given in 1940

LONDON, Nov. 28. (AP)—A communique broadcast from Vichy tonight said the French fleet at Toulon had been scuttled on instructions issued at the time of the armistice of 1940 and that the suicide of the warships was preferable to "letting them be taken over by any foreign power whatever."

NIGHT CLUB IN RUINS—Boston City firemen inspect ruins of the Cocoanut Grove, Back Bay area night club, after a devastating fire destroyed it last night, killing, injuring and trapping hudreds of merrymakers. (AP) Wirephoto

Rising Toll May Hit 400

Hospitals Crowded With Victims of Blaze; Flames Flash as National Anthem Opens Show; Many Merrymakers Jump to Safety or Death

BOSTON, Nov. 29 (Sunday.) (AP) — Fire which flashed swiftly among Saturday night merrymakers in the Cocoanut Grove night club in the Back Bay district killed an estimated 260 and injured scores of others and some officials at the disordered scene estimated the death toll might rise still higher.

Newsmen counted 210 bodies at the city's Southern Mortuary and 50 more at the Northern Mortuary.

A night club manager who was in the Cocoanut Grove when the fire broke out estimated there might have been as many as 1000 persons in the building at the time.

POSSIBLE DEAD ESTIMATED AT 400

As officials tried desperately to gain a true estimate of the dead, an unofficial compilation made at police headquarters placed the possible dead at above 400. The possibility existed, however, that some of the bodies counted in hospitals might have been counted again at the morgues.

In addition to those at the Northern and Southern Mortuaries, the Massachusetts General Hospital reported 65 dead, Peter Bent Brigham Hospital 22 and other hospitals counted bodies numbering up to 15.

ALL OF CITY'S FACILITIES CALLED

All bodies were believed removed from the one-and-a-half-story building by 1:15 a.m., three hours after the first alarm, which was followed by four others and calls for all available ambulances, police cars and physicians. Soldiers sailors and Coast Guardsmen assisted in carrying out the dead.

Eyewitnesses said a cloud of smoke burst among the dancers just as the orchestra prepared to play the "Star Spangled Banner," opening the floor show. Some said the blaze apparently originated in the kitchen, in the cellar, and spread swiftly to the Melody Room, a lounge also below street level.

MERRYMAKERS LEAP FROM ROOF

Some of the trapped night clubbers leaped from the roof and landed on parked automobiles. Others fled the burning building, their clothing aflame.

Surrounding communities sent ambulances, and beach wagons, private cars and virtually all types of usable vehicles were used to move the injured to hospitals. Large express vans, with policemen riding the running boards, helped carry bodies to the city's two principal morgues.

Soon after midnight, while firemen still tried to quell the flames enough so that all the bodies could be recovered, a call was made for all medical examiners in the State to report.

INTERIOR GUTTED

The interior of the low stucco front building was gutted. Lined with cloth hangings that were clustered at the ceiling, the interior apparently flamed up in a burst and dozens who tried to rush for the doors were trapped.

In a steady stream bodies, fantastically twisted, were carried from the still-smoking door of the night club into a garage directly across the street. Automobiles were hurriedly shifted to make room for the blanket-covered forms.

The bodies were lined up in symmetrical rows and virtually the entire floor was covered with gray-blanketed forms, some with knees raised, some with shoes missing, some with smoke-blackened hands hanging over the sides

Turn to Page 11, Column 1

American Bombers Rip Jap Solomons Bases

Concentrated Attack by Planes Destroys Buildings and Sets Fire to Enemy Airdrome

WASHINGTON, Nov. 28. (U.P.) American bombers from Guadalcanal have smashed an important Japanese supply base in the Solomons and heavily blasted a major enemy airdrome, the Navy announced today.

The attacks were carried out while United States ground forces on the island were continuing mopping-up activities west of Henderson Field, apparently in preparation for a drive to exterminate the poorly supplied and meagerly reinforced Japanese troops on Guadalcanal.

ALL BUILDINGS DESTROYED

In the most recent patrol activities reported by the Navy, American patrols on Friday (Solomons time) killed 50 Japanese and captured several machine guns west of Point Cruz. Point Cruz is about six miles west of the Guadalcanal airfield in the direction of Cape Esperance, where most of the enemy's forces on the island are believed to be concentrated.

The air attacks were launched against the Munda area of New Georgia Island, about 185 miles northwest of Guadalcanal, and the enemy's Kahili airdrome near Buin on Bougainville Island.

In the attacks on Munda, carried out Nov. 23 and 24 (island time) "all buildings in the vicinity were destroyed," the communique said.

At midnight on the night of Nov. 26-27 seven Army Flying Fortresses scored 16 hits on the runway at Kahili and started large fires without encountering enemy opposition. Kahili is one of the air bases from which the Japanese had been launching long-range fighters and bombers against American positions on Guadalcanal.

The Navy attached considerable importance to the raids on Munda. The first was mentioned in a communique on Nov. 25 which said that American fighter planes and dive bombers attacked the supply base, smashing a warehouse. That raid was followed up with another on Nov. 24 which left not a single structure standing.

NUISANCE RAIDS BY FOE

During the night of Nov. 27 two enemy bombers dropped bombs near the mouth of the Lunga River on Guadalcanal but, the Navy said, "no damage was suffered." It was the third successive night in which the Japanese carried out nuisance raids, presumably to break up the rest of American forces and to keep American planes confined to the vicinity of Guadalcanal.

Airmen from Guadalcanal have been carrying out intensive night patrol activity for the dual purpose of preventing Japanese night landing attempts and of keeping enemy planes pinned to

Turn to Page 6, Column 2

Rationing Hits More Articles

Coffee on List Today; Gasoline Tuesday; Others May Follow

With coffee being added to the list of rationed commodities today and gasoline scheduled to follow on Tuesday, Southern Californians, along with the rest of the nation, are beginning to feel the pinch of wartime living more acutely than ever before.

And yesterday local Federal officials admitted that the scarcity of meat, butter and eggs—three commodities which form the basis of most housewives' menus—is becoming a more serious problem daily.

COFFEE SALES RESUMED

This morning America will have its customary cup of coffee, but there'll be no warmups or refills.

Retail coffee sales, frozen for a week to allow stores to stock up, will be resumed. Each customer 15 years old or more possessing a sugar ration book will be permitted to purchase one pound. This amount must last each consumer until Jan. 3, 1943—at a rate of one cup per day.

The last eight stamps in the sugar ration book have been earmarked for coffee purchases, in the following sequence: No. 27 and 28; 25 and 26; 23 and 24, 21 and 22 and 20.

Stamp No. 27 will be torn off by the retailer for the first pound you buy. Validation periods and unit value of stamps following No. 27 have not been determined.

ADVANCE BUYING HIT

In order to conserve present coffee stocks, Office of Price Administration officials warned the public not to purchase beyond immediate needs. Use of one stamp at a time for the family allowance was urged.

"Anyone possessing more than one pound per adult will be violating the regulations if he purchases more coffee with the stamps in his sugar book," the O.P.A. warned.

"Further, consumers will be required to account for excess supplies when Ration Book No. 2 is issued."

Most war price rationing boards in Southern California will remain open today to continue the processing of requests for supplemental gasoline ration-

Turn to Page 3, Column 5

IN THE 'TIMES' TODAY

SUNDAY NOVEMBER 29, 1942

REMEMBER THIS

No thought that makes life worthier will ever die.

The War Fronts

RUSSIA—Moscow jubilantly announced a new offensive in the north against the Nazis, saying 10,000 German troops were killed, five divisions routed, 300 populated places liberated and wide gaps broken in enemy lines 90 miles from old Latvian border. Page 1.

MEDITERRANEAN—French submarine, survivor of Toulon, arrived in Spain, indicating more may have escaped; rumors fly on Nazi reprisals against French Cabinet and naval officers. British sank nine Axis vessels supplying Tunisia forces. Allied land offensive mounting. Page 1.

SOLOMONS—American bombers destroyed all buildings in Munda area of Japanese-held New Georgia Island in Solomons. United States ground patrols killed 50 more Japanese on Guadalcanal. Page 1.

NEW GUINEA—New Jap naval force maneuvering off New Guinea. Enemy counterattacks crushed in Buna sector. Page 6, Part I.

Georgia Signed for Rose Bowl; Notre Dame Beats Trojans

The University of Georgia Bulldogs triumphed over Georgia Tech, 34 to 0, yesterday and voted shortly after the victory to play in the Rose Bowl game on New Year's Day.

Western opponents of the Bulldogs will not be named until after the game between the U.C.L.A. Bruins and Southern California Trojans on Dec. 12.

The Bruins were idle yesterday while a crowd of 95,100 persons, largest of the season, saw Notre Dame whip Southern California, 13 to 0.

Stanford, just about the hottest team on the Coast in recent weeks, walloped St. Mary's Preflight, 28 to 13.

Boston College surprisingly was beaten, 55 to 12, by Holy Cross, which enabled Tulsa to end the season as the only undefeated major school in the country.

[For further details see Sports Section.]

ALL THE NEWS ALL THE TIME
Largest Home Delivered Circulation
Largest Advertising Volume

Los Angeles Times

EQUAL RIGHTS
LIBERTY UNDER THE LAW — TRUE INDUSTRIAL FREEDOM

IN THREE PARTS—34 PAGES
Part I—GENERAL NEWS—22 Pages
Times Office: 202 West First Street
Times Telephone Number MAdison 2345

VOL. LXII — CCC — MONDAY MORNING, APRIL 26, 1943 — DAILY, FIVE CENTS

L.A. IN BLACKOUT FOR 56 MINUTES

Easter Hailed by Thousands

Southland Worshipers at Sunrise Services Pray for Nation's Fighters

BY JAMES WARNACK

Lifting her golden wings against the night and rising from the shadows into light, victorious Faith yesterday found her voice and filled the ear of Morning with songs that echoed through the Southland from the mountains to the sea.

While battles raged on foreign fields, as America's manhood fought to maintain the liberty sacred to our nation's heart, thousands of men, women and children assembled in safety on hilltops and in flowered glens to pray for their defenders and to offer the tribute of devotion to the champion of human freedom, the Christ of the Resurrection.

Wakened by Easter bells in the temples of their souls, the devotees arose long before dawn and wended their way to nature's temples, domed by purple, star-studded skies and carpeted with verdant spring, interlaced with ribbons of floral loveliness. Yet all of that beauty, which forced itself upon the attention of the multitude, was only a symbol of the glory of the One whose praises the people had come to sing.

Multitude at Bowl

Outstanding among Southland services was the one at Hollywood Bowl, attended by more than 25,000 worshipers, many of whom arrived between midnight and 4 a.m. They filled the seats and sat in the aisles and under the fir, cypress and deodar trees that line the sides of the vast amphitheater. Shortly before sunrise, following the rendition of Grieg's "Morning" by Dr. Roy Reid Brignall, organist, Paul Palmer addressed the audience, giving instructions as to how to behave in case of a possible aerial attack by Christendom's foes.

On the north rim of the Bowl stood six young women in white, flowing robes. They were Inice Millican, Evelyn Barton, Sylviamay Barnett, Betty Hooper, Grace Hall and Iris Kennelley. They placed silver trumpets to their lips and sent the notes of Meineke's "Gloria Patri" reverberating among the hills.

Wild Birds Carol

Flying above the great shell that overarches the stage and, flitting in and out among the 30,000 calla lilies that adorned the scene of service, the wild birds caroled their springtime joy.

Addressing the heavenly Father, Dr. R. A. Young, pastor of Rosewood Methodist Church, voiced the gratitude of the assembly for the privilege of worshiping and prayed for "a new America, a new Europe and a new world in which all peoples may be free." That was followed by the singing of "The Lord's Prayer," to the musical setting by Josephine Forsyth, rendered by the Lutheran Choral Union of Southern California, directed by Dr. John B. Nield, with harp obbligato by Private Gail Laughton, organ accompaniment by Dr. Brignall and with Gordon Ruud at the piano.

Scripture Reading

Scripture reading by Rev. Robert Kerstetter, pastor of Hollywood Lutheran Church, was followed by Granier's "Hosanna," sung and played by Irving Berlin's "This Is the Army" chorus and orchestra, with Sergt. Clyde Turner directing

Turn to Page 6, Column 1

Americans Serving Abroad Attend Church

BY THE ASSOCIATED PRESS

In churches and on battlefields throughout the world, Christians yesterday marked Easter with prayer and music.

American servicemen and women, sent across the seas by war, attended services in London, in Jerusalem, in towns and cities of countries strange to them, or marked the church holiday individually or in small groups at their battle stations.

In Jerusalem, along streets and steps worn by the tread of millions of pilgrims, American fighting men joined the throngs at the Church of the Holy Sepulchre for a pontifical high mass celebrated by Archbishop Francis J. Spellman of New York, Catholic military vicar for United States armed forces.

Sunrise Service.

Hundreds of soldiers of all ranks greeted Easter with a traditional sunrise service in London's Hyde Park, with the message of resurrection preached from a simple pulpit. Participating was Bishop Adna W. Leonard of Washington, D.C., representing 31 Protestant denominations. Later he conducted a morning service at an air base and then went to St. Paul's Cathedral for vespers.

In England the church bells, silenced with the fall of France, pealed their Easter message. The bells, reserved as signals of invasion, had been permitted to ring only twice before since the summer of 1940.

Moscow Churches Crowded

Thousands of worshipers thronged Moscow's 26 churches open for observance of Easter, flocking to the churches in greater numbers than at any time since before the revolution. Some women fainted in the crush.

Pope Pius XIII celebrated mass in the presence of the Diplomatic Corps, the Vatican radio reported, but did not make an expected radio broadcast.

HOUSEWIVES HAD 700,000,000 CANS AT RATION START

WASHINGTON, April 25. (AP) — American household stocks of canned goods at the recent start of rationing totaled about 700.000.000 assorted cans it was learned today. This was more than a month's national supply. About 650.000.000 cans were penalty-free under the five cans per person rule, but 54.000,000 cans over the limit were reported voluntarily by holders, who consequently surrendered 432,000,000 blue points, at the rate of eight points for each excess can.

U.S. Carrier Ranger Sunk, Nazis Claim

Vessel Declared Torpedoed in Convoy in North Atlantic

BY THE UNITED PRESS

A German special high command communique broadcast by the German Transocean Agency asserted yesterday that a German submarine had sunk the 14,500-ton United States aircraft carrier Ranger in the middle of the North Atlantic.

The broadcast, recorded by the United Press in New York, said the Ranger was guarding convoy lanes across the Atlantic.

The asserted sinking was attributed to a submarine commanded by one Lieut. Comdr. Von Buelow.

Planes on Board

A second Transocean broadcast said that the Ranger had 50 planes aboard.

(The Navy Department at Washington said it had been apprised of the broadcast but had no other comment.)

The Ranger was laid down Sept. 26, 1931, and completed in

Illustrated on Page 2

June, 1934, at Newport News Shipbuilding Co., Newport News, Va.

According to Jane's Fighting Ships, the aircraft carrier's displacement is 14,500 tons with an over-all length of 769 feet.

Carries 1788 Men

Built at a cost of almost $20,000,000, the authoritative naval book said, the Ranger carries 72 aircraft, of which four squadrons are bomber fighters and the remainder amphibians. Her normal complement, according to Jane's, is 1788 men, including flying personnel, of whom 162 are commissioned officers.

The Ranger's arms include eight five-inch, 38-caliber dual-purpose guns and 40 smaller weapons. She is powered by gear turbines and is understood to be capable of about 35 knots' speed.

Cafe Ceilings Set for May 1

SAN FRANCISCO, April 26. (AP)—A ceiling on restaurant prices in the three Pacific Coast States was ordered today by the Office of Price Administration, effective on May 1.

The regulation, covering all eating places, stipulates that no food item, beverage or meal can be sold for more than the highest price in the seven-day period of last April 4 through April 10. Food and drink may be sold at lower than ceiling prices, however.

Regional Administrator Frank E. Marsh announced the price freeze.

Italian Fleet Doesn't Worry British Admiral

CAPETOWN (Union of South Africa) April 25. (AP)—Admiral Sir James Somerville said in an interview today that should the Italian fleet attempt to cover a withdrawal of Axis troops from Tunisia, "I personally have the greatest confidence that we shall be able to dispose of it adequately."

LIEUT. GEN. M'NAIR WOUNDED IN AFRICA

Chief of All U.S. Army Ground Forces Hurt Watching American Drive in Tunisia

WASHINGTON, April 25. (U.P.)—Lieut. Gen. Lesley J. McNair, 59-year-old commander of all United States ground forces and sometimes called the "brains of the American Army," was disclosed today to have been seriously wounded on Friday during the American occupation of Djebel Ainchouna on the Northern Tunisian front.

WOUNDED IN TUNISIA—Lieut. Gen. L. J. McNair, ground forces chief. (AP) Wirephoto

Col. R. Ernest Dupuy, chief of the War Department's news bureau, said during his weekly radio broadcast that the hard-bitten but soft-spoken McNair was wounded in the fighting for the city, astride the Sedjenane-Mateur road in the mountains of North Tunisia.

Firsthand Glimpse

He said the general, on an inspection tour in North Africa, was getting a firsthand glimpse of the "thunderbolt he had forged during the past two years"—the men and equipment that have been welded into a powerful striking force under training technique laid down by McNair.

The War Department had formally announced that McNair, one of the "big four" of the Army general staff, was wounded at the Tunisian front on Friday, April 23, but said the exact circumstances were not known. Officials would not go beyond the announcement's statement that McNair was on an inspection trip and had been wounded.

Dupuy described the attack and capture of Djebel Ainchouna as the "highlight" of the Allied offensive in the Bizerte-Tunis area and added:

Gen. Lear Called

"In this fighting, Lieut. Gen. Lesley J. McNair, commanding Army ground forces, at present at the front on an inspection of the thunderbolt he has forged during the last two years, was seriously wounded April 23."

McNair's duties in Washington will be taken over temporarily by Lieut. Gen. Ben Lear, 63-year-old commander of the 2nd Army who, nearing the retirement age, was scheduled to relinquish that post on May 1 for assignment to other duties.

As chief of United States ground forces in all theaters where American boys are stationed, McNair has been responsible for making them fit for the toughest war the United States has ever fought. He was placed in charge of all troops—except airmen and those in the Services of Supply—in March, 1942, when the War Department streamlined its general staff into three compact, co-ordinated divisions; ground forces, air forces and supply forces.

Mild-Mannered

While mild-mannered in appearance, McNair is hard-boiled and ruthless with his officers. It is his belief that "it's plain murder to send boys into battle under incompetent officers."

"You can't live with your conscience and you can't win that way," he told friends, according to an article published last January.

And he is equally insistent the men under his command have a real fighting spirit. In a recent radio address beamed to all

Turn to Page 4, Column 1

Kiska, Munda Bombed Again

WASHINGTON, April 25. (U.P.) Hard-hitting American airmen, carrying on their aerial offensive against Japan at both ends of the long Pacific battle front, have again blasted Jap-held Munda in the central Solomons and, despite bad weather, bombed and strafed much-battered Kiska in the Aleutians, the Navy reported today.

Avenger torpedo and Dauntless dive bombers, presumably operating from Henderson Field on Guadalcanal, smashed at the Jap base at Munda to destroy buildings, start large fires and set off at least one heavy explosion. The raiders were escorted by Grumman Wildcat fighters.

In the Aleutians, Army twin-engined Lockheed fighters fought their way through bad weather to Kiska to bomb and strafe enemy installations. It was the 114th raid on the enemy outpost since the first of April.

Fortresses Deal Heavy Punches in Pacific

ALLIED HEADQUARTERS IN AUSTRALIA, April 26 (Monday.) (AP) — Flying Fortresses, ranging along the north coast of New Guinea from Wewak to Saidor, delivered heavy punches for Gen. MacArthur's air force in limited Easter Sunday operations.

The huge B-17's left plumes of heavy black smoke trailing aloft from the Wewak Airdrome after a 26-minute predawn attack. Then they proceeded to Madang where they strafed the town and installations. A similar visit was paid the Saidor area. All of these operations were before daybreak.

Airdrome Hit

Late in the afternoon a single Liberator attacked the Madang Airdrome, starting fires, while a lone B-24 bombed the dock area at Finschhafen and a formation of A-20's bombed and strafed enemy positions near Mubo.

Medium bombers attacked the town of Timika, Dutch New Guinea, and Dobo in the Aroe Islands. Four enemy fighters attempted interception over Dobo but all were driven off and one of them was damaged.

News of Convoy

Meanwhile a spokesman for Gen. MacArthur said that a Japanese convoy, which was attacked by a Liberator bomber April 24 some 300 miles north-northeast of Wewak, apparently had continued on a westward course and had gone beyond the range of Allied bombers.

THE WORLD'S WAR FRONTS

AFRICA—Lieut. Gen. Lesley J. McNair, chief of United States ground forces, wounded on Tunisia front. Meanwhile French troops take vital hill while British engage in savage battle with tanks. Page 1.

BERLIN—German radio claims, without confirmation from any source, submarine sinking in Atlantic of United States aircraft carrier Ranger. Page 1.

RUSSIA—Berlin admits Reds have seized mountains rimming Black Sea port of Novorossisk. Page 2, Part I.

PACIFIC—American bombers again attack Munda, in Solomons, and Kiska, in Aleutians. In New Guinea Flying Fortresses deliver heavy punches to five Japanese bases. Page 1.

French Seize Vital Tunisia Hill Position

Allied Infantry and Armor Hammer at Foe on 140-Mile Front

ALLIED HEADQUARTERS IN NORTH AFRICA, April 25. (AP)—French troops seized Djebel Mansour, strategic hill position 10 miles southwest of Pont du Fahs, the French announced today, while Allied armor and infantry kept hammering at German positions all along the mountainous, 140-mile Tunisian front.

Djebel Mansour, scene of bloody fighting earlier in the Tunisian campaign, was evacuated by the Germans after "lively pressure" from French troops intensified in the last 24 hours, a French communique declared, and one spokesman said it might be the first indication that the Germans are starting evacuation of their southern positions. The hill is the key to high defenses the Germans held on the northern end of the Grand Dorsal, which formed a salient into Allied-held territory.

Savage Battle

North of this French advance, General Sir Harold Alexander has thrown British armor into a savage battle with two German tank divisions southeast of Goubellat, a headquarters spokesman said.

(The London radio, in a broadcast recorded in New York by C.B.S., asserted that the 8th Army on the Nazi southern front has forced a new advance, driving along the coastal plain "for about 12 miles from Enfidaville, and is now within striking distance of Bou Ficha.")

(The German-controlled Paris radio said Allied tank assaults by the 1st Army on a "gigantic scale" have driven wedges into the Axis lines. Lieut. Gen. K. A. N. Anderson, 1st Army commander, is "throwing masses of tanks into the fighting," this broadcast declared.

Allied Gains Reported

(A Berlin broadcast recorded by the Associated Press reported that a "big and violent battle on the eastern front of the German-Italian line of defense in Tunisia is continuing with unabated force," and said that reports indicated that "at some place or other the Anglo-American attack had certain local successes.")

The French reported they are advancing farther eastward from Djebel Mansour, in conjunction

Turn to Page 4, Column 3

Allied Flyers Shot Civilians, Say Nazis

BY THE ASSOCIATED PRESS

The German radio, broadcasting a Vichy dispatch, declared last night that United States and British pilots had machine-gunned and killed French civilians, including women and children, who were flying in five transport planes from Tunisia to Italy on April 18.

This was the date that Allied fighters attacked a huge Axis aerial convoy off Cap Bon in Tunisia, downing 58 transports and 16 of their protecting fighters.

Nazi Leaders Back Killing of Captives

BY THE ASSOCIATED PRESS

The Berlin radio last night quoted official German sources as saying that they backed Japan's execution of American airmen who raided Tokyo.

However, the broadcast recorded by the Associated Press did not indicate that Germany is planning to take similar steps, even though the official Foreign Office organ Deutsche Diplomatische Korrespondenz was quoted as commenting that "the increase of air terrorism against Germany" from Allied bases in Britain "also is the work of the American command."

Targets Later Found to Be Friendly Cause Sixth Raid Alert Here

Los Angeles last night underwent its sixth air-raid alert and radio silence of the war when "unidentified targets" later found to be friendly plunged the city and its environs into a 56-minute blackout.

The blackout was ordered by the Los Angeles Air Defense Wing at 8:30 p.m. and the "all clear" signal was given at 9:26 p.m.

There were several reports that heavy gunfire was heard in the San Pedro area during the blackout.

Bright flashes that illumined the sky in the harbor district and led many observers to believe that lead actually was being thrown were attributed to several power transformers which blew up when overloaded by the sudden electricity shutoff occasioned by the blackout.

An underground transformer in downtown San Pedro exploded and blew out a man-hole cover, the sheet of flame setting fire to a parked automobile.

An official communique from the Fourth Air Force said:

"An air-raid alarm and radio silence was ordered in the Los Angeles area tonight by the Los Angeles Air Defense Wing when unidentified targets were detected.

"The all clear was given when the targets were identified as friendly.

Planes in Air

"In the Los Angeles area the yellow alert was ordered at 8:19 p.m., the blue alert at 8:26 p.m., and the red and radio silence at 8:30 p.m. The all clear was given at 9:26 p.m."

A number of planes were seen overhead during the blackout, but were operating with their running lights on and were presumed to be friendly. The tapering fingers of giant Army searchlights probed the heavens.

Although the blackout was ordered only 11 minutes after the yellow alert was flashed, mobilization of military, police and civilian defense units went ahead speedily and throughout the alert ticked like a Swiss watch.

Made 'Ghost Town'

With the first mournful sound of the air-raid sirens lights began going off all over the metropolitan area and within a few minutes Los Angeles was virtually a "ghost town."

Effectiveness of the blackout ranged from "perfect" to "about 98 per cent" to "very good" in various sections of Los Angeles.

The confusion which marked the last red alert—ordered in mid-afternoon March 16 of this year—was absent, authorities declared. Motorists and pedestrians with rare exceptions obeyed the regulations and eased the task of thousands of auxiliary police who patrolled the downtown streets and neighborhood areas.

Many Minor Accidents

Gayly dressed Easter promenaders in downtown Los Angeles were shepherded into air-raid shelters and theaters by air-raid wardens as the blackout transformed the heart of the city into a series of pitch-dark canyons.

During a 30-minute span Georgia Street Receiving Hospital received 75 traffic accident calls, most of them of a minor nature involving pedestrians who failed to heed blackout regulations.

"Much of the success of the blackout was because of increased effectiveness of the air-raid warning system recently augmented by the addition of 18 sirens," said George Hjelte, executive officer of the Los Angeles Citizens Defense Corps.

'Times' Whistle Blows

The steam whistle atop the Times building, which recently was added to the system after a test toot which startled citizens as far as a mile away, came through with flying colors in its first trial "under fire."

Hjelte said that for the first time the sirens were sounded more than once three two-minute signals being given at one-minute intervals.

The Defense Corps—130.000 strong—was found on the alert and every one of the 13 controls—the main city control and 12 subcontrols—were fully manned, Hjlete reported.

Work Smoothly

At least one string of illuminated street lights marred the defense setup. Persons living on Occidental Blvd. between Beverly Blvd. and Sixth St. complained that the lights there remained on during most of the blackout.

Sheriff Biscailuz and Capt. Harry Seger, night chief of po-

Turn to Page A, Column 4

U.S. and Finland May Break Off Relations Today

STOCKHOLM, April 25. (AP)—Mounting indications from sources usually reliable pointed tonight to a break in diplomatic relations between the United States and Finland, perhaps tomorrow.

Reports from Helsinki that German sources seemed confident that the Finns would string along with the Axis added impetus to the belief in many quarters that a rupture is imminent.

Cancels Appointment

Reports that relations already had been broken were described as "premature" by a high Finnish Foreign Office source in Helsinki. This informant disclosed that United States Charge d'Affaires Robert Mills McClintock had made an appointment for 4 p.m. today to discuss an important matter, and then in the afternoon had canceled it.

McClintock and a code clerk are the only members of the United States Legation staff remaining in the Finnish capital, the others having gone to Stockholm late last week.

McClintock's wife arrived in Stockholm today.

While the Finnish public expressed anxiety over the possibility of a break, a source close to the government said that "the Americans cannot expect us to tie a noose around our own necks."

Still on Job

Finland is the only country fighting with the Nazis in which the United States maintains a Legation. Relations recently are understood to have been continued in the hope that the Finns would settle their differences with Russia and withdraw from the war.

McClintock at Helsinki told the Associated Press just before midnight tonight that "I am still on the job." He declined, however, to comment further on developments.

Hope Abandoned for Swedish Sub

STOCKHOLM, April 25. (AP)—The Swedish Navy announced tonight that all hope had been abandoned for the crew of 33 aboard the submarine Ulven, missing off the Swedish coast near Marstrand since April 16.

'I BOMBED TOKYO' BEGINS TOMORROW IN 'THE TIMES'

Tomorrow, the Los Angeles Times will start publishing the eyewitness story for which the world has waited for more than a year—the story of the bombing of Tokyo as told by a man who had a bomber's-eye view of what happened.

Lieut. Charles L. McClure was the navigator of one of the bombers which made this epic flight. Day after day, starting tomorrow, his account of what the five men in his bomber plane saw and experienced will take you from the day he learned he was to go on a special mission until the day his plane cracked up in China, where for days the men suffered incredible hardships eluding their Jap pursuers.

IN THE 'TIMES' TODAY

MONDAY APRIL 26, 1943

REMEMBER THIS

Repentance without reform signs no passport to heaven.

ALL THE NEWS ALL THE TIME
Largest Home Delivered Circulation
Largest Advertising Volume

Los Angeles Times

EQUAL RIGHTS
LIBERTY UNDER THE LAW
TRUE INDUSTRIAL FREEDOM

IN THREE PARTS — 40 PAGES
Part I — GENERAL NEWS — 18 Pages
Times Office: 202 West First Street
Los Angeles 53, Calif.
Times Telephone Number MAdison 2345

VOL. LXII CC* WEDNESDAY MORNING, JUNE 9, 1943 DAILY, FIVE CENTS

City, Navy Clamp Lid on Zoot-Suit Warfare

Sporadic Clashes Follow Rioting; Police Patrols Tour Battlegrounds

Illustrated on Page B

Throughout tense hours last night the zoot-suit war was held to sporadic clashes by a combination of strong police patrols and a Navy order listing Los Angeles as a restricted area for men of the Navy, Marine Corps and Coast Guard.

Nearly 1000 uniformed and special officers took up assigned positions throughout the downtown and East Side sections of the city at dusk. Others patrolled the streets in cruising cars, keeping a throng of sight-seers moving.

Crowds were dispersed almost as soon as they gathered and few youths in zoot suits were seen as groups of soldiers moved through the district with the watchful eyes of men looking for trouble.

Sailor's Nose Broken

One sailor, Harold Tabor, 32, was beaten by a group of zoot suiters at 103rd and Graham streets and treated at Georgia Street Receiving Hospital for a broken nose. George Lorigo, 19, of 9533 Wilmington Ave., was arrested on a battery charge in connection with the assault.

Lewis D. English, 23-year-old zoot-suit wearer of 844 E. Fifth St., was arrested by Officer R. F. Brady for carrying a 16-inch razor-sharp butcher knife "for protection" and a 16-year-old lad was taken into custody for carrying an iron bar and a knife.

Two southbound Pacific Electric cars loaded with sailors were stoned at 109th St. in Watts. None of the Navy men was injured, although a missile struck J. Mainwaring, conductor on the rear car, a glancing blow.

A shot was fired through a window of another train, outbound from Watts. No one was hit.

Dr. H. A. Rue, 625 S. Lorena St., reported to police that a group of Coast Guardsmen brought one of their number to his office to be treated for stab wounds. The physician gave the name of the injured man to police. The Guardsmen departed when the wounds were treated.

M.P.'s Patrol in Groups

Military police patrols roamed the streets on foot and in jeeps, augmenting the work of city police. Many women and girls strolled the sidewalks with soldier escorts and the bars were crowded with servicemen awaiting the sound of a police whistle or a scuffle.

Only a sprinkling of sailors was seen, however, as the ban ordered by Rear Admiral D. W. Bagley, commandant of the 11th Naval District, went into effect.

Admiral Bagley issued the "precautionary measure" as a result of clashes between Navy men and the youths.

The official Navy announcement described the sailors as acting in "self-defense against the rowdy element," and defined the order as applying to all Navy personnel except those granted special authorization by commanders of naval stations in this area.

Military Police Active

There was no similar action by the Army, although military police were again acting in close co-operation with naval shore patrols.

Under conditions of the Navy order, commanding officers are given the right to grant liberty to Navy men on travel status, to those working at posts within the city and to men residing in the area. They can also allow liberty to men in special cases, such as illness or family responsibilities, and to men on leave from other zones.

"It's entirely up to the judgment of the station commander," a Navy spokesman said.

"However," he added, "it is ad-

Turn to Page A, Column 4

Over 600 Nisei at Poston Found Openly Disloyal

About 630 American-born Japanese over the age of 17, now at the Poston (Ariz.) relocation center, were found to be openly disloyal or of questionable loyalty to the United States, the Dies subcommittee learned at its hearing yesterday in the Federal Building.

Of that number, 450 American-born answered "No" to the question: "Will you swear allegiance to the United States and forswear allegiance to the Emperor of Japan or to any other foreign power?"

The balance of the 630, or 180, gave a qualified answer to the question, such as "I'm neutral" or some other evasion.

Nisei Total 11,000

Among the 630 there were 606 men and 24 women.

The men at Poston who were born in the United States and who are now over the age of 17 number about 3600. In all there are about 11,000 American-born, or Nisei, Japanese at Poston, counting them in all ages from babies up. Not many are much over 30.

The information was given the committee by Ralph M. Gelvin, associate director at Poston for the War Relocation Authority.

Gelvin told the committee that the administration at Poston was very much surprised at the number of Nisei who said "No" to the question.

Gelvin was on the witness stand all day. The committee consists of Representatives John Costello, chairman, Karl E. Mundt of South Dakota and Herman Eberharter of Pennsylvania. The hearing will be continued today when other officials at Poston are expected to be called.

Placed on 'Stop' List

The question on loyalty was part of a general questionnaire which was submitted to the Japanese by the W.R.A. in efforts to determine who could be released from the center to work on the outside. There

Turn to Page 4, Column 1

SLASHED—Donald J. Jackson, 20, sailor, who was attacked by zoot-suit gang.

President Hints Additional Taxes May Be Needed

WASHINGTON, June 8. (AP)—President Roosevelt today said he intends to sign the pay-as-you-go tax bill soon and hinted at a new administration request for additional taxes, possibly heavier excise levies on cigarettes, tobacco and whisky.

At the same time he did not exclude the possibility of compulsory savings as a means of closing what was termed an inflationary gap in the economic system. The pay-as-you-go tax measure imposing a 20 per cent withholding levy, he intimated, will not be adequate to wipe out the gap.

Plans Made for July 1

The Treasury, he told a press conference, is getting ready to put the new withholding tax measure into effect July 1.

The request for more taxes will be made before Congress recesses for the summer, he indicated, but added that he was not ready to say whether the $16,000,000,000 in taxes and compulsory savings recommended to Congress last January is being boosted.

Later, Chairman George of the Senate Finance Committee disclosed that he and Chairman Doughton of the House Ways and Means Committee had talked with Secretary Morgenthau about the possibility of a new tax bill and would confer with him again June 15.

Opposes Sales Tax

The President asserted he thought everybody realizes we have a gap in savings that causes a change in prices. There cannot be any economic change in the country, he added, except to close that gap by taxes or compulsory savings.

Mr. Roosevelt made it plain that he still opposes a general sales tax, remarking that such a levy hits the poorer people.

Not all excise taxes are a sales tax, however, he added. He said England had increased excise taxes on cigarettes, tobacco and liquor, yet Britishers were consuming about as much tobacco and liquor as before. He said this was an excellent way of closing the gap.

CITY GOES FIVE DAYS WITHOUT TRAFFIC DEATHS

For five days there have been no traffic fatalities in Los Angeles, and Deputy Chief of Police Bernard R. Caldwell set about analyzing the situation to discover why.

Yesterday he reached the conclusion that additional supervision of traffic made possible by working traffic officers on overtime shifts has slowed down traffic and reduced the number of accidents. The policy will be continued as a test, Caldwell said.

IN THE 'TIMES' TODAY

WEDNESDAY JUNE 9, 1943

REMEMBER THIS

Too much contentment produces termites, too much discontent hornets.

Hoover Urges Reforms on Food Front

Nine-Point Program With Wickard Acting as Chief Demanded

NEW YORK, June 8. (AP) A demand for consolidation of all authority over food production, with the Secretary of Agriculture as food administrator, headed a nine-point war food program outlined tonight by former President Hoover.

The former President, who recalled his own experience as World War I food administrator, said in a broadcast speech at a meeting of the American Farm Bureau Federation that a program such as he outlined would be "the only road that leads to the defeat of inflation, to decreased hardship in our homes, to assured support of our Allies and to peace for mankind."

Changes Needed

Declaring that drastic changes in the national policy would be needed to meet a decline in food supply in the face of a demand that "is dangerously rising," Hoover said his program would be the "only one course which will clear up this muddle of uncontrolled food prices, local

The text of Mr. Hoover's address, in large part, will be found on Page 13, Part I.

famines, profiteering, black markets and stifled farm production."

He advocated:

1—Consolidation of all authority over food production and distribution under "one single responsible administrator."

2—Decentralization of work under State, municipal and county administrators, because "in no other way can farmers' and consumers' needs be adjusted to our various local conditions."

More Man Power

3—An increase of farm man power to levels higher than before the war, and planting of "40 or 50 million acres more in 1944 than this year."

4—Addition of great amounts of agricultural machinery to handle the additional acreage, replacing the one-year supply of machinery which he said was used up "through suppression of manufacture."

5—Abolition of the system of retail and wholesale price ceilings, so that price fixing would begin "as near as possible to the farmer," with profiteering controls by regulation of trades proceeding from there on.

6—Establishment of a farmers' war committee on prices, and abandonment of "so-called parities" for the war.

Simplify Rationing

7—Simplification of rationing by "decreasing the number and variety of articles rationed," exclusion of nonessential food from rationing, and balancing consumption to production through rationing.

8—Establishment of war committees in all processing and distribution trades. They should be given major responsibilities in keeping the flow of food moving to the right spots.

9—Avoidance of subsidies, which he termed "delayed aggravation" which would not stop inflation.

Air Hospitals Carry 30,000

CHICAGO, June 8. (AP)—The flying hospitals of the Army Air Forces have carried 30,000 seriously wounded men out of combat zones with only two deaths in transit.

These hospitals of the air, something new in war, are one reason for the low death rates of American wounded.

These records were given at the American Medical Association house of delegates today by Brig. Gen. David N. W. Grant, chief flight surgeon of the Air Forces.

Gen. Grant said that helicopter planes are being built experimentally to pick wounded right out of the woods and fields on the fighting fronts.

British Bishop Dies

LONDON, June 8. (AP)—Rt. Rev. John Francis McNulty, 63, Roman Catholic Bishop of Nottingham, died tonight. Dr. McNulty was nominated a bishop in 1932.

F.D.R. Warns Enemy on Gas; Invasion Near, Says Churchill

Allies Winning U-boat War, Commons Told

LONDON, June 8. (AP)—Winston Churchill, as though raising at last the bright signal that will send the invading Allied armies plunging forward, told the world today that amphibious attacks of "a peculiar complexity and hazard on a large scale" are very near at hand in the European theater — operations already "fitted into their proper place in relation to the general war."

All is in readiness for this grand assault, he made clear in a vigorous and heartening report to Commons in which he declared the Allied submarine position is getting better and better by the day and suggested,

Text and highlights of Mr. Churchill's address will be found on Page 8, Part I.

although throwing this out with his customary conservative qualifications, that the prospective defeat of the U-boat might mean the moral and actual defeat of the Germans.

Proud and Confident

The Prime Minister stood proud and confident before Commons—reflecting, as he had put it in another connection, that "mellow light of victory" which he saw playing over the Allied cause—and gave to the members the most confident review in the years of his war leadership.

Telling of an American-British strategy and unity of war purpose "brought into full focus and punch" in the Washington negotiations recently concluded with President Roosevelt, Churchill thus proclaimed that the time of decision is now at hand:

Has Good Hopes

"It is evident that amphibious operations of a peculiar complexity and hazard on a large scale are approaching.

"I can give no guarantee any more than I have done in the past of what will happen . . . Yet all the same I have good hopes that neither the Parliament nor the Congress of the United States will find themselves ill-served by their forces, whether in the British Isles or on the African shore."

More than once he made it plain that this coming offensive, grand though its conception,

Turn to Page 8, Column 7

Japanese Warned of 100 Years War

BY THE UNITED PRESS

Eiji Amau, head of the Japanese board of information, was quoted by the Tokyo radio yesterday as saying that Japan must win the war this year or "it will remain for us to do so during the next 100 years."

The broadcast to Japanese areas was recorded by Federal Communications Commission monitors. It said the occasion for Amau's "instructional address" to the information board was Japan's imperial receipt day.

DOCKWEILER SON REPORTED TAKEN PRISONER BY JAPS

Reported missing in action in the Philippines for more than a year, Lieut. Comdr. George V. Dockweiler, son of Isidore Dockweiler, yesterday was reported to be a prisoner of the Japanese.

According to information received by the family from Admiral Ernest J. King, the 40-year-old naval officer's location of imprisonment has not yet been made known.

Young Dockweiler was graduated from Annapolis in 1924. He was on duty at Cavite, P.I., at the outbreak of the war and later was moved to Corregidor and finally to Cebu. He was captured on Negros Island, the report stated.

News of Lieut. Comdr. Dockweiler's imprisonment was received by his wife Jeanne.

RAID ON ITALY ISLE REPULSED, SAYS AXIS

Commando Landing at Lampedusa Foiled and Allied Ships Sunk, Enemy Announces

LONDON, June 8. (AP)—Rome and Berlin reported today that British commandos assaulted the tiny turtle-shaped island of Lampedusa Monday night and were repulsed in the first attempt of Allied forces massed in North Africa to invade Italian soil in the Mediterranean.

Allied military and naval quarters were silent on enemy accounts of the operation which—if true—appeared nothing more than a minor-scale probing for bigger blows to come.

Despite the attempts of the Italian and German high commands to magnify the action, it was regarded in some London quarters as possibly only a forerunner of a series of widespread operations which might precede the main strike.

Landing Attempted

"The enemy attempted a landing on the island of Lampedusa," said the Italian communique, as recorded here in a broadcast. "The attempt was carried out by British units. It was promptly repulsed by our defenses which sank several enemy naval vessels."

German broadcasts considerably amplified this account of the attack on Lampedusa, a barren bit of desert 120 miles south of Sicily and 70 miles east of the Tunisian coast which is reported to have been the original uninhabited isle of Shakespeare's "The Tempest."

D.N.B., official German news agency, said it was a "serious effort" by about five companies of commandos, and the German communique said it was an attempt to occupy the seven-mile-long island "by a coup de main."

Force Wiped Out

The communique implied that the attempt had gained at least some initial success by declaring that the forces which landed were wiped out.

Asserting the attempt had failed "100 per cent," D.N.B. said "if the Allies by this attempt intended to test the resistance of Italian troops when they are defending their home soil, then the Italians have stood the test in a brilliant manner."

Lampedusa, one of the Pelagie group, which includes Lampione and Linosa, is the southernmost of the Italian steppingstones dotting the Mediterranean between Tunisia and the European mainland. It is about 80 miles south of the air track which Allied bombers have been

Turn to Page 6, Column 3

Mussolini Girds Fleet for Invasion by Allies

LONDON, June 8.—Expecting that the heaviest United Nations invasion thrust in the Mediterranean will be pushed through Sardinia and Corsica, Premier Mussolini is understood here to be concentrating his strongest naval squadron in ports of the Ligurian Sea. He is reported to have ordered his navy to fight gun to gun with the powerful Allied forces when they move into these waters to open a bridgehead on the strategic islands.

Italy's battleship strength is now believed to comprise the 35,000-tonners, Impero, Roma, Littorio and Vittorio Veneto. This heavy armor is supported by three modernized and refitted battlewagons of the Cavour class, 16 first-class cruisers and probably 45 destroyers.

Sub Losses Heavy

The Italian navy's loss in submarines is known to have been heavy, and experts would be surprised if they are able to muster more than 70 to meet an Allied attack.

With all enemy craft driven behind the mine fields in the Aegean, Adriatic and Ligurian seas, and with no necessity to patrol the North African coast, the United Nations, it is believed, can mass three full battle squadrons to take care of Mussolini's fleet.

The morale of the Italian navy is known to have grown steadily worse since the Battle of Matapan. There, and in the Battle of Sartivento, the Italian crews cracked as soon as the British navy's metal began to burst over them. The gunners were thrown into a panic. Their marksmanship, even with their heavier caliber guns, was some of the worst in modern naval warfare.

Under Nazi Prodding

But Mussolini and his henchmen ever since El Alamein have been under ceaseless Nazi prodding. They are believed to have so purged and stiffened the crews that the biggest naval battle of modern times can be anticipated as the opening phase of any invasion of the islands or the Italian mainland.

Douglas El Segundo Workers Balk Union; Vernon for C.I.O.

Workers at the Douglas Aircraft Co.'s El Segundo plant yesterday voted against selecting any union organization as the employee bargaining agent.

At the small Vernon subplant of the main Santa Monica plant, however, employees gave a majority vote to the C.I.O.'s United Auto Workers.

Percentage of Votes

The vote at the El Segundo plant, as certified by George Yager, National Labor Relations Board field agent, was 44.7 per cent for no union, 39.3 per cent for the International Association of Machinists, lately withdrawn from the A.F.L., and 16 per cent for the United Auto Workers, C.I.O.

Total votes were not disclosed for reasons of military security.

The vote at Vernon was 60.9 per cent for the U.A.W., 25.2 per cent for no union and 13.9 per cent for the I.A.M.

At El Segundo, 88.2 per cent of the eligible employees voted. At Vernon the figure was 85 per cent.

As a result of the election the U.A.W., having received a majority at the Vernon plant, will be certified as the bargaining agent for that plant.

At El Segundo the present situation — that of nonunionization—will prevail unless a new election is ordered between the nonunion group and the second highest group, the I.A.M.

A company spokesman issued this statement after learning of the Vernon vote:

"Results of the voting at our Vernon location, which the company has maintained is not an appropriate unit but merely a temporary overflow from our main plant at Santa Monica, seem to us to have little significance because the total of votes cast there represents less than one-half of 1 per cent of our employees."

THE WORLD'S WAR FRONTS

LONDON — Churchill declares all is in readiness for grand assault against Continent. Page 1, Part 1.

AFRICA — Axis reports British commando attack on Italian island of Lampedusa. Page 1, Part 1.

RUSSIA — Nazis claim 550,000 Russians slain in 45-day Western Causasus battles; Germans repulsed below Kharkov but city of Gorki again pounded by planes. Page 7, Part 1.

CHINA — Threats to Chinese rice bowl declared removed. Page 9, Part 1.

SOUTH PACIFIC — MacArthur planes rake Jap ships and air bases. Page 9, Part 1.

New Threat of Retaliation Hurled at Axis

WASHINGTON, June 8. (U.P.)—President Roosevelt disclosed today the Axis powers are making preparations that indicate they may resort to gas warfare, and sternly warned the Axis armies and peoples in Europe and Asia that such action would be countered by the Allies immediately "by the fullest possible retaliation."

He pledged that the Allies will not resort to gas warfare unless the Axis powers do so first. If they turn loose on mankind "such a terrible and inhumane weapon," he added, "we promise to any perpetrators of such crimes full and swift retaliation in kind, and I feel obliged now to warn the Axis armies and the Axis peoples, in Europe and in Asia, that terrible consequences of any use of these inhumane weapons on their part will be brought down swiftly and surely on their own heads."

Full Retaliation

In such an event, he said, the Allies will visit the "fullest possible retaliation on munitions centers, seaports and other military objectives throughout the whole extent of the territory of such Axis country."

It was Mr. Roosevelt's third—and strongest—antigas warning since the war began.

Aside from its plain-spoken purposes, his gas warning was regarded as another move in the strategy of bringing heavy pressure on the populations of Axis countries at a time when the full impact of Allied invasion forces is about to be exerted.

Reports Heard

In a blunt statement given out at his semiweekly press conference, he said that from time to time since the war started there have been reports one or more of the Axis nations "were seriously contemplating use of poisonous or noxious gases or other inhumane devices of warfare."

"I have been loath to believe that any nation, even our present enemies, could or would be willing to loose on mankind such terrible or inhumane weapons," he said.

"However evidence that the Axis powers are making significant preparations indicative of such an intention is being reported with increasing frequency from a variety of sources."

He said gas warfare had been outlawed by the general opinion of civilized mankind and that this country had not used such inhuman weapons "and I hope we never will be compelled to use them."

We Won't Use Gas First

He said categorically that "we shall under no circumstances resort to the use of such weapons unless they are first used by our enemies."

Then, reiterating in substance last year's warning to Japan, he said:

"I want to make clear beyond all doubt to any of our enemies contemplating a resort to such desperate and barbarous methods that acts of this nature committed against any one of the United Nations will be regarded as having been committed against the United States itself and will be treated accordingly."

Mr. Roosevelt declined to discuss forthcoming military operations in Europe or elsewhere but there was accumulating evidence that momentous military undertakings were at hand.

Talks With Marshall

Gen. George C. Marshall, Army Chief of Staff who returned only yesterday from a mission to North Africa, conferred for more than an hour with President Roosevelt and it was speculated that they went over the final plans for the imminent Allied invasion of Europe.

Commenting on Churchill's statement today that the Allies were preparing to launch "amphibious operations of peculiar complexity," the President said, "I should say that was a conservative statement."

ALL THE NEWS ALL THE TIME
Largest Home Delivered Circulation
Largest Advertising Volume

Los Angeles Times

EQUAL RIGHTS
LIBERTY UNDER THE LAW — TRUE INDUSTRIAL FREEDOM

IN THREE PARTS — 40 PAGES
Part I — GENERAL NEWS — 18 Pages
Times Office: 202 West First Street
Los Angeles 53, Cal.
Times Telephone Number MAdison 2345

VOL. LXII — CC — TUESDAY MORNING, JULY 27, 1943 — DAILY, FIVE CENTS

ITALY PEACE BID REPORTED

City Hunting for Source of 'Gas Attack'

Thousands Left With Sore Eyes and Throats by Irritating Fumes

Illustrated on Page B

With the entire downtown area engulfed by a low-hanging cloud of acrid smoke yesterday morning, city health and police authorities began investigations to determine the source of the latest "gas attack" that left thousands of Angelenos with irritated eyes, noses and throats.

Yesterday's annoyance was at least the fourth such "attack" of recent date, and by far the worst.

Visibility was cut to less than three blocks in some sections of the business district. Office workers found the noxious fumes almost unbearable. One municipal judge threatened to adjourn court this morning if the condition persists.

Gets Unanimous Consent

Warning that Los Angeles soon would become a "Deserted Village" unless the nuisance were abated, Councilman Carl Rasmussen demanded that the Health Commission make a report on what could be done about it. His suggestion received the unanimous consent of the Council.

Chemists and engineers of the City Health Department announced after a preliminary investigation that irritating fumes are emanating from a new synthetic rubber plant and that steps are being taken by the plant to eliminate this condition as soon as priorities and war necessities will permit.

"A spot check of all industrial establishments capable of producing irritating gases and smokes is being made by health department inspectors," said Dr. George M. Uhl, city health officer, "The Police Department is also co-operating by reporting any unusual concentrations or sources of these fumes.

Gas Accumulation

"This condition is caused by an accumulation of gases and fumes from industrial stacks and vehicle traffic. Until these gases have been isolated and identified, specific control measures cannot be initiated. However, no permanent or serious injury may be expected, and the investigation will be continued until all sources of the gases and their identity have been established," Dr. Uhl declared.

The Board of Public Works requested City Engineer Lloyd Aldrich to have several engineers in his department who are considered expert on gases to study the problem in an effort to find a remedy.

Although thousands of persons coughed, cried and sneezed, attaches of the Georgia Street Receiving Hospital said nobody applied there for relief.

By noon the fumes had been virtually dissipated.

AS MANY WILL VERIFY, IT WAS 93 ON SUNDAY

Angelenos sweltered in a maximum temperature of 93 degrees on Sunday, the Weather Bureau disclosed yesterday.

It was the hottest day since Oct. 21, 1942, when the maximum was 95, the bureau said.

Sunday's heat was believed to have caused the death by prostration of Della De La Rosa, 8, of 431 Temple St., according to physicians in General Hospital.

Elsewhere in the Southland, Sunday brought a top temperature of 124 degrees in Imperial Valley, the highest there since 1914; Riverside reported 107, while San Gabriel and Burbank recorded 101 maximums.

Jury Indicts 30 in Coal Strikes Under New Law

PITTSBURGH, July 26. (AP)—In the first action under the newly enacted anti-strike law, a Federal grand jury today indicted 30 persons on charges of conspiracy and fomenting strikes in connection with recent unauthorized work stoppages in Southwestern Pennsylvania coal fields.

The indictments followed nearly two weeks of investigation by the grand jury, called July 14 while more than 12,000 miners were idle and after steel production had dropped because of a lack of coal to fire blast furnaces.

Officials of Unions

Of the 30 persons indicted five were presidents of local unions of the United Mine Workers, one a local ex-president, one a local vice-president, one a checkweighman, 10 local committeemen and one local recording secretary. Others were members.

Five indictments, embracing a total of 32 counts, charged 28 persons specifically with "combining, conspiring and confederating together to interfere by strike and other interruptions with the operations" of mines operated by the government. The other two were miners and were charged with coercing miners to absent themselves from work.

Knowledge Imputed

The indictment said those named "well knew" the mines were in possession of the United States and that continuous operation was necessary "for successful prosecution of the present war."

The grand jury was convened after agents of the Federal Bureau of Investigation had gone into the coal fields to determine causes of the walkouts which continued after the United Mine Workers' policy committee and President John L. Lewis had ordered the men back to work. The mines returned to almost normal operation almost simultaneously with start of the investigation.

The jurors heard 99 witnesses, including a number of U.M.W. district officers and F.B.I. agents. Besides those indicted, the jury linked "divers other persons whose names are unknown" to the alleged conspiracy.

U.S. Forces Race Italians to Messina

Routed Military Rabble in Sicily Offering Little Fight

BY DANIEL DE LUCE

ALLIED HEADQUARTERS IN NORTH AFRICA, July 26. (AP)—American infantry and tanks swept along the north coast of Sicily today in close pursuit of the Italian military rabble falling back with hardly a fight toward the Messina bridgehead.

Marshal Pietro Badoglio's reassumption of command of Italian forces under King Vittorio Emanuele caused no pause in the flight of remnants of his Sicilian garrison toward the two-mile-wide strait separating the island from the mainland.

United States 7th Army units have captured Termini, 20 miles east of Palermo, it was officially announced, but are already far east of that north coastal port in their dash toward Messina, and have taken 7000 more prisoners, including six Italian generals and one admiral, in their mopping up of Western Sicily.

Hurls in Division

Nazi Field Marshal Gen. Albert Kesselring threw a resurrected 29th Motorized Division into the hopeless struggle in Eastern Sicily, apparently hoping that it and two and a half other German divisions already engaged would be able to delay the Allies long enough to establish a new defense line for besieged Europe.

Whether this new line would be in Southern Italy, despite Mussolini's collapse, or be somewhere north in the Po Valley, Hitler's headquarters itself may not yet have decided.

The new American advances on the northern flank promised to turn the Messina bridgehead into a second Cap Bon, where the last Axis remnants were trapped in Tunisia.

Canadians Advance

Attacking in the central sector against another resuscitated German division—the 15th Armored Division—the Canadians pressed forward indomitably. Their most recent gains, however, have not yet been announced officially.

Turn to Page 4, Column 4

News Hailed by Prisoners

WHITE SULPHUR SPRINGS (W.Va.) July 26. (AP)—Col. Frank A. Hunter, commanding officer at the Ashford internment camp, today said that the Italian prisoners of war appeared anything but downcast at the news of Mussolini's "resignation."

The prisoners' ranks, swollen by new arrivals from the battle fronts, were cheerful as they went about their work, Col. Hunter stated.

One internee's cap bore in Italian the legend: "I told you so."

WELCOME AMERICANS—Cheering natives of Palermo, Sicily, crowd around on American car when it enters captured city. Waving Sicilian boys jump aboard "bandwagon."
(AP) Wirephoto from United States Army Signal Corps by radio.

Treanor Feels Italians Upset Allied War Plans

BY TOM TREANOR, Times Staff Representative

ALLIED FORCE HEADQUARTERS, NORTH AFRICA, July 26.—It's hard to know whether you're afoot or on horseback since Mussolini quit.

He quit so suddenly it amounted to aggressive action.

Expectations of an orderly logical timetable defeat of Italy are jarred as by a block buster. Everything's guesswork and confusion whether we will be in Rome before Labor Day or whether the Germans will fight us the whole route.

The inescapable conclusion is that Mussolini lost control of the army or he would still be in power.

If the army feels so badly about the war that it throws the Duce out the window, presumably it will shortly throw the war out the window, too.

Can't Find Answer

Then the question becomes whether the Germans want to go on with a war in Italy.

There's one thing certain. You can't find the answer here today.

But the answer is certainly in Rome and Berlin and they can't keep it secret long the way we're bombing and attacking.

We'll know soon, maybe day after tomorrow. It doesn't appear too likely the Germans will want to fight.

I know this isn't what I wrote yesterday but they got me up in the middle of the night like it was a four-alarm fire and said "Mussolini's quit." I instantly started writing from North Africa how Mussolini's resignation in Rome would affect the war in China.

That's what you call looking at the war with mirrors. You're bound to get some distortions and have to make some reservations afterward. It's just lucky I don't have to take something completely back instead of modifying a bit and putting in an on-the-other-hand to the effect that the Germans may very well decide they can't waste the man power and machines to defend Italy.

Not Sticking Neck Out

And on the other hand I'll add they may decide they are. No use sticking your neck out the way I did the first night when I was thinking in terms of Chungking. Got my eye off the ball a little.

One of the speculations here where we have been indulging in a good old-fashioned orgy of speculation for the past 36 hours is whether Italy is apt to swing wide left. The Italians were always told that Fascism was their shield against Communism.

The shield has been destroyed. We ought to know whether it was shielding them from Communism or whether it was

Turn to Page A, Column 1

Elated Italians Expect Peace, Reports Indicate

BERN, July 26. (AP)—The Italian people went wild with joy on hearing of the downfall of Mussolini and the end of more than 20 years of Fascism and years of preparation for war, reports reaching Bern said today.

The only Italian newspaper arriving at Chiasso on the Swiss frontier, the Gazzetta del Sport published in Milan, declared that cheering throngs had burst into the streets as soon as they heard the radio announcement, and despite the blackout paraded through the streets of Rome and invaded the empty halls of the Palazzo Venezia from whose balcony Il Duce had harangued them for a score of years.

An impromptu parade formed and there were demonstrations against Fascism with shouts of long life to Italy's King, to Marshal Pietro Badoglio and the army.

One parade went to the Quirinale where the people shouted for the King. Others demonstrated at the War Ministry, acclaiming the army, and in various other parts of the city in front of newspaper offices. The Gazzetta del Sport reported

Turn to Page 3, Column 6

Rome Radio Ends Lessons in German

ALGIERS, July 26. (U.P.)—Radio Rome today announced that it is discontinuing, effective now, its daily morning lesson in the German language.

ITALIANS KNOW ALLIED PEACE PRICE, HULL SAYS

WASHINGTON, July 26. (U.P.) Secretary of State Hull, hailing the downfall of Benito Mussolini as the first major step in the early and complete destruction and eradication of Fascism, said today that if Italy wants peace the Allied price is still unconditional surrender.

Italy has not yet made a bid for peace, but if and when she does the conditions will be those laid down by President Roosevelt and Prime Minister Churchill at Casablanca for all Axis nations.

Cautious Approach

Hull made this plain by telling his press conference there has been no contact between the United Nations and Marshal Pietro Badoglio who, as Il Duce's successor, would be most likely the source of any Italian peace bid. Nor has the question whether the United Nations would deal with the House of Savoy come up in his conversations with President Roosevelt and the War Department, he said.

Obviously jubilant over Sunday's historic turn in events, Hull nonetheless took a cautious approach in discussing the Italian upheaval and said in effect the Allies would have to follow a wait-and-see policy.

'Military Work to Do'

He said he did not know the attitude of military leaders regarding King Victor Emmanuel and that since the war still is in progress it would be better to wait until the question actually arises.

He also said no particular consultations are in progress with Great Britain about events in Italy and for the present there was not so much to be talked about.

Further military developments must be awaited, he said, suggesting the questioning was getting too far ahead of events.

He said he felt that the very timely and appropriate ending of Mussolini is the first major step in the early and complete destruction and eradication of every vestige of Fascism both nationally and internationally. For a long time, he said, he has been convinced that Fascism car-

Turn to Page 3, Column 4

THE WORLD'S WAR FRONTS

Badoglio Orders Home 26 Divisions in France, Greece and Yugoslavia

LONDON, July 27 (Tuesday.) (AP)—A Reuters Stockholm dispatch today said preliminary negotiations for an armistice between Italy and the Allies began in Vatican City last night. The Bern correspondent of Svenska Dagbladet was the source of the report. There was no confirmation whatever.

While negotiations were going on in the Vatican, it was said that the German Ambassador to Rome, Hans Georg Viktor von Mackensen, was holding a series of talks with Marshal Badoglio.

An Italian and German communique on the Von Mackensen-Badoglio talks is expected shortly, the dispatch said.

LONDON, July 27 (Tuesday.) (U.P.)—Marshal Pietro Badoglio, heading a non-Fascist Cabinet, imposed martial law throughout Italy yesterday and was reported to have started a sweep of key Fascist leaders, while new political groups demanded that Italy be taken out of the war and that those responsible for the nation's condition be punished drastically.

The London Daily Telegraph reported that the Italians had recalled 22 divisions from Yugoslavia and Greece and four from France for the defense of Italy.

There was no authentic news of Benito Mussolini, whose departure from power brought a quick reaction from some portions of the Italian press and a rebirth of political activity which had been held in check by Fascism for almost a generation. One report said Il Duce was under arrest at a villa outside Rome, along with Carlo Scorza and other high Fascists.

Want to Quit War

The renewed political activity was revealed in copies of the Italian newspaper Stampa of Turin arriving in Bern, Switzerland. Stampa printed on the front page a manifesto signed by the National, Christian Democracy, Communist, Liberal Reconstruction and Socialist parties which demanded heavy punishment for "those persons responsible for grave damage done our nation."

At the same time the parties warned Badoglio that the Italian people want to get out of the war that Fascism forced upon them, not continue it as he had said would be done when he took over from Mussolini on Sunday.

Also received at Bern were copies of the Corriere Della Sera of Milan which praised the fall of Mussolini and said "we are finally free." This newspaper's editorial pleaded for Italians to avoid hasty vengeance, saying that those responsible will be brought to terms in due time.

Reports from Bern said that Italians in the northern part of the country believed Badoglio's statement that the war will continue was merely made to give time in which to reach an understanding as to how an evacuation of the large German forces in Italy should be carried out.

A Bern dispatch told of anti-Fascist demonstrations in several Italian cities, with mobs burning Mussolini's old Fascist headquarters, attacking his newspaper office in Milan Sunday night.

Il Duce Reported Interned

The Bern radio reported unusual diplomatic activity at Vatican City, where the Pope was said to have conferred with foreign representatives and the Papal Nuncio to Italy. Bern also heard that Mussolini had been interned in a village near Lake Como.

The new Cabinet, headed by Badoglio as chief of staff, included Raffaele Guariglia, Ambassador to Turkey and former envoy at the Vatican and in Argentina, as Foreign Minister and retained only one former Minister, Leonardo Piccardi, as Minister of Corporations.

Guido Rocco, known as an ardent nationalist, was made Propaganda Minister, but most of the new Cabinet members appeared to be bureaucrats or men who would follow the lead of Badoglio and King Victor Emmanuel.

Other reports reaching here from Switzerland stated that workers in Northern Italy had threatened to strike unless Fascist party members were removed from industrial staffs and organizing committees. It was said that many Fascist officials already had been removed and placed under protective arrest.

Hitler Hops to Berlin

A Daily Mail dispatch datelined on the German frontier said tonight that Adolf Hitler was reported on reliable authority to have flown to Berlin today from his high command headquarters on the eastern front.

Bern heard direct reports from Italy that Mussolini's newspaper at Milan had been sacked, that his one-time private headquarters there had been burned and that various

Turn to Page A, Column 4

IN THE 'TIMES' TODAY

TUESDAY JULY 27, 1943

REMEMBER THIS

Paganism lowers a God to a man; Christianity raises a man to a God.

ALL THE NEWS ALL THE TIME

Largest Home Delivered Circulation
Largest Advertising Volume

EQUAL RIGHTS

Los Angeles Times

LIBERTY UNDER THE LAW — TRUE INDUSTRIAL FREEDOM

IN THREE PARTS

PART I — GENERAL NEWS

Times Office: 202 West First Street
Los Angeles 53, Cal.
Times Telephone Number MAdison 2345

VOL. LXIII — CC *** — TUESDAY MORNING, JUNE 6, 1944 — DAILY, FIVE CENTS

INVASION!

WHERE ALLIES ARE STRIKING—Arrows indicate the ports and coastal regions where Allied armies of invasion were reported swarming ashore in France early this morning.

Allied Landings Begun in France, Eisenhower Says

SUPREME HEADQUARTERS, ALLIED EXPEDITIONARY FORCE, June 6 (Tuesday.) (A.P.)—American, British and Canadian troops landed in Northern France this morning, launching the greatest overseas military operation in history with word from their supreme commander, Gen. Dwight D. Eisenhower, that "we will accept nothing except full victory" over the German masters of the continent.

The invasion, which Eisenhower called "a great crusade," was announced at 7:32 a.m. Greenwich mean time (12:32 a.m., Pacific War Time) in this one-sentence Communique No. 1:

"Under the command of Gen. Eisenhower, Allied naval forces supported by strong air forces began landing Allied armies this morning on the northern coast of France."

It was announced moments later that Britain's Sir Bernard L. Montgomery, hero of the African desert, was in charge of the assault.

Landing Points Undisclosed

The locations of the landings were not announced.

Eisenhower himself wished Godspeed to the parachutists who were the first to land on the enemy-held soil of France.

For three hours previous to the Allied announcement the German radio had been pouring forth a series of flashes reporting that the Allies were landing between Le Havre and Cherbourg along the south side of the Bay of the Seine and along the north coast of Normandy.

This would be across the Channel and almost due south of such British ports as Hastings, Brighton, Portsmouth and Bournemouth.

The Germans also said parachutists had descended in Normandy and were being engaged by Nazi shock troops.

Berlin said the "center of gravity" of the fierce fighting was at Caen, 30 miles southwest of Le Havre and 65 miles southeast of Cherbourg.

Caen is 10 miles inland from the sea, at the base of the 75-mile-wide Normandy Peninsula.

Heavy fighting also was reported between Caen and Trouville.

One of Berlin's first claims was that the first British parachute division was badly mauled.

Gen. Montgomery, hero of the African desert, was leading

Turn to Page A, Column 1

Invasion—and 'The Times'

This is D-Day. The greatest continuing news story in the history of man has begun—and will continue until Victory. Americans, and all the people of the earth, now eagerly await every new development, watch every Allied move and Nazi countermove.

The detailed story of invasion, complete with all the available maps and pictures, will be brought to Times readers with the speed, thoroughness and accuracy that have always made The Times the West's most dependable . . . and depended upon . . . newspaper!

ALL THE NEWS ALL THE TIME
Largest Home Delivered Circulation
Largest Advertising Volume

Los Angeles Times

EQUAL RIGHTS
LIBERTY UNDER THE LAW — TRUE INDUSTRIAL FREEDOM

IN TWO PARTS
PART I—GENERAL NEWS
Times Office: 202 West First Street
Los Angeles 53, Cal.
Times Telephone Number MAdison 2345

VOL. LXIII CC* SATURDAY MORNING, AUGUST 26, 1944 DAILY, FIVE CENTS

THREE VICTORIES WON IN FRANCE

WELCOME—American Army jeep is center of crowd of excited Parisians as they celebrate arrival of first Allied troops in liberated French capital yesterday. (AP) Wirephoto

French and Yanks in Paris Force Nazis to Surrender

Battle in Streets Won but Sniping Continues; De Gaulle Entry Cheered

LONDON, Aug. 26 (Saturday.) (U.P.)—Allied troops and frenzied civilians, battling shoulder to shoulder in crowded, bullet-swept streets, smashed the organized German resistance in Paris yesterday, forcing the commander of the Nazi garrison to surrender. Scattered sniping continued through the night but these disorganized units were swiftly being liquidated, it was indicated.

Crowds of Partisans, summoned to the barricades early in the day by the French Forces of the Interior, followed the course of the battle through the streets, screaming the "Marseillaise" between bursts of gunfire from Allied tanks and the guns of German forces, dispatches from the capital said.

As Paris rose, and Allied tanks rumbled in, the plight of the Germans, isolated in a city aflame with patriotism, became more and more precarious.

Germans Surrender

Finally, a report of the Paris radio said, the German commander surrendered to the commander of the F.F.I. and to Brig. Gen. Jacques LeClerc, whose French 2nd Armored Division was the first Allied force to enter the city.

The German chief agreed to tell his commanders to cease firing and hoist the white flag; to collect weapons intact at a predetermined spot until they were disposed of.

German army forces which received the orders and disregarded them were to be regarded as guerrillas, no longer under protection of the laws of war, the surrender terms said, but those who fought on because they did not know of the order were guaranteed humane treatment.

Sniping Continues

It appeared clear that not all German troops were aware of the order, or that some disregarded it. Late radioed reports from the city said snipers continued their fire into the night.

Some of the resistance, it was indicated, came from pro-Nazi French groups. One radioed report described the fighting as a "revolution."

Wildly celebrating Parisians, kissing every American in sight, following the course of skirmish so closely that they blocked the passage of armored forces, practically ignored the bullets.

De Gaulle Arrives

Gen. Charles de Gaulle, symbol of French resistance and who was in command of the French forces which plunged into the city, made formal entry into the city at 7 p.m., the dispatches said.

He promised Parisians in an address broadcast by the Paris radio the battle against the Teuton would continue until every German was forced from the soil of France; that the only Germans left in France would be prisoners or dead.

A B.B.C. correspondent, Robin Duff, said that the Germans in Paris were gone after a hard and bitter fight, and the only ones remaining were "lying quiet," But other reports indicated bursts of fighting went on, and it appeared that some opposition

Turn to Page 8, Column 3

Romanians Join in Reds' Record Blow at Nazis

LONDON, Aug. 26 (Saturday.) (AP)—Two Russian armies driving a mile an hour toward the heart of Romania yesterday reached the Galati Gap defenses at Tecuci and the Danube River delta at Kiliya.

The six-day Romanian offensive has cost the enemy nearly 205,000 killed and captured, Moscow announced early today.

In perhaps the greatest defeat yet inflicted on the Axis in a comparable period, the Russians also encircled 12 German divisions of more than 60,000 men southwest of fallen Chisinau, capital of the Romanian province of Bessarabia. Thirteen thousand of the Germans already have surrendered in two days, and the remainder are being annihilated, said the Moscow radio bulletin.

Thousands of Romanians were abandoning the struggle against the Russians and turning to fight the Germans, dispatches said, as the 2nd and 3rd Ukrainian armies under Gens. Rodion Y. Malinovsky and Feodor I. Tolbukhin linked up for a quick drive on Bucharest, within 112 miles of Soviet columns which seized Tecuci on the Barlad River.

Take 550 Places

A total of 550 towns and villages were swept up by the two armies, and the capture of Tecuci also found the Russians within 92 miles northeast of the bomb-wrecked Ploesti oil wells. Gen. Malinovsky's troops now were at the Galati Gap, a 45-mile stretch of defenses prepared along the Putna, Siret and Barlad rivers just above where those streams empty into the Danube.

To the southeast, a Soviet mid-

Turn to Page 2, Column 6

Romania Reported Told to Pay $600,000,000

NEW YORK, Aug. 25. (AP) Charles Davila, former Romanian Minister to the United States and now personal representative of Romania's new Minister of State, said today he had been informed that terms of Romania's surrender included payment of $600,000,000 indemnity.

The surrender terms, Davila said he had learned, also provide that Romania shall cede Bessarabia and Northern Bukovina to Russia, areas claimed by Russia as legally part of its territory for several years.

(AP) Wirephoto

LISTED DEAD—Field Marshal Gen. Guenther von Kluge, German chief in France, reported killed.

Von Kluge, Nazi Chief in France, Reported Killed

STOCKHOLM, Aug. 26 (Saturday.) (AP)—Field Marshal Gen. Guenther von Kluge has been killed, the newspaper Dagens Nyheter said today on the basis of information received from Germany.

Circumstances of his reported death were not known here and the newspaper had no additional details. (There was no immediate confirmation of this report in either Axis or Allied official quarters.)

Von Kluge, 61, had held command of the German armies on the western front since July 6, when he succeeded Field Marshal Gen. Karl Rudolph von Rundstedt.

Von Kluge rose through the regular army channels and attained prominence in the 1939 Polish campaign.

Transferred to the west in 1940, he led the German 4th Army through French fortifications and helped drive the British back across the Channel.

Long Beach Pilot Bags Six Planes

A U.S. FIGHTER BASE, ENGLAND, Aug. 25. (AP) — A Mustang squadron commanded by Lt. Col. John P. Randolph, Schertz, Tex., destroyed 19 landplanes, 10 seaplanes and damaged at least 20 other craft today in attacks on a German airfield and a seaplane base north of Berlin.

Lt. Joseph Mansker, 420½ Cedar St., Long Beach, Cal., destroyed six planes in the attack.

THE WORLD'S WAR FRONTS

FRANCE—Patton's tanks take Troyes far east of Paris in smashing drive as Allied troops compel surrender of Nazis in Paris. Page 1, Part I. Cannes and Antibes fall to Southern France invading forces. Page 8, Part I.

RUSSIA — Soviet armies smash deep into Romania; thousands of Romanian troops turn on Germans. Page 1, Part I.

PACIFIC — MacArthur bombers smash five Jap merchantmen and leave cruiser heavily damaged. Page 1, Part I. Central Pacific planes hit Bonins, Wake, Ponape, Nauru and Jap bases in Marianas and Carolines. Page 2, Part I.

CHINA — Japs open new drive. Page 2, Part I.

Troyes, 130 Miles From German Frontier, Falls; Yanks May Be in Reims

BY DREW MIDDLETON
New York Times

SUPREME HEADQUARTERS, ALLIED EXPEDITIONARY FORCE, Aug. 26 (Saturday.)—Three resounding victories have been won along the 200-mile long front in Northern France.

Armored patrols of the 3rd Army in an advance of 23 miles have rumbled into Troyes, the great road and railroad center 130 miles from the German frontier. Bridgeheads across the Seine south of Paris have been widened, the enemy has been driven from Montereau, 10 miles east of Fontainebleau and is retreating hurriedly from the area northeast of Montargis taken by other American forces late Thursday.

French and American troops have penetrated into the center of Paris and liberation of the city and the wiping up of remnants of the Nazi garrison are almost completed. Aside from its tremendous effect on French morale Allied occupation of Paris, the most important communications center in France, is a military triumph of the first magnitude.

Drive Nazis Into Seine

Finally far to the west, British, American and Canadian forces are driving remnants of the German 7th Army pell-mell into the Seine. The Elbeuf pocket has replaced that of Falaise as a German graveyard. Enemy forces are now contained in an area of less than 300 square miles with the Seine on the east and the north, the Risle River on the west and a steadily advancing Allied line to the south.

There is a German report, as yet unconfirmed here, that the Americans have reached the cathedral city of Reims, 80 miles northeast of Paris.

While field guns and tanks search forests for fleeing Germans, hundreds of medium and light fighter-bombers are scourging Germans seeking to escape across the Seine.

The battle has become a race for Seine crossings with the Allied forces confident that they will have killed, wounded or captured at least 40,000 of the enemy before they reach the Seine.

Planes Pound Brest

Between 3 and 4 o'clock yesterday the great port of Brest, obstinately defended by the Germans since the first United States troops reached its outskirts nearly three weeks ago, was hammered by 300 Marauders and Havocs of the 9th Air Force. A general land assault may be in full swing against this Breton port whose importance grows as each new advance complicates an already imposing Allied supply problem.

German strong points and forts, the naval port and arsenal were attacked by nine waves of medium and light bombers whose crews reported "good results."

The Allied air forces played a major role in yesterday's operations against German troops trying to cross the Seine. Although the weather was far from ideal in this area fighters and fighter-bombers of the 9th Fighter Command destroyed 158 trucks and 54 tanks and damaged 50 other tanks in 500 sorties flown up to 6 p.m. yesterday. Two direct bomb hits were scored on a vital bridge across the

Turn to Page 8, Column 4

Bombers Leave Jap Cruiser Sinking and Bag Five Vessels

GENERAL HEADQUARTERS, SOUTHWEST PACIFIC, Aug. 26 (Saturday.) (AP)—Mitchell bombers, attacking at mast height, probably sank a Japanese light cruiser and destroyed five medium freighter-transports near Manado, Northern Celebes, headquarters reported today.

The attack was made Thursday by the medium bombers during their ceaseless hunt for Jap shipping withdrawing from the Philippines-Halmahera line.

Cruiser Explodes

When last seen the cruiser had exploded in the stern, was blazing from end to end and had a 20-degree list. The communique said the warship was believed to be sinking.

A headquarters spokesman said the freighter-transports averaged between 2000 and 3000 tons. Two other vessels of this class were damaged. An estimated 40 luggers and barges were riddled with machine-gun bullets.

All were at anchor off Manado, Jap headquarters some 250 miles due west of Halmahera.

There was no interception and all the Allied planes returned.

Halmahera Hit

This was the heaviest assault in weeks against shipping at Celebes. The gangling island has been named by Gen. Douglas MacArthur as one link in the curving supply line from the Philippines to Ceram behind which Jap heavy shipping has been confined.

In another assault Thursday Liberators hit Halmahera, southern steppingstone to the Philippines, with 59 tons of bombs. A big ammunition dump was blown up. The attack was centered around the Lolobata airdrome area, in the northern part of the island. The Japanese again failed to offer interception to this fourth in a series of heavy raids on Halmahera.

Rubber Director Dewey Hits Nelson as 'Sniper'

Assails W.P.B. Chairman's Statement: 'Program Completed—All but Getting Tires'

WASHINGTON, Aug. 25. (U.P.)—War Production Chief Donald M. Nelson, target of a blistering attack from within his own agency, came under fire from a new quarter tonight when retiring Rubber Director Bradley Dewey accused him of engaging in "typical Washington sniping."

Dewey's blast was prompted by Nelson's statement to the Senate war inestigating committee, made public yesterday, that the rubber program "was completed—all but getting the tires."

Nelson left town this morning on a Presidential mission to China.

Revamping Seen

Some two hours later, President Roosevelt raised doubts that Nelson would resume his duties as W.P.B. chairman when he returns from the Orient, and it appeared likely that a complete change in the high command of the dissension-torn W.P.B. was in the making.

There were reports that when Nelson returns from China he may be "kicked upstairs" and become a sort of roving commercial ambassador r the White House. In that case it was expected the W.P.B. chairmanship would go to Lt. Comdr. J. A. Krug, whom Mr. Roosevelt directed last night to "take over and run" the W.P.B. in Nelson's absence.

Nelson's Comment

Dewey's was the second attack against Nelson within 24 hours. He said in an interview that Nelson's testimony was typical of the type of "sniping" that led to the resignation yesterday of W.P.B. Executive Vice-Chairman Charles E. Wilson, who said he had been "constantly pilloried" by Nelson's personal staff.

Wilson, in his attack yesterday, also charged that it was Nelson—not he—who had delayed reconversion planning through a policy of "manana"—putting things off until tomorrow.

Dewey's ire was aroused by remarks which Nelson made in a closed session before the Senate committee.

Questioned by the committee about Dewey's resignation—which becomes effective Sept. 1.—Nelson had said that to call the rubber program completed now would be "like the Army saying they are completed except for the shooting."

Dewey said it was such "word-twisting" that "has made many good Americans unwilling to give services that otherwise would be of value to the country and the conduct of the war."

He pointed out that his directive from President Roosevelt required him to provide synthetic rubber, but that the job of making the tires was the responsibility of the W.P.B.

Turning Out Surplus

Dewey emphasized that, in announcing recently he would resign because his job was done, he never had said the job of providing tires was done but rather that the synthetic rubber plants are turning out surplus rubber.

The problem of providing man power and tire cords to make

Turn to Page 4, Column 1

TEMPERATURE 84 HERE YESTERDAY

It was both cooler and warmer at the ground level yesterday than on the Federal Building roof where official temperature is recorded.

Highest temperature on the roof was 79, on the ground 84. Lowest temperature on the roof was 57, on the ground 56.

The Weather Bureau predicted clear weather with little change in temperature for Los Angeles and vicinity today. Tomorrow will be slightly cooler.

Willkie Would Defer Parley With President

WASHINGTON, Aug. 25. (AP)—Wendell Willkie, saying that President Roosevelt has invited him to a conference, took the attitude today that he would prefer to wait until after the election.

Nothing definite has been done toward arranging a meeting.

Willkie, in New York, confirmed reports of the Presidential invitation after Mr. Roosevelt, at his news conference here, said he had been in communication with Willkie.

Receives Two Letters

Willkie said he had no contact with the President other than two letters written to him by Mr. Roosevelt. Mr. Roosevelt last Friday told reporters at his press conference that as far as he knew there was nothing to reports that he had written to Willkie.

The disclosures followed several days of rumors that the White House was making overtures to the 1940 G.O.P. Presidential nominee for a conference on foreign policy.

The reports had attracted more attention from the standpoint of politics than from foreign affairs, since Willkie has kept silent on what role, if any, he intends to take in the Presidential election campaign.

Willkie left little doubt, however, that if he does see the President before the election their talks will be completely divorced from partisan matters.

Statement Interpreted

After Mr. Roosevelt acknowledged in response to questions at his news conference that he had been in private contact with Willkie, the latter told newsmen in New York:

"It is true Mr. Roosevelt has written me asking that I confer with him. Naturally I would much prefer that no such conference occur until after the election. But if the President of

Turn to Page 4, Column 3

IN THE 'TIMES' TODAY

SATURDAY AUGUST 26, 1944

REMEMBER THIS

The more we find to laugh about, the less there'll be to squabble over.

Jones Favors U.S. Food Stock Pile Disposal in Europe

New York News

WASHINGTON, Aug. 25.—War Food Administrator Marvin Jones disclosed at a House postwar committee hearing today that this country, overpessimistic about the needs of liberated areas, has built up tremendous food stock piles in Europe which should be disposed of overseas after the war to prevent a disruption of the home market.

Italy, he said, required less food than we had anticipated. North Africa got into production very quickly. France, he said, we are finding in "good" shape.

Revealing that some Italians had buried their wheat and planted grass over it to hide it, Jones remarked:

"Let the Italian keep his wheat buried. He will, anyway, if he thinks he can get something out of Uncle Sam."

Food, he said, should be treated like any other war surplus, "such as the fighter planes bristling with guns."

"We have to go on producing full speed, right up to the last minute," Jones explained, "even if we should think the war would end in 10 days."

The Weather

United States Weather Bureau forecast for Los Angeles and vicinity issued last night: Partly cloudy early this morning with occasional light drizzle some sections but becoming clear by midforenoon, clear tomorrow; somewhat warmer this afternoon and again tomorrow; windy in exposed areas today. Highest temperatures yesterday, 73; lowest, 62.

Los Angeles Times

IN TWO PARTS

PART II—LOCAL NEWS

TIMES OFFICE
202 West First Street
Los Angeles 53, Cal.

VOL. LXIII CC MONDAY MORNING, SEPTEMBER 18, 1944 CITY NEWS—EDITORIAL—SOCIETY

By The Way

with

BILL HENRY

WASHINGTON.—No history of this city could be considered complete without at least one column on the ebullient laundryman and pigskin impresario, Mr. George Preston Marshall. No other town has anybody quite like him.

PERSONALITY—Mister Marshall is a man of dual split personality. Not only does he double as a highly successful cleaner-man and all-time top pro football promoter but he likewise splits his activities between Southern California and Washington. He married one of our prize gals, Corinne Griffith, and lives as much of the time as possible down at Rancho Santa Fe and insists on bringing his football team to Southern California every winter, thereby combining business with pleasure. He is persistently heckled by the sports writers, whose barbs bounce from his well-bank-rolled personality without making a dent.

SUCCESS—How, for instance, are you going to insult a guy whose football team will have played to 235,000 customers before the season even starts? When needled about getting a few thousand bucks out of a football game at the Coliseum, Mister Marshall remarks that the Army Air Forces Relief Fund got some $70,000 from the game and asks what's wrong with that. He also calls attention to the fact that the customers rarely, if ever, squawk at the brand of entertainment provided by his football team.

CLASS—When you go to see Mister Marshall here in Washington you have to be careful to select the entrance which is the office of the Washington Redskins. If you happen to walk into the laundry entrance you may have your pants and coat snatched off you and returned cleaned and pressed before you can locate the manager to enter a complaint. If you walk into the football office you will get nothing but a pitying look from Mister Sid Carroll, who suspects you—he suspects everybody of the same thing—of wanting to buy season tickets to the Redskins' home games. He hasn't any to sell. He disposed of 18,000 season tickets some months ago and that's all they sell in advance.

OFFICE—To get to Mister Marshall's office you go through a picture gallery of action pictures of the Redskins and of Mister Marshall in sundry poses with sundry celebrities, then shuttle down a hallway and into the sanctum of the big chief. That's just what it is, too. There is an oil of an Indian chief by Balink, a totem, a genuine unduplicated Indian blanket, a big Alaskan mask and sundry other items, most of which, says Mister Marshall, were picked out by Mrs. M., who is considerable of an expert on the subject. Not the least decorative item on the wall is a picture of Mrs. M. by James Montgomery Flagg.

BUSINESS—The Redskins' big chief has one of those interoffice whatnots through which come mysterious messages from the outer guardians and most of the time he is engaged in long-distance conversations with somebody. Mister Marshall is generally credited with talking more minute-miles than anybody in the world. He wins all arguments by the simple method of keeping right on talking and paying no attention whatever to what his opponent may be saying. Mottoes on pillows say "Never Complain—Never Explain" and "Don't Worry—It Never Happens."

ATTENDANCE—Last year he played six games at home. Capacity at Griffith Stadium is slightly over 34,000. Total attendance of 206,540 indicates that every game was a complete sellout. He played to 119,000 in games "away" and to 145,000 before the season opened—total 470,000. This year he thinks the Redskins will play to 235,000 before the season opens and 350,000 during the season, which will put them well over the half-million mark. Asked if he thought there were enough players for all the new professional leagues, Mister Marshall said, "There are enough players, but probably not enough customers." Well, Mister Marshall should know about that!

Hear Bill Henry, Monday through Friday, KNX, 5:55 p.m.

Leaders Urge V-Day on Job

Shipyard and Plane Officials Stress Task of Defeating Japan

Victory day in Europe will be observed here as a day of thanksgiving and firm rededication to pressing war against Japan as vigorously as busy production lines can make it, if we are to keep faith with the men who have died and those who must fight on for complete peace.

This attitude is being expressed by Los Angeles industrial, educational and religious leaders regarding actual war production needs, as well as the will-to-win final victory over the Axis, which might be interrupted by proposed celebrations of the Nazis' defeat in carnival spirit.

"We have been wanting and working a long time for the defeat of Hitler and his gangster horde," said Donald W. Douglas, president of Douglas Aircraft.

Halfway to Victory

"While we will all be mighty happy on that rapidly approaching V-Day, we would do well to remember then that the job is still only half done.

"Rather than celebrate in the holiday spirit, it would be far more appropriate for Americans on the home front to give thanks to the Almighty for our partial victory and then to pitch in with renewed vigor to knock out the Nips in a hurry."

Production of P-51 Mustang fighters will continue as usual at North American Aviation's Inglewood plant in a company decision backed by the four unions at the plant.

"Collapse of Germany," said Factory Manager R. E. Dawe, "will not be a time for celebration, but rather a time to renew our pledge to stay on the job until this war is won—and it won't be won until the Japanese, too, are defeated.

"We cannot shut down this plant for even one shift as long as Americans are fighting our enemies. The planes we build in that time can save hundreds of lives. They must be built."

Shipyards to Work

In the shipyards, too, are vessels which, if construction is cut even for a day, will make their rendezvous with victory too late.

"The 30 transports now being built by Calship are so important to the American drive against the Japs," said John A. McCone, president, "that this yard must take no holiday to celebrate the fall of Germany. These ships must be delivered on schedule or the Pacific war timetable will be delayed."

Growing sentiment that final victory over the Germans, seen by the Allied top command as being achieved before Oct. 31, should be a day of even more serious effort, rather than a tem-

Turn to Page 2, Column 7

Hotels and Cafes Plan to Keep Observance Dry

Hotel and restaurant men of Los Angeles have perfected plans for observation of V-Day which will make the downtown district as quiet as a month of Sundays. This is being done to emphasize the solemnity of the end of the European war.

The Southern California Hotel, Restaurant and Tavern Association, whose members comprise 90 per cent of the industry, have agreed to close all beverage services beginning with receipt of the news and through the following day. Some restaurants also will close their meal services.

WAR-BOOMED INDUSTRIES BLAMED FOR FUMES

SMOKE FACTORY—The smoke from this lead smelting plant is held partly responsible for the smoke in the city.

CONTRIBUTING FACTOR—Another example of the smoke producers blamed for the acrid fumes in the city.

SHARES THE BLAME—Diesel trucks such as this add considerably to over-all cloud that hangs in skies.

Times photos

THIS DOESN'T HELP, EITHER—Phyllis Fraser, 548 S. Kingsley Drive, stands beside her incinerator, thousands of which do their daily bit toward making the smoke cloud.

City 'Smog' Laid to Dozen Causes

Autos, Chemical Plants, Sewers All Contribute, Experts Report

BY RAY ZEMAN

Why has Los Angeles been plagued by more irritating smoke and noxious fumes this year than ever before in its history?

Is it becoming a second Pittsburgh?

Are the fog, haze, fumes, gases, vapor, soot, dust and smoke due to the tremendous impounding of water in Lake Mead?

Has some eerie climatic cycle swung to lash the Southland with repeated irritants?

Questions like these are on everyone's lips nowadays. Health officers, investigating committees, engineers and public officials are analyzing the problem with their fingers crossed. They're happy about one thing—Los Angeles depends on gas, electricity and oil instead of coal for fuel.

Practically all agree that Lake Mead's water has no more effect on atmospheric conditions in Los Angeles County than a glass of water would on the speakers' table on the stage of Shrine Auditorium. Practically all agree that no weird "20-year cycle" is to blame.

Yet, here's how the experts themselves describe the mess which some have called smog (smoke and fog:)

"A community of more than 2,000,000 people is shut up in a vast room with doors and windows closed and into this room is poured the smoke and fumes from a thousand stacks, from tens of thousands of home incinerators, from hundreds of thousands of autos and trucks, poisonous vapors from chemical plants, stenches from packing houses, sewers and glue factories, lachrymating gases from refineries and burning rubbish heaps—a hellish cloud that fills the room and is indifferent to municipal boundaries."

That's the report not from crackpot or eccentrics but from the County Fumes and Smoke Commission, composed of two private citizens, Al S. Waxman and C. E. Van Der Oef, and three college professors, Dean R. E. Vivian of the University of Southern California School of Engineering, Dr. W. Roy Newsom, Whittier College professor of chemistry, and William Howard Clapp, California Institute of Technology professor emeritus in machine design.

Bird's-eye View

To get a bird's-eye view of what happens when a "tourists' paradise" shifts from fifth place in industrial production ($1,200,000,000 in 1939) to second place in the nation ($8,500,000,000 in war contracts today) The Times sent a reporter and photographer to Mt. Wilson.

As they traveled up Angeles Crest Highway they could see why the Altadena Property Owners' League is crying, "Pure air is as important as pure water."

On a typical day—not on one when the "smog" is so intense that downtown Los Angeles is in a daytime dimout—the dirty banks of air were drifting onto the San Gabriel Mountains and filtering into the canyons.

The huge masses of ugly haze hid the war-booming industrial area below—aircraft, metal working, food processing, high-octane gasoline, wood products, shipbuilding, rubber and many more whose dollar output is treble Pittsburgh's and second only to Detroit's today.

Shame, Says Astronomer

In a box seat for this sunshine paradox is Joseph Hickox, Mt. Wilson Observatory astronomer.

From a platform 150 feet high in a sun tower atop the 5710-foot peak he commands—or did command—a panoramic view unsurpassed.

"It's a shame," was his terse summary.

"It never has been so thick, so muggy, so dirty in all the history of the observatory."

He explained that the haze increased gradually every summer until 1943, when it intensified noticeably in the valley below. In 1944 the haze-fumes-dust-smoke menace multiplied many times over.

"The foggy appearance used to be at 1500 to 2000 feet," Hickox said. "Now we're practically always submerged in it."

He pointed to the crest of the surrounding haze, a brownish "frosting" at about 7000 feet forming an umbrella over the grayish-black masses.

Old Baldy Obscured

"Day after day it's like this," the astronomer related. "We used to be able to see Mt. San Jacinto, Palomar and all the way to Point Loma. Now sometimes we can't even see Old Baldy from here."

Needless to say, all this was with the naked eye. Now the haze intermittently blocks both day and night work of the observatory's nine telescopes. At night the valley lights reflect on the dust in the air and occasionally fog photographic plates. This is especially true on long exposures up to 40 hours, when faint stellar objects fail to show up because of the local reflections.

Temperature Inversion

Why doesn't the haze drift away?

Hickox and weather men have different ways of describing the "temperature inversion."

"The dust and smoke particles in the air each form a nucleus on which water condenses," Hickox said. "A higher layer of warm

Turn to Page 10, Column 1

Lana Turner's Ex-Mate and Turhan Bey Scuffle

Lana Turner, blond film star, was the "cause d'affaire" of the latest Hollywood battle Saturday night when her ex-husband, Stephen Crane, and Turhan Bey, young Turkish actor, grappled with each other at a Beverly Hills house party, an eyewitness disclosed yesterday.

The "battle" started, witnesses said, when Crane objected to Miss Turner wearing a diamond ruby ring he had given her in honor of their year-old daughter, Cheryl Christine.

Bey, current escort of the screen glamour girl, and Crane exchanged words on the dance floor.

One word led to another, as it usually does at Hollywood parties, and the two men stepped into the garden and began wrestling, witnesses reported.

Crane received a black eye when he struck his head against a pipe Bey was smoking. After tussling a few seconds the two fell to the ground, with Bay suffering scratches when he struck his head against a heavy bush.

Bey's mother said her son had a bruise on his forehead.

Spectators separated the pair and the "battle" was over.

The ring was later turned over to a friend, it was reported, and Bey and the actress left the party.

Miss Turner divorced Crane Aug. 21 on the ground that he behaved in a "sullen manner" and "nagged" her, causing her to become too thin to appear before motion-picture cameras.

Known as the original Hollywood sweater girl, Miss Turner has reportedly been in Bey's company in recent weeks.

BATTLE—Lana Turner and ex-mate, Stephen Crane.

Ferry Planes Forced Down

Two Ferry Command flight officers escaped injury late Saturday night when they crash-landed with small planes they were flying in the vicinity of Temple City.

Pilots of the planes were reported by Ferry Command officers at the Long Beach Airport as Flight Officer Leland S. Fraley, 21, Piedmont, Cal., and Flight Officer Norman J. Fowler, 21, of Millville, N.J. Neither officer was hurt and the planes were only slightly damaged, according to reports.

2nd Lt. Calvin R. Gintz of the Ferry Command group stationed at Long Beach was reported confined at the San Bernardino Station Hospital with injuries incurred when his plane assertedly crashed in the Forest Home area late Friday night.

Plans Completed for Toy Exposition

Completion of plans for its first annual "California Toy Show," merchandising event to be held here next spring in the interests of this area's growing toy industry and expected to attract hundreds of buyers from all parts of the country, was announced yesterday by the Los Angeles Chamber of Commerce.

Woody C. Klingborg, chamber departmental executive who will manage the event, said wholesalers and retailers are showing increased interest in the originality of design and motion in toys produced in Southern California.

Rain and Speed Blamed in Five Traffic Deaths

Rain-dampened pavement and too much speed, according to police, combined in two similar traffic accidents yesterday which took a total of four lives. A pedestrian injured last Friday, was the fifth traffic death of the day.

In one accident two sailors were killed and their girl companions seriously injured when an automobile in which they were riding turned over four times after skidding 305 feet on wet pavement at Hawthorne Ave. and Rosecrans Blvd.

Woman Killed

The two sailors killed were Machinist's Mate 2nd Class Milton Buffington, 23, a Seabee, and Machinist's Mate 3rd Class Gordon Kennedy, 21, Long Beach.

Anna Dickerson, 20, of 409 E. Redondo Blvd., Inglewood, who was reported by investigating officers to have been at the wheel of the speeding automobile when the accident occurred, was taken to Los Angeles General Hospital with a crushed right arm and a possible skull fracture. The other injured girl was Juanita Rouse, 23, of 420 E. Redondo Blvd., Inglewood, who was treated at the Southwest Industrial Hospital for severe lacerations and sent home.

Fatally Injured

In another accident, Jerry H. Butler Jr., 25, of 1811 Belmar Place, Santa Monica, the driver, and his girl, companion, Freddie May Jones, 17, of 417 Bay St., Ocean Park, were fatally injured.

John Hightower, 11, of 616 Westminster St., Venice, who received critical injuries in the accident which occurred at Pico Ave. and 31st St., Santa Monica, told police the driver of the car took his hands off the steering wheel to light a cigarette while the car was traveling at approximately 70 miles an hour.

Alice McClear, 70, 2623 S. Normandie Ave., died in California Hospital yesterday morning of injuries received Saturday when she was struck by a car driven by George M. Gray, 53, 1572 W. Adams Blvd. Gray was not held.

Struck down Friday night while crossing S. Figueroa St. at Ninth St., Andrew Seaborg, 73, of 251 S. Bixel St., died last night at General Hospital. He was struck by an automobile driven by Charles L. Spedale, 43, of 1735 W. 38th Place, police said. Spedale was not held.

Sessions to Open on Tuberculosis

Planned for workers and trainees, the 67th Institute for Tuberculosis Workers will begin a series of 11 daily sessions today in Bridge Hall on the University of Southern California campus at 9:30 a.m.

Sponsored by the National Tuberculosis Association in co-operation with the Graduate School of Social Work of S.C., the morning and afternoon meetings will feature subjects of case methods, treatment, nursing, medical-social service, child health and public education, as well as special programs and history of the movement.

Baby Scalds Self Fatally

Scalding burns on both feet received when he turned on the hot water while playing in the bathtub at his home last Thursday resulted in the death at General Hospital yesterday of Terry E. Kennedy, 15 months of 649 Santa Clara St., Venice.

According to the baby's parents, Mr. and Mrs. Lloyd Kennedy, he was treated for second-degree burns on his feet at a hospital immediately after he was scalded and then taken home. The next day, however, his condition became serious and he was taken to the General Hospital.

ALL THE NEWS ALL THE TIME
Largest Home Delivered Circulation
Largest Advertising Volume

Los Angeles Times

EQUAL RIGHTS
LIBERTY UNDER THE LAW — TRUE INDUSTRIAL FREEDOM

IN TWO PARTS
PART I — GENERAL NEWS

Times Office: 202 West First Street
Los Angeles 53, Cal.
Times Telephone Number MAdison 2345

VOL. LXIII — CC — THURSDAY MORNING, OCTOBER 26, 1944 — DAILY, FIVE CENTS

U.S. DEFEATS ENTIRE JAP NAVY

Battleship, Carrier Sunk; 7 Others Damaged

Dewey Vows Integrity in White House

G.O.P. Leader Lists 'Devious Methods' Used by New Deal

BY WARREN B. FRANCIS
Times Staff Representative

CHICAGO, Oct. 25.—Repeating the battle cry, "He asked for it—here it is!" Gov. Thomas E. Dewey tonight delivered one of the most vigorous indictments of the campaign against President Roosevelt and the New Deal.

In a broadcast speech before 30,000 persons in the stadium where he accepted the nomination nearly four months ago, Dewey observed that Mr. Roosevelt "is now talking in this campaign about 'fraud' and 'falsification.' Then, after listing a number of examples of Mr. Roosevelt's "devious methods," he said:

"Is it any wonder that when the White House speaks, the first question the people ask is not whether the news is good or bad, but 'Is it true?'"

Will Restore Honesty

"The new administration," he said, "will once again restore honesty and integrity to the White House so that its spoken word can be trusted."

He charged that "for a thousand dollars laid on the line to finance the fourth term drive" the administration "boldly offers for sale 'special privilege,' including the special privilege of assisting 'in the formulation of administration policies.'"

He quoted from a letter dated last Oct. 16, which he said was written from a letterhead of the National Democratic campaign headquarters, Little Rock, Ark., and signed by H. L. McAlister and Sam J. Watkins, State finance directors, inviting the recipient to join the "One Thousand Club," by the payment of $1000 to the Democratic campaign fund.

Letter Quoted

Dewey then read what he said was the following quotation from the letter:

"Members of this organization undoubtedly will be granted special privilege and prestige by party leaders. These members will be called into conference from time to time to discuss matters of national importance and to assist in the formulation of administration policies."

A cheering crowd, by all odds

Turn to Page 8, Column 1

Dewey Address Rebroadcasts Set

Gov. Dewey's talk from Chicago last night will be rebroadcast today as follows: 6:15-6:45 a.m., KECA; 12:30-1 p.m., KMPC; 1:30-2 p.m., KMTR.

MAY RETURN — Dr. Clarence A. Dykstra, who may become provost at U.C.L.A.

Dr. C. A. Dykstra May Be Named U.C.L.A. Provost

The nomination of Dr. Clarence A. Dykstra, former Los Angeles educator and administrator and now president of the University of Wisconsin, for appointment as provost for the Los Angeles campus of the University of California, may be made by Dr. Robert Gordon Sproul, president of the University of California, at a meeting of the Board of Regents of the university at the California Club tomorrow.

Appointment of someone to fill the post left vacant by the death of Dr. Earle R. Hedrick Feb. 3, 1943, is known to be considered a matter of increasing urgency by alumni groups and other leaders of the university, and action by the regents was considered likely tomorrow.

Leading Possibility

While Dr. Sproul is known to have been considering several of the university faculty members and three or four other eastern educators as nominees, it was reported to several friends of the university yesterday that Dr. Dykstra is the leading possibility for the appointment.

Dr. Sproul last night admitted that he had been considering Dr. Dykstra "among several possibilities for the nomination" and indicated that nomination and appointment of a provost is likely to be the chief order of

Turn to Page 12, Column 2

All Must File New Tax Form

Every employee in Southern California, as well as the rest of the nation, must file a new withholding tax exemption certificate by Dec. 1, Harry C. Westover, Collector of Internal Revenue for this district, announced yesterday.

To facilitate the procedure, more than 2,000,000 forms have been mailed to employers throughout the Southland, who, in turn, will hand them to employees.

Allied Pincers Closing In on 70,000 Nazis

Power Drives Seize 'S Hertogenbosch and Smash Into Tilburg

ALLIED SUPREME HEADQUARTERS, PARIS, Oct. 26 (Thursday.) (U.P.)—Allied armies, in a series of power drives gaining up to eight miles on a 100-mile front, yesterday broke the back of German resistance in Southern Holland and tightened a squeeze on possibly 70,000 enemy troops which belatedly wheeled north, hoping to escape across the bridgeless Maas Estuary.

Using flame throwers, the British 2nd Army captured 'S Hertogenbosch except for a knot of resistance in the southwest corner of that road hub, smashed into the outskirts of Tilburg, 12 miles to the southwest, and surged ahead in no less than seven columns.

Canadians Capture Fort

To the west the Canadian 1st Army captured Ft. Frederick-Hendrik after a bitter three-day battle, clearing the south bank of the Schelde Estuary, and shot six miles up the neck of Beveland Peninsula, north of the Schelde, against weak opposition. The latter drive resulted in the capture of Rilland, six miles west of Woensdrecht on the mainland.

The Canadians also advanced five miles up the west coast northeast of Beveland and began outflanking the road center of Bergen Op Zoom.

Nazis Escape by Ferry

Only rear guard resistance was encountered in these drives, indicating that the 10,000 or so Germans commanding the Antwerp passage from the north are trying to withdraw toward Rotterdam from island to island by ferry.

Between the main Canadian and British drives a new British push began rolling toward the city of Breda in the center of the Dutch front. Advancing two miles from positions established some time ago north of Baarle Nassau, the British are only about five miles from Breda.

It was estimated that up to 70,000 Germans are on the move

Turn to Page 5, Column 3

Two Ration Changes Told

WASHINGTON, Oct. 25. (U.P.)—Ration point values for meats, butter and processed foods will continue unchanged, with two exceptions, during November, but more top-grade meats will be available on the civilian market, the Office of Price Administration announced tonight.

Only changes from the October ration charts will affect applesauce, reduced from 50 to 30 points per No. 2 can, and packaged spaghetti and macaroni dinners, slightly decreased in value.

The new one-month ration period will begin Sunday.

(AP) Wirephoto

U.S. NAVY BLOWS IN WESTERN PACIFIC—Arrows indicate U.S. aerial blows in the Western Pacific, including 3rd Fleet carrier action and an attack on Kyushu by Superfortresses. In the Philippines area the U.S. Navy won its greatest victory when two Jap naval forces entered the Sibuyan and Sulu seas while a third moved south from Formosa.

Progress of Philippine Naval Battle at Glance

BY THE ASSOCIATED PRESS

Out of a welter of reports, here briefly appears to be the still-developing situations in the Philippines-Formosa naval-air battles:

The Japanese sent two fleet groups eastward against invaded Leyte in the Central Philippines. A third fleet group moved down from Formosa.

Although outnumbered, Vice Adm. Thomas C. Kinkaid split up his 7th Fleet to engage the two groups moving toward Leyte.

Adm. William F. Halsey's 3rd Fleet carrier planes took on the third group approaching from Formosa.

Kinkaid's forces won and sizable results have been announced. Reports are somewhat meager on the Formosa action, although Adm. Chester W. Nimitz has reported from Pearl Harbor the definite sinking of a large Nipponese carrier and two others damaged.

Of the two groups Kinkaid took on, here is what happened:

One group moved out of the Sulu Sea through the Mindanao Sea, passed through Surigao Straits and approached Leyte Gulf from the southwest. A 25-minute naval battle, plus carrier-plane attacks, occurred. The Japanese fleet withdrew to the southwest, leaving a Yamasiro class battleship sinking and several cruisers and destroyers sunk.

The second Japanese group, moving through the Philippine inland sea of Sibuyan, sailed between Luzon and Samar and was engaged off the east coast of Samar. It was attacked with gunfire, then by planes of Kinkaid's escort carriers, supported by flyers from another American task force, forcing it to flee north.

ARCTIC PORT CAPTURED AS RUSS ENTER NORWAY

LONDON, Oct. 25. (AP)— The Red army invaded Norway today and captured the prize Arctic port of Kirkenes and 30 other communities at the northern end of the front, completed the conquest of Transylvania in the south, and won 13 strong points in East Prussia from the counterattacking Germans.

The Moscow communique and two orders of the day from Marshal Stalin announced these successes, but did not confirm a German high command announcement that the Russians had launched a new offensive northwest of the Narew River between Warsaw and East Prussia.

Towns in Arc Taken

Moscow said only that Russian and 1st Polish Army units took 11 small towns in a narrow arc immediately northwest of Warsaw below the Narew, and dismissed this action as merely "of local importance."

The invasion of Norway and the clearance of Transylvania were presented by the Russians as the day's top news, both being heralded by orders of the day from Stalin and victory salutes from Moscow's cannon.

In addition, Moscow announced capture of another 50 populated centers in the mountains of Eastern Czechoslovakia northeast and southeast of Mukacevo, and the repulse of large German forces trying to break out of the tight pocket in Southwest Latvia above Liepaja.

The invasion of East Prussia

Turn to Page 4, Column 3

THE WORLD'S WAR FRONTS

PACIFIC—Japanese navy defeated, seriously damaged and routed in battle with U.S. Fleet; enemy loses at least one battleship and one aircraft carrier with five battleships and two carriers damaged. In Philippines American troops invade Samar; forces on Leyte smash nine miles inland. Pages 1 and 2.

WESTERN FRONT—German resistance near collapse in Southern Holland under Allied drives that gain up to eight miles. Page 1.

EASTERN FRONT—Red army captures Norwegian port of Kirkenes; reopens battle for Warsaw and completes liberation of prewar Romania. Page 1.

Victory Told by Eyewitness

[Following is the first eyewitness account of the naval battle which ended in a great American victory yesterday.]

BY RALPH TEATSWORTH

ABOARD ADM. KINKAID'S FLAGSHIP OFF PHILIPPINES, Oct. 26. (U.P.)—The Tokyo Express rammed into the American Navy Limited today.

The pride of Japan was wrecked so badly it may never make another long run. It was the day our Navy had dreamed about for more than a year.

Concentrated Hell

It was 17 hours of concentrated hell, and the most amazing thing about the battle was that our Pacific flight carrier force—which nobody thought could deliver such a terrific punch—held off the bulk of the Japanese fleet all day and had it on the run all afternoon.

When evening came and most of the pieces of the huge naval puzzle had been fitted together, a Navy spokesman announced:

"The enemy has been decisively defeated with heavy losses. Our Fleet is without serious losses and fit to fight tomorrow."

Minimum Losses Told

It is yet too early to ascertain accurately the destruction and damage wrought on the Japanese fleet, but the enemy's minimum losses are estimated at one Yamasiro class battleship sunk, one battleship knocked out and probably sunk, three battleships damaged severely, several cruisers and destroyers sunk, three cruisers and several destroyers damaged.

Tomorrow—Gallup Poll

Times readers may again learn the nation-wide opinion of voters on Presidential candidates in tomorrow's Times. A complete 48-State Gallup Poll report on voting sentiment at this time will be published tomorrow. One more survey will be made prior to election. Gallup Poll reports appear exclusively in The Times in Southern California.

Enemy Loses Cruisers and 150 Planes in Most Crushing Defeat of War

U.S. PACIFIC FLEET HEADQUARTERS, PEARL HARBOR, Oct. 25. (U.P.)—The Japanese navy has been defeated, seriously damaged and routed in the Philippines in momentous engagements with the United States Fleet which have cost the enemy at least one battleship and one aircraft carrier sunk, at least five battleships and two carriers heavily damaged, and several cruisers and destroyers sunk, it was announced today.

Complete details of the engagements have not been received and the battle is continuing.

The news of the great American naval victory—possibly the greatest of all time—was disclosed in a series of dramatic announcements and eyewitness accounts which told of furious aerial engagements between carrier planes and with warships of both fleets firing broadsides at each other in close contact.

Halsey Reports to President

Adm. William F. Halsey, commanding the U.S. 3rd Fleet which won one part of the victory, reported to President Roosevelt:

"The Japanese navy in the Philippines area has been defeated, seriously damaged and routed by the United States Navy in that area."

Gen. Douglas MacArthur said in a special statement: "The Japanese navy has received its most crushing defeat

Illustrated on Page 3, Part I

of the war. Its future efforts can only be on a dwindling scale."

Adm. Ernest J. King, commander-in-chief of the United States Fleet, said that virtually the whole Japanese fleet was involved in the series of actions, which extended from the mid-Philippines invasion zone to the waters between the Northern Philippines and Formosa.

(Gordon Walker, broadcasting from Leyte Island for Mutual Network, quoted a naval spokesman as saying that practically every major ship in the Japanese navy, with the exception of carriers, has been either sunk or damaged.)

Down 150 Jap Planes

At least 150 enemy planes have been shot down, and probably the total will prove above 200.

The United States has lost the 10,000-ton light aircraft carrier Princeton and several PT boats sunk and several escort carriers and destroyers damaged.

MacArthur reported the loss of an American escort carrier. Presumably this was not the Princeton, which is a full-fledged carrier.

At the same time MacArthur announced that his troops had invaded Samar, third largest island of the Philippines, while on Leyte the Americans drove nine miles inland to seize Burauen.

The enemy battleship known sunk was of the 29,300-ton Yamasiro class mounting 12 14-inch guns in its main batteries. It was in one of two Japanese battleship formations which attempted to attack MacArthur's invasion forces in the Leyte Gulf. Both formations were ripped by Vice-Adm. Thomas C. Kinkaid's 7th Fleet supported by Australian cruisers and carriers of Vice-Adm. Marc A. Mitscher's fast task force.

Large Carrier Sunk

The enemy carrier known sunk, a large one, was destroyed by carrier-borne planes of Halsey's 3rd Fleet off the Northern Philippines.

Damage done to the enemy is not yet known in full.

MacArthur reported that Monday, Pearl Harbor time—Tuesday, Philippines time—the Japanese attempted a big aerial attack on his invasion fleet. The enemy planes swept over the Leyte Gulf just after dawn. Carrier planes intercepted them, broke up their formations and defeated them. Fifty-three enemy planes were destroyed by planes and anti-aircraft guns.

Tuesday, Pearl Harbor time—today, Philippines time—two Japanese fleets moved in to attack MacArthur's invasion zone.

One went in from the south through the Surigao Strait south of Leyte. The other went in through the San Bernardino Pass north of Leyte and adjacent Samar.

Enemy Fleet Routed

In the Surigao force were two Japanese battleships, a heavy cruiser, a light cruiser and four destroyers. Kinkaid moved in with his combat ships and carrier planes. The enemy fleet was routed. The battleship was sunk early in the engagement.

Several of the cruiser and destroyer units were sunk. Every ship in it was sunk or damaged and carrier planes continued to attack its beaten remnants as they fled. In this engagement several American PT boats were sunk or

Turn to Page 2, Column 4

WHO SAID THIS?

"When the treachery of Pearl Harbor came, we were not ready."—From the speech of Sen. Alben Barkley placing in nomination the name of Franklin D. Roosevelt for the Presidency, Chicago, July 20, 1944.

Sen. Barkley now seeks to keep Mr. Roosevelt in office 16 years.

IN THE 'TIMES' TODAY

THURSDAY OCTOBER 26, 1944

REMEMBER THIS

A kiss is a kiss but indiscriminate kisses are not real kisses.

ALL THE NEWS ALL THE TIME
Largest Home Delivered Circulation
Largest Advertising Volume

Los Angeles Times

EQUAL RIGHTS
LIBERTY UNDER THE LAW — TRUE INDUSTRIAL FREEDOM

IN TWO PARTS
PART I — GENERAL NEWS
Times Office: 202 West First Street
Los Angeles 53, Cal.
Times Telephone Number MAdison 2345

VOL. LXIV — CC* — SATURDAY MORNING, MARCH 24, 1945 — DAILY, FIVE CENTS

PATTON'S MEN STORM OVER RHINE

New Move for Peace in Studio Strike

Heads of Factions Involved in Walkout Confer on Issues

Carrying new hope for a possible early sudden termination of the strike, principals in the A.F.L. motion-picture strike situation conferred yesterday for some hours but came out of their conference uncommunicative as to any positive result.

In the conference were President E. J. Mannix of the Association of Motion Picture Producers, Inc., President Richard A. Walsh of the International Alliance of Theatrical Stage Employees and head of the non-striking element, and President Herbert Sorrell of the Conference of Student Unions, under whose banner the strikers are on the picket lines.

Nothing Accomplished

Reports that representatives of the Federal government attended the conference were denied. No participant wished to relate what took place in their meeting except to say that, in the words of one, "nothing decisive was accomplished."

It is believed in some quarters that Big Bill Hutcheson, national first vice-president of the American Federation of Labor, has it within his power to bring an immediate end to the strike and he is being urged from many quarters, including the War Labor Board, to do so.

Hutcheson is head of the Carpenters' Union and W.L.B. has been trying to get him to send an order down the line to his union here to quit the strike. Without the support of the carpenters, the strike would fail, it is believed.

Joe Cambiano, a vice-president of the Carpenters' Union, and James Skelton, business representative of its local, are leaving tonight for Washington to confer with Hutcheson.

The Screen Actors' Guild went overwhelmingly antistrike yesterday in the quarrel, over which picket lines have kept several thousand workers out of their jobs in major studios for two weeks.

How They Voted

The first 3117 guild votes showed 3029 against observing the strikers' picket lines and in favor of keeping their union's no-strike contract and 88 for observing the picket line for a sympathy strike.

Other ballots were being totaled but guild officers said the indications are indisputably that the antistrike position will prevail. The A Class in union membership, which includes stars, voted antistrike, 731 to 10. The A juniors voted antistrike 2298 to 78.

Teamsters Opposed

The powerful Teamsters' Union, which handles studio transportation, a considerable item, early lined up its members against the strike and hurled a defiant notice to the strikers by way of an unusual display in its official publication yesterday.

Entitled "To Whom It May

Turn to Page 2, Column 7

WATER BARRIER ON BERLIN ROAD CROSSED

(AP) Wirephoto

ASSAULT BOAT—A soldier of Gen. Patton's 3rd Army guides assault boat as he and comrades crossed Moselle River near Coblenz a few days ago in drive which overran Saar and was followed by crossing of Rhine. In just such boats 3rd Army was ferried across Rhine River Thursday night.

Nazis Say Other Crossings Made on 215-Mile Front

PARIS, March 23. (U.P.)—Lt. Gen. George S. Patton's famed 3rd Army troops have stormed across the Rhine and established a solid, expanding bridgehead on the direct road to Berlin—265 miles away, it was announced tonight, as Berlin reported that other Allied forces are crossing the historic river barrier at other points along a 215-mile front.

German reports placed Patton's crossing at Oppenheim, 10 miles south of Mainz, and said also that other crossings were being made in the north by Field Marshal Sir B. L. Montgomery's massive striking force of three Allied armies. Allied headquarters admitted that advance patrols had crossed the Rhine and were battling the Germans in the northern sector. It was likely that Montgomery would throw the full might of his armies against the Rhine within the next 24 hours.

Patton's crossing—second historic forcing of Germany's great river barrier—was made at 10 p.m. Thursday. Within 25 minutes, Patton sent thousands of veteran troops over the river in hand-paddled assault boats. Snipers were quickly eliminated, and the Yanks began moving inland.

Offensive Unchecked

Only once did German artillery attempt to challenge the men who had collapsed German resistance in France and who had come fresh from another great victory in the Saar. But that artillery burst was insignificant and Patton's men were unchecked.

A few enemy planes came over the bridgehead at dawn, about eight hours after the first crossing, but by then the foothold was solid and troops and materiel were swinging over the river in great numbers. The river was packed with ferry vessels.

With Patton across at a point about 70 miles south of Lt. Gen. Courtney H. Hodges' 1st Army at Remagen, the whole Rhine east bank may soon be swarming with Allied troops.

Near Darmstadt

Patton's troops are less than 10 miles from the Hessian capital of Darmstadt, with a population of 72,000, at the point of crossing described by Berlin. Darmstadt lies in the wooded Main River valley only 13 miles south of the great industrial and transportation center of Frankfort on the Main.

German reports said 3rd Army troops also were attempting to span the Rhine on a great superhighway bridge four miles north of Ludwigshafen and were making other assault preparations in the area of Worms, 15 miles south of Oppenheim, but these were not confirmed by Allied sources.

German resistance along the Rhine has been so utterly crushed in the flaming 10-day Battle of the Saar, where the German 1st and 7th armies lost more than 100,000 prisoners alone, that Patton used neither air nor artillery preparation to span the river.

Flat Valley Ahead

At his point of crossing Patton is 265 miles from Berlin, four miles less than Lt. Gen. Courtney H. Hodges' 1st Army in the Remagen bridgehead. His drive into the Reich's inner fortress, however, can follow the flat main river valley and need not battle through mountains such as hem in Hodges' 1st Army.

Less than eight miles ahead of Patton's eager troops is the great six-lane Mannheim-Berlin superhighway, built especially by Adolf Hitler to send Nazi tanks roaring against the Allies in the west. There is no doubt Patton will lose little time in getting his famed armored divisions rolling along the road toward the Reich capital.

Bradley Confident

Berlin said that American shock troops tried to cross the Rhine at Duesseldorf and at another point six miles south of Cologne, claiming that both attacks were repulsed. Another crossing also was attempted near the Ruhr to the north, the German reports said, without giving details.

These German reports, coupled with the increasingly urgent tone of front dispatches describing Allied preparations, left little doubt that Montgomery's armies would storm the river within the next 24 hours if they have not already done so.

Indicative that crossings may be under way was a confident statement by Gen. Omar N. Brad-

Turn to Page 4, Column 4

EYEWITNESS TELLS OF CROSSING RHINE

Patton's First Group Had Been Across River 20 Minutes Before Nazis Started Firing

[Edward D. Ball of the Associated Press was the only correspondent to make the night crossing of the Rhine with the U.S. 3rd Army and for the first 12 hours of the operation was the only correspondent eyewitness. He tells about it in the following dispatch.]

BY EDWARD D. BALL

EAST OF THE RHINE, March 23. (AP)—The 3rd Army stormed across the Rhine at 10:25 p.m. last night without loss of a man and without drawing a single shot from the Germans until a good 20 minutes after the crossing was made good.

By dawn today a solid bridgehead was driven into Hitler's inner fortress against opposition that still was spotty and erratic despite some artillery and mortar fire. Most of the enemy weapons were soon silenced.

Bridgehead Established

Within eight hours Lt. Gen. George S. Patton's forces had completely established a firm bridgehead in the greatest over-water assault since Normandy.

At the first crack of day a couple of Messerschmitt 262 jet-propelled planes came over the bridgehead and promptly were knocked down.

The operation, which had been planned and rehearsed for months, went off far smoother than anyone could have hoped.

The Germans simply were caught by surprise and by the overwhelming weight of American arms.

Patton's Rhine-conquering exploit followed one of the greatest armor and infantry thrusts in military history—the tremendous sweep through the Saarland.

Together these successes appeared to be decisive blows against the Germans. The elated doughboys, who three weeks ago were urging the Russians on to Berlin, now nominated themselves for the job of taking the German capital.

Amazing Sight

The Rhineland never saw a more amazing sight than last night's. Probably it never will. For miles back the roads were lined with trucks and other vehicles struggling up the hills.

Hundreds of conveyances of all kinds which had pulled up just out of sight of the river during the day stood silent and shadowy in the moon-splashed fields and along the edges of woods near the Rhine. Engineers who had spent back-breaking months at home preparing for this show were on hand to help get the vehicles across.

For months columns of trucks with their tons of assault boats had been edging toward the front at night and hiding out by day.

Sometimes they got in the way of swearing tankmen and played hob with traffic.

On Spot When Needed

Along toward the end of the 3rd Army's recent sensational spurt to the Rhine they lagged uneasily behind, but they put on a spurt and were on the spot last night when needed.

For some of the doughboys

Turn to Page 4, Column 1

Senate Rejects Williams, Giving F.D.R. Rebuff

WASHINGTON, March 23. (AP) The Senate rebuffed President Roosevelt today with a 52-to-36 rejection of his nomination of Aubrey Williams as Rural Electrification Administrator.

Thirty-three Republicans and 19 Democrats joined to blackball the ardent New Dealer for a job which in the early postwar period may involve lending up to $1,000,000,000 to finance rural electric lines.

Voting for confirmation were 31 Democrats, 4 Republicans and Sen. La Follette (Prog.) Wis.

Victory Fete Planned

President James G. Patton of the National Farmers Union announced that the organization will hold a "victory dinner" in honor of Williams Wednesday. He said Mrs. Roosevelt has accepted an invitation to speak.

Patton said it will be a "victory dinner" because "this is just the first battle, and it has shown us what is necessary to victory." He said there will be a "total war of issues to decide whether this country is to conduct itself for the people instead of vested interests and racial bigots."

Williams, commenting on the Senate action, said "it is time for the people to look into what is happening" here.

Opposition Group

It was the first time since 1939 that a Presidential nominee, other than for postmaster, has been rejected by the Senate. That rejection was of a nominee for U.S. Attorney in Nevada.

The Democrats who opposed

Turn to Page 3, Column 2

State Tax Cut Backers Lose First Skirmish

BY CHESTER G. HANSON, Times Staff Representative

SACRAMENTO, March 23.—Abandoned by 11 of their own number, Republicans in the Assembly lost the first major skirmish in their fight to preserve the cuts in State taxes.

The Assembly adopted, 41 to 39, an amendment to the tax bill by Edward O'Day of San Francisco and other Democrats which would give California cities and counties $57,000,000 of State funds for postwar construction of public works.

Threat to Program

The Republican leadership objected to the amendment as not germaine to the tax bill and as launching a new principle under which cities and counties would be cut in on State tax funds. It would throw Warren's entire tax program out of line, according to Assemblyman Walter Fourt, who is handling the bill for the Governor.

Because it does not affect the tax cuts as such, the amendment afforded an easy out for some of the wavering Republicans or for those who believe in the principle of using State tax revenues to finance projects in local political subdivisions.

Here is the vote on the amendment:

Republicans for: Carey, Clarke, Denny, Dickey, Johnson, Kraft, McCollister, Niehouse, Price, Stream and Thorp (11.)

Democratic Vote

Democrats for: Anderson, Beal, Beck, Bennett, Berry, Brady, Brown, Burkhalter, George Collins, Debs, Dekker, Clayton Dills, Ralph Dills, Doyle, Dunn, Emlay, Fletcher, Gaffney, Haggerty, Hawkins, Heisinger, Kilpatrick, King, Lowrey, Mission, McMillan, O'Day, Robertson, Rosenthal, Thomas (30.)

Republicans against: Armstrong, Boyd, Burke, Burns, Butters, Call, Sam Collins, Davis, Erwin, Field, Fourt, Gannon, Geddes, Hollibaugh, Knight, Leonard, John Lyons, Maloney, Miller, Sheridan, Sherwin, Stephenson, Stewart, Thompson, Thurman, Waters, Watson, Weber, Werdel, Wollenberg, Charles Lyon (31.)

Democrats against: Allen, Crichton, Crowley, Evans, Guthrie, Middough, Pelletier and Sawallisch (8.)

Democrats Cheer

As the close vote showed up on the scoreboard, the Democrats cheered. They got their amendment, but more important, they got more delay.

Assemblyman Call (R.) Redwood City, immediately gave notice that on the next legislative day he will move to reconsider the vote by which the O'Day amendment was adopted. That will be Monday, so that final Assembly action on the tax bill must wait at least until then.

Earlier in the day the Assembly was warned to keep the tax spenders close to the taxpayers.

The warning was sounded by Rolland Vandegrift, legislative auditor, as he testified before the Assembly sitting as a committee of the whole in considering Assembly Bill 272, which continues the tax reductions inaugurated two years ago. Vandegrift was called by the opposition to the Governor's tax-cut program.

"When officials of cities and counties propose to spend money which has to be raised by levying city and county taxes they approach the matter with much greater caution than when they are to spend money which they

Turn to Page 3, Column 4

Japs Sink U.S. Escort Carrier Bismarck Sea

GUAM, March 24. (AP)—Japanese planes, which counterattacked U.S. amphibious forces off Iwo Jima the night of Feb. 21, sank the U.S.S. Bismarck Sea, an escort carrier, Adm. Chester W. Nimitz announced today.

The Bismarck Sea, a 10,200-ton vessel, was the 11th U.S. carrier listed as lost in the war. Ten of the 11 have been lost in the Pacific. Six of the flattops were escorts, one was a light carrier and four were full carriers.

Nimitz said "most" of the Bismarck Sea's personnel—estimated at 1500—were rescued, but Capt. John Lockwood Pratt, the skipper, told war correspondents in an interview that "many" of his men were killed in explosions caused by Japanese aerial torpedoes and by the fires which followed. He said many others were killed in the water by Japanese pilots,

Turn to Page 2, Column 5

Tokyo Reports U.S. Carriers Hit Okinawa

SAN FRANCISCO, March 23. American carrier planes raided Okinawa in the Ryukyu Islands, midway between Japan and Formosa, Friday and Saturday (Tokyo Time,) Radio Tokyo reported tonight.

The enemy report, unconfirmed by the Navy at Guam which disclosed earlier in the week a two-day strike by Vice-Adm. Marc A. Mitscher's carrier aircraft at Southern Japan, said 230 planes made Friday's raid.

Okinawa is a Jap naval and air base.

Earlier, Radio Tokyo, in claiming a "pursuit" of Mitscher's fleet from Southern Japan, placed the task force east of Okinawa on Wednesday.

Jap Inland Sea Bases Heavily Hit by Fleet

GUAM, March 24. (U.P.)—Further reports from the 5th Fleet on the carrier attacks on Japan this week disclose extensive damage to air installations at many Jap bases along the Inland Sea and 731 enemy planes were destroyed or damaged. Adm. Chester W. Nimitz did not give any further information on losses suffered by the Jap fleet in the Inland Sea. He listed 281 aircraft shot down, 275 destroyed on the ground and 175 probably destroyed or damaged on the ground.

BERLIN BATTLE REOPENED BY RUSSIA, NAZIS CLAIM

LONDON, March 24. (AP)—Berlin said last night that the Red army had reopened the battle for the German capital while Moscow announced that Russian forces had split the Nazi defenders of the prize Baltic ports of Danzig and Gdynia.

Waves of Russian infantry and tanks were reported by the enemy to have broken through Berlin's Oder River line and to have swept six miles beyond captured Kuestrin to within 31 miles east of the capital.

Artillery Bombardment

A 90-minute artillery bombardment, followed by attacks by hundreds of Soviet dive bombers, preceded the assault which smashed to Golzow on the main Kuestrin-Berlin trunk railroad. There, an enemy front report said, a German counterattack stalled the drive but the Russians struck again in a swaying, indecisive battle.

"The major Russian offensive against Berlin is immediately at hand," said a Berlin report to the German-controlled S.T.B. Agency in Stockholm.

The German radio said Marshal Gregory K. Zhukov's 1st White Russian Army had thrown 72,000 troops and 400 tanks into the battle west of Kuestrin. Other enemy broadcasts said Russian scouting was spreading all along the middle Oder from Kuestrin 45 miles south to Guben, and in London it was believed Zhukov had massed 100 divisions, perhaps more than 1,200,000 men, for a climactic lunge to Berlin.

Significantly, Moscow's war bulletins reported a sharp jump in enemy tank and plane losses. Along the entire eastern front, Moscow said, 156 German tanks and 149 planes were destroyed. More than 4200 prisoners were taken in East Prussia, at Danzig and Gdynia and in Silesia.

At the southern end of the eastern front Marshal Ivan S. Konev's 1st Ukrainian Army reached the frontier of Moravia in pursuing enemy forces from Upper Silesia into the Sudeten Mountains.

Simultaneously, Berlin said, a four-day Red army offensive south of the Danube River in Hungary had reached Komarom, key to Bratislava and Vienna, 54 and 84 miles to the west, and Red air force heavy bombers blasted the Hungarian rail town of Papa.

NAZIS PRINT OBITUARIES, THEN FLEE TO HAVENS

BERN, March 23. (AP) — Weltwoche, a Swiss weekly, today reported many "dead" were coming back to life from Germany. These are Nazis whose "obituaries" were published in papers and now are reappearing under assumed names to avoid the war criminals list.

The paper declared that four weeks after his death notice in Germany, S.S. Leader Olaf Fickert was seen on the streets of Barcelona—but under another name, Wilhelm Kleinert. Another case listed was that of Hitler Youth Staff Member Helmut Moeckel, reported "accidentally killed." Moeckel is under the protection of Alvarez Serrano, leader of the Spanish Militia College, the paper said.

Labor Director Robert Leitner blew himself to a "funeral" Jan. 26 in Prague which party, state and Wehrmacht leaders attended while newsreels of the procession were taken—but the "deceased" traveled through the country under the name of George Hanauer with new papers and a new beard, Weltwoche asserted.

S.S. Men Karl Heinz von Duffais, Hans Steudemann and S.S. Fuehrer Frick went to Buenos Aires under phony names, the paper continued.

"It is so customary in party circles to indulge in 'painless death,' to disappear from the war criminal list, that people no longer believe the real death notices," the paper said.

FATHER STABS SON, KILLS SELF IN TRY TO HALT WEDDING

ROCK ISLAND (Ill.) March 23. (U.P.)—Carl Swicker Jr., 23, was married today eight hours after his father wounded him and killed himself in an effort to prevent the wedding.

The ex-serviceman, bearing knife wounds in his neck, chest and hands, married his 18-year-old sweetheart, Jacqueline Brown, on schedule at 2 p.m. His mother attended the ceremony.

Before he died, Carl Swicker Sr., 58, told police he had committed the knifings "to prevent my son from getting married."

THE WORLD'S WAR FRONTS

WEST FRONT—Patton's troops cross Rhine. Page 1, Part I.

EAST FRONT — Soviets crash Berlin's immediate defenses, drive to outskirts of Golzow, 32 miles from the city. Page 1.

PACIFIC — Navy announces carrier Bismarck Sea sunk off Iwo Jima; Japs say carrier fleet attacking Ryukyu Islands. Page 1. MacArthur troops take town eight miles from Baguio. Page 2.

FEATURES INDEX

MacArthur's Men Dig Out Enemy on Luzon—

American troops are battering away at enemy resistance points on Luzon as Gen. MacArthur's drives to clean up the Philippines continue. Read what infantrymen and airmen as a team are doing on Page 2, Part I.

On Other Pages:

EXTRA

LATEST WAR NEWS

Los Angeles Times

VOL. LXIV Two Parts *** FRIDAY MORNING, APRIL 13, 1945 DAILY, FIVE CENTS

ROOSEVELT DEAD!

Cerebral Hemorrhage Proves Fatal; President Truman Sworn in Office

Yanks Near Suburb Area of Berlin

Troops Cross Elbe and Junction With Russians Seems Close

PARIS, April 12. (U.P.)—American 9th Army tank forces crashed over the Elbe River today and were reported approaching the suburban area of Berlin tonight. One semiofficial report placed the Yanks within 49 miles of the Reich capital.

A strict security blackout, lifted temporarily to reveal that the 9th Army's 2nd Armored Division had bridged the Elbe in the Magdeburg area, hid movements of the tank forces beyond the river—last natural barrier before Berlin.

Rumors and speculation of all kinds swept throughout the world as the Battle of Berlin neared its climactic stage. One wholly unconfirmed report said that Allied paratroopers had landed only 16 miles from the Reich capital in the path of the advancing Americans.

Charging in from the east, the Russians were meeting fierce resistance on the approaches to Berlin, Radio Moscow said, but in the west the American tanks were believed speeding along virtually unopposed down the homestretch.

Junction Seems Near

A junction between the Americans and Russians seemed near. Secretary of War Stimson said in Washington that the east-west forces now are 75 miles apart at some points.

At the same time, the American 3rd and 1st armies swept on across the waist of Germany to within 19 miles of the Czechoslovakian border and 129 miles of the last known Russian positions along the Neisse River.

Lunging from 30 to 46 miles in the past 24 hours, Lt. Gen. George S. Patton's armor overran Weimar, birthplace of the German republic which Adolf

Turn to Page 4, Column 3.

PRESIDENTS NAMED EVERY 20 YEARS DIE IN OFFICE

NEW YORK, April 12. (AP) President Roosevelt's death today carried on an American tradition that Presidents elected at 20-year intervals die in office. The list includes:

1840—William Henry Harrison.
1860—Abraham Lincoln.
1880—James A. Garfield.
1900—William McKinley.
1920—Warren G. Harding.
1940—Franklin D. Roosevelt.

DEATH COMES—Franklin D. Roosevelt, the 31st President of the United States, died unexpectedly today of a cerebral hemorrhage at his summer cottage at Warm Springs, Ga. The end came on eve of victory in Europe.

Ship Blows Up; Hundreds Die

ROME, April 12. (AP) — An American Liberty ship loaded with aerial bombs blew up in Bari Harbor at noon Monday, killing or injuring possibly 1867 Italian civilians and an unstated number of American and British servicemen, an Italian government spokesman announced today.

Only two persons who were aboard the ship at the time were reported to have survived. They were Italian civilians who were blown clear. The identity of the ship was not disclosed

Tentatively the Italian spokesman placed the toll of Italian dead at 267 and the injured at about 1600.

U.S. SUBMARINE SCAMP AND LARGE LCS LOST

WASHINGTON, April 12. (AP) The submarine Scamp and a large support landing craft have been lost in the Pacific, the Navy announced today.

The submarine was reported overdue from patrol and presumed lost, and the LCS (L) (3)—49 was lost in the Philippines as the result of enemy action.

Normal complement of a submarine is about 65 officers and men and of a landing craft of the type about 45.

No Casualty Report

There was no report of casualties on the landing craft.

The submarine was under command of Comdr. John C. Hollingsworth, son of Mr. and Mrs. J. C. Hollingsworth of Emory University, Ga. Comdr. Hollingsworth is listed as missing in action.

The landing craft was skippered by Lt. Harold W. Smith, Decatur, Ala. The Navy said Lt. Smith had no casualty status.

The announcement brought to 284 the total of naval vessels lost since the start of the war from all causes, including 227 sunk, 46 overdue and presumed lost, and 10 destroyed to prevent capture.

42 Submarines Lost

The Scamp was the 42nd submarine lost, of which 36 have been reported overdue and presumed lost, four known sunk and two destroyed to prevent capture.

The Scamp was commissioned Sept. 18, 1942.

Yanks Storm Bohol Island

MANILA, April 13. (AP)—Veteran Americal Division Yanks landed Wednesday on Bohol Island, last of the Central Philippines still in enemy hands, under cover of naval and air bombardment, Gen. Douglas MacArthur reported today.

Bohol is directly north of Mindanao.

Maj. Gen. William H. Arnold's Americal troops landed at Tagbilaran, on the southwestern shore, and quickly drove inland "in an endeavor to secure control of the entire island before the surprised enemy could rally his strength," MacArthur said.

Emergency Cabinet Session Summoned; Parley Plan in Doubt

WARM SPRINGS (Ga.) April 12. (U.P.)—Franklin D. Roosevelt, President for 12 of the momentous years in this country's history, died at 3:35 p.m. C.W.T. (1:35 p.m. P.W.T.) today in a small room in the "little White House" here.

Mr. Roosevelt had been in Warm Springs—which he liked to call his "second home"—since March 30. The week preceding he had spent at his home in Hyde Park, N.Y.

He was 63 and had served as President longer than any other American.

Less than three hours after the President died, Harry S. Truman was sworn in as 32nd President.

With the President at the time of his death of cerebral hemorrhage were Comdr. Howard G. Breunn and Dr. James P. Paulin of Atlanta.

Death Announced to Press

News of Mr. Roosevelt's death came from Secretary William D. Hassett. He called in three press association reporters who had accompanied the President here and said:

"It is my sad duty to inform you that the President died at 3:35 of a cerebral hemorrhage."

Simultaneously the news was telephoned to the White House in Washington and announced there, too.

In Washington, where the news of the President's death at first produced shocked disbelief, officials immediately wondered what effect the tragedy would have on the many domestic and international projects the President was guiding.

Whether it would cause postponement of the United Nations security conference at San Francisco remained to be seen. No one knew in the confusion of the tragic moment.

But the conference was perhaps the project closest to the President's heart, and there was some belief that in tribute to him the United Nations would carry it through.

Planned to Open Conference

He had planned to open the conference in person—to lay before the United Nations his own ideas for world peace.

The President had spent a leisurely two weeks in Warm Springs. And at no time was there any indication that he was sick, beyond the fact that he had not made his usual visits to the Warm Springs swimming pool where in 1924 he began his lifelong battle to overcome the withering effects of infantile paralysis.

Almost daily during his stay he took long automobile rides in the soft Georgia spring sun and had been keeping up constantly with developments in Washington and abroad

Turn to Page 2, Column 1

For President Roosevelt's obituary and account of his career, see Page 6, Part I.

Truman Takes Oath of Office as President

WASHINGTON, April 12. (AP) Harry S. Truman of Missouri was sworn in as 32nd President of the United States today at 7:09 p.m. E.W.T. (4:09 p.m. P.W.T.)

Solemnly he repeated the oath of the nation's highest office less than three hours after Franklin Delano Roosevelt died of a cerebral hemorrhage at Warm Springs, Ga.

Truman is 60.

It was a moment of significance to America and a warring world. The transition in the nation's leadership came when Allied might was nearing victory in Europe and when preparations for permanent peace even now are under way.

Must Shape the Peace

To Truman, onetime Missouri county judge, falls the tremendous task of shaping that peace so largely patterned by Roosevelt.

Truman, his hand on a small black Bible whose pages were edged in red, repeated the oath after Chief Justice Harlan Fiske Stone.

The scene was the Cabinet room in the executive offices of the White House, where, for more years than any other President, Mr. Roosevelt had presided over momentous meetings of his key advisers.

They were there tonight to watch the slender, gray, former Senator from Missouri inducted into the highest office.

Truman read the oath from a

Turn to Page 2, Column 3

Reds Say Hitler, Goebbels Took Own Lives

BY THE ASSOCIATED PRESS

The Soviet official communique last night quoted a high Nazi official in conquered Berlin as stating that Adolf Hitler, Propaganda Minister Joseph Goebbels and the chief of the German general staff, Gen. Krebs, committed suicide before the capital fell.

No details whatever were given as the communique, delayed well past midnight, recounted the fall of Berlin with capture of 70,000 troops, and then went on:

"Also taken prisoner were Hans Fritsche, first deputy of Goebbels in propaganda and the press; Press Chief Flick, and Government Counselor Heinrich Dorsch.

"During interrogation Dr. Fritsche stated that Hitler, Goebbels and the newly appointed chief of the general staff, Infantry Gen. Krebs, had committed suicide."

This report by the Russians was the third version in 24 hours of how Hitler died although there was general agreement in all Allied capitals that he actually is dead.

Supreme Allied headquarters in Paris hurled the lie at the German story of his purported heroic death, quoting Heinrich Himmler as saying that the Fuehrer had died or was dying of a cerebral hemorrhage.

In Washington President Truman said he had it on the best authority that Hitler was dead, but didn't know how the death occurred.

Presumably a thorough checkup was being made by Russian troops in the ruined buildings of Berlin, but the Soviet communique made no mention of such a search.

Inclusion of the Fritsche statement in so formal a document as a communique indicated that the Russians placed credence in the suicide report.

Only Tuesday night the Nazi Hamburg radio said that Hitler had died "a hero's death" in the Reichschancellery in Berlin, "fighting to the last breath" against the Russians and that Grand Adm. Karl Doenitz had been appointed by Hitler as the new fuehrer.

The new report that Hitler was dead, by his own hand, came as the grim U-boat boss, Doenitz, issued a "fight-on" battle cry to the dwindling and rent forces still clinging to Hitler's tattered swastika banner.

Goebbels, Hitler's shadow and closest adviser since the earliest days of the Nazi party, apparently made good—by the Russian account—a statement in his last radio address that he would rather commit suicide than live in Germany "under the Bolshevik terror."

There remained the question of how far Adm. Doenitz could succeed in his announced plan to carry on a fight.

But Doenitz won pledges of support for continuing the war from commanders in Norway, Denmark and the southern section of the eastern front as he seized control of Germany's military and diplomatic machinery.

A German officer captured by Canadian forces declared that Doenitz had ordered all German troops facing the western Allies to cease fighting and withdraw to the east to oppose the Russians, but there was no confirmation of the report.

One of the new Fuehrer's first acts, the Hamburg radio said, was to dismiss Foreign Minister Joachim von Ribbentrop and replace the former champagne salesman with Count Ludwig Schwerin von Krosigk, former Rhodes scholar who served as Finance Minister throughout the Hitler regime and was a large factor in German preparations for launching and sustaining the war.

Beyond Doenitz's belligerent statement upon assuming command, there was no definite indication whether he would swing to immediate peace or to continued resistance, but after his first day's reign as Hitler's successor

Turn to Page 2, Column 7

ALL THE NEWS ALL THE TIME
Largest Home Delivered Circulation
Largest Advertising Volume

IN TWO PARTS
PART I — GENERAL NEWS
Times Office: 202 West First Street
Los Angeles 53, Cal.
Times Telephone Number MAdison 2345

VOL. LXIV | CC* | THURSDAY MORNING, MAY 3, 1945 | DAILY, FIVE CENTS

BERLIN CAPTURED BY RUSSIANS

1,000,000 Italy and Austria Nazis Surrender

British Troops Ready to Take Over Hamburg, Declared Open City

ROME, May 2. (AP)—The German and Italian Fascist armies of Col. Gen. Heinrich von Vietinghoff-Scheel in Northern Italy and Western Austria, numbering nearly 1,000,000 men, surrendered unconditionally today to the Allies, opening the way for an unhindered Allied march through an extensive part of the Nazi mountain redoubt within 10 miles of Berchtesgaden.

The surrender documents, ending the bloody 20-month Italian campaign, were signed Sunday at the royal palace at Caserta, near Naples, and became effective at 12 noon Italian time, 5 a.m. Pacific War Time, today.

Two German plenipotentiaries signed for Germany in the presence of American, British and Russian officers.

Approximately 20,000 square miles of German-held territory including all of Northern Italy to the Isonzo River in the northeast and the Austrian provinces of Vorarlberg, Tyrol, Salzburg and parts of Carinthia and Styria were surrendered to the Allies.

Redoubt Lopped Off

The action not only uncovers the southern approaches to Germany but lops off the southwestern end of the so-called German national redoubt and turns the right flank of Col. Gen. Von Lehr, commanding enemy troops in the Trieste area and Northern Yugoslavia. New Zealand troops of the British 8th Army and forces of Marshal Tito's Yugoslav army already have joined 14 miles northwest of Trieste which has been occupied by the Yugoslavs.

It was rumored in Rome tonight that Gen. Von Vietinghoff will surrender himself and his staff to Field Marshal Sir Harold Alexander, Allied commander-in-chief in the Mediterranean, tomorrow.

Alexander's Message

Field Marshal Alexander in an order of the day to Allied troops said that "today you stand as victors of the Italian campaign. You have won a victory which

Turn to Page 4, Column 3

LONDON, May 3. (U.P.) The Hamburg radio announced early today that British troops have occupied Hamburg, the London Exchange Telegraph Agency reported.

LONDON, May 3. (AP) — Hamburg has been declared an open city, the Hamburg radio announced today, and British forces under Lt. Gen. Sir Miles C. Dempsey will enter the port at noon today.

The broadcast was made in the German language in the name of Secretary of State Ahrendt.

It decreed a curfew for the entire population and declared that restrictions on civilian movements depended upon "the behavior of the population."

Hamburg is Germany's third city. It had a prewar population of 1,682,220.

Field Marshal Montgomery's forces for some time have been massed along the Elbe River opposite Hamburg and had made a crossing to the east side of the river in the Hamburg area.

North Germany Split Into Three Parts

PARIS, May 2. (AP)—Northern Germany was split into three pockets today by the British capture of Luebeck—where Himmler sued unsuccessfully for peace—and an American junction with the Russians on the Elbe 60 miles northwest of fallen Berlin.

At the same time, the bottom fell out of the southern redoubt with a German unconditional surrender in Northern Italy and Western Austria to Allied armies in Italy.

The U.S. 3rd and 7th armies raced 20 to 30 miles through cracking enemy lines and virtually completed the subjugation of Bavaria, with the 3rd Army 16 miles from the great Austrian stronghold of Linz and possibly 40 miles from a junction with the Russian southern army.

Final Hours of Reich

In the final hours of a dying Reich, the 7th Army flushed the most important military captive

Turn to Page 2, Column 2

(AP) Wirephoto from Signal Corps Radiophoto

VON RUNDSTEDT AS PRISONER—Two military police of the U.S. 7th Army are shown guarding Field Marshal Karl Gerd von Runstedt, left, former supreme German western front commander, his son, Lt. Hans G. von Rundstedt, center, and a medical attendant, following capture at a small town five miles from Munich.

Hannegan Gets Walker's Post

WASHINGTON, May 2. (AP)—In the first shift in the old Roosevelt Cabinet, President Truman today announced the resignation of Postmaster General Frank C. Walker and the selection of Robert E. Hannegan to succeed him.

Walker, 59-year-old New York lawyer and theater chain operator, will leave the Cabinet voluntarily June 30.

Robert E. Hannegan

Hannegan, 41-year-old Missourian who ran Franklin D. Roosevelt's fourth-term campaign, will take over his new job July 1 if confirmed by the Senate. He will retain the Democratic national chairmanship.

Walker resigned April 16. The President accepted tne resignation "reluctantly and grudgingly."

Hannegan issued a statement thanking the President and praising Walker.

"I have never known a finer man," he said.

Truman Calls for 10% Slash in War Spending

WASHINGTON, May 2. (AP)—President Truman today recommended a 10 per cent slash in war spending and pledged further economies as the military situation improves.

The Executive proposed a $7,365,000,000 cutback in shipbuilding and a $95,689,300 reduction in eight war agency budgets. In addition he abolished the Office of Civilian Defense effective June 30 and asked that its $369,000 budget request be rescinded.

Mr. Truman said he was impelled by "favorable progress of the war." He sent his recommendations to Congress with the advice that all Federal activities "will be continually reviewed to achieve economies where they will not interfere with the prosecution of the war."

Apply to 1946 Budget

The reductions will be applied to the 1946 budget, submitted by President Roosevelt. As it stands now the budget calls for $70,000,000,000 for war expenditures and $13,103,000,000 for normal functions.

Recommendations for cuts were:

Maritime Commission—repeal of appropriation of $3,100,000,000 and $4,265,000,000 in contract authorizations.

Office of War Information—$12,100,000.

War Production Board—$8,891,000.

Office of Censorship—$4,800,000.

Office of Defense Transportation—$3,300,000.

Petroleum Administration for War—$345,000.

Federal Security Agency—$43,710,400.

War Manpower Commission—$9,339,900.

Office of Scientific Research—$13,200,000.

Old Age Aid Increased

One increase was suggested, $15,000,000 to the F.S.A. for increased State aid to old-age assistance programs.

The shipping cutback, the President said, doesn't affect present construction, for which there is adequate funds and authority. There is no need, he said, for the additional ships contemplated in the budget.

Volunteer organizations in lo-

Turn to Page 8, Column 2

Postwar Tax Revisions Considered by Truman

WASHINGTON, May 2. (AP) President Truman disclosed today he is discussing the possibility of postwar tax revisions with Treasury Secretary Morgenthau. He said he had no information on what trend taxes may take after VE-Day.

Fight Senseless, Says Rundstedt

BY HOWARD COWAN

SOUTHERN BAVARIA, May 2. (AP)—Thin-lipped Field Marshal Gen. Karl Rudolf Gerd von Rundstedt, Germany's top military strategist taken prisoner by American troops south of Munich, told his captors today it was senseless for the Reich to fight any longer.

Advised of the reported death of Adolf Hitler, the cold Prussian aristocrat commented without elaboration: "Adm. Doenitz has been in charge for some time."

Bade Hitler Good-by

Von Rundstedt said that he went to Berlin March 10 to bid Hitler farewell and that the Fuehrer seemed to be in good health then, but was "shaking like he had the palsy."

He said Field Marshal Albert Kesselring was somewhere in Bavaria and Field Marshal Walther von Model was either dead or captured.

The man who directed the German armies at the peak of their success and again just before they sank to the depths of defeat was captured by a young American lieutenant on his first combat assignment.

Surprised at Home

The field marshal was surprised at his home in the little spa of Bad Toelz, about five miles from Munich, just after he had finished dining with his family last night.

The capture was made by Lt. Joseph Burke and a detachment from Co. A, 141st Regiment, 36th Infantry Division. A 7th Army announcement said it was Lt. Burke's first combat assignment since he received a battlefield command three weeks ago. Taken prisoner with the field marshal were his son and aide, Lt. Hans Gerd von Rundstedt; a driver and a medical aid man.

THE WORLD'S WAR FRONTS

GERMANY — Berlin captured by Russians; German garrison of 70,000 surrenders unconditionally. British troops drive 50 miles to Baltic; Denmark completely sealed off. Page 1.

ITALY — German armies in Northern Italy and Western Austria surrender unconditionally; almost 1,000,000 men lay down arms. Page 1.

PACIFIC — Australian forces land on Tarakan Island of Dutch Borneo; advance toward Japanese airdrome; U.S. troops open fierce drive on Okinawa. Page 4.

SOUTHEAST ASIA—British troops land on Southern Burma in amphibious operation; advancing toward Rangoon. Page 4.

Germans' Great Baltic Bases of Warnemuende and Rostock Also Taken

LONDON, May 2. (U.P.)—Red army troops captured Berlin today, crowning their three-year comeback from the desperate days before Moscow with a triumphant victory in the last great all-out battle of the European war.

Marshal Joseph Stalin announced that 70,000 haggard survivors of the garrison of the flattened, ruined capital of the defeated Nazi Reich laid down their arms, and the largest metropolis ever stormed had fallen after a siege of only 11 days.

The details of Berlin's last few hours still were to be told, including what the Russians found when they captured the ruined pile of the German Chancellery where, according to the Germans, Adolf Hitler died a "hero's death."

Great Naval Bases Fall

Announcing the historic victory one day after the May Day holiday, Stalin hailed the entire Red army and navy on the capture of "the center of German imperialism and the nest of German aggression."

Along with Berlin, fell Germany's big Baltic naval bases of Rostock and Warnemuende where Russian troops drove close to a junction with the British 2nd Army east of Hamburg. As a crowning humiliation to German arms, the Russians captured Fehrbellin, 22 miles northwest of Berlin, where the Prussians under Frederick William won a great victory over the Swedes in 1675.

What will doubtlessly prove the final big-scale offensive of the most horrible of wars started with reconnaissance thrusts from Oder River bridgeheads 30 miles east of Berlin in mid-April. It swelled into irresistible force with more than 1,000,000 men supported by perhaps the greatest tank and artillery concentrations of the war.

In three weeks of thundering battle, the avenging 1st White Russian and 1st Ukrainian armies, veterans who had turned the tide at Moscow in 1941 and at Stalingrad a year later, riddled the defenses of Berlin, which were the mightiest ever erected around a city.

They smashed into the Greater Berlin city limits in a frontal assault April 21 and four days later, streaking through the German flanks, encircled the blazing capital by linking up spearheads in the Potsdam area. From that moment on it was just a question of how long the fanatic defenders would hang on in the cauldron of the inner city.

Take Thousands of Prisoners

Among the last areas to hold out were Hitler's Chancellery on the Wilhelmstrasse, the Brandenburg Gate area just north of the Chancellery, the Potsdamer Platz in the geographical center of the city, the government quarters along Unter den Linden, Friedrichstrasse and Leipzigerstrasse, and the Tiergarten west of these streets. Old Berlin landmarks were reported unrecognizable among piles of rubble and blackened steel.

Not only did the Germans lose their Fuehrer and their capital, in the battle for Berlin, but almost 400,000 men of the Wehrmacht's thinning legions were captured or killed in the last 11 days alone. The total included 120,000 captured and 60,000 killed in a huge pocket just southeast of the city as well as the 70,000 survivors of the garrison. Nine generals were taken in the final mop-up.

Berlin was violently defended to the end by S.S. fanatics and, as their numbers thinned, by Volkssturm militia, Hitler Youth and even "death battalions" of women.

After the formal surrender by the commandant, Gen. Wesling, it took six hours to round up all the defenders from the basements and stone ruins where they had manned their firing points in a hell of bombs and shells.

Berlin fell 3 years, 10 months and 10 days after German armies, flushed with their victories in France and the

Turn to Page 2, Column 4

Living Index Here Hits Wartime High

Rising prices in food, clothing and miscellaneous items have brought the Bureau of Labor Statistics cost of living index to a new wartime high in Los Angeles, it was announced yesterday.

Latest figures put the overall increase at .4 per cent during the 30-day period ending March 15, with food up .6 per cent and clothing .1 per cent higher than was reported in the previous period.

Costs of goods and services listed among miscellaneous items advanced .3 per cent, according to the bureau's estimates, which do not include advanced housing costs except as reflected in rent ceilings.

FEATURES INDEX

Navy Transports Land 2959 Internees Here—

After three years in Jap prison camps, 2499 freed internees yesterday arrived on Navy transports at San Pedro. For details of their joy on arrival turn to Page 1, Part II.

On Other Pages

EXTRA!

9 A.M. FINAL

Los Angeles Times

9 A.M. FINAL

VOL. LXIV ★★★ MONDAY MORNING, MAY 7, 1945 DAILY, FIVE CENTS

V-E DAY!

War Is Just Half Over!

(Editorial)

VE-Day has arrived.

Organized resistance by Germany is ended. Allied lives have paid the terrible price of suppressing the mad terror unleashed by Adolf Hitler. Germany herself is paying the awful penalty of having been led into a depravity of cruelty almost unequaled in the world's history.

Yet now our task is not finished. We are but at the halfway mark. Japan still remains, the Japan which raped Manchuria in 1931, leaped upon China in 1937, indulged in the infamy of Pearl Harbor in 1941.

We have no time to dwell long upon the past. We must look ahead to total victory and the building of a new and safer world order upon the ruins of the old.

Yet so titanic a victory as was signalized by the arrival of V-E Day—Victory-in-Europe Day—cannot pass without a backward glance at the blood upon the hands of the aggressors and at the long rows of white crosses of those brave men of ours who finally have made this surcease possible. The world should not soon forget the execrable name and the loathsome acts of Adolf Hitler. It should not forget the fair promises, and the red stains upon the soil of Poland and Czechoslovakia and Norway and France and Belgium and the Netherlands and all the other innocent countries when those fair promises were treacherously broken.

Those memories should help to safeguard us against too great a complacency again.

We should not forget the valor of our men and women, our Allied men and women of all nationalities and all creeds. We should enshrine the names of Stalingrad and Tobruk, and Casa Blanca, and Sicily and Normandy, and a thousand others. For they speak of what suffering and faith and triumph can mean. We should never forget those names.

And then there are Eisenhower, and Patton, and Hodges, and Montgomery and a host of others whose leadership made victory possible.

There is the bridge at Remagen. There is the pierced Siegfried Line. There are the paratroopers and the infantry and the flyers and the artillerymen and the tank battalions.

They all bespeak a courage that knew no limit, a spirit that conquered all adversity.

While this victory in Europe, then, is an occasion justifying fervent rejoicing, the American people must not forget that we have a job to do in the Pacific, and that will not be finished until Hirohito's armed savages have been deprived of their capacity for rapine, murder, robbery and other forms of aggression.

It was the Jap sneak attack on Pearl Harbor, made at a time when their smirking diplomats were bowing and scraping at Washington, that formally began this war so far as the United States is concerned, and only the complete collapse of the Japanese can end it.

The stupendous task of moving men, planes, guns, tanks and stores from Europe to the Pacific war fronts now confronts the Allies.

There must be no letdown at home.

The final victory can be achieved quickly only by a united effort on the part of the armed forces and the civilian population.

Germany is beaten.

Let us see to it now that a like fate speedily is visited upon Japan.

Stores Will Be Open Today

According to plans previously announced by the Downtown Business Men's Association, downtown stores will be open today as usual. In that announcement it was stated that "there will be no store closing except if the news of victory comes while the stores are open."

BULLETINS ON SURRENDER

LONDON, May 7. (AP) — Adm. Karl Doenitz has "ordered the unconditional surrender of all fighting German troops," a broadcast on the Flensburg wave length said today. The statement, attributed to German Foreign Minister Ludwig von Krosigk, was broadcast to the German people.

LONDON, May 7. (AP) — Reuter's in a Moscow dispatch said today that it was reported without confirmation that the bodies of German Propaganda Minister Joseph Goebbels and his family had been found in an air raid shelter near the Reichstag Building in Berlin.

LISBON, May 7. (AP) — Portugal severed diplomatic relation with Germany yesterday on the ground that there no longer is a legal government in the Reich. German Minister Adolf von Hallen was notified of the Portuguese government's decision as he was leaving the legation chapel after memorial services for Adolf Hitler.

MOSCOW, May 7. (AP) — Russian troops, systematicall, examining the bodies found in the Nazi Chancellery in Berlin, have not yet reported finding Adolf Hitler or Joseph Goebbels, although the bodies of many members of the general staff, leading Storm Troopers and high-ranking Nazis — all suicides —have been found. The Russians still believe that the report of Hitler's death is a Nazi trick, and that the Fuehrer is in hiding.

LONDON, May 7. (AP)—In obvious anticipation of an early announcement of VE-Day, pennants and flags were being strung across the fronts of hotel and office buildings in many parts of London today. For the first time since the war began, factory signals sounded their whistles this morning to mark the start of the working day. The whistles previously had been banned to prevent confusion with air-raid warnings.

Nazis Surrender Unconditionally to Allied Powers

REIMS (France) May 7 (A.P.)—Germany surrendered unconditionally to the western Allies and Russia at 2:41 a.m. French time today.

The surrender took place at a little red school house which is the headquarters of Gen. Eisenhower.

The surrender which brought the war in Europe to a formal end after five years, eight months and six days of bloodshed and destruction was signed for Germany by Col. Gen. Gustav Jodl. (Jodl is the new chief of staff of the German army.)

It was signed for the supreme Allied command by Lt. Gen. Walter Bedell Smith, chief of staff for Gen. Eisenhower.

It was also signed by Gen. Ivan Susloparoff for Russia and by Gen. Francois Sevez for France.

(A sour note came from the German-controlled radio at Prague. A broadcast monitored by the Czechoslovak government offices in London said the German commander in Czechoslovakia did not recognize the surrender of Adm. Doenitz and would fight on until his forces "have secured free passage for German troops out of the country.")

LONDON, May 7. (AP) — German broadcasts today said "all fighting German troops" had surrendered unconditionally, and the world waited for an official Allied announcement expected from the Big Three capitals.

Adm. Karl Doenitz has "ordered the unconditional surrender of all fighting German troops," the broadcast said.

This statement, attributed to German Foreign Minister Ludwig Schwerin von Krosigk, was broadcast to the German people:

"German men and women! The high command of the armed forces has today, at the order of Grand-Adm. Doenitz, declared the unconditional surrender of all fighting German troops."

The broadcast was recorded by the British Ministry of Information. There was no Allied confirmation.

Earlier, Grand-Adm. Karl Doenitz had ordered his German submarine crews to cease hostilities today. In a broadcast order of the day over the Flensburg radio, Doenitz told the submarine crews: "Crushing superiority has compressed us into a very narrow area. Continuation of the struggle is impossible from the bases that remain," and the B.B.C. has broadcast news of the surrender of Norway.

Sympathy Goes to Soldiers

"After almost six years struggle we have succumbed," the Krosigk broadcast said.

"Our sympathy firstly goes out to our soldiers. Nobody must deceive

Turn to Page A, Column 1

ALL THE NEWS ALL THE TIME
Largest Home Delivered Circulation
Largest Advertising Volume

Los Angeles Times

EQUAL RIGHTS
LIBERTY UNDER THE LAW — TRUE INDUSTRIAL FREEDOM

IN THREE PARTS
PART I — GENERAL NEWS
Times Office: 202 West First Street
Los Angeles 53, Cal.
Times Telephone Number MAdison 2345

VOL. LXIV — CC ★★★ — THURSDAY MORNING, AUGUST 9, 1945 — DAILY, FIVE CENTS

RUSSIA ATTACKS JAPAN

SECOND ATOMIC BOMBING!

New Missile Hits Nagasaki, Great War Plant Center

GUAM, Aug. 9. (U.P.)—The second mighty new atomic bomb to rock Japan fell on the teeming war city of Nagasaki at noon today and first reports indicated that the attack was as successful as the explosion that devastated Hiroshima.

The 11th largest city of Japan, Nagasaki, was struck by the same type of weapon which crushed buildings like match boxes at Hiroshima and killed almost every living thing within its range.

For the second time in four days Japan felt the stunning effect of the terrible weapon.

Gen. Carl A. Spaatz, commander of the Strategic Air Forces, announced the second use of the atomic bomb in a brief special communique which said:

"The second use of the atomic bomb occurred at noon of Aug. 9 at Nagasaki. Crew members reported good results. No further details will be available until the mission returns."

Jammed War Plants Great Target

How destructive is the atomic bomb had been grimly demonstrated at Hiroshima. In Nagasaki's jammed shipyards and war plants, the most terrible explosive force ever loosed by man would find greater targets than those used for the first war test of the bomb.

Nagasaki has a population of more than 250,000. It is located on Kyushu, Japan's southernmost home island.

Tokyo said disastrous and utter ruin struck Hiroshima Monday when a lone Superfortress unleashed the first new bomb on the important imperial army base. It appeared probable that Nagasaki also has been turned into a desolate area of destruction.

Hiroshima Casualties May Reach 200,000

Sixty per cent of Hiroshima's built-up area was leveled Monday and as many as 200,000 of that city's 340,000 residents perished or were injured under the impact of history's greatest explosion.

There was little doubt that the second atomic bomb blast would prove every bit as effective as the first.

The second bomb fell on Nagasaki, site of great shipbuilding yards, while Japan still sought to survey the seared and blistered corpses—"too numerous to count"—scattered amid the wreckage of what once was Hiroshima.

Testifying to the magnitude of Hiroshima's disaster, the enemy reported that as late as Thursday morning—four days after the attack—they still were unable to ascertain the full extent of damage inflicted by the parachute-borne bomb.

A special meeting of the Japanese Cabinet was called at the residence of Premier Baron Kantaro Suzuki to hear a preliminary report on the devastation, but there was no in-

Turn to Page 2, Column 4

(AP) Wirephoto

TRUMAN'S ANNOUNCEMENT—President Truman as he announced to newsmen in White House office yesterday that Russia had declared war on Japan. Secretary of State Byrnes is seated in foreground and to his right is Adm. William D. Ledhy.

Truman Report on Radio Today

WASHINGTON, Aug. 8. (AP)—President Truman will report to the nation on the Potsdam conference over all radio networks at 7 p.m. (Pacific War Time) tomorrow in a 30-minute speech.

Presidential Secretary Charles G. Ross said today the speech, which probably will be shortwaved abroad, will go into greater detail than the Big Three communique issued at the close of the meeting July 26.

Associates of the President indicated that his address probably will mention the new and revolutionary bomb used for the first time against Japan.

Mr. Truman worked on the speech today as well as on a mass of other paper work which accumulated during his month-long absence. He held his calling list to a minimum, including brief conferences with Sens. Hatch (D.) N.M., and Kilgore (D.) W.Va., and Secretary of War Stimson. The Stimson conference was devoted to further discussion of the atomic bomb.

Russia's declaration of war on Japan heightened speculation that Congress may be called into session before its scheduled date of Oct. 8.

Broadcast Schedule on Truman Speech

President Truman's speech will be carried locally on the following stations from 7 to 7:30 p.m.: KECA, KNX, KFWB, KMPC, KHJ and KFI.

Rebroadcasts of the speech will be made on KFI at 11:30 p.m. to 12 m., and KFWB at 12m. to 12:30 a.m. KMTR will rebroadcast the speech today at 9:06 p.m. and tomorrow at 12:06 a.m.

Temperature Rises to 87 Degrees

The thermometer downtown yesterday rose to 87 degrees, highest since Monday when the temperature fell to 82 from a week-end point of 90.

Generally clear weather was predicted for Southern California today, except for early morning fog along the coast.

President Given Credit for Russian War Move

WASHINGTON, Aug. 8. (U.P.)—Russia declared war on Japan today at the request of President Truman.

The President's part in bringing Russia's vast might into the Pacific war was revealed by Secretary of State Byrnes three hours after Mr. Truman summoned newsmen into his office at 3 p.m. and made this brief announcement:

"Russia has declared war on Japan—that's all."

Mr. Truman gave no details.

Proposed at Potsdam

But Byrnes disclosed that the President had proposed a Russian declaration of war at the recent Big Three conference at Potsdam.

Hailing the Russian action, Byrnes said it "should materially shorten the war and save the loss of many lives."

He warned the Japanese that there is "still time—but little time—to save themselves from the destruction which threatens them."

Washington hailed Mr. Truman's announcement as meaning that the war, already shortened by the atomic bomb, was nearing its end.

Typical Congressional reaction was summed up in these words: "It won't be long now."

Some Congressmen believed the end might be a matter of days.

Byrnes said the President pointed out to Soviet Premier Stalin various sections of the Moscow declaration of 1943 and the new United Nations security charter. Byrnes said these sections led Mr. Truman to believe that Russia would be justified in declaring war.

He quoted the statement Mr. Truman made to Stalin at Potsdam, the last paragraph of which said:

"It seems to me that under the terms of the Moscow declaration and the provisions of the charter . . . it would be proper for the Soviet Union to indicate its willingness to consult and co-operate with other great powers now at war with Japan with a view to joint action on behalf of the community of nations to maintain peace and security."

May Disclose More

Mr. Truman may enlarge upon this disclosure when he reports to the nation by radio tomorrow night. He also will discuss the atomic bombing of Japan Sunday, and there was speculation that he may take the occasion to issue a new ultimatum to the Japanese.

His announcement of the Russian declaration came with dramatic suddenness.

Earlier in the day, there were indications that "something big" was brewing at the White House.

At midmorning while the President was receiving latest reports of the atomic bombing from Secretary of War Stimson, Undersecretary of State Grew interrupted the conference long enough to deliver a small sheaf of papers to the President. Soon afterward, Mr. Truman held a lengthy conference with Byrnes.

Message Is Mystery

What message was contained in the sheaf of papers still remains a mystery. But it was evident that tney did not concern the Russian declaration inasmuch as Presidential Secretary Charles G. Ross disclosed

Turn to Page A, Column 1

REDS NOW ELIGIBLE FOR $1,000,000,000 LEND-LEASE HELP

WASHINGTON, Aug. 8. (AP) — Russia automatically became eligible for $1,000,000,000 in lend-lease aid when she declared war against Japan, Foreign Economic Administration officials disclosed today.

Since the defeat of Germany she has been receiving only limited supplies under lend-lease via Siberia.

However, Foreign Economic Administrator Leo Crowley had foreseen the possibility that Russia would declare war against Japan when Congress appropriated additional funds for the program last June.

At his urging it approved a provision that $1,000,000,000 of the $4,385,000,000 budget would be allotted for supplies to Russia in event she joined the Allies in the Pacific.

Soviet's Far Eastern Army of 1,000,000 Strikes Blow Soon After War Declaration

CHUNGKING, Aug. 9. (U.P.)—Soviet Russia's Far Eastern army of more than 1,000,000 men early today launched a broad attack across the Manchurian border, gaining several miles in the first hours of the attack which began only a short time after the Russian declaration of war became effective, it was learned today.

The Russian operation was carried out in the strictest secrecy, though it was known that the attack was concentrated on three main points.

Japanese broadcasts announcing the start of hostilities said the Russians opened their drive along the eastern Soviet-Manchuria border, paced by bombing planes.

The Americans were informed of Russian tactical plans before the assault was launched.

The Russian deployment by the trans-Siberian railway meanwhile was described by informed sources as a "tremendous logistic feat," indicating that battlewise troops from the German front had been shuttled 8000 miles across Siberia to go into action against the crack Japanese Kwantung army.

Attack Comes as Surprise

These sources were surprised that the Russians attacked today as they believed Soviet participation possibly was awaiting outcome of negotiations between Premier Marshal Josef Stalin and Chinese Premier T. V. Soong. The declaration was not expected for another week, it was said. It was believed use of the atomic bomb might have hastened it.

The idea now is to pile up one catastrophe on another for the Japanese in order to induce them to surrender as quickly

Full page of pictures on Page B.

as possible. The highest sources here were most optimistic that the end of the war would come soon.

These sources said that liaison between the Americans and the Russians was the closest in history.

Earlier, Japanese broadcasts said that Russia's mighty Far Eastern army began hostilities at 12:10 a.m. Manchurian time, beginning their attack only nine minutes after Moscow's declaration of war became effective.

Attack Reported by Hsinking

A Kwantung Japanese army headquarters communique issued at Hsinking reported the attack and said that the Red Air Force was in action against strategic points in Manchurian territory behind Japanese lines.

The swift attack by the Red army, paced by bombers of the Far Eastern Air Force, climaxed 14 years of undeclared hostilities between Russia and Japan which started when the Japanese invaded Manchuria. It completed the encirclement of Japan by Allied forces to spell a quicker doom for Japanese militarists, and for the first time brought into a declared war Japan's crack Kwantung army of 2,000,000 men.

A Kwantung army headquarters communique issued at Hsinking and recorded here by United Press reported the attack, and also announced that the Red air force already was bombing strategic points in Manchukuo territory behind Japanese lines.

No details of the attack were given, but presumably the Russians would drive west from the Vladivostok area into Japanese-held territory north of the tip of Korea. Vladivostok is only about 20 miles east of the border, separated from the Japanese by fortified positions along the rugged and mountainous terrain.

Far Eastern Red Army Always Ready

The communique made it clear that ground forces had opened the attack—part of the Soviet's Far Eastern army of more than 1,000,000 finely equipped troops who were never called into action against Germany but remained along the border, a constant threat to Japan.

Although the brief communique announcing opening of hostilities did not locate the fighting, it was believed the Russians would strike out as quickly as possible from the Vladivostok region, which is highly vulnerable to air attack since it is so close to the border.

The whole population and most of the industries of the Soviet Far East are concentrated on the frontier, with the

Turn to Page A, Column 3

Molotov Reveals Jap Peace Bid as He Declares War

MOSCOW, Aug. 8. (AP)—Long columns of singing Red army men tramped through the heart of Moscow tonight, 45 minutes after the Soviet radio announced to the people of Russia that the nation would be at war with Japan at one second after midnight.

People filed out of buildings and apartments to cheer the marching soldiers of the Red army, whose force is being turned against the Japanese, the Soviet government said, at the request of the Allies to speed "universal peace."

Hirohito's Request

Foreign Commissar Molotov disclosed that Emperor Hirohito had asked the Soviet Union to mediate "about mid-July" in the war in the Pacific, but added that Tokyo's rejection of the Potsdam unconditional surrender ultimatum caused the proposals to "lose all significance."

Molotov said the Emperor's request was transmitted through a special Japanese mission in the Soviet capital.

The Foreign Commissar said President Truman, Winston Churchill, then Prime Minister, and Clement Attlee, who succeeded Churchill, had been informed.

A high foreign diplomatic source said tonight this was one of two such moves the Japanese had made.

The streets of Moscow were fairly full of civilians and soldiers when the news broke, but many citizens chose to stick close by their radios in anticipation of word of the first action

Turn to Page A, Column 4

THE WORLD'S WAR FRONTS

RUSSIA—Russia declares war on Japan and attacks Japs on Manchukuo border. Page 1, Part I.

PACIFIC—U.S. 3rd Fleet swings back into action with 1000-plane carrier raid on Northern Honshu. Page 1, Part I.

AIR WAR—Second atomic bomb dropped on Nagasaki; Japan says every living thing dead at Hiroshima. Page 1, Part I.

CHINA—Japanese in South China retreat as other enemy forces guarding Hengchow captured three towns. Page 2, Part I.

HALSEY'S PLANES DEAL JAPAN ANOTHER BLOW

GUAM, Aug. 9. (U.P.)—Adm. William F. Halsey's powerful U.S. and British 3rd Fleet returned to action against the Japanese homeland at dawn today, hurling more than 1000 carrier planes against Northern Honshu in a devastating blow coinciding with Russia's declaration of war against Japan.

The attacks are continuing more than nine hours after the first carrier-based planes roared in over Japan to break an 11-day news blackout of the 3rd Fleet.

Navy bombers and fighters ripped up Japanese shipping, airfields and other military targets in the northern portion of the main enemy island.

Targets Not Announced

Specific targets were not announced but it was reported they included "hidden" airfields where the Japanese air force has been lying under camouflage, attempting to conserve its strength for the all-out defense of the homeland.

The carrier assault followed an unprecedented series of B-29 strikes which sent nearly 400 Superfortresses against four Japanese targets within 24 hours yesterday. The B-29's rained incendiary and demolition bombs on Fukuyama and Yawata, the Nakajima aircraft plant in To-

Turn to Page 2, Column 3

FEATURES INDEX

Atomic Bomb Effects Don't Surprise Nazis—

Former Nazi leaders interned at Mondorf were not surprised at the effects of the atomic bomb in Japan and one declared the Nazis had feared its earlier development and use on Germany. Turn to Page 3, Part I.

On Other Pages

ALL THE NEWS ALL THE TIME
Largest Home Delivered Circulation
Largest Advertising Volume

Los Angeles Times

EQUAL RIGHTS
LIBERTY UNDER THE LAW — TRUE INDUSTRIAL FREEDOM

IN TWO PARTS
PART I — GENERAL NEWS
Times Office: 202 West First Street
Los Angeles 53, Cal.
Times Telephone Number MAdison 2345

VOL. LXIV ★★★ WEDNESDAY MORNING, AUGUST 15, 1945 DAILY, FIVE CENTS

PEACE!

Japs Accept Allies' Terms Unreservedly

WASHINGTON, Aug. 14. (U.P.)—President Truman announced tonight that the Japanese government has accepted the surrender terms without qualifications.

He made the announcement at a press conference. He read a statement which said:

"I deem this reply a full acceptance of the Potsdam declaration which specified the unconditional surrender of Japan. In the reply there are no qualifications."

The President also revealed that he had named Gen. Douglas MacArthur the supreme commander to receive the Japanese surrender.

Meanwhile, he said, Allied armed forces have been ordered to suspend offensive operations.

VJ-Day will not be proclaimed until after the formal signing of the surrender terms by Japan.

The three Allies in the Pacific war—Great Britain, Russia and China—will be represented at the signing by high ranking officers.

The Japanese government's message accepting the Allied terms said that Emperor Hirohito is prepared "to authorize and insure the signature" by the Japanese government and the imperial general headquarters of the necessary terms for carrying out provisions of the Potsdam declaration.

Hirohito Will Obey Allies

"His Majesty is also prepared to issue his commands to all the military, naval and air authorities of Japan and all the forces under their control wherever located to cease active operations, to surrender arms and to issue such other orders as may be required by the supreme commander of the Allied forces of the execution of the above-mentioned terms."

The President did not say where the surrender terms will be signed but it has been reported ceremonies will take place aboard a battleship or at Okinawa.

Truman did say that arrangements are now being made for the formal signing at the "earliest possible moment."

The President, attired in a blue double-breasted suit, blue

Turn to Page 2, Column 8

President Declares Two-Day Holiday--Wednesday and Thursday

WASHINGTON, Aug. 14. (U.P.)—President Truman tonight declared a two-day holiday, tomorrow and Thursday, for all Federal employees in Washington and throughout the country.

He told a press conference that the reason for two days was the employees had not had a chance to celebrate the last surrender on VE-Day.

Air Onslaughts Continue Around Clock on Japan

GUAM, Aug. 15. (AP)—Allied aerial onslaughts on Japan continued in nonstop around the clock fury today with bombing, strafing and rocketing planes accentuating Allied demands for acceptance of surrender terms laid down for Nippon.

More than 800 Marianas-based Superfortresses have dropped 6000 tons of demolition and fire bombs into the home islands in the past 24 hours.

The B-29 raids were under way even as Tokyo radio yesterday said an answer to the Allied note of Saturday was en route, and the raids continued into the early hours today. Two hundred Iwo-based fighters gave escort.

Gen. Douglas MacArthur's communique from Manila today reported the strongest Japanese interception attempt over Korea met in weeks by Pacific Air Forces pilots.

The communique said 16 were downed and two probably by more than 40 Thunderbolts on the Korean mission Monday. The interception was over Meijo on the west central coast, where an important airdrome is located. One Thunderbolt was lost.

Headquarters of the Army Strategic Air Forces indicated

Turn to Page 2, Column 7

ALL THE NEWS ALL THE TIME

Los Angeles Times

EQUAL RIGHTS — LIBERTY UNDER THE LAW — TRUE INDUSTRIAL FREEDOM

PART I—GENERAL NEWS

VOL. LXV — CC — WEDNESDAY MORNING, OCTOBER 2, 1946 — DAILY, FIVE CENTS

Rioting Marks Film Strike; 16 Injured and 13 Arrested

Mob of 400 in Battle With 200 Officers

Illustrated on Page 3, Part I

A yelling, cursing mob of 400 motion-picture strikers and sympathizers battled nearly 200 deputy sheriffs and police for 15 hectic minutes yesterday at the Metro-Goldwyn-Mayer studio in Culver City. Hundreds of bystanders witnessed the scene.

Scores of men were knocked down with sticks, bottles, bricks and fists. One deputy, knocked down, was kicked into unconsciousness before fellow officers with drawn, cocked guns rescued him.

Blood streaked from battlers' faces as the fighting spread over a long Culver Blvd. block in front of the studio's south and main gate. The street was slippery with mud and in some spots with blood.

Nine Deputies Treated

Nine deputies, one in a grave condition and another with broken ribs, were treated in hospitals. Seven strikers, all with reportedly lesser injuries, also were treated in hospitals. Thirteen strikers were hauled off to the Culver City Jail. All were charged with defying a Superior Court order that restricted picketing operations.

While the fighting was at its height, Dep. Dean W. Stafford of the Vermont Ave. substation was separated from fellow officers by a gang of 12 or more of the strikers.

A blow with a bottle against the side of Stafford's face knocked him to the ground and fellow officers said at least a dozen strikers jumped on him and kicked him into unconsciousness.

Aid Called for

The Sheriff's loud-speaker called for officers to go to his aid. Two broke through, drew their revolvers, cocked them and, calling out warnings to the threatening mob, held it off until other deputies ran up. They dragged the prostrate Stafford from under the running board of an auto and carried him to an ambulance.

Dep. Gilbert O. Leslie, first officer to reach Stafford, told newsmen:

"I saw he was cut off from the rest of us and a crowd was bearing down on him. They were yelling, 'Kill him! Kill him!' and 'Get that ——' He went down and they were beating him with bottles and clubs. He was unconscious but they kept it up.

Condition Serious

"I was in plain clothes and the only way I could help him and hold them off until others arrived was to draw my gun. I have no prejudices in the strike but I saw the danger to one of us and it was the only thing I could do to save a life."

Stafford, 28, was taken to Culver City Hospital where his condition was said to be serious from internal injuries, shock, lacerations and bruises.

Another injured deputy was Sidney E. Vance, who apparently was hit with a bottle that broke and cut his eye so badly that officers said he may lose it.

Dep. John L. Deane was clubbed so badly on the side that several ribs were broken and he was otherwise injured. Other officers who were injured and treated for various lesser injuries were Sgts. Charles E. Irvin and F. W. Hunter and Deps. Horace W. Gard, Homer T. Riddle, John J. Dowd and William D. Sells. They were treated at the studio first aid hospital.

Among the latter's injuries

Turn to Page 2, Column 7

FEATURES INDEX

New Class to Train for Rocket Navigation

New class at U.C.L.A. offers students chance to learn rocket navigation. See Page 1, Part II.

On Other Pages

Harbor Tied Up Again by Two Unions' Pickets

Two C.I.O. unions' picket lines yesterday tied up Los Angeles Harbor again after the port had enjoyed four days of freedom from strike paralysis since A.F.L. and C.I.O. picket lines shut it down Sept. 4.

Waterfront Employers' Association said about 25 ships were made idle by the new lines. The strikers said no Navy, Army or other craft in repair yards will be affected. The strikers also arranged for a certain amount of time within which ships with perishable cargo may unload.

At 6 a.m. the C.I.O. Marine Engineers' Beneficial Association put on its pickets and at 1 p.m. the C.I.O. International Longshoremen's and Warehousemen's Union put out its lines. Activity was halted.

Anker Petersen, port agent of the A.F.L. Masters', Mates' and Pilots' Association, said skippers will remain aboard the struck ships, but probably not the mates.

To Honor Picket Lines

Harlan Snow, business agent for the A.F.L. Sailors' Union of the Pacific, said the A.F.L. crews abandoned ship. Both A.F.L. men made it plain that their unions will observe C.I.O. picket lines.

The C.I.O. Committee for Maritime Unity, embracing the I.L.W.U., said the seven unions in the committee would honor the picket lines.

Both of the two picketing unions are striking for higher wages and other contract changes, the engineers on an all-coast basis and the longshoremen on a West Coast basis.

Way Seen Paved for Ship Strike Settlement

WASHINGTON, Oct. 2 (Wednesday.) (AP) — Union officials said early today the Maritime Commission has assured them it will enforce on all coasts any working conditions, including union security provisions, agreed upon between the unions and East Coast ship operators.

Officials of the government and the A.F.L. and C.I.O. unions of ship officers who are on strike to obtain their demands expressed confidence this would pave the way for an early settlement of all issues and an end to the current tie-up.

Transit Tied Up by Strike

TACOMA, Oct. 1. (AP)—Failure of eleventh-hour conciliation efforts today led to walkout of 323 Tacoma Transit Co. employees over an alleged contract violation, leaving 75,000 patrons without transportation.

Columbus Streetcars Halted by Walkout

COLUMBUS (O.) Oct. 1. (AP)—A strike by 615 operators and maintenance men halted streetcar and bus service in Ohio's capital today, forcing 300,000 riders to seek other transportation.

Chicago Commuter Trains Hit by Strike

CHICAGO, Oct. 1. (AP)—Commuters from some of Chicago's western suburbs, accustomed to riding the 200 daily electric trains of the Chicago, Aurora & Elgin Railroad had to use other means of getting to and from their jobs today as a strike stopped service.

CARDS TROUNCE BUMS, 4-2; IN FIRST PLAY-OFF

St. Louis defeated Brooklyn, 4 to 2, yesterday in the opening game of their three-game play-off series to decide the National League pennant winner for 1946.

A disappointing crowd of 26,012 showed up at Sportsman's Park, which has a capacity of 34,000, and watched their Cardinals pounce on five Dodger pitchers for an even dozen hits. Howie Pollet, ably supported by his teammates, hurled the triumph, allowing eight hits to the Bums.

There'll be no game today, allowing the clubs traveling time to get to Brooklyn, where the series resumes tomorrow.

For complete details, including description by The Times' Al Wolf, see Sports section.

Second Storm Hits Southland; Utilities Suffer

The season's second storm yesterday swept most of Southern California, bringing rainfall up to 1.55 inches in some outlying suburbs, interrupting power line and telephone service and benefiting produce growers throughout the county.

As the .37 of an inch rainfall brought the downtown area's season total to .39 of an inch, compared with last year's .04 and a normal of .22 of an inch, the Weather Bureau yesterday predicted partly cloudy and slightly warmer weather today.

La Crescenta Doused

Yesterday's rain, close on the heels of Sunday's widespread showers, left La Crescenta with 1.55 of an inch precipitation, as compared with last year's .01 of an inch. Other outlying areas reporting heavy rain included Altadena, 1.02 of an inch; La Canada, .97 of an inch for a 1.01 season total; Sierra Madre, .89, 1.01; San Bernardino, .81; Santa Monica,

For Southland rainfall totals turn to Page 2, Part I.

.71; Mt. Wilson, .98; Palos Verdes, .50, and Culver City, .35.

While heat-parched ground quickly absorbed the runoff in most areas, small rivers of water swept across highways bordering mountain areas, particularly Foothill Blvd., although no serious traffic congestion was reported.

The Southern California Telephone Co. reported that service on 2885 lines was interrupted when 168 rain-soaked cables were made inoperative. Company officials said that this figure is considered below normal considering the dry condition of cable sheathing which had not been replaced due to wartime shortages.

About 50 light and power consumers in the Pasadena area were without service for an average of two hours Monday night, it was reported.

Minor Earthquake Felt at San Jose

SAN JOSE, Oct. 1. (AP)—An earthquake of minor intensity was felt here and in neighboring communities today. Dr. Albert J. Newlin of Santa Clara University said it was recorded at 11:23:12 a.m. and originated 30 or 40 miles from Santa Clara.

Navy Plane Sets Mark of 11,236 Miles

Australia-to-Ohio Flight Made in 55 Hours and 18 Minutes

COLUMBUS (O.) Oct. 1. (U.P.) — The Truculent Turtle did it. The blue Navy patrol bomber with its four-man crew and a kangaroo landed at Port Columbus today to set an all-time record for long-distance flight from Australia, 11,236 miles in 55 hours and 18 minutes.

The Turtle is a U.S. Navy Neptune P2V, built by Lockheed.

Out of its hatch tumbled the four Navy officers who manned the two-engine craft on its Pacific-hopping flight — Comdr. Thomas C. Davies, Cleveland, O.; Comdr. W. S. Reid, Washington; Comdr. E. P. Rankin, Sapulpa, Okla., and Lt. Comdr. R. H. Tabeling of Jacksonville, Fla.

They were grinning and appeared ready to go on. In fact, the Navy was so sure that they might climb back into the plane and take off again that it ordered them officially grounded.

Ordered to Land

Davies, who commanded the ship, said the Turtle had enough gasoline left for a try at Washington, D.C., but "we were ordered to land here, so we did."

Davies, acting as spokesman for the crew, said the worst part of the trip was when they hit icing conditions off the West Coast and had to change course.

"We were on instruments from about 200 miles off the coast last night until we broke clear at Ogden, Utah," he said. "When we came out of that soup we had about a thousand pounds of ice on our wings. One engine quit, but came back in 30 seconds."

Tail Wind Over Utah

Their only contact for a long period was the Williams (Cal.) radio range, he said.

After they hit good weather and a tail wind over Utah, it became merely a question of how

Turn to Page 2, Column 4

Army Flight Project Distance Eclipsed

WASHINGTON, Oct. 1. (AP) The Navy's Truculent Turtle plane, on its trip from Australia, eclipsed at Des Moines, Ia., the distance of the Army's projected Hawaii-Cairo flight. At that point the Turtle had flown approximately 10,660 miles.

The Army's B-29 Dreamboat on the planned flight across the Arctic from Hawaii to Cairo would cover approximately 10,200 miles. The Dreamboat is still awaiting favorable weather conditions for its trip.

Northeast Hit by Snowstorm

BY THE ASSOCIATED PRESS

An early October snowstorm swept down from the polar regions across the Northeastern States yesterday, damaging late fall crops, snapping power and communication lines and blocking highways.

New York, Vermont and New Hampshire were hit hardest by the icy gale which chased the mercury down to 30 degrees and toppled trees in some places with gusts up to 55 miles an hour.

Maine, Massachusetts and New Jersey reported snow flurries and heavy rains.

Frost was reported Monday night in Illinois, Iowa, Missouri, Wisconsin, Indiana, Kentucky, Ohio and Michigan.

Eisenhower Gets Rooms in Castle

CULZEAN CASTLE, AYRSHIRE (Scotland) Oct. 1. (U.P.) Gen. Dwight D. Eisenhower today moved into an ancient castle complete with massive rock walls, battlements, and blood-filled traditions.

Scotland, in a gesture of gratitude, gave him apartments among the high towers of Culzean Castle overlooking the Firth of Clyde. Eisenhower arrived by plane after a tour of American military establishments in Germany.

AIRLINER PARTS SHOWER ON HOME OF ANGELENO

It rained airplane parts last night on and around the home of George M. Jordan, at 932 S. Sierra Bonita Ave.

Three rumpled pieces of fabricated aluminum, part of an engine cowling lost from a commercial transport plane flying over the Jordan home, fell. One piece struck the roof of the Jordan home, causing minor damage. Another narrowly missed striking a visiting daughter of Jordan's, Mrs. Thomas Ware of Wilmette, Ill., who was on the sidewalk near the house. The third piece fell into the back yard of a neighbor, Paul C. Hill, of 933 S. Masselin St.

The cowling was dropped from an American Airlines transport as it was flying from the Los Angeles Municipal Airport to the Lockheed Air Terminal. Airline officials said such cowlings are made of sheet aluminum and measure about 12 feet in circumference. They are not functional parts of a plane, and are removable for purposes of engine inspection.

Wilshire police gathered up the three crumpled pieces, took them to the station and labeled them "Found Property."

Goering and 10 Other Hitler Chiefs Must Hang in 15 Days

(AP) Wirephoto

DESPAIR STRIKES NAZIS—Hermann Goering, left, condemned to death, and Rudolf Hess, sentenced to life imprisonment, bow heads hopelessly as they learn their fate.

Von Papen One of Three to Be Acquitted

Illustrated on Page 3, Part I

NUERNBERG, Oct. 1. (U.P.) Hermann Goering, Joachim von Ribbentrop and 10 other Nazi arch-conspirators were condemned today to hang within 15 days for their World War II crimes.

Martin Bormann, Hitler's deputy fuehrer, who was among the 12 sentenced to die, has been missing since the Nazi surrender. He was tried in absentia.

Seven other top Nazis were given sentences ranging from 10 years to life imprisonment and three—Franz von Papen, Hjalmar Schacht and Hans Fritzsche—were acquitted despite a Russian dissent.

Defense attorneys announced appeals for clemency to the Allied Control Council for Germany, but there appeared no chance whatever of any of the condemned escaping.

Given Life Terms

In addition to Goering and Ribbentrop, those condemned to hang were Julius Streicher, Field Marshal Wilhelm von Keitel, Ernst Kaltenbrunner, Alfred Rosenberg, Hans Frank, Wilhelm Frick, Fritz Sauckel, Col. Gen. Alfred Jodl, Arthur Seyss-Inquart and Bormann, who is believed dead.

Rudolph Hess, Grand-Adm. Erich Raeder and Walther Funk were sentenced to life imprisonment. Baldur von Schirach, the Nazi youth leader, and Albert Speer, munitions maker, were sentenced to 20 years. Constantin von Neurath, former Foreign Minister, was given 15 years. Grand-Adm. Karl Doenitz, commander-in-chief of the German navy, was sentenced to 10 years.

Russian Dissents

Von Papen, Schacht and Fritzsche were acquitted on all charges and freed. They were given documents permitting them to live as free men anywhere in Germany, provided they are not rearrested for trial under the de-Nazification laws.

Soviet Judge Iola T. Nikichenkos, Russian member of the tribunal, dissented from the three acquittals and also the life imprisonment sentence for Hess and the acquittal of the German high command as a group. He wanted Hess sentenced to death and the high command convicted.

Defense attorneys announced also that appeals will be filed for seven defendants given prison terms as well as for those sentenced to hang.

Execution Oct. 16

The Allied Control Council, which assumed jurisdiction over the defendants as soon as the sentences were imposed, announced in Berlin that the criminals will be permitted four days—until Saturday night—to file their clemency appeals with the secretariat of the military tribunal.

It was learned reliably that if

Turn to Page 4, Column 2

U.S. Plans Crackdown to Ease Meat Shortage

WASHINGTON, Oct. 1. (AP)—Government action to ease the meat shortage bobbed up as a possibility today as the Agriculture Department reported that production is only 27 per cent of what it was a year ago.

Indications that the administration is considering steps to increase supplies for home dinner tables and hospitals came from two sources—Rep. Spence (D.) Ky., chairman of the House Banking Committee, and Secretary of Agriculture Anderson.

Spence said that he "gathered the impression" at a conference with President Truman today that the government may "take some remedial action" to increase supplies. He said he is not at liberty to discuss what the action might be.

Seizures Suggested

Secretary Anderson had earlier suggested that the government might requisition livestock arriving at markets. He raised this possibility in an address to a group of New Mexico cattlemen at Albuquerque.

Spence said that during his visit to the White House he had talked to Mr. Truman about the O.P.A. and the "dissatisfaction of the people" with it.

Evidence that supplies are improving very little was provided by an Agriculture Department report that meat produced by Federally inspected slaughterers last week totaled only 80,000,000 pounds compared with 292,000,000 in the corresponding week last year.

Officials Mum

While both Spence and Anderson raised the possibility of government action, meat authorities at the Agriculture Department professed to have no knowledge of this.

They said there appeared to be only three ways of increasing supplies: Lifting of controls, raising price ceilings to encourage the marketing of more grass-fattened cattle, or government requisitioning of meat animals from farms.

Meanwhile, the Army said today that 2,000,000 pounds of meat in a Boston cold storage plant "is part of the last remaining reserves held by the Army" and would be shipped to the European theater within the next two weeks.

Huge Stores Found

In New York Mayor William O'Dwyer said tonight his operatives had turned up 13,312,880 pounds of meat. A force of 225 police, health and market inspectors found the meat in cold storage plants, refrigerator railroad cars and slaughter houses, O'Dwyer said. In addition, they found 15,946,808 pounds of poultry.

The Mayor ordered the search last night, declaring he would use the findings as a basis for recommendations to relieve the meat scarcity.

No recommendations accompanied tonight's brief statement.

New Yorkers in normal times eat about 3,800,000 pounds of meat a day. At this rate, the supplies uncovered by the Mayor would last less than four days—if they were diverted to retail channels.

Bob Hope 'Papa' to Two More

CHICAGO, Oct. 1. — The Bob Hope family increased 50 per cent today with the adoption of William Francis (Kelly) Hope and Honora Avis Mary (Nora) Hope from the Cradle, Evanston (Ill.,) foundling home.

Mrs. Hope appeared before County Judge Edmund K. Jarecki here in the first step to make the adoption legal. She will return April 9 for the final papers.

The Hopes have two other Cradle babies, Linda, 7, and Anthony, 6. The babies adopted today are less than one year old.

CHOCOLATE AND COCOA PRICES RAISED BY O.P.A.

WASHINGTON, Oct. 1. (AP)—O.P.A. today ordered a 27 per cent boost in manufacturers' ceiling prices for chocolate and cocoa, effective tomorrow.

Wholesalers and retailers will be allowed to pass the increase along as soon as they receive chocolate and cocoa at the higher rates.

The agency also raised growers' ceiling prices on oranges today, but said consumer costs should not increase because the boost amounts to only a fractional part of a cent a pound.

The agency increased California oranges 12 cents for a 75-pound container while Florida oranges were raised 6 cents for a 90-pound container. Most of the increase was attributed to higher cost of containers, but O.P.A. said California was allowed a larger increase because of higher costs.

O.P.A. also raised ceiling prices of cloth for window shades, oilcloth and other coated and combined fabrics at manufacturing levels as of tomorrow.

CHEWING GUM PRICE CONTROL OFF

WASHINGTON, Oct. 1. (AP) O.P.A. kicked chewing gum out from under price control today with the explanation that it is not important to the cost of living, and, furthermore:

"If equitable price controls were to be maintained a new ceiling price would have to be established at a level somewhat above that which is likely to result in a free market."

Hull, Believed Dying, Appeals for World Peace

WASHINGTON, Oct. 1. (U.P.)—Former Secretary of State Cordell Hull, critically and perhaps mortally ill in Bethesda Naval Hospital, appealed to the world's statesmen tonight to settle their international differences and avert the "incalculable disaster" of another war.

His dramatic plea for peace and world unity was issued on the eve of his 75th birthday anniversary from the hospital bed where his life seemed to be ebbing away as a result of a stroke suffered last night.

At midnight the Navy issued an official bulletin that the statesman's condition remains serious.

Anniversary Message

Written as an "anniversary message" shortly before his sudden attack, the statement carried a forceful appeal for preservation of the international peace structure he fought to build and maintain through 12 troubled years at the helm of American foreign policy.

"Not since the darkest days of the war has it been so necessary as now for the United States, Great Britain, the Soviet Union, China and France to work together," the Tennessee statesman said.

Co-operation Needed

"A special responsibility still rests on these nations . . . achieving and maintaining . . . unity and co-operation must continue to be the predominant duty of statesmanship.

"No matter how laborious the task, if the large nations can agree and act together to that end, then there is hope that our military victories of a year ago will be turned into enduring peace. Incalculable disaster would result if these nations should become irreconcilably divided, either within or among themselves."

County Smog Curb Sought

Direct action by the County to reduce Los Angeles and Vernon smog wafted into Pasadena by way of the Arroyo Seco was demanded yesterday by nearly 500 Crown City residents at a mass meeting in the Pasadena City Hall.

A suggestion by I. A. Deutch, county air pollution control officer, that Pasadena adopt an ordinance outlawing faulty incinerators and offending industries was met with the assertion that Los Angeles and Vernon factories are the chief offenders.

Robert E. Dawson, chairman of the city's board of directors, pointed out that Pasadena would take steps to abate local smog-producing nuisances if they could be located by Deutch.

Reds Blame Chinese War on Marshall

LONDON, Oct. 1. (U.P.)—The Moscow newspaper Trud declared today that "American mediation" by Gen. George C. Marshall, special United States envoy to China, resulted in the Chinese civil war, in which fighting is going on on a larger scale than at any time since 1927.

The Trud article by Commentator Alexandrov, distributed in London by the Russian news agency Tass, was the strongest Soviet attack on United States policies in China since Prime Minister Stalin declared on Sept. 24 that American troops in China were a "danger to peace."

Trud said that Generalissimo Chiang Kai-shek used not more than 100 divisions out of 290 in the offensive against the Japanese.

"Now," the newspaper said, "217 out of 241 divisions, or 86 per cent of all Kuomintang troops, are taking part in the offensive against the democratic districts of China."

ALL THE NEWS ALL THE TIME

Los Angeles Times

EQUAL RIGHTS — LIBERTY UNDER THE LAW — TRUE INDUSTRIAL FREEDOM

PART I—GENERAL NEWS

VOL. LXVII — CC ★ — THURSDAY MORNING, DECEMBER 11, 1947 — DAILY, FIVE CENTS

France Rebukes Russia Over Note

Half of Police Work Caused by Drunks!

Officers Disclose Scope of Problem at Crime Hearing

Executive police officials and other top law enforcement men yesterday scored drunkenness as giving rise to more than 50 per cent of all police activity and added that arrests for that cause among women are steadily mounting.

Appearing before the Governor's special crime study commission in the State Building, Los Angeles Police Chief Horrall said that the city's average jail population now is 1705. Proposed new jail facilities would bring total prisoner capacity to 3506.

Recognized as Disease

Following Horrall, Asst. Chief Joseph Reed said that police now recognize alcoholism as a disease which the department is not equipped to treat.

For this reason, Reed declared, arrests for drunkenness follow the pattern of release of the prisoner "when he or she sobers up." They are thereafter allowed to return to former haunts, a fact which the Assistant Chief decried.

"Most of the time of approximately 1700 policemen, one-half of the police force, is taken up with problems connected directly to drunkenness," Reed disclosed. "Many of these inebriates have been arrested 60 or 70 times.

Females Grow Worse

"There is a tremendous increase in drunkenness among females and this rate is growing steadily."

Reed advocated a State-wide program for the treatment of alcoholics.

"It is recognized that narcotic users are medical cases," he told the commission. "Addicts are treated by medical methods. Alcoholism, as seen by the working police officer, is as bad or worse than narcotic addiction."

Other Witnesses

Other witnesses included Chairman Raymond V. Darby of the Board of Supervisors; Kenneth Lynch, Deputy District Attorney; Undersheriff A. C. Jewell and Donald Redwine, Assistant City Attorney of Los Angeles.

Virtually all emphasized present overcrowded conditions in local jails, a fact which causes inadequate correctional treatment being administered to many, particularly among juveniles.

Darby brought out that there are now 1200 persons on parole in Los Angeles and Orange counties, with the large majority in this county.

Burdette J. Daniels was commission chairman at yesterday's session. Members sitting at the hearing included John M. Zuck, county probation chief; Sheriff John Loustalot of Kern County; Mrs. Sumner Spaulding, Dr. Milton Chernin of Stanford University, Frank Cane and Richard A. McGee, director State Department of Corrections.

Huge Plane Makes Safe Snow Landing

FARGO (N.D.) Dec. 10. (AP)—One of Northwest Airlines' huge Martin 202's made a belly landing on the snow west of the Fargo Airport today. None of the four crew members was injured.

The plane had taken off from the airport when one engine began to smoke and the pilot attempted to return to the runway, but failed to make it.

FEATURES INDEX

$300,000 Damages Won in Turf Film Suit

Telefilm, Inc., wins $300,000 damages against Harry M. Warner, cinema executive, and officials of Hollywood Turf Club for asserted theft of secret processes used in filming horse races. Page 2, Part I.

EARTH MAY GO THROUGH NEW COMET'S TAIL

SYDNEY (Australia) Dec. 10. (AP)—Dr. Richard Woolley, director of the Commonwealth Observatory in Canberra, today said it is possible that the earth will pass through the 40,000,000-mile tail of a strange new comet which has flamed across the southern skies for the last two nights.

"Observations in the next few days will show if and when this can be expected," Woolley said. "If it occurs, there will be a harmless but spectacular shower of meteorites."

The earth passed through the tail of the great comet of 1861, according to the Encyclopaedia Britannica, but no phenomenon was noticeable "beyond the diffused glare."

He said he is convinced that the comet is one which never before had been recorded.

Woolley described the comet as the brightest he has ever seen and said it is more spectacular than the famous Halley's comet—last seen in 1910.

Plane Carrying 29 Crashes in Labrador Waste

ST. JOHN'S (N.F.) Dec. 10. (AP)—A ground search party tonight reached the wreckage of a U.S. Army transport plane which crashed in rugged country north of Goose Bay, Labrador, last night with 29 military men aboard.

The rescue party, without radio equipment, was unable to give word of the fate of the occupants of the big four-engined ship.

The fact the search group had reached its goal was reported to Goose Bay by scouting aircraft and relayed to the U.S. Army base command here, 550 miles southeast of the Goose Bay air base.

Earlier reports that flares had been sighted near the crash, eight miles northwest of the base, and a man seen waving from the wreckage led to belief that at least one of the 10 crew members and 19 military personnel had survived. Whether these included any high-ranking officers was not known.

Storm Hampers Aid

Whether the flares were lighted by the vanguard of the ground rescuers—or by survivors—was not definitely known.

A helicopter borne by a special plane from Patterson Field, Dayton, O., arrived at Goose Bay tonight to assist in bringing survivors out of the icy wilderness. Officials said air rescue attempts would be postponed until dawn because of hazardous conditions where the plane crashed.

The C-54 Skymaster crashed within five minutes after taking off from Goose Bay last night with a cargo of mail and military equipment for Westover Field, Massachusetts.

Tops Again 63 in Cool Spell

The Los Angeles earmuff market continued bullish yesterday as the mercury failed to rise above 63 degrees for the second straight day while the minimum dropped to 39, one degree below Tuesday's 40.

Temperatures that sagged close to the danger point in the citrus belt yesterday threatened to drop even lower this morning, requiring scattered firing in the Pomona, Azusa, Whittier, Santa Paula, Redlands and Corona districts, the Pomona Frost Warning Service announced.

Forecast for Los Angeles today and tomorrow was variable high thin cloudiness, with slowly rising daytime temperatures but continued cool nights.

Curb on Powers of Peers Approved

LONDON, Dec. 10. (AP)—The House of Commons approved tonight a bill curbing the powers of the House of Lords by requiring the peers to act on Commons-approved legislation within one year instead of two years as at present.

The vote was 340 to 86. The bill now goes to the House of Lords for action.

BOOKED, FINGERPRINTED IN CONTEMPT OF CONGRESS CASE

Times photo

SURRENDER—Charged with contempt of Congress, nine Hollywood men gave themselves up to U.S. Marshal yesterday. From left, Robert Adrian Scott, Edward Dmytryk, Samuel Ornitz, Lester Cole, Herbert Biberman, Albert Maltz, Alvah Bessie, John Howard Lawson and Ring Lardner Jr.

Film Men Surrender in U.S. Contempt Case

Nine Arraigned Here Previous to Trial; One Missing Defendant Will Appear Today

Six Hollywood writers, two directors and one producer charged with contempt of Congress for refusing to state whether they are Communists, yesterday surrendered to U.S. Marshal Robert E. Clark.

After being fingerprinted and booked by the Marshal, the defendants were taken at once to U.S. Judge J. F. T. O'Connor's court, where they were arraigned. Bond for each was fixed at $1000.

Dalton Trumbo Absent

Only one defendant was missing in the group of 10 men. He is Dalton Trumbo, who is isolated on his ranch near the Ridge Route in a mountainous district where he has no telephone. Atty. Robert W. Kenny promised to have him in court today.

After hearing arguments by U.S. Atty. James M. Carter urging expedition of the removal hearing, Judge O'Connor ordered the defendants to present arguments today through their lawyers opposing removal to the District of Columbia for trial on the contempt of Congress charge.

Early in the arguments presented to the court, Atty. Kenny stated that he intends to exhaust every legal resource available to the defendants in opposing their removal to Washington for trial.

Kenny said he had no statement to make and that the defendants wished to make no statement other than the remarks he made in the courtroom.

In these remarks Kenny indicated that he questions the constitutional right of the Congressional committee to ask a question demanding of a witness their beliefs such as being or once having been a member of the Communist party.

Defendants who surrendered in court are Albert Maltz, Samuel Ornitz, John Howard Lawson, Ring Lardner Jr., Lester Cole and Alvah Bessie, all writers; Herbert Biberman and Edward Dmytryk, directors, and Robert Adrian Scott, producer.

All defendants posted bonds and were released.

British Film and Stage Stars Back 10 Rebels

LONDON, Dec. 10. (AP)—Fifteen British stage and screen personalities, among them Vivien Leigh and Sir Laurence Olivier, offered congratulations today to American movie men who refused to testify before the House Committee on Un-American Activities investigating Communism in Hollywood.

The message was sent in a letter to William Wyler, Hollywood executive and chairman of the Committee for the First Amendment.

The signatories, including Sir Alexander Korda, Michael Redgrave and Robert Donat, said "we find ourselves completely at a loss to understand why so many of our fellow artists, technicians and screen writers have been subjected to an inquisition."

"We extend our sympathy and our congratulations to all those who refuse to submit themselves to this examination of their private beliefs and opinions," the letter added.

"The undersigned represent widely differing political views, but we are all united in upholding the right of the artist to work in an atmosphere of freedom in any country regardless of what his own private political opinions may be."

Child Wields Cake Turner, Kills Cousin

A 14-month-old baby died in Pasadena Emergency Hospital last night a few hours after he was struck in the head by a pancake turner wielded by his cousin, also 14 months old, police reported.

The victim was Joseph W. Diaz, son of Joseph and Mary Diaz of 3139 Alameda St., Pasadena. Little Alice Vasquez, the cousin, was visiting at the Diaz home and the two children were playing in the kitchen while the parents sat in the living room.

Hearing a child scream, Mr. and Mrs. Diaz rushed into the kitchen to find their baby bleeding from a severe head injury and his cousin holding the pancake turner, they told police.

GO SLOW ON BANNING OIL EXPORTS, TRUMAN ASKS

WASHINGTON, Dec. 10. (AP)—President Truman wants Congress to think it over carefully before taking any action to prohibit shipments of oil abroad. Otherwise, he says, the country may suffer.

Mr. Truman gave this advice to Chairman Welch (R.) Cal., of the House Public Lands Committee, in a letter made public by Welch.

Welch and Chairman Butler (R.) Neb., of the Senate Public Lands Committee had joined in asking the President to ban oil exports as a means of conserving petroleum reserves at home.

Welch said Mr. Truman's reply "does not answer the problem."

"Situations such as these have to be approached with extreme caution, as you know, and as the House committee discovered when they began raising a fuss about $22,000,000 worth of goods being shipped to Russia before they knew that we bought $26,000,000 worth of good from Russia which were indispensable to us," the President wrote.

"I think you will find the interchange of oil products is practically in the same class and I'd suggest you give the matter a thorough look before you start to take action for which the country may suffer."

G.O.P. Will Seek Voluntary Curbs to Halt Inflation

WASHINGTON, Dec. 10. (AP)—A Republican anti-inflation program based on voluntary controls and prohibiting price fixing was put into legislative form today and scheduled for House consideration next Monday.

It was introduced late today by Chairman Wolcott (R.) Mich., of the House Banking Committee. Wolcott said the committee expects to approve the bill tomorrow.

The bill, intended as a substitute for the compulsory control powers President Truman had asked, was drafted after a meeting of Senate and House Republican leaders.

Major Provision

Major provisions of the measure:

It would permit and encourage industry to enter into voluntary agreements for the allocation of general transportation facilities, for the prevention of grain speculation, for livestock marketing and for the allocation and inventorying of basic consumer goods. The agreements would be subject to Presidential approval and industries entering into them would be exempt from prosecution under the antitrust laws.

It would extend export control authority now vested in the President and put on the President the responsibility for determining what part of domestic production can be exported without jeopardizing the domestic economy.

Would Tighten Credit

It would extend existing authority of the President to allocate rail transportation facilities, such as boxcars.

It would tighten credit by increasing from 25 per cent to 40 per cent the gold reserves behind currency issued by Federal Reserve banks and from 25 per cent to 35 per cent the gold reserves Federal Reserve banks must carry to support deposits of commercial banks.

The entire proposed law would expire March 1, 1949.

Taft Explains

Sen. Taft (R.) chairman of the Senate Republican steering committee, said that omission of consumer credit controls from the G.O.P. measure does not necessarily preclude action.

This is a prime point in the administration's 10-point pro-

Turn to Page 2, Column 1

Strike Authorized by Radio Directors

NEW YORK, Dec. 10. (AP)—The New York local of the Radio Directors Guild (A.F.L.) has authorized a strike Jan. 1 against the N.B.C., C.B.S. and A.B.C. networks and Station WOR, New York outlet of Mutual.

The guild is asking a weekly minimum of $250 for staff directors, compared with $100 at present, and similar adjustments in other classifications. William Sweets, local president, said the guild is seeking to remedy what he called "gross inequities" in the radio directors' pay situation.

British Report U.S. Will Handle Both Reich Zones

London Sources Say Agreement Reached on Control of Economic and Money Policies

LONDON, Dec. 10. (AP)—Authoritative government sources said tonight that the United States and Britain have reached agreement which would give the United States virtually complete control over economic and financial policies of the American and British zones of Germany.

A text of the document revising last year's pact for economic fusion of the two zones was said to have reached London from Washington at about the same time as U.S. Secretary of State Marshall asserted that the Soviet Union is taking $500,000,000 annually in German assets out of the Russian-occupied zone. He demanded that these withdrawals stop within three weeks.

Marshall for Showdown

Launching his first offensive in the Foreign Ministers' council meeting, the American diplomat made a bid for a showdown on the issue of reparations, which may make or break the present conference within a matter of days.

In reference to the Soviet demand for $10,000,000,000 in reparations from Germany out of current production, Marshall said:

"I wish it to be clearly understood that the United States is not prepared to agree to any program of reparations from current production as a price for the unification of Germany."

The British Foreign Office was not available for official comment on the report of the tentative agreement between the United States and Britain. But earlier a spokesman said word of conclusion of the Washington negotiations—they have been going on for several weeks—is expected hourly.

U.S. May Take Over

Control of economic and financial policies of the merged zones in Germany would be in direct proportion to each country's contribution to a common budget, the informants said.

This would mean that the United States would assume virtually complete economic and financial control over the two areas, as American negotiators have agreed to take over all of Britain's dollar commitments un-

Turn to Page 6, Column 2

General Strike Starts in Rome

ROME, Dec. 11 (Thursday.) (U.P.)—Rome's first general strike in 26 years got under way today despite futile government-union negotiations which extended nearly two hours beyond the midnight strike deadline.

The Communist-controlled Rome Chamber of Labor ordered the strike of more than 500,000 workers, even though union officials discussed a compromise offer until 1:45 a.m.

How successful the strike will be is a question mark. Transportation workers quit almost immediately after the midnight deadline and bus and streetcar service was halted.

Officials of the minority Christian Democratic Union—the labor segment of the Premier's governing party—denounced the strike as a "Communist imposition" and appealed to its members to work.

Communist leaders said they will post shop committees in all plants to prevent any back-to-work movement.

Free Trip Back Offered Reds

HARTFORD (Ct.) Dec. 10. (AP) The Connecticut Secretary of State's office approved papers today organizing the American Anti-Communist League, whose slogan is a "free one-way ticket to Moscow."

Albert B. Epstein, a restaurant cashier and one of the founders, said the league will give a "free, first-class, one-way ticket to Moscow" to any American Communist who renounces his citizenship and promises to "go to Russia and stay there."

FILMS SPED TO THEATER SCREEN BY TELEVISION

New York Times

NEW YORK, Dec. 10.—Theater-size motion pictures comparable in quality with ordinary newsreel films, made in 66 seconds by aiming a film camera at the screen of a television receiver, were demonstrated today for the Television Broadcasters Association.

The system, developed by Paramount Pictures, is said to reduce greatly the time lag between the shooting of special events with the usual optical cameras, their processing and subsequent showing in theaters.

It was said also to present the future possibility of exposing most motion picture films right in the centrally located processing plants, using a television camera at the "on location" remote spots, and relaying the scenes via microwave radio from location to processing depots.

The films comprised three rounds of the Louis-Wolcott championship fight televised last Friday night from Madison Square Garden and several scenes of the Theatre Guild's play, "The Late George Apley," televised on Sunday. The films thus made from television were clear. They were projected over the usual film-projecting machine onto a screen about 10 by 12 feet in size. Some 300 guests at the clinic viewed the demonstration. They represented television interests from coast to coast.

'Violence' of Wording Brings Snub

PARIS, Dec. 10. (U.P.)—France today returned as "unreceivable" a Russian note breaking off trade talks. The French action was a diplomatic rebuke far stronger than rejecting the note, a Foreign Ministry spokesman said.

The government's action, climaxing a series of reprisals between the two nations, brought France into closer harmony with the west than at any time since World War II.

Premier Schuman, in a nationwide radio address aimed at consolidating his victory over the Communist party, warned workers that a higher standard of living depends on the success of the Marshall plan.

American Aid Needed

"With American aid," he said, "we can hope for a progressive amelioration of our living standard."

Schuman did not mention the Soviet note, which ordered a French repatriation mission to leave Russia and canceled scheduled trade negotiations aimed at giving France 300,000 tons of desperately needed wheat and other cereals.

Schuman's government in instructing Charge d'Affaires Pierre Charpentier in Moscow to return the note to the Soviet Foreign Ministry, said, in effect, that it did not deem it worthy of consideration.

'Violence' Cited

A Foreign Ministry spokesman said the note was snubbed because of the "violence" of its phraseology and the "false basis on which objections were made."

Technically, the spokesman said, the French in effect have informed the Russians that the phraseology is unacceptable and

Head of French mission in Russia assails own government in crisis. For details see Page 9, Part I.

if they want to rephrase and send it back "in a normal, diplomatic manner," the French government will reply.

He said France objects to publication of the note in Moscow before it was received by the government. He added that the terms themselves are "unacceptable."

Workers Return

Schuman spoke to the nation as workers streamed back to most industries in response to yesterday's order by the General Confederation of Labor (C.G.T.) In the northern coal mines, however, where the Communists are particularly powerful, thousands remained on strike and many miners were beaten up when they tried to enter pits.

Schuman promised speedy action toward settlement of economic and social problems "in so far as our situation permits," but he warned that strikes have made the country's financial condition desperate.

Second in Month

The government's rebuff of Russia was the second in the last month. Earlier, France rejected a Soviet protest over a French police raid on a Russian repatriation camp near Paris. Soviet ire was aroused further when France expelled Russian citizens for alleged subversive activities in connection with recent disorders.

French newspapers, except for L'Humanite, were unanimous in denouncing Russia for canceling the trade talks. Most papers said the Soviet action was in retaliation for the government's strong antistrike measures, which broke Communist plans for a general strike.

Russ Report Progress in British Trade Pact

LONDON, Dec. 11 (Thursday.) (AP)—The Soviet news agency Tass said today an agreement was reached "on all main points" in the first stage of the British-Russian trade negotiations in Moscow.

The dispatch, distributed here by the Soviet monitor, said Sir Maurice Peterson, British Ambassador to Russia, will continue the negotiations begun by Harold Wilson, president of the British Board of Trade.

Gandhi as He Carried on Spiritual Crusade for Peace in India to Death

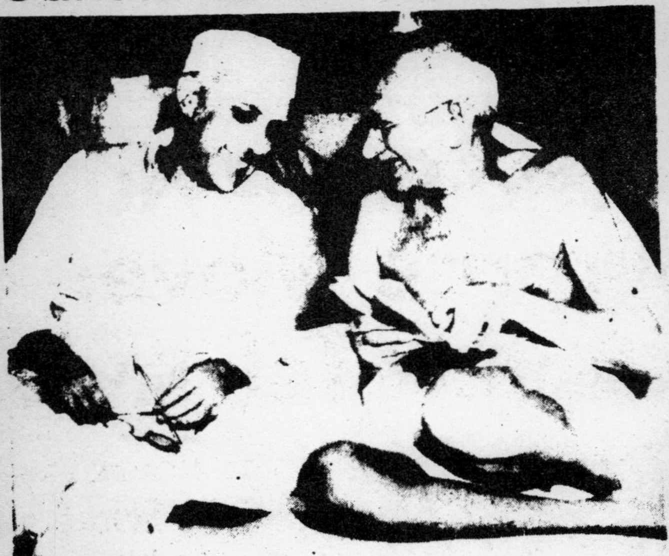

(AP) Photo

INDEPENDENCE LEADERS—Jawaharlal Nehru, at left, Prime Minister of India and Gandhi's "heir" is pictured with the Mahatma. Nehru was beside Gandhi when he died.

(AP) Wirephoto

SALUTING AUDIENCE—Gandhi presses his hands in attitude of prayer as he salutes Bombay crowd of 100,000.

(AP) Wirephoto

FAST FOR PEACE—Wearing a loin cloth and shawl, Gandhi squats before microphone in New Delhi to deliver prayer meeting discourse during his recent fast to enforce peace.

ALL THE NEWS ALL THE TIME

Los Angeles Times

EQUAL RIGHTS — LIBERTY UNDER THE LAW — TRUE INDUSTRIAL FREEDOM

PART I—GENERAL NEWS

VOL. LXVII CC ★ SATURDAY MORNING, JANUARY 31, 1948 DAILY, FIVE CENTS

Civic Works Face Threat of Strike

A.F.L. Plans Shutdown Monday in Drive to Unionize Workers

Officials of A.F.L. building trades unions yesterday threatened to shut down more than $50,000,000 of public works being carried on by Los Angeles Municipal Water and Power Department and by Los Angeles County at its Pomona Fairground.

Hundreds and possibly more than 1000 men may be thrown out of work by the strikes if they are carried out as threatened. The object of the strikes is to force unionization of all men on the jobs.

Monday is the day the union leaders have set for the strike to begin on the municipal jobs. No date has been announced for the walkout proposed on the county job. The two works programs are not related, other than that A.F.L. building craftsmen are employed on each.

Hits Construction Work

At the municipal department offices, it was said that "as far as we know" the strike set for Monday will not in any way interfere with the city providing water and power as usual. It will interfere only with construction jobs "intended to help Los Angeles keep pace with its rapid growth."

The walkout order that went out yesterday to all A.F.L. building tradesmen on the municipal jobs, directing them not to appear for work Monday, went to the several hundred employees of private contractors on the Harbor Steam Plant and Baldwin Hills Reservoir.

Both union men for the contractors and civil service men in the department employ work together on those jobs. Under the strike order the union men will be forbidden to work longer with the nonunion department employees.

May Affect Other Jobs

Other jobs that are expected to be affected, by reason of some department employees' belonging to one of the striking unions, include the Manhattan Pumping Project, construction work on Distributing Station 49, Station F, Station 28 and on a number of smaller jobs throughout the municipal system.

The total number of depart-

Turn to Page 6, Column 1

Visit of Three House Guests of Judd Disclosed

Three men were overnight guests at the home of George T. Judd Sr., 55, Pasadena financier, two days before his stabbed body was found Thursday in his home, police were informed yesterday as they undertook questioning of barroom habitues in the Pasadena area.

R. A. Elliott, contractor of 701 Poppy Field Drive, Altadena, told Det. Lt. Cecil H. Burlingame of the Pasadena homicide detail that Judd telephoned him at home last Tuesday night.

"He said he wanted me to send him a plumber to fix a broken shower head," Elliott reported. "He said that three men had stayed at the house overnight and that one of them had broken the fixture."

View of Police

Police expressed belief the murderer probably was a chance acquaintance of the victim, who resided at 840 Seco Drive, Pasadena. Relatives and friends told investigators the $35,000-a-year bond and mortgage company executive had no particular women friends since the death of his wife a year ago.

"We are not looking for a woman in the case," Burlingame said.

Judd's body, clad in shorts and lying on a bed, was found by his daughter, Mrs. Mary Mikel, 1522 Morada Place, Altadena. Mrs. Mikel first told police she peered through a window and thought her father was asleep early Thursday.

'Tidied Up' Glasses

Returning later, she said originally, she entered the house and learned he was dead. Believing it to be a natural death, she said she "tidied up" by washing two highball glasses she

Turn to Page 6, Column 2

FEATURES INDEX

Fights and Sabotage Peril Olympic Games

Two American bobsleds were sabotaged, hockey players engaged in fist fights and other untoward incidents threaten to wreck the Winter Olympic Games which just opened at St. Moritz, Switzerland. Page 9, Part 1.

On Other Pages

Paris Fire Ruins 2000 Tons of Food

PARIS, Jan. 30. (AP) Fire today destroyed a warehouse filled with approximately $5,000,000 worth of food and clothing. Police said a disgruntled former worker might have set it.

Included in the loss were 2000 tons of goods from the American Friendship Train. The relief supplies had been stored in the French social aid warehouse in suburban Charenton.

(AP) Wirephoto

RECENT PHOTO—This picture of Orville Wright was taken at rare interview.

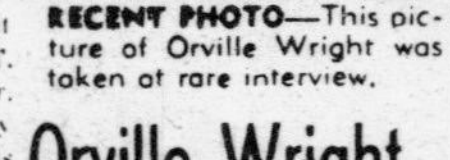

Orville Wright Succumbs at 76

DAYTON (O.) Jan. 30. (AP) The co-inventor of the airplane, 76-year-old Orville Wright, died tonight in his sleep under an oxygen tent at Miami Valley Hospital.

The aged pioneer who put wings on the world died of a lung congestion and a heart disease.

Four persons stood at his bedside at the end. They are Mr. and Mrs. Horace A. Wright, Mrs. H. S. Miller and Nurse Delyle Meyers. Horace Wright is a nephew and Mrs. Miller a niece of the dead inventor.

Couldn't Foresee Uses

Wright, whose dreams of flying changed man's way of life, once said: "Quite obviously, Wilbur (his late brother with whom he invented the heavier-than-air machine) and I could not foresee what awful use could be made of the airplane. But, it is

Turn to Page 4, Column 1

It Stays Dry and Cool With No Rain Seen

Ten-Day Ban Put on Imperial County Citrus Shipments

Southern California yesterday remained cool and, to farmers and citrus growers, aggravatingly dry. And the weatherman promised no rain today, although he offered hope for next month.

A 10-day ban on citrus exports from Imperial County was clamped on yesterday by B. A. Harrigan, County Agricultural Commissioner, who tentatively set loss from cold and drouth at $500,000.

Preliminary estimates from the Coachella Valley placed vegetable crop damage at 20 per cent. Riverside County Agricultural Commissioner William H. Wright said no embargo will be placed on shipments but that they will be watched for damaged produce.

Elsinore Level Falls

At Elsinore residents of the valley planned a mass prayer meeting to appeal for rain as the Lake Elsinore water level fell to the danger point. Loss of citrus in the valley caused by cold weather was unofficially estimated at 33 per cent of the crop.

Reporting that a storm heading south "ran out of water" over Northern California, the Weather Bureau predicted variable high cloudiness over the Southland today with patches of early fog along the coast line tomorrow. Slightly cooler and locally windy weather in the mountains and interior regions also was forecast.

The 25-degree downtown temperature range of Thursday was duplicated yesterday but moved

Turn to Page 8, Column 1

Streetcar Riders to Pay Higher Fares Beginning Tomorrow

Higher rates for public transportation patrons in some zones will become effective tomorrow as scheduled.

The California Public Utilities Commission in San Francisco yesterday denied a request that the increases, granted on an interim basis, be deferred pending further study.

The request for deferment was made by the Los Angeles City Council, which expressed by resolution the belief that the fare increases were "unjust and unreasonable." The Council asked for further time to study the facts.

The commission said it would continue studies of service and operating results but that the transit companies had been losing money and this situation had to be remedied.

About 85 per cent of the streetcar and bus riders travel on the inner zone bounded by Hollywood Blvd., Coliseum St., La Brea Ave, and the downtown area.

In this zone cash fares of 10 cents and token fares of three for 25 cents remain in effect while weekly passes go up from $1.25 to $1.50. In the same zone 10-ride school-ticket books will sell for $2.40.

In most of Zone 2, beyond the inner zone limits, cash fare will be 15 cents and the school-ticket books $3.60. No changes will be made in fares in some sections south of the inner zone.

In Zone 3, generally defined as beyond Inglewood, Bell, Huntington Park and South Gate, single cash fares will be 20 cents.

Transfers will be interchangeably honored by L.A.T.L. street cars and busses and Pacific Electric cars when issued on 10-cent cash fares.

Terrible Conflict Brewing Over Gandhi Assassination

(AP) Wirephoto

MISSING—Air Marshal Sir Arthur Coningham of Britain, aboard missing plane.

Mediterranean to Get Marines

NORFOLK (Va.) Jan. 30. (AP) Approximately 1000 United States marines will be sent shortly to the Mediterranean, 5th Naval District headquarters announced today.

The marines, the announcement said, are "replacements" and "will not augment the total number of marines now in the Mediterranean area."

The announcement said:

"About 1000 marines stationed at Camp Lejeune, N.C., will embark at Norfolk today aboard the carrier Philippine Sea for Quonset, R.I.

"At Quonset they will be reassigned to the carrier and other vessels for participation in Atlantic Fleet exercises in the Caribbean.

"After the exercises the marines on the assigned vessels will depart for the Mediterranean, where the ships will relieve on station a similar number of naval vessels."

Plane Crash Kills Navy Reservists

Two 25-year-old ensigns were killed yesterday when their Navy (SNJ) trainer crashed in the surf at San Clemente Island, it was announced by Los Alamitos Naval Air Station, where the reservists took off on a temporary duty flight.

They were identified as Arthur F. Berger Jr., pilot, of San Diego, and Emery Papp of Imperial Beach. Berger leaves his mother and Papp his widow and one son.

The bodies of both men were recovered after the ship smashed into the water.

Airliner Carrying Air Marshal of Britain Missing

HAMILTON (Bermuda) Jan. 30. (AP) U.S. planes and ships scoured the sea near Bermuda tonight in search of a missing British plane carrying 31 persons, including Air Marshal Sir Arthur Coningham. Hope faded for the safety of the passengers on the flight from the Azores. Everything depended on whether the four-engined luxury airliner might still be afloat.

Clouds hampered U.S. Coast Guard ships and Army and Navy planes in the hunt for the Star Tiger, a Tudor IV operated by the British South American Airways Line. It was due at Kindley Field, Bermuda, at 10:30 p.m. yesterday.

Planes Search Sea

Fifteen U.S. service planes and two British South American Airways planes were searching the area.

In London the British Ministry of Civil Aviation said the big airliner was "presumed lost." The Ministry said a public inquiry will be held.

A B.S.A.A. line official said the situation "looks black."

Most of the 25 passengers and six crewmen are British.

Sir Arthur Coningham was an R.A.F. hero in World War II. He served with the British 8th Army in North Africa and formed the first tactical air force in French North Africa in 1943. He also took part in Italian operations.

Sir Arthur, 52, a native of Brisbane, Australia, headed the R.A.F.'s flying training command.

A fighter pilot himself who had battled Germans in World War II, Sir Arthur commanded the Second Tactical Air Force on the Continent from January, 1944, until the Nazi collapse.

SHIRLEY TEMPLE, NOW 19, BECOMES MOTHER OF GIRL

Shirley Temple, since Sept. 19, 1945, Mrs. John Agar, yesterday gave birth to a 7-pound 6-ounce daughter at Santa Monica Hospital, their first child.

The 19-year-old former child film star was resting well, said her physician, Dr. William C. Bradbury. Agar, 26, said the infant will be named Linda Susan.

Shirley was born in the same hospital 20 years ago next April 23.

The Agars reside in what was once Shirley's doll house on the Brentwood estate of her parents, Mr. and Mrs. George Temple. The play building was enlarged for the bridal couple.

Bloody Rioting Breaks Out; Killer Hidden to Prevent Lynching as Nehru Asks Calm

NEW DELHI, Jan. 31 (Saturday.) (AP)—An assassin killed Mohandas K. Gandhi, India's apostle of peace, at prayer time last night. The 78-year-old Mahatma, or Great Souled One, was cut down by the bullets of a young Hindu for what police called political reasons.

The news crossed India's troubled continent swiftly and bloody rioting broke out in Bombay, perhaps the forerunner of terrible conflict. Fifteen were reported killed and 54 injured in fighting between Hindus and Moslems.

Gandhi, the little Hindu who led India to her independence, died soon after two bullets crashed into his body as he was about to start his evening prayer meeting. The shooting occurred in the gardens of spacious Birla House, home of a leading industrialist.

Assailant Grabbed and Beaten

The assailant was grabbed and beaten by Gandhi's worshipers. To police he gave several aliases, but he was booked under the name of Nathuram. He is 25. He is not a refugee from communal riot areas but police explained that some Hindus strongly disagree with Gandhi's hatred of violence.

Police said he tried to kill himself before his pistol was taken away. He was swiftly removed to a secret place to prevent a lynching.

All night long hundreds of Gandhi's faithful kept a vigil outside Birla Mansion. Crowds jammed roads leading to it. Today they will follow the body on foot over the more than five miles it will be carried to a Hindu burning ground, on the Jumna River for cremation.

A five-wicked Hindu oil lamp lighted the space where the frail man lay in death. At midnight Jawaharlal Nehru, India's Prime Minister and foremost leader in the Indian dominion after Gandhi, appealed to the crowds to be calm.

Nehru Asks Body Lie in Peace

There were shouts to bring the body out for view. Nehru, sobbing, asked the people to disperse, saying, "At least let the body be in peace."

Soon after the shooting the body was carried to a second floor veranda of the Birla House where Gandhi was staying and where he died. The couch on which the body lay was tilted and floodlighted so that many could view the face.

At Madras 200,000 milled about newspaper offices clamoring for more information of the assassination.

Widespread looting, arson and stabbing started in Bombay two hours after news of the assassination was received. Police fired scores of times at Hindu-Moslem rioters and troops were sent into the city. Transport and business were brought to a standstill In other cities tense crowds filled the streets but an uneasy peace prevailed.

Gandhi was still weak from the six-day fast he broke Jan. 18 in behalf of peace among warring Hindus and Moslems when he walked onto the prayer meeting grounds at Birla Mansion. He was leaning heavily on the shoulders of Manu and Ava Gandhi, his nieces.

A crowd of about 500 gathered round. Suddenly a young, stoutly built man in a military-like jacket pulled out a pistol

Turn to Page 2, Column 3

ALL THE NEWS ALL THE TIME

Los Angeles Times

EQUAL RIGHTS
LIBERTY UNDER THE LAW
TRUE INDUSTRIAL FREEDOM

PART I—GENERAL NEWS

VOL. LXVII — C C ★ — SATURDAY MORNING, MAY 15, 1948 — DAILY, FIVE CENTS

Jewish State Recognized By U.S. in Surprise Move; Air Raiders Bomb Tel Aviv

Planes Patrolling Meat Strike Area

Minnesota Troops Mobilized to Prevent Recurrence of Violence

SOUTH ST. PAUL, Minn., May 14 (U.P.)—National Guard combat planes patrolled packing house areas tonight while ground troops mobilized to prevent a recurrence of strike violence climaxed when 200 men smashed into one meat plant armed with knives and clubs.

Gov. Luther Youngdahl ordered the Guard mobilized after three days of mounting tension in the bitter strike of CIO United Packinghouse Workers. Union lines thinned out under new union orders to picket peacefully while troops assembled at armories to be outfitted.

The invasion of the Cudahy plant at Newport occurred early today when the group of about 200, armed with clubs, knives and hammers, smashed the lock on the plant gate and surged inside.

The abducted workers, some of them badly beaten, were carried by autos to county roads and released. Hours after the attack, Cudahy officials said that all 30 of them had been accounted for.

Other Peace Efforts

Meanwhile, reports of other attempts to settle the prolonged and bitter strike came from Evansville, Ind., where a district director of the union said that a conference of high union officials will be held at Chicago tomorrow to consider a government settlement proposal.

The union's international headquarters confirmed that the union executive board will meet tomorrow, but said it has no knowledge of any settlement proposal.

The mobilization of the National Guard was made at the request of two sheriffs who signed petitions stating that they are "unable, with the forces at our command, to enforce law and order and protect life and property."

Number Undisclosed

There was no indication how many troops would be summoned to duty. Presumably they will be sent to the main Swift & Co. plant in South St. Paul and to the Cudahy plant in Newport.

Hours after the mobilization order was issued, troops still had not entered any of the strike areas. They were jamming armories, however, to be outfitted.

Word that the Guard had been ordered mobilized spread quickly along picket lines in South St. Paul and Newport.

"How will they use it?" was the question heard most frequently.

Officer's Comment

A policeman said that "if they're going to close up the plant and order everyone off the street, then everything will be calm.

"But if they use the Guard to open up the picket lines," he said, "there may be trouble."

Police Cars Rushed to Kansas City Plant

KANSAS CITY, Kan., May 14 (AP) — All police cars in service were dispatched to the Armour & Co. plant tonight following a report of trouble involving strikers there, but Police Lt. Lester Riley said everything was under control when the police arrived. Bricks were thrown at a motorcar driven by a postal messenger seeking to deliver a special delivery letter at the plant, police said. "A large crowd" of strikers was reported near the plant.

Hawaii Alert After Quake in Aleutians

Fear of Tidal Wave Sends Islanders Hurrying to Hills

SEATTLE, May 14 (AP)—Tidal wave alerts sent shoreline residents in Hawaii streaming into the hills and caused precautions to be taken in the Aleutians following an earthquake west of Dutch Harbor in the Aleutians.

However, as hours passed without a sign of the waves, authorities expressed belief that the danger was over.

The only report of the quake being felt on the water came from the motor vessel Square Knot 100 miles or less northwest of Umnak Island. It reported "a severe earthquake with a violent bouncing motion experienced on a smooth sea."

Stations Alerted

On the basis of the report the Ketchikan Coast Guard Base alerted all Coast Guard stations in the Aleutians against possible tidal waves.

The same report, relayed to Hilo in Hawaii, which lost 175 persons in a tidal wave in 1946, caused a rush to higher ground. Swimmers were warned away from beaches and the military services were alerted. The alert later was canceled.

Equipment Moved

In the Aleutians, also, equipment at Coast Guard stations was moved to higher ground and all personnel alerted. However, several hours after the original quake, messages from such points as Ft. Glenn, Nikolsky, Cape Sarachef and Scotch Cap reported no sign of tidal waves.

It was at Scotch Cap off Unimak Island that 10 Coast Guardsmen were lost in the tidal waves which also hit Hawaii. The waves destroyed the Scotch Cap lighthouse installation.

Hawaiians Flee to Hills on Tidal Wave Alarm

HILO, Hawaii, May 14 (AP)—A tidal wave alert sent shoreline residents fleeing to the hills today but the alert later was canceled.

Honolulu police, who had issued the first warning when a severe earthquake hit the Aleutians, said the alert was rescinded on the advice of Seismologist Laurie R. Burgess that any tidal wave would have hit the islands by 7 p.m. and the hour passed with no disturbances.

Burgess said he was advised by the Navy station at Adak, in the Aleutians, that there had been no tidal wave there.

This capital of the island of Hawaii was devastated by a tidal wave that took 175 lives in the islands in 1946.

Sen. Vandenberg Guarded After Threat by Phone

WASHINGTON, May 14 (AP)—Sen. Vandenberg (R) Mich., was guarded by Capitol police late yesterday and this morning after his office received an anonymous telephone call that "he'd better circle round."

Arthur Vandenberg Jr. said his father, frequently mentioned as a Presidential possibility, "is not the least bit alarmed."

He said the Capitol police insisted on giving the Senator a guard until noon today.

Phone Call to Office

This is the story related by young Vandenberg:

About noon yesterday, a stenographer in Vandenberg's office answered the telephone and a voice said:

"This is the guard. Tell Arthur he'd better circle around. He'll know what I mean."

Young Vandenberg called the guard to see what the call meant—but the guard denied making the call.

"At that point," said Vandenberg Jr., "the guard became alarmed.

"They insisted father have a guard during the rest of the day. The guard stayed on duty until noon today."

He said, "We don't consider there is any cause for alarm."

Speed Sought on Missile Ships Work

WASHINGTON, May 14 (AP)—Secretary Sullivan asked Congress today to let the Navy speed work on guided-missile ships and a giant 65,000-ton aircraft carrier.

He testified before a House Armed Services Subcommittee in support of a bill which would allow the Navy to stop construction of 13 ships and divert approximately $300,000,000 to vessels of newer types. The 13 ships already have cost $197,000,000, Sullivan said.

The Navy wants to quit work on one battleship, the Kentucky, a large cruiser, the Hawaii, seven destroyers, two destroyer escorts and two submarines, Sullivan said.

"Other ships have a higher priority because of the more immediate operational need for them in the event of an emergency," he explained.

The Kentucky and the Hawaii are to be turned into guided-missile ships.

Summer's Here; Warmest May 14

Yesterday's low of 55 and high of 82 deg. gave Los Angeles its warmest May 14 since 1937.

What's more, the weatherman predicted the weather today will continue in the same pleasant vein—clear and continued warm.

However, the weatherman cocked his weather eye at a storm brewing 700 miles off the Northern California coast last night and said if it travels east, the Southland's temperature will drop tomorrow.

Other warmish spots in the Southland yesterday were Burbank, 85; Long Beach, 81; Pasadena, 84; San Gabriel, 86; Imperial, 102, and Blythe, 102.

Britain to Sell Milk Unrationed

LONDON, May 14 (AP)—The Ministry of Food tonight announced the unrestricted sale of milk for three weeks beginning Sunday. It will be the first time in nearly 10 years of rationing for milk to go on the free list. High milk yields due to good weather permitted the relaxation, the Food Ministry said. The usual weekly adult ration is 2½ pints.

DRUG BRINGS ON SNOOZE OF THE 300

CHAMBERY, France, May 14—When bugles sounded reveille at the Joppet Barracks at daybreak the entire garrison of 300 soldiers of the 90th Alpine Battalion remained in their cots, snoring in different keys.

Sergeants bounded into the dormitory and snapped orders to get up but the men continued to sleep peacefully. Then officers appeared and tried to arouse the men but without success.

A medical officer was summoned and discovered the entire battalion had been drugged. Thieves placed an opiate in the soup last night and stole the wallets and valuables of the soldiers as they slept. They got 50,000 francs ($200) in cash and 20 watches.

FEATURES INDEX

Inflation Checked, Congress Report Hints

Congressional Economic Committee in formal report hints that inflation has been checked, and in 16-point program urges that business adopt modest profit policy and that labor take a reasonable wage attitude. Page 6, Part I.

On Other Pages

Slight Hope for 31 in Congo Air Crash

BRUSSELS, May 14 (AP)—A spokesman for the Belgian Airlines (Sabena) said tonight "there is little chance" of survival for 25 passengers and crew of six aboard a DC-4 plane which crashed in the Belgian Congo yesterday.

The plane crashed 20 miles from Libenge. No news reached Brussels tonight from rescue teams trying to reach the wreckage. A searching plane spotted the wreckage. The plane was on the regular Belgian Congo-Belgian route.

(AP) Wirephoto

CELEBRATION—Haim Shertok, 14, son of Moshe Shertok, Foreign Minister of new Jewish state, looks out of window of Jewish Agency in New York, and watches Zionists dancing in street to celebrate Zionist flag raising.

Attack Comes After British End Mandate

Casualties Reported in All-Jewish City; Planes Unidentified

TEL AVIV, Israel, May 15 (Saturday) (AP)—Air raiders bombed this all-Jewish city at dawn today only a few hours after the new Jewish state of Israel had been proclaimed.

First reports said casualties were one dead and six injured.

Tel Aviv Airport workers said Jewish fighters drove off the attacking planes, which they said appeared to be fighter-bomber types.

Six bombs fell at the edge of the airport, near the power and light station. Casualties were suffered when one bomb smashed a building. Tel Aviv was under complete blackout all night.

The attacking planes were not identified as to nationality.

Britain surrendered her 25-year-old mandate over Palestine at midnight and one minute later Israel officially came into existence.

Threat of Invasion

The newly born Jewish state faced an immediate threat of blood as Arab nations of the Middle East, awaiting the end of the mandate to launch their regular armies on an invasion of the Holy Land, poised troops on its frontiers and sent probing forces across the border.

The Egyptian government announced last night it has ordered its army to enter Palestine. A Cairo newspaper said two columns of regular Egyptian troops knifed their way across the frontier at dawn yesterday. Syrian and Lebanese troops were camped on the northern frontier awaiting an expected zero hour today.

Defense Pledged

Leaders of the new Israel promised, however, that its militia, Haganah, will defend the Jewish nation against the bloodiest Arab attacks.

The death of the British mandate was signalized by the departure of Sir Alan Cunningham, High Commissioner, from Haifa in a royal navy cruiser.

Cunningham's departure caused little excitement among Haifa's Jews, who control most of Palestine's largest seaport. The British fired a few rockets and searchlights played over the cruiser as it steamed from the port.

The chief function of the British now in Palestine is to complete the evacuation of their troops which has been ordered by Parliament by Aug. 1.

A hint of trouble to come was seen in Tel Aviv last night when

Turn to Page 2, Column 2

White House Promises More Action in Effort to End Palestine Strife

WASHINGTON, May 14 (U.P.)—President Truman, who had abandoned the U.S. partition plan for Palestine, tonight dramatically announced U.S. recognition of the Jewish state of Israel 20 minutes after it came into existence.

At the same time, the President's spokesman, White House Secretary Charles G. Ross, announced the determination of this country to continue its efforts to obtain a truce in Palestine between the Arabs and Jews and to appeal to the new Jewish state to support United States efforts to stop the fighting.

Mr. Truman's brief statement announcing recognition of Israel said:

"This government has been informed that a Jewish state has been proclaimed in Palestine, and recognition has been requested by the provisional government thereof.

"The United States recognizes the provisional government as the de facto authority of the new state of Israel."

U.N. Delegates Amazed

Mr. Truman's decision had been kept a top secret of the highest level for two days. Even many officials of the State Department were surprised by the announcement.

News of the recognition amazed United Nations delegates in New York. No delegation was more surprised than that of the United States.

American officials, plugging to the last for a temporary United Nations regime in Jerusalem and a United Nations mediation program for all of Palestine, disclosed they had received no advance notice of President Truman's plans. [Editor's note: President Truman was praised by Democratic Chairman McGrath at a Young Democrats' dinner for his recognition of Israel. See Page 4, Part I.]

The immediate reaction was that the speedy action was taken to beat Russia to the gun.

U.S. Firm on Policy

Officials here have felt that the Russians might rush to recognize the "facts" as soon as Britain's mandate expired and the Jews proclaimed the existance of a new sovereign state.

Ross said creation of the new Jewish state and U.S. recognition will in no way lessen this government's effort to bring about a truce between warring Arabs and Jews.

"We hope that the new Jewish state will join with the Security Council Truce Commission in redoubled efforts to bring about an end to the fighting which has been, throughout the United Nations consideration of Palestine, a principal objective of this government," he told reporters.

There was no immediate ex-

Turn to Page 2, Column 3

Jews Here Pray for Peace as Nation Is Born

Illustrated on Page 2, Part I

Solemnity marked the observances by Jews in Los Angeles yesterday of the proclamation and recognition of the new State of Israel.

Jubilation was lacking as Jews halted at 3:01 p.m. to pray for peace in the wartorn Holy Land.

Instead, a spirit of solemnity pervaded the temples and synagogues of the city. The ceremonial shophar (ram's horn) was blown before a gathering of children at Temple Talmud Torah, 247 N Breed St.

Israel Flag Unfurled

It was here that the new flag of Israel—blue and white with the Star of David in the center—was unfurled for the first time in Los Angeles by Samuel Dubin, sexton.

And in another part of the city, Rabbi Jacob Kohn, of Temple Sinai, dean of the graduate school of the West Coast Branch of the Jewish Theological Seminary, declared from his pulpit:

"Creation of the new state marks not only a milestone in Jewish history, but in the civilization of the Near East and perhaps of the Western World."

Special sabbath services will be conducted today in all Jewish places of worship in Los Angeles—to commemorate the independence of the new State.

Supplies for Palestine

When the 10,000-ton steamship Sorol clears Los Angeles Harbor tomorrow for Palestine she will carry 120 tons of food, medical supplies and clothing for the new Jewish state, plus the blessing of Southland Jewry. Shipboard ceremonies were conducted yesterday by Jewish lay and religious leaders in celebration of dispatching the cargo, all of which was collected in a local drive.

Rabbi Osher Zilberstein, president of the Los Angeles Orthodox Rabbinate; Charles Brown, president of the Los Angeles Jewish Community Council, and Theodore Strimling, chairman of the local Zionist Emergency Council, conducted the rite.

Strimling said American recognition of Israel "is the most important event in the history of the Jewish people. We hope the United States will use its power, prestige and material resources to help this young state take its rightful place among the nations of the world."

Stassen, Dewey Agree to Radio Debate on Reds

PORTLAND, Or., May 14 (U.P.)—Presidential Aspirants Harold E. Stassen of Minnesota and Gov. Thomas E. Dewey of New York agreed today to air their views on Communism "before the whole American people" on a nation-wide radio debate Monday night.

Both agreed on an hour-long discussion from 7 to 8 p.m. PDT over the four major networks.

Dewey hurled the final challenge before the May 21 Oregon primary as he rode into Portland from a speaking tour along the Columbia River.

He said he considered Stassen's proposal to outlaw the Communist Party "so dangerous and destructive to the security, safety and freedom of our nation that I have accepted it as the issue of the Oregon campaign."

Stassen met Dewey's demand as he campaigned up-State at Bonneville Dam. He had been holding out for a public debate on "all the issues involved in the Presidential race."

Dewey said he is willing to debate in a radio studio, with Stassen to take the first 20 minutes, himself the next 20 and then to divide 16½ minutes between them for rebuttal.

At Bonneville, Stassen said that while the issue would be confined to Communism, he felt that the question "involves the whole matter of the American system."

Dewey Beats Stassen in New Jersey Primary

TRENTON, N.J., May 14 (U.P.)—Gov. Thomas E. Dewey nosed out Harold E. Stassen in write-in votes in New Jersey's primary election last April 20, it was disclosed today. Secretary of State Lloyd B. Marsh revealed that Dewey received 3714 write-in votes to 3123 for Stassen. Their names did not appear on the ballot.

Russia Warns Greece

LONDON, May 14 (AP)—Tass, the Soviet news agency, said today Russia has protested to Greece against the execution of rebels and has warned they must stop.

A Farewell to Her Appendix! Doctors Tell It With Music

New York Times

NEW YORK, May 14—A musical interpretation of the emotional tribulations of a young woman about to undergo an appendectomy was presented here last night when "The Hospital," a suite by Dr. Herman M. Parris, Philadelphia physician and composer, received its premiere in Hunter College Auditorium.

Appropriately enough, it was the Doctors' Orchestral Society of New York, a symphony orchestra made up of more than 75 doctors and persons affiliated with the medical profession, whose musical instruments described the patient's farewell to her appendix. Ignace Strasfogel, formerly with the New York Philharmonic Orchestra, conducted.

Beginning with the patient's entrance into the hospital, the suite—a descriptive work in 10 movements—narrated an operative saga from the apprehensive history-taking by an intern to the patient's joy at going home.

Muted strings were used to symbolize the patient's silent prayers before going to the operating room. Woodwinds and brasses depicted the bustle and activity in the surgeon's theater. Classical tonal patterns were merged with the modern to describe the surgeon himself and the young woman's fantasies under anaesthesia.

The music brought a shock of recognition to the appendixless among the listeners.

STOCK GAINS FASTEST IN EIGHT YEARS

NEW YORK, May 14 (AP)—Stocks took a frenzied whirl upward today in the fastest trading in eight years.

Gains of $1 to $7 a share for principal issues boosted total market value of listed stocks by around $1,700,000,000.

Traders who base their stock purchases on chart theories touched off the surge of demand for shares.

This came when the Dow-Jones industrial average punched its way through the high of last summer. This gave a long-awaited signal which Dow theorists said confirmed existence of a primary bull market in which a long price rise may be expected.

A total of 3,840,000 shares changed hands, largest total for any day since May 21, 1940.

Princess Elizabeth Urges Pool of British-French Resources

PARIS, May 14 (AP)—Princess Elizabeth today called on Britain and France to "look well beyond their own frontiers" if they would escape destruction and preserve their common way of life.

"We must work for the breakdown of prejudices born of narrowminded nationalism," the heiress apparent to the British throne said in an address at the opening of an exhibition of the history of Britons in Paris.

She spoke in French before French, British dominion and other notables. She urged that France and Britain take the lead in pooling resources.

"No country is morally self-sufficient, any more than it is economically self-supporting," she said. "Therefore we must be ready to throw into the common pool the gifts and virtues which are our treasured heritage."

The Princess and Prince Philip, her consort, arrived in Paris earlier today for a four-day stay. They were closely guarded after rumors of a plot to kidnap or kill her.

President Vincent Auriol welcomed them to France at the Elysee Palace and conferred the Grand Cordon of the Legion of Honor on the Princess.

With a smile, he delegated his further ceremonial powers "to your illustrious husband." Protocol for such a ceremony requires that the donor kiss the recipient on each cheek.

Elizabeth apparently did not grasp the President's reference. Philip was perhaps too flustered to plant the kisses on his bride.

PART 1

EQUAL RIGHTS

Los Angeles Times

LIBERTY UNDER THE LAW — TRUE INDUSTRIAL FREEDOM

ALL THE NEWS
ALL THE TIME

VOL. LXVII — CC ★ — THURSDAY MORNING, NOVEMBER 4, 1948 — DAILY, SEVEN CENTS

Truman's Victory Grows After Tightest Contest in 32 Years

Upset Follows Desertion by Factions of Own Party

BY THE UNITED PRESS

Harry S. Truman won the Presidency of the United States and a solidly Democratic Congress yesterday in one of the most astonishing political upsets in history.

He won against impossible odds after the tightest Presidential race in 32 years.

Counted out long ago by the public opinion polls and deserted by his own party's left and right wings, the man from Missouri jumped into the lead on the first scattered returns Tuesday afternoon and never was headed.

The race ended at 11:14 a.m. (9:14 a.m. PDT) when New York's Republican Gov. Dewey conceded defeat.

The news was flashed to the far corners of the earth and into a Kansas City hotel room where Mr. Truman was waiting.

He grinned and hugged his brother, J. Vivian Truman.

"I just want to deserve the honor," he said.

Thus the Democratic regime that Franklin D. Roosevelt swept into power in 1932 and passed to Mr. Truman on his death in 1945 was extended again and will cover a span of at least 20 years.

Returns Still Coming

Returns still were coming in from outlying districts across the land. But the President was 1,500,000 votes ahead of the 46-year-old GOP challenger in popular votes and 28 States with 304 electoral college votes were in his grasp.

That was 38 more than a winning majority of the 531 electoral college votes.

Mr. Truman and his Vice-Presidential running mate, Sen. Alben W. Barkley of Kentucky, were in.

Dewey Won't Run Again

And Dewey, a 15-to-1 shot on election eve to reverse the defeat he suffered at the hands of Franklin D. Roosevelt in 1944, probably had come to the end of the political trail. Twice beaten at the polls, he said he will never seek the Presidency again.

Crushed with him in the stunning Truman victory were the southern States Rights rebels led by Gov. J. Strom Thurmond of South Carolina and the left-wing New Dealers who followed Henry A. Wallace's Progressive Party banner.

The President, who fought his way to the Democratic nomination at Philadelphia last June against the red-hot opposition of party leaders who dubbed him a hopelessly weak candidate, confounded all the advance dope.

He broke into the big State strongholds that Dewey had counted on. When Dewey swept up New York's big bag of 47 electoral votes, the President bounced back and grabbed off the supposedly Republican prizes of Illinois, Ohio, Wisconsin, Massachusetts and Washington State.

It was Henry A. Wallace's defection from the Democratic camp that cost Mr. Truman the Empire State. The Progressive Party candidate polled more than 500,000 voter in New York. Mr. Truman trailed Dewey in the State by only 50,000.

Not since the Wilson-Hughes campaign of 1916 has a President been elected without carrying New York.

He topped off that astounding performance by jumping out in front in California, the home State of Dewey's Vice-Presidential partner, Gov. Warren.

Mr. Truman poured on another surprise by running ahead of his

Turn to Page A, Column 1

HOUR OF VICTORY—President Truman, grinning broadly, waves to crowd gathered outside Kansas City hotel in acknowledgment of smashing victory. (AP) Wirephoto

LATE TALLY ON POPULAR VOTE

Associated press returns from 122,083 of the country's 135,867 voting units late last night showed the popular vote:

Dewey	20,371,674
Truman	22,229,400
Wallace	1,028,391
Thurmond	862,429
Total	44,491,891

HOW STATES VOTED

These are the latest returns on the vote for the Dewey-Warren and Truman-Barkley tickets as compiled by the Associated Press:

States—	Total Precincts	Precincts Reporting	Popular Vote Dewey	Popular Vote Truman	Indicate Electoral Vote (D)	(1
Alabama	2,408	1,110	20,570	....	(X)	(X
Arizona	438	364	45,075	59,101	..	4
Arkansas	2,217	1,541	36,516	110,992	..	9
California	16,802	13,775	1,475,223	1,533,153	..	25
Colorado	1,704	1,522	208,017	225,174	..	6
Connecticut	169	169	438,226	422,228	8	..
Delaware	261	261	69,633	67,921	3	..
Florida	1,523	1,268	172,983	243,762	..	8
Georgia	1,736	1,318	68,745	228,953	..	12
Idaho	834	775	99,502	105,395	..	4
Illinois	9,231	9,215	1,934,933	1,985,263	..	28
Indiana	4,056	3,809	773,260	765,963	13	..
Iowa	2,474	2,474	488,933	523,502	..	10
Kansas	2,772	2,549	353,933	295,026	8	..
Kentucky	4,066	3,863	323,495	446,003	..	11
Louisiana	1,884	824	48,729	73,659	(X)	(X)
Maine	622	617	149,551	111,148	5	..
Maryland	1,347	1,347	293,929	285,834	8	..
Massachusetts	1,879	1,611	784,170	955,038	..	16
Michigan	4,193	4,042	993,027	958,595	19	..
Minnesota	3,738	2,859	367,119	504,459	..	11
Mississippi	1,725	1,000	3,661	11,208	(X)	(X)
Missouri	4,635	4,472	625,245	881,834	..	15
Montana	1,142	898	83,370	101,336	..	4
Nebraska	2,024	1,980	256,503	218,161	6	..
Nevada	301	301	29,102	30,568	..	3
New Hampshire	298	289	117,872	103,901	4	..
New Jersey	3,707	3,707	973,629	894,791	16	..
New Mexico	884	781	70,947	94,218	..	4
New York	9,959	9,959	2,837,848	2,782,555	47	..
North Carolina	1,959	1,675	213,648	418,368	..	14
North Dakota	2,272	1,565	89,121	72,819	4	..
Ohio	9,710	9,597	1,428,211	1,442,333	..	25
Oklahoma	3,701	3,655	263,132	446,147	..	10
Oregon	1,861	1,258	123,837	102,167	6	..
Pennsylvania	8,292	8,292	1,901,160	1,751,186	35	..
Rhode Island	266	266	134,892	188,619	..	4
South Carolina	1,296	975	5,101	30,498	(X)	(X)
South Dakota	1,950	1,459	88,499	81,900	4	..
Tennessee	2,300	2,259	191,396	254,694	..	12y
Texas	254	253	213,962	578,085		23
Utah	901	885	122,972	147,969	.	4
Vermont	246	246	76,066	45,594	3	..
Virginia	1,755	1,722	171,942	200,320	.	11
Washington	3,457	2,769	265,006	329,660	..	8
West Virginia	2,785	2,745	308,473	424,633	..	8
Wisconsin	3,143	3,113	584,854	644,452	..	12
Wyoming	681	648	45,656	49,945	..	3
Totals	135,858	122,083	20,371,674	22,229,400	189	304

(X)—Indicated Thurmond electoral vote, 38.
(Y)—Note—Two votes in doubt between Truman and Thurmond.

(For Thurmond and Wallace votes see Page 6, Part I.)

Transit Lines Get Straight 10c Fare

Tokens Eliminated and Cost of Weekly Passes to Be $1.75

Elimination of three-for-a-quarter tokens by the Los Angeles Transit Lines and raising of weekly passes from $1.50 to $1.75 were authorized by the State Public Utilities Commission yesterday.

Stanley M. Lanham, LATL director of planning, said the change will be made effective Nov. 21.

In authorizing a straight 10-cent fare, the Commission took note of the company's contention that it would suffer a $500,000 annual loss under previous rates.

Passes Convenient

LATL spokesmen before the Commission originally sought complete elimination of the weekly pass. However, witnesses at rate hearings set forth that passes are a great convenience and strongly desired by the public.

Fare hike petitions by the company were based on increased costs assertedly caused by a 5-cent wage rise and pension plan for employees put into effect last June.

A Commission study found those same rates would yield an annual profit of 0.7%. The Commission today said this was not a reasonable return and the company's plea for an increase was justified.

In contesting the increase, spokesmen for the city of Los Angeles said the old rates provided 2.36% profit.

The Commission today also authorized certain bookkeeping changes for the company.

STATE JOB OFFICE DROPS OFFICE JOBS

Department to Lay Off Total of 400; Move Protested by 200 Affected Here

Unemployment trouble within its own ranks beset the State Department of Employment here yesterday.

Faced with the announcement that more than 400 department workers will be laid off throughout the State system, with more than 200 layoffs in the Los Angeles division area five offices, the affected workers protested the move.

Their complaints were based on the fact that the layoffs were being made on a "horizontal" rather than a "vertical" level—that firings were confined to the lowest-pay bracket of civil service Grade 1, rather than spread out among higher grades and lower groups alike.

Budget Reduction Blamed

In explanation, R. J. Wade, spokesman for Area Director H. R. Harnish, said that efficient operation of the State Employment Service made it necessary to confine layoffs to the "group which fills the lesser technical positions."

"I can understand there are people who are hurt in this move," he said. "And there is no doubt that the layoffs will impair our efficiency. But the whole thing is due to an enforced budget reduction. I don't see how we could do otherwise."

The people whose jobs ended yesterday were chiefly in three groups, Wade said: personnel interviewers, unemployment claims examiners and employment security assistants. All were in civil service Grade 1.

Employees Complain

One complaining employee, discharged yesterday, said she knows workers laid off who had 12 years of service with the department while others who were retained, were on temporary civil service ratings, or had but one or two years of service.

Wade said the move will come as a "crippling blow" to the service, which is entering a period of greater activity with California employment due for its slack season.

City and County Feud Seen on Gasoline Fund

A feud between the city and county over the distribution of state gasoline tax monies appeared in the offing yesterday.

Mayor Bowron disclosed that hostilities are under way when he met informally with a group of City Councilmen.

The Mayor made it plain that he is considerably irked by receipt of a letter from the office of Wayne Allen chief administrative officer for the county, saying in substance that unless salaries of members of the city's engineering staff are reduced to conform with those paid by the county that the county will withhold payment of gasoline tax funds to the city.

Mayor's Comment

"If county officials are going to use this money to dictate what salaries we shall pay our employees they have no right to control these trust funds," the Mayor told the Councilmen.

He intimated that it might be well to advocate a change in the law which gives the county exclusive control over distribution of the State gasoline tax funds, which are confined to street and highway construction.

The Mayor said that some county salaries are higher than city salaries.

THE WEATHER

U.S. Weather Bureau forecast: Scattered cloudiness today and tomorrow. Warmer today with high near 70. Windy tomorrow. Highest temperature yesterday, 61; lowest, 56.

Tribunal Drops 38 of 55 Charges Against Tojo

TOKYO, Nov. 4 (Thursday) (AP) Hideki Tojo, who led Japan to war, and 24 other Jap leaders were cleared today of 38 of the 55 counts in their war crimes indictment.

The international military tribunal dismissed the 38 specifications as either duplicates or not within its jurisdiction. The principal charges remain, however. These accuse the defendants of responsibility for the Pacific war.

The 11-nation court held it lacked authority to try the defendants for "conspiracy to murder," a decision also reached at Nuernberg. In effect, it eliminated counts dealing with each separate act of alleged Jap aggression.

The ruling came shortly after the tribunal reconvened to begin the ponderous task of pronouncing judgment on the men who once ruled an empire.

The defendants will not hear their fate immediately. Sir William Webb of Australia, tribunal president, is not expected to complete the judgment reading—1575 pages totaling 300,000 words—before Nov. 11.

The courtroom was packed with spectators as Sir William started reading. Twenty-two defendants were in the prisoners' box facing the bench. Three others were in the hospital.

The defendants, called a "criminal militaristic clique" by the prosecution, include three other former Premiers beside Tojo, and six members of Tojo's Pearl Harbor Cabinet. Their two-year-long trial ended last April 16.

STOCKS DROP $2 TO $7, BUT GRAINS RISE

NEW YORK, Nov. 3 (AP)—Selling orders poured in from all sections of the country today following the surprise Truman victory, sending leading stocks down from $2 to $7 a share on the New York Stock Exchange.

But dealers in most commodities took the Truman victory as a bullish omen. In Chicago wheat, oats and rye were bid higher. Cotton prices advanced on the New York market.

The Truman victory caught the Stock Exchange traders far off base. It was as much as three hours before some of the big name stocks opened on the market. Traders said this was almost unheard of.

Today, 3,230,000 shares changed hands, against 1,220,000 Monday.

California's 25 Votes Go to Truman

Gov. Warren Fails to Carry Own State for First Time

Back in the Democratic fold after swinging in and out of the Republican column, California yesterday added its 25 electoral votes to President Truman's winning tally as a near-final tabulation of State returns from Tuesday's election showed that GOP Vice-Presidential Nominee Earl Warren had failed to carry his home State for the first time in his political career.

With 13,775 of the State's 16,802 precincts reported, President Truman had 1,533,153 votes; Gov. Dewey, 1,475,223, and Henry Wallace, 144,704.

Back to Work

Warren himself took gracefully the defeat, which he and Gov. Dewey suffered.

"The election result," he said, "should be cheerfully accepted by everyone as the voice of the people. The important thing is to get back to work, put our shoulders to the wheel and attempt to help solve the great problems confronting the nation."

Warren promptly followed his own advice by leaving his political headquarters in San Francisco by automobile for the State Capitol at Sacramento, where he said he would plunge immediately into the task of preparing the State budget for submission to the California Legislature in January.

The California Governor wired congratulations and good wishes

Turn to Page 5, Column 4

Baby Misses Death in Fall From Auto

Twenty-month-old Marvin LeRoy Wagner fell from an automobile traveling more than 30 miles an hour yesterday and apparently suffered only three large head bumps and pavement burns.

The child's father, Howard E. Wagner, 2663½ E Colorado St., Pasadena, told Pasadena Emergency Hospital attendants the baby landed on his head and rolled on the pavement, narrowly being missed by oncoming cars.

Wagner said he believes the baby accidentally opened the rear door.

The accident occurred on Washington St. between Allen Ave. and Foothill Blvd..

FEATURES INDEX

Three Companies Sign With Union Oil Strikers

Three major oil companies have signed new agreements with various components of the striking CIO Oil Workers Union. Page 1, Part II.

On Other Pages:

THIS SHOULD BE OF INTEREST

Dr. Gallup and Other Pollsters Explain All

NEW YORK, Nov. 3 (AP)—It was precisely as President Truman predicted:

The faces of the poll takers were red today, the day after election.

The President said the polls, which proved statistically he was beaten before the ballots were cast, were wrong. "Sleeping polls" he called them.

And wrong they were.

Not since 1936, when the Literary Digest poll picked Alf Landon over Franklin D. Roosevelt (final official result: Roosevelt won 46 States to 2), have the polls taken such a whipping.

Gallup Explanation

At 6 a.m. today, with Truman's popular vote more than 1,300,000 ahead of Dewey's, a spokesman for the Gallup Poll issued this statement:

"In the closest Presidential race since the Hughes-Wilson election in 1916, all public opinion polls—national, State and local—have underestimated the Democratic strength.

"President Truman staged a strong upsurge in the closing days of the campaign to recapture votes previously lost to Henry A. Wallace.

"The polls, without exception, showed a steady decline throughout the campaign in Wallace's following, but on election day his support skidded sharply.

"Polls earlier in the year showed that what votes the Progressive candidate would receive would come almost entirely from the Democratic Party.

Election Held Nightmare

"Over 3,000,000 voters remained undecided on their Presidential choice right up to the week before election. Obviously, substantial numbers of these undecided voters cast their ballots for President Truman."

Dr. George Gallup, director of the poll which had predicted a Dewey victory, himself a little later said:

"This is the kind of a close election that happens once in a generation and is a nightmare to poll takers.

"Everyone is asking, 'What happened? Why did all the polls underestimate Truman's strength.'

Turn to Page 4, Column 2

SEMIOFFICIAL RETURNS TABULATED FOR COUNTY

Following are semiofficial Los Angeles city and county returns from Tuesday's election as tabulated by Registrar of Voters Hite up to the time his office closed for the night late yesterday:

PRESIDENT

4023 Precincts out of 6558

Dewey (R)	462,388
Truman (D)	486,160
Wallace (IPP)	61,638
Watson (Proh.)	4,466

CONGRESS

12th District

228 Precincts out of 661

Nixon (R, D)	47,899
Rice (IPP)	6,203

13th District

211 Precincts out of 497

Poulson (R)	26,745
Healy (D, IPP)	25,151

14th District

304 Precincts out of 634

Braden (R)	17,996
Douglas (D)	40,787
Moore (IPP)	1,341

15th District

287 Precincts out of 719

McDonough (R, D)	51,015
Omerberg (IPP)	9,877

16th District

236 Precincts out of 818

Jackson (R)	30,563
Patterson (D, IPP)	26,166

In the 17th Congressional District there was no contest, Congressman Cecil King having been re-elected at the primaries.

18th District

135 Precincts out of 804

Bradley (R)	14,068
Doyle (D)	14,604
Moffatt (IPP)	1,454

19th District

141 Precincts out of 423

Quigley (R)	7,962
Holifield (D)	22,219
Berman (IPP)	672
Weiss (Ind.)	326

20th District

260 Precincts out of 982

Hinshaw (R, D)	50,699
Esterman (IPP)	11,558

21st District

343 Precincts out of 411 in San Bernardino County.

Lathrop (R)	32,564
Sheppard (D)	43,170
Louks (IPP)	1,611

21 Precincts out of 60 in Los Angeles County.

Lathrop (R)	16,371

Turn to Page 3, Column 3

Congress Sweep Puts Democrats in Firm Control

BY THE UNITED PRESS

The victorious Democratic Party last night solidly nailed down its control of the 81st Congress to which President Truman will submit a far-reaching domestic and foreign program.

Democrats held both the House and Senate by decisive majorities after ousting influential Republicans in the greatest Congressional upset since Franklin Delano Roosevelt was swept into office for his third term.

To this Congress, which will convene next Jan. 3, Mr. Truman will submit the program he had promised the voters—repeal of the Taft-Hartley Labor Relations Act, and enactment of anti-inflation, housing and other so-called social legislation.

Margin in Senate

By electing 24 Senatorial candidates, the Democrats held a commanding margin of 54 to 42 seats in the Senate. They took over 9 seats held by the Republicans and held on to 15 of their own seats, which were at stake, including four the GOP had hoped to take.

But the GOP suffered an even more stunning reversal in the House. There the Democrats had already captured 255 seats and were leading for eight more. The Republicans were definitely in possession of 161 and leading for 10 others.

At least 70 Republican House seats were taken by the Democrats in their victory march. Republicans were able to capture

Turn to Page 3, Column 6

Light Drizzles Spatter City

Spotty, intermittent light drizzles spattered portions of the Southland yesterday under lowering skies that held the thermometer to a 5-degree spread—from 56 to 61.

Misty precipitation began registering traces in the downtown area at 6:15 a.m. and continued at intervals throughout the day.

Measurable rainfall reported included .02 inch at San Pedro, .05 at Pomona and Covina, and .01 at Compton, Gardena, Hermosa Beach, Lomita and Palos Verdes.

The Weather Bureau ordered small craft warnings hoisted along the coast from Point Conception to Oceanside until 9 p.m. today. West to northwest winds of 20 to 30 m.p.h., with locally stronger gusts, are anticipated.

PART 1

Los Angeles Times

EQUAL RIGHTS · LIBERTY UNDER THE LAW · TRUE INDUSTRIAL FREEDOM

ALL THE NEWS ALL THE TIME

VOL. LXVIII | C C ** | WEDNESDAY MORNING, JANUARY 12, 1949 | DAILY, SEVEN CENTS

BELATED WHITE CHRISTMAS—Barbara Oates, 14, and Judy Rolfe, 11, ski down Altadena's Christmas Tree Lane. Times photo

Snow Falls for Third Night, Tangling Southland Traffic

Mountain Areas Isolated With Steep Grades Iced

Los Angeles and environs dug out of Monday's snowstorm only to be faced by another series of flurries and showers yesterday and last night that further tangled traffic and heaped additional havoc on Southland citrus orchards.

The almost unprecedented cold wave which has brought snow for three straight days found outlying suburbs and portions of Los Angeles itself whitened yesterday morning by a night-long fall of flakes.

Three full pages of pictures of Southland snow will be found on pages B, 2 and 3, Part I. Other weather news on pages A and 4.

Later in the day and on into last night the snow continued to fall in San Fernando Valley and foothill communities along the Sierra Madres and Verdugo Hills.

Fourteen inches of snow piled on Ventura Blvd. near Woodland Hills in the Chalk Hills area, Sheriff's deputies radioed. They also appealed to Ventura County for a snowplow to clear the road there and on Calabasas Grade late last night.

Call for Chains

Authorities warned that travel along almost all foothill thoroughfares required tire chains.

Slight comfort was to be gained from the Weather Bureau's evening forecast, which saw occasional showers today and tomorrow with slowly rising daytime temperatures. There will be continued, but scattered snow flurries in foothill sections, the weatherman added.

The intermittently heavy fall of snow throughout the Southland yesterday stalled street and highway traffic in various areas for hours.

Foothill Cars Snarled

And last night the earlier snarls of skidding, snow-blinded cars and trucks promised to be repeated as the new snow began falling shortly before dusk.

Foothill Blvd. through the Altadena-Tujunga district was jammed part of the night with cars unable to proceed through nearly 6 inches of snow.

Roads into San Fernando Valley west of Cahuenga Pass were reported dangerous because of frequent flurries.

Thoroughfares leading into the Santa Monica Mountains from Pacific Coast Highway were said to be nearly impassable. Sheriff's and California Highway Patrol cars were unable to answer calls to some isolated mountain sections when they encountered snow on steep grades.

Frost Warnings Out

As motorists fought slushy streets, citrus growers in some portions of the orchard belt wearily prepared to fire heaters again. The Weather Bureau's frost warning service pointed out that many spots would be safe from freezing tonight, but warned of temperatures of 27 at Whittier, Rialto and Colton; 28 at Canoga Park, Riverside, Redlands, San Juan Capistrano and Santa Paula; 29 at Pomona, Azusa, Cucamonga and in the Santa Rosa Valley, and 30 at Chatsworth, San Gabriel, Pacoima, El Centro and Indio.

Yesterday's maximum temperature was 47 deg. at 12:45 p.m. The morning low was 32 deg. at 5 a.m.

The snowfall in Los Angeles' Civic Center measured .3 of an inch in depth, but intermittent showers, which incidentally removed the snow rapidly, added .56 of an inch to the rainfall table for a seasonal total of 2.87 inches to date, in contrast to 1.92 inches on this date last year.

Driveways Blocked

Thousands of motorists, particularly in the foothill communities, found themselves unable to get out of their driveways in the morning because of snow which ranged from four inches in Pasadena to eight in La Canada.

The Ridge Route between Los Angeles and Bakersfield was blocked by heavy snow despite nightlong efforts of sand truck gangs.

During the day only automobiles equipped with chains were permitted to tackle the snowy grades. Trucks and busses were held back while snowplows attempted to reopen the road.

Blizzard Blocks Road

A blizzard at sundown yesterday blocked the highway completely, forcing all traffic back at Castaic.

Other highways closed included Highway 6 through Mint Conyon, Cajon Pass and the Weldon Canyon Road.

Many county and rural schools were closed yesterday. Some bus drivers who toured their pickup routes without finding more than two or three students promptly retraced their courses and delivered the children back home. Other children escorted to school by parents were immediately dismissed.

Long Beach Snow

Long Beach residents saw a night during which snow, rain, sleet, hail, thunder and lightning succeeded one another.

When the storm was interrupted in the morning, Long Beach had recorded .40 of an inch of rain, for a season total of 3.10 inches. Last year at this time Long Beach had received 1.82 inches. And no snow.

San Pedro Outer Harbor, the Marine Exchange and Fishermen's Dock were without light or power for an hour and a half last

Turn to Page 2, Column 7

THE WEATHER

U.S. Weather Bureau forecast: Partly cloudy with occasional showers today and tomorrow, with scattered snow flurries in foothill sections tonight. Slowly rising daytime temperatures with high today near 50. Highest temperature yesterday, 47; lowest, 32.

Icy Storm Grips Most of Nation

Rain, Sleet and Snow Extend From Coast Across Midwest

CHICAGO, Jan. 11 (U.P.)—Rain, sleet and snow stretched tonight from the cold Southern California fruitlands across ice-crippled areas in the Central States and into Ohio.

Ice cut communication and power lines in thousands of places and disrupted highway travel in Northern Texas, Southeastern Kansas, almost all of Missouri, parts of Oklahoma and Iowa, and in Central Illinois, Indiana and Ohio.

Skies cleared over Northern Great Plains States, plagued by two blizzards in the past week, and relief finally reached Gordon, Neb., isolated for 10 days by huge drifts. Planes crossed other parts of Nebraska to drop food, medicine and supplies in many marooned areas.

Power Shortage in Northwest

A severe cold gripped the Pacific Northwest, freezing the water power sources and plunging Idaho, Utah, Washington, Oregon and Montana into an electrical power shortage. In the Cascade Mountain area, the Weather Bureau predicted temperatures as low as 10 and 20 degrees below zero, with the cold continuing until the end of the week.

The East Coast enjoyed generally fair weather with temperatures in the 70's and 80's in the Southeastern States.

The Southwestern Bell Telephone Co. at St. Louis reported 145 towns in Missouri and Oklahoma cut off from all long distance communications. The company said 1000 telephone poles were down and 10,000 wire breaks due to ice will have to be repaired in the two States.

Capital Isolated

Jefferson City, Missouri's capital, was isolated from outside telephone calls.

Even heavier snows fell in Northern Arizona. At Flagstaff 33 inches fell in a 52-hour period to pile more than 40 inches on the ground. The Flagstaff Weather Bureau said there was no letup in sight.

In Nebraska, an air lift of planes from the Strategic Air Command, the National Guard, Civil Air Patrol and private owners was in full operation on mercy flights. The cargo was blood plasma, baby food, bread, canned milk, medicine, coal and baled hay for livestock. The fleet included Army helicopters from Lowry Field, Denver, and ski-equipped private planes.

Farms and ranches around North Platte, Neb., indicated their needs to inspecting airplanes by spreading one blanket on the snow for food and two blankets to signal the need for medicine.

SNOW CLOAKS CATALINA WITH WHITE MANTLE

Southern California's snowy coastal plains and foothills had a similarly snowy bastion offshore yesterday.

Santa Catalina Island was crowned with white—nearly eight inches of snow that drifted in to mantle 2100-foot Blackjack Peak and other summits and canyons throughout the island.

The storm drove the resort land's wildlife, including boar, goats and buffalo, to shelter under scrub pine and in old Indian caves.

School children, many of whom had never seen snow before, were taken in buses to cavort in the floating white fall.

Vehicular traffic to Catalina Airport was blocked by drifts and air transportation was suspended.

Federal Aid in Crop Loss Held Remote

BY WARREN B. FRANCIS
Times Staff Correspondent

WASHINGTON, Jan. 11—Slim prospects were seen today in government circles for Federal financial aid to Southern California fruit growers, truck farmers, flower raisers and other agriculturists hit by the recent unusual freezes which have brought a deluge of pleas to Congress members for help.

Only limited Federal funds are available for such purposes and much red tape will have to be cut before these are released to help stricken areas.

Up to Congress

The best chance of getting Federal help appears to hinge on action of Congress, since existing laws do not appear to cover such unusual situations.

Lack of detailed information about the extent of damage and nature of loss is a big hurdle which is keeping California legislators from introducing bills which would authorize government agencies to make loans to persons who lost all or large parts of their crops.

Special Legislation Needed

Reps. Phillips (R) of Banning and Sheppard (D) of Yucaipa doubted whether Congress will vote any appropriations until an inventory has been made of the extent of crop damages.

The Agriculture Department advised Rep. Sheppard, chairman of the California delegation, that it will require special legislation be-

Turn to Page 4, Column 5

PENSION RUSH SEES 9000 FILE CLAIMS

Board Authorizes Hiring of 190 Clerks to Handle Unexpected Heavy Paper Work

An unexpected flood of nearly 9000 applications for places on State pension rolls for the needy aged under Proposition 4 yesterday caused the Board of Supervisors to authorize hiring 190 additional clerks to handle the paper work.

County Supt. of Charities Arthur J. Will, in requesting the increase to his staff, said the department had estimated a maximum of only 3750 applications during January.

Forms Filled Out

Already, in the first six working days of the month, 8969 oldsters filled out the forms that may qualify them to draw the $75 monthly maximum authorized by the amendment approved by voters last Nov. 2.

Will pointed out that all new applications are from the ranks of the aged, inasmuch as blind pensioners already are on the rolls.

He said that apparently many of the current applicants are individuals who are "taking a gamble" that they are eligible for aid under the liberalized provisions of the new law.

May Reach 18,000

He estimated that at the present rate as many as 18,000 persons who have never before received pensions may seek to get on the remittance list before the end of January.

Some 200 extra workers hired to process applications when the local program got under way two weeks ago are being swamped in the avalanche of filings. The 190 newly authorized employees will go to work immediately, Will said.

No Peril Indicated for Federal Funds

SACRAMENTO, Jan. 11 (AP)—The Legislative Counsel's office said today that provisions of Proposition 4 will not imperil Federal funds for California's old age and blind security programs.

The Federal government has held up its January check to the State. Officials in Washington said they wanted to get a clarification of California's new welfare department setup. State aid, however, has been paid from other State sources.

The Legislative Counsel, in an opinion requested by Sen. George J. Hatfield, Merced County, said nothing in Proposition 4 conflicts with Federal regulations.

Woman Killed by Propeller of Big Airliner

A woman passenger, dashing to board a moving American Airlines DC-6 plane at Municipal Airport before midnight yesterday was fatally injured when struck by whirling propellor blades.

She was pronounced dead on arrival at a private hospital in Inglewood. Police said a ticket in possession of the woman indicated her to be Miss H. Crawford, and that her destination was New Orleans. No other identification was available at the time.

Airline authorities said the woman dashed out from an employees' gate into the ramp area after calling out: "That's the plane I'm supposed to take."

Two Children in Fire Caught by Fireman

NEW YORK, Jan. 11 (U.P.)—An off-duty Brooklyn fireman on his way to visit friends today caught two small children dropped from a blazing third-floor apartment.

Walking down a Brooklyn street, Fireman George Mayer looked up to see smoke pouring from the third floor of an apartment building. Mrs. Ida Thompson, 30, shouted that she and her two sons were trapped by a fire.

Mayer called to her to drop the children to him—20 feet below. Mrs. Thompson dropped Nathaniel, 3, and then Cornelius, 18 months. Mayer made perfect catches.

The fireman then enlisted two passers-by to help him catch Mrs. Thompson. They successfully broke her fall and she suffered only minor injuries.

Florida Train Leaves Rails

GROVELAND, Fla., Jan. 11 (AP) At least 20 persons were hurt when the Seaboard Airline Railroad's New York-to-Miami Orange Blossom Special derailed tonight 14 miles southwest of here.

A highway patrolman reported that all cars of the 15-car train were off the rails and most of them overturned.

EIGHT LOYALTY OATH SIGNERS LABELED RED

Eight city workers who took the loyalty oath admitted past or present Communist affiliations, Joseph W. Hawthorne, general manager of the Civil Service Department, said yesterday. At the same time four more municipal employees, discharged or suspended for refusal to take the oath, appealed to the department for hearings on their ousters.

At a conference yesterday Mayor Bowron and City Councilmen discussed the cases of those who said they had belonged to the Communist Party, but reached no decision on what action may be taken.

The four who appealed for reinstatement are:

Ola R. Pacifico and Frances Schwartz, Health Department nurses; Carrie L. Dick, Water and Power Department clerk, and Margaret Haskell, city library employee who was suspended.

New Television Hookup Opens

NEW YORK, Jan. 11 (AP)—Television tonight extended the range of its vision from the Atlantic to the Mississippi over an area with a quarter of the nation's population.

In a historic ceremony, the East Coast and Midwest television networks of the American Telephone & Telegraph Co.'s Bell System were joined with the opening of a new link between Philadelphia and Cleveland.

For the first time, St. Louis residents could watch a television show in Washington, or New York or Boston residents could see a program in Chicago. It was a giant stride toward coast-to-coast television which, however, may still be four or five years away because of the expense, technical problems and great distances involved.

'Golden Spike' Fete

The "golden spike" ceremony made it possible to telecast simultaneously to 17 cities with more than 30 stations—or better than half the nation's total.

The four television networks—ABC, CBS, Dumont and NBC—gave viewers a sampling of things to come with 15-minute shows each.

Gov. Warren Outlines Health Insurance Plan

BY CHESTER G. HANSON, Times Staff Representative

SACRAMENTO, Jan. 11—Gov. Warren today disclosed details of his compulsory health insurance plan and said he has more hope than he had as to his previous plans that it will be approved by the Legislature.

The plan calls for all persons under unemployment insurance in the State, together with their families, to be insured against what is termed "catastrophic illness." In general, that is any illness that requires hospitalization.

The plan would be financed by a payroll deduction of 1% by the employee and 1% by the employer.

The patient would have, Warren said, absolutely free choice of physician and hospital. The physician or hospital does not have to participate in the plan—they can refuse to handle a patient under the State plan.

The State would pay, within certain limits to be specified, whatever it cost the patient for hospitalization—medical care and laboratory fees and the like.

Details of the plan are to be worked out in the bill to be presented by Sen. Salsman.

Warren said he does not think it fair or accurate to dub the plan socialized medicine as it is not Socialism. He said he is as opposed as anyone could be to Socialism and regimentation.

FEATURES INDEX

Grand Jury Dismissed; Race Track Betting Hit

The 1948 county grand jury was excused from duty yesterday after submitting a final report in which it denounced legalized pari mutuel betting at horse race tracks. Page 1, Part II.

On Other Pages

CHEST APPEAL IN EMERGENCY BRINGS GROWING RESPONSE

Los Angeles residents made huge strides yesterday toward erasing a $1,800,000 Community Chest goal deficit with contributions of $134,600 at the end of the first full day's campaigning.

Announced Tuesday were gifts of $75,000 representing results tallied at the end of the first few hours. A final tally at the close of the day showed another $59,600, according to Edwin R. Valentine, campaign chairman.

Valentine expressed complete optimism about the eventual success of the four-day emergency appeal which ends tomorrow. He stated:

"I have never seen the people of Los Angeles so conscious about a Community Chest campaign in this city's history."

Some people were sending in more in extra pledges than they had sent during the regular campaign, according to Valentine.

And while it was still too early to measure final results, the campaign chairman feels that all signs point to the community preserving its reputation for taking care of its needy through adequate support of the Community Chest.

Word has been received from Lindsley F. Kimball, national president of the United Services Organization in New York City, expressing deep concern over the situation. USO is scheduled to receive a $150,000 allocation if the $7,550,000 goal is reached.

"Can we still depend on Los Angeles for its share? Reduction in our appropriation would mean retrenchment of programs planned for veterans in hospitals and new selectees. Trust you make it," Kimball wired.

Eddie Cantor will turn "disk jockey" over KFWB at 6:30 p.m. tomorrow to aid the appeal. Cantor will join Frank Bull on his "America Dances" program in a two-hour show.

Volunteers are being hampered somewhat in their efforts by the snow and unusual weather conditions, Valentine said. All people who have not been contacted are urged to send their contributions to Chest headquarters, 729 S Figueroa St., or to any branch bank.

Total contributions now stand at $5,884,736. Original goal, in behalf of 159 health, welfare and recreation organizations, was set at $7,550,000.

[Hundreds of children may face malnutrition if emergency Chest drive fails. For details see Page 1, Part II.]

The Community Chest Needs Your Support---Give Now

PART 1

Los Angeles Times

EQUAL RIGHTS
LIBERTY UNDER THE LAW — TRUE INDUSTRIAL FREEDOM

ALL THE NEWS
ALL THE TIME

VOL. LXVIII — CC ★ — TUESDAY MORNING, MARCH 1, 1949 — DAILY, SEVEN CENTS

Truman Asks More Millions for Needy

Up to $100 Monthly Per Couple Plus Medical Expenses Proposed

WASHINGTON, Feb. 28 (AP)—The Truman administration asked Congress today for $200,000,000 to $250,000,000 a year to help provide home relief for all needy—including cost of medical care.

This would be added to the present $1,000,000,000 the Federal government spends on direct assistance to dependent children, the blind and the needy aged.

The reaction on Capitol Hill was noncommittal for the most part.

Chairman Doughton (D) N.C., of the House Ways and Means Committee declined to forecast the outcome one way or the other.

Arthur J. Altmeyer, Commissioner for Social Security, opened before Doughton's Committee the administration's arguments backing President Truman's proposals for a vast expansion of the general social security program. He dealt with relief for the poor first.

Poorhouse Abolished

Social security has abolished the poorhouse, Altmeyer said, and he set as the new objective: "preventing destitution."

To this end he said Mr. Truman wants Federal financial aid extended to all needy people, in a Federal-State money-matching system—up to $100 a month for a needy couple plus $20 for each additional person in a needy home.

Moreover, Altmeyer proposed special attention to the medical needs of the poor. He testified:

"To enable States to make medical care available to needy persons, we believe that Federal participation should be extended to payments made directly to individuals and agencies furnishing medical services and supplies to public assistance recipients."

5,000,000 Get Aid

Altmeyer said 5,000,000 Americans now receive some kind of public assistance. Such direct relief is apart from the old age and survivors insurance benefits paid for in special payroll taxes by workers and their employers.

This direct aid amounts to almost $2,000,000,000 a year in Federal, State and local funds. The 5,000,000 include 2,500,000 needy old people, 1,700,000 persons in families receiving aid to dependent children, 86,000 blind persons, and 800,000 other needy persons. The Federal government does not participate in the aid to the 800,000 unclassified other needy.

Altmeyer argued that $200,000,000 to $250,000,000 a year more should be contributed by the Federal government to extend relief to all needy, including physically and mentally handicapped and jobless persons not covered by unemployment insurance.

WAR ON FILIBUSTER OPENED IN SENATE

WASHINGTON, Feb. 28 (U.P.)—The administration opened its antifilibuster fight in the Senate today under orders from President Truman to see it through even though it holds up his entire legislative program.

The order could provoke the greatest filibuster in the nation's history and seems certain to aggravate the split between the President and southern Democrats on the civil rights issue.

Mr. Truman gave his Senate leaders the go-ahead at a White House conference. Senate Democratic Leader Scott W. Lucas said the President told them to see it through to the bitter end and not to lay aside the filibuster fight for anything else. Lucas had proposed to sidetrack the battle so important bills wouldn't bog down.

Challenge Accepted

Southern Democrats who would have agreed to Lucas' program accepted the President's challenge.

They said they are prepared to talk indefinitely against the filibuster-curb which could wreck their chances of blocking civil rights legislation.

The civil rights measures, including antilynch, antipoll tax, antisegregation and antidiscrimination in jobs, are major planks in the President's Congressional program.

The filibuster fight began when Lucas called up a Rules Committee resolution to change the rules of Senate debate. It would permit the Senate to limit debate on any business by a two-thirds vote. The existing rule provides for a limitation by two-thirds vote on legislation itself but not on preliminary motions to take up bills. The new resolution is intended to close that loophole.

The first day's debate ended with Sen. Walter F. George (D), Ga., thundering the South's opposition. The Senate then recessed until tomorrow.

George, second only to Sen. Kenneth D. McKellar (D), Tenn., in Senate seniority, was the lead-off for the Southerners.

He denounced the proposed rules change as an interference with State's rights and a thinly veiled scheme to push through civil rights legislation.

He protested a "grant of power" which "may be used some day "to do a great wrong."

"The Federal government did

Turn to Page 10, Column 2

99 PRISONERS QUARANTINED

Ninety-nine prisoners and two police officers yesterday were under quarantine at City Jail following discovery of a case of diphtheria.

Dr. George M. Uhl, City Health Officer, said the quarantine will be removed Friday if no others fall ill. The victim is Gordon Hart, 49, held on a misdemeanor charge, who was taken to General Hospital.

Most of the prisoners under quarantine were serving misdemeanor sentences, police said.

Scattered Rains Fall Across Southland Area

Rain Figures on Page 2, Part I.

Clouds and sun played hide and seek in the Southland yesterday as some scattered showers fell to add to a rainfall table now far above last year's for the season but still below normal.

More rain was predicted for today and tomorrow, however. The weatherman forecast clouds and showers for Los Angeles and vicinity, with snow above 6000 feet in mountain areas.

Chief Forecaster A. K. Showalter said chances for a thunderstorm in the metropolitan area are better in March than any other month and that chances also are best then for getting 1.25 inches of rain here.

Weather Odds

In his forecast for the month he gave the following weather odds: 2 to 1 that March rainfall will exceed 1.25 inches and be less than 3 inches; 6 to 1 that it will be less than 6 inches and 20 to 1 that March will not produce the 8 inches needed to bring rainfall up to normal.

The week-end rain amounted to .45 inch here to make the February total 1.41 inches and the season total 6.31 inches, compared with a 10.88-inch normal and a 3.21-inch season total for last year.

Showalter predicted that maximum March temperatures in the Imperial and Coachella valleys should exceed 80 deg. on some days, with a few days over 90 deg.

"In the coastal valleys and along the coast," he said, "afternoon maximum temperatures are likely to remain near 70, with only a slight chance of the extreme for the month going above 86. Minimum temperatures will be near 40 in the coastal valleys, but in the high 40s along the coast and over the Imperial and Coachella River valleys.

Clouds or Fog

"March is not a typically sunny month and the majority of the days can be expected to have clouds or fog during at least a portion of the days in all sections from the mountains westward to the coast.

"Low clouds and fog can be expected to dissipate before 11 a.m. in the coastal valleys and by noon along the southern coast. But along the central coast, there is a good chance of low clouds continuing until afternoon."

Temperatures downtown, yesterday ranged from 49 to 61 deg.

REDS SHOWER LEAFLETS ON PRINCESS ELIZABETH

LONDON, Feb. 28 (U.P.)—Communists showered Red propaganda leaflets on Princess Elizabeth, the future Queen of England, and her husband, the Duke of Edinburgh, at a preview of the "Ideal Home" Exhibition here today.

The leaflets were hurled from the gallery. Police said they "interviewed" the two men who threw the leaflets and released them. One had shouted, "Homes for the workers, not for the rich!"

The royal couple ignored the leaflets and the scuffling in the gallery. They said they were especially interested in the exhibits because they are now furnishing their new London home, Clarence House.

ULCERS ACTING UP? LEARN TO RELAX

Doctor Finds Highest Incidence Among Wealthy Executives, Lowest Among Wives

When a woman becomes head of a business or a man loses a bet on a horse race ulcers are apt to result, according to Dr. Andrew C. Ivy, vice-president of the University of Illinois Professional Colleges, Chicago.

The former head of medical research for the United States Navy yesterday addressed 1500 physicians attending the postgraduate assembly of the College of Medical Evangelists.

The ideal method of treating ulcers, he indicated, would be for patients to alter their entire outlook on life by changing their occupations or moving to an environment where tensions would be minimal. "Unfortunately," he added, "this isn't possible for eight out of every 10 patients."

Styles Change

"At the dawn of this century, more young women had ulcers than men because of the style of tight lacing," said Dr. Ivy. "As early as 1776 the practice caused women to be the principal sufferers. Campaigns against tight corsets, however, changed the picture. At present, many more men than women are afflicted.

"The highest incidence is among wealthy executives subject to constant pressure and strain. The lowest incidence is among these men's wives. It was found in England that there is a high incidence among laborers and their wives.

Learn to Relax

"X-rays show us that about 10% of men have stomachs which become very tense and pour out acid during special strains. If you criticize medical students who are standing in front of an X-ray apparatus, the stomachs of 90% of them can be seen to drop. They aren't so apt to get ulcers as the 10% whose stomachs tighten. This seems in line with the finding that 10% of all men will suffer from some form of ulcers between the ages of 18 and 60. They tend to be the ones who are outwardly poised, but inwardly tense.

"The most important thing to

Turn to Page 12, Column 3

Unemployed Reported on Rise in State

SACRAMENTO, Feb. 28 (AP)—A rising curve of unemployment and a leveling off of some business activities were reported to Gov. Warren and his council today.

James G. Bryant, Director of Employment, said 411,000 were jobless in California last month. Employment was down 131,000 compared to the preceding month but the figure still was 5000 above mid-January 1948.

Farm unemployment was increasing yet did not reach the low level of a year ago.

FEATURES INDEX

Telescope May Have Reached Universe Edge

The 220-inch Hale telescope on Palomar Mountain, pushing out into hitherto unexplored realms of space, already may have penetrated to the outermost limits of the universe, scientists disclosed. Page 1, Part II.

On Other Pages

WRONG TURN

50 Injured as Trolleys Collide

More than 50 persons were injured, 30 of them seriously enough to require hospital treatment, when two "5" cars crashed at 12th and Main Sts. last night.

Flying glass, shattered in both cars by the force of the impact, cut more than a score of passengers while others suffered wrenched backs, arms, legs and less serious injuries.

The accident occurred as one car operated by Motorman W. E. Matthews, proceeding south on Main St., missed a switch and started to turn into W 12th St., colliding almost head on with the other car, which was going north.

Motormen Unhurt

Neither Matthews nor J. P. Aaron, 306 Rodger Young Village, motorman of the other car, was injured although the operator's vestibules of both cars were damaged.

Five ambulances were sent from the Georgia Street Receiving Hospital within minutes of the crash, and picked up the injured, most of whom were able to walk. Several, in a hysterical condition, had to be carried to the ambulances.

Noise Heard Blocks

The noise of the crash could be heard for blocks and hundreds of spectators swarmed about the scene. Neither car was derailed by the crash and both were able to proceed to the barns under their own power.

At Georgia Street Receiving Hospital, every available doctor, intern and nurse was pressed into duty to treat the injured who thronged the emergency room.

Virtually all of the injured were able to leave after treatment, although one woman was held for observation.

Air Lift Costs $119,702,600

WASHINGTON, Feb. 28 (AP)—The Berlin Air Lift has cost the United States taxpayer $119,702,600 in the past eight months, the Air Force estimated today.

The Air Lift began June 26, and since then the United States Air Force and Navy planes have flown in a total of 780,963 tons of supplies. They have made 87,757 flights.

Joe E. Brown Ill, Opening Called Off

PHILADELPHIA, Feb. 28 (U.P.)—Joe E. Brown, popular stage and screen comedian, was stricken ill today and was forced to cancel the opening of the play "Harvey" at a theater here tonight.

Physicians diagnosed his illness as a virus infection and ordered him confined to his hotel suite.

PE Seeks to Replace Cars With Busses on 11 of 17 Lines

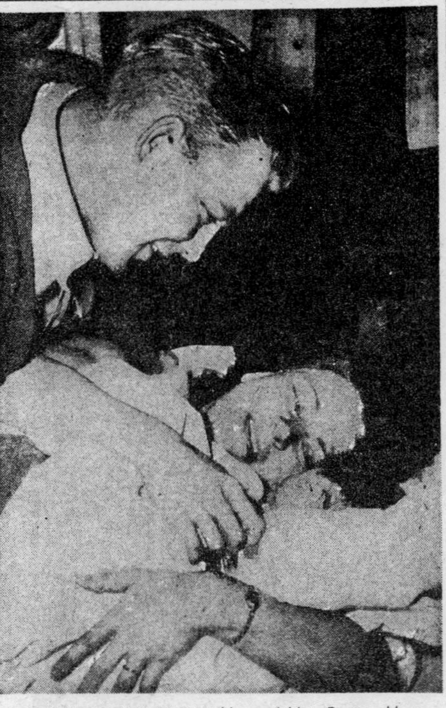

THEY LOST, AND WON—Mr. and Mrs. Benton Moore and brand-new daughter. The couple raced the stork in a car, ambulance, stretcher and elevator, but the bird overtook them at Georgia Street Receiving Hospital. Times photo

Proposed Plan Will Cut Losses, Company Says

The "big red cars" may soon go the way of the horse and buggy here, if the Pacific Electric Railway Co. has its way.

The company yesterday asked permission of the State Public Utilities Commission to replace trolleys with busses on 11 of its 17 present streetcar routes.

The application said the proposal is part of a $4,500,000 modernization program. The program is designed to eliminate operating losses, the company said, and to improve service without an increase in passenger fares.

No date is set for a hearing. Under customary procedure, the PUC will allow ample time for opponents to prepare their cases.

May Oppose Request

And many communities, including the city of Los Angeles, will probably oppose the application. Only last fall Los Angeles and 11 other Southland cities announced their intention to battle a proposal to substitute busses for streetcars.

Under the application, surviving rail lines will be rerouted in some cases and operated with one-man service in others. In several areas passenger transportation will be discontinued entirely, since PE routes are paralleled by other public carriers, the application said.

Replacement Proposed

A company spokesman said 151 of the system's 246 miles of passenger trackage will be abandoned under the plan. Removal of rails, he said, will depend on terms of the company's franchises with the various communities involved.

The spokesman said the plan calls for purchase of 200 busses to replace an equal number of streetcars. Abandoned trolleys, 53 of them the wooden type, will be either sold or salvaged.

He emphasized that all figures are estimates, subject to time and local variations.

The plan, he summed up, will leave 225 trolleys available for operation to San Pedro, Long Beach and the Watts district to the south, and to Beverly Hills via Hollywood Blvd., Glendale-Burbank and San Fernando Blvd.

Busses will replace streetcars on these routes: Pasadena Short Line; Pasadena Oak Knoll; Monrovia-Glendora; Sierra Madre; El Monte-Baldwin Park; Sierra Vista local; Venice Short Line, and Santa Monica Blvd.-West Hollywood.

Abandoned entirely will be rail lines to Santa Ana, Newport Beach and Van Nuys beyond North Hollywood. Bus service between Tarzana, Woodland Hills and Northridge will also be discontinued for lack of patronage, according to the application.

Lines Transfer Asked

The company's petition also asked these lines be transferred to another operator: Van Nuys-San Fernando, Van Nuys-Canoga Park, North Hollywood, North Hollywood-Studio City-Sherman Oaks and the Birmingham Hospital Leg of the Van Nuys-Birmingham Hospital line.

The program envisages that all rail service on Hill and Main Sts. downtown be discontinued. The cars to Beverly Hills, Glendale-Burbank and San Fernando Blvd. will operate from Subway Terminal as usual.

Losses Cited

O. A. Smith, president of PE, said the plan stems from an intensive year-long study. He said the company, despite a fare boost last year, had an operating loss for 1948 of $2,300,000.

PE and the Los Angeles Transit Lines joined in asking for separation of jointly owned lines. This concurrent application proposes that PE take over and operate Wilshire Blvd. limited and express service, Sunset Blvd. and Fairfax Ave. lines. The LATL will operate PE's motor-coach lines, including local service on Wilshire Blvd. between downtown and Fairfax Ave.

BIG BIRD OVERTAKES THEM

Stork Beats Elevator, Ambulance and Auto

Her father's automobile, a police ambulance, hospital elevator, and finally a wheeled stretcher all figured as conveyances in the arrival of the daughter of Mr. and Mrs. Benton L. Moore early yesterday.

Mrs. Moore, en route to St. Vincent's Hospital from the family home at 11208 La Grange Ave., tugged at her frantic husband's sleeve as their car neared Wilshire Division police station. Moore made a quick stop and the party went on, faster, by ambulance. The stork drew apace on the three-story elevator ride at Georgia Street Receiving Hospital and finally flapped the little girl into the world as the stretcher rolled through the third-floor vestibule.

The harried Moores, who then departed by ambulance for St. Vincent's, had no name for their daughter, and didn't even know her weight.

Dr. Maurice Steinman and his aides attended the mobile event.

STORE TEETH GOOD TO STOP BULLETS, TOO

SAULT ST. MARIE, Ont., Feb. 28 (AP) — Police said George Hatfield put the barrel of a .22-caliber rifle in his mouth and pulled the trigger.

The bullet ran around the inside of his false teeth and came out of his mouth.

Dr. J. E. Grimby, who treated Hatfield for a cut tongue, said the man was alive because:

The bullet was 10 years old.

The false teeth were in its way.

The teeth were wrecked.

Six New York City Baking Companies Suspend Work

NEW YORK, Feb. 28 (AP)—It'll be crackers instead of bread and cake in many New York homes today as a result of the shutdown of six major baking companies which make 70% of the city's wrapped bread and cake.

An official of the New York State Food Merchants Association said that several other companies still are producing white bread.

A strike order by the AFL Teamsters Union against the Continental Baking Co.—effective last midnight—led the five other companies to suspend operations.

THE WEATHER

U.S. Weather Bureau forecast: Partly cloudy today, becoming cloudy with rain late this afternoon and tonight. Showers tomorrow. Slightly warmer today, with high near 64. Cooler tomorrow. Highest temperature yesterday, 61; lowest, 49.

Child Rearing Failure Laid to 'Fool Parents'

SAN FRANCISCO, Feb. 28 (AP)—The chief reason for failure in child rearing, said a Duke University specialist today, may be described in three blunt words: "damn fool parents."

The speaker was Dr. Leslie B. Hohman, neuropsychiatrist and author of numerous texts on child behavior. He was participating in a question and answer session at the conference of the International Council for Exceptional Children.

"They won't let you teach until you have had a good education," he remarked, "but you can have children with not a day of education."

Average parents "do not enjoy spending time with their children while they are learning," and hence are to blame for the children's failures, he declared.

Editor-Poet Towne Dies

NEW YORK, Feb. 28 (AP)—Charles Hanson Towne, 72, editor, poet and author, died tonight.

Towne had been editor of Harper's Bazaar, Smart Set magazine and McClure's magazine. He also conducted a daily literary column in the old New York American.

Pope Names Observer

New York Times

ROME, Feb. 28—Pope Pius XII appointed a permanent observer of the Holy See to the Food and Agriculture Organization of the United Nations in the person of Msgr. Louis Ligutti, secretary-general of the National Catholic Rural Life Conference of the United States.

FIVE MORE CLERICS CONFESS FOR REDS

SOFIA, Feb. 28 (AP)—Proceedings speeded up in Bulgaria's spy trial today as five more Protestant churchmen pleaded guilty and asked for a chance to work for the Communist-controlled government.

Their confessions were entered at the rate of one every 45 minutes. So routine has the pattern of self-denunciation become that spectators in the courtroom dozed.

Eight defendants in all have entered pleas of guilty to charges of spying for the United States and Britain, treason and black market money dealings since the trial began Friday. Seven others still must plead.

Those who appeared on the stand today were the Rev. Georgi Chernov, 46; the Rev. Lambri Mishkov, 41; the Rev. Georgi Vassev, 48; the Rev. Haralan Popov, 41, and the Rev. Ioncho Drianov, 41. Vassev is a Baptist and Mishkov a Congregationalist. The other three belong to the Pentecost Church.

Chernov testified he and other pastors had delivered information to American on Russian troop movements and on military and economic developments.

He said he had been ordered to collect espionage data by Cyril Black, former secretary in the United States political mission here. He claimed he had talked with Black during the period from November, 1944, to the middle of 1945.

American and British authorities in Sofia have rejected all charges made by the defendants in their court relations. (Black, now a professor at Princeton University.

Turn to Page 6, Column 4

Clay Advisers May Leave Germany With General

BERLIN, Feb. 28 (AP)—Gen. Lucius D. Clay disclosed tonight that he has asked to be retired from his duties as United States Military Governor of Germany.

It appears there may be a complete change in American administration here by early summer. Clay's retirement would certainly be followed by wholesale resignations among the top advisers in the military government.

Three generals have been mentioned as possible successors. They are: Gen. Mark Clark, former Military Governor of Austria; Lt. Gen. Walter Bedell Smith, who has asked to be relieved of his post as Ambassador to Moscow, and Lt. Gen. Albert C. Wedemeyer.

No Action on Request

Clay told a news conference in Frankfurt that he had no information about who might succeed him. He pointed out that Washington had not yet acted on his retirement request, submitted several months ago. The general asked to be freed from his duties here "at the earliest moment the government felt it could release me."

In Washington Secretary of the Army Royall said today no decision had been made either on Clay's retirement or on the appointment of a successor.

Symbol of Resistance

Clay has become a symbol of resistance to Soviet pressure in Germany. This has been one of the chief factors in the general's staying here.

Even now the Russians would propagandize Clay's retirement as a victory for them. However, the air lift to blockaded Berlin symbolizes American policy at present, and Clay's retirement would not have the adverse effect on German morale now it would have had last year.

Authoritative sources revealed that consideration is being given to the meeting of the American, British and French Foreign Ministers to hammer out a detailed co-ordinated policy for the Western German state.

PART 1

Los Angeles Times

EQUAL RIGHTS

LIBERTY UNDER THE LAW — TRUE INDUSTRIAL FREEDOM

ALL THE NEWS ALL THE TIME

VOL. LXVIII | IN FOUR PARTS | CC ★ | MONDAY MORNING, MAY 23, 1949 | 52 PAGES | DAILY, SEVEN CENTS

New Rioting Flares in Berlin Rail Strike

Jeering Mob Stones 200 Soviet Guards

BY DANIEL DE LUCE

BERLIN, May 23 (Monday) (AP)—New rioting flared today in Berlin's railway strike and the American military commander called a meeting with the French and British commanders to "deal with the intolerable situation."

Shooting broke out early today in the railyards a few hundred yards west of the Charlottenburg station. British sector police said 25 Communist strikebreakers stormed a signal tower and transformer plant occupied by anti-Communist strikers and drove them out.

Red Guards Stoned

Just after midnight a crowd of 1000 jeering strikers and sympathizers stoned about 200 guards of the Soviet-controlled railway system who had barricaded themselves in the Zoo Station, about a mile from the Charlottenburg Station. Both stations are in the British sector. The crowd was pushed back by British sector police.

Brig Gen. Frank Howley, the American commandant in Berlin, asked his colleagues to meet later today.

"This intolerable situation requires our attention," he said. "This is no longer just a matter between the Soviet-controlled Reichbahn (railroad) management and the workers. The management has used strikebreakers and armed police and threatened to discharge permanently all strikers."

Strike in Third Day

The strike went into its third day. Sporadic clashes yesterday between armed Soviet sector railway police and the strikers and sympathizers had wounded and injured at least 20 persons. West Berlin police said there had been no deaths from the rioting.

There were unconfirmed reports that the Allied commandants would order their troops to assume control of all rail installations in Western Berlin. The headquarters of the American Armored Constabulary Squadron said it had received no alert order.

The strike started over demands by the workers that they be paid in west marks instead of east marks, which have one-fourth the value of west marks.

Hit By Red Paper

The official Soviet army newspaper here, Taegliche Rundschau, called the suspension of traffic due to the strike "a criminal act against West Berlin." It described those who have been trying to break the strike as "duty-true" rail workers who have been the target of rowdies and West Berlin police.

Howley and British Maj. Gen. G. K. Bourne, in whose sectors all strike violence has been concentrated, met informally last night with Ferdinand Friedensburg, acting Lord Mayor of Western Berlin.

It was reported unofficially the Western Berlin government would go on record as requesting Allied intervention.

One possible action by the Kommandatura—the three power governing body—would be to order the Soviet-controlled railway police from installations in Western Berlin and make the

Turn to Page 9, Column 3

SOVIET ZONE POLICEMEN GIVE UP TO WESTERNERS

BERLIN, May 22 (AP)—Fifteen Russian-controlled police, tired of firing on fellow Germans, voluntarily surrendered to western sector police and turned in their arms. The strikers had told them the Soviet Union and its German backers were working against Germany.

The policemen who surrendered had been on duty at the Charlottenburg Station, scene of the day's most serious outbreak. They had watched their fellow officers fire into a crowd of 300 strikers.

The strikers had been cleared from the station earlier. They surged back, however, and tried to storm a train bringing men, women and children from the Soviet sector to occupy elevated railway stations already wrested from the strikers.

Big Three in Paris Chart United Front

BY WES GALLAGHER

PARIS, May 22 (AP)—Big Four Foreign Ministers who meet here tomorrow to seek a German settlement may seize a favorable opportunity to explore a broader armistice in the cold war, diplomats said today.

Those explorations might deal with Greece, Austria, China and the atomic question. At best, however, they would be only on an informal basis.

The Foreign Ministers of the United States, Britain and France completed their preconference strategy meetings today.

In an hour and a half they gave final approval to a series of recommendations for a united western front in the negotiations with Soviet Foreign Minister Vishinsky on Germany. Germany is the only subject on the formal agenda.

Advisers Meet

The recommendations had been prepared in week-long meetings by the leading political and economic advisers of U.S. Secretary of State Acheson, British Foreign Secretary Bevin and French Foreign Minister Schuman.

The nature of the joint policy and strategy will not unfold until after the conference opens.

However, authoritative sources indicated it will include these basic points:

A firm stand in support of the West German state.

Opposition to any Russian proposal for withdrawal of occupation troops.

Attempt to secure an iron-clad agreement with Russia on Berlin.

Demand that Eastern Germany hold a free democratic election under four-power control before East German representatives are recognized as bargaining agents.

Demand that postwar changes in Germany's eastern frontiers—in favor of Poland—be considered provisional until confirmed by a peace conference.

Favors Short Session

Determination not to allow the conference to be used as a Soviet propaganda sounding board. The American delegation favors ending the meeting in three weeks unless a definite agreement is in sight by then.

In general, the western Foreign Ministers are agreed not to compromise on any proposal which would promote Communism in the west. They feel that the rapid economic and political recovery of West Germany and East Germany's decline have put them in a strong bargaining position.

One western source summed it up:

"Before we were always seeking some compromise to reach an agreement. This time the shoe is on the other foot."

Crash of Hot-Rod Racers Kills Three, Injures One

"Hot rod" racing at El Mirage Dry Lake, 20 miles west of Victorville, brought death yesterday to three Los Angeles men. Two of the men died instantly and the third died in an ambulance on the way to the San Bernardino County Hospital.

A fourth man was seriously injured.

The men who died were Rulon McGregor, 21, of 5860 S Grand Ave.; Robert Fadave, 22, of 5129 S Van Ness Ave., and Jackson R. Pendleton, 21, of 3874 S Sycamore Ave. Seriously injured was John Cuthbert, 18, of 5763½ S Western Ave.

According to a report to the San Bernardino County Sheriff's office, McGregor, returning to the starting point after completing a run on the speed course, crashed into the side of a racer driven by Fadave.

Dep. County Coroner Edward P. Doyle said that the information given him was to the effect that both cars were traveling between 60 and 90 miles an hour when they hit.

Fadave had completed three runs by himself and had picked up Pendleton and Cuthbert. McGregor and Pendleton were instantly killed. Fadave died in the ambulance.

Cutnbert was taken to the San Bernardino County Hospital. He is to be transferred to the Queen of the Angels Hospital later.

FORD CO. INSPECTOR SLAIN BY SHOTGUN

WINDSOR, Ont., May 22 (U.P.)—A Ford Motor Company inspector was slain by a shotgun blast through a kitchen window of his home early today in a shooting similar to the attempt on the life of Walter P. Reuther, president of the CIO United Auto Workers' Union.

William D. Allen, 37, was killed by an unidentified assailant as he sat at the kitchen table drinking coffee and reading a newspaper. His murderer jammed a shotgun through the window screen and fired into Allen's head at a distance of seven feet.

Reuther was shot in a similar manner April 20, 1948. He was standing in the kitchen of his home, eating a late evening snack, when a shotgun blast through a window hit him in the side and arm. The union leader still carries his arm in a brace.

Police said there was no apparent connection between the shooting and the present Ford strike.

They also discounted theories that Reuther's assailant, who is still at large, was involved in the Allen shooting.

Allen was alone in the kitchen. His wife Del and their small child Lorraine, 10, were asleep at the time. The killer fired from a small veranda outside the window.

Allen died two hours later at Grace Hospital. Police said his family could give no motive for the crime, and Allen's assailant left no clues.

FEATURES INDEX

Archery, Ancient Sport, Flourishes

Hundreds of archers from California and other States take part in tournament sponsored by Desert Bow Hunters at Barstow. See Page 4, Part I.

On Other Pages

New Areas Blasted by Tornadoes

Week-End Toll 46 Dead, 229 Injured; Damage in Millions

BY THE ASSOCIATED PRESS

A new blast of tornadoes and windstorms broke out in widely scattered areas of the country yesterday. The storms followed on the heels of a series of twisters which whipped the Midwest Saturday night.

They raised the week-end death toll to 46, and the number of injured to more than 229. Property damage ran into millions.

Illustrated on Page 3, Part I.

More than 900 homes were smashed, trees were ripped up by their roots and communications lines were severed.

Saturday Victims

Most of the dead were victims of the Saturday night twisters which tore at sections of Missouri, Indiana, Illinois, Iowa, and Kentucky.

The dead included: 21 at Cape Girardeau, Mo.; 8 at Shelburn, Ind.; 5 at Wood River, Ill.; 4 at Palestine, Ill.; two at Terre Haute, Ind.; 1 at Clay City, Ind., and 1 each at Clarksville, Bessville and Cabool, Mo.

Yesterday a young mother was killed in Somerset, Ky., where a severe storm caused property damage estimated at near $750,000.

Man Electrocuted

A Johnstown (Pa.) man was electrocuted when he tried to dislodge a wire blown down on the sidewalk during a storm. Damage here was estimated in the thousands.

Two tornadoes struck yesterday in Abilene, Tex., and its surroundings, injuring four persons and flattening half a dozen homes. A wind, hail and rain storm injured two more persons near Texarkana and damaged houses and barns.

Another twister battered crops at Hawley, 10 miles north of Abilene.

A storm described as a "baby tornado" hit near Reading, Pa., last night, cutting off electricity in more than a dozen communities. Roofs were whipped up and trees flattened by the winds.

West Virginia Hit

Another violent storm hit Charleston, W.Va., leaving an estimated damage of hundreds of thousands of dollars. No one was injured.

Zelienople, Pa., felt the force of a twister Sunday which tore down trees, lifted roofs, and cut off electricity. There were no casualties.

Heavy winds bore down on scattered sections of Western and Central Pennsylvania, blowing down or uprooting hundreds of trees. Altoona reported it had one of the worst storms in years. Large hailstones accompanied the wind in many places. There were no injuries.

Hailstones as big as baseballs pelted Lynchburg, Va., yesterday. Pedestrians scurried for cover,

Turn to Page 12, Column 3

Bakers Strike Threat Ended by Wage Pact

A threatened strike at 19 baking companies here was averted when members of Bakers Union 37 accepted a pay rise offer by the Baking Industry Council, it was announced yesterday by Robert F. Callender, industry spokesman.

The industry offered pay increases of 10 cents an hour in most categories and 5 cents an hour in a minor department. Earlier union members had given executive committee power to call a strike, but instructed the executive board to continue negotiations which culminated in yesterday's agreement.

Bakery wages, before the increase, range from 92 cents an hour for inexperienced work to a high of $1.90 an hour.

THE WEATHER

United States Weather Bureau forecast: Mostly clear today and tomorrow except patches early morning fog near coast. High today near 87, slightly cooler tomorrow. Highest temperature yesterday, 87; lowest, 55.

Forrestal's Suicide Leap Brings Inquiry by Navy

SCENE—Broken line shows path body of former Secretary of Defense Forrestal took in death plunge from 16th floor to ledge of Naval Hospital, Bethesda, Md. Arrow points to room from which he walked to jumpoff spot. (AP) Wirephoto

Ex-Defense Chief Left Unattended in Hospital

WASHINGTON, May 22 (AP)—Former Defense Secretary James Forrestal committed suicide today, plunging from a high hospital window.

In his room he left a book of Greek poetry, a page opened to a quotation saying "when reason's day sets rayless—joyless—quenched in cold decay, better to die and sleep."

The 57-year-old Forrestal was found dead on a third-floor ledge below the 16th floor window from which he had dropped at a nearby naval hospital in suburban Bethesda, Md.

A cord from a bathrobe was found knotted tightly about the neck.

Navy Orders Inquiry Tomorrow

The Navy quickly ordered a board of inquiry to study the case. It will begin work tomorrow. The order was issued by Rear Adm. Morton D. Willicutts, chief medical officer at the hospital.

Apparently the board's job will be to determine, among other things, why Forrestal was left unattended long enough for him to reach the window. He entered the hospital seven weeks ago in a condition described as nervous exhaustion resulting from overwork. He recently was reported greatly improved.

Official Statement

An official statement by the hospital said:

"Mr. James Forrestal took his own life at the U.S. Naval Hospital, Bethesda, Md., at 2 a.m., by climbing out of window adjacent to his room on the 16th floor.

"He was dressed in a dressing gown with the sash from the gown wrapped around his neck. The noise from falling body was heard by nurse on seventh floor and immediately reported. The body was found on the roof of the passageway of the third floor. He was wearing a wrist watch which is still running.

"He was recently believed improving, was allowed visitors by his own request and free use of the telephone. The book, 'An Anthology of World Poetry,' was lying on the radiator beside his bed and had been opened to the poem, 'Chorus From Ajax,' dealing with death and the grave."

President Shocked and Grieved

President Truman was "inexpressably shocked and grieved" when told of the death of his former high-ranking Cabinet officer. He said, "This able and devoted public servant was as truly a casualty of the war as if he had died on the firing line."

Forrestal was admitted to the hospital April 2 in "a state of excessive fatigue" and suffering nervous exhaustion. This was only five days after he left the Defense Secretary's post.

Lately he was reported steadily improving. He had gained weight and seen visitors. President Truman dropped in May 6 and chatted with him, the White House said.

When he arrived, Forrestal was assigned what normally was a double room in the tower of the skyscraper building. However, the room had been converted into a suite. An orderly or doctor customarily was on duty and at the time of the suicide a doctor was in the next room, authorities said.

Declined Usual Sedative

The large windows in Forrestal's room were enclosed with heavy wire screening, locked down. Across a corridor is a diet kitchen.

From the official statement and from subsequent comment by Rear Adm. Leslie Stone, commandant of the hospital, this is what appears to have happened:

Forrestal earlier in the evening had declined to take his usual sedative.

At the moment when no one was present, he left his room, using a door opening directly onto the corridor and avoiding the exit through the second room of the suite where the doctor was located.

Suicide Plan Not Clear

He crossed the corridor to the diet kitchen, removed the cord of his bathrobe and knotted it tightly about his throat. (It was unclear immediately whether he may have contemplated attaching the cord to a radiator and then leaping from the window to hang himself—or whether he actually did tie it only to have it jerk loose. Nor could it be determined before autopsy whether any degree of strangulation occurred before his body plummeted down to the narrow offset at the third floor.)

Navy nurses and corpsmen were on duty throughout the hospital.

The poem which Forrestal apparently read in the last moments of his life was the brooding, tragic "Chorus From Ajax" by Sophocles, great Grecian poet of tragedy.

It cries of despair . . . "comfortless, nameless, hopeless—save in the dark prospect of the yawning grave" . . . "The deeds that he hath done seem hostile all to hostile eyes" . . . "Better to die, and sleep the never waking sleep, than linger on, and dare to live, when the soul's life is gone."

Talking to reporters, White

Turn to Page 2, Column 3

FLAGS LOWERED FOR FORRESTAL

WASHINGTON, May 22 (U.P.)—President Truman today proclaimed a period of national mourning for former Defense Secretary James Forrestal.

He directed that as a mark of respect to the former Cabinet officer's memory, the national Flag be displayed at half-staff on all public buildings, naval stations, ships at sea and at military installations until after Forrestal's funeral.

SENATOR DEMANDS LILIENTHAL GET OUT

Hickenlooper, Who Supported Atomic Chief's Appointment, Attacks His Management

WASHINGTON, May 22 (AP)—Sen. Hickenlooper (R) Ia., today demanded that David E. Lilienthal resign as chairman of the Atomic Energy Commission for "incredible mismanagement." Lilienthal promptly replied that the nation's atomic "pre-eminence" is the answer to the Senator's "vague and ungenerous wholesale indictment."

Hickenlooper said "our atomic program is suffering from equivocation, misplaced emphasis and waste" since Lilienthal took over two and a half years ago.

Hickenlooper is the ranking Republican member of the Senate-House Committee on Atomic Energy and was its Chairman during the last GOP-controlled Congress. He fought hard for Lilienthal's confirmation when the latter's qualifications were challenged on the Senate floor two years ago.

Sharp Contrast

Lilienthal said that in sharp contrast to the situation when the civilian commission took over, production of atomic weapons is secure, raw material supplies have increased and morale has been restored.

He made no direct reference to Hickenlooper's demand that he resign. Nor did he mention the Senator's charge that he had "sneered" at Congress' concern over the disappearance of a quantity of uranium-235.

The Senator took issue with the Commission as to the significance of that disappearance. The Commission said no theft or loss was involved and that the quantity would not be helpful to an enemy.

Hickenlooper said the amount was "a vast quantity" so far as scientists are concerned.

He added that Lilienthal was wrong when he said earlier there was no suspician of theft or espionage.

"This is completely untrue,"

Turn to Page 9, Column 5

Mercury Hits 87; Beaches Busy

Southland beaches yesterday basked in the weather spotlight as temperatures in downtown Los Angeles reached a peak of 87 deg.

Thousands of persons flocked to the beaches, despite recurrent rip tides in many sections. Lifeguards at the Hermosa-Redondo-Manhattan beach area reported 161 rescues and exceptionally strong rip tides set whirlpools eddying to snare unwary swimmers.

Zuma Beach also reported moderately strong rip tides with 10 rescues reported. One of these rescues was a triple-save, effected by Lifeguards William Jay and Nate Shargo. They pulled from the water Joanne Gilbert, 19, of 838 E Providence St., Burbank; Isabel Corbett, 22, of 79 Olmsted Drive, Glendale, and Bob Levand, 23, of 500 N Paula St., Glendale.

Artificial resuscitation was necessary to revive John Goldston, 27, of 2552 Ellendale Place, after he was rescued off 14th St. in Hermosa Beach, where at one time 15 persons were endangered in a rip-tide whirlpool.

Yesterday's minimum temperature downtown was 55. The Weather Bureau predicted fair weather for today and tomorrow.

Sen. Watson's Widow Dies in Washington

WASHINGTON, May 22 (U.P.)—Mrs. James E. Watson, widow of the Indiana Senator who figured prominently in national politics in the turbulent days of 1929-1933, died here tonight.

COLOR PRINT OFFER DETAILED

Details of The Times' color print offer appear on Page 4, Part III.

Color print coupon is published on Page 2, Part I.

Eight Escape Death as Two Cars Explode

Five women and three children miraculously escaped serious injury yesterday although they were seated in two automobiles that exploded in fire after an accident at Los Angeles St. and Sunset Blvd.

Witnesses told police flames from gasoline spilled in the accident shot higher than the tops of the buildings surrounding the old Plaza and Olvera St.

Officers J. V. Redmond and G. N. Riley said the explosion occurred some minutes after the accident. Either a cigarette was carelessly tossed into the spilled gasoline or it was ignited by the exhaust of a passing car, they believed.

Crash at Stop

They said an automobile driven by Claude Frazier, 27, of Santa Paula, containing five adults and two children, crashed into the rear of an automobile driven by James Kitchen, 1611 N Orange Drive, which had stopped for a traffic light.

Frazier and Kitchen and a third man, Charles Huber, left the cars to examine the damage.

Gasoline in a great pool was spread over the intersection.

Frazier told the officers suddenly everything erupted in flame and smoke.

"Like a volcano," he said.

Saved by Strollers

Sunday Plaza strollers and the three men rushed to the cars and pulled from the flaming wreckage:

Kitchen's wife Anita and their 13-year-old daughter Barbara Jean from the first car.

Frazier's wife Verna; his mother, Mrs. G. M. Frazier; Huber's wife Mildred, all of Santa Paula, and Mrs. Evelyn Milton and her two children, Maxine, 2, and Billy, 5, of Baytown, Tex., in the second car.

Mrs. Anita Kitchen was taken to Georgia Street Receiving Hospital for treatment for a bruised head received when the explosion drove her against the automobile roof.

Seven fire-fighting companies under Batt. Chief Ralph Watson answered the call.

PART 1

Los Angeles Times

EQUAL RIGHTS
LIBERTY UNDER THE LAW — TRUE INDUSTRIAL FREEDOM

ALL THE NEWS
ALL THE TIME

VOL. LXVIII | IN FIVE PARTS | CC ★ | THURSDAY MORNING, JULY 21, 1949 | 72 PAGES | DAILY, SEVEN CENTS

ALL-OUT WAR OPENED ON GANGS

Rioting Breaks Out in Hawaii Strike

Pickets and Nonstrikers Battle; Governor Summons Legislature

HONOLULU, July 20 (U.P.)—Violence flared in the first major outbreak in the Hawaiian water-front strike today.

Three policemen and 26 men were injured when massed pickets of the CIO longshoremen's union and nonunion stevedores clashed.

Police, called out for the third time in the history of the dock tie-up, took 38 of an estimated 300 pickets off to jail after an offshoot of about 200 of them broke through the gates of a newly formed stevedoring company and began smashing windows in protest to employment of nonunion dock gangs.

Held Without Bail

Those arrested were held without bail.

Police Capt. Eugene Kennedy said the raid by about 300 pickets was directed by loudspeaker from an ILWU sound truck.

"Get the cops first," was one of the instructions broadcast, Kennedy said.

Members of the striking International Longshoremen's and Warehousemen's Union attacked as the nonunion stevedores were climbing aboard busses to take them to a pier where the Isthmian freighter, Steel Flyer, is being unloaded.

Strikers and nonstrikers milled around. Fist fights broke out in various groups. Clubs were swung. Police charged into the fray and ultimately separated the two groups.

Special Session Called

At the same time, Territorial Gov. Stainback announced he has called a special session of the Hawaiian Legislature for next Tuesday to "consider such legislation as shall be deemed necessary to meet the present waterfront emergency and such other legislation as shall be deemed in the public interest."

The less seriously injured included 16 nonunion men, the three policemen and six union men.

Seven stevedoring company employees and one policeman were injured seriously enough to require hospitalization.

Despite the fight, more than 100 nonunion dock hands went to work on the Steel Flyer and the company reportedly planned to unload another Isthmian freighter, the Steel Scientist, next.

Police Reinforced

The new company, Hawaii Stevedores, Ltd., was formed two weeks ago and the ILWU charged it was organized for the purpose of strike breaking.

Only five policemen were on hand when the riot started but 30 reinforcements arrived within a few minutes and managed to end the battle in about 20 minutes.

Company President Ray Adelmeyer estimated that more than 200 strikers were in the attacking party. Three got through the gate in the fence surrounding the small office building on Ala Moana Blvd. and started swinging fists, he said.

As if by signal, he said, the rest of the strikers scrambled over the fence and moved in swinging fists and clubs and throwing bricks through the windows. Eight windows in the office were broken and windows were also smashed in eight automobiles owned by company officials and employees.

[For Kyle Palmer's article on Hawaiian strike turn to Page 10, Part I.]

A-BOMB HER SECRET TOO, CANADA SAYS

OTTAWA, July 20 (U.P.)—Canada, on the basis of information already in her possession, could go ahead and make an atom bomb on her own if she wanted to, acting Prime Minister C. D. Howe told a press conference today.

"We could make a bomb if we wanted to—maybe not as good as the American one—but a good bomb, nevertheless," he said.

Howe emphasized, however, that Canada is not interested in producing atom bombs, but rather in converting atomic energy to peacetime uses.

Making Good Progress

"We're making good progress in our research (mainly at Chalk River, Ont.) and those are the important fields for us," he added.

Howe made his comments in reply to questioning on Canada's attitude towards the current top-secret atomic energy discussions of United States officials in Washington.

Exchanging Information

With respect to the talks, Howe said:

"We have nothing to say about them. We certainly haven't provoked the meetings because Canada has asked for no information on atomic energy from the United States.

"We're still selling uranium ores to the United States, and we're still exchanging certain classified information on atomic research and developments," Howe said.

THIS IS REAL NEWS!

Civics Teacher Wants to Pay More Taxes

The Board of Equalization got the surprise of its life yesterday when a taxpayer asked an increase .instead of a reduction in his property assessment.

He is George K. Roth, instructor in American history and government at John Muir College, Pasadena. Outlining the reasons for the unusual request, he told the Board:

"Last year I made a protest about the inaccurate figure of $25 assessed on my lot on Seaview Ave. This year it was increased to $400. That is not enough. It is still not equalized with surrounding values.

"The lot is worth $1000 on today's market and should be assessed at $500. There is no reason for any taxpayer to try to avoid taxes rightfully owed."

After listening to Roth's argument, Board Chairman Leonard J. Roach said:

"The only thing we are interested in is whether your lot was evaluated by the assessor on a basis comparable to surrounding properties."

This is exactly what was done, Asst. Assessor Jack Hartman assured the Board.

FEATURES INDEX

Ground Broken for New $25,000,000 Plant Here

Ground is broken for new $25,000,000 Lever Bros. Co. plant at Anaheim-Telegraph Road and Washington Blvd. Page 1, Part II.

On Other Pages

TARGETS—Only an hour after this picture was made in the predawn yesterday as Mickey Cohen, right, and Harry Cooper left Continentale Cafe on Santa Monica Blvd., the two went down in a heap as gunmen opened up on them outside Sherry's Restaurant, 9030 Sunset Blvd. Cooper, special agent whom Atty. Gen. Howser had ordered as a bodyguard for Cohen, was badly wounded. Cohen's right shoulder was torn by a shotgun slug.
Times photo

Board Delays SP Rail Strike

SAN FRANCISCO, July 20 (AP) J. J. Corcoran, general chairman of the Brotherhood of Railway Trainmen, announced today that in accordance with President Truman's creation of an emergency board, the strike called against the Southern Pacific Railway was being postponed 60 days.

This would be 60 days from the date originally set for the strike—Friday, July 22, Corcoran said.

The President created the emergency board to investigate the dispute between the Brotherhood and the railway.

Mercury Hits 85 Third Day

It hit 85 again downtown yesterday—for the third consecutive day. But desert areas did not fare so well temperature-wise.

Away from the moderating ocean breezes, Silverlake shimmered and baked at 112 deg., El Centro at 109 and Indio at 111. Daggett reported 103 deg. and Bakersfield 99.

Smog again plagued the Civic Center, with visibility ranging from 2 to 5 miles most of the day. Humidity was higher than earlier in the week—55% at noon. Look for fog and low clouds early today, with slightly warmer weather this afternoon, the forecaster said.

U.S. FAMILY INCOME RISES 14% IN YEAR

WASHINGTON, July 20 (U.P.)—Family income in 1948 rose to a median of $3320 but only $3000 was left after Federal income taxes, the government estimated today.

The 1948 level was nearly 14% above the 1947 median of $2920, and compared with $2600 in 1946, according to a Federal Reserve Board survey.

New England Storm Takes Seven Lives

BOSTON, July 20 (AP)—Southern New England sweltered all day through temperatures that reached as high as 99 deg. and then, in an abrupt change, was lashed tonight by a triple-threat storm of lightning, rain and hail.

At least seven deaths were reported as a result of the storm.

Rain, wind and hail caused damage that may run as high as $1,000,000 to the expensive Connecticut Valley tobacco crop.

Fires caused by lightning damaged scores of buildings.

In Salem, Mass., a bolt flashed into a group of tanks containing 400,000 gallons of gasoline and fuel oil. The fires it started brought out all available fire-fighting equipment and for a time threatened a nearby tenement district.

HOWSER EX-AIDE FACES U.S. CHARGE

Lentz Accused of Offering Witness Cash in Attorney General's Suit Against Pearson

Walter H. Lentz, former chief investigator for Atty. Gen. Howser, yesterday was arraigned before a U.S. commissioner at Fresno on a complaint charging him with interfering with and obstructing justice in connection with Howser's libel suit against Columnist Drew Pearson.

The complaint was issued by U.S. Commissioner Frank Lerrigo at the request of U.S. Atty. James M. Carter, who charged that Lentz had "caused money to be offered" to James Thomas Mulloy of Fresno "to influence Mulloy's testimony" in a libel suit Howser had brought against Pearson.

Payment Charged

The suit was based on the alleged quotation of a charge by Mulloy, which the latter reiterated in a U.S. District Court deposition in Washington, to the effect that he, Mulloy, once gave Howser an envelope containing 12 $100 bills which he had received from a Long Beach bookmaker.

The charges on which the complaint was issued are to the effect that Lentz sought, by offers of money, to have Mulloy change this story, Carter said at Fresno yesterday. He would not elaborate further, however, on how much money Lentz "caused to be offered" to Mulloy or the source of the information leading to issuance of the complaint.

Lentz resigned last Dec. 31 with Howser's official blessing. The Attorney General at that time issued a statement saying, "I wish him well in his new anticipated venture. His resignation at this time is of his own election." The private venture, Lentz disclosed some weeks later, was opening of a private detective agency with headquarters in Long Beach.

Went With Howser

Lentz, former Long Beach police chief, was named by Howser as head of his investigative staff as District Attorney in October, 1944.

When Howser became Attorney General, Lentz resigned from the District Attorney's staff here to head the Attorney General's special agents.

THE WEATHER

United States Weather Bureau forecast: Night and early morning low clouds and fog otherwise clear today and tomorrow. Little change in temperature. High today near 84. Highest temperature yesterday, 85; lowest, 64.

Shooting of Cohen Stirs Huge Man Hunt; Howser Tells of Tip-off

Law enforcement agencies rallied against a bold upsurge of gangsterism in Los Angeles yesterday following the shotgun wounding of Mobster Mickey Cohen and three other persons in the Sunset Strip.

While a man hunt spread for the gunmen who blasted at the local underworld kingpin, an aroused citizenry demanded protection against the rising tide of crime typified by the gangland assassination attempt.

Developments included:

1—A top-level "policy" conference called by Atty. Gen. Howser in the State Building and attended by Sheriff Biscailuz, Chief of Police Worton, Dist. Atty. Simpson, Undersheriff Arthur C. Jewell, Sheriff's Inspector Gordon Bowers, Asst. Chief of Police Joe Reed, Dep. Chief Thad Brown, Asst. Atty. Gen. Kenneth Lynch, Asst. Atty. Gen. Mike Riordan, Chief Special Agent George Griffin, Asst. Dist. Atty. John Barnes and Herbert R. Van Brunt, of the Governor's Commission for the Study of Organized Crime.

[Other news and pictures of Cohen shooting on Pages 2, 3, 4, 5, 6 and 7, Part I.]

Commission's Aid Sought

2—A demand by Councilman Kenneth Hahn that the Crime Commission be requested to work with Worton to "provide the public fullest protection."

3—Announcement by Harry A. Lawson, foreman of the grand jury, that the panel may subpoena Howser to learn why he requested the Police Department, Sheriff's office and the District Attorney's office to "lay off" Cohen while he was accompanied by a State Department of Justice special agent.

4—Disclosure by Howser that his office had "specific information" of a plan to assassinate Cohen and was investigating extensively gangsterism and matters pertaining to the jury's vice inquiry.

5—Announcement by Adm. William E. Standley, chairman of the Crime Commission, that a meeting of that group will be called "as soon as possible" to consider circumstances surrounding the assassination attempt.

6—Persistent reports that Cohen, at liberty under $100,000 bond after indictment on conspiracy charges several weeks ago, is the target of "eastern interests" which are attempting to "move in" on Los Angeles.

7—Queen of Angels Hospital, where the wounded persons are under treatment, last night received a telephoned warning to "be on guard—we're going to get Mickey tonight." Although the threat was discounted by detectives, three homicide squad officers were assigned to the hospital a short time later.

Others Wounded

Cohen and his companions were shot outside Sherry's Restaurant, 9039 Sunset Blvd., at 3:55 a.m. Also wounded in the fusillade of slugs were:

Harry Cooper, 39, special agent for Howser assigned to guard Cohen a week ago. The former California highway patrolman received a slug in the liver and was reported in a serious condition.

Edward (Neddie) Herbert, 35, a Cohen henchman who escaped 11 shots from a gangland 45-caliber pistol last June 22. He was wounded in the kidney and spleen and was reported critical and in severe shock.

Woman's Condition Critical

Following surgery to remove his spleen, Herbert was reported in better condition, with a chance for life barring unforeseen complications.

The wounded henchman's wife arrived by plane from the East late last night and was met at Los Angeles Airport by Cohen's wife.

Mrs. Dee David, also known as Dee Davis, 26-year-old doctor's assistant and acquaintance of Cohen. She received three

Turn to Page 5, Column 1

WOUNDED GANG LEADER ADMITS HE IS SCARED

Mickey Cohen, wounded mob leader, gazed at the ceiling of his heavily guarded room in Queen of Angels Hospital last night and frankly admitted he is scared.

"I'm scared not only for myself, but for everyone around me—my wife, my friends, and even the law," he declared. "I don't know what to expect next. I wish I did."

Asked what he will do when he is able to leave the hospital, Cohen said he has no plans.

"I don't know what people want from me. Every time I've been shaken down lately I've had the feeling I was a 'sitting duck.'

"It would have been so easy for someone in a car to drive by and mow us all down.

"I hope I don't come any closer to death than I did this morning."

PART 1

Los Angeles Times

EQUAL RIGHTS
LIBERTY UNDER THE LAW — TRUE INDUSTRIAL FREEDOM

ALL THE NEWS
ALL THE TIME

VOL. LXVIII — IN FOUR PARTS — C C — FRIDAY MORNING, SEPTEMBER 30, 1949 — 48 PAGES — DAILY, SEVEN CENTS

KING'S NEPHEW WEDS—Posing for wedding picture at reception in St. James's Palace, London, are Earl of Harewood and bride, the former Marion Stein, Viennese commoner. Left to right are: Dowager Queen Mary; her daughter, the Princess Royal, mother of the bridegroom; the Earl and his bride; King George VI, Harewood's uncle; Hon. Gerald Lascelles, younger brother of the bridegroom and best man; and Queen Elizabeth.
(AP) Wirephoto

Horrall and Wellpott Freed in Vice Inquiry

Ex-Police Chief Acquitted of Perjury; Three Officers Still Must Face Trial

Two of five police officials indicted as the outcome of the county grand jury's vice graft investigation were freed of all charges, one by acquittal and one by dismissal without trial.

They are C. B. Horrall, retired Chief of Police charged with perjury, and Lt. Rudy Wellpott, former head of the administrative vice detail charged with perjury and bribery. Both were freed by Superior Judge Stanley N. Barnes.

Three other defendants face trial on the true bills. Sgt. E. V. Jackson, charged also with perjury and bribery, was denied dismissal with Wellpott on the ground that grand jury testimony of Brenda Allen, Hollywood panderer, provided sufficient basis for a hearing.

He was ordered to trial Nov. 14 before Judge Barnes.

Reed and Wisdom to Be Tried

Asst. Chief of Police Joseph F. Reed and Capt. Cecil M. Wisdom, named on perjury accusations with Horrall, were ordered to trial Nov. 9.

Judge Barnes, ruling favorably on a motion to quash the indictment against Wellpott, inferentially criticized the grand jury for returning the indictment with insufficient evidence and overstepping its legally constituted authority.

The jurist read all of the 2140-page grand jury transcript, he said, not only because of its importance to the community, the Police Department and the defendants, but because "there existed considerable difference of opinion between two law-enforcement bodies in this county."

"I speak of the grand jury and the District Attorney's office," he added.

The jurist commented that the "authority of the grand jury and its limitations are set up in the Penal Code and in Appellate Court decree." This gives the grand jury authority to indict, he continued, "when the evidence, if unexplained and uncorroborated, would warrant consideration."

These legal tenets provide for the exercise by the grand jury of judicial discretion within certain rules but does not allow arbitrary discretion, Judge Barnes remarked.

Such evidence, however, must be valid evidence, said the jurist, not any evidence whether incompetent, irrelevant or otherwise.

"Hearsay evidence is obviously not valid evidence within the rule," he observed.

Brenda Denies Bribery

Judge Barnes noted that Miss Allen, star witness before the grand jury, specifically denied to that body that Wellpott took money from her or had any transactions whatever with her. This, he added, was in marked contrast to her testimony involving Jackson and Sgt. Charles Stoker, suspended vice squad officer whose story of corruption touched off the jury's inquiry.

"There is no valid evidence that Wellpott was bribed," Judge Barnes said.

In denying a motion to quash Jackson's indictment, the jurist expressed doubt that Miss Allen could be considered an accomplice in bribery as charged by Russell Parsons, attorney for both Wellpott and Jackson.

Thus Miss Allen's testimony against Jackson provides a

Turn to Page 8, Column 1

MERCURY HITS 91 AS SMOG RETURNS

Heat and smog returned to plague Los Angeles yesterday—the former in moderation, the latter to an eye-smarting degree.

Peak 91 deg. temperature was hit at 1 p.m. Visibility downtown, around three miles most of the morning, was able to push only to four miles by midafternoon.

Beach areas were clear most of the day, the weatherman reported, forecasting clear and continued warm weather today. Clouds are expected tonight and cooler weather is in prospect for tomorrow.

Too Early for Rain

Forecaster A. K. Showalter, issuing his month-end roundup, reported 2-to-1 odds in favor of his fall and winter being wetter than any of the five preceding years.

"It still is too early to open the rainy season," he said cautiously, "but we can concede October about one chance in seven of producing more than one inch of rainfall and offer 10-to-1 odds that the month will produce measurable rainfall.

"October can be expected to have one or two days with strong desert winds, followed by warm days and clear, cool nights. Over the inland areas there is a good chance for sunshine during the month, but close to the coast there should be at least five mornings with thick fog."

THE WEATHER

U.S. Weather Bureau forecast: Clear and continued warm today. Clouds tonight. Cooler tomorrow. High today 88. Highest temperature yesterday, 91; lowest, 59.

MISS EUROPE GRANTS MALES LOOK LIKE CARY

ROME, Sept. 29 (AP)—Miss Europe of 1949, Juliette Figueras of Arles, France, today implied that American women don't know how lucky they are.

The 20-year-old brunet beauty had this to say about American men: "They're so strong and handsome. Nearly all of them seem to look like Cary Grant, my favorite movie actor."

Jobless Pay Frauds Bring 23 Convictions

Twenty-three persons were prosecuted by the Fraud and Investigation Section of the Department of Employment in local courts during the month of August for violation of the Unemployment Insurance Act.

Supervising Investigator R. C. Truesdale announced all cases resulted in convictions. Twenty-two cases involved claimants who accepted unemployment insurance benefits while gainfully employed and carried sentences ranging from probation to six months in the County Jail.

These criminal actions resulted in the recovery by the Department of $2650 paid in illegal claims. Truesdale urged anyone having knowledge of claimants drawing unemployment insurance benefits when not entitled to them to report to the Fraud and Investigation Section, Department of Employment, 1100 S Flower St.

Army Plane Crash Told

McCLEARY, Wash., Sept. 29 (U.P.)—An Army plane with three men aboard crashed four miles northeast of here after shearing off 1000 feet of treetops.

The craft apparently attempted to make an emergency landing on the McCleary airstrip, an unlighted emergency field.

Bookie 'Bumped' in Street Killing

DALY CITY, Cal., Sept. 20 (U.P.) Martin D. Breslauer, described by police as a "lay-off bookie," was executed here tonight in a typical gangland "ride" slaying.

A witness to the murder said Breslauer was shot down by two men who hustled him out of the rear seat of a sedan and pumped a bullet into him as he "hollered for help."

Investigating police said Breslauer had $3800 in his pockets when they examined his body. His own car was parked only a few feet from the scene of the killing.

Opera Singer Dies

CHICAGO, Sept. 29 (AP)—Madame Rosa Olitzka, 76, Metropolitan Opera Company contralto, died today of a heart attack.

Commoner Married to British Earl

LONDON, Sept. 29 (U.P.)—Marion Stein, Austrian refugee born in a room over a tobacco store in Vienna, was married to the wealthy Earl of Harewood, 11th in line for the British throne, today in a ceremony exceeded in pomp and popular excitement only by the wedding of Princess Elizabeth two years ago.

Wearing her royal mother-in-law's wedding veil, the pretty, 22-year-old pianist walked down the aisle of St. Mark's Church on the arm of her father, an employee of a music company, as the King and Queen and nearly all the rest of the royal family nodded their approval.

Cook Attends

The wedding guests ranged from the ruler of the British Empire to an old Viennese woman who cooked for the Stein family before they were forced to flee Austria in 1938 because of Hitler's racial laws.

Throngs of curious, cheering Britons broke through police lines for a glimpse of the girl who had captured Britain's handsome, blond, 26-year-old Earl of Harewood as she left her family's modest flat to become a countess and live like a queen in a royal palace.

Even King George, Queen Elizabeth and the Princesses Elizabeth and Margaret took a back seat as the crowds of persons who had started gathering at midnight wished the newlyweds "good luck."

FEATURES INDEX

Brooklyn Dodgers Grab Lead in Pennant Race

Brooklyn Dodgers grab lead in National League by winning double-header from the Boston Braves while St. Louis Cardinals lost to the Pittsburgh Pirates. The New York Yankees and Boston Red Sox remained tied for the American League pennant flag as both their games were rained out. Page 1, 2nd Section, Part I.

On Other Pages

Commons Backs Labor Cabinet

Vote of Confidence on Devaluation Won; Churchill Attacked

LONDON, Sept. 29 (U.P.) — The House of Commons tonight gave the Labor government a vote of confidence on its devaluation of the British pound sterling. The vote for the government motion was 342 to 5. The Conservatives and Liberals abstained.

The negative votes were cast by Communists and Independent Laborites.

Growing Reports

But the result, which was a certainty because of the big Labor majority in the House, did not quell the growing reports that the government will call a general election this autumn.

The expected vote came after a three-day debate during which the Labor government rejected opposition demands for early elections and suggested that Conservative Leader Winston Churchill "retire from public life."

The government motion gave approval to devaluation, to the agreements reached at the Washington conference and to the Socialist government's policy of maintaining full employment and the social services.

Churchill's motion of "no confidence" was defeated 350 to 212. It would have placed full blame for devaluation on "four years financial mismanagement" by the Laborites.

Challenge Rejected

Churchill called for an early election. But the Laborites temporarily rejected the challenge and turned instead to a bitter attack on Churchill.

Minister of Health Aneurin Bevan, a former coal miner and a bitter foe of Churchill, led the attack against the wartime Prime Minister in the debate.

The election flavor continued through the debate tonight to the last speaker, Prime Minister Attlee.

He denounced Churchill for his personal attack on Chancellor Sir Stafford Cripps and said Churchill stooped to "pettiness and meanness."

"But it will not harm the Chancellor," Attlee said. "It will devalue the right honorable gentleman (Churchill). Mr. Churchill's only suggestion was 'vote for me.'"

Attlee got a rousing cheer when he rose. His address was milder than that of Bevan.

Personal Attack

Bevan hurled a vitriolic personal attack at Churchill, denouncing him for offering "flatulent generalities" in his attack yesterday on the government and describing the Conservative leader as a discredited man who would be "flung aside like a soiled glove" if his party regained power.

"I welcome the opportunity for pricking this bloated bladder of lies upon the poignard (dagger) of truth," Bevan shouted, amid laughter from the Labor benches.

Meat Prices Decline 4%

CHICAGO, Sept. 29 (U.P.)—The American Meat Institute today reported a downward trend in retail meat prices.

Reports from Chicago retailers showed a price decline of 4% this week compared with last week, the AMI said.

Baby Girl Almost Drowns as Mother Answers Doorbell

A year-old baby almost drowned in a bathtub yesterday when her mother answered a doorbell.

The mother, Mrs. Martha A. Connor, pulled the drain plug to answer the call at her home, 1113 Pacific St., Santa Monica.

She thought her baby Kathleen would be all right for a few moments, but a washcloth plugged the drain. When Mrs. Connor returned the child was unconscious, face down in the water.

A neighbor, Mrs. Ann W. Summers, 1107 Pacific St., used artificial respiration for six minutes and the baby was conscious when firemen arrived.

PUZZLE CONTEST

Full details, rules and prize list of the Fun and Fortune contest appear on Page 2, Part II of today's Times.

Tokyo Rose Held Guilty by Treason Case Jury

MAN HURLED 20 FEET BY PLANE SEAT EJECTOR

A March Air Force Base crew chief was in Long Beach Naval Hospital yesterday with painful injuries received Wednesday when he accidentally triggered the ejector seat in a jet fighter and was blown some 20 feet in the air.

Explosion of the 37-mm. shell that arms the seat hurled Tech. Sgt. Vincent J. Didio, 30, through the half-open canopy and dropped him on the concrete flight apron in a shower of plexiglas.

He received a fractured shoulder, broken ribs, a compound fracture of the left knee and numerous cuts on the left leg.

Base spokesmen said Didio is attached to the 94th Fighter Squadron and explained he was working on the F-86 seat when the accident occurred. The seat is designed to hurl a pilot clear of the plane for an emergency bail-out aloft.

Normally a pilot could not accidentally trigger the mechanism because of a sequence procedure necessary to explode the charge, they said.

Didio's condition is reported "satisfactory."

Prison Term --or Death-- Awaited

SAN FRANCISCO, Sept. 29 (U.P.)—Mrs. Iva Toguri (Tokyo Rose) d'Aquino was found guilty of treason tonight.

A six-man, six-woman jury convicted the 33-year-old American-born defendant on one count of betraying her native land by broadcasting to GIs in the Pacific that they were "orphaned" by the sinking of their ships. The jurors had argued the case four days.

For turning traitor by becoming a Radio Tokyo wartime disk jockey, the defendant faces a minimum sentence of five years in prison and a $10,000 fine, or a maximum of death.

Sentence Awaited

She will be sentenced Oct. 6. The defense announced it will appeal the verdict.

In a poll of the jury all but one of the jurors answered "yes" without hesitation to the question: "Is that your verdict?"

Mrs. Flora E. Covell, Piedmont (Cal.) housewife, choked first and was told to "speak up." She answered "yes" in a strained voice.

The prosecution had never demanded the death penalty. It was believed unlikely that U.S. Judge Michael J. Roche would levy the extreme penalty against her. No convicted traitor has ever been put to death under the Federal law, although John Brown, of Harper's Ferry, was hanged under military law.

Iva Breaks Down

The verdict was delivered with stunning abruptness in a courtroom that had expected the jury to retire again for the fourth night.

The Los Angeles-born defendant, a zoology graduate of UCLA, stiffened momentarily as Court Clerk James Welsh read the jury's verdict finding her guilty of Overt Act 6—broadcasting concerning the loss of Allied shipping in Leyte Gulf.

Then she wilted completely and tears filled her eyes. The composure she maintained throughout the long trial with but two exceptions—both breakdowns under cross-examination—had been shattered during the long ordeal of waiting for the decision.

Loses Weight

She had lost about 30 pounds, from 130 down to 98. She was very pale as she was led out of court and back to the U.S. Marshal's office.

Judge Roche dismissed the jurors with the complimentary remark that they had shown "great sincerity, diligence and hard work."

The jury refused to disclose any details of the long deliberation.

Jury Foreman John Mann said the jurors had agreed among themselves to keep secret the results of balloting and how the jury stood at any time.

Jury Spokesman Robin Stevenson explained the technique that had kept the deliberators going so long. "We evolved a formula of law to apply to each overt act and then applied it," he said.

'BIG STEEL' PLANTS RESIST DEMANDS

Small Company Signs Pact With CIO as Deadline Nears for Industrial Halt

PITTSBURGH, Sept. 29 (U.P.)—One small independent steel company signed an agreement with the United Steelworkers Union today but the industry's giants continued to hold out through a 2½-hour negotiation session today.

CIO President Philip Murray interrupted the meeting to report that Portsmouth Steel Co., Portsmouth, O., employing some 4000 workers, had agreed to union demands for insurance and pensions financed entirely by the employer.

No Progress to Report

Murray said that Portsmouth alone, as of tonight, stood as the company whose furnaces will be making steel if Friday night's deadline should pass without agreement with Big Steel. Already picket lines are forming and production is slowing to a halt throughout the country.

The union delegation came out of the meeting with no progress to report. Big steel representatives who followed had no statement.

During a two-hour session tonight United States Steel and the Steelworkers Union failed to reach agreement on their welfare plan differences, but agreed to meet with Federal mediators tomorrow.

Before Deadline

Federal Mediation Service Representatives William Margolis and Peter Seitz asked for tomorrow's session—14 hours before the 12:01 a.m. Saturday deadline for a strike.

Murray said Portsmouth had "gone down the line" and agreed to a 10-cents-per-hour-per-man, company-financed insurance-pensions plan. If a "better" agreement is reached with big steel, he said, the Portsmouth employees will share in the advantage.

At New York Joseph P. Molony, USW negotiator with Bethlehem and other companies, said he thought the Portsmouth agreement might be "helpful" in later conferences with employers.

Even the most optimistic observers, however, could see no basis for hope that the industry as a whole would give up its

Turn to Page 6, Column 1

Senate Votes Pay Boost for Top Officials

WASHINGTON, Sept. 29 (AP)—The Senate tonight passed, 52 to 14, a bill to boost the pay of Cabinet members and other top level government officials.

It goes to the House which has approved a bill calling for generally larger salary increases for some 240 key executives.

Mr. Truman had urged Senate approval of the House bill.

The Senate bill, calling for increases totaling about $700,000, would raise the pay of Cabinet officers to $22,500. They now get $15,000. The House voted $25,000.

The heads of Federal agencies and undersecretaries of departments would get increases bringing their salaries to $15,000, or $5000 less than the House approved.

By 39 to 28, a Senate group lost a fight to amend the bill by requiring President Truman to slash Federal spending 5 to 10%.

Ray C. Wakefield Dies in Capital

WASHINGTON, Sept. 29 (AP)—Ray C. Wakefield, 54, a member of the Federal Communications Commission from 1941 to 1947, died here today.

Wakefield was a member of the old California Railroad Commission, predecessor of the Public Utilities Commission, for years. He was commission president for a time and was active in formulating many new rate-making policies.

NEW KIND OF GIVEAWAY PROGRAM

Capital Visitor Doles Out $13,000 Merely 'to Help Some Poor People'

WASHINGTON, Sept. 29 (U.P.)—Police were busy today rounding up the more than $13,000 which Cornelius La Roy gave away to taxicab drivers and waitresses because he wanted to help "some poor people I thought needed it."

They had collected $6100 and had promises of more.

Police began the collection campaign after La Roy, a 39-year-old Lansing (Mich.) machinist, was ordered to a mental hospital to find out what impulse led him to scatter $100 bills throughout the capital and two nearby States.

But La Roy can't understand what the fuss was about.

"I just wanted to help some poor people," he said.

In Kalamazoo, La Roy's brother Robert said Cornelius had been ill about two years. He said Cornelius had disappeared two weeks ago and this was the first word of him.

Police began checking on La Roy after they were informed that two sight-seeing cab drivers, who never had that kind of money before, were flashing $100 bills in front of their friends.

The trail led to Cabbie John Joseph Brennan, 42, who admitted La Roy had given him $7000 and that he had used $3500 as a down payment on a house.

Brennan got his house deposit back, dug down in his pocket and came up with a total of $6150 which he returned to police.

Then a second cab driver, James Spart, said La Roy had agreed to give him $1000 to drive him around the capital this week.

La Roy's itinerary, he said, included Reading, Pa., and Luray, Va., where his passenger handed out $100 tips.

Spart agreed to turn in "what's left" of his fare tomorrow.

Police said La Roy told them he also gave $5000 to still another cabbie "to buy a bus." He has not been located.

La Roy also helped Laurel race track in nearby Maryland to the tune of $1800. He lost the money on the horses.

PART 1

Los Angeles Times

EQUAL RIGHTS

LIBERTY UNDER THE LAW — TRUE INDUSTRIAL FREEDOM

ALL THE NEWS
ALL THE TIME

VOL. LXIX | IN FOUR PARTS | CC ★ | WEDNESDAY MORNING, JANUARY 18, 1950 | 52 PAGES | DAILY, SEVEN CENTS

$1,500,000 in Cash Taken by Bandits

Another Million Left Behind in Brink's Office in Boston

BOSTON, Jan. 17 (AP)—More than $1,500,000 in cash was stolen tonight and another million left behind because the bandits couldn't carry it in one of the biggest robberies in the nation's history.

Seven Halloween masked gunmen, obviously well rehearsed, pulled the holdup at Brink's, Inc., a money transportation firm, on the water front.

Police Supt. Edward W. Fallon, at an emergency meeting of high-ranking police officials, said:

"Over $1,000,000 was stolen tonight and they missed at least as much more because they couldn't carry it away."

Two Cars Waiting

While the seven robbers were in the firm's office, two accomplices sat behind the steering wheels of automobiles at the curb.

Boston police broadcast a 14-State alarm for two men described as former Brink's employees. It asked police to pick up for questioning Stanley Kobak, 230 Huntington Ave., Boston, and Edwin Bradshaw, 12 New Cross Ave., Somerville. No other identifying details were given.

Bradshaw later went voluntarily to police headquarters and answered questions. He was not held.

The gunmen entered the office at 7:10 p.m., opening six locked doors to get there. Police said they opened the doors "probably with a passkey."

A company spokesman said several employees have passkeys and "possibly some former employees still have them."

Fallon inspected the robbery scene and sharply criticized the firm for the "poor security it takes to protect such huge sums of money."

Jolice Capt. John D. Ahearn of the special service squad said the robbery "was so neatly executed it must have been engineered by the cream of Boston's crime world."

John Morley, representative of the National Surety Corporation, said the loss is "fully covered" by insurance. He said a syndicate of underwriters insures Brink's against theft, fire, burglary and other risks.

FBI May Act

Agents of the FBI said they were making a "preliminary investigation" to determine if any Federal law was violated by the robbers.

Of the sum left behind, Fallon said, $880,000 included the payroll of the General Electric Co. and $120,000 from Filene's Department Store.

The manager of Brink's, Herbert Humphrey, said "no accurate picture of the loss can be made before tomorrow."

The money, all in paper bills, was scooped from an open vault into two laundry bags brought

Turn to Page 13, Column 1

REPORT TO SENATE SAYS—

Secret Guns Make U.S. Almost Air Raid Proof

WASHINGTON, Jan. 17 (U.P.) The Senate Armed Services Committee has been informed that this country possesses spectacular new weapons, including self-aiming antiaircraft guns, capable of creating an almost impenetrable defense against supersonic planes.

The information was in a report sent to his Committee colleagues by Sen. Henry Cabot Lodge Jr., (R) Mass., a World War II combat officer and now a member of the Army Reserve. The letter was made available today by a Senatorial colleague.

Lodge's conclusions were based on his recent tour of duty at the Ft. Bliss (Tex.) Anti-Aircraft and Guided Missiles Center.

Success Seems Impossible

He did not contend that the nation is absolutely secure against air attack but he said it is difficult to see how one could succeed where the new weapons are available. He said that applies to supersonic as well as more conventional planes.

He said guided missile developments would make military-operations like the Normandy invasion impossible in the future, underscoring the necessity of doing "everything we can" to hold Western Europe because it might be impossible to wrest it from an occupying enemy.

He said there is a "strong feeling" in military circles that Russia is lagging behind the United States in guided missiles but there is no "precise, factual basis for this feeling."

He said the Army's new antiaircraft weapons can detect planes flying 1000 miles an hour at 80,000 feet while they still are 175 miles away, giving defending forces a full 10-minute warning to ready their antiaircraft guns and get interceptors into the air.

New 'Sky-Sweeper' Gun

As a defense against surprise attack by low-flying bombers, he said, the Army has its new "sky-sweeper" gun which literally makes the skies untenable.

Taken together, he concluded, the equipment "satisfies one that no enemy plane will ever come out of this network alive."

He also revealed that infantry divisions soon will be equipped with new twin 44-millimeter antiaircraft guns mounted on a tank chassis as an added protection against enemy planes.

"There is no indication here to commit the classic military error of 'fighting the last war,'" Lodge said in summation. "Everything at Ft. Bliss points sharply and rapidly to the future."

Landings on Wide Basis

In ruling out future operations patterned after the Normandy invasion, Lodge pointed out that the mass Allied landings were made in a relatively limited area.

"A target as large as Omaha Beach, for example, could be rendered untenable by weapons which have been developed," he said.

USS Missouri Fast in Mud; Army Called In for Rescue

Illustrated on Page 3, Part I

NORFOLK, Va., Jan. 17 (U.P.) The battleship Missouri's first cruise under a new skipper ended ingloriously on a mudbank in Hampton Roads today, and the Army hurried to the rescue when the Navy failed to free her.

Sixteen tugs strained at the 45,000-ton Big Mo, the Navy's only active battleship, during the day. She only wallowed deeper in the mud.

Tonight the Navy called off the attempt to free the Missouri and decided to wait until early tomorrow, when a dredge manned by Army engineers is scheduled to arrive from Baltimore.

The Navy had hoped to refloat her with the aid of tugs at high tide tonight. It spent the day getting the stranded pride of the Fleet ready for the big pull.

Tons of supplies and heavy movable equipment were taken off, and 40,000 barrels of fuel oil were siphoned out, but that was not enough.

Comdr. John Paul Preston, public information officer of the Atlantic Fleet, said the Missouri might have to give up the rest of her oil, her ammunition and most of her 71 officers and 1400 men before being dug out of the mudbank by the Army dredge.

The Missouri fought in the Pacific. It sailed into Tokyo Bay and the empire of Japan surrendered on its deck. But today the ship failed to clear its home port. It was aground 1.7 miles from Old Point Comfort Light, near Thimble Shoals.

The skipper, Capt. William D. Brown of Jacksonville, Fla., was taking the battleship out on a routine training cruise to Guantanamo, Cuba, his first voyage since he assumed command last Dec. 10.

MOTHER DIES AT SON'S WEDDING ON RADIO

A La Mesa mother collapsed yesterday while watching her son's wedding on a nationwide radio broadcast, dying a few minutes later following a heart attack.

The son, Donald Barnes, 24, exchanged vows with Frances Mary Dermody, 21, formerly of Roxbury, Mass., before he learned his mother, Mrs. Dorothy Barnes, 49, was dead.

Mrs. Barnes, wife of Lawrence Barnes, was attending the American Broadcasting Co.'s Bride and Groom program when she was stricken. Carried to a nearby room, she was pronounced dead.

Row Rages on Plan for Hydrogen Bomb

WASHINGTON, Jan. 17 (AP)—A raging undercover fight over whether to build a hydrogen-powered superatomic bomb tonight threatened to engulf scientists, military experts and administration figures in an open eruption.

Out of all the hush-hush discussion about a new weapon dwarfing the original atom bomb into almost pea-shooter proportions, at least one new fact emerged:

Before any final decision is made to go ahead with the hydrogen bomb, the Senate-House Atomic Committee plans another review of its possibilities, both from the military and moral points of view.

Moral Issue Raised

That is a sign of how serious the underground scrapping has become, since there had been hints earlier that the Committee was about ready to recommend that the government go ahead with the hydrogen bomb in order to beat Russia to its tremendous punch.

Among persons with some inside knowledge of the problems involved and the various currents of talk about a hydrogen bomb, this additional information is a matter of fairly general agreement:

Military men want the bomb. They figure Russia is going to get it, so we should try to get it first.

Some atomic scientists and others are reluctant to work on the new bomb. They consider it morally wrong to develop a weapon which might destroy lives and lands on a scale incomparably greater than the A-bombs of World War II.

Some key civilians in the administration lean toward the idea we should develop the hydrogen bomb to keep ahead or abreast of Russia.

Cheaper Than A-Bomb

There is some thought that a hydrogen bomb could be perfected in a year or so; that present atomic bomb plants could be used in the process, and that the bill might be around $200,000,000 compared with the $2,000,000,000 estimated for the first A-bomb.

The clinching decision on building a hydrogen bomb must rest with President Truman. But some scientists and some Congressmen believe the issues involved are so stupendous that the American people should have a chance to learn of them and make their views known before the signal is given to go ahead.

Tydings' View

Sen. Tydings (D) Md., Chairman of the Senate Armed Services Committee, told reporters today he would like to see world-wide disarmament with respect to all mass-killing weapons but only under a rigid system of inspection.

The United States must keep on working for an agreement, he said, but meanwhile "we must be stronger than any possible opponent."

Broadened Benefit Asked for Old Age

WASHINGTON, Jan. 17 (AP) The administration renewed its fight for a vast expansion of the Social Security system today amid signs that some increase in coverage, benefits and taxes will be written into law this year.

Arthur J. Altmeyer, the Social Security administrator, asked Congress to extend old age insurance benefits and taxes until they cover practically all of the nearly 60,000,000 persons gainfully employed in the United States. Old age insurance now covers about 35,000,000 workers.

Coverage Extended

The House has already approved a bill which would raise this total to 46,000,000, bringing in self-employed persons, many domestic servants and employees of local and State governments.

Altmeyer did not mention all of the additional trades and professions he would like to see brought into the system. But he recommended specifically that 5,500,000 farm operators and farm workers be covered.

Altmeyer testified before the Senate Finance Committee, whose ranking Democrat and Republican have both predicted that increased benefits and broader coverage will be approved by the Senate and enacted into law this year.

Tax Rise Urged

Altmeyer recommended not only that coverage be broadened. He proposed also that benefits be increased more than they would be under the House bill. And he urged that Social Security taxes be collected on the first $4800 of a worker's annual income, instead of only on the first $3000 as at present.

The last proposal drew fire from Republicans.

Sen. Taft (R) O., argued the effect of it would be to make higher income workers carry a large part of the cost for the lower income workers. He contended those who paid taxes on larger incomes would not get back at retirement what they had put in.

Altmeyer said that workers paying taxes on income above $3000 would receive higher bene-

Turn to Page 10, Column 1

Draft Hearing Set

WASHINGTON, Jan. 17 (AP)—The House Armed Services Committee will start hearings Friday on President Truman's request that the preacetime draft be extended.

FEATURES INDEX

Hogan and Snead Set for Title Golf Match

Ben Hogan and Sam Snead are ready to fight it out today at 12:30 p.m. in the play-off for the Los Angeles Open Golf title at Riviera Country Club. Page 1, Sports Green Sheet.

On Other Pages

Government Will Buy Pork Products to Bolster Prices

WASHINGTON, Jan. 17 (AP)—The Agriculture Department announced today that it will buy pork products in an effort to bolster sagging hog prices.

It said its purchases for the time being will be limited to bacon, smoked hams and smoked picnic shoulders.

Officials said hog prices this week are slightly below a level that would give producers a national average farm price of $14.90 for 100 pounds during January—a support average promised last year.

The support program is designed to assure farmers an average of 90% of parity through March, 1950. Parity is a legal standard for measuring farm prices, declared by statute to be equally fair to farmers and consumers.

In his recent budget report to Congress, President Truman estimated the government might have to buy $90,000,000 worth of pork during its fiscal year ending next June 30.

Name Check Hints Doom of Bowron Recall Attempt

Many Signatures Invalid; Petition Errors Disclosed

Out of a flurry of fast and confusing action on the local political front yesterday came one salient fact:

The recall movement against Mayor Bowron is apparently doomed.

What most political observers described as a death blow to the anti-Bowron forces was dealt shortly after noon by City Clerk Walter Peterson when he announced semiofficially that the recall petitions obviously will fall far short of the number of valid signatures required for a special election.

Less Than 50%

Out of some 90,000 signatures already checked, only 40,000—or less than 50%—were found to be good, Peterson reported. And there are, he added, some amazing discrepancies.

For special election 89,497 valid signatures are needed. The recall petitions contained a total of approximately 130,000 names.

Under election laws, those sponsoring petitions of this type have 10 days in which to make up a deficiency in the number of required signatures after the City Clerk has certified to the City Council that the initial petitions did not contain sufficient signatures.

Meanwhile, in the crammed courtroom of Superior Judge Paul Nourse, a legal hearing to halt official counting of the petitions' signatures was begun.

Doubt Expressed

Although brought about by pro-Bowron forces, this action would give those opposing the Mayor more time to attempt to obtain additional valid signatures inasmuch as the City Clerk cannot make his certification to the City Council until the hearing ends.

Informed sources said that, despite this advantage, it is extremely doubtful if the anti-Bowron faction can make it.

"The recall movement is as good as dead," astute politicians predicted.

The hearing was launched amid complete confusion which reached its zenith when a news photographer was arrested and sentenced to jail by Judge Nourse for assertedly violating the jurist's order barring photography in the courtroom.

Two hours later—after being treated to lunch in the City Hall cafeteria—the photographer was returned to the courtroom where Judge Nourse dismissed the contempt charge, admitting that he, the judge, had erred in ordering the arrest inasmuch as he was convinced that he had adjourned court before the photograph was made.

On still another front, the District Attorney's office—at the request of the City Clerk and the City Attorney's office—was busy investigating numerous glaring "errors" in the recall petitions.

Denies He Signed It

Among these was the astonishing coincidence that one petition carried the purported signature of Harry W. Chapman, chief deputy registrar of voters, in whose offices at 808 N Spring St. the petitions were being checked!

"Hell, no, I didn't sign it!" exploded Chapman. In a matter of minutes a District Attorney's investigator was interviewing Chapman about the phony signature.

In a supplemental answer which the City Clerk filed in a taxpayer's Superior Court suit to halt the expensive counting and certification of the recall petitions, it was stated that:

1—Many of the purported signatures were written by the same person and persons.

2—Many of the purported signatures actually were in alphabetical order!

The suit was filed by Mrs. Frances Cassidy, a taxpayer, of 3872 Hubert St.

Injunction Sought

Represented by a battery of attorneys (Austin Clapp, Ralph Golub, Herbert Bent, James C. Sheppard and E. Talbot Callister) Mrs. Cassidy seeks an injunction against further counting of the recall petitions on the

Turn to Page 4, Column 2

ALIVE—C. James Cooper, 53, aboard Coast Guard boat after his rescue seven miles off Point Fermin. Cooper clung 41 hours to the keel of his overturned skiff—two days of a frantic struggle for life on a tossing sea.

Times photo

MAN ADRIFT AT SEA TWO DAYS RESCUED

Fisherman Clings to Overturned 14-Foot Skiff Until Spotted by Coast Guard Plane

Rescue for C. James Cooper, 53-year-old machine operator from Bell Gardens who went fishing Sunday morning in his 14-foot skiff, came yesterday just in the nick of time.

He was spotted, clinging to the keel of his capsized boat as it drifted seven miles off Point Fermin, by a Coast Guard search plane from San Diego.

The plane alerted the sport-fishing boat Pierpont and directed it to the surface rescue by dropping a string of smoke bombs. Cooper was transferred from the Pierpont to Coast Guard Patrol Boat 83320 and landed at the base in San Pedro.

All-Night Ordeal

The time of his rescue was 11 a.m.—43 hours after his skiff had capsized 18 miles south of San Pedro when struck by a heavy swell on the windward side as he leaned over the lee side to boat a rock cod he had just caught.

Cooper managed to crawl up on the keel, which kept his head and shoulders above water—except when breaking waves doused him.

All that night he clung to the rolling and pitching derelict, confident that morning would bring speedy rescue.

Visibility was poor due to haze, and his plight remained undiscovered.

Unseen By Ships

Several ships passed in the distance during the day, and though he waved frantically with one arm while clinging to the boat with the other, and yelled himself hoarse, he remained unnoticed.

Monday night was cold and foggy. The sea kicked up fearsomely at times. His tiny craft bobbed crazily on the wave crests and lurched soggily in the troughs.

He thought of praying — and

Turn to Page 4, Column 5

Detroiters Burned by Brandy Blast

DETROIT, Jan. 17 (AP) — A number of prominent Detroiters were severely burned tonight by a flash fire that followed the explosion of a "coffee diablo" tankard at a union dinner.

The injured included Malcolm W. Bingay, editorial director of the Detroit Free Press, Detroit Recorder's Judge Joseph A. Gillis and Circuit Judge Ira W. Jayne. Bingay and Gillis were reported in serious condition.

Recorder's Judge John J. Scallen, who aided the injured, said brandy was being poured into the flaming coffee.

Alcohol fumes apparently collected when the air became charged, causing the explosion.

Flaming liquid sprayed over the diners seated within 20 feet. Flames shot 10 feet into the air.

The diners, guests of a union at the AFL Labor Temple, were seated around a U-shaped table. The flames shot into the faces of the most seriously injured.

THE WEATHER

U.S. Weather Bureau forecast: Partly cloudy today and tomorrow with fog near the coast. Slightly warmer with high today near 68. Highest temperature yesterday, 66; lowest, 44.

Warren Hopes to Avoid Asking New State Taxes

SACRAMENTO, Jan. 17 (AP)—Gov. Warren today expressed the hope he will not have to ask for any new taxes when he submits the 1950-51 budget to the Legislature in March.

The Governor said he is "hopeful" that no new taxes will be needed, but that it is not a certainty.

"That is what we are striving for," he added.

Warren said at his news conference all State departments are being pressed "very hard" for an economical budget.

He said all departmental budgets will be ready by the end of the month, but that he could not yet reach any over-all conclusions on the relationship of revenues and expenditures for the next fiscal year.

Drop in Revenues

The Governor added, however, "there is no doubt that our revenues have fallen off."

The office of the legislative auditor recently estimated there would be a $33,000,000 gap between revenues and expenditures by July 1, 1951.

Asked to comment on reports of possible moves in the Legislature to dip into the State's post-war building funds, Warren reiterated his opposition to any use of those funds except for the purposes for which they were built up.

"I consider those funds are in trust . . . and should be used for hospitals, universities and colleges and all our other institutions which have outgrown their plants."

About Proposition 2

Warren again stated his belief that the switchover in administration of the State's pension program will be accomplished smoothly when Proposition 2 goes into effect March 1.

He said he does not believe there will be any especial problems for the State in qualifying for Federal pension subsidies.

Warren had no comment on Los Angeles County Supervisor Raymond Darby's statement he may run for Governor.

PRESIDENT OUTRUNNING RED IN FINLAND VOTING

HELSINKI, Jan. 18 (Wednesday) (U.P.) — President Juho K. Paasikivi, target of recent Soviet press attacks, appeared certain today to win re-election in Finland's first Presidential elections since 1937.

With only a few scattered districts still to report, official returns gave Paasikivi 868,693 or 58.9% of 1,477,007 votes counted. Mauno Pekkala, Communist candidate, had 316,999 or 21.4%, while Urho K. Kekkonen, Agrarian, trailed with 291,315 or 19.7%.

Election officials said that only about 1,500,000 of the nation's 2,500,000 eligible voters braved the Arctic cold, which saw the temperature drop to 22 below zero in Northern Lapland.

Paasikivi, who took office four years ago to help negotiate the Soviet-Finnish peace treaty, made only one campaign speech —on New Year's Day. In it, he said he had done more than any other living Finn to maintain cordial relations with Russia.

But reliable informants said earlier that Paasikivi's government has drafted a friendly, but firm note to the Soviet Union, informing the colossal neighbor that most of the 56 alleged Russian war criminals have fled Finland and cannot be returned.

PART 1

Los Angeles Times

EQUAL RIGHTS
LIBERTY UNDER THE LAW — TRUE INDUSTRIAL FREEDOM

FINAL EDITION
ALL THE NEWS ALL THE TIME

VOL. LXIX | IN TEN PARTS | CC ★ | SUNDAY MORNING, JANUARY 22, 1950 | 188 PAGES | SUNDAY, 15c

Hiss Convicted in Perjury Case

Faces Possible Penalty of 10 Years and $4000 Fine

NEW YORK, Jan. 21 (UP)—A Federal court jury of eight women and four men decided today that Alger Hiss, former State Department "bright young man" who sat behind President Roosevelt at Yalta, lied when he denied being a Communist spy within the government in 1938.

The jury of the second Hiss perjury trial returned its guilty verdict 23 hours and 38 minutes after it received the case. It spent nine hours and 16 minutes in actual deliberation.

The jury in the first Hiss perjury trial reported last July 8, after 14 hours and 44 minutes of actual deliberations, that it could not agree.

The first trial lasted 27 days. The verdict in the second trial came on the 40th court day.

The decision was the jury's answer to what had become one of the most intriguing questions of 1948, '49 and '50: Who lied?

Guilty on Two Counts

The jury decided that Whittaker Chambers, the arch accuser of Hiss and star government witness in both trials, was telling the truth when he said that Hiss as an assistant to an Assistant Secretary of State in 1938 had stolen State Department secret documents in wholesale fashion.

Chambers said he was a courier for an underground Communist apparatus in prewar Washington and Hiss had given the documents to him for delivery to a Russian spy agent.

The jury found Hiss guilty on both counts of the two-count indictment. The maximum sentence possible on each count is five years imprisonment and a $2000 fine or a total of 10 years imprisonment and a fine of $4000. It is believed, however, that the sentences for the two counts will be made concurrent, which is customary in Federal courts.

Sentencing Wednesday

Judge Henry W. Goddard set Wednesday for sentencing. Meanwhile Hiss was permitted to go free under his $5000 bail.

Hiss had denied giving documents to Chambers in February and March, 1938, and had denied ever seeing Chambers after Jan. 1, 1937. The denials were the basis of the two counts in the perjury indictment.

The three-year statute of limitations prevented a Federal grand jury from bringing an espionage indictment against Hiss, 45-year-old Harvard graduate, who had begun a 13-year distinguished government career as law secretary to the late Supreme Court Justice Oliver Wendell Holmes and who had sat as secretary-general of of the U.N. charter conference in San Francisco.

Hiss and his wife left the courthouse at 3:05 p.m., his arm linked with that of his wife, Priscilla, who had sat beside him at both trials. Mrs. Hiss' face

Turn to Page 10, Column 2

AFTER VERDICT—Alger Hiss, his face grim, pictured walking from Federal Courthouse in New York with wife at side, following guilty verdict against him. (AP) Wirephoto

ANCHOR PLAN MAY RELEASE BIG MO

Latest Scheme to Rescue Stuck Battleship Feb. 2 Involves Heavy Beaching Equipment

NORFOLK, Va., Jan. 21 (AP)—The Navy plans to use heavy beaching gear on the next attempt to tug the Missouri, the nation's only active battleship, off a Chesapeake Bay shoal. In Washington, Navy officials announced plans for an investigation and a naval court of inquiry on how and why the Big Mo ran aground.

The Navy will make the next try at freeing the ship on Feb. 2.

Failing in three attempts to haul the battleship free with a fleet of tugs, salvage officers dug deeper into their bag of tricks today and came up with the announcement that heavy beaching gear will be used. This is how it works:

Ten or 12 four-ton anchors will be placed 1000 yards astern of the ship. Each anchor, its cable drawn fiddle-tight from the immobile Missouri, will exert a pulling force of 80 tons, a naval spokesman explained.

800-Ton Force

Thus, a pulling force of some 800 tons will be exerted on the 45,000-ton warship. The spokesman said that this, plus the deep trench an Army dredge has carved in the shoal about the ship, plus removal of her fuel oil, ammunition and provisions, plus submarine pontoons under her stern, may even cause the Missouri "to slide off the shoal by herself."

Feb. 2 was selected for the next attempt to haul the Missouri loose as that is the earliest date that will bring the most favorable high tides. An earlier try will be made, however, should northeast winds throw tides two feet above normal into the bay.

NAVY OFFERED B-36 HELP IN EXTRACTING MO

WASHINGTON, Jan. 21 (AP)—The plight of the battleship Missouri reportedly prompted a grinning offer from the commander of the Air Force yesterday to haul the big battle wagon out of the mud with B-36 bombers.

Senators who lunched with the chiefs of staffs of the armed forces said a good-natured revival of the air-power-versus-sea-power dispute was set off by Gen. J. Lawton Collins of the Army.

Collins suggested solemnly that perhaps the Air Force had dropped phony buoys into Chesapeake Bay to lure the Missouri onto a mudbank.

Gen. Hoyt S. Vandenberg, Air Force Chief of Staff, denied it. Just to prove that their is "complete unification" among the armed forces, he said, "I'm even willing to attach some B-36s to the Missouri and yank her out by air power."

The ribbing was directed at Adm. Forrest P. Sherman, Chief of Naval Operations. Senators reported that a sad grin was Sherman's only contribution to the discussion.

Wits (jg) Offer Plenty of Advice on Missouri

WASHINGTON, Jan. 21 (UP)—The Navy would be mighty pleased if all the wits who are offering suggestions on how to free the stranded battleship Missouri would go to Hampton Roads and do the job themselves.

One anonymous group of Air Force veterans recommended that the Mighty Mo be painted orange and left in the mud as a practice target for the B-36s.

President Truman, for whose home State the ship was named and who personally ordered it kept in commission when some Navy people wanted to put the Mighty Mo in mothballs, had nothing to say.

But Rep. F. Edward Hebert (D), La., a member of the House Armed Services Committee and a stanch Navy supporter in the unification row, said with a grin that he suspected Pentagon politics in the incident.

"It's in keeping with the apparent policy of the Defense Department to beach the Navy," said Hebert.

Violent Quake Rocks Chile

SANTIAGO, Jan. 21 (UP)—A severe earthquake shook the entire area of Central Chile from Valparaiso to Temuco today. No casualties have been reported, but city populations were thrown into a panic.

American Lost on Pacific Ship

MANILA, Jan. 22 (Sunday) (UP)—Twelve persons, including an American, were reported missing today in the sinking of the 234-ton Filipino ship Isidrito Wednesday off the Southern Philippines. The Philippine Red Cross identified the American as Frank McCarthy, manager of the Cosmos Lumber Co. of Cebu.

'DID I DO ALL RIGHT?'

Heroine, 5, Rescues Boy From Icy Waters

DOVER, O., Jan. 21 (AP)—Five-year-old Vivian Sue O'Brien rescued a 6-year-old playmate today after he plunged through an ice-covered hole into 10 feet of water and then asked her mother:

"Did I do all right?"

Her mother, Mrs. John O'Brien, suggested that she might have called for adult help. Vivian replied:

"But, Momie, I couldn't leave him. I had to pull him out. There were bubbles coming up."

Vivian and John Christman were playing near a 20-foot square hole which the Russ Engineering Co. used in testing pumps. Their fathers were working in a building 200 feet away.

John fell through thin ice into the 10-foot-deep water.

Vivian ran 75 feet to a building where she found 8 feet of half-inch wire cable.

She threw the cable to the boy, and then, bracing herself on a water pipe, hauled him to shore. Vivian weighs only 50 pounds, and it took all her strength to tug her 52-pound playmate to safety.

Vivian then ran to their fathers for help.

John, son of Mayor and Mrs. Bernard J. Christman of nearby Bolivar, later was pronounced by a doctor to be "in good shape."

Mrs. O'Brien, who is employed in the company's office, tried to get Vivian to talk to a reporter on the telephone tonight, but the little heroine was too bashful to even take the receiver and listen.

When her mother told her she was a heroine it didn't make much of an impression. She just asked what "heroine" meant.

Vivian told her mother she did not know beforehand the cable was beside the building. She went looking for something when all she could see of John were his waving hands and the top of his hat.

SMOG AND FOG JOIN TO VEX SOUTHLAND

Los Angeles and environs had another smoggy day yesterday and harbor areas were draped with dense fog. However, the weatherman had good news for smog haters.

He predicted that air movement early this morning will move some of yesterday's polluted air out of the area. That, and a lessening of pollution in the air from industry should mean better visibility, he said.

As for fog, he predicts that coast areas and the southern sections of Los Angeles will have the stuff at least during the night and morning.

Visibility Reduced

Yesterday's blanket of warm air that hovered over Los Angeles from 9:15 a.m. throughout most of the day cut down visibility to as low as one mile.

In harbor areas, the Marine Exchange reported visibility zero from midnight until late afternoon. Four ships, among them the around the world American President Lines President Polk, remained offshore, unable to penetrate the fog barrier.

Other ships were the tanker Ticonderoga and the freighters Pacific Fortune and the Captain John D. P. Six of 12 ships inside the harbor and due to sail in the morning were still warped to their berths in the afternoon.

Bus and Auto Crash

A bus-auto crash at 9th and Pacific Ave., San Pedro, resulted in minor injuries to five persons.

To top everything, pilots in the Long Beach Harbor pilot house were jolted from their slumbers when the 50-foot fishing boat View Point crashed over the rocks into the structure. No injuries were reported and the tug Pacific Rocket pulled the boat out of the house and to dry dock for survey of damage.

THE WEATHER

United States Weather Bureau forecast: Mostly sunny today and tomorrow with variable high thin cloudiness and night and morning fog near the coast and in southern sections of the city. Little change in temperature. High today near 72. Highest temperature yesterday, 72; lowest, 51.

U.S. Backs Down in Berlin to Avert New Blockade

Western Police Ordered Out of Seized Railway Building

BERLIN, Jan. 21 (UP)—The United States backed down in the face of a threatened new Soviet blockade of Berlin today and gave back to the Russians a disputed railway administration building in the American sector.

It was the first time that the Americans have retreated in a major Berlin dispute with the Russians since the Soviets imposed their 11-month blockade on Western Berlin in the spring of 1948.

It had been rumored in Berlin that Maj. Gen. Maxwell D. Taylor's backdown was prompted by pressure from his superiors. But U.S. High Commissioner John McCloy, who arrived at Mitchel Field in New York tonight, said "I doubt it" when asked whether Washington had prompted the action.

Sees Eased Situation

McCloy said he was not fully informed on the matter, having left Germany Friday. But he said he believed the U.S. backdown would "ease the situation."

Taylor's order was scarcely issued when Soviet propaganda organs began trumpeting the Soviet "victory."

"Taylor sounds retreat," the Soviet-licensed news agency ADN said as five Russian-directed railway police marched into the building and slammed shut the iron gates on an American property control official.

Gen. Taylor, Berlin's American commandant, ordered West German police out of the building and returned it to the Soviet-controlled railway administration.

Seek Empty Rooms

West German police seized control of the building Tuesday on American instructions so that its 600 empty rooms could be used for the benefit of space-short Western Berliners.

The Soviets and their East Berlin Communist associates hinted broadly that they might reimpose their blockade of Western Berlin in reprisal.

Taylor said the Soviets used the seizure of the building as "an excuse to harass the residents of Western Berlin, to threaten reprisals against rail workers, and generally to disturb the peace of the city."

"Unfortunately," he said, "the unreasonable and provocative attitude of the Soviets and of the Reichsbahn (the Soviet-controlled railway administration) makes it appear probable that the hardships which they intend to impose outweight the benefits arising from the American plan.

"The 600 office rooms are not worth the threat of a new blockade."

Cut Train Service

The Soviet-run railway cut elevated traffic in Berlin by more than 50% in reprisal, and Soviet zone officials threatened that interzonal rail traffic between Berlin and Western Germany would be affected.

Today, many truck drivers going to and from Berlin were stopped and questioned. Some of them were turned back as Soviet frontier guards applied many of the tactics that preceded imposition of their 1948 blockade.

On Thursday Taylor rejected a formal Soviet demand for evacuation of the building and said the police are "there to stay."

Now, he said, "we are bending over backward."

Socialism Out of Tune, Says Churchill

Ex-Prime Minister Makes Appeal for Change by Voters

LONDON, Jan. 21 (AP)—Winston Churchill declared tonight that Socialism is out of tune with the times and is the "weakest defense against Communism." Socialist restrictions have paralyzed Britain and blocked her path to recovery, he said.

In his first 1950 campaign speech, broadcast from his home at Westerham, the 75-year-old Conservative Party leader urged British voters in the Feb. 23 general election to spurn the Labor Party's bid for a return to power after almost five years' rule.

The speech was transmitted by the government-owned BBC and rebroadcast in the United States and elsewhere.

Hits Socialist Policy

The opening salvo of the Conservative campaign was not in the doughty wartime Prime Minister's usual rousing style, however.

Speaking slowly, as if to weigh his words, he claimed credit for some of the social services which the Labor government has put into effect. But he declared the "Socialist policy of equalizing misery and organizing scarcity" might bring results the like of which "we have never yet suffered or even imagined."

The issue, he said, "is whether we should take another plunge into Socialist regimentation" or regain the "freedom, initiative and opportunity" that once won for Britain "glorious ascendancy."

Now on Decline

"Socialism has been found in all European countries, in bond or free, to have been the weakest defense against Communism," he asserted.

Declaring that except in Scandinavia Socialist parties were on the decline throughout Europe outside the Iron Curtain, he said:

"In taking another lurch into Socialism at this juncture, we should be moving contrary to the general trend and tide of reviving European society.

"Still more should we be out of harmony with the states and nations of the English-speaking world, the British Dominions and the United States."

He recalled that New Zealand and Australia, two of the Dominions, "have recently shaken themselves free" after a prolonged trial of Socialist governments.

He defined Socialism as a "mistaken political philosophy and largely obsolete mode of thought" which believes in an "all-powerful state which owns everything, which plans every-

Turn to Page 13, Column 1

HIROHITO'S DAUGHTER SAYS SHE'S BROKE

TOKYO, Jan. 21 (UP)—Emperor Hirohito's eldest daughter and her husband, one-time Premier Prince Higashikuni, are broke a lot of the time, she confessed today.

Mrs. Morihoro Higashikuni, 25, made her first public speech, consoling the families of Japanese nationals still held in the Soviet Union.

Mrs. Higashikuni, whose husband was reduced from a nobleman to a commoner by the new constitution, said that he received a year-end bonus from his employers, the Bank of Japan. But the Higashikunis were so far from making ends meet, Hirohito's daughter said, that they had to use the bonus to wipe out the red ink in the family budget instead of for a present.

Finns Reject Accusations in Soviet Note

HELSINKI, Jan. 21 (AP)—The Finnish government tonight rejected Soviet charges that it has been harboring war criminals wanted by Russia.

Replying to Moscow's note of Jan. 1, the Finns said they are holding for questioning four of the 55 persons specifically listed by the Soviet government. But the Finns did not promise to deliver them to Russia.

The Finnish reply said an investigation is being made as to whether they ought to be extradited to Russia under provisions of the 1947 peace treaty. The answer declared Finland is striving loyally to fulfill provisions of that treaty but also is bound to observe international laws guaranteeing the rights of individuals—presumably a reference to the right of asylum of political refugees.

Three Made Citizens

Of the four persons detained, three have become Finnish citizens since the war and one is a stateless person who has lived in Finland since 1933.

The Finnish note was delivered tonight by Finnish Minister Karl Sundstroem in Moscow, a Foreign Office communique said, three weeks after Soviet Deputy Foreign Minister Andrei Gromyko accused the Finnish government of harboring 300 war criminals of Soviet origin. Gromyko listed 55 persons accused of the "most serious" crimes against Russia whose extradition he demanded.

He accused Finland of supplying them with false names and documents and thereby violating her 1947 peace treaty and her 1948 pact of friendship and alliance with Russia.

The Soviet demand was made just as Finland's presidential campaign was warming up and was regarded by observers here as an effort to put political pressure on the country in behalf of Finland's Communist Party.

In the election of presidential electors, President Juho Paasikivi won easily against Communist and Agrarian candidates.

FEATURES INDEX

Girl's Father Denies King Stole Her Love

Narriman Sadek, 16-year-old Egyptian girl, never was formally engaged to Saki Hashem, U.N. worker, and never loved him, according to her father, Hussein Fahmey Sadek Bey, and King Farouk had nothing to do with breaking off the affair. Story on Page 12, Part 1.

On Other Pages

RUSS SPEAKER SEES WORLD PEACE HOPE

MOSCOW, Jan. 21 (UP)—Premier Stalin, flanked by the top men of Russia and China, heard the Lenin memorial speaker declare at the Bolshoi Theater tonight that capitalism and Communism can live peacefully side by side.

The occasion was the 26th anniversary of the death of Nikolai Lenin. The principal speaker was Peter N. Pospelov, editor of the Communist Party newspaper Pravda and director of the party's Institute of Marx-Engels-Lenin.

Pospelov praised the growing prosperity of the Soviet Union; he predicted the inevitable doom of capitalism; he derided America's China and atomic policies; he called British Field Marshal Montgomery a "bloody cannibal."

Hopeful for Peace

But he ended on a note of optimism, on the possibility of the peaceful coexistence of the two systems — capitalism and Communism.

Lenin, he said, postulated the possibility and the Soviet people today are not departing from Lenin.

The Soviet foreign policy is based on the coexistence of the two systems, Pospelov said.

This theme was stressed by Deputy Premier and Politburo Member G. M. Malenkov in his speech on Stalin's birthday Dec. 21. It has been stressed again and again in recent Soviet utterances.

The annual service at the Bolshoi opened with President Nikolai Shvernik presiding over the notables.

Stalin, V. M. Molotov and Malenkov and the other members of the party's political bureau sat in the first row of seats behind a baize-covered table in the center of the enormous stage. Behind them was a giant, black-bordered portrait of Lenin.

Foreign guests included Chinese Communist Leader Mao Tze-tung, Chou En-lai, Premier of the Peking regime, and representatives of the People's Democracies.

Derides U.S. Policy

His mention of the triumph of the Chinese revolutionaries and the name of Mao brought a tumultuous applause from the audience.

American intervention in China, even with $6,000,000,000, he said, was not able to crush the Communists. American policy collapsed there, he said, just as did her atomic monopoly.

Radio Moscow reported that Pospelov said: "The illusions regarding the imaginary atomic monopoly of the United States have collapsed. It has been established that the Soviet Union, which heads the camp of peace and Socialism, has possessed the atomic weapon since 1947."

Hon. Police Joyfully Perform Duty, Hunt Dishon. Girl Without Falsies

TOKYO, Jan. 21 (UP)—Japanese police, armed with an intriguing description, today prowled the art studios in search of "The Bosom," a 22-year-old model accused of robbing artists after posing for them in the nude.

Authorities sent out a special warning to artists and art students to keep an eye out for Model Hatsu Kawaguchi after three prominent Japanese artists complained she had robbed them of money and clothing.

Instead of the usual "wanted" photograph, the Japanese press splashed reproductions of a full length nude painting of Miss Kawaguchi by complaining Artist Usaburo Ihara.

Readers generally agreed with the artists' description.

Kenichiro Maeno, chief of the Arasaka district police, said he didn't anticipate any trouble in spotting the model. "She has an unusual figure for a Japanese girl," he said.

He said he believes many of the model's victims failed to report her because they were ashamed of admitting they had been taken in.

The suspect's usual method of operation, he explained, is to seek employment with an artist as a nude model, "gain his confidence," and then disappear within a week, taking money and other valuables.

The Police Chief admitted that the rising popularity of "falsies" in Japan would complicate the problem of finding the suspect, but added: "I'm sure our trained observers can put the finger on the right girl."

He said the search for the girl has spread all over Tokyo, with every policeman anxious to "make the pinch."

PART 1

Los Angeles Times

EQUAL RIGHTS · LIBERTY UNDER THE LAW · TRUE INDUSTRIAL FREEDOM

ALL THE NEWS ALL THE TIME

VOL. LXIX | IN FOUR PARTS | CC | TUESDAY MORNING, FEBRUARY 7, 1950 | 56 PAGES | DAILY, SEVEN CENTS

Southland Rain Sets Seven Year Record

Stores Flooded, Autos Trapped as Heavy Downpour Chokes Streets

Illustrated on Page 3, Part I

Rain—in quantities that the Southland has been needing for seven years—fell yesterday and boosted the season total here to 8.82 inches, .30 inch above normal.

This total, swelled by the 1.32 inches that fell in the current storm, was the highest since that for the comparable season ended Feb. 6, 1943, when 10.04 inches of rain had fallen, the Weather Bureau said. Last season's to date was 5.05 inches.

To all growers and water conservationists the rain was an unmixed blessing.

Stores Flooded

But for some motorists, householders and merchants, it was too sudden.

In Downey, Norwalk, Venice and Hawthorne, ground floors of stores were flooded. In the latter, marooned merchants and customers were removed by boats. Lifeguards also used boats to carry stranded motorists to dry ground from stalled cars in the West Los Angeles and Venice areas.

Water seeped through floors of new houses along Sawtelle Creek, below National Blvd.

Car Swept Away

In the San Fernando Valley floodwaters swept an automobile along 40 feet from its parking place and dashed it into a bridge, and caused new sewer lines to sink, resulting in street cave-ins.

Boiling Chino Creek inundated State Highway 71, closing it to traffic between Pine St., at the south end of Ontario, to Corona, for the storm's duration.

Today and tomorrow will be partly cloudy, according to the weatherman, with occasional drizzles early this morning in Los Angeles and scattered showers over the mountains and along the coast.

One of the heaviest floods yesterday was in the vicinity of the Berryman Ave.-Culver City Blvd. intersection, near the Culver City-Los Angeles city line, where several cars were trapped at around 3:30 a.m.

Lifeguards from Venice responded to an emergency call and removed the motorists from their cars with dories. The water subsided after the rain tapered off and permitted cars to be moved as traffic, rerouted for several hours by police, was resumed over the highway.

Boats also were at a premium in the Broadway-Hawthorne Blvd. area, where houses and stores were flooded. Water ran more than 30 inches deep at the intersection, flooding stores six inches deep. Max Isaacs, owner of a five-and-ten-cent store at 129 N Hawthorne Blvd. was still busy by midafternoon trying to clean floors to reopen for business.

Stocks Damaged

Also flooded were a drug store and a food market, both on the west side of Hawthorne Blvd. at Broadway. Ray Lazare, owner of the drug store, estimated water damage up to $1000 and Julius Kraft, market manager, figured damage to his stock would more than top that figure.

Worst flooding in Inglewood was at Freeman Ave. and Hillcrest Blvd., Phil Baily, assistant to the City Manager, reported.

Pile-ups of traffic due to stalled cars also were reported at Jefferson and Centinela Blvds. and at Sepulveda Blvd. and Slauson Ave., with water running three feet deep at the latter location.

Turn to Page 4, Column 5

SENATE FIGHT OPENS ON ARIZONA PROJECT

BY WARREN B. FRANCIS, Times Staff Correspondent

WASHINGTON, Feb. 6—Suggestions that Arizona might seek Federal funds to build the $738,000,000 Central Arizona reclamation project even if the U.S. Supreme Court rules water is not available to rescue the Phoenix plateau "is an insult to Congress," Sen. McFarland (D) Ariz., declared today in opening floor discussion on the long-fought authorization bill.

Warning that no further compromise is possible, McFarland launched the final round in the drive for Senate approval of the measure with the O'Mahoney-Millikin rider—termed inadequate by Californians—allowing court test of conflicting claims to Colorado River water, with assertions his State is "fighting for her very existence."

Basin State Rights

The co-author of the controversial measure virtually turned down in advance any possible moves by the California Congressional delegation to sidetrack the CARP authorization pending a positive Supreme Court finding that Arizona is entitled to additional water from the main stream of the Colorado.

As on every previous occasion, he maintained firmly during a 90-minute speech that the rights of all Colorado River Basin States are "fully protected."

McFarland voiced confidence that the Supreme Court eventually will rule in Arizona's favor but contended California cannot obtain judicial review of the 28-year-long interstate dispute until Congress authorizes construction of the "rescue project" and thus presents "a justifiable issue."

Knowland Challenge

The only challenge to McFarland's argument—most of which was heard by fewer than a half-dozen Senators—was from Sen. Knowland (R) Cal.

Knowland sought to raise issues about the financial soundness of the Arizona project, the asserted Arizona attempt to "break up the yardstick" used for years to judge the feasibility of reclamation proposals, and the possibility that Congress would be committed to build the Parker Dam pump-lift and Phoenix aqueduct regardless of the outcome of expected litigation.

Question of Validity

Admitting the legislation extends indefinitely the time during which water users would be expected to repay the cost of irrigation works, McFarland vehemently denied the bill sets any precedents.

When Knowland inquired whether the CARP authorization would still be valid in event of a

Turn to Page 6, Column 1

New Jersey Republican Elected in Thomas' Place

HACKENSACK, N.J., Feb. 6 (AP)—The Republican Party today held onto the Congressional seat vacated by the jailed J. Parnell Thomas, electing William B. Widnall, 43-year-old State Assemblyman to the post.

Widnall coasted to a 2-to-1 victory over his Democratic opponent, George T. English, in the special election in New Jersey's 7th Congressional District.

The election was called to name a replacement for Thomas in the traditionally GOP district.

Complete unofficial returns gave Widnall 32,224 votes to 15,711 for English.

The House post has been vacant since Jan. 2 when Thomas resigned. The GOP Congressman relinquished the office after being sentenced to six to 18 months in prison and fined $10,000 for padding his office payroll and accepting kickbacks. Thomas, who once headed the House Un-American Activities Committee, now is serving time in the Federal correctional institution in Danbury, Ct.

The winner of today's election—first Congressional election in the nation this year—will serve until the end of 1950. The full two-year term will be filled in November's elections.

PUZZLE CONTEST

Correct solutions to Puzzles 61 to 65 of the recent Fun and Fortune contest are published on Page 2, Part IV of today's issue.

NEW POSTWAR JOBLESS PEAK REACHES 4,480,000

WASHINGTON, Feb. 6 (AP)—The nation's jobless increased to 4,480,000 in January—highest since the war.

Secretary of Commerce Sawyer, announcing the figure today, blamed the rise in unemployment on bad weather, the holidays and the normal "midwinter lull in trade and outdoor work."

"It is noteworthy," he said, "that industrial employment did not appear to be materially affected. A year ago, industrial layoffs were an important factor in the rise of unemployment."

The figures showed unemployment jumped 991,000 during the last month.

Simultaneously, the number with jobs dropped by 1,609,000 to a total of 56,947,000. Officials explained that the full force of the decline in jobs did not show up in unemployment figures because many who lost jobs dropped out of the labor market—at least temporarily.

Figures covering the week ended Jan. 14 showed unemployment had risen 1,816,000 over the last 12 months.

TRUMAN INVOKES TAFT-HARTLEY ACT

President Moves to Halt Fuel Crisis as Soft-Coal Miners of Nation Join Strike

WASHINGTON, Feb. 6 (AP)—The nation's soft coal miners struck today and President Truman immediately put the Taft-Hartley Act in motion on a speed-up basis to try to force them back to work next week.

Nearly 400,000 of John L. Lewis' United Mine Workers staged the midwinter walkout, forcing a showdown after 10 months of contract bickering over the union's demand for higher pay, bigger welfare funds and other concessions.

National Emergency

The nation has two weeks of coal on hand. President Truman found a national emergency was here.

Seeking a no-strike Federal court injunction against the union, he started up the Taft-Hartley machinery by naming a three-man board of inquiry. He directed it to report not later than next Monday.

When it brings him the facts of the coal dispute, Mr. Truman can at once send Atty. Gen. McGrath into court to ask for an order directing the union to halt the strike for 80 days.

Whether the miners will obey this injunction is the next big question. Lewis himself raised this doubt Saturday when he told Mr. Truman in a cryptic message:

"It is questionable whether one could postulate that such mass coercion (use of the Taft-Hartley Law) would insure enthusiastic service from grateful men."

Failure to Conform

This was followed by cries from the mining field today of "No contract, no work."

Failure to conform with a court order can be punished as contempt. The UMW and Lewis have been fined twice for this offense, a total of $2,130,000.

There was one strong hope for peace in spite of the complete failure of contract negotiations. This hope lay in the make-up of the Taft-Hartley fact-finding board named by Mr. Truman. These men are veteran labor arbitrators. They are:

David L. Cole, Paterson (N.J.) lawyer, chairman. He headed a similar board in 1948 which settled a bitter contract argument between Lewis and the operators by getting them together. This headed off an injunction.

Dispute Arbiter

John Dunlop, Harvard University Business School, who has been the arbiter between the AFL building trades department

Turn to Page 12, Column 4

There'll Be No German Army, McCloy Warns

BY WALDO DRAKE
Times European Bureau

STUTTGART, Feb. 6—"There will be no German army or air force," John J. McCloy told the German people here today in his first major statement of policy since he assumed office as U.S. High Commissioner five months ago.

McCloy spoke from the stage of the same Stuttgart theater where former Secretary of State Byrnes first stated the U.S. policy on postwar Germany on Sept. 6, 1946. Byrnes threw down the gauntlet to the Soviets and said, "As long as there is any occupation army in Germany, American armed forces will be a part of that occupation army."

Avoids One Issue

McCloy today courageously faced every issue except the Russian situation. He told Germans that the United States' main purpose here is to help Germany achieve political and economic independence along democratic lines by close association with the free peoples of Western Europe.

"By such action," he said, "Germany can acquire a world position which no amount of German political maneuvering between two great world powers could ever create.

"Germany cannot be allowed to develop political conditions or a military status which would threaten other nations or the peace of the world. That means," he explained, "that there will be

Turn to Page 16, Column 4

Ice Cream Soda Fracas Goes to Court

READING Pa., Feb. 6 (AP)—A 25-cent ice cream soda went to court today.

The sweet dish is the main ingredient—and the cause—of a $22,500 damage suit filed in Berks County Court by Harry C. Specter of New York City.

On the defense are a restaurant owner and his wife, Mr. and Mrs. Leroy Reber, the couple who served the soda.

Specter charges he purchased a chocolate ice cream soda, which lacked sufficient ice cream. A fracas resulted. Specter was jailed, then fined.

Now he's suing "for injuries suffered to his reputation" and for "being taken to City Hall in a patrol wagon."

The soda was advertised to contain two dips of ice cream. But Specter alleges that it had "no more ice cream than would fill a flat teaspoon."

Bus-Car Crash Hurts 24

MIAMI, Feb. 6 (AP)—Twenty-four persons were injured today when a Miami Transit Co. bus and an automobile collided.

FEATURES INDEX

Boycott on Television Voted by Wrestlers

Wrestlers who participate in bouts at Olympic Auditorium, Hollywood Legion Stadium, Ocean Park and South Gate Arenas have voted to boycott those clubs if they continue to televise the shows. Page 1, Sports Section.

On Other Pages

Mystery Pair in Car Hunted in Bombing of Cohen Home

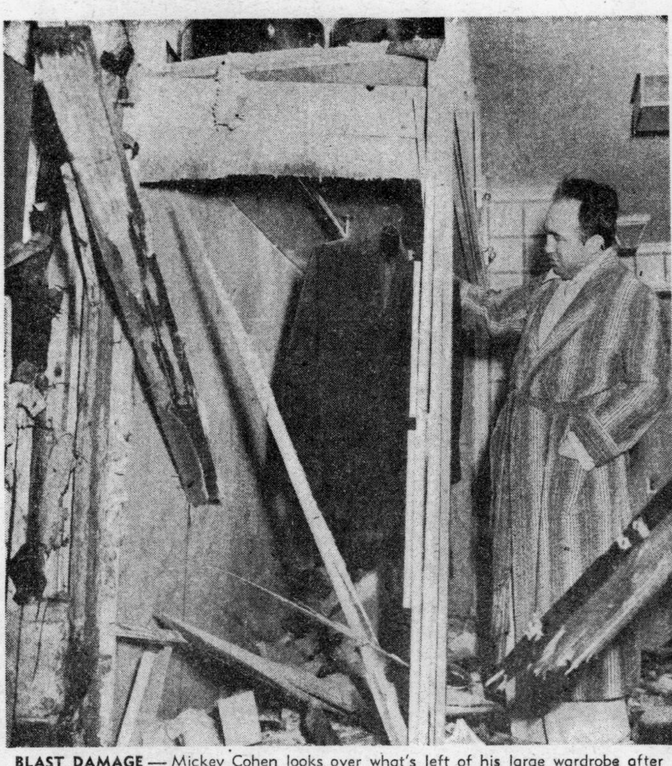

BLAST DAMAGE — Mickey Cohen looks over what's left of his large wardrobe after bomb shattered part of his Brentwood home and damaged neighboring residences. Times photo

None Injured as Dynamite Wrecks Room

Illustrated on Page 3, Part I

Two men seen driving a dark automobile in the vicinity of Mickey Cohen's West Los Angeles home, at about the time a terrific dynamite blast shattered one room of the gambler's house and rocked the neighborhood, were hunted last night.

No one was hurt in the blast which shattered windows, damaged roofs and imperiled a score of sleeping adults and children in homes along Moreno Ave., just off San Vicente Blvd.

Cohen, his wife LaVonne and their maid were in other rooms in the house when the explosion occurred at 4:15 a.m. The shock was felt as far away as seven miles.

Statement by Chief

Chief of Police Worton issued a statement in the afternoon, a short time after Cohen had denied he had any idea who might have tried to kill him or any idea why.

"There are several leads that are under investigation," Worton said. "A dark automobile with two unidentified men has been placed in the immediate vicinity of that area in the early hours."

The chief declined to amplify. He said "it would appear that the bomb used might have been a service-type charge." This was at variance with his criminal investigation division men who said the explosive probably was from 25 to 30 sticks of dynamite.

Effects of Blast

The blast blew off a corner of the house, heaved up the foundation, and weakened walls and partitions.

Cohen escaped death by a matter of minutes.

After spending part of the evening at the Mocambo, he and his wife returned home at 12:30 a.m. They retired about an hour later, Cohen told investigators.

At 4:10 a.m. the electronic alarm guarding the Cohen home sounded. Cohen jumped out of bed and ran to the bar, off the den, where is installed the apparatus indicating which of the several photo-electric cell beams around the house had been tripped.

Dog Asleep

It was the front one, aimed from side to side across the semicircular driveway. Cohen, equipped with a flashlight, he told police, went into the dressing room he had used as a bedroom until a few months ago, at the southeast corner of the house, and peered out.

He smelled something burning, he said later, but could see nothing suspicious, so he turned off the floodlights and went back to bed.

Even his Boston bull Toughie, asleep in a basket in the room, had not stirred.

Windows Shattered

At 4:15 a.m. the house heaved in the terrific explosion. Windows and mirrors were shattered, doors and cabinets wrecked and broken, and the house filled with acrid smoke and the dust of powdered plaster.

In the house besides the Cohens was their maid, Kathryn Jones. Also in the menage is their boxer dog, Mike. None was injured.

Cohen estimated damage at $50,000 and said he believes his insurance covers the loss.

The natty gambler, who is on trial for conspiracy in connection with the beating of a radio repairman in the Wilshire district last year, said he didn't

Turn to Page 3, Column 7

Workers Ready for Walkout in Southland

Southern California members of the CIO Communications Workers of America are ready for the nationwide strike of their members that could mean a shutdown of the Bell telephone system tomorrow at 6 a.m.

Don Matheson and Walter Hofer, presidents of the locals, held meetings last night with their picket captains here and in San Diego in preparation for the walkout. They said they had no information of any postponement such as has been proposed by Cyrus Ching in Washington. Ching is head of the Federal Mediation and Conciliation Service.

Thousand Involved

The two striking locals are Divisions 6 and 18. They comprise less than 1000 Southern California workers of Western Electric Co., whose employees are in the WE sales and installation divisions. WE employees do installation work for Pacific Telephone & Telegraph Co. in Southern California.

At union headquarters it was said that it has not been determined yet whether the union will picket all PT&T places or only those in which WE is doing installation or other work.

Another division of the same union embraces about 10,000 employees of the PT&T Southern California system. Spokesmen for that division said its members will not go through any picket lines set up by the divisions that are scheduled to strike WE.

Silent on Picket Lines

Another 10,000 PT&T Southern California employees belong to the independent Federation of Telephone Workers. Its officials have not disclosed whether their members will observe CIO picket lines. In it are telephone operators.

However, this union officially observed the 1947 strike of other telephone workers. The others then were in an independent union that later became the CIO CWA.

PT&T officials said they will use every effort to continue phone service despite the strike if it begins as scheduled. During the 1947 walkout, they maintained almost uninterrupted local service and there was little impairment of long distance service.

Telephone Union Asked to Postpone Walkout

U.S. Mediator Urges Intensified Effort to Reach Settlement During 16-Day Truce

WASHINGTON, Feb. 6 (AP)—Cyrus S. Ching, government mediation chief, today called on the CIO telephone workers to put off their nationwide strike until Feb. 24 and told both sides that they "must" reach a prompt settlement.

With the walkout set for Wednesday, Ching spoke out for intensified bargaining. He warned that a strike might have international consequences by damaging the national economy and our prestige abroad.

Poll Under Way

Joseph A. Beirne, president of the union, wired Ching tonight that its executive board was being polled on Ching's proposal. He promised a reply as soon as the voting is completed. The large board is widely scattered.

Ching's gravely-worded statement—delivered as negotiations in New York appeared to be hopelessly deadlocked—told both the communications workers and the Bell Telephone System that failure to agree would risk their own freedoms. Ching said:

"The consequences may not be limited to a temporary inconvenience to the public.

Hints Congress Action

"Many of the freedoms which both sides presently enjoy and are enjoyed by employers and unions, generally, will be endangered by a demonstration of an absence of sound and stable management-labor relations in the critical communications industry."

Ching appeared to be hinting that a strike shutting down the telephone network of the nation, vital to the economy and national defense, might force Congress to pass legislation extending beyond the telephone industry.

Ching asked company and union to say by noon tomorrow whether they will co-operate in his request for a 16-day delay and a report by Monday, Feb. 20, on the results of stepped-up negotiations.

Integral Part

The strike threat directly applies to 100,000 workers. Union leaders say another 200,000 would be involved because they would refuse to pass picket lines. Because of the far-flung extent of the operations, a union leader said that any decision to delay the walkout will have to be made before tomorrow.

"We could not possibly call off the strike within 24 hours," said this official, Ernest Weaver, president of the installation division of the union.

This branch of the CWA was involved in the New York talks. It is an integral part of the telephone setup, with 11,000 workers in 43 States.

WARNER PROPERTY

Offer of $4,500,000 for Ranch Reported

Negotiations are under way for sale of the 1000-acre horse ranch of Harry M. Warner in San Fernando Valley for development as business and residential property, it was reported yesterday.

Harold J. Perkins, land developer of 7218 Melrose Ave., said he has offered the film magnate $4500 an acre, or approximately $4,500,000 in cash, for the property. The cash would be payable within one year.

Warner is in the East. His personal representative, J. C. Yoss, would neither confirm nor deny the Perkins offer.

"Negotiations concerning the sale of the Woodland Hills property have been under way for some time," Yoss said. "While negotiations are pending, they will of necessity be done in strict confidence."

The land lies north of Ventura Blvd. and east of Topanga Canyon Blvd., with three-quarters of a mile frontage on Ventura Blvd. A survey is being made for a major business development along the Ventura Blvd., Topanga Canyon Blvd. and Canoga Ave. frontages, Perkins said.

THE WEATHER

U.S. Weather Bureau forecast: Partly cloudy today and tomorrow. Occasional drizzles early this morning. Slightly warmer afternoons. High today near 62. Highest temperature yesterday, 60; lowest, 53.

PART 1

Los Angeles Times

EQUAL RIGHTS · LIBERTY UNDER THE LAW · TRUE INDUSTRIAL FREEDOM

ALL THE NEWS ALL THE TIME

VOL. LXIX | IN FOUR PARTS | CC ★ | WEDNESDAY MORNING, JUNE 28, 1950 | 58 PAGES | DAILY, SEVEN CENTS

U.S. JETS HELP PUSH BACK REDS

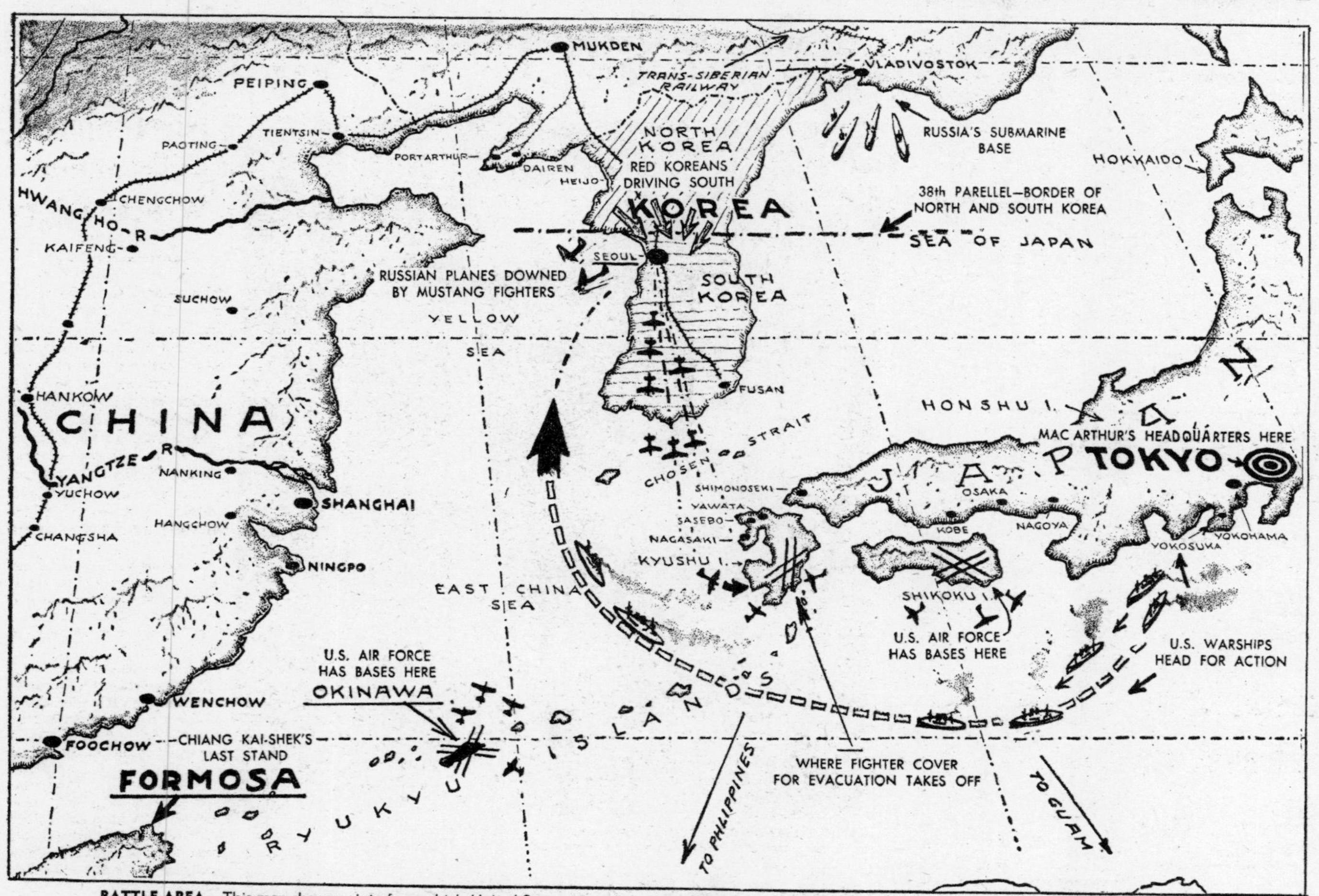

BATTLE AREA—This map shows points from which United States is sending air and naval assistance to Southern Korea fighting northern Communist invasion.

Map by Times Staff Artist Charles Owens

Korea Invading Force Bombed and Strafed; South Holding Seoul

[Additional news and pictures on Korea situation on Pages 2, 4, 5, 6, 7 and 8, Part I.]

TOKYO, June 28 (Wednesday) (AP)—South Korean troops, backed by bombing and strafing U.S. jet fighters and light bombers, today drove the Communist invaders out of Seoul, reliable reports said.

Gen. MacArthur's headquarters announced that 500-pound bombs were rained down on the troops from the Communist north who plunged Korea into civil war with an invasion Sunday.

The swift jets and attack bombers of MacArthur's command were thrown into the swaying battle at the express orders of President Truman, who acted to halt now a conflict leading the world to the brink of war.

An advance echelon of MacArthur's general headquarters was set up in South Korea. His generals were in continuous conference.

Headquarter's latest summary of the situation said southern troops still held Seoul and the capital was quiet. A concentration of about 40 North Korean armored vehicles was reported several miles to the north.

It declared the situation on the front was "substantially unchanged."

The summary declared the initial northern advantage of "surprise and shock action" had been eliminated and the invaders had run into "considerable difficulty in their various attempts to resume the offensive."

Red Forces Rolled Back

It made no further mention of U.S. air or sea activity.

A Moscow broadcast had said that the northerners knifed into Seoul, capital of the U.S.-sponsored South Korean Republic, at four points this morning.

But an American informant said that later reports indicated a southern counterattack had thrown the tank-led troops from the Red north all the way back to the key city of Uijongbu.

This city sits astride the invasion valley 12 miles north of Seoul. Southern Korean reports yesterday said the city had been recaptured. Accounts early today indicated the Reds had swept back through the city and on to the limits of Seoul.

The American informant, who said he was in communication with the South Korean army, declared the counterattack pushed the northerners out of Seoul at about 11:30 a.m.

If all accounts are correct the Reds were in Seoul twice. MacArthur's headquarters said armored elements reached the city yesterday. Later, Korean reports said the Reds were driven back as far as 20 miles from the city yesterday. But today's reports again put the Communists back in the city this morning until they were pushed north.

Naval Units in Action

Somewhere along South Korea's sea frontiers the U.S. naval units based in Japan also were in action.

Despite this, Kim Yong Ju, Korean Minister in Tokyo, said the northerners had landed on an unspecified section of the southeast coast. He added that it was "expected" these invaders would be repulsed.

Kim last communicated with Seoul late last night. At that time, he said, he was informed that North Korean fighters had bombed and strafed Seoul several times.

Breaks in communications with Seoul left in doubt whether President Syngman Rhee and his government still were in the capital. The Moscow radio said Rhee had fled and there was rioting in Seoul. There was no confirmation.

MacArthur's brief headquarters announcement of U.S. warplane attacks said:

"Headquarters of the Far East Air Force announced today that F-80s and B-26s are carrying 500-pound bombs on bombing and strafing missions. The airplanes are armed with 50-caliber machine guns."

Jet Fighters Carry Bombs

The sleek U.S. jet fighters can carry two 500-pound bombs. The light bombers have a larger capacity. The jets do not carry rockets when on bombing missions, but have banked rows of 50-caliber machine guns. On strafing runs they use both rockets and machine guns.

Korean reports said bombers had attacked Communist tanks. It was the north's tank superiority that eased the 30-mile push down the Uijongbu Valley to Seoul.

Key American air bases in Japan were under wartime precautions. Antiaircraft guns, long set up, were ready for instant action. Pilots, ground crews and all officers were on wartime alerts for any emergency.

All information was being analyzed carefully to see whether security was involved as headquarters moved to a wartime basis.

While there was no confirmation, some military quarters expressed nervousness over the abrupt cut in communications to Seoul this morning.

The missions against the Reds were confined to territory south of the 38th parallel which divides North and South Korea.

The Korean Minister said the 10 Mustang fighters turned over to South Korean pilots by the United States also are in battle.

Gen. MacArthur's headquarters issued a terse announce-

Turn to Page 2, Column 8

HIGH-FIGURE BUDGET ADOPTED BY COUNTY

New Tax Rate of $1.78½ Indicated When Supervisors Approve $261,412,865 Program

A record-setting county budget of $261,412,865 for the fiscal year, 1950-51, was adopted yesterday by the Board of Supervisors.

The final figures reached a total less than $100,000 under the preliminary budget estimate despite pleas of taxpayers for cuts of some $7,000,000 during recent public hearings.

Rate Goes Upward

Based on the budget compilation, the new tax rate was placed at $1.785 a $100 of assessed valuation, an increase of 18.5 cents over last year's $1.60 rate.

Although the $1.785 rate is not the highest in county history, next year's total property assessments, which will be made to meet the current budget needs, are expected to soar to new heights.

The Supervisors restored $200,000 to the new budget for free chest X-ray programs after having deleted the sum from the preliminary tabulation.

'Relatively Small'

Spurred by Supervisor Roger W. Jessup, who declared that inasmuch as the county "now spends something like $9,000,000 to treat tubercular patients," the $200,000 for a preventive program "seems relatively small," a majority of the Supervisors rallied behind the support move.

Supervisors Leonard J. Roach and William A. Smith voted against the measure, with Supervisors John Anson Ford and Raymond V. Darby approving it.

The fund will be spent by the Los Angeles County X-Ray Foundation for completion of some 3,000,000 chest examinations this year.

Mercury Here Hits 83 With Visibility Good

Temperature and visibility rose together in Los Angeles yesterday, with the mercury climbing to a noon maximum of 83 deg.—one higher than on Monday. Visibility increased from 1¾ miles at 9 a.m. to 10 miles by 3 p.m.

The forecast was for late night and early morning fog and low clouds, but otherwise clear. It was expected to continue "warm and smoggy" today, with a high of near 88.

The five-day forecast called for increasing night and morning low clouds beginning tomorrow, with temperatures falling from slightly above normal for late June to near or slightly below normal.

Normal temperatures will range from 72 along the coast to 78 in Los Angeles and from 80 to 92 deg. in the coastal and intermediate valleys.

However, it will be the other way around in the interior valleys and desert regions during the same period. Maximum temperatures will range from the low 90s in the higher valleys to 105 to 110 deg. in the Imperial, Coachella and other lower valleys, according to the forecast.

THE WEATHER

U.S. Weather Bureau forecast: Cloudy nights, foggy sunrises, smoggy mornings and clear and warm afternoons today and tomorrow. High temperature today, 88 degs. Highest temperature yesterday, 83; lowest, 56.

ATOMIC PROGRAM SET FOR 'WHATEVER' COMES

WASHINGTON, June 27 (AP)—Rep. Durham (D) N.C., vice-chairman of the Senate-House Committee on Atomic Energy, said today, "The atomic energy program is set for whatever we have to do."

Durham made the statement to reporters in commenting on President Truman's order for aid to Korea. He called the order "the only thing to do."

Liner Passengers Saved After New York Collision

NEW YORK, June 27 (UP)—The American luxury liner Excalibur collided head on with a freighter in the harbor today and began to sink, but her 114 passengers, headed for a 43-day Mediterranean cruise, were removed safely.

Her crew of 130 aided the crews of Coast Guard and civilian craft in removing the passengers from the 9644-ton cruise ship. The operation was completed less than an hour after the Excalibur and the 5146-ton Danish freighter Colombia collided in the narrows separating upper and lower New York Harbors.

No Serious Injuries

The Coast Guard said there were no serious injuries among those on the Excalibur or aboard the Colombia, which carried a crew of 35.

As the rescue operation proceeded almost in the shadows of lower Manhattan's skyscrapers, tugs eased the sinking Excalibur to the Red Hook Flats off Brooklyn, where she was beached in 32 feet of water about 10:35 a.m. The collision occurred at 9:35 a.m.

The bow of the Danish freighter broke into flames but fire boats extinguished them quickly.

Crew members, questioned at the dock by newsmen, charged that the Excalibur was proceeding through the narrows at an excessive speed which they estimated at 10 knots.

A passenger, Harold G. Karnes of Los Angeles, an employee of the Near East Development Co., said most of the passengers seemed more disturbed that they had to repack their luggage.

"My wife and I had just finished unpacking everything and we had to load it all back into the suitcases again," he said. "I figure we just weren't supposed to go."

Lt. and Mrs. Edward W. Samuell and children, Dorothy and Sally, of Santa Barbara, were among the passengers.

Man-Hole Cover, Blown Into Air, Cuts Power Line

A man-hole cover, flung 50 feet into the air by a sewer gas explosion, severed a 15,000-volt high-tension line last night, making lights flutter weirdly for five minutes at Inglewood, Hawthorne and Hermosa Beach.

Many of the area's residents, nerves raw from threat of war, thought hostilities had opened.

Hawthorne police said their switchboard was besieged with calls from persons excitedly demanding to know if there had been a surprise attack.

Auxiliary equipment was quickly put to use and service returned to normal as repair crews worked on the damaged wire.

Evacuee Ship in Distress

Tokyo, June 28 Wednesday, (UP)—Japanese maritime security board reported today that an American ship with 600 evacuees from South Korea was in distress in heavy seas. A Japanese rescue ship was reported enroute to the scene.

No other information was immediately available.

FEATURES INDEX

20 Take Examinations for Chief of Police

Twenty candidates for Chief of Police of Los Angeles yesterday began taking oral examinations before a City Civil Service Commission board. Page 1, Part 2.

On Other Pages

Truman Orders Planes and Ships to Aid Korea

Pravda Charges 'Direct Act of Aggression' Against Northern Reds and Communist China

WASHINGTON, June 27 (AP)—President Truman today dispatched American warships and planes to help embattled South Korea and drew a taut line against the spread of Communist aggression in the Far Pacific.

In the first Russian reaction to the order, the Communist Party organ, Pravda, charged the United States with a "direct act of aggression against the Korean People's Democratic Republic and the People's Republic of China." The editorial was broadcast by Moscow Radio and heard in London by the Soviet monitor.

The President's historic order, committing the United States in the strongest terms since World War II, also directed the U.S. 7th Fleet to protect Formosa against any invasion from Red China.

He directed that American military aid be speeded up to the Philippines and Indo-China.

The President acted two days after the Russian-backed North Koreans launched an invasion of South Korea, which is supported by the United States.

Bursts of Applause

"The attack upon Korea makes it plain beyond all doubt that Communism has passed beyond the use of subversion to conquer independent nations and will now use armed invasion and war," Mr. Truman said.

The President's dramatic action, greeted with bursts of applause on Capitol Hill, was keyed with other swift-breaking developments in the Korean crisis.

Secretary of Defense Johnson told newsmen the President's order does not commit this country to send any land troops into action.

Asked if mobilization will be required in the United States, Johnson replied tersely: "At the moment, no."

Senate Majority Leader Lucas (D) Ill., announced in the Senate that negotiations are under way to get other nations to join the United States in armed support of South Korea. Congressional leaders of both parties swung quickly behind the President in support of his momentous decision.

Termed Aggression

The Pravda editorial said:

"Truman's statement and actions, unprecedented in international relations of the postwar period, constitute further evidence that American ruling circles no longer restrict themselves to preparation for aggression but have gone over to direct acts of aggression."

"But have they not gone too far?" the newspaper asked.

The editorial charged that the U.S. government, "with its inherent disregard of international

Turn to Page 2, Column 4

EXTENSION OF DRAFT POWER FOR YEAR VOTED

WASHINGTON, June 27 (AP)—Senate-House conferees today voted a one-year extension of the President's existing power to draft young men.

In quick order the House voted, 315 to 4, to ratify the extension. The Senate agreed to vote on the measure tomorrow.

The extension also would empower the President to order the National Guard and all reserves to immediate active duty.

The Senate-House group obviously acted because of the tense Korean situation.

They junked previous restrictions voted by the Senate and House upon Presidential authority to induct man power.

Sen. Byrd (D) Va., one of the conferees, said the previously deadlocked lawmakers had quickly agreed today that this is no time to have the world think there is a dispute here over such a matter.

Previously the House had voted a two-year extension of the peacetime Draft Act requiring registration of young men 18 through 25 years. It retained in the hands of Congress the authority for inductions or actual drafting.

The Senate had voted a three-year extension also retaining "trigger control" over actual drafting when Congress was in session.

PART 1

Los Angeles Times

EQUAL RIGHTS
LIBERTY UNDER THE LAW — TRUE INDUSTRIAL FREEDOM

ALL THE NEWS
ALL THE TIME

VOL. LXIX — IN FIVE PARTS — C C — THURSDAY MORNING, NOVEMBER 2, 1950 — 92 PAGES — DAILY, SEVEN CENTS

TRUMAN ASSASSINATION FOILED; TWO SLAIN

AFTER SHOOTING—Police and spectators crowd around entrance of Blair House, temporary residence of President Truman and his family, after Puerto Rican assassins attempted to kill President. Wounded gunman lies on steps after battle. His companion was killed and a White House policeman was fatally shot. Three were wounded. (AP) Wirephoto

Puerto Rican Rebels and Police Battle at Doors of Blair House

BY BILL HENRY

WASHINGTON, Nov. 1 — Two trigger-happy Puerto Ricans bent on the assassination of President Truman today turned peaceful Pennsylvania Ave. in front of the temporary White House into a daylight shooting gallery.

After 30 seconds of frenzied excitement during which half a hundred shots were fired, one of the would-be assassins, Griselio Torresola, lay dead on the Blair House lawn and his partner, Oscar Collazo, 37, and three White House policemen lay wounded. One of the latter, Pvt. Leslie Coffelt, 40, died in emergency hospital.

Truman Awakened by Shots

Hugh E. Baughman, chief of the Secret Service, said Collazo told Secret Service agents:

"We came here for the express purpose of shooting the President."

Maj. Robert J. Barrett, superintendent of the metropolitan police, announced tonight that Collazo had been booked on a murder charge.

Baughman said that police protection for Mr. Truman would be increased until an investigation has been completed.

President Truman, meanwhile, had been asleep in an upstairs bedroom of the Blair House. Awakened by the shots,

Full page of pictures on Page 3, Part I

he stepped gingerly to the window, since he was attired only in his underwear, and was promptly waved away by a vigilant policeman who spotted him from a sidewalk.

A moment later the President was joined by Mrs. Truman who had also been awakened by the firing, but they remained inside the Blair House. Half an hour after the shooting the President, with no visible indication of nerves, was whisked away to an engagement at the Arlington National Cemetery where he delivered a brief eulogy to the late British Field Marshal Dill.

Scene of Mad Confusion

When I arrived on the scene a moment or two after the shooting, Collazo was lying at the foot of the stairs leading into the Blair House and Torresola on the lawn behind the hedge.

White House police were administering first aid to the three wounded officers and the entire area was the scene of mad confusion.

The shooting took place at approximately 2:20 p.m. Washington time when traffic on the sidewalk in front of the White House and in the street was quite heavy. How so many shots could have been fired without striking any of the passers-by is a miracle almost impossible to explain.

What happened was this:

The two Puerto Ricans, one of whom carried on his person two letters signed by Pedro Campos, head of the Puerto Rican Nationalist Party which this week staged an unsuccessful revolution, had been in Washington for a couple of days, having come here from New York.

Suspicious Click Heard

One of them, Collazo, today sauntered past the police pillbox just east of the Blair House, passing Officer Davidson of the White House police and Floyd Boring, a Secret Service man who frequently acts as driver for the President.

Thirty feet away Pvt. Donald T. Birdzell, 41, of the White House police, was standing at his post under the canopy at the foot of the stairs leading to Blair House. This is the entrance and exit normally used by President Truman and he was due to leave for the services at Arlington within a few minutes.

Birdzell heard a suspicious click, turned just in time to receive the first bullet from Collazo's P-38. Birdzell, seeking to draw the fire away from the Blair House, ran toward the curb where he fell with both knees shattered by the assailant's bullets.

Drops in Pool of Blood

Meantime, Davidson and Boring pulled their guns and Collazo dropped in a pool of his own blood at the foot of the Blair House stairs. He was shot through the body, but is expected to live.

Accounts are not clear as to whether or not Torresola came from across the street or from the other direction. In any event, he leaped the barrier to the Blair House lawn firing his German Luger at the officers occupying the pillbox at the west end of the building.

Torresola also wounded Joseph H. Downs, 44, who is in a critical condition tonight.

Someone, presumably either Coffelt or Downs, ended Torresola's career with a bullet through the head.

Quick Action Praised

Baughman was high in his praise of the quick action of both the White House police and Secret Service personnel on the scene.

He said that the Secret Service had been aware of the activities of the Puerto Rican Nationalists, but that the two men who participated in today's shooting were strangers to his organization.

He said that if the authenticity of the notes from Campos

Turn to Page 2, Column 1

RED TRAP CATCHES U.N. FIGHTING FORCE

More Than Four Divisions Put on Defensive by Chinese and Koreans Firing New Rockets

SEOUL, Nov. 2 (Thursday) (AP)—Chinese and North Koreans attacked today with rockets, howitzers and self-propelled guns in Northwest Korea, trapping some retreating United Nations units and putting more than four divisions on the defensive.

A U.S. 1st Army Corps spokesman, acknowledging for the first time that Chinese troops are fighting in that sector, said the situation was "very serious."

Hard fighting also was in progress in Northeast Korea but on a smaller scale. Chinese troops had been reported previously in this area.

Russ-Built Planes

Russian-built jet planes, which fought sky battles yesterday over the northwest battle front, appeared again briefly today. American pilots said they saw similar jets in the air across the Manchurian border above the Chinese Communist city of Antung.

The ground attacks, unleashed in strength last night, were being pressed on the right flank of a U.S. 24th Division armored column trying to push quickly to the Manchurian border. It advanced four miles today to within 15 air miles of the frontier.

The column, driving up a west coast road beyong Charyongwan, was headed for the Korean border city of Sinuiju, across the Yalu River from Antung. It slammed through resisting Reds and beat off two counterattacks today.

Yanks Encircled

The sector of greatest peril for U.N. forces was around Unsan, some 60 miles east of the advancing American column.

U.S. 1st Cavalry Division elements were surrounded last night and remained encircled today. A 1st Corps spokesman said it was a regiment. A U.S. 8th Army spokesman referred to it as a battalion.

Other 1st Cavalry troops were trying to fight their way to the rescue of the isolated group.

A battalion of the South Ko-

Turn to Page 6, Column 2

Stassen Will Answer Truman Campaign Talk

WASHINGTON, Nov. 1 (AP)—Republican leaders today tapped Harold Stassen, 1948 Presidential aspirant, to reply for their party to President Truman's Saturday night campaign speech.

The GOP National Committee announced that Stassen will speak over the Mutual network at 10:30 p.m. (EST), 7:30 p.m. PST) Saturday—immediately after Mr. Truman concludes a four-network broadcast.

Stassen will speak from New Haven, Ct.

They turned to Stassen, president of the University of Pennsylvania, after Sen. Vandenberg (R) Mich., begged off from undertaking the job. Vandenberg's office in Grand Rapids, Mich., said he told GOP leaders he was sorry but he could not do it because of doctor's orders. His health has been poor for months.

Republicans indicated they probably would retain only one radio network, probably Mutual, because of the cost. A single hookup would cost about $15,000 compared with the more than $50,000 the Democrats planned to lay out for four radio networks plus a television line-up for Mr. Truman.

THE WEATHER

U.S. Weather Bureau forecast: Mostly clear today and tomorrow. Warmer today with a high near 90. Highest temperature yesterday 83 deg.; lowest, 55.

Landlord Here Raises Rent as Test of Power

In a bold move to test the right of Housing Expediter Tighe E. Woods to refuse to decontrol rents here, Frank W. Babcock, Los Angeles apartment house owner, served notice on 106 tenants yesterday that their rents will be boosted sharply on Dec. 1.

Babcock's attorneys previously announced that he would take the lead in challenging Woods' position in the bitter rent battle here. The landlord subsequently filed suit against the Housing Expediter to compel him to sign the rent decontrol resolution passed by the Los Angeles City Council last July 28.

Advice Given Owners

Quickly following Babcock's action, the Apartment, Hotel and Motel Association of California late yesterday advised Los Angeles apartment house owners to serve 30-day notices regarding rent raises or evictions to tenants immediately.

Babcock is a member of the association and his attorney, Austin Clapp, also represents the organization.

"We feel certain," said Willard Smith, vice-president of the association, "that there will be a

Turn to Page 10, Column 1

FEATURES INDEX

Dr. Lindstrom Awarded Divorce From Bergman

Dr. Peter Lindstrom is given a divorce in Superior Court here from Ingrid Bergman, the proceedings bringing forth some new and startling revelations. Page 1, Part II.

On Other Pages

George Bernard Shaw Dies at English Cottage

94-Year-Old World-Renowned Dramatist and Wit Passes After Saying, 'I Want to Sleep'

AYOT ST. LAWRENCE, Eng., Nov. 2 (Thursday) (AP)—George Bernard Shaw, one of the modern age's greatest dramatists and its most caustic critic, died today at the age of 94.

DIES — George Bernard Shaw, famed playwright and wit, succumbs at 94. (AP) photo

The white-bearded Irish-born sage, whose wit was renowned throughout the world for a half century, succumbed at 5:05 a.m.

"Oh, Nancy, I want to sleep," Shaw told Virginia-born Lady Astor, who was at his bedside during his last hours.

Shaw's death was announced to newsmen by his housekeeper, Mrs. Alice Laden.

Wearing black, she appeared at the gates of the cottage, Shaw's Corner, and told the reporters: "Mr. Shaw is dead."

Prayers Offered

Vegetarian, teetotaling Shaw, who professed himself both a Communist and an atheist, was visited in his last hours by an Anglican clergyman who said final prayers for the old sage's soul.

"It is wrong to say that he was an atheist," said the minister, the Rev. R. G. Davies. "He believed in God."

Shaw lapsed into his final coma yesterday at 3 a.m. and never regained consciousness. Operated on seven weeks ago for a broken thigh, suffered when he slipped and fell in his garden, Shaw grew steadily weaker. A bladder ailment aggravated his condition.

Lights burned for two nights in Shaw's Corners, the red brick

Turn to Page 12, Column 1

MANCHURIA COLOR MAP TO APPEAR NEXT SUNDAY

The North Korean battleground and the vast reaches of Manchuria beyond are presented in great detail in a full-page color map to be published in next Sunday's Times.

With U.N. forces driving close to the Korea-Manchuria border and untold numbers of Chinese Reds poised for entrance into the battle, the area covered by the Times map looms as a source of war headlines in the very near future.

The full-page color map of Manchuria and North Korea will appear exclusively in The Times next Sunday.

U.N. Keeps Lie in Post Over Russ Protest

NEW YORK, Nov. 1 (AP)—The U.N. General Assembly today extended Secretary-General Trygve Lie's term for three more years despite a Soviet bloc threat not to deal with him.

By a vote of 46 to 5 with 7 abstentions, the Assembly supported the United States position that Lie should be kept in office as an expression of confidence for the way he handled the Korean case.

Led by Vishinsky

Before keeping Lie in the $40,000-a-year job, the Assembly rejected a Soviet resolution to toss the matter back to the Security Council which had failed to agree on a candidate after a month of consideration. The vote on the Russian proposal was 9 in favor, 37 against and 11 abstaining.

An Iraqi resolution to refer the issue to a seven-member committee for a two-week study also was rejected. The vote on this was 15 for, 37 against and 7 abstaining.

The Assembly action came after a day and a half of de-

Turn to Page 7, Column 4

Bombs Set Off in N.Y. Office of Puerto Rico

NEW YORK, Nov. 1 (U.P.)—Two bottle bombs, commonly called "Molotov cocktails," were thrown into offices of the Puerto Rican government shortly after noon today.

The two bottles, filled with gasoline, were tossed into the first floor offices of a four-story building which contain the local offices of the Department of Labor of Puerto Rico. They burst into flame and burned fiercely, but soon burned out. No one was injured. The damage was not extensive.

The bottles were hurled by an unidentified man described as about 45 years old, of dark complexion and short and stocky stature. It was believed a local repercussion of the Nationalist uprising in Puerto Rico.

1951–1960

PART I

Los Angeles Times

EQUAL RIGHTS

LIBERTY UNDER THE LAW — TRUE INDUSTRIAL FREEDOM

ALL THE NEWS ALL THE TIME

VOL. LXX — IN FOUR PARTS — C C ★ — WEDNESDAY MORNING, APRIL 11, 1951 — 68 PAGES — DAILY, SEVEN CENTS

TRUMAN FIRES MACARTHUR

Hayden Names Reds in Hollywood

Film Star, Marine Veteran, Was in Party Seven Months, He Says

WASHINGTON, April 10 (U.P.)—Movie Actor Sterling Hayden, World War II marine veteran, testified today he joined the Communist Party in a burst of misguided emotion in June, 1946, but quit in disgust seven months later.

The actor, who ticked off the names of several members of his Hollywood cell including former Actress Karen Morley, said he returned from highly dangerous war service with Marshal Tito's Yugoslav partisans imbued with the idea of righting the world's wrongs.

Hayden, ex-husband of Screen Actress Madeleine Carroll, told the House Un-American Activities Committee it was in this mood he was recruited into the party by a woman named Bea Winter, then secretary to his agent, Berg Allenberg. He said she now is employed by Sam Spiegel, independent producer.

Names Given

The actor, second Hollywood figure to confess former Red affiliations, also revealed he had handed investigators a list of film colony persons he believes "by conjecture" to be Communists. He refused to tell reporters how many he had listed.

Rep. Moulder (D) Mo., told Hayden he was satisfied "you gave honest testimony—I have concluded that you are an intensely loyal American citizen." Hayden thanked him.

But Rep. Kearney (R) N.Y., said he was not satisfied with Hayden's testimony that he could not remember more persons at Communist cell meetings. Kearney said he could go to an Elks lodge meeting and "tell you at least 15 people who had been there."

The first witness in the committee's revived Communism-in-Hollywood hearings were Larry Parks, leading actor in "The Jolson Story," who likewise admitted he was a onetime Communist Party member who later repented. Two other previous witnesses, Actor Howard di Silva and Actress Gale Sondergaard, refused to answer questions and were threatened with contempt prosecution.

When Hayden concluded the committee recessed until tomorrow when it will question Actor Will Geer, one of some 40 other figures of screen, radio, stage and television subpoenaed by the group.

Back Lot Workers

Hayden said he attended a series of party meetings at which a principal subject was the 1946 studio workers strike. He was told, he testified, that it would be very helpful if the Screen Actors Guild, of which he was a member, could be lined up behind the walkout.

Hayden, who plays he-man roles and has had a career rivaling a movie scenario, said most of his cell members were "back lot workers" such as carpenters

Turn to Page 9, Column 1

Recording of Truman Phone Talks Revealed

Investigators Disclose Sen. Tobey Has Transcriptions of Two Calls on RFC

WASHINGTON, April 10 (U.P.)—Sen. Charles W. Tobey (R) N.H., has told Senate investigators he has recordings of two telephone conversations with President Truman about the RFC investigation, it was learned tonight.

In the first conversation, Mr. Truman reportedly told Tobey that RFC records show some Congressman had gotten fees for getting loans from the Reconstruction Finance Corp.

But in the second conversation, which one informed source said Tobey originated, the President told the Senator he had been mistaken about the fees to Congressmen.

Part of One Talk

Tobey made the disclosures at a secret meeting of the RFC investigating subcommittee headed by Sen. J. William Fulbright, (D) Ark., it was learned.

According to informed sources, Tobey caught only part of the first conversation with Mr. Truman on an office recording device. One source said Tobey told the subcommittee he recorded all of the second one.

Members of the subcommittee declined to comment on the reports. Tobey, a former member, was not immediately available.

Exact dates of the two conversations with the White House were not established. However, the first phone call from Mr. Truman was believed to have been made shortly after the President demanded from the RFC copies of all correspondence regarding RFC loans written by Senators and House members.

The second conversation was reported to have been held some time later.

Truman's Statement

Mr. Truman announced after getting the letters from the RFC that he had found no evidence of "illegal influence" in the files.

Tobey made the phone recording disclosures in the same meeting at which the subcommittee heard private testimony from Sen. Wheeler (D) Mont., about a call to Tobey at the request of White House Aide David K. Niles.

Wheeler testified he asked Tobey to "go easy on" Donald S.

Turn to Page 6, Column 5

UMT SETUP PLAN SHELVED BY HOUSE

WASHINGTON, April 10 (U.P.) The House ignored an eleventh-hour appeal from Defense Secretary Marshall today and voted against setting up a universal military training program at this time.

On a series of voice votes the chamber approved amendments to its UMT-draft bill which would put the training program on a stand-by basis and require passage of another law when, and if, Congress decides UMT should go into effect.

A proposal by Rep. Barden (D) N.C., which would kill UMT outright, may come up for a vote tomorrow. The Barden measure would retain only the draft features of the administration measure—lowering the draft age from 19 to 18½ and extending the term of service from 21 to 26 months.

Shortly before the vote Marshall urged Congress to give the administration a free hand in setting up UMT whenever it thinks the world situation calls for it. He told a news conference he was afraid Congress would "emasculate" the training program.

The amendment to put the UMT program on a stand-by basis was offered by sponsors of the UMT-draft bill in an effort to ward off outright rejection of UMT. They believed their proposal assured passage of the bill.

DRIVERS FACE ARREST IF AUTOS SMOKE

Police action against drivers of motor vehicles exuding smoke from exhaust pipes was authorized yesterday by the Board of Supervisors.

The county governors, for the first time in the battle against smog, invoked a section of the State Vehicle Code which provides that "no motor vehicle shall be operated in a manner resulting in the escape of excessive smoke, gas, oil or fuel residue."

The county board ordered that deputies be appointed by the Sheriff from among personnel of the Air Pollution Control District office here. The deputies will be vested with arrest powers.

Under State law violators are subject to misdemeanor charges carrying penalties of $500 fine or six months in jail.

Jury Indicts Walker for Cook Slayings

An indictment charging Lawrence J. Walker, 20, with the murders of Richard and Doris Cook and five other felonies was returned by the Riverside County grand jury in a special session yesterday.

The Cook couple, both 18, were murdered in desert wastelands near Lake Mathews, Riverside County, last March 26. Cook's body was found beside his automobile on Cajalco Road at 11:25 a.m. that day. Mrs. Cook's body was not found until two days later, being located near an abandoned quarry 11.4 miles east of the spot where her husband was slain.

Hear 14 Witnesses

Yesterday's indictment was returned by the grand jury after two-and-a-half hours' deliberation that followed testimony by 14 witnesses.

The true bill was returned before Presiding Judge John G. Gabbert, who remanded Walker to Riverside County Jail without bail. Judge Gabbert ordered Walker arraigned at 9:30 a.m. today.

At a press conference immediately prior to the grand jury meeting yesterday, Dist. Atty. William O. Mackey announced that full information regarding evidence gathered by investigators from his office, the Riverside County Sheriff and the Riverside Police Department, will be outlined by him at another conference today.

Evidence Kept Secret

The evidence, much of it circumstantial, heretofore has been jealously kept secret by investigators and Mackey.

In addition to the two murder charges, Walker is accused of kidnaping and attempting to criminally attack Mrs. Cook; kidnaping and criminally attacking Mrs. Betty Maund in Riverside, and assault with deadly weapon on Sgt. James Hicks, Mrs. Maund's escort.

Thirteen witnesses appeared before the jury in rapid-fire order, but the jury visited another wit-

Turn to Page 12, Column 1

FEATURES INDEX

$1,000,000 Given for Missionaries' Home

A Chinese who attributes his success to his missionary education has written a $1,000,000 check to finance a Duarte home for retired missionaries. Story on Page 1, Part 2.

On Other Pages

Red Rallying Base Blasted by U.N. Guns

Foe Nearly Cleared From South Korea as MacArthur Goes

TOKYO, April 11 (Wednesday) (AP)—U.N. forces had the Reds cleared out of all South Korea except for one small northwest fragment today—their last day under Gen. MacArthur's command.

As reports of new allied successes arrived from Lt. Gen. Matthew B. Ridgway's 8th Army headquarters, announcement came from Washington that President Truman had removed MacArthur from all his commands in favor of Ridgway.

The announcement, first heard here over Army radio, struck headquarters like a thunderclap.

Out on the battlefield in Korea, allied planes and artillery were reported to have wiped out Chorwon, the rallying center of three Chinese Red armies in West-Central Korea.

Reds Abandon Town

East of the Hwachon power site the Reds were reported to have abandoned the town of Inje. Inje, four miles north of the 38th parallel and 25 miles east of the town of Hwachon, is in a sector where the Reds have been putting up a stiff fight.

Allied ruining of Chorwon deprived the Reds of one of their most important supply and assembly centers. Artillery began pounding Chorwon three days ago.

Gen. MacArthur's intelligence officers estimated last week that the Reds were massing up to 500,000 men in the Chorwon-Kumhwa-Hwachon triangle for an expected counteroffensive.

But MacArthur's midmorning communique said his U.N. forces held the initiative all across Korea yesterday and scored gains.

Turks Cross River

Just north of the 38th parallel on a highway leading up to Chorwon Turk'sh infantry crossed the Hantan River yesterday. Brushing aside light Red resistance, the Turks seized a hill southeast of Yonchon, 13 miles southwest of Chorwon.

Chinese and North Korean Reds now have been driven back

Turn to Page 2, Column 4

Eight Airmen Die as Glider Pickup Fails

FAIRBANKS, Alaska, April 10 (AP)—Eight airmen perished today in the crash of an Air Force C-54 in a glider pick-up attempt.

Witnesses said the four-engine transport exploded and burst into flames after striking the south runway of Ladd Air Force Base. There was no chance for any of the men aboard to escape.

Tonight the names of three of the eight victims were released by the Air Force. They were: Capt. George H. Wood, pilot, Battle Creek, Mich.; Capt. Bernard W. Stark, navigator, East Orange, N.J., and Staff Sgt. George W. Hollister, crew chief, Herington, Kan.

'MR. ROBERTS' RULED OUT AS TOO TOUGH FOR GIS

FRANKFURT, April 11 (Wednesday) (U.P.)—The United States 7th Army has ruled that the seagoing language of the play "Mr. Roberts" is too rough for the ears of soldiers.

A GI production of the Broadway hit was to have appeared in Frankfurt, but it was canceled by the Army "for technical reasons." One officer admitted that objections were made to the language used in the play.

The GI show already had played to audiences in Heidelberg and Stuttgart before it was canceled for Frankfurt. Officials would not say who objected to the play's language, but there were hints that "some general's wife" was responsible.

The Army chaplains' corps insisted it had no hand in the matter.

In New Orleans, Joshua Logan, who wrote the stage version of the popular book, said: "I spent four and one-half years in the Army and I consider the dialogue of 'Mr. Roberts' mild in comparison to the true speech of servicemen . . . I cannot believe it is too strong for the ears of the United States Army."

OUSTED—Gen. Douglas MacArthur, forced out as allied commander in Far East by President Truman, who said the general was unable to support U.S. policies in Asia.

General's Ouster Stuns U.S. Officers and Japs

MacArthur Staff Members Bitter at Truman Action; Commander Keeps Silent

TOKYO, April 11 (Wednesday) (AP)—A small brown envelope with "flash" printed on it in red carried to Gen. MacArthur today the news that he had been fired from his commands by President Truman.

It was delivered to the five-star general by a senior aide, Col. Sid Huff.

Huff said MacArthur received the news without comment. He indicated the general had no forewarning that he was being relieved.

The general said he would have no statement immediately.

The message came as a Signal Corps communication about the time the Army radio announced MacArthur was finished as commander.

MacArthur got the news while at lunch with his wife, Sen. Warren Magnuson (R) Wash., and William Sterns, of Northwest Airlines. He was joined a few minutes later by his 13-year-old son Arthur.

Relayed by Embassy

The American Embassy got the news and reporters relayed it to Gen. MacArthur's honor guard. Guardsmen flocked around their recreation room in stiff silence.

One captain remarked: "I won't believe it until I see it on paper."

Sgt. Phillip Oberst, the guard at the gate, said: "Boy, they sure made a big mistake."

The Embassy was strangely silent despite the scurrying of reporters and movements of headquarters staff cars as the news was confirmed.

MacArthur himself was at his American Embassy residence for his customary afternoon rest. He was not immediately available.

Staff officers, discussing the report of the impending action a few minutes before the historic White House news conference, all said they did not believe the Prsident would take such a step.

The report spread quickly

Turn to Page 2, Column 2

Visibility Cut by Drizzles, Fog and Smog

Drizzles, fog and smog yesterday held Los Angeles visibility to three-fourths of a mile at 8 a.m. and two miles at 4 p.m.

The haze and smoke lifted slightly in the afternoon, with the maximum visibility measuring 2½ miles at 2 and 3 p.m. Temperatures ranged from a low of 56 deg. at 6:54 a.m. to a high of 64 at 3:14 p.m.

The Weather Bureau forecast cloudy skies during the nights and mornings and hazy afternoons for today and tomorrow. Warmer temperatures are expected for today, with a high near 68.

Barbara Hutton Has Virus Attack

NEW YORK, April 10 (U.P.)—Woolworth Heiress Barbara Hutton is in a "serious condition" with a virus attack in a Manhattan hospital, it was learned tonight.

Intimates of Miss Hutton said, however, that the latest physician's bulletin indicated "some improvement" and that there was "no reason to believe that she won't pull through."

THE WEATHER

U.S. Weather Bureau forecast: Cloudy nights and mornings today and tomorrow, with partly cloudy skies and hazy sunshine in the afternoons. Warmer today, with a high today near 68. Highest temperature yesterday, 64; lowest, 56.

General to Lose All Commands at Once; Ridgway Is Successor

WASHINGTON, April 11 (AP)—President Truman early today forced Gen. MacArthur from all his commands.

The President said he had concluded that MacArthur "is unable to give his wholehearted support" to United States and United Nations policies.

Mr. Truman immediately designated Lt. Gen. Matthew B. Ridgway as MacArthur's successor as supreme commander, allied powers, commander in chief, United Nations command; commander in chief, Far East; and commanding general, U.S. Army, Far East.

In a statement, Mr. Truman asserted that "military commanders must be governed" by policies and directives of the government and "in time of crisis, this consideration is particularly compelling."

New 8th Army Chief Named

The President appointed Lt. Gen. James A. Van Fleet to succeed Ridgway to take over active command of the 8th Army.

Announcement of the almost unprecedented dismissal of the hero-general was made at a rare news conference at

For full page of pictures showing Gen. MacArthur in various phases of his military career, turn to Page 3, Part I.

the White House at 1 a.m. (EST). The time was fixed to coincide as nearly as possible with the delivery to MacArthur at Tokyo of the order relieving him of his commands, "effective at once."

The White House released, with the President's statement, a memorandum purporting to show differences between MacArthur's statements and action and Presidential policy.

Order Made Effective at Once

The President's order, telegraphed to MacArthur over the Army network, was brief and pointed:

"I deeply regret that it becomes my duty as President and Commander in Chief of the United States military forces to replace you as supreme commander, allied powers; commander in chief, United Nations command; commander in chief, Far East; commanding general, U.S. Army Far East.

"You will turn over your commands, effective at once, to Lt. Gen. Matthew B. Ridgway. You are authorized to have issued such orders as are necessary to complete desired travel to such places as you select.

"My reasons for your replacement will be made public concurrently with the delivery to you of the foregoing order, and are contained in the next following message." (This referred to the President's statement.)

Aftermath of Differences

The President's action came as the aftermath of a series of differences with MacArthur over policy in the Far East and raised prospects that MacArthur might return to this country to deliver a series of blasts against the administration, probably under auspices of Republican supporters of the general.

These differences embraced not only the question of MacArthur's sympathy with the administration's policy but also fundamental views toward the struggle against Communism.

MacArthur is on record in favor of waging a more vigorous war in Asia. He said the west was fighting Europe's battles in the Far East.

The general wanted to bomb Red Chinese bases in Manchuria and also wanted Nationalist Chinese troops released from Formosa to fight the Reds, possibly in a second front on the mainland.

The Truman administration felt these policies could lead to all-out war with China. This was the view of many U.S. allies, who regarded Europe as the critical area and wanted to concentrate defenses there.

The President's statement asserted that Gen. MacArthur's place in history "as one of our greatest commanders" is fully established.

"The nation owes him a debt of gratitude for the distinguished and exceptional service which he has rendered his country in posts of great responsibility," the President's statement said.

"For that reason I repeat my regret at the necessity for the action I feel compelled to take in his case."

Secret Directives Made Public

Aware of political reverberations certain to follow in the wake of his action, the President made public a series of heretofore secret directives tending to show how MacArthur failed to follow administrative foreign policy.

These included one from the Joint Chiefs of Staff to MacArthur and other commanders on Dec. 6, 1950, embracing a Presidential order that "no speech, press release, or other public statement concerning foreign policy

Turn to Page 2, Column 8

PART 1

Los Angeles Times

EQUAL RIGHTS
LIBERTY UNDER THE LAW TRUE INDUSTRIAL FREEDOM

ALL THE NEWS
ALL THE TIME

VOL. LXX IN THREE PARTS C C SATURDAY MORNING, OCTOBER 27, 1951 32 PAGES DAILY, 10c

Churchill Party Holds 26-Seat Majority in House of Commons

Yanks Down Two Red Jets, Cripple Three

Ground Action Slows; Committees Bargain at Peace Parley

U.S. 8TH ARMY HEADQUARTERS, Korea, Oct. 27 (Saturday) (AP) — American jets shot down two more Russian-made MIG-15s yesterday in the continuing series of flashing dogfights over Northwest Korea. Three Red jets were reported damaged.

Ground action slowed while subcommittees bargained at the Panmunjom truce talks, but some allied gains were made in Western and Central Korea.

Although relatively minor, the fighting was bitter—some of it hand-to-hand.

Total Brought to 13

The two Russian-made jets shot down by U.S. F-86 Sabre jets Friday brought to 13 the number the 5th Air Force has listed as blasted out of the Korean skies in six straight days of air battles. Thirty-five Red jets have been reported damaged.

Allied losses for the period were reported as two fighters and four B-29 bombers shot down and six B-29s damaged.

On the battle front, allied infantrymen made minor gains in the west against stubborn Chinese Red resistance. The 8th Army reported the Chinese were shoved off some high ground northwest of Yonchon.

Allies and Reds Fail to Select Truce Line

MUNSAN, Korea, Oct. 27 (Saturday) (AP)—Allied and Communist truce negotiators today for two hours grappled without success with the problem of where to draw a cease-fire line across Korea.

A dispatch from Panmunjom, where subcommittees of the truce team are meeting, quoted Brig. Gen. William P. Nuckols as saying there was "very little, if any progress." Nuckols is spokesman for the United Nations command.

There was cause for some optimism, however. The Communists had abandoned their demand that the line hew to the 38th parallel. Apparently the allies still were sticking to their demand for a line roughly following the present battlefront.

Issue Clarified

The line which the Reds did suggest at yesterday's subcommittee meeting in Panmunjom was quickly rejected by the United Nations negotiators "because it does not provide military protection for our troops."

However, Red failure to insist on the old 38th parallel boundary was the most important development since the truce talks began last July 10.

For the first time it lifted the issue out of the political arena and placed it where the U.N. said it always belonged—in the military field.

ENVOY REPORTS U.S. GAINS IN RUSS RELATIONS

WASHINGTON, Oct. 26 (AP) — Ambassador Allan G. Kirk said after a talk with President Truman today that relations with Soviet Russia show "signs of turning in our favor."

Kirk expressed the opinion that "relations are not quite as tough as they were," but he added:

"We have to continue to be firm and consistent in our policies."

The envoy, home from Moscow for consultations, had a half-hour meeting with Mr. Truman at the White House. Kirk said they discussed the situation in Russia in general terms.

Kirk told reporters he based his feeling that relations are turning in favor of the United States and the west on the attitude of his government and the United Nations. He said that "we know what limits to set."

Delayed Test of A-Bomb Seen Serious

BY GENE SHERMAN
Times Staff Representative

LAS VEGAS, Oct. 26—Bitter, blustery weather caused cancellation of the second nuclear detonation in the current atomic test series at the Nevada proving ground early this morning.

Now behind schedule, the Atomic Energy Commission alerted this desert community for an atomic air drop over the Yucca Flat test site on a 50-50 chance that prevailing unfavorable weather would clear sufficiently by dawn to allow the operation.

Delay Serious

When it did not, the drop was canceled and it remained doubtful whether the detonation would occur before Sunday or Monday morning at the earliest.

The fact that the AEC for the first time alerted for a test on a tentative basis indicated the seriousness of the present program's delay.

The usual procedure calls for a definite go-ahead decision, which nevertheless is subject to revision at the last minute if weather turns unfavorable or if any one of a multiplicity of details goes wrong.

50-50 Chance

This morning's decision, relayed through the Civil Aeronautics Administration at midnight, was converse in that it depended upon obviously impossible weather turning favorable at the proper time. The AEC's meteorologist gave this possibility a 50-50 chance, and rather than to lose even that chance the commission scheduled a "possible" drop.

The test series was thrown off schedule a week ago when a planned detonation failed because of a mechanical fault in complicated electrical circuits. After Monday morning's now famed midget blast weather conditions deteriorated rapidly.

High winds blew down tents at Camp Desert Rock where 5000 troops of the Army's 3rd Corps await their role in the tests. Rain, snow and low-lying gray clouds blanketed the blast area.

One of the principal safety concerns of the AEC is the protection of Nevada's population

Turn to Page 5, Column 1

McCracken Sentenced to Gas Chamber

One of Attorneys, George Chula, Gets Term for Contempt

BY ED MEAGHER
Times Staff Representative

SANTA ANA, Oct. 26 — Henry Ford McCracken, convicted slayer of 10-year-old Patricia Jean Hull, was sentenced to the gas chamber here today in Superior Judge Robert Gardner's courtroom and one of his attorneys, George H. Chula, was given a five-day jail term for contempt of court.

McCracken took it placidly. He stood with arms folded across his chest, a slight figure wearing the same cotton shirt and jail-scrounged, high-water trousers that made up his courtroom costume through almost five months of trials.

He didn't flinch when Judge Gardner prefaced his passing sentence with a short, incisive personal judgment of McCracken's crime.

'Overwhelming Evidence'

"You have been proven guilty," said Judge Gardner, "of a most inhuman crime on the most overwhelming amount of evidence that has marked any case in my courtroom."

The judge then reviewed with great skepticism McCracken's story that made up his principal defense—a fantastic tale of a talking dog and other hallucinations designed to make it appear that he killed the child in his Buena Park motel cabin while in the throes of a dream.

The judge, too, curtly pointed out that he had stooped to impugn the moral character of his 10-year-old victim. Then he passed sentence.

Deputies quickly handcuffed the 34-year-old guitar player and hustled him back to his cell in the Orange County Jail.

As the barred door to the jail was swinging open for his entrance, McCracken turned. His eyes were moist. He said:

Monroe Contempt Dropped

"I still say I'm not guilty."

Judge Gardner's finding Chula in contempt did not come as a surprise. Both Chula and his associate, James C. Monroe, were under contempt citations.

In Monroe's case, however, Judge Gardner said that he had carefully gone over the transcript and had determined that Monroe's occasional failures to obey court rulings were not willful.

"I cannot say the same to you, Mr. Chula," said the judge.

He referred then to numerous statements and actions by Chula that he found to be contemptuous. In particular, he pointed to Chula's examination of a psychiatrist during McCracken's sanity trial.

Judge Gardner said he twice admonished Chula not to ask

Turn to Page 3, Column 1

V FOR VICTORY—Waving with his famous victory symbol, Winston Churchill, the new Prime Minister, who had listened to voting trends in a suburb, joined jubilant Conservative Party headquarters workers at Abbey House, London, when results assured party's return to power after six years of Socialist Labor rule. (AP) Wirephoto

5 Contests Remain to Be Decided

LONDON, Oct. 26 (AP) — King George VI restored Winston Churchill to the Prime Ministry tonight as the victor in a hard-fought election which ends six years of Socialist Labor rule. Churchill pledged to work for better times.

The Conservative Party, led by Churchill, won 319 or more seats in the 625-seat House of Commons, and thereby majority control and the right to name the new government. However, its popular vote was about 1% less than that of the Laborites in yesterday's general election.

293 Seats for Labor

With five seats still unaccounted for, Clement R. Attlee's Labor Party had 293 seats, the Liberals five and others three, giving the Conservatives a majority of 26 seats over the Laborites. In addition, the Liberal Party members are more likely to vote with the Conservatives.

Of the five still uncounted districts, two have been Conservative, one has been held by Labor and one by the Liberals. The fifth seat is vacant because the candidate died during the campaign. It was a Labor seat and probably will remain so in a by-election to be held Nov. 8.

With Liberal support, and the seats remaining as they are, Churchill probably will have a working majority of 29 to 30 seats.

Churchill, 77 next month, returns to No. 10 Downing St. as the oldest Prime Minister Britain has had since Liberal William Gladstone, 85, resigned in 1894.

King Sees Churchill

The King is still ailing from a lung operation, but he received Churchill and Attlee individually at Buckingham Palace. Attlee went first to resign his positions as Prime Minister and First Lord of the Treasury. Churchill followed to receive the King's appointment, which gives him the "last chance" he sought to work for peace.

Churchill and his chief deputy, Anthony Eden, began considering a Cabinet list for approval by the King. Most of the new Ministers will be members of a "shadow Cabinet" kept in existence during the Conservatives' six years on the sidelines. Eden is slated to succeed Laborite Herbert Morrison as Foreign Minister.

Session Date Set

The new Cabinet probably will take office Monday. The new Parliament will meet Wednesday to elect a Speaker. It will hold its first formal session Nov. 6.

The Labor Party polled the

Turn to Page 4, Column 2

10-YEAR L.A. DRAFT DODGER SUSPECT HELD

William Collier, 38, of Los Angeles, was being held in Springfield, Ill., yesterday on charges of having evaded the draft since 1941, according to wire dispatches.

Federal Bureau of Investigation officers said that Collier was arrested in a rooming house in the Illinois city. He was placed in the Federal section of the Springfield City Prison.

Richard H. Hosteny, agent in charge of the Springfield FBI office, said that Collier registered for the draft in Los Angeles in 1941 and then disappeared. He added that Collier moved from one city to another, "always keeping just a jump ahead of us" and working as a laborer and truck driver.

Dock Strike May Cut Off Holiday Goods

NEW YORK, Oct. 26 (UP)—The 12-day-old dock strike bit into the nation's economy today, threatening a nationwide shortage of some items for the Thanksgiving and Christmas holiday trade.

In addition to putting a crimp in holiday business, the strike already has caused a shortage of Scotch whiskey and bananas and threatens a coffee famine.

The New York Board of Trade asked President Truman to invoke the Taft-Hartley Law against the strikers and proposed to Gov. Dewey and Gov. Alfred Driscoll of New Jersey that they ask that the President declare a national emergency and "enforce the existing Federal law."

The strike was called in protest against a contract already ratified by the union, the insurgents demanding that the agreement be renegotiated in an attempt to win an additional 15-cent hourly pay raise.

The strike spread to Philadelphia, where about half of the 2500 longshoremen in port today refused to handle any cargo diverted from New York.

Explosion Rips Aircraft Plant, Worker Injured

An explosion heard more than a mile away last night ripped open a Douglas Aircraft Co. subsidiary plant at 4900 Cecilia St. in the Bell district and sent one workman to Maywood Hospital with a broken collarbone.

The injured man, Edward J. Evers, 20, of 9461 S Walker St., Cypress, was hurled 40 feet when an oven used for baking paper honeycomb insulation material exploded. Eleven other workers nearby escaped injury.

Wall Blown Out

The blast sent the oven door spinning through the roof, blew out a 100-foot section of wall and part of the roof and started a fire which destroyed some of the paper stock.

Damage to the building and materials was estimated at $25,000 by Asst. County Fire Chief Ted Loggins.

Four county fire companies extinguished the blaze. Members of one engine company said they heard the blast a mile and a half away.

Bomb Blast Feared

Residents nearby said they thought it was a bomb explosion. Mrs. William Given, 39, of 4907 Cecilia St., her daughter Marcia, 11, and her mother-in-law, Mrs. Jennie Given, said they observed civil defense rules by staying away from windows and lying down on a bedroom floor.

The building is about 500 feet long and is constructed partly of reinforced sheet metal and partly of stucco. It was acquired by the Douglas company about six months ago for manufacture of the insulating material.

TOUGH TASK SEEN FACING CHURCHILL

Attlee Successor Must Spur Britons to Far Greater Production in Shops and Mills

BY WALDO DRAKE, Times European Bureau

LONDON, Oct. 26—Whether it is because Attlee made a tactical error in picking St. Crispin's Day or whether Liberals helped Conservatives to victory, it is now a certainty that Churchill and his staff of young men have been selected to guide the British nation back toward stability from which it has widely drifted under six years of Socialist rule.

The narrow margin of 29 seats which the Conservatives will have in the new House of Commons fails to indicate the grave difficulty of the struggle Churchill must undertake in trying to spur his countrymen to much greater productive efforts in shops and mills.

Labor Still Strong

The fact that although beaten by circumstances the Labor Party will at least equal the Conservatives' popular total of 14,000,000 votes is an ominous reminder that trade unions have preserved the monolithic solidarity which Churchill must somehow shake from their present lethargic practices into extraordinary output.

The Laborites' syndical solidarity was again demonstrated by the return to Parliament of demagogic Aneurin Bevan and

Turn to Page 4, Column 1

City Receives Touch of Crisp Fall Weather

Los Angeles got a quick touch of crisp fall weather yesterday in the wake of the season's first storm.

The minimum temperature of 50 deg. at 5:45 a.m. was the lowest reading since last May 4. The high was 68 deg. at 1:11 p.m.

Some other Southland cities recorded cold mornings, too. Santa Barbara had a minimum of 44; San Bernardino, 42; Palmdale, 35; San Pedro and Newport, 50, and Riverside, 43.

However, the crisp weather and the clouds are expected to be gone today. The Weather Bureau predicted sunny skies and rising temperature.

Quake Felt in Long Beach

The Long Beach area felt its second successive earthquake yesterday at 12:50 a.m. There was a small shock Thursday at 5:45 a.m.

Police received scores of calls from persons in the Lakewood area and the shock was felt at Long Beach Airport. Both shocks were recorded at California Institute of Technology Seismological Laboratory.

British War Craft Banned From Canal

CAIRO, Oct. 26 (AP) — The Egyptian government today declared a ban on British warships in the Suez Canal but the French operating company said it will defy any orders to interfere with canal transit.

A tense quiet prevailed along the British-held canal except for propaganda moves.

Egypt's announcement on warships was made by Foreign Minister Mohammed Salah El Din at a news conference. He sketched a policy of noncooperation with Britain, the United States and France, and indicated Egypt was too weak in arms to fight an organized war to get rid of the British.

In the canal zone Egyptians were reported circulating propaganda pamphlets at Port Said, Ismailia and Port Suez. They lambasted the British and called for a boycott by labor, food suppliers and other Egyptians.

The British command countered with an Arabic-language news sheet called the Canal Arab News for Egyptian laborers.

S.F. Dock Battles Seen as Firm Defies Union Strikers

SAN FRANCISCO, Oct. 26 (AP)—Attorneys for the Isthmian Steamship Co. disclosed today that the company has hired AFL longshoremen to unload three strike-bound ships here.

The action was seen as a forerunner of possible waterfront violence.

Harry Bridges' Independent Longshoremen's Union, which has held exclusive jurisdiction here since the mid-1930s, has announced it will not stand for an invasion by AFL dockworkers.

THE WEATHER

U.S. Weather Bureau forecast: Clear today and tomorrow. Warmer afternoons. High today near 72. Highest temperature yesterday 68 deg.; lowest, 50.

FEATURES INDEX

Camp Pendleton Chief Scores Senate Critics

Maj. Gen. Oliver P. Smith of Camp Pendleton cites marines' bravery in Korea as his answer to Senate committee's criticism of morale at post he commands. Story on Page 5, Part 1.

On Other Pages

Crash Kills Industrialist, Wife and Daughter-in-law

WASHINGTON, Oct. 26 (UP).—A wealthy Ohio industrialist-sportsman and two members of his family plunged to their death in the Potomac River today while trying to land their private plane for a visit with Gen. Marshall.

The plane crashed in two feet of water just short of a National Airport runway, killing Thomas Holden White, 57, of Chagrin Falls, O., his wife Kathleen and their daughter-in-law, Mrs. Robert York White.

White, a friend of the former Defense Secretary, was at the controls of the single-engine cabin craft. They had taken off earlier today from the private airport of David S. Ingalls near Chagrin Falls, an exclusive Cleveland suburb.

Ingalls is manager of Sen. Taft's campaign for the Republican presidential nomination and White has been working in his behalf.

Marshall, who became acquainted with White when both were on the Pan American World Airways board of directors, said he was "very distressed" by the tragedy.

Marshall's military aide said White was going to call on the general at his Leesburg (Va.) home but did not plan to be a house guest.

White was a scion of the family which established the White Motor Co. and the White Sewing Machine Co. He leaves his father, Winsor T. White, 85, millionaire Cleveland industrialist.

ACCUSED OF PERJURY

Fired Symphony Chief Denied Entry to U.S.

NEW YORK, Oct. 26 (AP) — French-born Emmanuel Rosenthal, fired yesterday from his $15,000-a-year post as conductor of the Seattle Symphony Orchestra, today was excluded from the United States on grounds involving moral turpitude.

P. A. Esperdy, acting district director of the Immigration and Naturalization Service here, said after a hearing it was decided to deny Rosenthal admission to the United States on the grounds that he "admitted committing perjury, a crime involving moral turpitude concerning his marital status prior to entry."

Rosenthal arrived here Oct. 13 accompanied by Claudine Pillard Verneuil, known in Seattle as Mrs. Rosenthal. Both were detained by the immigration authorities and placed on parole.

The immigration authorities first became interested in Rosenthal and Miss Verneuil, a singer, when it was learned that Mme. Lucie Troussier Rosenthal of Paris had said she still is married to the conductor and had never divorced him.

In Seattle the symphony board had considered the effect of these developments on public acceptance of Rosenthal's orchestral stewardship this year and also its effect on the orchestra's program, which has been delayed because of the immigration hearing.

Aaron Frosch, attorney for Rosenthal, told the immigration hearing today that he will appeal the decision to the Naturalization Service at Washington, D.C.

PART 1

Los Angeles Times

EQUAL RIGHTS

LIBERTY UNDER THE LAW — TRUE INDUSTRIAL FREEDOM

ALL THE NEWS
ALL THE TIME

VOL. LXXI | IN FOUR PARTS | C C | SATURDAY MORNING, JANUARY 19, 1952 | 34 PAGES | DAILY, 10c

WEATHERMAN SAYS SOUTHLAND STORM OVER

HOMES FLOODED—Air view shows floodwaters in Artesia, where hundreds were evacuated, thousands placed in danger by waters that were 3 feet deep in some homes.

Times photo by Paul Calvert

Street Waters Recede; Loss Set at Millions; More Deaths Counted

The storm that cost the Southland at least eight lives and millions of dollars in damage is ended, the U.S. Weather Bureau said last night.

Coincidentally, the city's Civil Defense and Disaster Corps declared Los Angeles' flood emergency "under control" and closed its disaster control center.

A soggy, groggy Southland was thankful.

Metropolitan Los Angeles last night had returned to normal. Downtown streets were clear. Stores and shops did business as usual.

[More storm news and photos on Pages A and B and 2 and 3, Part I. Rainfall figures on Page 3.]

As the disastrous 3.98-inch rain ended, A. K. Showalter, Weather Bureau chief here, predicted less than .75 inch of rainfall for today.

Originally an Alaskan storm was reported headed here. Showalter amended this report to say the "simple cold front will not be a major threat to Southern California."

"It will produce only light rain, less than .75 inch in all areas," he said in announcing the official forecast for Los Angeles and vicinity:

"Partly cloudy today and tomorrow, but mostly cloudy Saturday night, with some moderate showers. Rainfall amount one-half to three-fourths of an inch. Not so cool Saturday night."

Rain Foreseen for Coastal Areas

The long-range forecast for the coastal and mountain areas predicted intermittent rain with "occasional" heavy rain through Wednesday.

Of the storm total of 3.98 inches, 3.17 inches fell within the 24 hours ending at 4 p.m. yesterday. This raised the Los Angeles seasonal total to 17.21 inches of rain, compared with a normal of 6.33 inches. At this time last year the total was 3.51 inches.

While the work of repairing storm damage and clearing away debris continued, Mayor Bowron and Rear Adm. Robert W. Berry, director of the Civil Defense and Disaster Corps, declared an end to the emergency.

Berry Praises Thousands of Volunteers

The disaster control center operated on a 24-hour basis for two days. Earlier, County Manager Arthur J. Will ordered his department heads to remain available for a "potential disaster."

Operation of the control center proved the need for better disaster communications, now under study, Berry observed.

"It also proved the city is ready, willing and able to function in the performance of its duty to its citizens," he added. "We thank the countless thousands of volunteers who worked in every capacity."

Dr. Uhl Declares Water Supply Safe

Transportation, communications, housing and shelter divisions of the corps carried the burden of the emergency, he said.

Dr. George M. Uhl, city health officer, and Samuel Morris, general manager of the Department of Water and Power, emphasized that the city's water supply is safe to drink.

The announcement was prompted by a health hazard caused when 1000 cesspools in the San Fernando Valley area collapsed under torrential downpours. Their contents flooded onto streets and sidewalks.

"Surface waters of the flood are unsafe," Dr. Uhl said. "But the city's drinking water is still safe and will continue to be safe.

Reservoirs Supplied From Deep Wells

"The city water system reservoirs are supplied from aqueducts and from deep-well pumping, not from surface waters," he explained. "The department keeps checking the water supply constantly, and the water is chemically treated as needed to keep it absolutely safe for drinking purposes."

Although deaths attributed directly to the storm totaled eight, many others were blamed indirectly on the violent weather. These included traffic deaths caused by slippery streets and poor visibility.

Possibly a score of deaths in Southern California could be

Turn to Page 2, Column 2

GOP HEARS STASSEN, EISENHOWER PLEAS

Sen. Lodge Presents Case for General; Minnesota Ex-Governor Speaks for Self

BY KYLE PALMER, Times Political Editor

SAN FRANCISCO, Jan. 18—More concerned with the in-fighting between representatives of rival Presidential candidates than with plans for party success in November, members and guests of the Republican National Committee took time out from official business today to listen to speeches in behalf of Gen. Eisenhower and Harold E. Stassen.

U.S. Sen. Lodge of Massachusetts presented the case for Eisenhower at a luncheon, taking quick advantage of inept remarks made yesterday in an address by David Ingalls, manager of Sen. Taft's candidacy, and Stassen spoke for himself at considerable length during the dinner hour.

Eisenhower Spokesman

Eisenhower was described by Lodge as the one individual whom the Republicans definitely can elect and if elected as a leader most likely to build security at home and organize a durable peace in the world.

Taking cognizance of inferential slaps by Ingalls at other GOP Presidential aspirants, Lodge said, "Let us not take cracks at each other now which will endanger co-operation" in November. "For my part, I promise that I shall speak for my candidate, but I will never attack or take sly digs at any other candidate."

Lodge then diplomatically complimented California's Gov. Warren on the Governor's address of welcome at yesterday's opening meeting.

Stassen, outlining in detail his proposed policies on foreign relations and domestic affairs, more or less followed Lodge's lead in warning against a destructive fight among Republicans.

Mentioning Warren, Eisenhower and Taft by name, he said that while he has "some sincere differences of view on future policy of our party and of our country with these men," he entertains "a very high regard for each and every one" of them.

Nevertheless, Stassen challenged both the Eisenhower and Taft claims of decisive delegate strength.

Tribute to MacArthur

One of the biggest outbursts of applause in the course of Stassen's speech occurred when Stassen pulled a surprise insert in his prepared speech as follows:

"One of the first things I would do as a Republican President would be to wipe out the

Turn to Page 8, Column 1

Churchill OKs Top Navy Post for U.S.

WASHINGTON, Jan. 18 (AP)—Prime Minister Churchill today yielded to the appointment of an American as supreme allied naval commander in Atlantic waters but won a promise of a million tons of scarce U.S. steel for Britain.

The steel will be exchanged for British tin and aluminum, badly needed in America's rearmament program.

Surprise Concession

Churchill's acceptance of an American to head the North Atlantic Treaty naval forces came as something of a surprise concession during his farewell conference with President Truman at the White House.

Navy quarters said the most logical choice as the new "seagoing Eisenhower" would be Adm. Lynde D. McCormick, now commander of the U.S. Atlantic Fleet. He served in both the Atlantic and Pacific during World War II.

Agreement on the NATO command was reached last year but was held in abeyance because of Churchill's opposition. The British will now inform

Turn to Page 6, Column 1

Council Votes to Place Housing Issue on Ballot

Bowron Offers Assurance He Won't Veto Ordinance for Election Consolidation

Unanimous action of the City Council yesterday practically assured voters of an opportunity to pass on the highly controversial question of public housing at the coming June 3 election.

Without a dissenting vote, the Councilmen adopted a resolution asking the Board of Supervisors to permit the municipal issue of public housing to be presented to the electorate at the coming State primary election.

Bowron Won't Veto

Mayor Bowron gave assurance that he would not veto an ordinance calling for the consolidation of the special municipal election with the State election. Previously, there had been some speculation that he would veto such an ordinance because of his doubts as to whether the matter could be placed legally before the voters.

The ordinance must be approved after the Board of Supervisors grants the city the privilege of participating in the State election.

There was a practically unanimous expression of opinion among the Councilmen yesterday that, despite their own personal convictions on the matter, the people should have the final say.

Support Urged

Councilman Ernest E. Debs, long-time supporter of public housing but not too happy with the way the projects are planned for his district, asked other pro-public housing Councilmen to join in putting the matter on the ballot.

"Let's make it unanimous," he said. "This is still a government of the people, by the people and for the people."

Councilman L. E. Timberlake, one of those most active in support of the subsidized housing,

Turn to Page 4, Column 1

Reds Charge U.N Planes Strafed Truce Convoy

PANMUNJOM, Korea, Jan. 19 (Saturday) (U.P.)—The Communists charged today that allied planes strafed a properly marked Red truce delegation convoy Friday afternoon in violation of a joint agreement.

The Communists apparently made no official claims that anyone was killed or wounded but Communist newsmen said two Communists were wounded.

Red Newsmen's Version

Red newsmen said four F-80 Shooting Star jet fighters strafed a marked convoy of three Red vehicles—two trucks and one jeep.

United Nations negotiators told the Communists bluntly today that the United Nations will not agree to any truce supervision plan which does not restrict military airfield construction during an armistice.

Maj. Gen. Claude Ferenbaugh of the U.N. truce delegation reported that no progress was made during today's hour-and-40-minute session of the truce supervision subcommittee.

Chinese Maj. Gen. Hsieh Fang had asserted yesterday restrictions on airfields would violate sovereign rights. He added scornfully that surrender of such rights "may be all right for some running dogs" of the United States—but not for North Korea.

BENEFITS TOP STORM LOSSES, LEADERS SAY

In spite of the vast damage to Los Angeles from the week's rainstorms, the benefits will far outweigh the losses.

This was the conclusion yesterday in statements made by Mayor Bowron and Samuel B. Morris, general manager of the Department of Water and Power.

Morris pointed out that increase in power from Hoover and Davis Dams and the increased water supply, especially in the Colorado River basin, will far exceed the losses due to the storm.

Mayor Bowron said that the storm, while serious, is not a disaster.

"It is serious and has claimed some lives and injured persons and property, but it is under control and every city division has met its responsibility in a practical and efficient manner," he said.

British Cruiser Opens Fire on Port Said

PORT SAID, Egypt, Jan. 18 (U.P.)—The British cruiser Liverpool opened fire on Port Said tonight following a four-hour gun battle in the city between British troops and Egyptian guerrillas.

No damage was reported immediately. The cruiser fired its guns intermittently toward the city from its anchorage in the Bay of Tina.

(In London, the British Admiralty duty officer said he had heard no official report of the incident. He said several British warships were on duty in the area.)

One Egyptian was killed and one injured in the exchange of gunfire in the city.

Guerrillas Attack

Egyptian guerrillas launched an attack from two directions on a British camp in the Port Said gulf area. British forces started firing field guns when their troops tried to force their way out in amored cars, but were forced back into the camp by machine-gun fire.

Egyptian guerrillas also attacked a British officer in Port Fuad, directly across the Suez Canal from Port Said, which lies at the north end of the waterway.

Truman Stirs Speculation He Will Seek Re-election

WASHINGTON, Jan. 18 (AP)—Democrats who hope President Truman will run for re-election got a little more grist for their mill today when a House member quoted Mr. Truman as saying, "I never quit under fire or ran away from anything."

Rep. Sieminski (D) N.J., said the President made that comment while they chatted at the White House today.

Asked if he thought the President would do so, Sieminski told newsmen:

"If there is a fight and he's asked to join, he'll fight—he'll never quit—that's my opinion."

Some politicians believe that one of the factors influencing Mr. Truman's decision will be the increasing criticism of his administration on grounds of corruption.

Sieminski, a veteran of the Korean fighting said he told the President "I hoped he would run again, and of my admiration of him as my leader." He quoted Mr. Truman as replying:

"From precinct captain to President, I have served the people to the best of my ability and I'm a lobbyist for the people. I never quit a fight or ran away from anything."

FEATURES INDEX

Industrial Employment Hits New High in L.A.

Industrial employment in the Los Angeles metropolitan area reached a record total of 517,900 in December. Story on Page 1, Part 2.

On Other Pages

Marines Ask More Men for First Half of 1952

WASHINGTON, Jan. 18 (AP)—The Marines have increased their draft requirements for the first six months of this year, requesting 36,750 men. Gen. Lemuel C. Shepherd Jr., told the House Armed Services Committee today.

THE WEATHER

U.S. Weather Bureau forecast: Partly cloudy today and Sunday but mostly cloudy tonight with some moderate showers. Rainfall amount .50 to .75 inch. Not so cool tonight. Highest temperature yesterday, 57; lowest, 47.

RED COUNTERSPY STORY TO START TOMORROW

A thrilling story of danger, of counterespionage within the Communist underground's high command, begins tomorrow in The Times.

It is the story of Herbert A. Philbrick, a patriotic American who for nine danger-packed years posed as a Communist, rose to high position in the party and managed, at great personal risk, to keep the FBI fully informed despite constant Red surveillance.

In "I Led Three Lives" Philbrick tells how, as a private citizen, he fell victim to a Communist ruse; how he went to the FBI about it and of his subsequent triple life as citizen, pseudo Communist and counterspy. Read every dramatic installment beginning tomorrow in The Times.

PART 1

Los Angeles Times

EQUAL RIGHTS — LIBERTY UNDER THE LAW — TRUE INDUSTRIAL FREEDOM

ALL THE NEWS
ALL THE TIME

VOL. LXXI | IN FOUR PARTS | CC ★ | THURSDAY MORNING, FEBRUARY 7, 1952 | 72 PAGES | DAILY, 10c

GEORGE VI MOURNED; ELIZABETH FLIES HOME

Tempers Fly High at Reds' Trial Here

Attorney's Remarks Set Off Charges and Countercharges

Courtroom tempers flew high in the Communist conspiracy trial yesterday when a defense attorney denounced a "witch-hunting grand jury" and predicted the prosecution will use "stool pigeons."

Asst. U.S. Atty. Norman N. Neukom leaped to his feet when Defense Atty. Leo Branton Jr. said the government will call many FBI agents and other "stool pigeons."

"We're arguing now," Neukom said in protest to Branton's opening statement to the jury in U.S. Judge William C. Mathes' court.

Branton withdrew his comment but Neukom was on his feet again when the defense attorney called the Federal grand jury a witch-hunting group.

Told to Continue

Despite the prosecution's objection, Judge Mathes instructed Branton to continue.

Later the judge admonished another defense attorney, Ben Margolis, to tone down the word "lie" to something like "willful falsehood" when referring to the prosecution's case. U.S. Atty. Walter S. Binns stormed that Margolis sounded as if he were testifying instead of presenting an outline of his case.

California's top Communist, William Schneiderman, joined Branton, Margolis and Atty. A. L. Wirin in presenting opening statements in the trial of the 15 Red leaders.

Wirin said, "the defendants admit they are affiliated with the Communist Party. They are proud of their membership in the Communist Party."

Different Versions

He then contended that the main question is whether the jury will believe the prosecutors' version of what Marxism and Leninism stand for or the defendants' version.

Wirin insisted that Marxism and Leninism are a "vast body

Turn to Page 20, Column 1

Breeze Hikes Visibility to 70 Miles

A light breeze yesterday kept skies clear of smog and raised visibility to 70 miles during the morning and 60 miles most of the afternoon.

Yesterday's high temperature was 80 deg. at 1:34 p.m., with a low of 53 at 4:36 a.m.

Other high temperatures for local stations were: Culver City, 84; Long Beach, 83; Torrance, 82; UCLA, 81, and Pasadena and San Gabriel, 80.

The Weather Bureau forecast increasing high cloudiness today and tomorrow, with a high of 78 today.

KING'S LAST PICTURE — Bareheaded and hair whipping from breeze, King George walks with Queen Elizabeth ,and Princess Margaret to plane to see the then Princess . Elizabeth off on world tour. This is the last-known picture made of British monarch. (AP) Wirephoto

U.N. Yields Ground on Exchange of Prisoners

Truce Negotiators Drop Demand That Communists Include Civilians in Swap

MUNSAN, Korea, Feb. 7 (Thursday) (AP)—U.N. command negotiators today dropped their demand that excess prisoners of war in allied hands be exchanged for displaced civilians now in Communist territory.

Under the original proposal, the allies wanted to exchange prisoners of war on a man-for-man basis. The Reds had said they held 11,559 allied troops.

Then the allies wanted to exchange the rest of the Red troops they hold—some 121,000—for displaced civilians in Communist hands.

Firm on Repatriation

While staff officers now negotiating the prisoner exchange issue gave ground on the POW-civilian swap, they held firm to the principle of voluntary repatriation. They insist that no one can be sent back to the other side against his wishes.

In a nearby tent at Panmunjom where another group of staff officers is drafting truce supervision agreements, the Communists narrowed the gap on rotation of troops. The Reds agreed to rotation of 25,000 monthly, exclusive of those on rest and recuperation leaves or temporary duty.

Minimum Figure

The U.N. command still insisted that 40,000 was its rock-bottom figure.

The allies made no reply to a new Communist peace plan which ignored South Korean and injected Formosa and other tense Far Eastern issues into final settlement of the Korean war.

The Reds yesterday called for a high-level political conference within 90 days after an armistice is signed to settle all Asian problems related to peace in Korea.

(Gen. Ridgway, supreme allied commander, was in Korea but the purpose of his visit was not indicated.)

Rules for UMT Sent to House Floor for Action

WASHINGTON, Feb. 6 (AP)—The House Armed Services Committee completed a set of operating rules for universal military training today and recommended it to Congress, but left the starting date to future decision.

The vote of approval, reported as 27 to 7, sends the legislation to the House. Rep. Vinson (D) Ga., Armed Services chairman, plans to have the bill ready for a House test soon. Opponents are claiming they can kill it.

Provisions of Bill

Basically the plan calls for six months of military training for all eligible males soon after their 18th birthdays, followed by seven and a half years in the reserves. In full operation the program would take in some 800,000 boys a year.

The program could not take effect until Congress by law or the President by executive order had ended the present draft of youths below the age of 19 or had reduced their term of service. After that happened the UMT program could be started by the President or Congress.

The bill specifies that none may be called up without his consent for more than 30 days of

Turn to Page 10, Column 1

Asbury Transit System Given Boost in Fares

The Asbury Rapid Transit System, operating between Los Angeles, Pasadena, San Fernando, Culver City and Burbank, yesterday was granted fare raises effective next Feb. 25.

The State Public Utilities Commission gave the company a temporary 3-cent hike, pending acquisition of tokens and fare box equipment. The temporary order will expire in six months.

During the interim, present 10-cent rides go to 13 cents, 15-cent to 18-cent, 20 to 23 cents and 25 to 28 cents.

After the lapse of the six-month period the 10-cent fare will go to 15 cents or one 12½ cent token, the 15-cent fares to 20 cents or token plus 5 cents, 20-cent fare to 25 cents or token plus 10 cents, 25-cent fare to 30 cents or token plus 15 cents.

No tokens will apply to the following adult fares, which will go up permanently on Feb. 25: 30-cent to 33 cents, 35-cent unchanged, 39 to 42, 43 to 46 and 48 to 51.

Present 30-ride commutation book will go from $5.40 to $6.20; 30-ride commutation book (for longer rides) from $6.75 to $7.55; the 12-ride deal from $3.25 to $3.60.

School ride books remain unchanged.

The company sought in its original application for straight fare boosts of 5 cents, with no tokens.

THE WEATHER

U.S. Weather Bureau forecast: Increasing high cloudiness today and tomorrow, with a high of 78 today. Cooler tomorrow. Highest temperature yesterday, 80 deg.; lowest, 53.

FEATURES INDEX

Brannan Ousts Two in Grain Loss Scandal

Secretary Brannan fires two Agriculture Department officials as a result of stored grain losses scandal. Story on Page 19, Part 1.

On Other Pages

Kansas City Fares Hiked to 20 Cents

KANSAS CITY, Feb. 6 (AP)—Streetcar and bus riders will have to pay the nation's highest basic cash fare—20 cents a ride—in Greater Kansas City beginning Sunday.

The Kansas Corporation Commission at Topeka today granted the Kansas City Public Service Co. a temporary emergency fare increase. Missouri authorities previously approved the rise.

The single cash fare will go from 15 to 20 cents.

NEW QUEEN OF ENGLAND — Proclaimed officially Queen Elizabeth II on the death of her father, Britain's new ruler is speeding homeward from Africa. (AP) Wirephoto

ELIZABETH IN TEARS OVER KING'S DEATH

Princess Regains Composure and Proves She's Every Inch a Queen, Royal Source Says

NAIROBI, Kenya Colony, Feb. 6 (AP)—The slight young Princess who has been trained since childhood for the responsibilities of the British crown headed home sorrowfully as a Queen tonight to take up the royal duties left her by her father's sudden death.

Princess Elizabeth burst into tears when her husband, Prince Philip, the Duke of Edinburgh, broke the news from London of King George VI, but soon regained her composure.

"She was every inch a Queen," a source at the royal lodge told reporters.

Cutting short a projected five-month, 30,000-mile royal tour that was to have taken them on to Ceylon, Australia, New Zealand and other British regions, Elizabeth and the Duke are going home by plane.

The couple flew tonight from Nairobi to Entebee, Uganda, and transferred there to a four-engined airliner.

The 25-year-old Queen, Britain's first woman ruler since Victoria reigned 51 years ago, is due to reach London tomorrow.

It was only last Thursday that she left London, bidding goodbye to the King after earnestly scanning his tired, lined face. She and the Duke were substituting for him on the tour because of the ill health that had plagued him in recent years.

Only a few hours before news of the King's death was radioed from London, Elizabeth and her husband had returned to the royal lodge from a thrilling night in big-game country. White hunters and the Duke were armed.

Their greatest thrill came when an elephant, one in a herd of 46, roved to within 12 yards of the Princess, screened from her only by low bush.

Truman Praise of Caudle Before Firing Revealed

WASHINGTON, Feb. 6 (U.P.)—President Truman wrote T. Lamar Caudle less than a month before firing him that it was men like Caudle that made it "possible to carry on in this job," it was disclosed tonight.

The letter was made public by the White House after its existence was disclosed by Ned Brooks, radio commentator.

Presidential Press Secretary Joseph Short said the letter was written Oct. 19, before Mr. Truman received the information which resulted in Caudle's dismissal as Assistant Attorney General for activities "incompatible" with his duties. Caudle was ousted Nov. 16.

Short said the Chief Executive received a report about Caudle early last summer but it was not until after Nov. 1 that he "had the verification of those at-first-unsubstantiated reports."

Short said Mr. Truman's letter to Caudle was written after Caudle wrote the President Oct. 17 "paying him a compliment and passing along a compliment from Jess Larson (General Services Administrator)."

The text of the President's letter:

"Dear Mr. Caudle:

"I can't tell you how very much I appreciate your good letter of the 17th.

"I certainly enjoyed the visit to Winston-Salem and was glad to have the opportunity to tell the world some things that needed to be said.

"Men like you and Jess Larsen make it possible to carry on in this job.

"Sincerely yours, Harry Truman."

ADVERTISEMENTS GIVE IDEA OF TWO DOLLAR DAYS' VALUES

Downtown Dollar Days will be celebrated both tomorrow and Saturday so that the public can have a choice of shopping days. A preview of the unusual values to be offered will be found in this morning's Times with pages of advertisements by co-operating merchants listing and describing their outstanding bargains. Tomorrow's Times, too, will publish many pages of advertisements featuring the Downtown Dollar Days' values to be offered tomorrow and Saturday by leading stores.

Britain Makes Ready for Reign of Queen; Nations Show Respect

Illustrated on Page 3, Part 1

LONDON, Feb. 6 (AP)—Britain's steady, beloved monarch, King George VI, died in his sleep today. His elder daughter thus became Queen Elizabeth II, Britain's first woman ruler since Victoria reigned 51 years ago.

The new Queen heard the unexpected news in Kenya, one of the remnants of the once-mighty British Empire, but set out at once by plane for home and the responsibilities of the throne.

Her four-engine silver and blue Argonaut had an escort of Lancaster planes carrying land and sea rescue gear. The royal plane is due in London at 4:30 p.m. today.

The King's death plunged Britain and the commonwealth into mourning. Flags all over the world dipped to half staff. Even the Russians made this gesture of respect in Berlin.

Turbulent Years of Reign

George's reign spanned 15 years of turbulent history. He saw Britain lose much of the empire upon which, it had once been said, the sun never set. He saw it come to austerity, privation and near bankruptcy. He saw his countrymen stand against and help to conquer the bloody thrusts of Hitler and the Japanese. For his own part, he refused to leave embattled England with his gracious Queen, Elizabeth, and their two daughters, Elizabeth and Margaret.

Worn and wearied by persistent illness, he died at the royal estate at Sandringham, where he was born 56 years ago. His valet, John MacDonald, discovered the body when he took the King his usual early-morning tea. Queen Elizabeth and Princess Margaret were immediately awakened and told the news and a radio message was dispatched to Princess Elizabeth, in Kenya on a royal tour.

World Gets News of Death

The news was given to the world some three hours later. It was a shock, even though it was widely known that the King was not in good health. Only yesterday he had been rabbit hunting on the Sandringham estate and there was no hint that his condition was any worse than usual.

Coronary thrombosis—a blood clot—was believed to have been the immediate cause of death. Last September surgeons removed the King's cancerous left lung. Two years before that he underwent an operation to relieve a circulatory ailment in one of his legs. His face was haggard and lined in recent months and his condition had caused concern to his subjects.

Britons the length and breadth of the islands wept and paid the King tribute today in five simple words:

"He was a good man."

London Goes Into Mourning

Londoners slipped into churches, black-bordered newspapers gripped in their hands, to think and to pray. Shopkeepers ripped bright displays from their windows and replaced them with more somber things. In one there was a massive portrait of King George, surrounded by the purple of mourning.

Many donned black ties and somber suits. Crowds stood before Buckingham Palace, where the blinds were drawn. The British Broadcasting Corp. shut down for the day after announcing the King's death, except for news bulletins and weather reports. The Stock Exchange closed, as did courts and many businesses.

At Westminster Abbey the bells tolled for two hours; Great Tom, the hour bells at St. Paul's Cathedral, tolled once a minute from 11:50 a.m. to 12:50 p.m. Restaurant and hotel operators posted bans on dancing. As night fell, London was quiet and the streets were nearly deserted.

Announcement in 11 Words

The official daily court circular from Buckingham Palace gave just 11 words tonight to the death of George:

"The King passed peacefully away in his sleep early this morning."

It is expected the King's body will be taken tomorrow to Westminster Hall in London, where by tradition British monarchs lie in state after death. The hall, one of the oldest buildings in London, adjoins the Houses of Parliament.

First Since Victoria

Under law, at the moment of her father's death, Princess Elizabeth, 25, became Queen—the first reigning British Queen since Victoria and the seventh since William the Conqueror. There is a superstition in England that Britain waxes fat and prosperous under a Queen, a superstition dating back to the days of the first Elizabeth 350 years ago.

But because Elizabeth II is away from England, the nation actually has no constitutional head. She is expected to touch down on English soil again tomorrow. Her first official act probably will be to declare a period of court mourning for her father.

At her side will be her husband, 30, to whom she may grant the title Prince Consort Philip. They were married in Westminster Abbey Nov. 20, 1947.

Heir to Throne

Their son, 3-year-old Prince Charles, becomes heir to the British throne and probably will be granted the title of Prince of Wales.

His baby sister Anne becomes second in line.

The machinery for putting Elizabeth formally on the throne already is started. The Accession Council drafted a

Turn to Page 2, Column 1

PART 1

Los Angeles Times

EQUAL RIGHTS
LIBERTY UNDER THE LAW — TRUE INDUSTRIAL FREEDOM

ALL THE NEWS
ALL THE TIME

VOL. LXXI | IN FOUR PARTS | CC | MONDAY MORNING, MARCH 17, 1952 | 68 PAGES | DAILY, 10c

Three Dead, Heavy Property Damage Left in Wake of Storm

WIND DAMAGE—Mrs. Beatrice Goodfriend surveys damage when a freak tornado blew down the building onto three cars inside. The sudden gale, which caused other damage in Santa Monica, followed a violent thunderbolt, heard early Sunday morning. Times photo

Rain Total of Season 24.41 Inches

Illustrated on Page 3, Part 1

The season's third big storm headed eastward yesterday, leaving in its wake three persons dead and huge property damage throughout the Southland.

The storm delivered 2.28 inches of rain in downtown Los Angeles, some of which fell late in the afternoon following lightning, thunder and hail during the morning. The season's total rose to 24.41 inches. Last year at this time 6.43 inches had fallen compared with a normal of 12.66 inches.

Skies to Be Cloudy

Today and tomorrow will see partly cloudy skies, the Weather Bureau said, with a high temperature this afternoon near 58. Snow flurries may continue in the mountains.

Sheriff's deputies said two men died of carbon monoxide poisoning. A third was drowned at the peak of the storm.

A three-truck caravan en route to a Standard Oil Co. well on Pine Mountain Saturday morning was marooned on a nine-mile stretch of road between the Ventura-Maricopa Highway and the well.

Truck Covered

Death from the carbon monoxide poisoning took Raymond Funderburk, 27, and Lewis McConna, 42, of Taft, after the truck they occupied, with the motor running, was covered with snow. Five others received medical treatment.

The men were rescued by a special squad organized by Sheriff's deputies. Treated at the hospital in Taft for carbon monoxide poisoning were Frank Gilkey, 42; Charlie McPherson, 38; Phillip Herboldsheimer, 31; Olious Hubbert, 40, and Holly Van Baugh, 36, of Taft.

Engines Running

Sheriff's deputies said the men were overcome by the fumes from running engines. The two men who died were in the lead truck. The others were rescued by the party led by bulldozers and snowshoed searchers. They were taken to the hospital in a weasel truck.

Newhall Sheriff's deputies Saturday reported the death of Harvey E. Myrick, 60, who was pinned beneath his tractor and drowned when it overturned as he sought to drive it across the rushing Santa Clara Wash, one-quarter mile from Solamint Junction near Newhall. He drowned in three feet of water.

The Weather Bureau said yesterday's rain fell as the storm left unstable air which allowed clouds to build up to shower strength.

Blizzards and landslides closed many highways, roads and streets throughout the Southland during the fury of the storm.

Others Marooned

An undetermined number of persons were marooned along the eastern end of Angeles Crest Highway. At least a dozen snow slides, one 250 yards long and an estimated 40 feet deep, sealed off the area early yesterday.

Searches were conducted throughout the day to locate Division of Highways workers and television station personnel who had driven up the highway for snow scenes. It was fear for a time that they had been buried in one of the numerous small avalanches.

Late last night, however,

Turn to Page 2, Column 2

'Baby Tornado' Spreads Damage in Santa Monica

Garage Blown Onto Cars, Chimney Wrecked as Freak Windstorm Follows Thunderbolt

A freak "twister" of wind following a violent thunderbolt in Santa Monica early yesterday blew down a hollow-tile garage building onto three cars, knocked over a brick chimney and fireplace, shattered windows and toppled boats in several boat-building yards.

It whirled one half-completed skiff through the air like a football pass.

The thunderclap itself was so loud that it wakened sleepers throughout the Santa Monica Bay area.

Wakened by Wind

Mrs. Beatrice Goodfriend, 1532 3rd St., Santa Monica, owner of the wrecked garage, timed the "baby tornado" at about 12:30 a.m.

"I was wakened by a sudden roar of wind," she said. "I looked out of my window and saw a long streak of lightning with forks on it. Then the house started to shake and a terrific crash came, like thunder. Then the rain came in a regular cloudburst."

The tile walls, roof beams and shingled top of the garage collapsed onto the automobiles belonging to Paul Johnson, 206 Broadway; Benjamin Cohen, Carmel Hotel, and C. W. Carey, 203 Broadway, all of Santa Monica.

In the same block a large plate glass window, 12 by 14 feet, in the display room of an automobile agency at Colorado Ave. and 2nd St., was blown in upon a new $3100 car.

Also in the same block, a brick chimney and fireplace crashed down at the home of Jack Wilson, 1543 3rd St. Nearby, a large outdoor advertising sign was demolished.

Boat Blown on Man

At 1520 2nd St., across from the automobile agency, three skylights were blown off a roof and a plate-glass window was shattered.

Small boats in a number of Santa Monica boatbuilding yards were blown through the air.

Joe Quigg, 26, of 1321 19th St., Santa Monica, received an ankle injury when the wind blew down a sailboat upon which he was working. He said that a half-completed skiff came sailing through the air aimed at his head.

"I ducked," said Quigg.

In the same yard a 40-foot boat belonging to Larry North, 728 Montana Ave., received $500 damage when it was blown sideway 30 feet against a quonset hut. Other boats in the yard also were damaged.

31 Marooned by Avalanche at Mine Rescued

By a Times Correspondent

BISHOP, March 16 — Rescue teams late today reached the U.S. Vanadium Corp. mine 15 miles northwest of here and carried 31 persons to safety from their avalanche-wrecked homes.

Thundering slides which virtually demolished the mine's mill shortly after 9 a.m. yesterday also swept portions of most of the houses into the steep-walled canyon and momentarily buried a number of residents.

Two power stations of the California Electric Power Co. also were covered with snow from a series of slides. The terminal of a mine tram at the 11,000-foot level was destroyed by another avalanche and buildings at the Tungstar Mine, some distance down Pine Creek Canyon from the Vanadium Corp. mine, were wiped out.

Find Concrete Refuge

The 31 took refuge in a reinforced-concrete room built into the side of the mountain until rescuers reached them today. They obtained food from a nearby boarding house which escaped damage.

Men, women and children were taken out of the slide-menaced area in a snow tractor loaned by the Navy's weather observation station on White Mountain Peak, far across the Owens Valley.

In one instance a slide tore away most of one home—leaving only the bedroom, in which three youngsters lay seriously ill of pneumonia. Another house was demolished except for the kitchen, where rescuers found Mrs. Gill Simmons standing atop the stove.

There were several reports of

Turn to Page 2, Column 1

Marine Busses Still Stranded in Snowdrifts

Two busses loaded with Camp Pendleton-bound marines yesterday were reported still marooned in deep snow between Bridgeport and Sonora Junction on Highway 395.

The marines, en route south from a winter camp at Pickel Meadows in the Sierra Nevadas, carried arctic equipment and apparently were in no danger.

Rotary plows continued to cut away heavy snowdrifts in the highway, which has been closed to traffic by the California Highway Patrol for two days, to get to the busses.

Four other busses also stalled, but were able to depart for Camp Pendleton before they were caught by the deep drifts.

TIMES TO PRINT PRIVATE PAPERS OF VANDENBERG

Few men in recent years have had the opportunity afforded the late Arthur H. Vandenberg to observe the trend of national and world events. From his seat in the Senate, where his stature as a statesman and leader of foreign policy increased steadily during the final decade of his life, Vandenberg helped to shape the course of history. As a leading American delegate to United Nations conferences, he met and dealt with the leaders of all nations.

Now—for the first time—his private letters, diaries and journals will be published, to bring readers of the Los Angeles Times a new insight into events and personalities of major significance today. For the timeliest and most revealing story of the 1952 election year, read "The Private Papers of Senator Vandenberg," beginning Wednesday in The Times.

U.N. Reports Progress in Truce Talks

Greatest Gains in Two Months Made on Supervision Issue

MUNSAN, Korea, March 17 (Monday) (AP)—Allied and Communist negotiators made some headway yesterday on secondary ground rules for a Korean armistice. It wasn't much, but an allied spokesman still rated it as "the most progress in two months."

The harmonious tenor of yesterday's truce supervision meeting had its discordant counterpart in a blistering Communist note asking a "responsible" account of last Thursday's Koje Island prison outbreak.

The note was delivered in the staff officer meeting on prisoner exchange. It quoted Gen. Nam Il, senior Red delegate: "Such barbarous massacres would not be further tolerated." Twelve North Korean prisoners were killed and 26 wounded in the outbreak between rival POW groups.

Charge Camp Attacked

At today's meeting Red negotiators charged that an allied plane attacked a North Korean prisoner of war camp Sunday morning and wounded a British soldier.

Col. Tsai Cheng Wen, Chinese delegate, called the alleged attack part of the continual murder by the allies of prisoners held by both sides.

The meeting lasted an hour and 34 minutes. Nearby, staff officers arguing truce supervision met for an hour and 52 minutes. Both groups will meet again tomorrow.

Provisions Listed

The Reds' tentative acceptance of the United Nations command "package" proposal on truce supervision was regarded as a significant step forward. It had five provisions:

1—The U.N. command would reduce from six to five the number of ports of entry available to each side.

2—The Chinese and North Koreans would drop their demands for inspection of secret military equipment.

3—The Communists would agree that the words "in Korea" be inserted in pertinent paragraphs, thus strictly limiting an armistice to the Korean peninsula.

4—The allies would drop a request that neither side mass military forces to post a threat.

5—Reports on the location of major military units would not be required.

Progress Reported

"It was the most progress in two months," commented U.S Col. Andrew J. Kinney, allied staff officer. "The day's work does clear the issues down to naming the (specific) ports of entry and the question of the Soviet Union. It removes the bulk of the remaining issues."

The allies have flatly rejected Communist nomination of Russia as one of six neutral nations which would police an armistice.

Van Fleet Sees No New Snags in POW Rioting

TOKYO, March 16 (AP)—The service newspaper, Stars and Stripes, today quoted Gen. James A. Van Fleet, U.S. 8th Army commander, as saying he doesn't think Thursday's outbreak of violence at Koje Island will create any new snags in the Panmunjon peace talks.

BATTLESHIP WISCONSIN HIT OFF KOREA COAST

TOKYO, March 17 (Monday) (U.P.) — Communist guns shelled the battleship Wisconsin Sunday.

United Press Movietone Correspondent Tom McCallen reported from aboard the Wisconsin that the 45,000-ton battlewagon flagship of the U.S. 7th Fleet, received her first hit in two wars. A shore battery scored a direct hit that caused minor damage to a deck and injured three crewmen, none of them seriously.

The Wisconsin was shelling enemy rail lines along the East Korean coast when she was hit and had destroyed one train and sealed eight railway tunnels when the lucky shot landed.

BOMBS RIP HOMES IN W ADAMS AREA

Flying Glass From Blasts Perils Residents; Planted Explosives Rock District for Mile

Bombs, set off simultaneously, shattered two West Adams district homes early yesterday and rocked an area a mile around.

While no one was injured, flying glass narrowly missed many asleep in nearby homes.

The bombs were planted in front of 2130 and 2135 S Dunsmuir Ave., and set off shortly after 4 a.m. by a timing device. Damage to the homes was estimated at $5000.

Family Asleep

Asleep in the home at 2130 S Dunsmuir Ave. were William Bailey, 33, a science teacher at Carver Junior High School; his wife Willa, 30, and their son, William Jr., 12. The Baileys are Negroes.

In the other home were Ralph Martinez, 25, a studio worker, and John W. Potts, 32, restaurant owner. Police reported they said they were renting the home and were planning to move out shortly because of an increase in rent.

Police pointed out that some Negro families have been living peacefully in the area for at least a year.

FBI Aid Asked

Police Chief Parker announced later in the day that he is almost certain that those responsible for the outrage were the same persons who had bombed residences at 2308 and 2437 S Dunsmuir Ave. on July 25, 1951.

He has asked the FBI to work with police detectives in investigating the crimes.

Bailey told investigators that his boxer dog Dana had awakened him at 4 a.m. but quieted down shortly. A few minutes later the bomb exploded. After the blast the dog disappeared.

The Baileys moved to their home early in January and had received no threats, Bailey told officers. However, the former owner had notified police of hav-

Turn to Page 2, Column 6

Bus Upset Kills One, Injures 40

AMERICUS, Ga., March 16 (U.P.)—A crowded Trailways bus was flipped completely over in a field today in a six-way collision that killed one person and injured 35 to 40 others, the State Highway Patrol reported.

An automobile crashed into a line of standing cars and rebounded into the path of the oncoming bus. The bus, traveling toward Atlanta with 37 passengers, struck the automobile and then bounded across a ditch, rolled over and landed on its wheels. The driver of the automobile was killed.

Five Ford Local Union Officers Ousted as Reds

DETROIT, March 16 (AP) — Five union unit officers named as Communists before the House Un-American Activities Committee here were removed today from their posts in Ford Local 600 by an administrative board of the CIO United Auto Workers.

The administrative board was named Saturday to take over the huge local, after UAW President Walter P. Reuther accused its officers of permitting Communists to infiltrate their ranks. The board was directed to remove any local officers it found to be "members of or subservient to any political organization, such as the Communist, Fascist or Nazi organizations . . . ."

Those Fired Named

The board announced its decision today to take over the local's headquarters tomorrow. But Carl Stellato, local president, and members of his immediate staff theoretically have not been removed and continue to serve pending any decision otherwise by the administrative board.

Those fired from their union offices today were listed by the board as:

Paul Boatin, chairman of the motor building unit; John Gallo, recording secretary of the motor building unit; Dave Moore, vice-chairman of the gear and axle building unit; Nelson Davis, vice-chairman of the Dearborn Iron Foundry unit, and Ed Lock, chairman of the plastics building unit.

Named as Communists

All were named as Communists by witnesses before the House Un-American Activities Committee, whose hearings here last week set off the UAW action. All were called as witnesses, but none would answer questions regarding Communist affiliations, if any.

Winchell Stricken; Cancels Broadcast

NEW YORK, March 16 (AP)—Walter Winchell became ill and did not make his usual broadcast tonight.

The American Broadcasting Co., which carries the columnist's weekly radio broadcast, said he became ill "just before air time and went to bed."

1750 Federal Workers Seen in Red Union

Communist Activity of Leaders Disclosed in McCarran Report

Chicago Tribune Press Service

WASHINGTON, March 16. Approximately 1750 government employees are members of a Communist-dominated union, a Senate Internal Security Subcommittee reported today.

These Federal workers, concentrated in the Post Office Department, the Veterans Administration and the Bureau of Engraving of the Treasury Department belong to a union which was expelled from the CIO in 1950 as a subsidiary of the Communist Party, the report stated.

The union, the United Public Workers of America, has a total membership of 35,000 scattered through Federal, State, city and county organizations.

Testimony Made Public

Chairman McCarran (D) Nev., made public testimony taken in executive sessions which disclosed the Communist activities of the union leaders. He said the rank and file appeared to be unaware of the nature of their leadership.

Abram Flaxer, 47, national president of the union, was described in the report as "one of the tried fanatics" of the Communist Party. Flaxer, born in Lithuania, was identified in testimony as a card-carrying Communist.

The union's secretary-treasurer, Ewart Guinier; director of negotiations, Alfred Bernstein and two executive committee members, Jack Bigel and Mrs. Rose Russell, were also identified in testimony as Communists. Flaxer refused to testify on the ground that he might incriminate himself. The subcommittee recommended Flaxer's prosecution for contempt of Congress because he refused to produce union records.

Membership Divided

About 500 members of the union are employed in the Bureau of Engraving of the Treasury, where the nation's currency is printed, the report revealed, adding that union membership in the Post Office Department is close to 1000 and the Veterans Administration accounts for most of the remainder.

The union's annual income is approximately $119,000 and part of this fund has gone to the support of Communist organizations and fronts, the subcommittee reported.

A number of the union's members were found in the headquarters of the Immigration and Naturalization Service of the Department of Justice in New York City. These workers have participated in picket lines protesting the deportation of aliens with which the immigration service is concerned.

World Bank's Oil Mission to Iran Fails

TEHERAN, March 16 (AP)—The World Bank's attempt to get Iranian oil flowing again to the West broke down tonight in a deadlock with the Iranian government.

A bank mission, headed by Hector Prudhomme, loan officer, will pay a farewell call on Premier Mossadegh tomorrow morning and return later this week to the United States.

In a broadcast over the Teheran radio tonight, Ali Shayegan, a member of Iran's joint oil board, said: "Negotiations are now ended."

Shayegan said the government and the bank had failed to agree on the use of British technicians, the bank's position in operating the industry, and the price for the oil. Mossadegh has refused to permit any of the ousted British technicians of the British-controlled Anglo-Iranian Oil Co., whose properties in Iran were nationalized last year, to return to this country.

British Jet Clips Time to Australia

DARWIN, Australia, March 16 (Reuters)—A British Canberra jet bomber today flew from England to Australia in 20 hours 20 minutes flying time, clipping three hours from the record held by the first Canberra to fly to Australia in 1951.

Woman Author Seized With $50,000 Cash From Reno Burglary Loot

RENO, March 16 (AP) — FBI agents today arrested a woman in Flagstaff, Ariz., with $50,000 of the $1,500,000 Redfield burglary loot. Other agents pulled from an abandoned mine shaft near here the safe stolen from the L. V. Redfield home Feb. 29.

Mrs. Marie Jeanne D'Arc Machaud, arrested in Flagstaff after leaving the California Limited bound for Chicago, was the fingerwoman in the case, officers indicated. She is the sixth suspect under arrest—two women and four men.

Mrs. Machaud, 36, an artist and short-story writer, had been a guest in the home of Millionaire La Vere Redfield on several occasions, they said.

When FBI agents picked her up, she had not only the $50,000 identified as Redfield loot, but also was carrying 28 pieces of jewelry and a thick packet of securities.

Reno FBI Agent-in-Charge D. K. Brown said "in a general way the jewelry answers the description" of the loot. He added that "checks are under way" to determine if the securities also are part of the Redfield loot.

Mrs. Machaud, known here as Jeanne Michaud, had lived in Reno about two years. She was traveling under the name of Mrs. Arthur Grant when arrested. She is a native of St. Agathe, Quebec.

Only a few hours earlier, FBI men and Reno police pulled Redfield's battered green safe from a 35-foot shaft in the desolate Hot Springs area, 10 miles south of here. Its door had been smashed off.

They refused to say how they discovered the safe's hiding place. There was speculation that one of the four men held for the burglary had been persuaded to talk. John Triliegi, 37, nabbed in Milwaukee yesterday, was intensively quizzed. Arrested with Triliegi was Frank Sorrenti, 36.

Also held are Louis (Firpo) Gazzigli, 44, ex-prize fighter and Reno gambling club bouncer; Robert Young, 46, ex-convict, and Mrs. Leona Mae Giordano, 38, Reno gambling girl and cocktail waitress, who was arrested in Los Angeles.

THE WEATHER

U.S. Weather Bureau forecast: Partly cloudy today and tomorrow. Slightly warmer this afternoon with high near 58. Highest temperature yesterday, 53; lowest, 42.

FEATURES INDEX

French Trial Begins for Madame Bluebeard

France's version of "Arsenic and Old Lace" comes to life in medieval French village as Mme. Marie Besnard is tried for the murder of 11 persons. For details, see Page 5, Part II.

On Other Pages

EXTRA

LATE NEWS

Los Angeles Times

9 A.M. FINAL

VOL. LXXI | IN FOUR PARTS ★ | MONDAY MORNING, JULY 21, 1952 | 60 PAGES | DAILY, 10¢

BIG QUAKE ROCKS L.A.

Steel Peace Talks Again Break Down

Four-Hour Parley Unsuccessful in Ending Long Industry Tie-up

New York Times News Service

PITTSBURGH, July 20—White House-sponsored efforts to settle the seven-week steel strike broke down again tonight.

A four-hour joint conference between industry and union leaders failed to end the tie-up

Illustrated on Page 13, Part I

that has slowed down the de- companies met privately later this afternoon and decided they had no new proposal to offer Philip Murray, president of the CIO United Steel Workers.

This double-barreled setback fense program and brought idleness to 1,500,000 workers in steel and related industries.

Representatives of major steel did not halt the peacemaking activities of Dr. John R. Steelman, Acting Director of Defense Mobilization, who had induced the parties to make a fresh try at settling their dispute over union security today.

Race Against Deadline

Steelman kept in touch by telephone with union and management committees far into the night. He was racing to beat a 10 a.m. deadline set by Murray for a meeting of the union's 175-man wage policy committee here tomorrow.

In the absence of a settlement the committee is virtually certain to reinstate many of the Murray group's earlier wage and union shop demands. For the record this would wipe the slate clean of all the tentative understandings that have been reached in weary weeks of secret negotiations and put the dispute back where it was when the Wage Stabilization Board handed down its steel recommendations last March.

RADIO AND TV SCHEDULES ON CONVENTION

Television coverage of the Democratic convention today is scheduled to start at 7 a.m. when KNXT (2) comes onto the screen. KNBH (4) follows at 7:30 a.m., KTLA (5) at 9 a.m. and KECA (7) and KFMB (8) at 9:30 a.m. KNBH plans a special telecast at 4 p.m., returning to the screen at 6 p.m. with KNXT. At 6:30 p.m. KTLA, KECA and KFMB will all be on.

Radio coverage has been scheduled as follows: KMPC, 9:05 a.m.; KHJ, 9:20 a.m.; KFI, KNX and KECA, 9:30 a.m.; KHJ, 11 a.m.; KMPC, 2:05 and 3 p.m.; KNX, 4 p.m.; KHJ, 5 p.m.; KMPC, 5:20 p.m.; KNX and KECA, 6 p.m.; KFI, 6:30 p.m.; KHJ, 7 p.m.; KMPC, 7:45 p.m.; KNX, 8 p.m., and KHJ, 9:15 p.m.

GET FULL CONVENTION COVERAGE IN THE TIMES

They're off and running at Chicago!

The Democratic National Convention begins today and the race for the Presidential nominee to oppose the Republican candidate, Dwight D. Eisenhower, is under way.

The Times is presenting the most complete and brilliant coverage of the convention in Southern California. So that you may get the behind-scene story as well as the minute-by-minute news developments, five members of The Times' own staff are in Chicago—the same five who gave Times readers such comprehensive coverage of the Republican convention.

These experts are L. D. Hotchkiss, editor of The Times; Kyle Palmer, Times political editor; Bill Henry, Times columnist and analyst; Chester G. Hanson, veteran political writer, and Warren B. Francis of The Times Washington Bureau.

In addition, The Times' leased wire will bring special dispatches from the convention floor written by James Reston and Anne O'Hare McCormick of the New York Times and Ruth Montgomery of the New York Daily News. Analyses by Walter Lippmann, Holmes Alexander and other writers on the staffs of the Chicago Tribune, New York Daily News and New York Times will supplement this fine coverage.

The full reports of the Associated Press and United Press and the pictorial service of the Associated Press Wirephoto will round out this impressive coverage of the convention. Follow the dramatic events daily in The Times.

Democrats in Search of a 'Moses'

BY KYLE PALMER
Times Political Editor

CHICAGO, July 20—Accustomed to 20 years of taking orders, asking no questions and voting as directed, delegates to the "wide open" 1952 Democratic National Convention were looking for a party Moses here today as they swarmed into town for tomorrow's opening convention session.

Milling around hotel lobbies and conference rooms, huddling in spur-of-the-moment parleys and looking in vain to their leaders for enlightenment and guidance, the hosts of Democracy appear bewildered and perturbed.

Even their top spokesmen are unsure.

The powerful organization built in the name of Franklin D. Roosevelt and continued successfully by Harry S. Truman seems leaderless, rudderless and aimless.

Little Support

None of the candidates for the party's nomination for President has managed to accumulate anything more than personal or section support, with the possible exception of Sen. Kefauver. And there are indications his following may drift away.

President Truman probably could settle the whole matter by coming out for Vice-President Barkley.

The very fact that the President does have a preference, which to date he has coyly declined to make public, adds to the general atmosphere of hesitation and confusion.

Obviously, 20 years of regimentation under the Roosevelt-Truman regime has robbed the Democrats of self-reliance and initiative. The delegates have plenty of enthusiasm and, despite the heat, are almost as noisy as heretofore.

Donkey Saddled

Here is the traditional donkey, saddled, bridled, all dressed up and ready to go, but the reins hang limp and the saddle is empty.

Democratic leaders generally appear to believe they have a pretty good chance to win the November election, but they haven't come within striking distance of agreeing on a ticket.

Barkley appears to have latent

Turn to Page 2, Column 3

OPENING PROGRAMS AT DEMOCRAT CONVENTION

CHICAGO, July 20 (AP)—The program for Monday's opening-day sessions of the Democratic National Convention follows:

Morning session: 9:30 a.m., PDT

Call to order, Chairman Frank E. McKinney of the Democratic National Committee.

Invocation, Samuel Cardinal Stritch.

Address of welcome, Mayor Kennelly of Chicago.

Convention call, read by Mrs. Dorothy Vredenburgh, secretary of the national committee.

Addresses: Gov. Adlai E. Stevenson of Illinois; Sen. Paul H. Douglas of Illinois; J. M. Arvey, national committeeman for Illinois; Mrs. Elizabeth A. Conkey, national committeewoman for Illinois.

Evening session: 6 p.m., PDT

Invocation, J. Ralph Magee, retired Methodist Church Bishop.

Address by McKinney.

Appointment of committees.

Keynote address by the temporary convention chairman, Gov. Paul A. Dever of Massachusetts.

EISENHOWER MAY OPEN DRIVE HERE

DENVER, July 20 (AP)—Gen. Eisenhower may make his first major speech as the Republican Presidential nominee at the Veterans of Foreign Wars national convention opening in Los Angeles Aug. 3.

The General's campaign headquarters here today said he has received an informal invitation to address the convention and will decide within the next few days whether to accept.

Eisenhower already has agreed to speak at the American Legion's national convention at Madison Square Garden in New York Aug. 25.

The General is slated to return to Denver Wednesday or Thursday from Fraser, Colo., where he is vacationing at the Rocky Mountain cattle ranch of an old friend, Aksel Nielsen.

Members of the General's political staff who have been charting campaign plans in his absence have been at work on a far-reaching study of domestic issues likely to figure in the campaign. The results of the study will be put before Eisenhower when he returns from his vacation.

During his campaign for the GOP nomination the General acknowledged in several instances that he was unable to

Turn to Page 6, Column 3

Showdown on Sectional Strength Delayed a Day

CHICAGO, July 20 (AP)—The Democratic National Committee tonight cut the ground from under a drive to force an opening day showdown between northern and southern strength at the party convention.

The committee juggled the first session program, with the effect of delaying until Tuesday a fight over seating of two contested delegations, both anti-Truman administration, from Texas and Mississippi.

Taken out of the program was the adoption of temporary rules—the point at which the fight was to be made.

Harriman and Kefauver forces had indicated they would seek a showdown then.

One of the party advisers who

Turn to Page 4, Column 2

Nevada Favors Russell

CHICAGO, July 20 (U.P.) The 10-vote Nevada delegation will be predominantly for Sen. Russell on the first ballot at the Democratic National Convention.

FEATURES INDEX

Cal. Caucus Fist Fight Breaks Out

BY CHESTER G. HANSON
Times Staff Representative

CHICAGO, July 20—The first meeting of the California delegation to the Democratic National Convention in the Palmer House tonight was marked by a brawl in which fists flew and police were called to clear the meeting hall.

The ruckus was no fault of the Californians but resulted when their meeting was invaded by about a dozen men said to be connected with the Presidential campaign efforts of Herbert C. Holdridge.

Meeting Invaded

The Californians had gathered in the Crystal Room, their meeting place in the hotel, for the caucus and were waiting for the meeting to be called to order by Chairman George Miller Jr. when suddenly an uproar broke out at the rear of the large room when these men entered.

They demanded that they be heard and there were some shouts about the delegation being fraudulently selected for Kefauver, to whom the delegation is pledged.

Many of the delegation arose and immediately engaged the invaders physically by trying to throw them out. Fists flew and the place was in an uproar. Somebody called the police and a squad arrived immediately from downstairs.

One delegate, Rex Whittemore of Bakersfield, a 200-pounder, chose one of the big boys who invaded the place. "You look about my size," Whittemore explained and squared off at one of the invaders.

Uses Brass Knuckles

He said before he knew it his intended victim slipped on a pair of brass knuckles and let Whittemore have one on the collarbone, cutting his neck. The police restored comparative order and before the meeting was resumed the entire hall was cleared out and only delegates and alternates and the California visitors were permitted to re-enter.

After the brawl over the Holderidge intruders was settled, the delegates heard a few words from Kefauver, who told them of his great appreciation for the tremendous vote he received in California and of its great effect on his campaign over the rest of the nation.

Wrangle on Tickets

The delegates then resumed the wrangle that covered nearly two hours over how tickets to the convention were to be distributed to guests.

After an anxious plea from

Turn to Page 4, Column 3

Heaviest Jolt Since 1933 Breaks Water Mains; Wires Down

BULLETIN!

Dep. Sheriff Art Cross of Tehachapi reported that there are five known residents of the city killed in the earthquake that struck Southern California this morning.

Cross said that as far as he knows none of the inmates of the Women's Prison there were killed in the quake but that all were brought down to the mezzanine floor of the building.

Ralph Kreiser, Times correspondent in Bakersfield, reported that two water towers fell in the city of Bakersfield and many of the downtown streets are flooded. No loss of life has been reported in that desert city.

The Paloma gas field, 22 miles south of Bakersfield is reported burning. Many of the buildings in Bakersfield had windows broken and there was a large explosion in an automobile agency but no one was reported in the building at the time.

An earthquake of a major intensity hit Southern California at 4:51 a.m. today and a series of minor shocks continued to rock the Southland for an hour after.

First reports from all sections of the city were of broken water mains, high tension wires down but at this report, 5:25 a.m., no structures have been reported down.

Streets were reported crowded with daylight traffic, and persons throughout the Los Angeles area jammed the sidewalks after the first minute-long roll was felt.

Reports from up and down the coast were that the quake was the heaviest since the March 10, 1933, earthquake in which more than a hundred persons lost their lives.

Seismologists at the California Institute of Technology reported at 5:30 this morning that from their instruments they could not immediately tell or estimate the intensity of the slow rolling quake.

At Georgia Street Receiving Hospital a woman is in critical condition. Police say she went out onto her front lawn to sweep aside high tension wires which had fallen and she was severely burned.

Windows and plaster in buildings throughout the city fell.

All power is virtually out in the Valley and in a number of other parts of the city.

BARRICADES PLACED

Barricades were thrown up in about five places where pavement had sunk in the streets.

They were also placed around the Security Title Insurance Building at 530 W 6th St., a 15-story building which is reported to have been damaged extensively within. Until the

Turn to Page 2, Column 1

PART 1

Los Angeles Times

EQUAL RIGHTS

LIBERTY UNDER THE LAW — TRUE INDUSTRIAL FREEDOM

ALL THE NEWS
ALL THE TIME

VOL. LXXI | IN FIVE PARTS | CC★ | WEDNESDAY MORNING, NOVEMBER 5, 1952 | 72 PAGES | DAILY, 10c

EISENHOWER BY A LANDSLIDE

Stevenson Concedes After GOP Wins 30 States

California Carried by Republicans for First Time in 20 Years

Latest State-wide election figures early today gave Eisenhower 1,145,198 and Stevenson 896,346 with 10,787 precincts reporting, 5582 of them in Los Angeles.

Carrying California into the Republican column for the first time in 20 years and piling up a State lead that mounted toward 300,000, Gen. Dwight Eisenhower and Richard Nixon swamped the Stevenson-Sparkman ticket yesterday as voters piled up the greatest ballot total in the State's history.

Not only winning California's 32 electoral votes in their triumphant stride, the GOP Presidential nominees apparently carried several Republican Congressional candidates to victory in districts hitherto regarded as safe for Democratic nominees.

Eisenhower won in Los Angeles County by more than 145,000 in partial returns that indicated a probable majority here of 200,000 and ran ahead of Stevenson in some Southern California areas by as much as 10 to 1.

Stevenson Strongest in North

Democratic Presidential Nominee Stevenson made his best showing in San Francisco and in several other northern districts.

His California campaign director, State Sen. Miller, conceded defeat when a tabulation of returns from approximately half of the State's 20,746 polling places showed the Republican ticket safely in the lead.

Victory for Nixon as Eisenhower's running mate will result in a Senatorial vacancy when the young Republican Vice-Presidential nominee resigns to take his oath of office next January.

Gov. Earl Warren, who will appoint Nixon's successor, has not indicated his probable choice.

Knowland From North

The next junior United States Senator from this State will come from Southern California, as the senior U.S. Senator, William F. Knowland of Oakland, won both the Republican and Democratic nominations in the June primaries.

Knowland received a tremendous confidence vote in Tuesday's balloting.

Reversal of California's allegiance in National party politics was most pronounced in the southern end of the State, although many districts where

Turn to Page A, Column 3

County Vote Backs Schools and Veterans

Approval of propositions calling for additonal support for public schools, together with bonds for purchase of veterans' homes and farms featured yesterday's election in Los Angeles County.

In this respect the county was in line with reports from the rest of the State.

The voters appeared to have approved a change in the matter of showing party registration on the primary ballot but the move to bar cross-filing in California primaries was failing through a principle of priority of election returns.

Bonds Win Easily

The voters gave approval to Proposition No. 1, the veterans' bond issue, by an overwhelming margin, as they always have.

The schoolteachers flew their victory flag in the breeze last night as returns showed the voters approving Proposition No. 2, increases in State contributions, by a 2-to-1 vote.

Proposition No. 3, one of the most controversial on the ballot, exempting privately owned and parochial schools from taxation, was leading by a small margin on the face of incomplete returns.

The voters gave a good margin of approval to both propo-

Turn to Page 6, Column 4

NEW PRESIDENT—Dwight D. Eisenhower swept to impressive victory in yesterday's national election, the first Republican to be named to the White House in 20 years.

SHARES VICTORY—Sen. Richard M. Nixon of California was elected to Vice-Presidency in smashing Republican win to end two decades of Democratic domination.

General Cracks Solid South to End Long Rule by Democrats

BY THE ASSOCIATED PRESS

Gen. Eisenhower won the Presidency by a landslide yesterday and brought to a crashing end the 20-year era of Democratic political reign.

Eisenhower even split the South.

Down to defeat went Gov. Stevenson of Illinois. The Democratic nominee conceded it was all over after at least 30 States with 356 electoral votes had gone Republican After the concession the Eisenhower winnings had piled up to a fairly certain 39 States with a total of 453 electoral votes. Only 266 of the total of 531 are needed for victory.

"My fellow citizens have made their choice . . . and I gladly accept it," Stevenson said.

Praising Eisenhower as a great leader in time of war, the beaten Governor read a statement at Springfield, Ill., urging all Americans to unite behind the winner.

"I urge you all to give Gen. Eisenhower the support he will need," Stevenson said. "With a united people, with faith in democracy . . . we shall move forward with God's guidance . . . in freedom and dignity and peace."

As Stevenson spoke the fateful words of concession, this was the scope of the Eisenhower sweep:

Ike had ripped Virginia and Florida away from the traditionally Solid South and was leading in Texas and Tennessee. He had captured Oklahoma and Maryland along the border and was out front in Missouri.

Carries Big Vote States

New York, New Jersey, Ohio—all big vote States—were solidly in the GOP column. So were Illinois and California. Michigan and Pennsylvania were moving in that direction.

Farm States—many of those that sealed President Truman's upset victory four years ago—swung to the GOP. And the victory surge rolled westward to the coast.

Stevenson was ahead in a mere nine States with 89 electoral ballots — Alabama, Arkansas, Georgia, Louisiana, Mississippi, North Carolina, South Carolina, Kentucky and West Virginia.

At one mighty blow Eisenhower had demolished political ramparts which had securely sheltered Franklin D. Roose-

Turn to Page A, Column 7

Stevenson Calm as He Concedes Defeat at Polls

SPRINGFIELD, Ill., Nov. 5 (Wednesday) (AP)—Gov. Stevenson conceded victory in the election to Gen. Eisenhower.

The Leland Hotel ballroom was crowded when Stevenson entered at 1:40 a.m. (EST) and the room burst into cheers. The people set up a chant of "We want Stevenson."

The Governor was smiling and he laughed when the crowd started to chant. He wore a dark-blue double-breasted suit and a red tie. He appeared relaxed and completely at ease.

Stevenson said:

"It is traditional for Americans to fight hard before an election.

"It is traditional also to close ranks after an election."

Wires Congratulations

He said: "The people have rendered their verdict and I gladly accept it."

Stevenson said he had sent a wire of congratulation to Gen. Eisenhower.

Stevenson urged all those who had supported him to give their support now to the General.

"That which unites us as American citizens is far greater than that which divides us as political parties," Stevenson added.

Latest Los Angeles City and County Vote Returns

PRESIDENTIAL

5582 Precincts Out of 8148

Eisenhower (Rep.)	689,024
Stevenson (Dem.)	541,982

CONGRESS

16th District — 58 Precincts out of 467

Jackson (R)	2,988
Harter (D)	1,946

17th District — 189 Precincts out of 788

Finch (R)	6,667
King (D)	8,265

18th District — 351 Precincts out of 634

Hosmer (R)	1,403
Kennick (D)	1,346

21st District — 70 Precincts out of 785

Hiestand (R)	2,409
Burkhalter (D)	1,555

22nd District — 299 Precincts out of 524

Holt (R)	10,939
McHenry (D)	7,195

25th District — 32 Precincts Out of 788

Hillings (Rep.)	1,902
Sayre (Dem.)	297

SUPERVISOR

2nd District — 483 Precincts Out of 1043

Roach	16,858
Hahn	19,934

STATE PROPOSITIONS

3134 Precincts Out of 8148

1—Veterans Bonds	
Yes	78,883
No	13,330
2—Public School Funds	
Yes	59,563
No	34,464
3—School Taxation	
Yes	57,396
No	45,383
6—Oaths of Office	
Yes	57,654
No	25,116
7—Party Affiliations	
Yes	54,421
No	25,127
10—Public Funds	
Yes	39,716
No	44,663
11—Aged Aid	
Yes	46,311
No	53,673
13—Cross-Filing	
Yes	46,267
No	38,548
24—School Bonds	
Yes	57,268
No	19,426

COUNTY PROPOSITIONS

A—Supervisors' Pay Increase — 3134 Precincts out of 8148

Yes	45,771
No	23,464

B—Flood Control Bonds — 3134 Precincts out of 8113

Yes	57,146
No	17,151

ASSEMBLY

42nd District — 15 Precincts Out of 311

Marsh (Rep.)	308
Jolley (Dem.)	297

47th District — 137 Precincts Outof 238

Stewart (Rep.)	1,374
Johnson (Dem.)	512

37th District — 90 Precincts Out of 238

Conrad (Rep.)	2,757
Schwartz (Dem.)	1,758

61st District — 60 Precincts Out of 372

Lindstrom (Rep.)	3,242
McMillan (Dem.)	4,371

Turn to Page A, Column 6

Gen. Eisenhower Pledges His Best as President

NEW YORK, Nov. 4 (AP)—Gen. Eisenhower, swept to a smashing victory by America's voters, promptly pledged tonight that as President he never will give "short weight" to his new responsibilities.

Addressing a wildly cheering crowd at his campaign headquarters, the Republican President-elect told his audience he had sent his Democratic opponent, Gov. Stevenson of Illinois, the following telegram:

"I thank you for your courteous and generous message. Recognizing the intensity of the difficulties that lie ahead, it is clearly necessary that men and women of goodwill of both parties forget the political strife through which we have passed and devote themselves to the single purpose of a better future. This, I believe, they will do."

Reply to Stevenson

Eisenhower's telegram was in reply to one he received a short time earlier from Stevenson, conceding the election.

The General's appearance in the packed Grand Ballroom of the Commodore Hotel touched off a thunderous ovation which went on for several minutes before he was able to speak.

Smiling happily, Eisenhower waved to the crowd again and again.

The General said that it is "trite to say that this is a day of dedication rather than triumph" and added that he is "indeed as humble as I am proud of the decision" of the American people.

Stating that he recognized the weight of responsibility of his new office, Gen. Eisenhower pledged:

"I shall never in my service

Turn to Page 6, Column 1

State-by-State Returns in Presidential Election

Following is the State-by-State vote for President as compiled by the Associated Press:

STATE—	Total Precincts	Precincts Reporting	Stevenson	Eisenhower	Indicated Electoral Vote D.	R.
Alabama	2,505	1,942	217,327	124,700	11	..
Arizona	505	310	53,551	82,135	..	4
Arkansas	2,382	1,242	99,058	68,035	8	..
California	20,746	10,591	789,450	1,014,893	..	32
Colorado	1,650	316	41,388	64,105	..	6
Connecticut	169	169	481,482	610,989	..	8
Delaware	276	191	40,990	43,215	..	3
Florida	1,684	1,343	374,960	476,744	..	10
Georgia	1,725	759	253,389	117,879	12	..
Idaho	865	458	52,019	100,748	..	4
Illinois	9,680	6,291	1,284,723	1,367,005	..	27
Indiana	4,202	2,455	557,884	743,104	..	13
Iowa	2,481	1,389	261,111	448,080	..	10
Kansas	2,851	1,277	90,113	211,870	..	8
Kentucky	4,135	2,654	346,056	333,700	10	..
Louisiana	2,118	914	192,685	187,662	10	..
Maine	625	617	118,545	232,622	..	5
Maryland	1,428	1,411	389,452	489,955	..	9
Massachusetts	1,967	1,087	581,873	656,858	..	16
Michigan	4,480	1,023	229,722	386,264	..	20
Minnesota	3,791	1,046	268,622	300,598	..	11
Mississippi	1,790	1,396	143,226	98,389	8	..
Missouri	4,771	3,137	481,893	525,165	..	13
Montana	1,137	349	49,938	52,935	..	4
Nebraska	2,067	482	31,07	80,775	..	6
Nevada	244	170	9,152	15,241	..	3
New Hampshire	297	290	99,218	155,819	..	4
New Jersey	3,840	3,080	843,940	1,079,764	..	16
New Mexico	893	291	36,150	43,904	..	4
New York	10,348	10,181	3,044,648	3,851,975	..	45
North Carolina	2,036	1;763	563,138	471,740	14	..
North Dakota	2,301	355	15,804	37,904	..	4
Ohio	10,877	4,613	646,649	833,347	..	25
Oklahoma	3,860	3,468	360,168	420,120	..	8
Oregon	2,269	967	52,474	98,289	..	6
Pennsylvania	8,439	7,027	1,725,871	1,904,682	..	32
Rhode Island	284	284	193,152	200,551	..	4
South Carolina	1,563	1,426	165,126	154,380	8	..
South Dakota	1,950	1,393	55,454	108,157	..	4
Tennessee	2,400	2,059	268,147	271,397	..	11
Texas	254	242	723,129	829,369	..	24
Utah	969	471	62,180	101,476	..	4
Vermont	246	246	43,220	109,239	..	3
Virginia	1,792	1,722	255,043	330,532	..	12
Washington	4,381	300	35,457	40,324	..	9
West Virginia	2,841	1,481	234,531	220,214	8	..
Wisconsin	3,224	2,036	356,218	554,369	..	12
Wyoming	677	325	11,063	20,711	..	3

Rule of New Congress Hinges on Close Races

Republicans Gain Five Seats in House and Take Lead in Nine Crucial Contests

WASHINGTON, Nov. 5 (Wednesday) (AP)—Republicans made gains early today in a tough battle to give Dwight D. Eisenhower a GOP Congress, but the outcome still was in doubt in both House and Senate.

Two Senate seats now held by Democrats, in Connecticut and Maryland, were captured by Republicans. But this still was one short of the net gain of three needed to assure GOP control of that branch in the 83rd Congress.

In the House the Republicans had gained five seats. But they needed a pickup of 16 to win a majority there.

The Senate race, where the Democrats had a mathematical edge before the voting began, promised to be exceedingly close.

Win 13 Senate Races

Nineteen Senate races had been decided. The Republicans won 13 of them. But that left the Senate tally 41 to 39 Democratic because the Democrats will have 35 holdovers and the Republicans 26 in the new Congress.

Of the 16 races in doubt, Republicans were leading in nine and Democrats in seven. If the candidates who were leading proved to be the victors. the Senate would be tied, 48 to 48, on the basis of old party labels. That could leave control up to Sen. Wayne Morse of Oregon, who identifies himself now as an independent.

Hinges on Close Race

The Senate race appeared to hinge on close contests in Kentucky, New Mexico, Wyoming, Missouri and Nevada, and possibly other States.

These Democratic incumbents were trailing: Ernest W. McFarland of Arizona, the majority leader; Joseph O'Mahoney of Wyoming; Thomas Underwood of Kentucky and Blair Moody of Michigan.

But these Republican Senators also were behind: James P. Kem of Missouri, Zales Ecton of Montana, Harry Cain of Washington and Henry Cabot Lodge of Massachusetts.

Sen. Joseph R. McCarthy of Wisconsin, who became a top campaign issue because of tactics in pressing charges of Communist infiltration into the Federal government, was well ahead in his bid for re-election.

The Democrats clung to an edge in the House with over half of the 435 seats decided, but many of the marginal districts were yet to be heard from.

FEATURES INDEX

HAHN AHEAD OF ROACH IN RACE FOR SUPERVISOR

On the face of incomplete but fairly indicative returns at midnight last night, City Councilman Kenneth Hahn appeared to be assured victory over Supervisor Leonard J. Roach, in the 2nd Supervisorial District.

Hahn, popular with the younger element and tied to the George McLain influence in the district took an early lead as the returns rolled in and piled it up as the night wore on.

Roach, who has served several terms as Supervisor, would have to enjoy a considerable reversal in trend if he was to overtake the lead established by Hahn.

This was the only contest in the Supervisors' offices in yesterday's election, the others having been settled in the primary last June.

THE WEATHER

U.S. Weather Bureau forecast: Increasing high clouds today with considerable cloudiness tonight and tomorrow and a chance of a few scattered light showers tomorrow. High today about 80. High yesterday, 88; low, 62.

Supervisor Darby Dies After Blow by Irate Property Owner

PART 1

ALL THE NEWS ALL THE TIME

VOL. LXXII | IN FOUR PARTS | CC ★ | FRIDAY MORNING, MARCH 6, 1953 | 64 PAGES | DAILY, 10c

STALIN DIES; MYSTERY VEILS SUCCESSOR

Supervisor Darby Dies After Blow

Man Who Struck Him Booked; Autopsy Blames Hemorrhage

Supervisor Raymond V. Darby, 56, died of a brain hemorrhage yesterday afternoon, two hours and a half after he was staggered by a blow from an irate property owner at a Board of Supervisors meeting.

At 8:50 p.m. the property owner, Samuel H. Emerson, 50, of 4121 Wilshire Blvd., walked into the Hall of Justice offices of Dist. Atty. S. Ernest Roll, who had sought him for questioning.

Emerson was booked in County Jail on suspicion of manslaughter following a two-hour-long conference in Roll's offices. The booking was made jointly by Sheriff's Sgt. Herman Garbe and Police Sgt. Harry Hansen of the homicide detail.

The property owner's lawyer, Walter C. Harbert, said he expects to obtain a writ of habeas corpus for Emerson's release from jail this morning.

Stroke Suffered

Mr. Darby suffered a stroke 10 minutes after being hit on the chin and collapsed unconscious in his private office.

At the Georgia Street Receiving Hospital oxygen was administered and feverish preparations were made to relieve the pressure of the brain hemorrhage by tapping the spinal cord but Mr. Darby never recovered consciousness.

A post-mortem was performed last night by Chief Autopsy Surgeon Frederick D. Newbarr, Dr. Richard O. Myers and Brain Specialist Cyril Courville.

After stating that no bruises were found, the autopsy report said death was caused by a "massive spontaneous hemorrhage into the brain stem." Other significant findings, the report added, included the presence of "chronic hypertensive arterial sclerotic cardiovascular disease."

Emotional Distress

Elaborating on the report, Dr. Newbarr added:

"The emotional distress and excitement incident to the episode was of such a nature that it materially raised the already elevated blood pressure, thus putting additional strain on diseased blood vessels and leading to the brain hemorrhage."

Coroner Ben H. Brown announced that an inquest will

Supervisor Darby

be held at 10:30 a.m. Tuesday. Mr. Darby's body was taken to Pierce Bros. Inglewood Mortuary.

Roll said no formal complaint will be issued against Emerson until after the inquest.

Witnesses said Emerson clipped Mr. Darby on the chin with his right fist in the Supervisors' room at 1 p.m.

Zoning Request

More than 50 persons were attending a hearing in which Emerson and his wife, Mrs. Jari P. Emerson, 35, were asking for zoning changes on their subdivision near Palmdale.

Ironically, Mr. Darby was the only one of the five Supervisors who voted in favor of the Emersons' request. He apparently disagreed with their purpose but felt they were within their legal rights.

As the meeting ended, Mr. Darby said to the Emersons:

"All you want to do is sell this land to a lot of suckers."

Apology Demanded

Mrs. Emerson, seated among the spectators, leaped to her feet and cried, "That is not true. I demand an apology."

Mr. Darby made no apology but, as is often his custom, walked to the railing separating board members from spectators and said, "I would like to talk to you."

Witnesses said he asked Mrs. Emerson: "Why did you attack me? I want to know why you attacked me in this way."

Mrs. Emerson answered, "I think you were very much out of line."

At this point accounts differ. Mrs. Emerson insists that Mr. Darby looked at her and said,

Turn to Page 2, Column 3

WARREN WILL NAME DARBY SUCCESSOR

Under State law, Gov. Warren will appoint a successor to serve out the remainder of Supervisor Darby's term, which has about three and a half years to run.

Kenneth Sampson, chief field deputy for Darby, will temporarily discharge formal duties of the office until the Governor acts.

Sampson, 47, entered county service in 1926 when he joined the Regional Planning Commission. He resigned in 1931 but returned in 1936 after a period in private business. In 1943 he transferred to the County Manager's office where he remained until four years ago.

High of 80 Deg. Equals 16-Year Record for Date

The temperature rose to a summerlike 80 deg. yesterday and the Weather Bureau announced it was the hottest March 5 since 1937 when a similar high was reached.

The 80-deg. high was recorded at 12:08 p.m. It was by no means the highest for this year, the weatherman pointed out. Five days in February the temperature reached 80 deg. and once it touched 85.

The highest temperature for this date was 87 deg., which was measured back in 1899.

Clear skies are forecast for today with a top temperature of 80. Yesterday's lowest temperature was 49 deg.

Based on the Weather Bureau forecast of strong inversion and easterly winds in the morning, the Air Pollution Control District predicts eye irritation and crop damage in the central and western portions of Los Angeles.

Decks Clear for Ouster of Democrats

Eisenhower Order to Give Agency Heads Firing Authority

WASHINGTON, March 5 (AP) — President Eisenhower cleared the decks today for ousting at least several hundred holdover Democratic officials from their government jobs.

Gen. Eisenhower directed that an executive order be drafted immediately "to provide the heads of agencies with greater freedom in determining" who should occupy a number of jobs now under Civil Service protection.

Several Hundred Involved

White House Press Secretary James C. Hagerty said this would make it possible to fire the present holders of the jobs concerned. All of the jobs, in some degree, are policymaking posts. The White House announcement said the action "will not involve more than several hundred positions."

There have been complaints that when the new Republican administration went into office, it found that in many agencies the new chief could appoint only a handful of the top policymakers.

Gen. Eisenhower also told the Civil Service to review the whole question of employees in Schedule A of the Civil Service rules. Schedule A jobs are those of a policymaking nature.

Job Freeze Hit

Hagerty said a number of officeholders who should have been put in Schedule A, and thus made subject to dismissal at the administration's pleasure, instead were "frozen" in their jobs by the Roosevelt and Truman administrations.

This was done, Hagerty said, by extending them the job protection that should be extended only to career Civil Service employees.

"Such actions," the White House statement said, "undermine the foundations on which a genuine career service should be built. A Civil Service system is not an end in itself. It is a method for obtaining more efficient administration."

Lurline Sails After Wage Dispute Ends

SAN FRANCISCO, March 5 (U.P.)—The Matson liner Lurline, with 720 cheering vacation-bound passengers aboard, finally sailed for Honolulu today after being held at the pier for 24 hours by a CIO radio operators' wage dispute.

The luxury liner cast off at 3:50 p.m., an hour after the Pacific Maritime Association announced it had agreed to the radiomen's demand for a 9.5% pay hike.

The settlement was a victory for the union which had been fighting for wage parity with East Coast operators.

The announcement by J. Paul St. Sure, president of PMA, said the agreement gave both the CIO American Radio Association and the AFL Masters, Mates and Pilots Union the full 9.5% raise, retroactive to last Monday, with additional retroactivity subject to arbitration.

THE WEATHER

U.S. Weather Bureau forecast: Mostly clear today and sunny with scattered high cloudiness tomorrow. Local fog near the coast late tonight and early tomorrow. High today near 80. Cooler tomorrow afternoon. High yesterday, 80; low, 49.

DICTATOR PASSES—Joseph Stalin, Premier of Russia, who died of a brain hemorrhage, after lingering for four days, shown in familiar salute in more active days. (AP) Wirephoto

Controls Lifted on Bread, Autos and Appliances

WASHINGTON, March 5 (U.P.) The government today scrapped price controls on bread, automobiles, laundry services and virtually all home appliances such as refrigerators and stoves. Only two market basket items—coffee and beer—were left under ceilings.

Price officials predicted the sweeping decontrol order probably will mean price increases n bread, automobile parts, some appliances and laundry and dry cleaning services, including diaper service. The order affected goods representing an estimated $25,000,000,000 in annual sales.

Fifth Decontrol Order

It left less than 4% of the items on the government's cost-of-living index still under price controls. It was the fifth in the step-by-step program to decontrol all prices by April 30 when the present control law expires.

The National Automobile Dealers hailed the order and hinted there will be no over-all increase in car and truck prices. They said used cars have been selling below ceiling and that production of new automobiles "has met if not exceeded" demand.

The order came as President Eisenhower told a news conference he is gratified to see that the administration's decontrol program has brought little evidence of anyone trying to gouge consumers or force up prices. He said he is convinced the people are ready to be considerate and moderate.

No Increase Expected by L.A. Bakeries

Spokesmen for leading Los Angeles bakeries said yesterday they anticipate no raise in the price of bread and pastry with the removal of price controls.

A Helms Bakery official said bakery products in this area have been selling below ceiling for some time.

Ed Mills, vice-president of Van de Kamp's Holland Dutch Bakers, said his company anticipates no change in present prices.

Population Set at 158,448,000

WASHINGTON, March 5 (AP) The Census Bureau estimated today that the population of the United States on Jan. 1, this year, was about 158,448,000.

This was an increase of 2,698,000 in 1952—the biggest jump of any year in the nation's history.

Soviets Hint Malenkov Will Succeed Stalin

Premier's Policies to Be Carried Out by Party Leadership, Pravda Editorial Says

LONDON, March 5 (U.P.) — Russian Communism hinted broadly today that Joseph Stalin's policy will be carried on "under the tried leadership of the party" and that Georgi M. Malenkov might be its headman.

The Soviet party's first political statement on the possible successor to Stalin was published as a front page editorial in its official organ, Pravda, a few hours before Moscow announced the death of the Russian Prime Minister.

Plans which determine "the prospects and ways of our progress," it said, "are based on the laws of the national economy, on the science of the Communist society structure, which have been evolved by Comrade Stalin."

It attributed that pronouncement to Malenkov, bracketing him with Stalin and Nikolai Lenin, the father of Communism, as the only three men mentioned by name.

Mention Held Significant

The mention of Malenkov, secretary of the party and a highly regarded prospect for Stalin's mantle, seemed significant to those familiar with Soviet indirection and innuendo.

The forward-looking policy of which he spoke at the 19th party congress in Moscow last October was one of peaceful coexistence with the capitalist world, on the theory that capitalism finally would fall apart on its own.

The statement dwelt through-

Turn to Page 4, Column 4

Eisenhower Renews Offer for Russ Talk

WASHINGTON, March 5 (U.P.) President Eisenhower today again offered to meet Soviet leaders personally if it would help promote peace and the administration asked the Senate to rush confirmation of the new Ambassador to Russia.

The twin developments highlighted the second day of efforts here to evaluate the new situation in the Kremlin and get ready for anything that may happen as a result of Premier Stalin's death.

The State Department asked the Senate to speed confirmation of Charles E. Bohlen as Ambassador to Moscow in order to have a seasoned diplomat available for on-the-spot analysis. The Senate Foreign Relations Committee agreed to vote on the nomination Tuesday. Bohlen in an expert on Russian affairs.

Gen. Eisenhower told his third news conference he would meet with the new Soviet lead-

Turn to Page 10, Column 5

FEATURES INDEX

Longer Lives Credited to Stomach Removal

Mayo Clinic surgeon, in address here, says persons who have their stomachs taken out successfully live longer than the rest of the population. Story on Page 1, Part 2.

On Other Pages

Vishinsky Calls Death Great Blow

GLEN COVE, N.Y., March 5 (AP) — Soviet Foreign Minister Andrei Y. Vishinsky said tonight the death of Joseph Stalin was a blow to all humanity.

Reached by telephone at his country retreat on Long Island, the Kremlin's diplomatic chief said:

"With great sorrow I confirm the death of Prime Minister Stalin. It is a great blow to all of the Soviet people and to all humanity. The name of Stalin is immortal."

Vishinsky, who was prosecutor for Stalin at the purge trials of the 30s which eliminated many of Stalin's enemies, said he will leave for Moscow tomorrow.

Premier Succumbs to Brain Hemorrhage After Four-Day Battle

LONDON, March 6 (Friday) (AP) — Joseph Stalin died last night behind the 12-foot-thick walls of Moscow's Kremlin. He dominated a third of the world's peoples as the most powerful dictator in history.

The Prime Minister of the Soviet Union and the supreme chief of the Communist Party succumbed at 9:50 p.m. (10:50 a.m. PST), four days after suffering a brain hemorrhage.

He had been in coma since he was stricken Sunday

(Full page of pictures on life of Stalin, Page 3, Part 1)

night and his condition grew progressively worse. Yesterday his 10 physicians said his heart was faltering.

The announcement of his death was broadcast from Moscow at 4:07 a.m. Moscow time today—more than six hours after his doctors had given up their struggle.

Official Soviet Announcement

The official announcement said:

"The heart of the comrade and inspired continuer of Lenin's will, the wise leader and teacher of the Communist Party and the Soviet people—Joseph Vissarionovitch Stalin—has stopped beating."

There was no immediate indication from Moscow who was taking over control of the country. The announcement was issued in the name of the Communist Party's Central Committee, the Council of Ministers and the Presidium of the Supreme Council. All these are organs which Stalin dominated and among those next to him in power have been Georgi Malenkov, L. P. Beria, V. M. Molotov and Nicholas Bulganin.

As if appealing for unity, the official statement said: "In these sorrowful days all the peoples of our country are rallying even closer in a great fraternal family under the tested leadership of the Communist Party created and reared by Lenin and Stalin."

The most prominent leader of the Communist Party, next to Stalin, has been Malenkov.

Points to Increased Might

The announcement was, in effect, an order of the day.

It declared the armed might of the Soviet Union is growing, "for a decisive rebuff to any aggressor," but insisted the U.S.S.R. policy is one of peace and international collaboration. It called for the "development of businesslike relations with all countries."

There was no mention at any place of any of Stalin's lieutenants—Malenkov, Beria and so on.

It did not even bear the name of the nominal President of Russia — Nikolai Mikhailovich Shvernik, since 1946 president of the Presidium of the Supreme Soviet (Parliament).

Stalin's fatal illness became known on Wednesday, more than two days after he was stricken in his Kremlin apartment. An official announcement issued from the Ministry of Health and signed by the 10 physicians said Stalin "had

Turn to Page 6, Column 1

MOSCOW PUTS ON BLACK

Russian Workers Grim as They Hear of Death

BY EDDIE GILMORE

MOSCOW, March 6 (Friday) (AP)—It has happened — the thing that the average Russian never let enter his mind. Joseph Stalin has died in the Kremlin.

This correspondent heard the news—that Stalin had died at 9:50 p.m. (Thursday) after four days of illness—as he was riding through Moscow's snowy streets. The announcement came over the car radio. The driver, a former Soviet army man, was stunned. He could hardly drive the car to the central telegraph office, where all telephone calls to the outside world must be placed.

Russian Workers Grim

A trickle of tears rolled down his cheeks.

"Excuse me," said the driver. "He was a real person."

That probably sums up what is in the heart of many Soviet citizens.

At the telegraph office all the Russian workers were grim. To some, Stalin's death was like the death of one's father.

Even before dawn, people began putting black-bordered flags on Moscow's buildings. They were everywhere—on the big downtown structure of the Council of Ministers, which the 73-year-old Stalin headed, and on small wooden houses in the suburbs.

As Russians Knew Him

The Russians began talking of Stalin as they knew him. There was the time he directed a battle from a little hut close to the front—this hut has become a historic place and painters have put it on canvas. His early life was not easy. He was arrested many times as a revolutionary against the Czar, and banished to Siberia. There were times when he was cold and hungry. But he came to be, said the Russians, the best known man in the world.

(This material was telephoned from Moscow to London several hours after the Moscow radio had announced Stalin's death. At this point the phone connection was broken.)

PART 1

EQUAL RIGHTS

Los Angeles Times

LIBERTY UNDER THE LAW — TRUE INDUSTRIAL FREEDOM

ALL THE NEWS
ALL THE TIME

VOL. LXXII | IN FOUR PARTS | CC ★★ | WEDNESDAY MORNING, MAY 27, 1953 | 64 PAGES | DAILY, 10¢

POULSON ELECTED MAYOR

Auditorium and Airport Bond Propositions Lag

Russ Execute Four as Spies for U.S.

Ministry Claims Parachutists Admitted American Assignments

MOSCOW, May 27 (Wednesday) (AP)—The Soviet Ministry of Internal Affairs announced today that four spies who confessed they had dropped by parachute on the Ukraine with assignments from the American Intelligence Service had been tried and executed.

The Ministry said the four had confessed they were dropped in the Ukraine the night of April 26 from an unmarked four-engine American plane for diversionist, terrorist and espionage assignments.

The Ministry, in a special communique, said the four were executed by a firing squad. They were identified as Alexander Vasilievich Lakhno, Alexander Nikolaevich Makov, Sergi Iozisimovich Gorbunov and Dmitri Nikolaevich Remiga.

The communique gave this account of the incident:

"On the night of April 26, 1953, there was received by the Ministry of Internal Affairs of the U.S.S.R. information of a violation of the Soviet frontier and the appearance over the territory of the Ukrainian Republic (one of the member republics of the U.S.S.R.) of a foreign airplane of unknown nationality.

Parachutists Named

"It was established that from the above named plane there were dropped parachutists—agents of a foreign intelligence service.

"As a result of measures taken by the Ministry of Internal Affairs of the U.S.S.R, there were searched out and arrested two parachutists who gave their names as Vasili Vasilievich Vasilchenko and Leonid Nikolaevich Matov.

"The caught parachutists confessed that they were diversionists dropped on the U.S.S.R from abroad by the American Intelligence Service with diversionist, terrorist, and espionage assignments.

"The diversionists declared they were dropped the night of April 26, 1953, on territory of the Ukrainian Republic in parachutes from an American four-motored plane without recognition markers."

Assumed Names

The communique said Vasilchenko and Matkov admitted they were using fabricated surnames given them by the American intelligence. They said their real names are Alexander Lakhno, with the spy nickname of Alec, and Alexander Nikolaevich Makov, with the spy nickname Pete.

Judging from the names, all four were of Ukrainian or Russian origin.

The communique said Lakhno, Makov and Gorbunov were "active accomplices of the German-Fascist occupiers and betrayed the Soviet people" during World War II. After the war, the communique said, all four of the alleged spies had fled to West Germany and found "new masters and protectors in American intelligence organs."

ROSENBERGS DENIED STAY OF EXECUTION

WASHINGTON, May 26 (U.P.) Chief Justice Fred M. Vinson today denied a request by condemned atomic spies Julius and Ethel Rosenberg for a stay of execution to give them time for a fourth appeal to the Supreme Court.

Vinson's action does not prevent attorneys for the Rosenbergs from going ahead with their appeal anyway. But they have no assurance an execution date will not be set that would come before the high court could rule. The appeal must be filed by June 9.

May Have Time

The Justice Department, which opposed the request for a stay, said any new date for the Rosenbergs to pay the death penalty in Sing Sing Prison's electric chair likely would be after June 15.

The department said this would give the Supreme Court ample time to rule on a new appeal without a stay.

Vinson did not issue any opinion or statement with his rejection of the petition. He merely wrote the word "denied" on the papers that were submitted to him.

The Rosenbergs are expected to be sentenced when notice of the high court's rejection of their third appeal reaches the trial court, probably Friday.

New Plea to President

Sentenced to death more than two years ago for conspiracy to slip atomic secrets to Russia, the couple have been spared so far through a series of appeals to the Supreme Court and a petition for Presidential clemency, which President Eisenhower rejected.

In New York the National Committee to Secure Justice in the Rosenberg Case announced it has sent a new plea to Gen. Eisenhower. It said that "newly discovered documents in the case warrant, we believe, an act of clemency at this time."

SON OF EARL BROWDER RECEIVES FELLOWSHIP

NEW YORK, May 26 (AP)—In awarding a fellowship to Dr. Felix Browder, son of former Communist Leader Earl Browder, the John Simon Guggenheim Memorial Foundation first determined that he is not and never was a Communist, the foundation reported today.

Dr. Browder, an instructor in mathematics at Boston University, is a registered Democrat.

A statement from the foundation said the foundation trustees were confident that the American people will agree that Dr. Browder, "as an able and loyal young American," was entitled "to have his opportunity for development."

The statement described the 25-year-old Browder as a brilliant mathematician.

L.A. Transit Strike Near, Union Warns

Riders Told to Expect Walkout Sunday Midnight

Threat of a strike against the Los Angeles Transit Lines grew stronger yesterday with a union announcement warning the public to "make other arrangements for transportation next week."

The union statement, issued through Henry Crawford, president of Division 1277, AFL Transportation Union, said that no settlement is in sight although negotiations are continuing with the company. The union, comprising motor coach and streetcar operators, has authorized a strike against the company beginning on midnight Sunday, May 31.

Accuses Company

Crawford charged that the company was not considering making any offer other than renewal of the present agreement. He said that the union, at the company's request, had withdrawn certain demands in order to facilitate an agreement, but that the company had refused to make any concessions on major issues in dispute.

"In the light of the present impasse and with the imminence of the strike deadline, the first business of the union now is to prepare for an orderly strike and for the protection of our members and their families," he said.

The company had no comment on Crawford's statement.

Negotiations Stalled

W. J. Bassett, secretary of the AFL Central Labor Council, sat in on a negotiation session with company representatives yesterday. Union spokesmen described the session as "unproductive."

In the San Gabriel area members of the same union were planning to meet either tomorrow or Friday with government conciliators in an effort to avoid a strike set for Sunday midnight against the Foster Transportation Co. which serves Alhambra, San Gabriel and Monterey Park.

Approximately 18 drivers are seeking a 10-cent hourly wage increase, according to Ray Gregg, business agent, who said the company had proposed a wage cut instead.

Bomber Lost on Flight to Southland

VANCOUVER, B.C., May 26 (U.P.)—A four-engine Royal Canadian Air Force Lancaster bomber with 10 men aboard was unreported on a flight to San Diego, Cal., today and search planes fanned out over the stormy Southern Oregon coast where the plane was last reported.

The U.S. Coast Guard said the last report from the plane placed it over Newport, Or., at 3:20 a.m. It was en route from Vancouver Island with several other bombers.

The brightly painted red and silver plane had enough fuel to remain aloft only until 1 p.m., the Coast Guard said.

Four U.S. Coast Guard, two Air Force and three Canadian air force planes were searching the Southern Oregon and Northern California coastlines for the plane. Search planes were flying out of the airport at North Bend, Or.

There were thunderstorms and heavy showers in the vicinity today.

VICTORY SIGN—Rep. Norris Poulson, shown as he claimed victory in Mayoralty election. Shortly thereafter, Mayor Bowron conceded the Congressman had won. Times photo

Whirlwind Hits Factory in Van Nuys

A whirlwind yesterday blew off a section of roof from a Van Nuys clothing factory, while other "dust devils" plagued various San Fernando Valley communities.

Henry Strum, owner of the factory at 14620 Arminta St., said the wind blew in with great force, ripping off a 300-foot section and frightening his 20 employees.

Spinning dust devils in other San Fernando Valley areas caused no damage.

Early voters shivered yesterday in the coldest dawn of the month—49 deg. Record low for the year was a frosty 38 deg. March 2. The high was 68.

FEATURES INDEX

Man Seriously Hurt by Barracuda Attack

A fisherman, seriously injured when attacked by a deadly barracuda off Lower California, has been flown to a San Diego hospital. Story Page 28, Part 1.

On Other Pages

Forget U.N. in Korean War, Taft Suggests

U.S. Should Operate on Its Own if Present Truce Talks Fail, Senator Tells Conference

New York Times News Service

CINCINNATI, May 26—In an address of major significance, Sen. Taft of Ohio, the majority floor leader, declared tonight that the United States "might as well forget the United Nations as far as the Korean war is concerned."

"I think we should do our best now to negotiate this truce, and if we fail, then let England and our other allies know that we are withdrawing from all further peace negotiations in Korea," Taft added.

"I believe we might as well abandon any idea of working with the United Nations in the east, and reserve to ourselves a completely free hand."

Son Reads Address

Taft's address was read by one of his sons, Robert A. Taft Jr., a Cincinnati attorney, to some 700 guests at the silver anniversary dinner of the National Conference of Christians and Jews in the Netherland Plaza Hotel.

Taft himself has been a patient in the Holmes Memorial Hospital here since Sunday, when he arrived from Washington where he had been receiving treatment for a hip condition in the Walter Reed Hospital. His condition was reported good today.

In a wide-ranging consideration of U.S. foreign policy, Taft's address also observed that he believes in the United Nations, "but not as an effective means to prevent aggression" and suggested that a conference should be called to obtain amendment of the U.N. charter.

There seems to be no "satisfactory solution" for any foreign policy problems now con-

Turn to Page 11, Column 5

Reds Request Meeting of Truce Group

MUNSAN, May 27 (Wednesday) (AP) — The Communists requested a meeting of U.N. and Red liaison officers at Panmunjom today. The U.N. command arranged immediately to send liaison officers to the truce talks village.

The Communists gave no reason for calling the liaison officers together. The usual reason for such a meeting is for delivery of a verbal or written message from one side to the other.

The liaison session was called during a recess in full-scale negotiations until June 1.

More news of truce efforts and Korea war on Page 11.

Avalanche Buries Snowplow; 1 Dead

GLACIER PARK, Mont., May 26 (AP)—An avalanche smashed a snowplow off a 2000-foot cliff today, killing one man, injuring a second and burying a third who was dug out alive after eight hours.

A fourth man was believed caught in the slide that roared over a section of Glacier National Park's Going-to-the-Sun Highway. William Whitford, 45, an Indian, was killed.

Burkhalter, Wilkinson and Wiener Ahead in Race for City Council

Rep. Norris Poulson is Los Angeles' next Mayor.

Mayor Bowron conceded the election of the Congressman at yesterday's municipal general election after vote tabulations showed Poulson had a decisive lead.

Poulson's final majority appeared likely to be between 35,000 and 50,000.

The Mayor and Poulson met in the City Hall late in the evening as the trend in the voting established conclusively that the Congressman had ended the Mayor's 15-year reign in the City Hall. Bowron conceded victory to his opponent.

The new Mayor will take office July 1.

Results of the race for Mayor, bitterly fought for months, were watched intently by thousands interested in the fate of tax-subsidized public housing in Los Angeles. Poulson has promised that he will end the half-finished $110,000,000 housing program if elected and Bowron had sponsored the program. Public housing was main issue in the campaign.

Three Lead for Council

In the three City Council races, Everett Burkhalter, former State Assemblyman, took an early lead over Ben O'Brien, young attorney, in the 1st District race.

In the 3rd District, Robert Wilkinson was piling up a margin of victory over Laurence O'Rourke.

In the 5th District, Rosalind Wiener, 22-year-old recreation director and the only woman in the Council races, went ahead of Elmer Marshrey, tax consultant and public accountant.

Airport Issue Lags

Proposition A, the $33,255,000 airport bond issue, was below the necessary two-thirds majority and Proposition B, which would have provided a civic auditorium, while running stronger than Proposition A, still lacked the needed two-thirds.

Four of the five proposed City Charter amendments appeared to be carrying.

The measure which trailed was Amendment 1, providing for reorganization of the Board of Public Works.

The charter amendments required only a simple majority for passage.

Salary Measure Ahead

Amendment 2, requiring City Council approval for salary raises for municipal department heads, was away to a substantial lead which continued to grow.

Amendment 3, giving the Traffic Commission City Char-

Turn to Page 2, Column 8

ELECTION RETURNS

Following are the latest returns from yesterday's city election as tabulated by City Clerk Walter E. Peterson:

MAYOR

2500 Precincts out of 3641

Poulson	193,658
Bowron (Inc.)	169,750

CITY COUNCIL

District No. 1

135 Precincts out of 241

Burkhalter	11,807
O'Brien	7,480

District No. 3

97 Precincts out of 261

Wilkinson	7,401
O'Rourke	5,839

District No. 5

182 Precincts out of 244

Wiener	15,148
Marshrey	13,980

PROPOSITIONS

(Require two-thirds vote for passage)

2500 Precincts out of 3641

A—Airport Bonds	
Yes	187,884
No	129,048
B—Auditorium Bonds	
Yes	203,770
No	123,566

AMENDMENTS

(Require only majority vote for passage)

2500 Precincts out of 3641

1—Director of Board of Public Works	
Yes	142,851
No	152,202
2—City Salary Fixing	
Yes	156,066
No	119,940
3—Traffic Commission	
Yes	185,982
No	99,460
4—Commissioners' Pay Increase	
Yes	157,873
No	122,723
5—Records Disposal	
Yes	196,802
No	84,819

Bowron Concedes, Congratulates Poulson

Mayor Bowron late last night conceded the election to Rep. Norris Poulson. He issued the following statement:

"I congratulate my opponent on his victory. I wish him every success in the opportunity he has to carry forward the traditions of honesty, integrity and clean government which the people of Los Angeles so richly deserve.

"To the many citizens and good friends who supported me in the heartfelt belief that my re-election would be to the best interest of the city we all love—my most sincere appreciation.

"To all my fellow citizens—thank you very much for your confidence and assistance throughout the past 14 years, trying years of both peace and war, during which we have seen Los Angeles achieve greatness, not only in size but in the kind of government of which we can justly be proud.

"It has been a great honor to serve this city and its people. I will always consider it a privilege to assist in the betterment of our community in whatever capacity I may serve.

"My dream is to see our city continue to grow, and to prosper, until it is acknowledged as the greatest in this nation.

"To this end, I urge all of you—all of my fellow citizens, regardless of creed, or race, or political affiliation—to remain active and alert in the unceasing fight we must always carry on to assure ourselves and our children of the best government we can devise."

THE WEATHER

U.S. Weather Bureau forecast: Generally sunny today and tomorrow but scattered high cloudiness at times. Slowly rising daytime temperatures. High today near 70. Yesterday's high, 68; low, 49.

PART 1

Los Angeles Times

EQUAL RIGHTS

LIBERTY UNDER THE LAW — TRUE INDUSTRIAL FREEDOM

ALL THE NEWS
ALL THE TIME

VOL. LXXII — IN FOUR PARTS — CC ★★ — TUESDAY MORNING, JUNE 2, 1953 — 64 PAGES — DAILY, 10c

Tremendous Crowds Hail Queen Along London Coronation Route

CROWD GREETS CORONATION DAY — Dawn of Queen Elizabeth's coronation day saw this crowd gathered before Admiralty Arch in Trafalgar Square, London. Square is one of key spots in coronation procession.

(AP) Wirephoto via radio from London

Millions Gather for Rites

Illustrated on Page 3, Part I

LONDON, June 2 (Tuesday) (AP)—Roaring, cheering crowds totaling hundreds of thousands of persons jammed the gorgeously panoplied streets of London today for the coronation of Queen Elizabeth II.

The vast, seething mass of humanity took little heed of cold winds and rain squalls.

Over half a million had braved the night long 44-deg. temperatures at places they had staked out along the six-mile coronation procession route. Fully 3,000,000 people were expected to be packed tight along the route.

Reports from Buckingham Palace said the Queen reached her great moment in a calm, serene mood which contrasted strongly with the joyous hysteria sweeping her capital city.

Told of Everest

Just before midnight she received a most unusual "coronation gift"—news that a British expedition had conquered the world's highest mountain, Everest, reaching 29,002 feet above the snowy Himalayas on the Nepal-Tibet frontier.

The thermometer read 46 deg. and some spectators along the route of the procession wrapped themselves in heavy blankets.

Deep-throated roars of "We want the Queen" rose from the throngs outside the palace. The crowds there reached 50,000 at times.

But the Queen and her family did not appear.

Elizabeth had been expected by many to go to Westminster Abbey, ancient scene of the actual crowning, to pray just as did her late father, King George VI, on his coronation eve 16 years ago.

Stays With Family

But she elected to stay close to her family.

Over the palace fluttered a single red and gold flag, the Queen's own standard, telling all that the Queen was there.

It contrasted sharply with the enchanting magic of the 1000-yard-long Mall, triumphantly arched and emblazoned with banners, bunting and myriad lights.

Over the entire six-mile coronation route, winding through the heart of the world's biggest city like a dazzling necklace, were tens of thousands of other watchers.

They sang such songs as "Tipperary" and "Land of Hope and Glory." Girls and boys danced. Mothers cradled young children in their arms against the cold.

At places impromptu jazz bands blared out in lively song, adding to the festive mood.

Trafalgar Square was a great mass of surging, cheering and singing people.

Down the length of stately Whitehall to Westminster Abbey pavemtns were packed 10 and 20 deep with people from

Turn to Page 2, Column 3

Rhee Agrees to Eisenhower Plan

'We Must Accept Anything U.S. President Wants,' Says Leader

SEOUL, June 2 (Tuesday) (AP) — President Syngman Rhee disclosed today he had received a three-point message from President Eisenhower, and added: "We must accept anything that the U.S. President wants."

"Common sense and wisdom require that we co-operate with the United States at any cost," Rhee said, without saying what Gen. Eisenhower had told him.

The 78-year-old Republic of Korea leader's statement indicated that South Korean opposition to the secret U.N. command proposal for bringing an armistice in Korea is lessening.

Rhee also said he is looking for someone to take the place of Maj. Gen. Choi Duk Shin as the South Korean delegate on the U.N. armistice negotiation team.

Details Declined

Rhee declined to elaborate on his apparently conciliatory statement. He spoke to correspondents at a parade of the British Commonwealth Division honoring the coronation of Elizabeth II.

Nor did he make it precisely clear whether he is ready now to accept the allied truce proposal, to which he and his government had expressed vigorous opposition.

South Korea's Prime Minister yesterday had threatened a break with the allies and a go-it-alone policy for South Korea but deferred action until after Thursday's critical truce session.

The Communists are expected to reply to the allied proposal at Thursday's meeting.

Agreement Sought

A South Korean source said Rhee had sent a "compromise" plan to President Eisenhower through U.S. Ambassador Ellis O. Briggs after South Korea's violent opposition to the United Nation's latest truce proposal threatened to disrupt the Panmunjom talks.

South Koreans said Gen. Eisenhower must sign an agreement with South Korea before Rhee agrees to any truce. The agreement would provide:

1—The United States again would come to South Korea's assistance in event of another Communist invasion.

2—The United States would continue military aid to the South Korean government after a truce.

3—The United States would guarantee a large-scale economic rehabilitation program far greater than assistance now given to South Korea.

Although drastic, the Rhee proposal was far less drastic than steps threatened earlier by the South Korean government.

Knowland for All-Out Korea War

WASHINGTON, June 1 (AP) — Sen. Knowland (R) Cal., tonight said if truce negotiations with the Communists collapse the United States should expand the Korean fighting and take the "calculated risk" of war with Russia.

Supporting proposals made by Sen. Taft (R) O., and rejected by President Eisenhower, Knowland said he does not believe the allied armistice offer to the Communists will produce a "truce with honor" because it would leave Korea divided.

Favors Fund Threat

In his appearance on a radio show, Reporters' Roundup, the chairman of the Republican policy committee said he supports a proposed rider to the money bill for the State, Commerce and Justice Departments which would cut off U.S. contributions to the United Nations if Red China is seated on the Security Council.

The Senate, considering appropriations sections of the measure, put off debate on the proposed rider until tomorrow or possibly later.

If truce talks fail, Knowland said, he believes the United States should bring more Republic of Korea divisions into being, throw a complete blockade around Red China "and lift the restrictions on our Air Force."

He was asked if this might not risk Russian entry into the war.

"I think no one would take additional steps unless you recognize that that was a calculated risk and a possibility," he replied. "I merely say to you that at some point along the line we are going to have to determine where the line is going to be drawn."

He said he would prefer that

Turn to Page 12, Column 3

Survey Finds L.A. Teachers Doubt Board

Result of Opinion Poll in School System Disclosed

Although the morale among the teachers of Los Angeles is generally good, 75% of them lack confidence in the Board of Education and 92% say they need more time to give individual help to their pupils.

That was the disclosure made last night by Lyle M. Spencer, president of Science Research Associates, Chicago, in reporting the results of the teacher opinion survey conducted throughout the Los Angeles school system.

Cost $20,000

Of the 14,000 teachers who participated in the survey on March 17, 89% feel that local pressure groups are too influential in decisions by the school board and 76% believe board members can do more to assure fair treatment of teachers.

Spencer made his report before a throng of some 1000 persons in the Board of Education Auditorium. The opinionaire, which cost $20,000, was designed to measure teacher reaction to every phase of the educational program.

"From the strongly worded comments it is evident that lack of confidence in the board is widespread," Spencer said. But he added:

"This opinion does not apply only to the present board. These teachers are reacting to the sum total of their experiences with school boards, including the one which collapsed in scandal."

The inventory, first of its kind ever given in a large metropolitan school system, was turned over to the board by Science Research Associates in fulfillment of its contract. It took up eight large volumes and 515 charts.

55% Satisfied With Pay

"From the more than 2,000,000 responses to the 150 questions asked anonymously we concluded that the teachers of Los Angeles are 'deeply concerned with the welfare of their pupils,'" Spencer said.

The poll showed that 55% of the teachers are satisfied with their pay; 88% feel their immediate superiors are fair; 75% believe the over-all curriculum is on the right track; 95% feel their work is worth while, and 82% say they are doing the work they like best.

One of the most critical areas is in the field of individual instruction, Spencer said, explaining:

"The teachers feel that the most underprivileged children in Los Angeles are the bright ones. They're the ones we're doing the least for, whereas we should be doing the most for them because they are the future leaders of the community."

Contact Need Stressed

Lack of enough direct communication with employees is probably the biggest problem, said Spencer. He pointed out that only 27% of the teachers understand their retirement benefits and that many apparently are not aware of the School Board's problems.

"In our attitude studies of employees in business concerns across the country, he said,

Turn to Page 18, Column 5

Britons Conquer Mt. Everest as 'Gift' for Queen

LONDON, June 1 (AP)—A British expedition has climbed hitherto unscaled Mt. Everest, the world's highest peak, planting the Union Jack on the icy peak as a coronation "gift" for Queen Elizabeth II, Buckingham Palace announced tonight.

Word that the party, fighting the snows and icy blasts on the world's rooftop, had reached their goal in a third attempt within a month reached the palace tonight, a spokesman said.

The party which succeeded where 10 previous formally organized expeditions had failed was headed by Col. John Hunt. Two men of his party—New Zealander E. P. Hillary and a famous Sherpa tribesman guide, Tensing Bhutia—reached the more than 29,000-foot-high snow-peaked summit May 29.

Hunt's message said, "All is well."

The British party failed in two attempts in late May to climb the mist-shrouded peak, where snow, ice and bone-chilling winds had thwarted many other efforts.

WEATHER BLUSTERS, THEN CLEARS UP

Early Multitudes Soaked, but Storm Moves On to Leave Skies Bright for Great Day

BY WALDO DRAKE, Times European Bureau

LONDON, June 1—A plague of showers late today thoroughly soaked thousands of spectators who preempted vantage points along the Mall and Trafalgar Square for the coronation procession. Later the skies cleared.

Shortly before midnight tonight the streets along the route were so jammed with people that police might as well have shut the great barrier gates which later closed off the entire parade area.

Government spokesmen insist that less than 250,000 visitors have come to London for the coronation but the city seems to have at least doubled its normal 10,000,000 population this last week—so overloaded are all restaurants, theaters, streets and means of communication.

$300,000,000 Event

It is too bad that in the honors the Queen gave to hundreds of her subjects this morning she could not have given some credit to the London Underground (subway, in American) which has done a remarkable job in transporting masses of visitors in and out of Central London this past week.

The real miracle, though, has been the manner in which the great event has captured the interest of the entire free world to such an extent that 30,000 Americans are in London and no less than 20,000 loyal subjects of Elizabeth have come all the way from Australia.

Spokesmen claim the government is spending less than $3,000,000 on decorations and facilities for the coronation but it is estimated that an additional $25,000,000 has been spent by private interests for London's coronation dress.

Experts say that about $300,000,000 will be spent in the sterling area by visitors for their passage to and during their coronation visits in Britain.

A bright round of social events for American visitors was climaxed tonight by the garden party of U.S. Ambassador and Mrs. Aldrich at their Kensington residence.

London Thrills as Excitement Rises Swiftly

BY EDWIN SCHALLERT
Times Staff Representative

LONDON, June 1 — A newspaper headline here says "London Bulges," and there's no doubt about that. The huge city is practically breaking out at the seams.

Underground trains follow fast after each other to take care of the crowds, and busses and taxis proceed hither and yon in a sort of wild melee.

Yet, out of this chaos by degrees comes complete order as gates are shut along the route the Queen takes and those within the confines are unable to move without special permission.

London is becoming the most thrilled and thrilling city in the world.

Huge Choir to Sing

The great heart of its events is Westminster Abbey. Hither comes Queen Elizabeth with her husband, the Duke of Edinburgh, to be received by the Earl Marshal, the Duke of Norfolk, on the steps of the Annex. Here, also, she is met by the officers of state and, climactically, by the Archbishops of Canterbury and York and other bishops assisting in the ceremonies.

Within a quarter of an hour the procession enters the Abbey itself, with the Queen joining and proceeding to her chair of estate near the altar while an estimated 400 choristers sing:

"I was glad when they said unto me
We will go into the house of the Lord . ."

This is followed by "Vivat Vivat Regina Elizabeth" chanted by a huge choir.

Then the service itself unfolds in a full panoply of formality and grandeur, mingling the spiritual rites of the Church of England with the ceremony

Turn to Page 2, Column 7

ASSEMBLY PASSES INCOME TAX CUT

SACRAMENTO, June 1 (AP)—The Assembly today passed and sent to the Senate administration bills increasing the tax on beer and hard liquor and raising the State personal income tax exemption enough to relieve 800,000 Californians of having to pay the tax.

Backed by Warren

The tax shift plan was offered by Assemblyman Marvin Sherwin (R) Piedmont, with the blessing of Gov. Warren. Opponents called it politically motivated.

But Sherwin said the beer and liquor industries have not been carrying their share of the tax burden and that income taxpayers in the lower brackets are entitled to some relief.

The vote was 51 to 13 in favor of upping the tax on hard liquor from 80 cents to $1.50 a gallon. The beer-tax bill was passed by 42 to 27. It would double the 2-cent-a-gallon tax on the beverage.

$4900 for Couples

Personal income tax exemptions would be raised by $1400 to $4900 for couples and $3400 for single persons. All told an estimated $17,250,000 in taxes would be shifted from income taxpayers to beer and liquor.

Boy on School Field Hit by 10-Pound Steel Ball

A 15-year-old boy was struck in the head by a 10-pound steel ball yesterday as he ran across the shot-put ring on the athletic field at John Marshall High School.

The youngster, John Barrett of 948½ Hyperion Ave., was taken to General Hospital with a depressed skull fracture. His condition was described as critical.

Police said the boy had been playing volleyball nearby and that he ran into the shot-put area to retrieve a ball that had bounced out of bounds.

It happened just as another boy, Don Josephson of 3768 Glen Feliz Road was heaving the shot.

THE WEATHER

U.S. Weather Bureau forecast: Considerable cloudiness at times today and tomorrow with a few brief sprinkles likely in the foothill sections but partly sunny afternoons especially near the coast. Little change in temperatures. The high today, near 68. Highest temperature yesterday, 64, lowest, 54.

City Gets Rain---but Only Trace

A trace of rain fell in Los Angeles yesterday between 10:25 and 10:45 a.m., and the Weather Bureau forecast a few brief sprinkles in foothill sections today.

With only a month to go, rainfall for the season in Los Angeles measures far under last year's total and also well below the normal for this date.

Thus far 9.40 inches has been recorded, compared to 26.21 on this date last year and a normal for this time of 14.47 inches.

Based on a Weather Bureau forecast of a high inversion and gentle to moderate air movement, the Air Pollution Control District predicted there will be no eye irritation or crop damage today.

Blast Burns Woman in Powder Plant

A 43-year-old woman suffered third-degree burns over most of her body yesterday in an explosion at the Bermite Powder Plant near Saugus.

The victim, Miss Marie P. Thomas of Saugus, was taken to the Newhall Community Hospital, where her condition was described as grave.

Deputy sheriffs said she was working near a machine known as a tetro pellet compressor, a device used in making explosives, when it blew up and engulfed the room in flames.

The damage was estimated at $2000. Firemen were unable to determine what caused the machine to explode. Mrs. Thomas was the only one near the compressor.

Tropic Storm Off Key West Growing

MIAMI, Fla., June 1 (AP)—A tropical storm with the characteristics of a hurricane formed today 200 miles west of Key West, and moved slowly northward up the Gulf of Mexico on a course paralleling the Gulf coast.

Wind velocity reached 65 m.p.h., just 10 miles under hurricane force.

Three Killed, Two Hurt in Spectacular Crash

By a Times Correspondent

MURRIETA, June 1—Three persons were killed and two critically injured late this afternoon in a spectacular collision at U.S. Highway 395 and Webster Road.

Five other persons have lost their lives and 40 have been seriously injured in traffic accidents at this same intersection, which was opened last October.

According to the Highway Patrol the three persons killed yesterday have been tentatively identified as Frank Kamesar and his wife Tania of 2816 Wellington Road, Los Angeles, and an unidentified woman said to be a neighbor of the Kamesars.

Injured Hospitalized

Critically injured, officers reported, were Mrs. Lillian Morrison, 30, of San Diego and a sailor, Whaylon O. Fisher, 32, stationed aboard the USS Sirios in San Diego. Mrs. Morrison and Fisher were rushed to Hemet Hospital in ambulances and later transferred to Norco Naval Hospital in Corona.

Officers said the Kamesar car apparently failed to make a stop at Highway 395, which is a freeway, and was struck broadside by Mrs. Morrison's vehicle.

The intersection is located on a hill and has a blind corner. It has been the object of much criticism because of the blind corner and recurrence of serious accidents.

Stock Prices in Sharp Drop

NEW YORK, June 1 (AP)—Stock market prices dropped as much as $3 or more a share today, wiping an estimated $1,800,000,000 from quoted valuations.

Traders cited the international situation and the possibility that the excess profits tax may be continued as contributing to the decline. Government bonds and commodities fell to new lows, which also may have unsettled the stock market.

Bowron in Hospital for Rest, Checkup

Mayor Bowron is expected to leave St. John's Hospital, Santa Monica, today. He entered the hospital last Friday for a rest and checkup.

He went into the institution following a strenuous election campaign and is under the care of Dr. John Sharpe of Beverly Hills. Mayor Bowron intends to return to work today, his office reported.

FEATURES INDEX

State's Road-Building Program Endangered

It was pointed out yesterday in Sacramento that the attitude of the Senate may kill chances for continuation of California's vast highway-building program. Story on Page 20, Part 1.

On Other Pages

FULL PAGE COLOR PORTRAIT OF ELIZABETH (SEE PAGE 1, PART 3)

PART 1

ALL THE NEWS
ALL THE TIME

VOL. LXXII | IN FIVE PARTS | CC | WEDNESDAY MORNING, JUNE 3, 1953 | 68 PAGES | DAILY, 10c

NEW-CROWNED QUEEN HAILED

CROWNED QUEEN—Elizabeth II, Queen of Great Britain and Head of British Commonwealth of Nations, sits solemnly upon throne in Westminster Abbey after coronation. She wears heavy St. Edward's crown, ritual crown of England. At right is Bishop of Bath and Wells; at left, Bishop of Durham. Others are not identified.

(AP) Wirephoto via radio from London

Military Pageantry and Dramatic Ritual Thrill Spectators

BY WALDO DRAKE, Times European Bureau

LONDON, June 2—The spell of enchantment which has gripped London for the past week burst out this morning in a glorious pageant which carried Queen Elizabeth to and from her crowning in Westminster Abbey.

Any eyewitness for whom this tremendous spectacle did not send shivers of pride and wonderment up and down his spine was not human.

No other place on earth could have produced such a magnificent display of military color and precision nor such a moving demonstration of Christian and patriotic devotion to a sovereign and her realm.

Much of the ponderous dramatic ritual of the Queen's consecration and encrownment in Westminster Abbey dates back a thousand years from the days of England's Saxon kings or from the rule imposed by William the Conqueror.

Anyone who witnessed the earnest, heartfelt devotion of all participants today—from millions of spectators who suffered hours of waiting on curbstones in heavy rains, to marching troops from all corners of the earth, and to richly robed peers who pledged their allegiance to Elizabeth at the Abbey altar—cannot doubt that this British monarchy will stand on these same secure foundations of Christian faith for another thousand years.

Even though the lengthy ritual in Westminster Abbey was the most dramatic religious event possible in the British Protestant world it must bow to the Queen's triumphal homeward procession through Central London as undoubtedly the most magnificently military and regal pageant ever enacted.

Canadian Brigade

Among 30,000 troops and 47 military bands which took part, first honors for precision undoubtedly were captured by a contingent from the Canadian 27th Infantry Brigade, which is on occupation duty in Northern Germany.

Second to the Canadians were both battalions of the Grenadier Guards in red tunics and giant black bearskin shakos.

Among mounted contingents from all over the world the greatest applause was won by red-coated Royal Canadian Mounted Police. It was a field day for Canada, for in the evening the most spectacular performers among a flight of 168 Royal Air Force jet fighters that passed above after the Queen had returned to Buckingham Palace were two squadrons of F-86 Sabre jets which Canada donated to the RAF.

Spectators Soaked

Rain held off until after the Queen had reached Westminster Abbey at 11 o'clock but from then on until just before she returned to Buckingham Palace at 5 o'clock, 2,000,000 spectators along the streets and in uncovered stands were thoroughly soaked by a barrage of heavy showers.

So were 10,000 red-jacketed guardsmen and sailors and airmen who lined the six-mile route for nine unbroken hours from 8 o'clock.

The royal procession was led out from Buckingham Palace at 9:20 o'clock by four open carriages containing visiting rulers of Elizabeth's realms overseas.

In the first carriage was the majestic smiling figure of the Queen of the Tonga Islands wearing a simple heliotrope gown. With her rode the be-

Turn to Page 5, Column 3

'Long Live Queen,' Cries Abbey Crowd

Homage Vowed to Elizabeth During Coronation Service

BY EDWIN SCHALLERT
Times Staff Representative

WESTMINSTER ABBEY, London, June 2—"God save Queen Elizabeth! Long live Queen Elizabeth! May the Queen live forever!"

This solemn shout within the hallowed walls of Westminster Abbey today proclaimed the homage of the British people for their new sovereign, Elizabeth II. And it was the tribute in which most people joined in spirit who attended the historic and regally glorious ceremony in the great coronation church.

On Imperial Throne

The new Queen sat on the Imperial Throne as a huge conclave from all over the world shouted its acclaim of Elizabeth Regina.

She had received the crown of St. Edward, the Scepter, the Orb with Cross and the Rod with Dove in earlier ritual.

Even the Archbishop of Canterbury vowed his allegiance as part of the homage. The Queen's husband, the Duke of Edinburgh, followed. Then came peers of the land to the throne to touch the crown and pledge their loyalty to the much-beloved young woman who had become officially their ruler.

England is filled with portraits of Elizabeth II. They may be found on every street corner, in every store window, adorning a multitude of homes.

Zenith of Glory

All these pictures were superseded and became as one picture today — that of the still young daughter of the late George VI in the zenith of her glory as she knelt in adoration on various faldstools or sat in the Chair of Estate or King Edward's Chair or the Imperial

Turn to Page 7, Column 4

8 MORE PAGES OF NEWS, PHOTOS

Two full pages of coronation picture on pages B and 3. Other stories and photos of colorful and dramatic ceremony will be found on pages A, 2, 3, 4, 5, 6 and 7.

FEATURES INDEX

Transit Lines and PE Seek New Fare Boosts

Officials of the Los Angeles Transit Lines and the Pacific Electric Railway disclose that they will seek new fare boosts in an application to be filed this week. Story on Page 1, Part 2.

On Other Pages

U.N. COUNTERATTACKS BEAT BACK FIERCE DRIVE BY 4000 KOREA REDS

SEOUL, June 3 (Wednesday) (AP)—Determined allied counterattacks early today smashed back the last of some 4000 Korean Reds who overran several hilly outposts on the eastern front yesterday.

It was the heaviest fighting on the eastern front in more than a year.

The U.N. command communique reported the Republic of Korea 12th Division attacked in predawn darkness around Luke the Gook's Castle and, by 6:30 a.m., had cleaned the Communists out of all positions.

Communist casualties in the fighting yesterday were estimated at more than 1100.

The U.N. command reported the tempo of fighting had not lessened on the east-central front, with allied troops hurling back probing assaults by two

Turn to Page 9, Column 2

Eisenhower's Report on Air

President Eisenhower's Report to the Nation will be telecast on KNXT (2), KNBH (4) and KECA (7) at 6:30 p.m. tonight. Radio stations KFI and KGFJ carry it at 6:30; KNX at 7 p.m.; KHJ at 8 p.m. and KECA, 9:30 p.m.

THE WEATHER FORECAST:

U.S. Weather Bureau forecast: Mostly clear today and tomorrow but patches of early morning low clouds along coast. Slightly warmer today with high about 74. Yesterday's highest temperature, 71; lowest, 50.

Big 3 Delay Bermuda Meet

PARIS, June 2 (AP) — The French Foreign Office said today the Western Big Three conference at Bermuda will be postponed from mid-June to the latter part of the month.

The Foreign Office said British Prime Minister Churchill suggested the delay yesterday.

EXTRA

RACE RESULTS

Los Angeles Times TRUE INDUSTRIAL FREEDOM

PICTORIAL

VOL. LXXII IN THREE PARTS ★★★ SATURDAY MORNING, JUNE 20, 1953 42 PAGES DAILY, 10c

ROSENBERGS DIE

Pair Executed for Atom Spying

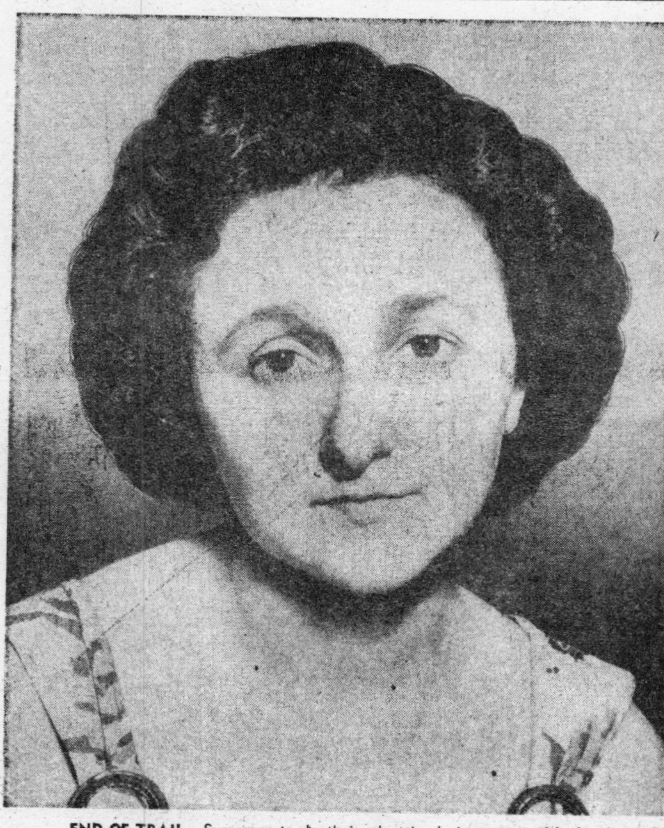

END OF TRAIL—Summons to death in electric chair came swiftly for Atom Spies Ethel and Julius Rosenberg after stay was revoked and clemency was refused.

Supreme Court and Eisenhower Reject Couple's Last Pleas

OSSINING, N.Y., June 19—Atom Spies Julius and Ethel Rosenberg died in Sing Sing Prison's electric chair shortly before sundown today. The executions followed quickly after the Supreme Court set aside a stay of execution granted Wednesday by Justice William O. Douglas and President Eisenhower's refusal to grant them clemency.

SING SING PRISON, N.Y., June 19 (U.P.) Atom Spies Julius and Ethel Rosenberg were ordered electrocuted late today for betraying their country's secrets to Russia and threatening the lives of millions by bringing the world closer to an atomic war.

The Justice Department set the time for the doomed couple's death in Sing Sing Prison's electric chair after a day of suspense in which the U.S. Supreme Court denied their final appeals and President Eisenhower again refused executive clemency.

Warden Wilfred Denno announced first the husband and wife espionage team would be put to death in the gray-walled prison's death chamber "before sundown," which comes at 8:30 p.m. (5:30 PDT) today at Sing Sing.

Later he said the first execution would come at 8 p.m. EDT, with the second a few minutes later.

Spend Time Together

The Jewish Sabbath starts at sundown, and the plans to execute the couple before that time, instead of at the traditional 11 p.m., were announced after the prison rabbi said he would ask the Rosenbergs if they wanted to request a delay until tomorrow night.

The Rosenbergs spent their last afternoon together and then ate a dinner of regular prison fare—hard-boiled eggs, macaroni salad, orange marmalade and tea.

At 5:30 p.m. the two were separated and prepared for the electric chair. The prison barber went to Mrs. Rosenberg's cell, about 200 yards from the high-ceilinged, windowless death chamber in this prison, 41 miles north of New York City on the east bank of the scenic Hudson River.

Rosenberg was taken to a pre-execution cell, about 40 feet from the electric chair.

Eisenhower Statement

President Eisenhower said the Rosenbergs had "immeasurably" increased the chances of an atomic war. They "may have condemned to death tens of millions of innocent people all over the world," he said.

The order for the Rosenbergs' electrocution came only a few minutes after Gen. Eisenhower acted.

The execution was to have been held last night but the Rosenbergs got a temporary reprieve in a stay of execution issued by Supreme Court Justice William O. Douglas.

The Rosenbergs, doomed for participating in the activities of an international spy ring that handed over vital United States atom secrets to the Russians, were the first U.S. civilians ever to be sentenced to death for espionage in peacetime.

They were sentenced in April, 1951, by U.S. Judge Irving R. Kaufman, who said their crime was "worse than murder." That crime was handing over to the Rus-

Turn to Page 4, Column 8

WEST BERLIN'S RED OFFICES WRECKED

Anti-Communist Mob Storms Party Building; Soviets Rush Reinforcements in East Sector

BERLIN, June 19 (U.P.)—Anti-Communist demonstrators stormed the Communist Party offices in West Berlin tonight as the Soviets rushed tank and troop reinforcements to the East sector in a frantic effort to end the three-day-old uprising.

A crowd of 500 West Berliners, inflamed at the ruthless "firing squad justice" across the heavily guarded border, stormed the Communist Party headquarters on West Berlin's busy Schlosstrasse tonight and tried to set fire to the building.

They wrecked the offices, smashed furniture and threw furniture and papers out of the windows. Police prevented their burning the building and dispersed the crowd.

Paralysis Spreads

Martial law and firing squads failed to halt the paralysis gripping the eastern part of the city and there were reports of serious food shortages brought on by disruption of communications. Small children were reported without fresh milk.

Long lines of people queued for meager food rations, and the Red radio issued appeals against hoarding.

West Berlin authorities confirmed that a wave of mass arrests of workers had begun in both East Berlin and throughout the Soviet zone. Prisons were reported jammed with "hundreds" of strikers and suspected ringleaders of Wednesday's bloody uprising.

FEATURES INDEX

Fallbrook Couple Adopt Five Children

An airline pilot of Fallbrook and his wife have completed adoption of five children. Story on Page 3, Part 1.

On Other Pages

20 Injured as Fireworks Blast Levels Factory

FT. WORTH, June 19 (AP)—A tremendous noon-hour explosion leveled a Ft. Worth fireworks storage plant on the northwest outskirts of the city, injuring about 20 persons. No one was killed.

The blast damaged about 100 houses in the residential area and sent grass fires speeding through the drought-dry countryside, near the vast Carswell Air Force Base.

Ten persons were in the fireworks plant, but only one of them was hurt.

Residents Injured

Most of the injured were residents who lived nearby, some in the swanky Beverly Hills addition. One modern $40,000 home about two blocks away was burned to the ground.

Firemen from eight departments, more than 100 city policemen, and dozens of ambulances raced to the scene after four major blasts splintered the Wilfong Fireworks Co.'s masonry building.

The factory was stocked to the rafters with fireworks for the Fourth of July trade.

TRUCE DELEGATES FACE CRUCIAL TALK

Reds Demand Session as Communist Radios Charge Connivance by U.S. in POW Escapes

MUNSAN, June 20 (Saturday) (AP)—Communist and allied truce delegates meet today on Red demand in a crisis-laden session that may determine the immediate fate of the Korean war armistice.

Angry Communist broadcasts indicated a stormy session as a result of South Korea's defiant release of nearly 26,000 anti-Red Korean prisoners of war.

Communist radio stations in China and North Korea accused the U.S. Army of "connivance" in the mass escapes.

Full-Dress Session

The Reds yesterday curtly demanded a full-dress truce session at Panmunjom today and the allies agreed.

Peiping Red radio ominously said the chief Red delegate, North Korean Gen. Nam Il, had "an important subject to discuss" with the allies.

The radio at Pyongyang, capital of North Korea, declared that the release of the POW's "will surely change the plans for an early Korean armistice." The Communist broadcast said the prisoner breakout indicated the United States and South Korea had signed a "secret agreement" to boycott any plans for an early armistice.

Observers here expected the Communist reaction to the prisoner escapes to be bitter. With the 26,000 prisoners gone, the POW compounds now contain only about 21,000 of the 47,000 captives which the United Nations had said would forcibly resist return to Communism. Of those remaining more than 14,000 are Chinese.

The truce, more than two years in the making, has hinged on disposal of the reluctant prisoners. The armistice draft, almost ready for signature, provides for turning over the prisoners refusing repatriation

Turn to Page 5, Column 5

THE WEATHER

U.S. Weather Bureau forecast: Low clouds this morning but sunny and slightly warmer this afternoon. High temperature today near 75. Highest temperature yesterday, 69; lowest, 60.

Clouds Clamp Cool Damper as Summer Nears

Low threatening clouds put a damper on the city yesterday but the weatherman said they might vanish in time for the official start of summer tomorrow.

The winter-like overcast held temperatures down below the 70s and restricted visibility to a maximum of 15 miles.

Rain on Coast

No rain was reported in the Los Angeles area but showers fell along the Southland coast—Chula Vista recording .02 inch, Del Mar, .06, La Jolla, .05 and La Mesa, .01.

The Weather Bureau said some low clouds can be expected this morning but the weather will be sunny and warmer this afternoon. The improving trend, it was indicated, probably will continue tomorrow when summer officially begins.

"It looks like we're in for some good summer weather—at last," the weatherman said. "We'll still get some morning clouds but there will be much more sunshine before noon and in the afternoons."

The Air Pollution Control District said no eye irritation or crop damage is expected from smog today.

EXTRA

LATE NEWS

Los Angeles Times

9 A.M. FINAL

VOL. LXXII | IN FOUR PARTS | MONDAY MORNING, JULY 27, 1953 | 60 PAGES | DAILY, 10c

CEASE-FIRE!

REDS WARNED THEY MUST KEEP PLEDGE

Polygamy Cult Jailed in Arizona

Governor Orders Raid on White Slave Community

BY MARVIN MILES
Times Staff Representative

SHORT CREEK, Ariz., July 26—An entire community of 122 polygamists, excommunicated Mormons, in this remote, shabby Eden, was raided an hour before dawn today by more than 100 State patrolmen and deputy sheriffs under an insurrection proclamation by Arizona's Gov. Howard Pyle to clean up what he called a foul and ruthless conspiracy dedicated to white slavery.

Arizona authorities here said they believe the Governor's action involves the first insurrection proclaimed in the United States in half a century. It required one of the largest police operations in State history.

Move in Darkness

Midnight roadblocks and monitored telephones cut off all outside communication with this communal farm village lying astraddle the Arizona-Utah border in the desolate strip area north of the Grand Canyon—while the long auto caravan of raiders rolled over miles of primitive muddy plateau roads under cover of darkness.

The cavalcade of armed officers swept into Short Creek shortly after 4 a.m. under a full-moon eclipse as a warning blast of dynamite was set off on the nearby Vermillion Cliffs by a sentinel posted to alert the community.

Defense Shouted

The raiders had expected to take the Short Creek sect by surprise, but they in turn were surprised to find a group of some 30 men — including the cult's three executive elders — massed on the grassy courtyard of the schoolhouse singing Mormon hymns and "America."

One group of officers, led by Sheriff Frank Porter, directing

Turn to Page 6, Column 1

FEATURES INDEX

Operation Olive Branch!

Signing of Truce Halts Guns but Permanent Peace Not Yet Certain

PANMUNJOM, July 27 (Monday) (AP) — The United Nations and the Communists finally signed the hard-bargained Korean armistice today, ending 37 months of war, but both top commands quickly warned their troops that a truce did not necessarily mean a peace.

The Chinese Communists in Peiping immediately broadcast a claim that the Red forces had won a glorious victory."

By terms of the armistice signed at 10:01 a.m. today (6:01 p.m. Sunday, PDT), the guns were to cease firing not later than 10 p.m. tonight (6 a.m. Monday, PDT). But even as the signing took place the war had slowed to a standstill. There was only sporadic artillery fire.

The main ceremony was a cold, 10-minute formality in Panmunjom by Lt. Gen. William K. Harrison, American representing the United Nations command, and Gen. Nam Il of North Korea, representing the Chinese and Korean Reds.

Shortly afterward, Gen. Mark W. Clark, United Nations supreme commander, countersigned the 18 documents—nine copies for each side—and issued a warning

Other armistice news on Pages 2, 3, 4, 5, 9, 11 and 12.

statement to his forces. Clark said the armistice does "not mean an immediate or even early withdrawal" from Korea.

"It does mean that our duties and responsibilities during the critical period of the armistice are heightened and intensified rather than diminished," he said.

"The conflict will not be over until the governments concerned have reached a firm political settlement.

"Meanwhile, we remain — in strength — a reminder to the enemy and his emissaries that our might and power stand behind the pledges of the United Nations to defend the Republic of Korea against any aggressor."

Gen. Maxwell D. Taylor, 8th Army commander, warned similarly that the armistice was "just a suspension of hostilities, which may or may not be preparatory to permanent peace."

The Chinese and North Korean commanders, Gen. Peng Teh-huai and Marshal Kim Il Sung, were due to countersign the truce documents somewhere in North Korea. Meanwhile the Peiping Red radio broadcast the Red command's order of the day to cease firing at 10 p.m.

Reds Claim Glorious Victory

The order said the Reds had won "a glorious victory" but warned them to "guard against aggressive and disruptive actions from the other side."

Ignoring the North Korean invasion of the South on June 25, 1950, and the Chinese intervention Oct. 25, 1950, the Communist order of the day said the Red troops had fought heroically "for three years against aggression and in defense of peace."

The normal signing ceremony by Harrison and Nim Il was a cold and silent one in this hamlet near the 38th parallel, where the war began and near which the stalemated armies have been locked for two years past.

They met in a jerry-built but ornate structure with an Oriental pagoda roof in this war-ruined wayside village of Panmunjom which the Koreans called, "The Inn With the Wooden Door."

Signers Separate in Silence

They began at 10:01 a.m. and finished exactly 10 minutes later. They separated in silence, but not before exchanging one long, searching look.

The strokes of their pens on the 18 copies of the armi-

Turn to Page 2, Column 4

PART 1

Los Angeles Times

EQUAL RIGHTS
LIBERTY UNDER THE LAW — TRUE INDUSTRIAL FREEDOM

ALL THE NEWS ALL THE TIME

VOL. LXXII | IN THREE PARTS | C C | SATURDAY MORNING, AUGUST 22, 1953 | 38 PAGES | DAILY, 10c

U.S. Has Big Lead Over Russ in H-Bomb Race, Experts Say

Free World Will Retain Atom Weapons Superiority, Congressional Group Told

WASHINGTON, Aug. 21 (U.P.)—The Senate-House Atomic Energy Committee asserted today, after a secret briefing by Central Intelligence agents, that the United States is well ahead of Russia in both hydrogen and atomic bomb developments "and will continue to be."

The committee's statement came as Civil Defense Administrator Val Peterson warned that the Soviet H-bomb explosion means "we must prepare a better and bigger civil defense—much sooner than many realize." If an attack comes, he said, it will be "on a scale undreamed of in any past war."

Deputy Defense Secretary Roger M. Kyes also cautioned that the Russian blast emphasized that "these are critical days."

Secret Meeting

The Congressional committee met for more than an hour with officials of the Central Intelligence Agency, which presumably has ways of checking on Russian military secrets. Afterward, Chairman W. Sterling Cole (R) N.Y., said in a brief statement that "the United States, and thus the free world, is and will continue to be in a pre-eminent position" in both A-bomb and H-bomb developments.

Cole also indicated that President Eisenhower and his top military and civilian advisers are not particularly alarmed by Moscow's Aug. 12 H-bomb test.

Not Alarmed

He said the President and other administration officials had advised committee members there was "no reason" why they should not go ahead with an African survey trip scheduled to start Sunday.

Cole said the committee was "fully informed" by CIA officials on the Soviet explosion, but no details were made public.

The highly secret briefing was given by Lt. Gen. C. P. Cabell, acting CIA director, and H. I. Miller, another CIA official.

In addition to Cole, Sens. Guy Cordon (R) Or., and Richard B. Russell (D) Ga., and Rep. Thomas A. Jenkins (R) O., attended the emergency session which the chairman called soon after disclosure of the Soviet explosion.

WEDDING BELLS—Earl Warren Jr., son of Gov. Warren, and Miss Cleo Patricia Kent of Sacramento, both 23, obtained marriage license in Santa Monica yesterday. Times photo

Housing Sites Offered City at Low Price

Chavez for Sale at $1,279,203 and Rose Hills for $243,744

Bargain prices were quoted to the city yesterday if it wants to exercise its priority to purchase the Rose Hills and Elysian Park Heights abandoned public housing sites.

In a letter to Councilman John C. Holland, chairman of the Veterans Affairs and Public Housing Committee, George A. Beavers Jr., chairman of the City Housing Commission, said that the city could acquire the 212-acre Rose Hills site for $243,744.35 and the 230-acre Elysian Park Heights (Chavez Ravine) site for $1,279,203.87.

This is in conformance with terms of a recent agreement devised by Mayor Poulson to curtail Los Angeles' unwanted $110,000,000 public housing program by 60%. The city, under the agreement, has six months to buy the sites, if it wants to, at cost of the bare land.

Spent Much More

Actually, the CHA spent several millions more in acquiring the sites by condemnation and demolition but this cost has been absorbed by the Federal government.

In his letter to Councilman Holland, Beavers commented as follows:

"The price (at which the sites are offered the city) was determined by taking the appraised value of the land (exclusive of improvements) and prorating it against the price paid by the Authority for each parcel."

Resolution Adopted

The City Council already has adopted a resolution offering either of the locations as a site for a new State college, and a State public works group is due in Los Angeles Sept. 1 to pass upon the proposals.

Councilman Holland said yesterday, however, that, in addition, he intends to immediately introduce a resolution before the Council asking for a survey by the Recreation and Park Department to determine the value of the onetime public-housing projects for park purposes.

"These sites are big enough for three or four golf courses which the city needs badly and which not only would be self-supporting but return a profit," said Holland.

NEW MOROCCO SULTAN NAMED BY PRO-FRENCH

RABAT, Morocco, Aug. 21 (AP)—Moulay Mohammed Ben Arafa, the candidate of pro-French Berber chieftains, was proclaimed Sultan of this French North African protectorate today to succeed his exiled nephew, the nationalist-minded Sidi Mohammed Ben Youssef.

(The Arab-Asian bloc in the United Nations unanimously decided to ask the Security Council to intervene in the Moroccan situation. The chairman of the 16-nation group, Faried Zeineddine of Syria, indicated France's removal of the Sultan would be described as a threat to peace. The call for a holy war echoed again in Cairo. The 1000-year-old Al Azhar, Islam's highest religious institution, urged Moslems throughout the world to "start a crusade against France.")

Many Moroccans have been seen crying since the French government exiled Ben Youssef yesterday to Corsica and opened the way for the enthronement of Arafa. The Moslems of Morocco have been divided recently in their loyalties to the point of rioting. But the fighting mood was not evident today.

MOSSADEGH FACES DEATH, HINTS SHAH

Returning Iran Ruler Says Justice Will Be Done in All Traitor Cases

BAGDAD, Iraq, Aug. 21 (AP)—The triumphant Shah of Iran, brimming with imperial anger, declared tonight that Premier Mohammed Mossadegh is an evil man and hinted that the aged nationalist might face the death penalty.

Shah Mohammed Reza Pahlevi, who arrived in Bagdad today on the first leg of his journey back to Iran's fabled Peacock Throne, told an interviewer he was not sure whether Mossadegh, as a civilian, would be condemned to death. But a soldier would be shot for such activities, he added.

Called Most Serious

"The crimes of Mossadegh are the most serious a person can be responsible for," the Shah said, adding that under the Iranian constitution the highest crime is armed resistance to the government.

"The case applies perfectly to my former Premier," he continued . . . "Mossadegh is an evil man who wanted only one thing out of life: power at all costs. To accomplish this end he was ready to sacrifice the Iranian people and he almost succeeded. Thank God my people finally understood him!"

The first thing he would do on his arrival back in Teheran—he is due there tomorrow—will be to make sure that "justice will be done" in the cases of all traitors.

To Name Government

Then he said he would appoint an Iranian government, studying suggestions submitted to him by his new Premier, Gen. Fazollah Zahedi. Thereafter, he said, he would meet with the foreign Ambassadors to his country, obviously meaning

Turn to Page 5, Column 5

FRENCH END STRIKE AND DEFY RED PLEA

PARIS, Aug. 21 (U.P.)—The united front of French labor, which for 17 days has defied the economic reforms program of Premier Joseph Laniel with a crippling series of nationwide strikes, cracked wide open today.

Laborers, by the tens of thousands, began streaming back to work in nationalized industries and civil services in defiance of Communist pleas for a continuation of the work stoppages enforced by 2,000,000 workers. At their peak, last week, the strikes affected 4,000,000 men.

The collapse of the strike followed an agreement, reached at dawn today, between non-Communist union leaders and representatives of Premier Laniel's Cabinet.

Reds Claim Sellout

Laniel backed away from his "get tough" attitude toward the strikers and watered down his government economies program with a promise that no new cutbacks and retrenchments would be attempted in government posts until the unions have been consulted.

Communist union bosses shouted "sellout" but their voices were ignored.

The government action won it a delay until next Monday in a Socialist-Communist fight to have the National Assembly recalled from vacation to consider the strike and government economy policies. The Assembly steering committee voted to put off until Monday a decision on whether the Assembly will be recalled. Most observers now believe it will not.

Laniel's Cabinet appeared to fear that if the Assembly was reconvened in a special session the present government would be ousted. Therefore they surrendered to the strikers' demands.

However, new strikes appeared to be springing up as the workers in public utilities, transportation systems and postal and telegraph employees began to return to work.

Accept Agreement

A few hundred Bordeaux postmen, who started the nationwide walkout 17 days ago in protest at tighter pension restrictions, set the pace for the return to work as well.

The Socialist-led letter carriers voted to accept the agreement reached between union leaders and government officials early today. One hour later they were back on the job and the return-to-work movement was under way.

Thousands of workers were reported disgruntled by what they said were minimum concessions by the government, but they voted to end the strike because they did not want the responsibility of converting an industrial dispute into a political fight to the finish.

M'CARTHY OPENS RED HEARING HERE

Only One Witness Questioned at Closed Session on Alleged Communistic Ties

Sen. McCarthy, chairman of the committee investigating asserted infiltration of Communists into governmental agencies and departments, yesterday opened a two-day hearing in the Federal Building.

The only witness to be interrogated at yesterday's closed session in connection with the Red activities was William Taylor, identified as a former functionary in the Washington (D.C.) Communist Party and for the past few years a resident of Los Angeles.

Following the session, Sen. McCarthy announced that he had subpoenaed Taylor to appear at an open session at 10:30 a.m. today.

Tells of Questions

Taylor said after leaving the hearing that he had been asked whether he knew Edward M. Rothschild, employee of the Government Printing Office in Washington, who recently was discharged after he refused to answer questions about the "leak" of government secrets to Russia.

Taylor said that he had never known Rothschild and had never worked for government agencies in Washington.

He said that he had also been asked about other persons of whom he had no knowledge and that he had stood on his constitutional rights in refusing to answer questions by Sen. McCarthy and Roy M. Cohn, chief counsel of the subcommittee.

Taylor was accompanied to the hearing by his attorney, John T. McTernan, and following his appearance before McCarthy issued first a written statement and later made some oral remarks.

In his written statement, Taylor said:

"The secret hearing was the same old McCarthyism trying to frighten people with star chamber sessions about the alleged misdeeds of government employees and spy stories.

"Perhaps they are preparing to railroad a few more innocents to their death in order to intimidate people from protesting against war, the high cost of living and Jim Crow."

At a morning press conference McCarthy had said that while here he also would consult with mining men who are interested in the question of stockpiling certain strategic metals. He said that the old administration had launched and followed a policy of importing as much of those mate-

Turn to Page 6, Column 4

M'CARTHY PROBE TO BE TELECAST

Television Station KTLA (5) announced last night that it will originate a "pool" telecast of the McCarthy hearings from 10:30 a.m. to 12:30 p.m. today. (A pool-telecast means that other local TV stations will be able to hook into KTLA's telecast for the live transmission of the hearings, if they so desire.)

Warren's Son Gets License for Marriage

Earl Warren Jr., son of the Governor, and Miss Cleo Patricia Kent, both 23 years old and both residents of the State capital, obtained a marriage license yesterday at Santa Monica.

They said the wedding is scheduled for Sept. 4 in Sacramento, where they met six years ago while both were students at McClatchy High School.

Staying at Ranch

Young Warren, whose father and mother are now in Europe, has been staying at the Uplifters' Ranch in Rustic Canyon with his brother Bob. He said he was interested in farming, particularly in cattle raising. He was graduated from the University of California at Davis in 1952.

The bride-to-be is the daughter of Lisle G. Kent of 1050 49th St., Sacramento. She is a graduate og San Jose State College, where she studied commercial art. She has been working as a department store fashion coordinator.

It will be the first marriage for each.

The couple originally announced their engagement last May. They said they planned to be married in the First Baptist Church, Sacramento.

TEST RUN

Door-to-Door Tax Evader Hunt Set Here

Chronicle News Bureau

SAN FRANCISCO, Aug. 21—A door-to-door search for income tax evaders in Los Angeles will start within the next week to 10 days, Regional Commissioner M. A. Fremming of the Bureau of Internal Revenue disclosed here tonight.

Fremming said orders for the check will be given to the bureau's Los Angeles director Monday morning.

Bureau agents will seek to find tax evaders in all brackets—including the lower ones. Those the bureau feels are guilty of willful evasion will be prosecuted criminally, even if the amount owed is less than $100, Fremming said.

Check in Major Cities

The check is being ordered in major cities throughout this region, which comprises the eight Western States, Alaska and Hawaii.

In the Los Angeles area, Fremming said, a two-week test run will be held first, taking in a sampling of "several hundred" persons. From this the bureau hopes to find in what brackets and occupations it should concentrate its efforts. Agents will then call at thousands of homes and business concerns throughout the city.

Similar checks in eastern cities have shown that some 13% or 14% of persons contacted have failed to file returns.

High of 82; Breeze Brings Pleasant Day

Pleasant, sunny weather should prevail over most of Southern California this week end.

The weatherman forecast generally clear skies except for night and morning low clouds and local fog near the beaches.

The County Air Pollution Control District foresaw no eye irritation or crop damage from smog today or tomorrow.

The mercury reached a high of 82 at 12:35 p.m. yesterday and there was enough breeze to keep the atmosphere reasonably pleasant. Humidity ranged from 95% at 1:30 a.m. to 49% at 2 p.m.

BEATS WHITE HOUSE AIDE

Stassen Wins 2 Cents on Own Aptitude Test

WASHINGTON, Aug. 21 (AP) It looks as if Harold E. Stassen, head of the foreign aid program, has won 2 cents from C. D. Jackson, special assistant to President Eisenhower.

Today both men took the aptitude test Stassen has ordained for the 1700 employees of the Foreign Operations Administration—with Jackson betting Stassen a pair of pennies that he would get a better score.

Both Stassen, an ex-college president, and Jackson, former publisher of Fortune Magazine, got 38 questions right out of 45 on the reading comprehension test.

But Stassen answered 52 of 70 questions correctly on the public affairs test, while his White House rival got only 49.

Here's a sample question: Read the following paragraph and then select the alternative below which is best supported by the quotation:

"More patents have been issued for inventions relating to transportation than for those in any other line of human activity. These inventions have resulted in a great financial saving to the people and have made possible a civilization that could not have existed without them."

This means that transportation:

1—Would be impossible without inventions.

2—Is an important factor in civilization.

3—Is still to be much improved.

4—Is more important than any other activity.

5—Is carried on through the Patent Office.

Right answer: No 2.

Paratrooper Saves Buddy as Chute Fails

FORT CAMPBELL, Ky., Aug. 21 (AP)—Military authorities said a quick-thinking paratrooper sergeant saved the life of a fellow trooper whose parachute collapsed today during a training jump.

Both soldiers dropped several hundred feet to safety on the sergeant's parachute.

The Public Information Office said Sgt. Richard N. Cleaver of Niagara Falls, N.Y., saved the life of Pfc. Harold D. Lovell, Oklahoma City, Okla. Both are members of the 11th Airborne Division.

Here is the way the PIO said it happened:

Cleaver and Lovell were among 106 men participating in a mass practice jump.

Lovell's parachute collapsed and he fell into the lines of Cleaver's parachute. Cleaver grabbed the collapsed canopy and held on until both men landed.

"Something fell through my suspension lines just after I got my opening shock after the jump," the Sergeant said. "There was a wad of silk in my face, so I grabbed it and held on."

FEATURES INDEX

Boy Scientist Seized in Caltech Lab Raids

A brilliant boy scientist, 16, and three teen-age companions were in custody yesterday accused of stealing $3000 worth of scientific apparatus in raids on California Institute of Technology laboratories. Story on Page 2, Part 1.

On Other Pages

Baldwin Hills Oil Work Curtailed to Protect Homes

Curtailment of further oil development in the Baldwin Hills area was ordered yesterday by the Board of Supervisors to safeguard residential use of the region.

Within about 30 years, current oil production in the hill district will have exhausted sources already tapped, it was pointed out. This pumping will be allowed to continue but no new wells may be drilled within 500 feet of existing residences.

WALDO DRAKE REPORTS ON ITALY CRISIS

Tomorrow in the Sunday Times, read the first of two articles dispatched from Italy by Waldo Drake of this newspaper's European Bureau. Developments of world-wide significance are attached to the present-day situation in Italian politics and economics. Whether the country goes completely Communistic, Fascist or becomes a firm keystone of democracy could well be decided by today's events.

In his forthcoming series, Waldo Drake gives his analysis based on facts uncovered at the source—after three weeks and 3000 miles of travel through Italy.

Be sure to see the Sunday Times this week end for a profound study of an important subject—the Italian crisis by Waldo Drake, with helpful photographic illustrations.

Compromise Reached in Sheet Metal Dispute

Dispute between sheet metal contractors and union workers in the Los Angeles area was compromised last night, subject to a union membership vote Monday morning, a spokesman for the contractors announced.

If the compromise settlement is approved, more than 500 sheet metal shops in Los Angeles, Orange, Riverside and San Bernardino Counties, employing more than 4000 members of AFL Sheet Metal Workers Local 108, will go back to work Monday after two weeks of inactivity.

Penalty Plan Dropped

To reach the compromise, the union dropped its insistence on a five-cent penalty on contractors belonging to the Sheet Metal Contractors Association of Southern California.

In return, the contractors agreed to a 22-cent package deal for the contract year ending April 30, 1954, and to a 16-cent increase (15 cents an hour in wages and one cent for the welfare fund) from May 1, 1954, to April 30, 1955.

Extension of the contract period will eliminate the need for negotiations next April, it was pointed out.

The compromise agreement will be submitted to the membership of Local 108 at 8 a.m. Monday in Embassy Auditorium.

THE WEATHER

U.S. Weather Bureau forecast: Mostly clear today and tomorrow but patches of late night and early morning low clouds near the coast. Little change in temperature. High today 82 Civic Center and 74 at the beaches. Yesterday's high, 82; low, 60.

PART 1

Los Angeles Times

EQUAL RIGHTS
LIBERTY UNDER THE LAW — TRUE INDUSTRIAL FREEDOM

ALL THE NEWS
ALL THE TIME

VOL. LXXIII | IN FOUR PARTS | CC ★ | TUESDAY MORNING, MARCH 2, 1954 | 60 PAGES | DAILY, 10c

FANATICS SHOOT FIVE IN CONGRESS

Knight Gives Budget to Legislature

Can Be Financed Without New Taxes, Members Told

BY CHESTER G. HANSON
Times Staff Representative

SACRAMENTO, March 1. Gov. Knight for the first time since he took office appeared before a joint session of the Legislature today and presented the lawmakers with a budget to pay the costs of running the State for the next fiscal year beginning July 1.

The budget total was for $1,423,000,000. This can be financed, he said, without any additional taxes or higher tax rates.

"It's a tight budget," said Sen. Ben Hulse (R) El Centro, who is about ts tough as any legislator in these parts when it comes to budget matters.

Features Outlined

Knight read his message accompanying the budget in which he outlined some of the salient features and commented upon the significance of various items or policies.

Although he told the lawmakers his debut is about $6,000,000 less than the budget of Gov. Warren for the current year, budget fans with their pencils began arguing that Knight was comparing an unknown quantity with a more or less known quantity.

"This budget does not require additional taxes," Knight told the legislators. "It is built on strict economy and demonstrates that it is possible to maintain high standards of essential public services without heavy increases in expenditures . . . This is one of the few budgets in our State history which calls for a net reduction in expenditures.

Wants to Tap Fund

"In spite of the fact that proposed expenditures have been curtailed wherever possible, the total outgo for the State's general fund will exceed the revenues estimated to be received during the year by $76,456,000. I propose that this deficiency be met by utilizing a portion of the reserve funds which have been set aside in earlier years."

Further to save, the Governor was forced to trim proposed expenditures for construction of State buildings drastically—from $93,000,000 down to $33,000,000.

For increased allowances for the operations of State institutions Knight allowed about $6,000,000 for the Department of Mental Hygiene to care for about 3600 more patients, making a total budget for that department of about $64,000,000. For the California Youth Authority an additional $2,300,000, for a total of about $9,000,000 or about 33% increase over the current year. The Department of Corrections will receive about $2,700,000 more, for a total of about $21,000,000 figuring an additional 1036 more prisoners.

The 11 State colleges will get

Turn to Page 10, Column 4

Puerto Rico Assassins Open Fire on House From Visitors Gallery

WASHINGTON, March 1 (AP)—Four fanatics seated in the House gallery today suddenly shouted, "Free Puerto Rico!" waved their flag and then fired at least 20 wild pistol shots that wounded five Congressmen.

One Congressman, Alvin M. Bentley (R) Mich., was so seriously wounded that he was given only an even chance of survival.

Dr. Charles White, who helped operate on Bentley, said: "The operation was a success. Bentley has a 50-50 chance. He is now in the hands of the Lord."

Another Congressman had a shoulder wound and three were hit in the leg.

Confess to Shooting

Two gunmen and their woman companion, Puerto Ricans from New York City, were seized on the spot. Police Chief Robert V. Murray said tonight that they have confessed the shooting and have implicated a fourth.

The wounded Congressmen:

Bentley, 35, hit in the left side below the heart. The bullet went on through and came out the right side.

Ben F. Jensen (R) Ia., 61, struck in the left shoulder.

Clifford Davis (D) Tenn., 56, shot through the upper calf of his right leg.

Kenneth A. Roberts (D) Ala., 41, bullet struck left leg while he was seated. It entered above the knee and came out below.

George H. Fallon (D) Md., 51, shot in the hip.

More news and pictures of shooting in Congress on Pages 2 to 10, Part I.

Police identified the Puerto Ricans as members of the Nationalist Party of Puerto Rico. Two other members of the party tried to assassinate President Truman in 1950.

Police Chief Murray said these three had admitted the shooting:

Mrs. Lolita Lebron, 34; Rafael Concel Miranda, 25, and Andres Figueroa Cordero, 29.

Murray said Mrs. Lebron has just been divorced.

Edgar E. Scott, deputy chief of detectives, said that Mrs. Lebron had said Irving Flores, 27, of New York also was a member of the group. But Scott said Flores had not admitted he was present at the shooting.

Witness to Participation

"Flores ducked out in the confusion," Scott said, "but we have a witness (Mrs. Lebron) to his participation."

The four were arraigned before U.S. Commissioner Cyril S. Lawrence tonight and held in total bond of $400,000 or $100,000 each to cover five charges each of felonious assault with intent to kill.

U.S. Atty. for the District of Columbia, Leo A. Rover told Lawrence two of the five Congressmen are in very serious condition and that there was a grave possibility one or both might die.

Dr. Joseph Young, chief of Casualty Hospital medical staff said at midnight that Bentley was holding his own and expected no early change in his condition.

The Congressman was visited by his wife, an expectant mother, and his mother, Mrs. Helen Wicker of Ann Arbor, Mich. Mrs. Bentley said her husband recognized both and talked coherently with them.

Young, describing Bentley as a "right sick man," said

Turn to Page 2, Column 7

CAPTURED—Capitol police hold three persons in custody after five Congressmen were wounded by shots from House gallery. The woman was identified as Lolita Lebron, and the men, being held with feet off the ground, are Rafael Miranda, in dark suit, and Andres Cordero, in light suit, with coat half off. All three are said to be members of Nationalist Independence Party, extremist Puerto Rican group.
(AP) Wirephoto

WARREN APPROVED AS CHIEF JUSTICE

Senate Voice Vote With No Audible 'Noes' Ends Delay Caused by Unevaluated Charges

WASHINGTON, March 1 (U.P.)—Former Gov. Earl Warren of California was confirmed as Chief Justice of the United States today with a minimum of Senate debate and no audible opposition.

The voice vote ended a bizarre weeks-long delay during which Chairman William Langer (R) N.D., of the Senate Judiciary Committee, released "unevaluated" charges against Warren.

There was no delay today. Senate Republican Leader William F. Knowland and Sen. Thomas H. Kuchel (R) Cal., made brief speeches praising Warren.

Then, with about half of the 96 members present, the Senate confirmed Warren by a voice vote. There were no audible "noes."

Warren has been serving under a recess appointment since last October when President Eisenhower named him to succeed the late Chief Justice Fred M. Vinson. The President sent the formal nomination to the Senate early in January.

The nomination was tied up for weeks in a Senate Judiciary Subcommittee, which Langer also heads.

Snow Hits Kentucky, Tennessee and Ohio

BY THE ASSOCIATED PRESS

A heavy March 1 snowstorm, riding on strong winds, piled drifts over a wide area of Ohio, Kentucky and Tennessee and took at least five lives.

Much of the Eastern Seaboard received heavy rain, and a new cold wave slipped southward over the Canadian border into the Northern Plains.

London, Ky., in the State's southeastern mountain region, received an official 17¾ inches of snow. Cleveland had 14 inches, and a foot or more fell in the Kingsport area of Eastern Upstate Tennessee.

The snow and wind snapped hundreds of overhead wires, cutting off power and telephone service in Eastern Kentucky and Tennessee localities. Traffic was snarled by drifts which blockaded highways.

In several of the heavy snow areas, schools remained closed.

The snow extended into Western Pennsylvania and West Virginia.

Snow turned Colorado highways into icy death traps for four persons.

The cold air mass brought daytime temperatures of 5 below zero as far south as Northern Colorado and to many points in the Northern Plains and Upper Mississippi Valley.

New Mexico watched its worst dust storm since the 1930s come rolling out of the northeast last night.

U.S. Starts New Series of Atomic Tests in Pacific

WASHINGTON, March 1 (U.P.) The United States has begun a new series of atomic tests in the Far Pacific with the explosion of "an atomic device," the Atomic Energy Commission announced today.

The tests, which will continue for several weeks, are expected to include the explosion of the world's first "practical" hydrogen bomb.

AEC Chairman Lewis L. Strauss, announcing the beginning of the new series of tests, merely said the "atomic device" was detonated in the AEC's Pacific proving ground in the Marshall Islands.

Twice as Violent

The tests, under strictest secrecy, are being conducted by Task Force 7 under the command of Army Maj. Gen. Percy W. Clarkson. The task force has been at the Eniwetok-Bikini proving ground for several weeks.

The experimental H-bomb that is expected to be tested was understood to be roughly twice as violent as the H-bomb "device" that obliterated an island on Nov. 1, 1952.

The AEC, before today's official announcement, had said nothing about the new tests. It has been understood unofficially, however, that the first test explosion would be a large atomic blast.

The new H-bomb test apparently is scheduled for the third or fourth week in March. It probably will be set off on the ground and blow one or more of the Bikini islets out of existence.

REGISTRATION OF VOTERS SET AT 2,317,638

A total of 2,317,638 Los Angeles County citizens have registered to cast ballots in the June 8 primary election, Registrar of Voters Benjamin S. Hite disclosed yesterday. In 1952, 2,510,666 registered to vote.

Of the total 1,244,237 signed as Democrats and 969,303 as Republicans. Independent Progressive Party listings are 4735 and miscellaneous 3801, while 92,000 declined to state party affiliations.

Included in the miscellaneous category are seven members of the Communist Party, one Whig and a number who are affiliated with the Vegetarian Party and the Constitution Party, Hite said.

Hite emphasized that registration deadline is next April 15 at 5 p.m.

March Slips In Like Lamb With 68 High

March may go out like a lion but it came in like a lamb yesterday ranging from a low of 51 deg. at 5:24 a.m. to a high of 68 deg. at 2:25 p.m.

The Weather Bureau predicted today will be about the same, with fog in early morning, hazy sunshine in the afternoon and a high temperature of about 70.

The Air Pollution Control District said the smog will irritate eyes lightly in the central and coastal areas during the morning and will extend to

Turn to Page 12, Column 5

Two Injured in Richfield Building Fire

Fire roared up an elevator shaft in the Richfield Building at 555 S Flower St. last night, spreading smoke throughout the top three floors of the building.

Charles S. Jones, president of the company, estimated damage at $50,000, primarily to the building's No. 3 elevator and elevator shaft.

The downtown fire attracted a large crowd of 9 p.m. strollers and snarled traffic along W 5th, W 6th and Flower Sts. Extra police officers were dispatched to the scene to reroute traffic.

Short Circuit Blamed

The flames were touched off when a wire short-circuited near a can of lacquer thinner being used by painters refinishing the building's elevators at the third floor level.

One of the men, Charles Mora, 28, of 1633¼ S Trinity St., was treated for first and second degree burns of the right arm and hand.

A second, Alfonso Tellis, 37, of 9703 Maplewood Ave., Bellflower, received minor burns of the right hand. He was treated at the scene by Fireman Harry Stires.

THE WEATHER

U. S. Weather Bureau forecast: Variable high cloudiness today and tomorrow with late night and early morning fog and low clouds and hazy mid-day sunshine. Not much change in temperatures. High today near 70. Highest temperature yesterday, 68; lowest, 51.

Rep. Holt Helps Disarm Man Firing From Gallery

Rep. Joe Holt (R) Van Nuys, said yesterday that when the shooting began in the House of Representatives he raced to the gallery and helped police hold and disarm one of the gunmen.

Speaking over long-distance telephone with his San Fernando Valley office, Holt said that he saw bullets hit near Floor Leader Charles L. Halleck (R) Ind., and California Reps. Glenard P. Lipscomb, Patrick J. Hillings and Robert Wilson.

Hillings Sees It

In another long-distance telephone conversation, an eyewitness to the shooting, Rep. Hillings (R) Arcadia, said:

"At first we thought it was some sort of a monstrous joke—someone setting off firecrackers in the House.

"Then someone shouted, 'Hit the deck!' We fell to the floor. I could hear the bullets hit the table over our heads.

"I looked up and saw a woman in the gallery firing a heavy gun with both hands. Two men also were firing.

"They were shouting: 'Free Puerto Rico! Free our country!' We could hear them quite plainly.

"Rep. Halleck had just finished a speech favoring a unilateral pact on the admission of Mexican farm laborers. Leslie Arends, the House majority whip, was seated beside him at the leadership table.

"Congressman Glen Lipscomb of Los Angeles and Bob Wilson of San Diego and I also were at the leadership table because of California's special interest in the Mexican labor problem.

"None of us have any doubt that the leadership table—with Halleck and Arends—was the primary target of the assassins. If the three of us and the two leaders hadn't been on the floor, we would have been hit. Later we found bullet holes in the table and chairs around us.

Minutes Drag

"The minutes seemed to drag into hours as the shooting went on. I saw the girl trying to reload. She couldn't, but one of the men did and started firing again.

"I saw the girl drop her gun and grab a flag and start waving it.

"Finally, someone, I think it was a page boy, crashed through and grappled with them.

"Then they were surrounded by people."

FEATURES INDEX

Poor Books Blamed for Pupils' Troubles

Inadequate textbooks and not enough of them cause of Los Angeles school children having trouble with arithmetic, principals indicate in report to Board of Education. Story on Page 23, Part I.

On Other Pages

PART 1

Los Angeles Times

EQUAL RIGHTS — LIBERTY UNDER THE LAW — TRUE INDUSTRIAL FREEDOM

ALL THE NEWS ALL THE TIME

VOL. LXXIII — IN FOUR PARTS — C C — TUESDAY MORNING, MAY 18, 1954 — 60 PAGES — DAILY, 10c

Supreme Court Outlaws Segregation in Schools

Unanimous Vote Told by Warren

BY ROBERT T. HARTMANN
Times Washington Bureau Chief

WASHINGTON, May 17—The Supreme Court today outlawed racial segregation in the public schools.

Chief Justice Warren wrote and delivered the court's unanimous opinion in the long-pending legal test, brought on behalf of Negro school children in Kansas, South Carolina, Virginia and Delaware.

"We conclude that in the field of public education the doctrine of 'separate but equal' has no place," the court ruled. "Separate educational facilities are inherently unequal."

Reverses Old Doctrine

The historic decision reversed as unconstitutional the doctrine of "separate but equal facilities" for racial groups which the Supreme Court set forth in 1896.

Warren's 12-page opinion combined four cases accepted by the Supreme Court in 1951. A second, similar ruling struck down segregation in the District of Columbia.

Separation Doomed

Although, technically, today's rulings apply only to the four States and the District of Columbia, and further legal delays may be encountered before public school segregation is formally outlawed throughout the land, the Supreme Court's broad application of the 14th Amendment appeared to doom separation of pupils on racial grounds as surely as Lincoln ended slavery in the United States.

Chief Justice Warren took note, however, of the delicate problem of implementing the court's ruling by deferring, until the Supreme Court's next term in October, the issuance of any decrees.

Further Argument

Attorneys General not only of the States concerned but of all 21 States requiring or permitting segregation in public education (together with Brownell, on behalf of the Federal government, and counsel for the Negro plaintiffs) were invited to present further argument on two points:

1—Should the court order Negro children admitted forthwith to schools of their choice?

2—Should the court exercise its equity powers to permit "an effective gradual adjustment" from existing segregated systems to a system not based on color distinctions?

Claims the Same

The four State cases carried to the Supreme Court differed in circumstances but in each the appellants claimed that racial segregation, whether required or permitted by State laws, violated the equal protection clause of the 14th Amendment. This became a part of the Constitution after the Civil War.

The case originating in the

Turn to Page 6, Column 3

FREE PARKING—Ocean tides yesterday swept into the already flooded city of Peabody, Mass., five miles from the sea, after water from a burst dam had caused much damage, such as shown above, with parking meters nearly submerged. — UP Wirephoto

Order May Cut Off McCarthy Inquiry

Week's Recess Taken as President Bars Disclosure of Aides' Talk

WASHINGTON, May 17 (AP) — President Eisenhower brought the McCarthy-Army hearings to an unexpected, dramatic halt today — for a week at least, and maybe forever.

Taking a personal hand, the President issued an order forbidding Army witnesses to testify about the role of White House and other high officials in the televised controversy between Sen. McCarthy (R) Wis., and civilian Pentagon chiefs.

McCarthy cried "Iron Curtain!" Democrats raised a protest of "whitewash." And in the end the Senate Investigations Subcommittee voted to recess the public inquiry until next Monday to see if the Chief Executive would withdraw or modify his secrecy clampdown.

[Condensed transcript of hearing begins on Page 10, Part I.]

Mundt Optimistic

Acting Chairman Mundt (R) S.D., declared there is nothing about the recess which "even remotely implies a discontinuation of these hearings" for good. The Democrats, however, said it looked to them as if the hearings may well have blown sky high—unless the President should change his mind.

The chances of President Eisenhower doing this appeared pretty slim.

The President said in today's secrecy order, issued to Secretary of Defense Wilson, that his stand was taken "to maintain the proper separation of powers between the executive and legislative branches of the government in accordance with my responsibilities and duties under the Constitution."

Language Conclusive

And he said, too, in language that left little if any room for backtracking:

"This separation is vital to preclude the exercise of arbitrary power by any branch of the government."

And so ended—for the time being at least—18 days of unprecedented, nationally televised hearings that brought day after day of testimony from Secretary of the Army Stevens and Army Counselor John G. Adams—but only brief, incidental trips to the witness stand by their main antagonists, McCarthy and his chief counsel, Roy M. Cohn.

Adams Silenced

Specifically, President Eisenhower's order forbade Adams—who was still on the witness stand when the breakup came—to give any further details of a Jan. 21 meeting of White House and other top-level officials which led to the Army's head-on collision with McCarthy.

At the Jan. 21 meeting, in addition to Army Lawyer Adams, were Sherman Adams, assistant to President Eisenhower; Atty. Gen. Brownell; Dep. Atty. Gen. William P. Rogers; Henry Cabot Lodge Jr., chief U.S. delegate to the United Nations and a part-time White House aide, and Gerald Morgan of the White House staff.

McCarthy contended he will be unable to present his case unless he can find out—and put on the record—what took place at that meeting and any subsequent meetings at which the Army's course of action might have been planned.

Bitter Protest

The Wisconsin Senator, who bitterly protested the President's secrecy order, said he must determine whether his real foes were Stevens and Adams or persons higher up in the administration.

"You can't go on (with the hearings) with that order in effect," he told reporters. "When the President has it explained to him what he signed, I am sure he will revoke it.

"I would like to know who

Turn to Page 8, Column 4

McCarthy Letter Studied for Violation of Law

WASHINGTON, May 17 (AP)—Atty. Gen. Brownell said officially today the Justice Department is considering "possible violations of the criminal law" in the preparation and dissemination of a document Sen. McCarthy presented May 4 in the McCarthy-Army hearings.

Brownell made the disclosure in ruling that no part of the document should be declassified from its confidential category.

McCarthy Stand

McCarthy's document was two and one-quarter pages long in the form of a "letter" signed with the name of FBI Director J. Edgar Hoover. Hoover reported he never had written such a letter but that its subject matter and parts of its language were identical to a confidential FBI memorandum of the same date. It dealt with an investigation for possible subversives at Ft. Monmouth, N.J.

McCarthy refused to say how he got the letter, except that it came from an Army intelligence officer who was worried by the Army's handling of the Ft. Monmouth situation. He maintained it was identical with the FBI memo, except that security information had been deleted.

Letter to Mundt

Brownell was asked May 13 at a news conference whether the Justice Department was investigating the case of the intelligence officer.

His ruling today, in a letter to Chairman Mundt (R) S.D., went further. It said:

"The department has under consideration at the present time possible violations of the criminal law as a result of the referral of the transcript of the hearings to the department by your subcommittee."

NATIONALISTS SINK RED GUNBOAT OFF FORMOSA

TAIPEI, May 17 (UP)—A Nationalist Chinese destroyer sank a Communist Chinese gunboat in the Straits of Formosa with gunfire today and chased nine others under the protection of Red shore batteries, the Defense Ministry announced.

The action was the fourth such naval battle in the past week as bitter air and naval fighting broke out all along the China coast.

The Nationalist Defense Ministry said the destroyer engaged an entire flotilla of Communist gunboats and scored several hits, sinking one. It did not identify the destroyer.

REDS STAND FIRM AT PEACE SESSION

Secret Meeting at Geneva on Indo-China Discourages French Hopes for Compromise

BY WALDO DRAKE, Times European Bureau

GENEVA, May 17 — There was no comfort for the western world in today's first secret session on peace for Indo-China.

After a Franco-Viet-Minh exchange over the breakdown of plans for evacuation of French and Viet-Namese wounded from Dien Bien Phu, Russian Foreign Minister Molotov made some caustic observations which were discouraging to French hopes that the Communists might show some spirit of compromise on Viet-Minh's demands for a concurrent military and political settlement for all Indo-China prior to the cease-fire which the French want so badly.

Nine foreign ministers, with three subordinates each, will again meet in restricted session on Indo-China tomorrow afternoon but the only progress expected is a further inexorable drift toward either deadlock or capitulation to a compromise armistice on the Communists' terms.

Brings Gloom

Prime Minister Churchill's reassurance to his Parliament today that Britain will make no commitments for defense either in Indo-China or in Southeast Asia until results of the Geneva Conference are determined left as much gloom in the United States delegation as did last night's cynical newscast by Radio Moscow.

Moscow Commentator Lev Chougin said the western powers' calculations for peace in Indo-China will be unsuccessful because the Communist powers are unified behind Viet

Turn to Page 8, Column 2

French Chiefs in Hanoi Plan New Strategy

HANOI, May 18 (Tuesday) (UP)—An emergency military mission headed by French Chief of Staff Gen. Paul Ely arrived here by air from Paris tonight to map strategy against a threatened new mass assault by the Communists in Indo-China.

Ely was accompanied by Gen. Raoul Salan, former French supreme commander in Indo-China, and Gen. Pierre Pelissier, deputy chief of staff of the French air force.

Military Survey

The emergency mission was believed to have brought instructions to the French commander in Indo-China, Gen. Henri-Eugene Navarre, to concentrate some 260,000 of his troops in the Red River Delta area for the defense of Hanoi.

Such a move was expected to mean abandoning by regular French Union forces of some outlying posts and leaving their defense to the home guard.

The French mission will survey the military situation in Indo-China following the fall of Dien Bien Phu.

France's high command today offered the Communists new concessions in an effort to get the stalled evacuation of French wounded from Dien Bien Phu rolling again.

Await New Reply

Earlier today the French called off the lagging mercy mission. They announced that at midnight they would resume bombing convoys on the highway eastward from Dien Bien Phu.

The Reds were accused of using the immunity of the evacuation agreement to shift armed forces toward Hanoi for a threatened drive against this northern capital.

Four hours before the deadline, the high command broadcast a new proposition to the Communists. Officials said the bombing planes likely would be held up until the enemy answered. French planes stood by, ready for action if the new move failed.

The French proposal, broad-

Turn to Page 8, Column 4

Drugstore Owner Shot by Bandit

The operator of an East Side drugstore was wounded in the right arm last night when he slugged a shaky bandit armed with what he thought was a toy gun.

Frank Meyer, 47, co-owner of Wabash Drugs, 3025 Wabash Ave., was treated at the scene for a flesh wound.

Meyer said the slender bandit, who appeared to be about 27 years old, walked up to the counter at 9:20 p.m. as he was closing the store. The bandit forced him back in the store and demanded his wallet.

"He started shaking and pointed what looked like a toy gun at me," Meyer said. "I grabbed his arm and shoved the gun down and then hit him with a right cross."

The bandit began shooting as the drugstore owner tried to grab his arm. The nervous man fired a second shot which struck an icebox and fled.

Tornado Races Through Town in New Mexico

LOVINGTON, N.M., May 17 (UP)—A small tornado tore through the northwest part of this small Southeastern New Mexico town late tonight, but did little damage and no persons were injured.

Lovington police said the tornado went through the town about six blocks from the business district. The only damage reported was an overturned automobile.

Heavy rains accompanied the brief twister and several basements were flooded. It was the third tornado to pass through the Lovington area in the past two days.

Earlier a small tornado hit the ground about 30 miles northeast of Socorro, N.M., but did no damage.

YWCA Board Protests Loyalty Oath Requirement to Get Tax Relief

The board of directors of the Los Angeles Young Women's Christian Association is on record as protesting the signing of a loyalty oath as a condition of gaining tax relief as a welfare institution, it was revealed yesterday.

The board approved the signing of the oath but attached a letter of protest to the affidavit sent to the County Assessor's office, it was learned.

Counters U.S. Ideals

The letter, according to Harold Levy, public relations director for the YWCA, states, in essence, that such an oath conflicts with Christian convictions by discrediting the integrity of the YWCA, one of the "finest and most idealistic institutions by making an attempt to test loyalty by word instead of deed."

He added that the letter also pointed out that the oath is "really counter to national ideals because it creates a pattern of interference by the state with the church and agencies of the church."

Lynn D. Mowat, executive director of the Community Chest, which contributes largely to the YWCA, said the Chest is aware of the YWCA's loyalty oath protest.

"But it hasn't been taken up by the Chest yet," he said, "because we feel the board probably will withdraw its protest. Apparently there never was any question on the part of the YWCA directors of signing the oath. They base their protests on philosophical and religious grounds."

Meeting Slated Today

Mowat said an informal meeting between Chest officials and some of the YWCA directors is scheduled to be held today to discuss the situation.

Levy said the board voted to sign the affidavit under protest last March 18, following a meeting in which every member of the group expressed her opinion. He said the vote was a close one.

"Then, he continued, at request of six members of the 40-woman board, a special meeting was called March 31 to reconsider the loyalty oath protest. At that time, he said, a motion to rescind the protest was voted down, again in a close contest.

THE WEATHER

U.S. Weather Bureau forecast: Low clouds and drizzles this morning; mostly sunny in afternoon; little change in temperature. Highest temperature yesterday, 72, lowest, 56.

Plane Warning Marks Wilson's Visit to Troops

SEOUL, May 18 (Tuesday) (UP)—Unidentified warplanes—presumably Communist—caused a red alert today as Defense Secretary Wilson toured a U.S. front-line division.

The alert was sounded at 10:10 a.m. in the area south of the armistice zone and was still in effect more than an hour later.

With Gen. Taylor

Wilson was visiting the U.S. 2nd Division in the company of 8th Army Commander Gen. Maxwell Taylor at the time the alert sounded.

The defense chief will fly to Pusan tomorrow to confer with Gen. James A. Van Fleet, who is touring the Far East as President Eisenhower's special representative.

Temperature Levels at 72; Drizzles Seen

Drizzles during the morning hours were forecast for today by the U.S. Weather Bureau, with mostly sunny skies in the afternoon.

The temperatures yesterday remained in a moderate range, hovering from 56 deg. at 5:18 a.m. to 72 at 2:05 p.m.

The Air Pollution Control District predicted the possibility of some eye irritation in the foothill area only today because of an inversion near 1500 feet which will lift but not break.

DRIVERS GET WARNING ON BUMPER-RIDING

SACRAMENTO, May 17 (AP)—The California Highway Patrol warned summer drivers today to be aware of "bumper-riding"—following too closely the car in front.

"Don't throw your passengers through the windshield by striking the rear of the car ahead," cautioned Commissioner B. R. Caldwell.

He suggested that drivers allow at least one car length distance from the car ahead for every 10 miles of speed.

Tides Swirl Five Miles Inland on Flooded City

Peabody (Mass.) Streets Already Covered From Dam Break When Ocean Joins Assault

Illustrated on Page 2, Part I

PEABODY, Mass., May 17 (UP) — Ocean tides swept into this already flooded city five miles from the sea today, swirling through a 15-block downtown area.

Three feet of water covered streets in the center of town, where floods from a broken dam caused more than $1,000,000 damage yesterday. However, police said not much more damage was expected from today's tides.

Mayor Philip C. O'Donnell warned residents to boil all drinking and washing water because of pollution from dyestuffs which had been stored in the cellars of local leather plants. More than 42 pumping engines were in operation to help drain the city's flooded basements.

Scores of families were routed from their homes yesterday when a mill pond dam gave way, flooding the downtown area as much as eight feet in some places. No serious injury was reported and no fire despite fears that the floods would explode untended factory boilers.

The millpond water had been rising steadily during 10 weeks of runoff from heavy rains. Motorboats, skiffs, Coast Guard helicopters and an amphibious "duck" were pressed into service to take stranded residents of flooded areas to higher ground.

Jet Trainer Wreck Found; Two Killed

Wreckage of a Navy jet trainer which crashed Saturday, killing a Marine captain and a Navy lieutenant eight miles northwest of Santa Paula, was reached yesterday by a Navy ground party from Point Mugu.

The victims are Capt. J. L. Barr of Santa Barbara and Lt. S. L. Kruger of Sunnyvale, both stationed at Corpus Christi, Tex.

The crashed plane was first spotted from the air Sunday afternoon by a Civil Air Patrol pilot based at Oxnard, and a CAP ground crew reached the spot early yesterday.

Missing since Saturday, when it was en route from Corpus Christi to the Oxnard Air Force Base, the plane crashed on Sulphur Mountain, approximately eight miles from Santa Paula.

New Chessman Execution Date Delayed 60 Days

SAN RAFAEL, Cal., May 17 (AP)—Legal action today assured that it would be 60 days or more before a new execution date could be set for Caryl Chessman, 32-year-old kidnap-attacker and author of a death row autobiography.

Over the protest of Chessman's attorney, Berwyn Rice, affidavits signed by the trial judge holding that the typewritten trial records were accurate was accepted by Superior Court Judge Thomas F. Keating. Keating then gave Rice until 10 a.m. Friday to reply.

Judge Keating last week intervened less than 24 hours before Chessman, Los Angeles "lovers' lane bandit" was to be executed and set today for a hearing on a writ of habeas corpus.

Clarence Linn, Assistant Attorney General, said he thought Judge Keating would rule on such a writ either Friday or Monday.

Rice induced Judge Keating to stay Chessman's execution by arguing the typewritten trial records were inaccurate.

Observers of the proceedings here thought that if Judge Keating grants the habeas corpus writ it would mean another hearing on Rice's claims of an inaccurate transcript.

Roll Asks Ruling to Effect Execution

Dist. Atty. Roll yesterday asked Atty. Gen. Brown to petition the State Supreme Court

Turn to Page 12, Column 4

FEATURES INDEX

$50,000 Violin Found; Negotiations Secret

Mysterious negotiations have ended in the recovery of a $50,000 Stradivarius violin reported stolen five years ago. Story on Page 2, Part 1.

On Other Pages

New Times Telephone Numbers
- MAdison 5-2345 for all calls except those concerning classified advertising.
- MAdison 9-4411 for all classified advertising calls.

Los Angeles Times

EQUAL RIGHTS — LIBERTY UNDER THE LAW — TRUE INDUSTRIAL FREEDOM

PART I
ALL THE NEWS ALL THE TIME

VOL. LXXIII | IN FOUR PARTS | CC★ | WEDNESDAY MORNING, JULY 21, 1954 | 68 PAGES | DAILY, 10c

Armistice Signed Ending Fighting in Indo-China

AT GENEVA—French Premier Pierre Mendes-France, right, chats with Viet-Minh Foreign Minister Pham Van Dong, left, at French headquarters in Geneva shortly before signing of cease-fire agreement to end eight-year-old war in Indo-China. French aides, Guy de la Tournelle, with glasses, and George Boris, join in talk.
(AP) Wirephoto by radio from Paris

Viet-Nam to Be Split in 2 Zones

BY WALDO DRAKE
Times European Bureau

GENEVA, July 21 (Wednesday) —French Premier Mendes-France won his country a signed armistice in Indo-China early today but in disengaging France from a ruinous eight years of Communist rebellion he has left western democracies a new nest of vipers on their open Asian flank.

Pending a Communist reversal at a final plenary session late today this French-Viet-Minh agreement provides that Viet-Nam will be "temporarily" partitioned near the 17th parallel during an indefinite "cease-fire" period while French Union forces withdraw from the northern half of the country and leave it to Ho Chi-Minh's Viet-Minh armies.

Red Evacuation

Similarly Viet-Minh forces in the southern French-held remnant would be evacuated during the 10-month period left for the French to evacuate the Red River port of Haiphong.

This means the eclipse of French influence in the Far East while for the Viet-Minh the "cease-fire" in Viet-Nam is merely another step in a vast enterprise whose objective is the conquest of all of Indo-China, perhaps less by armed forces in the future than by internal subversion.

His Pyrrhic victory undoubtedly will make Mendes-France a national hero in France, but it leaves France with only two equally ominous alternatives in Indo-China:

Firstly—she can massively fortify Southern Viet-Nam as a redoubt with the help of U.S. military and economic aid. This might incur immediate reaction by the Communists, particularly in reprisals against French enterprises and forces before they can be evacuated from the Red River Delta.

Alternative Course

Secondly—France might encourage reconcilation between the Viet-Minh and Bao Dai's anti-Communist regime in Viet-Nam. This certainly would incur the displeasure of the United States which already considers Mendes-France's truce as a formidable victory for Asiatic Communism on its march toward Singapore.

The truce agreement places Bao Dai's Viet-Nam government in a pathetic, untenable position since his Foreign Minister, Tran Van Do, has been

Turn to Page 6, Column 4

Washington Glum and Mum Over Indo-China

Dulles Holds Meeting With Eisenhower as Geneva Reports Flow In on Partitioning

BY ROBERT T. HARTMANN, Times Washington Bureau Chief

WASHINGTON, July 20—As the Iron Curtain today enveloped another part of Asia with the anxious acquiescence of Europe, there was no rejoicing in the capital of the United States.

The official mood here can be described as glum—and mum.

Secretary of State Dulles was closeted with President Eisenhower for nearly an hour this afternoon as reports from Geneva brought assurance of a cease-fire truce partitioning Indo-China.

Highest-ranking official to offer comment during a day of watchful waiting was Defense Secretary Wilson, who told a press conference that the truce "isn't anything I enthuse too much about."

Typical Comment

Wilson's comment, qualified by his assertion that the Geneva accord is perhaps the best answer "at the moment" to the Indo-China problem, was typical.

Dulles canceled his customary Tuesday morning press conference. It was reported he wanted to keep in readiness for communication with Undersec-

Turn to Page 9, Column 1

Roy Cohn Out as M'Carthy Counsel

Senator Transfers Surine to His Personal Staff to Prevent Fight

WASHINGTON, July 20 (AP)—Sen. McCarthy (R) Wis., today reluctantly accepted the resignation of Roy Cohn as chief counsel of the Senate Investigations Subcommittee and transferred Donald A. Surine, another aide who has been under fire.

The moves came in advance of a showdown session of the subcommittee, a majority of whose members had demanded a "house cleaning" of the staff.

Surine, a former FBI agent, was one of two McCarthy subcommittee assistants who have been refused clearance by the Defense Department to handle secret matters. The other, Thomas LaVenia, was kept in his post, at least temporarily.

Accuses Democrat

McCarthy announced that Surine was being transferred from the post of assistant counsel to the subcommittee to McCarthy's Senate office payroll.

Praising Surine in a statement, McCarthy accused an unnamed Democratic committeeman of using an affidavit of "a jailed white slaver in an attempt to discredit Mr. Surine." No details were given.

This maneuvering beat to the punch members of McCarthy's subcommittee bent on a staff shake-up.

The upshot was that when six of the seven subcommittee members met over a steak lunch in the old Supreme Court chamber in the Capitol Building there was nothing that could be done about firing Cohn or Surine. And a decision on LaVenia was put off until a report comes in from the Defense Department regarding its refusal to grant him security clearance for handling secret correspondence.

McCarthy confirmed to reporters that both Surine and LaVenia have been refused such clearance. He said he has asked Secretary of Defense Wilson for the reasons why the two men were not cleared. He added that he plans to seek Surine's return to the subcommittee staff when a reply comes in.

However, a spokesman at the Pentagon said the Defense Department would not give McCarthy any reasons for denying the clearances. The spokesman said Wilson has written McCarthy a letter explaining that the Defense Department's stand is based on confidential information.

Aside from Cohn, Surine and LaVenia, all of the other 22 men and women on the staff were confirmed in their jobs by the subcommittee, including Chief of Staff Francis P. Carr. There had been reports Carr also was on the way out.

All Votes Unanimous

McCarthy said all the votes today were unanimous. So the big blowoff over the staff failed to come off. Now, McCarthy said, he is going to continue an investigation of alleged Communists in defense plants.

Along with McCarthy, Cohn was a principal in the famed McCarthy-Army hearings.

As for Surine and LaVenia, several members didn't like the idea of having men on the staff who had been denied Defense Department clearance. In addition, some members were aware that a Senate committee reported in 1951 that Surine's testimony contained "an apparent willful and knowing misstatement of a material fact relating to the circumstances of the termination of his services with the Federal Bureau of Investigation prior to his employment by Sen. McCarthy."

In advance of today's meet-

Turn to Page 23, Column 1

DIES—Ex-Sen. Blair Moody of Michigan died at 52 following heart attack.
(AP) Wirephoto

Ex-Sen. Moody of Michigan Dies at 52

ANN ARBOR, Mich., July 20 (AP)—Former U.S. Sen. Blair Moody, 52, died today at University Hospital.

The death of the former Washington political writer came as a shock to his followers, who had believed he was recovering from an attack of virus pneumonia and soon would resume his campaign for the Democratic nomination as U.S. Senator in the August primary.

Moody's death left Patrick V. McNamara of Detroit unopposed for the Democratic nomination to run against Republican Sen. Ferguson.

Suffers Reversal

Dr. Cyrus C. Sturgis, head of the department of internal medicine at University Hospital, said Moody "had extensive involvement of the lungs. He had been doing very satisfactorily. Then suddenly he suffered a reversal."

Moody, a former Washington correspondent for the Detroit News, was appointed to the Senate by Gov. Williams in 1951 to fill the vacancy caused by the death of Republican Sen. Arthur H. Vandenberg. He was defeated in his first attempt at election in 1952 by Charles W. Potter, then a Republican Congressman from Michigan.

Moody parlayed a reputation as a global reporter and "man about Washington" to a seat in the U.S. Senate.

Appointment Surprise

Michigan politicians said that Gov. Williams had been impressed for many years with Moody's knowledge of Washington and when Williams had to select a successor to the late Sen. Vandenberg, he reached into the nonpolitical sphere of journalism and chose Moody, to the surprise of most of Michigan and the anger of much of the Democratic Party.

Moody's tenure in the Senate was brief—about 18 months.

Democratic Gov. Williams, in Beaver Island, Mich., on a vacation, made plans to return by plane immediately to Lansing, the capital. The Governor ordered a 30-day period of mourning with flags on all public buildings to be flown at half-staff.

Moody was born in New Haven, Ct., Feb. 13, 1902. He attended public schools at Providence, R.I., and was graduated from Brown University in 1922. He had been a nine-letter athlete there and a member of Phi Beta Kappa. He came to Detroit in 1923. He was married and had three children, Blair Jr., Christopher and Robin.

Bill Boosting Roll of Social Security OKd

Senate Committee Votes to Add on 7,000,000 More

WASHINGTON, July 20 (AP)—A bill to bring about 7,000,000 more Americans under Social Security, at the same time increasing benefits and the taxes to pay for it all, was approved by the Senate Finance Committee today.

Chairman Millikin (R) Colo., said the measure would be ready for the Senate floor early next week. The House has already passed its version of the legislation.

As the bill came out of the Senate committee, it was only a partial victory for President Eisenhower. It gave him almost exactly what he asked for in higher benefits and Social Security taxes. But it eliminated coverage for about 3,500,000 persons, chiefly farm operators and professional persons, whom the President wanted brought in.

Increase of $5

The bill provides for a minimum increase in benefits of $5 a month for all 5,000,000 aged now on the Social Security rolls and the same minimum raise for all those retiring in the future.

However, the formulas for future benefits would be revised so that the increases could amount to as much as $35 a month.

The annual amount of wages subject to Social Security taxes would be $4200 effective Jan. 1, 1955, under the bill, as compared with $3600 under the present law.

This means a $12 tax increase for each covered individual earning $4200 or more next year, and the same for his employer.

Extends Coverage

The Senate version of the measure would extend coverage on a voluntary basis to about 3,500,000 State and local government workers and 260,000 ministers, and on a compulsory basis to 2,600,000 additional farm hands, 250,000 domestic workers, 100,000 industrial home workers and 50,000 persons in the fishing industry.

The minimum Social Security payment now is about $25 a month. This is boosted to $30 under the bill.

The maximum payment of $85 to an individual would go up at once to $98.50 under the bill. In the future the ceiling would be $108.50.

Breezes Rout Heat Wave; High Only 83

Temperatures tumbled from their six-day 90-deg. maximums to a high of 83 yesterday as westerly breezes ended the heat wave with clearing skies and there was promise of more cooling for today.

The city's maximum yesterday was reached at 1:54 p.m., when visibility in the Civic Center had reached more than 12 miles. The day's minimum was 68, recorded at 6:57 a.m.

Today's forecast is for mostly clear weather but with some early morning low cloudiness. The high temperature is expected to be near 83.

In 70s at Beach

Beach communities enjoyed temperatures in the 70s with pleasant breezes, clear skies and water temperatures near 70. There was a light chop to the sea surface. But temperatures in the San Fernando Valley were still high, with 90 recorded at Van Nuys and 88 at San Fernando.

Relative humidity for the day ranged from 86% at 1 a.m. to 50% at 2 p.m.

Based on the forecast, the Air Pollution Control District predicted there will be no eye irritation today, pointing to a high inversion and normal air movements.

Heat Eases in Midwest, Holds Farther South

BY THE ASSOCIATED PRESS

Cool Canadian air brought a brief respite yesterday to the Midwest from a two-week-long heat wave which claimed at least 287 lives and mounting crop, livestock and poultry losses.

But, farther south, the oven-like temperatures and drought continued. Ponca City, Okla., and Salina, Kan., marked up 104 deg. at midday. Emporia, Kan., reported 103.

Indiana Storm

A wind and rain storm hit Ft. Wayne, Ind., last night. One farmer was crushed to death when his barn was flattened. The tower of radio station WANE, atop a 14-story building, was doubled over so that the tip of the tower was at the first-floor level.

High winds, rain and hail and lightning struck Ohio. At Zanesville, a hailstone measured a whopping 8½ inches in circumference.

The U.S. Weather Bureau's weather and crop survey indicated serious damage to corn and some other crops in Kansas, Missouri, Nebraska and the southern portions of Iowa, Illinois and Indiana from heat and dryness of the last week.

Wide Area of Storms

A wide area of thunderstorms extended from the Oregon coast east to the Alleghenies, with some light rainfall touching northern parts of the hard-hit agricultural area.

In Missouri Gov. Phil M. Donnelly's drought emergency committee urged that the whole State be declared a disaster area. The committee recommended reinstatement of the Federal meat-buying program to help stabilize the price of commercial grade livestock and that grain held by the Commodity Credit Corp. be made available for stock feed.

The heat and lack of moisture has killed poultry and hogs by the thousands in Illinois and Missouri.

BUTANE EXPLOSION SETS $85,000 FIRE

Illustrated on Page 3, Part I

Blazing butane that turned a La Habra Heights oil drilling site into a half-acre of towering flames did upwards of $85,000 damage yesterday before the spectacular fire was brought under control by 15 fire companies.

No one was injured.

A violent explosion of the butane that leaked from a hose as it was being transferred from a tank truck to permanent tanks at the drilling site set off the fire.

Can't Stop Leakage

Sheets of flames roared 150 feet in the air, higher than the lofty drilling rig and sheer cliffs that pocket the drilling site, which has an official address of 1497 N Cypress St., La Habra Heights.

Desperate attempts of Lloyd R. Parrish of 7357 Walnut St., Hollydale, driver of the butane tank truck, to stop the leakage of the highly inflammable gas as he was pumping it from his truck to two stationary tanks at the drilling site proved futile. Realizing the imminent danger as the gas vaporized and spread over the area, Parrish sprinted for his life, shouting warnings to drillers.

Within seconds, the blanket of gas enveloped mud-pumping machinery beside the drilling rig, a spark ignited it, and the whole area was a vast field of sky-high flame.

A total of six petcocks on the butane truck and the two storage tanks it was loading were blown out and from them six fingers of the blazing butane reached hungrily heavenward.

Five Autos Burned

Exploding gasoline tanks of five automobiles owned by drillers and parked within the area of the holocaust added to the confusion. All five were burned to metal shells.

The estimated damage included $50,000 for the butane truck, the two permanent tanks and the lost butane they contained; $15,000 to the soundproof encasement of the drilling rig; $15,000 to the mud-pumping machinery which ignited the gas, and at least $5000 for the five totally destroyed automobiles.

Still flaring skyward when the 15 fire companies from three different Fire Departments raced to the scene, the flames were "fogged" down within 30 minutes and confined to the butane tanks.

35 Acres of Mint Canyon Brush Burned

Fire burned over about 35 acres of brushland two miles north of Solemint Junction in Mint Canyon yesterday before it was brought under control.

The blaze was centered in Forest Park west of U.S. Highway 6. It was the second fire in the area within a 24-hour period. Earlier flames believed started from a defective butane stove destroyed a house occupied by Edward Rogers east of the highway and burned 35 acres of watershed.

County firemen under the direction of Asst. Chief Roland Percey dispatched eight units to the latest fire.

Poor Man's Kon-Tiki Voyage Ends; Quintet Decide to Abandon Raft

The adventure of The Five Gentlemen of Ventura, who put to sea on a raft, came to an end yesterday when the skipper of the Coast Guard cutter Morris radioed that the crew of the Rubber Bomb Sneaky — the poor man's Kon-Tiki—had decided to abandon their craft.

The message, received at 4:33 p.m. at Coast Guard headquarters in Long Beach, said four members of the raft's crew had been taken aboard the press boat Hawk and were being returned to Port Hueneme. The fifth crew member was aboard the Morris and was to be taken to Santa Barbara.

The Morris skipper said he was dismantling the raft before leaving because it was a menace to navigation.

The five had sailed from Ventura at 2:15 p.m. Sunday, bound for Santa Catalina Island with a cargo of cold beer and sandwiches. Their craft was built of 100 inner tubes lashed together and wired to a wooden platform. It carried emergency radio equipment, a 15-horsepower outboard motor and a canvas tent "to keep the beer cool."

At the time of sailing the raft was reported to have six crew members: Johnny Strobel III, 22-year-old father of four children; Jerry Straughan, 22; Kenny Kiuke, 20; Dick Davidson, 21; Jimmy Wills, 19, and Bill Shoemaker, 20, all of Ventura. The Morris reported, however, only five men aboard when they were persuaded to abandon their odyssey.

The raft was first sighted, 40 hours after sailing time, by the Yellowtail, a patrol boat for the Department of Fish and Game, wallowing in the waves 12 miles southeast of Anacapa Island and 12 miles offshore from Port Hueneme. It had covered only 20 miles in 40 hours.

Capt. William McGuire, skipper of the Yellowtail, radioed that the crew of the elastic ark looked "wet, bedraggled and discouraged." However, they spurned any assistance and declared, "We're doing fine."

Even after the Morris reached them it took an hour before the argonauts could be persuaded to abandon their voyage.

Burning Airliner Lands; 38 Safe

WASHINGTON, July 20 (U.P.) A Trans World Airlines Constellation made a safe emergency landing at National Airport today after one of its four engines caught fire in the air.

The plane's 33 passengers and five crew members were removed from the plane uninjured.

The plane was TWA's Flight 9 to Los Angeles, first stop Dayton, O.

Stronger Truman Takes Auto Ride

KANSAS CITY, July 20 (AP) Former President Truman took his first automobile ride today since leaving Research Hospital, where he underwent surgery for removal of his gall bladder and appendix June 20.

FEATURES INDEX

Jury Told It Cannot Subpoena Tax Returns

Dist. Atty. Roll yesterday reported to the grand jury that it could not subpoena State income tax returns of public officials unless there is sufficient charge involving a false or fraudulent return. See story Page 1, Part 2.

On Other Pages

Police Climb to Rescue Scouts Ill on Mountain

Mounted police and Sheriff's deputies late last night began a tortuous ascent of the east slope of Mt. San Jacinto near Palm Springs to rescue a group of Boy Scouts, two of whom were reported ill. The hikers also were said to be out of water.

Word of the plight of two Scout leaders and four Scouts from the Balboa-Newport Beach area was carried to Palm Springs police just after dark last night by two of the Scouts who managed to make their way down the rugged, precipitous mountain. The pair, Dennis Cole, 13, of Newport Beach, and Gary Soule, 13, of Costa Mesa, told police their companions had run out of water 12 hours earlier and that two boys needed medical attention.

A short while later Scoutmaster Lewis E. Cock, of 124 27th St., Newport Beach, and his son, John, 13, also managed the descent. Cock said the group, members of Troop No. 5 of Newport Beach, left Idyllwild Saturday for what was to be a two-day hike bringing them out on the desert just north of Palm Springs. He identified those still in the mountains as Arthur Remley, 37, of Balboa, district Scout commissioner for the Balboa-Newport area; Remley's son, Charles, 13; Dan Pierce, 14; Wayne Watson, 13; Gerry Giles, 12, and David Gibson, 12.

He said Giles and Gibson became ill yesterday, apparently suffering from dehydration and convulsions.

Palm Springs Police Chief John S. Davis said his mounted police, under Capt. Warren Coble, and the Riverside Sheriff's mounted unit, under Lt. J. T. Williams, were making the rescue effort.

THE WEATHER

U.S. Weather Bureau forecast: Mostly clear today and tomorrow but late night and early morning low clouds. Little change in temperature. High today about 83 deg. Highest temperature yesterday, 83; lowest, 68.

New Times Telephone Numbers
- MAdison 5-2345 for all calls except those concerning classified advertising.
- MAdison 9-4411 for all classified advertising calls.

Los Angeles Times

PART I
ALL THE NEWS ALL THE TIME

VOL. LXXIII | IN FOUR PARTS | CC | FRIDAY MORNING, DECEMBER 3, 1954 | 80 PAGES | DAILY, 10c

Pope Pius' Condition Grave; Heart Weakened by Collapse

WORLD FEARS FOR LIFE—Pope Pius XII, in a grave condition after collapse, is shown during audience last week at summer papal residence at Castel Gandolfo.
(AP) Wirephoto

People Over World Pray for Recovery

Illustrated on Page 3, Part I

VATICAN CITY, Dec. 3 (Friday) (AP)—Pope Pius XII has suffered a severe collapse with a weakening of his heart. Early today there was grave anxiety for his life.

Through the night Romans gathered in St. Peter's Square and knelt on the cobblestones to pray for recovery of their Pope and Bishop.

The Vatican's vicar general, Clement Cardinal Micara, urged the world's 425,000,000 Roman Catholics to join in the prayers.

Family at Bedside

Members of the Pope's family, the Pacellis, were near his bedside in his simple white-walled bedroom.

Dr. Riccardo Galeazzi-Lisi, physician to the 78-year-old Pontiff, was constantly at his side. He had made emergency X rays and called in a surgeon for consultation.

Up to shortly before dawn there was no further word on the Pope's condition. No lights showed from the Papal Palace or the Pontiff's apartment at that time.

The Pope had been ill before in the nearly 16 years he has headed the church, but never so gravely.

This illness—starting as a recurrence of the gastritis and hiccuping that sapped the Pope's strength last winter — became serious last week end. His collapse yesterday weakened his heart and there also was an indication that his condition was aggravated by an ulcer.

Unable to Eat

He was extremely weak and had been unable to take any food by mouth for several days. His physician yesterday afternoon described the Pope as conscious and completely lucid. But apparently he was unconscious for a time after his collapse.

One Rome newspaper said he had asked for extreme unction, the sacrament administered to Catholics in danger of death. But the Vatican press office denied that Pius had asked for the last sacrament.

Word of Cheer

In the hushed corridors of vast Vatican palace, church dignitaries waited anxiously.

At midnight Msgr. Angelo Dell 'Acqua, substitute Secretary of State, had a word of cheer with the announcement, "The situation is unchanged. There is nothing new."

But highly placed sources made it clear the Pope's condition was indeed serious.

Cardinal Micara announced the Pope would be unable to attend the closing ceremony

Turn to Page 7, Column 1

Senate Rebukes McCarthy, Closes

GOP Members Split as Session Votes Condemnation, 67 to 22

BY ROBERT T. HARTMANN
Times Washington Bureau Chief

WASHINGTON, Dec. 2—Sen. McCarthy stood condemned by his colleagues tonight as the Senate adjourned the special censure session which split its Republican members into two angry camps.

The final vote was 67 to 22 on a much-amended resolution in which the word censure nowhere appears.

[For roll call votes on McCarthy issues see Page 12, Part I.]

Neither is there any trace left of the original second count condemning McCarthy's treatment of Brig. Gen. Ralph Zwicker as a witness in the Peress investigation. The Senate rebuked him only for his conduct toward Senators and two Senate committees.

Californians Opposed

There were 22 Republicans, including California's Senate Majority Leader Knowland and Sen. Kuchel, opposing censure to the bitter end.

And there were 22 Republicans, including the instigator of the action, Sen. Flanders of Vermont, and all three GOP members of the Watkins committee, who joined with a solid bloc of 44 Democrats and Sen. Morse (Ind.) Or., in voting censure.

McCarthy, who with his vote might have kept a majority of Republicans on his side, merely voted present.

His last-ditch defenders took what comfort they could from the legislative legerdemain by which the Zwicker charge never came to a vote and the word censure wound up missing. But Vice-President Nixon, who presided over the climactic day of parliamentary maneuver, refused to rule directly on Sen. Bridges' inquiry contending that it was "not a censure resolution" as finally adopted.

Nixon said the printed title of the resolution used the term "relating to the conduct of the junior Senator from Wisconsin, Mr. McCarthy," and that further interpretation was up to each individual.

Later, when asked if he felt censured, McCarthy laughingly said: "Well, it wasn't exactly a vote of confidence."

Opinion of Watkins

Sen. Watkins (R) Utah, chairman of the select committee, said he doesn't know the difference between the two words and that some people think condemn is a stronger expression. The three previous censure actions in Senate annals did not invariably imply the word censure.

Watkins declined to comment on the outcome. Earlier, on the specific charge that McCarthy had abused the select committee and its 67-year-old chairman, the Senate had voted 64-23. On this preliminary roll call Sen. Case abstained as "a party in inter-

Turn to Page 12, Column 3

NEW STATE TAXES CALLED IMPERATIVE

SAN FRANCISCO, Dec. 2 (AP)—State Finance Director John M. Pierce called today for additional taxes next year to meet an expected $100,000,000 deficit in Gov. Knight's 1955-56 budget.

"A revenue deficiency of more than $100,000,000 is in

For other news of State Chamber sessions see Page 18, Part I.

prospect," Pierce told the 27th annual meeting of the State Chamber of Commerce.

The alternative to more taxes, Pierce explained, is using the remaining State reserves which he said should be preserved as a "cushion against unforeseen emergencies." The reserves are estimated to be about $100,000,000.

Pierce already has said he favors a 2-cent-a-pack cigarette tax along with other tobacco levies which he said would raise about $38,000,000 annually. His speech gave no indication as to the sources for the additional taxes.

Cutback Advocated

A cutback in expenses rather than more taxes was proposed by Legislative Auditor A. Alan Post, who said his office will present a balanced budget for next year without any new taxes.

Post's staff reviews Gov. Knight's proposed budget, then makes recommendations to the Legislature.

"By more intensive cost review and by amending some basic legislation creating expenditure obligations, it should be possible to balance the next budget without additional taxes," Post said. He added that if more revenue is needed, taxes should be increased "only as absolutely required."

COMPLY WITH U.S. LAW

Loyalty Oath Changed for School Employees

The Los Angeles Board of Education unanimously adopted a new loyalty oath for school employees yesterday after hearing objections from three speakers.

The new pledge, more specific than the one now in use, places the city school districts in compliance with the recently enacted Federal Communist Control Law and the California Dilworth Act.

Protests Voiced

Daniel G. Marshall, representing the Rev. A. A. Heist's Citizens Committee to Preserve American Freedoms; Eason Monroe of the American Civil Liberties Union, and Frank K. Holly, a social studies teacher at Jefferson High School, appeared at yesterday's board meeting to protest against the oath.

Herschel Griffin, executive secretary of the Affiliated Teacher Organization of Los Angeles, spoke in support of the loyalty pledge. "The overwhelming proportion of teachers in Los Angeles," Griffin said, "are not intimidated and not afraid, but they will be happy when the necessity for this sort of thing comes to an end."

Affects 28,000

More than 28,000 school employees—from board members and superintendents on down—must sign the oath to keep their jobs.

They must guarantee that they do not knowingly belong to the Communist Party or its successor, that they will not support a foreign government in event of hostilities against the United States, and that they will not engage in any of the activities noted while employed by the public schools.

TO END SMOG: POUR WATER ON IT, HE SAYS

A proposal to eliminate smog by dumping tons of water on the city from aircraft was made yesterday to city officials.

Kenneth D. Dills, 10803½ Blix St., North Hollywood, said in a letter that the downpour of water would break a hole in the inversion layer of air and allow smog to escape in an updraft.

"There would be some kind of reaction even if it only results in watering the City Hall lawn," Dills wrote.

Smog Panel Asks Ban on Incinerators

The back-yard incinerator, a panel of experts agreed yesterday, must go.

Expressed in various ways, this opinion was given yesterday at Pasadena's Huntington-Sheraton by air pollution control leaders from major cities across the nation.

Sponsor of the two-day conference on incineration, rubbish disposal and air pollution is the Southern California Air Pollution Foundation. More than 60 experts on the related subjects are in attendance.

The two best methods of rubbish disposal, it was agreed, are municipal incineration or cut and fill, although there are drawbacks to both.

Cut and Fill Method

No really acceptable design has been evolved for a municipal incinerator, it was pointed out, and cut and fill is necessarily limited by the amount of available land.

But it was upon the back-yard incinerator that the smoke and haze men heaped abuse.

"We've never had them in Philadelphia," said Abraham Michaels, chief of refuse disposal and plant operations for the City of Brotherly Love.

"But we did have open burning dumps and the Philadelphia people decided they'd have to be replaced by municipal incinerators. By next fall all of our rubbish will be incinerated."

Michaels was asked what he thought Philadelphians

Turn to Page 4, Column 2

Buffer Puts Auto Washer in Hospital

Clifford Berry, 45, of 2810 Leeward Ave., found out the hard way yesterday that one should not use an electric buffer while standing on wet pavement.

Berry, a cook, was buffing his car after he had washed it in front of his home. The cord became tangled and wrapped around his arm and the rotating part of the buffer, which, in turn, produced a 110-volt shock in Berry's body.

His wife Thelma rushed to his aid, turned off the buffer, called the police and an ambulance arrived soon after. Berry was removed to Georgia Street Receiving Hospital and treated for shock.

Hod Carrier Escapes Death in 16-Story Fall

LOUISVILLE, Ky., Dec. 2 (AP)—Hod Carrier Richard L. Garth, 51, survived a 16-story fall today.

He was aboard a construction elevator that was released for a free drop from the 21st floor of the Martin Brown Building being built in downtown Louisville.

The elevator operator learned at the last minute Garth was aboard and started braking the car at the fifth floor level. Usually he lets it fall free to the third floor.

Garth suffered only minor cuts and bruises.

Blockade Act of War, Says Eisenhower

Declares He Would Consult Congress on Such Action

BY DON SHANNON
Times Washington Bureau

WASHINGTON, Dec. 2—President Eisenhower today declared that a blockade of Red China would be an act of war and that he would lay the problem before Congress before taking such a step.

The President said he agreed with Senate Majority Leader Knowland that their much-publicized differences were more of method than principle. He said he acknowledged the right of any individual to differ violently and persistently. But, he said, in frequent discussions with Knowland he had found little between them at the time in philosophy on foreign or domestic policy.

At the opening of his press conference the Chief Executive spoke for several minutes on the 13 American prisoners of war sentenced as spies by the Communist Chinese.

Same Feelings

"A President experiences exactly the same resentments, the same anger, the same kind of sense of frustration almost, when things like this occur to other Americans, and his impulse is to lash out," the President said.

"In many ways the easy course for a President, for the administration, is to adopt a truculent, publicly bold, almost insulting attitude," he said. "That would be the easy way for this reason: those actions lead toward war."

He conceded that war automatically unifies our people.

"The nation closes ranks behind the leader. The job to do becomes simply understood—it is to win the war. There is a real fervor devel-

Turn to Page 23, Column 1

Doomed Man, Guard Foil Break by Four

CHICAGO, Dec. 2 (UP)—Four desperate criminals made a break for freedom late today in the Cook County Jail and were fought off by a guard and a prisoner under death sentence for murder.

Police reinforcements also arrived to help quell the disturbance.

Guard Jack Fahey was escorting prisoners back to their cells when he was leaped upon by the four, who fought to get his keys.

Fahey fought with them and was aided by Paul Krump, who is awaiting outcome of an appeal from a death sentence for murder. Another guard sounded an alarm.

The prisoners were restrained and forced back into their cells.

FEATURES INDEX

City Traffic Group Urges District Parking

The City Traffic Commission yesterday moved closer to solving the city's parking problems by urging establishment of community shopping district parking. See Page 1, Part 2.

On Other Pages

More Ports Hit in West Coast Ship Strike

SAN FRANCISCO, Dec. 2 (AP)—The creeping paralysis of the West Coast radiomen's strike began spreading through Pacific Coast ports today, delaying the sailing of several vessels and forcing changes in schedules for others.

The Matson Line freighter Hawaiian Forester and the ship Sulphur Mines both were tied up in Portland by American Radio Association pickets as they prepared to sail. The Hawaiian Forester had unloaded a cargo from Hawaii and was ready to sail when it was picketed. The Sulphur Mines also was loading cargo when the picket showed up and work stopped.

Christmas Tree Cargo

In San Francisco the Matson Line Hawaiian Packer, ready to sail for Hawaii with a cargo including 100,000 Christmas trees, remained at its dock when radiomen refused to sign on and the other unions refused to move the ship without a union radioman.

Meanwhile Federal Mediation Commissioner George Hillenbrand said, "We're moving in on this waterfront dispute" and immediately made separate contacts with the disputing parties preparatory to trying to get them together.

No Pickets Seen at Los Angeles Harbor

There were no picket lines in evidence at Los Angeles Harbor yesterday and all vessels were being worked under normal conditions, a spokesman for the Pacific Maritime Association reported.

Vessels being loaded and unloaded included six of PMA members, the spokesman said. Five more ships are due to tie up here within the next three days.

The Washington, operated by the State Steamship Co., was scheduled to sail at 6 a.m. today for Yokohama.

Five Found Alive After Two Days in Lost Plane

Two on Craft Perish; Copter Rescues Survivors on New Hampshire Mountainside

Illustrated on Page 3, Part I

BERLIN, N.H., Dec. 2 (AP)—A young stewardess and four men were hoisted by helicopter from a frozen, desolate mountainside today—45 hours after an airliner crashed killing two of the plane's personnel.

The Northeast Airlines DC-3 was discovered this morning by searchers as it nestled in a forest of ice-coated evergreen trees. The search had gone on during all the daylight hours since the plane was reported overdue Tuesday noon on a flight from Boston to Berlin.

Fatalities Identified

Dead were the copilot, George McCormick, 37, of West Hurley, N.Y., and John McNulty, 39, of Boston, a flight superintendent. They were crushed against the windshield as the big ship nosed into the side of Mt. Success, seven miles due east of Berlin and one mile from the Maine border.

The crash occurred at an altitude of 3362 feet near the

Turn to Page 6, Column 1

Blast Kills Rescuer and Injures Three

LEAVENWORTH, Kan., Dec. 2 (AP)—A would-be rescuer was killed and three persons injured, one critically, in a series of gas explosions that rocked an 8-unit apartment building during a fire this afternoon.

The dead man was identified as Matt Kennedy, 30, a spectator, who had gone to the assistance of Mrs. Carl Gonser, about 60, operator of the apartment building. She was knocked down on a back porch by the second of the series of three explosions.

The third explosion buried Kennedy in debris.

Firemen succeeded in rescuing Mrs. Gonser after working 25 minutes to clear the wreckage. She suffered fractures of both legs and possible internal injuries. Hospital attendants described her condition as very critical.

Two firemen were injured, neither seriously.

TWO DAYS TILL WOMEN OF YEAR LISTING

There are only two more days until the Times Women of the Year for 1954 will be announced. Watch for this special four-page section in Sunday's Times.

Weatherman Says, Uh-- It MAY Rain, He Says

Hope apparently springs eternal in the Weather Bureau's breast — rain is once again forecast for Los Angeles.

Last night's prediction by Forecaster G. W. Kalstrom calls for cloudy weather today and tomorrow "with chance of a few showers."

Earlier in the day, any possibility of precipitation was written off by the weatherman after a storm center appeared stalled off the coast.

Another disturbance southbound from the Gulf of Alaska, however, changed the weather picture and produced another — the third in as many days — forecast of rain.

The mercury yesterday ranged between 51 deg. at 4:19 a.m. and 70 at 1:17 p.m. Relative humidity was 68% at 4 a.m. and 37% at 12:45 p.m. Visibility varied from 30 miles at 8 a.m. to five miles at 1 p.m., then rose to 12 miles at 4 p.m.

With a forecast of a surface inversion and variable winds today, the Air Pollution Control District predicted some eye-irritating smog in the central and foothill areas.

THE WEATHER

U.S. Weather Bureau forecast: Partly cloudy today and tomorrow with chance of few showers in west portion. Little change in temperatures. Highest temperature yesterday, 70; lowest, 51.

New Times Telephone Numbers
• MAdison 5-2345 for all calls except those concerning classified advertising.
• MAdison 9-4411 for all classified advertising calls.

Los Angeles Times

EQUAL RIGHTS · LIBERTY UNDER THE LAW · TRUE INDUSTRIAL FREEDOM

PART 1
ALL THE NEWS ALL THE TIME

VOL. LXXIV | IN FOUR PARTS | CC | THURSDAY MORNING, APRIL 14, 1955 | 84 PAGES | DAILY, 10c

First Child in L.A. Gets Polio Vaccine

Shipments Pour In for Treatment of 200,000 in Schools

In a dress rehearsal for the inoculation of more than 200,000 school children with the new Salk antipolio vaccine, a 9-year-old girl yesterday received the first shot in the Los Angeles area.

Karen Kain, daughter of Mr. and Mrs. Aaron Kain of 9608 Bartley Ave., Whittier, was administered the primary injection by Dr. Harvey Shipper at St. John's Hospital in Santa Monica.

The vaccine was a part of the first shipment to arrive here. It came aboard an American Airlines plane from Detroit and was quickly trucked to the Parke, Davis & Co. warehouse at 164 W Jefferson Blvd.

Smiles in Pride

Karen cried briefly in anticipation of pain before Dr. Shipper injected her in the right arm. But she quickly smiled in pride when the simple operation had been accomplished.

Karen's father is warehouse superintendent for the drug firm which made arrangements for the "rehearsal" inoculation here.

A large number of Salk vaccine shipments followed throughout the day from manufacturing firms in the East and Middle West. The Cutter Laboratories in Berkeley trucked a shipment here for transshipment by air to Phoenix.

Four Priorities

Meanwhile, as preparations went forward for the free inoculation of all first and second-grade pupils in the county, beginning Monday, a County Medical Association committee on the vaccine made a series of recommendations relative to the distribution and administration of the Salk serum.

They suggested four priority classifications:

1—For preschool children above 12 months, all other children through the eighth grade and for expectant mothers.

2—For junior and senior high school students, all teenagers.

Adults 20 to 30

3—Adults in the 20-30 age bracket and infants less than one year old.

4—All of the remaining adult population.

Dr. David B. Kuris, chairman of the committee, said these priorities were set up in relationship to incidence of polio in the various age groups.

He said that the association has requested the pharmaceutical houses to allocate their supplies of the vaccine directly to doctors during this preliminary period when supply exceeds demand.

He said the doctors themselves would assume the responsibility to observe the priority classifications in administering the vaccine.

Dr. Kuris said the price of the vaccine to doctors would be from $4.20 to $4.50 for the series of three shots. List

Turn to Page 2, Column 2

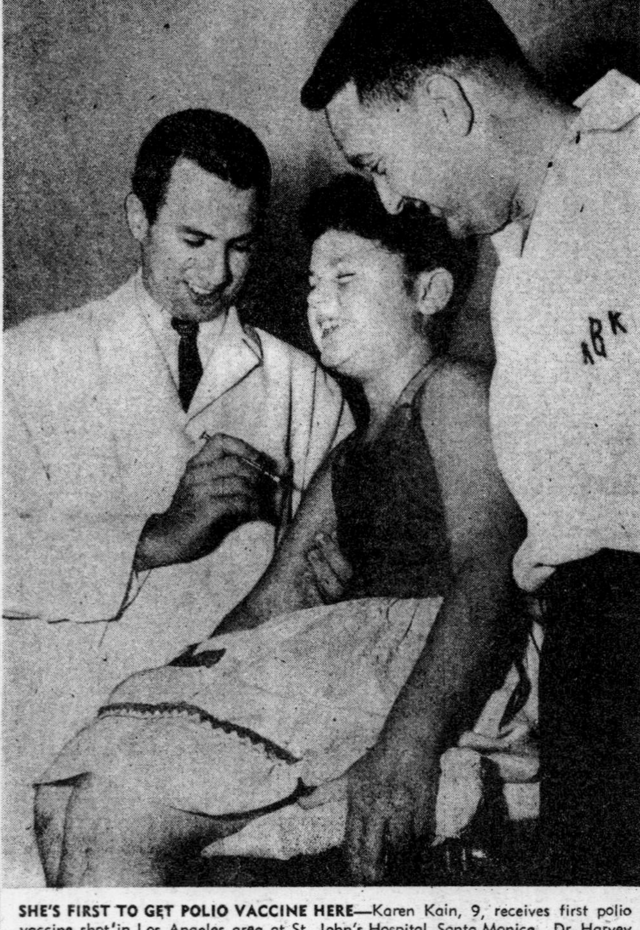

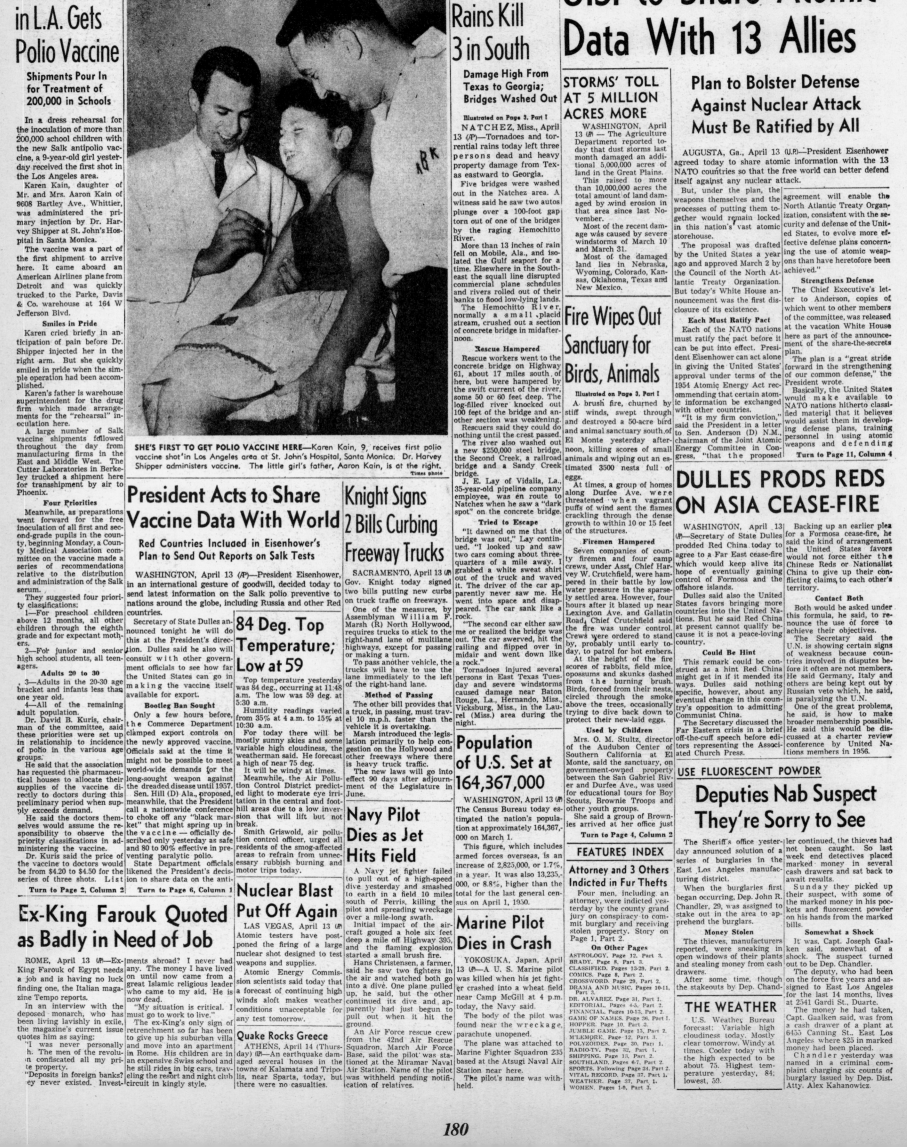

SHE'S FIRST TO GET POLIO VACCINE HERE—Karen Kain, 9, receives first polio vaccine shot in Los Angeles area at St. John's Hospital, Santa Monica. Dr. Harvey Shipper administers vaccine. The little girl's father, Aaron Kain, is at the right. Times photo

President Acts to Share Vaccine Data With World

Red Countries Included in Eisenhower's Plan to Send Out Reports on Salk Tests

WASHINGTON, April 13 (AP)—President Eisenhower, in an international gesture of goodwill, decided today to send latest information on the Salk polio preventive to nations around the globe, including Russia and other Red countries.

Secretary of State Dulles announced tonight he will do this at the President's direction. Dulles said he also will consult with other government officials to see how far the United States can go in making the vaccine itself available for export.

Bootleg Ban Sought

Only a few hours before, the Commerce Department clamped export controls on the newly approved vaccine. Officials said at the time it might not be possible to meet world-wide demands for the long-sought weapon against the dreaded disease until 1957.

Sen. Hill (D) Ala., proposed, meanwhile, that the President call a nationwide conference to choke off any "black market" that might spring up in the vaccine — officially described only yesterday as safe and 80 to 90% effective in preventing paralytic polio.

State Department officials likened the President's decision to share data on the anti-

Turn to Page 6, Column 1

84 Deg. Top Temperature; Low at 59

Top temperature yesterday was 84 deg., occurring at 11:48 a.m. The low was 59 deg. at 5:30 a.m.

Humidity readings varied from 35% at 4 a.m. to 15% at 10:30 a.m.

For today there will be mostly sunny skies and some variable high cloudiness, the weatherman said. He forecast a high of near 75 deg.

It will be windy at times.

Meanwhile, the Air Pollution Control District predicted light to moderate eye irritation in the central and foothill areas due to a low inversion that will lift but not break.

Smith Griswold, air pollution control officer, urged all residents of the smog-affected areas to refrain from unnecessary rubbish burning and motor trips today.

Ex-King Farouk Quoted as Badly in Need of Job

ROME, April 13 (AP)—Ex-King Farouk of Egypt needs a job and is having no luck finding one, the Italian magazine Tempo reports.

In an interview with the deposed monarch, who has been living lavishly in exile, the magazine's current issue quotes him as saying:

"I was never personally rich. The men of the revolution confiscated all my private property.

"Deposits in foreign banks? They never existed. Investments abroad? I never had any. The money I have lived on until now came from a great Islamic religious leader who came to my aid. He is now dead.

"My situation is critical. I must go to work to live."

The ex-King's only sign of retrenchment so far has been to give up his suburban villa and move into an apartment in Rome. His children are in an expensive Swiss school and he still rides in big cars, traveling the resort and night club circuit in kingly style.

Nuclear Blast Put Off Again

LAS VEGAS, April 13 (AP) Atomic testers have postponed the firing of a large nuclear shot designed to test weapons and supplies.

Atomic Energy Commission scientists said today that a forecast of continuing high winds aloft makes weather conditions unacceptable for any test tomorrow.

Quake Rocks Greece

ATHENS, April 14 (Thursday) (UP)—An earthquake damaged several houses in the towns of Kalamata and Tripolis, near Sparta, today, but there were no casualties.

Knight Signs 2 Bills Curbing Freeway Trucks

SACRAMENTO, April 13 (AP) Gov. Knight today signed two bills putting new curbs on truck traffic on freeways.

One of the measures, by Assemblyman William F. Marsh (R) North Hollywood, requires trucks to stick to the right-hand lane of multilane highways, except for passing or making a turn.

To pass another vehicle, the trucks will have to use the lane immediately to the left of the right-hand lane.

Method of Passing

The other bill provides that a truck, in passing, must travel 10 m.p.h. faster than the vehicle it is overtaking.

Marsh introduced the legislation primarily to help congestion on the Hollywood and other freeways where there is heavy truck traffic.

The new laws will go into effect 90 days after adjournment of the Legislature in June.

Navy Pilot Dies as Jet Hits Field

A Navy jet fighter failed to pull out of a high-speed dive yesterday and smashed to earth in a field 10 miles south of Perris, killing the pilot and spreading wreckage over a mile-long swath.

Initial impact of the aircraft gouged a hole six feet deep a mile off Highway 395, and the flaming explosion started a small brush fire.

Hans Christensen, a farmer, said he saw two fighters in the air and watched both go into a dive. One plane pulled up, he said, but the other continued its dive and apparently had just begun to pull out when it hit the ground.

An Air Force rescue crew from the 42nd Air Rescue Squadron, March Air Force Base, said the pilot was stationed at the Miramar Naval Air Station. Name of the pilot was withheld pending notification of relatives.

Tornadoes, Rains Kill 3 in South

Damage High From Texas to Georgia; Bridges Washed Out

Illustrated on Page 3, Part I

NATCHEZ, Miss., April 13 (AP)—Tornadoes and torrential rains today left three persons dead and heavy property damage from Texas eastward to Georgia.

Five bridges were washed out in the Natchez area. A witness said he saw two autos plunge over a 100-foot gap torn out of one of the bridges by the raging Hemochitto River.

More than 13 inches of rain fell on Mobile, Ala., and isolated the Gulf seaport for a time. Elsewhere in the Southeast the squall line disrupted commercial plane schedules and rivers rolled out of their banks to flood low-lying lands.

The Hemochitto River, normally a small placid stream, crushed out a section of concrete bridge in midafternoon.

Rescue Hampered

Rescue workers went to the concrete bridge on Highway 61, about 17 miles south of here, but were hampered by the swift current of the river, some 50 or 60 feet deep. The log-filled river knocked out 100 feet of the bridge and another section was weakening.

Rescuers said they could do nothing until the crest passed.

The river also washed out a new $250,000 steel bridge, the Second Creek, a railroad bridge and a Sandy Creek bridge.

J. E. Lay of Vidalia, La., 35-year-old pipeline company employee, was en route to Natchez when he saw a "dark spot" on the concrete bridge.

Tried to Escape

"It dawned on me that the bridge was out," Lay continued. "I looked up and saw two cars coming about three-quarters of a mile away. I grabbed a white sweat shirt out of the truck and waved it. The driver of the car apparently never saw me. He went into space and disappeared. The car sank like a rock.

"The second car either saw me or realized the bridge was out. The car swerved, hit the railing and flipped over in midair and went down like a rock."

Tornadoes injured several persons in East Texas Tuesday and severe windstorms caused damage near Baton Rouge, La., Hernando, Miss., Vicksburg, Miss., in the Laurel (Miss.) area during the night.

Population of U.S. Set at 164,367,000

WASHINGTON, April 13 (AP) The Census Bureau today estimated the nation's population at approximately 164,367,000 on March 1.

This figure, which includes armed forces overseas, is an increase of 2,825,000, or 1.7%, in a year. It was also 13,235,000, or 8.8%, higher than the total for the last general census on April 1, 1950.

Marine Pilot Dies in Crash

YOKOSUKA, Japan, April 13 (AP)—A U. S. Marine pilot was killed when his jet fighter crashed into a wheat field near Camp McGill at 4 p.m. today, the Navy said.

The body of the pilot was found near the wreckage, parachute unopened.

The plane was attached to Marine Fighter Squadron 235 based at the Atsugi Naval Air Station near here.

The pilot's name was withheld.

U.S. to Share Atomic Data With 13 Allies

Plan to Bolster Defense Against Nuclear Attack Must Be Ratified by All

AUGUSTA, Ga., April 13 (U.P.)—President Eisenhower agreed today to share atomic information with the 13 NATO countries so that the free world can better defend itself against any nuclear attack.

But, under the plan, the weapons themselves and the processes of putting them together would remain locked in this nation's vast atomic storehouse.

The proposal was drafted by the United States a year ago and approved March 2 by the Council of the North Atlantic Treaty Organization. But today's White House announcement was the first disclosure of its existence.

Each Must Ratify Pact

Each of the NATO nations must ratify the pact before it can be put into effect. President Eisenhower can act alone in giving the United States' approval under terms of the 1954 Atomic Energy Act recommending that certain atomic information be exchanged with other countries.

"It is my firm conviction," said the President in a letter to Sen. Anderson (D) N.M., chairman of the Joint Atomic Energy Committee in Congress, "that the proposed agreement will enable the North Atlantic Treaty Organization, consistent with the security and defense of the United States, to evolve more effective defense plans concerning the use of atomic weapons than have heretofore been achieved."

Strengthens Defense

The Chief Executive's letter to Anderson, copies of which went to other members of the committee, was released at the vacation White House here as part of the announcement of the share-the-secrets plan.

The plan is a "great stride forward in the strengthening of our common defense," the President wrote.

Basically, the United States would make available to NATO nations hitherto classified material that it believes would assist them in developing defense plans, training personnel in using atomic weapons and defending

Turn to Page 11, Column 4

STORMS' TOLL AT 5 MILLION ACRES MORE

WASHINGTON, April 13 (AP) — The Agriculture Department reported today that dust storms last month damaged an additional 5,000,000 acres of land in the Great Plains.

This raised to more than 10,000,000 acres the total amount of land damaged by wind erosion in that area since last November.

Most of the recent damage was caused by severe windstorms of March 10 and March 31.

Most of the damaged land lies in Nebraska, Wyoming, Colorado, Kansas, Oklahoma, Texas and New Mexico.

Fire Wipes Out Sanctuary for Birds, Animals

Illustrated on Page 3, Part I

A brush fire, churned by stiff winds, swept through and destroyed a 50-acre bird and animal sanctuary south of El Monte yesterday afternoon, killing scores of small animals and wiping out an estimated 3500 nests full of eggs.

At times, a group of homes along Durfee Ave. were threatened when vagrant puffs of wind sent the flames crackling through the dense growth to within 10 or 15 feet of the structures.

Firemen Hampered

Seven companies of county firemen and four camp crews, under Asst. Chief Harvey W. Crutchfield, were hampered in their battle by low water pressure in the sparsely settled area. However, four hours after it blazed up near Lexington Ave. and Gallatin Road, Chief Crutchfield said the fire was under control. Crews were ordered to stand by, probably until early today, to patrol for hot embers.

At the height of the fire scores of rabbits, field mice, opossums and skunks dashed from the burning brush. Birds, forced from their nests, circled through the smoke above the trees, occasionally trying to dive back down to protect their new-laid eggs.

Used by Children

Mrs. O. M. Stultz, director of the Audubon Center of Southern California at El Monte, said the sanctuary, on government-owned property between the San Gabriel River and Durfee Ave., was used for educational tours for Boy Scouts, Brownie Troops and other youth groups.

She said a group of Brownies arrived at her office just

Turn to Page 4, Column 2

FEATURES INDEX

Attorney and 3 Others Indicted in Fur Thefts

Four men, including an attorney, were indicted yesterday by the county grand jury on conspiracy to commit burglary and receiving stolen property. Story on Page 1, Part 2.

On Other Pages

DULLES PRODS REDS ON ASIA CEASE-FIRE

WASHINGTON, April 13 (AP)—Secretary of State Dulles prodded Red China today to agree to a Far East cease-fire which would keep alive its hope of eventually gaining control of Formosa and the offshore islands.

Dulles said also the United States favors bringing more countries into the United Nations. But he said Red China at present cannot qualify because it is not a peace-loving country.

Could Be Hint

This remark could be construed as a hint Red China might get in if it mended its ways. Dulles said nothing specific, however, about any eventual change in this country's opposition to admitting Communist China.

The Secretary discussed the Far Eastern crisis in a brief off-the-cuff speech before editors representing the Associated Church Press.

Backing up an earlier plea for a Formosa cease-fire, he said the kind of arrangement the United States favors would not force either the Chinese Reds or Nationalist China to give up their conflicting claims to each other's territory.

Contact Both

Both would be asked under this formula, he said, to renounce the use of force to achieve their objectives.

The Secretary said the U.N. is showing certain signs of weakness because countries involved in disputes before it often are not members. He said Germany, Italy and others are being kept out by Russian veto which, he said, is paralyzing the U.N.

One of the great problems, he said, is how to make broader membership possible. He said this would be discussed at a charter review conference by United Nations members in 1956.

USE FLUORESCENT POWDER

Deputies Nab Suspect They're Sorry to See

The Sheriff's office yesterday announced solution of a series of burglaries in the East Los Angeles manufacturing district.

When the burglaries first began occurring, Dep. John R. Chandler, 29, was assigned to stake out in the area to apprehend the burglars.

Money Stolen

The thieves, manufacturers reported, were sneaking in open windows of their plants and stealing money from cash drawers.

After some time, though the stakeouts by Dep. Chandler continued, the thieves had not been caught. So last week end detectives placed marked money in several cash drawers and sat back to await results.

Sunday they picked up their suspect, with some of the marked money in his pockets and fluorescent powder on his hands from the marked bills.

Somewhat a Shock

It was, Capt. Joseph Gaalken said, somewhat of a shock. The suspect turned out to be Dep. Chandler.

The deputy, who had been on the force five years and assigned to East Los Angeles for the last 14 months, lives at 2541 Gardi St., Duarte.

The money he had taken, Capt. Gaalken said, was from a cash drawer of a plant at 6455 Canning St., East Los Angeles where $25 in marked money had been placed.

Chandler yesterday was named in a criminal complaint charging six counts of burglary issued by Dep. Dist. Atty. Alex Kahanowicz.

THE WEATHER

U.S. Weather Bureau forecast: Variable high cloudiness today. Mostly clear tomorrow. Windy at times. Cooler today with the high expected to be about 75. Highest temperature yesterday, 84; lowest, 59.

PART 2

Los Angeles Times

LOCAL NEWS
EDITORIALS — OPINIONS

VOL. LXXIV Times Classified Advertising Number, MAdison 9-4411 CC MONDAY MORNING, JULY 18, 1955 Times Office: 202 West First Street, Los Angeles 53, Calif. MAdison 5-2345

BY THE WAY with BILL HENRY

GENEVA, July 17 — On this eve of the first session of the Big Four conference reporters dined and conferred. Between mouthfuls, correspondents speculated gloomily about the prospects of peace and appropriately enough this Sunday saw the impending proceedings fervently bathed in blessings offered by the local clergy and even the visiting evangelist, Billy Graham.

PROSPECTS — Goodwill is always the watchword on these preliminary occasions, as inevitable as the soft music from the orchestra before the curtain goes up on a summer theater idyll. While all seemed serene and peaceful among the diplomats there was wild confusion and excitement at the Maison de la Presse, an imposing pile on the left bank of the Rhone which is dedicated at least temporarily to the activities of the writers' ring at this conclave. Diplomatic meetings attract an amazing assortment of deep-thinking types whose specialty is speculation in advance and second guessing in retrospect of such affairs. There are, of course, the usual workaday reporters and photographers but they aren't much different from normal types. The diplomatic correspondents, however, are really in a class by themselves.

WORKROOM — The Maison de la Presse has a large lobby and after you have fought your way inside by flashing a green document carrying your picture you find yourself in a two-story room about the size of a basketball court. About a third of the area is covered by a horseshoe-shaped bar surrounded by Cafe de la Paix-type iron tables at which those unable to stand while swapping rumors are enabled to carry on this fascinating occupational pastime in a sitting or semirecumbent position. Others, unable to get near the bar or sit down, mill around whispering the latest tidbit, greeting fellow members of their fraternity and waiting for the occasional broadcast announcement that some new press release is ready.

CELEBRITIES — Quite a batch of publishers of American newspapers have taken this occasion as an excuse for casting an executive eye on the doings of their underlings while at the same time charging off a European vacation as a business expense. The most imposing types here, however, are the professional diplomatic writers who wear Homburg hats, striped pants, canes and a knowing expression—all except, of course Mme. Genevieve Tabuis, a French lady correspondent of advanced years whose black dress and white hair are so well known at diplomatic gatherings that nobody would dare open such an occasion without checking to see that she is on hand.

LOCAL COLOR — Nearly everybody is impressed by the efficiency of the Swiss authorities who are the world's leading exponents of the iron fist beneath the velvet glove. They are the soul of hospitality but insist that everything be correct. No such items as White House passes mean anything over here. The Swiss have a pass of their own which carries the picture of the holder. Some chap forgot to countersign mine this morning and within half an hour the efficient Swiss police had noted this on the duplicate, sternly called this to the attention of the culprit and sent him scurrying around town until he caught up with me and affixed his signature in the proper place. The big news of the day is all small stuff: no golf for Eisenhower while here; the Swiss press scored a clean scoop on their American counterparts with the discovery that Mrs. Eisenhower's name is Mamie Geneva Doud Eisenhower; many Chinese-appearing individuals in the Soviet delegation. Latest gag-rumor many say Georgy Porgy Malenkov must be the real boss of Russia because he stayed home to mind the shop. More seriously, the "pecking order" of the Soviet hierarchy seems established by the way they descended from the airplane—Bulganin first, followed by Khrushchev, Molotov and Zhukov.

FLAG RISES—Old Glory goes up over Disneyland at dedication ceremonies. Camera looks down Main St., where all stores are replicas of the early 1900s.

ALL ABOARD — Walt Disney pulls Gov. Knight and F. G. Gurley, president of the Santa Fe Railroad, aboard Santa Fe train at the opening of Disneyland at Anaheim.
Times photo

OFF THE SCREEN—Real live characters get ready for opening day: Patty Thomas as Mickey Mouse; Bob Street, Mad Hatter; Herb Lurie, March Hare; Betty Scott, Peter Pan, and Betty O'Kelly, Donald Duck, make a reality out of fantasy.

INTO FANTASYLAND — Youngsters rush across drawbridge and through castle at invitational premiere of Disneyland yesterday. Stampede into Fantasyland developed when it opened after other attractions.
Times photos

IN A STEW—Dick Morneau of Los Angeles finds out how cannibal's pot feels, even without fire.

Dream Realized--- Disneyland Opens

$17,500,000 World of Fantasy Dedicated to Children and Hope

BY JERRY HULSE

Once-upon-a-time-land — that magical land of fantasy and faraway places in the minds of little children—became a dream come true yesterday.

It came true at the world premiere opening the new $17,500,000 Disneyland—land of childish dreams and adult hopes—in Anaheim.

Snow White lives. Donald Duck quacks. Captain Hook stalks the paths of Never Never Land.

These and other characters from the pages of ageless fairy tales came to life yesterday in the miracle of Disneyland's Fantasyland.

Time in Reverse

Time spun backward in this once-upon-a-time setting, back to the difficult days of America's pioneer past and daring exploits of the King of the Wild Frontier—Davy Crockett.

Davy Crockett lives again in a place called Frontierland, a land dedicated to the ideals, dreams and exploits that created America.

Stagecoaches jogged over the Painted Desert. Indians attacked. A river boat—the Mark Twain — moved lazily down the Mississippi.

In Frontierland, America's brave past was re-created.

Dreams of Youth

But its pioneer history was contrasted by a startling visit to Tomorrowland—a land that may well be a prediction of things come true near the year 2000. A rocket shot forth to the moon, filled with squealing little boys and girls. And those adults young enough in mind to recapture the happy dreams of youth.

Youngsters caught in this dreamland discovered these adventures as they strolled happily down a path that led from this world of reality into Disneyland's wonderful world of dreams.

Adventureland

There was a place called Adventureland, where they rode an explorer boat down tropical rivers. Plastic crocodiles snapped. Lions roared. Tigers growled. The shore was lined with tropical flowers. Wild birds cried from the treetops.

This happy world of wonders within a troubled world came to life with magic wandlike suddenness when Walt Disney stepped off the Santa Fe and Disneyland train accompanied by Gov. Knight.

From there Disney strolled to the Town Square at the head of Main St., U.S.A. His dedication address was simple.

"All who come to this happy place—welcome," he said.

"Here age relives fond memories of the past . . . and here youth may savor the

Turn to Page 26, Column 1

ROUND THE BEND—Stern-wheel paddle boat brings back days of Tom Sawyer and Huck Finn as it pulls away from landing to the delight of huge Disneyland crowd.

DISNEYLAND OPEN DAILY 10 A.M.-10 P.M.

Disneyland will open to the public today. It will be open from 10 a.m. to 10 p.m. through the summer months.

A year's work — and $17,500,000 — went into construction of Disney's attraction. The park is located just off the Santa Ana Freeway at Harbor Blvd. in Anaheim.

Disneyland spreads across 160 acres of land formerly occupied by orange groves.

Times Telephone Numbers
- MAdison 5-2345 for all calls except those concerning classified advertising.
- MAdison 9-4411 for all classified advertising calls.

Los Angeles Times

EQUAL RIGHTS
LIBERTY UNDER THE LAW — TRUE INDUSTRIAL FREEDOM

PART I
ALL THE NEWS ALL THE TIME

VOL. LXXIV — IN FOUR PARTS — CC* — WEDNESDAY MORNING, SEPTEMBER 14, 1955 — 72 PAGES — DAILY, 10c

L.A. Suffers Worst Smog Crisis; Another Alert Today Predicted

AT SMOG'S PEAK—With Stephen M. White statue on Hall of Records lawn in foreground, City Hall is dimly seen yesterday at peak of city's densest smog.
Photo by John Malmin. Times staff photographer

Ban on Industry and Traffic Threatened; Disaster Unit Stands By

Illustrated on Page 3, Part I

The densest smog on record grayed Los Angeles for hours yesterday, threatening closure of industry and curtailment of traffic as ozone concentration came within a shade of reaching the second alert stage for the first time.

Another smog assault was forecast for today by the Air Pollution Control District. The prediction was based on a Weather Bureau forecast of another 1000-foot inversion that probably will not lift.

The APCD said there will be moderate eye irritation in the central area between 9 a.m. and 12:30 p.m. and heavy irritation in the foothill districts between 11 a.m. and 2 p.m.

The APCD evaluation staff said another first stage alert probably will be called today and urged that householders postpone all backyard burning or other smog-producing activity until the inversion lifts.

As residents dabbed at their watering eyes yesterday, officialdom's leaders, admittedly alarmed, waived political differences.

Police Co-Operation

Gov. Knight, called in Sacramento, placed the California Disaster Committee on an alert stand-by basis.

Mayor Poulson ordered Chief of Police Parker to cooperate in enforcing Air Pollution Control District emergency regulations and, for the initial time, Los Angeles Police Department officers were directed to halt residents from burning combustible waste or from operating backyard incinerators.

The Board of Supervisors, at request of Smith Griswold, APCD director, called an extraordinary session, meeting as the APCD Board, with the Emergency Action Committee in attendance.

Truckers Comply

APCD inspectors in radio cars stood by each oil refinery, ready for the calling of a second alert stage and orders to close down the oil industry's plants.

The City Hall's emergency clinic treated five persons for severe eye irritation.

Trucking associations complied with an APCD request to curtail activities as much as possible. And the city's fleet of trucks was withdrawn from the streets by Mayor Poulson's order.

A first alert stage was called by the APCD at 10:23, when the ozone reading was .56 in downtown Los Angeles and .50 in Vernon.

Second Alert Defined

It was to last for three hours and nine minutes, until 1:32 p.m., when ozone concentrations had fallen well below the one-half part per million parts of air at which first

Turn to Page 2, Column 7

Heat Holds Grip on Area; High of 93

The September hot weather continued yesterday, as the mercury climbed to a peak of 93 deg.

The high reading was recorded at 1:14 p.m., after a gradual rise from the official low temperature of 67 deg., reported at 4:08 a.m.

Relative humidity, fairly high for this time of year, made the heat seem even more torrid. The humidity ranged from a peak of 70% at 5:30 a.m. to a low of 21% at 10:20 a.m.

For today the weatherman promised some relief from the heat — the temperature, he predicted, will rise only to about 88 deg. in downtown Los Angeles.

TEMPERATURES

Midnight	71	11 a.m.	91
1 a.m.	71	Noon	92
2 a.m.	71	1 p.m.	92
3 a.m.	70	1:14 p.m.	93
4 a.m.	68	2 p.m.	93
4:08 a.m.	67	3 p.m.	90
5 a.m.	68	4 p.m.	88
6 a.m.	69	5 p.m.	86
7 a.m.	72	6 p.m.	82
8 a.m.	75	7 p.m.	80
9 a.m.	84	8 p.m.	76
10 a.m.	88	9 p.m.	75

Germany Agrees to Russian Pact

No Secret Deals, Adenauer Says; Gets Pledge on Captives

MOSCOW, Sept. 14 (Wednesday) (AP)—Chancellor Konrad Adenauer gave emphatic public assurance to the West today that in agreeing to set up diplomatic relations with the Soviet Union, he had not surrendered any of West Germany's obligations to NATO and the Western European Union.

Adenauer also told a news conference shortly before taking off for Bonn:

"I want to declare emphatically that no secret deal or pact of any kind were made between us and the Soviet government."

Resume Diplomatic Ties

In a surprise finish to the Chancellor's five-day visit to the Soviet capital, he and Soviet Premier Bulganin announced in a joint communique last night that they had agreed to establish formal relations between their governments.

The communique made no mention of Germans still held prisoner by the Soviets but Adenauer said today the Russians had promised to return them to Germany.

The Chancellor added that he expected these releases to start almost immediately after his delegation returned to Bonn. Some, he said, would be amnestied while others would be turned over to the West German government to be dealt with according to German law.

Hope for Others

A German press spokesman said those prisoners with homes in West Germany will be turned over to the Bonn government, while those with homes in East Germany will go to the Communist East German regime.

Adenauer's words indicated that the agreement covered only the 9626 Germans Bulganin said during the conference were in Soviet jails as convicted war criminals. Bulganin said these were all the Germans still held by the Soviets, although the West Germans contended earlier 100,000 or so were not accounted for.

Adenauer reiterated at his news conference that "we Germans are convinced there are still many other Germans—not only soldiers—who are still unable to leave the Soviet Union." He continued:

Promise to Investigate

"Both Bulganin and Soviet Communist Party Chief Nikita Khrushchev said they did not know of any of these but they promised to investigate and said if any such were found, they would be handed over in the same way as the so-called war criminals.

"We believe the Soviets will keep this promise, and we hope these other detained Germans also will be able to return to their homeland."

The communique was issued after the close of four days of talks here between Adenauer and Soviet leaders.

"Today is a big day in the lives of the Soviet people as it is in the lives of the German people," a Soviet spokesman declared.

The decision ends the estrangement between Bonn and Moscow that has existed since World War II.

The German press officer, Bonn's U.N. Ambassador

Turn to Page 10, Column 3

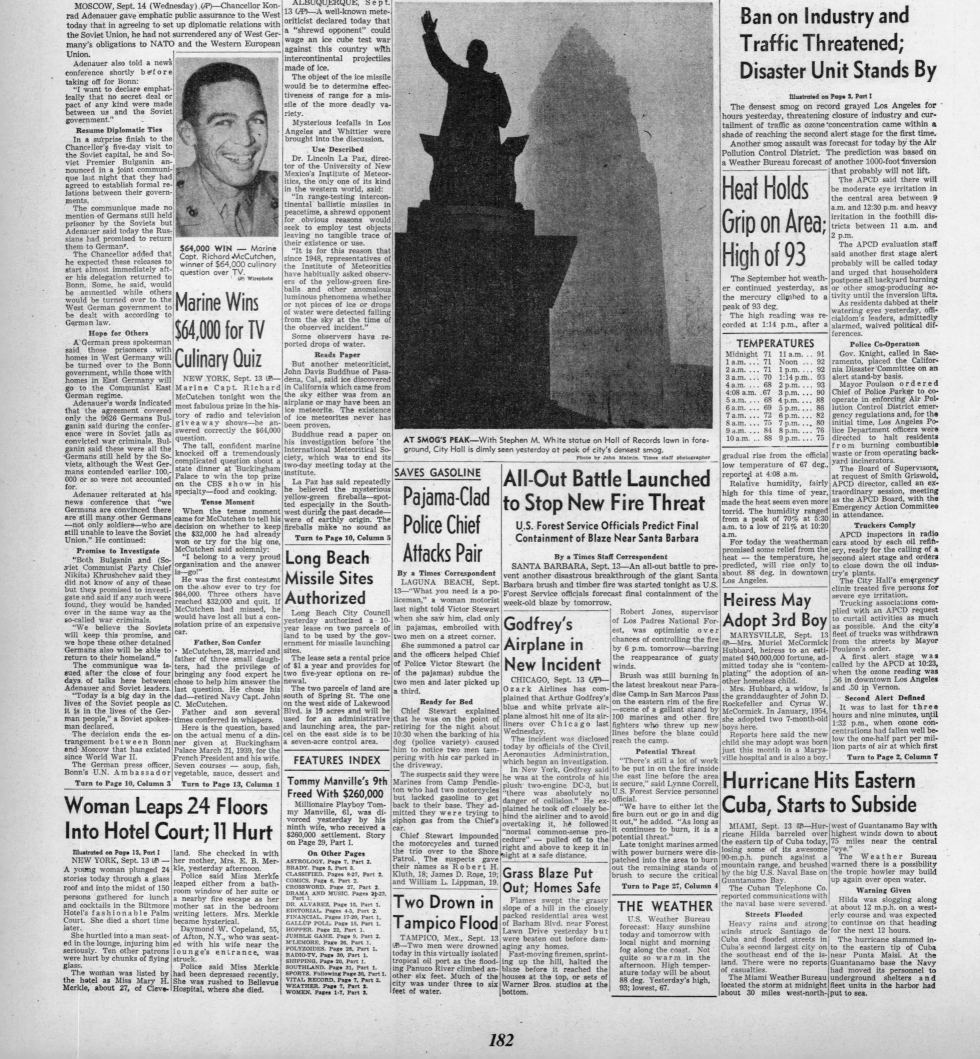

$64,000 WIN — Marine Capt. Richard McCutchen, winner of $64,000 culinary question over TV.
(AP) Wirephoto

Marine Wins $64,000 for TV Culinary Quiz

NEW YORK, Sept. 13 (AP)—Marine Capt. Richard McCutchen tonight won the most fabulous prize in the history of radio and television giveaway shows—he answered correctly the $64,000 question.

The tall, confident marine knocked off a tremendously complicated question about a state dinner at Buckingham Palace to win the top prize on the CBS show in his specialty—food and cooking.

Tense Moment

When the tense moment came for McCutchen to tell his decision on whether to keep the $32,000 he had already won or try for the big one, McCutchen said solemnly:

"I belong to a very proud organization and the answer is—go!"

He was the first contestant on the show ever to try for $64,000. Three others have reached $32,000 and quit. If McCutchen had missed, he would have lost all but a consolation prize of an expensive car.

Father, Son Confer

McCutchen, 28, married and father of three small daughters, had the privilege of bringing any food expert he chose to help him answer the last question. He chose his dad—retired Navy Capt. John C. McCutchen.

Father and son several times conferred in whispers.

Here is the question, based on the actual menu of a dinner given at Buckingham Palace March 21, 1939, for the French President and his wife. Seven courses — soup, fish, vegetable, sauce, dessert and

Turn to Page 13, Column 1

EXPERT SAYS:

U.S. May Face Ice Cube War

ALBUQUERQUE, Sept. 13 (AP)—A well-known meteoriticist declared today that a "shrewd opponent" could wage an ice cube test war against this country with intercontinental projectiles made of ice.

The object of the ice missile would be to determine effectiveness of range for a missile of the more deadly variety.

Mysterious icefalls in Los Angeles and Whittier were brought into the discussion.

Use Described

Dr. Lincoln La Paz, director of the University of New Mexico's Institute of Meteoritics, the only one of its kind in the western world, said:

"In range-testing intercontinental ballistic missiles in peacetime, a shrewd opponent for obvious reasons would seek to employ test objects leaving no tangible trace of their existence or use.

"It is for this reason that since 1948, representatives of the Institute of Meteoritics have habitually asked observers of the yellow-green fireballs and other anomalous luminous phenomena whether or not pieces of ice or drops of water were detected falling from the sky at the time of the observed incident."

Some observers have reported drops of water.

Reads Paper

But another meteoriticist, John Davis Buddhue of Pasadena, Cal., said ice discovered in California which came from the sky either was from an airplane or may have been an ice meteorite. The existence of ice meteorites never has been proven.

Buddhue read a paper on his investigation before the International Meteoritical Society, which was to end its two-day meeting today at the institute.

La Paz has said repeatedly he believed the mysterious yellow-green fireballs—spotted especially in the Southwest during the past decade—were of earthly origin. The fireballs make no sound as

Turn to Page 10, Column 5

Long Beach Missile Sites Authorized

Long Beach City Council yesterday authorized a 10-year lease on two parcels of land to be used by the government for missile launching sites.

The lease sets a rental price of $1 a year and provides for two five-year options on renewal.

The two parcels of land are south of Spring St. The one on the west side of Lakewood Blvd. is 19 acres and will be used for an administrative and launching area, the parcel on the east side is to be a seven-acre control area.

SAVES GASOLINE

Pajama-Clad Police Chief Attacks Pair

By a Times Correspondent

LAGUNA BEACH, Sept. 13—"What you need is a policeman," a woman motorist last night told Victor Stewart when she saw him, clad only in pajamas, embroiled with two men on a street corner.

She summoned a patrol car and the officers helped Chief of Police Victor Stewart (he of the pajamas) subdue the two men and later picked up a third.

Ready for Bed

Chief Stewart explained that he was on the point of retiring for the night about 10:30 when the barking of his dog (police variety) caused him to notice two men tampering with his car parked in the driveway.

The suspects said they were Marines from Camp Pendleton who had two motorcycles but lacked gasoline to get back to their base. They admitted they were trying to siphon gas from the Chief's car.

Chief Stewart impounded the motorcycles and turned the trio over to the Shore Patrol. The suspects gave their names as Robert H. Kluth, 18; James D. Rose, 19; and William L. Lippman, 19.

All-Out Battle Launched to Stop New Fire Threat

U.S. Forest Service Officials Predict Final Containment of Blaze Near Santa Barbara

By a Times Staff Correspondent

SANTA BARBARA, Sept. 13—An all-out battle to prevent another disastrous breakthrough of the giant Santa Barbara brush and timber fire was started tonight as U.S. Forest Service officials forecast final containment of the week-old blaze by tomorrow.

Robert Jones, supervisor of Los Padres National Forest, was optimistic over chances of controlling the fire by 6 p.m. tomorrow—barring the reappearance of gusty winds.

Brush was still burning in the latest breakout near Paradise Camp in San Marcos Pass on the eastern rim of the fire—scene of a gallant stand by 100 marines and other fire fighters who threw up new lines before the blaze could reach the camp.

Potential Threat

"There's still a lot of work to be put in on the fire inside the east line before the area is secure," said Lynne Correll, U.S. Forest Service personnel official.

"We have to either let the fire burn out or go in and dig it out," he added. "As long as it continues to burn, it is a potential threat."

Late tonight marines armed with power burners were dispatched into the area to burn out the remaining stands of brush to secure the critical

Turn to Page 27, Column 4

Godfrey's Airplane in New Incident

CHICAGO, Sept. 13 (AP)—Ozark Airlines has complained that Arthur Godfrey's blue and white private airplane almost hit one of its airliners over Chicago last Wednesday.

The incident was disclosed today by officials of the Civil Aeronautics Administration, which began an investigation.

In New York, Godfrey said he was at the controls of his plush two-engine DC-3, but "there was absolutely no danger of collision." He explained he took off closely behind the airliner and to avoid overtaking it, he followed "normal common-sense procedure" — pulled off to the right and above to keep it in sight at a safe distance.

Grass Blaze Put Out; Homes Safe

Flames swept the grassy slope of a hill in the closely packed residential area west of Barham Blvd. near Forest Lawn Drive yesterday but were beaten out before damaging any homes.

Fast-moving firemen, sprinting up the hill, halted the blaze before it reached the houses at the top, or sets of Warner Bros. studios at the bottom.

THE WEATHER

U.S. Weather Bureau forecast: Hazy sunshine today and tomorrow with local night and morning fog along the coast. Not quite so warm in the afternoon. High temperature today will be about 88 deg. Yesterday's high, 93; lowest, 67.

Heiress May Adopt 3rd Boy

MARYSVILLE, Sept. 13 (AP)—Mrs. Muriel McCormick Hubbard, heiress to an estimated $40,000,000 fortune, admitted today she is "contemplating" the adoption of another homeless child.

Mrs. Hubbard, a widow, is the granddaughter of John D. Rockefeller and Cyrus W. McCormick. In January, 1954, she adopted two 7-month-old boys here.

Reports here said the new child she may adopt was born just this month in a Marysville hospital and is also a boy.

Hurricane Hits Eastern Cuba, Starts to Subside

MIAMI, Sept. 13 (AP)—Hurricane Hilda barreled over the eastern tip of Cuba today, losing some of its awesome 90-m.p.h. punch against a mountain range, and brushed by the big U.S. Naval Base on Guantanamo Bay.

The Cuban Telephone Co. reported communications with the naval base were severed.

Streets Flooded

Heavy rains and strong winds struck Santiago de Cuba and flooded streets in Cuba's second largest city on the southeast end of the island. There were no reports of casualties.

The Miami Weather Bureau located the storm at midnight about 30 miles west-northwest of Guantanamo Bay with highest winds down to about 75 miles near the central "eye."

The Weather Bureau warned there is a possibility the tropic howler may build up again over open water.

Warning Given

Hilda was slogging along at about 12 m.p.h. on a westerly course and was expected to continue on that heading for the next 12 hours.

The hurricane slammed into the eastern tip of Cuba near Punta Maisi. At the Guantanamo base the Navy had moved its personnel to underground shelters and fleet units in the harbor had put to sea.

Woman Leaps 24 Floors Into Hotel Court; 11 Hurt

Illustrated on Page 13, Part I

NEW YORK, Sept. 13 (AP)—A young woman plunged 24 stories today through a glass roof and into the midst of 150 persons gathered for lunch and cocktails in the Biltmore Hotel's fashionable Palm Court. She died a short time later.

She hurtled into a man seated in the lounge, injuring him seriously. Ten other patrons were hurt by chunks of flying glass.

The woman was listed by the hotel as Miss Mary H. Merkle, about 27, of Cleveland. She checked in with her mother, Mrs. E. B. Merkle, yesterday afternoon.

Police said Miss Merkle leaped either from a bathroom window of her suite or a nearby fire escape as her mother sat in the bedroom writing letters. Mrs. Merkle became hysterical.

Daymond W. Copeland, 55, of Afton, N.Y., who was seated with his wife near the lounge's entrance, was struck.

Police said Miss Merkle had been depressed recently. She was rushed to Bellevue Hospital, where she died.

FEATURES INDEX

Tommy Manville's 9th Freed With $260,000

Millionaire Playboy Tommy Manville, 61, was divorced yesterday by his ninth wife, who received a $260,000 settlement. Story on Page 29, Part I.

On Other Pages

Two Drown in Tampico Flood

TAMPICO, Mex., Sept. 13 (AP)—Two men were drowned today in this virtually isolated tropical oil port as the flooding Panuco River climbed another six feet. Much of the city was under three to six feet of water.

Times Telephone Numbers
• **MAdison 5-2345** for all calls except those concerning classified advertising.
• **MAdison 9-4411** for all classified advertising calls.

EQUAL RIGHTS

Los Angeles Times

LIBERTY UNDER THE LAW — TRUE INDUSTRIAL FREEDOM

PART I
ALL THE NEWS ALL THE TIME

)L. LXXIV — IN THREE PARTS — CC ★ — SATURDAY MORNING, OCTOBER 1, 1955 — 46 PAGES — DAILY, 10c

isenhower akes First)fficial Step

Return to Command Starts With Signing of Two Documents

DENVER, Sept. 30 (AP) — resident Eisenhower to-ight took the first small but nomentous step in a long narch back toward active ommand of the government y signing two Federal doc-nents.

The action, taken by the esident from his hospital d after another day of en-ouraging progress in recu-eration from his heart at-ack, came at 8:27 p.m.—a few ours short of a week from ie time he was stricken.

Bulletin on President

Tonight's medical bulletin, 10 p.m., said:

"The President's condition ontinues to progress satis-ictorily without complica-ons. The President had a omfortable day. He again en-oyed music and was read to or a short period in the after-oon. The oxygen tent has ot been used for the last 36 ours.

"The President continues be on a 1600 calorie diet a ay as previously an-ounced."

A medical technician and a urse read to the Chief Executive from Sir Arthur onan Doyle's "Sir Nigel."

For dinner, the President ad a "very small" T-bone teak, a small baked potato, a roiled tomato, some lettuce, slice of honey-dew melon nd buttermilk.

The signing of the docu-uents, providing for promo-ion of State Department For-ign Service officers, was the rst business transacted by e Chief Executive since last iday, the eve of his attack.

Writes Full Name

Originally White House offi-ials had said President Eisen-ower merely would initial ie two papers. Instead, using pen from his desk at the mporary White House here, e wrote his full name on ich.

His bed was elevated slight-to permit this action.

The documents were laid efore the President by his ersonal physician, Maj. Gen. loward M. Snyder.

The promotions were in the orm of recess appointments, equiring Senate approval aft-r it meets next January, for 17 Foreign Service officers 'ho are moving up to high-r ranks. There were 78 on ne list, 39 on the other.

Signature Lighter

A member of the White louse staff said Gen. Snyder uggested to the President ow he should sign the pa-ers.

The President replied in a ocular vein: "I know more bout it than you do, How-rd."

The White House staff nember said the President's ignature was lighter than ual and that he held the

Turn to Page 5, Column 3

FRENCH WALK OUT—Antoine Pinay, left, France's Foreign Minister, and members of French delegation walk out of U.N. General Assembly Building in New York City after the Assembly voted to take up the Algerian question. At right is Ambassador Herve Alphand, permanent French representative to the United Nations. (AP) Wirephoto

Caliber of Eisenhower's Team Impresses Nixon

Everyone in Administration Dedicates Self to Guiding Program, Vice-President Says

BY ROBERT T. HARTMANN
Times Washington Bureau Chief

WASHINGTON, Sept. 30—Vice-President Nixon's out-standing impression of the week since President Eisen-hower was stricken has been the caliber and teamwork of all administration leaders.

"Every member of the Cabinet, everyone in the ad-ministration has dedicated himself to seeing that the administration's program goes forward and that every action taken is as close as possible to the way President Eisenhower would have wished it if he were here," Nixon said.

Nixon made his reflections at an informal luncheon he gave in honor of the Gover-nor-designate of the Virgin Islands, Walter A. Gordon of Berkeley, and Mrs. Gordon.

UC Classmates

Most of the guests were Cal-ifornians and many were for-mer classmates of Gordon at the University of California, where he won football fame on the "Wonder Team" of 1918 and continued as an as-sistant coach until 1943.

Speaking earnestly and showing some of the strain he has been under during the last week, Nixon welcomed Gordon to the "Eisenhower team" and said he has always been impressed by the caliber of men who have come to Washington to work on it.

"I had appreciated these

Turn to Page 5, Column 7

France Bolts U.N. Because of Algeria Crisis

UNITED NATIONS, N.Y., Sept. 30 (AP)—French Foreign Minister Antoine Pinay and the entire French delegation walked out of the United Na-tions Assembly today after that body had voted to take up the Algerian question.

By a margin of one vote, the Assembly rejected the rec-ommendation of its 15-nation steering committee that the Assembly skip the issue for this session. The vote was 28-27 in favor of rejecting the committee recommendation. There were five abstentions.

One-Vote Margin

Over bitter French opposi-tion, the Assembly decided by a margin of one vote to place the highly controversial ques-tion on its agenda.

What the Assembly actual-ly did was reverse a decision of its 15-nation steering com-mittee to turn down an Alge-rian debate. The vote was 28 in favor of the debate, 27 against and five abstaining.

Pinay immediately took the floor and said France would regard any action taken by the Assembly on Algeria as null and void. He added:

"I do not know tomorrow what will be the relations be-tween France and the United Nations."

The French delegation then rose and left while the As-sembly went on with other business.

Storm-Fanned Blaze Wrecks Japanese City

TOKYO, Oct. 1 (Saturday) (AP)—Typhoon winds whipped a holocaust through the city of Niigata today in Japan's worst fire since the B-29s of World War II.

This morning, with water pressure failing, firemen be-gan dynamiting rows of houses in an effort to starve the inferno that devoured 1200 buildings and houses in its first seven hours.

Six hours and 40 minutes after it started police re-ported the fire had been brought under at least tem-porary control.

No deaths have yet been reported but early scanty re-ports listed 12 injured.

The U.S. Air Force has a base about five miles from Niigata, but Far East Air Forces headquarters said no U.S. airmen were injured.

Meanwhile, the season's worst typhoon swung toward Northern Japan after leaving at least 31 dead, 241 injured and 41 missing on Kyushu, Shikoku and Western Honshu islands.

Millionaire Says He'll Wed Frances Langford

MILWAUKEE, Sept. 30 (AP)—Ralph S. Evinrude, million-aire Milwaukee industrialist and yachtsman, says he will marry Singer Frances Lang-ford, perhaps "within a cou-ple of months."

Evinrude, who is in New York, was quoted by the Mil-waukee Journal today as say-ing the engagement was an-nounced to friends at a Nan-tucket (Mass.) party.

THE WEATHER

U.S. Weather Bureau forecast: Hazy sunshine today and tomorrow with night and early morning clouds and fog. High to-day near 77. Slightly cool-er tomorrow. Highest temperature yesterday, 74; lowest, 52.

Dodgers Beat Yankees, 8-3, in 3rd Game

Erskine, Larsen Clash on Mound in Series Today

BY AL WOLF
Times Staff Representative

EBBETS FIELD, Brook-lyn, Sept. 30 — Johnny Po-dres was right and Bob Tur-ley was wrong in today's duel of pitching unpredicta-bles. So Brooklyn's Dodg-ers are back in this World Series as bona fide partici-pants instead of New York Yankee stooges.

Podres made his 23rd birth-day an especially memorable occasion by southpawing the National League champions to an 8-3 victory, which also was his first in Series compe-tition.

Dodgers' Task Tough

So there'll be no Yankee sweep, which loomed as a dis-tinct possibility following the first two games. But the Dodgers still face a mighty stiff assignment. They must win three out of four now—and the best they've ever done in this annual tourna-ment is three out of seven.

Carl Erskine, who has beaten New York twice while bowing but once in previous Series—he set an all-time rec-ord by fanning 14 Yanks in one 1953 game—got Manager Walt Alston's nod to keep the rally rolling at this same park tomorrow.

His opposition will come from Don Larsen, a freshman in Series competition.

Winning Records

Both right-handers posted winning records this season, Erskine finishing 11-8 despite protracted arm trouble which prompted Alston to hold him out of the first three games, and Larsen winding up 9-2 after spending much of the summer farm-handing at Den-ver.

This afternoon's win, the most decisive ever scored in Series play by a Brooklyn

Turn to Page 1, Pt. 3, Col. 3

Air Force Grounds All C-47 Planes

WASHINGTON, Sept. 30 (AP)—The Air Force today grounded all C-47s, work horses of the transport fleet since World War II, because of the possible use of a clean-ing and preservative com-pound in a few fuel tanks.

The compound could clog fuel lines under certain con-ditions, the Air Force said.

At the Pentagon the Air Force said the decision to ground the two-engine trans-port planes was made after a routine inspection by the Air Materiel Command and that the action taken was precautionary.

Base commands were au-thorized to free their C-47s for use as soon as they check their planes for the use of the compound.

FEATURES INDEX

Peron's Romance With Teen-age Girl Told

Argentine police tell story of Juan Peron's romance with teen-age girl. Story on Page 3, Part 1.

On Other Pages

Texas Town Hit by Flood

CLARKSVILLE, Tex., Sept. 30 (AP)—A flash flood, fed by 10 inches of rain in three hours, washed down a six-block wide strip through the center of this Northeast Texas town of 4500 tonight, as high as the tops of pumps in filling sta-tions.

County Judge Gavin Wat-son said so far there had been no reports of injuries. He said about 75 persons who live in the two-mile long strip along Boggy Creek were homeless and property damage would be high. Watson said he saw five houses washed down the street.

Strike Hits Port

BREMEN, Germany, Sept. 30 (AP)—A wildcat strike of 2500 part-time dock workers who demanded more pay threat-ened tonight to paralyze Bremen's port. Almost 50 ships were tied up in the har-bor.

Rubbish Quiz Hears of 'Pressure' on Cities

Bell Police Chief, Mayor of Maywood Describe Difficulties on Contracts

Two Southland cities were victimized in a struggle for power among rubbish contractors, it was charged yester-day at an Assembly committee hearing in the State Building.

City officials of Maywood and Bell named Andrew V. Hohn, rubbish contractor who figures prominently in the current grand jury bribery in-quiry, as a central figure in the struggle.

They told the Assembly In-terim Committee on Govern-mental Efficiency and Econo-my that Hohn had boasted that he would force rival con-tractors to "eat" their rubbish—that he was "tougher and bigger" than they.

Resulted in Indictment

Hohn's testimony before the grand jury that he paid two $5000 bribes resulted in indictment of Supervisor Her-bert C. Legg's chief deputy, George Turner, and Theodore Hamlin, a rubbish dealer.

Before hearing the new rev-elations concerning Hohn, the Assembly committee acceded to a grand jury request that certain persons involved in the bribery investigation—in-cluding Legg, Turner, Ham-lin and Hohn — not be called as witnesses, lest they be cloaked with immunity.

Members of the committee, taking note of suggestions that they might be getting "cold feet" and might "whitewash" someone, agreed that they did not want to be placed in that position.

Maywood Mayor Testifies

Yesterday's testimony con-cerning Hohn came first from Mayor Ben Lang of Maywood, who described for the commit-tee the troubles his city en-countered in rubbish disposal about a year ago.

He said the long-time hold-er of a contract for disposal of Maywood's garbage and rubbish wanted more money, and canceled the contract. The city then advertised for new bids.

Mayor Lang said the Pacific Waste & Disposal Co., op-erated then by John Gevor-kian and Bill Makerdishian, submitted the low bid of $1950 a month. Among higher bid-ders was Hohn, at $3570, he said.

The contract was awarded to Pacific Waste & Disposal Co., which immediately en-countered difficulty in finding a place to dispose of the gar-bage and rubbish, Mayor Lang testified. Even with the help of the city, he said, the com-pany could find no place in Los Angeles County which would accept its loads.

Introduced to Hohn

Shortly before the company was to begin operations, the Mayor went on, he was intro-duced to Hohn.

"I told him, 'You seem to be the fly in our ointment,'" May-or Lang testified. "He brag-gadociously told me that he certainly was.

"He said, 'Those two Arme-nians might get the first two loads of garbage on but they won't get them off. They'll have to eat it. I know May-wood and Bell is going to pay more for their garbage pick-up. I'm tougher and bigger

Turn to Page 13, Column 1

KILLED — Actor James Dean, 24, dies in auto crash near Paso Robles.

James Dean, Film Star, Dies in Auto Crash

James Dean, 24, one of Hol-lywood's brightest new mo-tion-picture stars, was killed early last night in a head-on collision at the rural town of Cholame, about 19 miles east of Paso Robles, the California Highway Patrol reported.

The young actor met death in his German-built Porsche sports car while en route to road races at Salinas. Patrol-men said Dean was dead on arrival at the Paso Robles War Memorial Hospital fol-lowing the crash at the inter-section of State Highway 41 and U.S. 466.

Mechanic Injured

His mechanic, identified by the CHP as Rolph Wuether-ich, about 27, of Hollywood, suffered a fractured jaw, frac-tured hip and body lacera-tions. He was described as in "moderately serious condi-tion."

The CHP office at San Luis Obispo said a car driven by Donald Turnupseed of Tulare made a left turn on Highway 41 while traveling east, col-liding almost head on with Dean's tiny sports car. Inves-tigators said Turnupseed suf-fered minor injuries.

An attending physician was quoted as saying Dean died instantly at about 5:30 p.m.

Turn to Page 2, Column 3

Forest Fire Burning Along 3-Mile Front

By a Times Correspondent

SAN BERNARDINO, Sept. 30—Flames still burned along a three-mile line of forest and brush in mountains here to-day after blackening 2800 acres since Wednesday.

Don J. Lewis, public infor-mation official for the U.S. Forest Service, said thus far it has cost an estimated $75,-000 to fight the blaze. He add-ed that it is hoped the fire can be controlled by 10 a.m. to-morrow.

Flames today were reach-ing from Shea Mountain to Coxey Ranger Station.

"Two-thirds of the perim-eter is in excellent shape now and safe," Lewis said.

At the outset the fire came within five miles of the east-ern slope of Lake Arrowhead.

Heiress Has Cold

PARIS, Sept. 30 (AP)—Ameri-can Heiress Barbara Hutton, who arrived in Paris last night with Baron Gottfried von Cramm, German tennis player, amid rumors they might soon marry, remained in her room at the Ritz Hotel today with a cold.

FIRST 'SMOG RED' ALERT CALLED HERE

The Los Angeles area ex-perienced its first "Smog Red" alert yesterday as the ozone count in Pasadena climbed from .56 to .65, highest ever recorded there.

Temperatures were au-tumnlike and breezes helped clear the air by 1:27 p.m. when the alert, called at 12:07 p.m., was canceled. Under Smog Red conditions, all open burning is banned and indus-try and the public are urged to curtail the use of cars and trucks.

Eye Irritation Seen

The Air Pollution Control District predicted moderate eye irritation this morning in the central area, with smog moving into the northeast and foothill zones after noon. The forecast said the smog may reach the "red" stage again.

The ozone count for Los An-geles reached .44, according to the APCD. The first alert stage is called when the count ex-ceeds .50 part of ozone per million parts of air. Until yesterday, the high count in Pasadena had been .60, set last Aug. 29.

The Weather Bureau pre-dicted fog and low clouds for today with hazy sunshine.

77 Deg. Forecast

The day's maximum tem-perature will be near 77. Yesterday's temperature ranged from 52 at 6:52 a.m. to 74 at 12:15 p.m. Relative hu-midity was 47% at 11:20 a.m. after a high of 100% at 2:30 a.m.

The bureau noted that Oc-tober should bring the first two days of rain and some sudden temperature changes. There will be several foggy days, three or four more se-vere smoggy days and 17 clear days.

Crippled Plane Lands in Sea; Ship Saves Crew

SAN FRANCISCO, Sept. 30 (AP)—A Catalina flying boat with one of its two engines disabled made an emergency landing in the open sea 530 miles southwest of San Fran-cisco today and its four crew-men were taken aboard a freighter.

Hamilton Air Force Base, whose rescue planes sped to the scene, reported that the flying boat alighted undam-aged in nine-foot swells.

An Air Force rescue plane radioed that it appeared the freighter, the Harry Cul-breath, was trying to take the flying boat aboard. The Cata-lina's pilot, Capt. Clark Dixon of Danville, Cal., was able to taxi the plane along-side the freighter.

The ship, en route from Pusan to Gulf ports, was re-portedly heading for Long Beach.

In addition to Capt. Dixon, the Transocean Air Lines crew which was ferrying the plane from Guam to Oakland consisted of Copilot Chris Angelos of Palo Alto, Navi-gator Bob Adgerly of Soquel, Cal., and Engineer Russell Varner of Agana, Guam.

About 1000 miles out of Honolulu one of the engines stalled. Capt. Dixon then was just beyond the point of no return.

He gradually lost altitude, first dropping to 2000 feet, then to 1000, as his speed cut to a little under 100 m.p.h.

Eisenhower Could Run, Misquoted' Doctor Says

3OSTON, Sept. 30 (AP)—Dr. aul Dudley White, famous rt specialist who attended sident Eisenhower, said ght, "I would have no ob-on whatsoever to his run-g again."

r. White issued the state-t in Boston because of ssible misinterpretation" statement he made today he NBS television show oday."

During that program Dr. hite said that if he were esident Eisenhower he ouldn't want to run" for a ond term.

n a voluntary statement to press tonight Dr. White d: "I would like to respond, answer to many questions ning today, concerning the ssible misinterpretation of ecent comment of mine.

"I indicated that I, person-ally, as Paul D. White, would have no great desire to under-take such a strain as that im-posed upon a President of the United States of America.

"This remark could, and probably already has been, interpreted as meaning that I would give such advice to the President.

"Far from it.

"If the President has a good recovery, as he seems to be on the way to establishing, and if he desires to continue his present career — which would be, of course, to the great benefit of this country and the world at large — I would have no objections whatsoever to his running again.

"But that remains still for the future to decide."

Times Telephone Numbers
• MAdison 5-2345 for all calls except those concerning classified advertising.
• MAdison 9-4411 for all classified advertising calls.

Los Angeles Times

EQUAL RIGHTS — LIBERTY UNDER THE LAW — TRUE INDUSTRIAL FREEDOM

PART 1
ALL THE NEWS
ALL THE TIME

VOL. LXXV | IN FOUR PARTS | CC ★★ | THURSDAY MORNING, JULY 26, 1956 | 84 PAGES | DAILY 10c

Liners Collide at Sea: 2000 Aboard

Stassen-Nixon Rift Puts Chief on Spot

Disarmament Aide Seeks to Goad Newsmen to Quiz President

BY ROBERT T. HARTMANN
Times Washington Bureau Chief

WASHINGTON, July 25—Harold Stassen said today he will halt his Herter-for-Vice-President activity when and if President Eisenhower publicly picks Richard Nixon as his running mate.

Thus Stassen, for whom the cabinet-rank job of disarmament assistant was created by President Eisenhower, put his boss squarely on the spot.

The President repeatedly has termed it improper for him to dictate to the Republican National Convention, even in regard to his own candidacy. This is a political tradition even Franklin D. Roosevelt (who gave Stassen his first Federal job) dared not ignore.

Goaded to Questions

Stassen, either in desperation, misapprehension or sustained by knowledge not yet available to most mortals, continued to goad reporters into putting the question to the President direct.

Press Secretary Hagerty said the President probably will hold a news conference next Wednesday, his first since June 6. He definitely will not meet the press this week.

This delay served as artificial respiration for Stassen's dying cause. He labored diligently to keep it alive with frequent press briefings, radio and television interviews and teasers of things to come. These included:

1—A barrage of charges against Republican National Chairman Leonard Hall, who was portrayed by Stassen as author of a plot to stop Stassen.

May Publish Poll Result

2—A tentative promise to make public his private polls—which he asserted showed Nixon the weakest of eight potential running-mates, including Stassen. He said the polls are being continued by a private professional group, but declined to identify it.

3—An assertion that other members of the group he claims are behind him in fi-

Turn to Page 8, Column 3

Jordan and Israel Trade Heavy Fire

JERUSALEM, July 25 (AP) Jordan and Israel forces exchanged heavy fire today in the Judean Hills west of Jerusalem and minor shooting incidents erupted on the Syrian and Egyptian frontiers.

Six Jordanian soldiers, one civilian and the Jordan member of the Mixed Jordanian-Israeli Armistice Commission were wounded in a series of four clashes in the Jerusalem area, center of rising tension over a succession of Arab-Israel incidents. There were no reports of Israeli casualties.

Observer Wounded

Another United Nations truce observer, Swedish Col. Erik Helge Thaalin, was wounded. He is the third U.N. casualty in two days of efforts to end shootings and mine incidents along the tense frontier that marks a narrow neck of Israel jutting into Jordan territory in Palestine. Jordan reported its member of the Mixed Armistice Commission, Capt. Mohammed Barghouti, also was wounded.

Israel, blaming the Jordanians for the incidents and for the shot which struck the U.N. observer, protested to the Mixed Armistice Commission. An Israeli Foreign Ministry spokesman called the incidents a "cease-fire breach by Jordan."

CONGRESS HOPES TO QUIT IN FEW DAYS

WASHINGTON, July 25 (AP) Legislators quickened their pace today and their leaders predicted the 84th Congress would adjourn within two or three days.

The possibility that the final gavel might even fall as early as tomorrow night was raised by Sen. Johnson of Texas, Democratic leader, though others were not so optimistic.

Johnson said a Thursday windup was possible after Senators agreed to suspend rules and take up a catch-all $2,315,000,000 appropriation bill, which they passed and sent to conference.

Republican Leader Knowland of California predicted adjournment possibly Friday or Saturday.

SOMETHING TO STAND ON

Bookie Suspect Has Leg Full of Money

When vice-squad officers haul Ralph W. Pattison, 55, into court Aug. 14 for a preliminary hearing on three felony counts of bookmaking, they're confident they'll have a leg to stand on—Pattison's.

When he was arrested at a hot-dog stand he operates at 1606 S Maple St. after Officers Jeffrey Holms and Joel Powell reportedly overheard him taking a bet over a pay phone at the stand, Pattison vehemently denied he was a bookie.

"If I was a bookie, I'd have money, wouldn't I?" he demanded.

Although they could find no money on Pattison, the officers took him to the City Jail. It was there that a thorough search disclosed that Pattison was carrying $3233 in cash — hidden in a neat little compartment in his wooden leg.

After arraignment on a felony complaint issued by the District Attorney's office, Pattison was freed under $500 bail and ordered to appear for preliminary hearing Aug. 14.

And officers will testify about all the money he was walking around with or, that is, on.

IN COLLISION—This is the Italian luxury liner Andrea Doria which collided in the fog with the liner Stockholm off Nantucket Island last night. The Italian ship, built in 1953, had 1134 passengers aboard.

Marine Saved From Sea in Secret Weapons Test

Bomber Pilot Rescued After 16 Hours in Ocean Off Catalina; Second Man Sought

A marine bomber pilot was rescued from the cold sea off Santa Catalina Island early yesterday after a night-long ordeal that began when he parachuted from his plane while on a secret weapons-testing mission.

A second marine was still missing in the fog-shrouded water and aircraft and boats of three military services suspended an all-day search when darkness descended.

Three Coast Guard cutters, a Coast Guard amphibious plane, five Marine Corps helicopters and various Air Force planes had conducted the day-long search.

Saved by Teen-agers

Master Sgt. George V. Mikkelsen, 38, a square-jawed veteran of 16 years' service, was pulled from the sea 3½ miles west of Santa Catalina by 11 teen-agers aboard a Sea Scout boat taking part in a search for the missing plane.

Mikkelsen's wife, Dorothy, and children, Mike, 4, and Melanie, 5, live at 1315 S Doreen Way, Santa Ana. His parents are James and Mable Mikkelsen of 1325 Victoria Drive, Modesto.

In Water 16 Hours

Marine Corps officials refused to identify the second man until relatives were notified.

Mikkelsen was in the water 16 hours after his AD-5 attack bomber developed "op-

Turn to Page 25, Column 1

House Votes to Cite Miller for Contempt

WASHINGTON, July 25 (AP) The House today voted contempt citations against Arthur Miller and seven other persons. Miller is the New York playwright who recently married Marilyn Monroe.

The action sends the citations to the Justice Department for possible prosecution. Penalty in case of conviction in Federal court can be as much as a year in jail and $1000 fine.

All eight persons cited were accused by the House Committee on Un-American Activities of refusing to answer questions.

Now in England

Miller now is in England where Miss Monroe is making a movie.

In addition to Miller, those cited were Otto Nathan, New York, executor of the estate of the late Albert Einstein; Peter Seeger, Beacon, N.Y.; William E. Davis, St. Louis, Mo.; John W. Simpson, St. Louis; Mrs. Anne Yasgur Kling, St. Louis; Elliott Sullivan, New York, and George Tyne, New York.

Appears at Hearing

Miller told the committee, at a hearing June 21, that he was never a Communist, never advocated the overthrow of the U.S. government, and is now strongly anti-Communist. But he acknowledged that he had been affiliated at times with organizations which have been cited as Communist fronts and attended "meetings of Communist Party writers in 1947."

Sirens Will Get Test Tomorrow

Col. Richard F. Lynch, director of the municipal Office of Civil Defense, announced yesterday that the city's siren system at 10 a.m. tomorrow will participate in State-wide air raid tests.

FEATURES INDEX

Share-the-Ride Fight on Smog Wins Backing

Share-the-ride program to combat smog wins support of varied industries. Story on Page 1, Part 3.

On Other Pages

Downpours Hit Towns in Southland

Thunderstorms that have been pounding mountain and desert areas of Southern California in recent days moved into the lowlands yesterday and drenched several towns with downpours that at times reached near cloudburst proportions.

Riverside was soaked with 1.26 inches of rain yesterday. Trees were shattered by lightning and several power poles and transformers were knocked out. One residential street was closed by floodwaters, but no injuries were reported.

Other communities reporting more than an inch of rain were Yucaipa 1.05, Lytle Creek 1.01, and Upland 1.15.

Communities Hit

The rare summer storm swept on Glendora, dropping almost half an inch of rain in five minutes. The runoff rushed into nearby San Dimas. A similar five-minute downpour gave Claremont .25 of an inch and lightning hit two power transformers at noon and disrupted electric service in much of the city.

In Pomona a rumbling thunder barrage heralded a half-hour rainstorm, and at San Bernardino .30 of an inch of rain overflowed gutters and caused power interruptions. Ontario measured .12 of an inch shortly after noon.

Flooded Road

Similar torrential rains were reported in desert areas where Daggett and Barstow received an inch of precipitation within a matter of minutes. Las Vegas, Nev., got 1.32 inches during a two-hour period.

A flash flood on Highway 6 at Red Rock Canyon 20 miles north of Mojave yesterday washed out the highway in two places and forced closing

Turn to Page 4, Column 7

THE WEATHER

Light eye irritation today. No morning burning permitted.

U.S. Weather Bureau forecast: Variable high cloudiness with mostly sunny days today and tomorrow. Local fog and low clouds near coast night and early morning hours. Little change in temperatures. High today near 84. High temperature yesterday, 85; low, 63.

ON SHIP — Actress Ruth Roman was a passenger on Andrea Doria, involved in collision in the Atlantic.

Ruth Roman, Son Reported as Passengers

Illustrated on Page 3, Part I

BOSTON, July 25 (AP) — Screen Actress Ruth Roman was reported among passengers aboard the Andrea Doria, as was the Mayor of Philadelphia, Richardson Dilworth.

Miss Roman, whose home is at 436 N Rockingham Road, Brentwood, (Cal.) was accompanied by her son, Richard Hall. Mayor Dilworth's wife was with him on the ship.

Also listed as passengers aboard the Italian Lines vessel were Camille Cianfarra, New York Times correspondent in Spain, and F. M. Thie-

Turn to Page 11, Column 1

Passengers Abandon Italian Luxury Ship Off Nantucket Island

BOSTON, July 26 (Thursday) (AP)—Two luxury ocean liners, the Swedish Stockholm and the Italian Andrea Doria, crashed in a dense Atlantic fog off New England late last night. Three hours later the Coast Guard intercepted this message: "The Andrea Doria has begun to abandon ship."

The Coast Guard reported that there were about 2000 passengers on both vessels.

Less than five minutes after the Andrea Doria's message, one of the rescuers that had raced to the scene radioed that it had taken the first lifeboat of survivors on board. The message came from the Cape Ann, a fruit ship.

There was no indication as to casualties.

At least eight Coast Guard cutters and two passenger liners were at the scene attempting to help some 1500 passengers and crewmen abandon the Andrea Doria, which was listing badly. The crash occurred 45 miles south of Nantucket.

Navy Dispatches Rescue Ship

Two Navy destroyers were being readied at Boston to rush for the scene. Two more destroyers and two fleet tugs were being dispatched from Newport, R.I.

The Doria listed its condition as "danger immediate." It radioed it was listing so badly lifeboats could not be lowered.

The passengers reportedly were using ladders to go over the side of the stricken ship. There were no indications that any passengers had jumped into the water.

Passenger liners at the scene included the huge luxury craft Ile de France and the smaller Cape Ann.

The Coast Guard said the Andrea Doria has requested medical assistance.

The Coast Guard said it did not need to send special medical aid from Boston because of medical facilities and doctors aboard most of the vessels it had already dispatched to the scene.

The request for medical assistance was the first indication there may be injuries as a result of the collision.

Was Due in N.Y. Today

The first SOS flashed from the stricken Andrea Doria, a 29,000-ton Italian liner out of Genoa, about 11:30 p.m. The ship was due to dock in New York City today with 1134 passengers aboard.

Minutes later, the Coast Guard said, the Stockholm, operated by the Swedish American Line, sent out a distress signal.

The Coast Guard said the Stockholm, a 12,600-ton, 510-foot motor ship, had its bow "stove in" and its No. 1 hold flooded. But the vessel appeared to be in less danger than the stricken Italian ship, built in 1953.

The Stockholm was outward bound. It left New York yesterday for Goeteborg.

The Stockholm messaged the Coast Guard early today that she could proceed to New York, indicating she was still watertight.

Escort Back Sought

The Stockholm asked the Ile de France:

"If you are going there (to New York) with passengers from the Andrea Doria, could we keep company?"

The Coast Guard said the Ile de France radioed back:

"Will proceed to New York full speed when all men rescued. Please ask another ship. My schedule imperative."

The Coast Guard said the Andrea Doria reported at 2:55 a.m.:

"Unable to use our boats. Passengers leaving ship by assistance of other ships."

The Andrea Doria sailed on her maiden voyage from Genoa, Italy, on Jan. 14, 1953. When she was introduced into transatlantic service Italian Line officials said she

Turn to Page 11, Column 1

Swaps Sets His Fourth World Record in Hollywood Park Sunset 'Cap

BY PAUL ZIMMERMAN
Times Sports Editor

Swaps added a fourth world's record to his amazing list of performances at Hollywood Park yesterday when he won the $110,500 Sunset Handicap, under restraint, with a remarkable time of 2:38 1-5 for the mile and five-eighths.

That clipped one and three-fifths seconds off the previous mark set by Ace Admiral in this same event seven years ago. In addition to his record shattering performances, Swaps also has a tie for a world's mark this year.

It was a wire-to-wire triumph in a race where he gave 21 or more pounds to the eight other starters. Only once did Jockey Bill Shoemaker let Swaps have his head and that was at the top of the home stretch when the chestnut colt built up such a lead that he was a winner by four and a quarter lengths over Honeys Alibi, eased up. Blue Volt was third.

Swaps paid $2.20 to win, the only spot opened to wagering in the race for the 43,442 enticed to the track by probably the greatest thoroughbred of all time. The victory was worth $64,000 to the Rex C. Ellsworth stable and increased the 4-year-old's earnings to $765,150.

With everything else badly beaten except perhaps for Honeys Alibi, Shoemaker let Swaps have his head briefly off the final turn. The great thoroughbred, carrying 130 pounds, might well have made a complete shambles of the race, and the world's record, had not Shoemaker eased him off after gaining a lead of six lengths.

(Other details of race and photos in Sports Section.)

Times Telephone Numbers
• MAdison 5-2345 for all calls except those concerning classified advertising.
• MAdison 9-4411 for all classified advertising calls.

Los Angeles Times

EQUAL RIGHTS
LIBERTY UNDER THE LAW — TRUE INDUSTRIAL FREEDOM

FINAL
ALL THE NEWS ALL THE TIME

VOL. LXXV IN FIFTEEN PARTS—PART ONE CC★★ SUNDAY MORNING, NOVEMBER 4, 1956 330 PAGES Copyright, 1956, by the Times-Mirror Company SUNDAY 20c

RUSS ATTACK HUNGARY, OUST NAGY

Polls Indicate Eisenhower Re-election

Democrats Given Edge to Continue Control of Congress

BY W. H. LAWRENCE
© New York Times News Service

NEW YORK, Nov. 3 — Surveys indicate that President Eisenhower and Vice-President Nixon will be re-elected Tuesday by comfortable majorities of both the popular and electoral votes.

The outlook, at the same time, is for continued Democratic control of Congress, unless there is a big swing behind the entire Republican ticket as a result of the outbreak of war in the Suez Canal area

Probable Results

Reports from New York Times correspondents, who have investigated political sentiment in the 48 States indicate these probable results:

For President Eisenhower—27 States with 285 electoral votes, or 19 votes more than required for a majority of the 531-member electoral college.

For Adlai Stevenson—Seven States with 76 electoral votes.

Leaning toward President Eisenhower — eight States with 99 electoral votes.

Leaning toward Stevenson—six States with 71 electoral votes.

As the campaign was drawing to a close, the Suez crisis appeared to be making votes for the Republicans. But it still seemed doubtful that President Eisenhower's margin would be as great as it was in 1952 when his popular vote plurality reached 6,621,242.

Carried 39 States

Four years ago, the President carried 39 States with 442 electoral votes. Stevenson carried nine States with 89 electoral votes.

This year teams of Times correspondents found President Eisenhower far more popular than the party he heads. The fact that he ended the Korean war and had kept the nation out of any other foreign conflicts was the reason most frequently given for pro-Eisenhower votes even before the sudden outbreak of hostilities in the Suez area.

Reports from Times correspondents placed these 27 States, with their indicated electoral votes, in the Eisenhower column:

Arizona, 4; California, 32; Colorado, 6; Connecticut, 8; Delaware, 3; Idaho, 4; Illinois, 27; Indiana, 13; Iowa, 10; Kansas, 8; Maine, 5; Maryland, 9; Massachusetts,

Turn to Page 14, Column 4

The March of Freedom

(An Editorial)

Informed of the main issues involved, and prepared to render a verdict that all will accept, millions of voters two days hence will go to the polls.

They will choose a President and Vice-President of the United States, elect a Congress and name hundreds of State and local officials.

To an extent greater in all probability than at any time in their history the American people will make decisions affecting not only their own welfare and security but that of many of the other peoples of the world.

Here, where men are free and where our institutions, firmly established, stand as the bulwark of our freedom, we may vote for whom we please and for the political philosophy we prefer.

In this process a free press is our best assurance that information will be made available without distortion and that editorial opinion will be given without fear.

Thus public opinion is formed, and thus the processes of our government are shaped and directed.

The election contest now drawing to its conclusion has been energetic, controversial and complex.

As a newspaper believing in the fundamental principles of the Republican Party, and being independent of any individual or factional influence within the party, The Times supports the Republican viewpoint and, for the most part, Republican nominees.

In this campaign The Times has given the Democratic Presidential nominee, Adlai Stevenson, and his running mate, Sen. Estes Kefauver, full opportunity to state their case in its news columns. On its editorial page The Times has expressed its assessment of the utterances of all the opposing candidates.

With few, if any exceptions The Times has remained convinced that the issues as discussed by President Eisenhower clearly show him to be a much sounder and greater leader, a better and surer hope for our security and welfare tnan Mr. Stevenson.

In this campaign the Democrats have been seeking issues because they sought and failed to find a leader.

The Times regards Mr. Stevenson's philosophy in 1956 as no improvement over the brand that lost him the election in 1952, and would regard his election to the Presidency as a misfortune bordering upon national calamity.

President Eisenhower, Vice-President Nixon and their associates in the national administration have given the people an effective, able, honest and devoted administration. In the relatively short time he has been in office President Eisenhower has done much, but his program is not completed.

It will be in the best interests of the people not only to re-elect the President but also to give him a working Republican majority in both the houses of Congress.

President Can't Work Full Time—Stevenson

Democratic Candidate Asks if Nation Wants Nixon as Its Commander in Chief

CHICAGO, Nov. 3 (AP)—Adlai E. Stevenson said tonight that President Eisenhower "now lacks the energy for full-time work at the world's toughest job." And he asked whether this nation wanted Vice-President Nixon as its Commander in Chief.

Text of Adlai Stevenson's Chicago speech begins on Page 20, Part I. Excerpts from his statement on natural resources begins on Page 24, Part I.

This was Stevenson's last major speech of the campaign. And in his remarks to a nationally televised rally of 19,000 persons in Chicago's Stadium he hit out again at a "part-time" President, and then referring to Nixon, he asked:

"Do you want this man as Commander in Chief to exercise power over war and peace?"

Stevenson said the Republicans have only one thing to offer, President Eisenhower.

And he raised questions of

Turn to Page 12, Column 1

Egypt Claims First Rebuff to Invasion

Allies Deny Repulse, Ignore U.N. Plea; 'At War,' Says Cairo

LONDON, Nov. 4 (Sunday) (AP)—Egypt claimed today Britain and France tried to land troops on the Suez Canal yesterday and were repulsed with losses by shore guns.

The British and French denied this.

The final statements through Saturday midnight from the British and French said their warplanes still were preparing the way for their land forces to start the offensive. Appeals from the U.N. for a softer course were brushed aside.

In Washington, the Egyptian Embassy released a statement received from Cairo, saying:

"We are at war with Britain and France."

Counters Claim

This apparently was intended to counter British-French references to the fighting as a police action.

President Nasser declared in a speech in Cairo:

"Egypt was always a grave for invaders. All empires collapsed whenever they invaded Egypt. We will fight and we will never surrender . . .

"We are waiting for the British and French in the canal and Nile delta."

Massing of Syrian, Iraqi and Jordanian troops in Jordan posed the threat of a second front on Israel's eastern border.

Israeli Advance

The Israelis said on the western front their advance patrols had reached the Suez Canal.

The main Israeli force was reported about nine miles from the waterway and moving freely throughout the Sinai Peninsula where fighting has ended.

An Israeli spokesman said thousands of prisoners had been taken, but most Egyptian officers had fled, leaving their units to be captured in Sinai.

Prime Minister Eden told the nation in a TV address that Britain and France acted to prevent a greater conflict in the Middle East.

He said he will make certain Israeli troops quit Egypt

Turn to Page 3, Column 3

Gusty Winds Will Increase Fire Danger

Clear skies and mild temperatures gave the Southland an ideal fall day yesterday but there were warnings of a high fire danger in mountain and foothill areas.

Under smogless skies, visibility stretched out to seven miles in early afternoon while the mercury climbed to a comfortable 71 deg. at 1:15 p.m. Relative humidity ranged from 51% at 12:30 a.m. to 14% at 1:15 p.m.

The Weather Bureau said a moderate sand storm condition existing in canyon areas will bring gusty northeasterly winds and increase the fire hazard today. Skies will be clear and free of smog.

THE WEATHER

No smog today. Morning burning permitted.

U.S. Weather Bureau forecast: Mostly clear today and tomorrow. Little change in temperature. High today about 72. Yesterday's high, 71; low, 50.

Dulles Undergoes Surgery; Eisenhower Active in Crisis

Secretary Stricken Suddenly

BY DON SHANNON
Times Washington Bureau

WASHINGTON, Nov. 3—Secretary of State Dulles today emerged in "good condition" from two and a half hours of abdominal surgery in which a perforated section of the upper colon was removed.

The 68-year-old Secretary was taken to Walter Reed Army Hospital this morning suffering from what was believed to be acute appendicitis.

President Informed

President Eisenhower was immediately informed of the result of the operation. The Chief Executive, who is sticking close to the White House to keep a continuous eye on foreign developments, was in steady contact with State Department aides.

The correct diagnosis was not known until after the operation was completed by Maj. Gen. Leonard D. Heaton, commanding officer of the hospital and surgeon who successfully operated on

Turn to Page A, Column 2

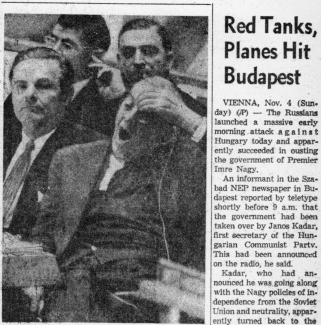

SHOWS STRAIN—Secretary of State Dulles yawns wearily in this, the last photo taken of him before he underwent emergency surgery. Occasion was the U.N. debate on the cease-fire resolution in Egypt crisis. At left is Ambassador Henry Cabot Lodge Jr.
(AP) Wirephoto

Red Tanks, Planes Hit Budapest

VIENNA, Nov. 4 (Sunday) (AP) — The Russians launched a massive early morning attack against Hungary today and apparently succeeded in ousting the government of Premier Imre Nagy.

An informant in the Szabad NEP newspaper in Budapest reported by teletype shortly before 9 a.m. that the government had been taken over by Janos Kadar, first secretary of the Hungarian Communist Party. This had been announced on the radio, he said.

Kadar, who had announced he was going along with the Nagy policies of independence from the Soviet Union and neutrality, apparently turned back to the Russians.

Heavy firing had been reported at the Parliament Building where the Nagy government had been installed. Nagy's fate was not known.

Attack Without Warning

The Austrian press agency said, without stating its source of information, that the Parliament Building had been occupied and Nagy taken prisoner with other members of his government.

Earlier, Soviet tanks, troops and planes made a general attack on Hungary without warning.

Premier Nagy in Budapest appealed to the world for help.

He spoke in an excited voice over Budapest radio.

The plea was broadcast in several languages.

"Soviet troops have opened an attack on Budapest at dawn with the clear intention to overthrow the lawful, democratic government of the Hungarian People's Republic," he said.

Troops Fighting

"Our troops are engaged in fighting the Soviets for right and freedom! The government is at its place!

"This we bring to the information of the Hungarian people and the entire world!"

Fierce fighting swept through Budapest, already burned and scarred by the anti-Soviet rebellion.

The Russians seized the military delegation commissioned by Nagy to negotiate for the withdrawal of all Soviet troops from Hungary.

After assuring rebel leaders only 48 hours ago that

Turn to Page 7, Column 1

U.S. Protects Hungarian Cardinal

UNITED NATIONS, N.Y., Nov. 4 (Sunday) (AP)—Ambassador Henry Cabot Lodge Jr. announced today that Josef Cardinal Mindszenty had taken refuge in the American Legation in Budapest.

Lodge made his disclosure at a dramatic predawn meeting of the U.N. Security Council which was called hurriedly to deal with the Soviet military attacks in Hungary.

The U.S. delegate read the Council details of the Soviet attack, as reported by the U.S. Legation.

Lodge said:

"If there ever was a time when action in the United Nations could literally be the life or death of a whole nation, this is the time."

U.N. Assembly Orders Mideast Police Force

Hammarskjold Told to Submit Plan in 48 Hours; Council Meets on Hungary

UNITED NATIONS, N.Y., Nov. 4 (Sunday) (AP)—The U.N. Assembly early today ordered Secretary General Dag Hammarskjold to submit a plan for an emergency international force to secure and supervise a cease-fire in the Middle East. The U.N. Security Council was called into a dramatic early morning session to take urgent action on the new Soviet military attacks on Hungary.

The Assembly voted 57-0 to approve a resolution presented by Canadian Foreign Secretary Lester B. Pearson and quickly seconded by U.S. Chief Delegate Henry Cabot Lodge Jr., calling for an international force. Nineteen countries abstained, including the Soviet bloc.

Set Deadline

The Assembly asked Hammarskjold to submit the plan for the U.N. force within 48 hours.

Just before the vote on the Canadian resolution, Pearson explained to the Assembly that no country will be listed on the force without its consent. It was also agreed that none of the countries involved in the fighting now—Britain, France, Israel or Egypt — will be asked to serve.

The Assembly then ap-

Turn to Page 3, Column 6

UCLA Upsets Stanford, 14-13; SC Beats WSC

UCLA rocked the Pacific Coast Conference race for the Rose Bowl bid by handing Stanford a stunning 14-13 defeat before 76,505 fans yesterday at the Coliseum and favored SC came from behind to defeat Washington State, 28-12, at Pullman, Wash.

As the nation's college football teams headed into the November homestretch, it appeared Oregon State and Minnesota had the inside track to the Rose Bowl.

Oregon State Wins

Oregon State went to the top of the PCC standings along with ineligible UCLA by beating Washington, 28-20. In another PCC clash Oregon upset California, 28-6.

Minnesota beat Pittsburgh in a 9-6 nonconference thriller; Michigan defeated Iowa by a 17-14 score. Elsewhere in the Big Ten Ohio State tripped Northwestern, 6-2; Michigan State trounced Wisconsin, 33-0, and Illinois tied with Purdue, 7-7.

Oklahoma, the nation's No. 1 ranking team, trailed Colorado, 7-19, at the half but rallied for a 27-19 victory, its 36th win in a row.

(Details in Sports Section)

FEATURES INDEX

Times Lists Tuesday Vote Suggestions

The Times' recommendations for Tuesday's balloting on candidates and propositions are listed today on Page 1, Part 2. The marked sample ballot form may be clipped and taken to the polls for reference.

On Other Pages

CRAWL MILE TO SUNLIGHT

50 of 113 Buried 42 Hours in Mine Without Food Brought Out Safely

SPRINGHILL, Nova Scotia, Nov. 3 (AP)—Fifty of the 113 men trapped in a coal mine explosion here for 42 hours walked or were carried alive to the surface today. More were known to be still alive deep in the mine tunnels.

Official reports at noon said there were 59 known survivors.

Four hours later, Mine Manager George Calder said the exact number who survived is still unknown. He said it was a false hope to expect that all the men still below the surface will be brought up alive.

Preliminary reports from rescue teams and miners now hospitalized indicated that at least 23 were killed in the blast that wrecked surface buildings and filled most of No. 4 Cumberland pit with flame, gas and rubble.

Charles Burton, the first miner to reach sunlight, said he thought about 40 were dead in the rock-filled shafts.

When announcement was made that the first survivors had been reached relatives keeping vigil at the pithead shouted for joy. Automobiles, with horns blaring, raced through this mining town of 8000. Nearly every family in the community was involved in the disaster.

Most of those reaching the surface walked out without assistance.

Burton said the men in his section of the mine began walking and crawling to the surface Thursday night. Today they met rescue crews on the way down.

Getting out meant crawling up a 30-degree slope for almost a mile.

Burton said the survivors had nothing to eat after Thursday noon, and no water except dirty mine water sucked from soaked rags.

At All Saints Hospital, doctors said the rescued men were in surprisingly good condition. Many walked about, talking with happy relatives.

STORY OF SANE IN MENTAL INSTITUTIONS WILL BE TOLD

"California's State mental hospitals are teeming with the sane . . ."

With this shocking statement, Veteran Times Reporter Jerry Hulse will unfold a heart-wrenching story of California's "unwanted," the thousands of sane, useful people who are confined to mental institutions merely because they are old.

Reporter Hulse has unearthed a depressing manifestation of the 20th century: The age of grandma-in-her-rocker at home is gone. Instead, an increasingly compassionless society has deprived many of its elder members of the inherent right to a dignified old age and a dignified death.

Hulse's articles will pull no punches on this subject, but they also will point out a few examples where whole communities have taken steps to solve this heart-breaking problem.

Be sure to read "The Unwanted." It starts next Sunday, Nov. 11, in The Times.

Times Telephone Numbers
- MAdison 5-2345 for all calls except those concerning classified advertising.
- MAdison 9-4411 for all classified advertising calls.

EQUAL RIGHTS

Los Angeles Times

LIBERTY UNDER THE LAW — TRUE INDUSTRIAL FREEDOM

PART 1
ALL THE NEWS
ALL THE TIME

VOL. LXXV — IN FIVE PARTS — CC* — WEDNESDAY MORNING, NOVEMBER 7, 1956 — 84 PAGES — DAILY 10c

EISENHOWER LANDSLIDE!

President and Sen. Kuchel Win in California

Record Vote Cast in State; Proposition 4 Loses by Wide Margin

California voters marched in unprecedented numbers yesterday to give President Eisenhower and Vice-President Nixon a smashing victory.

And only by a slightly smaller majority they voted to send Republican U.S. Sen. Thomas Kuchel back to Washington.

At 1 a.m., with 12,336 precincts of 24,984 reporting, the count stood:

Eisenhower 865,131
Stevenson 713,515

In the Senatorial race at the same time, 12,345 precincts reported:

Kuchel 747,093
Richards 651,848

On the basis of returns available at midnight it was estimated that in excess of 85% of the State's more than 6,400,000 voters went to the polls.

A whopping total of 5,500,000 votes was indicated.

In giving the State's 32 electoral votes to the Republican ticket California voters showed substantial disregard of a heavy Democratic lead over Republicans registered for the Tuesday balloting.

Below 1952 Margin

President Eisenhower's indicated majority in this State is expected to fall below the 700,000 majority he piled up in his contest with Adlai Stevenson here in 1952, but the Eisenhower victory of 1956 was mounting rapidly toward a probable 500,000 majority as returns continued to pour in.

On the basis of incomplete but fairly comprehensive returns the voters approved all of the various bond proposals on the ballot.

Proposition 4 Loses

Defeat by a wide margin was given Proposition 4—the controversial oil conservation measure.

Democratic leaders of the State had expected Los Angeles County to give the Stevenson-Kefauver ticket and Democratic Senatorial nominee Richard Richards a strong lead in this area.

And this trend was indicated in early returns, but as more comprehensive reports

Turn to Page 14, Column 2

All But Two of State's House Members Safe

All but two of California's members of the House of Representatives apparently swept to victory in yesterday's general election.

One incumbent who at a late hour still was battling for his political life was Republican Rep. Leroy Johnson of Stockton. He was opposed for re-election by Democratic Assemblyman John J. McFall of Manteca in the 11th Congressional District.

Baldwin in Trouble

The other was Republican Rep. John F. Baldwin Jr. of Martinez, who was opposed by H. Roberts Quinney of Vallejo, a Democrat.

Also to be decided was a neck-and-neck race between Jacqueline Cochran Odlum, Indio Republican, and D. S. Saund, Westmorland Democrat, for the 29th Congressional District at left vacant by the retirement of Republican Rep. John Phillips of Banning.

Three Unopposed

In the 20th Congressional District, where another vacancy was created by the death of Republican Rep. Carl Hinshaw, Assemblyman H. Allen Smith, a Republican of Glendale, was the apparent victor over Eugene Radding, a Democrat.

Three Representatives, all Democrats, were unopposed and were re-elected automatically. They are Reps. Clair Engle of Red Bluff,

Turn to Page 11, Column 1

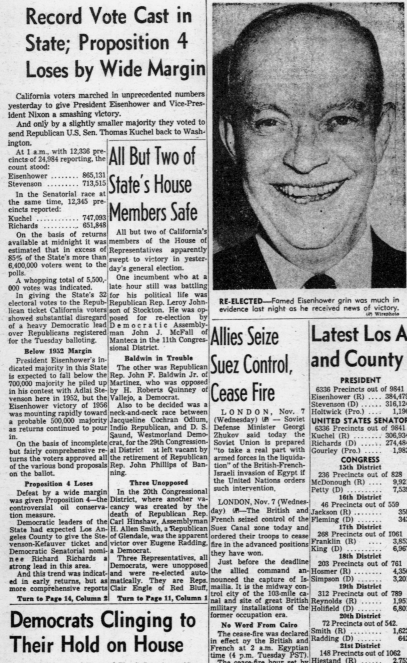

RE-ELECTED—Famed Eisenhower grin was much in evidence last night as he received news of victory. (AP) Wirephoto

ON WINNING TEAM—Vice-President Nixon again wins as Republicans piled up an impressive victory.

Allies Seize Suez Control, Cease Fire

LONDON, Nov. 7 (Wednesday) (AP) — Soviet Defense Minister Georgi Zhukov said today the Soviet Union is prepared "to take a real part with armed forces in the liquidation" of the British-French-Israeli invasion of Egypt if the United Nations orders such intervention.

LONDON, Nov. 7 (Wednesday) (AP)—The British and French seized control of the Suez Canal zone today and ordered their troops to cease fire in the advanced positions they have won.

Just before the deadline the allied command announced the capture of Ismailia. It is the midway control city of the 103-mile canal and site of great British military installations of the former occupation era.

No Word From Cairo

The cease-fire was declared in effect by the British and French at 2 a.m. Egyptian time (4 p.m. Tuesday PST).

The cease-fire hour set by Britain and France passed without official word from Cairo that Egypt had accepted.

Egyptian officials would not even say if their forces

Turn to Page 10, Column 5

Latest Los Angeles City and County Returns

PRESIDENT
6336 Precincts out of 9841

Eisenhower (R)	384,479
Stevenson (D)	316,124
Holtwick (Pro.)	1,196

UNITED STATES SENATOR
6336 Precincts out of 9841

Kuchel (R)	306,934
Richards (D)	274,484
Gourley (Pro.)	1,982

CONGRESS

15th District — 236 Precincts out of 828	
McDonough (R)	9,921
Petty (D)	7,539
16th District — 46 Precincts out of 559	
Jackson (R)	358
Fleming (D)	343
17th District — 268 Precincts out of 1061	
Franklin (R)	3,852
King (D)	6,967
18th District — 203 Precincts out of 761	
Hosmer (R)	4,356
Simpson (D)	3,201
19th District — 312 Precincts out of 789	
Reynolds (R)	1,951
Holifield (D)	6,801
20th District — 72 Precincts out of 542.	
Smith (R)	1,622
Radding (D)	642
21st District — 148 Precincts out of 1062	
Hiestand (R)	2,752
Stethem (D)	1,357
22nd District — 109 Precincts out of 717	
Holt (R)	3,273
Glasband (D)	2,221
23rd District — 165 Precincts out of 815	
Calvin (R)	1,726
Doylt (D)	4,023
24th District — 320 Precincts out of 639	
Lipscomb (R)	7,675
Porter (D)	5,022
25th District — 482 Precincts out of 1144	
Hillings (R)	6,523
Sobieski (D)	4,030
26th District — 293 Precincts out of 924	
Gibbons (R)	5,076
Roosevelt (D)	12,076

COUNTY SUPERVISOR
5th District
140 Precincts out of 2177

Jessup	1,807
Dorn	7,645

JUDICIAL
Superior Court, Office No. 28
3500 Precincts out of 9841

Bowron	41,128
Call	33,300

STATE MEASURES
3500 Precincts out of 9841

1—Veterans Bonds	
Yes	63,975
No	14,005
2—School Bonds	
Yes	63,897
No	12,205
3—State Construction Program	
Yes	55,263
No	16,203
4—Oil Conservation — 6336 Precincts out of 9841	
Yes	82,341
No	250,325
5—Beverage Establishments	
Yes	32,616
No	48,384

COUNTY MEASURES
3500 Precincts out of 9841

A—Juvenile Bonds	
Yes	49,652
No	13,308
B—Harbor Hospital Bonds	
Yes	48,004
No	13,811
C—Yacht Harbor Bonds	
Yes	38,815
No	19,009
D—Coroner	
Yes	46,426
No	11,716

Turn to Page 11, Column 7

President Hails Victory of New Republicanism

BY ROBERT HARTMANN
Times Washington Bureau Chief

WASHINGTON, Nov. 7 (Wednesday)—President Eisenhower today hailed his triumphant re-election as proof that "modern Republicanism has now proved itself and America has approved of modern Republicanism."

The President, accompanied by Mrs. Eisenhower, and Vice-President and Mrs. Nixon, appeared at a GOP victory rally in the Sheraton Park Hotel here about 15 minutes after Adlai Stevenson concluded his televised statement conceding the election to the Chief Executive. He made no mention of his twice-defeated Democratic foe.

President's Pledge

President Eisenhower concluded his victory statement with this pledge:

"With whatever talents the good God has given me, with whatever strength is in me, I will continue to work for 168,000,000 Americans here at home and for peace in the world."

With the victorious standard-bearers to enjoy their moment of victory were the President's son and daughter-in-law, Maj. and Mrs. John

Turn to Page 12, Column 1

457 to 74 Electoral Victory for President; Stevenson Concedes

BY THE ASSOCIATED PRESS

Dwight D. Eisenhower won re-election to the Presidency early today by the massive, overwhelming vote of a nation that heard and heeded his pledge of peace and prosperity.

Deep beneath an avalanche of Eisenhower victory votes were buried the Presidential ambitions of Democrat Adlai E. Stevenson—now and probably for all time.

Stevenson conceded at 1:20 a.m. EST a defeat that had been obvious and inevitable almost from the moment the ballot counting from yesterday's election got under way.

Control of Congress, now in Democratic hands, still dangled in tantalizing doubt.

Leading in 41 States

But for President Eisenhower there was a clear-cut, resounding vote of confidence from the great American electorate—and one of the most crushing landslide victories in the nation's political history.

The soldier-statesman became the first Republican to win a second term since William McKinley did it in 1900—56 years ago. McKinley was assassinated soon after his re-election.

The nation's Presidential picture at 4:00 a.m. (EST) stood at (popular vote): Eisenhower, 23,487,647; Stevenson, 17,215,529 in 96,833 of 154,844 precincts.

President Eisenhower led in 41 States with 457 electoral votes, Stevenson in seven with 74. Needed to win, 266.

Stevenson conceded his defeat in these words, addressed to President Eisenhower:

"You have won not only the election, but also an ex-

Turn to Page 16, Column 1

Democrats Clinging to Their Hold on House

Party Waging Nip-and-Tuck Battle to Keep Control of Senate in Many Seesaw Races

WASHINGTON, Nov. 7 (Wednesday) (UP)—Democrats clung tenaciously to their control of the House today and waged a nip-and-tuck battle with Republicans for continued leadership of the Senate.

On the basis of returns which were still far from complete, and with reversals always possible in close contests, Democrats had won or were leading in enough House races to give their party a working majority.

At 2 a.m. Republicans had elected nine Senators and the Democrats 12. Of 14 races still undecided, Republicans were ahead in seven and Democrats in seven.

30 GOP Holdovers

Republicans will have 30 holdovers in the new Senate and Democrats 31. If all undecided races were to go nally as they were inclining at 2 a.m., the new Senate would be controlled by the Democrats, 49 to 47.

However, the balance had swung back and forth repeatedly during the night as first one candidate and then another pulled into the lead. Especially hot was the seesaw race between Democratic Sen. Wayne Morse and former Interior Secretary Douglas McKay in Oregon.

Clements Trails

In New York, former Rep. Jacob K. Javits, Republican State Attorney General, defeated Democrat Robert F. Wagner Jr. for the seat now held by Democratic Sen. Herbert H. Lehman.

In Pennsylvania, Democrat Joseph Clark Jr. held a marginal lead over GOP Sen. James H. Duff.

In Kentucky, Sen. Earle C. Clements, the Senate Democratic whip, was a consistent underdog during long hours of counting in his race with

Turn to Page 5, Column 4

FEATURES INDEX

Heart Attack Fatal to Actor Paul Kelly

Actor Paul Kelly, 57, stricken with heart attack, dies. Story on Page 1, Part 3.

On Other Pages

THE WEATHER

Light to moderate smog today. Morning burning prohibited.

U.S. Weather Bureau forecast. Generally clear today and tomorrow. Not much temperature change. High today near 90. Highest temperature yesterday, 91; lowest, 55.

Stevenson Congratulates President on Victory

CHICAGO, Nov. 6 (AP) — Adlai E. Stevenson conceded tonight his second defeat for the Presidency.

Here is the text of a telegram sent by Stevenson to President Eisenhower:

"You have won not only the election, but also an expression of the great confidence of the American people. I send you my warm congratulations.

"Tonight we are not Republicans and Democrats, but Americans.

"We appreciate the grave difficulties your administration faces, and as Americans, join in wishing you all success in the years that lie ahead."

Talking to a group of volunteers at the Conrad Hilton Hotel, Stevenson said:

"I want to express my respect and thanks to a gallant partner in this great adventure—Estes Kefauver."

Stevenson went on to say:

"I wish there was some way I could properly thank you, one by one. I wish there was some way I could make you feel my gratitude for the support, the encouragement,

Turn to Page A, Column 4

State-by-State Returns in Presidential Election

BY THE ASSOCIATED PRESS

States—	*Voting Units	Units Rptng.	Popular Vote Eisenhower	Popular Vote Stevenson	Indicated Electoral Vote R	Indicated Electoral Vote D
Alabama	2,847	2,120	149,329	209,564	..	11
Arizona	521	150	69,683	40,252	4	..
Arkansas	2,396	837	31,346	44,317	..	8
California	24,984	12,336	865,131	713,515	32	..
Colorado	1,790	100	20,909	10,155	6	..
Connecticut	169	169	709,395	404,209	8	..
Delaware	336	315	92,328	75,162	3	..
Florida	1,782	1,212	512,308	361,097	10	..
Georgia	1,780	794	159,654	279,587	..	12
Idaho	893	45	8,012	4,778	4	..
Illinois	9,588	3,411	759,089	667,477	27	..
Indiana	4,384	1,975	628,643	429,713	13	..
Iowa	2,488	639	142,879	109,982	10	..
Kansas	2,976	891	136,174	72,976	8	..
Kentucky	4,056	1,667	300,875	240.807	10	..
Louisiana	2,040	669	98,760	81,048	10	..
Maine	630	627	249,024	101,978	5	..
Maryland	1,289	1,203	512,777	344,372	9	..
Massachusetts	1,963	708	424,066	338,066	16	..
Michigan	5,171	936	324,881	254,010	20	..
Minnesota	3,859	532	169,231	162,891	11	..
Mississippi	1,820	1,335	49,273	112,251	..	8
Missouri	4,560	2,846	490,294	481,318	13	..
Montana	1,081	20	1,242	762	4	..
Nebraska	2,103	336	46,562	23,771	6	..
Nevada	347	25	4,888	2,559	3	..
New Hampsh.	297	195	75,411	34,677	4	..
New Jersey	4,155	3,046	1,166,155	628,289	16	..
New Mexico	915	195	36,649	26,496	4	..
New York	11,132	7,900	2,907,857	2,052,533	45	..
N. Carolina	2,055	1,544	392,003	436,235	..	14
North Dakota	2,318	209	15,941	8,590	4	..
Ohio	12,097	2,035	345,573	195,424	25	..
Oklahoma	3,212	2,18[illegible]	262,729	233,129	8	..
Oregon	2,532	189	16,235	12,000	6	..
Penn.	8,808	5,275	1,425,990	1,245,079	32	..
Rhode Island	293	293	220,962	160,507	4	..
S. Carolina	1,580	1,470	74,455	130,335	..	8
S. Dakota	1,968	244	11,511	10,959	4	..
Tennessee	2,500	2,470	422,639	412,392	11	..
Texas	254	201	469,011	378,571	24	..
Utah	1,029	123	28,721	13,857	4	..
Vermont	246	219	77,354	26,890	3	..
Virginia	1,876	1,675	323,004	216,496	12	..
Washington	4,782	59	5,393	4,149	9	..
W. Virginia	2,810	943	143,621	125,154	8	..
Wisconsin	3,349	1,901	505,782	327,787	12	..
Wyoming	683	106	3,567	1,889	3	..

* Precincts except: Connecticut and Vermont, towns: Maryland and Ohio, places: New Jersey and New York, districts: Alabama, boxes, and Texas, counties.

Los Angeles Times
EQUAL RIGHTS — LIBERTY UNDER THE LAW — TRUE INDUSTRIAL FREEDOM

PART 1
ALL THE NEWS
ALL THE TIME

VOL. LXXVI — IN FOUR PARTS — CC ★ — FRIDAY MORNING, FEBRUARY 22, 1957 — 72 PAGES — DAILY 10c

Brooklyn Dodgers Buy L.A. Angels

Wrigley Sells Field and Franchise; Transfer to City in Future Seen

BY FRANK FINCH

Presaging an ultimate move to Los Angeles, the Brooklyn Dodgers yesterday bought Wrigley Field, the Los Angeles Angels, their territorial rights and Pacific Coast League franchise from P. K. Wrigley for an estimated $3,000,000.

Terms were not announced, but a Dodger official conceded that the transaction, whereby Wrigley's Chicago Cubs acquired the Ft. Worth franchise in the Texas League from Brooklyn, involved "a seven-figure sum."

Dodger Farm Team

Transfer of the Angel franchise to new ownership is subject to approval by the directors of the Coast League, a mere technicality. The directors are expected to vote early next month.

For the present, Brooklyn will operate the Angels as its No. 1 farm club, funneling the cream of its excess talent here, but Dodger President Walter O'Malley left local fandom with great expectations.

"It is my considered opinion that Los Angeles will be major league baseball by 1960," O'Malley declared at the Dodgers' training camp at Vero Beach, Fla.

He said even if the Dodgers didn't move here he wouldn't stand in the way if another big-league club drafted this territory "as long as we would be fully compensated."

Big Bank Account

There is $4,000,000 in the Dodger treasury which is earmarked for new stadium construction, Brooklyn having sold Ebbets Field and its Montreal park site last year.

The Dodgers, O'Malley said, want to spend the money as their share of a new downtown sports center in Brooklyn, but little progress

Turn to Page 1, Pt. 4, Col. 7

U.S. Missile Slips 'Leash,' Runs Wild

ALAMAGORDO, N.M., Feb. 21 (AP) — A Matador guided missile escaped its ground controls here today and roared northwest over New Mexico toward Colorado and Utah.

Holloman Air Development Center officials, from where the missile was fired, said it probably went down "somewhere in Western Colorado."

The missile did not carry an explosive warhead and was equipped only with instruments, officials said.

Fuel for One Hour

At Colorado Springs, Continental Air Defense Command officials expressed belief the missile landed in an isolated mountain area in Western Colorado or Eastern Utah.

A spokesman said if the missile caused damage when it landed the damage would have been reported. The missile had fuel for an hour, so it would have come down about 11:12 a.m.

The missile was launched at 10:12 a.m. and reportedly escaped electronic guidance eight minutes later.

It was the second runaway missile in three months for the Air Force. One of the missiles was fired from Florida in December and disappeared in the direction of Brazil. It was never found.

Reported Sighted

There were several reported sightings in Utah of today's missile as it streaked northward from New Mexico. None was confirmed.

Two jet interceptor planes from Utah's Wendover Air Force Base, sent aloft to intercept the wayward missile, returned to their base after vainly searching for the Matador. Jets in New Mexico and Utah also were ordered aloft.

BABY RESCUED—Marvin Gilmore leans from the window of a burning home in Camden, N.J., to drop a 9-month-old baby into the arms of spectators waiting on sidewalk. Gilmore earlier saved three other children. He later escaped himself. (AP) Wirephoto

Eisenhower's Appeal Rejected by Israelis

L.A. TOPS 41 STATES IN CAR REGISTRATION

Motor vehicle registrations in Los Angeles metropolitan area last year reached a record total of 3,114,774, a 5.8% increase over the 1955 figure.

The figures, compiled by the Los Angeles Chamber of Commerce research department, showed the area led 41 individual States in passenger car registrations and accounted for 47% of the vehicles registered in California.

Automobiles in the metropolitan area numbered 2,610,436, trucks 281,481, and other vehicles 222,857.

Refuse to Withdraw From Gaza

JERUSALEM, Israeli Sector, Feb. 21 (AP)—Israel refused tonight to bow to President Eisenhower's appeal to withdraw immediately behind the armistice lines. But Prime Minister David Ben-Gurion insisted the door is still open for negotiations.

Addressing Parliament after a critical Cabinet meeting, Ben-Gurion declared anew that Israel must have guarantees of freedom of navigation in the Gulf of Aqaba, plus security against raids from the Gaza Strip.

Seeking Further Talks

"No matter what may happen, Israel will not submit to restoration of the status quo in the strip," he said. Before last October's invasion Egypt controlled the strip, formerly a part of Palestine, under the 1949 armistice terms.

Ben-Gurion said Israel is seeking further negotiations to reach an understanding with the United Nations and with the United States.

Ambassador Abba Eban, returning tomorrow to Washington, will convey the Israeli government's position. He had been summoned home to give a firsthand report to Ben-Gurion and the Cabinet.

President Eisenhower last night called on Israel to meet U.N. demands that Israel withdraw from Gaza and from the Sharm El Sheik area at the mouth of the Gulf of Aqaba. He in effect held over Israel the threat of U.S. backing for punitive sanctions by the United Nations.

The 70-year-old Israeli Prime Minister told Parliament:

"We hope the door is not closed to further discussion. The government has decided to make a further effort to reach an understanding with the United States."

'Has No Need'

He said of the Aqaba Gulf coast:

"Israel has no need and no desire to occupy the desolate coastal strip of the (Tiran) straits. But she cannot withdraw from the area without effective security guarantees that the Egyptian dictator's acts of violence against her shipping—which the United Nations has tolerated for years—will not be repeated."

He made these proposals for Aqaba and Gaza:

"The government of Israel considers it essential that the U.N. emergency force should be stationed on the coast of the straits to safeguard freedom of navigation of Israeli shipping until peace is concluded with Egypt . . .

"As for the Gaza Strip, it

Turn to Page 8, Column 3

Knowland Says Position on Israel Is Unchanged

Three State Congressmen Back President on Sanctions; Four Take Senator's Stand

BY DON SHANNON, Times Washington Bureau

WASHINGTON, Feb. 21—Congressmen today took opposing points of view in reaction to President Eisenhower's speech to the nation last night calling on Israel to withdraw from the Gulf of Aqaba and the Gaza Strip or face U.N. sanctions.

The President himself added no comment to the debate that his speech touched off. The White House silence was at least partly due to a sore throat which has troubled President Eisenhower since his inauguration last month.

Knowland Comment

Senate Minority Leader Knowland (R) Cal., most vocal opponent of U.N. sanctions against Israel, commented in the wake of the President's speech:

"Nothing the President said last night changes my position. However, it was an excellent presentation of this government's position."

Knowland pointed out that "what he said relative to the importance for the survival of the United Nations of not having its resolution ignored applied equally well to the Soviet Union in the Hungarian situation." The Senator repeated that he does not oppose U.S. efforts to induce Israel to withdraw from Egypt.

"I am still opposed to the application of sanctions against Israel if they (the United Nations) are not prepared to apply them to other nations."

Johnson Also Unchanged

Senate Majority Leader Johnson (D) Tex., also remained unchanged in his opposition to pressure against Israel alone in the Mideast controversy.

In the House, Minority Leader Martin (R) Mass., strove for a neutral stand, commenting:

"Naturally we hope it (the

Turn to Page 9, Column 1

EISENHOWER GIVEN X RAY OF SINUSES

WASHINGTON, Feb. 21 (AP)—President Eisenhower had an X ray taken of his sinuses at Walter Reed Hospital today in connection with an examination for a cough. His doctor reported the X rays showed the sinuses were clear.

The President was at the hospital about 15 minutes.

White House Press Secretary Hagerty told newsmen that Maj. Gen. Howard M. Snyder, President Eisenhower's physician, refers to the cough as tracheitis and that the President is using a spray. Tracheitis is an inflammation of the windpipe.

Two Killed as Jet Crashes Near School

Illustrated on Page 3, Part I

HERTFORD, N.C., Feb. 21 (AP)—A pilotless Navy jet fighter crashed into a school bus garage here, fatally injuring a mechanic, and exploded barely 300 yards from a school where 550 pupils were in class. The pilot jumped to his death before the crash.

The disintegrating F3H Demon jet fighter careened toward the school but blew apart in the garage where two mechanics were at work.

One of the mechanics, J. Van Roach, 57, died several hours later. The second man was in critical condition with burns suffered in the crash but is expected to live.

The pilot, Ensign William W. Bell, Longton, Kan., bailed out but his parachute apparently did not open.

Coffee Price Cut Planned at Wholesale Level

NEW YORK, Feb. 21 (AP)—Major coffee roasters today announced reductions in the wholesale price of their regular and instant coffees, effective Monday.

Standard Brands, Inc., cut its Chase and Sanborn pressure-packed coffee by 3 cents a pound and instant coffee by 5 cents for a 6-ounce jar.

General Foods Corp. posted similar price reductions.

Living Cost Sets Record for Fifth Month in Row

Further Increase Expected for February; Food Bill Predicted to Pass Last Year's

WASHINGTON, Feb. 21 (UP)—The government's cost-of-living index rose to a new record high again last month for the fifth month in a row and a further rise is expected this month, it was announced today.

At the same time, the Agriculture Department predicted that the average American's 1957 grocery bill will average "a little higher" than last year although food consumption will remain about the same.

The report was issued by the Labor Department's Bureau of Labor Statistics. It said a .2% rise between December and January left the government's price index at 118.2% of the 1947-49 base period.

Expects Further Rise

As a result, some 1,400,000 workers in the automobile, farm equipment and aircraft industries will get an automatic penny-an-hour wage raise March 1. Their wages are tied to the index.

In discussing last month's price rise, Evan Clague, chief of the statistics branch, said he expects living costs to continue "to creep up like this again in February."

Films' Rhonda Fleming Hurt in Car Crash

Actress Rhonda Fleming was injured yesterday when her car collided with another near Pico and Sepulveda Blvds. in West Los Angeles.

The actress told officers she was driving west on Pico Blvd. in the middle lane when a car driven by John M. Ramsey, 17, of 2946 Midvale Ave., drove out of a filling station and head on into her car. She said her vision was obscured by a large van which was in the lane to her right and slightly ahead of her.

She was taken in an ambulance to Santa Monica Receiving Hospital and treated for cuts and bruises on her knees and elbows and a cut on the nose.

Crippled U.S. Plane Lands 42 Safely

MCMURDO SOUND, Antarctica, Feb. 22 (Friday) (AP)—A U.S. Air Force Globemaster headed for New Zealand with 42 men aboard was forced back here today by engine trouble.

The 92-ton transport plane landed smoothly on the ice runway on three of its four engines. It was high over the ice sea separating this snow-swept continent from New Zealand when carburetor trouble developed 743 miles out.

The 34 passengers were going home at the end of the U.S. Antarctic operation Deep Freeze II.

Unusually Long Test of Sirens Set for Today

An unusually long test of attack warning sirens will be made at 10 a.m. today, the Office of Civil Defense reminded residents.

A steady tone lasting one minute will be followed by a minute of silence and then two minutes of a warbling sound.

Residents are requested to send post cards to the OCD at Los Angeles 51, reporting their location and telling if they heard the sirens.

Joan at Stake Gets Singed in Film Scene

LONDON, Feb. 21 (AP) — The scene in which Joan of Arc is burned at the stake turned out to be almost too realistic today for Actress Jean Seburg. Fire burning around the feet of the American actress blazed up too high at a London movie studio where Otto Preminger is filming "St. Joan."

Somebody turned the gas too high and there was nothing the actress could do. She was chained to the stake and her screams were part of the script.

Extras shouting "Burn her" failed to realize Miss Seburg's plight until firemen dashed up with fire extinguishers. She suffered slight burns.

Pope Receives Envoy Zellerbach

VATICAN CITY, Feb. 21 (AP) — Pope Pius XII received James D. Zellerbach, new U.S. Ambassador to Italy, in private audience today and congratulated him on his appointment.

City's Record School Rolls Catch Planners Short on Teacher Needs

The growth of the Los Angeles city schools, boasting a massive and record enrollment of 555,971, caught the system's planners short yesterday in their estimates of anticipated registration for the spring semester and number of new teachers needed.

Superintendent of Schools Ellis A. Jarvis posted the new all-time high mark and at the same time informed the Board of Education that 2147 more students enrolled this month than predicted by principals, personnel and budget division authorities.

He said 63 teachers are needed in the elementary schools for regular classes and eight teachers for special training rooms for slow learners, in addition to 143 new teachers already on the job. Another 29 instructors should be available for further increases, he said, setting the total at 100.

William Brown, chief of the system's personnel division, said the estimate made for enrollment in the elementary division for this term was 276,644 but that 278,791 somehow popped up, throwing the schedule off considerably. Brown and Jack Crowther, budget director, aid Jarvis in second-guessing future needs in the vital employment picture.

Board Member Paul Burke said the pattern of growth in the past simply deviated this time—upward—and upset the estimates which in previous years were close to the actual figures.

The record enrollment includes 39,125 students on half-day or short sessions, 12,372 of them in San Fernando Valley elementary schools.

THE WEATHER

No smog today, morning burning permitted.

U.S. Weather Bureau forecast: Variable cloudiness but mostly sunny today and tomorrow. Little change in temperature. High today about 65. Yesterday's high, 65; low, 51.

Sun Peeks Out—More Expected

Considerable sunshine—rather than the sprinkles predicted—emerged from a partly cloudy sky yesterday and the weatherman forecast more of the same for today.

Temperatures yesterday ranged from a low of 51 deg. at 5:51 a.m. to a high of 65 at 12:28 p.m. Relative humidity was 80% at 5:30 a.m. and 49% at 12:28 p.m.

$2174 Tax Lien Names Chessman

SAN QUENTIN, Feb. 21 (AP) — The government has filed an income tax lien for $2174 against Convict-Author Caryl Chessman, it was disclosed today.

The lien is on income from his writings while in San Quentin Prison's death row.

Krishna Menon Reported Better

NEW YORK, Feb. 21 (AP)—The condition of India's roving Ambassador V. K. Krishna Menon was described today as better. Menon, 59, collapsed yesterday during a U.N. Security Council session.

King Saud Ends Visit in Morocco

RABAT, Feb. 21 (AP)—King Saud of Saudi Arabia flew to Tunisia today after a three-day Moroccan visit.

Klondike Kate of Yukon Gold Rush Fame Dies

SWEET HOME, Or., Feb. 21 (AP)—Klondike Kate, 77, died at her home here today.

Her real name, Mrs. Kate Rockwell Matson Van Duren, was known to her neighbors, but it was as Klondike Kate, the dance hall girl of Dawson City, that she had a continent-wide acquaintance.

No meeting of sourdoughs throughout the Pacific Northwest was complete without her and she filled the hours with reminiscences of the 1900 gold rush into the Yukon Territory.

Kate Rockwell was born near Oswego, Kan., in 1880. She went to New York as a stage-struck girl and later trouped through the country with touring groups. She was 20 years old when she found herself in Seattle with the gold fever at its height.

She took a ship north and later was fond of telling of her life in the dance halls where miners with gold in their pokes paid high prices for a dance and a sip of champagne with her.

For the past 45 years Oregon had been her home.

Her first husband was John Matson, a sourdough, who died many years ago. She was married to her present husband, William L. Van Duren, 10 years ago.

FEATURES INDEX

Art Aragon Convicted in Fight-Fixing Case

Golden Boy Art Aragon found guilty of offering bribe to boxing opponent. Story on Page 2, Part 1.

On Other Pages

Times Telephone Numbers
• MAdison 5-2345 for all calls except those concerning classified advertising.
• MAdison 9-4411 for all classified advertising calls.

Los Angeles Times

EQUAL RIGHTS — LIBERTY UNDER THE LAW — TRUE INDUSTRIAL FREEDOM

PART 1
ALL THE NEWS
ALL THE TIME

VOL. LXXVI | IN FOUR PARTS | CC ★★ | WEDNESDAY MORNING, SEPTEMBER 25, 1957 | 80 PAGES | DAILY 10c

Troops Patrol Little Rock; President Fears Anarchy

Eisenhower on Air, Offers Conciliation; Guards Federalized

BY ROBERT HARTMANN
Times Washington Bureau Chief

WASHINGTON, Sept. 24. President Eisenhower tonight told the nation he ordered U.S. troops into Little Rock to prevent anarchy and mob rule "under the leadership of demagogic extremists" opposed to school integration.

The President spoke a few hours after he ordered ground and air units of the Arkansas National Guard into Federal service to cope with the crisis. He also

[Text of President's Speech on Page 10, Part 1; Text of his Proclamation on Page 13, Part 1.]

authorized use of Federal troops to deal with the situation.

The Chief Executive took his dramatic action in an executive order declaring that his proclamation yesterday, demanding a cessation to the obstruction of justice, had not been obeyed.

Offer of Conciliation

Seeming to speak more in sorrow than anger, the President held out one more offer of conciliation in his radio talk. He confidently called upon the citizens of Arkansas "to assist in bringing to an immediate end all interference with the law and its processes."

"If resistance to the Federal court orders ceases at once," the Chief Executive told the nation over all major networks, "the further presence of Federal troops will be unnecessary and the city of Little Rock will return to its normal habits of peace and order."

"And," he added grimly, "a blot upon the fair name and high honor of our nation in the world will be removed."

Paratroopers on Duty

As President Eisenhower spoke from his White House office crack paratroopers of the Regular Army's 101st Airborne Division already were patrolling the streets of strife-torn Little Rock, under orders to prevent any further obstruction of Federal court orders to integrate the Central High School.

The Chief Executive flew here from his Newport vaca-

Turn to Page 14, Column 1

LITTLE ROCK, Sept. 24 (AP) — The Army flew 1000 battle-equipped regulars into Little Rock today and prepared to activate all Arkansas' National Guard to enforce Federal school integration following orders from President Eisenhower.

The planes loaded with soldiers landed at midafternoon at Little Rock Air Force Base. An officer called the City Hall, asked for and got permission to enter the city and for a police escort to handle the traffic.

President Eisenhower took decisive action after racial violence and riots swept small parts of the city yesterday and last night.

The President federalized the Arkansas National Guard and the State Air National Guard.

Out of State Control

His action placed the 9900 Guardsmen under Army control and took them out of State control.

Helmeted paratroopers from the famed 101st Airborne Division took up stations around Central High School tonight while hundreds of Little Rock people looked on.

There was no immediate reaction from the crowd.

The troops rolled in convoy from Little Rock Air Force Base shortly after dark.

At Ft. Campbell, Capt. Ivan Worrell, division public information officer, confirmed that a total of 1000 soldiers had been flown to Little Rock but said there was no word from Washington on whether more would be sent.

Force Divided

The total force split—one group going to the high school and the other to the National Guard Armory at Little Rock.

The high school's handsome, stone facade was lighted and the lights from the jeeps and the 2½-ton trucks, carrying the paratroopers, gave the scene almost a wartime look.

A number of Negro paratroopers were seen in the trucks.

However, it appeared that they were being assigned to duty away from the high school.

Confers With Police

A trailer, marked "explosives," and a weapons carrier came with the paratroopers.

The paratroopers wore battle dress.

Col. William A. Kuehn, commander of the troops at the high school, conferred with Asst. Police Chief Gene

Turn to Page 2, Column 6

JET CRASHES BUILDINGS—Wreckage of National Guard jet plane lies strewn on ground after plane hit second floor of house, shown by arrow, and crashed flaming into other buildings at 16433 Chase St. Both pilots of the T-33 were killed in crash. The occupant of the house suffered only minor injuries.
Times photo

GOMULKA THREATENS WAR IN BORDER STRIFE

WARSAW, Sept. 24 (AP)—Wladyslaw Gomulka, Poland's Communist Party chief, has warned that the only alternative to permanent recognition of Poland's disputed border with Germany is war.

Gomulka said Poland must build its armed forces and system of alliances to guard against what he called the "great danger for Eastern Europe" by a rearming West Germany.

Gomulka spoke at an automobile works in Warsaw and his speech was distributed tonight by the Polish Press Agency.

MIDEAST TENSIONS BLAMED ON RUSSIA

U.S. Note Lays Responsibility for Crisis to Soviet, Reaffirms Pledge on Independence

WASHINGTON, Sept. 24 (AP)—The United States laid to Russia "primary responsibility" for Mideast tensions and reaffirmed its determination to preserve independence in the area today.

In a note to the Soviet Foreign Ministry, similar to others being delivered by France and Britain, the State Department declared that Soviet arms shipments "set in motion a chain of events leading to the present dangerous situation."

The U.S. note deplored a previous Soviet note as "offensive in tone" and said it "cynically distorts" U.S. actions in the Middle East.

Impeded Efforts

It charged Soviet propagandists have impeded efforts to relax tensions and solve Middle East problems.

The American note cited the Middle East resolution, adopted by Congress this year, which pledged military-economic aid, including U.S. troops if requested, to Middle East countries subjected to Communist aggression.

"There should be no doubt," the U.S. note said, "that the government of the United States intends to carry out the national policy set forth in this resolution."

Latest in Exchange

The note was the latest in a series of diplomatic exchanges this year between Russia and the big western powers concerning the Middle East.

On Feb. 11, Russia proposed that the United States, Britain, France and Russia issue a joint statement opposing use of force in the Middle East.

The United States replied

Turn to Page 8, Column 3

AEC Reports Russ Fired Big Nuclear Blast

WASHINGTON, Sept. 24 The Atomic Energy Commission announced that the Soviet Union set off a large nuclear explosion today north of the Arctic Circle.

The commission said the force of the explosion was measured in megatons—or millions of tons of TNT.

While not stated by the AEC, the strength would indicate a hydrogen bomb. The yield of hydrogen bombs is measured in megatons, while that of atomic bombs is customarily measured in kilotons, or thousands of tons of TNT.

Maneuvers Held

The location of the explosion raised the possibility that the test was conducted in connection with the Soviet naval maneuvers in the Barents Sea above the Arctic Circle.

The AEC announcement was issued shortly after the official Soviet news agency Tass said in a broadcast over Radio Moscow that as part of the training of Soviet military forces atomic and hydrogen weapons had been exploded. The Tass announcement said the explosions were carried out "in nonpopulated localities and at great heights."

The explosion was the first to be announced by the AEC as taking place "north of the Arctic Circle." In 1956 President Eisenhower disclosed that Russia had two atomic testing grounds—in Southwest Siberia north of India and Pakistan, and the Barents Sea area.

Mrs. F. D. R. Will See Khrushchev

MOSCOW, Sept. 24 (AP) — Mrs. Franklin D. Roosevelt has received an invitation to visit the Communist Party Leader, Nikita Khrushchev, at his Yalta vacation home. She is flying there Thursday.

U.N. Assembly Shelves Red China Bid for Seat

Lodge Recalls American Losses in Korea; Vote Is Rebuff for India and Russia

UNITED NATIONS, Sept. 24 (AP)—The General Assembly decided tonight to shelve for another year the question of seating Red China in the United Nations.

The action was a rebuff for India and the Soviet Union, which had led an attempt to get the issue placed before the 82-nation Assembly for a full debate.

By a vote of 47 in favor, 27 against and seven abstentions, the Assembly adopted a U.S. proposal to postpone considering Communist China's membership in the United Nations at least until the fall of 1958.

Recalls Korea Cost

On an identical resolution last year, the vote was 47 to 24 with eight abstentions.

Voting against shelving the question were the Soviet bloc, the Scandinavian countries, and several Asian and Middle East nations including Syria and Egypt.

U.S. Delegate Henry Cabot Lodge said the United States "suffered 140,000 casualties in Korea, of which 35,000 were deaths, and these were almost all inflicted by the Chinese Communists, and that is something it is only human for us to remember."

Red Bases in Mideast?

Earlier, British Foreign Secretary Lloyd said there is reason to believe the heavy Soviet arms shipments to the Middle East may be intended to stock forward bases for the Soviet Union itself.

He told the Assembly that Britain views the situation in Syria "with grave concern." He also expressed concern over the bitter propaganda war being waged by the Russians against the governments of Iraq, Iran, Lebanon and Jordan.

Downtown Rubber Plant Hit by Fire

A rubber plant in downtown Los Angeles was hit last night by a roaring fire which sent a cloud of greasy, black smoke across the city's warehouse section.

Six Fire Department companies under Asst. Chief Pat Ferguson were called out to fight the blaze in the United Rubber Corp. building at 821 Traction Ave.

Flames Visible

Flames were visible in the Civic Center a few blocks away.

Fireman Harry J. Lambert, 36, Engine Company 6, was treated at the scene after receiving a cut nose from flying glass.

The fire in the one-story concrete block structure was brought under control in about 20 minutes with damage only to the rubber material inside and the roof. Cause of the blaze was undetermined.

The rubber plant is in a warehouse and light manufacturing section of the city near 3rd and Alameda Sts.

Sheik's Son Wins $8000

NEW YORK, Sept. 24 (AP) — Kamal Monsour, the son of an Arab sheik, won $8000 tonight on the CBS television show $64,000 Question.

Monsour who arrived in this country from his home in Israel two weeks ago, answered questions on Islam, Christianity and Judaism. He will return to the program next week.

Coy, Former FTC Chief, Dies

INDIANAPOLIS, Sept. 24 (AP)—Wayne Coy, 53, former chairman of the Federal Communications Commission, suffered a heart attack and died tonight.

PAY RAISED AT NORTH AMERICAN

A pay raise of 3 cents an hour for its 20,000 hourly and weekly employees in Southern California was announced yesterday by North American Aviation, Inc.

Designated as a "cost-of-living allowance," the pay boost goes into effect Oct. 28 and is based on the consumer price index for last Aug. 15.

Salaried employees are not affected.

Four Die as Bomber Hits Ohio House

Illustrated on Page 3, Part 1

DAYTON, O., Sept. 24 (AP) An Air Force B-26 twin engine bomber, coming in for an emergency landing at Wright-Patterson Air Force Base here, plunged 70 feet into a suburban housing development today, killing four persons and injuring at least one.

The plane ripped sections from two houses and demolished a third.

Engine Trouble

Air Force officials said the medium-sized bomber developed engine trouble immediately after takeoff and was returning to the base.

Killed instantly in the crash, Air Force officials reported, were the plane's pilot and copilot and two occupants of the demolished house.

The Air Force withheld names of the crew members pending notification of next of kin, but the other dead were identified as Mrs. Mildred Van Zant and Walter Joseph Geisler, reported to be Mrs. Van Zant's brother-in-law.

Egypt Seizes Israeli Ship

PORT SAID, Egypt, Sept. 24 (AP)—Egyptian authorities said an Egyptian coast guard patrol craft today intercepted an Israeli fishing vessel in Egyptian territorial waters 90 miles east of Port Said and brought it to this Mediterranean port.

Carrier Midway Will Sail Again

BREMERTON, Wash., Sept. 24 (AP)—The aircraft carrier Midway will be recommissioned here Monday after being modernized at a cost of $50,000,000.

More than 1400 sailors were scheduled to arrive here tomorrow to join the crew of the carrier.

Two Pilots Killed as Jet Crashes Home

A Sepulveda housewife stood frozen in her kitchen as she watched a T-33 National Guard jet strike her home killing both pilots late yesterday.

The plane occupants were identified as Capt. Joseph C. Bryant, 28, of 941-E W Huntington Drive, Arcadia, and Lt. Edison B. Gaston, 32, of 2423 Patricia St., Los Angeles.

The plane of the 115th Fighter-Interceptor Squadron took off from Van Nuys Airport, plowed into high-tension lines and then crashed into the home at 16433 Chase St.

This is one of the few homes still occupied in the area being cleared north of the airport for extension of the runway.

Strikes Guest House

After hitting the second-story section of the home, the plane then crashed through a guest house, bath house, garage and storage shed—all on the same property.

Flames spread across each of the structures.

The sole occupant of the house at the time of the crash—Mrs. Beatrice Stone, 42—told this story:

"I was sitting in the kitchen and saw the plane coming. It was already flaming. The flames were shooting out all around.

"I sat stunned. It seemed

Turn to Page 21, Column 2

L. B. Mayer Goes Back to Hospital

Motion Picture Producer Louis B. Mayer, 72, who returned to his home last Sept. 16 after six weeks of confinement at Stanford Hospital, San Francisco, for treatment of severe anemia, is in UCLA Medical Center for additional treatment.

Mayer spent only three days at home, where a hospital room was set up, when he was taken to UCLA for blood and platelet transfusions. (A platelet is a small, colorless corpuscle concerned in coagulation of blood and contraction of a clot.)

A hospital spokesman said Mayer's condition is satisfactory.

150 WILL WIN IN FUN CONTEST

One hundred fifty Times and Mirror-News readers will win new wealth in the $35,000 Fun for All Contest. Full details are on Page 6, Part III of today's Times.

Ladd, Olivia de Havilland Suffer Burns

CEDAR CITY, Utah, Sept. 24 (AP)—Members of a Hollywood movie company, including Film Stars Alan Ladd and Olivia de Havilland, suffered minor but painful burns today when a gust of wind blew flames at them during a barn-burning scene.

In addition to Ladd and Miss De Havilland, Ladd's 10-year-old son David and three studio technicians suffered burns. The actors were behind controlled gas fires in the barn scene when a gust of wind swept the flames at them, dropping embers among the group.

De Scaffa Ultimatum

MEXICO CITY, Sept. 24 (AP) — Officials said Actress Francesca De Scaffa will be fined and deported unless she voluntarily leaves Mexico by tomorrow.

Temperature Sizzles Up to 90 Deg. With Eye-Stinging Pall of Smog

Temperatures sizzled up to 90 deg. yesterday in an eye-stinging pall of smog.

Both heat and smog will return today. The predicted high is 88 deg. The Air Pollution Control District said a smog alert is possible.

It was 100 in Van Nuys, 97 in Burbank and 95 in Pasadena.

The high was at 12:36 p.m. It was the hottest since last Aug. 27, when the high was 92, and the 28th time this year that temperatures have reached or topped 90.

Although there were many complaints of smog, the Air Pollution Control District said that ozone readings were fairly low. The highest was .30 part of ozone per million parts of air in the downtown, Rivera and Azusa districts. Although the smog was worse, the ozone readings were much lower than those of Monday.

An alert is declared when the reading reaches .50 part. The APCD said an alert is possible today. There has been only one this year—last July 31.

The low temperature yesterday was 63 at 5:23 a.m. Relative humidity reached 81% at 5 a.m., but dropped to 33% at 12:36 p.m. Fog which had been predicted arrived on schedule, but blanketed only some coastal sections.

Morning fog is predicted again today. The afternoon will be generally clear.

THE WEATHER

Smog today. Possible alert. No burning until 4 p.m.

U.S. Weather Bureau forecast: Generally sunny today and tomorrow but late night and early morning fog along the coast. Little change in temperatures. High today, 88. High yesterday, 90; low, 63.

INDEX OF FEATURES

A's in L.A.? That's in Works Too!

Walter O'Malley and his Dodgers may be beaten to the punch in landing L.A. as major league territory. Del Webb is reported ready to sell Yankee holdings and bring the Kansas City A's here. Story in Sports Section.

ON OTHER PAGES

Times Telephone Numbers
• MAdison 5-2345 for all calls except those concerning classified advertising.
• MAdison 9-4411 for all classified advertising calls.

Los Angeles Times

EQUAL RIGHTS · LIBERTY UNDER THE LAW · TRUE INDUSTRIAL FREEDOM

PART 1
ALL THE NEWS
ALL THE TIME

VOL. LXXVI | IN FOUR PARTS | CC ★ | SATURDAY MORNING, OCTOBER 5, 1957 | 44 PAGES | DAILY 10c

Russia Launches First Earth Satellite 560 Miles Into Sky

'Moon' Carried Up by Multiple Rocket; Radio Signals Heard

MOSCOW, Oct. 5 (Saturday) (AP) — The Soviet Union announced today it has the world's first artificial moon streaking around the globe 560 miles out in space. A multiple-stage rocket launched the earth satellite yesterday, the Russians said, shooting it upward at about five miles a second.

They said the satellite, a globe described as 23 inches in diameter and weighing 185 pounds, can be seen in its orbit with glasses and followed by radio through instruments it carries.

In New York radio signals on the wave length of the Soviet moon—sounding as a deep "beep, beep, beep"—were picked up by electronic engineers of the National Broadcasting Co. The British Broadcasting Corp. in London reported similar reception.

Victory for Russia

In thus announcing the launching of the first earth satellite ever put in a globe-girdling orbit under man's controls, the Soviet Union claimed a victory over the United States. The two big powers had been in a hot but mainly secret race to be first to probe space with spheres laden with instruments.

The Moscow announcement said:

"The successful launching of the first man-made satellite makes a tremendous contribution to the treasure house of world science and culture . . .

Space Travel Predicted

"Artificial earth satellites will pave the way for space travel and it seems that the present generation will witness how the freed and conscious labor of the people of the new Socialist society turns even the most daring of man's dreams into reality . . ."

In a special bulletin early this morning the Soviet Tass agency said the Russian moon "is now revolving around the earth at the rate of one circuit every hour and 35 minutes.

The launching occurred just three months and four days after the opening of the International Geophysical Year.

In Cambridge, Mass., officials at the Smithsonian Astrophysical Observatory said that sightings of the satellite had been reported last night by moonwatch stations across the country, including Whittier, Cal., Terre Haute, Ind., and Columbus, O.

Will Launch More

The observatory is the central point for collection of data on satellite observation by teams of "moon-watchers" in many parts of the world.

The Russian broadcast said the Soviet Union plans to launch several more earth satellites in the next year. It declared the development will open a way for travel to the planets.

Moscow said the satellite is fitted with steel radio transmitters continuously sending signals earthward on the 15 and 7.5-meter wave lengths and easily received by a broad range of amateur sets. Its announced weight of about 185 pounds is more than eight times the weight of a projected U.S. earth satellite.

Moscow described the signals as of about 3/10 of a second long with a pause of the same length. The two frequencies alternate in signaling, Moscow radio said.

The broadcast said Soviet satellites planned later will

Turn to Page 4, Column 1

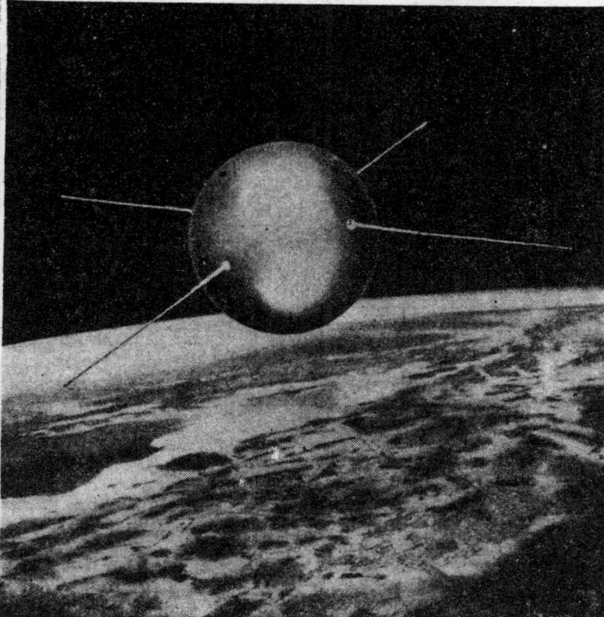

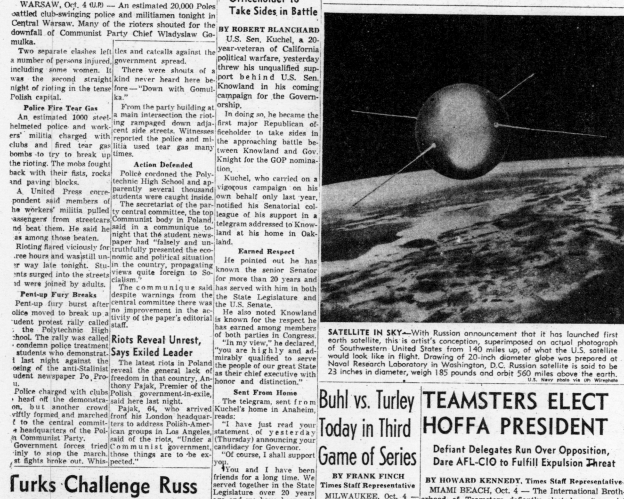

SATELLITE IN SKY—With Russian announcement that it has launched first earth satellite, this is artist's conception, superimposed on actual photograph of Southwestern United States from 140 miles up, of what the U.S. satellite would look like in flight. Drawing of 20-inch diameter globe was prepared at Naval Research Laboratory in Washington, D.C. Russian satellite is said to be 23 inches in diameter, weigh 185 pounds and orbit 560 miles above the earth.
U.S. Navy photo via (AP) Wirephoto

Polish Capital Swept by Riots

20,000 Battle Police and Militia, Shouting 'Down With Gomulka'

WARSAW, Oct. 4 (U.P.) — An estimated 20,000 Poles battled club-swinging police and militiamen tonight in Central Warsaw. Many of the rioters shouted for the downfall of Communist Party Chief Wladyslaw Gomulka.

Two separate clashes left a number of persons injured, including some women. It was the second straight night of rioting in the tense Polish capital.

Police Fire Tear Gas

An estimated 1000 steel-helmeted police and workers' militia charged with clubs and fired tear gas bombs to try to break up the rioting. The mobs fought back with their fists, rocks and paving blocks.

A United Press correspondent said members of the workers' militia pulled passengers from streetcars and beat them. He said he was among those beaten.

Rioting flared viciously for three hours and was still under way late tonight. Students surged into the streets and were joined by adults.

Pent-up Fury Breaks

Pent-up fury burst after police moved to break up a student protest rally called at the Polytechnic High School. The rally was called to condemn police treatment of students who demonstrated last night against the closing of the anti-Stalinist student newspaper Po Prostu.

Police charged with clubs to head off the demonstration, but another crowd swiftly formed and marched it to the central committee headquarters of the Polish Communist Party.

Government forces tried vainly to stop the march. Fist fights broke out. Whistles and catcalls against the government spread.

There were shouts of a kind never heard here before—"Down with Gomulka."

From the party building at a main intersection the rioting rampaged down adjacent side streets. Witnesses reported the police and militia used tear gas many times.

Action Defended

Police cordoned the Polytechnic High School and apparently several thousand students were caught inside.

The secretariat of the party central committee, the top Communist body in Poland, said in a communique tonight that the student newspaper had "falsely and untruthfully presented the economic and political situation in the country, propagating views quite foreign to Socialism."

The communique said despite warnings from the central committee there was no improvement in the activity of the paper's editorial staff.

Riots Reveal Unrest, Says Exiled Leader

The latest riots in Poland reveal the general lack of freedom in that country, Anthony Pajak, Premier of the Polish government-in-exile, said here last night.

Pajak, 64, who arrived from his London headquarters to address Polish-American groups in Los Angeles, said of the riots, "Under a Communist government, those things are to be expected."

Kuchel Gives Support to Knowland

First Major GOP Officeholder to Take Sides in Battle

BY ROBERT BLANCHARD

U.S. Sen. Kuchel, a 20-year-veteran of California political warfare, yesterday threw his unqualified support behind U.S. Sen. Knowland in his coming campaign for the Governorship.

In doing so, he became the first major Republican officeholder to take sides in the approaching battle between Knowland and Gov. Knight for the GOP nomination.

Kuchel, who carried on a vigorous campaign on his own behalf only last year, notified his Senatorial colleague of his support in a telegram addressed to Knowland at his home in Oakland.

Earned Respect

He pointed out he has known the senior Senator for more than 20 years and has served with him in both the State Legislature and the U.S. Senate.

He also noted Knowland is known for the respect he has earned among members of both parties in Congress.

"In my view," he declared, "you are highly and admirably qualified to serve the people of our great State as their chief executive with honor and distinction."

Sent From Home

The telegram, sent from Kuchel's home in Anaheim, reads:

"I have just read your statement of yesterday (Thursday) announcing your candidacy for Governor.

"Of course, I shall support you.

"You and I have been friends for a long time. We served together in the State Legislature over 20 years ago and we have been colleagues in the U.S. Senate these last five years.

"All the members of the Senate, Democrats as well as Republicans, have the highest respect for you. In my view, you are highly and admirably qualified to serve the people of our great State as their chief executive with honor and distinction."

Turks Challenge Russ to Drop Mideast Policy

Firmly Deny Plotting to Attack Syria; Suggest Moscow Stop Sending Arms

ANKARA, Oct. 5 (Saturday) (AP) — Turkey today sharply rejected Soviet charges of planned aggression against Syria and challenged Moscow to abandon its own Middle East policy.

The Turkish government released the text of a letter from Premier Menderes to Soviet Premier Bulganin.

"This country (Syria) is arming itself speedily and far beyond its logical defensive needs," Menderes said.

"Or rather it perhaps is being turned into an armament depot eventually to be used by others.

"If establishment of the true friendship based on mutual trust between our two countries is desired, as you in your message," the Turkish leader said, "discontinuance of a policy pursued in the Middle East, and especially in Syria, would greatly contribute to this end."

Menderes' letter was in reply to one from Bulganin Sept. 13, accusing Turkey of threatening to provoke a third world war by massing troops on the Syrian border.

The Turkish note said, "On this occasion we wish to state once again and most finally, we do not have the smallest aggressive aim toward any of our neighbors."

Other Mideast news on Page 5, Part 1.

Coty Bids Mollet Form New Cabinet in France

PARIS, Oct. 4 (AP)—Socialist Guy Mollet, who set a postwar record by holding the Premier's office for 15 months, was virtually drafted by President Coty today to try to form a new government.

He said neither yes nor no when asked to be Premier, but promised the President to see what support he could rally. He will not give a definite answer until Sunday.

He did not think much of his prospects. He told reporters he did not think it would be possible to form a Cabinet. He said he had finally agreed to try only on the President's insistence.

Coty took action on the fourth day of the crisis, which broke Monday when Premier Bourges-Maunoury was defeated on his Algeria home rule bill.

The same political figures who had visited Coty during the past three days started filing in and out of Mollet's office.

Since the two previous crises have been provoked by the center groups in the National Assembly, Mollet sought assurances of their support before agreeing to move ahead. There was little chance he would get them.

THE WEATHER

No smog today.

U.S. Weather Bureau forecast: Scattered cloudiness but mostly sunny today with high near 75. Partly cloudy and slightly cooler tomorrow with chance of showers. Yesterday's high, 75; low, 59.

Cool Weather Continues as High Hits 75

Cool weather continued yesterday as temperatures ranged from 59 deg. at 5:24 a.m. to 75 deg. at 12:36 p.m.

There will be little change today.

Scattered clouds are predicted for today, with the weatherman forecasting possible showers for tomorrow.

Relative humidity yesterday ranged from 86% at 4 a.m. to 45 % at 12:36 p.m.

There was little smog. There will be none today, the Air Pollution Control District said.

Three Men Swept to Deaths by Slide on Highway

SEATTLE, Oct. 4 (AP) — A great chunk of mountainside fell away late today on the main roadway across the Cascade Mountains east of here, sweeping three men to their deaths and injuring another.

The slide poured across U.S. Highway 10 on what is known as the Snoqualmie Pass Highway.

The men who died were identified as Clarence Sluetter, 35, a State Highway Department road crew foreman of Snoqualmie Pass summit; Knute Johnson, about 40, a construction worker of Roslyn, Wash., and Carson R. Mundis, a truck driver from Yakima.

Buhl vs. Turley Today in Third Game of Series

BY FRANK FINCH
Times Staff Representative

MILWAUKEE, Oct. 4 — New York's world champions remain a 6-7 choice to retain their title as World Series warfare resumes here tomorrow, but today it was tough to find a single Yankee rooter in this stronghold of beer, bratwurst and the Braves.

"We're definitely going to win the Series now," writes Red Schoendienst, a local journalist who also plays second base for the Braves.

"We'll take the Yanks in three straight," promises Fanny Flugle, our favorite female taxi driver.

Sunny Weather

Brisk, sunny weather, in the high 60s and with a moderate wind that is expected to help the right-handed hitters, looms for the tussle which will break the 1-1 deadlock that exisits since the opening skirmishes in New York.

It'll be Bob Buhl (18-7) for Milwaukee against an-

Turn to Page 1, Pt. II Col. 3

Nixon Secludes Self in Florida

MIAMI, Oct. 4 (UP)—Vice-President Nixon was vacationing in seclusion today at an ocean front hotel on Biscayne Key.

A close friend said Nixon was "tired and just wants to take it easy."

TEAMSTERS ELECT HOFFA PRESIDENT

Defiant Delegates Run Over Opposition, Dare AFL-CIO to Fulfill Expulsion Threat

BY HOWARD KENNEDY, Times Staff Representative

MIAMI BEACH, Oct. 4 — The International Brotherhood of Teamsters defiantly elected controversial James R. Hoffa its president here today over the weak opposition of two reform candidates.

Results of the first roll-call vote — 1208 for Hoffa, 313 for William A. Lee, Chicago, seventh-ranking vice-president, and 140 for Thomas J. Haggerty, secretary-treasurer of a Chicago milk wagon drivers' local — gave Hoffa a 2½-to-1 margin and justified his victory predictions. He needed only a plain majority of the 1753 eligible delegates.

Mandate Seen

Hurdling in one jump the gap between ninth vice-president and the $50,000-a-year top job in the giant Truckers Union, Hoffa took the election result as a mandate to dare the AFL-CIO to carry out its threat to expel the Teamsters from the ranks of organized labor.

The AFL-CIO had given the Teamsters until Oct. 24 to dump Hoffa, retiring President Dave Beck, Vice-President Frank W. Brewster of Seattle and Sidney L. Brennan of Minneapolis in response to charges by the AFL-CIO ethical practices committee that the Teamster leadership was substantially dominated by corrupt influences.

Hoffa, in an acceptance speech, was quick to convert the convention's defi-

Turn to Page 6, Column 1

State of Siege Proclaimed in Buenos Aires

BUENOS AIRES, Oct. 4 (AP)—The Argentine government, troubled by labor unrest, announced tonight it has declared a state of siege in Greater Buenos Aires. This is a modified form of martial law.

The Interior Ministry said the state of siege was decreed to prevent possible sabotage in connection with strikes.

The military guard around the cable office, where employees are on strike, was increased tonight.

Labor sources asserted that about 150 labor leaders had been arrested under the state-of-siege setup.

Author Michener Among 13 on Ditched Plane

AGANA, Guam, Oct. 4 (UP) A U.S. Air Force C-47 transport plane ditched in the Pacific two miles north of Iwo Jima today but all 13 persons aboard, including Author James Michener, escaped unhurt.

The Air Force said the twin-engine plane had engine failure shortly after taking off from Iwo, where it stopped to refuel on a flight from Guam to Japan.

$35,000 CONTEST DETAILS INSIDE

New entries in the $35,000 Fun for All contest close one week from today. Details of the competition appear on Page 8, Part 2 of today's Times.

THREE-SECOND VIEW

2 Whittier Watchers Briefly See Satellite

Illustrated on Page 4, Part I

Two members of the Whittier Amateur Astronomers Association, alerted last night as part of Operation Moonwatch, reported sighting the Russian satellite launched yesterday.

Paul Nemecek, 39, of 7727 Glengarry Ave., Whittier, and Eugene Enyard, 39, of 1256 Cedar Grove Ave., Whittier, said they sighted the satellite moving in a northeast to southwest direction about 8 p.m.

The association manned 10 special satellite observing telescopes for more than three hours last night at the Whittier College Observatory on College Hill east of the campus.

The scanners watched a narrow strip of the sky from north to south with special wide-angle, low-magnification telescopes. They said the satellite passed through their field of vision in about three seconds. They were reluctant to discuss their find until they received clearance from the Smithsonian Astrophysical Observatory at Cambridge, Mass.

Observatories at Griffith Park, Mt. Wilson and Mt. Palomar last night reported their astronomical equipment was inadequate to track the satellite.

Spokesmen said it was too close to the earth and moving too fast for large telescopes to follow in their narrow fields of vision.

INDEX OF FEATURES

Pittsburgh Defeats SC Trojans, 20-14

Pittsburgh's Panthers defeated the winless Southern California Trojans, 20-14, before 43,489 football fans at the Coliseum last night. Story in Sports Section.

ON OTHER PAGES

AIR FORCE PLANES COLLIDE; 2 KILLED

RACE RESULTS

VOL. LXXVII IN FOUR PARTS ★★★ SATURDAY MORNING, FEBRUARY 1, 1958 46 PAGES DAILY 10c

HUGE NEW RUSSIAN SPUTNIK RUMORED

Deadlock Persists in TV Strike Negotiations

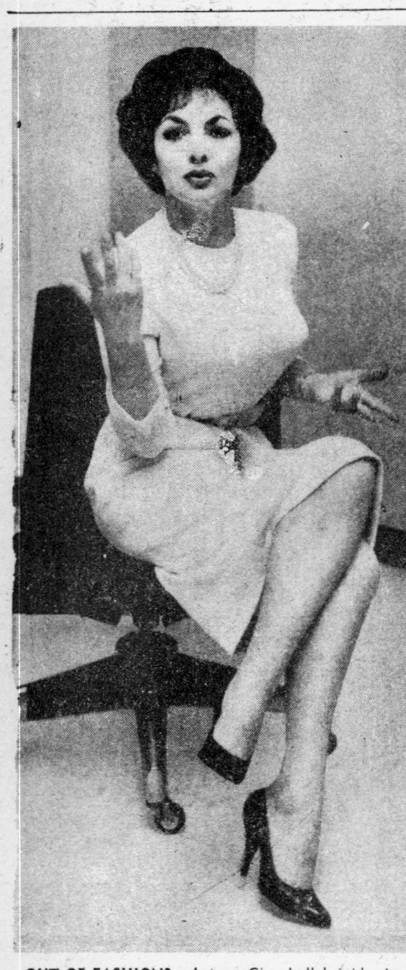

OUT OF FASHION?—Actress Gina Lollobrigida, in New York after flight from Paris, appears indifferent to criticism of Paris paper, which pointed out that fashion czars now have flattened the bust, taken a hike in the hemline and loosened the belt.
Story on Page 5, Part I (AP) Wirephoto

Two Killed in Mid-Air Collision of Bombers

One Plane Crashes While Other Makes Safe Landing on Foam at George Air Base

An Air Force B-26 me-ium bomber crashed about miles east of Barstow sterday after colliding th another B-26 in a flight five.

The Air Force said both w members of the hed plane were killed. ir bodies were returned George Air Force Base yesterday by helicop-

he second plane was aged in the air collision made a safe landing at rge Air Force Base, ut 75 miles from the ne of the collision.

The plane was landed on foam-covered strip, with e of its two propellers feathered and its landing gear up.

The Air Force said its two crew members were not injured.

They were identified as 1st Lt. William Suzich, pilot, and Technical Sgt. Tygart, engineer.

Both were taken to the George AFB hospital for observation.

Names of the two men killed in the crash of the other plane were temporarily withheld.

The crash occurred shortly before 11 a.m. The five craft, attached to the 4th Tow Target Squadron, were on a routine training flight

Turn to Page 6, Column 3

Talks Go On Near Deadline

A nerve-wracking countdown was in progress yesterday at the Hollywood and Burbank studios of the National Broadcasting Co. and American Broadcasting Co. toward the 9 p.m. deadline of a strike threatened by 750 technical and engineering employees.

Negotiations between the two networks and the National Association of Broadcast Employees and Technicians (NABET) were continuing in Boston in hopes of reaching agreement on a new contract.

On Standby Duty

At the studios here, special crews of supervisory personnel went on standby duty to maintain television and radio broadcasting in the event the talks should fail and the union should call on its membership to stop work.

NBC and ABC spokesmen said the networks intend to keep their programs going despite the strike threat. There was some question whether live shows over the week end would be affected.

In Boston, NABET said its course would be determined "by what happens in the remaining hours." The union hinted that if the companies "get down to business," negotiations would be continued until an agreement is reached.

750 May Picket

A NABET spokesman here said 400 members at NBC and 350 at ABC have received their picket assignments.

NBC has its West Coast headquarters at Sunset Blvd. and Vine St. and its color television studios at 3000 W Alameda Ave., Burbank. ABC's KABC-TV studio is at Prospect Ave. and Talmadge St. and its KABC radio station is at 1539 N Vine St.

In response to a NABET demand for a 15% wage boost, the companies reportedly offered 3% and rejected the union suggestion for a four-day, 32-hour work week.

Negotiators also discussed the complicated problem of work jurisdiction relating to the introduction of video tape, a new process which is expected to replace film in telecasting.

THE WEATHER

No eye-irritating smog today.

U.S. Weather Bureau forecast: Variable high cloudiness today. Chance of rain tonight. Little change in temperatures. High, 72. Rain probability, 30%. High yesterday, 72; low, 49.

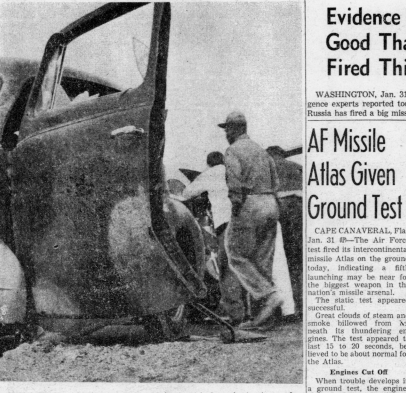

CRASH SCENE—Ambulance attendants, behind wrecked car, load a victim of a head-on crash near Palmdale that killed one and injured four, one critically.
Story on Page 1, Part III Times photo

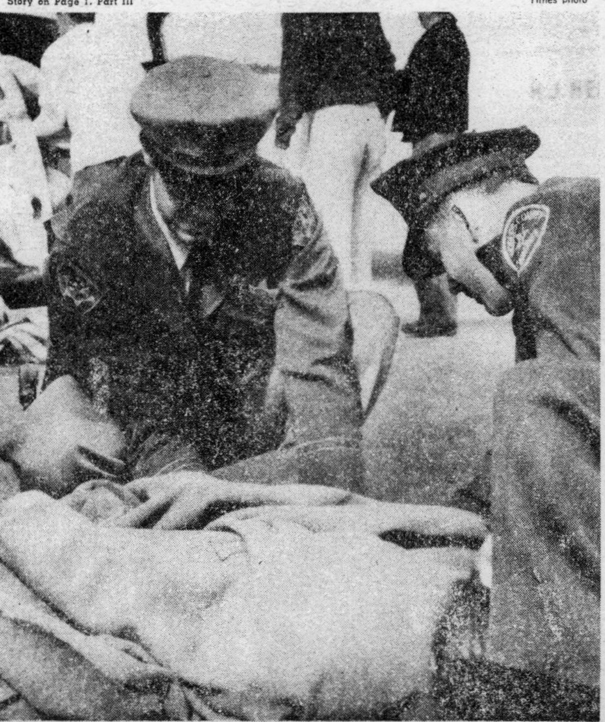

KILLED IN COLLISIO—Officers cover body of Lloyd Bradfield, 17, Culver City youth who died in crash near Palmdale as he returned from a hunting trip.
Times photo

Evidence Reported Good That Soviets Fired Third Missile

WASHINGTON, Jan. 31 (AP) — Government intelligence experts reported today they had some evidence Russia has fired a big missile into outer space.

They said this missile might have thrust a third and bigger Soviet satellite into the heavens but they acknowledged they were not sure.

No government department or agency was willing to say on the record that it knew positively the Soviets had launched what was described as a very large missile.

Pretty Good Evidence

These authorities, however, who usually keep close check on Soviet developments, said evidence they have received seems pretty good to them.

This information became available a few hours after these and other officials reported the Soviets were about ready to fire a missile.

The speculation was mainly about a new Soviet earth satellite but did not rule out other possibilities, including an attempt to hit the moon.

Guarded remarks of a number of officials here, plus the refusal to comment by other usually well-informed sources, lent an air of expectancy in key government departments.

One informant said he was personally prepared for a Moscow announcement that "a new, bigger and fancier satellite" had been put into orbit.

Long Expected

Some authorities long have expected the Soviets to launch such a satellite quickly after the United States finally succeeded in putting its first baby moon into the heavens.

The Soviet aim, they said, would be to blanket news of the American achievement by boasting about a more impressive one of their own.

The willingness of some officials to talk about Soviet missile operations, previously a topic they kept mum about, appeared to indicate:

1—The Eisenhower administration is seeking to beat Moscow to the punch in announcing to the world any new Soviet satellite or missile success. This advance American tip would blunt the world-wide impact.

2—The information was being leaked as part of a psychological warfare operation. The idea would be that

Turn to Page 4, Column 6

AF Missile Atlas Given Ground Test

CAPE CANAVERAL, Fla., Jan. 31 (AP)—The Air Force test fired its intercontinental missile Atlas on the ground today, indicating a fifth launching may be near for the biggest weapon in the nation's missile arsenal.

The static test appeared successful.

Great clouds of steam and smoke billowed from beneath its thundering engines. The test appeared to last 15 to 20 seconds, believed to be about normal for the Atlas.

Engines Cut Off

When trouble develops in a ground test, the engines are cut off immediately.

The Atlas test was only part of a sudden spurt of activity at the nation's missile testing center, but there was no word of when another satellite-launching try will be made.

As the Air Force took the wraps off the Atlas for the ground test the Army erected a second big missile beside its Jupiter-C satellite carrier which has been grounded by strong winds in the upper atmosphere.

The 100-ton Atlas, a gleaming white giant which towered above telephone poles near it on the cape, is one of two Atlases believed standing on the cape.

A test firing usually takes place a week to 10 days before actual launching. But the flight test could be delayed if trouble was encountered during the static run.

New Zealand Hit by Sharp Quake

AUCKLAND, New Zealand, Jan. 31 (AP)—An earthquake smashed shop windows and damaged buildings today in Dannevirke, a town of 4000 population in Northern New Zealand. There were no reports of casualties.

INDEX OF FEATURES

BIG LEAGUE CROWD—Wide-angle view of Coliseum shows part of the 78,672 paid baseball fans who jammed stadium yesterday to cheer the Los Angeles Dodgers during their opener here with San Francisco Giants.
Times photo

Times Telephone Numbers
- MAdison 5-2345 for subscriber service calls and all other calls except those concerning classified advertising.
- MAdison 9-4411 for all classified advertising calls.

Los Angeles Times

PART I
ALL THE NEWS
ALL THE TIME

VOL. LXXVII | IN FIVE PARTS | CC | SATURDAY MORNING, APRIL 19, 1958 | 54 PAGES | DAILY 10c

78,672 See Dodgers Win; City Gives Team Big Welcome

Russ Accuse U.S. of Near Attacks

A-Bombers Sent Toward Soviet Almost Started War, Envoy Says

MOSCOW, April 18 (U.P.)—Russia today accused the United States of sending planes with atomic and hydrogen bombs toward Soviet borders on alert missions and of bringing the world to "within a hairbreadth" of war on several occasions. It demanded United Nations Security Council action to ground the flights.

A statement read by Soviet Foreign Minister Gromyko at an unusual news conference said the Soviet Union is ready to take "instant measures" if U.S. Strategic Air Command planes approach Soviet territory. Soviet U.N. Delegate Arkady A. Sobolev in New York demanded a Council meeting tomorrow.

Bartholomew's story on Page 4, Part I.

Tonight U.S. Delegate Henry Cabot Lodge, U.N. Security Council president for April, summoned the Council to meet Monday afternoon to consider the Soviet complaint.

"A Council debate on these new charges would demonstrate that the Soviets are using the technique of the 'big lie' to incite fear among the peoples of the world," a U.S. delegation spokesman said.

Based on Dispatch

In Washington the White House said Gromyko's charges that the U.S. bombers endanger peace are "not true." The State Department denied Gromyko's assertions that the U.S. procedures are provocative.

Gromyko referred in his statement to the "report of the American news agency, United Press," which described "Strategic Air Command procedures in dealing with suspected targets that appear on radar.

(The dispatch was written April 7 by United Press President Frank H. Bartholomew who made personal visits to SAC headquarters in Omaha.

(The U.S. Defense Department in Washington said the

Turn to Page 4, Column 4

Ex-President Hoover Taking Hospital Tests

NEW YORK, April 18 (UP) Former President Hoover, 83, is in Harkness Pavilion of Columbia Presbyterian Medical Center undergoing tests of an undisclosed nature, the hospital announced today. There was no indication of his condition.

Mr. Hoover was admitted to the hospital yesterday, a hospital spokesman said, after consulations with his private physician.

Charles Niess, night superintendent of the Pavilion, would give no information other than to say Mr. Hoover was on the 10th floor of the 12-story building and that a bulletin would be issued some time tomorrow.

Went Fishing Recently

There has been no indication to the public that Mr. Hoover has been ailing. He recently went on a Florida fishing vacation, and in February he gave a major address at Valley Forge, Pa., in accepting a Freedoms Foundation award of $5000 and a George Washington Honor Medal for "wisdom and devoted service.

The former President has made his home in the Waldorf-Astoria Towers most of the time since he left the White House. His sons live in California and there was no indication that they planned to come here because their father was in the hospital.

Anderson Sees Deficit of 3 Billion

Treasury Chief Reiterates Stand Against Tax Cuts

BY ROBERT HARTMANN
Times Washington Bureau Chief

WASHINGTON, April 18—Secretary of the Treasury Anderson today predicted a Federal deficit of well over 3 billion dollars for the current fiscal year ending June 30.

Reiterating his cautious stand on tax cuts in an address before the American Society of Newspaper Editors, Anderson said government spending is likely to rise to 78 billion dollars in fiscal 1959 and revenues may continue to fall short of expectations.

Praise for Congress

"These figures as to deficits give us concern," the Treasury Secretary stated. "They do not warrant pessimism."

Anderson, the administration's chief advocate of a "wait-and-see" policy on tax reduction, warned against "the theory that some single dramatic action will automatically be all that is required to assure lasting business recovery." He praised the "attitude of statesmanship" of Democratic and Republican leaders in Congress in holding off on cutting taxes without prior bipartisan consultation.

Psychology Stressed

"We are not headed for a depression but for new horizons of progress," he assured the nation's editors. "So long as we are free to make our own decisions the most important single factor in our economic system is the continuity of confidence."

The Treasury chief stressed the psychological factor involving millions of individual decisions in the current economic slump. Illustrating the secondary role

Turn to Page 3, Column 1

BILLION-DOLLAR WORK RELIEF PROGRAM VOTED

WASHINGTON, April 18 (AP) — The House Ways and Means Committee today approved a billion-dollar unemployment relief program.

Backed by the Democratic committee majority, the plan calls for Federal financing of 16 weeks of additional unemployment payments for workers who exhaust their benefits under the existing program.

The new program also would provide for an entirely new Federal program of unemployment relief for some 1,800,000 workers not now covered.

Rep. Byrnes (R) Wis., a member, said the committee proposal "embarks this country on an absolute dole."

"The Federal Treasury is left wide open, and nobody has any idea what it will actually cost," Byrnes said.

WATER DEADLOCK SOLUTION REFUSED

Fifth Attempt to Compromise on Issue and Pass Budget Rejected by Assembly

BY ROBERT BLANCHARD, Times Staff Representative

SACRAMENTO, April 18—A fifth attempt to end the legislative deadlock over water that has held up passage of the 2-billion-dollar State budget for 24 days failed today when the Assembly voted down a compromise offered by a two-house conference committee.

The Senate previously had approved the measure, 31 to 5.

Most of the opposition to the latest compromise came from Southern California legislators who protested that it committed too much money to Northern California water projects without any indication that the Southland would get water from them.

Extra Funds Included

The compromise would have called for a budget of $2,045,034,372, including $48,940,972 for support of the State Department of Water Resources and the development of water resources.

It differed from previous proposals mainly in that it

Turn to Page 2, Column 2

12-Day Strike of Technicians Ended at CBS

Technicians ended a 12-day strike against Columbia Broadcasting System yesterday, voting in a national referendum to accept a new three-year labor contract for higher wages and settlement of jurisdiction and job security issues.

The International Brotherhood of Electrical Workers said its 1300 CBS employees voted by a 7-to-4 margin to accept contract terms and start returning to work at once in Hollywood and seven other cities where the network operates television and radio facilities. The strike started April 7.

Officers of IBEW Local 45 in Hollywood, speaking for 330 members, said pickets were pulled away from CBS installations yesterday afternoon, with radio division personnel reporting for duty at midnight. Television division personnel are to re-

Turn to Page 6, Column 3

THE WEATHER

Light eye irritation along foothills today.

U.S. Weather Bureau forecast: Low clouds and fog night and early morning hours but sunny afternoons today and tomorrow. Little change in temperatures. High today about 75. Rain probability, zero. Yesterday's high, 72; low, 58.

L.A. Beats Giants, 6-5, in Opener

BY PAUL ZIMMERMAN
Sports Editor

San Francisco found the range of short left field at Memorial Coliseum yesterday, but not well enough, as the Dodgers made their first home stand a successful one, 6 to 5, before a pleased National League record-breaking crowd of 78,672.

In addition to this being the greatest outpouring of humanity in the history of the senior circuit, the gathering also broke major-loop marks for both an opener and a single game in season.

Hank Sauer, who lives only a few miles south of the Coliseum, was the Giant who found left field most to his liking. The Inglewood slugger hit one home run over the screen at 275 feet and another beyond, at 340.

Gray Finds Range

Dick Gray also found the range for the Dodgers with a 340-foot homer to left.

Smart, careful Carl Erskine got credit for the victory, but he wasn't around at the end. After Jim Davenport smashed a double high off the left-field screen to lead off the ninth, he departed in favor of Clem Labine.

Willie Kirkland promptly tripled to deep center and had Davenport not failed to touch third, the game would have gone into extra innings because Willie Mays singled Kirkland home before Clem Labine extinguished the fire.

L.A. Takes Lead

The Dodgers took the lead in the third when they got help with a walk and an error to augment singles by Duke Snider and Charlie Neal.

Sauer's first homer tied things up in the fourth but Los Angeles drove Giant starting hurler Alan Worthington to cover in the fifth, scoring three runs on a pair of hits, a pass and a bobble.

Bob Schmidt's triple to center and a wild pitch gave the Giants their third run in the sixth. Sauer's "cheap" homer in the eighth, brought the count to four.

Labine terminated festivities in the ninth.

Enthusiastic Crowds Jam Broadway to Cheer for Players

BY ART RYON

Los Angeles really did it yesterday.

It gave its Dodgers the goldarnedest, warming, howling, confetti-filled, big league welcome it has ever accorded anyone.

And the Dodgers responded by winning their home opener, 6-5, before 78,762 in the Coliseum, a figure that broke four baseball records.

Other news and pictures of Dodgers welcome on Pages A and B, Part I and in Sports Section.

This is supposed to be the city that won't turn out for a parade.

Ha!

Enthusiastic thousands lined Broadway to shout welcome and encouragement to members of the team that was, at last, satisfying the city's long thirst for major league baseball.

Broadway Crowded

No, the thousands didn't line Broadway.

They crowded it.

They swarmed into the street, leaving bare passage room for the motorcade of open cars that carried the uniformed Dodgers. The players rode two to a car, their names bannered on the side.

Los Angeles had never seen them before. But it had heard and read of them. And, as each pair passed, the friendly greetings roared out: "Hi, Duke!" . . . "Next time, Newk!" . . . "Coupla home runs today, eh, Gil?"

The baseball players, obviously overwhelmed by the size and warmth of the reception, tried their best to respond.

City Hall Welcome

"Hey," a fan shouted to Pitcher Ed Roebuck, "when do you play the Yanks?"

"Next fall!" he yelled back.

The jubilance began with the official civic welcome on the Spring St. steps of the City Hall at 10:30 a.m.

This was no stuffy affair.

The crowd, which eventually swelled to about 5000, began gathering early.

Also there early, astride a horse, bursting out of a Dodger uniform, and shouting through a megaphone was James (Foghorn) Murphy. He set the tenor of the occasion.

As he used to be in San Francisco many years ago when Jack London gave him his nickname, Foghorn was supposed to announce, "Baseball today!"

But he blew his lines.

Instead, mistaking himself for an umpire, he kept bawling, "Play ball!"

But nobody minded.

When they piled from a special bus, the Dodgers were given a rousing cheer.

Gay Senoritas

As they took their seats on the steps, gaily costumed senoritas from Olvera St. swirled among them, yanking off their caps, and cracking their heads with cascarones — confetti-filled eggshells.

Somebody put a serape and huge, beaded Mexican sombrero on Walter O'Malley.

"Play ball!" bawled Foghorn.

Two fellows in a tiny three-wheeled automobile raced up and down the street honking the horn and waving blue and white Dodger pennants.

Over at the side, the Police Band was playing "California, Here I Come."

Reporters did quick kneeling interviews with Warren Giles, president of the Na-

Turn to Page A, Column 3

50 Called to Testify on Charges That Judges Vie for Wedding Fees

State process servers swooped through the Civic Center yesterday with summonses calling for more than 50 witnesses to appear at an executive session of the Legislative Joint Judiciary Committee on Administration of Justice Monday and tell what they know about marriage procedures of certain judges.

From the State Capitol in Sacramento, Sen. Edwin J. Regan of Weaverville, chairman of the committee, issued the following statement:

"Investigators for the committee have received information alleging that certain employees have been directing couples desiring to be married to certain judges. For this they assertedly have received gratuities. We are holding a closed meeting to provide protection for these witnesses and screen them from political reprisals."

Locally it was learned that among those subpoenaed to the Monday hearing are Fred G. Fink, clerk, and W. D. Fisher, a deputy sheriff serving as bailiff in the courtroom of Superior Judge George A. Dockweiler.

Also served are Herbert Shaffer, clerk, and Albert Morris, a deputy city marshal serving as clerk in the court of Municipal Judge Ida Mae Adams.

Subpoenas were also served on practically the entire corps of elevator operators in the Hall of Records headed by Chief Starter Fred Clark. Others served were Norma Stovall, Eugene

Turn to Page 6, Column 1

INDEX OF FEATURES

Lana Consults Psychiatrist on Daughter

Actress Lana Turner confers with psychiatrist on problems facing daughter. Story on Page 1, Part 3.

ON OTHER PAGES

Times Telephone Numbers
• MAdison 5-2345 for subscriber service calls and all other calls except those concerning classified advertising.
• MAdison 9-4411 for all classified advertising calls.

Los Angeles Times

EQUAL RIGHTS
LIBERTY UNDER THE LAW — TRUE INDUSTRIAL FREEDOM

PART I
ALL THE NEWS
ALL THE TIME

VOL. LXXVII — IN FOUR PARTS — CC — WEDNESDAY MORNING, APRIL 23, 1958 — 80 PAGES — DAILY 10c

Big Bunker Hill Project Wins Approval of U.S.

GREEN LIGHT—A beaming Mayor Poulson, on left, and Sen. Kuchel (R) Cal., look on in the Washington office of Albert M. Cole, Federal Housing Administrator, as he gives his approval for the huge urban renewal plan for Bunker Hill. (AP) Wirephoto

Loan and Grant Due for City

The Federal government yesterday gave Los Angeles a green light for its Bunker Hill redevelopment plan, which envisions an ultimate total investment of some $315,000,000.

Approval of the program to clear the 130-acre hilltop area in downtown Los Angeles to make way for an ultramodern business and apartment section was given in Washington by Albert Cole, administrator of the Housing and Home Finance Agency.

Under the plan, the Los Angeles Community Redevelopment Agency will receive a $57,504,203 Federal project loan for clearing and preparing the site, of which $15,469,203 ultimately will become an outright grant.

Offers Received

Gross project cost was set at $64,863,805 and the net project cost — after the cleared land has been sold to private developers — at $22,078,805.

The local agency's one-third share will be $7,359,602, to be supplied through tax allocation bonds which will be paid off only from the excess of tax revenues which will be realized from the redeveloped land.

It is estimated that private enterprise will invest $250,000,000 to erect office buildings, hotels, apartment houses, motels, stores and parking facilities. Offers of commitments have been received from several developers.

Needs Council OK

The plan still must clear the City Planning Commission and the City Council. If all goes well, it is anticipated that bond money will be available to begin purchasing property early next year and construction on the first cleared sites will start in about two years.

Mayor Poulson, who flew to Washington with City Council President John S. Gibson and CRA Chairman William T. Sesnon Jr., hailed the plan as "a shot in the arm" to stimulate business conditions.

"We are proposing to spend money and put people to work on something we need and ought to have, something that represents a sound investment in better living, better business and a better community," the Mayor said.

'Proud of Progress'

With the Los Angeles officials at ceremonies in Cole's office were Sen. Kuchel (R) Cal., and Urban Renewal Commissioner Richard L. Steiner.

"Los Angeles today stands on the threshold of attaining some of the great rewards of sound urban renewal," Cole said. "You and the people of Los Angeles

Turn to Page 2, Column 7

Air Tragedy Brings Call for Action

Transport Pilots Report Jet Stunting Near Nevada Route

BY MARVIN MILES
Times Aviation Editor

LAS VEGAS, April 22—The exhaustive task of analyzing yesterday's tragic air collision began here this morning as the death of 49 persons reverberated in Washington demands for rigid control of air space.

Meanwhile reports of jet aerobatics and military flights close to scheduled transports on the airway near Las Vegas were under investigation.

Both American and Continental Air Lines captains reported "close" military flights in the vicinity, while medical authorities were still removing the ripped and charred bodies from the blackened wreckage of a United Air Lines DC-7 that collided with an F-100F Super Sabre.

Jet Aerobatics

Walter Plett, regional director for the Civil Aeronautics Administration, said American Airlines Flight 43 reported jet aircraft performing aerobatics in or near the airway at a distance of five miles, while the Continental flight reported jet flights within 2000 feet.

The Continental flight, he said, was recalled to Las Vegas, where the crew was to be questioned closely on the report.

In Washington there were angry demands for a single Federal authority with absolute control over air space and moves to separate civilian and military flying.

The House Appropriations subcommittee that controls appropriations for the Commerce Department and the CAA opened its own investigation of the crash and sent

Turn to Page 4, Column 4

PRACTICE TORPEDO HIT CRIPPLES DESTROYER

SAN DIEGO, April 22 (AP)—The Navy disclosed tonight that the submarine Bugara scored a direct torpedo hit today on the destroyer Yarnall with a dummy warhead and sent the ship limping back into port.

Read Adm. Frank W. Fenno, commander of the Pacific Fleet Cruiser-Destroyer Force, said there were no injuries. The practice torpedo hit the destroyer amidship at the waterline.

Fenno's statement said unarmed torpedoes used in training exercises are supposed to pass under the target ship.

Plane With 74 Aboard Forced Down by Blaze

Trans World Airliner Makes Precautionary Landing After Engine Ignites Over Desert

A Trans World Airlines Super Constellation with 74 persons aboard made a precautionary landing at George Air Force Base yesterday after one of its four engines caught fire over the Mojave Desert.

The airliner, carrying 69 passengers and a crew of five, had taken off from International Airport here less than an hour before the fire broke out. It was bound for Kansas City.

Airline officials said the plane, TWA Flight 42, radioed the Civil Aeronautics Administration tower at Daggett at 10:12 a.m., reporting the No. 4 engine afire.

Capt. James Roe of Kansas City, who had turned the plane around and was heading west, asked permission to make an emergency landing at Daggett but was advised to proceed to George AFB, 40 miles nearer Los Angeles.

Fire Put Out

Capt. Roe set the plane down at 10:38 a.m. as a precautionary measure, an airline spokesman said, although crew members had extinguished the fire before the plane reached George AFB.

Passengers traveling on the Kansas City-bound airliner remained at the Air Force base until another plane, dispatched from here, picked them up.

Flight 42, the airline said, departed from International Airport at 9:15 a.m. The plane had left San Francisco at 7 a.m.

Tito Advises Kremlin Not to Interfere

Yugoslav Leader Defies Moscow on Boycott

LJUBLJANA, Yugoslavia, April 22 (AP)—President Tito tartly advised Moscow today to abandon attempts to force this country's Communist Party into a Kremlin-designed mold.

The Yugoslav leader's defiance of the Kremlin brought to their feet the 1700 delegates to the party's seventh congress. The hall rocked with applause each time Tito emphasized a difference between Yugoslav and Soviet ideology.

Tito's four-hour speech was a sharp retort to Moscow's boycott of the congress. Tito did not mention the boycott specifically.

Russians Stung

Tito's 35,000-word speech, distributed in advance to the delegates, said Yugoslav-Soviet relations were improving on the basis of the 1955 Belgrade-Moscow declaration after Nikita Khrushchev's pilgrimage of apology to this country. In delivery, Tito changed this to read that relations "until today were developing very successfully."

The Russians obviously have been stung by this turn of events. In Moscow today Peter Pospelov, a Soviet Party theoretician, lambasted the Yugoslav party's draft program being considered here. He called it "a document aimed at weakening the unity of the Communist and workers' parties, at weakening the unity of the Socialist (Communist-ruled) countries."

Root of Quarrel

At the root of this new quarrel, apparently, is a Yugoslav feeling the Russians reneged on a promise to recognize "different roads to Socialism."

Tito reminded the Russians that Stalin's inflexible and bellicose foreign policies had brought the Atlantic alliance into being. Here he touched a live nerve. Originally, the draft program under discussion at the congress denounced both military blocs, NATO and the Red Warsaw pact alike.

Later, in a gesture of appeasement, the Yugoslavs said the Warsaw pact was justified because NATO came first.

But the Russians would

Turn to Page 8, Column 4

LACC Faculty Assembly Hits Teaching by TV

BY DICK TURPIN
Times Education Editor

Faculty members at Los Angeles City College, birthplace of local closed-circuit educational television, launched a bitter attack yesterday on the medium as an encroachment on their profession.

In a report sent to offices of the Board of Education, the Faculty Assembly, by a 22-to-4 vote, condemned the experimental program as fruitless, too impersonal for good learning and a bad use of good ($70,000 annually) money.

Dr. Walter Varnum, who prepared the report, said faculty members wish to reiterate their stand of a year ago that the Board of Education "redirect" this program "from television to more useful channels."

Called Too Costly

Dr. Varnum, head of the junior college's psychology department, labeled the educational TV project, in the second year of a three-year pilot study, as too costly, a false effort to meet the teacher shortage and a devitalized way to teach.

The faculty spokesman declared instructors would not oppose television if it is used as an educational aid such as motion pictures. They just want it placed in "proper perspective," he added.

Miss Edith Clark, assistant superintendent in charge of junior colleges, said the reported vote represented a small segment of the 325-member staff and was not an expression of the entire faculty. When she sees the report, she said, there will be an official comment.

In an evaluation report of the program at City College last fall, made by Dr. George Goody, School Board evaluator, the program, re-

Turn to Page 20, Column 1

L.A. Has 79 Deg. High; Cooler Today

It was only 79 deg. yesterday—at 10:55 a.m.—and the high today will be only about 74, the Weather Bureau said.

The low yesterday was 61 at 4:56 a.m. Relative humidity was 97% at 4 a.m. and 49% at 10:45 a.m.

In addition to cool weather, today should see an end of eye-irritating smog, the Air Pollution Control District said.

Admiral Burke in Navy Hospital With Cracked Rib

WASHINGTON, April 22 (AP) — Adm. Arleigh Burke, Chief of Naval Operations, is under treatment at the Naval Hospital in Bethesda, Md., for a cracked rib he suffered Sunday.

A Defense Department statement said:

"He took a spill over some rocks at his estate near McLean, in Fairfax County, suffered skinned legs and a cracked rib, is recuperating nicely and expects to be back in a day or two."

Full-Scale Inquiry on Chavez Deal Scheduled

Assembly to Open Investigation Here May 15 on Negotiations With Dodgers

BY ROBERT BLANCHARD, Times Staff Representative

SACRAMENTO, April 22—Plans for full-scale investigation into all dealings between the city of Los Angeles and the Dodgers were disclosed today by Assemblyman Ralph Brown (D) of Modesto, chairman of the Assembly Committee on Governmental Efficiency and Economy.

Brown said the inquiry, which will be held in Los Angeles May 15 and 16, is being made in response to a request from the City Council which adopted a resolution on March 26 asking the Legislature to look into the negotiations between the city and the Dodgers for the Chavez Ravine site.

Reasons Given

The Governmental Efficiency and Economy Committee was selected for the investigation at the request of Assemblyman Don Anderson (R) of Monterey Park in whose district Chavez Ravine is located.

Anderson said he picked that committee because Brown, the chairman, and Assemblyman John Busterud (R) of San Francisco both live outside the Los Angeles area and, representing different political faiths, can be expected to conduct a

Turn to Page 17, Column 1

100-Foot Ball Will Give U.S. Moon Secrets

WASHINGTON, April 22 (UP) — Government scientists disclosed plans today for firing a 100-foot aluminum foil ball to the vicinity of the moon in an effort to uncover some of the secrets of the earth's only natural satellite.

The plans for the moon shot were disclosed by Dr. Hugh L. Dryden, director of the National Advisory Committee for Aeronautics, nucleus of the President's proposed new space agency. He said the huge inflatable ball is under development.

Carried by Rocket

He explained that the nine-pound ball will be carried the 238,000 miles to the moon in a rocket and inflated near the moon's surface. He said the inflated ball either will circle the earth in the path of the moon's orbit or orbit the moon itself.

Dryden said the silver ball will be visible from the earth. He indicated that the behavior of the ball would give scientists valuable clues about the nature of outer space near the moon and about the moon itself.

Explorer I Radio Set Still Sending

The low-power radio of Explorer I satellite, launched Jan. 31, still is telemetering cosmic information back to earth, an official of Caltech's Jet Propulsion Laboratory said yesterday.

Dr. Norman F. Jacobson, JPL engineering group supervisor, said the tiny radio is giving information on cosmic rays, cosmic dust impacts and internal and skin temperatures of the satellite.

The transmitter was designed to last only two months and already has exceeded this period by three weeks, Dr. Jacobson told the Society of Motion Picture and Television Engineers at the Ambassador.

FLAG INSULT CHARGED

Britain's Lady Docker Barred From Monaco

MONTE CARLO, April 22 (AP) — Britain's Lady Docker today got the boot from Monaco. Prince Rainier's government charged she insulted the royal family and the country's flag.

The order does not apply to Lady Docker's industrialist husband, Sir Bernard. The government considered him merely an onlooker.

The Monacan order also bars Lady Docker from the adjacent French Riviera. This is possible under a 1918 agreement with France.

It was expected that at least one of the fun spots in the French Riviera, Cannes, will find a loophole. The Dockers spend a lot of money and they unload plenty of it at Cannes.

The government charged Lady Docker tore up a paper Monacan flag because her [illegible]n was not permitted to at[illegible]nd the christening reception Sunday for Prince Albert, newborn son of Prince Rainier and Princess Grace.

Reached at Cannes, Lady Docker told reporters "I never intend to go back to Monaco anyway" but if the ban is extended to Cannes "I will call in my lawyers."

The spotlight is nothing new for Lady Docker, who has made headlines for activities ranging from playing tiddlywinks to driving around in a gold-plated car.

Told that the palace is returning the Dockers' christening gifts, which cost more than $1000, Sir Bernard said:

"I am delighted. I hope an apology comes with them."

THE WEATHER

No smog today.

U.S. Weather Bureau forecast: Mostly sunny today and tomorrow but coastal cloudiness this morning. Windy and a little cooler today with high near 74. Probably a little warmer tomorrow. High yesterday, 79; low, 61.

Hoover Still Better; Gets Out of Bed

NEW YORK, April 22 (UP)—Former President Hoover, 83, today continued his recovery from an operation for removal of his gall bladder last Saturday.

A medical bulletin issued at Harkness Pavilion said:

"Mr. Hoover had a good day. He was up a couple of times, walked both times, and sat in his chair. He read the newspapers and some of the telegrams he has received."

A hospital spokesman said that Mr. Hoover was very anxious to resume work on several books. He said an adjoining hospital room has been converted into a sitting room-workshop.

Anti-British Riots Flare on Malta

VALLETTA, Malta, April 22 (AP) — Anti-British demonstrations flared today among Maltese stirred by the resignation of Don Mintoff, their Laborite Prime Minister.

Mintoff resigned last night. He had failed in an effort to get Britain to promise more financial assistance to Malta to offset unemployment expected when the British carry out plans to close the big royal naval base.

Threat of Flood in Oregon Grows

PENDLETON, Or., April 22 (AP)—Sandbag levees grew around scores of houses south of here today as McKay Creek continued to rise and rain came down.

National Guardsmen ordered 41 families out of their homes in the threatened area late last night.

INDEX OF FEATURES

Dodgers Win Night Game From Cubs

Dodgers take early lead, defeat Chicago Cubs, 4 to 2, in night game before 39,459. Story on Page 1, Part 4.

ON OTHER PAGES

Cancer of Lung Deaths Rise Told

GENEVA, April 22 (AP) — A rise of 10% or more in the number of deaths from lung cancer over a five to six-year period was reported today by the U.N. World Health Organization.

The report said fatalities from cancer of respiratory system are increasing more rapidly than any other single cause of death, particularly in Western Europe.

Officer Loses Bouts With Fire and Deer

The forces of nature seem to be in league against Pasadena Police Officer Walt Kilgore.

Monday his motorcycle burned up from under him. He watched a new pair of $8 cyclists' gloves go up in smoke with the machine as his radio kept demanding that he cover the fire.

Yesterday came another indignity. Two deer wandered down into the heavily settled area above Brookside Park and Kilgore was dispatched to handle the situation.

He trapped one of the animals and tried bulldogging it for the Humane Society.

In the ensuing bout the deer escaped injury but one sharp horn stripped the officer of his pants. Amused fellow officers and bystanders provided him with decent covering for a quick trip to the station.

Today he is keeping a wary eye out for meteorites, flash floods and tornadoes.

Times Telephone Numbers
• MAdison 5-2345 for subscriber service calls and all other calls except those concerning classified advertising.
• MAdison 9-4411 for all classified advertising calls.

Los Angeles Times

EQUAL RIGHTS · LIBERTY UNDER THE LAW · TRUE INDUSTRIAL FREEDOM

PART I
ALL THE NEWS
ALL THE TIME

VOL. LXXVII | IN FOUR PARTS | CC ★ | MONDAY MORNING, JUNE 2, 1958 | 76 PAGES | DAILY 10c

De Gaulle Named Premier; Reds Battle Police in Streets

Asks Powers to Run France for 6 Months, Amend Constitution

PARIS, June 2 (Monday) (AP) — Gen. Charles de Gaulle held the reins of power in France again today. His first official act was to ask the National Assembly for a free hand in running the country for the next six months.

The Assembly last night approved De Gaulle's bid to become Premier by a 329-224 vote. There were bitter words in the Assembly and Communists fought police in street demonstrations against him, but De Gaulle won.

Communists and other leftists opposed to his return marched to the heart of Paris shouting "No to De Gaulle." They were dispersed by the helmeted security police.

Following through swiftly, he asked the Assembly to give him a new short-cut procedure for amending the constitution and to extend special power measures which his predecessors have had for dealing with the 3½-year-old Algerian rebellion.

Text of De Gaulle's address to Assembly on Page 11, Part 1.

Within minutes, the Assembly reconvened to receive the texts of three government bills. They were referred to committees and a floor debate was scheduled.

Rule by Decree

The "blank check" legislation sought by De Gaulle would give his Cabinet power to rule France by decree for six months.

At the end of that period all interim measures would be filed with the Assembly for ratification.

One committee, showing some hostility to the powers demanded by De Gaulle, summoned the four Deputy Premiers named by the general to testify on the full powers measure.

Called in at 3 a.m. were Pierre Pflimlin and Guy Mollet, bother former Premiers, and Louis Jacquinot and Felix Houphonet-Boigny.

The action of the Committee of Universal Suffrage in summoning such high figures to a hearing at that hour was virtually unprecedented.

Although it appeared possible the committee might oppose De Gaulle's request, the Assembly can overrule the committee.

The Interior Committee approved the routine request for special powers in Algeria.

As Parliament received the bills, De Gaulle's aides sent out word that he wants rapid approval so he can fly to Algiers early this week in an effort to restore governmental order in Algeria.

De Gaulle was moving to steer France on a course he

Turn to Page 10, Column 1

FACES ASSEMBLY—Gen. Charles de Gaulle addresses French National Assembly in Paris in a six-minute speech asking for confirmation as Premier. He then retired to his hotel and the Assembly, after heated debate, voted confirmation. (AP) Wirephoto via radio from Paris

CENSORSHIP ENDS SWIFTLY

PARIS, June 2 (Monday) (AP) — Premier De Gaulle lifted French censorship at midnight Sunday night.

It was one of his first acts. Censorship had been imposed by the Pflimlin government after the May 13 Algerian uprising.

It applied to all news and pictures distributed in France. Censorship was not used on dispatches and photographs sent abroad.

5-HOUR DODGERTHON

Notables Back Prop. B on TV

Illustrated on Page 3, Part I

Swarms of sports, film, night-club and television personalities paraded before a KTTV audience last night in support of Proposition B on a five-hour telethon climaxed at International Airport with a roaring welcome to the home-coming Los Angeles Dodgers.

The Dodgerthon, viewed by an estimated 1,800,000 persons, was staged to emphasize that a yes vote for Proposition B is the best way to keep the Dodgers here.

A king-size half-hour traffic jam clogged avenues to the airport where the Dodgers, fresh from a 1-0 victory over the Chicago Cubs, landed in a United Air Lines plane at 9:45 p.m.

7500 Greet Team

Wives, fans, citizens committee members, city officials and cameramen, an estimated 7500 in all, mobbed the returning team.

Star performer at the telethon staged earlier in KTTV studios was the cigar-puffing boss of the Dodgers, Walter O'Malley.

O'Malley said that he will do everything in his power to keep the Dodgers in Los Angeles regardless of the outcome of tomorrow's election.

Proposition B asks Los Angeles voters to approve a contract between the city and the Dodgers for use of Chavez Ravine as the site for a modern baseball park.

Contract Approval

O'Malley said he wished to explain the significance of the contract between his baseball organization and the city so that voters would have the correct information on which to base their vote.

He answered a number of questions from baseball fans. Among his answers were:

There is no idea in the minds of Dodger executives that the club will move from Los Angeles. "We have to stay here 30 years," he quipped, "to get our money back at least."

O'Malley said he had no idea how much revenue major league baseball is bringing into Los Angeles, but "baseball fans have spent $35,000,000 in Milwaukee since the Braves moved there."

The Dodgers in Chavez Ravine may ease the tax burden in Los Angeles,

Turn to Page 7, Column 1

U.S. HOLIDAY AUTO DEATHS CLIMB TO 349

BY THE ASSOCIATED PRESS

With millions still on the highways last night, the traffic death toll climbed to 349 in the final hours of the three-day Memorial Day week end.

Traffic was lighter in many areas, due to rainy weather, than safety officials anticipated. Late last night they expressed cautious optimism the deaths would not exceed the record traffic toll of 369 counted for the three-day Memorial Day week end in 1955.

The National Safety Council estimated prior to the week end that there would be 350 traffic deaths.

Five More Die in Week-End County Traffic

TRAFFIC TOLL
Yesterday's deaths—7
1958 county total—333

Five more persons were killed in traffic accidents yesterday, bringing the Memorial Day week-end death toll in Los Angeles County to 10.

Two others, injured in collisions prior to the holidays, died in Los Angeles hospitals yesterday.

The latest fatality was a Santa Monica man who was killed about 9 p.m. last night by a hit-and-run driver.

The victim, George M. Earl, 72, of 2013 18th St., was killed while attempting to cross Pico Blvd. at 18th St. in the beach city. He was pronounced dead on arrival at Santa Monica Hospital.

Hit by Sports Car

Police said he was struck by an expensive sports car which was going east at a high rate of speed.

William J. Pierce Jr., 18, of 17202 Elgar Ave., Torrance, lost his life in a predawn head-on collision yesterday at 190th St. and Hawthorne Blvd., Torrance.

Pierce's car collided with a car driven by Jack Pherigo, also 18, of 3944 182nd St., Torrance.

Pherigo and his two passengers, Jerry Rocha, 18, of 3808-B 174th St., and Patrick Frattarole, 17, of 2614 W 181st St., were taken to

Turn to Page 4, Column 2

Californians Go to Polls Tomorrow

State Secretary Foresees 70% Vote in Primary

California voters will go to the polls tomorrow to indicate their preference of candidates for Governor, State constitutional offices, U.S. Senator, members of the House of Representatives and the State Legislature and numerous other State and local offices. They also will express their opinion of various issues on the ballot.

Secretary of State Frank Jordan, in an optimistic frame of mind, is predicting 70% of the State's 6,280,000 voters will cast their ballots in the primary election.

Los Angeles County Registrar of Voters Benjamin S. Hite, however, is more conservative. He is predicting a 60% turnout.

Local Concern

Although the main candidates for Governor, Republican U.S. Sen. William F. Knowland and Democratic Atty. Gen. Edmund G. Brown, are expected to win their respective nominations with ease, considerable Statewide interest has been aroused by the contests involving Knowland's Senate seat and Brown's Attorney Generalship.

Locally, the electorate is most concerned over Proposition B, which would ratify a contract between the city and the Dodgers for the use of Chavez Ravine as the site for a modern major league baseball park.

In the U.S. Senate race, although there is a scattering of other candidates, the voters are watching with interest the outcome of the battle between Gov. Knight and Mayor George Christopher of San Francisco for the Republican nomination. Rep. Clair Engle of Red Bluff is

Turn to Page 6, Column 3

Beach Crowd Kept Down by Overcast

A dreary overcast during the morning and cooling breezes yesterday scared off an expected holiday weekend jam of beach visitors from Playa del Rey to Zuma Beach.

The high temperature downtown was 76; the low, 60. Relative humidity was 85% at 5 a.m. and 49% at 2 p.m.

Lifeguards described crowds as average for a Sunday but below normal for a holiday week end.

The forecast for today called for more clouds this morning, becoming partly cloudy in the afternoon. High temperature will be near 77 deg.

Khrushchev Asks Haste in Nuclear Tests Talks

Suggests Experts Confer on Policing Within 3 Weeks and Report Back Quickly

MOSCOW, June 1 (UPI) — Soviet Premier Khrushchev has agreed with President Eisenhower's proposal to open technical talks within three weeks on a suspension of nuclear tests, it was disclosed tonight.

The Communist Party newspaper Pravda, in its Monday edition made available tonight, published a letter Khrushchev sent to President Eisenhower in which the Premier stated Russia's readiness to open such conversations.

The Premier was replying to a May 24 note from President Eisenhower which itself was an answer to a note on test suspension Khrushchev had written two weeks previously.

Message Delivered

Khrushchev's latest message was delivered to the State Department in Washington yesterday. The State Department refused to disclose the contents of the three-page note, but officials described it as a favorable response to the President's bid to scientific talks next month.

The Premier's letter, as reported by Pravda, signified agreement with the President's call for talks to start within three weeks on methods of enforcing and policing an international nuclear test suspension.

Khrushchev declared he was eager, along with the

Turn to Page 13, Column 2

1000 Flee as Tank Car Blast Kills 2

MT. PULASKI, Ill., June 1 (UPI)—One thousand of this Central Illinois town's 1500 residents were evacuated today after a railroad tank car exploded, killing two trainmen and causing an estimated million dollars property damage.

A score of townspeople were injured in the blast. Police earlier ordered all residents to leave but, after the flames were extinguished, evacuated only those whose homes were most seriously damaged.

Gov. Stratton ordered 200 National Guardsmen into the area and directed that a 200-bed Civil Defense hospital unit be set up to house some of those evacuated.

Leftist Groups Pour Into Paris and Clubs Fly

PARIS, June 1 (UPI)—Communists and other leftists opposed to Gen. Charles de Gaulle as Premier clashed with riot police in the center of Paris today. The police held the upper hand.

Demonstrators streamed into Paris on foot, busses, subways and cars from the industrial outskirts. They came by the thousands, singing the Marseillaise and carrying the French flag.

"Down with De Gaulle," they cried. "Long live the republic."

The police, guided by radio from helicopters, met the mobs as they swarmed in from many directions. The demonstrators flailed with their sticks; the police answered with heavy clubs.

Other Disorders

Three persons were known to have been seriously injured.

The police tactics were to keep the demonstrators from massing in great strength at any one point.

Smaller disorders were noted elsewhere in France.

Demonstrations broke out in Rouen, in Northwestern France, and in Avignon in the south, but were quickly quelled.

The Paris marchers were joined by thousands more in a half dozen of the capital's main squares.

In the Place de la Republique, in the northern indus-

Turn to Page 2, Column 6

Death Asked for Father-in-Law, Brother of Saud

DAMASCUS, June 1 (UPI) A military prosecutor today asked a three-man military tribunal to pass death sentences in absentia on King Saud's father-in-law, Asad Ibrahim, and his brother, Majed Ibrahim.

The two were charged with plotting a coup d'etat in Syria against the United Arab Republic at the instigation of King Saud of Saudi Arabia.

Italy's Stromboli Volcano Erupting

STROMBOLI, Italy, June 1 (Reuters)—Stromboli Volcano began erupting today, hurling molten lava into the air amid a series of earth-shaking explosions. The lava streamed down one side of the island volcano into the sea.

U.S. Bids for Friendly Relations With French

White House Statement Raises View That President Will Seek De Gaulle Meeting

WASHINGTON, June 1 (UPI) The Eisenhower administration made a bid tonight for "intimate and friendly relations" with the new crisis government of France under Gen. Charles de Gaulle.

The use of that phrase in a White House statement fed speculation that when the time is right President Eisenhower will seek a personal meeting with the new French Premier, a wartime associate. The President said last week he had liked De Gaulle.

Relief Obvious

The White House statement was issued to newsmen at Gettysburg, where the President is spending the week end.

It was the first formal U.S. government comment on the French crisis since it developed.

There was obvious relief in official quarters here that De Gaulle had finally come to power as Premier, an action which the White House and State Department had considered for some days to be inevitable if political chaos was to be avoided in France.

Uncertain About Policies

At the same time there was deep and worrisome uncertainty in official quarters over De Gaulle's policies now that he has charge of the destiny of France.

Secretary of Defense McElroy said, however, he sees no need for any changes in NATO defense plans because of De Gaulle's rise to power.

"We will deal with him in the same way as we have dealt with previous Pre-

Turn to Page 11, Column 4

INDEX OF FEATURES

No Contracts for United Auto Workers

A half-million automobile workers are without union coverage for first time in 17 years as Ford and Chrysler fail to agree on new pacts. Story on Page 2, Part 1.

ON OTHER PAGES

Plane Lands Safely in River Bed

A pilot brought his four passengers to a safe landing in the Los Angeles River bed yesterday after his plane developed engine trouble en route to International Airport from Riverside.

The pilot, Donald C. Hart, of 3925 Everest St., Riverside, landed in sand and shallow water near the Downey Road bridge. Hart's passengers, flying to make connections with an airliner, completed the journey by taxi.

Yachtsman Killed by Gas Fumes on Cruiser, 5 Saved in Sea Drama

One yachtsman was killed and five others narrowly escaped death early yesterday when the 30-foot cabin cruiser they were aboard became saturated with deadly carbon monoxide fumes off Santa Catalina Island.

All aboard the vessel could have died but for a dramatic air-sea rescue carried out jointly by the Coast Guard and the Avalon Air Transport Co., police indicated.

Names of Victims

The fatality of the tragic week-end cruise was Wilton McComb of 2000 Miramar St., Los Angeles. Rescued were Dale Weaver, same address, and M. C. Hawkins, 36, of 217 Loma Drive, co-owners of the craft; Miss Donna Barton, 33, of 187 S Alvarado St.; William Dunlap, 34, of 426 S Lucas St., and Michael Jaszczyzyn, 37, of 10336 Strathern St., Sun Valley.

Miss Barton was reported in a "good" condition last night in Harbor General Hospital. The others were released after treatment.

Police pieced together this story of the tragedy from the survivors:

The cruiser, R-Mis-Take, left Avalon at 6:15 a.m. to return to the mainland. Weaver and Hawkins were on deck, the other passengers were sleeping below.

Weak Cry Heard

The craft was well under way when Weaver heard a weak cry for help from Miss Barton. Weaver went below and found the cabin filled with exhaust fumes. He shut off the engines and radioed the Coast Guard for help.

Those below deck had become unconscious and the two men carried them topside. Before the last person

Turn to Page 2, Column 7

THE WEATHER

No smog today.

U.S. Weather Bureau forecast: Considerable cloudiness today and tonight but partly sunny this afternoon and mostly sunny after midmorning tomorrow. Not much change in temperatures. High today near 77. High yesterday, 76; low, 60.

Cardinal Stepinac Out of Danger

ZAGREB, Yugoslavia, June 1 (Reuters)—Cardinal Stepinac, titular head of the Roman Catholic Church in Yugoslavia, today was said to be out of danger. The Cardinal has been critically ill with a rare blood disease aggravated by acute thrombosis and pneumonia.

Times Telephone Numbers
- MAdison 5-2345 for subscriber service calls and all other calls except those concerning classified advertising.
- MAdison 9-4411 for all classified advertising calls.

Los Angeles Times

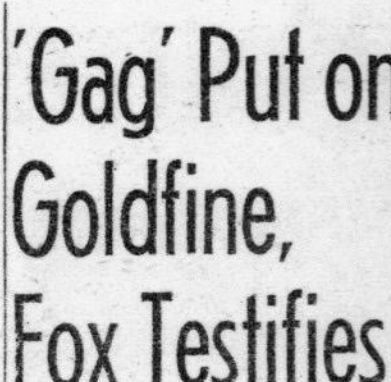

PART I
ALL THE NEWS ALL THE TIME

VOL. LXXVII | IN FOUR PARTS | CC ★ | TUESDAY MORNING, JULY 1, 1958 | 76 PAGES | DAILY 10c

ALASKA VOTED 49TH STATE BY SENATE

SPURNED NEW NAME

Cheryl's Court Secrets Aired

BY JACK JONES

Cheryl Crane, Lana Turner's 14-year-old daughter who stabbed to death Johnny Stompanato on April 4, courageously turned down a proposal that she hide from publicity in another community behind a false name, it was learned yesterday.

She told a judge she'd rather keep her name and fight it out."

This disclosure is in a transcript of the secret April 24 Juvenile Court proceedings in Santa Monica.

Wished to Retire

The previously closed record also brought into the open an apparent custody struggle between Miss Turner and her former husband, Stephen Crane, with its account of a dispute as to whether he has contributed money toward Cheryl's keep.

And it revealed a sad wish of the glamorous actress that she could retire from the spotlight . . . the glare" only she had enough money saved so that she would not have to perform again.

Father Appeals

The record was lodged in the District Court of Appeal yesterday in connection with the appeal by Crane, Cheryl's father, of Superior Judge Allen T. Lynch's ruling making her a ward of the court.

Judge Lynch will rule Sept. 25 on possible revision of the girl's status.

As a ward of the court, she is currently living with her grandmother, Mrs. Mildred Turner, under direct supervision of Probation Officer Mrs. Jeanette Muhlbach.

It was during a discussion of Lana's ability to support Cheryl that the actress made known her unhappiness with the attention awarded a Hollywood star.

Judge Lynch asked her if she hoped to continue in her present employment.

'Only Work I Know'

"A great part of me would like very much not to continue," said Miss Turner, "only because of the . . . spotlight, the glare, that is not only on me but anyone in this business.

"However, the fact that it is the only work that I know, and that I have been the sole support of my daughter and my mother . . . I quite obviously . . . I wish I could say . . . that I had enough put away that I wouldn't have to work. I don't. I must continue working."

The transcript quotes the judge as saying:

"I am interested very much in this girl's future, and she's got to be placed some place, in my opinion, where this, all this publicity, isn't going to just be heaped

Turn to Page 23, Column 1

KEEPS NAME — Cheryl Crane rejects proposal that she hide behind false name to avoid publicity. Times photo

'Gag' Put on Goldfine, Fox Testifies

Adams Told Him to Stop Talking, House Quiz Hears

WASHINGTON, June 30 (AP)—John Fox testified today Sherman Adams obviously ordered Bernard Goldfine to "keep his mouth shut."

Fox said the order followed a Goldfine statement that Adams "isn't letting me down."

Fox, a controversial Boston business promoter, didn't retreat an inch from previous testimony that in Adams' presence Goldfine proposed "a drink to Mr. Adams," who "never lets his friends down."

Testimony Called False

Adams, President Eisenhower's top aide, has called the testimony utterly false.

Fox enlarged on it today. He told a House subcommittee that after Goldfine, Adams' friend and benefactor, proposed the toast, Adams took him off in a corner and "quite obviously admonished him not to talk too much."

The place and time, Fox repeated, were Goldfine's suite at the Sheraton-Carlton Hotel here on May 10, 1955. At the time, Goldfine was in trouble with the Federal Trade Commission over complaints that contents of textiles manufactured by the wealthy industrialist were mislabeled.

Fox also said today he intends to file a libel suit

Turn to Page 19, Column 4

VICTORY CHEERS—Congressional backers of Alaska Statehood bill and Alaska Gov. Mike Stepovich celebrate its passage over 49-star Flag outside Senate chamber. From left, Sens. Church (D) Ida., and Kuchel (R) Cal.; Stepovich; Sen. Jackson (D) Wash.; Wally Hickel, GOP chairman for Alaska; and Sens. Watkins (R) Utah and Neuberger (D) Or. The men smiling in background are not identified. (AP) Wirephoto

Bill Gets Approval by 64-20

WASHINGTON, June 30 (UP)—The Senate tonight voted to make Alaska the 49th State. The roll-call vote was 64-20.

Acceptance of the House-passed bill left only the requirement of Presidential approval and acceptance by Alaskans of the bill's terms to extend the Union to a point 55 miles from Russian Siberia.

The bill would permit Alaska to take its place late this fall or early in the winter as the first new State since the 1912 admission of Arizona and New Mexico. Its two Senators and lone House member could take their seats in the Congress in January.

Bigger Than Texas

Extension of Statehood to Alaska will add to the United States an area roughly one-fifth the size of the existing 48 States and two and one-half times that of Texas.

It will end the Territorial status which has been Alaska's since it was acquired from Russia in 1867 for $7,200,000.

Alaskans for the first time will be permitted to cast their vote for President and Vice-President, have voting representation in the Congress and elect their own Governor and State officers. Proponents of Statehood have been battling since 1916 when the first bill was introduced.

Southern Opposition

Passage of the bill on the sixth day of Senate debate came over the opposition of a determined group of Senators, largely from the South, who argued that Alaska is not prepared for Statehood from the standpoint of either economy or population.

They pointed also to Alaska's geographical location, and said the overstepping of Canada to extend Statehood to a noncontiguous area would be a precedent for admission of other offshore areas, such as Hawaii, Puerto Rico or Guam.

Conservative View

Reports linking southern opposition to the civil rights issue and fears that Alaska's admission would lead to election of Senators unfriendly to the southern stand were denied by Sen. Russell (D) Ga., in one of the final appeals made against the bill.

Russell said opposition stemmed from the higher percentage of southern Senators who are traditionalists and who are opposed to "change for the sake of change." He noted that some of Statehood's most ardent advocates—for Hawaii as well as Alaska—were from the South.

During debate, Statehood supporters cited Alaska's ad-

Turn to Page 6, Column 1

L.A. to Reduce Electric Rate Again Today

The fifth successive rate reduction in less than a year will be effected today when Los Angeles electric bills are lowered to 1956 basic levels, the Water and Power Commission announced yesterday.

"We are able to pass these savings along to the people of Los Angeles because our power production costs have dropped by $6,000,000 annually and are reflected automatically under the fuel adjustment clause formula," said J. C. Moller Jr., president of the commission.

Escalator Formula

Under an escalator formula approved by the City Council last year, customers' bills go up or down according to what it costs the department to operate its power plants.

Moller said the department has been able to lower its charges despite generally higher costs because of increased supplies of low-cost Hoover Dam power in addition to savings in fuel oil purchases and higher operating efficiencies. These resulted largely from increased rainfall this year and more abundant water power.

Rebels, Army Trade Blows Near Beirut

BEIRUT, Lebanon, June 30 (AP)—Government forces and mountain tribesmen fought a seesaw battle in the hills overlooking Beirut today after the rebels drove closer to the capital than ever before.

Followers of young Rebel Leader Kamal Jublatt made a surprise dawn push into the hills between Chemlan and Kayfoun, only five miles from Beirut International Airport.

Government forces counter-attacked. The rebels fell back from two hills.

U.S., Russian Delegates Map Nuclear Talks

GENEVA, June 30 (AP)—Russian and American scientific officials got together amiably today and predicted success for East-West nuclear talks opening here tomorrow.

The statement cleared away any lingering suggestion Soviet delegates might not attend the conference on ways of detecting nuclear weapons testing. The findings could be put to practical use if a world-wide ban on nuclear weapons is never agreed upon.

Two-Hour Talks

Prof. Yevgeni K. Federov, head of the Soviet delegation, met for two hours with Dr. James B. Fisk, U.S. delegation leader. They agreed the conference will deal solely with means for detection of any cheating that might be tried under a ban.

In addition to the United States and Russia, countries with representatives at the conference are Britain, France, Canada, Czechoslovakia, Rumania and Poland.

High Court Strikes Out State Tax Loyalty Oath

7-1 Decision Upholds Religious Groups and Veterans in Their Refusal to Comply

BY DON SHANNON, Times Washington Bureau

WASHINGTON, June 30—The Supreme Court today declared unconstitutional the California non-Communist oath required of religious groups and veterans seeking State tax exemptions.

Seven justices approved the decisions striking down California's loyalty oath for taxpayers. Justice Clark dissented and Chief Justice Warren, who was Governor of the State at the time the constitutional provision was adopted, did not take part in the decision.

Justice Brennan, delivering the lengthy majority

Other Supreme Court news on Pages 2, 10 and 13, Part 1.

opinion in the appeals of two Northern California veterans who refused to sign the oath to win the veterans' property tax exemption, said:

"For the purpose of this case we assume without deciding that California may deny tax exemptions to persons who engage in the proscribed speech for which they might be fined or imprisoned. But the question remains whether California has chosen a fair method for determining when a claimant is a member of that class."

The chief defect of the California law, Brennan said, was the requirement that the veteran bear the burden of proof that he is not a person advocating the overthrow of the government, despite the State's

Turn to Page 13, Column 1

Postage-Due Letters Now Cost 5 Cents

Beginning today any mail delivered without the proper amount of stamps on it will cost the householder 5 cents besides the amount of postage due, it was announced yesterday by Postmaster Olesen.

The new charge results from a bill passed in Congress last April and is designed to defray a portion of the cost involved in handling postage-due mail, Olesen said. Under the new act, the fees for returning "dead letters" and first-class parcels to senders has been increased from 5 cents to 10 cents.

On Aug. 1 postal rates on most mail will be increased to 4 cents an ounce for first-class mail, 7 cents an ounce for air mail letters, 5 cents an ounce for air mail postal and postcards and 3 cents an ounce for regular postal or postcards.

Juneau's Bell Rings Out 49 Times at News

Forty-nine jubilant peals of a bell resounded throughout the streets of Juneau, Alaska, yesterday to notify residents of the Territorial capital that Alaska had finally reached the end of its trouble-strewn road to becoming the nation's 49th State.

The glad tidings were sounded shortly after 4 p.m. on Juneau's replica of the Liberty Bell which stands in front of the Federal Office Building, later to become the Capitol Building of the State of Alaska.

Bonfire and Parade

The Times telephoned Juneau last night to get a firsthand account of the residents' reaction to the news that the Senate had given final Congressional approval to Statehood for the vast northern Territory.

Joe Kirkbride of the city's newspaper, Empire, said the ringing of the bell was followed by impromptu parades of cars whose drivers heralded the victory with wildly honking horns.

Work came to a halt in the Territorial Office Building as

Turn to Page 7, Column 1

Twenty-One Quiz Girl Ties Again

NEW YORK, June 30 (UPI) — Elfrida Von Nardroff kept her title as television's highest quiz show winner tonight by tying a school official for the fifth time.

Miss Von Nardroff, 32, and Robert Leicester of New York could not defeat each other on the NBC-TV program Twenty-One. They will return next week. Miss Von Nardroff, who has won $253,500, and Leicester answered questions on the Civil War, theater and quotations.

Sunny Day Brings High of 81 Deg.

Sunshine and a trace of smog were the weather yesterday.

Downtown Los Angeles had a high temperature of 81 deg. at 2:16 p.m., following a low of 63 at 2:53 a.m. High relative humidity was 86% at 3 a.m. The low was 45% at 2:15 p.m. Smog was measurable in the early afternoon.

FAMILY OF 8 SPLIT

Girls' Kidnap of Baby to Halt Adoption Fails

Two teen-age Sun Valley girls who Sunday kidnaped their baby brother in an attempt to block plans to put him up for adoption apparently found their efforts wasted.

"The boy has to go," the girls' father, Lyle Hill, 43, insisted moments after his family of eight children was reunited late yesterday. "There just isn't enough money to go around."

The situation came to light Sunday shortly after Sandra Hill, 16, and Genevieve (Gigi) Hill, 13, overheard their parents making plans to take 20-month-old Michael Hill to an adoption agency.

The two girls fled from the modest house at 10433 Arminta St. "to a little hideout" and there they decided to keep their baby brother themselves.

"We asked mother (Mrs. Virginia Marie Hill, 42) if we could take Mike to the movies," Sandra said, "and she agreed to drive us into Burbank. I wrote a note and left it in the car saying that Mike could not be taken away."

The two girls left the movie shortly after it started and, carrying Mikie, walked back to the "hideout" where they had hidden some diapers, a blanket and a can of plums. They then caught a bus into Hollywood and dis-

Turn to Page 2, Column 6

THE WEATHER

Light to moderate eye irritation today.

U.S. Weather Bureau forecast: Low cloudiness spreading in from the coast in late evening through early morning hours but mostly sunny days otherwise today and tomorrow. Not much change in temperatures. High today near 82. Yesterday's high, 81; low, 63.

INDEX OF FEATURES

Zsa Zsa Cancels Party for Trujillo

Zsa Zsa Gabor cancels her Beverly Hilton party for Gen. Rafael Trujillo Jr., but the general denies reports of a rift between them. Story on Page 1, Part 3.

ON OTHER PAGES

Queen Dons Tin Hat, Enters Mine

DUNFERMLINE, Scotland, June 30 (UPI)—Queen Elizabeth put on overalls and a miner's tin hat today and went down a 1600-foot coal mine shaft near Dunfermline. Elizabeth, accompanied by Prince Philip, splashed through puddles.

Eisenhowers Wed 42 Years Today

WASHINGTON, June 30 (AP) — Tomorrow is the 42nd wedding anniversary of President and Mrs. Eisenhower. In reply to reporters' questions, White House Press Secretary Hagerty said he had no information on celebration plans.

Soviets Have No ICBM, Army Secretary Says

BY GRAHAM BERRY, Times Science Editor

FT. BLISS, Tex., June 30.—Army Secretary Brucker said tonight Russia has no intercontinental ballistic missile and that her intermediate range missile has less range than our own.

He also told a news conference after a talk before 400 industrial and military leaders at Ft. Bliss Officers Club, "I have seen nothing on the other side to believe that they have solved the nose cone re-entry problem as we have."

He referred to the Jupiter missile firings in which the nose cone was recovered by our Navy.

He added that Caltech's Jet Propulsion Laboratory and the Army Ballistics Missile Agency are working on one or two lunar probes.

This is the Juno project, for which JPL has received $2,850,000.

The Secretary emphasized that the United States has and will continue to maintain air and space defenses that can match any enemy's known capabilities.

Brucker said the Nike Hercules missile system is being developed to defend American industrial areas. This is a more powerful model of the Nike.

These systems have already been installed at Washington, New York and Chicago, he reported.

Story on Army missile exhibition on Page 2, Part 1.

Times Telephone Numbers
• MAdison 5-2345 for subscriber service calls and all other calls except those concerning classified advertising.
• MAdison 9-4411 for all classified advertising calls.

Los Angeles Times

EQUAL RIGHTS
LIBERTY UNDER THE LAW · TRUE INDUSTRIAL FREEDOM

PART 1
ALL THE NEWS
ALL THE TIME

VOL. LXXVIII · IN FOUR PARTS · CC ★ · SATURDAY MORNING, JANUARY 3, 1959 · 42 PAGES · DAILY 10c

RUSSIA FIRES ROCKET TOWARD MOON

108,000 Miles Out, Soviet Says; Lunar Expedition Planned

MOSCOW, Jan. 3 (Saturday) (AP)—The Soviet Union fired a multi-stage rocket toward the moon yesterday. An announcement early today said the final stage was 108,000 miles out and on target with the speed required to put it in the vicinity of the moon.

The rocket is due in the vicinity of the moon early tomorrow, Moscow time (about 8 p.m. today PST). Already it has traveled farther than any object man has sent from the earth.

In view of these developments, Moscow radio announced, Russian scientists will make preparations to equip an expedition to the moon "which would establish an observatory and an intermediary base there for a future space flight."

The broadcast in English gave no details about the expedition.

The rocket was reported today to have reached "second cosmic speed," which the Russians said insured that it was in interplanetary flight. "The rocket continues its flight toward the moon," Moscow radio said.

Won't Come Back

The highest that a man-made object has been lofted from the earth before this was a U.S. Air Force moon shot which went 71,300 miles before plunging back to the earth.

The Soviet rocket shows no signs of coming back, the Russians indicated. Moscow radio said that instruments on it were working reliably and everything seemed to be going fine.

The nose cone carries the Soviet flag, the announcement said, and in addition to many instruments the rocket carries special equipment designed to create the sodium cloud of an artificial comet. This is to permit it to be observed and photographed.

The Russian announcement immediately raised speculation that Soviet science has reached a stage at which a man could be successfully launched into orbit around the moon. The size of the final stage was regarded as more than adequate for a man to eat, breathe comfortably and even stretch his legs.

Dramatic Report

Moscow Radio called the newest shot "the first successful interplanetary flight" almost before the multi-stage rocket left the earth's atmosphere.

It said the super Sputnik was heading moonward after being fired off by a multi-stage rocket which can reach a cosmic speed of 11.2 kilometers (7 miles) a second.

A dramatic account tracking the rocket out of Soviet Russia flashed abroad over the Moscow wavelength. It said the rocket had flashed eastward across the borders of Soviet Russia, had climbed across the Hawaiian Islands and was moving rapidly away from the earth over the Pacific Ocean.

None of the broadcasts thus far has stated whether the rocket was aimed directly at the moon or intended to go around it.

Over-all Weight Not Told

The over-all weight of the rocket was not mentioned. Tass said the "last stage" weighed 1,472 kilograms (3,245.2 pounds) without the fuel and was equipped with a special container inside of which were various measuring apparatus. The weight of the equipment was given as about 796½ pounds.

(The total launching weight of the rocket must have been about 250 tons, the chairman of the British Interplanetary Society said in London.

(Leslie Shepherd told an interviewer this was about five times the launching weight of the Juno rocket used

Please Turn to Pg. 3, Col. 7

BOOTED OUT—One of signs carried by parading Castro followers in Havana shows deposed President Batista being kicked off island by victorious rebel chief. (AP) Wirephoto

NEARLY 50 DIE IN HAVANA FIGHTING

Tanks, Armored Cars Used in Hot Battles Between Castro Men, Die-Hard Batistans

HAVANA, Jan. 2 (AP)—A blood-wet battle of tanks and guns ushered in the occupation of Havana by Fidel Castro's field troops today. From 40 to 50 men were believed killed in a three-hour fight between Castro forces and diehard Batistans within sight of the Presidential Palace.

Meanwhile, the city awaited the arrival of Manuel Urrutia, the man Castro has proclaimed provisional President.

Estimates of the wounded ranged up to 450.

Batistan groups numbering several hundred were apparently crushed. But the action may portend even more vicious fighting.

Americans Sail

The ocean-going ferry City of Havana sailed tonight for Key West, Fla., with nearly 500 American citizens aboard.

The U.S. Embassy announced the vessel will return tomorrow night to pick up any other Americans who want to get out of Havana. Three U.S. warships and two auxiliary vessels stood off the Cuban coast ready to take out any other Americans, if necessary.

Speaking of a purported

Please Turn to Pg. 2, Col. 5

New Contract Believed Near in Pilots Strike

WASHINGTON, Jan. 2 (UPI)—Top representatives of American Airlines and the striking air line pilots' union were reported near agreement tonight on a new contract that would end a 14-day-old walkout.

Sources close to the negotiations said they believe a settlement will be reached, perhaps tomorrow, at bargaining sessions being conducted at National Mediation Board headquarters.

American President C. R. Smith and Claren N. Sayen, head of the Air Line Pilots Assn., resumed talks this afternoon at the invitation of Board Chairman Leverett Edwards.

Scores of Reds Reported Held in Syria, Egypt

CAIRO, Jan. 2 (AP) — Communists estimated to number 200 have been arrested in Syria and Egypt in the first two days of the new year, authoritative sources said today.

It was the biggest action so far in the anti-Communist campaign kicked off by President Nasser of the United Arab Republic in a speech Dec. 23. He denounced Reds as enemies of Arab unity and promoters of Zionist and imperialist objectives.

'Small Frogs'

(Similar news came from Beirut, where an unconfirmed report from just across the border placed the total arrested by Syrian police at 600 Communists in Damascus, Aleppo, Homs, Hama and other cities.)

Apparently the big Communist fish slipped out of Nasser's net. The list of those arrested in Syria did not include Syria's top Communist, Khaled Bagdash. One Egyptian source described the Reds now in Syrian custody as "all small frogs."

Reliable informants said that in Egypt alone at least 180 Communists are known to have been picked up in the last 48 hours.

Marathon Talks Set in Store Tie-up

State Conciliator Orders Both Sides Into Session Today

BY HOWARD KENNEDY
Times Labor Editor

State Conciliator Edward Peters ordered marathon sessions starting today in hope of a quick break in the contract deadlock which yesterday closed 1000 Los Angeles area food markets.

Peters instructed negotiators for the Food Employers Council and the Retail Clerks Union to appear at the Ambassador at 10:30 a.m. and "be prepared to stay."

The development followed a day of futility in the grocery dispute which idled 16,000 clerks and by Monday may bring layoffs to nearly 5000 allied workers.

No Pinch Felt

A snap survey yesterday indicated housewives had not yet felt the pinch of the work stoppage. At least, there were no complaints. Some 4,000 smaller stores and about 400 markets which signed interim agreements with the union were open and busy.

The tone of the contract stalemate was underlined by the union yesterday when it reportedly filed one general and two specific charges of apathy against the FEC with the National Labor Relations Board.

Union's Charges

The principal charge by the clerks was that the FEC had "refused to produce financial statements and/or records so that the union may evaluate its bargaining requests for a wage increase and fringe benefits."

The union also complained that the FEC was trying to "frustrate . . . the collective bargaining process."

Negotiators met yesterday at the Ambassador with Peters to explore what compromises are possible between the union's demand for an 82.4-cent hourly increase in wages and fringe benefits and the employers' offer of 50 cents over a five-year contract period, plus

Please Turn to Pg. 5, Col. 1

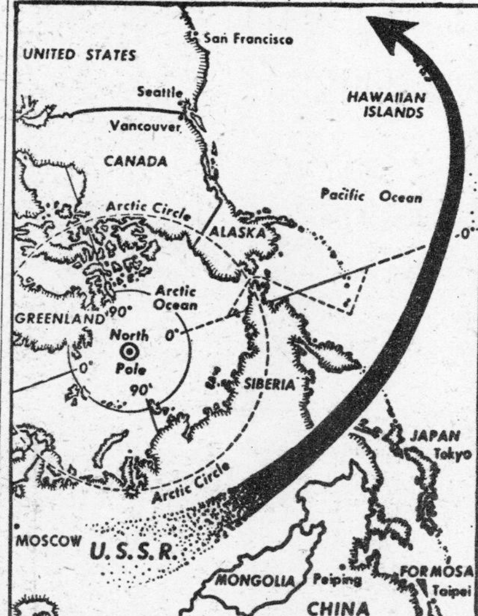

RUSSIAN ROCKET—Arrow indicates trajectory of rocket Russia launched toward moon. Moscow said it is due to reach target at 8 p.m. today (PST). (AP) Wirephoto map

Knight's Final Word: 'Ain't Mad at Nobody'

Outgoing Governor Gives Valedictory; Warns Against Attempts to Weaken Office

SACRAMENTO, Jan. 2 (AP)—Gov. Knight told his final news conference today he'll leave office Monday with no regrets and no grudges. "I ain't mad at nobody," he said.

With this lighthearted valediction, the outgoing Republican Governor coupled a serious warning against any further attempts to weaken the powers of the State's chief executive officer.

Refers to Senate

Knight referred to the tendency by the Senate to require more and more of the Governor's appointments to be subject to confirmation. He said this worked no hardship on him, but that he could foresee the time when the Senate could be powerful enough to dictate to the Governor.

Knight on Monday will wind up a quarter of a century in office—11½ years as a Superior Court judge in Los Angeles, seven as Lieutenant-Governor and five as Governor.

He said he has no plans after Monday, except to take a rest and play some golf for a month or so. After that, he indicated he'll go into business of some kind. He

Please Turn to Pg. 6, Col. 2

L.A.-to-Tokyo Flight Treaty Reported Near

BY DON SHANNON
Times Washington Bureau

WASHINGTON, Jan. 2 — The United States and Japan today were reported near agreement on a new bilateral treaty which will permit direct air service between Los Angeles and Tokyo.

Rep. Craig Hosmer (R) Long Beach, said the pact, which has been under negotiation in Tokyo for more than a year, will enable Los Angeles passengers to fly direct to Tokyo via Honolulu. Los Angeles passengers will also be able to travel to South America aboard Japanese air lines. The new agreement will not include service to Mexico or Central America, however.

Present Agreement

Under the existing air agreement between the United States and Japan, JAL is authorized to serve San Francisco and Seattle but has never activated the Seattle-Tokyo route. Two U.S. carriers now serve Japan

Please Turn to Pg. 2, Col. 2

Newly-Born Baby Stolen From Hospital

NEW YORK, Jan. 2 (AP) — A newborn baby was kidnaped tonight from St. Peter's Hospital in Brooklyn, police reported.

Police said the kidnaper was an unidentified blond woman, about 30.

The infant was born at 9:17 p.m. and was reported kidnaped two minutes before midnight.

The baby's parents are Mr. and Mrs. Frank Chionchio, who live in the Ft. Hamilton section of Brooklyn. Chionchio is a lawyer.

The infant was one of nine laying in bassinets in a room adjacent to the maternity ward.

Gusty Winds Buffet Coast; Storms Due

Gusty winds — advance guard of a weather front expected to bring rain and snow showers, freezing temperatures and dust storms to some Southern California areas today — began buffeting the Southland coast last night.

Small-craft warnings were hoisted from Point Conception to Oceanside at 8 p.m. yesterday as the U.S. Weather Bureau forecast northwest winds to 30 m.p.h.

The Weather Bureau said snow flurries are possible in the mountains today, and a few light showers are expected on the south coast. The high in Los Angeles will be about 60, the Weather Bureau said, and temperatures will be colder tonight.

Holiday Traffic Toll Rises to 211

BY THE ASSOCIATED PRESS

Traffic deaths across the country over the four-day New Year's holiday rose to 211 early today.

The rate of fatalities from motor vehicle accidents dropped to slightly more than three an hour.

THE WEATHER

No smog today.

U.S. Weather Bureau forecast: Partly cloudy at times today and tomorrow. Gusty north winds. Cooler today with high about 60. Colder tonight. Yesterday's high, 65; low, 52.

Caltech Alters Station to Track Russ Rocket

Crews from the Caltech Jet Propulsion Laboratory last night were making hurried modifications at the Jet Lab's Goldstone Tracking Station near Barstow so Russia's moon rocket can be followed by radio signals.

The tracking station, with its 85-foot dish antenna, was set to follow United States space probes operating on a 1,000-megacycle band and could not track the Russian lunar rocket which reportedly is transmitting on 19.995 and 19.997 megacycles and 183.6 megacycles.

It was necessary to install a more discriminating receiver, JPL officials said, in order to receive signals from the Russian rocket.

Although the Defense Department said it knew of Russia's moon shot before the Moscow radio announcement, JPL had no advance knowledge of the space probe and was faced with assigning special crews to night work at Goldstone to properly modify the radio telescope system.

They expected the work would be completed in time to start tracking the Soviet rocket when it rose above the eastern horizon this morning. Officials added that the probe should be directly above Southern California about 7 a.m. today.

For several hours yesterday Caltech scientists considered using the institute's three radio telescopes at Bishop for tracking duties, but these, too, would have required modification and the idea was abandoned in favor of the Goldstone operation.

Studio Bars Young Jack Warner as Family Feud Breaks Into Open

A stormy Hollywood family feud appeared to be in full blast yesterday when 42-year-old Jack M. Warner, son of Producer Jack L. Warner, told reporters that he was barred from the lot at Warner Bros., the studio his father heads.

Earlier this week, the studio announced officially that young Warner was being released from his position as vice-president in charge of production of commercial and industrial films. Warner subsequently issued a statement that he had not terminated his association with the company and expected to report to work yesterday morning.

"He was barred from the lot," Mrs. Barbara Warner, wife of the executive, told The Times.

There were studio rumors that he had been bodily ejected but Mrs. Warner had no comment to make on them.

She repeated that her husband had not resigned nor had he been released from his job at the studio.

"This has nothing to do with his work," she said. "This is strictly a family matter."

Meanwhile, at the studio there was no comment concerning a family feud but simply a reiteration of the statement that Jack M. Warner was no longer with Warner Bros. A spokesman, however, said that young Warner's office was not on the Warner Bros. lot but across a street from it.

The studio announced that young Warner was being replaced by his former assistant, David DePatie.

Earlier in the day, young Warner told reporters: "I went out to the studio this morning just like a normal business day and was denied admittance to my office . . . I have practically grown up in this studio. I have worked here almost all of my life—except for five years in ETO during World War II."

Feud or no feud, resignation or no, workmen yesterday were removing Warner's name from his office door.

INDEX OF FEATURES

Deputy Involved in Coroner Fight Quits

Assistant who recently filed misconduct charges against Coroner Curphey resigns. Story Page 1, Part 3.

ON OTHER PAGES

Times Telephone Numbers:
MAdison 9-4411—Classified Advertising.
MAdison 5-2345—For all other calls.
Circulation—Largest in the West:
484,000 Daily; 878,000 Sunday.

Los Angeles Times

EQUAL RIGHTS
LIBERTY UNDER THE LAW · TRUE INDUSTRIAL FREEDOM

FINAL
ALL THE NEWS
ALL THE TIME

VOL. LXXVIII · IN FIFTEEN PARTS—PART ONE · CC · SUNDAY MORNING, FEBRUARY 22, 1959 · 318 PAGES · Copyright, 1959 by the Times-Mirror Company · Beyond 75-Mile Zone, Price 25c · SUNDAY 20c

Macmillan in Moscow, Fears War by 'Muddle'

APPROPRIATE HEADGEAR — Britain's Prime Minister Macmillan, left, not to be outdone by his Russian hosts, wore light gray fur hat on arrival at Moscow's Vnukovo airport yesterday. Khrushchev, at right, and his interpreter were on hand to meet the visitor. Macmillan's fur headgear wowed the Russian crowds.
(AP) Wirephoto via radio from Moscow

Russ Hear Appeal for Accord Aid

MOSCOW, Feb. 21 (UPI) British Prime Minister Macmillan opened summit talks with Soviet Premier Khrushchev today by appealing for greater East-West understanding lest the big powers "muddle" their way into a suicidal war.

The two chiefs of state plunged into the first of a series of discussions on such world problems as Berlin and Germany almost immediately after Macmillan arrived aboard a British Comet jetliner from London to a rigidly formal welcome.

Khrushchev Jovial

Khrushchev, in jovial mood, said at the airport he looked forward to useful talks. Macmillan said his 10-day mission is to seek better understanding between the world power blocs.

At a Kremlin reception later, Macmillan amplified his remark in a speech that ranged generally over major issues and reduced them to the basic fear that a war in the nuclear age could destroy the world.

He reminded the audience that for more than 10 years with only intermittent "thaws," the East and West have been "confronting each other with ever more terrible instruments of destruction."

Macmillan Wish

"I wish with all my heart that this competition would cease," he said.

"It is not that we fear acts of calculated aggression, and I hope that you do not. In modern conditions such aggression, between the great powers, at least, would be suicidal folly.

"At the same time it is impossible to hide from ourselves the dangers of a war by miscalculation or by muddle. That indeed would be a calamity for us all."

In off-the-cuff remarks directly to Khrushchev at a two-hour banquet in St. Catherine's Hall of the Kremlin, Macmillan said East and West should concentrate on "the things that unite us rather than the things that divide us" to give the world peace.

Peace Sought

"Let us try to guide the world through the next generation in peace," he said.

Khrushchev in return said he considered Macmillan's visit a result of "this thaw" in the cold war.

The two statesmen toasted each other and their respective countries.

Macmillan, making the first summit contact between East and West since the So-

Please Turn to Pg. 9, Col. 1

Crash Near Oceanside Kills Seven

Parents, Three Children Among Victims in Wreck

Four adults and three children were killed yesterday in a five-car collision on Highway 101 about 3½ miles north of Oceanside, during a heavy rain.

The tragedy almost wiped out the family of Arnold David Boatner, 34, of 9071 Timothy Lane, Garden Grove, with the only survivor of four children, Danny, 9, being sent to the Oceanside Hospital in critical condition.

Others Badly Hurt

Three other Garden Grove children and one adult, driver of a third car in the pileup, all are in critical condition.

Dead in addition to Boatner are his wife, Elois, 28, daughters, Becky, 8 and Evon, 4 months, and a son, David, 11; Bernard William Patterson, 36, of 2317 Sycamore St. Anaheim, and a Los Angeles woman, Carmen Casillas, 1831 Sichel St.

California Highway Patrolman Albert Scott said a car going north and driven by Patterson, a chemist travelling alone, crossed into the southbound lane hitting head-on a pick-up truck driven by Boatner, which was carrying nine persons, seven of them children.

Scott said that a car going south driven by Lazaro Samudio, 50, of 522 N Soto St., plowed into the rear of the pickup truck. Samudio's sister-in-law, Miss Casillas, died and Samudio was injured seriously.

Children Injured

The chain reaction continued when a car said to be driven by Owen Patrick Rafferty, 32, of 2728 S La Cienega Blvd., and also going south, sideswiped the Samudio car, then bounced across the highway to collide with the northbound car of M/Sgt. Robert O. Burton of Camp Pendleton.

Officers said neither Rafferty nor Burton was injured.

The critically injured children traveling with the Boatner family, besides Danny Boatner, were Tommy Steele, 11, of 12151 Ditmore

Please Turn to Pg. 12, Col. 5

BOMBER-FIRED ATOM MISSILE SEEN BY 1960

WASHINGTON, Feb. 21 (UPI) — The Air Force is planning to bolster U.S. retaliatory power with a revolutionary ballistic missile that can be fired from bombers, it was disclosed today.

A highly placed official said the first of the high-speed, nuclear-tipped weapons may be ready by late summer 1960.

They will have a range of more than 1,000 miles and will zoom from beneath the wings of the bombers.

The project is known as Bold Orion.

Philadelphia Favored as GOP Convention City

Democrats Meet Friday to Confirm L.A. as Site of Nomination Despite Protests

© New York Times News Service

WASHINGTON, Feb. 21—Philadelphia suddenly has emerged as a favored 1960 convention site for Republicans, and also may be threatening Los Angeles as the choice for the Democratic meeting.

A shift in GOP sentiment toward Philadelphia became known from talks among Republican leaders who previously had leaned toward Chicago. The question will be settled at a national committee meeting here early in April.

The Democratic National Committee meets here next Friday with a recommendation from its site subcommittee that the party hold its next nominating convention in Los Angeles the week of July 11, 1960. But the recommendation will be opposed by a group including Gov. Davi' L. Lawrence of Pennsylvania, Jacob M. Arvey of Chicago and Carmine De Sapio of New York. Chicago and New York are strong contenders, as is Philadelphia.

Butler Confident

One problem of the Lawrence-Arvey-De Sapio group is that each of the three leaders favors his own city and it will be difficult for them to pool their strength against the forces backing the site subcommittee selection. Paul M. Butler, Democratic national chairman, is confident the Los Angeles selection will be upheld.

Republican and Democratic leaders said sentiment for Chicago is declining. Both expressed disappointment with the Chicago presentation in bidding for the convention site.

Western Democrats favor Los Angeles to open the 1960 campaign in the "backyard" of Vice-President Nixon, who is the front runner for the GOP presidential nomination next year.

Time a Factor

Opponents of the Los Angeles choice argue that in a hotly contested convention the three-hour difference in time between New York and Los Angeles would greatly reduce the probable viewing and listening audience for night-time Democratic sessions. This problem did not arise at the 1956 San Francisco convention because the renomination of President Eisenhower and Vice-President Nixon was assured.

Republican leaders said they had given little consideration to the convention bids of either Los Angeles or New York, because the selection of the Southern California city would seem to favor

Please Turn to Pg. 9, Col. 4

Singer Dropped Over Racket Quiz Publicity

NEW YORK, Feb. 21 (UPI)—Singer Tommy Leonetti said today he was dropped as a guest star on tonight's "Dick Clark Show" after publication of testimony before the Senate rackets committee that his former manager had tried to force jukebox suppliers to push his records.

"This kind of publicity could be very bad for my career, and I want to be treated fairly," Leonetti said.

The 28-year-old singer from Cliffside, N.J., had been scheduled to appear on the Clark show today on the ABC-TV network. He was to have plugged his new recording of "Moonlight Serenade."

Press Agent

Leonetti's press agent Frances Kaye said the singer arrived here last night after appearing at a Heart Fund benefit show in Providence, R.I., and learned this morning he had been dropped from the program.

She said ABC promised to put him back on the variety show "after this cools down."

Charles Reeves, executive producer of the Clark show, said Leonetti will appear on the program at a later date. He said it often is necessary to drop scheduled acts. There was no need to substitute for Leonetti tonight because the program was "jammed" with talent, he added.

"The program change (dropping Leonetti) was in complete agreement with

Please Turn to Pg. 14, Col. 3

New Storm Sweeps in Heavy Rain

Up to 1.38 In. Falls Along Coast; Clearing Forecast

Heavy showers dumped up to 1.38 in. of rain over Los Angeles coastal areas and lighter intermittent rainfall inland yesterday as the latest Pacific storm swept over the Southland. From 6 in. to a foot of new snow covered most mountain resort areas.

But except for a few scattered showers near the mountains today, the storm

Rainfall figures Page 2, Part I.

will leave only clouds and continued cool temperatures, the weatherman said. Snow level will be about 3,000 feet today.

Los Angeles received .36 in. of precipitation yesterday, bringing the season's total to 4.92 in., as compared with 11.40 in. last year and 9.88 in. normal to date.

Records 1.38 In.

But in the coastal areas, Torrance recorded 1.38 in. and Hermosa Beach received 1 in. Other high-rainfall districts were Rolling Hills, 1.10 in.; Manhattan Beach, .90; Redondo Beach, .85 and Lynwood, .67.

In Orange County, 1.29 in. of rain fell at Huntington Beach and Seal Beach recorded .99 in.

Mountain temperatures remained below the freezing mark through the day with the resultant snow fall whitening the hills as low as the 2,000-foot level.

Rockslide Loosened

Rains loosened a rockslide which closed one lane of Malibu Canyon Rd. five miles north of Pacific Coast Highway and State Division of Highway crews were clearing it away last night.

Rain threatened the homes of Michael Kidd, Broadway choreographer, 9121 Alta Credo Dr., in Coldwater Canyon, and Mrs. Vera Kaplan, 9052 Wonderland Park Ave., Laurel Canyon, whose back yards were under tons of decomposed granite sliding down in last Monday's downpours.

Kidd piled some 250 sandbags against the creeping

Please Turn to Pg. 2, Col. 2

Eisenhower Returns From Visit to Mexico

'Goodwill Trip Called 'Highly Successful'; President Spends 20 Minutes With Dulles

BY DON SHANNON, Times Washington Bureau

WASHINGTON, Feb. 21—President Eisenhower today returned from his goodwill visit to Mexico's President Lopez Mateos, which the White House described as "highly successful."

Three hours later, the President paid a 20-minute call on Secretary of State Dulles at Walter Reed Army Hospital, where the secretary is under treatment for cancer.

Dulles had just received his second one-minute radiation treatment, which doctors said was "well tolerated," with no adverse after effects. He received his first exposure to the hospital's 1,000,000 volt X-ray machine yesterday and was reported to have spent a comfortable night.

Longer Exposures

The treatment, which sometimes produces nausea or weakness, is designed to arrest the abdominal cancer discovered after the secretary underwent surgery for the repair of a hernia Feb. 13. The X-ray therapy will continue with exposures up to five minutes if initial treatments are tolerated.

The President flew nonstop from the Mexican resort, canceling a projected stopover at Augusta, Ga., because of cold weather. Before his departure the President closed two days of informal conferences with Mexico's chief executive by agreeing to joint U.S.-Mexican construction of the Diablo Dam on the Rio Grande.

Press secretary Hagerty told reporters that President Eisenhower came home with "the feeling that he has a friend" in Lopez Mateos and that co-operation between

Please Turn to Pg. 8, Col. 3

Brazil Puts OK on Mrs. Luce as New U.S. Envoy

RIO DE JANEIRO, Feb. 21 (AP)—A Brazilian official said today the U.S. government has asked for approval of Mrs. Clare Boothe Luce as ambassador to Brazil. She formerly was ambassador to Italy.

Augusto Frederico Schmidt, an adviser to President Kubitschek, said the request came this morning, and Washington was informed immediately that Mrs. Luce is acceptable. U.S. Embassy sources would not comment.

White House Uninformed

Presidential Press Secretary Hagerty said in Washington the reports about Mrs. Luce were "news to the White House."

Mrs. Luce would succeed Ellis O. Briggs, who has been ambassador to Brazil since July, 1956. He is a career diplomat who also has served in the Dominican Republic, Uruguay, Peru, Korea and Czechoslovakia.

U.S. Can Meet Berlin Test, General Says

WASHINGTON, Feb. 21 (AP)—The Army chief of staff says the United States has all the strength necessary to resist force in Berlin "if we are willing to mobilize it and do so in time."

"Mobilize the entire nation?" asked Sen. Long (D-La.).

"Yes," replied Gen. Maxwell D. Taylor at a secret hearing on Feb. 2. "You cannot play around in this business unless you have a lot of blue chips in your pocket. This is unlimited poker."

The exchange was included in testimony made public tonight by the Senate disarmament subcommittee.

Taylor Questioned

Long, questioning Taylor about Western ability to maintain its position in West Berlin, referred to earlier testimony Soviet bloc conventional forces greatly outnumber those of the West and said:

"But I heard you make the statement a moment ago that, as it stands now, you do not have any blue chips to give away."

Taylor replied, "We do not, with standing forces," but "we have a mobilization base, in proved reserve forces and so on." This was an apparent reference to reserve and Guard forces in ad-

Please Turn to Pg. 9, Col. 1

German Ship Sinks; 11 of Crew Saved

LONDON, Feb. 21 (AP)—The 1,180-ton German motor vessel Helene B. Schupp sank in the North Sea tonight, radio messages heard here said.

A Danish fishing vessel picked up 11 men, the radio message said and one man was still missing.

The Blaavand radio at Esbjerg, Denmark, reported earlier the German craft was in trouble in the gale-whipped North Sea off Jutland's west coast.

Janet Blair Gets $2 Million Job

NEW YORK, Feb. 21 (AP)—Janet Blair, singer and dancer, has been signed to a five-year $2 million contract by NBC, her agent said today.

Martin Baum, the agent, said Miss Blair will replace Dinah Shore next summer and have a new TV show next season.

Doctors Give Gen. Marshall 50-50 Chance

FT. BRAGG, N.C., Feb. 21 (UPI)—Physicians treating Gen. George C. Marshall for two strokes and pneumonia today gave the famed soldier-statesman "a 50-50 chance" for recovery.

Doctors expressed concern that another stroke might occur. But they said Marshall was "progressing as satisfactorily as can be expected." They said the prognosis "still must be guarded."

Marshall spent a more restful night and was more alert today. He was being nourished by fruit juice fed by a feeding pump.

Hayden Schooner Puts Into Marquesas Port

The 65-year-old schooner carrying actor Sterling Hayden and his four children on a voyage to the South Pacific in defiance of a court order has put in at Taiohae in the Marquesas Islands, it was reported yesterday.

United Press International said word had reached Papeete, Tahiti, that the vessel Wanderer had arrived at Taiohae Feb. 12. Tahiti is 950 miles south-southwest of the Marquesas.

According to dispatches, it was believed that recent bad weather had prevented the swashbuckling actor from continuing at once on the voyage to Papeete, his destination when he sailed from Sausalito Jan. 18.

On board the vessel, in addition to the actor and his four children, were eight men, five women and three other children. Their father, Phillip Africa, is the Wanderer's first mate.

Word of the vessel's arrival in the Marquesas lifted any doubt that Hayden had defied a court order prohibiting him from taking the children on a proposed 'round-the-world film making trip because of the Wanderer's age and alleged frailty.

The 42-year-old actor was

Please Turn to Pg. 15, Col. 4

Edith Piaf Ailing, Takes Time Off

NEW YORK, Feb. 21 (UPI)—Doctors said today French Singer Edith Piaf, 43, is suffering from a bad reaction to arthritis medication but will be able to return to her nightclub appearances in a few days.

Miss Piaf was forced to call off her appearances at the Waldorf-Astoria Hotel Thursday night. She was given a blood transfusion, her manager, Eddie Elcort, said.

THE WEATHER

No smog today.

U.S. Weather Bureau forecast: Partly cloudy today and tomorrow. Continued cool. High today about 58. Yesterday's high, 50; low, 45.

INDEX OF FEATURES

Finnegan in Upset Victory at Santa Anita

Neil McCarthy's Finnegan wins San Felipe Handicap, a bitter stretch duel with favored Tomy Lee in race for 3-year-olds at Santa Anita. See the Sports Section.

ON OTHER PAGES

13 SOLVE BAFFLER

The Baffler was beaten by 13 contestants last week, and surrendered $2.200 to his victors.

He's back again today on Page 6, Part 1A, with more dilemmas and a fresh prize jackpot for those who can outsmart him.

TIMES TODAY OFFERS WEALTH OF FEATURES

There's something for everyone in today's Sunday Times. And here are some notable news features deserving of your immediate interest:

The Times begins publication today of the startlingly true story of a young woman missionary who lived among the very primitives who speared her husband to death. Graphically illustrated with jungle pictures, "Faith Beyond Fear" begins on Page B. This is a gripping account of how missionary Elisabeth Elliot and her 3½-year-old daughter worked among the savage, stone-age Auca Indians in the remote Ecuadorian jungle of South America.

In the final installment of the "Our Southernmost Counties" series today, reporter Ray Hebert takes an appraising look at Los Angeles County. This illustrated report is on Page 1, Part II.

To provide space for the photomontage of Los Angeles County scenes illustrating Hebert's story, Bill Henry's "By the Way" column has been moved (for today's issue only) to Page 2, Part II.

The poignant life story of famed aviator Ar Earhart, second in the series of "17 Women Can't Forget," will be found on Page 10, Pa

Times Telephone Numbers:
MAdison 9-4411—Classified Advertising.
MAdison 5-2345—For all other calls.
Circulation—Largest in the West:
484,000 Daily; 878,000 Sunday.

Los Angeles Times

EQUAL RIGHTS
LIBERTY UNDER THE LAW
TRUE INDUSTRIAL FREEDOM

PART I
ALL THE NEWS
ALL THE TIME

VOL. LXXVIII | IN FOUR PARTS | CC★ | FRIDAY MORNING, MARCH 13, 1959 | 84 PAGES | DAILY 10c

HAWAII WINS APPROVAL AS 50TH STATE

Macmillan Stills Fears of Adenauer

Agrees to Parley on Central Europe Troop Limitation

BONN, March 12 (UPI) British Prime Minister Macmillan told Chancellor Adenauer here today that Britain was willing to negotiate a limitation of armed forces in Central Europe without creating a military vacuum in the area.

A spokesman for Macmillan outlined the British position tonight after the prime minister conferred for three and one-half hours with Adenauer in the latter's office.

Apprehension Allayed

Informed diplomatic sources indicated that Adenauer's apprehension about British intentions in Central Europe, particularly marked since Macmillan's trip to Russia, might have been allayed as a result of Macmillan's remarks today.

Macmillan and his party arrived here almost at the moment that Soviet Premier Khrushchev flew back to Moscow from East Berlin after a week-long East German visit that left little change in his basic demand that the western allies leave West Berlin.

In a statement on his arrival, Macmillan declared that the West must stand by its principles in dealing with the Soviets but added, "We must not be inflexible in our methods."

Conditions Not Improved

Adenauer told Macmillan that "since your last visit here a couple of months ago, world conditions have once more changed substantially, and, I must say, have not improved."

After today's conference British Foreign Office spokesman Peter Hope told newsmen that his government desired a limitation of armed forces in some area of Europe yet to be defined.

"We are not studying disengagement," the spokesman said. "By disengagement, we understand a separation of forces which would create a military vacuum."

Similar Views

Felix von Eckardt, West German press chief, said that the limitation of armed forces the British sought was similar to the controlled disarmament the West German government favored.

The British spokesman said that limitation of forces, as his government viewed it, "should involve no discrimination against any weapon or nation."

Other Berlin news on Page 6, Part 1.

CELEBRATING VICTORY—Women in Honolulu pineapple cannery raise cheer and slogan on hearing Congress had voted statehood. (AP) Wirephoto by cable from Honolulu

House Vote Sends Bill to Eisenhower; Signature Pledged

BY ROBERT T. HARTMANN
Times Washington Bureau Chief

WASHINGTON, March 12—Only President Eisenhower's pledged signature stood between Hawaii and its 40-year dream of statehood as Congress approved its admission today.

The House voted 323 to 89 to adopt the Senate version of the bill passed last night and sent the long-delayed legislation to the White House.

Hawaii will become the 50th state when all the formalities are completed, probably not before fall. Like Alaska, which joined the Union Jan. 7, it will add another star to the American Flag and the 49-star ensign to be officially unfurled over Ft. McHenry for the first time July 4 soon will become a collector's item.

President Eisenhower was reported delighted with the overwhelming House action after two days of debate, but the White House set no date for the signing ceremony. Hawaii's territorial Gov. Quinn arrived in the capital last night for the momentous roll calls which climaxed the Pacific outpost's long fight for full representation.

The first Hawaiian statehood bill was introduced in 1919 but it and subsequent measures never succeeded in winning passage by both House and Senate.

When Speaker Rayburn announced the final vote, congressmen on both sides of the aisle applauded. Both parties endorsed statehood in their 1956 platforms but most of the last-ditch opposition came from southern Democrats.

Backed By Rayburn

"My congratulations to Hawaii," Rayburn said in a statement swinging his potent support to the bill. "I opposed this in the past when I felt Hawaii was not ready for statehood. Now, however, the situation has changed and I welcome statehood because the territory deserves membership in the Union and will be an asset to the United States."

Vice-President Nixon issued this statement:

"This is a great day for Hawaii but an even better day for the United States. As one who has long favored statehood for Hawaii, I am particularly pleased today to be able to welcome her as the 50th state in the Union. Hawaii has served a long 'apprenticeship' as a territory and has more than met the traditional tests for statehood.

"She has been politely pa-

Please Turn to Pg. 13, Col. 3

HAPPY FOLK

Whingding Tossed by Islanders

BY JACK JONES
Times Staff Representative

HONOLULU, March 12. Hawaii's normally unmoved populace threw a whingding today as air raid sirens shrieked the signal that the House of Representatives had passed the bill making the aloha territory the 50th state.

Full page of pictures on Hawaii on Page 3, Part I. Other news and pictures on Pages 2, 12, 13 and 14, Part I.

Luau-shirted and muumuu-draped residents strolled into the streets of downtown Honolulu, Waikiki and most island villages following a triumphant telephone call from territorial Gov. William F. Quinn in Washington, D.C.

Riotous Din

Church bells, ships bells and automobile horns set up a riotous din to begin a planned two days of hysteria.

But other than a jamming of traffic, a scattering of serpentines and a cloud of confetti, the initial celebration was not quite what the Honolulu Police Department had been expecting.

Buildings along King and Bishop Sts. were afiutter with streamers and huge signs reading 50.

Palm-decorated cars honked through the streets. The wilder island rites got under way at dusk and Honolulu police were in no mood to stifle the enthusiasm—short of a major rampage.

Street dancing took place at Iolani Palace, Kalakaua Ave., Wahiawa and several other centers.

A massive bonfire was touched off on Sand Island in Honolulu Harbor. Ha-

Please Turn to Pg. 14, Col. 1

Nasser Woos Iraqis, Denounces Their Chief

Premier Kassem Hit as Trying to Spread Red Terrorism Across Arabian World

DAMASCUS, March 12 (AP)—President Nasser wooed Iraq's people today and denounced their premier as a man trying to spread a communist reign of terror across the Arab world.

Nasser renewed his attack on the premier, Abdel Karim Kassem, in a biting discussion of the Mosul rebellion before flag-waving student demonstrators at the Presidential Palace in Damascus.

He denied Bagdad charges that his United Arab Republic, which links Egypt and Syria, inspired Col. Abdel Wahab Shawaf's nationalist revolt last week end against the leftist-inclined Kassem regime.

Reason for Revolt

Instead, he said, the revolt sprang from opposition of Iraq's people to "a reign of communist terror and persecution of free officers and Arab nationalists in Iraq."

"Kassem was trying to drive a wedge between the Iraqi people and the UAR," he said, "assuming that by this policy he would divide the Arabs to strengthen communism in the Arab world and bring it under communist terror, as in Iraq"

He accused Kassem of opening Bagdad to Syrian Communists fleeing the recent anti-Red campaign within the UAR. Kassem offered them haven, he said, in a vain belief that

Please Turn to Pg. 11, Col. 1

Assembly Balks at Repeal of Loyalty Oath

SACRAMENTO, March 12 (AP) — With its Democratic majority split, the Assembly today refused to repeal a loyalty oath law, even though it can't be enforced.

Eight Democrats joined the solid 33 Republican minority in the 41-39 vote against repeal of a 1953 law requiring loyalty declarations from all persons or organizations claiming property tax exemptions.

Unconstitutional

The law made a false declaration a felony, but last June the U. S. Supreme Court found it unconstitutional. The court said the law violates due process by placing the burden of proof of loyalty on the taxpayers.

The Democratic caucus made repeal a party objective last week. The 1958 Democratic platform opposed all oaths of non-disloyalty.

Assemblyman S. C. Mas-

Please Turn to Pg. 18, Col. 5

Storm Slams Northeast and Leaves 15 Dead

BY THE ASSOCIATED PRESS

The worst snowstorm of winter struck a savage blow at the Northeast yesterday, just nine days before the advent of spring. It also hit the Midwest and south to Virginia.

By nightfall the storm was tapering off but not before it had claimed at least 15 lives. Most of the deaths resulted from heart attacks induced by the strain of shoveling snow.

Deaths were reported in Ohio, New Jersey, Connecticut, New York, Rhode Island, Vermont and Massachusetts.

Up to 14 in. of snow, followed by sleet and rain, lashed an area from Indiana to Virginia and Maine.

Highways Tied Up

Hazardous driving conditions tied up many of the East's highways.

As one storm center moved in from the west, a second came off the Virginia coast. Winds up to 60 m.p.h. whistled in with the snow. Tides ranged 2 to 3 ft. above normal.

Western Maryland and upstate New York measured 14 in. of snow. West Virginia and Western Massachusetts had a foot. New Jersey got up to 10 in. Ohio had 7 in., Indiana, 6.

Air travelers were grounded in Cleveland, Boston, Buffalo, Rochester and New

Please Turn to Pg. 7, Col. 1

BROWN SIGNS RIGID SPEED LIMIT BILL

SACRAMENTO, March 12 (AP) — Gov. Brown today signed into law a rigid 65-m.p.h. speed limit for California highways, effective next Jan. 1.

The present prima-facie limit of 55, permitting drivers to go faster if they can prove it's safe, will be junked. This is the first major part of Brown's legislative program to reach his desk.

"I am anxious that this law be given aggressive enforcement just as soon as it goes into effect," Brown said.

Average Man Saves 6 Cents Out of Dollar

WASHINGTON, March 12 (AP)—The average man had his own antirecession program, it developed today. He not only balanced the 1958 family budget but built up a surplus.

Mr. Average tucked away 6 cents out of every take-home dollar. It was a record saving rate surpassed only during World War II, when goods were so scarce Americans could not find much of anything to buy.

The consumer's tight-money policy was a bit rough on the automobile and appliance makers, but it built up a tidy family reserve against possible layoffs or shortened hours.

This national nest egg grew by $18 billion last year, in the kind of savings which are easily turned into cash, the Federal Home Loan Bank board reported.

The increase represents a reserve of buying power on which the government's economists now rely heavily to keep the business recovery rolling.

Population of City Reaches 2,406,000

Los Angeles has a population of 2,406,000, an increase of 162,099 since a special U.S. census was taken in February, 1956, and at the present rate of growth should reach 3 million by 1970, City Planning Director John E. Roberts said yesterday.

The city's population has increased 436,000 since the 1950 census, an average of almost 50,000 a year. This gain in less than a decade is greater than the entire population of Oakland or Portland, Ore., Roberts said.

Roberts said the city's studies show that Los Angeles has made the largest percentage gain in growth among the 10 largest U.S. cities from 1900 to 1958.

The city's population has increased 2,242% in that period, from 102,479 in 1900 to 2,406,000 now, against 569% for second-place Detroit, 135% for New York, 124% for Chicago and 73% for San Francisco.

Improving Economy

Roberts also pointed out that the end of the economic recession during 1958 resulted in the resumption of Los Angeles' normal growth rate.

The quarterly population estimate, made by the Planning Department and co-operating city agencies, showed that several of the trends in the city's growth pattern also responded to the improving economy of the area.

In San Fernando Valley,

Please Turn to Pg. 4, Col. 6

Santiago de Cuba Shaken by Quake

SANTIAGO DE CUBA, March 12 (AP) — A strong earth tremor shook this easternmost city of Cuba today.

No damage or casualties were reported.

Ding Dong Daddy Gets on Wrong Track Again by Taking 17th Bride

The Ding Dong Daddy of the D Car Line is off on the wrong track again.

Francis H. Van Wie, 69-year-old ex-trolleyman who achieved notoriety and jail by marrying 16 women without 15 divorces, appeared yesterday to have hitched himself to yet a 17th bride in violation of conditions of his seven-year probation for bigamy.

The latest bride, 73-year-old June Pucket Van Wie, said yesterday in Sacramento that she had just learned of his flamboyant past and would ask an annulment.

She sued for divorce the previous day on grounds of desertion. She said she and Van Wie were married June 15, 1957, in Lodi, and lived together about a year before the ex-motorman disappeared.

Mrs. Van Wie said she had asked her attorney to drop the divorce suit and ask for an annulment on learning her husband's true colors.

Meanwhile, Van Wie's whereabouts was unknown either to her or the Los Angeles Probation Office.

Probation Officer Glen Reed, who has handled Van Wie's case since he was placed on probation Dec. 2, 1952, by Superior Judge Jesse J. Frampton here, disclosed that the court had revoked probation last Feb. 6 and issued a bench warrant for his arrest.

The revocation was based on Van Wie's failure to make a regular monthly report to the probation office as required. Reed said also that a marriage contracted during the probation period, which still has eight months to run, would also be grounds for revocation.

Van Wie was convicted of bigamy in marrying Mrs. Amelia Pritchard, 73, without first divorcing Mrs. Mary Abba Van Wie, 67.

He served six months in the County Jail and honor farm before being placed on probation with orders to keep out of the matrimonial wilderness for seven years.

Mrs. Van Wie No. 17 said the short, plump Lothario "led me to believe he had only been married once before."

Carl Sandburg Ordered to Bed

FLAT ROCK, N.C., March 12 (UPI)—Poet Carl Sandburg, 81, was ordered to bed for at least two weeks by his physician today because of physical exhaustion and laryngitis.

His wife said Sandburg "is just worn out" from a recent series of lectures.

House Votes to Extend Draft

WASHINGTON, March 12 (AP) — Legislation extending the draft law four years was speeded to President Eisenhower today by the House.

By voice vote and without debate, the House approved a Senate amendment to a bill which passed the House last month. The amendment dealt with the pay of doctors and dentists in the armed services.

Temperature Soars to 87 for Year's Highest

Los Angeles' temperature soared to a 1959 record high yesterday.

It was just like summer as the mercury, unmindful of the month, hit 87 deg. at 1:36 p.m., making it the warmest March 12 on record and the warmest day this year.

In fact, the weatherman said, it hasn't been that warm since last Dec. 3, when the temperature reached 89.

It was warmer in other nearby communities. Long Beach had a high of 90 deg.; San Gabriel, 89; Northridge, 88, and Burbank, Montebello, Pasadena and Santa Ana each recorded highs of 87.

Actually, the weather yesterday was just as fine as it was hot. Visibility stretched out to 30 miles in midafternoon and relative humidity ranged from a dry 25% at 6 a.m. to an even drier 13% at 1:10 p.m.

The low temperature was 59 at 5:21 a.m.

The Weather Bureau said it will be clear today but not quite so warm—about 80. As for smog, there will be some eye irritation in the central and coastal areas but none elsewhere.

INDEX OF FEATURES

Pinch of Salt All You Need, Doctor Says

A pinch of salt a day is all a heathy person needs, doctor declares. Story on Page 1, Part 3.

ON OTHER PAGES

Duce's Son Freed of War Charge

FLORENCE, Italy, March 12 (AP)—Benito Mussolini's son Vittorio today was acquitted of a charge of deserting the Italian air force in World War II

The military court verdict brought cheers from a crowd of 200 sympathizers who surrounded the 42-year-old son of Italy's late Fascist dictator. Some kissed him.

THE WEATHER

Smog today.

U.S. Weather Bureau forecast: Mostly sunny today and tomorrow but increasing night and morning coastal fog. Cooler days. High today 80. Yesterday's high, 87; low, 59.

Times Telephone Numbers:
MAdison 9-4411—Classified Advertising.
MAdison 5-2345—For all other calls.
Circulation—Largest in the West:
497,873 Daily; 893,792 Sunday.

EQUAL RIGHTS

Los Angeles Times

LIBERTY UNDER THE LAW — TRUE INDUSTRIAL FREEDOM

PART 1
ALL THE NEWS
ALL THE TIME

VOL. LXXVIII | IN FOUR PARTS | CC | WEDNESDAY MORNING, SEPTEMBER 16, 1959 | 92 PAGES | 2† | DAILY 10c

COOL, POLITE RECEPTION GIVEN TO MR. K

Man Hurls Bomb, Kills 6 at School

Hits Children at Play; 19 Hurt in Explosion

HOUSTON, Sept. 15 (UPI) — A demented tile setter and ex-convict threw a powerful suitcase bomb into a crowd of children playing at Edgar Allan Poe Elementary School today.

Police Capt. Weldon Waycott said the bomb killed six persons, including the man who made it and his 7-year-old son Paul.

It also killed two other pupils and a teacher and a custodian, who were trying to drive off the tile setter, Paul Harold Orgeron.

Waycott said 19 persons were injured. They were all pupils, except Mrs. R. E. Doty, the principal, who lost a leg.

Identified by Note

Orgeron, Waycott said, was identified from fingerprints taken from a man's hand, papers in his wallet and from a note on the schoolyard that was signed P. H. Orgeron.

The note said:

"I want Bobby (name illegible) Orgeron, mother of my son, Dusty Paul Orgeron. I want to return my son to her. I have tried hard to get the police department to return my son to her.

"I do not believe I can get killed without others getting killed around me, and I mean my son will get killed, too."

Pupils Identified

The pupils who were killed were Bill Hawes, 8, and Johnny Fitch, 7. Fitch was the grandson of Vice Adm. Aubrey W. Fitch, who was second in command to the late Adm. William Halsey during the Pacific fighting in World War II.

The custodian was James A. Montgomery and the teacher was Mrs. Jennie Kolter, who taught the second grade and had just taken the children out to play.

As the group approached, Orgeron yelled "stay away from here or I'll blow you to pieces."

Someone went to get Montgomery, who arrived and rushed the man. The man threw the bomb, which exploded almost instantly. It

Please Turn to Pg. 11, Col. 3

AIRLINER CARRYING 36 CRASH LANDS

PLATTSBURGH, N.Y., Sept. 16 (AP) — An Eastern Airlines plane with 36 persons aboard made a belly landing early this morning amid a shower of sparks on a foam-covered runway.

Officials at Plattsburgh Air Force Base said it appeared no one was injured.

The starboard engine of the twin-engine Martin 404 caught fire during the landing but then quickly went out.

The plane, flight 28 from New York City to Massena, N.Y., landed after circling almost five hours in the air over the airfields at Glen Falls and at Plattsburgh.

Congress Ends, Avoids Russian Visit

WASHINGTON, Sept. 15 (AP) — A battle-weary Congress broke for home today a scant six hours before the arrival of Soviet Premier Khrushchev.

By adjourning its eight-month session, Congress avoided a possibly embarrassing dilemma over whether to invite the Russian leader to address it.

The end of this longest session in eight years came at 6:24 a.m. EDT. At that time, the Senate had been working for nearly 21½ hours and the House had been sitting off and on for almost 18½ hours.

Major Actions

Before scattering for home until next January, Congress took these major actions:

1—Voted to extend the life of the Civil Rights Commission for two years beyond Nov. 8 and to provide $500,000 in funds to carry on its work for the rest of this fiscal year ending next June 30.

2—Appropriated $3,225,815,000 for foreign aid during this fiscal year—$704,182,000 less than President Eisenhower originally asked. In reaching a pre-dawn compromise, conferees cut $56 million from the original Senate total and increased the House figure by $39 million.

Seeds of Battle

In the final hours, the Senate planted the seeds of what promises to be a searing battle over broad civil rights legislation at the next session starting Jan. 6.

Senators seeking such legislation won an understanding from Democratic and Republican party leaders that a showdown fight on the issue will be waged starting about mid-February.

Sen. Richard B. Russell (D-Ga.) said he now could see no way to sidestep the showdown, which could split the Democratic Party in a year when it will be battling the Republicans for control

Please Turn to Pg. 15, Col. 4

Day Cool, Cloudy With High of 78

Partly cloudy skies and an absence of desert winds yesterday gave the Los Angeles Basin its second day of respite from blistering heat.

The temperature leveled off at 78 deg. at 12:49 p.m. after a morning low of 63 at 3:05 a.m.

Aside from morning low clouds, lovely weather will return again today.

SERIOUS MOMENT—Russia's Premier Khrushchev and President Eisenhower, hat over heart, display serious expressions as the U.S. and Soviet anthems are played at airport after the premier's arrival. (AP) Wirephoto

200,000 See Parade With Little Cheering; Talks Start at Once

BY ROBERT T. HARTMANN
Times Washington Bureau Chief

WASHINGTON, Sept. 15—Soviet Premier Khrushchev was greeted today on his arrival in the United States with military pomp by a strangely unsmiling President Eisenhower and a coolly courteous crowd of some 200,000 undemonstrative Americans.

Alighting nearly an hour late from his giant TU-114 turboprop airliner, the Soviet leader called for developing harmony between the two nations as "relations between good neighbors."

President Eisenhower, for his part, assured Khrushchev that "because our people do want peace and because they are the decisive influence in the basic actions of our government, aggression by this nation is an impossibility."

Urges Visitor to 'See for Himself'

He called upon Khrushchev to see for himself that Americans have no ill-will toward any other people, covet no territory or power, and do not seek to impose their will on any other nation.

"I most sincerely hope that as you come to see and believe these truths about our people there will develop an improved basis on which we can together consider the problems that divide us," the President told his guest.

There were no serious incidents along the 15-mile route from Andrews Air Force Base, swarming with ex-

More news and pictures of Khrushchev arrival on Pages 2, 3, 4, 5, 12, 13, 15 and 16, Part 1.

tra security officers. Apparently all that most of the curious citizens wanted to do to Mr. K was take his photograph.

The world's No. 1 Communist was not bashful about his country's successful lunar probe, promptly presenting President Eisenhower with a replica of the hammer and sickle insigne reportedly planted on the moon. But he stressed its peaceful scientific aspect and even attempted a little joke about it, saying he was sure the United States would soon duplicate the Soviet feat.

"The Soviet pennant, as an old resident of the moon, will welcome your pennant, and they will live together in peace and friendship as we both should live together on earth in peace and friendship," he declared.

"War does not promise anyone any good. We have come to you with an open heart and good intentions."

After nearly two hours of afternoon talks, described in a joint communique as "friendly and frank," the White House announced that the President and Khrushchev will meet for three more days of serious discussion at nearby Camp David Sept. 25-27, when the Soviet visitor returns from his cross-country tour.

Agreement to Talk More

The only agreement announced today was "agreement that the discussions should continue in this spirit to seek ways to achieve a better understanding."

As suspected, Khrushchev showed up for the formal White House dinner tonight without the white tie and tails explicit in such invitations. But Mrs. Khrushchev wore an evening gown.

He wore a dark business suit, as he did all day, with his Order of Lenin medal on the left lapel and two smaller Red decorations on the other lapel. Before joining the 100 other guests, the President and First Lady met with the hKrushchevs in their private upstairs quarters.

At the end of the afternoon talks, Mr. Eisenhower and Khrushchev were alone with their interpreters for about 13 minutes.

Previously, the conference in the President's office in-

Please Turn to Pg. 5, Col. 1

DeSapio Wins Re-election by Slim Margin

NEW YORK, Sept. 15 (AP) Carmine G. DeSapio, fighting to retain control of Tammany Hall against an organized insurgent group led by big-name Democrats, won re-election by a narrow margin tonight as Democratic leader of his home district.

Insurgent leaders claimed victory for anti-Tammany candidates in seven other Manhattan districts but their strength was not believed to be sufficient to strip DeSapio of his leadership of Tammany Hall.

Unofficial returns gave DeSapio an edge of less than 600 votes over Charles E. McGuimness, a 38-year-old corporation lawyer backed by the insurgent group led by former Sen. Herbert H. Lehman, former Air Force Secretary Thomas K. Finletter and Mrs. Franklin D. Roosevelt. They accused DeSapio of "boss rule" and said this gave the Republicans a ready-made issue last year which led to Nelson A. Rockefeller's victory over Gov. Averill Harriman.

SIGHT LIKELY FOR WOMAN BLIND 36 YRS.

After 36 years of blindness a Texas woman possibly will see again following a corneal transplant to both of her eyes during a surgery which occurred last Sunday at Burbank Hospital.

The woman, Mrs. R. L. Harris, 49, of Ft. Worth, flew here Saturday after her doctor had been informed that a pair of eyes donated by a heart attack victim in San Diego was available.

Doctors said it still is too early to determine whether the operation is a success, but indications are that normal vision will be restored.

Bonn President Takes Oath

BONN, Sept. 15 (AP)—Heinrich Luebke was sworn in today as West Germany's second president.

Russian Premier Tours Capital Aboard Copter

President Takes Red Boss Aloft to See Washington Homes, Cars, Golf Courses

BY DON SHANNON, Times Washington Bureau

WASHINGTON, Sept. 15—Premier Khrushchev today took President Eisenhower's suggestion that he "fly along in my chopper" and inspect housing, American-style traffic jams and golf courses.

Mr. Eisenhower expressed his hope at a press conference last month that the Soviet visitor could see that "the fine, small or modest homes that Americans live in are not the unusual or the exception as he seemed to think the sample we sent over to Moscow was."

Rush-Hour Traffic

Today, as the two heads of state rode from the airport to the city, the President proposed the helicopter trip and the 65-year-old Khrushchev accepted what was believed to be his first flight in a helicopter.

The President's Marine Corps Sikorsky S-58 was brought to the White House lawn at 5:23 while he and his guest were completing private talks in the oval Presidential office.

A few minutes later, Mr. Eisenhower escorted Khrushchev across the lawn and assisted him and his interpreter into their places.

Khrushchev Waves

With Khrushchev waving happily from his seat at the right window, the Presidential seal emblazoned below, the helicopter roared off at 5:30 p.m. After a quick trip over the Capitol, the party had a look at the avenues along the Potomac River, choked with rush hour traffic.

The aircraft, followed by two other helicopters carrying security guards and newsmen, crossed the Poto-

Please Turn to Pg. 16, Col. 1

GRIN, CHARM MISSING

Eisenhower Stern as Premier Clowns

Times Washington Bureau

WASHINGTON, Sept. 15. For a man whose contagious grin is world-renowned, President Eisenhower appeared unusually stern and serious today in all his public appearances with Soviet Premier Khrushchev.

He was painstakingly polite, but never turned on what has come to be the legendary Eisenhower charm as he usually does with official visitors. At times he seemed almost trying not to smile.

The ebullient Mr. K, however, after a few nervous minutes at the start, began living up every minute of his first day in America.

A consummate scene-stealer, he used his black Homburg as a prop to attract the battery of news photographers all through President Eisenhower's welcoming remarks. The sun was shining uncomfortably in his eyes, nobody can deny, but his experiments with the hat (comically duplicated by Gromyko) had to be seen to be believed.

Finally he tossed his hat over the brass stanchion on the dais as blithely as he flouted all known rules of White House dinner attire at the end of his biggest day.

But those who have witnessed him in Russia figure he was just warming up, actually amazingly subdued by President Eisenhower's proximity. Wait, these experts say, until Khrushchev takes his show on the road.

Man Carrying $11,000 Drops Dead on Hill St.

A man with more than $11,000 cash in his pockets collapsed and died yesterday on the sidewalk at 2nd and Hill Sts., police reported.

From papers on his person he was identified as Demos K. Keremes, 70, believed to be in the stock brokerage business, of 1230½ San Fernando Rd.

There is no such address, however, and the victim is not known at the Jewel Lithograph Co., 1230 San Fernando Rd.

Police said he carried $11,042.76 cash, mostly in denominations of $100, $50 and $20, plus three gold pieces with face values of $10, $20 and $2.50 and two bank books showing about $20,000 on deposit.

Also found in the pockets of his ordinary brown business suit were a book of Angel's Flight tickets and an Irish Sweepstakes ticket. Although he carried an Auto Club of Southern California card, the club said he is not listed on its membership roll.

THE WEATHER

Light smog today.

U.S. Weather Bureau forecast: Considerable cloudiness in night and morning hours but mostly sunny in afternoons today and tomorrow. High temperature today near 80. A little warmer tomorrow. Yesterday's high, 78; low, 63.

KHRUSHCHEV TALK ON TV AND RADIO

Premier Khrushchev's address to the National Press Club in Washington will be televised today by Channel 7 at 10:30 a.m. (repeated at 10 p.m.), Channel 4 at 11:30 a.m. and Channel 2 at 1:30 p.m. (repeated at 8 p.m.) Radio stations KABC, KFI and KNX will air the speech at 10:30 a.m.

INDEX OF FEATURES

Walk in 10th Wins for Dodgers, 8-7

Bases loaded walk in 10th gives Dodgers 8-7 victory over Braves, while Giants defeat Cincinnati to keep two-game lead in pennant chase. See story in Sports.

ON OTHER PAGES

Times Telephone Numbers:
MAdison 9-4411—Classified Advertising.
MAdison 5-2345—For all other calls.
Circulation—Largest in the West:
523,626 Daily; 913,042 Sunday.

Los Angeles Times

EQUAL RIGHTS · LIBERTY UNDER THE LAW · TRUE INDUSTRIAL FREEDOM

PART I
ALL THE NEWS
ALL THE TIME

VOL. LXXIX 4† IN FIVE PARTS CC WEDNESDAY MORNING, NOVEMBER 9, 1960 KTTV (Channel 11) 92 PAGES DAILY 10c

KENNEDY NEARING VICTORY

Nixon Concedes 'If Present Trend Continues'

Democrats Leading in California

BY KYLE PALMER
Political Editor

U.S. Sen. Kennedy slowly piled up a 76,000-vote lead over Vice President Nixon Tuesday night and if this trend continues will capture all 32 of the state's electoral votes.

On a statewide basis, returns from 13,016 out of 30,682 precincts gave Kennedy 1,046,281 votes to Nixon's 969,369.

In Los Angeles County, where the counting stopped shortly after midnight, Kennedy led the Vice President, 480,561 to 421.895, in returns from 5,796 out of 11,851 precincts.

State wide, Prop. 1, with 11,472 precincts out of 30,682 reporting, was leading with 637,734 yes and 617,745 no votes. Prop. 15, with 11,552 precincts reporting, had 361,857 yes votes and 703,692 no votes.

Kennedy jumped into the lead at the outset both in Los Angeles County and in the state and slowly built up his margin.

Strong in Big Cities

He ran particularly strong in the bigger cities, including San Francisco, Oakland, Sacramento and Fresno and trailed Nixon only in San Diego.

The voting turnout in California, where the Democrats outnumber the Republicans, 1,295,330 to 2,926,408, was extremely heavy throughout the state, but particularly so in Los Angeles County where a record shattering 90.35% of the 3,011,379 voters went to the polls. This smashed all records for any county in the state.

Little Prejudice Seen

As pre-election polls indicated, New York gave Kennedy a heavy majority, and Nixon's anticipated victory in Texas vanished as the Democratic ticket picked up a majority there.

Catholic Kennedy not only ran ahead in areas where Catholics represented heavy vote percentages, but his showing in Protestant areas indicated little evidence of religious prejudice.

Statewide returns from slightly more than 10% of California's 30,682 precincts indicated seeming defeat for Proposition No. 15—the so-called Bonelli plan for reapportionment of the State

Please Turn to Pg. 6, Col. 3

(AP) Wirephoto

Times photo

CANDIDATES CAST VOTES—Sen. Kennedy, Democratic nominee for President of the United States, emerges from voting machine in a Boston library, while Vice President Nixon, GOP candidate for highest office, uses ballot box at East Whittier polling place.

Senator Takes N.Y., Ahead in Tex., Penn., Runs Strong in Dixie

WASHINGTON (AP)—Sen. John F. Kennedy swept so close to the Presidency early today that practically everybody except the GOP high command proclaimed him the victor.

And while Nixon clutched at hopes that belated tallies in such vital states as Michigan, Illinois and his own California could swing things his way until 12:15 a.m., he then issued a statement saying:

"If the present trend continues, Sen. Kennedy will be the next President of the United States."

His wife, Pat, wept on TV before viewers coast to coast.

Trails Popular Vote

At that instant, Nixon actually was ahead of Kennedy in the number of states won or in which he was leading — but not in the number of vital electoral votes that decide the Presidency. And Kennedy held only a slender edge in the popular, nationwide vote of the millions of Americans.

With 269 electoral votes needed for victory, Kennedy had bagged or was ahead in 24 states with 335; Nixon had taken or was leading in 25 states with 188.

The popular vote was going Kennedy's way, too:

Kennedy 26,196,143 (50.9%).

Nixon 25,290,310 (49.1%).

So, while the outcome was pretty much in the cards once the first substantial returns rolled in, the results were by no means a massive, overpowering landslide for Kennedy.

The senator simply scooped up states with more people and more electoral votes, just as he had set out to do.

Kennedy's press secretary, Pierre Salinger, said that the Democratic candidate was going to bed without making a statement.

Vice President Nixon and his Republican supporters weren't giving up. They were hoping that, with the pop-

Please Turn to Pg. 16, Col. 1

Democrats Nail Down Control of Congress

Victory in Senate Never in Doubt; 219 House Seats Won While GOP Counts 104

WASHINGTON (UPI) — The Democrats retained control of both houses in the new 87th Congress today.

Never in doubt, Democratic control of the Senate was assured in the election results before 10 p.m. Tuesday.

The Democrats passed the 219 seats needed to continue their rule in the House and were leading for 49 others. Republicans had won 104 and were leading for 65.

It was clear on this basis that Democrats in the new House would exercise a majority control of about 100 votes, not too far short of their present maggin.

The indicated Senate breakdown was 65 Democrats to 35 Republicans.

Democrats shortly before midnight Tuesday were assured of 57 Senate seats in the new Congress, including 43 holdovers. They were leading for eight additional seats, including two currently held by Republicans in Iowa and South Dakota, for a possible total of 65.

Republicans, with 23 holdover seats, had captured five seats and were leading for six, including one now held by a Democrat in Wyoming, for a possible total of 34 seats.

In the House, with much of the vote still to be counted, Democrats had lost seven seats to the Republicans — two in Indiana, two in Con-

Please Turn to Pg. 7, Col. 1

Nixon Fails to Concede, but Comes Close

BY ROBERT HARTMANN
Times Washington Bureau Chief

Vice President Nixon, who said that since boyhood he "never wanted to be left behind," early Wednesday conceded that "if the present trend continues" he had finished second in this century's hardest fought Presidential election.

Waving with his left hand while his right tightly encircled his wife, Pat, who was choking back tears, the California - born candidate appeared at 12:15 a.m. in the Ambassador ballroom to urge his hard-core supporters to give their support to the next President of the United States and pledged his own wholeheartedly.

Then, still smiling, he told the crowd that he had had

Please Turn to Pg. 6, Col. 1

Outlook 'Very Good,' Robert Kennedy Says

BY DON SHANNON, Times Washington Bureau

HYANNIS PORT, Mass. (AP) Sen. Kennedy's brother said Tuesday night the outlook for his election "is very good."

Robert F. Kennedy, campaign manager, emerging from his command post at the Kennedy home, said:

"I think things are going very good, I must say," Kennedy declared. That was after Kennedy's press headquarters announced that Connecticut state chairman John Bailey had forecast a margin of 75,000 to 100,000 votes for Kennedy in Connecticut.

Pierre Salinger, the senator's press secretary, said in a statement:

"We are very encouraged by the returns in Connecticut and grateful for the margin the people of Connecticut have extended to Sen. Kennedy."

Sen. Kennedy himself said nothing but he visited his brother's command post to go over returns with Robert.

The senator spent the longest day of his long pursuit of the Presidency waiting in his white - shingled summer house for the election results.

The Democratic candidate, who ended the campaign with a riotous home-coming parade and rally in Boston Monday night, voted there Tuesday morning. He was

Please Turn to Pg. 16, Col. 6

INDEX OF FEATURES

French Army Revolt Over Algeria Feared

Unrest in France and Algeria increases as a revolt by French officials against President De Gaulle's policies threatens to spread to the army. See Page 8, Part 1.

ON OTHER PAGES

LATEST L.A. CITY, COUNTY RETURNS

PRESIDENTIAL

5796 Precincts out of 11,851

Republican

Nixon Lodge	421,895

Democratic

Kennedy Johnson	480,561

CONGRESS

15th District — 331 Precincts out of 890

McDonough (R)	13,081
Martell (D)	13,219

16th District — 59 Precincts out of 688

Bell (R)	2,649
Pacht (D)	1,781

17th District — 613 Precincts out of 1,418

Coffee (R)	7,534
King (D)	15,172

18th District — 241 Precincts out of 841

Hosmer (R)	10,553
Ahern (D)	4,426

19th District — 345 Precincts out of 925

McWilliams (R)	3,969
Holifield (D)	14,638

20th District — 178 Precincts out of 593

Smith (R)	3,343
Sadler (D)	1,837

21st District — 507 Precincts out of 1,384

Hiestand (R)	11,288
Brown (D)	7,963

22nd District — 295 Precincts out of 944

Blanchard (R)	4,678
Corman (D)	4,893

23rd District — 200 Precincts out of 969

Schwartz (R)	2,167
Doyle (D)	7,302

24th District — 154 Precincts out of 656

Lipscomb (R)	7,240
Hass (D)	5,293

25th District — 394 Precincts out of 1,546

Rousselot (R)	8,062
Kasem (D)	8,219

26th District — 335 Precincts out of 997

McIntyre (R)	4,874
Roosevelt (D)	15,058

STATE MEASURES

5,786 Precincts out of 11,851

1. Water Resources Bond

Yes	370,232
No	261,469

2. Assembly Terms

4,036 Precincts out of 11,851

Yes	58,810
No	69,897

5. Compensation of Legislators

Yes	55,088
No	69,141

6. Golf Course Tax

Yes	82,020
No	53,102

10. Administration of Justice

Yes	83,658
No	30,060

11. Veterans Tax Exemption

Yes	93,149
No	54,583

15. Reapportionment

Yes	256,252
No	201,635

COUNTY QUESTIONS

"A" County Employees in Politics

3,551 Precincts out of 11,851

Yes	41,980
No	64,913

"D" Bonds—School

4,200 Precincts out of 11,851

Yes	46,843
No	17,042

"E" Bonds—Junior College

3,899 Precincts out of 11,851

Yes	44,490
No	17,797

State-by-State Returns in Presidential Election

BY THE ASSOCIATED PRESS

State—	Voting Units	Units Reporting	Popular Vote Nixon	Popular Vote Kennedy	Electoral Vote R	Electoral Vote D
Alabama	3,293	2,468	168,396	237,500	..	5
Alaska	300	7	104	106	..	3
Arizona	654	307	128,657	99,068	4	..
Arkansas	2,389	1,573	86,728	111,223	..	8
California	30,682	11,837	856,814	927,784	..	..
Colorado	1,914	681	139,071	112,493	6	..
Connecticut	169	169	566,497	656,494	..	8
Delaware	356	351	95,555	98,354	..	3
Florida	1,969	1,727	735,061	687,129	10	..
Georgia	1,826	943	184,790	297,317	..	12
Hawaii	240	99	27,216	25,296	3	..
Idaho	886	241	36,077	32,920	4	..
Illinois	10,015	3,750	630,535	965,899	..	27
Indiana	4,299	2,693	803,164	687,473	13	..
Iowa	2,488	934	243,562	197,484	10	..
Kansas	2,961	1,148	193,222	127,132	8	..
Kentucky	3,533	2,426	461,166	429,464	10	..
Louisiana	2,114	1,240	112,404	232,144	..	10
Maine	630	351	107,798	76,616	5	..
Maryland	1,338	1,336	481,697	559,971	..	9
Massachusetts	1,984	693	224,376	487,594	..	16
Michigan	5,074	2,014	578,934	745,218	..	20
Minnesota	3,766	493	162,573	205,535	..	11
Mississippi	1,828	1,424	41,926	71,466	..	..
Missouri	4,371	3,514	622,530	697,722	..	13
Montana	1,080	33	3,574	2,566	4	..
Nebraska	2,129	376	43,189	24,120	6	..
Nevada	451	101	23,654	21,508	3	..
N. Hampshire	301	219	84,854	71,558	4	..
New Jersey	4,291	3,767	1,173,678	1,223,694	..	16
New Mexico	979	301	59,523	57,606	4	..
New York	11,793	8,832	2,423,042	2,962,365	..	45
N. Carolina	2,089	1,726	496,188	586,859	..	14
N. Dakota	2,311	456	32,825	26,311	4	..
Ohio	14,076	7,240	1,075,492	970,206	25	..
Oklahoma	3,224	2,936	449,187	319,558	8	..
Oregon	2,896	358	35,966	28,313	6	..
Pennsylvania	9,044	6,956	1,741,945	1,951,448	..	32
Rhode Island	467	467	144,953	257,158	..	4
S. Carolina	1,602	1,578	183,321	193,295	..	8
S. Dakota	1,890	459	27,107	21,988	4	..
Tennessee	2,699	2,510	507,403	434,727	11	..
Texas	254	231	742,298	789,032	..	24
Utah	1,128	298	52,529	38,052	4	..
Vermont	246	242	92,437	63,657	3	..
Virginia	1,947	1,825	367,578	322,928	12	..
Washington	5,200	177	16,287	12,839	9	..
West Virginia	2,751	1,975	278,668	327,634	..	8
Wisconsin	3,476	2,336	599,380	578,343	12	..
Wyoming	673	178	6,602	5,248	3	..

1961–1970

Times Telephone Numbers:
MAdison 9-4411—Classified Advertising.
MAdison 5-2345—For all other calls.
Circulation—Largest in the West:
523,626 Daily; 913,042 Sunday.

Los Angeles Times

EQUAL RIGHTS — LIBERTY UNDER THE LAW — TRUE INDUSTRIAL FREEDOM

ONE OF THE WORLD'S GREAT NEWSPAPERS

VOL. LXXX 3† IN FIVE PARTS—PART ONE CC WEDNESDAY MORNING, JANUARY 4, 1961 KTTV (Channel 11) 108 PAGES DAILY 10c

U.S. BREAKS OFF RELATIONS WITH CUBA

Legislators Given Program by Brown

No Need for New Taxes Seen; Education Placed in Top Spot

BY ROBERT BLANCHARD
Times Sacramento Bureau Chief

SACRAMENTO—Gov. Brown Tuesday submitted to the Legislature a wide-ranging program which he said can be financed without any increase in taxes.

Although the program contained something for everyone, Brown termed the improvement of education "the number one goal of my administration."

The governor made his recommendations at a joint session of the Senate and the Assembly in the Assembly chamber.

The recommendations covered a multitude of subjects, including education, the administration of justice, social welfare, public health, election law reforms, the reorganization of state government, labor-management relations, natural resources, growth and development problems.

Studies Urged

In many instances, the governor actually made no recommendations to the Legislature but "commended" to its study several reports such as those turned in by commissions on narcotics, juvenile delinquency and metropolitan area problems.

In the field of education, the governor called for the adoption of new requirements for teaching credentials which would play down so-called method or how-to-teach courses and reduce the types of credentials from 40 to five basic types, an increase in the expenditures from the state bond fund for local school construction from $10 million to $12 million a month, a $200,000 appropriation to help speed the reorganization of school districts and the creation of a new medical school in San Diego under the supervision of the University of California.

Although he urged the

Please Turn to Pg. 14, Col. 1

Filibuster Fight Opens Congress

WASHINGTON (UPI)—The Democratic-controlled 87th Congress formally convened Tuesday and promptly plunged into a liberal-conservative battle over potential barriers to President-elect Kennedy's legislative program.

Shortly after the House and Senate opened for business at noon, Senate liberals won a favorable ruling from Vice President Nixon, the presiding officer, and launched two drives to strengthen the Senate's anti-filibuster rule.

But action was blocked at least until today by Sen. Russell (D-Ga.), leader of southern senators who have used the filibuster to head off civil rights bills. The maneuvering produced a sharp exchange between Russell and Nixon, the first of the fledgling session.

House Move Hangs Fire

Hanging fire in the House was a liberal move to purge conservative Rep. William M. Colmer (D-Miss.) from the powerful rules committee. The aim is to make it easier to pry Kennedy's economic-welfare bills out of the committee, now dominated by a group of conservative Republicans and Democrats.

Democratic leaders indicated they planned to press ahead with the Colmer purge. Without objecting, they allowed the House to adopt rules of procedure that left Colmer's ouster as the only solution to liberalizing the rules committee.

One of the first measures introduced in the House was a bill embodying Kennedy's proposals for aiding economically depressed areas. Rep. Gray (D-Ill.) said he and Sen. Douglas (D-Ill.) had agreed to sponsor the priority legislation.

House Republicans were

Please Turn to Pg. 20, Col. 1

Central Treaty Group to Meet

ANKARA, Turkey (AP)—The Central Treaty Organization (CENTO) Tuesday announced that its military committee will meet here Jan. 24-26. Officers representing Britain, the United States, Turkey, Iran and Pakistan are expected.

Fiery Crash on Freeway Kills Driver

Illustrated on Page 3, Part I

Charles M. Lockard, 36, of 404 N Danehurst Ave., Covina, was killed instantly Tuesday night when his car went out of control on the San Bernardino Freeway at Citrus St. crossed the divider and crashed head-on into a westbound truck and trailer, California highway patrolmen reported.

The impact ruptured the truck's fuel tank spilling fuel oil over the highway which then burst into flames. Truckdriver Clyde Ryan, 40, of 17756 Owen St., Fontana, fled from the flaming cab without injury.

The flashback spread to the victim's car. Highway patrolman George D. Madsion attempted to rescue him but was driven back by the flames.

$15 Million in County Pay Boosts Predicted

Salary boosts for about 40,000 county employees that will cost $15 million a year were predicted Tuesday by Supervisor Chairman Ernest E. Debs as part of his forecast for 1961.

For the first time, he said, the county "will become a $600 million operation," when its new basic budget soars beyond that figure. The budget has been nudging the half-billion mark for the past two years.

In his New Year statement, the board chairman prophesied that the county would need more money to meet the growing demand for public services, but insisted that the Board of Supervisors "would do everything possible to keep the tax rate from going up."

The county already has become the largest in the nation from a standpoint of money collected and spent, Debs said.

Key Laos City Recaptured, Rebels Say

But King Deals Major Diplomatic Setback to Reds

VIENTIANE (UPI)—Communist-led Laotian rebels claimed Tuesday night they had recaptured the key central Laotian town of Xieng Khouang in a major victory and sent spearheads driving toward southern Laos.

While the Communists were reporting new successes, King Savang Vathana dealt them a major diplomatic and propaganda setback by convening parliament for a three-day session to invest pro-western Prince Boun Oum as premier.

One broadcast from the clandestine Communist Pathet Lao radio said forces under paratroop Capt. Kong Le "annihilated" an entire company of pro-western Laotian paratroopers dropped on the Plaine des Jarres to try to win Xieng Khouang from the reds.

Outside Aid Seen

Xieng Khouang, in the center of a complex of airfields, is a key military position in the defense of Laos and blocks the Communist approaches to the rest of Southeast Asia. American military officials said any such rebel victory must have been achieved with outside help.

The rebel radio reported control of all of Xieng Khouang Province and said columns of troops were moving on the provincial capitals of Savannakhet and Thakhet in southern Laos while other guerrillas were active around Pakse and along the colonial road leading to South Viet-Nam.

The pro-western government earlier Tuesday had claimed capture of the Xieng Khouang stronghold but admitted heavy fighting raged around the town in a seesaw battle. The Communist "voice of Laos" radio said Red forces had encircled and wiped out the paratroopers reported by the government to have taken the city.

The communists also claimed the capture of 200 other pro-western soldiers plus 1,000 rifles, many artillery pieces and vehicles and

Please Turn to Pg. 6, Col. 1

U.S. Holiday Traffic Toll Reaches 338

BY THE ASSOCIATED PRESS

Traffic accidents across the nation took a toll of 338 lives during the long New Year's holiday weekend. California recorded 42 traffic deaths.

The number of persons killed on streets and highways during the 78-hour observance that ended at midnight Monday (local time) was the lowest for a three-day New Year's holiday since 1953 when 317 deaths were counted.

The National Safety Council had estimated 340 lives might be lost in traffic during the holiday.

FINANCIAL REVIEW APPEARS TODAY

The Times annual business review and forecast section, featuring major categories of the Southland and national economies, appears today in Part 2.

Because the financial review takes up the entire Part 2, the Family Section starts on Page 16, Part 3.

POLICE GUARD EMBASSY—Two Washington policemen stand guard at Cuban Embassy. Police were assigned to embassy Tuesday night after U.S. broke ties with Cuba. In driveway is American auto carrying diplomatic license tags. (AP) Wirephoto

Belgian Police Battle Strikers With Sabers

Illustrated on Page 3, Part I

BRUSSELS (AP)—Police with sabers and clubs fought strikers in Brussels and other major cities Tuesday as Parliament opened debate on the object of the workers' wrath—a rigid economy program.

Socialist leaders of the general strike, now in its third week, defiantly called for more mass rallies in the streets today.

Ignoring appeals to call off the strike, the Socialists tried to scrap the austerity program in Parliament after hearing Premier Gaston Eyskens denounce the mass walkout as political. The Conservative coalition beat down the Socialist motion, 121-83.

Barricades Manned

State police manned barbed wire barricades around Parliament buildings and military police guarded the corridors as the deputies and senators, ending a Christmas recess, took up the crisis.

As they debated, mass protest rallies called by the Socialists erupted in disorders in the capital, in Antwerp, in Namur and elsewhere.

Mounted state police charged unruly strikers with sabers in Brussels' Place Rogier, a mile from the Parliament buildings.

Nine thousand marchers trudged through the capital's main streets — but stayed clear of Brussels' neutral zone housing Parliament and the Palace.

Other than for two outbreaks of stone and torpedo throwing, the demonstration had been the most orderly so far held in the capital

Please Turn to Pg. 7, Col. 1

Cuba Calls On U.N. to Prevent U.S. 'Attack'

Castro Aide Tells Security Council Chief That It May Come in Matter of Hours

UNITED NATIONS (UPI)—Cuba Tuesday night asked the U.N. Security Council to prevent a U.S. attack which it said may follow "in a question of hours" after the break of diplomatic relations.

The council was scheduled to meet today to take up earlier Cuban charges of the alleged U.S. invasion threat. It was the second such session called by Cuba in the past six months, and had been scheduled before the diplomatic rupture.

Foreign Minister Raul Roa, in a note to the council president, said "news agencies" reported U.S. destroyers would go to Havana to pick up U.S. embassy personnel.

In Washington, the Navy said Tuesday night that commercial transportation would be used for the evacuation of all Americans forced to leave Cuba by the break in diplomatic relations.

(It denied reports that two destroyers based in Key West had been put on two hour alert and said the Navy had not been asked to participate in the evacuation.)

Spying Charged

"Complying with instructions of the revolutionary government of Cuba, I express to your excellency our deep concern with this action . . . which according to reliable reports will lead to direct military aggression against the government and people of Cuba in a question of hours, with grave danger to the peace and security of the world," Roa's note said.

Roa said the United States broke off relations because of "evidence" in the hands of Premier Castro's government that the majority of the personnel of the U.S. embassy in Havana "was en-

Please Turn to Pg. 5, Col. 2

Kennedy Had Advance Word of Cuba Break

PALM BEACH (UPI)—A spokesman for President-elect Kennedy said Tuesday night Kennedy had been informed, "in advance" that the U.S. intended to break off diplomatic relations with Cuba.

But press secretary Pierre Salinger said Kennedy would have no comment on the development at this time.

Salinger said Kennedy received word of the break in relations with Cuba from Dean Rusk, who will be secretary of state in the Kennedy administration.

The President-elect will fly to New York today for a series of top-level conferences with members of the new administration.

Kennedy apparently is keeping hands off the Cuban situation because President Eisenhower is still chief executive in charge of foreign policy. Apparently he feels

Please Turn to Pg. 5, Col. 1

Eisenhower Assails Castro; 3 Americans Arrested in Havana

HAVANA (UPI)—The U.S. Embassy Tuesday night urged American citizens to "depart from Cuba immediately" following the break in diplomatic relations and the seizure and detention of three Americans.

Two American embassy staff members and another U.S. citizen were detained Tuesday night.

Stewart H. Adams, U.S. Treasury representative at the embassy, Miss Frances Simopolous, an embassy secretary, and Tony Ferrente, of Los Angeles, were questioned on charges that Adams' Cuban maid tried to take furniture out of Adams' rented house in violation of the Cuban urban reform law. Ferrante had been in the dairy business here; his property was seized recently by the Cuban government.

Release Expected

The Americans were expected to be released today. Their arrests were the only known cases Tuesday night.

There are an estimated 2,000 Americans living in Cuba outside the U.S. Naval base at Guantanamo Bay, where an additional 4,700 servicemen and dependents live.

The Cuban government radio reacted angrily to the break, but Acting Foreign Secretary Carlos Olivares, after conferring with Premier Castro, told newsmen Americans would not be harmed.

Government Quoted

"The revolutionary government, consequent with its policy of respecting human rights and in keeping with customary international practice, reiterates every manner of assistance to United States citizens resident in this nation, whether they have diplomatic status or not," he said.

The Cuban government announced it had asked Communist Czechoslovakia to take charge of Cuban affairs in Washington.

Charge d'Affaires Daniel J. Braddock issued a statement offering to help transport all Americans in Cuba to the United States "unless com-

Please Turn to Pg. 5, Col. 1

WASHINGTON (AP)—The United States broke off diplomatic relations Tuesday night with the left-leaning, boisterous regime of Fidel Castro in Cuba.

The break came at 8:30 p.m. when President Eisenhower issued a statement saying:

"There is a limit to what the United States in self-respect can endure. That limit has now been reached."

The dramatic announcement severed relations that have existed since the turn of the century when the United States went to war and helped the Caribbean island win its independence from Spain.

Castro's Charge

Castro has charged that the Spanish-American War merely shifted Cuba from the political domination of Spain to the economic domination of the United States.

In his statement Mr. Eisenhower gave as the reason for the break an ultimatum delivered by Cuba Tuesday morning. In it, Cuba demanded that the United States limit its personnel in its embassy and consulate in Havana to 11 persons.

President-elect Kennedy was informed of the decision to break relations with Cuba before it was announced.

Russian Arms

Although the Cuban note ordering the U.S. Embassy staff in Havana reduced was given as the specific cause of the break, the United States has shown growing concern and anger in the last year as Prime Minister Castro has moved closer to the Communist orbit of Soviet Russia.

Just three days ago, on the second anniversary of his seizure of power, Castro paraded Russian military equipment through the streets of Havana.

Press Secretary Hagerty would not elaborate on Mr. Eisenhower's statement except to point out that Secretary of State Herter in a note to Cuba had said the United States would ask Switzerland to assume diplomatic and consular represen-

Please Turn to Pg. 2, Col. 3

KEEP HANDS OFF NAVY BASE, CASTRO WARNED

WASHINGTON (UPI)—A State Department spokesman Tuesday in effect warned Castro to keep hands off the big U.S. naval base at Guantanamo Bay — the target of a mounting attack by the Cuban premier and his propagandists.

White House press secretary Hagerty refused to answer questions as to whether the United States would defend its naval base at Guantanamo Bay from possible Cuban attack.

"I am not going to answer any hypothetical questions," he said.

But State Department press officer Joseph Reap said the United States intends to keep its naval base, to which it has treaty rights for an indefinite time.

"This has no effect at all on the base," Reap said.

Other officials said in this connection that a break in diplomatic relations has no effect on treaty obligations.

Action Not Expected to Affect U.S. Retention of Guantanamo Base

WASHINGTON (AP)—Defense officials saw little likelihood Tuesday night that the formal severance of diplomatic relations with Cuba would have any immediate effect upon U.S. retention of the naval base at Guantanamo Bay.

This view was based upon a series of treaties and agreements between Cuba and the United States dating from shortly after the liberation of Cuba during the Spanish-American War.

These treaties provide specifically that the area on the southeast coast of Cuba comprising the base shall remain under U.S. control providing that annual lease payments are made and that the United States continues to use the area for the military purposes set forth in the agreement.

The treaties further set no terminal date. Under the wording of the agreement, the only way that the United States could be legally dispossessed at Guantanamo Bay would be for the government in Washington and the administration in Havana to agree upon an abrogation of the treaties.

Adm. Arleigh Burke, chief of naval operations, has repeatedly and forcefully declared in recent months that the United States would take all measures to protect its interests at Guantanamo Bay.

The administration, following recommendations by

Please Turn to Pg. 2, Col. 4

THE WEATHER

Light smog today. U.S. Weather Bureau forecast: Mostly sunny today and Thursday. Patchy fog along coast tonight and Thursday morning. Little change in temperature with the high near 72 deg. High Tuesday, 70; low, 45.

INDEX OF FEATURES

Frank Lane Moves to Kansas City Post

Frank Lane, known as the "Trader Horn" of baseball, swaps jobs. He quit the Cleveland club and was signed as general manager of Athletics. Story, Sports Section.

ON OTHER PAGES

Times Telephone Numbers:
MAdison 9-4411—Classified Advertising.
MAdison 5-2345—For all other calls.
Circulation—Largest in the West:
557,037 Daily; 1,001,396 Sunday.

Los Angeles Times

EQUAL RIGHTS
LIBERTY UNDER THE LAW
TRUE INDUSTRIAL FREEDOM

ONE OF THE WORLD'S GREAT NEWSPAPERS

VOL. LXXX 2† IN FOUR PARTS—PART ONE CC WEDNESDAY MORNING, APRIL 12, 1961 KTTV (Channel 11) 88 PAGES DAILY 10c

RUSSIA SENDS FIRST MAN INTO SPACE

Eichmann Lawyer Calls Trial Illegal

Three-Judge Panel Listens to Arguments on Rights of Israel

Illustrated on Page 3, Part I

JERUSALEM (AP) — The trial of Adolf Eichmann entered its second day today with opposing attorneys waging a legal battle over the authority of a Jewish court to try the onetime Gestapo leader.

Eichmann, accused of directing the wartime extermination of millions of Jews, entered the modernistic courtroom in the Jerusalem Community Center, eight minutes before the three-judge panel convened the session.

As soon as the judges were seated, Chief Justice Moshe Landau announced:

"I hereby order the arrest of the accused until the conclusion of the trial before this court."

After this legal formality, Justice Landau ordered Atty. Gen. Gideon Hausner to continue with arguments he began Tuesday against the challenge to the court's authority presented by the defense counsel, Dr. Robert Servatius.

Shows No Emotion

Eichmann's pale face showed no emotion Tuesday as the Israeli court read off a roll of crimes portraying him as a mastermind in the methodical extermination of millions of Jews.

Then, behind the bulletproof glass of the prisoner's dock, the onetime Gestapo bureaucrat listened with Teutonic stiffness while his attorney pictured him as no more than a tool "dragged" into his actions by the Nazi state.

The trial's opening day ended with legalistic questions still unresolved. Eichmann himself had spoken only a single word — and

Please Turn to Pg. 23, Col. 1

Reds Influence U.S. Decisions, Welch Charges

BY GENE BLAKE

Communists have been "heavily influencing all major decisions in our government since 1941," Robert Welch, head of the John Birch Society, told a capacity crowd of more than 6,000 Tuesday night in Shrine Auditorium.

Speaking for an hour and one-half under auspices of the Freedom Club of the First Congregational Church, Welch said the Communists have been gaining through a "principle of reversal."

This principle, he indicated, has been one of winning objectives while ostensibly favoring something else.

Threats 'Phoney'

"Ever since 1945 or 1946 or perhaps earlier," Welch said, "our government has been the greatest single force supporting the Communist advance while pretending to oppose that advance."

The threat of military force on the part of the Soviet Union is "phoney" and has been used only as an "excuse" for socialization

Please Turn to Pg. 2, Col. 4

'Strike' on U.N. Called by DeGaulle

Says France Will Shun 'Enterprises' of World Body

PARIS — President de Gaulle Tuesday declared a virtual strike by France against the United Nations.

In one of the harshest indictments he has ever made against the United Nations, De Gaulle said France does not wish to participate either by her men or her money in any present or possible enterprise of this organization—or of this disorganization."

In response to a question, he confirmed his country's refusal to contribute to the costs of the U.N. Congo force. A foreign office spokesman said that in this context he referred to present or future military enterprises although the word military did not figure in the actual text.

Calls for Reform

De Gaulle called for the U.N.'s reform as well as that of the Atlantic Alliance. He made it clear that the question of the alliance would be a major subject of discussion between himself and President Kennedy during the latter's visit at the end of May. De Gaulle also served notice that France would continue to build up her atomic armaments.

President De Gaulle indicted the United Nations for no longer resembling what it was or ought to have been at the start. He said the Security Council had only five great powers at the beginning but there were now other powers elected in turn as well as "an undetermined number of delegations" attending debates according to the subject under discussion. The General Assembly was a deliberative body, he said, which was supposed to debate only those questions submitted to it by the Council.

'Scandalous Meetings'

He asserted that the Assembly "had taken all powers and it can deliberate on everything without and even against the advice of the Security Council which is thus dispossessed of its prerogative."

U.N. meetings "are no longer anything but tumultuous and scandalous meetings where there is no means of organizing an objective debate," he said.

He spoke scornfully of the U.N.'s present ambitions "to intervene in all kinds of subjects and this is true in particular for its functionaries." Although he did not name any functionaries, he appeared to be referring to

Please Turn to Pg. 13, Col. 1

SOVIET SPACEMAN—This photo, released by an official Soviet agency, shows a Russian astronaut in full space equipment training for ride into orbit. Moscow radio made the announcement of a successful manned space trip.

UPI Photo

Red Astronaut Still Orbiting Earth, Tass News Agency Reveals

MOSCOW (UPI)—Russia announced a successful launching of a man into space today.

The astronaut is still in orbit, the Tass News Agency said.

A Moscow radio announcer broke into a program and said in emotional tones:

"Russia has successfully launched a man into space. His name is Yuri Gagarin. He was launched in a Sputnik named Vostok which means east."

Moscow radio reported that when Gagarin was over South America he radioed: "The flight is normal. I withstand well the state of weightlessness."

The radio announcer said the Sputnik reached a minimum altitude of 175 kilometers (109½ miles) and a maximum altitude of 302 kilometers (187¾ miles).

Weighs Over Five Tons

The announcer said the weight of the sputnik was 10,395 lb., or slightly over five tons.

The announcement came at 10 a.m. today (11 p.m. Tuesday, PST).

It said everything functioned normally during the flight.

Constant radio contact is being maintained between earth and the sputnik, Moscow radio said.

The announcer said the duration of each revolution around the earth is 89.1 minutes.

The title of the announcement as aired over Moscow radio was "the first human flight into the cosmos."

Moscow radio, which was quoting the Tass news agency statement on the launching, said that Gargarin "is feeling well" and that "conditions in the cabin are normal."

Major in Air Force

As soon as the Moscow announcement was made, Russians began to telephone each other congratulations.

The first astronaut is a major in the Soviet air force and is believed to be a test pilot.

The Tass announcement said the launching of the multi-stage space rocket which carried the Sputnik into orbit was successful.

After attaining the first escape velocity, it said, and the separation of the last stage of the carrier rocket, the space ship went into free flight on a round-the-earth orbit.

Reports of the launching of a Soviet space man had been reported repeatedly in Moscow for 24 hours.

The London Daily Worker and other sources had said the Soviets sent a man into space last Friday and brought him back alive.

Believe Earlier Try Failed

Many persons in Moscow were convinced after today's announcement that another flight into space was attempted on Friday and there is speculation that something may have gone wrong.

The announcement of the first flight into space was repeated three times after which the normal radio program of music was resumed.

The radio also aired patriotic songs.

The announcement said the condition of the navigator is being observed by means of radio telemetering devices and television.

Space navigator Gagarin, the announcement went on, withstood satisfactorily the placing of the satellite ship into orbit and at present feels well.

The system which insures the necessary vital conditions in the cabin is functioning normally.

The Vostok is continuing its flight in orbit, the announcement said.

Details of the reported flight were cabled from Moscow by the chief correspondent of the London Daily Worker, the British Communist Party newspaper.

The report by Worker correspondent Dennis Ogden

Please Turn to Pg. 11, Col. 1

SENATE GROUP OK'S $1.25 MINIMUM PAY

WASHINGTON (AP)—President Kennedy's minimum wage bill, shredded by the House last month, emerged from a Senate committee Tuesday with almost all his pet provisions intact.

By a 13-2 vote, the labor committee voted to raise the minimum wage, now at $1 an hour, to $1.25 an hour and to extend that minimum to 4 million more workers.

Committee approval came in two hours. But the bill's path may not be so easy from now on.

Sen. Barry Goldwater (R-Ariz.), one of the committee members who voted no, said opponents would make their main fight against the bill on the floor of the Senate.

The bill goes to the floor Thursday. Senate Democratic leader Mike Mansfield of Montana said he hoped the Senate would pass it by Friday night.

Senate Republican Leader Everett M. Dirksen of Illinois, who joined Goldwater in voting against the bill in committee, agreed with Mansfield that Friday night approval was possible.

It was on the floor of the House last month that Mr. Kennedy received a major legislative defeat when a coalition of Republicans and southern Democrats, by a single vote, rejected an administration-backed minimum wage bill.

Instead, the coalition sub-

Please Turn to Pg. 15, Col. 5

Kennedy Will Press for Equal Job Rights

WASHINGTON — President Kennedy Tuesday declared his intention to "end job discrimination once and for all" as he addressed the first meeting of a committee on equal employment opportunity headed by Vice President Johnson.

"There is no intention to make this a harsh or unreasonable mandate for those sincerely and honestly seeking compliance, nor is there any intention to compromise the principle of equality in employment," the President said. "American citizens unjustly denied the opportunity to work for the government or those doing business with the government will have that opportunity."

Meany Named Head

Johnson announced following the White House meeting his appointment of five subcommittees — three of them aimed at the reluctance of labor unions in some areas to admit Negroes to their ranks.

A subcommittee on skill improvement, training and apprenticeship will be headed by George Meany, president of the AFL-CIO; a subcommittee on vocational education will be headed by Secretary of Health, Education and Welfare Ribicoff; and one on promotion and

Please Turn to Pg. 20, Col. 1

U.S. Boosts Supplies to Loyal Laos Forces

Rusk Admits Concern Over Russian Arms Airlift as Reds Delay Reply on Cease-Fire

WASHINGTON (UPI)—The State Department said Tuesday it is concerned that the Russians are still supplying arms to Laotian Communists while delaying a reply to western cease-fire proposals.

At the same time, Secretary of State Rusk said, the United States is increasing its supplies to the pro-western forces "to a degree." He did not specify whether the increased U.S. buildup is in reply to the continuing Soviet airlift.

Moscow Parley

Soviet and British diplomats met in Moscow last week to work out final details for a joint cease-fire call in Laos. Some diplomats had expected the Russians to issue the call last weekend.

But with no official Soviet action in sight, State Department spokesman Lincoln White said "a further delay in working out a cease-fire would be a matter of very serious concern. You certainly don't have a cease-fire now."

White's statement reflected U.S. fears that Russia is stalling on the cease-fire negotiations while building up the Pathet Lao Communist forces. The monsoon season is due in Laos in a few weeks. It will hamper supply activities.

One source said Monday the Russians have tripled their airlift recently. White said only that "we view an increase in Soviet arms deliveries . . . with concern in view of the efforts going on to achieve a cease-fire."

He said the United States is consulting on this with its allies in the Southeast Asian Treaty Organization.

There were reports the United States is considering sending a strong statement to the Russians through U.S. Ambassador Llewellyn Thompson.

Rusk reviewed the Laotian crisis in an appearance before the Senate Foreign Relations Committee.

He said to reporters afterward that U.S. aid to the Laotian government forces is

Please Turn to Pg. 12, Col. 3

Too Much Spotlight on Caroline, Too Little Privacy, First Lady Says

WASHINGTON (UPI) — Mrs. Jacqueline Kennedy expressed concern Tuesday that the public attention showered on her 3-year-old daughter Caroline eventually may change her.

Mrs. Kennedy, who stressed that her role as First Lady is second to her job as a mother and wife, said it is hard to raise children in the White House because "there is so little privacy."

The President's 31-year-old wife said her active blond child has not been affected by the White House spotlight so far because she is too small.

"But someday," she added, "she is going to have to go to school, and if she is in the papers all the time that will affect her little classmates and they will treat her differently. That is why I am so anxious—we always treat her the same, but it is how other people treat her because they have read about her."

Mrs. Kennedy discussed the matter in a television interview (NBC-"JFK No. 2)", the first she has granted since becoming First Lady. The show was filmed March 24 with commentator Sandor Vanocur sitting beside Mrs. Kennedy by the fireplace in the Green Room.

Asked whether the White House was a "very good place to raise children" and whether her life had changed, she replied:

"It is rather hard with children. There is so little privacy . . . for instance I wanted to take my daughter to the circus last week, and I decided I shouldn't because I would ruin it for her.

"I worked so hard to make her ballet school a private

Please Turn to Pg. 15, Col. 1

THE WEATHER

Smog today.

U.S. Weather Bureau forecast: Low clouds early today becoming sunny in late morning and afternoon. Gusty winds Thursday. High today about 70. Tuesday's high, 74; low, 52.

INDEX OF FEATURES

Dodgers and Angels Win Opening Games

The Dodgers beat the Phillies, 6-2, in opener here before 50,665, and Angels made their debut in Baltimore with 7-2 victory over the Orioles. See Sports Section.

ON OTHER PAGES

L.A. Scientists Hail Russ Flight as No. 1 Space Age Achievement

BY MARVIN MILES
Space-Aviation Editor

Soviet success in orbiting an astronaut was regarded by Southland scientists early today as the most significant event of the space age "and also the most predicted."

This was pointed out by such scientists as Dr. William Pickering, director of Caltech's Jet Propulsion Laboratory, operated for the National Aeronautics and Space Administration, and Dr. Albert Hibbs, chief of the jet lab's division of space sciences.

While the Russian astronaut was flying over South America, Dr. Pickering predicted the re-entry would be made either on the first or 17th pass.

Hibbs pointed out that the significance of man's orbit is attested by the top priority assigned such a goal in the U.S. Mercury program, now some nine months behind the Russians.

The Soviet feat will be applauded by the world while the United States is still several weeks away from sending a Mercury astronaut on a short ballistic flight some 290 miles down the Atlantic Missile Range and to an altitude of about 150 miles.

The scientific world has long expected the Russians to orbit a man and as America's Redstone shot neared it was competently and confidently predicted that the Russians would have their man in orbit before this nation could get off its preliminary flight.

Scientists also pointed out that the weight of the Russian capsule—10,395 lb.—as contrasted to the Mercury capsule's 2,000 lb.—marked the margin of victory for the USSR.

With vastly less booster power at its command, this country at present can expect to launch no more than one ton into orbit with a man aboard.

This severely limits the safety and recovery systems that can be carried aboard and demands extensive trials and proof of operation be-

Please Turn to Pg. 11, Col. 1

Times Telephone Numbers:
MAdison 9-4411—Classified Advertising.
MAdison 5-2345—For all other calls.
Circulation—Largest in the West:
557,037 Daily; 1,001,396 Sunday.

Los Angeles Times

EQUAL RIGHTS
LIBERTY UNDER THE LAW
TRUE INDUSTRIAL FREEDOM

ONE OF THE WORLD'S GREAT NEWSPAPERS

VOL. LXXX 2† IN FIVE PARTS—PART ONE CC SATURDAY MORNING, MAY 6, 1961 KTTV (Channel 11) 54 PAGES DAILY 10c

FIRST U.S. ASTRONAUT SHOT INTO SPACE

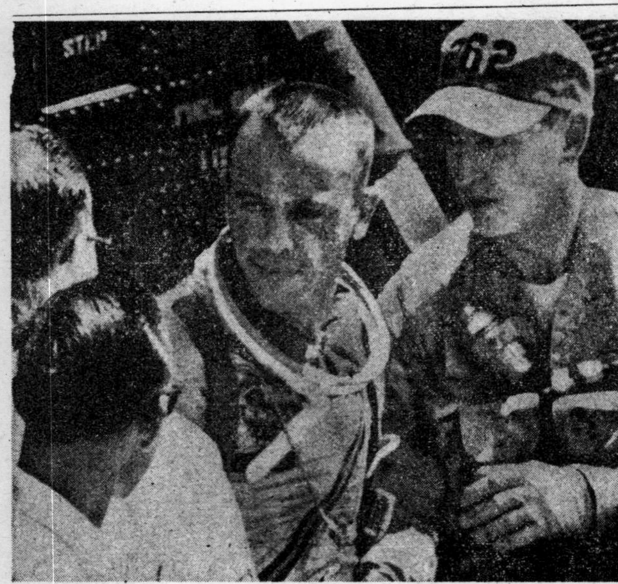

'WHAT A RIDE'—Comdr. Alan B. Shepard Jr., center, still wearing his space suit, is congratulated by crew of aircraft carrier Lake Champlain after his historic flight. The first words he uttered when picked up were, "What a ride!" (AP) Wirephoto

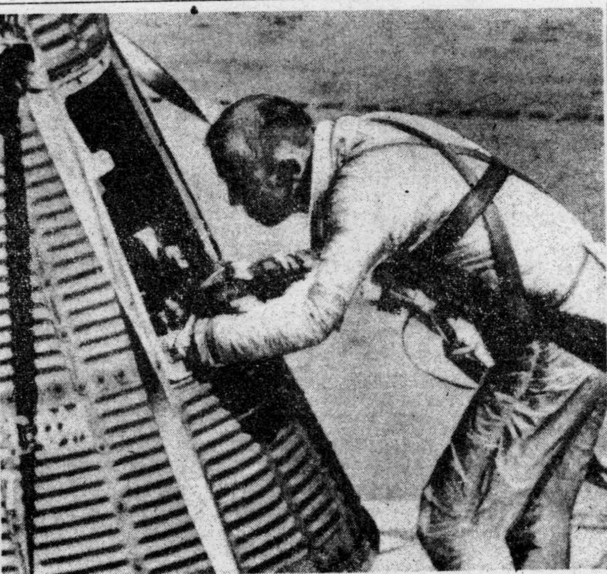

NOW WHERE'S THAT HELMET?—Astronaut Alan B. Shepard Jr., on deck of carrier Lake Champlain, looks into space capsule for the helmet he wore during his historic ride and left behind when he was picked up at sea by a helicopter. —UPI Telephoto

Shepard Hits Peak Altitude of 115 Miles in Ride Over Atlantic

BY MARVIN MILES, Times Space-Aviation Editor

CAPE CANAVERAL—Astronaut Alan B. Shepard Jr. was rocketed 115 miles above the earth in a flawless sub-orbital flight Friday and recovered safely 302 miles down the Atlantic Missile Range to become America's first man in space.

Climax of the dramatic flight came when the astronaut was lifted unharmed and grinning from his floating 3,000-lb. capsule by a Marine helicopter within five minutes after his space craft parachuted into the sea three miles from the carrier USS Lake Champlain.

His first words: "What a ride!"

The 37-year-old Navy commander jumped jauntily from the helicopter to the carrier's flight deck just 26m.

Full page of pictures on astronaut on Page B. Other stories and pictures on Pages A, 3, 4 and 5, Part 1.

after he was hurled aloft (at 9:34 a.m. EST) by a bellowing Redstone missile. He hit a top speed of 5,160 m.p.h. in the historic flight that subjected him to five minutes of weightlessness.

Constant Progress Report

The blue-eyed, brown-haired astronaut was in communication with Cape Canaveral throughout the mission, reporting pressures and procedures in the laconic, unemotional voice of the test pilot — a step-by-step account that boosted tension here almost to the bursting point until he radioed:

"Main recovery chute open."

His words brought unusual cheers from hundreds of newsmen who just a few moments before had been almost silent in appreciation of the courage of the man and the dangers he faced in riding 33 tons of brute speed into space.

The astronaut was sealed in the nine-ft. top-shaped space capsule for 3 hrs. and 24 mins. before launch when a series of holds, one of them for almost an hour, for an inverter problem, another for weather, delayed the shot, which had been scheduled for 7 a.m.

Shows Cheerful Patience

But, despite the long wait in the cramped quarters of the space craft—where he lay strapped on his back with his legs in the air somewhat in the manner of a man who has fallen over in a chair — Shepard was cheerfully patient on the radio and doctors said instruments in the capsule detected no evidence of nervousness.

Shortly after launch he interrupted his technical reports to exclaim:

"What a beautiful view."

At another point he reported that, although cloud cover partially obscured the view through his periscope, he could see the Atlantic coast line as far north as Cape Hatteras, 582 miles distant.

And when a special medical team hurried up to him on the carrier after the recovery, Shepard cracked:

"I don't think you're going to have much to do."

Report by Army Medic

Army Capt. Jerry Strong, one of the doctors aboard the ship, reported:

"There is nothing we can determine that is in any way abnormal. He appears to be in excellent physical condition and fine spirits."

Later, following an extensive examination by doctors and a psychiatrist at Grand Bahama Island, Shepard was declared to be "in excellent shape and health."

The nation's first manned step into the cosmos came 23 days after Russia orbited Maj. Yuri Gagarin. It was followed with intense interest on television and radio by millions of early risers throughout the country who

Please Turn to Pg. 4, Col. 1

Kennedy Studies Sending Troops to South Viet-Nam

Decision Will Await Johnson's 2-Week Asian Fact-Finding Tour

BY DON SHANNON, Times Washington Bureau

WASHINGTON—President Kennedy said Friday he is considering the advisability of sending U.S. soldiers into South Viet-Nam if such action becomes necessary to save that country from Communist domination.

But he told his press conference this is an issue which can await a two-week Asian fact-finding tour by Vice President Johnson which begins Tuesday. The trip will include South Viet-Nam, Thailand, the Philippines, India and Pakistan.

"The vice president will consult with top government officials and conduct discussions on the highest levels relating to the situation in those countries," Mr. Kennedy said.

No Plans on Cuba

In a response to a question as to whether the United States will continue to train and arm Cuban exiles here or elsewhere, the President said:

"We have no plans to train Cuban exiles, as a Cuban force in this country, or in any other country, at this time. There are of course, Cubans who live in this country who have the opportunity to serve in the armed forces of the United States, but if your question means are we planning now to train a Cuban force . . . we are not now training and are not now planning to train a Cuban force of the kind that your question would suggest."

(Just before the afternoon news session, Dr. Miro Cardona, chairman of the ill-fated Cuban Revolutionary Council, conferred with the President for 25 minutes. A White House statement said they discussed "ways of assisting the Cuban refugees and exiles now in this country" and the President arranged for Cardona to meet with Secretary of Health, Education and Welfare Ribicoff.)

Other 'Bright Spots'

Mr. Kennedy announced that U.S. negotiator Arthur H. Dean is returning Friday to Geneva for resumption of the nuclear test ban talks. The President observed that the Soviet Union is now considering a U.S.-British proposal for a treaty "and we hope it will do so in a positive manner, as of course we are most anxious to secure an agreement in this vital area."

Asked if, aside from the successful space probe, there are any bright spots on the international horizon, the President listed as "grounds for encouragement" the fol-

Please Turn to Pg. 7, Col. 1

Red Demands Stymie Truce Talks in Laos

BAN HIN HEUP, Laos (UPI)—A one-hour meeting between government delegates and pro-Communist rebels at this thatched truce village 50 miles north of Vientiane ended Friday in frayed nerves and anger. Results were practically nil.

It was Panmunjom all over again with the Communist Pathet Lao negotiators acting like arrogant victors. They objected to the procedure, raised unexpected demands and then refused to discuss terms of a formal cease-fire.

The meeting began 20 minutes late and when it did get under way the Pathet Lao leaders began heaping abuse on the government representatives and raising doubts as to their competency.

They demanded a higher-ra[illegible]ing "permanent" gove[illegible]nt delegation be sent o[illegible] Sunday.

Delegates Objected

When the government delegation moved back across the rickety bridge over the Nam River, past barbed wire barricades and heavily armed guards, the members were weary and dejected. They sent word back to Vientiane by helicopter for new instructions.

A government source said the meeting was marred by angry Communist demands that the Laotian army be pulled back from the Nam River and that helicopters ferrying government negotiators fro[illegible] Vientiane be grounded because they flew over rebel positions while coming in for a landing.

Laotian rebel Capt. Kong Le, the paratrooper who touched off the Laotian crisis last December by overthrow-

Please Turn to Pg. 15, Col. 4

TORNADO RIPS TOWNS, 14 DEAD, 40 HURT

BY THE ASSOCIATED PRESS

A tornado ripped through southeastern Oklahoma late Friday, killing at least 14 persons.

At least 40 other persons were injured by the twister.

The tornado first hit Reichert, a community of 25 persons, before it struck and destroyed half of Howe, a town of 500 persons seven miles to the south. Churches, homes and business buildings were destroyed in the two hill-country towns.

Ten were reported dead at Howe and four at Reichert.

City Pay Rise Approved by Council Units

BY GENE HUNTER

Across-the-board pay raises for 14,000 city employees were approved Friday by two City Council committees.

The wage increases will cost $4,762,403 next fiscal year.

The council had acted previously to raise pay for policemen and firemen by 11%, costing $6,565,416.

If the entire council approves the salaries recommended Friday by the personnel and finance committees, total cost for fiscal year 1961-62 will be $11,327,819.

Councilman Edward R. Roybal said he expects to bring Friday's joint committee report before the council Wednesday or Thursday.

Will Act for Rundberg

He will act in place of Councilman Karl L. Rundberg, personnel committee chairman, who will be on a three-week vacation.

If passed by the council,

Please Turn to Pg. 16, Col. 3

Kennedy-Khrushchev Talks Urged by Nixon

Former Vice President Believes Meeting Might Dispel Illusion of U.S. Weakness

BY EARL MAZO
Herald Tribune News Service

CHICAGO—Former Vice President Nixon said Friday that President Kennedy should meet soon with Premier Khrushchev to prevent any rash, war-provoking move by the Communists that might stem from a belief that the administration talks big but won't act.

Normally, Nixon said, conferences between heads of government should be held only after adequate preparations. He added, however, that a Kennedy-Khrushchev meeting is justified now because the Soviet chief may be operating under a 'terribly dangerous delusion" based on the recent American setbacks in Cuba and Laos.

"It would be helpful if Khrushchev saw that he is dealing with a man (whose failure to act) in Cuba and Laos does not mean he will allow the United States to be pushed around," Nixon said. "Mr. Kennedy is the only one who can tell him."

The Nixon comment was in reply to a question from the floor following a luncheon speech to the Executives' Club of Chicago.

Chides Kennedy

Earlier, Nixon chided the man who defeated him last year — and the Kennedy administration — for not matching with deeds their "exceptionally high standard for words."

Nixon said, "The lesson of Laos, the lesson of Cuba is this: We must never talk bigger than we are prepared to act. When our words are strong and our actions are timid, we end up appearing aggressive and weak at the same time."

"We can't wish away the problem by brushing off nations like Cuba and Laos as 'unimportant peripheral areas,'" he said.

If the small nations get the idea the United States doesn't think they're important enough to fight for,

Please Turn to Pg. 6, Col. 1

Russia Offers Back-Handed Compliments

MOSCOW (UPI) — Soviet journalists greeted America's man in space Friday with a barrage of back-handed compliments and reminders that Russia did it first—and better.

Soviet ballistics expert Georgi Pokrovsky said the U.S. man-in-space program still lags roughly two years behind that of the Soviet Union.

"Today's flight is in some measure like those of June, 1959, in the Soviet when we launched and recovered animals from rockets," he said. "The result and the scientific interest is about the same."

News on Radio

The Russians received their first word of America's successful manned space flight in a normal radio news program an hour and 23 minutes after the event.

The announcer did not

Please Turn to Pg. 3, Col. 8

Kennedy Plans to Ask Tax Reduction Program

WASHINGTON — The Kennedy administration plans to lay before Congress next year a tax-reform program that will include reduction of individual income taxes. Treasury Secretary Dillon told the House Ways and Means Committee of the plan Friday but gave no details.

He made it clear, however, that taxpayers with high inc[illegible]mes would probably be [illegible]ong the chief beneficiaries [illegible] a reduction in rates. "I [illegible]hink those in high brackets deserve relief," he said under questioning.

Dillon was quizzed for nearly three hours, mainly by Republican committee members, as he completed three days of testimony on the tax-revision legislation now being sought by the administration.

The pending proposals include $1.7 million a year in special tax credits for business enterprises to encourage modernization and expansion of plant and equipment. To offset most of the resulting revenue losses to the government, tax laws on foreign income, business expense accounts and stock dividends would be revised, and withholding taxes on dividends and interest would be imposed.

President Kennedy requested the legislation April 20 as the forerunner of a long-range tax program.

122 Aboard First Plane From Cuba

MIAMI (UPI)—The first commercial flight from Cuba since Fidel Castro proclaimed the country a "Socialist" state four days ago arrived here Friday jammed to capacity with 122 passengers.

First reports indicated six Americans were aboard. One couple was identified as Mr. and Mrs. L. M. Johnson.

INDEX OF FEATURES

Largest Home Crowd Sees Angels Lose

Before 17,801 Wrigley Field fans, the Yankees make their official West Coast debut a winning effort in defeating L.A. Angels, 5-4. Story on Page 1, Part 2.

ON OTHER PAGES

Epochal Flight Means More Than Soviet Union Feat, Says Scientist

Because it was not done in secrecy, Friday's sub-orbital space flight by a United States astronaut means more to the world than the Soviet Union's orbital flight, Dr. Joseph Kaplan, UCLA physicist and a leader in world scientific circles, believes.

"I don't want to live in a world where science advances so rapidly that the man in the street doesn't know what's going on," declared Dr. Kaplan, who is vice president of the International Union of Geodesy and Geophysics.

"I like the way the United States is proceeding, telling the public what is going on. It marks a great contrast to the secrecy and small amount of information from the USSR. We are setting a fine example for the world.

"In the long run, the United States will contribute more to the world program in space, even if we do come in second place occasionally.

"I'm one of that group of scientists who considers placing a man in space an extremely important scientific experiment.

"But to me the most significant thing of this particular shot . . . is the fact that it takes men's minds and eyes away from troubles and comparatively trivial problems, such as Laos and Cuba, and points out in the sky to what they are capable of doing.

"We are possibly going into a second renaissance of science, art and literature."

Commented Dr. William H. Pickering, director of the Jet Propulsion Laboratory which Caltech operates for

Please Turn to Pg. 3, Col. 3

THE WEATHER

No smog.

U.S. Weather Bureau forecast: Mostly cloudy today and Sunday but some afternoon sunshine. Scattered morning drizzles likely. High today 65. Friday's high, 68; low, 55.

Times Telephone Numbers:
MAdison 5-4411—Classified Advertising.
MAdison 5-2345—For all other calls.
Circulation—Largest in the West:
554,871 Daily, 989,283 Sunday.

Los Angeles Times

EQUAL RIGHTS
LIBERTY UNDER THE LAW — TRUE INDUSTRIAL FREEDOM

ONE OF THE WORLD'S GREAT NEWSPAPERS

VOL. LXXX 5† IN FOUR PARTS—PART ONE CC THURSDAY MORNING, JUNE 1, 1961 KTTV (Channel 11) 88 PAGES DAILY 10c

YORTY ELECTED MAYOR IN CLOSE RACE

Kennedy, De Gaulle Agree on Need to Defend Berlin

CLOSEUP OF PRESIDENTS—President Kennedy and his host, President de Gaulle, stand side by side after the U.S. Chief Executive's arrival in Paris. (AP) Wirephoto via radio from Paris

Laos and Africa Also Discussed at Paris Parley

BY WALDO DRAKE
Times European Bureau

PARIS—President Kennedy and Gen. de Gaulle began their epochal three-day meeting Wednesday with full agreement on the necessity of defending the freedom of Berlin.

Because they were meeting in strictest secrecy nothing further was disclosed about their two talks Wednesday except that they also discussed the problems of Southeast Asia and Africa and the stalemated Laos peace conference in Geneva.

The obvious compelling reason for their secrecy is

Bill Henry's column on Kennedy in Paris, Page 1, Part 3. Other news and pictures, Pages 2 and 3, partial text Page 23, Part 1.

that neither wants to disclose his intentions to Prime Minister Khrushchev before Mr. Kennedy meets him in Vienna next Saturday.

Khrushchev's shadow must nonetheless plague their thoughts today and Friday as they tackle the thorny problems of De Gaulle's refusal to commit France's military resources to NATO's integrated defense of Europe and his insistence on separate development of France's independent nuclear weapons system.

Disagreements Seen

They are expected to terminate their five separate talks in disagreement on these two subjects. Nor are they likely to reach accord on De Gaulle's two major demands: that Anglo-American nuclear weapon secrets be shared with France; and that the United States and Britain join France in a superdirectorate of worldwide military and political strategy.

The White House spokesman said Wednesday night the two meetings at the Elysee Palace were conducted in a cordial atmosphere of mutual respect. Only their interpreters were present as the two Presidents talked in two armchairs, seated in front of a low table in a corner of De Gaulle's small workroom, known as the Golden Salon.

Distinguished Envoy

President de Gaulle's interpreter is a distinguished French diplomat, Claude Lebel, now minister-counsellor of the French Embassy in Washington. President Kennedy alternately used two State Department

Please Turn to Pg. 23, Col. 3

Paris Gives Rousing Welcome to Kennedys

Thousands Line Streets as President and First Lady Arrive; Reception at Palace

BY DON SHANNON, Times Washington Bureau

PARIS—Parisians gave a rousing welcome to President Kennedy Wednesday, beginning with applause and cheers along his flag-decked route into the city and ending with a gala reception at the glittering Elysee Palace.

Mr. Kennedy and his wife Jacqueline were greeted at Orly Airport by French President De Gaulle, who stood smiling and bareheaded in the chill wind on the airstrip.

Hundreds of thousands of Parisians lined the streets from the airport to Paris, cheering and shouting "Vive Kennedy" as the car carrying the Kennedys passed.

The highlight of the day, aside from the discussions between the two presidents, came Wednesday night at the gilt and crystal, museum-like Elysee Palace.

Cream of Society

Besides the official party, the guests included such illustrious French names as Prince and Princess De Polignac, Baron and Baroness De Rothschild, and Marquis De Rochambeau, descendant of the general who fought in the American Revolution.

At least 2,000 members of the cream of Paris society, U.S. and French officialdom

Please Turn to Pg. 2, Col. 4

Khrushchev Tells His Aims

VIENNA (AP)—Soviet Premier Khrushchev declared Wednesday night he will strive personally for a relaxation of world tensions when he meets here with President Kennedy.

This was reported by Prague radio in describing Khrushchev's arrival in Bratislava, Czech city only 30 miles from Vienna. He was met at the station by Antonin Novotny, Czech president and Communist Party chief, and Premier Vilem Siroky.

Khrushchev was greeted by large crowds. He told them:

"I am on my way to Vienna to meet with President Kennedy. I do not want to make a prior judgment on the meeting but I will strive for a relaxation of world tensions and to secure peace."

Romance With a Nation: President Out to Woo Affection of France

BY ROBERT T. HARTMANN, Times Washington Bureau Chief

PARIS—When a Frenchman wants to say you are right, he literally says "you have reason." This is no accident of idiom, but a clear clue to French character.

French civilization has exalted reason above all the virtues and Paris is a temple to this cult, which has spread around the world to influence such dissimilar men as President Kennedy and, one hopes, Premier Khrushchev. All Frenchmen, even when they are being most unreasonable, do homage to reason itself.

It is possible that Mr. Kennedy and Gen. de Gaulle reasoned with one another in their private talks Wednesday. Both are very good at the use of their respective languages, and the topics they discussed—Berlin, Southeast Asia and Africa—all lend themselves to reasonable argument. But since nobody was present except the official interpreters—men picked for discretion as well as linguistic skill—all the authoritative sources can only speculate what they really told each other.

In his public comments, however, the American President gave evidence of his awareness that there is much more to the French character than reason alone, that the heart has reasons which reason does not know. So Mr. Kennedy did not reason with France but rather wooed the French people and their formidable president as one would woo a desirable but difficult woman.

He did not lecture the French, as the late Secretary of State Dulles did, nor did he speak as Presi-

Please Turn to Pg. 28, Col. 1

SLAIN — Rafael Trujillo, Dominican Republic dictator, who was slain. (AP) Wirephoto

U.S. Aid Called 'Last Hope' in Halting Reds

WASHINGTON (AP)—Secretary of State Rusk testified Wednesday that America must spend $4,806,000,000 on foreign aid to meet Communist aggression. "We can afford to do what has to be done," he said.

Those who oppose foreign aid, Rusk told the Senate Foreign Relations Committee, "must accept the consequences of their opposition."

"They must understand," he continued, "that, if they succeed (in killing the program), they deny the peoples in the emergent societies their last great hope for independent development and therefore condemn them to the high probability of Communist servitude — and us to Communist world encirclement."

First Witness

Rusk was the first administration witness for President Kennedy's $4,806,000,000 foreign aid bill.

Most committee members gave Rusk and the bill a friendly reception, but Sen. Morse (D-Ore.) said: "I am going into this program sentence by sentence and item by item."

Morse said the United States cannot continue to waste money as he said it

Please Turn to Pg. 18, Col. 1

Dominican Strongman Trujillo Slain

Assassination Team Reportedly Headed by Retired General

Illustrated on Page 3, Part I

SAN JUAN, Puerto Rico, (AP) — Assassins have shot and killed Rafael Leonidas Trujillo, the Dominican dictator, the Dominican government announced Wednesday.

The death of the 69-year-old strongman—dictator for 31 years and a storm center in inter-American relations—was announced in Ciudad Trujillo, his capital.

The communique gave no details except to say Trujillo fell victim to an atentado (assassination) during the night.

Revenge Motive Seen

(The National Broadcasting Co. reported in New York that a disgruntled army general seeking revenge carried out the assassination.

(In a telephone call from Ciudad Trujillo, NBC correspondent John Hlavacek said Trujillo was shot from ambush by a band of seven men headed by Gen. Juan Thomas Diaz.

(One of the assassins was killed and several others captured, Hlavacek reported. But Diaz and several survivors escaped to the mountains, where the general is reported to have 1,000 troops loyal to him.

(Hlavacek said the assassination was not believed to be connected with an impending coup but with a grudge Diaz bore against the dictator.

Slain in Automobile

(The exact motive is unknown, but Hlavacek said Diaz is believed to have acted to avenge some wrong done by Trujillo to members of his family.)

Trujillo was in his chauffeur-driven limousine on his way to his summer home at San Cristobal when the assassins struck.

In Mexico City, Dominican exiles speculated that a long-awaited revolt has erupted in the Dominican Republic. Juan Romero Ulloa, secretary-general of the Dominican revolutionary group, said a general uprising had

Please Turn to Pg. 4, Col. 4

2 GENERALS SENTENCED FOR ALGERIAN REVOLT

PARIS (AP)—A special military court Wednesday night sentenced ex-Generals Maurice Challe and Andre Zeller to 15 years in prison for heading the April military insurrection in Algeria.

The prosecution had asked life imprisonment instead of death for the two.

The public prosecutor asked the court to show its indulgence by sentencing them to the life term, equivalent to 20 years.

Prosecutor Antonin Besson pointed out that Challe himself ended the four-day insurrection by his act in surrendering. He never ordered the use of force and tried to avoid bloodshed.

"That is why I ask indulgence for him," Besson said. "If you do not grant it, you would be putting him in the same case as (ex-Gen. Raoul) Salan who sought to prolong the rebellion."

Zeller, 63, was formerly army chief of staff, and Challe, 55, was formerly the supreme commander in Algeria and later commander in chief of North Atlantic Treaty Organization forces in Central Europe.

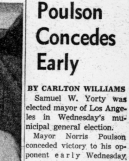

INDEX OF FEATURES

Objection Made on Cancer Cure Statements

Some local cancer authorities have objected to U.S. Surgeon General's statements on drug that cures some cases of a rare form of cancer. Story on Page 1, Part 3.

ON OTHER PAGES

ELECTED MAYOR — Samuel W. Yorty, conceded victory in Wednesday election by Mayor Poulson, and Mrs. Yorty emerge from booths after voting. Times photo

Yorty Hails Election as People's Victory

Mayor-Elect Greeted by Large Crowd as He Arrives at His Campaign Office

Samuel W. Yorty, Los Angeles' mayor-elect, told a cheering crowd at his Wilshire Blvd. campaign headquarters Wednesday night that "this is the first real people's victory in the 35 years that I have lived here."

Yorty, accompanied by his wife and son Bill, 13, arrived at a late hour in the company of television commentator George Putnam and was greeted by an overflow throng who interrupted his victory statement with frequent cheers.

"I don't blame you for your shouting," Yorty declared. "We have been silenced for so long that we deserve to shout."

Yorty, who won against Mayor Poulson after a particularly bitter campaign, praised the support he said he received from many small community newspapers, radio and television commentators — as opposed to the four metropolitan newspapers.

"This is your victory more than mine," Yorty told his audience of more than 500, "and we proved that democracy does work."

The second-floor campaign headquarters at 3335 Wilshire Blvd. was jammed with jubilant supporters and outside more hundreds milled about.

ELECTION RESULTS

MAYOR

4000 Precincts out of 4,712

Samuel Yorty	232,394
Norris Poulson (Inc.)	217,994

CONTROLLER

4000 Precincts out of 4,712

Charles Navarro	281,766
Dan O. Hoye (Inc.)	136,604

CITY COUNCIL

District No. 3

200 Precincts out of 358

Thomas D. Shepard	15,843
Norbert B. Moffat	9,971

District No. 7

225 Precincts out of 343

Ernani Bernardi	14,513
J. Howard Hardy	12,021

CHARTER AMENDMENTS

1—Fire-Police Pensions

4,000 Precincts out of 4,712

Yes	248,693
No	156,978

2—City Pensions

4,000 Precincts out of 4,712

Yes	229,837
No	172,298

3—Harbor Commissioners

4,000 Precincts out of 4,712

Yes	249,850
No	132,631

Russ Turn Down Test Ban Offer

GENEVA (UPI) — The Russians brushed aside as inadequate Wednesday the formal Western proposals for a reduction in the number of annual on-the-site inspections under a nuclear test ban treaty.

The United States and Britain formally submitted in treaty language their plan to cut the proposed inspections from 20 to 12.

But Soviet chief delegate Semyon J. Tsarapkin immediately turned it down.

THE WEATHER

No smog.

U.S. Weather Bureau forecast: Cloudy with few sprinkles this morning. Mostly sunny this afternoon and Friday. High today 68. Wednesday's high, 65; low, 57.

Poulson Concedes Early

BY CARLTON WILLIAMS

Samuel W. Yorty was elected mayor of Los Angeles in Wednesday's municipal general election.

Mayor Norris Poulson conceded victory to his opponent early Wednesday evening when the count was only one-quarter finished.

With 4,000 of the city's 4,712 precincts counted, Yorty held a 15,000 vote lead. From the very first count, the former Democratic congressman polled about 52% of the vote and the edge varied but little throughout the evening.

Approximately a half million votes were cast.

If the trend continued, Yorty appeared to be a probable winner by a narrow margin of 20,000 or 25,000 votes in the entire city.

Sees Vote Trend

"The trend is established and I don't think anything will change it," said Poulson when 2,000 precincts had been reported.

This view was not entirely embraced at that time by Martin Pollard, the mayor's campaign manager.

"The situation is not encouraging but I am not ready to concede yet," said Pollard late in the evening. "The vote count is too close at this time."

The mayoral contest was a nip-and-tuck affair from the time the polls closed. Yorty went ahead from the start but for a considerable time was unable to establish a telling lead.

Yorty will take office July 1 for a four-year term. The mayor's salary is $25,000 a year.

Third Term Bid

Poulson, 65, was trying for his third four-year term as mayor. Throughout the campaign he was hampered by a severe case of laryngitis which made speaking and television engagements difficult.

While the mayoralty race was close, City Councilman Charles Navarro coasted to an easy victory over Dan O. Hoye, incumbent city controller, seeking re-election. Navarro took a 2-to-1 lead over Hoye in the early returns and maintained this edge throughout the night.

Bernardi Leads

In the 3rd Councilmanic District in the San Fernando Valley, Thomas D. Shepard, former City Council field secretary, apparently was winning over Norbert B. Moffatt, member of the Planning Commission.

In the 7th District, also in the San Fernando Valley, Ernani Bernardi, home builder, was leading J. How-

Please Turn to Pg. 9, Col. 2

Proud of Eight Years in Office, Says Poulson

Mayor Poulson, who said "I am proud of the eight years I served," conceded victory to Samuel W. Yorty Wednesday night.

The mayor issued a formal statement at 9:50 p.m. before a gathering of about 50 campaign workers in his headquarters at 3173 Wilshire Blvd.

"The voters of Los Angeles have decided there shall be a new mayor to guide the affairs of the city for the next four years," he said.

In a barely audible voice, which he had blamed on a stubborn case of laryngitis throughout his campaign, Mayor Poulson said:

"I am proud of the eight years I served in that capacity—proud of the progress and growth of Los Angeles under my administration.

"Your new mayor faces a tremendous responsibility. The future progress of our great city depends upon the men and women he will appoint to assist him in the task of administering our city government for the benefit of all the people."

Despite the bitterness of the campaign and the many charges hurled back and forth between the two candidates, Mayor Poulson

Please Turn to Pg. 9, Col. 2

Times Telephone Numbers:
MAdison 9-4411—Classified Advertising.
MAdison 5-2345—For all other calls.
Circulation—Largest in the West:
552,797 Daily; 982,435 Sunday.

Los Angeles Times

EQUAL RIGHTS — LIBERTY UNDER THE LAW — TRUE INDUSTRIAL FREEDOM

ONE OF THE WORLD'S GREAT NEWSPAPERS

VOL. LXXX 2† FIVE PARTS—PART ONE CC TUESDAY MORNING, NOVEMBER 7, 1961 KTTV (Channel 11) 80 PAGES DAILY 10¢

FIRE BURNS 250 HOMES

WALL OF FLAME—Burning homes form a wall of flame in Bel-Air. House at right is at 1757 Roscomare Rd.; left center, 1751 Roscomare. Far left, a garage burns. Times photo

3,500 in Western Section Flee Worst Blaze in L.A. History

The worst fire in the city's history burned out of control early today in the parched Santa Monica mountains, routing more than 3,500 persons and burning an estimated 250 homes.

Nine additional homes were destroyed in a separate blaze raging unchecked in the Topanga Canyon area only about four miles west from the major fire in the Bel-Air-Brentwood area.

Firemen feared the two huge blazes would be whipped together by high winds and spread south into the lush Pacific Palisades area.

The two brush fires have blackened approximately 7,000 acres of valuable watershed.

High Winds to Continue

City Fire Chief Miller said he saw no hope of containing the baze until the erratic winds die down — and the outlook for that was gloomy.

The U.S. Weather Bureau predicted continued high winds, low humidity and warm temperatures for today.

Damage to homes — not counting landscaping and watershed —was estimated by the city fire department in excess of $6,000,000.

Gov. Brown in Sacramento declared Los Angeles County a disaster area and Mayor Yorty declared a state of emergency.

Most of the destroyed and threatened homes were in the $50,000 to $250,000 class, including many occupied by such personalities as former Vice President Nixon, Zsa Zsa Gabor, Joe E. Brown, Fred MacMurray and Burt Lancaster.

Nixon said after fleeing the blaze:

"I have seen trouble all over the world, but nothing like this."

At 1:15 a.m.—17 hours after the fire broke out—the perimeter of the Bel-Air-Brentwood fire extended from Benedict Canyon west to near Sunset Blvd. on the South, west to Sullivan Canyon and north to Mulholland Dr.

The Topanga Canyon blaze burned in a rectangular shape extending from Mulholland Dr. on the north to within a mile of Fernwood on the south where about 100 homes were threatened. The western edge was Topanga Canyon and Santa Ynez Canyon was the eastern edge. It erupted at 1 p.m.

About 5,000 acres have been blackened in the Bel-Air-Brentwood fire and 2,000 acres at Topanga.

Extremely low humidity of 5%, winds blowing in gusts up to 60 m.p.h. and a record three-year dry spell fed the rampaging blazes which spread faster than firemen could set up lines to combat them.

Nearly 2,000 in Battle

Chief Miller said the Bel-Air-Brentwood fire was the "worst fire in the city's history in terms of the number of homes burned and their value."

The previous record blaze was the Laurel Canyon fire of 1959 which destroyed 38 homes.

Nearly 2,000 firemen were thrown into the desperate fight against the flames and the U.S. Forest Service late Monday night asked Ft. MacArthur for an additional 250 trained firefighters to report at 7 a.m. today.

A Ft. MacArthur spokesman said they will probably be Navy men from Point Magu and Port Hueneme, since that many men are not available at the fort.

All state and federal firefighters throughout Califor-

Please Turn to Pg. A, Col. 6

3 PAGES OF FIRE PICTURES

Other news and pictures of fire disaster on Pages A, B, 2, 3, 4, 5, 16, and 17, Part 1.

EAST, WEST POLICE IN TEAR GAS FIGHT

Battle Starts When Workmen Begin to Demolish Red-Built Wire Fence in Berlin

BERLIN (AP)—West Berlin police and East German border guards engaged in a tear gas battle Monday as West Berlin workmen tore down a 300-yard Communist-built wire fence along the border.

The exchange started after the workmen, accompanied by 12 West Berlin policemen and a French officer, refused the East German guards' order to leave the fence, which was a foot inside Western territory.

West Berlin police said the East Germans then started throwing tear gas grenades and brought up two armored personnel carriers and 60 border guards. Another 200 East German guards could be seen in reserve.

Return Gas Grenades

The West Berlin police returned the hail of tear gas grenades and under the cover of the gas barrage, the workmen went about their task. About 150 grenades were thrown, an equal number by each side.

The wire fence had been put up long before the Communists erected a second fence on their side in building the barricade through the divided city. At least one East German has been reported caught between the two fences and hauled back to the Communist sector.

During the night a refugee touched an alarm wire on the East German border and set off flares. He was fired at but managed to get safely into the French sector.

Tear Gas Used

At Heinrich Heine Strasse, leading into the British sector, two men were less lucky. They were almost through the sewage system into the West when they were heard by East German guards who forced them out with tear gas and arrested them.

At Checkpoint Charlie, on Friedrichstrasse—the scene of East-West battles of nerve the last two weeks — all was quiet.

American and Russian tanks lay in encampments

Please Turn to Pg. 8, Col. 1

Kennedy Starts Round of Talks With Nehru

BY JOHN H. AVERILL
Times Washington Bureau

WASHINGTON — President Kennedy and Prime Minister Nehru opened a round of talks on world problems in New England Monday and then flew to Washington for a more formal welcome to the Indian leader.

The 44-year-old President first greeted the 70-year-old prime minister at Newport, R.I., a favorite Kennedy vacation retreat where the Chief Executive and his wife and small daughter had spent the night.

After a private luncheon for Nehru, followed by a round of conversations, the leaders of the world's two largest democracies flew to Washington aboard the Presidential jet.

White House Press Secretary Salinger said Mr. Kennedy and Nehru concentrated the first four hours of talks "generally on the problems of Southeast Asia."

More Meetings Set

Nehru, who arrived in New York Sunday for a nine-day U.S. visit that will take him to Los Angeles next week, meets again with the President this morning for another round of talks.

On their arrival at Andrews Air Force Base from Newport, Nehru and Mr. Kennedy were greeted by Vice President and Mrs. Johnson, Secretary of State and Mrs. Rusk and diplomats of the British Commonwealth nations.

The President told the prime minister in a welcom-

Please Turn to Pg. 6, Col. 3

Hot, High Winds Play Havoc in Southland

Trees and Power Lines Blown Down as Powerful Gusts Lash Three Valleys

Hot winds lashed much of the Southland for the second day Monday, blowing down trees and power lines, smashing windows and whipping flames into the worst fire in the city's history.

Areas hit hardest were the San Fernando, San Gabriel and San Bernardino Valleys, where gusts ranged from 50 to 76 m.p.h.

Powerful gusts kicked up clouds of sand and dust, forcing closure of a number of roads to traffic. Small boats were tossed around like corks in harbor and channel areas.

Electric power failures caused by downed transmission lines were reported over widely scattered areas.

Center of Trouble

The Southern California Edison Co. said most of its problems were around Pomona and Santa Ana on Sunday. Extra maintenance crews had to be rushed in from other areas to handle distress calls.

As winds picked up Monday toward Santa Monica and Oxnard, reports of additional power failures were building up, a spokesman said.

Automobile traffic on city streets was snarled by faulty control signals and debris which littered the roadways in the early morning. Motorcycle officers in the San Fernando Valley were ordered to leave their vehicles at home because of hazardous road conditions.

At least 100 trees were re-

Please Turn to Pg. 14, Col. 3

36 Killed as Storm Batters Greek Capital

ATHENS (AP)—A battering, driving storm that a rescue worker described as "a Biblical deluge," hit Greece's capital with torrential rains, hail and hurricane-force winds Monday, taking at least 36 lives and leaving 4,500 homeless.

Many victims drowned in their beds when flood waters swirled into low-lying apartments, flooding them to the ceiling.

The worst storm in memory here struck before Greeks aroused themselves for the start of a new work week. Basement apartments were submerged, 450 homes collapsed, and wooden shanties at the edge of the city folded like pasteboard cartons. The rivers Cephisus and Iissus rose from their beds and surged through Athens and its suburbs. Athens was left a sea of mud.

Athens police headquarters said 36 had drowned, 11 were missing, 350 were injured — 84 of them serious-

Please Turn to Pg. 13, Col. 3

Property Loss Worst Since S.F. in 1906

The National Fire Underwriters reported that Monday's fire here represented the worst property destruction for a single California community since the San Francisco fire of 1906.

The board said in San Francisco that property losses will be paid promptly — within a week, in most cases. It urged homeowners to take three specific steps in submitting claims to their independent agent or insurance broker:

1—Notify the agent or broker immediately of the property loss.

Immediate Repairs

2—Effect immediate repairs to avoid additional damage from weather. (It noted that the cost of such repairs would be paid by the covering insurance company.)

3—Consult with the agent or broker about additional living expenses necessitated by the property loss, since many policies include a living expense clause where an individual or family is forced out of a home.

Congo Troops Assault Women, Beat Priests

LEOPOLDVILLE (UPI) Central Congolese soldiers raped at least 18 European women and beat scores of nuns, priests, school teachers and other whites during a two-day reign of terror in Luluabourg, refugees from the capital of Kasai Province reported Monday.

At least 132 soldiers were reported arrested by Maj. Gen. Mobutu's elite commando units as a result of the rampages last week — described by the refugees as the worst since the army mutiny last year which triggered the exodus of Europeans from the Congo.

Sources here said the soldiers, members of the regular army garrison at Luluabourg, ran amok the nights of Nov. 1 and 2 in defiance of their officers. Commando units were flown in from their base at Thysville to restore order and discipline.

A civilian plane brought 25 women and children here from Luluabourg Monday. They said they had previously been refused exit permits by the provisional president of Kasai Province who wanted to prevent Europeans from leaving their jobs.

The trouble started last Thursday night when Congolese army troops began a search for what they said were "illegal" radio transmitters relaying information to the secessionist Katanga Province.

"They took all the men to the Pax Hotel as prisoners and then assaulted the women," a refugee said.

The refugees bitterly complained against the failure of the United Nations to protect them.

Hurricane Perils Disabled Ship

MIAMI (UPI) — Hurricane Jenny, 10th tropical storm of the season, blew into the Atlantic Monday with top winds of 75 m.p.h. endangering the disabled ore ship Venore near Bermuda.

The Miami Weather Bureau located the storm center about 740 miles east-southeast of Bermuda. It was moving west at 18 m.p.h.

INDEX OF FEATURES

N.Y., New Jersey Voters May Show Trends

Politicians will watch New York City and New Jersey voters today for trends which could carry over into the nationwide balloting in 1962-64. Story Page 6, Part 1.

ON OTHER PAGES

County Declared Disaster Area; Extra Pumpers Rushed Into Battle

Los Angeles County was declared a disaster area Monday night by Gov. Brown because of its fires.

His action followed similar declarations by Mayor Yorty and Supervisor Debs.

Yorty said Fire Chief Miller asked for the state of emergency declaration.

"All city forces are being made available to Chief Miller to combat the conflagration," Mayor Yorty said. "This is the biggest fire in the city's history."

After Debs acted, Donald McLarnan, regional director of the Small Business Administration, said money, at 3% interest, will be available to rebuild or replace homes and businesses damaged or leveled by the fire.

Brown ordered 20 pumpers from the California Disaster Office and 25 State Forestry trucks rushed into the battle. Two crews from the California Conservation Camps were dispatched to the scene and 2,000 more men were ordered to stand by.

In Los Angeles, on Yorty's orders, the city's civil defense control center in Police Headquarters was activated by Chief Parker, chairman of civil defense, and Joseph M. Quinn, civil defense director.

Quinn said all equipment and manpower requested by Miller were being drawn from city departments, neighboring cities, the county and the state. Quinn emphasized that no civil defense volunteers are being called to duty because regular emergency forces are adequate to do all that can be done.

Mayor Yorty established his line of communications on the fire situation between his home, where he is recuperating from an eye operation, and the police headquarters control center.

THE WEATHER

No smog today.

U.S. Weather Bureau forecast: Mostly clear today and Wednesday, strong gusty northeast winds below the canyons decreasing late today. Continued warm with high temperature near 85. Monday's high, 83; low, 64.

Times Telephone Numbers:
MAdison 9-4411—Classified Advertising.
MAdison 5-2345—For all other calls.
Largest Circulation in the West

Los Angeles Times

EQUAL RIGHTS
LIBERTY UNDER THE LAW
TRUE INDUSTRIAL FREEDOM

ONE OF THE WORLD'S GREAT NEWSPAPERS

VOL. LXXXI 2† SIX PARTS—PART ONE CC WEDNESDAY MORNING, FEBRUARY 21, 1962 KTTV (Channel 11) 110 PAGES DAILY 10c

GLENN BACK SAFELY AFTER THREE ORBITS

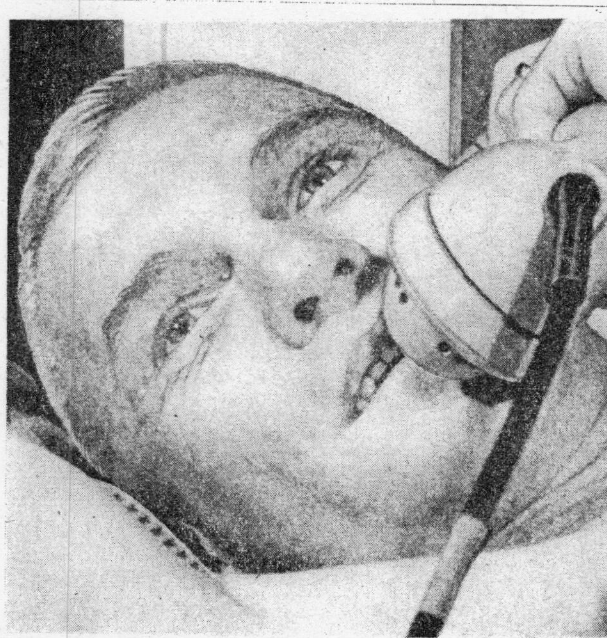

TALKS WITH PRESIDENT—Astronaut John Glenn talks with President Kennedy by phone aboard destroyer Noa after he and space capsule were recovered at sea.
NASA photo via (AP) Wirephoto

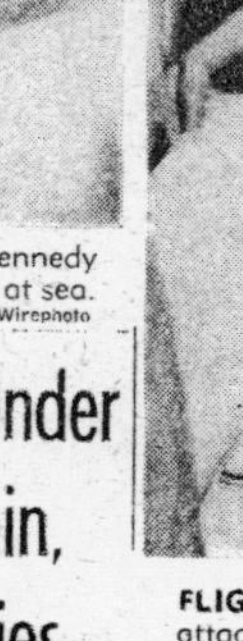

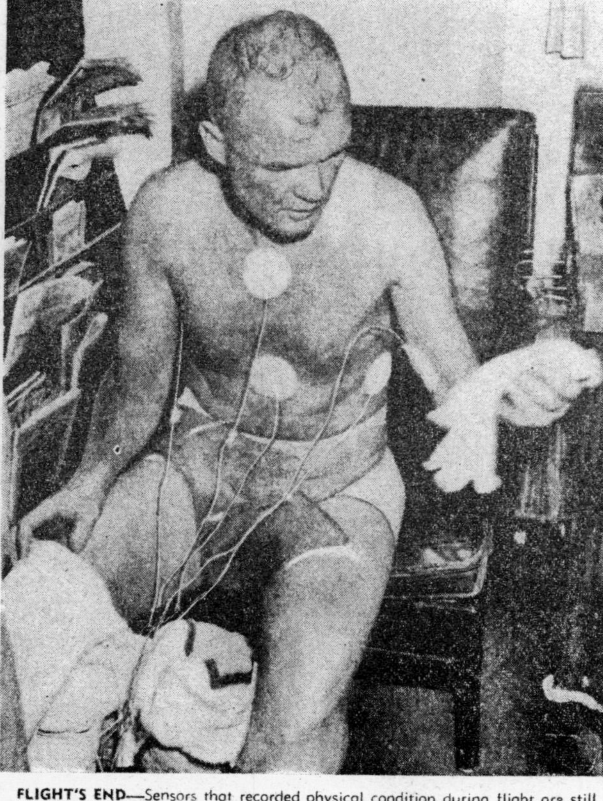

FLIGHT'S END—Sensors that recorded physical condition during flight are still attached to John Glenn's body as he gets out of his space suit aboard destroyer.
U.S. Navy photo via UPI Telephoto

Controls Capsule Manually During Much of Mission

BY MARVIN MILES, Times Space-Aviation Editor

CAPE CANAVERAL—Astronaut John H. Glenn Jr. streaked through three orbits of the earth Tuesday in his Friendship 7 spacecraft and was recovered unharmed in the Atlantic. The dramatic flight gripped the nation in intense excitement for 296 minutes as Glenn reported calmly from space and controlled his capsule manually for much of the mission.

Breathless televiewers across the country watched the thunderous, long-awaited launch that hurled the titanium capsule into the airless cold of space at 17,545 m.p.h. and three times from Tuesday into Wednesday and back again while Glenn flew weightless and soared to a peak altitude of 162.3 miles near Australia.

Friendship 7 flashed over Southern California on its last orbit, beginning its long fall from space that ended with a bullseye parachute descent into the Atlantic just five miles from the destroyer USS Noa in the Atlantic 156 miles east of Grand Turk Island.

2 FULL PAGES OF PICTURES

Other news and pictures of orbit flight on Pages A, B, 2, 3, 4, 5, 6, 7, 9, 10, 11, 12, 14, 15 and 19, Part 1.

The capsule splashed gently into the sea at 11:43 a.m. (PST), four hours, 56 minutes after launch at 6:47 a.m. (PST) and was sighted in descent by the Noa which raced to the scene from her position some 50 miles from the main rescue ship, the carrier USS Randolph.

The capsule was plucked from the sea and hauled aboard the Noa 21 minutes later and there was some difficulty in clearing a way for Glenn to exit from the top of the space craft.

While helping in the exit operation, the exuberant astronaut reported from inside the capsule that he was in excellent condition—a report that was verified shortly when he crawled onto the deck with a broad, freckle-faced grin after exploding the capsule's hatch open to get out of the space craft.

Withstands Rigors of Weightlessness

The astronaut apparently withstood the rigors of extended weightlessness with ease and there were no adverse physical reports during the flight either from Glenn himself or from military doctors who followed his reactions by means of telemetry during the long mission. Only major problem was a malfunction in the spacecraft's automatic stabilization and control system that forced Glenn to "fly by wire"—control the capsule manually—for most of the flight instead of relying on his auto-pilot.

But he repeatedly reported he was having no difficulty in maintaining the capsule's attitude as he desired and radioed that the spacecraft handled easily and smoothly under manual control which actuated electronic signals to attitude control jets in the capsule.

This malfunction was believed possibly the same that caused the return of Enos, the chimpanzee, from orbit after two circles of the earth, and Glenn's handling of the situation emphasized the reason for man in space.

Skinned Knuckles Only Injury

The only injury he sustained in the hazardous mission—several skinned knuckles—occurred in blowing the hatch.

Glenn was transferred by helicopter to the recovery carrier USS Randolph where he was given a preliminary physical checkup. He then was flown to Grand Turk Island for a 48-hour rest and physical examination.

Earlier it was indicated he would fly to Washington after the two-day rest for presidential honors, public acclaim and a national press conference.

However, the White House indicated late Tuesday that President Kennedy will fly here Friday to honor Glenn. There was no indication whether there will be a

Please Turn to Pg. 14, Col. 1

BABYSITTER'S BODY FOUND IN DESERT

Lancaster Girl Stabbed in Back, Throat and Buried in Shallow Grave in Sand

The body of missing babysitter Donna Marie Frislie, 14, stabbed in the back and slashed on the right side of her throat, was found Tuesday afternoon in a shallow grave in the desert 22 miles east of Palmdale.

"The vicious character of the wounds lead us to feel this may have been a revenge killing," said Floyd W. Rosenberg, chief of sheriff's detectives. "We think the murderer may have been someone she knew. She was not sexually molested."

Donna Marie Frislie

Donna Marie's grave was only a thin layer of sand hastily spread over her body by her murderer.

Her blond hair and the Capri pants and black sweater she was wearing when she disappeared from a Lancaster home Feb. 12 were visible through the sand.

Weird Shadows Cast

On one foot was a black flat shoe with a black buckle and a black strap. Its mate was with a small number of her possessions in the house from which she mysteriously vanished.

Floodlights put up by deputy sheriffs Monday night to help the coroner and detectives in their investigations cast weird shadows among the Joshua trees on the cold desert. Sand around the grave was screened for clues.

Det. Lt. George Walsh said wide tire tracks and some footprints were found around the makeshift grave.

A 5-in. snowfall Monday obliterated part of the tire tracks, but, Walsh said, there was hope enough remained for laboratory experts to make impressions.

The grave was off a side road, about six miles from the nearest main highway, No. 6 to Pearblossom.

The body was found at 1:40 p.m. by John Ganaway, 28, of 1617 E Ave. I, and Frank E. Diller, 73, of 20538 E Ave. Q-12, Lancaster, while they were visiting an abandoned gold mine in rock

Please Turn to Pg. 23, Col. 1

Trapped Under Auto in Rain, Woman Dies

Los Angeles Rainfall: Storm, 1.93 in.; Season 17.64 in.; Last year to date, 3.99 in.; Normal to date, 10.11 in.

Mrs. Roberta O'Keefe, 50, former wife of radio star Walter O'Keefe, drowned in raging runoff water during Tuesday night's storm.

She had been visiting Mrs. Howard Reinheimer, 1131 Coldwater Canyon Dr., Beverly Hills, and was returning to her car when she apparently lost her footing, police said.

Rain figures on Page 22.

She was trapped under her car by the torrential runoff waters pouring down the hilly canyon street at curb level.

Downtown Los Angeles escaped with relative light showers Tuesday while some areas were drenched with more than 2 in. of rain in heavy thunderstorms. Downtown received only .22 of its 1.93 storm total Tuesday.

The rain eased off to sporadic showers in most Southern California areas during the evening, but in the San Gabriel Valley points and in the Santa Barbara area the showers were steady.

3.76 in. at Santa Barbara

Some representative rainfall figures included Santa Barbara, 3.76; Lake Arrowhead, 3.75; Monterey Park, 2.73; Temple City, 2.56; Whittier, 2.38; San Bernardino, 1.89; Santa Monica, 1.64, and Santa Ana, .72.

But the weatherman promised storm-fatigued Southern Californians relief today with only a few thunderstorms and light showers.

Less than an inch of rain was predicted by U.S. forecasters.

Beverly Hills police found the body of a toy poodle in Mrs. O'Keefe's purse in a

Please Turn to Pg. 22, Col. 6

Kennedy to Astronaut: 'Really Proud of You'

Space Is New Ocean U.S. Must Sail and Conquer, Chief Executive Says to Nation

BY ROBERT THOMPSON, Times Washington Bureau

WASHINGTON—President Kennedy, speaking for a grateful America at the triumphant end of a long and anxious vigil on Tuesday, told Lt. Col. John Glenn Jr.: "We are really proud of you."

And to the nation itself, the Chief Executive declared that space is the "new ocean" that the United States must sail and conquer—"in a position second to none."

Mr. Kennedy, who tracked the astronaut's daring orbital flight by television and telephone for eight tense hours, talked with Glenn moments after he emerged from his space capsule aboard the destroyer Noa.

One-Minute Call

The President notified the sturdy Marine hero in a one-minute telephone conversation at 4:10 p.m. (1:10 p.m. EST) that he will fly to Cape Canaveral on Friday to congratulate him in person.

In addition, the Chief Executive said he expects Glenn to come to Washington on Monday or Tuesday to receive the nation's applause. Glenn will be honored at ceremonies in the White House and in Congress and during a parade down Pennsylvania Ave.

Vice President Johnson will fly to the Bahama Islands to escort the astronaut to Cape Canaveral on Friday. Glenn probably will be awarded the Distinguished Service Medal of the National Aeronautics and Space Administration, which Mr. Kennedy conferred on Comdr. Alan Shepard last year after he became America's first man in space.

'Proud of You'

"Listen, colonel, we are really proud of you," said Mr. Kennedy after making telephonic contact with the astronaut. "And I must say you did a wonderful job."

"Thanks, Mr. President," responded Glenn.

"We are glad you got

Please Turn to Pg. 6, Col. 3

'I Couldn't Feel Better,' Glenn Exclaims

GRAND TURK, Bahamas (UPI)—Lt. Col. John H. Glenn Jr. stepped jauntily back on dry land Tuesday after his three-orbit trip around the earth and said "I couldn't feel better."

"It was a long day—and a very interesting one, too," he added.

The 40-year-old astronaut landed at 9:11 p.m. EST on this tiny British island where an Air Force tracking station is located.

Dressed in Coveralls

Glenn, dressed in blue coveralls and wearing sneakers, was in the co-pilot's seat of a twin-engined Navy patrol plane which brought him here from the carrier Randolph where he had been taken after being picked up at sea by a destroyer Tuesday afternoon.

A crowd of about 100 greeted Glenn at the landing strip and applauded him as he stepped into a waiting truck and rode off to a hospital built especially for "debriefing" of Project Mercury astronauts.

Back-up astronaut M. Scott Carpenter was one of

Please Turn to Pg. 9, Col 1

INDEX OF FEATURES

Smog Study on Animals Under Way

The nation's largest study to determine effects of smog on 6,000 experimental animals is under way in Los Angeles, Burbank and Azusa. Story on Page 1, Part 2.

On Other Pages

The cartoon Peanuts appears regularly on Page 4, Part 1.

Britain Stays With U.S. for Nuclear Deterrent

BY WALDO DRAKE, Times European Bureau

LONDON — Britain's expected decision to take refuge for another five years under America's nuclear-weapons umbrella is confirmed by the defense white paper which Minister of Defense Harold Watkinson submitted to Parliament Tuesday.

The document continues the policy enunciated by the Macmillan Government in 1957:

To develop a separate British nuclear deterrent, as a measure of national prestige, but at the expense of the pressing conventional warfare needs of British armed forces throughout the world.

Watkinson said the British deterrent, which "is by itself enough to make a potential aggressor fear that our retaliation would inflict destruction beyond any level which he would be prepared to tolerate," would be maintained throughout the 1960s by using Britain's obsolete "V" bomber aircraft. These aging bombers would be reinforced with "stand-off" air-launched ballistic missiles. These would include the U.S. Douglas-built Skybolt and the British-built Blue Steel.

The remainder of Britain's

Please Turn to Pg. 20, Col. 1

KENNEDY PARLEY ON RADIO, TV

President Kennedy's news conference will be televised today at 4 p.m. on Channels 2 and 4 and at 5 p.m. on Channel 7. Radio coverage will air at 2:05 p.m. on KFI, 8:15 p.m. on KNX, 9 p.m. on KWKW (in Spanish) and 11:30 p.m. on KABC.

Southlanders Go Wild, Bells Ring Hailing Success of Orbital Flight

Los Angeles, like the nation, went wild over the successful orbiting of Col. John H. Glenn Jr.'s space capsule Friendship 7.

Church bells rang when word was flashed that the capsule had been lowered to the decks of the destroyer Noa at 12:04 p.m. (PST) . . . that Glenn was in excellent condition after his historic flight.

Babies were being named after the astronaut.

Millions of Southlanders awakened to the launching of the Atlas-Mercury space vehicle at 6:48 a.m.

At the moment of blast-off a rash of minor traffic accidents occurred on freeways and city streets.

Motorists honked their horns, rolled down car windows and shouted to those in passing vehicles:

"He did it. He blasted off."

Little work was accomplished in downtown offices from the time Glenn went into orbit until the Friendship 7 was brought aboard the destroyer—an interval of four hours and 56 minutes.

At offices equipped with TV receivers, space was at a premium.

Transistor radios carried by pedestrians, clutched by pupils and teachers in thousands of classrooms, and propped up on office desks kept proud Angelenos in

Please Turn to Pg. 19, Col. 1

THE WEATHER

United States Weather Bureau forecast: Variable cloudiness and occasional showers today with a few thunderstorms likely. High 56. High Tuesday, 54; low, 46.

Times Telephone Numbers:
MAdison 9-4411—Classified Advertising.
MAdison 5-2345—For all other calls.
Circulation—Largest in the West:
772,439 Daily; 1,120,153 Sunday.

Los Angeles Times

EQUAL RIGHTS
LIBERTY UNDER THE LAW — TRUE INDUSTRIAL FREEDOM

ONE OF THE WORLD'S GREAT NEWSPAPERS

VOL. LXXXI 2† SIX PARTS—PART ONE CC TUESDAY MORNING, OCTOBER 2, 1962 KTTV (Channel 11) 86 PAGES DAILY 10c

NEW RIOT QUELLED; GEN. WALKER SEIZED

Brown and Nixon in Violent Clash

Two Candidates Differ Sharply on Many Issues in TV Exchange

BY RICHARD BERGHOLZ AND CARL GREENBERG
Times Political Writers

SAN FRANCISCO — Gov. Brown and Richard M. Nixon clashed violently Monday in a "joint press conference" that almost turned into a full-fledged debate.

It ran the gamut from communism to the death penalty, and touched on the John Birch Society, governmental spending and welfare chiseling.

And it marked the first time that Nixon, Republican candidate for governor, publicly discussed in detail the $205,000 Hughes Tool Co. loan to the former Vice-President's brother, Donald, in 1956.

The televised confrontation between the Democratic governor and his GOP challenger — both of whom wore frozen smiles throughout most of the exchange — took place at the annual United Press International Editors and Publishers Conference.

Undergo Questioning

Each candidate made a brief opening statement and then underwent questioning by editors and publishers. For whatever significance may be drawn from it, Nixon appeared to get most of the applause from the audience of about 600.

On the question of subversives control, Brown said he doesn't believe in "political control of the University of California in any shape, form or manner," and places his confidence in the UC Board of Regents, which adopted a rule prohibiting any Communist from speaking on the campus.

But Nixon immediately countered that as a member of the Board of Regents, a governor has a responsibility to provide leadership, and he got heavy applause when he reaffirmed his stand that any one who refuses to answer questions by agencies investigating subversives should be barred from campus appearances.

Opposed to Birchers

Asked whether he is "proud" of Reps. John Rousselot and Edgar Hiestand, Los Angeles County Republicans who are members of the right-wing Birch Society, Nixon declared he has made his position abundantly clear —that his opposition to the society is not changed.

"I am not endorsing any candidate for federal office," he said. "I am running only for state office. I am running in the independent tradition of California.

"I'd like to put a question to Gov. Brown. On his ticket are (John) O'Connell and (Philip) Burton, two assem-

Please Turn to Pg. 3, Col. 2

Plane Chartered in L.A. Crashes; 8 Lose Lives

Airliner, Believed Carrying Employees of Martin Co., Falls to Earth at Santa Maria

Los Angeles Times News Service

SANTA MARIA—At least eight persons were killed Monday night when a chartered airliner from Los Angeles crashed south of the airport here.

The plane, believed carrying employees of the Martin Aircraft Co., was identified as a Center Airways plane from Hawthorne Airport.

The aircraft, a twin-engined De Havilland Dove, sliced into tall eucalyptus trees bordering the south end of the Santa Maria Public Airport and plunged nose down to the ground.

Witnesses said the aircraft was destroyed and everyone aboard was killed instantly. Eight bodies were recovered from the wreckage.

Sheriff's deputies were digging beneath the wreckage to see if there were other victims.

Officials of the Martin Aircraft Co. rushed to the scene, but declined to answer questions.

One report said that Martin employees had flown to Los Angeles earlier Monday on a scheduled airline, then transferred to the charter plane.

A number of Martin employees work at Vandenberg Air Force Base near Santa Maria.

Several residents in the area south of the airport told investigators they were alerted by the sound of a low-flying aircraft about 8:30 p.m. They said the engines appeared to be functioning.

The plane hit the top of a stand of trees about 75 ft. tall.

The Federal Aviation Agency said there was a broken layer of clouds at 500 ft. and visibility was 7 mi.

The bodies were taken to C.P. Magner Furneral Home, Santa Maria.

Dodgers Lose Opener, Meet Giants Here Today

By a Times Staff Representative

SAN FRANCISCO—Willie Mays hit two home runs and Billy Pierce hurled a three-hitter as the San Francisco Giants crushed the Dodgers, 8-0, in the opening game of a best-of-three playoff for the National League pennant here Monday.

The Dodgers, faced with elimination if they lose today at Dodger Stadium, will pitch either Stan Williams (13-12) or Don Drysdale (25-9) against Jack Sanford (24-7). If Drysdale goes he will be making his fourth appearance in 9 days.

Mays homered off Sandy Koufax with two out and Felipe Alou on base in the first inning and it was all Pierce needed as the slump-ridden Dodgers stretched their scoreless string to 30 innings.

Mays, who put his club in the playoffs with a homer Sunday, hit another off Larry Sherry in the sixth.

If the Dodgers win today the third game will be played at Dodger Stadium Wednesday. If they lose the Giants will oppose the New York Yankees in the first game of the World Series Thursday in San Francisco.

Details in Sports Section

BEFORE ARREST — Former Maj. Gen. Edwin A. Walker is marched away at bayonet point by U.S. troops after refusing to leave riot scene at Oxford. He later was arrested on charge of inciting rebellion.

UPI Telephoto

Taylor Takes Over Top U.S. Military Post

BY ROBERT HARTMANN
Times Washington Bureau Chief

WASHINGTON — Gen. Maxwell D. Taylor, advocate of conventional forces in the nuclear age, took over the nation's top military job Monday as the U. S. Army faced its gravest internal test since the Civil War.

The 61-year-old four-star general, recalled from retirement 18 months ago to serve as President Kennedy's personal military representative, was sworn in as chairman of the Joint Chiefs of Staff by Atty. Gen. Kennedy in a White House ceremony witnessed by the President.

Record Praised

Mr. Kennedy praised Taylor's broad experience and combat record in World War II and Korea. He said Taylor "comprehends and divines" the complex military problems facing the country.

Taylor in turn pledged that he would "align the military strength of the United States" behind the President's policies. In moving to the Pentagon, he will have statuatory authority to serve, as he has informally, as chief military adviser to the commander-in-chief. He said he knows of no plan to name a successor to his White House post.

Taylor succeeds Gen. Lyman L. Lemnitzer, who goes to Paris to relieve retiring Gen. Norstad as supreme allied commander of European NATO forces. Earlier, Mr. Kennedy presented Lemnitzer with a second Oak Leaf Cluster in lieu of a third Distinguished Service Medal.

Wheeler Takes Oath

Completing the formal reshuffle, Gen. Earle G. Wheeler took the oath as Army chief of staff, the post Taylor held in the Eisenhower administration before requesting retirement in 1959. Thereupon Taylor wrote a book — "The Uncertain Trumpet" — criticizing the Eisenhower administration's alleged overemphasis on

Please Turn to Pg. 11, Col. 1

THE WEATHER

Moderate to heavy smog today.

U.S. Weather Bureau forecast: Low clouds and fog during night and early morning hours with sunny afternoons today and Wednesday. High today 82. High Monday 81; low 60.

EMBARRASSED, DEFIANT

Oxford Reacts Deeply to Moment of Shame

BY GENE SHERMAN
Los Angeles Times News Service

OXFORD, Miss.—A single American Flag flew in the central Government Square of this besieged college town Monday.

It fluttered from a sidewalk staff at the curb in front of an apparel shop that caters to the coeds of Ole Miss.

Mrs. William Baker, a soft - voiced citizen of Oxford who owns the shop, gazed with saddened eyes across the rubble littered square now occupied by the federalized National Guard.

"I fly it every day," he said. "I celebrate every day because I love my country and the heritage it gives us."

Symbolically, the red indicated, as did all the meters in town: "Violation."

There is tragic, grieving sadness today in Oxford which is occupied in the upcompromising literal sense by the U.S. Army.

Depends on View

Not since it was burned during the Civil War has it been voiolated so thoroughly but the source of the violation depends upon the viewpoint being expressed.

For some, the registration of James H. Meredith as, it is euphemistically noted, "the first known" Negro to attend class at the University of Mississippi is the ultimate violation.

For others, the disgrace of being the scene of ruthless mob violence that caused death and injury over an incident they feel could have been avoided is the ultimate violation.

Whatever the viewpoint, Oxford has known its moment of shame and the purging of that shame will take a long time.

The normally quiet ante

Please Turn to Pg. 2, Col. 1

Double-Cross on Meredith Move Claimed

BY ROBERT THOMPSON
Los Angeles Times News Service

WASHINGTON — Atty. Gen. Kennedy Monday laid out a detailed account of Gov. Ross Barnett's alleged role in the dramatic events leading up to Sunday night's fatal rioting at the University of Mississippi.

Kennedy claimed it was clear that somewhere he and President Kennedy were double-crossed.

The attorney general stated publicly that Mississippi state police were ordered away from the Ole Miss campus twice during the deadly tumult, despite Barnett's pledge that they would maintain law and order.

Patrolmen in Cars

At one point, while the campus was under siege, 50 patrolmen were found a quarter of a mile away sitting in their cars, he said.

Kennedy also disclosed that it was Gov. Barnett himself who arranged for Negro James Meredith to enter the campus under state police protection Sunday night.

The attorney general, deeply angered by Barnett's continued defiance of feder-

Please Turn to Pg. 2, Col. 6

U.S. Transfers Gen. Walker to Prison Hospital

SPRINGFIELD, Mo. (AP)—Former Maj. Gen. Edwin Walker, charged with insurrection against the United States, was taken to the U.S. medical center for federal prisoners in Springfield, Mo. Monday night.

Several U.S. marshals stepped off a border patrol two-engine plane with Walker at the Springfield Airport, walked him quickly to a waiting car and sped away to the medical center.

Bystanders were not allowed to approach the group.

The controversial Texan was charged with leading a charge of students against U.S. marshals at the University of Mississippi Sunday night.

Walker was arrested at a roadblock in Oxford, Miss., at noon. He waived preliminary hearing when arraigned before U.S. Commissioner Omar Craig, who set Walker's bond at $100,000.

Hospital Center

The medical center is maintained by the Federal Bureau of Prisons to treat prisoners with either physical or mental ills. Federal judges often send accused persons to the center for psychiatric study to determine whether they are sane enough to stand trial.

Dr. Russell Settle, warden of the center, declined to say what the staff would do with Walker.

When officers took Walker into custody on the outskirts of Oxford, Miss., Walker told

Please Turn to Pg. 2, Col. 3

Reds Accused of Spying Leave U.S.

NEW YORK (UPI)—Two Soviet United Nations diplomats, asked to leave the United States for engaging in espionage activity with a U.S. sailor, left for home Monday night.

The pair, Evgeni N. Prokhopov and Ivan Y. Vyrodov, left by plane from Idlewild International Airport for Moscow.

The two were picked up by FBI agents last Friday and charged with receiving secret information from Navy yeoman first class Nelson Cornelious Drummond. The enlisted man now is being held in $100,000 bail on an espionage charge.

U.S. Pours Troops Into Mississippi as Arrests Rise to 215

OXFORD, Miss. (AP)—Hordes of combat-ready troops clamped rigid control on this seething southern town Monday night after the enrollment of James Meredith, a Negro, ended segregation at the University of Mississippi.

Bent on smothering continued riots that took two lives Sunday night and led to Monday's arrest of former Maj. Gen. Edwin A. Walker, helmeted troops patroled with loaded rifles and fixed bayonets.

The Army named Lt. Gen. Hamilton Howze of Ft. Bragg, N. C., to head the massive buildup of nearly 10,000 army troops. Observers said appointment of the three-star general may mean there will be more soldiers in the state than were ever assembled in peacetime.

Military police and infantrymen patroled Oxford with loaded rifles and fixed bayonets. They imposed tight security measures on the Ole Miss campus.

For the most part, quiet settled over Oxford as night fell. The darkness ended a day marred by a downtown riot quelled by rifle fire into the air and tear gas.

Other news and pictures on Mississippi developments on Pages A, B, 2, 13, 14, 15 and 16, Part 1.

Soldiers permitted no outsiders on the grounds. They searched everyone entering the gates. They kept the numbers of milling students under 100 — scattering them.

Scattered arrests persisted into the night. Soldiers broke out tear gas to quash a new demonstration of about 30 brick-throwing students near a fraternity house. Troops caught a man wearing a white-hooded garment to his waist and carrying a home-made gas mask.

Federal forces arrested at least 39 persons Monday night—most of them youths taken in custody at campus roadblocks. The total brought the arrest number to 215 since the rioting began last night. Many have since been turned loose.

Walker, who Sunday night lead a charge of students against federal marshals on the Ole Miss campus, was arrested on four counts including insurrection against the United States.

He was flown to the federal medical center at Springfield, Mo.

Walker also was present during skirmishing at Courthouse Square Monday in Oxford. The controversial Texan, who led the troops in the Little Rock school desegregation crisis in Little Rock in 1957 and said later he was on the wrong side then, was taken into custody at noon at a roadblock in Oxford.

At the capital in Jackson, Gov. Ross Barnett, who once vowed to go to jail rather than see Ole Miss integrated, blamed the disorder on the marshals. He said they were "inexperienced, nervous and trigger happy."

Barnett Version of Violence

In a television statement Monday night, Barnett said the marshals fired tear gas point blank at state highway patrolmen, who he said were successfully moving back a crowd of students. Someone tossed a pop bottle. The marshals opened up, Barnett said, adding that five patrolmen were treated for effects of the gas.

"This was the direct cause of violence on the campus," he charged.

Earlier, Barnett, under an 11 a.m. deadline today to purge himself of contempt of court charges, called for an end to violence. Law and order must prevail, he said in a broadcast, "even though our state has been invaded by federal forces."

Before that Barnett had urged everyone to remain in his home community. To those from other states, he

Please Turn to Pg. A, Col. 4

CRISIS AT GLANCE

BY THE ASSOCIATED PRESS

James H. Meredith enrolled in University of Mississippi under bayonetted rifles of the federal government, becoming the first Negro knowingly enrolled at the university at Oxford, Miss.

Violence broke out anew in downtown Oxford; troops fired over heads of angry mob.

New outbreak came after lull in night-long rioting in which two persons—a newsman and an Oxford resident—were killed.

Atty. Gen. Kennedy announced in Washington the arrest Monday of former Army Maj. Gen. Edwin Walker on charges of inciting a rebellion or insurretion. Walker was taken to the U.S. Medical Center for federal prisoners in Springfield, Mo.

Arrests in Oxford jumped to 215 and officers said some taken into custody lived as far away as 500 miles.

Gov. Barnett went on radio and television Monday to plead for the end of violence and restoration of "law and order" at Oxford and on the University of Mississippi campus. He blamed U.S. marshals for the violence.

Sen. Eastland (D-Miss.) directed the Senate Judiciary Committee to investigate the Mississippi rioting.

INDEX OF FEATURES

U.S. Insists on Aerojet-General Strike Delay

Labor Secretary Wirtz insists on a delay of threatened strike at Aerojet-General Corp. Story on Page 1, Part 2.

ON OTHER PAGES

Times Telephone Numbers:
MAdison 5-4411—Classified Advertising.
MAdison 5-2345—For all other calls.
Circulation—Largest in the West:
772,439 Daily; 1,120,153 Sunday.

Los Angeles Times

EQUAL RIGHTS
LIBERTY UNDER THE LAW — TRUE INDUSTRIAL FREEDOM

ONE OF THE WORLD'S GREAT NEWSPAPERS

VOL. LXXXI 2† SIX PARTS—PART ONE CC TUESDAY MORNING, OCTOBER 23, 1962 KTTV (Channel 11) 84 PAGES DAILY 10c

BLOCKADE OF CUBA ORDERED

U.S. Forces Ordered on War Footing

Reportedly Told to Sink Arms Ships Violating Blockade

BY WILLIAM MacDOUGALL
Los Angeles Times News Service

WASHINGTON — The United States, grimly facing the threat of a missile attack from Cuba, ordered its armed forces Monday night to prepare for the possibility of war.

The action, a Defense Department spokesman said, was taken on orders of President Kennedy after discovery that sites for missiles capable of hitting nearly every major American city are operational or under construction in Cuba.

Moves Ordered

Steps ordered, the unimpeachable source said, include:

1 — Directions to U.S. forces to sink, if necessary, any ships loaded with Cuban-bound offensive weapons.

Such a drastic measure, he indicated, will be started within a day or two if those ships insist on continuing on to Cuba.

2—A world-wide alert of American armed forces, including the Strategic Air Command, to the possibility of retaliation by the Russians or Cubans.

Armada Deployed

3—Deployment of a vast armada of U.S. airplanes and ships to the Atlantic and Caribbean to assure effectiveness of the blockade.

4—Reinforcement of the naval base at Guantanamo Bay, Cuba, and evacuation of all families from that encircled post.

The official bluntly warned that the United States has no way of intercepting and destroying the Communist missiles — which are capable of carrying nuclear warheads—and declared "we will face losses" as the result of action ordered.

Areas threatened immediately by medium range missiles which have been identified from the air cover a 1,200-statute-mile radius from Havana, and include New Orleans, St. Louis, Washington and New York City.

L.A. Within Range

Soviet technicians, however, are also building sites from which intermediate range missiles could be shot 2,500 statute miles, the official indicated.

That radius would include Los Angeles, Chicago and Toronto, and would extend

Please Turn to Pg. 17, Col. 3

INITIAL U.S. STEPS IN MEETING CRISIS

Los Angeles Times News Service

These are the initial steps President Kennedy says are being taken in the crisis over Cuba:

1—A blockade on all offensive military equipment under shipment to Cuba. All ships of any kind bound for Cuba, from whatever nation or port, will, if found to contain cargoes of offensive weapons be turned back. If necessary the quarantine will be extended to other types of cargoes.

2—Continued and increased close surveillance of Cuba and its military buildup.

3—"It shall be the policy of this nation to regard any nuclear missile launched from Cuba against any nation in the western hemisphere as an attack by the Soviet Union on the United States requiring a full retaliatory response upon the Soviet Union."

4—The U.S. naval base at Guantanamo, Cuba, has been reinforced, dependents of military personnel there have been evacuated and additional military units have been ordered on an alert basis.

5—An immediate meeting of the organ of consultation under the Organization of American States, "to consider this threat to hemispheric security . . ." has been asked.

6—An emergency meeting of the U.N. Security Council has been asked to be "convoked without delay to take action against this latest Soviet threat to world peace."

7—Soviet Premier Khrushchev has been called on to "halt and eliminate this clandestine, reckless and provocative threat to world peace and to stable relations between our two nations."

MESSAGE ON CUBA—President Kennedy delivers radio and television address in which he told the nation that Cuba is being placed under naval blockade. (AP) Wirephoto

Kennedy Says U.S. Will Attack Soviet if Island Fires Missiles

BY ROBERT THOMPSON
Los Angeles Times News Service

WASHINGTON — President Kennedy ordered a blockade of Cuba Monday night to halt the buildup of Soviet-made missiles that could inflict mass destruction on every nation in the Americas.

The President announced that the United States will turn back ships hauling offensive weapons to the Communist-ruled island. He also pledged full retaliation against the Soviet Union if a single nuclear missile is fired from Cuba against any nation in the Western Hemisphere.

The United States will not shrink from the threat of nuclear war to preserve the peace and freedom of the hemisphere, Mr. Kennedy said over nationwide radio and television.

Text of President's address begins on Page A. See editorial on Page 4, Part 2.

He directed the armed forces to "prepare for any eventualities" if Russia does not cease shipping offensive military equipment to Fidel Castro's "imprisoned island."

U.S. ships and planes immediately moved into position in the Caribbean to enforce the blockade. They had orders to shoot if necessary.

The Navy announced at San Juan, Puerto Rico, that its 40 ships, 20,000 men and aircraft assembled for annual Caribbean maneuvers have started Cuban blockade duties.

The first test may come soon. A Defense Department spokesman said a Soviet bloc convoy was in the Atlantic headed for Cuba.

Warning to Khrushchev

Mr. Kennedy also warned Soviet Premier Khrushchev not to attempt to intimidate the United States by aggression against Communist-isolated West Berlin. Any hostile move against the safety and freedom of the people of West Berlin or any other area to which the United States is committed "will be met by whatever action needed," Mr. Kennedy said.

In a personal letter to Khrushchev, Mr. Kennedy detailed the U.S. position on Cuba and also left the door ajar for a Soviet-American summit conference.

Mr. Kennedy indicated to the Soviet leader that he might be willing to meet with him once Khrushchev has reversed his policy of turning Cuba into an aggressive Communist missile base.

Ambassador Given Letter

The President's letter was handed to Soviet Ambassador Anatoly Dobrynin by Secretary of State Rusk shortly before the President went on the air. A copy of the letter was delivered simultaneously at the Soviet Foreign office in Moscow by U.S. Ambassador Foy Kohler.

In the gravest hour of his Presidency, Mr. Kennedy told the world that the peace and security of the Western Hemisphere have been jeopardized by construction in Cuba of bases for Soviet nuclear warhead missiles.

Within the last week, he disclosed, U.S. surveillance has discovered that sites are being constructed for medium range ballistic missiles that can carry a nuclear warhead more than 1,000 nautical miles and for intermediate range ballistic missiles that can carry their devastation twice that far.

In addition, the President said, the Cubans are uncrating and assembling Soviet-made jet bombers.

As additional steps to meet the crisis in the Carib-

Please Turn to Pg. 18, Col. 1

Kennedy Cancels Plan for Trip to California

Johnson Also Will Halt Campaign Activity; Cuba Now Believed Dead as Political Issue

BY JOHN H. AVERILL
Los Angeles Times News Service

WASHINGTON — President Kennedy, armed with pledges of bipartisan support in the Cuban crisis, has canceled all political appearances for the balance of the 1962 campaign. This includes a scheduled two-day visit to California this weekend.

Announcing this Monday night, White House Press Secretary Salinger said neither the President nor Vice President will make any further political statement before the Nov. 6 elections.

While Salinger didn't amplify it was obvious that by halting what up to now has been the most vigorous off-year campaigning by any President yet, Mr. Kennedy hopes to remove Cuba as a political issue.

Now Out of Bounds

Until the President's dramatic talk to a nationwide television audience Monday night, Cuba was shaping up as perhaps the paramount issue of this year's state and congressional elections.

But Mr. Kennedy's pledge of firm action, coupled with prompt assurances of support from leaders of both parties, appeared to put Cuba pretty much out of bounds as Republican campaign ammunition. However, there still were GOP taunts that the administration should have acted sooner.

The Chief Executive had scheduled an intensive two-day stumping of California this coming weekend in behalf of the re-election campaign of Gov. Brown and other Golden State Democratic candidates.

In addition to California, the President also had been plannng stops in Wyoming, Utah, Idaho and Oregon and return trips to Pennsylvania, New York, Connecticut and Michigan. All these, too, have been scrubbed.

Throughout his political barnstorming of the eastern half of the country during the last three week ends, Mr. Kennedy has encountered repeated heckling over his handling of Cuba. There have been indications that the heckling has got under his skin.

GOP Vows Support

While it is too early to say whether his actions Monday will stop all political talk on Cuba, there was an immediate change in the way politicians discussed it.

Typical was the statement issued by GOP congressional leaders immediately after the President's broadcast.

"Americans will support the President on the decision or decisions he makes for the security of our country," the statement said.

It was signed by Senate Minority Leader Dirksen (Ill.) and Sens. Hickenlooper (Ia.), Saltonstall (Mass.) and Wiley (Wis.), by House GOP Leader Halleck (Ind.) and Reps. Leslie C. Arends

Please Turn to Pg. 16, Col. 1

U.S. Resolution to Be Offered in U.N. Council

BY LOUIS B. FLEMING
Los Angeles Times News Service

UNITED NATIONS—The United Nations Security Council probably will meet this morning in urgent session to consider a four-point action program proposed by the United States to halt the armed buildup in Cuba.

U.S. Ambassador Stevenson sent a letter Monday evening to the council chairman requesting the Security Council meeting. Ironically, the chairman is Valerian A. Zorin of the Soviet Union, against which the action program is directed.

The letter was delivered while President Kennedy was addressing the nation by radio and television, outlining a program of national action against Cuba and the Soviet Union. A second copy was sent to Acting U.N. Secretary-General Thant Monday evening.

Zorin Silent

There was no immediate comment from Zorin. A spokesman for the Soviet mission to the U.N. said no announcement regarding the Security Council meeting is expected before this morning.

The United States will propose a resolution to the Security Council:

1—Calling for the im-

Please Turn to Pg. 13, Col. 1

Cuba Mobilizes Forces; Castro to Speak Today

Hundreds of Thousands of Men Called Up in 'Few Hours,' Havana Radio Says

KEY WEST, Fla. (AP) — All of Cuba's military forces have been mobilized as a result "of the news from the United States," Havana Radio said today.

The broadcast said the order was issued by Prime Minister Castro who will address the nation later today.

"Our combat units rapidly placed themselves on a fighting basis," said the radio.

Thousands Mobilized

The announcement, monitored in Key West, came a few hours after President Kennedy proclaimed a naval blockade against Cuba.

"Hundreds of thousands of men were mobilized in the course of a few hours," the broadcast said.

Well-informed neutralist sources in Havana predicted that the U.S. arms quarantine of Cuba will put Soviet Premier Khrushchev on the defensive — and cause serious repercussions.

Predict Berlin Action

They predicted a new Soviet blockade of Berlin and other strong Soviet counter measures — perhaps at such flashpoints as Laos, South Viet-Nam and Formosa.

A semi-official Havana television commentator called the blockade an act of war.

"The blockade measures are not only an act of war . . . but also a provocation for tragic world events," declared the commentator, Luis Gomez Wanguemert. He said the United States appears not to be heeding the Soviet Union's guarantees to defend Cuba.

One neutralist informant called President Kennedy's measures shortsighted. He said that with "the hot potato having been thrown over to Khrushchev," Kennedy's measures may turn the Soviet leader away from his avowed policy of peaceful coexistence to the more rigid and drastic cold war line of the Communist Chinese.

U.S. Warships Seen

It was said in some circles that if the Kennedy proclamation is carried out to the letter and the Communists try to maintain their present sea traffic to Cuba, the situation could result in "war, global or local."

Meanwhile, passengers arriving in Havana from Miami reported late Monday that they saw five warships, presumably American, steaming about a third of the way from Florida to Cuba. The distance from Key West, Fla., to the north coast of Cuba, is about 90 miles.

Crowd Gathers Silently on Street and Listens Intently to President

BY PAUL WEEKS

Half a dozen self-conscious men stood and watched the closing love scene of a movie before the President of the United States' image flashed on the screen. They fidgeted from foot to foot.

The manager of the Southern California Music Co., with 10 sets in his show window all tuned to the same station, turned up the volume on the speaker outside at 737 S Hill St. as the President came on.

The half-dozen magically grew to 25 or 30, then 50, then upward of 75.

They didn't talk. They listened, They didn't cheer. They didn't grimace. They stood mostly with arms folded or with hands in pockets. It was as if each were standing there alone, unaware of the crowd around..

Busses of home-going commuters rumbled by, and the crowd strained forward as one not to miss a word by the President.

Illustrated on Page B

Inside the store, clerks and customers alike hugged more TV sets.

"There's no business," said the manager. "We expect none. We want them to hear."

One man nodded his head in approval of the President's words. But most stood silent. They wore business suits and ties. They wore workmen's denims. There were Anglos, Mexicans, Negroes, Orientals side-by-side. There were housewives with shopping bags.

There was Joseph E. Berntsein, 71, a cane-carrying veteran of World War I; Thomas Forman, 26, a government major at UCLA; George Pine, 64 a retiree, and Tillie Axler, 63, a housewife.

There were dozens more. Nameless. They wanted to

Please Turn to Pg. 17, Col. 1

INDEX OF FEATURES

Skillful Rescue Saves 102 on Ditched Plane

A skillful rescue saves 102 persons aboard a military-chartered plane that ditched off Alaska. Page 3, Part 1.

ON OTHER PAGES

Navy Dependents at Guantanamo Rushed to U.S. on Short Notice

NORFOLK, Va., (AP) — Hundreds of U.S. Navy dependents were flown to Norfolk Monday night from the Guantanamo Naval Base in Cuba.

Five Marine Corps turbo-jet troop transports landed 321 evacuees at the Norfolk Naval Air Station. The evacuees included a number of U.S. Civil Service employees.

The dependents, carrying heavily loaded suitcases, were taken in busses to the Little Creek naval amphibious base where they were housed in a three-story barracks building.

A naval spokesman said it was "reasonable to assume" that the Guantanamo evacuees, estimated to total 3,000, were being landed also at other Navy and Marine installations on the Atlantic seaboard.

In the barracks at Little Creek, women and children milled around. Rooms were assigned. Cribs were provided.

Sailors at the base did everything from rocking babies to sleep to mixing formulas. Navy wives came in to tend children while harried mothers grabbed a bite to eat or called relatives across the country.

The evacuees said they were given 10 minutes notice of their evacuation at 11:50 a.m. Monday. A sample: "Pack one bag each and get ready to leave."

Trucks took them to the

Please Turn to Pg. 16, Col. 1

THE WEATHER

Moderate to heavy smog today.

U.S. Weather Bureau forecast: Night and morning low clouds and fog with hazy sunshine in the late morning and afternoon today and Wednesday. High today near 75. High Monday, 79; low, 58.

Los Angeles Times

LARGEST CIRCULATION IN THE WEST: 761,481 DAILY; 1,110,295 SUNDAY

VOL. LXXXII 2† SIX PARTS—PART ONE CC THURSDAY MORNING, AUGUST 29, 1963 110 PAGES DAILY 10c

Kennedy Signs Bill Blocking Rail Strike

Congress Speeds Measure Calling for Arbitration; Work Rules Canceled

WASHINGTON (AP)—There will be no railroad strike.

Congress passed legislation Wednesday requiring arbitration of the dispute that threatened to shut down the nation's rail lines at midnight. President Kennedy signed it a short while later.

Even as the measure was being hurried from the Capitol to the White House:

1—Secretary of Labor W. Willard Wirtz announced the railroads had withdrawn controversial new work rules.

2—The railroads issued a statement saying they share "the nation's relief over the lifting of the strike threat."

3—The unions described the compulsory arbitration measure as "a backward step" but said they would "co-operate fully with the intent of the law."

Maintain Schedules

"Only time will tell whether Congress has changed the course of labor-management relations," the chiefs of the five unions said in a statement.

The railroads lifted orders canceling trains which could not have reached their final destinations before the midnight strike deadline. Instead, regular schedules were maintained.

Mr. Kennedy signed the bill at 6:15 p.m. as thousands of civil rights marchers streamed out of the capital after a day-long rally.

The President said the measure "reaffirmed the essential priority of the public interest over any narrower interest."

He noted both sides have said that questions not involved in the arbitration procedure can be settled "by good faith collective bargaining."

The two key issues which will go to arbitration involve elimination of jobs affected by technological advances.

Mr. Kennedy said the lopsided congressional votes on the bill constitute "the firmest assurance that free collective bargaining is not being eroded."

The President said those who voted for the measure acted to eliminate the strike threat "that would cripple the economy . . . without weakening for the future, the structure of collective bargaining."

Submit to Arbitration

He said the new law is based on actions taken by the opposing parties in the rail dispute — notably by agreeing on Aug. 16 that the two central issues should be submitted to arbitration.

Thus, he said, Congress was able "to confine its action to implementing, in effect, what is essentially a private and voluntary decision."

Mr. Kennedy said he signed the bill "with the

Please Turn to Pg. 28, Col. 1

Two of 25 Rescued in Utah Mine

Eight Found Dead; Five Reported Alive Behind Barricade

MOAB, Utah (AP) — Eight dead miners were found Wednesday night after two of seven known survivors were brought up safely from a mine where an explosion trapped 25 men more than 2,700 ft. underground.

Two rescue teams, however, were unable to reach the five miners reported alive and barricaded behind debris about 2,100 ft. into one of two tunnels which extend laterally and downward from the main shaft.

The five were reported alive by the two men rescued earlier Wednesday.

Frank Tippie, head of the potash division of the Texas Gulf Sulphur Co. mine, said, "In covering the tunnel, the rescue workers observed eight bodies. We don't know what the situation is behind the barrier."

Rescuers Forced Back

Tippie said three bodies were found near the main shaft (apparently the same ones spotted by the two rescued miners), three more about halfway down the 3,000-ft.-long tunnel, and two more separately in smaller connecting tunnels near the main shaft.

The rescue teams only probed the tunnel to the 1,500-ft. mark, then were forced to turn back when they ran out of oxygen.

Asked how the situation looked, Tippie replied:

"Well, when you find eight bodies, it doesn't look good."

Tippie said the rescuers didn't have time to find out whether the men died in the blast, suffocated, or were poisoned by carbon monoxide or other gasses.

Water Rises in Shaft

He also said the rescuers were not certain the five barricaded men were getting compressed air through pipes hooked up to their blockade.

Tippie reported water was rising in the main shaft, but was not backing up into the tunnels. Rescue operations were suspended for 90 minutes while electricians tried to start the first of two pumps to remove the water.

Tippie said the water presented no danger, but made rescue operations difficult.

The finding of the eight bodies, plus the two rescued men and the five reported behind the barricade, ac-

Please Turn to Pg. 23, Col. 1

ASSEMBLY—View from top of Lincoln Memorial shows civil rights marchers around memorial and Washington Monument pool. (AP) Wirephoto

200,000 TAKE PART IN CAPITAL MARCH

Negroes and White Sympathizers Demand Across-the-Board End of Discrimination

WASHINGTON (AP) — In a great, dramatic demonstration, more than 200,000 Negroes and white sympathizers massed before the Abraham Lincoln Memorial Wednesday and demanded across-the-board abolition of race discrimination.

Then, after the "march for jobs and freedom," President Kennedy asserted that "the cause of 20 million Negroes has been advanced" by the gigantic, orderly assemblage.

After conferring with 10 march leaders at the White House, Mr. Kennedy issued a statement pledging a continued drive for civil rights legislation, for the removal of job barriers, for better education and full employment.

Pour Into Capital

By special train, plane, buses by the thousands, private automobiles — and even in some cases on foot—the marchers poured into the capital. As they headed homeward Wednesday night, the small army of police and National Guardsmen mustered to cope with feared disorder could report that only three arrests had been made—and not one of these was a demonstrator.

Though the temperature was a balmy 84 and a cool wind stirred, many marchers fainted by the wayside.

Other news and pictures of Washington march and related subjects on Pages 2, 3, 8, 9, 10, 12, 13, 14, 15, 16 and 17, Part 1.

More than 1,700 were treated at first-aid tents or hospitals for ills such as ribs fractured in the crush, headaches and insect bites.

Gathering around the Washington Monument, the great sea of humanity moved toward the Lincoln Memorial, which enshrines the marble statue of the man who freed the slaves 100 years ago.

Chant Rights Hymn

Softly, as they went, they chanted the familiar civil rights hymn:

"Deep in my heart I do believe . . . some day we shall overcome."

And a forest of placards moved with them. Some of these struck a religious note.

"God of wisdom, God of power, can America deny freedom in this hour?"

Others were more down-

Please Turn to Pg. 14, Col. 1

Condemn Syria for Murders, U.S. Asks U.N.

UNITED NATIONS (AP) — The United States called on the U.N. Security Council Wednesday to vote the "strongest condemnation" against Syria for the ambush slayings of two Israeli farmers Aug. 19.

U.S. Ambassador Adlai E. Stevenson told the 11-nation council that the evidence gathered by U.N. observers supported Israel's charges that the murders were carried out by a Syrian raiding party.

"For us," he said, "the course this body should follow is clear. In all justice and in the interest of law and order in international affairs, we believe this reprehensible act of murder . . . deserves the strongest condemnation.

"Only then can it be made clear that outrages of this kind cannot pass without the stern disapproval of the international community."

Cease-Fire Observed

Stevenson spoke after U.N. Secretary-General U Thant had told the council that U.N. observers, inspecting the Israeli-Syrian border area, had found no concentrations of military forces. He said both sides were observing a U.N. cease-fire.

Council members have all the known evidence in the ambush slaying of two Israeli farmers north of the Sea of

Please Turn to Pg. 27, Col. 5

U.S. Determined Nhus Must Go, Reports Say

S. Viet-Nam Military Coup Seen as Only Answer if Diem Defies Policy on Ouster

BY JOSEPH FRIED

Exclusive to The Times from the New York News

SAIGON—The United States has decided that President Ngo Dinh Diem must get rid of his powerful brother and sister-in-law, Ngo Dinh Nhu and Mme. Nhu, or leave office himself, top sources told this correspondent Wednesday.

This was described as official U.S. policy after the Diem government's suppression of Buddhist opposition.

Despite U.S. pressure, however, there were no signs that Diem would bow. U.S.-South Viet-Namese relations have sunk to their lowest point and show no sign of improving.

Heads Secret Police

Nhu, who is head of the secret police, is regarded by U.S. officials as having masterminded the crackdown on Buddhists and students, despite a statement signed by military leaders that they had taken the initiative.

Barring the departure of the Nhus, American officials see a military coup against the regime as the only alternative.

Such a development would pose the danger of civil war, or at least chaos, thereby imperiling the war against the Communist Viet Cong in which 14,000 American "advisers" are participating.

Diem regime assails U.S. State Department stand. Story on Page 5, Part 1.

Senators Study Timetable for Test-Ban Treaty

WASHINGTON (AP)—The Senate Foreign Relations Committee conducted Wednesday what one member called a spirited closed-door discussion over a timetable for action on the limited nuclear test-ban treaty.

Chairman J. William Fulbright (D-Ark.) set up another executive session for today and said he has hopes the committee will approve the pact then without attaching any reservations.

Sen. George D. Aiken (R-Vt.), like Fulbright a proponent of the treaty, said there were some suggestions that the committee ought to call additional witnesses. He said another question was raised as to whether the committee should wait until the Senate preparedness subcommittee, which has

Please Turn to Pg. 25, Col. 1

$5 Billion Space Bill Approved by Congress

Compromise Measure, $362 Million Less Than Asked for, Covers Moon Project

WASHINGTON (AP)—A bill to authorize a $5,350,820,400 civilian space program for the current fiscal year was passed Wednesday by Congress and sent to President Kennedy.

The House acted first, 248 to 125, and the Senate then completed congressional action on a voice vote.

It was a compromise of bills passed previously by the two branches and included $1,147,400,000 for the Apollo project designed to send a man to the moon and bring him back alive by 1970.

The final version was about $362 million less than the President requested, $160 million less than the Senate had voted earlier and $147 million more than the House originally approved.

It includes $3.9 million to start building a controversial electronic research center originally planned for the Boston area, but none of the money could be committed until space committees of the Senate and House have reviewed detailed plans.

Large allotments in the measure, most of them subject to financing in a later bill, include $42,175,000 for communications satellites, $194.4 million for the geophysics and astronomy program, about $285 million for new facilities at Cape Canaveral, Fla., and $110,196,000 for new facilities at the Mississippi test location.

Before passing the bill by roll call vote, the House defeated 200 to 176 a motion to return it to a conference committee with instructions to hold the total to the original House figures.

Kennedy Sees Leaders, Lauds Historic March

BY ROBERT THOMPSON

Los Angeles Times News Service

WASHINGTON — President Kennedy lauded the massive march for freedom Wednesday as a significant contribution to all mankind, but warned its leaders that "a very long way" lies ahead in the fight for civil rights.

During a 75-minute White House conference with 10 Negro and white leaders of the historic demonstration, Mr. Kennedy emphasized that meaningful civil rights legislation can be attained this year only with "very strong bi-partisan support."

On behalf of the administration, he pledged to battle for his sweeping civil rights bill and legislation to provide Negroes with new opportunities in employment, job training, and vocational education.

The march leaders reported to newsmen that their conference with Mr. Kennedy was friendly, co-operative and "very satisfactory."

The President, who watched the vast interracial demonstration on television from time to time during his busy day, met with the leaders at 5 p.m.

He congratulated them upon orderliness which resulted from their detailed preparations for the march.

"One cannot help but be impressed with the deep fervor and the quiet dignity that characterizes the thousands who have gathered in the nation's capital from across the country to demonstrate their faith and confidence in our democratic form of government," said the President.

The great outpouring of eloquence and emotion on

Please Turn to Pg. 8, Col. 1

Fire Quelled in Bouquet Canyon Brush

A brush fire, apparently touched off by youngsters sneaking a smoke while on a picnic, Wednesday night blackened 120 acres in Bouquet Canyon, eight miles northeast of Newhall.

About 275 firefighters, aided by three helicopters and three air tankers, controlled the blaze at 8 p.m.

A U.S. Forest Service spokesman said the fire apparently was caused by four youngsters, 10 to 12. It was a mile away from the 2,700 acres charred by a blaze two weeks ago.

Another brush fire Wednesday night blackened about 10 acres in the 7000 block of Foothill Blvd. in Tujunga. It was quickly brought under control.

INDEX OF FEATURES

Tax for Rapid Transit Stirs Heated Clash

Chairman Warren M. Dorn of the Board of Supervisors and C. M. (Max) Gilliss, MTA director, clash over tax financing of rapid transit. See Page 1, Part 2.

ON OTHER PAGES

Kuchel Rips Arizona Water Plan, Proposes Wider Study of Problem

BY WILLIAM MacDOUGALL

Los Angeles Times News Service

WASHINGTON — Sen. Thomas Kuchel (R-Cal.) accused Arizona Wednesday of "trying to jam down our throats" legislation which would vastly alter the distribution of water in the arid southwest.

Protesting against hearings on a bill to set up the Central Arizona Project, Kuchel asked the Senate Interior Reclamation Subcommittee to consider the water problems of the entire area, not one state at a time.

He granted that Arizona faces a crisis because of growing water shortages, but warned his Senate colleagues:

"Don't write off the crisis in one state (California) with 17 million people. The honest thing is to consider them (the states) together."

Kuchel then urged that no further hearings be held until after Secretary of the Interior Stewart Udall submits a final southwest water plan to Congress, probably early next year.

Udall, who released a preliminary plan Monday for $1.9 billion worth of area water developments by 1975, has asked the governors of the five lower Colorado River basin states to comment on the report within 90 days.

Sen. Carl Hayden (D-Ariz.) is seeking approval of the Central Arizona Project—one part of the overall plan—in advance of action on the entire program, however.

The project would divert 1.2 million acre-feet of water

Please Turn to Pg. 21, Col. 8

THE WEATHER

Moderate to heavy smog today.

U.S. Weather Bureau forecast: Night and morning clouds but mostly sunny today and Friday. High today, 87. High Wednesday, 87; low, 62.

EXTRA

Los Angeles Times

LARGEST CIRCULATION IN THE WEST: 761,481 DAILY; 1,110,295 SUNDAY

RACE RESULTS

VOL. LXXXII FOUR PARTS—PART ONE ★★★† SATURDAY MORNING, NOVEMBER 23, 1963 60 PAGES DAILY 10c

KENNEDY DEAD

Assassin Flees After Shooting

ONE MINUTE BEFORE DEATH STRUCK—President John F. Kennedy rides in Dallas motorcade with Mrs. Kennedy, right, and Gov. and Mrs. John Connally of Texas about one minute before bullets hit. (AP) Wirephoto

Shocked Nation Mourns Death of Kennedy

BY THE ASSOCIATED PRESS

The nation reeled in stunned disbelief Friday at the news that President Kennedy had been shot and killed by an assassin. Business came to a near standstill from coast to coast.

Is it true? a New York judge asked.

How did it happen? was another question.

But the big question in those first numbing moments of the momentous news from Dallas, Tex., was:

"Is he alive?"

More than an hour passed before the feared answer

Please Turn to Pg. 9, Col. 1

Stock Marts Close Down

NEW YORK (UPI)—News of the assassination of President Kennedy brought the nation's market activity to a standstill Friday.

The major stock exchanges closed. The commodity exchanges suspended operations or closed. The Securities and Exchange Commission asked what probably already was a fact when its request was issued—that all broker-dealers stop trading over the counter.

FIGURES IN HISTORIC DRAMA—President Kennedy speaking to Ft. Worth crowd Friday morning. Behind him are Gov. Connally, left, who also was to be hit by sniper, and Lyndon B. Johnson, soon to become the new President. (AP) Wirephoto

JOHNSON TAKES OATH

DALLAS (AP)---A furtive sniper armed with a high-powered rifle assassinated President John F. Kennedy Friday. Barely two hours after Mr. Kennedy's death, Lyndon B. Johnson took the oath of office as the 36th President of the United States. Mr. Kennedy was shot through the head and neck as he rode through Dallas in the Presidential limousine in what had been a triumphal motorcade.

When the shots were fired at about 12:30 p.m. and the Chief Executive slumped forward, Mrs. Kennedy turned in the seat ahead of him and cried, "Oh, no," in anguish and horror.

She tried to cradle his head in her arms as the limousine took off at top speed for Parkland Hospital where Mr. Kennedy died about half an hour later.

The assassin had not been apprehended late Friday afternoon.

However, police held a 24-year-old Ft. Worth man for questioning in the assassination. He was identified as Lee Harvey Oswald, an ex-Marine who was a prime suspect in the killing of a Dallas policeman after the President's assassination.

Mr. Johnson, who was Mr. Kennedy's Vice President, automatically succeeded to the Presidency.

The New Chief Executive tok the oath of office at about 2:30 p.m. (CST). For the first time in history, the oath was administered by a woman—U.S. District Judge Sarah T. Hughes.

Mr. Johnson was sworn in aboard the Presidential jet transport—Air Force One—at Dallas' Love Field. He then flew to Washington to take over the government which Mr. Kennedy had directed since Jan. 20, 1961. Mr. Kennedy's body was aboard the plane.

The same volley of shots that killed the President struck Gov. John Connally of Texas, who was riding beside Mr. Kennedy.

Like Mr. Kennedy, the stricken Connally was sped to Parkland Hospital and wheeled into surgery for an emergency operation. The Democratic governor was struck in the body and wrist.

Mr. Kennedy, who was 46, was cut down by a flurry of bullets shortly after his open-topped car had left the Dallas business district, where thousands had massed 10 and 12 deep along each curb to cheer him and Mrs. Kennedy.

This was the first Presidential assassination since 1900 when a half-crazed gunman shot William McKinley at close range during a reception in Buffalo, N.Y.

Mr. Kennedy was the first President to die in office since Franklin D. Roosevelt succumbed to a cerebral hemorrhage in April, 1945.

The Secret Service, the Federal Bureau of Investigation and Dallas police swung into action within seconds and launched what was perhaps the biggest, determined manhunt in the nation's history.

A number of suspects were picked up during the next few hours.

Mr. Kennedy was administered the last rites of the Roman Catholic Church shortly after he was carried into Parkland Hospital. He was the nation's first Catholic President.

Emergency treatment given the dying President was described for newsmen by two physicians, Drs. Kemp Clark, 38, and Malcolm Perry, 34.

Dr. Perry said Mr. Kennedy suffered a neck wound —a bullet hole in the lower part of the neck. There was a second wound in Mr. Kennedy's head but Perry

Please Turn to Pg. 6, Col. 1

EXTRA

Los Angeles Times

LATE NEWS

LARGEST CIRCULATION IN THE WEST: 761,481 DAILY; 1,110,295 SUNDAY

VOL. LXXXII | SIX PARTS—PART ONE | ★★★† | MONDAY MORNING, NOVEMBER 25, 1963 | 76 PAGES | DAILY 10c

OSWALD SLAIN!

Accused J.F.K. Killer Hit in Jail

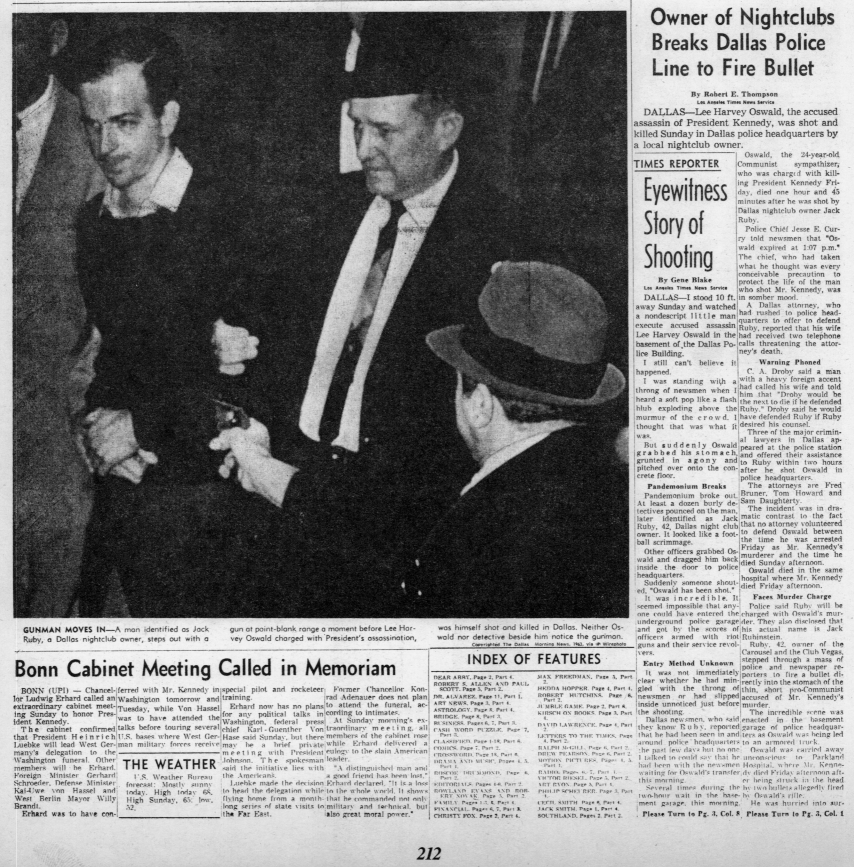

GUNMAN MOVES IN—A man identified as Jack Ruby, a Dallas nightclub owner, steps out with a gun at point-blank range a moment before Lee Harvey Oswald charged with President's assassination, was himself shot and killed in Dallas. Neither Oswald nor detective beside him notice the gunman.

Copyrighted The Dallas Morning News, 1963, via AP Wirephoto

Owner of Nightclubs Breaks Dallas Police Line to Fire Bullet

By Robert E. Thompson
Los Angeles Times News Service

DALLAS—Lee Harvey Oswald, the accused assassin of President Kennedy, was shot and killed Sunday in Dallas police headquarters by a local nightclub owner.

Oswald, the 24-year-old Communist sympathizer, who was charged with killing President Kennedy Friday, died one hour and 45 minutes after he was shot by Dallas nightclub owner Jack Ruby.

Police Chief Jesse E. Curry told newsmen that "Oswald expired at 1:07 p.m." The chief, who had taken what he thought was every conceivable precaution to protect the life of the man who shot Mr. Kennedy, was in somber mood.

A Dallas attorney, who had rushed to police headquarters to offer to defend Ruby, reported that his wife had received two telephone calls threatening the attorney's death.

Warning Phoned

C. A. Droby said a man with a heavy foreign accent had called his wife and told him that "Droby would be the next to die if he defended Ruby." Droby said he would have defended Ruby if Ruby desired his counsel.

Three of the major criminal lawyers in Dallas appeared at the police station and offered their assistance to Ruby within two hours after he shot Oswald in police headquarters.

The attorneys are Fred Bruner, Tom Howard and Sam Daughterty.

The incident was in dramatic contrast to the fact that no attorney volunteered to defend Oswald between the time he was arrested Friday as Mr. Kennedy's murderer and the time he died Sunday afternoon.

Oswald died in the same hospital where Mr. Kennedy died Friday afternoon.

Faces Murder Charge

Police said Ruby will be charged with Oswald's murder. They also disclosed that his actual name is Jack Rubinstein.

Ruby, 42, owner of the Carousel and the Club Vegas, stepped through a mass of police and newspaper reporters to fire a bullet directly into the stomach of the thin, short pro-Communist accused of Mr. Kennedy's murder.

The incredible scene was enacted in the basement garage of police headquarters as Oswald was being led to an armored truck.

Oswald was carried away unconscious to Parkland Hospital, where Mr. Kennedy died Friday afternoon after being struck in the head by two bullets allegedly fired by Oswald's rifle.

He was hurried into sur-

Please Turn to Pg. 3, Col. 1

TIMES REPORTER

Eyewitness Story of Shooting

By Gene Blake
Los Angeles Times News Service

DALLAS—I stood 10 ft. away Sunday and watched a nondescript little man execute accused assassin Lee Harvey Oswald in the basement of the Dallas Police Building.

I still can't believe it happened.

I was standing with a throng of newsmen when I heard a soft pop like a flash blub exploding above the murmur of the crowd. I thought that was what it was.

But suddenly Oswald grabbed his stomach, grunted in agony and pitched over onto the concrete floor.

Pandemonium Breaks

Pandemonium broke out. At least a dozen burly detectives pounced on the man, later identified as Jack Ruby, 42, Dallas night club owner. It looked like a football scrimmage.

Other officers grabbed Oswald and dragged him back inside the door to police headquarters.

Suddenly someone shouted, "Oswald has been shot."

It was incredible. It seemed impossible that anyone could have entered the underground police garage and got by the scores of officers armed with riot guns and their service revolvers.

Entry Method Unknown

It was not immediately clear whether he had mingled with the throng of newsmen or had slipped inside unnoticed just before the shooting.

Dallas newsmen, who said they know Ruby, reported that he had been seen in and around police headquarters the past few days but no one I talked to could say that he had been with the newsmen waiting for Oswald's transfer this morning.

Several times during the two-hour wait in the basement garage, this morning.

Please Turn to Pg. 3, Col. 8

Bonn Cabinet Meeting Called in Memoriam

BONN (UPI) — Chancellor Ludwig Erhard called an extraordinary cabinet meeting Sunday to honor President Kennedy.

The cabinet confirmed that President Heinrich Luebke will lead West Germany's delegation to the Washington funeral. Other members will be Erhard, Foreign Minister Gerhard Schroeder, Defense Minister Kai-Uwe von Hassel and West Berlin Mayor Willy Brandt.

Erhard was to have conferred with Mr. Kennedy in Washington tomorrow and Tuesday, while Von Hassel was to have attended the talks before touring several U.S. bases where West German military forces receive special pilot and rocketeer training.

Erhard now has no plans for any political talks in Washington, federal press chief Karl-Guenther Von Hase said Sunday, but there may be a brief private meeting with President Johnson. The spokesman said the initiative lies with the Americans.

Luebke made the decision to head the delegation while flying home from a month-long series of state visits to the Far East.

Former Chancellor Konrad Adenauer does not plan to attend the funeral, according to intimates.

At Sunday morning's extraordinary meeting, all members of the cabinet rose while Erhard delivered a eulogy to the slain American leader.

"A distinguished man and a good friend has been lost," Erhard declared. "It is a loss to the whole world. It shows that he commanded not only military and technical, but also great moral power."

THE WEATHER

U.S. Weather Bureau forecast: Mostly sunny today. High today 68. High Sunday, 65; low, 52.

INDEX OF FEATURES

Los Angeles Times

LARGEST CIRCULATION IN THE WEST. 812,147 DAILY; 1,149,295 SUNDAY

VOL. LXXXIII 2† FIVE PARTS—PART ONE CC WEDNESDAY MORNING, AUG. 5, 1964 86 PAGES

DAILY 10c

U.S. PLANES BOMBING N. VIETNAM PORTS

FBI Unearths Three Bodies in Hunt for Rights Workers

Identification Checks Slated in Mississippi

JACKSON, Miss. (AP) — The FBI Tuesday night found three bodies buried in graves at a dam site near Philadelphia, Miss., where a trio of civil rights workers vanished six weeks ago.

Roy Moore, chief of the FBI office in the Mississippi capital, said his agency is "fairly certain" the bodies are those of the missing workers but he cannot be positive until laboratory tests are made.

The bodies were discovered in graves in a wooded area about six miles southwest of Philadelphia. The only word the FBI received was by radio from its agents.

Will Seek Killers

Gov. Paul Johnson, informed by Washington of the discovery, said in a statement, "If these are the bodies of the three civil rights workers who have been missing several weeks, the investigative forces of the state of Mississippi will exert every effort to apprehend those who may have been responsible for their deaths."

Gov. Johnson said that "outstanding pathologists of the University of Mississippi medical center will make positive identification of the bodies."

The governor said the FBI told him the bodies were located on a farm southwest of Philadelphia near the Neshoba County Fairgrounds.

Find Dam

When the searchers first combed the area, Gov. Johnson said he was told, they found what appeared to be a fresh dam thrown up to catch water in a low area.

Later, it was noticed that the dam had collected no water despite several showers in the area.

An investigation of the dam was ordered and the excavation uncovered the bodies in the fill of the dam.

Tests Scheduled

Moore said he had talked with Mississippi officials and the bodies would be taken to the University Medical Center in Jackson for identification tests.

"Word should come any minute" on when the bodies will be taken out, Moore said. "We are moving fast."

The three, Andrew Goodman, James Early Chaney and Michael Henry Schwerner, were last seen

Please Turn to Pg. 11, Col. 1

NINE FRENCH MINERS HAULED UP TO SAFETY

Illustrated on Page 3, Part I

CHAMPAGNOLE, France (AP) — Nine French miners imprisoned for eight days deep in the collapsed chambers of a limestone mine were hauled safely up a rescue shaft Tuesday, ready for a party with red wine and champagne.

Military ambulances sped them to a Champagnole hospital for checkups and any treatment they might need. The miners appeared to be in relatively good condition.

Andre Martinet, the mine foreman, was among those who walked from the special aluminum capsule which hauled them, one at a time, from their prison 270 ft. below.

Even those placed on stretchers managed smiles and weak waves to the hundreds of relatives and villagers clustered around the rescue site.

Martinet had been a tower of strength to his men during uncertainties of their ordeal.

Only doubt about the fate of five other men who had been down in the Mt. Rivel mine when it collapsed dimmed the otherwise festive air which spread through the village in eastern France.

Weary drilling teams continued work toward another section of the mine where tapping sounds have been heard.

Brown Names Salinger to Engle's Senate Seat

Former White House Press Secretary Scheduled to Be Sworn In Today

BY JERRY GILLAM
Times Staff Writer

SACRAMENTO — Gov. Brown Tuesday appointed Pierre Salinger to serve out the unexpired term of the late U.S. Sen. Clair Engle.

The former White House press secretary is scheduled to be sworn into office today at 12:15 p.m. in Washington, D.C.

Engle, 52, died last Thursday of a brain tumor after two operations. He was buried Monday in his hometown of Red Bluff.

Won Primary

A native San Franciscan, Salinger, 39, won the Democratic nomination for Engle's seat in the June 2 primary election, defeating State Controller Alan Cranston in a close contest.

Salinger faces former film actor George Murphy, the Republican nominee, in the Nov. 3 general election.

The appointment was announced by Brown at a press conference also attended by Salinger.

With Salinger at his side, Brown declared:

"In appointing a new U.S. senator from California, I do so aware of my great responsibility as governor to appoint a man who can represent the 18 million people of our state and move on in the fight for peace in the world.

"The man I am appointing already has been selected by the Democratic Party, so my choice is really not a difficult one.

"I have known Pierre Salinger for 21 years. He is a young man . . . Few governors have been so fortunate to have had a situation like this made to order for appointment of a U.S. senator.

"It gives me great pleasure to announce to you the appointment of Pierre Salinger."

Johnson's Approval

During his brief speech, the governor also said President Johnson has put his personal stamp of approval on Salinger as the new Senate appointee.

Mr. Johnson, Brown said, telephoned him Monday at the mansion to express his sorrow at Engle's death, adding he didn't want to dictate Brown's choice but, "I hope you will give me a U.S. senator who is progres-

Please Turn to Pg. 2, Col. 4

Murphy Will File Suit on Salinger Selection

BY CARL GREENBERG
Times Political Writer

George Murphy, Republican nominee for U.S. senator, said Tuesday night he will sue today to set aside Gov. Brown's appointment of Democratic nominee Pierre Salinger to the post.

But, by the time Murphy's petition for a writ of mandate from the Superior Court is filed the governor and his appointee will be in Washington.

And, with Salinger's oath as a senator expected to be administered at noon, a hearing on the petition not expected until about Aug. 17 and the Senate the judge of its own membership, there was puzzlement as to just what a superior judge in a state court could do about it.

Murphy, who charged the appointment "smacks of the wheeling and dealing of political bosses and conspirators who run the state's affairs," said his petition will ask that Brown recall the appointment on the grounds it was illegal under the state elections code.

He notified President Johnson of his plans and reiterated his contention that Salinger is a resident of Virginia.

In response to another wire that Murphy sent Brown, the governor said he acted on the basis of an opinion from his legal adviser, Atty. Gen. Stanley Mosk, holding the appointment "valid and proper."

Mosk's opinion went beyond that—actually it held:

1—"The ultimate decision as to whether or not a particular person shall be seated

Please Turn to Pg. 7, Col. 4

32 Injured in Illinois Train Derailment

CARBONDALE, Ill. (AP)— At least 32 persons were injured Tuesday as the last six cars of the Illinois Central passenger train City of Miami derailed 12 miles south of Carbondale.

None of the injured was seriously hurt.

The derailed cars carried an estimated 100 passengers. The cars left the track on a curve and were dragged about 500 ft. before the train came to a halt. All of the cars remained upright.

The train left Chicago at 9:45 a.m. carrying 263 passengers and was destined for Miami.

There was no immediate determination of the cause of the accident.

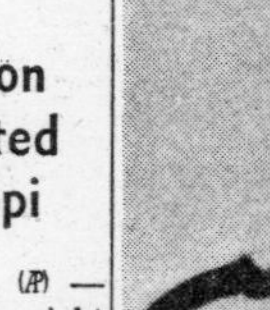

PRESIDENTIAL BROADCAST—President Johnson broadcasts radio-TV address to nation Tuesday night on hostile action taken against U.S. ships in Tonkin Gulf. He said he had ordered U.S. military forces to take action against the Reds. (AP) Wirephoto

U.S. Acts to Prevent 'Major' Error by Reds

Washington Officials Say Move Does Not Signify Desire to Step Up Vietnam War

BY RICHARD RESTON
Times Staff Writer

WASHINGTON — Top government officials said Tuesday night that the U.S. decision to attack North Vietnamese installations was made in an effort to prevent a "major mistake" by the Communist side in the Southeast Asian crisis.

Highly informed sources said this country's response did not indicate an American desire to escalate the anti-Communist war in South Vietnam. The U.S. response, said officials, was tailored specifically to the attack of North Vietnamese torpedo boats on American destroyers cruising in the Gulf of Tonkin.

President Johnson set the tone of U.S. policy in his nationally televised speech:

"Yet our response, for the present, will be limited and fitting. We Americans know, although others appear to forget, the risks of spreading conflict—we still seek no wider war."

Misunderstood U.S.

U.S. officials clearly felt that the attacks on American ships in international waters indicated that both North Vietnam and Communist China were in serious danger of misreading the U.S. position in Southeast Asia—that is, U.S. determination to stand firm against the Reds.

Such a mistake on the Communist side, these officials declared, would inevitably lead to precisely the kind of escalation the United States is now trying to prevent.

"We must get them (Communists) to understand that they have to leave their neighbors alone or face major trouble in Southeast Asia," informed sources said.

Response Prompt

This statement was the crux of the U.S. message delivered to North Vietnam by American fighter - bombers Tuesday night. It was felt that the American response had to be delivered immediately before North Vietnam overstepped the acceptable bounds again.

Meanwhile, the United States asked Tuesday night for an urgent meeting of the U.N. Security Council this morning to inform the coun-

Please Turn to Pg. 16, Col. 3

Johnson's Viet Stand Backed by Goldwater

BY DON IRWIN
Times Staff Writer

NEWPORT BEACH—Sen. Barry Goldwater gave President Johnson his complete backing on the Vietnam crisis Tuesday night.

Goldwater, before boarding a chartered plane Tuesday night for Washington, said:

"I told him I thought all Americans would stand behind his decision."

The President apparently held up his statement until he had a chance to read it to the Republican Presidential nominee.

Mr. Johnson made three attempts to reach Goldwater by radio telephone while the GOP candidate was cruising Tuesday afternoon near Santa Catalina Island. The connection was so poor that the call was not completed until Goldwater landed.

Calls White House

The senator called the White House at 7:07 p.m. after he had reached his suite at the Balboa Beach Hotel.

Later, Goldwater issued the following statement through his press secretary, Edward K. Nellor:

"I am sure that every American will subscribe to the actions outlined in the President's statement. I be-

Please Turn to Pg. 16, Col. 1

Johnson Orders Raids After American Ships Again Are Attacked

BY ROBERT J. DONOVAN
Times Washington Bureau Chief

WASHINGTON — The United States early today was bombing PT boat installations on the shores of North Vietnam with carrier-based planes and was reinforcing its forces in Southeast Asia and the Western Pacific.

These actions of potentially enormous — but hopefully limited—consequences were announced by President Johnson in a television speech Tuesday night in response to a second North Vietnamese PT attack on U.S. destroyers in the Gulf of Tonkin.

In addition to the military measures the President announced that:

1—The United States would "immediately and urgently" bring the North Vietnamese aggression before the U.N. Security Council.

2—He would submit to Congress immediately a proposed resolution "making it clear that our government is united in its determination to take all necessary measures in the support of freedom and in defense of peace in Southeast Asia."

Text of President's speech on Page 3, Part 1.

The action, permissive in nature on the part of Congress, will be similar to the Eisenhower Doctrine in the Middle East and the Formosa Resolution passed during the Eisenhower administration. Congress is expected to act swiftly.

Before making his statement over television from the White House, Mr. Johnson read it on the telephone to Sen. Barry Goldwater, the Republican Presidential nominee, who is vacationing at Newport Beach, Cal. The senator later issued a statement saying:

"I am sure that every American will subscribe to the action outlined in the President's statement. It is the only thing he can do under the circumstances. We cannot allow the American Flag to be shot at anywhere on earth if we are to retain our respect and prestige."

U. S. Vessels Undamaged

The President's historic and highly dramatic television appearance came hours after North Vietnam PT boats had attacked the destroyers Maddox and C. Turner Joy, though without inflicting damage or casualties. The first attack occurred early Sunday when PT boats attacked the Maddox.

The second attack, the President said, "required me to order the military forces of the United States to take action in reply.

"Repeated acts of violence against the armed forces of the United States," he continued, "must be met not only with alert defense, but with positive reply. That reply is given as I speak to you. Air action is now in execution against gunboats and certain suporting facilities of North Vietnam which have been used in these hostile operaitons."

Later at the Pentagon Secretary of Defense Robert S. McNamara supplied greater detail about the nature of the attacks and the addition of reinforcements.

Results are Uncertain

While it is the President's fervent hope and the continuing aim of U.S. policy to avert a major war, there can be no certainty where military measures of this sort will lead. The great danger is that North Vietnamese action and U.S. counter-action could start an upward spiral, or "escalation," as the Pentagon calls it, that would end in a large war, possibly involving Communist China.

"It is a solemn responsibility to have to order even

Please Turn to Pg. 3, Col. 4

Military Reinforcements Rushed to Southeast Asia, McNamara Says

BY TED SELL
Times Staff Writer

WASHINGTON— Defense Secretary Robert S. McNamara revealed early today that "substantial military reinforcements" are moving toward Southeast Asia and that "replacement deployments" to the far Pacific from the United States have been ordered.

McNamara spoke at a suddenly called Pentagon press conference after President Johnson told a national television audience that U.S. aircraft had been ordered to strike at North Vietnam.

The defense secretary refused to reveal what North Vietnamese targets were attacked. He said the attack was under way as he spoke.

McNamara said the strikes from the aircraft carriers Ticonderoga and Constellation were aimed at "the bases from which" Communist torpedo boats had attacked U.S. destroyers and at "certain supporting facilities" for those bases.

In response to questions, McNamara said the additional targets were located near the torpedo boat bases but were "separated geographically."

Although McNamara indicated that military forces in the United States had been alerted for movement, he said no additional alert orders have been issued for the nuclear armed missiles and bombers of the Strategic Air Command such as occurred during the 1962 Cuban missile crisis.

McNamara said U.S. planes used conventional explosives—not nuclear weapons. He said all the targets were located in North Vietnam, a disclaimer of the possibility that the targets included nearby bases on the Communist Chinese island of Hainam.

"Support facilities" pre-

Please Turn to Pg. 16, Col. 1

THE WEATHER

Light to moderate smog.

U.S. Weather Bureau forecast: Mostly sunny today and Thursday but night and morning clouds near coast. High today near 88. High Tuesday, 87; low, 64.

INDEX OF FEATURES

'Slowdown' Reported in Health Department

Reports that city health workers who transferred to similar county jobs are being ordered to "slow down" cause uproar before supervisors. See Page 1, Part 2.

ON OTHER PAGES

Los Angeles Times

LARGEST CIRCULATION IN THE WEST, 812,147 DAILY, 1,149,295 SUNDAY

VOL. LXXXIII 2† FIVE PARTS—PART ONE CC MONDAY MORNING, AUG. 24, 1964 98 PAGES DAILY 10c

BINOCULARS FOR BEATLES—Ardent youngsters display their emotions as they watch performance of Beatles at Hollywood Bowl. Many of the fans in the crowd of more than 18,700 had binoculars.

Times photo

Democratic Conclave Opens Today; Dixie Clash Grows

BOB KENNEDY RESIGNS POST IN DELEGATION

ATLANTIC CITY (AP) — Atty. Gen. Robert F. Kennedy resigned Sunday from the Massachusetts delegation to the Democratic National Convention.

Kennedy submitted his resignation in a telegram sent from his McClean (Va.) home to Gov. Endicott Peabody, chairman of the Massachusetts delegation. The resignation had been expected as a preliminary to his expected entry into the race for the U.S. Senate from New York.

Peabody told a news conference he will ask the delegation to approve Mrs. Joan Kennedy, wife of Sen. Edward M. (Ted) Kennedy of Massachusetts, as the replacement for her brother-in-law. Sen. Kennedy was listed on the temporary roll of the Massachusetts delegation, but a spinal fracture suffered in a plane crash makes it impossible for him to attend.

"It is my belief that Massachusetts should have a Kennedy in its delegation," Peabody said. "Many of these delegates, four years ago, chose John F. Kennedy as their nominee and still support his aims and ideals."

Alabamans Spurn Loyalty Oath; Two Mississippi Delegations Pose Crisis

BY DAVID KRASLOW
Times Staff Writer

ATLANTIC CITY — Democratic Party leaders faced a crisis on the eve of the national convention Sunday night because of the failure to resolve a bitter contest between two Mississippi delegations.

They also faced a hassle with another southern state, Alabama, on the issue of the Alabama delegation's party loyalty.

The convention's Credentials Committee deferred until today action in the emotion-charged Mississippi dispute. But the committee voted, as had been expected, to require the Alabama dele-

Illustrated on Page 3, Part I

gates, as a condition of being seated at the convention, to sign pledges to support the national Democratic ticket in the November election.

Most of the Alabama delegates, who have backed a slate of unpledged Presidential electors, voted against signing the party loyalty pledges.

However, the Alabama delegation decided to hang onto credentials badges issued to them before the loyalty pledge was requested, apparently with the intent of trying to enter Convention Hall tonight for the convention's opening session.

Fight in Prospect

When Eugene (Bull) Conner, Alabama national committeeman and former police commissioner of Birmingham was told police may bar his state's delegates who have not signed the pledges, he said:

"Let them move tomorrow and let's see if we can't jump them."

The failure of the committee to decide, during

Please Turn to Pg. 2, Col. 7

BY ROBERT J. DONOVAN
Times Washington Bureau Chief

ATLANTIC CITY — The Democratic National Convention will open today with President Johnson in firm control of everything except the potentially disruptive issues of the seating of the Mississippi and Alabama delegations.

With respect to the Vice Presidential nomination Mr. Johnson maintained absolute authority. While he continued to keep his choice a secret, speculation turned mostly toward Sen. Hubert H. Humphrey of Minnesota, who seems to be the favorite of most convention delegates.

Until the President has spoken, however, other contenders cannot be ruled out. Among the others being talked about here are Sen. Eugene McCarthy, also of Minnesota, Sen. Mike Mansfield of Montana, the Senate majority leader, and Sen. Edmund S. Muskie of Maine.

Nomination Wednesday

Beyond the choice of the Vice Presidential nominee and the quarrel over the seating of Mississippi and Alabama delegates, the convention looks like a fairly cut-and-dried affair.

Sen. John O. Pastore (D-R.I.) will deliver the keynote address at the opening session in Convention Hall tonight, seting the tone for the Democratic attack this fall on Sen. Barry Goldwater and the Republicans.

The Democratic platform, taking shape pretty much as the President wishes, will be adopted Tuesday. On Wednesday Mr. Johnson will be nominated by acclamation, and his running mate will be formally ratified by the de-

Please Turn to Pg. 6, Col. 1

Major Planks Drafted for Democrat Platform

Document Pledges Reduction in Excise Taxes and Enforcement of Civil Rights

BY VINCENT J. BURKE
Times Staff Writer

ATLANTIC CITY—A drafting panel finished work Sunday night on all major planks of the 1964 Democratic platform. The document pledges reductions in excise taxes next year and promises "effective" federal enforcement of the civil rights law, if local communities fail to comply with its provisions.

The domestic planks—last to be drafted by a 17-member executive committee — still must be approved by the full Platform Committee which has more than 100 members.

The draft, which will be placed before the full committee for ratification today, includes a condemnation of tactics of the Ku Klux Klan, the John Birch Society, the Communist Party and other extremist groups of the right and left.

Issues Not Mentioned

It takes no position on the controversial Supreme Court decisions dealing with reapportionment of state legislatures and with prayer in public schools. The Republican Party platform approved last month in San Francisco called for amendments to the Constitution in both areas.

The draft platform would put the Democratic, as well as the Republican Party, on record in support of excise tax cuts.

In describing how Democrats would administer the civil rights law, the drafters came up with language that was satisfactory to both northern liberals and to at least some southern moderates.

The plank pledged "fair and effective enforcement, if there is default."

The decision to make the pledge of federal enforce-

Please Turn to Pg. 8, Col. 1

Federal Farm Control Rapped by Goldwater

WASHINGTON (AP)—Sen. Barry Goldwater said Sunday President Johnson's farm program is "based on increased government intervention and centralized management," and called for a voluntary system of agricultural price supports.

The Republican Presidential nominee outlined in general terms what he called "the foundations upon which I would . . . hope and trust the Congress might build a truly effective program . . ."

"The Republican Party is the farmer's party," the Arizona Senator said in a statement issued at the suggestion of Sen. Carl T. Curtis (R-Neb.).

Orderly Marketing Goal

"Farmers have in the past supported Republican candidates at every level of government because the GOP has traditionally stood for responsible fiscal policies, a sound peace through preparedness, and at the same time has recognized the very complex special economic problems facing American farmers."

Goldwater promised "sympathetic understanding

Please Turn to Pg. 13, Col. 4

STIFF ATOM ARMS PLANK PREPARED

BY RICHARD RESTON
Times Staff Writer

ATLANTIC CITY — Democratic platform drafters declared Sunday that the President of the United States alone must be responsible for all decisions affecting the nation's use of nuclear weapons.

The Democratic Platform Committee said, "Control of the use of nuclear weapons must remain solely with the highest elected official in the country . . ." This was regarded by observers as criticism of the Republican Presidential nominee, Sen. Barry Goldwater.

Goldwater has suggested that the supreme allied commander of NATO be given greater authority over the use of tactical nuclear weapons. At the Republican National Convention in San Francisco last month, the liberal and moderate wings of the party led a drive to put the GOP on record favoring the President's retaining sole control over the use of all nuclear weapons.

Goldwater forces successfully blocked the drive.

Sunday the Democratic committee released the foreign policy and national security sections of the

Please Turn to Pg. 11, Col. 1

Student Mob in Vietnam Attacks U.S. Army Billet

Rocks Hurled Through Windows; New Violence Erupts in Cities

SAIGON (AP)—A mob of about 2,000 students and other persons hurled rocks through the windows of a U.S. Army billet in Da Nang, the second-largest city of South Vietnam today, shouting anti-government and anti-American slogans.

Violent demonstrations also were in progress in Hue and Saigon.

The new disorders followed invasion of the government radio station in Saigon Sunday by a student mob howling for President Nguyen Khanh's ouster. The students smashed furniture and windows with torn-down barricades.

High School Target

About 1,000 students attacked a high school run by French Roman Catholic priests in Hue, 400 miles north of Saigon. The mob smashed windows and destroyed furniture, despite the pleas of several priests.

In Da Nang, farther down the coast, students were joined by cyclo (pedicab) drivers and others persons in a wild, marching demonstration. Several civilians were injured and hospitalized, but police did not interfere.

There were no reports of any American casualties.

AP Office Guarded

In Saigon, meanwhile, about 400 students were meeting in various parts of the city, and planned to march on the government information ministry. Violence was expected.

In anticipation that marchers might also move on the Associated Press bureau, a contingent of police was stationed outside the AP office.

The student mob Sunday demanded civilian rule in South Vietnam.

At the University Students Union, leaders charged that the students were under the control of extremists and that the majority of students in Saigon did not support them.

The students massed in front of the radio station after an anti-government rally to demand a retraction for a broadcast that said a group of students who met with Khanh Saturday agreed with his explanation of his regime's policies.

Police Flee for Cover

The station's director refused to meet them in the street. Then the monsoon downpour struck and the students surged through the wooden barricades and entered the doors and windows of the station.

Unarmed police and some military personnel fled for cover of trees outside but they obviously were under orders not to block the students.

Inside, the students smashed windows with

Please Turn to Pg. 16, Col. 1

Hurricane Kills 14, Injures 100 on Guadeloupe

SANTO DOMINGO, Dominican Republic (AP) — Cleo, a killer hurricane that left at least 14 dead, 100 injured and $50 million damage on Guadeloupe, lashed the island of Hispaniola with gales Sunday night. The storm's 140 m.p.h. winds were expected to hit later.

Cleo churned just south of the Caribbean island on a course that would batter the southwestern Dominican Republic and then the entire south coast of Haiti, not yet recovered from last year's hurricane Flora.

Jamaica was also in Cleo's path, and the Weather Bureau said winds of hurricane force would probably begin spreading into the island tonight.

Plantations Wiped Out

There was a chance that Cuba, also smashed by Flora, might get a taste of Cleo.

Cleo wiped out entire sugar and banana plantations on Guadeloupe. In the capital city of Basse Terre alone, more than 1,000 persons were homeless. Officials said several hundred homes were demolished and more than 10,000 others badly damaged across the islands.

Electricity was out to most sections, and roads were blocked with debris. Officials of the seven-island, French possession said it was the worst hurricane since 1928.

Another victim of Cleo's fury was a U.S. Navy hurricane hunter plane flying only a few hundred feet off

Please Turn to Pg. 18, Col. 3

18,700 Shriek for Beatles at Show in Bowl

BY JACK SMITH
AND
LANCE BRISSON
Times Staff Writers

The Beatles, England's answer to the Revolutionary War, gave their long-heralded performance Sunday night in Hollywood Bowl and escaped with their lives.

With 18,700 teen-age fans shrieking hysterically, not

Illustrated on Page B

much of the mop-haired quartet's singing could be heard. It seemed to be enjoyed, however.

After a half-hour performance, the Beatles left the stage at 10 p.m. and darted directly to a compact car parked alongside. They sped away, leaving most of their fans disconsolately watching a black limousine parked behind the Bowl as a decoy.

Car Roof Caved in

About 60 ran to the closest gate and clambered for a vantage point on the car of a commercial photographer. The roof and hood were caved in.

The Bowl's first aid station reported only three fainters for the entire evening.

Harried police hore the brunt of the irrepressible young people's antics. They fought a losing battle trying to herd them off private property around the amphitheater and untangling a huge traffic jam as parents arrived to pick up their charges after the show.

There were no untoward incidents, although the sight of ticket-takers wearing army helmets presaged

Please Turn to Pg. 21, Col. 1

Bridge Falls; Four Dead, 18 Missing

CIUDAD BOLIVAR, Venezuela (AP)—More than 100 persons plunged about 50 ft. to the rocks and rapids of the Caroni River Sunday when a footbridge crowded with teachers on a picnic collapsed.

Four bodies were recovered and 18 persons were listed as missing. There was no immediate indication of the extent of the injuries of other persons or how many were hurt.

A helicopter aided rescue teams patrolling downstream.

Authorities said the bridge was 98 ft. long and about 2 ft. wide.

MACARTHUR SPECIAL TO START NEXT WEEK

On December 10, 1941, General Douglas MacArthur sent an urgent and secret message from Manila to the Army Chief of Staff in Washington.

"A golden opportunity now exists for a master stroke while the enemy is engaged in over-extended initial air effort," the message concluded.

What was the master stroke—and why did MacArthur's dispatch go unanswered?

Next Sunday, Aug. 30, The Times will begin an 18-part condensation of General Douglas MacArthur's "Reminiscences," his own life story, completed just before his death last April.

In daily installments, one of America's great soldiers reveals secrets of military operations never before told. He traces his full career, from West Point to the conflicts of his last years. Don't miss this important autobiography, beginning Aug. 30 in The Times.

THE WEATHER

Light to moderate smog today.

U.S. Weather Bureau forecast: Sunny today and Tuesday with night and morning low clouds and fog along coast. High today 88. High Sunday, 86; low, 63.

INDEX OF FEATURES

Rams Trade Jon Arnett to Chicago Bears

The Rams trade star halfback-end Jon Arnett to the world champion Chicago Bears for two offensive linemen and a defensive backfield man. Story in Sports Section.

ON OTHER PAGES

Running Mate Must Carry Heavy Campaign Burden, Humphrey Says

ATLANTIC CITY (UPI)—Senate Democratic whip Hubert H. Humphrey said Sunday night President Johnson's running mate will "have to carry a good deal of the burden of the campaign" because the people want the President at work in the White House.

Humphrey, apparent front-runner for the job, made the statement during a television appearance with Sen. Eugene McCarthy, his Minnesota colleague and a top rival for the Democratic Vice Presidential nomination.

Both senators said they had not discussed their chances with Mr. Johnson. They said the President had known them as fellow lawmakers for years and didn't need them to tell him of their qualifications or shortcomings.

The Chief Executive surprised the two senators with a telephone call of congratulations immediately after their joint appearance on the program ("Meet the Press"—NBC). Mrs. Johnson also spoke to the Vice Presidential contenders.

"We got a passing grade," Humphrey said afterward. "He (Mr. Johnson) was pleased with the entire show."

Both Humphrey and McCarthy made clear they would be willing to give up their Senate posts if Mr. Johnson taps one of them. McCarthy, interviewed first, said "it's a matter of obligation." Humphrey noted that Mr. Johnson gave up the Senate leadership in 1960 for the Vice Presidential nomination and said he "knew what he was doing."

Humphrey did not attempt to outline the probable course of Mr. Johnson's

Please Turn to Pg. 6, Col. 5

Los Angeles Times

LARGEST CIRCULATION IN THE WEST. 812,147 DAILY, 1,149,295 SUNDAY

VOL. LXXXIII | 2† FIVE PARTS—PART ONE | CC | MONDAY MORNING, SEPT. 28, 1964 | 96 PAGES | DAILY 10c

OSWALD'S CAPTURE—Lee Harvey Oswald, second from right, struggles with police outside the Texas Theater Nov. 22 after his arrest. This photo was included as an exhibit in the Warren Commission report naming Oswald alone as the killer of President John F. Kennedy and Patrolman J. D. Tippit.

WARREN COMMISSION REPORT:

Oswald Acted Alone in Kennedy Assassination

Historic Crime Found Free of Foreign or Domestic Conspiracy

BY ROBERT E. THOMPSON
Times Staff Writer

WASHINGTON—Lee Harvey Oswald, in a solitary act of violence free of foreign or domestic conspiracy, assassinated President John F. Kennedy in Dallas on Nov. 22, 1963, the Warren Commission ruled Sunday.

The seven-member panel concluded unanimously that Oswald, the murdered 24-year-old Marxist, planned and executed the "cruel and shocking" slaying of Mr. Kennedy without assistance from any individual or group.

Oswald probably was driven to the historic crime, the commission said, by his "overriding hostility" toward

Text of the summary and conclusions of the Warren Commission report starts on Page A. Text of rumors and findings starts on Page C.

society and his "capacity to risk all in cruel and irresponsible actions."

But, since Oswald was dead, the commission said it could not make "any definite determination" of the motives of the assassin nor could it judge his "legal guilt" or sanity.

However, the panel said, it was satisfied that "it has ascertained the truth concerning the assassination of President Kennedy to the extent that a prolonged and thorough search makes this possible."

There is no evidence, the commission reported, to substantiate theories that Oswald or his killer, Dallas night club owner Jack Ruby, were associated or involved in any kind of plot.

Nor could the commission find a relationship between Oswald's Communist associations and the murder of Mr. Kennedy. Oswald had gone to the Soviet Union in 1959 and was a fervent partisan of Communist Cuba.

The commission also said in an 888-page report that there "was nothing to support speculation" that Oswald was associated in any way with the Federal Bureau of Investigation, the Central Intelligence Agency or any other U.S. government agency.

In addition, the panel said:

"In its entire investigation the commission has found no evidence of conspiracy, subversion or disloyalty to the U.S government by any federal, state or local official."

Reports Gleaned From Interviews

These determinations were based upon an exhaustive, 10-month assessment of "all available evidence" and the "reasoned judgment" of all its members, the commission said.

Since President Johnson appointed the bipartisan commission last Nov. 29, its members and staff have studied 2,300 reports from the FBI and 800 from the Secret Service based on some 26,550 interviews of persons having information of possible relevance to the assassination.

Under the chairmanship of Chief Justice Earl Warren, the commission's members are: Sen. Richard B. Russell (D-Ga.), Sen. John Sherman Cooper (R-Ky.) Rep. Hale Boggs (D-La.), Rep. Gerald Ford (R-Mich.), former CIA Director Allen W. Dulles, and New York banker-diplomat John J. McCloy.

They concluded that Oswald, from a sixth-floor window in the Texas School Book Depository building, fired the rifle shots which killed Mr. Kennedy and seriously

Please Turn to Pg. 9, Col. 1

Flaws Found in Security Procedures

Secret Service, FBI and State Dept. Receive Criticism

BY DON IRWIN
Times Staff Writer

WASHINGTON — The Warren Commission has found that security arrangements around the late President John F. Kennedy were "inadequate" and proposes reforms to augment and tighten procedures for Presidential protection.

In the voluminous report it submitted to President Johnson Thursday and made public Sunday, the commission found nothing to reflect on the "courage and devotion to duty" of the Secret Service agents who had primary responsibility for Mr. Kennedy's safety when he was killed by an assassin's bullets last Nov. 22 in Dallas.

Inspection Laxity

But the panel found numerous flaws in procedures that were the foundation of that protection. In criticism that took in not only the Secret Service but the Federal Bureau of Investigation and the State Department, it reported:

1—That the Secret Service placed undue reliance on "standard procedures in use for many years." While the report said that most advance preparations for the Kennedy visit were "soundly planned," it criticized the service for not inspecting buildings along the President's motorcade route and dissented from the Secret Service position that it is "not practical" to make such checks on out-of-town Presidential trips. It held that the service relied on inadequate information and failed to establish effective working procedures with other intelligence and protective agencies.

No Names Listed

2—That files kept by the Protective Research Section of the Secret Service to locate potential attackers of the President listed no names in the Dallas-Ft. Worth area at the time of Mr. Kennedy's visit to Dallas.

3—That the Secret Ser-

Please Turn to Pg. 8, Col. 1

FINDINGS AT A GLANCE

By Associated Press

Here in brief are important finding of the Warren Commission's report on the assassination of President John F. Kennedy:

Lee Harvey Oswald and Jack Ruby acted as loners; there was no conspiracy, domestic or foreign.

Secret Service measures to guard the President were insufficient. Also the FBI failed to tip the Secret Service to Oswald's presence in Dallas.

Dallas police committed errors in the events that led up to the killing of Oswald by Ruby; news media must also "share responsibility for the failure of law enforcement which occurred in connection with the death of Oswald."

Methods for protecting Presidents must be drastically modernized.

British Papers Term Warren Report Honest

LONDON (AP)—The Warren report on President John F. Kennedy's murder won general acceptance in British editorials today as a competent and honest document holding dire lessons for the free world.

Among first commentaries, the only criticism came from the Communist Daily Worker, which called it a whitewash.

News dispatches from Washington headlined the report's criticism of the FBI and Secret Service, long regarded here as models of their trade.

Vulnerability Stressed

Other headlines and editorials stressed the vulnerability of a democratic head of state—something pointed out by the late President himself on the morning of his assassination.

This vulnerability has special meaning here since later this month Queen Elizabeth II is due to tour Canada. Officials believe her life may be in danger there from French Canadian separatists.

The London Times, independent, set the tone of most non-Communist comment by calling the report "thorough, painstaking, voluminous, frank and above all scrupul-

Please Turn to Pg. 6, Col. 4

Troops Leave Saigon After Tension Eases

SAIGON (AP) — Airborne troops and marines loyal to Premier Nguyen Khanh's regime began drifting back to their posts from Saigon Sunday as the threat of a new military coup seemed to ease. But soldiers still held key points in the capital.

There were two other tension-easing developments in this nation torn by Communist guerrilla warfare and an uprising of the Montagnard tribesmen in the central highlands:

Elected Chairman

Phan Khac Suu, a major foe of the late President Ngo Dinh Diem's government, was elected chairman of a new high national council that is supposed to lead the nation back to civilian rule. Student opposition to military rule was a major factor in rioting this summer.

And a fleet of 50 U.S. Army helicopters flew out 60 Vietnamese military and civilian hostages from the main rebel camp at Buon Sar Pa near the border of Cambodia.

The regime made their

Please Turn to Pg. 29, Col. 3

Train Crash Kills Four; Dozens Hurt

MONTGOMERY, Ill. (AP)—At least four persons were killed and dozens injured late Sunday night when a Chicago, Burlington & Quincy passenger train crashed head-on with a Rock Island Line passenger train standing still on a siding in Montgomery.

A Burlington spokesman said the two-man engine crew of the Rock Island train were among those killed along with a crewman on the Burlington train. Montgomery is located about 40 miles west of Chicago.

Union Orders Picketing at Three Market Firms

177 Stores of Von, Food Giant, Stater Bros. Selected as First Retail Targets in Strike

Teamster Union officials ordered picketing to begin at midnight Sunday against three supermarket chains and the warehouse of a fourth and predicted food shortages will develop as an inevitable result.

The action was taken on the 15th day of the food industry strike-lockout involving the teamsters and 56 members of the Food Employers Council.

Union attorney Charles Hackler said Teamster locals not involved in the strike-lockout are pledged not to cross the picket lines. This will end deliveries from processors directly to markets in the four chains — and will cut off milk, bread and meat supplies as well, union officials said.

177 Stores Affected

The action is being taken against 177 Von, Food Giant and Stater Bros. stores and against the wholesale operation of Safeway Stores, Inc.

Teamsters in Safeway's creamery, bakery and meat plant, which supply Safeway markets, remained on their jobs during the strike-lockout but now won't cross the picket lines, union officials added.

More than 1,000 Teamster members turned out for a briefing session and picket assignments Sunday at union headquarters, 846 S Union St.

Hand Out Pamphlets

The pickets will hand out pamphlets in which the union contends the markets "illegally locked out teamsters regardless of the fact that such action is illegal."

The picketing, the union literature reads, is "for the sole purpose of protesting the store's unfair practices and inducing it to let its

Please Turn to Pg. 31, Col. 1

2 Sides Seek Speedy End to Strike at GM

DETROIT (AP) — Negotiators for General Motors and the United Auto Workers met for two hours Sunday seeking avenues that might lead to quick settlement of a strike which has cut off the flow of GM's 1965 automobiles.

Deadlocked issues weren't debated anew, only the mechanics of how they should be taken up.

Afterward, the two sides said they would meet again this morning and that procedures had been set up for further bargaining on non-economic union demands that caused the walkout of more than 250,000 GM workers last Friday.

Local Demands, Too

UAW President Walter Reuther told newsmen that efforts would be made to settle some 18,000 local at-the-plant demands at the same time that negotiations are proceeding on a national contract.

Asked if there appeared to be a possibility of settling the nationwide strike before the end of the week, Reuther replied that such a possibility existed—but he declined to make a flat prediction.

Reuther said reaction among workers on the picket lines has been one of "overwhelmingly enthusiastic support" around the country. "They've been pushed around long enough," he said.

GM and the UAW reportedly have reached virtual agreement on an economic package paralleling the ones accepted by the union from Ford and Chrysler. Reuther said these were worth 54

Please Turn to Pg. 21, Col. 8

Group Picked to Help Draft Safety Steps

JOHNSON CITY, Tex. (AP) — President Johnson appointed Sunday a four-man committee to advise him "on the execution of the recommendations of the Warren Commission."

The commission which investigated the assassination of President John F. Kennedy recommended action to tighten the protection of Presidents and to make killing a President or a Vice President a federal crime.

Members of the committee are:

Secretary of the Treasury Douglas Dillon, acting Atty. Gen. Nicholas Katzenbach, Director John A. McCone of the Central Intelligence Agency, and McGeorge Bundy, special assistant to Mr. Johnson for national security affairs.

No Chairman Named

The President named no chairman for the committee. However, it was understood that Dillon, as the ranking member of the panel, would have general supervision over the group.

The panel he selected presumably will canvass the possible need for further measures to be taken to increase protection for the President.

And it was possible that the committee would explore the key question, raised by the commission, as to whether all or part of the protective functions of the Secret Service should be turned over to some other agency.

TIMES STARTS SERIES BY JOHNSON TODAY

One of the most important political series to be published in The Times this year, "My Hope for America," by President Johnson, begins on Page 2, Part 1, in today's issue.

The Johnson series is appearing as a part of The Times' comprehensive campaign coverage and as a matter of general news interest. The Times earlier published a series based on Barry Goldwater's new book, "Where I Stand."

In "My Hope for America," the President presents his viewpoints on nuclear responsibility, NATO strength, the war on poverty and other national and international issues.

THE WEATHER

U.S. Weather Bureau forecasts: low clouds and local fog in the early morning hours otherwise mostly sunny. High today 77, low 62; high Sunday 75, low 64.

INDEX OF FEATURES

Music Center Site Dedicated Before 3,500

Distinguished gathering of 3,500 pays tribute to "a dreamer and a dream come true" as Music Center site is dedicated to Mrs. Norman Chandler. See Page 1, Part 2.

ON OTHER PAGES

Assassination Termed Act of Man 'Alienated' From the Real World

BY VINCENT J. BURKE
Times Staff Writer

WASHINGTON — President John F. Kennedy's assassin was "profoundly alienated from the world in which he lived."

That was one of the big differences between Lee Harvey Oswald and most other men, the Warren Commission reported Sunday.

Unable to find a satisfactory, rational explanation for the assassination, the commission attempted to delve posthumously into Oswald's mental outlook and character.

It found that Oswald was "moved by an overriding hostility to his environment," whatever it happened to be.

"He was never satisfied with anything," the commission reported. "His wife . . . thought that he would not be happy anywhere, only on the moon, perhaps.'"

Since Oswald is dead, the commission said it could reach no definite conclusions as to whether he was "sane" under prevailing legal standards.

Summarizing its conclusions, the commission said:

"Many factors were undoubtedly involved in Oswald's motivation for the assassination, and the commission does not believe that it can ascribe to him any one motive or group of motives.

"It is apparent, however, that Oswald was moved by an overriding hostility to his environment. He does not appear to have been able to establish meaningful relationships with other people.

"He was perpetually discontented with the world around him. Long before the assassination he expressed his hatred for American society and acted in protest against it. Oswald's search for what he conceived to be the perfect society was doomed from the start.

"He sought for himself a

Please Turn to Pg. 14, Col. 1

Los Angeles Times

LARGEST CIRCULATION IN THE WEST. 812,147 DAILY, 1,149,295 SUNDAY

VOL. LXXXIII 2† SEVEN PARTS—PART ONE CC FRIDAY MORNING, OCT. 16, 1964 122 PAGES

DAILY 10¢

KHRUSHCHEV STRIPPED OF ALL POWER

Labor Holds Thin Lead in Britain

Final Outcome Expected to Give Party Majority of 10-17 Seats

BY GENE SHERMAN
Times Staff Writer

LONDON—Labor looked like a winner in Britain's general election Thursday—but only barely. There remained the slight chance the Tories might tip the scales—at least enough to make a Socialist government awkward.

When British ballot counting ended for a five-hour break at 3 a.m. today, Labor had a solid edge in contests decided.

Returns from 428 of 630 parliamentary districts showed:

Labor Party ....246 seats.
Conservatives ..180 seats.
Liberal Party .. 2 seats.

Percentages of the total popular vote: Labor 46%, Conservatives 43%, Liberals 11%.

At 5 a.m. today computers indicated a leftward swing of 3.9% and experts predicted a Labor majority of 17 seats in the House of Commons.

This was by no means a unanimous opinion. Lord Blakenham, chairman of the Conservative Party, went to bed predicting victory when the northern constituencies are counted, but conceding it would be close.

Wilson Encouraged

Prime Minister Sir Alec Douglas-Home, who led his party from chaos a year ago to the brink of victory, made no public statement.

Harold Wilson, leader of the opposition, declined to claim victory, but said the results in more than half the constituencies were "moderately encouraging."

In the absence of a uniform national trend which would materially change the country's voting pattern, experts were at a loss to predict the final result. The election was marked by narrow vote margins in many of the country's 630 constituencies, and recounts were demanded by some candidates.

AHEAD—Harold Wilson, whose Labor Party was leading in British voting. UPI photo

Key to victory for Labor had been a 50-seat gain by the time ballot counting paused for five hours at 3 a.m.

But that goal fell short by two.

The prospect of a sketchy victory—perhaps a majority in Commons of less than 10 seats—was disturbing to the Socialists who had confidently predicted a majority of from 20 to 30 seats.

When the counting ended, Labor had won 246 seats, the Conservatives 180, and the Liberals 2.

Len Williams, Labor Par-

Please Turn to Pg. A, Col. 1

President Comments on Jenkins

Declares Question About Conduct of Aide Never Raised

WASHINGTON (AP)—President Johnson said Thursday night he had never had any information before late Wednesday that "had ever raised a question" about the personal conduct of Walter Jenkins.

The President made this statement as Goldwater forces stepped up their "scandal" accusations against the Johnson administration and said that the Jenkins moral case raises grave issues of national security.

Jenkins, long-time confidant and top aide to Mr. Johnson, resigned suddenly Wednesday. It was disclosed that Jenkins had been arrested on Oct. 7 on a charge of "disorderly conduct (indecent gestures)" and that he had been arrested five years before on a charge of "disorderly conduct (pervert)." In both cases he forfeited collateral.

Public Interest Put First

The President disclosed he had asked for and received Jenkins' resignation Wednesday. He also said he had asked FBI director J. Edgar Hoover to make an immediate and comprehensive inquiry on the case and reported promptly "to me and the American people." The President noted that in any such case, "the public interest comes before all personal feelings."

Jenkins is now in George Washington University Hospital suffering from what his doctor called "extreme fatigue."

The President in his statement Thursday night, issued on his return from a political campaign swing in New York state, said no information or report had ever come to him before Wednesday that would raise a question about Jenkins' personal conduct.

Cites Fine Record

Taking cognizance of the 25 years that Jenkins has been in his employ except for military service during World War II and a brief fling in politics on his own, Mr. Johnson said:

"No man I know has given more personal dedication, devotion and tireless labor."

The President said, "For myself and Mrs. Johnson, I want to say that our hearts go out with the deepest compassion for him and for his wife and six children—and they have our love and prayers.

The President's statement was, in effect, a reply to an

Please Turn to Pg. 2, Col. 4

RUSSIAN BOSSES, NEW AND OLD—Leonid I. Brezhnev, left, and Nikita S. Khrushchev, listening to proceedings in the Soviet Parliament last July 15 when Brezhnev gave up figurehead job of president to become Khrushchev's deputy. Now Khrushchev is out of power and Brezhnev commands top post in the party. UPI Telephoto

Brezhnev Appointed Party Chief; Kosygin Becomes New Premier

BY HENRY SHAPIRO
UPI Staff Writer

MOSCOW — In a drastic move that caught the world by surprise, the Soviet Union's Communist Party has stripped Nikita S. Khrushchev of his posts as premier and party chief.

To replace him, the party's Central Committee elected two of his top lieutenants:

Leonid I. Brezhnev, who became the first secretary of the Communist Party and thus the most powerful man in Russia.

Alexei N. Kosygin, who was named chairman of the Council of Ministers, or premier.

No Praise for Khrushchev

Khrushchev bowed out with uncharacteristic silence and without receiving a single word of official praise for his 11 years of power and a lifetime of service to the Communist Party.

The end of Khrushchev's leadership of the Soviet Union was announced Thursday by Tass, the official Soviet news agency. The action relieving him of his duties was taken Wednesday by the Central Committee of the Communist Party while he was away at his Black Sea vacation retreat.

The official announcement that came while a wave of rumors about the government shakeup swept through Moscow said Khrushchev had asked to be relieved. The reason: "his advanced age and deterioration of his health." Khrushchev is 70 but he had appeared as full of bounce as ever and showed no signs of physical wear and tear.

Shock Wave Around Globe

In world capitals the news that Khrushchev was out came as a shock. Even the foreign diplomatic corps in Moscow, usually alert to the slightest shift in Kremlin politics, confessed surprise.

Although surprised, most diplomats saw the Soviet shift as the result of his failure to solve Russia's mounting tide of problems at home and abroad. But they foresaw no immediate major changes in Soviet policy toward the West.

One U.S. diplomat saw the switch as "merely a change of personalities, not a change of policies."

Khrushchev's heirs, many of them saved from the terror of Joseph Stalin by Khrushchev, are not expected to turn back the political clock to despotism. Khrushchev had been first party secretary since 1953 when Stalin died. He took the premiership in 1958.

Generous Pension Expected

To all appearances Khrushchev bowed out peacefully, and it was expected that he would be given a generous government pension to live on quietly for the rest of his life.

But the quiet life will be strange to the pudgy Communist boss. Gone will be the days of pounding a shoe on a desk of the U.N. General Assembly, of breaking up the 1960 Paris conference with a violent denunciation of President Dwight D. Eisenhower, of throwing a temper tantrum in Los Angeles because he was not allowed to go to Disneyland. Gone will be the Khrushchev who blasted open a dam site in Egypt, looked a gift horse in the mouth in Hungary, who postured at the Berlin Wall, and who surprised giggling Parisian housewives with his early morning visit to a dairy shop.

One certainty in the present uncertainties of Moscow is that Khrushchev's successors will be less colorful. Both lack his flair for the dramatic, his bubbling and mercurial personality.

Another certainty was that Khrushchev's disap-

Please Turn to Pg. B, Col. 4

UAW, American Motors Reach Contract Accord

But Some Workers Strike at Midnight Deadline Before Pact Is Announced

DETROIT (AP) — American Motors Corp. and the United Auto Workers Union announced today they had reached agreement on a new national economic contract that will carry forward the industry's only profit-sharing plan.

The new national agreement was announced jointly by Edward L. Cushman, American Motors vice president, and Douglas A. Fraser, the UAW's AMC chief, at 1 a.m.—an hour after the strike deadline.

"Unfortunately," Cushman said, "American Motors operations already had been shut down, I understand, at its authoritative plants in Milwaukee and Kenosha, Wis."

Asked if this meant strikes were under way, Fraser interjected, "When he says shut down, we mean strike."

Union sources said 1,000 midnight shift workers at Kenosha, where Rambler car assembly is concentrated, did not report for work, and that another 500 stayed away from their jobs on the third shift at Milwaukee.

While having reached agreement on a national level contract that includes profit-sharing, both Cushman and Fraser said in a joint announcement "many knotty local-level problems still exist, and we're going to keep working on them tonight."

Cushman, speaking for himself and Fraser, declined to disclose any details of the profit-sharing plan.

Cole Porter, 71, Dies in Hospital After Surgery

BY CHARLES DAVIS JR.
Times Staff Writer

Cole Porter, 71, one of America's great song and musical comedy writers, died Thursday night in St. John's Hospital, Santa Monica.

He was admitted to the hospital Sept. 22 with a high fever and underwent surgery for a kidney ailment Tuesday. Death came at 11:05 p.m. Thursday.

Porter wrote the music and lyrics for scores of songs that became all-time favorites, such as "Night and Day," "Begin the Beguine," "What Is This Thing Called Love?" "In the Still of the Night," "I've Got You Under My Skin," and "I Get a Kick Out of You."

Other Porter hits included "Don't Fence Me In," "My Heart Belongs to Daddy," "Let's Do It," "You're the Tops," "You Do Something to Me," "All Through the

Please Turn to Pg. 18, Col. 1

Alexei N. Kosygin UPI Wirephoto

Russian News Triggers Rush to Sell Stocks

NEW YORK (AP) — The stock market Thursday weathered the worst wave of selling since the Kennedy assassination and by the close had about halved its steepest losses. Trading was heavy.

The Dow Jones industrial average, which was off 11.23 at its worst, closed with a net loss of 6.74 at 868.44. Standard & Poor's 500-stock index lost .54 and closed at 84.25.

Early Losses Pared

Nervous selling by small investors and traders on reports of a change in Russian government leadership triggered the selloff.

Losses running as much as 2 or more points among key stocks were pared to a maximum of a point or so for most issues.

Volume was 6.59 million shares compared with 4.65 million Wednesday.

Of 1,366 issues traded, 944 fell and 199 rose. New highs for the year totaled 37 and new lows 21.

Details on Page 11, Part 3.

Showers, Lightning Hit Basin; Power Cut Off

Scattered showers, many accompanied by thunder and lightning, peppered the Los Angeles basin and other areas of Southern California Thursday.

There were a few reports of minor damage to power circuits from lightning and short circuits.

A Department of Water and Power line was hit at Santa Monica Blvd. and Glendon Ave. in West Los Angeles, knocking out service for a brief period near Santa Monica and Westwood Blvds. Some telephones in the area also were affected.

A 115,000-volt Southern California Edison Co. transmission line was short circuited in Banning and power was off for an hour near Hemet when wires were hit by lightning.

A thunderstorm poured .22-inch of rain in less than 30 minutes on El Centro and Calexico early Thursday. Streets were flooded from curb to curb for a time and children were late to school as traffic piled up.

The Imperial County agricultural commissioner's office said some damage to new plantings of lettuce and sugar beets is anticipated.

The heaviest recorded rainfall was .57-inch at War-

Please Turn to Pg. 30, Col. 1

Jenkins Case Hurts Johnson Drive; Soviet Shakeup May Offset Harm

BY LAURENCE BURD
Times Staff Writer

WASHINGTON — The Walter Jenkins case struck President Johnson's election campaign amidships, with heavy damage, just when it seemed to be cruising smoothly toward victory in November.

Disclosure that Jenkins, long-time top aide and confidant to Mr. Johnson, was twice arrested on morals charges, plays right into the hand of GOP Presidential nominee Barry Goldwater's campaign against "moral decay" in the Johnson administration from the White House down.

Political strategists of every stripe agree that the Jenkins episode, standing alone, would cost the Johnson ticket a good many votes in November.

But, by one of those twists of fate, the damaging impact on Mr. Johnson of the Jenkins case could be offset, at least in part, by a completely unrelated development 5,000 miles away—in Moscow.

The surprise replacement of Russian Premier Nikita S. Khrushchev a day after the Jenkins case erupted Wednesday, poses new global uncertainties.

Although it is too early to tell whether the Moscow shakeup could presage an East-West crisis, its occurrence less than three weeks before the U.S. election is amost sure to have an impact on the voting here.

If the past is any guide, the backlash from Moscow is likely to help Mr. Johnson politically more than Goldwater. The majority of American voters traditionally tend to rally in time of global crisis or uncertainty to the incumbent administration as a safer haven than a new team of leaders.

Republicans will seek to make political capital out of both the Jenkins episode and the Moscow shakeup, but they have a much more salable issue in the Jenkins case.

Former Vice President Richard M. Nixon signaled

Please Turn to Pg. 24, Col. 1

INDEX OF FEATURES

Cardinals Win World Series From Yankees

Cardinals complete their dramatic drive to the World Series championship by defeating the Yankees, 7-5, in seventh game played at St. Louis. See Sports Section.

ON OTHER PAGES

THE WEATHER

Light to moderate smog today.

U.S. Weather Bureau forecast: Some night and early morning clouds but mostly sunny today and Saturday. High today, 79. High Thursday, 76; low, 59.

Washington Sees Shift as Struggle for Power

BY RICHARD RESTON
Times Staff Writer

WASHINGTON — Official sources here interpreted Soviet Premier Nikita S. Khrushchev's sudden retirement Thursday as the result of an apparent internal power struggle triggered by mounting policy problems both at home and abroad.

Washington is clearly not accepting Moscow's explanation that Khrushchev voluntarily had asked to be "relieved of his duties." The dramatic Soviet announcement said the Russian leader stepped down because of "advanced age and deterioration of his health."

Officials do not see at this time a significant shift in Russian Cold War policy, which might have a direct bearing on Soviet-American relations. Nevertheless, it is too early for Washington's diplomatic community to predict the long-range impact of the Soviet power shuffle.

Although the Johnson administration indicated that health could have been one factor in Khrushchev's departure, it is convinced that the Soviet leader has not had full and effective control of his administration in recent years.

The political shift caught Washington by surprise, but the administration was calm and in no way alarmed by what was described as an "in-house transfer of power." There was, for example, no

Please Turn to Pg. 11, Col. 1

Los Angeles Times

LARGEST CIRCULATION IN THE WEST. 817,087 DAILY; 1,144,326 SUNDAY

VOL. LXXXIV 2† SIX PARTS—PART ONE CC WEDNESDAY MORNING, APRIL 7, 1965 106 PAGES DAILY 10c

Mayor Yorty Re-elected! Wyman Faces Runoff

End to Red Berlin Curbs Demanded

West Also Studies Possible Reprisals for Harassment

BERLIN (AP)—The Western allies demanded Tuesday night an immediate end to harassment of the Berlin lifeline after Soviet jets buzzed U.S. and French airports and the East Germans again temporarily closed the autobahn.

The war of nerves sharpened as the hour approached for today's meeting of the West German parliament in Berlin, long-divided city coveted by both East and West Germans as the capital of a future united Germany.

Measures Weighed

(In Washington, a four-power western task force weighed possible reprisal measures against the Russians and East Germans if squeeze plays continue against ground and air traffic into Berlin, which lies 110 miles behind the Iron Curtain.

(The task force is made up of the ambassadors of West Germany, Britain, France and Assistant Secretary of State William Tyler.

(Among retaliatory measures that could be taken if Communist pressure continues on Berlin communications are restrictions on movement of Soviet military personnel in Frankfurt and West Berlin.

(Soviet authorities Tuesday clamped travel restrictions on the staff of the U.S. mission in Potsdam, limiting it to movement along certain roads in East Germany.)

Erhard Firm

Arriving in Berlin for the Bundestag meeting, Chancellor Ludwig Erhard told reporters, "We will not bow before terror."

The parliamentary meeting, first in Berlin in seven years, was allowed by the Western allies as an election year favor to the Bonn government.

After a day of Soviet-East German road stoppages and airport buzzings, the U.S., British and French commanders sent identical protests to Gen. Petr K. Koshevoy, Soviet commander in East Germany.

Place Responsibility

He was told Soviet authorities would be held "responsible for any possible consequences of interference with the Allied right of access to Berlin either in the air or on the ground."

The East Germans claimed they and Soviet forces were maneuvering west of Berlin and this necessitated closing the autobahn.

Russian tanks tore along East Germany's express highways Tuesday, pushing traffic off the road.

The U.S. protest note, signed by Gen. Andrew O'Meara, said:

"The attempt to interfere with Allied communications

Please Turn to Pg. 8, Col. 3

BRITAIN PLANS HUGE BOMBER DEAL WITH U.S.

Exclusive to The Times from a Staff Writer

WASHINGTON—Defense Secretary Robert S. McNamara announced Tuesday that arrangements have been made for Great Britain to buy, if she so desires, $1 billion worth of American-built F-111 tactical bombers.

The Pentagon disclosure followed the official announcement in the British Parliament that England is scrapping her own program to build the costly TSR-2 airplane, which would have performed the functions planned for the F-111.

This government's award of the prime contract for the F-111, then called the TFX, to General Dynamics Corp. was the subject of a year-long congressional inquiry in 1962-63.

McNamara's carefully worded announcement did not say a definite deal had been made for the British purchase. He said the two-country agreement "gives Britain the option" of buying F-111s to meet her "world-wide defense responsibilities."

Neither the English nor American announce-

Please Turn to Pg. 12, Col. 1

Britain Raises, Reforms Taxes in Labor Budget

Measures Affect All Segments of Society, Designed to Impress Foreign Creditors

LONDON (AP)—Stiff taxes and tax reforms affecting the workingman's beer and the stockholder's profit were brought in Tuesday by Britain's Labor government.

They were designed to impress Britain's foreign creditors with the nation's sacrifices to get out of the red in world trade once and for all.

The taxes were presented in the annual budget — the government's statement of revenues, taxes and economic policy—presented by Chancellor of the Exchequer James Callaghan in a two-hour and five-minute speech to the House of Commons.

Every segment of society will be affected. A beer in a pub will cost a penny more. A businessman will not be able to deduct any of his business entertainment for taxes, except when trying to sell British products to foreign buyers.

Callaghan also announced increases, effective today, on cigarets, tobcco, wines, whisky and gin.

An income tax boost announced last fall also goes into effect this week.

Blot Excess Spending

The aim of these consumer taxes is to blot excess spending power out of the economy and reduce home demand, thus forcing British manufacturers to look for export orders abroad.

Callaghan said the new taxes, combined with an already announced increase in postal rates and a cut in expenditures, will bring the government an extra $700 million this year.

The background to the budget is last year's massive payments deficit of $2 billion. Half was created by Britons buying more goods abroad than they sold. The other half represented money sent abroad by British

Please Turn to Pg. 12, Col. 3

U.S. to Spend Millions for Vietnam Ports

BY JACK FOISIE
Times Staff Writer

SAIGON—The U.S. government has embarked on a multimillion-dollar program of developing 12 ports along the South Vietnam coast for handling ocean-going ships, it was learned Tuesday.

Envisioned as a long-range program to improve the embattled country's peace-time economy, it now has become a crash project because of the danger that Communist Viet Cong guerrillas will isolate cities and towns through control of roads and the cutting of coastal railroads.

The first step in this rapidly implemented effort will be the signing of a $300,000 contract Thursday between the South Vietnamese government and a Los Angeles architectural engineering firm —Daniel, Mann, Johnson & Mendenhall.

L.A. Firm in Line

The initial contract is for a feasibility study. But the California company is in line for millions of dollars of follow-up work.

Sven B. Svendsen, vice president and international manager of the Los Angeles firm, 300 Grenola St., Pacific Palisades, is here to sign the company's phase of the program.

Only the ports of Saigon and Da Nang in the north now handle big ocean freighters. And Da Nang harbor still is not back to normal following heavy silting by last fall's floods.

Improved navigational

Please Turn to Pg. 14, Col. 1

U.S. Against Auto Smog Device Law

Administration Sees Hope of Voluntary Control by Industry

BY ROBERT C. TOTH
Times National Science Correspondent

WASHINGTON — The Johnson administration Tuesday came out "at this time" against a proposed law to require California-type exhaust control devices on all new cars in the nation next fall.

The surprising stand, disclosed by James M. Quigley, assistant secretary of the Department of Health, Educatin and Welfare, drew sharp questions from senators on the subcommittee before which he testified on the bill.

"Why is what is good for California not good for the rest of the country?" asked Sen. Edmund S. Muskie (D-Me.), chairman of the air and water pollution subcommittee and one of 22 senators sponsoring the bill.

"It may be," Quigley replied but he said he preferred to give the auto industry a chance to put the devices on cars voluntarily. The industry is against the bill which would require the devices on all new cars sold six months after its passage.

Sharp Reaction

If the industry does not act, and if the California system works there and on test government cars, only then should a law be passed making the devices mandatory, he said.

(In Los Angeles, Supervisor Warren Dorn, chairman of the county's Air Pollution Control Department, branded the Johnson administration stand "shocking — almost unbelievable." He said the position announced by Quigley is "a complete reversal of everything HEW has stated up to this moment.")

Asked if California had moved on the basis of "inadequate" study, Quigley replied that "as a layman, I would say yes."

He acknowledged later that announcement of the opposition to the devices at this time is a follow-up to a recent statement by President Johnson. The gist of Quigley's testimony was cleared by the White House's Budget Bureau last weekend.

Promised Discussion

In a February message to Congress on conservation, Mr. Johnson spoke of the high toll of air pollution from cars and he promised to "institute discussions" with the auto industry and others aimed at eliminating or substantially reducing pollution from motor vehicles.

If the President had not proposed the conference, Quigley was asked later by a reporter, would he have supported the bill on mandatory car devices? "I don't know." he said after a long pause.

This latest twist in the auto-air pollution problem which is now beginning to

Please Turn to Pg. 24, Col. 1

WINNING SMILES—Mayor Samuel W. Yorty and Mrs. Yorty stand in front of election return board at City Hall after his triumph over Rep. James Roosevelt.
Times photo by Larry Sharkey

Six Council Incumbents Swept In

BY RICHARD BERGHOLZ
Times Political Writer

It was an across-the-board sweep for Mayor Samuel W. Yorty.

The 55-year-old chief executive won a smashing victory in Tuesday's municipal primary election and a new four-year term as leader of the nation's third largest city.

Yorty, who came out of political exile four years ago to topple the then Mayor Norris Poulson, swamped Rep. James Roosevelt (D-Los Angeles), his major challenger, and six other opponents in a convincing demonstration of political strength.

Heaviest Vote

The mayor not only turned back the spirited challenge of the 57-year-old son of the late President Roosevelt, but he also racked up a majority of all votes cast in the city primary which saw the heaviest vote turnout in history.

On the basis of unofficial returns from 4622 precincts out of 5055 in the city, Yorty had 196,342 and Roosevelt had 113,509.

Throughout most of the early counting, Yorty was getting approximately 58% of all votes cast. Six other mayoral candidates failed to poll enough votes to challenge the front-runners or to throw the results into the runoff category.

Election law provides that a runoff at the May 25 general election isn't necessary if a candidate runs up a majority of all primary votes.

Incumbents Winning

While the mayor was swamping his opponents in early returns, most of the seven incumbent city councilmen seeking new four-year terms were also running well ahead and were headed for victory.

Councilmen Louis R. Nowell of Sunland, Thomas D. Shepard of Woodland Hills, Ernani Bernardi of Van Nuys, Gilbert W. Lindsay of Los Angeles, Karl L. Rundberg of Pacific Palisades and John S. Gibson Jr. of San Pedro all appeared to have clinched re-election without runoff.

But Councilwoman Rosalind Wiener Wyman in the 5th District was having a tough fight with six opponents and appeared to be headed for a run-off.

Mrs. Wyman, who had been marked by Yorty for

Please Turn to Pg. 3, Col. 6

Committees OK Bills on Education, Medicare

Actions Mark Milestones in Progress of Great Society Program Through Congress

BY DON IRWIN
Times Staff Writer

WASHINGTON—President Johnson won major victories at both ends of the Capitol Tuesday as his education and Medicare bills cleared committees for consideration today by the Senate and the House.

The $1.3 billion school-aid bill was approved by the Senate Labor and Public Welfare Committee without the change of a comma in the 80-page measure which passed the House March 26. Some GOP amendments will be offered, but Democratic leaders hope to push the bill to final passage unchanged and have it on the President's desk by the end of the week.

Package Approved

Almost simultaneously, the $6 billion-a-year package of welfare benefits that includes health care for the aged under Social Security was approved, 10 to 5, by the House Rules Committee. It will be the principal business of the House for the balance of the week.

Taken together, Tuesday's two committee actions mark a milestone in the progress of the President's Great Society program through the

Please Turn to Pg. 20, Col. 1

Alabama Faces Loss of Millions in School Aid

BY DAVID KRASLOW
Times Staff Writer

WASHINGTON — The Alabama public school system may lose millions of dollars in federal aid because it has not taken "adequate steps to desegregate," the U.S. Office of Education said Tuesday.

U.S. Commissioner of Education Francis Keppel, in a letter to Austin R. Meadows, Alabama superintendent of schools, said the state has not complied with the 1964 Civil Rights Act. He warned that there is "grave concern" whether federal aid to the school system can be continued.

Bans Federal Aid

The new civil rights law bars federal aid to states or communities that practice racial discrimination. Local school districts and state school officials must file statements pledging compliance with the law.

Keppel said compliance statements filed by Meadows and about 100 of the state's school districts do not come close to satisfying the law's requirements on desegregation.

Keppel urged the State

Please Turn to Pg. 5, Col. 3

State Senate Redistricting Plan Unveiled

BY JERRY GILLAM
Times Staff Writer

SACRAMENTO — Southern California would gain majority control of the State Senate under a revised Senate reapportionment bill unveiled Tuesday.

Under the proposal, Sen. Stephen P. Teale (D-West Point) said Los Angeles County would be entitled to 12 senators.

The county now has only one senator to represent a population of 7 million residents.

Orange, San Diego, San Francisco, Alameda and Santa Clara counties would be entitled to two senators. These counties also now have a single senator.

The 12 Los Angeles senators would run at large within the county boundaries.

The total membership of the Senate would remain at 40.

This was the first disclosure of details for the Senate reapportionment plan.

Teale said his plan has the

Please Turn to Pg. 33, Col. 1

ELECTION RESULTS

MAYOR

4,622 Precincts out of 5055

Yorty (Inc.)	196,342
Roosevelt	113,509
McGee	16,555
Ware	844
Bolger	658
Chrisoheris	430
Coover	236
Hawthorne	392

CITY COUNCIL

District No. 1

212 Precincts out of 324

Nowell (Inc.)	7,336
Skowron	1,935

District No. 3

190 Precincts out of 322

Shepard (Inc.)	6,256
Morris	2,736
Slocum	390

District No. 5

156 Precincts out of 349

Edelman	2,286
Wyman (Inc.)	2,271
Teichner	1,764
Halper	1,500
Biren	825
French	381
Lertzman	84

District No. 7

156 Precincts out of 323

Bernardi (Inc.)	4,484
McIntyre	1,608
Brown	854
Carasso	336
Simmons	226
Frailich	123

District No. 9

142 Precincts out of 355

Lindsay (Inc.)	3,829
Calderon	1,811
Valencia	432
Brooks	136

District No. 11

228 Precincts out of 355

Rundberg (Inc.)	6,060
Braude	2,467
Rogers	2,366
Eells	1,008

Please Turn to Pg. 3, Col. 1

Six Yanks Die in Battle; Viet Cong Loss Heavy

SAIGON (AP) — A fierce three-day battle in the swampy rice fields south of Saigon ended Tuesday night with 276 Viet Cong killed and 33 captured, U.S. military spokesmen reported today. Six Americans died in the action.

U.S. B-57 jet bombers pounded Communist positions with tons of explosives during the first major encounter with Red guerrillas in months in the Mekong Delta paddies.

Four U.S. servicemen perished when their helicopter exploded after a hit by Viet Cong machine gun fire.

South Vietnamese forces lost 16 men killed and 69 wounded in the water and air assault near Vinh Loc, 130 miles southwest of Saigon in the heart of Ca Mau Peninsula, government officials said.

The twin-engine American B-57 Canberras flew 16 strikes in support of the ground forces, while Vietnamese Skyraiders also blasted away in the Ca Mau battle zone.

There was no announcement of any further raids on Communist North Vietnam in the bombing operations started two months ago.

The four helicopter crewmen died while they were

Please Turn to Pg. 15, Col. 1

Red Suspects Rounded Up at Da Nang

DA NANG, South Vietnam (UPI)—South Vietnamese military police today seized 143 suspected Viet Cong agents in raids around this coastal city—site of the biggest U.S. air base in South Vietnam.

Police were led to the Communist agents by a condemned Viet Cong terrorist who turned informer just before he was to die.

Vietnamese officials said at least six of the suspected Red agents had incriminating documents in their possession when captured.

The terrorist who talked was given a few more hours of life. His execution was rescheduled for 1 p.m. today. It was the third time in three days that his execution has been changed.

The agent, Le Dua, was arrested Sunday night in the restaurant of a hotel crowded with American troops. He was carrying a transistor radio stuffed with high explosives.

Will Resign Disputed Union Post, Carey Says

BY ROBERT J. DONOVAN
Times Washington Bureau Chief

WASHINGTON — James B. Carey announced Tuesday that he would resign as president of the International Union of Electrical Workers.

Twenty-four hours after the Labor Department had asserted that his re-election was due to a miscount and "false reporting" of votes, Carey also said he was debating whether to resign as a member of the AFL-CIO Executive Council and secretary-treasurer of the federation's industrial union department.

Carey's downfall grows out of a union election in which Secretary of Labor Willard Wirtz said there was "misconduct" of a "serious nature."

At the press conference where Carey announced that he would submit his resignation to the executive board of the IUE here today, he disclaimed any knowledge of a miscount of votes. He said he was "deeply shocked" by charges of irregularities.

The Labor Department had announced on Monday

Please Turn to Pg. 35, Col. 1

THE WEATHER

U.S. Weather Bureau forecast: Cloudy with occasional showers today and Thursday. High today, 62. High Tuesday, 62; low, 48.

Los Angeles Times

LARGEST CIRCULATION IN THE WEST. 817,087 DAILY; 1,144,326 SUNDAY

VOL. LXXXIV 2† FIVE PARTS—PART ONE CC TUESDAY MORNING, JUNE 8, 1965 90 PAGES DAILY 10c

ASTRONAUTS LAND--BOTH IN GREAT SHAPE

MISSION ACCOMPLISHED—Edward H. White II, at left, and James A. McDivitt salute after boarding the carrier Wasp at the end of successful Gemini 4 flight. UPI Wirephoto

Gemini 4 Hits Ocean 44 Miles From Carrier to End 4-Day Flight

BY MARVIN MILES
Times Aerospace Editor

HOUSTON — Gemini astronauts James A. McDivitt and Edward H. White II landed safely and in great physical shape in the Atlantic at 10:12 a.m. (PDT) Monday to end America's longest manned space flight — 97 hours, 56 minutes and 30 seconds after launch from Cape Kennedy last Thursday.

Less than an hour after their 4,600-pound spacecraft splashed into a sunlit sea about 44 miles short of the recovery carrier Wasp, they were taken aboard by a Navy helicopter.

Smiling and waving, they stepped onto the deck in their silvery spacesuits and received a thunderous roar of welcome from the officers and men of the Wasp. Sailors threw their white hats into the air and the Wasp's band heralded their achievement with a spirited march.

Though their faces were unshaven and drawn, neither astronaut showed any evidence of weakness after the four grueling days of weightlessness in the cramped little spaceship.

Full page of pictures on Page 3, Part 1. Other news and pictures on Pages 2, 16, 17, 18 and 20.

They both seemed to be in excellent health and acknowledged the cheers of the ship's crew with broad grins and thumbs-up signals.

They were greeted by Rear Adm. William McCormick, chief of the naval recovery force; Capt. J. W. Conger, skipper of the Wasp, and flight surgeons. They walked down a red carpet into the sick bay to undergo medical checks. McDivitt wisecracked, "I knew we'd end up in a hospital."

The Gemini partners posed for photographers and then walked with their arms around each other's shoulders to the sick bay. They walked erectly without any sign of stiffness from their confinement in close quarters. They climbed down steep ladders without help.

Help Each Other Out of Heavy Suits

McDivitt and White did not ask for anything but acknowledged they were hungry and thirsty. They helped each other out of their heavy spacesuits, and one report described them as being like "two big-game fishermen back from the sea with the biggest catch of all."

Doctors reported that White became slightly seasick as Gemini 4 bobbed in the waves. They also said McDivitt and White, after 62 orbits, appeared in "every respect" in the same condition as Virgil (Gus) Grissom and John W. Young after the three-orbit Gemini 3 flight, except one—"they had beards."

While the painstaking medical examinations were under way, Gemini 4 was hoisted aboard the joyous carrier at 12:30 p.m. (PDT). The marine honor guard which had greeted the astronauts snapped to attention.

Symbols Clearly Visible on Side

Despite the intense 3,000-degree heat which Gemini 4 had generated in its plunge into the atmosphere, the American Flag painted on one side and the words "United States" on the other were plainly visible.

The two men were brought to the Wasp aboard a twin-turbined Navy helicopter less than 38 minutes after their capsule parachuted into the sea 396 miles east of Cape Kennedy.

The left hatch opened and McDivitt emerged first as the spacecraft bobbed gently in a light, choppy sea. He stood, stretched, sat down, then stood once more as if unlimbering after four days of being cramped in the small cabin.

The pair were hoisted to the copter separately in slings from life rafts. They had clambered onto the raft

Please Turn to Pg. 2, Col. 7

Estes Conviction Upset Because of TV Coverage

Supreme Court Rules His Rights Were Violated During Texas Trial on Swindling

BY JOHN H. AVERILL
Times Staff Writer

WASHINGTON—A sharply divided Supreme Court reversed the 1962 swindling conviction of Billie Sol Estes Monday on grounds that the televising of his Texas court trial violated his constitutional rights.

However, the court's 5-4 opinion apparently stopped short of outlawing the televising of all criminal trials in the two states that permit it —Texas and Colorado.

The reversal of the state court conviction does not affect Estes' conviction in federal court at El Paso, Tex., on charges of mail fraud and conspiracy. He is serving a 15-year prison term for that conviction.

Opposes Television

The court majority, in an opinion written by Justice Tom C. Clark, made clear it opposes the televising of any criminal proceeding on grounds that it deprives the defendant of his constitutional right of due process of law.

But one of the dissenters, Justice William J. Brennan, said only four of the five justices in the majority voted to prohibit televised criminal trials, whatever the circumstances.

For this reason, Brennan said in a separate opinion that he did not regard Monday's decision as a blanket prohibition against the televising of state criminal trials.

Brennan based this on the position taken by Justice John M. Harlan, who concurred with the majority, but said in a separate opinion that the Estes case was a "highly sensational affair."

Wait Appropriate Case

Harlan implied that he might take a different view in a case involving a less notorious trial.

He said the resolving of such a question should "await an appropriate case."

"The court should proceed only step by step in this unplowed field," Harlan wrote.

"The opinion of the court necessarily goes no farther, for only the four members of the majority who unreservedly join the court's opinion

Please Turn to Pg. 5, Col. 4

House Group Gets Plea on Military Pay

Exclusive to The Times from a Staff Writer

WASHINGTON — Defense Secretary Robert S. McNamara Monday urged the House Armed Services Committee to discard its own military pay bill in favor of an administration proposal which the committee chairman has called "disgracefully inadequate."

McNamara asked the committee to approve "without any reservation whatever" a $446.6 million a year serviceman's pay raise proposed by President Johnson.

The defense secretary said the bill, which would give an across-the-board raise of 4.8% to officers and men with more than two years of service, is "fair to our military personnel . . . and fair to our taxpayers."

Criticized by Rivers

The administration bill was introduced last Wednesday by Committee Chairman L. Mendel Rivers (D-S.C.), who, while offering the bill, criticized it as inadequate.

Rivers and 33 of the other 37 members of the committee introduced their own pay bill last March 3. It would give an average 10.7% military pay raise and cost, according to Rivers' figures, $832.3 million a year in active duty pay or $1.05 billion when pay for retired servicemen, Coast Guard and Geodetic Survey personnel and others is included.

Before the public hearing opened, defense officials criticized the Rivers' pay proposal. They said it actually would cost $1.5 billion a year and be "a waste of the taxpayer's money."

Doubt Proposal

The same officials said they doubted the Rivers proposal would be able to pass both the Senate and House when and if it comes to a floor vote.

In presenting this testimony, McNamara told the committee:

"We should not delude ourselves that we can ever adequately compensate our uniformed personnel for the unique hazards and hardships of the military profession—the risk of death or injury in combat, the long and frequent family separations,

Please Turn to Pg. 21, Col. 1

Taylor in Washington for War Consultation

Declines Predictions on Viet Conflict, but Sees 'Advance Here, Regression There'

BY TED SELL
Times Staff Writer

WASHINGTON—U.S. Ambassador Maxwell D. Taylor returned from Vietnam Monday for what he called another "periodic consultation" with President Johnson and other officials on the conduct of the war in Southeast Asia.

Taylor, arriving for his fourth consultation in less than a year, declined to comment specifically on developments in Vietnam. But he told newsmen at Andrews Air Force Base the situation there represented an "advance here, a regression there."

Taylor left open the question of greater combat roles for U.S. forces in Vietnam, although he added that the American military on the scene are "going to do their duty." But he said he was not going to try to predict the future.

Less Decision-making

However, State Department officials indicated there would be less decision-making during this visit by Taylor than in connection with any of his previous visits.

State Department press officer Robert J. McCloskey expressed no surprise at reports that 15,000 more American troops were on their way to Vietnam.

McCloskey also redefined the combat role of U.S. troops in Vietnam to include the carrying out of aggressive patrols in which Communist guerrillas are sought out and cleared from the perimeters of U.S. defense installations. Main responsibility for fighting the Viet Cong remains with the Vietnamese, but Americans do not have to wait for hostile fire before acting in a positive way in the areas they are defending.

At about the time Taylor was talking to newsmen, Defense Department officials were reporting that the Viet Cong have still-uncommitted reserves which can be thrown into new offensive action. The Communists recently have employed greatly beefed-up forces to score a number of major successes against Vietnamese government troops in recent weeks.

New Units Unidentified

But the Pentagon hedged on the question of whether the fresh units were South Vietnamese guerrillas or units from the regular army of North Vietnam.

Defense officials insisted only one North Vietnamese battalion has been confirmed as present in South Vietnam but admitted "there could be others" not yet confirmed in action.

Under military intel-

Please Turn to Pg. A, Col. 3

INVITED TO RANCH

'Well Done,' Johnson Tells Gemini Pair

WASHINGTON (AP)—President Johnson telephoned a "well done" to the Gemini astronauts Monday and invited them to his Texas ranch this weekend.

Alternately joking and serious, the President expressed a hope and a prayer that the time will come "when all men of all nations will join together to explore space together and walk side by side toward peace."

"And you two outstanding men," he said, "have taken a long stride forward in mankind's progress and everyone in this nation and, I think, in the free world, feels in your debt."

Major James A. McDivitt and Maj. Edward H. White II thanked the President from the other end of the connection aboard the recovery ship USS Wasp. The two-way conversation was carried by radio and television networks.

Something for Them

Mr. Johnson told the two spacemen, in inviting them to Texas this Friday or Saturday, that "I've been saving a little something for you."

He presumably referred to some type of award he plans to confer on the two men who he said have written their names in history "and in our hearts."

"We're all in this country very proud of you," Mr. Johnson said. "And I think the entire world is grateful for what you've done and particularly for your safe return."

In an apparent effort to put the two men at ease, the President said:

"Maj. White, there are several million people in this country who've been wondering for three days what you were doing to Jim's

Please Turn to Pg. 17, Col. 4

High Court Overturns Anti-Birth Control Law

BY THOMAS J. FOLEY
Times Staff Writer

WASHINGTON—The Supreme Court Monday struck down an 1879 Connecticut law barring the use of contraceptives.

It did so in a 7-2 decision reversing the conviction of two persons for aiding and abetting violation of the law by operating a birth control clinic in New Haven.

The two are Estelle T. Griswold, executive director of the Planned Parenthood League of Connecticut, and Dr. C. Lee Buxton, chief of the Yale Medical School's department of obstetrics. They deliberately had opened the clinic in 1961 to challenge the state law.

The court recognized that the 86-year-old law generally has been ignored and that no one is prosecuted in the state for violating the law.

But the majority opinion, written by Associate Justice William O. Douglas, noted that the Connecticut law applies to married persons as well as others and therefore "concerns a relationship lying within the zone of privacy created by several fundamental constitutional guarantees."

Douglas cited several previous cases in which the First Amendment guaranteeing the right of free speech and association has been construed to include many other rights, including those "where privacy is

Please Turn to Pg. 14, Col. 1

HUNGARY STOPS RADIO TO HELP ASTRONAUTS

WASHINGTON (AP)—The Hungarian Communist government suspended a Budapest radio broadcast Monday to help the U.S. Gemini astronauts return safely to earth, it was learned Monday night.

U.S. officials said that because the Hungarian broadcasts on 1.016 megacycles might interfere with base-to-ship communications during the critical splashdown period, the State Department Monday morning put in an urgent request with the Hungarian legation that they be suspended for three hours.

The legation in Washington immediately called the Hungarian foreign ministry and a few minutes later Bela Szilagyi, deputy foreign minister, informed the legation here that his government complied with the request.

American officials commended the Hungarian authorities for their speedy co-operation.

THE WEATHER

U.S. Weather Bureau forecast: Cloudy today and Wednesday with drizzles this morning. High today, 70. High Monday, 67; low, 59.

Lazy Wait in Capsule Ordered at Flight's End

BY ROBERT C. TOTH
Times National Science Correspondent

HOUSTON — Astronauts James A. McDivitt and Edward H. White II, if they followed orders, were sitting with feet propped up on the instrument panel of their spacecraft Monday while waiting for recovery forces.

That seemingly incongruous ending to their four-day space flight was in retrospect rather fitting, for everything after White's extraordinary 20-minute space walk on the first day was anticlimatic.

There were some brief moments of suspense during the last three and a half days of the mission but none of danger, according to officials of the National Aeronautics and Space Administration.

White had to work hard to get back into the spacecraft after the fuel in his jet gun ran out and as he reached for the ship his heart was beating the fastest of any time during the flight—178 times a minute compared to his normal 50.

The bulky hatch took considerable effort to close—exertions which added to thos[e] outside the vehicle could e[x]plain why White slept c[on]siderably subsequently [in] the flight.

NASA officials said [the] hatch problem might [have] been caused by "va[cuum] welding" of the meta[l] and its jamb. In extr[a]boratory vacuums,

Please Turn to Pg.

Los Angeles Times

LARGEST CIRCULATION IN THE WEST. 830,118 DAILY, 1,177,588 SUNDAY

VOL. LXXXIV 2† FIVE PARTS—PART ONE CC FRIDAY MORNING, AUGUST 13, 1965 88 PAGES DAILY 10c

7,000 IN NEW RIOTING; TROOPS ALERTED

HANGING ON—Demonstrators cling to the sides of moving troop train at Berkeley in protest to the U.S. buildup in Vietnam. As the train moved slowly the demonstrators were pulled to ground by police. UPI Wirephoto

USIA FILMING JOHNSON LIFE, SENATOR CHARGES

WASHINGTON (UPI) — The U.S. Information Agency is filming the life of President Johnson in a movie called "A President's Country," the Senate was told Thursday.

Sen. John J. Williams (R-Del.) charged that USIA has already spent $80,000 on the movie designed to show the President's contributions to the country.

The movie came up during floor debate on the appropriations bill for the State, Justice and Commerce departments when Williams offered an amendment to bar the use of USIA funds for the film.

The amendment was shouted down on a voice vote after Sen. John L. McClellan (D-Ark.) argued that it would prevent the USIA from making a movie about any dead or living American statesman.

The Williams amendment stipulated that no USIA funds could be used for a movie production in this country with an American public official

Please Turn to Pg. 7, Col. 3

Police Move Against Mobs; Shops Looted; Shootings Reported

BY JACK McCURDY and ART BERMAN

Five hundred National Guard troops were poised to move into the Watts area Thursday after more than 7,000 persons rioted for the second straight night in violence which spread to the nearby Willowbrook district.

Shotgun-armed officers moved into a portion of the riot-torn district shortly before midnight, dispersing many of the demonstrators.

Rioters were reportedly firing guns at policemen and civilians as bands of Negro youths and adults roamed the turbulent neighborhoods. Hundreds of householders telephoned police seeking protection.

Many Fires Burn Unchecked

Police said fires from markets and liquor stores, overturned cars and debris were burning unchecked along Avalon Blvd. between Imperial Highway and 120th St.

Store windows were being smashed by rocks and widespread looting was taking place, officers said.

Gas-filled bottles made into Molotov cocktails reportedly were being hurled into cars and crowds and a number of motorists said they were dragged from their cars and beaten by groups of Negroes

The rioting spread to the Willowbrook district in county territory shortly before midnight when officers requested tear gas to control a crowd of some 300. Three cars were reported overturned and police were being fired upon from apartment houses at Imperial Highway and Parmelee Ave.

Long-range Tear Gas Guns Sent

Long-range tear gas guns were sent to the area but permission was not immediately granted for their use.

Numerous automobiles were reported burning throughout the eight-block area and motorists who were beaten by the mobs sought sanctuary in nearby homes.

Fire trucks and ambulances were unable to enter the area to fight the fires and pick up the injured because of the danger from flying rocks, bricks and fire bombs.

The Fire Department and hospitals reported receipt of many false reports designed to lure vehicles into the riot area.

Two police cars were unaccounted for for two hours at midnight.

More than 350 city police, deputy sheriffs and California Highway Patrol officers attempted to seal off the area at 113th St., 120th St., San Pedro St. and Stanford Ave.

One newsman said the intersection of Imperial Highway and Avalon Blvd. was "a mass of fire trucks, police cars, overturned automobiles."

Officers reportedly were taking refuge in doorways and behind cars with drawn revolvers.

Rioters Continue to Hurl Objects

Throngs of rioters continued to hurl objects at the police amid the sound of gun shots.

At least seven policemen and two firemen were treated at Central Receiving Hospital for injuries. More than 40 civilians were treated for injuries at Oak Park Hospital.

Some 15 rioters were arrested.

Maj. Gen. Charles A. Ott Jr., commanding general of the 40th Armored Division of the National Guard, said his 10,500-member division has been alerted by Gov. Brown and a brigade of 500 men was on standby orders to move in.

He said an "emergency task force" could be quickly assembled.

Plans call for the division to leave for a two-week summer training session Saturday morning, but he said men will be left behind if police request it.

"It looks very explosive—much worse than Wednes-

Please Turn to Pg. 3, Col. 1

Singapore to Seek Indonesia Friendship Tie

BY ED MEAGHER
Times Staff Writer

SINGAPORE — Newly independent Singapore put out friendly overtures to Indonesia Thursday in its campaign to survive in the complex politics of Southeast Asia.

Foreign Minister S. Rajaratnam told a press conference that this new island-nation is aiming at some kind of friendly relationship with Indonesia and at putting an end to Jakarta's "crush Malaysia" campaign.

But he said these would not be done at the expense of giving up British military bases here.

The friendly overtures, which were not unexpected in the wake of Singapore's expulsion from the Federation of Malaysia last Monday, could mean resumption of this port city's rich $500 million annual trans-shipping trade with Indonesia. This ended abruptly two years ago when Jakarta started its "crush Malaysia" campaign.

Hopes for Amity

Rajaratnam said that amid a good deal of trial balloon comments on the subject by both nations, it appeared that Indonesian leaders would be prepared to establish some kind of relations with Singapore, some with a view to settling the "crush Malaysia" issue.

"As far as we are concerned," the foreign minister said, "Singapore is out of Malaysia and therefore technically cannot be included in the 'crush Malaysia' campaign. At the same time, we are not going to be a party to any scheme that would da-

Please Turn to Pg. 16, Col. 1

Second U.S. Jet Downed by Missile Near Hanoi

Mobile Rocket Unit Blamed as Navy Plane Is Hit Outside Range of Known Fixed Sites

SAIGON (AP)—A surface to air (SAM) missile downed a U.S. Navy Skyhawk over North Vietnam Thursday at a point outside range of the known fixed sites ringing Hanoi, a U.S. spokesman announced. The implication was that a mobile unit fired it.

The spokesman said the pilot was missing and presumed dead.

It was the second U.S. plane apparently shot down by a missile.

The missile issue revived as large American and Vietnamese ground forces lifted the 70-day siege of Duc Co and launched operations to clear Viet Cong from a broad strip of South Vietnam's central highlands between Pleiku and the Cambodian frontier. Aircraft again landed supplies at the Duc Co air strip and flew out dead and wounded.

Mekong Delta Battle

Elsewhere the heaviest ground action seemed to center in the Mekong Delta about 95 miles southwest of Saigon. Big government and Viet Cong units were engaged at that point, 15 miles below Can Tho. Reports from the field said the troops estimated they killed 156 guerrillas and confirmed 90 of these by body count. Government casualties were described as light.

The Skyhawk fell 19 days after a U.S. Air Force Phantom jet fighter was shot down northwest of Hanoi by what briefing officers said appeared to be a surface to air missile.

The U.S. Air Force followed up loss of the Phantom with a 46-plane raid that pilots said destroyed one missile site and damaged an-

Please Turn to Pg. 19, Col. 1

Saigon Wanted U.S. Troops, Johnson Says

BY RICHARD RESTON
Times Staff Writer

WASHINGTON — President Johnson, at a swearing-in ceremony for Henry Cabot Lodge as the new U.S. ambassador to South Vietnam, made it clear Thursday that American troops are in Vietnam only at the request of the Saigon government.

The President said the United States "would never undertake the sacrifice these efforts require if its help were not wanted and requested."

Embarrassing Issue

Mr. Johnson's remarks were aimed at prying the administration loose from an embarrassing controversy touched off by Lodge's recent appearance before the Senate Foreign Relations Committee.

Lodge reportedly told several senators in secret session that U.S. troops would remain in South Vietnam even if a future Saigon regime requested their withdrawal.

The President firmly rejected this thesis, as the

Please Turn to Pg. 18, Col. 1

Police Rout 300 in Troop Train Protest

BERKELEY (UPI) — Policemen using riot sticks Thursday shoved and hauled 300 demonstrators from the path of a troop train carrying soldiers bound for the Far East.

Two persons were arrested and three suffered minor injuries in the fourth such incident in a week by demonstrators protesting U.S. policy in Vietnam.

Many of the college-age protesters outflanked the 50 patrolmen assigned to the demonstration and clung to hand rails outside the 20-coach train. But they were tossed off before the train reached the Oakland Army Terminal, main West Coast embarkation point for South Vietnam.

Woman Falls Down

One unidentified woman missed her footing as she tried to get on the Santa Fe Railway train to distribute anti-Vietnam war leaflets to the soldiers. She fell to the roadbed and was struck by a spring box under the carriage, which hurled her away from the wheels of the slow-moving train.

Several demonstrators sat down on the tracks as the train approached. They were seized by plainclothesmen who grabbed them by

Please Turn to Pg. 18, Col. 1

House OKs $3.2 Billion Public Works Measure

Bill Wins Approval After Republican Efforts to Reduce Funds Are Rejected

WASHINGTON (AP)—The House passed a $3.25 billion public works development bill Thursday after beating all attempts to cut it.

The measure has been labeled by its sponsors as a long step toward wiping out pockets of unemployment and subnormal income in almost every state.

Opponents, mainly Republicans, branded it a "boondoggle" and said it would not accomplish the claimed objectives.

Voting for the bill on the final roll call were 215 Democrats and 31 Republicans; against it were 45 Democrats and 93 Republicans.

Amendments Lumped

In a final gesture, Republicans lumped some of the rejected amendments into a package and forced a roll call. They lost by a vote of 224 to 163, with 48 Democrats and 115 Republicans supporting the move and 214 Democrats and 10 Republicans opposing it.

The Senate passed the bill June 1 after adding $750 million to the amount proposed by President Johnson. The House made no change in the money total but approved committee alterations which the Senate is expected to accept without much argument.

The bill is an authorization measure spelling out the scope of the program but not financing it. A separate appropriation would be needed to put it into operation.

Sponsors of numerous amendments made only token fights as it became apparent that administration forces, with some Republican

Please Turn to Pg. 7, Col. 4

Senate Group Approves Bill on Union Shop

BY THOMAS J. FOLEY
Times Staff Writer

WASHINGTON — The administration-supported move to wipe out state laws barring the union shop easily leaped its first Senate hurdle Thursday, winning approval by a labor subcommittee on a 7-1 vote.

The group made one change in the House-approved bill, adding a provision to exempt from any union shop agreement all persons who object to joining a union on religious grounds.

But the bill ran up against a jam of other administration-backed bills in the full Labor Committee and Sen. Pat McNamara (D-Mich.) said he did not know when that body could take it up.

Labor Confident

Organized labor, which has made repeal its No. 1 legislative target, is confident that the Senate will approve the bill by a relatively safe margin.

The conscientious objector amendment was vigorously and successfully opposed in the House. Administration strategists reasoned that if this amendment — which they did not really object to —were approved, it would be easier for opponents to tack on other amendments, some of which labor is against.

Present strategy calls for letting the religious amendment ride through the Senate and then asking the House to accept it. The ad-

Please Turn to Pg. 8, Col. 1

Small Post Besieged by Viet Cong Odd Prize in Long, Bitter Battle

BY JACK FOISIE
Times Staff Writer

DUC CO, South Vietnam—It is a strange prize, this government outpost over which the Communist Viet Cong and Vietnamese forces have fought this past week.

Duc Co is a block square of muddy red soil in which the defenders — 12 Americans and more than 100 Vietnamese and aboriginal Montagnard soldiers—all live underground. The camp is surrounded by multiple strands of barbed wire, staked knee-high. In these fields of wire are mines that can be detonated electrically by the defenders in their underground bunkers. Where no mines are sown, there are punji sticks — the dagger-sharp shafts of dried bamboo that can effectively stop the charge of the barefooted or canvas-shoed attackers.

For the past week, said Capt. Edward T. Richards of Fayetteville, N.C., the threat of attack made sleep at night unwise. But instead of charges by hordes of Viet Cong, for which Richards and other American Special Forces men were prepared, the enemy chose only to harass them by constant mortar fire. This effectively kept everyone underground, save for those involved in the counter-mortar fire put out from an open pit by the defenders in their attempts to zero in on the Viet Cong mortar positions.

"How can you find the mortars out there?" asked the 33-year-old Richards.

He let his arm sweep the dazzling green-matted forest around him.

"They could set up a tube (mortar) in a small clearing, fire a few rounds and then move it somewhere else."

While the men at Duc Co hung on, a column of more than 1,000 Vietnamese marines, paratroopers and oth-

Please Turn to Pg. 2, Col. 3

TRIBUTE—President Johnson sits before enlargement of the Herbert Hoover memorial stamp after signing law setting up a Hoover historic site in Iowa. UPI Telephoto

President Signs Bill Establishing Historic Site at Hoover Birthplace

BY DON IRWIN
Times Staff Writer

WASHINGTON — Before a heavily Republican audience, President Johnson paid tribute Thursday to former President Herbert Hoover as an exponent of nonpartisanship in the White House.

"This house and this government and this society . . . really belong to no party because the partisan spirit is an alien spirit to America," Mr. Johnson told the gathering invited to watch him sign a bill establishing a national historic site at Mr. Hoover's birthplace in West Branch, Iowa.

Absent from the ceremony, although they had been invited, were the five living former Republican Presidential candidates, from Alf M. Landon to Barry Goldwater.

Mr. Johnson read a telegram from former President Dwight D. Eisenhower, who said he had a previous commitment to attend the opening of the Professional Golfers Assn. tournament at Ligonier, Pa. The last GOP President was represented by his brother, Dr. Milton Eisenhower.

The White House did get off the invitations somewhat belatedly, by telegram and telephone Wednesday. That might have been a factor in the absences.

Mr. Johnson cited Gen. Eisenhower, along with Mr. Hoover, as Republican Presidents who have "raised

Please Turn to Pg. 10, Col. 1

THE WEATHER

Light smog today.

U.S. Weather Bureau forecast: Variable cloudiness with considerable sunshine today and Saturday. High today, 90. High Thursday, 92; low, 72.

Los Angeles Times

LARGEST CIRCULATION IN THE WEST. 830,118 DAILY; 1,177,588 SUNDAY

VOL. LXXXV 3† EIGHT PARTS—PART ONE CC THURSDAY MORNING, DECEMBER 16, 1965 146 PAGES DAILY 10c

GEMINIS IN FIRST SPACE RENDEZVOUS

TWO'S COMPANY—Drawing shows meeting of Gemini 6 and 7 in space as astronauts maneuvered to within 10 feet of each other at 17,540 m.p.h.
Times drawing by Russell Arasmith

Two Capsules Meet 6 to 10 Ft. Apart in 17,540 M.P.H. Flight

BY MARVIN MILES
Times Aerospace Editor

HOUSTON—Gemini 6 and 7 spaceships met an incredible 6 to 10 feet apart in a dramatic rendezvous Wednesday at the climax of an 83,000-mile chase around the earth.

The two capsules kept their space date over the Mariana Islands north of Guam at an altitude of 187 miles while both were streaking around the planet at about 17,540 m.p.h.

The meeting was the first rendezvous of manned craft in space.

It also marked the first time the United States has had two capsules aloft at the same time and the first time any nation has had four astronauts in orbit simultaneously.

Takes Space Exploration Lead

There seemed to be no doubt that the success of the rendezvous mission has placed America well ahead of Russia in manned space exploration.

Communications problems blurred reports from the two spacecraft during the critical rendezvous period and controllers here were tense and concerned as they watched the seconds tick by with no direct report from the two Geminis.

Then, 5 hours, 54 minutes after the second spacecraft was launched from Cape Kennedy, Gemini 6 pilot Thomas P. Stafford reported in an utterly calm voice:

"We're 120 feet apart and sitting."

In successive murky transmissions, Gemini 6 command pilot Walter N. Schirra Jr. explained:

"We jockeyed into position at about 120 feet."

Gap Continues to Get Narrower

"What's your range (separation distance) now?" Mission Control here asked.

"About 20 feet."

Later, he said:

"We're down to about 10 feet."

Mission Control said the distance apparently was between 6 and 10 feet, with the spacecraft nose-to-nose while hurtling around the earth.

It was far better than space officials had dared hope for. The flight plan called for a 20-foot separation, but early expressions of confidence indicated the range might be narrowed "to a few feet."

The rendezvous was achieved a minute or two after both spacecraft streaked out of darkness into sunlight.

And in the historic space meeting both capsules apparently were inverted—crews head down in weightlessness—with Gemini 6 flying in front, blunt end first and looking aft, while Gemini 7 trailed, facing forward.

Close Enough to See Beards

So close were the two spaceships that the crew of each could look into the windows of the other. They joshed about chewing gum and the length of beards on Gemini 7 astronauts Frank Borman and James A. Lovell Jr.

"There seems to be a lot of traffic up here," said Schirra in Gemini 6.

"Call a policeman," advised Borman in Gemini 7.

By the time the two Geminis had raced across the Pacific in close formation, Schirra was jockeying his spacecraft at various angles to Gemini 7 at distances of 20 to 50 feet.

He reported seeing a mysterious length of dangling strapping that has flicked on Gemini 7 occasionally in

Please Turn to Pg. 2, Col. 6

U.S. Bombs Power Site in Hanoi-Haiphong Area

Raid Knocks Out Plant Vital to Military, Spurs Speculation of Intensification of War

BY RUBEN SALAZAR
Times Staff Writer

SAIGON—U.S. Air Force jet bombers Wednesday knocked out a steam-run power plant in North Vietnam's Hanoi-Haiphong industrial complex. The raid led to speculation that Washington has undertaken another intensification of the war against the Communists.

An Air Force spokesman said about six Thunderchief F-105 jets hit the plant at Uong Bi, 14 miles northeast of Haiphong. The spokesman said direct hits and secondary explosions from 12 tons of 3,000-pound bombs left the site a mass of rubble.

The coal-burning, 24,000-watt capacity plant supplies 15% of North Vietnam's electrical energy and is the primary source of power for the Hanoi-Haiphong area. The spokesman said the plant was of vital military importance as a source of power for factories producing arms and equipment. But he said only the plant was hit, not the industries it powered.

Blackout Reported

The spokesman said the plant "is producing nothing tonight," adding that "at least parts of Hanoi and Haiphong are blacked out."

(In Washington Secretary of Defense Robert S. McNamara said the bombing of the North Vietnamese power plant near Haiphong "is representative of the type of attack we have carried out and will continue to carry out," the Associated Press reported.

(That was his answer to a question by newsmen who asked him if the latest strike against the North Vietnamese power generating system was part of the "hard steps" which President Johnson recently indicated might be taken.

(McNamara preferred to answer that question only by his statement about the type of attacks being carried out.

Explains Objective

(McNamara once more explained the overall objective in the air attacks on targets in North Vietnam—to destroy munitions which go to the Viet Cong in the south.

(He said the power plants in the Hanoi-Haiphong area furnish electrical energy for the manufacturing of munitions.)

One F-105 was reported shot down by conventional ground fire during the raid. But the pilot was able to bail out into the Gulf of Tonkin and was rescued minutes later.

The Air Force identified the pilot as Capt. Harry D. De Witt of Moscow, Ida. He suffered a broken leg and facial cuts but was reported in good condition.

The Air Force emphasized that this is not the first time

Please Turn to Pg. 6, Col. 1

26th District Congress Seat Won by Rees

BY RICHARD BERGHOLZ
Times Political Writer

Democratic State Sen. Thomas Rees breezed to an easy victory in the 26th Congressional District special election Wednesday.

The 40-year-old lawmaker, running in the heavily Democratic district, trounced Dr. Edward Marshall, 27-year-old Republican nominee.

Returns from all 465 precincts showed:

Rees	40,575
Marshall	27,696

The election fills the vacancy created by the resignation Sept. 30 of former Rep. James Roosevelt (D-Los Angeles) who had represented the district since 1954. Roosevelt accepted an appointment as U.S. representative on the U.N. Economic and Social Council.

Topped 7-Man Field

Rees picked up where he left off at the Nov. 23 primary election to fill Roosevelt's seat. At that test, the state senator topped a seven-man field but failed to get a majority of all votes cast.

So the runoff Wednesday was between Rees and Marshall, who finished third in the primary but made the finals because he was the only Republican in the race.

This time it was easier for Rees, who had a tight primary election tussle with Beverly Hills Councilman Leonard Horwin, also a Democrat.

From the first returns

Please Turn to Pg. 32, Col. 1

AT FIRST MEETING

'Lot of Traffic Here' Breaks Space Silence

HOUSTON (AP)—"There seems to be a lot of traffic up here," said Walter M. Schirra Jr. from the Gemini 6 spacecraft.

"Call a policeman," answered Frank Borman from Gemini 7.

With those words, history was made—the first face-to-face meeting of two manned spacecraft.

"You're up close," commented Schirra.

"I can see your lips moving," replied James Lovell Jr., pilot of Gemini 7.

"I'm chewing gum," Schirra said.

"Oh, OK," said Lovell. "Can you see Frank's beard, Wally?"

"Yeah. I can see yours too—better right now."

"How's the visibility?" asked Lovell. "Is it pretty bad at this time?"

'I See You .....'

"Yeah, it's pretty bad. I see through the window and see you fellows inside."

The Canary Islands tracking station first told Borman and Lovell that Gemini 6 had achieved orbit.

"Roger," said Borman. "We didn't get to see the lift-off, but we saw them coming up."

Talking with the Canary Islands a few minutes later, Schirra asked, "How's the 7

Please Turn to Pg. 25, Col. 1

Maugham Dies at 91 in His Riviera Villa

NICE, France (AP) — W. Somerset Maugham, a great English story teller and craftsman who roamed the world for material, died early today at his Riviera villa. He was 91 and doctors days ago realized he could not recover from a recent fall.

At the end, however, when all hope was gone, he was taken from the British-American Hospital to die in the villa, his secretary and companion of years, Alan Searle, said in announcing the death this morning.

The feeble Maugham suffered the fall last Friday, was taken to the hospital Saturday and given only hours to live after a medical consultation Sunday.

Rallied for a Time

He rallied for a time but weakened Wednesday and arrangements were made to let him die at his beloved villa, La Mauresque.

Doctors said he suffered a stroke that produced a nervous ailment afflicting blood vessels and a heart specialist told newsmen Saturday he believed the condition would lead to death "within two or three days at maximum."

On Sunday, doctors reported Maugham's condition was aggravated by a rise in temperature and pulmonary congestion. Dr. Georges Rosanoff, the author's physician, said then his brain was no longer supplied with blood, "but the heart is still holding out."

One of the most prolific authors of his time, Maugham turned out 25

Please Turn to Pg. 22, Col. 1

Gemini 6 Ends Its Jinx With Perfect Launch

BY ED MEAGHER
Times Staff Writer

CAPE KENNEDY—Gemini 6 shook off past failures here Wednesday and rose flawlessly from lift-off to perfect insertion into orbit.

Calm but jubilant, astronauts Walter M. Schirra Jr. and Thomas P. Stafford, who twice before sweated out Gemini 6 countdowns in vain, could even joke as they began pursuit of astronauts Frank Borman and James A. Lovell Jr. in Gemini 7 for an unprecedented rendezvous in space.

"For the third time, go!" Schirra is reported to have cracked just before lift-off.

Cool Confidence

That may have set the tone of cool confidence that prevailed the rest of the way—in the spacecraft, in Mission Control and among those on the ground here.

Almost 13 minutes into the flight, while moving across the Atlantic in their spacecraft, Schirra cracked that the only problem he could see "is a little smoke on my window which might be some of that Florida haze or fog."

On Sunday, Gemini 6 fizzled in a lateral bellowing of smoke. But it shot upward

Please Turn to Pg. 24, Col. 3

City Asking U.S. for $12 Million to Give Jobs, Schooling to 2,000

BY ERWIN BAKER
Times Staff Writer

Federal funds are being sought by the city to employ and partially educate 2,000 jobless and currently unemployable adult males from East Los Angeles and south-central poverty areas.

Mayor Samuel W. Yorty said Wednesday the proposal, to put jobless family men to work on beautification and improvement projects, would cost $12 million a year. The city cannot afford it without federal anti-poverty fund help, he said.

The plan calls for 34 hours of work a week and six hours in self-improvement classes through the city school system's adult-education program for each enrollee.

At his weekly press conference, the mayor frankly admitted: "We are trying to find city employment at federal expense.

"This is really useful work. We are not trying to make work. These are things we really want to do, but can't afford in the city budget."

The program, Yorty said, would be designed to train the men for jobs available in private industry so they will be able to work permanently.

He called such a plan "the only real hope" of solving the unemployment problem.

Yorty's proposal will be submitted to the Economic and Youth Opportunities Agency for funding through the Office of Economic Opportunity and the Manpower Development and Training Act.

The education provision, he said, would be for basic and remedial courses for high school credits.

The mayor said enrollees—with priority going to family men who have been employed more than six months and whose unem-

Please Turn to Pg. 34, Col. 1

THE WEATHER

U.S. Weather Bureau forecast: Variable cloudiness through Friday with occasional light showers today. Continued cool. High today, 58. High Wednesday, 58; low, 39.

SIGNS OF SUCCESS—Alan B. Shepard, the first American in space, exults at his post at Cape Kennedy as Gemini 6 lifts off and heads for historic meeting in space. Shepard is Gemini 6 crew director.
(AP) Wirephoto

Los Angeles Times

LARGEST CIRCULATION IN THE WEST. 845,150 DAILY, 1,184,384 SUNDAY

VOL. LXXXV 3† SIX PARTS—PART ONE CC WEDNESDAY MORNING, NOVEMBER 9, 1966 108 PAGES DAILY 10c

REAGAN TRIUMPHS! FINCH ALSO WINS

GOP Scores Heavily in Congress and Governor Races

Democrats Lose Senate Seats in Illinois, Oregon, Tennessee and Up to 45 Seats in House

BY LAURENCE BURD
Times Staff Writer

WASHINGTON — In a striking comeback from their 1964 losses, the Republicans scored heavy gains in House, Senate and governors' races in Tuesday's elections.

Although the GOP increases were not enough to win numerical majorities in Congress or the 50 statehouses, they cut deeply into Democratic dominance and raised a caution sign against President Johnson's Great Society welfare programs.

Based on returns and projections early Wednesday, the Republicans appeared headed for a net gain of perhaps 45 seats in the House. This would reduce the former 295-140 Democratic majority to the neighborhood of 250-185 and give the GOP House contingent, in tandem with conservative southern Democrats, a strong anti-administration base.

Resistance to Johnson Seen

The extent of the resistance that the House elections spell for Johnson programs in 1967-68 was clear from the political complexion of House winners and losers. A late tabulation by NBC's Electronic Vote Analysis found that 26 House incumbents "mostly in favor" of Great Society programs were defeated, while 20 of those newly elected are "mostly opposed" to it. This could mean a swing of 46 House votes against key Johnson domestic programs.

In contrast to their House gains, where many Republican victors over Democratic incumbents are conservatives, Republican moderates scored a hatful of the party's key victories in Senate and governorship races. An exception was in California where GOP conservative Ronald Reagan won the governorship going away.

The Republicans, with moderates stealing the show, captured formerly Democratic Senate seats in spotlight races in Illinois, Oregon and Tennessee. As of early Wednesday, the Republicans had not yielded any of their previously held Senate seats to Democrats.

The GOP's three-seat Senate pickup in 35 races gave them 36 senators to 64 for the Democrats, compared to a 67-33 Democratic hold before Tuesday and results in some races are still undecided.

The GOP achieved an even greater victory in governorship races. With California's Reagan leading the surge, Republican candidates took at least six statehouses formerly in Democratic hands, while losing two GOP governors' chairs to the Demo-

Please Turn to Page 28, Col. 1

PARTY SCORE FOR NATIONAL OFFICES

Associated Press returns at midnight Tuesday showed:

SENATE:	Dems.	Reps.
Elected	14	14
Leading	3	4
Holdovers	47	18
Total	64	36
Unreported 1		
OLD SENATE:	67	33
Needed for majority 51		
HOUSE:		
Elected	227	158
Leading	22	28
Totals	249	186
OLD HOUSE:	295	140
Needed for majority 218		
GOVERNORS:		
Elected	10	16
Leading	4	5
Totals	14	21
Unreported races 3		
OLD LINEUP:	33	17

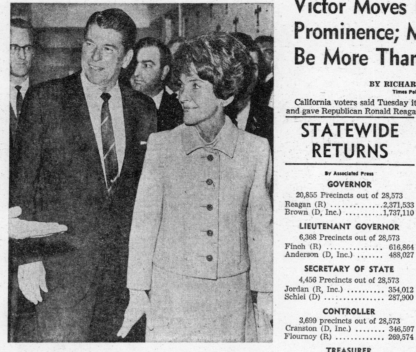

GREETINGS FOR THE WINNER — A hand is outstretched to smiling Ronald Reagan and his wife, Nancy, as they arrive at the Biltmore Hotel. They went to their suite, then later appeared before Republican throng.
Times photos by Larry Sharkey

Victor Moves Into National Prominence; Margin May Be More Than Half-Million

BY RICHARD BERGHOLZ
Times Political Writer

California voters said Tuesday it is time for a change in Sacramento and gave Republican Ronald Reagan a smashing triumph in the race for governor.

The 55-year-old Reagan making his first try for public office, turned back the third-term bid of Democratic Gov. Brown, a veteran of 23 years of public office.

With 20,855 of the state's 28,573 precincts reporting, the count stood:

Reagan 2,371,533
Brown 1,737,110

Reagan, whose victory vaults him into national political prominence, also spread his coattails for other GOP nominees, and there was evidence that they were broad enough to upset a number of veteran Democratic office-holders.

Robert H. Finch, Los Angeles lawyer and GOP nominee for lieutenant governor, pulled ahead of Democratic incumbent Glenn M. Anderson and the Democrat conceded defeat at 10:45 p.m.

With 6,368 of the state's 28,573 precincts reporting, the count stood:

Finch 616,864
Anderson 488,027

Other Democrats who had been swept into statewide office eight years ago when Brown scored a million-vote triumph also were having tough fights.

And in any number of races for congressional and state legislative offices, Republicans were running stronger than had been expected.

Reagan jumped into the lead from the very first returns and never looked back.

Even before the polls closed in Los Angeles and other major counties in the state, television computer experts had declared Reagan a sure winner. They said his margin of victory would run more than 55% of the total vote—which may mean a half-million vote edge or more by the time all the tabulations are completed.

It was a long and difficult night

Please Turn to Page 3, Col. 1

STATEWIDE RETURNS

By Associated Press

GOVERNOR
20,855 Precincts out of 28,573

Reagan (R)	2,371,533
Brown (D, Inc.)	1,737,110

LIEUTENANT GOVERNOR
6,368 Precincts out of 28,573

Finch (R)	616,864
Anderson (D, Inc.)	488,027

SECRETARY OF STATE
4,456 Precincts out of 28,573

Jordan (R, Inc.)	354,012
Schlei (D)	287,900

CONTROLLER
3,699 precincts out of 28,573

Cranston (D, Inc.)	346,597
Flournoy (R)	269,574

TREASURER
3,699 precincts out of 28,573

Betts (D, Inc.)	312,831
Priest (R)	277,633

ATTORNEY GENERAL
3,699 precincts out of 28,573

Lynch (D, Inc.)	334,822
Williams (R)	238,631

PROPOSITION 1A
Constitutional Revision
3,338 precincts out of 28,573

Yes	355,398
No	140,409

PROPOSITION 16
Obscenity
4,062 precincts out of 28,573

No	363,329
Yes	243,861

Reagan's Task Force Swiftly Acts to Establish GOP Regime

BY CARL GREENBERG
Times Political Editor

Gov.-elect Ronald Reagan's new Republican administration swiftly began taking shape Tuesday night as California voters sounded Democratic Gov. Brown's political requiem.

A "Major Appointments Task Force," headed by former oil company president A. C. Rubel of Los Angeles, quietly at work since a week ago, started its labors in earnest.

It presaged the sweeping changeover of key cabinet officials and department heads that will take place when Reagan takes the reins of government on Jan. 2 and the 61-year-old Brown steps down from the office he has held for two four-year terms.

The actor-businessman's election represented the sentiments of a electorate captivated by the 55-year-old Reagan's pledge of a state government geared to strict economy, strict law enforcement, and a minimum of interference in their lives.

But, it also bespoke their tiredness of Brown, their anger over the Rumford housing act Reagan has said should be repealed and their agreement with Reagan that it was "time for a change."

The election of Reagan's running mate, Robert H. Finch, as lieutenant governor, over the Democratic incumbent, Glenn M. Anderson, who billed himself in campaign literature as the "quiet fighter," assured Reagan of a strong right arm

Please Turn to Page 33, Col. 1

Brooke Victorious in Massachusetts

BY TOM FOLEY
Times Staff Writer

BOSTON — Massachusetts, which has written so much American political history for more than three centuries, added a new chapter Tuesday by electing Negro Republican Edward W. Brooke as the first U.S. senator of his race since Reconstruction.

Brooke, the state's 47-year-old attorney general, triumphed over former Gov. Endicott Peabody to succeed Republican Sen. Leverett Saltonstall, 73, who did not seek reelection.

The vote, with 1,041 of the state's 2,055 precincts reporting:

Brooke 464,596
Peabody 337,783

Peabody conceded Brooke's election at midnight when it was clear that he would carry heavily Democratic Boston by only about one-third of the 75,000-vote margin the

Brooke overcame even the strong efforts of the brothers Kennedy, Sen. Edward of Massachusetts and

Please Turn to Page 23, Col. 5

L.A. COUNTY RETURNS

Unofficial returns for Los Angeles County:

GOVERNOR
9,544 Precincts out of 13,154

Reagan (R)	972,812
Brown (D, Inc.)	671,900

LIEUTENANT GOVERNOR
2,305 Precincts out of 13,154

Finch (R)	105,520
Anderson (D, Inc.)	74,171

SECRETARY OF STATE
1,733 Precincts out of 13,154

Schlei (D)	74,128
Jordan (R, Inc.)	68,229

CONTROLLER
1,569 Precincts out of 13,154

Flournoy (R)	70,731
Cranston (D, Inc.)	62,050

TREASURER
1,247 Precincts out of 13,154

Priest (R)	68,168
Betts (D, Inc.)	61,674

ATTORNEY GENERAL
1,218 Precincts out of 13,154

Lynch (D, Inc.)	61,216
Williams (R)	49,594

PROPOSITION 1A
Constitutional Revision
1,313 Precincts out of 13,154

Yes	57,965
No	22,912

PROPOSITION 16
Obscenity
1,261 Precincts out of 13,154

No	43,452
Yes	42,477

Please Turn to Page 35, Col. 1

GOP's Gains Spark Interest in 1968 Presidential Campaign

BY ROBERT J. DONOVAN
Times Washington Bureau Chief

WASHINGTON—The solid Republican gains won Tuesday make it perfectly clear that the 1968 Republican Presidential nomination will be worth fighting for.

The Republican Party, on the strength of nationwide returns, has come back a long way from the depths of Barry Goldwater's 1964 debacle.

While the Democrats, of course, remain the majority party in Congress and in the country at large, the two-party system — abnormally weakened two years ago—has been greatly strengthened.

Furthermore, the outcome of several elections produced a strong crop of men who will either be Republican contenders or kingmakers in 1968. Among them are Michigan Gov. George Romney, Sen.-elect Charles H. Percy of Illinois and California Gov.-elect Ronald Reagan. Richard M. Nixon, to be sure, is a part of this company even though he was not running for anything this year.

In addition, New York Gov. Nelson A. Rockefeller's decisive victory raises some practical questions as to whether he will be as far removed from the 1968 race as he has said he would.

Long before Tuesday it was apparent that troubled times lie ahead

Please Turn to Page 28, Col. 4

MAJOR RACES AT A GLANCE

How the top personalities fared in Tuesday's election:

ALABAMA—Mrs. Lurleen Wallace (D) defeated Rep. James D. Martin (R) for governor, succeeding her husband. (Story on Page 23.)

ARKANSAS—Winthrop Rockefeller (R) was leading Jim Johnson (D) for governor. (Story on Page 24.)

GEORGIA—Rep. Howard (Bo) Callaway (R) pulled ahead of Lester G. Maddox (D) in a gubernatorial race so close it may ultimately have to be decided by the state legislature. (Story on Page 23.)

ILLINOIS—Charles H. Percy (R) defeated Sen. Paul H. Douglas (D) for senator. (Story on Page 22.)

MARYLAND—Spiro T. Agnew (R) defeated George P. Mahoney for governor. (Story on Page 22.)

MICHIGAN—Gov. George Romney (R) won reelection, defeating Zolton Ferency (D); Sen. Robert P. Griffin (R) defeated G. Mennen (Soapy) Williams (D) for senator. (Story on Page 22.)

NEW YORK—Gov. Nelson R. Rockefeller (R) won re-election, defeating Frank D. O'Connor (D). (Story on Page 23.)

OREGON—Gov. Mark O. Hatfield (R) defeated Rep. Robert B. Duncan (D) for senator. (Story on Page 3.)

Leaders of Erhard's Party Move to Oust Him

BY OSGOOD CARUTHERS
Times Staff Writer

BONN—The chiefs of Ludwig Erhard's Christian Democratic Party demanded Tuesday night that a decision be made on his successor as West Germany's chancellor before the end of this week.

The presidium of the party, its highest organ made up of all the provincial chairmen and top federal officers, called on its deputies in Parliament to choose from among four specific candidates.

The deputies, meeting as the "parliamentary faction," were ordered to choose from the four named and to discuss no other possible candidates. They were told to keep voting until they reached an absolute majority on one of the candidates.

Those named came as no surprise to West Germans who have been following the two-week crisis over Erhard's leadership. They are Eugen Gerstenmaier, president of the lower house of Parliament or Bundestag; Rainer Barzel, the party's parliamentary chief; Kurt Georg Kiesinger, minister president of the state of Baden—Wurttemberg; Gerhard Schroeder, the present foreign minister.

The decision was made in the presence of the harassed Erhard who, as the leader of the party, was named to head the commission to assist the new candidate in his negotiations aimed at reforming the now-shattered coalition government. Also taking part in this commission will be the Bavarian wing of Erhard's party, the Christian Social Union headed by Franz-Joseph Strauss.

The new candidate will have to induce the Free Democrats to return to the coalition from which they bolted two weeks ago, ostensibly

Please Turn to Page 13, Col. 3

THE WEATHER

U.S. Weather Bureau forecast: Mostly sunny today and Thursday with patchy fog early this morning. Increasing clouds Thursday. High today, 66. High Tuesday, 59, low, 49.

FEATURE INDEX

Los Angeles Times

LARGEST CIRCULATION IN THE WEST. 845,150 DAILY, 1,184,384 SUNDAY

VOL. LXXXVI 2† FIVE PARTS—PART ONE CC MONDAY MORNING, JANUARY 30, 1967 96 PAGES DAILY 10¢

CAPSULE'S CHARRED INTERIOR—View through hatch of the blackened Apollo spacecraft and the couch that was occupied by Edward H. White II when he and his fellow astronauts were killed by fire. (AP Wirephoto)

Jury Finds Baker Guilty on 7 Counts

He Could Draw 48-Year Term, $47,000 in Fines

BY DON IRWIN
Times Staff Writer

WASHINGTON—Bobby Baker, who tried to build a fortune while he was the secretary to the Senate's Democrats, was found guilty Sunday of the full catalog of crimes for which he was indicted a year ago.

Baker, 38, stood expressionless in the half-empty U.S. district courtroom as a poll of the jurors reaffirmed conviction on seven counts of tax evasion, larceny and conspiracy that could bring maximum penalties of 48 years in prison and $47,000 in fines.

The poll completed an anticlimactic six-minute court session that ended the three-week trial. The pallid, balding defendant lit a cigaret with a shaking hand. His daughter, Dorothy, sobbed in her place beside her mother, also named Dorothy, and brother on one of the courtroom's oak benches. The Bakers walked together to an adjoining empty courtroom.

Defense Will Appeal

Defense counsel Edward Bennett Williams told reporters that the defense is "of course going to the appeals court and all the way to the Supreme Court, if necessary.

"This has always been our intention," the visibly weary Williams said. "We will execute our intention."

Across the court, government prosecutor William O. Bittman told another group of reporters: "I think that the verdict is fully justified by the evidence—absolutely—and a victory for law enforcement generally."

How complete that victory may be rests with the appeals process. Williams has a week to move for a new trial, and he is also free to petition U.S. District Judge Oliver Gasch to set the verdict aside.

Judge Gasch, meanwhile, will not impose sentence until he receives a probation report on Baker, who is presently free on $5,000 bond. Probation reports normally take two weeks to process but sentencing could be deferred by defense motions that may be filed in the meantime.

Avoids Direct Comment

The tall, soft-spoken judge avoided any direct comment on the verdict, emphasizing that it had been "entrusted to the judgment of the jury."

"Essentially, it was a question of credibility," he told reporters in a brief interview. "If the defense was believed, it could have been a verdict of not guilty. If it was not believed, it could have been a verdict of guilty. And credibility is strictly a question for the jury."

The jury foreman, John M. Buchanan, substantiated the judge's point. He told a reporter the jury reached its decision because it did not believe Baker's testimony that $99,600 paid to him in 1962 by

Please Turn to Page 6, Col. 3

SYSTEM REMAINS ON TRIAL DESPITE GUILTY VERDICT

BY ROBERT J. DONOVAN
Times Washington Bureau Chief

WASHINGTON — Bobby Baker stands convicted, but the system on Capitol Hill that spawned the conditions in which he parlayed a $19,612 Senate job into holdings once estimated at $2 million remains on trial.

The kingpin of influence peddlers, the pal and protege of Senate nabobs like Lyndon B. Johnson and the late Robert S. Kerr (D-Okla.) finally got his comeuppance Sunday at the hands of a U.S. district court jury.

The trial, however, only raised new suspicions about influence peddling, money passing and shadowy deals over legislation.

Baker wasn't the only influence peddler in the complex world of the U.S. Senate any more than

Please Turn to Page 7, Col. 1

MANY DOUBTS

Credibility Test Failure Brought Baker Conviction

Exclusive to The Times from a Staff Writer

WASHINGTON — Bobby Baker was convicted because he flunked his credibility test with the only people who ultimately counted: the six men and six women, all present or former government workers, who sat as the jury at his trial.

John M. Buchanan, 35, the jury foreman, said Baker's total of 12 hours on the stand had left the jury dubious on many points. It was especially concerned, he said, with Baker's contention that he gave the late Sen. Robert S. Kerr (D-Okla.) the entire $99,600 in payments from savings and loan men. The government had accused Baker of stealing at least $80,000 of the money. Baker said Kerr loaned him $50,000 of the total.

Notes Use of Friendship

"One of the undercurrents in the entire thinking of the jury," Buchanan said, "was how Baker used the friendship of his deceased friend, Sen. Kerr, to point the finger of possible bribery."

To "a number of jurors," Buchanan said, this was "a despicable thing to do." Jurors also felt, he said, that there were "fabrications by the defense." Even though they were impressed by the emotional summation delivered Friday by defense counsel Edward Bennett Williams, he said, they "looked to the evidence, not the oratory."

Lenzie G. Barnes, a postal clerk who served as juror No. 5, said he simply felt that Baker's testimony showed "fabrications all through it."

The government had "a very convincing case," Barnes said, citing

Please Turn to Page 6, Col. 6

U.S. Arms Sales Seen as Blow to Aims Abroad

Senate Group Questions Pentagon Tactics Among Underdeveloped Nations

BY TOM LAMBERT
Times Staff Writer

WASHINGTON—A Senate committee staff study suggested worriedly Sunday that the Pentagon's busy and successful arms salesmen overseas may be jeopardizing some of this country's foreign relations and international policy goals.

The Pentagon's weapons sales abroad totaling "some $6 to $7 billion in the past four years," the study suggested, do not jibe with this country's hope of ending the arms race in the underdeveloped world.

That race may be only a "walk" in some underdeveloped regions, the study acknowledged, but it may speed up if it is not slowed down.

The underdeveloped nations, the study implied, should spend their money on non-military development programs instead of airplanes and tanks.

Some U.S. Allies Angered

Additionally, the study continued, the Pentagon's intensive arms-selling efforts abroad are angering some American allies, notably the British and West Germans.

Further, the study said, American weapons sold to some countries have figured in "a series of international crises" in Kashmir and the Middle East, and might be involved in others in Latin America in the future.

The study, prepared by the Senate Foreign Relations Committee's staff, wound up with this conclusion:

"It is incumbent upon the United States to reappraise the adequacy of the present machinery of policy control and legislative oversight governing the sale of arms."

Or, in less bureaucratic language, "the United States must take another searching look, from all angles, at this whole arms-selling business."

The arms sales worries voiced by the Foreign Relations Committee's staff may be voiced again later when its parent body starts reviewing American policies abroad. American arms commitments overseas are only one of the concerns of the committee chairman, Sen. J. William Fulbright (D-Ark.).

McNamara Not Apprehensive

Sunday's staff study on U.S. arms sales abroad was issued only a few days after Defense Secretary Robert S. McNamara discussed that subject in his annual defense posture statement.

And while the Senate staff was worried about such sales, McNamara evinced no undue apprehension over them.

No arms sale abroad is approved, he said, if it threatens "peace or stability" or endangers any "foreign policy consideration" held or sought by the United States.

Further, he said, each proposed sale is reviewed "at the highest levels of government," and approved only if "it is in our best national interest and that of the (purchasing) country concerned."

The volume of U.S. arms sales abroad is as imprecise, complex and uncertain as some of the transactions involved, the Senate staff study indicated, and its authors were uneasy and perplexed about those

Please Turn to Page 18, Col. 1

Devastated Cockpit Complicates Job of Apollo Investigators

BY JACK NELSON
Times Staff Writer

CAPE KENNEDY—The fire that swept Apollo 1 and killed three astronauts devastated their cockpit, complicating the job of a board of inquiry, an inspection trip by newsmen revealed Sunday.

The board, meanwhile, continued to pore over evidence in its search for the origin of the spark that ignited the fire.

Killed Friday night during a test 'f the Apollo for a scheduled Feb. 21 light were Air Force Lt. Col. Virgil (Gus) Grissom, 40, veteran of Iercury and Gemini flights; Air 'orce Lt. Col. Edward H. White II, , America's first space walker emini 4), and Navy Lt. Comdr. ger B. Chaffee, 31, who had never ide a space flight.

Board Has Key Role

On the findings of the board of inuiry will rest much of the fate of merica's drive to land astronauts the moon before 1970.

If the board finds human error or a elatively simple mechanical failure aused the fire, the first blastoff of an Apollo spacecraft may not be delayed for more than several months.

If the trouble turns out to be a major design problem in the Apollo system, the postponement could be six months to a year and could so cripple the Apollo project as to delay the first lunar flight beyond this decade.

An inspection of the Apollo by two newsmen representing all news media here showed that the flash fire left the cockpit a darkened, dingy hull, its walls covered with slate-gray deposits of smoke and soot and its floor covered with blackened,

Please Turn to Pg. 10, Col. 1

Yugoslav Embassies in U.S., Canada Bombed by Terrorists

By United Press International

Terrorists bombed two Yugoslav embassies and four consulates in the United States and Canada early Sunday in well-coordinated raids that one diplomat blamed on anti-Tito exiles who fled Yugoslavia with Hitler's armies in 1945.

No injuries were reported in the bombings at the embassies in Washington and Ottawa and the consulates at Toronto, San Francisco, New York City and Chicago. But a fireman died of a heart attack while inspecting damage in New York, and a child was thrown from his bed by the embassy blast in Washington.

Police set up guards around the Yugsolav consulate in Pittsburgh, the only one in the United States and Canada to escape the bombings. The Pittsburgh consulate occupies the 16th floor of a 25-story apartment building. The other consulates and the embassies are at ground level.

Secretary of State Dean Rusk expressed his regrets to Yugsolav Ambassador Veljko Micunovic in Washington. The State Department called the bombings "outrageous and senseless acts of terrorism (that) can only be condemned by the American people."

No White House Comment

The White House had no comment.

Micunovic delivered a formal protest to Undersecretary of State Nicholas D. Katzenbach at the State Department Sunday afternoon.

The note called for "the most energetic investigation and the punishment of the perpetrators of these crimes, as well as undertaking of all necessary measures by the U.S. government and the authorities of the individual states, measures which would render impossible similar terrorist activities in the future."

The ambassador said after the 45-minute meeting that Katzenbach had assured him everything possible would be done to "prevent repetition of such madness."

Katzenbach also said the United States will make prompt compensation for damages to the Yugsolav

Please Turn to Page 19, Col. 1

U.S. Copters Strafe 200 Viet Sampans, Killing 31 Civilians

SAIGON (AP)—Three U.S. helicopters, responding to gunfire from below, strafed a fleet of 200 sampans on the Bassac River in the Mekong Delta Saturday night and early Sunday. A U.S. spokesman said today some women and children were among 69 Vietnamese civilians killed or wounded.

The spokesman said 31 Vietnamese were killed and 38 wounded by the attack of the night-flying helicopters 78 miles southwest of Saigon. He said there was no breakdown on the number of women and children among the casualties.

He said the civilians told interrogators they were moving out in sampans in violation of curfew hours because of numerous Viet Cong in the area.

Copters Gunfire Targets

The helicopters attacked the sampans after being fired on by automatic weapons from at least three positions—two in the sampans and one on the river bank, the spokesman said.

The U.S. spokesman said the circumstances of the incident still were not clear. He gave this account:

Late Saturday night, a flight of three gunship helicopters made an armed reconnaissance of the south bank of the Bassac River.

Intelligence reports had indicated that a Viet Cong main force unit was in the area and had been observed two nights earlier.

The helicopters encountered 200 sampans attempting to cross the river during curfew hours. The curfew in the area prohibits river or

Please Turn to Page 15, Col. 3

Rain Expected in Southland Today

Drizzles followed by rain are expected to moisten Southern California today and Tuesday.

"There's a 50-50 chance you'll get measurable rain in your back yard" tonight and Tuesday morning, forecaster John Frazee said Sunday.

He predicted the rain would amount to less than a quarter-inch in most areas. Mountains and foothills may receive more, he said, but skies should begin to clear by Tuesday afternoon.

Frazee said the precipitation was being generated by a small front which spun off a larger one to the north, where rain and strong gusty winds raked points as far south as Santa Maria.

The Weather Bureau predicted the temperature will reach a high of 65 at the Civic Center today, one degree above Sunday's high. Light smog was forecast for the basin.

Snow averaging two feet deep in the Angeles National Forest attracted 166,000 visitors over the weekend.

FOUND GUILTY—Bobby Baker leaving in car with wife, Dorothy, after being convicted by a jury in Washington. He is presently free on bond. (AP Wirephoto)

Pro-West Sato Party Returned to Power by Japanese Voters

TOKYO (AP)—Prime Minister Eisaku Sato's pro-Western Liberal Democratic Party was returned to power today in elections climaxing a hard-fought campaign that centered on charges of corruption.

Three former Sato cabinet ministers under public fire for a variety of indiscretions were reelected with wide margins to the ruling lower house.

Exposure of these indiscretions, coupled with charges of corruption against other government party members, had produced an anti-government outcry that resulted in dissolution of the house.

Displaying deep-rooted strength, the Liberal Democrats went easily over the simple majority hump of 244 of the 486 seats in the House of Representatives. They were still moving ahead with 389 seats unofficially decided.

Counting continued for the remaining 97 seats in Sunday's elec-

Please Turn to Page 16, Col. 1

THE WEATHER

Light smog today.

U.S. Weather Bureau forecast: Local drizzle this morning with 50% chance of some light rain tonight and Tuesday. High today, 65. High Sunday, 64; low 52.

FEATURE INDEX

Los Angeles Times

LARGEST CIRCULATION IN THE WEST, 845,150 DAILY, 1,184,384 SUNDAY

VOL. LXXXVI 2† FIVE PARTS—PART ONE CC FRIDAY MORNING, JUNE 9, 1967 104 PAGES

DAILY 10c

EGYPT AND SYRIA ACCEPT CEASE-FIRE

Assembly Votes Record Budget of $5.154 Billion

Members Quarrel Over Increased Taxes Called Necessary to Pay for It

BY RAY ZEMAN
Times Sacramento Bureau Chief

SACRAMENTO — The Assembly approved a record $5.154 billion budget by a 64-14 vote Thursday, but it quarreled over higher taxes needed to pay for it.

"This budget is now $818 million out of balance," said Assembly Minority Leader Robert T. Monagan (R-Stockton.)

"We don't have before us a sufficient revenue program to finance it."

Assembly Speaker Jesse M. Unruh (D-Inglewood) blamed Gov. Reagan for the budget, which would be the largest for any state in the nation's history.

He pointed out that the revised total of $5,154,264,128 is far larger than the $4.6 billion program Reagan proposed Jan. 31.

"Now we're going to have to raise taxes about $500 million more than if he had stayed with his original budget," Unruh told the Assembly.

Democrats Join in Approval

However, Unruh and 25 other Democrats joined the Assembly's 38 Republicans in voting for the "consensus" budget. All 14 no votes were cast by other Democrats.

The Senate Finance Committee is completing work on the upper house's own budget bill. If the Senate approves this, both measures will be submitted to a two-house conference committee for compromise.

A similar conference committee may have to settle the stalemate over a tax bill.

Acting chairman Hugh M. Burns (D-Fresno) of the Senate Governmental Efficiency Committee scheduled an executive session for 9 a.m. Monday on the governor's $1.07 billion tax proposals, introduced through Sen. George Deukmejian (R-Long Beach).

Burns hopes for a committee vote on this measure next Wednesday, but he said Thursday, "The chances are it will be amended considerably."

Amendment Proposed

When Chairman Robert W. Crown (D-Oakland) of the Assembly Ways and Means Committee submitted the mammoth budget bill on the lower house floor Thursday, Monagan proposed an amendment.

This would permit State Finance Director Gordon P. Smith to make the 24.8% cuts necessary to balance the budget if the Legislature fails to provide sufficient revenues.

Crown promptly protested. He explained this would transfer the budget blue-penciling job from an elected governor to an appointee.

Unruh quickly swept into the fray. He blamed Reagan for blocking the $1.5 billion tax measure proposed by Assemblyman John G. Veneman (R-Modesto), which would

Please Turn to Page 12, Col. 1

ISRAELI HERO—Gen. Moshe Dayan, center, Israel's defense minister, walks in old Jerusalem after its capture from Jordanian forces. With Dayan, hero of the 1956 Suez war, are Brig. Gen. Uzi Narkiss, on left, commander of central front, and Maj. Gen. Izhak Rabin, chief of staff.
(AP) Wirephoto

Israel Attacks U.S. Navy Ship in Error; 10 Die

Government Apologizes Immediately After Jets and PT Boats Hit Vessel

BY TED SELL
Times Staff Writer

WASHINGTON — Israeli jets and torpedo boats mistakenly attacked a U.S. Navy communications ship in the eastern Mediterranean early Thursday, killing 10 American sailors and wounding about 100, 20 seriously.

Israel promptly apologized—almost within minutes of the attack. The apology said the attack on the USS Liberty, which was flying U.S. colors, resulted from an error by Israeli forces.

The incident occurred at 5:05 a.m. PDT, shortly after the Liberty took up station 15 miles off the north coast of the Sinai Peninsula and 90 miles southwest of Tel Aviv.

Israeli jets first made six strafing runs. Twenty minutes later, three torpedo boats attacked. They launched at least two torpedos. One struck the starboard side of the Liberty.

No Danger of Sinking

The Liberty reported extensive but superficial topside damage and that some of the forward deck spaces had been damaged. But the ship was in no danger of sinking.

One immediate result of the attack was a sudden message on a teletype hot line linking Washington and Moscow.

The United States advised Moscow that the 6th Fleet aircraft carriers America and Saratoga, operating several hundred miles north of the attack scene, were launching aircraft to check on the incident, but with no hostile intent. Russian ships have been shadowing the 6th Fleet.

Pentagon officials said the America launched four A-4 Sky Hawk jet bombers and the Saratoga put four propeller-driven A-1 Sky Raiders into the air, with fighter support. But Tel Aviv's apology was flashed to the fleet before the aircraft reached the attack scene, and they returned to the carriers.

Ship's Guns Open Fire

Reports from the scene said the Liberty opened fire with the ship's machine guns in an apparent effort to detonate an approaching torpedo. The ship's only armament is four .50-caliber machine guns.

Immediately after the attack, the Liberty began steaming northward at eight knots to rendezvous with two 6th Fleet destroyers, the Massey and the Davis. Aboard the destroyers were a doctor and medical corpsmen. The Pentagon said the Liberty has one doctor and two corpsmen. It was not known if they were among the casualties.

The Liberty has a crew of 15 officers, 279 enlisted men and three civilian technical experts to assist with complex communications equipment.

At the time the attack report was received, Secretary of State Dean Rusk was on Capitol Hill, briefing the Senate Foreign Relations Committee on the Mideast situation. He cut the session short and rushed to the White House.

Rusk delivered a speedy protest to Avraham Harman, Israeli ambassa-

Please Turn to Page 20, Col. 5

Agree to Halt 4-Day Conflict After Blitz by Israeli Forces

By Associated Press

Egypt accepted a cease-fire Thursday—and broke the bitter news to its own people—in the face of Israel's air and tank blitz that smashed President Gamal Abdel Nasser's forces back to the Suez Canal in four days of fighting. Syria also announced later that it had accepted the cease-fire.

The official Damascus radio said an emergency session of the Council of Ministers decided to take Syria out of the conflict.

Since the outbreak of the Middle East conflict Monday, Israel's tough and highly mobile troops and airmen had destroyed Arab air power and routed Egyptian armor in the Sinai Desert, reopened the blockaded Gulf of Aqaba, and seized long-coveted areas of the Holy Land.

Jordan bowed out of the conflict Wednesday.

With Egypt and Syria joining Jordan in accepting the truce, one of the shortest wars in history seemed about over.

Nasser Remains Silent

Nasser, who yearned to lead the Arab world, was silent in the face of the debacle — his second humiliation as president in 11 years at the hands of Israel's air and desert legions. He was also a loser to Israel as a field soldier in the war of 1948.

The semiofficial Egyptian newspaper Al Ahram said Nasser would address the nation today.

Egyptians were bitter as the news was broken to them by the official Cairo radio.

"This means we have shed our blood in vain," said one in Cairo.

These were the developments in what seemed the closing hours of the war:

In New York, U.N. Secretary General U Thant told the Security Council Thursday afternoon that Egypt had accepted the cease-fire appeal issued by the council Tuesday and repeated Wednesday.

In Cairo, the United Arab Republic military high command told of continued fighting and of a battle with Israelis "unprecedented in its ferociousness" in a communique apparently preparing the people for news of disaster. Then, Cairo radio later broadcast the announcement of the cease-fire.

In Damascus, the Syrians, who had been most vociferous in support of the war, kept up belligerent broadcasts until the official radio beamed out the news of the cease-fire.

In Washington, the Pentagon reported that Israeli jets and torpedo boats mistakenly attacked a U.S. Navy communications ship in the eastern Mediterranean, killing 10 American sailors and wounding about 100, 20 seriously.

In New York, the report of Egypt's acceptance came five minutes before the close of stock trading and promptly set off a rush of buy orders. The Dow Jones industrial average, which had been down slightly, spurted to a 4.01-point gain for the day and closed at 873.20. Prices continued to advance in heavy trading on the Pacific Coast Stock Exchange, which closed two hours later.

Earlier in the day, an Israeli spokesman in Tel Aviv declared Israeli tanks and troops had smashed stubborn Egyptian resistance in a series of five battles in the Sinai Desert.

Accepting the cease-fire, Egypt made no reference in the Security Council to Soviet Union demands

Please Turn to Page 20, Col. 1

FINAL BATTLES — Map shows five sites in Sinai Desert where Israel said it defeated Egyptian tanks Thursday. Cross marks position of U.S. ship hit by Israel.
(AP) Wirephoto map

Secret Peking Paper Forebodes Maoists' Final Spiral of Collapse

Article by a Member of Red Guard High Command Tells in Great Detail How Disaster Is Likely to Come About

BY ROBERT S. ELEGANT
Times Staff Writer

HONG KONG—The Communist regime of Mao Tse-tung is spiraling rapidly toward final collapse under conditions already predicted in detail by a senior Red Guard chieftain in a secret publication which has just become available in Hong Kong.

All the news from China — official, semiofficial, wall poster and clandestine—points to the conclusion that a new ad hoc structure of limited power is rising on the nearly total wreckage of the Maoists' own power. Its chief component is a pragmatic and informal alliance between regional, provincial and local officials of the Communist Party and the People's Government —the "power-holders following the capitalist road," in Maoist terminology — and the People's Liberation Army.

The total situation and the inescapable trend are quite clear, though specific details are obscured by two factors: (A) The ever-rising obstacles to investigation amid the chaos of almost complete anarchy; and (B) the fact that Chinese regimes never collapse all at once like the wonderful one-horse shay, but rather decay at different rates in different places until they finally blow away.

It is, nonetheless, becoming increasingly plain that the foundation of Maoist power has already been riven beyond repair. It is today no longer a matter of the Mao inner circle seeking to retain their personal positions by abandoning their extremist policies, but a matter of their fighting a desperate rear-guard action to save their political lives.

That action is most unlikely to be successful.

All Components Apparent

All the components of a traditional dynastic collapse are already apparent in Communist China:

Worsening food shortages and transportation breakdowns; the disappearance of any effective nationwide authority and the defection of peace-keeping units like the Public Security Forces; the breaking away of major administrative units—like the Southeast Region, the Northeast Region and Honan Province, among others—and workers' disruption of vital facilities like the railroads; widespread armed clashes arising

Please Turn to Page 9, Col. 1

Egyptian Truce Action Comes as Stunning Surprise in U.N.

BY LOUIS B. FLEMING
Times Staff Writer

UNITED NATIONS—The United Arab Republic, in a sudden change of policy, accepted the Security Council's appeal for a cease-fire in the Middle East War Thursday. Syria accepted a similar cease-fire several hours later.

Word of Egypt's acceptance came as a stunning surprise in the midst of a council meeting. It was a surprise for the Egyptian diplomats as well as for all the others in the crowded council chamber.

It was in the council chamber under these circumstances that Israel, through its foreign minister, Abba Eban, received the first official indication from Egypt that Israel's military campaign had been victorious.

The Egyptian decision set the stage for peace on two of the three battle fronts. The third was pacified with Syria's acceptance.

Israel Tuesday had accepted the cease-fire subject to reciprocity and, on Wednesday, Jordan had agreed. By Wednesday night, relative calm reportedly had settled on the Israeli-Jordanian battle line.

The U.A.R. acceptance of the cease-fire came as the United States and the Soviet Union were offering divergent resolutions on the Middle East crisis to the Security Council.

The United States sought to bring unanimous acceptance of the cease-fire while setting in motion peace

Please Turn to Page 24, Col. 1

Senators Rebuff House, Approve Prompt Action on Apportioning

BY JOHN H. AVERILL
Times Staff Writer

WASHINGTON—In a rare rebuff to its sister chamber, the Senate refused Thursday to give House members a four-year reprieve from the Supreme Court's decision that congressional districts be apportioned on a one-man, one-vote basis.

At the urging of the Kennedy brothers, the Senate passed a bill that would limit the population variance among congressional districts to not more than 10%, effective with next year's elections.

By its surprise action, the Senate rejected terms of a House-passed bill that would have permitted a 30% variance between the population of a state's smallest and largest districts through the 1968 and 1970 elections. After that, the variance would have dropped to 10%.

At the urging of New York congressmen, the Senate Judiciary Committee raised the population variance figure to 35% through 1970.

The revised bill now goes back to the House, where prospects for acceptance of the Senate version are regarded as dim. House opponents of the Senate bill are certain to argue that the Senate's action:

1—Violates the congressional tradition that one chamber makes no major changes in legislation that solely affects the other.

2—Would require 33 states to redraw the boundaries of their congressional districts before next spring's primary elections.

This latter argument was employed by Sen. Sam J. Ervin Jr. (D-N.C.) in opposing an amendment by

Please Turn to Page 7, Col. 1

FEATURE INDEX

ARMS POLICY UNDER REVIEW

U.S. Expected to Urge Restraint by Israel

BY ROBERT J. DONOVAN
Times Washington Bureau Chief

WASHINGTON — The United States is expected to urge Israel to forego demanding a harsh and humiliating settlement from the defeated Arabs.

At the same time this country will use whatever influence it can to promote some satisfactory form of international guarantee of the existence and territorial integrity of Israel.

Meanwhile, as was forecast earlier in the week, the Pentagon began a review of its entire program of supplying arms to the Middle East as a means of terminating the mischievous arms race in that part of the world.

As the fighting between the Israelis and Arabs ended Thursday, new information became available concerning the course upon which President Johnson embarked at the outset of the crisis.

Behind this course lay one cardinal fact: Despite various propaganda statements issued from Washington and Moscow there was genuine concern in both capitals that the Middle East friction might grow until it embroiled the United States and the Soviet Union.

It seemed clear to American officials early in the crisis that the Soviet Union as well as the United States was eager to avert any such confrontation. This opinion was reinforced by the friendly and candid

Please Turn to Page 21, Col. 3

THE WEATHER

Light smog today.

U.S. Weather Bureau forecast: Mostly cloudy night and morning hours with scattered drizzles in foothill sections becoming partly sunny today and mostly sunny Saturday afternoon. High today, 68. High Thursday, 66; low, 60.

Los Angeles Times

LARGEST CIRCULATION IN THE WEST, 861,350 DAILY, 1,212,983 SUNDAY

VOL. LXXXVII 2† SIX PARTS—PART ONE CC FRIDAY MORNING, APRIL 5, 1968 118 PAGES DAILY 10¢

Dr. King Shot to Death in Memphis

Rights Leader Slain as He Talks to His Aides; White Sniper Sought

BY NICHOLAS C. CHRISS and JACK NELSON
Times Staff Writers

MEMPHIS—Dr. Martin Luther King was shot to death by a sniper here Thursday. The 1964 Nobel Peace Prize-winner, America's leading exponent of nonviolence in the civil rights movement, was shot as he stood on the second floor balcony at a motel, talking to aides in a parking lot below.

He was rushed to St. Joseph's Hospital, where he was pronounced dead of a bullet wound in the neck.

Police said the shot apparently came from a brick building directly across the street from the Lorraine Motel, where Dr. King was staying.

An all-points bulletin was issued for the assassin, described by witnesses as Caucasian, about 6 feet tall, between 26 and 32 years old, about 165 pounds, wearing dark clothing.

Dr. King's aides told police a man answering that description fled from the building across the street a few moments after the fatal shot was fired. Police said later they had no definite lead on the assassin.

Rifle Dropped to Ground

They said he jumped into a car parked near the building, dropping a rifle, fitted with a telescopic sight to the sidewalk as he ran. The car sped away.

Memphis Police and Fire Director Frank C. Holloman, at a press conference early today, identified the rifle "which we think was used to kill Dr. King" as a 30-06 Remington pump action model with a telescopic sight.

He said the rifle and suitcase were found in an entryway a short distance from the hotel at 420 S. Main Street that the suspect checked into between 3 and 3:30 p.m. Thursday.

Holloman said the rifle was immediately turned over to the FBI.

Holloman said he had "certain new evidence" that would help to identify the assassin, but did not reveal it. Nor would he reveal the name under which the suspected assassin registered at the hotel.

A five-square-block area of the city surrounding the motel was sealed off quickly by police and sheriff's deputies, but police said the car escaped the blockade. Police and civilian vehicles were reported in pursuit of a speeding automobile headed for the Memphis suburb of Millington.

Holloman appeared on television a few minutes after Dr. King was pronounced dead to appeal for order. He asked all citizens to stay off the streets because of "this volatile situation."

Guardsmen Move Into City

Gov. Buford Ellington immediately ordered 4,000 national guardsmen into the city, and Mayor Henry Loeb announced a curfew at nightfall. All police and sheriff's deputies were called to patrol duty.

Nevertheless, incidents of violence, including fire bombings and shooting, were reported within an hour after the Negro leader's death was announced.

Mayor Loeb later declared a three-day period of mourning for Dr. King.

Paul Hess, assistant administrator of St. Joseph's Hospital, said Dr. King died of the wound in the neck. He said doctors in the emergency room were unable to stop the bleeding despite immediate surgical efforts.

Please Turn to Page 6, Col. 1

ON HIS LAST MARCH—Dr. Martin Luther King locked arms with two aides as he led a protest march last Thursday in Memphis that ended in violence and looting. The Nobel Peace Prize-winner escaped injury that day but was fatally shot Thursday as he stood on balcony of his Memphis motel. (AP) Wirephoto

Johnson Delays Departure for Hawaii Meeting

Assassination of Dr. King Prompts Change in Plans for Vietnam Conference

BY TOM LAMBERT
Times Staff Writer

WASHINGTON — President Johnson late Thursday postponed his departure for a Honolulu conference on Vietnam strategy pending developments in the slaying of Dr. Martin Luther King.

Several hours before he was scheduled to board his plane for a flight to California en route to Hawaii the President was informed of Dr. King's assassination in Memphis. After expressing his shock and appealing for understanding in a televised comment at the White House, the President said, "I am postponing my trip to Hawaii until tomorrow."

The President had planned to fly to California Thursday night, spend the night at March Air Force Base near Riverside and have a breakfast meeting with former President Dwight D. Eisenhower this morning before continuing on to Honolulu. The departure times and the possibility of the Eisenhower visit are now uncertain.

Delay on Decision

George Christian, White House press secretary, said "We'll get up tomorrow and make a decision on departure."

However, there was speculation that in view of the situation Mr. Johnson might not go to Hawaii at this time.

In Honolulu the President is scheduled to meet with U.S. officials from Saigon, including Ambassador Ellsworth Bunker and Gen. William C. Westmoreland, U.S. commander in Vietnam, to discuss strategy.

He also is scheduled to meet with South Korean President Park Chung Hee, who reportedly is uneasy about Hanoi's willingness—and Washington's agreement—to talk about "unconditional cessation of bombing and all other war acts" by the United States as a possible step toward peace negotiations.

It was not known if South Vietnamese President Nguyen Van Thieu would go to Honolulu. He also is said to be uneasy about the forthcoming American-North Vietnamese meeting.

Caution Against Optimism

While the President was described as cheered by Hanoi's offer, Washington officials cautioned against any undue optimism that the offer indicated a peace settlement was in prospect.

The President's decision to delay his trip came at the end of a hectic day in which he:

—Flew to New York for the investiture of Roman Catholic Archbishop Terence J. Cooke as the successor to the late Francis Cardinal Spellman.

—Conferred at U.N. headquarters with Secretary General U Thant.

—Returned to Washington to talk with Ambassadors W. Averell Harriman and Llewellyn E. Thompson, his Vietnam negotiators.

Mr. Johnson received a standing ovation in St. Patrick's Cathedral at Archbishop Cooke's investiture. He

Please Turn to Page 13, Col. 1

North Viet Premier Warns of Hard Line at Conference Table

Exclusive to The Times from the Washington Post

PARIS—The premier of North Vietnam has warned that Hanoi will take a tough and uncompromising line in peace talks with the United States.

He made it clear that his government believes it will be bargaining from a position of strength in terms of both the military situation and the political ferment in the United States.

But he said that Hanoi is "in no hurry" to achieve its ultimate objective—a reunified Vietnam under a "truly original" Communist government.

In a three-hour conversation with a correspondent of the French newspaper Le Monde, Pham Van Dong said, "We will be as firm in negotiations as we have been on the battlefield."

Washington Kept Informed

He also indicated that Washington has been kept regularly and fully informed of North Vietnamese thinking during the long march toward the conference table and through a much more extensive exchange of information than Washington has been willing to admit.

The interview was granted before President Johnson's Sunday announcement of a cutback in the bombing of North Vietnam and his new invitation for negotiations. However, the approved text which Le Monde published was officially released by the Hanoi government on Tuesday, after Mr. Johnson's announcement.

The Le Monde correspondent, writing from Hanoi Thursday, said that Hanoi's decision for preliminary talks with the United States should be interpreted as a North Vietnamese estimate of American weakness, not a sign of failing Communist resolve.

COURT OVERTURNS IMPEACHMENT OF PANAMA PRESIDENT

PANAMA (AP)—Panama's supreme court ruled today that the impeachment process against President Marco A. Robles was illegal.

A majority opinion held that the president had been deprived of his constitutional rights during the process that culminated with his conviction and dismissal by the National Assembly March 24.

The court voted 8-1 for the president.

The court was acting on an injunction, issued on behalf of Robles, which challenged the legality and constitutionality of the impeachment process.

No immediate comment was available from the political opposition, but the National Guard, Panama's army, has backed the president.

The opposition, which controls the assembly, charged Robles with unconstitutional activity on behalf of the government candidate in the May presidential election.

McCarthy Would Cut Powers of FBI, CIA, Draft Boards

BY CARL GREENBERG
Times Political Editor

BERKELEY — Sen. Eugene J. McCarthy said Thursday that if he becomes President he will check the power of the Central Intelligence Agency, the Federal Bureau of Investigation and draft boards under Gen. Lewis B. Hershey.

In the first speech of his California primary campaign, the Democratic presidential candidate declared the three agencies "need to be somewhat altered—they have become almost independent sources of power."

The Minnesota senator, who arrived here from Washington and will fly to Los Angeles today, addressed a crowd of students in UC Berkeley's Greek Theater that campus police estimated at from 10,000 to 15,000.

There was a large contingent of Peace and Freedom Party adherents, armed with placards, in the stands, and McCarthy experienced heckling that his staff said was somewhat rougher than any to which he has so far been subjected.

His Toughest Attack Yet

McCarthy's attack on the CIA, FBI and the draft boards was the toughest he has made since he became a candidate.

When he referred to the draft boards and mentioned the name of Gen. Hershey, Selective Service director, the students gave him the loudest burst of applause of his entire speech.

"Since this is a government of men as well as laws, I have in mind to make some changes," McCarthy said.

The Greek Theater appearance was followed by an address late Thursday night to 3,000 guests at a fund raising dinner in the San Francisco Hilton.

The senator's arrival at San Francisco International Airport shortly before noon was in marked contrast to the reception for his opponent in the primary, Sen. Robert F. Kennedy of New York, when he arrived there on March 23.

Kennedy was virtually mobbed. McCarthy was greeted by about 200 persons, including a sprinkling of bearded Peace and Freedom repre-

Please Turn to Page 3, Col. 2

Humphrey All but Says He Will Enter Presidential Race

BY THOMAS J. FOLEY
Times Staff Writer

PITTSBURGH—Amidst cries of "Tell us now, Hubert," Vice President Humphrey all but announced his candidacy for the Presidency Thursday to a labor audience.

"I know what your quest is, what your thoughts are," Humphrey told 3,500 persons at the Pennsylvania AFL-CIO convention, "and I am not one to walk away from a decision. It will come in due time."

Humphrey insisted he had not made up his mind, but his demeanor and his hints belied his protest. And the reception did little to discourage him.

His entrance brought a 10-minute demonstration with a band marching in the aisles playing the University of Minnesota's fight song and "Chicago," the site of this year's Democratic National Convention.

The crowd chanted "We want Humphrey" and "Sock it to them, Hubert," and the Vice President smiled benignly.

I. W. Abel, president of the 1.1-million member United Steel Workers Union, who canceled a scheduled trip to Texas to listen to Humphrey, endorsed the Vice President, telling him "go, Mr. Humphrey, go—we are with you."

It was clear that the Vice President was ready to go but was not

Please Turn to Page 24, Col. 3

President Condemns Violence, Says U.S. Is Shocked, Saddened

By Associated Press

President Johnson said Thursday night America was "shocked and saddened" by the assassination of Dr. Martin Luther King.

The President went on to condemn violence, lawlessness and divisiveness.

In a brief, solemn message to the nation, Mr. Johnson disclosed that because of the slaying in Memphis he had canceled plans for a political appearance Thursday night and postponed until today his scheduled midnight departure for Hawaii and a Vietnam strategy conference.

The President appeared in the doorway of the White House offices, stern-faced, and spoke on all television and radio networks.

"America is shocked and saddened by the brutal slaying tonight of Dr. Martin Luther King," Mr. Johnson said.

"I ask every citizen to reject the blind violence that has struck Dr. King, who lived by nonviolence.

"I pray that his family can find comfort in the memory of all he tried to do for the land he loved so well. I have just conveyed the sympathy of Mrs. Johnson and myself to his widow, Mrs. King.

"I know that every American of goodwill joins me in mourning the death of this outstanding leader and in praying for peace and understanding throughout this land.

"We can achieve nothing by lawlessness and divisiveness among the American people. It is only by joining together and only by working together can we continue to move toward equality and fulfillment for all of our people.

"I hope that all Americans tonight will search their hearts as they ponder this most tragic incident."

Mr. Johnson was to have attended a Democratic fund-raising dinner at

Please Turn to Page 8, Col. 1

THE SECRET SEARCH FOR PEACE

Wilson Switch at U.S. Behest Blamed for Lost Opportunity

BY DAVID KRASLOW and STUART H. LOORY
Times Staff Writers

WASHINGTON—With the White House dictating the moves on the transatlantic cable, British Prime Minister Harold Wilson switched and toughened a Vietnam peace proposal he had given, just hours before, to Soviet Premier Alexei N. Kosygin last year.

The switch forced by President Johnson occurred in London during the evening hours of Feb. 10, 1967. It deeply embarrassed Wilson and may have confused Kosygin and President Ho Chi Minh of North Vietnam.

Some informed critics of Mr. Johnson's Vietnam policies feel the London switch, along with a personal letter the President had sent to Ho two days before, may have ruined a promising opportunity for negotiations 14 months before this week's breakthrough.

The switching in peace terms came at the climax of a weeklong effort by Wilson and Kosygin to end the war in Vietnam.

While their talks were under way, the United States was secretly dealing with the North Vietnamese in face-to-face contacts in Moscow.

Shortly before the White House dictated the peace message change to Wilson, a draft of the President's letter to Ho was toughened and delivered through the Moscow channel. American officials later conceded privately that the substituted terms in the letter could be read as an ultimatum.

Wilson, who thought he was being kept fully informed by Washington during his talks with Kosygin, was not given the text of the letter.

Please Turn to Page 10, Col. 1

FEATURE INDEX

THE WEATHER

Night and morning coastal low clouds, otherwise partly cloudy today. Variable high clouds Saturday. Light smog today. High today and Saturday near 74. Low Saturday near 54. High Thursday, 75; low, 53.

Complete weather information on Page 23, Part 3.

HARRIS SURVEY

Nixon Trails 3 Democrats in Wake of Johnson Withdrawal

BY LOUIS HARRIS
© 1968, Washington Post Co.

In an initial nationwide test made this past Monday and Tuesday, Richard M. Nixon now runs behind Sen. Robert F. Kennedy (D-N.Y.), Sen. Eugene J. McCarthy (D-Minn.) and Vice President Humphrey.

It must be concluded that the withdrawal of President Johnson from the race has dealt a heavy, although perhaps temporary, blow to Nixon's efforts to establish a reputation as a Republican winner.

Here are the high points of a telephone interview this week, after the President's dramatic withdrawal, of a national cross section of voters surveyed earlier in their homes:

—Sen. Kennedy is ahead of Nixon by 41% to 35%, with former Alabama Gov. George C. Wallace receiving 8% of the vote.

—Sen. McCarthy now holds a comparable 39% to 33% edge over Nixon, with Wallace taking 10%.

—Vice President Humphrey, still undeclared when the survey was conducted, heads Nixon by 35% to 34%, with Wallace capturing 12%.

—Voters interviewed were still reacting with surprise to the President's dramatic announcement, as evidenced by the fact that the undecided vote rose sharply from a level of 7% to 10% ten days earlier to 16% to 19% in this survey.

The biggest gainer appears to be Sen. McCarthy, who dramatically has turned a 9-point deficit to a 6-point lead over Nixon. The Minnesotan picked up 5 points, while the former Vice President slipped a full 10 points. Among Republicans and independents, McCarthy runs strongest of any Democrat against Nixon.

Kennedy widened his previous 5-

Please Turn to Page 24, Col. 1

Los Angeles Times

LARGEST CIRCULATION IN THE WEST, MORE THAN 950,000 DAILY; MORE THAN 1,250,000 SUNDAY.

VOL. LXXXVII 5† FIVE PARTS—PART ONE CC WEDNESDAY MORNING, JUNE 5, 1968 104 PAGES DAILY 10c

KENNEDY SHOT; CONDITION IS CRITICAL

Wounded in Head, Leg at Victory Fete; Suspect Arrested

Israeli Jets Rip Jordan as New Fighting Erupts

Ambassadors of Nations Trade Charges at U.N.; Two Claims Vary Widely

By Associated Press

Israeli jet fighters attacked Jordanian positions Tuesday while Israeli and Jordanian artillery crews fired thunderous barrages across the Jordan River like those of the Mideast War that began a year ago today.

Ambassadors of the two countries traded charges at the United Nations.

Jordanian sources said fighting south of the Sea of Galilee lasted more than eight hours. They said the area was quiet at 9 p.m. and reported nearly 100 Jordanian and about 45 Israeli casualties.

Most Serious Since March

The outbreak was the most serious since March 29, when Israeli planes dive-bombed Jordanian gun emplacements that Israelis said were used to harass farmers across the cease-fire line.

Officials in Jordan said the Israelis fired first Tuesday in a "surprise attack." Israeli spokesman said the attack was in reply to the shelling of six Israeli cooperative settlements.

"We hope that this will teach Jordan the lesson once and for all that the shelling of settlements and army positions is taboo," Maj. Gen. Haim Bar-Lev, Israel's chief of staff, told a newsman.

Bar-Lev said Jordanian forces began by shelling an Israeli army position, then turned their guns on civilian targets. He said there were no attempts to negotiate a cease-fire because Jordanian units appeared to have been put out of action.

Widespread Fires in Fields

Ambassador Muhammad H. El-Farra of Jordan said at the United Nations the shooting set off raging forest fires around the Jordanian city of Irbid, focus of much of the battle. Associated Press correspondent Rodney Pinder reported from Israel that widespread fires were started in ripe wheatfields on both sides of the river.

Yosef Tekoah, Israel's U.N. Ambassador, said three farm people were killed and six wounded in "a large-scale Jordanian assault." He said it became necessary "to order Israeli aircraft to take action in self-defense to silence the sources of fire."

In Amman, a government communique reported casualties on both sides as 32 Jordanian civilians and three soldiers killed, 52 Jordanian civilians and 10 soldiers wounded and an estimated 45 Israeli soldiers killed or wounded.

Please Turn to Page 10, Col. 1

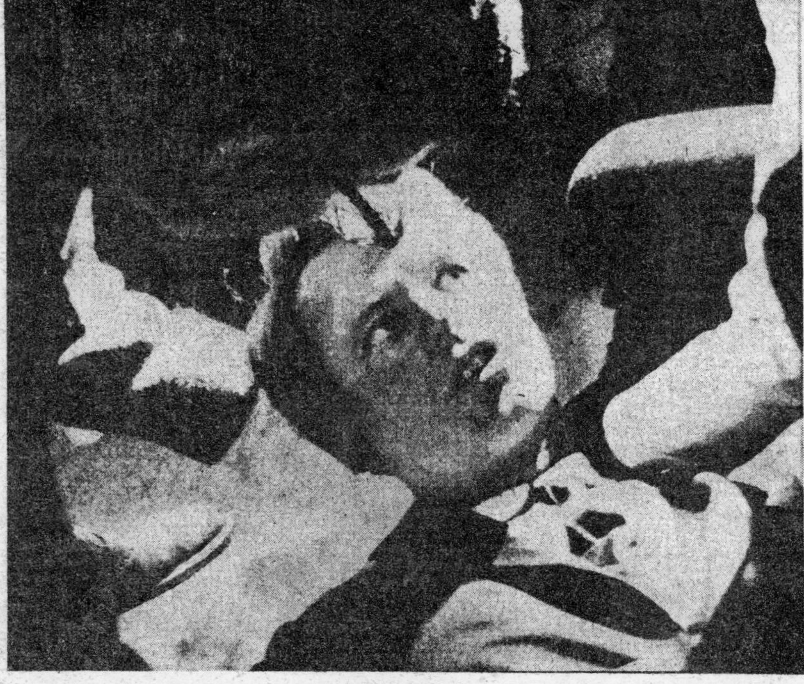

MOMENTS AFTER SHOOTING—Sen. Robert F. Kennedy on floor of Ambassador after he was struck down. Times photo by Boris Yaro

Senator Attacked at Hotel; Bodyguard Captures Gunman

BY DARYL E. LEMBKE
Times Staff Writer

Sen. Robert F. Kennedy was shot in the right ear early this morning in a kitchen of the Ambassador only a few moments after he had made a victory statement after capturing the California Democratic presidential primary.

The New York senator's condition was listed as critical at Good Samaritan Hospital, where he was in the intensive care unit.

A suspect in the s hooting was arrested minutes after the shots were fired and was taken to the police administration building downtown under heavy guard. The suspect was not identified.

Inspector Robert Rock of the Los Angeles police said that only one suspect was involved. Rock said there was no reason to believe more than one person was involved.

The police also have the gun that fired the shots, Rock said.

Witnesses nearby said Kennedy's head was covered with blood and a woman standing nearby was also splattered with blood.

Also shot was Paul Schrade, UAW official. The extent of his injuries was not known.

The shooting occurred at 12:20 a.m.

Shouts, Screams Fill Hall

Shouts and screams filled the packed hall as the call went out over the public address system for a doctor. Three came to Kennedy's aid as his campaign assistants pleaded for his supporters to be calm and clear the hall.

The senator appeared to be in great pain, but conscious.

As he was lifted into the police ambulance, Kennedy was heard to say:

"Oh, no! No! Don't . . .!"

Mrs. Kennedy whispered to him, apparently trying to comfort and reassure her husband. Then she entered the ambulance, doors were closed behind them and the vehicle sped away.

Kennedy was taken first to Central Receiving Hospital, then was transferred to Good Samaritan, his head wrapped in bandages.

Eyewitness account on Page 23, Part 1.

Back in the hotel, shocked and silent members of the Kennedy party gathered in small groups around television sets, attempting to clarify their own memories of the event.

Others left in tears.

Leaving Ambassador

Kennedy was leaving the Ambassador to attend a party at the Factory in the aftermath of his victory in the Democratic primary.

His path through the kitchen was taken on the spur of the moment.

The assailant fired at the senator at close range and began spraying bullets around the kitchen, witnesses said.

William Barry, a former FBI agent, who is Kennedy's bodyguard, grabbed the gun from the man and wrestled him to the floor.

Roosevelt Grier, the football player, then sat on the assailant until police officers arrived.

Please Turn to Page 23, Col. 8

Kennedy Wins Race; Rafferty Apparent Victor Over Kuchel

BY RICHARD BERGHOLZ
Times Political Writer

A late surge of votes from Mexican-American and Negro precincts—particularly in Los Angeles County—made Sen. Robert F. Kennedy the winner in California's Democratic Presidential primary battle Tuesday.

Sen. Eugene McCarthy of Minnesota, Kennedy's major rival in the key primary contest, said he was "reconciled" to a Kennedy triumph. But he said he intended to keep fighting for the party nomination at the Chicago convention Aug. 26.

On the Republican ballot, Dr. Max Rafferty, state superintendent of public instruction, appeared to have ended the political reign of Sen. Thomas H. Kuchel of Anaheim.

The Senate GOP whip and a veteran of 15 years on Capitol Hill ran up leads in Northern and Central California.

But the late surge of votes from Southern California wiped out the Kuchel margin and, on the basis of vote projections, appeared to have swept the conservative Rafferty to an impressive victory.

Rafferty Vote Projection

NBC analysts said their projection of the vote showed Rafferty would get 52% of the Republican vote, and Kuchel would get 45% with the balance going to lesser-known candidates.

The Democratic race for the U.S. Senate nomination was never in doubt.

Former State Controller Alan Cranston easily outdistanced four lesser-known opponents from the very start of the vote-count. For Cranston, it was a political comeback after his defeat two years ago by the current state controller, Republican Houston I. Flournoy.

Cranston hac tried for the Democratic nomination for U.S. senator in 1964 but was defeated by Pierre Salinger, who then lost to Republican George Murphy in the finals.

Returns were badly delayed in Los Angeles County, where the old-style paper ballot voting system was changed this year to the IBM-Votomatic punchcard system.

Delays in transporting the punchcard ballots from the precincts to the 93 collection centers and then to the computer counters were blamed for the breakdown in tabulations.

And in Fresno County, a programming error in computers was blamed for a breakdown that made

Please Turn to Page 23, Col. 3

L.A. COUNTY RETURNS

PRESIDENTIAL DELEGATION

Democratic

1,077 out of 6,924 Precincts

Kennedy	88,891	51%
McCarthy	68,442	39
Lynch	18,193	10

Republican

1,077 out of 6,924 Precincts

Reagan	69,759	100%

U.S. SENATOR

Democratic

1,077 out of 6,924 Precincts

Cranston	84,097	53%
Beilenson	48,109	30
Buchanan	11,378	7
Bennett	9,508	6
Crail	4,839	3

Republican

1,077 out of 6,924 Precincts

Rafferty	62,181	58%
Kuchel	42,478	39
Ware	1,230	1
Jones	864	1
Cammack	787	1

CONGRESS

13th DISTRICT

Democratic

4 out of 53 Precincts

Sheinbaum	204	47%
Horwitz	154	35
Cole	80	18

13th DISTRICT

Republican

4 out of 53 Precincts

Teague (Inc.)	473	100%

17th DISTRICT

Democratic

22 out of 394 Precincts

Anderson	1,459	32%
Tucker	1,167	25
Gibson	860	19
Hayward	425	9
Frantz	377	8
Griffin	167	4
Pipersky	70	2
Van Petten	67	1

17th DISTRICT

Republican

22 out of 394 Precincts

Howard	443	34%
Blatchford	419	32
Sciarrotta	255	20
Hooper	100	8
Berry	84	6

Please Turn to Page 22, Col. 1

STATEWIDE RETURNS

PRESIDENTIAL DELEGATION

Democratic

5,749 out of 21,301 Precincts

Kennedy	303,965	44%
McCarthy	297,449	43
Lynch	89,401	13

Republican

5,679 out of 21,301 Precincts

Reagan	296,348	100%

U.S. SENATOR

Democratic

5,613 out of 21,301 Precincts

Cranston	360,066	61%
Beilenson	116,916	20
Bennett	55,306	9
Buchanan	43,536	7
Crail	17,246	3

Republican

5,624 out of 21,301 Precincts

Kuchel	244,446	55%
Rafferty	186,232	42
Jones	3,920	1
Ware	5,590	1
Cammack	5,452	1

Kennedy Shooting May Alter Nature of '68 Campaign

BY ROBERT J. DONOVAN
Times Washington Bureau Chief

The shooting of Sen. Robert F. Kennedy at the moment of his California primary victory could change the whole nature of the 1968 campaign.

If he should recover in time to continue his quest for the Democratic Presidential nomination, public sympathy could fan the fires of his support to a degree that would diminish Vice President Humphrey's current lead.

If Kennedy is disabled and cannot continue the race, the result would approach a national crisis.

Stability of Politics

If the United States has reached a point where candidates for the Presidency are retired by gunfire, the stability of the American political process is in jeopardy.

If Kennedy was not safe in the midst of his followers, what security would there be, say, for Richard M. Nixon in crowded streets or Humphrey in a typical mob scene in an airport?

In this new disorder in America, with its already grim landmarks in

Please Turn to Page 26, Col. 1

KIDNAPING, ROBBERY ON SUBWAY

Reporter Indicts Himself and Passengers for Doing Nothing

BY BRIAN D. BOYER
Exclusive to The Times from the Chicago Sun-Times

CHICAGO — Two men who claimed they were police officers kidnaped the father of four children from a subway Monday while half a dozen persons watched without attempting to assist him.

The victim, Eddie Martin, 38, was then robbed of $300 in wages and savings in a station vestibule.

The kidnaping and the robbery should not have happened, if the train conductor and Martin's fellow passengers had done their duty—or police had been guarding the train.

I know, because I was one of the witnesses who lacked courage and resolve at the critical moment. I was one of the six passengers, confused and fearful of "getting involved," who rode with Eddie Martin and the two thugs.

Martin was not hurt but he could have been injured or killed.

What happened and what didn't happen is an indictment of myself and my fellow citizens, who found it all too easy to watch danger stalk and capture the other guy.

I boarded the mostly empty train at 2:07 a.m. on my way home from work.

Facing me in the seat across the

Please Turn to Page 34, Col. 1

THE WEATHER

Light smog today.

Heavy night and morning low cloudiness with partial afternoon clearing today and Thursday. High today and Thursday near 73. Low Thursday near 59. High Tuesday, 70; low, 63.

Complete weather information on Page 8, Part 2.

FEATURE INDEX

Southland elections on Page 9, Part 2.

TRANSPORTING OF CARDS DELAYED

Flow of Ballots to Computer Bogs Down

BY JOHN KENDALL
Times Staff Writer

Two major breakdowns in plans to use a new electronic voting and tabulating system disrupted Tuesday's primary election in Los Angeles County.

The initial vote count, in tabulating summaries for news media, ran more than an hour behind the old-fashioned manual counting system.

The reason: delays at polling precincts in verifying and certifying the punch card ballots before they were transported to 93 checking centers throughout the county.

The vaunted electronic devices, capable of tabulating 14,000 ballots a minute, virtually stood idle for more than two hours after the polls were closed.

A report that the computer equipment had broken down, causing the delay was denied by a spokesman for International Business Machines at a computer center on Wilshire Blvd.

Except for absentee ballots, the punch card ballots failed to arrive in bulk for processing until about 10:30 p.m., he said.

Earlier, hundreds of voters were confused by another breakdown — late delivery of sample ballots. Many said they never received their sample ballots at all.

It was the first time punch card ballots were used throughout Los Angeles County and tabulated on electronic data processing equipment.

An administrative analyst for the county said sheriff's officers moved on schedule in transporting ballots from the 93 checking centers to the computer centers.

"We just didn't get them for an hour or more because they were held up at the polling precincts," he said. "Precinct clerical workers had no prior experience in handling cards and probably spent more time than planned in verifying that the number of ballots corresponded with the number of voters who signed polling sheets at their precincts."

The delay in tabulating Los Angeles County's vote caused suspense to build up throughout the nation during the night, because the county's returns were expected to be decisive in the race between Sens. Eugene J. McCarthy and Robert F. Kennedy for the Democratic presidential nomination.

Please Turn to Page 28, Col. 3

Los Angeles Times

LARGEST CIRCULATION IN THE WEST, 958,124 DAILY, 1,269,931 SUNDAY.

VOL. LXXXVII 4† SEVEN PARTS—PART ONE CC THURSDAY MORNING, AUGUST 29, 1968 146 PAGES DAILY 10c

HUMPHREY NOMINATED ON 1ST BALLOT

Kidnaper Seizes Son of Banker in Beverly Hills

Gunman Posing as Worker Flees With Boy, 4, After $250,000 Ransom Demand

BY ART BERMAN and JOHN KENDALL
Times Staff Writers

The 4½-year-old son of a Beverly Hills banker was kidnaped from the family home Wednesday morning by a gunman who demanded ransom of $250,000 in $20 bills.

The abduction occurred only a few blocks from the home where another $250,000 kidnaping took place a year and a half ago. That case is still unsolved.

Curly-haired Stanley Stalford Jr., son of the board chairman of Fidelity Bank, was taken from his mother Wednesday by a man who fled in the family's Cadillac, police said.

By late Wednesday, there was no word on the child's fate. Police said they had found the getaway car abandoned, but would give no further details.

Beverly Hills Police Chief Clinton H. Anderson said the parents, Mr. and Mrs. Stanley M. Stalford, were anxious to pay off the ransom.

Wore Only Bathing Suit

The boy, an only child, wore only a bathing suit when he was abducted.

The kidnaper, dressed in aluminum hard hat and blue work clothes, gained access to the Stalford residence on N. Palm Drive by posing as a workman.

He told Stalford's wife, Joanne, that he had to check electrical circuits in connection with a renovation project on a house next door.

Once inside, the man brandished a revolver with a six-inch barrel, tried unsuccessfully to get cash, bound Mrs. Stalford and fled with the boy.

"I'm going to take the child with me," he was quoted as saying. "I'll contact your husband later. I want $250,000 in $20 bills."

The gunman warned Mrs. Stalford not to call police, and it was only by accident that his department learned of the kidnaping, Anderson said.

Mother Reported Hysterical

Mrs. Stalford made her way to a telephone and called her husband, but was too hysterical to explain the situation, the chief said.

The husband thought the boy might have fallen into the pool, Anderson said.

Stalford called the Fire Department for an ambulance, and a police car routinely joined in responding to the call.

Officer Tom Rhodes said he heard screams coming from the house and, when no one answered the front door, he broke in through a side screen door.

He said he found Mrs. Stalford lying in a hallway, tape still on her wrists and legs, and screaming: "My son's been kidnaped!"

Rhodes got a description of the getaway car, notified the police station and word quickly was flashed on police teletypes and radios.

Please Turn to Page 30, Col. 1

John Gordon Mein
(AP) Wirephoto

U.S. Ambassador Assassinated in Guatemala Ambush

GUATEMALA CITY (AP) — U.S. Ambassador John Gordon Mein was shot to death Wednesday in an ambush of his limousine on a main thoroughfare of this violence-ridden Central American capital. The unknown assassins escaped.

In a swift strike, apparently involving both a car and a truck, the 54-year-old career diplomat was cut down as he tried to escape after the ambushers stopped his chauffeur-driven car.

The midafternoon shooting occurred a few blocks from where two U.S. military attaches, Col. John Daniel Webber and Capt. Ernest A. Monric, were slain in a similar attack last Jan. 16 during a wave of terrorism by both rightists and leftists. A Communist-led insurgent group claimed credit for those two murders.

Attache Describes Slaying

Richard Knowles of Waterloo, Iowa, the embassy's press attache, gave this account of the assassination of Mein:

Mein and his Guatemalan chauffeur were en route from home to the embassy when a car pulled up in front of the limousine. At the same time a truck pulled up behind the limousine. Two men got out of either the car or truck, or both, and forced the chaffeur out of the limousine.

Mein then tried to flee and was cut down by a burst of machine-gun fire. The attack occurred at 3:05 p.m. on Avenida de la Reforma, one of the main streets leading downtown from a fashionable suburb.

The ambassador's life had been threatened previously by the Revolutionary Armed Forces, a Cuban-backed Communist terrorist group.

In Washington, a State Department spokesman said the United States "will request the government of Guatemala to conduct a full investigation of all the circumstances of the tragedy." A spokesman said President Johnson, Secretary of

Please Turn to Page 4, Col. 4

Chicago Police Charge, Club Crowd at Hotel

Tear Gas Hits Humphrey as Attack Routs Hundreds of Protesters, Bystanders

BY RICHARD T. COOPER
Times Staff Writer

CHICAGO—City police hemmed several hundred demonstrators and bystanders against a wall of the Democratic National Convention's headquarters hotel Wednesday night and flailed them with nightsticks, ignoring a deputy police superintendent who was shouting orders to stop the attack.

The incident was the most violent of a continuing series of eruptions in the downtown area around the Conrad Hilton, convention center for the Democratic Party.

An air of tension and disorder continued in the area into the early morning hours. National Guard troops, with fixed bayonets, flooded the area at midnight, and at 1 a.m. busloads of delegates from the convention hall returned to find double rows of troops forming a square in front of the Hilton.

Jeeps with machine guns were drawn into some intersections, and a crowd of 4,000 milled through the area.

Roving Bands of Protesters

Earlier, tear gas had been used in an attempt to control roving bands of protesters.

Hundreds of passersby and hotel guests were caught by the gas and flying police riot sticks. Vice President Humphrey, whose 25th-floor suite windows let in the gas, had to rush into a shower to bathe away the stinging fumes.

More than 100 persons were injured and more than 150 arrested in dozens of clashes, police officials said.

Protesters set harassing fires in trash baskets along downtown streets, and, shortly before 11 p.m., a chemical bomb flooded the Hilton lobby with nauseating vapors, virtually clearing it.

Sen. Eugene J. McCarthy, who witnessed the incident in front of the Hilton from his 23rd-floor suite, went down to inspect conditions on the street just before midnight, accompanied by 18 Secret Service agents.

A spokesman said the senator was "extremely concerned about these

Please Turn to Page 2, Col. 5

Eisenhower Taken Off Critical List

WASHINGTON (AP)—Doctors for former President Dwight D. Eisenhower said Wednesday night they no longer consider his immediate condition as critical.

But his overall situation following his seventh heart attack Aug. 16 is serious, they said.

In response to questions from reporters the doctors said it is not yet possible to say whether Gen. Eisenhower will be able to lead a relatively normal life.

The doctors at the Army's Walter Reed Hospital said:

"Because of the extent of Gen. Eisenhower's underlying coronary artery disease, his present condition must still be considered serious, albeit not necessarily critical at this time. The long range outlook is still

Please Turn to Page 12, Col. 1

HE'S IN!—Vice President Humphrey leaps to his feet in front of a television set in his hotel as he sees himself win the nomination.
(AP) Wirephoto

Delegates Reject Peace Plank in Victory for Johnson Policies

BY RICHARD BERGHOLZ
Times Political Writer

CHICAGO—The Democratic Party, in a convulsive effort to resolve its differences over Vietnam war policy, Wednesday decided to commit its candidates to the basic policies of President Johnson.

The decision came when the convention delegates voted 1,567 3/4 to 1,041 1/4 to reject a so-called peace plank which asked for an unconditional halt to bombing of North Vietnam and phased disengagement from the military operations in South Vietnam.

After turning back the challenge of the end-the-war advocates in the party, the delegates then approved a national party platform which takes a more cautious stance on war policy.

In terms of significance to the presidential campaign this fall and the degree of enthusiasm Democrats might be expected to show for it, the vote-rich states of California and New York went for the minority plank by overwhelming margins, Pennsylvania went 92 1/4 to 35 1/4 for the majority plank and Michigan divided 52 to 44 for the minority view.

Back Majority View

Illinois, under the heavy hand of Mayor Richard J. Daley of Chicago, cast its vote 105 to 13 for the majority plank and Texas, under the leadership of Gov. John B. Connally, cast all of its 104 votes for the majority view.

The decision, acted out in more than three hours of tension-packed debate on the convention floor, didn't come easily.

There were repeated chants of "stop the war" from the dissidents. There were angry charges of "appeasement" hurled at the peace plank advocates. And there was a wearing of black armbands and the singing of "We Shall Overcome" by

Please Turn to Page 2, Col. 1

McCarthy Predicts Humphrey Will Be Defeated by Nixon

BY KEN REICH
Times Staff Writer

CHICAGO — Sen. Eugene J. McCarthy (D-Minn.), still indicating it would be unlikely that he would support Vice President Humphrey for President this fall, predicted Wednesday that Richard M. Nixon would win the election.

The Minnesota senator, calling Humphrey a "total" backer of the Johnson Administration's Vietnam foreign policy, conditioned support for the Vice President on acceptance by Humphrey of a Dovish position on the war.

McCarthy added he would have nothing further to say about his position on Humphrey for about two weeks, but indicated he thought the possibility of Humphrey changing his war stand was almost nil.

Asked who he expected to win in November, McCarthy replied:

"I have said the Republicans will win this year."

McCarthy later called Humphrey and congratulated him on winning, but still refused to say if he would support the Vice President.

In an afternoon interview with

Please Turn to Page D, Col. 5

Scene Perhaps Most Violent in U.S. Politics

BY ROBERT J. DONOVAN
Times Washington Bureau Chief

CHICAGO—Vice President Humphrey was nominated for President by the Democrats on the first ballot Wednesday night in perhaps the wildest and most violent and bitter convention scene in American history.

Against a background of street fighting raging downtown, delegates in the convention booed, shook fists, yelled, shoved and turned Chicago's Mayor Richard J. Daley into the personification of a villain.

The roll call was preceded by a brawl on the floor over a security check of a delegate's credentials and by clashes downtown between antiwar demonstrators and police and national guardsmen in which tear gas blew into Humphrey's 25th floor suite in the Conrad Hilton Hotel. He was seized by coughing and sneezing.

Not even thought of for the Democratic nomination five months ago, the Vice President rolled to victory over his closest rival, Sen. Eugene J. McCarthy of Minnesota—a political phenomenon who changed the political climate of the country but could not change the political machinery of the party.

Tabulation of Votes

The balloting was as follows:

Humphrey	1,761 3/4
Sen. McCarthy	601
Sen. McGovern	146 1/2
Rev. Phillips	67 1/2

The outcome never had been in doubt after the earlier collapse of a movement to draft Sen. Edward M. (Ted) Kennedy, whose refusal to run left Humphrey impregnable.

Clubbings, arrests, unpatriotic gestures and police, police and more police outside the convention hall and boos and antiwar chants inside not only marked the day on which the Democrats nominated their candidate, but defined the nature of the problem that lies ahead of him in the campaign. The old political warhorses, Humphrey and Nixon, will be running in a different kind of America this fall.

Typical of the fervid feeling in the convention, a Colorado delegate, Robert Maytag, raised thunderous applause when he interrupted the nominating proceedings and asked the chair:

"Is there any rule under which Mayor Daley can be compelled to suspend the police state terror in Chicago, perpetrated this minute on kids in front of the Conrad Hilton?"

Daley Shouts at Ribicoff

Moments later the mayor was on his feet shouting, booing and shaking his fist at Sen. Abraham A. Ribicoff of Connecticut on the podium. While nominating Sen. George S. McGovern of South Dakota, the suave, mild-mannered Ribicoff had infuriated the Chicago mayor by saying that if McGovern were President, it would not have been necessary to bring the "Gestapo" and National Guard to the city for the convention.

When reporters crowded around Daley, he ordered security guards to push them back up the aisle. Even as the mayor was on his feet a crescendo of boos rolled through the hall.

Please Turn to Page 18, Col. 1

Assembly in Prague Refuses to Approve Moscow Accord

PRAGUE (AP)—The Czechoslovak National Assembly refused to ratify the Moscow accord Wednesday and declared the Soviet-led occupation illegal.

The National Assembly urged the reformist government to seek an early deadline for withdrawal of the Soviet bloc troops as Soviet armored cars patrolled the streets and soldiers guarded the doors of newspaper offices, radio and television studios and the office of the national news agency.

The eight-point National Assembly resolution stated:

—Continued occupation of Czechoslovakia is "illegal and violates the United Nations Charter and the Warsaw Treaty."

—The Czechoslovak delegation is thanked for its efforts at Moscow to "remove the present abnormal situation in the country."

—The National Assembly is convinced that Czechoslovakia must remain in the socialist community.

—The National Assembly is convinced that the Czechoslovak army is able to defend the country's western borders without foreign assistance and calls on the government to insist on a firm date for the withdrawal of the foreign armies as soon as possible.

—The National Assembly demands that all government organs and mass media be allowed to resume normal free activities. It demands the release of all persons illegally arrested by Czechoslovak or foreign security organs since the beginning of the occupation.

The National Assembly insists on uncompromising pursuance of the principles proclaimed in the reformist action program of the Communist Party and the program of the legal government. The democratization process should be continued without interference.

Please Turn to Page 9, Col. 1

FEATURE INDEX

NEGATIVE DECISION HIS OWN

Frantic Efforts to Draft Kennedy Disclosed

BY D.J.R. BRUCKNER
Times Staff Writer

CHICAGO—Sen. Edward M. (Ted) Kennedy's decision Wednesday morning to stop a draft movement on his behalf at the Democratic National Convention was entirely his own.

Ultimately, it was for personal reasons, as his official statement said. But it was a personal decision that involved the trust, and possibly the power, of leaders of some powerful political forces. These leaders had asked him repeatedly to give some overt sign that he would be willing to run this year for the Presidency.

Among the men seeking the sign were Sen. Eugene J. McCarthy of Minnesota, Mayor Richard J. Daley of Chicago and Jesse M. Unruh, Speaker of the California Assembly.

Apparently Unruh was the most public leader of the draft-Kennedy movement and Daley was its most powerful. McCarthy came late to it, waiting until Tuesday evening to offer the full weight of his support to a draft movement for Kennedy. The movement was still possible at midnight Tuesday, but it died a few hours later.

Finally, it was the personal feeling of the 36-year-old Massachusetts senator that this was the wrong year for him to run, that the circumstances were wrong for a draft at this convention and that, personally, he did not want to get into the fight, which led him to make a "final, firm" decision, which was "not subject to further consideration," against accepting the presidential nomination.

Under the personal feeling, of course, there is a complex series of

Please Turn to Page 20, Col. 1

THE WEATHER

Moderate to heavy smog today.

Sunny today and Friday with high both days near 96. Low Friday near 66. High Wednesday, 93; low, 68.

Complete weather information on Page 19, Part 3.

Los Angeles Times

LARGEST CIRCULATION IN THE WEST, 958,124 DAILY, 1,269,931 SUNDAY.

VOL. LXXXVII 2† SEVEN PARTS—PART ONE CC WEDNESDAY MORNING, NOVEMBER 6, 1968 120 PAGES DAILY 10¢

NIXON EDGING CLOSE TO MAGIC 270

Carries California; Cranston Leading Senate Contest

Southland Votes Decisive in President Race

BY RICHARD BERGHOLZ
Times Political Writer

Republican Richard M. Nixon rode a late surge of Southern California votes to an all-important victory early Wednesday in the fight for California's 40 electoral votes.

A strong showing in Los Angeles, Orange and San Diego counties, which account for more than half the state's votes, pushed Nixon to a hard-fought victory over Democratic Vice President Hubert H. Humphrey in the state.

Third-party candidate George C. Wallace never developed into a major force in California.

Returns from 4,851 precincts, 22% of the state's 21,590 precincts, showed:

Nixon	747,102
Humphrey	721,681
Wallace	117,026

The Nixon triumph still didn't push the native Californian over the 270 electoral-vote mark, the margin he needed for the national victory.

The powerful Republican showing in Southern California apparently made it uncertain whether Democrat Alan Cranston could claim the U.S. Senate race over Republican Max Rafferty, the state superintendent of public instruction.

Returns from 4,581 precincts, 22% of the state's 21,590 precincts, showed:

Cranston	831,798
Rafferty	697,168
Jacobs	19,476

Cranston, former state controller, jumped into an early and commanding lead in the race, bolstered by a strong showing in Northern California.

But Rafferty was expected to pile up a big edge in Orange and San Diego counties and was making a horse race of it in Los Angeles County after trailing through most of the early count.

Only an hour after the polls closed, NBC said Cranston would win, and CBS agreed shortly afterward.

Cranston claimed victory in a speech to his supporters at the Biltmore before midnight.

Rafferty, however, refused to concede defeat from his headquarters at the Ambassador and said he would withhold any further statement until later today.

As the national vote count progressed through the night, it became more and more evident that neither Nixon nor Humphrey was in a position to claim victory until California's big haul of 40 electoral votes were decided.

Agonizingly Slow Count

And the California vote count was agonizingly slow getting started.

First Nixon, then Humphrey took the lead in the California balloting.

The Republican ran surprisingly strong in such normally Democratic areas as Alameda County, Sacramento County, Fresno County and San Bernardino.

Los Angeles County—where 38% of the state's voters reside — gave Nixon an early lead but inconclusive lead.

But returns from Orange and San

Please Turn to Page 18, Col. 1

BACK IN NEW YORK—Richard M. Nixon and wife Pat in car after arrival on flight from California. UPI Wirephoto

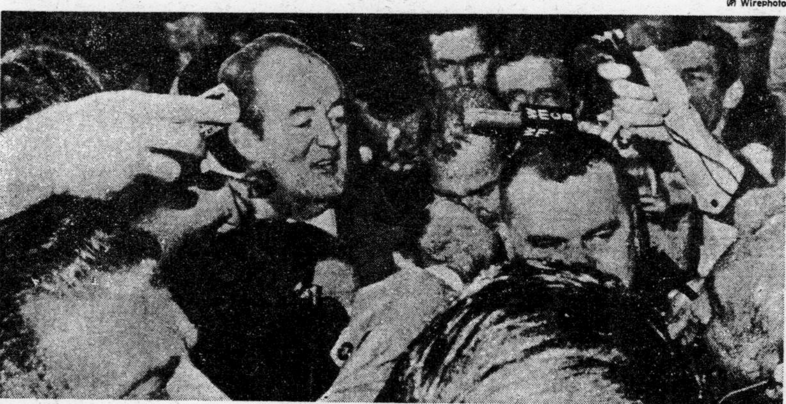

SPIRITS HIGH—Vice President Humphrey is engulfed in crowd at Minneapolis election headquarters. UPI photo

Humphrey Runs Tight Race but Odds Favor Republican

BY ROBERT J. DONOVAN
Times Washington Bureau Chief

NEW YORK—Richard M. Nixon forged ahead early today in another hair-raising presidential election finish as he wrested California and apparently New Jersey from Vice President Humphrey.

He also was making a strong finis in Ohio. Thus it seemed increasingly likely that Nixon would be elected, ending Democratic control of the White House that has lasted for 28 of the last 36 years.

Final results from Ohio, Illinois and Texas may not be known until later today, so the outcome remains inconclusive and it is still possible that neither candidate will emerge with the 270 electoral votes needed for victory. Such a deadlock would be due to the votes drained away from the two major party candidates by George C. Wallace, who nevertheless did not run nearly so well as expected.

If Nixon's late lead does hold up and puts him in the White House, however, he will possess a most bewildering mandate because of the nearly dead heat in which the popular voting resulted.

Humphrey Optimistic

In Minneapolis, Vice President Humphrey, still exuding optimism, went to bed before it was evident that California was going to Nixon.

"At best," he said, "it is a donnybrook. Anything can happen."

Throughout the evening Nixon never left his 36th floor suite at the Waldorf-Astoria Hotel in New York.

In a race reminiscent of the Kennedy-Nixon cliff-hanger of 1960 and the Truman-Dewey thriller of 1948, the popular votes with 75% counted stood early today as follows:

Nixon	22,653,987 or 43%
Humphrey	22,608,830 or 42%
Wallace	7,851,763 or 15%

The electoral vote totals were:

Nixon—238 in 29 states.

Humphrey—166 in 12 states and the District of Columbia.

Wallace—45 in 5 states.

The odds however, favored Nixon to win a majority in the electoral college, as he won California's pivotal 40 electoral votes.

The California victory for Nixon coupled with wins in Ohio (26) and Illinois (26) would put him over the magic 270 figure.

If the final returns should give neither Nixon nor Humphrey 270 electoral votes, a delay of weeks might ensue before the identities of the new President and Vice President are known.

The issue might be decided when the presidential electors—the Electoral College—vote on Dec. 16, if enough of the Wallace electors should shift either way to give Humphrey or Nixon the needed votes.

But if the Wallace electors should stick with their candidate, preserving the deadlock, the House of Representatives next January would have to choose a President for the first time since 1825. The Senate would choose the Vice President. The two could be of different parties.

All along the route of this selection process, however, there might be lawsuits or legislative attempts to revise procedures, with the result that any number of unforeseeable developments might occur.

Seeds of Crisis

The situation would hold the seeds of a grave political constitutional crisis at the very time, for example, when the Vietnam negotiations are entering a delicate stage.

Potentially the most ominous element in the picture is Wallace's announced intention of bargaining with each of the two major parties for his votes in the Electoral College. Playing kingmaker, his purpose would be to throw the election in the Electoral College to whichever party would agree—if one would—to further his program.

Humphrey won New York, Michigan, Massachusetts, Connecticut, Washington, Rhode Island, West Virginia, Maine, the District of Columbia, Hawaii, Maryland, Minnesota, Pennsylvania, California and New Jersey.

Nixon won Oregon, Idaho, Wyoming, Nevada, Utah, Colorado, New Mexico, North Dakota, South Dakota, Nebraska, Kansas, Iowa, Oklahoma, Wisconsin, Indiana, Kentucky, Tennessee, Virginia, North Carolina, South Carolina, Florida, Delaware, New Hampshire, Vermont, Montana, Arizona and Alaska.

Wallace carried Arkansas, Louisiana, Mississippi, Alabama and Georgia.

Please Turn to Page 28, Col. 1

16 Valley State Students Face Court in Occupation of Building

Police Meet With Leaders of Sit-in Demonstration and Ask Voluntary Surrender; Reagan Hails School's Action

BY JOHN DREYFUSS and DIAL TORGERSON
Times Staff Writers

Swift retribution was launched Tuesday by police and college administrators against students accused of forcibly occupying a building at San Fernando Valley State College.

Paul Blomgren, acting president of the college, said students who took part in the occupation will be suspended. Police Chief Tom Reddin said those who broke laws will be arrested and prosecuted.

Later, two police community relations officers urged 16 suspects allegedly linked to criminal acts to surrender voluntarily.

Police indicated there may be other suspects.

The request for voluntary surrender of suspects was made at a three-hour meeting with leaders of the Black Students Union at Northridge Hall. The meeting was recessed at 8:30 p.m.

"We are maintaining close contact with the BSU and feel our discussions so far have been leading in the right direction," Police Inspector John McAllister said.

"Our investigation is continuing and arrests—either on a voluntary or involuntary basis—will be made with all possible dispatch."

Earlier, Blomgren's office said 12 students had been suspended and five others subjected to undisclosed "disciplinary action."

The acting president's prompt action was commended by Gov. Reagan—and, on campus, by the Associated Students Senate.

The occupation occurred Monday at the administration building of the big Northridge campus.

Forty to 50 members of the BSU, to dramatize what they termed a "racist attitude" on the part of physical education instructors, took control of the fifth floor of the administration building. More than 100 others, some of them members of Students for a Democratic Society

Please Turn to Page 8, Col. 1

Democrats Rebuff GOP's Attempt to End Congress Rule

BY VINCENT J. BURKE
Times Staff Writer

NEW YORK—Democrats Tuesday rebuffed far more easily than they had anticipated a Republican attempt to end their 14 year rule over Congress.

Voters apparently gave Republicans no more than half a dozen of the 30 additional seats they needed to win control of the House.

Republicans scored a net gain of four to six seats in their battle for Senate control, but that still leaves Democrats with a majority of close to 3 to 2 in the new Senate.

With the result still uncertain in 91 of the 435 House races, an NBC computer projection indicated that the lineup in the new House would be: Democrats, 245, Republicans, 190. That would be a GOP gain of two seats over the present House lineup.

In gubernatorial races, Republicans captured Democratic-held statehouses in Indiana and Vermont and were heading toward party gains in governorship races in Iowa and New Hampshire. But Democrats unseated Republican Gov. John Chafee of Rhode Island and were leading in battles for GOP-held statehouses in Montana and New Mexico.

As for the new Congress, the prospective result is that the conservative-bent House will be a trifle more conservative and the liberal-tinged Senate will be somewhat less liberal.

It has been the House, where a

Please Turn to Page 33, Col. 1

U.S. and Hanoi Delay Formal Talks; Saigon Continues Snub

BY ARTHUR J. DOMMEN
Times Staff Writer

PARIS—The United States and North Vietnam Tuesday postponed today's scheduled formal session of the Paris talks in the absence of a delegation from Saigon.

They agreed, though, to continue discussing procedures for the widened talks on Vietnam which they both have accepted.

Neither side saw any useful purpose in holding a formal meeting today without representatives of the Republic of Vietnam, which refuses to attend, informed diplomatic sources said.

Mrs. Nguyen Thi Binh, the leader of the advance delegation of the South Vietnam National Liberation Front, which arrived in Paris Monday, told a packed press conference her delegation was prepared to begin work "as from tomorrow, Nov. 6."

But North Vietnam did not insist on holding to the Wednesday date, the sources said, and the first meeting of the widened talks was put off without fixing a new date.

The United States views the coming talks as two-sided, but North Vietnam and the NLF view them as four-cornered. The Republic of Vietnam has not given its agreement to participate at all.

"We continue to consult with the government of the Republic of Vietnam in this matter and are hopeful its delegation to these

Please Turn to Page 6, Col. 1

FEATURE INDEX

THE WEATHER

Patchy clouds and fog late nights and early mornings today and Thursday with some increasing high cloudiness, but fair and slightly warmer afternoons. High today and Thursday near 74. High Tuesday, 69; low, 52.

STATEWIDE RETURNS

PRESIDENT

4,851 Precincts out of 21,590

Nixon (R)	747,102	47%
Humphrey (D)	721,681	45%
Wallace (AI)	117,102	7%

U.S. SENATE

4,851 Precincts out of 21,590

Cranston (D)	831,798	54%
Rafferty (R)	697,168	45%
Jacobs (PF)	19,476	1%

State Measure No. 1A
Tax Exemption

6,697 Precincts out of 21,590

Yes	1,174,201	58%
No	852,814	42%

State Measure No. 1
Constitutional Revision

7,120 Precincts out of 21,590

No	1,056,703	55%
Yes	855,053	45%

State Measure No. 2
Taxation—
Publicly Owner Property

7,120 Precincts out of 21,590

Yes	1,034,563	52%
No	968,159	48%

State Measure No. 3
State College Bonds

7,120 Precincts out of 21,590

No	1,125,454	54%
Yes	971,541	46%

State Measure No. 4
Personal Income Taxes

5,921 Precincts out of 21,590

Yes	824,282	50%
No	832,320	50%

Please Turn to Page 27, Col. 4

L.A. COUNTY RETURNS

PRESIDENT

3,481 Precincts out of 7,086

Nixon (R)	621,873	48%
Humphrey (D)	588,428	46%
Wallace (AI)	72,358	6%

U.S. SENATE

3,481 Precincts out of 7,086

Cranston (D)	646,927	51%
Rafferty (R)	603,215	48%
Jacobs (PF)	16,873	1%

CONGRESS

13th District

15 Precincts out of 59

Teague (R) Inc.	4,244	68%
Sheinbaum (D)	2,009	32%

17th District

159 Precincts out of 403

Anderson (D)	31,013	52%
Blatchford (R)	28,219	47%
Dobbs (PF)	690	1%

19th District

215 Precincts out of 432

Holifield (D) Inc.	48,629	64%
Jones (R)	25,352	33%
Cook (AI)	1,996	3%

20th District

307 Precincts out of 539

Smith (R) Inc.	79,933	70%
White (D)	31,906	28%
Clarke (PF)	1,751	2%

Please Turn to Page 26, Col. 1

EXTRA

MONDAY

FINAL

COMPLETE RACING

Los Angeles Times

LARGEST CIRCULATION IN THE WEST, 975,491 DAILY, 1,308,711 SUNDAY.

VOL. LXXXVIII | FIVE PARTS—PART ONE | MONDAY MORNING, JULY 21, 1969 | 84 PAGES | Copyright © 1969 Los Angeles Times | DAILY 10c

WALK ON MOON

'That's One Small Step for Man... One Giant Leap for Mankind'

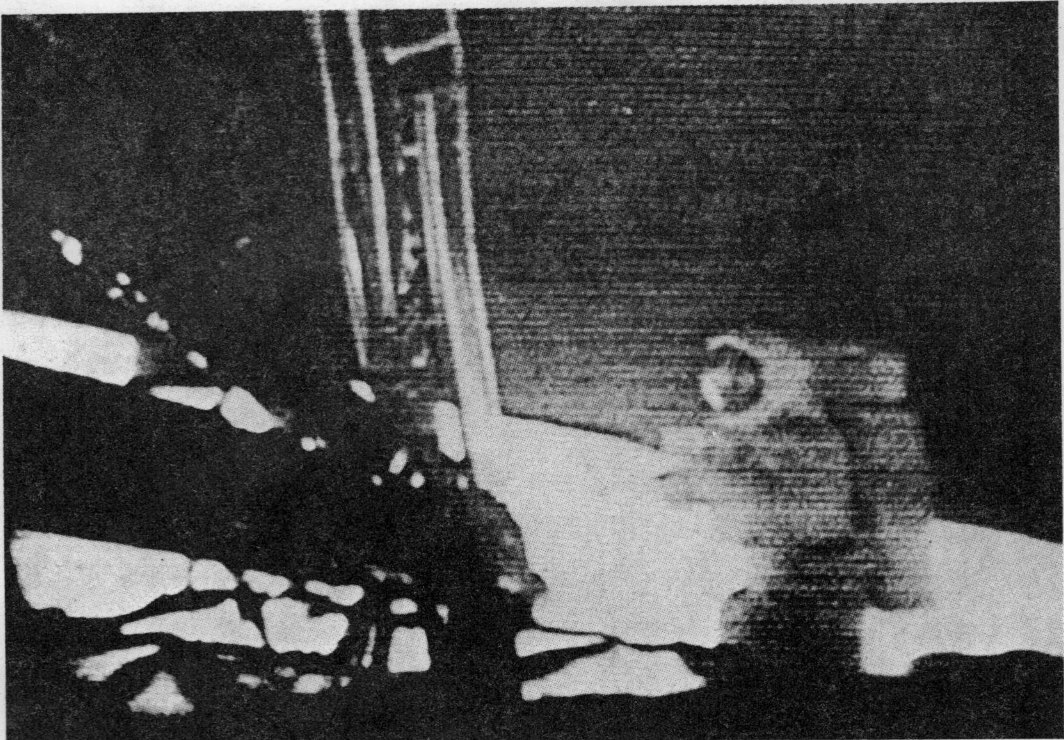

TAKING A WALK—Neil A. Armstrong, wearing life-support backpack, steps on lunar surface after descending the ladder of the spacecraft.

PLANTING THE FLAG—Armstrong and Edwin E. Aldrin Jr. setting Stars and Stripes on the moon. Reflecting light, left, is a landing leg.
UPI Wirephotos

Armstrong Beams His Words to Earth After Testing Surface

BY MARVIN MILES and RUDY ABRAMSON
Times Staff Writers

HOUSTON—U.S. astronauts stepped onto the surface of the moon Sunday and explored its bleak, forbidding crust in man's first visit to another celestial body.

Apollo 11 Commander Neil A. Armstrong climbed slowly down the ladder from the spaceship Eagle, and became the first man to set foot on the lunar surface.

As Armstrong swung his left boot to the surface of the moon at 7:56 p.m., PDT, he gave millions of spellbound television viewers words sure to live in history:

"That's one small step for man . . . one giant leap for mankind."

Nearly seven hours earlier, Armstrong had averted possible disaster by taking full manual control of the vehicle on landing, selecting a safe spot for man's first landing on the moon.

Much of the civilized world watched and listened as Armstrong and fellow explorer Edwin E. Aldrin Jr., who followed him down the steps about 20 minutes later, collected rocks which may reveal the oldest secrets of the solar system.

Collins Waits, Listens

Waiting and listening in lunar orbit was the third member of the Apollo crew, command module pilot Michael Collins.

As he took his first steps on the lunar surface, Armstrong could be seen in remarkably clear television pictures taken by a camera attached to the lunar module descent stage. He described what he found.

He said the surface "appears fine-grained, almost like a powder. I can kick it up loosely with my foot. I only go in maybe an eighth of an inch."

Armstrong said the lunar module's round footpads penetrated the surface only one to two inches.

At first the black-and-white pictures were silhouettes, but then as Armstrong moved away from the ladder his bulky life support pack could be discerned. In almost no time Armstrong was moving around the surface rapidly—quickly adapting to the lunar environment.

The spacecraft commander went to work on his first major assignment, the gathering of a contingency sample of lunar soil. This is a "quick grab" of sample material, about two pounds, retrieved with a butterfly net-type device.

The contingency sample was planned to assure that at least some lunar material would be brought back to earth if for any reason the astronauts had to launch from the moon in an emergency.

At one point he said he had penetrated the surface six to eight inches with the sampler and told Mission Control, "I'm sure I could push it in further."

Practices Several Jumps

Aldrin was down on the surface of the moon at 8:16 p.m. with an athletic drop of what appeared to be about three feet. He then immediately practiced several jumps to determine the effect of the moon's weight gravity on his balance and coordination.

Mission Control here asked Armstrong if he foresaw any difficulty transferring equipment back and forth between the surface and the lunar module cabin in the top stage of the spacecraft and his cryptic reply was "Negative."

As soon as Aldrin was on the surface, both men could be seen by the television audience working near the ladder which was mounted on the lander's forward leg.

One of the first tasks of the two men after Armstrong gathered the contingency sample and stowed it in a bag in his spacesuit pocket, was to

Please Turn to Page 10, Col. 1

TALKS TO ASTRONAUTS

Heavens Have Become Part of Man's World, Nixon Says

WASHINGTON — For two minutes Sunday night, President Nixon spoke via radiotelephone to his farthest flung countrymen—American astronauts in the moon's Sea of Tranquility—and told them:

"Because of what you have done, the heavens have become part of man's world and, as you talk to us from the Sea of Tranquility, it inspires us to redouble our efforts to bring peace and tranquility to the earth."

Those were the official words of the President of the United States, speaking from the august Oval Office of the White House.

A few minutes earlier, Mr. Nixon, like television viewers all over the world, sat in a smaller, private, more informal office and watched astronaut Neil A. Armstrong climb down from his moon landing ship to set the first human feet on the moon.

The President, his eyes fixed on the set, said:

"It's an unbelievable thing. Fantastic."

Col. Frank Borman, who commanded the Apollo 8 Christmastime voyage around the moon, was with the President when Armstrong took his walk. He provided the President with a running commentary and explained the technicalities of the mission.

Why, Mr. Nixon wanted to know,

Please Turn to Page 8, Col. 3

Los Angeles Times

LARGEST CIRCULATION IN THE WEST, 975,491 DAILY, 1,308,711 SUNDAY.

FINAL
ONE OF THE WORLD'S GREAT NEWSPAPERS

VOL. LXXXVIII 2† TWENTY-ONE SECTIONS—SECTION A CC SUNDAY, AUGUST 10, 1969 468 PAGES

SUNDAY 35c

'ALL ARE STARS'

Air Controllers: Elite Fraternity of Action Men

BY JACK SMITH
Times Staff Writer

". . . You don't think about it as human lives. You couldn't take it. To me it's just a blip; just a target; just another airplane."—Louis Perry.

". . . There are times . . . when things start closing in on you. But there's always a way out. That's what you're paid to think of—a way out."—Charles Moore.

". . . You've got to stay ahead of it, or you can't stay with it."—Jean Paul Roger.

Louis Perry, Charles Moore and Jean Paul Roger are all in the same line of work. They are traffic controllers at Los Angeles International Airport, second busiest commercial airport in the world.

They are part of a 70-man crew which works around the clock at International, 365 days a year, controlling the approaches, landings, takeoffs and departures of 1,800 to 2,100 aircraft every 24 hours.

On an average, 60,000 lives are in their hands daily—each for a few critical minutes—more than 20 million in a year.

Elite Fraternity

They belong to an elite fraternity. There are only 8,100 journeyman air traffic controllers in the country, making it among the most exclusive of callings.

(About 5,000 controllers, most of them members of the Professional Air Traffic Controllers Organization, are said to be planning mass resignations unless work loads are eased, training is improved and pay is raised.)

Like most of their colleagues, Perry, Moore and Roger are in their 30s. The job takes young eyes and ears, young nerves, young reflexes and a young man's physical stamina. It burns most men out by 40.

Controllers at International make $14,000-$19,000 a year, well above the national average, plus overtime and holiday pay. But some feel "just compensation can only go so far" for unrelenting pressure and irregular work shifts.

At International the controllers work eight-hour, 22-man shifts, divided between the tower cab, 13 stories above the runways, and the 12th-story radar room "downstairs."

Each Minute Something New

Access to these sanctuaries is by key only. The occasional authorized visitor finds himself in an atmosphere of quick efficiency; but he feels the undercurrent of tension and excitement.

Perhaps there is no "typical" day at International. Each 24 hours brings its own unique problems or emergencies. It was a "normal" situation one morning last week for example: Overcast. Ceiling 1,200. Visibility three miles with haze and smoke. Wind 15 knots.

The difficulty was the wind was blowing the wrong way; from the southeast. Los Angeles International is laid out for a prevailing west wind. It gets an east wind only a few days a year and almost never in summer.

"We've got to turn the whole airport around," the tower cab crew chief explained. "Everything gets slowed down."

Eight controllers were at work in the 20x20 foot tower cab, with its 360-degree view of the airport. Charles Moore, standing in the

Please Turn to Page 2, Col. 1

SOUTHLAND WELCOME — President Nixon waves to friends in crowd as he and Mrs. Nixon arrive at Orange County Airport. The President plans a month's stay at home in San Clemente.
Times photo by Steve Fontanini

Nixon Arrives, Sets Up Summer White House in San Clemente

Greeted by Crowd at Orange County Airport; President Picks Up 5-Year-Old Boy Who Falls Off Fence in Crush

BY STUART H. LOORY
Times Staff Writer

President Nixon established a White House-by-the-sea Saturday on a cypress-shaded bluff overlooking the Pacific in San Clemente.

The Chief Executive's airplane touched down at Orange County Airport at 4:27 p.m. Mr. Nixon and his wife, Patricia, were greeted by a Flag-waving, cheering crowd estimated by local police at 8,000.

Normally, the President, on visits to Southern California, has landed at El Toro Marine Air Station. But for this one-month visit, local Republican leaders convinced him he should give the people a chance to greet him at a public place.

On hand to greet the President were Dr. Arnold Beckman, an old friend and chairman of the board of California Institute of Technology; Victor Andrews, Republican national committee finance chairman for California, and O.W. (Dick) Richards, a long-time Nixon campaigner. The group handed Mrs. Nixon a large bouquet of yellow roses while the Santa Ana High School Band played "California Here I Come."

A Navajo Welcome

The Disneyland band also was present as well as a contingent of Navajo Indians carrying a sign that said, "Ya Ta Hey, President Nixon," meaning welcome.

The President walked along a hurricane fence shaking hands and then, standing on a small cargo truck, made a short speech.

He said:

"We want to thank all of you for giving us such a wonderful welcome home to California and my home county, Orange County."

Then, noting the large crowds he had drawn on his recent round-the-world tour, he said, "However great they were, there's nothing like coming home."

Continuing in that vein, he said: "To bring the summer White House back to Orange County, my home county—that's one of the happiest things of all."

Then, before boarding Marine One, his helicopter, for the trip to San Clemente, he once again shook hands along the fence. Among those greeting him was Ralph G. Hand of Long Beach, a World War II Marine Corps officer who had known Mr. Nixon when they were both stationed at Vella LaVella, a South Pacific island.

The President also met 5-year-old Ted Garrison, son of Mr. and Mrs.

Please Turn to Sec. B, Page 2

Welfare Reform Seen by Nixon as a Moral Necessity

BY VINCENT J. BURKE
Times Staff Writer

WASHINGTON — For President Nixon, extension of cash assistance to the working poor seems to be a moral issue—a matter of right and wrong.

That was how he presented it to a nationwide TV audience Friday night. And that, according to Administration sources, was how he put it privately when he overrode the opposition of a majority of his Cabinet in approving the Administration's new welfare reform program.

If enacted, the controversial plan would assure a minimum income to every family in which the father is willing to work. It would extend supplementary cash to boost income of low-earning families with children.

The payments would account for about $2.2 billion of the total $4 billion first-year cost of the program. The program also would provide $700 million in cash relief to state and county governments by having the federal government take

Text of President Nixon's welfare speech Section B, Page 4.

over a bigger share of existing welfare costs. California's state and county governments would get $178 million of this savings.

On Wednesday morning Mr. Nixon presented his plan to the Cabinet members, who were assembled along with top White House aides as overnight guests at the presidential retreat at Camp David.

According to two men who attended the briefing, only three Cabinet members applauded the proposal: Secretary Robert H. Finch of the Department of Health, Education and Welfare, Secretary George P. Shultz of the Labor Department and Donald Rumsfeld, chief of the Office of Economic Opportunity (a Cabinet member although his agency does not have departmental status).

Other Cabinet members protested against the cost, the philosophy, the

Please Turn to Sec. B, Page 6

State Lawmakers Adjourn With Tax Reform Unresolved

BY TOM GOFF
Times Sacramento Bureau Chief

SACRAMENTO—The Legislature wrapped up early Saturday a generally lackluster, albeit sometimes explosive, 1969 law-making session, more noteworthy for what it did not do than for its accomplishments.

Its principal failure—and the one for which it probably will be remembered—was its inability to solve the knotty problem of tax reform.

A general overhaul of the state's burdensome and complex tax system was the principal goal of Gov. Reagan and the lawmakers themselves when the session opened last January.

It didn't get past first base.

The Legislature, to be sure, passed a Reagan-sponsored one-time limited 10% income tax cut, effective only next year.

Called 1970 'Vote Bait'

Democrats labeled it "vote bait" for next year's election, using money which could better have been spent for other purposes.

The lawmakers also gave to business and industry a two-year doubling of the present 15% exemption in the tax on business inventories, also sought by the governor.

However, the massive problems of the protesting home owner and the property tax, the cries from hard-pressed local governments for new sources of revenue, and the long-needed equalization of the tax burden for the support of schools all were left for another day.

Politics was largely responsible for the failure of tax reform.

Minority Democrats, groping for an effective posture in the unfamiliar role of being out of power for the first time in a decade, were more destructive than constructive.

Please Turn to Page 20, Col. 1

'RITUALISTIC SLAYINGS'

Sharon Tate, Four Others Murdered

BY DIAL TORGERSON
Times Staff Writer

Film star Sharon Tate, another woman and three men were found slain Saturday, their bodies scattered around a Benedict Canyon estate in what police said resembled a ritualistic mass murder.

The victims were shot, stabbed or throttled. On the front door of the home, written in blood, was one word: "Pig."

Police arrested the only one left alive on the property—a 19-year-old houseboy. He was booked on suspicion of murder.

Killed were:

—Miss Tate, 26, a star of "Valley of the Dolls" and wife of Roman Polanski, director of "Rosemary's

Sharon Tate
Times photo

Related story, pictures on Page B.

Baby." She was eight months pregnant. He is in England.

—Abigail Folger, 26, heiress to the Folger's Coffee family.

—Jay Sebring, 35, once Miss Tate's fiance, a Hollywood hair stylist credited wih launching the trend to hair styling for men.

— Voityck Frokowski, 37, who worked with Polanski in Polish films before they came to Hollywood.

—Steven Parent, 18, of El Monte, who left his home Friday morning after telling his family he was going to "go to Beverly Hills."

A maid, Mrs. Winifred Chapman, went to the sprawling home at the end of Cielo Drive at 8:30 a.m. to begin her day's work. What she found sent her running to a neighbor's home in a state of shock:

In a white two-door sedan in the driveway was the body of the young man, slumped back in the driver's seat, shot to death.

On the lawn in front of the ranch-style home was the body of Frokowski.

Twenty yards away, under a fir tree on the well-trimmed lawn, was the body of Miss Folger, clad in a nightgown.

In the living room, dressed in underwear—bikini panties and a brassiere—was Miss Tate. A bloodied nylon cord was around her neck. It ran over a beam in the open-beam ceiling and was tied around the neck of Sebring, whose body lay nearby.

Over Sebring's head was a black

Please Turn to Page 18, Col. 1

Wreckage of Gamblers Special Found on Side of Mt. Whitney

BY WILLIAM J. DRUMMOND
Times Staff Writer

The wreckage of the long-sought Gamblers Special — a DC-3 which vanished with 35 persons aboard Feb. 18 near the California-Nevada border — has been found on the northeast side of Mt. Whitney, the Air Force said Saturday.

The debris was sighted at 9:36 a.m. Friday by Bakersfield pilot Stanford Dow and his wife, Johnadene, about 10 miles west of Lone Pine, Calif., at an elevation of 11,900 feet. Mt. Whitney, the highest point in the United States outside Alaska, is 14,495 feet high.

Dow told The Times that the DC-3 apparently slammed into a sheer rock wall, disintegrated and slid down the surface. All aboard must have perished instantly, Dow said.

The heavily loaded liner left the Hawthorne, Nev., Airport for Burbank and Long Beach just before a turbulent snowstorm struck the deserts and mountain ranges in its path.

Heavy snows fell, off and on, for 10 days after the plane disappeared, hampering attempts to locate the missing craft. By the time the weather cleared enough for a careful aerial search, up to 40 feet of snow covered higher regions of the rugged borderland.

Aboard the craft were three crew members—pilot, copilot and stewardess—and 32 passengers returning from a five-hour visit to Hawthorne's El Capitan Casino.

Thousands of man-hours were spent searching for the craft. Some sightings were reported, but when followed up, they proved false.

However, on Saturday spokesmen for rescue and recovery teams at Hamilton Air Force Base identified the wreckage found by the Dows as that of the Gamblers Special.

Dow, owner of Gold Seal Aviation in Bakersfield, said he had been searching for the DC-3 continually over the past five months. He estimated that he had logged 22 hours aloft in his Cessna 172 in searching for the lost aircraft.

Please Turn to Sec. B, Page 7

$30 MILLION IN NEW CUTBACKS FEARED

Schools Face Another Big Deficit Next Year

BY JACK McCURDY
Times Education Writer

Despite budget slashes, a record property tax increase and a boost in state aid, Los Angeles city schools face another whopping spending deficit next year which is likely to result in cutbacks more damaging than those enacted during the past few months.

Preliminary estimates indicate the 1970-71 school budget will have to be cut by another $30 million to $35 million to bring it into balance with anticipated income.

Curtailments will probably have to be made in the most vital areas of the school program, such as reducing teaching staff and increasing class size or reducing the length of the school day.

Noninstructional activities—such as health services, custodial and maintenance programs, extracurricular activities and equipment purchases—received the major blow in cutbacks to balance the 1969-70 budget at $690 million.

But school officials believe that these support services have been pared almost to the minimum.

They have been reduced to such a low level, budget planners argue, that further cuts: (1) will not save the volume of funds needed to balance next year's budget and (2) could render support services largely ineffective in providing the necessary backup support for operation of the regular instructional program.

The two prime targets of conservatives, voluntary bussing of minority students to predominantly white schools and the urban affairs office to improve community relations, are two such support programs.

Both could be eliminated at a savings of no more than $500,000.

School administrators point out that 85% of the school district's budget is devoted to salaries of district personnel and that this figure may be closer to 90% after this year's curtailments.

Of this total, about 70% to 75% is composed of salaries for teachers and other certificated employes such as administrators.

Officials estimate that at least 8% to 10% of the budget must be devoted to expenditures outside of salaries to provide the basic services to keep classrooms operating.

Thus, it seems probable that the salary section of the budget will have to be tapped in some way if $30 million to $35 million must be trimmed, officials agree.

Class size in the elementary grades is prescribed by the state, preventing local districts from reducing the pupil-teacher ratio from present levels.

Please Turn to Page 22, Col. 1

THE WEATHER

Light to moderate smog through out the basin today.

U.S. Weather Bureau forecast: Mostly fair today and Monday. Chance of thundershowers over the mountains in the afternoons. Little temperature change. High today, 93.

High Saturday, 92.

Complete weather information on Section C, Page 6.

IN TODAY'S TIMES

U.S. Opens 3rd Cambodia Drive

TUESDAY

FINAL

RACING ENTRIES

Los Angeles Times

LARGEST CIRCULATION IN THE WEST, 982,075 DAILY, 1,317,220 SUNDAY.

VOL. LXXXIX SEVEN PARTS—PART ONE | TUESDAY MORNING, MAY 5, 1970 | 108 PAGES | DAILY 10c

4 STUDENTS SLAIN

IN KENT, OHIO—National guardsmen advance during clash in which four students were killed. UPI Wirephotos

Troops Open Fire on Ohio Campus

KENT, Ohio (UPI)—Four students were shot to death on the Kent State University campus Monday when national guardsmen, believing a sniper had attacked them, fired into a crowd of rioting antiwar protesters. At least 11 persons were wounded, three critically, before order was restored. The university was shut down for at least a week.

The town of 18,000 was sealed off and a judge ordered the university's 20,000 students to leave the campus by noon Tuesday. By late Monday night only 300 students, most of them foreign students, remained as 800 guardsmen patrolled in convoys of jeeps and personnel carriers armed with .50-caliber machine guns.

Students and National Guard officials gave different versions of what triggered the gunfire, but the guard admitted no warning was given that the troops would begin firing their M-1 semiautomatic rifles.

The battle was the most violent campus confrontation since the antiwar movement began. The trouble started when about 1,000 demonstrators, defying an order not to assemble, rallied on the commons at the center of the tree-lined campus. Guardsmen moved in and fired tear gas grenades at the mob, which broke and ran.

The protesters then regrouped and confronted about 300 guardsmen on a practice football field. The students, now numbering 1,500, charged down a hill and pelted the troops with rocks. Guardsmen exhausted their supply of tear gas. Students, who tossed back the canisters, surrounded the troops on three sides.

Believes Sniper Fired

Then, according to S. T. Del Corso, state adjutant general, "a sniper opened fire against the guardsmen from a nearby rooftop."

Del Corso, who was in Columbus, the state capital, maintained contact with the troops through Brig. Gen. Robert Canterbury, who commanded the guard force on campus. Canterbury said the students were given no warning before the shooting started.

Student eyewitnesses said they did not hear any gunfire before the guardsmen began shooting.

"All of a sudden," said one male student," some of them turned around, faced the crowd of students and started firing. A coed said she saw several guardsmen drop to their knees and fire from a kneeling position.

Please Turn to Page 6, Col. 1

WAR SITUATION AT A GLANCE

The stock market took a heavy beating Monday, reacting to concern over U.S. action in Cambodia. The Dow Jones industrial average dropped 19.07. Part 3, Page 9.

The Vietnam peace talks in Paris hung in the balance as the result of the U.S. Cambodia action. Page 18.

The Senate Foreign Relations Committee said the Cambodian invasion was "constitutionally unauthorized." Page 11.

U.S. troops swept through Cambodia's Fishhook toward what was believed to be a major Communist headquarters base. Page 22.

Soviet Premier Alexei N. Kosygin called for "vigorous measures" to get the U.S. out of Indochina. Page 19.

Official Washington, however, noted that Kosygin gave no indication of any Russian action to counter the United States. Page 19.

For Red China, U.S. action was "frantic provocation." Page 16.

Large S. Viet-U.S. Force Opens Third Cambodia Offensive

SAIGON (AP)—Thousands of American and South Vietnamese troops launched a third offensive into northeast Cambodia today, seeking to smash more North Vietnamese base camps and sanctuaries, the U.S. command announced.

The American command said the operation was kicked off early this afternoon in the Se San base area, about 50 miles west of Pleiku, in the Central Highlands.

A spokesman said troops of the U.S. 4th Infantry Division and the South Vietnamese 22nd Infantry Division were participating in the operation.

(Their target is a highlands bivouac area that long has served as an entry point for the Ho Chi Minh Trail into Vietnam, United Press International said. It lies just south of the point where the borders of Laos, Cambodia and South Vietnam meet.

(Communist troops operating from this area have besieged several border Green Beret camps in the course of the war.

All Sanctuaries Are Targets

Defense Secretary Melvin R. Laird said in Washington Saturday that all North Vietnamese and Viet Cong sanctuaries along the full length of the border would be attacked by the allies.

There are numerous enemy base camp areas in Cambodia from the western Mekong Delta to the area north of Saigon which are outside the areas attacked last week by allied troops.

The two earlier allied drives, one into an area known as the Parrot's Beak and the other into an area called the Fishhook, have accounted for 2,171 North Vietnamese and Viet Cong killed. U.S. losses were given as 16 killed and South Vietnamese deaths were put at 151.

The new operation is taking place in rugged, mountainous jungle 160 miles north northeast of the Fishhook area where another task force of more than 8,000 Americans launched the first U.S. offensive into Cambodia last Friday.

IN CAMBODIA—American soldiers try to spot enemy through rubber trees in the Fishhook region.

Hopes Rise for End to Teacher Strike

BY HARRY BERNSTEIN
Times Labor Writer

The Los Angeles teachers' strike started its fourth week Monday, amid rising hopes that the walkout will be over by this weekend.

A possible delaying effect on the hoped-for settlement was avoided Monday when Superior Judge Stevens Fargo agreed with another Superior Court judge that the strike is illegal and issued a preliminary injunction to that effect, but delayed action at least until May 18 on contempt of court charges against strike leaders.

This means United Teachers of Los Angeles President Robert Ransom, Vice President Larry Sibelman, Executive Secretary Don Baer and Assistant Executive Secretary Roger Segure can devote full time to seeking a settlement instead of to the court proceedings.

A UTLA spokesman said the preliminary injunction issued Monday against the strike will be appealed on constitutional grounds.

The hopes for a quick end to the strike are based on the belief that UCLA law Prof. Benjamin Aaron will come up Thursday with a contract proposal acceptable both to the

Please Turn to Page 26, Col. 1

DEATH ON THE CAMPUS—A [illegible] ms over the body of a student shot at Kent State University. UPI Wirephoto

New U.S. Air Raids Halted Over North, but Option Remains

BY TED SELL
Times Staff Writer

WASHINGTON—A new bombing campaign against North Vietnam was publicly declared ended Monday but defense sources said privately that a new policy giving field commanders increased authority on launching air strikes remained in effect.

The formal announcement, by Daniel Z. Henkin, assistant secretary of defense for public affairs, was that three heavy strikes against Communist supply areas just north of the border with South Vietnam were "all that were planned." Henkin said that with the strong attacks, the operation had "terminated."

Henkin, chief spokesman for the Defense Department, said there had been no change in the U.S. policy of protecting American reconnaissance flights.

But on Sunday, equally well-informed Pentagon officials said the policy had in fact been changed, permitting far more massive retaliatory bombing of North Vietnam.

Under the old policy, fighter escorts could attack only whatever single antiaircraft positions fired on reconnaissance planes.

It was made clear over the weekend, in connection with the expansion of the raids, that that policy no longer held. If antiaircraft positions in any military base area fired, escorts could attack both that position and any military targets associated with it.

That expansion of authority, Pentagon sources said Monday, has not been revoked. White House officials,

Please Turn to Page 13, Col. 1

THE WEATHER

U.S. Weather Bureau forecast: Night and morning low clouds with local drizzles but hazy afternoon sunshine today and Wednesday. High today, 70. High Monday, 80; low, 55.

Smog report and complete weather information in Part 2, Page 4.

INDEX TO THE TIMES

Page 2, Part 1

Los Angeles Times

LARGEST CIRCULATION IN THE WEST, 982,075 DAILY, 1,317,229 SUNDAY.

VOL. LXXXIX † SEVEN PARTS—PART ONE CC THURSDAY MORNING, AUGUST 27, 1970 144 PAGES DAILY 10c

ATOMIC SHIP

The Savannah: $100 Million White Elephant

BY NICHOLAS C. CHRISS
Times Staff Writer

GALVESTON, Tex.—Her name is Savannah, and once she was a belle of such distinguished heritage and beauty that she attracted worldwide attention.

As the world's first atomic-powered commercial ship, the Savannah, a gleaming white and blue showpiece, was to usher in a new sea age and demonstrate to the world this country's desire for the peaceful uses of nuclear energy.

Today, 11 years after she was christened by Mamie Eisenhower at Camden, N.J., the Savannah lies tied up in caretaker status at Pier E of the Todd Shipyards Nuclear Division here.

There is talk of turning her into a fish processing ship, putting her on runs to the Canal Zone or placing her in mothballs.

Trouble From the First

Almost from the day the Savannah was aborning in design she has had difficulties.

First she was supposed to be a tanker. But the Eisenhower administration, which conceived her, decided the Savannah should be a passenger ship. Then she was made later a cargo ship which could not compete with today's container cargo ships. She never overcame her schizoid personality.

In her prime, the Savannah, named after the first steamship to cross the Atlantic in 1819, was plagued by fears that wherever she sailed an accident or collision might result in the spread of radioactive material.

Japan has never allowed the ship into its ports. And even now, when the Savannah docks abroad or at home, elaborate negotiations and plans are made over her berthing and how to evacuate nearby populations should an accident occur.

What went wrong?

"She was, after all, an experimental prototype," said Cecil Benson, the ship's master in Galveston, where she has been docked since July 29.

Not Competitive

"She was not built to be competitive, but to gain experience and learn the difficulties of nuclear-powered sailing," he said. Benson also pointed out that for all the precautions taken, there has never been a hint of a nuclear accident.

He believes that the expense of building and maintaining the ship—more than $100 million so far—is little enough price to pay for maritime progress compared to the billions spent on space exploration.

"We compete with the Russians in space, arms and other things, why can't we compete with them with a maritime fleet," Benson said.

(The Russians have one nuclear-powered vessel, the icebreaker Lenin, and 50 nuclear-powered submarines. The West Germans have a nuclear-powered test ship. The Japanese are building one. The U.S. Navy has 91 nuclear-powered war ships.)

Benson and men like Hoyt Haddock, executive director of the AFL-CIO Martime Committee, and Robert Giblou, the designer, believe the Savannah has never had an adequate chance.

Please Turn to Page 28, Col. 1

LIB LISTENER—City Councilman John Ferraro puts hand to head during speechmaking at hour-long ceremony in council chamber that was conducted in honor of women's liberation movement.
Times photos by Joe Kennedy

Mideast Role With Russ Seen by U.S.

2-Power Force Would Replace U.N. Observers

BY STUART H. LOORY
Times Staff Writer

SAN CLEMENTE—The United States envisions a permanent role for itself and the Soviet Union in cooperating to keep peace between Arabs and Israelis in the Middle East.

High-placed Nixon Administration sources made this known for the first time in a briefing for Western states news media executives at the Western White House Monday.

Although few details were disclosed of just what the involvement

Israel trying to divert peace talks, Egypt charges. See Page 5, Part 1.

would be, it was apparent from a transcript of the briefing, released for publication today, that the Nixon Administration had in mind a Soviet-American force of military observers that would replace the present, moribund U.N. force made up of troops from smaller, neutral countries.

The major-power observer force would be the mechanism through which the United States and Soviet Union would guarantee the terms of a permanent peace settlement. It would go into effect after a settlement.

The major-power role, the sources said, would be supplementary to an agreement reached between Israel and Egypt and Jordan, and would only be undertaken if all three parties agreed to it, the sources said.

The ground rules under which the transcript was released forbid direct quotation of the sources as well as their identification even though, at one point, a network television crew was allowed into the briefing to take silent film footage of one of the sources answering questions.

The film was for a forthcoming television show on the subject "What Is the Real Henry Kissinger?" Kissinger is the President's assistant for national security affairs.

The briefing also revealed more clearly than ever before the extent to which the United States has guaranteed Israel's security during the present 90-day cease-fire, which, the Administration hopes, will ultimately lead to successful peace negotiations. The negotiations, directed by Swedish Ambassador Gunnar V. Jarring, got under way at the United

Please Turn to Page 8, Col. 1

ARAB COMMANDOS TOLD BY NASSER TO FACE REALITY

BY WILLIAM TUOHY
Times Staff Writer

CAIRO—Egypt's President Gamal Abdel Nasser has told commando leader Yasser Arafat that the Palestinian commandos must begin to face up to reality in planning their future.

This is the essential message that the Egyptians have been passing to the Fatah leader and other commandos during a series of talks in Cairo and Alexandria.

Reliable sources here place a good deal of significance on the talks.

For underneath the official pronouncements of sweetness-and-light, the cold fact is that for the first time a major Arab leader—Nasser—has talked turkey to a commando leader—Arafat.

Nasser warned Arafat against publicly decrying Egypt's participating in the peace talks at the United Nations, reliable sources say.

He suggested to the guerrilla

Please Turn to Page 8, Col. 3

NOT EXACTLY A TRIUMPH

L.A. 'Women's Lib' Marchers Greeted by Cheers and Jeers

BY LEE DYE
Times Staff Writer

Scores of women who believe they stand second best in the battle of the sexes took to the streets of Los Angeles Wednesday as part of a nationwide commemoration of the 50th anniversary of women's suffrage.

But rather than being a victory celebration over the passage of the 19th Amendment in 1920, the day's events were aimed at the future.

There were very few indications that the gals made much headway on the local scene.

The Los Angeles City Council—11

Women around the nation declare their independence. Page 16, Part 1.

men and one woman—devoted an hour to the celebration, but the men were clearly annoyed and bored. They walked in and out of the chambers and some complained that the normal time set aside for such matters is only 10 minutes, not an hour.

During the day's activities, the feminists made repeated attempts to persuade other women to join their one-day strike and to boycott stores.

"Show them we have power," they shouted as they marched down Broadway. "Don't buy anything today."

But many women, startled by the appearance of the marchers, rushed into stores.

The women were heckled by a few as they marched down Broad-

Please Turn to Page 3, Col. 2

IN CHARGE—Councilwoman Pat Russell presides over the council's meeting. With her is Charlene Pfalzgraf, the sergeant at arms for the day.

Growers Losing $500,000 a Day in Lettuce Strike

BY HARRY BERNSTEIN
Times Labor Writer

SALINAS—Growers in this fertile farm center of California were losing up to $500,000 a day by Wednesday and more than 10,000 workers were idled by the strike of Cesar Chavez' farm workers union.

Herb Fleming, a major grower here and chief spokesman for the growers' association, predicted, however, that "our losses will start going down quickly as our workers recognize that we will protect them from the lies, the threats and the intimidations of those characters in that union."

Fleming referred to Chavez' AFL-CIO United Farm Workers Organizing Committee, not the Teamsters Union, which by Wednesday was closely allied with the growers in their struggle with UFWOC.

He said half those idled were field workers and half were production workers put out of work by the harvesters' walkout.

Down to One-Fourth

Government estimates showed that on Wednesday, the third day of the most massive strike in U.S. farm labor history, this valley's lettuce production was down to about 62 railroad carloads of the normal 250.

The slowdown in lettuce production continued to send wholesale prices skyrocketing, going up to $6 a crate in some areas of the state compared to $1.75 before the strike.

In Los Angeles, retail prices rose somewhat, from 29 cents a head on Monday to about 39 cents by Wednesday.

If the strike remains effective, the retail markets will feel the full impact by the end of this week as supplies on hand are sold out.

But the growers joined with the Teamsters Union in predicting that the strike has already started to diminish.

"We've got about 40% to 50% of the people back to work and we are signing them up as fast as they re-

Please Turn to Page 32, Col. 1

Lockheed Passes Senate Test for $200 Million in Extra Funds

BY JOHN H. AVERILL and ROBERT E. WOOD
Times Staff Writers

Lockheed Aircraft Corp. cleared a major hurdle Wednesday in its efforts to win congressional approval of an extra $200 million fund to continue the controversial C-5A cargo plane program through next June.

In a crucial floor vote, the U.S. Senate defeated an amendment that would have deleted the $200 million extra authorization from the pending $9.2 billion military procurement bill. The vote against the amendment by Sen. William Proxmier (D-Wis.) and Sen. Richard S. Schweiker (R-Pa.) was 48 to 30.

Burbank-based Lockheed has claimed that the money is needed to assure production of more than 30 of the big Air Force planes. The Air Force now plans to buy a total of 81 C-5As which would be produced at the Lockheed plant in Marietta, Ga.

Lockheed and the Defense Department are in disagreement on charges totaling almost $1 billion for work on the C-5A and three other big defense production contracts.

The $200 million government financing is also crucial to Lockheed's ability to get needed bank loans. The company has been negotiating for months with a group of 24 major U.S. banks for a big loan.

"There isn't any cut and dried understanding on this to my knowledge," a Lockheed spokesman said Wednesday, "but a favorable vote on the $200 million is certainly not going to hurt the status of those negotiations."

James K. Dobey, executive vice president of one of the banks—Wells Fargo—said Wednesday the group "is still working out" loan arrangements for Lockheed. Passage of the $200 million federal assistance, however, will "trigger some

Please Turn to Page 34, Col. 1

NEW FACES ON BARROOM FLOOR

Shure, and 'Tis No Fit Place for a Colleen, That M'Sorley's

BY RICHARD DOUGHERTY
Times Staff Writer

NEW YORK—"I don't know what the world is comin' to," said Gene Nolan to the man beside him at the bar. "All this long hair on the lads so you can't tell if they're boy or girl. Nuns marryin' priests. I saw a young priest on the TV the other night and he was with a divorced woman. And now we got the women comin' in here. Is it a conspiracy, do you suppose?"

By *here*, the 65-year-old Nolan, who emigrated from County Galway a half-century ago, meant McSorley's Old Ale House, which last week was required by law to open its doors to women for the first time in its 116-year history.

"Do they want to work with a pick and shovel?" asked Nolan's companion. "Well, let 'em. What the hell, they do it in Russia. But what they're doing in here is beyond me. Most of 'em don't like beer, anyway, and ale is even worse."

He drained his stein, wiped his mouth with the back of his hand and departed, casting a disapproving glance at three young women seated at a table near the door.

"Yes," said Daniel O'Connell Kirwan, the thin, dark-haired young proprietor of the nation's oldest continuously operating saloon, "it's been a shock to many of our older patrons. But things are settling down. The first two days when the militant ladies were in here were the hardest."

And so, as the nationwide women's strike for equality was observed Wednesday with parades, demonstrations, shop stoppages and the like, McSorley's was gradually adjusting

Please Turn to Page 16, Col. 1

Index to The Times

Thurmond's Hometown: School Integration Achieved Smoothly

BY KENNETH REICH
Times Staff Writer

AIKEN, S.C.—After months of careful planning, public school integration was completed smoothly and with surprising enthusiasm Wednesday in the hometown of Sen. Strom Thurmond (R-S.C.).

Nine thousand students, about two-thirds of them white and one-third black, flocked to the city's schools. In contrast with many other Southern communities, whites even showed up en masse in formerly all-black schools.

Three-fourths arrived by school bus, although school officials said total bus mileage had actually declined under the district's voluntary integration plan.

The first stage of the plan was completed last year with the geographic zoning of elementary schools. Wednesday, all 9th and 10th graders were enrolled in the formerly black high school, and all 11th and 12th graders in the former predominantly white high school. Integration also came to the junior highs.

The successful integration in the home of one of the Senate's most inveterate foes of the concept was widely credited to a determined local leadership. Less than 20 miles away, in Augusta, Ga., integration this week had been accompanied with protest, turmoil and white boycotts.

Please Turn to Page 36, Col. 1

THE WEATHER

U.S. Weather Bureau **forecast:** Mostly sunny today and **Friday** but some variable high **cloudiness.** Patchy coastal low clouds **early** Friday. High today, 83. High Wednesday, 86; low, 69.

Complete weather information and smog report in Part 2, Page 4.

Russ Power Play Seen in Egypt

TUESDAY **FINAL**

RACING RESULTS-ENTRIES

Los Angeles Times

LARGEST CIRCULATION IN THE WEST, 982,075 DAILY, 1,317,220 SUNDAY.

VOL. LXXXIX FIVE PARTS—PART ONE TUESDAY MORNING, SEPTEMBER 29, 1970 90 PAGES DAILY 10c

SOUTHLAND'S FIRE DEATHS RISE TO 8

Gamal Abdel Nasser
UPI Wirephoto

Nasser, Force for Unification in Arab World, Dies at 52

CAIRO (UPI)—President Gamal Abdel Nasser of Egypt, the unifying leader of a divided Arab world and the greatest figure in its modern history, died of a heart attack Monday at 52. His death raised the possibility of further strife in an area already deep in crisis.

Nasser was stricken at Cairo Airport while saying farewell to the ruler of Kuwait, Sheik Sabah al-Salim al-Sabah, one of the Arab leaders who had attended the summit conference Nasser called to end the civil war in Jordan.

A medical report signed by five doctors said Nasser suddenly complained of feeling dizzy and weak and began perspiring profusely. At

With Nasser's death, the Arab world has lost its only real hero of the 20th century. Page 5, Part 1.

3:15 p.m. Cairo time he was taken by car to his home in a Cairo suburb where he died at 6:15 p.m.

"A number of doctors arrived immediately and found his excellency to be suffering from an acute heart attack which resulted from a blockage of the heart artery," the medical bulletin said.

"All necessary medical aid was administered to his excellency, including the use of equipment to regulate the heartbeat. But God's will was stronger and he gave up the ghost at 6:15 p.m. during the administration of this aid."

Vice President Anwar Sadat, in accordance with the constitution, was declared acting president until a new chief of state can be chosen. House Speaker Habib Shukair said today that the National Assembly would elect a new president within 60 days with the approval of two-thirds of the members. Shukair made the statement after a joint meeting of the higher Executive Committee of

Please Turn to Page 7, Col. 1

Russ Expected to Fight for Power in Egypt

BY ROBERT C. TOTH
Times Staff Writer

WASHINGTON—American officials forecast Monday that after several weeks of mourning, post-Nasser Egypt will suffer a power struggle in which the Russians, with their huge investment at stake, will play a major role.

The death of the relatively moderate Gamal Abdel Nasser will further destabilize the Mideast for some time, it was said. The already fragile hopes for a regional peace settlement have further dimmed.

Anti-Israeli rhetoric in Cairo is sure to increase as the new Egyptian regime consolidates itself, using the only rallying cry available, American sources said. But it was not certain that Nasser's successors would break the American-initiated cease-fire along the Suez Canal before it expires Nov. 7.

'Not Bad News' for Israel

Israel feels that Nasser's death is not bad news, according to diplomatic sources, because no Egyptian leader could be worse. Israel does not see any coming divisiveness among the Arab states as working against its interests since that prevents another united military effort as in 1967.

Further polarization of the Arab world must be expected, the diplomatic sources said, with the gap between the leftist regimes (like Syria and Iraq) and the conservative governments (like Saudi Arabia and Jordan) growing much greater.

There is no Arab leader on the horizon, whether in Egypt or beyond, who could bring together all parties in another Jordan crisis, for example.

The Palestinian guerrillas are now in disarray, but with Nasser gone they will be less restrained when they regain their strength. King Hussein of Jordan, despite his victory on the battlefield, sits less secure on his throne now.

No successor to Nasser, even if inclined to continue the cease-fire with Israel, will feel secure enough for some time to embark on substantive peace negotiations under the American plan, according to some analysts.

Please Turn to Page 6, Col. 5

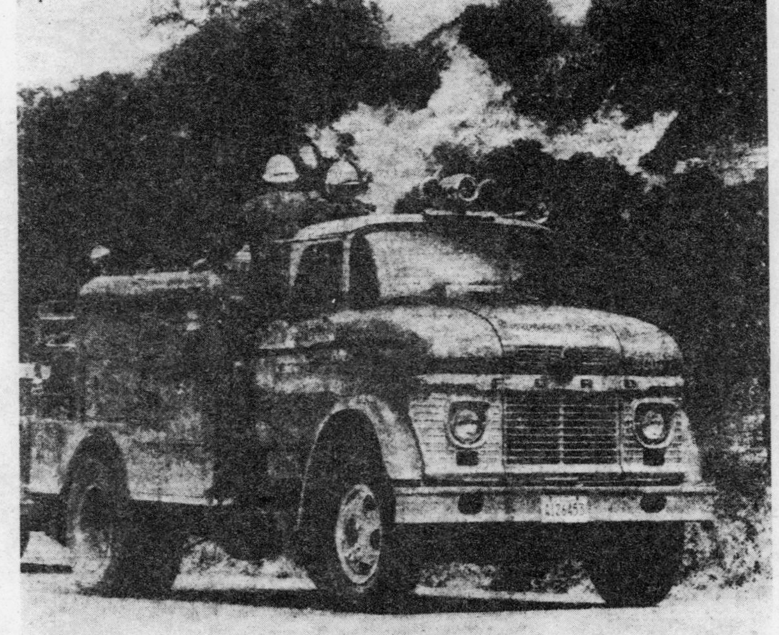

ON THE ROAD—Fire truck pulls up on highway near Descanso in San Diego County to survey flames billowing up above hill. The small town was periled by the blaze but the firemen saved it.
Times photo by Boris Yaro

5 Men Killed in Crash of Helicopter

BY DIAL TORGERSON
Times Staff Writer

Five men were killed in the San Gabriel Canyon fire Monday as fire fighters began to win a four-day battle against fires throughout the Los Angeles Basin.

The deaths of four U.S. Forest Service fire fighters and a helicopter pilot when their craft crashed into a burned-over area of the Angeles National Forest brought to eight the number killed since the fires erupted Friday.

Forest Service officials said the five-seat Alouette helicopter, on charter from Western Helicopters of Rialto, was delivering the fire fighters to fire lines when it crashed. The cause was not immediately learned and identification of the victims was withheld.

General Situation Improves

A fire broke out in the foothills of Arcadia early today when a building caught fire and the blaze spread to nearby brush. Residents in the area near Wilderness Park were alerted, but firemen contained the blaze quickly.

At other fires, the situation improved.

Winds diminished, and firemen were able to contain two big fires and almost contain a third in the Los Angeles-Ventura County area.

Five new fires sprang up Monday—three almost surely the work of arsonists—but firemen were able to knock them down.

No new Santa Ana gales are expected, and firemen said lines cut around the fires would hold.

Massed men and equipment, backfiring and countless air drops by helicopters and planes halted a surge of flames from moving into often-threatened Topanga Canyon Monday.

Please Turn to Page 25, Col. 1

Second Major Fire Breaks Out in Hard-Hit San Diego County

BY WILLIAM ENDICOTT
Times Staff Writer

A second major fire erupted in San Diego County late Monday and moved swiftly southward, threatening to link up with a blaze already called the worst in California history.

Fire officials said the newest fire, which broke out in the Middle Peak area of Cuyamaca State Park, destroyed two homes along Boulder Creek, then raced over 10,000 acres of a heavily wooded but uninhabited area.

By late evening, it had moved to within three miles of the little mountain community of Alpine, where residents had just moved back into their homes after the first fire roared through the southern edge of the town Sunday night.

Fire officials said they hoped to establish a line between the south side of the new blaze and Alpine.

Winds that gusted up to 60 m.p.h. earlier in the day eased during the night, raising hopes that the fire could be stopped before it reached Alpine or the burned-over section of the larger fire.

The fire erupted just as firemen were beginning to breathe more easily about the massive blaze that started Saturday in the Cleveland National Forest.

More than 2,000 men, including marines from Camp Pendleton, had battled for three days to halt its progress and there were indications late Monday that they were having some success.

Erratic winds turned the flames back northward early Monday and forced evacuation of the small community of Descanso about 20 miles east of El Cajon, but a fire line held and the town was saved.

By late Monday, more than 185,000 acres had been consumed and at least 250 homes destroyed, but fire officials said the blaze had "laid down" and was staying within its 120-mile perimeter.

Shortly before midnight, a State

Please Turn to Page 18, Col. 1

Nixon Cancels U.S. Naval Show, Pays Tribute to Nasser

BY STUART H. LOORY
Times Staff Writer

ABOARD THE SARATOGA — President Nixon Monday canceled a display of American naval power in the Mediterranean scheduled for today out of respect for Gamal Abdel Nasser. Mr. Nixon also praised the Egyptian leader.

Shortly after announcing the cancellation, Mr. Nixon issued the following statement:

"I was shocked to hear of the sudden death of President Nasser. The world has lost an outstanding leader who tirelessly and devotedly served the causes of his countrymen and the Arab world.

"This tragic loss requires that all nations, and particularly those in the Middle East, renew their efforts to calm passions, reach for mutual understanding and build lasting peace. On behalf of the American people, I extend deep sympathy to

Please Turn to Page 10, Col. 1

Dos Passos, Giant of Literature, Dies

Exclusive to The Times From Reuters

BALTIMORE—John Dos Passos, a Portuguese immigrant's grandson who became one of the giants of 20th century American literature, died here Monday at 74.

Death was attributed to a heart ailment that had troubled him during the past three years.

Born in Chicago, Mr. Dos Passos had a migratory childhood. He lived in England, Washington and Virginia and visited Mexico and Belgium with his parents.

Mr. Dos Passos acquired a love of the sea through the novels of Frederick Marryat, and planned for a while to attend Annapolis. He wound up at Harvard, though, along with E. E. Cummings and Gilbert Seldes, and graduated cum laude in 1916.

He went to Spain to study architecture but when the United States entered World War I he signed on as an ambulance driver.

Please Turn to Page 13, Col. 1

Index to The Times

THE WEATHER

U.S. Weather Bureau forecast: Sunny with some high clouds today and Wednesday. High today about 90. Cooler Wednesday. High Monday, 93; low, 71.

1971–1980

EXTRA

Los Angeles Times

LATE SPORTS

LARGEST CIRCULATION IN THE WEST, 982,075 DAILY, 1,317,220 SUNDAY.

VOL. XC | FIVE PARTS—PART ONE | ★★★ | TUESDAY MORNING, JANUARY 26, 1971 | 72 PAGES | DAILY 10c

MANSON VERDICT

ALL GUILTY!

NEWS SUMMARY

THE WORLD

UGANDA OUSTER—Apollo Milton Obote was ousted as president of Uganda in a military coup but loyal units evidently are continuing resistance. (See Page 2, Part 1.)

CAMBODIA CURFEW—New attacks in Phnom Penh streets and on the airport, and an attempted bombing of the South Vietnamese Embassy, brought a dusk-to-dawn curfew in the city. (See Page 2, Part 1.)

MIDEAST TALKS—The State Department said the Administration was encouraged by the tone of peace talks in the Middle East, and called for an extension of the cease-fire. (See Page 2, Part 1.)

THE NATION

OVERPROFITS CHARGED—The agency charged with eliminating excess profits on defense contracts reported that private contractors overcharged the government by nearly $33.5 million in fiscal 1970. (See Page 2, Part 1.)

REVENUE PLAN—The two top members of the House Ways and Means Committee told President Nixon they still opposed his revenue-sharing proposal but they promised committee hearings. (See Page 2, Part 1.)

MORTON DEFENSE—Rep. Rogers C. B. Morton, nominated to head the Interior Department, defended his allegiance to environmental protection. (See Page 2, Part 1.)

CITY AND STATE

OIL SPILL HEARING—A Coast Guard hearing into the tanker collision which spilled 840,000 gallons of oil into the ocean and San Francisco Bay opened with questioning of Capt. Harry H. Parnell of the Arizona Standard. (See Part 2, Page 1.)

SUICIDES UP—The suicide rate among Los Angeles County youths has taken a sudden surge upward, the Suicide Prevention Center reported. (See Part 2, Page 1.)

BUSINESS-FINANCE

MARKET KEEPS GOING — The stock market maintained its winning streak Monday in heavy volume, though not matching Friday's record. The Dow Jones index advanced 4.31 points to close at 865.62.

See Financial Section

SPORTS

FANS HIT JACKPOT—A group of 25 horse racing bettors in New Zealand will share in a jackpot worth $716,776 as a result of their horse, a 50-1 shot, winning a special jackpot race.

See Sports Section

AFTER THE VERDICT—Charles Manson, looking calm, is led back to cell after being found guilty of murder in Tate-La Bianca killings.

Times photos by Bruce Cox

CONVICTED—Seemingly cheerful, co-defendants, from left, Patricia Krenwinkel, Susan Atkins and Leslie Van Houten after verdict.

First-Degree Conviction on 27 Counts

BY JOHN KENDALL
Times Staff Writer

Charles Manson and three of his "girls" were convicted Monday on all 27 counts of first-degree murder and conspiracy to murder in the seven Tate-La Bianca killings 18 months ago.

The long-haired, bearded Manson and the three denim-clad young women had sat quietly, seemingly without tension, as the court clerk took 20 minutes to read the jury's 27 verdicts.

As the jury started to leave the courtroom Manson called to Superior Judge Charles H. Older:

"We are still not allowed to put on a defense?

"You won't outlive that, old man—dad—hey, dad—look at the truth over here—hey!"

Older ordered removal of the defendants and as he was being led away, he said, "You will not outlive that, old man."

The seven men and five women in the regular jury panel filed into the courtroom at 11:42 a.m. after nearly

Manson—the family, trial highlights, the jury. Page 3, Part 1.

43 hours of deliberation on nine days. They wore sober expressions but were not grim.

"Mr. Tubick, has the jury reached a verdict?" Older asked Herman C. Tubick, the foreman.

"Yes, you honor, we have," the mortician replied.

Older took several minutes to check the order of the verdicts, then asked the clerk, Gene Darrow, to read them.

What he read amounted to this:

Manson, 36, Susan Atkins, 22, and Patricial Krenwinkel, 23: Guilty of first-degree murder and conspiracy to murder in the deaths of Sharon Tate, Abigail Folger, Voityck Frykowski, Thomas John (Jay) Sebring, Steven Earle Parent and Leno and Rosemary La Bianca on Aug. 9-10, 1969.

Jury Ordered Polled

Leslie Van Houten: Guilty of first-degree murder and conspiracy to murder in the killings of the La Biancas.

Judge Older ordered the polling of the jury and each juror confirmed his verdict.

As the jurors filed out of the room, Miss Van Houten leaned over to "Katie" Krenwinkel and said, "Look how sad they all look."

The penalty phase of the trial, also expected to be lengthy, will begin Thursday.

Heavy security was imposed on the Hall of Justice courtroom when the verdicts were announced.

Four uniformed women bailiffs stood behind the three seated women defendants. Five male bailiffs stood near the table where Manson sat. One of the bailiffs had his hands on the back of Manson's chair.

There were perhaps a dozen other sheriff's deputies and police officers on both sides of the court railing. Five uniformed deputies stood along the wall in the spectators' section.

Please Turn to Page 12, Col. 1

39 Missing in Hospital Rubble

WEDNESDAY

FINAL

RACING RESULTS-ENTRIES

Los Angeles Times

LARGEST CIRCULATION IN THE WEST, 982,075 DAILY, 1,317,220 SUNDAY

VOL. XC | FIVE PARTS—PART ONE | WEDNESDAY MORNING, FEBRUARY 10, 1971 | 94 PAGES | DAILY 10c

DAY OF DISASTER

Quake Leaves 42 Dead, 1,000 Hurt; Periled Dam Forces 40,000 to Flee

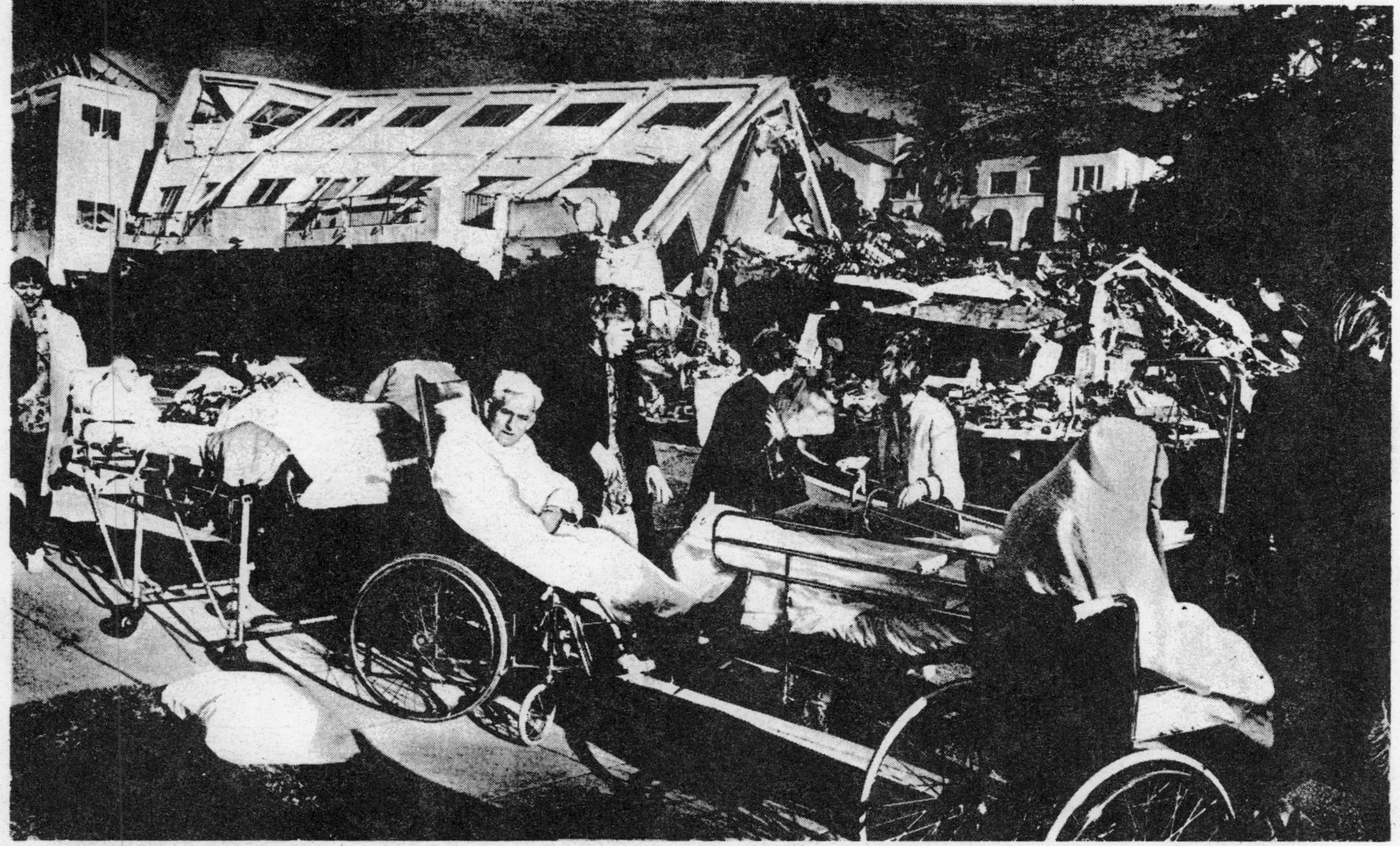

EVACUEES—San Fernando Veterans Administration Hospital patients wait in the open for evacuation to other facilities as ruins of buildings are searched for quake victims.
Times photo by Bruce Cox

12 Freeway Bridges Fall, Snag Traffic

By The Times Staff

The worst earthquake since 1933 struck Southern California a massive blow 42 seconds after 6 a.m. Tuesday, awakening millions to a day of disaster:

Forty-two persons were dead.

Perhaps as many as 1,000 were injured.

At least 39 persons remained missing in debris of a Veterans Hospital near Sylmar—one of two hospitals where buildings collapsed, causing 19 of the known deaths.

Damage was estimated in hundreds of millions of dollars.

Police ordered 40,000 persons to evacuate a San Fernando Valley area beneath a threatened dam.

Twelve overpass bridges fell into freeway lanes. One killed two men, crushing their pickup truck like a stepped-on toy. Four main arteries were closed.

Lights failed as the first quake struck and bright flashes from exploding power transformers cast a blue light in the predawn sky.

Hundreds of Gas Line Fires

Broken gas lines touched off hundreds of fires. City firemen answered 456 alarms in the first eight hours. As morning came, smoke from a score of major blazes rose into the sky.

At least 427 buildings in the city reportedly sustained some structural damage; 42 were damaged badly enough to force evacuation.

Aftershocks continued. By late evening there had been at least 16 big ones.

Many Los Angeles city and county schools were closed.

The quake—worst since 120 persons were killed March 10, 1933—was so frightening that eight of its victims died of heart attacks.

The quake was centered southeast of Newhall, almost at the spot where two earthquake faults—the San Gabriel and the Soledad Canyon—meet near the junction of the Golden State Freeway and California 14.

It registered 6.5 on the Richter scale. It was the most intense temblor since a 7.7 quake in 1952 near Tehachapi. That quake, in a more isolated area, claimed 12 lives.

Gov. Reagan declared Los Angeles County a disaster area and flew to Burbank to make an inspection trip. President Nixon made a similar announcement and ordered Vice President Agnew to California for an inspection trip.

Some looting was reported and 9 arrests for looting were reported in city areas. Units of the California

Please Turn to Page 2, Col. 3

Apollo Lands Right on Target, Carrying Trove of Knowledge

BY MARVIN MILES
Times Aerospace Writer

HOUSTON—Apollo 14 scorched back into earth's atmosphere Tuesday and parachuted safely into the South Pacific within less than a mile of its target area. It was the best splashdown yet of a manned space flight.

"Welcome home from the moon," the helicopter carrier New Orleans radioed the spacemen on the water.

"Thank you, sir," replied Alan B. Shepard, a Navy captain.

The landing that ended man's third successful expedition to the moon came at 1:05 p.m. PST, 900 miles south of American Samoa and about four miles ahead of the New Orleans which took the astronauts aboard about 50 minutes later.

Behind them in their bobbing spacecraft lay the scientific treasure they had brought from the moon, 96 pounds of lunar rocks and soil taken from the Fra Mauro highlands, plus

Pictures, related stories. Part 1, Pages A, 3, 6 and 7.

pictures snapped on the long voyage.

All three crewmen — Shepard, Edgar D. Mitchell and Stuart A. Roosa—were reported in good condition. They walked with steady stride to their trailer-like mobile quarantine facility from the pickup helicopter.

They wore plain dark coveralls, traditional flight crew caps and filter masks passed to them in the spacecraft by Navy swimmers.

Even before the doctor aboard the quarantine trailer could start his examination of the astronauts, they were pressed by ship's officers into

Please Turn to Page 3, Col. 3

THE WEATHER

National Weather Service forecast: Fair today and Thursday with patchy late night and early morning coastal fog. High today, 85. High Tuesday, 82; low, 48.

Complete weather information and smog report in Part 2, Page 4.

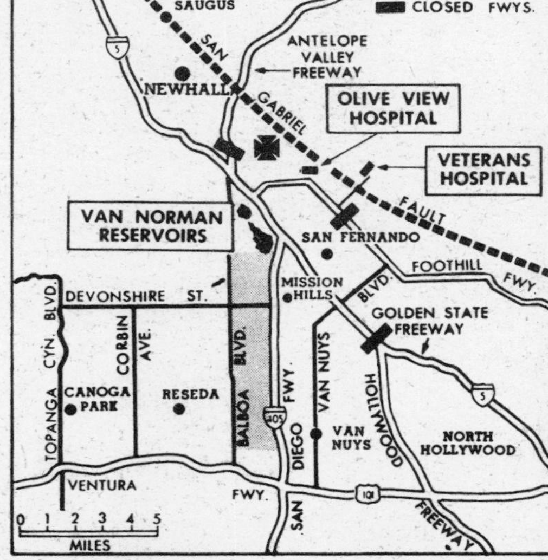

HARD HIT—Cross locates earthquake epicenter on San Gabriel Fault near two badly damaged hospitals. Shaded portion of map shows the area below Van Norman Lakes ordered evacuated. In addition to three freeways indicated as being closed, fourth freeway, the San Diego, also was reported as being partially closed.
Times map by Patrick Lynch

39 STILL MISSING IN HOSPITAL RUINS

BY JIM STINGLEY and LEE DYE
Times Staff Writers

Two buildings at the Veterans Hospital near Sylmar crashed in a pile of rubble during the quake Tuesday, claiming an uncounted number of lives and transforming the hospital into a scene of heartbreak and devastation.

By early today, at least 25 dead had been counted, with fears that the toll might reach many times that. Thirty-nine persons, including 11 members of the staff, were still reported missing.

But indications were that some of those people were still alive and might still be saved.

Please Turn to Page 18, Col. 1

THE QUAKE AT A GLANCE

Downtown skyscrapers rode out the quake but older buildings were hard hit. Part 1, Page 2.

Antelope Valley was isolated by collapse of overpasses. Part 1, Page C.

Quake was stronger than one in Long Beach disaster. Part 1, Page C.

Medical disaster planning brought swift aid to injured. Part 1, Page 2.

Public utilities were disrupted by broken lines and mains. Part 1, Page 20.

Los Angeles Unified District schools will stay closed today. Part 1, Page 2.

Reporter's story of first moments after the "rumble." Part 1, Page C.

Endangered reservoir dwarfs old one in Baldwin Hills. Part 1, Page C.

Los Angeles Times

FINAL
ONE OF THE WORLD'S GREAT NEWSPAPERS

LARGEST CIRCULATION IN THE WEST, 982,878 DAILY, 1,317,220 SUNDAY.

VOL. XC † TWENTY SECTIONS—SECTION A CC SUNDAY, MAY 2, 1971 424 PAGES SUNDAY 50c

VOLUME DROPS

The Telegram Is Becoming Part of Past

BY STANLEY O. WILLIFORD
Times Staff Writer

Western Union telegrams, as most Americans have known them for 119 years, are vanishing.

These are perhaps ignoble times for a once vital institution whose history started when Samuel F. B. Morse sent the first public telegram —"What hath God wrought?"—in May, 1844.

Slightly more than a century later, Western Union had more than 30,000 agencies and was sending more than 200 million telegrams annually. The volume today is less than half that number.

In years past, the telegram traveled in almost every conceivable form, including the radiogram, cablegram, candygram, flowergram, sing-o-gram, Santagram, bunnygram and cigargram among others.

It was heralded as the fastest means of written communication, a dependable 24-hour alternate to the once-a-day mail delivery.

The company gained a beloved reputation. It would go to any lengths to make a customer happy.

Efforts to 'Get Your Man'

Some offices adopted the slogan, "Get your man."

A messenger, it was written, once climbed 90 feet into the air to deliver a wire of encouragement to a flagpole sitter. Another descended two miles below the earth's surface to notify a coal miner he had become a grandfather.

There are tales of how boats with a messenger aboard would overtake ships at sea to deliver a telegram. Or how the wire would be flashed ahead to the next stop in an effort to catch an addressee who had just caught a train.

The company was once the nation's largest employer of boys. It was a prestige job.

Among the alumni of its blue-suited brigade were Thomas A. Edison, Andrew Carnegie, George M. Cohan, Steve Brodie, Jack Dempsey and Gene Autry, who delivered the singing variety.

Sideline Services Offered

For the right price, messengers could be hired to hunt fireflies, walk dogs around the block, cook breakfast, press a pair of pants, be a fourth at bridge, provide an escort for the evening, teach bike riding, throw rice at a bridal couple, bid by proxy at an auction sale . . .

Today the disappearing messenger is usually an older man with a number of years on the payroll, worried that he may be the next man the company lets go.

Worse, there is a growing fear among some Los Angeles employes of the Western Union Telegraph Co. that the telegram is being purposely destroyed by the company.

They charge the company is abandoning the task of providing telegraph service to the general public for bigger profits in dealing with private businesses.

These employes, who wish to remain anonymous, are supported by William B. Foglesong, president of Local 48 of the United Telegraph Workers.

In letters to Sens. John V. Tunney and Alan Cranston, Foglesong has urged a congressional investigation.

Please Turn to Page 20, Col. 1

WON'T HAPPEN AGAIN—Station Master Ken T. Bradley checks watch as City of Los Angeles, which was discontinued in takeover of passenger trains by Amtrak, arrives late on one of last runs.
Times photo by John Malmin

GOODBY CITY OF LOS ANGELES

Famed Trains Arrive at End of Line in Switch to Amtrak

BY CHARLES D. WOOD
Times Staff Writer

The City of Los Angeles died today.

So did the Capital Limited, Pocahontas, Texas Eagle and the Wabash Cannon Ball.

For decades these streamliners were the way to go—providing you weren't in a hurry. Unfortunately, most people today are in a hurry, so they climb aboard a jet.

The trip to Chicago takes three or four hours, not counting time to and from and in and out of airports.

For the City of Los Angeles—a deluxe passenger train that for 35 years sped between Chicago and here—the running time was a heady 39 hours and 45 minutes.

That was when Mae West, John Barrymore, Herbert Hoover were among its regular passengers.

But in recent years the streamliner wasn't quite as streamlined as it once was. As other trains died over the years, more stops were added to its schedule. At the end, the running time for the City of Los Angeles was up to 46 hours and 20 minutes.

National Agency Takes Over

The National Railroad Passenger Corp., a quasi-governmental entity, officially took over operation of most U.S. railroad passenger service on Saturday.

It was something of a shaky start. NRPC first had nicknamed itself Railpax but a spokesman said a lot of people didn't like the name and at the last minute it was renamed Amtrak.

Saturday the new rail system made an on-time debut.

The first train from Washington to New York City arrived at Penn Station two hours and 40 minutes after it left the nation's capital, right on schedule.

A lot of senators didn't like the wholesale reduction of passenger trains—to 182 from 360—and attempted to block the take-over at the last minute but the attempt failed.

The government took over the financially troubled passenger railway service in hopes of "revitalizing" the ailing industry, Secretary of Transportation John A. Volpe said Saturday during inauguration ceremonies in Washington.

Please Turn to Page B, Col. 2

Muscovites Parade in Rain and Sleet

BY HARRY TRIMBORN
Times Staff Writer

MOSCOW—Tens of thousands of Muscovites paraded through Red Square Saturday in a May Day spectacle that should result in Siberian exile for the weatherman as a counterrevolutionary provocateur.

He dished up virtually every atmospheric unpleasantry for the Soviet Union's Day of Celebration of Labor, a Socialist tradition dating back to 1889.

There was rain, snow, sleet, thunder and lightning and plunging temperatures. Random shafts of sunlight briefly pierced the heavy overcast to tantalize the paraders and spectators with the promise of clearing weather. But the dark clouds quickly reformed ranks to keep the sun away.

The brooding, gray skies robbed the spectacle of much of its color. Big, bright artificial flowers, colorful balloons, multihued placards and the miles of red banners and bunting that blanketed the city could not lift the gloom.

Please Turn to Page 6, Col. 1

Pentagon Deploys Troops Near Capital as Protesters Mass

BY STUART H. LOORY
Times Staff Writer

WASHINGTON — The Pentagon alerted several thousand soldiers and marines and moved riot-equipped military police into the Washington area Saturday as the capital girded for the massive three-day effort to close down the federal government in protest to the war.

The precautionary action, taken in response to a request of the Justice Department, came while as many as 45,000 young people lounged near the Potomac River for a night-long rock concert.

First the Pentagon said it had moved elements of the 519th Military Police Batt. from their post at Ft. Meade, Md., 35 miles away, to Ft. Myer, Va., near the Pentagon.

A few hours later, a statement was issued saying it had "raised the readiness status of several thousand troops and associated airlift." Units involved in that announcement are based at Ft. Lee, Ft. Eustis and Ft. Belvoir, Va., Ft. Bragg, N.C., and Ft. Meade.

Marine Brigade Arrives

At 10 p.m., the Pentagon announced the arrival at Ft. Myer of a battalion of 850 marines from Quantico, Va. The unit is to remain in readiness to assist local authorities if requested. The marine base at Camp Lejeune, N.C. was added to the readiness list.

By then, the crowd in West Potomac park had attracted thousands of curious motorists and forced park police to divert traffic because of the traffic jam.

After two weeks of continuous antiwar demonstrations, the nonviolent effort to bring the government to a halt will come Monday with attempts to block traffic leading into the city and particularly to shut off access to the Pentagon.

Demonstrators are scheduled to start moving from the Washington

Please Turn to Page 18, Col. 1

President Indicates Help for Lockheed

Also Will Seek Federal Projects for West to Ease Unemployment

BY WILLIAM J. DRUMMOND
Times Staff Writer

SAN CLEMENTE — President Nixon indicated strongly Saturday that he would ask Congress to guarantee large private loans to salvage the ailing Lockheed Aircraft Corp.

In a press conference on the lawn of the Western White House, the President also said he would seek to channel future government spending programs to California, Oregon and Washington to alleviate unemployment brought about by curtailed defense spending.

His Administration's decisions on future government contracts, said Mr. Nixon, will give California and the Pacific Northwest "special consideration."

However, he added, "it doesn't mean that we regionally are favoring one part of the country over another, but this part of the country has suffered the most from the turn from a wartime to a peacetime economy."

Decision Due This Week

The decision on Lockheed will be made Tuesday or Wednesday, the President said. But Mr. Nixon added:

"Lockheed is one of the nation's great companies. It provides an enormous employment lift to this part of the country. And I'm going to be heavily influenced by the need to see to it that Southern California, after taking the disappointment of not getting the SST . . . does not have the additional jolt of losing Lockheed.

"That gives you an indication of which way I'm leaning. On the other hand if the Secretary of the Treasury comes in and gives me strong arguments to the contrary, I'll look in the other direction," Mr. Nixon said.

Treasury Secretary John B. Connally has already endorsed the idea of loan guarantees for Lockheed.

On April 27, Connally appeared before a Senate subcommittee on appropriations and asked for government backing of $250 million in loans to Lockheed. This sum is part of the $700 million the Burbank based firm says it needs to produce the L-1011 TriStar air bus.

Banks had already put up $400 million but were balking at further loans without government guarantees against losses should Lockheed renege on repaying.

'Save Lockheed and Jobs'

"What we're trying to do is save Lockheed and save 25,000 to 30,000 jobs to keep this country's largest defense contractor from going into receivership," Connally said.

Speculation on Mr. Nixon's position had been current since his breakfast meeting Friday with former British Prime Minister Harold Wilson. It was the financial troubles of the British firm, Rolls-Royce, makers of the engine for the air bus, that brought Lockheed close to financial ruin.

Mr. Nixon was asked Saturday if it was proper for the government to bail out multimillion-dollar corporations if they got into predicaments through mismanagement.

The President responded that it was Rolls-Royce's failure and not any mismanagement by Lockheed that imperiled the TriStar.

Please Turn to Page 12, Col. 1

Red China Steps Up Efforts to Expand Influence in Mideast

BY WILLIAM TUOHY
Times Staff Writer

BEIRUT—Red China is making a determined effort to strengthen its influence in the Middle East, diplomatic sources here report.

The effort includes exchanging ambassadors, developing trade relations, providing construction experts, and supplying arms and military advisers for insurgent movements in the area.

One reliable source here estimates that China has provided about $225

Rogers starts Mideast quest in Saudi Arabia. Section A, Page 3.

million in aid to the Arab states. But this still falls far short of the Soviet Union's nearly $2 billion in aid.

The Chinese appear to be particularly active in the diplomatic field, the sources say.

In March, Red China established relations at the ambassadorial level with Kuwait, and reportedly is considering making diplomatic ties with Turkey, Lebanon and Iran—all of which recognize Nationalist China.

A trade agreement between China and Kuwait is expected to follow the appointment of an ambassador to Kuwait.

Kuwait recognizes Nationalist China but the Nationalists have decided to break off relations because of the "present deplorable development."

Thus Peking's achievement in Kuwait is regarded as a considerable diplomatic feat by observers here.

In the past six months, China has established diplomatic ties with Canada, Italy, Equatorial Guinea, Cameroon, Ethiopia, Nigeria, and Chile.

Ideologically, China has made progress in the Middle East by calling for the elimination of the state of Israel, which Moscow is committed to recognizing.

And Red China has been all-out in its support of the Palestinian com-

Please Turn to Page 4, Col. 1

Nation Beginning to Find Ways to Solve the Problem of Drugs

BY JOHN BARBOUR
Associated Press Writer

SAN FRANCISCO—Why can't we solve the drug problem? It's somehow a frustrated silent-majority, middle-America question.

A youth in a free clinic in Seattle replies: "What problem?"

A doctor treating addicts in San Francisco ponders a moment and murmurs, "That's a good question."

A drug cop in Washington says defensively, "Law enforcement can't do the whole job. But we've made a lot of progress in the last two years."

And a parent in New York persists, "Why can't we solve the drug problem?"

The drug problem. Tintype visions of Oriental opium dens, or young American kids with their backs flat up against a wall and their heads nodding, or dark rooms and dirty needles, or adolescents with a dance in their eyes, a faster dance than usual. Or the up-and-down escalator of the mind, or the exciting kid in school who gives bad habits a good name. A kaleidoscope of misconceptions and realities, one worse than the other.

Not a bad question: Why can't we solve the drug problem?

We are solving the drug problem, but there are no easy answers.

Only the frustration of realizing that you cannot have a cop on every street corner, you cannot stamp out every opium poppy in the world, you cannot open every package or

Turkey pledges measures to limit opium growing. Section A, Page 3.

frisk every tourist or search every ship and plane that comes to the United States. You cannot put the heel to the throat of every youngster who tries marijuana.

It took a long time for drugs to become everybody's problem. Drugs were a buried sin, hidden in the Negro ghetto, the beatnik haven. They suddenly exploded on middle class

Please Turn to Sec. B, Page 7

IN TODAY'S TIMES

KEPT CANCER SECRET

Playwright Says He Erred in 'Playing God' to Dying Wife

ROCHESTER, N.Y. (AP) — Playwright Robert Anderson says he did not tell his wife she had cancer even though he knew about it four years before her death, and instead "played God . . . trying to arrange her life." Now, he says, he knows he was wrong.

Anderson, author of "Tea and Sympathy" and "I Never Sang for My Father," was speaking Saturday at a conference on death held by Rochester General Hospital in cooperation with the University of Rochester school of medicine in an effort at stripping away the taboos surrounding death.

"It would have been easier, far, far less lonely, if she had known," Anderson said. "I would want to know. The complicated ruses, deceptions, explanations, were incredible."

"I'm quite sure I deprived my wife of the right to share her dying with someone else," he said. "I played God for four years, trying to arrange her life in a way I thought she would want to lead it in her last years, but actually might not have led it if she had known they were her last years."

Anderson, his voice near breaking at times, told the psychiatrists, medical workers, clergymen, social workers and nurses about the death of his wife, Phyllis, 15 years ago from cancer.

Please Turn to Page 16, Col. 1

THE WEATHER

National Weather Service forecast: Considerable cloudiness with chance of scattered light showers today and Monday. Overnight low 52; highs today and Monday 64. Light eye irritation in all but coastal areas of the Los Angeles Basin.

Complete weather information in Section C, Page 4.

Schools to Get Citizen Councils

TUESDAY

FINAL

RACING
RESULTS-ENTRIES

LARGEST CIRCULATION IN THE WEST, 1,009,519 DAILY, 1,208,209 SUNDAY.

Los Angeles Times

VOL. XC | FIVE PARTS—PART ONE | TUESDAY MORNING, JUNE 29, 1971 | 82 PAGES | DAILY 10¢

WINNERS--LOSERS

Ellsberg Indicted, 30 Death Sentences Upset, Ali Cleared, Joe Colombo Shot

Condition of Crime Figure Held Critical

BY JOHN J. GOLDMAN
Times Staff Writer

NEW YORK—A gunman disguised as a photographer shot and critically wounded Joseph A. Colombo Sr. Monday as the reputed organized crime leader was making final arrangements in Manhattan's Columbus Circle to lead his big Italian-American Civil Rights League in a unity rally.

While spectators in the crowd of thousands ran in panic, three police officers wrestled the black gunman to the ground. He fell mortally wounded, apparently by bullets from Colombo's bodyguards or possibly by a companion's pistol. Colombo sprawled face up on the ground, amidst fluttering red, white and green bunting. It was a quick, sudden spasm of violence.

Son Stunned by Shooting

The 48-year-old founder of the Italian-American Civil Rights League —which has gained notoriety by its almost nightly picketing of the FBI's headquarters in Manhattan—was rushed by ambulance to nearby Roosevelt Hospital. One of his sons, Joseph Jr., stood stunned in blood-stained clothes outside the operating room while a team of surgeons worked to save his father.

After a five-hour operation, Dr. Irwin Hanson, the neurosurgeon, said Colombo was in a coma and in critical condition. He said it was "too early to tell whether or not he would live." The operating team removed a bullet from Colombo's brain and another from his neck. A third bullet remained lodged in his left jaw.

The surgeon said it would be "a week or two" before the extent of brain damage could be determined.

The assailant, identified by police as Jerome Johnson, 24, was dead on arrival at the hospital. Police said he had a criminal record.

Please Turn to Page 10, Col. 1

GETS WORD — Muhammad Ali in Chicago after draft evasion conviction was overturned.
AP Wirephoto

Ali Wins Reversal of Draft Sentence

Exclusive to The Times from a Staff Writer

WASHINGTON—Former heavyweight champion Muhammad Ali Monday won a Supreme Court reversal of his draft-refusal conviction. The court held that the Justice Department "was simply wrong as a matter of law" in the case.

In an 8-0 decision, the court said that "there is absolutely no way of knowing" whether Ali had been denied a conscientious-objector exemption on legal grounds.

Ali, who was sentenced to five years in prison and fined $10,000 in 1967 for refusing to be inducted, met with newsmen in Chicago shortly after a grocery-store owner hugged him and told him of the decision.

"I've done my celebrating already. I said a prayer to Allah," said Ali, who sought exemption from the

Please Turn to Page 12, Col. 1

Court to Rule on Legality of Executions

BY RONALD J. OSTROW
Times Staff Writer

WASHINGTON — The Supreme Court Monday agreed to rule whether the constitutional guarantee against cruel and unusual punishment bans the death penalty.

At the same time, the justices reversed the death sentences, but not the convictions, of 30 persons, including Richard Speck, who was found guilty of slaying eight nurses in Chicago five years ago.

Supreme Court limits aid for parochial schools. Part 1, Page 5.

The principal reason cited for reversing the death sentences was an earlier court ruling against keeping foes of capital punishment off juries without determining that their opposition would influence their judgment in all cases.

In addition, the court vacated the convictions pending further proceedings of nine other persons who had been sentenced to death.

The justices agreed to rule on the challenge of cruel and unusual punishment, a question on which capital punishment opponents have long been trying to win high court review, in four varied cases, including that of a Ventura man convicted in 1966 of raping and murdering two women.

Could Determine Fate of 600

The decision in the four cases, which will be heard during the court's next term opening in October, could determine the fate of more than 600 persons under death sentence in the United States. Ninety-nine are in California.

In what appeared to be an indication that the justices would prefer suspending executions until their decision, the court held up issuing a final order rejecting appeals in two capital punishment cases decided May 3.

One is the 1967 conviction of Dennis McGautha for murdering a Los Angeles grocer. McGautha's appeal, attacking the discretion allowed juries in imposing the death penalty, was turned down by the court 6 to 3.

But then, asking the justices to reconsider, McGautha raised the cruel and unusual punishment challenge.

The defendant in the Ventura case is Earnest James Aikens Jr., who was convicted of raping and murdering Mrs. Kathleen Nell Dodd in 1962 and Mrs. Mary Winifred Eaton three years later.

Please Turn to Page 12, Col. 3

HAWK AND DOVE—Two photos show change in attitude toward Vietnam war of Daniel Ellsberg. At top he appears in combat garb with weapon during tour as a civilian in Vietnam. Below, with his wife, Patricia, he is met by newsmen in Boston on Monday.
AP Wirephotos

Ex-Pentagon Adviser Gives Up in Boston

BY GENE BLAKE and JACK NELSON
Times Staff Writers

Within hours after he publicly acknowledged that he leaked top-secret Pentagon papers to the press, Daniel Ellsberg was indicted here Monday on charges that he had unauthorized possession of the documents and converted them to his own use.

A federal grand jury accused Ellsberg, 40, a onetime Hawk turned Dove, of stealing copies of a study entitled, "United States—Vietnam Relations, 1945-67." The theft occurred in about September and October, 1969, when Ellsberg was a government consultant at Rand Corp. in Santa Monica, according to the indictment.

Meanwhile, the U.S. Supreme Court postponed its scheduled adjournment to consider whether the government may pursue its suits to ban further publication of the leaked documents. A ruling is expected soon, possibly today.

Surrenders in Boston

Ellsberg, now a senior research associate at the Center for International Studies at Massachusetts Institute of Technology, surrendered on a federal warrant to the U.S. attorney in Boston. He arrived at the federal building in a taxi with his wife, Patricia, and attorney Charles Nesson a few minutes before the 10 a.m. time Nesson had announced he would surrender.

Although he faces a possible 10-year prison term and $10,000 fine on each of two counts, Ellsberg nevertheless was smiling and buoyant. He told newsmen in a sidewalk interview that he hoped publication of the documents would help end the Vietnam war.

Looking among the scores of newsmen and about 200 supporters and spectators surrounding him outside the federal building, Ellsberg said:

"I wonder if there are many people who wouldn't think that 10 years in prison is a very cheap price if they contribute to ending this war."

In Congress, the top-secret Vietnam study was delivered in sealed

Please Turn to Page 6, Col. 1

House Rejects End-War Move; Compromise Proposal Expected

BY THOMAS J. FOLEY
Times Staff Writer

WASHINGTON — The House Monday rejected a Senate-passed proposal urging President Nixon to end the war within nine months—but by the smallest margin to date against any Vietnam withdrawal plan.

The vote was 219 to 176 against an amendment to the draft extension bill sponsored by Sen. Mike Mansfield (D-Mont.) in the Senate and, carried to the House by Rep. Charles W. Whalen Jr. (R-Ohio).

The margin would have been closer but for a pledge by House Armed Services Committee leaders, who promptly began to work out differences on the draft bill with their Senate counterparts. The committee leaders promised to come back to the House with a compromise on the Mansfield amendment.

House GOP Conference Chairman John B. Anderson of Illinois, said he and a group of other Republicans were ready to vote for the Mansfield amendment until the compromise pledge was made. The number of votes in this group was put at 10 by one Republican.

Anderson said he was hoping for a declaration of policy by Congress to end the war although without a specific date.

A White House aide said the Administration hoped to head off more end-the-war amendments in the House by compromising with a policy statement that members could point to that they voted for, rather than against.

Although House and Senate conferees began work immediately on settling differences between the two versions of the draft bill, there was

Please Turn to Page 12, Col. 1

THE WEATHER

National Weather Service forecast: Some early morning low clouds and fog, otherwise sunny today and Wednesday. High today, 80. Slightly warmer Wednesday. High Monday, 76; low, 62.

Index in Part 1, Page 2

BOARD OF EDUCATION RULING

Citizen Councils Ordered for L.A. Schools

BY JACK McCURDY
Times Education Writer

Citizen advisory councils at each of Los Angeles city's 625 schools were ordered by the Board of Education Monday in completing action on the district's long-pending decentralization program.

The move to provide a measure of community control by lay citizens over school affairs is widely considered as the most important part of the plan to decentralize operations of the huge school district.

Under the program, advisory councils will share authority with principals over functions of individual elementary, secondary, adult and occupational schools.

The majority of members on newly created councils are required to be elected from among students' parents by balloting in communities served by the schools.

The new policies go further than ever before in giving lay citizens some direct control over schools on the local level at the expense of professional educators in the district.

The exact powers of the councils were left unclear, however.

The advisory bodies are empowered to assess the "education needs" of students and to establish program priorities, both of which significantly expand their present authority.

But the plan says their purpose is only to "advise" principals, who remain "responsible for decisions" in operating the schools.

In the past, advisory groups have been recommended by the district's central administration, but their formation by principals has been slow.

The district claims that 70% of the elementary and 90% of the junior and senior high schools now have advisory groups in some form.

Please Turn to Page 21, Col. 7

Council Votes Raise for 17,000

THURSDAY
FINAL

RACING
RESULTS-ENTRIES

Los Angeles Times

LARGEST CIRCULATION IN THE WEST, 1,009,319 DAILY, 1,203,209 SUNDAY.

VOL. XC SEVEN PARTS—PART ONE THURSDAY MORNING, JULY 1, 1971 132 PAGES DAILY 10¢

Court Unleashes Press

SECRETS ANYONE?

TURKEY MOVES

Opium Fields: Bumper Crop May Be Last

BY WILLIAM TUOHY
Times Staff Writer

AFYON, Turkey — It's harvest time in Afyon, and the white and purple poppy blossoms are losing their petals, exposing the green, plum-sized opium pods to ripen in the sun.

This year's harvest on the 4,000-foot-high Anatolian Plateau is expected to be a bumper crop.

It also might be the last.

Turkey, leading source of the opium-derivative heroin channeling illegally into the United States, agreed Wednesday to eradicate the production of poppies by late next year.

But 75,000 farm families in central Turkey, to whom opium is their livlihood, may never understand, even though President Nixon promised aid—estimated to run $10 million over several years—to wean them to other crops or pursuits.

Sell Opium to Government

"Our life is built on growing poppies," said 40-year-old Lutfi Yeldiz, in the nearby village of Kumartas. "We produce our opium and sell it to the government. They say they use it for medicine . . .

"We have heard in the newspapers that America is against opium, but we do not know why. I don't understand what you mean by drug addiction."

As Yeldiz says, legally produced opium is sold through government agencies to worldwide pharmaceutical firms which convert it to morphine and codeine to help the sick and injured.

But the same raw opium, illegally trafficked and refined into heroin, eventually finds its way into the veins of countless thousands of addicts. President Nixon Wednesday said more than 60% of the heroin peddled in the United States comes from Turkey, and he credited this nation with a "statesmanlike and courageous" decision.

Means Little to Farmers

Such high-level statements mean next to nothing, however, to farmers like Yeldiz. Wearing the traditional garb of dark suit, vest and cap, he says:

"If the government tells me not to plant poppies, it would be like saying that I can't eat bread. I could not obey such an order and live."

And a fellow farmer says:

"Opium is our best crop and we can't worry about other people's problems."

In the provincial capital, sitting beneath a portrait of the late Kemal Ataturk, the founder of modern Turkey, an agricultural official said: "This year 27,000 families are growing opium in this province. The people have been growing opium here for centuries. It would be very, very difficult for these conservative and illiterate farmers to switch to other crops."

The opium plant is enormously rewarding to the farmers of Afyon.

In addition to gathering the raw opium, the farmers use the leaves for salad greens. They eat or bake bread with poppy seeds. They press the rest of the seeds into cooking oil.

Please Turn to Page 28, Col. 1

Council Rejects Yorty Veto of Pay Increases

17,000 City Employes Will Get 5.5% Boost; Mayor Upheld in Denial of Police, Fire Hike

BY RICHARD WEST
Times Staff Writer

Los Angeles city councilmen Wednesday overrode Mayor Sam Yorty's veto of a $12.4 million pay raise for 17,000 city civilian employes.

An attempt to override the veto of a $6 million raise for 10,000 policemen and firemen failed.

In vetoing the pay raises, the mayor left open the possibility that he would reverse his position—or even approve a much larger raise for policemen and firemen—if the council adopts new revenue measures.

The raise for civilian personnel will go into effect today, the first day of the 1971-72 fiscal year.

But action on police and fire pay apparently must await council efforts to find $39 million in new revenues to balance the city's $577.4 million budget for this fiscal year.

The veto of the 5.5% increase for civilian employes was overridden by a vote of 13 to 1. Councilman Billy G. Mills cast the only negative vote.

The attempt to override the veto of the 3.75% raise for the uniformed services failed to carry on a vote of 8 for and 5 against. Overrides require 12 affirmative votes. The ordinance was sent back to committee.

The council took its actions in the afternoon after the mayor had vetoed the measures Wednesday morning.

Yorty's main reason for rejecting the ordinances, he said in messages to the City Council, is that the council has failed to adopt revenue measures necessary to pay for the increases.

The mayor said he also vetoed the raise for civilian employes because the council refused to grant increases to department managers and their chief assistants.

The city attorney's office, Yorty told the council, gave an opinion even before the ordinance was passed that it would "probably not be upheld if subjected to a legal challenge."

The City Charter requires paying prevailing wages to civilian employes.

The mayor advised the councilmen, "It would be more prudent to enact ordinances approved by the city attorney as to legality."

Another reason for his veto of the 3.75% raise for uniformed personnel, Yorty said, is that the council rejected a recommendation from the city administrative officer that policemen and firemen be given a 7.8% raise under existing procedures for adjusting annual salaries.

Please Turn to Page 20, Col. 1

TRACKED HIM AROUND WORLD

29-Year Search Ends as Pole Finds Slayer of Grandfather

BY TOM LAMBERT
Times Staff Writer

JERUSALEM — Sigmund Gorson's long and bitter search has ended. His sworn promise to a dead man has been fulfilled. The hunt is over. He is preparing to go home.

For 29 years, Gorson has been tracking relentlessly the slayer of his grandfather, clubbed to death one mournful winter day in Poland. This week Gorson found him in Israel.

"I feel like a stone weighing a million pounds has been lifted from my heart," he said wearily Wednesday by telephone from a Tel Aviv hotel.

"Vengeance? No, I wasn't seeking vengeance. I am not a violent man. I wanted justice for my grandfather, who was like God to me. It is now up to the Israeli authorities what to do next."

Followed Hitler Sweep

Gorson's search began after Hitler's armies swept into Poland, and into the industrial city of Lodz. The Germans killed Gorson's father, mother and three sisters.

But they spared Sigmund, then 17 years old, tall and husky, because there was work for young men. Sigmund went to live with his grandfather.

Then middle-aged, Moshe Jacobovitz was a coal distributor, hauling fuel in a one-horse cart to the Lodz ghetto residents. Sigmund became his helper.

One bone-chilling winter day in 1942 Jacobovitz halted his car briefly in front of a battered house in which lived three orphan girls he and Sigmund had been helping. Sigmund tucked several lumps of coal into his pockets and slipped off the cart to give them to the girls.

The Jewish house warden spotted the theft, tore the coal away from the boy and began flailing him with a club. He broke Sigmund's jaw. When Jacobovitz jumped off the cart to intervene, the warden turned on him and clubbed him unconscious. Sigmund dragged his grandfather home.

"He never recovered conscious-

Please Turn to Page 29, Col. 1

Four Papers Resume Their Series on War

Exclusive to The Times from a Staff Writer

NEW YORK—The New York Times and the Washington Post, acting under a favorable U.S. Supreme Court ruling Wednesday resumed publication today of their separate series based on the secret Pentagon study of the Vietnam war.

Two other newspapers affected by the case took similar action.

The New York Times' article published for today's editions said the Pentagon study showed that President John F. Kennedy transformed the "limited-risk gamble" of the Eisenhower administration into a "broad commitment" to prevent Communist domination of South Vietnam.

Feared 'Neutralists'

The Post reports appearing this morning featured an account of how the Kennedy and Johnson administrations in 1963 and 1964 feared that pro-French "neutralist" interests in Saigon might force the United States to quit Vietnam without victory.

Much of the information in the New York Times and Washington Post articles had been published before in newspapers—including the Los Angeles Times—not enjoined from printing information based on the Pentagon documents.

The New York and Washington papers had been forced to halt their series two weeks ago by government-obtained court orders.

But in a 6-3 ruling Wednesday, the Supreme Court held that the government had not met the burden of proving that national security would be harmed by disclosure of the Pentagon papers.

Others Also Resume

Also resuming publication in this morning's editions were the Boston Globe and the St. Louis Post-Dispatch. Neither was directly involved in the case before the Supreme Court, but both had been under federal court order not to publish further stories on the Pentagon study.

In its new article, the New York Times said the secret Pentagon study disclosed that President Kennedy knew of and approved plans for the military coup d'etat that overthrew President Ngo Dinh Diem in 1963.

"Our complicity in his overthrow heightened our responsibilities and our commitment" in Vietnam, the study found according to the New York Times.

The paper went on to say that, although Mr. Kennedy resisted pres-

Please Turn to Page 14, Col. 1

JUBILANT — Mrs. Katharine Graham, Washington Post publisher, and Arthur O. Sulzberger, New York Times publisher, hail court decision.
AP Wirephotos

Vote-at-18 Measure Now in Constitution Thanks to Ohio

COLUMBUS, Ohio (AP)—The voting age in all elections was lowered to 18 years Wednesday night when Ohio ratified the 26th Amendment to the U.S. Constitution, fulfilling the requirement that 38 states do so to make it law.

The Ohio House, with 99 members, ratified the amendment 81 to 9, a day after the Senate passed it 30 to 2.

House Speaker Charles Kurfess ruled out of order fellow Republican Rep. Jim Thorpe, who loudly objected to the quick action as the vote was taken electronically.

The North Carolina and Alabama legislatures approved the amendment earlier in the day.

Alabama Gov. George C. Wallace withheld his signature from the measure, hoping to time it so his state would be the one to carry the amendment over. However, Lt. Gov. Jere Beasley of Alabama and legislators in Ohio said a governor's signature was unnecessary.

The amendment attracted some opposition in the Ohio Legislature, where some felt that such a question should be put to a public vote. Ohio rejected a proposal two years ago to

Please Turn to Page 27, Col. 1

Ruling Backs N.Y. Times, Wash. Post

BY RONALD J. OSTROW
and LINDA MATHEWS
Times Staff Writers

WASHINGTON — The Supreme Court Wednesday freed the New York Times and the Washington Post to resume publishing articles on the Pentagon's top secret Vietnam war study, rejecting the government's claim that national security would be imperiled.

In a 6-3 ruling, the court held the government had failed to introduce sufficient proof to justify interfering with the First Amendment guarantee of a free press.

The decision was so splintered—each justice wrote his own opinion—that it provided only limited guidelines for the government or the press in any future cases. But it left

Supreme Court text on Page 16. Related stories on Pages 14, 15, 17.

open the possibility that the court could uphold prior restraint of the press under other circumstances.

Both the New York Times, which has been under court order not to publish the articles since June 15, and the Post, which has been restrained since June 19, said immediately they would publish more on the study in today's editions.

The Boston Globe and the St. Louis Post-Dispatch, which were challenging restraining orders in lower courts, made similar announcements.

The high court ruling, its final action before adjourning until October, took the form of an unsigned, 207-word order. Those backing it were Justices Hugo L. Black, William J. Brennan Jr., William O. Douglas, Thurgood Marshall, Potter Stewart and Byron R. White.

Justice John Marshall Harlan, backed by Chief Justice Warren E. Burger and Justice Harry A. Blackmun, dissented, criticizing the majority for being "almost irresponsibly feverish" in handling the case and for substituting its judgement of national security for that of the President.

Two Decisive Votes

The Stewart and White votes were decisive because they had sided with the three dissenters last Friday in continuing to restrain the two newspapers while the court decided the case. The other four members of the majority had favored erasing the publication bans without even hearing arguments.

Both Stewart and White conceded that publication of the so-far unidentified material in the top secret study of the origins of American involvement in the Vietnam conflict would do some harm to the national interest.

"But I cannot say that disclosure of any of (the documents) will surely result in direct, immediate and irreparable damage to our nation or its people," said Stewart. "That being so, there can under the First

Please Turn to Page 17, Col. 6

Index to The Times

THE WEATHER

National Weather Service forecast: Late night and early morning coastal low clouds but mostly sunny today and Friday. High today near 80. High Wednesday, 77; low, 59.

Complete weather information and smog report in Part 2, Page 4.

REVIEW

COMPLETE N.Y. STOCKS

Los Angeles Times

RACING ENTRIES

LARGEST CIRCULATION IN THE WEST, 1,009,519 DAILY, 1,208,209 SUNDAY.

VOL. XC | SIX PARTS—PART ONE | ★★★ | MONDAY, SEPTEMBER 13, 1971 | 96 PAGES | Copyright © 1971 Los Angeles Times | DAILY 10c

PRISON STORMED

9 Hostages, 28 Convicts Killed

Whew! Now It's Smog, Blackouts With Fierce Heat

BY DIAL TORGERSON
Times Staff Writer

Stagnant air, thick with smog, and fiercely hot, settled on Southern California today. The heat wave's toll:

—The entire Los Angeles power system neared a crisis level with hundreds of power outages in scores of communities.

—Over-100-degree heat forced the early closure of school for 75,000 pupils in San Bernardino and Riverside counties.

—The Air pollution Control District called a county-wide fir first stage smog alert at 12:30 p.m., when the ozone level reached .55 parts per million parts of air in the west San Gabriel Valley. It was the first smog alert of the year.

—No immediate relief was in sight. The stagnant air mass was expected to remain nearly stationary for at least 24 hours.

The long-range forecast called for temperatures in the 90s or better through Friday. At 1 p.m. today the temperature reached 103 degrees at the Civic Center with a high of 105 predicted.

Demands on Power

Millions sought relief from the oppressive heat with home air conditioners, coolers and fans, bringing the threat of what the Department of Water and Power called "selective interruption."

Said Floyd L. Goss, chief electrical engineer and assistant manager of the Department of Water and Power:

"This is an unprecedented heat wave. We may exceed our generating capacity. We may be forced to ask for voluntary curtailment of the use of power. If that doesn't work we may be forced to drop service to certain areas until the load on our capacity drops."

All major hospitals and police and fire units have back-up emergency service. The Department of Water and Power said the first areas blacked out—if it becomes necessary—would be residential.

Right Up to Capacity

"The capacity of our system is 3.5 million kilowatts," Goss said. "Our prediction of the load on our service is 3.5 million kilowatts."

A fire broke out in dry brush and heavy grass in Glendale just north of Eagle Rock Reservoir shortly before noon and burned over 35 acres before being contained.

Firemen from the Glendale, Los Angeles and Los Angeles County departments fought the blaze in the foothills where Figueroa St. ends in Scholl Canyon. Units from Pasadena stood by in the event assistance was required.

FEATURE INDEX

FLEEING TEAR GAS—As tear gas swirls around Attica, N.Y., State Prison, one guard guides another away to receive first aid. AP Wirephoto

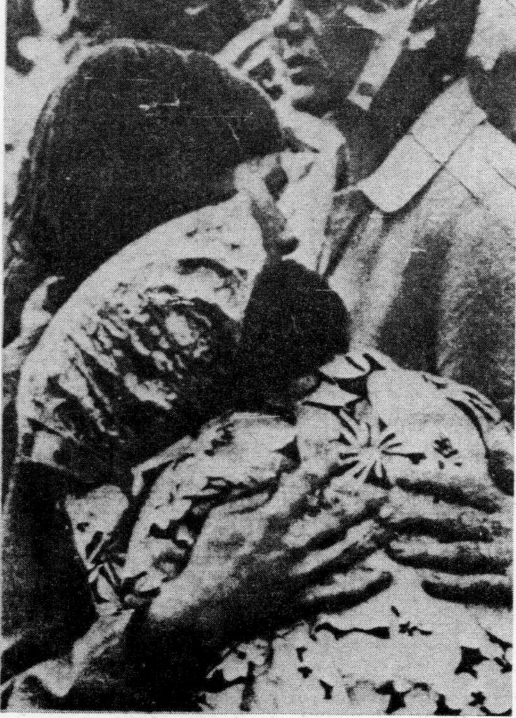

FEARFUL RELATIVES—Relatives of the hostages comfort one another during tense wait as police stormed into the stronghold. AP Wirephoto

NO CHOICE—State Correction Commissioner Russell G Oswald tells need for massive assault on insurgent inmates. AP Wirephoto

AWAITING NEWS—Apprehension and grief are reflected in the faces of friends and relatives as troops aided by helicopters dropping tear gas force their way into prison in bid to free hostages. AP Wirephoto

Attica Under Control; 29 of Guards Freed

ATTICA, N.Y. (UPI)—Nine hostages were slain by inmates and 28 convicts were killed by gunfire today when 1,700 state troopers, national guardsmen and sheriff's deputies stormed the Attica Correctional Facility to end one of the bloodiest revolts in the nation's prison annals.

A prison guard who died Saturday after he was thrown out of a window brought the death toll to 38.

The assault under the cover of two helicopters dropping tear gas liberated 29 of the 38 guards and civilian employes held captive by the inmates for five days.

Thrown Into Pit

Eight of the surviving hostages were thrown into a pit and doused with gasoline but at the last minute the convicts decided not to set them afire.

Some of the dead hostages had their throats slashed. One was shot to death.

The attack was ordered by State Correction Commissioner Russell G. Oswald—with Gov. Nelson A. Rockefeller's consent—after the inmates rejected an ultimatum to release the hostages.

A spokesman for Rockefeller said some of the hostage guards and civilian prison employes had been killed hours before the all-out assault on the lone cellblock still in convict hands. The governor called them "cold-blooded killings" by revolutionary militants.

Taken Back to Their Cells

Five hours after the massive assault on the gray-walled prison began, the entire 54-acre facility was under police control. Troopers and guardsmen systematically returned the 1,000 inmates—mostly blacks and Puerto Ricans—who took part in the revolt to their cells.

"We were so near death so many times, it's unbelievable," said Capt. Elmer Huehn, one of the freed hostages. "They held a knife to my throat. But the Puerto Rican guy didn't have the heart to do it. Some of the others weren't so lucky."

Oswald said the decision to storm the prison was made after he learned the insurgents were arming themselves with zip guns and knives made in a captured prison workshop. At the same time, he said, the prisoners were filling underground tunnels with electrically triggered explosives, and power was shut off to prevent them from setting off the charges.

"It became apparent to me that the situation was rapidly deteriorating, and it was evident the prisoners were not going to cooperate," Oswald said. "Their behavior was not too much different than their behavior on the streets, where several were convicted of manslaughter and murder."

Ignore Amnesty Demand

The convicts had threatened to kill their hostages if their demands for amnesty were not met. Authorities ignored the amnesty demand and ordered the attack.

"Surrender peacefully. You will not be harmed," a bull horn blared to the prisoners. "Surrender the hostages. Surrender the hostages. Lie down on the floor and put your hands on your head."

The attack on the prison came without warning. Rockefeller had signed the executive order calling up the National Guard hours earlier, but it was not announced.

Los Angeles Times

LARGEST CIRCULATION IN THE WEST, 1,009,519 DAILY, 1,208,209 SUNDAY.

VOL. XC | 2† FIVE PARTS—PART ONE | CC | TUESDAY MORNING, OCTOBER 26, 1971 | 84 PAGES | DAILY 10c

U.N. Seats Red China, Ousts Taiwan in Defeat for U.S.

Vote of 76-35 With 17 Abstentions Ends 22-Year Battle in Assembly

BY DON SHANNON
Times Staff Writer

UNITED NATIONS—The United States took a stunning defeat Monday as the U.N. General Assembly beat down delaying efforts and pushed through the Albanian resolution seating Communist China and ousting Taiwan. The vote was 76 to 35 with 17 abstentions.

Just before midnight, Secretary General U Thant sent a cable to the Ministry of Foreign Affairs in Peking transmitting the vote and text of the resolution.

The action climaxed a 22-year battle over China's U.N. representation, highlighted by a major U.S. effort in recent weeks to prevent the ouster of the Taiwan government.

Immediately before the vote, Nationalist Chinese Foreign Minister Chow Shu-kai strode to the speaker's rostrum and said in a voice of controlled fury that in view of the "frenzied and irrational" actions of the members, the Republic of China had decided to take no further part in the proceedings.

Vows to Continue Struggle

"We shall continue on the outside the struggle for the ideals on which the United Nations was founded but which the General Assembly has now betrayed," Chow declared.

An earlier key vote Monday, which foreshadowed the passage of the Albanian resolution, was on the U.S. proposal that the expulsion of Taiwan be considered an "important question" requiring a two-thirds majority. It was defeated by a vote of 59 to 55 with 15 abstentions.

U.S. officials had confidently predicted that they would win a simple majority on this issue and many observers had believed the results would end in a deadlock with no action in this session of the assembly.

African and Communist bloc delegations burst into cheers and clapped rhythmically as the electric scoreboard crept toward rejection of the "important question" proposal.

Further delaying action by Saudi Arabia's veteran Ambassador Jamil M. Baroody went down by heavy margins and the Albanian resolution itself was then overwhelmingly passed.

The final vote meant the collapse of the tactic—that of the "imporant question"—which the United States has used for 20 years to block the entry of Communist China.

This year the "important question" was applied by the Americans and their allies not to the admission of Peking but to the expulsion of Taiwan. The Albanian resolution—approved by Peking—embodied both actions in a single motion which its sponsors refused to split.

A warning signal of the U.S. defeat came earlier Monday when a Saudi Arabian motion to put off decision of the issue until today was beaten by 56 to 53 with 19 abstentions. Despite the fact that U.S. and allied strategists claimed earlier that further delay would help their cause, the ballot followed the same lines as that on the important question, with the exception that in the vote to postpone the decision there were four more abstentions.

Please Turn to Page 16, Col. 1

Presidential adviser Kissinger leaves Peking. Part 1, Page 18.

JUBILATION ON THE FLOOR—U.N. delegates reacting to vote to seat Red China and oust Taiwan. *AP Wirephoto*

BLAMES HIMSELF

Bush Stunned by Action, Calls It a Moment of Infamy

Exclusive to The Times from a Staff Writer

UNITED NATIONS—U.S. Ambassador George Bush, speaking to newsmen after the U.S. defeat in the General Assembly, called the vote a "moment of infamy."

"The only issue before the assembly was whether the General Assembly would expel the Republic of China, the functioning authority of 14 million people," he said. "The decision to deprive the Republic of China of representation in our opinion was a serious mistake."

The stunned ambassador was asked if he foresees a cutoff of U.S. funds to the United Nations, which constitute one-third of the operating budget. He replied:

"There are strong feelings in Congress. I suspect there was more unanimity in the House and Senate on wanting to see the Republic of China stay in the United Nations than on any issue in a long, long time. To underestimate the feeling on this subject in the country would be a serious mistake."

Smiling ruefully, he added:

"I am tremendously disappointed and looking desperately for somebody to blame and I can't find anybody else but me."

Refuses to Speculate

Bush refused to join the "guessing game" about what will happen when Peking arrives here, and said the United States has not yet made a decision about the seating of Peking in the Security Council, where the United States has a veto. But he pointed out that the U.S. dual representation plan offered the seat to the mainland government while keeping Taiwan in the assembly.

At another press conference, Taiwan's Foreign Affairs Minister Chow Shu-kai, who led his delegation from the General Assembly, said when the Chinese Communist regime took its seat in the world body "it will transform the United Nations into a Maoist front and a

Please Turn to Page 20, Col. 1

IN THE FACE OF DEFEAT—Nationalist Chinese Foreign Minister Chow Shu-kai, front, and Ambassador Liu Chieh as outcome of the U.N. vote became apparent. Man, rear, is not identified. *AP Wirephoto*

2 MONTHS LATER

'New Normalcy' Slowly Returning at San Quentin

BY PHILIP HAGER
Times Staff Writer

SAN QUENTIN—"It started, for us, around 3 yesterday afternoon when shots rang out . . .

"Following the shots (sounded like three to me) we heard a commotion in the yard, saw two convicts running, heard a shout of 'he has a gun' and all hell broke loose . . ."

Thus wrote an inmate here to a friend the day after the escape incident of Aug. 21, the day three guards and three inmates—including black militant George Jackson—were killed.

Jackson was shot by a guard as he dashed from the maximum-security adjustment center. The other five died inside the adjustment center and six inmates have been charged with murder in their deaths.

Attorney Also Charged

An Oakland attorney, Stephen M. Bingham, similarly charged as a conspirator who smuggled a pistol to Jackson in the prison visiting room, is still being sought by authorities.

Now, a little more than two months later, San Quentin is slowly returning to what one correction official called a "new normalcy."

"It will have to be a 'new normalcy,' because we don't want that to happen ever again," said the official. "It cost six lives and whether they were guards or inmates they were all human beings."

In the days after the incident there were repeated searches and heavy restrictions on the 2,800 inmates here. Gradually, most have been returned to their regular routine and work assignments.

There have been no major in-

Please Turn to Page 26, Col. 1

Ousted Mitchell Aide May Have Broken Bank Laws, Report Says

BY KEN W. CLAWSON
Exclusive to The Times from the Washington Post

WASHINGTON — Atty. Gen. John N. Mitchell dumped his chief enforcer of criminal laws 10 days ago after the Federal Deposit Insurance Corp. reported that Will Wilson may have violated federal banking laws in a Texas stock fraud scandal.

The FDIC report called for an investigation of Wilson's role in bank loans and stock purchases for Ted Bristol, an FDIC bank examiner who has since been indicted. The report was the first indication that Wilson may have been involved in banking law violations while a private lawyer for Houston financier Frank W. Sharp.

Wilson, who has retained his Georgetown residence here since he resigned Oct. 16 as assistant attorney general in charge of the Justice Department's criminal division, maintained Monday he had done nothing illegal.

He said the FDIC report, which he was shown, "didn't seem all that important to me," but he added, "it did seem important" to Mitchell and Dep. Atty. Gen. Richard G. Kleindienst when they convinced him to step down.

The FDIC report questioned whether Wilson actually was unaware of the governmental post held by Bristol when $10,000 worth of stock was purchased for Bristol's wife on Feb. 20, 1968.

The report called for an investigation into Wilson's role in the stock purchase, and also whether Wilson was unaware that he was paying for electronic surveillance of bank examiners in late 1967 when he spent $2,500 of his own money, later reimbursed by Sharp, to "Construction Consultants, Inc."

Justice Department sources said Monday that Wilson's role in these and other aspects of the Sharpstown State Bank fraud was under investigation by a federal grand jury in Houston. Wilson said he had not been called by the grand jury.

A total of eight men, including Bristol and three other former banking examiners, were indicted Sept. 29 on charges of scheming with Sharp to defraud the government. The indictments said the conspiracy

Please Turn to Page 9, Col. 1

Jumbo Jet Hijacked to Cuba; 237 Aboard

N.Y. Airliner Carrying 3 Sky Marshals, FBI Agent

MIAMI (UPI)—An American Airlines Boeing 747 with 237 persons aboard—including three sky marshals and an FBI agent—was hijacked to Cuba Monday night during a flight from New York to Puerto Rico.

The jumbo jet, carrying 221 passengers and 16 crew members, landed safely in Havana at 9:58 p.m. It was the second 747 hijacked to Cuba.

A Federal Aviation Administration spokesman in New York said a man armed with a gun took a stewardess hostage in the first class lounge about an hour after the jet, Flight 98, left Kennedy International Airport in New York at 6:45 p.m. bound for San Juan.

The pilot, O. R. Selmela., notified American Airlines and the FAA "by prearranged signal, not voice com-

Please Turn to Page 7, Col. 2

Way Open for Europe Security Talks, Pompidou Tells Brezhnev

PARIS (UPI)—French President Georges Pompidou told Soviet Communist Party leader Leonid I. Brezhnev Monday the road is clear for a European security conference—long sought by Moscow—now that the Big Four powers have reached agreement on the status of West Berlin.

Brezhnev said the Soviet Union had no objection to including the United States and Canada in the conference.

Pompidou said that in light of the accord on Berlin by the United States, Great Britain, France and the Soviet Union, "we think that nothing stands in the way . . . to opening at Helsinki of the multilateral phase of preparing the conference."

Brezhnev, in his first official visit to a Western nation, arrived here earlier in the day to a lukewarm public welcome.

The French position had been there would be no European security conference before an accord on West Berlin. Pompidou's statement appeared to mean France was satisfied the accord would go through despite problems between East and West Germany on its detailed implementation.

Observers viewed Pompidou's approval of a European security conference as a move that would enable France to seize leadership of the project in Western Europe in advance of the December meeting of North Atlantic Treaty Organization foreign ministers. At the semiannual meeting the matter will be of primary consideration.

Pompidou's action, observers believe, is out of step with stated policies of other Western powers, whose interest in the security conference has been characterized by caution and an explicit desire to move slowly.

The French backing for the idea of preparing a European security conference came at a banquet at the

Please Turn to Page 12, Col. 1

Canada, Russia agree to hold trade expansion talks. Part 1, Page 12.

Agnew Calls for War Support; Veterans Day Protest Fizzles

WASHINGTON (AP)—Vice President Agnew led Veterans Day observances Monday with a call for support of President Nixon's war policies, while an antiwar demonstration in the capital fizzled in the rain.

But peace forces claimed that a protest near Ft. Hood, Tex., brought the largest number of arrests of active-duty GIs in any single incident of the peace movement.

Police at Killeen, Tex., said at least 100 persons were arrested near the big Army base. The U.S. Servicemen's Fund said 125 soldiers and 25 civilians and veterans were arrested.

The arrests were made as the demonstrators tried to march after being denied a permit.

In Washington, rain and lack of a crowd washed out the planned start of an antiwar campaign. A rally on the Washington Monument grounds and a march on the White House were put off until today.

Agnew got in his speech at Arlington National Cemetery earlier in the day before the heavy rain started, but only a sparse crowd sat through the dark gray drizzle to hear him.

Later the peace groups scattered from the monument grounds, where only about 300 had gathered. Workshops were held Monday evening in a local church after civil rights activist Hosea Williams and antiwar advocate Dr. Benjamin Spock addressed the groups.

Please Turn to Page 10, Col. 1

THE WEATHER

National Weather Service forecast: Mostly sunny today and Wednesday, but increasing clouds Wednesday. High today, 72. High Monday, 65; low, 48.

Complete weather information and smog report in Part 2, Page 4.

Index to The Times

MOON ROCKS REVEAL HISTORY

Sun One of Stablest Stars, Unchanged in 4 Billion Years

BY THOMAS O'TOOLE
Exclusive to The Times from the Washington Post

WASHINGTON — The sun that gives us heat and light appears to be one of the most stable stars in the universe, essentially unchanged since the earth and moon were formed more than 4 billion years ago.

These conclusions have been reached by scientists comparing satellite measurements of solar particles the last 10 years with the record of the sun's rays left etched on the moon rocks brought back to earth by Apollo astronauts.

"We have found to our surprise," said Dr. James R. Arnold of the University of California at San Diego, "that the average values for the sun are the same today as they were millions of years ago. The sun has not changed very much, if it has changed at all."

Many scientists expected some change in the sun, if only because so many stars in the universe go through violent periodic change. Some stars explode, others flicker on and off and some just collapse.

The measurements of satellites orbiting the earth outside the atmosphere have told scientists what kinds of particles stream from the sun and in what intensities they pour into space, even during storms on the sun's surface.

These satellites have pretty much detailed what happens during an entire solar cycle of 11 years, which is the time it takes for the sun to boil up and quiet down before boiling up again.

Please Turn to Page 8, Col. 1

Los Angeles Times

LARGEST CIRCULATION IN THE WEST, 1,009,819 DAILY, 1,200,209 SUNDAY.

VOL. XCI 2† FIVE PARTS—PART ONE CC TUESDAY MORNING, MAY 9, 1972 94 PAGES

DAILY 10¢

NIXON ORDERS N. VIETNAM PORTS MINED

Confronts Soviet Union With Shipping Blockade

Jets Carry Out Initial Phases of Mining Mission

Operation Seeks to Deny Missiles, Artillery and Tanks to Communist Units

BY GEORGE McARTHUR
Times Staff Writer

SAIGON—An armada of American ships and warplanes today began the blockade of North Vietnam as ordered by President Nixon. But there were few immediate details on what precise measures were being taken.

Three hours after President Nixon spoke, the U.S. command announced:

"United States Navy aircraft are carrying out the orders of the commander in chief.

"The initial phases of the mining operation have been successfully accomplished.

"All planes have returned safely.

"One MIG aircraft was shot down during the operation. We have no further details at this time."

"I cannot talk about current operations," reported the spokesman for the U.S. 7th Air Force which has as one major mission the blocking of the rebuilt northeast rail line between Hanoi and China. This is the major route for Chinese aid to North Vietnam.

Letter to U.N. Council

Military sources would not reveal when the mining of North Vietnam's harbors and coastal inlets began, but a U.S. letter to the U.N. Security Council said it began at 9 a.m. today, Saigon time. The letter said the mines would activate at 6 p.m. Thursday (3 a.m. PDT).

The major port affected, of course, was Haiphong. Since the 1968 U.S. bombing halt, however, the North Vietnamese have restored some port facilities at Hon Gai and at Cam Pha and at river entrances to Thanh Hoa, Vinh and Dong Hoi farther down the coast. In addition, the North Vietnamese have some facilities for bringing in smaller loads off lighters at some points on the coast.

Heavy cargo such as tanks, surface-to-air missiles and big artillery pieces, however, can only come through Haiphong.

Presumably, the Navy intends to turn away most ships in the relatively narrow entrance to the Gulf of Tonkin—a stretch of about 175 miles already blanketed by American radar screens.

So far as is known there are no Russian warships now in the area although several merchant ships were in the area and a Russian radar-trawler always patrols near the U.S. 7th Fleet.

The major Air Force target is the

Please Turn to Page 3, Col. 1

SOME FINANCIAL ANALYSTS FEAR FOR U.S. ECONOMY

BY ROBERT E. WOOD
Times Staff Writer

President Nixon's order to cut North Vietnam's supply lines could bring about a major setback for the American economy, several economists said Monday night.

The first reaction of security analysts was that stock prices, too, would continue—at least for a time—the downtrend already under way because of unfavorable Indochina war news.

The economists expressed fears that the newest war measures could swiftly undercut the nation's growing recovery in employment and personal income if it leads to a prolonged confrontation between this country and the Soviet Union.

"In the very short term, at least until we know more about what's going to happen, it's a sure bet to create tremendous uncertainty in the public's mind," said Robert T.

Please Turn to Page 19, Col. 1

War Escalates Into a Direct Showdown Between U.S., Russ

BY DAVID KRASLOW
Times Washington Bureau Chief

WASHINGTON — For years American and Soviet leaders tiptoed around the Vietnam war in an effort to keep that treacherous problem from fouling relations between the two superpowers.

Now President Nixon, facing the possibility of a humiliation in Indochina which he concluded would be too damaging to America's standing as a world leader, has escalated Vietnam to a cosmic issue involving direct confrontation between Moscow and Washington.

If Vietnam ever was a peripheral question, it no longer is.

The President's direct challenge to the Soviet Union as the primary supplier of the armaments North Vietnam is relying upon in its "go-for-broke" invasion of South Vietnam entails a drastic shift in priorities in Washington-Moscow diplomacy.

Mr. Nixon's decision probably has created a situation in which there now has to be some big power movement on the Vietnam issue before the Russians and Americans can proceed further with such questions as strategic arms limitations, a European security conference and increased trade.

The summit conference scheduled to begin May 22 in Moscow which Mr. Nixon announced with such fanfare some months ago as another giant step in his journey for peace is jeopardy.

Please Turn to Page 11, Col. 1

ORDERED SEALED OFF—Haiphong Harbor and the mouth of the Cua Cam River in view taken by U.S. Navy reconnaissance plane. UPI photo

Says Measures Are Needed Because of Hanoi's Arrogant Rejection of All U.S. Offers

BY ROBERT C. TOTH
Times Staff Writer

WASHINGTON—President Nixon Monday announced that North Vietnam is being cut off from sea and rail supplies—its harbors mined and blockaded—to deprive it of the weapons of war.

He thus confronted Soviet leaders with a test of will implying clearly that Russian ships may be stopped by American vessels or sunk by American mines if the Soviet Union continues to attempt to supply North Vietnam by sea. And he clearly jeopardized his summit meeting with Soviet leaders due to start in Moscow in two weeks. No immediate reaction was forthcoming from Moscow.

Mr. Nixon demanded the return of U.S. prisoners of war and a cease-fire throughout Indochina to stop his portentous actions to isolate North Vietnam—but he promised total withdrawal of all U.S. forces from South Vietnam within four months thereafter.

The President also implied that the United States would withdraw from negotiations and leave a peace settlement to both Vietnams to work out.

Less than two weeks ago Mr. Nixon told the American people that Hanoi was making "its last desperate gamble," and the same might now be said of his fateful moves.

Almost 10 years after the Cuban missile blockade which brought the world to the brink of World War III, Mr. Nixon was attempting to force

Text of Nixon address on Page 8. Other stories, photos, map on Page 3.

Moscow to stop shipment of tanks, artillery and other sophisticated offensive weapons which, he said, made Hanoi's invasion of South Vietnam possible.

Mr. Nixon told the nation in a 17-minute radio-television address that his orders to mine and blockade North Vietnamese ports were being implemented as he spoke. All vessels in affected ports—recently reported to be about 29 Soviet and other Communist ships—will have three daylight periods to get out safely before the mines are activated Thursday at 3 a.m. PDT.

After that, any ships attempting to enter or leave will do so "at their own risk," Mr. Nixon said.

"These actions are not directed at any other nation," he said. Countries with vessels in the threatened ports were notified in advance of the action, he added.

The sole purpose of the moves is "to protect the lives of 60,000 Americans who would be gravely endangered in the event the Communist offensive continues to roll forward, and to prevent the imposition of a Communist government (on South Vietnam) by brutal aggression," the President said.

The risk of a Communist takeover of Saigon has increased because of Hanoi's invasion, Mr. Nixon conceded. And while the United States offered "to talk about every conceivable avenue toward peace" through negotiation, he said, Hanoi has responded with "arrogance and insult," it has "arrogantly refused to negotiate," choosing rather to escalate the war.

Mr. Nixon particularly addressed the Soviet Union, which he said the United States respects as a great power with the right to defend its own interests when threatened.

'60,000 Americans Are Threatened'

"The Soviet Union in turn must recognize our right to defend our interests. No Soviet soldiers are threatened in Vietnam (but) 60,000 Americans are threatened. We expect you," he told Moscow, "to help your allies, and you cannot expect us to do other than to continue to help our allies."

He called upon the Russians to do as the United States has done—to help its allies only to defend themselves, not to launch invasions. Otherwise peace "would be seriously jeopardized," he said.

He reminded the Russians of significant progress in recent negotiations on nuclear arms limitations, on trade and other issues.

"Let us not slide back toward the dark shadows of a previous age," he said.

The two superpowers are on the threshold of a new relationship serving both their own interests and world peace, he said.

"We are prepared to continue to build this relationship," he told the Russians. "The responsibility is yours if we fail to do so."

At the end, Mr. Nixon calmly asked the American people for the strong support they have always given their President "in difficult moments."

"You want peace. I want peace," he told the nation. "But you also want

Please Turn to Page 3, Col. 2

U.S. Political Leaders Split Over Wisdom of Nixon's New Move

Reagan: 'Only Course'; McGovern: 'Flirtation With War'; Humphrey: 'Unpredictable Danger'; Ford: 'The Only Way'

Exclusive to The Times from a Staff Writer

Presidential candidates, members of Congress and public officials appeared to be as sharply divided as ever on President Nixon's Vietnam policies Monday evening after his announcement that the United States would mine the sea lanes to North Vietnam.

In Nebraska, Sen. George McGovern of South Dakota and Hubert Humphrey of Minnesota, on the eve of their primary election battle there, issued separate statements criticizing the decision.

McGovern said it was "reckless, unnecessary and unworkable. It is a flirtation with World War III." Later he said he would return to Washington and buy television time to rebut the Nixon announcement.

Humphrey, announcing that he was suspending his campaign activities and returning to Washington to meet with leaders of Congress, said the President's course "is filled with unpredictable danger. It offers no real hope for ending the war nor protecting American forces."

In contrast, Gov. Reagan, who is Mr. Nixon's reelection chairman in California, praised the President's action, saying it was "the only course which can bring peace and the return of our prisoners."

Gov. George Wallace of Alabama, campaigning in Lansing, Mich., said, that he would not make an assessment of Nixon's announcement "until I think it through for a while."

He said he would pray for its success in serving peace as he would for the action of any President.

Congressional response to the President's decision split largely along party lines.

House Republican leader Gerald Ford of Michigan called it "the only way to end the Vietnam war," while Sen. Edward M. Kennedy (D-Mass.) saw in it a lesson unlearned: "Peace cannot be bought at the cost of greater war . . . his decision is ominous, and I think it is folly."

Muskie Fears Confrontation

Presidential candidate Sen. Edmund S. Muskie (D-Me.) said Mr. Nixon was setting up a major confrontation with Russia and China and in doing so "jeopardizing the major security interests of the United States."

Rep. Leslie C. Arends, House Republican Whip from Illinois, said Mr. Nixon's "bold action . . . demands nothing less than total national unity if we are to prevail over a foe counting on internal dissent to defeat the United States."

Sen. Alan Cranston (D-Calif.) said: "The President offered a prescription for more war, more American deaths, more Vietnamese deaths, plus a brand new danger: collision with the Soviet Union. I wish North Vietnam would accept his proposals

Please Turn to Page 14, Col. 3

Nixon Becomes 4th President Since 1945 to Challenge Russ

BY JULIAN HARTT
Times Staff Writer

Richard M. Nixon is the fourth American President since World War II to face the Soviet Union in a showdown confrontation.

Presidents Harry S Truman in the Berlin airlift of 1948, and John F. Kennedy in the Cuban missile crisis of 1962, matched the Russians' final ante and won. President Dwight D. Eisenhower, in the U-2 spy plane case of 1960, was caught by circumstances and forced to throw in his hand, neither winning nor losing.

The first major East-West encounter began early in 1948, when a Russian army newspaper demanded the Western powers leave Berlin, 110 miles inside East Germany. Gen. Lucius D. Clay, American commander in Berlin, and Undersecretary of State Robert A. Lovett retorted that U.S. troops would stay as long as any others.

The Russians began tightening their squeeze on West Berlin Mar. 30, giving 24 hours notice they would start searching all rail and highway traffic from the West for spies and "illegal" cargo. Two days later, the embargo was extended to all rail, highway and barge traffic in either direction.

The U.S. took to the air, along with the British and, later, the French. Under a 1945 four-power agreement, a 20-mile-wide air corridor was unrestricted and Tempelhof airport in the American sector was available. Gen. Clay said "any American who is nervous" could leave West Berlin, but none of the 10,000 there did.

The Russians moved scores of tanks and thousands of troops into the Soviet sector. The first day's operations brought in 15,000 pounds of food, enough to feed the Americans a few days. Cargo, more than half of it coal for heating and power.

Please Turn to Page 8, Col. 1

FEATURE INDEX

THE WEATHER

National Weather Service forecast: Fair today and Wednesday except for late night and early morning coastal low clouds. High today, 74. High Monday, 72; low, 56.

Complete weather information and smog report in Part 2, Page 6.

NIXON'S VIETNAM ACTION AND TERMS, AT A GLANCE

WASHINGTON (UPI)—Here at a glance are the measures President Nixon said were being implemented as he addressed the nation Monday night:

—"All entrances to North Vietnamese ports will be mined to prevent access to these ports and North Vietnamese naval operations from these ports."

—U.S. forces will "take appropriate measures within the internal and claimed territorial waters of North Vietnam" to block delivery of supplies.

—"Rail and all other communications" will be severed "to the maximum extent possible."

—Air and naval strikes against military targets in North Vietnam will continue.

—Mr. Nixon said these four actions were not directed against any other nations. "Countries with ships presently in North Vietnamese ports . . . will have three daylight periods to leave in safety . . ." he said.

—The President said the actions would cease when all American prisoners of war were returned and there was an internationally supervised cease-fire in Indochina.

—Withdrawal of all American forces should be completed within four months after these conditions are met, he said.

—The President urged the Soviet Union to continue to build the new relationship that has developed between the United States and Moscow. "The responsibility is yours if we fail to do so," he said

Los Angeles Times

LARGEST CIRCULATION IN THE WEST, 1,009,519 DAILY, 1,208,209 SUNDAY.

VOL. XCI 2† FIVE PARTS—PART ONE CC | TUESDAY MORNING, MAY 16, 1972 | 84 PAGES | DAILY 10¢

Wallace Shot, Paralyzed in Both Legs; Suspect Seized

WITH WOUNDED HUSBAND—Cornelia Wallace kneels over Alabama Gov. George C. Wallace just after he was felled by a gunman in Laurel, Md. This photo is from TV film taken by CBS News. UPI Wirephoto

MOMENT OF SHOOTING—Man wearing dark glasses fires pistol pointblank at the Alabama governor in this photo made by CBS News. The gunman, identified as Arthur Herman Bremer, 21, of Milwaukee was wrestled to the ground by policemen and citizens. UPI Wirephoto

Bullets Wound Three Others at Maryland Rally

BY THOMAS J. FOLEY
Times Staff Writer

LAUREL, Md.—Alabama Gov. George C. Wallace was shot and wounded Monday when he walked into a crowd of supporters to shake hands at a political rally here. Bullets also hit a Secret Service agent, an Alabama state trooper and a woman campaign worker.

The attack on the 52-year-old Democratic presidential candidate was believed made by a single gunman. A suspect, Arthur Herman Bremer, 21, a white man from Milwaukee, was captured.

Physicians said Wallace could be paralyzed permanently from the hips down.

"He (Wallace) has a bullet lodged in the spinal canal at the level of the first lumbar vertebra," said Dr. James G. Arnold, professor of neurosurgery at the University of Maryland, who was called in as a consultant.

"He is paralyzed in both lower extremities. What chance he has of a return of function in the lower extremities cannot be predicted, but the outlook is not favorable.

"When his general condition warrants it, the bullet will be removed."

Bullet Perforates Stomach

Arnold said one bullet entered Wallace's side and perforated his stomach and another lodged in the spinal column. There were other bullet wounds in the right shoulder and right arm, he said.

Dr. James G. Galbraith, professor of neurosurgery at the University of Alabama, added:

"There's no assurance he can regain the power in his lower extremities, but it's in the realm of possibility . . . It would be unusual to regain the complete use of his extremities."

Galbraith said an operation to remove the bullet in the spinal column would be attempted when Wallace could be turned onto his abdomen, to which several tubes are now attached.

"It might be a matter of several days," Galbraith said. "But he's tough. He's a very healthy specimen and I think he'll pull through."

Five Surgeons in Attendance

A team of five surgeons began working on Wallace in Holy Cross Hospital, Silver Spring, at 6 p.m. EDT, two hours after the shooting, and he was wheeled into a recovery room at 10:35 p.m.

However, Dr. Joseph Shannow, a vascular specialist who assisted with the surgery on Wallace, said it was difficult at this time to ascertain the extent of the injury to the spinal cord.

"At this point we must observe further," he said. "But there is a potential paralysis from the lower hips down. He has a weakness of the lower extremities. It could be permanent. It could be transient."

But barring complications, Shannow said, "a good recovery is expected."

Reporters asked Shannow whether Wallace could continue his political career if he should be permanently paralyzed.

"If worse comes to worst," the doctor said, "he would have the

Please Turn to Page 11, Col. 5

Suspect Must Have Been Sick if He Is Involved, Father Says

He Reports That Son Never Mentioned Wallace in His Presence; Milwaukee Neighbors Describe Youth as Loner

BY FRANCIS WARD
Times Staff Writer

MILWAUKEE—The father of the young man accused of shooting Alabama Gov. George C. Wallace said Monday night that if his son "is involved in this crime . . . he must have been awfully sick."

William Bremer, 58, met newsmen in the kitchen of the family's downstairs duplex on the city's near south side.

Bremer said his son never mentioned anything about Wallace in his presence.

"He was a Humphrey man, like myself," he said.

Ted Bremer, 34, one of the three brothers of Arthur Bremer, 21, who was taken into custody after Wallace was shot in Laurel, Md., said, "He was incapable of this."

Ted said Arthur's only political involvement to his knowledge was in a local Democratic ward.

William Bremer, a truck driver for the same company for 30 years, said his son had never had a gun while he was home. Arthur had been living alone in an apartment on the city's near west side.

Mrs. Bremer stayed in the living room while her husband talked to newsmen in the kitchen. Bremer said she had tried to get her son to return home but that he had wanted to be by himself.

Arthur was described by neighbors as "a loner" who "stayed pretty much to himself and didn't talk much."

Bremer lived in a small, sparsely furnished three-room apartment on the second floor of a three-story brick building at 2433 W. Michigan Ave., near the campus of Marquette University.

Several of his neighbors said he had few if any close friends. One young man who refused to give his name described him as an introverted, quiet person who "just came and went . . . and that's all."

Please Turn to Page 11, Col. 3

Wife Optimistic on Governor's Recovery

Exclusive to The Times from a Staff Writer

SILVER SPRING, Md.—Cornelia Wallace, still wearing her blood-splattered yellow skirt, walked into a second-floor press room at Holy Cross Hospital and made a brief statement over network television late Monday night.

Accompanied by the Wallace children, George Jr. and daughters Peggy Sue and Bobby Jo, Mrs. Wallace said:

"I just wanted to tell you myself that the governor is in very good condition, that he has suffered a serious injury to his abdomen, but it's cleaned out and he's out of surgery; he's in his room."

Dr. Hamilton Hutchinson, Wallace's personal physician, told reporters at the hospital at 11:45 p.m. EDT that the governor ran the risk

Please Turn to Page 8, Col. 3

WITNESS DRAGS GUNMAN TO GROUND

A Handshake, a Shove—and Shots Ring Out

Exclusive to The Times from a Staff Writer

LAUREL, Md.—Crane operator Ross Speigel, 46, still wearing his green denim work clothes, arrived with his wife at the Laurel Shopping Center 90 minutes before George C. Wallace was to speak.

Rain, which had fallen throughout Monday morning, had ceased, but the sky remained menacing. Despite the gray weather, a gathering crowd already was vying for choice spots around the speakers' platform.

Speigel and his wife pressed forward, edged into the front row and planted themselves alongside a blond young man wearing a Wallace button and dark lenses over his eyeglasses.

Although Speigel had no way of knowing it at the time, slightly more than two hours later the young man would raise a revolver and fire at the Alabama governor, and, split seconds after that, Speigel would be struggling to subdue the blond gunman.

During their long wait for the governor's arrival, neither Speigel nor his wife said anything to the young man nor did he speak to them.

Speigel later would remember noticing nothing remarkable about him, only that he appeared to be of average height and weight and that he appeared to be in his early 20s.

When the presidential candidate finally arrived and mounted the platform, the young man remained silent. He did not join in the rousing cheers and scattering of boos that greeted the governor.

Wallace began to speak almost at once, and the Speigels, Laurel residents, paid the man alongside them no further attention, although both would recall later that he neither applauded nor heckled the speaker.

When Wallace finished speaking, he quickly descended from the platform, started to walk to his right toward the limousine in which he had arrived, then hesitated.

The cluster of spectators, among whom the Speigels stood, called to Wallace, pleading that he come over to shake hands.

The governor acceded and plunged into the crowd, grasping the hands of those in the front row with his right hand and reaching over with his left to touch those in the second row.

Please Turn to Page 10, Col. 1

Saigon to Repeat Hit-and-Run Raids Behind Red Lines

BY RUDY ABRAMSON
Times Staff Writer

WASHINGTON—South Vietnamese marines transported by U.S. helicopters probably will launch more—and larger—attacks behind enemy lines similar to their quick counteroffensive in Quang Tri province last weekend, Administration sources said Monday.

For the time being, the sources said, hit-and-run attacks by a few marine battalions to frustrate planned North Vietnamese offensive thrusts are considered more effective than would be any attempt to retake and hold territory

The brief counterattack into South Vietnam's northernmost province Saturday came at the time when intelligence indicated the North Vietnamese were about to trigger their expected push against Hue.

In their effort to frustrate preparations for that attack, the 1,500 South Vietnamese marines killed about 250 enemy soldiers, knocked out three enemy tanks, captured three 130-mm. artillery pieces and opened an escape route for 1,000 refugees, according to their reports.

Military sources said the North Vietnamese efforts to organize for an assault on Hue also have been set back by heavy air strikes by U.S. B-52 bombers. Reports from the battlefield indicated that two North Vietnamese regiments—one in the 304th Division and another in the 308th Division—have been decimated by the B-52 attacks.

Sources indicated Monday that future helicopter-borne marine attacks behind North Vietnamese positions could come in the Central

Please Turn to Page 14, Col. 1

BLOCKADE STAYS UNTIL U.S. POW'S FREE, NIXON SAYS

WASHINGTON (UPI)—President Nixon Monday promised wives of prisoners of war and servicemen missing in Indochina that he will maintain the blockade of North Vietnam until the prisoners go free, one of the women told newsmen.

Mr. Nixon met for about 30 minutes with a three-woman delegation from the National League of Families of American Prisoners and Missing in Southeast Asia. All three said they were reassured by the meeting.

"He said the harbors will stay mined until the prisoners are released," said Mrs. James B. Stockdale, the spokeswoman for the group.

Please Turn to Page 14, Col. 3

Moscow Trip 'On,' Says Mrs. Nixon

WASHINGTON (AP) — First Lady Mrs. Richard M. Nixon said Monday "It's no secret" about the Moscow summit trip — "It's on."

She gave the first firm word from the White House that the presidential summit meeting had not been postponed or canceled and also said that she and the President would be departing on Saturday morning for Salzburg, Austria, the first stop on a four-country, two-week journey.

There had been some doubt about the meeting taking place, in view of Russian opposition to President Nixon's order to mine North Vietnamese harbor entrances.

Pravda, the Communist Party newspaper, published Tass news agency dispatches Monday from New York and London saying that

Please Turn to Page 14, Col. 1

Patrols by S. Viet Units Ease Enemy Pressure on Hue

BY GEORGE McARTHUR
Times Staff Writer

SAIGON — South Vietnamese troops today moved in force through the 1,500-foothills west of Hue, continuing aggressive patrols that have recaptured Fire Base Bastogne and pushed Communist forces back beyond rocket range of the old imperial capital.

Following a marine sweep into enemy territory in Quang Tri province north of Hue over the weekend, the forays into the foothills of the Annamite range west of Hue have considerably bolstered the city's defenses and the morale of the defenders.

"This is not a counteroffensive," an American spokesman said, "but it's the next best thing. We are certainly disrupting the North Vietnamese timing."

In addition to moving back on Bastogne without opposition Monday, the South Vietnamese sweeps uncovered more than six tons of munitions in two caches.

Hundreds of Shells Found

One cache included several hundred shells for the big 130-mm. guns that the North Vietnamese are attempting to edge up to Hue's outer defense ring. The shells were uncovered in a foothill area only 10 miles from Hue—well within the 17-mile range of the big guns that Hanoi has used so effectively in the seven-week offensive.

With the recapture of Bastogne, 12 miles southwest of Hue, and the continuing sweeps in the area, however, the North Vietnamese are pushed well back from the effective rocket range of six to eight miles—though the defense line is porous and hit-and-run attacks always are possible.

American warplanes are now flying 24-hour cover over Hue to guard against use of the 130-mm. guns from dug-in positions back in the mountains. The planes are equipped with electronic and other gear to pinpoint the muzzle flashes of the big guns.

"They know we are up there and they are keeping quiet for the moment," an adviser said. "But we know they are trying to get the guns into place."

South Vietnamese headquarters reported that the recapture of Bas-

Please Turn to Page 16, Col. 1

SBA Launches Major Inquiry Into Disaster Loan Program

BY ROBERT RAWITCH
Times Staff Writer

The Small Business Administration took the first major step Monday toward reforming its beleaguered disaster loan program.

It has launched a sweeping investigation of the entire disaster program admittedly as a result of a series of articles published in The Times.

The articles charge widespread abuse of the program and mismanagement by the agency that resulted in possibly millions of dollars going to thousands of persons who did not deserve it.

Earlier in the day the General Accounting Office, the audit arm of Congress, said it would conduct its own investigation of the SBA's handling of last year's earthquake loans.

The SBA also faces the possibility of several congressional probes in the next few months.

The Nixon Administration has proposed legislation which would remove the disaster home loan program from the agency's authority and eliminate the controversial $2,500 "forgiveness clause" in its loans.

Although never outwardly denying The Times' charges, the SBA had claimed allegations of misuse of funds and poor management were exaggerated.

But the SBA's decision for a thorough review of the program was viewed even within the agency as an admission that its problems were worse than initially conceded.

Earlier U.S. Senate hearings

Please Turn to Page 20, Col. 1

THE WEATHER

National Weather Service forecast: Night and morning low clouds with hazy afternoon sunshine today and Wednesday. High today, 75. High Monday, 80; low, 58.

Complete weather information and smog report in Part 1, Page 22.

FEATURE INDEX

Los Angeles Times

LARGEST CIRCULATION IN THE WEST, 1,026,499 DAILY, 1,210,556 SUNDAY.

FINAL
ONE OF THE WORLD'S GREAT NEWSPAPERS

VOL. XCI 2† TWENTY SECTIONS—SECTION A CC SUNDAY, JUNE 18, 1972 422 PAGES

SUNDAY 50c

The L.A. Media Area---Where McGovern Lost

Correlation May Indicate Senator Is Vulnerable on Economics and Welfare

BY ROBERT A. JONES
Times Staff Writer

On a map showing the results of the June 6 presidential primary, the counties voting for Sen. Hubert H. Humphrey (D-Minn) cut a wide swath across Southern California.

It indicates that California decidely did not conform to old political boundaries in the primary won by Sen. George S. McGovern (D-S.D.).

Humphrey country, centered in Los Angeles County, spread south to conservative Orange County but stopped abruptly at equally conservative San Diego County.

It then spread north to Ventura but stopped at Santa Barbara.

At first glance, the map confused McGovern aides here, largely because it contradicted results in other state areas. But then somone noticed that the area of loss coincides with what is called the "L.A. media area."

Greater Vulnerability Seen

The discovery has worried the McGovern people considerably, for it seems to indicate that the South Dakota senator is far more vulnerable to attacks on his economic and welfare policies than they had believed possible.

"As soon as you get outside the L.A. media area, the vote goes back consistently for us," said Pat Caddell, McGovern's principal pollster.

The critical difference between Los Angeles and other areas, they say, is the profusion of newspapers and television stations in the Los Angeles basin which "saturated" the final days of the campaign with charges by Humphrey that McGovern's aerospace cuts would cost thousands of jobs and that his welfare program would be enormously expensive.

Campaign coverage in other areas of the state was not nearly so detailed, nor were there so many overlapping boundaries of communications media that often produced repetition in the Los Angeles area.

TV Spots in Last Week

In addition, the Humphrey campaign could not afford to buy heavy television advertising in most areas of the state. But in Los Angeles there was a series of pointed, critical television spots that ran often in the last week.

Miles Rubin, McGovern's Southern California finance chairman, said:

"There was a conscious decision not to counterattack (to the Humphrey charges). I believe tne people read that as a 'no response' from the McGovern camp, and it hurt us. I don't think we would make the same decision in the fall."

However, the success of the Humphrey attack in this area has also raised fears over the validity of the McGovern positions.

One McGovern strategist said:

"Look at it this way. We won in nearly every section of the state, but then we had almost no organized opposition.

"In Los Angeles, the one place where the media could offset some of our own organization by publiciz-

Please Turn to Section B, Page 4

LOOKING IN ON THE ACTION—Two parent volunteers work with the children in the kindergarten room of the Golden View Elementary School in north Huntington Beach. Picture was taken through a hole in the free-form ring that surrounds the main meeting area of the classroom.
Times photo by John Malmin

Court Orders Poll on Pilot Walkout

Seeks to Find What Effect Delay of Strike by U.S. Crews Would Have

WASHINGTON (AP)—A federal appeals court directed the Air Line Pilots Assn. Saturday to poll its affiliates in 38 nations to determine the effect of a delay by U.S. pilots in a planned one-day work stoppage scheduled for Monday in protest against skyjackings.

ALPA lawyers protested that any delay would "give the kiss of death" to the scheduled protest against what the pilots see as lack of international cooperation to curb air piracy and extortion. But they said they were going ahead with the poll.

An ALPA spokesman said lawyers were trying to find the president of the International Federation of Airline Pilots Assns., Ola Forsberg of Finland, to inform him of the court request. The IFAPA isssued the strike call. Forsberg was reported en route from New York to Helsinki.

Report Findings to Court

The spokesman said ALPA is to report its findings to the court as soon as possible and then the judges would determine what action they will pursue. The court recessed for the night late Saturday and told attorneys to be ready for possible action in the case today.

The three-judge court made its request while hearing an appeal by the carriers' Air Transport Assn. from a U.S. district court refusal to grant an injunction against American participation in the stoppage.

The 24-hour shutdown, scheduled to start at 11 p.m. today PDT, could, at maximum effectiveness, affect about 31,000 U.S. pilots, about 50,000 more in 63 other pilots organizations in the world and cause losses in the millions of dollars.

(The ALPA believes the strike will stop nearly all the 15,000 flights made daily in the United States, affecting up to 550,000 persons, Reuters said.

(According to figures issued by the Air Transport Assn., that could mean a loss of $23 million in ticket sales and seriously delay cargo and mail shipments.)

However, there was no unanimity in pilot acceptance of the protest walkout. And several companies obtained injunctions barring participation by their own employes. Several foreign nations indicated their airlines would not join in the demonstrations.

Says He Lacked Jurisdiction

Earlier Saturday, U.S. Dist. Judge George L. Hart Jr. held that he lacked jurisdiction to grant the restraining order asked by the ATA, and the carriers' group immediately appealed his decision.

The ATA said a U.S. District Court in Manhattan had restrained the International Assn. of Machinists from participating.

The machinists, who represent maintenance personnel for most airlines, had backed the stoppage and their participation could have tied up aircraft even for those airlines whose pilots had decided against the stoppage.

President Nixon had no direct comment but at the Florida White House in Key Biscayne Press Secretary Ronald Ziegler said the work stoppage was not the best way to fight hijackings. He added:

"We do not need a dramatic gesture to focus our concern on hijacking. We recognize the problem and have taken steps to combat it, and are taking further steps."

Please Turn to Page 12, Col. 1

L.A. Jobs Easier to Find—and Computers May Help Even More

Countywide System Will List Openings That Have Remained Vacant Because of Gap in Communications

BY HARRY BERNSTEIN
Times Labor Writer

The chances of unemployed workers finding jobs in California have improved significantly in the past few months, and there are even some shortages of workers in certain job categories.

But the experts are not ready to start predicting a return to the good old days of, say, 1956, when only 3.2% of the California work force was unemployed, compared to today's 5.9%.

The statistics do show, however, that the hunt for jobs these days is not as tough as it has been for the last two years or so. And the state officials who help the unemployed find work are cautiously optimistic about even greater improvements in the next few months.

Still Serious Problem

And, the experts say, as more and more areas of California start using the new computerized "job banks" to match job vacancies with job hunters, there should be further progress in the effort to ease the still serious unemployment problem.

In job bank cities, each state employment service office gets a fresh computer-printed list of job openings every day. And on Sept. 1, Los Angeles County will put its own multimillion-dollar job bank into operation

The job bank is designed to help bring about a better distribution of work. That is, if an employer in Van Nuys needs a waitress or a cook, he should be able to fill the job more easily through the job bank because the opening will be announced almost instantly in every employment office in the county.

This one aspect of the program alone could make it well worth the $7.1 million the Los Angeles job bank will cost, according to some state officials.

For instance, the unemployment rate now in South-Central Los Angeles is estimated to be running around 20%. That office of the state's Human Resources Development Agency gets pleas for help from up to 1,800 job hunters every month.

But the South-Central office can place only 300 people in jobs, since most of the work force there consists of unskilled or semiskilled blacks or other minorities.

On the other hand the Van Nuys office of HRD is having trouble filling several categories of jobs, such as cooks, waitresses, shipping clerks, salesmen and assemblers, and the South-Central office might be able to help out.

Distance Factor Cited

Right now, though, the Van Nuys office makes little effort to get word of its job vacancies to South Central Los Angeles, or to the Compton office of HRD, which also has a high unemployment rate.

The usual explanation is that the distances involved are too great to allow much interchange of information about job openings.

"Workers cannot travel that far from the poverty communities because of the transportation problems," one official contended.

But when the computers start operating Sept. 1, the employer who wants help will be able to draw from every part of the county, and the job hunter can decide for himself whether he wants to travel.

Please Turn to Page 17, Col. 1

PARENTS HAPPY

School District Bucking Trend to Achieve Success

BY JACK McCURDY
Times Education Writer

In this tumultuous time of attacks on public education, is it possible that some school districts are quietly educating children, keeping parents happy and providing an imaginative program at a cost that doesn't bankrupt the taxpayers?

There is one that seems to be doing almost everything right—Ocean View Elementary District in Huntington Beach. Consider the record:

—Three tax and bond elections have been won in the last three years—and by an overwhelming margin to boot—while most districts in the state and nation have met with mounting failures.

Downward Trend

—Student achievement in reading has been boosted consistently to an above-average level, despite a downward trend throughout California as a whole.

—Schools have been opened to parents and other citizens to an unusually large degree in contrast with the uneasy superficiality of most public school contacts. The result has been powerful community support for the district and a feeling among many parents that they have some control over school affairs.

—The district has built modernistic "open structure" school buildings (without permanent interior halls or walls) at lower costs and has also pioneered other innovations, such as the use of noncredentialed teachers, year-around schooling and a private-

Please Turn to Page B, Col. 1

Civil Service 'Spoiled System' Blasted in Nader Team Report

BY MIKE CAUSEY
Exclusive to The Times from the Washington Post

WASHINGTON—Consumer crusader Ralph Nader issued a 500-page-plus report Saturday blasting the federal bureaucracy and calling for a system that would allow public officials to be sued, fined or fired for failing to do their jobs.

The document, "The Spoiled System," which Nader says is his "most important," pictures the civil service as a sometimes timid, sometimes arrogantly vicious institution operating under an intentionally dull, drab cover. He says it will get worse unless taxpayers and concerned employes are given the legal clout to make it run scared.

Nader likens the daily workings of government to a giant pool of quicksand that permits the mediocre to rise and either sinks or soils many dedicated professionals.

Most of the criticisms are directed at the Civil Service Commission, the government's personnel office, which Nader says is all-important but escapes general notice because it lacks political sex appeal.

The report is the result of nearly two years of work by a team headed by attorney Robert Vaughn, who works with Nader's Public Interest Research Group.

It contains criticism of and recommendations to improve four major areas of the commission's responsibility: employe appeal rights, inspections of other agency operations, investigations of workers and would-be employes, and equal employment.

Vaughn, a 30-year old Oklahoman and graduate of Harvard law school, said the report came out of hundreds of hours of interviews with top federal officials, records, court cases and sometimes "tearful" encounters with employes who have been wrecked by the system.

Commission Chairman Robert E. Hampton said his agency had received only one copy of the book-

Please Turn to Page 6, Col. 1

MEDAL OF HONOR WINNERS

After Heroism, What? Depths for Some, Routine for Others

BY H. D. QUIGG
UPI Staff Writer

WASHINGTON — Harry S Truman, an old soldier and a right good man, said on several occasions while presenting the Medal of Honor that he would rather have it than be President.

Last year, the House of Representatives wanted to give him the award. Mr. Truman declined, saying that the medal was for military valor and he didn't deserve it.

Holders of America's top military award for heroic bravery are a group of men surely among the elite of history. The medal hangs from the neck in solitary distinction. On one recent occasion it seemed to hang like an albatross.

About the time former President Truman was writing his refusal letter to the House, the tragedy of Sgt. Dwight Hal Johnson surfaced in Detroit. A Medal of Honor holder for "a magnificent display of courage" in Vietnam, he was shot and killed while trying to rob a grocery.

Johnson, raised on public welfare in a black ghetto, couldn't find a job when he came home. Then came the medal, and he wept at the White House when he got it. He was lionized, made public appearances for the military, dined with big people, went into heavy debt, began taking psychiatric treatment at an Army hospital.

At his tragic death, it was suggested that the medal should automatically carry a $10,000 annual pension.

The law does provide that holders of the medal may on application get a special pension of $100 a month. This, though, is empty largess for nearly two-thirds of the Medal of Honor winners for Vietnam. They died in actions for which they were

Please Turn to Section B, Page 6

FEATURE INDEX

ONE A FORMER CIA EMPLOYE

Five Held in Plot to Bug Democratic Office

BY ALFRED E. LEWIS
Exclusive to The Times from the Washington Post

WASHINGTON—Five men, one a former employe of the Central Intelligence Agency and three who are natives of Cuba, were arrested Saturday in what authorities described as an elaborate plot to bug the office of the Democratic National Committee here.

The men, all wearing rubber surgical gloves, were surprised at gunpoint at 2:30 a.m. by three plainclothes officers of the Metropolitan Police Department's tactical squad.

They were captured inside a small sixth-floor office at the plush Watergate Hotel. The Democratic National Committee occupies the entire sixth floor.

Police said the men had with them at least two sophisticated devices capable of picking up and transmitting oral and telephone conversations. In addition, police found lockpicks and door jimmies and almost $2,300 in cash, most of it in $100 bills with the serial numbers in sequence.

The men also had with them one walkie-talkie, a short-wave receiver, 40 rolls of unexposed film and two 35-mm. cameras.

There was no immediate indication as to why the five suspects would want to bug the Democratic National Commitee offices, or whether they were working for any other individuals or organizations.

In court Saturday one suspect did say the men were "anti-Communists," and the others nodded agreement. The operation was described in court by prosecutor Earl J. Silbert as "professional and clandestine."

One of the suspects is a locksmith by trade. Many of the burglary tools found at the Democratic National Commitee offices appeared to be packaged in what police said were burglary kits.

A spokesman for the Democratic National Commitee said records kept in the offices are "not of a sensitive variety," although he added there are "financial records and other such information."

Police said two ceiling panels in the office of Dorothy V. Bush, secretary of the Democratic Party, had been removed.

Her office is next to the office of Democratic National Chairman Lawrence F. O'Brien. Presumably it would have been possible to slide a bugging device through the panels in that office to a place above the ceiling panels in O'Brien's office.

Please Turn to Page 3, Col. 1

THE WEATHER

National Weather Service forecast: Night and morning low clouds with hazy sunshine after noon today and Monday. Highs today and Monday, 78. High Saturday, 82; low, 66.

Complete weather information in Section C, Page 4.

Los Angeles Times

LARGEST CIRCULATION IN THE WEST, 1,026,499 DAILY, 1,210,556 SUNDAY.

VOL. XCI 2† SIX PARTS—PART ONE CC FRIDAY MORNING, JUNE 30, 1972 106 PAGES

DAILY 10c

HIS LIFE SPARED—Elmer Branch, 19, one of three condemned prison inmates whose sentences were removed by the Supreme Court's decision on the death penalty, sits in Death Row cell in Huntsville, Tex. Branch had been sentenced to die for raping a 65-year-old white woman in 1967.

Wirephoto

Supreme Court Strikes Down Most Death Penalty Laws

Ruling Allows Capital Punishment When Mandatory in Certain Crimes

BY LINDA MATHEWS and RONALD J. OSTROW
Times Staff Writers

WASHINGTON—The Supreme Court Thursday struck down as "cruel and unusual punishment" virtually all of the nation's death penalty laws, apparently sparing the lives of 600 condemned prisoners.

But the 5-4 ruling stopped short of outright abolition of capital punishment, leaving intact at least three state laws and one federal statute that make the death penalty mandatory for certain crimes.

The majority ruling, expressed in five separate opinions, left the door open for Congress and state legislatures to enact additional death sentence laws. Such laws could survive under the ruling if they made capital punishment mandatory or severely limited through rigid guidelines the discretion of judges and juries in deciding whether to impose the penalty.

Only two justices—William J. Brennan Jr. and Thurgood Marshall—supported total abolition of capital punishment.

Agreement in Three Cases

The only point that all five justices in the majority agreed on was that the penalty had been unconstitutionally imposed in the three cases under review. Those appeals involved two rape convictions, one from Georgia and one from Texas, and a conviction for a Georgia murder that took place during a house burglary. The defendant in each case was black.

In addition to Brennan and Marshall, the majority included Justices William O. Douglas, Potter Stewart and Byron R. White.

Chief Justice Warren E. Burger and the other three justices named by President Nixon—Harry A. Blackmun, Lewis F. Powell Jr. and William H. Rehnquist—dissented. They said the majority exceeded the bounds of judicial power and interfered in a matter that they said should be left to the people and their elected representatives.

The court also vacated the death sentences in appeals of 117 other prisoners, sending the cases back to lower courts for resentencing. Those appeals included at least two men convicted of killing police officers.

The decision appeared to affect all 600 persons on Death Rows across the country because none of them was sentenced under a law that made the death penalty mandatory, according to Douglas B. Lyons. He is

Please Turn to Page 20, Col. 1

CALIF. INITIATIVE IN DOUBT; PRAISE AND ANGER VOICED

BY RICHARD WEST
Times Staff Writer

California reaction to the U.S. Supreme Court's decision on the death penalty Thursday ranged from anger and tirades against the court to satisfaction and praise for the ruling.

The decision raised the question of the legality of an initiative on the November ballot to restore the death penalty in the state. Its status, however, still is not clear.

Some lawyers specializing in criminal law admitted that at this time they did not know just what the decision meant.

Los Angeles Police Chief Edward M. Davis told a news conference that the decision was an "absurdity" that violates any "plain, simple country boy's interpretation" of the Constitution.

Please Turn to Page 20, Col. 5

M'Govern Loses 153 Delegates From California

But Credential Committee Action Will Be Appealed to Floor of Convention

BY THOMAS J. FOLEY
Times Staff Writer

WASHINGTON—The Democratic Party's credentials committee voted Thursday to strip Sen. George S. McGovern of 153 of his 271 California delegates, setting up at least a temporary roadblock in his drive for the party's presidential nomination.

A coalition of supporters of other major candidates approved a challenge to California's winner-take-all primary.

The vote was 72 to 66 with California's 10-member McGovern committee delegation unable to vote.

McGovern strategists immediately announced they would bring the issue to the convention floor in the opening session July 10.

They talked of a possible court suit in the meantime, but Washington attorney Joseph L. Rauh, who defended against the challenge, indicated the McGovern forces were more likely to depend on winning the issue on the convention floor.

'Rotten Steal,' McGovern Says

An obviously angered McGovern emerged from the Senate floor after hearing of the result and called it "an incredible cynical rotten political steal . . . a corrupt spiteful deal."

McGovern also indicated he would not support the Democratic ticket if he is denied the nomination, saying, "I couldn't possibly support a convention that would sustain this shabby backroom dealing . . . I wouldn't have any part of any convention nominee who would support this." Sen. Hubert H. Humphrey, who would get 104 of the 153 votes, took heart from the committee vote and expressed surprise at the tone of McGovern's comments. The Minnesotan said, "If I were as far ahead as George, I wouldn't get so mad."

He disclaimed sole support for the challenge, declaring "This has not been a Humphrey operation alone. If there had been only Humphrey votes there, we wouldn't have had a prayer."

Please Turn to Page 18, Col. 1

ELUSIVE 'GOOD LIFE'

Paradise Lost? Swedes Fear for Welfare State

BY JOE ALEX MORRIS JR.
Times Staff Writer

STOCKHOLM — Something is happening to this Scandinavian paradise.

—Sweden's lower classes have been moved from the cities to the countryside, only to find themselves in concrete warrens, while the good life is back in the cities where the wealthier remained.

—The machinery of the cradle-to-the-grave welfare concern for everyone is beginning to creak, and the tax structure to support it actually encourages joblessness in some cases.

—The country is approaching zero growth rate and the industrial labor force actually is declining.

—The gross national product is virtually stagnant, and industry is looking to cheaper labor abroad rather than within high-cost Sweden to expand.

Reviewing Socialist Trend

Against this background, Swedes are beginning to examine the values of the seeming abundance about them, attained under Social Democrat political leadership that has fascinated the world for four decades.

They are proud of their per capita income of $4,000 a year, and the most equitable distribution of real wealth in any country.

No one earthshaking event has brought about this universal reappraisal. It is a combination of factors that have jarred the Swedes as they consciously try to project into the decades ahead.

Please Turn to Page 12, Col. 1

U.S. and Hanoi to Resume Paris Talks July 13, Nixon Announces

Tells Press Conference Viet War Can Be 'Ended Well Before' Term Is Over if Enemy Negotiates Seriously

BY ROBERT C. TOTH
Times Staff Writer

WASHINGTON—President Nixon Thursday announced a resumption in the Paris peace talks July 13 "on the assumption that the North Vietnamese are prepared to negotiate in a constructive and serious way."

If such negotiations do occur, he told a televised press conference, the war can be "ended well before Jan. 20," when his current presidential term expires.

He claimed during the conference, his first in that forum in more than a year, that American mining of North Vietnamese waters and intensified bombing of its land has "completely turned around" the Hanoi offensive in the south.

On other matters, the President said:

—He would have recommended a $15 billion a year crash program to increase U.S. strategic weapons systems if the recent arms agreements with the Soviet Union had not been reached.

—He will wait until the Republican convention is near to announce his vice presidential choice. But he reiterated his previous high praise of Spiro T. Agnew.

"I almost said Vice President Connally," he admitted at one point, however, referring to Texas Democrat John B. Connally.

—He opposes Senate efforts to tack a 20% hike in Social Security benefits onto the pending bill to extend the ceiling on the national debt. But he repeated his proposal to raise Social Security payments 5%.

—That the rise in "real spendable income" in the past year was 5% after taxes and inflation, compared to an average of 1% during the 1960s. But he acknowledged that unemployment remains stubbornly high at 5.9% of the work force.

—He inferred from reading Chief Justice Warren E. Burger's dissent in Thursday's Supreme Court decision that there is room in the ruling for limited applications of the death penalty. He said that he hopes the ruling will not prohibit capital punishment in federal kidnaping and hijacking cases and that the death penalty would serve as a deterrent against such crimes.

On the peace talks Mr. Nixon said: "We would not be returning to Paris

Please Turn to Page 9, Col. 1

More Food Prices Put Under Controls

Nixon Lifts Exemption for Some Unprocessed Items

BY PAUL E. STEIGER
Times Staff Writer

WASHINGTON—President Nixon Thursday tightened his price-control program slightly by removing part of the exemption for unprocessed foods.

The action, signaling a rejection of Price Commission requests for tougher moves, was not expected to have a major effect on the cost of living.

The affected products—raw eggs, fresh fruits and vegetables, and raw seafood—account for only 2½% of the average family's budget and 11% of the average food budget. Meat and poultry prices, already partly subject to price controls, were not affected.

The President's action, accomplished by an executive order, makes the previously exempted food products subject to Price Commission rules after their first sale.

From the beginning of the price control program, all raw food products have been exempt from control, their prices determined by

Please Turn to Page 18, Col. 1

Many Will Go but Few Will Be Seated

BY RICHARD BERGHOLZ
Times Political Writer

There are going to be more would-be California delegates at the Democratic National Convention in Miami Beach next month than from almost any two states combined. But a lot of them are not going to be seated.

As a result of the credentials committee ruling in Washington Thursday knocking out California's winner-take-all primary results June 6, here is the prospective lineup in Miami Beach:

—All 271 California delegates pledged to Sen. George S. McGovern of South Dakota are planning to be on hand when the convention opens, despite the committee's decision that only 118 of them can be seated under a proportional division of the delegate strength.

—All 104 of the proposed delegates pledged to Sen. Hubert H. Humphrey of Minnesota plan to be present and demand credentials.

Please Turn to Page 18, Col. 3

Newsmen Must Answer Queries of Grand Juries, Court Decides

BY JACK NELSON
Times Staff Writer

WASHINGTON — The Supreme Court ruled 5 to 4 Thursday that newsmen have no First Amendment right to refuse to answer questions of grand juries.

The ruling, by Justice Byron R. White and President Nixon's four appointees to the court, opens the way for federal grand juries and most state grand juries to compel newsmen to divulge confidential sources.

Strong dissenting opinions criticized the decision as damaging to news gathering, inhibiting to editors and reporters, and as an invitation for state and federal authorities to "undermine the historic independence of the press by attempting to annex the journalistic profession as an investigative arm of government."

In the majority opinion, Justice White dismissed such criticism and wrote that the First Amendment "does not invalidate every incidental burdening of the press that may result from the enforcement of civil or criminal statutes of general applicability. Under prior cases, otherwise valid laws serving substantial public interests may be enforced against the press as against others, despite the possible burden that may be imposed."

White's majority opinion went beyond the issue of grand juries, addressing an issue not raised in the cases under review and giving Supreme Court sanction to additional press restrictions.

"Despite the fact that news gathering may be hampered," White wrote, "the press is regularly excluded from grand jury proceedings, our own conferences, the meetings of other official bodies gathered in

Please Turn to Page 23, Col. 1

S. Vietnamese Troops Reported Six Miles From Quang Tri City

SAIGON (AP)—A 20,000-man South Vietnamese task force pushing northward in a drive to recapture enemy-held Quang Tri province continued to encounter moderate resistance Thursday. Some South Vietnamese forces were reported as close as six miles from Quang Tri city, capital of the province.

Government officers and senior U.S. advisers seemed optimistic. One American said the counteroffensive was going better than anticipated. "We thought it would be a damn tough nut," he said. The North Vietnamese have had almost two months to consolidate their hold on South Vietnam's northernmost province, which they captured May 1.

Military spokesmen in Saigon reported at least 328 North Vietnamese killed in the first two days of the operation. South Vietnamese losses were reported as six dead and 34 wounded. Three enemy tanks were destroyed and one was captured after the North Vietnamese crew abandoned it with the engine running, the spokesman said. A long-range artillery gun, howitzers and antiaircraft guns also were reported captured.

South Vietnamese marines were moving on Quang Tri city from the southeast and paratroopers from the southwest.

More than 1,000 more South Vietnamese marines were committed to the drive Thursday in two combat assaults aboard U.S. Marine Corps helicopters, and were moving in from the northeast.

With the fresh troops, government forces formed a rough east-southwest arc, between 6 and 12 miles from Quang Tri city.

(The three-pronged advance was supported by what allied military sources called the greatest concentration of American firepower since the Korean war 20 years ago,

Please Turn to Page 11, Col. 1

FEATURE INDEX

THE WEATHER

National Weather Service forecast: Hazy sunshine today and Saturday but some night and morning coastal low clouds and fog. High today, 90; Saturday, 85. High Thursday, 89; low, 64.

Complete weather information and smog report in Part 2, Page 4.

SAME SIZE AS MOON AT FIRST

Earth Born in 10,000-Year 'Instant,' Two Scientists Say

BY GEORGE GETZE
Times Science Writer

The earth was born in an "instant"—an instant of perhaps fewer than 10,000 years, Caltech geophysicists have suggested.

Not only was it born very quickly, but early in the earth's history it was only about as large as the moon and had a similar composition, according to Don Anderson, director of the Caltech seismology lab, and Thomas Hanks, a research fellow.

Their concept of the birth of the earth explains several phenomena over which scientists have argued. It explains why the earth has a solid inner core and a molten outer core, Anderson and Hanks report in the current issue of Nature, the world's most prestigious scientific journal.

The Caltech seismologists said that after the earth grew to its present size part of its radioactive nucleus may have melted its way through intermediate layers and come to the surface to form the primitive land masses.

Anderson and Hanks' theory relies on the temperatures at which different metals solidify from a gas, and assumes that these minerals united in the order in which they became solids.

It is believed that the solar system grew out of hot whirling gases about five billion or so years ago. As these extremely hot gases cooled, the first compounds to solidify were those rich in calcium, aluminum, titanium, uranium and thorium.

Please Turn to Page 26, Col. 1

Los Angeles Times

LARGEST CIRCULATION IN THE WEST, 1,026,499 DAILY, 1,210,556 SUNDAY.

VOL. XCI 2† SEVEN PARTS—PART ONE CC WEDNESDAY MORNING, SEPTEMBER 6, 1972 120 PAGES

DAILY 10¢

9 OLYMPIC HOSTAGES DIE IN SHOOT-OUT

CONFRONTATION—Munich official points to watch during talk with helmeted figure on deadline for terrorists' demands. Right, a hooded terrorist on Olympic Village balcony. (AP Wirephotos)

Police Kill 4 Arab Guerrillas and Capture 3

BY JOE ALEX MORRIS JR.
Times Staff Writer

MUNICH—Nine Israeli hostages and four Arab terrorists died in a blaze of gunfire and explosions at an airport near here early today, climaxing a dramatic episode in which the Arabs seized the Israeli team's residence in Olympic Village here.

The bloodbath came after West German police opened fire on the Arabs as they were in the process of transferring the hostages from helicopters to a waiting transport plane. Two other Israelis died earlier Tuesday in shooting at the village itself.

All the Israeli's were members of their country's Olympics contingent.

Three other Arabs were captured in a wild post-midnight chase at the Furstenfeldbruck airport, some 30 miles west of here. One other was unaccounted for, officials said.

At least 16 persons died in the day of terror including a German policeman who was killed in the fray.

First Suspension of Games

The tragedy caused the first suspension in the history of the modern Olympic Games and cast in doubt the future of the $657 million Munich Olympiad.

The shocking news of the death of all the Israeli hostages was broken at a 3 a.m. press conference in the Olympics Press Center. Government officials said that sharp-shooters positioned at the airport had opened up in bad visibility as the terrorists prepared to herd their bound prisoners from two helicopters that had brought them from the Olympic Village.

The terrorists, having fallen into a trap, opened up in turn and sprayed the two helicopters where the hostages still sat with gunfire and grenades.

Olympic press chief, Hans Klein, said it had been impossible to count the number of bodies inside the wreckage of the helicopters but authorities at one time had a slender hope that one or two hostages may have escaped.

Arabs Promised Flight

The decision to open up on the Arabs came after they had been promised a flight to an Arab capital with the hostages. But as government spokesman Conrad Ahlers put it: "It was not the government's intention to allow the hostages to leave German soil for an unknown fate."

The slayings could affect the future course of the Olympic Games. Earlier, nervous West German officials had indicated the hostages had come through the fire fight, and on this basis it had been decided to resume the Games this afternoon.

But after the airport shoot-out, the president of the West German Olympic Organizing Committee, Willi Daume, announced he would ask the International Olympic Committee to meet today to decide whether the games should continue. The Olympics could be over.

Both Bavarian Interior Minister Otto Me.k and Federal Interior Minister Hans Dieter Genscher earlier expressed their conviction that cer-

Please Turn to Page 10, Col. 1

U.S. ITEMS TOO SCARCE

Saigon Black Market Finds Itself Compelled to Diversify

BY JACQUES LESLIE
Times Staff Writer

SAIGON—Like any company that finds its business no longer lucrative, Saigon's black market is diversifying.

Once almost everything that surfaced in the black market was American-made and shipped to Vietnam intended to be sold to American GIs. Most of the goods were either stolen from Saigan docks or U.S. Army PXs. Black market vendors could take pride in the variety of brands of each product they offered as well as the prices, which were always competitive with the PX.

Now with the drastic drop in American troops, the supply of American products is drying up. So black market vendors have turned to Japanese and Vietnamese goods. One vendor who previously sold only American items says that two-thirds of his products are Japanese and Vietnamese.

Not What It Wrs

Vendors agree that business is not what it used to be.

Most of the Japanese products have reached the black market illegally, thus avoiding an import tax, which for some products is several times the original value.

The vendors themselves do not take part in the illegal import transactions. They are supplied by middlemen, who visit them each day offering to sell them whatever products they have available. The other day a middleman approached a vendor and offered to sell a pair of pliers for a little less than $1. The vendor agreed but asked if the middleman had anything else to offer. The middleman had run out.

Before, the vendor bought about $25 worth of products a day from the middleman. Now, because the middleman's supply is reduced, the vendor buys only about $10 worth a day.

Saigon's black market area is referred to as the "sun market," an apt name, for the market is entirely outdoors, with goods spread along sidewalks in an area of several blocks.

Protected by Ponchos

Vendors and products are protected from the sun only by ponchos and canvas liners held up by ropes and poles. They are just high enough to allow most Vietnamese to walk under comfortably. But taller Westerners have to stoop as they go by.

As Americans walk through, Vietnamese children often pester them to buy plastic bags—on which they seem to have cornered the market. Vendors, who are mostly betel-chewing women, point to their products, and say with suddenly charming smiles, "You buy this?" Prices are determined by bargaining and Americans are notoriously bad bargainers.

In addition to the loss of American products, the black market has been hit by inflation.

Vendors who six months ago sold several different brands of American detergent in both family-size and regular-size boxes now sell only one brand, and that in small boxes

Please Turn to Page 17, Col. 1

20-FOOT BREAKERS FORCE CLOSING OF COUNTY BEACHES

BY DICK MAIN
Times Staff Writer

Breakers up to 20 feet high from tropical storm Hyacinth forced closing of most south-facing beaches in Los Angeles County late Tuesday after lifeguards rescued hundreds of persons from riptides and an extremely stormy surf.

The closures, extending from Manhattan Beach to Zuma Beach, were the most extensive put into effect in recent history, lifeguards said.

They came after the National Weather Service issued a small craft warning at 1:30 p.m. from Point Conception to Oceanside. At 5:45 p.m. the warning was extended from Oceanside to the Mexican border.

A bulletin issued at the Eastern Pacific Hurricane Center in San Francisco reported the storm was

Please Turn to Page 3, Col. 2

Berrigan Sentenced for Mail Smuggling

HARRISBURG, Pa. (AP)—Imprisoned antiwar priest Philip Berrigan was given a two years' sentence Tuesday for smuggling mail in and out of prison. A Roman Catholic nun, described as his ally in an alleged plot to kidnap a presidential adviser, was sentenced to one year—also for mail smuggling.

At the same time, the government said it would not seek new trials for Father Berrigan and other members of the so-called Harrisburg Seven on the conspiracy charges upon which a jury deadlocked last April.

Former U.S. Atty. Gen. Ramsey Clark, a member of the Berrigan defense, said the sentences would be appealed.

Father Berrigan, 48, who is serving a six-year term for destroying draft board files in Maryland in 1968, was sentenced to two years on each of four counts of smuggling. But U.S. Dist. Judge R. Dixon Herman ruled

Please Turn to Page 25, Col. 1

FEATURE INDEX

Fence-Scaling Wasn't Unusual ---but Then the Shooting Started

Night Workers at Olympic Village Post Office Saw Arabs Sneak In, but Athletes Had Often Done It After Curfew

BY SHIRLEY POVICH
Exclusive to The Times from the Washington Post

MUNICH—The night shift workers at the Olympic Village Post Office merely nudged each other and pointed to the fence climbers outside, in the dim light of the early dawn.

No great to-do about that. It happened all the time in the village—those agile Olympic athletes scaling the 6-foot fence to bypass the gatekeepers and sneak back to their dorms after violating curfew.

You couldn't tell an Arab from a blond Scandinavian in the half light of 5 a.m., especially if he was dressed in those long sweat suits favored in Olympic Village.

This time they were not just a couple of kids sneaking home. "They all were carrying those big Adidas or Puma bags," a postal worker said later.

A common sight in the village those carryall bags. Big enough to conceal a snub-nosed machine gun, if necessary.

As for getting over the fences, "there's never any trouble about that," said another athlete, a cyclist from Holland.

"Two nights ago my friend and I slung our bikes over the same fence before we crawled over and got back to the dorms," he said.

The first shots rang out in Building 31. That's where the Israeli team was living, on the first two floors. The third and top floor was occupied by a part of the East German Olympic contingent.

A knocking from the outside door of one of the four first-floor rooms aroused Dr. Weigel, an Israeli team physician, who partially opened the door. "You're an Arab, go away," he screamed.

The leader of the Arab terrorists fired through the door instantly killing Moshe Weinberg, 33-year-old

Please Turn to Page 12, Col. 4

Spitz Hastens Trip Home After Killings

LONDON (UPI)—American superswimmer Mark Spitz flew into London from Munich Tuesday because of the kidnaping and killing of Israeli team members at the Olympics by Palestinian guerrillas.

Airport sources said he was staying overnight and would fly to his home in California today.

Spitz, a Jew, arrived aboard a British European Airways flight from the German city. He said his departure was premature but that "I had not planned to stay up to the end of the Games."

He declined to comment on the

Please Turn to Page 11, Col. 1

ARRIVES IN LOS ANGELES

McGovern Campaign Tactics Resemble Nixon's in 1968

BY JULES WITCOVER
Times Staff Writer

The McGovern campaign entourage that flew into Los Angeles Tuesday in two remodeled jetliners bears a close resemblance to the Nixon campaign entourage of 1968—and the resemblance is not just physical.

The physical similarity is of course the most apparent. The candidate's plane, a United Air Lines 727, has been redesigned inside to provide a comfortable front cabin with sofa, table and telephone system, just as President Nixon's was four years ago.

McGovern deplores the killing of Israeli athletes. Part 1, Page 32.

There, Sen. George S. McGovern, as did Mr. Nixon in 1968, enjoys the privacy of his staff, while members of the press sit in comfortable first-class seats to the rear.

The Nixon campaign actually had three planes—one for the candidate and staff, one for the reporters and a third for TV cameramen, technicians, photographers and their heavy equipment.

The McGovern group has two jets, the candidate's called The Dakota Queen II after McGovern's World War II B-24 bomber, and one for the TV cameramen, technicians and some spill-over reporters.

Aboard the Dakota Queen II a rear compartment houses office and secretarial equipment on which press aides reproduce and distribute texts of McGovern's remarks in advance of most stops—also a 1968 Nixon pattern.

Please Turn to Page 31, Col. 1

JIM MURRAY

Olympics' New and Tragic Event---Murder

MUNICH—I stood on a rooftop balcony on the Connollystrasse in the Olympic Village Tuesday and witnessed an Olympic event Baron de Coubertin never dreamed of and the purpose of which is as arcane to me as the discus, the team foil, the hammer, individual epee or Greco-Roman wrestling.

An Arab rifle team, arriving late, scorned the small bore rifle, three positions, the free pistol (silhouette) and introduced a new event to the Olympic program—murder.

Dead were Moshe Weinberg, Yosef Romano, both 33, and, maybe, the Olympic Games, age 30 centuries.

There was great concern the Olympic Games were getting too costly and they are. When they start costing lives, there's a new name for them—and its not "games."

They became a forum for political protest in 1968 and now they've become a forum for political assassination. Maybe they'll bomb the next one.

Eight guys with hate in their hearts and guns in their hands have turned this whole billon-mark festival into a Middle East incident. They have hijacked the Olympics.

I arrived at the village at 9:30. Most of the non-German-speaking people still had no inkling that the Olympic Games were in the hands of an unofficial, non-sanctioned committee.

The Germans, who had not halted eight armed, homicidal uncredentialed terrorists, now proceeded to solve the problem by barring journalists armed with dangerous pencils.

But the Germans are undone by their own thoroughness in this Olympics. Obviously under instructions not to betray any officiousness reminiscent of you-know-who and his brown-shirted you-know-whats, they have dressed their cops in powder blue suits with white caps as if they were on their way to punting in the park with their picnic baskets. Underneath the pansy costumes were guys who were just as tough and muscular as the rubber truncheon crowd of 1936, but the impossibility of 250 guards sealing off 10,000 people is apparent. The Germans, as usual, had trouble with their occupation.

Inside the Olympic Village, the athletes treated the whole event as just another heat in the high jump. Bicyclists bicycled. Runners ran intervals. Occasionally, a crowd would wander out to the checkpoint on the

Please Turn to Page 12, Col. 2

THE WEATHER

National Weather Service forecast: Cloudy today with a few showers and chance of isolated thundershowers, decreasing this afternoon and tonight. Fair Thursday. High today, 88; high Thursday, 80. High Tuesday, 90; low, 71.

Complete weather information and smog report in Part 2, Page 4.

THE NEXT FOUR YEARS---WHAT YOU CAN EXPECT FROM NIXON

BY JOHN F. LAWRENCE
Times Washington Bureau Chief

WASHINGTON—President Nixon is determined in the next four years to leave an imprint of responsible conservatism that will outlive his Administration.

It is more than campaign talk, say his top advisers. They avoid the word "conservative" because of its head-in-the-sand connotations and because Mr. Nixon never has been afraid to embrace liberal programs when he believed it to be necessary.

However, the events they foresee in the coming term—a strong economy, an end to the war and its divisive influence at home—should enable Mr. Nixon to pursue more closely the aims he brought with him to office in 1969.

There were those who urged him then to begin trimming some of the so-called Great Society programs he believed were failing. "But you just couldn't do it then, you didn't dare have that kind of wrench" because of the unrest in the country, explains one White House aide.

Now Mr. Nixon speaks confidently of "the 'new majority' that is forming not around a man or a party, but around a set of principles that is deep in the American spirit."

The nation's big problems are still there—poverty, pollution and congestion. But if Mr. Nixon is right, they must be dealt with under new priorities with broad support. Atop the list, in Mr. Nixon's view, is less federal involvement in solving local problems, an extension of his belief that a strong private economy can do more than public programs to meet the nation's needs.

Critics of this approach say it will fail. Mr. Nixon cannot permit enough economic boom to provide jobs for many of the chronically unemployed without renewing the inflation he has spent two tough years fighting, they contend.

Nevertheless, interviews with many of his top advisers and Cabinet officers leave little doubt that in his second term the President can be expected to:

—Limit spending and if he cannot avoid a tax increase altogther, bring the federal budget more nearly into balance.

—Make a strong effort to reorganize the federal bureaucracy, renewing a proposal to consolidate seven cabinet-level departments into four, forcing department heads to operate more in unison with presidential directives and trimming government payrolls.

—Make good on a long-term pledge to shift more of the decision-making on public programs to state and local authorities, substituting general federal support for specific grants-in-aid.

—Use changes in tax laws to meet pressing problems, such as the need to ease the burden of inflation on the elderly, encourage private industry to battle pollution and make American goods more competitive in world markets.

—Shift within a few months from the present wage and price control system to a strong set of standby regulations and mechanisms, letting a tight fiscal policy bear the burden of restraining inflation.

—Continue to expand programs to fight crime and drug abuse, including more federal aid to local law-enforcement bodies and an effort to shift the balance of courtroom procedure away from what some say is too much protection for suspected criminals.

The President's most delicate settlement in Indochina will enable him to focus on modernization of the military and its deterent capabilities. But with military salaries rising as part of the switch to an all-volunteer army, that means a rise in defense spending. Critics will be quick to point out the contrast with his attitude toward social legislation.

Please Turn to Page 22, Col. 1

Los Angeles Times

LARGEST CIRCULATION IN THE WEST, 1,026,499 DAILY, 1,210,556 SUNDAY.

VOL. XCI † FIVE PARTS—PART ONE CC WEDNESDAY MORNING, NOVEMBER 8, 1972 104 PAGES

DAILY 10c

LANDSLIDE VICTORY FOR NIXON

Busch, Dorn and Hayes Leading; Proposition 14 Losing

California Gives President His Biggest Victory

BY RICHARD BERGHOLZ
Times Political Writer

California-born Richard Nixon made it three in a row in his home state Tuesday, running up his biggest and most impressive victory to capture 45 electoral votes.

Thus, he not only kept the state in step with the rest of the nation's voters, but he helped wipe out the memory of his most humiliating defeat exactly 10 years ago when he ran for governor.

On the local level, voters gave early leads to three Los Angeles County

State, Los Angeles and Orange counties returns. Part 1, Page 23.

officials who were seeking new four-year terms against heavy opposition—Dist. Atty. Joseph P. Busch and County Supervisors Warren M. Dorn and James A. Hayes.

But the slowness of the computerized vote count made trends late in developing.

Also on California's presidential ballot with Mr. Nixon and Sen. George S. McGovern were Rep. John G. Schmitz of Santa Ana, running on the American Independent Party ticket, and Dr. Benjamin Spock, the Peace and Freedom Party candidate. They did not constitute a significant force in the balloting.

The vote, with 5,415 of the state's 23,766 precincts reporting:

Nixon 1,118,038—55%
McGovern 856,604—43%
Schmitz 50,733—2%
Spock 16,196—0%

While the President was sweeping the state, it quickly became apparent there was not going to be any great across-the-board Republican triumph in California.

Most of California's Democratic and Republican congressmen seeking reelection appeared to be winning new two-year terms. And of the five new seats awarded the state on the basis of decennial reapportionment, Republicans were winning

Please Turn to Page 32, Col. 1

THE WINNING TEAM—President Nixon and his running mate, Vice President Agnew, appear before supporters at victory celebration in Washington after Sen. George McGovern conceded defeat.
UPI Wirephoto

President Sweeps 47 States; Democrats Control Congress

BY JULES WITCOVER
Times Staff Writer

WASHINGTON—President Nixon, riding a personal landslide in at least 47 of the 50 states, swept into a second term Tuesday night, smothering Democratic challenger George S. McGovern.

Only Massachusetts and the District of Columbia, with 17 electoral votes between them, escaped the President's grasp, with Minnesota still up for grabs early today and only scant returns in from Alaska.

The Democrats, however, retained control of Congress. They lost some ground in the House but appeared to hold a 20 to 25-seat edge. In the Senate, the Democrats increased their margin to 57-43.

In every corner of the country, at every economic level and among various ethnic, religious and racial groups, Mr. Nixon exceeded Republican norms in winning the "four more years" he had campaigned for only sparingly this fall.

The vote, with 72% of all ballots counted:

Nixon	35,046,267 or 62%
McGovern	21,206,701 or 37%

Electoral vote totals were Nixon 508 in 47 states and McGovern 17 in one state and the District of Columbia. Results in two states were not determined.

Trailing far back were the American Party candidate, lame-duck Rep. John G. Schmitz of California, and the People's Party candidate, Dr. Benjamin Spock. Between them they were getting less than 1% of the vote.

The President, speaking from the White House after his election was certain, expressed his appreciation and commiserated with McGovern on his loss. It was exactly 10 years ago that Mr. Nixon, after losing the California gubernatorial election, had told the press that "you won't have Dick Nixon to kick around anymore."

Noting his overwhelming victory, Mr. Nixon told the television audience that "a huge landslide margin means nothing at all unless it is a victory for America." It will not be such a victory, he said, "unless in

Please Turn to Page 20, Col. 1

4 GOP Incumbents Out; Democrats Add 2 Seats in Senate

BY JOHN H. AVERILL
Times Staff Writer

WASHINGTON — With voters splitting their tickets in massive numbers, the Democrats increased their dominance of the Senate Tuesday by picking up two additional seats.

Four Republican incumbents, including veteran Sens. Margaret Chase Smith of Maine and Gordon Allott of Colorado, were defeated in the surprising Democratic tide.

In addition, the Democrats won Senate seats in Kentucky and South Dakota vacated by retiring Republicans.

For their part, the Republicans ousted one Democratic incumbent, Sen. William B. Spong Jr. of Virginia, and picked up Senate seats in New Mexico, North Carolina and Oklahoma, where Democratic incumbents were not running.

But the GOP victories were more than offset by losses as the Democrats stretched their Senate majority to 57 to 43. In the 92nd Congress they held a 55-45 edge.

At the same time, the Republicans whittled the Democrats' margin in the House, so that overall the 93rd Congress should be more receptive to President Nixon's programs than its predecessors.

Although many key races remained undecided, indications where that the Republicans would gain 15 to 20 seats. That falls fare short of the 39 the Republicans needed to wrest control of the House from the Democrats.

The Senate outcome was a severe disappointment to President Nixon

Please Turn to Page 21, Col. 2

Hayes, Dorn and Busch Take Lead Over Their Challengers

BY BILL BOYARSKY
Times Political Writer

First returns gave incumbents the lead Tuesday night in the climax of one of Los Angeles County's stormiest elections.

As he was expected to do, Supervisor James A. Hayes moved to a substantial early lead over Los Angeles City Councilman Marvin Braude in the 4th District, which stretches the length of the county's coastline and runs inland to areas around Compton and Torrance.

But Dist. Atty. Joseph P. Busch and Supervisor Warren M. Dorn of the 5th District held narrower leads over their foes.

Absentee ballots put Busch ahead of Dep. Dist. Atty. Vincent T. Bugliosi in a contest that ended in bitterness between the two.

Dorn was ahead of Baxter Ward, the former television news anchorman, in the huge 5th District, which reaches from Pasadena through the San Fernando Valley and into the Antelope Valley and the desert around Lancaster.

With returns just trickling in, only one candidate, Hayes, ventured a preliminary victory statement.

"These early returns are highly encouraging and make us feel very elated at the outset," he said. "I can't predict whether the same percentage will continue but I am confident it will be near that percentage when the final ballots are tallied."

The election was an unusual one in county history. In the past, incumbents won easily, seldom facing stiff challenges. This year, challenges were plentiful and strong.

And they based their campaigns on controversial issues, generally trying to portray their foes as too favorable to special business interests who contributed to their campaigns. Incumbents responded vigorously and counter-attacked.

If there was an overriding issue in the two supervisorial races, it was how to best preserve the remaining undeveloped land in Los Angeles County, a subject that was discussed in both the 4th and 5th supervisorial districts.

Hayes said that the election will mean a change in county policy toward land development.

"As far as the supervisors were concerned, I think the fact of almost unrestricted building and unre-

Please Turn to Page 12, Col. 1

Feature index and weather box appear in Part 1, Page 2.

'GREAT TASKS' AHEAD

President Accepts Victory With Call for National Unity

BY ROBERT C. TOTH
Times Staff Writer

WASHINGTON—President Nixon accepted his greatest victory Tuesday night with a call for national unity after the bitterness of the campaign, declaring that "a huge landslide margin means nothing at all unless it is a victory for America."

Mr. Nixon said he had "never known a national election when I would be able to go to bed earlier than tonight."

Speaking from the Oval Office in the White House shortly after Sen. George S. McGovern conceded defeat in a telegram and on television, the President then went to a rally of his campaign workers at the Shoreham Hotel.

Mr. Nixon had not watched the election returns on television until after his victory was assured. He had dined early with Mrs. Nixon and their daughters and sons-in-law, after which he retired to the Lincoln sitting room and received reports by phone from his staff and from state campaign headquarters around the country, his aides said.

With his familiar yellow legal pad at hand, he jotted down notes for his victory statement. Occasionally he was visited by David Eisenhower and Edward Cox as the Nixon ladies watched television returns in their quarters.

McGovern's congratulations to Mr. Nixon were more formal than warm. He promised his "full support" of efforts for peace abroad and justice at home, and concluded with "best wishes to you and your gracious

Please Turn to Page 21, Col. 4

Death Penalty Approved; Coast Environmental Plan Winning

BY WILLIAM ENDICOTT
Times Staff Writer

Californians voted overwhelmingly Tuesday to restore the death penalty and, by a narrower margin, appeared to be approving an initiative designed to protect the state's scenic coastline from unrestricted development.

Still incomplete returns also showed heavy support for a measure to prohibit schools from busing children for integration.

A well-publicized $156 million bond issue for expansion of University of California health science and medical school facilities also was winning approval.

But voters appeared to be rejecting most other major propositions on their lengthy ballot, including measures to legalize marijuana, place a limit on property taxes, abolish the governor's veto on state employe salaries, toughen antiobscenity laws and regulate farm labor relations.

Voting on the farm labor initiative, however was extremely close.

Campaigns in support of or in opposition to many of the 22 ballot measures were marked by controversy. Charges of deception, fraud and forgery were more the rule than the exception. Even Gov. Reagan got into the act.

The nine initiatives alone touched an equal number of emotional nerves—property taxes, state employe and Highway Patrol salaries, the death penalty, obscenity, marijuana, coastline protection, busing, farm labor.

Special interests spent millions of

Please Turn to Page 17, Col. 1

MAJOR RACES AT GLANCE

How the top personalities fared in Tuesday's election:

—**Sen. Margaret Chase Smith**, 74, a 23-year symbol of the GOP from Maine, lost to Rep. William D. Hathaway, 48.

—**John D. (Jay) Rockefeller IV** was defeated in bid to unseat Republican Gov. Arch A. Moore Jr. in West Virginia.

—**Sen. Claiborne Pell** easily retained his seat in a race against former GOP Gov. John H. Chafee in Rhode Island.

—**Winston M. Blount**, former postmaster general in the Nixon Administration, failed in his bid to turn out Sen. John J. Sparkman (D-Ala.).

—**Illinois Gov. Richard B. Ogilvie** trailed in his race against Democrat Daniel Walker.

—**Sens. Charles H. Percy** (R-Ill.) and **Walter F. Mondale** (D-Minn.), mentioned as possible presidential contenders for their parties in 1976, both won reelection easily.

—**Sen. Robert P. Griffin** led Democratic challenger Frank J. Kelley in a Michigan Senate race revolving around the busing issue.

—**Texas Sen. John G. Tower**, defeated Barefoot Sanders, a Democratic protege of Lyndon B. Johnson.

—**Christopher (Kit) Bond**, a Republican, won the Missouri governorship from Edward L. Dowd to become the nation's youngest state chief executive at 33.

—**The 1976 Winter Olympics** were left in doubt when Colorado voters approved a constitutional amendment barring the use of state funds for the Denver games, and city voters did the same.

Los Angeles Times

LARGEST CIRCULATION IN THE WEST, 1,026,499 DAILY, 1,210,556 SUNDAY.

FINAL
ONE OF THE WORLD'S GREAT NEWSPAPERS

VOL. XCII 2† SIXTEEN PARTS—PART ONE CC SUNDAY, JANUARY 28, 1973 400 PAGES

SUNDAY 50c

FACE TO FACE—U.S. Secretary of State William P. Rogers, seated in center facing the camera, heads the American delegation during the first Vietnam peace agreement signing session in Paris. In the foreground, with backs to camera, is the delegation from North Vietnam.
AP Wirephoto

Vietnam Foes Sign a 'Fragile Peace'

13-Year Conflict Ended by Cool Paris Ceremony

BY DON COOK
Times Staff Writer

PARIS—A few minutes before 4 o'clock Saturday afternoon, Paris time, the signing of the Vietnam peace agreement was completed. Nine hours later a cease-fire went into effect to end 13 years of military conflict in South Vietnam.

The "fragile peace," as it is already characterized, was signed in two stages at morning and afternoon sessions. The site was the splendidly ornate setting of the ballroom of the Hotel Majestic International Conference Center where the peace talks began in May, 1968.

The atmosphere was one of strict protocol, cool and businesslike, devoid of any speechmaking or statements, handshaking or public cordialities.

The morning signing in which all four parties took part—the United States, North Vietnam, the South Vietnam government and the Viet Cong Provisional Revolutionary Government—lasted 18 minutes.

Cool Glasses of Champagne

The afternoon session, with only the United States and the North Vietnamese participating, took only 11 minutes.

After each signing, the chief delegates left the ballroom for a smaller salon where cool glasses of champagne were drunk, out of sight of television cameras and reporters.

It was as if all four combatants in the long conflict were mutually agreed that the occasion should be as muted and anticlimactic as possible after the exhausting, cruel, divisive and now ultimately inconclusive struggle which has cast such a deep shadow not only over the participants but the entire world.

Before the cease-fire took effect at midnight Greenwich time (4 p.m. Saturday in Los Angeles; 8 a.m. today in Vietnam), the first acts of implementing the agreements already had taken place. The North Vietnamese and the PRG delegations in Paris formally handed over to the United States a list of all American prisoners of war which they hold, and all those Americans they have identified who are listed as missing in action.

Under the agreement, repatriation of all POWs and withdrawal of all American forces from South Vietnam is now to be completed within 60 days.

Meanwhile, the United States formally announced in Washington that

Please Turn to Page 16, Col. 1

OTHER STORIES ON WAR, AFTERMATH INSIDE THE TIMES

—In the Southland peace was greeted by a few church bells—and silence. Page 3.

—North Vietnamese sources say U.S. jet transports will airlift Hanoi troops to South Vietnam to help enforce the cease-fire. Page 11.

—Hanoi has indicated it would favor a U.N. role in the reconstruction of Vietnam. Page 14.

—The final day of the war had its full measure of agony and killing. Page 17.

—Saigon faces peace with a mixture of pessimism and cautious hope. Page 18.

—In the final days of the war the International Control Commission was about the nearest thing to a laughingstock that the tragic conflict provided. Page 18.

THOUSANDS OF LIVES CHANGED

Truce in Vietnam---It Holds Special Meaning for Veterans

It was 4 p.m. in California Saturday when the cease-fire came to Vietnam.

The moment marked by the end to war had a special meaning here for thousands whose lives it had changed forever—the veterans.

Some fought and some fled. Some wasted valuable years and some came home scarred for the rest of their lives. Some came back to seek or find a better life than they had known before.

This story was compiled by Times reporters Dial Torgerson, Robert Jones and Robert Kelton.

Most of them have blended unobtrusively with the civilian population, just as did their fathers and uncles after wars of the '40s and '50s.

But when it finally came, Saturday's cease-fire meant something more and different to those who had served: the Vietnam veterans among us.

Unemployment among veterans is now down to 5.5%, only slightly greater than the 5.2% rate for the entire work force, the government says. But the Labor Department statistics don't reflect the anguishes of men like Mike Grijalva, beset with a vast gap between hopes and achievements.

The day of the Vietnam cease-fire was no day of rest for Mike Grijalva, 27, who had balconies to wash and a driveway to hose down as part of his job as manager of the seven-unit apartment where he lives in El Sereno.

"I get $30 off the price of the apartment for being the manager," he said, "and in my spot, I need it."

He and his wife, Olivia, have a daughter, Monique, 4, and expect another child next summer. He must find a way to pay for the new baby while continuing in school and working, when the job is there, as a printer.

He wants to be a social worker. But he is honest with himself about his chances:

"At the rate I'm going, I'll be 30 by the time I'm through school. I'm not fooling myself. I know I may never make it.

"I have no resentment. I'm not bitter. I realize where I'm at, what I'm up against. I don't want to be a millionaire. All I want is to get a home, and to have it so my children can get an education. I want to be working a press four years from now.

"I don't want to have to get up in the morning, and think about that monotonous job waiting for me, and say to myself, 'Jesus, here I go again.' "

Special Chicano Problems

Grijalva is a Chicano. The Chicano vets must cope with their own special class of problems, Grijalva said.

"It started in school," he said. "When I was in Woodrow Wilson High the advisers were putting my Anglo friends into the academic courses, and mine would say, 'Mickey,' or 'Miguel, why don't we put you down for a coupla hours of wood shop?'

"We had this myth that only the Anglo kids went to college. We were always programmed for the industrial arts. Know why I went into the Army? I was afraid to go to college. Afraid I didn't belong there. Nobody ever gave me any encouragement, told me I could make it.

"The recruiting sergeant told me how when I got out I'd be trained for a civilian job. I was in communications, went to Vietnam and Korea, got married while I was in the service, and when I got out, at 21, I found there was no way—I mean no way—I could use my Army training.

Please Turn to Page 3, Col. 1

UCLA WINS 61ST GAME IN ROW, SETS BASKETBALL MARK

Exclusive to The Times from a Staff Writer

SOUTH BEND, Ind. — UCLA's Bruins set an all-time college basketball record of 61 straight wins here Saturday afternoon, easily beating Notre Dame, 82-63.

The victory came in the same arena where the Bruins last lost, Jan. 23, 1971.

UCLA, now 16-0 this season, took control at the start behind Bill Walton's all-around play and Keith Wilkes' shooting in a game of rousing contact played before a roaring, sellout crowd at Notre Dame's Convocation and Convention Center.

Wilkes had 20 points, Walton and Larry Farmer 16 each and Walton grabbed 15 rebounds as UCLA broke the record of the Bill Russell-led University of San Francisco teams of the 1950s.

Details in Sports Section

Military Draft Ends Five Months Early

WASHINGTON (AP)—Secretary of Defense Melvin R. Laird announced Saturday the end of the military draft.

His action, placing the nation's armed forces on an all-volunteer footing for the first time in nearly 25 years, came five months ahead of President Nixon's goal.

In a message to senior defense officials, Laird said:

"With the signing of the peace agreement in Paris today, and after receiving a report from the secretary of the Army that he foresees no need for further inductions, I wish to inform you that the armed forces henceforth will depend exclusively on volunteer soldiers, sailors, airmen and marines."

Laird's decision canceled plans to draft about 5,000 men before next

Please Turn to Page 9, Col. 1

First 183 Names on POW List Released; Suspense Continues

By Associated Press

A good-news telephone call was the thing wanted most in hundreds of American homes Saturday as nerve-wracked families of American men missing in action awaited word on the fate of their loved ones.

And Colleen Henderson of Milwaukee got such a call. She learned that her husband, Air Force Capt. William Henderson, is a prisoner of war. He has been missing since April, 1972.

"I was just going nuts," Mrs. Henderson said. "I still don't believe it."

The Defense Department Saturday night released the first 183 names on the list of U.S. military servicemen held by North Vietnam while the State Department announced that civilian American prisoners will be freed. There was no indication how many servicemen were on the list turned over by Hanoi Saturday.

Believed Held Longest

One of the names released was that of the prisoner believed to have been held longest in North Vietnam, Navy Lt. Comdr. Everett Alvarez of Lafayette, Calif., who was one of the first pilots to fly an attack against the north. He was shot down Aug. 5, 1964, on his first mission over North Vietnam.

The Pentagon provided only names, branch of service and ranks of the men. Additional information, such as hometowns, comes from files of POW organizations and from reports by families already notified. Here is the list:

1. Brudno, Capt. Edward A., Air Force, Harrison, N.Y., Quincy, Mass., captured October, 1965.
2. Collins, Major Thomas Edward, AF, Jackson, Miss., captured October, 1965.
3. Sehorn, Capt. James Eldon, AF, Forest Grove, Ore., date of capture unknown.
4. Henderson, Capt. William J. AF, not named in previous public lists.

Please Turn to Page 12, Col. 1

Cease-Fire in South Vietnam: Hope and Continued Shooting

BY GEORGE McARTHUR
Times Staff Writer

SAIGON — The appointed hour marking a cease-fire in South Vietnam arrived today accompanied by church bells ringing in the towns and cities and continued shooting in many parts of the country.

There was no high drama, but the hope for peace was painfully real. Many people stood motionless at 8 a.m. (4 p.m. PST Saturday) for one minute of government-ordered silence. At the end, they frequently turned to one another and stated the hope that the cease-fire was real.

The official end of the shooting—if indeed it was real—was obviously going to be messy and drawn out. At the appointed hour, shooting was still in progress in many areas—notably the far north below the demilitarized zone and along the so-called invasion corridor leading from Saigon northwest to Tay Ninh province and War Zone C.

Tan Son Nhut Airport remained on red alert after an early morning shelling or rocket attack and military headquarters reported that just before the cease-fire hour Communist gunners were shelling or rocketing air bases at Da Nang, Pleiku, Can Tho and possibly elsewhere.

At least one American was killed in the last flurry of noise and battle.

Until his relatives were notified, he was identified only as an American officer. He thus wrested questionable recognition as the last American to die from Air Force Sgt. John Rucker, killed by a rocket in Da Nang two days ago. When the final killed in action figures are in—depending on official Pentagon record keeping—the unnamed American officer will probably be No. 45,-941.

Please Turn to Page 19, Col. 1

SHAKESPEARE'S MISTRESS REPORTED IDENTIFIED

Bard's 'Dark Lady' Brought Into Light

BY ROBERT R. KIRSCH
Times Book Critic

LONDON — The dark lady of Shakespeare's sonnets was no fantasy of the poet's imagination—nor was the person a young man, as some critics have suggested—but rather was a married woman with whom he had a very real, ultimately tragic love affair.

She was the half-Italian, half-English daughter of a musician at the court of Elizabeth I, according to Dr. A. L. Rowse, renowned authority on Elizabethan history.

In an exclusive interview with The Times, Dr. Rowse, fellow of All Souls College, Oxford University, and the Huntington Library, San Marino, says he has documentary evidence for the historical identity of the dark woman and will reveal her name and pedigree Monday.

The dark woman in Shakespeare's "Sonnets" has been a mystery to scholars for centuries.

She was, in real life, apparently a mystery to Shakespeare also—but more than that, a source of torment.

"A woman coloured ill," with raven brows and mournful eyes, she proved an unfaithful mistress. She even took his best friend, "a man right fair," as a lover, thus making Shakespeare's loss double: love and friendship.

"My reason, the physician to my love,/ Angry that his prescriptions are not kept,/Hath left me . . .," he wrote.

Finally, there is only bitter resignation. She has broken oaths to him, but he tells her that he, too, has broken oaths: "Oaths of thy deep kindness,/Oaths of thy love, thy truth . . "

Rowse made his discoveries in the manuscript diary of Simon Forman, a garish, sometimes scandalous astrologer and physician, who was a contemporary of Shakespeare.

The Forman diaries are not newly discovered, but they are voluminous, written in Latin and English,

Please Turn to Page 10, Col. 1

THE WEATHER

National Weather Service forecast: Increasing clouds today with chance of rain Monday. High today, 70. Low, 45.

Complete weather information in Part 2, Page 4.

FEATURE INDEX

Last U.S. Jet on Final Bombing Mission Returns Safely to Base

BY THOMAS W. LIPPMAN
Exclusive to The Times from the Washington Post

BIEN HOA AIR BASE, South Vietnam—It was 6:40 p.m. Saturday when Marine Lt. Thomas V. Boykin put his A-4 Skyhawk fighter-bomber down on the runway.

Boykin's plane was the last—the last plane in the last bombing mission by the last U.S. combat air group in the country. For the Americans in South Vietnam, the war was over.

There would be other air strikes during the night, flown by Air Force crews from Thailand and Guam. But in South Vietnam, where the United States once had 500,000 troops, Boykin was the last American to be sent into combat.

The 26-year-old resident of Baton Rouge, La., stepped from his plane to be doused with water by waiting ground crewmen celebrating the end of the war. He said his flight over a battle near Can Tho, in the Mekong Delta, had received some small-arms fire from Communist troops on the ground but had not been hit.

"I'm glad it's over," he said.

Marine Air Group 12's two squadrons of single-engine jets stood silently in their revetments. Each evening since last May, when MAG-12 was brought in from Japan to to bolster the U.S. air power that

Please Turn to Page 13, Col. 1

AFTER THE PROTESTS OF 1960'S: WHAT NEXT?

"Police Battle Antiwar Activists" . . . "Student Sit-in Paralyzes Campus" . . . "200,000 Civil Rights Demonstrators March on Washington." Such were the headlines of the 1960s, when the shouts and violence of the protest movement were rocking America. What did the demonstrators accomplish, if anything? Is their movement now dead? How do the activists themselves view the future? The Times examines such questions in today's Opinion Section.

Ziegler Offers an Apology

PART 1, PAGE 3

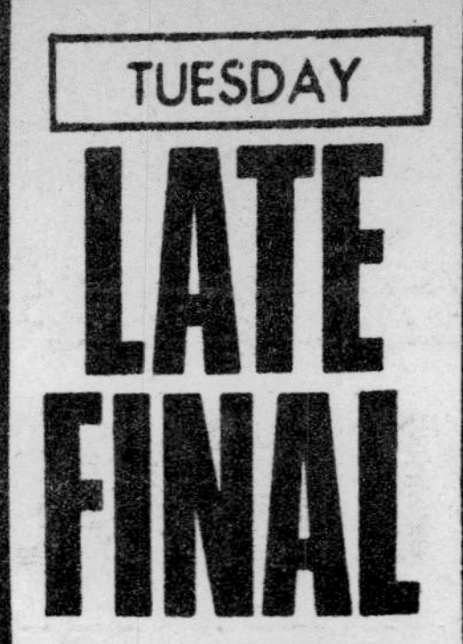

COMPLETE N.Y. STOCKS

Los Angeles Times

LARGEST CIRCULATION IN THE WEST, 1,026,499 DAILY, 1,210,556 SUNDAY

VOL. XCII FIVE PARTS—PART ONE ★★★ TUESDAY, MAY 1, 1973 92 PAGES DAILY 10c

KNEW OF BURGLARY, EHRLICHMAN SAYS

Stocks Dip

NEW YORK (AP)—Stock market prices opened strongly higher today, took a deep nose dive, then began a rapid recovery at the announcement that President Nixon would make an announcement on the economy Wednesday. The Dow Jones industrials closed off 0.22 at 921.21.

Details in Part 3, Page 7

FBI Guarding Files of Three Departing Aides

WASHINGTON (UPI) — FBI agents moved into the White House and the next door Executive Office Building today to "maintain presidential papers" in the offices of three top aides to President Nixon who resigned Monday.

The agents, wearing visitor's passes, were spotted near the offices of H. R. Haldeman, outgoing chief of staff; John D. Ehrlichman, Mr. Nixon's domestic adviser, and departing White House legal counsel John W. Dean III.

FBI agents also were posted near the mailroom in the EOB, where Mr. Nixon has a hideaway office.

Aides said that presence of the FBI agents was an "orderly procedure to maintain presidential papers and in no way reflects on the integrity of the departing advisers."

"It's a procedural step," they said.

Expected to Stay a Week

Haldeman and Ehrlichman were on the job today and are expected to remain at least a week more while they gather their belongings and ease the transition to lower echelon staffers as Mr. Nixon ponders the organization of the White House without those two closest assistants.

White House Press Secretary Ronald Ziegler meantime told reporters that the President may decide not to replace Haldeman and Ehrlichman. He said Mr. Nixon was considering restructuring his staff but had not yet given this any detailed study.

White House officials said the move to safeguard the files was decided on Monday after consultations between Atty. General - designate Elliot L. Richardson, acting FBI Director William D. Ruckelshaus and acting White House Counsel Leonard Garment—all picked within the past four days to succeed men swept from office by the rising tide of the Watergate scandal.

White House observers could not recall the FBI ever being posted on White House guard duty, which traditionally falls to the Secret Service. Spokesmen conceded the move was to protect both presidential papers and files needed for the Watergate investigation.

Related stories in Part 1, Pages 2, 3, 7.

PLEASANT STROLL—A smiling President Nixon and West German Chancellor Willy Brandt walk toward the White House after Brandt's arrival today 10 minutes late, from nearby Blair House.
(AP) Wirephoto

HAND-IN-HAND—Olympic swim champion Mark Spitz, 23, and his bride-to-be Susan Weiner, 21, leave the courthouse in Santa Monica. Spitz says they will be married next Sunday in Beverly Hills.
Times photo by George R. Fry

ROMAN RALLY—Thousands of workers, many waving red flags, jam the Square of St. John in Lateran during traditional May Day demonstration.
Story in Part 1, Page 3
(AP) Wirephoto

Ellsberg's Lawyer Asks for Dismissal

BY GENE BLAKE
Times Staff Writer

Former White House aide John D. Ehrlichman knew of the burglary of the office of Daniel Ellsberg's psychiatrist, it was revealed today by the judge in the Pentagon Papers case. The judge took under submission a motion to dismiss all charges against Ellsberg and co-defendant Anthony J. Russo.

U.S. Dist. Judge Matt Byrne released an FBI interview of Ehrlichman conducted last Friday, in which Ehrlichman said he had told convicted Watergate bugging conspirators G. Gordon Liddy and E. Howard Hunt Jr. not to commit such burglaries again.

He also said he had assigned Liddy and Hunt to undertake a White House injuiry into the leak of the Pentagon Papers.

Defense attorney Leonard Boudin made an impassioned plea for dismissal of the indictment against Ellsberg and Russo. He referred to the FBI report as "this dreadful paper" and said it was the "shame of the government of the United States."

Byrne said in denying the dismissal motion that it could be renewed later or "I may renew it myself."

He then ordered the trial to proceed while the government continues to submit reports on its investigation of the burglary.

Got Report Monday

The judge had received the FBI report of the interview of Ehrlichman on Monday. He ruled today that it contained "exculpatory" material—that is material tending to show the innocence of the defendants.

Byrne ordered the report turned over to the defense and Boudin read from it at length during his argument on the motion to dismiss.

The FBI report said Ehrlichman was contacted in his office in the executive office of the President to be questioned about any knowledge he might have on the burglary.

FBI agents said he recalled that sometime in 1971 the President had expressed an interest in the problem of unauthorized disclosure of classified information. He said the President asked him to make inquiries independent of the FBI.

Ehrlichman assumed this responsibility along with Egil Krogh Jr., a White House assistant, and David Young, of the National Security Agency, the report said.

"A decision was made by them to conduct some investigation in the Pentagon Papers' leak matter 'directly out of the White House' and G. Gordon Liddy and E. Howard Hunt were designed to conduct this investigation," the report said.

Ehrlichman knew that Liddy and Hunt had conducted their investigation in the Washington, D.C., area, the report continued, and that during the inquiry they were going to the West Coast to follow up on leads.

Ehrlichman assertedly told the FBI agents there was an indication that Ellsberg had "emotional and moral problems." He said Liddy and Hunt were to prepare a "psychiatric profile" of Ellsberg.

Los Angeles Times

LARGEST CIRCULATION IN THE WEST, 1,026,499 DAILY, 1,210,556 SUNDAY

VOL. XCII 3† SIX PARTS—PART ONE CC WEDNESDAY MORNING, MAY 30, 1973 100 PAGES DAILY 10c

BRADLEY DEFEATS YORTY IN LANDSLIDE

FAMILY JOY—City Councilman Tom Bradley is hugged by daughters Phyllis, 28, left, Lorraine, 29, rear, and wife Ethel after returns showed him to be winner of mayor race over Sam Yorty.
Times photo by Rick Browne

L.A. Becomes Largest U.S. City to Elect a Black Mayor

BY BILL BOYARSKY
Times Political Writer

City Councilman Tom Bradley, son of a black sharecropper, was elected mayor of Los Angeles by a landslide in Tuesday's election, driving Mayor Sam Yorty out of office after 12 tempestuous years.

Bradley's defeat of the 63-year-old Yorty exceeded the hopes of supporters who had been encouraged by favorable public opinion polls but remembered how Yorty came from behind to win four years ago. Bradley's victory margin was greater than Yorty's had been in 1969.

In the end, Yorty, who had survived scandals and the Watts riot, was a victim of his supporters' indifference. He said not enough voters in the white, blue-collar San Fernando Valley precincts that were Yorty strongholds showed up at the polls to vote.

But Pollster Mervin Field told The Times that even if Yorty's backers had turned out in the numbers they did in 1969, he would have had to get about 90% of their votes to win.

Helped by White Backlash

Bradley's aides said that the 55-year-old former police lieutenant also was helped by white backlash to a campaign mailing signed by Yorty bluntly appealing to whites to vote against a black man. Such tactics, they said, reminded people of the political tactics revealed in the Watergate scandal.

With 3,168 of 3,169 precincts reporting, the vote was:

Bradley	431,222	56.33%
Yorty	334,297	43.66%

The campaign thus ended with the election of a black man to be chief executive of the nation's third largest city. Never before had a Negro been elected mayor of such a large city, one with a black population of only between 15% to 18% among 2.8 million residents.

In defeat, Yorty—always a hard scrapper—blamed his Valley supporters for his defeat and said of Bradley: "The change, if it takes place, will be a very radical one and there'll be a lot of people who wish they went out to vote. That's my prediction."

He did not concede, however, saying only: "The trend at the moment doesn't look very good."

"We want Bradley. We want Bradley," the happy crowds shouted at the Bradley headquarters, at a party that overflowed a large room at the Los Angeles Hilton.

Smile Happily at Crowd

Bradley and his wife, Ethel, smiled happily at the crowd. Nearby was a key man in his victory, City Councilman Joel Wachs, whose revelations of how Mayor Yorty had accepted an insurance policy financed by political funds was a major boost to the Bradley campaign in the last week.

Bradley seemed overcome with emotion, and found it difficult to talk.

"We've come a long way," he said.

"The spirit here tonight almost calls for an emotional kind of speech to you but this moment of history is so heavy in drama that it hardly requires that we build your emotions tonight," said Bradley, who rose from Poly High, to UCLA, to the Los Angeles Police Department, to his own law office and then to the Los Angeles City Council.

"Next stop the White House,"

Please Turn to Page 3, Col. 4

Pines Defeats Arnebergh for City Attorney

BY KENNETH REICH
Times Political Writer

Thirty-four-year-old Burt Pines—a political unknown when he announced his candidacy six months ago—swept by 20-year incumbent Roger Arnebergh Tuesday to be elected Los Angeles' new city attorney.

In nearly complete vote totals in the municipal election, Pines ran ahead of winning mayoral candidate Tom Bradley, and got 58.3% of the vote to Arnebergh's 41.7%.

Even though Pines had emerged as the favorite in the last days, the size of his triumph was a surprise. It marked a stunning first victory for a man who may one day aspire to an important role in state politics.

With 3,168 precincts of 3,169 reporting, the results were:

Pines	418,856
Arnebergh	299,212

Speaking from his election night headquarters at the Wilshire Hyatt House, a jubilant Pines declared:

"We've come a long way in this campaign since people thought we were crazy.

"It's a great day in Los Angeles. We're beginning something new in Los Angeles. We've shown you can talk sense to the people and they will respond."

Pines said in an interview that he planned no wholesale firings of present deputy city attorneys.

"Everybody there is going to start off on an even foot and not be prejudged," he said.

Pines also reiterated a campaign pledge that he would not seek more than two four-year terms as city attorney.

"I think that should be the limit," said the man who had just beaten a five-term incumbent. "I think that's enough and then a person ought to be out and bring new leadership in."

Please Turn to Page 3, Col. 1

OFFICERS YOUNGER, WELL TRAINED

'Big-Bellied Sheriff' Gone in Small Town Police Revolution

BY TED SELL
Times Staff Writer

ROCKWOOD, Tenn. — "When I first came here, there was just two old policemen, one to rattle the doorknobs on the stores at night and one to do traffic during the day. Both old men."

Rockwood's chief of police, Cecil W. Strade, 55, chief for two years and a Tennessee state trooper for 32, was immaculate in his blue uniform, wearing the four stars of a chief, an expert pistolman's badge, an American Flag patch on his shoulder, as he talked of the changing standards of small-town police forces in the last 30 years.

"I got 11 men, including myself," Chief Strade said. "All but one of the men are young, less than 30. They all been to school. You got to have that now. They go to the district attorney's school and learn police work."

Straddles U.S. Highway 27

Rockwood's population is 5,345. It straddles U.S. Highway 27 and has a steel smelter. It is a depressing town, with clouds of yellow smoke from the smelter. Just to the south are fragrant farmlands with beautiful horses and a close-by community, Dayton, where the Scopes trial was held to determine if teachers could teach Darwin's theory of evolution.

Through an open door, the town's two fire engines were being serviced by firemen. All the firemen are auxiliary policemen. At Chief Strade's right hand, a radio alternately whispered and yelled.

It was tied into a communications network largely financed by the Justice Department's Law Enforcement Assistance Administration.

There has been a revolution in law enforcement in small U.S. cities during the last 30 years—and almost no one has noticed.

The revolution has come mostly in individual training and in availability of more new equipment.

Some Old Ills Remain

But some of the old ills remain—largely in the form of relatively low pay and, more importantly to officers, political control of the departments by part-time city officials who are full-time businessmen and who often expect favors.

Few of the small cities afford civil service-type tenure for their lawmen. Most are employed at the discretion of the chief or the city council. And firing can come quickly.

But the stereotype of the "big-bellied sheriff" with a gun on his hip, as referred to in a current popular song ("The Night the Lights Went Out in Georgia"), is patently out of date in most small towns—in the South as well as elsewhere.

And even police officers cannot pinpoint a reason why that is so.

The LEAA likes to say that it is because the Nixon Administration has poured $2.4 billion into law and

Please Turn to Page 10, Col. 1

FOUND FLOATING ON BACK

Boy, 11, Who Cannot Swim Survives 15 Hours in Lake

Exclusive to The Times from a Staff Writer

LAKE ELSINORE—George Perez, 11, can't swim and he may never challenge Mark Spitz for swimming honors but if the Olympics ever add a marathon floating event he ought to be an odds-on favorite.

He spent 15 hours Monday night and Tuesday morning floating on his back—bobbing and drifting in Lake Elsinore while 25 Riverside County sheriff's deputies and volunteer divers searched for his body.

The county coroner's office had even assigned him a number in the morgue.

George disappeared Memorial Day while wading in the lake with his 12-year-old brother. There was no hope.

But when a water-skiing party discovered the chubby boy—still afloat, but somewhat waterlogged—near the center of the lake early Tuesday, all George wanted was some milk and cake.

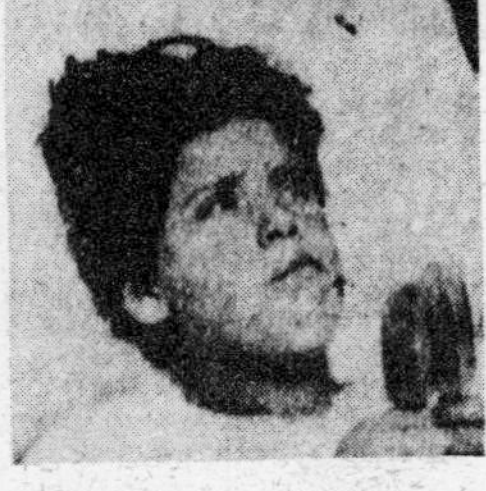

George in the hospital
Times photo

"I just did what they told me in school," was how he explained his survival.

The epochal float began, deputies

Please Turn to Page 24, Col. 1

Domestic Spy Plan Was Carried Out, Inquiry Sources Say

WASHINGTON (UPI) — A White House plan to use secret agents to spy on American radicals was ostensibly canceled, then carried out later by an interdepartmental undercover team inside government, sources close to the Watergate investigation said Tuesday.

Two sources, one of whom said he had seen the plan, reported it was the text of the plan that ousted Counsel to the President John W. Dean III locked in a safe-deposit box and later turned over to a federal judge. The text, classified top secret, has not been released.

Asked to comment on the report, White House Dep. Press Secretary Gerald Warren would not go beyond a lengthy statement in which President Nixon last week discussed the Watergate scandal.

Mr. Nixon at that time referred to a domestic-intelligence plan that he said was withdrawn without being implemented in July, 1970, after FBI Director J. Edgar Hoover objected to the proposal.

Please Turn to Page 4, Col. 4

8 POWs Accused of Collaborating

WASHINGTON (UPI)—A commander of U.S. prisoners of war formally accused eight young enlisted men Tuesday of collaborating with the North Vietnamese while in captivity.

Air Force Col. Theodore W. Guy filed formal charges against the five Army men and three marines, alleging their misconduct while he was the senior American in a POW camp outside Hanoi known as the Plantation.

The Pentagon has followed a general policy of allowing the issue of alleged misbehavior among the 566 returned military POWs to die quietly.

Guy, of Tucson, Ariz., has said that some POWs obtained special privileges by telling the North Vietnamese of the activities of the other prisoners. In some cases other POWs were tortured as a result of the alleged collaboration, according to Guy.

Please Turn to Page 7, Col. 4

THE WEATHER

National Weather Service forecast: Night and early morning low clouds and local fog, otherwise fair today and Thursday. Highs today, upper 70s; Thursday, mid-70s. High Tuesday, 83; low, 66.

Complete weather information and smog report in Part 2, Page 4.

Gasoline Tax Boost Under Study by U.S.

Would Save Fuel, Serve as a Brake on Economy

BY PAUL E. STEIGER
Times Staff Writer

WASHINGTON—The Nixon Administration may ask Congress for an increase in the 4-cent-a-gallon federal tax on gasoline, Treasury Secretary George P. Shultz said Tuesday.

Shultz did not mention a figure, but other government sources said a boost of 1 to 10 cents a gallon was being considered.

The advantage of such a move is that it would tend to curtail use of the increasingly scarce fuel and also serve as a brake on the current headlong economic boom, according to Dep. Treasury Secretary William E. Simon, whose responsibilities include petroleum matters.

The disadvantage, Simon said, is that a gas tax boost would hit poor people harder than wealthy ones, since poor persons usually pay a higher proportion of their incomes for gasoline.

Shultz and Simon made their comments in response to questions from reporters at a day-long briefing on Administration economic policies by

Please Turn to Page 11, Col. 1

FEATURE INDEX

Stevenson, Lorenzen Defeat Challengers in Council Races

BY DOUG SHUIT
Times Staff Writer

Two incumbents up for reelection in Los Angeles City Council races won second terms in Tuesday's election.

Councilman Robert J. Stevenson, whose 13th District covers the Central Los Angeles area from Highland Park to Hollywood, easily defeated his conservative opponent, Irving L. J. Kasper, with 56.4% of the vote.

The vote, with 230 out of the district's 230 precincts reporting:

Stevenson	27,231
Kasper	21,062

Councilman Donald Lorenzen squeaked by opponent Joy Picus in San Fernando Valley's 3rd District with 50.5% of the vote.

The vote, with 216 out of the district's 216 precincts reporting:

Lorenzen	27,572
Picus	27,026

The strong Stevenson vote was the biggest surprise of the two races.

The liberal candidate, he had to beat back an aggressive campaign by Kasper, a retired Los Angeles police lieutenant, that was based primarily on his indictment in 1970 in connection with a Chinatown gambling case.

"It's an overwhelming victory," Stevenson said at his Hollywood campaign headquarters. "I think it owes to the fact that I've kept my office open to the people. Once you get to election night, if you stick with the people, you get their votes."

Almost equally surprising was the vote for Mrs. Picus — a former League of Women Voters official who was running as a liberal-moderate against a conservative in what is considered a conservative district.

Both first-term councilmen topped the voting in the April 3 primary but were forced into runoffs when a total of 13 candidates figured in the balloting. Four challengers ran against Lorenzen; seven against Stevenson.

The campaign in the 13th District, which ranges from the middle-class

Please Turn to Page 17, Col. 1

JUDGE 'WANTS THEM PENNILESS'

Four Stripped of Assets for Defrauding Noncom Clubs

BY GENE BLAKE
Times Staff Writer

U.S. Dist. Judge Warren J. Ferguson made certain Tuesday that former Army Sgt. Maj. William O. Wooldridge and three other men will never benefit financially from their scheme to defraud noncommissioned officers' clubs in Vietnam.

Instead of imposing prison terms, Ferguson took the novel step of ordering the men to perform charitable work without salary and to sign over virtually all their present and future assets—including one defendant's home—to the government.

"I want the defendants penniless," the judge told them. "I just want to make sure you don't have anything."

Ferguson conceded the sentence was "unusual," but told the defendants that their crimes were unusual. One of the defense attorneys, Bruce I. Hochman, said he thought the sentence was illegal, but all agreed to accept it.

Wooldridge and three other former Army sergeants, William E. Higdon, Theodore D. Bass, and Seymour Lazar, had pleaded guilty to charges growing out of a Senate subcommittee investigation which revealed that the clubs had been systematically looted of hundreds of thousands of dollars by a "khaki Cosa Nostra."

Higdon conceded that he had deposited over $300,000 in a secret Swiss bank account.

Ferguson questioned the four men closely in an attempt to determine if any organized crime group in this country was tied in with the operation. All denied any knowledge of any such connection.

The judge had delayed sentencing the men until they had a chance to testify before the Senate subcommittee. He noted that they had done so.

Please Turn to Page 24, Col. 1

EXTRA

Los Angeles Times

LARGEST CIRCULATION IN THE WEST, 1,036,911 DAILY, 1,226,132 SUNDAY

VOL. XCII SEVEN PARTS—PART ONE ★★★ WEDNESDAY, OCTOBER 10, 1973 122 PAGES DAILY 10c

AGNEW RESIGNS

Fined $10,000, Gets Probation

Stocks Dive

NEW YORK (AP)—The stock market plummeted in the last hour of trading today with the news that Vice President Agnew had resigned and pleaded no contest to a charge of income tax evasion. The Dow Jones average closed off 13.62 at 960.57.

Details in Part 3, Page 11

Iraq Joins Mideast Fighting as Jordan Calls Up Reserves

From Associated Press

Israel said its jets attacked Damascus airport and other targets deep in Syria and Egypt today as Iraq announced its forces had joined the fighting in a major widening of the war.

Jordan, a 1967 combatant that has stayed out of the current fighting, called up its reserves.

Communiques reported armored battles in the Golan Heights and the Sinai Peninsula as the new Arab-Israeli struggle moved into its fifth day.

Israeli reports said Syrian forces had been pushed back from the Golan Heights and that Israeli troops were advancing Syrian territory.

A communique broadcast by Cairo radio said the Egyptian forces "are improving their advance positions east of the Suez Canal under air cover while the enemy forces continue to retreat eastward."

Tel Aviv and Damascus reported savage air clashes over the Golan Heights battleground and during the Israeli raids on targets in the Syrian heartland. Each side claimed the other suffered heavy losses.

President Nixon met with congressional leaders in Washington and won their support for his efforts to halt the war.

The President said later that the United States was "trying its best" to mediate the "very dangerous" situation, but he gave no indication of headway.

Without giving details, Mr. Nixon said the United States was playing "a responsible role, very fair to both sides."

Senate Majority Leader Mike Mansfield of Montana said after the White House session that the question of U.S. arms for Israel is "always under advisement" but that it did not arise in his talk with Mr. Nixon.

Iraq's announcement that its air and land forces were fighting on both fronts made it the third major Arab country to enter the fight against the Israelis in the fourth broad Arab-Israeli conflict since 1948.

The Beirut newspaper An Nahar reported Iraq had committed 18,000 troops and 100 tanks along with an undisclosed amount of air power to back Syria on the Golan front and Egypt in the Sinai battle.

QUITS—Vice President Agnew resigned today and then pleaded no contest to income tax evasion. (AP) Wirephoto

ISRAELI POW'S—Cairo newspapers ran this photograph of what were said to be Israeli prisoners of war captured in the fighting and being held at a camp near the Egyptian capital city. (AP) Wirephoto

Pleads No Contest to Tax Count; Nixon to Pick Successor

WASHINGTON (AP)—Vice President Agnew resigned today, his historic decision announced by a weeping staff secretary.

Agnew then pleaded no contest in federal court in Baltimore to a single count of federal income tax evasion.

The Vice President, his face drawn and hands trembling, entered the plea before U.S. District Judge Walter E. Hoffman. Hoffman told the Vice President he considered the no-contest plea the equivalent of an admission of guilt.

Hoffman sentenced Agnew to the maximum $10,000 fine and placed him on probation without supervision for three years.

President Nixon acknowledged the resignation with "a sense of deep personal loss." Mr. Nixon pledged to consult with the nation's leaders and move promptly to nominate a successor.

Agnew left the courthouse at about 2:40 p.m., stepping into a limousine for an unknown destination. Agnew told newsmen the Justice Department has not been fully prosecuting witnesses in his case.

Witnesses against him had received either full or partial immunity, Agnew said.

Waving to bystanders, he drove off.

He had attended a hearing in which he and Atty. Gen. Elliot L. Richardson were seated in a courtroom for about 30 minutes.

Richardson personally asked Judge Hoffman to spare Agnew a prison sentence. The attorney general said the no-contest plea and the resignation were punishment enough.

Agnew had been under investigation in connection with alleged political graft dating back to his days as county executive in the mid-1960s, and later as governor of Maryland.

Agnew denied all allegations save that of income tax evasion. He also had been under investigation for bribery, extortion and conspiracy.

Richardson said the Justice Department had agreed to the single-count plea in an arrangement that included the Vice President's resignation.

Agnew's resignation means President Nixon will submit to Congress a nominee to succeed the Vice President. The Nixon nominee would take over the Vice Presidency upon approval by both houses of Congress.

In a statement to the court, Agnew said his decision to resign "rests on my firm belief that the public interest requires swift disposition" of his case.

Agnew entered his plea of no contest to a criminal information filed by U.S. Atty. George Beall.

Agnew said that had an agreement not been reached with the government, and had he been indicted, the case would have dragged on for two or three years and "intense media interest in the case would distract public attention from other matters of national importance."

Richardson announced in the Baltimore courtroom that the Justice Department had recommended Agnew not be imprisoned on grounds that his resignation and conviction on the tax charge served as sufficient punishment.

The criminal information said Agnew filed a false joint income tax return for 1967 showing income of $26,099 and that he owed taxes of $6,416 while in fact his income was $55,599 carrying taxes of $19,967.47.

Richardson told the court that the investigation of kickbacks in Maryland politics during the time Agnew was governor and Baltimore County executive produced evidence which "establishes a pattern of substantial cash payments to the defendant (Agnew) during the period when he served as governor of Maryland in return for engineering contracts with the state of Maryland."

Payments by a leading unidentified figure in one large engineering firm began in the early 1960s and continued into 1971, Richardson said.

Agnew also had been under investigation in connection with bribery and extortion accusations.

"I categorically deny assertions of illegal practices on my part by government witnesses," Agnew declared.

Mrs. Lisa Brown, Agnew's secretary, told the Associated Press of the resignation. She said she was speaking on behalf of J. Marsh Thomson, press secretary to Agnew.

She was in tears.

Secretaries at Agnew's office in the Executive Office Building said there would be no further comment immediately.

Mrs. Brown said only:

"The Agnew staff has just returned from a meeting in which we were informed that the Vice President has resigned as of 2 o'clock this afternoon."

President Nixon was in his Oval Office when word of Agnew's resignation swept through the capital.

There was no indication whether he was meeting with anyone.

Agnew sent Senate Democratic leader Mike Mansfield his letter of resignation: "Today I have resigned as Vice President of the United States. Thank you for the many kindnesses you have extended to me. I will always treasure my days of service with you and with the U.S. Senate."

A Vice President's only constitutional responsiblity is to preside over the Senate.

Mansfield told reporters, "I think he is making a tragic mistake. I think he should have stayed in the ring."

Press Secretary Ronald Ziegler said the resignation became official at 2:05 p.m. EDT when Agnew, following established legal procedures, presented a one-sentence letter of resignation to Secretary of State Henry A. Kissinger. The letter was delivered in Kissinger's White House office, and said:

"I hereby resign the office of Vice President of the United States, effectively immediately.

"Sincerely, Spiro T. Agnew."

Los Angeles Times

LARGEST CIRCULATION IN THE WEST, 1,036,911 DAILY, 1,226,132 SUNDAY

VOL. XCIII 2† FIVE PARTS—PART ONE CC TUESDAY MORNING, FEBRUARY 26, 1974 76 PAGES DAILY 10¢

SOVIET SWINDLERS

Ruble Rip-Off Artists Thrive on Comrades

BY MURRAY SEEGER
Times Staff Writer

MOSCOW — Mikhail Akimovich bade his wife and daughter farewell at the Leningrad railroad station recently and then lingered in the huge Komsomol Square, not anxious to return to his empty apartment.

"Let me share your loneliness," a blonde girl 20 years younger said to Mikhail. A few minutes later they were comfortably settled in his flat when the doorbell rang.

With that Mikhail Akimovich was introduced into the shadowy world of the Moscow underground that specializes in various kinds of swindles and thefts.

Americans these days would call such characters rip-off artists and police used to call them bunko operators or swindlers. In Russian they are called "plutee" or "moshenikee" (rogues) and they are one of the biggest problems of the Soviet police.

Despite what is probably the world's largest anticrime force, the Soviet Union cannot halt the operations of fast-ruble-and-kopek cheaters and perpetrators of all kinds of frauds, some of which can be traced to the pre-Communist era.

These criminals take advantage of the immensity and impersonality of the Soviet system as well as the naivete of their individual victims. Take Mikhail Akimovich as an example.

Before he could answer the bell on that romantic evening, his young companion, Valentina, jumped to the door and let in her associate, Georgy Lapochenock, a photographer and ex-convict.

They had spotted a good pigeon because after tying and gagging Mikhail they collected 5,000 rubles worth ($6,440) of cash and valuables.

In tracking down Lapochenok, police found that he had formed a ring that specialized in using taxicabs for robberies. One variation on this racket was a card game called "Olympic pip."

The driver and his partner would watch for a traveler going to an airport and offer to play the game to kill time on the road. In 30 or so minutes, the operators could pick up as much as 200 rubles ($258).

A taxicab was also the favorite working area for Alexander Nikolayevich, who introduced himself to Moscow newcomers as a manager at the GUM store, the shopping mecca for many visitors from out of town.

In the most friendly, casual way, "Sasha" offered to help the visitors to buy anything they wanted, even such rarities as a fur coat and a carpet.

He met his customers at a subway station the next day, took nearly 1,000 rubles ($1,300) and walked with them to the third floor of the GUM. Telling them to wait, Sasha disappeared behind a door and never came back.

When the police finally caught Sasha, there were 32 witnesses who had paid him the equivalent of $13,000, a fortune in Soviet terms.

Paying for something that is never delivered is one of the most common Russian frauds. The victims are often country people who come to the

Please Turn to Page 8, Col. 1

AFTER PLEADING GUILTY—Herbert W. Kalmbach, the President's personal lawyer, leaves federal court in Washington. AP Wirephoto

Kalmbach Pleads Guilty, Could Get 3 Years in Vote Fund Case

Attorney Admits Inducing Illegal Expenditures in Congress Races; Also Offered Ambassadorship in Return for Donation

BY RONALD J. OSTROW
Times Staff Writer

WASHINGTON — Herbert W. Kalmbach, a personal attorney for President Nixon, pleaded guilty Monday of having promised an ambassadorship in return for $100,000 in campaign contributions and to violating the Federal Corrupt Practices Act.

Kalmbach, 52, his normally tan complexion wan and his eyes deep-set as he stood before U.S. Dist. Judge John J. Sirica, was permitted to remain free pending completion of a presentencing report.

The Southern California lawyer, whose firm has offices in Newport Beach and Los Angeles, faces a maximum of three years' imprisonment and $11,000 in fines for the violations, which occurred in 1970.

In a letter to Kalmbach's attorney, Watergate special prosecutor Leon Jaworski said the negotiated plea would "dispose of pending or potential charges" relating to the Watergate coverup, campaign contributions from milk producers, "other contributions from persons seeking ambassadorial appointments" and any charges arising from grand jury testimony Kalmbach had given.

(When asked at his Monday evening press conference about Kalmbach's ambassadorship offer, Mr. Nixon said he had not been consulted about it.

("Ambassadorships have not been for sale to my knowledge," he said. "Ambassadorships cannot be purchased, and I would not approve an ambassadorship unless the man or woman was qualified—clearly apart from any contributions."

(Mr. Nixon said he had looked into who at the White House had been responsible for approving the ambassadorship offer relayed by Kalmbach. He did not disclose any results of his inquiry.)

Jaworski added that Kalmbach still was subject to prosecution for false testimony or "any serious offenses . . . of which this office is presently unaware."

The Corrupt Practices Act violation involved Kalmbach's role in a

Please Turn to Page 11, Col. 1

Britain Trade Deficit Largest in Its History

Heath Foes Instantly Use Report as Club in Election

BY TOM LAMBERT
Times Staff Writer

LONDON—Only three days before a general election is to decide the future government of Britain, Prime Minister Edward Heath's regime announced Monday the greatest foreign trade deficit in the nation's history. The announcement was immediately picked up by the opposition Labor Party and the minority Liberal Party—the latter has been gaining in the opinion polls—as a new bludgeon against the Conservatives.

The Trade and Industry Department and Central Statistical Office disclosed that Britain, under Heath's management, had plunged about $873 million into the red in its foreign trade account last month. Revenues from tourism, shipping and insurance should, however, lower that total somewhat.

Liberal Party leader Jeremy

Please Turn to Page 7, Col. 1

Nixon Foresees No Quick End to Gas Shortage

'Crisis' Over but 'Problem' Remains, President Says; Energy Bill Veto Vowed

BY ROBERT C. TOTH
Times Staff Writer

WASHINGTON — Declaring that the energy "crisis" is past but that the "problem" remains, President Nixon predicted Monday night that lines at gasoline stations "will become shorter in the spring and summer." He foresaw no drop in gasoline prices until supplies picked up.

He did not predict a quick end to the Arab oil embargo, which helped cause the shortage, but he indicated that if it was not lifted soon, American-led efforts to get a peace settlement in the Mideast would lag.

Mr. Nixon told his news conference that there was a "much better than even chance that there will be **no need for gas rationing.**" Such **rationing would add 17,000 to 20,000 "federal bureaucrats"** to the government payroll and cost $1.5 billion, he said.

And he threatened to veto the current energy bill now passing through Congress because of its price-rollback feature. Cutting gas prices, he said, would be popular but would lead to more shortages and longer gasoline lines.

In his 38-minute news conference, his first in four months, the President had the following to say on other matters:

—The economy: "We will bring inflation under control as the year goes on, but I would not underestimate the problem." Controls have been tried but have not worked, he said. The country is going through a "downturn," but "not a recession," he said, predicting an upturn in the last half of the year.

—The resignation of former Vice President Spiro T. Agnew: "I am not going to join anyone else in kicking him while he is down." The President said that Agnew had "rendered dedicated service in all the assignments" given to him. Mr. Nixon did not mention that the Justice Department had alleged that Agnew had continued to accept payments from Maryland contractors while he was Vice President.

—Deportation of Alexander Solzhenitsyn from the Soviet Union: The President said he was an admirer of the Russian writer but that breaking relations with the Russians would not help dissidents like the Nobel Prize winner. Before So-

Please Turn to Page 16, Col. 1

Nationwide Traffic Toll Declines 23%

WASHINGTON (AP)—Deaths on the nation's highways were reduced 23% in January, the first month of the national mandatory 55 m.p.h. speed limit, James P. Gregory, administrator of the National Highway Traffic Safety Administration, reported Monday.

He said there were 853 fewer deaths on the road last month than in January a year ago.

"Before the advent of the energy crisis we were predicting a significant increase in fatalities for 1973," Gregory told the Senate Commerce Committee.

Instead, he said, there was a reduction in November, followed by a larger drop in December.

In December, he said, all states had fewer fatalities than they had a year before. But the decrease was three times as great in those 18 states that had lowered their speed limits than for those that had not, Gregory said.

Please Turn to Page 18, Col. 2

FEATURE INDEX

Odd-Even Gas Plan in L.A. County OKd

Mandatory Program Announced by Reagan Includes Municipalities

BY RAY ZEMAN
Times County Bureau Chief

Gov. Reagan announced a mandatory "gasoline marketing" plan Monday which is expected to limit sales on the basis of odd-even license plate numbers beginning Friday throughout Los Angeles County, including incorporated cities.

At a news conference with the Los Angeles County Board of Supervisors, the governor said he will use his disaster powers to implement the plan in any county which declares that an emergency exists.

Chairman Kenneth Hahn said he will introduce a resolution today for supervisors to declare such a crisis in Los Angeles County. He said he is confident of unanimous support.

"I also believe supervisors of Orange, Riverside, San Diego, Ventura, San Bernardino and Imperial counties will do the same soon," Hahn predicted.

"Chairmen of their boards or representatives were all at a gasoline conference with state officials in the Serra Building today," he said. "They all said some plan like this must be adopted."

Reagan said the gasoline panic is comparable to a major fire, flood, earthquake or other disaster under which he can exercise emergency power if a county requests it.

The program then would be applicable not only to unincorporated areas of a county but to all cities within it.

"We will lift it at any time the supervisors say the emergency has ended," Reagan explained.

He also disclosed that California has been allocated an additional 21 million gallons of gasoline for the remainder of this week.

Reagan was notified of the emergency allocation by John W. Weber, assistant administrator of the Federal Energy Office.

The stopgap supply, described in a telegram as a "one-time, emergency allocation of inventories," doubles the amount of gasoline at Reagan's disposal for alleviating fuel shortages in hardship areas of the state.

There have been three such emergency allocations made to about 26 other states since Feb. 9, but this is the first special allocation to California.

The order stipulates that if any of the 21 million gallons remains at the end of this month, the state can carry the remainder forward into March, with no deduction from the March allocation.

The telegram also stated that gasoline suppliers must notify the Federal Energy Office in Washington by telegram of "their compliance with this directive within 48 hours."

The order is significant because in some of the earlier one-time allocations to states there was no such followup requested and some suppliers held onto the gasoline.

Twenty-one gasoline companies, including all of the major ones, were notified by telegram of the special allocation.

Full details of Reagan's new marketing plan are being drafted for release in Sacramento today.

The plan incorporates much of Supervisor James A. Hayes' proposed modification of Oregon's odd-even license plate program which the Los Angeles County Board of Supervisors unanimously endorsed Thursday.

Reagan's proposal called for:

—Sales on odd-numbered days to motorists whose license plates are

Please Turn to Page 3, Col. 2

Has Rejected Jaworski Request for Testimony, Nixon Discloses

BY ROBERT L. JACKSON
Times Staff Writer

WASHINGTON—President Nixon said Monday night that he had rejected a request by special prosecutor Leon Jaworski to testify under oath before a federal grand jury probing the Watergate scandal.

Mr. Nixon told a nationally televised news conference that he had made a counter offer to Jaworski—that instead of testifying he answer written question from Jaworski. The President said Jaworski turned down that idea.

With much of his press conference focused on the Watergate case and the impeachment inquiry by the House Judiciary Committee, Mr. Nixon expressed the view that a President can only be impeached for committing a criminal offense.

And, he added: "I do not expect to be impeached."

The President's opinion on impeachable offenses, which he said was supported by the Constitution, by White House counsel and by "a number of other constitutional lawyers," conflicts with a finding last week by the staff of the House Judiciary Committee.

The committee staff filed a report saying that impeachable offenses need not be criminal offenses, and that a President could be impeached for "undermining the integrity of office, disregard of constitutional duties and oath of office, arrogation of power, abuse of the governmental process (and) adverse impact on the system of government."

The Justice Department last week made public an analysis that concluded that a President is clearly impeachable for criminal offenses but less certainly so on broader charges of political misconduct.

As in his State of the Union message on Jan. 30, Mr. Nixon again was vague about his precise degree of cooperation with the Judiciary Committee.

Please Turn to Page 16, Col. 6

Douglas Refuses to Disqualify Himself in Gas Price Hearing

BY LINDA MATHEWS
Times Staff Writer

WASHINGTON—Supreme Court Justice William O. Douglas, ignoring accusations of personal bias against the petroleum industry, refused Monday to disqualify himself from a major gas regulation case.

Shell Oil Co. had asked Douglas to take himself out of the case because of a speech in which the justice charged the oil companies with creating the energy crisis for their own profit.

Shell petitioned the other members of the court also, asking that they take the unprecedented step of forcing Douglas to disqualify himself if he did not do so voluntarily.

Both requests were turned down by the high court Monday in a brief unsigned order that said: "The motion of Shell Oil Co. to recuse Mr. Justice William O. Douglas is denied."

At stake in the case are the prices that producers of natural gas in the southern Louisiana area charge to interstate pipelines. Although rates established by the Federal Power Commission and approved by the U.S. Court of Appeals in New Orleans had included some incentives for future exploration, several oil companies complained to the high court that they were too low.

Their appeals are to be argued later this spring, with opinions to be issued by June.

In its motion, Shell quoted news accounts of a speech Douglas had made Jan. 28 at the University of Mississippi law school. Douglas was quoted as saying "the oil industry keeps the supply of oil and gas low enough to boost prices" and blocks development of other energy sources.

Please Turn to Page 18, Col. 2

FALL OF NIXON CONFIDANT

Blows to Family, Reputation Hurt the Most

BY KENNETH REICH
Times Political Writer

Not too many months ago, Herbert W. Kalmbach traveled the nation and the world soliciting large contributions for the reelection of President Nixon.

By his own account, he raised more than $10 million for the President's 1972 campaign. In 1968, he raised $6 million.

In his role as Mr. Nixon's personal attorney, Kalmbach was entrusted with extremely sensitive missions for the President. He arranged the purchase and refurbishing of the President's San Clemente estate in 1969 and 1970. He helped draw up Mr. Nixon's will.

Reports—which for a long time Kalmbach, who habitually shunned publicity, did not publicly deny—circulated that the Newport Beach lawyer was one of the five men closest to the President.

Those days, before the Watergate scandal, were happy and fulfilling ones for Kalmbach. The law firm he had founded prospered. When he traveled abroad, he often stayed in American embassies. In California and national Republican circles, he was a figure of immense prestige.

But beginning with the Watergate break-in and the disclosures that ensued, Kalmbach's life changed.

He was linked with payments of thousands of dollars of alleged "hush" money to the original Watergate defendants in 1972; with the hiring of Donald H. Segretti, who was later convicted of campaign sabotage, with soliciting contributions from milk producers and with arranging allegedly excessive Secret Service expenditures on the San Clemente estate.

Kalmbach's tribulations reached new intensity Monday when he pleaded guilty to a felony charge relating to a Republican congressional campaign committee for which he helped raise $3.9 million in 1970 but which had no chairman or treasurer, and guilty to a misdemeanor charge of promising a European ambassadorship for $100,000 in campaign contributions that same year.

The guilty pleas could subject him to disbarment and a prison term of up to three years.

It was learned Monday that Kalmbach had resigned his senior partnership in the Los Angeles and Newport Beach law firm of Kalmbach, DeMarco, Knapp & Chilling-

Please Turn to Page 11, Col. 1

THE WEATHER

National Weather Service forecast: Fair today and Wednesday except for low clouds or fog tonight and early Wednesday. Highs both days near 70. High Monday, 82; low, 53.

Complete weather information and smog report in Part 2, Page 2.

Gas Lines---a New Life-Style

SATURDAY

FINAL

RACING

RESULTS-ENTRIES

Los Angeles Times

LARGEST CIRCULATION IN THE WEST, 1,036,911 DAILY, 1,226,132 SUNDAY

VOL. XCIII | FOUR PARTS—PART ONE | SATURDAY MORNING, MARCH 2, 1974 | 74 PAGES | DAILY 10c

CHARGES DISPUTE NIXON ON PAYOFFS

New Gold Fever Undercuts Value of Paper Money

BY RONALD L. SOBLE

Times Staff Writer

Is paper money passe?

You'd think so amid the current worldwide near-panic flight from paper currencies into gold.

The world's major international gold markets—London, Zurich and Paris—are swamped with speculative buy orders for the precious metal.

Gold bugs have driven up the private market price from approximately $90 an ounce three months ago to above $180, a record level.

Americans can't legally purchase gold bullion. But Americans have the gold fever too and are sharing in the bonanza through sharply increased investments in gold mining stocks, gold coins, and mutual funds that specialize in gold extraction companies.

Serious inflation on a worldwide scale is the main stimulant behind the unprecedented gold frenzy, most economists agree.

The gold speculator is betting that the world's major industrialized nations will be unable to control the inflation which continues to erode the value of paper money.

The oil crisis and political uncertainty in some countries, including the Watergate-impacted United States, also are credited with driving up gold demand.

This is nothing new, of course. Gold has a history of attracting investors during times of stress.

Two devaluations of the dollar have placed the official price of gold at $42.22 an ounce, the level agreed upon by the world's central bankers.

But this is a far cry from the private market situation.

Americans are putting their dollars into a host of gold-related investments on an unprecedented basis.

Gold mining stocks are enjoying spectacular prosperity and have suddenly become the darlings of Wall Street. One Wall Street analyst said that some investors wake up, ask their broker for the London gold price fixing and then run out and buy more gold mining issues.

Others are investing in the proliferating gold funds.

John C. van Eck started his New York-based International Investors Inc. fund in such a manner in 1968, concentrating primarily in South African issues. It is now one of the nation's leading gold funds with assets soaring from $68 million as recently as last December to its current level of $125 million.

Who's buying gold stocks?

Deson Sze, a vice president and gold expert with Harris, Upham & Co. Inc., says they're coming from all walks of life—rich and of moderate means, young and old.

"It's almost a sort of gold fever," says Sze. "People have lost their confidence in paper currency."

If there is any trend, says Sze, it is that the small investor who has stayed away from the stock market is putting his dollars into gold mining issues and gold coins.

Please Turn to Page 4, Col. 1

WORKERS' FATIGUE FORCES DELAY IN HEARST FOOD PLAN

BY PHILIP HAGER

Times Staff Writer

SAN FRANCISCO—Resumption of the Hearst free-food program will be delayed until Tuesday because of the physical exhaustion of its volunteer workers.

A. Ludlow Kramer, who heads People in Need for Randolph A. Hearst, said Friday volunteers were so fatigued by the previous day's effort to distribute more than 25,000 bags of groceries that they could not resupply outlets for today's scheduled reopening.

Kramer told a news conference the program, through which Hearst hopes to free his kidnaped daughter, will operate Tuesdays and Fridays instead of three days a week as planned.

Please Turn to Page 16, Col. 3

Israeli Pullback Plan Fails to Get Syrian Approval

BY WILLIAM J. COUGHLIN

Times Staff Writer

BEIRUT—The outcome of possible negotiations between Israel and Syria on troop disengagement on the Golan Heights remained in doubt early this morning after a meeting of more than four hours between Syrian President Hafez Assad and U.S. Secretary of State Henry A. Kissinger.

The official Syrian news agency said Assad had "not accepted" Israeli suggestions on disengagement, which Kissinger brought from Tel Aviv Friday, but American officials with Kissinger said negotiations would continue.

Kissinger, who arrived at the Damascus airport Friday night, took the Israeli proposal for disengagement directly to a meeting with President Assad. There were no detailed reports on their discussion but the Syrian news agency said efforts toward a peace settlement would continue.

Whether Kissinger would postpone his scheduled departure this morning for Saudi Arabia and Jordan was not known immediately. But it was expected that he would meet again with Assad.

Please Turn to Page 3, Col. 1

FEATURE INDEX

A TOTAL LOSS—Firemen battle blaze at the Vendome Liquor and Wine Shops, 327 N. Beverly Drive but the building was a complete loss. All of Beverly Hills' fire equipment and six units from Los Angeles fought the fire. One fireman was injured.

Times photo by Boris Yaro

Confusion, Long Lines Mark Beginning of Odd-Even Plan

BY NARDA Z. TROUT

Times Staff Writer

Long lines and much confusion generally dominated the first day of the emergency gasoline distribution plan in Los Angeles Friday as hundreds of motorists with odd-numbered plates—and some with even-numbered plates—had their day at the pumps.

The program, proposed by Gov. Reagan, went into effect one minute after midnight in some counties as the outlook for gasoline availability this weekend remained bleak.

The first day of the plan came as many retailers announced their deliveries of March allotment gasoline will not come until next week, and as gasoline prices jumped 1.5 to 6 cents a gallon.

The Automobile Club of Southern California said only one station in 100 is expected to be open Sunday in the Los Angeles metropolitan area.

Today — the first day for drivers with even-numbered plates to get gasoline—only 50% of the stations are expected to be open.

Chairman Kenneth Hahn of the Los Angeles County Board of Supervisors told a midafternoon news conference that "the key" to success for the program was supplies of gasoline adequate to meet the public's minimum needs. Without enough gasoline, Hahn said, "this plan will not be worth 5 cents."

The director of the state Office of Emergency Services, who ordered the plan into effect in counties requesting it, expressed a similar view at the same news conference, in the county gasoline control center in the Hall of Records.

Herbert R. Temple Jr. said he came here from Sacramento on the first day of the program because "Los Angeles had the recipe for implementing this plan" and this is "where the action is."

Please Turn to Page 17, Col. 1

Jury Challenges Haldeman's Story, Backed by President

BY JACK NELSON

Times Staff Writer

WASHINGTON — The Watergate conspiracy indictment Friday challenged President Nixon's account of his discussions about the raising of a million dollars in hush money for the original Watergate defendants.

Mr. Nixon and his former chief of staff, H. R. Haldeman, have contended that the President told John W. Dean III it would be "wrong" to raise the money for that purpose.

The indictment charged that Haldeman's testimony to that effect before the Senate Watergate committee had been false.

Mr. Nixon, who has refused to appear before either the grand jury or the committee, had made a statement similar to Haldeman's at a press conference and described Haldeman's testimony as accurate.

Although the indictment appeared to be carefully drawn to exclude any reference to Mr. Nixon by name, the document's allegations tended to corroborate parts of Dean's testimony linking the President to knowledge of the coverup.

The indictment included another count against Haldeman, accusing him of having falsely testified that Dean had not told Mr. Nixon that former White House aide Jeb Stuart Magruder had lied to the Watergate grand jury.

Dean testified before the Senate committee that he had informed the President of Magruder's perjury in a general discussion about measures being taken to cover up the Watergate break-in and burglary.

Fund raising, the Magruder perjury and other coverup activities were discussed with the President at meetings at the White House on March 13 and March 21, 1973, Dean told the Senate committee. The Watergate prosecutor has tape recordings of those meetings.

When Mr. Nixon, in a press conference on Aug. 22, 1973, vouched for

Please Turn to Page 21, Col. 1

Six Ex-Nixon Aides, Lawyer Indicted in Watergate Coverup

BY ROBERT L. JACKSON and RONALD J. OSTROW

Times Staff Writers

WASHINGTON—A federal grand jury indicted six former Nixon Administration officials and a Republican campaign lawyer in the Watergate coverup Friday and submitted a secret report containing findings on President Nixon's alleged role.

It was the most sweeping single indictment of former government officials in U.S. history and represented only the first in a series of such charges to be returned by Watergate-related grand juries here.

Those charged with conspiring to obstruct justice in the Watergate investigation were H. R. Haldeman and John D. Ehrlichman, formerly Mr. Nixon's two top assistants; former Atty. Gen. John N. Mitchell; former White House aides Charles W. Colson and Gordon C. Strachan; Robert C. Mardian, former Justice Department internal security chief, and Kenneth W. Parkinson, an attorney hired by the Nixon reelection campaign to handle Watergate matters.

Haldeman, Ehrlichman, Mitchell and Strachan also were charged with one count each of obstructing justice and lying to either FBI agents, grand jurors or the Senate Watergate committee about their knowledge of the coverup. Colson and Parkinson also were charged with one count each of obstructing justice.

In handing up the 24-count indictment to U.S. Dist. Judge John J. Sirica, the grand jury foreman, Vladimir N. Pregelj, also gave him a sealed brown envelope, bearing a red-and-white address label.

Though no comment was made in court about the envelope's contents, it was learned that it contained the grand jury's findings about Mr. Nixon's alleged role in the case, plus a recommendation on how to handle the material. Some expect Sirica eventually to forward the report to the House Judiciary Committee, which is considering impeachment of the President.

Sirica, with spectators in the packed courtroom straining forward in their seats, broke the envelope's seal with a letter opener and removed only what seemed to be a cover letter.

Please Turn to Page 18, Col. 1

IT'S EARLY TO RISE TO GET THE PRIZE

The Gas Line---a New Southland Life-Style

BY ROBERT KISTLER

Times Staff Writer

Every morning they come, in eerie predawn lines like supplicant honeybees to be nourished by their queen.

An hour, sometimes more, before the service station opens, the motorists are already there.

Some nap. Some read. Some do their nails. Some wander about, chatting with other "strangers in the night."

Some simply stare at their windshields and listen to the man on the radio tell of the new day's next impending crisis, disaster or holocaust.

They are part of the newest, and sometimes bizarre, wrinkle in the Southern California life-style: the gasoline line.

And, because the line leaves its mark on those who are forced to endure it, the once lowly, if not taken for granted, service station has now become one of society's prime focal points.

In addition to the church, the domino parlor, the neighborhood bar, or the beauty shop as social institutions, there are now Chevron, Shell

Please Turn to Page 10, Col. 1

THE WEATHER

National Weather Service forecast: Intermittent rain this morning, with scattered showers through Sunday. Highs both days in the 60s. High Friday, 70; low, 56. Chance of rain this morning, 80%.

Complete weather information and smog report in Part 3, Page 7.

India Explodes Nuclear Device

SATURDAY FINAL

RACING RESULTS-ENTRIES

Los Angeles Times

LARGEST CIRCULATION IN THE WEST, 1,036,911 DAILY, 1,226,132 SUNDAY

VOL. XCIII FOUR PARTS—PART ONE SATURDAY MORNING, MAY 18, 1974 78 PAGES

DAILY 10c

SLA HIDEOUT STORMED, 5 DIE

HOUSE ABLAZE—Los Angeles policeman with bullhorn runs across street toward spectators as fire rages in house on E. 54th St.

House Burned; Charred Bodies Due to Be Identified Today

BY AL MARTINEZ and ROBERT KISTLER
Times Staff Writers

Five hundred law officers stormed a suspected hideout of the terrorist Symbionese Liberation Army in South-Central Los Angeles Friday, and five occupants died in the battle. The house was destroyed in flames.

The furious gunfight began at 5:50 p.m. and lasted almost two hours. Thousands of rounds of ammunition sprayed the air and at least seven canisters of tear gas were fired.

All five bodies were burned beyond recognition near the rear of the house and police were unable to say whether they were members of the SLA.

Two of the dead were known to be women.

Los Angeles County Coroner Thomas Noguchi said that autopsies on all five of the dead were scheduled for 9 a.m. today.

Immediate identification was impossible, he said, because of the charred condition of the bodies. The FBI was rushing medical and dental records to Los Angeles to aid in the identification.

There were unconfirmed reports that two of the dead were Donald David DeFreeze — the SLA's "Cinque," founder of the "army"— and Camilla Hall, one of its members.

Flak-jacketed members of the Los Angeles Police Department, the FBI, the California Highway Patrol and the Sheriff's Department, acting on a tip, mounted the huge raid against the one-story stucco house at 1466 E. 54th St.

Their attack came a day after three suspected members of the SLA were involved in a shootout at an Inglewood sporting goods store. It was the first appearance of the "army" in Los Angeles.

Friday afternoon's battle was a scene from a war.

Automatic gunfire poured from the house and officers—ducking behind cars, trees and power poles—returned the fire with deadly precision.

Houses next door and across the street were riddled by bullets. A pall of tear gas choked police and newsmen alike. The battle was carried live on television.

No one was able to say exactly what caused the fire in the house, but officers believed that it was set by the tear gas canisters fired through the windows. A house and apartment building on either side of the besieged structure were gutted by flames.

For awhile, those inside the embattled home held a hostage whom they apparently released about 30 minutes before the gunfight ended.

She was identified as Christine Johnson, 35, and suffered puncture wounds in the back and a burned right forearm. She was taken to California Hospital.

Miss Johnson had run from the house, screaming, "They held me, they held me." Police quickly rushed her away during the height of the battle.

The woman said she lived in the house, but there was at least one conflicting report.

Mary Carr, 52, told officers her daughter, Minnie Lewis, 33, had allowed the five persons to spend the night there after they had offered to pay her $100.

Mrs. Carr said her daughter lived in the house, and that when the mother went to check on her Friday she saw a white woman with a pistol on her hip.

"I went back to see what was going on," Mrs. Carr said. "A white lady had a belt on with a pistol. She slapped at her side and smiled up at me."

Mrs. Carr left the house and notified police.

The army of officers moved in at 5:50 p.m. and shooting began almost immediately. Miss Johnson ran screaming from the house at 6:15.

Please Turn to Page 22, Col. 1

India Becomes 6th Nation to Explode Nuclear Device

From Reuters

NEW DELHI—India has exploded a nuclear device, the Indian Atomic Energy Commission announced today.

India thus became the sixth country to explode a nuclear device. The others are the United States, the Soviet Union, China, Britain and France.

The announcement said the underground experiment at a depth of 330 feet was part of its program of the study of peaceful nuclear explosions.

The government wanted to keep itself up-to-date with this technology, particularly its use in mining and earth-moving operations, the announcement said.

The commission said India had no intention of producing nuclear weapons and reiterated its strong opposition to the military use of nuclear explosions.

The site of the explosion was not stated.

RUN FOR COVER—Policeman wearing gas mask rushes two women neighbors to safety during battle.
Times photos by Jack Gaunt

POLICE SURROUND STUCCO HOUSE

Silence, Then Gas, Bullets

BY RICHARD WEST and JOHN MOSQUEDA
Times Staff Writers

Silence suddenly settled over the shabby neighborhood of Victorian-type houses, stucco bungalows and small apartment houses in South Central Los Angeles Friday evening.

Although half a block away, you felt you could hear the footsteps of the policeman who, wearing a flak jacket and carrying a tear-gas gun, glided along the 1400 block of E. 54th St.

He dropped to one knee almost directly in front of the yellow stucco bungalow at 1466 and fired a tear-gas round through the front window.

Then he scrambled to his feet and ran for his life.

As soon as he was out of the way, scores of policemen and FBI agents started pouring bullets into the house.

That was the start of a gun battle which left five suspected members of the Symbionese Liberation Army dead, the house they were holed up in burned to its foundations and the dwellings on both sides of it gutted.

Please Turn to Page A, Col. 5

THE WEATHER

National Weather Service forecast: Partly cloudy today and Sunday. Highs both days, 65 to 72. High Friday, 68; low, 58.

Complete weather information and smog report in Part 3, Page 14.

Los Angeles Times

LARGEST CIRCULATION IN THE WEST, 1,043,479 DAILY, 1,238,066 SUNDAY

VOL. XCIII 2† SEVEN PARTS—PART ONE CC WEDNESDAY MORNING, JULY 10, 1974 110 PAGES DAILY 10c

Panel's Tapes Quote Nixon: 'Save' Coverup, 'Stonewall It'

Show Numerous Differences With His Transcripts

BY JACK NELSON
Times Staff Writer

WASHINGTON—President Nixon urged "stonewalling" and "coverup" plans for the Watergate scandal, according to transcripts of presidential conversations released Tuesday by the House Judiciary Committee.

The documents showed numerous differences from Mr. Nixon's edited transcripts, involving presidential comments about perjury, stonewalling, coverup plans and the raising of money for Watergate defendants.

In the context of the presidential conversations, stonewalling apparently meant refusing to divulge information. The term was used in discussing plans for Watergate witnesses to take the Fifth Amendment or to say they could not recall certain facts.

The committee transcripts, based on White House tape recordings, quote Mr. Nixon as discussing the need to "save" a coverup plan and as saying to then White House counsel John W. Dean III and former Atty. Gen. John N. Mitchell:

". . . I don't give a shit what happens. I want you all to stonewall it, let them plead the Fifth Amendment, cover up or anything else, if it'll save it—save the plan. That's the whole point . . ."

Those quotes come from a committee transcript of a March 22, 1973, conversation, the day after Mr. Nixon says he first learned of the Watergate coverup from Dean. The comments are missing from transcripts Mr. Nixon edited before releasing them to the committee and the public last April 30.

The differences include omissions, additions and changes in wording and punctuation, with the committee transcript almost invariably putting Mr. Nixon's knowledge and comments about the Watergate

Partial text of transcript, Page 10.

coverup in a more damaging light.

The nature of the differences and the pervasive pattern of them in crucial segments of presidential conversations "leave only one inference that can be drawn — that the changes in the White House transcripts were done deliberately," a committee source said.

The differences probably will be cited in a proposed article of impeachment alleging that Mr. Nixon participated in the Watergate coverup, the source said.

Presidential Press Secretary Ronald Ziegler accused the Judiciary Committee of "dribbling out" its impeachment evidence in a "hypoed public relations campaign . . ."

Ziegler said also that "a negative twist" could be put on some of the phrases used by Mr. Nixon if looked at in isolation . . . You cannot take sections of these transcripts and draw conclusions from them.

"What the Judiciary Committee

Please Turn to Page 14, Col. 1

12 Indicted Here in Crackdown on Organized Crime

Action Will 'Put Mafia Out of Business' in L.A., Federal Attorney Says

BY BILL HAZLETT
Times Staff Writer

Indictments one government attorney said "puts the Mafia out of business" in Los Angeles were returned Tuesday by a federal grand jury against 12 suspects in a massive crackdown on organized crime.

A widespread pattern of extortion, loansharking and racketeering was revealed in the seven-count indictment, which was based on a yearlong investigation by the Justice Department's Organized Crime Strike Force and a special team of FBI agents.

Attorney Richard P. Crane Jr., who heads the strike force, said the probe uncovered a scheme to extort "protection" money from a Woodland Hills restaurant through threats of labor trouble and stink bombs.

He said efforts to shake down local bookmakers and gamblers and to force protection payoffs from at least two small publishing firms also were discovered.

In one instance, the indictment said, the suspects set up a phony bookmaking operation—which supposedly lost money—to bilk one of their would-be partners out of $62,500.

In several others they are accused of using threats in efforts to collect gambling debts, including $7,500 reportedly owed to a Chicago bookie called "Big Herbie."

One local bookmaker, investigators said, was "sweated" in a steambath until he agreed to come up with $300 a week in protection money from his gambling venture.

The investigation, which started in May, 1973, was handled by FBI agents and detectives from the Los Angeles Police Department's Organized Crime Intelligence Division, Crane said.

It involved keeping close surveillance on several of the suspects and

Please Turn to Page 19, Col. 1

KISSINGER FLIES HOME TO TESTIFY AT BREAK-IN TRIAL

BY RUDY ABRAMSON
Times Staff Writer

WASHINGTON—Having spent a week briefing European leaders on the state of affairs between the United States and the Soviet Union, Henry A. Kissinger flew home under subpoena Tuesday to testify at the trial of former White House aide John D. Ehrlichman.

He did not wish to do so. Indeed, his attorneys tried in vain to persuade U.S. Dist. Judge Gerhard A. Gesell to quash the subpoena. It was not in the public interest, they said, to take the secretary of state away from his mission of building ties with European allies so he could appear at a trial growing out of the Ellsberg break-in.

While that was the argument made by Kissinger's lawyers several days ago in seeking to quash the subpoena, they later worked out an arrangement with the court that permitted the secretary to complete his European mission as scheduled Tuesday and testify today.

Please Turn to Page 20, Col. 1

Two Admit Ellsberg Break-in, Say They Considered It Legal

BY RICHARD T. COOPER
Times Staff Writer

WASHINGTON — Convicted Watergate burglars Bernard L. Barker and Eugenio R. Martinez admitted Tuesday that they had broken into the office of Daniel Ellsberg's psychiatrist but said they thought government authorities ordered the "surreptitious entry."

"I was sure at that time that I was acting under legal orders and I still believe so today after some of the testimony I've heard," Barker said, testifying in his own defense at the Ellsberg break-in trial.

Barker, who described himself as the "team leader" on the break-in, said he thought he was working for "a legally constituted organization with its headquarters in the White House. And that represented to me, not being a lawyer, a proper authority."

Martinez, who said his assignment had been to photograph documents from the files of Beverly Hills psychiatrist Lewis J. Fielding, asserted that the Sept. 3, 1971, break-in might have been illegal "for a normal person" but was not for White House agents.

Barker and Martinez, whose predawn arrests with three others inside the Democratic National Committee's headquarters in June, 1972, touched off the Watergate scandal, have argued repeatedly that they considered themselves legitimate government agents. They were convicted of the Watergate burglary

Please Turn to Page 19, Col. 7

TRASH TOO?

Pipeline Paving Tourists' Way to Arctic Wilds

BY DARYL LEMBKE
Times Staff Writer

DIETRICH CAMP, Alaska—A red fox trots nonchalantly along the partially completed roadbed of the new highway, unaware that it is being observed from a helicopter hovering over this construction camp above the Arctic Circle.

The Dall sheep munching peacefully on the side of the 5,000-foot peaks surrounding Dietrich Valley and the moose sloshing along the lakeshores on the valley floor also are oblivious to their fate. Little do they realize that they soon will be stalked by shutter-snapping tourists.

Construction of the 800-mile oil pipeline from the top of Alaska to the ice-free port of Valdez is not only going to send huge quantities of oil south. The highway being built as a haul road for the pipeline will also carry vacationers north, possibly as early as 1977 or 1978.

That means that before the end of the decade, a new status symbol in travel for the adventurous and curious will be piling the family in the car and taking a spin to the Arctic Ocean at the North Slope.

Even now, the mighty Yukon River that slants across Alaska is being bridged for the first time. Work is also proceeding rapidly at this and 10 other camps on a two-lane highway that will open up one of the nation's last wilderness regions. The road extends 360 miles through virtually uninhabited territory from the Yukon north to the Arctic Ocean. From the Yukon south, a road already exists along the remainder of the pipeline route.

Completion of the highway north of the Yukon will make it possible for Joe, Jane and the kids in Los Angeles, Akron or Pensacola to motor to that until recently unknown and mysterious place, Prudhoe Bay on the North Slope.

That is a prospect that conservationists would rather not contemplate. To them, it conjures up visions of tourists in sports shirts tooling blithely through grizzly bear country, pulling trailers and tossing beer cans out of the window. They can envision hunters leaving the highway and carving out a destructive path across the fragile tundra in tracked, cleated "all-terrain" vehicles. They can even conceive of hot-dog stands springing up along the Fairbanks-to-Prudhoe Bay highway.

Others maintain that such fears are unwarranted and that the possibilities are breathtaking for opening up the heretofore inexcessible northern third of Alaska to both tourism and mineral development, through that man-made wonder, the road.

Practically no advance planning seems to have been done on accommodating tourists in large numbers, either along the highway as it winds its way north of the Yukon over the Brooks range, or after they arrive at the treeless North Slope. There are many unanswered questions and the time for making decisions is not unlimited.

Please Turn to Page 17, Col. 1

Earl Warren in 1971. (AP) Wirephoto

Earl Warren Dies at 83; Chief Justice for 16 Years

Ex-California Governor Led Supreme Court That Was in the Vanguard of Social Change

WASHINGTON (AP)—Earl Warren, the former California governor who served for 16 years as chief justice of the United States, presiding over a Supreme Court that was in the vanguard of social change, died Tuesday night. He was 83.

Mr. Warren, who retired from the court five years ago, died at Georgetown University Hospital. He had been hospitalized since July 2, suffering from congestive heart failure and coronary insufficiency.

During Mr. Warren's service as chief justice, the Supreme Court issued a stream of momentous decisions that wrought major changes in American society and politics. Among them was the unanimous ruling Mr. Warren himself wrote that banned racial segregation in public schools.

A hospital official said Mr. Warren died at 8:10 p.m. of cardiac arrest. His wife, Nina, and one of his daughters, Nina Elizabeth Bryan, were with him at the time.

A Supreme Court spokesman said that Justices William O. Douglas and William J. Brennan had visited Mr. Warren during the afternoon and stayed until 5:30 p.m. Mr. Warren had wanted them to stay on, but they felt they should not, given his condition, the spokesman said.

Mr. Warren retired in June, 1969, after 52 years of public service as a prosecuting attorney, three-time governor of California, twice aspirant for the Republican presidential nomination, once nominee for Vice President, and finally chief justice.

Mr. Warren ranked with John Marshall and Roger Taney as one of the three most important chief justices in the nation's history.

He headed the Supreme Court as it outlawed school segregation, imposed the "one man-one vote" doctrine on the states and altered police and trial procedures to safeguard the rights of defendants.

In Marshall's time, the court first asserted its authority to pass judgment on the laws of Congress. The Marshall Court played a major role in strengthening the federal government.

The Taney Court, in the middle of the 19th century, was in the crossfire between the federal government and the states and had to deal with the controversial slavery question.

The Warren Court dealt with the

Please Turn to Page 16, Col. 1

THE MIGHTY TREMBLED

Warren Cautious-- but Also a Fighter

BY CARL GREENBERG

Nearly a quarter-century ago, a reporter covering a boring political luncheon in Santa Cruz doodled on the PRESS sign at his table.

On the dais a *few* feet away sat Earl Warren. He stared straight ahead, grim-faced, as an interminable list of speakers droned through "brief remarks." Mr. Warren was to be *the* speaker that day—if the others ever got through.

The reporter, bolstered by a couple of martinis, transformed his doodle on the PRESS sign into "CLEANING and PRESSING, 75c-$1 Sats. and hols." He had a waiter deliver it to Mr. Warren.

The man who was to win three terms as governor of California stared at the sign placed before him. It seemed an eon. The reporter shuddered. What a fool he had been.

Twenty minutes later the waiter returned the sign to the press table. On the back was a penned request:

"Please call for two pairs of pants. Earl Warren."

Earl Warren played things close to the vest.

In his gubernatorial days, political correspondents sat in front of Mr. Warren at his desk—a San Quentin Prison-made product — and questioned him.

Please Turn to Page 18, Col. 1

Annapolis Ousts 7 in Cheating Probe

ANNAPOLIS, Md. (AP)—The superintendent of the U.S. Naval Academy said Tuesday that seven sophomores have been ousted and 13 other students and a navigation instructor have been disciplined in the school's biggest cheating incident in nearly 60 years.

The announcement by Vice Adm. William P. Mack capped a six-week investigation begun in May after the instructor reportedly provided advance answers to a navigation course final exam taken by about 900 of the approximately 4,000 academy students.

Mack, who refused to identify any of the persons involved, said answers to about 30% of the exam were given to one or two sophomores, who then distributed the data to some classmates.

An unidentified midshipman alerted authorities, who swept through the examination room collecting chart and table books, some of which had test answers written in them, according to Mack.

The superintendent said that 61 midshipmen were investigated by

Please Turn to Page 8, Col. 3

POLICEMEN EARN $15,100

S.F. Street Cleaners' Wages Will Go to $17,059 Annually

BY PHILIP HAGER
Times Staff Writer

SAN FRANCISCO—Clad in orange vests and pushing heavy bristle brooms, they endure the fog, wind and rain to sweep the paper, bottles, cans and other refuse from city streets.

The lonely task of San Francisco's 160 street cleaners might seem unattractive to some. But whatever its shortcomings, it's a job that in this city within a year will be paying $17,059 annually, officials said Tuesday.

The pay increase is scheduled to go into effect next June, putting the city street sweepers far ahead of police patrolmen ($15,100), librarians ($12,500) and registered nurses ($13,600), among others.

The San Francisco street sweepers' pay will substantially exceed salaries for comparable positions in other major U.S. cities. In New York, the job pays $12,886; Philadelphia, $9,143 and Boston, $8,695. Their salaries will approach, but not exceed, operators of heavy, motorized street sweepers, who now receive $17,160 annually here. San Francisco's street cleaners currently make $13,208 annually.

In Los Angeles, street cleaners and other city laborers will be receiving up to $10,700 annually next July and operators of motorized sweepers up to $15,700.

The disclosure of the pay raises scheduled for street cleaners brought new calls for reform of what critics call an unbalanced and inequitable pay system for city employes—a system one official calls "a hodgepodge of special interests."

Under the city charter, the salaries of certain city workers—including

Please Turn to Page 3, Col. 1

FEATURE INDEX

THE WEATHER

National Weather Service forecast: Some night and morning low cloudiness but mostly sunny today and Thursday. Highs today in mid 70s; Thursday in low 80s. High Tuesday, 75; low, 61.

Complete weather information and smog report in Part 2, Page 4.

BEATE KLARSFELD GETS 2 MONTHS

Nazi Foe's Jail Term Aids Her Drive on War Criminals

BY JOE ALEX MORRIS JR.
Times Staff Writer

COLOGNE, West Germany—Nazi hunter Beate Klarsfeld was sentenced to two months in jail Tuesday for trying unsuccessfully to spirit a former SS officer back to France to serve out a war-crimes life sentence. But she accomplished her purpose of getting the legal wheels rolling again here against old Nazi war criminals.

Mrs. Klarsfeld, the 35-year-old non-Jewish German wife of a French Jew, has been on trial here after returning voluntarily to Germany to face the charges of attempting to kidnap Kurt Lischka, the former SS security police commander in occupied Paris. Lischka had been sentenced to life imprisonment by a French court for his role in shipping perhaps 100,000 French Jews to Nazi concentration camps and eventual death.

As she sat down before Chief Judge Victor Henry de Somoskeoy to hear the summation of her celebrated case, a phalanx of French newsmen rose in respectful greeting.

"Les amis sont la," one of them told her. "The friends are here."

Outside the red brick courthouse, in the shadow of Cologne's famous Gothic cathedral, a handful of German anti-fascists and French survivors of Nazi oppression waited to get in. Some of the Frenchmen wore medals. Many carried signs saying it was a crime to be trying Beate Klarsfeld while countless old Nazis were running about free on West German streets.

Please Turn to Page 4, Col. 4

EXTRA

THURSDAY

LATE FINAL

Los Angeles Times

LARGEST CIRCULATION IN THE WEST, 1,045,479 DAILY, 1,236,06c SUNDAY

VOL. XCIII ★★★ EIGHT PARTS—PART ONE THURSDAY, AUGUST 8, 1974 144 PAGES Los Angeles Times Copyright © 1974 DAILY 10c

NIXON QUITS

Will Explain Decision on TV Tonight; Ford to Take Office Friday Morning

Stocks Dive 12.6 Points

Details in Part 3, Page 12.

Solemn-Faced Ford Waves Press Aside, Consults Kissinger

From Times Wire Services

WASHINGTON—Vice President Ford emerged solemn-faced from a meeting with President Nixon this morning and strode across the street to seclusion in his own office in the Executive Office Building.

He did not speak to reporters clustered on the lawn in a light rain.

Ford had been summoned to the White House after completing a Medal of Honor award ceremony in nearby Blair House. Reporters swarmed around him as he left there, but he only shook his head at their shouted questions.

After conferring with Mr. Nixon, Ford called Secretary of State Henry A. Kissinger and they talked for 10 minutes, according to a Kissinger aide. They arranged to meet later in Ford's office.

One friend of Ford was asked to compare the changeover after the assassination of John F. Kennedy to the administration of Lyndon B. Johnson with the current situation.

"It's no secret there was no love lost between the Johnson-Kennedy staffs," he said. "That's not the case here. There has been some friction, but generally they have been working closely together."

Ford has specifically decided to ask White House chief of staff Alexander Haig to stay on, he said.

Presidential Press Secretary Ronald Ziegler "will go fairly fast," the Ford associate said.

Ford would be the first U.S. President not chosen by popular election. He was selected by Mr. Nixon on Oct. 12, 1973, to replace Spiro T. Agnew, who resigned after pleading no contest to a charge of tax evasion.

Ford was sworn in as Vice President on Dec. 6 and has spent much of his time since then traveling around the country in an effort to unify and rally the scandal-shattered Republican Party.

Ford reportedly had told his staff Thursday to begin writing an inaugural speech and drawing up a list of potential vice presidential nominees.

That normally talkative staff was either hard to reach or unable to respond to questions. But the night before, press aide Paul Miltich denied that the staff had been told to prepare for the Presidency.

RICHARD M. NIXON President 1969-1974

President, Vice President Hold 70-Minute Meeting

From Times Wire Services

WASHINGTON — President Nixon told Vice President Ford today that he was resigning the Presidency, a White House aide said. The President will address the nation at 6 p.m. PDT today.

Congressional sources said the President's resignation—first in the 198-year history of the Republic—would be effective at 9 a.m. PDT Friday. Ford would become President immediately.

House Democratic Whip John McFall of California said he was told that Ford would take the oath of office Friday afternoon.

Mr. Nixon called Ford for a 70-minute meeting in the Oval Office late in the morning to tell the Vice President of his momentous decision and arrange for the orderly transfer of executive power, according to a White House aide who asked not to be identified.

Mr. Nixon will meet with bipartisan congressional leaders later in the day before this evening's broadcast, Press Secretary Ronald Ziegler said in an emotional appearance before newsmen at the White House.

Deputy Press Secretary Gerald L. Warren said Mr. Nixon would appear on television as President of the United States, apparently discounting the possibility of a resignation before 6 p.m.

Ziegler, his voice choked with emotion, made only a brief announcement on the day's plans, and did not confirm the resignation.

Ziegler said it was a difficult time, then announced:

"The President of the United States will meet with various members of the bipartisan leadership of Congress here at the White House early this evening.

"Tonight at 9 o'clock, the President of the United States will address the people of the United States by radio and television from the Oval office."

Then he turned from the rostrum, answering no questions.

As his meeting with Mr. Nixon ended this morning, Ford crossed the street to the Executive Office Building and conferred with his chief aid, Robert Hartman, and a spokesman said he showed no strong emotion. "He is a strong personality. He adjusts well to new situations," the aide said.

Ford was a veteran Michigan congressman and House Republican leader when Mr. Nixon elevated him to the Vice Presidency. This followed Spiro T. Agnew's resignation and conviction on a felony charge stemming from a kickback scheme in Maryland.

Under the Constitution, Ford will designate his own Vice President, subject to congressional confirmation.

As the Watergate scandal overwhelmed his Presidency, it was reported that Mr. Nixon's closest aides joined scores of Republican leaders in urging him to step down.

One source said White House staff chief Alexander M. Haig urged resignation. Another source said Secretary of State Henry A. Kissinger argued that America's foreign policy required an immediate end to the crisis of confidence gripping the government.

One official said Mr. Nixon's family—wife Pat and daughters Julie and Tricia—opposed resignation on grounds their husband and father was innocent of wrongdoing.

With the President in shirtsleeves, the family gathered for a private dinner in the White House Wednesday night. While sources said they were unable to precisely pinpoint the moment of decision, they said they believed it came after that dinner and the meeting with Kissinger.

Within moments after Ziegler's emotional appearance before the press, his assistants began distributing a flood of formal White House announcements as the machinery of the President ground out its last acts.

There were nominations of circuit and district judges, an appointment to the International Pacific Salmon Fisheries Commission, an annual report on trade agreements and the signing of two bills among the 14 announcements.

Ford canceled a schedule 12-day trip to the Western United States and Hawaii to support Republican candidates.

"I'm aware of the intense interest of the American people concerning developments over the last two days," Ziegler said, his voice quavering and speaking very slowly. "This of course has been a very difficult time."

Pressure for Mr. Nixon's resignation built up following his disclosure Monday of materials that showed he attempted to thwart an early phase of the FBI investigation of the Watergate break-in and was told of probable high-level involvement by aides in the scandal.

Mr. Nixon conceded this was damaging information that he should have disclosed earlier and said he realized the House would surely impeach him. By Tuesday, all 10 Republicans who had opposed articles of impeachment voted by the Judiciary Committee had all switched and announced they would vote for impeachment.

Crowds stood behind the large iron fence in front of the White House today trying to get a glimpse of history. Television newsmen standing outside the White House trying to broadcast were surrounded by people.

Los Angeles Times

LARGEST CIRCULATION IN THE WEST, 1,045,479 DAILY, 1,236,066 SUNDAY

VOL. XCIII † FOUR PARTS—PART ONE CC SATURDAY MORNING, AUGUST 10, 1974 74 PAGES DAILY 10c

PRESIDENT FORD SAYS 'NIGHTMARE OVER'

Europe Churches Coping With Tourists, Thieves

More Guards, Television, Electronic Gadgets Used to Protect Priceless Art

BY RUSSELL CHANDLER
Times Religion Writer

VATICAN CITY — A uniformed guard, standing in the central control room of the Vatican museums, scans a battery of TV screens, watching for unusual movement among the crowds of tourists.

In Kent, 56 miles from London, 70 lay guides augment a regular staff of 60 clerical chaplain-guides to control the tourists at Canterbury Cathedral.

These are but two examples of the security measures being used to stem the sharply rising numbers of thefts of religious art objects and to handle the tourists swarming into Europe's major cathedrals and historic religious centers.

"It's a trend," said Walter Persegati, a precise man with gray crew-cut hair who is secretary and treasurer of the Vatican museums. "A curator has to think not only about thieves but also vandals who want to destroy art forms in order to call attention to political ideas and world problems."

"Thefts here, like everywhere in the world, are up," added Dr. Deoclecio de Campos, director general of pontifical monuments, museums and galleries.

Italy has been especially hard hit by thieves and vandals who concentrate on religious art.

Last year, 8,520 works of art were stolen, almost a third more than in 1972. About 25% of the thefts were from churches and cathedrals.

In the past 15 years, 104,000 gravesites in and around Rome have been stripped of marble.

This June, Italy's bishops ordered a nationwide, parish-by-parish inventory of all church valuables. The lists, containing photographs and detailed descriptions, will be circulated among national and international police to aid in a crackdown on those who are stripping Italy of its art heritage.

Hundreds of small churches in Italy contain millions of dollars of art works. Though burglar alarms and electronic devices are slowly being installed, most churches are relatively unprotected.

Please Turn to Page 5, Col. 1

GM PLANS $480, 9.5% HIKE ON 1975 MODELS

General Motors Corp. Friday announced a $480 average price increase—about 9.5%—on its 1975 model vehicles. It was believed to be the largest single price hike in GM history. Part 3, Page 8.

CEREMONY—Gerald R. Ford takes oath as 38th President with wife Betty at his side in the East Room of the White House. Administering the oath is U.S. Chief Justice Warren E. Burger. UPI Wirephoto

U.S. LIFE BARELY PAUSES

Power Transfer: No Surging Mobs, No Frenzied Speeches

BY JOHN F. LAWRENCE
Times Washington Bureau Chief

WASHINGTON — "My fellow Americans, our long national nightmare is over. Our Constitution works; our great republic is a government of laws and not of men. Here, the people rule."

With those words, the 38th President of the United States answered those who have been telling America for months that its system of government was somehow being jeopardized, that the office of the Presidency faced permanent damage.

It was an answer, too, to those who had characterized the long months of Watergate as a political struggle, as two political parties in something approaching mortal combat.

It was clear that President Ford believed that the nation had suffered a tragedy, but it was equally clear that he saw it a tragedy not of a government or of an office but of a man.

Most of the week, unusual crowds had been gathering at the north gate of the White House, some with unfriendly signs, others part of a national organization that called itself bipartisan and claimed to be defending the Presidency.

Most of the people, however, were there just to look, to participate in their own way in the moment, the awesome shift in power taking place within the White House, their White House.

The quiet mood of that crowd said much about the transfer of power in this country. It spoke of contrast with the picture of surging mobs, shouted slogans and frenzied speeches from balconies that accompany so many sudden shifts of power in so many other lands.

Inside the White House, the ceremony was incredibly simple, as always, designed to remind the central figure in it that his power flows primarily from a document written years ago, not from the crowd of the moment.

As the 38th President turned to the official gathering in the East Room to speak, it became clear once again what differentiates the American Presidency from positions that bear the same title in other countries.

It was that Gerald R. Ford had no need to go to the balcony to rally the crowd, to call out the military to rebuild the power of a shattered government. Political opponents he had—some with ambition to stand where he stood. But enemies he had not.

Please Turn to Page 21, Col. 1

Nixon Bids Tearful Farewell to Cabinet and Personal Staff

BY RICHARD RESTON
Times Staff Writer

WASHINGTON — At 9:31 a.m. Friday the White House public address system made the usual announcement for formal presidential appearances: "The President of the United States and Mrs. Nixon."

At first there was a hush, but then applause, a prolonged standing ovation that went on for five minutes. The red-coated Marine band in the main White House lobby trumpeted the traditional tribute of "Hail to the Chief."

Mr. Nixon and his wife, Pat; their two daughters, Julie and Tricia, and their sons-in-law entered the gold and white East Room.

Mr. Nixon would remain the 37th President of the United States for only another 149 minutes. This was to be the final public act of his shattered Presidency, a Presidency that had died the night before in resignation precipitated by scandal.

He came to bid a final, emotional farewell to his Cabinet and personal White House staff.

"You are here to say goodby to us, and we don't have a good word for it," Mr. Nixon said. "The best is au revoir. We will see you again."

As the final minutes of his Presidency waned, Mr. Nixon fought for composure, choking back tears and fighting to keep his voice from breaking.

Please Turn to Page 19, Col. 1

Connally Pleads Innocent to Bribery

BY WILLIAM L. CLAIBORNE
The Washington Post

WASHINGTON—Former Secretary of the Treasury John B. Connally pleaded not guilty Friday to charges that he accepted a $10,000 bribe for recommending that the Nixon Administration increase milk price supports.

In a confident, booming voice that has become an emblem of his 27 years in politics, Connally startled a crowded courtroom by declaring, "If there is any doubt, I plead not guilty to all counts."

His statement came after one of the government prosecutors at the arraignment in U.S. District Court asked whether Connally had yet entered a plea, which he had done earlier in response to a pro forma question by Chief U.S. Dist. Judge George L. Hart Jr.

Connally, 57, was reportedly former President Richard M. Nixon's first choice to replace his resigned Vice President, Spiro T. Agnew, last October. But Mr. Nixon was persuaded by Republicans in Congress, who were suspicious of Connally's presidential ambitions and his recent conversion from the Democratic Party, to choose Gerald R. Ford, then the House GOP leader, instead.

Please Turn to Page 11, Col. 1

Pledges Openness, Honesty, Candor in His Administration

BY RUDY ABRAMSON
Times Staff Writer

WASHINGTON—Gerald R. Ford, 61, was sworn in as President of the United States at noon Friday and solemnly declared minutes later: "Our long national nightmare is over."

The former Michigan congressman, who became Vice President just last December, was installed officially as the nation's 38th Chief Executive two hours after Richard M. Nixon had flown away from the White House grounds by helicopter.

Legally, Mr. Ford had been President for 25 minutes before the presidential oath was administered by Chief Justice Warren E. Burger. Under the 25th Amendment to the Constitution, he was given the powers of the Presidency at 11:35 a.m., when Mr. Nixon's letter of resignation was handed to Secretary of State Henry A. Kissinger.

The letter, delivered by White House chief of staff Alexander M. Haig Jr., said only: "Dear Mr. Secretary, I hereby resign the Office of the President of the United States."

In a moving 10-minute address after his swearing in, the new President sought to begin immediately

Full page of pictures. Part 1, Page 20.

wiping away the tarnish of the Watergate scandals that had destroyed the Nixon Administration.

"I believe that truth is the glue that holds government together," he said, "not only our government, but civilization itself. That bond, though stained, is unbroken at home and abroad.

"In all my public and private acts as your President, I expect to follow my instincts of openness and candor with full confidence that honesty is always the best policy in the end.

"My fellow Americans, our long national nightmare is over."

Immediately after the ceremony in the East Room of the White House, where Mr. Nixon earlier in the day had said his tearful goodby, Mr. Ford plunged into an uninterrupted series of meetings to set his Administration in motion.

He conferred with congressional leaders, met with several groups of ambassadors from allied nations, talked briefly with the White House senior staff, called in his chief economic advisers and organized a transition team to lead the organization of the Ford White House.

He called a Cabinet meeting for this morning and announced plans to appear before a joint session of Congress Monday.

The new President sought not only to put Watergate behind but to assure U.S. allies that the country's foreign policy would go on uninterrupted.

"To the peoples and the governments of all friendly nations, and I hope that could encompass the whole world," he said, "I pledge an

Please Turn to Page 21, Col. 1

A SOMBER CROWD

'God Bless America' They Sing as Nixon Family Comes Home

BY BILL BOYARSKY
Times Political Writer

As a large, sad crowd softly sang "God Bless America," Air Force One taxied to a stop Friday and Richard M. Nixon, now a private citizen, came home to California.

He and his wife, Pat, stepped out of the presidential jet into the bright noon sun of El Toro Marine Corps Air Station in Orange County, apparently pleased by the cheers of a crowd estimated by reporters at 4,500.

Halfway across the nation, Mr. Nixon had ceased being President. It was the last time he would ride as the boss on the big plane he had dubbed "the Spirit of '76" in honor of the bicentennial celebration he had hoped would be a triumphant climax to eight years in the White House.

The Nixons walked down the red carpeted steps after waving a greeting, followed by their daughter Tricia and her husband, Edward Cox.

"We want Nixon, we want Nixon," the audience shouted, some waving American flags. He hesitated, then walked to a microphone and spoke.

It was, in a sense, a notice that he would not withdraw from the world.

"It is appropriate for me to say, very firmly, that having completed one task does not mean that we now just sit in the marvelous California sun," Mr. Nixon said.

And, at a later point, he said, "I am going to continue to work for peace among all nations. I am going to work for opportunity and understanding among our people in America."

There was no reference to Watergate. Instead, he spoke of the founding fathers in a way reminiscent of speeches he had made as President and candidate.

"We will celebrate the 200th anniversary of our country in 1976 and you want that to be a year of greatness—what this country was born for, what we came into this world for 200 years ago, for something far greater than to just make something for ourselves in a selfish way," Mr. Nixon said.

Please Turn to Page 18, Col. 1

THE RETURN—Richard M. Nixon, wife Pat and son-in-law Edward F. Cox wave to crowd at El Toro air station as they walk to helicopter for flight to San Clemente. Center, Tricia Nixon Cox. UPI Wirephoto

Rain Ends Midwest Drought; Crop Losses Run in Billions

From United Press International

The nation's breadbasket was drenched with rain Friday, breaking a drought that had caused crop losses running into the billions of dollars.

"The dry spell for this area is over," Fred Ostby of the National Weather Service said. "It looks like there are more opportunities for showers and thunderstorms through the Plains down into Texas . . . There's a lot of moisture available, and it looks good for additional rains."

Nearly an inch of rain fell in Tulsa, Okla. Over an inch fell in Ohio and Nebraska. Almost 2 inches fell in southeast South Dakota and the Texas Panhandle.

Government and state officials, farmers and ranchers assessed the situation, hoping that the moisture had come in time to salvage at least half the soybean and grain sorghum crops.

Most of the drought-stricken states, including Kansas, Missouri, Illinois, Oklahoma, North and South Dakota, Texas, Nebraska and Ohio, conceded that corn crops were about lost.

"The rain should help the pastures and it could give the beans a boost but as far as the corn in the drought area is concerned, it is already damaged," said Robert Watson, chief of the administrative division of the Agriculture Stabilization and Conservation Service for Iowa.

Please Turn to Page 6, Col. 1

THE WEATHER

National Weather Service forecast: Night and morning low clouds with sunny afternoons today and Sunday. Highs both days in the low 80s. Lows in mid 60s. High Friday, 80. Low, 67.

Complete weather information and smog report in Part 3, Page 7.

FEATURE INDEX

Los Angeles Times

LARGEST CIRCULATION IN THE WEST, 1,045,479 DAILY, 1,236,066 SUNDAY

VOL. XCIII 3† SIX PARTS—PART ONE CC MONDAY MORNING, SEPTEMBER 9, 1974 96 PAGES

DAILY 10¢

FORD GRANTS NIXON ABSOLUTE PARDON

Ex-President Concedes Mistakes but Admits No Legal Guilt

Pardon Won't End All Nixon Legal Problems

He Still Faces Possibility of State Charges, Loss of Right to Practice Law

BY LINDA MATHEWS
Times Staff Writer

WASHINGTON — The historic pardon granted to Richard M. Nixon was intended to be "full, free and absolute," to use President Ford's words, but it will not automatically solve all of the former President's legal problems.

Despite the pardon, Mr. Nixon can be prosecuted for any state crimes he may have committed in California or Florida, where some Watergate-related transactions occurred. He can still lose his right to practice law. He can still be sued civilly by private citizens who claim to have been damaged by his official actions.

And what may prove most significant, particularly to people who desire some final accounting of the former President's role in the Watergate scandal, Mr. Nixon almost certainly will have to testify at the upcoming trial of former aides and associates.

All the pardon accomplishes, by itself, is to absolve Mr. Nixon of responsibility for any "offenses against the United States" that he "has committed or may have committed" during his term in office.

The phrase "offenses against the United States," which President Ford invoked several times, springs from the clause of the Constitution that authorizes presidential pardons and reprieves.

According to law professors and criminal attorneys interviewed by The Times, the constitutional phrase acts also as a limit on the President's pardon authority. It makes clear, they said, that he can pardon only for federal crimes and cannot involve himself in prosecutions brought under state laws.

Although the legal authorities be-

Please Turn to Page 13, Col. 1

TIME TO REFLECT—President Ford appears to be deep in thought as aides receive comments on decision to pardon Richard M. Nixon. From left are William Timmons, John Marsh, Alexander Haig and Robert Hartmann (partially hidden). Photograph was taken minutes after Ford announcement. UPI Wirephoto

Press Secretary Cites Problem of Credibility, Quits in Protest

BY DON IRWIN
Times Staff Writer

WASHINGTON—President Ford Sunday granted former President Richard M. Nixon "a full, free, and absolute" pardon for "all offenses against the United States" that Mr. Nixon may have committed during his Presidency.

President Ford said that he was taking the unprecedented action after prayerful consideration because he believed Mr. Nixon had "suffered enough" and because he believed "many months and perhaps years" must pass before Mr. Nixon could receive a fair trial in the post-Watergate atmosphere.

"During this long period of delay and potential litigation, ugly passions would again be aroused and our people would again be polarized in their opinions, and the credibility of our free institutions of government would again be challenged at home and abroad," Mr. Ford said in the televised address.

The President signed the pardon as he ended his 10-minute speech, one month to the day after Mr. Nixon became the first American President to resign his office.

Mr. Ford said he was acting in response to the dictates of his conscience. For the same reason, J.F. terHorst, his press secretary and first White House appointment, announced his own resignation within hours after the President's speech.

"The President acted in good conscience and I also found it necessary to resign in good conscience," terHorst said in a statement.

"I knew my credibility as White House spokesman would be difficult to sustain . . . in the absence of a

Presidential statement on Page 12; Nixon's response, political reaction, Page 13; text of proclamation, Page 15. Related stories on Page 3.

like decision to grant mercy to persons of lesser station in life," he said.

President Ford's decision, which aides said he had reached after a week of intense consideration that included negotiations with Mr. Nixon through intermediaries, was promptly accepted by the former President in a statement issued from San Clemente.

In retrospect, Mr. Nixon said, "I can see clearly now that I was wrong in not acting more decisively and more forthrightly in dealing with Watergate, particularly when it reached the stage of judicial proceedings and grew from a political scandal into a national tragedy."

Although he conceded that his "mistakes and misjudgments" have contributed to the belief that his "motivations and actions . . . were intentionally self-serving and illegal," Mr. Nixon at no point in his 250-word statement admitted criminal guilt.

Mr. Ford's decision to absolve his predecessor roused mixed reactions

Please Turn to Page 12, Col. 1

Nixon Declares He Will Bear Burden the Rest of His Life

BY KENNETH REICH
Times Political Writer

Former President Richard M. Nixon, responding Sunday to President Ford's absolute pardon for any and all federal offenses committed while he was President, conceded he had made "mistakes and misjudgments" in the Watergate scandal but admitted no legal guilt.

"That the way I tried to deal with Watergate was the wrong way is a burden I shall bear for every day of the life that is left to me," Mr. Nixon concluded in a statement read to reporters by Ronald Ziegler, the former White House press secretary, in San Clemente.

An hour before Mr. Ford announced the pardon, about 7 a.m. PDT, the former President left his San Clemente estate by automobile for the Palm Springs area. Some sources told The Times he would stay several days at the private estate of his friend and political contributor, Walter H. Annenberg, the U.S. ambassador to Great Britain, but one source said he would return by today.

The 200-acre-plus estate, shielded from outside scrutiny by a 6-foot-high barbed wire fence, high oleanders and gates guarded 24 hours a day, provides Mr. Nixon with privacy. He had taken advantage of it several times during his Presidency.

The former President reportedly was accompanied by his wife, Pat, and his military aide, Lt. Col. Jack Brennan.

About 10 minutes after President Ford made his announcement, Ziegler read this statement by Mr. Nixon:

"I have been informed that President Ford has granted me a full and absolute pardon for any charges which may be brought against me for actions taken during the time I was the President of the United States. In accepting this pardon, I hope that his compassionate act will contribute to lifting the burden of Watergate from our country.

"Here in California, my perspective on Watergate is quite different than it was while I was embattled in the midst of the controversy while I was still subject to the unrelenting

Please Turn to Page 11, Col. 1

Knievel Jump Has Abysmal Ending—But He Survives

BY CHARLES MAHER
Times Staff Writer

SNAKE RIVER CANYON, Ida.—And there was Evel Knievel, twisting slowly, slowly in the wind, his rocket ship descending by parachute into the canyon he was supposed to leap.

And so the great Snake River Canyon leap hit rock bottom, but the star lives on.

Knievel was bleeding from cuts on his nose and face when interviewed briefly about an hour after the jump, and he said his knees "were a little busted up." But he appeared otherwise sound.

The Sunday afternoon was warm, cloudless and windy and the liftoff spectacular, but it was apparent before the steam-powered Sky-Cycle X-2 reached the top of its steep, 108-foot takeoff ramp that something was wrong.

Please Turn to Page 16, Col. 1

Agreement Lets Nixon Retain Almost Total Control of Tapes

He'll Have Access to All Documents and Right to Destroy Them Eventually but They Will Be Available for Court Use

BY RICHARD T. COOPER
Times Staff Writer

WASHINGTON — Former President Richard M. Nixon and the Ford Administration have agreed that Mr. Nixon's White House tapes will be preserved temporarily under an elaborate double lock-and-key system for possible use in court, it was announced Sunday.

Under the agreement, however, Mr. Nixon may order destruction of any of the tapes after five years and all of the tapes will be destroyed automatically in 10 years or on the former President's death, whichever comes first.

The agreement, negotiated at President Ford's request and announced along with the pardon, gives the government physical possession of the tapes and Mr. Nixon's White House papers, but the former President retains almost complete control over access to the material.

The tapes and documents will be stored in a special facility near Mr. Nixon's San Clemente estate. Access will require use of two keys, apparently for two separate locks. "One key, essential for access, shall be given to me alone," Mr. Nixon insisted; the other key will go to the government.

The provision for destruction of the controversial tapes was made "to guard against the possibility of the tapes being used to injure, embarrass, or harass any person and properly to safeguard the interests of the United States," Mr. Nixon said in

Please Turn to Page 14, Col. 1

ISRAEL-JORDAN ACCORD ON PULLBACK REPORTED

Israel and Jordan have agreed to a disengagement of forces on the Jordan River and a turnover of part of the West Bank to Jordanian administration. Part 1, Page 7.

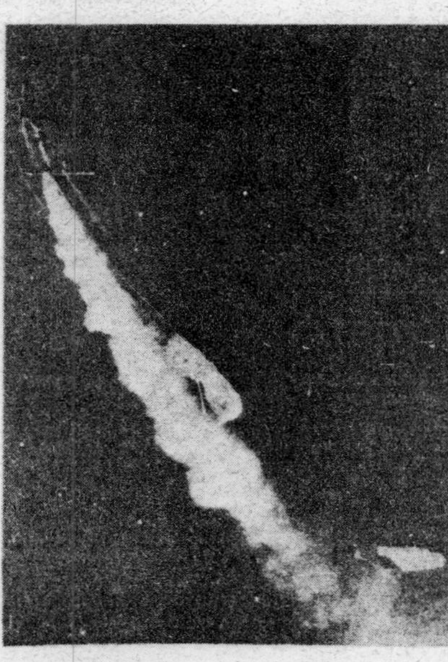

LEAP THAT WASN'T—Evel Knievel's Sky-Cycle ascending, left, and bouncing off ledge, right, on way to bottom of canyon. In left photo, drogue parachute that deployed too soon is seen in the lower right-hand corner, with main chute already following. Designer took blame for the failure. UPI Wirephotos

Nixon Health Called Factor in Decision

BY HOWARD SEELYE
Times Staff Writer

President Ford's reference to the health of Richard M. Nixon in his pardon statement Sunday again raised questions about the former President's physical and emotional conditions.

Despite outward signs that his health and mental conditions are good, knowledgeable sources in Washington confirmed Sunday that fear for Mr. Nixon's health had played an important role in Mr. Ford's decision to pardon the former President.

One source, who asked not to be identified, said that "many old friends (of Mr. Nixon) did contact

Please Turn to Page 13, Col. 3

FEATURE INDEX

'SHORT CIRCUIT' CHARGED

Action Raises Questions on Prosecution of Former Aides

BY RONALD J. OSTROW and ROBERT L. JACKSON
Times Staff Writers

WASHINGTON—The foreman of the Watergate coverup grand jury said Sunday that President Ford's pardon of Richard M. Nixon had "short-circuited" his panel's investigation and contended it would satisfy only Mr. Nixon.

Meanwhile Mr. Ford's action raised questions as to whether former aides to Mr. Nixon could be prosecuted fairly for alleged offenses for which the former President was pardoned.

The grand jury foreman, Vladimir N. Presgelj, told of his disappointment over the pardon shortly after it was learned that special prosecutor Leon Jaworski had not given jurors any new evidence against Mr. Nixon.

At the time of the pardon, Jaworski was still far from making a decision on whether to prosecute the former Chief Executive, knowledgeable sources said, although the grand jury previously had named Mr. Nixon an unindicted coconspirator in the coverup case.

Pregelj, 46, a government trade analyst, said no new grand jury action against Mr. Nixon had been imminent.

"The question was primarily in the hands of Mr. Jaworski," he said. "It was his decision first whether to car-

Please Turn to Page 9, Col. 1

THE WEATHER

National Weather Service forecast: Night and early morning low clouds, otherwise sunny today and Tuesday. Highs both days in the 80s. High Sunday, 83; low, 67.

Complete weather information in Part 1, Page 15.

Los Angeles Times

LARGEST CIRCULATION IN THE WEST, 1,045,479 DAILY, 1,236,066 SUNDAY

VOL. XCIII 2† SEVEN PARTS—PART ONE CC WEDNESDAY MORNING, NOVEMBER 6, 1974 122 PAGES DAILY 10c

BROWN VICTOR; RAPID TRANSIT LOSING

Democratic Sweep Gains 40 House Seats, 4 in Senate

9 Governorships Also Taken Away From the Republicans

BY PAUL HOUSTON
Times Staff Writer

WASHINGTON—Democrats headed for a landslide gain of more than 40 House seats Tuesday, made substantial gains in the Senate and took away at least nine Republican governorships.

Republican losses in the House threatened to match the 47 lost by the GOP in 1958, another nonpresidential election year in the midst of an economic slump.

As one indication of this surge, Democrats were elected to the House for the first time this century in certain districts in Illinois, New York, Massachusetts and New Jersey.

Close ties to former President Richard M. Nixon turned out to be political handicaps. Four Republican members of the House Judiciary Committee who had voted against his impeachment were defeated, as was Rep. Earl Landgrebe (R-Ind.), who had protested Mr. Nixon's innocence even after his resignation.

Meanwhile, Democrats wrested away four Republican Senate seats, with three races undecided.

Democrats won nine governorships held by Republicans and gave up three, with one race undecided. A Republican won the South Carolina governorship for the first time since Reconstruction. In Maine, neither the Democratic nor Republican candidate won, both falling to the "Longley for Maine" party of Independent James B. Longley.

The Democrats' 248-187 majority in the House swelled dramatically. Whether it would approach the gains necessary for a "veto-proof" House as sought by labor unions—and warned against by President Ford as he campaigned for beleaguered Republicans in 20 states—remained to be determined by final returns.

The GOP suffered its most telling losses in the Midwest, where their 66-53 majority evaporated, particularly because of the loss of five seats in Indiana and at least three in Illinois, two in Iowa and two in Wisconsin.

The GOP suffered big losses in New Jersey and New York also.

In late evening returns, the Republicans had picked up only two seats, one vacated by a retiring Democrat in Florida, the other held by Democratic incumbent Frank E. Denholm of South Dakota.

Please Turn to Page 18, Col. 3

HOUSE AND SENATE, GOVERNOR TALLIES

Late returns from Times wire services showed:

SENATE	DEMS.	REPS.
Elected	22	7
Leading	3	2
Holdovers	38	28
Total	63	37
Current	58	42

Needed for control: 51

HOUSE	DEMS.	REPS.
Elected	262	115
Leading	30	28
Total	292	143
Current	248	187
Unreported:		

Needed for control: 218

GOVERNORS	DEMS.	REPS.	OTHER
Elected	26	4	0
Leading	4	0	1
Holdovers	9	6	0
Totals	39	10	1
Current	32	18	0

THE NEXT GOVERNOR—Edmund G. Brown Jr., winner of the gubernatorial race, talks with newsmen at his headquarters in the Convention Center shortly before making his victory speech.
Times photo by Rick Meyer

Cranston Wins Easily; Dymally Apparent Choice Over Harmer

BY RICHARD BERGHOLZ
Times Political Writer

Democrat Edmund G. Brown Jr. trailed at the beginning, come on strong and finally won a hard-fought battle for governor in Tuesday's statewide election.

The 36-year-old secretary of state, whose father is the former Democratic governor who lost to Republican Gov. Reagan eight years ago, had to go almost two hours into the vote-counting before he edged ahead of his 45-year-old Republican opponent, State Controller Houston I. Flournoy.

But the Brown surge was inexorable and returns from Los Angeles County, where the Democrat was pulling more than 57% of the vote, finally made the victory inevitable.

Returns from 5,111 of the state's 24,265 precincts showed:

Brown (D)	884,871	53%
Flournoy (R)	778,732	47%

While Brown was struggling hard for his triumph, U.S. Sen. Alan Cranston, the Democratic incumbent, had a cakewalk in his battle with Republican State Sen. H. L. (Bill) Richardson of Arcadia.

Returns from 5,114 of the state's 24,265 precincts showed:

Cranston (D)	829,659	65%
Richardson (R)	443,656	35%

Brown told The Times shortly before 11 p.m. that "it looks good," and he acted like a winner but stopped short of declaring victory.

He mingled with a crowd of his supporters at the Convention Center and said he wanted "to savor this victory, to let it permeate."

"I've been working at this for some time. I want to enjoy it."

There was nothing but silence from the Flournoy camp at the Century Plaza.

The battle was a lot closer than Brown and some of his backers had expected. A Democratic sweep of the ballot had been their goal, and they expected a smashing Brown triumph at the top of the ticket to carry a lot of other Democrats to victory.

The CBS computer analysis called the Brown victory only 33 minutes after the polls closed, and ABC was not far behind. But NBC, claiming incomplete information from its bellwether precinct, held off for more returns before picking a winner.

While Cranston was having an easy time and Brown was having a relatively hard time, it quickly became clear that a Democratic sweep was going to be difficult to achieve.

Here were the standings in the other statewide races:

Lieutenant governor—Democratic state Sen. Mervyn Dymally of Los Angeles apparently defeated Republican John L. Harmer of Glendale, a

Please Turn to Page 3, Col. 3

L.A. County and statewide returns are in Part 1, Page 20; other election stories in Part 1, Pages 3, 21, 22, 23.

MAN ON THE MOVE

Brown: Where Is He Going, How Far, How Fast?

BY TOM GOFF
Times Sacramento Bureau Chief

California's governor-elect, Democrat Edmund G. Brown Jr., is a young man on the move.

One of the problems facing Californians now that they have elected him governor, however, is that there is no certainty as to just where, how far or how fast he's going to move or whether he'll either be willing or able to take the state along with him.

Brown, 36, has pledged publicly to serve the state as governor for the full four-year term to which he was elected.

He probably intends to do just that.

But the nature of the man, his ambition, the speed with which he has moved so far so fast, leaves the nagging feeling that political promises such as that are made to be broken.

Given the opportunity two years hence, the question remains, will the "new spirit" Brown has promised to take to Sacramento be ready once again to move on?

Whatever the future may hold, Brown will move into the governor's office in January. Things from that point on will be different than they have been for the past eight years.

But probably not as totally different as many of those who supported him might think.

Brown is liberal in some areas. He opposes the death penalty. He would liberalize laws on marijuana. He would give legal sanction to the right of public employes to strike.

In other areas he appears to be as conservative as the man he will succeed, Republican Gov. Reagan.

He believes punishment should fit the crime, short of execution, of course—and that hard, swift justice will go far to end crime in the streets.

He frowns on psychology, generally, as a hoked up substitute for religion.

He believes welfare is a poor substitute for work.

He has vowed repeatedly to be frugal to the point of parsimony in the spending of state dolliars.

He has accused Reagan of being

Please Turn to Page 24, Col. 1

GOP Founders in Riptides of Watergate, Pardon, Economy

BY ROBERT SHOGAN
Times Political Writer

WASHINGTON — The nation's voters Tuesday savagely punished the Republican Party for the sins of Watergate, the Nixon pardon and the hardships of the economy, and left the Democrats with a large share of the burden for shaping the future.

By the time the last ballots were being counted early today the Republicans still controlled the White House—but not much else of political significance.

The turnout was typically low for an off-year election but apparently not as low as some pollsters had predicted.

With half the nation's precincts reporting, NBC calculated that about 43% of the eligible voters had gone to the polls, about half a percent below the 1970 rate.

But the Democratic tide was relentless. It swept across every region of the country, every level of government — House, Senate and governor's mansion—and every age group.

In the states of the Old Confederacy, on which had been lavished the attention of former President Richard M. Nixon's Southern Strategy, hopes for an emerging Republican majority suffered a bitter setback. The Republicans lost Senate seats in Kentucky and Florida along with the governorship of Tennessee.

In the House and Senate the Democrats added to their already considerable majorities.

Few seriously contended that this would constitute a "veto-proof" Congress, a threat President Ford had unsuccessfully relied on during the

Please Turn to Page 16, Col. 1

Transit Tax Trailing in Early Tally; Vote to Block Dam Close

BY JERRY GILLAM
Times Staff Writer

A proposed 1-cent sales tax increase to help finance a multibillion dollar Southern California rapid transit system appeared to be losing by a narrow margin, early Los Angeles County election returns showed Tuesday.

At the same time, incomplete returns reflected a very close statewide race for Proposition 17, the wild and scenic rivers initiative, designed to block a controversial Northern California federal dam project.

Three Los Angeles County Charter amendments involving Civil Service and salaries were in trouble but a fourth was being approved. So was a Los Angeles city proposal relating to Civil Service status for certain exempt employes working in the mayor's office.

Proponents of Proposition A argued it represented a "last chance" to give the Southland a combination of superior bus lines and a high-speed commuter train network to relieve traffic congestion and reduce air pollution.

Opponents claimed the plan was too vague, too expensive and too uncertain because it relied on huge federal monetary subsidies that might or might not be forthcoming in the future.

The sales tax would go up from 6 to 7 cents starting Jan. 1. This would raise about $205 million a year initially for public transportation improvements.

Please Turn to Page 20, Col. 7

EDELMAN HOLDING SLENDER LEAD IN SUPERVISOR RACE

BY DOUG SHUIT
Times Staff Writer

Voters went to the polls Tuesday to fill central Los Angeles County's 3rd District seat on the county Board of Supervisors, breaking a lock on the seat held for the last 16 years by Supervisor Ernest E. Debs.

Los Angeles City Councilman Ed Edelman, who based his campaign on the need for sweeping reforms in county government, took an early lead in the balloting, with only a small percentage of the votes counted.

His opponent, fellow Los Angeles City Councilman John Ferraro, trailed him by a margin of about 1,000 votes.

Edelman, 43, and Ferraro, 50, were thrown into their bitterly contested

Please Turn to Page 27, Col. 1

L.A. Sniper Wounds Man, Fires at Police

Los Angeles police sealed off an area around 18th St. and Manhattan Place Tuesday night, seeking a sniper who wounded one young man in a supermarket parking lot and later fired several more shots at a police car.

The wounded man, who was not immediately identified, was taken to West Adams Hospital where he was in critical condition with a bullet wound in the head.

Police said the first volley of shots was fired at about 8:45 p.m. from an office building on 18th St., and was apparently aimed at a group of young men standing in the parking lot. Only one was hit.

Several police cars arrived in the area in response to the shooting report and several more shots were fired. No one was hit. Officers surrounded the area, near Western Ave. on 18th St., and began to search the neighboring buildings.

Kissinger Pledges U.S. Help on Food, Asks Aid of Oil Nations

BY WILLIAM TUOHY
Times Staff Writer

ROME—Secretary of State Henry A. Kissinger, in the keynote address before the World Food Conference Tuesday, promised that the United States would make a "major effort" to forestall a world food crisis.

Kissinger proposed the establishment of an international system of nationally held grain reserves "at the earliest possible time" to supply food to needy nations and keep prices stable.

He also said that the oil-exporting nations have a "special responsibility" in financing food imports to developing nations because "many of them have income far in excess of that needed to balance their international payments or finance their economic development."

Kissinger spoke at the opening session of the conference attended by about 1,000 delegates from more than 100 nations under the auspices of the Food and Agriculture Organization of the United Nations.

To underscore the seriousness of the conference, first proposed by the United States, Kissinger took time off from his diplomatic rounds with Italian political leaders and Pope Paul VI, to present his views.

Then he flew to Cairo for another session of Middle East peace negotiations.

Earlier he had driven through heavy rain to the Vatican for a meeting with Pope Paul to discuss the Middle East, with particular emphasis on the future of Jerusalem and its holy places.

Please Turn to Page 11, Col. 1

FEATURE INDEX

THE WEATHER

National Weather Service forecast: Fair today and Thursday. Highs today in mid 70s; Thursday, upper 70s. High Tuesday, 71; low, 50.

Complete weather information and smog report in Part 3, Page 22.

MAJOR RACES AT A GLANCE

OHIO—Former astronaut John H. Glenn Jr. (D) won a Senate seat, and incumbent Gov. John J. Gilligan (D) and former Gov. James A. Rhodes were in a nip and tuck battle for governor.

NEW YORK—Sen. Jacob K. Javits (R) won reelection to a fourth term, defeating former U.S. Atty. Gen. Ramsey Clark (D). Rep. Hugh L. Carey (D) defeated incumbent Gov. Malcolm Wilson (R).

COLORADO—Gary Hart (D) defeated incumbent Sen. Peter H. Dominick (R).

ARKANSAS—Rep. Wilbur D. Mills (D) won reelection.

INDIANA—Sen. Birch Bayh (D) stood off a strong challenge by Indianapolis Mayor Richard G. Lugar to win reelection.

SOUTH DAKOTA—Democrat Sen. George S. McGovern defeated Leo K. Thorsness (R), a former prisoner of war.

CONNECTICUT—Rep. Ella Grasso (D) became the first woman in the nation to be elected governor in her own right.

MASSACHUSETTS—Michael S. Dukakis (D) defeated incumbent Gov. Francis W. Sargent (R).

KANSAS—Sen. Robert Dole (R) narrowly won reelection over William A. Roy (D).

SOUTH CAROLINA—State Sen. James B. Edwards defeated veteran Democratic Rep. William J. Bryan Dorn to become South Carolina's first Republican governor in 100 years.

FLORIDA—Richard Stone (D) won over Jack Eckerd (R) for the U.S. Senate seat vacated by Republican Edward J. Gurney.

MICHIGAN—Gov. William G. Milliken (R) won reelection.

ALABAMA—Incumbent Gov. George C. Wallace (D) won an unprecedented third term.

Los Angeles Times

LARGEST CIRCULATION IN THE WEST, 1,045,479 DAILY, 1,236,066 SUNDAY

THURSDAY LATE FINAL

VOL. XCIV SEVEN PARTS—PART ONE ★★★ THURSDAY, APRIL 3, 1975 120 PAGES DAILY 10c

Ford Blames President Thieu

Stocks Off

From Times Wire Services

NEW YORK—The stock market drifted lower again today in an atmosphere of continuing caution over the federal budget deficit and its potential impact on the economy.

The Dow Jones average of 30 industrials closed down 8.37 at 752.19.

New York Stock Exchange volume was 13.9 million shares compared with 15.6 million Wednesday.

Complete tables in Financial Section

Connally Called Milk Price Hike 'Political'—Tape

WASHINGTON (UPI)—Former Secretary of the Treasury John B. Connally urged ex-President Richard M. Nixon to boost price supports for raw milk "on the basis of the political aspects of it," according to a White House tape played today at Connally's bribery trial.

"Uh. I'm not trying to talk about or discuss at any great length the, the economics of it, but as far as the politics are concerned, looking to 1972, uh, it appears very clear to me that you're going to have to move, uh, strong in the Midwest, you're going to have to be strong in rural America," Connally told the former President.

"I wouldn't judge it on a moral basis," Connally told Mr. Nixon, "I judge it on the basis of the political aspects of it."

The conversation took place March 23, 1971, two days before the Department of Agriculture reversed itself and increased the price support for raw milk from 80% to 85% of parity.

The Connally trial is in its third day in U.S. District Court. He is charged with accepting bribes of $10,000 from milk producers for his help in obtaining price-support increases.

Present at the meeting were John D. Erhlichman, Mr. Nixon's No. 2 aide; Agriculture Secretary Clifford Hardin; Budget Director George P. Schultz and three other aides.

Connally dominated the first part of the 30-minute meeting with long statements about the political advantages of helping the dairy farmers.

"These dairymen are organized, they are adamant, they're militant," Connally said.

"And just remember, when you talk about food prices now, and bleed for the consumer," Connally said, "that today, food prices in the United States, are cheaper than they've ever been in the history of this nation in terms of . . . hours of work to feed a family."

Wednesday's proceedings in Connally trial, Part 1, Page 14.

Deputy Resigns After Shooting

BRIDGEPORT—The Mono County sheriff's deputy who accidentally shot a 19-year-old store employe to death in a robbery March 9 has resigned from the force.

Sheriff Bill Evans announced today the resignation of Tom Stoneburner, 30, effective Wednesday, for "personal reasons having to do with the death of Kathleen M. Delhay."

As a result of Stoneburner's resignation, Evans announced that an inquiry related to Stoneburner's actions has been terminated.

Stoneburner, son of the Mono County treasurer-tax collector, was not publicly identified until five days after the girl was slain.

The county's grand jury reportedly declined by a "split vote" to indict Stoneburner. The girl was fatally wounded by a shotgun blast as she lay bound and gagged in a restroom as deputies, including Stoneburner, searched the rear of the store for two suspects.

The indicted pair—found hiding in the rafters after the shooting—are Michael Dean Busby, 23, and Gene Berkeley Waters, 30. They face a preliminary hearing April 11.

YF-16 Gains in Contest for Europe Deal

From Times Wire Service

BRUSSELS—Defense ministers of Belgium, Denmark, the Netherlands and Norway agreed today that General Dynamics' YF-16 "has undisputed advantages" over other fighter planes competing for what could become the biggest series of contracts in aviation history.

But the four NATO ministers said there were still "industrial and economic aspects" that could tip the choice another way.

qThe ministers, in a communique issued at the end of a three-hour meeting, said they would urge their governments to make a final choice before the end of this month.

The four countries are planning to order a total of 350 planes to replace their obsolete Lockheed F-104G Starfighters. The total purchase would run about $2 billion.

The other main contenders for the European contracts have been the French Mirage and the Swedish Viggen. The Norwegians and Danes were previously reported favoring the American plane, with the Belgians pressing for the Mirage and the Dutch undecided.

The four countries have agreed to try to maintain effeciency and keep down costs by choosing the same type of plane, but because of strong sentiment in the Belgian government to buy the French plane there had been doubt that the agreement would hold.

"The ministers agreed that, from the point of view of operational qualities and program costs, the YF-16 has undisputed advantages over the other contending aircrafts," the communique said.

JOBLESS RATE TO HIT 9%—SIMON

WASHINGTON (UPI)—Treasury Secretary William E. Simon told a congressional joint economic subcommittee today he believed the unemployment rate would go to 9% in the second half of this year but would be dropping before 1975 is over.

Unemployment reached 8.2% in January and February. The March figure, to be announced Friday, is expected to be subtantially higher. But Simon was upbeat about the economy as a whole, saying, "We are more certain about the recovery than we were at any time in the past."

PROMISED LAND — Vietnamese orphans crowd windows of World Airways plane as it flies them to their new homes in the United States. The children landed in Oakland to begin new lives.

Story in Part 1, Page 3

AP Wirephoto

Brown Campaign Reportedly Gathered 'Embarrassing' Data on Primary Foes

BY ROBERT FAIRBANKS
Times Staff Writer

SACRAMENTO—A top aide to Gov. Brown recently told a private gathering that the Brown campaign developed politically embarrassing information about Brown's major opponents in the Democratic primary election and reportedly promised to use it if the opponents launched personal attacks on Brown, The Times has learned.

The purported statements came from A. Thomas Quinn, the manager of Brown's successful gubernatorial campaign and now the governor's special assistant for environmental protection.

According to persons at the meeting, Quinn said Brown's strategists had identified San Francisco Mayor Joseph Alioto and former Assembly Speaker Bob Moretti as Brown's major opponents in the June, 1974, primary and had sent persons to investigate their backgrounds.

Quinn, who was not available for comment, did not describe the information that was gathered. But one person at the meeting said he recalled Quinn's mentioning studies of land and property management records in Alioto's case.

The Times has learned that the information developed regarding Moretti concerned campaign contributions and has been used by the People's Lobby in its unsuccessful attempt to block state Senate confirmation of Moretti's appointment to the Energy Resources and Conservation Commission.

Brown appointed Moretti to the $37,212 per year job last February, after Moretti had been saying publicly for weeks that he wanted a job with the new administration.

When told of Quinn's reported remarks, Moretti said the attorney general's office had sent five investigators to examine his campaign contribution reports and found nothing wrong.

Moretti also declared he was never told that the Brown forces were examining his activities or had developed any potentially damaging information about him. However, he did not rule out a possibility that someone on his staff may have been told.

The Times has learned that the information was presented to a member of Moretti's staff.

Moretti said the governor told him, before appointing him to his present job last February, that he (Brown) had seen the Moretti material and had found it—in Moretti's words—"without merit."

However, Moretti continued, Brown said a copy of the material had already gone to Ed Koupál, director of the People's Lobby, who made a copy before giving the original back. (Koupal has since said he received the information last May.)

The private meeting was held March 20 at the Clift Hotel in San Francisco as part of a study project being conducted by the California Journal, a magazine that specializes in state government affairs.

BIG TROUBLE — Truck driver Donald W. Clark, 57, of San Jose, had his first accident in 30 years today—and it was a lulu. No one was injured but part of his load of sunflower seeds, a Volkswagen and a pickup truck were scattered along the Golden State Freeway. Also involved in the three-way collision were VW driver Luis M. Luarca, 61, of Burbank, and pickup truck driver James A. Vaughn, 26, of Simi Valley.

Times Photo by R. L. Oliver

'Disaster' Laid to Pullback

From Times Wire Services

SAN DIEGO—President Ford said today that South Vietnamese President Nguyen Van Thieu had ordered a poorly planned and unnecessary pullback that led to startling Communist successes, news executives reported after listening to Mr. Ford at a private meeting.

In a speech after his noon press conference, Mr. Ford said the United States had suffered serious setbacks in Indochina and the Middle East and described the situation in Vietnam as "a disaster of incredible proportions."

The news executives said Mr. Ford stated that President Thieu made a unilateral decision to withdraw, the South Vietnamese military commanders had been unprepared, and no account had been taken of the mass of refugees clogging the roads.

The abandonment of millions of dollars worth of American military equipment in the headlong retreat by Saigon's troops was an unbelievable tragedy, the President was quoted as saying.

At the press conference, the President said he had ordered all available U.S. naval ships to stand off Indochina to do everything to assist refugees in the "great human tragedy in progress there.

He also ordered giant C-5 transports to fly to Saigon to pick up 2,000 South Vietnamese orphans and children already adopted by American families.

Mr. Ford said he had ordered the federal government to "cut red tape and other bureaucratic obstacles preventing these children from coming to the United States."

"This is the least we can do, and we will do much, much more," Mr. Ford pledged.

He said he remained optimistic that South Vietnam would prevail over the Communists, "despite the sad and tragic events that we see unfolding."

Asked whether he felt the fall of South Vietnam and Cambodia would affect U.S. national security, Mr. Ford said: "At present I do not anticipate the fall of South Vietnam and I greatly admire and respect the fight the pople and government of Cambodia are putting up . . .

But, he said, America's allies around the world cannot help but feel insecure about the reliability of U.S. commitments to stand by them and he repeated his assurances that the United States would remain a trustworthy ally everywhere.

"Let me say to our European allies: we are going to stand behind our commitments to NATO and we are going to stand behind our commitments to our other allies around the world."

In a speech prior to the press conference, referring to setbacks in Southeast Asia, Mr. Ford said despite events in Vietnam, "no allies or time-tested friends of the United States should worry or fear that our commitments to them will not be honored."

Speaking at a White House-sponsored conference here on energy and the economy, Mr. Ford said, "The current confusion and changing situation in Southeast Asia" should not undermine the faith of allies in the United States.

"We stand ready to support ourselves and defend our allies as surely as we always have," the President said.

In these "sad and troubled times," he said, "what is essential now is that we keep our nerve and our essential unity as a powerful but peace-loving nation."

FEATURE INDEX

Los Angeles Times

LARGEST CIRCULATION IN THE WEST, 1,045,479 DAILY, 1,236,066 SUNDAY

VOL. XCIV FIVE PARTS—PART ONE 82 PAGES TUESDAY MORNING, MAY 13, 1975 CC †† DAILY 10c

Cambodia Seizes U.S. Freighter, Crew of 39

Ford Demands Release, Hits 'Act of Piracy'

BY DON IRWIN and OSWALD L. JOHNSTON
Times Staff Writers

WASHINGTON—An unarmed U.S. freighter was fired on and seized early Monday in the Gulf of Thailand by a Cambodian gunboat that then took the vessel and her crew of 39 into port.

President Ford denounced the seizure as "an act of piracy" and ordered the State Department to demand that Cambodia's new revolutionary government immediately release the freighter, the Mayaguez, or face "the most serious consequences."

The captain of the seized vessel was identified by the owners as Charles T. Miller of Fountain Valley, Calif. They said that many of the crew members were from California, including Second Mate Jared C. Myregard of Van Nuys and Third Mate Burton Coombes of Richmond.

The White House announced the incident at 1:50 p.m. EDT—about 10 hours after first word was received here—without revealing details of the approach to be used to recover the vessel.

Before the announcement, Mr. Ford discussed the incident for 45 minutes with the National Security Council and later went over the few known facts with key members of Congress.

Pentagon sources said that the aircraft carrier Coral Sea and several other ships had been ordered to sail for the Gulf of Thailand. Such ship movements are standard procedure when trouble occurs.

Congress reacted with concern to the seizure of the first U.S. vessel taken over by a foreign power since North Korean warships captured the spy ship USS Pueblo in January, 1968. Some members urged use of force to recover the Mayaguez, but others agreed with Sen. Jacob K. Javits (R-N.Y.) that Americans "should keep our shirts on and see if they return the ship."

White House Press Secretary Ron Nessen denied that the Mayaguez was linked in any way with espionage. A State Department source said the ship carried a general cargo, about half of it consisting of "military vans" —containers carrying military materiel, but not arms or munitions.

An informed source said there would be no need for the United States to have a Pueblo-type intelligence ship in waters off Cambodia since American installations in Thailand can pick up any information available to such spy vessels.

Nessen said the ship, owned by Sea-Land Service Inc. of Edison, N.J., was believed to have been steaming from Hong Kong to a port in Thailand. Other officials said it was bound for Sattahip, a naval port adjoining the U.S. air base at Utapao, Thailand, when it was seized and apparently escorted into the Cambodian port of Kompong Som.

Fragmentary radio messages from the ship said the encounter took place in the Gulf of Thailand about

Please Turn to Page 10, Col. 1

CAMBODIA · Tonle Sap · Phnom Penh · Kompong Som · Saigon · Gulf of Thailand · South China Sea

Where ship was seized. Times map

Donations for Israel: 'Seven Lean Years'

Recession, Corruption Sharply Cut Worldwide Fund-Raising Efforts

BY WILLIAM J. DRUMMOND
Times Staff Writer

JERUSALEM—Prime Minister Yitzhak Rabin's disturbing prophecy of "seven lean years" for Israel is swiftly coming to pass, as donations by Jews around the world to Israeli projects have shown a sharp downward trend.

Hospitals, universities and other philanthropic institutions which rely on support from abroad are feeling a severe financial pinch, which most fund-raisers attribute to the economic recession in the United States and Western Europe.

Another explanation for the fund-raising problems, according to other responsible sources, is spreading disillusionment among Jews living abroad because of recent revelations of corruption in the Jewish state.

Among the bigger scandals uncovered were the financial problems of the government-backed Israel Corp. involving irregularities amounting to $22 million. Michael Tzur, former head of the corporation, was convicted last week of 14 charges of fraud, bribery and breach of trust. He could get up to 22 years in prison.

Former banker Yehoshua Bension was convicted of stealing $47 million from the now defunct Israel-British Bank while he was its head.

Then in late April, the previously above reproach defense establishment was touched by scandal when two businessmen were arrested on charges of paying large sums to Defense Ministry officials to obtain contracts.

"The reports of immorality, corruption, bribery, embezzlement and other related crimes . . . are creating havoc in the hearts and minds of North American Jews," said Bernard Morris, national executive director of the Canadian Assn. for Israel Labor.

"Fine and generous donors of gifts to Israel are obviously entertaining second thoughts about making contributions to their favorite Zionist causes," said Morris. "Considerable numbers of regular donors in Canada are withholding their commitments until some satisfactory answers are forthcoming on whether their money is being used for legitimate purposes, or whether it is being siphoned off by Israel's bureaucrats for all kinds of nefarious self-enriching schemes."

Whatever the explanation, the well-organized worldwide mechanism of Israel fund-raising campaigns is not producing the results it used to.

The central instrument for channeling contributions from the United States to Israel for social services and welfare is the United Jewish Appeal. Through it, donations from the 934 separate UJA organizations reach Israel.

Officials here reported a "discrepancy" of $86 million between what had been allocated by American Jewry to the UJA for overseas programs and the actual cash receipts over the past two years.

This is said to be the largest such shortfall in the UJA's long history. It indicates that donors are not paying off their pledges at the rate they used to.

Campaign officials added, however,

Please Turn to Page 4, Col. 3

SIGHTSEEING—Russian sailors from two visiting destroyers look over the scene in Boston during a tour. Visit of the Soviet warships was the first to a U.S. port since World War II. Meanwhile, two U.S. Navy destroyers reciprocated with courtesy call at Leningrad harbor. Story in Part 1, Page 17 AP Wirephoto

Korea A-Arms Use an Option, General Says

BY SAM JAMESON
Times Staff Writer

SEOUL—The United States would consider using tactical nuclear weapons in case of an outbreak of war in the Korean peninsula, a top American military commander said here Monday.

The U.S. officer, who asked not to be named, made it clear in an interview that he did not expect North Korea's Communist dictator, Kim Il Sung, to launch an all-out attack upon South Korea at this time.

But he also indicated that if such an attack should occur, a recommendation urging use of tactical nuclear weapons would most likely be made by the U.S. command here to the White House.

The highly placed commander was asked what role "the most powerful of American weapons" played in U.S. contingency plans against an all-out attack by North Korea. Although the question was worded indirectly to allow the officer to avoid violating American policy forbidding the discussion of the location of nuclear weapons, the commander replied:

"I'm an 'attack nuke' man myself."

Then he elaborated:

"The United States armed forces has kept a whole array of tactical nuclear weapons in its inventory, recognizing that the decision as to whether they will ever be used is a decision only the commander-in-chief can make, recognizing that more emotion surrounds this in the whole military equation than anything else, and recognizing there is a school of thought that persists today that the first use of nuclear weapons starts an uncontrollable spiral.

"Having said all that, the tactical nuclear capability constitutes one option available to U.S. and allied decision makers."

The officer pointed out that "as good military professionals, we plan against the contingencies we may be called upon to exercise." But he said an all-out war on the Korea peninsula in which either China or the Soviet Union—or both Communist giants—participated directly would "really pose some tough decisions for Washington to make."

Please Turn to Page 16, Col. 1

Soviet Tactics Imperil Detente, Kissinger Warns

From Times Wire Services

ST. LOUIS—Secretary of State Henry A. Kissinger warned Monday that Moscow's readiness to exploit strategic opportunities and its expansion of military power around the world "constitutes a heavy mortgage on detente" and jeopardizes new trends in Soviet-American relations.

"The United States is determined to maintain the hopeful new trends in U.S.-Soviet relations on the basis of realism and reciprocity," he said. "But it is equally determined to resist pressures or the exploitation of local conflict."

Kissinger also warned that any reduction of the United States' protective role throughout the world would increase the danger of nuclear disaster through the proliferation of nuclear weapons.

In a statement to the World Affairs Council of St. Louis, a local civic group, Kissinger spelled out an agenda for American foreign policy, calling for active participation in world affairs in the aftermath of what he called "the tragedy of Vietnam."

"The fact that we failed in one endeavor," he said, "does not invalidate all others.

"If in the aftermath of Vietnam we flee from responsibility as uncritically as we rushed into commitment a decade ago, we will surely find ourselves in a period of chaos and peril that will dwarf all previous experience."

Kissinger said "this Administration considers our allies and friends our first priority."

In a brief news conference after his speech, Kissinger said "an atrocity of major proportions is going on" in Cambodia.

He called the situation "a tragedy," and confirmed reports that 3 million residents of Phnom Penh have been forcibly evacuated and marched toward rural areas, and also that hospitals were cleared of patients.

In his warning on nuclear weapons he referred to "the Indian nuclear explosion of a year ago" and said it

Please Turn to Page 16, Col. 1

L.A. Wins 20-Year Fight on Disputed Water Rights

State High Court Rules Most of Underground San Fernando Valley Supply Belongs to City

BY DARYL LEMBKE
Times Staff Writer

SAN FRANCISCO—Partly because of an award made by Spain's King Charles III when the pueblo of Los Angeles was founded in 1781, the city of Los Angeles Monday won a 20-year battle with Glendale and Burbank for underground water rights.

The state Supreme Court unanimously awarded most of the water under the San Fernando Valley to Los Angeles, reversing a 1968 Superior Court decision granting almost a third of it to the other two cities.

The high court let stand that portion of the 1968 ruling that rejected Los Angeles' claim that the pueblo title to water also extended to the Sylmar basin, northeast of the city of San Fernando, and to the Verdugo basin, east of the Verdugo hills.

"This was a very monumental case that will affect water rights all over California," said Ralph Wesson, an assistant Los Angeles city attorney and a spokesman for City Atty. Burt Pines. "It changes the water law in California and affects a lot of pending cases."

Monday's ruling will force Glendale and Burbank to stop pumping from the San Fernando Valley section of the upper Los Angeles River area. They will have to replace that water with a higher-priced supply from the Metropolitan Water District.

Burbank and Glendale city officials were unable to immediately calculate how much the average water bill will go up but the boost is expected to be substantial. Glendale, for example, is now importing about 40% of its water from the MWD, which gets that

Please Turn to Page 22, Col. 1

Democrat Energy Bill Clears Panel

Could Hike Gas Taxes, Inefficient-Auto Prices

BY RICHARD T. COOPER
Times Staff Writer

WASHINGTON—A divided, dissatisfied and weary Democratic majority on the House Ways and Means Committee gave final approval Monday to a much-modified energy bill that could raise gasoline taxes, increase prices for inefficient cars and impose import quotas on oil.

The measure, adopted 19 to 16 with four Democrats joining the committee's 12 Republicans in opposition, would offer tax credits to private citizens for insulating their homes and other incentives to various segments of the energy industry.

Committee Democrats refused to include in the bill a windfall profits tax on the oil industry, because the House Commerce Committee has not decided what to do about price ceilings on U.S. oil production and because approval of such a plan now could strengthen the Ford Administration in its efforts to remove existing controls.

The Administration wants a windfall profits tax formula as a companion to its plan to decontrol oil

Please Turn to Page 6, Col. 1

Saigon Bishop Urges Concord

SAIGON (AP)—The Roman Catholic archbishop of Saigon, Nguyen Van Binh, has called on South Vietnamese Catholics to put forth "maximum efforts to rebuild the nation and contribute to national reconciliation and concord so as to create a thorough mutual understanding."

A communique from the archbishop was read at the Saigon cathedral during the Sunday morning Mass, a report from Saigon said Monday.

"A new page of history is open to the population of Vietnam," he said. "Since April 30, peace has returned to Vietnam, pushing death and misfortune back to the past.

"Together with our compatriots, we joyfully greet peace and participate in the common life of the whole population.

"We Catholics must actively realize our civic duties under the guidance of the Provisional Revolutionary Government. What we can do immediately is to contribute to the stabilizing of the situation. What is impor-

Please Turn to Page 15, Col. 1

Number of Doctors Fired in King Strike Rises to 38

BY TENDAYI KUMBULA
Times Staff Writer

A strike by young interns and residents at Martin Luther King Hospital that led to firing of 21 doctors over the weekend and the firing of 17 more Monday night went into its seventh day today with both sides issuing conflicting reports about whether the walkout was losing or gaining strength.

Hospital officials indicated they would continue to fire all interns and

State Senate approves third medical malpractice insurance bill, Part 2, Page 8.

residents who absented themselves for three consecutive days without an approved excuse.

Tony Tripi, a spokesman for the county Department of Health Services, said he thought the strike was weakening.

He said of 129 King Hospital interns and residents, 35 never participated in the strike, 31 others returned to their jobs over the weekend and 21 were on authorized vacations.

He said only 42 were still officially on strike. Of that number 38 have been fired.

Dr. Martha Flowers, one of the strikers, said about 40 of the intern and resident physicians were still out. But she also said that even some of those who had returned to duty were still offering active support to the strike in their off-duty hours.

"At this time we are still optimistic," she said. "Things are going fine. So far we have been getting fairly good receptions from the community and we intend to stand firm."

Another striker, Dr. Judith Schwedes, said:

"The strike seems to be gaining

Please Turn to Page 18, Col. 1

FEATURE INDEX

THE WEATHER

National Weather Service forecast: Fair today and Wednesday with a chance of patchy fog near the coast in the mornings. Highs both days in the low 80s. High Monday 80; low, 56.

Complete weather information and smog report in Part 2, Page 4.

PREMIER SIGNS EDICT

Communist Takes Over Laotian Armed Forces

BY JACQUES LESLIE
Times Staff Writer

VIENTIANE, Laos—Laotian rightists have been deprived of their last significant asset as control over the royal Lao armed forces was shifted to a Communist Pathet Lao official.

The shift means that the Pathet Lao will face virtually no resistance as they move toward establishing full control over Laos. Nevertheless, it is thought that at least the facade of the coalition government in which rightists and the Pathet Lao have shared power since 1973 will be maintained.

(In Washington, White House Press Secretary Ron Nessen said President Ford has no present plans to evacuate the 1,000 Americans now in Laos, despite tightening regulations that require certain formalities before foreign citizens may leave.)

Laotian Premier Souvanna Phouma signed an edict turning over control of national armed forces to Khammouane Boupha, vice minister of defense. This follows the resignation announced Saturday of rightist Minister of Defense Sisouk na Champassak, who left office under great pressure from Laotian leftists.

Under the September, 1973, protocol to Laos' peace agreement, control of ministries was divided equally between rightist and Pathet Lao officials. In ministries such as Defense, where a rightist was supposed to be minister, a Pathet Lao official was named vice minister.

The agreement also called for the two armies which had opposed each other during 11 years of war—the

Please Turn to Page 14, Col. 1

Los Angeles Times

LARGEST CIRCULATION IN THE WEST, 1,037,963, DAILY, 1,244,713 SUNDAY

VOL. XCIV SIX PARTS—PART ONE 120 PAGES FRIDAY, SEPTEMBER 19, 1975 MORNING ★ FINAL DAILY 15c

PATTY HEARST CAPTURE

NORSE SPIRITS

Aquavit-- Water of Life, Way of Life

BY DON COOK
Times Staff Writer

OSLO—In Scandinavia, aquavit is not merely "the water of life," it is part of the way of life.

With modest ingenuity and patience—both of which Norwegians possess in abundance—it is possible to convert a sack of potatoes, 40 gallons of water, 20 pounds of sugar and a couple of pounds of yeast into a suitably potable gallon-and-a-half of raw aquavit spirits.

Going on from there to create something palatable as well as potable is another problem. But Norwegians as well as Swedes are spurred to artistic heights by the fact that aquavit, distilled, enriched and matured by the state monopolies in the two countries, costs an astronomical price of up to $20 a bottle in the government stores.

The Norwegian Vinmonopolet, which has controlled, produced and bottled all legal aquavit in Norway since 1927, offers its customers a dozen different varieties. There are about 20 commercially bottled aquavits in all of Scandinavia, and anyone at a loss for conversation up here can always get things rolling by asking, "Which is your favorite aquavit?"

Sooner or later, usually sooner, the ensuing debate will settle down to an argument between the lovers of Norwegian Linie aquavit against all the rest.

The particular flavor—as well as the mystique—of Linie aquavit (pronounced lean-ya) lies in the fact that it has aged in oak sherry casks for an average of three years before it is bottled and sold.

At least six months of that time has been spent on a voyage in the casks across the equator and back in a Norwegian ship of the Wilhelmsen line, on regular cargo runs between Norway and Australia. Thus, this aquavit has crossed the line and hence its name.

It is a reassuring comfort to Norwegians in a changing world—and to anybody else who has taken to an ice-cold glass of Linie with its carmel-brown color and light, somewhat sweetish first taste, and smooth, fiery descent afterwards—to know that there are usually about 400,000 liters of the stuff at seas at any one time, rocking away to maturity on the voyage to Australia and back.

About 20 casks of 500 liters each go aboard every Wilhelmsen line ship sailing from Norway, and when it finally reaches the bottles, the back of each label bears the name of the ship and the dates of the voyage, to be read through the contents.

Please Turn to Page 18, Col. 1

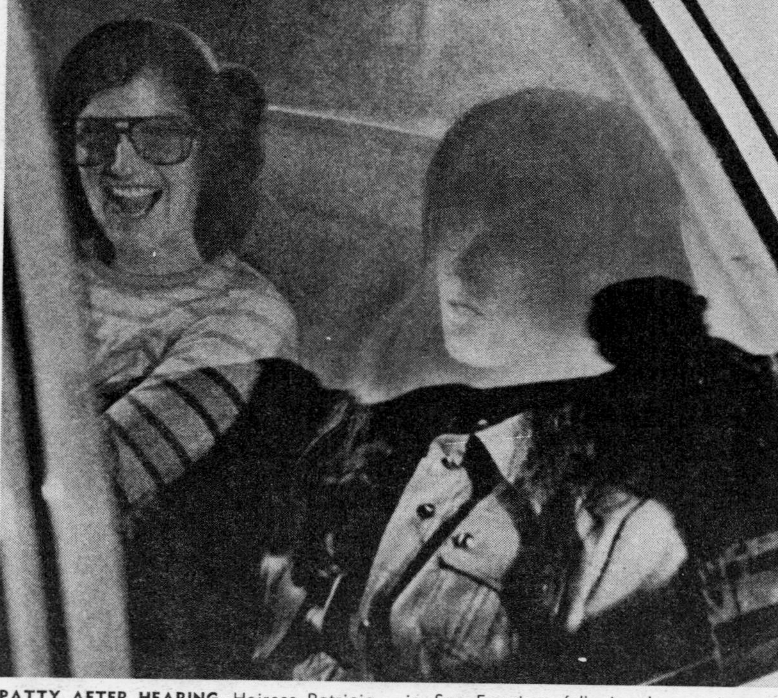

PATTY AFTER HEARING—Heiress Patricia Hearst, left, in back seat of a U.S. marshal's car in San Francisco following her arraignment. Woman seated beside her was not identified.
AP Wirephoto

Fugitive Heiress and 3 Companions Seized Without a Fight in S.F.

BY ROBERT KISTLER
Times Staff Writer

SAN FRANCISCO—Newspaper heiress Patricia Hearst and her three fugitive companions were captured without a fight here Thursday, ending one of the longest and most bizarre manhunts in American history.

None of the fugitives was armed when arrested. Only one tried briefly to resist.

The sudden, yet almost casual apprehension of the four—by agents of the FBI and San Francisco police—provided a whimper ending to the violent history of the Symbionese Liberation Army.

Charles W. Bates, the FBI agent who headed the 19-month nationwide manhunt for Patty—both as kidnap victim and terrorist "soldier"—gave this account of the captures:

—At 1:15 p.m., William Harris, 30, and his wife, Emily, 28—both wearing jogging clothes—were arrested in front of a home at 288 Precita Ave. in the city's Mission District.

Emily, upon seeing agents, started to run but was quickly placed under arrest.

—At 2:25 p.m., Patty and Wendy Yoshimura were arrested inside a house at 625 Morse St. in the outer Mission District, about three miles southwest of where the Harrises had been captured.

The locations of the arrests range from two to five miles south of the city's Civic Center where, among other agencies, the FBI maintains its headquarters. The area of both arrests is essentially residential, populated by lower- and middle-income families.

Both Harrises, like Patty, are avowed members of the SLA, the small terrorist band that first bored into the public mind when it claimed "credit" for the November, 1973, assassination of Marcus Foster, Oakland's black superintendent of schools.

Catherine Hearst, told of her daughter's arrest about 25 minutes afterward, said "God has answered our prayers. Today everything is wiped out—all the despair. I'm terribly happy."

Randolph A. Hearst, president of the San Francisco Examiner, said he is not worried about his daughter's legal problems.

"After all, she was a kidnap victim, you know," he said. "I know there will be some hassles and some rough times in store, probably a bumpy road. I don't see that there is anything to worry about, though."

While authorities would provide only sketchy details on what had led them to the quartet after all this time, Bates told reporters that agents had begun a "check" of the Precita Ave. home two days ago.

The check, he said, was not the result of a tip, but "just digging out people on the periphery who might have information."

Later Thursday, a 27-year-old house painter, Stephen F. Soliah, was arrested near where Patty was captured. The FBI said he would be charged with harboring a fugitive. No further details were available.

Bates said there might be additional arrests in the case soon, presumably of persons believed to have given assistance to Patty and her comrades. Bates did not elaborate.

The house at which the Harrises were arrested had been placed under surveillance at 2 p.m. Wednesday, Bates said, and agents had sighted the couple on at least one occasion. Why agents chose not to arrest them at the time was not explained.

While federal sources said they did not know whether either of the houses contained weaponry of the kind frequently stockpiled by the SLA at past "safe houses," Police Inspector Gary Kern said the Harris dwelling contained three automatic rifles, two shotguns, several handguns and 40 pounds of explosives, plus two gas masks.

Whether any armament also was taken from the house in which Patty had been living was not immediately determined.

Please Turn to Page 3, Col. 1

This story was prepared with the assistance of Times Staff Writers Kathy Burke, William Endicott, Philip Hager, Jeff Hansen, Eleanor Hoover, Daryl Lembke and Patt Morrison.

Patty Hearst in 1972
AP photo

FBI Bldg.

The Harrises Captured 288 Precita Ave.

Miss Hearst and Miss Yoshimura Captured 625 Morse St.

Times map by Patrick Lynch

CIA Fooled U.S. on Tet Offensive, Ex-Agent Says

BY RONALD J. OSTROW
Times Staff Writer

WASHINGTON—A former CIA expert on the Viet Cong charged Thursday that "corruption in the (U.S.) intelligence process" caused America to be taken by surprise by the 1968 Tet offensive in Vietnam.

Samuel A. Adams, who left the Central Intelligence Agency in 1973, told the House Intelligence Committee that in the months before the offensive "U.S. intelligence had deliberately downgraded the strength of the enemy army to portray the Viet Cong as weaker than they actually were."

"Although our aim was to fool the American press, the public and the Congress, we in intelligence succeeded best in fooling ourselves," Adams said.

Referring to testimony last week before the committee on the failure of American intelligence to predict the 1973 Mideast war, Adams said that the astonishment at Tet differed in a key respect.

Other intelligence surprises, he said, stemmed from negligence or misreading evidence, but "the Tet surprise stemmed in large measure from corruption in the intelligence process."

Adams, describing himself as the CIA's principal Viet Cong analyst for seven of his 10 years with the agency, said he found documents at the agency's headquarters in 1966 that

Please Turn to Page 10, Col. 5

QUIET TENANTS

Patty Seized in District Where Trouble's Rare

BY DARYL LEMBKE
and TED THACKREY JR.
Times Staff Writers

SAN FRANCISCO—The neighborhood where Patricia Hearst and Wendy Yoshimura were arrested was just another quiet San Francisco-style slice of semisuburbia until Thursday afternoon.

"And now," said Winston Amberg, who lives next door to the two-story duplex at 625 Morse St. where the two young women were found, "all of a sudden we're famous!

"Every cop in town, half the FBI and I don't know who else is going in and out. All the school kids are camped out there in front. We've got a stream of cars going past, rubbernecking—and I'll swear I saw a tour bus a few minutes ago.

"And you know . . . I never saw a thing!"

Neither did any of the girls' other neighbors.

The news that they had been living in close proximity with the fugitive newspaper heiress and Miss Yoshimura came as a complete surprise.

For Mrs. Kay Good, who lives diagonally across the street, it was a little more than that.

"It was a shock, I'll tell you!" she said. "Why—I can remember when they moved in, a week ago last Tuesday. I ought to. I mean . . . I gave them the key!"

Mrs. Good explained that she has known Joseph Prill, who owns the duplex, and her son had cleaned the rugs in the living room and bedroom later occupied by the two fugitives.

"Mr. Prill had been trying to sell the place," she said. "He wanted $50,000 for it, I think, and he was re-

Please Turn to Page 21, Col. 4

Boost in Steel Prices Opposed

BY PAUL E. STEIGER
Times Staff Writer

WASHINGTON—In its toughest-worded assault yet on an industry's price-raising plans, the staff of President Ford's Council on Wage and Price Stability reported Thursday that steel companies were flush with profits and held that their planned Oct. 1 price increase was not justified.

The 85-page staff report assailed in detail every one of the arguments the industry has advanced to support a price boost.

In addition, in a letter accompanying the report, the council's acting director, George C. Eads, said his staff was prepared to fight planned moves by Amerian steel companies aimed at winning government protection from the competition of low-cost steel imports.

"While we must protect ourselves against unfair foreign competition, there is a tendency on the part of many industries to consider *all* foreign competition 'unfair,'" Eads said. "Domestic firms cannot be allowed to take advantage of their

Please Turn to Page 8, Col. 1

GOVERNMENT IN DILEMMA

19 Die as Armed Bands Control Heart of Beirut

BY JOE ALEX MORRIS JR.
Times Staff Writer

BEIRUT—The Lebanese capital Thursday was plunged deeply into the sectarian warfare that had been spreading throughout the country.

Armed bands took over the center of the city after the worst night of shooting and bombings in this year's fourth round of civil strife in Lebanon. At least 19 persons were killed.

The main commercial district never opened for business. Internal security forces were nowhere to be found outside the port district, and the Lebanese parliament was in a no-man's-land crackling with sniper fire.

Shooting continued into Thursday night despite a call for a late afternoon cease-fire.

The situation differed from that in Tripoli—a northern city and Lebanon's second largest—in that armed groups of Moslem and left-wing forces here did not take over the entire city. Beirut's Christian districts are as heavily armed as their Moslem counterparts.

The government appeared to be hopelessly caught in the middle. Prime Minister Rashid Karami, a conservative Moslem whose "government of national salvation" was installed two months ago to end the first three rounds of sectarian warfare, was torn between demands to call in the army and pressure from the Moslem community against it.

(Reuters news agency quoted informed sources as saying Karami had threatened to resign rather than call in the army.)

Late Wednesday Karami announced formation of a committee of national reconciliation. A few hours later, however, sharp fighting broke out, not only in Beirut's suburbs, as has become usual, but downtown.

In one of the worst incidents, a

Please Turn to Page 16, Col. 5

FEATURE INDEX

THE WEATHER

National Weather Service forecast: Some late night and early morning fog and low clouds near the coast, otherwise fair today and Saturday. Highs both days near 82. High Thursday, 87; low, 69.

Complete weather information and smog report in Part 3, Page 12.

Los Angeles Times

LARGEST CIRCULATION IN THE WEST, 1,037,963 DAILY; 1,244,713 SUNDAY

VOL. XCIV EIGHT PARTS—PART ONE 150 PAGES THURSDAY MORNING, OCTOBER 9, 1975 CC† DAILY 15c

Inflation of 5% to 7% Appears Here to Stay

Economists Differ in Explaining How Rate Got 'Built Into' System

BY JOHN F. LAWRENCE
Times Economic Affairs Editor

The one good thing about a bad recession is that it is supposed to kill inflation.

After nearly a year of bad recession, however, prices keep going up. The rate has slowed appreciably to about 7%, but the experts are saying it won't slow much more. Instead, the nation will have to live indefinitely with inflation of at least 5% and probably as much as 7%. That is more than twice what was considered healthy just a few years ago.

"We have roughly a 6% rate of inflation built into the system," said Edgar R. Fiedler, until recently the U.S. Treasury's top economist and now a vice president of the Conference Board, a New York business research organization. "It took us a decade to get into this situation so if we ever do get out, it's certainly going to take an equally long time."

How does an inflation rate get "built in"?

Talk to a dozen economists and you'll get more than a dozen explanations (some give you a choice of two). Their confusion is a none-too-encouraging backdrop for what is likely to be a major election-year debate about federal economic policy.

Critics of business have been grumbling for years that some companies have become so big and powerful they don't have to cut prices even in the worst of times. The current inflation is further evidence to them of the need for government controls.

Then there is a group—and it includes President Ford—that sees inflation as "made in Washington," a result of years of too much federal spending.

Other experts see the problem in less sinister terms. They insist that the continuing rise in the cost of living is the result of nothing more than society's preference for stability and long-term economic growth. Hence, it is a necessary evil and one that Americans get used to.

If the economists offer little consensus on the point, at least an examination of some of their arguments sheds a little light on why inflation persists.

Big Business Theory

Those who place most of the blame on American industry point to such things as the recent steel price hikes at a time when demand is slack. The law of supply and demand dictates that prices should fall as companies scramble for customers.

Instead, the critics say, big companies in many basic industries raise prices based on how much profit they think they should make, regardless of demand. They figure most of their competition is in the same boat and will do likewise. They probably base their profit target on such things as how much other major industries are making and how much it costs to attract the capital they need to grow.

Please Turn to Page 24, Col. 1

L.A. WELCOME—Japan's Emperor Hirohito and Empress Nagako are greeted at planeside at the airport here by Gov. Brown and Mayor Tom Bradley. Emperor is shaking hands with Mrs. Bradley.
Times photo by John Malmin

Hirohito and Bradley Toast Each Other at Banquet

Mayor Cites Pride in U.S.-Japanese Partnership; Emperor Waves to Crowd of 1,000 at Music Center

BY JOHN DREYFUSS and LEE HARRIS
Times Staff Writers

Japan's Emperor Hirohito and Los Angeles Mayor Tom Bradley drank champagne toasts to each other Wednesday, with Bradley citing pride in the Japanese-American partnership established "over the years."

The toasts terminated a banquet in the Dorothy Chandler Pavilion of the Music Center where Bradley was host to the 74-year-old emperor, Empress Nagako, 72, and about 520 invited guests.

Before the banquet, Hirohito walked slowly along a red carpet on the pavilion balcony, carefully mounted three steps to a special platform, and waved to a crowd of about 1,000 persons below.

He was accompanied to the platform by the empress and Mayor and Mrs. Bradley.

The crowd, which gathered beneath Japanese and American flags flying side by side in the Music Center Mall, responded by applauding, cheering and vigorously waving miniature American and Japanese flags.

Several persons in the gathering carried signs in English and Japanese protesting "U.S.-Japanese intervention in Korea," and the "Japanese economic invasion into the Third World."

After the Music Center Luncheon the royal couple toured Disneyland for about an hour and 10 minutes Wednesday afternoon where they were greeted by Mickey Mouse.

The couple was also welcomed by Snow White, the Seven Dwarfs and

Please Turn to Page 3, Col. 1

5 Die in Spanish Terrorist Attack

All Apparently Slain by Police; Raiders Escape

BY DON COOK
Times Staff Writer

MADRID—Five Spaniards died Wednesday apparently from police bullets during a terrorist attack on a Barcelona police station.

At the same time, the news from Paris that an assistant military attache of the Spanish Embassy there had been shot and wounded added to the grim, repressionist mood which is now dominating the attitude of the Spanish government.

It is a mood, moreover, which is widely supported by Spanish public opinion—a mixture of indignation and pride which has been reinforced by anti-Franco, pro-terrorist demonstrations and diplomatic activities in Western Europe and the rest of the world.

In the Barcelona incident, it apparently was police bullets that brought death to five people, including two policemen.

A car sped by a police station in the mainly working-class Verneda section of the city. Terrorists opened fire from the automobile with submachine guns.

Police, a bit trigger-happy after 15 police killings in Spain in the last three months, returned the fire. But

Please Turn to Page 12, Col. 1

House Votes Approval of Sinai Teams

But Gives President No Power to Send New U.S. Troops to Mideast

WASHINGTON (AP)—The House gave overwhelming approval Wednesday night to a plan that commits 200 American technicians to monitor the Sinai peace accord.

Before final assent, the House approved an amendment specifying that the resolution approving the technicians gives the President no power to introduce U.S. military force into the Middle East that is not already there.

The commitment of U.S. technicians was approved 341 to 69 and sent to the Senate where final action on the plan was put off until Friday.

The military force amendment, introduced by Rep. Bob Eckhardt (D-Tex.), was approved 124 to 71. It was accepted by supporters of the resolution—including Rep. Wayne L. Hays (D-Ohio)—who said it would now prevent President Ford from using military forces to rescue the technicians should that be essential.

Congressional leaders had hoped to give the resolution final approval by Thursday, but the Senate put off final action until Friday.

Congress should make clear, Eckhardt told the House, that it was not writing anything comparable to the Gulf of Tonkin Resolution that committed U.S. forces to the Vietnam war.

He said, "We want to make it clear we have not given blanket authority to go to war as a nation."

The House also overwhelmingly rejected a two-year limit on the technicians' stint in the Sinai.

Any danger of the technicians involving the United States in a Middle East war "is very remote," House International Relations Committee Chairman Thomas E. Morgan (D-Pa.) told the House.

An almost identical resolution, including the condition that technicians be pulled out immediately if war erupts, is scheduled for Senate consideration today and Friday.

The House also approved on a voice vote an amendment by Rep. Mario Biaggi (D-N.Y.) requiring the President to report on the feasibility of ending the U.S. technicians' involvement by replacing them with people from other nations.

Morgan said the technicians would be protected by 5,000 U.N. troops in the buffer zone and Rep. Dante B. Fascell (D-Fla.) said they'll be the first to know of war. "We think they'll be smart enough to get out of the way."

Please Turn to Page 13, Col. 1

Health Plan Seen Failing in Britain

Doctors Say the System Is Heading for Collapse

LONDON (AP)—Leading doctors said Wednesday that Britain's 27-year-old socialized medicine system was headed for collapse.

The president of the Royal College of Surgeons urged Prime Minister Harold Wilson to order an investigation.

Sir Rodney Smith, head of the royal college, said inefficiency coupled with an exodus of doctors seeking better pay in other countries have brought the National Health Service to the brink of irreparable damage. He said the condition of the system also has resulted in fewer young persons entering the field.

"You can't accept this without a progressive slide in standards, and that means, quite simply, that more patients will die or have an unsuccessful operation," Smith said. "We are not running out of time in this respect. We have run out of time."

Discontent within the medical profession was brought to a head by the Labor government's decision to phase out the 1% of state hospital

Please Turn to Page 14, Col. 1

Ford Would Curb U.S. Regulation of Airlines

Wants to Give Carriers Power to Raise or Cut Rates, Kill Routes, Initiate New Ones

BY GAYLORD SHAW
Times Staff Writer

WASHINGTON—President Ford, declaring that the "present promotional and protectionist regulatory system" needs reform, urged Congress Wednesday to inject more competition into the airline industry by sharply curtailing government controls.

He sent to Capitol Hill legislation that would give airlines freedom to raise fares 10% annually or to slash them up to 40% without the now-required approval of the Civil Aeronautics Board.

James C. Miller III, a senior White House economist, told reporters that, if the President's plan were adopted, fares on heavily traveled cross-country routes such as Los Angeles to New York might fall 20% to 30% and "overall rates will decline on an average of 15% to 20%."

Administration officials said the legislation would also make it easier for new airlines to enter the business and for existing carriers to start service to additional cities or to abandon routes.

Mr. Ford's proposal, the second of a three-part package of legislation to reduce federal regulation of transportation, faces an uncertain fate in Congress.

The Air Transport Assn., representing all major domestic airlines, strenuously opposes the measure. Soon after it was made public by the White House, the association charged that Mr. Ford's plan would "cause a major reduction or elimination of scheduled air service to many communities and would lead inevitably to increased costs to consumers."

On the other hand, Sen. Edward M. Kennedy (D-Mass.), who was chairman of congressional hearings on the airline industry last spring, said that he welcomed the "extremely constructive initiatives by the Administration."

"I am personally convinced that the airline industry needs far more healthy competition," Kennedy said in a statement, adding that he would work "with the Administration in a bipartisan effort to improve and enact this important legislation."

In his message to Congress, Mr. Ford said that his plan was intended to ensure the best possible air service at the lowest possible cost.

"We must make sure that the industry responds to natural market forces and to consumer demands rather than artificial constraints of government," the President said. "For many Americans, air travel has become a luxury too expensive to afford," he added.

Administration officials were reluctant to predict precisely how the President's proposals would change air travel. But Paul McAvoy, a member of Mr. Ford's Council of Economic Advisers, said it could spur airlines to offer a wider variety of services at differing costs—"red-eye (late night) service, no lunch service, no drink service . . . off-peak and no frills service"—which could substantially cut ticket prices.

For their part, airline spokesmen contend that the Administration's proposals would strip many small and medium-size cities of air service

Please Turn to Page 26, Col. 1

LEVIES MIGHT RISE

Tax Plan Cheers GOP but It Could Backfire

BY PAUL E. STEIGER
Times Staff Writer

WASHINGTON—Republicans in the Administration and Congress are ecstatic over President Ford's surprise proposal for a big tax cut in January provided Congress first commits itself to trimming $28 billion from federal spending nine months later.

They believe the Ford plan has suddenly put Democrats on the defensive on the key issues of taxes, spending and economic recovery, just in time for the start of the 1976 election season.

But signs are emerging that the artful proposal could backfire on Mr. Ford if—as now seems probable—congressional Democrats ignore the President's demand for an advance commitment to hold down spending, vote a tax cut of their own and then dare Mr. Ford to carry out his threat to veto it.

Such a veto, if sustained, would cause everyone's taxes to rise Jan. 1 because personal income tax reductions enacted in March will expire at the end of this year unless extended by law.

Democrats contend privately that Mr. Ford ultimately will shrink from such a veto, not only because the voters would be displeased with an increase in their tax bills but because failure to at least extend the current one-year tax cuts would risk short-circuiting recovery from the recession.

Moreover, the Democrats argue, even if the President did carry out his veto threat, there is a good chance the veto would be overridden. Either way, Mr. Ford would suffer serious political embarrassment, they contend.

One of the Administration's economists, Asst. Treasury Secretary Sidney Jones, inadvertently gave credence to the Democratic arguments Wednesday. He acknowledged at a press conference aimed at promoting the Ford proposals that, if the tax reductions were not extended into next year, the recovery could well start to sputter.

The key, Democrats and Republicans agree, is whether the Ford Administration can convince the public of the importance of Mr. Ford's insistence that any extension or expansion of the 1975 tax cuts be tied to congressional endorsement, in ad-

Please Turn to Page 20, Col. 1

CONTROVERSIES CITED

Ward Blocking Real for DA Post, Sources Claim

BY DOUG SHUIT
Times Staff Writer

Supervisor Baxter Ward put up the roadblock that killed the immediate chance of U.S. Dist. Judge Manuel L. Real winning the district attorney's appointment Tuesday, according to reliable sources in the county Hall of Administration Wednesday.

Real reportedly came closer to getting the appointment than any of the other candidates during a 3½ hour closed-door session of the five-man Board of Supervisors.

But Ward, it is said, became the pivotal figure when sentiment appeared to be moving toward Real's appointment.

The supervisor reportedly raised a series of questions about controversies in Real's background, some extending into the 1960s.

And, after calling Real in for private questioning, the board adjourned without making a decision.

According to reports, Real apparently answered the questions satisfactorily—at least to some supervisors. Ward so far has refused to comment on the matter.

For his part, Real also has refused to comment.

Despite the questions raised during the closed-door meeting, Real was said Wednesday still to be one of the top contenders for the appointment.

Ward's posture on Real is said to be of critical importance when the board meets again today to take up the appointment.

In addition to the importance of his vote, it is said that a chief concern is that a district attorney opposed by Ward will come under the same kind of fire that Ward directed at the previous district attorney—the late Joseph Busch, whose death June 27 left the vacancy the board is now trying to fill.

Please Turn to Page 29, Col. 1

FEATURE INDEX

THE WEATHER

National Weather Service forecast: Increasing high clouds today with considerable cloudiness tonight and Friday and a 20% chance of occasional light rain. Highs today in the mid 70s and on Friday near 70. High Wednesday, 73; low, 55.

Complete weather information and smog report in Part 3, Page 10.

'DAMN EASY TO GET OUT'

GI Who Deserted in '70 Returns for Discharge

BY DAVID LAMB
Times Staff Writer

FT. DIX, N.J.—The lanky soldier—wearing corduroy jeans, a faded plaid shirt and a gold neck chain his friends in Canada had given him for good luck a few days earlier—ambled into the provost marshal's office and looked around for a brief, awkward moment, apparently not quite sure whether to salute or shake hands.

He set his book of Ernest Hemingway short stories and his shaving kit on a bench and seemed to be trying to ignore a herd of butterflies taking flight in his stomach. He approached a lieutenant dressed in starched Army fatigues and said quietly: "I'm John Schafer. I'm here to surrender."

The lieutenant, Hank Pitcher, has watched dozens of Vietnam deserters pass through his office in recent months. "Usually," he said, "they just get tired of running, tired of looking over their shoulder." The lieutenant introduced Schafer to Sgt. Charles Tallmadge in an adjoining office.

"Okay, John, I'm going to read you your rights under article 31 of the Uniform Code of Military Justice," Tallmadge told Schafer. "Then I've got some questions for these forms. You don't have to answer them if you don't want to but it's just stuff like the color of your eyes and when you left your unit. There's nothing incriminating in any of these here forms. They're just to get your paperwork moving."

Thus did Schafer—one of 10,500 men listed as deserters by the Department of Defense—end his exile of more than five years in Canada and return this week to settle his accounts with the U.S. Army. Like most of his peers, he found little personal merit in President Ford's clemency offer and preferred instead to

Please Turn to Page 16, Col. 1

Los Angeles Times

LARGEST CIRCULATION IN THE WEST, 1,037,963 DAILY, 1,244,713 SUNDAY

VOL. XCV SEVENTEEN PARTS—PART ONE 416 PAGES SUNDAY MORNING, MARCH 14, 1976 ★ SUNDAY 50c

'HUB' BYPASSED

Dying Hopes Give St. Louis the Blues

BY RICHARD T. COOPER
Times Staff Writer

ST. LOUIS—Once the proud gateway to half a continent, with hopes of becoming capital of the entire nation, rich in history, wealth and attainment, St. Louis has become a city puzzled by the mystery of how its dreams of greatness vanished between cup and lip.

"The center of North America, if not the world and civilization! The great focus of the West and Southwest . . . We burn one third of our steamboats, destroy one tenth of the wealth of our citizens in one night, kill one tenth by cholera—try our hand at burning again—all only to show how much we can stand without succumbing."

Another in an intermittent series of articles on American cities that played a significant role in the development of the nation.

In those heroic terms did Dr. George Engelmann, a leading physician and amateur botanist, see St. Louis in 1843, shortly before he and others decided that a city destined for such greatness should have a botanical palace to rival London's Kew Gardens.

Both then and later, considerable evidence seemed to exist for Engelmann's expansive assessment. It is only recently that the good doctor's faith in the city's recuperative powers has come to seem more relevant.

During the colonial era, while Boston and Philadelphia were squabbling over tea parties, St. Louis had begun establishing dominion over the Rocky Mountain fur trade and the future riches of the midcontinent. Though successively under French and Spanish authority, the merchant princes of St. Louis sent men and money to help the 13 Colonies throw off British rule.

Later, St. Louisans like to recall, theirs was a busy commercial center when wild onions still grew in the future streets of Chicago. Outfitter of Conestoga wagon trains, preeminent port for Mark Twain's paddle-wheelers, pivotal factor in the Civil War, then bourgeoning industrial center—St. Louis seemed fated for perpetual glory.

Yet somewhere between cup and lip there was the proverbial slip. Despite all it was and all it expected to become, St. Louis as much as any major city in America has seen dreams of greatness dissolve into stagnation and decay.

With its inner city mauled by poverty and crime, its suburbs preoccupied with their own mounting problems, many of its factories gone and the region's economy lagging behind the rest of the nation in vigor, many in St. Louis wonder what went wrong.

Was it inevitable, a rush of history that lifted St. Louis and now has dropped it? St. Louis University urbanologist George D. Wendel sees things pretty much that way:

"We have played our role in history," he said in a recent interview. "History has passed us by. We are not going to die. We are just going to plod along."

Or might things have been made to turn out better? Was St. Louis at least partly a victim of poor planning, short-sighted leaders and a genteel impulse toward self-satisfaction that even now causes many St. Louisans to scorn the hurly-burly of fierce competition with other cities?

Stanley Goodman, chief executive officer of the St. Louis-based May Co. department stores, is one of those who think the city and its leaders must shoulder part of the blame.

"It's important to understand what is in the childhood of a place," Good-

Please Turn to Pt. 1-A, Pg. 4

FEATURE INDEX

PREVIEW—A traffic control officer had to be put on duty at the Overland Ave. on-ramp to the Santa Monica Freeway—where the wait can be more than 12 minutes—last week; and the Diamond Express system has not yet started. Pedestrian on median seems to be surveying situation.

Times photo by George R. Fry

Freeway Car-Pool Lane Starts Monday; Controversy Swirls Around Experiment

BY RAY HEBERT
Times Urban Affairs Writer

Commuting may never be the same again on the Santa Monica Freeway, California's busiest.

For many of the freeway's 240,000 daily users, a drastic change takes place Monday when the Santa Monica's two fast lanes—one each way—become exclusive roadways for buses and car pools during rush hours.

It marks the first time a project of this type—taking lanes away from regular traffic for special use—has been tried on a major highway in the United States.

'Pity the poor freeway . . . and the people who use it," a regular Santa Monica Freeway commuter moaned. "The whole thing sums up bureaucratic stupidity."

But transportation experts see it differently. They believe that funneling high occupancy vehicles into the freeway's fast lanes will go a long way toward improving traffic in the heavily traveled corridor between the Westside and downtown Los Angeles.

However, they are apprehensive about confusion and accidents as the new program, called the Santa Monica Freeway Diamond Express, gets under way. Giant white diamonds have been painted on the fast inbound and outbound lanes to designate their preferential status.

Inspector Michael O'Leary, supervisor for the California Highway Patrol's Los Angeles area, is predicting a 10% to 12% increase in accidents because of more congestion on the freeway.

And, Los Angeles City Traffic Engineer S. S. Taylor believes accidents will jump as much as 10% on adjacent surface streets, as motorists, unable to get on the freeway, try alternate routes.

However, California Department of Transportation engineers are more optimistic. With the traffic controls, such as metered on-ramps, that exist now, they believe accidents will be kept to a minimum.

These exclusive lanes mean that the freeway, a guinea pig among freeways since its completion 10 years ago, is being subjected to yet another experiment in a series of pilot projects that have annoyed, frustrated and angered many motorists.

The demonstration programs have included huge electronic signs installed in the freeway's median strip, puzzling assortments of smog testing devices mounted on overpasses and metered on-ramps where motorists have to wait, sometimes up to 15 minutes, to get on the freeway.

In the program starting Monday, drivers alone or with only one passenger must stay out of the freeway's two speed preferential lanes fast lanes during the eight busiest traffic hours of the day. Their choices are to fight traffic squeezed into the remaining lanes, use surface streets, take a bus or join a car pool.

The idea of taking lanes away from regular traffic and designating them for bus and car pool use is unique, especially on a freeway as busy as the Santa Monica. The route ranks among the three most heavily used in the nation, carrying only slightly

Please Turn to Page 8, Col. 1

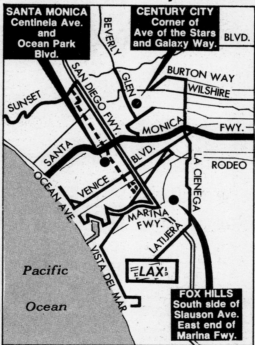

SANTA MONICA Centinela Ave. and Ocean Park Blvd.
CENTURY CITY Corner of Ave of the Stars and Galaxy Way.
FOX HILLS South side of Slauson Ave. East end of Marina Fwy.
BEVERLY BLVD.
BURTON WAY
WILSHIRE
SUNSET
GLEN
SAN DIEGO FWY.
SANTA MONICA FWY.
VENICE BLVD.
RODEO
LA CIENEGA
OCEAN AVE
MARINA FWY.
LATIJERA
VISTA DEL MAR
LAX
Pacific Ocean

OPTION—Three rapid transit district park-and-ride lots and extra bus lines offer driver options in Diamond Express experiment.

Times map

OLD-FASHIONED POLITICS

Backers, Not Issues, Key to Illinois Voting

BY GEORGE SKELTON
Times Political Writer

CHICAGO—When a Chicago steelworker goes to the polls Tuesday, the deciding factor in his vote for President may be whether the ward boss has sent a new garbage can over to his house.

"Give a guy a garbage can and he'll vote any way ya want. It's amazing. He thinks you've given him a million dollars," said a city worker who delivers garbage cans at election time for the Democratic machine.

What kind of garbage can?

"A 55-gallon drum. Guy like you could sit in it," a machine lieutenant told an inquiring reporter.

Downstate, a farmer's decision on whether to vote for President Ford or to help rescue Ronald Reagan's sinking candidacy may hinge on the price of soy beans, but probably not on detente.

Weighty issues are not the most important factor in Tuesday's Illinois primary. The most important factor is who's supporting whom.

An illustration of how issues are regarded here was provided by the machine-backed candidate for governor, Secretary of State Michael J. Howlett. He told a reporter:

"Issues are bull. I have to get the Democrats to vote for me. I'm not going to do that by talking about issues."

Illinois is not a haven for ideologues. It is a haven for patronage-oriented, ward-based, old-fashioned machine politics, the last of its kind.

And, once again, the machine, controlled by Chicago Mayor Richard J. Daley, is having a distorting influence on the process of selecting the next presidential nominee of the Democratic Party.

The Republican Party structure also is strong, but there is no greased, overbearing machine. What exists is called "the organization." And it overwhelmingly backs Ford, giving him a big leg up on Reagan.

It is essential to keep in mind these basics of Illinois politics in order to understand the real meaning of Tuesday's results.

The nation's fourth major presidential primary is significant for these reasons:

—Regardless of what he says publicly, Reagan badly needs a victory in the state of his birth to restore credibility to his campaign. He has yet to win a primary and the odds are heavy against him here. Ford could deliver the fatal blow, whether Reagan acknowledges it or not, by piling up the 2-to-1 landslide margin his Illinois chairman has predicted.

"My ambition is to finish off Reagan here," said Ford chairman Richard B. Ogilvie, who was governor of Illinois at the same time Reagan was governor of California.

—Jimmy Carter, former governor of Georgia, has now won major Democratic primaries in the Northeast and the South—New Hampshire and the South—even though he lost in Massachusetts. A triumph here would not only continue but increase his substantial momentum. It also would demonstrate that he is a Southerner who can carry a large non-Southern state populated by a cross-section of voters ranging from farmers to factory workers to fat cats.

—Alabama Gov. George C. Wallace is Carter's chief rival here. Democratic leaders say that Wallace cannot win the nomination because he is unacceptably divisive. But he can influence the nominating con-

Please Turn to Page 20, Col. 1

Beleaguered Palestinian Arabs Try to Regain Unity

BY JOE ALEX MORRIS JR.
Times Staff Writer

BEIRUT—The Palestinian Arabs, whose star has risen rapidly at the international level with a series of victories at the United Nations, ironically find themselves increasingly beleaguered in the Middle East.

Now they are trying to bury their differences and restore a semblance of unity in their ranks to stem the steady erosion of their position in the Arab world.

Three major developments have prompted the Palestinian concern:

—Last summer's Sinai disengagement agreement between Egypt and Israel, which brought an almost total break between the Palestinians and Cairo.

—The Lebanese civil war, which has cost the Palestinians both heavy casualties and some of the freedom of movement they enjoyed in the country.

The rapprochement of Syria, heretofore the Palestinians' main backer, with Jordan, a country with which the Palestinians have a long history of bitter enmity. This is the Palestinians' most serious concern.

The more than 3 million Arab Palestinians are in a quandary. Jordan's King Hussein surrendered all claim to represent them at the Rabat Arab summit of 1974, which designated the Palestinian Liberation Organization as the legitimate Palestinian power. But the PLO is unacceptable to Israel, which rules the Palestinian homeland. And what, the Palestinians are asking, are the Syrians up to?

Since 1948, when it all started, the struggle of the Palestinian Arabs to regain their homeland has gone mainly in reverse. In 1967, Israel took over the West Bank and Gaza, the last remaining pieces of old Palestine still in Arab hands.

Since 1967, Palestinian political

Please Turn to Page 11, Col. 1

Lebanese Rebel Warns President

BEIRUT (UPI)—The rebel military commander of Beirut warned President Suleiman Franjieh Friday that he would be guilty of "negligence toward the nation" if he did not resign and hinted the army might attack the presidential palace.

Brig. Gen. Aziz Ahdab, commander of the Beirut military garrison and self-appointed "provisional military governor of Lebanon," issued the warning as the 24-hour deadline he set for Franjieh's resignation passed. The president and troops loyal to him still held out at Baabda Palace.

"After the warning by the national and corrective movement to His Excellency the president, instructing him to resign or be regarded as no longer in office, the movement now regards any further hesitiation as negligence towards the nation for which the president will bear the full consequences," Ahdab said.

Franjieh, a Christian, earlier remained adamant against resigning, terming it only "stupid talk."

Ahdab did not indicate whether his troops now intended to move against Baadba Palace, seven miles southeast of Beirut. But political observers intrepreted this as the threat behind the communique.

RUSS HOPE TO DOUBLE PRODUCTION

Caspian Caviar Makes a Comeback

BY ROBERT C. TOTH
Times Staff Writer

BAKU, Azerbaijan, U.S.S.R.—After years of falling output, the "black pearls of the Caspian"—caviar—are becoming more plentiful these days.

Two years ago a visitor was unable to buy the gray-black delicacy here on the shores of the Caspian Sea, from which virtually all caviar comes. But this year it was available, for about $5 a mouthful.

A small sign, perhaps, but it supports the claims of Soviet fish specialists who have been furiously restocking the sea with sturgeon, pushing conservation rules and cross-mating the various species of the fish to get a hybrid that matures faster. Caviar is the roe, or eggs, of sturgeon.

The director of the Sturgeon Scientific Research Institute, T. Astakhova, told the local newspaper here in January that the Caspian's sturgeon population is now about 200 million, or back to the level of the 1930s.

More than three-fourths of those fish are still too young or too small to harvest commercially, but as they mature, she predicted, caviar production will double in "the near future." World output now stands at about 350 tons annually.

Which brave soul in history first ate the gelatinous stuff—slimy to touch and a bit salty to taste—is unknown. Early Roman writings mention a fish egg delicacy, but the first clear references to caviar by name come from the 16th century—in the banquet menus of Rabelais' "Gargantua" and in Shakespeare's "Hamlet."

It had been a popular dish in Russia for many centuries, and is still eaten here with folksy abandon—smeared thick over butter on rich white bread. It became broadly accepted in Europe and America only within the last 100 years.

By that time the sturgeon—a lumbering, hideous but harmless fish, once very common in European rivers—was fast becoming a rare species. Today, some still live in the Black Sea, where they account for the small Romanian and Bulgarian caviar industry, but more than 90% of the world's sturgeon live here in the landlocked salty Caspian.

The sturgeon favor the southern shore, which is Iranian, and before the revolution, Russian entrepreneurs bought exclusive fishing rights for it there. (Iranians, for religious reasons, shun fish without scales.)

Most "Russian caviar" for years was really the Iranian product sent out under a Russian label.

A measure of the decline of Caspian sturgeon is that in the early years of this century, 40,000 tons per year was caught. By 1936 the catch fell to 21,500 tons and in 1956 it was 15,000 tons.

In recent years it has ranged as low as 11,000 tons, according to an article in "Kommunist."

The primary reason given for the decline is the dropping level of the sea itself. In the last half a century it has fallen 10 feet due to diversion of incoming river waters for irrigation and a gradual sinking bottom in places.

Please Turn to Pt. 1-A, Pg. 3

STATUS OF NATION'S BANKS EXAMINED

America's banks have weathered tough times economically in recent years but remain basically sound. Nevertheless, the recent publication of "problem lists" raises issues, some of which are discussed on Page 5 of Opinion.

- Reform Sought
- Banks Must Venture
- Secrecy May End

Los Angeles Times

LARGEST CIRCULATION IN THE WEST, 1,020,479 DAILY, 1,289,183 SUNDAY

VOL. XCV FIVE PARTS—PART ONE 78 PAGES TUESDAY, AUGUST 10, 1976 MORNING ★ FINAL DAILY 15c

Harrises Guilty of Kidnaping

Also Convicted of Holdup, Theft but Not Assault

BY JOHN HURST and WILLIAM FARR
Times Staff Writers

Symbionese Liberation Army members William and Emily Harris were both found guilty Monday of two counts of kidnaping, one count of armed robbery and two counts of auto theft by a Superior Court jury in its ninth day of deliberations.

The Harrises were acquitted of six charges of assault with a deadly weapon.

But with swarms of allegations of prejudice and misconduct surrounding the verdicts, the jury remained sequestered pending questioning of the jurors today by Superior Judge Mark Brandler.

The auto theft convictions represented a reduction by the jury from a stiffer charge of armed robbery of the automobiles.

One of the kidnaping counts also represented a reduction by the jury from the more serious charge of kidnaping for the purpose of robbery.

But the jury found that the Harrises were armed with a deadly weapon and used firearms in kidnapings and used firearms in the armed robbery.

These findings could add years to their sentences. Judge Brandler set sentencing for Aug. 30. Chief defense attorney Leonard Weinglass plans to appeal, but said the Harrises would not seek probation.

The jury reached its verdict as controversy continued to rage over possible jury prejudice and allegations by the defense of misconduct by jurors, sheriff's deputies and Brandler.

In an extraordinary decision, Brandler, after questioning one juror about the prejudice allegations, ordered the entire jury to return to court this morning for further inquiry.

After admonishing the jurors not to discuss the case with anyone prior to today's hearing and then asking the news media to wait for one more day

Please Turn to Page 3, Col. 2

Governments Cut Services to Save Funds

BY ROBERT E. DALLOS
Times Staff Writer

NEW YORK—Because the Detroit Institute of Fine Arts let go 22 of its guards, it can now open fewer than half of its 101 galleries.

In St. Louis hospitals, preventive maintenance has been stopped and repairs are done only when something breaks down.

Fairfax County, Va., will begin charging for textbooks when school opens next month.

South Dakota employes cannot travel out of state on business.

These examples illustrate an important trend sweeping the nation. Rich or poor, big or small, states, counties and cities are trimming budgets by reducing services.

Public reaction, according to officials in a number of cities, ranges from apathy to a little grumbling.

"The public is apparently beginning to accept them (cutbacks) as inevitable and necessary," said a spokesman for Wayne County, Mich.

Everything from garbage collection to fire protection, from street paving to after-school sports, is facing the ax. Many of the services being cut are things that citizens had come to take for granted.

"With the exception of a few financially untroubled cities in the South, such as Houston," said Thomas Muller, director of land use evaluation of the Urban Institute, "government officials everywhere are realizing that they must either reduce spending or increase taxes, and higher taxes are not palatable right now. So the question is: 'Where do we cut back?' "

New York City's fiscal crisis has made headlines around the country and the things its citizens are having to do without have become well-known. School days are shorter, museums and libraries have cut back hours and operations, police are making fewer arrests, and free language lessons for immigrants have been discontinued.

Residents of other communities are experiencing similar cutbacks.

In Detroit, all athletic programs will be cut out when schools open in the fall; first graders will be put on half-days (three hours), a move that educators say will have serious long-term effects on the children, and 15 schools will be closed down.

Wayne County, Mich., has eliminated a successful crime-fighting operation—the sheriff's helicopter patrol. The sheriff used to operate two helicopters to spot crimes in progress on highways and, in cities and parks. Total savings from the cut—$200,000.

In most cases it is not that fewer dollars are being spent for services but that inflation has reduced the dollar's buying power. And there are places where cutbacks were necessary in any case.

Please Turn to Page 10, Col. 1

HURRICANE BELLE—Satellite view taken at 4:30 p.m. EDT of spiraling cloud mass centered about 150 miles south of New York City. Storm was moving on the city and its Long Island suburbs.
AP Wirephoto

Hurricane Belle Hits Long Island

NEW YORK (AP)—Hurricane Belle, packing winds of 90 m.p.h., roared onto Long Island only five miles from the New York City limit this morning after sending giant waves crashing over Atlantic City's famed boardwalk.

The National Weather Service said the eye of the hurricane crossed the island of Long Beach on Long Island's southern shore at 1 a.m. Gusts of more than 80 m.p.h. lashed southern Connecticut and gale-force winds battered other areas of New England.

The season's first hurricane lost some of her punch just before landfall but still downed trees and power lines and brought heavy rains and wind that threatened low-lying areas with floods.

The National Weather Service in Boston reported that Belle's top winds had dwindled from 110 m.p.h. to 90 m.p.h. in less than four hours.

"It's gradually weakening," a forecaster there said. "It is further west than we expected and it's two or three hours behind schedule."

At least 55,000 customers were without electric power and fallen trees blocked roads as Belle hit the Connecticut coast, where most residents left their coastal homes earlier for emergency shelters.

As the hurricane drove inland, it claimed its first direct victim, a woman who was killed by a falling tree on the north shore of Long Island. She had come out with her husband to watch the storm over Long Island Sound. He was seriously injured.

The majority of the New York City area's 18 million residents escaped the full fury of the hurricane, although beset by howling winds and torrential rains. Flash-flood warnings were in effect north of the city and across the Hudson River in northern New Jersey.

Please Turn to Page 6, Col. 1

'Understanding' With Russ on A-Test Limits Revealed

BY OSWALD JOHNSTON
Times Staff Writer

WASHINGTON—Under an unpublicized "understanding" with Moscow worked out over the past two years, both the Soviet Union and the United States would be allowed to exceed the 150-kiloton limit on underground nuclear weapons tests once or twice a year, according to a Ford Administration document before the Senate.

The understanding on "mistakes," as they are officially described, amounts to a separate and, until now, confidential addendum to the Threshold Test Ban Treaty. The treaty, negotiated and signed in 1974, is awaiting Senate ratification.

Under the treaty as originally negotiated and made public two years ago, underground weapons tests over 150 kilotons in yield (equivalent to 10 times the Hiroshima bomb) would be banned.

But the "mistakes" understanding would allow each side "one or two slight, unintended breaches per year," which "would not be considered treaty violations."

The disclosure of what appeared to be a technical loophole in the treaty came after a report last week that the Russians conducted a weapons test July 4 that might have exceeded the 150-kiloton force.

News of that explosion was held closely in the Administration for weeks after it was apparent that the test might have violated an informal Soviet promise not to conduct tests above the treaty threshold during the period before the treaty was ratified and in full effect.

The "mistakes" understanding was initiated by the Russians and was described in a lengthy document sub-

Please Turn to Page 16, Col. 1

STUDENTS LAUGHED AT AMIN'S SON

Army Rape of Uganda University Told

BY DIAL TORGERSON
Times Staff Writer

NAIROBI, Kenya—Makerere University in Kampala, Uganda, once one of Africa's best schools, has been at least temporarily destroyed as a functioning institution by two attacks by President Idi Amin's troops, who reportedly killed scores of students and wounded hundreds.

The raids assertedly were ordered by Amin himself, apparently in a fury because students laughed at his son, Taban.

Students who were not jailed, hospitalized or slain have dropped from sight to escape the wrath of Amin, who also is chancellor of the university.

The toll is a closely kept secret but reliable reports now reaching Nairobi and other African capitals indicate that:

—At least 20 students were killed. One source said there were 102 bodies at the morgue at Mulago Hospital, which is surrounded by soldiers to hide the exact number of fatalities.

—At least 700, and perhaps 1,000, students were injured. Many coeds were raped. Some who resisted had their breasts slashed with bayonets. Some students were thrown off third- and fourth-floor balconies.

—An estimated 500 students were arrested.

Amin told a Swedish reporter who reached him by telephone that a British press report of the alleged massacre was "lies from beginning to end . . . everything in Uganda is peaceful," Reuters reported from Stockholm.

Information officials in Uganda referred questions to the university, where phones either were not answered or were out of order.

Events leading to the bloodshed last Tuesday and Wednesday began earlier this year.

A Kenya coed at Makerere, Esther Chesire, was arrested by security men at Entebbe Airport in February and, it is believed, later killed. Amin made a show of appointing a commission to investigate the case. Summoned before the commission in June was Therese Bukenya, a mathematics lecturer and housemother of the

Please Turn to Page 15, Col. 1

THE WEATHER

National Weather Service forecast: Low clouds night and morning hours, otherwise sunny today and Wednesday. Highs both days near 80. High Monday, 80; low, 61.

Complete weather information and smog report in Part 2, Page 2.

Mystery Disease in '74 Reported

BY HARRY NELSON
Times Medical Writer

HARRISBURG, Pa.—Nineteen cases of an illness with symptoms similar to the "Legion fever" hit persons attending a convention of the Independent Order of Odd Fellows in Philadelphia two years ago, a Center for Disease Control physician disclosed Monday.

There were three deaths among the Odd Fellows, some of whom were staying at the same hotels that housed the American Legion convention last July 21-24, according to Dr. David W. Fraser.

Fraser is in charge of 20 Center for Disease Control epidemiologic intelligence service members in Pennsylvania investigating the Legion outbreak, which has killed 27 persons and produced a flu-like illness in 128 others.

He said the Odd Fellows' outbreak came to light only recently when members of that fraternal organization alerted health officials about it after hearing of the American Legion cases. The cause of the outbreak is unknown, he said.

Please Turn to Page 17, Col. 1

FEATURE INDEX

Judge Orders Diamond Lane Project Halted

BY RAY HEBERT
Times Urban Affairs Writer

U.S. Dist. Judge Matt Byrne Monday ordered the Santa Monica Freeway's disputed Diamond Lane project halted at 7 p.m. Friday until the California Department of Transportation makes environmental studies of the project.

Caltrans has estimated such studies would take nine months to one year to complete.

"It's out of operation Friday night," the judge said.

Ruling in a case challenging the state's environmental preparations for the Diamond Lanes, he said he wanted the freeway returned to the status quo that prevailed before the project started March 15.

This means that all signs and symbols identifying the freeway's high-speed inside Diamond Lanes will be removed and all traffic—not just buses and car pools with three or more persons—will be permitted to use the lanes during peak periods.

Within four hours, as news of the judge's order spread, scores of homeward-bound motorists began using the Diamond Lanes in violation of the law. The California Highway Patrol was quoted as saying its officers would not ticket violators—those driving alone or with only one passenger in their cars.

After Byrne's ruling, Joseph Montoya, a representative of Caltrans' legal division here, said the state agency plans to ask the 9th Circuit Court of Appeals to stay the judge's order for 20 days.

But this cannot be done until Byrne formally signs the order, which he is expected to do Thursday.

However, Montoya suggested optimistically that the Diamond Lanes could remain in operation or might be shut down for a day at the most if the stay is granted.

The Caltrans attorney appeared concerned about getting a ruling on the stay as soon as possible to avoid problems in shutting down the lanes and possibly opening them again.

Such an off-and-on situation, if it should occur, would create confusion and more turmoil on the part of the freeway's regular and two-persons-to-a-car commuters, those car poolers

Please Turn to Page 3, Col. 5

RUNNING MATE RULE PROPOSED BY REAGAN AIDE

BY ROBERT SHOGAN
Times Political Writer

KANSAS CITY—In a surprise maneuver, Ronald Reagan's campaign manager Monday proposed a change in Republican convention rules to require a presidential contender to disclose his choice for a running mate before the roll is called on the presidential nomination.

The resolution offered by John P. Sears III, executive vice chairman of Citizens for Reagan, was aimed at upsetting President Ford's front-running drive to nail down his party's nomination when the convention formally opens here next week. It was promptly and resoundingly defeated by a voice vote of the Republican National Committee's rules committee, which has a heavy preponderance of Ford supporters.

Please Turn to Page 7, Col. 1

GOP SWEETNESS FLEETING

Calm Before the Storm Prevails in Kansas City

BY BILL BOYARSKY
Times Political Writer

KANSAS CITY—The days ahead, the Republican national chairman said, require "a deep sense of understanding and a spirit of cooperation. God bless you."

Mary Louise Smith, the chairman, looks and talks like the president of a women's club—the sedate kind of club that was more popular in the days before the women's movement.

Tall, thin and usually smiling, she was dressed in a brown jumper and a high-necked light brown blouse Monday as she opened a meeting of the Republican National Committee's rules committee.

In a week, the GOP National Convention would open. Monday the party leaders were on the scene for preliminary meetings. The rules committee met at the Continental Hotel, an old structure not far from a row of tawdry go-go bars.

All day Sunday, the politicians and the reporters had arrived at Kansas City International Airport. The politicians lined up for baggage and rental cars, greeting each other like fraternity boys returning to school after summer vacation.

Monday they began work on a platform and complicated party rules —and it quickly became evident that Mrs. Smith's pleasant words would have no effect on a political party that is in Kansas City for a fight.

This is a party struggling for survival after Watergate and more than a decade of fierce division between

Please Turn to Page 8, Col. 1

Los Angeles Times

LARGEST CIRCULATION IN THE WEST, 1,020,479 DAILY, 1,289,183 SUNDAY

VOL. XCV | SIX PARTS—PART ONE | 130 PAGES | THURSDAY, SEPTEMBER 9, 1976 | MORNING ★ FINAL | DAILY 15c

MAO TSE-TUNG DIES

China's Party Chairman, 82, Ill Several Months

TOKYO (AP)—Mao Tse-tung died today, the official Chinese news agency Hsinhua announced. Hsinhua said the chairman of the Chihese Communist Party died about 16 hours before the announcement, at 12:10 a.m. Peking time.

He was 82 and had been in failing health for many months.

Hsinhua said Mao's death was due to "the worsening of his illness and despite all treatment, although meticulous medical care was given him in every way after he fell ill."

The nature of Mao's final illness was not announced. He stopped receiving visiting foreigners in June although Chinese officials continued to say that he remained busy with affairs of state.

Only last week Hsinhua said a conference of earthquake relief workers was held in Peking under his "attention."

Mao Tse-tung in 1972
AP Wirephoto

His death was expected to intensify the power struggle that has been under way in Peking for years and that has been waged with new intensity in the eight months since Premier Chou En-lai died.

There has been no indication of who would succeed the acknowledged supreme leader of the People's Republic of China since it was founded on Oct. 1, 1949.

Apparently the next man in line is Premier Hau Kuo-feng, who was named both premier and first vice chairman of the Communist Party only five months ago.

That development came in the latest of Mao's many battles against opponents of his policy of continual revolution to do away with all vestiges of capitalism and the bourgeois class in China. Hua was elevated over First Vice Premier Teng Hsiao-ping, who foreign observers had considered certain to succeed Chou. Instead, he was fired—by Mao, according to Peking's official announcements—and accused to trying to restore capitalism in China.

Mao was a soldier, classical poet, historian and Marxist philosopher who placed his faith in China's peasants. A peasant's son himself, he put them in the vanguard of the Chinese Communist revolution.

His armies, raised and operating from rural bases, crushed the Nationalist forces of Generalissimo Chiang Kai-shek in the bloody civil war, clearing the way for the proclamation of 1949 of the Chinese People's Republic.

In the tumultuous years which followed, Mao continued to build on the peasant base, pouring 500 million of

Please Turn to Page 31, Col. 3

CHEMICALS

Where Does Benefit End, Risk Begin?

BY ROBERT GILLETTE
Times Science Writer

Julian P. Heicklen, a professor of chemistry at Pennsylvania State University, thinks he has a better idea.

Rather than obliging consumers to spend billions of dollars on automotive pollution controls, Heicklen proposes that American cities spend a few hundred million dollars each year to fumigate the urban air with a chemical that prevents formation of smog.

The chemical Heicklin has in mind is diethylhydroxylamine, or DEHA, a volatile industrial liquid used mainly in synthesizing rubber.

During the last three years, Heicklin's experiments have shown that DEHA "scavenges" the short-lived fragments of molecules called free radicals that propel the airborne chemistry of smog. DEHA, at least in the laboratory, thereby interrupts the chemical chain reaction that muddies the air.

Heicklen predicts that merely by spraying 20,000 or so gallons of the liquid over the entire Los Angeles basin every day during the smoggiest months, there would no longer be smoggy months in Los Angeles. Other cities, he says, would require less-intensive fumigation.

Needless to say, the idea has met with some skepticism from other environmental scientists.

"Some of them just go bananas when you mention the idea," Heicklen said. "They cannot discuss it rationally. It's as if I'm in league with the devil, that I'm going to poison us all."

Bizarre as the idea may sound, it is a serious proposal from a respected chemist. And for all anyone knows, it might actually work. But an unfortunate flaw has emerged:

When rats were exposed to high levels of DEHA, some developed thyroid abnormalities while others produced a breakdown product in their urine that is known from laboratory tests to cause genetic damage.

"It's a very serious problem and it may eliminate DEHA from consideration," Heicklen said with a sigh.

Safer chemicals may be found, though. And he adds that the risks may be small when measured against the benefits of clean air and splendid views of the mountains: "There are always tradeoffs in these things."

In a way, Heicklen's tradeoff is a symbol of an age of technological risk and benefit. Often the two not only are interlocked but are nearly impossible to measure.

This point was made time and again as several thousand chemists and engineers trooped into a meeting

Please Turn to Page 26, Col. 1

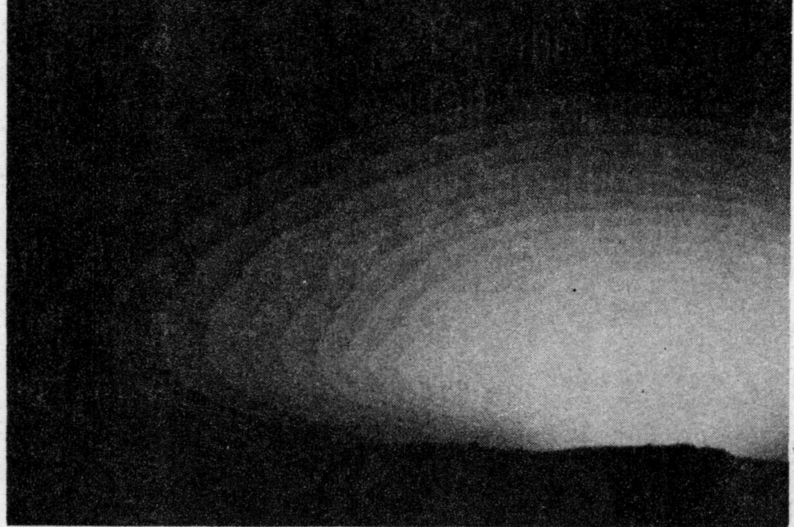

SUNSET ON MARS—This view of the sun sinking below Mars' horizon was photographed by Viking 1. Wavy effect is the result of light striking particles in the planet's atmosphere.
AP Wirephoto

Ford Counts on 'Big State' Strategy to Defeat Carter

BY RICHARD BERGHOLZ
Times Political Writer

WASHINGTON—In the inner sanctum of the President Ford Committee, behind all of the public relations doublespeak indigenous to campaigning, the cold-eyed view of the next 54 days is:

"We're behind, but we can win it. More than that, Jimmy Carter can lose it."

The consensus of the key men who plan and carry out the President's drive for a Nov. 2 election victory is based, they say, on field reports from staff workers throughout the country and on extensive polling by professionals William Teeter and Richard Wirthlin.

This is what the Ford campaign strategy is based on:

The eight key states where polling has been completed—New York, New Jersey, Pennsylvania, Ohio, Michigan, Indiana, Illinois and Wisconsin—all are adjudged "winnable" and it is entirely reasonable to expect Ford to "do well" in the entire group.

(When it comes to defining what constitutes "doing well," the Ford strategists say that is a tightly held secret and they will not divulge how many of the eight states must be won to reach their real expectations.)

In the three big states where polling has not yet been completed—California, Texas and Florida—Ford has a "fighting chance."

Those 11 states account for 269 electoral votes. It takes 270 to win. Neither man is going to win all 11, the Ford people believe.

After those 11 states are accounted for, there remain 39 states and the District of Columbia, and it is out of this group that the figures come that are used by the Ford campaigners to make up their campaign strategy.

What it amounts to, said Stuart Spencer, deputy campaign committee chairman and head of the political

Please Turn to Page 11, Col. 1

Charge Against Dole in Error

WASHINGTON (AP)—Claude Wild Jr., the former Gulf Oil Corp. lobbyist who is a central figure in a federal investigation of illegal campaign contributions, said Wednesday that he erred in claiming he gave $2,000 in 1970 to Sen. Robert J. Dole, the Republican vice presidential candidate.

Wild apologized to Dole and repudiated his earlier statement that he had given Dole the money from a legal Gulf "good government" fund in 1970 to pass on to other GOP Senate candidates.

"I have been in error and consequently have done a serious disservice to Sen. Dole," Wild said.

Dole accepted Wild's explanation, calling the matter "an unfortunate incident." And, he added, "We're moving ahead with the campaign."

Wild's statement did not mention a second, potentially more serious, allegation concerning the question of whether Dole received illegal Gulf funds in 1973 through Senate Minority Leader Hugh Scott of Pennsylvania.

Please Turn to Page 10, Col. 1

New Aviation Policy Aims at Reduced Fares

BY ROBERT A. ROSENBLATT
Times Staff Writer

WASHINGTON—The Ford Administration Wednesday issued a new international aviation policy calling for cheaper charter flights to foreign countries and for the abandonment of unprofitable routes by U.S. airlines.

Without naming Pan American World Airways, Inc., the Administration statement also suggested that U.S.-based international carriers be given permission to fly some domestic routes. Pan Am, suffering severe financial problems, would be the prime beneficiary of such a change in government policy.

The "old rhetoric" requiring competition among several U.S. carriers on the same route must be changed, Secretary of Transportation William T. Coleman Jr. told a news conference. "There may already be 10 foreign competitors on the route."

Rather than force U.S. carriers to fight each other for the same foreign market, Coleman said, the airlines should be encouraged to drop unprofitable routes.

If a particular route is vital to the national interest, service should be supported with a direct subsidy, according to the new Administration policy. This would reverse the traditional system under which airlines are expected to use profitable routes to subsidize the cost of service that runs a deficit.

A variety of proposals were contained in the 31-page document issued by President Ford, the first comprehensive statement of international aviation policy since 1970. Coleman and Charles W. Robinson, deputy secretary of state, discussed the new policies at a crowded press briefing.

The Civil Aeronautics Board regulates the airline industry. Policies outlined Wednesday will become the Administration's official position in arguments before the CAB and in ne-

Please Turn to Page 12, Col. 1

Conferees Tentatively Increase Minimum Tax

BY PAUL E. STEIGER
Times Staff Writer

WASHINGTON—Reacting to growing resentment to the use of income tax loopholes by the rich, a House-Senate conference committee tentatively agreed Wednesday to increase tax collections from 300,000 of the nation's wealthiest households by more than $1.2 billion a year.

The conferees did so by tentatively voting to curtail tax shelters used by

The Senate voted to end automatic cost-of-living increases for federal retirees. Part 1, Page 5.

investors in the entertainment, oil and gas, and sports industries, and to expand and increase the present so-called 10% minimum tax.

Tax shelters are investments set up to generate artificial losses through accounting devices. These paper losses are then subtracted from other income to reduce the amount on which taxes are paid.

The 10% minimum income tax, first enacted in 1969, was intended to assure that nearly all citizens above the poverty line pay at least some taxes every year. The conferees voted to move closer to this goal by widening its coverage and raising the rate to 15%.

These actions, which came as the conferees moved into the final stages of resolving differences between House and Senate versions of the measure, sharply increased the chances that the big bill ultimately will become law.

The committee adjourned late Wednesday. It was expected to finish action on the measure today.

Liberals had complained that the Senate version of the bill, in particu-

Please Turn to Page 15, Col. 1

FROM QUIET ANGER TO FAMILIAR SMILE

Trip North Reveals Insights Into Carter

BY BILL BOYARSKY
Times Political Writer

PITTSBURGH—Jimmy Carter stood in front of the old bookbinding plant with nobody around to shake his hand.

The Democratic presidential candidate loves to shake workers' hands in front of factories early in the morning. It gives him a feeling of contact with the people and he thinks it also gets him votes.

But this time, in Scranton, east of here, his staff had chosen a plant that does not have many employes. Besides, there were so many cameramen and reporters around Carter that it was difficult for anyone else to reach him. And his aides had placed him and some local candidates behind a barricade.

Carter turned to Greg Schneiders, one of his top assistants, and, in the icy manner he has when angry, said, "Greg, what are you suggesting we do?"

Schneiders and an assistant press secretary, Rex Granum, tried to explain it was an attempt to have the workers reach Carter in an orderly manner.

Carter pointed out the obvious: "Nobody's coming through."

Finally, disgusted with what he obviously considered the incompetence of his crew, the old Navy submarine officer took command of the operation himself.

"Come on through," Carter said to the workers, gesturing for them to walk by. "Work your way through."

It succeeded and things finally started going well.

It was an example of some of the foulups in a campaign swing through industrial Pennsylvania. There were good moments, too. The incident showed the strengths and weaknesses in Carter's effort to capture the important state of Pennsylvania.

The trip also showed something about Carter—about how he gets quietly furious on bad days and how he can quickly change into the familiar smiling Georgia country boy at the first sign of success.

The first day, in Philadelphia, was mixed. Philadelphia had never been Carter's town. It was a weak spot in his successful Pennsylvania primary campaign in April. The maverick Democratic mayor, Frank Rizzo, who has control of the local machine, opposed him then.

The archdiocese had insisted that abortion be a major part of a discussion Carter was to have in a Catholic church with community groups. Car-

Please Turn to Page 14, Col. 1

THE WEATHER

National Weather Service forecast: Considerable cloudiness today and Friday with a slight chance of showers and isolated thundershowers. Highs both days near 87. High Wednesday 92; low, 70.

Complete weather information and smog forecast in Part 2, Page 4.

FEATURE INDEX

Team Inspecting Pipeline Was Misled, Report Says

BY RICHARD T. COOPER
Times Staff Writer

WASHINGTON—A special government fact-finding team that visited the Alaska pipeline last July to check on complaints of continued environmental and construction problems was given a highly misleading impression of prevailing conditions, House investigators charged Wednesday.

Whereas the high-level government officials were shown a bustling work site at which quality-control activity was vigorous and special precautions were being taken to protect weather-sensitive welding operations, actual conditions on most of the 800-mile-long project are quite different, the investigators contended.

Instead of moving ahead on schedule and in compliance with federal quality standards, they asserted, the pipeline continues to be plagued by work-stoppages, breakdowns and substandard construction that threaten to delay completion of the line by as much as a year.

The pipeline, which is eventually to carry about 2 million barrels of crude oil a day from the Prudhoe Bay oil field on Alaska's North Slope to a shipping terminal at Valdez, is now scheduled for completion in mid-1977.

Both federal officials and executives of the Alyeska Pipeline Service Co., the consortium of major oil companies which is building the line, vehemently denied the charges, which are contained in a staff report of the House energy and power subcommittee of the Committee on Interstate and Foreign Commerce.

Kent Frizzell, undersecretary of the Department of the Interior, which shares government responsibility for the pipeline with the Department of Transportation, said the report "is full of conjecture, unsub-

Please Turn to Page 18, Col. 1

Los Angeles Times

LARGEST CIRCULATION IN THE WEST, 1,020,479 DAILY, 1,289,183 SUNDAY

VOL. XCV SEVEN PARTS—PART ONE 110 PAGES WEDNESDAY MORNING, NOVEMBER 3, 1976 CC †† DAILY 15c

CARTER IS VICTOR IN TIGHT RACE

Hayakawa in Early Lead; Prop. 13 and 14 Losing

DOWN TO THE WIRE—Jimmy Carter talks with brother Billy in the Carter peanut warehouse in Plains. Right, President and Mrs. Ford arrive at the White House after voting in Grand Rapids.
AP Wirephotos

Senate Seat Hanging in the Balance

BY TOM GOFF
Times Sacramento Bureau Chief

Aging semanticist S.I. Hayakawa took an early lead Tuesday in his fight to unseat Democratic U.S. Sen. John V. Tunney but a computerized sampling of Californians as they left the polls indicated Tunney would win reelection.

With about 6% of the vote counted, Hayakawa, the Republican candidate, was running ahead of Tunney by about 53% to 44%. Minor candidates were picking up about 3% of the vote.

The early returns were heavy with absentee ballots, however, and absentee voters traditionally favor Republican candidates.

And with 95% of the vote still to be counted it was far too early even to establish a trend.

The computerized sampling of voters, conducted by NBC and the Los Angeles Times, found that Tunney was running, in that sample, ahead of Hayakawa by about the same ratio that the challenger was leading in the very early vote count.

Although no projections were made, the indications were that Tunney should win the election by about that ratio.

Both candidates were highly optimistic as the long vote count began.

Tunney, who awaited the results surrounded by campaign aides and contributors in a 12th floor suite at the Hyatt Airport Hotel, was not even deterred by the early tallies—mostly absentee voters—which showed Hayakawa leading by a narrow margin.

"That's good for us," he told a reporter, "because Republicans tend to be absent more when they vote."

Tunney has been predicting he would win by at least 8%. Tuesday night he said he would "settle right now for 1%."

"I must say," he commented, "that no matter how well you're doing, there's a sense of anxiety . . . Maybe I'm superstitious but I don't like to feel elated."

Hayakawa, who awaited the results with his wife in a suite at the Century Plaza Hotel, declared as the polls closed that the heavy turnout of voters "is not going to hurt me one bit."

"The more they turn out," he told a reporter, "the better it looks because I have a very strong following

Please Turn to Page 3, Col. 3

Edition-Time Returns

NATIONAL

PRESIDENT

	Vote	%
Carter	35,399,937	51
Ford	33,338,442	48

STATEWIDE

PRESIDENT

24,440 Pcts.; Rptg. 14,796

	Vote	%
Carter	2,301,532	50
Ford	2,241,237	48
SENATE		
Tunney	2,125,314	49
Hayakawa	2,122,228	49
Prop. 13—Greyhound racing		
No	3,377,428	75
Yes	1,106,283	25
Prop. 14—Farm labor relations		
No	2,762,896	61
Yes	1,758,488	39

COUNTYWIDE

PRESIDENT

7,981 Pcts.; Rptg. 6,034

	Vote	%
Carter	916,081	50
Ford	870,863	48
SENATE		
Tunney	791,412	51
Hayakawa	736,228	47
Prop. 13—Greyhound racing		
No	666,126	75
Yes	220,765	25
Prop. 14—Farm labor relations		
No	498,331	56
Yes	392,780	44
County Mayor—A		
No	458,698	57
Yes	346,306	43

Captures Electoral Vote Lead

BULLETIN

Jimmy Carter was elected President in a close race with Gerald Ford Tuesday and will become the first President from the Deep South since Zachary Taylor's election in 1848.

BY JACK NELSON
Times Washington Bureau Chief

Jimmy Carter swept the South Tuesday and won key victories in border states and the Northeast as he closed in on the 270 electoral votes needed to defeat President Ford.

Most tabulations showed Carter near the magic number. By 10 p.m. PST almost all counts showed him well over 200 electoral votes—CBS with 267, NBC with 235. CBS gave Ford 71 electoral votes, NBC 126.

Ford had hoped to cut into Carter's Southern base but managed to carry only Virginia out of the 11 states of the old Confederacy. Nationwide, Ford trailed the Democratic former governor of Georgia badly, not only in electoral votes but by about 1.5 million in the popular vote.

Carter's chances of winning were boosted by an unusually heavy turnout that disproved forecasts of widespread voter apathy.

The Republican President clung to the hope that final returns in some states with large numbers of electoral votes might yet salvage a victory. However, Carter was ahead with 22% of the vote counted in California, which has the nation's highest number of electoral votes—45.

Late Tuesday night James A. Baker, Ford's campaign director, expressed disappointment that the President had failed to crack the South. He said the President would need three out of four key states—Michigan, Ohio, Texas and Pennsylvania—to win.

Shortly after Baker spoke, Carter was projected as the winner in Pennsylvania.

Patrick Caddell, Carter's chief pollster, said, "We've won it—I think."

Ford, watching returns at the White House, reportedly had lost his voice in heavy campaigning in recent days. The mood at the White House was described as less than joyous.

At the same time, Carter and his aides were highly optimistic.

Carter's lead, beginning with the first Southern returns, grew steadily throughout the night.

Besides being established the early winner in the South, by 10:15 p.m. PST he had been declared the winner by most tabulations in Delaware, the District of Columbia, Kentucky, Maryland, Massachussetts, New York, Rhode Island, West Virginia, Wisconsin and Pennsylvania.

He was leading in enough other states to go over the 270 electoral vote total if the leads held up, according to both the Associated Press and United Press International.

In piling up his margin, Carter benefited from an unusually high degree of Democratic solidarity.

The NBC/Los Angeles Times poll of more than 15,000 persons after they had voted Tuesday showed that

Please Turn to Page 16, Col. 1

Carter Orders Aide to Ready Victory Speech

BY KENNETH REICH
Times Political Writer

ATLANTA—Jimmy Carter ordered his speech writer, Pat Anderson, to prepare a victory statement Tuesday night, but concern was evident among some Carter workers as victory in the big Northern states remained tantalizingly out of reach with midnight approaching.

Carter was ensconced in his 15th-floor suite at the Omni International Hotel in downtown Atlanta watching the returns and greeting friends. Across the street a capacity crowd of 25,000 persons awaited his eventual appearance in a trade center.

Earlier, as he flew into Atlanta from south Georgia, Carter had talked with reporters as if he were already a winner.

He spoke about how he would go about choosing a Cabinet and he criticized major polls for "taking a dive" by calling the race between him and President Ford too close to call.

Carter was apparently encouraged by advance information on a network poll of voters leaving polling places that showed him running ahead.

At the beginning of the evening, Carter aides were talking about returning to Carter's hometown of Plains and a big victory celebration there fairly early.

But as the night wore on, the big states remained close and a faint gloom and exasperation began to permeate the Carter ranks. There was some talk even that Ford could win the electoral college while losing the popular vote, and Carter could

Please Turn to Page 9, Col. 1

Dog Racing, Farm Labor Issues Appear Defeated

Early Returns Show Greyhound Proposal Losing by More Than 3-1, Union Initiative by Almost 2-1

BY WILLIAM ENDICOTT
Times Staff Writer

California voters Tuesday were overwhelmingly rejecting a controversial proposal to legalize pari-mutuel betting on greyhound racing and appeared to be defeating a bitterly disputed farm labor initiative sponsored by Cesar Chavez.

Early returns showed the greyhound racing measure going down to defeat by more than a 3-1 margin and the farm labor initiative losing by almost 2 to 1.

Although Californians decided Tuesday on 15 ballot measures, most of the interest was reserved for just those two.

Proposition 14, the farm labor measure, was by far the most emotional issue on the ballot. It pitted growers against Chavez and his United Farm Workers of America.

It also was viewed as a test of the continuing popularity of Gov. Brown, who endorsed the measure and, through an expensive advertising campaign, pleaded with Californians to vote for it.

Essentially, the measure would rewrite the state's 1975 farm labor law, which guaranteed farm workers the right to secret ballot union elections, and it would prohibit changes without another vote of the people.

The effect would be to take the farm labor issue largely out of the hands of the Legislature. Indeed, the initiative was drafted in a reaction to this year's six-month legislative deadlock over funding for the state Agricultural Labor Relations Board.

Most of the growers' fury was directed at a so-called access rule which now is an administrative regulation of the board.

Under terms of the initiative, the rule, which permits union organizers to enter farms without growers' permission, would become a permanent part of the law.

The growers portrayed the rule as a violation of property rights, and their well-financed campaign was based on the slogan "Protect Property Rights."

The campaign was fought on many fronts, including the presidential campaign trail. Democratic nominee Jimmy Carter endorsed Proposition 14. President Ford took no position, but his running mate, Sen. Robert J. Dole, said he was against it.

Brown, who guided the landmark 1975 law through the Legislature, said the initiative would bring stability to the tense and bitter issue of

Please Turn to Page 18, Col. 1

LINEUP BY PARTY IN NEW CONGRESS

BY UNITED PRESS INTERNATIONAL

The preliminary standings of the 95th Congress.

SENATE—51 necessary for control.

	Rep.	Dem.	Other
Elected	9	19	1
Leading	2	2	0
Holdovers	26	41	0
New total	37	62	1
Present	38	61	1

Reps. won 5 Dem. seats, leading for 2 Dem. seats.

Dems. won 6 Rep. seats, leading for 1 Rep. seats.

HOUSE—218 necessary for control.

	Rep.	Dem.	Other
Elected	111	241	0
Leading	36	44	0
New total	147	285	0
Present	145	290	0

Reps. won 7 Dem. seats, leading for 8 Dem. seats.

Dems. won 4 Rep. seats, leading for 5 Rep. seats.

A Tired Ford Has Dinner With Family and Friends

BY RUDY ABRAMSON
Times Staff Writer

WASHINGTON—As the Eastern polls began closing Tuesday night, bringing Gerald R. Ford within hours of a verdict on his tenure in the White House, the tired candidate had a quiet dinner with persons who had shared his race to catch Jimmy Carter.

He had come back from the hustings, back from a sentimental journey home just in time to catch an hour's sleep and do some paper work in the Oval Office before settling back with the rest of the country to see finally what had happened in American politics this fall.

Far up Connecticut Ave., north from the White House, the Washington Republican establishment gathered in a large hotel ballroom to party and await the returns, knowing they would not see their leader until the outcome was certain—one way or the other.

The White House was strangely still, considering the Presidency was at stake on the chilly night. Most of the staff had gone to the uptown party to watch the returns. A few television crews puttered with their equipment under an elm tree on the lawn.

About 7:30 p.m.—well after dark—vice presidential nominee Robert J. Dole and his wife Elizabeth were chauffered through the southwest gate and around to the south portico.

In the residence wing of the mansion, they joined the Fords, former Democratic Rep. Edith Green, and Mr. and Mrs. Joe Garagiola for dinner.

After dinner, the group, which also

Please Turn to Page 13, Col. 5

FEATURE INDEX

County Mayor Proposal Trails

First Returns Show Reform Plans Losing

BY BRUCE KEPPEL
Times Staff Writer

Los Angeles County voters were deciding Tuesday whether to rewrite significantly their 64-year-old government Charter.

The major issues on which the county's cost-conscious voters cast their ballots: and the first, very sketchy returns:

—Proposition A, which would create an elected county mayor to exercise the executive powers now held by the five-member Board of Supervisors: Trailing.

—Proposition B, which would increase the membership of the legislative Board of Supervisors to nine (and take effect only if the county mayor proposal also was adopted): Trailing:

—Proposition F, which would carve Canyon County out of Los Angeles County's northwest triangle. (It required majority votes in both the

Please Turn to Page 18, Col. 1

THE WEATHER

National Weather Service forecast: Sunny today and Thursday with highs today in the mid 90s and Thursday in the low 90s. High Tuesday 94; low, 62.

Complete weather information and smog forecast in in Part 3, Page 9.

Democrats Keep Control of Senate

Hartke, McGee, Moss, Montoya, Buckley Out

BY JOHN H. AVERILL
Times Staff Writer

WASHINGTON—Despite the loss of four veteran incumbents, the Democrats easily retained their 22-year domination of the U.S. Senate in Tuesday's elections.

They appeared certain to maintain, if not increase, their current 62-38 margin in the upper chamber of Congress.

In balloting that produced unusually heavy casualties among senators of both parties, at least seven incumbents were defeated.

The losers included Democratic veterans Vance Hartke of Indiana, Gale W. McGee of Wyoming, Joseph M. Montoya of New Mexico and Frank E. Moss of Utah. Also defeated were Republican Sens. J. Glenn Beall Jr. of Maryland and William E. Brock III of Tennessee and Sen. James L. Buckley (R-Cons. N.Y.), each of whom was seeking a second six-year term.

Buckley's New York race against Democrat Daniel P. Moynihan captured national attention. A soft-spo-

Please Turn to Page 11, Col. 1

KEY RACES AT GLANCE

How the top candidates and issues fared in Tuesday's election:

—Sen. Vance Hartke (D-Ind.), seeking a fourth term, was defeated by Republican Richard Lugar, a former mayor of Indianapolis.

—Sen. Joseph M. Montoya (D-N.M.) was defeated by Republican Jack Schmitt, a former astronaut who went to the moon in 1972.

—Sen. William E. Brock (R-Tenn.) lost to Democrat James Sasser, a former Tennessee state Democratic chairman.

—Sen. James L. Buckley of New York, a Conservative-Republican, was defeated by Democrat Daniel P. Moynihan, former ambassador to the U.N.

—John D. Rockefeller IV, a Democrat and nephew of the Vice President, was elected governor of West Virginia, defeating ex-Gov. Cecil H. Underwood.

—Republican James Thompson was elected governor of Illinois, defeating Michael Howlett, Chicago Mayor Richard Daley's hand-picked candidate.

—Sen. Harry F. Byrd Jr. of Virginia, an independent, defeated Democrat Elmo R. Zumwalt, a former chief of naval operations.

—Democrat Dixy Lee Ray, former chairman of the Atomic Energy Commission, was elected governor of Washington, defeating Republican John Spellman.

—A proposal to allow casino gambling in Atlantic City, N.J., was approved by New Jersey voters.

—Sen. Gale W. McGee (D-Wyo.) was defeated by Republican Malcolm Wallop.

—Sen. Frank E. Moss (D-Utah) was defeated by Republican Orrin G. Hatch.

—Rep. Allan T. Howe (D-Utah), who was convicted of trying to buy sexual favors from decoy policemen, lost to Republican Dan Marriott.

Los Angeles Times

LARGEST CIRCULATION IN THE WEST, 1,020,479 DAILY, 1,289,183 SUNDAY

VOL. XCVI | FOUR PARTS—PART ONE | 82 PAGES | SATURDAY, DECEMBER 18, 1976 | MORNING ★ FINAL | DAILY 15c

BLAST RIPS OIL TANKER

At Least 5 Killed, 50 Hurt in L.A. Harbor Explosion

SHATTERED VESSEL—Oil tanker Sansinena was ripped in two by blast at Los Angeles Harbor. Bow juts from water at left of photo. The stern section, at right, is illuminated by helicopter searchlight. Coast Guard cutter is stationed near tanker's bow.

Times photo by Jack Gaunt

Windows Shattered as Far Away as 21 Miles

BY RICHARD WEST
Times Staff Writer

An 810-foot tanker blew up at Los Angeles Harbor Friday night, hurling crewmen into the water and then sending a carpet of flaming fuel oil rolling over their bobbing heads.

Five men were killed—bits and pieces of two of the bodies showered down on a dock—and 50 other persons, including 25 civilians were burned or injured by the explosion which shook Southern California coastal areas with the intensity of an earthquake.

The survivors were brought to seven harbor area hospitals with their bodies covered with oil. Nurses swabbed off the goo with towels soaked in acetone to get at the burns and injuries.

The explosion was so tremendous that it broke the 70,000-ton Sansinena in half, shoving the fore and aft sections 150 feet apart, and heaved the entire superstructure of the vessel up on the dock in San Pedro.

The blast at 7:40 p.m. was felt as far away as Dana Point, 45 miles to the south. It broke windows in Costa Mesa, 21 miles away, and rattled dwellings in Glendale and the Hollywood Hills.

Flames from the burning Sansinena, a Liberian-registered vessel under charter to the Union Oil Co., at one time shot more than 1,000 feet into the air.

They were fed by 20,000 barrels of bunker fuel oil which the ship had just taken aboard at Pier 46 and what was left of 507,000 barrels of light crude oil the ship had been unloading since Thursday morning.

The fire was contained at 11 p.m. Friday.

The Coast Guard reported a few minutes after the blast: "She's completely engulfed in flames except in the fantail. We're taking people off there. There are people in the water."

Firemen, Coast Guardsmen, county lifeguards and other rescue workers arriving at the scene found the vessel a roaring inferno with both the bow and the stern sticking 40 feet up the air.

Some of the survivors were taken off at the stern while others were plucked from the water by rescue craft which braved waves and swells of burning oil to get to them.

Teams of divers will be sent down today to search the hulk for more bodies.

Gaylee Hermosillo, a nurse who lives in the harbor area and rushed to the scene to see if she could help, said she counted 23 men pulled from the water by Coast Guard and county lifeguard boat crews.

"We saw a flash and came straight down," Mrs. Hermosillo said. "It was like a mushroom . . . flames hundreds of feet in the air."

Another man who arrived in the area shortly after the blast said he saw a body that had been blown apart lying on the dock.

Please Turn to Page 26, Col. 1

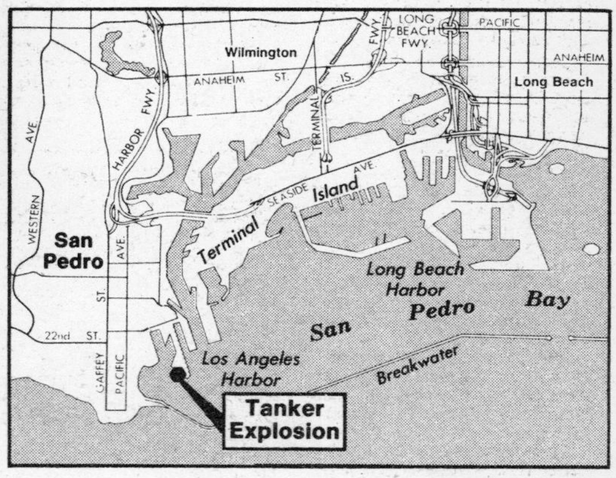

Times map by Don Clement

FALLING METAL—About 20 minutes after blast, part of ship's structure, top left, collapses.

Times photo by Bart Everett

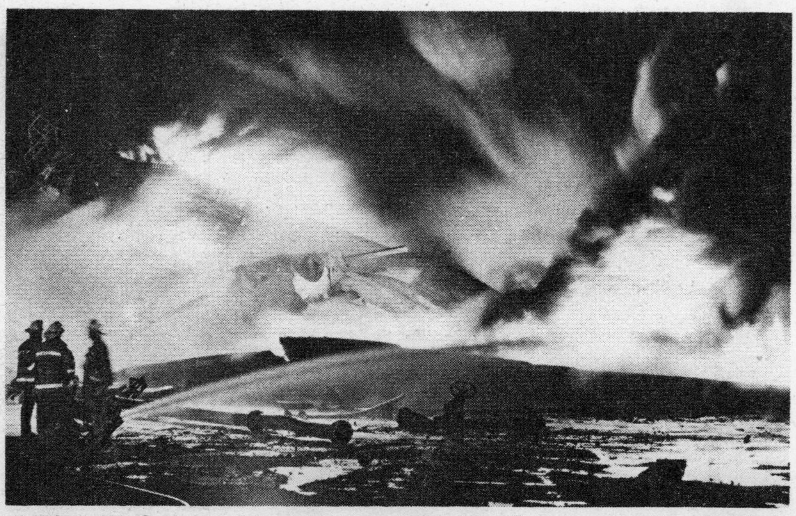

HARBOR INFERNO—Sheets of flame light sky as tanker burns. Firemen pour water on the inferno.

Times photo by Robert Lachman

SEASONAL SPURT

Bank Robbers Get Busy at Christmastime

BY JOHN A. JONES
Times Staff Writer

Right behind Santa's helpers with their jingling bells and curbside collection boxes comes the not-so-merry jingle of another seasonal money-raising effort: bank robberies are on the rise again.

It always gets worse around the holidays, bank officials say. And for reasons they can't pin down, it seems worse than ever in California, especially in the Los Angeles area.

Bank robberies have been declining nationwide during the last two years, according to FBI statistics. The FBI counted 1,837 robberies at commercial banks, mutual savings banks, savings and loan associations and credit unions in the six months ended last June 30. That was down from 1,977 in the previous six months and from 2,203 in the first half of 1975.

But California did not join that trend. The state had 535 robberies in the first half of this year, up from 406 in the first half of 1975.

"California is the bank robbery capital of the world," said Charles Kneller, a former Glendale deputy police chief who now works as chief security officer for the Glendale Federal Savings & Loan Assn.

It is not so much the Bonnie and Clyde type of operation, with hoodlums taking over a bank branch and cleaning out the tellers plus the vault. Mostly it's a lone, not-too-bright bandit who points a gun—or a toy gun, or just pretends to have a gun—at one teller and leaves with a few hundred dollars and less than one chance in five of getting away with it.

He is almost certain to leave behind a high-quality photographic portrait

Please Turn to Page 28, Col. 1

THE WEATHER

National Weather Service forecast: Fair today and Sunday with local fog early today and tonight. Highs both days in the mid 60s. High Friday 76; low 51.

Complete weather information and smog forecast in Part 3, Page 11.

Oil Price Rise Will Hold at 5%, Saudi Official Says

BY JOE ALEX MORRIS JR.
Times Staff Writer

DOHA, Qatar—The price of oil will increase by only 5% on Jan. 1, Saudi Arabia's Oil Minister Ahmed Zaki Yamani predicted Friday. This was the amount demanded—and set—by

U.S. economists believe the two-price oil formula arrived at by the oil cartel will not work. Part 1, Page 14.

Saudi Arabia, the biggest producer in the international petroleum exporting cartel, during a dramatic and tension-filled ministerial meeting here.

Eleven of the 13 members of the Organization of Petroleum Exporting Countries challenged Saudi dominance of the organization and raised their prices by 10.4% effective Jan. 1 and another 5% effective July 1.

President Ford and President-elect Jimmy Carter praised Saudi Arabia and the United Arab Emirates for holding their increases to 5%. Ford said the action by the 11 other OPEC members ignored their responsibility to the "plight of the world's poorest societies."

Carter withheld comment on the 10.4% increase and confined himself to thanking the Saudis.

Yamani was confident that Saudi Arabia's dominant position, plus internal divisions within the majority faction, eventually would force their prices down. "I think the increase in the world price of crude oil won't be more than 5%," he said.

To force the Saudi price upon the others, Yamani revealed that his country will increase production. Until now, Saudi Arabia has limited its

Please Turn to Page 22, Col. 1

FEATURE INDEX

Los Angeles Times

LARGEST CIRCULATION IN THE WEST, 1,020,479 DAILY, 1,289,183 SUNDAY

VOL. XCVI FIVE PARTS—PART ONE 76 PAGES MONDAY, MARCH 28, 1977 MORNING ★ FINAL DAILY 15c

JUMBO JET DISASTER

550 Die as 747s Collide on Runway

HOLOCAUST—Fireman directs water at the burning wreckage of a 747 jet in the Canary Islands in one frame of CBS television film. AP Wirephoto

304 Californians Aboard as Pan Am, KLM Planes Crash in Canary Islands

From Times Wire Services

SANTA CRUZ DE TENERIFE, Spain—Two Boeing 747 jumbo jets flown by Pan American World Airways and KLM Royal Dutch Airlines collided and burned Sunday on a foggy airport runway in the Canary Islands, killing as many as 550 people in the worst disaster in aviation history.

All 249 passengers and crew aboard the KLM plane were killed, KLM President Sergio Orlandini said in Amsterdam.

Latest reports indicated at least 300 died aboard the Pan American 747, which was a charter flight originating in Los Angeles where all but 14 of its passengers boarded Saturday. The other passengers boarded in New York. The Pan Am jet carried 378 passengers and 16 crew members. A total of 304 of the passengers were from California. All the passengers aboard the Pan Am plane were to board a ship in Las Palmas for a 12-day cruise of the Mediterranean.

The death toll on the Pan Am 747 was not officially confirmed.

The Spanish news agency Cifra quoted Santa Cruz airport officials as saying a total of 570 persons died.

Police and medical workers worked in stormy weather today recovering the remains of the victims and trying to identify them. Corpses were being piled in an airport hangar. Police, soldiers and firemen had recovered 522 bodies Sunday.

The Civil Guard said this morning a final toll would not be available for several hours. "The bad weather is slowing things down considerably," a spokesman said. The airport was closed because of the weather.

Neither plane was scheduled to be in Santa Cruz de Tenerife when the collision occurred. Both had been diverted there from Las Palmas in the Canaries after a bomb exploded at the Las Palmas airport lounge. The planes were preparing to fly back to Las Palmas when the collision took place.

A Pan Am spokesman said its plane was taxiing toward its takeoff point when it crossed a runway and was hit by the KLM airliner.

But KLM's Orlandini said, "The Dutch jumbo jet was taking off on the runway. The Pan Am plane was turning onto the runway at a fast speed and hit the KLM plane midships."

A Pan Am spokesman in New York said that the copilot of its plane, R. L. Bragg, called from a hospital in Santa Cruz and said, "Visibility was poor and suddenly there was another aircraft and a collision."

Bragg said that V. F. Grubbs, the pilot of the plane, also survived the crash, the spokesman reported. The copilot was believed to have a broken leg.

"You couldn't see the runway from the airport building, the fog was that thick," said Eduardo Urbano, a Santa Cruz resident who arrived at the airport after the collision.

Urbano said parts of both planes and bodies were scattered over the runway and "a wing broke off from one plane that was in flames."

In a telephone interview, the administrator of the Santa Cruz General Clinic said 18 Americans were admitted there and two were in critical condition.

Seventeen other Americans were admitted to a second local hospital and they were all in fair to good condition, a doctor reported.

The crash occurred at 4:40 p.m. (8:40 a.m. PST).

The worst single airline crash on record was that of a Turkish DC-10 near Paris in March, 1974, in which 346 people perished.

The most disastrous air collision was over Zagreb, Yugoslavia, Sept. 10, 1976, when 176 persons were killed in the crash of a British Airways plane and a chartered Yugoslav airliner.

Sunday's accident was the first at Santa Cruz since Dec. 3, 1972, when 155 persons died in the crash of a chartered Spanish airliner.

Please Turn to Page 14, Col. 1

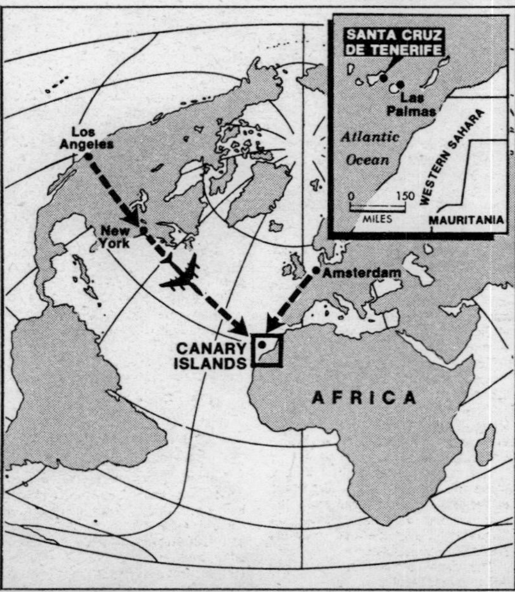

DEATH FLIGHTS—Routes of planes that crashed in the Canaries. Times map by John Snyder

'It Was Like Being in an Oven'

L.A. Survivor Describes Ordeal of Fire, Smoke After Crash

BY JACK JONES
Times Staff Writer

A Marina del Rey man Sunday described how he survived the flaming collision of two Boeing 747s in the Canary Islands, crawling through a shattered jet hulk so filled with fire and smoke he could hardly breathe.

John Charles Amador, 36, an Immigration and Naturalization Service hearing officer, telephoned his father, former wire service reporter Charles Amador, to let him know he had come through alive.

As relayed by his father, the younger Amador told of staring in horror as the other big jet bore down on the Pan American World Airways plane while the latter waited to take off from the fog-shrouded airport at Santa Cruz de Tenerife.

Amador and his apartment mate, Howard Harper, were in the second row of the first-class section as the Pan American plane moved toward takeoff position across a runway.

Amador said he looked out the window and realized the KLM plane was bearing down on them—a few inches off the ground and approaching at takeoff speed.

Amador said he could only hope that the other plane would simply shear off the Pan American jet's tail—but there was a thunderous explosion as the collision came mid-plane and the American craft was torn in three parts.

The forward portion of the plane, where Amador and Harper were seated, was torn loose and fell forward into fire. Amador said he began crawling forward but realized that the section was tipping farther, so he retreated.

"It was like being in an oven," he told his father. He said he thought he was going to be roasted in the flaming wreckage. The smoke was so thick he could catch his breath only in an occasional whiff of air.

Amador told his father he was inside the plane for what seemed like 5 minutes while men and women screamed and clawed to get to the windows and away from the flames.

Explosions knocked out some of the windows and Amador managed to get through one and drop to the ground, where he landed on his back.

Although he had thought that Harper was right behind him, his friend was nowhere in sight when Amador fell clear. The aircraft captain would not let him try to get back to the wreckage to find Harper, Amador said. There was no immediate word on Harper's fate.

Taken to a hospital in Santa Cruz, Amador was treated for abrasions and gashes on his arm and released to stay in a hotel with other survivors.

"I'm absolutely praising the Lord and so is the wife," said the senior Amador, for whom long hours of waiting for news had ended.

Another survivor was Jim Naik, 37, of Cupertino in Santa Clara County.

Please Turn to Page 15, Col. 1

Partial List of Survivors Provided by Two Hospitals

SANTA CRUZ DE TENERIFE, Spain (AP)—The Santa Cruz General Hospital listed these Americans as having been admitted after the collision of their Pan American plane Sunday with a Dutch airliner. Hometowns were not available:

Larry Walker
Philip Walker
Karen Anderson
Diana Brown
Richard Sennet
Kay Sennet
Homer Culbert
Maurice Reynolds
Madelaine Reynolds
Edward Lamb
Miss Liberty, first name not available
Mary Berkley
Jim Naik
Elsie Naik
Floyd Elck
Rime Enelcht

Survivors' names, gathered by KFWB radio in Los Angeles, of those admitted to the hospital Residentia Sanitaria. Spellings may be approximate:

Patricia Daniels
Elinda Daniels
Suzanne Dondoan
Byron Ellerbrock
Grace Ellerbrock
Ken Sox
Victor Grubbs
John Charles Amador
Maria Anderson
Dick Bowman
Cleo Brusco
John Combs
Luisa Combs
Isabel Lord
Charles Miller
Antonio Monde
Harold and Grace McGowan
Ethel and Simon Meyer
Maurice Magamte
Carolina Hopkins
Warren Hopkins
Edward Hesse
Paul Heck
Carla Johnson
John Jackson
Maria Jacodeck
Dorothy Kershaw
Dorothy Keya
Beth Moore
Charles Feikstass
Steve Sparacino
Toshio Tannemura
Jordan and Enid Tartikoss
Mario Tyzber
A. H. Trumbull
Mrs. Water, first name not available
Norman Williams
George Warns
David Welley
Laura and Herbert Waldripp

WATER SERVICES

Drought Makes Entrepreneurs' Business Bloom

BY WILLIAM ENDICOTT
Times Staff Writer

SAN FRANCISCO—Before the calamitous water shortage gripped Northern California, Joe Smith was a mechanic.

"I was in a garage all day, working on cars and breathing carbon monoxide fumes," he said. "It was awful."

But because of the water shortage, Smith, 32, now is out of the garage and into the open air, operating the Green Garden Water Service in Marin County and offering to "put a smile in your garden" with water he trucks in from wells in neighboring Sonoma County.

Water savings in area households can be almost painless. Part 1, Page 3.

He is typical of a growing number of water entrepreneurs—including water witchers, inventors and an 11-year-old boy—who have turned up in recent weeks to cash in on the drought and prove that even in adversity there is potential for profit.

"Everybody needs water," said Ed Nichols, 35, a San Rafael water witcher who for $35 will visit your property and give you his opinion as

Please Turn to Page 18, Col. 1

FEATURE INDEX

THE WEATHER

National Weather Service forecast: Cloudy with a chance of a few light showers in the early morning hours. Gradual clearing and increasing winds of 15 to 30 m.p.h. will develop toward the afternoon and dissipate late tonight. Highs today and Tuesday will be in the mid 60s. High Sunday 66, low 49.

Complete weather information and smog forecast in Part 2, Page 4.

CLOSING N.Y. STOCKS

Los Angeles Times

LARGEST CIRCULATION IN THE WEST, 1,020,987 DAILY, 1,309,677 SUNDAY

TUESDAY LATE FINAL

VOL. XCVI SIX PARTS—PART ONE 102 PAGES TUESDAY, AUGUST 16, 1977 LATE ★★ FINAL DAILY 15c

ELVIS PRESLEY DIES

LATE NEWS

Stock Rally Flops

From Times Wire Services

NEW YORK—The stock market declined slightly today, abandoning the rally attempt it began late in Monday's session.

The Dow Jones average of 30 industrials closed off 4.85 at 869.28.

New York Stock Exchange volume was about 19.3 million shares compared with 15.7 million Monday.

Tables in Financial Section

Ex-Official Gets 7 Years

ST. LOUIS (UPI)—Former Missouri House Speaker Richard J. Rabbitt today was sentenced to seven years in prison and fined $18,000 on his conviction in federal court on 15 counts of mail fraud, extortion and attempted extortion.

Rabbitt, who faced a maximum sentence of 135 years in prison and $51,000 in fines, promised to appeal his sentence, saying, "I still maintain I'm innocent and will prove it. This is round one."

Oil Spill Closes Pipeline

FAIRBANKS, Alaska (UPI)—An oil spill flooded a pumping station and caused a shutdown of the trans-Alaska pipeline, authorities said today.

The spill Monday night at Pump Station 9 on the 800-mile pipeline caused the black crude to overflow in the station's main pump building, said John Ratterman, spokesman for Alyeska. The oil overflowed from a sump in the station and an automatic fire alarm system was activated.

Deodorant Type Banned

WASHINGTON (UPI)—The Food and Drug Administration today ordered aerosol deodorants containing zirconium off the market as possible causes of lung tumors.

The FDA's final order, ending nearly three years of controversy over the metal's role in lung disease, said millions of consumers could be exposed to unnecessary risk by using deodorant sprays containing zirconium.

Lebanon Fighting Flares

From Reuters

BEIRUT—Fighting flared in south Lebanon again today and Palestinian leader Yasser Arafat said stepped-up Israeli military activity in the area was to blame.

Arafat said he had sent an urgent cable to Mahmoud Riad, secretary general of the Arab League, informing him of the gravity of the situation in the south.

175 Arrested in Soweto

JOHANNESBURG, South Africa (AP)—Police today shot and wounded an 18-year-old youth in the segregated black township of Soweto and arrested 175 students as officers raided five schools, police reported.

A police spokesman said the raids were designed to "clean up" at schools where students had taken over from teachers and were allegedly using classrooms for political meetings. The police used dogs in some of the raids.

DESERT DOWNPOUR—Motorist inspects his car in downtown Palm Springs after resort had over two inches of rain. Community has no drainage system and depends on runoff to the desert.

AP Wirephoto

Singer Succumbs in Memphis

MEMPHIS, Tenn. (AP)—Elvis Presley, the Mississippi boy whose country rock guitar and gyrating hips launched a new style in popular music, died this afternoon at Baptist Hospital, police said. He was 42.

Presley was taken to the emergency room of Baptist Hospital in serious condition this afternoon, suffering from what hospital officials said was respiratory distress.

Presley was taken from his Graceland mansion to the hospital.

Presley's gyrating hips were only mildly suggestive compared to most of today's rock performers. But when he appeared on the Ed Sullivan Show in the late 1950s fears that his sexuality seemed too overt caused him to be shown only from the waist up.

His shake, rattle and roll showmanship with such million-sellers as "You Ain't Nothing but a Hound Dog," "Heartbreak Hotel," "Blue Suede Shoes" and "Love Me Tender" kept teen-aged girls sighing.

He performed with slicked-back hair, sideburns and a perpetual sneer.

Ford Throws Support Behind Panama Accord

VAIL, Colo. (AP)—Former President Gerald R. Ford today threw his support behind a new Panama Canal agreement announced by the Carter Administration. Ford labeled the pact "an important step forward" and called for prompt approval by the U.S. Senate.

Following a lengthy briefing at his vacation retreat, Ford said he was "absolutely convinced it's in the national interest of the United States that the treaty be approved."

The agreement, which would cede control of the canal to the Panamanian government at the end of this century although ensuring continued neutrality, was announced last week, the culmination of 16 years of negotiations.

Ford's backing was an important boost for the Carter Administration, which faces an uphill struggle in getting the agreement approved over the objections of conservative senators.

Ambassador Sol Linowitz, who took part in the final negotiations, and Air Force Gen. George Brown had flown to Vail earlier in the day and spent about 90 minutes at Ford's vacation home.

Asked if he would try to pressure conservative Republicans to support the measure, Ford said he would "do what I can," and expressed "hope my endorsement will be helpful."

U.S. JUDGE RULES STUDENT CAN SIT OUT FLAG PLEDGE

NEWARK, N.J. (AP)—A federal judge today declared a state law requiring students to stand during the pledge of allegiance is unconstitutional. He said a student could remain seated as long as he or she "doesn't whistle, drum, tap dance or otherwise be disruptive."

Dist. Judge H. Curtis Meanor ruled in the case of Debbie Lipp, 16, of the affluent New York suburb of Mountain Lakes.

On May 16, she was suspended from classes as a sophomore at Mountain Lakes High School because she sat while others saluted the flag. She said her reason was that the phrase "with liberty and justice for all" is "a lie."

Meanor's ruling applies only to that part of the law requiring students to stand. He said another section, barring disruptions during the pledge, was constitutional and remained in force.

OFFICER, INMATE

Love Blooms in Florida Prison

COCOA, Fla. (UPI)—Florida prison officials have a love story on their hands. A female corrections officer has fallen in love with an inmate and they want to get married.

Michael Ryan, sentenced to prison in March, 1975, for six months to five years for grand larceny and aggravated assault, was sent to the newly opened Brevard Correctional Institution where he began working in the dining room and met correctional officer Donna L. Knapp.

"It was poor judgment on my part to fall in love with an inmate because the system frowns on personal involvement," Miss Knapp says, "but love is an emotion which is not any worse than the hate that is given to those inmates."

Prison officials investigated the relationship in January, 1977, and found there had been no "type of physical contact, nor was there any breach of security involved," according to a letter written by Ryan.

After the investigation, Miss Knapp transferred here and was put on a leave of absence.

Ryan was transferred to the River Junction Correctional Institution in northern Florida, and later to Carryville, following the investigation. He was denied parole in June and will not see a parole officer again until December.

Miss Knapp said she has been discriminated against as a woman and claims her involvement with Ryan already has "jammed" her time for getting out of prison.

Food Poisons 1,200

TOKYO (AP)—More than 1,200 people in northern Japan have suffered symptoms of food poisoning over the last four days, apparently after eating raw shellfish and crabs, local authorities reported today.

Brezhnev Refers Positively to U.S. Peace Feelers

MOSCOW (UPI)—In the first positive response to peace feelers from President Carter, Soviet President Leonid I. Brezhnev said today he will "willingly look for mutually acceptable solutions" to issues between the two superpowers.

In a ceremony welcoming visiting Yugloslav President Tito, Brezhnev referred to Carter's recent Charleston, S.C., speech and said "compared with the previous moves by the U.S. Administration, these statements sound positive.

"If there is a wish to translate them into the language of practical deeds, we will willingly look for mutually acceptable solutions."

The remarks were Brezhnev's first public statements in response to the Carter speech of July 21.

In that address, Carter referred to the "yearning for peace that is in the bones of us all. I am absolutely certain that the people of the Soviet Union who have suffered from war feel this yearning. It is up to all of us to help make that unspoken passion into something more than a dream."

Carter said the responsibility "falls most heavily on those like President Brezhnev and myself who hold the power of war in their hands."

Brezhnev, in his speech today, criticized so-called "imperialist circles" for unleashing a "hostile propaganda campaign against socialist countries, a campaign that is actually conducted in the spirit of the Cold War."

The Soviet press has been particularly critical of the Carter human rights campaign and what it considers a stepup in the arms race through the development of new weapons.

"The point is that the hostile campaign is used as a smokescreen for another round of the arms race," Brezhnev said.

"This connection has become particularly obvious after the United States adopted a decision to develop the production of cruise missiles and to allocate funds for the neutron bomb."

Brezhnev's remarks came during a ceremony in which Tito was awarded the Order of the October Revolution.

Brezhnev, in a rare show of respect, broke off a Crimean vacation and flew back to Moscow to welcome Tito to the Soviet Union today on an eight-day official visit.

More Floods Due in Desert; 50% Odds of L.A. Rain

BY JACK JONES
Times Staff Writer

Imperial County residents and desert travelers were warned today that Doreen, a Baja California hurricane downgraded to a tropical storm, was about to hit the area with a possible 6 inches of rain.

Heavy rains on Monday washed out highways and flooded some homes.

With thousands of motorists stalled by a washout on Interstate 15 near Baker on the way to Las Vegas and with two Salton Sea communities struck by flooding, the National Weather Service posted a rain warning from the high desert to the Mexican border through tonight.

A flash flood watch was declared for all mountain and desert areas.

Los Angeles itself, already having muggy and tropical weather, had an increasing chance of showers up to 50% tonight and Wednesday. The high temperature was expected to be 90 degrees.

The Monday night storm already had washed out part of the pavement on Interstate 15, cutting off travel to Las Vegas and stacking the motels and coffee shops of Barstow and other desert communities with stranded motorists.

By midmorning, however, Caltrans reported that northbound and southbound cars were being allowed through on two open lanes in alternating groups.

There were early reports by the California Highway Patrol that Interstate 40 between Barstow and Needles was closed because of flooding, as was U.S. 90 north from Needles. But Caltrans said it had no such information.

Imperial County sheriff's communications supervisor Kenny Dukes said the major problems Monday night and early today were in the Salton Sea area—at Bombay Beach, Niland and Palo Verde.

Dukes said that about 15 county roads remained closed this morning, that California 86 on the west side of the Salton Sea from Brawley to Palm Springs was open only to motorists with emergencies and that Interstate 8 from El Centro to San Diego was just "passable."

California 111 on the east side of the Salton Sea and California 78 west to the Borrego Springs area were closed, Dukes said, with water "running across most of them."

Despite those reports, the Salton Sea communities did not appear to be hard hit.

Flooding had been reported officially in both the El Centro and Brawley areas, but there were no accounts of evacuations or injuries there.

Please Turn to Page 19, Col. 1

FEATURE INDEX

18-WHEEL RIG ON 50-MILE RAMPAGE

Trucker Has Own Demolition Derby

JACKSON, Tenn. (UPI)—A wild trucker "drove over" three police cruisers with his 18-wheel tractor trailer rig today and sideswiped at least 20 other cars and trucks during an "incredible" two-hour, 41-minute chase that covered 50 miles.

Two of the tractor trailers he hit were disabled.

Jim Henderson, information officer of the Tennessee Highway Patrol, said the trucker finally was stopped in Jackson when the windows were shot out of his cab.

"He came out fighting and it took five officers to subdue him," Henderson said.

He identified the truck driver as Melvin Davis, 36, of Philadelphia. Davis was checked into Madison County General Hospital for observation.

The saga began at about 1:30 a.m. when the highway patrol dispatcher in Jackson received a call from another trucker that he saw a trailer rig "weaving all over the road" between Nashville and Jackson.

The dispatcher sent trooper Lynn Allen to investigate.

"Allen stopped the truck east of Jackson and pulled him over and told him he would have to go into the rest area and the man told him he would not," Henderson said.

"He rolled to the next exit and started back up the interstate toward the east. When Allen caught up with him, he ran the trooper off the road," he said.

"Allen shot out one of his tires but he kept going," according to Henderson.

The patrol spokesman said that many cars and trucks joined the chase for about 25 miles into adjoining Henderson County.

By this time other police units from both Henderson and Madison counties had joined in the pursuit.

Henderson said Davis "ran over" Allen's patrol car and across the median, heading back west toward Jackson. He said Allen was in the car but was not injured. His car was demolished.

Henderson said four big tractor trailer rigs joined together with the use of citizens' band radios in a "rolling roadblock" in an attempt to aid officers.

Still the truck moved on down toward Jackson. A roadblock composed of the trucks and two patrol cars was waiting for the truck in Madison County.

"He just drove over two patrol cars. He would stop, back up and run into them and finally he drove over them," Henderson said.

"He finally stopped after officers shot out the glass in his cab. He came out fighting and it took five officers to subdue him," Henderson said.

Henderson quoted Davis as saying "I guess you know who I am." He said the officers didn't.

THE LATEST WEATHER

Tropical Storm Doreen is moving north from Baja California, bringing heavy rain to San Diego and Imperial counties as well as to the Mojave Desert. Los Angeles, muggy and cloudy, with the high today near 90 degrees and in the upper 80s on Wednesday, has a chance of showers increasing from 30% this afternoon to 50% tonight and Wednesday.

RACING RESULTS-ENTRIES

Los Angeles Times

LARGEST CIRCULATION IN THE WEST, 1,020,987 DAILY, 1,309,677 SUNDAY

MONDAY MORNING FINAL

VOL. XCVI SIX PARTS—PART ONE 112 PAGES MONDAY, NOVEMBER 21, 1977 MORNING ★ FINAL DAILY 15c

BEGIN OPENS BORDERS TO EGYPT

Sadat Recognizes Israel

PROS, CONS

Equal Rights Amendment: Is It Needed?

BY PHILIP HAGER
Times Staff Writer

WASHINGTON—True or false: Under the Equal Rights Amendment, women would be subject to the draft, separate public schools for boys and girls would be abolished and men would have the same right to alimony as women.

The answer: True, according to most legal authorities.

True or false: Under the amendment, prohibitions on homosexual marriage would be overturned, unisex public restrooms wonld be mandated and separate college dormitories for men and women would be prohibited.

The answer to all these questions is False, according to the same authorities.

But confident as authorities are on these questions, based largely on the stated intent of Congress in approving the amendment, confusion and uncertainty still surround the ERA, and authorities concede that nobody can know for sure all the ramifications before such an amendment has gone into effect and has been interpreted and applied by the courts, legislators and government officials.

The operative section of the amendment is stated simply: "Equality of rights under the law shall not be denied or abridged by the United States or by any state on account of sex."

At first, the amendment seemed destined for quick ratification. State after state rushed to approve it. But now, as the deadline of March, 1979, approaches with the amendment at least three states short of the 38 required for ratification, it seems stalled by a growing controversy over what it would do.

Meanwhile, the Supreme Court in recent decisions has extended constitutional protection against sex discrimination, raising the question of whether the proposed amendment would make any difference.

Amid the debate, there is widespread agreement on one point: there will be plenty of lawsuits over sex discrimination for years to come, whether the amendment is adopted or not.

If it is adopted, the lack of specifics in its language would, over the years, provide the flexibility judges like so that they can shape the law to changing times. But in the short run, they will have plenty of interpreting to do.

"The language of the ERA is written in the same grand manner in which many constitutional gurantees have been written," a UCLA law

Please Turn to Page 9, Col. 1

TALK OF PEACE—Egyptian President Anwar Sadat delivers historic address to Knesset in Jerusalem at left. At right, Israeli Prime Minister Menahem Begin gestures while giving his reply as Sadat listens at his side. Sadat said he made trip at "great risk."

AP Wirephotos

But Leaders Are Firm on Differences

BY DIAL TORGERSON
Times Staff Writer

JERUSALEM—Only slight cracks appeared Sunday in the stone-wall deadlock between Egypt and Israel as Anwar Sadat and Menahem Begin debated war and peace before the Israeli Knesset and the world.

In his historic speech to the country's lawmakers, the Egyptian president offered Israel firm recognition as a Middle East state, something he has never done in such a public forum.

In his reply, the Israeli prime minister said he was opening his borders to Egypt and called for meetings between Israel and the Arab confrontation states prior to a Geneva peace conference—a position similar to that of Egypt and one that could expedite the move toward Geneva.

But hopes that a dramatic breakthrough would be announced were

Text of Sadat and Begin speeches, Part 1, Pages 20 and 21. Related stories on Pages 18, 22 and 24.

dashed when Sadat and Begin spoke. Basically, the positions spelled out by the two leaders followed the line each side has held as Geneva peace talks seemed to be pending.

Both leaders came to Sunday's debate in the Knesset hoping to give the best presentation possible of diametrically opposed positions on which each has refused to waver.

—On Israel's occupation of the formerly Arab-held land taken in the six-day war of 1967:

Sadat—"We insist on complete withdrawal from the territories."

Begin—"We will never again put our people in jeopardy. It is our duty to defend them. They will never be put within range of fire for annihilation."

—On Jerusalem, site of Jewish, Moslem and Christian shrines, consolidated under Israeli rule by the 1967 advances:

Sadat—". . . (Israeli) withdrawal from Arab Jerusalem, city of peace. It is inadmissible that anyone should conceive of Jerusalem within the framework of annexation or expansionism—it should be a free and open city to all believers."

Begin—"Ever since this has become a city joined together, this is a city open to all believers of any faith. We can assure the world of Islam and the Christian world that access will be free."

—On the Palestinians:

Sadat—"There can be no peace without the Palestinians. The Palestinians are the crux of the entire problem."

Begin—"We must make peace with all our neighbors, Egypt, Jordan, Syria and Lebanon . . ."

And here he was interrupted by

Please Turn to Page 16, Col. 1

Women's Parley Supports Free Abortion Choice

BY WILLIAM ENDICOTT
Times Staff Writer

HOUSTON—The National Women's Conference endorsed free choice on abortion and an end to discrimination against lesbians Sunday as antifeminist delegates charged that the conference had been "orchestrated" to stifle dissent.

The antifeminists tried through procedural moves to slow the progress of the conference, but with less than 20% of the approximately 2,000 delegates, they were having little success.

Having gone on record late Saturday in favor of the Equal Rights Amendment, the delegates turned Sunday to other conference proposals, including the abortion and lesbian rights issues, which had been billed as the most volatile and potentially divisive of the conference.

Ironically, however, there never was much doubt that they would be approved. A "Pro-Plan Caucus" that represents the majority of delegates endorsed them last week.

Please Turn to Page 5, Col. 1

WANTED: INVITATION TO CAIRO

Critical Test of Sadat's Mission Expected Today

BY LOUIS B. FLEMING
Times Staff Writer

JERUSALEM—The leaders of Egypt and Israel go into their final day of contacts today with no clear indication whether the momentum of their peacemaking was slowed down by the differences emphasized in their Knesset speeches Sunday.

If the private talks are paralleling the public presentations, the gulf remaining between the two nations is great.

The critical test will come today. If there is no invitation for Prime Minister Menahem Begin to visit Cairo, there will be deep disappointment among the Israelis.

"We will be very glad to continue the momentum," Aryeh Naor, secretary of the cabinet, told reporters Sunday after the cabinet had received Begin's report on his first conversations with Anwar Sadat, the Egyptian president. Implicit in Naor's comment was the need for Egyptian agreement in order to move ahead.

Regardless of what comes of the closing round of talks today, there remains the possibility of reconvening the Geneva peace conference. But the agenda for such a meeting has not been clarified by Sunday's speeches in the Knesset.

President Sadat indicated that the sensitive issues of greatest importance to Israel were not open to negotiation. Israel must withdraw from all the territories taken from the Arabs in the 1967 war, including East Jerusalem, he said. And the creation of a Palestine state is a "sublime objective" that is essential if there is to be permanent peace, he said.

Prime Minister Begin insisted that all issues be negotiable. But any reading of Israeli views would suggest how difficult, if not impossible, it would be to consider returning East Jerusalem or the West Bank of the Jordan River.

Both leaders did agree on the end of the state of belligerency as an important goal, but it was listed as "first and foremost" by Begin and last on a five-point peace list spelled out by Sadat.

For those who had expected something new, there could only be disappointment with the formal speeches. The Egyptian delegation that attended the Knesset session appeared to reflect that disappointment. And many Israelis, after the euphoria of Sadat's dramatic arrival Saturday night, showed disappointment that Sadat was still insistent on the return of the occupied territories.

Please Turn to Page 17, Col. 1

Wrath of Arabs Raises Question of Sadat Survival

BY JOE ALEX MORRIS JR.
Times Staff Writer

CAIRO—Egyptian President Anwar Sadat told the Israeli parliament Sunday that he came to the Jewish state at "great risk."

Even as he spoke, crowds in Damascus, Syria, were shouting "kill the traitor!"

The reaction raised the question of whether Sadat could survive the wrath that his historic mission to Israel has generated.

At home, Egyptians watched Sadat and Israeli Prime Minister Menahem Begin on television for the second day. But it was the start of Bairam, the Moslem festival marking the end of the holy pilgrimage season, and a festive air had replaced the drama of Sadat's arrival Saturday in what most people here still think of as the enemy heartland.

The speeches told them little more than they already knew. Sadat's peace package was seen as mainly a repetition of well-known Arab principles for a settlement. And Begin's

Please Turn to Page 23, Col. 1

NATURAL POLITICIAN

Chiang Outshines His Father as Taiwan Ruler

BY LINDA MATHEWS
Times Staff Writer

TAIPEI, Taiwan—Typhoon Vera was still battering Taiwan one morning last summer when Premier Chiang Ching-kuo slipped out of bed at 5 a.m. to inspect Taipei's stricken neighborhoods and commiserate with shopkeepers whose inventories had been ruined by floodwaters.

The next morning, he was up again before dawn to survey the damage at the ravaged northern port of Keelung. He took one look at the harbor, clogged with sunken fishing boats and twisted docks, and ordered relief work to be expedited so that the port could be reopened to the oceangoing freighters that are Taiwan's lifeline to the outside.

It was the kind of performance that has become Chiang's trademark in his five years as premier and has established this stocky, bespectacled son of the late Gen. Chiang Kai-shek as the island's undisputed ruler.

For most of his life, the 67-year-old Chiang Ching-kuo (pronounced Tiang Ting-gwa and commonly known here as C.C.K. lived in the shadow of his formidable father. But by combining shrewd economic policy with shirtsleeve political tours of the countryside, where he slurps noodles

Please Turn to Page 7, Col. 1

THE WEATHER

National Weather Service forecast: Variable high cloudiness today and Tuesday, with highs both days near 70. High Sunday 65; low 48.

Complete weather information and smog report in Part 3, Page 14.

FEATURE INDEX

PARTY'S OVER IN JERUSALEM

Letdown Replaces the Earlier Euphoria

BY DON A. SCHANCHE
Times Staff Writer

JERUSALEM—The air of almost hysterical exhilaration that seized this ancient city when President Anwar Sadat arrived was clouded with a feeling of letdown Sunday night, like the hangover of a mildly over-indulgent evening.

After Sadat and Prime Minister Menahem Begin reasserted their old and so far irresolvable positions at the Knesset, both the Israelis and their Egyptian guests appeared to reawaken from the euphoric jag of the night before.

"Begin won. He responded in the only way he could after Sadat's speech," said an Israeli woman, an American immigrant, who only the night before had viewed Sadat as the likely harbinger of peace at last in the Middle East.

The tone had changed on both sides.

"I was disgusted," a senior Egyptian diplomat said after listening to Begin's unbending response to Sadat's reassertion of the Arabs' basic bargaining demands.

The official had been observed in the distinguished-guest gallery of the Knesset during the Begin reply, his head in his hands. He was asked whether he had been pressing his earphones to hear better the simultaneous translation of the Hebrew language speech, or whether he had been crying. "Just say we were disappointed," he

Please Turn to Page 18, Col. 2

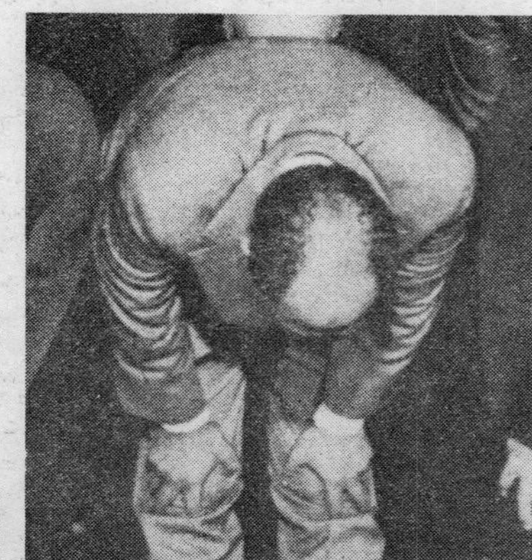

Anwar Sadat bows in prayer at Al Aqsa Mosque.

AP Wirephoto

RACING RESULTS-ENTRIES

Los Angeles Times

LARGEST CIRCULATION IN THE WEST, 1,020,987 DAILY, 1,309,677 SUNDAY

THURSDAY MORNING FINAL

VOL. XCVII SEVEN PARTS—PART ONE 146 PAGES THURSDAY, FEBRUARY 16, 1978 MORNING ★ FINAL DAILY 15c

Spinks Dethrones Ali

Contractors in Dogfight Over Defense Work

BY TOM REDBURN
Times Staff Writer

High above the Nevada desert, an Air Force fighter pilot located a "Russian" fighter on his radar. By computer, he fired a simulated missile at the enemy plane—in reality a small F-5E flown by an American pilot as if it were a Soviet MIG jet.

On the ground experts followed the imaginary missile to its target. Unfortunately for the Air Force pilot, who was flying an F-15, the most advanced fighter in the military inventory, the missile arrived one second too late to prevent the "Russian" pilot from firing his missile in return. Under real conditions the enemy plane would have been in flames but its missile would have continued on to the twisting F-15.

According to the computer monitoring this dogfight, both pilots were killed and both planes destroyed.

In Hawthorne, Calif., Bethpage, N.Y., St. Louis and Ft. Worth, where the Pentagon's newest four fighters are being built by Northrop Corp., Grumman, McDonnell Douglas and General Dynamics, corporate executives have been watching the results at Nevada's Nellis Air Force Base with intense interest.

For while their planes have been battling to prove their worth in the sky, a larger struggle is going on among military contractors in Washington, D.C., and in foreign capitals for a piece of the more than $100 billion in fighter contracts that Western nations are expected to parcel out in the next few years.

And probably double that sum will be spent to acquire all types of military aircraft.

Yet despite the staggering sums of money involved, $200 billion will not be enough to support every U.S. defense contractor that wants to continue building military airplanes. The coming struggle to stay in the defense business has set off a wild game of musical chairs being played for huge stakes. Thousands of jobs, billions of dollars in money for local economies and perhaps a few political futures depend on the outcome.

In the Northeast, politicians have been bitterly complaining about declining defense spending in the region. Even members of Congress who favor military budget cuts have gotten in the act.

"Nobody likes building weapons of war," liberal Rep. Thomas J. Downey (D-N.Y.) said. "But if we have to do it why can't we build these weapons on, say, Long Island?" Downey's district is near Grumman Corp.'s facility on Long Island, which employs 25,000 persons and builds the Navy's F-14 Tomcat.

From California, Thomas V. Jones, chairman of Northrop Corp., the de-

Please Turn to Page 20, Col. 1

DETHRONES ALI—Leon Spinks is lifted by his handlers after ending Muhammad Ali's long reign as heavyweight boxing champion with a 15-round split decision in Las Vegas. The gap-toothed Spinks, a 24-year-old ex-marine, won the title in only his eighth professional fight.
AP Wirephoto

Scores Shocking Upset in Only Eighth Pro Fight

From Times Wire Services

LAS VEGAS—Leon Spinks, turning tiger in the final rounds Wednesday night, scored boxing's most shocking upset since Muhammad Ali won the heavyweight championship from Sonny Liston in seven rounds on Feb. 25, 1964. He ended Ali's reign as champion in a split decision.

Ali was bleeding from the mouth most of the fight as he grew old in the ring at the age of 36 and succumbed to the relentless pursuit of the 1976 Olympic light-heavyweight gold medalist.

Spinks, a 24-year-old ex-marine with just seven previous professional fights, refused to run out of gas. In an exciting 15th round, he landed a combination of left and right punches to the head at the bell that sent Ali stumbling to his corner, his face a mask of pain and weariness.

At the final bell, Spinks' cornermen jumped into the ring and began celebrating. As it turned out, the celebration was not premature.

Judge Art Lurie, the first scorer announced, scored the fight 143 to 142 for Ali. But the other two judges voted for Spinks—Howard Buck 144 to 141 and Lou Tabat 145 to 140.

Spinks said he was willing to give Ali a return match, although there was no provision for it in the contract for Wednesday's fight. Spinks received $350,000, by far his biggest purse. Ali made $3.5 million in losing the title.

Ali, conserving his strength and picking his spots with head punches, seemed to be in command after 10 rounds.

But Spinks would not be denied.

In the 13th round, Spinks scored with a left-right to the head and, as Ali visibly tired, the challenger landed several other good lefts.

In the 14th, Ali, his left eye swelling, tried to stem the tide with his famous jab. But Spinks kept coming and hurt Ali with a vicious left hook midway in the round. He followed it with a right-left and an uppercut in a flurry just before the bell, outpunching the champion in that exchange.

The St. Louis native is the most professionally inexperienced heavyweight champion in history. Only one man ever fought for the title with fewer pro fights. That was Pete Rademacher, who was stopped in six rounds by Floyd Patterson in 1957 in what was Rademacher's pro debut.

Details in Sports Section

Coal Strike Talks Resume at Request of White House

Nation 'Looking to You' to Reach Settlement, Carter Tells Negotiators; Utilities Cut Service

BY BRYCE NELSON
Times Staff Writer

WASHINGTON—Striking mine workers and soft-coal operators resumed contract negotiations under White House auspices Wednesday night with President Carter warning them that the country "is looking to you men" to reach a settlement.

The President spoke for five minutes to the combined negotiating teams—five representing the coal companies and 10 the United Mine Workers union—and then left it up to Secretary of Labor Ray Marshall to serve as the top federal representative at the talks.

"I am not a mediator and don't intend to become one," the President told the two sides, according to White House Press Secretary Jody Powell. Carter added, however, that he would return to the negotiating scene if needed.

Also sitting in on the negotiations, which Carter called a test of the collective-bargaining system, was Wayne L. Horvitz, director of the Federal Mediation and Conciliation Service. The negotiations are being conducted in the Roosevelt Room of the White House.

Marshall reported later that the session, lasting more than an hour, "went very well." He said the discussions were devoted to procedural questions and added that bargainers would hold substantive talks beginning this morning at the Labor Department.

Marshall said the mood of the session was good but discussions became "heated" at times.

The press was barred from the opening session but Powell gave reporters a brief summary of the President's remarks.

The White House also announced that Carter would meet today with governors from 12 states most affected by the coal strike to discuss ways to alleviate the effects of the 72-day-old walkout, which has idled 160,000 miners, cut coal production by two-thirds and caused power curtailments

Please Turn to Page 15, Col. 3

Rhodesians Reach Accord on Plan for Majority Rule

From Times Wire Services

SALISBURY, Rhodesia—Black and white Rhodesian leaders announced agreement Wednesday on the major constitutional points for a transfer to black-majority rule in Rhodesia and said they expected to set up a transitional government soon.

The breakthrough, which paves the way for a multiracial administration to phase out white-minority rule in this breakaway British colony, came during the 37th session of talks that began Dec. 2 on an "internal settlement."

The "internal settlement" bypassed black nationalist guerrillas fighting the white Rhodesian government from outside the country. Guerrilla leaders immediately denounced the accord and said their armed struggle would continue.

But in Salisbury, harmony was the keynote. In an unprecedented gesture of black and white accord, Prime Minister Ian Smith and nationalist leaders strode side by side across the lawn of a suburban mansion to make the announcement.

It was the first time that Smith, who declared unilateral independence for Rhodesia from Britain on Nov. 11, 1965, had met reporters alongside nationalist leaders dedicated to ending 90 years of white supremacy in this country of 6.8 million blacks and 268,000 whites.

"We are very happy," said Bishop Abel Muzorewa, whose United African National Council had deadlocked

Please Turn to Page 12, Col. 1

Begin Urges U.S. to Reconsider Jet Sales to Arabs

BY DIAL TORGERSON
Times Staff Writer

JERUSALEM—Prime Minister Menachem Begin Wednesday urged the Carter Administration to reconsider its sale of advanced jet fighters to Arab countries, arguing that the warplanes would turn Saudi Arabia into a "confrontation state."

Within hours, the Carter Administration rejected Begin's appeal.

In a speech to the Knesset, Israel's parliament, Begin also said that he would go to Washington for a three-day visit early next month.

The U.S. refusal to reconsider the warplane sales "will not affect the prime minister's plans to go to Washington," an aide said, adding, however, that it was a "fair presumption" that Begin would continue to urge a review of the sales to the Arabs when he gets to Washington.

The Begin visit, during which he will meet with President Carter and other U.S. officials, is not "a crisis visit," an Administration spokesman said in Washington, comparing it to Carter's recent private, problem-solving conference with Egyptian President Anwar Sadat.

The White House also announced Wednesday that Israeli Foreign Minister Moshe Dayan would discuss Middle East issues with Secretary of State Cyrus R. Vance in Washington today. Dayan, who is on a U.S. tour, will pay a courtesy call on Carter after having lunch with Vance, the announcement said.

In his Knesset speech, Begin said

Please Turn to Page 7, Col. 1

Carter Declares Storm a Disaster

BY RICHARD WEST
Times Staff Writer

President Carter Wednesday declared a "major disaster" in eight Southern California counties as a result of last week's storms, permitting the use of federal money for rebuilding and relief activities.

Gov. Brown, who had requested the declaration, said in Sacramento that the latest estimate of damage for the affected area is between $45 million and $50 million.

Eligible for the aid are individuals, municipalities and public entities such as sewage, water and conservation districts in Los Angeles, Kern, Orange, Riverside, San Bernardino, Santa Barbara, Tulare and Ventura counties.

Much of the aid will be in the form of low-interest loans to owners of homes, businesses and farms that were damaged, free temporary housing for the homeless and assistance payments to those temporarily unemployed as a result of the disaster.

Federal money also will be provid-

Please Turn to Page 26, Col. 3

Haldeman Views on Nixon, Watergate and Kissinger

Beginning Monday, The Times will publish a five-part series of articles from H. R. Haldeman's memoir, "The Ends of Power." In his own words, Haldeman, White House chief of staff during the Nixon Presidency, gives an insider's views of the Watergate break-in, the 18½-minute erasure of the White House tapes, Nixon's dark side and Henry Kissinger's insecurities. The Washington Post in the following story reports on portions of the book.

WASHINGTON—H.R. Haldeman, Richard M. Nixon's closest aide during his White House years, believes Nixon "himself caused those burglars to break into" the Watergate. Later, when the historic White House coverup was unraveling, Haldeman is convinced it was the President who personally attempted to erase incriminating parts of his secret tape recordings.

Haldeman, currently in prison, consigns the role of the Watergate "heavy" to Charles W. Colson. And he ascribes much of the motivation for installing the fateful White House tape recorders to Nixon's concern over "the unpredictable Henry Kissinger," whom Haldeman depicts as a scheming, conspiratorial figure.

The President knew that Kissinger was keeping a log of everything they discussed, and he wanted a rival record of his own. According to Haldeman, Nixon had become aware that Kissinger was "given to second thoughts on vital matters" they had discussed in private.

It was Kissinger, Haldeman says, generally confirming other accounts, "whose anger at leaks really started the 1969 FBI national security wiretapping." And it was Kissinger who pressed Nixon to fight the publication of the Pentagon Papers.

But it is Haldeman's picture of Nixon, as sketched in his forthcoming book, "The Ends of Power," that commands the most attention. The latter two-thirds of the book was

Please Turn to Page 14, Col. 1

VIOLENCE STUDY RESULTS

PTA Names 'Best' and 'Worst' of TV Programs

BY LARRY GREEN
Times Staff Writer

CHICAGO—In its continuing war on what it considers objectionable television program content, the National PTA Wednesday released its first list of the prime-time shows it considers the 10 worst and 10 best.

Ten months after the 6.4 million-member Parent-Teacher Assn. had put the three networks "on probation," its fall season monitoring project found a decrease of violence in some prime-time programming. But it reported an increase in violence in movies shown on television.

In addition, the Chicago-based association served notice on the networks that "sex is not an appropriate or acceptable substitute for violence in series, specials or movie selections during children's viewing hours."

CBS was given the highest rating by the association, ABC was ranked second and NBC received the lowest rating.

The 10 programs rated "poorest in overall quality," although in no particular order, were: Soap, the Redd Foxx Show, Three's Company and Welcome Back, Kotter, all on ABC; NBC movies and that network's Man From Atlantis; and CBS movies plus that network's Kojak, Maude and Busting Loose. Of the 10, Busting Loose, Man From Atlantis and the Redd Foxx Show have been canceled.

"These shows were selected for a variety of reasons, including offensively portrayed sexuality and violence, stereotyping of women and minorities and general lack of program quality and entertainment value," the PTA said in a statement.

Cited for "objectionably violent content" were NBC's movies, Police Woman, Rockford Files, Bionic Woman and Man From Atlantis; CBS's Kojak and CBS movies; and ABC's Charlie's Angels, Six Million Dollar Man and Starsky and Hutch.

"Violence is still a pervasive factor in TV programs, according to PTA members," the association reported.

Please Turn to Page 18, Col. 1

FEATURE INDEX

THE WEATHER

National Weather Service forecast: Partly cloudy this morning and fair this afternoon through Friday. Highs both days in the mid to upper 60s. High Wednesday 63; low, 44.

Complete weather information and smog forecast in Part 1, Page 22.

RACING RESULTS-ENTRIES

Los Angeles Times

LARGEST CIRCULATION IN THE WEST, 1,034,329 DAILY, 1,332,875 SUNDAY

WEDNESDAY MORNING FINAL

VOL. XCVII EIGHT PARTS—PART ONE 134 PAGES WEDNESDAY, APRIL 19, 1978 MORNING ★ FINAL DAILY 15c

2nd Panama Treaty Ratified

PARENTS SHARE

Swedes Give Fathers Leave for Childbirth

BY MURRAY SEEGER
Times Staff Writer

STOCKHOLM, Sweden—"Hoa" Dahlgren, the weightlifter, Janne Carlsson, the popular singer, and Per-Olf Edin, a labor economist, have one thing in common: They are among the new fathers taking advantage of one of the Sweden's more unusual social welfare programs, paternity leave.

Sweden's first non-Socialist government in 44 years, despite an economic recession and a pledge to reduce swollen public spending, has expanded the pioneering program that gives fathers an equal claim to stay home with their children as the mothers have had.

In recent weeks, the government has mounted a promotion campaign to get more fathers to take advantage of the role-switching program.

Billboards and movie shorts featuring Dahlgren and Carlsson, both popular personalities, have been used to publicize the idea of "Daddy's on childbirth leave."

But Edin, a 37-year-old economist for the big Metal Workers Union, is more typical of the men who support the idea.

"I think it is a very good reform, good on a personal basis, good for the father, good for the wife, and good for the child," he said during an interview in his apartment near central Stockholm.

"It is also good for my work for I get a better idea of household problems from actual experience—this is the real world. Most men in Sweden are too tied to their work. This gives us a chance to separate ourselves from the job a little bit."

Katharina, now one year old, is the first child for Edin and his wife, Sonya, an editor.

Between them, the Edins took a total of seven months of leave. Then Mrs. Edin left her job to spend more time with the girl.

"We decided to give the baby all our attention for her first year. Diapers and shopping are no problem—I've really enjoyed it," Edin said.

Please Turn to Page 15, Col. 1

PROFIT-TAKERS END WILD MARKET RALLY

Profit-takers moved into the stock market Tuesday, selling off some of the securities bought during the wild rally Friday and Monday. Trading was still heavy at 38.95 million shares but well below the record 63.5 million traded Monday. The Dow Jones index of 30 industrials dropped 6.85 to 803.27.

Details in Financial Section

256 ARRESTED IN CRACKDOWN ON FENCING

BY TENDAYI KUMBULA
Times Staff Writer

Local and federal law enforcement officers Tuesday said they had arrested 256 persons and recovered $42 million worth of property and contraband during an extensive 22-month antifencing drive.

Los Angeles County Sheriff Peter J. Pitchess told a Hall of Justice news conference that "Operation Tarpit" was the most successful antifencing operation ever conducted in the United States.

He said 33 undercover sheriff's deputies and FBI agents, operating on a $450,000 federal Law Enforcement Assistance Administration grant, had cooperated on Operation Tarpit since last July.

Please Turn to Page 32, Col. 7

Supreme Court Bars Release of Nixon Tapes

BY PHILIP HAGER
Times Staff Writer

WASHINGTON—White House tape recordings played at the 1974 Watergate coverup trial may not be released for public broadcast or commercial reproduction, the Supreme Court ruled Tuesday.

In a legal victory for former President Richard M. Nixon, the justices held 7 to 2 that if the tapes are ever released they should be released through the General Services Administration after government archivists sift through all 42 million documents and tapes to decide which ones will be made public.

As a result of the ruling, the public will not be able to listen to the tapes played at the trial for some time—perhaps years. Had the court voted to approve the immediate release of the tapes, they probably would have been available for broadcast and purchase within months.

The justices rejected contentions by broadcasters and a recording company that because the tapes already had been played in open court—and heard by spectators and reporters—they should be made available for copying. The broadcasters had argued that actually hearing the tapes—with voice inflections, pauses and interruptions—would increase the public's understanding of the case.

Nixon's lawyers had argued that release of the tapes for broadcast and commercial use would violate the confidentiality of presidential decision-making and intrude on his and his family's privacy.

The lawyers said the tapes—containing 22 hours of conversations—could be distorted through cutting, erasing and splicing. Or, they said, the tapes might end up being exploited by disc jockeys and satirists or be-

Please Turn to Page 13, Col. 1

DELIGHT—Panamanians take to the streets after U.S. Senate vote on canal treaty. In background is poster of Gen. Omar Torrijos.
AP Wirephoto

MONTHS OF STRUGGLE END

For Carter, With Victory Comes Welcome Relief

BY RUDY ABRAMSON
Times Staff Writer

WASHINGTON—For the Carter Administration, the dramatic end of the Panama Canal debate Tuesday evening brought not a climactic moment of political triumph, but a desperately yearned-for arrival of blessed relief.

After months of struggle, President Carter escaped potential disaster with the Senate's 68-32 vote to ratify the canal treaty. After 13 years of negotiation, after riots in Panama and simmering ill-will across Latin America, the U.S. Senate grudgingly agreed to slowly transfer the famed canal to the country it crosses.

Seeking to put his leadership imprint on U.S. foreign policy, Carter sent the two treaties with Panama to the Senate last Sept. 16 in the face of a national tide of opposition.

Carter came to the Presidency with minimal foreign policy experience, facing not only the perennial Middle East crisis but also a stalemate in strategic arms limitation talks with the Soviet Union and an explosive situation in Africa that was complicated by Soviet and Cuban involvement.

With new Panama Canal treaties apparently within reach after 13 years of negotiations, the new Administration last year saw an opportunity to establish Carter's foreign policy credentials and project an image of mastery that would improve his chances of handling more difficult diplomatic challenges down the road.

As it turned out, however, Carter found the treaties an extremely difficult political plum to pick. Beset by domestic political problems that

Please Turn to Page 30, Col. 1

Note Found, Lake Combed for Moro

BY LOUIS B. FLEMING
Times Staff Writer

ROME—A communique purportedly from the ultraleftist abductors of Aldo Moro said Tuesday that the former Italian premier had been killed and his body dumped in an icy, mile-high mountain lake.

Following receipt of the message signed by the Red Brigades, officials searched Lake Duchessa, about 70 miles northeast of Rome, until dusk but could find no clues.

However, a new search was begun at an abandoned quarry six miles from the lake, using floodlights. Police reported they had received information that two persons were seen throwing a large object into the water-filled quarry a few days ago.

The search at the lake will be resumed today.

Officials said that the communique appeared to have been prepared with the typewriter used for six earlier Red Brigades messages, and therefore was thought to be authentic. It came only three days after the terrorists had announced that Moro had been condemned to death by a "people's court."

Meanwhile, some officials said that

Please Turn to Page 6, Col. 1

FEATURE INDEX

Carter Hails 'New Era' After Close Senate Vote

BY JOHN H. AVERILL
Times Staff Writer

WASHINGTON—The Senate, with only a single vote to spare, completed approval of the Panama Canal treaties Tuesday, signaling the end of an era that began 75 years ago when President Theodore Roosevelt acquired the land to build an ocean-linking waterway.

After months of controversy and bitter national debate, the Senate approved the second of the two treaties by a vote of 68 to 32—one vote more than the two-thirds majority required by the Constitution for approval of a treaty.

The vote, with all 100 senators again present, was identical, senator for senator, to the one on March 16 when the first treaty was approved. That treaty binds the United States and Panama to guarantee the permanent neutrality of the canal when control of it is transferred to Panama at the beginning of the year 2000.

The treaty approved Tuesday provides the mechanism by which Panama gradually will take over control of the canal during the next 22 years.

Immediately after the vote, President Carter announced that Panamanian leader Omar Torrijos had informed him that Panama would accept both treaties in their final form—despite conditions and reservations attached to them by the Senate.

Text of ratification resolution, abridged treaty text, Page 24. Other stories, Pages 20, 28 and 30. The Senate roll call, Page 25.

The President, who threw the full weight of the White House into the fight, expressed delight with the outcome and said: "We have a clear right to do what is necessary to defend the Canal and keep it open—but not to interfere with the internal affairs of Panama."

The Senate vote was the most significant victory of Carter's Presidency and he hailed it as signaling "a new era" for the United States in its relations with Latin America and the rest of the world.

Although the historic roll call on the second treaty turned out to be the same as the first tally, the outcome was in doubt up to the last because of threatened defections by three senators—Republican S. I. Hayakawa of California, and Democrats James Abourezk of South Dakota and Howard W. Cannon of Nevada.

Voting for the treaty were 52 Democrats, including Sen. Alan Cranston of California, and 16 Republicans, including Hayakawa. Opposed were 10 Democrats and 22 Republicans.

Abourezk and Cannon voted for the second treaty, as they had for the first, after winning concessions from the Administration and the Senate leadership.

Despite days of anguish and suspense by both sides before Tuesday evening's vote, the roll call was something of an anticlimax when it finally came. Word had seeped out several hours earlier that the threats of defections had evaporated and that the ranks of treaty supporters remained intact.

The galleries were jammed and most senators were on the floor as the roll call began, but the electric tension that characterized the first treaty vote in March was missing.

Senate Majority Leader Robert C.

Please Turn to Page 26, Col. 1

Torrijos Tells Nation Treaty Is Acceptable

BY LEONARD GREENWOOD
Times Staff Writer

PANAMA CITY—Panamanian leader Omar Torrijos Tuesday night declared "my mission is completed" as thousands of his countrymen rushed into the streets of this capital to cheer the U.S. Senate's ratification of the second Panama Canal treaty.

Gen. Torrijos, obviously relishing the outcome, told a press conference, "The treaty is acceptable as it is. We can live with this treaty. It is proper."

But had the Senate rejected the treaty, he said, "we would have begun a struggle for liberation and possibly by tomorrow morning the canal would not have been in operation . . . We are capable of destroying it . . ."

Torrijos and nearly everyone else in Panama had listened to radio broadcasts of the 68-32 vote that will turn the vital waterway over to Panama at the turn of the century.

In a television address, Torrijos called the vote a triumph for Panama. He announced immediate restoration of full political freedoms, which had been abridged since he came to power in a coup 10 years ago.

Most of the country's 1.8 million people already were celebrating. Fireworks filled the air and waiting bands played Caribbean music in the main plaza. Hundreds of celebrators raised bottles to toast the historic moment.

There was only one altercation between rival youth groups—one opposing the treaties, the other celebrating them—but they were separated swiftly by Panamanian National Guardsmen.

"For us, this is a moment of great emotion," Torrijos told his nation. "I feel proud that my mission is completed.

"I did not want to leave this problem to future generations, obliging them to live through the moments of shame that I have lived through."

As for the controversial additions to the treaty, Torrijos told his citizens, "I can assure you with all sincerity that there is nothing in the treaties which justifies intervention here."

He then asserted that he had never intended to return to the negotiating table had the Senate failed to ratify the second treaty.

"I never considered negotiation the only way out," he said. "We were going to take the route of violent intervention."

Please Turn to Page 23, Col. 1

Couple Seized in Slaying of Girl, 12, and Brother, 18

BY JUDITH MICHAELSON
Times Staff Writer

A 28-year-old Los Angeles couple—themselves the parents of an 8-month-old girl—were arrested and booked Tuesday as suspects in the double slaying of a young brother and sister in their home on a quiet street in Santa Monica the afternoon before.

John William Zimmerman, an unemployed roofer, and his wife, Merrilee Claire—described by neighbors as ordinary people who played Ping-Pong in their front yard—were accused of stabbing and bludgeoning the children to death.

The victims, who apparently discovered the suspects ransacking their home, were Brian Dean, 18, a senior at Santa Monica High School, and his sister, Vriana, 12, an honor student at Lincoln Junior High School.

Dean—eldest of three children of James S. Dean, an insurance broker, and his wife, Martha, a Pasadena school librarian—would have been 19 Tuesday.

The father discovered the bodies when he arrived home from work.

"It was a brutal murder. I'll leave it at that," said Det. Charles Wilson, the investigator in charge of the case, at a press conference outside Santa Monica police headquarters after the bookings Tuesday afternoon.

He refused to describe the weapons, but other police sources said several knives and blunt instruments were found in the Dean home on 16th St. They were taken to the police laboratory for investigation.

"It was pretty grisly," said Det. Kelley Leftwich, who saw police photos of the victims Tuesday morning.

Meanwhile, police left open the possibility that one or more persons besides the Zimmermans may have been involved. There were unconfirmed reports a third suspect was being sought.

Police declined to say whether they found any drugs in the small rundown

Please Turn to Page 3, Col. 1

QUESTIONS AND ANSWERS ON PACTS

Steps to Implement Treaties Remain

BY JOHN H. AVERILL
Times Staff Writer

WASHINGTON—With the Senate's approval Tuesday of the second Panama Canal treaty a number of steps remain before the documents go into effect.

Among other things, Congress must pass implementing legislation and leaders of the two countries must play a variety of roles as the future of the canal is shaped in the United States and in Panama.

Here is a question-and-answer report on the situation:

Question. What do the treaties do?

Answer. The one approved Tuesday, known as the Panama Canal Treaty, details the conditions and means by which Panama, in gradual stages, will take over ownership and control of the canal on Jan. 1, 2000. The other, approved last month and known as the Treaty Concerning the Permanent Neutrality and Operation of the Panama Canal, commits the United States and Panama to guarantee the canal's permanent neutrality after Panama takes over at the end of 1999.

Q. Now that the Senate has approved the two treaties, what happens next?

A. U.S. ratification of the treaties will be complete when President Carter signs the resolutions of ratification that were approved by the Senate. The next step will be for the United States and Panama to exchange treaty documents, the instruments of ratification. The exchange will take place in Panama and the two treaties will go into effect six months later. The effective date will not be before Oct. 1, 1979, unless Congress enacts implementing legislation before March 31, 1979.

Please Turn to Page 18, Col. 1

THE WEATHER

National Weather Service forecast: Fair today and Thursday except for some patchy fog and low clouds Thursday morning. Highs today in the upper 70s and Thursday in the mid 70s. High Tuesday 79; low, 54.

Complete weather information and smog forecast in Part 1, Page 32.

Los Angeles Times

LARGEST CIRCULATION IN THE WEST, 1,034,329 DAILY, 1,332,875 SUNDAY

VOL. XCVII EIGHT PARTS—PART ONE 176 PAGES THURSDAY MORNING, JUNE 29, 1978 CC † DAILY 15c

RICH PAST

Spain Keeps Sherry Dry, Exports High

BY STANLEY MEISLER
Times Staff Writer

JEREZ DE LA FRONTERA, Spain—Since the death of the dictator Francisco Franco and Spain's transition to democracy, exports of sherry are higher than ever.

Are democratic drinkers trying to give Spain a pat on the back? To anyone in the sherry business, the question is a bit ridiculous.

Inhaling deeply and sipping a glass of his company's dry fino sherry, Jose Ignacio Domecq, 64, one of the sherry aristocrats, tried to reply.

"We are selling a little more," he said, "but because of our efforts, not because of the political system."

There is a mystique about sherry, about its taste and the way it is produced, that seems to transcend politics. Democratic drinkers, in fact, never deprived themselves of sherry in the past out of any distaste for Franco's fascism.

During the Spanish Civil War, the Republican air force never bombed the sherry country even though Franco used it as a base for troops being brought up from North Africa. During World War II, Britain ignored Franco's sympathy for Adolf Hitler and used precious foreign exchange to buy small quantities of sherry to bolster home front morale. After the war, the diplomatic boycott of Franco failed to stop a boom in sherry sales.

Sherry, or *Jerez*, as it is known in Spanish, comes from a tiny nub of land in southwestern Spain. All the vineyards cover an area only 20 miles long and 15 miles wide. Some kinds of sherry are produced elsewhere in the world, some in the United States, but, as far as the Spanish are concerned, the only true sherry is produced here.

In 1960, a court in England, the country that consumes the most sherry, ruled that only Spanish sherry could be labeled with the term sherry alone. Other sherries would have to be labeled according to origin—South African sherry, Cyprus sherry, British sherry and so on.

The ruling, of course, did not affect the United States, and California and New York vintners can label their product when sold in the United States simply as sherry. But the Spaniards insist that the product is not the same.

Wine of some kind has been produced in the Jerez area for 3,000 years. In fact, according to a letter written by a Roman counsul in the 2nd century, wine from the area was then being exported to Rome and to the northern reaches of the empire. The northern reaches, what is now England and Holland, are still the main customers for sherry exports.

Laughing at this parallel between antiquity and modernity, Manuel de Domecq-Zurita, the director of public relations for the Pedro Domecq Co., the largest producer of sherry here, said recently, "It's interesting to see that modern marketing doesn't count."

The word "sherry" has an interesting etymology. The town in the center of the wine area, conquered by many throughout the ages, was known as Xera by the Greeks, Ceret by the Romans, Seret by the Goths, Sherris by the Arabs and Xeres and finally Jerez (pronounced Hereth) by the Spaniards. After Alfonso the Wise

Please Turn to Page 6, Col. 1

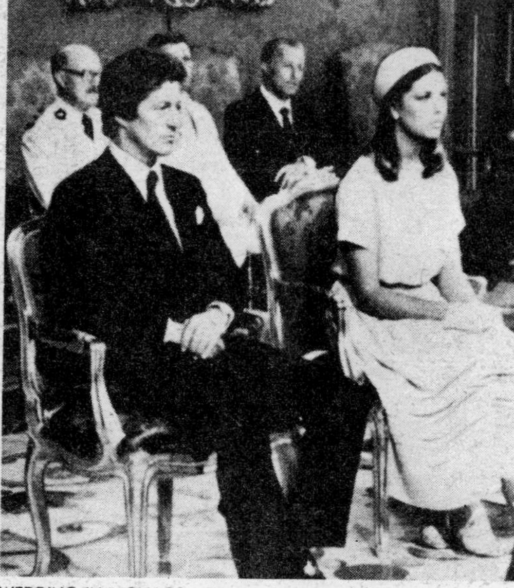

WEDDING IN MONACO—Princess Caroline and Paris playboy-financier Philippe Junot as they were married in a civil ceremony in the same palace room where their parents, Prince Rainier III, and film star Grace Kelly, were married 22 years ago. Monaco Palace released this photo; the press was barred from the rites.
STORY IN PART I, PAGE 26 AP Wirephoto

Bakke Wins but Justices Uphold Affirmative Action

Historic Ruling Strikes Down Davis Quotas

BY PHILIP HAGER
Times Staff Writer

WASHINGTON—In a historic decision, the Supreme Court ruled Wednesday that Allan Bakke must be admitted to the UC Davis medical school, concluding that he was denied admission unlawfully because he is white.

But, significantly, the court also held that universities may constitutionally give blacks and other members of minority groups special consideration through admissions programs that do not employ rigid racial quotas.

By a vote of 5 to 4, the justices struck down a UC Davis special admissions program that set aside 16 of 100 medical school openings a year for blacks, Chicanos, Asians and American Indians.

Excerpts of justices' decisions Page 23. Other stories Pages 16, 17, 18.

In another 5-4 vote, the court said that race could be taken into account as one of several factors in a flexible, individual admissions program—such as one employed by Harvard College—aimed at ensuring diversity in the student body.

The decision climaxed the biggest civil rights issue to come before the court since the school desegregation cases of 1954. At stake Wednesday were classic competing claims: Bakke, a 38-year old civil engineer from Los Altos, Calif., charged that he had been rejected in favor of less-qualified minority applicants to the medical school. The university defended its program as the only effective way to make up for pervasive and deep-seated discrimination against minorities.

In 1976, the California Supreme Court upheld Bakke, saying the Davis program violated the equal protection clause of the Constitution by denying him admission on the basis of race.

In their ruling, the U.S. justices were widely divided, issuing six separate opinions—none of which was joined in full by a court majority. As they often do, they cited different reasons for their votes on the key issues in the case.

Ironically, the court's holdings in the case permitted both critics and supporters of "affirmative action" programs to claim at least a qualified victory.

Bakke, in a statement issued through his attorneys, said he was pleased and, after five years of waiting, that he looked forward to entering medical school in the fall.

The conservative Young Americans for Freedom, one of several groups supporting Bakke, expressed satisfaction with the ruling. Executive Director Ron Robinson said that the court had "taken an important step in eliminating the practices of reverse discrimination and quotas."

On the other side, Jack Greenberg, director-counsel of the NAACP Legal Defense and Education Fund, noted

Please Turn to Page 17, Col. 1

Modifications Seem Certain in State System

BY DON SPEICH
Times Education Writer

The U.S. Supreme Court's Bakke decision means that most of the special admissions programs in California's law and medical schools will continue to operate.

However, many will have to undergo modifications to satisfy the guidelines contained in the court's long-awaited decision, according to legal experts familiar with the programs.

The net effect of these modifications—which will result in some schools relying less on race as an admissions factor than they have in the past—might well be fewer minorities admitted to law and medical schools in the future.

The only program expected to undergo drastic change is the one at UC Davis medical school. This is because the program—unlike virtually any other in the state—has been based on a rigid quota system that sets aside 16 of 100 slots in each first-year class for minorities.

Other medical schools and most law schools use a more flexible method of admissions, under which the number of minorities admitted varies from year to year.

Higher education officials across the state Wednesday obviously were pleased by the Supreme Court's majority opinion that race could be used as a factor—but not the sole factor—in determining admissions.

UC President David Saxon said he was "extremely happy" with the court's decision and said that with the exception of UC Davis, the university would not have to make any major changes in its admissions programs.

Under questioning from reporters during a news conference at UC's headquarters in Berkeley, Saxon did say that the ruling would make it "more difficult for minorities to gain admission," adding later, "We hope we can maintain our current level of minority enrollment."

Asked how UC would use race as a factor without employing the out-

Please Turn to Page 22, Col. 1

A smiling Allan Bakke arrives home from work after ruling.
AP Wirephoto

LONG DREAM

Intense Desire to Be a Doctor Spurred Bakke

BY DAVID JOHNSTON
Times Staff Writer

The sun had yet to rise on the quiet street lined with pepper trees where Allan Paul Bakke lives with his wife and two children in Los Altos, Calif., when reporters and photographers from across the nation began to mass in his front yard.

They had gathered after a news service had reported that the court might act on Wednesday.

By sunrise many of the reporters had grown impatient. One rapped loudly on the front door of Bakke's unpretentious ranch-style home in the affluent suburb 40 miles south of San Francisco and shouted, "Come on out, Bakke."

But inside the house all was quiet and by 9:15 a.m., two hours after the court acted, the press corps had eased its vigil and moved across the street.

Calmly, Bakke opened his front door and strolled to his mustard-colored Volkswagen in the driveway. He had already climbed in and shut the door before the press corps came running up.

Grinning broadly, perhaps as much at the court's decision as at his outlasting the reporters he has consistently refused to speak with, Bakke put his car in gear and drove off to his $28,623-a-year job as assistant chief of the equipment engineering branch

Please Turn to Page 16, Col. 1

HIGH COURT REFUSES TO SUSPEND PROP. 13

State Justices Agree to Hear Challenges but Final Decision 'Could Be Weeks, Could Be Years' Away

BY WILLIAM ENDICOTT
Times Staff Writer

SAN FRANCISCO—The California Supreme Court agreed Wednesday to hear the legal challenges to Proposition 13 but refused to stay its July 1 effective date.

That means the controversial measure to slice property taxes in the state almost 60% will be implemented on schedule Saturday.

But a final decision on whether the court will uphold the measure or overturn it, according to a court source, "could be weeks, could be years" away.

The court, in a three-paragraph order, said simply that "the request for a stay in the operation of Article XIII-A (Proposition 13) of the California Constitution is denied."

But the order also noted that "the court has concluded that the resolution of the issues raised in these petitions will require further briefing and full argument."

Therefore, further written briefs by both proponents and opponents involved in the Proposition 13 case were directed to be filed by July 24.

Oral arguments were scheduled for Aug. 11.

After that, the court will take the matter under submission and later issue a decision. It is under no time deadlines.

The order was signed by all seven justices—Chief Justice Rose Elizabeth Bird and Associate Justices Mathew O. Tobriner, Stanley Mosk, William P. Clark, Frank K. Richardson, Wiley W. Manuel and Frank C. Newman.

There was no explanation of why the court has taken so long to reach the basic decision of whether it would assume jurisdiction of the Proposition 13 challenges.

The first of nine suits against the measure was filed just hours after voters had overwhelmingly approved the tax-limitation initiative in the June 6 primary election.

But ruling on Proposition 13 is apt to prove a politically sensitive issue for at least four of the justices whose

Please Turn to Page 10, Col. 3

Conferees Meet on State Budget

BY JERRY GILLAM
Times Staff Writer

SACRAMENTO—A Senate-Assembly conference committee began negotiating Wednesday in an effort to write a $15.2 billion state budget to send to Gov. Brown.

But continuing disputes on state employe pay raises, Medi-Cal abortion funding and government spending limits all but guaranteed that it will not get to him by Saturday, the start of the new fiscal year.

State Controller Ken Cory has announced he will stop paying bills and signing paychecks unless a budget is passed by both houses of the Legislature and signed into law by the governor by next Wednesday.

Senate President Pro Tem James R. Mills (D-San Diego) and Assembly Speaker Leo T. McCarthy (D-San Francisco) said they would push for floor votes by Monday.

There were hundreds of differences between the Senate and Assembly versions of the huge spending program.

Please Turn to Page 28, Col. 1

Begelman Gets Fine, Probation

BY BILL FARR
Times Staff Writer

Former Columbia Pictures President David Begelman, his conduct described as "bizarre" by a prosecutor and "almost a death wish" by the judge, Wednesday was fined $5,000 for forging $40,000 in studio checks.

Burbank Superior Court Judge Thomas C. Murphy also placed the film executive on three years' probation and accepted his offer of making a movie on the drug dangers of "angel dust" (PCP) as a public service.

Murphy was in agreement with Dep. Dist. Atty. Sheldon Brown, defense lawyer Richard Rogan and the Probation Department that time in custody was not warranted in Begelman's case.

"I'm not going to send you to jail because I don't think it is warranted," Murphy said. "And I am not going to send you to jail just because you are Begelman."

Commenting further on his decision not to impose a jail or prison term, Murphy said:

"It is an unusual case; it really be-

Please Turn to Page 27, Col. 1

COMEDIAN ADDRESSES WEARY LAWMAKERS

Legislators Take Hope, Laugh at Selves

BY BILL STALL
Times Staff Writer

SACRAMENTO—With all the sound and fury over Proposition 13, it was the first time in weeks that the California Legislature had truly been silent—particularly when waiting to listen to someone else.

But Bop Hope really is a person who commands attention and needs no introduction (but got one anyway—a long one). And the men and women of government—often the butt of many jokes—waited in suspense for the old master to speak Wednesday.

With a timing and understated manner that any politician would marvel at, Hope did it again, as he always does:

"Proposition 13 used to be the sort of thing you'd hear from a girl at the bar . . ."

"But I can't tell you what a kick it is to be in Sacramento, the home of my money . . ."

"The governor was very nice. He sent his chauffeur for me and I must say it's the first time I ever rode on a bicycle built for two . . ."

Hope with Gov. Brown and Assemblyman Herschel Rosenthal.
AP Wirephoto

"And I just wanted to tell you, I just wanted to visit this chamber because this is where you make the laws and it's very seldom a victim returns to the scene of the crime."

Even the governor, not usually a fount of merriment, laughed.

Hope was in Sacramento to perform at the local Music Circus and he

Please Turn to Page 3, Col. 2

MINORITIES BENEFIT, TOO

Court's Ruling Viewed as Civil Rights Victory

BY JIM MANN
Times Staff Writer

WASHINGTON—Allan Bakke will go to medical school. Symbolically, he has registered a triumph for all white persons who believe they have been harmed by special programs giving preference to blacks and members of other racial minorities.

But in practical terms, Wednesday's Supreme Court decision amounted in a number of ways to a substantial victory for civil rights forces.

Although the high court ruled that the admissions program used by the University of California's medical school at Davis went too far, a majority of the court also endorsed other admissions programs that give preference to racial minorities without setting aside specific places for them.

Furthermore, the court decision was qualified in such a way that its immediate impact will be felt only in the field of higher education. The ruling will not directly affect affirmative action programs in the field of employment, and it will not affect school desegregation cases or legislative reapportionment.

Justice Lewis F. Powell, Jr., who cast the deciding votes in the Bakke case, wrote that he believed the law, facts and court decisions concerning employment discrimination, voting

Please Turn to Page 20, Col. 1

FEATURE INDEX

THE WEATHER

National Weather Service forecast: Low cloudiness in the late night and morning hours with sunny afternoons today and Friday. Highs today in upper 70s and Friday in the low to mid 80s. High Wednesday 75; low, 59.

Complete weather information and smog forecast in Part 3, Page 15.

RESULTS-ENTRIES

Late Racing

Los Angeles Times

MONDAY

Morning Final

CIRCULATION: 1,034,329 DAILY / 1,332,875 SUNDAY MONDAY MORNING, AUGUST 7, 1978 MF / VOL. XCVII / 80 PAGES / Copyright 1978 Los Angeles Times / DAILY 15c

Pope Paul VI Dies at 80

Stricken by Heart Attack; Led Church for 15 Years

BY LOUIS B. FLEMING
Times Staff Writer

VATICAN CITY—Pope Paul VI, the Roman Catholic Pontiff for 15 years, died Sunday night at his summer residence outside Rome, just hours after suffering a heart attack. He would have been 81 next month.

The frail Pope was confined to bed at Castel Gandolfo Saturday with arthrosis, a severe form of arthritis, according to a statement issued by his doctors. It was the second time this year that he had been forced to cancel public appearances for health reasons, but no unusual concern was attached to the announcement.

The heart attack came at about 5:30 p.m. Sunday (8:30 a.m. PDT) while the Pope was celebrating Mass from his bed with his personal secretary, the Rev. Pasquale Macchi.

Cardinal Jean Villot, the Vatican secretary of state who became interim head of the church upon the Pope's death, was summoned immediately to the bedside. He was joined by the Right Rev. Giuseppe Caprio, now acting secretary of state.

The heart condition was said to have been aggravated by pulmonary edema, a seepage of fluid into the lungs, and the Pope was given oxygen.

Vatican sources said that up until an hour before his death, the Pope was lucid and had been praying, according to Associated Press. At that point, he apparently started to become dizzy, but he signaled to Villot,

Other stories and photos in Part 1, Pages 14, 15 and 16.

Caprio and Macchi to continue praying.

Death came to the spiritual leader of 700 million Roman Catholics at 9:40 p.m. and was announced 15 minutes later in the Vatican pressroom adjacent to St. Peter's Square.

"With profound anguish, I must announce the death of the Pope at 2140 hours this evening," the Rev. Pierre Franco Pastore, an assistant Vatican press spokesman, said.

Almost immediately after the Pontiff's death, elaborate arrangements were begun for the period of mourning, funeral and burial at St. Peter's Basilica. By early today, however, no dates had been set.

By tradition, there will be an official nine-day mourning period. The body will lie in state for three days inside the Basilica. Then it will be enclosed in a coffin and placed in a crypt and Masses will be said for the remaining six days of the mourning period.

Paul succeeded the colorful Pope John XXIII on June 21, 1963, becoming the church's 262nd Pontiff. Paul carried out the reforms of the 1962-65 Vatican Council opened by Pope John and later became the church's most widely traveled leader.

Please Turn to Page 15, Col. 1

Pope Paul VI, who died at summer home, shown in 1977 photo. AP Photo

THE CONTENDERS

Who Will Be Selected to Replace Paul?

From Times Wire Services

VATICAN CITY—Pope Paul VI's successor will be elected by the 115 Roman Catholic cardinals who are less than 80 years old, meeting in a conclave in Michelangelo's Sistine Chapel in the Vatican.

The successor is likely to be an Italian, but some veteran Vatican observers think chances for a non-Italian Pope are the best in this century. An American would not be an impossibility.

In theory, the cardinals could choose a bishop, priest or even layman to fill the shoes of Peter, the fisherman. They never do. A cardinal always wins.

Only 46 of 262 popes have been non-Italians. The last was Hadrian VI of Holland who reigned for 21 months in 1522-23. He was booed by Roman crowds on election day.

Three Italians and three foreigners are mentioned as frontrunners to succeed Pope Paul VI.

Italians are still considered to hold an edge because 27 of the 115 voting members of the College of Cardinals are Italians.

The Italian bloc of cardinals is the largest, followed by the American one, which has 10 voting members under the age of 80, the age at which cardinals lose their voting privilege under a decree issued by Paul. There are 15 cardinals over the age of 80.

The leading Italian contenders are:

—Cardinal Sergio Pignedoli, 68, president of the Secretariat for Non-Christians. He is known as a progressive and has spearheaded new relationships with Islamic and other creeds prevalent in the Third World. He has had very little pastoral experience, however.

—Cardinal Sebastiano Baggio, 65, prefect of the Congregation for Bishops, a consummate diplomat who served in Latin America and in Europe. Baggio has also had pastoral experience and has the advantage of being identified neither with the con-

Please Turn to Page 14, Col. 5

BRONX 'JUNGLE'

Rehabilitated Housing a Costly Failure

BY ROBERT SCHEER
Times Staff Writer

Four-year-old Carmen had fallen from the fifth-floor tenement window and the congressman walked up the stairs to pay his respects. He could have used the elevator, but its floor was covered with urine.

The light fixtures on each landing were ripped out, there were huge gaping holes in the sheet-rocked hallways, the walls were covered with the foulest graffiti, and it was necessary for Rep. Robert Garcia, who represents this South Bronx district, to sidestep the feces in the hallway.

The mother was not at home; she was with her child, who was in critical condition at the hospital. But kids "from somewhere" had already burglarized the apartment.

Welcome to Jose de Diego-Beekman housing project, where upwards of 6,000 people live in the largest government-subsidized effort at rehabilitated housing in the country.

The federal government has allocated $234 million this year for similar efforts at rehabilitating older buildings around the country. The case of Diego-Beekman illustrates some inherent weaknesses in this federal program to aid the poor and the cities.

This is one of an occasional series of articles by Robert Scheer examining urban decay in the United States.

Five short years ago, Diego-Beekman was billed as a showcase project, with fancy graphic numerals outside each of the renovated five- and six-story tenements. It was nationally celebrated as a model for urban renewal.

There is not much disagreement that the showcase has become a jungle. The hallways are dark, muggings and burglaries frequent. Small children found playing in the rubble of burned-out buildings that surrounds the project and provides its playing area tick off accounts of the latest rape, child molestation or knifing.

The promised recreational area—a community center—is shut down, a security problem, management says. The washers and dryers tenants say were promised for each unit never materialized. Instead, there is a private laundry owned by a management official who is in charge of tenant selection.

No great claims are made for tenant selection, which is said by management officials to have broken

Please Turn to Page 10, Col. 1

BAR CONSIDERS MORAL ISSUES OF TEST-TUBE BIRTH

BY JIM MANN
Times Staff Writer

NEW YORK—Could a test-tube baby sue a scientific researcher on grounds that his conception had been a mistake? What would happen if poor women began to agree, for a fee, to bear children for wealthy families?

What if couples asked scientists to separate sperm cells in an effort to make sure that the test-tube babies they were planning would be boys?

Those were a few of the many problems raised Sunday as a group of scientists, lawyers and educators at the American Bar Assn.'s annual convention here wrestled with the moral and legal problems raised by the recent birth of a baby conceived through fertilization in a British laboratory.

That birth, and other recent scientific developments, caused one biologist here to tell the lawyers that "you

Please Turn to Page 4, Col. 4

Democrat May Challenge Carter, Kennedy Says

BY RONALD J. OSTROW
Times Staff Writer

WASHINGTON—Sen. Edward M. Kennedy (D-Mass.), in a change of mind, said Sunday he now believed it was "possible" that President Carter would be challenged by a Democrat if he sought reelection.

But Kennedy, appearing on ABC-TV's Issues and Answers, said he had no intention of seeking the Democratic presidential nomination in 1980, despite a sharp split with Carter over national health insurance.

Kennedy said he had changed his mind about a forecast he had made earlier this year—that Carter would not be challenged because of the President's declining standings in the polls. He did not specify who he thought might oppose Carter.

But Kennedy, who often tops Carter in presidential popularity polls, said that he thought Carter would be renominated and reelected and that he had "every expectation" of supporting him.

Kennedy, who favors a broader national health program than the Administration and one that would not hinge on a variety of economic measures, said his differences with Carter were fundamental.

In other areas, however, he said Carter had shown "strong leadership." He blamed the Democratic Congress' susceptibility to "very special interest groups" for the poor showing of the Administration's legislative program.

Please Turn to Page 6, Col. 1

Urban League President Bitterly Assails Congress

BY AUSTIN SCOTT
Times Staff Writer

The president of the National Urban League lashed out bitterly at Congress Sunday, calling it "callous," "intransigent" and "do-nothing" on issues vitally important to minorities and the poor.

Vernon E. Jordan Jr. also called for a "massive coalition" of black and brown voters to stave off what he called ". . . the full fruition of a national backlash against the poor and minorities" by electing more sympathetic politicians.

Jordan said he sees a "basic reneging on the promises of the 1960s" in a broad and continuing pattern of national and local developments "deeply subversive of the interests of the poor and America's minorities."

He labeled it a "new negativism," which he said manipulates legitimate worries over high taxes, inflation and urban problems and also subtly plays on irrational class and racial fears in an attempt to weaken the government, push blacks out of cities and end affirmative action.

It represents, he said, ". . . an America that has lost its capacity for caring and sharing, an America that has lost its compassion for the least among us, an America that doesn't want to be reminded of the ideals that made it great."

The points were made in a keynote speech Jordan delivered to the League's 68th annual conference, being held in the Los Angeles Convention Center.

In his keynote speech to last year's conference, Jordan provoked President Carter's anger by criticizing the Administration for not fulfilling his campaign promises to minorities and the poor.

This time, he said, "we note significant improvement" from the Administration. "We still have some criticisms to make, but there are also strong positives to stress." This time Congress caught the full fury of a speech which said over and over again that America has lost the commitment to morality and justice that civil rights leaders were able to build on in the 1960s.

"It is disgraceful that a nation with 40 million poor people crying out for food, jobs and homes should have its

Please Turn to Page 18, Col. 4

Gloom Pervades Vance Mission

BY DIAL TORGERSON
Times Staff Writer

JERUSALEM—Secretary of State Cyrus R. Vance heard nothing new Sunday on the first stop of his new Middle East mission, and aides said he might cut short his planned visit to Egypt.

Gloom pervaded the Israeli segment of the trip, which is now being described not as an attempt to resume the stalled peace talks between Israel and Egypt but as a fact-finding mission.

The talks here, with Prime Minister Menachem Begin and other Israeli leaders, had not been expected to break the deadlock. Egyptian President Anwar Sadat said that to do so will require new concessions from Israel.

Please Turn to Page 8, Col. 1

'CLEAR MORAL BEACON'

Leaders Salute Pontiff's Efforts, Achievements

From Times Wire Services

World and religious leaders Sunday praised Pope Paul VI for his efforts toward world peace and his sensitivity to the troubles that racked his church during his reign as leader of the world's Roman Catholics.

President Carter said the Pope was "a man whose life and works have served me personally as a source of great moral inspiration. As a man of peace and profound spirituality, he will be greatly missed, not only by all Roman Catholics but by all people."

"The voice of Paul VI serves as a clear moral beacon to a troubled world," Carter said. "With his passing, we have all been deprived of a strong voice for reason, for moderation, and for peace."

Queen Elizabeth II, touring Canada, issued a statement through Buckingham Palace in London praising the Pope's "untiring effort" to "promote peace throughout the world." She ordered all government buildings in Britain to fly flags at half mast.

British Prime Minister James Callaghan, visiting Wales, sent a message to the Vatican noting the Pope's "deep concern for humanity."

Evangelist Billy Graham said, "Pope Paul presided over the Roman Catholic Church when it was going through one of the most critical periods in its history. In one sense, he witnessed a revolution within the Roman Catholic world that has developed for several decades. In another sense, he sought to give that revolution direction and guidance. I believe history may show he was one of the most significant Popes in modern times."

Robert J. Marshall, president of the Lutheran Church in America—the nation's largest branch of Lutherans—said, "It is a time for remembering

Please Turn to Page 16, Col. 1

FEATURE INDEX

THE WEATHER

National Weather Service forecast: Fair today and Tuesday, continued warm and humid. Highs today and Tuesday near 90. High Sunday 93; low, 69. High Aug. 6 last year 85; low, 65. Record high for Aug. 6 was 101 in 1884; record low was 50 in 1883.

Complete weather information and smog forecast in Part 1, Page 18.

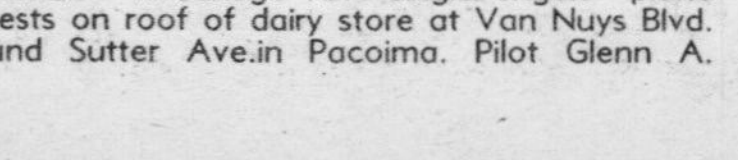

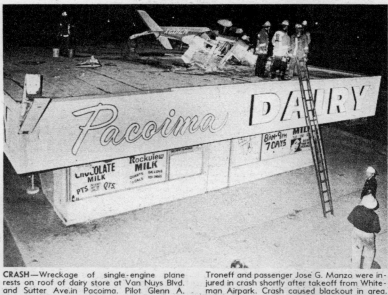

CRASH—Wreckage of single-engine plane rests on roof of dairy store at Van Nuys Blvd. and Sutter Ave. in Pacoima. Pilot Glenn A. Troneff and passenger José G. Manzo were injured in crash shortly after takeoff from Whiteman Airpark. Crash caused blackout in area. Times photo by Boris Yaro

ENTRIES
Late Racing

Los Angeles Times

TUESDAY
Morning Final

CIRCULATION: 1,034,329 DAILY / 1,332,875 SUNDAY | TUESDAY, NOVEMBER 21, 1978 | MF / 116 PAGES / Copyright 1978 Los Angeles Times / DAILY 20c / Designated Areas Higher

'STARTED WITH BABIES'

Jones Ordered Cultists to Drink Cyanide Potion

MASS DEATH—Bodies are everywhere in this air view of the Rev. Jim Jones' Peoples Temple encampment in the Guyana jungle.
AP Wirephoto

Jones, 409 Cultists Found Dead

Police Discover Mass Suicide and Murder Victims

BY LEONARD GREENWOOD
Times Staff Writer

GEORGETOWN, Guyana—The bodies of the Rev. Jim Jones and at least 409 of his followers were found by Guyana officials Monday after a weekend of horror and killing at an American religious commune in the jungles of this South American nation.

Commune members had shot and killed Rep. Leo J. Ryan (D-Calif.) and four other Americans at a jungle airstrip Saturday. The bodies were reported to be victims of a mass suicide pact, though some had been murdered.

✓ The Rev. Jim Jones and his Peoples Temple had friends in high political places, partly by providing volunteers for election campaigns. Page 3.

✓ Dozens of former followers of Jones have sought refuge in Berkeley and some talk about the horror which Peoples Temple brought to their lives. Page 3.

✓ Jones and his flock were neither strangers nor friends to the people of isolated, sparsely populated Guyana. Page 20.

The Guyana Ministry of Information said that by midafternoon Monday soldiers reported counting the bodies of 163 women, 138 men and 82 children. A police spokesman said later that the toll was 409 and that bodies were still being found.

By dark, police and soldiers had found only 12 survivors from among the estimated 500 to 900 who had fled into the bush. All of the settlers were believed to be Americans, most from California.

Guyana officials said the victims appear to have died of poisoning in a mass suicide pact, but some of them had been shot with rifles and automatic weapons.

U.S. attorney Mark Lane, one of the few survivors of the mass killing to reach this capital so far, told the Los Angeles Times in an interview Monday night, "There was no mass suicide. It was mass murder, planned to look like mass suicide."

Guyana army officers returning to Georgetown Monday night told nightmare tales of bodies piled in the sect's community center and the stench of death under the tropical sun.

Officials said Jones, a former San Francisco city official who founded the Peoples Temple Christian Commune, had been shot and near him were the bodies of his wife and one of his children, who had apparently been poisoned.

Lane, who agreed to represent the community only a few weeks ago in the face of growing criticism in the United States from relatives of people who lived there, said poison was taken into the community center hall Saturday night. Then the sect members, surrounded by armed men, some of whom had modern automatic weapons, were persuaded or ordered to take the poison.

"They lined up women, even little children, to take poison. It was crazy. This was not suicide, it was poison or a bullet."

Events at the commune last Saturday are still confused, and there are very few known survivors. Those who have reached Georgetown have been put under protective custody by the Guyana authorities, Lane said.

But Lane himself, who went to the commune last week with Ryan and a party of U.S. journalists, lawyers and

Please Turn to Page 22, Col. 1

DEATH VAT—Tub that contained Kool-Aid mixed with cyanide rests on wooden sidewalk at Jonestown near bodies of victims.
AP Wirephoto

VIP CLIENTELE

U.S. Air Force —Blue Chip Airliner Fleet

BY NORMAN KEMPSTER
Times Staff Writer

WASHINGTON—When President Carter badly needed another vote to extend the deadline for ratification of the Equal Rights Amendment last month, he dispatched an Air Force jet to Denver to whisk Sen. Floyd K. Haskell (D-Colo.) to the Senate floor.

When Secretary of State Cyrus R. Vance traveled to New York earlier this month to discuss Middle East peace plans with Israeli Prime Minister Menachem Begin, he went by Air Force jet.

When Defense Secretary Harold Brown took a week off to bask in the sun of Puerto Rico during the last New Year's Day holiday, he also made the trip in an Air Force jet.

To the public, the Air Force consists of nuclear bombers, supersonic fighters and ocean-spanning missiles. But it is also a passenger airline—one of the nation's smallest, but one of its most luxurious.

Known officially as the 89th Military Airlift Group, the airline flies only 16 jet aircraft, but its blue-chip service puts most commercial airlines to shame. Its on-time dependability record is an amazing 99.5%. In-flight meals are cooked from scratch in the back of the planes, using the best fresh meats and produce available. Most seats are spaced comfortably well apart.

There's one catch: it is tough to get a reservation.

The only regular customers are the President of the United States, the Vice President, members of the Senate and House, members of the Cabinet, generals, admirals and—rarely—civilian subcabinet officers, colonels and others of equal military rank.

The problems of the 89th verge on the exotic. Several years ago, Secretary of State William P. Rogers stopped in Afghanistan on the way home from a globe-spanning trip.

Several State Department staff members took the occasion to purchase colorfully embroidered sheepskin coats which they stowed in a closet aboard the Air Force plane.

Too late the souvenir hunters learned that the tanning agent used on the coats contained camel urine. "Once those coats got warm," one passenger recalled, "they put out an unbelievable smell."

The best-known task of the 89th is transporting the President. The blue, white and silver Air Force One jet is the flagship of the Air Force's passenger fleet. Two of the 16 planes in the 89th are assigned full time to the White House.

If he wished, a President could loan

Please Turn to Page 8, Col. 1

FEATURE INDEX

Miller Asks U.S. Austerity in Inflation Fight

BY WILLIAM J. EATON
Times Staff Writer

WASHINGTON—Federal Reserve Chairman G. William Miller Monday called for three or four years of government austerity—without any major new federal programs—to combat inflation and "wring it all out" of the economy.

In past anti-inflation drives, Miller said, the federal government has relaxed stringent monetary and budget policies too soon to conquer the price spiral.

"This time we've got to finish out the war," Miller told reporters at a breakfast meeting.

He warned of "difficult times" ahead. But he said there was no foreseeable danger of depression even if President Carter's anti-inflation program failed to achieve its goals.

"There is no reason, based on economic realities, to have a recession," Miller said. "If we listen to the clamor, the noise and the pessimism, we can talk ourselves into a recession, which would be foolish."

Miller's view conflicted with a statement last week by Alfred E. Kahn, the President's chief inflation fighter, who said that unchecked inflation would lead to a "deep, deep depression."

President Carter said later that a depression or recession was a possibility only if his anti-inflation efforts ended in complete failure.

But Miller scoffed at the thought of a depression like the one that paralyzed the U.S. economy in the 1930's.

Miller said the federal government should adopt tight budgets, run a tight monetary policy and continue

Please Turn to Page 9, Col. 4

REP. DIGGS RECEIVES 3-YEAR PRISON TERM

Rep. Charles C. Diggs Jr. (D-Mich.) was sentenced to three years in prison for mail fraud by a judge who rejected arguments that Diggs belonged in Congress, not in jail. Part 1, Page 9.

Gunmen Prevented Escapes

BY CHARLES A. KRAUSE
The Washington Post

PORT KAITUMA, Guyana—When the Rev. Jim Jones learned Saturday that Rep. Leo J. Ryan (D-Calif.) had been killed but that some members of the congressman's party had survived, Jones called his followers together and told them that the time had come to commit the mass suicide they had rehearsed several times before.

"They started with the babies," administering a potion of Kool-aid mixed with cyanide, Odell Rhodes recalled Monday when I revisited Jonestown to view the horrifying sight of 405 bodies—men, women and children, most of them grouped around the altar where Jones himself lay dead. (Later reports put the known death toll at 409.)

Rhodes is the only known survivor of Jonestown who witnessed a part of the suicide rite before escaping. He was helping Guyanese authorities identify the dead.

Most of those who drank the deadly potion served to them by a Jonestown doctor, Lawrence Schact, and by nurses, did so willingly, Rhodes said. Mothers often would give the cyanide to their own children before taking it themselves, he said.

But others who tried to escape were turned back by armed guards who ringed the central pavilion where the rite was carried out, Rhodes said. They were then forced to drink the poisoned Kool-aid, and shortly after that the mass killings began, Rhodes said.

"It just got all out of order. Babies were screaming, children were screaming and there was mass confusion," he said.

It took about five minutes for the liquid to take its final effect. Young and old, black and white grouped themselves, usually near other family members, often with their arms around one another, waiting for the poison to kill them.

Please Turn to Page 21, Col. 1

Ryan Aid Raps Probe of Cult

BY ROBERT BARKDOLL
Times Staff Writer

WASHINGTON—Rep. Leo J. Ryan's top aide charged Monday that State Department officials had conducted only a superficial investigation into a Guyanan cultist settlement whose members killed the congressman and four other Americans Saturday.

American consular officials in Guyana insisted that the commune "was benign and reasonable despite (contrary) information we had" from relatives of commune members and those who had defected, according to Joe Holsinger, the slain congressman's administrative assistant.

"The U.S. Embassy reported: 'From

Please Turn to Page 24, Col. 1

THE WEATHER

National Weather Service forecast: Rain likely today and Wednesday morning. Partly cloudy and locally windy Wednesday afternoon. Highs both days near 60. High Monday 64; low, 54. High Nov. 20 last year, 65; low, 48. Record high for Nov. 20 was 88 in 1954; record low, 37 in 1906.

Complete weather information and smog forecast in Part 1, Page 26.

RESULTS-ENTRIES

Late Racing

Los Angeles Times

SATURDAY

Morning Final

CIRCULATION: 1,034,329 DAILY / 1,332,875 SUNDAY — SATURDAY, DECEMBER 16, 1978 — MF / 88 PAGES / Copyright 1978 Los Angeles Times / DAILY 20c / Designated Areas Higher

U.S. Has Full Ties With China

Cleveland Defaults; Mayor Plans Layoffs

Mayor Dennis Kucinich speaking to Cleveland City Council. AP Wirephoto

Half of Firemen, Police, Sanitation Workers May Go

BY BOB SECTER
Times Staff Writer

CLEVELAND—This city plunged into financial chaos today when feuding politicians refused to back off from a high-stakes game of fiscal chicken, forcing the city to default on its debts.

Mayor Dennis J. Kucinich said he was drawing up tentative plans to lay off half the city's policemen, half of the fire department as well as half of the street and sanitation workers on Monday as a result of the failure.

By failing to meet a midnight deadline Friday for repaying or refinancing $15.5 million in notes held by six Cleveland banks, Cleveland became the first major American city since the Great Depression to plunge into default.

The final blow came in an 11th-hour City Council meeting convened by Kucinich just before the deadline. Despite his warnings of dire consequences for months and years to come, the council refused to pass a Kucinich program designed to restructure city finances.

Asked if the city was in default when midnight passed without council action, the mayor's press secretary, Andrew Juniewicz, said, "It appears as if it is."

The council chamber was packed with Kucinich supporters and foes who repeatedly punctuated the meeting with cheers and catcalls.

Aware that default was imminent, the normally flamboyant Kucinich made no attempt to be conciliatory in his last-minute plea that the council reconsider its opposition to his financial program. He also lashed out at the last-minute offer from Cleveland Trust, one of the creditor banks, to bail the city out of its financial problems if the city would agree to sell a public utility.

"I'm wondering if Cleveland Trust . . . is so corrupt that they're trying to buy off a whole city," Kucinich said. "It's a totally dishonest offer which indicates the Cleveland Trust philosophy that everyone has a price. I don't believe the city of Cleveland can be made available to the highest bidder."

The late night confrontation capped a frantic day of scheming and screaming by city leaders who made minor overtures toward compromise but refused to budge on fundamental differences.

Those differences centered on the future of the city-owned Municipal Light Plant, an aging facility that funnels cut-rate power to about one-fifth of the city's residents. Most Clevelanders get their power from the privately owned Cleveland Electric Illuminating Co., which wants to buy MLP.

Kucinich, who pledged during his campaign for mayor last year never

Please Turn to Page 12, Col. 1

Israeli Cabinet Rejects Egypt's Latest Proposal

BY DIAL TORGERSON
Times Staff Writer

JERUSALEM—The Israeli cabinet Friday rejected both Egypt's newest peace proposal and a pointed U.S. suggestion that Israel accept it.

Prime Minister Menachem Begin said that Israel hoped negotiations would continue. But officials said there seemed to be no chance of a treaty being signed by Sunday, the Dec. 17 deadline set at the Camp David Mideast summit in September.

Begin insisted that Egypt bore the "total responsibility for the failure to reach an agreement by Sunday."

After Friday morning's special cabinet session, he issued a measured statement citing hardening of the Egyptian position and emphasizing Israel's willingness to accept the original treaty draft worked out in Washington at Blair House.

"These demands are inconsistent with the Camp David framework," he said of the Egyptian proposals, "and, therefore, are unacceptable to Israel and (are) rejected by it."

Begin chided the United States, saying, "We would like the United States not to keep a one-sided attitude . . . We ask the United States government to keep objectivity and allow for negotiations."

He also rejected the U.S. interpretation of the Egyptian proposals, refusing to accept the American version that Egypt had softened rather than hardened its stand.

The cabinet rejected a White House statement that Israel was now responsible for the outcome of peace,

Please Turn to Page 6, Col. 1

Order Against Yule Cross at L.A. City Hall Upheld

BY PHILIP HAGER
Times Staff Writer

SAN FRANCISCO—Striking down a 30-year-old custom, the state Supreme Court Friday upheld an order forbidding the lighting of windows of the Los Angeles City Hall tower in the form of a cross at Christmas and Easter.

Citing state constitutions provisions requiring separation of chuch and state, the court by a vote of 5 to 2 affirmed a preliminary injunction issued by Superior Court Judge Norman R. Dowds in January, 1976.

The court majority rejected claims by Los Angeles city officials that the display of the cross was not a religious tribute to Christianity but instead an interfaith gesture of goodwill to all mankind.

Chief Justice Rose Elizabeth Bird, in a separate concurring opinion, expressed concern with the "church-like appearance" of a cross prominently displayed on City Hall. She said she thought the display violated both the state and federal constitutions as an impermissible entanglement of government and religion.

Ms. Bird observed that by authorizing an illuminated cross on the building, the city could not justifiably deny requests to place other religious symbols there, too.

"It does not take foresight to see that this situation is fraught with dangers of political divisiveness," she wrote. ". . . Once the tower of City Hall is converted into a giant calendar, marked with symbols such as the Latin cross, the Jewish Star of David, the Moslem crescent and star, the

Please Turn to Page 31, Col. 6

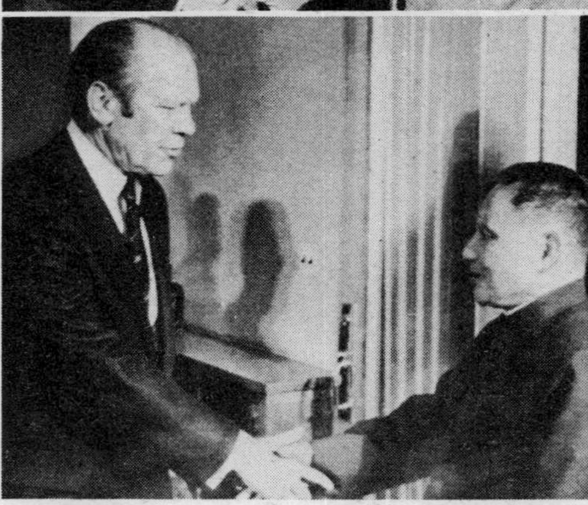

PAVING THE WAY—Former President Nixon, top, met with the late Mao Tse-tung in Peking in February, 1972, and former President Ford conferred with Vice Premier Teng Hsiao-ping in 1975. AP Wirephotos

China Concessions Called Key to Normal Relations

BY LINDA MATHEWS
Times Staff Writer

HONG KONG—Concessions by the Chinese made possible the normalization of Sino-American relations, a step that had been stalled for years by dispute over Taiwan, according to diplomats here and in Peking.

Although they regard Taiwan as an integral part of China, the Peking leaders decided to go ahead with normalization despite the stated intention of the United States to continue selling arms to the Nationalist Chinese government on Taiwan, 100 miles off China's eastern coast.

Peking did not accede to that American intention, and Chinese Premier Hua Kuo-feng stressed China's objection to such sales in his news conference in Peking today as the joint communique was announced.

Hua said that during the U.S.-China negotiations leading up to the normalization agreement, the two sides differed on the arms-to-Taiwan question. The United States said it would continue to sell limited amounts of arms to Taiwan after normalization, Hua told newsmen.

But the Chinese leader added: "We can absolutely not agree to this . . . The continued sale of arms to Taiwan by the United States does not conform to the principles of normalization and would be detrimental to the peaceful solution of the issue of Taiwan . . . Nevertheless, we reached agreement on the joint communique."

Although it did not block the normalization agreement, the Taiwan arms issue could be an irritant between Washington and Peking as they establish full relations.

In a somewhat smaller concession, China did not dispute President Carter's stated hopes for a peaceful solution of the Taiwan question, and approved of continued U.S. cultural and commercial links with the island.

China's willingness to yield on such issues and its eagerness to establish

Please Turn to Page 23, Col. 1

Taiwan Opposes Talks With China

From Times Wire Services

TAIPEI, Taiwan—Nationalist Chinese President Chiang Ching-kuo today ruled out negotiations with mainland China following the establishment of diplomatic ties between Washington and Peking.

Chiang said the Republic of China (Taiwan) "shall never give up her task of recovering the mainland and delivering the compatriots there. This firm position shall remain unchanged."

Chiang was informed of the U.S. decision by U.S. Ambassador Leonard Unger before it was officially announced.

The Taiwan leader said in a statement: "The decision by the United States to establish diplomatic relations with the Chinese Communist regime has not only seriously damaged the rights and interests of the government and people of the Republic of China (Taiwan), but also had tremendous adverse impact upon the entire free world."

The joint announcement made in Washington amd Peking was broad-

Please Turn to Page 24, Col. 1

THE WEATHER

National Weather Service forecast: Considerable cloudiness today and Sunday. Highs both days in the mid 60s. High Friday, 68; low, 46. High Dec. 15, last year, 65; low, 53. Record high Dec. 15, 84 in 1939; record low, 36 in 1878.

Complete weather information and smog forecast in Part 1, Page 31.

FEATURE INDEX

Diplomatic, Military Links With Taiwan to Be Severed

BY JACK NELSON
Times Washington Bureau Chief

WASHINGTON—The United States and the People's Republic of China announced Friday that they will establish full diplomatic relations, a move that may substantially alter the strategic balance between the United States and the world's other superpower, the Soviet Union.

The surprise development not only terminates American diplomatic relations with Taiwan but also unilaterally breaks the 1954 Mutual Defense Treaty with that old American ally. The move has profound international and domestic implications.

President Carter announced the move, which caused consternation in Taiwan and the Soviet Union, in a hurriedly arranged speech on nationwide television Friday night.

"Yesterday, the United States of America and the People's Republic of China reached this final historic agreement," Carter said. "On January 1, 1979, our two governments will implement full normalization of diplomatic relations."

In a joint communique, the two governments announced that they will exchange ambassadors and

Texts of U.S. statements on China accord. Pages 22, 29.

establish embassies on March 1, 1979. And the United States acknowledged "the Chinese position that there is but one China and Taiwan is part of China."

In a separate statement, the United States said that on Jan. 1, it will notify Taiwan "that it is terminating diplomatic relations and that the Mutual Defense Treaty between the United States and the Republic of China is being terminated in accordance with the provisions of the treaty."

"The United States continues to have an interest in the peaceful resolution of the Taiwan issue and expects that the Taiwan issue will be settled peacefully by the Chinese themselves," it said.

President Carter said, however, that this country will maintain "commercial, cultural and other relations without official governmental representation."

Technically, one year's notice is required to terminate the Mutual Defense Treaty with Taiwan and thus it will remain in force legally until Jan. 1, 1980. This apparently will mean that U.S. military supplies may continue to flow to the Nationalist Chinese during that period. The broad effect of the one year's notice is likely to be minimal, however.

The United States also announced that it will be withdrawing its remaining military personnel, now fewer than 1,000, from Taiwan within four months.

Carter, obviously exhilarated, also announced that Vice Premier Teng Hsiao-ping of the People's Republic of China has accepted his invitation to visit here at the end of January.

"His visit will give our governments the opportunity to consult with each other on global issues and to begin working together to enhance the cause of world peace," Carter said.

Please Turn to Page 29, Col. 1

GETTING READY—President Carter in the Oval Room of the White House before his speech. AP Wirephoto

Goldwater Calls Carter's Decision 'Cowardly Act'

WASHINGTON (AP)—Sen. Barry Goldwater (R-Ariz.) accused President Carter Friday night of "one of the most cowardly" presidential acts in history for his decision to extend diplomatic recognition to China and break with Taiwan.

Former President Gerald R. Ford said that, based on his understanding of Carter's move, "I approve of the action to be taken by the Carter Administration."

Sen. Alan Cranston (D-Calif.) called Carter's a courageous decision and a positive step toward world peace.

Sen. Richard Stone (D-Fla.) called Carter's move "a slap in the face to our staunch friend and ally, the Republic of China, and to the Congress."

Goldwater, keynoting a conservative outcry, threatened to sue Carter if the Administration breaks the U.S. defense treaty with Taiwan without congressional approval.

Since 1950, when the United States severed diplomatic relations with mainland China after the Communists took power, Washington has recognized the Nationalist Chinese administration on Taiwan as the government of China.

In the waning days of the last Congress, the Senate voted 96 to 0 for a resolution declaring that Carter should consult Congress before extending diplomatic recognition to Peking.

With Congress in adjournment, Carter conferred with a group of House and Senate leaders Friday evening, shortly before his nationally broadcast and televised announcement of the new policy toward China.

Cranston, the Senate Democratic whip, said he applauded the decision. "This is a very positive step toward

Please Turn to Page 28, Col. 3

CLOUD OVER ARMS TALKS

Moscow's Reaction May Be the Most Important

BY OSWALD JOHNSTON
Times Staff Writer

WASHINGTON—The first shock waves of the sudden decision by the Carter Administration and the Peking leadership were felt in Taiwan. But the most important reverberation may be in Moscow.

As early reports of President Carter's pending announcement swept through this capital Friday afternoon, even strong advocates of Washington-Peking relations were taken by surprise. The conventional wisdom had been that full relations would be restored eventually but not this year. The strategic arms treaty being negotiated with the Soviet Union was thought to have priority.

Now, thanks to intense hostility among Senate conservatives to what they consider abandonment of an ally in Taiwan, ratification of an arms treaty may be doomed. And the Russians, on the eve of a new round of strategic arms negotiations, likewise may harden their position, making a treaty that much more difficult to attain.

"A big move toward China now will ruin this Administration with the Soviets and with Congress too," observed a seasoned foreign policy analyst who has long advocated a go-slow approach to relations with Peking. "It could wash out SALT altogether. But what do we gain from it?"

The reason for Carter's action now

Please Turn to Page 28, Col. 1

Los Angeles Times

CIRCULATION: 1,034,329 DAILY / 1,332,875 SUNDAY — TUESDAY, MARCH 27, 1979 — CC†/110 PAGES / Copyright 1979 Los Angeles Times / DAILY 20c / Designated Areas Higher

BEGIN, SADAT PLEDGE NO MORE WAR

JOINED IN PEACE—Egypt's Anwar Sadat, President Carter and Israel's Menachem Begin just after the White House treaty signing. AP Wirephoto

Carter Also Signs Treaty to End a Generation of Egyptian-Israeli Hostility

BY OSWALD JOHNSTON
Times Staff Writer

WASHINGTON—President Anwar Sadat and Prime Minister Menachem Begin Monday put their names to an Israeli-Egyptian peace treaty that pledged an end to a generation of war between their two nations.

President Carter, presiding over the event as host and as the mediator who had made agreement possible, signed the pact as a witness in a brief ceremony on the North Lawn of the White House. The signing, a full six months after the Camp David summit, was a climax to negotiations so difficult and uncertain that details were still being hammered out in the final hours.

In contrast to the euphoria and high drama of the Camp David signing ceremony last September, Monday's ceremony was formal, almost austere, reflecting the fragile hope that the treaty can point the way to a comprehensive peace between Israel and the rest of the Arab world.

Most of the Arab nations have already condemned the treaty, and Carter, Begin and Sadat, in brief statements that looked apprehensively to the future even as they extolled the present, could hear the intermittent chants of Palestinians demonstrating against the agreement.

"We have no illusions," Carter said in his own evocation of the hard negotiations that lie ahead before the next stage envisaged in the treaty can be achieved—agreement on the political future of the Palestinians in the occupied territories of the Gaza Strip and the West Bank of the Jordan River.

"We realize that difficult times lie ahead," Sadat said in his speech, describing the treaty as "only the beginning of peace. Other steps remain to be taken without delay or procrastination."

"Let there be no more wars or bloodshed between Arabs and the Israelis," Sadat said.

"No more war," Begin said in his address. ". . . *Shalom, salaam*, forever."

Begin dwelt more on the present success than on future negotiations. He cited the four wars between Egypt and Israel in 30 years, praised Sadat for his courage in seeking an end to hostilities and referred to peace as "the cornerstone of cooperation and friendship."

The last substantive negotiation between Egypt and Israel took place Sunday night at the summit level, when Begin and Sadat, meeting at the Egyptian Embassy here, struck the last compromise on key issues that made the signing possible.

Text of treaty, Page 14. Related stories, Pages 16-25.

At that 11th-hour session, Sadat agreed to let Israel keep the Sinai Peninsula oil fields seven months after treaty ratifications, rather than yielding them to Egyptian control in six months as the Egyptians had been demanding. Egypt also dropped its requirement that Israel stop pumping oil from the fields as soon as the treaty is ratified.

In return, Begin agreed to a hurry-up schedule in Israel's evacuation of El Arish, the oasis town on the Mediterranean known as the capital of the Sinai. Earlier, Israel had agreed to return El Arish four months after ratification. Now the town will be in Egyptian hands after two months.

In its main lines, the treaty follows

Please Turn to Page 16, Col. 1

THE KARAYIMS

Castle Warriors —Ancient Stock Fades in Russia

BY DAN FISHER
Times Staff Writer

TRAKAI, U.S.S.R.—Only 150 Karayims are left here in the ancient capital of Lithuania. But a visitor can easily pick out the houses where they live.

According to centuries-old tradition, their homes have only three first-floor windows facing the street. The first, it is said, is for God. The second is for the grand duke. And the third is for the inhabitants.

Today, however, the windows are mostly unused. The God of the Karayims is fading from memory, his church shuttered and untended. The political masters of Lithuania now operate out of Moscow's Kremlin, not in the 15th-century castle of the grand duke. And the Karayims themselves are rapidly disappearing, their small but distinctive nationality a victim of age and intermarriage.

"I can't comprehend how our language, our customs and our religion can cease to be," mused 66-year-old Simyon Kharchinko, a Karayim who works as a ticket-taker at the restored, nearly 600-year-old castle.

Yet Kharchinko's oldest son committed the almost unpardonable sin of marrying outside his nationality. "I don't know if she's Polish, Byelorussian, or what," the old man said of his daughter-in-law. "I just know she's not one of us."

The Karayims are descended from the Khazars, a Turkic-speaking people whose empire in the second half of the first millenium after Christ was

Please Turn to Page 10, Col. 1

Supreme Court Widens Discretion in Sentencing

State's Justices Reject Contention That Legislature Intended Only the Crime, Not Criminal, to Count

BY PHILIP HAGER
Times Staff Writer

SAN FRANCISCO—In a decision that widens judicial sentencing discretion, the state Supreme Court ruled Monday that trial judges can make the punishment fit the criminal, as well as the crime.

The court, by a 6-1 vote, rejected the contention that the Legislature, in abandoning the old indeterminate sentencing system, intended to restrict judges to considering only the crime when weighing aggravating or mitigating factors in imposing sentences.

The justices upheld rules adopted by the state Judicial Council, the administrative arm of the courts, that permit trial judges to consider "facts relating to the defendant" as circumstances in aggravation or mitigation of a crime.

Under the ruling, judges, in deciding whether to impose a maximum sentence, will be able to weigh such aggravating factors as a defendant's pattern of violent conduct, increasing seriousness of crimes or poor record on probation or parole.

Similarly, personal mitigating factors could be considered in imposing a minimum sentence on a defendant.

Three state appellate court justices, specially appointed to hear the issue before the Supreme Court, joined with Justices William P. Clark, Stanley Mosk and Frank K. Richardson to form the majority.

Appellate Justices Norman H. Elkington, Wakefield Taylor and Robert Francis Kane served on the case in place of Chief Justice Rose Elizabeth Bird and Justices Mathew O. Tobriner and Wiley W. Manuel, all three of whom had a role in the adoption of the rules. Ms. Bird and Tobriner were on the 22-member council when the rules were approved and Manuel was a member of an advisory committee that proposed the rules.

The court's lone dissenter, Justice Frank C. Newman, said he believes the decision flouts an intent by the Legislature to achieve uniformity of sentencing by tailoring punishment to fit the seriousness of the offense, not the background of the offender.

"The Legislature clearly has pronounced that the punishment should

Please Turn to Page 11, Col. 1

Judge Bars Story on H-Bomb, Cites National Security

BY BOB SECTER
Times Staff Writer

MILWAUKEE—A federal judge blocked publication of a magazine article Monday after the government contended it would reveal vital secrets on how to build a hydrogen bomb.

U.S. Dist. Judge Robert Warren, saying national security interest sometimes outweighed First Amendment guarantees of a free press, issued a preliminary injunction barring the Progressive, which is published in Madison, Wis., from printing the article, titled "The H-Bomb Secret."

"In the short run," Warren said in making his ruling, "one cannot enjoy freedom of the press, freedom of speech or freedom of religion unless one first enjoys the freedom to live."

Warren's decision was believed to be the second case in which U.S. courts have exercised prior restraint on a publication. The first instance was in June, 1971, when the federal government obtained temporary restraining orders against the New York Times, the Washington Post and other newspapers, prohibiting their further publication of articles based on the Pentagon Papers, a Pentagon analysis of U.S. involvement in the Vietnam war.

On June 30, 1971, the Supreme Court in a 6-3 decision upheld the newspapers' right to publish.

Editors of the self-styled radical magazine, which has a circulation of 40,000, said they would appeal Warren's decision to the 7th U.S. Circuit Court of Appeals in Chicago.

Please Turn to Page 7, Col. 1

Arafat Vows to 'Chop Off Hands' of 3 Peacemakers

From Times Wire Services

Much of the Arab world seethed with hatred and sorrow Monday, the day of peace for Egypt and Israel.

Palestinian leader Yasser Arafat vowed to "chop off the hands" of "the stooge Sadat, the terrorist Begin and the imperialist Carter."

"This is my worst day since I left my home in Palestine in 1948," a Palestinian tailor, Mohammed Khaldi, told a reporter in Beirut. "I wish I were dead rather than be alive and witness this stigma and disgrace."

Effigies of President Carter, Israeli Prime Minister Menachem Begin and Egyptian President Anwar Sadat went up in flames in Palestinian refugee camps in Beirut and elsewhere in Lebanon.

Palestinians staged general strikes in the Israeli-occupied West Bank of the Jordan River and Gaza Strip to protest the Israeli-Egyptian treaty.

In Jerusalem, an explosive device apparently thrown by Arab guerrillas, went off inside a hotel during the treaty signing ceremonies in Washington and injured a number of people.

In Tehran, Iran, protesters seized the Egyptian Embassy and four employes as hostages but said they would not be harmed.

A mob stormed the Egyptian Embassy in the Persian Gulf oil state of Kuwait, smashing doors and windows.

Protesters occupied the offices of Egypt Air in Damascus, Syria.

In other world capitals, Palestinians, other Arabs and sympathizers paraded, staged sit-ins and rallied to denounce the signing of a treaty that ends 30 years of war between Israel and Egypt but leaves Israel in control of some occupied Arab lands and does not meet Arab demands for an independent Palestinian homeland.

Arab states led by Syria and Iraq pressed their diplomatic campaign for pan-Arab economic and political sanctions against Egypt.

The government press in Algeria launched an all-out attack on the ac-

Please Turn to Page 19, Col. 1

LAND THAT TREMBLED NOW BOOMS

Warnings From Quake of '64 Ignored by Alaskans

BY WILLIAM ENDICOTT
Times Staff Writer

ANCHORAGE—It was 15 years ago today, March 27, 1964, at 5:36 p.m. that an earthquake the likes of which had never been recorded on the North American continent struck Alaska with unremitting ferocity.

But despite the heavy toll of victims—114 dead—and widespread damage—estimated at $350 million—most Alaskans treat the experience as a historical oddity.

Warnings not to rebuild in high-risk areas have been virtually ignored. The word "earthquake" was stricken from the municipal development plan adopted by the Anchorage Assembly (city council) just a few years ago.

A secretary pleaded with a reporter who said he was planning an anniversary story on the earthquake, "Oh, why do you want to remind people of that?" And Wilda Marston, wife of a local real estate agent, flatly refused to talk about the experience of coping with an earthquake that registered 8.6 on the Richter scale.

"I really don't like to go through the whole thing," she politely told a caller. "It was a devastating experience, but we've made a satisfactory recovery. I'd just like to forget about it."

For others, it is unforgettable.

Fifteen years ago, Myrtle Stalnaker

Please Turn to Page 8, Col. 1

Arco to Open 2nd Alaskan Oil Field

Output Will Alleviate Loss of Iranian Crude

BY LINDA GRANT
Times Staff Writer

In a move hailed by energy experts, Atlantic Richfield Co. said Monday that it would develop a second major oil field on Alaska's North Slope.

The facility will be capable of producing about 60,000 barrels a day by 1982, or roughly 6% of the U.S. shortage caused by the disruption of Iranian oil production.

"That's good news for the United States," a spokesman for one major oil company said. "It's one of the reservoirs we counted on to keep Alaskan production high during the 1980's."

Los Angeles-based Arco, one of the three major North Slope producers, said it would spend about $350 million in an initial phase to develop the Kuparuk oil reservoir.

Although this first step is an exclusively Arco venture, the company said that other producers holding leases in the Kuparuk field may eventually join Arco in the development. Total investment by the group

Please Turn to Page 9, Col. 3

FEATURE INDEX

MICHIGAN STATE WINS NCAA TITLE

Michigan State ended Indiana State's bid for a perfect season and won the NCAA basketball championship with a 75-64 victory Monday night at Salt Lake City. Indiana State had won 33 consecutive games before losing in the title game. (Details in Sports Section)

HEARTFELT APPLAUSE, CHANTED PROTEST

Pact Sealed by a Vigorous Handshake

BY RUDY ABRAMSON
Times Staff Writer

WASHINGTON—A second after Egyptian President Anwar Sadat and Israeli Prime Minister Menachem Begin signed their historic peace treaty Monday and President Carter had added his own signature as a witness, Carter quietly said, "Let's have a handshake."

Smiling broadly, the three shook hands vigorously while 1,200 invited guests rose and began to applaud. After 30 years of intermittent warfare, after heartbreaking failures of peace negotiations, a formal pledge at last was signed—a pledge saying, in effect, that Egypt and the modern state of Israel together would surmount their deep-seated enmity and try to lead the volatile Middle East to peace.

It was a joyous afternoon on the North Lawn of the White House, complete with anthems and airs by the Marine Corps Band. But there was a striking absence of the euphoria that swept the United States, Israel and Egypt last September after Carter, Sadat and Begin had met in seclusion for 13 days at Camp David, emerging with a framework for a peace accord and a December deadline for completing it.

The more serious mood Monday was underlined by the fact that Carter took the initiative to suggest the handshake after the signing, and by his remark, a few minutes later: "We have no illusions. We have hopes, dreams, prayers, yes—but no illusions."

In the same spirit, the President was host to a festive dinner for 1,300 guests in a huge red and gold circus tent erected last week on the South Lawn of the White House.

"The way is long and hard, but peace is on the way," Carter said. "We share a vision of the time when all the people of the Middle East may turn their energies to the works of life."

Raising his glass of California champagne, Carter borrowed a word common to Hebrew and Arabic and toasted his guests and "the cause we all serve: *Salaam; shalom;* to peace."

The long-awaited treaty was signed in front of the stately North Portico, the ceremonial entrance to the White House.

Although the spring sun was bright, a chill wind stirred the yellow forsythia, the budding tulip trees and the American elms taking on their first tinge of green.

Beyond Lafayette Park, across Pennsylvania Ave., bells pealed at St. John's Church, an early 18th-century sanctuary almost as old as the White House itself. As the invited guests arrived for the ceremony, many of them had no outer coats, although the temperature was in the upper 40s and the wind gusted to nearly 30 m.p.h.

Please Turn to Page 23, Col. 1

THE WEATHER

National Weather Service forecast: Rain likely today, increasing tonight and Wednesday. Gusty winds both days. Highs today about 60 and Wednesday in the mid to upper 50s. High Monday, 67; low, 55. High March 26 last year, 89; low, 59. Record high, March 26, 89 in 1978; record low, 39 in 1907.

Complete weather information and smog forecast in Part 3, Page 11.

RESULTS-ENTRIES

Late Racing

Los Angeles Times

SATURDAY

Morning Final

CIRCULATION: 1,034,329 DAILY / 1,332,875 SUNDAY   SATURDAY, MARCH 31, 1979   MF / 80 PAGES / / DAILY 20c / Designated Areas Higher

Confusion Near Nuclear Site

PRECAUTIONS IN HARRISBURG—Some homes, foreground, that were evacuated after accident in nuclear plant. Domed structure between the cooling towers is the reactor building. At right, children leave one of the schools ordered closed by the governor.

AP Wirephotos

Evacuation of Some Advised

BY BRYCE NELSON
Times Staff Writer

HARRISBURG, Pa.—Gov. Richard L. Thornburgh Friday advised all pregnant women and preschool children living within five miles of the disabled Three Mile Island nuclear power plant to leave the area, but late Friday night he ruled out a general evacuation of the area "at this time."

He also ordered 23 schools in the five-mile radius closed.

After the tensest day since Wednesday's plant accident, Harold Denton, director of operations for the U.S. Nuclear Regulatory Commission, somewhat eased the mounting worries of local residents when he said there was "no immediate danger to the public" and said the chance of a dreaded meltdown of the reactor's core was "very remote."

NRC officials in Washington had said for the first time on Friday that there was a slight possibility of such a meltdown.

Thornburgh said at a news conference Friday evening that he was canceling his advice to people living within 10 miles of the plant to remain indoors, but would retain his recommendation that pregnant women and small children move from the area within the five miles of the plant.

Thornburgh had advised the women and children to leave after he received reports that an unplanned, "uncontrolled" release of radioactive gas had been made from the plant for more than two hours early Friday. Two other releases of gas were reported later in the day, all of which were caused by excess gas produced by the nuclear fuel rods damaged in Wednesday's accident. Thornburgh said that relatively low levels of radioactivity were being recorded.

The reports of the radioactive gas emissions and the governor's recommendations prompted large numbers of people to leave towns near the plant on Friday.

Denton, who was sent by President Carter to the site Friday, said that Wednesday's breakdown was "easily the most serious accident in the reactor program" and said "we've never had such extensive fuel damage" in a power plant accident.

Denton said the immediate problems were to try to cool down the reactor, parts of which are now at 600 degrees Fahrenheit, and to attempt to dissipate a large gas bubble over the reactor core (but inside the containment vessel) that could expand and prevent water from flowing to cool the hot reactor fuel elements.

Denton said that from three to five workers at the plant had been exposed to more than three rems of radioactivity during the accident, the limit that the NRC allows a worker in a three-month period. But he said no one had more than five rems exposure, the limit for a year.

Speaking at the press conference, Denton described a meltdown as "the

Please Turn to Page 13, Col. 1

Anxiety Spreads in Area

BY PENNY GIRARD and ELLEN HUME
Times Staff Writers

LONDONDERRY TOWNSHIP, Pa.—Dennis Murray had never before pumped as much gas in one day, and a friend at the bank next door told him, "People are drawing their money out of the bank to get out of town."

Friday was a day of anxiety and confusion for many of the 20,000 persons living in this and other small towns within a five-mile radius of the crippled Three Mile Island nuclear plant, as officials contemplated issuing evacuation orders.

Many residents left voluntarily throughout the day, after clouds of radioactive steam burst from the plant in three separate incidents Friday.

Shortly after news of the first incident reached adjacent Middletown about 9:30 a.m., policemen with bullhorns combed the town, urging pregnant women and preschool children to leave the area.

"We were besieged by parents coming up here to take their children home," Wendell Poppy, principal of the Londonderry Township Elementary School, said. His school was among 23 closed Friday because of the nuclear accident. "Many families told us they were going to stay with relatives, or leave the area," he said.

In Harrisburg's state capitol building, 10 miles from the plant, some employes left their jobs early after a worker had set off an unauthorized civil defense siren at 11:15 a.m. One left a note saying, "Tell the boss I left because I'm scared."

Those who had no relatives to stay with ended up at the Hershey Sports Arena 12 miles northeast of the plant, where the Red Cross set up cots for 500 persons Friday night. By late af-

Please Turn to Page 9, Col. 1

Car Bomb Kills Key British Figure

From Times Wire Services

LONDON—A senior member of the British Parliament who served as the Conservative Party's spokesman on Northern Ireland was assassinated Friday by a car bomb while leaving the House of Commons.

Airey Neave, 63, who was also a celebrated British war hero and a close adviser and friend of Conservative Party leader Margaret Thatcher, was killed as he drove up the exit ramp of the House of Commons underground garage inside Parliament's Westminister Palace.

Terrorist factions of the Irish Republican Army immediately claimed responsibility for the death of Neave, an outspoken supporter of strong security measures in Ulster. He would have become Northern Ireland secre-

Please Turn to Page 6, Col. 1

NO EASY WAY

Oil Decontrol: a Nightmare for President

BY NORMAN KEMPSTER
Times Staff Writer

WASHINGTON—On Dec. 17, 1975, while Jimmy Carter was lining up votes in Iowa precinct caucuses that started him on his way to the White House, Congress fashioned a political time bomb. Now the President is about to see it explode.

It was on that day that the Senate and House passed legislation that extended price controls on crude oil through May 31, 1979, and authorized the President to retain the controls, either at existing or reduced levels, for another 28 months at his discretion.

Presidents sometimes dream of being given authority to act without congressional approval, but the decision on whether to extend, reduce or eliminate oil price controls has given Carter nightmares.

According to Administration officials, Carter has made his choice: to order a gradual decontrol of crude oil prices and to call on Congress to enact an excess-profits tax on oil companies.

That choice is not likely to dispel the nightmares. It might even provoke some new ones, because the action seems guaranteed to produce far more criticism than praise for the President. The costs of decontrol—including higher prices at the gasoline pump—will be painfully obvious almost at once. The benefits will be far more subtle, will require months or even years to take hold and cannot be measured with precision.

But the alternative steps which Carter considered—and discarded—also had the potential for causing the public pain. Removal of the controls would raise prices and aggravate in-

Please Turn to Page 14, Col. 1

THE WEATHER

National Weather Service forecast: Mostly fair with some cloudiness today and Sunday. Highs both days in the mid 60s. High Friday, 64; low, 48. High March 30 last year, 67; low, 58. Record high March 20, 89 in 1934; record low, 36 in 1892.

Complete weather information and smog forecast in Part 2, Page 5.

Teamsters Reported Near Pact That Bends Guideline

BY WILLIAM J. EATON
Times Staff Writer

WASHINGTON—The Teamsters Union was reported on the verge of a guideline-bending settlement with the trucking industry Friday night that would end the threat of a national truck strike this weekend.

Union and management negotiators reached substantial agreement on a money package providing increases in wages and benefits totaling more than 9% in the first year of a three-year contract, reliable sources said.

Bargaining continued on other issues amid rising optimism that a settlement would be reached well before the deadline of midnight tonight.

The Carter Administration's willingness to loosen its wage-price guidelines was a crucial element in the negotiations, the sources said.

"I think they are going to settle," said a White House official who has been closely monitoring the Teamsters contract talks.

However, the proposed settlement breached the softened 7% wage guideline, according to a source close to the contract talks, and provoked objections from high officials in the Administration.

The money package was nearly 2% above the revised standard, the source said, even when part of the wage increase was exempted from the calculations because of the Administration's efforts to head off a strike.

By Administration figures, the source said, the settlement was priced at about 24%. Industry sources estimated the package cost at 30% or more over three years.

The outcome of the bargaining is critical for President Carter's anti-inflation program, since negotiations in the rubber, electrical, auto and other industries will be using the Teamsters settlement as a pattern.

If the trucking increase amounts to 30%, it would tend to set a 10% annual target for other labor negotiators.

Negotiators for the Teamsters and Trucking Management, Inc., the bargaining arm of the trucking industry, reportedly agreed on the following terms:

Please Turn to Page 17, Col. 1

Petitioners Can Use Private Shopping Sites, Court Rules

BY PHILIP HAGER
Times Staff Writer

SAN FRANCISCO—persons circulating political petitions are entitled to solicit signatures in privately owned shopping centers, the state Supreme Court ruled Friday by a vote of 4 to 3.

The court majority, sidestepping a ruling by the U.S. Supreme Court, said the state Constitution guarantees that right—even if a shopping center does not discriminate in barring such activity and even if there are adequate alternatives for seeking signatures elsewhere.

The court's dissenters accused the majority of overriding property rights guaranteed by the U.S. Constitution and of asserting state rights over federal rights in violation of constitutional principles.

The majority, in an opinion written by Justice Frank C. Newman, overruled a previous state Supreme Court decision upholding shopping center owners in a similar case. And it found that a U.S. Supreme Court decision upholding a shopping center in Oregon still left room for the state court to assert free speech rights based on the state Constitution.

Its ruling, the majority indicated, applied only to shopping centers—where large numbers of the public congregate—and not to individual homeowners or businesses. And soliciting, it suggested, could still be regulated as to time, place and manner.

"By no means do we imply that those who wish to disseminate ideas have free reign," Newman wrote.

But, the majority concluded, the state Constitution " . . . protects speech and petitioning, reasonably exercised, in shopping centers even when the centers are privately owned."

The majority took note of the growth of suburbs in California and the unique role of the shopping cen-

Please Turn to Page 19, Col. 1

3 More Firms Cut Gasoline Supplies for April by 5%

BY TOM REDBURN
Times Staff Writer

With crude oil in shorter supply, many big oil companies are further curtailing gasoline deliveries to the nation's dealers.

Mobil, Shell and Chevron said Friday they would reduce April allocations to their dealers 5% below March levels. Texaco and Exxon made the same announcement earlier in the week.

Meanwhile, industry sources said some Southland stations have used their entire March allotments of fuel and only about one-third are expected to be open Sunday. That could inconvenience those who plan extensive driving this weekend.

"Our shortfall in April will be about 10% of our crude oil requirement," a Shell Oil spokesman said Friday, "and we have little room to further reduce our inventory."

Next month, Shell, the second largest supplier of gasoline in California, will sell dealers in Western states only 90% of the gasoline they received in April, 1978. Shell's allocations in March were 95% of last year's levels.

Standard Oil Co. of California, which sells gasoline under the Chevron label, will cut allocations in April to 95% compared to March's 100% allocations. Exxon and Mobil are taking the same action, while Texaco is cutting allocations to 85% from March's 90% level.

Total deliveries of gasoline, in most cases, will be about the same as during April, 1978, however, because of new outlets added since last year and various changes in government requirements to supply essential users

Please Turn to Page 16, Col. 1

FEATURE INDEX

Libyans Reported Battling to Hold Kampala for Amin

BY DAVID LAMB
Times Staff Writer

NAIROBI, Kenya—Libyan forces made a final—and apparently futile—attempt to save the capital of Uganda Friday as 20,000 soldiers trying to topple the regime of President Idi Amin shelled Kampala with heavy artillery and prepared for a ground attack, Western and African sources said.

The Libyans took up positions on the front lines in the Kampala suburbs after remnants of Amin's shattered army were reported to have broken and fled in the wake of an eight-hour artillery barrage that left sections of the capital in ruins.

Western diplomatic sources said it was doubtful that the Libyan resistance, which they described as a token defense, would be enough to save either Kampala or the Amin regime from the attackers. By Friday night, tens of thousands of Ugandans had fled and Kampala was a virtual ghost town.

The attacking forces have nearly tripled in size to 20,000 men with an influx of Ugandan dissidents joining the ranks of Ugandan exiles and Tanzanian troops during the past week, sources said. The attackers were on the doorstep of downtown Kampala Friday night, delaying their final attack to give foreigners and civilians an opportunity to leave the capital, Uganda's government in exile said and Western diplomats confirmed.

The presence of Libyans on the front lines indicated that the Tripoli government had taken over much of the five-month-old war from Amin's crumbling regime. Tanzanian sources said that a Soviet-made Tupolev-22 bomber flown by Libyan pilots took off from Nakasongola, 50 miles north of Kampala, late Thursday and attacked the Tanzanian town of Mwanza on the shore of Lake Victoria.

The plane dropped five bombs,

Please Turn to Page 5, Col. 1

RESULTS-ENTRIES
Late Racing

Los Angeles Times

SATURDAY
Morning Final

CIRCULATION: 1,057,611 DAILY / 1,344,660 SUNDAY — SATURDAY, MAY 26, 1979 — MF / 94 PAGES / Copyright 1979 Los Angeles Times / DAILY 20c / Designated Areas Higher

270 on L.A.-Bound Jet Die

A PALL IN CHICAGO—Black smoke covers scene of DC-10 jetliner crash at O'Hare airport. Foreground, a piece of landing gear.
AP Wirephoto

No Survivors in Fiery Crash at Chicago

BY BOB SECTER and TOM PAEGEL
Times Staff Writers

CHICAGO—A Los Angeles-bound American Airlines DC-10 jetliner jammed with 257 Memorial Day Holiday travelers and 13 crew members crashed and burned shortly after takeoff from busy O'Hare International Airport Friday afternoon.

There were no survivors, authorities said, in the worst air disaster in U.S. history. An airline spokesman said 130 of the victims were from Southern California.

The toll of 270 was revised downward from 272 early today when authorities discovered that two persons whose names were on the passenger list had not boarded the plane.

Additional crash pictures and stories, Part 1, Pages 24-28.

Among those killed in the crash were Richard P. Schuster, director of development for Caltech in Pasadena, and Playboy magazine Managing Editor Sheldon Wax, his wife, author Judith Wax; Vicki Haider, the magazine's fiction editor, and Mary Sheridan, administrative director of the organization's international publishing division.

The dead also included two widely known book publishers: Henry Regnery, vice president of the Regnery-Gateway Publishing Co. of South Bend, Ind., and Stephen Greene, president of Greenemont Books of Brattleboro, Vt.

At least two persons on the ground were injured when the wide-bodied jumbo jet—which dropped its left engine onto the runway as it lifted off—plunged nose first into a vacant field about a mile north of the airport shortly after 3 p.m. CDT.

Witnesses said the aircraft erupted into flames and a pillar of smoke rose nearly 200 feet into the air. Black smoke continued to billow over the crash site for several hours as rescue teams pored over the rubble—at first looking for survivors, later marking the locations of bodies with flag-topped stakes they drove into the ground.

The plane went down in an unincorporated area of Cook County near Elk Grove Township, narrowly missing three large mobile home parks

Please Turn to Page 26, Col. 1

Times map

Schlesinger—'the Man You Love to Hate'

BY ROBERT A. ROSENBLATT
Times Staff Writer

WASHINGTON—For once in these turbulent times, Rep. Jerry M. Patterson (D-Calif.) knew almost instantly that he had done the right thing. Convinced that California was being short-changed on gasoline, Patterson had filed a legal complaint against James R. Schlesinger, the secretary of energy.

The response from Patterson's constituents was quick and it was positive. As one Santa Ana voter put it in a pungent postcard, "Right on, Jerry,. Sue the bastards!"

Where other members of President Carter's Cabinet are concerned, messages like that are rare. Almost nobody seems to get mad enough to sit down and cuss out the secretary of commerce, for example, or the man in charge of the Labor Department. But James Rodney Schlesinger, the nation's fourth energy czar and first head of the newly created Energy Department, is something different.

As gasoline lines, ever higher prices, and threats of heating oil shortages next winter send waves of bitter emotion surging across the country, Schlesinger is becoming the federal incarnation of the old silent movie villain—"the man you love to hate."

Consumer advocates accuse him of fronting for the big oil companies. Big oil companies accuse his army of 18,000 bureaucrats of hobbling U.S. petroleum output. And demands for his resignation are a glut on the market.

So vociferous is the criticism that Carter was moved to remark at a recent Cabinet meeting that being secretary of energy these days seemed to be even tougher than being President.

The man at the center of this firestorm is a large, white haired, pipe-smoking, Harvard-trained economist who often spends his weekends bird-watching with some of his eight children and whose utter self-confidence sometimes leads to charges of arrogance.

Under Presidents Nixon and Ford, Schlesinger, now 50, served variously as chairman of the Atomic Energy Commission, director of the Central Intelligence Agency and secretary of defense before taking the energy post under Carter.

Beyond the rhetoric of his critics there are serious questions to be asked about Schlesinger's performance thus far. How well does he discharge his duties as policy-maker, as chief administrator of a $10.8 billion-a-year agency, as field marshal for Carter's programs in Congress, and as chief Administration spokesman on one of the nation's most vexing problems?

The record, perhaps inevitably, is mixed. Even his critics concede that Schlesinger's intellect is formidable. And many acknowledge that he fore-

Please Turn to Page 14, Col. 1

Carter Concedes Shortcomings but Defends Policies

BY ROBERT SHOGAN
Times Political Writer

WASHINGTON—President Carter acknowledged his limitations as a politician Friday but nevertheless told Democratic Party leaders that he will campaign "in every precinct in this country" if he becomes a candidate for reelection in 1980.

The somber and frustrated tone of the President's remarks to the Democratic National Committee seemed to reflect recent setbacks he has suffered. But he left scarcely any doubt that he intends to run again and that he plans to rely on some of the same themes that won him the White House in 1976 and that have remained the foundation of his Presidency.

As he has often in the past, Carter blamed many of his problems on "well financed and powerful special interests," which, he charged, have "twisted and pulled Congress in every direction."

He conceded that he has shortcomings and that he has advocated unpopular policies but implied that, in the long run, these are virtues rather than faults.

"I have made mistakes, but I have made and I will continue to make decisions without fear which call for you and for your states to make some sacrifice," Carter declared. "I will never duck any decision which is vital to the welfare of the nation just because the popularity polls might go down."

Please Turn to Page 20, Col. 1

L.A. Prices Shoot Up 2% in April, Most in 32 Years

U.S. Rise is 1.1%; Higher Costs of Food, Homes, Gasoline Cited; Annual Inflation Rate Now 13.2%

BY WILLIAM J. EATON
Times Staff Writer

WASHINGTON—Consumer prices in the Los Angeles area shot up by 2% in April, the biggest monthly increase in nearly 32 years and almost double the national rise of 1.1%, the government reported Friday.

Soaring prices of gasoline, food and home-ownership accounted for the increase in Los Angeles and the rest of the nation, the Labor Department said.

Consumers in the Los Angeles area paid about 10% more for gasoline in April than in March, compared to a 6% increase for the United States as a whole, the department said.

Food and beverage prices were up by 1.5% in Los Angeles but only 0.9% for the nation, while housing costs leaped by 1.9% in Los Angeles and rose by 1.1% nationally.

For blue-collar workers the inflation news was even worse—the index of goods and services that urban wage earners buy was up by 2.2% in the Los Angeles area.

The Labor Department said that nationally the buying power of a typical worker in a family of four had declined by 4.5% in the last year and by 2.5% in April alone. The decline has occurred because prices are rising faster than wages, the department said.

In Los Angeles, the overall price increase was the largest since a 2.5% advance in September, 1947, when prices exploded after the removal of World War II controls.

In the past, Los Angeles prices have gone up more slowly than the national inflation rate. During the last 12 months, prices have increased by 10.4% in the United States as a whole but by 9.6% in the Los Angeles area.

The Labor Department index for the Los Angeles area covers Los Angeles, Long Beach, Anaheim and the surrounding metropolitan area.

Consumer prices for San Diego will not be available until next month.

The 1.1% rise in the national consumer price index in April lifted 1979 inflation to an annual rate of 13.2%—almost double the 7.4% that President Carter had forecast for this year.

White House officials held out little hope of relief for shoppers until the final half of 1979. Alfred E. Kahn, the chief White House inflation fighter, said that the government could not do "a hell of a lot" about it.

The latest consumer price report dealt another blow to President Carter's anti-inflation program, which was started last October in hopes of lowering the rate of price increases.

The Bureau of Labor Statistics said that the consumer price index had gone up at an annual rate of 11.4% in the first six months after Carter's program began, compared to a 9.5% rate for the preceding six months.

"The April (price index) proves that the program is a flop," AFL-CIO President George Meany said in a

Please Turn to Page 18, Col. 1

Partial List of Air Crash Victims

From Times Wire Services

NEW YORK—Here is a partial list from American Airlines of victims aboard Flight 191, which crashed on takeoff from O'Hare International Airport at Chicago Friday, killing all 270 aboard:

Crew

Capt. Walter H. Lux, based in Chicago.
First Officer James R. Dillard, based in Chicago.
Flight Engineer Alfred F. Udovich, based in Chicago.

Flight Attendants

Catherine Hiebert, 39, based in Los Angeles.
Carol M. Ohm, 34, based in Los Angeles.
Linda L. Bundens, 31, Poway.
Barbara M. Burns, 32, Chula Vista.
James T. DeHart, 28, San Diego.
Linda Marie Prince, 29, Canyon Lake.
Michael W. Schassburger, 36, Coronado.
Nancy T. Sullivan, 32, La Jolla.
Sally Jo Titterington, 33, Bonita.
Carmen Fowler of San Diego.

Passengers

Washburn, Rebecca, Long Beach.
Vanberkhoot, P., Los Angeles area.
Mon, R., Los Angeles area.
Stogel, L. Los Angeles area.
Kuykendal, Dr. D., Los Angeles area.
Kuykendal, Mrs. D., Los Angeles area.
Keeney, H.F., Los Angeles area.
Blake, Stephen, Los Angeles area.
Valle, Dr. R., Los Angeles area.
Charisse, Shiela, Los Angeles area.
Tyne, Mrs. M., Los Angeles area.
Tramell, P., Los Angeles area.
Conner, J., Los Angeles area.
Nordhaus, J., Los Angeles area.
Kamhi, M., Los Angeles area.
Halodoff, P., Los Angeles area.
Harrison, Mrs. W., Los Angeles area.
Files, William, Diamond Bar.
Adams, Jeff, Los Angeles area.
Cady, T., Los Angeles area.
Lent, R.E., Los Angeles area.
Leiman, L.K., Los Angeles area.

Please Turn to Page 28, Col. 1

Florida Executes Killer Spenkelink

BY JEFF PRUGH
Times Staff Writer

STARKE, Fla.—John Arthur Spenkelink became the first person to be executed against his will in the United States in 12 years Friday morning when he died in Florida's electric chair.

A reporter who was among 32 witnesses said that Spenkelink—a 30-year-old California prison escapee convicted of killing a fellow drifter in 1973—appeared to receive three surges of high voltage electricity. The first, at 10:12 a.m., was said to have caused his hands to clench and his legs to jerk.

After two minutes, the reporter said, a physician unbuttoned Spenkelink's white shirt, listened through a stethescope placed against his chest, then stepped back. Two minutes later, the doctor repeated the procedure.

Finally, at 10:18, the physician examined the body a third time and peeled back the black rubber hood over the head to shine a small light into the eyes. The doctor then nodded to David Brierton, the prison superintendent.

It was all over.

Please Turn to Page 12, Col. 1

Court Upholds Juveniles' Rights in Search, Seizure

BY PHILIP HAGER
Times Staff Writer

SAN FRANCISCO—Police may not search a juvenile's personal property without a warrant, even if his parents consent to the search, the state Supreme Court ruled Friday by a vote of 5 to 2.

The court, adding to an ever-growing list of juvenile rights, struck down a search of a toolbox belonging to a 17-year-old Canoga Park boy. His parents, suspecting he was selling marijuana in the neighborhood, had called police to investigate and permitted them to search his bedroom and open the toolbox. Inside, they found nine bags of the contraband.

The court majority rejected the contention that, because parents are responsible for their children, a police search with only parental consent is reasonable and constitutional.

"It would be incongruous to conclude that parents, for good reason or no reason, may summarily waive their child's right to search and seizure protections," Justice Frank C. Newman wrote for the majority.

". . . Justice should not be compromised by well-intended aims to correct transgressing youths, and the rehabilitative value of treating juveniles with fairness must not be underrated."

In dissent, Justice William P. Clark said the decisions violated the "parents' rights to care for, discipline and control their minor children." And, in a separate dissent, Justice Frank K. Richardson said parents had both a responsibility and a legitimate purpose "in seeking to ferret out the existence of any criminal activity conducted in any part of their home."

In its ruling, the court invoked state constitutional guarantees against unreasonable search and seizure. Already, under both federal and state court decisions, youths in juvenile court proceedings enjoy many of the constitutional rights adults do in regular criminal proceedings—in-

Please Turn to Page 10, Col. 1

FEATURE INDEX

THE WEATHER

National Weather Service forecast: Late night and early morning low clouds, otherwise fair through Sunday. Highs today near 78 and Sunday near 80. High Friday, 77; low, 58. High May 18 last year, 70; low, 51. Record high May 18, 103 in 1896; record low, 47 in 1916.

Complete weather information and smog forecast in Part 1, Page 29.

WITNESS DESCRIBES CRASH

'. . . Bang—and Then Just a Huge, Red Ball of Fire'

From Times Wire Services

CHICAGO—Tom Ring, 27, was working at a junkyard near O'Hare International Airport Friday afternoon when he looked up and saw the huge shape of a crippled American Airlines DC-10.

"I looked up, I saw one engine gone. I knew it was going . . . When it missed that (nearby) tower by 10 feet, I knew it was going," Ring said.

Ring said the plane was "going 45 to 50 m.p.h. at the most . . . just barely missed us. There was one engine gone from the plane. It just veered with the left wing down and hit. It was terrible! What can I say?

"The pilot tried hard to steer away from an area where there was a gas station and a lot of junked cars. He tried hard and he did it.

"Me and a carpenter went over the fence, but there was nothing we could do. The fire was too intense. You couldn't go into it to get anyone out."

The plane exploded after hitting the ground, killing everyone on board.

Even after emergency crews arrived at the site, the Rev. Matthew McDonald, chaplain for the Chicago Fire Department, said the heat was too intense to get close enough to perform last rites.

John Wayne, a passenger on an Ozark Airlines flight arriving as the American aircraft was departing, said, "It went over some trees—bang—and then just a huge, red ball of fire. It looked like it pretty much nosed in."

Robert Anderson, a motorist who saw the crash, said, "I looked up and I could plainly see the plane was banking. It was almost vertical and I almost started to scream because I knew it would not come out of it. It continued almost upside down. As it impacted, flames shot out to where I thought my face was going to be

Please Turn to Page 27, Col. 3

CLOSING PRICES
N.Y. Stocks

Los Angeles Times

TUESDAY
Late Final

CIRCULATION: 1,057,611 DAILY / 1,344,660 SUNDAY — TUESDAY, OCTOBER 23, 1979 — LF / 126 PAGES / Copyright 1979 Los Angeles Times / DAILY 25c

FLOWN TO N.Y. HOSPITAL

Shah Has Cancer

State Dept. Reveals His Condition

From Times Wire Services

NEW YORK—Shah Mohammed Reza Pahlavi, deposed ruler of Iran, has been admitted to New York Hospital-Cornell Medical Center, and a State Department spokesman in Washington said today the shah had cancer and a blocked bile duct.

The spokesman, who asked not to be identified, gave no further details.

Meanwhile, department spokesman Hodding Carter III said the length of the shah's stay in the United States will depend on his medical condition.

Carter said the United States had been in prior contact with Iranian authorities about the U.S. decision to permit the shah to travel to this country. He stressed that the United States believes the shah no longer has a claim to authority in Iran.

Pahlavi, who arrived in New York unannounced late Monday night, was lodged in three private rooms on the 17th floor of the hospital's Baker Pavilion. He was tightly guarded by his own security forces, hospital spokesman Ray Rebhann said.

Rebhann said the shah was undergoing tests which would continue through the day. No word on the condition of the exiled former ruler was expected until Wednesday morning, at the earliest.

He would not describe the symptoms of the shah's sickness, but did say that he could not be described as desperately ill.

The 59-year-old shah, looking ill and apparently having trouble walking, arrived at New York's LaGuardia Airport from Mexico at about 10:30 p.m. Monday aboard a small chartered jet.

An airport aide said he was accompanied by a woman believed to be his wife, Empress Farah, and by about a dozen aides and two Doberman pinschers.

The shah immediately got into a limousine that was part of a 12-car motorcade and drove off to Manhattan.

A hospital spokesman said the shah was admitted to the facility on Manhattan's East Side at 11 p.m. and was listed in serious condition.

Iran's Foreign Ministry in Tehran reported earlier today that it had information the shah was suffering from terminal cancer.

Seven hours after the shah's arrival, one of his senior advisers released a statement which did not reveal the shah's ailment.

"His imperial majesty has come to the United States to undergo extensive medical examinations at New York Hospital. The shah and members of his family are optimistic that the outstanding medical care available in the United States will diagnose his ailment and provide a cure," the statement from Robert F. Armao said.

The shah, who will be 60 years old on Friday, has no known history of serious illness. He is an avid skier and an enthusiastic pilot. When he left Tehran in January, he piloted his own jet.

Shah Mohammed Reza Pahlavi
AP Wirephoto

LATE NEWS

Dow Declines as Rally Ebbs

From Times Wire Services

NEW YORK—The Dow Jones industrial average posted its 11th loss in the past 12 sessions today as the stock market failed to make an early advance stand up.

The Dow Jones average of 30 industrials closed off 2.30 at 806.83.

New York Stock Exchange volume was about 33.2 million shares compared with 45.2 million Monday.

Tables in Financial Section.

2 Bodies Found in Palos Verdes

Two men were shot to death and tossed off a 40-foot cliff near Portuguese Bend early this morning after what appears to have been a robbery.

Sheriff's deputies said the men carried no identification and their pants pockets were turned inside out. One of the victims was about 60, the other in his mid-20s. The bodies were found near the intersection of Peppertree Drive and Palos Verdes Drive.

Begin Survives Ouster Votes

JERUSALEM (AP)—Israeli Prime Minister Menachem Begin outlasted a barrage of no-confidence motions in the Knesset (parliament) today with the support of former Foreign Minister Moshe Dayan who resigned from the government.

Five motions were offered in an attempt to oust the Begin government and they were defeated 59 to 47 in a single combined vote.

Gas Rationing Bill Approved

WASHINGTON (UPI)—The House today passed and sent to the White House a bill allowing President Carter to develop a standby gasoline and diesel fuel rationing plan, but requiring the approval of Congress to actually implement it. The bill, which passed the Senate 77 to 18 last Wednesday, was given final approval by the House, 301 to 112.

Woman Loses Freedom Bid

ISTANBUL, Turkey (AP)—A Turkish judge today rejected a defense plea for the release of an 18-year-old Tracy, Calif., woman, Loretta Dooley, jailed on charges of drug smuggling. The judge ruled it "inappropriate" to release the former American Field Service exchange student.

Court to Hear Taiwan Appeal

WASHINGTON (UPI)—A federal appeals court today granted the government's request for an early hearing of a lower court order that President Carter cannot unilaterally terminate the mutual defense treaty with Taiwan.

The U.S. Court of Appeals for the District of Columbia set Nov. 13 for arguments on whether Carter overstepped his authority in terminating the treaty without the approval of Congress.

Japanese May Buy Into Kaiser Steel

Sale of Large Part of Assets Under Study

OAKLAND (AP)—Kaiser Steel Corp., which has suffered a string of losses it blamed partly on foreign steel imports, said today it is discussing the possible sale of "a substantial portion of the company's assets" to a Japanese steel maker.

Kaiser said it is holding the talks with Nippon Kokan K.K., Japan's second largest steel producer and one of the five largest in the world. Kaiser's principal facility is at Fontana, Calif.

Kaiser said discussions are in an early state and gave no details as to prices or assets that might be included.

The announcement said technical teams from the two companies are now visiting each other's plants.

Kaiser, the nation's ninth-largest steel maker, has reported 13 consecutive quarters of losses from its steel-making operations. The company has run into problems with its integrated steel-making facility at Fontana.

"NKK brings to these discussions considerable financial strength and technical expertise. We at Kaiser Steel operate the West Coast's only integrated steel mill, one which contains the most modern steel-making shop in the United States," said Edgar F. Kaiser Jr., the company's president and chief executive officer.

"We have entered these discussions to see if by combining the strengths of each company, we might be able to arrive at an agreement which works to the long-term benefit of all the parties involved," Kaiser added.

The company said it expects that it would be a number of weeks before the discussions might result in any agreement.

An agreement, if reached, would be subject to a definition of the assets to be included, prices and terms of sale. It would need approval of the governments of Japan, the United States and the state of California.

ROYAL SCREAM—Julie Deanne Raatz, 18, a freshman at Pasadena City College, shrieks with joy upon being named 61st queen of Pasadena Tournament of Roses in ceremonies today.
ADDITIONAL PHOTO PART 1, PAGE 3
Times photo by Cal Montney

Kreisky Backs Talks With PLO

From Reuters

VIENNA—Austrian Chancellor Bruno Kreisky said today he would advise President Carter to begin talks with the Palestine Liberation Organization.

Kreisky, who left for the United States today, said in an interview he would tell Carter when they meet on Friday in Washington that the Egyptian-Israeli peace treaty had not solved the Palestinian problem.

He said negotiations for autonomy for the West Bank also offered no real solution because the Palestinians wanted their national identity back and autonomy did not give it to them.

"One cannot let their refugee status last forever," he said.

FEATURE INDEX

'Killer' SALT Amendment Rejected by Senate Panel

WASHINGTON (AP)—The Senate Foreign Relations Committee voted 8 to 7 today to reject a "killer" amendment to the strategic arms limitation treaty that would have asserted the right of the United States to match the Soviet Union's strength in heavy nuclear-tipped missiles.

The vote was the closest test to date of the committee's willingness to forgo adopting amendments that almost certainly would force new negotiations with the Soviet Union and possibly delay the arms control process for years.

Three Democrats joined four Republicans in voting for the amendment, which was offered by Senate Republican leader Howard H. Baker, Jr.

In more than two hours of debate, Baker contended that U.S. SALT II negotiators failed to live up to Senate instructions to negotiate a treaty imposing equal limits on both sides.

He said the fact that the Soviet Union is allowed to retain 308 heavy SS-18 intercontinental ballistic missiles of enormous destructive power unbalances the treaty against the United States.

But Baker readily acknowledged that the United States has never sought to build heavy missiles and is not likely to do so even if given permission under the treaty.

White House counsel Lloyd Cutler concurred, saying American military leaders believe that U.S. strategic forces divided into air, sea and land components are sufficient to deal with the Soviet Union without matching its strength in heavy missiles.

"We would oppose Sen. Baker's amendment as unnecessary and not confirming any military advantage on the United States," Cutler said.

Sen. Frank Church (D-Ida.) the committee chairman, said: "There is just no going argument for this proposal except, for those who oppose the treaty itself, its end effect would be to kill the treaty."

Voting for the amendment were Baker and Sens. Edward Zorinsky, (D-Neb.), Richard Stone (D-Fla.), and John Glenn (D-Ohio), Richard G. Lugar (R-Ind.), Jesse Helms (R-N.C.) and S. I. Hayakawa (R-Calif.).

Last week the committee voted 9 to 6 to kill a Baker amendment that would have placed the Soviet Backfire bomber under SALT II limits.

THE LATEST WEATHER

The Southland experienced variable high cloudiness and slightly cooler temperatures today with more of the same expected Wednesday. The high today will be in the low 80s and in the upper 70s Wednesday, the National Weather Service reported. The low tonight will be in the 60s.

Man Mistakes Son for Burglar, Fires Fatal Shot

A 20-year-old man was shot to death by his father early today in their Encino home after the older man apparently mistook his son for a burglar.

Police said Stephen Saunders returned home unexpectedly from his night-shift job and his father, Maxwell Saunders, a dentist, was awakened by noises.

Maxwell Saunders grabbed a handgun and went to his son's room. He fired once, hitting Stephen in the back, authorities said.

The younger man was pronounced dead by city paramedics.

Police did not arrest the father, although an investigation is continuing. "There was no criminal intent," said Lt. Les Coil, a West Valley homicide detective. "It was one of those lousy tragedies."

Nixon Serene in Face of Ouster, Goldwater Says

WASHINGTON (UPI)—Richard M. Nixon was "serene, confident, cheerful" five years ago as three congressional leaders walked into the White House to tell him he could not avoid impeachment, Sen. Barry Goldwater says.

"He acted as though he had just shot a hole-in-one," Goldwater writes in a new book. "I had never seen him so relaxed."

Goldwater, a leader among conservative Republicans, had been "commissioned" by his colleagues to call on Nixon and ask that he resign.

But it was at Nixon's invitation that Goldwater, joined by Senate and House GOP leaders Hugh Scott and John J. Rhodes, went to the Oval Office.

Goldwater says resignation was not mentioned outright by anyone at the meeting.

Although Nixon had just told the nation he would not step down, he resigned a little more than 24 hours after the Goldwater meeting, effective at noon the following day—Aug. 9, 1974.

In his book "With No Apologies," Goldwater says Nixon reminisced, made complimentary remarks about his predecessor, Lyndon B. Johnson, and spoke of his affection for Dwight D. Eisenhower.

"And then, almost casually, he asked me how things stood in the Senate," Goldwater recalls. "I told him he could count on about 12 votes, perhaps as many as 15. No more. And that it would take 34 votes to defeat the impeachment charges in the Senate."

"The magnitude of the situation brought tears to my eyes," Goldwater says. "The President knew what he must do. Thank God he did not require us to spell out the message we carried.

"When we left, he was smiling."

RESULTS-ENTRIES

Late Racing

Los Angeles Times

MONDAY

Morning Final

CIRCULATION: 1,057,611 DAILY / 1,344,660 SUNDAY — MONDAY, NOVEMBER 5, 1979 — MF / 98 PAGES / Copyright 1979 Los Angeles Times / DAILY 25c

U.S. Embassy in Iran Seized

Fall Fox Hunt: Good ol' Boys Keep It Going

BY RUDY ABRAMSON
Times Staff Writer

EAGLEVILLE, Tenn.—The first faint light of morning was just beginning to backlight the rolling hills off to the east when a long string of pickup trucks went down a gravel road past the tiny Emmanuel Church of Christ and stopped in a field of sage grass.

Presently, wire cages in the backs of the trucks were opened and the valley began ringing with an ungodly cacophony of barking, baying and yelping from about 150 hounds in pursuit of a red fox. Tennessee's famed One Gallus Fox Hunt was under way.

By the time the sun peeped over the trees, the hounds had already covered miles through soybean fields, stands of scrub cedar, pastures marked with outcropped limestone, across barbed-wire fences and in and out of tangled underbrush. They had aroused slumbering farmers, frightened chickens and generally stirred up the countryside between Eagleville, Rockvale and Versailles.

An early morning mist was rising, and with it intermittent clouds of dust, as the hunters who had unleashed their dogs careened around the backroads in their pickups, trying to figure out where the fox had taken the hounds.

For awhile the race headed straight for Willie Manire's house. A sleepy-eyed Manire came out on his front porch just in time to hear somebody yell: "They're driving that fox, buddy, they're driving that fox," and to see half a dozen pickups take off in a cloud of dust.

Put aside the Virginia hunt country image of a red-coated Jacqueline Onassis jumping a fine-blooded horse over a stone fence behind a pack of English hounds nipping at the tail of a fox. Forget the whole gentlemanly notion of brunch and Bloody Marys and riding to the hounds.

This is not the sport of kings—it's the sport of good people like Tom B. Toombs and Butler Smith and Brit Gammon and Judge Jim Warren and Roscoe, Raymond, Robert and Roy Frost.

They are people who have loved their fox hounds as they have loved their families. When Judge Jim Warren's father sent him off to Hampden-Sidney College in Virginia back in the 'teens, the boy took his hounds to school with him. Butler Smith says he is convinced that if all fathers paid as much attention to their daughters' romances as fox hunters pay to their female hounds, "we'd have a better class of people."

For more than half a century now, hunters have been coming here from Tennessee, Kentucky, Alabama,

Please Turn to Page 9, Col. 4

AUTUMN IN L.A.—On a clear day, with winds blowing away the haze, Sunday sailors take to the water in Marina del Rey. Temperatures were in 60s and 70s, and even predictions of rain could not dampen spirits. Marina condominiums are in background.

Times photo by Joe Kennedy

Students Hold 60 Americans

From Times Wire Services

TEHRAN, Iran—Moslem students stormed the U.S. Embassy in Tehran Sunday, seized about 60 Americans and vowed to stay there until the deposed Shah of Iran is sent back from New York to face trial.

A student spokesman told a news conference inside the embassy that about 90 Americans had been seized along with 10 Iranians. However, the State Department in Washington said there probably are only 59 American hostages, but "we can't be precise."

In the shrine city of Qom, a spokesman for Iran's revolutionary leader, the Ayatollah Ruhollah Khomaini, said the occupation of the embassy had the ayatollah's personal support.

There were no reports of casualties in the takeovers of the embassy building, although witnesses said several of the attackers were armed.

One student said 15 women were among the hostages.

Revolutionary guardsmen at the embassy gates did not try to intervene during the attack, which came as tens of thousands of people marched through the streets of the Iranian capital on the first anniversary of the shooting of students by Shah Mohammed Reza Pahlavi's security force at Tehran University.

Western diplomatic sources said Charge d'Affaires Bruce Laingen, who heads the U.S. mission here, was not among the Americans seized by the students. They said he was in touch throughout the day with Iranian Foreign Minister Ibrahim Yazdi, who had just returned from an official visit to Algiers.

The Foreign Ministry, in a statement reported by the official Pars news agency, said:

"Today's move by a group of our compatriots is a natural reaction to the U.S. government's indifference to the hurt feelings of the Iranian people about the presence of the deposed shah, who is in the United States under the pretext of illness.

"If the U.S. authorities respected the feelings of the Iranian people and understood the depth of the Iranian revolution, they should have at least not allowed the deposed shah into the country and should have returned his property."

The students showed reporters embassy files captured in the raid. They said staff members had been trying to burn documents when the embassy was taken over.

(In Washington, the State Department said it had expressed concern to Iranian leaders about the safety of the American hostages and was assured that they are "safe and well.")

The embassy takeover followed a series of virulently anti-American speeches by Khomaini, Iran's de facto head of state, who said recently that he hopes reports that the shah was dying of cancer were true. The deposed monarch is receiving treatment in New York for cancer.

Please Turn to Page 7, Col. 1

Workers' Votes Avert Strike at Supermarkets

BY HARRY BERNSTEIN
Times Labor Writer

Southern California meat cutters Sunday overwhelmingly approved terms of their new three-year contract, but while a slight majority of the Teamsters voted to reject their agreement, there will be no strike against supermarkets today.

A spokesman for the Food Employers Council said the strike, which was scheduled to start today, was averted because under the Teamsters Union constitution the agreement will become effective anyway unless management's last offer is rejected by a two-thirds majority.

This is because of the union theory that a successful strike cannot be called unless the overwhelming majority of the union's membership supports it.

The strike would have affected 7,500 Southern California supermarkets and would have directly affected 20,000 butchers and Teamsters and indirectly involved 60,000 clerks, who are members of the United Food and Commercial Workers Union, which represents the meat cutters, too.

Afterwards, Robert K. Fox, president of the Food Employers Council, said that the "important conclusion of our negotiations with the Teamsters

Please Turn to Page 23, Col. 5

Weighty Issues Riding on a Short Ballot Tuesday

BY RICHARD BERGHOLZ
Times Political Writer

The ballot is short but the issues are very big in Tuesday's special statewide election.

California's voters will pass on four ballot measures that could have a lasting effect on the state's political and educational system.

One—Proposition 4—would attempt to put a curb on state and local government spending. It is the followup to Proposition 13, the property-tax cut measure which won big on last year's ballot. And, like its predecessor, it got on the ballot because enough Californians wanted it, through the initiative process.

Another, Proposition 1, would touch on the most sensitive of school issues these days—court-ordered busing to achieve racial balance.

The measure, put on the ballot as a constitutional amendment by the Legislature, would seek to slow down or limit court-ordered busing by requiring California courts to stay within the guidelines of the federal Constitution as spelled out by the U.S. Supreme Court.

Two other less controversial constitutional amendments round out the statewide ballot.

Secretary of State March Fong Eu predicts about 42% of the state's 10,006,957 registered voters will cast their ballots. Polls will be open from 7 a.m. to 8 p.m.

Mrs. Eu said she believes the turnout will be primarily from those voters who, election after election, cast their ballots without a great deal of urging.

And she is basing her turnout prediction in part on a National Weather Service forecast last week that called

Please Turn to Page 18, Col. 1

Salvador Junta Can't Deliver

BY LAURIE BECKLUND
Times Staff Writer

SAN SALVADOR, El Salvador—Idealistic young military officers who staged a "humanist coup" three weeks ago have been unable to deliver the vast reforms they promised and are in danger of losing control over the new junta they put in power, sources in and around the new government say.

Right-wing security forces have launched brutal tank and machine-gun attacks on leftist demonstrators, killing at least 45 persons last week alone. These actions have successfully torpedoed the image of what was supposed to be a human rights-oriented government.

Old guard military officers, working with a corrupt elite who ran this country through military rule for 47 years, are expected to attempt a countercoup within the next few months.

Furthermore, middle-of-the-road military officers who were brought into the new government by the young coup planners are pulling rank on the junior officers in fear that they may go too far with their reforms.

Seven young military officers, who have never publicly identified themselves, spawned the coup more than six months ago. After ousting the rightist president, Gen. Carlos Hum-

Please Turn to Page 16, Col. 1

Begin Rebukes Israeli Official for Comment on PLO

BY DIAL TORGERSON
Times Staff Writer

JERUSALEM—Prime Minister Menachem Begin on Sunday reprimanded the head of Israel's delegation to the Palestinian autonomy talks for suggesting that Israel might under certain circumstances talk to the Palestine Liberation Organization.

At the regular weekly cabinet session, Begin took Interior Minister Yosef Burg to task for saying in London last week that if the PLO changed its charter and its terrorist tactics it could become "a suitable negotiating partner."

In what Israel radio termed a "severe reprimand," Begin reminded Burg that government policy is not to deal with the PLO "under any conditions." A cabinet minister who attended the session said Burg was also "raked over the coals" by a number of his colleagues.

Begin lashed out at Burg—considered to be one of his staunchest supporters—in an effort to stifle any suggestion from within his government that Israel might moderate its inflexible rule against talking to the PLO. Israel bases its refusal on the PLO's call for the elimination of Israel, a position spelled out in the PLO National Covenant, or charter.

Please Turn to Page 24, Col. 1

BAN ON TOXAPHENE AT ISSUE

Cattle Deaths Stir Pesticide Debate

BY RONALD B. TAYLOR
Times Staff Writer

"Toxaphene is the epitome of a dirty pesticide. If you were to invent something undesirable . . . you would have invented toxaphene."

—N. Kim Hooper, Department of Biochemistry, UC Berkeley.

"Toxaphene is relatively safe . . . It is not a serious threat to man or the environment."

—Paul Schwartz, U.S. Department of Agriculture.

CHICO, Calif.—In a cold, driving rain cattleman George Neary stood bare-headed among the dead and dying cows and calves on his 4,300-acre ranch. Angrily, he cursed the government veterinarians who had sprayed his cattle with a pesticide called toxaphene.

That was last winter. In the ensuing months, the Neary cattle death controversy—known officially as "High Level Episode 6-TEH-79" by the Environmental Protection Agency—has helped to stir a national controversy over toxaphene among government officials, farmers, agribusiness executives and environmentalists.

At issue is whether the EPA will ban or sharply restrict future use of what is now the most widely used insecticide in the nation.

The toxaphene controversy has also raised disturbing questions about how effectively state, federal and local officials meet their responsibilities for regulating chemicals that pose potential threats to the health and safety of millions of persons.

It is estimated that farmers annually apply from 40 million to 100 million pounds of this chlorinated hydrocarbon—a chemical cousin of now-outlawed aldrin, dieldrin and DDT.

More than one billion pounds of toxaphene have been manufactured since it was put on the market by Hercules, Inc., in 1947, according to University of California at Berkeley research scientists. It is used on cotton, vegetable crops and on livestock to control parasites.

On March 16, 1979, after six years of research, the National Cancer Institute reported: "Toxaphene has caused liver cancers in male and female mice . . . . Test results also suggested that toxaphene causes thyroid cancers in rats."

Beyond the cancer institute findings, very little is known about toxaphene's chemical makeup or what happens to it after it is released into the environment, even though toxaphene has been used extensively for about 30 years.

Research scientists are still baffled by the compound's complex structure. Toxaphene is made from turpentine that has been extracted from pine

Please Turn to Page 11, Col. 1

THE WEATHER

National Weather Service forecast: Fair today but mostly cloudy tonight and a chance of showers Tuesday. Highs today in the low 70s and Tuesday in the upper 60s. High Sunday, 70; low, 55. High Nov. 4 last year, 80; low, 51. Record high Nov. 4, 96 in 1980; record low, 41 in 1886.

Complete weather information and smog forecast in Part 1, Page 22.

FEATURE INDEX

ESPOUSES CONSERVATISM

Sen. Church Seeks to Reverse Image at Home

BY GAYLORD SHAW
Times Staff Writer

IDAHO FALLS, Ida.—One day earlier, Sen. Frank Church (D-Ida.) had been the center of attention in a packed Capitol hearing room, presiding as the Senate Foreign Relations Committee debated amendments to the strategic arms limitation treaty with the Soviet Union.

Senate Republican leader Howard H. Baker Jr. of Tennessee, noting that under the treaty the Soviets could have 308 heavy missiles but the United States could have none, proposed language giving the two superpowers parity.

Administration officials argued that U.S. strategy was built around smaller, more mobile missiles and that they had no intention of ever producing such large missiles. Church agreed. He helped to engineer a close committee vote defeating Baker's amendments.

Now, as he taped a weekend public affairs program in the drafty studios of television station KIFI ("serving Idaho Falls, Pocatello and Blackfoot"), Church skillfully steered an interviewer toward topics more palatable to voters in eastern Idaho's potato country.

"I'm a big pusher of gasohol," he said, explaining that the mixture of gasoline and alcohol could help meet America's energy needs. Besides, he added, expanded gasohol production could open up new markets for Idaho farmers.

"Potatoes," he said earnestly, "are very good alcohol producers."

The two scenes, a day apart, give glimpses of the two worlds of Frank Church.

In one, as chairman of the most prestigious committee in Congress, Church is an international figure, consulted and courted by Presidents and prime ministers. In the other, as an embattled incumbent seeking ree-

Please Turn to Page 8, Col. 1

RESULTS-ENTRIES
Late Racing

Los Angeles Times

SATURDAY
Morning Final

CIRCULATION: 1,057,611 DAILY / 1,344,660 SUNDAY SATURDAY, APRIL 26, 1980 MF / 94 PAGES / Copyright 1980 Los Angeles Times / DAILY 25c

IRAN MISSION—STEP BY STEP

Tense Day, Tragic Night

Priority Back to Sanctions and Diplomacy

By OSWALD JOHNSTON and NORMAN KEMPSTER
Times Staff Writers

WASHINGTON—With the failure of its bid to rescue the American hostages, the Carter Administration returned Friday to its long-struggling program of political and economic sanctions against Iran in an atmosphere of deepening pessimism that any solution to the crisis is in sight.

Deputy Secretary of State Warren M. Christopher met Friday afternoon with ambassadors from allied and friendly nations of Europe, Asia and the Pacific and urged them to put into effect the sanctions agreed to by the European Common Market earlier this week.

But senior Administration officials, including Defense Secretary Harold Brown and ranking policy makers at the State Department and White House, did not pretend to expect the situation to improve with the passage of time.

The "balance of forces in Iran," Christopher is understood to have told the ambassadors, now favors the Muslim extremists who have thus far thwarted every U.S. initiative to reach a peaceful solution to the hostage crisis.

"We see a deterioration of the situation in Tehran," another senior State Department official said. "There seems to be some likelihood of an unraveling; the tensions between Iran and Iraq are not promising to the hostages."

In his own meeting with reporters on a day of feverish briefings in this harried capital, Brown made plain his belief that the rescue mission—with its acknowledged high risk of failure and of bloodshed for both rescuers and hostages—had to be undertaken because diplomatic efforts such as the pressure campaign to which the Administration now is returning had no chance of success.

"All diplomatic efforts so far had failed," the defense secretary said. "There was no reason to believe that the hostages would be released at any time in the foreseeable future."

Brown and other officials explained that crucial weather factors—high winds, short nights and high temperatures—will rule out any second attempt at a rescue until next fall at the earliest.

Thus, while refusing for the record to rule out other military options—such as mining Iranian harbors or im-

Please Turn to Page 30, Col. 1

PENTAGON BRIEFING—Secretary of Defense Harold Brown, left, and Gen. David Jones, head of the Joint Chiefs of Staff, as they detailed to reporters the attempted rescue of the hostages.
Associated Press photo

Rescue Attempt's Failure Laid to Copter Breakdowns

8 Dead Left Behind in Raiders' Evacuation; Iran Warned by Carter Against Harm to 50 Hostages

By WILLIAM J. EATON and DON IRWIN
Times Staff Writers

WASHINGTON—A daring dark-ness-to-dawn attempt by a special 90-man military team to rescue 50 U.S. hostages in Tehran—which left eight American soldiers dead in a flaming crash Friday—was aborted when three of its eight helicopters could not go on.

The team was forced to evacuate, leaving the eight dead inside the burning wreckage on a desert salt lake, without ever getting closer than 300 miles to Tehran.

President Carter, saying the commando-style raid would have had an "excellent chance of success" if it had gone off as planned, warned Iran that the United States will continue to hold it responsible for the hostages' safety.

In Tehran, the hostages remained unharmed, despite earlier threats by their militant captors to execute them if the United States employed military force to achieve their freedom. The Ayatollah Ruhollah Khomeini warned that the hostages would be killed if Carter tries another "silly maneuver."

In Washington, Defense Secretary Harold Brown insisted that a military option still is available to the United States. Privately, however, U.S. officials discounted additional use of force in the 174th day of the hostage crisis Friday.

Carter stressed the "humanitarian" goal of the hand-picked, 90-man unit from the Army, Navy, Marines and Air Force that embarked on the rescue effort from the aircraft carrier Nimitz in the Arabian Sea and from undisclosed land bases in the Mideast.

Texts of remarks by President Carter and Defense Secretary Harold Brown in Part I, Pages 34-35.

He said there was no combat and that no Iranians were injured in the episode.

Disclosure of the military mission, however, stirred wide repercussions in the presidential election campaign, in Congress, in European capitals and in Iran. There were these developments:

—While most leaders of Congress backed the President's high-risk plan, a few claimed that he had flouted a

Please Turn to Page 29, Col. 1

Some U.S. Allies Disturbed; Others Are Sympathetic

By FRANCIS B. KENT
Times Staff Writer

Some U.S. allies were clearly upset Friday by President Carter's abortive effort to rescue the American hostages in Iran, but others expressed sympathy. The Soviet Union, however, charged that it was an "armed provocation" that could have triggered a Mideast war.

Tass, the official Soviet news agency, said the move "showed once more that the present master of the White House could not care less about his fellow citizens and is prepared to sacrifice their lives for his election interests."

Allied comments ranged from understanding to open criticism:

—Japan's Foreign Minister Saburo Okita described the action as "regrettable" and "impossible to understand."

—Britain's deputy foreign secretary, Sir Ian Gilmour, spoke out against criticism being expressed in Parliament and added: "I do not condemn the action. This is the time for allies to stick together."

—Prime Minister Menachem Begin of Israel: "I was very sorry about the mistake. It can happen to anybody."

—Prime Minister Odvar Nordli of Norway: "I fully understand the American action because it was aimed solely at freeing the hostages. No nation can sit idle and let this continue."

Some European leaders coolly declined to comment Friday on the American operation. But the heads of the nine countries that make up the European Common Market are scheduled to meet Sunday in Luxembourg, and the subject is certain to come up.

Only four days ago, on Tuesday, the Common Market countries voted unanimously—but under pressure from Washington—to impose economic sanctions on Iran unless the hostages are freed by May 17.

Please Turn to Page 26, Col. 1

Rescue Effort Started Out Smooth but Then Misfired

By RUDY ABRAMSON
Times Staff Writer

WASHINGTON—The call to the White House came at 3:15 p.m. EST.

Several hours earlier, the United States had launched a bold effort to rescue the 50 Americans in their 173rd day of captivity at the U.S. Embassy in Tehran. And so far all had gone smoothly.

Now Secretary of Defense Harold Brown was on the phone from the Pentagon across the Potomac River with an urgent message for Zbigniew Brzezinski, President Carter's national security adviser. The situation was turning sour.

Two of the eight RH-53 Sea Stallion helicopters in the rescue force were out of commission. One had become lost in a dust storm as the armada lumbered low across the Iranian desert, and had turned back to the aircraft carrier Nimitz in the Arabian Sea. The other had made a forced landing and had been abandoned after its crew was rescued.

Now the rest of the force had landed at its rendezvous point 300 miles from Tehran, but shortly after its arrival a busload of Iranians had come down the road and had been taken into custody.

On top of that, a truck loaded with gasoline had come by, and when the Americans shot out its engine to bring it to a stop, the driver, who apparently was a smuggler, had jumped into a sedan that had been following the truck and had escaped into the desert night.

Brzezinski took the disturbing report to President Carter's Oval Office down the hall, and after a hurried review of the situation, they decided the mission would continue.

It was quiet for a while.

Brown called back with a report on refueling operations, which were proceeding normally, and it appeared the super-secret mission would successfully reach the point for a final surprise thrust toward the captured embassy.

But at 4:35 p.m., Brown was on the telephone again; another helicopter had been lost, this one to a failure of hydraulic equipment, leaving only five choppers to sweep into Tehran with 90 members of the anti-terrorist strike force and bring them back out with the 50 hostages.

"I think we have an abort situation," the defense chief said gravely.

Less than a half hour later, a dejected Jimmy Carter called off the mission—an operation he once had publicly declared impossible but had come to believe provided the only real hope of getting the hostages out of Iran in the foreseeable future.

It was an effort conducted in such secrecy that most of those taking part had only a glimmer of what was happening, and it ended in failure and tragedy three hours before anyone but the participants ever learned of it.

Even when Carter ordered the effort abandoned just before 5 p.m. in Washington, there remained a chance that the rescue force could be with-

Please Turn to Page 33, Col. 1

Another Raid and Hostages Will Die, Captors Declare

By DON A. SCHANCHE
Times Staff Writer

TEHRAN—The militants at the U.S. Embassy said Friday they will not harm their American hostages despite the abortive American attempt to free them but warned that "if Carter wants to commit stupid, incompetent acts, he will have the bodies of the spies (hostages) and all his satanic agents buried in Iran."

The Ayatollah Ruhollah Khomeini repeated the militants' warning concerning the likely deaths of the hostages in the event of another military attack and also disputed White House and Defense Department claims that all the survivors of the failed rescue effort had escaped.

"I am warning Carter that, if he commits another stupid act, we will not be able to control the youths who are now guarding the hostages, and he will be responsible for their lives," Khomeini said in a statement issued by his office Friday night.

"If this group had attacked the nest of espionage (the U.S. Embassy), all of them and the spies as well would have gone to hell," he said.

The supreme leader of Iran also said that, contrary to U.S. announcements, more than eight Americans died in the ill-fated attempt to reach Tehran from the east-central Iranian desert. "We think there are dozens," he said. "Dozens of them lost their lives and dozens are wandering in the desert." Washington has stated that no Americans were left behind during the withdrawal.

Foreign Minister Sadegh Ghotbzadeh also said he believed that at least some of the American raiders were at large in the desert near Robat-e Khan, where a winding desert road cuts through virtually unin-

Please Turn to Page 32, Col. 1

Caspian Sea
Ashkabad
U. S. S. R.
Mashhad
0 50 100
MILES
Tehran
I R A N
Qom
DASHT-E KAVIR (SALT DESERT)
Herat
AFGHANISTAN
Robat-e Khan
Tabas
Posht-e Badam
DASHT-E LUT DESERT
Esfahan
Yazd

TRAGEDY IN THE DESERT—U.S. rescue mission was aborted between Yazd and Tabas.
Times map by Russell Arasmith

Candidates Line Up Warily With Carter on Iran Raid

By WILLIAM ENDICOTT
Times Staff Writer

"Victory has a million fathers and defeat is an orphan," a strategist for George Bush said, summing up the political opportunity now afforded candidates trying to take the White House away from President Carter.

Although the immediate reaction Friday to the abortive attempt to rescue the American hostages in Iran was one of support for the President, there were signs that such shows of national unity would soon evaporate in the heat of political campaigning.

After saying he "unequivocally" supported Carter, Bush, for instance, quickly tried to turn the rescue failure to his political advantage by adding that the United States has "seen what it's like . . . to have a President who had no experience in foreign affairs at all. And now we're being asked on the Republican side to think that if (Ronald) Reagan is nominated, that's OK, too."

And Rep. John B. Anderson of Illinois, now running for President as an independent, charged that the "timing of this mission was unfortunate. It came just at the moment that

Please Turn to Page 33, Col. 1

FEATURE INDEX

THE WEATHER

National Weather Service forecast: Considerable cloudiness today and Sunday but partly sunny this afternoon. Highs today near 65 and Sunday near 63. High Friday, 68; low, 52. High April 25 last year, 77; low, 54. Record high April 25, 94 in 1898; record low, 42 in 1882.

Complete weather information and smog forecast in Part III, Page 10.

RESULTS-ENTRIES
Late Racing

Los Angeles Times

MONDAY
Morning Final

CIRCULATION: 1,057,611 DAILY / 1,344,660 SUNDAY MONDAY, MAY 19, 1980 MF / 98 PAGES / Copyright 1980 Los Angeles Times / DAILY 25c

15 Dead in Miami Rioting

Mt. St. Helens Erupts; 6 Killed

By GAYLORD SHAW
Times Staff Writer

VANCOUVER, Wash.—Mt. St. Helens exploded Sunday in an awesome volcanic eruption that caused at least six deaths and widespread damage across the Pacific Northwest.

Described by geologists as the largest volcanic eruption in historic times in the contiguous United States, the breakfast-time explosion literally blew apart the northern flank of the summit in the Cascade Range 50 miles northeast of here.

The force of the explosion was so great that large trees 10 to 15 miles from the mountain were flattened by the blast wave.

The explosion was heard 200 miles away, and it was followed by clouds of steam and ash that reached 12 miles into the stratosphere, where winds carried the debris as far as Montana.

Pyroclastic flows—mixtures of gas and superheated rock—sped down all sides of the mountain and scores of forest fires were reported.

Mud flows, some reportedly traveling at 80 m.p.h., surged into creeks and rivers, causing floods that wiped out bridges and at least one lumber camp, forced the evacuation of entire communities and closed Interstate 5 between Seattle and Portland.

The death toll was reported by Phil Cogan of the Federal Emergency Mobilization Agency. He said five of the fatalities had been confirmed by the Washington State Patrol and the

Related stories in Part I, Pages 4, 14.

sixth was a pilot who flew into utility wires near Yakima, Wash., during poor visibility caused by clouds of volcanic ash.

All airports in Washington state subsequently were closed.

The five victims found near the mountain "were in their cars, and the deaths apparently were due to heat from mud and ash flows," Cogan said.

There also was concern about the fate of Harry Truman, the 84-year-old operator of a lodge at Spirit Lake, just below the northern flank of the mountain. For weeks, Truman had steadfastly refused to leave the lodge where he had spent more than five decades, and government pilots who flew a reconnaissance mission Sunday afternoon radioed back that Spirit Lake is now "all boiling ash and gas—no longer as we knew it."

Although the mountain had been sputtering with volcanic activity since March 27, Sunday's massive eruption came with little warning.

At about 8:30 a.m. seismographs at the U.S. Geological Survey Command Center here recorded an earthquake registering 5 on the Richter scale.

Within minutes, local, state and federal offices were flooded with accounts of the huge explosion, which reportedly was felt as far away as Vancouver, B.C., 200 miles to the

Please Turn to Page 12, Col. 1

SONGWRITERS

Tin Pan Alley Dead End for Most Today

By JOHN. J. GOLDMAN
Times Staff Writer

NEW YORK—It is well past midnight and somewhere in an attic in Small-Town America a struggling songwriter is bent over a battered upright piano. Smoke from a smoldering cigarette drifts through lamplight and across the sheet music.

The night has been a sleepless one for the composer, who sits, searching for the last eight bars. Finally, in the first light of dawn, the right words and melody come.

Now there is another scene. Enter the songwriter pounding on doors, playing his tune for skeptical publishers. Suddenly, when all seems lost, an executive leaps up from behind his desk. "I love it. I'll take it," he says, and another hit record enters production.

Nurtured by countless movies, the romantic notion of the songwriter remains firmly lodged in America's cerebrum. But it is only a notion: The music business is a rough, narrow track these days, even for the most talented. Those *doo-wah* days when a pickup group could harmonize its way to gold records clearly are gone—if they ever existed.

Instead, more songwriters are competing for fewer opportunities. At last count 19,000 songwriters belonged to the American Society of Composers, Authors and Publishers. Most fail to make a living at their craft.

"It's a tough business," says Stanley Adams, ASCAP's president for 24 years. "When you take a grand overall average, you'd be surprised how many songwriters have earned a decent living. People always have an idea, you have a hit and you are set for life and you are a millionaire. These are old wives' tales."

"The main difference is, years ago artists were always looking for material from songwriters," says Marvin Hamlisch, a successful composer. "The change today is, most of the important artists write their own

Please Turn to Page 8, Col. 1

VOLCANIC BLAST—Mt. St. Helens vents a massive cloud of ash, smoke and debris in its most violent eruption since becoming active March 27, bringing floods, fire and death.
Associated Press photo

165 Injured in 2 Nights of Violence

By JEFF PRUGH
Times Staff Writer

MIAMI—Sniper fire and widespread arson and looting Sunday forced authorities to order a dusk-to-dawn curfew and call in 1,100 National Guard troops here. As racial violence continued for a second night the death toll grew to 15, with 165 persons injured.

Police said that fires, burglaries and looting increased Sunday in the wake of Saturday's night-long rioting. Personal violence declined, although five Miami-area police officers were wounded Sunday by snipers.

"In some sections of Miami, we do not have control," Miami Police Chief Kenneth Harms said late Sunday at a press conference. "We have sent fire units in, accompanied by police officers, and they've had to withdraw because of sniper fire and other acts of violence directed against them."

All public schools in Dade County were ordered closed today, as were most private and parochial schools. Bus service throughout the county was stopped indefinitely. Downtown businesses closed. Liquor and firearms sales were banned.

The uprising began Saturday evening when thousands of blacks angrily protested a not-guilty verdict that cleared four white former policemen who had been accused of the beating death of Arthur McDuffie, 33, a black Miami insurance executive, last Dec. 17.

In an attempt to defuse the crisis, U.S. Atty. Atlee Wampler said Sunday that he will ask a grand jury here Wednesday to level federal charges of civil rights violations against the four—Alex Merrero, Ira Diggs, Michael Watts and Herbert Evans.

Wampler asked for all evidence in the seven-week trial, which a judge had called a "ticking time bomb" before he moved it across the state to Tampa because of pretrial publicity here. Dade County State Attorney Janet Reno, whose office prosecuted the case, said that she will comply with Wampler's request.

In explaining his decision, Wampler said Sunday: "The Justice Department and the FBI division here have constantly been on top of the investigation and the prosecution, which in my opinion was very ably handled. Sometimes things in the administration of justice just go awry."

Meanwhile, fires raged in the city's northwest section and downtown Sunday, darkening the skyline with columns of smoke that resembled tornado funnel clouds.

Florida Gov. Robert Graham ordered 1,100 National Guardsmen, 300 state highway patrolmen, four helicopters and an armored personnel carrier into the city to help local law-enforcement officers quell disturbances.

"I ask my fellow Dade Countians to do your part to stop the violence and hatred between black and white Floridians," Graham said in a statement in which he urged compliance with the 8 p.m.-to-6 a.m. curfew.

"Black Americans, as well as white Americans, have worked long and hard since the days of the first civil rights marches to secure a fair portion of the American dream for all our citizens. I am proud to count myself

Please Turn to Page 16, Col. 1

Iran Puts Afghans on Its Islamic Unit

By TYLER MARSHALL
Times Staff Writer

ISLAMABAD, Pakistan—In a blatantly anti-Soviet move, Iran on Sunday admitted eight Afghan rebel leaders to its delegation currently attending the Islamic foreign ministers' conference.

Although Iran has consistently condemned the Soviet invasion of Afghanistan, the seating of six representatives from Peshawar-based rebel groups plus two from the Iranian city of Qom is viewed as a major shift in policy away from the Soviet Union.

"It commits them irrevocably against the Russians on the Afghan issue," a senior Pakistani delegate summed up.

Iran's Foreign Minister Sadegh Ghotbzadeh said the decision means that Iran is fully committed to the

Please Turn to Page 11, Col. 1

Poor Squeezed Hardest by Housing Shortage in L.A.

By AUSTIN SCOTT
Times Staff Writer

The room costs $260 a month and is barely longer and wider than two beds placed end to end. At one time, because of the housing shortage in Los Angeles, eight people—four adults and four children; two unrelated families—called it home.

Tables, chairs and beds are crammed so tightly together that there is almost no space for walking or playing. Possessions—blankets, clothes, toys for the children, a TV, a portable stereo—are piled high on every surface, and spill over onto more tables and chairs that line the tiny bathroom.

A single unshaded light bulb bounces harsh shadows off the green, gold and purple wallpaper that was someone's whim. It was so crowded when eight people called the room home that one man slept in his car every night, while his wife slept with relatives.

The crowding eased a bit last month when the man who slept in his car moved out, taking his wife with him. Now there are only six people crammed into that one-room apartment.

They would like a larger place, they say. But this was the best they could afford when they were forced out of their much larger, $160-a-month apartment because the building was being demolished.

It cost them $567 just to move into

Please Turn to Page 3, Col. 4

LINKS SEEN WITH NEW RIGHT

Evangelicals Seeking to Establish Political Force

By JOAN SWEENEY
Times Staff Writer

With evangelical television preachers as salesmen, a movement is under way to weld "born-again" Christians into a powerful political force.

This vast flock would be mobilized on behalf of "moral" issues and conservative candidates.

However, some leaders of mainline Protestant groups object that the issues around which the born-again Christians are rallying coincide less with biblical morality than with conservative political views. They also point with concern to links between these religious groups and the New Right.

The number of evangelical Christians in the United States is now estimated at about 40 million. So the potential of these leaders, particularly ministers boasting large TV and radio audiences, for reaching voters and raising money is enormous.

And some of them hope to shepherd not only fundamentalists, evangelicals and charismatics, but conservative Catholics, Orthodox Jews and Mormons into their political fold.

The "Washington for Jesus" rally last month, which drew 200,000 persons to the nation's capital, was seen by some observers as a manifestation of born-again Christians' growing political interest.

The event's organizers insisted that its sole purpose was prayer, not politics, but they took pains to call it to the attention of congressmen, and in a city as numbers-conscious as Washington, a group drawing 200,000 on a *Tuesday* was regarded as a political

Please Turn to Page 20, Col. 1

FEATURE INDEX

Africa's One-Time Rio a Ghost Town

By DAVID LAMB
Times Staff Writer

LUANDA, Angola—It's hard to believe now, but only a few years ago Luanda was known as the Rio de Janeiro of Africa. And Angola was full of prosperity and abundance. Ask a Portuguese what life was like here then and he will smile, close his eyes and blow a kiss.

When Angola was a Portuguese colony, he will say, it was a far better place to live than Lisbon, with weekends spent on the beach eating fresh lobsters and prawns, shops stuffed with gourmet foods and the latest European fashions, luxury high-rise apartments overlooking the bay, summer homes at Lobito and Luanda—ah, Luanda . . .

Luanda had 170 nightclubs and restaurants. It was built on hills that rose gently from the bay, the sidewalks were paved with mosaic tile, and the streets were wide and lined with trees. There were parks everywhere, neatly clipped and ablaze with flowers. The skyline, from the 25-story President Hotel to the 17th-Century Dutch fort a few miles away, was like nothing anywhere else in Africa. There was no more striking urban view on the entire continent.

As recently as 1972, Angola grew 90% of its own food and was the world's fourth-largest coffee producer. It had oil, diamonds and iron—and its annual industrial production topped $40 million. It had 17 radio stations, 16 newspapers and 15 magazines.

But all that was before the Portuguese empire — and Angola—col-

Please Turn to Page 5, Col. 1

THE WEATHER

National Weather Service forecast: Morning low cloudiness clearing to hazy sunshine in the afternoons today and Tuesday. High today about 70 and Tuesday in the upper 60s. High Sunday, 74; low, 60. High May 18 last year, 81; low, 57. Record high for May 18, 95 in 1896; record low, 45 in 1916.

Complete weather information and smog forecast in Part IV, Page 5.

RESULTS-ENTRIES

Late Racing

Los Angeles Times

TUESDAY

Morning Final

Circulation: 1,043,028 Daily/1,289,314 Sunday

Tuesday, December 9, 1980

MF/136 pages/Copyright 1980, Los Angeles Times/Daily 25¢

Beatle John Lennon Slain

Shot Down Outside New York Apartment

TONY BARNARD / Los Angeles Times

John Lennon, who was shot to death in New York, is shown during a Los Angeles interview in 1974.

Associated Press

The Beatles in 1965: from the left, Ringo Starr, Lennon, Paul McCartney and George Harrison.

Man Termed 'Screwball' Held in Death of Singer

By JOHN J. GOLDMAN, *Times Staff Writer*

NEW YORK—Former Beatle John Lennon, 40, who led a revolution in popular music that captured the imagination of an entire generation, was shot to death Monday night outside his exclusive Manhattan apartment house.

He was rushed to Roosevelt Hospital, less than a mile from the Dakota, the famous apartment building where he lived with his wife, Yoko Ono. Doctors pronounced him dead at the hospital.

Police announced early today that Mark David Chapman, 25, of Hawaii had been charged with murder. Chief of Detectives James Sullivan said Chapman had arrived in New York about a week ago and had been seen near the apartment building at least three times in recent days.

Sullivan said Chapman had gotten Lennon's autograph when the Lennons left the Dakota about 5 p.m. and had waited outside until they returned six hours later.

Sullivan declined to speculate on a motive for the shooting. Earlier, police had described the suspect as "a local screwball" and "a wacko."

Had Handgun

Police said Lennon and his wife arrived at 10:50 p.m. in a limousine from a recording studio and had just stepped out of the car when the gunman approached them.

"Mr. Lennon?" the man said, drawing a .38-caliber handgun from under his coat.

He opened fire without waiting for an answer.

Lennon, struck in the chest, back and shoulder, staggered from the sidewalk into a small vestibule of the apartment used by the doorman.

The aghast doorman looked at the gunman.

"Do you know what you just did?" he shouted.

"I just shot John Lennon," the gunman responded, throwing down the handgun.

Lennon's wife was not injured.

Police Officer Anthony Palmer was one of the first to arrive at the Dakota. He said it was quickly apparent to him that Lennon had to be

Ted O. Thackrey wrote the biographical material for this article.

rushed to the hospital without waiting for an ambulance.

"I made the decision," Palmer said. "We had to get him out of there. . . ."

Police Officer James Moran, who was in the patrol car that took Lennon to Roosevelt Hospital, said the singer was semiconscious during the ride.

He said he asked the former Beatle if he were John Lennon and Lennon nodded, moaning.

At the hospital, a physician said Lennon was dead by the time he arrived, and efforts to resuscitate him were unsuccessful. He said there had been "a significant" loss of blood from the bullet wounds.

Palmer rode to the hospital in a squad car with Yoko Ono.

He said she was distraught and kept asking, "Tell me he's all right . . . ."

As the news spread, more than 1,000 Beatles fans gathered outside the Dakota, some of them listening to Beatles music on tape recorders.

Please see LENNON, Page 16

Associated Press

A distraught Yoko Ono being escorted from the New York hospital.

Breast Cancer

Some Trying Surgery as a Preventive

By EDWIN CHEN
Times Staff Writer

At age 30, Sharon Hughes took a monumental gamble that she hopes will save her life.

She underwent a double mastectomy in hopes of virtually eliminating her chances of getting breast cancer. She didn't have any signs of the disease at the time.

"I know I couldn't handle breast cancer mentally," said Hughes, who lives in San Diego County. "And I didn't want to spend the next 10 to 15 years worrying about it. I haven't regretted it at all."

Hughes had been plagued by lumps in both breasts since she was 21. Not all women with lumps—known as fibrocystic disease—are likely to get cancer. But Hughes had learned that her type of the disease, atypical hyperplasia, is considered a precursor of breast cancer. When the lumps grew especially large and painful last year, she became alarmed.

A Growing Trend

In choosing to go ahead and have most of her breasts removed, Hughes joined a small but growing number of women opting for a controversial procedure called the prophylactic mastectomy. Many of these women have been told they have a high risk of getting breast cancer because of family history or because of their own breast tissue patterns.

In a prophylactic mastectomy, most of the breast tissue is removed and replaced with plastic or silicone implants. The skin and nipple remain, as do the chest wall muscles and the lymph nodes.

Physicians have argued for decades about how best to *treat* cancer of the breast, which is the most common malignancy among American women. Each year breast cancer kills 34,000 women and is detected in 100,000 more. In 25% to 50% of these cases the malignancies will already have spread at the time of diagnosis, making successful treatment difficult.

What makes prophylactic mastectomies so controversial is that they are an attempt to *prevent* cancer in cases where malignancy has not yet been diagnosed. Many physicians oppose the removal of any organ until there is microscopic evidence of malignancy. Some physicians also question the precision of the criteria used to select candidates for prophylactic mastectomies.

"There is a whole bag of worms in this situation," said Dr. Jerome F.

Please see SURGERY, Page 17

Brezhnev Assailed Over Policy in Afghanistan

By TYLER MARSHALL, *Times Staff Writer*

NEW DELHI—Soviet President Leonid I. Brezhnev arrived here Monday and was quickly confronted by some tough words from Indian President Neelam Sanjiva Reddy about Soviet policy in Afghanistan.

"We in India remain opposed to any form of intervention, covert or overt, by outside forces in the internal affairs of the region," Reddy said at a banquet for Brezhnev. The words clearly alluded to the Soviet involvement in Afghanistan.

Although the official reception given the 73-year-old Soviet leader was warm, the motorcade bringing him from the airport into the city had to detour around a hostile demonstration, and smaller protests were staged at the Soviet Embassy here and at the Soviet consulate in Calcutta.

Brezhnev is here for a three-day state visit, and it is believed that this is the first time that a note of dissent has greeted a Soviet leader in India. The two countries maintain close and friendly relations.

At the banquet, Reddy called for a political settlement of the crisis in Afghanistan, which was invaded by Soviet troops last December.

Although Reddy's remarks represent more an underscoring of India's existing policy than a toughening of its stance, it is considered sig-

Please see BREZHNEV, Page 14

Gasoline Prices Climbing; More Increases Seen

By LYDIA CHAVEZ
Times Staff Writer

Gasoline prices, which late last summer fell for the first time in 18 months, have started to climb again and analysts now expect prices to increase at the rate of 1.5 cents per gallon per month through October, 1981.

The average retail price of gasoline increased by more than half a cent a gallon in the last month, according to the Lundberg Letter, which surveys more than 14,000 stations across the country.

Wholesale prices have jumped even more—1.5 cents a gallon in the last month. However, instead of passing the full increase on to consumers, dealers have had to swallow the bulk of the wholesale increases because of lagging demand.

Jose Espadas, the owner of a Los Angeles Chevron station, said he has had to cut his profit margin to remain competitive.

Profit Margin Down

"I've had to let go of one of my employees and my margin has dropped by 6 cents (to 10 cents a gallon) in the last couple of months," Espadas said. "We're just not pumping as much gas as we used to."

However, like Espadas, who said he plans a price increase in January, dealers now appear to have cut their operating margins as far as practicable and will begin passing

Please see GASOLINE, Page 24

High Zimbabwe Official Released in Murder Trial

From Times Wire Services

SALISBURY, Zimbabwe—Edgar Tekere, Zimbabwe's minister of manpower who was accused of the murder of a white farmer, was freed Monday on a legal technicality even though the African nation's High Court found that he and his bodyguards were indeed responsible for the man's death.

Tekere, a leader of more radical elements within Prime Minister Robert Mugabe's governing party, escaped conviction under a law—revoked since his arrest in August—that shielded government officials from prosecution if the crimes they committed took place "in good faith" to suppress terrorist activity.

Judge John Pittman, a white jurist who was born in South Africa,

Please see ZIMBABWE, Page 12

'A Little More Freedom'

Guarded Sympathy Shown by Muscovites for the Poles

By ROBERT GILLETTE, *Times Staff Writer*

MOSCOW—"*Molodtsi, eti Polyaki*," said the middle-aged Muscovite, a retired professional man who by no means thinks of himself as a dissident. "Good fellows, these Poles."

It was a quick, candid remark, meant to convey a certain admiration for millions of Polish workers who have begun to stand up for themselves and to demand from their socialist state a higher standard of living and a greater voice in their own destiny.

Such sentiments are expressed discreetly and guardedly in the Soviet Union, where—if the word filters along to the wrong co-worker, neighbor or acquaintance—the consequence can be an invitation for a chat and a warning from the KGB security police.

Despite the risks, after five months of turmoil in Poland that has touched every level of society and severely shaken the ruling Communist Party there, sympathetic vibrations can occasionally be heard here.

"Really exciting things are going on in Poland," one young intellec-

Poland's army hints it may have to intervene in unrest. Page 15.

tual who has friends in Warsaw said. "They have gotten a little more freedom for themselves."

These and similar expressions of empathy for Poles appear to be largely confined, however, to the better-educated elite in Moscow and a few other large cities, where at least some of the Soviet Union's relatively privileged people keep

Please see SYMPATHY, Page 14

The Weather

National Weather Service forecast: Clear today and Wednesday with highs today near 68 and Wednesday near 70. High Monday, 68; low, 45. High Dec. 8 last year, 81; low, 59. Record high Dec. 8, 92 in 1938; record low, 30 in 1978.

Complete weather details and smog forecast in Part III, Page 11.

INDEX

U.S. Is Closer to Hostage Terms, Iran Official Says

From Reuters

TEHRAN—The Speaker of the Iranian Parliament said Monday that the United States has moved closer to meeting Iran's terms for freeing the 52 American hostages.

Hashemi Rafsanjani's remarks at a routine news conference were couched in cautious language but stirred the first hope of progress for some time on the issue of the hostages, who spent their 401st day in captivity Monday.

"America has made it clear that it has made some advance in the implementation of our demands. The (U.S.) answer was previously ambiguous, but now it (the United States) has almost made it clear that it is ready to meet these demands," he said.

"In the past, America accepted our four conditions in principle, and this time it has made clear steps in implementing them. In our view, it has got further towards a solution."

Rafsanjani would not give details of the latest U.S. answer to Iran's conditions, which was handed over last week. Diplomats said the ambiguities of translating from the Persian made it hard to gauge from his remarks the extent of change in the U.S. stance.

Iran's four conditions are that Washington promise to unfreeze Iranian assets, return the wealth of the late Shah Mohammed Reza Pahlavi, void all private and public lawsuits in the United States against Iranian property and not to interfere in Iran's affairs.

Washington's first response to the terms was considered unclear by the Iranians, and a second message was delivered in Tehran by Algerian intermediaries last Thursday.

Iran has been studying it since then while the Algerians wait in a

Please see IRAN, Page 9

1981–1989

Los Angeles Times

Circulation: 1,043,028 Daily / 1,289,314 Sunday | Wednesday, January 21, 1981 | CC† / 106 pages / Copyright 1981, Los Angeles Times / Daily 25¢

The Hostages Fly to Freedom

Reagan Takes Office, Asks 'National Renewal'

Associated Press

Reagan takes oath from Chief Justice Warren Burger; with them, Mrs. Reagan, Sen. Mark Hatfield, the outgoing President and Mrs. Carter.

First Action Is a Federal Job Freeze

By JACK NELSON
Times Washington Bureau Chief

WASHINGTON—Ronald Reagan assumed office as the nation's 40th President Tuesday with a passionate call for an "era of national renewal" and a pledge not to compromise on his promises to cut taxes and reduce the size of the federal government.

In his first official act as President, less than an hour after being sworn in, the former California governor signed an order imposing a federal hiring freeze that he said "will eventually lead to a sizable reduction in the federal work force."

"It is time for us to realize that we are too great a nation to limit ourselves to small dreams," declared Reagan, who during the 1980 campaign said President Carter had too limited a view of the nation's potential.

Not Doomed to Decline

"We're not, as some would have us believe, doomed to an inevitable decline," he said. "I do not believe in a fate that will fall on us no matter what we do. I do believe in a fate that will fall on us if we do nothing. So with all the creative energy at our command, let us begin an era of national renewal."

Inaugurated as the American hostages were being freed in Iran, Reagan also had a warning for international terrorists. He declared that no weapon against them is so formidable as one employed by Americans—"The will and moral courage of free men and women.

"Let that be understood by those who practice terrorism and prey upon their neighbors."

Reagan made no direct reference to the hostages in his forcefully delivered, 19-minute Inaugural Ad-

The text of President Reagan's Inaugural Address. Page 16.

dress. But the high drama of their release dominated the conversations of many of the thousands who turned out to watch the inaugural ceremonies and parade under cloudy skies and in almost spring-like weather.

The planes carrying the hostages to freedom took off from Tehran just a few minutes after the President completed his speech.

Reagan began his speech with a tribute to Carter—the man he crushed in a landslide vote Nov. 4—for his efforts in carrying on the tradition of assuring an orderly transfer of authority.

"Mr. President," Reagan said, "I want our fellow citizens to know how much you did to carry on this tradition. By your gracious cooperation in the transition process, you have shown a watching world that we are a united people pledged to

Please see REAGAN, Page 15

Speech Displays Enthusiasm for Nation's Future

By GEORGE SKELTON
Times Staff Writer

WASHINGTON—More than anything else, Ronald Reagan's Inaugural Address Tuesday illustrated the self-confidence and philosophical conviction that have fueled his extraordinary political career.

There were the catch-phrases that all speechwriters bleed for, of course—a "new beginning" and an "era of national renewal."

But this speech was most striking for its skilled, faultless delivery and straightforward message of unabashed enthusiasm for America's future.

Nation Gets Good Look

It was vintage Reagan. The former California governor has given thousands of speeches in his 14-year political career, but probably none any better. And it offered the nation a good look at its new President.

What Americans saw was a leader with exceptional skills at communicating with the public. Certainly not since John F. Kennedy, and before that Franklin D. Roosevelt, has the country had a President who could match Reagan's skills in front of a microphone or camera.

In Reagan's case, these skills also extend to an unsurpassed stage presence and physical self-confidence—attributes obviously developed

Please see ADDRESS, Page 15

Country Band Plays 'Dixie'

Carter Returns Home to a Hero's Welcome

By ELEANOR RANDOLPH and JEFF PRUGH, *Times Staff Writers*

PLAINS, Ga.—In a cold, dreary rainstorm that seemed tailored for a man who had resoundingly lost his presidency, private citizen Jimmy Carter returned home Tuesday to a hero's welcome.

A country band played "Dixie," a crowd estimated at 3,000 cheered and Carter wearily but happily danced cheek-to-cheek with his wife, Rosalynn, on a wooden platform, where one red-white-and-blue banner read "Welcome Home, Jimmy" and another read "Welcome Home, Hostages."

Exhausted but publicly upbeat, Carter assured his friends and supporters that the last dramatic day of his presidency had been emotional but not unduly sad.

Carter used the makeshift platform on Main Street to make his first public statement on the freeing of the hostages, announcing that shortly before landing in Georgia at 3:35 p.m. he learned officially that the Americans had cleared Iranian airspace and were finally free.

'Prisoners No More'

"It's impossible for me or any of us to realize how they feel on that plane because they realize they are hostages no more, they are prisoners no more," Carter said to the wildly enthusiastic crowd. "And they are coming back to this land that we all love."

Carter, who was scheduled to leave Plains before dawn this morning to fly directly to Weisbaden, Germany, on behalf of President Reagan, offered several rounds of praise to the Algerians, Reagan, the families of the hostages, the men who died in the abortive raid last year and finally to the American people.

"The Algerians in the last few weeks have been the real heroes," said Carter, who added that American diplomats were expected to make a special trip to Algiers to thank the hostage negotiators.

Test of 'National Will'

To the crowd huddled under umbrellas and large hats, Carter also said: "I thank my successor for the care with which he approached this issue." He also called the hostage crisis a "test of our national wisdom, as well as our national will."

"My thoughts at this moment are with the families of the hostages," Carter said, "but also with those who risked and who gave their lives on a desert in Iran (in the aborted rescue attempt last spring). Their pride and patriotism must not be forgotten . . ."

He went on to thank the American people, who voted him out of office almost three months ago. He called them "proud people, not naturally patient, who have stood by me through these 14 months."

Please see CARTER, Page 24

52 Americans Welcomed in West Germany

By HARRY TRIMBORN
Times Staff Writer

WIESBADEN, West Germany—The freed 52 American hostages arrived in West Germany shortly before dawn today on the final stop in their long journey home from 14½ months of captivity in Iran.

A cheer went up from a crowd as the first of two U.S. Air Force transports touched down at 6:44 a.m. (9:44 p.m. Tuesday PST) at a U.S. military air base near Frankfurt.

The plane, its navigation lights flashing, taxied slowly toward the welcoming crowd, which raised a large banner proclaiming, "Welcome Back to the U.S.A."

The first C-9A transport rolled to a stop at 6:49 a.m. The door swung open, revealing a sign saying, "Welcome Back to Freedom."

Laingen First Off

At the foot of the ramp to greet the freed hostages were former Secretary of State Cyrus R. Vance and Walter J. Stoessel Jr., the U.S. ambassador to West Germany. L. Bruce Laingen, the highest ranking diplomat among the hostages, was first off the plane.

The hostages all were wearing Air Force parkas with fur-trimmed hoods to ward off the 23-degree cold.

The second plane, carrying half of the freed hostages and former De-

Please see GERMANY, Page 7

Grateful U.S. Celebrates Release

By GAYLORD SHAW
and OSWALD JOHNSTON
Times Staff Writers

WASHINGTON—Free at last, the 52 American hostages who endured so much for so long at the hands of taunting Iranian kidnapers traveled with tears and laughter Tuesday night toward a nation that never forgot them during their 444 days of captivity.

The flight to freedom began 33 minutes after Ronald Reagan assumed the presidency from Jimmy Carter, who had devoted his last hours in office to turning national humiliation into what he called "this day of joy and thanksgiving."

First the journey was to Algeria, the North African nation that acted as middleman in negotiating the agreement exchanging frozen Iranian gold and bank deposits for the hostages' release. Then, with holiday dinners of turkey and the trimmings en route, it was on to a U.S. military hospital in Wiesbaden, West Germany, for several days of rest before the 50 men and 2 women—most of them diplomats and military personnel—headed home.

Church Bells and Sirens

And from the beginning of their odyssey, all across a thankful land Americans joined in spontaneous celebration with silent prayers, the pealing of church bells and a cacophony of sirens and honking horns.

"They're Free! They're Free!" flashed a huge sign in New York's Times Square. The torch atop the Statue of Liberty was lit. So was Washington's National Christmas Tree, symbolically dark during two trying holiday seasons.

America's first glimpse of the freed hostages came via satellite

Related hostage stories on Pages A, B, C, D, 4, 5, 6 and 8.

television transmissions when they stepped from an Algerian airliner in Algiers eight hours after leaving Tehran amidst shouts of "Down with America" from their militant captors.

There were 52 faces wreathed in smiles in Algiers—and animated talk and laughter—as some flashed "V for Victory" signs. The first two off the plane—political officer Elizabeth Ann Swift and cultural attache Kathryn L. Koob—wore in their hair the yellow ribbons that at home had symbolized a nation's hope for their safe return.

The chief U.S. negotiator, Deputy Secretary of State Warren M. Christopher, repeatedly received warm hugs as he stood on a rain-slicked airport tarmac. "We are very glad to be here, believe me," said Robert C. Ode, at 65 the oldest of the hostages.

Christopher, who four years ago

Please see HOSTAGES, Page B

Formal Dress, Up-Kicking Heels Mark GOP Day of Joy

By RUDY ABRAMSON, *Times Staff Writer*

WASHINGTON—With three days of determined celebrating already behind them, Republicans from across the land began congregating at daybreak Tuesday to cheer their man, Ronald Reagan, into the White House.

They were still kicking up their heels in the wee hours, long after the nation's capital ordinarily rolls up its sidewalks.

Washington had fun Tuesday as it does only once every four years, on the days when it inaugurates a President.

By 7:30 a.m., the faithful were taking their places along historic Pennsylvania Avenue, the inaugural parade route. They were waiting for front-row seats at the West Front of the Capitol, where the swearing-in took place, and staking out choice vantage points in standing areas. Some of them carried portable radios to keep up with developments in the hostage crisis.

By the time Ronald and Nancy Reagan and George and Barbara Bush went off to services at St. John's Episcopal Church, across Lafayette Park from the White House, party activists had gathered

Please see DAY, Page 14

Associated Press

Elated hostages arriving in Algiers include, from left, Barry Rosen, Donald Cooke and Kathryn Koob; two others are not identified.

The Weather

National Weather Service forecast: Variable high cloudiness today. Mostly cloudy tonight and Thursday. Highs today about 68 and Thursday about 65. High Tuesday, 70; low 56. High Jan. 20 last year, 69; low 43. Record high Jan. 20, 82 in 1912; record low, 30 in 1883.

Complete weather details and smog forecast in Part IV, Page 11.

I N D E X

Los Angeles Times

Circulation: 1,043,028 Daily/1,289,314 Sunday — Monday, March 30, 1981 — LF/78 pages/Copyright 1981, Los Angeles Times/Daily 25¢

Reagan Shot

Assassin's Bullet Lodged in Chest; 3 Others Wounded; Gunman Seized

Associated Press

Two Secret Service agents shove President Reagan into limousine after he was hit in chest by an assailant's bullet in Washington.

President Undergoes Surgery at Hospital

From Times Wire Services

WASHINGTON—President Reagan was shot in the chest by a gunman today outside a Washington Hotel. He was reported conscious and in "good" condition before doctors started to operate to remove the bullet at George Washington University Hospital. One lung was partially collapsed.

Three other men were hit, including presidential press secretary James S. Brady.

Presidential aide Lyn Nofziger said, "The president was shot in the left chest. The bullet did not hit the heart."

The Secret Service said John Warnock Hinkley, Jr., 22, of Evergreen, Colo., was arrested. Secret Service spokesman Jack Warner said the suspect had fired a .38-caliber revolver.

A Secret Service agent, Timothy J. McCarthy, was shot in the chest. A city policeman also was wounded and was reported in critical condition at the Washington Hospital Center.

Vice President George Bush, en route from Fort Worth to Austin to address the Texas legislature, was ordered to fly directly back to Washington.

Nofziger, asked if Reagan's wound is serious, replied, "Obviously a wound in the chest is a serious wound."

But he said Reagan had not lost consciousness and had walked into the hospital talking to his companions.

Four or five shots were fired at close range by the gunman, and the Secret Service immediately shoved Reagan into the waiting limousine.

Brady's condition was not immediately known, but he was taken to George Washington Hospital bleeding profusely from the head.

Nancy Reagan, who was not with the President at the hotel, rushed to the hospital to be with her husband.

A television cameraman who was near the alleged assailant said Brady was shot in the forehead. The cameraman said the gunman "just opened up and started firing" about 10 feet from Reagan.

The burst of gunfire sounded as Reagan left the Washington Hilton Hotel after addressing a union convention. The President strode smiling from the hotel and walked toward his limousine a few paces away. He turned to acknowledge the shouts of "Mr. President" from newsmen seeking to question him.

Then came the burst of gunfire.

Momentarily Stunned

Reagan appeared momentarily stunned. Secret Service agents drew their pistols as others hustled Reagan into the limousine. One shot apparently hit the automobile before Reagan got into it, blasting a hole in the rear window.

The scene outside the hotel was one of pandemonium. There were shouts from security men and a crowd quickly gathered at the hotel, about a mile from the White House.

Secret Service agents and police pinned the apparent assailant to the ground.

Reagan is the sixth U.S. President in this century who was the target of an assassination attempt. Two of the six, William McKinley and John F. Kennedy, were killed.

The shots fired at Reagan today marked the first assassination attacks since Sara Jane Moore and Lynette (Squeaky) Fromme, tried to shoot President Gerald R. Ford in separate incidents in northern California in September, 1975.

Associated Press

James S. Brady, President Reagan's press secretary, who was wounded at Washington hotel.

Neither Ford nor anyone else was injured in that incident, which was remarkably similar to today's attempt against President Reagan.

Moore, who is still serving a prison sentence, was waiting across the street when Ford emerged from the St. Francis Hotel and fired a single shot at him as he walked to his limousine.

She was quickly subdued by bystanders.

Moore later pleaded guilty to charges of attempting to assassinate Ford. She was sentenced to life imprisonment.

Fromme was found guilty of attempted assassination of the President and is serving a life term.

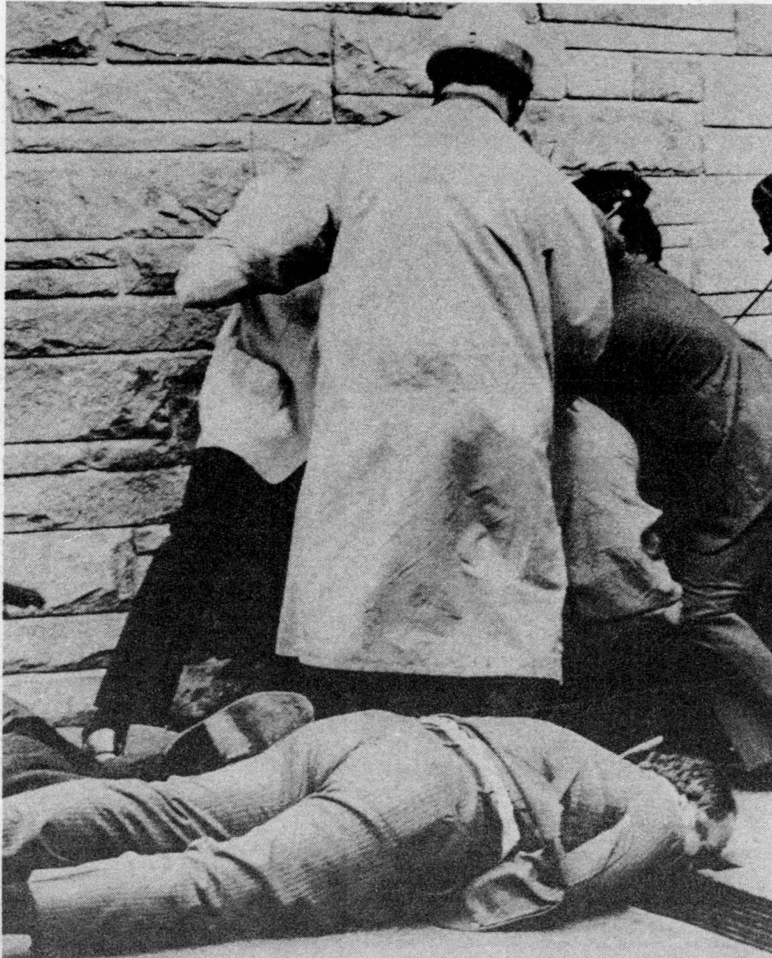

Associated Press

James S. Brady, President Reagan's press secretary, lies wounded as police wrestle with gunman.

N.Y. Stock Exchanges Halt Trading

NEW YORK (UPI)—The New York Stock Exchange and the American Stock Exchange stopped trading today after the assassination attempt on President Reagan. Prices were in a tailspin at the time.

Trading diminished rapidly after the shooting in which presidential Press Secretary James A. Brady and two other men also were wounded.

The Dow Jones industrial average, which had risen more than six points over the 1,000 level in the early afternoon, was off 2.88 points to 991.89 when trading was halted at 3:22 p.m. EST.

The Pacific Stock Exchange and the Toronto Stock Exchange also halted trading.

3 Austrians Called Spies

VIENNA (AP)—Acting on a tip from a Romanian defector, the Foreign Ministry has suspended three employees suspected of espionage activities, officials said today. The names of the three were not disclosed.

THE LATEST WEATHER

Gusty northwest winds swept the Southland today, ranging from up to 20 m.p.h. in the Los Angeles area to 35 m.p.h. or more in the mountains. A travelers advisory was issued for the winds in the mountains through this evening. Los Angeles Civic Center temperatures were expected to peak in the mid-70s on Tuesday.

Troops Attack Hijacked Jet

BANGKOK, Thailand (AP)—Thai troops today attacked a hijacked Indonesian jetliner parked on an airport runway here with 55 hostages and five armed hijackers aboard, witnesses said. It was not immediately known if anyone was hurt.

Hours earlier the Thai government announced Indonesia had agreed to free 80 political prisoners as demanded by the hijackers who seized the plane in Indonesia Saturday and diverted it here.

The soldiers put ladders up against the fuselage and climbed to the wings, witnesses said. Short bursts of machine gun fire were heard as two doors were forced open. No activity could be seen inside the aircraft as all but one of the soldiers entered.

EXTRA

Los Angeles Times

Circulation: 1,043,028 Daily / 1,289,314 Sunday | Wednesday, May 13, 1981 | LF / 120 pages / Copyright 1981, Los Angeles Times / Daily 25¢

Pope Shot 3 Times, Rallies After Surgery

LATE NEWS

Dow Subdued After Shooting

From Times Wire Services

NEW YORK—The stock market showed a subdued response to the shooting of Pope John Paul II today. The Dow Jones index of 30 leading industrial stocks, which was off a fraction in early trading, fell more than three points after news of the assassination attempt reached the trading floor. By late in the session, however, the Dow industrials had regained that loss and were up 0.54 to 971.36 at 3 p.m. EST. Gainers held a 4-3 lead over losers in the broader tally of New York Stock Exchange-listed issues.

Because of the shooting of the Pope, The Times will not carry closing New York stock prices in today's Late Final edition. Tables in the Business section relflect prices as of 2 p.m. EST.

State Closes Perris Hospital

RIVERSIDE (AP)—The state Department of Health today suspended the operating license of a Perris hospital where 25 elderly persons died under mysterious circumstances and immediately closed the facility.

Four patients, the only ones in the hospital, were transferred to other nearby medical facilities, said Deputy Atty. Gen. James Lahana.

Body of IRA Faster Held

BELFAST, Northern Ireland (AP)—British authorities today refused to turn the body of IRA hunger striker Francis Hughes over to members of his family unless they drop plans to take it through Roman Catholic West Belfast for a hero's farewell, Sinn Fein, the IRA's political arm, reported.

French Stocks Bounce Back

PARIS (AP)—French stock prices, which collapsed after Socialist Francois Mitterrand's presidential election victory, rebounded in heavy trading today.

The market, which had dropped 20% in the two days of trading since Mitterrand's election, responded with a strong rally, averaging 9% for the issues quoted.

THE LATEST WEATHER

Continued fair skies with mild temperatures were forecast for Los Angeles Thursday by the National Weather Service. The downtown high should be in the mid-70s after an overnight low in the low 60s.

Public Flocks to Churches to Pray for Pope

From Times Wire Services

Shock quietly was succeeded by fervent prayers today as word spread of the shooting of Pope John Paul II. Churchgoers flocked to special services where they were asked to "pray your hearts out for our pontiff."

"I'll pray for him," was the reported reaction of President Reagan, still recovering from a bullet fired by a would-be assassin.

Reagan called Cardinal Terrence Cooke in New York and "expressed the sorrow of the American people and expressed his personal concern" for the Pope, Deputy White House Press Secretary Larry Speakes said.

Special Masses

Special Masses were scheduled all over California and the 4.8 million Roman Catholics in the state were urged by their bishops to go to church sometime during the day to pray for the Pope.

"The urgency . . . is prayer," said Cardinal Timothy Manning, archbishop of the Diocese of Los Angeles. "That's our commerce, to pray for the man and for peace all over. This is just a sign and a symbol of that kind of insanity plaguing our world today."

Manning celebrated a special Mass for the Pope at noon in the downtown Los Angeles St. Vibiana's Cathedral. But he said, "We're going to ask all the churches to have special Masses."

Though the identity of the assailant was unknown at the time he talked to reporters, Manning suggested that he was "one of many who are victims of a strange insanity that pervades the world today . . . with violence as the only means to vent their anger or whatever it might be."

Programming Interrupted

As television networks broke off regular programming to go on the air with news of the attack on the Pope, people gathered grim-faced around TV sets—repeating the pattern set only six weeks ago when Reagan was shot.

At New York City's St. Patrick's Cathedral, crowds gathered. A murmur of shock and cries of "Oh, God" arose from worshipers at the noon Mass when they were told the Pope had been shot.

"I have some dreadful, tragic news to tell you," The Rev. Charles Mahoney said before beginning Mass. "Pope John Paul II was shot just a few minutes ago. . . . We want you today to pray your hearts out for our pontiff."

INDEX

Associated Press

Pope John Paul II, who was shot today in St. Peter's Square.

Overwhelmed by Mobs

Pontiff Has Shrugged Off Threats Since 1978

From Associated Press

Pope John Paul II has shrugged off death threats and braved mobs who nearly overwhelmed him with love as he has traveled around the globe since becoming pontiff in 1978.

The Pope has been protected by such diverse groups as an anti-terrorist force with submachine guns in Ireland and police wielding special tennis rackets in Japan.

The Swiss Guard of the Vatican, founded in 1505, acts as the personal guard of the Pope. Its members are recruited from the Roman Catholic cantons of Switzerland.

John Paul has also frequently been accompanied by a personal bodyguard, Bishop Paul C. Marcinkus, a 6-foot-3, 58-year-old former football player from Cicero, Ill. The bishop also often escorted Pope Paul VI, serving as advance man for his travels. He was credited with saving Paul when he was attacked during a 1970 visit to the Philippines.

John Paul visited six countries in 1979 alone. His travels have taken him to South America, Asia, Africa, the United States and Europe.

On Feb. 16 this year, a bomb exploded at the national stadium in Karachi, Pakistan, killing one person only minutes before Pope John Paul II arrived to say Mass. The dead man was later identified as a follower of the late Pakistani Prime Minister Zulfikar Ali Bhutto. The Pope apparently did not learn of the incident until after he reached the stadium.

The same Asian tour included visits to the Philippines and Japan. In Manila, a 17-year-old wearing a T-shirt with the slogan "I Love You" frightened observers by rushing toward the Pope in the stadium at Santo Tomas University. The youth kissed the Pope's hand and got a papal embrace in return before he was led away by police.

It was in the Philippines that a knife-wielding Bolivian painter tried to stab Pope Paul VI in 1970.

Everywhere John Paul II has gone there have been crowds, mostly friendly, but potentially dangerous because of their size.

Nearly a year ago, on July 7, 1980, crowds of slum-dwellers in Salvador, Brazil, broke through security lines and surged toward the Pope. John Paul, his white cassock spattered with mud, was forced to duck into a bus reserved for the papal party to escape the crush.

Turk Suspect Seized in St. Peter's Square

From Times Wire Services

VATICAN CITY—Pope John Paul II was hit by three bullets today fired at close range before 18,000 horrified people in St. Peter's Square by a man said to be an escaped killer from a Turkish prison.

The Pope underwent emergency surgery and was said by Vatican officials to be in satisfactory condition after being hit in the left hand, right arm and lower stomach.

The most serious wound was in the stomach and caused intestinal lesions. No vital organs were hit, the Vatican said.

The pontiff's heart and lungs were working well as he underwent surgery more than two hours after the attack, said Dr. Luigi Candia, medical director of the Gemelli Policlinic.

Doctors said the Pope is expected to survive.

The Vatican said a small part of the 60-year-old Pope's intestine was removed in the surgery, during which he received a transfusion. Vatican radio said the Pope was "serene and calm" before the operation, which began at 5:55 p.m.—8:55 a.m. PDT.

Police said the shots were fired from a 9-millimeter pistol by a 23-year-old man who identified himself as a Turkish national and kept repeating, "I couldn't care less about life." Police said he gave his name as Mehmet Ali Agca and told them he was a student at the University for Foreigners at Perugia, north of Rome. However, the university said no such student is enrolled.

Associated Press

Mehmet Ali Agca, the suspect, shortly after his arrest in Rome.

Two Women Wounded

A man with a similar name escaped from a Turkish jail in November, 1979, after admitting the assassination of a moderate Turkish newspaper editor. However, there was no immediate confirmation that the suspect in the shooting of the Pope and the escaped man were the same.

First reports from Italian police sources said two men were seized and a third was being sought in the shooting, but officials later made no mention of any suspect except the 23-year-old who identified himself as Agca.

Police said in addition to the 60-year-old Pope, two women were wounded by the four or five bullets fired in St. Peter's Square. One was identified as Ann Odre of Buffalo, N.Y. She was not in serious condition, police said.

In Buffalo, friends said Mrs. Odre, a widow, was a tourist on a two-week trip to Italy that included "a chance to talk to the Pope." Her party was led by Msgr. Donald Szostak, the rector of St. Joseph's Cathedral, who had been a papal chamberlain in 1977.

"We heard two shots. A terrible quiet fell over the crowd. Then all of a sudden screams and yelling began. People were pushing and shoving. The Pope slumped over. Guards were running after people," said Betty Holsten of Minneapolis, Minn., who was in the square.

The Vatican radio appealed to the faithful around the world to pray for the Pope, whose 61st birthday is Monday.

Vatican radio said the pontiff had been driven through St. Peter's Square in his Jeep and was about to leave the Jeep to start a general audience when shots were heard.

The pontiff collapsed into the arms of his aides as the Jeep returned inside the Vatican at high speed, the radio said.

Seconds later an ambulance followed by a car with Vatican dignitaries carried the Pope to the Gemelli Policlinic, Rome's most modern hospital.

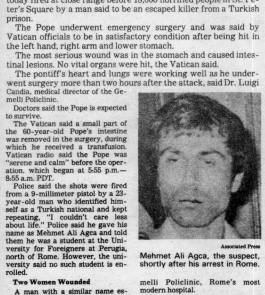

The Roman Catholic Church in the Pope's native land expressed "deep shock" over the shooting and said "the whole church of Poland is praying for his speedy return to health."

Warsaw television interrupted its regular program to report the assassination attempt, and Warsaw radio carried a bulletin a few minutes earlier.

In a dynamic 30 months on the throne of St. Peter, Pope John Paul II has used his brand of personal magnetism to bolster the Roman Catholic Church and proclaim its traditional values.

Unflaggingly energetic, the 60-year-old Polish-born pontiff has consistently delivered his message on travels around the world—a triumphal return to Poland, a visit to the United States, a tour of Africa or island-hopping in the Philippines.

John Paul has spoken out eloquently and forcefully against violations of human rights, denounced economic exploitation and spent time with the poor, the sick and the young.

But he has warned against effecting social change through violence and told priests not to meddle in politics.

Strong on Family Issues

On family issues, he has strongly reaffirmed the church ban on artificial birth control, divorce, abortion and polygamy.

He says that the church, "as a good mother," will aid its children "in difficult times."

After the reforms of the 1960s and the turbulence of the 1970s, John Paul's papacy for the 1980s and beyond appears aimed at clamping down on excesses, tightening the ranks and making sure no doubt among Catholics as to where the Pope stands.

A number of Popes early in the church's 2,000-year history were killed and are regarded by Catholics as martyrs, including St. Peter.

New York Stocks

Los Angeles Times

Late Final

Circulation: 1,081,050 Daily / 1,340,743 Sunday

Monday, June 21, 1982

LF† / 92 pages / Copyright 1982, Los Angeles Times / Daily 25¢

Israelis Bombard West Beirut

LATE NEWS

Dow Up, Then Down

From Times Wire Services

NEW YORK—The stock market relinquished a broad advance today as continued fears about interest rates overshadowed news that the recession may be nearing an end.

The Dow Jones average of 30 industrials closed down 1.33 at 789.95.

New York Stock Exchange volume was about 50.37 million shares compared with 53.8 million Friday.

Tables in Business Section

ERA Beaten in Florida

TALLAHASSEE, Fla. (AP)—The Florida Senate today defeated the equal rights amendment on a 22-16 vote, further reducing any chance it might still have of being added to the U.S. Constitution.

The Senate defeat, its fifth in 10 years, effectively nullified the 60-58 endorsement ERA received earlier today in the Florida House. The amendment, which would prohibit discrimination based on sex, has a June 30 deadline for passage by three more states.

Hunger Strike Ends

MOSCOW (AP)—Yuri Balovlenkov ended a 43-day hunger strike today after Kremlin authorities promised that he could leave the Soviet Union and live with his American wife in the United States.

"She is very happy!" exclaimed Balovlenkov, a 33-year-old computer programer, minutes after he broke the news by telephone to his wife, Elena, a nurse in Baltimore, Md.

$5.5-Million Jackpot

HARRISBURG, Pa. (AP)—A suburban Philadelphia mother of four has won $5.5 million by buying a $1 Pennsylvania Lotto ticket, making her the largest lottery jackpot winner in the nation, officials said today.

Lottery Bureau director Lynn Nelson identified the winner as Dorothy Thomas, 52, of Havertown, a western suburb of Philadelphia. Nelson said Thomas is a customer service representative at Girard Bank. Her husband, John, is an employee of the Postal Workers Credit Union in Philadelphia. They have two sons and two daughters.

Iran War to Continue

LONDON—The Ayatollah Ruhollah Khomeini said today that Iran will continue the Persian Gulf War until all its demands are met, despite Iraq's decision to withdraw its invasion force, Tehran radio said. The revolutionary leader said Iraq's announcement that it was withdrawing was a plot.

Georgia Inmates Riot

SAVANNAH, Ga. (UPI)—Angry inmates at the Coastal Correctional Institute at Savannah took over a prison building today, setting fires and throwing burning material out windows. The disturbance spread to at least four other cellblocks.

There were no injuries reported, and officials said no hostages were taken. The inmates, who issued a list of 10 demands, were not known to have any weapons.

Gibraltar Talks Put Off

From Reuters

LUXEMBOURG—British Foreign Secretary Francis Pym said today that Spain and Britain have agreed to postpone negotiations over the future of Gibraltar, at Spain's request.

This means that Spain's frontier with the British rock colony will not be reopened Friday as originally planned.

Heir to the British Throne

Princess Di Gives Birth to a Son

From Times Wire Services

LONDON—The Princess of Wales gave birth today to a boy, who will be second in line the the British throne, Buckingham Palace announced.

Charles had kept vigil at his wife's side, waiting in the five-story wing of the hospital for the birth of the child who may one day succeed him on the British throne. The baby, second in line of succession after Charles, is the most truly English heir to the monarchy in more than 400 years.

The baby was the first born to a Prince and Princess of Wales in 77 years, and in line to become the most English monarch since King James I reigned from 1603-1625, according to experts at Debrett's Peerage.

Diana, a descendant of four English kings, became the first English bride of an heir to the throne in 303 years when she and Charles were married at St. Paul's Cathedral July 29, 1981.

The scene outside the hospital took on a carnival atmosphere as thousands waited in intermittent rain. Hawkers sold strawberries and cream to spectators, some of whom said they had been at the hospital in West London since before dawn.

London bobbies manning the hospital entrance accepted flowers and greeting cards from delivery-men, who arrived in a steady flow.

Queen Kept Informed

Queen Elizabeth II went ahead with a scheduled tour of a Royal Air Force base at Wittering, Cambridgeshire, but kept in touch with Diana's progress through a special hotline radio link between the hospital and her Andover aircraft.

In the past, royal mothers gave birth in palaces or mansions, and the queen was said to have favored the privacy of Buckingham Palace for the arrival of her third grand-child. Three of the queen's four children were born there, and her only daughter, Princess Anne, was born at Clarence House, the official London residence of the Queen Mother.

But the royal surgeon-gynecologist reportedly argued in favor of St. Mary's, where medical backup equipment would be available in the event of an emergency. Princess Anne had her two children in the private wing of the state-run hospital.

Charles returned home Sunday afternoon after reviewing a British parachute regiment in France, crossing the English Channel by helicopter in 90 minutes.

His wife greeted him at Windsor Castle, 30 miles west of London, and Press Assn., the British news agency, said she drove their car on the return trip to London.

Associated Press

The Princess of Wales, who gave birth to a baby today in London.

1,235 Nuclear Protesters Arrested at Livermore Lab

LIVERMORE, Calif. (AP)—Police in riot gear arrested 1,235 anti-nuclear protesters who attempted today to block entry to the Lawrence Livermore Laboratory, one of the nation's foremost nuclear weapons development facilities.

About 3,500 demonstrators, many in wheelchairs and some carrying banners, had shown up by late morning at the 640-acre facility about 50 miles east of San Francisco.

A coalition of about 200 anti-nuclear groups said they planned to stage a three-day blockade at the laboratory. Up to 5,000 demonstrators were expected.

There was no violence today. Those arrested, including many who went limp and had to be dragged away, were charged with obstructing traffic, a misdemeanor.

About 55% of Staff on Duty

Jack Kahn, associate director of the lab, said about 55% of the staff was on duty, somewhat below normal for a weekday. He said employees had been told to try to get to work but not to jeopardize their safety.

The demonstrators denounced the University of California's role in nuclear weapons development. The university operates the lab under contract with the government.

The facility conducts tests on most U.S. nuclear weapons research and design projects, along with its sister lab in Los Alamos, N.M.

The California Highway Patrol attempted to defuse the protest by diverting traffic off nearby freeways around the frontage roads leading to the laboratory. However, traffic jams increased as more and more people attempted to reach the lab, which employs 7,300 people.

About 120 officers from the Highway Patrol, the Alameda County Sheriff's Department and the Livermore Police Department were on hand.

The Livermore Action Group and its subgroups dedicated to nuclear disarmament want the Livermore installation converted to peaceful uses.

More than 1,500 anti-nuclear activists signed up to be arrested voluntarily during the demonstration, said Bob Cooper, a spokesman for the demonstrators.

Trained on Berkeley Campus

About 500 people were trained Sunday in non-violent protest methods on the University of California campus at Berkeley.

The training, which focused on various civil disobedience techniques, pitted demonstrators pretending to be police officers against other protesters, who were dragged off to a "booking area."

The protesters try to conduct at least one demonstration at the lab each month. About 250 people had been arrested at the facility this year before today.

4 Plead Guilty to Coup Attempt in Seychelles

VICTORIA, Seychelles (AP)—Four foreigners pleaded guilty today to treason in last November's bungled attempt by mercenaries to overthrow the Seychelles government, court officials said. Two others pleaded innocent.

Treason carries a maximum penalty of death by hanging in this Indian Ocean republic, and the charge can be applied to foreigners as well as Seychelles citizens.

Fond of Pertini

I'm in Love, Nancy Jokes

WASHINGTON (AP)—Nancy Reagan joked today that she had fallen in love with Italian President Sandro Pertini during her recent trip to Europe with President Reagan.

The First Lady described Pertini, an octogenarian, as "a darling little man," and said, "I may be in love" with him.

Her remarks were made during a White House luncheon for Senate wives.

The President's wife also said the entire 10-day, four-nation trip was wonderful, and their stay at Windsor Castle "just extraordinary and wonderful. And they (the British Royal Family) are so warm and so easy and all of them have such a wonderful sense of humor."

She seemed amazed as she described preparations for a white-tie dinner at the castle in the Reagans' honor.

"They had a man walk on the table with irons to press out the creases in the tablecloths," she gushed. "And they had a man with pillows on his feet walking down the tables placing the candelabra."

"There were so many memories and so many incidents I could tell you about," she said. "You are just lucky I didn't ask you over for a slide presentation."

20 Killed in Non-Stop Barrage

From Times Wire Services

BEIRUT—From land and sea, Israeli gunners unleashed a non-stop bombardment of Palestinian positions and residential areas of encircled West Beirut today, killing at least 20 people and hitting a hospital in one of the heaviest barrages of the two-week-old war.

The Palestine Liberation Organization reported "many casualties" as the shells, at one point whining overhead every three or four minutes, crashed into Palestinian camps and tenements. In mostly Muslim Lebanese neighborhoods of West Beirut, 77 people were wounded, Lebanese police reported.

The PLO said the Israeli gunners scored a direct hit on the Acre hospital of the Palestinian Red Crescent near the four-lane highway leading to Beirut's paralyzed international airport.

The PLO said two patients under treatment for earlier injuries were killed and 13 others, including five children, were injured. It called for "urgent international action to prevent further Israeli barbarism."

While diplomatic efforts to save the city stalled, the Israelis launched their biggest attacks on the Beirut area since declaring a cease-fire 10 days ago, and convoys of Israeli troops were reported moving toward the Lebanese capital from the south.

Begin in Washington

Israeli Prime Minister Menachem Begin, meeting with President Reagan in Washington, has said Israel has no plans to take the capital.

Israeli gunboats and ground artillery meanwhile pummeled refugee camps and residential neighborhoods as well as Palestinian strongholds in Muslim West Beirut.

One shell fell just a few yards from the Commodore Hotel, headquarters for most of the foreign journalists covering the war.

Police sources said a shell landed in the garden of the Soviet Embassy compound in West Beirut, slightly injuring two diplomats.

Begin said Sunday that the Soviets had asked Israel to guarantee the safety of their embassy and had been assured that the diplomatic headquarters would not be harmed.

Israel also shelled Syrian positions to the east of the capital. Israeli forces, which have reportedly destroyed about 300 Syrian tanks in the war, said they had knocked out four more in a sudden exchange of fire.

Guerrillas Are Trapped

The new violence renewed fears that Israeli forces surrounding Beirut might launch an attack on the city, where about 6,000 Palestine Liberation Organization guerrillas are trapped.

Travelers from the south reported seeing major Israeli troop movements northward, including row after row of orange-red Israeli city buses carrying soldiers in the direction of Beirut.

They said they saw 120 Israeli tanks and armored cars around Damour, 13 miles south of Beirut, and another 70 heavy armored personnel carriers moving north from Sidon to Damour.

Tens of thousands of Beirut residents cowered in basement shelters or fled to the city's eastern sector to escape the artillery, armor and naval fire.

The Palestinians claimed that Israeli ground forces used the covering shellfire to launch a long-expected assault against the guerrillas' West Beirut stronghold, but were beaten back. The Israeli command in Tel Aviv said, however, that the shelling began after guerrillas fired first.

Israel had promised to hold off its threatened onslaught against the PLO's West Beirut nerve center to facilitate U.S. special envoy Philip C. Habib's peace efforts, but the promise evidently did not apply to shelling.

THE LATEST WEATHER

Considerable low cloudiness was predicted through Tuesday for Los Angeles, but the National Weather Service said clearing will occur in mid-afternoon and early evening. Early-morning drizzle is expected in some areas. The high should be near 70.

Cornered in Backyard of Home

Police Kill 6-Foot Bear in Granada Hills

By BILL BILLITER, *Times Staff Writer*

An apparently wild bear lumbered into the Granada Hills section of Los Angeles early today, scaring some residents and leading officers on a three-hour chase before being shot and killed.

The 6-foot, 350-pound animal, described as fast and agile, was tracked by an animal control officer and Los Angeles police on foot, in cars and in a police helicopter. It was cornered and shot about 4:40 a.m.

"An effort was made to capture the bear alive after it was cornered in a backyard, but it started to attack a police officer and Animal Control Officer Michael Fowble, and so it had to be shot," said Gary Olsen, district supervisor for the city Department of Animal Regulation.

No one was hurt in the bear hunt.

Olsen said the animal was a mature male black bear and apparently wild since it had burrs and ticks in its fur. He said it is possible that the bear was someone's escaped pet, but if so it was illegal. Bears cannot be kept as pets in Los Angeles, he noted.

Olsen said the bear was first sighted at 1:20 a.m. by Granada Hills residents near Bull Canyon. Officers found the animal about 3:45 a.m.

About an hour later, the bear was cornered in a backyard near Jellico Avenue and San Jose Street, close to Granada High School and just north of California State University, Northridge. Officers tried to lasso the bear, but when it lunged at them Police Officer Henry Izzo killed it with two shotgun blasts.

Olsen said the bear's carcass will be offered to a museum, possibly to be stuffed and used as an educational exhibit.

The bear was first spotted just below the Santa Susana Mountains, where it may have come from.

Are there more bears in those hills?

"If there's one, there are more," Olsen said. "Our wildlife officer is tracking in Bull Canyon to see if he can find more. But I don't think we'll see another bear. This is a very rare thing."

INDEX

Late Sports

Los Angeles Times

Morning Final

Circulation: 1,081,050 Daily / 1,340,743 Sunday | Thursday, December 2, 1982 | MF / 220 pages / Copyright 1982, Los Angeles Times / Daily 25¢

Man Given Artificial Heart

Horn of Long Beach

His Campus Is Also His Battlefield

By MAURA DOLAN, *Times Staff Writer*

A group of 10 men and women sat around a conference table in a room adjoining the campus office of Stephen Horn, president of California State University, Long Beach. Evangelical Christians and aides to conservative Republican legislators wanted Horn to remove a book about lesbian sex from a class reading list.

An aide to Assemblyman Dennis Brown of Signal Hill tried to explain that his dislike of the book did not mean he is naive or prudish.

"We've all read books like this at one time or another," said the aide, 27, in the kind of tone that is usually accompanied by a wink or a nudge.

Horn, who was allowing his deans and vice presidents to run the meeting, suddenly perked up.

"Young man, I am 50 years old and I have never read pornography," participants quoted the bespectacled, balding president as saying. "You are wrong to assume we have all read this kind of material."

Uncomfortable Silence

An uncomfortable silence settled over the room. The aide, taken aback, said nothing.

The meeting was typical of Horn's encounters with controversy. As always, he was doing the unexpected—throwing people off guard. The book, after a review, remained on the university's bookshelves.

Smart, politically shrewd and impatient with formal structure and bureaucracy, Horn has defied yearly speculation of an imminent departure and survived 12 years as chief executive of the largest and, in recent times, the most controversial of the 19 Cal State campuses.

He has fought with faculty leaders, taken swipes at the chancellor's office, seen his campus shelled by international publicity and managed, through it all, to keep his position intact.

Fostered Strong Ties

For all his problems, Horn also enjoys good relations with the student body and with the Long Beach community. City officials in Long Beach say Horn was responsible for integrating the campus into the community and fostering strong cooperation between the two.

In Sacramento, Horn is regarded as an effective lobbyist for his campus. During the 1970s, he successfully lobbied for new campus buildings and received them even when others higher on the chancellor's list of statewide priorities were declined.

"Steve Horn, it seems, has an ability to rise above the fray and escape into academia," said a member of the statewide Board of Trustees, disquieted by recent events on

Please see HORN, Page 3

Los Angeles Times

Sen. Edward M. Kennedy as he bowed out of presidential race.

Sen. Kennedy Won't Enter 1984 Race

By ROBERT SHOGAN, *Times Political Writer*

WASHINGTON—Sen. Edward M. Kennedy took himself out of the 1984 contest for the White House Wednesday, setting off a scramble among the remaining Democratic presidential prospects for the support that had made him a principal contender.

The Massachusetts senator's withdrawal, which he attributed to concern for his children, appeared to make former Vice President Walter F. Mondale the front-runner, at least for the time being.

Kennedy indicated that he was bowing to the wishes of his children—Kara, 22; Edward Jr., 21, and Patrick, 15. They reportedly were concerned that another presidential campaign would bring more attacks on his character and perhaps further threats against his life.

Might Run in 1988

"My first and overriding obligation now is to Patrick and Kara and Teddy," Kennedy said. "I will not be a candidate for the presidency of the United States in 1984."

In announcing his withdrawal, Kennedy made it plain that he intends to maintain his role as the Democratic Party's most vigorous spokesman for liberal goals. "The causes which have always been my concern I remain firmly committed to," he said.

And Kennedy hinted broadly that he might return to the presidential competition in 1988, if circumstances are favorable. "I don't think it's any mystery that I would like to be President," he said. "Actually, I enjoyed campaigning in Iowa in

Please see KENNEDY, Page 10

Many Homes Still Dark in Storm's Wake

By CATHLEEN DECKER and JACK JONES, *Times Staff Writers*

Weary workers cleared debris from storm-battered Southern California on Wednesday with efforts that ranged from the raking of suburban lawns to a massive attempt to restore downed electrical lines.

Tens of thousands of Southland homes remained without power late Wednesday, and utility company officials said that some homes will remain dark until Saturday.

At the height of the wind-packed storm, which slammed into Southern California at dawn Tuesday, more than 1.6 million homes lost power for varying periods.

Efforts to repair damage were hampered by persistent winds that continued Wednesday and also by the exhaustion of repair crews, some of whom had worked for 32 consecutive hours. Many workers were ordered to rest.

No Room for Error

"When you've got 12,000 volts in those lines, you only get one mistake," said San Diego Gas and Electric spokesman Fred Vaughn.

The storm's damage extended to Central and Northern California, where about 10,000 homes remained blacked out late Wednesday.

There were some isolated snow showers Wednesday over the Tehachapis as well as east of Inyokern, west of Palm Springs and northeast of San Diego, with light rainshowers elsewhere.

But mostly, Southern California was left with brisk, cold winds and high surf.

A building high-pressure system should bring fair skies today and Friday, forecasters said. And it should be a little warmer, with maximum readings in Los Angeles today from 62 to 66 degrees. There will be gusty northerly winds near the foothills.

Wednesday's Los Angeles Civic

Please see STORM, Page 3

House Votes to Halt FTC Rules on Professions

By PAUL HOUSTON, *Times Staff Writer*

WASHINGTON—The House Wednesday administered a large dose of relief to doctors, lawyers and other professionals, voting to exempt them from Federal Trade Commission enforcement of rules against price-fixing, boycotts and deceptive advertising.

By a vote of 245 to 155, the House attached the heavily lobbied amendment to a bill that reauthorizes funding for the FTC. Minutes earlier, the House had failed narrowly to pass a compromise amendment, supported by key Democratic and Republican leaders, that would have preserved most of the FTC's enforcement powers. That amendment lost, 208 to 195.

An analysis of that vote showed that 17 House members, including eight Californians, who received the legal maximum campaign contribution of $5,000 from the American Medical Assn., the chief lobbying force behind the exemption, voted for it. Only one $5,000 recipient—Rep. Carl D. Pursell (R-Mich.)—voted against the AMA.

The Senate Commerce Committee has voted a similar exemption for professionals in a companion FTC bill. But the measure faces a probable filibuster on the Senate floor that could kill it in this lame-duck session of Congress.

If the measure dies this year, it

Please see FTC, Page 8

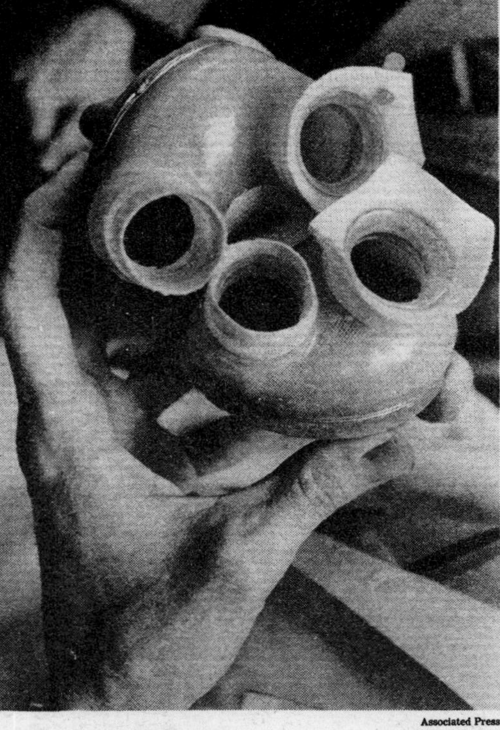

Associated Press

Model of artificial heart implanted by Salt Lake City surgical team.

Implant of Permanent Pump a First

SALT LAKE CITY (UPI)—Surgeons replaced the dying heart of a 61-year-old dentist today with the first permanent artificial heart implanted in a human.

The historic operation at the University of Utah was a last-ditch effort to save the life of Barney Clark of Seattle.

The second of two plastic pump chambers was snapped into place in his chest cavity about 3½ hours after the procedure began, officials said.

"Blood is actually flowing through the heart now," John Dwan, a spokesman for the University of Utah Medical Center, said as surgery drew to a close early today.

He said doctors had begun the painstaking process of weaning the patient from a heart-lung machine to the new heart.

Surgeons had to complete sewing up the connections to natural tissue before activating the artificial heart. That was to be done before the opening in the chest was closed.

If successful, the operation would mean Clark must be connected for the rest of his life by two tubes to an external air compressor running the implanted device.

'Bound to Bed'

Dr. Chase Peterson, university vice president for medical services, likened it to "life tethered to a grocery cart."

"He's now bound to a bed," Peterson said after surgery started. "Therefore he would have more movement if the operation is successful. He would be able to walk around his apartment."

The operation headed by Dr. William DeVries was moved up 9½ hours because Clark's condition was deteriorating rapidly. Peterson said his heart had slowed to "barely a quiver."

Peterson said the 6-foot 4-inch patient was conscious and alert when he visited with his family before being rolled into the operating room.

About two-thirds of the heart—the lower pumping chambers—were removed from Clark at 12:07 a.m. The heart's two upper chambers were left in place.

The artificial heart, called the Jarvik-7, is a double polyurethane pump that must beat 100,000 times a day to move oxygen-rich blood through 60,000 miles of vessels. If it failed, the man would be doomed.

Approved Project

Doctors cautioned before the surgery started that the chances of a full success were slim. The chairman of a university review board, which approved the project last year, said then that the first person to receive the artificial heart probably would not live for more than a few hours.

Dr. Willem Kolff, the inventor of the artificial kidney and head of artificial organ research at the university, said Wednesday he would consider the operation a success "only if the man is restored to a happy life."

Kolff described Clark Wednesday as a "bright, articulate, knowledgeable candidate who understands the importance of the operation and who wants to make a contribution to

Please see HEART, Page 4

Mexico's New President Urges 'Great Sacrifices'

By JUAN M. VASQUEZ, *Times Staff Writer*

MEXICO CITY—In one of the most somber inaugural addresses ever delivered by a Mexican president, Miguel de la Madrid declared Wednesday that Mexico finds itself in a grave crisis that will demand "great sacrifices."

"I cannot offer, in the immediate future, any substantial or rapid improvement in our situation," De la Madrid said in his 70-minute speech, which was largely devoted to the themes of economic recovery and public corruption.

Moments after donning the tricolor sash of office, the silver-haired chief executive warned his countrymen that neither help from abroad nor quick solutions could overcome the problems Mexico faces.

"I am aware that I assume office in difficult hours," De la Madrid said.

"Recovery will take time—at least two years. The first months of the government will be arduous and difficult. The situation demands it. Austerity is mandatory."

A crowd of about 2,500 legislators, federal officials, foreign diplomats and invited guests sat in attentive silence throughout the speech in Mexico's new congressional building. Leaflets placed on each seat asked the audience to withhold all applause until the end.

Some scattered applause was heard when De la Madrid mentioned the accomplishments of his predecessor, Jose Lopez Portillo. Then, however, the new president launched into a grim survey of the economic and social problems faced by his country. He portrayed Mexico as practically bankrupt, burdened by government corruption and marred by social inequality.

The economy, he said, suffers from staggering inflation, zero growth, a lack of foreign exchange,

Please see MEXICO, Page 13

U.S. Grants Big Loan to Brazil

By JACK NELSON, *Times Washington Bureau Chief*

BRASILIA, Brazil—President Reagan announced Wednesday a $1.23-billion government "bridging" loan to financially pressed Brazil and approved creation of a joint task force to study restoring a U.S. military assistance program that Brazil canceled in a bitter dispute in 1977.

The 90-day loan from the U.S. Treasury Exchange Stabilization Fund is intended to help Brazil cope with a serious liquidity problem in its massive foreign debt until it can draw money from the International Monetary Fund.

Treasury Secretary Donald T. Regan expressed confidence that Brazil will be able to repay the loan and said its approval should signal private banks that "the U.S. and Brazil are standing together at the time Brazil needs help."

"Everyone knows that Brazil is having problems," Regan told reporters at a briefing here. "Brazil is a great nation, has a great long-term future. Temporarily, it is in some type of straits. There is a pro-

Please see REAGAN, Page 14

Court Grants Accused Nazi Delay of Deportation Order

By CHARLES MAHER, *Times Staff Writer*

An ailing, aging, suspected Nazi war collaborator, who has resisted three decades of on-and-off government efforts to deport him, Wednesday won a federal court ruling that may allow him to live out his life in the United States.

A divided panel of the U.S. 9th Circuit Court of Appeals ruled that Andrija Artukovic, 83, a longtime resident of the Orange County beach community of Surfside, should have his deportation case reopened—a process Artukovic's attorney said could take five to 10 years.

Artukovic has "been in and out of the hospital with a heart condition," his attorney, Ronald H. Bonaparte said.

The accusations against Artukovic stem from the period during World War II in which Ante Pavelic, an avowed Fascist, took over much of Yugoslavia after its former government fell to Axis armies.

The Pavelic government, driven by extreme nationalism and adherence to the Roman Catholic church, renamed its territory Croatia and began purging Serbs and Jews.

Artukovic, who became Pavelic's minister of the interior, headed an elite military corps known as the Ustashi, which conducted the purge and controlled concentration camps.

Yugoslavian authorities later accused Artukovic of complicity in the execution of 750,000 Serbs and gypsies and 20,000 Jews during the war and sought to have him extradited for trial on 22 counts of murder. He emphatically denied the allegations and a U.S. commissioner turned

Please see NAZI, Page 18

INDEX

WEATHER

U.S. Weather Service forecast: Today—fair and a little warmer. Gusty northerly winds near the foothills. Friday—sunny and warmer.

Temperatures	High	Low
Wednesday	61	52
Today's forecast	mid-60s	near 50
Friday	upper 60s	near 50
Dec. 1 last year	72	50

Record high Dec. 1, 1972 85
Record low Dec. 1, 1880 38

Complete details, Page 15, Part IV.

U.S. Drafts Low-Cost Plan to Reduce Unemployment

By WILLIAM J. EATON, *Times Staff Writer*

WASHINGTON—The Reagan Administration is drafting a package of relatively low-cost proposals to try to reduce both long-term unemployment and the record level of joblessness among youths 18 to 24.

President Reagan has not yet seen the plans being drafted by Cabinet-level committees, but he has said that he intends to present a jobs program to Congress early next year.

Economic policy-makers in the Administration said the jobs proposals will be made in addition to the $5.5-billion-a-year highway and bridge repair program, financed by a 5-cent-a-gallon increase in the gasoline tax, which has bipartisan backing and would provide 320,000 jobs.

Reagan's jobs proposal would compete with a $5-billion public works measure being developed by House Democratic leaders that would provide 250,000 jobs.

Neither Reagan's approach nor the Democratic program would make a major dent in unemployment—11.6 million persons now are idle—but the political jockeying over the issue is expected to be intense when the 98th Congress convenes next month.

The Administration plans to use additional subsidies for employers, along with expanded job training, as the basis of its attack on unemployment.

The aim would be to encourage employers to hire young persons and to provide on-the-job training, either during summer vacations or year-round for dropouts and high school graduates.

Please see JOBS, Page 9

Late Sports

Los Angeles Times

Morning Final

Circulation: 1,081,050 Daily/1,340,743 Sunday · Tuesday, May 3, 1983 · MF/96 pages/Copyright 1983, Los Angeles Times/Daily 25¢

Quake Devastates Town

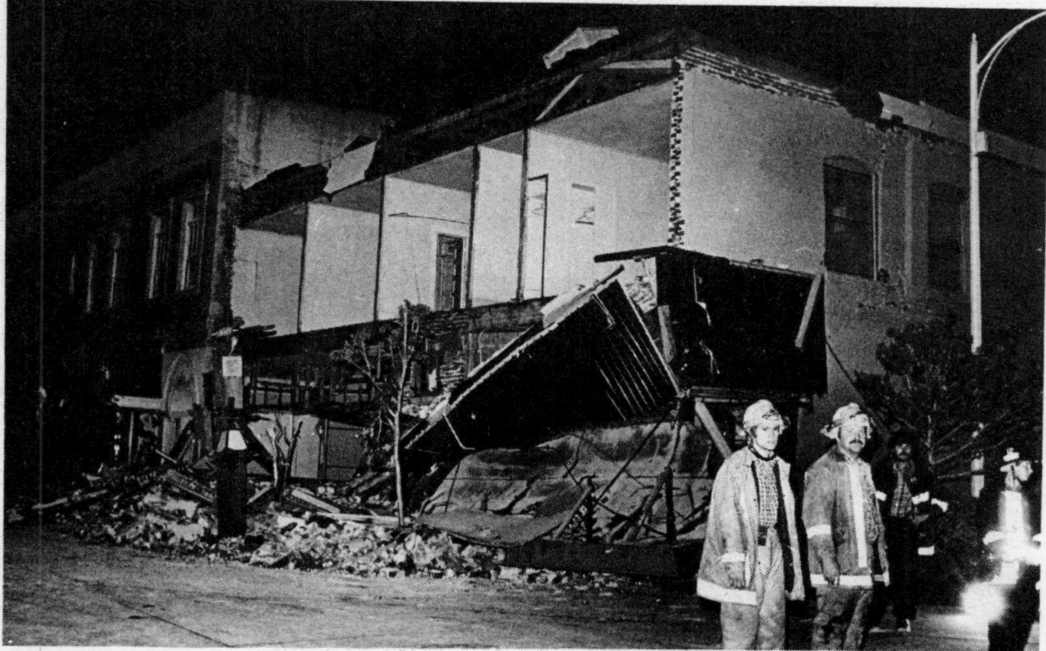

GARY FRIEDMAN / Los Angeles Times

Firemen survey the wreckage of a building in downtown Coalinga after a major earthquake caused its front wall to tumble into the street.

100 Buildings Collapse in Coalinga; 53 Injured

By ERIC MALNIC and TED THACKREY JR., *Times Staff Writers*

COALINGA, Calif.—A major earthquake hammered Central California Monday, turning this western San Joaquin Valley town into a disaster of collapsed buildings, hissing steam, broken glass and fires that towered 60 feet into the sky.

There were no immediate reports of deaths, although at least three people were believed to have suffered major injuries, 50 others were less seriously hurt and there was speculation that others might be buried in the debris.

Fresno County Emergency Services Department coordinator Roy Manning said at least 100 structures had been destroyed by the temblor, and added that of the city's 2,000 houses, virtually all had sustained damage of one kind or another.

He said the city's water supply was contaminated and should be boiled before use, but said the hazardous waste dump outside the city seemed to be untouched by the quake.

Emergency Status Declared

Gov. George Deukmejian declared a state of emergency, clearing the way for property tax relief and possible federal disaster aid as well.

Seismologists at the University of California, Berkeley, said the temblor evidently began at 4:43 p.m., lasted about 20 seconds, and was measured at 6.5 on the Richter scale—a major event, comparable to the ones that devastated Long Beach in 1933 and Sylmar in 1971.

They said the epicenter appeared to be about five miles northeast of Coalinga, which is a town of about 6,500 located 45 miles southwest of Fresno, and added that the main jolt was followed by a series of aftershocks occurring "every eight or nine minutes."

Snapped petroleum lines in nearby oil fields sent fires blazing through the rolling country outside the city, according to Charlotte Button of the state Department of Emergency Services, and clouds of steam were reported hissing from great cracks in the earth.

But Ardith Frederickson, wife of Coalinga's fire chief, said the worst damage was downtown.

Downtown Structures Collapse

In the Plaza, a complex of red-wood-and-brick structures built before World War II and recently renovated, she said at least "five buildings are down—many of them collapsed completely."

The biggest fire, she said, seemed to be at the Coalinga Inn—a landmark in the middle of the complex—which was "completely destroyed."

A helicopter pilot flying over the scene an hour after the first shock reported flames "leaping 40 to 50 feet into the air—it looks like the whole center of Coalinga's gone or going."

The city's airport was later closed to all but emergency aviation traffic, and remained so for nearly six hours. During that time, all aircraft were ordered to stay out of a 10-mile radius around the town.

Many homes in the oil and farming community were "just sitting at crazy angles," James Hodgins, 58, a lifelong resident, said.

"But I didn't see anyone really

Please see QUAKE, Page 3

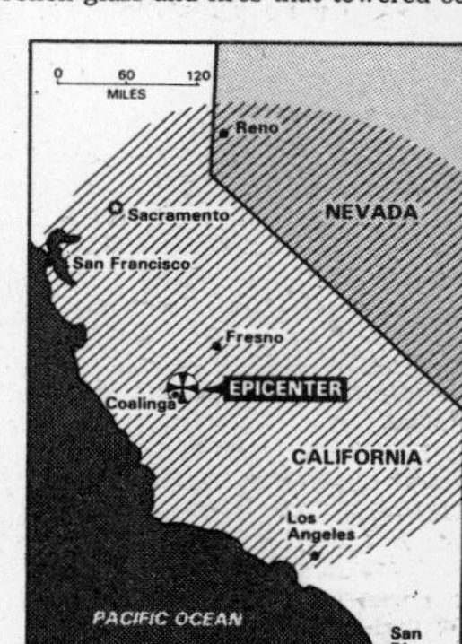

Los Angeles Times

'Hell of a Jolt'

Quake Wasn't End of World for Residents

By ERIC MALNIC and JACK JONES, *Times Staff Writers*

COALINGA, Calif.—In the blackness of Elm Street, littered with the rubble of shattered buildings, the people of this quake-devastated San Joaquin Valley town seemed almost relieved Monday night. They were just beginning to realize that it was not as dreadful as it might have been.

"I thought it was the end of the world," said Coalinga Police Department dispatcher Marilyn Roberts, who was at home when the earth began to shake at 4:43 p.m., "but it wasn't."

Authorities had the blacked-out town cordoned off Monday night and emergency workers were digging for possible victims under emergency lighting as fires continued to burn. Billowing smoke rose in the red glare of flares.

Walls Fall Into Streets

The red, blue and white lights of police, Fresno County sheriff's and California Highway Patrol cars flashed along the main street, where 20 to 30 buildings had collapsed or were heavily damaged.

Walls of the old brick structures had fallen outward into Elm Street downtown, exposing offices, many with furniture intact.

Some families were setting up tents in the yards of their homes, where porches had been torn away or were sagging. They illuminated their makeshift campouts with the headlights of their cars and camper vans.

Please see JOLT, Page 27

Temblor Probably Not Tied to Major California Faults

By GEORGE ALEXANDER, *Times Science Writer*

Monday's devastating Coalinga temblor had seismologists apprehensive because first reports seemed to place it close to the small, Central California community of Parkfield—starting point of the 1857 earthquake, the last giant shock to crack the San Andreas Fault in Southern California.

Earth scientists are understandably jumpy about tremors in that area because studies suggest that a segment of the state-long fault zone there breaks approximately every 150 years, give or take a few decades.

But as it turned out, Monday's earthquake was about 15 miles east of the San Andreas on an unknown and unmapped fault.

Kate Hutton, a Caltech researcher, said it is unlikely that the shock was connected to the better-known fault, which geologists say produces giant shocks of the sort that devastated San Francisco in 1906 and Southern California 126 years ago.

"We can't be absolutely certain of that," she said, "but we wouldn't think it would be."

Jerry Eaton of the U.S. Geological Survey in Menlo Park agreed.

Eaton and Hutton also said it is unlikely that Monday's temblor could trigger an earthquake on the San Andreas Fault, although again they said they could not flatly rule it out.

Instead, the earthquake—felt from Los Angeles to Sacramento and San Francisco and as far east as Nevada—appears to be an isolated incident on a kind of fault that has only recently come to the attention of geologists and geophysicists.

In a telephone interview from the geological survey headquarters at Reston, Va., geologist Darrell Herd said that the Coalinga quake could

Please see FAULTS, Page 27

Growing Trend

Mail Voting Puts Stamp on Politics

By PHILIP HAGER, *Times Staff Writer*

SAN FRANCISCO—Sixty years ago, the state of California took a first cautious step to permit voters to cast ballots by mail rather than by going to the polling place on election day.

Under legislation passed in the wake of an amendment to the state Constitution, absentee voting was permitted for those whose occupations or military duty took them away from their neighborhood precincts.

But since then, voting laws have been gradually liberalized—and a revolutionary change in the state's balloting process may be at hand. More and more, Californians are voting by mail, either in regular elections with absentee ballots or in special local elections where all balloting is done by mail.

The ballot-by-mail trend reached a new high here last Tuesday when Mayor Dianne Feinstein scored a smashing victory in a recall election. In all, 60,382 absentee ballots were cast, representing a record 36% of the total vote. The mayor, who had worked hard to build a big mail-in vote, won support from eight of every nine absentee ballots cast.

Please see VOTING, Page 26

Justices Ease Curbs on Nuclear Waste Disposal

By JIM MANN, *Times Staff Writer*

WASHINGTON—The Supreme Court, which last month upheld the authority of states to regulate nuclear power plants, served notice Monday that states still may not prevent out-of-state nuclear wastes from being transported or stored within their borders.

The justices left in effect two separate lower court rulings striking down state laws in Washington and Illinois that had barred nuclear storage facilities from accepting any nuclear wastes produced in other states. Both laws were passed in 1980 and were challenged in court by companies operating nuclear plants or storage facilities.

The court's action in the Illinois case was a major victory for Southern California Edison Co., which until 1980 had been sending spent nuclear fuel from its nuclear plant at San Onofre, Calif., to a storage facility operated by General Electric Co. at Morris, Ill., about 60 miles southwest of Chicago.

Will Resume Shipments

In a written statement, Southern California Edison said Monday that, as a result of the court's action, "Edison will be able to resume fuel shipments from its temporary storage site at the San Onofre Nuclear Generating Station to General Electric's facility at Morris." A company spokesman said it is not yet clear when these shipments will begin again.

The high court did not issue any opinion of its own Monday on the subject of nuclear wastes. Instead, it issued two brief orders refusing to review the lower court opinions, which found the Washington and Illinois laws unconstitutional. Technically, these actions end the two court cases without setting any precedent for future disputes over

Please see COURT, Page 19

State Vagrancy Law Voided as Overly Vague

By JIM MANN, *Times Staff Writer*

WASHINGTON—The Supreme Court ruled 7 to 2 Monday that California's vagrancy law, which gives police the power to stop suspicious-looking persons on the street and ask them to identify themselves, is unconstitutional.

In an opinion by Justice Sandra Day O'Connor, the high court held that the law must be struck down because it is overly vague and fails to spell out exactly what an individual must show or tell the police in order to avoid being arrested.

Under the law, persons who refused to show police "reliable" identification or "account for their presence" could be arrested for disorderly conduct.

"The concern of our citizens with curbing criminal activity is certainly a matter requiring the attention of all branches of government," O'Connor wrote for the court. "As weighty as this concern is, however, it cannot justify legislation that would otherwise fail to meet constitutional standards for definiteness and clarity."

The decision leaves California free to try to pass a new law that explains in detail what sort of identification police may demand. The high court left unanswered the

Please see VAGRANCY, Page 19

Machine Strips Mayor of Power in Chicago Coup

By LARRY GREEN, *Times Staff Writer*

CHICAGO—Just three days after the inauguration of black reform Mayor Harold Washington, white machine Democrats on Monday seized control of the City Council and rammed through rules and committee changes that effectively strip the new mayor of much of his legislative power.

Washington, who is five votes short of a majority on the 50-member council, declared the meeting an "illegal rump session" and called the political coup by 29 aldermen "illegitimate." His supporters said a court challenge is being considered.

"It appears that some members of the council are apparently experiencing a nervous reaction to the prospect of reform," said Washington, who had pledged during the divisive mayoral election campaign to dilute the machine's power.

Please see CHICAGO, Page 16

Bishops Stop Short of Call for Nuclear Freeze

By RUSSELL CHANDLER, *Times Religion Writer*

CHICAGO—America's Roman Catholic bishops, meeting here to prepare a controversial statement on war and peace, Monday approved wording that calls for a "halt" to the growth of nuclear arsenals—rather than just a "curb"—but does not endorse a specific nuclear freeze movement.

The 285 Catholic bishops are expected to give final approval to the 155-page document, "The Challenge of Peace: God's Promise and Our Response," today after they have considered several hundred proposed amendments. The letter, which has been in preparation for more than two years, then will become an official teaching document for the nation's 50 million Catholics.

Please see BISHOPS, Page 16

Growing Older in America

Jack Lemmon: 'I Think I Have a Lot of Kid in Me'

By JERRY COHEN, *Times Staff Writer*

This is another in a series about growing older in 20th-Century America. Not old. Merely older. These reports derive from conversations conducted over a yearlong period with the true experts on the subject, men and women experiencing life's inescapable process.

Jack Lemmon, the actor, is boyish-looking, although his skin is leathery, possibly the result of his devotion to the game of golf. His hair is dark but somewhat silvered, and his clear blue eyes are mischievous and expressive. He is a comparatively slight man, but his bearing suggests great physical vigor. He was asked as he sat in his Beverly Hills office how he felt about being 56.

I'm more aware, I guess, of my own mortality, let's say, than when I was young. But beyond that, not a great deal.

When I was in my 40s, I think I was a little—desperate is not the right word—a little more concerned about, "Gee whiz, two things: How much am I going to accomplish that I want? And how much have I accomplished?"

I'm less concerned. But I don't know why. But I'm less concerned. Now.

I must say that, on the whole, I think I've been very fortunate and I'm not unhappy, professionally, with what I've done. But in the last 10 years, a lot of good things have happened. And, also, I think I'm in good health. And I feel good.

I feel younger, I guess, than what

Please see LEMMON, Page 14

INDEX

WEATHER

U.S. Weather Service forecast: Today—some morning clouds, otherwise fair. Tonight—fair. Wednesday—morning clouds; mostly sunny afternoon.

	Highs	Lows
Monday	73	56
Today's forecast	75	56
Wednesday's forecast	72	58
May 2 last year	71	60

Record high May 2, 1929	89
Record low May 2, 1915	41

Complete details, Part II, Page 2.

Late Sports

Los Angeles Times

Morning Final

Circulation: 1,072,500 Daily / 1,358,420 Sunday — Thursday, June 16, 1983 — MF / 200 pages / Copyright 1983, Los Angeles Times / Daily 25¢

'Twilight Zone' Indictments

Underground Peril

Toxic Water —Legacy of Stringfellow

By ROBERT A. JONES,
Times Staff Writer

Nine years after the Stringfellow Acid Pits were closed by Riverside County, the site is almost pastoral. The dark lake of chemical solvents, pesticides and suspected carcinogens has been pumped dry. Small tufts of green are now appearing and Stringfellow is beginning to resemble nothing more dangerous than the cattle and horse pastures that dot the hills nearby.

But the scene is deceptive. Beneath Stringfellow, where no one can see it, the legacy remains. A plume of contaminated groundwater 3,000 feet long is snaking down Pyrite Canyon toward a major aquifer that feeds the town of Glen Avon and other communities in eastern Riverside County.

Within the plume are many of the ingredients from 18 years of toxic waste dumping at Stringfellow: trichloroethylene (TCE), a suspected carcinogen; chloroform; arsenic; lead; benzene and 16 other contaminants. Almost all are dangerous; almost any by themselves could mean the closure of the water basin if they reach the aquifer in sufficient quantity.

Yearly Speed

Pushed by runoff from nearby springs, the tongue of contaminants has been estimated to be moving at the leisurely pace of 250 to 400 feet a year. At that rate, if left unchecked, it will flow into the main aquifer of the Chino water basin in about five years.

Walking through the lower reaches of Pyrite Canyon, Penny Newman glanced downward and said, "It's (the plume) right here under our feet, but no one seems to know what to do about it or when."

Newman, a resident of Glen Avon who has led a citizens campaign urging speedier control of Stringfellow's aftermath, said she sometimes wonders if her community will become another sacrifice area to toxic wastes. "Can they solve this problem or will they just write us off as a loss?" she asked.

Dreaded Consequence

A plume of contaminants such as the one at Stringfellow is one of the most dreaded consequences of the nation's troubled toxic waste disposal program. The size and location of such plumes are difficult to define, even more difficult to eradicate, and the prospects for complete success in cleaning a polluted aquifer remain problematical. At Stringfellow, federal and state waste officials concede, many years of cleanup efforts will be required before the outcome is known.

And the cost of failure in dealing with such plumes can be very high. In Southern California, for example, approximately 60% of drinking water supplies comes from groundwa-

Please see PLUME, Page 3

Associated Press

Wants to go home—Sirhan Sirhan, convicted slayer of Sen. Robert F. Kennedy, told a parole board he'd like to return to Arab world in "unlikely" event of release. (Story, Page 18.)

Court Absolves Utilities of Nuclear Plant Debts

By TOM REDBURN and NANCY RIVERA, *Times Staff Writers*

The Washington state Supreme Court ruled Wednesday that utilities there are not responsible for their 70% share of the $2.25-billion debt owed on two nuclear power plants canceled by the beleaguered Washington Public Power Supply System.

The court ruled that the utilities, which had sponsored the projects, had no legal authority to sign the contracts launching them.

By leaving WPPSS—the consortium of Pacific Northwest utilities that was once involved in five nuclear power projects—with no means to pay off the debt, the ruling sets the stage for what is increasingly expected to be the largest default in the history of the municipal bond market.

'Devastating Decision'

"This is a devastating decision; it's just incredible," said Don Mazur, new managing director of WPPSS, which was building the plants for 88 public utilities in the Northwest and which was trying to force the utilities to honor their so-called "hell-or-high-water" contracts requiring them to pay for the nuclear projects whether or not they were ever completed.

The decision could cause investors to look more skeptically upon billions of dollars in bonds being used to finance other public power projects around the country. The Intermountain Power Project in Utah, sponsored in part by the Los Angeles Department of Water and Power, is one of several large power projects with a legal and financial structure similar to that of WPPSS. But a DWP official noted that the Intermountain project is in strong financial shape and should be able to weather any temporary investor concern.

"The magnitude of this default is

Please see NUCLEAR, Page 14

118 Injured by Poison Leak on Texas Campus

NACOGDOCHES, Texas (AP)—A cloud of insecticide leaked from a greenhouse at Stephen F. Austin State University Wednesday night, sending scores of injured and hysterical people to hospitals and forcing the evacuation of 1,500, authorities said.

About 118 people, including the mayor, were overcome by fumes or hysteria and were taken to the two hospitals in the east Texas city, officials said. About half were reported as being hysterical.

The very dense, 100-yard-wide cloud of the toxic chemical parathion caused many people to suffer eye and nose irritation, said C.E. Duffin, fire chief in this city of about 28,000 people about 175 miles southeast of Dallas.

Highly Toxic

Parathion is a deep brown to yellow liquid which turns into a gas in air. It is highly toxic when it contacts the skin, is inhaled or swallowed.

Nacogdoches Mayor A.L. Mangham was overcome by the fumes as he watched firemen hose down the greenhouse and was taken to Medical Center Hospital's intensive care unit, where he was listed in serious condition.

A college spokesman said that about 325 college students and 600

Please see POISON, Page 11

459 Arrested in $23-Million Police 'Sting'

By RICHARD WEST,
Times Staff Writer

A $100,000 investment by the U.S. Justice Department has returned a profit of $23.5 million in recovered stolen goods and 459 felony arrests in the biggest "sting" operation believed ever conducted anywhere, Los Angeles area law enforcement officials reported Wednesday.

Undercover officers, working out of their "Anything and Everything" store in Culver City for the last 11 months, recovered vehicles, guns, electronic and office equipment, counterfeit and stolen credit cards, travelers' checks and negotiable securities, including a $100,000 U.S. Treasury bond.

The front windows of the store bore the wording: "Wholesale Brokers" and "If We Can Sell It, We'll Buy It."

Please see STING, Page 18

Internee Losses Put at $6 Billion

By LEE MAY,
Times Staff Writer

WASHINGTON—West Coast Japanese-Americans interned during World War II suffered economic losses estimated as high as $6.2 billion, a federal commission said Wednesday.

The figure, announced by the Commission on Wartime Relocation and Internment of Civilians, was the highest of several estimates in a study conducted for it by ICF Inc., a Washington consulting firm.

The commission, authorized by Congress in 1980 to investigate the internment of 120,000 Japanese-Americans, is expected to make a recommendation Wednesday on whether the government should pay reparations to internees and their survivors. The panel is expected to recommend some compensation, and the new study gives support to that position.

Please see INTERNEES, Page 14

Director, 2 Others Face Charges in Film Deaths

By TED ROHRLICH, *Times Staff Writer*

Film director John Landis will be prosecuted criminally in connection with the helicopter crash that took the lives of actor Vic Morrow and two children on the set of the movie "Twilight Zone," The Times has learned.

"I understand the charges are involuntary manslaughter," said Landis' attorney, Harland Braun.

However, not even Landis will learn for certain the charges he faces until June 24, when the secret Los Angeles County Grand Jury indictment, returned against him Wednesday, is unsealed in court.

The grand jury also returned indictments Wednesday against George Folsey Jr., "Twilight Zone's" associate producer, and Dan Allingham, its unit production manager, it was learned.

John Landis

Four Days of Hearings

It could not be determined whether any other members of the film company were charged.

The grand jury issued its indictments after conducting four days of hearings into the deaths of the 53-year-old Morrow, Renee Chen, 6, and Myca Dinh Le, 7.

They died last July 23 in Saugus when a helicopter crashed on top of them as they were wading across a shallow stream in a mock Vietnamese village on the set of the soon-to-be-released film. The helicopter scythed to the ground after its tail rotor was struck by debris generated by a powerful special-effects mortar, which had been detonated under a hut.

Landis, Allingham and Folsey were told to report to court June 24 for their arraignments, at which time the district attorney's office will officially inform them of the charges they face, said Folsey's attorney, Roger Rosen.

Braun said of Landis, "He's stunned and disappointed at the charges and is convinced that when all the facts are out he'll be exonerated."

During its hearings, the grand jury heard testimony from a variety of witnesses, including the three men it charged.

Already Fined

The district attorney's office, which had asked the grand jury to conduct the hearings, could have sought involuntary manslaughter charges under the theory that evidence showed the deaths were the result of gross negligence and unlawful child endangering.

State agencies have already imposed heavy fines against Landis and others, including Warner Bros., the studio making the picture, for violation of safety and child-labor laws.

The Federal Aviation Administration has moved to lift the license of the helicopter's pilot, Dorcey Wingo, for "careless and reckless" flying. In addition, the parents of one of the slain children and the daughters of Morrow have filed wrongful-death suits.

Key questions the grand jury sought to answer in its probe were these:

—Who was responsible for placing the special-effects mortar?

—Was the power of the mortar blast greater than the film's special-effects crew has claimed?

Please see TWILIGHT, Page 18

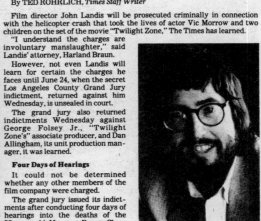

Abortion Right Reaffirmed by Supreme Court

By JIM MANN,
Times Staff Writer

WASHINGTON—In its most important pronouncement on abortion in a decade, the Supreme Court Wednesday strongly reaffirmed its 1973 decision that women have a constitutional right to end their pregnancies and struck down a far-reaching ordinance in Akron, Ohio, restricting that right.

Led by Justice Sandra Day O'Connor, an appointee of President Reagan, three dissenters on the court made a frontal attack on Roe vs. Wade, the 10-year-old ruling. The nation's first woman justice, who had not taken part in any of the court's previous abortion rulings, contended that the government has a "compelling" interest in protecting "potential human life" at all stages of a woman's pregnancy.

Powell Writes Decision

But O'Connor's effort, supported by Justices William H. Rehnquist and Byron R. White, fell short. The rest of the court pointed out that the Roe decision had been "considered with special care" before it was issued and said they abide by it as a precedent under the doctrine of *stare decisis* (Latin for "let stand what is already decided").

The 6-3 decision, written by Justice Lewis F. Powell Jr., appeared designed to lay to rest any speculation that the present Supreme Court will change its stance on abortion. The ruling was denounced immediately as a major disappointment by right-to-life groups and praised as a broad victory by groups supporting the right of women to choose an abortion.

Please see ABORTION, Page 16

Growing Older in America

A Salesman: 'I've Taken Pride in My Resilience'

By JERRY COHEN,
Times Staff Writer

This is another in a series about growing older in today's America. Not old. Merely older. These reports derive from conversations conducted over a yearlong period. The subjects' age and circumstances are the ones that prevailed at the time of the interviews.

Richard Tormey, at 52, describes his life as the "story of the man in the gray flannel suit." He explained that after graduating from the University of California and during the early years of his first job in the Pacific Northwest, "I had a great vision of grandeur." But after more than a quarter of a century of shifting from job to job in the marketing and advertising businesses, the vision disintegrated.

Today, he works out of his South Pasadena home, scratching up business for a consulting firm. He is a compactly built man with a pug nose, dark-brown hair and eyes and an unlined face. His first job collapsed when he was 32 and he sensed what he was to sense many times afterwards, that "things were starting to close in on me." When he was 40 and out of work still once more, he said:

I made an analysis at that point.

I felt at 25 your education should be completed. Then, I figured, 25 to 35, you can afford to look around and establish a track record. Thirty-five to 55, you should be managing, from a supervisional standpoint, or whatever.

In other words, if you're going to be in business, you should be running your own business or function-

Please see SALESMAN, Page 22

INDEX

WEATHER

U.S. Weather Service forecast: Today through Friday—late night and early morning coastal fog, otherwise fair.

	Highs	Lows
Wednesday	83	67
Today's forecast	86	65
Friday 's forecast	90	65
June 15 last year	72	59

Record high June 15, 1981	102
Record low June 15, 1892	48

Complete details, Part IV, Page 13.

Andropov Vows Military Buildup, East Bloc Control

By ROBERT GILLETTE, *Times Staff Writer*

MOSCOW—Communist Party leader Yuri V. Andropov warned Wednesday that the Soviet Union will continue to strengthen its armed forces and will never allow the West to achieve military superiority.

In a major policy address, Andropov, speaking to the Communist Party's Central Committee on his 69th birthday, also made clear that Moscow has no intention of loosening its grip on Eastern Europe but instead views closer economic and political integration with its neighbors as essential to their collective security.

The achievement of military balance with the West "is one of the important results of the last decades" and will not be surrendered, Andropov declared at the end of the Central Committee's two-day meeting.

"It required from our people and the peoples of other countries of the socialist community no small efforts and resources, and we shall not allow it to be disrupted," Andropov said in a speech outlining the Communist Party's long-range objectives.

He said the Soviet Union will do "everything possible" to ensure its security and that of its allies and

Shultz blames U.S.-Soviet tensions on the Kremlin. Page 7.

"will enhance the combat power of the Soviet armed forces."

The committee session produced several minor shifts in the party leadership but added no new members to the ruling Politburo, which has been depleted by deaths and retirements and now has 11 members. A meeting of the Supreme

Please see ANDROPOV, Page 6

Los Angeles Times

Sunday Final

Circulation: 1,064,392 Daily / 1,331,666 Sunday — Sunday, July 29, 1984 — CC† / 528 pages / Copyright 1984, Los Angeles Times / Sunday $1

JOE KENNEDY / Los Angeles Times

Thousands of competitors from nearly 140 nations fill the floor of packed Coliseum for the Olympic Opening Ceremony.

Spectacular Show Provides Dazzling Start for Games

Arrival of Flame Crowns Emotional Ceremony Before 92,655 in Coliseum

By PETER H. KING, *Times Staff Writer*

In a ceremony that balanced the spectacular with the poignant, the Los Angeles Olympic Games were declared open Saturday by President Reagan and crowned with a Grecian flame that had been passed hand-to-hand by thousands of Americans from New York City to the Coliseum.

The three-hour ceremony played on a full range of emotions, stunning the 92,655 spectators with a dazzling airborne entrance by a man riding only a rocket pack and leaving many deeply moved with a farewell sing-a-along that seemingly had the entire stadium clasping hands and swaying gently as one.

President Reagan, who at one point in the Americana-laden ceremony declared himself "bursting with pride," delivered the formal opening statement from a glass-enclosed booth high atop the southern rim of the Coliseum, his image projected for the spectators on a giant screen.

Words Rearranged

"Celebrating the XXIII Olympiad of the modern era, I declare open the Olympic Games of Los Angeles," Reagan said, reciting words dictated by the International Olympic Committee but rearranged slightly by the President.

Then, as shadows stretched across a Coliseum enlivened with sprays of flowers and a fresh coat of startingly colorful paint, Gina Hemphill, 26-year-old granddaughter of Olympic great Jesse Owens and one of the first torchbearers in the 9,000-mile transcontinental Torch Relay, entered the stadium at a full run with the Olympic flame.

She lapped the field, which was covered with athletes. And at the sight of the flame the competitors broke ranks and rushed forward to swarm around Hemphill—a response strikingly similar to that of millions of Americans who played witness to the 82-day Torch Relay.

The Rings in Flame

Hemphill then handed the torch to Rafer Johnson, a gold medalist in the decathlon at the Rome Games of 1960. Gripping the torch with one hand and balancing himself with the other, the 48-year-old Johnson scaled the steep grade of 99 steps that took him up the Coliseum peristyle.

He stood still for a moment, his face set sternly, then turned to display the torch to all sides of the stadium. Finally, after the dramatic interruption, he applied the flame to an apparatus that sent it shooting through five large Olympic rings and into the cauldron atop the Coliseum, where it exploded in triumph.

After seven years of preparations, the Games of the XXIII Olympiad—a mammoth undertaking challenged by financial restrictions imposed by wary taxpayers,

Please see GAMES, Page 3

OLYMPICS '84

For complete coverage of athletic competitions, see our special section, Olympics '84.

- Columnist Jim Murray sees the Opening Ceremony itself as a victory over the variety of obstacles that had threatened the Games. **Olympics '84. Page 1**
- In a pep talk to the U.S. Olympic team, President Reagan urges athletes to "do it for the Gipper." **Page 3**
- Transit officials are generally pleased that tens of thousands of spectators left their cars behind and boarded buses for the Olympic Opening Ceremony. **Page 3**
- Early Los Angeles civic leaders helped change the Coliseum from an eyesore into a two-time Olympic venue. **View, Page 1**

Relay Sparks Late Surge of Ticket Buying

By ROBERT WELKOS, *Times Staff Writer*

Ignited by the final hours of the Torch Relay, sales of tickets to Olympic events kicked into high gear Saturday—reaping a gold mine for some sellers who pocketed up to $1,000 per ticket from a public clamoring to experience the color and international drama of the Opening Ceremony.

"A week ago it was busy, but it wasn't as busy as it is now," said Curtis Lantello of Southern California Tickets. "I think some of these people saw them run the torch and got emotion built up in them and said, 'Hey, let's go to this event!' "

Olga Goldine and her daughter, Marlaina, both of Downey, stood outside the Coliseum Saturday hoping to find tickets, saying they hadn't been interested in the Games until the torch came through their city.

"It just fired us up and we haven't been down yet," she said.

Please see TICKETS, Page 17

Author! Author!

Pen Names: The Debate Is Renewed

By ANNE C. ROARK, *Times Staff Writer*

Pseudonyms are as old as literature itself. A mere listing of the pen names of the world's writers might well fill several scholarly volumes.

Mark Twain, O. Henry, Lewis Carroll—all were pen names. And the use of pseudonyms is not limited to fiction. Movie stars have acquired them. Journalists have appropriated them. So have historians, political commentators and people of all professions who have wanted to disguise their sex or their ethnic and cultural origins.

It is generally acknowledged that there are many legitimate reasons for a writer to acquire a new name and public persona. Nearly everybody's favorite example is George Eliot, England's great novelist of the 19th Century.

Debate Renewed

Had *she* (her true identity was Mary Ann Evans) not adopted the name of a man, critics agree, she might never have been published and surely would not have been taken seriously.

Yet the recent disclosure that the author of an acclaimed first novel, "Famous All Over Town," was not a young, underprivileged Latino from East Los Angeles, known as Danny Santiago, but a well-connected Anglo writer from Carmel, whose real name is Dan James, has renewed the debate on the ethics of using a false identity in writing.

Although few people would categorically condemn the practice, many have begun to question the

Please see PEN NAMES, Page 22

City Swept by Excitement

Games Open With a Rush of Good Cheer

By MARK A. STEIN, *Times Staff Writer*

Jeanette Arbogast Webb couldn't help it. As the band struck up the "Star-Spangled Banner" at the Opening Ceremony of the XXIIIrd Olympiad in the Coliseum Saturday, tears pooled in her eyes and then cascaded unchecked down her cheeks.

"I don't know what came over me," the Long Beach woman said after regaining her composure. "I was so proud."

Webb's tears of joy and pride were not shed in solitude, nor was she alone in her smile. Opening day of the 1984 Olympics released a rush of good cheer over the host city that swept into all but a few last pockets of cynicism and disinterest.

Troubles Crowded Out

The predicted traffic gridlock failed to materialize, bright blue skies belied the presence of smog, the temperature was relatively mild and spectators were friendly and well-behaved. Indeed, all of the troubles projected for the 3½-hour pageant were crowded out of town on the first day of the Games by enthusiastic celebrants.

"The weather is great, the ambiance is great, the people are great," said Nick Houtin of San Francisco, who viewed the ceremony from a standing-room-only spot tucked behind the side of the peristyle—one of the worst viewing areas in the stadium. "Overall, it is the event of a lifetime."

Actress Diane Keaton, no stranger to Hollywood pageantry, agreed. "It almost leaves you speechless," she said. "I can't find the adjectives to describe it."

Another actress, Dyan Cannon, said she came without eye makeup so she could cry.

"We were all embracing and crying," she said of her party. "I had many pals who said, 'We're going to get out of L.A. for the Olympics,' but every second of it was worth it. Every second of it."

Some said their enthusiasm did not blossom until only a few days—or a few hours—before the spectacular Opening Ceremony began.

"I will admit that I caught the fever at the last moment when I saw the runner with the torch," said one 42-year-old Santa Monica woman outside the stadium, echoing the sentiments of many.

The woman, who identified herself only as Gabrielle, was one of scores of people, many with signs,

Please see GAMES, Page 16

Flame Ends Its Journey in a Blaze of Glory

By TOM GORMAN and PATT MORRISON, *Times Staff Writers*

The remarkable cross-country relay of the Olympic flame, a journey that gave millions of Americans their only opportunity to experience the spirit of the Summer Games, completed its 82-day run Saturday evening in similarly remarkable and dramatic fashion.

Rafer Johnson, the most awesome athlete in the world 24 years ago and today a continuing champion of amateur sports, carried the flame up 99 steps and ignited a fuse that set afire the five Olympic rings just above him, at the peristyle end of the Coliseum. Moments later, the flame was funneled to the top of the torch, and the receptacle ignited with a whoosh, fueling the cheers of about 100,000 spectators and athletes.

Torch Passed

The 48-year-old Johnson turned and stoically faced the crowd, his chest heaving with exhaustion, as the setting sun's rays illuminated the scene beneath a soft blue evening sky.

Johnson had received the torch from Gina Hemphill, Olympic track legend Jesse Owens' granddaughter, who brought the flame onto the Coliseum floor. Her torch was modified to enhance the size and brilliance of the flame, which shone brighter than it had at any time in its cross-country relay.

The identity of the final torch carriers had been kept secret, and

Please see TORCH, Page 18

Battle-Weary Beirut Regains Its Composure

By CHARLES P. WALLACE, *Times Staff Writer*

BEIRUT—On a particularly humid recent evening, a Lebanese businessman invited a visitor onto his balcony to catch the whisper of a breeze that drifted lazily in from the Mediterranean.

As the setting sun sent streamers of gold and red into the cloudless sky, the kettle-drum rumble of distant explosions could be heard.

"Don't be afraid," the businessman said with a grin. "That's just the sound of fishermen throwing dynamite into the ocean. You see, we Lebanese have finally agreed to stop bombarding each other. But, please, don't ask for how long."

As the remark suggests, Beirut's weary residents have been grappling with a mixture of elation and anxiety since a cease-fire went into effect in the capital July 4.

Please see BEIRUT, Page 7

Brother Details Car Attack Suspect's Mental Problems

By LAURIE BECKLUND and BILL FARR, *Times Staff Writers*

The 21-year-old Inglewood man booked on suspicion of murder in a wild automobile assault that killed one and injured 57 in Westwood Friday night was "psychologically disabled" and had been seeing a psychiatrist for months, his older brother told The Times on Saturday.

Police said the suspect, Daniel Lee (Dannie) Young, revved up his car's motor and drove down a Westwood Boulevard sidewalk at full speed just before 9 p.m. Uninjured and calm, he was led away by police, leaving behind him a trail of battered bodies.

The dead person was identified Saturday as Eileen Deutsch, 15, of New York City. Twenty-one remained hospitalized Saturday, four in critical condition. In the confusion after the attack Friday, hospitals had initially indicated that the death count was three.

Police gave few details of their investigation, except to say that the bizarre incident was a deliberate attack and that it was apparently motivated by an attempt by Young, who had recently been jailed on a burglary conviction, to take revenge on police. They said there was no evidence that Young was under the influence of alcohol or drugs.

Please see ATTACK, Page 20

WEATHER

U.S. Weather Service forecast: Today through Monday—some late night and morning low clouds along the coast; otherwise clear.

	Highs	Lows
Saturday	86	71
Today's forecast	near 84	68-74
Monday's forecast	near 84	68-74
July 28 last year	84	66

Record high July 28, 1972 101
Record low July 28, 1883 52

Complete details, Part II, Page 6.

INDEX

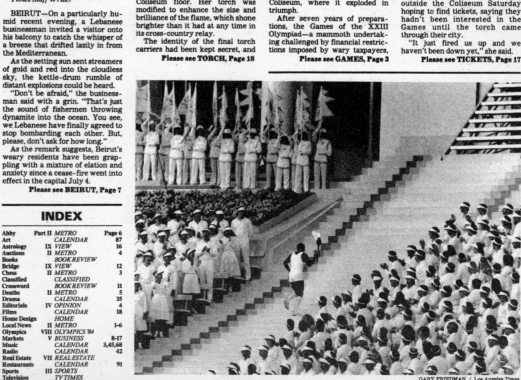

GARY FRIEDMAN / Los Angeles Times

Rafer Johnson, former decathlon gold medalist, dashes up steps on way to lighting Olympic flame.

Los Angeles Times

Circulation: 1,076,466 Daily / 1,346,343 Sunday | Monday, July 1, 1985 | CC†/ 88 Pages | Copyright 1985 / The Times Mirror Company | Daily 25¢

39 Hostages Freed, Start Home

47 Houses Lost in Fire at San Diego

Damage Estimated at $5.3 Million as Hundreds Flee; Other Areas Hit

By T.W. MCGARRY and TED THACKREY JR., *Times Staff Writers*

At least 47 homes were destroyed and four others heavily damaged Sunday as fire burst out of a steep, brush-filled canyon in the Normal Heights district eight miles northeast of downtown San Diego, forcing hundreds of residents to flee.

Damage was officially estimated by the county Emergency Management Office at more than $5.3 million, but was expected to climb. By 8:30 p.m., fire officials said the blaze was 95% contained with full control not expected before dawn.

San Diego Mayor Roger Hedgecock toured the 290-acre area of the blaze, called it the most destructive in the city's history, and asked Gov. George Deukmejian to declare Normal Heights a disaster area.

Winds Pose Problem

Firefighters fought erratic winds, low humidity and difficult terrain to contain the flames in temperatures that soared over the 100-degree mark in the afternoon.

There were no deaths and injuries were said to be minor. Several firefighters and residents who stayed and tried to fight the flames were treated at the scene for heat exhaustion, smoke inhalation, first- and second-degree burns and eye irritation.

Ambulances took at least five people to hospitals. These included two infants suffering from smoke inhalation, authorities said.

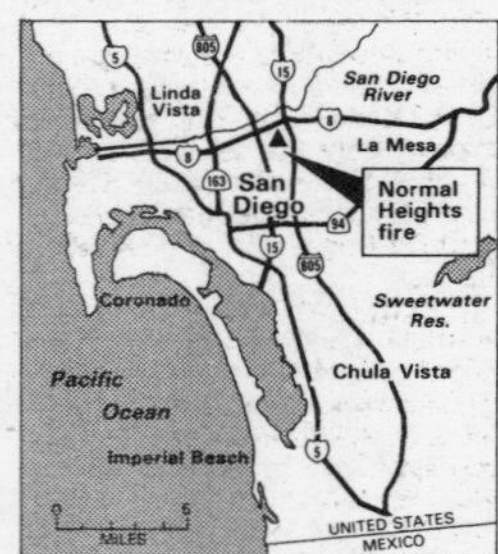

Los Angeles Times

The toll of misery and destruction mounted as night fell, reducing the winds that had fueled the flames but adding confusion and fear to the plight of those who had been driven from their homes.

Many of the evacuees were elderly, and were in house coats and slippers as they fled from the houses where some of them had lived for nearly half a century. A number of the evacuees were taken in by friends outside the threatened area; others went to an emergency shelter set up by the Red Cross.

By late evening, police and sheriff's helicopters were still in the area, hovering amid hot embers, wind and smoke, using loudspeakers to warn residents below of the spreading fire—and asking them

Please see FIRES, Page 3

Interest Surges

Enrollments Born Again at Bible Colleges

By ANNE C. ROARK, *Times Education Writer*

Carol Hulgus, the daughter of a United Mine Workers official, is an ambitious 22-year-old who is going out into the working world this spring armed with everything a new college graduate could want—from a nearly flawless academic record to a lucrative job offer from a prestigious corporation.

But Hulgus, who passed up both Princeton and the University of California, Berkeley, to attend school in Southern California, believes she has something going for her that is even more important than an impressive resume: She is a graduate of an evangelical college.

As far as she is concerned, Biola University, a little-known Christian liberal arts college 22 miles southeast of downtown Los Angeles, is one of the few places in the country that would let her combine her rather considerable academic and career aspirations (law school and an eventual position as a labor-management arbitrator) with her commitment to Christ.

Ever Greater Number

She is not alone in her thinking. Indeed, Hulgus is one of a growing number of determined young people who are attending Protestant evangelical colleges with the expressed purpose of taking their religion out of the church and into the classroom, the laboratory and the headquarters of corporate America.

This new interest in evangelical higher education has come as welcome, if somewhat unexpected, news to educators at liberal arts colleges in this country that consider themselves "Christ-centered" or fundamentalist in character.

As recently as five years ago, church-related colleges—long seen as the backwater of the academic world—were said to be on the verge of extinction. Enrollments were dropping, funds were drying up and some colleges were even closing their doors.

Please see COLLEGES, Page 20

Associated Press

Vice President Bush shakes hand of freed hostage Dr. Richard Moon at Frankfurt air base after Moon's arrival from Syria. Between them is another hostage, Father James McLoughlin.

Land Tired but Happy in Germany

By TYLER MARSHALL and CHARLES P. WALLACE, *Times Staff Writers*

FRANKFURT, West Germany—Thirty-nine American hostages arrived safely here early today after gaining their freedom in Beirut on Sunday, traveling to Syria in a Red Cross convoy and finally flying out of the Mideast in a U.S. Air Force plane.

Looking tired but happy, the men filed down the steps of the C-141 Starlifter that brought them to the U.S. Rhein-Main Air Base in Frankfurt from the Syrian capital of Damascus. Reaching the tarmac, some embraced waiting relatives and some wiped tears from their eyes.

Most of them raised their arms to the waiting crowd in a sign of triumph.

Conwell Offers Thanks

"We have a long list of people to thank," hostage Allyn B. Conwell of Houston had said late Sunday, speaking for all of the hostages at a news conference held in Damascus to express their gratitude to Syria's President Hafez Assad for helping to obtain their release. "I just wish they would all line up; I'd kiss every one of them."

Conwell said that none of the hostages seeks "retaliation or revenge" for the hijacking, which began June 14 when two fundamentalist Muslim gunmen hijacked TWA Flight 847 on a flight between Athens and Rome. The next day they murdered one of the American passengers.

He called for a "deeper understanding of the circumstances that led up to people taking a desperate act."

On hand to greet the hostages here was Vice President George Bush, who had broken away briefly from a seven-nation European tour to arrive in Frankfurt from Paris half-an-hour earlier than the hostages.

"You endured this cruel and painful experience with courage," Bush said. "America is proud of you."

Speaking into a microphone decorated with a yellow ribbon tied in a neat bow, the vice president said, "You are back, and America did not compromise her principles to get you back. Friends and neighbors joined to help your families in their terrible ordeal of waiting, showing the best of America. And today, as news of your release fills the air, we join your families in welcoming you."

The freed Americans shook hands with Bush and with a group of four U.S. senators, who had

Please see HOSTAGES, Page 4

INSIDE

Reagan 'Moment of Joy' Tempered by Missing 7

By JACK NELSON, *Times Washington Bureau Chief*

WASHINGTON—President Reagan, welcoming the release of the 39 American hostages from TWA Flight 847, Sunday demanded freedom for seven U.S. kidnap victims still held in Lebanon and served notice on terrorists that the United States will fight back against "cowardly attacks on American citizens and property."

The United States "will not rest until justice is done" to those who hijacked the TWA plane and killed 23-year old Navy diver Robert Dean Stethem, Reagan vowed.

In discussing future steps, however, Administration officials focused on plans for deterring terrorists rather than retaliating against the TWA hijackers. And one senior official said that inflicting retribution on Hezbollah, the radical Shia Muslim faction whose members are believed responsible for the Beirut crisis, is not feasible because innocent lives would be endangered.

Reagan, no doubt reflecting the views of millions of Americans who followed the release of the hostages on television, called the outcome "a moment of joy." But he cautioned that, as long as seven Americans remain in the hands of kidnapers in Lebanon, it was "no moment for celebration."

The President's toughly worded statement, which was televised from the Oval Office, contrasted sharply with the restraint he dis-

Please see REAGAN, Page 5

U.S. Says Syria Seeks Release of 'Other Seven'

By JAMES GERSTENZANG, *Times Staff Writer*

WASHINGTON—Syria has been trying in earnest to win the release of the seven Americans who were kidnaped in Lebanon before the TWA hijacking on June 14, and it eventually "may well be able to succeed," a senior Reagan Administration official said Sunday.

But the official, speaking on condition that he not be identified by name, sounded a pessimistic note about the seven Americans, who remained in custody Sunday even after the last 39 of the TWA hostages were freed.

Chance of 'Comfort'

In view of U.S. threats to retaliate against terrorists in Lebanon, the official said, the presence of the seven hostages may give the captors "the comfort that we may be deterred while Americans are at risk."

The official also confirmed that the Administration believes that the seven, kidnaped in West Beirut over the past 15½ months, were believed to be held by elements of the radical Hezbollah, or Party of God, although perhaps not the same faction that held some of the 39 Americans who were released Sunday.

He said that, although the freedom of the seven had always been a

Please see SEVEN, Page 6

FPPC Member—Conflict of Interest Questions Arise

By GEORGE REASONS, *Times Staff Writer*

The newest member of the state Fair Political Practices Commission—a man whose own public career has been marked by recurring conflict-of-interest questions—has been chosen to help revise the watchdog agency's conflict rules for public officials.

Redevelopment agency lawyer Michael B. Montgomery, appointed to the FPPC in March despite a controversial background, has been named to a two-man subcommittee by Chairman Dan Stanford to study and revamp the rules with particular emphasis on redevelopment agencies.

Montgomery, who has held a variety of local government jobs over the last 20 years, has been caught up in a number of conflicts between his role as the public's lawyer and his own personal business interests.

In the last decade, public records disclose, Montgomery has been involved in personal dealings with at least nine firms or individuals doing business with agencies Montgomery represented as a lawyer or elected official.

In 1980, Irwindale officials said, he resigned as legal counsel to that

Please see CONFLICTS, Page 18

Conflicting U.S. Impulses

Nation Facing Decisions on Handling of Terrorism

By DOYLE McMANUS, *Times Staff Writer*

WASHINGTON—The ordeal of 39 Americans held hostage in Beirut has ended, but a major national debate over how the United States should deal with such terrorism has only begun.

While the Reagan Administration's words still echoed the President's initial pledge of "swift and effective retribution" against terrorists, senior Administration officials on Sunday specifically ruled out any quick retaliatory strike against Hezbollah (the Party of God), the extremist Shia Muslim group believed responsible for the June 14 hijacking of TWA Flight 847.

And, despite 4½ years of painful experience with terrorism since taking office, the Administration finds itself still in the talking stage about even such relatively uncontroversial measures as tighter airport security and collective international action against regimes that cast a tolerant eye on terrorists.

Please see POLICY, Page 7

INDEX

WEATHER

U.S. Weather Service forecast: Today through Tuesday—fair.

	Highs	Lows
Sunday	100	70
Today's forecast	95-100	68-73
Tuesday's forecast	upper 90s	65-70
June 30 last year	85	68

Record high June 30, 1985	100
Record low June 30, 1894	49

Complete details, Part II, Page 2.

BOB GRIESER / Los Angeles Times

Smoke pours from burning homes on Cliff Place in the Normal Heights section of San Diego.

EXTRA

Los Angeles Times

Circulation: 1,076,466 Daily / 1,346,343 Sunday — Tuesday, January 28, 1986 — LF/ 82 Pages Copyright 1986 / The Times Mirror Company — Daily 25¢

Shuttle Explodes; All 7 Die

Teacher on Board as Challenger Blows Up on Liftoff

Associated Press

The seven-member crew of the space shuttle Challenger: from the left, front row, astronauts Michael J. Smith, Francis R. (Dick) Scobee and Ronald E. McNair; rear row, Ellison S. Onizuka, Christa McAuliffe, Gregory Jarvis and Judith A. Resnik.

Reagan Postpones Future Flights Pending a Probe

By MICHAEL SEILER and PETER H. KING, *Times Staff Writers*

KENNEDY SPACE CENTER, Fla.—The space shuttle Challenger exploded in a huge fireball less than two minutes after takeoff today, with all seven crew members—including New Hampshire teacher Sharon Christa McAuliffe—feared dead.

Airborne paramedics parachuted quickly into the calm waters off Cape Canaveral in a vain search for survivors. Though there was no immediate announcement on the fate of the crew, all were believed dead.

The disaster—the worst in the history of America's manned space program—came shortly after the Challenger blasted off on a cold Florida morning on the 25th shuttle mission.

Without warning, there was an explosion, either in one of the solid rocket boosters or in the main fuel tank, and the flames engulfed Challenger.

The shuttle, rocketing upward at more than 1,900 miles an hour, appeared to incinerate instantly, disappearing into a ball of yellow flame, tinged in red.

Little Remained

Television pictures provided by the National Aeronautics and Space Administration and replayed time and again to a stunned national audience by the networks showed only the smoky tracks of debris—what little remained of the shuttle and its booster rockets—plummeting into the Atlantic Ocean.

Missing and presumed dead were shuttle commander Francis "Dick" Scobee, 46, co-pilot Michael Smith, 40, and astronauts Judith Resnick, 36, Ellison Onizuka, 39, Ronald E. McNair, 35, Gregory Jarvis, 41, and McAuliffe, 37.

Late in the morning, President Reagan told the media that there will be no more manned space missions until the cause of the disaster is established. "I'm sure there will be no more flights," he said. "It's a horrible thing all of us have witnessed."

The President was described as stunned as he watched television replays of the disaster and he later postponed until next Tuesday the State of the Union message scheduled for delivery to Congress tonight.

Shock and Tears

Students at Concord High School in Concord, N.H., where McAuliffe taught, watched in horror on television monitors and reacted with a mixture of shock and tears as the shuttle disappeared in flame.

"I don't believe it happened," said one student, grimly. "Everyone's watching her and she gets killed."

Here at Kennedy Space Center, McAuliffe's husband, two children and parents stood arm-in-arm, silently watching the fireball in the center's VIP viewing platform.

A NASA official walked up to them and said, "The vehicle has exploded."

The teacher's mother, Grace Corrigan repeated the words as a question, "The vehicle has exploded?"

The family was quickly led away.

'A Major Malfunction'

As the disaster unfolded before spectators here, Steven Nesbitt, the NASA announcer on the launch, said "flight controllers here are looking very carefully at the situation," adding calmly that there appeared to be "a major malfunction."

Then a few minutes later he confirmed the worst fears of those watching:

"We have a report from (a) flight dynamics officer that the vehicle has exploded. The flight director confirms that. We are looking at, uh, checking with the recovery forces to see what can be done at this point."

As the contrails formed to the east of Cape Canaveral, a parachute appeared in the clear blue sky, giving spectators a small glimmer of hope. Challenger carried no parachutes or ejection devices for the crew.

Rescue personnel reacted as quickly as possible to the disaster. More than a dozen aircraft and small surface vessels, dodging falling debris, raced to the impact point 18 miles southeast of the launch pad.

As the minutes raced by, there was no word from NASA and what little hope there had been for news of survivors faded away.

No Immediate Explanation

NASA officials had no immediate explanation for the explosion, and it was not clear whether the explosion began in the two solid fuel booster rockets or the main fuel tank.

There was speculation that overnight temperatures of less than 28 degrees, which formed two-foot-long icicle on the launch pad, may have played some part in the disaster. The flight had been postponed two hours; one hour of the delay was attributed to possible danger from ice forming on the craft.

A NASA team inspected the boosters, main fuel tank and gantry area before the countdown was continued.

The explosion occurred one minute and 15 seconds into the flight at an altitude of 4.9 miles and the crew was just beginning to boost their engines up to full throttle, NASA officials said. There had been no indication of any problems from the crew on the radio.

"Challenger, go at throttle-up"—the order to go to full power—was given by Mission Control to the crew 52 seconds after liftoff.

Sense of Grief

Scobee's final words came back, "Roger, go at throttle-up." Telemetry from the craft simply stopped as the Challenger's huge main fuel tank, carrying 526,000 gallons of volatile liquid hydrogen and oxygen, burst into flame. Seconds later, there was nothing but twisting contrails in the clear morning sky, and a sense of grief building up around the country.

The shuttle was not equipped with ejection equipment to separate the crew from the burning craft. The first four shuttle launches had ejection seats, but the need for more room in the craft and increased confidence in the shuttles' reliability had convinced NASA officials to leave them off.

It was the 10th shuttle flight for the $1.1-billion Challenger and came 11 years and 1 day after the nation's only previous fatal space

Please see SHUTTLE, Page 2

Gets News During Oval Office Meeting

Disaster Stuns Reagan Into Silence

WASHINGTON (AP)—President Reagan halted an Oval Office meeting with top aides when he learned that the shuttle carrying the teacher he sent into space had exploded, and he stood in "stunned silence" as he watched a television replay of the fiery disaster.

Presidential spokesman Larry Speakes said Vice President George Bush and Reagan's national security adviser, Vice Adm. John M. Poindexter, interrupted the meeting between Reagan and senior aides to tell him of the explosion.

Reagan went immediately to his small study to watch developments on television.

"The President is concerned; he is saddened; he is anxious to have more information," Speakes told reporters at a briefing.

The spokesman added that "quite frankly, the President stood there in almost stunned silence as he watched the television."

Reagan had been scheduled to host a luncheon for television anchors and network White House correspondents in the Roosevelt Room near his office. But the principal anchors hastily left the White House when they learned what had happened, and Reagan, after first postponing his session with them, canceled to await further reports, leaving Chief of Staff Donald T. Regan to begin the luncheon meeting late.

Deputy White House Press Secretary Peter Roussel, who was present in the Oval Office while Reagan was being briefed for the meeting, said Bush and Poindexter walked in together.

He quoted them as saying, almost simultaneously, "We hate to interrupt, but we have this report." Roussel said one of the men then read a typewritten report of the explosion to Reagan.

Asked whether the subject of the teacher was brought up in those first moments, Roussel said, "Nobody even mentioned that."

Asked if the President said anything about Christa McAuliffe, the teacher on board the flight, Speakes said, "It was something that was on all of our minds, that it had the first teacher in space, the first civilian" on board.

During his 1984 reelection campaign, Reagan surprised the world when he announced that a teacher would be the first citizen-passenger to fly aboard the space shuttle. Last July, after a national competition during which 11,000 teachers applied, Bush announced at a White House ceremony that McAuliffe had been selected by the National Aeronautics and Space Administration from among 10 finalists.

Reagan to Speak on Shuttle, Not State of Union

WASHINGTON (UPI)—President Reagan's State of the Union address, scheduled for 6 p.m. PDT today, has been canceled because of the explosion that destroyed the space shuttle Challenger, White House spokesman Larry Speakes said. Instead, the President will address the nation on the tragedy, Speakes said.

He said that Reagan ordered Vice President George Bush to fly to Cape Canaveral later today to express his sympathy to the families of the shuttle astronauts.

White House Chief of Staff Donald T. Regan telephoned House Speaker Thomas P. (Tip) O'Neill at about 1:30 p.m. and said the President would like to postpone the State of the Union speech until next Tuesday, according to Christopher Matthews, O'Neill's spokesman.

United Press International

Contrail of space shuttle Challenger halts at explosion point shortly after liftoff from Kennedy Space Center this morning.

In VIP Seats, Parents Watch in Disbelief

From Times Wire Services

KENNEDY SPACE CENTER, Fla.—The parents of New Hampshire teacher Christa McAuliffe stared in utter disbelief today as they watched the shuttle Challenger explode and fall into the Atlantic Ocean. Then they wept.

Edward and Grace Corrigan of Framingham, Mass., watched the launch from a VIP viewing site three miles from Launch Pad 39B.

They cheered along with the rest of the crowd at the site as Challenger lifted off the pad and soared skyward. But their smiles and cheers turned to faces of horror as the orbiter blew apart about two minutes after launch.

Husband, Children at Cape

McAuliffe's attorney husband, Steve, and their two children, Scott, 9, and Caroline, 6, were also in the crowd watching at Cape Canaveral.

Also there were members of Scott's third grade class from Concord, N.H., displaying a large "Go Christa" banner.

They watched in stunned silence as the spacecraft blew apart.

A hushed, chilled silence fell over the crowd of viewers.

"O my God!" cried one woman.

"No! No! No!" pleaded another.

With looks of shock, the Corrigans watched as a bright orange ball of flame shot from the shuttle.

They continued to stare skyward in disbelief as streams of contrail and pieces of the shuttle fell toward Earth.

They stood silently, arm in arm, and remained standing together as the loudspeaker brought the bad news and a NASA official climbed a couple of rows into the bleachers, walked to them and said: "The vehicle has exploded."

A stunned Grace Corrigan looked back at him and repeated his words as a question.

"The vehicle has exploded?"

He nodded silently and the Corrigans were quickly led away.

Others at the viewing site walked away in silence. Some sobbed; others merely stared in horror. Schoolchildren, squealing with delight only seconds earlier, were sobbing uncontrollably.

THE LATEST WEATHER

Mostly cloudy skies with a slight chance of showers are forecast for Wednesday by the National Weather Service. The downtown high should be in the lower 70s after an overnight low of about 53.

Los Angeles Times

Circulation: 1,103,656 Daily/1,368,105 Sunday | Friday, January 23, 1987 | LF/ 136 Pages Copyright 1987/The Times Mirror Company | Daily 25¢

A Wild Day on Wall Street! Dow Up, Down 110 in 1 Hr.

LATE NEWS/STOCKS

Nicaragua to Free Guardsmen

MANAGUA, Nicaragua (UPI)—A government human rights panel said today 300 former national guardsmen jailed after Nicaragua's revolution in 1979 will be freed this month for "humanitarian reasons" and to correct "judicial errors."

The announcement by the government's National Commission for the Promotion and Protection of Human Rights involved 300 former soldiers in the National Guard that served as Nicaragua's army under former President Anastasio Somoza. Sandinista leaders and some independent observers charge that some guardsmen committed human rights abuses. But the United States contends that Nicaragua's leftist government jails political opponents.

Dollar Gains in Europe, Japan

LONDON (AP)—The U.S. dollar strengthened against the major currencies in quiet European trading today.

The rise followed Japanese press reports that U.S. and Japanese authorities were preparing to support the American currency after recent sessions when the dollar hit its lowest levels for several years. Earlier, the dollar closed in Tokyo at 153.25 Japanese yen, up from 152.40 on Thursday and from 153.10 last Friday. Later in London, the dollar exchanged at 152.80 yen. The British pound lost more than one cent against the dollar in London, trading at $1.5230 late today.

Reagan Attacks Iran Offensive

WASHINGTON (UPI)—President Reagan today condemned Iran's offensive in its war with Iraq and declared that the United States regards the expansion of the fighting as a "major threat" to its interests in the Persian Gulf.

In a written statement, Reagan said the United States remains "determined to ensure the free flow of oil through the Strait of Hormuz" at the mouth of the Persian Gulf. "We also remain strongly committed to supporting the individual and collective self-defense of our friends in the gulf, with whom we have deep and longstanding ties," Reagan said.

Judge Upholds N.C. Election

RALEIGH, N.C. (AP)—A Superior Court judge today refused to order a recount in the 6th Congressional District race, upholding the State Board of Elections' decision to declare Republican Rep. Howard Coble the winner by 79 votes.

Former Rep. Robin Britt, a Democrat who lost to Coble, had filed a lawsuit asking that all 144,579 ballots cast in the Nov. 4 election be recounted or that a new election be held. Britt charged there were massive irregularities in the vote tabulation, which showed Coble with 72,329 votes to Britt's 72,250.

Guard's Chilling Action Probed

MINNEAPOLIS (AP)—The head of the Minnesota National Guard today ordered an investigation into the use of fire hoses on about 300 demonstrators who turned out in subzero temperatures to protest Guard missions to Central America.

"It was ruthless," Dan Greenburg, 23, of Minneapolis said of the hosing Thursday night as temperatures dipped to minus 2 degrees, with a wind chill factor of 36 below zero, at Minneapolis-St. Paul International Airport. No injuries were reported. Adjutant Gen. James Sieben, commander of the Minnesota National Guard, said today he has requested an investigation of the incident, according to an advisory from the governor's office.

Police, Students Clash in Spain

MADRID (UPI)—Riot police firing rubber bullets, tear gas and water cannons clashed today with hundreds of rock-hurling students protesting plans to raise college fees and stiffen admissions procedures. Twenty-five people were injured, including a 15-year-old girl hit by police gunfire.

Two officers were caught in a hail of rocks and carried off on stretchers as the students battled in downtown streets, sending passers-by fleeing for safety. The violence broke out as about 150,000 students staged a two-mile march to protest the socialist government's education policies. The main body of the students demonstrated peacefully but trouble erupted when about 300 broke away and fought running battles with police. Police said at least four students were arrested.

Kidnapers Seize 2 More in Lebanon

BEIRUT (AP)—Kidnapers forced two more foreigners into a car at gunpoint today while Anglican Church envoy Terry Waite negotiated for a fourth day with captors of American hostages.

Police said they had unconfirmed reports that the latest kidnap victims were West Germans who called on their embassy in West Beirut minutes before they were abducted at 9:30 a.m. on Pavillon Street near Hamra, the Muslim sector's commercial district.

But Consul Rene Trager at the West German Embassy annex in Christian East Beirut said: "We don't think they are Germans. We are still checking."

Witnesses said the victims protested to their abductors in a foreign language, but the Arabic-speaking witnesses were unsure what language it was.

A perfume vendor, who identified himself as Abu Khalil, said he saw five men in a gray Mercedes car pull to a stop.

'All Sped Away'

"Three gunmen leaped out. One came to me and threatened to shoot me if I moved. The other two bundled the victims into the Mercedes, and all sped away," Abu Khalil said.

The Christian radio station Voice of Lebanon said early today that American captives Terry A. Anderson and Thomas Sutherland were expected to be turned over to Waite in east Lebanon's Bekaa Valley town of Baalbek. The report could not be verified.

The radio later said that the captors were making "stiffer demands" and that the Americans' release appeared to be in doubt. It did not elaborate.

The radio account said Waite was meeting in Baalbek with representatives of Hezbollah and Islamic Jihad, two pro-Iranian Shia Muslim groups. Hezbollah is the most militant Shia group in Lebanon. Islamic Jihad has claimed it kidnaped Anderson and Sutherland.

The Voice of Lebanon, the station of President Amin Gemayel's rightist Falange Party, has made inaccurate reports on Muslim happenings in the past.

Asks Sheik to Intervene

West German Ambassador Antonius Eitel, meanwhile, met Sheik Mohammed Hussein Fadlallah, the reputed spiritual guide of Hezbollah.

Eitel told reporters after a 45-minute meeting at Fadlallah's house in Muslim West Beirut that he asked him to intervene to rescue two West Germans abducted in the last week in the Lebanese capital. They are Rudolf Cordes, 53, seized last Saturday, and Siemens company engineer Alfred Schmidt, 47, abducted Tuesday.

Radio Lower Saxony, a private West German station in Hanover, said today that the brother of a Lebanese terrorist suspect detained in West Germany had ordered the kidnapings. It identified him as Abdul Hadi Hamadi, security chief for Hezbollah and brother of the detained suspect, Mohammed Ali Hamadi.

The United States is seeking Hamadi's extradition to face charges of air piracy and murder in connection with the June, 1985, hijack of a TWA jetliner to Beirut.

In Bonn, officials said today Chancellor Helmut Kohl's government is considering putting Hamadi on trial on explosives and forgery charges before extraditing him to the United States. The officials, who requested anonymity, said that would win time for the West German government to negotiate the freedom of the hostages.

Associated Press

Neither snow nor rain. . . .—Lisa Massarelli of Medford, Mass., is no letter carrier but she measures up to their standards today as she wipes off her face while fighting her way home through high wind and driving sleet from shopping in Boston.

Storm Lashes Great Lakes; Cold Chills Eastern Cities

From Associated Press

A new storm lashed the Great Lakes today with snow and wind that shoved windchill readings to as low as 70 below zero, while a cold wave meant more misery for cities from the Gulf Coast to New England digging out from a major blast of ice and snow.

Armies of plows and salt-spreaders were deployed along the Eastern Seaboard to clear highways and runways buried by the storm, which was born in the Gulf of Mexico on Wednesday night, became a blizzard in New England on Thursday night and moved into Canada this morning.

It left behind up to 20 inches of snow, forced schools to close from Mississippi to Maine, stymied travelers and brought much of the work of the federal government to a halt. Ten deaths were blamed on the storm.

National Airport in Washington, New Jersey's Newark International and New York's Kennedy and LaGuardia airports reopened this morning after being shut down Thursday.

Single Runways Open

A single runway at Boston's Logan Airport was open for departures early today. A runway opened at Philadelphia International Airport for arrivals and departures.

Winter's worst came today in the Great Lakes region, where icy winds moving across the warmer waters churned up snowstorms from Michigan to Indiana.

Northwesterly winds gusting to 47 m.p.h. knifed across Michigan. In Sault Ste. Marie, where temperatures fell to 20 below zero early today, the windchill factor was 60 below to 70 below, the National Weather Service said. Ten to 20 inches of snow was expected by tonight in the Upper Peninsula.

Blowing snow and cold turned many county roads in east-central Illinois into solid sheets of ice, police said.

At mid-morning, the temperature was zero in Decatur, but northwest winds made it feel like 34 below on bare skin. In Chicago, where the temperature was 1 degree above, the windchill index stood at 33 below.

In northern Indiana, blowing and drifting snow shut down some highways. South Bend accumulated 9.1 inches of snow by 7 a.m. as temperatures across the state dropped to their lowest levels of the season.

A mid-morning temperature of 2, plus a westerly wind of 21 m.p.h., created a windchill factor of 30 below in Indianapolis.

Readings in Minnesota ranged from 15 below in the south to about 35 below in the north.

Temperatures dropped in parts of the Deep South as soon as the skies cleared there Thursday, and extreme cold began moving into the Northeast today. In some states, officials again urged motorists to stay off the roads.

"The road crews need to get as much of the snow off the highways before the temperatures drop into the single digits tonight," said Maryland state police spokesman Chuck Jackson.

"We're concerned that the temperature is going to drop and we're going have the whole metropolitan area turn into an ice-skating rink."

Papandreou: Greece Won't Leave NATO

ATHENS (UPI)—Prime Minister Andreas Papandreou told Parliament today that Greece will not leave NATO and that he plans to renegotiate the presence of U.S. military bases in Greece.

During a debate on national defense, Greece's Socialist prime minister said, "We are not pulling out of NATO for reasons of national security and because with such a move, war with Turkey might become inevitable, and not because we believe in a future clash between East and West."

Papandreou said the agreement on the operation of U.S. military bases on Greek soil expires in December, 1988, and Greece is ready to negotiate a new agreement.

Greece's ruling Panhellenic Socialist Movement, or PASOK, came to power in 1981 on a platform calling for an end to the presence of U.S. bases in Greece. PASOK had also made Greece's withdrawal from NATO one of its objectives.

Papandreou, who in 1983 signed a five-year agreement on the bases, said he is going to negotiate a new agreement.

"Our negotiations will start from zero point," he said.

Constantine Mitsotakis, leader of the main opposition party New Democracy, said his party supports the presence of the bases but asked the government to negotiate "to draw benefits necessary for our defense."

THE LATEST WEATHER

Partly cloudy skies are forecast for Saturday by the National Weather Service. The downtown high should be in the mid-60s after an overnight low in the upper 40s.

Mormon Papers Dealer Admits 2 Bombing Deaths

SALT LAKE CITY (AP)—Mormon documents dealer Mark Hofmann pleaded guilty today to reduced charges of second-degree murder in the bombing deaths of two people and was sentenced to five years to life in prison.

The plea-bargain agreement closed the bizarre case without a trial and allowed Hofmann, charged with two counts of first-degree murder, to avoid the possibility of the death penalty.

Third District Judge Kenneth A. Rigtrup told Hofmann that given the "indiscriminate" nature of his crimes and his use of pipe bombs as murder weapons, he would recommend that Hofmann "remain incarcerated for life."

In addition to the five years to life sentence for one murder, Rigtrup sentenced Hofmann to 1 to 15 years in prison on the other second-degree murder plea.

Hofmann, 32, also pleaded guilty to two counts of theft by deception, for which he was sentenced to one to 15 years each.

Today's plea was entered nearly a year after Hofmann was charged with the pipe-bomb murders of Steven Christensen, 31, and Kathleen Sheets, 50, on Oct. 15, 1985.

Hofmann, a married father of three, was seriously injured the next day when a pipe bomb blew him out of his parked sports car in the downtown area. Investigators maintained the device had been triggered accidentally and named Hofmann as their prime suspect within days.

Prosecutors contended that Hofmann, who had maintained his innocence until today, turned to murder in a desperate attempt to cover up a scheme in which allegedly fraudulent historical documents were sold to the Mormon Church and other collectors for hundreds of thousands of dollars.

Christensen was killed about two hours before he was to inspect a purported cache of old documents written by early Mormon leader William McLellin with Hofmann and an attorney representing a potential buyer. Prosecutors contended Hofmann never had the McLellin collection.

Ends Off 43 on Historic Trade Spree

From Times Wire Services

NEW YORK—Stock prices careened like a wild roller coaster today, surging to unprecedented levels and then plunging in record-heavy volume that marked one of the most volatile days in Wall Street history.

The Dow Jones average of 30 industrial stocks, 64 points higher by early afternoon to the 2,209 level for the first time ever, tumbled more than 110 points within an hour. It then stabilized, rebounding briefly and headed down again, closing off 43.87 at 2,101.80. This was the fourth biggest one-day drop ever.

Volume was a record 302.39 million shares, compared with 188.86 million Thursday.

'It's Just Insane'

"I've never seen a day like this in my life. It's just insane," said Robert O'Toole, manager of over-the-counter trading at Shearson Lehman Brothers Inc. in New York. "We had a 110-point swing in the Dow. I've been in this business for 30 years and I've never seen that before."

Volume on the New York Stock Exchange surpassed 263 million shares as of 3 p.m. EST, easily topping the previous record of 253.12 million set Jan. 15.

The volatility came one day after the Dow Jones industrials rose a record 51.60 points. Broader market barometers also rose sharply, reflecting an enormous New Year interest in stocks over other investments.

Wary Investors Jump

Much of the advance has been attributed to buying by investors who had been wary about getting into the market during the New Year rally, but increasingly are afraid of missing out on a prolonged advance.

"There's a lot of money still out there, so that every time it (the market) backs off that money finds its way in here," said Hildegarde Zagorski, an analyst for Prudential-Bache Securities Inc.

Analysts also said some Wall Streeters may have been heartened when the West German central bank cut its discount rate by a half percentage point. Some economists believe the move could help stabilize the plunging dollar, thus lessening chances of high U.S. inflation.

Institutional Buying

Traders said institutions were doing most of the buying and investors seemed determined not to miss out on a rally that has boosted prices on all but one trading day this year.

"This market is rewriting the record books and everyone is saying it's a once-in-a-lifetime phenomenon," trader William Schneider of Kidder Peabody said.

"I get a sense that larger and smaller investors are just throwing money at stocks," said Chris Callies of Dean Witter Reynolds. Thursday's big advance showed "some sort of buying panic."

Technical analysts have been predicting a pullback to correct for the long string of gains.

"This (decline from the highs) might have been a shakeout, but the market's not going to give up this easily," Callies added.

Tables in Business Section

INDEX

EXTRA

Los Angeles Times

Circulation: 1,127,607 Daily/1,411,000 Sunday | Thursday, October 1, 1987 | LF/ 180 Pages Daily 25¢

6.0 Quake Rocks L.A.

At Least 3 Dead, Scores Hurt, Buildings Damaged

JOSE GALVEZ / Los Angeles Times

Rescuers survey the ruins of a building in the 100 block of South Fair Oaks Avenue in Pasadena that collapsed onto cars next door.

Cal State Student Dies, Man Trapped in Tunnel

By ERIC MALNIC, *Times Staff Writer*

A major earthquake rocked the Los Angeles metropolitan area at 7:42 this morning, killing at least three people, injuring scores of others, severely damaging dozens of buildings and forcing closure of two freeways in the Santa Fe Springs area.

Seismologists at Caltech said the quake measured 6.0 on the Richter scale—considerably less than the devastating Sylmar quake in 1971—and was centered in the Montebello-Whittier Narrows area. Scientists said it was not the "big quake" that is predicted for Southern California sometime in the next 30 years.

This morning's quake was felt as far away as San Diego, San Luis Obispo and even Las Vegas, more than 200 miles to the northeast.

Walls crumbled, windows shattered and ceilings collapsed in scattered locations throughout the metropolitan area. Telephone, radio and television systems were momentarily knocked out of service by the quake, and there were numerous reports of gas and water leaks.

Trapped in Elevators

Power outages trapped scores of workers in stalled elevators and thousands of early morning workers were ordered to evacuate downtown office structures.

City fire officials said a woman—not further identified—was killed when the wall of a building collapsed at the California State University, Los Angeles, campus.

A man buried under seven feet of earth in a tunnel being dug in the Eaton Canyon area above Pasadena was presumed dead, according to the Pasadena Fire Department. He was not immediately identified.

Another man, 35 years old, sustained severe head injuries and was reported near death at the Los Angeles County-USC Medical Center after the temblor reportedly threw him through a second-floor window in the Commerce area.

Boulder Injures Man

At least one person was seriously injured when a three-foot-by-four-foot boulder rolled down a steep hillside, crushing a vehicle on the Golden State Freeway transition road to the Harbor Freeway near Elysian Park.

California Highway Patrol spokesman Ernie Garcia said the injured person, whose identity and injuries were unknown, was taken to a downtown-area hospital. It was not known whether the victim was the driver or a passenger.

Emergency room spokesmen at County-USC Medical Center said they were swamped with earthquake injuries.

"We've had every kind of injury that can come in, and we're extremely busy with all kinds of problems from very bad to minor," he said.

Freeways Damaged

The quake forced the closure of the Santa Ana and San Gabriel River freeways in the Santa Fe Springs area at the height of the morning rush hour after Caltrans engineers noted major cracks in the San Gabriel River Freeway overpass and chunks of concrete tumbled onto the roadway. A major traffic tie-up resulted as commuters were diverted onto nearby surface streets.

Kate Hutton, staff seismologist at Caltech, said the quake, which was the strongest in the Los Angeles area since the Sylmar earthquake in 1971, appeared to occur along the Whittier Fault, a massive, subterranean crack in the earth that has been the source of a number of relatively minor temblors over the years.

She said tracking equipment recorded dozens of aftershocks this morning, but none approached the 6.0 magnitude of the initial quake.

One aftershock measuring 4.4 was registered at 7:45 a.m., followed by another at 8:12 a.m. By 8:30, there had been at least a dozen more between 3.0 and 3.5

The Richter scale is a measure of ground motion as recorded on seismographs. Every increase of one number means a tenfold increase in magnitude. Thus, a reading of 7.5 reflects an earthquake 10 times stronger than one of 6.5. An earthquake of 5 on the Richter scale can cause considerable damage, while one measuring 6 can cause severe damage.

The San Francisco earthquake of 1906, which occurred before the Richter scale was devised, has been estimated at 8.3 on the Richter scale. The 1971 quake here measured 6.4.

City workers had just begun reaching their downtown offices this morning when the quake struck.

File Cabinets Tumble

Lily Pruitt, 36, a management aide with the city Transportation Department, said she squatted on the floor of her office on the 13th floor of the Los Angeles City Hall as metal file cabinets crashed around her. She looked up to see small cracks open on the office walls.

When the first quake subsided, Harvey Lowe, 51, a material control storekeeper who was the designated civil defense warden for the floor, walked from desk to desk to make sure staffers were unhurt. Then he waited until 30 workers had gathered at the stairwell and then joined them.

On the way down, there were more shocks. As plaster rained down on them, the employees moved briskly, but there was no panic, Lowe said. "There wasn't anyone crying or hysterical," Lowe said. "But we all wanted out of there fast."

Cracks in City Hall

Large cracks were left in the City Hall facade. On the sixth floor, a fissure extended from a window facing south. On the building's east side, workmen gathered around a chunk of concrete that pushed out from the wall.

On the mall outside City Hall, Zachary Castleberry, 26, a transient from Augusta, Ga., had been sleeping in his shorts on an orange blanket unfurled on the grass. When the ground started to quiver, he sat up and watched the trees whip back and forth overhead.

"I thought they were fixing to fall," he said. Still, he sat there, dumbstruck. "It's probably another Mt. St. Helen's or something."

Castleberry watched as dozens of employees streamed out of the City Hall south exit. "They were all looking up as they came out," he said. "They looked like they had all saw ghosts."

Rescue Mission Damaged

Outside the Union Rescue Mission, 400 homeless were being served their morning meal when the shocks started. They dashed to the west side of the street as plaster and chunks of debris fell around them.

Bill Inglsey, 65, said he grabbed for a chain-link fence as an aftershock rattled the ground. Above him, a flock of startled pigeons flew off the shaking roof of the mission.

Daniel Shea, 26, a transient who had arrived in Los Angeles just three days ago from Ohio, was

Please see QUAKE, Page 2

Milling in Street for Hours

Hundreds Evacuate Downtown Buildings

By JUDY PASTERNAK and DEAN MURPHY. *Times Staff Writer*

Keun Bae Pak thought his end had come when the ground pitched beneath his feet while he poured water into the coffee maker at his downtown hamburger stand. But then the realization that it was merely the strongest earthquake he'd felt in 17 years in Los Angeles was followed by an afterthought: This could be good for business.

Indeed it was. Hundreds of employees were evacuated from the nearby State Office Building, the Times Mirror building, City Hall and storefronts along Broadway and Spring Street. Forced to mill in the streets for hours Thursday morning, they lined up five deep behind the five stools at Pak's Husky Boy stand on 2nd Street.

They talked of glass vases falling off tables and shattering, of computer terminals toppling over, of long cracks appearing in walls. And they shouted for Pak, his wife and his helper to serve them coffee or soda.

"The earthquake helped me," Pak said, showing off the bulging pockets of his green apron that signified bunches of dollar bills he hadn't had time to count. "I sold 10 times as many drinks as usual. And when they calmed down, they ate."

Damage appeared minor. But sirens blared as fire engines, some from as far away as Mission Hills, responded to alarms set off by broken water pipes. Burglar alarms also squalled at several stores. Queues formed at pay telephones as those forced outside called home or, in the case of lawyers with hearings, to the court.

Please see STREETS, Page 2

BOB CHAMBERLIN / Los Angeles Times

Helpless—Owners of the Aquarium store at 1714 S. Western Ave. grimace as they watch their store burn after earthquake.

THE QUAKE AT A GLANCE

Sun Valley
Van Nuys
Burbank
Glendale
Pasadena
Hollywood
Alhambra
Los Angeles
EPICENTER
Pomona
Montebello
Inglewood
Sante Fe Springs
Hawthorne
Compton
Fullerton
Carson
Torrance
Garden Grove
Long Beach
San Pedro
Santa Ana
Seal Beach
Irvine
Huntington Beach
Costa Mesa

PATRICK LYNCH / Los Angeles Times

- **Time:** 7:42 a.m.
- **Magnitude:** 6.0 on the open-ended Richter Scale. By comparison, the 1971 quake in Sylmar was listed as 6.4 on the Richter Scale; the 1906 quake in San Francisco was listed as 8.3.
- **Epicenter:** The Whittier Narrows area south of El Monte and north of Whittier, southeast from Pasadena. The quake and at least three aftershocks were felt as far away as Las Vegas, Ventura County and San Diego.
- **Deaths and Injuries:** Two dead, scores injured.

INSIDE TODAY'S TIMES

WEATHER: Variable clouds Friday. Civic Center high 96. Low tonight 69. Details: Part II, Page 5.

Caught in Political Hailstorm

Only nine months into his first term in Congress, brash California Rep. Ernie Konnyu finds himself in a political hailstorm. **Page 3.**

Reagan Faults Media

President Reagan said many in the news media and some lawmakers have been influenced by a "very sophisticated" Soviet disinformation campaign. **Page 4.**

Growth in Economy

The government's main barometer of economic activity nosed up—by 0.6%—for the seventh straight month. **Business.**

Los Angeles Times

Circulation: 1,127,607 Daily/1,411,000 Sunday | Monday, October 19, 1987 | LF/ 94 Pages

Daily 25¢

Bedlam on Wall St.

Dow Plunges 508; Record 604 Million Shares Sold

LATE NEWS/ STOCKS

No Progress in Mideast—Shultz

CAIRO (UPI)—Secretary of State George P. Shultz acknowledged today that he made no progress in reviving the stalled Middle East peace process while in the region but said Israel and Egypt showed a "genuine preoccupation with the importance of peace."

Shultz, speaking to reporters after a two-hour meeting with President Hosni Mubarak before flying on to London for talks with Jordan's King Hussein, said a commitment to peace should "help us find our way to the direct, bilateral negotiations that are the vehicle for peace."

AT&T Earnings Down, MCI Up

From Associated Press

American Telephone & Telegraph Co.'s earnings fell 5% and MCI Communications Corp.'s earnings rose 22% in the latest fiscal quarter, the long-distance companies said today.

AT&T said its earnings slid to $505 million, or 47 cents per share, in the three months ending Sept. 30, from $533 million, or 48 cents per common share, in the third quarter of 1986. MCI, the second-biggest long-distance phone company, said its third-quarter earnings jumped to $22 million, or 8 cents per share, from $18 million, or 6 cents per share, for the same 1986 period.

Hefty Driver Hoisted From Crash

From United Press International

Firefighters today used a stretcher hanging from a hook-and-ladder fire truck to rescue a 300-pound man who was seriously injured when his car crashed down a steep hill in the Santa Monica Mountains.

The unidentified man's car went off the side of West Encino Hills Drive, south of Encino, and plunged 50 feet down a steep embankment at 7:48 a.m. The man's girth caused firefighters problems, firefighters said. Once up the hill, the man was transferred to a helicopter and flown to UCLA Medical Center in critical condition with undisclosed injuries, they said.

Factory Use Steady at 81.2%

WASHINGTON (AP)—The operating rate at America's factories, mines and utilities remained unchanged in September at 81.2% of capacity, the highest level in three years, the government said today.

The Federal Reserve said that the operating rate showed no movement from the revised August level but was 2.4 percentage points higher than a year ago. So far this year, American manufacturers have enjoyed a significant upturn in activity as the weaker dollar has made U.S. goods competitive once more on overseas markets.

Goetz Sentenced to 6 Months

NEW YORK (AP)—Bernhard Goetz was sentenced today to six months in jail and five months probation on his conviction for illegal possession of the gun he used to shoot four youths on a subway almost three years ago.

The judge also directed Goetz to undergo psychiatric treatment, fined him $5,000 and ordered him to perform 280 hours of community service. "A non-jail sentence for Mr. Goetz would invite others to violate the gun law," state Supreme Court Justice Stephen G. Crane said. The maximum term Goetz could have received was 2⅓ to 7 years. The state Probation Department had recommended that he be spared prison.

U.S. Delays Decision on UNESCO

WASHINGTON (AP)—The State Department said today the election of a new director general of UNESCO to replace Amadou-Mahatar M'Bow of Senegal will not automatically lead to a U.S. decision to rejoin the organization, which it left in 1984 complaining of politicization.

UNESCO selected a former minister of education of Spain, Federico Mayor Zaragoza, to replace M'Bow during a weekend meeting in Paris. "We will assess rejoining UNESCO only when there is evidence of institutional, programmatic and structural reforms," State Department spokeswoman Phyllis Oakley said.

INSIDE TODAY'S TIMES

WEATHER: Morning low clouds, then mostly sunny Tuesday. L.A. high near 74. Low tonight 64. Details: Part II, Page 5.

Kirkpatrick Eyes White House

Conservatives may have found a champion in Jeane J. Kirkpatrick, who said she is considering a race for the GOP nomination. **Page 12.**

Twins Take 2-0 Lead

The Minnesota Twins took a 2-0 lead over the St. Louis Cardinals in the best-of-seven World Series with an 8-4 victory. **Sports.**

No Longer a Leg Up

Less leg room on commuter flights is just one more painful sign of the demise of regional airlines on the West Coast. **Business.**

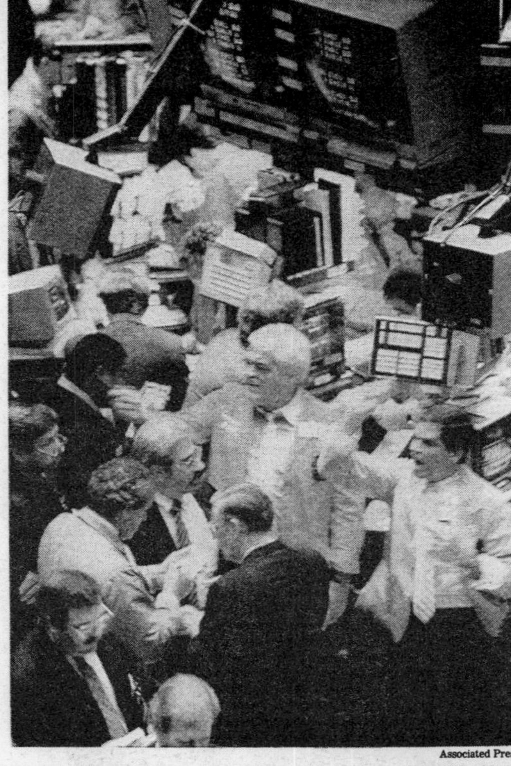

Associated Press

Down, down, down—Traders crowd the floor of the New York Stock Exchange on a day of frantic activity as market plunged.

Many Gains of Last 5 Years Wiped Out

From Times Wire Services

NEW YORK—Bedlam swept Wall Street today as the stock market selloff turned into a full-scale panic as the Dow Jones industrial index plunged 508.32 points—the worst one-day drop ever.

That represented a one-day loss of 22.4%, far larger than the 12.8% drop on Oct. 28, 1929, known as Black Monday. The Dow average's worst percentage decline ever was on Dec. 12, 1914, early in World War I, when it lost 24.4% of its value.

The Dow closed today at 1,738.74.

Trading was the heaviest ever recorded at the New York Stock Exchange: 604.4 million shares were traded, far exceeding the 338.48-million share record set Friday.

The plunge wiped out a big part of the gains amassed through the bull market of the past five years.

"I don't have words to describe this," said Suresh Bhirud, an analyst at Oppenheimer & Co.

"What we have is a full-scale financial panic," said Hugh Johnson at First Albany Corp.

Brokers said the market was caught up in a chain reaction of events that created what William LeFevre at Advest Inc. called "a terrible washout" as the trading week began.

Global Trend

Stock markets in Tokyo and London fell sharply in reaction to Wall Street's severe break last week.

On the Big Board, battered Dow stocks included IBM, off as much as 10½ at 124½ and General Electric, down 6¼ at 44½. The only issues on the gaining list were precious metal miners, reflecting the sharp rise in gold prices in reaction to the declines in financial markets.

Initially, the stock market edged to a fractional gain as investors tried to regroup after last Friday's disastrous fall.

But a further collapse in bond prices and the dollar knocked stocks into the minus column and the selling in the equity market gained momentum of its own.

U.S. bond prices tumbled in early trading today, although they later recovered much of their losses.

LeFevre said it appeared that mutual funds were being forced to sell stocks as their shareholders switched money out of stock funds and into safer money market funds.

In addition, he said, brokers were selling stocks from so-called margin accounts in which investors who bought stocks earlier with borrowed money declined to put up additional collateral.

World markets also had to contend with heightened tensions in the Middle East. The United States confirmed that it had attacked and destroyed an Iranian oil platform in the Persian Gulf.

Bhirud said computer program strategies that allow professional traders to transmit huge orders in a matter of moments exacerbated the rout in the stock market.

Bond prices also plummeted in early, active trading, hammered by the twin pressures of the falling dollar and the worst declines in Wall Street's history.

At mid-morning the Treasury's closely watched 30-year bond was down about 1¼ point, or $12.50 for every $1,000 in face value. Bond yields, which move inversely to prices, had soared to 10.32% from 10.17% late Friday.

"Really, it's a blood bath," said Elizabeth Reiners, a vice president of investment firm Dean Witter Reynolds. "All of the markets have fallen apart; there's confusion on every front."

Beside the psychological impact of the tumbling stock market, analysts said bond prices were also weakened by the declining dollar—which had fallen to about 141.55 Japanese yen at around midday in New York.

Reagan Discusses Plunge With Aides, but Isn't Alarmed

WASHINGTON (AP)—President Reagan, at swearing-in ceremonies for Commerce Secretary C. William Verity, made no mention of today's stock market plunge but said the U.S. economy is being bolstered by "substantial growth" in exports not reflected in recent government trade figures, widely viewed as the event that triggered the plunge.

Reagan noted that the current expansion has reached a record length for a peacetime recovery. "Leading indicators are sending a message: steady she goes," Reagan said.

White House spokesman Marlin Fitzwater said Reagan did discuss the plunging stock market with top advisers at lunch today.

Asked if the Administration is alarmed by the market's fall, Fitzwater said, "No. We feel the underlying economy is sound. On the other hand, it is a situation we have to watch."

U.S. Destroys 2 Iranian Oil Platforms in Gulf

MANAMA, Bahrain (AP)—The United States destroyed two Iranian offshore oil platforms in the central Persian Gulf today in retaliation for a missile attack on a U.S.-flagged tanker, U.S. officials announced.

White House spokesman Marlin Fitzwater said gunfire from four U.S. destroyers blasted "the two platforms at one location. They both collapsed."

Iran confirmed the attack and vowed "a crushing response."

Gulf-based marine salvage executives said Iranian tugboats were seen rushing to the Sassan and Rostam platforms, 30 miles apart, east of the Qatar peninsula and 60 and 75 miles south of the Iranian coast.

Platforms Ablaze

U.S. Defense Secretary Caspar W. Weinberger said the attack was confined to the Rostam platforms. However, shipping sources in the Persian Gulf and Iranian radio said the Sassan platform 30 miles away also had been attacked. They said the platforms were ablaze.

In Washington, the Pentagon said that no Americans were injured in the attack and that most of the 20 to 30 Iranians on the Rostam platforms abandoned them after being warned an attack was imminent.

The oil platforms, like other Iranian facilities in the gulf, are used as bases for Iranian helicopters and speedboats that attack neutral commercial shipping as part of the 7-year-old Iran-Iraq War.

Radio monitors said they heard an Iranian voice saying, "U.S. warship, U.S. warship, let me evacuate the injured before you shoot again."

Reprisal for Missile Attack

Today's attack was in reprisal for Friday's missile attack that injured 18 people on the U.S.-flagged Kuwaiti tanker Sea Isle City. The attack, which involved Chinese-made Silkworm missiles, was launched from the Faw peninsula, more than 300 miles north of the Rostam platforms.

In a statement, President Reagan said the attack was "a prudent yet restrained response to this unlawful use of force against the United States and to numerous violations to the rights of other non-belligerents."

He described the one-time oil drilling facility as "a military platform" and said it had been "used to assist in a number of attacks on non-belligerent shipping."

Weinberger told reporters in Washington: "We do not seek further confrontation with Iran but will be prepared to meet any further military escalation by Iran with stronger retaliation."

Another Platform Boarded

Later, the Pentagon said Navy SEAL commandos boarded another Iranian sea platform in the gulf after it had been abandoned by Iranian personnel and destroyed some radar and communications gear before departing.

Spokesman Fred Hoffman said the platform was situated about five nautical miles from the scene of the earlier attack by U.S. forces on two other platforms.

The third platform had not been selected as a target for U.S. naval gunfire, Hoffman said. But shortly after four Navy destroyers bombarded the first two targets, "it was noticed that boats were taking people off another platform," he said.

"After this platform was abandoned, U.S. Navy men went aboard, looked around, destroyed some radar and communications equipment and then left," he added.

Yugoslav President OK After Collapse

BELGRADE, Yugoslavia (AP)—President Lazar Mojsov collapsed today in Parliament and was carried from the assembly hall, but later reappeared and finished his speech.

Mojsov, 67, was in the middle of an address on Yugoslavia's economic and social crisis when he sat down and turned pale. A doctor had Mojsov carried from the hall, but 35 minutes later, the president re-entered the Parliament, sat down and finished reading his speech.

Blaming Dow Skid on Tax Plan 'Balderdash': Wright

WASHINGTON (AP)—House Speaker Jim Wright today dismissed as "balderdash" the Reagan Administration assertion that the work of Democrats on a tax-increase package pushed the stock market into a tailspin.

Treasury Secretary James A. Baker III, in a television interview on Sunday, said tax increase bills approved by House and Senate committees last week helped fuel the market fall last week in which the Dow Jones industrial average suffered its largest weekly decline since World War II.

"I think that the writing of these tax packages had a major effect in what's happened to the stock market over the course of the past three or four days," Baker said on NBC-TV's "Meet the Press." (Story, Part IV, Page 2.)

As the market continued to fall today Wright said blaming the tax bills was the Administration's way of pinning the blame elsewhere.

"I think that that's balderdash, utterly ridiculous," Wright (D-Tex.) told reporters. He said the market reacts favorably to evidence that Congress is trying to control the deficits that have added $1.3 trillion to the national debt since President Reagan took office.

Rep. William H. Gray III (D-Pa.) said the key to assuring the markets is substantial progress on reducing the deficit. But with Reagan unwilling to compromise with Congress, "the marketplace is lacking confidence that that is going to happen," he said.

Sen. Lloyd Bentsen (D-Tex.), chairman of the tax-writing Senate Finance Committee, blamed the market fall on the nation's trade and budget deficits and the Reagan Administration's failure to respond to the growing debts.

"The immediate cause of last week's stock market drop was the sharp jump in the prime rate. Interest rates shot up because of our persistent trade deficit and budget deficit and this Administration's refusal to develop policies to reduce them," Bentsen said.

"Anyone who says otherwise is out of touch with reality, living in a dream world," he added.

Los Angeles Times

Circulation: 1,136,813 Daily/1,421,711 Sunday | Monday, July 4, 1988 | CC†/ 92 Pages

Daily 25¢ / Designated Areas Higher

U.S. Downs Iran Airliner; 290 Dead

Navy Cruiser Mistakes Jet for Hostile F-14 Over Gulf

Beauty, Stealth Ability

Flying Wing Boomerangs Into Favor

By RUDY ABRAMSON, *Times Staff Writer*

WASHINGTON—It has titillated fliers and designers and eccentrics for half a century—an airplane fully contained within a sleek boomerang-shaped wing, an aesthetic tour de force, a flying wing.

Once it had a promising future on both sides of the Atlantic and then it faded away, the victim of aerial instability and lost government contracts. In America, it survived only among the artifacts of the Smithsonian Institution's Air and Space Museum, one tiny flying wing rescued from rust and dry rot by 11,000 tedious hours of work by experts.

But now there is promise of a renaissance.

Snowmobile Engine

In Nampa, Ida., one Gilbert Davis, haunted by flying wing pictures he had seen as a small boy, built a 950-pound plane with a wingspan of 35 feet. He outfitted it with a snowmobile engine and, though he had previously piloted nothing hotter than a Piper Arrow, he flew the wing successfully and repeatedly.

About a year ago, though, he took off overloaded, bound for an air show in Oshkosh, Wis., and wound up floating in the Snake River, the snowmobile engine still putt-putting like a motorboat. Davis came out of it with "nothing worse than a bruised ego."

Now the wing is being put back into flying condition and the pilot-designer is pressing onward with plans to market a Davis flying wing kit for $16,500, plus change. (Engine not included.)

In Chino, not far from Ontario airport, Ed Maloney, with a platoon of volunteers, including some who worked on flying wing bombers in the 1940s, is restoring a flying wing prototype to operating condition.

Built to Prove Concept

It is one of four 60-foot-wingspan models that aviation pioneer John K. Northrop built to prove the concept he had tinkered with since the 1920s. Maloney, the founder and president of the Planes of Fame aircraft museum at Chino, expects to see it in the air again in about two years.

"The flying wing never really died," said E.T. Wooldridge, an assistant director of the Smithsonian Air and Space Museum and author of a flying wing history, who lectures around the country on the trials and tribulations of the extraordinary design. "But now there is really a revival," he said.

The revival that brings hundreds of flying wing buffs out to hear Wooldridge's talks was fired anew

Please see WING, Page 20

Associated Press and United Press International

U.S. Navy cruiser Vincennes, left, its commander, Capt. Will C. Rogers III, center, and Airbus A-300 airliner of the type shot down by the Vincennes in the Persian Gulf. Above right, Adm. William J. Crowe Jr., chairman of the Joint Chiefs of Staff, explains incident to reporters.

Lawmakers Vow Probe and Warn of Retaliation

Fear Iranians Will 'Demand Pound of Flesh'; New Attacks on U.S. Policy in Gulf Expected

By SARA FRITZ, *Times Staff Writer*

WASHINGTON—Members of Congress on Sunday pledged to conduct a full inquiry into the destruction of an Iranian airliner by U.S. forces in the Persian Gulf and urged the Reagan Administration to brace for a new burst of Iranian terrorism directed at Americans around the world.

"They are going to demand their pound of flesh in return—anywhere in the world, not just in the Persian Gulf," Sen. Dale Bumpers (D-Ark.) predicted. "If that had been an American airline, we'd probably be in the process of declaring war on Iran right now."

The tragedy was certain to revive criticism of U.S. policy in the Persian Gulf, both in Congress and among U.S. allies. The assistant House majority leader, Californian Tony Coelho (D-Merced), said President Reagan should have anticipated such a disaster when he authorized the U.S. Navy to begin escorting reflagged Kuwaiti tankers in the gulf nearly a year ago.

"The Persian Gulf operation lacks definition and reason, and this kind of tragedy is the inevitable result," Coelho said. "If a retaliatory act of terror is Iran's response, who will remember this mission to protect commercial shipping or its purpose?"

Both House and Senate members called for immediate hearings—focusing particularly on the question of how the cruiser Vincennes' sophisticated Aegis missile defense system failed to detect the difference between an F-14 fighter and a large commercial airliner.

"We have been told the Aegis system is the greatest in the world and that this couldn't happen," said Rep. Pat Schroeder (D-Colo.), a member of the House Armed Services Committee. "If we're paying more for an expensive system and getting the same, we ought to know why."

Pentagon Briefing Due

Senate Armed Services Chairman Sam Nunn (D-Ga.) said the capabilities of the Aegis system would be one of the issues explored by his committee when it receives a briefing from Pentagon officials early this week.

"I believe we should reserve judgment until receiving further information and the answers to such key questions as follows: What was the ongoing operations situation, what intelligence did we have regarding any threats, what were the rules of engagement and the command decision-making chain for this situation, what are the technical capabilities of the Aegis system and how have we previously handled airline traffic in

Please see CONGRESS, Page 11

Tehran Assails Navy Attack as a 'Massacre'

By CHARLES P. WALLACE, *Times Staff Writer*

NICOSIA, Cyprus—Iran accused the United States of provoking Sunday's military confrontation in the Persian Gulf and called for international condemnation of Washington's "capital crime" of shooting down an Iranian civilian airliner.

The incident shows that the United States has "entered a more direct war with our nation," Prime Minister Hussein Moussavi declared, according to a dispatch received in Nicosia from IRNA, the official Iranian news agency.

'Abhorrence of Washington'

Moussavi warned that this "latest crime against the Iranian people would only further arouse the abhorrence of [Iranians] against Washington."

In a similar vein, Foreign Minister Ali Akbar Velayati declared: "The United States is responsible for the consequences of its barbaric massacre of innocent passengers."

IRNA's report did not say what actions Iran might take, but it said that the incident would bolster Iran's resolve in its long war with Iraq.

The news agency said that all 290 people aboard the Iran Air A-300 Airbus died when the plane was shot down shortly after it left the Iranian city of Bandar Abbas. July 4 was proclaimed a day of mourning throughout Iran.

In a broadcast monitored here, Tehran Radio said the downing of the airliner was "new evidence of America's crimes and mischief, crimes which expose America's

Please see IRAN, Page 7

'Proper Defensive Action' Amid Battle, Reagan Says

By JOHN M. BRODER and MELISSA HEALY, *Times Staff Writers*

WASHINGTON—A U.S. warship, mistaking a commercial Iranian airliner for a warplane, shot the jet down during a naval skirmish in the Persian Gulf on Sunday. Officials in Tehran said that 290 passengers and crew aboard Iran Air Flight 655 were killed.

President Reagan said officers aboard the American guided missile cruiser Vincennes, which was battling with several Iranian gunboats, believed the jetliner was an attacking Iranian F-14 fighter and fired two surface-to-air missiles at it at 10:54 a.m. gulf time. At least one of the missiles struck the A-300B2 Airbus, sending it into the waters of the Strait of Hormuz.

"This is a terrible human tragedy," Reagan said in a statement read by his spokesman Marlin Fitzwater. "We deeply regret any loss of life."

But Reagan insisted that the Navy's downing of the jetliner was a "proper defensive action" at a time when the Vincennes and another U.S. warship were already engaged in a sea battle directly beneath the airliner's path.

U.S. officials said the Vincennes warned the Iran Air flight seven

Other gulf stories, pictures are on Pages 7, 8, 9, 12 and 15.

times that it was entering a hostile zone, but the pilot did not respond.

"When the aircraft failed to heed repeated warnings, the Vincennes followed standing orders and widely publicized procedures, firing to protect itself against possible attack," Reagan said.

The Iranian news agency IRNA said that the attack on the airliner was "among the most horrendous crimes of its kind ever committed by America." Tehran Radio vowed, "We will not leave the crimes of America unanswered."

Iran Air Flight 655 is a twice-weekly half-hour flight from Bandar Abbas in Iran to Dubai in the United Arab Emirates, a route that normally takes it very close to the location of Sunday's hostilities on the Persian Gulf. It is popular with Iranian tourists and foreign technicians who use Dubai as a shopping center for consumer goods unavailable in Iran.

Airline sources said all but 40 of

Please see GULF, Page 12

Sophisticated System Failed to Identify Jet

By ROBERT W. STEWART, *Times Staff Writer*

WASHINGTON—The $525-million Aegis missile defense system used Sunday by the Navy to shoot down an Iranian airliner is among the most sophisticated weapons in the U.S. arsenal, but faced with an unidentified plane spotted so close and approaching so fast, it apparently was not sophisticated enough.

And the special characteristics of the Aegis system may prove to be a key factor in answering the central question posed by the tragedy: How could the U.S. ship, the cruiser Vincennes, fail to tell the difference between a two-man F-14 jet fighter and a commercial A-300 Airbus airliner that carried nearly 300 people?

'Electronic Indications'

At a press conference, Adm. William J. Crowe Jr., chairman of the Joint Chiefs of Staff, said the Vincennes picked up "electronic indications . . . that led it to believe that the aircraft was an F-14." He described the indications only as "electronic information which is classified and [which] I am not willing to discuss."

The Aegis system, for all of its elaborate capabilities, was not designed primarily for the close-in conditions and short reaction times that prevail in the gulf, according to military experts.

At close range, the Aegis is no more effective in identifying

Please see AEGIS, Page 10

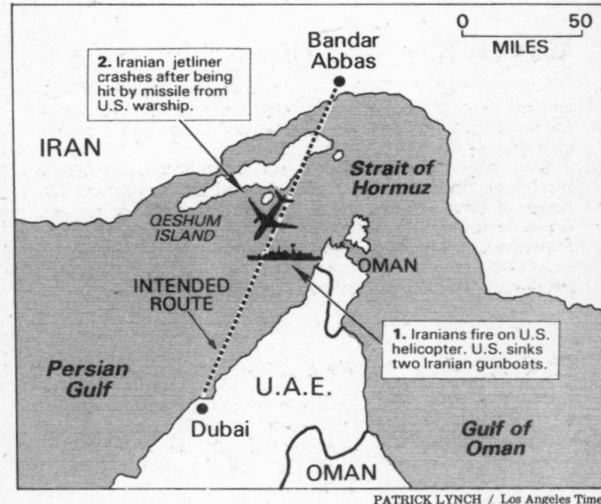

PATRICK LYNCH / Los Angeles Times

Climate for Wrongdoing Created

Scandal's Roots Traced to Basic Reagan Policy Goals

By DANIEL M. WEINTRAUB and MELISSA HEALY, *Times Staff Writers*

WASHINGTON—The massive procurement scandal now enveloping the Defense Department had its roots not only in the greed of individuals but in some of the Reagan Administration's most basic policy goals: cutting back the bureaucracy, encouraging free-market competition and restoring the strength and prestige of America's armed forces.

As applied to the Pentagon, the changes produced unquestionable benefits, but they also created conditions under which the incentives to cheat grew enormously even as traditional safeguards were being reduced.

The defense budget is so vast it has always been a prime target for abuses. But former Pentagon officials, defense analysts and members of Congress say the Reagan Administration unwittingly helped create a climate in which the opportunities—and temptations—rose dramatically for potentially dishonest or unscrupulous Pentagon employees, defense consultants and contractors.

"It's like driving down the highway at 80 miles an hour in your car and taking your hands off the steering wheel," said Gordon Adams, director of the Defense Budget Project. "It's crazy."

The factors contributing to the new environment included four separate but related Administration initiatives:

—First, when Caspar W. Weinberger became secretary of the Department of Defense in 1981, he

Please see DEFENSE, Page 16

INSIDE TODAY'S TIMES

WEATHER: Morning low clouds, hazy afternoon. Civic Center low/high today: 64/76. Details: Part II, Page 3.

Jackson Warns Party Leaders

Jesse Jackson strongly suggested that Democratic leaders should not take him and the votes he delivers for granted. **Page 5.**

Consider the Snowflake

The computer is being used to decipher snowflake patterns and to help form a theory of how snowflakes grow. **Metro, Page 4.**

Trade Reports: Be Wary

The up or down movements in the trade deficit can be false statistical changes with no ties to underlying realities. **Business.**

Political Debate Expands: Soviets in Happy Turmoil

By MICHAEL PARKS, *Times Staff Writer*

MOSCOW—Suddenly, political debate has exploded across the Soviet Union.

Debates are raging about government policies, about national priorities, about the very future of the country.

Feuds within the ruling Communist Party are flaring up. Leaders, and would-be leaders, are competing for public support. Alliances are being forged as reformers and conservatives maneuver for position.

New issue-oriented political groups are forming. Petitions, protests, rallies and even approved public demonstrations have become almost commonplace. The long-insipid Soviet press has a new zest with readers lining up by the dozens to buy the hottest newspapers and magazines.

And that great political bastion, the Communist Party, is undertaking a vast reorganization that will transform it from an inward-looking, *de facto* government back into a political party—still fully in charge but knowing it will have to canvass hard to win support.

The whole country seems to be in turmoil, and quite happily so.

"We've discovered politics, and it seems that it's better than sex," Yuri Glushko, 36, a research mathematician, commented Sunday. "Everywhere I go, people are talking politics, politics, politics. It's really becoming a national obsession. . . ."

Please see SOVIETS, Page 6

Los Angeles Times

Circulation: 1,118,649 Daily/1,433,739 Sunday | Tuesday, June 6, 1989 | CC†/ 104 Pages Copyright 1989/The Times Mirror Company Daily 25¢ / Designated Areas Higher

China Teeters on Edge of Civil War as Rival Forces Mobilize

Associated Press

A protester blocks a column of tanks in front of Beijing Hotel. After climbing aboard the lead tank, the man, apparently unharmed, was led away by friends, and the column proceeded.

Battle for Control of Beijing Seen

By DAVID HOLLEY and DANIEL WILLIAMS, *Times Staff Writers*

BEIJING—China teetered this morning on the edge of civil war, with troops presumed loyal to hard-line President Yang Shangkun in control of central Beijing but positioned defensively at strategic points in apparent anticipation of attack by rival forces.

Troops and armored vehicles were reported moving toward Beijing from the east, according to Western diplomats who said they appeared to be opposed to the troops of the 27th Army that killed hundreds or perhaps thousands of people while taking control of the center of the capital over the weekend.

A military attache in the British colony of Hong Kong, reached by telephone this morning, said the Chinese air force has joined the effort to wrest control of Beijing from the 27th Army. Infantry units of the air force landed at the Nanyuan military airport south of the capital Monday night and engaged in skirmishes with other military units at or near the airport, the attache said.

The air force believes that responsibility for the indiscriminate shootings in Beijing rests with the army, the attache said. The air force is headed by Wang Hai, who canceled a planned trip to Europe last week apparently to remain in Beijing during the intra-military feuding.

Other small-scale duels broke out between rival troops Monday, according to Western witnesses, only about one mile west of Tian An Men Square, now controlled by thousands of 27th Army soldiers with hundreds of armored vehicles.

Tanks Fan Out

At about 7 p.m. Monday, tanks accompanied by armored personnel carriers and truckloads of troops fanned out to points along the Second Ring Road that loops around the main part of the city. This area includes Tian An Men Square, the Great Hall of the People and Zhongnanhai, the red-walled compound from which China's leaders have traditionally ruled, and the city's older residential and commercial districts.

About 20 tanks continued to stand guard this morning at the Jianguomen bridge on the eastern side of the city, about half facing east in defensive positions. The others faced north, south and west to control access to the strategically important bridge, which crosses the Second Ring Road.

Please see CHINA, Page 9

■ **CHAOS AT THE TOP**
Diplomats said China's leadership has collapsed. Page 8
■ **RELATED STORIES**
World leaders shocked. Page 8
U.S. employees leaving. Page 8
Faxes keep lines open. Page 8
Hong Kong stocks fall. Page 11

Bush Halts Arms Sales Over China Repression

By JAMES GERSTENZANG, *Times Staff Writer*

WASHINGTON—President Bush suspended all U.S. military sales to China on Monday to protest the Chinese army's violent suppression of the pro-democracy movement.

"It is very important the Chinese leaders know it's not going to be business as usual," Bush declared in a press conference announcing his decision.

Bush's action, which also included a suspension of visits between U.S. and Chinese military leaders, won immediate praise across the political spectrum in Congress, where it was generally viewed as a sufficient response for the current situation.

$600 Million in Arms

The sales halt will affect more than $600 million in arms ordered by China from the U.S. government, as well as commercial military sales of an undetermined value, U.S. officials said.

"The United States cannot condone the violent attacks and cannot ignore the consequences for our relationship with China, which has been built on a foundation of broad support by the American people," Bush said.

However, he added, "this is not the time for an emotional response, but for a reasoned, careful action that takes into account both our long-term interests and recognition of a complex internal situation in China."

Bush seemed to have been moved by accounts of a Chinese man who halted a column of 10 tanks and 10 armored personnel carriers Monday near Tian An Men Square. He stood in front of the lead tank, climbed up on it and talked to someone inside, then climbed down and walked away.

Overcoming Repression

Referring to the incident, the President told reporters, "I believe the forces of democracy are so powerful, and when you see them, as recently as this morning—a single student standing in front of a tank, and then, I might add, seeing the tank driver exercise restraint—I'm convinced that the forces of democracy are going to overcome these unfortunate events in Tian An Men Square."

The President's move to suspend military sales was designed to take concrete, punitive action against the Chinese government for killing hundreds—and perhaps thousands—of Chinese students in breaking up pro-democracy demonstrations, while avoiding sweeping sanctions that would wipe out the last decade's improvements in Sino-American relations.

Stronger action that might harm the Chinese people or "the relationship he has worked so long on" with the nation would be counterproductive, an Administration official said.

Please see BUSH, Page 9

China Campuses Become Shrines for the Fallen

By DANIEL WILLIAMS, *Times Staff Writer*

BEIJING—Tearful students in the main classroom building of the Beijing Institute of Politics and Law filed past the battered corpse of a victim of the Tian An Men massacre.

He had been brought to the school, one of the centers for pro-democracy agitation, by rescuers who had commandeered a taxi.

No one knows who he was or where he came from. His body lay packed in ice, partially draped in a Chinese flag and surrounded by humble prayer wreaths with messages praising his heroism.

'Unknown Victim'

"This is the Unknown Victim," explained a young law student at the institute. "He stands for all the dead slaughtered by the army."

College campuses throughout Beijing were turned into memorial shrines for the dead on Monday. Students draped the gates of their schools in black and white bunting, the traditional mourning colors here, and hung banners bearing classical eulogies to the dead as well as political slogans of defiance in the face of military repression.

Please see MOURN, Page 10

Iran After the Imam

4 Who May Rule Steeled by Struggle

By ROBIN WRIGHT, *Times Staff Writer*

WASHINGTON—The scene at New York's opulent Waldorf-Astoria Hotel was surreal. In a formal ballroom, underneath elegant chandeliers, Iranian President Ali Khamenei was having breakfast with 15 American journalists.

Surrounding Khamenei was a squad of formidable, bearded Revolutionary Guards from the fearsome military unit made famous by its quest for martyrdom during the war with Iraq. And in the hallways just outside, U.S. Secret Service agents provided their own protection for a man whose government had officially dubbed the United States "the Great Satan."

The first moments of the meal were awkward. In 1981, Khamenei was nearly killed by a bomb hidden inside a tape recorder and placed on the podium as he gave a Friday prayer sermon. Since then, he has walked with a cane, and his right arm has dangled uselessly at his side. To help the Iranian president eat his breakfast, one of the Revolutionary Guards had to bend over him, like a parent over a child, and cut his cheese and cold cuts.

■ **IT'S IRAN'S MOVE**
President Bush calls on Iran to help free U.S. hostages. Page 5
■ **PICTURES:** Pages 2, 7

On Sunday, Iran's ruling mullahs, or clerics, named Khamenei to replace the revered Ayatollah Ruhollah Khomeini as the leader of Iran's revolution.

Whether he will survive in that role in unpredictable Iran is anybody's guess. But for now, the 49-year-old Khamenei has emerged as one of four Iranian leaders who are expected to play major roles in the struggle to fill the vacuum left by Khomeini.

And in a nation where violence has become an accepted form of political expression, Khamenei's close brush with death does not distinguish him. Two of the three other contenders for power have also been targets of assassins since Khomeini's revolution swept Shah Mohammed Reza Pahlavi from power in 1979.

Near-Misses for Rafsanjani

Hashemi Rafsanjani, 54, the Speaker of Parliament and the man widely predicted to become the real power during the revolution's next phase, was injured during a 1980 assassination attempt. A year later, he left a building less than three minutes before a bomb killed more than 70 people, including 10 Cabinet officials and 27 members of Parliament. Unconfirmed reports suggest that he has survived a series of further assaults over the past 18 months.

Ali Akbar Mohtashemi, the interior minister, has no left hand and only the thumb remaining on his right hand. He lost his hands and part of his face in 1984 when a book bomb detonated as he opened it at the Iranian Embassy in Syria, where he was then serving as ambassador.

Only Ahmed Khomeini, the ayatollah's son and chief of staff for 12 years, has remained unscathed, at

Please see RULE, Page 6

Crush Kills 8 at Rite for Khomeini

By WILLIAM TUOHY, *Times Staff Writer*

TEHRAN—Hundreds of thousands of Iranians struggled for a last glimpse of the Ayatollah Ruhollah Khomeini as he lay in state Monday, and in the wild expressions of mass grief, at least eight people were crushed to death and an estimated 500 others were injured.

In temperatures of more than 100 degrees, the crowd of mourners, estimated by some officials at 2 million, jammed into Moussalam Square, a huge area reserved for prayer meetings in north Tehran. Weeping, wailing and chanting, they pushed forward to see the body of

Please see IRAN, Page 14

Polish Election Loss Conceded by Communists

By CHARLES T. POWERS, *Times Staff Writer*

WARSAW—Poland's ruling authorities Monday conceded defeat to Solidarity in a humiliating electoral wipe-out for the Communist Party.

In the first free balloting in this country in more than 40 years, candidates backed by the Solidarity trade union were devastating their Communist-coalition opponents by margins of 70 to 75 percentage points.

"Solidarity got a decided majority," said a spokesman for the party, in effect acknowledging the opposition's landslide triumph two days before the official count is scheduled to be announced. "The results are genuinely unfavorable for the [party] coalition."

'Moving Toward Democracy'

In Washington, President Bush said the election results show Poland is "moving toward freedom and democracy."

"We haven't seen the final results, but Communist bureaucrats beware in Poland," Bush said at a news conference.

The early, and unofficial, returns released by Solidarity indicated that:

—Solidarity would capture all 100 seats in a newly constituted Senate.

—Solidarity candidates are likely to sweep nearly all of the 161 seats apportioned for open competitive elections to the Sejm, or Parliament.

—And the overwhelming majority, if not all, of the government's special "national list" of 35 unopposed candidates, who represent the government and party establishment, would fail to receive the 50% minimum vote for election to the Parliament.

Official results will not be ready until Wednesday, but the results released by Solidarity—although heavily weighted to urban areas such as Warsaw, Katowice, Krakow and Gdansk that represent

Please see POLAND, Page 12

'Surprising' Level of AIDS Reported in Young Teens

By ROBERT STEINBROOK, *Times Medical Writer*

MONTREAL—A surprising number of American teen-agers are becoming infected with the AIDS virus during early adolescence, the U.S. Centers for Disease Control reported Monday.

The findings, presented at the Fifth International Conference on AIDS, were part of the most complete report to date on "sentinel" hospital surveillance for AIDS virus infections. Federal health officials consider the ongoing surveillance project at a national sample of 27 urban hospitals one of the most accurate measures of the distribution of human immunodeficiency virus, or HIV, infections among different segments of the population.

The researchers also said they were disturbed by "epidemic proportions" of infections—6% to 8%—in surveys of presumably low-risk male and female patients from two of the hospitals, one in Newark, N.J., and one in the South Bronx, N.Y. The infection rates at the two hospitals were particularly high, about 20%, for men ages 25 to 44 hospitalized with conditions thought unlikely to be related to infection with HIV.

These rates reflect the fact that HIV infection has become a common problem for all residents of these poor urban communities, not just for members of identified AIDS risk groups, researchers said.

The report included the first cross-sectional data on infections in hospitalized adolescents. At hospitals from areas of the country with high numbers of AIDS cases, 1.4% of 15- and 16-year-olds tested positive for HIV, according to the CDC, and a few HIV infections were detected among youths ages 12 to 14.

Please see AIDS, Page 26

INSIDE TODAY'S TIMES

GORBACHEV ANGERED
Soviet leader Mikhail S. Gorbachev, angered by the pipeline disaster that killed hundreds of people, warned against incompetence. **Page 16.**

FEW VOTERS EXPECTED
The turnout in L.A.'s runoff election today is expected to be so low that the city clerk has decided he won't even try to forecast it. **Metro, Page 1.**

PRIME RATE FALLS
The nation's banks lowered their prime rate—the benchmark for many consumer and small-business loans—to 11% from 11.5%. **Business.**

WEATHER: Morning low clouds, hazy this afternoon. Civic Center low/high: 59/75. Details: Part II, Page 5.

■ INDEX ON PAGE 2

Chang in action Monday.

CHANG UPSETS LENDL
Michael Chang, hampered by muscle cramps in his legs and once employing an underhand serve, defeated Ivan Lendl in the French Open. **Sports.**

Job Bias Suit 'Death Knell' Seen in High Court Ruling

By DAVID G. SAVAGE, *Times Staff Writer*

WASHINGTON—The Supreme Court dealt a sharp blow Monday to minority workers' chances of winning job discrimination cases, ruling that employment policies that tend to concentrate non-white workers in low-paying jobs do not necessarily violate federal civil rights law.

In the 5-4 ruling, the court's new conservative majority backed away considerably from a landmark 1971 decision that had declared illegal seemingly unbiased employment policies, such as using a test to screen applicants, that had the effect of excluding blacks or Latinos.

That 18-year-old doctrine had provided a major impetus to businesses to establish affirmative action hiring programs to avoid being sued.

Monday's ruling will greatly ease that pressure on business, civil rights lawyers said, by making it far more difficult for plaintiffs to prove that an employer's policies discriminate against them.

The decision brought an unusually bitter dissent from the court's four liberals.

"One wonders whether the majority still believes that racial discrimination . . . is a problem in our society, or even remembers that it ever was," Justice Harry A. Blackmun wrote. He was joined by Justices William J. Brennan Jr., Thurgood Marshall and John Paul Stevens.

"It's devastating, a total change in the law," said E. Richard Larson, counsel for the Mexican American

Please see COURT, Page 19

■ **DEATH PENALTY LAW**
The court will hear a challenge to California's statute. Page 3